P9-DGS-823

THE COLLEGEVILLE BIBLE COMMENTARY

BASED ON THE NEW AMERICAN BIBLE WITH REVISED NEW TESTAMENT

General Editors

DIANNE BERGANT, C.S.A.

ROBERT J. KARRIS, O.F.M.

THE LITURGICAL PRESS

COLLEGEVILLE, MINNESOTA

NIHIL OBSTAT: Robert C. Harren, J.C.L.
Censor Deputatus

IMPRIMATUR: ✠ Jerome Hanus, O.S.B.
Bishop of St. Cloud
October 19, 1988

Printed in the United States of America.

Library of Congress Cataloging-in-Publication Data

The Collegeville Bible commentary.

Previously published in 36 separate booklets.

1. Bible—Commentaries. I. Bergant, Dianne.
II. Karris, Robert J.
BS491.2.C66 1989 220.7′7 88-27356
ISBN 0-8146-1484-1

CONTENTS

Preface vii

Abbreviations ix

Introduction to the Bible 3
Dianne Bergant, C.S.A.

OLD TESTAMENT

Genesis 35
Pauline A. Viviano

Exodus 79
John F. Craghan

Leviticus 115
Wayne A. Turner

Numbers 144
Helen Kenik Mainelli

Deuteronomy 196
Leslie J. Hoppe, O.F.M.

Joshua 229
John A. Grindel, C.M.

Judges 248
John A. Grindel, C.M.

1 and 2 Samuel 265
Paula J. Bowes

1 and 2 Kings 296
Alice L. Laffey, R.S.M.

1 and 2 Chronicles 321
Alice L. Laffey, R.S.M.

Ezra and Nehemiah 332
Rita J. Burns

1 Maccabees 370
Alphonse P. Spilly, C.PP.S.

2 Maccabees 395
Alphonse P. Spilly, C.PP.S.

Isaiah 411
John J. Collins

Jeremiah 453
Peter F. Ellis

Baruch 481
Peter F. Ellis

Amos 487
Carroll Stuhlmueller, C.P.

Hosea 496
Carroll Stuhlmueller, C.P.

Micah 509
Carroll Stuhlmueller, C.P.

Nahum 520
Carroll Stuhlmueller, C.P.

Zephaniah 524
Carroll Stuhlmueller, C.P.

Habakkuk 529
Carroll Stuhlmueller, C.P.

Ezekiel and Daniel 533
Toni Craven

Joel 578
Mary Margaret Pazdan, O.P.

Obadiah 586
Mary Margaret Pazdan, O.P.

Haggai 592
Mary Margaret Pazdan, O.P.

Zechariah 600
Mary Margaret Pazdan, O.P.

Malachi 625
Mary Margaret Pazdan, O.P.

Introduction to Wisdom Literature 634
Lawrence E. Boadt, C.S.P.

Proverbs 644
Lawrence E. Boadt, C.S.P.

Job 675
Michael D. Guinan, O.F.M.

Wisdom 701
John E. Rybolt, C.M.

Sirach 722
John E. Rybolt, C.M.

Psalms 754
Richard J. Clifford, S.J.

Song of Songs 789
James A. Fischer, C.M.

Ruth 797
James A. Fischer, C.M.

Lamentations 804
James A. Fischer, C.M.

Ecclesiastes 812
James A. Fischer, C.M.

Esther 822
James A. Fischer, C.M.

Jonah 828
Irene Nowell, O.S.B.

Tobit 832
Irene Nowell, O.S.B.

Judith 844
Irene Nowell, O.S.B.

NEW TESTAMENT

Matthew 861
Daniel J. Harrington, S.J.

Mark 903
Philip Van Linden, C.M.

Luke 936
Jerome Kodell, O.S.B.

John 981
Neal M. Flanagan, O.S.M.

1 John 1021
Neal M. Flanagan, O.S.M.

2 John 1028
Neal M. Flanagan, O.S.M.

3 John 1029
Neal M. Flanagan, O.S.M.

The Acts of the Apostles 1031
William S. Kurz, S.J.

Galatians 1069
John J. Pilch

Romans 1080
John J. Pilch

1 Corinthians 1100
Mary Ann Getty

2 Corinthians 1134
Mary Ann Getty

1 Thessalonians 1151
Ivan Havener, O.S.B.

Philippians 1160
Ivan Havener, O.S.B.

Philemon 1169
Ivan Havener, O.S.B.

2 Thessalonians 1172
Ivan Havener, O.S.B.

Colossians 1179
Ivan Havener, O.S.B.

Ephesians 1188
Ivan Havener, O.S.B.

1 Timothy 1200
Jerome H. Neyrey, S.J.

2 Timothy 1208
Jerome H. Neyrey, S.J.

Titus 1215
Jerome H. Neyrey, S.J.

James 1219
Jerome H. Neyrey, S.J.

1 Peter 1228
Jerome H. Neyrey, S.J.

2 Peter 1235
Jerome H. Neyrey, S.J.

Jude 1241
Jerome H. Neyrey, S.J.

Hebrews 1245
George W. MacRae, S.J.

Revelation 1265
Pheme Perkins

List of Maps 1301

PREFACE

Today we are witnessing an increased interest in the Bible. Women and men from all walks of life are enrolling in classes, attending workshops, and organizing study groups. Guided reflection on the biblical tradition is a fundamental component of evangelization programs such as the Rite of Christian Initiation of Adults (RCIA) and RENEW. Prayer groups look for leaders who can guide them beyond private interpretation into the spiritual depths of the tradition. People are searching for new insights and are turning to biblical scholars to provide them. Non-specialists are no longer satisfied with a merely devotional understanding of the Bible. They are asking literary, historical, and theological questions that require learned answers.

In an effort to address this need, The Liturgical Press commissioned thirty-four respected scholars to provide individual booklets that together would interpret the entire Roman Catholic canon. Utilizing the most recent critical methods and incorporating the fruits of contemporary scholarship, they brought to completion in 1986 the *Collegeville Bible Commentary*, a series of thirty-six booklets, each including questions for review and discussion. The wide selection of authors resulted in a variety of theological positions and methodological approaches, which contributed to the richness of the enterprise. There was a consistent attempt throughout to be sensitive to contemporary concerns. This project was completed in a little over five years, thus ensuring the up-to-date character of the interpretation. In 1988 the authors of the New Testament commentaries redid their works in the light of the revised edition of the New Testament of the New American Bible.

The present volume brings together the commentaries of all thirty-six booklets. Its comprehensiveness makes it an invaluable resource, enabling the reader to refer easily to the interpretation of any or all of the biblical books. Besides being used for Bible study, it can also serve as a reference for liturgy planning, homily preparation, and biblical prayer services. This volume is an admirable response to the injunction of the Second Vatican Council: "Access to sacred Scripture ought to be wide open to the Christian faithful" *(Dei Verbum,* no. 22).

DIANNE BERGANT, C.S.A.
General Editor, Old Testament Commentary

ROBERT J. KARRIS, O.F.M.
General Editor, New Testament Commentary

ABBREVIATIONS

OLD TESTAMENT

Gen	Genesis	Prov	Proverbs
Exod	Exodus	Eccl	Ecclesiastes
Lev	Leviticus	Song	Song of Songs
Num	Numbers	Wis	Wisdom
Deut	Deuteronomy	Sir	Sirach
Josh	Joshua	Isa	Isaiah
Judg	Judges	Jer	Jeremiah
Ruth	Ruth	Lam	Lamentations
1 Sam	1 Samuel	Bar	Baruch
2 Sam	2 Samuel	Ezek	Ezekiel
1 Kgs	1 Kings	Dan	Daniel
2 Kgs	2 Kings	Hos	Hosea
1 Chr	1 Chronicles	Joel	Joel
2 Chr	2 Chronicles	Amos	Amos
Ezra	Ezra	Obad	Obadiah
Neh	Nehemiah	Jonah	Jonah
Tob	Tobit	Mic	Micah
Jdt	Judith	Nah	Nahum
Esth	Esther	Hab	Habakkuk
1 Macc	1 Maccabees	Zeph	Zephaniah
2 Macc	2 Maccabees	Hag	Haggai
Job	Job	Zech	Zechariah
Ps(s)	Psalm(s)	Mal	Malachi

NEW TESTAMENT

Matt	Matthew	1 Tim	1 Timothy
Mark	Mark	2 Tim	2 Timothy
Luke	Luke	Titus	Titus
John	John	Phlm	Philemon
Acts	Acts	Heb	Hebrews
Rom	Romans	Jas	James
1 Cor	1 Corinthians	1 Pet	1 Peter
2 Cor	2 Corinthians	2 Pet	2 Peter
Gal	Galatians	1 John	1 John
Eph	Ephesians	2 John	2 John
Phil	Philippians	3 John	3 John
Col	Colossians	Jude	Jude
1 Thess	1 Thessalonians	Rev	Revelation
2 Thess	2 Thessalonians		

OTHER ABBREVIATIONS

NAB	New American Bible	RSV	Revised Standard Version
NEB	New English Bible		

THE
OLD TESTAMENT

INTRODUCTION TO THE BIBLE

Dianne Bergant, C.S.A.

An introduction to the Bible is not merely a preface to the entire work, something elementary or preliminary, leading up to the major part. It is primarily a theological discipline in its own right and normally examines the origin of the individual books of the Bible, the history of the canon, and the history of the textual tradition. This article, though not an introduction in this strict sense, does treat some of the issues that fall within the range of an introduction.

Since the introductions to the books of the Bible in this volume address questions pertaining to the origin of particular books, such information can be found within the respective commentary. In this article attention is given to the origin, growth, and development of the biblical traditions in general—traditions that ultimately comprise the canon of Sacred Scripture. Next, a sketch of the history of the canon is offered, followed by a survey of the textual witness. The tradition formation, the development of the canon, and the textual witness are topics that seem to follow one another logically. Since the Bible claims divine authorship, the role of God's activity in this process of composition is also discussed. Finally, the interpretative tools necessary for understanding the Bible are described.

At first glance the material treated in this article may appear to be esoteric and of interest only to the professional student of Scripture. Upon closer examination, however, it should become clear that many of the basic questions that the average person asks about the Bible are answered within these pages—questions such as: What books belong to the Bible? Why do some churches have more books than others? Which is the best version? What does the Bible really mean? The sections have been arranged in such a way as to answer some of these questions as they may arise.

Perhaps one of the first questions asked by the beginning student of Scripture is: What books belong to the Bible? Close on its heels is: Why do some churches have more books than others? These are questions that pertain to the CANON of the Bible, and they are addressed in the first section. Rather than merely provide the factual information about the canon and explain the role that authority played and continues to play in this area, the first section attempts to describe the growth of the Scriptures from their very beginnings up to the time of the later decisions to "close the canon." Our knowledge of the development of the traditions, be they religious, social, political, or literary, has aided us in our investigation of this process of growth and development. Our knowledge of the socio-political and religious histories of both ancient Israel and early Christianity has also made significant contributions in this area. It seems that the process of tradition formation was dynamic rather than static, a communal venture rather than an individual accomplishment, that is, it was the work of a historical community rather than of a single author.

In this same section attention is given to the question of biblical authority. What is it? Who has it? How did they get it? The importance of historical movements and particular events has been highlighted. Thus, the Bible is seen as growing as the people grow, changing as the people change, and becoming standardized as the people seek stability. Viewing the Scriptures from this perspective should help the reader appreciate the description of the Bible as "the word of God in human words."

Even a detailed look at the human dimension of the composition of the Bible cannot adequately answer the fundamental question about its nature as Sacred Scripture. How is it the word of God? How did God speak this word in the first place? How does God speak this word today? These questions touch on the topic of INSPIRATION, the focus of the second section. This section is quite a bit shorter because it presumes the description of tradition formation outlined in the preceding one. It presents an understanding of inspiration that regards it as dynamic and operative within ordinary human events and situations. Such a view in no way detracts from the authoritative claims of the Bible; rather, it expands the scope of divine activity and places the exercise of authority squarely within the context of the believing community.

The claim that the Bible is inspired influences how its truthfulness is perceived. Human comprehension is limited and human judgment is subject to error, but surely the word of God is trustworthy. Several attempts at solving the dilemma of dual (divine and human) authorship, and the strengths and weaknesses of each solution, have been advanced over the years. Some of them are discussed in this section.

Even the beginning student of the Bible is soon aware that a variety of editions of the Bible are available. Unless every member of a Bible study group is consulting the same edition, confusion could result. This confusion may result from different translations or from the use of different sources used in constructing a text. The third section offers a brief summary of the history of the TEXTS AND VERSIONS which have survived the ravages of time and which form the basis of present-day Bibles.

The meaning of the text is ultimately the most important question. To know how the traditions developed, to believe that they were inspired by God, to be able to recover early versions of them are of very little significance if they remain unintelligible. HERMENEUTICS provides tools and methods for interpretation. These tools and methods are described in the last section. As more and more people become involved in serious study of the Bible, easy explanations of the Scriptures are being questioned and sometimes even rejected. Bewilderment over conflicting interpretations still remains. In addition, the use of biblical passages to strengthen one's point of view has become very popular in the broader society, even when a contradictory interpretation is advanced by another. All this points to the need to understand ways of interpretation in order to judge the validity and the appropriateness of the use to which the Bible is being put.

In no way does this final section claim to cover all the interpretative approaches. Its intention is to explain the basic methods used in contemporary scholarship. The authors of the commentaries in this volume frequently identify the methods they have employed in their research. The definitions found in this section might throw some light on that research and thus on the findings offered by the respective authors.

As with any other work, another author might perceive the material under discussion in another way. One of the primary goals of the COLLEGEVILLE BIBLE COMMENTARY is to bring the findings of contemporary scholarship to the beginning students of Scripture. These findings may be very new to some, not so new to others. Because of the wide selection of authors, these commentaries offer a variety of theological positions and methodological approaches. There has been a consistent attempt to be sensitive to contemporary concerns. Although efforts have been made to refrain from referring to God in gender-specific language, the lack of consensus in this area is reflected in the different styles of the authors. The work undertaken here is offered as a part of the ongoing process of biblical interpretation.

THE CANON

CANON AND AUTHORITY

Even before opening the Bible to begin a study of its contents, the serious inquirer is faced with several basic questions. What is the Bible? How did the Bible acquire its present form? Who is responsible for the contents of the Bible? Why has the Bible endured over the centuries? Is the Bible relevant to the contemporary world? While well-known answers to these questions may come immediately to mind, one very important common denominator is frequently overlooked: each answer presumes some dimension of *authority*.

What is the Bible? It is a collection of religious traditions that are revered as sacred because they are inspired by God. The believing community's official recognition of the inspired character of these traditions has accorded them "canonical" status. This means that they enjoy an authoritative status possessed by no other traditions of the community.

How did the Bible acquire its present form? The history of its origin and development is long and complicated and will be treated later. Here it is enough to say that the traditions that have been incorporated into the Bible and the shape that they have taken were dependent upon choices made within the community, choices made by persons and groups having the authority to so choose.

Who is responsible for the contents of the Bible? Prominent lawgivers, prophets, and teachers whose names are mentioned in the texts themselves were not the only ones responsible for the biblical material; there were also editors and compilers who refined and selected material from the community's vast literary and theological treasury. They preserved what they thought were religious norms, and thereby they exercised a significant amount of authority within the community.

Why has the Bible endured over the centuries? Acknowledging that it contains material stemming from times of the distant past and from cultures so different from our own, one can only marvel at its perdurability. The reason lies in the fact that believers throughout the ages have continued to be convinced of its authoritative character. They, too, have regarded its contents as normative and have tried to fashion their lives in accord with it.

Is the Bible relevant to the contemporary world? This question is at the heart of most of the biblical debate of our time. One does not merely ask, *How* can the Bible speak to the modern world? but, *Can* the Bible speak to the modern world? The first query raises the question of interpretation; the second, the issue of authority. Does the Bible still have normative value for women and men today? It is not enough to say that it is inspiring. The point is: Is it inspired, and therefore authoritative?

When addressing the authoritative character of the Bible, one must deal with some quite distinct but interrelated questions: (1) Why did these traditions emerge and not others? (2) Who had the right to decide about them? (3) Is the Bible relevant and still normative?

Why these traditions?

This study must begin with a brief working description of "biblical tradition." Put quite simply, a biblical tradition is at root a statement about the self-understanding of ancient Israel and/or the early Christian community. It not only specifically defined them as they perceived themselves, but it directed the further development of their self-understanding.

The expression "God's people" can serve as an example. Our religious ancestors believed that they were "God's people," and this concept not only identified them but shaped the way they developed through history, and it kept explaining for them why they continued to survive. For them, being "God's people" meant that God had called them and was leading and protecting them. They believed that they were recipients of divine revelation, and their traditions were testimonies to this revelation. Such traditions can be called authoritative to the extent that they authentically express the basic self-understanding of the people.

Slightly differing and sometimes even quite different traditions could and did arise. Examples of such diversity include the two accounts of creation (Gen 1:1–2:4a and Gen 2:4b-25) and the several accounts of Paul's conversion (Gal 1:13-17; Acts 9:1-9; 22:6-11; 26:12-18). Different traditions did not necessarily cause undue tension within the community as long as the self-identity of the people was not threatened. However, when there was a crisis of identity, the survival of the group demanded that some kind of agreement be reached. This crisis of identity frequently ushered in a crisis of authority as well. Which of the various statements of self-understanding was authentic? Which traditions could draw together the dissipated forces within the community? These were the ones that would subsequently function as the normative version of the community's self-identity. They would serve as a kind of "canon," a kind of authority within the community. They would continue as such as long as they expressed the identity of the group.

Scholars agree that not all the sacred traditions of ancient Israel and/or of early Christianity have survived. Among those that have survived, not all enjoy the same degree of authoritativeness. This brief description of the dynamic process known as tradition formation explains why such is the case. As their experience of life and the events of history forced the people to search for meaning, they came to understand themselves and their relationship with God in terms of that history. Thus, traditions arose, developed, and often had to be refashioned as the circumstances of life demanded.

The ultimate explanation for the endurance of a tradition seems to have been its ability to remain fundamentally unchanged and yet applicable to new situations. If it could not be refashioned or retraditioned, it would cease to be authoritative and its revelatory value would be questionable. In a very real sense, biblical authority has always resided in the interaction between an authentic tradition and the living community.

Who decides?

To acknowledge the authoritative character of the process known as tradition formation is not to deny the role played by significant people within the community. Some people had to make very important decisions for the rest of the group. However, these significant people did not simply create religious understandings or teachings independently of the community. Some may have had unique creative insights, but whatever they brought forth had to be recognized and endorsed by the others as a valid interpretation of the communal faith. That explains why some of the proclamations of the prophets, for example, were not accepted immediately. The majority of the people may not have regarded their proclamations as authentic. In such instances it was often the disciples of the prophets who preserved the teachings. Only at a later date was the authoritative character of the pronouncements broadly recognized.

According to this view, a variety of forces were at work shaping and reshaping the religious consciousness and self-understanding of the people. This means that there was no single locus of authority. Some individuals and groups originated the traditions; others contributed to their development and reshaping; others were involved in determining their place and significance in the communal self-understanding. Those in leadership positions within the community may have authenticated the traditions, but it was the people who had to confirm this decision.

Is the Bible relevant and still normative?

This question can be asked by believer and nonbeliever alike. In either case, it will proceed from a particular understanding of the nature of the material and will elicit a different answer. Anyone can be profoundly moved by the inspirational quality of literature, religious or nonreligious. A believer, however, accepts the traditions of the faith-community as somehow binding. They are regarded as not only explaining the faith but as forming the members within that faith. They are the norms and standards that direct the lives of the believers. They exercise a type of authority over these people. *That* they do this is a matter of the obedient faith of the believing community. *Why* they do this is a question of inspiration. *How* they speak to a new situation is a concern of interpretation.

The canon, then, has to do with reference to authority. It is a statement from the past that continues to be operative in the present. As literature, it is a collection of the constitutive religious writings of the community. Believers hold that these writings had their origins in revelation and that as historical memory they continue to be a source of revelation today.

THE GROWTH OF TRADITION

The study of biblical tradition is a very complicated undertaking. It includes not only an analysis of the final or "canonical" testimony of the community but also a probing into the long and labyrinthian process that brought that testimony into being. It is not enough to view tradition as a completed statement. One should also appreciate the traditioning process that created and refined that articulation. A brief examination of this process will throw light on what might otherwise be very confusing.

One of the major characteristics of this transmission process was the community's constant interpretation and application of older traditions. Tradition growth was not merely the handing down of static formulations; it also included the repeated process of actualizing earlier material within new contexts. Changes in the political, social, or religious worlds necessitated new expressions of fundamental faith as well as the articulation of new insights. The interaction between historical events and forces within the community determined the shape of the tradition, a shape that might change at another time or in another place. This process might have continued to the present day had not several significant events compelled the community to endorse certain statements over others and to confer authority on them. The destruction of the Solomonic temple at the time of the Babylonian Exile (587–538 B.C.E.—Before the Common Era) was one such event. A second historical watershed was the destruction of the Herodian temple at the time of the emergence of early Christianity (70 C.E.—Common Era). Each of these catastrophes played a major role in the choice of which traditional materials were to be preserved, the specific arrangement of what was transmitted, and their subsequent interpretation as normative theology.

Everyone is familiar with the designation "the tribes of Israel." While scholars differ in their understanding of the history of the tribal origins, most agree that the earliest organization of the people was that of a loosely united federation of clans and tribes, each retaining its unique traditions and each fiercely loyal to its own chieftains and military leaders. The traditions that grew out of their experiences were probably preserved in poetic forms, while the stability of their social structures was safeguarded by their laws. These early traditions were embedded in sagas and other narratives, the details of which readily could and did change with retelling, while the core traditions remained intact.

This was a period of great fluidity (ca. 1200–1040 B.C.E.). Groups of people changed location and shifted social and political allegiance quite frequently. As diverse peoples amalgamated, their traditions were brought together into a common story. Although this common story now flows quite smoothly, the process of assimilation never completely erased characteristics that might identify one group from another. These characteristics can be detected upon careful study of the text.

The socio-political move from a federation of tribes to a nation under the administration of a king (ca. tenth century B.C.E.) called for a review of the relationship of the people with their God. The people were forced to scrutinize their religious traditions, restating some while reshaping others. Earlier tribal narratives were retold with a bias in favor of the monarchy. Since the contemporary situation influenced the way the past was understood, inevitably these new interpretations became part of the original narrative in such a way that details from different periods now comprised one story. This interpretative process explains why the tradition known as the Yahwist (J) is both a narrative epic of early Israelite history and a justification of the Davidic monarchy.

At still another time and from another perspective, the tradition now known as the Elohist (E) took shape. This was a retelling of basically the same story as that told by the Yahwist, but the concerns were not the same and so the focus was different. During this period prophets such as Amos and Hosea in the north and Isaiah in the south were also calling for a reevaluation of the current beliefs and practices of the people. Although some of this theology had probably already established itself with some degree of authority, much of it was still in flux.

When the northern kingdom fell to the Assyrians (722 B.C.E.), the traditions that had originated there were incorporated with those of the south. Thus, different portraits of the tribal ancestors were woven together into one; legal customs that operated within one community became part of the law of another. The selection, codification, and crystallization of these various traditions resulted in a rich and sometimes contradictory testimony to the action of God in the history of the nation. This testimony became the official story, the authoritative self-understanding, of the people. The messages of early prophets were probably proclaimed again and again as long as they could be adapted to the needs of the people. More than likely they were preserved by followers of the prophets, and these disciples were the ones who made the necessary yet appropriate adaptations.

The demise of the northern kingdom had its theological repercussions in the south as well. It became a catalyst for the retelling of the stories of the initial settlement of the land, stories that not only pointed to the reasons for the fall but also served as a warning to the south. There was a renewed attention to the Law and a resurgence of prophetic critique. These concerns and the subsequent reshaping of earlier traditions set the stage for both the Deuteronomistic (D) and Priestly (P) theologies.

As stated earlier, the destruction of the temple, the downfall of the monarchy, and the deportation of the people all played a part in the fashioning of traditions. This critical period of captivity probably forged the two major biblical portions known as the Law and the Prophets. Early historical, prophetic, and legal traditions were given the shape that has, for the most part, been handed down to the present time. The precise text of the primary history of Israel, including the Law, was then fixed and was not to undergo any further significant reinterpretation. References to the existence of a version of the Law and its importance in the postexilic community are found in Ezra 7:14 and Neh 8:1. The prophetic books such as Jeremiah and Ezekiel would still be somewhat expanded and revised as new material was added, but once this expansion and revision had ceased, the prophetic corpus was also accorded a kind of authoritative status. There is a second-century mention of this status in 2 Macc 15:9. The believing community now revered these traditions as normative for them. What the institutions of monarchy, priesthood, and prophecy had done in shaping the self-identity of the pre-exilic community, the authoritative traditions that emerged from the crucible of the Exile did for the self-identity of later Judaism.

These literary and theological books of material told the story of the people's beginnings, but they ended the story with the people on the threshold of the land of promise, thus proclaiming a message of hope for a nation looking to the future for a land of its own. The national history now described prosperity as contingent upon fidelity to covenantal commitment, thus explaining the nation's present plight as both a judgment for past failures and an incentive to future repentance. The prophetic material established the credibility of the major prophets as spokespersons for God. Their teachings were to be heeded. In this way the newly forged exilic community reactualized its normative traditions, preserving them for the future.

The needs of the postexilic community called for new and different religious traditions. Theological interpretations of events, prophetic pronouncements, sapiential reflections on life, didactic stories, hymns, and other cultic songs emerged as part of the religious treasury of the second temple period. The significance of these traditions was a focus of dispute within the community.

The Samaritans appear to have dissociated themselves from the returned community sometime around 300 B.C.E., and to this day those who remain faithful to the Samaritan tradition consider only the Torah, or Pentateuch, as inspired. The Sadducees of the early Christian era were descendants of this same point of view. Not until well into the Christian period did official Judaism decide upon the authoritativeness of the third section of the Scriptures, known as the Writings. By that time there were several collections of inspired material, each claiming a position of privilege within the community.

The spread of Hellenistic thought and language prompted the translation of the traditions into Greek. This version came to be known as the Septuagint (LXX) or Alexandrian version. The former name comes from a tradition which claimed that seventy (LXX) translators, working independently of one another, produced the same translation. The latter designation stems from the name of the city of its origin. This version contains some books not found in the Hebrew Bible. It seems that both the Hebrew and the Greek versions enjoyed the same prestige, each within different communities.

A third collection that has survived from this period belonged to a sectarian group known as the Essenes. Portions of their library have been found in the caves at Qumran, a settlement in the Judean desert. They appear to have included more books in their Scripture than did either the Septuagint or the more traditional Hebrew Scriptures of the time. The existence of these different "canons" is evidence of what was stated above about the diversity of religious traditions within the believing community. This diversity resulted from different life perspectives as well as different hermeneutical or interpretative ways of understanding the material.

The "event of Christ" constituted an impact not unlike that of other revelatory events in the history of "God's people" in that it forced the believers to seriously reexamine their beliefs. It was radically different, however, in several significant ways. It was not merely another revelation of God—believers insist that it was *the* revelation of God. For that reason earlier traditions may now be seen in an entirely new light. By this time Judaism was a religion of "the Book"; Christianity, on the other hand, is a religion of "the living Christ." The Gospels portray Jesus as claiming authority in his own right. He did not seem to place himself within the stream of traditional authority but called directly upon divine authority. Further, he explained the traditions of Israel in terms of himself. Clearly, Jesus, not the Bible, is the focus of authority here. Hence the ultimate question inevitably arises: What relevance does the Hebrew Bible have for the Christian experience and for Christian theology? This is a question that confronted the very earliest Christians and has confronted every generation of Christians since their time.

The first Christians, like Jesus himself, had been formed within the ancient biblical traditions. Thus, they accepted or rejected him in the light of those traditions. The Scriptures became the basis of their faith in him as Lord, and he became the focus through which they understood the Scriptures. A new religious group was born out of this faith in Jesus and this reinterpretation of the traditions. The new phenomenon was the source of conflict within the original community. Jesus' radical perspective was challenged by the religious authorities of his day. The Gospels have preserved recollections of this new interpretation (see Matt 5:17-48). His followers faced the same opposition. Stephen was stoned for this reason (see Acts 7), and Paul himself suffered for his preaching (see Acts 14:4f. and 19).

This new teaching of Jesus and its furtherance by his followers gave rise to a new tradition that soon enjoyed a prominence parallel to the Scriptures (see 2 Pet 3:2). This did not happen without internal strife, however. There were those within the Christian community who felt that the Law was not only irrelevant but was actually a hindrance. This attitude appeared most frequently in the Gentile churches established by Paul (see Gal 3:23–4:7). Others clung tenaciously to observance of the Law as necessary for themselves as well as for new converts. The Judeo-Christian communities, notably the church in Jerusalem and a group known as the Ebionites, represented this position (see Acts 15:1-4). Once again, the issue was the relationship of earlier traditions to a new revelation.

Various forces were at work during this period. The Christian community was expanding and assuming several different and flexible shapes. Within the Jewish community, of which many Christians were a part, the biblical traditions were moving toward a final shape. Books that were somehow associated with the great figures of the Hebrew past were given a prominence not accorded to other writings. All the criteria for making these decisions are not known to modern scholarship, and therefore much about the closing of the canon remains unclear. One thing can be said: Neither the collection of the Septuagint nor that of the Qumran became the official canon of the Jewish community. That is interesting, since studies have shown that the version most popularly used at this time was the Septuagint, especially among Christians. When they quoted from the older traditions, they usually cited the Greek version.

While the Jewish community may have made some decisions about its authoritative list, the Christian community, which drew on the same sources, certainly did not. Although there are references to "the law and the prophets" (Matt 5:17) and to "the law of Moses and the prophets and the psalms" (Luke 24:44), significant controversy continued well into the fourth century. It was not so much conflict with forces outside the community as it was internal strife that brought the question of canon to the fore again and again. Groups like the Gnostics and teachers like Marcion, who were later condemned as heretics because of their views of Christianity, had used their biblical interpretations, especially their rejection of the Hebrew Scriptures, as fuel for their theological arguments. Thus, both the Jewish and the emerging Christian Scriptures became the weapons in the fight over Christian orthodoxy.

The great second-century apologist Justin Martyr was one of the first to witness to the practice of reading Christian writings in conjunction with the Jewish Scriptures at liturgical services. Defense of the Scriptures was at the heart of his teaching. The early champions of the faith such as Irenaeus, Clement of Alexandria, Tertullian, Origen, and Eusebius all preserved canonical lists of Christian writings. Some of them agreed with each other, others did not. In the fourth century both the church in the West and the church in the East accepted a Christian list of twenty-seven books but did not adopt a standard for the Jewish Scriptures. That would have to wait for the Reformation and the Council of Trent's response to it.

THE SHAPE OF THE CANON

The long process of tradition formation and development that has been described here was finally brought to a close. This closure resulted in a normative version of the tradition which, as the recognized testimony to divine revelation, could henceforth enable the believing community to organize its life and verify its hope. A canon or standard was thus established in this normative version. The word "canon," it should be noted, has a long and complicated history. Originally meaning "reed," it came to signify something that acted as a norm, a measuring stick. In Christian usage it refers to a model or rule.

The final canonical forms of the biblical traditions attest to God's presence and revelation in the past experiences of the people. These forms became the rule or standard for determining revelation within the believing community in the present and in the future. They also provided a means of achieving unity within the faith. Born of the community, they were instrumental in the rebirth of that community generation after generation.

There are three major Jewish theories concerning the closing of the canon. Since most of the Hebrew Scriptures were in existence at the time of Ezra in the fifth century B.C.E., Ezra himself was credited with the completion of the collection. This tradition is legendary and enjoys little prominence today. A second theory holds that a group of leaders of the postexilic community, forerunners of what came to be known as the Great Synagogue, worked under the impetus of Ezra and established the canon. However, there is no evidence that a body resembling the Great Synagogue existed before the Middle Ages, and so this theory is also usually discounted. The third position, the one generally held today, suggests that it was not until the Christian era that the Palestinian Jewish community closed its canon. The town of Jamnia (also known as Jabneh) appears to have been the center of Pharisaic Judaism. Here the leaders of the community that had survived the fall of Jerusalem and the destruction of the temple built by Herod decided upon the list of inspired books.

Just as it was a particular interpretation of God's presence and revelation that had shaped the tradition, so it was another particular interpretation that eventually considered the canon closed. There is no certainty about the exact criteria followed in making these decisions. Knowledge of the sociopolitical and religious forces at work at that particular time may throw some light on this question, but much necessary information has been lost to history. However, some criteria can be assumed.

If the Scriptures do testify to divine revelation, then obviously the prophetic tradition, that bearer of revelation *par excellence*, played a significant role in the canonization of these Scriptures. Only those books that were believed to have originated before the termination of genuine prophecy were considered uniquely inspired. Liturgical usage was a second criterion. Books that gained prominence because of their cultic or liturgical function were also accorded canonical status. Adherence to these criteria yielded the tripartite Bible: the Torah, or Law (the first five books); the Prophets (the Former Prophets, or Historical Books; and the Latter or Writing Prophets); and the Writings (Psalms, Wisdom writings, the five liturgical scrolls, Daniel, and the postexilic history). These were the sacred books of Israel that "soiled the hands." This curious phrase indicates that after handling the above-mentioned scrolls, the reader's hands were to be washed in a ritual acknowledgment of the holiness of the traditions and the unworthiness of the reader.

As stated earlier, the Greek version that originated in Alexandria was probably the one in popular use at this time (ca. 90 C.E.). However, it was the older Hebrew version that was adopted by the Jewish community at Jamnia. Some believe that this choice was due to the rivalry that had developed between the Jewish and the Christian interpretations of some of the traditions as well as to the Christian practice of adding Christian writings to the collections. Other scholars hold that disputes within the Jewish community itself influenced the decision about the canon. At this time the Pharisees were in conflict with some of the more apocalyptically minded Jewish sects, and they took a stand in favor of a more conservative interpretation. (Apocalyptic was a very imaginative and symbolic way of interpreting the events of history. It frequently included a description of the future.) The time of Ezra, the time after the destruction of the first temple, was recalled at this, the time of the destruction of the second temple. At the time of Ezra apocalyptic and messianic speculation was eliminated, and the collection of books that came out of the Exile became the normative version. So the same selection occurred at the time of Jamnia.

The apocalyptic and messianic speculation did, however, serve the Christian need to come to grips with "the event of Christ." That was probably one of the reasons for the continued use by Christians of writings that were part of the Greek version. Whether Jesus and the disciples used the Hebrew or the Greek version is not clear. What is clear, however, is that the communities from which the Christian Scriptures were born quoted from the Greek, for the vast majority of the Christians of the first century were Greek-speaking Gentile converts. Since they did not believe that revelation had ended with the death of the last prophet but continued in Christ, they continued to use the more extensive Greek version.

It was not until the second and third centuries that the debates within Judaism precipitated a move by Christians to close their list of Jewish sacred books. By the fourth century the Western churches had accepted the decision of the North African councils and had adopted the Greek Bible. The Eastern churches, on the other hand, appear to have preferred the list drawn up by the Jews. These decisions were made by local or regional churches. It was the Council of Trent that finally decided upon the canon for the churches in union with Rome.

Since the Reformers rejected the authority of the papacy and its use of Scripture to authenticate some of its teachings, they looked to the Scriptures themselves as the norms for interpreting tradition and chose the shorter Jewish canon as their official list. The Roman church, in accepting the wider Greek canon, has preserved an authentic early church tradition and is consistent with that community's usage of certain books rejected by the Jewish community. The Protestant churches, in their retention of the shorter canon, have preserved a more ancient version. These ecclesiastical decisions have resulted in the lists given on the next page.

The story of the growth and development of the Jewish canon provides solid reasons for the threefold division of Law, Prophets, and Writings. But one can only conjecture about the reasons for the order of the Alexandrian canon: Pentateuch, History, Poetry, Prophets. Perhaps it can be traced to the fact that Hellenistic Jews were trained in Greek schools of rhetoric, where literature was studied according to literary types. Finally, there is an interesting theological feature in the differing orientations with which each collection concludes. In the Jewish canon the reader is left with an exhortation to go up to Jerusalem and to rebuild the temple (2 Chr 36:23), a message dear to every Jewish heart. The Alexandrian order, reflecting a messianic concern, ends with the promise to send Elijah the prophet at the inauguration of the day of the Lord's coming (Mal 4:5). Christians could easily see this as an appropriate transition to their own sacred traditions.

Those seven books about which canonicity was disputed (Judith, Tobit, 1 and 2 Maccabees, Wisdom, Sirach, and Baruch) are called "deuterocanonical" by Roman Catholics and "apocryphal" by Protestants, who frequently include them in a separate section at the end of their Bibles. The term "deuterocanonical" does not suggest a separate canonizing process so much as a deliberate canonical recognition deemed necessary because of controversy within the community. Initially "apocrypha" meant "hidden," implying that

JEWISH CANON	ALEXANDRIAN CANON
TORAH (LAW)	PENTATEUCH
Genesis	Genesis
Exodus	Exodus
Leviticus	Leviticus
Numbers	Numbers
Deuteronomy	Deuteronomy
PROPHETS	HISTORY
(Former)	Joshua
Joshua	Judges
Judges	Ruth
1-2 Samuel	1-2 Samuel
1-2 Kings	1-2 Kings
	1-2 Chronicles
(Latter)	Ezra-Nehemiah
Isaiah	Esther
Jeremiah	Judith
Ezekiel	Tobit
(12 minor)	1-2 Maccabees
Hosea	
Joel	POETRY
Amos	Psalms
Obadiah	Proverbs
Jonah	Ecclesiastes
Micah	Song of Songs
Nahum	Job
Habakkuk	Wisdom of Solomon
Zephaniah	Sirach
Haggai	
Zechariah	PROPHETS
Malachi	*(Major)*
	Isaiah
WRITINGS	Jeremiah
Psalms	Baruch
Job	Lamentations
Proverbs	Ezekiel
Ruth	Daniel
Song of Songs	
Qoheleth	*(Minor)*
Lamentations	Hosea
Esther	Amos
Daniel	Micah
Ezra-Nehemiah	Joel
1-2 Chronicles	Obadiah
	Jonah
	Nahum
	Habakkuk
	Zephaniah
	Haggai
	Zechariah
	Malachi

the message of these books was hidden from the majority of the community and understood only by the truly wise. Gradually the term took on a negative meaning because the orthodoxy of the books was suspect. Today the word "apocryphal" merely refers to writings that may be profoundly religious and inspirational but not canonical. Though absent from the Hebrew canon, the deuterocanonical or apocryphal material was considered part of the Jewish (and therefore also the Protestant) religious literature and was frequently used in liturgical settings.

There is another group of religious writings that, although not considered canonical by either Jewish or Christian communities, greatly influenced both. In them can be found the background for such themes as the kingdom of God, the Son of Man, the resurrection of the dead, the teachings about angels and demons. These intertestamental works (writings from the period between the times of the Old and the New Testaments), frequently apocalyptic in character, were in a rather fluid state between 200 B.C.E. and 100 C.E., and sometimes enjoyed the same respect as did some of the "Writings" that eventually became canonical.

A large number of manuscripts from this group of writings have been discovered at Qumran, a Jewish community that shared many of the same apocalyptic and messianic hopes as did the early Christians. The intensity of these widespread hopes explains the popularity of this kind of literature, which include such works as the Book of Enoch, the Book of Jubilees, the Testaments of the Twelve Patriarchs, the Sibylline Oracles, the Assumption of Moses, to name but a few. Because their proclaimed authorship is questionable, these works have often been referred to by Protestants as "pseudepigrapha"; because of their somewhat esoteric nature, Catholics call them "apocrypha." Actually, neither term is really satisfactory, but, because of traditional usage, the designations stand.

The rise of Christian writings to the status of Scripture is easier to trace than that of the Jewish writings because witnesses to their influence can be found in the writings of the "apostolic teachers" of the early Christian centuries. Their authority rested not so much on the fact that they were the traditions of the earliest Christians as on the fact that they preserved the authentic "Jesus tradition." It was the words of Jesus that were authoritative. Paul called upon this authority when teaching about the final coming (1 Thess 4:15) and the institution of the Lord's Supper (1 Cor 11:23ff.). Although the oral tradition may have been preferred, the need for Christian writings soon became obvious. With the founding of Christian communities at great distances both from Jerusalem and from one another, written communication became necessary. As the apostles became dispersed and the eyewitnesses to Jesus began to die, the need for authoritative written testimonies increased. These testimonies became the building blocks of the Christian Scriptures.

These Scriptures themselves existed as individual works long before they were collected into fixed groups. The earliest known writings were the letters of Paul. They might have been lost to history had not someone collected them and circulated this collection throughout the church. Scholars have suggested that the compiler was the author of Ephesians, who wrote that letter under Paul's name and sent it as a general introduction to the entire collection. Whatever the case may be, even before the end of the first century an early Christian writer called Paul's letters "true inspiration" (1 Clement 47:3) similar to the Hebrew Scriptures (see 2 Pet 3:15-16). The great teachers of the second and third centuries—Ignatius, Polycarp, Tertullian, and Origen—all knew of Paul's letters and acknowledged their authority. Even Marcion, a Gnostic who repudiated the entire Jewish tradition, considered Paul as prominent. He devised a canon that consisted only of ten Pauline letters and the Gospel of Luke.

The first reference to a "Gospel tradition" appears toward the middle of the second century; a short time later Justin Martyr mentions a Gospel reading as part of Sunday worship. While there may have been earlier hints that the "Jesus tradition" was enjoying the same authority as the Hebrew tradition, this is the first clear evidence of a new canon growing up beside the traditional one.

One cannot but ask: Why four Gospels? Why not just one, as Marcion had suggested? And if more than one, why only four out of the many that were composed in the first centuries of the Christian period? Even Luke tells us that "many have undertaken to compile a narrative . . ." (1:1). Modern scholarship claims that this variety of Gospels reflects the diversity and pluralism within early Christianity and the adaptation of the Gospel tradition to new and different Christian communities.

A careful study of the apocryphal Gospels may explain why the church rejected most of them, but it does not answer the question about the fourfold Gospel tradition. Different answers have been put forward, all somewhat hypothetical. Some say that since apostolic origin was a criterion for canonization and all four Gospels could claim such origin (Matthew and John were among the Twelve; Mark was associated with Peter, and Luke with Paul), all four had to be accepted. Irenaeus thought that since there were four world regions, four major winds, four covenants in the Hebrew tradition, there should be four Gospel witnesses as pillars of the church. Others suggest that Marcion's rejection of every Gospel but Luke's played a part in the decision in favor of a fourfold Gospel tradition. Whatever the reason, by the end of the second century the collection of four Gospels was accepted everywhere but Syria, where a harmonized account known as the Diatessaron of Tatian continued as authoritative until the fifth century.

By the end of the second century a new two-part canon was taking shape. It consisted of a fourfold Gospel canon and a collection of apostolic writings. The status of several of the apostolic writings was the subject of controversy down through the fifth century. Although the early church citations and lists were the two main criteria for determining the authoritativeness of the Christian Scriptures, it is clear that there was not yet universal agreement. These diverse early church lists may reflect nothing more than the custom of each author's local church. If this was the case, the extent of the agreement that one finds is quite significant.

The earliest official or ecclesiastical list still in existence is called the Muratorian Fragment and is thought to be representative of late second-century Roman usage. The fact that Irenaeus, Polycarp, Clement, and Tertullian were all in basic agreement with it points to its catholicity. Twenty-two of the twenty-seven books of our canon were included in this listing.

At the beginning of the third century, Origen further classified the books then in use. Having traveled widely, he was able to compare the lists of various churches in different regions, categorizing them as: (1) "acknowledged"—four Gospels, thirteen Pauline letters, Acts, two other non-Pauline epistles (later called "catholic," because they are more like encyclicals intended for the whole church rather than for individual communities as the Pauline letters were); (2) "disputed"; (3) "false."

In the fourth century Eusebius categorized the writings in a similar fashion. However, it was Athanasius whose list included all and only those books that comprise our canonical Christian testament. In addition to the canonical books, he listed some of the writings that had been included in several earlier lists and suggested that they would be good for reading. The Latin church was influenced by this Greek decision, and, subsequently, several North African councils sanctioned the same list of twenty-seven books. Although there was general agreement throughout both the Greek and the Latin churches, it came about as the result of decisions made by provincial synods, not by an ecumenical council. The canon grew out of the common usage of the Christian communities.

While the West had canonized four Gospels, the Syrian church clung to the Diatessaron until the fifth century. It never completely accepted all the catholic epistles or the Apocalypse. The Ethiopic church, on the other hand, enlarged its canon. Thus, the church in the East continued to revere a different Christian Bible.

As already mentioned, several other early Christian works were often considered canonical well into the fifth century. These were: 1 and 2 Clement, the Epistle of Barnabas, the Didache, and the Shepherd of Hermas. It is still not clear in every instance why they were not included in the final listing.

Certain factors seem to have been gradually accepted for determining which books should be considered canonical and which books should not. First among these factors was apostolic origin. The work had to be associated with an apostle or with someone from the apostolic age. Second, there had to be a catholic or universal dimension to the message. This requirement did not deny that some of the writings were originally intended for individual communities, but it demanded that the message speak to all. Third, the teaching had to be in accord with the basic rule of faith and not propose some esoteric message. There is no direct evidence that these were the criteria used to determine canonicity; however, books seem to have been rejected because they deviated seriously from just this kind of criteria.

The church now had a twofold canon which, it believed, was inspired by God and which attested to God's presence and revelation in the past experiences of the people. Further, it cherished this twofold canon as the rule or standard for determining revelation within the believing community in the present and in the future.

INSPIRATION

INSPIRATION AND AUTHORITY

The Bible has been defined as a collection of religious traditions that are revered as sacred because they are inspired by God. In the preceding section we examined the process of tradition growth and development, showing how the ebb and flow of Israel's history significantly influenced it as it reshaped and reinterpreted the tradition, and how decisions about canonicity brought an end to this creative process.

Up to this point the focus of this study has been on human authorship. The communities first of ancient Israel and then of early Christianity, believed that God had been revealed in their midst through the events of their history. The Bible is a collection of those traditions that were cherished as authentic and enduring testimonies of God's revelation. By canonizing these testimonies, the community declared that, while God may be revealed in many ways, there is a unique relationship between revelation and these sacred Scriptures. This relationship is spoken of in terms of inspiration and divine authorship. Those who in any way contributed to the writing of the Bible were inspired by God. Thus, the Bible boasts both human and divine authorship.

The present consideration of biblical inspiration begins with a passage from the Bible itself: "All scripture is inspired of God and is useful for teaching—for reproof, correction, and training in holiness" (2 Tim 3:16). Here the word "inspired" can mean either "breathes" God or "is breathed of" God. While the community does indeed believe that the Scriptures continue to communicate God's word to us today (breathes God), it is the passive sense of the verb that is traditionally preferred: the Scriptures have been "breathed of" God. This idea recalls the familiar prophetic theme of the breath or spirit of God, that dynamic manifestation of God's action in the world.

It is no wonder, then, that biblical inspiration has often been understood as akin to prophetic inspiration or prophetic possession. However, if one uses the prophetic model of inspiration to understand biblical inspiration—as many people have done in the past and some continue to do in the present—one may tend to assume that each individual book can be traced back to one author who was inspired or whose words were inspired. The process of tradition formation that has been discussed in these pages rejects such a notion of authorship and finds the model inadequate and misleading.

Besides presuming single authorship, the prophetic model frequently minimizes the role played by human reflection and creativity. At times God is depicted as taking possession of the imagination and thought of the individual, and sometimes even as dictating the ideas and the very words. There can be little doubt about the difficulty in balancing the roles of the human and the divine in this kind of joint undertaking. But it is better that a difficulty stand unresolved than that the contribution of either partner in this venture be underestimated.

Without denying the unique role played by certain individual members of the community, the present study has suggested that it was really the community itself that gave birth to the sacred traditions. If this is the case, and if these traditions are indeed inspired by God, then it is within the community, and not merely in select members of that community, that inspiration is operative. Those who first recognized the action of God within their history and then developed a tradition to testify to that action, those who later reshaped that tradition in order that it speak to a new community at a new time, and those who set the tradition down in its final form were all communities inspired by God. From this perspective, the biblical text itself is not seen as the initial expression of inspiration; rather, this text is the written form that has since become normative. The Bible represents one point in the long process of divine inspiration. It was preceded by the inspired growth and development of religious traditions, and it frequently has been followed by the inspired reinterpretation of those traditions.

Before proceeding to a discussion of the process of inspiration, we must pose a crucial question: Just *what* is inspired? Is it the author? And how is this last question answered if one thinks that the community rather than select individuals authored the Bible? Are the words inspired? But then, *which* words? Would it be the ones used in the first expression of the traditions, words that probably have been lost in history? Or the words of the final text, in the original languages? And what about translations? And further, which versions of the translations? These are all very important questions and will not be neglected, but a more fundamental question has to do with the way inspiration operates within the community. The other questions will be addressed within that context.

Our earlier discussion about the formation of tradition will serve as the framework for this discussion of inspiration. Not every event left a lasting mark on the consciousness of the community. Only those events that helped to shape and refine their fundamental faith became central to the tradition. A particular event itself may have been either momentous or outwardly insignificant. It was the religious meaning of the event that was cherished and handed down from generation to generation. Those who had the actual experience saw it as contributing to their identity and to their life. By transmitting this formative tradition to others, they were inviting these others to be formed by the tradition just as they had been. Thus, there was a dimension to the tradition that was continually formative.

Now, if it was the dynamic power of God that fashioned a people in the first place, what but the same dynamic power could continue this process of formation? It must be noted here that a mutual formation was taking place: As the community formulated the tradition, so the tradition formed, that is, influenced, the self-identity of the community. The dynamic force operative in the development of the people was God's self-disclosure. The dynamic force operative in the development of the tradition was God's inspiration. Thus, it should become apparent that to limit inspiration to but one moment in this development is to confine God's activity to that moment.

Difficult as it may be, it is possible to trace the development of a tradition. The same cannot be said about tracing the movement of inspiration. The former is a verifiable human endeavor; the latter is by definition a divine activity and calls for, and is accessible only by means of, faith. A community of faith believes that God is revealed in its midst and communicates with the people through their religious traditions. These traditions will be revered as inspired as long as God is perceived as speaking through them. Since the dynamic faith of the community claims that God is not bound to the past but brings the power of the past into the newness of the present with an openness to the future, then, correspondingly, God's inspiration must be seen as ongoing. To the extent that a tradition continues to be open to God's communication, it can be said to be inspired. Traditions that originated in the past must continue to speak to the active presence of God in the ongoing life of the community. The Bible *was* inspired, for during its growth and development it continually formed a believing community. The Bible *is* inspired, for it has not ceased to perform this same wonder, giving witness even to this day to the community's origin and continually awakening it to its purpose.

INSPIRATION AND TRUTH

When one claims that God is the author of the Bible, one is thereby making a statement about its truthfulness. Surely the word of God is trustworthy. God would not deceive the community, nor would God allow the community to be led astray by either the ignorance or the limited perspectives of the human authors. In following this train of thought, many people have insisted that the Bible is inerrant, or free from all error. Such a claim raises several difficult questions.

How does one explain differing and even contradictory traditions? (Human beings were created after the plants and animals appeared—Gen 1:12, 21, 25, 27. Human beings were created while the earth was still uninhabited—Gen 2:5, 9.) Must one adhere to a perception of the universe that is contrary to scientific findings? (Light itself was created before the heavenly bodies that give off light—Gen 1:3, 16.) Can one reconcile conflicting chronology in the Gospel story? (Jesus cleansed the temple at the beginning of his ministry during one of his several visits to Jerusalem—John 2:13-17. The cleansing occurred during his only visit, which took place just before his death—Matt 21:12-17; Mark 11:15-19; Luke 19:45-48.)

Efforts to explain the inconsistencies found within the Bible have resulted in various methods of interpretation. Those who have opted for fundamentalist interpretations have frequently spurned historical and scientific evidence and have adopted the literal sense of the text, claiming that there are no real inconsistencies, for God can do even the impossible if need be.

Another approach attempts to reconcile the theory of inerrancy with the discrepancies present within the text. The Scriptures are taken quite literally until one comes upon a difficult passage. Then, believing that God's revelation can be neither illogical nor inaccurate, the interpreter concludes that what appears to be an inconsistency is really meant to be interpreted allegorically. Thus, what could otherwise be seen as discordant is harmonized.

A third way of resolving the dilemma is to make a decision about the kind of truth the Bible is intended to reveal. Biblical scholars have done just that, distinguishing between historical and/or scientific truth and religious truth—not an easy decision to make. Historical, scientific, and religious references are found to be intertwined. It is not always clear why the authors expressed ideas as they did. If their historical and scientific references are not to be understood as accurate expressions of theological truth, were they merely the best literary and figurative constructions available? Or is the very human, very limited understanding of reality simply the platform from which they launched their profound theological search for God and upon which the drama of God's loving involvement unfolded? However these questions are answered, one must decide which guidelines are to be followed when making the distinctions mentioned. Attempting to focus on what in the text is truly theological, critical biblical scholarship has taken great pains to be as honest as possible in applying literary and historical methods of research. In this way it has thrown new light on the question of the truthfulness of the Bible.

At this juncture something should be said about what is meant by "truth." Is it to be understood as something akin to honesty, integrity, the antithesis of deception? Or does it also imply precision, accuracy of fact, freedom from mistake?

Contemporary scholarship insists that the Bible is indeed inspired by God, but inspired through the natural process of the growth and development of tradition. Since the Bible is not merely the record of God's word but also of the human response to that word, the character of human authorship cannot be disregarded. Obvious discrepancies and apparent contradictions may be attributed to human error, but they may also result from those interpretations and reinterpretations produced by the living community over generations of tradition development. Both the needs of a specific community of faith and the particular insights it had into its religious tradition may also have influenced the quality or limitation of theological expression that emerged from the transmission of tradition. One would certainly not reject as either inadequate or in error the theology of Isaiah or Jeremiah simply because the prophets did not refer to or believe in the Trinity or in life after death.

The biblical traditions have been described as testimonies. The focus of the last section was on the very human composition of those testimonies. The issue in this section is the relationship between the testimonies and the revelation of God to which they testify. This relationship has been understood in significantly different ways, depending upon how one has come to understand inspiration. Those who hold that the words are inspired are more likely to revere the Bible itself as revelation. Others who believe that God is revealed primarily in the events of history are more inclined to regard the Bible as the interpreted testimony to those events. According to this latter view, the Bible is a witness to revelation. The basic difference between these two views, in essence, is the difference between what is said and what is meant. While both perspectives are indeed aspects of the same reality, they most certainly are not identical. Knowing what the Bible says is not the same as knowing what the Bible means.

A study of tradition development indicates that what the community cherished was not primarily some specific expression of the tradition but rather the fundamental meaning of it. Were this not the case, the community consistently would have resisted any attempt at reformulation.

As stated earlier, the dynamic force operative in the development of the people was God's self-disclosure. The dynamic force operative in the development of the tradition was God's inspiration. The Bible claims to be not only a testimony to God's self-disclosure and to the community's transformation in the past, but also a unique occasion for a comparable disclosure and transformation in the present. To the extent that this claim is verified again and again, the truthfulness of the Bible can be affirmed. It is not so much the accuracy of the words but rather the power of the message that bears witness to its truthfulness. The same Spirit that was operative in the formation of the Scriptures continues to bear witness to its truthfulness and to convince us of its inspired nature. Therein lies the authority of the Bible.

TEXTS AND VERSIONS

Anyone beginning the study of the Bible is quickly aware of the number of versions that are available. Why are there so many? Which one is the best? Questions such as these touch upon another very complicated but fundamental issue of biblical investigation—that of textual criticism. This particular aspect of biblical scholarship will be examined in some detail in the section on interpretation, or hermeneutics. Here attention will be given to the various texts themselves rather than to the method of examining them.

There are several reasons for the variety of biblical versions. The most obvious one is a difference in translations. One language does not easily lend itself to a literal translation in another, and translators have to make decisions about the choice of words and phrases used. Some translators made one choice, others make another; hence different translations result. This issue will be addressed at greater length below.

Another reason for some of the differences is scribal error. We all know how easy it is to make mistakes when transcribing something. If we add to this very human, very common occurrence the fact that scribes had to work long hours with manuscripts written in languages seldom their own, then the repetitions, omissions, and mistranslations are understandable. Only by pursuing the meticulous task of comparing various texts (and this is a task of textual criticism) can one correct some of these errors. As more of the ancient texts are found, more corrections can be made.

These two explanations presume that there was one common biblical version, and from this came different translations, some of which had suffered from occasional scribal error. A third reason given for the variety of translations has implications that reach deeper into the tradition. Scholars believe that even though there may have been lists indicating which books were included in the canon of inspired writings, in many cases there was not one fixed, standard text. Rather, several very similar but still different versions of the tradition were in existence. This explanation would account for some of the real discrepancies found in the modern versions.

Until recent times the earliest available complete editions of the Hebrew version of the Old Testament could be traced back no further than the fifteenth century. We know now that these editions were based on a very limited selection of manuscripts, some of which are no longer available to us for study. The earliest Greek versions containing both Testaments date from the fourth century; some fragments of books are even older. Archaeological discoveries of the twentieth century have brought the number of these manuscripts or fragments of manuscripts to the thousands. They have been classified on the basis of both material used (papyrus or parchment) and the style of writing (block-lettered uncials or cursive minuscules).

Papyrus came from a tall, reed-like plant that grows abundantly along the Nile River. It was the customary stationery of the Mediterranean world. The stem was cut lengthwise and the strips laid side by side to form a layer. The layers were then laid at right angles and pressed together to form a sheet. After being dried, they were glued together to form a scroll, which was then rolled around a stick. Scrolls averaged about thirty-five feet in length. At some time during the second century the church began to use a new format. Sheets of papyrus were sown rather than glued together, thus producing a kind of book that has come to be referred to as a "codex." While it was relatively inexpensive, papyrus became brittle with age. Hence a new, costlier, but more durable material gradually came into use. The skins of sheep and goats, once they were scraped and dried, were found to provide a smooth surface for writing. This parchment, or vellum, as it is called, soon became the most commonly used material.

Most of the early texts that have been preserved were written in large blocklike letters. This is true not only of the Hebrew, whose script was relatively square, but of the Greek as well. The influence of ancient Greek inscriptions that used only capital letters (uncials) is recognized in early Greek manuscripts. For this reason, these manuscripts have come to be known by the same name—uncials. This form of block-writing was prominent until the ninth century, when cursive script came into popular use. This script enabled the scribes to copy manuscripts much more quickly and thus to make more copies available. These more numerous copies, however, were not necessarily easier to read. Cursive script, like its uncial counterpart, gave its name to a manuscript form—minuscule.

TRANSMISSION OF OLD TESTAMENT TEXTS

The first edition of the Old Testament that can in any way be called critical did not appear until the sixteenth century. Along with the complete text, it included a system of markings that represented vowel sounds (Hebrew is a consonantal language), an Aramaic paraphrase of the Hebrew text (Targum), and some of the traditional medieval Jewish commentary. This edition was a marked improvement over those that preceded it. They were based on earlier manuscripts which, as contemporary critical scholarship has shown, were quite limited in comprehension and inferior in legibility and accuracy. The sixteenth-century edition became the norm for most of the Hebrew Bibles until 1929, when members of a German Bible Society published a very sophisticated critical edition. This work, which has undergone periodic revision, continues to enjoy a place of prominence in some circles today. This German edition includes mention of variant readings as well as citations from the Septuagint.

Two discoveries in Egypt at the turn of the century offered the scholarly world a preview of things to come. It was customary in many medieval synagogues to store copies of the sacred texts in a specially designated room, since these texts were not to be destroyed, even when they ceased to be useful. In a Cairo synagogue one such room, or *geniza*, was found to contain a treasury of eleventh- and twelfth-century manuscripts, including several biblical variants. In addition to the biblical and liturgical content of the manuscripts, the material revealed a primitive system for facilitating pronunciation. Studying these findings, scholars have been able to trace the development of vowel pointing, a procedure originally intended to aid public proclamation, which eventually became part of the Hebrew language.

The second discovery was a papyrus manuscript dating from about 150 B.C.E. and containing the Ten Commandments and a liturgical passage from the sixth chapter of Deuteronomy. These findings would have to await the revelation of the Dead Sea Scrolls before their value could be properly assessed and appreciated.

The year 1947 proved to be a milestone in the world of text criticism. In that year ancient scrolls were discovered in caves in the vicinity of the Dead Sea. The first finds occurred at a place known as Qumran. Manuscripts dating as far back as 250–175 B.C.E. were uncovered. Other fragments were found up and down the region of the Dead Sea well into 1964. About 190 manuscripts or fragments have been discovered in sites that date back to the first and second centuries of the Common Era. A comparison of the variant texts shows that the Jewish communities of this time had not yet standardized their traditions. They may have reached some agreement about which books were inspired, but they also tolerated a great diversity of textual expression.

This extensive material has not yet been completely translated and evaluated. Nonetheless, any critical edition of the Hebrew Scriptures must take into account the knowledge gleaned from these findings if it is to be considered a fully reliable version of the Old Testament.

The history of the Greek version of the Old Testament is no less complicated. As mentioned earlier, the tradition about the seventy scholars working independently yet producing identical translations is now considered legendary. Comparisons of early Hebrew manuscripts with Aramaic Targums and Greek versions have provided invaluable insights. At the same time, such comparisons have left scholars with many new questions. One of the first questions to be addressed is: Was the Greek translation made from the particular Hebrew version that eventually became the standard version known as the Masoretic Text? According to the study of the transmission of the text summarized above, the answer is no. The Masoretic Text, though a careful reconstruction from early manuscripts, does not claim to originate before the Common Era. In addition, the standardization of the Hebrew version apparently did not take place before the second century of that era. The Greek or Alexandrian version, on the other hand, claims a third-century B.C.E. origin. Most likely there was no unified Hebrew tradition used by the translators.

The translation itself shows textual inconsistencies. Most scholars agree that the books of the Pentateuch probably achieved comparative standardization during the postexilic period. That might be true not only of the content but also of the textual form. This standardization could explain why the translation of this material appears to be quite consistent with and faithful to a Hebrew text very similar to the one behind the Masoretic Text. The same is not true of the translation of the other books of the Old Testament; this process probably developed over a period of two hundred years. Since there was no standardization of the Hebrew, there would be no uniformity in the Greek.

One is led to ask a second question: From what was the Greek translated if not from a standardized Hebrew text? There were probably many sources. The first to be considered is the variety of Hebrew renderings which existed along with those that ultimately became the standard texts but which were not themselves included in that group. Translation of the Greek back into Hebrew and a comparison of that Hebrew with the Masoretic Text have led scholars to believe that some of the Hebrew tradition behind the Septuagint is older than that behind the Masoretic Text.

A second source came from the liturgical texts of the community. As Greek became the language of the people and knowledge of Hebrew became less and less common, the people devised a way of translating the Hebrew sounds into Aramaic. In this way they could still pray the Hebrew while reading it in Aramaic. These transliterations were known as Targums. They, too, provided biblical material that could be used in a Greek translation.

Finally, the New Testament itself has thrown some light on this question. As noted earlier, most of the citations from the Old Testament that are found in the New Testament were taken from the Greek version. Retranslating them back into Hebrew has, in some cases, uncovered a version more in line with the Samaritan Pentateuch than with any other extant Hebrew source.

These three examples suggest that when the biblical traditions were being translated into Greek, whatever Hebrew versions were in use at that time and in that place by that community were the ones that were translated. Because the Hebrew tradition was rather fluid, the Greek version would be no less variant.

The second century saw the Christians and the Jews in heated controversy. The Christians frequently used the Septuagint in their arguments, and this led the Jews to reject that version and to produce new translations of their own. Three of those translations played a role in text criticism that their authors and proponents could never have imagined. The third-century Christian writer Origen produced a sixfold version of the Old Testament called the Hexapla. He arranged his material in six parallel columns in this order: (1) the Hebrew consonantal text that was standard in the second century; (2) a Greek transliteration of the Hebrew; (3) Aquila's Greek version (one of the Jewish translations); (4) Symmachus' Greek version (another Jewish translation); (5) the Septuagint; (6) Theodotion's Greek version (the third Jewish translation). This monumental work has survived in fragments as well as in citations of it made by various early Christian writers.

Of all of the versions of the Old Testament, it was the Septuagint that served as the basis for the major manuscripts. These major manuscripts are the uncial codices that have come down from the fourth to the tenth centuries.

TRANSMISSION OF NEW TESTAMENT TEXTS

Within the last century archaeological findings have unearthed papyrus fragments of New Testament manuscripts that date as early as the second century. Prior to that time the oldest available copies of the New Testament were the great uncial codices mentioned above. There are four major witnesses and several less important works in this category: (1) Codex B or Vaticanus, so named because it has been preserved in the Vatican Library, is probably the oldest, dating from the fourth century. Though it must have once included the entire Greek Bible, it is missing certain sections today. (2) Codex א or Sinaiticus is the only version containing the entire New Testament. Although it, too, dates to the fourth century, it was relatively unknown until the nineteenth century, when it was found at the Monastery of Saint Catherine on Mount Sinai—hence the name. (3) Codex A or Alexandrinus is a fifth-century work. Like the other manuscripts, it is now incomplete. It may have received its name from the city Alexandria, renowned for its school of biblical interpretation. (4) Codex D or Bezae dates from the fifth or sixth century. It lacks an Old Testament as well as some New Testament material. It is a polyglot Bible, that is, it is written in more than one language. The Greek and the Latin are given on facing pages. The work is named after Theodore Beza, the successor of John Calvin.

One other codex might be of interest. It is Codex C or Ephraemi Rescriptus. The very name tells us that rewriting *(rescriptus)* has occurred. The earlier writing, probably a fifth-century Bible, was scraped off, and the skin was reused in the twelfth century to preserve some of the writings of Ephraem. Such was the fate of many biblical manuscripts. This codex is a famous example of reused manuscripts, called "palimpsests."

As mentioned earlier, the ninth century saw a kind of revolution in writing. Cursive (running hand) began to replace uncial (block) writing. This resulted in a new and quite extensive category of biblical manuscripts that date from the ninth on into the eighteenth century.

In addition to the uncial and minuscule manuscripts, another source of information about the New Testament tradition is evidence from early theological works. Early church writers, such as Eusebius and Clement, cited the Scriptures in their writings. Examination of these citations has been invaluable for text criticism.

Not until the sands of Egypt yielded their papyrus treasures in the late nineteenth century were scholars able to reconstruct a New Testament text that dated earlier than the fourth century. Some of the fragments that have been recently found can be traced to the second century, only a century or less away from the original composition. Although only fragments have been found, they show that at least in second-century Egypt there was no dominant type of New Testament text.

Finally, the importance of ancient liturgical texts is beginning to be appreciated. Since worship played such an important role in forming believers in the biblical tradition, these texts should be very enlightening. Because the study of lectionaries is only in its initial stage, no definite statement can be made at this time about their contribution to the study of the text.

With all the various text sources—uncials, minuscules, citations from early church writers, lectionary readings—how is one to decide on a single text? Certainly the reconstruction of a complete New Testament is more than a subjective selection from various manuscripts. One of the most famous responses to that question is a version known as the Textus Receptus (TR), or "Received Text." The phenomenon of printing perhaps more than the excellence of scholarship brought this work of a printer-editor to the public. Until recently, versions that grew out of this edition remained prominent for many Protestant Christians. However, current scholarship has furnished us with more manuscript evidence, and therefore a truer reconstruction of the text is possible.

One way this has been accomplished is by a process of classifying all the data into categories of families of texts. The quality of the Greek used, the literary style employed, and the content are all evaluated in this process. Once this has been done, editors can confine themselves to manuscripts with similar characteristics as they attempt to reconstruct the text. In the late nineteenth century the New Testament texts were classified into four main groups:

1) Neutral texts were thought to be the earliest and purest forms. They were free from emendations and deliberate reinterpretation, and were considered the common tradition of the entire Eastern church.

2) Alexandrian texts were named for the literary center in Egypt. These texts had considerable style and polish.

3) Western texts were preferred by the Western Christian writers and were clearly edited and interpolated to reflect that bias.

4) Syrian texts were marked by a combination of readings from the other groups. They showed great similarity to the Byzantine tradition.

New archaeological discoveries and diligent reexamination of these categories have resulted in refinements in the classifications. Collation and evaluation of the material have not yet been completed, and so scholars do not yet have all the information necessary to arrive at a consensus regarding the groupings. The present study does not require more detailed information about this field. It is enough to know that steps have been taken to enable scholars to work with a particular textual tradition and thus arrive at as good a text as possible.

This brief summary of the history of the transmission of texts and of the discovery of new evidence is intended to provide some initial explanation for the many versions of the Bible. If contemporary editions appear to be saying quite different things, the reason may be that they have originated from different textual sources. One edition might base its translation on evidence derived from an uncial manuscript, while another judges the Qumran reading as superior. A good critical edition will identify its sources so that the enlightened reader will know from which text tradition the reading has come.

ANCIENT VERSIONS

As both the Jewish and the Christian religious traditions spread into new areas, the need to translate the original languages became obvious. We have already seen that it was this need that prompted the creation of the Septuagint and other Greek versions. It also led to the formation of Aramaic paraphrases known as Targums. Gradually the original Hebrew and Greek manuscripts of both Testaments, as well as the Septuagint and the Targum versions, were translated into other ancient languages. Chief among these were Syriac, Latin, Coptic, and Ethiopic. Some of these ancient versions continue to play significant roles in the study of the early Bible.

We all know from a study of ancient history that after Alexander the Great conquered the world in the fourth century, Greek culture and the Greek language began to dominate the ancient world. What we may have overlooked is that since about the fifth century B.C.E., Aramaic remained the international language of the Fertile Crescent. This situation endured well into the Common Era. Targums began to appear in the last centuries B.C.E. and on into the medieval period. They continue to be a source of Jewish study today.

In addition to the Samaritan Pentateuch, the Targums, and the Masoretic Text, the *Syriac* writings also stem from the Hebrew version rather than from the Septuagint. Two works from this tradition will be noted. Mention has already been made of Tatian's Diatessaron, the harmonization of the four Gospel accounts into one narrative. This document was the official Syrian Gospel until the fifth century. That same century saw the wide acceptance of a Syriac version of the Old and New Testaments. This Bible is really a blending of several sources. The Old Testament was probably based on the Hebrew version, but with Targumic and Septuagint influences. The New Testament shows several Syrian characteristics. This Bible is known as the Peshitta, the "simple" version.

The most widely known *Latin* version is Jerome's Vulgate, which was the authoritative text of the Roman Catholic Bible from the time of the Council of Trent until recently. Although Jerome was undoubtedly influenced by the Septuagint and some Latin versions stemming from it, the Old Testament section of the Vulgate is a translation from the Hebrew. The New Testament, however, does come from Old Latin versions. Some scholars think that Jerome revised only the Gospels, leaving the rest of the rendition for someone else to complete.

Coptic is an Egyptian language written in the Greek alphabet. This fact would render translation from the Greek much easier than from the Hebrew version of the Old Testament. The Coptic Bible itself does not derive from one tradition but from several recensions, or editorial revisions. This makes the quality of the work rather uneven. As is often the case, the New Testament is more consistent than the Old, probably because fewer New Testament sources were used, and those that were employed were more standardized.

The language of Ethiopia, like Hebrew and Aramaic, is a Semitic language. However, the Old Testament of the *Ethiopic* Bible derives from the Greek version, not the Hebrew. In fact, it is one of the most reliable witnesses to the unrevised Septuagint. The New Testament is the section that shows the most revision and is consequently discounted as a reliable version.

MODERN ENGLISH VERSIONS

The past few decades have seen a proliferation of new English versions of the Bible. A noteworthy development of the ecumenical period in which we live is the interconfessional character of the committees working on the translating and editing of such projects.

One of the most memorable facets of Martin Luther's revolt was the priority he placed on biblical interpretation and the accusations he hurled at the Catholic church for its use (or, according to him, its misuse) of the Scriptures. From that time until the recent past, the Bible has been seen as a kind of measuring stick for one's orthodoxy, each side of the dispute deciding upon the criteria of measurement. While the Protestants encouraged personal reading of the Scriptures and accepted a certain amount of private interpretation, the Catholic church discouraged and even forbade the practice.

It was with great caution that the first English version of the Bible appeared in print. The New Testament appeared at Rheims in 1582, followed by the Old Testament at Douay in 1609. These were the works of English Roman Catholic scholars who had been exiled or fled from their homeland because of religious persecution and settled in France. This version, the Douay-Rheims retained exclusive authoritative status in the Catholic church until 1943, when Pope Pius XII issued the encyclical *Divino Afflante Spiritu*, encouraging Catholic scholars to return to manuscripts written in the original languages in an effort to produce new translations. The Douay-Rheims version of Latin Vulgate manuscripts was in accord with the Council of Trent's designation of that version as authoritative. About 150 years after its appearance, it was revised to bring the English in line with the development that the language had undergone. With the exception of that one revision, the Douay-Rheims remained standard until recent times.

Although the first English Bibles produced by Protestants appeared sometime in the fourteenth century, the one that enjoyed the greatest prominence for the longest time was the King James Version (KJV). It was commissioned by King James I of England and completed in 1611. A careful study of the text reveals that the committee relied heavily on several existing translations, the Rheims New Testament included. Because the Vulgate version was superior to many of the Greek codices available at that time, and because the King James Version was based on editions that relied on the inferior Textus Receptus, which utilized those Greek manuscripts, we can easily see why the King James Version underwent a major revision. The original edition was called the Authorized Version (AV), and the revision, which appeared about 250 years later, came to be known as the Revised Version (RV). The King James Version is renowned for its eloquence and lyrical quality. Quotations from this work have been woven into much of the music and literature of the English-speaking world. The beauty and artistry with which this has been done contribute to the difficulty many people have experienced in accepting a new revision of the text.

Since most of the manuscript discoveries occurred well after the appearance of the King James Version and its Revised Version, a new and even more comprehensive revision seemed in order. Some claim that the Revised Standard Version (RSV), which appeared in 1946, is in fact a new translation because the committee that produced it used all of the new text evidence that was available. Others contend that because the committee was instructed to stay as close to the King James tradition as possible, it must rightly be called a revision. Whatever the case may be, despite initial fundamentalist reaction against relinquishing the King James Version, the Revised Standard Version finally established itself as one of the best English versions of the time. Although the work was done under Protestant auspices, the Revised Standard Version received Catholic ecclesiastical approval in 1966 and has continued to be used by Catholics in educational as well as liturgical settings.

Another edition that has been quite popular in recent years is the Jerusalem Bible (JB), which appeared in 1954. Most of the translation was done from the original languages, yet it was carried out under the direct influence of the French version, *La Bible de Jérusalem*, thus producing what some have called a translation of a translation. This edition is replete with introductions, explanatory notes, and cross references, making it a helpful tool for study.

In 1970 several denominations of the British Isles published the New English Bible (NEB). The project was not bound to any prior biblical version or tradition. It was free to avoid unfamiliar non-English idioms in favor of modern expressions. Evidence from the latest archaeological finds was used, and variant readings are often cited in footnotes. Some of the English is more British than American, but this is to be expected from a British work that attempts to bring the best biblical witness to a contemporary audience.

Finally, the major American Catholic effort at translation has been the New American Bible (NAB). What was begun in 1941 as the Confraternity of Christian Doctrine (CCD) Version was eventually published in 1970 under the new title. Going directly to the best manuscripts in the original languages, the translating committee, which included Protestant scholars, left behind the strictures placed upon Catholic biblical scholarship by the Council of Trent.

All the versions reviewed here have strengths and weaknesses. Some are especially concerned with refinement of translation, and when critical choices have to be made, they tend to sacrifice points of fluency in favor of fidelity to the original. Others opt for a smooth-flowing rendition, forfeiting precision of translation. Still other readings are quite colloquial, a feature which might be beneficial for certain communities but which also limits the version to those groups.

A final point should be made. The Revised Standard Version and the New American Bible are being replaced by new translations. These new versions will be new translations, not revisions of the respective versions. Thus, new and ever more accurate readings of the biblical texts are being produced in order to bring the word of God closer to the people of God.

HERMENEUTICS

INTERPRETATION

One of the most exciting and challenging issues in contemporary biblical study is that of interpretation, or hermeneutics. Not only has it captured the imagination of scholarship, but it has also caused considerable confusion for the general public. Just what precisely *does* the Bible mean? Among the many conflicting interpretations, which one is right? Which school of interpretation or which particular scholar is one to follow? A closer look at this complex and controversial issue, while it certainly will not answer all these questions with satisfaction, may throw some light on the sources of some of the confusion about the meaning of the biblical text.

We must remember that the Bible, as a basic literary reality, is a form of communication comprised of three principal components: a sender or author; a message or text; and a receiver or audience. Historically, as long as the communication recorded in the biblical texts remained within the community of its origin, the audience required very little interpretation. Most of the audience belonged to the same world of meaning as did the author. It was only when a particular biblical message was carried into another world of meaning that extensive efforts of interpretation became necessary. Inevitably, different understandings resulted, depending primarily upon whether the major interpretative focus was principally on the sender, the message, or the receiver.

The message

It seems that throughout the earliest centuries of Christianity the primary focus of most interpretations was on the message. Hence, the interpretative task was to translate this message into the new world or worlds of meaning. By the Middle Ages four distinct types of interpretation of the message had been developed. They have survived the march of time and continue to influence the way many people today understand the Bible. They are: the literal, the allegorical, the moral, and the eschatological. Since these specific designations may be unfamiliar to the reader, a brief look at each will provide some understanding.

The *literal* sense of a text usually refers to a meaning that the words themselves convey. In this case the text is accepted at face value. Such an understanding implies that the audience immediately grasps all the nuances of the language in the very manner intended by the author. This understanding may be readily available whenever both author and audience share the same world view. However, an audience that holds a very different world view will not so easily grasp the author's intention. The elusiveness of the literal sense becomes obvious when we reflect, for example, on how quickly the meaning of words changes. Parents of teenagers frequently stand dumbfounded as they listen to their children speak an English that has absolutely no meaning for them. Basically, the two worlds of meanings—that of the parents and that of their teenagers—simply do not coincide completely; thus they cannot understand one another fully.

Rigidly literal or fundamentalistic interpretations of biblical texts often fail to take into account the undeniable change and development of language. Biblical fundamentalists seem reluctant to recognize that the world of meaning, the world view of the biblical texts, is not the same as the contemporary one. Add to this the fact that the Bible is the product of a different culture and a different time, and the need for interpretation is magnified. The literal sense of the Bible, then, while it may seem the most reasonable and likely one, is not always arrived at with the ease that some claim.

The *allegorical* sense of Scripture, especially prominent in the early centuries of the Christian era as well as in the Middle Ages, opens the Bible to a myriad of interpretations. According to this approach, the text really intends to say something other than that which its literal wording suggests. The contention is that deeper mystical meanings lie hidden beneath the words. Actually, these alleged deeper meanings usually originate from outside the biblical text itself and are brought to it by interpreters who read meanings into the images and actions of the text from their own world view. For example, the story of Mary of Bethany listening to Jesus while Martha prepares a meal was allegorically interpreted to mean that the contemplative life symbolized by Mary is a higher call than the active life symbolized by Martha. Yet, this was hardly a concern of the original author. Thus, there can be as many allegorical interpretations of one text as there are interpreters with their various points of view. Hence, while a text may yield a rich breadth of meanings, these may seem arbitrary, subjective, and remote from the more immediately apparent message of the text.

In the *moral* sense, the text is understood primarily in terms of the spiritual life of every individual believer. For example, anyone and everyone is Abraham called into a new relationship with God. The political liberation of ancient Israel is understood as really describing the personal freedom that salvation brings to the soul of the individual believer. Although this method of interpretation has frequently been employed by spiritual writers to nourish the interior lives of religious persons, it has serious deficiencies. The Bible's communal sense is frequently lost, and social responsibilities are often overlooked. The historical references are minimized in importance, and the text sometimes seems to be forced to fit an interpreter's predetermined format.

The fourth approach is called *eschatological.* It refers to the spiritual meaning of the text as this pertains to the future heavenly or eschatological realities. According to this sense, the "promised land" is neither historical Israel, as a literal interpretation would indicate, nor the church of Christ, as an allegorical sense might suggest, nor the soul of the redeemed Christian, as the moral sense would assert. It is the future kingdom of heaven. This kind of interpretation, which was so common in the later Middle Ages and well into the modern era, tended to minimize the importance of life in this world. Everything was focused on the next life. Like the moral sense, this manner of understanding principally served the devotional lives of the people. Whether it did justice to the biblical text is an altogether different question.

As stated earlier, these four senses of Scripture continue to influence the way many people today understand the Bible. Some of the current confusion may stem from the diverse perspectives employed in the individual approaches as well as from any mixture of the four. Traces of all these approaches frequently surface in contemporary preaching and are prominent in certain contemporary devotional literature.

The sender

One outgrowth of the Reformation was a persistent attempt to avoid any trace of dogmatic or theological bias in the interpretation of the Bible. Many of the Reformers were particularly critical of the manner in which (they alleged) the Roman church was dealing with the Bible. They insisted that the Bible was being misused to bolster official doctrine not at all rooted in the Bible, and demanded that the original meaning of the text rather than a subjective or denominational interpretation be sought.

This concern brought a halt to the allegorizing tendencies of much of biblical scholarship. While this style of interpretation persisted among Roman Catholics, most Protestant scholars and communities began to stress the historical background of the Bible. Thus began the historical-critical movement, that is, a broad enterprise among predominantly Protestant biblical scholars to seek for the meaning of a biblical text by pursuing a careful investigation and analysis of its historical background. It was not until very recently that this movement gained prominence in

Catholic circles. It had been encouraged since the time of Pope Pius XII (1943) and was given broad endorsement at the Second Vatican Council (Dogmatic Constitution on Divine Revelation).

The focus had now shifted from the multiple meanings of the message or text to the "real" meaning intended by the author. Thus, the biblical scholar now had to be as informed as possible about the circumstances surrounding the origins of the writings. Their historical, cultural, and religious settings took on new importance. The sources employed in their composition, the audiences for which they were intended, and the purposes they were to serve became the subjects that occupied the attention of interpreters.

The results of this shift in method were numerous. The Scriptures, while always recognized as inspired, began to be appreciated as human expressions of the faith of a people. From this human perspective, contemporary women and men could now see their ancient counterparts as being engaged in the very same struggles of life as they themselves were and are. They began to read the biblical narratives with renewed enthusiasm. Biblical theology came to occupy a significant place in their lives. They sought to respond to God's presence in their own history, as their ancestors of biblical times had done. The biblical revival ushered in by the historical-critical movement undoubtedly brought new life to the church.

The study of Scripture quickly became a very sophisticated undertaking. Those untrained in the method frequently grew discouraged with both its demands and some of its first fruits. Some felt that the very foundation of their faith was now being shattered by findings that did not square with their own devotional, allegorical, moral, or eschatological interpretations. Those who did acquire some facility in the approach and could appreciate its value, however, soon had to acknowledge its inadequacies. They could see that it was not enough to know the theology of the past. The questions they were grappling with had to do with the applicability of the biblical message to the present: Does biblical theology have any relevance for our day? If so, how is one to translate into the present a theological message of another era, another culture, another world view?

These questions led scholars to look beyond historical criticism and to turn to the issue of hermeneutics, or interpretation. But even this turn did not seem to be enough. More radical and more comprehensive questions were surfacing. Did revelation only occur thousands of years ago? Are we merely to reenact in our lives the saving events of the past? A second significant interpretative shift was about to take place.

The receiver

Attention is now being focused on the receiver, or the audience. This means that the contemporary interpreter and the act of interpreting have now become the objects of the analysis. The historical-critical method assumes that an objective understanding of the original meaning is possible. Such a position ignores the fact that the interpreter comes to the text with historical and religious biases. The new methods of interpretation admit that the way the text is understood depends to a large extent upon the socio-political and religious perspectives of the interpreter. Thus, for example, people from a situation of political, economic, or religious oppression will view the Bible quite differently than will those from a secure and comfortable vantage point.

This new approach is only in its infancy and therefore cannot yet be adequately evaluated. However, some very exciting and challenging results have already been achieved. Women and men are beginning to appreciate their own lives as the stage wherein revelation, as authentic as that revelation described in the biblical texts, is taking place. Biblical spirituality is no longer concerned exclusively with the individual. It has reclaimed its communal dimension.

CONTEMPORARY HERMENEUTICS

Another way to approach the question of interpretation is to distinguish between what the Bible *means* and what the Bible *meant.* As mentioned earlier, this is no problem when the authors and the audiences share the same worlds of meaning. It becomes an issue when cross-cultural and/or cross-generational communication no longer guarantee a common understanding. The professional scholars engaged in contemporary hermeneutics span a wide spectrum of positions regarding the major focus of these two poles. Some hold that the *real* meaning is that intended by the original author (what the Bible *meant*). Others contend that once a piece of literature leaves the hands of the author, it enjoys a life of its own, independent of authorial intention (what the Bible *means*). Most contemporary hermeneutical approaches can be found somewhere between these two poles, bridging the gap between the authorial intention and a present-day context.

Scholars today refer to authorial intention (what the Bible *meant*) as the literal sense. It is important to be clear as to the precise meaning of this designation. This way of understanding takes the words at face value, but it takes them as they were intended by the original author(s) or editor(s), not primarily as they have come to be understood today. A fundamentalist reading of Scripture understands the words in a literal sense too, but it ascribes contemporary meaning to them. The presupposition operative in this approach, though often unconsciously, is that today's world of meaning is identical with that of the ancient writers. A fundamentalist position claims to be able to arrive at the literal meaning merely by reading the text. Critical scholars, on the other hand, insist that extensive, precise historical analysis is required if the authors' world of meaning is to be unlocked. This critical analysis encompasses a large number of distinct but related methodologies. The principal ones will be discussed below.

Concentration on what the Bible *means* has led many scholars into studies that are less historical and more literary in character. Various literary theories have been examined and employed in biblical interpretation. This trend has led to further analysis of literary forms, study of the meaning of symbols, and probing into the very nature of language itself as a means of communication. Unlike historical studies, which strive to learn more about the world of the author in order to discover the original meaning, literary studies inevitably open the text to a plurality of meanings.

Without denying the importance and validity of each of these two approaches, many scholars believe that neither one is sufficient in itself. They insist that the Scriptures are more than literary works—they are also inspired tradition of an ongoing believing community. Thus, the literal sense plays a normative role in helping the present-day community come to an understanding of its identity and to an appreciation of the kind of lifestyles that should flow from that identity. If this is true, however, then different historical and/or cultural contexts will reinterpret and restate these biblical traditions in various ways. The result will be a plurality of valid meanings. The challenge of contemporary hermeneutics is to devise a method that will take both of these approaches into consideration. Such a method will be equipped to faithfully transmit the inspired tradition. Thus, a particular valid expression of the meaning of the text will function as the word of God, forming a new people into a community of believers.

HISTORICAL-CRITICAL APPROACHES

The phrase "historical-critical method" or "historical criticism" has been used so loosely and erroneously that the designation has become ambiguous and the usefulness of the interpretative approach has been questioned. As understood here, it is an approach that employs every available historical tool in an attempt to reconstruct history and to understand the documents which that history produced. Its goal is historical, and it works toward that goal critically and systematically. It seeks to understand and to interpret but not to judge the findings.

The nineteenth century saw a broadscale revolution in historical consciousness and the birth of a new historical theory. This led to the development of critical tools for studying the past. Sacred texts could not escape the critical eye of this kind of investigation. Soon believing communities were torn between the excitement of new discoveries, new interpretations, and new challenges to faith and the fear that what was exciting was also a potential threat to that faith. What had been cherished as "truth" was now questioned as "myth." Longstanding practices were viewed as irrelevant and lacking historical foundations.

Although there are still people who reject this critical approach as "faithless," it has come to be generally accepted. However, this acceptance does not imply that the historical methods have answered all the questions of interpretation. As a matter of fact, scholars now are becoming more and more convinced of their inadequacy. They are beginning to realize that more was expected of these methodologies than they could offer. The approach may succeed at addressing the historical issues, but it certainly is not adequate to uncover the theological issues. Realizing this, scholars continue to employ these historical methods, but not in a manner exclusive of other critical approaches.

Both biblical research and biblical spirituality are indebted to the historical approach. It has provided the believing community with critical editions of the Bible that far outstrip earlier editions in textual reconstruction and translation. It has thrown light on the life and history of both ancient Israel and early Christianity. It has brought the people of those times into sharper focus, enabling the reader to see them as real people whose concerns and dreams can be understood. It has revealed the depth of faith and the complexity and power of the religion of the believing communities.

Textual criticism

The function of textual criticism is twofold: (1) to reconstruct the original wording of a biblical text; (2) to trace the transmission of that text down through the centuries. The first goal is an impossible one. Since the autograph, or original copy, of every book of the Bible has been lost, the best that scholars can do is to reconstruct the text from manuscripts that are available. This task guarantees no historical certainty because of the inconsistency that exists in the manuscript material. It is by comparing manuscripts that scholars develop what is called a "critical text." This is a hypothetical reconstruction, usually accompanied by extensive footnotes (called critical apparatus) that indicate the manuscript sources of the passages as well as alternative readings. Modern translations are based on just such critical texts.

The second goal is also achieved by a comparison of texts, but with a different end in view. Reconstruction is a move backward toward one reading; the history of textual transmission is a search forward for variant readings that will enable the scholar to trace the change and development that took place. Origen's sixfold work called the Hexapla may well be the earliest attempt at such a textual criticism. It provides evidence of the changes that occurred as the text developed.

Since no manuscript contains the original text, all are more or less corrupt. The question is not which reading is reliable but in which way it is reliable. Every text reflects the period of history and the specific community from which it originated and within which it survived. Critical examination of the text and comparison with the variant texts tell us something about that period of history and that particular community. The translations reviewed in the previous chapter perform that same function. They reveal the particular stage of critical scholarship at which the community has arrived, the current stage of the language into which the text has been translated, and frequently some theological issues that the community must address.

This particular discipline requires expertise not only in the original languages but in related languages as well. Literature from cultures other than the biblical communities is studied in order to understand these biblical communities in the broader context of their respective worlds. While few people may devote themselves to this kind of research, the findings that derive therefrom must be considered by both translator and interpreter. Before any other interpretative step can be taken, the best possible rendition of the text must be established.

Much of the history of textual criticism, as well as explanations of the major manuscript sources and traditions, has been discussed in the previous section and need not be treated here.

Literary criticism

The term "literary criticism" is understood in at least three different ways. (1) In the classical sense it is the critical approach to the study of the literature. The structure, form, and language are analyzed. Such critique was brought to bear on biblical material, and as early as the time of Origen it led scholars to question the supposed authorship of some of the biblical books. (2) With the rise of historical consciousness in the nineteenth century, historical questions were being asked about literary differences, and the discipline came to be called "source criticism" by some. (3) Recently scholars have again been asking questions of a more literary nature, questions dealing with the relationship of content to form and with the philosophy of language.

Literary criticism in the traditional biblical sense actually grew out of a textual study. After noticing the use of different names for God in the Book of Genesis, an eighteenth-century scholar discovered literary patterns in that book. He concluded that the book had been composed of various preexisting sources. Eventually the explanation for the composition of the Pentateuch came to be known as the "Documentary Hypothesis" (four sources were "discovered": the Yahwist, the Elohist, the Deuteronomic, and the Priestly). Similarly, the explanation for the differences in the gospel tradition was called the "Two-Source Hypothesis" (it maintained that the Gospel of Mark and a collection of sayings known as Q were used by both Matthew and Luke). Once scholars believed that there were various sources for the biblical texts, they began to ask questions about their origins, their life settings, and the reason for their composition. Literary criticism thereby became a historical discipline.

With all the questions that were answered, literary criticism also raised some new ones that it seemed unable to address. The door was open to a new discipline that would address those questions. (New literary criticism will be explained later.)

Form criticism

The function of form criticism is to get behind the sources identified by literary criticism and to discover the life situations out of which they grew. Literary or source criticism may well be interested in authorship, but it still identifies this author in the singular. Form criticism, on the other hand, is interested in the original settings in the life of the community. It discovers these settings by identifying and analyzing the typical forms of expression found within the existing literature. Although it begins as a literary approach, its intent is to discover the historical setting and the historical function of the forms in order to understand their pre-literary (oral) stage.

Ancient Israel was probably not a highly literate culture. Thus, its oral forms of communication were most likely quite conventional. This would mean that before they attained literary form, these forms achieved a quite consistent oral expression. Such expressions were very much a part of the ordinary life of the community. Recognizing and interpreting these forms is the first step in gaining insight into that life.

In order to accomplish their task, form critics first examine the structure of the text so as to isolate the individual units of which it is composed. These units are then classified according to genre, or literary type. This classification leads directly to conclusions about the setting. Setting here does not refer to geographic location or to specific dating; rather, it refers to sociocultural situations that may or may not include a particular social or religious structure. For example, a study of the psalms of lament can tell us much, while at the same time leaving many things unanswered. A lament points to a human situation that may or may not be identified. These psalms frequently speak of social corruption and oppression or national calamity, although they also complain of personal misfortune. We know that psalms were part of the temple liturgy, but their use was not restricted to that site or to official liturgy. Thus, a lament reflects human suffering, but it is not always specific about that suffering. It suggests liturgical practice, but it was not limited to formal ritual. It was associated with the temple, but its use was not restricted to that religious institution.

The final step in the analysis of a particular form is to determine just what the genre was meant to accomplish within the community. Was the lament intended to inspire confidence in God? To offer a legitimate avenue for complaint? To serve as an admission of guilt and an acknowledgment of repentance?

Form criticism may appear to some to be a negative process, breaking down the biblical story. In fact, its goal is positive: to reconstruct the oral tradition behind the literary narrative. The forms are seen as the remnants of the early tradition. Hence, matching the fabrics, blending the colors, and discovering the designs enable scholars to detect something of the original piece.

As literary criticism grew out of textual study, so form criticism addresses questions that literary or source criticism could not answer—questions about origins and settings and reasons behind composition. But, like its predecessor, this discipline also had its limitations. It may have been able to identify the forms of the literary work, but it could not explain how they became part of the whole. Form criticism could take the text apart but could not put it back together. It would take tradition criticism to do that.

Tradition criticism

Tradition criticism, or tradition history, as it is sometimes called, is an analysis of the history of the transmission process of the traditions. It is that discipline which traces the growth and development of traditions as this process was described in the first section of this article. While form criticism locates the life-settings of the units, tradition criticism attempts to describe what happened within those settings. It is interested in what shaped the tradition as it was preserved and handed down, and it seeks to trace this development. Hence the name tradition *history*. Although it is really concerned with the process of transmission, it does examine the tradition that is being transmitted, primarily the oral stage of that tradition. (Redaction criticism examines the literary stages of this development. Some scholars treat redaction as a step in the tradition-history approach.)

The recurrence of similar motifs or forms makes tradition criticism possible. Various examples are analyzed in order to detect significant differences. (This process differs from form criticism, which highlights similarities.) Having uncovered the differences, the next step is to ascertain whether or not these differences are the result of development and, if so, to hypothesize as to the cause of that development. It is difficult enough to reconstruct literary history. When one is exploring the oral stages of a tradition, there is even less solid evidence available, and scholars must be on their guard lest their reconstructions be far afield of what the text actually says.

As scholars discover why the believing community preserved the traditions in the forms that it did and why these traditions went through the changes that occurred, they are able to reconstruct the tradition history of the community. In addition to this, their study also uncovers information that can be called historical, in the strict sense of that term. Streams of tradition have been found to be associated with one or another community or group, for example, the prophets or the Lukan community. Examining these streams of tradition brings one into contact with that group, with its preferences, its strategies, and its influence. Frequently traditions are also associated with specific locations. Jerusalem is a case in point. The more one knows about the site, the better one is able to reconstruct the traditioning process that took place there. All of this can aid in the discovery of the socio-political as well as the religious dynamics at work in the growth and development of the traditions.

The fruits of tradition criticism can perhaps be more directly appreciated by the average believer than can the findings of other disciplines that have so far been described. They tell us how ancient Israel understood its history. (Because the traditioning process that resulted in the New Testament took place in a considerably shorter span of time, it is usually studied under the heading of redaction criticism. Tradition criticism has become primarily an Old Testament discipline.) It also shows how significant events in that history have become types for understanding other experiences; for example, Exodus typology is often used to describe the Exile. Finally, tradition criticism shows how Israel understood the revelation of God. It was within the very process of tradition formation that Israel discerned the activity of God. As the community struggled to retain the validity of its inspired traditions within new situations and at new times, it recognized the active and directive involvement of God.

Redaction criticism

Redaction criticism is devoted to the study of how written sources were used by an editor or redactor and what this interpretative editing says about the theological interests of the redactor. This discipline is like tradition criticism, for both are concerned to show how stages of development gave new shapes to the tradition. Redaction criticism, however, is concerned with the literary rather than the oral stages. As tradition criticism is primarily an Old Testament discipline, redaction criticism developed in conjunction with New Testament study. Its principal focus is on the final literary form, the form that has come down to us.

It has been in Gospel studies that redaction criticism has provided the greatest insights. By comparing episodes from one synoptic Gospel with parallels that appear in the other two Gospels, redaction critics are able to discern the theological point of view of the evangelist. In this way they have contributed to our knowledge of the theological history of early Christianity.

NEW CRITICAL APPROACHES

Over the years the critical methods summarized above underwent constant development and refinement. Within recent years, however, new areas of interest have been probed, new analyses have been employed, and new information has been gathered. This is true with regard to both the historical approach and the more strictly literary analysis.

Sociological approaches

Sociology has come to be understood in two distinct but related ways. In the broad sense, it is the study of society. This would include the social sciences, such as sociology itself, anthropology, economics, political science, etc. In the narrow sense, sociology is concerned with the origin, development, and patterns of social behavior.

Traditional historical criticism produced detailed studies of the social realities of ancient Israel and of early Christianity (sociology in the broad sense). Scholars focused on the structures of social life and used available research methods to gather the data. Archaeology was invaluable in this approach, providing artifacts, literature, and official documents that were scrutinized, classified, and interpreted. The unearthed findings were compared with similar material belonging to other ancient cultures. Although some comparative studies proved valuable, the material analyzed had been lifted from its unique social context and was presumed to have in its own context the meaning and importance of similar material in another context. In addition, the social theories of the day determined the framework of interpretation. Prominent among these theories was the evolutionary perspective that frequently equated change and development with growth and improvement. Thus, sociological investigations were focused on the development of religion and religious structures and not on the dynamic at play.

The turn of the century saw scholars asking sociological questions and developing sociological methods to answer them. The social sciences had come of age, and sociology in the narrow sense (the sense in which it will be meant henceforth) began to make its impact not only in scholarly circles but in the world at large. This new study encouraged biblical scholars to employ sociological approaches in their investigation of the Scriptures.

Sociological study of the Scriptures is still in its early stages, and so it is difficult to evaluate its contributions. However, significant insights have already come to light. An understanding of the social and political structures of ancient Israel have underscored the role that prophets played in critiquing that society and have furthered an appreciation of the prophetic message. Studies of first-century Roman society have shown the Christian church as a unique and challenging community of equals.

One of the branches of anthropology, a second sociological field, has had a profound impact on the literary study of the Scriptures. That branch is linguistics, or the study of the structure of language. Out of it has developed structural exegesis, or structuralism. Unlike the historical-critical methods, which investigate the historical process and seek to discover the original meaning of the text, structural methods search for the meaning within the language itself rather than within the historical event beyond the language. In this way they share the same focus as does the new literary criticism.

Perhaps one of the most important insights that sociological approaches have brought to biblical studies is the realization that not only does the text have a special social context or contexts out of which it grew, but the interpreters also operate with social biases. All contexts have assumptions and pre-understandings that must be admitted if there is to be any cross-cultural and/or cross-generational communication. Just as one cannot presume that language has the same meaning in every context, one cannot expect that social structures or dynamics always play the same roles.

Canonical criticism

A second new development in biblical study, known as canonical or canon criticism, is only a little more than a decade old. Its interest is the biblical text in its canonical or final form and the role which that form plays in the faith of the community. It seeks to trace the development of the canon from the beginnings of tradition formation through the stages of interpretation, the selection and organization of material in the formation of a biblical book, and the final decisions that determine canonicity. It differs from tradition criticism (which is interested in the same development) in that it is not concerned with the historical dynamics that shaped the tradition but with the hermeneutical methods that were employed in the shaping. This does not make canonical criticism just another historical method, for its goal is not historical but theological.

Since it was interpretation that brought earlier traditions alive in a new setting, a study of the principles of interpretation should uncover how this was done. Proponents of this approach believe that the methods employed in the formation of the Bible might well be used by contemporary believers as they seek to do the same thing that was done by their ancestors, namely, to bring earlier traditions alive in new settings. Thus, the Bible can be read not merely as literature but also as the Sacred Scripture that it is.

Although scholars acknowledge that interpretative principles were employed by the different communities throughout the stages of tradition growth and development, they do not have a clear record of them. Only by applying the methods of historical and literary criticism, the very methods that have been described here, can scholars hope to bring these principles to light. The more that is known about each stage of development, the easier it will be to discern the process of development and the principles that guided that process.

It is clear that context, whether sociopolitical or religious, plays a major role in this approach. One must attend to the context when analyzing the meanings of the past as well as when arriving at meanings for the present. When a tradition of the past encountered new concerns or a new context, it was reinterpreted according to some theological perspective. In a similar manner, if that tradition is to be shaped anew in an authentic and meaningful way, it behooves the interpreter to accurately comprehend the contemporary situation. One's view of reality will influence, if not determine, the shape that the tradition will take. For example, the covenant theme might be used to assure a comfortable society that its security is a sign of God's good pleasure and it has every right to cling to it. On the other hand, it might challenge that society to assume its responsibilities to the less fortunate and to redistribute its resources in the name of social justice. The deepest needs of the community (assurance or challenge) must be recognized.

Although still in its initial stages, this approach to interpretation has generated quite a bit of excitement. Many hope that it will be a way of bridging the gap between what the Bible *meant* and what the Bible *means* today.

New literary criticism

New literary criticism seeks to understand the Bible strictly as literature. The historical issues that relate the material to its origin are ignored. The world that interests this critic is not some world of the past but the imaginative world created by the literary piece itself. To understand this world, one does not consult archaeology, sociology, or source criticism but rather the language and forms used, the structures created, and the literary movements developed within the work. To say that the world of a literary piece is imaginative does not mean that it is unreal. Rather, it means that the work does not claim to describe reality as it is; it imitates reality. Its integrity is not determined by its historical accuracy but by its internal harmony.

If the imaginative world of literature is an imitation of the historical world of reality, then the components of which the world is fashioned are not historically real but stand for historical reality. They are all basically metaphorical, analogous to something else. Clues to what they represent are not found outside the work but within it. The interpretation of these clues is to be sought within the scope of the genre or literary form to which the piece belongs. Because a genre is not so much a set of meanings as it is a set of relationships, every literary piece is open to a plurality of interpretations. There is little if any external control over the interpretation, and so one must hold strictly to the patterns set by the genre. Although a literary work may allow for several different renderings, this does not mean that its analysis can be done in a haphazard manner or that it can mean anything the interpreter wants it to mean. For example, a play can have different interpretations, but its internal relationships set certain limits. The same is true for sonnets, limericks, parables, miracle stories.

This kind of literary criticism has itself undergone stages of development. At first texts were characterized as windows through which the interpreter could look to the meaning beyond. Later other critics saw them more as mirrors within which meaning was to be found. Contemporary critics choose to see the text functioning as both window and mirror. Its meaning is to be found within itself, but not in such a way as to confine the reader to it. Good literature takes the reader beyond itself. This interpretative approach enables the critic to discover what the text *means*, but with no regard for what it *meant*.

TOWARD DEVELOPING A WAY OF INTERPRETATION

Clearly, interpretation is more than just the gathering of information about a text (narrow historical criticism). It is an explanation of the meaning of that text. And when the text in question is revered as the sacred tradition of a believing community, a tradition that is somehow rooted in the self-identity of that community, some kind of historical continuity with that ongoing community seems essential for correct interpretation. The following is an example of how both historical and literary approaches can contribute toward developing a way of interpreting the biblical text as Scripture (sacred tradition) and not merely as literature.

Returning to the model of communication described at the beginning of this section, one can focus on the sender, the message, or the audience. Another way of understanding this triad is to speak of three worlds: the world out of which the text grew; the world created by the text itself; and the world of the reader. Each world is independent of the others. However, the world of the text is indebted to the world out of which it grew for its structure and for the fundamental meaning which that structure projects. This does not mean that the text is restricted to the original meaning and cannot generate a plurality of legitimate meanings. The new literary criticism has shown that this can be done. "Indebtedness to the world out of which it grew," as used here, means that the scope of the possible interpretations was broadly set by the original context. That world intended to articulate a message (the original meaning), and it fashioned the text in such a way as to communicate that message. For example, the prophets chastised the nation through the use of an oracle of judgment. That literary form (the oracle of judgment) limits the number of ways in which the literary piece can be interpreted.

Interpretation can be defined as the meeting of the world of the reader with the world of the text in a way that the meaning of the text takes hold of the reader. This meaning may or may not be the original meaning of the text—that will depend upon whether or not the interpreter used historical or literary approaches. According to the new literary criticism, with the exception of the choice of form and all the internal relationships that are intrinsic to that form, the world out of which the text grew need play no part in the interpretation. However—and this is a most important point—the Bible is a unique kind of literature. It is the inspired word of God. No believer will deny that it is revelatory, but is its revelatory character in any way dependent upon the original meaning? In other words, is the original meaning normative? And if it is normative, in what way? The present study contends that the original meaning is indeed normative, and it explains this normative quality in the following way.

Just as during its growth and development the tradition contributed to the shaping of a believing community, it has not ceased to perform that same wonder down through the centuries. That is, it has given witness to the community's identity and has continually awakened that community to its purpose. This took place in the process of the community's reshaping of the tradition as that tradition had been handed down to it. The interpretation or understanding of the tradition that the community received may not have been identical with the tradition's original meaning (fidelity to the covenant might call for different responses in different circumstances). However, the meaning received was the meaning that had been preserved for it and transmitted to it, and it was the meaning that the community considered the correct expression of its understanding of its own identity. It appears that throughout the process of tradition formation, the believing community exercised a good deal of creative freedom. This freedom was restricted, however, by the concept of self-identity that it inherited from the preceding generation. Although different generations may have understood and expressed this identity in various ways, they safeguarded its essence. Each generation had to grasp this essence and then restate it in ways that were expressive of its time. From this point of view, the original meaning can be understood to be normative, while subsequent meanings can also enjoy validity.

A point that must be kept in mind is the role played by the believing community in determining the validity or appropriateness of various meanings. The *community* is the carrier of the tradition. The *community* is the agent of creative reinterpretation. Thus, while the interpretation of the Bible as literature might be done by any critic, only the believing community can interpret it as revelatory Scripture, because the refashioning of tradition takes place within a believing community.

Interpretation has been defined as the meeting of the world of the reader with the world of the text. The reader brings a particular perspective or understanding of life to the text; the text articulates the community's received tradition. The meaning of that tradition is shaped by the reader's perspective and in turn takes hold of the reader. In this way the tradition gives witness to the community's identity and is itself reshaped in the process.

GENESIS

Pauline A. Viviano

INTRODUCTION

The Book of Genesis often confronts us as an antiquated work of literature containing stories of questionable value for our sophisticated civilized world. And yet, because it forms a part of the Bible, we feel that it should say something to us, something about God that transcends time and place. Part of the problem in finding meaning in the Book of Genesis is the vast distance between the world that produced Genesis—a pre-scientific, Eastern world—and our own world, characterized by a scientific, Western approach to reality. To understand the Book of Genesis, we must enter its world, determine what it meant in its time, and only then can we venture to say what it means now for our world.

In this commentary we will interpret the Book of Genesis against its historical background. To do so, we will draw upon the discoveries of archaeology and the critical tools of literary analysis. Before turning to the biblical text itself, however, we want to discuss how the Book of Genesis came to be written and the forms in which it is written.

The formation of the Book of Genesis

The Book of Genesis is the story of the prehistory of Israel. Israel became a nation only when it came to occupy and rule the land of Canaan. This nation came to identify itself as a federation of tribes in covenant with a God who had brought their ancestors out of Egypt and led them to the Promised Land. The Exodus was interpreted as the moment of birth for this nation. But as these tribes consolidated their traditions that spoke of the actions of God in their past, they began to realize that even before the time of the Exodus, God was at work leading them to that moment. The Exodus came to be viewed as the culmination of a process that started when God first called Abraham and promised to make him a great nation.

Eventually Israel began to view its own history in the context of world history, and joined to the story of its origins the story of the beginnings of the universe and the history of humanity in the primeval period. It is important to recognize that this process took centuries. Stories were told and retold, adapted and reinterpreted. They were given a new context and acquired new meaning. These stories grew and developed beyond their original telling until they found their way into the larger story of Israel's relationship to God. The Book of Genesis bears the imprint of this long process of growth.

Scholars began to pay close attention to the formation of the Pentateuch (the first five books of the Bible) when it was recognized that there were two different Hebrew names given to the Deity in the Book of Genesis, namely, Yahweh, the personal name of Israel's God, and Elohim, translated simply God. The presence of these different names in various stories coincided with differences in style and vocabulary in the stories in which they appeared. Contradictions within stories (for example, compare Gen 6:19 with 7:2), which had long puzzled scholars, were resolved when these stories were divided, on the basis of the use of the divine name, into what were originally two independent traditions or sources. Further support for this theory about two or more separate traditions is evident in the occurrence of two, and sometimes three, versions of the same story (Gen 12:10-20/ Gen 20/Gen 26:1-11).

By careful analysis of the data, scholars were led to conclude that there were at least four different authors who contributed to the formation of the Pentateuch. These are identified as the Yahwist (J), Elohist (E), Priestly (P), and Deuteronomic (D) authors, also referred to as "sources" or "traditions." Of these four authors, only the Yahwist, Elohist, and Priestly are to be found in the Book of Genesis; thus we will omit from our discussion the Deuteronomic source.

The YAHWIST source (J) is so called because it uses the name Yahweh (spelled *Jahweh* in German, hence the abbreviation J) for the Deity. The Yahwist is the earliest of the sources, originating in the tenth century B.C.E., the age of David and Solomon. The stories of the Yahwist tradition are characterized by a vivid folk-tale style and a colorful portrayal of characters, setting the Yahwist apart as an author of great skill. The author allows the actions of the characters to speak for themselves and rarely passes moral judgment on their behavior. The anthropomorphic presentation of God in the Yahwist tradition gives a very personal character to the Deity. For the Yahwist, God is actively involved in the history of humanity and, in particular, in Israel's history. The Yahwist begins the story with creation (Gen 2:4b-31), presenting the history of humanity as the background against which Yahweh calls Abraham and extends to him a promise that is fully realized only by the Exodus and the conquest of Canaan. The theme of promise and fulfillment is dominant in the Yahwist's presentation of patriarchal history.

The ELOHIST (E) uses the name Elohim for Israel's God until Exod 3:14, where the name Yahweh is revealed to Moses. This source is generally dated in the ninth century B.C.E. and is believed to have originated in the northern kingdom. The Elohist source has been so intertwined with the Yahwist that it is difficult to separate the two sources in all instances. Since the Elohist source has been subordinated to the Yahwist, what remains of the Elohist narrative is often incomplete. Where we do find a complete story, for example Gen 22, the Elohist is seen to be an author of some skill. The Elohist resorts to dreams and angels as means of divine communication rather than allowing direct contact with the Deity, as does the Yahwist. The Elohist is most noted for his moral sensitivity, which is evident in his attempts to justify, explain, or gloss over the misdeeds of Israel's ancestors. The Elohist begins his story in the patriarchal period, and can be found for the first time in Gen 20, though perhaps in fragmentary form as early as Gen 15.

The PRIESTLY author (P) also prefers the name Elohim for the Deity until the time of Moses (Exod 6). Though the actual writing of the Priestly work is to be dated during the period of the Babylonian Exile (ca. 550 B.C.E.), the sources used by this author come from a much earlier period. The Priestly style tends to be repetitive, and his stories are rigidly structured, giving a very solemn tone to his work. The Priestly author preserves the transcendent character of God by avoiding anthropomorphisms in his portrayal of the Deity. The Book of Genesis opens with the Priestly account of creation. This author is responsible for the genealogies that form the framework of the Book of Genesis. The chronological format imposed on the Pentateuch also derives from the Priestly author.

It is generally held that the Priestly author is responsible for the final editing of the Book of Genesis. It has been theorized that the Priestly tradition incorporates the earlier Yahwist and Elohist narratives. However, there is some evidence to suggest that a later redactor, or editor, actually combined the Yahwist, Elohist, and Priestly writings. This commentary will accept the presence of these three sources in the Book of Genesis and will often refer to the final form or context of a story. Whether that final form or context comes from the Priestly author or a later redactor will be left an open question.

Forms in the Book of Genesis

In interpreting the Book of Genesis, we cannot ignore the forms in which it is written. Interpretation rests upon form. If we hear a story that begins "Once upon a time . . . ," we have no difficulty in recognizing that the story is a fairy tale; we would never mistake it for history, because we know its form. But the forms of the Book of Genesis are no longer common knowledge. Scholars in this past century have delineated and identified the forms in the Book of Genesis. Since this commentary is built upon their work, it is important to "rediscover" the forms in the Book of Genesis.

Narrative is the primary literary classification that we find in the Book of Genesis. A narrative is simply a story. To refer to the form of the Book of Genesis as story is not to devalue the book nor to minimize in any way its theological significance. Indeed, Israel's most distinctive way of speaking of the Deity is to tell the story of God's acts in its life as a nation.

The dominant form of narrative in the Book of Genesis is the saga. Sagas are stories that have a basis in fact, but as the stories are transmitted, they are expanded and enhanced by non-factual elements. Sagas originate at an oral level combining tradition and imagination. It is not unusual to find reported in a saga the direct intervention of God in human affairs. In a saga the incredible is simply part of the flow of events. Sagas may explain why something is the way it is (etiological sagas), why something or someone has a particular name (etymological sagas), why tribes relate as they do (ethnological sagas), why certain places or actions are considered holy (cult sagas), or why a particular locale has unique characteristics (geological sagas). All of these types of sagas are evident in the Book of Genesis.

In the patriarchal sagas of Genesis, the world is seen in terms of families. Jacob is no longer Jacob, he is Israel; Esau is the father of the Edomites. The history of the relationship between these tribes becomes the story of the relationship between these brothers. The patriarchs are characters larger than life. They no longer represent historical persons but become the embodiment of the characteristics of their tribes.

Many individual sagas have been joined together to form the story of the patriarchs. These stories have become a part of a larger context, and so their original meaning is changed. As we work our way through the stories, we will pay particular attention to the levels of meaning acquired by a story as it became a part of the Book of Genesis.

Scholars continue to debate about the presence of myth in the Book of Genesis. Whether or not they find myth in Genesis depends upon their definition of myth. The common definition of myth as a story about gods and goddesses excludes myth from the Bible, because Israel accepts only Yahweh as its God. But myth need not be so narrowly defined. Myth is a way of thinking about reality. What distinguishes myth is that it speaks of reality symbolically in terms of interacting divine powers in the primal era. These powers continue to affect our world through the cult.

The dominant form of expression among Israel's neighbors was myth. It was inevitable that Israel would appropriate the mythological motifs of the ancient Near East. However, Israel did not simply absorb the mythology of the nations that surrounded it; their mythology was changed and adapted to suit Israel's distinctive view of God and the world. We will find, particularly in Gen 1–11, mythological motifs that Israel borrowed but transformed. There are other forms in the Book of Genesis, but we will attend to these in context in the commentary itself.

COMMENTARY

THE PRIMEVAL HISTORY

Gen 1:1–11:27

The first eleven chapters of the Book of Genesis are designated "primeval history" because they treat of the history of humanity, and not specifically of the history of Israel. The universalist perspective of the Yahwist is seen in the placement of Israel's history within the larger context of human history, beginning with creation. The Yahwist narrative is now introduced and supplemented by the traditions of the Priestly author, but the overriding theme is still that of the Yahwist: humanity, because of sin, moves further and further from its God.

THE PRIESTLY CREATION ACCOUNT

Gen 1:1–2:4a

The Book of Genesis opens with a highly structured, hymnlike account of creation by the Priestly author. Though there are similarities between this account and the Babylonian creation account, the *Enuma Elish,* the Priestly author has reinterpreted and rewritten the ancient myth to reflect Israel's distinctive theology. In contrast to the *Enuma Elish,* creation does not result from conflict. There is no war between the gods, there is nothing that opposes God. Instead, we are informed, in a carefully ordered sequence, that God creates the world solely by the power of the divine word.

1:1-25 The creation of the world. The opening verse identifies God as the main actor, and creation as the result of God's action. In addition, the opening verse tells us that prior to God's creative act the world was a formless mass, existing as a watery chaos. This description of the world is in agreement with the mythology of the ancient Near East. Notice that darkness exists—it is not created by God. The origin of darkness, which symbolized evil and terror in the ancient world, is left in mystery. The abyss was the primordial ocean, which had to be "harnessed" for creation to occur. Upon this watery chaos the wind of God begins to act. The Hebrew text literally reads "wind of God," not "mighty wind" as in the New American Bible (v. 2). While the translation "mighty wind" captures some of the sense of the original, it fails to take account of the fact that God is the source of this wind.

The Priestly account of creation is characterized by repetition. By using a framework that remains more or less constant for each day of creation, the author achieves a maximum of repetition, with enough variation to keep the account moving forward at a rhythmic pace. This rhythm gives the account its hymnlike quality. A tone of solemnity pervades the entire creation account. The repeated framework is as follows:

1. *Announcement:* "And God said . . ."
2. *Command:* "Let there be . . ."
3. *Report:* "And it was so . . ."
4. *Evaluation:* "And God saw that it was good . . ."
5. *Temporal framework:* "It was evening, it was morning . . ."

In addition to this structural pattern, the author correlates the acts of creation of the last three days with those of the first three days.

Day 1	Light
Day 2	Sky, separating the upper and lower waters
Day 3	Earth and vegetation
Day 4	Heavenly lights
Day 5	Birds and fish
Day 6	Land animals and humanity

The creation of light on the first day is correlated with what gives light on the fourth day. Correspondingly, the sky, which separates the upper waters from the lower waters, becomes the habitat of the birds, whereas the lower waters are filled with fish. Animals and humanity dwell on the earth and eat its vegetation. This highly schematized picture accentuates the orderliness of creation. Nothing is left to chance or whim, but all is well organized and proceeds as planned by the Creator.

The first act of creation is light, even though that which gives light, the sun and the moon, are not created until the fourth day. The author is not concerned with scientific fact but with an ordered universe, and light is necessary in order to see. The author may also be forced to put light first because in the *Enuma Elish* it is a property of the gods, emanating from them, and is mentioned first in that creation account. For our author, light is no longer a property of the gods but an element of the created world. God names the light "day," and the darkness "night" (v. 5). In ancient Israel, naming signified one's power over that which was named. God names the day and night because God above has authority over them. Likewise, God will name the sky and the earth and the sea. The light is seen as good, as is the entire created universe. A strong affirmation of the goodness of the created world pervades this account. The section concludes with the temporal framework, in which evening is mentioned first, then morning. This reflects ancient Israel's manner of keeping time—the day began at sunset.

God then creates the sky (vv. 6-8), which separates the waters above the heavens from the waters below. The cosmology envisioned by the author is one that he shared with the rest of the ancient Near Eastern world. Water surrounded the entire world and was held back only by the heavens above and the earth below. It threatened to overwhelm the earth, especially when storms and floods enveloped the earth. The sky was pictured as a bowl set upside down to keep the upper waters in place. This bowl had windows, allowing the rain, snow, or hail to reach the earth. The waters below appeared on earth as streams, lakes, and springs.

God puts limits on the expanse of water so that earth can appear. From the earth God calls forth vegetation that is able to reproduce itself ("with its seed in it," v. 11). Fruitfulness is not something dependent on the gods of fertility, but God has put the power of reproduction in vegetation itself. Here again the author shows a world that is not under the control of pagan deities.

Next God creates the lights and places them in the heavens. The author carefully avoids the terms "sun" and "moon," but uses instead the terms "greater light" and "lesser light" (v. 16). The sun and moon were considered deities in the ancient pagan world. By avoiding the use of these terms, the author is in effect saying, "See what other nations consider deities! They are nothing but a 'big light' and a 'little light' in the heavens." The sun and the moon are simply elements of the created universe, not gods to be worshiped.

The sky separating the waters above from the waters below is filled with birds, and the waters below with fish. On the sixth day animals and humanity are created to inhabit the earth, which was created on the third day.

1:26-31 The creation of humanity. The whole creation account has been leading up to the creation of humanity. A habitat has been created in which humanity will dwell; time has been created as a measure by which humanity will govern its life. And finally when all is ready, man and woman are created. Since the Priestly author describes the creation of humanity in more detail than the previous creative acts, and since this act is the last in the series, the author is indicating that humanity is the high point of all creation. The special character of this creation is underscored by the fact that only humanity is described as being created in the "image and likeness" of God (v. 26).

There are three problematic expressions in this section that often cause confusion and misunderstanding. Who are the "us" in Gen 1:26? What does it mean to be created in the "image" of God? What kind of creature is this "man" created both male and female?

The "us" in Gen 1:26 is not easily explained. Several theories have been advanced, but none is entirely satisfactory. Some scholars argue that the "us" is to be explained as an example of the "plural of majesty." The plural of majesty accounts for the fact that in Hebrew the word for God (*Elohim*) is in the plural but is found with a singular verb, indicating that it is meant to be taken as a singular noun. It is supposed that because God is so great and powerful, the ancient Hebrews spoke of their Deity in the plural. For these scholars, the "us" in Gen 1:26 is an instance of this plural of majesty.

Since there is no other language that uses a plural of majesty, other scholars prefer to find in the use of "us" a remnant of pagan mythology. In ancient Near Eastern myths the high god creates humanity in consultation with the heavenly council. The heavenly council is composed of the lesser gods who surround the high god and act as advisors. This may well be in the background, but since the author has avoided other pagan overtones, one wonders why less care would be taken here.

More recently it has been argued that the "us" of Gen 1:26 is to be understood as a rhetorical device without much significance. It is something like saying "Let's do it" after one has debated with oneself over a course of action. Possibly the problem of the "us" in Gen 1:26 will never be solved, but each of these theories is at least plausible, if not entirely satisfactory.

In order to determine what kind of creature the human being is, it is essential that we understand what is meant by the term "image." Often this has been taken to mean that humanity is endowed with a soul, and that the soul is in the image of God. This could not be further from the intent of the author of Gen 1. The view that the human person is composed of a body and a soul is a distinctly Greek idea; in fact, the Hebrew language does not even have a word for "soul." In what way, then, does humanity "image" God? In the ancient world, "image" was used to refer to a statue of the king that was sent to the distant corners of the kingdom where the king could not be present in person. This "image" was to be the representative of the king in that area. If we apply this to Genesis, to be created in the image of God is to be God's representative on earth. This is underscored in the very next sentence of verse 26, in which humanity is given dominion over the earth. As God is ruler of the heavenly realm, so humanity, as God's representative, is ruler of the earthly realm. This is a very exalted view of humanity.

The final problem in these verses arises more from the limitations of the English language than from the original Hebrew text. In Hebrew, *'adam* generally means "humanity." To refer to an individual male, Hebrew used another term. In Gen 1:26 the term is *'adam*, and so the text can be translated, "God created humanity in his image; . . . male and female he created them." Humanity is not created as some kind of androgynous being, but rather humanity consists of the male and the female. Together man and woman constitute humanity.

2:1-4a The hallowing of the sabbath. Sabbath rest is associated with the rest of God on the seventh day. In six days there have been eight separate acts of creation. The author has varied the framework noted above by placing two acts of creation on the third and sixth day, and is then able to maintain a six-day structure in spite of the fact that there are eight acts of creation. This is done to underscore the significance of the sabbath. The sabbath rest mandated in the commandments in the Book of Exodus (20:8) is here bound up with the very beginnings of the world; it is tied to the created order.

CONCLUSION

The Priestly account of creation is a theological reflection on the world that the author has experienced. It is a world wherein God is seen as a powerful Being, able to create by merely speaking a word. God is seen as standing outside the universe that is called into being. The Deity transcends the created order. Humanity is seen as the high point of creation. The world in which humanity lives has been organized by God, but as God's representative on earth, humanity is to be sovereign over the world.

THE YAHWIST ACCOUNT OF CREATION AND SIN, AND THE PRIESTLY GENEALOGY OF ADAM

Gen 2:4b–5:32

Though the Yahwist account of creation follows upon the Priestly account, it is actually the earlier of the two accounts. It is written in the style of a folk tale, without the repetition and carefully delineated structure that characterizes the Priestly account. Creation is *formed* by Yahweh, not called into existence by the power of the divine word. The focus in this story is not on the creation of the world as such, but on the relationship of man and woman to each other and to the world.

2:4b-9 The creation of "the Human." In this creation account, what exists prior to God's creative act is not watery chaos, as in Gen 1, but rather desert. The earth is viewed as barren for two reasons: there is no water, and there is no one to till the soil. The background of this creation story is clearly the experience of the farmer, for whom water and the tilling of the soil are necessary in order to bring forth vegetation from the earth. Water aids creation, whereas in Gen 1 water had to be confined for creation to proceed.

The first thing formed by Yahweh is "the Human." This is not to be understood as an individual named Adam; rather, "the Human" is the whole of humanity. That the author views this original creature as a representative of undifferentiated humanity and not as an individual is clear from the use of the definite article "the" before "humanity" in the Hebrew text.

The human creature is made from the ground. In Hebrew, "human" and "ground" are similar-sounding words *('adam, 'adamah)*, and so bear a special relationship to each other. This play on words is characteristic of the Yahwist author. By using two similar-sounding words, the author is able to focus the attention of the reader on the relationship between the two words. The relationship between humanity and the ground is thus underscored. The human creature comes from the ground and so depends upon it for life.

Yahweh breathes life into "the Human" and it becomes a "living being" (v. 7). In the past this has been interpreted as the creation of the soul, but, as indicated above, the Hebrew language did not have a word for "soul." "The Human" becomes a living being. Humanity lives because Yahweh's breath is in it; when Yahweh's breath leaves, it dies. Every breath of every person depends directly upon Yahweh. It should be noted that the animals are also living beings (2:19). Humanity and animals are living, breathing creatures. Humanity and animals are to be distinguished from each other by the fact that Yahweh speaks to the human creature but not to the animals. In addition, the human creature names the animals, thus signifying humanity's control over the animal world.

Once the human creature is formed, Yahweh proceeds to create a place in which humanity will dwell. This is unlike Gen 1, where the habitat was created first, and only later were people created to live in it. Here Yahweh creates a garden (v. 8), which resembles a park with trees, not a garden of plants and flowers. These park-like gardens were cultivated by great kings in the ancient Near East. They were a source of shade from the sun, the kind of place where a king could relax. This is Yahweh's garden, and Yahweh uses it in the cool of the evening to "relax."

The author mentions two trees that will function significantly in Gen 3, the tree of life and the tree of the knowledge of good and evil. The tree of life appears again only at the end of Gen 3, and thus it can be seen to play a marginal role in the story. The tree of life was a symbol of immortality in ancient Near Eastern mythology; it plays the same role in this story. As long as the first couple are in the garden and have access to this tree, their life is not threatened. Once they are expelled from the garden, they become subject to death. The tree of the knowledge of good and evil, by contrast, plays an integral role in the story that follows, and we will consider its symbolism in the context of that story.

2:10-14 The four rivers. It is commonly recognized that these verses interrupt the story of the Yahwist. They contribute nothing to the action of the story. Verse 15 seems to be the continuation of verse 9, not of verses 10-14. Moreover, this insertion contradicts what was said earlier in the text about the location of Eden (v. 8). According to this passage, Eden is located in the north, and the four great rivers that surround the world flow from it. Only two of the rivers can be identified—the Tigris and the Euphrates. The Pishon and the Gihon cannot be identified with certainty, but they probably refer to rivers in the same general area as the Tigris and Euphrates. The purpose of this insertion seems to be to link the garden of Eden with a specific geographical area in an attempt to historicize the story.

2:15-17 The command. The human creature is placed in the garden and given the task of cultivating and taking care of it. This echoes ancient Near Eastern mythology, in which humanity is created to do the work of the gods. A command not to eat from the tree of the knowledge of good and evil is given, without any explanation for this prohibition. It is simply stated that Yahweh has created humanity and has placed certain limits upon human activity.

2:18-24 The creation of woman. The motive given by Yahweh for the creation of woman is that "It is not good for the human to be alone." While this aspect of the story has often been interpreted as a reference to the social nature of humanity, what is really intended by the author is to account for the marriage relationship, as the concluding verse of the story indicates (v. 24). We must bear in mind that in presenting that relationship the author is writing from the perspective of the tenth century B.C.E. and presents the woman from that viewpoint. A woman's position was one of support to her husband. She is, in the literal translation of the Hebrew text, a "helper fit for him." In the Old Testament, "helper" means one who gives support or strength, one who enables others to fulfill their destiny. Frequently in the Old Testament, it is actually God who is called "helper" (Deut 33:7; Ps 33:20; 70:6; etc.). No one would argue that God is subservient to anyone. The story is not about the essence of woman, but about her dignity in the institution of marriage. Woman is intended to be one in whom man finds support and strength.

In contrast to the Priestly account, creation does not appear as an organized, step-by-step process. Rather, one thing is made, then another, until God is satisfied with the results. Like the human creature, the animals are formed from the ground and become "living beings" (2:19—the phrase "living beings" is curiously omitted in the NAB). The human creature and the animals share a common origin. They are distinguished from each other by the fact that the human creature names the animals, signifying authority over them. Moreover, as previously stated, Yahweh speaks to the human creature but does not address the animals.

Even though the human creatures and the animals are both living beings, the animals do not prove to be suitable as a "helper." A second time Yahweh attempts to form a suitable helper, and this time forms a woman from one of the ribs of "the Human," who is put into a "deep sleep" lest the act of creation be witnessed. The act of creation remains a divine mystery.

One of the most puzzling aspects of this passage is the fact that Yahweh forms the woman from a rib (v. 22). We have no parallels in ancient Near Eastern mythology, and what a rib may symbolize in the text is simply unknown. We do know that in the Sumerian language "rib" and "life" are the same word. The goddess of life is at the same time the "Lady of the Rib." It is interesting to note that at the conclusion of chapter 3 the man calls his wife "Eve," a form of the Hebrew word for "life," and recognizes that she will be the "mother of all the living" (3:20). The association of life and rib with woman may indicate that in the background of the story is something akin to the Sumerian wordplay.

When the woman is brought to the man (v. 23), he exclaims in poetic form that at last a suitable helper has been found. No longer is he alone. There is a wordplay between the terms "man" and "woman" in Hebrew *('ish, 'ishshah)* that highlights the special relationship between man and woman. Woman comes from man and so depends upon him. This is consistent with the position of woman in ancient Near Eastern society in the tenth century B.C.E. This passage has often been used to substantiate the view that woman is inferior to man and subservient to him. This is certainly not the intent of the author. It is clear that woman is not inferior to man. Her mysterious creation by God from human substance underscores the common nature she shares with man and the bond that unites them. That she is his "helper" does not indicate subservience.

Verse 24 is clearly the conclusion of chapter 2 and shows that our story is an etiology, a story about the past that explains a present reality. This story tells us why men and women are drawn to each other sexually and marry. The terms "leave" and "cleave" are covenant terms and suggest that marriage is here viewed as a covenantal relationship.

CONCLUSION

The Yahwist account of creation is much more local in scope than the Priestly account; it is concerned with the human relationship to the soil and the relationship between man and woman, not with the creation of a universe. Clearly drawn from an agricultural milieu, the story presents humanity as coming from the ground, and dependent upon the ground for life. In death humanity will return to the ground from which it came. Woman is the only suitable helper for man, since she is formed from human flesh. The attraction of the sexes and the institution of marriage are described as the natural destiny of man and woman, flowing from the way they were created. Yahweh, in turn, is not distant from creation but is directly involved in the act of creation and concerned about all creatures.

2:25–3:7 The sin of Adam and Eve. The final verse of chapter 2 is transitional and serves more to introduce the next story than to conclude the previous one. That man and woman are naked and yet feel no shame is more than a mere observation of their being undressed. As will be obvious later, their nakedness becomes a symbol of their relationship to God. At this time in the story, that relationship to God is still intact; thus nakedness does not cause shame. Only with the disruption of that relationship is their nakedness an embarrassment.

A new character is now introduced into the story—the serpent. This creature is characterized as being "cunning." This term carries connotations of craftiness and cleverness, and contrasts with the naiveté of the woman. In Hebrew, "cunning" *('arum)* forms a wordplay with "naked" *('arummim)*. This wordplay underscores the fact that man and woman become aware of their nakedness because of the cunning of the serpent. It should be noted that nowhere in this text is the serpent identified as the devil; this identification does not come about until the first century B.C.E. (Wis 2:24; Enoch 69:6).

What, then, does the serpent represent? In Canaan the serpent was associated with the fertility cults. We know that these cults were a constant source of temptation to Israel, and, as indicated in the Old Testament, Israel often succumbed to such temptation. The choice of a serpent to represent the tempter of humanity is the author's way of saying, "Don't get involved with serpents (that is, the fertility cults); they will only cause trouble, as they did for the first man and woman." It becomes a way of warning Israel to stay away from fertility cults.

The story of Gen 3 says nothing about the serpent's motives in tempting the man and the woman. Indeed, the source of evil itself is left a mystery in Gen 3. What the story does tell us is that the presence of evil in the world is due to humanity's decision to oppose God's command.

Many scholars have attempted to explain why the serpent engages the woman in conversation and not the man. Their answers range from interpreting woman as inherently weak, incurably curious, to viewing her as much stronger than man. If she can be made to sin, man will automatically follow. The text supports none of these views. It is clear that the author portrays both man and woman as listening to the serpent. She eats the fruit and gives it to the man "who is with her" (v. 6). The fact that woman is presented first can be explained as simply a literary device that keeps the story moving. The serpent is introduced first, then the woman, then the man. When God comes to the garden, the man is addressed first, then the woman, then the serpent. When God punishes them, the serpent is punished first, then the woman, then the man. This movement from serpent-woman-man, man-woman-serpent, serpent-woman-man maintains an even flow to the story and has no great significance beyond this fact. It is clear that the woman is included in God's command even though she is never the explicit recipient of that command (2:11, 17). And it is clear, as indicated above, that the man is with the woman during the whole temptation scene.

The temptation scene has all the characteristics of a universal picture of temptation. This is the way every human being is tempted. The serpent, with an opening question, insinuates that God has some ulterior motive for the command, that God is keeping something from humanity. The woman jumps to God's defense, but the serpent has succeeded in attracting her attention and proceeds with three half-truths: (1) "you will not die"; (2) "your eyes will be opened"; (3) "you will be like God, knowing good and evil" (vv. 4-5). It is true that when the man and the woman eat, they do not die, yet they become subject to death and will eventually die. It is true that their eyes are opened, but not in the way they anticipated. They are now aware, as they were not before, of a whole new area of human experience—the experience of guilt and shame. They know that they are naked. And finally, they become like God, knowing good and evil, but not in the way they had expected. To determine what it means to be "like God, knowing good and evil," we must attempt to explain the meaning of the symbol of the tree of the knowledge of good and evil.

There are many theories as to the meaning of the tree of the knowledge of good and evil in Gen 3. While some of these theories are attractive, they are generally based upon present philosophical positions that bear little relationship to what is actually at issue in the Genesis account. The question to which we must attend in dealing with this symbol is:

What does the expression "knowing good and evil" mean in this story? What kind of knowledge does God forbid?

To determine the meaning of this symbol is very difficult, for we have no comparable symbol in any other literature of the ancient Near East. Nor is the symbol, as such, treated elsewhere in the Old Testament. However, we do find the expression "to know good and evil" in the Old Testament. If we can discover what it means in other contexts, and then test that meaning in the Genesis context, it may be possible to find a plausible meaning of the tree of the knowledge of good and evil.

In Deut 1:39 and Isa 7:15, 16, the phrase "knowing good and evil" refers to a kind of knowledge not possessed by children. They are too young to "know good and evil." In 2 Sam 19:35, Barzillai refuses the king's offer that he return with him to Jerusalem by saying, "I am now eighty years old. Can I know good and evil?" The implication is that Barzillai as an old man is beginning to lose his faculties and so cannot be of service to the king. In 1 Kgs 3:9 and 2 Sam 14:17, the phrase "good and evil" is used (though not with the verb "to know") in the context of making wise judgments by the king on behalf of his people. In summary, we can say that to know good and evil entails the kind of knowledge required in order to make adult decisions on one's own behalf.

Does this definition make sense in the Genesis story? God places a limit on humanity. Humanity can know many things, but who is to decide what is best for humanity—the God who created humanity or the creature who was created? Chapter 3 of Genesis says that God wished to retain the knowledge of what was best for human creation. The problem is that humanity overstepped the limit imposed by God and appropriated that knowledge. Now humanity exists in the position of deciding for itself what is best. It defines itself in rebellion against its Creator.

Humanity does "become like God" in the sense that now it makes its own decisions as to what is best for itself, but it makes these decisions as creature, without the wisdom and vision of the Creator. Who knows what is best for the creature—the One who created it or the creature itself? Humanity makes its own decisions, but its decisions lack the breadth and depth of God's wisdom.

The most immediate consequence of the sin of the man and the woman is the consciousness of their nakedness, which they seek to remedy by sewing loincloths of fig leaves (v. 7). We see almost at once the futility of this gesture. In the ensuing dialogue between Yahweh and the man, we note that the man, rather than answering Yahweh's question "Where are you?," gives the reason why he hid—"because I was naked." The reason is appropriate, in spite of the fact that it appears to be untrue. He is not naked, he is clothed with fig leaves. However, in relationship to Yahweh, he is naked, that is, his relationship to Yahweh has been disrupted and remains so. Humanity cannot "cover up" its own guilt and shame and restore its relationship to Yahweh. It is Yahweh alone who can remove humanity's guilt and shame. This is symbolized at the end of the story (v. 21), when Yahweh makes garments for the man and the woman.

3:8-24 The consequences. The purpose of the interrogation of the man and the woman is to bring them to an admission of their sin. It is interesting to note the all too human response of the man as he blames the woman and indirectly even God ("the woman you put here," v. 12). The woman, in turn, blames the serpent.

The punishments that follow are expressed in poetic form and are thought to be older than the story in which they are now found. The story is seen, then, as an etiology explaining such things as the reasons why serpents crawl, why there is pain in childbirth, and why farming is so difficult. These punishments are drawn from the world in which the author lives. They reflect the environmental and social conditions found in ancient Palestine.

The ongoing struggle of humanity to survive against the attacks of venomous serpents is highlighted in the first curse (vv. 14-15). The pain associated with childbirth, incongruous with the great joy that surrounds the gift of life, is attributed to woman's participation in sin. That her husband would rule over her reflects the position of woman in ancient society (v. 16). The curse under which man works (vv. 17-19) testifies to the rocky soil and desert-like conditions of Palestine, which make farming so difficult in that region. But the story does not end on a negative note. The woman receives her name, Eve, and she will become the mother of all the living. In spite of sin and its consequences, life will go on. Yahweh makes garments for the man and the woman, thus "covering up" their guilt and shame. Yahweh's care of humanity does not cease because of sin, but continues in spite of sin. On Yahweh's initiative the relationship disrupted by sin is restored.

At the end of chapter 3 the tree of life assumes importance. It has not yet functioned as an integral part of the story, but now, because of sin, humanity is denied access to this tree and is expelled from the garden. Humanity is not able to seize the Deity's prerogative of immortality. This is ensured by stationing the cherubim at the gate. They function as guardians of the tree of life and prevent humanity from re-entering the garden. These cherubim are to be identified with the winged animals that stood as guardians at the entrances of palaces and temples in Assyria and Babylon. The fiery revolving sword represents lightning, which is often a symbol of God's wrath.

4:1-16 The first murder. The story of Cain and Abel follows upon the story of the sin of humanity and represents humanity's further alienation from Yahweh. The opening verses are transitional. They once formed the introduction to the genealogy that begins in verse 17, but now they serve to introduce the main characters of our story. Cain, whose name means "I have produced," is Eve's firstborn. The etymology of Abel's name is not given, but the Hebrew root of the name means "emptiness," and may refer to the very brief life of Abel. The separateness of these brothers is brought out only by the terse sentence that contrasts their professions: Cain is a farmer; Abel, a shepherd.

As the story unfolds, it moves quickly to the actual murder of Abel and Yahweh's judgment on Cain. Many details that would interest the modern reader are simply ignored. We do not know why Cain's sacrifice was not acceptable, nor how Cain discovers that his sacrifice did not please God. The story focuses on Cain's reaction, the subsequent murder of his brother, and God's judgment on Cain. Verse 7 suggests that Cain could have controlled his anger. Sin is presented figuratively as "lurking at the door" to take possession of him, yet Cain could still overcome sin by "doing well." He does not, and so bears full responsibility for his sin.

When interrogated by Yahweh, Cain lies and then addresses a sarcastic question to Yahweh (v. 9). He is worse than the first sinners, who sought merely to shift the blame. Cain's sin cannot be ignored. The blood of his murdered brother cries out to Yahweh. In ancient Israel it was believed that blood and life are inextricably bound. As life belongs to God, so too does blood.

The punishment of Cain is more severe than that of the first parents. He is banished from the soil, cursed to be a wanderer. As in chapter 3, the punishment of the sinner is not the final word. When Cain cries out against the severity of his punishment and states his fear that others may seek vengeance against him, Yahweh places a mark on Cain to protect him. Though Cain leaves the presence of Yahweh (v. 16), he is mysteriously under God's protection.

The story of Cain and Abel is only loosely connected with the preceding story of the fall in chapter 3. This story presupposes the existence of other people (v. 14) and an organized society in which there are distinct professions and in which a sacrificial cult has been developed. The story bears all the marks of having been reduced to the bare necessities. The concern of the passage rests entirely on Cain's sin and his subsequent punishment, leaving many unanswered questions. It seems likely that we are dealing with a story that once existed independently but has been adapted by the Yahwist to suit his particular purpose.

It has been suggested that the concern of the original story was the animosity between peoples of different backgrounds and vocations, specifically farmers and shepherds. In the story the pastoral way of life wins out over that of the farmer, as can be evidenced by Yahweh's acceptance of Abel's sacrifice. If this was the concern of the original story, it is no longer the primary concern of the Genesis story. Another way of accounting for the origin of the story is to see it as an account of the origin (etiology) of the Kenites. The Kenites were a tribe that worshiped Yahweh and yet never became a member of Israel.

They were smiths and metalworkers, and continued to live as a wandering tribe long after many nomadic tribes had settled. It is believed that the members of this tribe wore a sign or tattoo on their foreheads, setting them apart from other tribes. This story suggests that Cain is the founding father of this tribe, and the story is told to account for the distinguishing characteristics of the Kenite tribe.

Though certain elements of the story may help us to better ascertain its original intention, they no longer fully explain the Yahwist's use of it. It is this level of the story that is most important to the reader. For the Yahwist, the story illustrates humanity's inclination to sin. From the first sin in the garden onward, humanity continues to move away from Yahweh, becoming so hardened in sin that Yahweh regrets ever having created the human race (6:6). According to the Yahwist, it is against the backdrop of the increasing sinfulness of humanity that a people is eventually chosen through whom all of humanity will be reconciled to God (12:1ff.). Left to itself, humanity moves toward sin. Hope is found in Yahweh's ever-present mercy and in Yahweh's will to save.

4:17-26 The Cainite genealogy. While most of the genealogies in Genesis are attributed to the Priestly author, this Cainite genealogy is the work of the Yahwist. That this piece is a separate tradition not originally linked to the Cain and Abel story is evident in the surprising appearance of Cain's wife. Since no other people are mentioned, where did the woman come from? In the previous story Cain is cursed to be a wanderer (vv. 12, 16), but in this genealogy he is the builder of a city (v. 17) and the father of civilization. Similarly, whereas Abel was described as a shepherd (v. 2), in this genealogy Jabal is the father of shepherds (v. 20). This genealogy is introduced in order to account for the origin of cities and the development of civilization with its attendant professions. Its inclusion fills the gap in the story between the account of creation and that of the flood.

There are points of contact between this genealogy and the Priestly genealogy in Gen 5. Some of the same names are repeated (Enoch, Lamech), and some names are simply variations of names appearing in the Yahwist genealogy (Mehujael/Mahalalel; Methusael/Methuselah). It appears that both genealogies come from a common source that has undergone a long period of transmission. This would account for the differences in the spelling and sequence of names. Behind both genealogies stands the tradition of an antediluvian (pre-flood) list of the kings of Mesopotamia. The points of contact between these traditions and the Genesis genealogies will be noted in the commentary on Gen 5.

Inserted into the Cainite genealogy is a "boasting song" of Lamech (vv. 23-24). It is distinct from the genealogy both in form and content. It is probably included because Cain is mentioned in the last line. The song reflects the pride and arrogance of unbridled revenge, and it is used by the Yahwist as another example of humanity's sinfulness. The disobedience of the first parents has led to an ever-increasing rebellion of humanity against God—first murder, and now wanton vengeance. As civilization advances, so does humanity's rebellion.

A Sethite fragment is appended to the Cainite genealogy. Verse 25 is similar to verse 17, and with it we return to Adam. There is, as is typical of the Yahwist, a play on words: the word for "granted" sounds like "Seth." In contrast to the Cainite genealogy, which ended with the rebellion of humanity against God, this fragment states that now humanity began to call upon Yahweh. Consistent with Yahwist theology, the section ends on a positive note.

Much scholarly debate has centered on the fact that whereas Gen 4:26 states that humanity called upon the name of Yahweh from the time of Seth, the Priestly and Elohist traditions do not introduce the name until the time of Moses (Exod 6:2; 3:14). Since we are unable to reconstruct with any certainty the pre-history of Israel's traditions, it is impossible to reconcile these two traditions. It may be that the name Yahweh was known to a small group or tribe and only later became known to the whole people, but this is highly speculative.

5:1-32 The genealogy of Adam. The first two verses of this section recall the creation of humanity in the Priestly account (1:26ff.) and serve as a transition to the genealogy of Adam drawn from that source. The relationship of this genealogy to the Cainite genealogy was noted above and can be clearly seen in the following comparison. The order of names in the Yahwist genealogy has been changed to highlight the similarity between the two lists. The numbers to the left indicate the order of appearance in the text.

Gen 4:17-26(J)	*Gen 5:1-32(P)*
1. Adam	1. Adam
8. [Seth]	2. Seth
9. [Enosh]	3. Enosh
2. Cain	4. Kenan
5. Mehujael	5. Mahalalel
4. Irad	6. Jared
3. Enoch	7. Enoch
6. Methusael	8. Methuselah
7. Lamech	9. Lamech
10. [Noah]	10. Noah

These are essentially the same genealogies. The Yahwist's reference to Noah is found in Gen 5:39. The change in the order of names reveals the fluid nature of genealogical traditions; they could be rearranged to suit the purposes of the author.

There is no doubt that the genealogy in chapter 5 bears some relationship to the antediluvian list of the kings of Mesopotamia. In both lists the seventh position is of special significance. In the Mesopotamian list the name of the seventh king, Enmeduranna, is the same as the capital city that served as the center of worship of the sun god. This may explain why it is that Enoch, the seventh in the Priestly list, lives precisely 365 years, the same number as that of the days in a solar year. It was believed that the seventh king was taken into the company of the gods. This could explain the rather cryptic reference to Enoch's fate (v. 24). The last king in the Mesopotamian list, like Noah, who is the last person mentioned in the Priestly genealogy, has an important role in the story of the flood. There is no direct relationship between any of the names in the two lists, nor are any of the numbers the same. Indeed, in contrast to the considerable length of reign in the Mesopotamian list (18,600–64,800 years), the life span of the biblical patriarchs is remarkably short. Nonetheless, there are striking similarities.

The genealogy in Gen 5 is introduced by the phrase "This is the record of the descendants . . ." (in literal translation: "This is the book of the generations . . ."). Since succeeding Priestly genealogies begin with a similar formula, it is commonly believed that the Priestly author took the lists from a collection of genealogical tables called by scholars the "Book of Generations."

Consistent with the Priestly style seen in Gen 1:1–2:4a, the genealogy follows a strict pattern. It is composed of the following elements: (1) the age of *X* when his first son is born; (2) the number of years *X* lived after that birth; (3) the statement that *X* had other sons and daughters; (4) the age of *X* when he died.

As with the Yahwist genealogy, the purpose of this genealogy is to fill the gap between the accounts of creation and that of the flood. But in addition to this, some distinctly Priestly concerns are evident. The blessing and command to multiply given by God in Gen 1:28 are now realized. The image of God in which the first couple were created is passed on from generation to generation, so that all humanity is created in the image of God (v. 3). Enoch's fellowship with God (v. 10) will save him from the flood. The name Noah literally means "rest," but in verse 29 it suggests comfort or relief, anticipating Noah's future role.

THE STORY OF THE FLOOD

Gen 6:1–9:29

The Genesis story of the flood is remarkably similar to Mesopotamian flood accounts, especially the Babylonian version of the Gilgamesh Epic. Gilgamesh, the hero of that story, embarks upon a search for immortality that brings him to an ancient ancestor named Utnapishtim, who is immortal. As Utnapishtim recounts how he became immortal, we readily recognize parallels to the Genesis flood story. The story is as follows. The council of the gods decides to destroy humanity. Ea, the god of wisdom, appears to Utnapishtim in a dream and warns him of the coming disaster. He instructs Utnapishtim to build a boat to save himself and his family. Utnapishtim brings his family, wild and tame animals, and artisans with him aboard the boat. The gods unleash a storm that quickly gets out of control, and the gods themselves cower in fear in the upper spheres of heaven. When the storm ends, the boat rests on a mountain and Utnapishtim sends birds from the boat to determine the extent to which the waters have receded. Upon leaving the boat, the survivors of the storm offer a sacrifice pleasing to the gods, who in turn bless Utnapishtim and his family with immortality.

It is clear that the Genesis version is essentially the same story, but there are some significant differences. In the Genesis account there is no hint of polytheism. God, and only God, is in control throughout; the storm never gets out of control. The flood is not the result of whim but is sent as punishment for sin. Noah does not gain immortality but rather enters into covenant with God.

Unlike Gen 1–5, where the Yahwist and Priestly traditions are for the most part separate, in Gen 6–9 the two versions are extensively interwoven. This is evident in the duplications and contradictions in the story in its present form. The duplications are as follows: God observes the sinfulness of humanity (6:5/6:12); God decides to destroy humanity (6:7/6:13); God announces the flood (7:4/6:17); Noah is ordered to enter the ark (7:1-3/6:18-20); Noah obeys (7:5/6:22); Noah enters the ark (7:1-3/7:18ff.); all living creatures on earth die (7:22/7:21); the waters recede (8:1/8:3a); God promises never again to destroy creation by a flood (8:21/9:11). The contradictions in the text include: the number of animals taken into the ark (7:2/6:19-20; 7:15-16); the cause of the flood (7:4, 12; 8:2b/7:11; 8:2); the flood's duration (7:24; 8:2a, 3b; 8:13/7:4, 10, 12; 8:8-12). The differences in the two versions will become clear in the commentary that follows.

6:1-4 (J) The intermarriage of the divine and the human. This is no doubt one of the strangest stories in the Old Testament. It appears to be a shortened myth taken over by the Yahwist and rewritten to serve as an introduction to the account of the flood. The "sons of heaven" (literally, "sons of the gods" or "sons of God") are certainly gods and not angels, as is often assumed. In ancient mythology the sons of God were considered members of the heavenly council, lesser deities that were of service to the high god.

What seems to be at issue here is not licentious behavior but the intermarriage between gods and human beings. If we were to eliminate verse 3, the story could be seen simply as an etiology explaining a race of giants or superhuman heroes of old. Verse 3 leads us to interpret the action described in verse 2 as a great sin. The Yahwist uses the myth to illustrate the extent of sin; it even violates the boundaries between the heavenly and earthly realms. Interestingly, the punishment is directed against humanity, whose lifespan is shortened, and not against the gods, who initiated the action. This can be explained by recognizing that the Yahwist uses the story to introduce his version of the flood, the means by which humanity is punished for its wickedness.

6:5-8 (J) Yahweh's decision to destroy all living creatures. In this section the Yahwist calls further attention to the extent of sin. It is universal. Everything conceived in the human heart is evil. In Hebrew anthropology the heart is not primarily the center of the emotions but the source of intellect and will. All human thoughts and actions are evil. Yahweh's regret over creation gives a very human touch to the Yahwist's portrayal of God. Yahweh's resolution to destroy what has been created is in response to humanity's behavior, and as such is not an arbitrary decision. The flood is Yahweh's judgment upon humanity, but this judgment is balanced by Yahweh's will to save, which is signified in the preservation of Noah and his family. Yahweh's choice of Noah remains a mystery in the Yahwist version of the flood story.

6:9-22 (P) God's decision to send the flood, and instructions on building the ark. The formula "These are the descendants of . . ." indicates that we have returned to the Priestly author. Noah's righteousness is immediately noted; because of it he is preserved from the flood. God's choice is not a mystery, as is the case in the Yahwist story. It is not simply humanity that is corrupted but the earth itself. As in the Yahwist account, God's will to destroy is in response to sin. Typical of the Priestly author, we find great attention given to details, such as the construction of the ark and the dating of the flood. Noah is to take his family and male and female members of every species of animal into the ark, as well as enough food to feed them all for the duration of the flood.

7:1-5, 7-10, 12, 16b, 17b, 22-23 (J) Instructions to Noah and the coming of the flood. Omitted from the Yahwist version of the flood is the command to build the ark. It was probably deleted in favor of the Priestly version. In view of the statement in 7:1 that

Noah alone was found to be just, it is possible that the building of the ark serves as a test for him. He is instructed to bring seven pairs of clean animals and one pair of unclean animals into the ark, at obvious variance with Gen 6:19. For the Priestly author, the distinction between ritually acceptable and unacceptable (clean and unclean) animals cannot be made until ritual laws are introduced by Moses in the Sinai narrative. The Yahwist has no problem presenting sacrificial worship as part of humanity's earliest history (4:3-4; 8:20-22). The anthropomorphic style (depicting God in human terms) of the Yahwist author is evident in the depiction of Yahweh shutting the door of the ark (7:16b). Here the flood is the result of forty days and nights of rain. The Priestly account offers another explanation.

7:6, 11, 13-16a, 17a, 18-21, 24 (P) A reversion to primeval chaos. In the Priestly account the flood is not caused by rain but by the waters above the heavens joining the waters below the earth. In other words, the world returns to the watery chaos that existed before creation (1:2). The extent of the flood is far greater in the Priestly account, for it entails the destruction of the entire cosmos and a reversion to primeval chaos.

8:2b, 3a, 6, 8-12, 13b, 20-22 (J) The receding of the waters, Noah's sacrifice, Yahweh's promise. The waters remain on the earth a total of sixty-one days. Noah sends out birds to determine if the waters have receded sufficiently so that he can disembark. The use of birds by sailors for navigational purposes was not unknown in the ancient world. The Yahwist, in good storytelling style, builds the bird-sending motif to a climax by having Noah send out three birds, the last of which is successful. As in the Babylonian myth, a pleasing sacrifice is offered to God upon leaving the ark. The mythological overtones of the phrase "the Lord smelled the sweet odor" (v. 21) cannot be overlooked. The expression is drawn from a primitive notion that food offered to the gods was actually eaten by them. This idea was later rejected by Israel. In our story this detail serves to show that the sacrifice was accepted by Yahweh, and thus reconciliation with humanity was effected. As the Yahwist's story opened with Yahweh's reflection upon humanity (6:5-8), so it now closes with comparable reflections. Humanity is the same, "evil from the start" (v. 21), but humanity's wickedness will never again become the basis for Yahweh's destruction of the earth. The order of creation is assured by Yahweh.

8:1-2a, 3b, 4-5, 7, 13a, 15-19; 9:1-17, 28-29 (P) God remembers Noah. In the Priestly account the flood lasts a full year and ten days, and restoration entails a re-creation. The "wind of God" that begins to move over the waters echoes the "wind of God" that functioned similarly in Gen 1. The turning point in the story is God's remembrance of Noah. It is God's "remembering" that sets in motion this new act of creation. The bird-sending motif is not as successfully integrated into the Priestly story as it is in the Yahwist version. Indeed, it is God who tells Noah to leave the ark; Noah does not rely on information gained from sending out the bird.

God's first words to Noah and his sons are a reiteration of the blessing given at creation: "Be fertile and multiply." In the postdiluvian (post-flood) world, the blessing of procreation continues in effect. What is altered is humanity's relationship to the animals. Recognizing humanity's violent nature, God permits animals to be killed and eaten, but the blood, because of its association with life, which belongs to God alone, must not be eaten. The prohibition against the taking of human life continues in effect; interestingly, the reason given is that humanity is created in the "image of God." If God's law against murder is transgressed, it is humanity, not God, that bears the responsibility of punishing the crime. The ancient legal formula in verse 6 was probably originally intended to set limits to blood revenge.

The divine promise never to destroy the earth again by flood takes the form of a covenant in the Priestly conclusion to the story. A covenant was a way of regulating the relationships between individuals and groups in ancient society. This covenant is introduced by the Priestly author as an anticipation of the future covenant between God and Israel. The initiation of the covenant and the responsibility to keep it rests entirely with God. The rainbow is a sign of that covenant. It is a reminder to God of the pledge to preserve the world; it is a reminder to humanity of God's faithfulness and mercy.

The story concludes in 9:28-29. These verses reveal the Priestly author's concern with chronology. Verse 29 recalls the genealogy of chapter 5, which was interrupted by the story of the flood, and in turn provides a transition to the Table of the Nations in chapter 10.

9:18-27 (J) The curse of Canaan. Again we find the Yahwist adapting a story that originally served another purpose. The original story functioned as an etiology explaining the origin of viniculture and the discovery of the intoxicating effects of wine. As such, there is no moral judgment on Noah's condition; it is simply stated that he became drunk. The interest of the Yahwist is not in Noah's drunkenness but in the curse on Canaan and in the blessings on Shem and Japheth that resulted from their behavior toward their father during his drunken stupor. Exactly what Ham did to Noah is not clear, but certainly it involved more than merely looking upon his father's nakedness (see 9:24). Nor is it clear why Canaan is cursed when, according to the story, Ham is the guilty party. The phrase "Ham was the father of Canaan" (v. 18) is certainly intended to bring the curse into harmony with the story, but this does not really remove the difficulty.

The curse of Canaan and the blessings of Shem and Japheth seek to account for the relationships between the peoples who descended from these three ancestors. The Canaanites did become the slaves of the Israelites (descendants of Shem). The identification of the descendants of Japheth is not certain. Perhaps they are the Philistines, who did "dwell among the tents of Shem," or the Hittites, who disappeared from the land shortly after the arrival of Israel. In any case, they are presented as sharing in the overlordship of Israel in the land of Canaan.

THE NATIONS OF THE WORLD

Gen 10:1–11:27

10:1-32 Table of the Nations. The genealogy of Gen 10 is actually an extensive tabulation of the nations of the ancient Near East. It is basically the work of the Priestly author, as signaled by the generation formula, but it now contains some fragments drawn from the Yahwist. The principle of division among the nations is not race or language, but geographic boundaries and political affiliations. The order in which the sons of Noah are listed—Shem, Ham, Japheth—is reversed in the genealogy that follows, in order to present the ancestors of the Israelites in a climactic final position.

The descendants of Japheth inhabit the region north of the Fertile Crescent to the coastlands west of Palestine. Many of the peoples mentioned are Indo-Europeans, but it is not possible to identify them all with certainty. Among those whose identification is certain are the following: the Madai are the Medes, the Javan are the Greeks, the Kittim are the people of the island of Rhodes.

The descendants of Ham include African and Arabic tribes that inhabited the region surrounding the Red Sea, northeastern Africa, and the land of Canaan. Ethiopia (Cush), Libya (Put), and Egypt are well known among the nations mentioned. It is surprising to find the Canaanites, who were Semites, identified as descendants of Ham, but this probably reflects the fact that Egypt controlled the region prior to Israel's claim on the land. The inhabitants of the Asiatic side of the Red Sea are also listed. Many of these names are familiar as peoples displaced by Israel's conquest of Canaan.

The descendants of Shem are the peoples occupying the region of the Fertile Crescent and the Arabian Peninsula. The known nations include Elam, Assyria, and Aram.

A later editor inserted Yahwistic materials into this Priestly genealogy (vv. 1b, 8-19, 21, 24-30). These insertions are clearly separate from their surrounding material in form and content. The Nimrod insertion (vv. 8-12) takes the form of a story rather than a genealogy. The identification of Nimrod with any known hero of the past is difficult. He is credited with the founding of several great cities, which has led scholars to identify Nimrod with Tukulti-Ninurta I (thirteenth century B.C.E.), the Assyrian king who conquered Babylon. Most of the names in verses 21, 24-30 are intended by the Yahwist to be names of individuals, unlike the Priestly author's names, which stand for peoples. Eber is the eponymous ancestor of the Hebrews, that is, the one from whom they took their name. The origin and meaning of the wordplay on the name Peleg (v. 25) is lost.

Though there is much uncertainty about this Table of the Nations, its theological significance is clear. It shows the fulfillment of God's command to increase and multiply found in Gen 1:28 and reiterated to Noah in Gen 9:1. It also shows us that Israel is one among many nations. The choice of Israel by Yahweh does not rest on any special achievement or quality that Israel possessed, but only on God's gracious intervention in its history.

11:1-9 The tower of Babel. The Yahwist tells in story form what the Priestly author has presented in genealogical form in chapter 10. The story may have once been an etiology explaining the diversity of languages and nations. The Yahwist, however, uses it not only as an example of humanity's ongoing sin, but also as a counterpoint to the call of Abraham in Gen 12:1ff. The background of the story is Babylonian. Shinar is an ancient name for Babylon (Babel). The method of brickmaking is characteristic of Mesopotamia, not Palestine, which used stone for building. In spite of the Babylonian milieu of this story, we have not as yet found an actual parallel to this story in any ancient Near Eastern mythology.

The narrative can be divided into three parts: verses 1-4, verses 5-8, verse 9. The first part is a report in which humans are the actors; the second part is discourse in which Yahweh is the chief actor. The final verse is an explanatory supplement that includes a popular etymology of the name Babel and concludes the story. It leads us back to the beginning by reversal: the people were united and their language was one, now they are not.

The people build a city with a tower, and Yahweh punishes them. It is not clear exactly why they are punished. What did they do to force Yahweh's hand? The sin can be inferred from the motive given for building the city: "to make a name for ourselves, lest we be scattered" (v. 4). There is a double motivation. On the one hand, they wish to make a name for themselves on their own initiative, in obvious independence from Yahweh. On the other hand, they seek to avoid being "scattered," which was commanded by God when they were told to "fill the earth" (1:28; 9:1). In this story the people do just the opposite: they come together in one place, a city.

Commentators often focus on the "tower with its top in the sky" (v. 4) as a sign of the sin of pride and rebellion against God, but there is no reason to separate the tower from the city. Most ancient cities were built with watchtowers. "With its top in the sky" simply means that it was a very tall tower. There is no need to identify the tower as a Babylonian temple (ziggurat), as is commonly done. Even if the tower was at one time associated with one of these ancient worship sites, in our story no religious significance is given to the tower.

As is characteristic of the Yahwist stories, this one presents Yahweh very anthropomorphically and contains wordplays. Yahweh "comes down" to see what the people are doing, appearing almost jealous or afraid of the people's growing skills. It is presumed that the "us" whom Yahweh addresses (v.7) are members of the heavenly council (compare Gen 1:26; 6:2). There are wordplays between the Hebrew for "Babel" and "confusion," for "name" and "place." The people sought to make their "name" great, but "from that place," from "Babel," "confusion" arose.

Against the background of the Babel story the Yahwist presents the call of Abraham. The people sought to make their name great, but it is Yahweh who will make Abraham's name great (12:2). They are scattered across the face of the earth; Yahweh will choose one nation, and through that nation all nations on earth will be blessed. Left to themselves they pursue sin; now Yahweh will intervene, not in punishment as in the flood, but in saving love, using Israel to call them back.

11:10-27, 31-32 The genealogy of Abraham. This genealogy of the Priestly author is patterned on the one found in chapter 5, but the lifespans given are considerably shorter. There is an insertion from the Yahwist tradition in verses 28-30. These verses really introduce the Abraham narratives and so will be treated with the call of Abraham (12:1ff.). Some of the names mentioned are actually cities of northwestern Mesopotamia (Serug, Nahor, Terah, Haran), but it was not unusual in the ancient Near East to borrow a name from a place.

In both the Priestly (v. 31) and Yahwist (v. 28) traditions, the birthplace of Terah, Abraham's father, is Ur of the Chaldeans. The identification of Ur as the city of the Chaldeans is anachronistic—the Chaldeans had entered the Mesopotamian region only after the city had reached its peak, and consequently it could not have been connected with the Chaldeans at the time of Abraham's migration. Abraham's migration begins from Haran (11:31; 12:5), and the cultural background assumed in the patriarchal narratives is that of the northwestern Mesopotamian region, not the southern Tigris-Euphrates valley, where Ur was located. Both cities, Ur and Haran, worshiped the moon god, Sin, and there was regular travel between these two cities. The Ur insertions into the text probably reflect the ancient associations between the two cities.

CONCLUSION

The primeval history in Gen 1–11 is a blend of traditions that relates a history of sin that marred the goodness of God's creation. The superiority of humanity over the rest of creation is indicated both by the statement that man and woman are created in the "image of God" and by God's command that they are to have dominion over the world. But because of its continued disobedience against God, humanity is bound to the very earth from which it was formed. Left to itself, it becomes ever more deeply caught in sin. God's forbearance is shown when each divine chastisement is tempered by care, protection, and restoration. The first eleven chapters of Genesis are the background against which the history of salvation moves forward with God's call of Abraham.

THE PATRIARCHAL NARRATIVES

Gen 11:28–36:43

From the story that ended with the whole of humanity scattered across the earth, the Yahwist now narrows the focus to one individual and his descendants. In this complex of sagas the connecting link is the theme of the promise and its fulfillment. The earliest form of the promise may have been only the promise of a son, but as the tradition developed it was expanded to include many descendants, land, greatness as a nation, and blessing. The concern for a descendant occupies most of the Abraham cycle.

It is legitimate to ask historical questions of the patriarchal narratives, but we are cautioned against an oversimplified reconstruction of the lives and historical period of the patriarchs by the nature of the narratives as saga. Nevertheless, the field of archaeology has contributed to our knowledge of the history of the ancient Near East, and there is general agreement that in view of the lifestyle and customs reflected in the patriarchal narratives, the patriarchs are to be situated in the region of the Fertile Crescent in the second millennium B.C.E.

THE ABRAHAM CYCLE

Gen 11:28–25:18

11:28-29; 12:1-9 The call and response of Abram. There is little preparation given for the call of Abram. (Abram and Abraham are variants of the same name, as are Sarai and Sarah. The changes in their names occur in 17:5 and 15 to indicate their new relationship to God as a result of the covenant.) Only the briefest mention is made of the migrations of Terah and his family. It is interesting that Milcah's father is remembered, but not the more important Sarai. Sarai's barrenness is mentioned in anticipation of later narratives and makes all the more paradoxical Yahweh's promise of many descendants in 12:2.

The promise to Abram represents a new phase in the Yahwist narrative. Previously we moved within the realm of primeval history, the history of all humanity; now we center on an individual, soon to become a family, and finally a nation. The choice of Abram remains a mystery in the Yahwist story, resting solely on God's initiative. The promise is dominated by the term "bless" (five times). What Yahweh offers to Abram will prove to be a sign of divine favor and a source of happiness to Abram himself. To be a great nation, Abram will need descendants and land. Both these aspects of blessing are spelled out in more detail in the following narratives. Abram's fame will come as a result of his trust in Yahweh's actions, not, as in the case of the Babel story, by means of making a name for himself. The final element in God's promise, the promise that all communities of the earth will find blessing in Abram, probably meant that Abram would be taken as the exemplar of divine blessing (Gen 48:20). Eventually, it came to be understood that Israel would actually be the mediator or agent of God's blessing to the world (Sir 44:21).

The Yahwist gives us no information about Abram's reaction to Yahweh's promise nor any indication of Abram's motives in obeying God's command. It is simply stated that "Abram went as the Lord directed" (v. 4). We can infer Abram's unquestioning faith and obedience from his response. The subject of the faith will come up again and again in the Abraham cycle of stories.

The narrator deliberately records that Shechem was Abram's first stop, because this ancient Canaanite city became an early center of Israelite cult (Josh 24:1; 1 Kgs 12:1). The patriarchs Abraham and Jacob are frequently presented as establishing altars and worshiping God in ancient Canaanite cities in response to some experience of the holy in these cities. This is a way of explaining why these originally pagan cities became worship centers in Israel. The terebinth of Moreh (v. 6) was a sacred tree, indicating that an ancient cult already existed at Shechem prior to Abram's visit. Old Testament events of great significance often occur near sacred trees, which were believed to be special places for receiving divine communication. It is here that Yahweh promises to give Abram the land of Canaan. Beyond being a statement of fact, the phrase "the Canaanites were then in the land" (v. 6) points to the unusual character of the promise given to Abram. The land will be possessed and the promise fulfilled by his descendants, not during Abram's own lifetime.

As Abram continues to journey south, he stops between Bethel and Ai, other ancient Canaanite cities that become important in Israel. Again he builds an altar to Yahweh, though we are not told why. Abram's travels bring him to the Negeb region, which is especially associated with him.

12:10-20 The ancestress in danger. Soon after the promise of land (12:7), we find Abram traveling to Egypt because of a famine. It was not unusual for Semitic peoples to go to Egypt in search of food, as is evidenced in Egyptian records of the period. But in light of the promise of land, it does not put Abram in the best light. What is even more striking about the story is that the patriarch, in order to ensure his own safety, knowingly compromises his wife's honor. He fears that his wife's beauty will come to the attention of Pharaoh and that Pharaoh will kill him in order to take Sarai into the royal harem. He persuades Sarai to lie by saying that she is his sister so that his life will not be in danger. As Abram had predicted, Sarai's beauty comes to the attention of the Egyptians, and Pharaoh, assuming that Abram is her brother, bestows gifts upon Abram and takes Sarai into his harem. Yahweh intervenes by sending a plague on Pharaoh's house but does not punish Abram. Pharaoh reprimands Abram and sends him away under military escort.

The wife-sister motif in this story may reflect an ancient Hurrian practice in northern Mesopotamia by which a husband adopted his wife as his sister. This gave the husband greater control over the wife, but it also gave the wife protection and privileges beyond those given to the ordinary wife. Such a practice eventually died out, and the narrator of the story does not seem to be aware of it.

Essentially the same story is also found in Gen 20:1-18 (E) and Gen 26:6-11 (J), but with some variations in characters and incidents. The alterations in subsequent versions indicate a greater sensitivity to the moral overtones of the story. Abraham no longer lies, since Sarah is said to be his half-sister, and God intervenes before her honor is compromised. The narrator of Gen 12 does not seek to excuse Abram's behavior, but rather seems to take delight in his shrewdness. The story also shows that in spite of what Abram and Sarai do, they are under God's protection, and God will intervene to secure the future realization of the promise when it is placed in jeopardy.

The story and the context in which it is found presents some difficulties. How does Pharaoh know that the plague is sent because of Sarai? How does he learn that Sarai is Abram's wife? These questions are never answered. The mention of camels in verse 16 is certainly anachronistic, for camels were not domesticated until the thirteenth century B.C.E. Is one to suppose that Sarai is actually sixty-five years old in the story (see Gen 12:4b; 17:17)? These inconsistencies were not of importance to the narrator, though they bother contemporary readers. The narrator's interest is in God's intervention that redeems the situation.

13:1-18 Separation of Lot and Abram. Abram's journey, first to the Negeb and then, by stages, north to Bethel, was typical of nomads in search of pastures for their flocks. Their movements were governed by the need for grazing land, and they were often found moving about near cities. Both Abram and Lot are described as having large flocks, and they agree to separate to forestall future arguments between them over rights to pastureland. Their herdsmen have already begun to quarrel. Abram, though older and by rights the one who could choose first, very magnanimously defers to Lot. Lot picks the land that looked lush and fertile, the Jordan Plain, and settles near Sodom. Lot's choice is ironic, for this is a territory that will be destroyed by Yahweh. The events of Gen 19 are here anticipated by the narrator.

Verses 14-17 may not have been part of the original story, but they now serve as its climax. The promise of land parallels the promise given in Gen 12:2-3, 7; the promise of innumerable descendants is added. Abram's walking the length and breadth of the land is a symbolic act indicating that he is taking legal possession of it, even though it is not his (13:7). Abram finally settles near the terebinth of Mamre.

14:1-24 Abram and Melchizedek. There is universal agreement that Gen 14 is one of the most difficult chapters in the Book of Genesis. It is very different from the rest of the patriarchal narratives. It begins like a report from an ancient chronicle and is replete with historical and geographical details. Abram is pictured, not as a peaceful nomad, but as a commander of forces involved in a war. The sequence of events that flows from chapter 13 to chapter 15 is interrupted by chapter 14. It is impossible to determine the source of this chapter. Consequently, scholars speak of it as an insertion into the patriarchal narratives, independent of any of the sources (J, E, P).

There is considerable debate about the historical reliability of the chapter. Are the cities and kings that are named evidence of the antiquity and historical reliability of the passage, or is the author of this insertion merely imitating historical style? Can we identify with certainty the kings and cities mentioned in chapter 14? The answers to these questions are very complex and, while of interest, are beyond the scope of this commentary. Our concern in chapter 14 will center mainly on Abram and his meeting with Melchizedek.

Chapter 14 is composed of two distinct parts: verses 1-16, 21-24, and verses 17-21. It seems that Abram has been introduced into the first part of the chapter precisely because of his encounter with Melchizedek, which serves as the conclusion and climax of the chapter. The name Melchizedek means "Zedek [a god] is my king." The city of Salem is to be identified with the city of Jerusalem (Ps 76:2). That Melchizedek is both a king and a priest is not unusual—that was often the case in the ancient Near East. The god he worships, "God Most High, the creator of heaven and earth" (v. 19), was the head of the Canaanite pantheon and supreme over the other gods and the world. Melchizedek offers Abram bread and wine, which may simply have been refreshment but could have had some ritual significance; he also blesses Abram. Abram, for his part, identifies Yahweh with God Most High (v. 22) and accepts Melchizedek's blessing. There is some question regarding who pays tribute to whom (v. 20). The subject of the sentence in the Hebrew text is simply "he" and not Abram, as supplied in our text. The context would seem to indicate that it is Melchizedek who not only blesses Abram but also pays him tribute.

Many scholars see in this passage an argument in support of the reign of the Davidic dynasty and its assimilation of priestly duties. It is true that Melchizedek was seen as a prototype of the ideal Davidic king (Ps 110:4), but it goes beyond the text to say that Abram's acceptance of Melchizedek's blessing suggests that Abram's descendants will accept the Davidic dynasty. The inclusion of the passage probably reflects the author's interest in linking Abram with Jerusalem and its priest-king, and in the identification of Yahweh with the God in whose name Abram is blessed.

15:1-21 The covenant with Abram. A source analysis of chapter 15 is difficult. Some scholars have argued for the presence of the Elohist source in 15:1-6, but the consensus is that the entire chapter was composed by the Yahwist, in spite of several inconsistencies that point to a combination of sources. It is likely that the Yahwist author is drawing from several traditions and harmonizes them with only partial success.

The problems in the text are obvious. The covenant ceremony takes place at sunset in verses 12 and 17, yet in verse 5 it is already night. In verse 8 Abram expresses doubt, whereas his faith is emphasized in verse 6. Yahweh's name is revealed in verse 7 but is already known by Abram in verse 2. These inconsistencies are removed if we separate verses 1-6, 13-16, which are concerned with the issue of descendants, from verses 7-12, 17-21, which focus on a covenant ritual surrounding the promise of the land. Thus we have at least two separate traditions that make up this chapter, though they are interrelated in a carefully constructed passage.

The first six verses show elements drawn both from prophetic traditions and from the cultic sphere. The opening phrase, "this word of the Lord came to Abram," is recognized as a prophetic formula (compare Isa 1:1; Ezek 1:1; Amos 1:1) and suggests that the author sees in God's summons to Abram a call similar to that of a prophet. The cultic background of the passage is clear, for its structure is patterned after the format of cultic celebrations: God's self-manifestation (v. 1) is followed by a salvation oracle (vv. 4, 5) and a declaration of righteousness (v. 6). Yahweh's admonition against fear is not unusual, for in the ancient world an encounter with the Deity was understood as a terror-filled event. "Fear not" is often found in the Old Testament accompanying a manifestation of God (see Judg 6:23; Isa 41:10). The title "shield" is frequently used of God as protector and deliverer (see Pss 3:3; 18:2; 28:7, etc.). It is a title drawn from the cult, and this is its only occurrence in the patriarchal narratives. The reward that Yahweh promises to Abram is certainly to be read against chapter 14, where Abram returned home with no recompense.

Difficulties in the original Hebrew text make the translation of verse 2 uncertain. However, verse 3 is clear and parallels the content of verse 2: Abram is concerned that a servant born in his household will become his heir. The practice of a slave becoming the heir of a childless couple accords with the customs of Mesopotamia in the fifteenth century B.C.E., as confirmed by the discovery of legal texts from Nuzi. Yahweh's answer to Abram is not a mere reiteration of the promise of innumerable descendants, but specifically assures Abram that his own issue will be his heir. Abram's response is faith in Yahweh. He trusts Yahweh completely and sets aside his doubts and anxiety. His righteousness is affirmed on the basis of this response. His total reliance upon Yahweh puts him in right relationship to Yahweh.

Verse 7 begins with a second self-introduction of the Deity in language and form drawn from the cult. The promise now focuses on land, not descendants. The confirmation of Yahweh's promise of the land is secured in the covenant ceremony described in verses 9-11, 17-20. This primitive ritual and its significance are mentioned in Jer 34:18, and discoveries within the past century have shown that this manner of making covenants was widespread in the ancient Near East. Cutting the animal in two and walking between the separate pieces bound the parties in covenant. If they failed to keep the terms of the covenant, they were cursed to share a fate like that of the split animal. The birds of prey that swoop down upon the carcasses are probably to be interpreted as omens of evil, but the exact meaning of the portent is not clear. Abram falls into a deep sleep, a state of suspended activity, in which he can receive a divine revelation. The covenant ceremony concludes when a fire pot and a flaming torch pass between the severed parts of the animal (v. 17). Fire is often a sign of the presence of God, and this is certainly what it represents in this passage. Yahweh initiates the covenant and agrees to be bound to it. The final verses (vv. 18-21) specify the extent of the promised land, which corresponds to the extent of the Davidic empire under Solomon.

Verses 13-16 interrupt the description of the covenant ceremony. They explain why it is not Abram himself but his descendants who will possess the land. Yahweh is not lacking in power; rather, the Amorites are allotted a measure of time before they are judged by God. These verses show a theology of history in which Yahweh rules over history and brings about the fulfillment of the divine promise to Abram in that history.

Chapter 15 confirms God's covenant with Abram: he will have a son, he will have many descendants, and one day they will possess the land.

16:1-16 The birth of Ishmael. The story of the birth of Ishmael is primarily the work of the Yahwist. Only in verses 3 and 15-16 do we find insertions from the Priestly author. The Priestly insertions give the essentials of the story but lack the lively, dramatic character of the Yahwist story. Through the eyes of the Yahwist we glimpse the frustration and jealousy of Sarai, the arrogance of Hagar, and the passivity of Abram.

Actually the elements that make up the story are not as scandalous as they may appear to the modern reader. Sarai's proposal that Abraham impregnate her servant, Hagar (v. 2), was in conformity with the legal customs of Mesopotamia. A barren wife could give her servant to her husband so that children could be fathered. The children of the concubine were considered the legal offspring of the wife, just as Sarai states: "perhaps I shall have sons through her" (v. 2). It is certainly understandable that a servant who now shares the master's bed may assume a certain equality to, or even superiority over, the barren wife. The law provided for servants who "forgot their place," however, by specifying that they be returned to their former status of servant. This is precisely what happens in the story (vv. 4-6). Abram is following the law when he returns Hagar to Sarai's control. Nonetheless, Sarai's severity with Hagar exceeds the law and does not enhance her character.

Hagar, an Egyptian, flees south because of Sarai's harsh treatment. She is apparently on her way back to Egypt when she is met by the messenger of Yahweh (v. 7). There is no clear distinction between Yahweh and the messenger of Yahweh (v. 13); it is simply a way of indicating that a message comes from Yahweh and at the same time preserves Yahweh's transcendence over the created world. The messenger's words of assurance echo the promise given to Abram: Hagar will be the mother of many descendants (v. 10). The name Ishmael is explained by popular etymology as meaning "God hears." Yahweh has heard Hagar's cry and has come to her aid. The description of Ishmael that follows (v. 12) is etiological in character. Ishmael, the son of a proud and rebellious mother, becomes the ancestor of the desert tribes, known for their wild, free spirit and warlike nature. Israel does not forget that it is closely related to these peoples; they are offspring of the same father.

The final verses (vv. 13-16) are not entirely clear, but it seems that some connection is drawn between the name given to a well, "Well of living sight" (?), and the name given to Yahweh by Hagar, "God of Vision." In ancient times there may have been a sanctuary to this God at this place. "God of Vision" was the name of a deity worshiped in Canaan.

The interest of the Yahwist does not center on the etiologies in the story; rather, the episode is intended to show that the fulfillment of God's promise depends upon God alone, not on human inventiveness. By situating this incident between the promise and its fulfillment, the story delays the realization of the promise and thus heightens the suspense. The reader is drawn into the story: When will Yahweh fulfill the promise?

17:1-14 The covenant with Abram. The covenant with Abram, recounted by the Yahwist in chapter 15, is told here by the Priestly author. This account consists primarily of an address by Yahweh and lacks the human-interest quality so characteristic of the Yahwist. It is more theological in tone, telling us very little about Abram's personal reactions. The chronological details, the theological orientation, and the concern with circumcision are all typical of the Priestly author.

Like the Yahwist version, the passage opens with God's self-introduction. The name "God Almighty" (El Shaddai) has special significance for the Priestly author, who limits the use of this name for God to the patriarchal narratives; it thus becomes the distinctive name of God associated with this period (28:3; 35:11; 48:3). In the primeval history God was called Elohim; in the future God will be known to Israel as Yahweh (Exod 6:3f.). The meaning of the name El Shaddai is uncertain, but there is some evidence to support the view that it means "mountain god."

The covenant is portrayed, not as an oath taken by God, as in the Yahwist version, but as a contract. God will give Abram many descendants; Abram, for his part, is commanded to walk in God's presence, to be blameless, and to practice circumcision as a sign of the covenant between them. The change in Abram's name (v. 5) signals his new relationship to God and the new life granted by the covenant. The new name, Abraham, is said to mean "father of a multitude of nations," but actually the name is simply a variation of the name Abram, which means "my father [the god] is exalted."

Some new elements introduced into the Priestly account are to be noted. The covenant is made not simply with Abraham but also with his descendants, and it will be an everlasting covenant (v. 7). In addition, a new relationship with God forms part of the covenant: this God who makes covenant with Abraham will be his God and the God of his descendants. This anticipates the relationship between Yahweh and Israel that will be established at Sinai.

Circumcision only became an important sign of the covenant during the Babylonian Exile (586–538 B.C.E.); it is doubtful that it always had this significance for Israel. Circumcision was practiced in ancient Egypt and by the Semitic peoples that lived in Canaan. It was not practiced in Mesopotamia nor by the Philistines, whom Israel referred to as the "uncircumcised" (2 Sam 1:20). It is not clear why the practice of infant circumcision developed, since circumcision was associated with puberty rites in other cultures. Circumcision may originally have had some religious significance now lost to us, or it may have been done simply for hygienic reasons. The exiles living in Babylon took circumcision to be a sign of their religious identity over against the Babylonians, who did not practice the ritual. For the Priestly author, whose writing originated in the exilic community, circumcision becomes the sign of inclusion in the community that worships Yahweh. Circumcision is so important for this source that if one is not circumcised, he is not considered a member of the covenanted people (v. 14).

17:15-27 The birth of Isaac. The announcement of the birth of Isaac interrupts the account of the command to circumcise and its eventual enactment related in verses 23-27. In all three sources—the Yahwist, Elohist, and Priestly—Isaac is the child of promise, and the unexpectedness of his birth points to God's great power in making the impossible a reality. As Abram's name is changed to signal his new role, so too Sarai's new role as mother is accompanied by the change of her name (v. 15), even though Sarah is really only a dialectical variant of the name Sarai.

Abraham's reaction to the announcement of Isaac's birth to Sarah, who is well beyond childbearing age (ninety years old), is an understandable mixture of respect and disbelief; he shows reverence to God by paying homage, but he cannot help but laugh. The laughter motif is also found in the Yahwist and Elohist traditions. It explains Isaac's name, which means "laughter" in Hebrew. Abraham thinks of Sarah's advanced age and directs God's attention to Ishmael. God seems to have forgotten how old Sarah is, and Abraham offers God a way out, but God is not to be diverted. The promise will be fulfilled in Sarah's descendants, not Hagar's. Ishmael will not be forgotten. He too will become a great nation, but the covenant is to be with Isaac's descendants.

18:1-15 The announcement of the birth of Isaac. This is one of the Yahwist author's most delightful stories. The Yahwist draws upon a common folk-tale motif—a story in which strangers who have been treated hospitably turn out to be divine guests. They, in turn, reward those who have been gracious to them. With this motif, developed against the background of the custom of desert hospitality, the Yahwist interweaves the announcement of the birth of Isaac, and the story moves one step closer to the fulfillment of the promise.

The only real problem in the narrative is the relationship between Yahweh and the three strangers. The text states that Yahweh appeared to Abraham, and then, suddenly, Abraham sees three strangers. The shift back and forth between Yahweh and the three visitors continues throughout the story. It is difficult to determine what the author means. Is Yahweh one of the three, or do all three stand for Yahweh? Perhaps the author is drawing upon a tradition that was originally polytheistic and feels constrained to leave it unchanged. The Yahwist may have kept the ambiguity in the story to suggest the mystery that surrounds God's presence in the world.

It must be remembered throughout this story that Abraham is an old man and Sarah is an old woman. Though the exact ages of ninety-nine years for Abraham and ninety years for Sarah come from the later Priestly source, even the Yahwist considers both Abraham and Sarah to be advanced in years (v. 12). The setting of the story is the terebinths of Mamre, a holy place very appropriate for this divine visitation. Abraham is sitting in the entrance of the tent in the heat of the day, which is the only place to be in midafternoon when the desert sun scorches the earth, especially if you are an old, old man. The three visitors suddenly appear at this unusual time. Who would be out walking in the heat? Equally strange is the detail that says that this old man runs and bows profusely to the ground. All of Abraham's actions are in excess, suggesting that he suspects the divine character of his guests and hopes that by displaying his great hospitality he may exact a favor from them.

Abraham becomes extremely verbose, in contrast to his later behavior (v. 9). His offer of a morsel of bread ("little food" in our text) and a little water ("some water" in our text) is an understatement in the extreme, for he has Sarah bake nearly a bushel's worth of flour into bread, he has prepared the best steer from his herd, and, in addition, he serves curds and milk with the meal. This is not a drop of water and a crumb of bread but a banquet befitting a king. As a good host, Abraham serves his guests and, as was the custom, Sarah is not present, since women did not eat with the men. She is nearby in the tent, however, as is evident later in the story.

After the meal the strangers ask a question that could only have caused great shock to the storyteller's audience (v. 9). According to desert hospitality, a guest was given anything that was requested. This included taking his pleasure with the wife of the host. It was certainly rude to ask for the host's wife, but a guest could not be denied. The abruptness of Abraham's answer indicates his shock at their request. Sarah, who is listening near the entrance of the tent, finds the exchange quite humorous. She may have been a beauty in the past (12:10ff.), but now she is old.

The shocking request is not what it seemed at first, however, but serves to introduce the announcement of the birth of Abraham's long-awaited descendant. That the guests are aware of Sarah's laughter and inner thoughts must certainly have unnerved her, for she hastens to deny that she laughed. But the guests do not allow her denial to stand, and the final word of the story, "You laughed," would have reminded a Hebrew audience of the name of the promised child, Isaac, meaning "laughter."

18:16-33 Abraham's intercession for Sodom. This section was evidently not drawn from ancient traditions but was freely composed by the Yahwist. In it we find a rather developed theology presented in two short conversations. In the first (vv. 17-18), in terms reminiscent of the promise (12:2-3), Yahweh decides to tell Abraham of the judgment made upon Sodom. God's intentionality and actions, previously hidden, are now revealed to the chosen one, Abraham, in order that he might be able to teach his descendants about God's justice. Thus the destruction of Sodom takes on a special admonitory significance for future generations.

The second conversation is between Abraham and Yahweh. It is a rather entertaining example of Oriental bargaining at its best, but its underlying concerns are quite serious. The question of justice is at stake: Is it just to destroy the innocent, few as they may be, along with the vast majority who are guilty? Are the innocent important enough to forestall the punishment of the wicked? Tension in the encounter is created by Abraham, who, though deferential toward Yahweh, dares to enter into debate and continues to press Yahweh at each step of the exchange by boldly attempting to reduce the minimum number of innocent needed to save the city. Not only is Yahweh's patience revealed in the dialogue, but also Yahweh's great willingness to set aside punishment for the sake of the innocent few.

19:1-29 The destruction of Sodom. The story of the destruction of Sodom, though once an independent saga, is now well integrated into the Abraham cycle. The two messengers, who separated from Yahweh in 18:22, arrive in Sodom. The purpose of their visit is to determine whether the outcry against Sodom (18:20) is justified. Lot is found at the city gate, which was the usual gathering place for townsmen. Unlike chapter 13, where Lot was pictured as a herder and a nomad, he is now a city-dweller. He persuades the strangers to spend the night at his home. In the course of the evening, Lot's fellow townsmen come and demand that his guests be sent out to them so that they may take pleasure with them. It is clear that for the Yahwist, inhospitality, so serious in a nomadic society, and sexual perversion, against which there is a strong Old Testament bias, are the sins for which the city is condemned.

We are shocked by Lot's attempt to placate the townsmen by offering to give them his two virgin daughters for their pleasure, but it is unlikely that an ancient audience would have been as horrified. They would have seen in Lot's offer a noble attempt, even if extreme, to fulfill the demands of hospitality. Lot is unsuccessful, and he himself is rescued by the two guests, who strike the townsmen blind. The wickedness of Sodom is confirmed and its destruction is imminent. Lot and his family must flee to save themselves from the destruction. The weak and vacillating character of Lot is revealed in his hesitation to leave; he must be led out of the city (v. 16).

There are etiological motifs tied to the story. Lot refuses to flee to the mountains but wants to escape to a "small" city, Zoar (v. 20). The name Zoar means "little" or "insignificant." He is granted this favor, and Zoar is spared from judgment. Lot's wife becomes a pillar of salt when she turns to see the destruction, for they had been commanded not to look back. There are many salt formations surrounding the southern end of the Dead Sea; the story explains their presence and shows the consequences of disobedience.

The destruction of Sodom may be based on some actual violent natural disaster in the distant past, but this is impossible to verify. The concern of the Yahwist is to explain the destruction of the region as God's judgment upon sin. The final verse (v. 29) is a summation of the story and is attributed to the Priestly author.

19:30-38 The ancestry of the Moabites and Ammonites. This story deals with the ancestry of the Israelites' neighbors, with whom they recognized a certain kinship but who nevertheless were their enemies and were barred from ever becoming members of the covenant community (Deut 23:4). The story was probably originally told in praise of the actions of the ancestresses, who take extreme measures to ensure the continuance of the family line. They are certainly not ashamed of their actions, since their children proudly bear names that tell of their deeds: Moab ("From my father") and Ammon ("The son of my kin"). The Yahwist includes the story in order to disparage the ancestry of Israel's traditional enemies.

20:1-18 Endangering the ancestress a second time. This story is immediately recognized as a doublet of the Yahwist story in 12:10-20. There is universal agreement that it is to be identified as the product of the Elohist. In addition to the use of the Hebrew Elohim for the divine name, the Elohist's authorship is indicated by the use of dreams as a means of divine communication. The distinctive concerns of the Elohist are all the more apparent when contrasted with the earlier version. Whereas the Yahwist presented at some length Abraham's motives for passing off Sarah as his sister and explained how she came to be in Pharaoh's harem, these concerns are largely ignored by the Elohist, who focuses rather on Abimelech's guilt and deliverance. In spite of the fact that Abimelech acted in ignorance and consequently did not intend to do wrong, he is considered guilty. He has sinned by taking another man's wife into his harem, even if he acted unknowingly, and that act cannot go without some form of punishment. In this case it is Abraham, whose own guilt is overlooked, who will be able to intercede on Abimelech's behalf. Abraham, who has special access to God in virtue of his call, is depicted in the role of mediator and prophet.

There are other differences between the two accounts. It is not clear in the Yahwist's version whether Pharaoh actually had relations with Sarah, but the Elohist leaves no doubt that God intervened before Abimelech even touched her. Here Abimelech's gifts to Abraham stand as testimony to the honorableness of Abraham and Sarah. In the Yahwist's version gifts are given when Sarah is first taken into Pharaoh's harem. The Elohist's moral sensitivity is indicated by his attempt to justify Abraham's action, stating that Sarah was indeed Abraham's half-sister. Whereas the Yahwist allows the patriarch's behavior to speak for itself, the Elohist explains Abraham's actions in order to present a more honorable picture of his ancestor.

21:1-21 The birth of Isaac and the expulsion of Hagar and Ishmael. All three sources are found in this account of the birth of Isaac. The Yahwist version (21:1, 6b, 7) simply presents the birth of Isaac in Sarah's old age as the fulfillment of Yahweh's promise (18:10). Laughter is connected with Isaac's name because it is the response Sarah expects from her neighbors when they hear that she has given birth in her old age. In the Priestly version (21:2-5), Isaac's birth is also said to be the fulfillment of God's promise (17:21), but this author adds that Abraham named and circumcised the child according to God's command (17:19, 12). Regarding the Elohist version (21:6a), only the motif of laughter associated with the name Isaac is retained.

The child is called Isaac because of Sarah's joy (laughter) at his birth.

The Elohist narrative of Isaac's birth (vv. 8-21) is a duplicate of the story of the expulsion of Hagar and Ishmael found in the Yahwist version in chapter 16. But as one might expect, there are significant differences in this version. It is Sarah's jealousy, not Hagar's arrogance, that leads her to demand that Abraham expel the two. She fears that Isaac's future inheritance is threatened by Ishmael's presence in the home. Here Abraham reacts more strongly to Sarah's demand than in the Yahwist version, where he remained passive. He gives in to her demand only when God tells him to do so and when God assures him that Ishmael will be the father of a great nation.

The Elohist paints a very poignant picture of Hagar's departure and of her subsequent despair when lack of water threatens her life and that of the child. God intervenes through a messenger, and Hagar is assured of Ishmael's future and, by means of God's assistance, she finds water. Ishmael becomes the father of camel nomads (Ishmaelites), who lived in the wilderness between Palestine and Egypt. They lived by hunting and plundering, as indicated by the phrase "he became an expert bowman" (v. 21).

The Elohist story suppresses the etiological interests of the Yahwist version. It ennobles the figure of Abraham, and even Hagar is presented in a better light than in chapter 16. God directs the action by ensuring the future of both the child of promise and the child of Hagar.

21:22-34 Abraham and Abimelech at Beer-sheba. The passage contains two separate agreements between Abraham and Abimelech, and thus the question of separate sources arises. Some scholars attempt to find evidence in this passage of both the Yahwist and the Elohist; others suppose that one author, the Elohist, drew upon two separate traditions in the composition of the passage.

The first agreement (vv. 22-24, 27, 31, 32b, 34) is initiated by Abimelech and presupposes the events of chapter 20. Abimelech wants to be assured of Abraham's friendship and suggests a covenant as a guarantee of Abraham's loyalty. Abraham agrees. The covenant oath is sworn at Beer-sheba, a name meaning "well of the oath."

The nature of the second agreement (vv. 25-26, 28-30, 32a, 33) is quite different. Abraham initiates the covenant in response to a dispute over a well. The seven lambs accepted by Abimelech indicate that he recognizes Abraham's claim to the well. The place was called Beer-sheba, "well of the seven," because of Abraham's gift. The purpose of this account is to show that the well at Beer-sheba, a sacred place for Israel, originated with Abraham. Its cultic significance is suggested in verse 33. At Beer-sheba, Abraham calls upon "God the Eternal" (El Olam), a divine name used by the Canaanites and eventually given to Yahweh by Israel (see Ps 102:25, 28).

22:1-19 The sacrifice of Isaac. The story of the sacrifice of Isaac, generally attributed to the Elohist, is one of the great masterpieces of narrative art in the Bible. We are drawn into the action of the story from the very start and are held in suspense until the climax. We know, as readers, that what is recounted is a test for Abraham; thus we focus on Abraham's response and not on the horror of God's command. We are left to imagine Abraham's inner thoughts while the narrator tells us only what he does. We follow Abraham each step of the way as he complies with the divine command. We feel the silence as father and son walk together, coming closer with each step, to that moment of ultimate decision. We smile at Isaac's innocent question and sympathize with Abraham in his tender but evasive answer. We watch as each detail of that final moment unfolds, from the building of the altar to Abraham's poised knife, ready to claim his son's life. We wait expectantly until the angel intervenes, and finally we rejoice at the turn of events. Abraham has withstood the test, and Isaac still lives.

It is clear that the story is concerned with Abraham's great faith, which is expressed in his willingness to sacrifice his son, the child of promise, in accord with God's command. A connection between this story and human sacrifice is often made. Human sacrifice was commonly practiced among Israel's neighbors, and on a few occasions even in Israel, though it was forbidden (see 1 Kgs 16:34; 2 Kgs 3:27; 23:10). It may be that the story originally centered on a repudiation of the practice of human sacrifice. However, any earlier significance is now superseded by the motif of the testing of Abraham's faith.

The original conclusion of the story was verse 14, but a supplement was added (vv. 15-19) to link the story with the theme of promise, the dominant theme of the patriarchal narratives.

22:20-23 The genealogy of Nahor. This genealogy is attributed to the Yahwist. It lists the twelve sons of Nahor, who are Semitic (Aramean) relatives of Israel. The purpose of its inclusion is to prepare the way for the appearance of Rebekah (v. 23) in chapter 24.

23:1-19 Abraham's purchase of Machpelah. It is often argued that the Priestly author is responsible for this story, though the vividness of presentation reminds one of the Yahwist. The passage tells how Abraham bought a piece of land in Canaan as a place to bury his wife. In doing so, it provides us with another delightful glimpse at the art of Oriental bargaining.

Abraham is a sojourner in the land, and as such has only limited rights; he cannot own property legally. For Abraham to acquire property, the matter must be decided by the elders of the city. The Hittites with whom Abraham negotiates would not have been Anatolian Hittites, who were powerful in the sixteenth/fifteenth centuries B.C.E. but one of the many groups living in pre-Israelite Canaan. In the exchange each party attempts to outdo the other in courtesy. The Hittites are hesitant to sell land to a sojourner but will allow Abraham to bury Sarah in any of their burial sites. This is not what Abraham wants, and he purposely ignores their suggestion and indicates the precise piece of land he wants to buy. Ephron, the owner of the land, magnanimously offers to "give" Abraham not only the cave he wants but also the field where the cave is located. Abraham graciously refuses to take the land as a gift but insists that he will pay for it.

This exchange is entirely within the bounds of the convention of bartering. While Abraham could have continued bartering for a lesser price, he accepts Ephron's first offer. It is difficult to determine whether the four hundred shekels paid by Abraham was considered exorbitant, because the value of the shekel varied. The fact that it was Ephron's first offer, when he certainly expected Abraham to make a counteroffer, suggests that the price was high. By comparison, David pays only fifty shekels for a threshing floor and oxen (2 Sam 24:24). In verses 16-20 we find a formal contract of sale. Abraham achieves his objective—he now owns property in Canaan for Sarah's burial.

Though this chapter correctly reflects the legal and social customs of the ancient Near East, its purpose is not simply to record an event in the life of Abraham. Rather, Abraham's possession of a portion of the land stands as a pledge of the future possession of the land in its entirety.

24:1-67 Finding a wife for Isaac. This charming story is another instance of the superior storytelling art of the Yahwist. There is some evidence of compilation, but it does not affect the unity of the story. The repetition, which the modern reader finds tiresome, is typical of biblical narrative and does not really detract from the story. The theme of promise remains in the background. In the forefront is God's guidance, but this guidance is directed through the heart. God does not intervene directly.

Abraham, according to custom, must arrange for the marriage of his son. Since he is old and near death, he entrusts the task of finding a wife for Isaac to a servant, who functions more like a trusted steward than a mere servant. Abraham binds the servant by oath to carry out this mission, underscoring its supreme importance. The "thigh" of verse 2 is a euphemism for the genitalia, which were viewed as sacred because they were understood to be the source of life. The servant is not to let Isaac marry a Canaanite woman. This prohibition is meant to exclude the possibility of intermingling religions; it does not reflect a racial bias as such. Under no circumstances is Isaac to be allowed to return to Abraham's country (v. 6). Such a journey apparently was viewed as a turning back on God's promise of the land. The assurance is given that God will guide the entire enterprise and bring it to successful conclusion.

The story barely mentions the servant's lengthy journey to Haran but moves immediately to the search for a suitable wife. At a well outside the city, the servant places the success of his mission in God's hands and suggests a sign by which he will recognize God's choice. The sign of drawing water, not only for the servant but also for ten thirsty camels, is meant to reveal the character of the woman; only a generous and industrious woman would willingly draw the many gallons of water needed. Rebekah arrives (v. 15) and, unknowingly, carries out the requirements of the sign. For this she is showered with gifts, which are probably meant to be part of the bride price. The servant is even more certain of God's guidance when he discovers that Rebekah is the grand-niece of Abraham and she invites him to her mother's home. It seems clear from this reference to her mother's home and from the fact that all subsequent negotiations take place with Laban, her brother, that Rebekah's father is deceased.

Laban's character is revealed in his haste to invite this wealthy stranger to his home after seeing the expensive gifts Rebekah has been given. His greed will become even more apparent in the Jacob-Laban stories that follow. The servant is treated with all due courtesy, but the urgency of his mission compels him to relate his story before eating. This section repeats Abraham's speech in the opening scene, with one significant omission: the servant does not allude to Abraham's refusal to allow Isaac to go to his homeland, for this would probably offend Rebekah's family. Laban admits that God has directed the servant and agrees to the marriage. Appropriately, more gifts are given to seal the agreement (v. 53).

Custom demanded a period of celebration, but the servant wants to be on his way and suggests that he leave immediately with Rebekah. The family understandably objects, but the servant reminds Laban that Yahweh has been directing the mission and so there is no need for delay. Rebekah's feelings in the matter are now solicited, in accordance with ancient customs, which held that a woman's consent was necessary when her brother arranged the marriage or when that marriage meant that she would have to leave her homeland. In this instance both stipulations are operative. Rebekah agrees and is given an ancient blessing promising fertility and power over enemies in the future (v. 60).

The final scene shifts to the Negeb as the caravan is returning. The text is untranslatable, so we can only guess what Isaac was doing as he saw his future bride approaching. Rebekah veils herself, according to custom—the groom was not to see the bride until after the wedding. The passage ends with their marriage and subsequent love. The order of marriage first and love second reflects what was often the case with arranged marriages.

25:1-18 Abraham's death. This section combines genealogies of the Yahwist (vv. 1-6, 11b) and Priestly (vv. 12-18) sources with an account of Abraham's death (vv. 7-11a, P). It is hard to fit the opening verses, which tell of Abraham's marriage, with the previous story, wherein Abraham is old and certainly dies before Rebekah marries Isaac (see 24:65: Isaac is now the servant's master). This discrepancy is probably to be explained by the juxtaposition of Yahwist and Priestly stories that do not follow the same chronologies. Keturah, Abraham's second wife, becomes the mother of the Arabian tribes that inhabited southern Palestine and northwestern Arabia. The gifts given to these children by Abraham testify to his generosity but also safeguard the inheritance for Isaac.

Abraham dies after a full life. It is not surprising to find Ishmael present at his father's funeral (v. 9), for the Priestly author does not provide an account of Hagar's expulsion. Abraham is laid to rest in the family tomb (see ch. 23). The chapter concludes with the Priestly genealogy of Ishmael, who becomes the father of twelve tribes that occupy the northwestern Arabian wilderness. The promise given to Abraham about Ishmael (21:13, E) is seen as fulfilled.

THE JACOB CYCLE

Gen 25:19–36:43

The Jacob cycle of stories differs from the Abraham cycle in the inner coherence of the cycle. Only the thread of promise united the Abraham cycle; each segment remained a separate unit. In the Jacob cycle, in addition to the theme of promise that continues to run through these stories, we find the theme of the quarrel between brothers integrating these stories at a deeper level. Even the Laban cycle of stories, which may once have circulated apart from the Jacob-Esau stories, is now also related to this theme.

25:19-26 The birth of Esau and Jacob. With the Priestly genealogy (vv. 19-20) that introduces this passage, we move into a new phase in patriarchal history—the period of Isaac and Jacob. What starts as a genealogy of Isaac is interrupted by a story about the birth of Jacob and Esau, usually attributed to the Yahwist (vv. 21-26a). The story may seem out of place in view of what precedes and follows, but it is clearly presupposed in chapter 27.

The barrenness of Rebekah echoes the barrenness of Sarah, but its resolution is almost immediate, and the motif does not become a major theme of the Isaac-Rebekah traditions, as it did with the Abraham-Sarah traditions. As with Sarah, God intervenes and Rebekah becomes pregnant. Only a remnant of the cultic background of the passage is retained in the use of the words "entreat," "heard this entreaty," "went to consult," and "answered." The joy of Rebekah at her pregnancy quickly turns to despair at the struggle going on in her womb. The oracle (v. 23), which is certainly the focus of the entire passage, is both a reassurance and a cause for concern. That Rebekah is to be the mother of two nations is indeed a blessing; that one will surpass the other is not unusual. What causes trepidation is that they will be divided and that, quite apart from the ordinary course of events, the elder will serve the younger, which means a painful struggle between the two. This oracle becomes programmatic as the story of Jacob and Esau continues.

By a series of implied and explicit wordplays the narrator underscores characteristics of Jacob and Esau that form a part of the future behavior and relationship of these two brothers. Esau is "reddish" *('admoni)* and "hairy" *(se'ar)*; he later becomes the father of the Edomites, who live in the region of Seir. The statement that Jacob is gripping Esau's "heel" functions as a wordplay on Jacob's name as well as a sign pointing to his grasping nature and the fact that he will supplant his brother. The name Jacob is actually a shortened form of a name similar to Jacob-el, which means "may God protect."

25:27-34 Esau sells his birthright. The tension between the two brothers is exemplified in their different vocations. Esau is a hunter, a man of the field, and, by implication, wild and crude; Jacob is a shepherd, a tent-dweller, and therefore more civilized. The difference between the two brothers is further accentuated by Isaac's preferential love for Esau, and Rebekah's for Jacob.

The unfolding story shows Esau so concerned with immediate gratification that he loses all sense of proportion. For a mere pot of "red stuff" (v. 30) he sells his birthright, which was a double portion of the family inheritance. The narrator comments at the end that "Esau cared little for his birthright" (v. 34), which is certainly shown by his actions. There is no explicit criticism of Jacob's outright manipulation of his brother. Jacob clearly takes advantage of his brother by pushing him not only to sell his birthright for a bowl of lentils, but to make the deal irrevocable by forcing Esau to swear to it.

The character of Jacob is one of the most carefully developed in the patriarchal narratives. While the narrator refrains from making explicit moral judgments, he does show that Jacob's actions will lead him away from home, penniless, and at the mercy of Laban. God's choice of Jacob remains a mystery, but from the moment God appears to Jacob (28:10ff.) his character begins to improve.

26:1-35 Fragments about Isaac. There is little to unify this chapter except the presence of Isaac. Indeed, this is the only chapter devoted to Isaac, but most of its contents are duplications or echoes of stories about Abraham. With the exception of verses 34-35, which are from the Priestly source, the chapter is the work of the Yahwist.

The story found in verses 1-11 is another version of the story of the ancestress in danger (12:10ff.; ch. 20). This narrative is the least offensive of the versions and the least intriguing. For a second time famine is given as the reason for moving into a new territory, but this famine is clearly distinguished from the famine of Abraham's day. There is never any real threat to Isaac or to Rebekah. That she has been taken into Abimelech's harem may be surmised from the other versions but is never mentioned in this version. God is surprisingly absent. Abimelech sees Isaac "fondling" Rebekah (v. 8) and realizes their relationship is not that of brother and sister. Once again Isaac's name is the basis for a pun, since "fondling" and "laughter" are derived from the same Hebrew root. No gifts are given at the conclusion of the episode, but Isaac and Rebekah are guaranteed protection.

Isaac is twice the recipient of a divine appearance (vv. 2-5, 24) in which the promise given to Abraham is reiterated in nearly the same terms. Verse 5 is certainly an insertion from a later hand, for it speaks of Abraham's obedience in Deuteronomistic language. Like Abraham, Isaac built an altar at the site of God's appearance (v. 25).

God's blessing on Isaac is immediately realized in the abundance of the harvest and his growing wealth. The dispute over wells (vv. 15-25) was already found in the Abraham stories, and this seems to be a variant tradition of the same event, just as the covenant between Abimelech and Isaac (vv. 26-33) is a variant of the Abraham story (21:22ff.). Here we find yet another etymology of the name Beer-sheba (v. 33).

The Priestly addition (vv. 34-35) prepares for the events of 27:46–28:9. The conflict between Esau and Jacob is curiously missing from the Priestly tradition. What becomes a matter of contention in the household is Esau's foreign wives.

27:1-46 The blessing. The story of Jacob's deception, by means of which he receives the blessing intended for Esau, is a masterful blend of the Yahwist and Elohist sources, but it it impossible to separate the sources in this carefully structured and dramatic story. The scene opens with Isaac and his favorite son, Esau, then shifts to Rebekah and her favorite, Jacob. Following Jacob's deception, Isaac is again with Esau, and Rebekah with Jacob. Only in the central scene, the important scene in which the blessing is transferred, is the parent not with his or her favorite son.

In the opening scene Isaac, who is old and blind, wishes to bless Esau before he dies. In the ancient world, deathbed blessings were believed to be particularly effective, and the meal that was prepared and eaten prior to the bestowal of the blessing had a sacral character. Rebekah has overheard Isaac's words to Esau and devises a plan to have Jacob receive the blessing intended for Esau. Rebekah's scheme seems incapable of success, which only heightens the suspense in the following scene. Jacob's only fear is what will happen if he is caught in the deceit. Rebekah draws upon herself any curse that might be directed against Jacob, and he makes no further objection. In the central scene of the chapter, the suspense is heightened by each of Isaac's statements: "Which of my sons are you?"; "How did you succeed . . . ?"; "Come closer that I may feel you"; "Are you really my son Esau?" Only when Isaac finally smells his son does he become convinced of the lie and proceed with the blessing.

No sooner does Jacob depart than Esau enters (v. 30). The revelation of Jacob's deception greatly affects both Isaac and Esau, who respond in shock and grief. It was believed in the ancient world that a blessing or a curse, once spoken, had a life of its own and thus could not be recalled. The blessing given to Jacob is irrevocable; there is nothing Isaac can do to call it back. Esau recognizes the correctness of Jacob's name, for he has "supplanted" (another wordplay on the name Jacob) him twice—first in bartering for the birthright, and now in gaining the blessing. Esau begs for some kind of blessing, and though Isaac attempts to comply, his words sound more like a curse. Understandably, Esau bears a murderous grudge against Jacob, compelling Rebekah to send Jacob away for his own safety. Neither realizes that they will never see each other again.

The blessing given to Jacob assures him of future fertility of the land and lordship over his brothers. Esau's "blessing" is its opposite, but his subjugation to his brother is to be only temporary. Both of these oracles reflect upon the brothers as representatives of their respective nations, Israel and Edom. Edom became a nation before Israel but was later conquered by David and became a vassal of Israel. The Edomites frequently rebelled against Israel and eventually regained their independence.

Interestingly, the narrator refrains from making an outright moral judgment on the deception carried out by Rebekah and Jacob. The narrator cannot condemn Jacob, for he knows him to be the inheritor of the promise. The oracle has been spoken: the elder will serve the younger (25:23). Is Rebekah to be condemned for assisting in the fulfillment of the divine word? Is Isaac not going against God's word by wanting to secure the blessing for his elder son? The narrator leaves these questions unanswered; he only tells the story. Yet, in the very telling of that story, the narrator directs our sympathies to Esau as the innocent and aggrieved victim. Surely he gives us a hint of disapproval as he portrays the shattering effects of this deceit. The family is torn apart by it. It will be twenty years before Jacob returns home. He has not only grasped his brother's heel but has replaced his brother, at a tremendous cost.

27:46–28:9 Jacob leaves to find a wife. This passage of the Priestly author continues the story about Rebekah's dissatisfaction with Esau's marriages, a theme begun in 26:34-35. The motive for Jacob's departure in this tradition is quite different from that of the previous story. Jacob is not fleeing from Esau's wrath; rather, he leaves with his father's blessing to go in search of a suitable wife. The enmity between Esau and Jacob has disappeared. Indeed, Esau tries to imitate Jacob's good example and obtains a wife from his father's family. The issue of intermarriage between Jews and non-Jews was especially acute during the period of restoration (after 538 B.C.E.), when Israel was concerned with the integrity of its religious practices and purity of race.

28:10-22 Jacob's dream at Bethel. The story of the origin of Bethel as a sacred shrine serves as a link between Jacob's previous life in the land of Canaan and his future life in Haran. It is a combination of the Yahwist and Elohist sources, and continues the narrative of 27:42-45. In both versions of the story, Jacob has a profound religious experience at Bethel, which testifies to the holiness of the place.

The Elohist version (vv. 11-12, 17-18, 20-22) dominates the passage. Jacob, having fled from Esau's wrath, finds himself at a shrine, where he rests for the night, using a stone for a pillow. Characteristic of the Elohist tradition, the divine revelation comes in a dream. Jacob sees a stairway going from earth to the heavens and identifies it as the "gateway to heaven" (v. 17). It was believed in the ancient world that there were certain places on earth where the divine and earthly realms met. One such place was Bethel. Jacob recognizes the sacredness of the place; the stone itself he calls Bethel, that is, "house of God" (v. 22; our text has "God's abode"). Jacob consecrates the stone and sets it up as a memorial stone. Such memorial stones were Canaanite cult symbols of fertility and have been found at major cultic centers. When Israel conquered the land, it inherited Canaanite cultic sites with these stones but associated the cultic sites with events in the lives of the patriarchs, thereby eliminating the pagan religious significance of the stones, and used them simply as memorials.

The Yahwist version (vv. 10, 13-16, 19) uses the appearance of Yahweh as an opportunity to extend the promise of Abraham to Jacob (12:1-3). Yahweh is identified as the God of Abraham and Isaac, and assures Jacob of the divine presence and protection on his way. Yahweh is revealed as the God of the ancestors, that is, committed to a family or clan, not bound to a specific place or land.

The association of both Abraham (12:8; 13:3-4) and Jacob with Bethel shows Israel's preoccupation with this city. Bethel became an extremely important cultic center in ancient Israel (see Amos 5:5, 7:10-13; Hos 10:5). It dominated Israel's cultic life in the north from the time of the divided kingdom (1 Kgs 12:28-29) until it was destroyed during the period of Deuteronomic reform (2 Kgs 23:15).

29:1-14 Jacob's arrival in Haran. The Yahwist source dominates in this story of Jacob's arrival in Haran. He comes upon a well, presumably the same well where Abraham's servant found a wife for Isaac. Jacob, who has previously contributed little in the way of conversation, becomes quite loquacious in this passage. The author vividly portrays an eager young Jacob trying to engage the local, rather taciturn shepherds in conversation. The dialogue focuses on the shepherds' inactivity, which is explained by the fact that they are waiting to water their flocks, and cannot do so until the large stone covering the well is removed. Apparently the stone was meant to guarantee equal access to the limited supply of water in the well; only when all the shepherds were gathered could the stone be removed.

The conversation includes inquiries by Jacob about his uncle (vv. 5-6). In answer, the shepherds point to Rachel, Laban's daughter, who is approaching. When Rachel arrives, Jacob removes the stone from the well and waters Laban's sheep. This is a reverse of chapter 24, where Rebekah watered the servant's camels. Rolling back the stone, Jacob reveals his great strength, which impresses Laban when he hears about it. Jacob is overcome with joy upon meeting Rachel.

After Rachel relays the news of Jacob's arrival, Laban goes out to greet him. Laban's response, "You are indeed my flesh and blood" (v. 14), is ambiguous. It may express his pleasure at meeting Jacob, but it could also betray his disappointment at meeting this poor relative. Jacob comes to him, not with the wealth that accompanied Abraham's servant, but penniless. What can Laban do but offer Jacob his home? After all, he is family. In view of Laban's later treatment of Jacob, it is more likely that the expression is an indication of his disappointment.

29:15-30 The marriages. Motifs are introduced in verses 15-30 that become dominant in the stories that follow. These motifs are developed around the words "service" and "wages"—Jacob's service and the wages paid by Laban.

The question "Should you serve me for nothing just because you are a relative of mine?" (v. 15) begins the crafty and devious dealings that will characterize the relationship between Laban and Jacob. It sounds as if Laban is being magnanimous in offering to pay Jacob for his services, but in fact he is declaring the bond of family relationship (uncle-nephew) null and void. It is replaced by a lord-servant relationship.

Jacob suggests seven years of labor for the hand of Rachel in marriage; his labor would serve as the bride price. This custom of paying a bride price recognized a woman's usefulness and was meant to compensate the family for the loss of her labor through marriage. Laban's answer to Jacob is ambiguous. He never says that he will give Rachel to Jacob in marriage; rather, he says that he "prefers" to give "her" to Jacob than to an outsider (v. 19). The reason for his lack of clarity becomes obvious as the story unfolds.

For Jacob, who is in love with Rachel, the seven years pass quickly. When the time for payment comes, Laban gives the older daughter, Leah, to Jacob. A modern reader is often puzzled by Jacob's apparent "blindness" in failing to notice that his bride is not Rachel, but it was possible for such a thing to have happened in view of the marriage customs of that age. The bride was heavily veiled, and in the course of the wedding feast she was escorted in the darkness of the night to her husband's home. We can only assume that the darkness, the veil, and probably a dullness of the senses induced by the celebration prevent Jacob from realizing that the woman he has married is not Rachel. Jacob, who deceived a blind man (ch. 27), is himself treated by Laban as if he were blind. He is made to look even more foolish than Isaac, for he has sight and yet was easily deceived by Laban.

Jacob's indignation when he discovers his uncle's deception is dismissed by Laban. Laban says that it is against their custom "to give the younger before the first-born" (v. 26, in literal translation). This has to be meant as a direct affront to Jacob, who, though younger, had usurped the position of first-born in gaining his brother's birthright and blessing. Without giving Jacob time to respond, Laban suggests that when the week-long marriage festivities end, Jacob can marry Rachel, on the condition that he will continue to work for Laban another seven years. Jacob, destined to be a ruler (27:20), remains a servant in his uncle's home. Laban has used Jacob's love for Rachel against him, without giving thought to the position in which he has placed Leah. She not only becomes the unloved wife but is a constant reminder to Jacob of his uncle's deception.

29:31–30:24 The birth and naming of Jacob's children. A number of smaller units of the Yahwist and Elohist sources are joined together to form an integrated account of the birth and naming of Jacob's children. Popular etymology is freely used to draw out the relationship between the names of the children and the bitter struggle between Leah and Rachel for love and recognition in the home. Laban has created a situation in which Jacob finds himself married to two women, only one of whom he loves. Ultimately, God controls the course of events by making Leah fruitful and Rachel barren, but at the human level the story revolves around the jealousies of Leah and Rachel. Jacob's role in the story is largely confined to fathering children.

The paradox of the story centers on the position of the two women. Leah, as first-born, first wife, and first mother, should have the love and recognition of her husband, but Jacob loves the younger, Rachel. Rachel, though loved, is barren and fears the loss of Jacob's love because of her inability to give him offspring. With each son that Leah bears, Rachel becomes more and more desperate, even to the point of demanding children from Jacob. He reminds her that it is God who gives children. Consequently, Rachel's struggle is not only for love but also for the favor of God. Rachel, like Sarah before her (ch. 16), finally becomes a mother through her maid. Likewise, Leah gives her maid to Jacob when she has ceased to bear children for a time. This was according to custom (see ch. 16).

The story of the mandrakes (v. 14) reveals how much the domestic situation has deteriorated. Leah is denied access to her husband by a jealous Rachel. Leah barters for her rights and "hires" her husband for the evening. Jacob, who had become a "servant" of Laban for "wages," now becomes a "servant" to Leah for "wages" paid to Rachel. The wages are mandrakes, herbs believed to have magical powers and used as an aphrodisiac and as an aid to fertility. In this story, however, it is because of God's intercession that Rachel becomes pregnant. It is interesting to note that God remembers Rachel only after she has granted Leah access to Jacob's bed.

Of Jacob's daughters, only Dinah is mentioned, but no etymological association is given for her name, as in the case of the name of each son. The reference to Dinah may be an insertion meant to anticipate her story in chapter 34. The birth of Benjamin is not included here but is postponed until 35:17ff., possibly because Rachel dies in childbirth and her death would be out of context in chapter 30.

30:25-43 Jacob acquires great wealth. Though there is some evidence of multiple sources in this text, it is primarily the work of the Yahwist. The motifs of "service" and "wages," previously dominant, come to the fore once again. In chapter 29 Laban deceived Jacob and was able to get fourteen years of "service" in exchange for wives, his "wages." But Jacob learned his lesson well, and now he attempts to outwit the wily old Laban.

The conversation between the two is another example of the art of Oriental bargaining. Reminding Laban of his years of service, Jacob requests permission to leave. Laban, who wants Jacob to continue working for him, ignores Jacob's request. But he admits that he has benefited from Jacob's service and asks what wages Jacob wants. Jacob, in turn, ignores Laban's question and asserts his intention to provide for his own household. He even says that Laban does not have to pay, which is certainly an overstatement, since he immediately sets the wages for his continued service. Laban is taken in by Jacob's meager request. As payment, Jacob will take the dark sheep and speckled goats, which would have been very few animals, for sheep were generally all white and goats black. Laban agrees but seeks to undercut any loss by removing all abnormally colored animals from the flock and pasturing them a distance of three days' journey from the herd in Jacob's care. The distance works against Laban, for it gives Jacob a chance to carry out his plan unobserved.

Jacob's breeding practices are based on the ancient belief that what a mother experiences while pregnant is transmitted to the fetus. Jacob sets up tree branches that he has cut in order to expose their white center. The black goats look upon these branches while mating, and the white from the inner core of the branch is transferred to their offspring and so they produce speckled offspring. He makes the white sheep look at the dark goats in order to achieve the same results. He purposely uses only the best of the flock for his selective breeding, leaving Laban with a flock of weak and inferior animals.

Throughout the account of Jacob's breeding practices, there is a series of wordplays. The "poplar," the "white stripes," and the "white core" are words that in Hebrew sound like and relate to the name Laban and its meaning, "white." In a sense, Jacob is using his knowledge of Laban's nature (white) against him. Jacob, the one deceived (ch. 29), becomes the deceiver once again.

31:1-16 Jacob prepares to leave Laban. The most important differences between the Elohist version in chapter 31 and that of the Yahwist in the previous chapter concern the role of God and of Jacob. In this version it is Yahweh who initiates the action and not Jacob himself (vv. 12-13). God has protected Jacob from Laban's double-dealing, has caused Jacob to succeed in gaining wealth, and now commands him to return home. Jacob's meeting with his wives allows him to justify himself and to see whether his wives are in agreement. Throughout the story it is implied that Jacob is not free to leave his father-in-law with his wives and children, but it is not clear why this is the case. It may indicate that Jacob's marriage was an adoption-marriage, a custom in the ancient Near East. If this were so, Jacob would be considered an adopted son of Laban, and his wives and children would be considered Laban's property. Jacob's flight with his wives and children would then have been illegal.

Yahwist insertions into the text (vv. 1, 3) indicate that the attitude of Laban's sons caused Jacob to decide to leave. The Priestly author's contribution to the story is minimal. Indeed, there is only the brief notice that Jacob left to return home (v. 18).

31:17-35 Jacob's flight. The Elohist version continues to dominate the story, though the hand of the Yahwist appears now and then. Jacob's flight takes place while Laban is occupied with the annual sheep-shearing. Jacob is able to "deceive" Laban ("hoodwink," v. 20). When the Hebrew text is translated literally, it reads, "Jacob stole Laban's heart." (The heart in Hebrew anthropology was not the seat of the emotions but the intellect.) Jacob's action is paralleled by Rachel's theft in verse 19: "Rachel stole her father's household gods." Rachel's motives are not clear. The household gods, at least in Nuzi documents, represented the credentials of the true heir. Rachel may be attempting to secure a future claim to the inheritance, or she may simply be hoping to derive prosperity and blessing from them.

Before Laban overtakes Jacob, God appears to him in a dream and warns him not to harm Jacob (v. 24). This puts Laban in a very awkward position. He has arrived ready to do battle but can only fuss and fume. He can do nothing about Jacob's departure, but the theft of the household gods cannot be ignored. Jacob denies any knowledge of the theft and unwittingly pronounces the death sentence on his beloved Rachel. The suspense that builds up during Laban's search is dissipated the moment the reader discovers that the menstruating Rachel is sitting on the household gods (v. 34). There is something ironic about the "gods," revered as sacred, being protected by the ancient taboo of "unclean" associated with blood. Whatever the original significance of these gods, there can be no doubt that the author, for whom idols are nothing but wood and stone, is ridiculing the pagan belief in, and worship of, idols.

31:36–32:3 Jacob's covenant with Laban. Jacob gains an advantage when Laban fails to find his gods. He proceeds to detail his loyal service over against Laban's shabby treatment. Laban seems unimpressed by Jacob's speech, for he continues to assert his ownership of Jacob's wives and children and flocks, but he can do nothing because of God's warning.

The present form of the agreement that Laban and Jacob eventually reach is a combination of two separate covenants, one from the Yahwist source and the other from the Elohist. The covenant in the Yahwist version is a non-aggression pact between Aram and Israel. The sign of the covenant is a mound of stones, and the covenant is sealed by a meal. The Elohist version is drawn from a boundary agreement between Aram and Israel. The covenant is marked by a memorial stone and ratified by a sacrifice and a meal. In both covenants there are wordplays associated with the name of the place where the covenant was ratified. In the Yahwist story, Gilead is a play on the Hebrew word for "mound of stones"; in the Elohist version, Mizpah is so named because it sounds like the Hebrew for "memorial stone."

The episode concludes with Laban returning home and Jacob continuing his journey (32:1-2). Jacob immediately encounters God's messengers. This experience provides the name of the place, Mahanaim ("two camps"). The reason for including this fragment certainly must exceed the meaning of the word, but it is not clear what that purpose is. Does the encounter with God's messengers give Jacob the idea of sending "messengers" to Esau? Of dividing his family into two camps? Does it prepare for the mysterious being Jacob encounters in 32:23-33?

32:4-21 Jacob prepares to meet Esau. We continue to find a blend of the Yahwist and Elohist sources as the narrative moves toward Jacob's meeting with his brother Esau. In the Yahwist story (vv. 4, 14a), Jacob sends messengers to Esau, hoping to gain his favor. When the messengers report that Esau is coming with four hundred men, Jacob is understandably alarmed and divides the camp in order to avoid total disaster. Having taken practical measures, Jacob finally turns to God in prayer. His prayer reveals his state of anxiety as he appeals for God's help by reminding God of the promise.

In the Elohist's account (vv. 14b-22), Jacob seeks to appease his brother with many gifts. The Hebrew for "gifts" and for "camp" recalls the previous wordplay of verse 3 (Mahanaim); the frequent use of the word "face" anticipates the Peniel ("face of God," v. 31) episode that follows.

32:22-33 Jacob wrestles with God. This story, which delays Jacob's encounter with Esau, is generally attributed to the Yahwist.

Jacob, left alone after sending his wives, children, and possessions across the river, is attacked by a "man," with whom he struggles until dawn. Exactly who wins remains ambiguous. The "man" cannot prevail (v. 22) and resorts to wounding Jacob by magic, yet in verse 27 the "man" asks to be released, as if he cannot best Jacob. Jacob demands a blessing but is given a new name. When he asks his mysterious contender for his name, his request is brushed aside. Verse 29 suggests that Jacob won, but in verse 31 Jacob is surprised to have seen God and still be alive. Perhaps the ambiguity is maintained to avoid stating explicitly that Jacob won, for in this story the nocturnal attacker is eventually identified as God (v. 31).

The story incorporates elements drawn from very ancient sources. The theme that one must appease a river-god in some way in order to be allowed to cross a river is often found in ancient folklore. There is also the notion from ancient folklore that the power of certain supernatural beings is limited to nighttime; they must leave or be overpowered when dawn breaks. These ancient elements explain only one level of the story. They leave unanswered questions about the relationship of this story to the larger Jacob cycle.

There is no doubt that the story, in addition to preserving ancient folkloric elements, was given a distinctly Israelite bias. Jacob's struggle is remembered by means of his new name, Israel, which is explained by popular etymology as "one who contends with God." The city of Peniel also receives its name following upon Jacob's struggle, and again popular etymology becomes the vehicle of explanation (v. 31). Finally, the story accounts for the dietary rule that prohibited Israelites from eating the sciatic nerve in memory of Jacob's wounded thigh, but this law is not recorded elsewhere in the Old Testament and Israel did not observe it.

The Yahwist's interest in the story goes beyond any of the concerns mentioned thus far. The Yahwist shows that Jacob, the contender with Esau and Laban, is brought to contend with God's very self and henceforth will never be the same. The character of Jacob is profoundly altered by this experience. From this moment until his death, he is a person of honor and integrity. In addition, Jacob (now Israel) reveals in his life Israel's own struggle with God in living as the people of covenant.

33:1-20 The meeting of Jacob and Esau. It is generally assumed that the Yahwist source is responsible for this final scene in the narrative of Jacob's return to Canaan, though traces of the Elohist can still be discerned. The actual meeting of the brothers turns out to be rather anticlimactic. Jacob's extensive preparations and subservient gestures prove to be effective. Esau no longer wishes to kill him and even expresses great joy at Jacob's return (v. 4). Jacob, for his part, compares his meeting with Esau to his encounter with God (v. 10).

Jacob's subsequent conversation with Esau suggests, however, that neither really trusts the other. Jacob will not allow Esau or Esau's men to accompany him, but persuades Esau to go on without him. Then, rather than follow Esau, Jacob turns in another direction and proceeds to Succoth. Eventually Jacob moves on to Shechem. According to the Elohist insertion in verses 19-20, Jacob buys land in Shechem and sets up a memorial stone to El, the God of Israel. Shechem was a very ancient city, important from the earliest days of Israel's occupation of the land.

34:1-31 The rape of Dinah. This story is basically from the Yahwist but has been supplemented by Elohist fragments. Dinah is raped by Shechem, but he comes to love her and wants to marry her. Hamor, Shechem's father, speaking on his son's behalf, recommends to Jacob and his sons expanded intermarriage and commerce between the Shechemites and the Israelites. Jacob's sons agree to this, on the condition that the Shechemites first be circumcised. Hamor brings the matter before the Shechemites, convincing them that they would benefit economically through intermarriage with the Israelites. The Shechemites agree to submit to circumcision, and while they are recuperating from the operation, Simeon and Levi attack Shechem and kill all the men of the city. Jacob reprimands his sons, but he is motivated more by a fear of reprisal from the neighboring inhabitants than from any moral objection to his sons' method of revenge. Simeon and Levi show no remorse but justify their behavior in avenging the injustice done to Dinah.

The narrative may preserve in story form an actual attack on the city of Shechem by the tribes of Simeon and Levi. In addition, the story may serve to explain the eventual decline of the tribes of Simeon and Levi.

35:1-29 The end of the Jacob cycle. This chapter includes two stories from the Elohist: the story of Jacob's fulfillment of his vow to build an altar at Bethel (vv. 1-8) and the story of the birth of Benjamin (vv. 16-20). The summarization of the life of Jacob (vv. 9-15), the list of Jacob's sons, and the death of Isaac come from the Priestly source. The Yahwist's only contribution is the brief notice about Reuben in verse 22a.

According to the Elohist, Jacob returns to Bethel because of a direct command from God to fulfill the vow he took on his first visit to that city (28:10ff.). The preparations for the trip indicate that Jacob's journey is to be a pilgrimage and may reflect the actual practices later associated with pilgrimages in Israel. The ritual purification before leaving on a pilgrimage includes a formal renunciation of foreign gods and anything associated with pagan cult, such as earrings, which were cultic symbols, or amulets. Changing one's clothes is a common religious symbol of renewal. The "terror from God" (v. 5) that protects Jacob's family is a kind of inexplicable paralysis or panic that renders the enemy incapable of attack (1 Sam 14:15; Exod 23:27; Josh 10:10; etc.). Arriving in Luz, Jacob builds the altar in fulfillment of his vow and renames the place Bethel.

The birth of Benjamin (v. 17) is the fulfillment of Rachel's prayer when Joseph was born (30:24). She would have named the child "Son of my sorrow" (Benoni) because of her pain in bearing him, but Jacob renames the child "Son of my right hand" (Benjamin). In the ancient world it was thought that there was a mysterious relationship between a name and its bearer; a name could determine the destiny of its bearer. Rather than mark the life of the child by the sorrow surrounding his birth, Jacob wisely gives the child a name that suggests an honorable and successful future. The name Benjamin means "southerners" and probably refers to the original geographical location of the tribe. The site of Rachel's tomb is unknown. According to 1 Sam 10:2 and Jer 31:15, it is located in the territory of Benjamin, north of Jerusalem. Thus Ephrath cannot be Bethlehem (v. 19), which is in the territory of the tribe of Judah and south of Jerusalem.

The Priestly author's contribution to the traditions surrounding the patriarch Jacob are limited. They consist of little more than summaries of the earlier traditions found in the narratives of the Yahwist and the Elohist. The Priestly author mentions only what is considered theologically important, making note on the change of Jacob's name to Israel (v. 10) and reiterating the promise given to Abraham (vv. 11-12). The list of names of the sons of Jacob given by the Priestly author (vv. 22b-29) is similar to that found elsewhere in the Old Testament (49:1ff.; Num 26:5ff.; Deut 27:12ff.; 33:2ff.; etc.), but it conflicts with the story of the birth of Benjamin in verses 16-20. For this author, the birth of Benjamin takes place, not in Canaan, but in Mesopotamia, while Jacob is still living with Laban. The Priestly author, who recorded the death and burial of Abraham, now recounts the death and burial of Isaac. Both Jacob and Esau are present at their father's burial (as were Isaac and Ishmael at their father's), for in the Priestly account there has been no break in the relationship between Jacob and Esau.

The reference to the incest of Reuben (v. 22) is but a fragment of an account that must have included Jacob's reaction to Reuben's offensive behavior. It is alluded to again in 49:4, but without any further elaboration that might give us a more complete picture of the event.

36:1-43 The genealogy of Esau. At the conclusion of the Jacob cycle of stories a genealogy of Esau is inserted. This genealogy is actually composed of six distinct lists: (1) verses 1-8; (2) verses 9-14; (3) verses 15-19; (4) verses 20-30; (5) verses 31-39; (6) verses 40-43. The first and second lists are parallel and differ only at the beginning and end. The second list includes grandchildren whose names are repeated again in the third list. The fourth list names the descendants of the original clans that settled in the territory of Seir, later inhabited by the Edomites. These people are called Horites, the biblical designation for the Hurrians. But there is no archaeological evidence that the Hurrians occupied Edomite territory, and the names of the list are clearly Semitic; thus the identity of these ancestors is difficult to determine. The fifth list contains the names of the kings of Edom who reigned prior to the establishment of monarchy in Israel. The sixth list, the clans of Esau, duplicates some of the names of the second list.

It is difficult to determine the historical reliability of any of these lists. The Edomites came east in the thirteenth century B.C.E. with the Ammonites and Moabites. They became a nation before Israel but were conquered and made vassals of Israel by David in the tenth century B.C.E.

The patriarchal sagas begin with a call to venture forth to a strange land with nothing more than a promise. Israel saw in Abraham's journeys its own call to go forth trusting in God. Israel saw in the story of Abraham's faith a testimony to its own faith. Even in the questionable behavior of Jacob, Israel saw its own history. But more important, Israel recognized in these stories God's activity. It saw a gracious God who chose to intervene in our world through a people called to be a special people. This God did not choose a perfect people, but one that, for all its faults, was willing to listen and to follow, and was open to the intervention of the Deity in their lives.

THE JOSEPH STORY

Gen 37:1–50:26

The Joseph story is set apart from the other narratives in the Book of Genesis by its distinctive literary form. It is often referred to as a "novelette" because the narrative is a unified organic whole. From beginning to end, each segment of the story is integrated into the entire narrative. It has its own distinctive theme—peace in the family—but it is also brought into the larger complex of stories. We must be attentive to its unique character, and yet also see it in the context of the entire Book of Genesis.

There is general agreement that the Joseph story has been influenced by the wisdom tradition of Israel. One of the concerns of the wisdom tradition was the success of the individual in life. Success was achieved by diligence and self-discipline. It was important to learn appropriate behavior, self-control, and propriety in speech. In Israel, fear of God was also a necessary factor in attaining wisdom. Joseph embodies all of these characteristics and thus is presented throughout the narrative as a model of wisdom.

37:1-36 Joseph is sold into slavery in Egypt. The Priestly author's contribution to this chapter (vv. 1-2), as in the entire Joseph story, is minimal. Verse 1 is the Priestly author's conclusion to the Jacob story, and verse 2 begins the Joseph story. The Jacob stories began under the caption "These are the generations of Isaac . . ."; likewise, the Joseph story begins with a reference to the generations of Jacob. The Yahwist and Elohist sources, separate at first (vv. 3-4, J; vv. 5-11, E) have been combined to form the climax of the chapter (vv. 12-36, JE).

Each of the three sources gives its own reason for the hostility of the brothers against Joseph. In the Priestly tradition (vv. 1-2), Joseph brings "bad reports" of his brothers to Jacob. The content of the reports is not specified, but the statement reveals the tension existing between Joseph and his brothers. Jacob's partiality for Joseph is the cause of the dissension in the Yahwist tradition (vv. 3-4). The "long tunic" given to Joseph is a sign of Jacob's favoritism and further arouses the jealousy of Joseph's brothers. This garment was a special coat distinguished by its length and its sleeves, not its color. The older translation "coat of many colors" was based on the Greek text of the Old Testament, not on the Hebrew.

The Elohist (vv. 5-11) introduces into the Joseph story a dream motif that is found again in chapters 40 and 41. In the dreams there is no direct address; rather, the dream itself communicates its message when interpreted. The science of dream interpretation developed to assist in deciphering a dream. The ancients held that in some dreams there was a foreshadowing of the future, and this is the sense in which these dreams are to be understood. The obvious import of the dreams—that Joseph would rule over his brothers—further alienates Joseph from them.

Once the characters have been introduced and the situation delineated, the story is set in motion when Joseph is sent on an errand by Jacob to his brothers, who are pasturing their flocks at some distance from Jacob's settlement. The contradictions in the episode are traced to the presence of the two different sources, the Yahwist and the Elohist. In the Yahwist tradition the brothers plot to kill Joseph, but Judah intercedes and the brothers decide to sell Joseph to the Ishmaelites (v. 27). It is Reuben, in the Elohist narrative, who persuades his brothers not to kill Joseph but to place him in a cistern (vv. 21-22). He hopes to return later to save Joseph, but Midianite traders find Joseph and bring him to Egypt.

It is ironic that the brothers relay the news of Joseph's death by using the now bloodstained tunic of Joseph. It once signaled Joseph's privileged status; now it announces his death. Jacob's great grief is vividly portrayed, but rather than end on this tragic note, the scene shifts to Egypt and the sale of Joseph to Potiphar, an official of Pharaoh's court.

38:1-30 Judah and Tamar. Given the importance of the tribe of Judah in Israel's history, it is not surprising to find a story specifically about its founder. The problem with the story is its present location, for it interrupts the Joseph story. But as we shall see, there are some connections between this story and the context in which it is now found.

The story is attributed to the Yahwist, who telescopes an entire generation in a few verses. Judah separates from his brothers, marries a Canaanite woman, and sires three sons who reach marital age rather quickly. The eldest son, Er, marries a Canaanite woman, Tamar. For an unspecified reason he displeases Yahweh and dies. In the ancient world an unexpected death in the prime of life was believed to be caused by sin. According to the levirate law (Deut 25:5-10), Er's brother must marry his widow because Er died without fathering a child. The first son of this union would be legally recognized as the heir of the deceased brother. Judah, therefore, gives his second son, Onan, to Tamar. But Onan is unwilling to raise up a son for his brother and fails to complete the sexual act. Onan dies because he refused to fulfill his obligation to his brother; no moral judgment is passed on his sexual behavior (vv. 9-10). Judah, after losing two sons, is hesitant to give his third son to Tamar. Judah's failure to carry out his duty sets the stage for the next act, in which Tamar has the dominant role.

After his wife dies, Judah journeys to Timnah for the shearing of his sheep (v. 12). Tamar takes advantage of the situation, disguises herself as a prostitute, and seduces Judah. She insists on taking his seal and cord and staff as pledge of payment. The seal functioned as an ancient means of identification. A seal was incised with the special design of its owner and was worn around the neck by means of an attached cord. When Judah sends his servant with the payment, Tamar cannot be found. Rather than embarrass himself further by searching for the woman, Judah drops the matter.

Tamar, as expected, conceives a child by Judah (v. 18). Tamar's pregnancy is made known to Judah, who has jurisdiction in this case because Tamar is betrothed to his third son. He sentences her to death, the punishment for adultery, but at the crucial moment she produces his seal and staff, which identify him as the father of the child. Judah exonerates Tamar and admits that he is at fault for his failure to fulfill the levirate law.

The struggle in Tamar's womb (v. 29), like that of Rebekah (25:21-26), anticipates the future conflict between tribes as one child seeks dominance over the other. The name of each child is associated with the manner of his birth. Perez "pushes" ("breach" in the NAB) his brother out of the way in order to be the firstborn; Zerah gets his name from the "crimson" thread tied about his wrist by the midwife. Through Tamar's bold act, Judah's line is saved from extinction; from that line will come the greatest of the kings of Israel, David.

Few scholars find any connection between the story of Judah and Tamar and the Joseph story. It does appear to be an intrusion into a narrative otherwise concerned with Joseph and his fate. Nevertheless, there are points of contact that should be noted. The same formula ("please verify . . . he recognized") spoken by Jacob's sons to hide their guilt (37:32-33) is used by Tamar to uncover Judah's guilt (38:25-26). The payment of a kid (38:20) by the deceived Judah recalls the goat in whose blood Joseph's garment was dipped (37:31) to deceive his father, Jacob. Finally, Judah's exposure results from his sexual incontinence, whereas Joseph's continence in chapter 39 brings him through seeming defeat to ultimate triumph. The story permits the narrator to contrast the lives of Judah and Joseph; at the same time, it gives Joseph time to journey to Egypt.

39:1-23 The rise and fall of Joseph. The Yahwist narrative of the Joseph story continues by referring the reader back to the moment when Joseph was sold to the Ishmaelites (37:26-27, 28b). Upon arrival in Egypt, Joseph is sold as a slave to an Egyptian (identified as Potiphar in the Elohist tradition). Joseph soon rises to a position of trust, and the Egyptian is blessed with prosperity because of him. In the Yahwist's view, Joseph's success is due entirely to Yahweh. Yahweh's behind-the-scenes presence is felt throughout the Joseph story and gives it its distinctive theological character.

Verses 1-6 set the scene for the attempted seduction of Joseph by Potiphar's wife. The successful and handsome Joseph is noticed by Potiphar's wife. Joseph refuses her sexual advances, for the act of adultery would be a sin against the trust his master has placed in him and a sin against God. The woman is persistent in her demands, so much so that she seizes hold of Joseph one day, and he eludes her only by leaving behind his garment (v. 12). The garment is then used as evidence against him when she falsely accuses him of trying to seduce her. The punishment for adultery is death. Joseph is in the same position that he was in in chapter 37—facing a life-and-death situation. In chapter 37, instead of being put to death he was sold into slavery; in chapter 39, instead of being put to death he is sent to prison. As Joseph had become a trusted slave, so too in jail he rises to prominence and a position of trust. The advance, as before, is attributed to the presence of Yahweh in his life.

The motif dominant in this chapter, that of an indiscreet woman incriminating a man who refuses her advances, is common in world literature. It is interesting to note that one of the closest parallels to this story is an Egyptian version entitled "A Tale of Two Brothers." This story, except for its ending, is similar to the one in Genesis. This is not to suggest, however, that there is direct relationship between the two stories; rather, both find their origin in widely distributed folklore.

40:1-23 Joseph interprets the prisoners' dreams. A return to the Elohist tradition is signaled by the difference in Joseph's position in jail and the presence, once again, of dreams. In chapter 39 Joseph was put in charge of all the prisoners, but in chapter 40 he is depicted as a slave of two noble prisoners, the royal cupbearer and the baker. The cupbearer was the official keeper and taster of Pharaoh's wine, an important position held by the most loyal and trusted of officials. Likewise, the royal baker occupied a prominent position in Pharaoh's court.

As Joseph serves the two officials, he notices their distress and discovers that it stems from the fact that they cannot get anyone to interpret their dreams (v. 8). Dream interpretation was done by professionals in Egypt. In prison these two officials do not have access to dream interpreters. Joseph dismisses their problem by maintaining that dream interpretation belongs to God. After hearing the dreams, Joseph proceeds to interpret them. Both the cupbearer and the baker will have their heads "lifted up" (vv. 13, 19); for the cupbearer this means reinstatement in Pharaoh's court, but for the baker it means death. Within three days the dreams come true. Though Joseph has asked the cupbearer to bring his case before Pharaoh, the cupbearer forgets about Joseph until Pharaoh himself dreams. Thus Joseph remains in prison for two more years.

41:1-57 Joseph interprets Pharaoh's dreams. The Elohist source continues in this chapter until Joseph comes to power in Egypt, at which point the Yahwist version is intertwined with that of the Elohist. Joseph is brought to Pharaoh to interpret his dreams after "all the magicians and sages of Egypt" (v. 8) have failed. Pharaoh tells his dreams to Joseph, not merely repeating verbatim the account found in verses 1-7 but expanding and enhancing the retelling with added detail (vv. 17-24). Joseph, for his part, repeats that dream interpretation comes from God and then proceeds with his interpretation, which is shown to come true by the end of the chapter (vv. 53-57). The symbolism of the dreams fits in well with the Egyptian background of the story. Seven good years, represented by fat cows and healthy ears of grain, will be followed by seven devastating years of famine, depicted as gaunt, ugly cows and shriveled ears of grain. Joseph follows his interpretation with practical advice, which Pharaoh immediately accepts.

In the Elohist tradition Joseph is installed as master of the palace, which puts him in charge of Egypt's finances. According to the Yahwist, Joseph is appointed vizier of Egypt, an even higher office. Joseph is placed in charge of the administration of the land. The ceremony of installation authentically reflects the political and social customs of Egypt. The signet ring was the royal seal kept by the vizier, and the gold chain was probably a ceremonial emblem of office (v. 42). The robes of fine linen and the chariots indicate Joseph's noble status, as do the criers who run before his chariot.

Joseph is completely drawn into the Egyptian royal court. He is given an Egyptian name, Zaphenath-paneah ("God speaks and lives"), and an Egyptian wife. His new name and the fact that he marries the daughter of an Egyptian priest apparently cause no problems for the Yahwist, who simply records it as part of Joseph's new position in Egypt. During the time of prosperity two sons are born to Joseph and are given names that relate to his new life. His previous suffering is "forgotten," so his first child receives the name Manasseh; his present state of prosperity is echoed in the name of the second child, Ephraim, "God has made me fruitful" (vv. 51-52).

The Priestly author's only contribution (v. 46a) tells of Joseph's age. Thirteen years have elapsed since Joseph's entry into Egypt and his rise to power.

42:1-38 Joseph tests his brothers. This chapter is dominated by the Elohist source but is supplemented by a few fragments of the Yahwist (for example, vv. 27-28). The narrative returns to the theme of the relationship between Joseph and his brothers after depicting his rise to power in Egypt. The famine has spread to Palestine, causing Jacob to send his sons to Egypt, for he has heard that food is available there. He does not send Benjamin, Rachel's other son, who presumably has replaced Joseph in his father's affection.

Joseph's dreams (37:5-10) are fulfilled when his brothers bow before him (v. 6). He recognizes them, but they do not recognize him. He begins to play a game with them, the import of which becomes clear only as the story continues. Joseph accuses his brothers of being spies. In their eagerness to defend themselves, they reveal to Joseph what he wants to know about his family. He insists that they bring Benjamin to him to prove the truth of their claim that they are not spies. By this means Joseph can determine whether or not his brothers have changed. Do they bear the same jealous hatred against Benjamin that they once directed against him? They had subjected Joseph to an unknown fate; now he does the same to them.

At first Joseph insists that all the brothers must stay in prison while one of them returns to fetch Benjamin, but finally he keeps only Simeon in prison as a guarantee that the other brothers will return (v. 24). He returns their money to their bags; they will not discover it until later. The conflation of sources is revealed by the contradiction between verses 27 and 35. According to the Yahwist (v. 27), the money is found on the first day of the journey home, but in verse 35 it is found only when the brothers arrive at their destination. The chapter ends on the same note as chapter 37, the lament of Jacob for his favorite son.

43:1-34 The brothers return to Egypt. The tension begun in chapter 42 intensifies in chapters 43–44 until it is resolved in chapter 45. In the narrative of chapters 43–44, we return to the Yahwist source, which accounts for some of the irregularities in the story as it continues. Simeon, imprisoned in Egypt, seems to have been completely forgotten in the opening scene. It also appears that Jacob is only now informed of the condition of their return to Egypt. Only the hopelessness of their situation, coupled with Judah's vow to assure Benjamin's safety, convinces Jacob to allow Benjamin to accompany his other sons to Egypt. Jacob sends gifts with them, hoping to placate the Egyptian official who has so falsely accused his sons.

When the brothers arrive in Egypt (v. 16), everything seems to go well for them. The Egyptian official has provided a banquet for them. Simeon has been returned. Gradually their hesitancy is overcome. Their attempt to return the money found in their bags is brushed off. The money is mysteriously spoken of as a gift from God (v. 23). Though they approach the banquet with a certain wariness, it disappears when they see how Joseph treats Benjamin. Finally they begin to relax and enjoy the festivities. Upon seeing Benjamin, Joseph is overcome with emotion and must leave the room to regain control, yet he still does not reveal himself to his brothers.

44:1-34 Joseph's final test of his brothers. The seriousness of the game Joseph is playing is seen in the final test of his brothers. He instructs his steward to return the money of his brothers and to place his own silver cup in Benjamin's bag. One wonders why the money is returned, for it is never mentioned again in the story; the cup alone serves as incriminating evidence. This cup was a sacred object used for divination. Exactly how it was used is not certain. One possible way was to drop objects into the cup filled with liquid and decipher the resultant rippling of the liquid. Another possibility was to mix oil and water in the cup and examine the patterns created to find their meaning. That Joseph used such a cup does not seem to have bothered the narrator, but divination practices were forbidden in Israel (Lev 19:31; Deut 18:10-11).

The brothers have gone but a short distance when they are overtaken by Joseph's steward (v. 6). They are genuinely shocked when accused of theft. Proclaiming their innocence, they vow death to the thief and slavery for the rest of them if the cup is found in their possession. These extreme punishments are rejected by the steward and later by Joseph himself. The punishment will be slavery, not death, for the thief, and the rest of them will go free. By isolating Benjamin from his brothers, Joseph wants to see whether or not they will allow Benjamin to become a slave and seize the opportunity to go free themselves.

As expected, the cup is found in Benjamin's bag, and the brothers return to Egypt. After a harsh reprimand from Joseph, Judah issues an impassioned speech. We may be surprised that he admits their guilt (v. 16) so soon after maintaining their innocence, but Judah sees in their present situation God's judgment upon them for what they had done to Joseph. They are indeed guilty, but until now they have escaped detection and punishment. Judah's stress on his father's grief at the loss of Joseph and his great fear that Benjamin would not return home become the basis for his request that he take Benjamin's place. Through Judah's speech Joseph learns that his brothers have changed. The murderous hatred that caused them to get rid of him has been replaced by a self-sacrificial concern for Benjamin. Brothers who once were indifferent to their father's grief display great solicitude and will do what they can to spare him further sorrow.

45:1-28 Joseph reveals himself to his brothers. In this chapter the Elohist source is again intertwined with the Yahwist story, giving rise to doublets (vv. 3a/4b) and discrepancies (45:16ff./46:31ff.). But rather than distracting from the chapter, the blending of sources actually adds to the chapter's inner credibility.

With Judah's speech the game has gone as far as it can go. The climax has come—Joseph must act. He is overcome by emotion upon hearing Judah's appeal and decides to reveal his identity at last. His brothers' bewilderment opens the way for Joseph's second disclosure: "do not reproach yourselves . . . . God has sent me here ahead of you" (v. 5). The underlying theology of the Joseph story is made explicit. God has directed and guided the course of events. What the brothers meant as evil, God has redeemed. God is the one who sent Joseph to Egypt to preserve a remnant and to deliver Jacob's family. The terms "remnant" and "deliverance" (v. 7) become important Old Testament terms expressing Israel's conviction that God intervenes in its history and preserves it from total destruction.

Joseph acquits his brothers and they are reconciled (vv. 14-15). The brothers are "able to talk with him" (v. 15), showing how completely the situation of chapter 37 has been reversed (see 37:4). The tension that has been building since chapter 42 is finally resolved. The denouement will include telling Jacob the news that Joseph lives, Jacob's relocation in Egypt, and the meeting between Joseph and his father.

When the brothers reveal to their father that Joseph lives and holds a position of honor in Egypt, Jacob is understandably dumbfounded. But gradually he is convinced of the truth of their claim and decides to go to Egypt. No mention is made of the brothers' guilty deed, for it has been superseded by God's saving intervention.

46:1–47:12, 27-28 Jacob travels to Egypt and settles there. The Yahwist source dominates in the final scenes of the Joseph story, but the Elohist and Priestly authors also contribute to its conclusion. According to the Yahwist, Jacob decides to go to Egypt (45:28; 46:1a), but for the Elohist this trip is taken in response to God's command (46:2-4). This Elohist insertion is different in style and form from the Joseph story. It shifts the focus of the Joseph story from that of the relationship between brothers to Jacob's descent into Egypt, and incorporates the Joseph story into the larger picture of Israel's history as a preparation for the Exodus.

The genealogical insertion of the Priestly author (vv. 6-27) certainly existed independently of its present context. Benjamin, who was a child in the Joseph story, now has ten sons! The list appears to be a summary of the genealogy found in Num 26. The number "seventy" for the descendants of Jacob (v. 27) is arrived at only by including Jacob himself and Dinah among Jacob's descendants. The original purpose of this genealogy cannot be determined, nor is it clear what purpose it serves in the present context. The Priestly conclusion to this genealogy (47:27-28) has been displaced by the conclusion of the Joseph story.

Verse 28 resumes the story interrupted by the Priestly genealogy. The long-awaited meeting between Joseph and his father presents a moving picture. Jacob's joy is complete in being reunited with this son whom he believed to be dead (46:30).

The final scene of the Joseph story takes up the practical consideration of where in Egypt Jacob and his family are to settle. Joseph's diplomatic skills are shown in his instructions to his father and brothers in preparing them for the meeting with Pharaoh (vv. 33-34). The territory of Goshen would have offered suitable grazing land for Jacob's flocks, but would Pharaoh agree to settle these foreigners in an unsupervised border province? Joseph's insistence that the family represent themselves as shepherds is meant to assure Pharaoh of their peaceful intentions as well as to indicate that Goshen would be suitable pastureland away from the city. There is no extrabiblical support for the statement that "shepherds are abhorrent to the Egyptians" (v. 34), but the attitude of distrust between settled peoples and nomads is well attested.

The meeting between Pharaoh and Joseph's family goes better than anticipated. Not only does Pharaoh give them Goshen as the place to settle, but he also suggests that they be appointed superintendents of the royal herds (v. 5a).

The final scene, with Jacob before Pharaoh (vv. 5b-11), comes from the Priestly source. In a polite exchange between Pharaoh and Jacob, the patriarch describes his 130 years of life as "few and hard" (v. 9) in comparison with the 175 years of Abraham's life and the 180 years of Isaac's life. He refers to his life as that of a "wayfarer." The term is often used in the patriarchal narratives (17:8; 28:4; 36:7; 37:1) to describe the lifestyle of the patriarchs, for whom the possession of the land is given only in promise, a promise not fulfilled for generations.

47:13-26 Joseph's land policy. There is no logical connection between verses 13-26 (from the Yahwist) and the previous section; the passage would be more appropriately located following the account of Joseph's rise to power in chapter 41. The passage relates how Joseph's economic policies during the period of famine enabled the Egyptians to survive only by selling their land to Pharaoh and becoming serfs. Only the temple lands were exempt. The situation presented describes accurately the decline of the free peasantry in Egypt. However, the story is remembered, not for its historical interest, but for the picture of Joseph that it presents. He is a wise and capable administrator, able to deal effectively with each new crisis.

47:29–48:22 The blessing of Ephraim and Manasseh. The tradition of Jacob's last days is found in all three sources. In the Yahwist version (47:29-31), Jacob's dying request is that he be buried with his ancestors in Canaan. Jacob's insistence that Joseph take an oath (compare 24:2) that he will do as asked indicates the importance of this request. Burial in the family tomb was not simply a fitting end to one's life but signified a bond with one's ancestors. In addition, for Jacob, burial in Canaan represents a claim to the land and anticipates the day of his descendants' return from Egypt.

In the Elohist tradition (48:1-2, 7), Joseph is called to his father's bedside, repeating essentially the scene found in 47:29. The reference to Rachel's grave in 48:7 is certainly incomplete. Perhaps in the Elohist tradition Jacob requests to be buried with Rachel, unlike the Priestly tradition, in which Jacob is buried in the cave of Machpelah.

In 48:3-6 the Priestly author depicts Jacob's adoption of Joseph's sons, Ephraim and Manasseh, in terms reminiscent of the promise given to Jacob at Bethel (35:6, 9-12). The tribe of Joseph, early in its history (Judg 5; Num 26:5-51) split into two separate tribes, the tribes of Ephraim and Manasseh. They settled in the Samaritan mountains and became powerful tribes of the northern kingdom. The adoption scene is meant to show how Ephraim and Manasseh became tribal leaders even though they were not the natural sons of Jacob. By adoption Jacob makes his grandsons full members of the family (Israel) and equal to the other tribes.

A second version of the blessing and adoption of Manasseh and Ephraim is ascribed to the Yahwist (vv. 8-12). Manasseh and Ephraim are not simply adopted as sons, but the future position of the two tribes is indicated in the manner in which Jacob blesses them. Joseph seeks to place the elder under Jacob's right hand, the place of honor, but Jacob crosses his hands, so that the younger is given precedence over the elder. This is a common motif found in the Yahwist (Abel over Cain, ch. 4; Isaac over Ishmael, 17:19-21; Jacob himself over Esau, ch. 27; Perez over Zerah, 38:27-30), and reflects the future destiny of the two tribes, for the tribe of Ephraim will soon surpass the tribe of Manasseh and become the most powerful tribe in the northern kingdom.

The blessing itself is found in two forms: verses 15-16 and verse 20. Both forms use traditional blessing formulas. In verses 15-16 Jacob invokes God as the God of Abraham and Isaac, thus establishing a link between the God worshiped by his ancestors and the God he himself worships. He addresses God as "shepherd," a frequent Old Testament title that suggests God's concern for the people. The third title, "Angel," refers to Jacob's own experience of the Deity as deliverer. The blessing ensures numerous descendants and a glorious future for the tribes represented by Joseph's sons. The blessing of verse 20 is reminiscent of the promise to Abraham (12:3b).

The final verse of chapter 48 is not clear. It appears that Jacob gives a part of the land of Canaan to Joseph. The term translated as "Shechem," referring to the city, also means "shoulder" or "mountain slope." It is not clear which Jacob means, but the city itself is later associated with the tribes of Ephraim and Manasseh. If the city is meant, then the final phrase presents a problem, for according to chapter 34 Jacob condemned the violence of Simeon and Levi in Shechem. Perhaps a variant tradition of the conquest of Shechem forms the background of this verse.

49:1-27 The blessing of Jacob. In chapter 49, under the fiction of Jacob's deathbed blessing of his sons, we find a rather haphazard collection of sayings about the characteristics and future destiny of the twelve tribes. Some of the sayings are certainly ancient, but the poem itself cannot predate the tenth century B.C.E., for it speaks of the rule of the tribe of Judah, which occurred at that time. The text is corrupt and parts of the poem are untranslatable, compounding the problems of interpretation.

The tribe of Reuben disappeared early as an independent tribe. The saying of verses 3-4 explains its fall from prominence as retribution for Reuben's incestuous crime (35:22). Behind the curses of Simeon and Levi (vv. 5-7) stand the events recorded in chapter 34; the violence of their revenge against Shechem for the rape of Dinah is condemned. The text about Judah (vv. 8-12) is in part obscure. What is clear is the allusion to the future rule of Israel through the tribe of Judah (v. 10). Of the tribe of Zebulun, it is said only that it dwelt by the sea (v. 13). The tribe of Issachar is derided for allowing itself to be lured by the fertile plain, only to become slaves of the Canaanites (vv. 14-15). By a play on words (Dan comes from a Hebrew root meaning "to judge"), the tribe of Dan is praised for establishing justice in its own territory (v. 16). The serpent image in verse 17 is not meant to be derogatory but calls to mind the small tribe's victories over mighty enemies. The tribe of Gad is characterized as successfully defending itself against raiding bands of nomads (v. 19). The tribe of Asher occupied the fertile region north of Mount Carmel, which was noted for its rich produce (v. 20). The saying about Naphtali is obscure (v. 21). The blessing on Joseph (vv. 22-27) stands apart from the rest of the poem because of its distinctive form. It is the only blessing properly so-called, and it appears to be derived from a very ancient fertility blessing. In verses 25b-26a there are direct parallels to Canaanite blessings. The tribe of Benjamin is praised for its might (v. 28).

49:28–50:14 The death and burial of Jacob. The Priestly account of Jacob's deathbed scene (49:1a), interrupted by the "blessing" of chapter 49, is now resumed. It parallels the Yahwist's version of Jacob's request to be buried with his ancestors (47:29-31). The conclusion of the Priestly author (50:12-13) shows Jacob's sons carrying out his last request. According to this tradition, Jacob is buried in the cave of Machpelah, the burial site of Abraham and Sarah.

The death and burial of Jacob from the Yahwist source are found in 50:1-11, 14. The embalming of Jacob's body does not seem to have religious significance but is done simply to preserve the body for the long trip to Canaan. The long mourning period (v. 3b) and the presence of high Egyptian officials in the funeral procession (vv. 7-9) suggest that Jacob was given a kingly funeral. According to the Yahwist, Jacob was buried in the Transjordan (50:10-11).

50:15-21 Joseph assures his brothers. Joseph's brothers fear that he will take revenge upon them now that their father is dead. This scene gives the Elohist the opportunity before closing his story to reiterate the theology that underlies the story of Joseph. What they meant for evil, God meant for good. Joseph insists that what they did to him has been overshadowed and redeemed by God's saving will. They were but instruments in God's plan for the salvation of Israel.

50:22-26 Joseph's death. In the epilogue Joseph's last days are reviewed by the Elohist. Joseph's adoption of Machir's children provides a basis for this tribe's later standing within the Israelite confederacy (Num 32:39-40; Judg 5:14). Joseph's final words about the land of promise are significant. They indicate that though this story ends in a foreign land, the promise given by God to Abraham, Isaac, and Jacob will be fulfilled. The end of Genesis points to the destiny of Israel: they are to become the liberated people of Yahweh.

CONCLUSION

In the Book of Genesis we have moved from the moment of creation through a history of sin to the call of Abraham, of Isaac, of Jacob, and finally to Joseph and the tribes in Egypt. In these stories we have learned of God's relationship to the world and to Israel. We have learned of God as creator, as judge, as redeemer. We have met a God who accepts the weakness of humanity and continues to love, a God who guides and directs, a God who is able to bring good out of evil. Genesis is only the beginning of the story, the beginning of the acts of God. The story continues not only throughout the Old and New Testaments but in our own lives and our world.

EXODUS

John F. Craghan

INTRODUCTION

The significance of the Exodus

The Exodus or the going out from Egypt lies at the very heart of Israel's faith experience. The God who acted on her behalf was not an insignificant deity of the ancient Near East cut off from reality and relegated to the realm of mythical time. Rather, Israel's God dramatically entered the arena of real time and real people. As the introduction to the Decalogue puts it, "I, the Lord, am your God, who brought you out of the land of Egypt, that place of slavery" (Exod 20:2). To mention the name Yahweh means to conjure up the image of a totally involved deity. To utter that name is to provide an identity. Yahweh without the Exodus is no Yahweh at all!

The Exodus identifies not only Yahweh but also Israel. Israel emerges as God's people precisely in the Exodus. That event implies that the former Egyptian slaves were different from all their contemporaries. The Exodus with its covenant experience at Sinai distinguishes them as Yahweh's people. The going out, therefore, was a selection process. The author of Exodus 3:7 succinctly expresses that process in these words: "I will take you as my own people, and you shall have me as your God."

The biblical book that captures this twofold identity is the Book of Exodus. It is the biblical document par excellence for exposing Israel's roots. Israel realized that those roots lay outside the Promised Land. However, it is the glory of Israel's writers that her origins could be presented in such a powerful yet intimate way. The Book of Exodus is not simply the record of Israel's itineraries. It is her identity papers, the record of human interaction and divine grace, of human success and failure, and of divine assistance and forgiveness.

The experience captured in the Book of Exodus was never subject to a generation gap. By providing identity, this unique book did not stifle growth. Thus Israel could apply the memory of the first going out to varied but nonetheless precarious situations in her history. In the sixth century B.C.E. Second Isaiah could recount the return from Babylon to Jerusalem as a second Exodus: "In the desert prepare the way of the Lord! Make straight in the wasteland a highway for our God!" (Isa 40:3). In the second century B.C.E. the author of Judith described the overthrow of another threat to Israel's faith (Hellenism in the guise of Holofernes and his troops). Among other things he fittingly depicted his heroine after the manner of Israel at the Reed Sea: "For the Lord is God; he crushes warfare, and sets his encampment among his people; he snatched me from the hands of my persecutors" (Jdt 16:2). In the first century B.C.E. the author of the Book of Wisdom sought to resolve the problem of retribution for the just and the wicked in metropolitan Egypt. He adapted the Exodus experience and concluded: "For by the things through which their foes [the Egyptians] were punished they [the Israelites] in their need were benefited" (Wis 11:5).

No historical account

The Egyptian records are as silent as the Sphinx regarding this key event in Israel's faith experience. And this is hardly surprising. The Egyptian texts envision the greater honor and glory of Pharaoh. Moses' dealings with the handicapped leader of Egypt in the plagues would hardly contribute to the thrust of Egyptian historiography. Moreover, according to a widely accepted view, those involved in the Exodus were a typical phenomenon in the ancient Near East.

The Egyptian records speak of Apiru while those written in Akkadian (an eastern Semitic language) refer to Habiru. These 'Apiru/Habiru are often described as displaced people, disturbers of the peace, malcontents who harassed the ancient Near East during the second and third millennia. Not infrequently these 'Apiru/Habiru hired themselves out as mercenaries. It is also known that these Bedouin also provided a work force for Egyptian building campaigns.

The word "Hebrew" derives from "Habiru." However, one must bear in mind that "Habiru" is originally a sociological, not an ethnic, term. It is significant that "Hebrew" occurs in the Book of Exodus especially when the sojourn in Egypt and the Egyptian oppression are concerned (see 2:11). It is likely that a process of assimilation took place: ancestors of the Israelites who had freely gone down to Egypt later became assimilated to other 'Apiru/Habiru. Since such ancestors were seminomadic herders, they would obviously have resented a change in their lifestyle whereby they were reduced to a slave labor force.

Not only were there several entries into Egypt over the centuries but there were also several departures. The text itself reflects an awareness of several different routes. However, from the vantage point of Israel's faith experience there is only *the* Exodus. This is the going out led by Moses that also included the theophany at Sinai. It is likely that this group was relatively small. As this event was recited in worship and pondered by Israel's theologians, it gradually took on epic proportions. The small band grew in both size and importance. At the same time it was not simply a question of arithmetic enlargement. It was also a matter of faith perception. All Israel saw herself represented in the small yet expanding group that had managed to break free of Pharaoh's brickyards.

Setting of the Exodus

Although the biblical account provides no historical report in the modern sense of the term, there are some indications of the setting. Most authorities place the Exodus in the thirteenth century B.C.E. According to these authorities the Pharaoh who oppressed the Israelites was Ramses II, the great builder of the New Kingdom who reigned from 1290 to 1224 B.C.E. One reason for this view is the testimony of Exod 1:11 that refers to the supply city of Raamses. It is known that Ramses II set up his capital in the northeast corner of the Nile Delta and that the term "city of Raamses" was not used after 1100 B.C.E.

Although some would distinguish Ramses II, the oppressor of the Israelites, from his successor, the Pharaoh of the Exodus, on the basis of Exod 2:23, reliable authors still identify Ramses II as both the oppressor and the Pharaoh of the Exodus. According to this view the Exodus would have occurred around 1250 B.C.E. in an area northeast of present-day Cairo and west of the Suez Canal. At the same time one must frankly note the ongoing study of the Exodus and Conquest date. One recent study, for example, suggests dating these events in the fifteenth century B.C.E.

The type of literature

The Book of Exodus is popular literature. As mentioned above, it is not a sober scientific historical treatise. In the other direction it is the blending of different literary types to correspond to Israel's basic perceptions and attitudes. In the plagues there is clear evidence of legendary embellishment. In the crossing of the Reed Sea there is all the dramatization of an epic account. In the rubrics for Passover the effects of liturgy are obvious. In the Covenant Code (20:22–23:19) and the Priestly legislation (chs. 25–31, 35–40) the legal hand is at work. In 15:1b-18 the songwriter is present. The variety of literary types in this popular literature witnesses to the variety of human efforts to capture a central experience. Israel did it her way and the reader must be willing to accept this fact and thus be enriched in the process.

Given the centrality of the Exodus for Israel's faith, one should not be surprised to find a number of theologians at work. Exegetes usually point to at least three theologians in the composition of this work. The first is the Yahwist (= J) who writes in the tenth century B.C.E. during the heady days of the Davidic-Solomonic kingdom. The second is the Elohist (= E) who reflects a period of religious turmoil and syncretism in the eighth or ninth century B.C.E. The third is the Priestly Writer (= P) who struggles to offer a picture of hope during the debacle of the Exile in the sixth century B.C.E. It would be wrong for the reader to attempt to harmonize their sometimes conflicting views. Rather, the reader must allow such theologians the requisite freedom to interpret. Such a stance recognizes that these writers judged the past in the light of their present and with a view to the future needs of Israel. As the commentary will show, such writers had their prejudices—inspiration does not neutralize the human tendency to impose one's view. Ultimately one must be as open as the Bible itself. It canonized not one party line but indeed a variety of party lines.

New exoduses—new liberations

The Exodus story continues to have an impact today, especially in Latin America, the locus of liberation theology. For liberation theologians the chief task is to reread the text in a new light, that is, against the background of exploitation that has characterized so much of Latin American history. In their view the ancient story of Israel's bondage and subsequent deliverance is as timely as ever. It shows that liberation is a process, not an acquired result. It is an ongoing human concern to uncover the manipulation of fellow humans and to proffer the means of genuine human transformation.

The Exodus story also underlines the need for the emergence of ever new prophets after the manner of Moses. It points up the task of such prophets to make people aware of the real malaise from which they suffer. Such prophets, therefore, must articulate the absence of genuine freedom that modern society so heartily encourages. There are ever new Pharaohs whose claims to divinity must be unmasked. At the same time these prophets are bidden to speak a word of hope. They are called upon not only to transport their people from the brickyards but also to energize them to the radical possibility of a genuine existence where misery is known as evil and hope is recognized as attainable. Moses thus transcends the limitations of the thirteenth century B.C.E. to let God's Word have an ever new impact.

COMMENTARY

PART I: THE EXODUS FROM EGYPT

Exod 1:1–15:21

The first part of Exodus provides both the background for the departure and the actual start of the going out. The final editor of the book (perhaps writing around 400 B.C.E.) has pulled together the work of his principal sources (JEP) as well as some independent traditions. In a spirit of fidelity to these sources and traditions this final editor has chosen not to even out various repetitions and inconsistencies. Nevertheless he has attained a certain unity so that, despite these variations, there is a certain flow to his narrative.

In this first part of his work the final editor seeks to provide answers to the following questions: What brought about the misery experienced by the Israelites in Egypt? What are the credentials of the leader? How did this leader respond to God's call? In what ways did the leader attempt to deal with Pharaoh? What was the final catalyst that provoked the going out? How should Israel continue to celebrate this going out? What happened as Israel journeyed to the Reed Sea? How did God intervene at the Reed Sea?

1:1-7 Israel's growth. The background of this introduction is Gen 46:1-4. This passage sums up the past by referring to the patriarchs (Isaac and Jacob/Israel). It also anticipates the future: namely, Israel will become a great nation in Egypt and God himself will lead them out. At the same time this passage creates tension and raises a problem. What will happen to God's people when they do leave Egypt? But, more fundamentally, how can such a small group become a great nation?

P is the author of 1:1-7. Genealogies and lists are a favorite device of this writer (see Gen 5:1; 6:9). Moreover, the language of verse 7 reflects P's vocabulary ("fruitful," "numerous," "filled"). It is the fulfillment of the command in Gen 1:28: "Be fertile and multiply; fill the earth . . . ." Against the background of Exile this passage is intended by P to offer hope and encouragement to God's despondent people. Their temptation is to disparage the Promised Land and not return from Exile (see Num 14:1-3, 5-10, 26-38). In its present position this passage explains how the small group developed into such a significant number.

1:8-14 The oppression of God's people. This section consists of J (vv. 8-11) and P (vv. 13-14). P states in a rather straightforward manner the results of Israel's fertility, that is, their reduction to the slave labor of building. While this policy was only logical for the Egyptian autocratic state (compare Gen 47:13-26), it was totally opposed to Israel's tradition of freedom. J, however, is not content to register Egypt's usual attitude. He accentuates the threat that Israel posed and the opposite results of Egyptian oppression.

J notes the new policy of the Egyptian government. With the emergence of a new king (whom the tradition chooses to leave nameless) there is a new manner of dealing with the prolific Israelites. Thus the oppression is directly related to the political threat that such numbers imply. One can legitimately ask whether the imposition of slave labor is really calculated to achieve the reduction of the Israelite population. With a certain irony, however, J wryly observes that the Egyptian plan was counterproductive. Instead of limiting the population, the policy only succeeded in encouraging its growth.

1:15-22 The suppression of God's people. E is generally considered the author of this doublet, that is, the repetition of substantially the same account in a somewhat different form. (Here the author prefers "God" ['*elohîm*] to J's "Lord" [*Yahweh*]; he also designates the political ruler "the king of Egypt" whereas J opts for "Pharaoh."). Here the manner of defeating God's people is not by oppression—the slave labor of building—but by suppression—the killing of all the baby boys. While suppression would appear to be more apt than oppression for the purposes of population control, it flies in the face of political expediency. Rulers are not likely to deplete their labor force and thus endanger their building programs by killing off the supply of workers. However, in this popular literature it does provide a marvelous setting for resolving the dire situation. The final editor will link E's account with J's birth of the hero in the following chapter.

There are other indications of this popular literature. Although the birth rate is enormous, only two midwives are required to care for the deliveries. Although the Egyptians thought the king was divine and therefore remained secluded from the masses of the people, here two Hebrew midwives have direct access to divine Pharaoh. Moreover, their devious explanation of the increasing population (v. 19) and hence their ability to outwit the sagacious Egyptian monarch are also in keeping with the character of popular literature.

The episode reflects what many critics regard as a motif of the E author, the fear of God (see Gen 20:11; Exod 20:20). It is this emphasis on fear of God (v. 17) that leads to civil disobedience. But the civil disobedience in such a righteous cause is not without its reward. Not only does the nation continue to increase and multiply (v. 20) but so do the offspring of the two midwives (v. 21). Nevertheless, the chapter closes on an ominous note that sets the stage for the birth of the hero.

2:1-10 The birth of the hero. There is a natural propensity to know something about the birth and youth of the hero (compare the theologically oriented infancy narratives of Jesus in Matt 1–2 and Luke 1–2). Humans seek to find extraordinary signs that stamp the person as superhuman right from the moment of birth. For example, Hercules strangles a snake in his cradle. Here J accedes to the needs of his own audience.

The ancient Near East provides certain analogues. Sargon, the great Semitic king who reigned in the twenty-fourth century B.C.E., is described in a legend as follows. His mother placed him in a basket of rushes which she sealed with bitumen. She then cast him into the river upon which he floated until drawn out. There is also an adoption account in which a child is found and then given to a nurse who is paid to keep him for three years. Afterwards the child is adopted and trained as a scribe. It is not unlikely that J's account is also inspired by this adoption story.

The final editor has wisely chosen to connect this passage with E's account of the suppression and thus set the stage for Moses' legend. This arrangement results in having the villain, Pharaoh, caught in his own trap. It is not simply anyone who rescues the baby boy—it is the Pharaoh's own daughter!

Moses is an Egyptian name meaning "is born." In keeping with Israelite sensitivities the name of the Egyptian god is omitted. (Compare Thutmose, that is "the god Thut is born.") This form of Egyptian name was given to children born on the god's anniversary. There is further evidence of Moses' Egyptian background in the Egyptian names borne by members of his family (see 6:16 for Merari and 6:25 for Phinehas). It is also noteworthy that Reuel's daughters in 2:19 refer to the hero as "an Egyptian." However, apart from these notices there is no further information about Moses' background. To be sure, the interest of the Israelite audience lay elsewhere.

2:11-22 The flight to Midian. J, the author responsible for this episode, endeavors to show Moses as a person interested in his own people. He is bent upon foreshadowing or anticipating a problem that will appear later. This problem is the question posed by the Hebrew in verse 14: "Who has appointed *you* ruler and judge over us?" It is precisely this question of credentials that Moses will have to face shortly. Moses' flight to Midian also foreshadows or anticipates other happenings. Just as Moses has to flee to the desert, so too the people of Israel will head for the desert. Just as Moses encounters God at the mountain (3:1), so too the people of Israel will experience God at the mountain (19:18).

The land of Midian, Moses' home for the time being, is a desert area in the Sinai peninsula. In later traditions (see Num 25:6-9; Judg 6:1–7:25) these desert-dwelling Midianites will become the implacable enemies of Israel. In the present tradition, however, the Midianites and those associated with Moses are related tribes. (Reuel is a tribal name, not a personal name.) Chapter 18 will show how Moses learned many practical things from these Midianites.

J presents Moses as a man with a checkered background. Although J likes stories of wells, for example, Rebecca (Gen 24:15) and Rachel (29:10), he must introduce this lady at the well, Zipporah, as a non-Israelite. Thus Moses is an Israelite of the tribe of Levi (2:1) who is brought up as an Egyptian but who must then flee his Egyptian home only to meet non-Israelites, one of whom he marries. These are hardly the best credentials. Hence the lingering question: With such credentials, will Moses be able to offset the oppression/suppression in Egypt?

2:23-25 The Exodus as lament liturgy. This description is not merely a passing note in the overall story. The final editor has combined the long period of time (v. 23a—probably from E) with the miserable state of the people (vv. 23b-25—a P passage). This state is presented in lament language ("groaned and cried out"). (Note the repetition of this language in 3:7, 9; 6:5.) The verb "to cry out" is the typical expression of the poor and disenfranchised; it is a cry that God cannot ignore. Lament is linked to covenant (v. 25). In covenant theology the people's problem necessarily becomes God's problem; the people's frustration necessarily becomes God's frustration. Liberation always begins by recognizing the plight of the poor.

3:1-6 The burning bush. This scene is a combination of J and E, though mostly J. (E is present in parts of verse 1, for example, "Horeb, the mountain of God," and verse 4b.) This combination of sources is significant theologically, since it indicates the diversity and richness of Israelite tradition. No one tradition could claim an exclusive right to tell the whole story. (This combination of sources will be very evident in the rest of chapter 3.) One should also note that here (v. 1) Moses' father-in-law is Jethro, whereas in 2:18 it is Reuel. Unlike Reuel, Jethro is a personal name. (For further complications see Judg 1:16; 4:11.)

J probably chose the term "bush" (in Hebrew *s[e]neh*) in order to connect this scene with Yahweh's mountain (in Hebrew *sînai*). The burning of the bush is thus linked to the fire of the theophany of Sinai (see 19:18). Hence there is a close association of the Exodus and Sinai right from the very start. What emerges from this scene for J is the twofold dimension of awe and historical continuity. Awe is expressed in Moses' gesture of removing his sandals because of the intrinsic holiness of the encounter with Yahweh—Yahweh's presence sanctifies the ground. Consequently, Moses hides his face. Historical continuity is articulated in verse 6. The God who speaks to Moses has been active over the centuries in his concern for this people. The God of Moses is also the God of the patriarchs (see also 3:16).

3:7-15 The commissioning of Moses. This scene is intimately bound up with the divine revelation at the burning bush. The experience of God is thus related to Moses' function in Israel. Israel's theologians reflected the tradition that regarded Moses as a prophet. He was, therefore, one who spoke on God's behalf to the people of Israel—he was God's spokesperson (see Deut 18:15-20). Faithful to the perception of Moses' prophetic office, both J and E employ the literary genre of call narrative. (See Judg 6:11-21; Isa 6:1-13.) This is not intended to be a blow-by-blow account of what transpired in Midian. Rather, it attempts to communicate the meaning of God's choice for a given audience without excluding some type of original experience. The call narrative builds upon the human need for signs and reassurances.

Both J and E offer somewhat different versions of Moses' call. However, the basic structure is the same: (a) divine response to prayer that presupposes a given difficulty: 3:7 (J), 3:9 (E); (b) God's promise to save: 3:8 (J), 3:10 (E); (c) the commission: 3:16-17 (J), 3:9 (E); (d) Moses' objection: 4:1 (J), 3:11 (E); (e) overcoming the objection by a sign: 4:1-9 (J), 3:12 (E); (f) second objection: 4:10 (J), 3:13 (E); (g) God's final or quasi-final answer: 4:13-16 (J), 3:14-15 (E), 4:17 (E?).

Both J (3:7) and E (3:9) begin by noting the plight of the people in lamentation language ("cry"). In developing the divine promise to save, J and E stress different dimensions of Moses' office. In 3:8 (J) Yahweh is the one who intends to deliver the Israelites, while Moses in 3:16 (J) is dispatched to speak to the people. In 3:10 (E) Moses is sent specifically to bring the Israelites out of Egypt. Although the verb "to send" (vv. 10, 12, 13) designates the prophet as an envoy (see Jer 1:7; 26:12, 15), E appears to allot a much more substantial role to Moses.

J emphasizes not only Israel's deliverance from the Egyptians but also the goal of that intervention: entrance into the Promised Land. That land flows with milk and honey (v. 8). This expression is borrowed from mythology, depicting the land as a veritable earthly paradise. The reference to the Canaanites, Hittites, and others (vv. 8, 17) is to the pre-Israelite inhabitants of the land (for a seven-people enumeration see Gen 15:20-21; Deut 7:1). The Exodus, therefore, is not only a going out—it is also a going up, namely, into the land formerly inhabited by these nations.

The proofs demanded by Moses in the E tradition are significant. In verse 12 the sign to provide credentials for Moses before Pharaoh and Israel is that the people will later meet to worship God on this very mountain. This is an anomaly in the call narrative, since signs occur immediately, not at some point in the future. Perhaps the compactness of the E tradition is the reason for this anomaly.

Moses still needs further proof in approaching the Israelites (v. 13). In the E tradition this proof is the disclosure of the divine name (vv. 14-15). It should be pointed out that for J this disclosure of the name Yahweh (consistently translated "the Lord" in the NAB) demanded no special scene. From the very beginning of his narrative (Gen 2:4b) J uses the personal name Yahweh and in Gen 4:26 onwards presumes that this name is known by humans. Up to this scene in chapter 3, E has simply employed the general word "God" (*'elohim* in Hebrew—hence the distinction of divine names early became a key criterion in separating the J and E sources). As one might suspect, this scene is theologically central in E's scheme of things. (For P's use of divine names see 6:2.)

For Israel as well as for the ancient Near East, names implied real existence. Something was a reality when one knew its name. The name implied a dimension of intimacy. By knowing someone's name, one was on personal terms with that person. When one comes to the personal name of the God of Israel, however, there are two distinct issues.

The first issue is the etymology of Yahweh (actually the Hebrew text supplies just four consonants [YHWH]—the addition of the vowels *a* and *e* is already an attempt at interpretation). The solutions to this etymological problem are legion and no one suggestion commands the field. A popular view is that the divine name is really a causative form of the verb "to be." Hence "he causes to be" = "he creates." The second issue is the meaning that the author of the passage (E) intended. Here one stands on firmer ground, the context itself.

Verse 15 ("The Lord . . . has sent . . .") is the real answer to verse 13, since it provides the name that Moses asked for. Verse 14a ("I am who am") explains the name in terms of being: Yahweh's being means active participation and involvement. According to verse 10 the name means leading the people out of Egypt; according to verse 12 it means assisting Moses. Verse 14b ("I AM sent me to you") links verse 13 ("The God of your fathers has sent me") to verse 15 ("The Lord . . . has sent me"). Yahweh is committed to act on behalf of the people.

3:16-22 Expansion of the commission. In this section from J, Moses is first commissioned to assemble the elders (v. 16) and then to communicate the divine displeasure with the oppression of the Israelites. This commission is then expanded in verses 18-22. Not only Moses but also the elders are to approach Pharaoh (v. 18). This expansion is not a useless appendage. The author is preparing the reader for a twofold exodus: an exodus-flight and an exodus-expulsion. In verse 19 Pharaoh will not permit the people to go unless he is constrained; hence the people will be forced to flee. In verses 21-22 Yahweh will make the Egyptians well disposed toward the Israelites. Indeed, the Israelite women will even receive gifts of jewelry and clothing. Yahweh will so arrange matters that the Israelites finally will be expelled (see 12:35-36).

4:1-9 Moses' objection and subsequent signs. Like E in 3:11-12, J has his tradition of objection (v. 1) and signs (vv. 2-9). In order that Moses may authenticate himself to his people and thus substantiate his claims, there is the need of signs. The signs provided are a staff or type of magic wand (vv. 2-4) and a leprous sleight of hand (vv. 6-8). It is interesting to note that P will later use the J rod-turned-serpent tradition in a different context (7:9-12). In any event, the signs mentioned here are subsequently successful (4:31) and establish Moses' right to speak on behalf of Yahweh.

4:10-17 More objections, replies, and signs. J heightens the enormity of the task given Moses by formulating a second objection. Moses now maintains that he does not possess the wherewithal for public relations because he really cannot communicate (v. 10). Yahweh's reply focuses on divine omnipotence (v. 11). Yahweh promises to provide two things: (a) help in oral delivery and (b) assistance in content (v. 12). These concessions notwithstanding, J's call narrative continues with a final effort on Moses' part to evade his vocation and with a final reassurance on Yahweh's part to support the wavering candidate. There is a certain audacity here but an audacity consonant with the human penchant for escaping responsibility and passing it on to someone else (v. 13). Yahweh's reaction is anger, but, surprisingly, the anger is quickly suppressed, so that Aaron becomes Moses' prophet (vv. 14-15). Thus Moses is to function after the manner of Yahweh, and Aaron will be the divine spokesperson (v. 16; see Deut 18:18; Jer 1:9).

Concerning the staff (v. 17), one is naturally disposed to think of the J tradition in verses 2-4 where the staff is *a* sign given to Moses to authenticate his mission and dispose the people to accept him. Here, however, the staff is linked to *signs.* Perhaps this was originally part of the E tradition where here and now signs are lacking (see 3:12).

4:18-23 Moses' return to Egypt. With the exception of verses 18 and 20b this passage is from J. According to E, Moses made the return trip to Egypt by himself (v. 18; see 18:5), but according to J, Moses made this journey in the company of his wife and children (v. 20a). (The presence of Moses' wife and children will be important for the circumcision rite in verses 24-27.) In view of Pharaoh's reluctance to let Israel go (the exodus-flight tradition), J has Moses exercise the office of prophet in verses 22-23: (a) commission ("So shall you say to Pharaoh"); (b) messenger formulary ("Thus says the Lord"); (c) message ("Israel is my son, my first-born"). Pharaoh's refusal to heed the prophetic word anticipates the death of the first-born in the tenth plague (see 11:5).

4:24-26 The circumcision. The J scene, where Yahweh tries to kill Moses, seems linked to the J story of Gen 32:24-32, where Jacob wrestles with Yahweh. In both cases Yahweh suddenly appears in the night as a threatening demonic power. Jacob is on his way to the land of promise, but he must first confront his hostile brother Esau. Moses, too, has received a promise, but he must first confront the hostile Pharaoh.

The Egyptians did not practice circumcision, whereas the Hebrews apparently did. Although some see this scene as an apotropaic act on the occasion of a marriage—that is, designed to ward off all dangers on such an occasion—it is at least conceivable that Moses' lack of circumcision caused an infection. Zipporah's action would then have saved his life and have given rise to the expression "a spouse of blood." In any event, J has Zipporah circumcise her husband because, given the Israelite practice, it was not fitting for the great leader to be uncircumcised.

4:27-31 Meeting between Moses and Aaron. Aaron is a somewhat enigmatic character, yet this early tradition (J) seems constrained to associate him with Moses. In verse 30 it is Aaron who performs the signs, but according to the J tradition in 4:2-9, it is Moses who is to perform them. Nonetheless, the outcome is positive. In verse 31 the people are convinced and, rejoicing, they bow down and worship. J, however, feels compelled to express their fickleness or lack of real faith, for in the following scene the people will grumble. For J, the people genuinely believe in Yahweh and his servant Moses only in the aftermath of the Reed Sea event (see 14:31).

5:1–6:1 First audience with Pharaoh. Now that the Israelites have heard and accepted Yahweh's message as presented by Moses and Aaron, it is time to have the leaders approach Pharaoh with a view to negotiating their release from Egypt. This well-constructed J story consists of six scenes, five of them opening with a verb of action.

The first scene (5:1-5) begins with the report that "Moses and Aaron *went*." Verse 2 poses a question that the rest of the story will develop: Who is Yahweh? The three-day journey into the desert is probably connected with the exodus-flight tradition. According to the tradition preserved in chapters 15–19, there are only three days or camps between Egypt and Sinai (15:27; 16:1; 17:1; 19:2). This scene provides a realistic attitude toward a labor force, namely, not to allow the slaves to get away and so keep them at their work. Such an attitude rejects E's view of a suppression in 1:15-22.

The second scene (5:6-9) has Pharaoh speaking to the Egyptian taskmasters and the Hebrew foremen. (This deployment of foreign labor, whereby the taskmasters are Egyptian and the foremen members of the subject people, is historically accurate.) Unlike the rest of the scenes, here there is no verb of action, since one cannot expect the divine Pharaoh to go out to his underlings. The bricks in question are adobe—unburnt bricks dried in the sun.

The third scene (5:10-14) begins with a verb of action ("So the taskmasters . . . *went out*") and brings together the taskmasters, the foremen, and the people. The people are forced to look for straw while the foremen are flogged because the people cannot produce.

The fourth scene (5:15-19) has the Hebrew foremen before Pharaoh. Popular literature permits, indeed demands at times, the interaction of the divine Pharaoh with such underlings, in this case the depressed foremen. Once again the scene opens with a verb of action ("Then the Israelite foremen *came*"). However, the outcome of the meeting is less than what the foremen hoped for. The quota must remain the same but still no straw!

The fifth scene (5:20-21) focuses on the foremen and Moses and Aaron. Once again there is a verb of action whereby the foremen bump into the two leaders ("they . . . *came upon* . . . ."). The less than accidental encounter does not augur well for the two leaders. They are the recipients of nothing less than a curse: "The Lord look upon you and judge!" The start of Moses' grandiose plan is hardly optimistic, and the future looks dismal indeed.

The sixth scene (5:22–6:1) has Moses appealing to Yahweh. The verb of action in verse 22 (in Hebrew "and he *returned*") is expressed by the English adverb "again." The scene depicts a discouraged Moses, indeed a typical Moses, who will not cease to badger Yahweh with his complaints. One is hardly surprised, therefore, that he was hesitant about accepting his office. In any case, Moses learns that Yahweh will intervene dramatically. The reader is naturally set for the first plague. However, P chooses to review the call of Moses.

6:2-13 P's commissioning of Moses. Although P knew of J and E traditions of Moses' call in chapters 3–4, he opts to provide his own version of that call. In response to the people's lament in 2:23b-25 and in light of the setbacks in 5:1–6:1, the call of the prophet is the guarantee of support for God's chosen one and, at the same time, the overcoming of oppression/depression for God's chosen people.

For P it is a question of both continuity and discontinuity. The God who speaks to Moses is the same God who appeared to the patriarchs. However, there is a difference; that God did not reveal his personal name Yahweh to them. Instead, he employed "El Shaddai" (translated "God the Almighty," "God of the mountain," "God of the steppe," or "God of the breasts"). Unlike 3:14-15, this passage (see vv. 6-8) does not entail a personal honor for Moses that provides credentials. It is a special communication that looks to alleviating Israel's pain. For P there is only one covenant in question, the one made with Abraham in Gen 17. This scene, therefore, creates tension: the ancient promise and the present lack of fulfillment. That lack will now be addressed.

In commissioning Moses, P adopts the same basic call narrative as J and E: (a) divine response to prayer (v. 5); (b) God's promise to save (vv. 6-8); (c) the commission (vv. 9-11) (the commission to the people is only alluded to); (d) Moses' objection (v. 12, repeated in verse 30); (e) overcoming the objection (7:1-5).

Verses 6-8 are an oracle of salvation, a literary genre at home especially in the prophetic literature of the sixth century B.C.E. Against the background of P's setting of the Exile, such an oracle provides hope and lays a new foundation for Israel's faith. It shows that the God who judges is also the God who delivers. More important, this bestowal of grace is not bound up with the success of institutions in the past. Paradoxically, Israel's lack of success cannot defeat God.

The expression "I am Yahweh" is typical of P. This is royal style, such as is used at the beginning of royal inscriptions. It was taken over and used as a self-introduction in liturgy (see 20:2). It suggests that "I am here, present and acting." It is a formula that calls for responsive action on Israel's part. (See the Holiness Code in Lev 17–26, for example, 19:4.) For P as well as for the priestly school of theologians, God's interventions on behalf of Israel are clear clues to the identity of this God (see Ezek 20).

6:14-30 Genealogy of Moses and Aaron. P has interrupted the account of Moses' commissioning to insert this genealogy. (An indication of the insertion is the repetition of the last line before the insertion [see vv. 13 and 26-27].) Although some tend to find genealogies rather boring and hence skip over them, one should observe their usefulness. They represent a form of survival—the tribe, for example, takes care of all its members. They provide identity—they tell a person who he or she is. They indicate status—for example, they inform the king as to his lineage. They structure history—they are the parameters of human and/or divine activity.

Here it is clear that P is really interested in the tribe of Levi. He rushes past Reuben and Simeon to get to Levi (vv. 14-15—all three were Leah tribes [see Gen 29:31-34]). Both Moses and Aaron are sons of Amram (v. 20) and ultimately descendants of Levi. Although P makes Miriam the sister of both Aaron and Moses (v. 20), Exod 15:20 makes her the sister of only Aaron. (Note also the opposition of Aaron and Miriam to Moses in Exod 32 and Num 12.)

Originally "Levite" was a secular name, meaning "member of the tribe of Levi." Only at the end of a long process was it changed into a designation for a somewhat lowly person who performed menial cultic tasks (see 28:1-43). By emphasizing Aaron, P intends to establish a claim for the legitimacy of the group of priests that ultimately controlled the temple in Jerusalem. (P has passed over other ancient priestly families such as the Mushites mentioned in verse 19.) For P, therefore, this genealogy has served to provide identity and undergird the status of Aaron's descendants.

7:1-7 Reassurance and compliance. In answer to Moses' objection about his speaking abilities (6:13, 30), P has Yahweh reassure Moses that he will have a quasi-divine function (the Hebrew *'elohim* can mean someone other than God—see Ps 45:7 vis-à-vis the prophet Aaron). The outcome of divine intervention will be that Yahweh will actually lead Israel out of Egypt (vv. 4-5). However, this intervention will also provoke Egyptian recognition of Yahweh's real identity: "so that the Egyptians may learn that I am the Lord . . ." (v. 5).

The literal translation of the beginning of verse 3 is "But I will harden Pharaoh's heart."

For the biblical writers the heart was the organ of thinking and willing (see Isa 6:10; 29:13) that focused on the person as the thinking and willing subject. It should be noted that Exodus employs three different ways of expressing the hardening of Pharaoh's heart: (a) Pharaoh's heart was hardened (7:13, 14, 22; 8:15; 9:7, 35); (b) Pharaoh hardened his (own) heart (8:11, 28); (c) Yahweh hardened Pharaoh's heart (7:3; 9:12; 10:1, 20, 27). Exodus, therefore, admits both human freedom and divine omnipotence. Like the rest of the Bible, Exodus attempts no explanation of that admission.

Besides noting the compliance of Moses and Aaron in verse 6, P goes on to record the ages of the two leaders. This fits in with his overall chronological interests. After the forty-year wandering, P later mentions that Moses died at the age of one hundred and twenty (see Deut 34:7).

7:8-13 Introduction to the plagues. In this scene P mentions the first demonstration of Yahweh's power before Pharaoh, since for him this is the first meeting between Pharaoh and Yahweh's emissaries (for J see 5:1–6:1). As noted earlier, P has changed Moses' staff from an authenticating instrument before the people (see J in 4:2-4) to a permission-seeking device before Pharaoh. Not surprisingly, Aaron has a key role to play. As Yahweh foretold (see 7:4), Pharaoh refuses to comply, despite Aaron's serpent-consuming staff.

This introductory scene should serve as a guide of sorts in approaching the plagues. A staff turned into a serpent and a river changed to blood are indications of the world of folklore, not of scientific explanations. Nonetheless, interpreters have sought a so-called natural explanation of the phenomena. According to the *cosmic* interpretation, a comet made contact with the earth, bringing in its wake red dust, small meteorites, earthquakes, etc. According to the *geological* explanation, a violent eruption of a volcano in the fifteenth century B.C.E. caused a tidal wave the aftereffects of which brought about the plagues. According to a *third* view, there was a natural succession of catastrophes beginning with an exceptionally large flooding of the Nile in July and August and culminating with a sirocco in March or April that killed off the remaining first fruits, not the first-born.

Ultimately, however, one must conclude that the biblical writers had only an imperfect knowledge of Egyptian matters. For example, locusts (the eighth plague) are known both in Egypt and Israel. However, the red Nile (the first plague) and frogs (the second plague) are known only in Egypt, while hail (the seventh plague) is exceptional in Egypt but not in Israel.

The biblical account itself contains doublets and inconsistencies, thus precluding a scientific exposition and suggesting a popular-literature approach. Thus the fourth plague (the flies) is a doublet of the third plague (the gnats). Similarly, the sixth plague (the boils, an epidemic affecting livestock and humans) is a doublet of the fifth plague (the pestilence, that is, the livestock epidemic). With regard to consistency, one may raise some questions. If all the livestock were killed in the fifth plague (9:6), then how could they have been affected by boils in the sixth plague (9:10), hail in the seventh plague (9:25), and death of the first-born in the tenth plague (12:29)? If frogs already covered the land of Egypt (8:2), how could the magicians repeat the feat (8:3)?

Before moving on to the question of the literary arrangement of the plagues, one should note that the presence of E is doubtful in these accounts. Hence one speaks more cautiously of JE, a combination of the Pentateuch's earliest written sources, rather than further distinguishing them as J or E. As for distribution, the final editor has taken five plagues from JE alone (the fourth, fifth, seventh, eighth, and ninth), two from P alone (the third and sixth), and three from a combination of JE and P (the first, second, and tenth).

The differences between JE and P touch on several points. With regard to roles, JE has Moses appear simply as a prophet, whereas P has Aaron play the principal part, so that Moses is upstaged. Concerning formulae, JE has Moses employ the messenger formula, while P has Yahweh speaking to Moses, who then speaks to Aaron. Finally, in terms of character, for JE the plagues are genuine afflictions to chastise Pharaoh for refusing to let the people go. For P, however, they are signs and wonders that legitimate Moses and Aaron as representatives of Yahweh, not scourges as such. (Compare the plague of gnats [8:12-15—P] with that of flies [8:16-28—JE].)

The presence of the different biblical traditions raises some further questions: How did the final editor put everything together? Did he hope to attain something concrete? If so, what indications are there?

In seeking to answer these questions, one must keep two points in mind. First, the plague account really begins in 7:8-13 because this scene contains the same outlook and vocabulary as the plagues themselves. Second, the tenth plague (the death of the first-born) is excluded here, since its make-up and literary characteristics are different. The result is that there are ten episodes: the introduction in 7:8-13 and the nine plagues (7:14–10:29). Moreover, they are arranged concentrically so that the introduction, the first plague, etc., have counterparts of approximately the same length and with the same formula in the ninth plague, the eighth plague, etc. (Compare 8:12-15 with 9:8-12.) This concentric arrangement is not haphazard. It is intentionally designed to indicate definite progress as one reads the remainder of the story.

The plague account is not so much a series of devastations as it is a series of disputes between Pharaoh and Moses linked to the question in 5:2: "Who is the Lord that I should heed his plea to let Israel go?" The failure of Moses and Aaron in these dealings with Pharaoh is not decisive, since the story continues in the Reed Sea account. These plagues look to an even greater wonder at the sea.

7:14-25 First plague: water turned into blood. The final editor has combined JE (vv. 14-18, 20b-21a, 23-25) and P (vv. 19-20, 21b-22). According to JE it is the Nile, *the* river, that will be affected. Moreover, JE makes reference to the general death of the fish and the subsequent pollution. According to P, however, the waters of all Egypt are affected (v. 19), not just the Nile.

In terms of progress, one must note that the Egyptian magicians are able to match the feat performed by God's emissaries (v. 22). With regard to Pharaoh, the recognition demanded of him is relatively simple: "This is how you shall know that I am the Lord" (v. 17). As the plague account continues, there will be significant differences on both scores.

7:26–8:11 Second plague: the frogs. Both JE (7:26-29; 8:4-9a) and P (8:1-3, 11b) are unmistakably present in this account. As with the first plague, this episode reveals that the Egyptian magicians are still able to match the feats performed by Moses and Aaron (8:3). However, there are other differences. Now Pharaoh actively seeks out the intercession of Moses (8:15), although he remains adamant in the end (8:11). Besides, the recognition now demanded of Pharaoh is more embracing than 7:17: "That you may learn that there is none like the Lord, our God" (8:6).

8:12-15 Third plague: the gnats. In this account, which is solely from P, there is clear evidence of progress. Unlike the first two plagues, this plague is one which the Egyptian magicians are incapable of reproducing. In the magicians' report to Pharaoh there is the further observation: "This is the finger of God" (v. 15). However, as Yahweh had predicted, Pharaoh chooses not to let Israel go.

8:16-28 Fourth plague: the flies. This passage from JE seems to presuppose that the Egyptians are not very remote from the Israelites, since the former would be able to view the sacrifices offered by the latter (v. 22). This note is somewhat surprising, since the author claims a distinction for the Israelites, namely, that the plague will not affect the land of Goshen (v. 18). Hence the Egyptians and the Israelites do not live side by side. In any event, the animal sacrifices of the Israelites would upset the religious sensitivities of the Egyptians. Perhaps this is because animals had a conspicuous place in Egyptian religion or because the sacrifice of whole animals was not the usual practice among them. What is significant here is, first of all, the acknowledgment by Pharaoh "that I am the Lord in the midst of the earth" (v. 18). Thus Pharaoh is to admit that Yahweh is present in Egypt. Second, the permission for the three-day trip is for a point in the desert that is not too far away (v. 24). Once again Moses is to pray on behalf of the mighty ruler of Egypt. Clearly there is development in Pharaoh's character.

9:1-7 Fifth plague: the pestilence. In this JE account one must note that there is no negotiation between Pharaoh and Moses after the start of the plague, as in 8:21. However, in keeping with the preceding plague, there is the distinction between the Egyptians and the Israelites. The pestilence will strike Egyptian, not Israelite, livestock. One can see that in this account Pharaoh takes pains to be assured that this distinction is really so (see vv. 6b-7a).

9:8-12 Sixth plague: the boils. In this P account it is somewhat astonishing that Aaron plays a relatively minor role, that of Moses' assistant. In terms of development, what emerges is the downward spiral of the magicians. Although they were able to match the first two plagues, they were unsuccessful in the third and were forced to admit the work as God's doing. Here the final editor has so arranged matters that the magicians are singled out for their lack of uniqueness. They too suffer from the skin disease and are unable to stand in Moses' presence (v. 11).

9:13-35 Seventh plague: the hail. In this JE account there is an explanation given for the failure of the previous plagues to induce Pharaoh to relent. Yahweh has acted this way to show his power and to make his name resound throughout the earth (v. 16). One almost expects Yahweh's final and decisive act here and now. While even this plague does not bring Pharaoh to grant the necessary permission to leave, it does contribute to the unfolding character of the divine ruler of Egypt.

There is the notice in verse 14 that Pharaoh (as well as his subjects) is to confess that there is no one like Yahweh anywhere on the earth. This is followed in verse 27 by the *mea culpa* of Pharaoh: "I have sinned again! The Lord is just; it is I and my subjects who are at fault." This is truly a remarkable confession. Finally there is the statement that the plague of hail will induce an even greater confession, namely, that the earth is Yahweh's (v. 29). The God of Israel is receiving a more fitting recognition from the mighty Egyptian god, Pharaoh himself.

10:1-20 Eighth plague: the locusts. This JE account opens with an explanation of the hardness of heart of Pharaoh and his servants. This obduracy is calculated to demonstrate Yahweh's might and to provide an ongoing tradition of those exploits in the Israelite community (vv. 1-2). The author makes special mention of Moses' actual going to Pharaoh and dwells upon Yahweh's vexation: "How long will you refuse to submit to me?" (v. 3b). For the first time one learns that Pharaoh's servants are becoming exasperated to the point of urging their king to exercise restraint and so be reasonable (v. 7). The result of this intervention is that Moses and Aaron are recalled to Pharaoh's court (v. 8). In this scene, the author points out Pharaoh's suspicion that a conspiracy of sorts is underway, since Moses petitions for the whole Israelite community to take part in the desert worship (vv. 10-11).

The progress in depicting Pharaoh's change of character is found in vv. 16-17. After the speedy summons there is the clear protestation of sin: "I have sinned against the Lord, your God, and against you." Thus Pharaoh has advanced in his awareness of Yahweh's presence and power from the time of the first plague. After the customary request for forgiveness and the successful outcome of that request, there is nonetheless the concluding remark that Pharaoh remains adamant and so the people remain in Egypt.

10:21-29 Ninth plague: the darkness. Many connect this darkness with a typical Near Eastern phenomenon, the *khamsin.* This is a hot wind that blows off the desert in March and April, bringing darkness and a very oppressive atmosphere in its wake. In the biblical account such darkness takes on a more foreboding character inasmuch as it suggests the evil powers of chaos. Such a character matches the thrust of this JE account. There is exasperation leading to the breaking off of any further negotiations (v. 28). Pharaoh is now willing to let all Israel leave for purposes of worship (contrast 10:11), but not the livestock (v. 24). Moses reacts to such permission rather ironically. He points out that animal sacrifices are a part of their worship and hence required. However, since the sacrificial animals can be determined only upon arrival at the place of worship, it is, therefore, necessary to bring all the livestock along. Pharaoh's response to Moses' ironic request is the cessation of all further negotiations. An impasse has been reached, one which will result in Moses' death if he should attempt to appear once again before Pharaoh. To be sure, a new way must be found to force Pharaoh's hand.

11:1-10 Tenth plague: the death of the first-born. Given Moses' seemingly final appearance before Pharaoh, the reader expects a quick dash to the sea and then the trek in the desert. In other words, the writers up to this point have created suspense, and the reader naturally anticipates release of tension and denouement. To the contrary, there is another (and final) plague that is totally out of character with the previous nine. (Actually the scene at the Reed Sea does not presuppose the tenth plague.) The reader now becomes bogged down, not in a Sea of Reeds, but in a whirlpool of rubrics. There is the sudden command to prepare for liturgy, not the expected bolt for freedom. Presumably the biblical writers had a reason for the temporary demise of narrative and the exaltation of liturgy.

The death of the first-born does not come as a total surprise. In 4:23 Yahweh addressed Pharaoh through Moses in these terms: "If you refuse to let him (Israel, Yahweh's first-born) go, I warn you, I will kill your son, your first-born." Neither does the plundering of the Egyptians come as a complete surprise. In 3:21-22 the Israelites were assured that they would not leave Egypt empty-handed. However, 11:1-3 (either J or E), belonging to the exodus-expulsion tradition, assumes that this tenth plague is really the one and only plague. How else could the Israelites get silver and gold ornaments and clothing from the Egyptians? How else can one explain Moses' prestige with Pharaoh's servants and Egypt as a whole?

The literary arrangement of verses 4-8 (from J; verses 9-10 from P) suggests that this plague is not linked to the previous nine. J usually informs the reader that Moses is to speak to Pharaoh, but in verse 4 it is not clear to whom Moses delivers the divine message. Up to verse 6 the recipient seems to be Israel, but in verses 7-8 Pharaoh is addressed. At the end of verse 8 Moses leaves Pharaoh's presence in a rage. But according to 10:29 (JE) he was never again to appear before Pharaoh. Although some posit a historical link—an epidemic that struck the Egyptians and hence facilitated the departure of the Israelites—it is not unreasonable to conclude that the tenth plague has been contrived to connect with the feast of the Passover.

12:1-20 The Passover ritual. In this rubrical section P provides details for a feast that was already old among seminomadic shepherds of the ancient Near East. It was an offering by such shepherds for the welfare of their flocks when the tribe set out to search for new pasture grounds. This was in the spring and indeed at a very critical time in the life of the flock. This was the time when the young of the sheep and the goats would be born. Indications of the antiquity of the feast are the following: no priests, no sanctuaries, no altars.

Other details fit in with this pastoral background. The animal is roasted, not boiled (v. 9), since cooking utensils are at a minimum. Perhaps this explains why the bones are not broken (vv. 9, 46). The time is the twilight of the first full spring moon (v. 6). This coincides with the return of the shepherds to the camp on the brightest night of the month. The unleavened bread (v. 8) is the ordinary bread eaten by such shepherds, and the bitter herbs (v. 8) are the desert plants used by these shepherds for spices. The clothing and attire suit this background: "with your loins girt, sandals on your feet and your staff in hand, . . ." (v. 11). The blood rite (v. 7) is apotropaic in purpose, that is, the smearing of the blood on the tent poles is intended to ward off all danger to the members of the tribe and especially to the young about to be born. This danger is personified in "the destroyer" (v. 23). The blood, therefore, prevents him from striking humans and animals.

It is the blood rite that establishes the link between the tenth plague and the Passover. "The destroyer" is now subject to a new interpretation arising from Israel's history. Yahweh will go through the land of Egypt, striking down the first-born of both humans and beasts (v. 12). But when Yahweh sees the blood on the houses, "the destroyer" will not be permitted to strike. Rather Yahweh will "pass over" (v. 13).

While the etymology of "passover" is far from clear, the meaning of the term for Israel is abundantly clear. "To pass over" means "to spare, protect, deliver." What Israel did, therefore, was to interpret the ancient feast of seminomadic shepherds in terms of her own relationship with Yahweh. It was no longer the quest for a temporary pasture but for the final pasture, the Promised Land itself. The ancient feast with its focus on change lent itself admirably to interpreting the change in Israel's destiny. The shepherds were now a people in flight (v. 11). (For the unleavened bread in verses 14-20 see 13:3-10.)

12:21-28 Promulgation of the Passover. In this J passage (with the exception of P in verse 28) Moses approaches the elders, those leaders responsible for carrying out Yahweh's command. Here the emphasis is principally on the blood rite. Hand in hand with the sprinkling is the prohibition to go outdoors until morning (v. 22) because of the nocturnal devastation.

The rubrics in verses 24-27a are significant for Israel's abhorrence of any and every form of generation gap. Those taking part in the original Exodus and all subsequent Israelite communities are linked together in this pivotal experience. The question asked by the children in verse 26 is not one of mere historical interest. It is a contrived question designed to interpret the past in view of the present. To be sure, Yahweh spared the Israelites but crushed the Egyptians. But the happenings of the thirteenth century B.C.E. affect the present community: "When he struck down the Egyptians, he spared *our* houses" (v. 27a). To celebrate the Passover means to span generations and coalesce in an experience explaining and unifying the entire people.

12:29-39 Death of the first-born and departure. J, the author of these verses, follows up the exodus-expulsion tradition of 11:1-3. The death of the first-born has been so grave that Pharaoh summons Moses and Aaron at night (v. 31). There is no longer the hesitancy to keep the livestock from going along (v. 32; see 10:24). Indeed the devastation has been so severe that the Egyptians urge the Israelites to advance their timetable. The haste in this departure is reflected in the condition of the bread. The Israelites were so rushed that their dough was not leavened (v. 34), and, consequently, they had to be satisfied with unleavened loaves (v. 39). (P in verse 15 gave no reason why the people would eat such bread for seven days.) Finally, in keeping with the exodus-expulsion tradition, the Israelites asked the Egyptians for silver and gold articles as well as clothing. However, the despoiling went far beyond such limitations. The Israelites ended up by getting from the Egyptians whatever they wanted (v. 36).

J mentions the first destination and the number of people involved. Succoth lies thirty-two miles southeast of Raamses and is approximately in the middle of the isthmus between the Mediterranean Sea and the Gulf of Suez. J sets down the number as "about six hundred thousand men on foot, not counting the children" (v. 37). This would imply a population of some three million men, women, and children. While it is probable that the Hebrew word for "thousand" originally meant a subsection of a tribe and hence a total number of five thousand or six thousand, the epic nature of this popular literature emphasizes the larger number. "A crowd of mixed ancestry" (v. 38) suggests that non-Israelite elements of the slave labor force also departed Egypt in the company of Moses.

12:40-51 Chronology and further Passover regulations. In verses 40-41 P reveals his penchant for chronology. He calculates the sojourn of the Israelites in Egypt as a period of 430 years (see Gen 15:13). The complexity of the biblical data, however, demands greater precision. In view of such data this sojourn was not necessarily continuous, made by the same group, and comprising the entire people. From a theological viewpoint P reveals a God absorbed in the real life of his people. Yahweh acted at a precise moment in time. Consequently, Yahweh's keeping vigil at the moment must be reflected in Israel's keeping vigil on this occasion each year.

P also provides additional Passover regulations, relating chiefly to admission to the Passover celebration. (Such regulations presuppose a setting where Israel is already leading an agricultural existence in the Promised Land.) Transient aliens (v. 45) and hired servants (v. 45) are excluded; their existence in the land was not so firmly rooted. Resident aliens (v. 48) and permanent slaves (v. 44) may take part in the celebration, provided they have been circumcised (see Gen 17:13). The celebration is further depicted as a domestic one (v. 46) which "the whole community of Israel" (v. 47) is to keep. This is a favorite P expression stressing the organization of Israel, especially in the desert, and underlining those responsible within this organization.

13:3-10 Feast of Unleavened Bread. 13:1-16 has been judged to reflect the language of the Book of Deuteronomy. However, its language is more proto-Deuteronomic, that is, an incipient style that would eventually culminate in the more developed language found in Deuteronomy. In its present context, this tradition deals with two matters: (a) the redemption of the first-born (vv. 1-2, 11-16); (b) the feast of Unleavened Bread (vv. 3-10).

Unlike Passover, which required no sanctuary and was celebrated at home, Unleavened Bread was a pilgrimage feast that required the attendance of the adult male at the sanctuary (see 23:15). Whereas Passover was the feast of seminomadic shepherds, Unleavened Bread was the feast of farmers. The feast expressed newness, noting the beginning of the barley harvest (the first crop to be gathered). For the first seven days of this harvest, one had to eat bread made from the new grain. Such bread was unleavened or unfermented because it contained nothing of the previous year's harvest. Since this feast presupposes an agricultural environment, it was adopted by the Israelites (possibly from the Canaanites) only after their desert experience.

It was only later that the feasts of Passover and Unleavened Bread were joined together. This was probably around the time of King Josiah (the second half of the seventh century B.C.E.—2 Chr 35:17). Since both feasts occurred around the same time of the year and since both likewise made use of unleavened bread (but for different reasons—see 12:8), they were eventually combined.

Whereas J in 12:34 connects the unleavened bread to the haste of the Exodus, the author of 13:8 attaches a more personal note: "This is because of what the Lord did to *me* when *I* came out of Egypt." This flows from the concept of remembrance expressed in verse 3. To remember means to relive, to make actual/meaningful now. Hence the feast is not the static recalling of the past but the dynamic reliving of the past because of its repercussions on the present.

13:1-2, 11-16 Redemption of the first-born. It is interesting to observe that this tradition is not attached to the Passover account itself but to the deaths of the first-born of the Egyptians. Similarly, other texts (for example, 22:28-29) do not link the redemption of the first-born to the Exodus experience (v. 15).

The practice of "buying back" the first-born reveals Israel's concern for human life and her special treatment of the first-born. Although Israel was aware of the sacrifice of the first-born among her Canaanite neighbors, she revolted against such a practice (see Gen 22:1-19). Rather, she viewed the first-born both of humans and of animals as God's exclusive property. Consequently, they had to be bought back (see Luke 2:23).

After hearing that the Israelite must buy back his first-born, one tends to think that God's act of redemption is merely that—a buying back. One is prone, as a result, to limit God's redemptive action in Jesus as another instance of such buying back. However, this passage (and several others in Exodus) provides examples of the depth and the variety of biblical thought.

According to verse 3 Israel "came out." This verb is a legal term which Israel's storytellers have borrowed (see 21:2) to interpret the Exodus experience. In both verses 3 and 8 it is a going out of Egypt, and verse 3 adds "that house of slavery." Redemption for the Israelite is thus the acquisition of freedom, something particularly important to a seminomad.

Another term is the verb "to dismiss, let go." Against its legal background it means "to set free" (a favorite verb of J). For example, in 21:26-27 a master who mistreats his slave must set that slave free. The author of the present passage uses this verb in verse 15 and thus implies that Pharaoh is a slaveholder who refuses to emancipate his slaves. Redemption for the Israelites means being removed from the caprice of Pharaoh and thus regaining their integrity.

Another term is the verb "to bring out." Since Pharaoh has refused to set Israel free, Yahweh decides to bring them out. In the present context the verb is used four times (vv. 3, 9, 14, 16), three times with the phrase "with a strong hand." This conveys the powerful, miraculous way in which Yahweh liberates his people. (Most likely the phrase derived from the very graphic way in which Yahweh delivered Israel at the Reed Sea.) Redemption means, not merely a juridical act, but a dramatic intervention that results in victory for the oppressed and defeat for the oppressors.

Another term is the verb "to cause to go up." This verb is not concerned with slavery and setting free but looks to the future (see 3:8). It means going up to the land of Canaan and so it is the precise opposite of the going down into Egypt (see Gen 46:3-4). Although those taking part in the Exodus knew it as a going out, later generations saw it in terms of entering a new land, a going up. Redemption means that the Israelite has a home, a future.

Another term is the verb "to save." (The noun usually translated "salvation" is found in 14:13; 15:2.) The word is from the language of the courtroom, whereby the savior is always on the side of justice as an advocate or witness for the defense. In the prophet Second Isaiah, who sings of a second Exodus, Yahweh is a savior since he gets back his rightful property, Israel (see Isa 43:3). Redemption also means that Yahweh takes up the cause of those treated unjustly.

A final term is "to be a redeemer" (see 15:13). A redeemer is the family member responsible for the integrity of the family. For example, if family property is in danger of going to an outsider, the redeemer sees to it that the property remains in the family (see Ruth 4; Jer 32). The redeemer thus intervenes at crucial moments of family life. Redemption also means that God is identified as a member of the family interested in other members of the family. Redemption is much more than simply buying back.

13:17-22 Israel on the march. This section, consisting of E in verses 17-19 and J in verses 20-22, brings up the problem of the route of the Exodus. While the question must remain open, it is possible to offer a hypothesis, an effort to explain a number of the data contained in the biblical traditions. This hypothesis allows for two different routes by two different groups.

Although the New American Bible consistently refers to the Red Sea, the probable translation of the body of water connected with the Exodus is the Reed Sea or the Sea of Reeds. The reed in question is a papyrus plant that is known to grow in the marshes at the north of the Delta (not in the Gulf of Suez or the Gulf of Aqabah). Although this name suggests a comparatively small body of water, its localization is doubtful and not overly significant in dealing with the problem of the route of the Exodus. (The term "Red Sea" derives from the Greek translators of the Hebrew Scriptures. The term, however, includes even the Persian Gulf.)

The first route is the *northern* route. According to this itinerary, when the Israelites came out of Egypt, they would have gone directly east, that is, across the northern part of the Sinai peninsula to Kadesh Barnea. However, the E tradition in verse 17 notes that the Israelites did not take the way of the Philistines, that is, the way along the Mediterranean Sea connected with the northern route. Still, the mention of Raamses (1:11), Succoth (12:37), Etham (13:20), and Pi-hahiroth in connection with Migdol and Baal-zephon (14:2, 9—all from J with the exception of the last two) tends to support this northern route.

The second route is the *southern* route. According to this route the Israelites on leaving Egypt would have headed to the south or southeast to the lower part of the Sinai peninsula where they would have experienced the covenant making at Sinai. This would be the way of the desert mentioned by E in verse 18.

It is likely that these two traditions recall two different exodus experiences. Elements of the tribes of Reuben, Simeon, Levi, and Judah (the Leah tribes) were possibly the first to leave Egypt, taking the northern route. It is further likely that they are the group connected with the exodus-expulsion tradition that invaded the land of Canaan from the south (see the J tradition in Num 13:22-23; 14:24). Elements of the tribes of Benjamin, Ephraim, and Manasseh (the Rachel tribes) possibly left Egypt later under the leadership of Moses by means of the southern route. This group would have wandered in the desert, experienced Yahweh at Sinai, and invaded the land of Canaan from the east (the Jordan River). Furthermore, this group would be connected with the exodus-flight tradition. When the different entries into Canaan were combined in the final narrative, these different exodus experiences were united as well.

In verses 21-22 J distinguishes between a column of cloud by day and a column of fire by night. However, in 14:24 J has one column of cloud and fire. Despite this variation, what is clear is the experience of God's presence. The cloud/fire is Israel's perception of her God's participation in the key events of the Exodus and desert wandering. This cloud/fire manifestation is not unlike Yahweh's "angelic" presence (compare 3:2 with 3:4a).

14:1-10 Egypt's pursuit of Israel. The liturgical connection of Passover (and Unleavened Bread) with the Exodus by way of the tenth plague and the liturgical suture between the redemption of the first-born and the tenth plague have now come to a close. The narrative resumes the action of the nine plagues in chapters 7–10 and, after the exodus-expulsion interlude (see 11:1-3; 12:33-36), resumes the exodus-flight tradition (v. 5). The action now switches to the miracle at the sea, a military undertaking that does not presuppose the death of the first-born.

This section contains both P (vv. 1-4, 8-10) and J or JE (vv. 5-7) traditions. For example, according to P Israel is trapped in the wilderness but, more accurately, it is Pharaoh who is trapped into thinking thus. The reason P gives is that Pharaoh's absolute determination to pursue Israel will result in Yahweh's definitive reception of glory through Pharaoh and his army. In the JE tradition Pharaoh has changed his mind, realizing full well the loss of such an invaluable labor force.

What is common to both traditions is that they have interpreted the crossing of the sea in terms of a holy war. A holy war was not merely the encounter between two opposing forces; it was a religious undertaking. For Israel this meant that Yahweh fought for Israel, not Israel for Yahweh. (This view persisted until the time of David's "secular" army in the tenth century B.C.E.) A holy war has five elements: (a) sacrifices and oracles to consult Yahweh (by reason of the pillar of cloud/fire Yahweh already marched with Israel); (b) absolute confidence in Yahweh (see 14:31); (c) ritual purifications (see 19:14-15); (d) fear put into the enemy by Yahweh (see 14:24-25); (e) total destruction of the enemy (see 14:28, 30). What Israel's writers clearly understood was that their commander-in-chief was none less than Yahweh himself.

14:11-18 The conquest of fear. In verses 11-14 J takes up the all-too-human reaction to the pursuit of the Egyptians. It is the reality of fear that threatens to undermine the whole purpose of the Exodus. The people are tempted to prefer the resumption of slavery in Egypt to death in the desert. This murmuring motif is one that will reappear in Israel's wandering experience. Arguing from faith, Moses replies that such an either-or is invalid. Pressing the holy war theology, he makes a demand for renewed commitment (v. 13) and concludes with the assurance of victory. "The Lord himself will fight for you; you have only to keep still" (v. 14).

In verses 15-18 P responds to Israel's cry of frustration. Yahweh's action consists of giving directions that will ensure the safe passage of the Israelites through the sea. Thus Moses is to lift his staff, stretch out his hand, and divide the sea in favor of Israel. As predicted in verse 4, the obstinate Egyptians will pursue Israel into the sea. Their corpses will then become mute yet eloquent witnesses to Yahweh's power. The Divine Warrior will thus be duly acknowledged.

14:19-31 Two traditions for the crossing of the sea. The biblical traditions are unable to present a blow-by-blow account of what actually transpired at the Reed Sea because the required sources are wanting. However, Israel has chosen to interpret that event by dwelling on Yahweh's military prowess. Holy war theology enables the traditions in this section to unfold the picture of a God who thinks resolutely on behalf of the fleeing Israelites. Liberation means, not to be free *from* the ennui of Israel's laments, but to be free *for* the bewildered and beleaguered people.

According to J Yahweh manifests himself in two ways: (a) the angel of God (v. 19a) and (b) the column of cloud (v. 19b). Yahweh in the form of a divine messenger and in the form of a cloud now takes up a position between the Israelites and the Egyptians (v. 20). This position implies protection for Israel. Moreover, during the night Yahweh drives back the sea with a strong easterly wind (v. 21b), thus making possible a passage on dry land. Just before dawn Yahweh, present in the column of cloud and fire, startles the Egyptians with a glance that results in the loss of military discipline (v. 24). Yahweh's panic-creating glance is now followed by the clogging of the Egyptian chariot wheels, a gesture that leads to the sounding of retreat (v. 25). However, at dawn the sea resumes its normal depth. At this juncture Yahweh hurls the retreating Egyptians into its midst (v. 27b). The outcome is that Israel acknowledges Yahweh's intervention to the point of believing in Yahweh and his servant Moses (vv. 30-31).

According to P Moses stretches out his hand over the sea (v. 21a). The result is a very special miracle. Dry land appears for the safe passage of the Israelites with the water forming something resembling walls to their right and left (v. 22). At this point the Egyptian forces pursue the Israelites on the dry land (v. 23). At Yahweh's command Moses once again stretches out his hand over the sea (vv. 26-27a). The returning waters then engulf the entire Egyptian army (v. 28). P finally notes much more dramatically than J the Israelite passage on the dry land with the contained waters to the right and left (v. 29). In P Moses' gesture has replaced Yahweh's strong easterly wind.

15:1-21 The Song of the Sea. The earliest tradition about the crossing is found in this section (vv. 1-18, 21) that, unlike the J and P traditions, is in poetry, not prose. It is generally regarded as an independent tradition that has been fitted into its present position by means of vv. 19-20. On the basis of several criteria the poem may be dated around 1100 B.C.E.

This poem is based on an earlier (around 1400 B.C.E.) Canaanite poem that describes the battle between Baal, god of fertility, and Yamm, god of the sea. The outcome of the battle is that Yamm is overcome by Baal who in the next episode receives his temple/palace. In this biblical account Yahweh overcomes the Egyptians by creating a storm at sea that in turn capsizes their boats and leads to their death by drowning (vv. 8-10). (J's easterly wind [14:21b] has apparently been adapted from the poem's reference to Yahweh's strong wind in verse 10.) It is interesting to note that the poem focuses on the destruction of the enemy with only an allusion to the passage of the Israelites. However, the poem goes beyond the exploits at the Reed Sea to mention the effects of such destructive power on Israel's neighbors (vv. 14-16). Finally, the poem concludes by speaking of Yahweh's kingly possession of his sanctuary (v. 17). (This need not be limited to Jerusalem. It is a general formula to denote Yahweh's dwelling place in the wake of the successful battle.)

This crossing of the Reed Sea is obviously related to the ritual crossing of the Jordan in Josh 3–4. It is perhaps due to the influence of the Jordan crossing that the Reed Sea crossing shifted focus from Yahweh's military exploits over the Egyptians to the march of his people into the Promised Land (v. 13).

PART II: ISRAEL IN THE DESERT

Exod 15:22–18:27

These chapters offer a summary of Israel's desert experience. For example, they deal with Yahweh's protection in terms of providing food and drink (15:22–17:7), the defeat of Israel's enemies (17:8-16), the organization of the people (18:13-27). At the same time, these chapters foreshadow events that the Book of Numbers will exploit. Hence the reader is not taken by surprise when the entire desert generation with the exception of Caleb and Joshua is forbidden to enter the Promised Land, but condemned to wander in the desert.

These chapters also deal with the human symbol of wandering. This symbol reflects life as a search for meaning both on the level of individuals and community (see also *The Aeneid, Moby Dick, The Divine Comedy*). One is thus reminded of the Lukan Jesus who resolutely determines to make the journey to Jerusalem (Luke 9:51) and so capture the meaning of his own life and his community's by experiencing passion, death, and resurrection. In their present setting these chapters are the prelude to Israel's experience of covenant making at Sinai.

In the prophetic literature there are two different traditions of this period in Israel's history. First, there is the tradition of God's graciousness and Israel's generous response to that graciousness: "I remember the devotion of your youth, how you loved me as a bride, following me in the desert, in a land unknown" (Jer 2:2; see also Hos 2:17). Second, there is the tradition of Israel's rebellion against Yahweh that is captured in the murmuring motif so prevalent in the confrontation between Yahweh and Israel: "But the house of Israel rebelled against me in the desert. They did not observe my statutes, and they despised my ordinances that bring life to those who keep them" (Ezek 20:13). In Exodus and usually in Numbers the first tradition, God's graciousness, is primary while the second tradition, Israel's rebellion, is secondary. Israel's theologians were free to adapt the wilderness experience in order to explain later theological crises.

15:22-27 Grumbling at Marah. This episode consists of three traditions: P (vv. 22a, 27), J (vv. 23-25), and Deuteronomistic (v. 26). P provides information after the manner of an itinerary—departure and arrival from stopping place to stopping place. Thus Moses leads the people from the Reed Sea through the desert of Shur to Elim. Verse 26 applies the basic theology of the book of Deuteronomy to this incident at Marah. Obedience to Yahweh's will as expressed in his commandments and precepts will prevent disastrous consequences, such as the diseases inflicted by Yahweh on the Egyptians.

The J tradition emphasizes God's generosity in meeting the needs of the desert community. After three days of travel the community comes upon water at Marah which, however, because of its bitterness is not drinkable. The people's predicament leads to Moses' cry to Yahweh that, in turn, leads to Yahweh's remedy for sweetening the water. Although J speaks of the people grumbling against Moses (v. 24), there is no indication at all that the people are in rebellion. Moreover, the content of the people's complaint is far from clear. According to verse 25 it is Yahweh who puts Israel to the test, not vice versa (see 17:2). Thus, given a concrete need, Yahweh generously responds.

This scene together with 16:1–17:7 underlines the femininity of Yahweh. In the sociology of that day it was the task of the mother and wife to provide food and drink. Mother Yahweh, therefore, senses the needs of her children in their plight and takes the necessary steps to alleviate the situation. The Divine Warrior who overcame the mighty Egyptians at the Reed Sea is also the tender mother who quickly responds to family problems.

16:1-36 The quail and the manna. This account focuses on two realities of the Sinai peninsula. The manna is the secretion of two insects that live on the tamarisk tree. The substance drops from the tamarisk to the ground where it hardens somewhat in the night air. This delicacy of central Sinai is prized by the Bedouin for its sweetness. The quail migrate to Europe in the spring and return in the fall. When they land exhausted on the northwest coast of the Sinai peninsula, they can be easily captured. (For the quail as a replacement for the manna see Num 11:5-6, 31-33.)

P, who is the principal author in this account (J is probably to be found in verses 4-5, 29-32), chooses to elaborate certain "spiritual" dimensions. Thus in verses 17-21 there is just enough manna whether one gathers a large amount or a small amount. Moreover, any quantity kept over for the next day is summarily wormy and rotten. Similarly in verses 22-26 there is the link between the manna and the sabbath. Consequently, on the sixth day one may gather twice as much in order to observe the complete rest required on the seventh. Whatever is left over from the sixth day is then used for the seventh. Indeed, those who venture out on the sabbath to find manna are in violation of that sacred day—besides, nothing is to be found then (v. 27).

The original tradition in this episode was God's gracious care of the people in the desert. Given the grumbling mentioned in verses 2 and 7, one would expect that the sudden arrival of Yahweh's glory (v. 11) would involve a punishment of sorts for the rebels. Instead, in verse 12 Yahweh assures the people through Moses that their food needs will be met. If the people had rebelled against Yahweh, it would be rather surprising for Yahweh to accede to the demands of the rebels. The simplest explanation, therefore, is the invocation of the graciousness tradition: the people were hungry and Yahweh answered their petitions for bread and meat by supplying the manna and the quail (see Ps 105:40).

In view of the Exile and hence an explanation of that debacle as the rebellion of the desert generation, P has introduced the murmuring motif. This is expressed in the form of a death wish in verse 3: "Would that we had died at the Lord's hand in the land of Egypt, as we sat by our fleshpots and ate our fill of bread!" This death wish, however, contains the element of rejection of God's saving plan. By opting for an earlier death in Egypt, they are thereby rejecting the events that led to the present impasse, the Exodus. It is not hunger pangs but the theological despair that commands center stage on this level of the tradition. The reply of Moses and Aaron in verse 6 sustains this interpretation of their rebellion. It is a question of the God who brought them out of Egypt. The tradition of God's graciousness has thus been converted into the tradition of refusing to acknowledge that the God of Israel can indeed accomplish what he sets out to do.

17:1-7 Grumbling at Massah and Meribah. This is a J narrative that is introduced by P's itinerary in verse 1a. Like the J story at Marah, this episode has the primary tradition of Yahweh's graciousness to his needy people. Unlike the Marah tradition, this episode also contains the secondary tradition of Israel's contention with Yahweh over the matter of the Exodus.

If one omits the people's attack on Yahweh at the end of verse 2, the rest of that verse may be understood simply as a quarrel with Moses and a demand that he meet the needs of the people. Moses' cry to Yahweh in verse 4 is not unlike his demand in 14:15 (P) that results in a positive answer from Yahweh. Here the favorable reply is found in verse 5 where Moses is commanded to strike the rock with his staff. (Contrast the different interpretation in Num 20:11-13.) The outcome is that Yahweh once again meets the needs of his people—in this case the need for water. One should also observe that in verse 5 there is no indication of any punishment.

Verse 3 contains the secondary tradition of rebellion in this account. It is not really the thirst that is central. Rather, the thirst serves as a backdrop for impugning the value of the Exodus: "Why did you ever make us leave Egypt?" As in chapter 16, the Exodus is the object of attack because of the lack of water. On this level of the tradition there is the rejection of the divine plan.

One view of the origin of the J murmuring motif is that it is a polemic directed against the northern kingdom of Israel, specifically against the cult of Jeroboam I (931–910 B.C.E.) in Dan and Bethel (see 1 Kgs 12:26-33). This fresh orientation of the desert experience is intended to explain how the northern kingdom lost its rights to divine election and why the southern kingdom retained them (see Ps 78:67-72). Through the rebellion of the desert generation the north forfeited its election while the south preserved its status through the Davidic king in Jerusalem.

17:8-16 Battle with the Amalekites. It is refreshing to come upon a narrative extolling a great human accomplishment in the midst of the awesome display of divine power. This J narrative is a legend, a narrative whose purpose is to edify, in this instance to reflect upon the heroic stature of Moses. While salvation always involves the interplay of divine grace and human cooperation, it is reassuring to note a story where the limelight falls on the human protagonist.

Apart from the notices in verses 14-15 explaining Israel's implacable hatred of the Amalekites and the origin of a particular altar (such explanations are called etiologies), the entire movement centers upon Moses, not Yahweh. In verse 9 Moses commissions Joshua to make the battle preparations and adds that he (Moses) will take up his position on a nearby hill. While no details of the battle are given, there is an abundant description of Moses' contributions to the successful outcome. It is Moses' tenacity and steadfastness that win the day for Israel. The stamina displayed in keeping his hands raised, albeit with the support of Aaron and Hur (v. 12), is precisely what one would expect of such a giant. These heroic dimensions are captured by the expression "steady hands" in verse 12. The steadiness described in the account is the faithfulness shown in fulfilling an official task (see 2 Kgs 12:16; 22:7). It is the courage of this one man that turns the tide of battle. For all his failings Moses retains his image as hero and superman (see Deut 34:7, 10-12).

The Amalekites who controlled the caravan routes between Egypt and Arabia lived in the Negeb, the southernmost section of Israel (see 1 Sam 15:7). Since they are linked to the tribe of Judah and are quite likely associated with the exodus-expulsion tradition, the story is out of place here. However, as a portrait of the heroic qualities of Moses, it is indeed most apropos in its present position.

18:1-27 Meeting between Moses and Jethro. This chapter, the work of E, contains two scenes: (a) the meeting between Moses and his father-in-law that culminates in a covenant meal (vv. 1-12); (b) the decentralization of judicial authority in Israel that results in the appointments of "minor" judges (vv. 13-27). It is in the desert near the mountain of God (v. 5). Unlike the mountain of God in chapter 19, this mountain is not the scene of a theophany but of a meeting.

Jethro is hardly a new character in the story. In 2:11-22 J narrated Moses' marriage to his daughter. What is striking in the present account is E's concentration on Jethro. Although the latter does indeed bring his daughter and two grandsons to meet Moses (in 2:22 Moses has only one son, but see 4:20), the woman and the two sons play a rather unimportant role. In verse 7 Moses all but ignores his wife and family. Clearly Moses and Jethro are the central figures.

The meeting revolves around Moses' story of Yahweh's exploits (v. 8), Jethro's joy-filled reaction to the story (vv. 9-11), and a covenant meal with Jethro, on the one hand, and Aaron and the elders, on the other hand (v. 12). Although some see Jethro's declaration as an indication of his conversion to Yahwism (v. 11; see 2 Kgs 5:15), it is also likely that Jethro merely recognized that Moses' god, Yahweh, was more powerful than all other gods (see Josh 2:9-11). Although Jethro is called a priest (v. 1) and hence exercised a cultic office, there is really no firm basis for suggesting that he was a priest of Yahweh or that he shared his Yahwistic faith with Moses. In verse 12, as a matter of fact, Moses is conspicuous by his absence. Here Jethro accepts (rather than "brought" as in the NAB translation) the sacrificial offerings, thereby indicating his acceptance of a mutual relationship with the Israelites. Given the subsequent enmity between Midianites and Israelites, this tradition reflects an early friendlier association between the two groups.

Verses 13-27 presuppose a situation that developed after the desert experience, in a time when the population was large and sedentary. The distinction between the more important and less important cases (v. 22) indicates a decentralization of legal authority. According to some authorities it may suggest the judicial appointments during the time of King Jehoshaphat (871–848 B.C.E.—see 2 Chr 19:5-11). In any event, a subsequent situation has been read back into the desert experience and thus the later solution has been attributed to Moses. At the same time, however, the story provides another occasion for E to emphasize his fear of God motif (see 1:17, 21). Hence Moses is instructed by his father-in-law to select God-fearing men (v. 21). This basic orientation of fear of God will ensure the common good, especially by the avoidance of bribes (see Deut 16:19).

PART III: THE MAKING OF THE COVENANT

Exod 19:1–24:11

Covenants are part and parcel of human social life. Since humans are drawn into relationships with other humans, the terms of those relationships must first of all be clarified and then accepted. A covenant, therefore, is a relationship in which the moral bond between the parties involved is defined and then accepted. For example, in Gen 31:43–32:3 Jacob and Laban make a covenant. A significant element in that relationship is the sworn oath by both parties not to attack each other (31:52-53). Moreover, a pile of stones serves as a witness to the covenant (31:45-48). A ritual meal, finally, is also central to the relationship: "He [Jacob] then offered a sacrifice on the mountain and invited his kinsmen to share in the meal" (31:54).

An obvious difference between the Jacob-Laban covenant and the Sinai covenant is the position of Yahweh. Yahweh is not an equal partner to the covenant. Rather, Yahweh is the superior and Israel the inferior. Consequently, Yahweh is the one who commands, while Israel is the one who is expected to obey. Israel's pledged word to abide by the terms of the relationship is, therefore, essential to her existence as Yahweh's chosen people. Covenant life is by definition the constant challenge to ongoing fidelity.

Since the covenant on Sinai was *the* experience whereby this people became God's people, it is only natural to assume that the scene at the mountain would be the logical meeting place for a variety of interpretations of this relationship. The variety of traditions reflects Israel's unrelenting efforts to fathom her unique position with Yahweh. Hence Yahweh and Israel could be perceived in various ways. At the same time, these chapters witness to a certain conservatism. Israel was not content to employ one tradition and then discard it. Instead, Israel chose to retain different traditions because each of them preserved a distinct value.

In the midst of the distinctiveness of Israel's covenant traditions there is also a certain basic outline for most of them. First of all, there is the encounter with Yahweh who overawes his people. Second, there is the expression of Yahweh's will for this people. Moses is here the recipient of the terms of covenant existence. Third, Moses reports to the people the will of Yahweh as he received it. This basic outline is also a testimony to Moses' unique position as the covenant mediator.

19:1-2 The setting. P continues his itinerary (see 16:1; 17:1), this time noting that the Israelites have arrived at Sinai. P's next tradition will come only in 24:15b, so there is no tradition of covenant making on Sinai comparable to J and E. For P there is only the one covenant made with Abraham that still perdures (see Gen 17:13). Nonetheless Sinai will become P's ideal place for many of Israel's cultic traditions.

The exact location of Sinai is not known. For those who follow the southern route of the exodus-flight tradition the mountain in question is often identified as Jebel Musa (Mount Moses). The size of the mountain (7,647 feet) is often thought to be imposing enough for the importance of the traditions associated with the biblical narrative. At the base of this mountain in the Sinai desert, the Greek Orthodox monastery of St. Catherine's now stands.

19:3-8 Attitude toward the covenant. The tradition embedded in verses 3b-8 is an independent tradition drawn from the liturgy that is now introduced by verse 3a. Its purpose is to foster the proper attitude that should guide God's people. While it is clearly a proclamation, it is not a proclamation that provides precise rules of conduct. Rather, it is one which underlines the notion of word (verse 5: "if you hearken to my voice"). Israel is bidden to listen and thus act upon Yahweh's word. The use of direct address ("I" and "you") adds both solemnity and power. Indeed, Israel is to learn from God's mighty deeds against the Egyptians (v. 4) the nature of Yahweh and the serious responsibility to heed his word.

There are other dimensions too. There is emphasis on intimacy. Yahweh brings the people, not just to a given destination in the desert but to himself (v. 4). The covenant is specifically Yahweh's (verse 5: "my covenant"), and the people are uniquely his own. The Hebrew word translated "special possession" (v. 5) conjures up the notion of the personal private property of a king (see Deut 7:6; 14:2; 26:18). There is also a stress on Israel's holiness (v. 6), a characteristic by which she is removed from the realm of the profane. The expression "kingdom of priests" does not imply that every Israelite is a priest. Quite likely the totality of Israel is intended: a royalty of priests and a holy nation. Finally, there is the accent on liberty. Israel is not coerced to accept this relationship (verse 5: "Therefore, *if* you hearken to my voice"). In Israel, Yahweh is never a puppeteer who capriciously pulls the strings to control human behavior. Only a free response is a fitting response.

This liturgical tradition suggests an approach whereby Yahweh can be considered the overlord and Israel the vassal. There are hints of such a conception here, hints that would come to fruition in the Book of Deuteronomy where the model of covenant is that of a treaty, in which Yahweh is the overlord and Israel is the vassal. Israel could thus use political models to great advantage.

19:9-20 Two theophany traditions. This section contains the J and E traditions of the Sinai theophany—God's manifestation on the mountain. (Verse 9 is a gloss that ties together the previous tradition with J and E.) For J (vv. 10-11a, 12-13a, 14-16a, 18, 20) the theophany is that of a volcanic eruption. It is a literary depiction that does not demand that one search for a now extinct volcano somewhere in Arabia. For E (vv. 11b, 13b, 16b-17, 19) the theophany is that of a fear-producing storm.

In the J account it is Yahweh who selects Moses to hear the revelation and then share it with the people (v. 10). Moses is to prepare the people for a ceremony on the third day (vv. 11a, 15a—see also Hos 6:1-3 and 1 Cor 15:4 for the use of the third day in a covenant setting). The ceremony involves washing their clothing and continence (vv. 14b, 15b). While the mention of readiness (vv. 11a, 15a) is also part of holy war preparations, the accent is more on holy and less on war (see 7:14; 38:7). What is expected of the people is that they will respect the limits of the mountain (v. 12) since Yahweh will occupy it (v. 20). The power and majesty of this God are evident in the fire, smoke, and shaking of the mountain. It is the presence of this God that brings about the covenant. (The precise stipulations of this relationship are now found in chapter 34.)

In the E account it is the people who select Moses to be their spokesperson (20:19). It is the fear caused by the storm (v. 16b) that provokes their decision. It is also this fear that makes them willing to receive the will of the storm god. Unlike the J account, the E tradition has Moses organize a liturgical procession but one that will place the people at the bottom of the mountain (vv. 13b, 17b). The tradition also alludes to meeting this God in the setting of a holy war. The camp in verse 17 need not be limited to a nomadic camp; it is also a military camp. While the trumpet is a liturgical instrument (see Ps 47:6), it is also a military instrument used for purposes of warfare (see Judg 7:20; also Josh 6 where the ram's horn mentioned here in verse 13b is both liturgical and military). The Hebrew verb used in verse 17 ("they stationed themselves") also means to line up in battle array (see Judg 20:2). Israel at Sinai is thus God's militia, ready to accede to the will of this commander whose presence is also marked by the cloud over the mountain.

19:21-25 The holiness of the mountain. In this passage J continues the theme of the holiness of the mountain first mentioned in verses 12-13a. Realizing that the people will be tempted to see Yahweh, J has Moses urge the people to observe a reverent distance. Not only are the people in general to sanctify themselves (v. 10) but also the priests (v. 22). Although Aaron is allowed to accompany Moses in his ascent to Yahweh, the priests and the people are expressly forbidden (v. 24). Yahweh's turf must be respected.

20:1-17 The Ten Commandments. While the basic outline calls for the expression of the divine will following the encounter with Yahweh, the condition of the biblical text is still somewhat disconcerting. In the J text of 19:25 Moses goes down the mountain to speak to the people. Next, in 20:1 God communicates the Ten Commandments rather abruptly. This is, in turn, followed by the remark in the E text of 20:19 that God's direct speaking to them will result in death. Finally, in 20:22 Yahweh speaks directly to Moses.

Both the Ten Commandments and the Covenant Code (20:22–23:19) have been associated with the E tradition. Most likely they are not E's personal work but independent traditions inserted by E at this point. At a first stage, the fear experienced by the people (see E in 20:18) was the direct result of the storm theophany in chapter 19. Moses was consequently deputed to hear the entire revelation. At a second stage, because of the importance of the Ten Commandments, the people listened to this fundamental law. This listening led to their fear that, in turn, led to Moses' receiving the rest of the legislation (the Covenant Code). This second stage clearly enhanced the stature of the Ten Commandments since, unlike the Covenant Code, God communicated them directly to the people.

The form of the Ten Commandments is significant. It is a series of apodictic laws, that is, laws that impose a command directly on a person, obliging that person to perform (or refrain from performing) some action that the legislator judges to be desirable (or harmful). Apodictic laws admit two formulations: (a) third person, as in Deut 17:6—"No one shall be put to death on the testimony of only one witness"; (b) second person, as in Lev 18:8—"You shall not have intercourse with your father's wife." Although these apodictic laws are found rather exceptionally in the ancient Near East, they are characteristic of Israel. Moreover, second person formulations, insofar as they express the fundamental religious orientation of an entire people, are unique to Israel. There is, therefore, a dimension of intimacy, especially in these second person singular formulations, since Yahweh speaks directly to the individual Israelite. Such laws are grounded in a person, not an impersonal legislative system (note Gen 2:17). Although murder and adultery were already forbidden in the ancient Near East, the fifth and the sixth commandments are new laws.

With the exception of the first three commandments, the Ten Commandments are originally a form of tribal wisdom. Before being united in their present form, they circulated in different series of commands that the young of a tribe were expected to learn from their elders (see Lev 18; Tob 4; Jer 35). These tribal elders sought to provide for the common good, and their position lent authority to the sayings.

As is clear from verse 1, Yahweh is the person behind this legislation. He is, however, more than a tribal elder. He identifies himself as one who has acted on behalf of the community. Using the liturgical introductory formula ("I am"), the text insists on the centrality of Yahweh's role in Exodus. Israel is bound to these commandments, not only because they are for the common good but also because this God has intervened decisively in her life. (Note how Deut 5:15 uses the Exodus tradition as motivation for the sabbath observance rather than the creation tradition used here in verses 9-11.)

20:18-21 Moses' appointment as mediator. The fear originally attributed to the theophany (19:16b) is now related to the divine proclamation in the Ten Commandments. (The smoking mountain in verse 18 harmonizes the traditions of J and E.) In this E passage Moses is deputed to hear the rest of the revelation (v. 19). Not surprisingly, E accentuates the fear of God motif in verse 20; such fear will be a help in avoiding sin. E concludes here by mentioning Moses' ascent in verse 21, an ascent that he will expand in 24:12-15a.

20:22-26 Introduction to the Covenant Code. The legislation that Moses now hears by himself begins in 20:22 and concludes in 23:19. It is called the Covenant Code or the Book of the Covenant because in 24:3 the people agree to accept God's will, which is then specifically labeled in 24:7, "the book of the covenant." As with the Ten Commandments, E has borrowed an independent collection or independent collections which he inserts at this point in the Sinai theophany. While this section of Exodus may strike some readers as being overly legal and perhaps legalistic and hence dry, one should nonetheless search for the values that Israel perceived here. One such value is Israel's regard for the human person, a value that stands out when viewed against other ancient Near Eastern legal codes. Such an attitude stems from her religious convictions.

These opening verses continue the apodictic form of the Ten Commandments (verse 23 is in the plural, however, and verse 25 is a mixed form). Unlike the J and E traditions that associate God's presence in one form or another with the mountain, this independent tradition has God speak from heaven (v. 24). The prohibition against images stems from the fact that Yahweh could not be seen and hence could not be represented. The law of the altar (vv. 24-26) presupposes Israel's early life in the land. More than one sanctuary is permitted—in fact, as many as there were places where God's presence was recognized. An elevated altar is forbidden, since it may involve immodesty on the part of the sacrificer (see the precautions taken in 28:40-42).

21:1-11 The law for slaves. Verse 2 introduces the casuistic or case law section of the Covenant Code. (This section continues to 22:16.) This form of law was the typical law of the ancient Near East. By its nature casuistic law is pragmatic; it does not depend directly on any ethical principle. The subject is simply reminded of the unpleasant consequences that will follow a violation of the law. In terms of obligation, case law binds the judge or judges who act for the legislator. The very core of these laws is the solution: if such and such has occurred, then such and such is the outcome. Although these laws have a personalistic overtone because of their setting at Sinai, they are, apart from that important note, practical human lay laws written, for the most part, in the third person. (For an example of second person casuistic law, see 21:2.) Their background indicates a time in Israel shortly after the occupation of the land.

This section on slaves clearly distinguishes between slaves and slaveowners, although there are certain limitations on the slaveowners' rights. The word "Hebrew" in verse 2 originally meant "Habiru"—those displaced people and malcontents who harassed the ancient Near East. In its present usage, however, the term means "Israelite." The situation described in verse 4 implies that women are the master's possessions. Ideally (see Jer 34:8-22), the enslavement of Israelites is only temporary: six years for Israelite men (v. 2). (Deut 21:10-14 applies the same to Israelite women.) Verses 8-11 contain special legislation when there is a question of giving the female slave in marriage. In that case she enjoys certain rights as a wife.

21:12-17 Offenses punishable by death. Although this section contains a mixture of legal forms, what makes it a unity is its subject—attacks on human life that involve the death penalty. While verse 12 establishes a general principle, verses 13 and 14 make distinctions. In the case of unpremeditated homicide or accidental manslaughter ("an act of God"), asylum is provided in a sanctuary. In the case of willful murder, not even the sanctuary will avail. In reverence due to parents (vv. 15, 17), Israelite legislation is more demanding than that of the ancient Near East in general.

21:18-31 Laws regarding bodily injuries. Masters cannot dispose of their slaves at their mere whim. The cases mentioned in verses 20-21 and 26-27 indicate limitations on the masters' rights. Verses 23-25 enunciate the law of talion. This law intends to curb unbridled revenge by insisting on proportionate compensation. Slaves, however, do not enjoy this right because they receive only their freedom in compensation for the injury inflicted on them (vv. 26-27). Verse 32 is another indication of the plight of the slave. In the goring death of a slave, the culpably negligent owner is obliged to pay the master the current price for a slave.

21:33–22:14 Laws regarding property damages. Israel never exacted the death penalty for crimes against property, something that the more progressive western states did not acknowledge until the beginning of the last century. The general principle exemplified in this section is that an individual who has been wronged in his property is to be compensated. The compensation is penal in character and usually greater than the damage caused. Thus a man who steals an ox or a sheep and then slaughters or sells it must pay fivefold for an ox and fourfold for a sheep (21:37). A thief who cannot make full restitution for his crime is to be sold into slavery (22:2).

Verses 6-10 have to do with divine adjudication. According to verses 7 and 8, justice is administered before God, that is, in a holy place or a sanctuary. In the legal disputes expressed in these verses, the manner of adjudication is best explained by verse 10. The party or parties involved must swear by Yahweh. This procedure reflects the sacredness of the divine name; to disparage the name is to disparage the person.

22:15–23:9 Social laws. (Although verses 15-16 belong to the casuistic section of the Covenant Code, they are grouped here because of their content.) The legislation in 22:17–23:19 constitutes the apodictic section of the Covenant Code. What is noteworthy about many laws here is the ethical sensitivity to the demands of charity toward one's fellow Israelite. By insisting so often on the obligation of love, it transcends the Ten Commandments, which concern only the demands of justice.

The deflowering of an unbetrothed virgin implies serious financial problems for a father because it would be difficult for her to obtain a suitor. (For a father's worry over a daughter see Sir 42:9-14.) The law in 22:15 states that the seducer must marry her or, in the event of the father's unwillingness to give her, pay the customary marriage price for virgins. In Israel a certain double standard exists. It is the status of the woman that determines adultery, not the status of the man. If the woman is either betrothed or married, and therefore the property of another man, it is adultery. If the woman is neither betrothed nor married, it is not adultery, even if the man in question is married.

Both sorcery (22:17) and bestiality (22:18) involve the death penalty. Sacrifice to false gods (22:19), while a capital offense, is nuanced differently. Such a person is to be doomed—totally destroyed. Some think this destruction applies to his belongings as well.

The laws in 22:20-23 and 23:9 concern those who are legally helpless. Aliens (see 12:48) are foreigners who live in the midst of Israel and enjoy certain rights. Since they do not enjoy full civic rights on a par with Israelites, they are often victims of oppression. Verse 20 exhibits a peculiarity of Israelite jurisprudence, namely, exhortation. Israel not only states the law but often provides reasons for its observance. In this instance Israel is to recall her own precarious existence in Egypt and thus treat the alien appropriately. Since the economy depends on the male heads of the household, widows and fatherless (such is the meaning of orphan in this sociological context) are exposed to the greatest dangers. To counteract these dangers, the legislation in verses 22-23 insists on divine involvement. Yahweh will listen to the laments and take punitive action against the guilty. Israel's conviction is that a truly strong society provides for its weakest members.

Exhortation is also prominent in verses 24-26. A cloak taken in pledge must be returned before sunset because this cloak also serves as bedding. The cry of such a cloakless Israelite merits prompt action from Yahweh.

The material in 23:1-3, 6-8 looks to legal procedures. Those who compose Israel's popular courts are urged not to bear false testimony (v. 1), not to follow the majority view to the detriment of justice (v. 2), and not to accept bribes (v. 8). On the positive side, they are to acquit the innocent and condemn the guilty (v. 8). Since it is unlikely that one would tend to favor the poor in court action, some emend verse 3 to read: "You shall not favor a wealthy man in his lawsuit." In any event, verse 6 clearly advocates due concern for the needy in litigation. Unfortunately, Israel's prophets had to decry the manipulation of the poor in the administration of justice (see Isa 1:23; 10:2; Ezek 22:29; Amos 5:10).

The provisions of 23:4-5 focus on one's personal enemy (some would identify this enemy in terms of an actual or imminent legal dispute). Allegiance to the covenant Lord takes precedence over personal antipathies. Or better, such allegiance demands seeing one's enemy from a new perspective. In any event, straying oxen or asses are to be returned to the proper owner and an overburdened ass is to be helped up.

23:10-19 Religious laws. Verses 10-12 refer to the sabbatical year and the sabbath itself. According to verses 10-11 the fields, vineyards, and olive groves are to lie fallow every seven years. The poor are envisioned as the primary beneficiaries of this institution (see also Lev 25:2-7; Deut 15:1-3). The mention of the sabbath in verse 12 suggests that the sabbatical year is to take place at a fixed date. However, there is little positive evidence to document its actual observance. With regard to the sabbath, the law in verse 13 declares that slaves, aliens, and even beasts are to benefit from the day of rest. (The word "sabbath" in Hebrew suggests "to halt, stop." It is a day marked by rest when everyday activities stop.)

After mentioning the exclusive worship of God's name (and hence person) in verse 13, the Covenant Code considers the pilgrimage feasts to be observed in Israel, that is, feasts requiring male attendance at local sanctuaries. The feast of Azymes or Unleavened Bread celebrates the beginning of the barley harvest (see 13:3-10). It is here linked to the time when Israel came out of Egypt (v. 15). The feast of the grain harvest or Weeks that takes place about fifty days after Unleavened Bread (Pentecost) marks the end of the wheat harvest. Finally, the feast at the end of the year, also called Tents or Tabernacles, celebrates the ingathering of all the produce of the field. Since these three pilgrimage feasts are agricultural, they were celebrated only after the desert experience.

The Covenant Code concludes with several sacrificial injunctions. Since leavened bread implies a change, it may have been deemed unfitting for use in sacrifice (v. 18a). Since the fat of an animal is considered the choicest part (see Lev 3:17), its being kept overnight would result in spoiling (v. 18b). Because Yahweh is Israel's God, he is worthy of receiving the first fruits of the soil at the local sanctuary (v. 19a). The prohibition against boiling a kid in its mother's milk (v. 19b), once thought to be a cultic practice among the Canaanites, is not clear. It seems to be a pagan practice whose specifics are not yet known.

23:20-33 Behavior in the Promised Land. Some see this passage after the manner of Lev 26 and Deut 28—a list of blessings that flow from obedience to the terms of the code. Others regard it as a departure speech that is rather loosely linked to the code. Since these blessings are not closely joined to the preceding stipulations, the second view is to be preferred. (The source of the tradition is not clear, however.)

The passage is a departure speech that aims at encouraging the people during the early monarchy in the tenth century B.C.E. (see the boundaries of the Davidic-Solomonic kingdom in verse 31). It is thus a time when Israel is threatened by Canaanite ways, since she is now living side by side with Canaanites as members of the one people of Israel. God is present through his messenger (vv. 20, 23). Such presence will mean protection, even against overwhelming odds. However, God's military action will be only gradual (vv. 30-31). During this entire time allegiance to Yahweh and his covenant must be uppermost (vv. 21-22, 24, 32-33). Although they are to live with Canaanites, they are not to adopt their ways. It is obedience of this caliber that will bring about the blessings of abundance of food and drink, health, fertility, and a long life (vv. 25-26).

24:1-2, 9-11 Covenant making and the ceremonial meal. In the wake of the J and E traditions of the theophany and the subsequent legislation in chapters 20–23, there now come two more traditions of covenant making: (a) verses 1-2, 9-11 and (b) verses 3-8. Most likely they are independent traditions. In the form of ritual actions they provide yet two more views of response to God's initiative. Although 24:1 is rather clumsily appended to the J and E traditions, and although 24:3 breaks up the initial tradition, still they preserve great values in terms of covenant making, values that Israel took great pains to preserve.

In 24:1-2, 9-11 there is the celebration of a meal in God's presence. This very simple but profound scene is a very ancient tradition stemming from Israel's perception of Yahweh as tribal chief. By means of the meal, Yahweh takes the whole community, represented by the clan elders, into his family. The meal is the assurance and support given by the superior, Yahweh, to the inferior, Israel. What is striking is that the clan elders do not accept any particular stipulations. What they do accept is the protection afforded them by the tribal chief. Israel's specific response to that gesture would be developed in subsequent traditions.

24:3-8 Covenant making and the blood rite. Sacrifices (here communion sacrifices) effect covenant. In response to the people's willingness to accept Yahweh's will (v. 3; see also v. 7), Moses writes down the stipulations (v. 4). After reading "the book of the covenant," he sprinkles the people with half of the blood of the slaughtered animals. For Israel, blood is life. The sprinkled blood joins them to the blood splashed on the altar, which symbolizes God. A union has been created from this blood relationship. However, the terms for preserving that relationship are also spelled out. By living up to those terms, Israel is assured of her ongoing union with Yahweh. Unlike the ancient ceremonial meal, this manner of covenant making lays greater stress on the demands of the covenant God.

PART IV: INSTRUCTIONS FOR THE BUILDING OF THE SANCTUARY

Exod 24:12–31:18

After the final traditions of covenant making (24:1-11), Moses ascends the mountain with Joshua to receive the tablets. This departure will set the stage for the Golden Calf story in chapter 32. Sandwiched in between these two texts is P's account of Moses' receiving divine instructions for the construction of the desert sanctuary. While P clearly rejects any covenant at Sinai, he nonetheless finds this setting the ideal place for developing his cultic interests. Hence this section as well as chapters 35–40 may rightly be termed P's political document.

Recalling Israel's infidelity that provoked the sack of Jerusalem and subsequent exile in 586 B.C.E., P aims at underlining the nature of the restored community, a holy people. Concretely, holiness entails such institutions as priesthood, sacrifices, etc. But the institutions are designed to achieve one purpose—God's presence. While Sinai is not, for P, the place of covenant making, it is the place par excellence for Yahweh's manifestation.

While P makes the desert sanctuary a portable replica of the Jerusalem temple, it is wrong to regard all his cultic elaborations as a retrojection of that temple into the desert experience. As a matter of fact, P also employs older traditions, many of which are at home in ancient Canaanite religion. While P appropriates such Canaanite institutions, he also confronts them, imposing upon them a theology of God's presence consonant with Israelite faith.

24:12-15a Moses' ascent. This E passage expands the rather laconic statement of Moses' ascent in 20:21. Although it now introduces the P material, it originally served to position Moses on the mountain to receive the divine revelation (see 20:18-20). This revelation is linked to the tablets that Yahweh will write. (In P the tablets are written by God's finger [31:18], whereas in J Moses writes them down [34:28].) It is interesting to observe that in the ancient Near East only Israel pictured her God as drafting or dictating legislation. For E the cloud is also significant as marking God's presence (see 19:16b; 20:21). Finally, the notion of additional judges in verse 14 is in keeping with E's "minor" judges in 18:21-26.

24:15b-18 P's theophany. For P this brief scene is not only an introduction to chapters 25–31; it is also a profound theological statement of the significance of Sinai. Here he links the divine manifestation on Sinai with the construction of the sanctuary (40:17, 33b) and the execution of the first sacrifice (Lev 9:1, 23-24). Just as the cloud covers the mountain and Yahweh's glory settles there (vv. 15b-16a), so too the cloud covers the tent of meeting, and Yahweh's glory fills the sanctuary (40:34). In verse 16b Yahweh calls Moses on the seventh day, and in Lev 9:1 Moses summons Aaron, his sons, and the elders of Israel on the eighth day. According to verse 17 Yahweh's glory is viewed as a consuming fire, and according to Lev 9:24a fire comes from Yahweh's presence and consumes the sacrifice. There is thus a clear parallelism between the manifestation on Sinai and the first act of worship after that manifestation. Hence Sinai becomes the model for worship.

25:1-9 Collection of materials. P's concept of Yahweh's earthly dwelling borrows yet reinterprets ancient Canaanite traditions. In that religion El, the head of the pantheon, had a tent on a mountain where he issued authoritative decrees or oracles (see 33:7-11). In verse 9 Moses is instructed to make a copy of the tent on the mountain. There is thus a similarity of form between the deity's earthly dwelling and its heavenly model. P employs two names for Yahweh's place: (a) the more traditional "tent of meeting" (for example, 40:34) and (b) his own special archaic "the dwelling" (always capitalized in the New American Bible). By using the latter term, P understands the transcendent God of Israel who will meet with that people (see 29:42-43; 30:36). For P, Yahweh will take up a permanent abode in the midst of his people (compare 33:7-11).

Unlike J and E, P provides directions for setting up the sanctuary and furnishing it (see also 36:8-38). Despite P's elaborations, modeled after the Jerusalem temple, the basic reality is that of a portable sanctuary, a tent similar to Israel's own tents during the time of the desert. This is similar to the practice of ancient Bedouin tribes that carried a small sacred tent made of red leather. During their journeys such tribes could experience the presence of their gods, owing to the stone idols carried in the tent. In human experience the presence of one's god is judged to be imperative.

25:10-22 Plan of the ark. After the manner of the practice mentioned above, Israel can meet with her God because of the ark that was most likely housed by the tent. The ark is a rectangular wooden cabinet about four feet long, two and a half feet wide, and two and a half feet high that contains the stone tablets given to Moses by Yahweh (vv. 16, 21)—hence the name "ark of the covenant" or "ark of the testimony." (In the ancient Near East it was a common practice to deposit treaties in a sacred place with a view to reading them at stipulated times.)

Although J and E do not associate the ark with the tent, P goes on to add that the ark has a propitiatory flanked by two cherubim. The propitiatory is the gold plate on top of the ark that is associated with divine forgiveness. From above the propitiatory Yahweh can speak to Moses and thus to the Israelites. (For the role of the propitiatory on the Day of Atonement see Lev 16:15-16; note Rom 3:25.) It is likely that this propitiatory was a substitute for the ark, that is, the seat of God's presence or mercy after the ark itself was destroyed (see Jer 3:16). The original ark probably functioned as a support or a pedestal for Israel's invisible God (see Num 10:35-36). Once the ark reached the Promised Land, it served as Yahweh's throne or footstool (see 1 Sam 4:4). The two golden cherubim, lesser deities borrowed from Israel's neighbors, provided protection for the throne and thus suggested the presence of Israel's God.

25:23-40 The table and lampstand. The table contains the showbread (v. 30) that consists of twelve loaves of unleavened bread (see Lev 24:5-9), replenished every sabbath and reserved to the priests. This bread serves as a reminder of God's covenant with the twelve tribes of Israel. The lampstand or "menorah," although elaborately described, is somewhat baffling to scholars. In any event it is a candelabrum that holds seven lamps. Today the term "menorah" is used for one of the best-known symbols of Judaism, the seven-branched candelabrum. (For the ten lampstands in Solomon's temple see 1 Kgs 7:49.)

26:1-37 Instructions for making the desert sanctuary. In P's conception the desert sanctuary is a collapsible temple that is exactly one half the size of Solomon's temple (see 1 Kgs 6:2, 16-17). First of all, wooden frames form a rectangular building that is approximately forty-five feet long, fifteen feet wide, fifteen feet high, and open on the east (vv. 15-29). Second, sheets of finely woven materials are sewn together to make two large sheets. These sheets are joined together by means of loops and clasps and have the cherubim embroidered on them (vv. 1-6). Third, sheets woven of goat hair are stretched like a tent over the sanctuary. These sheets are slightly longer than those in verses 1-6 and are left hanging down on both sides (vv. 7-13). Finally, ram skins dyed red cover the whole building, and tahash skins (light leather hides), cover the ram skins (v. 14).

This passage also mentions two veils. There is a veil over the entrance to the sanctuary (vv. 36-37) and one between the Holy of Holies and the Holy Place (vv. 31-32). The latter veil is more costly than the former. Behind the veil in the Holy of Holies (the most holy or most sacred area) there stands the ark with the propitiatory (vv. 33-34). This is the area reserved to Yahweh. In the Holy Place are the lampstand and the table of showbread (v. 35).

27:1-8 The altar of holocausts. This altar is basically a hollow wooden box, about seven and a half feet long, seven and a half feet wide, and four and a half feet high that was plated with bronze. It is difficult to understand how it operated, since the heat from these whole-burnt offerings would destroy the altar. To resolve this problem, some suggest that stones are placed on top of the altar for burning (see 29:18). The four corners of the altar are provided with horns. These were significant for seeking asylum in the temple (see 1 Kgs 1:50; 2:28).

27:9-19 Court of the sanctuary. P now describes the rather elaborate courtyard for the desert sanctuary, approximately one hundred and fifty feet long, seventy-five feet wide, and seven and a half feet high (v. 18). A barrier of bronze columns and silver curtain rods (that hold linen curtains) sets off the court from all other areas. One is naturally reminded of Ezekiel's vision that pictured the temple surrounded by a wall "to separate the sacred from the profane" (Ezek 42:20).

27:20-21 Oil for the lamps. The pure olive oil is to come from the people but it is to be handled by the priests. The sanctuary light is obviously intended to be a perpetual reminder of Yahweh's presence in the desert sanctuary (see Lev 24:2-4).

28:1-43 The priestly vestments. Some knowledge of the history of the priesthood in Israel is useful, if not necessary, to appreciate P's political document. Priesthood properly so called did not appear until there was considerable development of the social makeup of the community. (Note the lack of priests for the Passover in 12:1-20.) With the rise of the monarchy two phenomena occurred: (a) rival sanctuaries and (b) increased centralization at the Jerusalem temple (see 1 Sam 2:27-36; 2 Sam 15:24-29). With Deuteronomy's doctrine of only one sanctuary, Jerusalem, the priests serving the country sanctuaries were put out of work (see Deut 12:4-14). These country priests, many of whom were descendants of Levi, became second-class citizens in the Jerusalem temple and were often the objects of charity, along with the widow, the fatherless, and the alien (see Deut 26:12). The only legitimate priests were the Jerusalem Zadokites—those descended from Zadok (see 1 Kgs 2:26-27; 4:2) who were not descendants of Levi. In order to fulfill the Deuteronomic ideal that all priests, regardless of lineage, should be descendants of Levi (see Deut 17:9), the originally non-Levitical Zadokites claimed to be a special group of Levites, namely, the Aaronites or those descended from Aaron. The outcome was that the Levites now became synonymous with inferior cultic employees who were subordinate to the sons of Zadok (see Ezek 44:10-31). In Exodus, P reflects the claim of the Zadokites to be Aaronites.

This chapter endorses the claims of the Zadokites (v. 1). It focuses on Aaron, allotting only verses 41-43 to the sons of Aaron. Here it is worth noting that there was no ordination of priests as such in the Old Testament. The word translated "ordain" in verse 41 is, literally, "to fill the hand," a phrase whose original sense is not evident. In any event, priests were made holy or sacred by reason of their work.

Of the vestments mentioned here the most interesting are the ephod and the breastpiece. Originally the ephod was a garment worn by the priests and attached to the breastpiece of decision (v. 15). This breastpiece of the same material as the ephod was a bag containing the sacred lots known as Urim and Thummim (v. 30). These lots provide "yes" or "no" answers for those seeking oracles from the priests (see 1 Sam 14:36-37; 28:6). With the ascendancy of prophetism, priests were no longer sought out to give oracles. In keeping with that development the Urim and Thummim, unlike the other priestly items, are merely mentioned and not elaborated. In the P description these originally oracular devices now contain stones engraved with the names of the twelve tribes (vv. 12, 29).

29:1-9 Investiture of the priests. This investiture involves three steps: purification, clothing, and anointing (see also Lev 8:1-38). As a result of the purification or washing, the priest is enabled to enter the realm of the holy (see 30:17-21). The rite of anointing the high priest (v. 7) probably arose only after the Exile when the high priest assumed a political position and consequently received the mark of royalty. (According to 28:41 and other texts all priests are anointed.) This passage concludes by unequivocally stating the Aaronite claims of the Jerusalem Zadokite priests (see also v. 44).

29:10-37 The sacrifices of priestly consecration. There are three different types of sacrifice in this elaborate description. First, there is the sin offering, the bullock (vv.

10-14). Since the offering is for the sins of the priests, they do not share in the victim. Second, there is the holocaust, the first ram (vv. 15-18). Third, there is the communion sacrifice, the second ram (vv. 19-26, 31-37). In verse 20 Moses consecrates the priests by rubbing the animal's blood on the extremities of the body of Aaron and his sons. In verses 24-25 Moses then puts parts of the victims in their hands, has them perform the office of waving them before Yahweh, and receives them back. As a result of this ritual gesture, Aaron and his sons are invested with priestly power. (Verses 27-30 interrupt the ceremony. They determine the offering due the priests and make provision for handing down the priestly vestments.) Next, the priests boil the flesh of this second ram and share it in a sacred meal. Since this meal is a holy meal in connection with their priestly consecration, lay persons may not join them (vv. 31-35). This section concludes by noting the length of the ceremony. The exceptional holiness of the altar (Yahweh's meeting place—see verses 43-44) is underlined in the rubric of a daily sacrifice of a bullock for this seven-day period (vv. 35-37).

29:38-46 Daily sacrifices. The daily sacrifice of two yearling lambs (vv. 38-42) leads into a profound theological statement by P (vv. 43-46). The consecration of the altar, the sanctuary, and the priests looks to God's ongoing presence in the midst of Israel. Specifically, this God who dwells among them is none other than Yahweh, who brought the Israelites out of Egypt. Israel's cultic institutions are thus rooted in the Exodus and in Sinai.

30:1-38 Further cultic ordinances. The altar of the incense (called the golden altar in 1 Kgs 7:48) is perhaps a later priestly insertion, since it should be logically mentioned in 26:33-37 and is not included in the incense-related episodes in the desert (see Num 16:6-7, 17-18; 17:11-12). Each morning and each evening (vv. 7-8) a priest removes pieces of coal with a shovel from the altar of holocausts, sprinkles powder on the coals, and places them on the altar of incense (see Luke 1:8-9). Verses 34-38 provide the mixture for this absolutely sacred perfume. On the Day of Atonement (v. 10) the high priest takes this life-saving smoke screen into the Holy of Holies and rubs the blood of the sacrificial animal on the horns of the altar of incense itself (see Lev 16:12-13, 18).

Census taking is construed as a dangerous undertaking (see 32:30-35; 2 Sam 24). Everyone, therefore, of twenty years of age or over, who seeks to be enrolled and wishes to avoid the census plague must make a contribution to the sanctuary of a half-shekel (vv. 11-16; see Neh 10:33-35). Such a religious precaution is a fitting offering to the upkeep of Yahweh's dwelling place.

Verses 17-33 enact further requirements for cultic personnel and objects. According to verses 17-21 the priests must employ the laver (see 2 Chr 4:6) for washing their hands and feet prior to entering the sanctuary and when officiating at the altar (all Moslems observe this rite before prayer in the mosque). Since there is no mention of the laver in 38:29-31 and since it logically belongs with the altar of holocausts in 27:1-7, it is very likely a later priestly insertion. In addition to the washing, the priests (v. 30) and all the sacred furniture (vv. 26-28) are to be anointed with a very special holy oil (vv. 23-25). These rubrics indicate the unique character of cultic personnel and objects. They must be removed from everything that smacks of the profane (vv. 32-33). For P, however, the holiness of the sanctuary with its personnel is intended to have a sanctifying effect on the entire people of Yahweh.

31:1-11 Choice of artisans. The construction of a god's temple is not a haphazard decision. In ancient Canaanite literature the construction of Baal's temple falls to a special craftsman god. Against this background P has Yahweh single out Bezalel and, as his assistant, Oholiab. P emphasizes that Bezalel's talent results from a divine spirit (v. 3; see also 35:31). This detail is central to P's plan of divine presence whereby the creation of the world, the construction of the desert sanctuary, and the erection of the sanctuary are interrelated. Thus God's spirit in Gen 1:2 is linked to the spirit-filled architect of the desert construction (v. 3), who is, in turn, linked to the spirit-filled leader of the occupation forces, Joshua (see Num 27:18; Deut 34:9).

A key structural element in P is the execution of a command given directly or indirectly by God (see 7:6; 12:28). As noted in 25:1-9, it is eminently important to have exact correspondence between God's plan and its execution. Thus the divine command communicated through Moses to the artisans (vv. 6, 11) will be carried out exactly. In chapter 39 that execution will be noted in a context that also links the construction of the sanctuary to the creation of the world.

31:12-18 The significance of the sabbath. Although P earlier connected sabbath observance with the manna (16:23-30), he now develops the meaning of that institution for Israel. As in the other traditions of the sabbath in Exodus, there is the mention of cessation of work (see 20:9; 23:12; 34:21) and of the link to creation (see 20:11). In this passage, however, P underlines the sign value (vv. 13, 17) and the covenant thrust (v. 16) of the sabbath. Since Yahweh sanctified the sabbath (Gen 2:3) and rested (Gen 2:2) in the aftermath of creation (here in verse 17 Yahweh refreshes himself), Israel acknowledges through its observance the Holy One in her midst. Israel thereby enters into the whole rhythm of creation, celebrating anew her bond with the creator God and the created world. Israel is sacred and given over to Yahweh (v. 13), just as the sabbath is sacred and given over to Yahweh (vv. 14, 15). Later (39:43) P will connect Yahweh's action of blessing on the seventh day with Moses' blessing of the artisans.

PART V: ISRAEL'S APOSTASY AND THE RENEWAL OF THE COVENANT

Exod 32:1–34:35

This section of Exodus bristles with enormous difficulties. The source division of chapters 32–33 is far from clear. The original event behind the story of the Golden Calf is not really apparent. Nevertheless, despair should not control the general interpretation of the final text. Though the history of the traditions in these chapters continues to be elusive, what does emerge with clarity is Israel's ultimate understanding of herself as a covenanted people. The multiplicity of traditions, moreover, points to the centrality of this episode for her self-understanding.

Not a few scholars are convinced that a real event stands behind the story of the Golden Calf and that it occurred during the wilderness experience. There may have been a group that opposed Moses and his ark of the covenant symbol. Such a group under the leadership of Aaron may have broken away from allegiance to Moses and insisted on a bull figure as their symbol of the divine presence. However, to be more specific is to go beyond the evidence.

It should be noted that the Golden Calf does not violate the prescription of the Ten Commandments regarding false images (20:4-5). That prohibition concerns the person of Yahweh, whereas the Golden Calf (actually a young bull) looks to an attribute of Yahweh—strength. Such bulls could serve as supports for Yahweh's throne (see the cherubim in 25:10-22). Israel's history, however, shows that the people did not always distinguish between the deity and the deity's attribute and so identified the young bull with Yahweh (see Hos 13:2).

Jeroboam I (931–910 B.C.E.), the first king of the northern kingdom, set up such a young bull image in the cities of Dan and Bethel (see 1 Kgs 12:26-32) as a cultic move against Solomon's temple. Jeroboam's use of these images suggests that they were already an old tradition. Hence Exod 32 need not be construed as directly condemning this king's cultic changes. However, it is likely that this chapter is an indirect condemnation of Jeroboam's cultic reforms.

In their present setting chapters 32–34 reflect a theology of covenant renewal. The elements in this theological construct are: (a) sin, which is generally apostasy; (b) punishment; (c) repentance; (d) restoration (see Num 13–14; Judg 3:7-11). This pattern is theologically significant. It implies that Yahweh chooses to reveal himself, not only through a people (which is indeed a plus) but also through a sinful people. In this respect Israel considers herself a refuge of sinners.

32:1-6 Making of the Golden Calf. The sin in this covenant renewal pattern is the desire of the people to get rid of Moses and so obtain a new leader (vv. 1, 4). This tradition is certainly non-priestly. In such traditions Aaron is never identified as a priest or an ancestor of priests; indeed, as here, he even opposes Yahweh's chosen leader (see Num 12:1-8). Aaron readily accedes to the wishes of the people, constructs the young bull image, and calls for a celebration involving holocausts and communion sacrifices (vv. 2-5). It is not really clear that the reveling in verse 6 is some form of debauchery. Israel's sin of apostasy consists in rejecting Moses as leader and hence in rejecting Yahweh.

32:7-14 Yahweh's wrath and Moses' mediation. Moses appears as a covenant mediator, one who intercedes for the people, here in the context of winning forgiveness that ultimately leads to covenant renewal. Israel, therefore, envisioned a special role of intercession whereby the relationship of the people to Yahweh was bound up with the relationship of certain endowed individuals to Yahweh. It is also interesting to observe that Moses is able to oppose the God of Israel and still not be labeled unloyal.

Yahweh's violent reaction is precisely the reverse of that envisioned by the young bull devotees. Yahweh plans to wipe this people out and begin anew (vv. 7-10). Moses begins his mediatory role by pursuing the argument of continuity in history. To have the people die in the desert would only provoke ridicule from Yahweh's enemies in Egypt. The action begun in Egypt should be carried on to completion. To abandon Israel now would be to renege on the promises to the patriarchs (vv. 11-13). In the end Yahweh allows the persuasive Moses to win the argument (v. 14).

32:15-24 Twofold destruction. The tablets play a significant part in this story. In verses 15-16 these tablets are unique. Although the custom was to have such inscriptions on only one side, these are on both sides. E's tradition is hinted at. (Joshua's presence in verse 17 has already been explained by E in 24:12.) The divine revelation which Moses was to have communicated to the people is now recast to tell the account of Israel's infidelity and so necessitate Moses' return to the mountain where he will receive new tablets. Although J has Moses inscribe the tablets (34:28), this tradition insists that God himself actually did the engraving (see also P in 31:18). The tradition, therefore, went beyond the ancient Near Eastern understanding of divine writing whereby a deity did not produce the document physically. Yahweh's writing, as a result, stresses their value and authority. In the other direction, the breaking of the tablets is the breaking of the covenant relationship between Yahweh and Israel. The action of the people in the construction of the young bull image results in the destruction of the covenant bond.

The destruction of the tablets is followed by the account of the construction and subsequent destruction of the Golden Calf. Although verses 21-24 make a feeble attempt to exculpate Aaron's role in verses 2-5, they are interesting from the standpoint of the making of cultic objects. In ancient Canaanite literature, for example, cultic objects acquired their desired form by themselves. The palace of Baal is completed after a fire has worked on the silver and the gold for six days. Aaron's reply in verse 24 that the image emerged by itself is thus readily intelligible. The destruction is even more interesting. According to verse 20 Moses employs mutually exclusive acts in undoing the image: burning and grinding. In ancient Canaanite literature Mot, the god of death, is undone in the same way. Anat, Baal's consort, burns, grinds, and scatters Mot. The final act of making the Israelites drink the image-polluted water (see also Deut 9:21) is similar to Anat's scattering of Mot's remains in the open fields where birds consume them. In Exodus the Golden Calf, like Mot, is utterly destroyed and made totally irretrievable.

32:25-29 The zeal of the Levites. There are two traditions for the punishment of the people. According to verse 35 Yahweh smites the people for their sinful action. According to verses 25-29 members of the tribe of Levi rally to Moses' call to arms and execute the Israelites who sacrificed to the Golden Calf, including their own relatives. This loyalty wins for them their priestly prerogatives (see Deut 33:9). This tradition does not condemn Aaron as the ancestor of the Aaronites. It expresses the reaction of the covenant-committed Levites who rejected the cult established by Jeroboam I at Bethel, one of the cities where this king erected a young bull image. This episode also condemns the action of the king in making priests from among the people who were not Levites (see 1 Kgs 12:31).

32:30-35 The atonement. This tradition stresses Moses' identity with the people. If Yahweh is unrelenting, then the mediator wishes to share the fate of the people. The concept of God's book was known in the ancient Near East and is at home in the notion of military conscription where the lives of those enrolled in the book were fraught with danger. In this section Israel adapts the tradition—an Israel that considers herself

God's army. At the time of a census (see 30:11-16) there was a rite of expiation (see "atonement" in verse 30) and the names of the Israelites were inscribed on tablets. Those so inscribed enjoyed the rights of a member of God's militia, for example, possession of the land and worship in the sanctuary. Anyone removed from the tablets was placed among the dead, that is, separated from the community.

33:1-6 Orders for the departure. This section pursues the thrust of 32:33-34, the continuation of the journey to the Promised Land with the aid of an angel. However, the angel in 32:34 merely affirmed Moses' leadership role. The basic issue here is the personal presence of Yahweh with Moses and the Israelites (vv. 2-3). An angel is not the same as Yahweh. This bad news is reiterated in verses 4-6 and is marked by a sign of Israel's repentance, the removal of all ornaments. The people now stand under God's judgment. One naturally wonders about the efficacy of Moses' mediation.

33:7-11 Moses and the Tent of Meeting. This tradition, which is generally ascribed to E, takes up the question of divine presence already broached in verses 1-6. However, the text itself is not a unity. According to verse 7 any Israelite can visit the tent. However, according to verse 8 only Moses visits the tent while the people remain at their own tents in awe. According to verse 11b an official resides permanently in the tent. Yet verse 11a presumes that the intimate dialogue between God and Moses precludes the presence of a third person. Verses 8 and 10 presume that the tent is placed in the middle of the camp (see P in 25:1-9). But verse 7 states that the tent is outside the camp and indeed at some distance from the camp.

It seems that E has introduced changes into an older tent tradition from Israel's desert experience in order to demonstrate that the tent theophany is a miniature reproduction of the revelation of Sinai. Both the mountain and the tent are outside the camp (v. 7; 19:17). In both cases the people remain at a distance (v. 8; 20:18). (In Hebrew the same verb is used for the people stationing themselves [v. 8; 19:17].) In both cases a cloud indicates the divine presence (vv. 9-10; 19:16ab). In both cases Joshua assists Moses (v. 11b; 24:13). Finally, in both cases Moses appears as God's intimate. Israel's relationship to Yahweh hinges in no small measure on this unique mediator.

33:12-17 Moses' intercession. This section is linked to Moses' position vis-à-vis Yahweh (v. 11a) and his order to lead the people on (v. 1a). According to verse 12 the implication is that an angel simply will not do. Appealing to his status as divine intimate, Moses argues on behalf of the people (v. 13). If the leader's status is genuine, the divine conclusion must be to provide for the people. Verse 14 shows that the appeal is successful. However, it is directed only at Moses. Still dissatisfied, Moses presses his case by demonstrating that divine intimacy is real only if the people are included (vv. 15-16). The community-directed argument of Moses finally obtains divine approval (v. 17). The significance of this argumentation should not be overlooked. It implies that the welfare of the covenant people (here their renewal as God's people) is grounded in the love and trust between the covenant God and the covenant mediator.

33:18-23 Preparations for theophany. With no little audacity Moses seeks further surety for his people, since the pronouncing of the divine name is the guarantee of presence and hence of compassion (for this compassion see 34:6-7). Divine name goes hand in hand with covenant. Because of the dangers connected with the direct display of God's glory, Moses is to be set in the hollow of a rock and covered by God's hand (vv. 21-22). The viewing of God's back (but not his face) is both the limit and the proof of Moses' intimacy, but of intimacy as related to the well-being of the people. (For Elijah's similar theophany see 1 Kgs 19:9, 11-13.)

34:1-9 The theophany. Most of this section is from J (vv. 1a, 2-4, 6a, 8). Indeed, together with most of the remaining material in chapter 34, this scene is the natural sequel of Moses' ascent of the mountain in 19:20 (J). In keeping with the basic outline of the covenant proceedings, an expression of God's will is expected in J's account. This expression has been removed from its natural place—after 19:20—because of Israel's infidelity in the Golden Calf incident. In other words, the expression of God's will in the initial encounter on the mountain in J has become the expression of God's will in the second encounter of covenant renewal. According to the pattern of covenant renewal, restoration is now in order. The making of new tablets symbolizes the making of a new covenant. (References to the former broken tablets in verse 1b and to the cloud in verse 5 are editorial touches to make the J account fit its new setting.)

J's theophany has, first of all, Moses cutting the tablets and ascending the mountain alone (vv. 1a, 2-4). Next, Yahweh passes before Moses (v. 6a). Finally, in deference to the divine presence, Moses bows down to worship (v. 8).

Verses 6-7 and 9 are the conclusion of Moses' mediatorial role begun in 33:12-23. The theophany announced in 33:19 now takes place. The cultic saying in verses 6-7 (see also 20:5-6) in its present position is a statement about divine forgiveness and divine punishment. The word translated "merciful" in verse 6 (also the verb "to grant mercy" in 33:19) derives from the Hebrew word for "womb." Thus Mother Yahweh demonstrates that compassion for Israel which a mother is expected to show the child of her womb. At the same time, Yahweh will not let the guilty escape (v. 7). Ultimately the request for forgiveness (v. 9) is grounded once again in the relationship that Moses enjoys with Yahweh. The covenant renewal can now proceed because Moses has identified with Israel.

34:10-26 The Dodecalogue. There is no mention of Israel's explicit response to Yahweh's overtures in this covenant renewal. Moses' intercession and the people's repentance seem adequate (see also 1 Sam 12:16-25). The opening verses (vv. 10-11) transcend the immediate setting by focusing on the dangers that will confront Israel in the Promised Land (note also 23:20-33). Sinai appears, therefore, as the apt place for anticipating those dangers by reason of the covenant bond that will distinguish Israel from her neighbors.

Although verse 28 speaks of the Decalogue or Ten Commandments, this series of laws is actually a Dodecalogue or Twelve Commandments. (The expression "ten commandments" in verse 28 is a later development.) The Dodecalogue is often labeled cultic or ritual in contradistinction to the ethical Decalogue (see the injunction for the pilgrimage feasts in verse 23 and the law of redemption in verses 19-20). However, the prohibitions of images (v. 17) and intermarriage with the Canaanites (v. 16) are patently ethical. Moreover, most of these commandments are second person singular formulations (see 20:1-17). For J, this collection creates a healthy tension in his theological approach. According to Gen 12:1-3, Israel is to mediate blessings to the conquered nations. But a pagan environment can pose problems in mediating those blessings. This Dodecalogue, therefore, is J's form of insistence on fidelity to the covenant God in a pagan setting (vv. 12-15). It is rightly called by some Yahweh's privilege law—a statement of Yahweh's prerogatives grounded in his character as the Jealous One (v. 15). The distinctiveness of Israel flows from the distinctiveness of her God.

34:27-35 The impact of theophany. J mentions the divine command to write down the terms of the covenant and the subsequent execution of that command on the mountain for a period comprising forty days and forty nights (vv. 27-28; see Deut 9:9,18; Matt 4:2). J then narrates Moses' gathering of the people and his enjoining on them all that Yahweh commanded on the mountain (vv. 31-32).

The tradition contained in verses 29-30, 33-35 deals with Moses' shining face. It is linked to Moses' mediatorial position already noted in chapters 33 and 34. According to the tradition, Moses must veil his face when he is not performing his official duties (vv. 33-34). Whatever the background of the veil itself, what is central to the biblical account is the radiant face of Moses insofar as it derives from God and is the symbol of his authority before God. The man who was rejected by the people (32:1, 4) is the man who restored them in covenant and who now fittingly wears the symbol of his divine office. (See Paul's application of this tradition in 2 Cor 3:7–4:6.)

PART VI: THE EXECUTION OF THE INSTRUCTIONS FOR THE BUILDING OF THE SANCTUARY

Exod 35:1–40:38

P now recounts the execution of the instructions given to Moses in chapters 25–31. It is tempting to construe chapters 35–40, together with chapter 34, as a type of restoration. Thus chapters 25–31 are a creation and chapters 32–33 a fall. In any event, P utilizes the Sinai setting to develop his theology of divine presence.

35:1–36:7 The start of construction and Israel's generosity. P's basic structure here is the execution of commands given directly or indirectly by God. Thus there are divine commands for: (a) the observance of the sabbath (35:1, including the prohibition against lighting fires, in verse 3); (b) the collection of materials (35:4); (c) the call for artisans (35:10); (d) the start of work on the project (36:1). P goes on to note that the Israelites generously respond to Yahweh's command (35:20-29). In fact, they are overzealous. Moses has to make a special appeal to stop the flow of contributions (36:2-6). The outcome is nonetheless an abundance of materials to complete the work (36:7). The spirit-endowed Bezalel and Oholiab (see 31:1-11) as well as the other artisans are also portrayed as responding to the divine command to execute all the work. It is rather interesting to compare this wholehearted response in P's ideal account with the reluctance to rebuild the temple after the Exile (see the prophets Haggai and Zechariah). The biblical record does not hesitate to register both the ideal and the real.

36:8–39:31 Execution of the divine instructions. With the exception of 38:21-31 this section details how the divine instructions communicated to Moses in chapters 25–31 were in fact carried out. There is a difference, however, in the sequence. While the ark with the table and the lampstand (25:10-39) heads the list of instructions because of their greater importance, the tent (26:1-37) comes first in the order of execution. In this way there is progress from the outside inward. In general, this section basically duplicates chapters 25–31, belaboring the point that the final product corresponds to the initial directions. For the tent cloth, coverings, wooden frames, and veils (36:8-38) see 26:1-29, 31-37. For the ark with the propitiatory, table, and lampstand (37:1-24) see 25:10-39. For the altar of incense (37:25-28) as well as the anointing oil and fragrant incense (37:29) see 30:1-6, 23-25, 34-36. For the altar of holocausts and the court (38:1-7, 9-20) see 27:1-19. For the priestly and other vestments (39:1-31) see 28:1-43.

In 38:8 P notes that the bronze laver (30:18-21) was made from the mirrors of the women who served at the entrance of the sanctuary. These women reappear in a gloss of 1 Sam 2:22. Just what function they performed is not clear. There is no evidence to suggest that they exercised an office in public worship.

The passage dealing with the amount of metal used (38:21-31) is a later insertion into the text. The sanctuary tax in verse 26 that draws on the first census of Israel (to be mentioned later in Num 1:45-46) apparently ignores the tradition of 35:21 and 36:3. According to this tradition Israel generously contributes on a voluntary basis. Verse 21 notes the position of Ithamar, son of Aaron, as head of the Levites. However, the Levites (see 28:1-43) are not instituted until Num 3:5-10 and Ithamar assumes his role as head only in Num 4:33.

39:32-43 Presentation of the work to Moses. Besides enumerating the finished cultic materials that are presented to Moses, this section is especially significant for P's theology of God's ongoing presence. By a subtle use of structures, P interconnects the creation of the world, the construction/erection of the desert sanctuary, and the establishment of that sanctuary in the Promised Land (for this last point see 40:1-33). Despite Israel's infidelity, God's plan will not be thwarted. The God who created in the beginning will continue to create in Israel's ongoing history. Cult, therefore, is the principal means by which the creative presence will be manifest among the Israelites.

P not only reintroduces his execution-of-command structure (see 35:1–36:7) but here he also embellishes it with a more solemn formulation. Verse 32b may be translated literally: "And the sons of Israel did [it] according to everything that Yahweh had commanded Moses. Thus they did [it]." Similarly verse 42: "According to everything that Yahweh had commanded Moses, thus the sons of Israel did all the work." P also brings in a second structure, successful completion of work (v. 32a). In addition P has Moses make a judgment on the people's work. Verse 43a may be translated literally: "And Moses saw all the work, and behold, they had done it." Right after this judgment, P has Moses bless the people (v. 43b).

The parallels with P's creation account are evident. In Gen 1:31 God looks at everything he has made and labels it very good. Gen 2:1 observes that the heavens and the earth and all their array are finished. After concluding the six days of creation, God blesses the seventh day (Gen 2:3). Since God cannot issue a command to God, the creation account does not allow for the execution-of-command structure. As mentioned earlier (31:1-11), the spirit at work in creation (Gen 1:2) is also operative in Bezalel, the chief engineer of the sanctuary construction.

40:1-33 The erection of the sanctuary. Here P minutely relates how Moses carries out Yahweh's instructions in setting up the desert sanctuary. Besides pinpointing the time (vv. 2, 17) and accentuating the privileges of the Aaronites (vv. 13-15), P takes pains to highlight the significance of the event by means of his structures. The execution-of-command structure is mentioned no less than eight times (vv. 16, 19, 21, 23, 25, 27, 29, 32). Indeed, verse 16 has the more solemn form of the structure, which may be translated literally: "And Moses did according to everything that Yahweh had commanded him, thus he did [it]." The structure of successful completion of work is also in evidence. According to verse 33 Moses finishes everything.

P links not only creation and the erection of the sanctuary but also the setting up of that sanctuary in the apportioned Promised Land. In Num 27:18 and Deut 34:9, P describes Joshua as the spirit-filled leader and the architect of Israel's plan of occupation. In Josh 14:5, when narrating the division of the land, P employs the more solemn form of the execution-of-command structure. It may be translated literally: "As Yahweh had commanded Moses, thus the sons of Israel did [it] and they divided the land." In the same book, P also uses the successful completion-of-work structure in narrating the final apportionment: (literally) "And they finished dividing the land." This final act, moreover, takes place in front of the tent at Shiloh. In keeping with the divine command to subdue the earth (Gen 1:28), P states in Josh 18:1 that the earth was indeed subdued. In the same text he notes that the community of Israel gathered around the tent which was set up in Shiloh. For P, therefore, the event at Shiloh looks back to Sinai, which in turn looks back to the first creation. God's abiding presence in the land is the sacrament of hope for P's despairing exiles. In the final analysis, the dull rubrics are charged with life.

40:34-38 The abiding presence. For P, Sinai is the model of worship. According to 24:15b-16a the cloud covers the mountain and settles there. Here, too, the cloud covers the sanctuary and Yahweh's glory fills it (v. 34). For P, therefore, the desert sanctuary captures the experience on Sinai and perpetuates it.

This tradition of the cloud's covering and settling is also the seal of approval on and legitimation of everything that Moses and the Israelites have done. Yahweh here takes possession of his sanctuary. This is also Israel's experience when Yahweh's glory fills Solomon's temple and the priests are unable to minister because of the cloud (see 1 Kgs 8:10-11). P's cloud theophany also anticipates Israel's ongoing trek through the wilderness. P's cloud, which now does duty for the tradition of the pillar of cloud and the pillar of fire (see 13:21-22; 14:19-20), also serves as a signal. It will indicate when and how long Israel will set up camp and when Israel is to strike camp (see Num 9:15-23).

In these concluding chapters, P reveals himself to be a truly pastoral theologian. For a people that experienced God's absence in the fall of Jerusalem and subsequent exile, P now proclaims the good news of God's presence. Aware that Israel is deprived of temple worship because she dwells in a foreign land, P announces that Israel will be restored to the land and indeed that the land will be sanctified by God's presence in the sanctuary. (For the conditions of return see Lev 26.) One thus returns to the gospel of creation. By careful and proper attention to cult, the Israelite is empowered to move from chaos to cosmos.

LEVITICUS

Wayne A. Turner

INTRODUCTION

This is a book about holiness. Known also as the third book of Moses, the Book of Leviticus is one volume in the five-volume work called the Pentateuch. The term Torah, which usually means law, but more exactly is teaching, instruction, or direction, refers to the message of this book. Even though we customarily refer to Leviticus as a book, it is better to call it one chapter in the whole story of the Torah. This chapter is about a holy God and a people called to be holy.

1. Holiness means wholeness

To understand this chapter in the Torah story we need to consider "wholeness" as one meaning of holiness. This is more than a play on words and is necessary to understand the Book of Leviticus. Wholeness, in a sense, describes the life of God. More precisely, wholeness describes our lives when they reflect the life of God.

The biblical meaning of holiness includes not only the mystery of God but also the creature's response to that mystery. "Be holy, for I, the Lord, your God, am holy" (11:44-45; 19:2; 20:7, 26). The root of the word holy means "to cut off, separate," referring to the separation of the holy from the profane (unholy). "Holy" refers to persons, places, or things approached or touched only under certain conditions of ritual purity.

"Wholeness" describes particularly the response of the people to the command "Be holy, for I, the Lord, am holy." For, while there is a certain wholeness to the idea of oneness, God alone resides in absolute oneness. There is also a certain oneness about wholeness, which can reflect what Genesis calls the "image and likeness of God" (1:26).

Wholeness, unlike oneness, has parts or components. It is in the proper ordering of the parts of life that wholeness comes about and serves the cause of holiness. For example, a jigsaw puzzle must be put together in a particular order. If even one piece is left over, the puzzle lacks wholeness and oneness.

As we read the Book of Leviticus, we must keep in mind that everything fits together in a proper order. This serves the wholeness that reflects the oneness of God who called the people to be holy. The simple order of obedience, ritual purity, and holiness is as valid today as when first presented by the Priestly writers. True obedience plants the seed of an authentic ritual that purifies and prepares for the life of holiness. Once this simple lesson-plan was recognized, the Levitical material took its shape. Then this book acted as the key piece for the Pentateuch and became the third book of Moses. The five books formed one complete account of divine-human relationship, with Leviticus as the very heart of the Torah.

2. The titles tell the story

The Hebrew titles of the five books of Moses spell out a theme that is repeated again and again in the Bible and in life itself—God creates, identifies, and calls people from the wilderness of this life into the one, complete (holy) life that is God's. These books act as the "entrance" to the whole Bible.

In the Hebrew Bible the first significant word of each book is the title for that book. In the Pentateuch the Hebrew titles make a logical statement of the divine-human experience. *In the beginning* (Genesis) God created; these are the *names* (Exodus), *and he called* (Leviticus) Moses *in the wilderness* (Numbers) to speak these *words* (Deuteronomy). Note the place of Leviticus; the *names* (Exodus) of those led out of slavery needed direction to follow their calling as a "kingdom of priests and a holy nation" (19:6), especially *in the wilderness* (Numbers).

When reading Leviticus keep in mind the "guideline character" of this chapter in the one story that makes up the Pentateuch.

3. The title

The title in Hebrew is one word meaning "and he called." Today the common title is the Latinized Greek name *Leviticus,* which describes activities of the Levites (priests) from the tribe of Levi. The Hebrew title points to a vocation-call in the instruction of the Torah. So when using *Leviticus,* it is well to keep in mind the Hebrew overtone of "calling" or "vocation."

This central theme of a call to holiness is found in the Code of Holiness (17–26). It possibly formed an original "manual of holiness" around which the final editors of the book gathered other priestly (Levitical) material.

4. Three codes of law (instruction) in the Pentateuch

Three such Codes of Law have been identified in the Pentateuch: the Sinai or Covenant Code, which is the oldest and found in the Book of Exodus (19–24); the Levitical Code of Holiness (Lev 17–26); and an updating of the Torah in the Deuteronomy Code (Deut 12–26). Even though these three are considered the Codes of Law, many other passages in the Pentateuch speak of legal regulations. In fact, the Levitical regulations are not only in the Book of Leviticus but also in the second and the fourth books of Moses, Exodus and Numbers. Actually, there is more mention of the Levites elsewhere in the Pentateuch than in the Book of Leviticus. Here we concentrate on the "call to holiness."

5. Leviticus—heart of the Torah

Leviticus not only teaches holiness; the book itself is an example of holiness. The orderly arrangement is our first evidence of the presence of holiness. A simple arrangement of the material can be an important witness to holiness. Note that the matter of sacrifices (chs. 1–7) leads naturally into the subject of those who offer them (chs. 8–10) with their dispositions of legal purity (chs. 11–16) and legal holiness (chs. 17–27)—such a simple arrangement and yet filled with importance and authority calling the people to follow the Torah.

The book is something like the simple but decisive presence of the heart in the human organism. Even when its presence and precision of function are taken for granted, it continues to beat for the good of the whole organism. The material assigned to Leviticus seems to have a similar relation to the whole Torah. Leviticus is the heart of the Torah, and the beat of this heart is called the Code of Holiness (chs. 17–26).

The depth and elegance of the simple arrangement of Leviticus is revealed, first in the pulsating rhythm of the repeated "And the Lord spoke to Moses." After the vocational call of Moses in chapter 1, almost every chapter begins with this same refrain. The repetition is also a reminder of the form of a legal document with its repetition of formal phrases, details, and directions. In fact, roughly corresponding to the above four areas of arrangement, some legal-minded commentators point to underlying detailed arrangements. Some find seven sets of decalogues in each section. They say that they are patterned after the Decalogue (Ten Commandments) given on Mount Sinai. Thus, Leviticus, as the heart of the Torah, reflects the fine design of a heart and the simplicity of one of its single life-giving beats.

The commandments were now to come alive in the lives of the newly-formed people. The heart of the new priestly nation must now begin to beat and carry out the instruction to be holy (19:2). This holiness is at work in the Torah and throughout the whole Bible. "Holy" and "sacred" and other related forms are used over a thousand times, with nearly one quarter of such references in Leviticus.

St. Jerome in a letter to the cleric Paulinus affirms the holiness of the book: "In the Book of Leviticus it is easy to see that every sacrifice, yes, almost every syllable and both the garments of Aaron and the whole order of Leviticus breathe heavenly mysteries." Years later another Scripture writer, Peter, encourages the vocational call of Leviticus: "So gird the loins of your understanding, live soberly, set all your hope on the gift to be conferred on you when Jesus Christ appears. As obedient sons, do not yield to the desires that once shaped you in your ignorance. Rather, become holy yourselves in every aspect of your conduct, after the likeness of the Holy One who called you; remember Scripture says, 'You shall be holy, for I am holy'" (1 Pet 1:13-16 quoting Lev 19:2). This same pulsating beat of holiness endures today in the vocational call of everyone.

6. The shape of Leviticus—date and authorship

Today we usually think of a book as having one or two authors and written over just a few years. However, the Bible is the history of the people of God written by many authors and editors over two thousand years. Just as we can expect many changes in the history of a people, we can expect changes in the documents that record that history. Scholars sometimes speak of a particular manuscript family when referring to various manuscripts.

We now recognize that some final editors were not just compilers, but were true authors. Editors also reshaped or added material along the way. In Leviticus the form of the material is *historical* and *legal*, dealing with the call to holiness. Much of the material, especially in the first chapters, is "liturgical," having been written and edited by Levites or priests and given the name "Priestly" (P).

The Book of Leviticus has a unique shape and fits into a larger unit of the Pentateuch. This larger unit extends from Exod 25 through Leviticus to Num 10. Every book of the Pentateuch has some sections written by P. The emphasis given by these writers and final editors focuses on the underlying need to be holy.

One gets the impression that Leviticus, though edited, was substantially preserved, rather than abbreviated, to form a synthesis of worship regulations. This might explain why the Bible reader often bypasses Leviticus with the expression "Oh, it's just a bunch of laws and regulations." This is a valid first impression, but the editors used this material to fill a need for guidance and completeness. The final editors intentionally gave a wilderness setting to Exodus, Leviticus, and Numbers. What could be more needed in the wilderness than a book on law (direction) and order?

Just as we recognize schools of writers, so we find today schools of scholars presenting various answers to dating, text, and authorship questions. For some, Moses is the author, while others hold that the book is postexilic (late fifth century B.C.E.). Yet another group stands a near-middle ground and gives a date around the eighth century B.C.E. Further, it may be that the final shape was not decided at any one of these times. Such theories should help the reader understand the final form of a biblical book.

It is in the final editing that the whole message is conveyed. The shape of the book at the time it is born into the holy life of the Bible is the time when its divine source of life (i.e., divine inspiration) is affirmed. All the oral and written traditions, development of thought and practice, writing, editing and reediting come together in the Bible to serve the one, holy God. Leviticus witnesses this presence of God.

In considering the wilderness setting of the Book of Leviticus, somewhere a prejudice against temple worship could have influenced the shaping of the material. This prejudice could have occurred more than once. Also, the dispersion of population and distance of travel affect ritual practice. It is further possible that there were those who were convinced that Yahweh should be a pilgrim God, not having a fixed abode in this world except in the Holy of Holies of the Tabernacle, an abode that could travel with them wherever they would go, even into exile.

This commentary seeks to affirm the Book of Leviticus as it is in the Pentateuch, since this is the result of the final editing. The ancient editors presented a particular coherence for the ingathering of all the materials and traditions. Sometimes that ancient part of Leviticus, the Code of Holiness (17–26), is attributed to an author called H who is earlier than any of the Priestly writers.

7. Levitical themes

A. *Read the directions.* One regulation in everyday life simply says, "Read the directions." Sometimes it is touched with irony when someone says, "When everything else fails, read the directions!" Reading the directions is, no doubt, the first thing to do when beginning a new project. This advice could act as a meditation for reading the Book of Leviticus. In a way Leviticus serves as the directions for the whole Torah.

Leviticus gives a simple direction for life. The direction is as important and enduring as the beat and pulse of the heart is to the body. It is found in the lesson plan of obedience, purity, and holiness. The order is important. We begin with an obedience that brings about purification. This combination, in turn, conditions one for the life of holiness. So the direction for living a holy life is in Leviticus, centered around the simple directive of chapter 19, "Be holy, for I, the Lord, your God, am holy."

The Holy One of Israel (Isa 1:4) is God and God's name is Holy (Lev 22:32). The people, too, are to be holy. This is the regulation of life: "Sanctify yourselves, then, and be holy. . . . Be careful, therefore, to observe what I, the Lord, who make you holy, have prescribed" (20:7-8; *see also* 22:31-33).

B. *Israel's responsibility to its neighbors.* To understand the Book of Leviticus, we must respect the neighborhood in which Israel lived and moved. We proceed with caution from what we know to search out the unknown. Sometimes we expect a greater responsibility (ability-to-respond) on the part of Israel than we should. This is often done by including all the people of the then known world into the circle of Israel's response to life. This approach tends to become a smothering, rather than a drawing-out experience. We need to know more about the people of that time before we transfer the biblical narrative into real life experiences and judge historical events.

The relationship of Israel with the Canaanite and other peoples into whose land they sojourned or moved is of prime importance. The discoveries at Ras Shamra (on the Mediterranean, dating from 1400 B.C.E.) and Ebla (75 miles northeast, dating from 2300 B.C.E.) shed some light on the neighbors of the people of the Bible (*see*, for example, Exod 23). However, much material is still in the stage of critical analysis and publication. The translations themselves take many years. Ras Shamra (Ugarit) was first excavated in 1929, and some parallels to Israel's language and literature both there and at Ebla (1968–1974) have been recognized.

C. *My holy name.* A more exact translation of "my holy name" is "the name of my holiness." In Hebrew "holiness" refers to a concrete reality for which the emphasis is intended. Another example, "my good day," is really "the day of my goodness." Hebrew places the emphasis where it belongs.

Another important difference is using the superlative to preserve a certain dignified identity. For "holiest," the Hebrew says "the Holy of Holies."

A third difference not to be overlooked when reading the Bible is that certain realities in Hebrew thought are not considered separate entities as they are in our Western thought. Ideas such as body and soul, blood and life, thought and action, are almost always considered the same reality. In Hebrew thought, for instance, there is no word for body. "Flesh" is used instead. Thus, "all flesh" is really every created living thing and is equivalent to "every living soul." Because blood and life are intimately associated, it is the blood of Abel that cries out to God from the soil (Gen 4:10). Nor are understanding and good apart from life itself, "Give me understanding (discernment), that I may live" (Ps 119:144). The expression "Adam knew Eve and she conceived Cain" means that they had intercourse (since there is no separation of body and soul, the action can be called a knowledge). It is sharing one's life with another in the action that truthfully (knowingly) expresses the oneness of God reflected in the man-woman creation.

Biblical thought does not really contain what we are accustomed to think of as a code of ethics. Thus, in speaking of the Torah we should avoid the Western term law. The Torah is not a system of laws. The Torah comes from God, to teach, regulate, instruct and distinguish. "Law," in our Western thought, makes it a mere code of ethics. The Bible says, "Oh how I love your Torah, it is my meditation all the day" (see Ps 119).

D. *A common language of cult activity in the ancient Near East.* Over the centuries various reasons have been given for ritual and dietary regulations. The historian Philo and the philosopher Maimonides believed that God gave some of the commands and regulations in order to serve as a self-discipline of the appetites. Philo says that Moses forbade pork, since it is the most delicious of all meats and that self-denial would curb one's self-indulgence. He forbade flesh-eating animals and birds in order to teach one to be gentle and kind. Sometimes analogies were made between physical and spiritual. Thus, the cud-chewing animals are permitted, since they help one grow in wisdom (by chewing over and over what one has learned). And the cloven-footed animals, because they have a divided hoof, help one know how to decide between ideas.

Regarding the prohibitions concerning food, we suspect that most ancient peoples used the trial-and-error method based on taste. What tasted good and did not make one sick was clean or good. What we call taboo was probably a scare tactic to keep people from being poisoned. The "good sign" encouraged people to eat properly. What were practical considerations for one people became directives based on religious beliefs for another and were handed on as traditions to succeeding generations. Much of what we call ancient myth was simply the stirrings of humans in seeking the source of life and how to survive in life. Nomadic, agricultural and, eventually, urban living, would inevitably bring change in outlook, custom, and religious practice. Just the natural change of the seasons and the struggle for food, which we sometimes refer to as acts of nature, influenced the shaping of desire, understanding, planning, and celebration of life.

We recognize a certain kind of common language used throughout the Near East in regard to religious belief and practice. Israel used this language also, but with a particular meaning and emphasis directed to the One Holy Yahweh.

When people began to settle in the land with an agrarian lifestyle and with food assured, the need to preserve a certain stability became dominant. Priests, prophets, kings, and queens established order to survive, not only as individuals, tribes, or small family groups but as nations. Thus the Bible is a two thousand-year-old record of a people establishing their identity in relation to their God and their neighbors.

We really do not know a great deal about the early development of cult and religious practice. Exegesis, which applies critical methods of study to Scripture with the help of other sciences, especially archaeology, has helped our understanding in some measure. We know very little about the actual ritual of the sacrifice and practically nothing about the prayers or the commentary accompanying the ritual action and the dietary laws. The Book of Leviticus is a listing of ritual regulations, rather than a detailed description of actual performance. We do not have records of what was prayed, said, or sung during the discharge of the regulations.

It is in service of the Holy One then that we live our life of holiness, and our first regulation is to re-establish the order of God's creation in oneself and community. "Be holy" is the core meaning of "Seder" ("everything in proper order") in the Passover celebration that continues to this day in Jewish-Christian religious practice. The heart of the Torah still beats in the Book of Leviticus. The repeated call of Moses and the people to holiness in the pulse of the Code of Holiness is heard and answered at the Passover meal.

COMMENTARY

PART I: RITUAL OF SACRIFICES

Lev 1–7

It is helpful to begin reading the Book of Leviticus at Part IV, Code of Legal Holiness (chs. 17–26).

The first seven chapters of the book speak of ritual regulations for offering sacrifices and seem to take for granted that the reader has already been introduced to basic ideas of Israelite holiness. Chapters 1, 2, and 3 deal with burnt offerings (holocausts); chapters 4 and 5 generally speak of atonement sacrifices, while chapters 6 and 7 give special regulations for the priests.

Now that the presence of God finds a place in the midst of the people, in the tabernacle constructed by Moses (Exod 26–40), Moses is called by God to tell the people how to recognize the presence of the holy. If we read the first three chapters together, we can see that the same order runs throughout and that the emphasis is on obedience, which is the beginning of holiness.

1:1 Moses is still the mediator. Verses 1 and 2 are connecting links to the second and fourth books of Moses (Exodus and Numbers). Throughout Exodus, Yahweh tells Moses, "Speak to the Israelites." This phrase follows through Leviticus and on into Numbers. It acts as an introductory phrase to various regulations of worship and as an assertion of Israelite solidarity. A dispersed people needs to rally around their one leader and mediator Moses to celebrate their unity and solidarity.

The Hebrew title of this book, translated "and he called," is the first word of chapter 1. The "and" keeps us in contact with the call of Moses to build the Dwelling (Exod 24:16). Now that the Dwelling is complete, Moses is to act as the mediator of the worship action (Exod 40:32 and Lev 1:2). God calls Moses to speak the rules of worship for the people to obey. Moses is the one mediator, and we are reminded again and again of the Torah instruction for the unity of the people under Moses.

1:3-9 To give oneself entirely to God. At first glance it seems that we are presented with just a number of ritual regulations. Our first impulse is to set them aside, turning away from the blood of the killing, the cutting-up and burning of animals. The stench of slaughter, squealing animals, and the choking smoke of carcasses in holocaust are repulsive to our Western atmosphere of liturgical banquet. We must consider, however, that this is the record of the people of God, a people who at this time in their history carried the painful memory of slavery in their very bones. And in view of the first law of the Sinai Covenant they needed to be weaned from the other gods to the one God Yahweh.

The incident of the worship of the molten calf along with the call to holiness on the part of the mediator Moses could have evoked some of the ritual response of the first chapters of Leviticus. Rituals attending animal sacrifice were not something new for their world. Their attempt, then, would be to return everything to Yahweh. The first command for the people is to divest the community of any alien allegiance and invest in the life of the one, holy God. The natural response would be to use the ritual practices already developed until a covenant relationship would dictate otherwise.

Disciplinary action because of infidelity seems also to have played a part in some of the ritual behavior. Whatever the history or initial reasons for some of the practices that seem so strange to us, the main purpose for including this material is to teach a lesson in obedience. The lesser member of a covenant relationship needs to learn this lesson first and witness to its exercise within the community in order to preserve the tradition. The accent is on an enduring obedience, since ritual expression can change its mode of expression. Without obedience there can be no life of holiness for the people.

One meaning of holiness is "wholeness." To be free from slavery and return to the Lord is to restore wholeness to life. Every corner of life needs to be continually examined and affirmed in the light of the call to wholeness. When this vocation is set to writing in the Hebrew way of thinking, it is no wonder that the song of Israel reaches our ears in a very concrete way, in what we might call fleshy terms (Exod 3:9; Lev 23; Deut 12:7). Just as it was the blood of Abel that cried out to God from the soil, so now the heart and flesh of this people cry out for the living God (Ps 84:3). Even the inner organs of the sacrificial animal are arranged in a special way and brought back in offering to the Lord of creation (Lev 1:8, 9, 13).

1:10-17 The sacrifice that goes up to the Lord. The three sacrifices of the bull (v. 5), the sheep or goat (v. 10), and the bird (v. 14) are described as holocausts (burnt offerings). The Hebrew verb simply means "to go up"; so the primary meaning of these offerings is to affirm the Lord as giver of the gift of life. The sacrifice is burnt up to the Lord. The smoke of the burning, along with the smoke of the sacred incense "going up" and covering up the smell of the slaughter, presents a sweet-smelling oblation to the Lord (Exod 30; Lev 1–8).

1:9, 13, 17 A sweet-smelling oblation. In Gen 8:21 the Lord smelled the sweet odor of Noah's offering and promised never again to doom the earth. In the Pentateuch God is spoken of in human terms, and for God to smell the sweet-smelling odor is like saying that God is pleased with the sacrifice. This idea of the "sweet odor" is often repeated in the Pentateuch: in Exod 29 the ram, the unleavened food, and the lamb become sweet-smelling oblations (see also Lev 1–8, 23, 26 and Num 15, 18, 28, 29). Also in the flood story of Mesopotamia "the gods are smelling the savor of the sacrifices." This show of approval was probably used in Canaanite cult and taken over by the Israelites from the time when it was believed that the gods received nourishment from the smelling or inhaling of the burning food. Even the accounts of cereal and peace offerings conclude in this same way, "a sweet-smelling oblation to the Lord" (Lev 2 and 3).

When the offering was wholly burned by the priest, a certain completeness, a holiness of the return of creation to the Lord, was expressed and experienced. It meant the same going-up or giving-up of self to God as a sweet-smelling oblation (1:4). Now the people had found a way to be wholly involved.

Note that usually the offerer performed the slaughter. The sprinkling, spilling, or splashing of the blood on the altar was reserved to the priests. The people brought the sacrificial victim to the entrance of the meeting tent where the whole community was included in the sacrifice action. There they were to accommodate and make holy the customs of the Canaanite people with whom they lived.

The Law given on Mount Sinai demanded complete obedience over the use of herd, flock, and grain (1–3). All creatures are included in "when any one of you." Even the poor, who otherwise might not be able to take part, can take from the turtledoves or pigeons plentiful in the area. Thus, Exod 19:6, "You shall be to me a kingdom of priests, a holy nation," could become a reality. By faithfully obeying these decrees, they would identify with the offerings and find favor as sweet-smelling oblations to the Lord.

Throughout Exodus, Leviticus, and Numbers, the Dwelling of the Lord is in the meeting tent. It is the place from which the call comes and it is the place of the sacrifice. In the offering the people and the priests are made holy by coming in contact with the presence of the Lord. The real and concrete thinking of the Hebrew mind speaks of the Lord calling from the meeting tent and of the people coming to the entrance of the tent in obedience (Lev 1:1-4). This action prepares for contact with holiness, and the sacrifice is not complete (holy) unless this condition is fulfilled (1:3; 3:8; 4:4).

2:11 Leaven or honey not to be burned. The offerings to be burned were already dead, but the action of yeast and the fermentation of the fruit syrup (included in the term honey) suggest something is still alive and, as such, could not be burned on the altar (2:11). In the Passover tradition (23) leaven was forbidden (Exod 12:15) and the people were to eat unleavened bread (*matzah*) for seven days (some say, in memory of the first seven days of the Exodus). One should also note that to carry unleavened bread is certainly a practical and secure way to keep wheat, barley, and oats when on a journey. It is also stated that they had to leave Egypt in a hurry and had no time for the leavening action (Exod 12:33, 34). To eat unleavened bread would be a reminder of the hurried departure. This custom was kept in the feast of Unleavened Bread (Exod 12:17).

This latter feast was joined with the Passover feast, wherein a lamb was sacrificed and the blood was put on the doorposts as a sign for the Lord to pass over these houses. People on the move need to take along something to eat. Thus, both feasts came together quite naturally. Today, however, just the bread celebration remains. The Passover victim for the Jew is remembered only in the shankbone of the lamb and the order (*seder*) of the celebration. Both memorials are fused into one, called the Passover Seder (Lev 23). Within the Code of Holiness of the Book of Leviticus, these pilgrim feasts have their own particular emphasis.

We have cautioned not to read into the text more than can be seen at present. We should not, however, overlook a call to holiness that is conveyed by the sacred writer. To err in either regard would do an injustice to the living Word of God. So, in the Hebrew way of thinking, everything had to be brought to the Lord. Every slaughter, even killing for food, needed to be holy. It had to be in some way interpreted as a sacrifice, a making holy, since the blood shed had to return to the source of its life, the Creator. Life is in the blood (17:14; 19:26). For the people of God and those with whom they lived or who lived with them, every mark of living had to fall into the circle of the Holy (Exod 23).

This people struggled to respond to their call to holiness (wholeness). Such a struggle is the drive and desire of life itself to which the desire to survive is related. The duty now was to cooperate in a covenant with the Holy One present in their midst (Exod 19) and to bring about a certain completeness to their life and language (Exod 23). A covenant arrangement necessarily includes the condition of obedience for the one party and a recounting for the other of the blessings and curses that will follow upon obedience or disobedience to the covenant (Lev 26).

2:13 The salt of the covenant. Salt was a symbol of the lasting covenant, since salt kept food from spoiling. In ancient times partaking of salt together was a sign of friendship and alliance. There may also be a Hebrew wordplay on the word for salt which is related to the word for king. It is to God and God alone that the first obedience belongs, and this is the meaning of covenant obedience.

3:3, 16 "All the fat belongs to the Lord." References to food for the Lord may be for the Israelites honest attempts to gather in the practices of their neighbors and to return everything, including health, property, and the general well-being of the whole community, to the one, holy Lord.

There is a sharing of food (2:10; 3:9-11, 14-16), and thus, the custom of eating with the gods is now included (accommodated, sanctified) in the expression of the relation between the one God and the people, brought on by the covenant obedience. Even today we cement relationships by inviting one to share in a meal. Here is an outward expression in the act of obedience. In Hebrew belief and practice the presence of a neighbor affirmed the presence of God in their midst.

Burning the fat on the altar may have played a role in determining that the fatty portion belongs to the Lord. On hot fire grease will flare up and produce a cloud of smoke, perhaps reminiscent of the column of fire during the night and the column of cloud during the day (Exod 13). The Hebrews may have taken this graphic reminder as divine indication that this part of the victim belonged to the Lord.

Thus the fatty portion on the altar would cause great excitement. In the cloud (Exod 13:21; 16:10; 19:9; 24:16; 40:34; Lev 16:2, 13; Num 12:5) and in the column of fire (Exod 13:21, 22; 40:38), the Lord revealed the divine presence. God came to speak to Moses and through him to the people. (See Matt 17:5; Acts 1:9; 2 Pet 1:17; Rev 14:14—in these New Testament references and in the Old Testament references cited above, both the Hebrew and the Greek words for cloud and splendor are wrapped up in the idea of appearance-revelation.)

A concluding comment to chapters 1, 2, 3. The orderly arrangement of the material in these first three chapters may have also served as a memory aid, the key words being holocaust, cereal, and peace. The order has a certain holiness (completeness) in presenting the account of the sacrifices.

Chapters 4 and 5 exhibit an order that revolves not so much around the object of the sacrifice as around the disposition of the offerer. Sin and guilt are the subject matter, along with atonement for sin committed out of ignorance (4:1-35), out of omission (5:1-13), or by commission (5:14-26). These situations seem to cover the possible dispositions of the sinner and the offerings that are needed to atone for the situations in the covenant relationship.

Chapters 4 and 5, sin and guilt offerings. In chapters 1, 2, and 3, sacrifices were brought out of obedience (because of the covenant), but willingly. In chapters 4 and 5 offerings of obligation are treated for those who are guilty of either unintentional (4:1-31) or intentional (5:1, 21-26) sins. In this covenant relation, since every action is in a relationship with God, every action is also related with everyone else involved in the same covenant. God is the source of life and the covenant is in a sense the return to life (Gen 2:7 and 6:17, 18). (The material is also summarized in Num 15:22-31.) The first person considered here is the priest who sins. The people are thereby also made guilty (Lev 4:3). Just as the priest offers on behalf of and along with the people, so the community is affected by other actions of the priest's life.

4:2 Inadvertent sin. All cases of ritual uncleanness which are unavoidable (for example, burying the dead) are included here. Note in Lev 4:1-12 that in the purification rite for a priest, the whole victim is disposed of outside the camp. Not even the hide is kept, to be given to the priest, as was the usual case (7:8). Now even the sanctuary is unclean, since the one who would usually receive the impurity of the people is himself unclean. There are other cases of inadvertent sin that affect the whole community (see Num 15:26, 27).

4:5-7 The blood rite. The angel of death passed over the houses on whose doorposts the blood of the Passover lamb was smeared (Exod 12:23). Here and in Lev 14:7 the blood is sprinkled before the Lord seven times. Some of the blood is put on the horns of the altar (Exod 29:12; Lev 8:15; 9:9). The sprinkling is a reminder of the blood of the covenant and its renewal (Exod 24:8). The smearing on the horns would remind one of every blood smearing: on the tent post in the field camp, the doorposts in the city, and on the altar at the foot of Mount Sinai. The basic idea was to ward off death and be attached to the source of life. In this case the intention is to be freed from the slavery of uncleanness, which divides the membership of the covenant, and to be restored as a full member of the human-divine community. The life that is in the blood is now returned to the Lord by actual contact with the altar. By this returning of life to the source of life, the individual, and thus the community, regains purity and the freedom to live again.

The whole community is affected by the impurity, even though it was committed by an individual. The reference to inadvertence is the attempt to cover every possible situation.

4:6 The blood is sprinkled seven times. Here and elsewhere (4:17; 14:7, 16, 27; 16:19; Num 19:4) the blood is sprinkled seven times. The number seven in ancient times was a sign of wholeness and completeness (holiness). Seven admits of a grouping of one flanked by two groups of three. Note the design of the menorah lampstand: a single center stem with two groups of three stems flanking the center. The menorah is the symbol of the perfect (holy) life. Many other examples could be cited in the use of seven as a sacred number. A primary example is the holy work of creation. God created the world in six days and then blessed the seventh day and made it holy (Gen 2:3). In Exod 31:15, the seventh day is a day of complete rest, sacred to the Lord.

5:1-26 Special cases. Here we sense the editors' insistence to include every possible situation of guilt and punishment, in reference not only to those asked to testify about a particular case but even to those who know anything at all about another's sin (impurity), but refuse to testify. These latter also have a community responsibility to speak up. Note that the Hebrew word for guilt contains not only the conscious aspect of guilt from acting contrary to law (Torah) or the omission of a particular regulation but even self-accusation and the acceptance of the penalty.

6:1-7:38 Answers to questions. Chapters 6 and 7 provide regulations that seemed to have developed from questions that came up while carrying out the basic ritual described in the first five chapters. For example, Where should this be done? What is the priest to wear? How should ashes be disposed of? What if the animal were wild and/or killed by a wild animal? As these questions were answered, they formed other regulations which eventually found their way into the Book of Leviticus. Additional regulations do not seem in any way to disturb the simple order of the first chapters. Note, however, the order that is preserved here. Chapter 6 deals with the material of chapters 1, 2, and 3 while chapter 7 gives some additions for chapters 4 and 5.

But we must stress that everyone and everything must be included in the covenant. Nothing can be omitted in the gathering-in of even the slightest ritual regulations; every possible life-situation must be ordered as construction material for purity and the eventual life of holiness.

In chapter 7 we first meet the punishment of being "cut off from the people" (7:20, 21, 25, 27; 17:4, 9, 10, 14; 18:29; 19:8; 20:3, 5, 17, 18 and on into the Book of Numbers). Lev 17:10 and 20:6 make it clear that God, rather than the priest or people, will measure out this punishment. Some commentators interpret this penalty to be a premature death. It seems that this penalty is simply a statement of fact of what happens when one party violates the covenant. The Hebrew phrase for making a covenant is "to cut a covenant." So, in the violation of a covenant, one cuts oneself off from the other. Besides the Hebrew wordplay, there is a good scare tactic in stating a fact. In eating the blood (17:10) and the wanton ways of the mediums (some may have been involved in neighboring blood rites, *see* 20:6), it would follow that this punishment would come from God, since the life is in the blood and God is the source of life. God would then be the immediate source of the punishment for the direct violation of life.

To avoid being cut off, in whatever way it could happen, is of special concern, for being excommunicated would not reflect the presence of the Holy One in the midst of the people. Later, in chapter 20, we see the necessity of preserving the unity of the family and a proper order to the whole of one's life in order to preserve the community as a unit. In the community, the oneness of God is reflected. Therefore, one must avoid ever being cut off. In fact, everything concerning one's own life (and thus the community's life) must in some way move in relation to the Holy One. Belief is practice.

The order of belief and practice is obedience (chs. 1–27), then purification through ritual (chs. 11–27) and finally, sanctification (chs. 17–27). It seems as simple as the example of one who takes a prescription, finds healing, and then enjoys good health. The secret is in the "order" of making holy. And one experience does not end where the other begins. Obedience is at work in purity, both obedience and purity are at work in sanctification, and all three are fully alive in the life of holiness. However, if we concentrate on just one or try to escape from one into another, we find our life to be only an endless request of obedience. This could explain why the Book of Leviticus is often neglected or even avoided (*see also* Introduction, no. 5, p. 116).

The overall arrangement in the book is very simple, but it is possible for the reader to become entangled in the many regulations and traditions. We need only witness the volumes upon volumes of legal transactions in our own court system with their varying decisions and changing regulations. Add to this the ease that oral traditions have of growing and changing of themselves. Then, even a long period of time may elapse before the oral traditions are written down. Finally we need to consider the time lapse of gathering the materials and the countless things that can happen between the gathering and the final editing. In the Book of Leviticus, the final editing seems to point to the very simple progression for living the life of holiness—obedience, purity, holiness.

PART II: CEREMONY OF ORDINATION

Lev 8–10

Chapters 8, 9, and 10 are a fitting place to introduce the dedication of the tabernacle and the ordination of the priest into the arrangement of the material for the Book of Leviticus. P, the Priestly writing, will continue later with the regulations for purity (chs. 11–16) and regulations for holiness (chs. 17–27). Even though the ordination ceremony and the dedication of the tabernacle have already been explained in Exod 29, they are introduced again to keep the proper order of the holiness theme.

At the same time, we can almost hear the rhythmic beat and repetition of the life flow of the people: the arrival at and covenant on Sinai (Exod 19–24); the revelation of God (Exod 19); the tabernacle construction and ceremony (Exod 25–28); the consecration of priests and altar (Exod 29); the sabbath law (Exod 31); the sin (Exod 32); Moses the mediator (Exod 33); the renewal of the covenant (Exod 34) and the giving of the sabbath law, with regulations for the construction of the tabernacle (Exod 35–40); the ceremony (Lev

1-7); the ordination of priests (Lev 8–10); the cleansing of the sanctuary, priests, and people (Lev 11–16); a new covenant life (Lev 17–27); and the revelation of God. This rhythmic beat is not just a meaningless repetition. Each time the statement of life is given in the heartbeat of the people.

Signs of life, maturing, and new insights are evident. The placing of chapters 1–7 where they are points out the necessity of obedience to the ritual of sacrifice. This ritual expresses both the desire for holiness and the conditioning element for purification. All this is antecedent to the life and practice of holiness (chs. 17–26).

8:1-36 The ordination ceremony. Moses is the mediator even of the priesthood (vv. 1-4). A more detailed description of the vestments and ceremonies has already been given in Exod 28–29. In keeping with the theme of Leviticus, the *order* to be followed in the ordination ceremony (vv. 5-33) is affirmed. Stress is put upon atonement for the altar and for the ones being ordained (vv. 15, 34), identifying them with the victim of sacrifice (vv. 22-31), rather than stressing their appointment by God through Moses (v. 35).

9:1-7 The octave (eighth day) sacrifice. The sacrifice completes the consecration of the priest. It consists of a combination of a calf-sin offering, a ram-holocaust (on the part of a high priest), and a he-goat sin offering. A calf and lamb for a holocaust, and an ox and ram for a peace offering, along with a cereal offering mixed with oil, are also offered on the eighth day. What a tremendous celebration that includes virtually all the sacrifices at which the priest later assists. The celebration is magnificent, for on that day, the "glory of the Lord was revealed to all the people" (v. 23; *see also* vv. 4, 6).

The writer or writers seem to convey two essential marks of the priesthood. First, as for the intercessory duty of the priest, every sacrifice needed to be brought forth to stand before the Lord. The priests were to intercede regarding decisions already made and ones for which understanding was needed. This is what making holy was all about—to be present to the presence of the Lord (9:5). The priest is to "keep in touch" with the Lord. The community had to present itself at the entrance of the tent and then come to the altar in the person of the priest (v. 7). The divine power could then be at work in the midst of the people, through the priest in touch with the presence of God. The second essential which the writers seem to be intent on was Moses as the mediator. He was the prophet to Pharaoh. He acted as the king in leading the people out of Egypt. He is now the high priest in the sacrifice and the ordination of those who will assist in sacrifice.

10:1-5 Death of Nadab and Abihu. Some have suggested that Aaron's sons Nadab and Abihu had filled their containers with fire that was not holy, that is, taken from a place other than the altar. Others say that their incense was not the clean mixture it should have been. Thus, they were punished with death by fire, a holy fire from the altar. Lightning could have struck them dead. Since they were at the altar at the time, the people would certainly interpret any happening as coming from the Lord.

10:9-10 Ability to distinguish. Whatever happened, the main point is brought out in verses 9 and 10, where Moses says that no wine or strong drink is to be taken before priestly duty at the meeting tent. "You must be able to distinguish between the sacred and profane." So, in the seven-day celebration, it could be that Aaron and his sons might have imbibed too much wine. Even though Nadab and Abihu could have been struck by lightning, it is possible that they put the wrong mixture on the fire, resulting in a flare-up and consequent asphyxiation (since verse 5 says they were buried in their tunics).

In view of other references in Exod 24 and Num 3, and aside from the Moses injunction to avoid on-the-job drinking of wine or other strong drink (10:9), we would do well to look further. The moment is very sacred: "Through those who approach me I will manifest my sacredness; in the sight of all the people, I will reveal my glory" (10:3). Abihu ("He is my father") and Nadab ("Na is generous") might also represent an earlier priesthood now replaced by the Aaronic and Levitical priesthood. The incident, then, is used here to introduce, in a literary but nonetheless real way, the new order (or at least the demise of the old). It is now through Aaron and his sons that both the new and the old are represented at the ordination ceremony (10:3). Other sacrifices of fire are forbidden. Recall in chapter 9, after the seven-day ordination ceremony, that on the eighth day the people saw the glory of the Lord coming forth in the form of fire from the Lord's presence. If lightning occurred, it would have given occasion for an explanation.

10:11 The priests are to teach the Torah. There is an interesting and added responsibility for the priest in regard to preparation for and maturing in holiness. He is to be a teacher of the Torah, "all the laws that the Lord has given through Moses" (v. 11—once again, an insistence on Moses as the mediator). The Hebrew word means both "to teach," and "to direct." The priest is to learn the proper direction (order) and then teach others. In English we have the fuller meaning in basically the same word, which now has the meaning of "disciple" and "discipline."

PART III: LAWS REGARDING LEGAL PURITY

Lev 11–16

The insertion here of the chapters on the priesthood is natural. Otherwise, obedience might be practiced for obedience's sake. Obedience has now become a response to the covenant relation through the mediation of the priesthood and continues to be alive in the purification-preparation (chs. 11–16) for holiness (chs. 17–27).

Now legal purity (chs. 11–15) will be explained and emphasized as a condition, along with obedience, for legal holiness that comes later (chs. 17–27). (Chapter 16 is a bridge-chapter for chapters 11–15 and 17–27.)

Recalling what has been said about Hebrew thought patterns, we can respect these regulations as alive, not simply as directions for life. They all point to and are part of the life of holiness or completeness—to be fully alive is to respect the power of the Creator of life. It seems that the final editors laid a very simple pathway to holiness. They realized that now was the time, in the whole body of the Torah, to mention this Levitical regulation. Without it, the Torah would be without a heart and its beat. The beat should be an evident sign of the presence of the Holy and the expression of the fullness of life, the Code of Holiness in 17–26 (chapter 27 is another bridge-chapter). Since the Book of Leviticus is the heart of the Torah, we refer to the Code of Holiness as the beat of that heart.

For those who are to become holy, the Lord says, "Speak to the whole Israelite community and tell them, 'Be holy, for I, the Lord, your God, am holy' " (Lev 20:7; Exod 31:13; and Lev 11:44). Obedience comes first (chs. 1–7); then the Lord manifests his glory to the people through the holy priesthood-group of the community (chs. 8–10). But before one can experience holiness, one must be clean (pure) (chs. 11–16). And since "cleanliness is next to Godliness," so purity which results from obedience to the law comes next to holiness. This is the material treated next on the way to holiness. Obedience, purity, and holiness cannot be separated any more than can body, blood, and soul. (In Hebrew thinking, these latter three are included in the one word "being.") It is important to consider this way of thinking if we are to understand the way the Levitical material conveys the meaning of holiness. Obedience is included in the understanding and experience of purity. The regulations now become more exacting. Purity conditions one for the Code of Holiness.

Since purity can come only from God, the presence of God must be in the midst of the people, above the ark (16:2). This is the place of atonement in which is contained the forgiveness and reconciliation which result in purity.

Chapters 11–16 tell how the condition of purity is established. The materials brought together in these regulations present a fit (pure) receptacle, "for-giving" of holiness. This last sentence contains the ideas of forgiveness and the condition needed for holiness. It is one thing to be forgiven, but it is another to live a life of holiness. The state of purity resulting from the forgiveness of God is the receptacle for the life of holiness; it is not the state of holiness. This is why, once a year, even to this day, atonement is made for all the sins on the feast of Yom Kippur, the Day of Atonement.

This explains the placement of the Code of Holiness (chs. 17–27) in the Book of Leviticus; there is an orderly progression to the fullness of life, the life of holiness (19:1-7). It also explains the placement of the bridge-chapter 16 with the Day of Atonement, the ongoing condition for the life of holiness. Later we will see how chapter 27 also becomes a bridge-chapter, following the presentation of the material on holiness.

Chapters 11–16 concern the clean and the unclean. Chapters 11 and 12 consider what is taken internally: clean and unclean food and the uncleanness of childbirth resulting in loss of blood (the seed was taken internally). What shows up externally on the skin or garments is the subject of chapters 13 and 14. Chapter 15 deals with what flows from within a person. The well-known chapter 16, giving the account of the Day of Atonement, is the important bridge-chapter connecting the clean (pure) and the holy.

11:1-23 Clean and unclean food: the dietary laws. Animals that may and may not be eaten are listed here: those of the land (vv. 1-8), of the sea (vv. 9-12), and of the air (vv. 13-19), and finally, those found in all three areas—insects and swarming creatures (vv. 20-23).

The dead bodies of the unclean must not be touched or else one becomes unclean (vv. 24-32). For the most part these regulations are repeated in Deut 14:3-20. Both in Leviticus and Deuteronomy the people are warned to make themselves holy and to keep themselves holy by simply avoiding certain foods (Lev 11 and Deut 14:3-21). However, a straightforward reason why certain foods cause uncleanness or defilement is not known. Simple obedience seems to be a good reason in view of Gen 2:16 wherein God initially said, "You are free to eat . . . except . . . ." Even today, there are certain foods permitted by Jewish dietary regulation, called *kosher*, which means "proper" to eat.

Sometimes assumptions are made concerning Israelite relationship with the cult practice of their neighbors. Even though some literary references have emerged, we need to be cautious and apply studied research for further evidence of real life associations. There seems to have been a common cult language used in the Near East. From this base every tribe or nation took what would best express their relationship with the presence of the Holy in the whole of creation (*see also* Introduction, 7. D).

The simple and clear thrust of this material in Leviticus seems to be that everyone and everything must be brought into the order and dominion of the one, holy God. The whole of creation had already been joined to God's order and dominion in the creation stories of Genesis; now the worship-life of the people is directed to that God. The Tabernacle had just been erected (Exod 40), and now the time had come for the "Levitical material" to go through the Holy Place in preparation for entry into the Holy of Holies. The experience of the divine-human relationship could be lived out even in the written record of this people. As St. Jerome remarked, "There is an odor of holiness about the book of Leviticus."

11:36 A spring or cistern remains pure. The purity of water was necessary, not only because drinking water was scarce but also because this water had not yet been drawn out by human hands. The water is holy because its present source is the ground (spring) or heaven (rain in the cistern).

12:1-8 Uncleanness of childbirth. The reason for this defilement is found in verse 7: "Thus, she will be clean again after her flow of blood." It is the flow of blood that defiles. (The life is in the blood and because the flow is recurrent, proper control cannot be maintained. Lev 15:32-33 mentions that men and women are treated alike.) They could only come to the entrance of the tent or, in another time, they were barred from the temple mound.

Today there is still a great deal of mystery and pain connected with menstruation and childbirth. We have unraveled some of the mystery, but the pain remains (Gen 3:16). At that time fear and taboo also played a part in the experience. The afterbirth might tend to make one think that some kind of punishment was being put upon a person. And, of course, there were the stories and taboos of neighbors. The rate of miscarriage may also have been high. This would accentuate the need to explain the disorder and call for a regulation concerning defilement and the need for purification.

The offering is made only after the flow stops (Lev 15:13-14, 28-29), so there is no question of practicing magic—a ritual performed in order to bring about some change.

12:2, 5 The doubling of purification time for females. This may have something to do with menstrual flow. Remember, the life is in the blood and every precaution must be taken to recognize God as the source of life.

13:4 Seven-day quarantine. This is probably a practical precaution in the case of skin disorder. Any change in the skin should take place by then so that the priest can decide about the purity of the person. The waiting is made holy by choosing seven days.

13:46 Living outside the camp. In some cases this means living alone. To live outside the camp came to be expressed as "outside the walls of the city," or sometimes in the case of temple regulations, "outside the temple mound," or in the wilderness, "outside the tabernacle community." One could come only to the entrance of the tent, as seen in chapters 12 and 15.

In view of the extensive treatment of skin disease in chapters 13 and 14, it seems that at the time there may have been an epidemic of unknown skin disorders. We do know without a doubt the importance of the blood as containing the life of every living body (17:11, 14). Today, the importance of a blood analysis is well-known as an indication of a person's general health. Likewise in Leviticus the slightest discoloration or bruise would need to be analyzed so that proper care would be taken to affirm the power of God in any flow of blood.

If we cut a finger, we know how easy it is to bring it to our mouth. The Hebrew word in the prohibition is "not to eat" (Lev 7:26; 17:10). Even though the prohibition may have had reference to some practice in the rituals of other peoples, its primary meaning should be considered as respect for life in recognition of the creator of life.

14:3 The priest goes outside the camp. The unclean person is not a part of the living community, but the priest can go to that person. However, to avoid defilement of the community, the priest must go outside to make his analysis. "Leprosy" here stands for any number of skin disorders.

14:4 The rite of purification. A vessel of fresh water is perhaps drawn from a spring or cistern by dipping clean pottery into the water. Fresh water is taken because the cleansing was outside the camp and its pure community. The blood from the one slain bird drips into the fresh water and receives proper care by contact with the water. The water can then be poured onto the ground and the vessel cleansed. The cedar wood (type used in the construction of the temple roof), scarlet yarn (blood color), and hyssop make a sprinkler. The hyssop is probably tied onto the cedar wood with the yarn. Everything is touched with the blood of the clean bird, for the life is in the blood. One of the birds stands for Israel (the afflicted person) about to reenter into the covenant relationship. The bird mediates the purification, since much of its life is spent flying between heaven and earth.

14:7 Purification through sevenfold sprinkling. Some references to sprinkling of the blood are found in Exod 12:22; 24:8; 29:21; Lev 4:6; 5:9, and reminds one of the Sinai Covenant. In fact, in Exod 24 the blood that is sprinkled on the altar and the people is called "the blood of the covenant." So now, at the renewal of the covenant, the blood is sprinkled. It is also a reminder of the Passover blood which freed the people from slavery. The slavery now is the skin disease, holding a person captive outside the camp.

In the ancient world, seven was a sacred number and considered a complete (holy) number. There were seven planets (five plus the sun and the moon) that had movement of their own among the fixed stars. Seven is one flanked by two groups of three; three was also a perfect number since it has a beginning, a middle, and an end (1-1-1). The sprinkling towards the Lord must be perfect, complete, holy; the sprinkling in atonement for the afflicted must also be complete (holy), since the skin infection is hardly ever in just one spot but in a number of different areas on the body. The purification must extend to the entire body of the leper; leaving one spot untouched would make the person unclean and further purification would be needed.

14:7 The second bird is set free. The bird is like the scapegoat, taking the leprosy away to a place of no return. Note the important ritual directive: one shall let the living bird fly away. First, the priest sprinkles the afflicted one. Then, as the purification takes place, one is handed the other bird. The purified one releases the (scape)bird. Thus the purification is completed. One can imagine the person feeling a real cleansing receiving the remaining bird from the priest and then releasing the infection along with the bird (a real carrier pigeon!) in the direction of the atoning God. Covenant life, wholeness, is restored for the individual with God and community. There is no question of magic, since the person is already healed when the rite of purification is performed (14:3). A parallel is the present-day rite of reconciliation, which deals with the leprosy of sin. The penitent approaches the rite of reconciliation, even though the sin is forgiven by an act of contrition. The priest mediates the sacramental (holy moment-um) ritual that affirms the forgiving and healing power of God present in the community and reconciles the person to the covenant-community relationship.

14:8 The one purified remains outside. One is inside the camp now, but outside the tent. This could mean outside the tabernacle or temple, since it was only on the eighth day that one was allowed to bring sacrifice into the temple.

14:9 The afflicted shaves again on the seventh day. The root ends of the hair have grown out and the ends of the defilement are cut off. The hair is cleansed and again washed. The reason may be more practical than symbolic, since by then a good decision can be made about the disorder.

14:10 The eighth-day offering. The ritual takes place in the temple. The ephah was about half a bushel, and a log was about two-thirds of a pint. The only type of offering not mentioned is the peace offering, since peace offerings were usually voluntary. The guilt offering would be required (see 5:14-26). Also, the one cleansed may have had to bring the guilt offering to make up for the absenteeism from temple ritual during the time of being cut off.

14:12-13 The wave offering. This action might better be described as a "lifting up" rather than a wave offering. Perhaps this is the lifting up of one's hands in the manner of the priest today at the offering of the bread and wine. It could refer to praying with hands lifted up. In any case the Hebrew word is related to the English "height." Verse 13 refers to the guilt offering as "most sacred," since the wholeness of every member of the covenant is affirmed.

14:14 Blood put on the tip of one's ear, thumb, and big toe. The ancients believed that access to one's life by spirits was made through these extremities—as in the case of unclean (5:2) or sacred (6:11). Blood was used to cleanse and to ward off the unclean or evil. Later we shall see the anointing over the blood with oil. This anointing would seemingly prepare for the purification and entrance of the good spirit. Today, during baptism, the tip of the ear and the mouth are touched in preparation for receiving and speaking the word of God.

In the ordination rite of the priest, the blood of the ordination ram is splashed on the altar (Exod 29:19-25 and Lev 8–9). The priest is consecrated to the Lord. The altar splashing is not mentioned here, since it is the guilt offering of lamb's blood that is sprinkled seven times before the Lord. A change in the direction of the ritual action, or the omission of a particular rite where one might expect it to be repeated, may indicate a meaning of the present ritual. Thus, every area of life can be covered with positive regulation. However, the precision of the Levitical regulation seems to make some readers shy away from these Torah instructions. But to others this precision offers an exciting treasure hunt.

14:17 Oil over the blood of the guilt offering. Putting the oil over the blood signifies the complete return to covenant life. The oil represents God at work in the individual and community life of the people. God gives life to the blood relationship. For a priest needing such purification, this ritual acts as a mini-reconsecration rite (see also 8:10). The covenant is renewed and all are ready for the life of holiness with its enduring and maturing obedience, purification, and holy conduct.

14:21 A poor leper's sacrifice. The reduced requirement of turtledoves rather than lambs makes the purification ritual easier on the poor. The emphasis is on the recognition of the covenant, not on the requirement of the offering. However, the requirement of the guilt offering seems to have remained the same for all, since the affirmation of both God and neighbor is involved. The same requirement for everyone openly expresses this involvement, even though the guilty party acted unwillingly or inadvertently (5:14-26).

14:33-57 Cleansing the houses. Like the individual in need of cleansing and purification, so the dwelling place of the individual. Recall that even the dwelling place of the Lord was in need of purification from time to time. On the Day of Atonement there was purification of every possible defilement that could have occurred throughout the previous year (16:16-19).

14:37 "Infection on the walls . . ." This seems to be mold and rust, but in view of verse 34 and in the opinion of some rabbis, it was considered a defilement sent in punishment for one's lack of faith. Mold and rust assured that some type of life must be present. Therefore, a regulation had to ensure proper recognition of the source of life and respect for the life itself.

Some types of defilement are unavoidable or accidental, and some occur even in the normal course of events (recurrent body flows and sickness). Some can happen while performing commendable acts (Lev 16:21-28; Num 19:7, 8, 10). The rabbis call these "defilements of the body."

The rabbis thought that sin occurs when the unclean and the holy, or the clean and the profane, are brought together in a spirit of disobedience—for example, the entry into the Holy Place by one forbidden to do so or eating clean food while one is in an unclean state. Obedience is still the key in a covenant relationship. God is the only one who can say, "I am the Lord."

Obedience is the key to purification and holiness. It may seem that the Book of Leviticus speaks only of *ritual* obedience, but the Code of Holiness points to the necessity of obedience in the *whole* of life. Lev 1–7 concern obedience. Chapters 11–15 express the purification that results from obedience. Then, and only then, will one begin to live a holy life.

15:13 One is to bathe in fresh water. Cleanliness contains a twofold idea: first, to be healed of a disease or purified from uncleanness (see 14:48, 49), and second, washed (in some cases, bathing in a stream or freshwater lake, or whatever assigned regulation) to establish the purification. The process is a mini-freedom from Egypt leading into the Promised Land.

16:1-34 The Day of Atonement. This chapter has a unique place in Leviticus because it acts as a bridge connecting the rite of purification and the life of holiness (chs. 17–26). It is the Lord who initiates the atonement. The Lord does this by demanding the purification of the Holy of Holies, which has been defiled by the deaths of Nadab and Abihu.

Then the rite of sanctuary purification is joined with the confession and removal of the sins of both priests and people (16:33). This latter purification takes place in what is called the scapegoat ritual. This joint celebration, along with the mortification of fasting (vv. 29-31), begins the life of holiness. On the Day of Atonement, the sanctuary and the nation celebrate the atonement feast.

16:1 Purification after the death of Nadab and Abihu. This is the place to refer again to chapter 10, since it sets the stage for sanctuary purification. Here is a known defilement of the sanctuary. Their corpses made the Holy of Holies unclean and in need of purification. Perhaps they had gotten too close to the propitiatory (seat of mercy) on the ark. There were certain regulations for making a proper entry into the Holy of Holies. Note how the first span of the bridge to holiness is constructed from some leftover material of chapters 11–15 and reaching back into chapter 10. This first span is set in place. God and nation are ready to obey the order of purification.

16:2-5 The propitiatory on the ark. This is the mercy seat of the Lord. The place of at-one-ment must be at the mercy seat of the Lord. It is the cover over the ark containing the Ten Commandments. The cleansing of the sanctuary with its consequent purification is now able to take place here. In Hebrew the very word for *cover* is related to the word for *atonement*. It means that the guilt is covered over or that atonement is payment for being reinstated.

16:3-21 The rite of purification. The gold and white vestments are interchanged, signifying the presence of God and the people at work together. Mutually they take part in the atonement action that removes all the defilement of the past year, even that which may have happened inadvertently. Together in the life of holiness a new year is begun for God and people (chs. 17–27).

So, this atonement chapter acts as the bridge where the two members of the covenant (God and the people) come together to celebrate the at-one-ness to be experienced in the Code of Holiness.

16:20-28 The scapegoat ritual: means of atonement. There are actually two goats and a ram for a holocaust. One goat is offered as a sin offering. By the laying on of hands, the other receives the sins of the community and is sent to carry them off to a place of no return. Azazel (perhaps "power of El") seems to be a wordplay on the subduing of a foreign god (demon).

One goat represents the action of the purification of the sanctuary (v. 20). The other represents the atonement of the people in what has come to be known as a scapegoat ritual. The goat is driven into the desert, the place of no return and also the place of "just desert." This latter wordplay on desert alters the entire meaning of the word.

With the additional span of removal and punishment complete, the bridge-chapter furthers its construction towards covenant renewal.

During the ritual Aaron changes from gold to white, back to gold, and to white again. Before and after each change there are ritual bathings. God and people are represented in the vestments. Ritual directs the priest to dress up in different costumes to portray different characters. The simple white lines were also a sign of humility and honest contrition flowing between the two members of the covenant. Actions like the vestment changing (16:4, 23, 24, 32) pave the way for the atonement that is in progress.

Today Yom Kippur or the Day of Atonement is celebrated with great faith in the at-one-ment of God and people. It is a very important day for the Jew who seeks reconciliation with other members of the community and then receives atonement from God (see also Matt 5:24). One of the readings of the Jewish atonement celebration today is Isa 57:14–58:14, which speaks of a real inner, moral renewal by fasting (Lev 16:29-31). Fasting is made genuine by going out to others, especially the poor and the unfortunate, and by concentrating on a change of life for all (vv. 29, 30). In Leviticus all are now ready for the change to a life of holiness.

PART IV: CODE OF LEGAL HOLINESS

Lev 17–26

This section in Leviticus emphasizes life more than ritual, but obedience to the command of God is still at work. The covenant arrangement is still to be preserved (17:2). God is to be recognized first (v. 4). If this is not carried out, one is to be cut off from those who wish to keep this life-covenant arrangement (v. 4). It is a whole new way of life (vv. 5-7). What is presented in the Code of Holiness (17–26) is for everyone (v. 8). We need to be in touch with regulations that have gone before, but we cannot forget the practice of obedience, and the bridge (Lev 16) must be kept intact (17:2, 4, 9). Obedience is still at work now, with emphasis on principle rather than regulation. It is this change that seems to encourage more people to read this section of Leviticus rather than chapters 1–16, which stress ritual obedience. Ritual conformity, practiced only for the sake of obedience, becomes a very heavy burden in time. However, obedience, along with purification, is required in order to be fully alive in the life of holiness. Now the obedience is to a life-style embodied in the Code of Holiness.

The difference between "sacrifice" and "sanctification" should be noted. Sacrifice is the "making holy" and sanctification can be the "living holy" of life. One's living-out of purification (chs. 11–16) through obedience (chs. 1–7) opens the way to sanctification (chs. 17–27).

We now come to the very beat of the heart in the Code of Holiness (chs. 17–27). "Be holy, for I, the Lord, your God, am holy." Even the flow of the accent in this English quotation of the central theme (19:2) has a pulsating rhythm.

These chapters offer directives for living a life of holiness. They were guidelines for the people of old as they are for the people of today.

We accept, then, the real life situation of our ancestors and rejoice in their liturgical activity, whatever the expression. We can imagine the closeness they had with life and death; their struggle with the animals being dragged to the entrance of the meeting tent or temple; the shame, exposure, inconvenience, and humiliation of being people who had to keep at a distance at a time when community care and support was so needed and who were obliged to call out, "Unclean, Unclean!" (13:45). What a variety of offertory processions to the Holy One! Then came the slaughter, with the spurting, sprinkling and smearing of blood, and the smell covered over by incense. Like a grand finale, the cloud suggested that the sounds of sin and death were then transformed into a chorus of praise of the presence of God in the midst of the people (26:11-13). One can almost hear the ram's horn (shofar) and the soothing sound of the lute that are now silent. There may be a certain "away from home" feeling in the hearts of all people today, but the holy message of Leviticus is alive and pulsating, in the expectation and excitement of the Holy One, the Messiah-Redeemer, who is to establish the everlasting dwelling place (Ps 43:3).

Here we are given laws, directives, morals, and morale that beat and pulsate to real life situations. Lev 26 will put the finishing touches on the covenant arrangement by detailing the rewards of obedience and the punishments of disobedience—specifics usually included in a covenant treaty. They were both an incentive and a scare tactic to assert the dominion of the king over the subject and to encourage the subject to follow the commands of the king.

Chapter 17. Scholars have discussed whether or not this chapter is a part of the Code of Holiness. Some think that chapter 17 acts as a bridge over all the material *preceding* the Code of Holiness, since there is mention of the offerings of Lev 1–3 as a prelude to Lev 18:5. There God is recognized as the source of the command to be fully alive.

The people were commanded to bring everything to the entrance of the meeting tent to be offered to the Lord (Lev 1:3, 2:2, 3:2, and corresponding to these commands are 17:4, 5, and 6). The priesthood (chs. 8–10) and purification (chs. 11–16) also parallel chapter 17. Because of these features, chapter 17 seems to assume a fitting role as the introduction to the Code of Holiness. The chapter could even have been an addition to the original little "Manual of Holiness." But we see more reason to accept chapter 17 as the original first chapter of the Manual of Holiness. The preceding chapters 1–16 could be expanded ideas, practices, and traditions of the original Code of Holiness.

In Lev 1–7 the emphasis was on obedience, simply because God commanded obedience. Chapter 17 gives reason why a person is to obey, and the command to obey assumes fuller import in the covenant relationship.

17:3, 8, 13, 15 The sacredness of blood. Everyone is commanded to recognize the source of life in the one, holy God. By respecting the life that is in the blood and acting out this respect through the ritual of putting the blood on the altar (17:11), the atonement (at-one-ment) of the people's lives is effected. The text says that the blood, as the seat of life, makes the atonement. This is interesting and understandable, since the presence of the Lord is believed to reside over the seat of mercy that covers the ark in the Holy of Holies. God, the source of life, is hidden in the blood, and the sin of the people is now hidden or covered by the atoning presence of God (16:13).

The Code of Holiness will be issued in chapter 18. It is an invitation to the human-divine marriage (18:5)—to partake of the fruit of the tree of life, to eat of it, and live forever the life of holiness. The final chapter of Leviticus will hint at the everlasting character of this life.

First, we have a final comment concerning the respect and use of blood. Many regulations concerning the blood were wrapped in the fate of the lifeblood of the bleeding animal. While Western thought tends to spiritualize life and reality (in the sense of constructing an ideal world) and to speak of death as disturbing proper order, for the biblical people everything was concrete. Blood was life, and the pouring out of blood was death, and death acted as a thief stealing life.

To be able to think as did the writers of Sacred Scriptures is crucial to understanding the Bible. The biblical people thought and expressed themselves in concrete terms. Since God chose to use this medium for the Divine Word to enter into the world, we need to be aware of this way of thinking.

For the Hebrew mind the Word of God was real, spoken as real as the greeting exchanged between neighbors ("The Lord spoke to Moses . . . , and from the meeting tent gave him this message . . ."). The life of the ancient Hebrews was lived in the presence of God. The language of Scripture reflects a people who thought, lived, and moved in a real world, and their God was very much a part of the real world. Their expression of what God had to say was also real. Truth, justice, and peace were not ideas, but living things. For the Hebrew, "Kindness and truth shall meet; justice and peace shall kiss. Truth shall spring out of the earth, and justice shall look down from heaven" (Ps 85:11-12).

Also, every slaughter of an animal, even if just for food, had to be a sacrifice (a making holy) or a sanctification (a living holy), since the animal victim enabled the offerer to continue living. God, the source of life, had to be recognized in some way. Thus when people were no longer in proximity to the altar, the first regulation of putting the blood on the altar was modified (Deut 12:24). It was to be poured out on the ground like water and could then return to the Lord.

17:13 The blood of the clean animal. In the case of a clean animal killed while hunting, the blood was to be buried. Similarly, a scribe who erred in copying the Sacred Scripture did not crumple the page and start over. Rather, he carefully extracted the infected portion of the scroll (as in a surgical procedure), encased it in a little casket, and buried it (as in a funeral). As the life is in the blood (v. 14), so the Spirit of Holiness is in the Holy Word.

Even though the putting of the blood on the altar was later modified in Deuteronomy and is not possible today (the temple was destroyed by the Romans in A.D. 70), the prohibition of eating blood has remained in Jewish practice to this day. The regulation could be changed only if God, the source of life, would invite people to eat the blood. So, the command would then be, "Eat my blood," which, in Hebrew thought would be, "Become one with my life."

18:1-30 The sanctity of sex. It follows from the affirmation of the source of life that any control over that life would need to follow the order (command) of the source of life. Covenant relation concerning life demands that the lesser partner (creature) takes direction (life and order) from the greater or source-partner (creator). Holiness in the control of life (sex) is to be found in the ordering which accords with God's plan. Not only does one have life (18:5) but one can also share in the control of life (18:3). This is the reason for the constant reminder that God is the source of life, "I am the Lord." The only authentic plan of living (Code of Holiness) is the plan of the "God who is" (Yahweh). Thus, the writer begins chapter 18 with the Lord saying to Moses, "Speak to the Israelites and tell them: I, the Lord, am your God" (v. 2). One can hear this beat of the heart of the Torah in 18:2-6, 21, 30; 19:2, 4, 10, 11, 13, 15, and elsewhere. Life is found by following God's plan (v. 5).

18:18 A bridge-verse. In the language of regulation the word sex stands for both male and female, even though each has a unique sharing in the control of the one life of God.

Verse 18 is a bridge-verse. It connects a list of incest prohibitions with a list of other "out-of-order" sexual relations. Lev 18:6-17 lists the disorderly acts of incest; then verse 18 says, "While your wife is still living, you shall not marry her sister as her rival; for thus you would disgrace your first wife." The second part of the verse refers to the disorder created in the life plan of God (in the Hebrew, Yah-God is mentioned as joined to the very life of the wife). This part also acts as a bridge to all the other disorders or immoral relations that are prohibited (vv. 19–23). The disorder implied in the first part of verse 18 results because a man already united to a woman violates the covenant arrangement, marries his sister-in-law, and creates a polygamous relationship. This disorder relates to incest and affects the community in which all, including the sister, should live the same holy life. The first part of the verse connects as a bridge to prohibitions of incest; the "disgrace" connects with other community disorders.

One should notice, for the sake of completeness, that the incest of father and daughter should not even have to be mentioned, but it is included in verse 6 and is accorded one of the pulsating phrases, "I am the Lord." In verse 22 the disorder is called an abomination, which in Hebrew means trying to make holy a union that cannot be completed in the real sense of the action. This is the reason why it is usually referred to as making a sacrifice to a strange god. The ordering of the source of life and the orderly plan of God within the covenant is cut off.

When the marriage invitation in chapter 18 is accepted by both parties of the covenant, the holy life takes on the renewed dimension of oneness along with completeness. To be at one in the Lord is the goal of the divine-human covenant.

In chapter 19 we need to be careful not to read into the text more or less than the writer or editors intended.

In chapters 17–26, the Code of Holiness (H), some material has vocabulary and unity of its own and is recognized by scholars as having a very early date. It, too, centers around the call of Israel to be holy. This Code may have been the core around which the final editors gathered other Priestly material. For these reasons this section is often referred to by the letter H. Ritual regulations are absent, and the text begins to talk in terms of principle and conduct. The tone is more ethical than ritual. The reader may feel more at home in this section of Leviticus. Here we have directives for living a holy life. Echoes of Genesis and Exodus commands are heard in the regulations of the Code of Holiness. For Adam and Eve in Gen 1:28, for Noah and family after the flood in Gen 8:17 and 9:7, and for all the people in Exod 20, "Eat and multiply," is the directive, "but do not divide by defilement for I, the Lord, am your God."

19:1-37 Various rules of conduct. The two basic rules of the divine-human relationship are found here—love of God and love of neighbor. That this twofold directive is alive and breathing today is witness enough to its enduring validity. Verses 2 and 18 give the commands "Be holy, for I, the Lord, your God, am holy" and "You shall love your neighbor as yourself."

In 20:1-8 and 20:9-21, the respective penalties are given for disobeying these commands. The remaining verses of chapter 20 spell out, in no uncertain terms, what will happen to the disobedient. In other words, ethically as well as ritually, the covenant relationship is still founded on obedience. This is a basic tenet of the covenant agreement and points to a proper order. Obedience to the order of covenant relations is the basis of accepting the rules of the life of holiness. The important question is not "Who's on first?" but "Who comes first?" Often we may think that holiness is achieved by giving up some part of life or by depriving one member of the covenant. However, to submit to the superior member of the covenant is the basic meaning of a covenant treaty.

The negative directives of chapter 18 were issued because at various times the people had taken direction contrary to the plan of holiness. Often, in assessing guilt, it is not the good or evil of the action that needs to be considered, but rather the order or manner of its performance. Examples abound in chapter 18. Intercourse is not forbidden in itself. What is forbidden are the disorderly situations that are contrary to the Code of Holiness and the life-giving power of the Creator.

What seems to be given as a penalty—the "vomiting of the people out of the land"—is simply a stated result of disorderly conduct similar to what happens in the case of a social stomach disorder. In chapter 26 we find that God, as the source of life, uses time itself to retrieve the divine order from the disorder caused by the human member of the covenant. This is an aspect of the everlasting covenant—God still gives us time to live and sustains us in life even when we choose to make fools of ourselves or even when we cut ourselves off from the covenant.

19:2 "Be holy, for I, the Lord, your God, am holy." This is the first rule of conduct in the life of holiness—to recognize God as the source of life. If we wish to live we must keep God's order. Holiness is of primary importance because God is first of all holy. In God, holiness (wholeness) and oneness are the same. We speak of the one, holy God. The secret to a full (holy) life is found in the Code of Holiness. The order is so simple that we are apt to overlook the meaning of command.

The order in God is perfect, since there is only one God. The oneness of God is a mystery, and in oneness there is no room for disorder. This monotheistic conception of life and the source of life in the world and in the history of the Israelite people is traced to the revelation to Moses in Exod 3:14: "I am who am." The divine drawing out of one leader (Moses) and one people (Israel) reflects a new monotheistic way of thinking. God is drawing out of the people the life of God present in their midst, in their very living. As the people were held in slavery, so the life of God in the people was held captive. The command to be holy completes the circle by drawing out and returning life to the source of life. "I am who am" is God's way of saying "I am the source of life."

Order is heaven's first law. The proper order comes first. The "One" comes first. God is the only One who can say "I am who am." So God comes first and the Book of Leviticus records the proper order. To be holy because God is holy is to accept God as the source of life.

In Lev 19:3 the next command in order is reverence for parents, since through them we come into covenant contact with God, the source of life. This is why reverence for parents and keeping the sabbath are joined together in the text. Filial reverence recognizes parents as the contact point with the reality of life and the Creator of the whole of life.

Both parents and sabbath are joined for another reason. God rested on the seventh day and made it holy (Gen 2:3). The sabbath is, then, a holy day for the whole family. Celebration of the prime source of life will, in proper order, include the secondary source (parents). The order cannot be reversed. There is a proper order to living the Lord's day. The regulation of the sabbath is, in its final analysis, the regulation of the tithe, which puts God first. The portion, one day in seven (the holy unity), is the tithe commanded by God (Lev 27:30).

19:4 "Do not turn aside to idols or make molten gods for yourselves." Note that the making of images is not forbidden, but to turn to molten gods or images used as objects of worship is forbidden. In fact, it is the Spirit of God who continues to move today in the creative talent of artists who try, in a particular ordering of creation, to express the image and likeness of God as the source of all life. In the Hebrew rendering of this rule of conduct (v. 4), there is a wordplay on "El," the name of the god of neighboring people (18:3). The same root word is used to express "dumb idols."

19:5-8 An acceptable peace offering. Peace is the tranquility of order. If order is kept, peace results. The peace offering should be eaten on the day it is offered or on the next day, but not on the third day for then it becomes refuse (unclean). One living the life of holiness profanes oneself by eating the three-day-old offering. The obvious reason, besides spoilage, is that order is not followed. It was directed that on the third day the remaining part was to be burned, not eaten. Recall that those peace offerings are better called welfare or well-being offerings. Thus the recognition of the source of life and the insurance of the well-being of the people are brought about by following the order. The very reason for the peace offering is to recognize the continuing presence of the divine as the source of life for the well-being of the people. To partake of unclean food profanes the sacred presence of the One who is the vital part of the community.

19:9 Sharing the harvest. Next in the life-order are those lives threatened by a lack of food. Those who have food and are able to acknowledge the source of life through the peace offering (thanksgiving for well-being) are really unable to give authentic witness to a life in holiness (completeness of the community) as long as there are those in that community who are poor. The regulation in verse 9 was established to give the poor the chance to live. This allows God as the source of all life to be at work in the whole community. Completeness and wholeness are what the life of holiness is all about.

The same rule is true in regard to the vines. The people are commanded to leave the grapes that have fallen (v. 10). This is God's way of giving them to the poor and the stranger. But they are not to leave anything for the fertility gods in payment for the crop, as was the custom of the land. "I am the source of all life; I, the Lord, am your God."

This latter exclamation is repeated several times in chapters 18 and 19. It appears that these chapters are a unit; perhaps they are the very first gathering of the materials into a manual of holiness. The exclamation "I, the Lord, am your God" is a clear reference to the first commandment of the Sinai Covenant Code and draws attention to the one God as the source of life. This recognition comes first in order (Exod 20:2-6; Lev 26:45). The repetition of the exclamation could have been used as a memory aid for the original manual. It could also mean that there were neighboring unacceptable practices (Lev 18:3; 20:23) well known to them at the time, and the frequent pauses in the text would make room for a litany-like response of short oaths of allegiance. The exclamation is the beginning of the first commandment. The community would continue, then, to publicly acclaim God, the Holy One, as the source of life.

19:16 "You shall not stand by idly when your neighbor's life is at stake." This regulation is joined to the command to avoid slander. No wonder, since the phrase used for slander means "to cut someone down by the spoken word." One can either stand in the way, stand by idly, or stand up to support the life at stake in one's neighbor. A witness to the truth can be an assertion of God as the source of life. In every circumstance we are obliged to weigh properly the life of our neighbor in the scale of justice. Therefore, if we accept the life of holiness we cannot stand by idly when falsehood is parading in the guise of truth for the destruction of life.

19:17, 18 "You shall love your neighbor as yourself." This and 19:2, "Be holy, for I, the LORD your God, am holy," are the most quoted verses of Leviticus. Later Jesus will join these two together in answering "Which commandment of the Torah is the greatest?" His answer will be "You shall love the Lord, your God with your *whole* heart, with your *whole* soul and with *all* your mind" (Matt 22:37 quoting Deut 6:5). "The second is like to it, You shall love your neighbor as yourself" (Matt 22:39 quoting Lev 19:18). If one is living the life of holiness, which is described by the use of *whole* and *all*, then, everyone is neighbor to each other in this life. However, there is a holy sequence. Love of God comes first and includes love of neighbor, but love of neighbor does not, of necessity, lead immediately to love of the Holy One.

In verse 19 certain mixtures are prohibited. In the attempt to reflect the oneness of God in the wholeness of community life, the Priestly writers list some disorderly arrangements: crossbreeding, sowing two different seeds (one atop the other), and the tension of incompatible threads. The result of crossbreeding can be monstrous; different seeds vie for the same ground and moisture; the purity of the fabric is lost and the unity of the weaving is gone.

19:20-22 Atonement for relations with a female slave. The affirmation of the one source of life and the reflection of this oneness in the community is of prime importance. Thus the seriousness of sexual disorder or disorder in the control of life (v. 20) is shown by the requirement of a ram guilt offering in reparation. The importance of recognizing and affirming the source of life is deeper than meets the eye. For example, the slave girl does not have a life of her own since she is not free. Supposedly she would win her freedom if she were put to death (the creature's relationship with God goes beyond life and death), and the justice of Yahweh would be satisfied. The question at hand is not only that justice be done but also that the holiness of life be preserved. The man in this disorderly sexual relation also has a life of his own. Thus through the guilt offering he is forgiven his sin (v. 22). She then keeps her "non-status," death is not affirmed, and the man is purified for life in holiness. The proper order of recognition of God as the source of life is not disturbed. The sanctuary is also involved (v. 21), since the text is talking about sex as the sacred control of life. The ultimate support of life-control (sex) must be a proper orientation (order in worship) to God, the source of life.

The sex act of humans outside marriage is out of order. There is an order to the use of sex. The coming together of two people in the act of sex forms one body (Gen 2:24). It is the two that choose to act as one. This new oneness can result in the affirmation of existing life and creation of life. When God blesses man and woman in Gen 1:28 with the command "Be fertile and multiply," God is inviting them to a deeper share in the divine oneness, a share in the very power of the one source of life to create new life. It is this added dimension of oneness that must be affirmed before the couple engage in sexual union—a oneness that in turn can become a source of life here on earth. This new affirmation of God as the one source of life also affirms the true role of the couple in the covenant relationship. This affirmation is what the marriage covenant is all about.

In the case of the slave girl, it must be remembered that she is already living with a man (Lev 19:20). This could mean that the oneness of the Source of Life is already recognized and affirmed. The man who now has sexual union with her is definitely acting out of order. Sexual union among humans, then, has to do with the proper ordering or control of life. First, the oneness of God as the one source of life is affirmed, and then the oneness of the couple as a secondary source of life follows.

19:23-25 Uncircumcised fruit. Fruit trees take time to mature and first fruits cannot be given to the Lord until the fourth year. Then the first fruits can be given to the Lord for that year's harvest as a thanksgiving offering. As the rite of circumcision brought a Jewish male into life-relationship with the covenant, so the fruit had to be looked upon as uncircumcised (v. 23) until the fourth year, when it was brought into the covenant. Only in the fifth year could the fruit be eaten.

19:32 Respect for the elderly. The verse states that to stand up in the presence of the aged is a way to show respect. The length of life is a gift of the Lord; respect for the length of life is reverence for the God of life. In other words, we are not looking at the person as such. The criterion for respect is not the wealth the person has accumulated nor fame attained, but simply the length of years. The time that the life-power of the Creator has been at work in the world, in the individual, and in the community must be respected in the life of holiness.

20:1-21 Penalties for various sins. There are two groups of penalties here, corresponding to the twofold commandment of love of God and love of neighbor. In verses 1-8 violation of the holy name (the name of holiness) is treated. In verses 9-21 love of neighbor, starting with one's parents, is considered. The penalty for transgression is, of course, real or symbolic death. To be cut off and to be put to death seem to come together in the meaning and the extent of the penalty. The Code puts the recognition of God as the source of life at the head of the list. It follows that one who acts contrary to the recognition is cut off from the whole of life; this is the meaning of death. To be holy means to be fully alive.

20:2 Capital punishment. Israel allowed capital punishment by stoning. It was carried out by the whole community. One who refused to recognize God as the source of life was cut off from the community and put to death by stoning. There is a reference here to Molech. The word is akin to the Hebrew word for king and may be a graphic way of explaining that God comes first. The sanctuary becomes defiled when the palace becomes the place of worship. If the king is put first, then the king becomes one's source of life. One is cut off from the life of the Holy One and is dead to life in holiness. If the king is called upon, Yahweh is not acknowledged as the source of life. God alone can say, "I am who am" (meaning of Yahweh). No wonder the Jews were disturbed when Jesus said, "I solemnly declare it: before Abraham came to be, I AM," and they picked up rocks to stone him (John 8:58, 59). The holy name is blasphemed in Lev 24:16, and the consequent punishment is stoning by the community. No longer is that person allowed to be a member of the community of people who are living the life of holiness.

20:9 Cursing one's parents. These penalties concern the regulations of chapters 17, 18, and 19. The sacredness of the parental relation heads the list. The other penalties concern the disorder of control of life (sexuality) and of relationships of family and neighbor. Cursing is making light of something. To not only refuse proper crediting but even to discredit the proper order is what convicts a person. One who curses his or her parents, forfeits life (v. 9). This, in turn, leaves little room for recognition of God as the direct source of life. Such a state results in death. One cannot cut off the source of life without experiencing death.

20:22-27 Land ownership. Identity is fixed when people have a place to call their own. God has set the land apart for the people, who are to set themselves apart from the customs of the neighbor (vv. 24, 26). They must recognize this order and actually bring it about by setting themselves apart, the clean from the unclean (20:25). Thus they assert the commanding position of Yahweh.

20:24 A land flowing with milk and honey. Exod 3:8 is referred to here. The secondary source of the milk is the cow, sheep, goat, or camel, but God is the primary source of the milk and of honey from bees (see Sir 39:26). Because of the scarcity of clean water, milk was their most important drink. The land of Canaan is *fat* or wealthy (one of the meanings of the Hebrew word for milk). It is truly a "land flowing with milk and honey." Bees were plentiful, and deposited honey in the crevices of rocks or in hollow trees, even in the wilderness. In verse 24 God is affirmed as the source of these life-sustaining foods.

In verses 1-21 the penalties for not recognizing relation with God and neighbor are listed. In verses 22-27 the proper order of obedience is identified. Through obedience both God and people maintain an identity which is founded on covenant faith, not on fortune-telling (20:27).

Chs. 21–22 Mediators, sacrificial banquets, and sacrificial victims. The identities of God and people have been established. For God the identity is in the ordering. For the people their identity is in the obedient response. It is appropriate to consider now the mediators of these covenant relations: Moses who directs the priesthood (21:1-24) and the victim of the sacrifice (22:17-33). The irregularities concerning priest and victim find a certain balanced presentation in the text. Many regulations required for the state of purification are restated in relation to the priest and the victim. These considerations act as an introduction for what is to come in chapter 23. Moses is still the mediator. His role might best be described as the lawgiver-high priest. He is the one to direct and guide Aaron's sons, the priests (21:1).

The irregularities of chapters 21:2–22:33, especially those of 21:16ff., may seem strange to us, but we must remember that today we know a great deal more about many of these maladies than did the biblical people. At that time, some irregularities were simply considered punishment from God. Judgments of impurity and profanation were often based on the person's inability to perform a particular action, as in the case of blind, crippled, and disfigured individuals.

Chapter 23 has a beauty all its own. It describes the life of holiness in terms of the feasts of Israel. The list begins with the sabbath rest (23:3). By keeping a day of complete rest God is recognized as the source of the life of holiness (Gen 2:3). The list continues with mention of Passover, Pentecost, New Year's day, the Day of Atonement, and finally the third pilgrim feast, the feast of Booths. The order in which these are presented is significant. The purpose of Leviticus is not to give a detailed instruction for festival observance but to draw attention to the need for these celebrations in order to give recognition to God's plan of life. "I am the Lord, your God," must be repeated every six days. The holy number was seven; thus the seventh day became the Lord's day. The seventh day represents the tithe of time that belongs to God.

23:1-44 Holy days. Throughout the Pentateuch there are calendars of holy days (Exod 23:14-18; 34:18-25; Lev 23; Deut 16:1-16). In Leviticus the three pilgrim feasts are mentioned: Passover-Unleavened Bread (23:4-14); the feast of Weeks or Pentecost (23:15-22); and the feast of Booths (23:33-44). New Year's day (vv. 23-25) and the Day of Atonement (vv. 26-32) are added. The sabbath heads the list (v. 3). God made the sabbath holy (Gen 2:3; see Exod 20:8-11 and Heb 4:4, 9). The listing is merely an announcement on the part of Moses (Lev 23:44). As long as one is a covenant member, every day is holy. Certain days, however, are designated by God, through Moses, to be celebrated with a holy assembly (23:1-3).

In ancient stories of other peoples, the sacred assembly took place among the gods. With Israel the Holy One initiates the gathering of the people (Lev 23:4; Exod 12:16). By gathering the major feasts into one place (in the Levitical material of the Pentateuch), the Priestly writers affirm the mediatorship of Moses in the celebrations of the people.

The order in which the list appears gives the reader a mosaic of the life of holiness in the world—the Holy One living in the midst of the people. The feast of Passover-Unleavened Bread celebrates freedom from slavery. Fifty days later, the end of the harvest and the offering of the first fruits begins with the celebration of Weeks (Pentecost). Then, there is one final look back at the wilderness with the feast of Booths, which commemorates the booth made from branches and the tent dwelling of the wanderings in the wilderness. It was also called the feast of Tabernacles, and since it was celebrated at the end of harvest time it received the name of Ingathering. Throughout this description of life, the beginning of each year is announced at a celebration, and every year the whole of life rejoices in the Day of Atonement.

The feast of Booths is mentioned at the end of the list. Its many names and its accent on dwelling show a development in its significance. No wonder that later Peter will want permission to erect three booths, one for Moses the lawgiver, one for Elijah the prophet, and one for Jesus the life-giver.

Chapters 23–25 should probably be read as a unit, since they speak of holy days, holy places and holy land. The days are holy (23:1-44) and the sanctuary lamp (24:1-4) and showbread (24:5-9) point to the holy meeting place. The sabbatical year (25:1-7) and the jubilee year (25:8-22) with redemption of property (25:23-55) deal with the holy land (25:1-22), property rights (25:23-38), and freedom (25:39-55). Chapter 23 describes the life of holiness with emphasis on the presence of the Holy One living in the midst of the people, whereas the sabbatical and jubilee celebrations of chapter 25, with their note of perfection in the holy number seven, seem to be looking beyond this life to the life of perfect holiness in God (the eternal Holy of Holies). Every seven years the whole land has a complete rest as a sabbath for the Lord (25:2-4). Then, in the jubilee life of perfection (seven times seven weeks of years), all shall return to their property (25:10, 13). But the Lord does not have a role in redemption of the land as the sanctuary had a role in purification (ch. 16) because God is the source of life and the owner of the land (25:23). Recall that God actually dwelt only in the cloud above the propitiatory seat of mercy in 16:2.

24:1-4 The sanctuary lamp. This repeats the regulations in Exod 27:20, 21. Exodus closes with Moses putting the lampstand in the meeting tent and arranging the bread on the table before the Lord (40:22-40). So now, at the close of Leviticus, the lamp and the table of display are arranged in the proper Levitical order. Here, however, the emphasis is not on the pure oil as in Exod 27, but on the presence of the Holy. (This is much like the symbolism of the tabernacle light in churches today.) When there is a light in the window, there is somebody home. So, the Holy One and the people who are to be holy are at home in the one covenant. The showbread, or the bread of display, represents the people (Lev 24:5-9), with six loaves in each of two piles on a small table. The piles are a reminder of the twelve tribes, like the two onyx memorial stones with the engraved tribal names as part of the priest's vestments (Exod 28:9-12). Thus, the Holy One and the people are present to each other by real signs of life. The oil is replenished (Lev 24:2) and the bread is kept fresh (24:8). For a life of holiness it is necessary to have an ongoing experience of the presence of each other—of the Holy One and the people who are to be holy.

24:10-23 Punishment for blasphemy and murder. What is holy can become profaned (the light is snuffed out when it should be burning) or the people can become defiled (the bread becomes unclean, stale). However, means will be given to affirm both the holy and the people or to redeem them from profanity or defilement (see ch. 25). In this life of holiness there is no atonement/redemption that can be made for the blasphemer (24:16) or for the murderer (Num 35:31). The reasoning is thus: the Hebrew word for blasphemy suggests a piercing, in some way, of the name of the Holy One. Piercing could bring about the flow of the lifeblood of the victim as in the case of murder. The life of God is in the Holy Name and the life of the human is in the blood, so by blasphemy and by murder, both God and human are pierced. The blasphemer and the murderer must be put to death.

There is also a wordplay in the text on the name Shelomith (24:10), a name similar to that of a neighboring goddess who was considered complete, holy. Such a substitution for the Holy One of Israel would be a blasphemy. The punishment for this violation would be stoning and consequent cutting off such an offender from the covenant of the life of holiness.

It is important to note that the text maintains the covenant arrangement (24:23). Moses is asked what to do about the blasphemer, but God is the Holy One who gives the command for the blasphemer to be cut off from the life of holiness (v. 14). Those who heard the blasphemy must join in, since they received the profanation through their ears. They are joined together in the life of the Holy One. By the laying on of their hands, they return the blasphemy to the offender and by stoning send it to death, a place of no return (24:14).

In chapter 25 the focus is on atonement, not in the sense of forgiveness but in the sense of at-one-ment, union resulting from full acceptance of the covenant relationship. The orderly arrangement of the Priestly material continues in these final chapters.

We can now see the atonement (ch. 16) effected in and reflected by the life of holiness (chs. 17–26). The celebration of the holy days (ch. 23) brings atonement for a more complete living (ch. 25) with the rewards and punishments attached to obedience or disobedience to the Code of Holiness (ch. 26). The two members of the covenant are reidentified and reaffirmed (ch. 24). Chapter 27 becomes another bridge-chapter but, unlike chapter 16, this bridge is only partially constructed.

25:1-22 Sabbatical and jubilee years. During the seventh year the land shall have a complete rest (25:4), a sabbath for the Lord. Even the land is holy and, as the Lord set aside the seventh day, so the land is affirmed as holy in the seventh year. In the seventh month of the forty-ninth year and continuing into the fiftieth year, the celebration is called jubilee, "the year of the ram's horn." We think of jubilation. On this Atonement Day the horn is blown to call the sacred assembly. The word for horn also has the meaning of removing the veil to see the beauty of the woman or to see the clear blue sky when the cloud is gone. Chapter 25:10 says, "You shall make sacred this fiftieth year, by proclaiming liberty in the land for all its inhabitants. It shall be a jubilee for you."

The people are free and return to their families (25:10). There is no more sowing or reaping (v. 11). If they obey, their dwelling is secure (not movable as in the wilderness, v. 18). The land will yield its fruit. They will have food in abundance so that they may live without worry (v. 19). There will be crops for three years, and even in the ninth year they will eat from the old planting because the eternal covenant in the life of holiness has begun.

In 24:17-21 we saw the legal aspect of the Code of Holiness in what is usually referred to as the law of retaliation or recompense—an eye for an eye, a tooth for a tooth, a life for a life, etc. Each of three Codes in the Torah mentions this human balance of justice (Exod 21:24; Lev 24:17-21, and Deut 19:21). As we continue in the Code, we begin to experience the justice of God at one with an unconditional love. A certain holiness begins to enter into real-life situations, given unconditionally by God. A certain stability and wholeness of every life relationship comes to those who, in obedience, recognize the one, holy God as the source of life and live according to the Code.

We are not dealing here with just memories or vain hopes. These are moral directives that give beat and pulse to real living. They are life-support dynamics of the celebration of the wholeness (holiness) of life. They are the vertebrae of the divine-human covenant. Slavery and exile are still the human condition of unfaithful covenant partners, but the enduring and sustaining presence of the Holy One is at work in the midst of the people (Lev 26:44, 45).

This is as far as the Book of Leviticus takes us in the Torah of the Holy One.

Some commentators refer to these later sections as a portrayal of an ideal life. This is true but the life of holiness was never meant to remain just an ideal. When the Torah was given, with Leviticus as its heart, the world received the plan of living a holy life.

The final form of the holiness begins to take shape. The remaining pieces will fall readily into place. This chapter in the five-volume work of the Law is about to complete its message.

Before we consider the partially constructed bridge (ch. 27), we need to look at a final note about the redemption of property in chapter 25 and the material in chapter 26, which was the standard way of closing a covenant treaty.

25:23-55 Redemption of property. The perfect (holy) calendar is presented in the first part of chapter 25, followed by the sacred activity of the holy jubilation year (vv. 23-55). The intended results of the Code were to be: Yahweh recognized as king (vv. 23, 55); wealth redistributed every jubilee (vv. 6, 7); families (v. 10), the land (vv. 2-4), and everyone enjoying liberty (vv. 10, 54); the land bearing fruit (v. 19) of itself (v. 11); all debts canceled (vv. 36, 37); the poor lifted up (vv. 25, 35, 39, 47, 48)—everyone and everything whole in the life of holiness. Note that the land remains the possession of the Holy One. "The land shall not be sold in perpetuity; for the land is mine, and you are but aliens who have become my tenants." (Later you may become my children but, for now you are my renters.) "Therefore, in every part of the country you occupy, you must permit the land to be redeemed" (vv. 23, 24). That is, if they live in the life of holiness, they must acknowledge Yahweh as the original owner, the source of life.

Yahweh had already ordered and taken part in the cleansing and purification of the sanctuary, the meeting tent and the altar, as well as the priests and all the people of the community (16:20, 33). Now a further order is given. Unlike the negative order in Gen 2:17 (see also Gen 3:22), "From that tree you shall not eat," there is the positive command to share in the life of holiness: "Be holy."

While we cannot with certainty sort out the various traditions woven together in Leviticus, we can see changing conditions in the story and can come to some conclusions as to its message at the time of the final editing. For example, walled cities and open-air villages are provided for here, and throughout Leviticus the traveling tabernacle is given emphasis. Such references suggest different chronological times in Israel's development. Yet, behind these observations and the ordered structure of the regulations and directives we see the truth of Lev 25:23: God is the owner of land and property; the people are but aliens who have become tenants.

25:25 Redemption of property. After recognizing that Yahweh owns the land and the property, the poor come first and this for the good of the family (vv. 23-28). As we read verses 23-55, it is as though the owner is preparing to buy back the dwelling in the midst of the people in the wilderness. Chapter 27 will expand this idea of the plan of redemption. Chapter 26 seems to say, "Take your choice, but there is only one correct choice if you want to live the life of holiness. If you choose obedience or disobedience, here are the respective consequences!"

26:3-13 "Live in accord with my precepts." If one gives obedience to these precepts of the life of holiness and the commandments (actually the Code of Holiness in chapter 19 includes the commandments of the Sinai Code in Exod 20), then all kinds of life-giving experiences will happen (vv. 3-13). "If you obey, I will set my Dwelling among you, and will not disdain you" (vv. 11-13).

26:14-46 Punishment for disobedience. If the community members are unfaithful, terrible things will happen (vv. 16, 17). If they still disobey, terrible things will happen to the world in which they live (vv. 19, 20). If they become defiant, things will get worse by seven times (each time in vv. 18, 21, 24, and 28 punishment is increased seven times over), until they will be forced to eat their own children (v. 29). This dire situation could happen in order to survive the siege of walled cities. In their defiant struggle to survive, they themselves would revoke the results (children) of their covenant with the Source of Life. A complete breakdown in the relations of God and people with the whole of life being overturned in death and exile (vv. 30-33) would occur.

26:34 The land shall retrieve its lost sabbaths. This is the built-in payment plan put there by God. While the people are in exile, the land rests. Everything comes to a standstill. The sabbaths must be kept and the precepts followed by the people, even though unwillingly. Sabbath payments are made to God and the people can do nothing about it. Verse 36 returns to the threat of verse 17. Finally, when "their uncircumcised hearts are humbled and they make amends" (v. 41), God will start over with the people. God is holy and remembers the covenant made with their ancestors (v. 42). Exile actually gives the land and the people time to rest (v. 43). The land became defiled when the people defiled themselves by their disobedience. Now both lie desolate, in reprieve for the land and in punishment for the people (v. 43), until time has elapsed equal to the sabbaths defiled. The land is holy because it also belongs to the Lord (25:23). Whenever the land is defiled (polluted), it lies desolate.

God's love is unconditional, since the Holy One does not allow the covenant to be voided, even though God is the only faithful one remaining (vv. 44, 45). This unconditional love is under, behind, and all around the Torah Law. The Book of Leviticus has now become the heart inserted into the Torah and, with its lively beat of the Code of Holiness, the People of God find themselves invited again to share in the life of the Holy One.

Throughout the reading of Leviticus, this simple outline has been stressed: obedience (chs. 1–27), purification (chs. 8–27) and holiness-sanctification (chs. 17–27). Obedience endures as a requirement. Obedience of the human partner of the covenant is requested by and made possible by God. The purification of the relationship reaches its anticlimax in the atonement chapter (Lev 16). Here the covenant partners meet and prepare for the climax of the covenant relationship in the life of holiness (Lev 27). Chapter 27 describes only the beginning of the perfect life, and for this reason is "an open-ended bridge-chapter." The perfect life of holiness is begun in the acceptance and practice of the Code of Holiness.

PART V: REDEMPTION OF VOTIVE OFFERINGS

Lev 27

It is understandable why many commentators treat this final chapter as an appendix to Leviticus. It gives the impression of an afterthought, added later because of its importance. The meaning of Lev 27 is so simple that it can be easily overlooked: It affirms God and people as faithful covenant partners. Its open-ended character suggests that the divine-human covenant is still in the stage of promise.

Some might be tempted to read into the text the fact that the Messiah-Redeemer had not as yet come as reason for the open-ended treatment. This would be an assumption beyond what is contained in Leviticus. The concentration is still upon God as creator of life and Moses as lawgiver-mediator presenting the rules of conduct of the Sinai Covenant. Leviticus has reaffirmed the Sinai Covenant in adding the new dimension of holiness in the sense of completeness. The people are now to become fully alive (holy).

The secret in understanding chapter 27 lies in the meaning of the vow and the tithe. It begins by vowing all of creation to God: persons (vv. 2-8); livestock (vv. 9-13); dwelling (vv. 14, 15); hereditary land (vv. 16-24). The chapter ends by returning everything to God in the tithe (vv. 26-34).

In the preceding chapter the divine partner of the covenant spelled out the results, good and bad, of the obedience or disobedience of the junior member. Here the Holy One respects the free will of the human partner and points the way of respect for the divine partner.

The practice of making a vow to a deity in order to receive a favor or cure is very ancient. However, we are dealing with a more basic idea: the holiness of life. The vow and its redemption, along with the practice of tithing, make possible the holy life. As a free-will offering, the vow affirms human life. The tithe affirms divine life.

In chapter 27 God affirms human free will and gives conditions whereby the votive offering can be redeemed. Everyone and everything in creation is considered. The meaning of vow goes to the very root of life. In a way every vow to God is a promise to live a holy life. God wills the creature to be fully alive, that is, holy. In Gen 1:26, 27 the creature is created in the image and likeness of God, able to assert its own freedom. The buying back of life in all of creation must be done according to God's terms. The priest sets the price, but the terms are according to the rules of the jubilee, God's life-giving celebration (vv. 17, 18, 21, 23, 24). God, then, remains the source of life and holiness.

Certain offerings cannot be redeemed: the first-born and, at the other end of life, those doomed to die (vv. 26-29). They affirm God as the ultimate source of life. There is a refinement here of the dedication of Exod 13. Every first-born that opens the womb among the Israelites, both of humans and beasts, belongs to the Lord. It cannot be the object of a vow (dependent on human free will). It still acts as a reminder of the death of the first-born of the Egyptians, who would not recognize Yahweh as the source of life (Exod 13:14-16). Death is still the human condition (Gen 3:19), but now the emphasis is on dedication and redemption.

27:28-29 "All human beings that are doomed." The Hebrew word for "doomed" in verse 28 also has the meaning of "dedicated," that is, "set aside for the Lord." God alone has control over the human being, animal, or land that has become most sacred (dedicated). In modern-day parallel, people on death row are doomed to die, but appeal can be made to the highest authority. Another meaning of the word is "people dedicated by solemn vow to God." In the order of holiness they are on "life's row." It is the will of the divine covenant member that all live. Life, not death, is the will of God. Death came into the world because of the *human* covenant member (Gen 3), and death is still present to the community of the human covenant members. However, the divine partner could play the role of the lesser member and then restore life to the human condition.

27:30-33 The sacredness of tithes. The above explanation is only partial. In an unfinished bridge-chapter we expect some partial answers. As in Gen 28, the vow and the tithe are now brought together in chapter 27 to affirm and ensure the continued presence of God. The tithe becomes the span of the bridge that we set in place, even though constructed of material belonging to the Lord.

We need to rethink our definition of tithe. We are not speaking of one-tenth as of multiples of ten. In the creation of the world, the tithe was the seventh day. Each of the six days of creation is made up of the created things of the previous day plus its own works. The seventh day was made holy (Gen 1:3). The seventh day in the creation blueprint became a miniature world, holy and complete, a fitting expression of the creator's gift of the world. The Lord's day is a holy day. It is the original form of the tithe. "Seventh" and "complete rest" are from the same Hebrew root. The seventh day is the day of completion.

Deut 14:22-29 puts the finishing touches on the understanding of tithing. "Each year you shall tithe all . . . then in the place which the Lord, your God, chooses as the dwelling place of his name you shall eat in his presence your tithe . . . . that you may learn always to fear [respect the source of life] the Lord, your God" (14:22-23). In verse 26, after making provision for everyone, Deuteronomy directs all to partake of the tithe and make merry with their families.

Deuteronomy continues the regulation "at the end of every third year, you shall bring all the tithes . . . for that year and deposit them in community stores, that the Levite . . . the alien, the orphan and the widow . . . may come and eat their fill" (14:28-29). Let everyone enjoy fully the life of holiness.

The payment of the tithe is in the eating of the meal together (the Holy One and the ones called to be holy) with the feeding of the poor so that all may have life to the full. This is the life of holiness, a life that is being lived today in the Eucharist-Passover, the celebration of the redemption of the First-born. Gathered with the writers of the Book of Leviticus on the partially constructed bridge to the Dwelling of the Holy Name, we begin to hear the song of celebration: "Holy, holy, holy is the Lord of hosts! All the earth is filled with God's glory!"

NUMBERS

Helen Kenik Mainelli

INTRODUCTION

The Book of Numbers, the fourth book of the Pentateuch, is so named because it contains two censuses of the Israelite tribes (1:20-46 and 26:5-51) and of the Levites (3:14-51 and 26:57-62). It also includes lists of various kinds, some with numbers: a list of the princes who assist with the census (1:5-15); a list of gifts brought for the dedication of the altar (7:10-83); a list of the scouts sent to explore the land (13:4-15); lists of offerings to be brought for feast days and festivals (28:1–29:38); and a list of the booty taken from the Midianites (31:32-52). While the name "Numbers" fits some of the content, it does not accurately suggest the story told in the book.

The story in Numbers begins in the desert of Sinai just after the covenant event and ends forty years later with the people waiting on the plains of Moab to enter the Promised Land. It is the story of the people of God as they journey through the wilderness for almost forty years under the leadership of Moses and Aaron.

The central issue is the presence of Yahweh with the people as they journey through the wilderness: God walks with them and directs their lives. The people, for their part, often grumble and rebel; they provoke divine judgment and seek forgiveness.

The Book of Numbers is the last part of the story that begins in the Book of Genesis with creation and continues in the Book of Exodus with the liberation and election of God's people. As we read the Book of Numbers, we will continually be reminded that this is but one piece of a continuous story identified as the primary history.

The organization of the primary history

The primary history is divided into eras: the ages of Adam, Noah, and the ancestors of Israel (Genesis); the era of Israel's movement from Egypt to Sinai (Exodus); and the era of Israel's movement from Sinai to the threshold of the Promised Land (Exodus to Numbers).

The Sinai event stands at the center. What begins in the Book of Exodus with Sinai continues in the Book of Numbers. All the directives in Num 1–10, for example, are communicated to Moses at Sinai.

Likewise, from Sinai there is a look backward to creation. The law of the sabbath, given at Sinai (Exod 31:12-17), links with the creation event (Gen 2:2-3).

The Priestly authors and their audiences

The primary history was put into final form in the sixth century B.C.E. by priests intent on the restoration of the temple cult. The work is therefore called "Priestly," or "P" for short. The authors were from the family of priests, the sons of Zadok, who secured leadership among the displaced people of the Exile (sixth century B.C.E.) and motivated this people to center its life on the worship of Yahweh. They wrote the history specifically to give the exiled Israelites hope and comfort based on memory of God's actions. They challenged the exiles to recall the events of old, especially the ways in which God was present among the people, led them, and provided for them in their formative years.

The priests wrote the story of *God with Israel* for people whose identity and faith, like ours, were questioned in the face of dramatic political, cultural, social, and religious upheaval. They stirred people to reach behind the collapsed institutions to that early time of God's love-relationship in covenant to discover again the benefits of dependence and obedience. The priests detailed the ways of God's presence in that early time so that people might rediscover God in their midst in new ways in a new age. The priests provided a word of hope and encouragement for all of us in our wilderness experiences that we might know that others have walked before us under the protection and guidance of Yahweh.

The priests handed down traditions from Israel's past. They were not authors who made up stories nor historians whose intention was to report past events. Rather, they were writers who collected ancient documents, lists, reports, and stories, which they edited and arranged into an account of *God with the people* that at once told the story of the past and addressed the needs of contemporary generations. They were writers who *remembered* the past and *handed down* essentials from tradition to provide a basis for the reidentification of God's people.

The Priestly theology

The selection and organization of traditional material in the narrative were determined by covenant theology. The priests traced the covenants from the beginning of Israelite history, and in so doing they emphasized the perpetuity of the relationship between God and the people. Yahweh's covenant is eternal. The covenant with Noah (Gen 9:1-17) and the covenant with Abraham (Gen 17:1-27) prepared the way for God's ultimate self-disclosure to Israel at Sinai, the covenant that endured to the Exile and beyond.

At Sinai the covenant issued in one benefit—the presence of Yahweh in Israel's midst. The glory of the Lord settled upon Mount Sinai and remained present with the people in covenant (Exod 24:16; 25:8). The Priestly writer chose his words very carefully. Here the verb translated "settled upon" means literally "to tent" or "to walk about among." This was not a presence in the static sense of nearness in a shrine. The priests remembered the days when Yahweh, present on the ark and in the tent, moved with the people. By linking together the idea of Yahweh's "tenting" or "moving among" with various covenant formularies, they make the theological point that is central to the whole narrative:

> I will *dwell in the midst* of the Israelites and will be their God. They shall know that I, the Lord, am their God who brought them out of the land of Egypt, so I, the Lord, their God, might *dwell among them* (Exod 29:45-46; see Lev 26:11-13 and John 1:14).

Special vocabulary used in the Priestly edition

Glory of the Lord is the distinctive designation for the God-self revealed in majesty and power. The Priestly source uses the term "glory of the Lord" whenever it speaks about God being actually present and manifest (see Num 16:19; 17:7).

Dwelling is the key word of Priestly theology. Derived from the verb "to tent" or "to walk among as a tent-dweller," this idea implies mobility and nearness as well as holiness and transcendence. It is the word chosen by the Priestly author to indicate the place of Yahweh's covenant presence and carries the idea that Yahweh is always present with the people (see Num 1:50-53). This special word encompasses all of the other designations for Yahweh's presence: the tent, ark, holy place, etc.

Meeting tent refers to the traditional place of divine-human meeting. This is the place where Yahweh meets and speaks with the people through Moses (Exod 29:42; Num 1:1; 2:2; 3:7-8, etc.). The Priestly tradition sometimes uses "meeting tent" as a metaphor for the Dwelling, the place where the glory of the Lord is revealed (see 16:19).

Ark is identified by the Priestly writer as the "ark of the covenant" (Num 10:33) and as the "ark of the commandments" (Num 4:5; 7:89). In early tradition the ark was the seat upon which Yahweh was believed to be invisibly present. This instrument of Yahweh's presence was reinterpreted by the priests as the container for keeping the covenant document. In the Priestly tradition the covenant is the Decalogue, or the tablets of the law (see Exod 25:16, 21, 22).

Sanctuary is used to talk about the most sacred place, the location of the ark and the meeting tent, where Yahweh dwells among the people. It is a general term for "holy place" and is used interchangeably with "Dwelling."

Community refers to the people of the covenant and the whole family of the people of God. The priests think of Israel as a congregation, in the sense of a people at worship. This community, which participates in cult and worship, will gain the blessings inherent in the eternal covenant (see Num 1:2, 16, 18; 3:7, etc.).

"I am Yahweh" is a recognition formula that identifies God as the liberator of the people from slavery in Egypt, and therefore as the God who has chosen Israel for a special relationship:

> I am Yahweh.
> I will free you from the forced labor of the Egyptians . . . .
> I will take you as my own people, and you shall have me as your God (Exod 6:6a, 7a).

The Priestly writer uses this recognition formula throughout the narrative to lead the people to recognize that the God Yahweh who acted in the past continues to be present and active on behalf of the covenant people (see Num 3:13, 45; 35:34).

Stylistic features in the Priestly edition

The priests present their material in such patterned ways that it will be helpful for the reader to be able to recognize some of the literary peculiarities. We divide this commentary into chapters, for example, on the basis of the Priestly writers' use of the journey formula. The content in the book is set into the various segments of the journey schema.

Journey formula. The march through the wilderness begins at Sinai and ends at Moab in a sequence of stages. At precise moments the Priestly author inserts the formula "they moved on from ________ and came to rest in ________" to indicate the movement from place to place. After the events in the wilderness of Sinai (Num 1:1–10:10), the people move from Sinai to the desert of Paran (10:12); from the desert of Paran to the desert of Zin at Kadesh (20:1); from Kadesh to Mount Hor (20:22); from Mount Hor to the desert east of Moab (21:10-11); and finally they move on to the plains of Moab (22:1), where they remain at the end of the book.

The journey from Sinai to Moab takes place in six stages. The journey from Egypt to Sinai also takes place in six stages. The journey formula occurs at Exod 12:37a; 13:20; 14:1-2; 15:22a; 16:1 and 17:1a. These twelve stages correspond to an ancient tradition about the journey which the Priestly writer preserves in Num 33:5-49.

God's word spoken and obeyed. Moses is presented in the Book of Numbers as an illustration of a leader who faithfully carries out God's word. It is helpful to notice the typical formulation: "The Lord said to Moses: 'Do such and such.' Moses, therefore, did such and such in accordance with the command the Lord had given him" (see Num 1:1, 18-19; 3:14-15, 40-42, etc.).

Cycle of rebellion, punishment, forgiveness. One of the Priestly writer's intentions is to illustrate the history of Israel's infidelity. To do this, he borrows traditions of unfaithfulness and sets the incidents into a predictable story pattern. Each story has these elements: (1) the people complain; (2) God becomes angry and punishes; (3) the people cry out for help; (4) Moses intercedes on behalf of the people; (5) Yahweh responds by giving relief from the punishment. This pattern occurs in the stories in Num 11:1-3; 12:2; 9-16; 17:6-15; 21:4-9.

OUTLINE OF THE BOOK

1:1–10:10
In the desert of Sinai: Preparations for the journey

10:11–22:1
On the journey from Sinai to Moab
Events in the desert of Paran (10:11–19:22)
Last stops along the way (20:1–22:1)

22:2–36:13
On the plains of Moab: Preparation for life in the land

COMMENTARY

IN THE DESERT OF SINAI: PREPARATIONS FOR THE JOURNEY

Num 1:1–10:10

These beginning chapters of the Book of Numbers describe events that take place while the people are camped at Sinai. They are being readied for the great march into the Promised Land. First, a census is taken (ch. 1), and the people are organized around the Dwelling, the presence of Yahweh among them (ch. 2). Next, there is a numbering of the Levites, whose principal duty is the care of the Dwelling (ch. 3), and a description of their duties (chs. 4 and 8). There follows a series of regulations that ensure the sanctity of the camp (chs. 5 and 6). There is then a listing of the offerings by the princes/leaders to serve the Dwelling in transport (ch. 7), with final preparations for the movement out of the camp: the lights are lighted in the Dwelling (8:1-4), and guidance is provided for the trek through the wilderness (9:15-23). The second Passover is celebrated to remember that a year has passed since the deliverance from Egypt (ch. 9), and the silver trumpets are blown to signal the march (10:10).

These chapters were set down by priests in the exilic period, when the community needed instructions regarding its present circumstance. It viewed itself as being once again in the wilderness and preparing for a return to the homeland. The vision of a community organized about the Dwelling encompasses at once that early first entry into the land of promise and this new time of waiting for the return to the land.

These first ten chapters contain remembrances about life in the wilderness. The traditions are ancient ones preserved by members of the Priestly school to construct ideally that early experience. More important to the priests is the message of hope contained in the memory of the past. The account presents the exilic community with a model that has Yahweh at the center and the people as a community at worship, organized around the Dwelling. The regulations given clarify responsibilities for priests, leaders, and people that they might be holy within the organization of the new community of faith.

1:1-3 The census. The scene is the wilderness at the foot of Mount Sinai, where Yahweh and Israel celebrated the unique relationship of covenant. There, according to Yahweh's command, Moses erected the Dwelling and placed the ark in the meeting tent on the first day of the *first* month in the second year after the Israelites came out of the land of Egypt (Exod 40:2, 17-19; see 19:1).

Yahweh speaks with Moses in this tent one month later, on the first day of the *second* month of this second year after the Exodus (v. 1), commanding him to take a census of the people. The command specifically states that the sons of Israel are to be registered individually, as well as according to their clan in the father's line (v. 2). Only males twenty years or older are to be counted. Twenty years is the age at which a male person becomes an adult, and therefore subject to the full range of religious duties, including participation in military service (v. 3).

The census marks the initial preparation for the great pilgrimage to the Promised Land. Yahweh has appointed Moses as leader of the grand march. Moses is to be the people's representative before God and the one through whom God speaks with the people. The formula "The Lord said to Moses" (v. 1) is repeated over eighty times in the book. The importance of Moses cannot be emphasized enough. In continuity with the Exodus tradition (Exod 24 and 32), Moses will be assisted in his leadership role by his brother Aaron: "You and Aaron shall enroll . . ." (v. 3). The dominant role of Aaron will unfold in the course of the book.

1:4-19a Moses' assistants: Twelve princes of Israel. To assist Moses and Aaron with the census, a man holding a position of authority in each tribal unit is designated to conduct the count in his clan (v. 4). These individuals hold authority that extends to all dimensions of life. They are "councilors," or representatives in the worshiping community, "princes" within the family, and "chiefs" over the military forces (v. 16). As representatives within the worshiping community, these leaders present offerings for the dedication of the altar (7:10-88). As princes in their respective families, they are responsible for order in the camp (2:3-31). As chiefs of the military forces, they lead the people as they embark on the journey from the wilderness of Sinai (11:13-28).

It is uncertain whether the names of the leaders of the tribes have survived from an early time or whether they are names of leaders from the period after the Exile. Since some of the names appear in 1 and 2 Chronicles (see 1 Chr 6:12; 7:26; 12:3, 10; 15:24; 24:6; 2 Chr 11:18; 17:8; 35:9, etc.), which come from the time when the temple was rebuilt, we assume that these men were actual leaders known to the priests and not a recollection of leaders from the time of the wilderness sojourn.

The list of the twelve tribes found in verses 5-15 is one of the important genealogies of the people and reflects the rules of protocol in tribal hierarchy. This list follows the sequence of names first recorded in Gen 35:22b-26 in the narration of the birth of Jacob's sons, with variations that reflect the needs of the later period. According to protocol, the sons of the legitimate wives always take precedence over the sons of the maids. The lists are as follows:

	Gen 35:22b-26	*Num 1:5-15*	
Jacob's sons by Leah:	Reuben	Reuben	Because in Numbers, the tribe of Levi is enrolled separately (see 1:47-54), Levi is omitted from the list.
	Simeon	Simeon	
	Levi		
	Judah	Judah	
	Issachar	Issachar	
	Zebulun	Zebulun	
by Rachel:	Joseph	Ephraim	To retain the count of twelve, the tribe of Joseph is divided into the two sons (see Gen 48:1).
	Benjamin	Manasseh	
		Benjamin	
by Bilhah, Rachel's maid:	Dan	Dan	
	Naphtali	Asher	
by Zilpah, Leah's maid:	Gad	Gad	In all lists where the sons of Joseph are listed separately, the names Naphtali and Asher reverse order for a reason unknown (see 13:4-15).
	Asher	Naphtali	

There is another pattern for the listing of the tribes that we will discuss when we comment on the arrangement of tribes in the camp and on the march (see ch. 2).

On the very day on which the Lord instructs Moses and Aaron to take the census, that is, on the first day of the second month (v. 18; compare v. 1), the assistants are named and the census begins. Every adult male is registered according to the Lord's command (vv. 18b-19; compare vv. 2-3). Thus the census takes place, with Moses, Aaron, and the tribal leaders responding obediently to God's word.

1:19b-46 Count of the twelve tribes. Rigid structure and formulaic expression characterize the Priestly narrative. The record of the census count is typical of the patterned language. Each of the twelve tribes, with its count of male members, is set forth in stylistic rhetoric that is nicely captured in our translation. Notice that the schematized recital has an introduction, "This is their census" (v. 19b), and a conclusion (vv. 44-45) that reiterates the formulas to indicate that God's command has been carried out exactly. The stylized presentation serves two functions: (1) it puts emphasis on the group included in the census—male adults capable of military service, registered in their individual tribes in their father's line; (2) it points up the names of the individual tribes and the size of each group.

The order in which the tribes are presented falls into the pattern we have described above. The only variation from the list given in verses 5-15 is the substitution of Gad for the tribe of Levi. The repetition of the precise pattern gives us a sense of the priests' reliance on traditional information in recounting the memory of that early time in the wilderness in order to sustain the faith of the people in their current passage from an exilic wilderness.

The total 603,550 in verse 46, as well as

the numbers given for the individual tribes, can hardly be historically accurate. What was remembered of that idyllic period in the wilderness was the multitude of ancestors who populated the land and the pride in national history that had its beginning in the Exodus-wilderness experiences. Memory of that glorious past, however idealized and exaggerated, nurtures a people for whom the hope for a future is built on memory of the past.

1:47-54 The Levites. Because the Levites are assigned the care of the sanctuary, they are not included in the census of those who are capable of military service (v. 47). Their duties are to carry the Dwelling, to care for it, and to camp around it (v. 50). They alone are allowed to take it down and set it up again as the people move from site to site. Death is the punishment for any non-Levite who approaches the Dwelling (v. 51). When the tribes are encamped around the Dwelling, the Levites form a kind of shield to insulate the people from the divine presence (vv. 52-53).

The Dwelling is the place where Yahweh is present with the people, a presence rooted in the covenant. The phrase "Dwelling of the commandments" (v. 50) points to the Dwelling as the place where the ark with the commandments is located. There is here a merging of the various traditions of God's presence in order to emphasize what has always been true: God resides in the midst of the people. This Dwelling, given to the care of the Levites, represents Yahweh's presence not concretely but by covenant relationship.

The task assigned to the Levites is the *service* of the Dwelling. In verse 53 the phrase "shall have charge" is from the verb meaning "to serve," which is used most frequently in contexts of worship. It means to do worthy service, to honor and care for that which is sacred. The Levites' task is a kind of continuous performance of worship.

2:1-34 Camp around the meeting tent. Now that the census has been completed, the focus changes to the arrangement of the tribes around the meeting tent. According to tradition, the meeting tent was that place where God communicated with the people through the mediatorship of Moses (see Exod 33:7-11). The meeting tent could be moved along with the people. Wherever the people moved, Yahweh's voice could always come to Moses. In the introductory address Moses' name precedes that of Aaron because Moses is traditionally the mediator at the tent as well as the designated leader of the people on the way to the land.

The word of the Lord comes to Moses and Aaron (v. 1) with the command that the people should encircle the meeting tent, leaving some distance between themselves and the tent, and should group themselves according to the clan and family divisions of the census (v. 2). The tribes are to be arranged in a precise formation, three on each side, around the meeting tent (see next page). The Levites are situated in the center to shield the Israelites from the tent of Yahweh's presence (v. 17a; see also 3:24, 29, 35, 38).

The east side of the camp is the most prominent, since it faces the rising sun in front of the tent. As we move clockwise from the east, we discover the relative status of the tribes. Priority is given to the tribe of Judah, and the least position is given to three tribes that trace their birth to the maids of Jacob's wives (see Gen 35:25-26).

The order of the tribes differs slightly from the lists of the census in 1:5-15 and 20-43. It begins with Judah rather than Reuben.

1:20-43	*2:3-31*
Reuben	Judah
Simeon	Issachar
Gad	Zebulun
Judah	Reuben
Issachar	Simeon
Zebulun	Gad
Ephraim	Ephraim
Manasseh	Manasseh
Benjamin	Benjamin
Dan	Dan
Asher	Asher
Naphtali	Naphtali

By grouping the tribes in triads, we can see that the Judah group is positioned ahead of the Reuben group in order of status. The variation is important because the tradition of the preeminence of Judah in the arrangement of the camp carries over into the order of worship (7:12-83) and into the order of march (10:14-28). With this order the Priestly author is reflecting an actual situation of his own day. The exiles originally came from the territory of Judah, and they return there to reestablish Jerusalem as the religious center for the

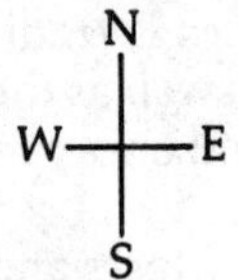

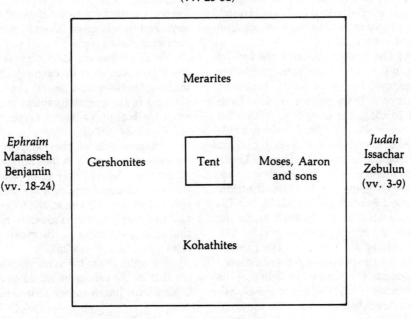

Dan
Asher and Naphtali
(vv. 25-31)

	Merarites		
Ephraim Manasseh Benjamin (vv. 18-24)	Gershonites	Tent	Moses, Aaron and sons	*Judah* Issachar Zebulun (vv. 3-9)
	Kohathites		

Reuben
Simeon and Gad
(vv. 10-16)

ARRANGEMENT OF THE TRIBES
AROUND THE MEETING TENT

people. The prominence of Judah thus suggests the importance of the southern region as the place where the people will establish themselves as well as the new temple for Yahweh's presence.

When the tribes move, they will move in precisely the designated order (v. 17b)—the Judah triad first (v. 9), the Reuben triad second (v. 16), the Ephraim triad third (v. 24), and the Dan triad last (v. 31). Each group consists of the males who have been numbered (v. 32), and each moves under the banner of the clan (v. 2). All this was done "just as the Lord had commanded Moses" (v. 34).

3:1-4 Priests distinct from Levites. This chapter opens with a genealogical formulary distinctive of the style of the Priestly writer: "The following were the descendants of so and so." This heading is typically used by the Priestly writer to mark off major periods in the history of God's people. From creation to the ancestors of Abraham, the formulary occurs five times to indicate major junctures (Gen 2:4a; 5:1; 6:9; 10:1; 11:10), and from the ancestors of Abraham to Jacob five more times (Gen 11:27; 25:12, 19; 36:1; 37:2). After the account of Israel's ancestors, the formulary is not used again until this place in Numbers, where we find the genealogy of the sons of Aaron, to whom the priests trace their ancestry. Thus, there is a conscious link from the priests back to the ancestors and, before them, to creation.

The name of Aaron comes before that of

Moses (compare 2:1) because here the Priestly writer is talking specifically about the descendants of Aaron, who exercise the duties of the priesthood. From this point on in Numbers, a distinction is made between the priests who are descended from Aaron and the Levites who identify with Moses. The appointment of the sons of Aaron to the duties of the priesthood is everywhere emphasized (see especially 17; 25:10-13; 27:12-23).

We note that the events recorded in Numbers are always linked back to the Sinai event. So, too, is the designation of the sons of Aaron linked to "the time that the Lord spoke to Moses on Mount Sinai" (v. 1b; compare Exod 24:1-2). Aaron had four sons: Nadab, Abihu, Eleazar, and Ithamar (v. 2; see also Exod 6:23), who were "anointed" and "ordained" to the priesthood (v. 3). Priests were anointed by the pouring of oil on their heads (Exod 29:7), the act by which they were dedicated to God (Lev 21:12). Ordaining means literally to "fill one's hand," that is, to give some task or responsibility in trust into someone's hands. The priests are entrusted with the good of the people who come to the presence of God. They are in charge of the liturgy, sacrifices, and feasts, the activities through which God's gifts of healing and life flow to the people. By being anointed and ordained, the priest is consecrated to carry out these responsibilities (see Exod 28:41).

Of Aaron's four sons, Nadab and Abihu died tragically in the wilderness of Sinai, leaving no descendants (v. 4a). This story can be read in Lev 10:1-5. The ancestry of Aaron was thereafter carried on by Eleazar and Ithamar (v. 4b). These two branches of the family can be traced through the time of David: Zadok from Eleazar, and Ahimelech from Ithamar (see 2 Sam 8:17; 1 Chr 18:16; 24:1-4). Eventually the line of Zadok rose to a position of prominence (see 2 Sam 15:24-29; 1 Kgs 2:35; Ezek 44:15-16). The designation of the sons of Aaron as a group assigned the special duties of the priesthood reflects, therefore, the actual practice from the tenth century on. The distinction between the priests and the Levites persisted into the time when the people returned from exile and after (see Ezra 2:36, 40; Neh 7:39, 43).

3:5-13 Levi's sons: assistants to the priests. In the remainder of this chapter, the Lord speaks to Moses alone (vv. 5, 11, 14, 40, 44). The concern is the Levites as distinct from the priests, and specifically as assistants to the priests (v. 6).

The Levites are traditionally identified as followers of Moses (see Exod 32:25-29), though actual descent from Moses is unclear. What is clear is the traditional status of the Levites as ministers to the priests and to the community. Only the sons of Aaron may function as priests (v. 10). The Levites are given to the priests as individuals "set apart" from the people Israel; they are "given" for Yahweh (v. 9; see 8:16; 18:6). They are to "discharge" the duties of Aaron and the community (v. 7) and to "have custody" of the furnishings of the meeting tent (v. 8). In both cases, the verb is "to serve," which more accurately means "to honor and care for something sacred." The Levites, then, would see that both priests and the community properly worship the divine presence (v. 7) by caring for the furnishings and overseeing the functions of the people at worship (v. 8).

The Levites are understood to be the property of Yahweh in place of the first-born of Israel (vv. 12-13). To commemorate Yahweh's claim on Israel, demonstrated with the death of the first-born of the Egyptians (v. 13a; Exod 11:4-8), the first-born of Israel belonged to Yahweh from that time on (v. 13b; Exod 13:2-16; 34:19-20). The Levites, as Yahweh's possession, act as substitutes for what is Yahweh's true right—the first-born of the other tribes. Yahweh has chosen the Levites, and they are given to Yahweh in place of the first-born (v. 12). The idea of being ransom for the first-born is discussed again in our commentary on 3:40-51 and 8:5-26.

3:14-39 Levi's sons: census and duties. We are once again invited to remember that these events are taking place in the wilderness of Sinai in accord with Yahweh's command (v. 14). The sons of Levi were excluded from being counted among the people of Israel in the census (see 1:47-48). As a sign that they are dedicated for service, a special census is taken of their numbers (v. 15). In their case, it is not males of twenty years or more, fit for military service that are counted (compare 1:3, 18, 45), but the entire male population from one month of age (v. 15b). This means that the Levites are "given" to Yahweh from birth, in the sense that they belong to Yahweh from the beginning of their existence. The indication of "one month" means that the infant has withstood the critical period of infancy and therefore has the potential for a full life. The Levites actually fulfill the duties assigned them only between the ages of thirty and fifty (see 4:3). Like all the Israelites, the Levites are registered by clans in their father's line (vv. 15a and 20b).

The listing of the names of the sons of Levi is intended to parallel that of the sons of Aaron in 3:2, though here the genealogical formulary is lacking. Obviously, the Priestly writer intends that the emphasis be on the priests, who are linked by the genealogical introduction to the ancestors and creation. The status of the Levites is secondary to that of the priests.

There are three sons of Levi, each of whom is named together with his descendants: Gershon, with his descendants Libni and Shimei; Kohath, with his descendants Amram, Izhar, Hebron, and Uzziel; and Merari, with his descendants Mahli and Mushi. This list of names in verses 17-20 corresponds to the data given in sections in verses 21, 27, and 33. While information about the descendants is scant, it is probable that they reflect persons as well as places. What the Priestly author has done is to put the traditional material about the Levites into a pattern of relationships that has a correspondence to the other Israelite tribes.

The information about the clans in each of the sections is presented in a patterned sequence. After the names in verses 21, 27 and 33, the count of each clan is given: Gershon numbers 7,500 (v. 22); Kohath numbers 8,300 (v. 28); and Merari numbers 6,200 (v. 34). The total of 22,000 is given in verse 39. These numbers have no purpose except to highlight the disparity in size between the Levites and the other tribes (1:20-43). If we remember that all Levites from one month old were counted, in contrast with the count of adult males only from the other tribes, the disparity is even more pronounced. The priests want the reader to be aware of the comparatively small number of Levites.

Next in each section, the Levitical clans are assigned to one of the compass points between the sanctuary and the tribes of Israel. They camp immediately around the Dwelling and thus function to protect and to atone in a mediatory capacity (see 8:19). The Gershonites are located on the west (v. 23); the Kohathites on the south (v. 29); and the Merarites on the north (v. 35b). The assignment to a specific compass point appears to be arbitrary. The favored eastern side, however, is reserved for Moses, Aaron, and the sons of Aaron (v. 38a). See the model on p. 150.

Each of the groups has specific duties in regard to the holy place. The sons of Aaron alone carry out the service at the sanctuary (v. 38b). The Levites attend to the appointments of the sanctuary. According to verses 25-26, the Gershonites tend to the tent itself, with all its curtains, hangings, coverings, and ropes. (Compare the description of the wilderness sanctuary in Exod 26; 27:9-16; 36:8-19, 35-38.) The Kohathites, according to verses 28b and 31, are charged with the care of the sacred contents of the wilderness sanctuary: the ark, table, lampstand, altars, utensils, and sanctuary veil. (These appointments are described in Exod 25; 27; 30:1-10; 37; 38.) According to verses 36-37, the Merarites attend to the frames, bases, poles, that is, those parts that secure the physical structure. (Read the elaborate descriptions of these physical features in Exod 26:15-37; 27:9-19; 36:20-34; 39:40.) Together with this division of assignments, we ought to recall the description of the Levitical duties given in 1:50-51, especially the Levites' role when the camp is broken and reestablished as the people move from place to place in the wilderness.

In each section there is also the name of a "prince" from each of the Levitical clans (vv. 24, 30 and 35a) to correspond to the listing of leaders from each of the Israelite tribes in 1:5b-15. Because these individuals are not mentioned again, their leadership function remains obscure. What is certain is the leadership of Eleazar, son of Aaron, who is identified as chief prince of the Levites (v. 32). It is to the priest Eleazar, the eventual successor to Aaron, that the Levites are accountable in the execution of their various duties (compare 3:6, 9a).

3:40-51 First-born of the Israelites. This section takes up again the matter introduced in 3:11-13—the Levites as substitutes for the first-born. Here the working out of the ransom is described in detail.

The presentation falls into the pattern of Yahweh's word (vv. 40 and 44), followed by the execution of that word (vv. 42 and 49-50).

Moses does exactly as the Lord directs him. He takes a census of the first-born males, those one month of age and over. These number 22,273 (v. 43). He then assigns the Levites as ransom for the first-born of Israel, and the cattle of the Levites as substitutes for the first-born cattle (vv. 41 and 45).

The number of the first-born males of Israel matches that of the Levites, with a difference of 273 (v. 46). The surplus can be ransomed by a sum of money given to the priests (v. 48). A price of five shekels, measured by the value of the temple shekel instead of the merchant shekel, provides a ransom for those remaining among the first-born (v. 49).

Such attention to detail points to the significance of the first-born, who were spared on that night when the first-born of Egypt died (see Exod 12:29). The first-born of every Israelite family in every succeeding generation remembers this event and therefore is himself spared. On account of this event, the first-born belongs to Yahweh (Exod 13:2, 12-25; 34:19-20).

The rationale for the Levites belonging to Yahweh is rooted in this tradition of the first-born belonging to Yahweh. By memory of this event, the people come to know Yahweh their God. The recognition formula "I am Yahweh" appears here: ". . . that the Levites may belong to me. I am the Lord" (v. 45b; see 13b). The connection between the delivery from Egyptian bondage and the dedication of the first-born provokes the realization that Israel is Yahweh's own, called into a unique relationship that endures forever. The dedication of the Levites witnesses to the nature of Israel's God as one who continues to act on Israel's behalf and who also demands dedication and service. (See p. 146 for a brief discussion of the recognition formula.)

4:1-33 Levitical duties defined. The word of the Lord is again addressed to Moses and Aaron, in that order (vv. 1, 17; see also 34 and 46). The command is to take a census of the subgroups of the Levites (vv. 2, 22, 29), those falling into the age bracket of thirty to fifty years old (vv. 3a, 23a, 30a).

The descriptions of the duties of each of the Levitical groups are set within the frame of the census command. Males of the designated age are assigned specific tasks in transporting the meeting tent. In each case the formulary "to undertake obligatory tasks" (vv. 3b, 23b, 30b) introduces the particular responsibilities. The verbs in this formulary emphasize *service*, in the sense of an army prepared to engage in battle together with the idea of *service* in worship. In their choice of words, the author underscores the seriousness of the Levitical duties. The specific tasks correspond to those assigned to the Levitical groups in 3:25-26, 31, 36-37. Here the emphasis is on the dismantling and transport of the tent and the sacred objects (compare 1:50-51).

The duties of the Kohathites are given first because theirs is the care of the most sacred objects (v. 4); presumably this gives them special status. Theirs is an unassuming task, however, for they may not touch the sacred objects nor even look upon them (vv. 15b, 18-20). Only after the priests have properly covered the objects (vv. 5-14), put the carrying poles in place (vv. 6b, 8b, 14b), or set the objects on litters (vv. 10b, 12b) are the Kohathites permitted to lift them (v. 15).

In this section, attention is diverted from the Kohathites to the priests, who alone may touch the sacred objects. First they cover the "ark of the commandments" with three layers: with the temple veil, skins, and an elaborate outer cloth (vv. 5-6). Only the ark, which contains the document of covenant with Yahweh, has a colored outer covering, making it stand out among the objects in transport. The other objects are each covered with a precious cloth and an outer skin covering (vv. 7-14). The Kohathites are not permitted, under pain of death, to touch anything but the handles of the carriers. It is the holiness and transcendence of God that are being emphasized in this reverential treatment of those objects that have a direct use in worship.

The priests and the Levites each have specific functions in regard to the sanctuary. The division of duties is uppermost in the mind of the author, who represents priestly families and who is writing this account at a time when the priests are dominant in the governance of the religious life of the people. The sons of Aaron alone have charge of the holy place, and Eleazar, in particular, has charge of the Dwelling (v. 16; compare 2:32 and 3:1-4).

The duties of the Gershonites and Merarites correspond to those assigned to them in 3:25-26 and 3:36-37, respectively. Here again the emphasis is on the transport of the holy place on the journey about to be undertaken. The Gershonites will carry all the cloths, coverings, skins, ropes, etc., that are part of the physical structure and its adornment (vv. 25-26). The Merarites will carry the boards, columns, pegs, etc., the wooden and metal parts that give the place shape or are used to secure it (vv. 31b-32a). As in the case of the Kohathites, these Levitical groups come under the direction of the priests (v. 27), and specifically under the supervision of Ithamar, the other son of Aaron (vv. 28 and 33; see 3:1-4).

The reader today cannot help but sense the reverence the Israelites had for the holy place and its appointments. Only the most precious cloths and the rarest of skins were suitable for covering the sacred objects (vv. 5-14). It is this regard for the place of worship and for the position of the priests in relation to the holy place that has influenced religious practice throughout history. Without minimizing the word of God, it is important to remember that this document comes from one period in history and reflects ancient practice. The truth contained here about the *presence of God* with the people for all time and in all places is sometimes lost in reading the detailed regulations. It is important for the reader to remember that the delimitation of duties and the distinction of roles point to the sacredness of the Presence among the people. This Dwelling of God in the midst of people cannot be limited to one mode, nor is it dependent on particular institutions. The whole point of this dramatic account is that *God is present* and continually reveals the God-self in ways that are meaningful in each new era of history.

4:34-49 Census completed. The results of the census commanded above (vv. 2-3, 22-23, 29-30) are summarized in this concluding section. Composed of repetitious formularies so characteristic of the Priestly writer, it states that Moses, together with Aaron, took the census of each of the Levitical groups (vv. 34, 38, 42), as the Lord had commanded (vv. 17, 41, 45). The males, registered by clans in their father's line, were those falling within the age limit for mandatory service—thirty to fifty years of age. (Contrast this census with that of all Levites in 3:15 and 40.) The total number of Levites designated for service in the transport of the meeting tent is correspondingly less than the total of all Levites who were registered (v. 48; compare 3:43).

Thus, the Levites, set apart for special service, are assigned tasks directly related to the sanctuary. As the people prepare to embark upon the journey through the wilderness toward the Promised Land, the Levites have the important duty of dismantling and carrying the physical structure of the Dwelling. All this elaborate preparation and designation of duties stresses the fact that the divine presence remains with the people and, indeed, accompanies them on their journey.

There is a pause in the preparations at this point as attention is focused on life within the camp. Because God dwells in the midst of the people, there is no place for anything unworthy of the all-holy God. At this juncture, therefore, the Israelites are given a series of laws pertaining to ritual and ethical purity (ch. 5) and laws concerning the nazirites, who dedicate themselves completely to the Lord (ch. 6).

5:1-4 Expulsion of the unclean. The laws given here are to ensure the cleanliness of the place where Yahweh dwells in the midst of the people (v. 3b; see Lev 15:31). These were laws that actually governed life in the land of Canaan, and they were especially important for the life of the postexilic worshiping community as mirrored in the organization and order of the wilderness camp. This place of the Lord's presence is a holy place. Everything unclean must be expelled; such things are incompatible with the holy place as long as they remain unclean (vv. 3-4).

According to customary law, the unclean were those with skin disease, those emitting a discharge from the genitals, and those who came into contact with a corpse (v. 2). These particular laws governed all the people but were especially rigid in regard to the priests (see Lev 22:4).

The skin disease, identified as leprosy, could be any variety of problems that are common in tropical climates. The distinctive factor is sores that are open and running. It is the discharge from the open sore that makes the diseased person ritually unclean. The laws that govern such disease are found in full in Lev 13–14. There we learn that several periods of seven days of quarantine, that is, exclusion from the camp, may be required before being declared clean (see Lev 13:4-6, 26-27, 31-34, 50-51; 14:8-9). Every disease, insofar as it is visible, is a contamination and therefore excludes the individual from the cultic community where Yahweh dwells (v. 3b).

The discharge refers to fluids from the sexual organs of both males (see Lev 15:1-17; Deut 23:10-15) and females (see Lev 15:19-30), whether such discharge is normal or linked with affliction. There is no provision for exclusion from the community in the Levitical laws; only in Numbers is such exclusion indicated. Exclusion from the community does not imply a negative attitude toward sex. It is rather the idea that all bodily discharges are defiling. They are incompatible with physical perfection and therefore unworthy of the holiness of God who dwells among the people (v. 3b). The prescribed purificatory rites for males and females were exactly the same, as was the required offering (see Lev 15:5-10, 19-24; 15:13-15, 25-30). Especially in this matter do the priests demonstrate a consciousness of the equality of the male and female person (v. 3a; see Lev 15:32-33).

The connection between death and evil was a strong one in antiquity, as it often still is today. It was believed that evil issued from a corpse, making anyone who came into contact with it unclean and therefore unworthy of the presence of God (v. 3b). According to the law, a person who touched a dead body was banned for the stipulated period of seven days (see Num 19:11).

5:5-10 Restitution for wrongdoing. This sets up a situation of wrongdoing in very broad terms. It specifies both the man and woman as possible offenders (v. 6a) and describes the offense as any transgression of human beings, that is, wrongs done to one another (v. 6b). This is a restatement of the law of restitution given in Lev 5:20-26.

In biblical teaching there is a direct connection between evils done within the human community and relationship with God (v. 6c). Love for God and love for neighbor are inextricably bound together. We have only to read the Decalogue (Exod 20:1-17 and Deut 5:6-21), the rules given for conduct within the community (Lev 19:1-37), prophetic speeches (Hos 4:1-3; Amos 5:21-24; Isa 1:12-16), or the New Testament (1 John 4:20-21; Matt 5:23-24; 23:34-40; 25:31-46) to be made aware that regard for the community's well-being is a direct expression of reverence for God.

According to the law, an individual who transgresses against another shall not only confess the wrong and compensate for the wrong done or the character defamed, but shall also make restitution in the value of one-fifth over and above the due amount (v. 7). Compensation plus one-fifth of that value is the standard restitution demanded in all cases (see Lev 5:16, 24; 22:14; 27:13, 27, 31). So sacred is the person in the community that any harm to an individual causes harm to the whole body. And so sacred is the community that any violation of its well-being demands restitution. God's presence within this community requires that nothing violate or disrupt the integrity of the common good, and when such occurs, restoration as well as restitution is required.

If this restitution cannot be paid to the one offended, it is to be paid to the next of kin (v. 8a). If there is no next of kin, the restitution belongs to the priests, who accept it as given to the Lord (v. 8b). This restitution is over and above the offering of a ram that is required as an expiation offering in atonement for sin (v. 8c; see Lev 5:14-26).

The place given to the next of kin tells us something about the solidarity of the community of God's people. The next of kin is the nearest male blood relative on the father's side of the family. Being the next of kin carries grave responsibilities to ensure the life of the immediate and extended family. If a woman becomes a widow and is childless, the next of kin has to marry her in order that the family line might flourish (Ruth 4). If there is threat of losing property that belongs to the family, the next of kin is required to buy it so that it remains in the family (Lev 25:25). If a family member becomes enslaved, the next of kin is responsible for securing that person's freedom (Lev 25:47-52). Just as the next of kin provides when life or property is threatened, so the next of kin becomes the recipient of goods when restitution cannot be made to a wronged party. That which was taken from a particular family is thus restored and compensated, and thereby the community is made whole within itself and with God.

Appended to this law governing restitution is a general statement about the "sacred contributions" or holy gifts that belong to the priests (vv. 9-10). This sacred contribution can be a reserved portion of the offering that the priest moves up and down in ritual action, or it can be the whole offering that an Israelite presents to Yahweh by lifting it up. In either case, the sacred contribution is that which is lifted up, and it belongs to the individual officiating priest.

5:11-31 Ritual for judgment. Another circumstance inappropriate to the place of God's presence is mistrust between husband and wife, described as jealousy (vv. 14, 30a). The case presents a husband who suspects that his wife has committed adultery (vv. 12-13, 29) and might therefore bear him a child that is not his own, but who has no concrete evidence and so cannot institute normal legal proceedings through the courts. The husband may resort to a trial by ordeal when there are no witnesses or other proof.

This is the only instance in the biblical literature where a ritual of ordeal is described in detail. The ordeal seems to have been used when the question of guilt or innocence could not be ascertained by the normal methods of making judgment. The accused person submits to some practice, such as drinking a potion or walking on fire. If he or she is unhurt, innocence is proven. Adultery was the offense for which the ordeal was most often invoked, as is suggested by the detailed description in this text. Deut 17:8-13, however, states that cases involving homicide, disputes over ownership rights, and personal assault may be settled by ordeal.

The case presented here is decidedly one-sided in that the man may accuse the woman, who then must bear the burden of the charge, while the man remains without guilt even when the accusation is groundless (v. 31). To be decided is the serious matter of paternity. The rite is designed to determine the legitimacy of the man's children.

The husband brings his wife before the priest with an offering of barley that has neither oil nor frankincense over it because "it is a cereal offering of jealousy" (v. 15). The dry grain signifies that the offering is an atonement for sin (see Lev 5:11-13). Oil and frankincense on the coarse grain would produce a sweet-smelling oblation, suggesting joy and bounty (Lev 2:1-2; 6:8).

The ritual for judgment follows. Essentially the woman stands before the Lord (vv. 16, 30b), a posture that brings God into the process of legal investigation. Her head is uncovered, a sign of disgrace and uncleanness, and she holds the cereal offering in her hands (v. 18). The priest meanwhile prepares the water by placing dust from the floor of the Dwelling into it (v. 17). This water is called "holy" because it is kept in the sanctuary. The addition of the dust increases the sacredness of the drink and its danger to the woman who will drink it. It is the drinking of this water, called "bitter," that decides innocence or guilt (v. 18c). Notice that reference is made to this water throughout verses 19, 22, 24, and 27.

The priest then puts the woman under oath to speak the truth (vv. 19a, 21a). The words pronounced by the priest cause the bitter water to be effective in confirming innocence (v. 19b) or guilt (vv. 20-22). The woman responds with "Amen, Amen," thereby agreeing with the effectiveness of the ordeal procedure. The curse itself is a euphemism for miscarriage or possibly sterility. "Thigh" is often used to mean the sexual organs. It is characteristic in accounts of judgment that the punishment is a reversal of the sin. If the woman has sinned by illicit intercourse, her punishment is the termination of the pregnancy (v. 27) or the inability to bear children. The opposite situation, described in verse 28, would be the ability to bear children.

Before the woman drinks, the words of the curse are written on, then washed off, the parchment into the water (v. 23) so that the words of the curse will be effective in themselves (v. 24). Last of all, the priest burns a handful of the cereal offering on the altar; the remainder of the cereal belongs to the priest (see Lev 2:2-3). Once the woman drinks the water, there are two possible outcomes (vv. 27-28): she is either proclaimed guilty and therefore unclean, or innocent and therefore clean.

6:1-21 Dedication of nazirites. In the context of preparation for the journey toward the land, where there will be the ideal community that has God dwelling among the people, we have noted the emphasis on the holiness and purity required of the believing community. The Priestly writer includes at this point a text about the consecration of individuals, both male and female (v. 2), underlining the sacredness and nobility of total dedication to the Lord. Such an individual is called a "nazirite," a term derived from the verb meaning "to set apart" or "to consecrate." A nazirite makes a vow of dedication to the Lord (v. 21) for a set period of time (vv. 4, 5, 6, 8, 12, 13).

The tradition of the nazirite was of long standing among the people of God. Samson (Judg 13:5) and Samuel (1 Sam 1:11) are thought to have been consecrated for life. The practice continued into the time of John the Baptist (Luke 1:15) and Paul the Apostle (Acts 18:18; 21:23-26).

Our text consists of three independent sections within the framework of verses 1-2 and 21. Verses 3-8 describe the conditions and laws that govern an individual who chooses to make a vow for a set period of time. Verses 9-12 outline the required purification if a person inadvertently becomes unclean. Verses 13-21 introduce the ceremonies to be observed when the period of the vow is fulfilled.

The nazirite assumes three restrictions when taking the vow of dedication. The obligations cover the matter of drinking and eating (vv. 3-4), the cutting of the hair (v. 5), and contact with the dead (vv. 6-7).

The nazirite is forbidden to consume the grape in any form—no drinking of wine, vinegar, or even grape juice (v. 3a), nor eating of grapes, raisins, the seeds or skins of the grape, or any part of the vine (vv. 3b-4). The abstention is from the grape, not from alcoholic drink as such. The grapevine represents urban culture, settled life, comfort, and high living—pleasures in opposition to faithful allegiance to Yahweh (see Amos 4:1b; 6:6).

Second, the nazirite does not put the razor to the hair of the head (v. 6). The growth of hair is a visible sign of consecration. Symbolic of integrity and dignity, the long hair dramatically distinguishes the individual as one who serves God in a special way (v. 7b).

Third, the nazirite never approaches the dead, not even the corpses of family members (vv. 6-7a). (On the uncleanness associated with contact with the dead, see the commentary on 5:1-3 and 9:11-22.) This law is stricter than in the case of the ordinary priest, who is exempted in the case of family (Lev 21:1-3); it is, however, comparable to the restrictions imposed on the high priest (Lev 21:11).

These practices set the nazirite apart as a continual reminder to the community of what total dedication of Yahweh should be. Apparently, in Amos' day the witness of the nazirites was so disturbing that the people tried to get them to break the vow (Amos 2:11-12).

The second section of the text addresses a situation in which the nazirite might accidentally become unclean by contact with a corpse (vv. 9-12). The hair, the sign of consecration, has thereby become polluted and must be shaved off (v. 9), and the period of dedication, now invalid, must be begun anew (v. 12). The period of purification, according to law, lasts seven days (v. 9b; see Num 19:11, 14, 16). Afterward the nazirite brings the simple offering of two birds, the offering required of the poor (v. 10; see Lev 5:7; 12:8; 14:22; 15:13-15). The priest offers one bird as a sin offering to restore the relationship with a holy God that has been interrupted by contact with that which makes one unclean; the other is offered as a holocaust, the sacrifice required of everyone coming before the Lord, and therefore must be completely consumed (v. 11). After the atonement has been made, the head of the nazirite is once again consecrated (v. 11b), and a guilt offering of a year-old lamb is made. This last is a kind of punitive fine paid to God for the loss of what is due. With the nullification of the vow, something that had properly belonged to Yahweh on the basis of the vow was lost. (See Deut 23:22-24 for the laws governing anyone who chooses to make a vow, and note the restrictions imposed on women in Num 30:4-16.)

The third section prescribes the ritual to be observed at the completion of the period of consecration (vv. 13-20). The instructions are addressed to the priest who will carry out the particulars of the ceremony. The individual comes forward to the meeting tent with specified offerings (vv. 13-15). After the priest has offered the sacrifice, the nazirite's head is shaved and the hair burned in the fire of the peace offering (vv. 16-18). The priest takes his share of the sacrificial gifts (vv. 19-20), and only then is the nazirite permitted to drink wine (v. 20c).

The full range of sacrifices indicates the solemnity of the occasion (vv. 14-15). The holocaust is offered by everyone who approaches the Lord; the sin offering is given in atonement for all violations committed, however unintentional. The peace offering is presented in thanksgiving together with cereal and drink offerings. This last suggests a banquet and signifies communion between God and the participant (vv. 16-17). The hair that has been cut is burned in the fire of the peace offering, signifying the destruction of that which had been consecrated to the Lord once it has served its purpose (vv. 18-19a).

In carrying out the sacrifice, the priest puts a share of the sacrifice into the hands of the one consecrated so that the portion may be formally presented to the priest (v. 19b) in a gesture of waving (v. 20a). This motion seems to represent the act of giving back to God from the bounty God has given. This share is part of the special gift presented to the priest. The usual gift due to the priest from every offering is the breast and the leg (v. 20b; see Lev 7:34 and Num 18:8-11). The nazirite is required to make the offerings prescribed, but other offerings may also be presented in accord with the individual's means (v. 21a).

With the completion of this ritual, the nazirite has fulfilled the period of vow and wine may be taken (v. 20c). The individual then resumes an ordinary life.

6:22-27 The priestly blessing. As a kind of interlude, unconnected with what precedes or follows, the Priestly author inserts a benediction formulary that is one of the oldest pieces of poetry in the Scriptures. Perhaps the blessing is placed here to show God's blessing on the people who live the holy life in accord with the regulations set forth in chapters 5–6.

The prayer itself (vv. 24-26) is positioned within a framework that begins with the typical "The Lord said to Moses." That the priests bless the people is seen as the Lord's will communicated through Moses (see Deut 10:8; 21:5). The specific reference to the Aaronic priesthood (v. 23a) reflects the postexilic time, when the principal duty of the priests in the sanctuary was to mediate the blessing, the wellspring of life that derives from Yahweh, the source of all life (see Pss 115:12-15; 118:26; 129:8; 134:3). At the installation of the priest, his first act was to raise his hand in blessing (Lev 9:1-24, esp. vv. 22-24). This strength for life that is mediated through the priests keeps alive the promise that through this people God's blessings flow to the world.

In the blessing, the name Yahweh is repeated three times and is the implied subject three more times. Pronouncing this name is itself an effectual blessing. Thus, the conclusion states that the priests "invoke my name upon the Israelites" (v. 27a). The Hebrew rendering is an unusual expression that literally states that they "put the name on" the people, rather than the expected "call on the name." This specific idiom would seem to imply a close relationship, an indication of God's ownership and protection. The Israelites are proclaimed to be Yahweh's property through the putting of Yahweh's name on them by the priests. The concluding statement "and I will bless them" (v. 27b) means, then, that when the priests put the divine name on the Israelites, Yahweh will indeed bless them.

The blessing itself is one of the finest pieces of ancient poetry. It is written in three lines, each with two parts, and in a complex metrical pattern that increases progressively in the number of words (three in the first line, five in the second line, and seven in the third line) and in metrical counts (ten, twelve, and fourteen, respectively). The blessing is addressed to "you" in the singular, meaning the whole of Israel as a corporate entity as well as each individual. This "you" is expressed three times as a direct object (vv. 24ab, 25b) and three times as the object of a preposition (vv. 25a, 26ab).

The first half of each line invokes Yahweh's personal act upon the people: "bless" (v. 24a), "let [your] face shine upon" (v. 25a), and "look kindly upon" (v. 26a).

To "bless" means to pour forth the continual and sustaining power of life that manifests itself as growth, increase, success, fertility, and prosperity (see Gen 24:34-36). Blessing derives from the essential divine being out of which arise the promises: "I will bless you; I will make your name great" (Gen 12:2); "I will be with you and bless you" (Gen 26:3).

To "let [Yahweh's] face shine upon" means to look with pleasure or favor. Clearly an anthropomorphism used metaphorically, reference to "face" implies the totality of divine goodness directed to the recipient of the blessing (see Ps 67:2). When Yahweh is gracious toward the people, they see Yahweh's face (Pss 31:17; 80:4, 8, 20). On the other hand, to express displeasure with the people, Yahweh declares, "I hide my face" (Ezek 39:23; see Isa 57:17).

To "look kindly upon" suggests the bestowal of divine love in gestures of favor and help. Yahweh's attention is directed toward the one who is dependent and in need of help (see Pss 33:18; 34:16; 1 Kgs 8:29, 52).

Each of these acts of Yahweh is followed

by a consequence of the blessing invoked. Yahweh will "keep" (v. 24b), "be gracious" (v. 25b), and "give peace" (v. 26b).

To "keep" means that in consequence of the blessing, Yahweh will protect Israel from the misfortunes that bring about the opposite of life and prosperity, such as childlessness, crop failure, threat from enemies. To "be gracious" means to show undeserved favor. As a consequence of Yahweh's face shining upon Israel, this people experiences the goodness that derives from the divine nature (see Exod 33:19; 34:6; Num 14:18; Deut 5:9-10). Finally, Yahweh "gives peace" as the consequence of looking kindly. The concept of peace is the summation of the act of blessing: "May the Lord bless his people with peace" (Ps 29:11). It is a term that means much more than freedom from war or discord. Peace is the state of being whole, of completeness, of happiness and harmony, so that a person is capable of a full and free development of life. Peace means the salvation that belongs to those whose lives are totally in harmony with God's will (see Ps 34:15; Isa 32:17). The purpose of Jesus' life was to bring peace (John 14:27; 16:33; 20:19, 21, 26).

7:1-88 Offerings of the princes. Chapter 7 returns to the preparations for the departure from Sinai after the interlude of the regulations governing life in the camp and in the community. There has been no passage of time from the date of the census (1:1, 18), which occurred exactly one month after the completion, erection, and consecration of the Dwelling (v. 1; Exod 40:2, 17; see the commentary on 1:1-3). The elaborate description of gifts creates a scene of dedication to the Lord as the tension heightens in the last preparations for the march (chs. 7–9).

The chapter is divided into two unequal sections. In the first, verses 1-9, the princes give wagons with oxen. In the second, verses 10-88, there is an elaborate listing of the gifts presented by each of the leaders.

The princes, the heads of the ancestral houses, are the same leaders of the people who assisted Moses with the census (v. 2; see the commentary on 1:4-19a). These men contribute six wagons and twelve oxen for use in the transport of the sanctuary (v. 3). The vehicles and animals will carry the sacred objects on the long journey through the wilderness.

In the stylistic pattern of Yahweh's word spoken and obeyed (vv. 4, 6), Moses is told to accept the offering and to assign the wagons to the Levites for use in carrying out their duties (v. 5). Moses gives two wagons with four oxen to the Gershonites (v. 7), whose responsibility is the tent itself and all the cloth hangings (3:25-26; 4:24-26); and four wagons with eight oxen to the Merarites (v. 8), who attend to the physical structure of the sanctuary (3:36-37; 4:31-32). Only the Kohathites, who take care of the most sacred objects, including the ark (3:28b, 31; 4:4-15), have to carry the carefully covered parcels on their shoulders (v. 9).

The remainder of the text (vv. 10-88) consists of Yahweh's command that the offerings brought by the princes for the dedication be presented on successive days (vv. 10-11); it gives a repetitive and detailed description of the gifts offered by each leader (vv. 12-83) and a final summary, with an accounting of the total number of gifts (vv. 84-88).

While the leaders are the same as those named as Moses' assistants in 1:5-15, their sequence corresponds to that of the tribes in the camp in 2:1-34 and again in the order of the march in 10:14-28 (see the commentary on 2:1-34). The privileged position of the Judah group reflects the importance of that tribe in the reestablishment of the religious center for the people who return from exile.

The gifts presented by each prince are identical in order and quantity. They are recounted in precise formulation, except for slight grammatical variation in verse 19. The only changes are in the names of the leaders and tribes. The princes bring gifts for all regular offerings—for the holocaust, the sin offering, and the peace offering. They also present silver plates and silver basins full of flour mixed with oil for the cereal offering, and a gold dish with incense. This exhaustively repetitive and detailed description of the offerings emphasizes the generosity of the leaders and has as its intention example and exhortation regarding provisions for the place of worship and its cultic celebrations. The text intentionally does not specify the offerings. The focus is not distracted from the liberality in giving.

The text concludes with a kind of accountant's report of the number of gifts presented on the occasion of the dedication of the altar (v. 84a). There is a precise listing of the numerous gifts (v. 84b), weights of the precious metals (vv. 85-86), and the number of each kind of animal offered (vv. 87-88) to reveal the extent of the princes' generosity in offering such gifts for the worship of God.

This display of gifts is a suitable conclusion to the preparation of the sanctuary and the worship therein. The Priestly writer's intention in re-creating this ideal scene in the wilderness is that it will be emulated in the postexilic community, where the people of Israel appropriately gather about the Presence among them, where everything unclean is purified, where total consecration is encouraged, and where the people tend to regular worship and contribute generously to the support of worship and the priests.

7:89 The voice. Appended to the description of the people of God gathered about the Dwelling in readiness for worship is a short piece that seems incomplete in itself but in reality concludes more than the particular chapter to which it is attached. The verse tells of Moses entering the meeting tent to communicate with the Lord (see Exod 33:7-11). Though Moses hears *"the voice,"* the message is lost to the reader. It is probable that the text is intended to convey the idea that the divine presence does indeed dwell in the holy place, and from there will speak to the people through Moses. The hearing of Yahweh's voice is the purpose of the entire preparation of the Dwelling.

At Sinai, where instructions for the construction of the Dwelling were communicated to Moses, the Lord promised that when the holy place was complete, "I will meet you . . . and from above the propitiatory, between the two cherubim on the ark of the commandments, I will tell you all the commands that I wish you to give the Israelites" (Exod 25:22). Our text is the direct fulfillment of Yahweh's promise.

The "propitiatory," sometimes called the "mercy seat," is a slab of gold set on top of the ark, where the covenant document is kept (see Exod 26:34). At either end of the propitiatory are facing cherubim, with wings extended in a kind of canopy over the ark. This is the highest place of atonement, where, on the Day of Atonement, the priest burns incense and sprinkles the blood of the sacrifice to cleanse the people from all their sins (Exod 25:17-22; 37:6-9). At this place the people turn again to the covenant and the hearing of the voice that bonds them with Yahweh.

8:1-4 The lampstand. Activities continue in readying the camp as the place where Yahweh is present and worshiped. In accord with the Lord's word (vv. 1, 3), Aaron sets up the seven lamps. This event culminates what had been commanded at Sinai. Instructions for the material and design of the lampstand were presented in Exod 25:31-40. Verse 4 corresponds exactly with that description. A detailed account of the making of the lampstand is given in Exod 37:17-24. Finally, the lampstand is set up against the south curtain of the meeting tent, opposite the table at the north end (Exod 40:22-25).

Emphasis in our text is upon the direction of the light "toward the front of the lampstand" (vv. 2-3; see Exod 25:37). This positioning of the wicks in the lamps of oil is necessary to focus the light in one direction. As the only source of light in the meeting tent, the wicks are set to cast light upon the table on which the bread of the Presence is placed (Exod 40:23).

8:5-26 Purification of the Levites. Continuing emphasis on complete dedication to Yahweh focuses our attention on the ritual for the consecration of the Levites. The text first outlines the rites as well as the purposes for the Levites' dedication in the pattern of God's word given (vv. 5-19) and obeyed (vv. 20-22), then designates the limiting age for Levitical service (vv. 23-26).

Earlier, in chapters 3 and 4, we learned about the census and duties of the Levites. Here the emphasis is on the Levites as a special offering to Yahweh. They "belong to Yahweh" (vv. 14, 16, 18); they are "taken from among the Israelites" (vv. 6, 14, 16, 18) and "dedicated" (vv. 16, 19) for service as a special contribution (vv. 11, 13, 15, 21; see the discussion below on the wave offering).

When the Levite reaches the age of service, he submits to a rite of purification (v. 7). He is first sprinkled with the "water of remission," that is, water that effects the forgiveness of sins. He then shaves the hair from his entire body, thereby removing all imperfection and rendering future growth pure and clean. Last of all, he washes his clothes to make them clean, just as the Israelites did at Sinai to ready themselves for the divine presence (Exod 19:10, 14).

These Levites are clearly distinguished from the priest who is consecrated with oil (Exod 29:7; Lev 8:12) and adorned with completely new garments (Exod 28:40-43; 29:8-9; Lev 8:13). The Levites are men taken from among the people to represent the people. To dramatize this representation, the Levites come before the assembled community. The people "lay their hands" upon them (vv. 9-10). The dedication of the Levites substitutes for the consecration of the first-born of every Israelite family (vv. 16-18; see 3:11-13, 40-51). The Levites thus serve in the place and in the name of the community. Their service in the care of the sanctuary is a kind of protection so that no harm will come to anyone who might approach the sanctuary unworthily (v. 19).

For the sacrifice, the Levites bring offerings for a holocaust and a sin offering (vv. 8, 12). Each Levite lays his hands on the head of the animals to demonstrate his giving of himself totally to God. The one bull and the cereal, like a banquet meal, symbolize union between Yahweh and the Levite, and are therefore wholly consumed. The other bull is offered to atone for sin.

The priest participates by offering the Levite as a "wave offering" (vv. 11, 13; also vv. 15, 21). The ritual for other occasions would be for the priest to put a share of the sacrifice into the hands of the offerer, who would return it to the priest. The priest would receive this share as the portion for his own use. The motion of this giving back and forth and to Yahweh resembles a waving. On this day of dedication the priest receives the Levite himself, who is given as the share from all Israel for the use and service of the priest (vv. 13-14; see 3:5-10). The Levite enters the service of the sanctuary as a subordinate to the Aaronite priests (v. 19). He belongs to Yahweh and takes care of the place where Yahweh dwells among the people.

The Levites engage in this special service of the sanctuary only during their prime years. The age limits given are between twenty-five and fifty years old (vv. 24-25). Apparently the time for initiation into service varies according to need and numbers of men available. In chapter 4, the age given for beginning service is thirty years old (vv. 35, 39, 43, 47); in other texts, twenty is given as the entry age (1 Chr 23:24; 2 Chr 31:17; Ezra 3:8). There are no variations for the age of retirement from service. Once the Levite has reached the age of fifty, he may assist the younger Levites in their work, but he may no longer be responsible for particular duties (v. 26).

9:1-14 The second Passover. A sense of excitement is created with a series of final preparations for departure from the wilderness of Sinai. It is the prescribed time for the celebration of Passover (vv. 1-5), which was first celebrated on the eve of deliverance from bondage in Egypt (see Exod 12–13). The legislation for keeping the feast is enjoined by Moses in the style of Yahweh's command (vv. 1-3), followed by obedient execution of the command (vv. 4-5). Moses commands the people to celebrate the feast when the same calendar date and time come around again, that is, at the beginning of the year in the month of Abib in the evening of the fourteenth day (vv. 2-3, 5; see Exod 12:2, 6, 18; 13:4; Lev 23:5).

The remainder of the text presents real-life situations that interfere with the observance of Passover. We find here an example of new instructions that become the precedent for subsequent practice. The people consult Moses regarding these problems, and Moses seeks direction from Yahweh to answer them (v. 8; see 15:34; 27:5; Lev 24:10-23 for other examples of seeking a decision from Yahweh).

The first situation is one of uncleanness. What should a person do who has become ritually unclean from contact with a corpse (v. 6; see 19:11-22) but who desires to participate in the feast (v. 7)? The instruction given in response includes another situation—that of a person who "is absent on a journey" (v. 10). While the case of uncleanness reflects the wilderness situation, this latter case suggests a later time when people traveled abroad and the practice of observing the feast in the central sanctuary prevailed (see Deut 16:2; Ezra 6:16-22).

The answer to these situations is the stipulation that a secondary feast might be celebrated one month later at the same time and in accord with all the laws for the feast (vv. 11-12; see Exod 12:8-10). According to this provision, one who is unclean might be purified, and one who is absent on a journey might be able to observe the feast on this later date. That this supplementary legislation was actually observed is evident in the case of Hezekiah. The Chronicler (2 Chr 30:1-5) records the occasion when Hezekiah invited the people from the northern tribes to Jerusalem for the feast. To accommodate the situation, the Passover feast was observed during the second month that year.

This provision must not be misconstrued, however, to exempt people from observance of the feast on the specified day for just any reason. From the tone of verse 13, only accidental circumstances or situations beyond one's control are legitimate exemptions. Those who excuse themselves from this community observance for reasons of neglect bring exclusion from the community upon themselves. The text says that they "shall be cut off from [their] people" (v. 13).

The second situation pertains to aliens or foreigners who wish to keep the feast. This is an issue that must have arisen time and again in the course of Israelite history. The problem is also addressed in Exod 12:43-49 in the regulations for the Passover feast. What we find in Numbers corresponds exactly. The stranger who has accepted circumcision, the one who "lives among you" (v. 14), meaning one who has accepted the God of the Israelites, may participate in the feast. There are no exceptions to the rules and regulations for these individuals, however. They will observe the feast in exactly the same manner as the natives.

9:15-23 The cloud and the Presence. The time has come for departure from the wilderness site. The great event at Sinai reaches its conclusion at this point. The Dwelling is now complete; it is filled with the "Glory of the Lord" and the "cloud settles down upon it" (Exod 40:34-35).

This cloud is the visible sign of the divine presence in the Dwelling. Where the cloud is visible, Yahweh is present. It manifests Yahweh "in the midst of this people" (Num 14:14). The cloud guided the people as they fled from Egypt (Exod 13:21-22), and it hid them from the approaching Egyptians (Exod 14:19, 24). When the cloud is visible over the meeting tent, Moses enters the tent to speak with the Lord (Exod 33:9-10; Num 12:5). This same cloud will determine Israel's movements on the long journey through the wilderness (Exod 40:36-38; Num 10:12). It hovers over the Dwelling by day, and at night it takes on the appearance of fire (vv. 15-16).

With the focus on Yahweh's presence in the midst of the people under the symbol of the cloud, the author stresses two points that are important for the generations of believers who will read or hear the story over and over again. The first is that the cloud determines the length of Israel's stay in a given place (vv. 19-22). Sometimes the stay is long; at times it is for a few days; sometimes it is only from evening to morning. The time of departure and the time for setting up camp are in no way self-determined. As the people embark on their journey, every phase of movement will be in response to the cloud.

Second, the point being made emphatically is that Yahweh speaks through the cloud. Two phrases emphasize that the Israelites obediently heed Yahweh's direction in the breaking and setting up of the camp. They move "at the bidding of the Lord" (vv. 18, 20, 23), an expression used seven times over; they "obey the Lord" (v. 19), and they "heed the charge of the Lord" (v. 23). Israel conforms totally to the will of God every step of the way on the long trek toward the land. The picture is of an ideal time when the people listen to the voice of God and comply willingly with God's instructions and commands.

10:1-10 Two silver trumpets. Our attention turns from the cloud as the Lord's guiding presence to the silver trumpets, the instruments used to assemble and move the community (v. 2). Known from the period of the postexilic community, the association of the trumpets with the wilderness generation reinforces the realization that the Priestly author intends to merge the ideal wilderness community gathered about the holy place with the worshiping community of the later period, when the people are being instructed in the ideals for living properly in the presence of a holy God.

These trumpets are blown in a sustained blast to give the signal for assembly. The specific verb "blown" is used in verses 3-4 and again in verses 7a, 8, 10 to indicate the type of signal. When both are blown, the entire community is being called to assembly (v. 3); when one trumpet is blown, only the leaders are being called (v. 4).

The signal for setting out, whether on a journey or into war, is a series of short, staccato-like notes. The silver trumpets are mentioned here because the people are ready to set out on the journey. The preparations that have been undertaken as described in the preceding chapters are now complete, and the people are ready to move forward under the guiding protection of Yahweh. When the first alarm is given, the Judah group on the east side of the camp marches out (v. 5); at the second alarm, the Reuben group, positioned south of the sanctuary, follows; then the Ephraim group from the west side of the camp; and finally the Dan group from the north side (v. 6; see ch. 2 for the arrangement of the tribes around the Dwelling). The tribes are readied to move out in an orderly manner and in the order of precedence.

The remainder of the text regulates the use of the trumpets once the people have come into "their own land" (v. 9a). It is the task of the priests to blow the trumpets (v. 8). This practice is frequently mentioned in the literature of the postexilic period (see 1 Chr 15:24; 16:6; 42; 2 Chr 7:6; Neh 12:35; 41). The trumpets are used to signal entry into battle (v. 9; see 2 Chr 13:12). They are blown most often to announce the observance of the various feasts, to summon the community to worship, and to express thanksgiving on joyous occasions (v. 10; see 2 Chr 5:12-13; 29:26-28; Ezra 3:10-11).

The text tells us that the reason the trumpet is blown is to cause God to "remember . . . and save" (v. 9b; see also v. 10b). The blowing of the trumpet is an act of prayer and dependence, a calling upon God to be present especially in situations of need and celebration.

This passage, and indeed the entire section in chapters 1–10, ends with the recognition formula, "I, the Lord, am your God" (v. 10c; see p. 146 for an explanation). It was Yahweh who invited Israel into the unique relationship that resulted in so many blessings. It is Yahweh who acts at this moment to be with the people, to lead them, protect them, and bring them safely to their own land.

ON THE JOURNEY FROM SINAI TO MOAB

Num 10:11–22:1

Up to this point the people have been encamped in the wilderness of Sinai. They now embark on a journey that will include a number of stops in the course of many years and will end on the plains of Moab, located across the Jordan River opposite the land of promise. This section begins with the departure from Sinai (10:12) and ends with the arrival at Moab (22:1). Throughout we will notice the journey formula and mention of various locations that make the reader aware of movement from site to site (10:12, 33; 11:35; 12:16; 20:1a, 22; 21:4, 10-20; 22:1). The Priestly writer uses a structure based on the tradition of the wilderness journey to support the record of events that happen along the way.

Many stories about the threat of danger, lack of food and water, tribal factions, and jealousies were passed down within the families who made the journey. These stories became the source from which our author gathered material to tell about the trials of the journey. The stories are found in chapters 11–14, 16–17, 20–21. Their narration is lively and very unlike the stylized language of the earlier chapters. These stories give the reader a glimpse of the very real struggles of people whom God had favored. They teach important lessons about the consequences for individuals and groups who turn from following God and the designated leaders. Directed at the community that is in passage from the wilderness of the Exile to their own land and in the process of resettlement and reorganization as a faith community, the stories provide lessons from history for future life.

Scattered throughout the narration of these chapters we find treasures of ancient poetry at 10:35-36; 12:6-8; 21:14-15, 17-18; 21:27b-30. These pieces survived from the time of the events they celebrate and allow the reader to hear what Israel itself sang, recited, and remembered.

As a kind of interruption to the dramatic action of these chapters, the author inserts some regulations in chapters 15, 18, 19. There is no apparent connection between the content of the narratives and these cultic regulations. They are directed to future generations, providing them with guidelines for living in a holy manner in the presence of a holy God.

Events in the Desert of Paran

(10:11–19:22)

10:11-28a Departure from Sinai. The departure from the wilderness is once again associated by date with the Exodus experience. After nearly a year's delay at Sinai—from the first day of the third month (Exod 19:1) to the twentieth day of the second month a year later (v. 11a)—and after final preparations that are telescoped to just nineteen days (compare Num 1:1), the signal is given for the beginning of the march.

The cloud covering the Dwelling rises from its place to signal movement from the camp (v. 11b; see the discussion on the cloud at 9:15-23). The cloud will guide the Israelites on the move until it settles in the desert of Paran, the first camping site on the continuing journey (v. 12). While the location is not certain, it is probable that this first stop was at Wadi Feiran, an oasis in the northern Sinai Peninsula south of the Negeb (see 13:17). The name Paran suggests that the author has the well-known Feiran oasis in mind.

The order of the march in verses 13-28 corresponds to the designated arrangement in the camp and the instructions for departure in 2:1-31, once again including mention of the leaders of the individual tribes. The Judah group from the east side of the Dwelling holds first place and leads the march (vv. 14-16). After them, the Levites, who transport the paraphernalia of the Dwelling, set out (v. 17; 2:17; see the duties of the Gershonites and Merarites in 4:21-33). Next come the three tribes headed by Reuben (vv. 18-20), followed by the sacred objects of the Dwelling carried by the Kohathites (v. 21; see 4:4-20). The sacred items are separated from the structure and coverings so that the tent might be readied at the new site in preparation for housing the ark, altar, table, and lampstand at the new campsite (v. 21b). The Ephraimite group follows the sacred objects (vv. 22-24), acting, no doubt, as a rear guard. Finally, as "rear guard for all the camps," the Dan group follows last of all (vv. 25-27).

10:28b-32 Moses' brother-in-law as guide. The very practical need for human wisdom on the journey through the wilderness balances the story that has focused exclusively on divine guidance. Moses asks his brother-in-law Hobab, a Midianite (v. 29a), to serve as "eyes" for the people, because he "knows where [they] can camp in the desert" (v. 31). The Midianites are nomads who live in the wilderness and know its routes and camping places. Hobab is from the clan of Zipporah, Moses' wife, who was, according to one tradition, the daughter of Reuel (see Exod 2:15-22). Elsewhere Jethro is the name of Moses' father-in-law (see Exod 3:1; 4:18; 18). The traditions agree that the father-in-law was a priest of Midian (Exod 2:16; 18:1).

In his bidding, Moses promises Hobab a share in the prosperity that the Lord has promised in the land (vv. 29b, 32). The implication is that those who associate themselves with the people of Yahweh share in the benefits that come as a result of Yahweh's covenant promise.

Hobab at first declines the invitation because he prefers to return to his own people (v. 30). This passage does not report Hobab's final answer. We presume his positive response, since Moses' relatives are mentioned among those who enter the land (see Judg 1:16; 4:11; 1 Sam 15:6. The Kenites named in these texts are part of the Midianite group).

10:33-36 The ark leads into the desert. Attention once again turns to the Lord's continual presence with the people. In the camp the cloud rested upon the sanctuary (v. 11), and on the march the cloud moves with the "ark of the covenant of the Lord" (v. 33) to lead the people forward. The ark, which traditionally was the portable seat of Yahweh's invisible presence, is specifically mentioned to show that Yahweh indeed moves with the people and leads them.

Inserted here is an ancient ritual cry that was recited over many years whenever the people of Israel engaged in warfare (see Pss 68:2; 132:8). One hymn is sung when the ark sets out with the troops (v. 35), another when it returns with them to the camp (v. 36). The hymns carry the tradition that Yahweh, the God of the armies, marches ahead to defeat the enemy.

The language of the hymn is clear. When the ark is moved, Yahweh arises and goes before the people to scatter their enemies. When the ark rests, Yahweh returns and sits enthroned in the midst of the troops.

According to tradition, the ark led the people through the wilderness, and it led the people into the land (see Josh 3:1-8). The ark remains with the people in the camp when they complain and prove themselves to be faithless.

11:1-3 Discontent at Taberah. No sooner have the people moved from Sinai than they do what they will do over and over again—they "complain in the hearing of the Lord" (v. 1). This first account of the people's discontent functions as a summary introduction in that it sets forth a pattern of behavior that will recur often in the stories of events in the wilderness. There is a predictable cycle of actions: the people complain (v. 1a); Yahweh's anger provokes punishment (v. 1b); the people cry to Moses to obtain relief (v. 2a); Moses intercedes on behalf of the people (v. 2b); Yahweh hears Moses' prayer (v. 2c).

There are actually two separate themes stressed in these stories. One theme is that of rebellion and punishment as characteristic of Israel's relation to Yahweh in the wilderness (see also Exod 14:11-22; 15:23-25a; 16:2-15; 17:1-7, though the telling in Numbers is highly stylized in comparison). The other theme is that of Moses as the intercessor to whom Yahweh responds with forgiveness and deliverance. This latter theme is especially important. Moses' unique leadership position and his authority are issues of such concern that the controversies regarding him are the basis for the stories in chapters 11–12 and 16–17.

The incident at Taberah is told to introduce the two major themes. There is no explanation of why the people complain nor any particulars about the fire sent as punishment. The cycle of rebellion and forgiveness moves quickly to the explanation for the name of the place (v. 3). The name Taberah derives from the verb "burn" or "consume." Stories were often told to explain the names of places. This feature is, in fact, a characteristic of the older stories (see, for example, Gen 16:13-14; 19:20-23; 21:31; 28:19-22; Exod 15:23; 17:7).

11:4-35 Complaint at Kibroth-hattaavah. Another incident, more complex in its structure, also ends with the explanation of the name of the place. Kibroth-hattaavah means "graves of greed" (v. 34). The story is about the people's complaint that they do not have enough meat in the wilderness. As a result, the people are fed with quail (vv. 4-9, 10, 13, 18-24a), and they also are punished for their greed (vv. 31-33).

Intertwined with the account about the craving for meat is a story about the sharing of Moses' leadership (vv. 11-12, 14-17, 24b-30). We will look at each story separately and consider how they are combined.

The account of the quail contains the elements of a typical complaint story. Two separate groups of people—the foreign element and the Israelites—complain about the lack of meat (v. 4). They long for the days in Egypt, when they enjoyed an abundance of fish and vegetables (v. 5). They are dissatisfied that all they have to eat is the manna, out of which they daily make loaves that taste like cakes with oil (vv. 6-9; see Exod 16:13-14, 31).

The "Lord became very angry" at the Israelites' display of greed (v. 10). Moses and Yahweh will each respond to the complaint. Rather than responding with intercession, Moses feels sorry for himself. He grieves that he alone must provide for the great multitude, saying, "Where can *I* get meat to give to all this people? They are crying to *me*" (v. 13). Moses presumes that it is his responsibility to find meat but expresses his inability to do so. Rather than seeking Yahweh's help, he shows resentment at the position in which he has been placed.

Yahweh, however, ignores Moses' lament and speaks to him in his capacity as mediator (vv. 18a, 24a). Yahweh responds, not to Moses' expressed concern, but directly to what the people have said. Yahweh makes plain that the people are in reality wishing to return to Egypt (vv. 18, 20b), thereby rejecting the Lord's deliverance. Yahweh instructs Moses to tell the people to "sanctify" themselves (v. 18), for they will receive meat in such abundance that they will become sick from it (vv. 19-20). Moses interjects again with a doubt about Yahweh's ability to provide the amount of meat that would be required to satisfy so many people (vv. 21-23).

In the fulfillment of Yahweh's word (vv. 31-34), Moses is conspicuously absent. Yahweh sends quail from the sea in great abundance. The people gather it (vv. 31-32), but before they can begin to eat it, Yahweh sends a plague to punish the greedy for their complaint (v. 33). Thus, the place was called "graves of greed," because those who were greedy were buried there (v. 34).

If we compare the elements in this story with those outlined in the incident at Taberah (vv. 1-3), it is obvious that Moses' response to the situation makes the difference. When Moses intercedes for the people, Yahweh responds with forgiveness (v. 2). In the incident of the quail, Moses' intercession is lacking, and the result is Yahweh's anger. By placing these stories side by side, the author is deliberately highlighting the effectiveness of Moses' intercession.

The lament of Moses (vv. 11-15) provides the link for the inclusion of the second story concerning the sharing of Moses' leadership. The issue raised by this lament is that he is burdened with the sole leadership of a people who are not his (vv. 12,14). Moses sees this as a punishment (v. 11), and his distress is so great that death is preferable (v. 15). Moses does not ask for help in leadership; he requests only the ultimate end of the burden.

Yahweh ignores Moses' death wish and takes up the matter of Moses' being *alone.* Yahweh instructs Moses to choose seventy elders and to bring them to the meeting tent (v. 16; see Exod 18:13-26 for the tradition regarding the selection of judges to help Moses with the care of the people). Yahweh will "take some of the spirit that is on [Moses] and will bestow it on [the elders], that they may share the burden" (v. 17). Moses does exactly as Yahweh has instructed (vv. 24b-25a). However, in the execution, a new element is added. In the sharing of Moses' spirit, nothing is said about sharing the burden with him (v. 25b). Instead, when the spirit rests on the elders, they prophesy (v. 25c). This story also supports the uniqueness of Moses' position as leader. Others may prophesy, but they cannot share the burden of the responsibility assigned to Moses—to communicate Yahweh's word and to bring the people safely into the land of promise (v. 12).

The theme of prophecy is continued in yet another story (vv. 26-30). Eldad and Medad, though not called elders, are among those chosen by Moses. Instead of going to the meeting tent with the seventy, they remain in the camp, where the spirit comes upon them also so that they prophesy (v. 26). Joshua, Moses' young assistant (see Exod 33:11), for some reason objects to this and pleads with Moses to stop them (vv. 27-28). Moses instead voices the wish that the "Lord might bestow his spirit" on all the people that they might all be prophets (v. 29). It is not Moses' spirit but rather Yahweh's spirit that is upon them. Moses approves of the distribution of Yahweh's spirit and is not concerned that his own prestige might be lost: "Are you jealous for my sake?" (v. 29). What appears to be a diminishing of Moses' position in the sharing of the spirit leads instead to a further delineation of Moses' uniqueness in chapter 12, a delineation that focuses the prophetic role.

Before the next story, there is a brief note about the people's move from Kibroth-hattaavah to Hazeroth (v. 35), the site of the next incident of rebellion.

12:1-16 Jealousy of Aaron and Miriam. Opposition to Moses comes from those closest to him. The tradition holds that Aaron and Miriam accompanied Moses from the time of the Exodus event (Exod 15:20-21; see Exod 6:20). Miriam and Aaron challenge Moses on two accounts: his marriage to a Cushite woman (v. 1) and his unique position as sole spokesman for Yahweh (v. 2). We have here another story that is told in the pattern of rebellion and eventual forgiveness through the intercession of Moses (see the discussion on 11:1-3).

The reason for the complaint that Moses has married a Cushite woman is obscure, since there is no evidence for a marriage other than with Zipporah, a Midianite (see Exod 2:15-22; 4:24-26; 18:2-3). If, however, the reference to Cush is actually a parallel to Midian, as in Hab 3:7, then the complaint is in opposition to Moses' marriage with a foreigner. There is, in fact, a tradition recorded in Num 25:6-18 that polemicizes marriage with Midianites, who are described as archenemies of Israel. This complaint reflects a strong anti-Moses bias because of his foreign wife.

In the second complaint Miriam and Aaron challenge Moses on the ground that they are prophets as well as he—"Does the Lord not speak through us also?" (v. 2). This opposition reveals resentment against Moses' exclusive role as mediator between God and the people. This issue was raised in the preceding story (11:26-30). If all people can be prophets, does Moses have a claim to uniqueness? The response and punishment are such that they both clarify (vv. 6-8) and affirm (vv. 13-14) the authority of Moses.

Moses makes no response to the complaints. The text states that he is the "meekest man on the face of the earth" (v. 3). This statement has been interpreted as a description of a person with personal honor and integrity of character. In spite of opposition, Moses will honorably stand by his responsibility as leader when he is called upon to intercede for Miriam (v. 13).

The response to the complaint comes directly from Yahweh in the form of an instruction (vv. 4-8) and a punishment (vv. 9-15). Overhearing the complaint, Yahweh summons Moses, Aaron, and Miriam to the meeting tent (v. 4), calls Aaron and Miriam aside (v. 5), and instructs them with a detailed account of the difference between Moses and a prophet (vv. 6-8). The words that Yahweh speaks express a tradition about Moses that survives in a piece of ancient poetry. The poem states that Yahweh communicates with the prophet in "visions" and "dreams" (v. 6), but with Moses, Yahweh speaks "face to face" and "plainly" (v. 8). Moses' relationship is more personal and intimate. He beholds the "presence of the Lord" (v. 8). He is thus set over all others as the peerless mediator of Yahweh's word. Aaron and Miriam stand rebuffed with the final question upholding the authority of Moses—"Did you not fear to speak against my servant Moses?" (v. 8b).

After this rebuke, Yahweh responds in anger (v. 9). Miriam is made snow-white with leprosy (v. 10). Aaron thereupon appeals to Moses for help and identifies with the punishment in his confession that both have sinned (v. 11). Moses prays for her healing and by his intercession wins Yahweh's forgiveness. Moses' authority receives legitimation and confirmation in the restoration of Miriam (vv. 14-16).

Miriam's leprosy is described as being "snow-white" (v. 9) and is compared to the appearance of a stillborn child (v. 12). She is fully restored after a period of seven days outside the camp (vv. 14-15a). To illuminate the situation, we look at the law pertaining to a leprous person in Lev 13:9-17. In summary, the law states that the leprous person is brought to the priest. If the leprosy covers the whole body and the body has turned white, the priest pronounces the leper clean. Miriam's whiteness and her confinement outside the camp for seven days point not to active but to burnt-out leprosy. Miriam was punished with a post-leprous condition. Her exclusion from the camp is for the period necessary to verify her cleanness.

During the period of Miriam's confinement, the people remain encamped at Hazeroth (v. 15b). Afterward they set out and settle in the desert of Paran (v. 16; see the discussion on 10:11-28).

Chapters 13–14 present the continuing drama of the people's rebellion, even when they are in sight of the Promised Land. These chapters are developed from a number of ancient traditions that the Priestly author weaves into one explanation for Israel's long sojourn in the wilderness. Though we have one story, we will approach the content in sections to facilitate reading.

13:1-24 Scouts enter Canaan. In accord with Yahweh's word (v. 1), Moses sends a delegation of scouts to explore the Promised Land (v. 2). The Israelites are encamped in the desert of Paran (v. 3a) at Kadesh (see v. 26), a well-known oasis located southwest of the southern tip of the Dead Sea. They are situated directly south of the Promised Land and in range of entrance. From this location Moses dispatches twelve leaders, one from each tribe, to look around (vv. 3b-16).

The names of the leaders are set in a tribal list that is a rather free arrangement of that in 1:5-15. The leaders are not the same as those appearing earlier (see also 7:12-83). And except for Caleb and Joshua, who play a major role in this story (13:30; 14:6, 24, 30), the leaders are not mentioned again by name. There is a special note that Moses has changed the name of Hoshea to Joshua (v. 16). Joshua, which means "Yahweh is salvation," is related to Hoshea, which means "salvation." Joshua receives his new name in preparation for his future role as successor to Moses (see 27:12-23). It is Joshua who will finally lead the next generation of Israelites into the land (14:30; see Deut 31:7-8; Josh 1:1-11).

The scouts are sent into the Negeb, a parched area south of Judah, to proceed into the highlands that run the length of central Canaan (v. 17). They reach Hebron, a city located about twenty miles south of Jerusalem, where three tribes are settled (v. 22; see Josh 15:14; Judg 1:20). The territory around Hebron has a reputation for its grapes, pomegranates, and figs. It is because of this that the place is called Wadi Eshcol, the "valley of the cluster," and the exaggerated story is told about two men required to carry the grapes (vv. 23-24).

One tradition says that the men scouted from the desert of Zin as far as Hamath (v. 21); that is, they went from the southern frontier to the northern limit of the land. The desert of Zin is part of the desert of Paran near

Kadesh (see 20:1; 27:14; 33:36), and Hamath, a pass near the Orontes, is located in Lebanon at the northern border of Israel's territory (see 34:8; Josh 13:5; Judg 3:3; 2 Kgs 14:25; Amos 6:14).

Moses instructed the scouts to secure information about the land and the people (v. 18), the towns and fortifications (v. 19), the terrain and the soil. He also told them to bring back some of the fruit of the land (v. 20).

13:25-33 Return of the scouts. After forty days, a stay of significant duration to adequately survey the situation (v. 25), the scouts return to Kadesh, where they report to Moses, Aaron, and the entire community and present them with the fruit (v. 26). They describe the land as flowing "with milk and honey" (v. 27), an expression that traditionally identifies the land as that promised by Yahweh (see Exod 3:8, 17; 13:5; 33:3, and frequently in Deuteronomy). But they quickly add that the inhabitants are powerful descendants of the Anakim, and the towns are well fortified (vv. 28, 31-33). A tradition prevailed that the Anakim were a numerous, tall, and strong people (see Deut 1:28; 2:21) who had to be defeated when Israel entered the land (Josh 11:21-22; 14:12, 15). That the population was mixed—Amalekites, Hittites, Jebusites, Amorites, and Canaanites (v. 29)—also accords with tradition regarding the inhabitants before the conquest. The Amalekites were encountered near Sinai (Exod 17:8-16); the Hittites were early inhabitants in Hebron (Gen 23:13-19); the Jebusites controlled Jerusalem (2 Sam 5:6-9). The Amorites were early inhabitants of Canaan who were later forced from the coastal plains and the Jordan valley to settle in the highlands. They were part of the indigenous Canaanite population. This latter group had settled in the fertile valleys and coastal region.

The scouts paint a fearful picture and recommend that the Israelites abort their attempt to enter the land because they will never survive the might of the inhabitants (vv. 31-33). The scouts thus challenge the guidance of Yahweh and the promise of the land to their ancestor Abraham. They, in fact, reject the land Yahweh is about to give them. Only Caleb encourages the people to proceed and expresses confidence in their success (v. 30). The interjection of Caleb at this point prepares for his role, along with Joshua, as one of the leaders who trusts the God of Israel (14:6-9). In tradition, the descendants of Caleb controlled the bountiful territory of Hebron and its surroundings (Josh 15:13-14; Judg 1:20). This story in Numbers provides an explanation of why Caleb and his descendants were favored with such a possession.

With the report from the scouts, the stage is set for the rebellion of the people. In this sense, the whole of chapter 13 functions as an introduction to the cycle of rebellion and forgiveness that follows in chapter 14.

14:1-10 The people's complaint. The whole community grumbles against Moses and Aaron on account of the report from the scouts (vv. 1-2a). The people reject Yahweh when they wish that they had never left Egypt. They are fearful of the disaster that awaits their families and themselves (vv. 2b-3). They conclude that it would be better to return to the security of bondage in Egypt, and they even decide to choose a leader of their own mind (vv. 3b-4).

Moses and Aaron respond by falling to the ground in helplessness (v. 5). Caleb and Joshua tear their garments in grief (v. 6). They appeal to the people, reminding them that the land is good (v. 7), that the Lord promised the land and will bring them to it (v. 8). They exhort the people to trust Yahweh who is with them (see Exod 33). And they remind the people that they need not fear the inhabitants, because "their defense has left them" (v. 9). The term "defense" is actually the word "shadow," which means literally that the inhabitants are left exposed and vulnerable to the ferocity of the sun, and metaphorically that Yahweh has removed the protection of their local gods. The inhabitants who have no protection will be "food for us," that is, they will be easily consumed.

The words of Caleb and Joshua are not heeded. The people rebel and threaten to stone them (v. 10a) and would have succeeded if Yahweh had not intervened. The "glory of the Lord appeared at the meeting tent" (v. 10b). The phrase "glory of the Lord" is always used by the Priestly author to express the revelation of Yahweh in power and majesty.

14:11-19 Punishment and Moses' intercession. Yahweh, manifest to all Israel, laments to Moses about the contempt of the people and their refusal to believe in spite of all the signs (v. 11). Yahweh announces the obliteration of the whole people and promises to start anew by creating a greater and mightier nation from Moses (v. 12).

Moses intercedes at this point and persuades Yahweh to set aside this harsh judgment (vv. 13-19). Moses pleads boldly, using Yahweh's reputation among the other nations as his argument (vv. 13-16). He asserts that Yahweh is known as a God in the midst of the people, a God who accompanies them by day and night. Should this people be annihilated, the nations will have cause to say that Yahweh did not have the power to bring them into the land and therefore killed them in the desert. Moses advises that Yahweh's honor and standing among the gods are at stake.

Quoting a confessional formulary from Exod 34:6-7, Moses suggests that the Lord's power will be better shown, not by killing, but by patience, kindness, forgiveness, and by just punishment of sin (vv. 17-18). Moses summarizes his request by asking that Yahweh forgive the iniquity of this people according to the greatness of the covenant love, just as Yahweh has forgiven them many times from Egypt until now (v. 19). Moses is pleading with Yahweh to preserve the covenant relationship that was made when Yahweh brought the people from Egypt. He thus appeals to Yahweh's covenant faithfulness and at the same time recognizes Yahweh's utter freedom to maintain or break off relationship with the people. The forgiveness that Moses asks is the preservation of relationship between Yahweh and the people, and the decision not to disinherit the present community by creating a new nation from Moses or from anyone else. Because Israel's only existence is relationship with Yahweh, there is room for punishment that does not include dissolution of the covenant.

14:20-38 The sentence. Yahweh answers Moses' prayer by announcing forgiveness (v. 20), that is, the continuation of the fundamental covenant relationship that is the basis of Israel's existence. But there is punishment also. In the strong language of an oath (v. 21; see also vv. 28, 35), Yahweh asserts that those who rebelled will be denied entry into the land on account of their infidelity: "not one shall see the land which I promised on oath to their fathers" (vv. 22-23). Only Caleb, who trusted the Lord's promise, will enter the land, and his descendants will inherit it (v. 24; see Josh 14:6-15). So also is Joshua spared the punishment (vv. 30b, 38; 32:12).

Yahweh continues with a description of precisely which members will be denied entry into the land: all those who "grumble against me" (v. 27) and those over twenty years old who were registered in the census (v. 29). Only the children, the next generation, will enter the land to enjoy it (v. 31). The Israelites are thus sentenced to remain in the wilderness for forty years, a year for each day of the scouting (v. 34). The children have to suffer the sin of their parents by languishing with them in the wilderness until the last of the generation has lived out a natural life (vv. 33, 35). While the community is being punished, Yahweh's covenant continues and endures.

There is a more immediate judgment on the scouts who instigated the grumbling by their discouraging report. They are struck with a plague and die (vv. 36-37).

This story of rebellion answers two questions. First, it gives the reason for Israel's prolonged stay in the wilderness, so that the whole generation that came from Egypt perished there. Because the Israelites rejected the land, they are rejected from entering the land. Second, it explains why Israel journeyed east to enter the land from the Transjordan rather than taking the more direct route from the south. The explanation given is that because the Amalekites and Canaanites live in the valleys, Israel must return south and travel the road that will take them around the Dead Sea (v. 25; see 20:14–22:1 for the details of the journey).

14:39-45 Unsuccessful invasion. Another story of rebellion arises from the issue of the route to be taken for entry into the land. It is an account of failure because of refusal to obey the word of God.

The people grieve when Moses tells them that they are to turn and head southward away from the Canaanites and Amalekites (v. 39; see vv. 25, 43a, 45). The people admit that they were wrong when earlier they listened to the report of the scouts (13:27-33; 14:1-4), and they resolve to head directly north into the foothills of Canaan (v. 40). Moses admonishes them that they are acting disobediently. He warns that failure is certain because the Lord is *not* in their midst (vv. 41-43). This headstrong people dare to set out without the presence of the ark, the leadership of Moses, and in opposition to the word of Yahweh (v. 44).

This is a story of failure. It demonstrates the consequences of acting apart from the word that is the basis for covenant relationship with Yahweh. Israel faces the enemy on its own counsel and is pursued as far as Hormah, a city located in the region of Beersheba (v. 45; the ultimate defeat of Hormah is reported in 21:1-3).

The long section in chapters 11–14 contains five stories of rebellion: the incident at Taberah, the greed for meat, the jealousy toward Moses, the rejection of the land, and the unsuccessful invasion. There follows an insertion of five ritual laws that have no apparent connection. All the instructions are intended for the guidance of the community when it has reached the land. The laws are thus future-oriented. They reflect modifications arising from everyday practice.

15:1-16 Secondary offerings. Every dimension of life belongs to Yahweh; therefore, all laws are directly attributed to Yahweh. Each directive is the Lord's explicit instruction (v. 1). Each focuses on the time when Israel will have entered the land (v. 2).

The first law outlines the quantities of grain, oil, and wine that are to accompany the "sweet-smelling oblation" given for the various sacrifices (v. 3). The phrase "sweet-smelling" means that the oblation is acceptable to the Lord. It is based on the idea that God smells and delights in the sacrifice presented on occasions of joy.

Each sacrifice, whether of a lamb (vv. 4-5), a ram (vv. 6-7), an ox (vv. 8-10), or goat (v. 11), should be presented with a proportional weight of cereal, oil, and wine. The quantities of cereal, oil, and wine increase with the size of the animal.

It is uncertain why a grain offering and a drink offering are to accompany each sacrifice. It could be the idea of providing a complete meal. It could also be the idea of giving from the natural resources of the land (see Deut 7:13). Whatever the meaning of the sacrifice, the text is concerned with giving God a full and acceptable offering.

There is an additional note which stresses that the instruction applies to the native and the alien alike (vv. 13-16). It states that the foreigner who has made a home among the Israelites has equal rights as well as the corresponding obligations. The detail of this note suggests that the presence of "resident aliens" is a matter of considerable concern. The principle of the law—"Before the Lord you and the alien are alike" (v. 15)—reflects a basic attitude of justice that witnesses to the authenticity of Israelite faith.

15:17-21 Offering from the first batch of dough. The second regulation belongs in the category of first things belonging to Yahweh (see Exod 13:11-16; Deut 26:1-2; Num 18:12-13). The text is focused on the future time in the land (vv. 18-19a) and applies to all future generations (v. 21a).

The regulation specifically identifies the cake made from the coarse grain taken from the threshing floor (v. 20). Since the whole harvest is a gift from God, the first dough made from the harvest grain belongs to God.

In the temple period, the cake made from the first dough was presented to the priest to eat. This offering symbolized the giving back to God from the abundance that was given. This offering was part of the priests' provisions (see 18:13; Lev 23:10-11).

15:22-31 Sin offerings. The third instruction is divided into two sections: the offerings for sin or violations that are "inadvertent" or unintentional (vv. 22-29), and punishment for willful sin (vv. 30-31).

In the case of the unintentional violation of instructions, separate provision is made for atonement when the community is involved (vv. 22-26) and when an individual is involved (vv. 27-29). Prescribed sacrifices (vv. 24, 27) are to be offered in atonement by the priest so that the sin committed unwittingly may be forgiven (vv. 25, 28). There is specific mention again that the regulation applies to the native and alien alike (vv. 26, 29).

When it is a case of deliberate sin, an "insult" to the Lord, no sacrifice can atone. The individual, native or alien, who has defiantly "despised the word" or "broken [the Lord's] commandment" has, in fact, chosen to be cut off from the community of God's people. The punishment for this person is separation from the community.

15:32-36 The sabbath-breaker. The fourth regulation is given as the solution to a specific behavior that is described. The people find a man gathering wood on the sabbath day (v. 32). They keep him in custody because there is "no clear decision as to what should be done with him" (v. 34). The case in point is an example of the way new regulations arose that would be normative for future similar situations (see the commentary on 9:6-13).

The law of the sabbath clearly states that work is forbidden (see Exod 20:8-11), and the death penalty is the prescribed punishment for breaking the law of the sabbath (see Exod 31:14-15; 35:2-3). What is unclear is the form of execution to be used in the case of deliberate violation of the law.

The answer given is that the man is to be stoned by the whole community outside the camp (v. 35). This person is thus excluded from the community symbolically by being led outside the camp as well as physically by the death sentence (v. 36). The strict observance of the sabbath took on greater importance after the Exile and continued into the time of Jesus (see John 9:16).

15:37-41 Tassels on the cloak. The fifth regulation makes the ancient practice of wearing tassels on the end of the outer garment a requirement with a specific meaning (see Deut 22:12). This practice survived into Judaism (Matt 9:20; 14:36; 23:5; Mark 6:56; Luke 8:44).

The tassels are attached with a violet cord (v. 38) and function to catch the eye. They thereby serve as a reminder of the Lord's presence and commands (v. 39). The external ornament is intended to continually remind the people that a holy God is among them and that to live in the presence of a holy God, they must observe the commandments by which covenant is preserved. Observance of the commandments is the mark of a holy people (v. 40).

The reason for observing the instruction is that Yahweh is present and will continue to be with a faithful people. The formulary "I, the Lord, am your God who . . . . brought you out of Egypt that I, the Lord, *may be* your God" (v. 41) is a reminder of the very basis of Israel's existence. It concludes the last instruction as well as the series of five instructions. The people are invited to obedient response to demonstrate loyalty to covenant. If the covenant relationship is broken, it is because Israel has turned from observing the word that the Lord has given for their direction since Egypt.

The section 16:1–17:5 picks up the theme of rebellion once again. This is one continuous narrative made up of two separate stories of rebellion: Korah and company against Aaron (16:1a, 2-11, 16-24, 32b, 35; 17:1-5), and the two Reubenites, Dathan and Abiram, against Moses (16:1b, 12-15, 25-32a, 33-34). Each story reflects ancient struggles for power that broke out again and again in the course of history. The Priestly tradition is responsible for knitting the two incidents into a continuous narrative of simultaneous rebellion.

16:1-11 Rebellion of Korah. The report begins with a presentation of the lineage of Korah, son of Izhar, son of Kohath, son of Levi (v. 1a; see Exod 6:17-25, esp. vv. 18, 21, 24). Generally, the longer the list of names, the more significant the individual. It is noteworthy that Korah is a Levite and belongs to the family of Kohathites, to whom is assigned care of the most sacred items of the sanctuary (see 3:27-32; 4:1-20). In the execution of their service, however, they are always subservient to the priest (4:15, 20).

Korah's rebellion undoubtedly arises from a long struggle for greater authority. The Kohathites are allowed to come near the holy vessels, but if they touch them, they will die. They carry them in transport, but only after the sacred utensils have been covered by the priests. Korah, a leader among the Kohathites, leads the rebellion against the authority of the priests. The tension between these groups will come to the forefront again at the very time when the document is being written down by the Priestly writer. There was a struggle to secure the priesthood by the Zadokites, descendants of Eleazar (see 3:1-4, esp. v. 4b; 1 Chr 24; Ezek 44:10-31). The story in Numbers reflects the supremacy of Eleazar and the Zadokites (17:1-5). The Levitic Korahites had to be content to be doorkeepers (1 Chr 26:1) and temple singers (Pss 42–49, 84, 85, 87, 88).

The story of Korah itself reflects two major conflicts. In one, Korah and the two hundred fifty conspirators maintain that the tribe of Levi, which includes Moses, Aaron, and their descendants, is not more sacred than the other tribes (vv. 2-3). They argue that because Yahweh is in the midst of the community, Moses and Aaron have no right to claim holiness for themselves above the rest. Each member of the community is holy because of

Yahweh's presence. A second conflict represents Korah and his followers as Levites who oppose the authority of Aaron and attempt to take the power of the priesthood for themselves (vv. 8-11). The Levites are not content with the special status assigned them in the service of the sanctuary but desire the full authority of the priesthood. These two very ancient and very real struggles—recognition of the holiness of each person and conflict over the privileged status of the priesthood—merge into one story of rebellion to which Moses responds.

Moses falls prostrate (v. 4); he does not intercede. Instead, he lets Yahweh decide who is the holy one and whom God chooses to come near (v. 5). This rebellion against the leaders is recognized as a rebellion against Yahweh to be resolved by Yahweh (v. 11).

Moses instructs Korah and his followers to prepare censers with fire and incense (vv. 6-7), an action reserved to the priest. Moses is telling Korah to take the priesthood and then see whom Yahweh will choose.

16:12-15 Rebellion of Dathan and Abiram. The lineage of Dathan and Abiram appears at the head of the chapter in the merging of the two separate stories. They are descendants of Jacob's first-born son Reuben (v. 1b; 26:5-8; Gen 35:23). The tradition of their rebellion is an ancient one that is recounted elsewhere (Ps 106:16-18 and Deut 11:6).

Dathan and Abiram represent the political faction that refuses to acknowledge the leadership of Moses. When they say, "We will not go" (vv. 12b, 14c), we are inclined to think that they might be leaders who conspired with the scouts in refusing to enter the land (14:1-4). Their concerns identify them. They lament having been brought from Egypt, and they fear perishing in the wilderness (v. 13a). They complain that Moses has set himself up as prince (v. 13b; see Exod 2:14). They complain, further, that Moses has not fulfilled his promise to bring them into a land where they will acquire fields and vineyards (v. 14a). As the ultimate insult, the rebels claim that Moses is deceiving them when they ask, ". . . will you also gouge out our eyes?" (v. 14b). This is an idiom for leading astray with false promises (see 1 Sam 11:2; Prov 30:17).

Moses responds angrily. He does not defend himself against the accusations but rather confesses that he has not harmed anyone (v. 15). The statement "I have never taken a single ass from them" is used to defend oneself against the charge of abuse of position (see 1 Sam 12:3; 8:16).

16:16-24, 35 Punishment of Korah. The story of Korah is resumed here, continuing from verse 11. Moses tells Aaron, Korah, and his supporters to each prepare a censer and to take his stand at the entrance to the meeting tent (vv. 16-17). The preparation of the censers is described in detail to emphasize the action of assuming the priesthood (v. 18). This is done in anticipation of judgment.

At this moment the "glory of Yahweh" is manifest in power and majesty before the entire community (v. 19). Moses and Aaron are instructed to separate themselves from the group about to be punished because they are exempt from judgment (vv. 20-21). They respond by falling down and pleading that the whole people of God might not perish on account of the sin of one group (v. 22). They address Yahweh by the old title "El," which is simply God, the Creator of life. They ask that God not destroy the life that has been given (see also 27:16). Yahweh thus exempts the community from judgment. The people are told to move away from the place (vv. 23-24). No sooner have they done this than fire bursts out from the Lord and consumes the rebellious individuals (v. 35). There is a note in 26:11 which states that not all descendants of Korah died.

This story settles once and for all the question of priestly authority. The object of Korah's rebellion was the desire and ambition to be a priest, to take the censer, the fire, and the incense and stand before the Lord. The Kohathites had been warned that they should not touch any of the sacred objects under pain of death (4:15, 20). Death by fire was foreshadowed in the taking of fire from the altar (compare the story in 3:1-4 and Lev 10:1-2).

The mention of Dathan and Abiram alongside Korah in verses 24 and 35 reflects the intent to make the two stories one. Korah's punishment occurred near the meeting tent. Reference to the Dwelling in these verses comes from the story of Dathan and Abiram, who, according to the following account (vv. 25-34), are punished near their own tents.

16:25-34 Punishment of Dathan and Abiram. This is the conclusion to the story of rebellion against the leadership of Moses. It picks up directly from verse 15.

Moses and the elders approach the defiant Dathan and Abiram (v. 25). Moses speaks directly to the community, warning them to separate themselves from the rebellious Reubenites, lest they also suffer punishment (v. 26). Dathan, Abiram, their wives and children stand outside their tents in expectation (v. 27). The scene is set for an act of judgment.

The word of judgment comes directly from Moses in confirmation of his authority and in refutation of any suspicion that he is acting on his own (v. 28). The judgment will be recognizable by the fact that death, "the fate common to all mankind," will not be from natural causes (v. 29). The Lord will do "something entirely new," that is, Yahweh will do an act of creation, so that they will die in a way that has been unheard of until this time (v. 30a). The earth will literally open up and swallow them and all their possessions (v. 30b).

No sooner has Moses spoken the word of judgment than his authority is vindicated in the sight of all. The earth opens, and those who refused to *go up* (vv. 12, 14), ironically, face the fate of *going down* to the nether world with everything belonging to them (vv. 31-33). Those who accused Moses of bringing them out of Egypt "to make [them] perish in the desert" (v. 13) suffer the fulfillment of their accusation. Dathan and Abiram disappear from the face of the earth and there is no evidence or trace of them. Mention that Korah's men suffer the same fate is made in verse 32b to knit the two accounts.

Quite understandably, all the Israelites flee in fear that the same thing might happen to them (v. 34). The story is told so that Israel might know the uniqueness of Moses in his call to lead the people from Egypt and into the land of promise.

17:1-5 A sign for the Israelites. This piece offers an explanation for the layer of copper that covers the altar, and it also foreshadows the succession of Eleazar as priest after Aaron (see 20:22-29). The word comes to Moses (v. 1) that Eleazar is to gather the censers that have been consecrated, and, after scattering the fire, he is to hammer them into plates to overlay the altar (vv. 2-3). Eleazar does exactly as the Lord commands (vv. 4-5). Because the censers have been made sacred at the cost of so many lives, they are to be protected from any abuse (see Exod 29:37; 30:29). The cover made from the consecrated censers would be a reminder that no person who is not a proper priest, a descendant of Aaron, should ever approach the altar. The cover stands as a warning of the consequences of any improper action.

17:6-15 The people grumble. Another story that contains the elements of the typical rebellion-forgiveness story (see commentary on 11:1-3) evolves out of the events of Korah's rebellion. The people grumble and blame Moses and Aaron for the death of so many of their compatriots (v. 6).

Yahweh appears in the usual manner and resolves to consume the entire community. Only Moses and Aaron are to be spared. Moses instructs Aaron to take his censer, fill it with fire from the altar, put incense on it, and make atonement for the people (v. 11). Aaron's intercessory action puts an end to the scourge, but not before a significant number of people have perished (vv. 12-15). Aaron the priest thus acts in the capacity of high priest, mediating healing and life from God. He stands "between the living and the dead" (v. 13); he makes intercession that effectively averts further destruction.

This story vindicates Aaron and his descendants and clarifies still further the role of the priest. The priest is consecrated for the good of the people. Through the priest the life-giving forces flow from God. For this mediatory task the priest is uniquely chosen. God's choice of the priestly family is based on the following legend.

17:16-26 Aaron's staff. The legend of the blooming of Aaron's staff is a delightful literary piece developed upon a wordplay. The Hebrew words for "staff" and "tribe" are exactly the same. The dead staff that bursts into life represents the tribe that God chooses and blesses for the service of the priesthood. The story is told to silence once and for all the "grumbling" (vv. 20, 25) against Aaron and his sons as the chosen of God.

The repetition of details in the word of God to Moses (vv. 16-20) carried out exactly (vv. 21-23) emphasizes the divine choice of the staff/tribe. In accord with Yahweh's direction, Moses requests that each prince representing one of the tribes bring a staff on which is written the prince's name. The name of Aaron is inscribed on the staff from the tribe of Levi (v. 18). The twelve staffs are then laid in the meeting tent in front of the commandments. Yahweh will signify the choice of tribe by a miracle.

The next day Moses enters the tent and finds that Aaron's staff has not only sprouted and sent out shoots but has blossomed and bears ripe almonds (v. 23). Moses brings all the staffs out for the people to see and returns each to its owner (v. 24). Aaron's staff, however, is returned to the meeting tent, where it will remain as a sign and a warning for future generations that the sons of Aaron are chosen to be the sole legitimate priests (v. 25).

17:27-28 Sacred objects. These verses are appropriately inserted as a transition between the preceding series of stories and the following clarification of priestly duties and rewards. The verses present the people crying out to Moses, as they have done so often when facing punishment (v. 27). In this instance they cry out in fear that all of them will surely die if they ever come near the Dwelling (v. 28). The concern expressed here reflects an actual question that caused disputes among the categories of priests. It is also a legitimate concern of the people who encamp about the Dwelling and know the punishment that befalls those who encroach upon the holy. The despair that resounds in the choice of verbs—"perishing," "lost," "die"—highlights the seriousness of the issue. The clarification of the duties of the priests and Levites that follows answers the concern.

18:1-7 Duties of the priests and the Levites. Only in this section is Yahweh's word addressed directly to Aaron (v. 1; see also vv. 8, 20). This is appropriate, since the instruction distinguishes the priests from the Levites and gives priority to the priests. The role of each is made clear. Aaron, his sons, and their descendants, as legitimate possessors of the priesthood, have sole responsibility for the sanctuary (v. 1). Only they may draw near the altar, perform the priestly functions, and touch that which pertains to the altar (vv. 1, 5, 7).

Death is the punishment for any layperson who comes near the altar (vv. 4b, 5b, 7b). The Levites, kin to the Aaronites, have been set apart in place of the first-born of Israel for the service of the sanctuary so that "no plague may strike among the Israelites should they come near the sanctuary" (see the commentary on 8:19). They are dedicated to the Lord and given as a gift to the priests (v. 6; see 3:5–4:49; 8:5–26). The Levites are to be assistants to the priests. Theirs will be the service of the priests and the holy place, but they may not touch the altar or the sacred objects (vv. 2-4).

The clear priority of the Aaronic priesthood over the Levites is defined in this text by the word "gift" (v. 6). The Levites are given as a *gift* to the priests, and the priesthood is given as a *gift* to Aaron and his sons. The ascendancy of the Aaronic priesthood was most pronounced in the period of the Exile and after.

18:8-20 Priests' share of the sacrifices. This is an elaborate description of the remuneration due to the priests and their families for their services on behalf of the people. The priests have no land or property; their sole possession is the God to whom they belong (v. 20; see Josh 13:14; 14:3-4). They therefore have a right to support from the people. What is offered to God in sacrifice belongs to the priests as their share (v. 8).

The priests have a share of all the most sacred offerings, be they cereal offerings, sin offerings, or guilt offerings. The only injunction is that their portion be treated as most sacred (vv. 9-10). They receive the breast and right leg from the wave offering (vv. 11, 18b). Also, the best of the oil, the new wine, and the grain presented as first fruits belong to the priests and may be consumed by members of their families (vv. 12-13). Theirs is whatever is "doomed," that is, whatever has been devoted to God and cannot be redeemed (v. 14). In early Israel, for example, everything taken in war belonged to God and had to be destroyed. In later years, what belongs to God is claimed by the priests, including all the first-born. The first-born sons and unclean animals are to be redeemed and the money presented to the priests. The first-born of the clean animals belong to the priests, except for the blood, which is splashed on the altar, and the fat, which is burned in the fire (vv. 15-18a).

The Lord promises all this to the priests and their families, both sons and daughters, as "an inviolable covenant to last forever" (v. 19). This very strong language reads literally "a covenant of salt." The phrase occurs again only in 2 Chr 13:5 in reference to the Davidic kingship. According to the priests responsible for both texts, only that which applies to the priests and to the family of David is guaranteed forever.

18:21-24 Tithes due the Levites. The Levites who attend the property of the sanctuary shield the people from danger (vv. 22-23a). They have no heritage of their own (vv. 23b, 24b) and therefore depend on the support of the people. The Lord designates that the tithes given as a contribution to the Lord be assigned to the Levites in return for their service (vv. 21, 24a). The tithe consists of one-tenth of the produce of the land, trees, and cattle (see Lev 27:30-33). The practice of presenting the tithe for the support of the Levites continued, with some variations, from early to postexilic times (see Deut 14:22-29; 12:17-19; 26:12; 2 Chr 31:4-6).

18:25-32 Tithes paid by the Levites. The tithes presented to the Levites for their support are to be looked upon as God's gift to them from the earth and the vineyard. The Levites, too, must tithe. Yahweh commands that they present a "tithe of the tithes" (v. 26) to the priests as their offering, as if from their own threshing floors and winepresses (vv. 27, 30). They are cautioned to offer the best part, so that they return to God the very best of that given to them (vv. 28-30, 32a). What remains can be eaten by themselves and their families—it is their remuneration for service. This food is sacred because it has been offered as a contribution to God. It must therefore be consumed, lest the Levite bring upon himself punishment for abuse of that which has been consecrated (vv. 31-32).

Besides distinguishing between the priest and the Levite, this chapter establishes the practice of providing support for those dedicated to God who carry out duties in service of the people.

Chapter 19 presents an ancient ritual that is entirely unrelated to the context other than the fact that it is carried out by a priest. The ritual has to do with cultic purity, specifically purification after contact with the dead.

19:1-10 Ashes of the red heifer. The animal to be used for the rite is a young red heifer which is without defect in the cultic sense and which has not been used for any other purpose (v. 2). It is to be given to Eleazar, taken outside the camp, and slaughtered in his presence (v. 3). The priest will take some of the blood on his finger and sprinkle it seven times in the direction of the meeting tent, presumably to signify total dedication (v. 4). The animal is then burned in its entirety before the priest, who adds to the fire some cedar wood, hyssop, and scarlet yarn (vv. 5-6). These items are understood to have a cleansing and purifying effect, and are used otherwise to purify lepers (see Lev 14:6-7). After the burning the priest and the one who has burned the animal are to wash their garments and bathe themselves. They remain unclean until evening, when they may reenter the camp (vv. 7-8).

Finally, a man who is clean from a cultic point of view gathers the ashes and stores them in a clean place outside the camp, so that they are available for use in the water of purification (v. 9a). The statement that the heifer is a sin offering (v. 9b) is strange, since the animal is not sacrificed or presented to God but is totally burnt and used to produce ashes for the purifying water sprinkled in rites of purification. The man who gathers the ashes also becomes unclean. He, too, must wash his garments and remain outside the camp until evening (v. 10). The ritual described here has no parallel. It carries magical overtones that suggest adaptation of a practice from the foreign environment.

19:11-22 Use of the ashes. The ashes are prepared specifically for use in the purification rites of those who have become unclean from contact with the dead. We saw earlier that contact with the dead is a means of defilement (5:2). The various regulations and rituals for cleansing this uncleanness are presented in this one place.

According to law, anyone who touches a corpse becomes unclean for a period of seven days. This individual must be banned from the camp lest the community be defiled. The unclean person is unworthy of the holy place where Yahweh dwells. To become clean, the person must be purified by being sprinkled with water on the third and seventh days (vv. 11-13).

There follows a listing of circumstances that bring about uncleanness (vv. 14-16). Anyone who enters a tent where there is a corpse, as well as those already in the tent at the time of the death, are unclean. So also is anything exposed to the dead, such as the contents of a jar that has been left open. A person does not have to touch the body. However, if anyone touches a corpse—even a part of it or the grave—that person is unclean. It does not matter whether the death was caused by natural or unnatural causes.

Instructions for purification are presented next (vv. 17-18). The unclean individuals are required to submit to a ritual of purification in which the ashes of the red heifer, mixed with fresh water, are sprinkled on them, their tents, and possessions. This is done by someone ritually clean, not necessarily a priest, on the third and seventh days. Those being cleansed then wash their garments, bathe themselves, and return to the camp in the evening of the day of purification. The person who sprinkles the water also becomes unclean and must therefore wash his garments and remain outside until evening.

An unclean person who does not submit to the purificatory rite remains unclean. Everything and everyone who comes in contact with this unclean person becomes unclean. This individual must be excluded from the community, being unworthy of the place where Yahweh dwells (vv. 20, 22).

It is probable that this reminder about ritual cleanness is added at this point to focus attention again on the community about to move forward on its journey to the land. This is a people among whom Yahweh dwells. Whether in the wilderness or in the land, only a ritually clean people is worthy of the presence of a holy God. Ritual cleanliness is, then, a sign of the people's fidelity to Yahweh.

Last Stops Along the Way (20:1–22:1)

20:1 Death of Miriam. After a long interval of struggles and rebellion, focus is again on the community encamped in the desert of Zin at Kadesh (v. la). This desert is part of the larger desert of Paran, from which the scouts were sent (see 10:12; 13:3, 21, 26). A sequence of events follows to mark the passage of time and the movement toward the land.

There is a brief note that Miriam died and was buried at Kadesh (v. lb; see ch. 12 and Exod 15:20-21). This is a reminder that because of the people's rebellion an entire generation will pass away before Israel moves on to the Promised Land.

20:2-13 Moses and Aaron punished. In a retelling of the Meribah incident (v. 13; see Exod 17:2-7), an explanation is offered of why Moses and Aaron are denied entry into the land. The reason develops from the event of contention over water. (Meribah means "contention" or "controversy.") The people quarrel with Moses and Aaron and accuse them of bringing the community from Egypt, where there was plenty of food, to the wilderness, where there is not even water to drink (vv. 2-5). All Moses and Aaron can do is turn to Yahweh, who at that moment is revealed to them at the entrance of the meeting tent and speaks to them (vv. 6-7). Yahweh instructs Moses and Aaron to take the staff, to assemble the people, and, in the presence of the community, to order the rock to give forth water for all to drink (v. 8).

There is a significant difference between the older story and the incident as told here by the Priestly writer. In Exod 17:5-6 Moses is told to strike the rock with the staff. Here Yahweh commands Moses and Aaron to "order" the rock, that by a miraculous occurrence in the presence of all, the "sanctity" (holiness) of Yahweh might be shown (vv. 12-13; see Isa 29:23). The Hebrew words for "sanctity" and for "Kadesh," the place of the present controversy, derive from the same root (see v. 1). It is to hint at this association that the point of Yahweh's sanctity is stressed.

However, the staff becomes the object of disobedience. It is identified with the staff of Aaron, which was placed before the Lord in the sanctuary (v. 9; 17:16-26). Rather than doing exactly as Yahweh has commanded, Moses asks the community a question that suggests doubt and lack of faith: "Are we to bring water for you out of this rock?" (v. 10). Using the staff, Moses subsequently strikes the rock not once but twice. The rock issues enough water for all to drink (v. 11), though Moses did not "order" the rock as Yahweh had directed.

Tradition holds that this infidelity is the reason for Yahweh's decision that neither Aaron nor Moses would enter the land (v. 12; see v. 24 and Ps 106:32-33). It is unclear, however, whether the infidelity is a lack of faith or an act of disobedience. Perhaps the lack of clarity is intentional so that the people will remember both. This story is told near the end of the journey to prepare for the designation of new leaders as well as to supply a reason for the need for new leaders. (See Deut 1:37; 3:26 and 4:21-22 for another explanation of why Moses is denied entry into the Promised Land.)

20:14-21 Edom's refusal. The easiest passage from Kadesh across the southern tip of the Dead Sea would be through Edom and Moab. To do this and to avoid conflict, Moses sends messengers to the king of Edom requesting permission to pass peacefully through his land (v. 14a). Moses appeals to the kinship between the two peoples (v. 14b), since Edom/Esau and Israel/Jacob are twin ancestors of the nations (Gen 25:21-26; 32:4; 33:1-17). Moses recounts the history of how Yahweh has led the people from Egypt to this place in the wilderness near the edge of Edomite territory (vv. 15-16). He promises that the people will not disturb their fields or vineyards nor drink any of their water. They will pass through the district on the royal road without deviating right or left (vv. 17, 19). The royal road, sometimes called the King's Highway, was an ancient, frequently traveled caravan route through Edom (see 21:22; Deut 2:27).

Edom refuses Moses' request twice and threatens attack if Israel attempts passage (vv. 18, 20; see Amos 1:11-12). Israel is then forced to travel southward as far as Elath on the Gulf of Aqaba to skirt the territory of Edom and to penetrate from the eastern desert. This story, rooted as it is in the tradition of dissension between the brothers, gives an explanation for embarking on such a circuitous route.

20:22-29 Death of Aaron. Before beginning the trek southward, the whole community moves to Mount Hor, which is located a short distance north of Kadesh on the border of Edom (vv. 22-23).

Yahweh's word spoken (vv. 23-26) and fulfilled (vv. 27-28a) once again indicates divine direction in the course of events. The word is very simple and clear. Aaron is about to die (v. 24; see 33:37-39), in fulfillment of the word given in 20:12. God commands that Moses install Aaron's son Eleazar as priest in succession to his father by transferring the robe from Aaron to his son (vv. 25-26, 27a, 28a; see Exod 39:1-31 and Lev 8:7-9 for a description of the robes and the installation ceremony). When this has been done, Aaron dies on the mountain and the community mourns him for thirty days (v. 28b). Of the first generation, only Moses remains to lead the people toward the land. Later Moses will die on a mountain and will be mourned for a thirty-day period (see Deut 34:1, 5-8).

21:1-3 Victory over Arad. This story explains the name Hormah, which is related to a Hebrew word meaning "doomed" (v. 3b; see Judg 1:17). In an earlier report the Israelites had attempted to enter Canaan from the south on their own initiative. They were routed by the inhabitants and chased back to Hormah (see 14:39-45 and Deut 1:41-46). The successful attack by the Canaanite king is a detail continuing from this earlier story (v. 1). A change of events occurs, however, when the Israelites turn to the Lord with the vow to "doom their cities" if Yahweh will deliver the Canaanites into their hands (v. 2). Because of this vow, Israel destroys the defeated Canaanite cities and calls the place Hormah, the "doomed" place (v. 3).

This story seems out of place, for the Israelites, who are heading southward, must travel north to Hormah. In an old list there is allusion to the event after the death of Aaron (see 33:40). Because the Priestly writer used that list as the basis for the present narrative, the story of Hormah is told here regardless of the geographical problem created.

21:4-9 The bronze serpent. This is a very old story that explains why a bronze serpent stood in the temple of Jerusalem. This figure was destroyed in the time of Hezekiah because of the worship that grew up around it (see 2 Kgs 18:4). Because of its ability to regenerate itself the serpent symbolizes life and was used as a fertility symbol from ancient times.

As we have the story, it is told in the formalized pattern of rebellion-punishment-intercession-forgiveness that has been used a number of times (see 11:1-3; 12:2-16; 17:6-15; 21:4-9). Our attention is turned once again to a rebellious people. Though this is a new generation and though they are within range of entrance into the land, they complain against God and Moses (v. 5a). The people have no sooner set out from Mount Hor and upon the road south toward the Gulf of Aqaba than they lose patience (v. 4). The complaint once again centers on food and drink and a longing to return to Egypt (v. 5b).

Yahweh responds immediately with punishment by sending serpents that bite the people, resulting in a great number of deaths (v. 6). The people turn to Moses for help. They confess that they have sinned and ask Moses to pray that Yahweh will remove the serpents from them (v. 7). Moses intercedes for them and receives instructions for bringing about an end to the suffering. He does exactly as Yahweh commands. He makes a bronze serpent and raises it on a pole. Anyone who looks at the serpent recovers (vv. 8-9). The healing of the bites is linked to obedience and to faith. And, ironically, the healing comes from a source like that of the punishment.

For the last time in the wilderness, Israel rebels and is forgiven. As the new generation advances toward the land, they walk in the footsteps of their ancestors who perished on account of their rebellion.

21:10-20 Journey around Moab. A remarkable piece, made up of a series of place names interspersed with fragments of ancient poetry, hastens the journey toward the plains of Moab, where the next events will take place. The movement is from the Arabah, the region south of the Dead Sea, through the Jordan Valley. The people reach the Wadi Zered, the boundary between Edom and Moab (vv. 11-12). From there they push on to the Arnon, a river dividing the territory of Moab from that of the Amorites (v. 13). The Amorite kingdom lies between Moab and Ammon. It is this territory that Israel will have to traverse to reach the Jordan (see vv. 21-32). All the sites named in verses 16, 18b, 19-20, as far as is known, are on the east side of the Dead Sea. Nahaliel is a valley a short distance north of the Arnon, and Pisgah is one of the peaks overlooking the plain where the Jordan River enters the Dead Sea.

Within the travel schema, there are two pieces of poetry (vv. 14-15, 17-18). The first of these is said to be from the "Book of the Wars of the Lord" (v. 14). Though the book is unknown otherwise, it is probable that there once existed a collection of songs celebrating victories from the early days of the settlement. The poem is included because it mentions the Arnon and verifies that this river formed the border of Moab. The other poem is a traditional song celebrating the springing up of well-water when the well was first dug. It was added in this context because of the place name Beer, meaning "well," and because the gift of water at any site in the wilderness was celebrated as a gift from God (see v. 16).

21:21-32 Victory over Sihon. The Amorite kingdom, with its capital of Heshbon, is located between Moab and Ammon. Its ruler Sihon had warred against Moab and had taken the entire plateau of Moab between the Jabbok River on the north down to the Arnon River, and from the desert on the east to the Jordan River on the west (v. 26; see Judg 11:22). Possession of this territory would put Israel within reach of the Promised Land. The defeat of the Amorites is therefore the first of the conquest stories.

According to the text, Moses sends messengers ahead to request passage through the land on the royal road. The alert reader recognizes immediately that the request parallels exactly that made to the king of Edom (vv. 21-22; compare 20:14, 17). Scholars believe that the Heshbon tradition is the older and that the Edom text was modeled after it.

Sihon, king of the Amorites, denies the request and engages Israel in battle at Jahaz (Jahzah). Israel defeats the forces of Sihon and takes possession of the entire land between the Jabbok and Arnon Rivers up to the territory of the Ammonites (vv. 24-26, 31-32). So significant is this victory that gives Israel possession of Canaanite land that the tradition of it is recorded again in Deut 2:24-37 and Judg 11:19-22.

Linked with this victory narrative there is also an ancient poem in verses 27-30 celebrating the victory. What is interesting is that the poem is a non-Israelite composition of great antiquity. The reference to Chemosh (v. 29a), the god of the Moabites, and the statement that Moab and the people of Chemosh are taken captive by the Amorite king Sihon suggest that this is the poem originally sung in celebration of the Amorite victory over Moab. The poem was appropriated by the Israelites without alteration and included as a reminder that the conqueror is now the conquered. This poem is quoted once again in a prophetic word against Moab (see Jer 48:45).

21:33-22:1 Victory over Og. Because the names of the kings Sihon and Og are associated in the tradition (Pss 135:11; 136:19-20), the story of Og's defeat follows immediately upon that of Sihon's defeat.

Bashan is the Amorite territory north of the Jabbok River. A fuller description of the confrontation with Og, king of Bashan, is given in Deut 3:1-11. Verses 1-3 of the Deuteronomy speech of Moses form the substance of the Numbers narrative. It is told as a story of Yahweh's victory (v. 34; see Deut 3:2-3a). As a sign of total dedication to Yahweh, the population is destroyed and the land is inhabited by the Israelites (v. 35; compare Deut 3:3b-6). With this victory Israel has gained control of the entire region outside the limits of Ammon, Moab, and Edom. Israel is now in possession of the entire Canaanite land of the Transjordan, separated from Canaan proper only by the Jordan River.

An itinerary formula concludes the section to summarize the final movement to the plains of Moab (22:1; see the discussion on the journey formula on p. 146). All the remaining events in the book take place while the people remain encamped here. Moses will die and be buried here (Deut 34:1-8), and from here Joshua will lead the people forth (see 27:12-23 and Deut 34:9).

ON THE PLAINS OF MOAB: PREPARATIONS FOR LIFE IN THE LAND

Num 22:2–36:13

The long journey from Sinai has spanned an entire generation. The length of the sojourn in the wilderness and the denial of entry into the land to Moses and Aaron are understood to be the consequence of infidelity to Yahweh's word. The deaths of Miriam and Aaron mark the passage of time to a new generation of adults. The people who survived the wilderness finally arrive, under the leadership of Moses, on the plains of Moab. The whole of the third part of the Book of Numbers takes place in Moab and focuses on the future life in the land of promise.

The content of this section is a mixture of traditions collected by the Priestly school from a variety of sources spanning the history of the nation.

The story of Balaam (chs. 22–24), the account of the unfortunate incident at Shittim (ch. 25), and the Midianite polemic (ch. 31) are very old narratives incorporated by the Priestly author. These accounts retain their original lively narrative and poetic style and therefore stand out against the formalized language of the legislation (27:1-11; chs. 28–30, 32, 35, 36) and lists (chs. 26 and 33).

The primary objective of this material is preparation for the future, when Israel will organize itself as a worshiping community of faith centered on Yahweh's presence in its midst. Questions about territorial possession and issues pertinent to inheritance of property are settled prior to entry into the Promised Land to forestall quarrels and divisions within the community. Laws for the observance of the major feasts guarantee an ordered religious life. Stress upon obedience to Yahweh's word reminds Israel that it alone can turn away from the covenant relationship. Observance of the law and the cult makes possible Yahweh's dwelling in the midst of this people forever.

When putting together this material, the Priestly author is reflecting upon Israel's history for the instruction of a people who are once again in a wilderness of exile and looking to the day when they can reenter the land of promise and reorganize themselves as a community of faith.

Chapters 22–24 contain a remarkable narrative complex, made up of a legend about a foreign prophet and told as the basis for a series of oracles that express Yahweh's blessing on the people of God. The setting for the narrative is the arrival of the Israelites on the plains of Moab. Frightened by the presence of the Israelites so near his borders, Balak, the king of Moab, seeks out the prophet Balaam to utter a curse on Israel. Balaam, however, presents himself as a prophet who speaks nothing else but Yahweh's word and therefore becomes a hero and model for all generations of Israelites.

Yahweh's word for Israel is one of blessing. Each of the oracles presents Israel as a people of election who have been wondrously blessed in the past and who will be victorious and prosperous in the future. The oracles are told at this juncture because of their content, which foreshadows what Israel will become in the land and provides an example of a truly obedient individual who is radically dependent on God's word.

22:2-14 Balaam summoned. The narrative begins with the introduction of one of the main characters, Balak, the king of Moab. He fears the Israelite forces encamped so near his borders. This is the army that defeated the Amorites, the people who had earlier defeated Moab (vv. 2-3; see 21:26). The Israelites are a numerous people who "cover the face of the earth" and who have demonstrated their strength (v. 6a).

Balak sends messengers from Moab and from Midian (vv. 4, 7) to hire Balaam to curse this enemy in order to make victory over them possible (v. 6a). The aim of the curse is to create a situation that will make defeat of the Israelites possible, that is, remove the protection of their God. To curse is to set one god against another and thereby unleash the destructive forces of the enemy God (see Jer 10:25; Pss 35:4-8; 79:6-7; 2 Sam 18:32).

Why the Midianites, neighbors from the desert south of Moab, are involved with Balak raises questions. Perhaps they are named here for the sake of continuity with the Peor and Midian incidents that follow, both of which are linked with Balaam in 31:8 and 16.

As the story goes, Balak involves Midian by pointing out the devastation of which Israel is capable, using the striking metaphor "as an ox devours the grass of the field" (v. 4). They seek out a foreigner, a reputed seer from the Euphrates valley in Mesopotamia, to utter a curse (v. 5a). This prophet, Balaam by name, is known to speak the word of God so effectively that Balak can be certain of the power of his word: "For I know that whoever you bless is blessed and whoever you curse is cursed" (v. 6b). Prophets such as Balaam were known in many of the countries of the ancient world from very early times. He can be compared to the earlier prophets of Israel, such as Samuel and Elijah, who were respected for their powerful word from God.

Following this introduction, there is a series of scenes that feature the prophet. In the first scene, verses 7-14, the messengers, with fee in hand, visit Balaam in his own territory (v. 7). From the perspective of those who solicit the prophet, Balaam is one of the diviners who deliver a message for pay. When a seer is paid for his services, as one would expect, he is more likely to utter words that the client wants to hear.

The response that the messengers receive for their offer, however, shows Balaam to be of a different disposition. He is a man who speaks only the word of Yahweh, regardless of the consequences and without reward. The messengers and the reader ought to take notice, for this Balaam, a foreigner from Mesopotamia, names Yahweh as the source of his word. Right from the start Balaam identifies himself as a prophet attentive to the God of the people upon whom Balak is seeking a curse. The stage is set for each of the scenes that follow.

Balaam invites the messengers to stay the night that he might inquire of Yahweh what to do (v. 8). The reader is privy to the conversation that takes place between God and Balaam. God asks Balaam to identify his visitors (v. 9). Obviously, these are individuals unknown to the God of Israel. Balaam answers by restating the request sent from Balak (vv. 10-11; compare vv. 5-6). God tells Balaam not to go with the messengers and not to curse the Israelites, because "they are blessed" (v. 12). This statement is the crux of the narrative. Because Yahweh has "blessed" this people, they are blessed; no word of curse will come upon them. The word "blessed" identifies Israel as a people to whom a unique identity has been given. The repetition of the phrase "out of Egypt" in this section (vv. 5, 11) points to the Exodus event as the foundation for Israel's life, the covenant relationship that unites Yahweh and Israel. Because of this unique relationship, Israel is blessed with greatness, prosperity, and the presence of Yahweh in their midst (vv. 3, 5, 11).

The telling point is that Balaam acts according to God's direction. His response to the invitation of the messengers is that Yahweh has refused to let him go (v. 13). He thus presents himself as a prophet who is faithful to the word spoken to him.

When the messengers report back to Balak, they do not mention that Balaam sought direction from Yahweh but say only that Balaam refused to come back with them (v. 14).

22:15-20 Second appeal to Balaam. Once again Balak sends messengers to Balaam. This time they are more numerous and more distinguished (v. 15). They entice Balaam with the promise of a handsome reward and anything he desires if he will come and put a curse on the Israelites (vv. 16-17).

Balaam's response indicates his total dependence on God's word in every instance. He says that regardless of what Balak will give him, "I could not do anything, small or great, contrary to the command of the Lord, my God" (v. 18). This warning given, Balaam inquires once again what Yahweh will command him (v. 19). That night, God comes to Balaam, gives him permission to accompany the messengers, and cautions him to do exactly as he is told (v. 20).

The focus of the narrative is Balaam's dependence at each step on word from Yahweh. God had earlier directed Balaam not to go; now Balaam is told that he may go. Earlier Yahweh had told Balaam not to curse this people; now Yahweh's word is simply "do exactly as I tell you" (v. 20).

22:21-35 The talking ass. An independent fable that is awkwardly fitted into the narrative follows. God has just told Balaam to go, but when Balaam goes off with the princes, God is angry at him for going (vv. 21-22a). At the end God again tells Balaam to go and to speak only what Yahweh tells him (v. 35). This is a return to the theme of the narrative. Within these literary parameters, a once independent fable about a talking ass is inserted to heighten the sense of the prophet's need to be attentive to Yahweh's direction.

According to the fable, Balaam travels from his home to an unnamed location. Because this journey is in opposition to what God has told him, an "angel of the Lord" blocks his way. Three times the ass sees the angel and responds appropriately; and three times Balaam beats the ass to force it to continue the journey (vv. 23-27). Only the ass sees what the seer does not see; it responds to the angel sent to prevent Balaam from continuing on a road that is contrary to God's intention.

In the next scene the animal and Balaam converse as if it were perfectly normal for them to be talking. The ass asks why Balaam has beaten it three times and points out that it has never before treated Balaam this way and would not this time had there not been a reason (vv. 28-30). The implication seems to be that Balaam ought to have trusted the perception of the animal against his own.

Then the seer sees what only the animal has previously seen. Balaam falls to his knees and bows to the ground before the angel of God (v. 31). The angel rebukes Balaam for his treatment of the animal and explains to him that the way is blocked because his journey is contrary to Yahweh's designs (vv. 32-33; see the use of this in 2 Pet 2:15-16). Balaam confesses that he has sinned and resolves to return to his home (v. 34).

The fable shows a Balaam who tries to act contrary to Yahweh's word. Yahweh, however, intervenes to reverse the action. This negative tradition about Balaam was one often remembered and restated to demonstrate the action of God for good (see Deut 23:5b-6; Josh 24:9-10; Mic 6:5; Neh 13:2).

22:36-40 Balaam arrives. The third scene in the narrative reports the first direct meeting between King Balak and Balaam. When Balak hears that Balaam is coming, he goes to the Arnon, the river separating Moab from the Israelites, to meet the prophet (v. 36). His greeting is more of a chiding that Balaam did not come promptly when summoned. Balak reminds the prophet that the rewards would be great (v. 37).

As an apology for his initial refusal, Balaam explains that he can speak only what God puts in his mouth (v. 38). Balaam's answer picks up the theme of the legend and further clarifies the prophet's dependence on Yahweh. The king hears for himself what Balaam has said about the source of his word, but he does not understand the implication of Balaam's reliance on Yahweh, the God of the Israelites.

The scene concludes with the king's sacrifice of animals, portions of which are sent to Balaam and those with him. Each of the oracles about to be spoken is delivered at a different site where animals have been sacrificed. The change of sacrificial scene separates one oracle from another.

22:41–23:12 The first oracle. Balak and Balaam go to Bamoth-baal, the high places of Baal, from which they can see some of the clans of Israel (22:41). Balaam there orders Balak to prepare seven altars and to offer sacrifice on each (23:1-2), the usual way to implore a deity. The prophet leaves Balak beside the altar, however, and goes aside to seek Yahweh. He announces to the king that if Yahweh meets him, he will report whatever Yahweh lets him *see*. God does meet him, "puts an utterance in [his] mouth," and tells him to go back to Balak and to speak the word (vv. 3-6).

In prophetic tradition the words "see" and "hear" (23:3; 24:4, 16) are often interchanged to express the means by which Yahweh's word is received (see Isa 1:1; 2:1; 13:1; Amos 1:1; Mic 1:1). Some of the prophets were visionaries who spoke the word out of the visions given to them (see Isa 6:1-13; Amos 7:1-3, 4-6, 7-9; 8:1-3; 9:1-6; Ezek 1-3).

Balaam returns to the altar, where he had left Balak and the princes, (v. 6) and speaks the oracle Yahweh has put in his mouth (vv. 7-10). While the oracle does not contain an explicit word of blessing, Balaam does not curse Israel: "How can I curse whom God has not cursed?" (v. 8). The oracle stresses that Israel is a people that lives apart from the nations; they are a unique people because they are Yahweh's own (v. 9). They are a people so numerous that they cannot be counted; they are like "dust" or "wind-borne particles" (v. 10a). This greatness is a sign of the blessing promised to Israel (see Gen 13:16; 28:14). Balaam ends the oracle by invoking a blessing on himself, that he and his descendants may be given such increase as Israel has received under God's blessing (v. 10b).

Balak is understandably distressed by Balaam's oracle (v. 11). Balaam retorts with a reminder that he can repeat only what Yahweh has put into his mouth (v. 21). Thus, Balaam consistently presents himself as one who depends totally on Yahweh for each word he will speak.

23:13-26 The second oracle. Balak and Balaam move to another site, the top of Pisgah (see 21:20), from which some of the Israelites can be viewed. There they prepare seven altars and offer sacrifice in anticipation of the curse (vv. 13-14). The circumstances of this meeting are told in the same pattern as the previous attempt to secure a curse.

The prophet tells the king to remain by his sacrifice while he goes apart for a meeting (v. 15). Yahweh meets Balaam once again, puts an utterance in his mouth, and sends the prophet back to Balak to speak accordingly (v. 16). Upon his return to Balak and the princes standing near the sacrifice, it is the king who names Yahweh as the source of the prophet's word: "What did the Lord say?" (v. 17). In answer, Balaam delivers the oracle of blessing on Israel.

When seeking oracles, it was the practice to persist until a favorable word was received. Balak does this, because he does not appreciate Yahweh's relationship with Israel. The Moabite king has no realization that Yahweh is a God who will never "change his mind" (v. 19). Yahweh has blessed Israel and the word given to Balaam to speak will always be a word of blessing (v. 20). No harm can come to Jacob/Israel because Yahweh-God, its King, is with it (v. 21). Israel's God has brought this people from Egypt, and the wonders that God will yet do on Israel's behalf cannot be imagined (vv. 22-23).

Two metaphors describe the nation of which Yahweh is an ally. Israel is called "a wild bull of towering might" (v. 22b), an animal with horns capable of goring the most powerful of enemies (compare Deut 33:17). And Israel has the strength of the "lioness" and the "lion," which do not rest until they have devoured their prey (v. 24; compare Gen 49:9; Mic 5:7). The oracle is a clear warning that Israel, supported by the power of Yahweh, can easily defeat Moab or any other nation.

After this oracle the king shows impatience with Balaam. He tells the prophet that if he cannot curse Israel, at least he should not bless it (v. 25). Rather than diminishing Israel's strength, Balaam has instead acclaimed the union between Israel and Yahweh, the source of its power and might.

Balaam's explanation shows once again why the narrative is told: Balaam is a man who "must do all that the Lord tells him" (v. 26). In this the prophet exemplifies a characteristic that is desirable for all Israel.

23:27–24:13 The third oracle. Though two attempts to secure a curse have been unsuccessful, Balak tries one more time. The pair move to the top of Peor and prepare a sacrifice on seven altars as before (23:27-30). This time, however, Balaam does not leave the king in order to inquire of Yahweh; he *sees* Yahweh's blessing on Israel immediately (24:1). Balaam stands forth, with the Israelite tribes in view, and the spirit of God comes upon him (v. 2). To say that the "spirit of God" comes upon someone is to ascribe to the recipient the onrush of power from God. Balaam is like other great figures through whom Yahweh acted for Israel, such as the judges (see Judg 3:10; 6:34; 14:6, 19); the prophets (see 1 Sam 10:10; Mic 3:8); and the kings (see 1 Sam 10:6, 10; 11:6; 2 Sam 23:2).

Balaam's oracle comes from one who sees the truth, because what the prophet sees and hears is Yahweh's word given to him (vv. 3-4).

The oracle emphasizes once again the strength and vitality of the Israelites. It speaks of the fullness of Israel's blessing and the power, prosperity, and life that flow from that blessing. So many and great are the tents of this nation that they are compared to the abundance of well-watered gardens and to the strength of the mighty cedars (vv. 5-6). There will be no end to their prosperity: their wells will flow with water; they will possess the lands all the way to the sea; and their king will dominate all others (vv. 6-7). Israel is described in its greatness, the result of the blessing promised to Abraham (Gen 12:2-3) and fulfilled in its becoming a nation (2 Sam 7–8).

On account of the covenant relationship rooted in the deliverance from Egypt (v. 8a), Israel has a vitality that can be compared to that of a wild bull that devours the nations like grass (v. 8b; compare 23:22) and to that of a lion and a lioness stalking their prey (v. 9a; compare 23:24). The message to Israel's neighbors is that this people is blessed because it is the people of Yahweh. For the nations to affirm the blessing would be to accept Yahweh as God and therefore come under the promise of blessing themselves. This would fulfill the promise "Blessed is he who blesses you, and cursed is he who curses you" (v. 9b; see Gen 12:3a). Because the king of Moab is intent on cursing Israel, the consequence for his nation is certain defeat.

Balak is extremely angry that Balaam has blessed Israel three times and dismisses him without reward and with the remark that the Lord is responsible for withholding the reward (v. 11), as if to ridicule Balaam because he obediently spoke God's word and did not try to earn a rich reward and honor by manipulating the word. To the end, Balaam is unmoved in his purpose. Remuneration does not matter, as he told the messengers earlier (v. 12; see 22:18). His sole motivation is to do what the Lord commands and to say what the Lord puts in his mouth (v. 13). Only one thing matters to him—not pleasing the host, not wealth nor honor, but only doing and saying what Yahweh commands.

24:14-25 The fourth oracle. Before going on his way, Balaam speaks an unsolicited word that announces Israel's ultimate victory over the peoples of the region. This is a most magnificent oracle spoken on the word of Yahweh (vv. 15-16), the culmination of the series of oracles. It promises the future rise of the nation—a "star" and "staff" from Jacob/Israel (v. 17a). These symbols for rulers and kings point to the Davidic monarchy (see Gen 49:10). The empire will include Moab and Edom, the peoples who denied Israel passage through their lands (vv. 17b-19; 20:14-21; 21:10-20; compare 2 Sam 8:11-12). The oracle proper ends at this point with the announcement of the defeat of the nations.

The oracle is expanded with a series of sayings that begin in the same way: "Upon seeing __________, Balaam gave voice" (vv. 20a, 21a, 23a). These sayings attack other nations that threatened Israel at various times throughout its history. "Amalek" (v. 20b) refers to the wandering tribes of the deserts of Sinai, who were traditionally the most hated of Israel's enemies. The Israelites faced the Amalekites when they first came from Egypt (Exod 17:8-13; Deut 25:17-19) and again as they sought to enter (14:43-45) and settle the land (Judg 3:12-13; 6:3, 33; 7:12; 10:12). The Amalekites were defeated under Saul (1 Sam 14:48; 15:2-9) and again under David (1 Sam 30:1-20; 2 Sam 8:12).

The reason why the Kenites are named among the enemy nations is not certain, for according to tradition the Kenites are ancestors of Moses (see Judg 1:16 and 4:11). The tradition also states that the Kenites lived among the Amalekites (see 1 Sam 15:6 and Judg 1:16). It is probable that because of their association with the worst of Israel's enemies, they face the defeat described in the oracle (v. 22). The first line of the oracle, verse 21b, obscure as it is in meaning, contains the words "smith" and "nest," both of which play on the sound of "Kenite" in the Hebrew. The poetic value carries more importance than the meaning.

Finally, the Ishmaelites, descendants of Abraham and the maidservant Hagar (Gen 16 and 21), are named among the enemies to be defeated (v. 23b; see Gen 16:12). The Ishmaelites, who dwelt in the wilderness of Paran (Gen 21:20-21), were scattered throughout the land from Egypt to Asshur (Gen 25:18), among the other neighboring foes (see Ps 83:7-8).

The victors in this case will not be the Israelites but rather the Kittim, who will also defeat Asshur (the Assyrians and Eber), the patronymic ancestor of the region that Abraham left for the land of promise (see Gen 10:21-25). "Kittim" is the name given to the people who settled the island of Cyprus (Isa 23:1, 12; Jer 2:10; Ezek 27:6). The Kittim were no doubt the Sea Peoples, the Philistines, who invaded lands along the Mediterranean Sea, including Canaan and that of other enemies of Israel. Reference here to the victories of the Philistines looks to their future role as provocateurs in the rise of the empire (see 1 Sam 4–6; 2 Sam 5:17-25) and their defeat by Israel: "He too shall perish forever" (v. 24b; Josh 13:2-3; 2 Sam 5:17-25; 8:12).

All the oracles, even those appended, are directed to the defeat of Israel's enemies and to the rise of Israel as a great nation. The oracles are fittingly recited at the moment of Israel's arrival on the plains of Moab to project from this place to the future possession of the land. The entire emphasis in the remainder of the book is on Israel's future life in the land. Even Balaam, as he is cast in this tradition, serves as a model for living faithfully by the word of God. As Balaam obeyed Yahweh's word, the result was blessing, and such is promised to an obedient Israel.

Chapter 25 contains two stories, verses 1-5 and 6-13, that have as their setting a place near the Promised Land. Both involve women, and both tell about Israelite infidelity and consequent punishment. These stories function as a foreshadowing of life as it will be when Israel enters the land (see Judg 2:10-23). They immediately follow the oracles of blessing to illustrate that the blessing is not automatic but rather is dependent on fidelity to the covenant relationship between Yahweh and Israel.

25:1-5 Worship of Baal of Peor. Ironically, what Balak was unable to do to Israel by curse, the people do themselves. Balak had hoped that the curse would effect vulnerability and destruction, the results of separation from God. This narrative recounts how the people turn from God and unleash upon themselves the anger of God and the punishment of death.

The incident takes place at Shittim (v. 1a; 33:49), the very place from which the Israelites would later depart to cross the Jordan into Canaan (see Josh 2:1; 3:1). The people have relations with the Moabite women, sacrifice to their gods, and eat the sacrifices (vv. 1b-2). This description suggests that the people took part in the fertility rites of Canaanite religion. The fertility god Baal was appeased by sexual acts and sacrifice in an attempt to guarantee productivity of the soil and procreation. These practices proved especially tempting to Israel in the Promised Land (see Hos 2:10, 15; 4:14) and were expressive of Israel's rejection of Yahweh (see Judg 2:13; 3:7; Deut 6:12-14; 7:5; 8:19, etc.). There were high places for Baal worship throughout the land. The name Baal of Peor refers simply to one of these places at Peor (v. 3a).

To turn to another god is to reject Yahweh and to arouse the anger of Yahweh, who is a jealous God (see Deut 4:24; 5:9; 6:15; Exod 20:5; 34:14-15). Because the people have indeed turned from Yahweh, Moses is commanded to have the leaders execute the guilty ones in the sight of the whole community (vv. 4-5). The usual punishment for violation of covenant unity is public hanging with the breaking of the bones (see 2 Sam 21:6, 9, 13). The word used for this punishment means also to alienate one from another (Jer 6:8; Exod 23:17-18). Thus, the consequence of alienation between covenant partners is the alienation of the members in the body.

25:6-15 Zeal of Phinehas. The second story carries the theme of infidelity and punishment, but its primary point of interest is the legitimation of the Zadokite priesthood, which claims descent from Eleazar through Phinehas (see Exod 6:25; 1 Chr 24:3a; 2 Sam 8:17).

There is no connection with the event at Peor, and parts of the story seem to be missing. The people are weeping at the entrance of the meeting tent (v. 6b), and a slaughter of Israelites is in process (v. 8b). There is no explicit mention of a plague, the usual punishment for sin, though it is certainly implied. And the nature of the sin is unclear. The story fragment tells only that an Israelite has brought a Midianite woman into the camp (v. 6a) and that when Phinehas, the grandson of Aaron, sees this, he pierces the two of them with his sword, thereby appeasing God's wrath (v. 11). To put the deed of Phinehas in bold relief, the names of both the man and the woman appear in the text, along with their ancestry. Both individuals were of noble descent (vv. 14-15).

The action of Phinehas gains him a reputation for zealousness for God's honor (v. 11; see Sir 45:23-24), and succession to the priesthood. Yahweh's word to Moses is a pledge of friendship with Phinehas and his descendants that bestows on them special rights (vv. 12-13; see the story of the Levites in Exod 32:25-29).

The presence of the Phinehas story in Numbers reflects the struggles among the groups of priests for position and power after the Exile. Though the Zadokite priesthood, descended from Phinehas, dominated from the time of the early monarchy, its position needs to be secured once again as the community looks forward to reestablishing itself in the land.

25:16-18 Vengeance on the Midianites. An appendix to the stories serves to knit the two preceding incidents together by claiming that the Midianite woman was responsible for the infidelity at Peor and by linking her death and the slaughter of the Israelites with the infidelity at Peor (v. 18).

This is the work of the Priestly author, who has another purpose in mind—to explain why the Midianites have become such enemies (v. 16), though traditionally they were friends and even related to Moses' wife (see 10:29). The continuation of this piece and the execution of the curse on the Midianites will follow in 31:1-18.

26:1-51 The second census. The Priestly writer links the new census with the narrative by referring to the slaughter (25:18b and 25:8-9), though the census is not the result of that punishment. Because a whole generation of Israelites perished in the wilderness, so that not one of those named in the first census remained except Caleb and Joshua, Yahweh orders Moses and Eleazar, who has succeeded Aaron (20:22-29), to take a register of those about to enter the land. This census takes place while the people are camped along the Jordan on the plains of Moab, in anticipation of entry into the land (v. 2; see v. 63).

The heading of the listing, those "who came out of the land of Egypt" (v. 4b), can be misleading. It is intended to show that the second census parallels and replaces the first taken at Sinai (compare 1:1, 19a).

The criteria for those registered are the same as for the first census. The count includes the men of twenty years or more who are fit for military service; they are listed by their father's lineage (vv. 2, 4; see 1:2-3, 18). The order of the tribes is the same as in the first census (1:20-43), except for Manasseh, who is listed before Ephraim (v. 28; compare 1:32-35). In this second list the individual clans are also named to emphasize the tribal structure, size, and ancestry in the postexilic time. (There are other lists of clans in Gen 46:8-25 and 1 Chr 2 with variations that reflect fluctuations in structure at different times in history.)

The purpose of the census list, as it is given here, is to determine the proportionate size of each group in preparation for the land assignment that will follow (vv. 52-56). A comparison between the numbers in the two lists reveals that while the totals do not differ dramatically—601,730 in 26:51 and 603,550 in 1:46—there is a marked change in the strength of individual tribes. Five tribes—Reuben, Simeon, Gad, Ephraim, and Naphtali—have decreased in size; and Simeon, which was the third largest in the first census (1:23), is now the smallest (v. 14). The greatest increase is registered by Manasseh (v. 34; compare 1:35), a fact that accounts for the transposition in order between it and Ephraim (v. 28; compare 1:32, 34). Judah holds its position as the largest of the tribes in both lists (v. 22; compare 1:27).

The list is made more interesting by the commentary in verses 9-11. This elaboration is placed here to account for the loss of particular clans. Dathan and Abiram (v. 9) perished because of their rebellion, as did the sons of Korah (see ch. 16). The reminder that not all the descendants of Korah died (v. 11) reflects a later period when the sons of Korah were active as singers (see the headings to Pss 42, 44–49, 84, 85, 87). The mention in verse 19 of the death of Er and Onan, sons of Judah, has the same effect. The loss of these clans is called to memory because they failed to abide by God's law. That story is told in Gen 38:6-10.

An opposite problem, the possibility of the extinction of a clan, is the reason for the comment on Zelophehad in verse 33. It states that this individual, the head of a clan, has five daughters but no sons. The problem that arises when there are only female heirs is dealt with in 27:1-11 and chapter 36.

26:52-56 Allotment of the land. The census is taken in preparation for the distribution of the land. Two principles upon which the allocation will be based are stated in this legislation. The land will be apportioned in accord with the size of the tribe (vv. 53-54); and the land will be distributed by lot (v. 55). A summary legislation attempts to reconcile the two principles by combining the two methods (v. 56; 33:54). The summary combines the human element of tribal size and the divine element of lot.

26:57-62 Census of the Levites. A separate census is taken of the Levites, just as it was earlier (3:17-39). The criterion for their numbering, as in the first census, is the time of their birth (v. 62a; see the commentary on 3:14-39). However, they are numbered separately in the first census because of their consecration for the service of the sanctuary (1:47-54); here it is because they receive no land for a heritage (v. 62b). This census is taken in preparation for the assignment of cities and land where the Levites might dwell in the land given to the tribes as a heritage (see 35:1-8).

The groups of Levites named in verse 57 are the traditional three: Gershon, Kohath, and Merari. They are listed here as the heads of clans rather than simply as the sons of Levi (compare 3:17) to emphasize that it is their descendants who will live in the assigned cities. The clans named in verse 58 are only five from the list given in 3:17-20. We can only speculate that these five Levitic clans were more prominent at the time this was written.

The ancestry of Amram, a descendant of Kohath, is traced in detail because from this line came Moses, Aaron, and Miriam (vv. 59-60; see Exod 6:20). Only the family of Aaron (v. 60) is given further mention. Recollection of the death of Nadab and Abihu accounts the loss of these families to their infidelity (v. 61; see 3:4; Lev 10:1-5) and indirectly points to Eleazar and Ithamar as the sole successors in the priestly line.

26:63-65 Census completed. A summary statement announces the completion of the census on the plains of Moab, as if to bring the reader once again to an awareness that the people are in readiness on the threshold of the land (v. 63). Those who are registered are the new generation who grew up in the wilderness while waiting for the death of their parents. They, together with Caleb and Joshua, were spared the judgment (v. 65; see 14:28-35).

27:1-11 Inheritance by daughters. This passage contains a legal question for which there is no solution in existing legislation. The matter, therefore, must be brought before the leaders of the community (v. 2), who in turn seek direction from Yahweh (v. 5). We have come across other such cases in 9:6-14 and 15:32-36. Each provides an example of new instruction for a specific situation, becoming a precedent for subsequent practice.

The case in point concerns the five daughters of Zelophehad of the tribe of Manasseh (v. 1; see 26:33), who are the sole descendants of their father. In ordinary circumstances the family land passes to the sons, who alone have the right to retain it and the family name. The daughters argue that their father's name will be dropped from the tribe just because he has no sons. With no male members to inherit the land, there will be no land ownership in the family, and the family name will no longer exist in the community. The daughters ask that they might inherit the land and thus keep alive their father's heritage and name (v. 4). Their argument is persuasive. They stress that though their father died in the desert, his death was not related to the judgment on Korah (16:16-24, 35). He died "for his own sin," which is to say that he came under the general judgment on rebellious Israel (see 14:26-35). There is, therefore, no reason that their father's name should be blotted out.

Moses' decision first answers the request of the daughters and then gives new general legislation pertinent to inheritance. The case is decided in favor of the daughters: they receive their father's inheritance and a place within the family by virtue of their inheritance (v. 7). The general legislation that follows provides that the family heritage be retained within the family even though there are no children (vv. 8-11a). The property never passes to the wife. If there are no sons, the land passes to the daughters in the family (v. 8); if there are no daughters, it is given to the man's brothers (v. 9), uncles (v. 10), or the nearest surviving relative in the clan (v. 11a). The legal norm stipulates that the land be retained in the family in the father's line (v. 11b) to ensure that no property is lost to a particular tribe, thus unbalancing the tribal holdings.

This particular legislation is of significance at this place in the narrative because the land in question belongs to the half-tribe of Manasseh that will settle in the Transjordan (v. 1; compare 32:39-42). The issue of land inheritance by the daughters of Zelophehad settles a territorial claim to land that will be assigned prior to crossing over the Jordan.

27:12-22 Joshua to succeed Moses. The time of Moses' leadership is drawing to a close. The scene patterns that of the death of Aaron in 20:22-26. Moses is told to go into the Abarim Mountains (v. 12) to Nebo, the place of his death, to view the Promised Land (see Deut 32:48-52; 33:47; 34:1-6). Before his death Moses is reminded that he is deprived of the land because of his infidelity in the wilderness (v. 14a). Mention of "the water of Meribah of Kadesh" (v. 14b) is meant to trigger memory of the incident. It involved a "contention" (Meribah) over water during which Moses was instructed to manifest Yahweh's "sanctity" (Kadesh) by commanding the water to come forth (see 20:2-13).

Moses' last concern is to provide a capable successor to lead the people. Addressing Yahweh as "God of the spirits of all," a title for the Creator (see also 16:22), Moses asks Yahweh to preserve the life of the nation by choosing a new leader for it (v. 16). This leader will, literally, "go out and come in," "lead out and bring in" the people, as a shepherd leads the sheep (v. 17). The role of the leader, though in succession to Moses, will be a new one. That is why Moses calls upon the Creator to bring about a new thing. The phrases "go out and come in," "lead out and in" are technical language for political and military leadership (see 1 Sam 18:13, 16; 29:6; Josh 14:10b-11; 1 Kgs 3:7), as is the shepherd reference (1 Kgs 22:17; Ezek 34:5-6; Zech 10:2-3; 11:8; 13:7). The successor to Moses will lead the people in the conquest battles and in the settlement of the land.

The man chosen for this task is Joshua, son of Nun, a man of spirit who has already demonstrated his God-given abilities for leadership (see 11:28; 14:6, 30, 38; compare Deut 34:9).

The commissioning ceremony has the effect of distinguishing the role of priest from that of political leader. Joshua stands in the presence of Eleazar the priest and the whole community (vv. 19, 22), where Moses lays his hands on him (v. 18), a sign of passing his authority on to his successor (v. 20). Joshua, however, is unlike Moses, who received instruction directly from the Lord (see 12:6-8). Joshua will seek direction through the priest, who will use the sacred lots, the Urim and Thummim, to obtain the Lord's decision (v. 21; see Deut 33:8; Exod 28:30).

In his commissioning, Joshua receives authority from Moses that the people might obey him (v. 20b); but in all other respects Joshua's role is different. The transition in leadership stresses the uniqueness of Moses' role in all of Israelite history; it also traces the distinction between the priestly and political powers to the time of Joshua. This last was a matter of particular concern in the time after the Exile (see Zech 6:12-13; 4:14; Ezek 45:17; 46:2).

Moses carries out the commissioning of Joshua exactly as Yahweh commanded him (vv. 22-23). The provision of a successor is complete and Moses' death is expected. The account of the death is separated, however, in the structure of the document so that Moses might complete the instruction of the people. All of the final legislation is thus attributed to Moses. The report of Moses' death is found in Deut 32:48-52 and 34:1-9.

Chapters 28–29 contain the regulations for public sacrificial worship to be carried out by the community in the land. The emphasis is on worship by the community as a whole and deals with daily, weekly, monthly, and yearly observances. These are regulations that the priests gathered in this one place and attributed to Moses. A comparable, though less detailed, list of observances is found in Lev 23.

28:1-2 General sacrifices. This introduction stipulates that at designated times food offerings will be presented to God. Burned upon the altar, they produce an odor pleasing to the Lord. The language speaks figuratively of God actually delighting in the aroma of the food presented. A "sweet-smelling oblation" is a metaphor for an acceptable sacrifice.

28:3-8 Each morning and evening. The morning and evening food offerings consist of two yearling lambs, one offered in the morning and one in the evening (vv. 3-4), along with a cereal offering (v. 5) and a drink offering (v. 7). The wine is poured out around the altar and the food is completely burned upon the altar as a sign of full dedication to the

Lord. This oblation is the required regular communal offering and the basic sacrifice to which all other offerings are added. As such, it was legislated at Sinai (see Exod 29:38-42). Reference to this Sinai tradition is made in verse 6.

28:9-10 On the sabbath. To set the sabbath day apart from all others, a food offering of lambs, cereal, and wine is presented in addition to the regular oblations. Thus, the sabbath offering is double that of a weekday.

28:11-15 At the feast of the New Moon. In the ancient calendar the day of the new moon marks a new beginning and is treated as a festival day. A sacrifice of greater quantity is required. In addition to the regular food offerings for each day (v. 15b), the sacrifice for this festive occasion consists of two bullocks, a ram, and seven lambs (v. 11), with proportionate amounts of cereal and wine for each of the animals (vv. 12-14; see the commentary on 5:1-16). In addition, a goat is sacrificed as a sin offering (v. 15). The offerings listed here are the usual oblations for all solemn occasions.

28:16-25 At the Passover. The feast of the Passover is celebrated on the fourteenth day of the first month of the year (v. 16; see 9:1-5 and Exod 12:2, 18); and the following day, called the feast of Unleavened Bread, is the beginning of the seven-day period during which only unleavened bread is eaten (v. 17). The first and seventh days of this week are sacred occasions for assembly when no work is done (vv. 18, 25). On each of the seven days the oblation appropriate for solemn festivals is offered (vv. 19-22; see vv. 11-15 above). This is in addition to the food offering required for each day (vv. 23-24).

28:26-31 At Pentecost. Seven weeks after the feast of Passover, the grain harvest is celebrated. Gifts of the harvested first fruits are brought to the temple as an offering (v. 26a; see Lev 23:9-22). This day is a sacred occasion on which no work may be done (v. 26b). The acceptable sacrifice for this solemn festival consists of the prescribed food offerings and sin offering for all such feasts (vv. 27-30; compare vv. 19-22, 11-15). These offerings are made in addition to the offerings required each day (v. 31).

29:1-6 On New Year's Day. The first day of the seventh month, also an occasion of the New Moon (see 28:11-15), marks the beginning of the New Year. This solemn feast is sometimes called the feast of Trumpets, because on it the trumpet is sounded (v. 1c; see the commentary on 10:1-10). No work is permitted on this sacred occasion (v. 1b), and the prescribed oblations for all such festivals are offered, except that only one bullock, rather than the usual two, is prescribed (vv. 2-5; see 28:11-15). That the offerings for the occasion are in addition to the oblations required for the monthly New Moon and for the daily offering (v. 6) accounts for the change in the number of animals required.

29:7-11 On the Day of Atonement. The tenth day in the same month as New Year's Day (v. 7a; compare v. 1) is the Day of Atonement, a day of fasting and self-denial. No work may be done on this day (v. 7b). The offering is the same as on New Year's Day, with one less animal (v. 8; compare v. 2) and the usual cereal (vv. 9-10) and sin offerings (v. 11a). The prescribed offerings for this day are in addition to that required for the atonement sin offering (v. 11b; see Lev 16 for the ritual of the scapegoat).

29:12-39 On the Feast of Booths. Exactly six months after Passover and the seven-day pilgrimage of Unleavened Bread, Israel celebrates another feast that lasts for eight days (v. 12; compare 28:16-17). The first and last days are sacred occasions on which no work is permitted (vv. 12, 35). This is a joyous celebration of the harvest, with pilgrimage and great sacrifices. On this day Israel remembers the time spent in the wilderness (see Lev 23:39-43).

The required food offerings for each day of the festival are listed in detail. On the first day thirteen bullocks, two rams, and fourteen yearling lambs are offered (v. 13). On each subsequent day the number of bulls decreases by one, while the number of other animals remain the same (vv. 17, 20, 23, 26, 29, 32). The proportionate offerings of cereal and drink accompany each animal sacrifice each day, and the sin offering is sacrificed each day in addition to the usual offerings required for every day (v. 16). On the eighth day (vv. 35-38) the prescribed sacrifice is the same as that required for the other festivals celebrated in the seventh month—New Year's (vv. 2-5) and the Day of Atonement (vv. 8-10).

The final comment in verse 39 concludes the whole of chapters 28–29. It is a reminder that the listing of offerings is the required sacrifice for each occasion. Individuals, however, may make offerings over and above these in accord with their own ability and desire.

30:1-17 Validity and annulment of vows. The total obedience of Moses is stressed with the comment in verse 1. It is placed here as a reminder that the regulations before and after must be obeyed by the faithful worshiping community.

This section deals only with the question of when vows or pledges made to God are binding. This legislation on vows clarifies a matter of authority and is, therefore, addressed to the heads of the tribes (v. 2).

A male person, having full authority, is always responsible for his own actions and must therefore fulfill the vow or pledge he makes (v. 3). A female person, on the other hand, has no authority of herself; she is dependent on her father before marriage and on her husband after marriage (see v. 17). Only a widow or a divorced woman, both of whom fall among the disenfranchised, retain responsibility for their own actions (v. 10). All other women come under the authority of men. The regulations in this chapter ensure that a woman will do nothing that might divest the family of property or progeny, the rights to which are retained by the male members. For example, a woman might vow a child to God (see 1 Sam 1:11), or make a pledge that would result in the loss of possessions.

The legislation is divided into three sections: laws governing the unmarried woman in her father's house (vv. 4-6); laws governing the woman who is under vow at the time of her marriage (vv. 7-9); and laws governing the married woman (vv. 11-13). In each case the situation for making a vow is the same. If her father or husband says nothing when he learns of the vow, the vow is valid and the woman must fulfill it (vv. 5, 8, 11-12). If, on the other hand, the father or husband disapproves of the vow, it is not binding. The voice of the man invalidates the vow and releases the woman from fulfilling it before the Lord (vv. 6, 9, 13).

The final section, verses 14-16, is meant to prevent a vow from becoming a matter of divisiveness in marriage. The husband's authority must be exercised upon hearing of the vow. The responsibility for failure to keep the vow falls upon the husband if he tries to invalidate it at a later time.

Chapter 31 reports a holy war against the Midianites as a prelude to the series of wars that Israel will fight to take possession of the land. In all instances a holy war ends in an ideal victory, because it is a war in which Yahweh participates.

The account of the war is followed by descriptions of the rites of purification and disposition of booty that have as their interest the ritual cleanliness and loyalty to God expected of a people who live with God in their midst. The actions following the battle are in compliance with regulations set forth in Numbers and witness to Israel's faith in Yahweh's covenant presence. This chapter is put together to illustrate the meaning of utter and uncompromising loyalty to Yahweh and to encourage those returning to the land from the Exile if they should run into difficulties in their attempt to reestablish themselves as a community of faith.

31:1-18 War against the Midianites. The narrator chooses as the context for the holy war the incident of the Midianite woman (25:6-15). Earlier this incident was linked with Peor (25:16-18), and here both the Peor and Midianite stories are linked with Balaam the prophet (vv. 8b, 16). Other points of contact are the priest Phinehas, who leads the battle against the Midianites (v. 6) and who, in the Midianite incident, demonstrated zeal for the Lord by thrusting his sword into the couple (25:7, 11-13); and mention of Zur, one of the five Midianite kings killed (v. 8a), who was also the father of the Midianite woman (25:15). The holy war is waged to fulfill the curse on Midian that followed from the affair with the Midianite woman (see 25:16-17).

The basis for a holy war is the understanding that an enemy of a people is an enemy of the god of that people. Thus the god would execute vengeance (v. 3b). In this context the technical word "vengeance" means the demonstration of power or use of force by legitimate authority against the enemy of that power and authority. For a reason that is unclear in the old story, the Midianites show themselves to be enemies of Israel and thus provoke a display of Yahweh's power. The ingredients of a holy war are the usual: a limited number of men take part in the battle (vv.

4-5): they rally behind the leader, who carries with him the sacred vessels and trumpets to sound battle (v. 6); and the victory is total (vv. 7-8). There is another description of a battle with the Midianites under the leadership of Gideon to which this account corresponds at many points (see Judg 6-8).

To signify complete possession by the victorious deity, all that is taken in battle belongs to Yahweh. For this reason the Israelites kill all the men (v. 7); they burn the towns and encampments (v. 10); and they present the women, children, livestock, and valuable items to Moses, the priest Eleazar, and the community (vv. 9, 11-12). But because of the circumstances that necessitated the war, Moses is angry that the lives of the women have been spared (vv. 13-16). He orders the death of all the male children and all the women except the virgins (vv. 17-18).

31:19-24 Purification after battle. Anyone and anything that comes into contact with a corpse is made unclean and must therefore submit to a ritual of purification (see ch. 19). Following the war with the Midianites, the combatants and everything with them must undergo the seven-day period of exclusion from camp and the ritual of sprinklings (v. 19). Perishable items, such as cloth, leather, goats' hair, and wood, are purified with them (v. 20). Materials that can withstand burning have to be cleansed in fire as well as in the purification water, whereas those materials that cannot withstand the fire are cleansed in the water alone (vv. 22-23).

On the seventh day, after washing their clothes, the soldiers are clean and may reenter the camp (v. 24).

31:25-42 Division of the booty. There remains the final disposition of all that is taken in battle. To signify its dedication to Yahweh, it is distributed proportionately in the community. Half is given to those who took part in the battle and half to the rest of the community, so that they, too, share in the glory and benefits of the victory (v. 27). From the distributed property, a portion is given to the priests and Levites as a contribution to the Lord (see ch. 18).

The amount assigned to the priests comes from the booty given to the combatants. They give one out of every five hundred of the people and livestock to the priest (vv. 28-29). The amount assigned to the Levites comes from the community's half of the booty. They are taxed at the rate of one out of every fifty persons and animals given to them (v. 30). The tremendous amount of booty taken in the war—a sign of the significance of the battle—is spelled out in great detail in the text: the total numbers of the spoils taken (vv. 32-35); the numbers of the half given to the combatants as well as that levied for the priests (vv. 36-41); and the numbers of the half given to the community, with mention that one-fiftieth belongs to the Levites (vv. 42-47).

31:48-54 Gifts of the officers. A final offering is presented by the officers of the campaign in thanksgiving for the safety of all the Israelites who engaged in the battle (v. 49). They pledge that each will contribute a precious article from the items they picked up on their own in the course of the battle (v. 50). The gold that the priests receive from the commanders is of great value (vv. 51-52). It is placed in the meeting tent as a portion freely offered to God (v. 54). The comment in verse 53 that the soldiers are allowed to keep their loot points up the free will and generosity of the officers in giving from their treasure. Placed in the sanctuary, the gold is a reminder that as God has spared the lives of all the warriors (compare 17:5), so God will remember Israel in the future.

Chapter 32 deals with the assignment of the Transjordanian land, the territory that the Israelites seized from Sihon (21:21-32) and Og (21:33-35) as they journeyed to the plains of Moab. Decisions in regard to the land are made by Moses in dialogue with the requesting tribes. The expected phrase "the Lord said to Moses" is noticeably absent in the telling. The fact that Yahweh does not speak and that God does not give the land suggests that the division of the people on two sides of the Jordan remains an unresolved issue. So important is this matter that its conclusion is narrated in full in Josh 1:12-18; 4:12-13; 22:1-8.

32:1-5 Request of Gad and Reuben. The tribes of Reuben and Gad request of Moses, Eleazar, and the leaders of the community that they might be given the land east of the Jordan for their inheritance. They argue that the region would be ideal for their livestock. And to make the request legitimate, they remind the leaders that this is land "which the Lord has laid low before the community of Israel" (v. 4). They are referring to the region extending from the Jabbok River south to the Arnon, land that the Israelites had taken from the Amorites (see 21:24).

The problem caused by the request is summarized in the statement "Do not make us cross the Jordan" (v. 5b). From Sinai and through the wilderness, the picture has been of *one people* journeying to enter *one land.* The granting of the request would mean a divided people in a divided land.

32:6-15 Moses' angry response. Moses' response to the idea of division within the community is immediate and passionate. He sees the request as a threat to all of Israel. The other tribes will be discouraged from going into the land the Lord has given them (v. 7). Moses accuses the Gadites and Reubenites of being "a brood of sinners" responsible for diverting the Israelites from entering the land and thus bringing the anger of God on the nation once again (vv. 14-15).

Moses invokes the incident (told in chapters 13–14) of the Israelites' failure to enter the land from the south (vv. 8-13). He claims that the behavior of the two tribes is like that of the spies who earlier discouraged the people. Just as Yahweh's anger caused Israel to wander for forty years until a whole generation died out, Yahweh will punish again. The result will be the ruin of the whole nation (v. 15b).

32:16-19 Compromise. The tribes of Gad and Reuben offer a compromise. Moses does not object to possession of the Transjordanian land; his concern and anger center on the unwillingness of these groups to cross the Jordan. The tribes therefore promise that they will accompany the Israelites into the land as the vanguard, that they will not return until every one of the Israelites has taken possession of his heritage, and that they will not claim a heritage for themselves in the land of Canaan (vv. 17a, 18, 19a).

The Gadites and Reubenites, however, make provision for themselves before helping the rest of Israel. Their promise of help is contingent upon their receipt of a heritage in the Transjordan (v. 19b) and on securing their families and animals before departure (vv. 16, 17b).

32:20-32 Agreement reached. Moses accepts the compromise proposed by the Reubenites and Gadites. The negotiations are settled in a sequence of four speeches.

In his acceptance Moses proposes the opposite of that suggested by the two tribes (vv. 20-24). He provides first for the entry and settlement of the Israelites in the land of Canaan, and only afterward for the establishment of the tribes in the Transjordanian territory.

The Gadites and Reubenites reaffirm their commitment (vv. 25-27). They reply that they, leaving their families and livestock behind, will indeed go across the Jordan to fight the battle before the Lord. They still put their own interests ahead of those of the rest of the Israelites.

Moses then instructs Joshua, the priest, and the leaders about the carrying out of the agreement (vv. 28-30). The settlement depends upon the good faith of the two tribes. If they cross the Jordan as combat troops and when the victory is complete, Joshua will give them Gilead as their property. But if they do not keep their promise to accompany and fight with the Israelites, they will be given a heritage in Canaan with all of Israel. Moses' instruction points to a *future* resolution of the situation. The request will not be honored if the Gadites and Reubenites do not keep their part of the bargain.

The two groups readily reply that they will do what the Lord commands (vv. 31-32). They thus perceive that Yahweh wills their actions. They reaffirm that they will cross the Jordan into the land of Canaan as troops before the Lord and that they will retain the property in the Transjordan. Their response is enthusiastic and religiously motivated.

32:33-42 Moses gives the land. It would seem that Moses is responding to the evidence of faith in the two tribes, for, contrary to his instructions in verses 28-30, he proceeds to give the land to the Gadites and Reubenites as well as the half tribe of Manasseh. The land distributed is that taken from Sihon, king of the Amorites, and from Og, king of Bashan (vv. 33; see 21:21-35). The land is not assigned by lot nor by tribal size, as the instruction clearly stipulates (see 26:52-56). In this sense the land falls outside that legitimately assigned to the Israelites.

The Reubenites and Gadites are assigned the territory of Sihon, the region south of the Jabbok River (vv. 34-38). The half tribe of Manasseh is given the land north of the Jabbok taken from Og. This land of Gilead was assigned to the Machir and Jair clans of the Manasseh tribe, which had invaded and settled in it (vv. 39-42; compare 21:33-35). It is because of this territorial possession prior to entry into the land that the case of land inheritance by women of the Machir line of the Manasseh family became an issue (27:1-11).

With this assignment of land, provision is made for the settlement of part of Israel. Other issues pertinent to designation of boundaries will also be settled by Moses before his death (chs. 34–36). The history of this time is presented in such a way that the future is seen as the fulfillment of Moses' leadership under the authority of Yahweh.

33:1-49 Stages on the journey. To both summarize and conclude the account of the journey through the wilderness, the Priestly author adds a very old record that lists the stations from Egypt to the plains of Moab (vv. 5-49). This is the same list used as the structure for the narrative account of the wilderness journey.

The formal introductory words echo the stylized heading that is characteristic of the Priestly author. "The following are the stages . . ." (v. 1a) is patterned after the heading "These are the generations . . ." (see Gen 5:1; 6:9; 10:1; 11:10; 11:27; 25:12, 19; 36:1; 37:2). The bold introduction highlights the importance of the list of stations that follows. Its significance is also underlined by the fact that Yahweh commands that Moses record it (v. 2).

The journey began at Rameses in Egypt (Exod 1:11; 12:37) with the celebration of Passover (Exod 12-13) at the time when Yahweh slew every first-born in the land of Egypt (Exod 12:29-30). The memory of the beginning out of Egypt in verses 3-4 comes from a song composed to celebrate the occasion.

The list of stations in verses 5-49 is much more detailed than the sequence of stops mentioned in the narrative. No tradition about many of the places was preserved, so the Priestly author employs the list in broad outline only.

The first segment goes *from Rameses in Egypt to the desert of Sinai* (vv. 5-14). This is the part of the journey told in the Book of Exodus from 12:37 to 19:2. Most of the places in the list occur also as headings in Exodus (see Exod 12:37; 13:20; 14:1-2; 15:22-25a; 16:1; 17:1a; 19:2). The events that took place at Sinai are related by the Priestly writer in Num 1:1 to 10:10.

The second segment outlines the journey *from Sinai to Kadesh* (vv. 16-36). This leg of the journey is recounted in Num 10:11 to 19:22. The limits of the journey are mentioned in the journey formula at 10:12, though in this text Kadesh is replaced by the desert of Paran, the name for the locality that includes Kadesh (see Num 2:16; 13:3, 26). Kibroth-hattaavah (vv. 16b-17a) appears in the narrative in connection with the quail story (11:34-35a); and Hazeroth (vv. 17b-18a) is the place where Aaron and Miriam rebelled against Moses (11:35b; 12:16). In the narrative, the desert of Paran is meant to include the whole range of places in the list not explicitly cited (vv. 18b-36).

The third stretch of the march goes *from Kadesh in the desert of Zin to Mount Hor* (vv. 36-40), places named in journey formulae at Num 20:1a and 22. The events are told in the relatively brief section of 20:1 to 21:9. The list in verses 38-39 is expanded with mention of two specific incidents that are part of the narrative: the death of Aaron (vv. 38-39; see 20:23-29) and the confrontation with the king of Arad (v. 40; see 21:1-3 and 14:39-45).

Finally, the Israelites traveled *from Mount Hor to the plains of Moab* (vv. 41-49). These places are named in the journey formulae at Num 21:10-11 and 22:1, headings that encompass the narrative material from 21:10 to the end of the book. In the narrative, the locality called the "desert fronting Moab on the east" (21:11) is cited to include the whole range of places named in verses 42-48a.

33:50-56 Rules for the conquest and division of Canaan. The effect of the list of stations is to bring the reader back to an awareness that the people remain on the border of the land. At this place Yahweh gives Moses more instructions concerning the future (v. 50). The first one deals with the taking and distribution of the land across the Jordan (v. 51).

The task before the Israelites is to drive out the inhabitants of the land and to destroy all the vestiges of their religion (vv. 52, 55a; see Deut 12:2-3). The conquest must be absolute. There are to be no non-Israelites remaining nor anything uncharacteristic of Israel's God. This is a land that Yahweh has given to Israel as an inheritance. It is a sign of the covenant relationship between Yahweh and Israel (v. 53). This relationship demands total love and loyalty.

The command is followed by a warning expressed in the typical conditional curse (see Deut 30:16-17). If the inhabitants of the land are permitted to remain, they will be a constant source of irritation and trouble (vv. 55; see Josh 23:13); and ultimately the removal from the land intended for the inhabitants will befall the Israelites themselves (v. 56). This last statement has special meaning for the people in exile who have been removed from the land. At issue is radical and uncompromising loyalty. Yahweh's land, as a theological idea, is the place for the faithful followers of Yahweh only.

Wedged into the instruction concerning occupation of the land is a repetition of the procedure for division of the land (v. 54; compare 26:52-56). That the land will be assigned "by lot" is repeated intentionally so that Israel might know that *Yahweh will give* the land, emptied of its inhabitants, for the possession of the families of Israel.

34:1-49 The boundaries. Yahweh's instruction for the future in the land continues with a description of the boundaries of the territory that will be given to Israel (vv. 1-2). An ancient boundary list is used for this idealized territorial description. The description does not correspond with the actual boundaries during any period after the tenth century B.C.E; it does correspond with the limits of Egypt's possession in Canaan in the thirteenth century B.C.E. as those limits are defined in the peace treaty between Egypt and the Hittites. The Priestly writer borrows this specific description of the land of Canaan because it includes only territory actually possessed by Israel, and because the eastern limit borders on the Jordan. For the purpose of the narrative, the writer is not interested in the land beyond the Jordan at this time.

The description of the southern boundary (vv. 3-5) is very similar to that of the southern border of Judah as presented in Josh 15:1-4.

The western boundary at the Great Sea (v. 6) is reminiscent of the idealized description in the promise statements, such as Gen 15:18 and Exod 23:31.

The description of the northern boundary (vv. 7-9) has only slight variations from the limits of the land as described in Ezek 47:15-17 and 48:1.

The eastern boundary, however, differs from the usual idealized extent of the land that would include territory on both sides of the Jordan (compare Ezek 47:18). The definition in verses 10-12 follows the line of the Jordan River and thus excludes the Transjordanian land.

The boundary at the Jordan is, of course, intentional, to indicate that the land in question is that to be divided among the "nine and one half tribes" (v. 13). The other two and one half tribes have already received their heritage on the eastern side of the Jordan (vv. 14-15; ch. 32). It is the land to be divided in the future that is highlighted.

To carry out the allotment of the land, Joshua and Eleazar are to be assisted by leaders from the individual tribes (vv. 17-18), in much the way that Moses and Aaron were assisted in the census (see 1:4-16). All the names of the leaders in verses 20-28 are new. Only Caleb (v. 19), who survived the wilderness period, has a place in tradition (see 14:6, 24, 30, 38).

The order of the tribes differs from any other, whether for the census or for the arrangement in the camp. Here the listing is governed by the geographical order in which each tribe holds land in Canaan, going from the south to the north (compare Josh 14–19). The nine and one half tribes that will occupy Canaan are grouped into the four southern tribes (vv. 19-22), the one and one half central tribes of the family of Joseph (vv. 23-24), and the four northern tribes (vv. 25-28).

35:1-8 Cities for the Levites. Because the Levites have no land for their inheritance, they are assigned cities in which to live and an expanse of land around the cities for their pastures (vv. 2-5). The cities and the land are to be appropriated from the tribes according to their size (v. 8). Forty-eight cities in all will be given to the Levites (v. 7).

We have here only the regulation for the assignment of cities and lands to the Levites. The apportionment that totals precisely forty-eight cities can be found in Josh 21:4-8. The land is to come from territory of all the tribes, including those in the Transjordan.

35:9-15 Cities of asylum. The cities of asylum are linked with the Levitical cities in verse 6. This verse states that of the forty-eight cities assigned to the Levites, six must be set aside as places where a person who takes a life unintentionally may find refuge (also v. 11). Three of these cities will be located in Canaan and three in the Transjordan (vv. 13-14). This regulation only specifies that such cities must be set aside; their names are given in Josh 20:1-9, especially vv. 7-8, and 21:21, 27, 32, 36, 38.

The cities are designated as places where all people, resident or alien (v. 15a), may seek refuge from revenge before they have had a chance to face trial (vv. 12, 15b) in cases where blood has been spilled. The law stipulates that a person who commits murder deserves death (Exod 21:12, 14). The death sentence is often carried out by the "avenger of blood" (v. 12), the nearest male relative of the deceased, before there is proof that the death was caused deliberately. The designation of cities of refuge represents a development in the law based on respect for human life. The legislation guarantees legal protection for an accused person.

35:16-34 Murder and manslaughter. The stipulations make clear which individuals have the right of asylum. The willful murderer is to be handed over to the avenger, the next of kin to the deceased, who is responsible for carrying out the death sentence (vv. 19, 21b). Willfulness is evidenced by a death-dealing weapon in hand (vv. 16-18) or when there is indication of hatred or enmity (vv. 20-21).

On the other hand, if death was caused accidentally (vv. 22-23), the community is required to protect the accused from the avenger (vv. 24-25a). After first determining that there was no intention to kill, the community will send the accused back to the city of asylum, where that person will stay safely until the death of the high priest (v. 25b). Loss of life is such a serious matter that, though it may have been caused accidentally, the person involved is nonetheless deprived of freedom. In fact, an accused person who leaves a city of asylum before the specified time can still be put to death by the avenger (vv. 26-28). Underlying this eagerness to take a life for a life is a keen sense of maintaining the balance of power in individual tribes. Intentional loss of life in one family calls for loss of life in the other.

Other norms govern the community when it is making decisions that justice might prevail and that both the accused and the community might be protected (v. 29). First, an accused person cannot be condemned to death except on the evidence of several witnesses (v. 30; see Deut 17:6; 19:15). Second, the condemned murderer may not substitute payment in place of suffering loss of life (v. 31); nor may a person relegated to a city of asylum buy release from the city (v. 32).

The demands seem very great. Israel is a society in which life is regarded as a precious gift from Yahweh. The shedding of blood desecrates the land—the very land in which Yahweh dwells in the midst of Israel, where Yahweh is present with the people in covenant. The land is not to be defiled for the simple reason that the God who is present with Israel is Yahweh, the God who brought Israel out of Egypt in order to dwell among them (v. 34; see Exod 29:45-46; Lev 26:11-13).

The chapter ends on a note that summarizes the theological focus of the Priestly work. All the preparations for entry into the land and all the legislation for living faithfully in the land have one motivation—to make Israel a holy place worthy of a holy God who is present in its midst.

36:1-12 Property of heiresses. The case brought to Moses for resolution in 27:1-11 created a problem that is presented here for consideration. The case has its immediate setting in the Machir clan of the tribe of Manasseh, which has already been assigned territory in the Transjordan. The leaders of that clan now come before Moses and Eleazar (v. 1) with the concern that the daughters of Zelophehad might marry into another Israelite family and thereby cause the loss of land to their father's tribe (vv. 2-3), for when a woman marries, all her possessions become the property of her husband. At issue is the diminishment of land allotted to the tribe under God's direction. The leaders add that the land would become the permanent possession of the husband's tribe in the jubilee year (v. 4; see Lev 25:8-34). The laws governing the jubilee year require that all land that has been sold be returned to its original possessor every fiftieth year. This law apparently does not affect land that has passed to another tribe as a result of marriage into the tribe.

The first ruling created a problem that requires modification. The new ruling does not negate the first decision, which gives women the right of inheritance when there are no male members. Moses offers the modification that Zelophehad's daughters may marry only into a clan within their own family so that no land will be lost to the family (vv. 5-7). The new legislation, then, becomes the precedent for all cases of inheritance by women so that each tribe might retain the inheritance allotted to it (vv. 8-9).

A final note is added with the announcement that the daughters of Zelophehad did marry within the clans of their father's family (vv. 10-12).

36:13 Conclusion. The Book of Numbers closes with a subscription to the rules and regulations gathered together in chapters 27–36. These were given while the people remained on the plains of Moab so that they might live faithfully when they enter the land Yahweh has given them and thus possess the land as a permanent inheritance.

DEUTERONOMY

Leslie J. Hoppe, O.F.M.

INTRODUCTION

Deuteronomy and the biblical tradition

The Book of Deuteronomy is certainly one of the most important and influential books in the Hebrew Scriptures. It provided the theological perspectives that dominated the Former Prophets (Joshua, Judges, Samuel, and Kings), now commonly known as the Deuteronomistic History of Israel. It exerted its influence over the final shape of a number of prophetic books, notably Hosea and Jeremiah. Indirectly it influenced the Chronicler's History of Israel (Chronicles, Ezra, and Nehemiah). The Temple Scroll of the Qumran community was basically an Essene reinterpretation of Deuteronomy. The New Testament cites or alludes to Deuteronomic texts almost two hundred times. Deuteronomy's reinterpretation of selected items of ancient Israelite law and history provided a model for the rabbis who produced the Mishnah and the Talmud. Finally, Deuteronomy's self-understanding as a written, authoritative document gave rise to the very concepts of Scripture and canon.

Deuteronomy stood at a pivotal point in the life of ancient Israel. Its pages preserved traditions that were ancient at the time of its own production. Some of the legal traditions handed on by the Deuteronomists had their origins in the pre-Israelite era of the ancient Near East. The Deuteronomists, however, were not antiquarians or even historians. Their purpose in preserving, transmitting, and reinterpreting ancient tradition was to provide Israel with some direction for its future at a time when that future was in great doubt. The Deuteronomists did their work well, for the phenomenon we know today as early Judaism was shaped in large measure by the Book of Deuteronomy. Their work, then, stood as the bridge between the religion of ancient Israel and the faith of early Judaism.

The meaning of Deuteronomy

Because of its obvious importance, the Book of Deuteronomy has attracted much attention over the years. Interpreters of the book have described it as a covenantal document, an example of Levitical preaching, a charter for religious revival, a response to the culture shock of foreign domination, an attempt at humanizing ancient laws, a call for cultic purity, and the basis for cult centralization. It has been disparaged as being morally simplistic and praised for its call for Israel to love God (Deut 6:5). The Deuteronomists have been called harsh and unsympathetic teachers as well as some of the greatest liberal theologians of all time. The diversity of these comments on, and characterizations of, Deuteronomy show how difficult it is to find a simple description for this very complex and sophisticated theological work.

Despite the complications presented by interpreters of Deuteronomy, the aim of the book was really quite simple. The Deuteronomists wanted to make ancient tradition speak again in a time of great crisis for Israel in order to help Israel survive that crisis. They saw that the great institutions of ancient Israel were dead or dying. The monarchy, prophecy, temple, and priesthood had all failed to prevent the nation from arriving at the brink of destruction, which was being caused by both internal and external forces. Deuteronomy suggested that Israel relearn the lessons of its formative years in the wilderness under Moses: obedience to the law of the Lord was the only way for Israel to secure its future. The meaning of Deuteronomy, then, was Deuteronomy itself. The book presented itself to Israel as the last hope: obey and live, or disobey and die (Deut 30:15-20).

The origins of Deuteronomy

There is no universal agreement as to the specific crisis that prompted the production of Deuteronomy. One of the longest held positions of modern biblical studies dates from the early nineteenth century and identifies the Book of Deuteronomy with the "book of the law" found in the temple by the high priest Hilkiah during the reign of Josiah (2 Kgs 22:8ff.). While the book includes much material that can be dated to the late seventh century B.C.E. and earlier, it is clear that Deuteronomy, in the form it now has, dates from the Babylonian Exile (587–539 B.C.E.). It was during the Exile that the remnant of the nation stood on the edge of extinction. In this life-or-death situation, the Deuteronomists presented Israel with the challenge of obedience to a written, authoritative book of the law and called for the nation to choose life (Deut 30:19). This exilic date for Deuteronomy does not eliminate the possibility that earlier traditions were used in the production of the book. On the contrary, Deuteronomy was the result of a conscious reinterpretation of ancient legal traditions for the sake of providing Israel with hope for the future.

Who were the Deuteronomists? From what circles did they emerge? Again, there has been a variety of answers to that question. At first, the prophets were presented as responsible for Deuteronomy, because at one time anything in the Hebrew Scriptures of ethical or theological value was ascribed to prophetic circles. But Deuteronomy does not treat the prophets very well (see the comment on 18:9-22).

Other interpreters have suggested that Deuteronomy reflects the preaching of the Levites. However, there are no examples of Levitical preaching in the Bible, so it is impossible to say that Deuteronomy is the product of such activity. In addition, the book consistently portrays the Levites as objects of charity, hardly a flattering self-portrait.

The sages of Israel have even been credited with the production of Deuteronomy, but they never even appear in the book that they supposedly composed and presented to Israel as the pattern for its life.

The one group that remains a possibility is the elders of Israel. These were the leaders of the community who were the traditional administrators of the very laws preserved in Deuteronomy. They were the principal guardians of ancient Israel's legal traditions. Why should they not be credited with Deuteronomy, the depository of these traditions?

Deuteronomy was composed in order to provide a new pattern of life for Israel in its land. During the Exile, Israel found itself outside that land, hoping to take possession of it once again. Deuteronomy came to light during the Exile. It was created by the elders, who considered themselves to be the custodians of Israel's ancient legal traditions. They took those traditions, altered them, developed them, enlarged them, and drew theological conclusions from them—all for the sake of providing Israel with a new pattern of life. It was this vision for a new life that gave the elders the impetus to create the Book of Deuteronomy.

Form and structure

Any analysis of Deuteronomy's literary form must begin with the book's connections with ancient Near Eastern treaty traditions. In the ancient world, treaties between nations followed a particular pattern, which usually included the following five components: (1) a title that identified the king offering the treaty; (2) a historical prologue, in which the king offering the treaty listed his beneficent acts toward the people accepting the treaty; (3) stipulations or demands made by the king offering the treaty; (4) a list of witnesses to the treaty, and occasionally provisions for storing and periodic reading of the treaty; (5) curses and blessings that would follow upon violation and observance of the treaty. Even a superficial reading of Deuteronomy will make it clear that there is a connection between Deuteronomy and the international treaty form.

At the same time, it is important to note

that Deuteronomy is not presented as if it were a treaty. It makes use of literary forms from the treaty tradition, but it is presented as a series of addresses given to Israel by Moses just before his death. Deuteronomy is Moses' testament to Israel, which is to take possession of the land of Canaan in a short while. It is not the text of a treaty or covenant. While the book may contain elements of the treaty form, it also contains material that cannot be included among such forms (see Deut 32–34).

In its present form, Deuteronomy is composed of four addresses given to Israel by Moses. The tone of these addresses is exhortatory. The book is meant to encourage Israel to obey the law. Moses portrays Israel as specially chosen by God to take possession of Canaan. Israel will maintain its hold on that land as long as it is obedient. (This commentary will follow the structure evident in the book itself, which divides the material into four separate addresses, each introduced by a formulaic expression which asserts that what follows are the words of Moses: Deut 1:1; 4:44; 29:1; 33:1.)

The exhortation to obedience is the core of Deuteronomy, but, as Deut 29:1 indicates, this exhortation was transformed into the text of a treaty or covenant between God and Israel. The ancient customs and laws that regulated the mutual relationships of the people became the test of their loyalty to God. The quality of intersocietal relationships within Israel became the barometer of Israel's relationship with God. Accordingly, for Deuteronomy, to know and love God means to love one's neighbors and do them justice. This, of course, is affirmed in the New Testament in a number of places, for example, Mark 12:29-31 and 1 John 4:7-12, 20-21. Thus, the elements of the ancient Near Eastern treaty tradition were introduced into the Book of Deuteronomy in order to give new value and importance to obedience. The effect of this transformation was to make one's love of neighbor the standard and test of one's love of God.

COMMENTARY

MOSES' FIRST ADDRESS

Deut 1:1–4:43

The scene of Moses' address to Israel is the region known as the plains of Moab, immediately east of the Jordan River. The time is just before the tribes are to take possession of the land promised to their ancestors. The context of these final words of Moses is an exhortation to obedience. This "testament" of Moses is his advice to Israel to heed the lessons of the past if it wants to secure its future. The lesson is simple enough: God expects complete loyalty from Israel; nothing less is satisfactory. Israel's trek through the wilderness after its departure from Egypt has taught it over and over again that loyalty is rewarded and infidelity is punished. Moses will now spend his last energies in trying to move Israel to the kind of obedience, loyalty, and commitment that will secure Israel's future in the land it will soon come to possess.

1:1-5 The preface to the first address. These verses function as a preamble, introducing not only the first of Moses' four addresses but also the entire book as well. They specify the persons involved in the events of the book, the scene of the action, and the exact time and purpose of the work. Deuteronomy purports to be the words of Moses addressed to all Israel. Here the book underscores the unity of the people of God, all of whom are subject to the divine will.

While the location where the address is given is specified with precision (vv. 1b-2), the exact location of all the sites mentioned is not known, though it is clear that the scene of the action is on the east side of the Jordan River.

Moses begins his first address to the tribes just before Israel is to cross the Jordan to take possession of the land promised to its ancestors. It is now forty years since the Exodus. Preliminary victories have already been won, but Israel, poised on the plains of Moab, hears Moses deliver a final plea for obedience as he makes the Lord's will absolutely clear to all Israel. The purpose of this exposition is to move Israel to renewed commitment.

1:6-18 The move from Horeb. Moses' first address begins with a direct quotation of

God's words at Horeb (Mount Sinai) calling Israel to begin the journey that will end with acquisition of the land that is to be the scene of its subsequent history. The dimensions given for the land (v. 7) reflect the promise made to Abraham (Gen 15:18) rather than any set of historical borders. This promise is now fulfilled as the land is shown to Israel and thereby passes into its possession. All that remains is for Israel to take physical possession of its inheritance. That, however, will be no easy task.

Verses 9-18 interrupt the account of Israel's departure from Horeb, which is resumed in verse 19. After arriving at Horeb, Moses foresaw the difficulties ahead and suggested that the people select leaders to share the burdens of leadership with himself (v. 13). Though Moses had played an indispensable role in leading Israel from Egypt to the threshold of the Promised Land, Israel reached a point in its life when others were to first share, and then finally take over, the responsibilities which up to that point Moses had had to bear alone. It is significant that Israel was to choose its own leaders. Any breakdown in the morale or loyalty of the people would be due to the decisions of these leaders. God could not be blamed, since Moses simply confirmed those leaders whom the people themselves presented to him.

Among the leaders confirmed in office by Moses were judges, who were specifically charged to administer justice without regard to the social and economic differences between the people who had disputes before them (vv. 16-17). Justice among Israelites was based on the premise of the equality of all Israelites. In fact, the mantle of equality was even placed on the shoulders of aliens residing among the Israelites (v. 16).

This section closes with the parenthetical note that Israel was fully instructed regarding its responsibilities in its new relationship with God (v. 18). Israel could not plead ignorance if it failed in that relationship.

1:19-46 Israel's failure at Kadesh-barnea. The journey from Horeb ended at Kadesh-barnea, a site in the south of Canaan. Kadesh-barnea was to serve as a base of operations from which the Israelite tribes were to begin the process of acquiring the land promised to them. It should have been the scene of initial victories; instead, it was the scene of Israel's first defeat. The nation was defeated because of its lack of confidence in God.

The people suggested that spies be sent to reconnoiter the land and its inhabitants (v. 22). The spies returned with glowing reports about the land, but with terrifying reports about the indigenous population of Canaan. The Israelites recoiled at the possibility of having to face the Canaanites in any type of armed conflict. Moses tried to encourage the people by reminding them of God's deliverance of Israel from Egypt and the guidance through the wilderness, but to no avail.

God's response was to allow the people just what they wanted—a safe haven outside the Promised Land. God would wait for the next generation to begin the settlement of Canaan. In addition, Moses was condemned to die outside the new land (v. 37). As the people's leader, he was most responsible for Israel's loss of faith. Only Caleb, Joshua, and the children of the rebellious generation would be spared the effects of the people's decision to remain outside Canaan.

After some time the people decided that they indeed wanted to take possession of Canaan, but it was too late. They were easily defeated by the Amorites. They had to live with the effects of their disobedience. Kadesh, not Canaan, was to be their home.

2:1-23 Peaceful transit through Edom, Moab and Ammon. In telling the story of Israel's experiences in Transjordan, the Deuteronomists assume that there was a peaceful transit through the areas that were not settled by the Israelite tribes. There was to be no conflict over these territories, since God had allotted them to their respective inhabitants at another time (vv. 5, 9, 19).

Other biblical traditions consider the populations of these territories to be related to the Israelites: in the case of the Moabites and Ammonites, through Lot, Abraham's nephew (Gen 19:36-38); and in the case of the Edomites, through Esau, the brother of Jacob (Gen 36:9).

Still other traditions preserve the memory of tensions that did exist between these people and the advancing Israelites. According to Num 20:14-21, Edom refused to permit the Israelites to traverse its territory, and Num 22–24 reports the attempt of Balak of Moab to obtain a curse upon Israel.

The most significant feature of the Deuteronomic tradition about Israel's relations with these peoples is the universalism which undergirds that tradition here. The God of Israel also gives the peoples of these Transjordanian countries the land they inhabit. Clearly, God's concern extends beyond the pale of Israel.

While Israel was spared conflict with these nations, according to Deuteronomy, Israel was locked in a conflict that took the lives of a whole generation of warriors. The enemy who caused Israel to suffer such a devastating defeat was none other than God (vv. 14-15). Israel's infidelity at Kadesh-barnea cost it dearly. Though God had fought for Israel against Pharaoh, God will just as easily turn against an unfaithful Israel. The Deuteronomists want to issue a warning: divine acts of deliverance in the past are no guarantee for the future! There is only one way Israel can look to the future with any hope, and that way is through obedience.

2:24–3:22 Conflicts with Sihon and Og. Though the historical presence of Israel on the east bank of the Jordan was short-lived, Deuteronomic tradition holds that the tribes of Reuben and Gad and two clans of Manasseh settled there. The tradition also assumes that the territory of these tribes was acquired in much the same way as were the lands west of the Jordan, where the other tribes settled—through armed confrontation with the indigenous population. The conflicts with the Amorites under Sihon and the people of Bashan under Og are presented as violent in the extreme (2:34; 3:6). Any conflict over the limited amount of arable land in the region had the potential for becoming very costly in terms of human lives, as are similar conflicts in the same region today. The intensity of these conflicts is not surprising, nor is the human tendency to attribute them to the divine will. The dark side of Israel's belief that it received the land as a gift from God was the practice of eliminating those who held a different belief.

Another theological issue raised by this text is the relation between the human and the divine wills. Sihon opposed Israel's entrance into his territory, but this came about because God hardened his heart (2:30). The victories that Israel won over Sihon and Og were the Lord's doing (2:33; 3:3), yet Israel's armies had to fight and defeat the forces of these two kings. The text seems to assert that both the divine and the human actions were necessary, but it does not deal at all with how the two were related.

Verse 11 is a parenthetical remark on the great size of Og's bed or sarcophagus, which was still to be seen in the Deuteronomists' day. In spite of Og's great power, his kingdom fell to an obedient Israel. Fidelity has a power that far outweighs military or political power.

The victories over Sihon and Og resulted in the distribution of their territories among the tribes of Reuben and Gad and among Machir and Jair, two clans of Manasseh. Since Sihon and Og defied the Lord (2:30; 3:1), they were defeated by the Lord's might. Their lands were now forfeit and passed to Israel. The allocation of the conquered territories was more than the settling of geographic boundaries. It was, first of all, a celebration of God's victory and a statement of belief in the divine origin of the territorial claims made by the tribes and clans named here. The same pattern—conquest followed by allocation of land—provides the basic outline of the Book of Joshua (conquest: Josh 1–12; allocation: Josh 13–21). The victories over Sihon and Og and the distribution of their land among the Israelite tribes were a harbinger of future victories on the other side of the Jordan.

The stipulations in 3:18-20 emphasize the unity of Israel, an important Deuteronomic theme. The militia of any tribe cannot rest until *all* the land of Canaan is acquired according to God's promise.

3:23-29 Joshua. Tradition locates Moses' grave outside the Promised Land (Deut 34:5). There then needs to be an explanation for this apparent injustice and for the eventual succession to Moses' position of leadership among the tribes. Regarding the former issue, the Deuteronomists opt for a solution that preserves Moses' integrity. Though he was personally innocent of any guilt, Moses was unfortunately caught up in the wake of infidelity that enveloped the whole generation of rebellion at Kadesh-barnea (1:26). This contrasts with the Priestly tradition, which accused Moses himself of a breach of faith that resulted in his exclusion from the Promised Land (Num 20:12). These two different explanations for the tradition about the grave of

Moses probably reflect the exilic debate between communal guilt and personal responsibility as an explanation for the presence of evil and suffering in Israel's life.

Another concern of the Deuteronomists is to demonstrate that the Mosaic office could continue beyond the death of Moses. Joshua was the first successor to Moses. There could then be others in the future who could do what Moses once did for Israel—transmit and interpret the divine will for Israel. If the law was to be the one guide for Israel's life in the land, Moses had to have legitimate successors who could provide Israel with access to the law and its interpretation (see Matt 23:2; *Pirke Aboth* 1:1).

4:1-40 The conclusion to the first address. Moses' first address concludes with a summary not simply of the foregoing material but of the entire Book of Deuteronomy. The material found here was incorporated into Deuteronomy during the Exile (587–539 B.C.E.), when circumstances forced Israel to reconsider the meaning of its relationship with God and to examine the status of that relationship.

The Book of Deuteronomy as a whole and this chapter in particular speak of the fundamental loyalty that is essential to Israel's unique relationship with God. Here the Exile is explained as one result of a serious lapse in that loyalty as manifested in Israel's disregard of the prohibition of images (vv. 25-27). The folly of serving other gods brought on the Exile (v. 28). Once Israel realizes what befalls those who are unfaithful, repentance is possible (vv. 29-30). Finally, the compassion of God does not allow Israel's infidelity to end the relationship that exists between God and Israel, since God remains faithful to the promise made to Israel's ancestors (v. 31). As disastrous as was Israel's disloyalty, it still did not mean the end of its relationship with God.

It is clear that obedience is the key to maintaining Israel's relationship with God, which is made tangible by its possession of the Promised Land. Five times this text speaks of the connection between obedience and possession of the land (vv. 1, 5-8, 14, 21-22, 40). The text uses the concrete example of the prohibition of images to show the results of disobedience (vv. 3-4, 15-26). When Israel disregarded God's commandments, disaster followed. Flouting the stipulations of the covenant (v. 13) resulted in Israel's exile from the land (vv. 26-27). The faith of the Deuteronomists leads them to expect that God will bring blessing from the curse of the Exile (v. 31) and restore Israel to an intimacy with God that is unparalleled (vv. 32-39).

Obedience, then, is the foundation of Israel's relationship with God, since it brings Israel closer to God than is thought humanly possible (v. 6). It is the uniqueness of Israel's God (v. 39) and of the covenant this God makes with Israel (v. 13) that makes Israel unlike any other people. To secure its future, Israel need only recognize what is so obvious and order its life according to the commandments. A life lived in obedience will bring not only renown (vv. 6-7) but also long life in the Promised Land (v. 40).

This text is a clear warning: disobedience arouses Israel's God, who does not tolerate infidelity. Disobedience will mean that God's power will be turned *against* Israel just as easily as it was once manifested *for* Israel (vv. 34-35). The key of Israel's future is the Book of Deuteronomy itself, since it is the collection of the "statutes and commandments" that Israel must obey to secure long life in the land (4:1, 40).

4:41-43 The cities of refuge. A complete presentation on the cities of refuge occurs in Deut 19, which makes no allusion to this passage. In Num 35:13-14 it is stated that three cities of refuge are to be set up on the east side of the Jordan. The three cities in question are named in Josh 20:8. Clearly, this text was added to its present context under the impression that these cities were established by Moses. This text probably would have fit better after Deut 3:12-17, in which Moses allots land to the tribes and clans that will remain in Transjordan. The exact location of these cities is unknown.

MOSES' SECOND ADDRESS

Deut 4:44–28:69

4:44-49 Introduction. Both the time and place of Moses' second address are specified. Moses gives this speech near Beth-peor (v. 46). This was the site of an infamous act of apostasy (Num 25). Here the Israelites had shown themselves ready to compromise the absolute fidelity that God expected of them. It was also within the borders of the new land that God had just given the tribes (Deut 2:24–3:17). Thus, Beth-peor is a reminder of God's graciousness, which overcame Israel's infidelity. The law that follows is to be the means of assuring that Israel will remain committed to the service of God alone. This speech is given by Moses after the initial victories of Israel over the Amorites (vv. 46-47). These latest demonstrations of God's graciousness should be a powerful stimulus to fidelity.

5:1–6:3 The Ten Commandments. With Israel standing in Transjordan, the promise made to the ancestors of the Israelite tribes is on the verge of fulfillment. The people who have been living by the promise now need to learn how to live with the fulfillment. The most dramatic shift in this transition is to learn that continued possession of the land is dependent upon fidelity to God. The initial acquisition of the land is the result of God's fidelity to the promises made to the ancestors of the Israelite tribes; now the Israelites need to respond to that fidelity if they wish to remain in their new land.

The Ten Commandments are to guide Israel in this transition from living by the promise to living with its fulfillment. The Decalogue provides Israel with a means to maintain a continuing relationship with God. These Ten Words, as Jewish tradition calls them, serve to pattern Israel's response to the God who brought it out of slavery in Egypt (5:6) and who is about to lead it into a new land. The commandments are restrictive in only one way: they call for Israel's uncompromising fidelity to the God who has fulfilled every promise made to Israel. They commit Israel to the exclusive service of God. This ensures that Israel will live and prosper in the land God is about to give it (5:33–6:3).

(Note: The numbering of the commandments here follows the Roman Catholic and Lutheran tradition. Other Christians and the Rabbis divide the prohibitions against false worship into two separate commandments [vv. 6-7 and 8-9] and unite the prohibitions of coveting into one [v. 21]. Another version of the Ten Commandments can be found in Exod 20:2-17.)

The first commandment (vv. 6-10) exemplifies God's passion for Israel's absolute fidelity. Once Israel settles in its land, there will be temptations to compromise the loyalty owed to God. The Israelites are looking forward to what will be a new experience for them—a life of freedom in their own land. What must not change for them is their commitment to God. Their whole life is to be determined by their relationship with the God who brought them out of Egypt. The prohibition of images (vv. 8-9) reminds Israel that its knowledge of God is to be gained from its experience of the reality of God that it encountered in the Exodus from Egypt and in the guidance in the wilderness.

The second commandment (v. 11) prohibits the attempt to harness with magic the power that the ancients believed was inherent in the divine name. In early Jewish tradition it became customary to avoid mentioning the divine name entirely. The God of Israel was beyond manipulation. God's name was not to be linked with any selfish human purpose. The commandment regarding the sabbath (vv. 12-15) imposes two obligations: to make the sabbath day holy (v. 12) and to cease work on that day (v. 13). The two obligations are related, since the day of rest provides the Israelites with the opportunity to remember their slavery in Egypt and their liberation by the power of God. The sabbath is to be a regular weekly reminder of Israel's dependence upon God.

The fourth commandment (v. 16) stands as a bridge between those that precede and those that follow it. The commandments deal with two kinds of relationships. The first three commandments focus on the relationship between God and Israel, while the last seven deal with the relationships that must exist within the Israelite community itself. Israel will be able to remain loyal to God as long as the people remain loyal to one another. The parent/child relationship is not only analogous to the divine/human relationship (1:31), but it is also the core relationship within the Israelite community.

This community will not be able to endure if human life can be taken for personal and illegitimate reasons, so murder is prohibited (v. 17). Murder ignores a person's status and worth as God's creature, and as such it is an attack on the Creator's prerogatives. Another threat to the life of the community is any threat to the binding commitment of faithfulness made by husband and wife. The sixth commandment (v. 18) aims to protect the marriage relationship. Infidelity is reprehensible to God, who is always faithful.

The seventh commandment (v. 19) is most probably concerned with crimes against persons rather than theft of property. Members of the Israelite community are not to turn against one another. For example, the slave trade is forbidden here. But in a wider sense, any action by which one human being takes control over the life of another is outlawed. Human beings are not to be manipulated but are to be given the freedom necessary to maintain a faithful relationship with God.

Another prerequisite for a healthy community is integrity and honesty in human relationships. The eighth commandment (v. 20) seeks to protect these values. The God who is faithful in every word and deed requires the same honesty in human relationships. Finally, the last two commandments (v. 21) prohibit coveting. Not only are actions disruptive to community life forbidden, but also proscribed are the desires that lead to such crimes. Self-interest must be kept in close check before it becomes the dominant force in a person's life. The position of the wife in the Deuteronomic form of this commandment differs from that of Exod 20:17, in which the wife is placed among the husband's property. Here the woman has a more favorable status.

The commandments come from God, but they are interpreted through Moses (vv. 22-33). Both the people and God choose Moses as the mediator of the law, which derives its authority from God and its applicability from Moses. Later, Deuteronomy will speak about the successors to the Mosaic office (18:15-19). But this text attests to the authenticity of Israel's encounter with God as mediated through a human being.

The section of the second address containing the Ten Commandments closes with a short exhortation that attempts to provide motives for obedience (6:1-3). The principal reason given is that obedience will lead to the fulfillment of the promises made to Israel's ancestors: a fruitful land and a numerous progeny. The Exile, which meant living outside the land and in numbers decimated by the war with Babylon, could be seen as nothing less than a course resulting from Israel's disobedience.

6:4-25 The love of God. The concern of this text is to promote obedience to a particular commandment: the prohibition of the worship of gods other than the Lord. The Israelites are preparing to enter a very prosperous land (vv. 10-11). Moses warns them against rashly concluding that the prosperity of the land is due to the beneficence of the gods worshiped by that land's indigenous population. Israel is never to forget what happened in Egypt (v. 12). The Lord's liberation of Israel from slavery in Egypt has forged a bond that must never be severed by Israel's service of deities worshiped by other peoples. Israel is not to divide its loyalties.

There are a variety of ways in which verse 4 can be translated (compare the rendering of the Revised Standard Version: "The Lord our God is one Lord"). Though each can be defended on linguistic and theological grounds, the New American Bible translation best fits this context, which emphasizes the exclusiveness of Israel's service of Yahweh. While this verse and its context underscore the loyalty that Israel owes to the Lord, this is not a statement of explicit monotheism. In fact, the possibility that other gods exist is implicit here. For Israel, however, there is only one God, and all of its energies are to be directed to the service of that one God.

Some may find it odd that verse 5 *commands* the love of God. The love envisioned here is the kind of deep loyalty and affection that Israel owes to the God who ended its cruel bondage in Egypt. Secondly, in Deuteronomy love is virtually synonymous with obedience. The image behind this injunction is the parent/child relationship, in which love and obedience are equivalent terms. The love that Israel owes God is all-encompassing. In fact, the entire Book of Deuteronomy is nothing else but a drawing out of the practical implications of verse 5. Jesus cited this verse when asked about the greatest commandment of the law (Matt 22:36-37; Mark 12:28-30).

The injunctions of verses 7-9 stress how total Israel's devotion to God's commands must be. Israel is to keep the commandments in mind at all times and under all circumstances. Early Judaism turned these metaphors into commands. Jews began the custom of wearing phylacteries (small leather containers holding tiny scrolls, on which were inscribed verses 4-9 as well as other biblical texts). Jesus' criticism of this custom assumes that obedience to this command was not always accompanied by the kind of total obedience envisioned by verse 5 (see Matt 23:5). Jews also began to attach a *mezuzah* (a small container holding a written biblical text) to the upper part of the right doorpost. Rather than establishing any specific customs, Deuteronomy is trying to insure that individual Israelites, their homes, and the entire community will be outstanding in their loyalty to God. The basis of this loyalty is God's liberation of Israel from slavery (v. 12) and God's insistence on fidelity (v. 14). There is no need to determine the strength of God's loyalty to Israel; that was tried once before, with disastrous results (v. 16; see Exod 17:1-7).

The last section of this passage (vv. 20-25) is simply a reprise of what has already been said. (Such repetitions are characteristic of Deuteronomy and lead some interpreters to locate the origins of the book in the situation of teaching and/or preaching.) At one time Israel was a slave of Pharaoh (v. 21). God freed Israel from slavery through a mighty display of power against Egypt (v. 22). The purpose of this gracious act was the fulfillment of the promises made to Israel's ancestors (v. 23). God now requires absolute loyalty from Israel, and this loyalty is Israel's only hope for the future (v. 24). Obedience, loyalty, and reverence are the keys to the kind of relationship with God that will preserve Israel's future (v. 25).

7:1-26 The nations. The Bible's pendulum swings back and forth with regard to the non-Israelite nations. At times the nations, too, will share in the blessings promised to Israel (Gen 12:1-3; Isa 42:1-4). They will be converted to the Lord (Isa 45:14-25; Jonah). At other times the nations are presented as Israel's implacable enemies, whose downfall is cause for rejoicing (Amos 1–3; Nahum).

This text is one of the harshest condemnations in the whole Bible, requiring Israel to annihilate the indigenous population of Canaan in the process of settling in the land promised to the ancestors of Israel (v. 2). Such a command is clearly abhorrent to the moral sensitivities of contemporary readers, but we should remember that this command was never carried out, nor was it ever intended to be. What, then, would have been the point of forbidding covenants and marriage with non-Israelite nations (vv. 2b-3)? This chapter represents a theological judgment on the nations, not a historical account of Israel's treatment of them.

While this theological judgment also is not very attractive to believers today, it reflects Israel's experience with the nations, especially Assyria and Babylon, which were serious threats to Israel's very existence at the time the Deuteronomic tradition was beginning to take shape. In these circumstances, Deuteronomy uses the strongest possible terms to mandate that Israel avoid any contact with the nations. The assumption behind such a prohibition is that cultural assimilation is just as great a threat to Israel's existence as is the political and military pressure being brought to bear upon Israel by the powerful nations warring against it.

7:1-5 Israel's enemies. Here the attitude toward the nations is unmistakably negative: every possible contact with them is to be avoided. No political agreements are to be made with them (v. 2b), for entering into such agreements would entail an explicit acknowledgment of the gods of the nations. While verse 3 may be directed at any type of intermarriage, the Deuteronomists more than likely have in mind marriages as political maneuvers (see 1 Kgs 11:1-8). These, too, inevitably involve explicit recognition of foreign deities. Finally, Israel is to destroy the appurtenances of the worship associated with these gods (v. 5). Adapting these to the worship of Yahweh, which apparently has been attempted (see 2 Kgs 18:4b), results in blurring the distinction between the God of Israel and the gods of the nations. Israel is to be committed to the service of Yahweh alone (Deut 6).

7:6-11 Holiness. The prohibitions regarding contact with the nations arose, not from any superiority on Israel's part, but because of Israel's election and the grave danger of Israel's failure to its responsibilities to God. Israel has been set apart from all other nations. The law was given to Israel in order to maintain that special relationship with God. The basis of this relationship is not Israel's inherent qualities but the divine love that focused its choice upon the least of all nations. People are to recognize Israel as God's choice because of Israel's love and obedience directed toward God. This fidelity will be rewarded, but quick retaliation will come to the unfaithful.

7:12-16 Blessing. God's fidelity is beyond question. The course of Israel's future, then, is largely dependent upon the quality of its adherence to the responsibilities that flow from its unique relationship with God. In a sense, the complete fulfillment of the promises made to Israel's ancestors depends upon Israel's obedience. Here Deuteronomy welds two covenantal traditions together. The unconditional promises made to Abraham, Isaac, and Jacob become bound to the conditional covenantal traditions related to Moses. The result of obedience is blessing, which is described here as abundance of life, prosperity, and well-being—a stark contrast to the conditions that afflicted those who experienced slavery in Egypt. But these blessings depend upon Israel's firm commitment to God and the preservation of its unique identity as the elect people of God.

7:17-26 Israel's victories. The nation of Israel ought to devote itself to obedience with reckless abandon. The metaphor used to illustrate this kind of obedience is Israel's armed conflicts with the population of Canaan. If Israel approaches these conflicts with absolute trust in God and total fearlessness in the face of human opposition, victory can be assured, for God will throw all Israel's opponents into a terrible panic, resulting in Israel's total victory. Verse 22 is an interesting bit of apologetic to explain why Israel's victories during the conquest were not complete. Judges 2:20-23 provides still another explanation: a few of Israel's enemies were allowed to survive in order to test Israel's faith.

8:1-20 A study in contrasts. Though Israel may eliminate external threats to the loyalty it owes to God, this does not mean that this loyalty is assured. There are also internal threats to Israel's commitment. These need to be identified. They may not appear to be as insidious as the worship of foreign gods, but in reality they are no less threatening to the allegiance that God expects of Israel. Moses now turns to these dangers from within and speaks of them by contrasting "remembering" and "forgetting," the desert and the arable land, human self-sufficiency and dependence upon God. These three contrasts are interwoven throughout this chapter, whose purpose is to keep Israel ever mindful of God.

Remembering the gracious acts of God in the Exodus from Egypt and in the guidance in the wilderness is basic to Israel's relationship with God, for such remembering is a stimulus to obedience. Remembering what God has done allows every generation to experience the reality and fidelity of God. Forgetting God leads inevitably to disobedience. The human will substitutes for the divine will. The claims of God are pushed to the sidelines of human awareness.

The contrast between the desert and the arable land does not intend to highlight the sterility of the former and the fertility of the latter; the contrast between the two lies in how the desert kept Israel from forgetting God, while the richness of the new land that Israel will possess can numb Israel to the divine presence. The wilderness was a place of testing as Israel learned to see its existence as totally dependent upon God. The harshness of life in the wilderness made it almost impossible to ignore divine nurture. To drive the point home even more dramatically, God cut off even the meager supply of food in the desert and had Israel live off manna, a miraculous source of nourishment. In the land of promise, Israel will have food in abundance, and then will come the inevitable temptation of believing that the abundance is the result of human efforts. In reality, divine providence supplies Israel's needs in both the wilderness and the new land.

God's purpose for Israel was achieved through human cooperation. Moses was the instrument God used to lead Israel out of Egypt and through the wilderness. The land of the promise is to be acquired through the leadership of Joshua and the efforts of the tribal militia. What begins with human cooperation can end with the pride of human self-sufficiency. Moses warns Israel that it can never afford to ignore the sustaining power of God, which may have been more evident in the wilderness but is just as much a reality in the arable land. Israel will be as dependent upon God in the new land as it was in the desert.

These three contrasts are intertwined with three commands calling for the fundamental, unswerving loyalty to God that is the hallmark of the Deuteronomic tradition (vv. 1, 11, 18). In each of these commands the word "today" emphasizes that every generation of Israel needs to remember God. Forgetfulness will lead to disaster.

The first command (v. 1) is the typical Deuteronomic call for obedience. It locates the motivation for obedience in the gifts of land and prosperity.

The second command (v. 11) is a more specific warning against ignoring the continuing role that God plays in Israel's life. Yahweh's sustenance of Israel is not limited to the wilderness period. Israel should broaden its horizons beyond that which is immediately known and experienced. Its prosperity in the land must not allow the reality of God to fade from its consciousness.

Finally, the third command (vv. 18-20) is a stern reminder of the consequences of "forgetting." It puts Israel on the same level as the nations that were not chosen to be God's own people. This, of course, would be the worst kind of disaster, for Israel is to remain a people with a unique relationship to God. But if Israel does not "remember" God, it will become easy to follow and serve the gods of the nations. Israel would then behave just as the nations it dispossessed behave. If Israel forgets God, it can look forward to being expelled from the land just as the nations were expelled.

9:1–10:11 Israel's stubbornness and God's grace. Another internal threat to Israel's relationship with God is Israel's belief in its own righteousness. Israel is, of course, totally dependent upon God's help in acquiring the land, but in order to reinforce the theme of Israel's unworthiness, Deuteronomy reminds Israel of its rebellion in the wilderness. Even as Moses was sealing the covenant between God and Israel, the people were worshiping an idol. The act of rebellion was enough to prompt God to destroy Israel. It was only through the intercession of Moses that Israel was saved from the full effects of God's anger so that the promises made to Israel's ancestors might be fulfilled.

9:1-6 The land as gift. Israel's victories over the Canaanites, represented by the Anakim (legendary giants), and their fortified cities will be due to God's power and fidelity. But because Israel itself will have to subdue the Canaanites (v. 3b), there will be the temptation to ignore God's help. In addition, the belief stated here (vv. 4-5) and in Gen 15:16 that the nations are being dispossessed because of their wickedness can easily be warped into a belief in Israel's righteousness. The truth is that Israel is no better than the nations. Despite all that God had done for Israel, the people were rebellious and stubborn in their refusal to serve God alone. The only reason Israel is favored over the nations is the oath that God swore to Abraham, Isaac, and Jacob (v. 5).

9:7-14 Rebellion. While Moses was in communion with God at Horeb, Israel turned to idolatry. At the very moment the covenant was being sealed, it was being broken by Israel. The irony is bitter. There could not have been a more inappropriate time for Israel to rebel, yet rebel is just what Israel did even as it stood at the very foot of God's mountain.

In verse 6 Moses called Israel a "stiff-necked" people; in verse 13 it is Yahweh who voices this condemnation of the people, along with the clear intention to destroy them. The wickedness of the nations led God to dispossess them; Israel's rebellion was now turning God against it as well. God's words to Moses in verse 14, "Let me be," were not taken by him as a prohibition but rather as an invitation to intercession. It is Moses who was able to turn God's anger from Israel, but before he began his intercession, Moses came down from the mountain and confronted the people who forgot their God.

9:15-21 The covenant is broken. Whatever the reason for the construction of the golden calf, Deuteronomy understands it as a direct breach of the command of God prohibiting false worship and the use of images. Moses' action in breaking the two tablets was not the result of an angry fit; he destroyed the tablets, which symbolized the covenantal bond between God and Israel, because Israel chose to destroy that relationship. As symbols, the tablets were robbed of all their significance when Israel constructed the golden calf. By not hesitating to include Aaron among the guilty (v. 20), the Deuteronomists are ready to indict the priesthood for helping Israel choose the way of rebellion.

9:22-24 More rebellion. Israel rebelled more than once. These verses mention four other incidents of rebellion in order to attest to Israel's rebellious character. This fatal flaw showed itself more than once during the wilderness period. Israel survived because of Moses' intercession, but what will become of Israel when there is no one like Moses to make intercession?

9:25-29 Moses' prayer. This prayer is another contrast drawn by the Deuteronomists. When speaking to Israel, Moses recalled the past to remind the people of their wickedness and disobedience. When speaking to God, Moses reminded God about the promises made to Israel's ancestors (v. 27) and of the gracious acts of salvation in the Exodus from Egypt (v. 29). Moses reminded God about the identity of the people destined for destruction: they are "*your* people and *your* heritage" (v. 25). They are the people whom God liberated from the slavery of Egypt. Moses was hoping that he could elicit from God another act of divine liberation. Israel needed to be freed from the debilitating effects of its own rebelliousness.

10:1-5 The ark of the covenant. To symbolize a renewed covenant between God and a rebellious Israel, the Lord authorized the manufacture of two new tablets. Once these had been inscribed with the Ten Commandments, they were placed in an ark, a wooden container used to hold these memorials of the covenant. Originally the ark was a symbol of the Israelite tribes' resistance to the Philistines (see 1 Sam 4:1b; 7:2). Later it was housed in the temple and was considered to be the footstool of God's throne and therefore symbolic of the divine presence (see Exod 25:1-22). In Deuteronomy the ark is simply a container for the tablets of the law. It is obedience to that law which guarantees God's favor, not any supposed presence of God in the temple.

10:6-9 An insertion. This text intrudes upon the story of Moses' intercession for the rebellious Israelites. Verses 6-7 reflect a somewhat different tradition about Aaron's death than is found in Num 20 and 33. Verses 8-9 give information found elsewhere in Deuteronomy (see 31:9, 25-26). The Levites were the ones who transported the ark when necessary. Two other Levitical functions are mentioned: their responsibility to lead worship and to bless the people in God's name.

10:10-11 The answer to Moses' prayer. Israel was not to be destroyed; the covenant was to be re-established. All this was the result of God's mercy and love. Divine justice called for Israel's annihilation. The Lord's fidelity to the promises made to Israel's ancestors and the Lord's willingness to hear Moses' pleas made the continued existence of Israel possible.

10:12–11:32 The great commandment. Before the Deuteronomists get into the specifics of the law for Israel's life in the land (chs. 12–26), they restate the great commandment, which calls for Israel's wholehearted love for God (10:12–11:25). Then, as a bridge to the specific commands, a warning is given (11:26-32), stating that the law has the potential of bringing a great blessing or a terrible curse upon the people. The requirements God makes of the nation have consequences. Israel's experience has shown quite conclusively that God is capable of fulfilling every promise made. If Israel wishes to secure its future in the land, loyalty to God and obedience to the law provide the only way to do so. Infidelity to the Lord and disregard of the commandments will bring disaster.

10:12-22 Israel's allegiance. The command calling for total commitment to God begins this transition to the Deuteronomic Code (chs. 12–26). In a variety of ways a single message comes through: the love of God is the centerpiece of Israel's response to Yahweh. This God is none other than the Creator of the universe, who freely chose to single out Israel's ancestors for special love. Israel's response is to include observance of rituals which celebrate that choice. Among these rituals is circumcision. But these observances must go beyond ritualistic activity to transformation of the spirit. Israel's entire approach to God must be overhauled (v. 16).

One way the people can show how seriously they take their election as the people of God is to accept responsibility for those members of the community whose social and economic status does not ensure their survival. In choosing Israel, God singled out a weak and powerless people to be the object of a unique love (Deut 7:7). In responding to that love, Israel must love the same kind of people God loves. Such a pattern of behavior will bring the complete fulfillment of the promises made by God to Israel's ancestors. One of those promises has already been fulfilled by the phenomenal growth in Israel's numbers (v. 22; see Gen 15:5-6). Another part of the promise, the gift of the land (Gen 17:8), still remains to be fulfilled. Israel's obedience will lead to the total fulfillment of all God's promises.

11:1-25 Memories. Here commands alternate with stories from Israel's collective memory to encourage obedience. Verse 1 begins this pattern. Its formulation of the basic command underlying the entire book introduces three lessons from the past that ought to promote obedience: the Exodus (vv. 2b-4), the wilderness experience (v. 5), and the affair of Dathan and Abiram (v. 6; see Num 16). These references to Israel's past provide both positive and negative illustrations of how God's grace and judgment affect the lives of the obedient and the disobedient. Remembering these great and terrible experiences is an education into the ways of God.

Verse 8 once again urges the people to keep the commandments of the Lord. In verses 9-12 a comparison between Egypt and Canaan provides the motivation for obedience. The Promised Land that awaits Israel is blessed by an abundance that rests on the provision of God. Egypt, by way of contrast, yields harvests only because of an irrigation system that is the work of human ingenuity and labor. The providential care of God over the land of Canaan is another inducement to obedience.

The thought of the previous section is carried on by verse 13, which calls for obedience as the means to ensure provision and prosperity from God in the future. God will provide the rain which, at the proper time, will bring success to Israel's agricultural endeavors. If Israel succumbs to the lies which assert that the land's fertility is guaranteed by other gods, Israel will find it impossible to survive in the land. The people will then have to learn the truth the hard way.

The last few verses of this section (vv. 16-25) are a concluding summary of Moses' address thus far. The main emphasis here is the obligations that God places upon Israel. These verses are a pastiche of admonitions given by Moses previously (see Deut 1:7-8; 2:25; 4:9-10, 38, 40; 6:2, 8-9, 17; 7:23-24). The repetition of this message underscores its importance: Israel's very existence is dependent upon its willingness to respond in kind to God's love.

11:26-32 The alternatives. Moses wants Israel to decide its future. He states the alternatives very clearly. The people can choose to be blessed, or they can choose to be cursed. Blessing is, of course, contingent upon Israel's obedience to the law. The detailed stipulations of that law are about to be presented to the people. Moses advises his audience that their acceptance of a life guided by the law is the only way they can expect the blessings promised to their ancestors. The law, then, is not simply a legal code to pattern Israel's behavior; it is the key to the fullness of life that awaits Israel on the other side of the Jordan River.

The last few verses (vv. 29-32) provide the outline of a ritual celebrating the relationship between God and Israel (a more detailed presentation of this ritual is given in Deut 27:1-26). The choice the people are called to make is really quite simple—it is a choice between Yahweh and other gods. Israel's choice is represented dramatically by a ritual celebrated near Shechem on the twin mountains Gerizim and Ebal. Israel knows that God has chosen it from all the nations of the world. Now it remains for Israel to choose Yahweh above all other gods. In reality, there is no real choice, but if Israel abandons Yahweh for what are really no gods, only misery and disaster will follow. If, however, Israel remains loyal to God, there is no limit to the expressions of God's love.

12:1-26:19 The Deuteronomic Code. Some of the laws found here are unique to Deuteronomy; most, however, are found in other codes, both Israelite and ancient Near Eastern. Deuteronomy's particular stamp may be recognized in its abiding concern for the poor, its humanization of older laws, and especially in its association of obedience with continued existence in the land. If the people wish to secure a future for themselves in the land God has provided, there is only one way—the way of obedience.

The term "code" is used rather loosely here. The Book of Deuteronomy is less a practical guide to legal matters than a recitation of traditional values and practices that the respected members of the community see as constitutive of the Israelite identity. There is no "logical" arrangement in this code, and, beginning with chapter 22, there is a succession of isolated laws that are not explained at any length; in fact, they seem to be unrelated to one another. This may confuse the contemporary reader.

Key words sometimes provide the connection between various laws, but sometimes this is not readily apparent in translation. In addition, the study of Hebrew rhetorical style is just beginning. Perhaps someday the "logic" of Deuteronomy's arrangement will become clear. Nonetheless, it is still important to remember that this book is not an exhaustive legal collection. It offers its readers a convenient summary of traditional practices and calls for their observance. The Deuteronomists are trying to inspire an attitude of submission and obedience. They are not necessarily concerned with providing the people with a complete code of law.

12:1-28 Centralization. The law requiring the centralization of Israel's sacrificial worship is unique to Deuteronomy and the literature dependent upon it. Previous legislation and practice envisioned such worship as taking place at any number of altars throughout the land (see Exod 20:24). Deuteronomy's departure from earlier usage is based on a concern for purity in Israel's cult and on the belief that a multiplicity of sanctuaries is incompatible with the worship of Israel's God. This concern for cultic purity and the desire for cultic unity are related, because both are founded on the recognition that Israel's God is not like the gods of the nations. The many local shrines that were once associated with the old Canaanite deities are unfit for Yahwistic worship. Those shrines have been replaced in favor of a single site chosen by the one God.

There are two other important dynamics in this passage that are characteristic of Deuteronomy: desacralization and humanization. Unlike the old gods of Canaan, the Lord is not a personified natural force; consequently, nothing in nature is sacred in itself. If a place becomes a medium of the divine presence, it is because of God's free choice rather than because of the site's inherent sacredness.

Second, this passage allows the slaughter of domestic animals for profane use (vv. 15, 20). Though blood is not to be consumed with the meat, it has no special sacred character and is therefore poured out like water (vv. 16, 24). The blood is to be offered to God (v. 27), probably as an acknowledgment of the divine sovereignty over life, which is symbolized by the blood.

Finally, Deuteronomy invests sacrifice with a twofold purpose. The first represents private religious concerns, such as the fulfillment of a vow (v. 7). A second purpose is more humanitarian in its orientation, providing the worshiper with an opportunity to share the blessing of the land, rejoice in the Lord, and offer help to the economically dependent (vv. 7, 12, 18).

In this passage there are repetitions, conflicting viewpoints, and differences in terminology, pointing to its complicated literary history. The original law regarding the central sanctuary can be found in verses 13-19. Later additions (vv. 2-7, 8-12 and 20-28) all agree to the restriction of worship to a single shrine, the choice of which is left to God alone.

12:1-7 Destruction of Canaanite sanctuaries. Centralization of worship is presented as the logical consequence of carrying out a previously given command to destroy Canaanite shrines and their appurtenances (v. 3; see Deut 7:5). Hills and shady trees were often chosen as sites for sanctuaries because they were associated with the divine by various Semitic peoples. The cultic activity that took place at these sites was unequivocally condemned as evil by the prophets (see Hos 4:3; Jer 2:20; Ezek 6:13).

The expression "designated as his dwelling" (v. 5) is a formula used by kings in the ancient Near East to indicate ownership. The Deuteronomistic History uses this same expression to refer to Jerusalem (1 Kgs 9:3; 11:36; 14:21; 2 Kgs 21:4, 7). Similarly, the expression "out of all your tribes" refers to Jerusalem in 1 Kgs 8:16; 11:32; 14:21; 2 Kgs 21:7. This implies that the place chosen by the Lord for the one sanctuary permitted is Jerusalem. Of course, Deuteronomy could not name the city, since Jerusalem was not incorporated into Israel until the time of David (see 2 Sam 5:6-12).

12:8-12 Centralization as the goal of Israel's pilgrimage. The Deuteronomists are very well aware that the requirement of a single sanctuary flies in the face of earlier, legitimate practices. This passage characterizes all those earlier usages as provisional. The "rest" that the Lord gives to Israel (see 1 Kgs 5:4; 8:36) inaugurates a new age marked by worship at one sanctuary chosen by God. Centralization of worship was apparently attempted by Hezekiah (2 Kgs 18:4) and Josiah (2 Kgs 23:8-9, 12-15, 20), but their attempts did not outlive them. Deuteronomy's goal of centralization of worship succeeded because the war with Babylon reduced the land under

Israelite control to Jerusalem and a few square miles surrounding it. Thus, the Deuteronomists made virtue out of necessity.

12:13-19 Some effects of centralization. The earliest of the laws about the central sanctuary is addressed to Israel in the second person singular, as is the case with most of the early Deuteronomic legislation. One consequence of this law is permission for profane slaughter of domestic animals. That becomes a practical necessity because ritual slaughter is to be limited to the central shrine. Even though the daily diet rarely includes meat, the slaughter of animals for food has to be disconnected from the cult. The Levites who minister at the shrines to be eliminated in favor of the one sanctuary are commended to the charity of the Israelites, as are other economically dependent groups (widows, orphans, and aliens: see Deut 12:12; 14:27-28; 16:11; 18:6-7; 26:11-12).

12:20-28 A limitation. The effect of verse 21 is to limit the rather broad permission of verse 25 regarding the non-cultic slaughter of animals for food. Such permission is restricted to sites whose distance from the central sanctuary makes ritual killing of the animals a practical impossibility. Verse 28 is a homiletical conclusion to the entire passage about the central shrine. Obedience is commended because it assures Israel of God's favor.

While the law of centralization is an important Deuteronomic innovation, the bulk of the book deals with legislation that neither requires nor even mentions centralization. Still, this innovation was a decisive moment in the life of ancient Israel. It offered a sense of unity and cohesion at a time when Israel's other institutions were dead or dying. Centralization of worship was indeed an innovation, but one that resulted from a fresh interpretation of the ancient cultic pattern of the wilderness. What was entirely feasible in Moses' day was never again realized by Israel until Deuteronomy. Under the influence of this book, centralization became the way to express the unique nature of Israel's God and Israel's unique relationship with the Divine.

12:29–13:18 The specter of infidelity. The unsympathetic treatment of the nations in Deuteronomy is not so much the result of a feeling of ethnic or cultural superiority by the Deuteronomists as it is the result of their fear that Israel is in very real danger of being lost forever in a sea of assimilation. If Israel is to have any future at all, it will be because of a clearly formulated self-definition manifested through distinctive cultural patterns that mark Israel as different from the nations. Certainly the most distinctive of those cultural patterns is Israel's religion, with its emphasis on loyalty to one, and only one, God. As a result of this concern, Deuteronomy is almost ruthless in its determination to ensure that Israel maintain its loyalty to Yahweh alone. This particular section deals with attempts at subverting Israel's allegiance and how these are to be handled.

12:29-31 Foreign religious rituals. Historians of religion are quite certain that much of Israel's cult was adopted from the religious rituals of Canaan, which were modified to conform with Yahwistic beliefs. For example, the agricultural festival of Passover took on a distinctively Yahwistic tone through its association with the Exodus (see Deut 16:1-6). In a similar fashion, the Israelite priesthood, sacrificial system, and even the Jerusalem temple derived from Canaanite patterns in use for a long time before Israel came into existence. But all this was lost in Israel's collective memory by the time Deuteronomy was written.

What the Deuteronomists have before their eyes is the temptation Israel faces: the desertion of Yahweh in favor of the gods of the conquered nations. To counteract this temptation, Deuteronomy recalls traditions associated with the settlement period (vv. 29-30) and reminds Israel of the disgusting nature of the religious rituals never adopted officially by Israel, such as child sacrifice (v. 31). The unremitting critique of non-Israelite religion is to overcome the impulse toward assimilation that threatens not only Israel's unique religious identity but also its very existence.

12:32–13:18 Internal threats. As severe as their critique of non-Israelite religions is, the Deuteronomists recognize that the most serious threats to the covenant come from within. The steps to be taken with regard to these threats show how seriously Deuteronomy takes the obligation of absolute loyalty to God.

Surprisingly enough, the first to come under scrutiny are the prophets (13:1-5). The enticement to apostasy can and has come from religious authorities such as the prophets. Deuteronomy betrays a real lack of confidence in those religious authorities by listing them as first among those who can lead Israel to compromise its allegiance to Yahweh. Of course, Deuteronomy presents itself as the authoritative word from God which, in effect, makes prophecy obsolete. The people can determine the divine will by consulting this written, authoritative document rather than by relying on human and fallible religious authorities who have the potential of leading them astray. Israel will never go astray by obeying the prescriptions found in Deuteronomy.

The loyalty Israel owes to God transcends every human bond, even that of the family (13:6-11). If a family member is an enticement to idolatry, Israelites loyal to God will not let familial love take precedence over the love they have for God. While this text makes use of legal language, its basic thrust is homiletical. It focuses on the value of allegiance to God rather than on the presentation of specific rules of conduct. It should be understood and interpreted as are similar passages in the New Testament, such as Matt 10:34-38 and its parallels.

A third internal threat can be an entire city that has gone over to the worship of other gods (13:12-18). From the perspective of the Exile, this is not simply a rhetorical exaggeration. The Assyrian and Babylonian conquests reduced Israel to a fraction of what it once was. All of Galilee and central Palestine was lost. From the perspectives of the Deuteronomists, those losses could be explained in only one way—Israel's disloyalty. If the remnant of Israel will not be engulfed by the nations, it will be because of a firm decision to foster absolute loyalty to the Lord.

According to Deuteronomy, Israel's continued existence is dependent upon maintaining its commitment to God. Any compromise is equivalent to communal suicide. The Deuteronomists make their point with shocking clarity and single-minded conviction. There is no room whatsoever for anyone within the community who fosters an attitude of apostasy. Israel's life and future hang in the balance. What choice does Israel have?

14:1-21 Holiness. At first glance the material of this chapter seems to have little to do with holiness. That is true if one defines holiness in terms of virtues to be acquired and vices to be avoided. From the Israelite perspective, holiness is a consequence of God's uniqueness. The God of Israel is not like the gods of the nation, and so those who serve this God cannot pattern their behavior according to the customs associated with the service of foreign gods. Israel is to be holy, that is, unique, as its God is holy.

Verses 1 and 2 prohibit the observance of mourning rites practiced in Canaanite religions. (Such rites apparently perdured throughout Israel's history, even into the exilic period—see Ezek 9:14-15.) Those mourning rituals are associated with the worship of the dying and rising god, reflecting the alternating agricultural cycles of infertility and fertility. For Israel, those cycles do not form an apt metaphor for Yahweh, whose rule over the cosmos is absolute. Israel is the Lord's own possession (v. 2). It is unthinkable, then, for the Lord's own people to observe foreign rituals.

The rest of this unit (vv. 3-21) deals with dietary laws. The origin of these observances is beyond recovery. Even the English translations of the names of some of the animals and birds listed here are no more than educated guesses. No matter what the origin of these laws may have been, their importance in the exilic and postexilic community cannot be overestimated.

Observance of these dietary laws helped early Judaism develop its identity. It effectively cut off socializing with non-Jews and thereby helped to fend off the impulse to assimilation. Gradually these dietary laws, as they were developed and enlarged in early Judaism, became so ingrained in the Jewish religious identity that the first Christians had a difficult time conceiving of the possibility of genuine religion without them (Acts 15:29; Col 2:21). The basic assumption behind these dietary laws is that the people of God cannot be like the people who worship foreign gods, and this distinction is to extend even to matters of diet.

Especially interesting is verse 21b, which prohibits the boiling of a kid in its mother's milk. (Later the rabbis extrapolated from this law the prohibition of eating dairy and meat products at the same meal.) This prohibition is unlike the others in this section, which deal with clean and unclean animals. There is some evidence that this law may be a conscious rejection of a particular Canaanite ritual, but the evidence is not sufficient to make a firm conclusion. In any case, all these laws remind Israel that its future depends on its willingness to keep away from anything that may be construed as compromising its commitment to God.

14:22–15:23 Israel's bounty. A basic Israelite belief was that though God gave the land to Israel, it really belonged to the Lord who gave it as a gift to Israel, in accordance with the promises made to Abraham, Isaac, and Jacob. An important consequence of this belief was a recognition of Israel's dependence upon God's bounty. The wealthy and the poor alike were to acknowledge God as the source of their sustenance. The legislation in this section describes some of the ways in which Israel chose to express this belief: the tithe, the year of release, the treatment of slaves, and the offering of firstlings.

Throughout this section Deuteronomy's particular regard for the poor is quite evident. In fact, Deut 15:4-5 claims that obedience could make poverty non-existent, but a more realistic assessment of Israel's potential for obedience recognizes the existence of poverty and the need for generosity on the part of the wealthy (15:11). This concern for the poor is one manifestation of a broader humanitarian bent within Deuteronomy. For example, Deut 14:22-27 implies that the purpose of tithing is to provide food especially for the poor. There is no mention of any sacral purpose for tithing, as an offering made for God's benefit. Even the use of the tithe as support for priests and Levites is ignored by Deuteronomy (compare Num 18:21-28). The Levites receive part of the tithe, not because of their priestly status, but because of their need as those without economic status (14:27, 29).

Finally, Deuteronomy makes practical accommodations in view of its expectation that there is to be only one sanctuary. Deut 14:25 speaks of turning the tithe into cash, which would obviate the necessity of transporting agricultural products over long distances to the central sanctuary. Similarly, while Exod 22:30 expects the sacrifice of the firstlings to take place eight days after birth, Deut 15:20 eliminates the necessity of frequent trips to the central sanctuary by stating that this sacrifice could take place anytime during the year.

The tithe (14:22-29) was an offering of a portion of agricultural produce originally intended for the support of sanctuaries and their personnel. It was a custom widely practiced in the ancient Near East. (Though the word "tithe" in Hebrew appears to be etymologically related to the word "ten," not all Hebrew philologists agree. They see "tithe" as related to the Ugaritic word for "libation, offering.") In the monarchic period, the king probably appropriated a portion of the tithe to support royal sanctuaries, such as the temple in Jerusalem. Deuteronomy ignores this use of the tithe. It simply provides the menu for a festal meal celebrated at the central sanctuary. Every three years the tithe is to be used locally for the welfare of the poor (14:28-29).

The law of release (15:1-11) reflects the Israelite practice of allowing the land to lie fallow at regular intervals (Exod 23:10-11). Obviously, the observance of such a practice would have been staggered throughout the land, but each time it was observed by an individual farmer, the fallow year made it difficult for those economically dependent upon agriculture. They would have found repaying their debts almost impossible. This law probably intended that debts not be called in during a farmer's fallow year, though later Jewish tradition required that the debt be forgiven rather than simply postponed. The "foreigner" spoken of in 15:3 is not the resident alien, who is somewhat integrated into the Israelite economic and agricultural system, but the traveling merchant or craftsman, who is not affected by the fallow year. The law makes it clear that no one is to take advantage of another's financial difficulties. The poor are to experience the generosity of their fellow Israelites (15:9-11).

One way to settle a debt is for debtors to work off their indebtedness. Verses 12-19 attempt to prevent abuses in this system. The service of the slave working off debts is to be limited. Male and female slaves have the same rights. When the service of slaves is completed, they are to be given financial support in order to ease their transition to freedom. To provide motivation for the observance of these humane regulations, Deuteronomy reminds its readers that they are descended from slaves. The Israelite who is working off a debt always remains an Israelite. The lender needs to remember the origin common to all (15:15).

The law regarding the offering of male firstlings (15:19-23) probably had its origin in rituals intended to ensure continued fertility by offering the firstlings to the gods. Deuteronomy upholds this practice adopted by Israel (see Exod 13:2), but once again the purpose of this action is not for the sake of supporting the sanctuary and its clergy; rather, it is to supply food for a festal meal.

Israel has experienced the wondrous power of the Lord to provide for all the people. Israel's response to this experience of God's abundance is to be a sharing through which both rich and poor can acknowledge their dependence upon God. Through their tithes the rich testify that God is the source of their abundance. By accepting the generosity of their fellow Israelites, the poor receive their support from God, who gives all Israel a share in the wealth of the land.

16:1-17 A calendar of feasts. This section deals with the pilgrimage feasts of Passover-Unleavened Bread, Weeks, and Booths. These feasts are known from other portions of the Pentateuch (Exod 23:14-17; 34:18-23; Lev 23; Num 28–29). Deuteronomy's particular stamp on the celebration of these festivals lies in transforming them into occasions of pilgrimage to the central sanctuary. For example, according to this text, the Passover meal must be eaten at the central sanctuary (vv. 5-6) rather than in the towns of the land, as was the previous custom (Lev 23:3).

The first feast, Passover-Unleavened Bread, is a combination of what were originally two separate observances. The Passover, marked by eating a lamb from the flock, probably originated among shepherds as they were changing pastures in the spring (Abib corresponds to March/April). The feast of Unleavened Bread probably originated among farmers as they renewed their supplies of leaven each year by first ridding themselves of the previous year's supply. These two feasts were joined already before the Deuteronomists began their work. Israelite tradition associated this feast with the Exodus from Egypt. Deuteronomy maintains this association but does not develop it in any significant way, except to insist upon its celebration at the central sanctuary.

The feast of Weeks derives its name from the way the time of its celebration is calculated. Since this feast is observed on the fiftieth day after Passover, the New Testament calls it Pentecost (Acts 2:1). It, too, originated as an agricultural festival, celebrating the grain harvest (see 15:9), which occurs in June. In rabbinic tradition this feast became associated with the giving of the law on Sinai, but no such association is made here. Verse 12 does remind the readers of Israel's slavery in Egypt in order to move them to obedience. Again, the principal concern of Deuteronomy is to encourage a pilgrimage to the central sanctuary for a festival of rejoicing for all to enjoy (v. 11).

The third feast is Booths, which is an autumnal agricultural feast celebrated at the conclusion of the harvest of dates, olives, grapes and other fruits. The name probably derives from the temporary dwellings that were erected in the orchards for the harvesters. Rabbinic tradition used this feast to commemorate Israel's time in the desert, when the people lived in temporary dwellings (tents). Again, this text makes no such allusion. The agricultural dimensions of this celebration are dominant here. In fact, there is no allusion at all to any element of the Exodus tradition. Deuteronomy simply describes the feast of Booths as the third pilgrimage feast to be celebrated at the central sanctuary.

The final two verses (15:16-17) summarize the obligation to make the three annual pilgrimages to the central sanctuary. Since these feasts celebrate the agricultural abundance of the land, it is appropriate that those making the pilgrimage come with offerings as a sign of thanksgiving for the bounty God has given them. This legislation as stated is quite impractical. It envisions the entire male population (at the very least) at the central sanctuary for each of these three festivals. The improbable scene becomes a bit more probable if this portion of Deuteronomic legislation is considered to have originated in the exilic or postexilic period, when Judah was reduced to Jerusalem and about twenty square miles surrounding it.

16:18–18:22 Israel's leaders. An important concern in Israel was the quality of its leadership. The Deuteronomists describe their expectations of those who are to hold specific offices: judge, king, priest, and prophet. What is most significant in Deuteronomy's presentation is the assumption that Israel's leaders, especially the king, are subject to the written, authoritative law found in the Book of Deuteronomy. The rule of the king is not absolute. All Israel's leaders are bound by the sacred traditions that find expression in Deuteronomy. This serves to limit the authority of the leadership class and makes it more responsible to the people as a whole. Deuteronomy clearly espouses belief in the value of limited government.

16:18–17:7 Judges and officers. Before the establishment of the monarchy, Israel's leaders were tribal elders for the most part. The elders were the leaders of important families and clans. They functioned in such a way as to prevent political power from being concentrated in the hands of a single person. With the rise of the monarchy, the influence of the elders waned, and their role in Israelite society was taken by officials appointed by the king. Verse 18 suggests official appointments made by some sort of centralized authority. It is difficult to be certain of all this because the Bible presents no theoretical account of Israel's social, political, and judicial institutions. In 2 Chr 19:5 there is mention of the judicial reforms of Jehoshaphat, who reigned in Judah during the ninth century B.C.E., so there is evidence for the appointment of judges by the central authority.

The role that the judges played in Israelite society was not confined to the judicial sphere. The judges were probably the equivalent of local governors responsible for the affairs of the district assigned to them. They exercised executive and legislative prerogatives as well as judicial ones. While the judges formulated policy, the officers were responsible for communicating and enforcing the decisions of the judges to whom they were responsible.

Deuteronomy is adamant about the integrity of the legal system, which was even more open to corruption in antiquity than is the case now. Judges supported themselves from their positions, and bribery was the easiest way to acquire a comfortable position. Verse 20 asserts that justice is the way to ensure prosperity for all. Harsh experience has taught Israel how destructive lapses in judicial authority can be.

At first glance the material in 16:18–17:7 seems to be intrusive in a context that deals with leadership. The concern of these verses is the purity of Israel's worship. What this section does, however, is to provide an example of how the judicial system operates (17:2-7) and samples of the matters that ought to concern the judiciary (16:21–7:1). Judges are to keep a keen eye on any attempts at introducing Canaanite religion practices into Yahwistic worship. Such attempts would be repulsive to God and destructive of Israelite society.

Second, the judges are to oversee sacrificial practices in order to ensure that Israel is taking this aspect of worship seriously. To offer inferior animals for sacrifice is nothing less than a mockery of the very purpose of such worship.

Finally, the judicial process demands integrity not only of those administering it but of all involved in it (17:6-7). No one can be convicted on the testimony of a lone witness. Witnesses have to be prepared to face the severest of penalties if their testimony proves false. All Israel is responsible for the integrity of the judicial system. The principal purpose of that system is to purge Israel of corrupting practices that threaten the very existence of the community.

17:8-13 The court at the central sanctuary. Deuteronomy makes provision for the handling of matters too involved for the local judiciary. The text does not make it clear who initiates the appeal, though Exod 18:13-23 suggests that appeals are made by local authorities. The central court is composed of priests and a judge. The inclusion of the former rests on the traditional expertise of priests in legal matters. The Deuteronomists probably introduce the judge as a way to break the exclusive control of the priests in such matters. The judgments of the central court are to resolve legal problems in a definitive way. Without such finality the judicial system would be too weak to be effective.

17:14-20 The king. The institution of the monarchy began as a response to the anarchy caused by the pressure brought to bear on the Israelite tribes by the Philistines (see 1 Sam 8–10). Because the beginnings of the monarchy were part of Israel's historical memory, this institution could not be mythologized, as it was in the other ancient Near Eastern cultures, as part of the divinely willed order of creation. Israel knew that the monarchy was established as a result of human initiative. This made Deuteronomy's approach to the monarchy possible.

Deuteronomy does not reject the monarchy as such. It is part of Israel's past and cannot be ignored; however, its role in Israel's future needs to be carefully understood. The king is not to imitate his counterparts in the ancient Near East by amassing a large standing army, by engaging in diplomacy through marriage, or by accumulating vast wealth. If Israel's God is unlike the gods of the nations, Israel's king has to be different as well.

For Deuteronomy, what makes Israel's monarchy unique is the subjection of the king to the law. Like every other Israelite, the king, too, is to order his life according to the Book of the Law. This is an important check on the monarchy's inherent tendency toward absolutism. Obedience to the law will lead to the maintenance of the king, while disobedience will surely lead to disaster. The king, like every other Israelite, is bound to the observance of the law. United in this observance, king and subjects are one people of God.

18:1-8 Priests and Levites. Priests and Levites as such are not discussed in Deuteronomy except when a layperson has some occasion to deal with them. The lone exception is this text. This is in marked contrast to the legislation of the Priestly writer. This passage tries to deal with the conflict over priestly rights—a conflict that raged between the priests of Jerusalem and the priests of the outlawed local shrines. The latter lost their source of income with the centralization of sacrificial worship mandated by Deuteronomy. The solution provided by verses 6-8 is completely impractical and was probably never put into practice (see 2 Kgs 23:8-9). Early in the postexilic era an accommodation was worked out by which the Levites became a type of second-rank clergy in the temple, while the priests of Jerusalem retained their exclusive position as those responsible for the conduct of the sacrificial cult (see Ezek 44:9-31). The end of the feud between these two groups, however, was not the achievement of Deuteronomic circles.

Some interpreters suggest that Deuteronomy was the product of Levitical circles. In light of this text, such an alternative seems unlikely, since the presumed authors of a book such as Deuteronomy would settle any disputes to which they were a party in their own favor. At the very least, they should have presented a more workable suggestion than is given here. In a few of the other times the Levites are mentioned in Deuteronomy, they are presented as objects of charity whose economic situation is so perilous that they need the help of their fellow Israelites (14:28-29; 16:11-14; 26:12). This is not a very flattering self-portrait by the supposed authors of Deuteronomy.

18:9-22 Prophets. Before the Deuteronomists discuss the role of the prophet, they deal with some of the mantic techniques that were obviously very popular in ancient Israel. According to the biblical tradition, there are three legitimate methods of divine-human communication: dreams (Gen 40); the Urim and Thummim (see the comment on 33:8-11 below); and prophecy.

The ancient Near East in general, and Mesopotamia in particular, was renowned for the variety of techniques developed to determine the divine will. Verses 10-11 mention a few of these. Deuteronomy rejects all of them as being incompatible with Yahwism. The chief objection to these techniques probably is not their use for determining God's will but rather their use in various rituals designed to manipulate the deity. Once the divine will has been determined, the ones making the inquiry would be given advice as to how they might change any decisions of the deity that might affect them adversely. The child sacrifice cited in verse 10 is likely one of the more gruesome rituals used with divination. From Deuteronomy's perspective, the God of Israel is above such gross manipulation. Use of divinatory techniques is the grounds justifying the Canaanites' expulsion from the land (v. 14). This ought to be warning enough for Israel.

Deuteronomy's treatment of the prophet does not lead to unqualified confidence in this form of leadership. Verses 15-19 apparently presume the continuance of the prophetic office, but who can claim to be another Moses (v. 15)? The text does not assume that there will be many prophets able to make this claim. Some interpreters suggest that this text testifies to the existence of a succession of prophets to an office of "the prophet." There is no direct evidence of such an office anywhere in the Bible. Its existence is unlikely.

Prophets are mentioned only twice in Deuteronomy—here and in 13:1-6. In both instances the prophets are presented as potential threats to the loyalty that Israel owes God.

Prophets are to be monitored very carefully, for they can lead, and presumably have led, Israel away from undivided service and obedience to the Lord (see Jer 28). The test for true prophecy given in verse 22 is quite impractical and of no use to anyone who has to make a decision regarding a specific case with any immediacy.

Deuteronomy can afford to be so negative about prophecy because it effectively eliminates its usefulness. If people want to know the divine will, all they need to do is study the Book of the Law, that is, Deuteronomy itself. The book's treatment of prophecy makes it highly unlikely that Deuteronomy arose amid prophetic circles, as some interpreters claim. At one time any text reflecting moral sensitivity was attributed to prophetic circles. Deuteronomy shares with prophecy a passionate concern for the ethical dimension of Israel's life with God, but it presents a singularly unflattering portrait of the prophet.

19:1-13 The cities of refuge. Though Deuteronomy itself does not use the term "cities of refuge," as does Num 35, both texts envision the same institution. Its origins are not easy to determine. Because the cities of refuge presuppose a transtribal identity, they must have been established some time in the latter part of the settlement period. On the other hand, the monarchy probably provided some sort of centralized authority to deal with the judicial determination of any killing as accidental or criminal. The cities of refuge, then, were an intertribal institution that attempted to restrain acts of revenge. Deuteronomy provides the theological support for this institution by asserting that it prevents the shedding of innocent blood and the consequent guilt, one effect of which would be the loss of the land (compare Gen 4:8-14).

In its presentation of the cities of refuge, Deuteronomy discusses both their use (vv. 4-10) and their abuse (vv. 11-13). As unfortunate as an accidental killing may be, its terrible effects will be multiplied if people rush to judgment and punish people responsible for accidental deaths as if they were murderers. Such a reaction would set off another act of "justice" and could thereby begin an unremitting cycle of killings. The cities of refuge provide the opportunity for a calm determination of guilt or innocence.

Unfortunately, the wrong people may take advantage of the sanctuary provided by these cities. The elders, who were the premonarchic dispensers of justice, must be vigilant to prevent a murderer from escaping justice. Those guilty of murder are themselves to be killed, because their shedding of innocent blood threatens the continued existence of Israel in the land. According to the religious perspectives of the Deuteronomists, the effects of a sin such as murder touch not only the one responsible for it but all those who seemingly acquiesce to it. By punishing the guilty individual, the community demonstrates its revulsion for the crime and thereby escapes any guilt and punishment flowing from it. While the cities of refuge help prevent the shedding of innocent blood, they must never become a way for the guilty to escape the consequences of their crimes.

19:14 The landmark. This is the Deuteronomic version of an ancient, pre-Israelite law found in other ancient Near Eastern law codes. Without the legal safeguards of deeds recorded and maintained by civil authorities, respecting landmarks is essential in avoiding disputes over territory. Deuteronomy adds its own typical flavor to this ancient law: the land was given by the Lord to its present owners. Attempts at expropriating it are nothing less than acts of rebellion against the Lord.

19:15-21 Witnesses. The integrity of the judicial system depends on the truthfulness of witnesses. What was decreed with regard to accusations of idolatry (17:6-7) is extended to all cases. When the veracity of witnesses is in doubt, appeal is to be made to the court at the central shrine (v. 17). The text does not describe the procedures used by the court to decide the issue of perjury. The focus here is on the punishment due to those guilty of lying in the course of judicial proceedings. The punishment for perjury corresponds to the punishment for the crime of which the false witnesses accused their fellow Israelites. In the end, evil will overtake those who plan evil for others. Verse 21 underscores this principle. Those who endanger the lives of the innocent by their perjury will find that their own lives are forfeit.

20:1-20 Rules for warfare. Deuteronomy has already dealt with the topic of war (see 7:1-26). This chapter provides additional legislation, which will be augmented by Deut

21:10-14; 23:9-14; 24:5; 25:17-19. All this attention to war may be offensive to modern sensibilities, but one cannot deny that ancient Israel acquired the land of Canaan, in part, through violent means. In fact, some interpreters believe that war was a cultic institution in the early years of Israel's history. The term "holy war" was coined to describe this institution. "Holy war" is a particularly infelicitous expression. It occurs nowhere in the Bible. It is doubtful that any manner of waging war was ever a fixed cultic pattern in Israel's history. The theology of divinely willed and directed wars was an ancient Near Eastern commonplace. What we read here and elsewhere in Deuteronomistic literature is an interpretation of Israel's battlefield experiences and memories. It hardly describes actual strategy and tactics.

A basic conviction of this ideology of warfare is that the outcome is determined in the heavens, where the gods of the warring nations fight one another for power and domination in the heavenly sphere. What happens on earthly battlefields merely reflects what has already happened in the heavenly realms. That is why the priest is the first to exhort those entering battle (vv. 2-4). That is why Israel's strength does not depend on numerical superiority or formidable weaponry. Deuteronomy reminds Israel that God fought against and defeated Egypt, a powerful empire, when Israel itself was powerless.

This chapter deals with three specific concerns regarding the conduct of war: exemption from military service (vv. 5-9); the treatment of enemy cities (vv. 10-18); and the protection of natural resources in time of war (vv. 19-20).

The laws specifying circumstances allowing for various exemptions from military service find many parallels in the laws of other ancient Near Eastern countries. Originally these exemptions recognized that people in "transition" were in a particularly vulnerable situation. The ancients spoke of that vulnerability in terms of subjection to demonic powers. There was no need to expose the entire army to these dangers, so those experiencing transitions in their lives were simply exempted from military service. Deuteronomy demythologizes those practices and allows for the same exemptions on purely humanitarian grounds. In addition, Deuteronomy exempts from battle all those whose faith is weak. In difficult circumstances their weakness could affect the whole army. It is better that they not be a part of the battle at all.

The treatment of enemy cities appears brutal, but what is described here (vv. 10-18) is not any more brutal than the practices of other nations in the ancient Near East. In interpreting these verses, it is important to remember that Deuteronomy is more ideological than realistic in its presentation of Israelite military policies. Israel is not in a position to conduct itself according to these prescriptions. Israel is more in danger of having its cities destroyed than its neighbors are.

No quarter is to be given to any Canaanite cities because of the dangers the Canaanites pose with regard to the absolute fidelity that Israel owes to God (vv. 16-18). That Israel's prophets consistently upbraided it for following the ways of the nations is proof enough that Israel did not engage in any full-scale extermination of the Canaanites. Though there were conflicts between the Israelites and the Canaanites, most of the latter gradually became assimilated among the Israelite population as Israel acquired hegemony over Canaan.

Finally, verses 19-20 indicate that Israel is not to implement a scorched-earth policy in its conflicts with other nations. Resources, especially those connected with food production, are to be preserved with care. Here Israel departs from the more common practice of the day, which witnessed the indiscriminate use of military destructiveness. Only that which threatens Israel's loyalty to God is to be treated without mercy; in other cases humanity and common sense ought to keep a rein on the destructive potential of war.

21:1–25:19 Miscellaneous laws. The next five chapters contain laws covering a wide variety of topics. They are not arranged in any particular order, but all serve to describe the pattern of Israel's life in the land. They all are supported by a single assumption: obedience to these laws will help Israel secure its future in the land.

21:1-9 The unsolved murder. This is another instance of Deuteronomy's adaptation of a practice that was probably pre-Israelite in origin. Ancient Near Eastern law codes held that the city nearest the site of an unsolved murder had to bear responsibility for the crime. The leaders of that community were required to perform a ritual that not only accepted responsibility for the crime but also deflected the guilt and punishment for the crime from the city. This practice reflects the strong ancient Near Eastern belief in group solidarity and the religious implications of a crime such as murder. Unless specific action was taken, the consequences of that crime had the potential of destroying innocent people.

The text describes a ritual that cannot be considered sacrificial, since Deuteronomy allows sacrifice only at the central shrine. The Levitical priests are simply mute witnesses rather than officiants. The ritual is conducted entirely by the elders of the city nearest the site of the unsolved murder. At the conclusion of the ritual, the elders pray that the guilt of the crime not be attached to their city nor to the nation as a whole. The words of this prayer transform the remnants of a magical rite into an act of obedience to the law and a petition for mercy. This Deuteronomic composition testifies to the belief that forgiveness is an act of God's grace, which cannot be manipulated by the performance of any ritual.

21:10-21 Family relationships. In the first two situations dealt with here (marriage with a female prisoner of war, vv. 10-14; and the inheritance rights of the first-born, vv. 15-17), the Deuteronomists assume the existence of polygamy. Though polygamy was practiced in ancient Israel, monogamy was far more common because of economic and social problems, such as those presented in this legislation. Later, for theological reasons, monogamy became the only form of marriage permitted in Judaism.

When an Israelite soldier wishes to marry a prisoner of war, he has to consider the woman's sensibilities and control his own impulses. First of all, the woman is to have time to deal with the shock of captivity, the separation from her family, and the integration into a new household. To allow for these transitions, the marriage is to be consummated only after one month. Once the former captive becomes the wife of an Israelite, she must be treated as his wife. In the case of divorce, she does not revert to her former status but is given the freedom due to any Israelite woman.

Laws of inheritance in the ancient world tended to favor the first-born. As a consequence, there developed the custom whereby a father selected his "first-born." This situation became especially complicated in a polygamous household. The Deuteronomists want to secure the rights of the actual first-born son, irrespective of the father's feelings toward him or his mother. No doubt conflicts like this one contributed to favoring the monogamous form of marriage.

Finally, the Deuteronomists deal with disputes that arise between parents and children (vv. 18-21). Because of the great respect due to the older generation in general, and parents in particular, rebellious young people put themselves into a precarious situation. The elders (v. 19) probably serve as mediators to calm the passions that might develop out of domestic squabbles. They prevent parents from becoming carried away by their anger with a recalcitrant son. The elders are permitted to let the full penalty of the law (v. 21) fall upon the "stubborn and rebellious" son only in cases where there are no other alternatives. The elders, then, serve as a societal safety-valve preventing family arguments from being blown all out of proportion.

21:22-23 Hanging. Hanging was not a form of capital punishment in ancient Israel. After some other form of execution, the criminal's body was put on public display as an object lesson to those who might threaten Israel's existence by their crimes. The Deuteronomists mercifully limit this gruesome spectacle by requiring burial on the same day as execution.

22:1-4 Respect for property. The principle behind this law is that a person's ownership of property does not cease when that property becomes lost. It is the duty of every Israelite to respect the property rights of all people. Another version of this law is found in Exod 23:4-5. Deuteronomy generalizes the beneficiary of the law from "your enemy" (Exod 23:4) to every Israelite, and the property concerned from livestock to every type of property. For Deuteronomy, these prescriptions do not arise from any abstract notion of property rights but from the conviction that Israel's future is dependent upon the ability of the people to remain united. Disputes over property can be nothing but divisive. Respect for others' property is one of the practical components of a genuinely effective communal spirit.

22:5 Transvestism. This law is more extensive than a simple prohibition of wearing the opposite sex's clothing. The Deuteronomists also have in mind ornaments, weapons, and other objects that pertain to one or the other sex. It is not possible to be certain whether this text forbids transvestism because of its association with homosexuality, which is proscribed by Lev 18:22, or because of possible links it may have with various Canaanite religious rituals. This prohibition also reflects a concern evident throughout the cultures of the ancient Near East to accept the distinctions that exist in nature. From the perspectives of antiquity, blurring these obvious distinctions is foolish, since they are present in nature for a good reason determined by the Creator.

22:6-7 Birds in the nest. Here the Deuteronomists show how ahead of the time they could be. This law, which is unique to Deuteronomy, accepts the possibility of raiding a bird's nest for food. While it allows the taking of eggs and the young, the text requires that the adult bird be freed. Such action precludes the possible extinction of a species in the quest for food. The adult bird is free to reproduce again, and thereby the survival of the species is ensured. Unrestricted hunting threatens the survival of the species.

22:8 The Deuteronomic building code. Roofs of homes in ancient Israel were part of the homes' living space. Roofs were used for entertaining, sleeping, and working. Here the Deuteronomists require the taking of simple safety precautions. Though the erecting of a parapet is an additional expense, it can prevent serious accidents and their consequences. In our culture these consequences would include lawsuits. In ancient Israel an accident resulting from negligence could set off a blood feud. Deuteronomy wants to prevent that.

22:9-11 Combinations. One of the recognized scholarly pursuits in the ancient world was the classification of natural phenomena. These verses probably reflect a concern to respect the differences in nature that these classification efforts brought to light. Elements that are separate in nature should not be combined by human efforts. Rabbinic Judaism took up and developed this Deuteronomic concern. An entire tractate of the Mishnah is devoted to the elaboration and application of the principle behind these verses.

22:12 Tassels. This is another bit of Deuteronomic legislation that became quite important in rabbinic Judaism. Matthew 23:5 testifies to the concern of Jesus' contemporaries over the observance of this law. It is still observed by modern orthodox Jews, who attach tassels to a special inner garment they wear. Again, the origin and purpose of this law are unknown. A similar law in Num 15:37-41 describes the tassels as reminders of the commandments that Israel is to obey. This is surely a later homiletic explanation of a custom whose original meaning was unknown even to the Priestly authors of Numbers.

22:13-29 Marriage and sexual relationships. The rest of this chapter is devoted to legislation regulating the expression of human sexuality. While the ancients were generally quite reticent about such matters, they did not regard human sexuality as an evil force that must be carefully controlled or suppressed. On the other hand, they were quite aware of how powerful a force human sexuality can be. What on the surface may be behavior between consenting adults can have important repercussions for the entire community. These matters must be handled prudently in order to maintain healthy relationships within the community.

The first case deals with the accusations against the virtue of a newly married woman by her disaffected husband (vv. 13-21). The case is spelled out in some detail, as compared with the others presented in this chapter. The values behind this law, as well as the law itself, do not immediately resonate with contemporary views regarding the role and status of women in society. In particular, the concern for the woman's virginity, without any concomitant concern for that of her husband, is inequitable. Second, the absence of any role for the woman in the forum where her future is being determined is unjust. This legislation underscores how different ancient Israelite society was from our own. While we may rightly reject some of the presuppositions behind this law, we ought to admire the concern it shows for the woman's rights in view of her husband's false accusations.

The cases envisioned by the rest of the chapter are not presented in as much detail as the previous case is. The value at stake in each of these cases is the prohibition of adultery (Deut 5:18). Because adultery involves a breach of the marriage relationship, the penalty is severe. (A betrothed woman is treated the same as a married woman, since both are committed to an exclusive relationship with a man.) The rape of a single woman (vv. 28-29) is treated differently because it does not involve the breach of any marriage relationship. This, of course, ignores the single woman's trauma resulting from a rape; it will not be any less severe than that of a married woman. The law does attempt to protect the raped woman's rights, but not in a way our culture finds acceptable.

The final law in this series (v. 30) forbids an incestuous relationship between a man and his father's wife. This law probably had in mind a man's stepmother, for it is doubtful that an explicit law would be needed to prohibit incest with one's natural mother.

23:1-9 Who is an Israelite? This legislation has a rather narrow view on full membership in the community of Israel. This attitude is understandable, given the situation in which Deuteronomy was written. It was a time when Israel's very existence was threatened by both internal and external forces. It is little wonder that the Deuteronomists were not in a very inclusivist mood as they dealt with the question of who should be admitted to full membership in the community.

While the Deuteronomists do not go so far as to withdraw the traditional protection accorded to the resident alien (see 1:16 and 10:18-19), still they draw the circle of full membership in the community very carefully—some might say too carefully. For example, the laws of verses 1-2 probably intend to bar people who are directly associated with the service of foreign deities. Verse 1 most likely envisions those who have had themselves castrated in order to participate in certain non-Yahwistic rituals. There also may be some cultic concerns behind the law of verse 2, which may refer to children conceived by a woman involved in Canaanite fertility rituals. Rabbinic tradition has understood this law as referring to children of incestuous relationships.

This interpretation may have been fostered by the permanent prohibition denying Moabites and Ammonites full membership in the Israelite community. Genesis preserves the tradition that both groups were offspring of the incestuous relationship between Lot and his two daughters (Gen 19:30-38). Deuteronomy, however, justifies its prohibition by adverting to traditions associated with Israel's entrance into Canaan (see Deut 2 and Num 22–24). The Deuteronomists show a bit more openness toward the Egyptians and the third Transjordanian nation, the Edomites. Individuals from both groups may be admitted to the Israelite community because the Edomites are kin through Jacob, and the Egyptians provided hospitality to Jacob and his family during a time of famine (Gen 25:24-26; 36:1).

At a later time, elements within early Judaism attempted to break the strictures of these laws. The Isaianic school especially is noted for its more universalist approach. In particular, Isaiah 56 should be pointed out as a later and more open approach toward some of the same groups mentioned here.

23:10-15 A sense of shame. Shame was a more powerful force among the ancient Israelites than it is among people of contemporary Western culture. These laws specify certain actions as expressions of that sense of shame. In a positive light, one can say that Deuteronomy here reflects ancient Israel's concern for dignity and hygiene. Deuteronomy wants to maintain these standards. Later the community at Qumran will be marked by a strong solicitude regarding these same issues. The practices of that community show a further specification of the general laws found here.

23:16-17 Escaped slaves. This law deals with slaves who have run away from foreign masters (no provision is made for slaves who have fled their Israelite masters). Escaped slaves who seek asylum in Israel are to be given protection. Usually international treaties provided extradition for runaway slaves. Deuteronomy does not envision the possibility of such agreements, because an international treaty is at least an implicit acknowledgment of foreign deities. While this law provides help for escaped slaves, its real intent is to preserve the sanctity of Israel's covenant relationship with Yahweh.

23:18-19 Cult prostitution. Sexual activity cannot be mythologized into a quasi-sacral rite that ensures divine favor, especially regarding fertility. That is what Canaanite rituals of fertility are all about. Sexual activity is human activity. Acting as if it were anything else implies a lack of faith in God, who is the one source of the land's fertility. Since cult prostitution is forbidden as evil, any monetary profit made from it is tainted and cannot be offered to the Lord.

23:20-21 Interest. The loans envisioned here have no resemblance to the loaning practices that are central to a modern capitalist economy. In the situation addressed by Deuteronomy, loans are used only as a means to escape economic disaster. To take advantage of partners in the covenantal community when they are in financial distress is incompatible with Deuteronomy's view of community. Loans made to those outside the community are another matter. God will give adequate provision to all Israel if the community is faithful to the law. There should be no need to supplement God's gracious bounty with interest earned on loans to brothers and sisters in financial need.

23:22-24 Vows. The making of vows out of religious devotion is not a required but a permitted form of piety. Once people commit themselves to some form of action by a vow, it is important that they fulfill the vow. Unfulfilled vows create an atmosphere in which it becomes acceptable to countenance failures in Israel's relationship with God. From Deuteronomy's perspective, such an attitude is disastrous.

23:25-26 Sharing God's bounty. Deuteronomy looks upon the fertility of the land as a gift given by God to all Israel. Individuals should be willing to share God's bounty with their fellow Israelites. The Deuteronomists are practical enough to recognize that such an attitude can be abused. The one who sowed the wheat and planted the vineyard is the one who should reap their harvest. Others may help themselves in time of need, but this right is limited by the property rights of those who own the field and vineyard.

24:1-4 Remarriage after divorce. This text does not legislate regarding divorce but simply accepts it as a matter of custom. Its concern is to forbid a man from remarrying his former wife if she has remarried and been divorced by another man. The reasons for this prohibition are not immediately clear, but perhaps the Deuteronomists are concerned that unrestricted divorces and remarriages serve to make divorce a legal form of adultery.

24:5 Another exemption for the military. This is an addition to the exemptions granted in 20:5-8. Similar exemptions are found among other ancient Near Eastern peoples. The transition from the single state to the married state was considered by the ancients as a time when a man is particularly vulnerable to attacks from evil powers. It would not make any sense to have such people in the army. Deuteronomy offers its own humane rationale for this exemption.

24:6 Collateral. If a lender requires a borrower to hand over collateral for a loan, it should not be a millstone, which is an essential piece of equipment in the home. Without it, grain cannot be ground to prepare bread, the staple in the ancient Israelite diet. Demanding such collateral would involve a genuine hardship for any family.

24:7 Kidnapping. The kidnapping described here does not involve holding someone for ransom but the sale of a person into slavery. It is treated as a capital crime because the victims of this crime are cut off from their communities, which are the source of their lives. The law protects the person who does not enjoy the safety afforded by family and wealth, since the victim of kidnapping would typically be a social outcast. No one, however, should be cut off from the covenantal community, no matter what his or her social or economic position may be.

24:8-9 Leprosy. This passage offers no guidance on how leprosy is to be treated. That is a matter for the priests. Deuteronomy's readers are advised to respect the expertise of the priests in this matter. The text probably presumes the existence of the Priestly legislation of Num 13–14 and specifically refers to the tradition about Miriam (Num 12:9-16). This is good evidence that the origins of Deuteronomy are to be found among the laity and that the Priestly source antedates Deuteronomy by a few years at the very least.

24:10-13 More on collateral. It is difficult enough to ask for a loan without having to deal with the hounding of creditors. The treatment of the borrower is to be marked by understanding, compassion, and charity. There is no excuse for adding to the burdens of the poor.

24:14-15 The wages of the poor. Deuteronomy is marked by a special concern for those whose economic status is marginal. Here the Deuteronomists require that the wages of the poor be paid each day, for the little they make is the only hedge their families have against hunger and want. Failure to pay the poor their wages will cause them to turn to the Lord for help. Since God hears the cry of the poor (Ps 69:34), the Lord's anger will be directed against Israel for its failure to consider the welfare of those in need.

24:16 Individual responsibility. This text seems to be opposed to that of Deut 5:9. Both texts contain important insights into the reality of crime and punishment. This text states unequivocally that each person is to be treated as an individual when it is a question of criminal responsibility. This means that the guilty individual must accept the criminal penalty for any breach of the law. The text of Deut 5:9 states that the nature of the criminal act is such that its effects cannot be confined to a single individual. For example, a parent's actions will inevitably affect the entire family. Punishment of a crime may be directed at individuals, but its repercussions will touch many more people.

24:17-22 Gleaning the harvest. Once again Deuteronomy's concern for the poor comes to the foreground. This legislation addresses the prosperous landowners and asks for some form of studied inefficiency in harvesting. That will allow the poor to survive without requiring them to accept obvious charity. They will have to work for their own support. The Deuteronomists remind the wealthy that all Israel would have the status of slaves were it not for God's mercy. One response expected from those who have benefited from God's goodness is compassion for those who do not have a full share in the community's wealth.

25:1-3 Corporal punishment. The Deuteronomists accept corporal punishment as one way to deal with the guilty. At the same time, they require specific safeguards to protect the ones undergoing punishment, because, despite their crimes, they are still Israelites. Punishment is to follow a legal trial. It is to be administered under the supervision of a competent authority and is to be limited to a specified number of lashes. Rabbinic tradition limited any whipping to thirty-nine lashes to avoid any possibility of breaking the requirement of verse 3 (see 2 Cor 11:24).

25:4 Concern for the ox. This is another law that is unique to Deuteronomy and shows to what extent this tradition went in its concern that all share in the land's God-given bounty. Even the oxen are not to be denied their fair share. The New Testament cites this passage as a justification for the practice whereby ministers of the gospel gained their support from their ministry (1 Cor 9:9; 1 Tim 5:18).

25:5-10 Levirate marriage. The custom described here (*levir* is Latin for "brother-in-law") was practiced in some form throughout the ancient Near East. The presumed origin of this custom lay in the desire of the patriarchal social system to keep the wealth (dowry) and fertility of the widow in the same patriarchal line. With the rise of urbanization and the devolution of the patriarchal extended family in ancient Israel, this issue became less important, though levirate marriage apparently persisted into the first century of the Common Era (see Matt 22:23-28; Luke 20:27-33). The elders can use their moral authority to encourage compliance with this ancient custom, but they cannot compel it (v. 8).

25:11-12 Mutilation as a penalty. Though mutilation was a common penalty in the ancient Near East, this is the only instance of such a penalty in the Bible apart from the *lex talionis* (Deut 19:21). In fact, some interpreters consider this an extension of the *lex talionis*, which, in this case, cannot be applied literally. While the wife's intention to save her husband from injury may be a good one, there are limits to the kind of action she can take on his behalf.

25:13-16 Trade laws. What kind of society could have any cohesion if every commercial transaction were suspect? Trust is a basic component of community life. Here the Deuteronomists require that those involved in trade adhere to honest business practices.

25:17-19 The Amalekites. By the time Deuteronomy was written, the Amalekites had already disappeared into the pages of history. The Deuteronomists imply that this was due to people who were obedient to the Lord's command. An additional implication is that Israel is to remember all that the nations did to it. That memory should help Israel avoid the disaster of assimilation, so that those nations will not achieve by Israel's cooperation what they cannot achieve by force of arms.

26:1-15 Two liturgies of remembrance. Ancient Israel's ritual was one vehicle for acknowledging its debt of gratitude to God who gave Israel a bounteous land. In paying that debt of gratitude, Israel also chose to remember a prior act of God on its behalf that was even more important than the gift of the land. That was the Exodus, which transformed Israel from a nation of slaves into a people set free. The two rites described here fuse both traditions of thanksgiving: gratitude for freedom and for the land.

Verses 1-11 deal with the annual tithe of agricultural products made by the grateful Israelite. The portrait the Deuteronomists paint here is that of a highly successful farmer who comes to the central sanctuary to present his tithe. His party includes not only his family but also the economically dependent Levites and resident aliens. The whole community benefits from the bounty God gives to Israel, and so all Israel is to be involved in the ritual of thanksgiving.

The heart of this passage is the confession that the Israelite makes as the offering is set before the Lord (vv. 5-10). The worshipers acknowledge their origins as a people without land or freedom. They can now present their tithes only because God took the side of their ancestors against the Egyptians and because God gave them a bountiful land as their new home.

Following the ritual, the whole group assembled by the wealthy farmer celebrated with a festal meal the bounty given by God. This is in accord with the typically Deuteronomic view of the elements of a sacrifice being used for a meal to be shared by the participants in the ritual.

Verses 12-15 deal with the triennial tithe, which is not brought to the central shrine but is to be used in each locality for the support of the poor. Instead of a profession of faith in God's gracious activity for Israel, the farmer offering the tithe makes prayerful assurances that he has been obedient to all stipulations regarding the offering of the tithe. The prayer ends with a petition for God's continued benevolence toward Israel, which is completely dependent upon God for its sustenance.

This passage marks Israel as distinct from its Canaanite neighbors, who see fertility as the outcome of skillful manipulation of divine powers. For Israel, fertility is a gift that can only be gratefully received. Israel's freedom, bounty, and future belong to God alone. Israel rejoices because of the gifts God has freely chosen to give it.

26:16-19 Recommitment. The Deuteronomic Code, which began with chapter 12, concludes with a mutual declaration of commitment made by both God and Israel. The people proclaim their allegiance to God, and through Moses God assures the people of the blessings that come to the obedient. The triple occurrence of "today" (vv. 16, 17 and 18) reflects a liturgical assembly at which Israel once again accepts the law as constitutive of its relationship with God. One effect of this relationship is Israel's great renown among the nations. A national life lived in accord with the divine law cannot help but reflect divine glory (v. 19). The substance of this ritual of recommitment or covenant renewal serves as the conclusion to the Deuteronomic Code as well as a transition to what follows: Moses' serious warning regarding the dire consequences that will come to a disobedient Israel.

27:1–28:69 Blessings and curses. Now the Deuteronomists turn to the future. For the law to have its beneficial effect, every generation will have to remember the law and its stipulations and be prepared to commit itself to that law. This address describes efforts to make certain that Israel will never forget that law but remain firmly committed to it.

27:1-8 The written law. These verses consider Deuteronomy as the written, authoritative law for Israel's life in the land. It is fitting, then, that copies of this law be left at significant sites connected with Israel's entrance into the land. A set of stones inscribed with the law are to be erected at the very spot where Israel crosses the Jordan. A second set of stones are to be left on Mount Ebal, where a great ceremony of covenant renewal is to take place.

This text indirectly preserves the memory of two Israelite shrines at which the entrance into the land was remembered in ritual. The first was at Gilgal, just west of the Jordan; the second was at Shechem, the town at the foot of Mount Ebal. The rituals at both these shrines celebrated not only Israel's entrance into Canaan but also the giving of the law, which became operative at the moment the people began to enter their new land.

27:9-10 Moses and the priests speak. These two verses are very significant from a theological perspective, for they assert that obedience to the commandments is to be Israel's response to its election. Obedience was not the reason why Israel became the elect people of God; Israel's election was an act of grace. Deuteronomic theology is usually caricatured as a theology of retribution that infuses a mentality of bargaining with God. Here it is quite clear that Deuteronomy holds that the basis of the divine-human relationship is an unmerited act of divine grace. It is because the Israelites have been chosen as the people of God that they are to obey the commandments.

27:11-26 A ritual on Mounts Gerizim and Ebal. Like the rest of this chapter, these verses reflect some sort of rite connected with the renewal of the covenant between God and Israel. Unfortunately, it is not possible to reconstruct the shape of that rite simply on the basis of what remains here. The image created by this text has the worshipers divided into two groups, each assembled on one of the two mountains that overlook Shechem. These two groups are to recite the blessings and curses associated with Israel's covenant with Yahweh. This ritual is probably meant to demonstrate Israel's free acceptance of the consequences flowing from the relationship established with God through the law.

The twelve curses in verses 14-26 provide a summary list of actions that are incompatible with Israel's status as the people of God. This list is certainly not exhaustive; it simply serves to remind the people that obedience to the law is to characterize the life of the nation. The people's response to each curse indicates their understanding and acceptance of the consequences that come to the disobedient.

There does not seem to be any unifying theme to the content of the curses, though some interpreters see the secrecy of the proscribed acts as a common element. If this is correct, the Deuteronomists are probably trying to avoid a type of legalism that identifies guilt with discovery. Here they may be saying that any action which disregards the law is an offense against God, whether that offense comes to the light of day or not.

The last curse is all-inclusive. It brings under God's curse the apathy and inactivity of those who know what the law requires but make no effort to obey. The term "this law" (v. 26) is another indication that this list of curses was composed at a time after Deuteronomy had been accepted as a written, authoritative document.

28:1-69 Blessings and curses. Many interpreters believe that the Deuteronomists consciously used covenant (international treaty) as a metaphor in presenting the relationship between God and Israel. While all the elements of the typical covenant form are not found in Deuteronomy, the three most important are. Chapters 5–11 are equivalent to the prologue of the covenant, which is an exhortation to fidelity based on what God has done for Israel. The stipulations of chapters 12–26 make up the core of the covenant, in which Israel's obligations to God are spelled out clearly. Finally, this chapter represents one of the concluding elements of the covenant, the blessings and curses. Here the consequences of fidelity and infidelity are stated with unmistakable clarity. As is the case with ancient Near Eastern treaties, the curses far outnumber the blessings. The covenant metaphor explains the relationship between God and Israel in a manner readily understandable to the ancient Israelites. In addition, it underscores the Deuteronomic presentation of the law as a loving response of Israel to the God who saved it from Egyptian slavery.

The sheer number of curses (vv. 15-68) as compared with the blessings (vv. 1-14) appears to belie the assertion that, for the Deuteronomists, obedience is a response of love. While some of these curses may have been introduced into this list after the Exile (for example, verses 36-68), the number of curses may simply be a rhetorical device to encourage Israel to obedience. For the Deuteronomists, many of these curses have already become a reality. They are trying to recommit the people to obedience, for their future depends upon faithful obedience.

In terms of form, verses 1-46 and 58-68 contain conditional blessings and curses. If Israel is obedient, it may expect God's favor; if Israel is disobedient, it may expect God's judgment. The election of Israel, though it was a matter of divine grace, does not exempt Israel from bearing the consequences of infidelity. Israel's relationship with God is dependent upon fidelity to the divine will as expressed in the law.

Verses 47-57 promise God's curses on a

disobedient Israel. There seems to be no question of "if Israel is disobedient." These verses presuppose the people's infidelity: "Since you would not serve the Lord, your God . . ." (v. 47a). This text apparently reflects the tragedy that befell Israel during the siege of Jerusalem and the other cities of Judah (597–587 B.C.E.). Verses 53-57 are particularly gruesome in their description of the horrors that accompany a lengthy siege. The consequences of disobedience are terrifying indeed.

One common thread running throughout the blessings and the curses is how these are related to the land. First and foremost, blessing means fertility of both the people and their land. The curses bring sickness, death, drought, disease, poor harvests, and a horrifying siege, followed by exile from the land and reenslavement in a foreign land. The land is God's great gift to a liberated Israel. Disobedience brings the reversal of all God's beneficent acts (vv. 60-68). As great as God's deeds for Israel were, they could be undone by an ungrateful people. This is the curse for disobedience, which is simply specified in verses 15-68.

Moses' second speech closes with a powerful call for Israel's fidelity. The intensity of language displayed in these curses shows how seriously Israel is to take its relationship with God. It is indeed a matter of life and death.

MOSES' THIRD ADDRESS

Deut 29:1–32:52

The major concern of this address is Israel's immediate future. Moses makes provisions for Joshua to assume the leadership of the tribes after his death. Equally important are the provisions made for storing the book of the law and for its periodic reading. The law is to be the guide in Israel's future existence in the land. Individual human leaders come and go, but the law endures as the most effective way to safeguard Israel's commitment to the Lord.

29:2-8 A call for fidelity. Moses' third address begins in a fashion that should be quite familiar by now—the recital of God's saving acts on Israel's behalf, from the defeat of Pharaoh (v. 2) to the defeat of Sihon and Og (v. 8). It continues in typical style with a plea for obedience, followed by a promise of prosperity in the new land (v. 9).

What makes this passage unique is the comment in verse 4 which asserts that Israel has not always been able to recognize God's presence in the events we consider "miraculous." This should be a reminder that God's saving deeds are not so unequivocal that they do not require faith on the part of those who experience them. If Israel is to recognize God's presence in its life, it will be because God supplies the kind of understanding and insight which can discern that presence.

29:9-14 Parties to the covenant. Here the Deuteronomists wish to include every generation of Israelites as partners in the covenant made with God. The obligation to fidelity falls not just on the people who experienced the Exodus and the guidance in the wilderness but on every generation. The covenant that Moses concludes between God and Israel involves not just those present at Horeb and Moab but those who are yet to be born and will likewise experience the benefits of God's goodness toward Israel.

29:15-20 A warning against false worship. The great commandment of the law is Israel's obligation to serve God alone. Moses repeats this central command here. Usually when Moses mentions Egypt, it is to remind Israel of its wondrous deliverance from slavery; here, however, Egypt serves as a model of the kind of false worship Israel is to avoid. The people will be tempted to abandon the service of God for that of foreign deities. If any of the people succumb to such a temptation, they may expect the severest of penalties. There can be no compromise whatever regarding the exclusive commitment God requires of Israel.

29:21-27 Consequences of disobedience. When people see the terrible effects of Israel's infidelity, they will have to be told the truth. Their first impulse may be to credit the gods of the nations who defeated Israel. They may conclude that a small nation such as Israel could not possibly withstand the onslaughts of powerful world empires. The real truth is that Israel's downfall was caused by its own failures to observe the stipulations of the Lord's covenant (v. 25). The consequences of these failures were defeat and exile. This constant emphasis on God's response to Israel's behavior emphasizes the personal nature of Israel's God. This was already revealed in the many acts of love that God has done for Israel's sake; it can also be revealed through the acts of judgment upon an unfaithful Israel.

29:28 A disclaimer. This verse is probably a gloss introduced into the text by a late editor. This, of course, does not affect its theological value in any way. Though there is no consensus on the meaning of the text, it may serve to acknowledge that Israel's God cannot be measured by the theological perspectives of the Deuteronomists, no matter how respected their views may be. What we have is a partial insight into the workings of the divine. While this insight is given for our sake, it should not serve to limit the prerogatives of God. This is as close as Deuteronomy gets to an acceptance of the relativity of human insight. The mystery of the divine always eludes our grasp.

30:1-14 Repentance. Human beings are not only limited in their ability to grasp fully the mystery of the divine, but the human will cannot make the kind of commitment that eliminates the possibility of unfaithfulness. This passage calls for Israel to return to the Lord after lapses. Repentance will bring restoration to the land from which Israel has been exiled (v. 4). Restoration will mean the complete reversal of the effects of infidelity. Not only will Israel be restored to its land, but it will enjoy a renewed prosperity. The only requirement is obedience—obedience that is the offshoot of Israel's love for God.

To prevent Israel from becoming discouraged by its failures, God will provide an inner source of commitment that was previously unavailable. Israel will no longer have to rely on its own strength but will receive a heart circumcised by God and fit for a renewed commitment (v. 6). Moses goes on to assure the people that obedience is not an impossible task. Israel's past performance may give rise to the view that the commandments are impossible to fulfill, but this text (vv. 11-14) presents obedience as a genuine possibility.

The law is designed as a guide to human life. It is not part of an inaccessible divine mystery (v. 12). To believe otherwise is nothing less than an attempt to evade responsibility. Second, the law is a practical guide to daily living. It is not some obtuse, rationalist system that is beyond most people (v. 13). The law is the way of life open to all.

30:15-20 The choice. The whole of Deuteronomy has been leading up to this dramatic choice that Moses sets before the people. These verses contain all the elements found in the rest of the book: commandments, blessing and curse, the appeal for obedience. After all has been said, the entire thrust of the book comes down to a choice that people need to make. Israel's future is dependent upon that choice. God's graciousness is not at issue. It is the response of Israel that causes its future to hang in the balance. Moses is not a neutral observer in the process; he is passionately concerned for Israel's future. That is why he virtually commands Israel to choose life (v. 19).

The life-and-death alternatives are broader than may be apparent to the contemporary reader. "Life" refers to that sphere of human activity under the protection of the divine; "death" refers to that sphere of human activity which is devoid of the divine presence. Death, then, is more than the cessation of physical life; it is existence outside the land, existence in the nether world of exile. Death is life without God. Life is *the* blessing, death *the* curse.

Good and evil here do not necessarily refer to moral choices. Good refers to the consequences of life with God: fertility, prosperity, and happiness. Evil refers to the consequences of life apart from God: exile, disease, and death. It is up to Israel to make one of two choices: (1) life with God, which brings blessing and good; or (2) life apart from God, which is nothing less than the curse of death. There are no other alternatives.

Moses calls upon the heavens and the earth to witness Israel's choice (v. 17). In ancient Near Eastern treaties, personified forces of nature were witnesses to the conclusion of a treaty, and it was presumed that they would deal with any partner to the treaty who proved unfaithful to its provisions. Israel, of course, demythologizes this aspect of covenant form, but it retains the idea of witnesses to the covenant by referring to the heavens and earth here.

Israel will find its true self by making a decision for life. The nation's very purpose is to love the Lord (v. 20). Every generation of Israel is to put itself in the place of those who were personally addressed by Moses, because all Israel needs to remember is that it has only two choices and that in making the right choice Israel will find "a long life" (v. 20).

31:1-8 Joshua, the successor of Moses. The Deuteronomists have already prepared their readers for the death of Moses and its significance for Israel's future (1:37-38 and 3:23-29). Though Moses was more than a heroic figure in the epic story of Israel's deliverance from Egypt and its guidance into the Promised Land, God, after all, was the actual liberator of and warrior for Israel (v. 3a). Moses is to die, but his death will not deprive Israel of the leadership it needs to settle the new land. Moses' role in Israel's life will be taken by Joshua. He is the one to lead Israel as it faces the crucial period of the settlement in Canaan.

31:9-13 Reading the law. While Moses' responsibility of providing leadership for the people is to be taken up by Joshua, there is to be a different arrangement regarding Moses' function as the people's teacher of the law. Moses has written the law and now gives it to the Levitical priests who carry the ark, which is the depository for the written document.

The written law is also given to the elders. The priests are given custody of the document, but the elders actually take up Moses' task of teaching the law. The elders were traditionally responsible for preserving the common life of the community through guiding its life and settling disputes in terms of traditional practices and values. The elders were the guardians of traditional legal lore not only in Israel but throughout the premonarchic societies of the ancient Near East. Here the elders are told to have the law read to the people periodically so that "they may hear it and learn it, and so fear the Lord . . ." (vv. 12, 13). This custom of public reading was the vehicle of covenant renewal.

There is no record of this command being fulfilled as prescribed here, though there was undoubtedly some ritual of recommitment. More important than the ritual itself is the expression of Deuteronomy's view that the Mosaic office is carried on in part by the elders, who handed down and administered the observance of ancient Israel's legal traditions.

31:14-32 Introduction to the Song of Moses. God's instructions to Moses concerning the song he is to compose and teach Israel (vv. 16-21) are framed by God's commissioning of Joshua. Again, provisions are being taken in view of Moses' imminent death (vv. 14, 16). Joshua is to provide Israel with the leadership it needs as it begins the settlement of Canaan. The song is to be a moral force touching Israel's conscience in the midst of the material blessing that the new land is to bring.

The determinism that marks verses 16-21 indicates their late introduction into this context. Israel's infidelity is not a possibility—it is inevitable. God's abandonment of the people in view of their infidelity is just as inevitable. These verses date from the Exile, when the full effects of Israel's rebellion and God's absence were being experienced by Israel. It is in the midst of this experience that the song will serve to remind Israel that what has happened to it is nothing but the curse that falls on the disobedient.

31:24-29 The book of the law. This is another attempt to deal with the loss of Moses. The law that he promulgated is to be preserved for future generations. Moses has written an account of the covenant that he has mediated between God and Israel. This written document, under the protection of the Levites, will be a perpetual reminder of the covenant. Moses calls the elders of the people and advises them of his own lack of faith in Israel's willingness to remain committed to God. Bitter experiences have shown the level of the nation's commitment. Again Moses calls upon the heavens and the earth to witness his final charge to Israel (v. 28). Moses' call for these witnesses is the link connecting this passage to the song that follows. The song begins with a similar invocation (32:1).

31:30–32:47 The Song of Moses. The Song of Moses is, in part, an indictment of Israel's infidelity to the covenant. It resembles the legal procedures used by an offended party in covenant to receive satisfaction from the offending party. The song begins with the summoning of witnesses (vv. 1-3). In this case it is the heavens and the earth that can testify that a covenant existed between God and Israel (see 30:19; 31:28). Next follows a statement of Israel's lack of commitment to the covenantal relationship (vv. 4-6). The prosecution begins with evidence of God's goodness toward Israel (vv. 7-14) and concludes with the evidence of Israel's apostasy (vv. 15-18). Finally, the people's guilt is declared and sentence is passed (vv. 19-25). Israel can expect total destruction in view of its total apostasy.

Following the trial, the song takes an abrupt turn in verses 26-27. God's enemies will misunderstand Israel's defeat. Those nations that cannot discern God's power at work in Israel's defeat will find themselves facing their own doom. The song encapsulates Israel's tragic history while affirming that the nation's defeat is not God's last word to Israel.

The song is a subtle corrective of a mechanistic application of Deuteronomic theology. From the perspective of the Exile, it is clear enough that Israel chose death rather than life. Here Deuteronomy makes a significant advance when it envisions blessing beyond the curse and proclaims a new life for Israel in spite of its infidelity. What begins with a sentence of death ends with a promise of new life.

32:48-52 The imminent death of Moses. These verses are an elaboration of Num 27:12-14, which come from the Priestly history of Israel. This is evident from the explanation that verse 51 offers for Moses' death outside the Promised Land. In Deut 1:32 Moses' fate is blamed on the people's sin and not on any personal failing of his own.

MOSES' FOURTH ADDRESS

Deut 33:1–34:12

The final component of Deuteronomy includes Moses' final testament to the tribes (ch. 33) and the account of his death (ch. 34). Moses' last words take the form of a blessing in which he foresees the fate of individual tribes (compare Gen 27 and 49). The final chapter does not come from the Deuteronomists, who wished to emphasize the continuity between the Mosaic era and every subsequent period in Israel's history. The thrust of the final chapter emphasizes a radical change that takes place with the death of Moses.

33:1-29 The blessing of Moses. The core of this text is the blessings Moses speaks upon individual tribes. These blessings are framed by a song of praise celebrating God's kingship and victories on Israel's behalf, as well as the gift of the land's prosperity (vv. 2-5, 26-29). It is through the conquest that Yahweh becomes the king of the Israelite tribes (v. 5). At this point the blessings begin.

The blessings name twelve tribes, though Simeon is missing (compare Gen 49 and Num 1:5-15). The number twelve is retained because the tribe of Joseph is divided into Ephraim and Manasseh. Apparently each tribal blessing existed independently, as evidenced by the diversity of their form and content. These independent sayings are brought together as a fitting climax to Deuteronomy. The last word spoken to the tribes is a word of blessing.

Of the particular blessings that call for specific comment, the blessing of Levi (vv. 8-11) stands out. The Thummim and Urim (v. 8) are lot oracles by means of which answers to yes-or-no questions can be ascertained. How these objects looked or how they were manipulated cannot be determined with certainty (see 1 Sam 14:18-19, 41-42; 23:9-12). Verse 10 shows that priests are more than cultic functionaries; they are also responsible for teaching traditional Israelite moral values.

34:1-8 The death of Moses. These final verses are an elaboration of what the Deuteronomists have written above in 3:27. The statement that Moses was buried "in the ravine opposite Beth-peor" might give the impression that a well-known grave site is indicated; however, the remark in verse 6b states that the exact spot of Moses' burial is unknown. Apparently by the time these words were written, the grave of Moses was no longer visited or even known, though the writers were aware of a tradition about the general area associated with Moses' death.

34:9-12 The conclusion. Here Moses is a unique, irreplaceable leader (compare Deut 18:18). In fact, verse 12 describes Moses in language usually reserved for God alone. Such a portrait could become oppressive. Though Moses is remembered as a great leader, others will have to take his place if Israel is to remain loyal to the covenant. Certainly the Deuteronomists consider themselves as continuing the role of Moses for their generation. Later, even Jesus will recognize the Pharisees' claim to the Mosaic office (see Matt 23:2). Jesus, too, believed that his mission was to fulfill "the law and the prophets" (Matt 5:17-18) and thereby bring Moses' task to completion. Thus, later generations that recognized Moses' special role in Israel's life also recognized that what Moses did for the first generation of Israelites, others must do for succeeding ones.

JOSHUA

John A. Grindel, C.M.

INTRODUCTION

The Book of Joshua is named after its chief actor, Joshua, the son of Nun. Joshua had been Moses' aide and succeeded him as the leader of the people. In Hebrew the name Joshua means "Yahweh saves" or "May Yahweh save."

The theme of the book is the occupation of the land west of the Jordan River. The book falls into three distinct sections: the conquest of Canaan (chs. 1–12); the division of the land (chs. 13–21); the return of the Transjordan tribes and the farewell of Joshua (chs. 22–24).

The Deuteronomistic History

In the Hebrew Bible the Book of Joshua is the first of what are termed the "former prophets," so called because of the importance of the prophetic word in the books. Today the book is usually seen as the first volume in what is known as the Deuteronomistic History. The Deuteronomistic History includes the Books of Joshua, Judges, Samuel, and Kings, and spans the period from the conquest of Canaan in the twelfth century B.C.E. down to the time of the Exile in the sixth century B.C.E. The Book of Deuteronomy is often considered the introduction to these books.

Our modern understanding of the larger Deuteronomistic History owes much to the work of a German scholar, Martin Noth. He was able to show that someone who shared the theological perspective, as well as literary style found in the Book of Deuteronomy, formed a continuous historical work by pulling together into a coherent whole many different units of material which were originally independent and came from various periods of Israel's history. The author drew from numerous written and oral sources, such as annals, kings' lists, and stories of different kinds. Some of the units were of substantial size, such as Josh 2–11. The author's own additions established an interpretative framework that linked the disparate material together and provided judgments on the events in the story. The editor's additions are especially found in punctuating comments—sermons and speeches put into the mouths of important characters at periods of significant transition in the story (e.g., Josh 1 and 24; 1 Sam 12; 1 Kgs 8), bridge passages, and summaries. Scholars debate whether one person produced this work or a school of writers. Most presume that the present edition was composed soon after the last event reported in it, namely, the release of the last Judean king, Jehoiachin, from a Babylonian prison in 561 B.C.E. Though most believe the work to have been composed in Palestine, others think that it was written in Babylonia.

While Martin Noth thought that there was only one edition of the work, written around 550 B.C.E., it is more common today to speak of two editions. The earlier first edition was probably written during the reign of King Josiah (620–609 B.C.E.). The later second edition, which was quite thorough, would have been compiled during the Exile in the sixth century. This commentary will explain the book from the perspective of the second edition, that of the exilic editor.

The Deuteronomistic History was not written just to preserve a memory of the past;

rather, its purpose was to give a theological explanation of the loss of the two kingdoms of Israel and Judah, and to provide a theological basis for a hope in the future. To understand the work it is necessary to see it against the background of the times in which it was written.

In 721 B.C.E. the Assyrians destroyed the northern kingdom of Israel; and in 587 B.C.E., the Babylonians destroyed the southern kingdom of Judah. When Jerusalem fell in 587 B.C.E., the city, with its magnificent temple and palace, was leveled, and the leaders of the people were led off into exile in Babylonia.

The period of the Exile was a time of despair and deep questioning on the part of the people. Yahweh had promised to watch over the people, and to protect and guide them; but now all had been lost. Why had the Lord allowed this destruction and the loss of everything? The people especially wondered if they were still the people of God, and if there were any basis for a hope in the future. Would God remain true to the promises made in the past despite all that had happened since? It was in this context that the Deuteronomistic History was written.

The author's purpose is to explain that Israel had lost all because of her sinfulness. The Lord had called the people to fidelity to the covenant, and had warned them of the consequences of infidelity, but the people had sinned. Hence, in exile they were experiencing the divine judgment. Israel had not been faithful to Yahweh, and her long history of sin justified the punishment she was enduring.

The work is also an exhortation to the people to repent and turn back to the Lord and to trust that God will keep the ancient promises. The people are to believe that as God responded positively to repentant people in the past, so will God now hear their cries and forgive them once again. All the ancient promises are still in force, though temporarily suspended because of the sinfulness of the people. At the same time these promises can serve as a basis for the future if the people will only repent.

The purpose of the Book of Joshua

In the context of the Deuteronomistic History the specific purpose of the Book of Joshua, with its emphasis on the conquest and division of the land, is to show the fidelity of God to the promises made in the past to the patriarchs and Moses—particularly the promise of the land. One of the chief themes found in the Pentateuch is the promise of the land. That promise is fulfilled in the Book of Joshua so as to engender in the people a trust in God's promises. Now Israel, in the midst of the Exile, can trust in God's continuing care and presence, and trust especially that the promise of the land remains in force. At the same time, obedience to the Law is important lest, having been forgiven and brought back to the land, Israel again bring down upon her head such destruction as she is now experiencing.

Historical accuracy

A question that is often raised regarding the Book of Joshua is just how accurate is it from a historical perspective, especially in terms of its reporting on the conquest of the land in the twelfth century B.C.E. This is not an easy question to answer. There are inconsistencies and contradictions in the book itself (compare 4:3 and 4:9; 8:3 and 8:12). What are we to think of the conflicting reports of the conquest of the land found in Josh 1–12 and Judg 1:1–2:5? While the picture presented in Joshua is that of a violent and complete conquest of the land by a united Israel, the picture painted in Judges is that of individual tribes or clans slowly taking their own land and settling down next to the Canaanites in the country. This latter picture is probably closer to the reality.

The author uses different kinds of material in the book, ranging from factual documents to legends. It is also clear that the author, writing over five hundred years after the events being presented, has chosen material so that it would stress a theological viewpoint. In addition, the author has interspersed speeches created out of this theological perspective throughout the work.

Archaeological evidence also raises questions concerning the historical reliability of some of the material in the book, especially the traditions about the cities of Jericho and Ai. While the Book of Joshua gives extensive reports about the conquest of these two cities, archaeological evidence shows that they were not occupied after the fourteenth century B.C.E., and that Ai had been destroyed about a thousand years before the Israelites entered the land.

In conclusion, then, it is clear that the story, as we have it in the Book of Joshua, is simplified, schematic, incomplete, influenced by the theological views of the author, and the result of compiling very diverse material. We will make some judgments about the historical accuracy of the individual stories as we continue this commentary.

It is interesting to note that most of the material in chapters 1–12 dealing with the conquest of the land seems to be associated with the territory of Benjamin (see ch. 18:11-28) and the sanctuary of Gilgal. It would appear that the traditions in the first part of the book were gathered together and handed on at the sanctuary of Gilgal. The tribal lists in chapters 13–21, on the other hand, all date from the period of the monarchy. While some of the lists incorporated here may go back to the time of David and Solomon in the tenth century, others, such as those in chapters 20 and 21, come from the period of Josiah in the seventh century. One must be careful in accepting too quickly the biblical story of the conquest and the division of the land at face value. The reality was much more complex. We must keep in mind that the author was more interested in bringing out the meaning and significance of the events reported than in reporting exactly what happened. For it is in the meaning of events that one learns of God, oneself, and what God demands of us.

The person and work of Joshua

Against the above background on the historical reliability of the material in the Book of Joshua the person and work of Joshua also becomes a problem. If one accepts the view presented in the Deuteronomistic History that the conquest was the result of a united military action, then Joshua, as the supreme commander of the Israelite forces, plays an important role. But when we know the conquest to have been a century-long process of internal revolution, slow infiltration, and occupation by individual groups, then the figure of Joshua is difficult to explain. What adds to the problem is that while the traditions of the conquest preserved in the Book of Joshua are from the tribe of Benjamin, Joshua was from the tribe of Ephraim.

What all of this shows is that the very complicated history of the conquest has been reduced in the Book of Joshua to a small group of typical stories which are now attributed to all Israel, but which originally came primarily from the traditions of the tribe of Benjamin. These exploits have now been attributed to Joshua, a well-known person who had been active either militarily or in resolving conflicts in the central hill country of Palestine.

COMMENTARY

PART I: THE CONQUEST OF CANAAN

Josh 1:1–12:24

1:1–2:24 Preparations. The book begins with a report on the preparations for entrance into the land of Canaan. First, there is the Lord's commissioning of Joshua (1:1-9), which is followed by Joshua's orders to the people (1:10-18) and the sending of spies across the river to reconnoiter the land, especially Jericho (2:1-24).

1:1-9 The commissioning of Joshua. This passage, like all of chapter 1, comes from the hand of the Deuteronomistic Historian (henceforth D) and forms the transition from the death of Moses (see Deut 34) to the conquest of the land. The passage picks up on and develops the original commissioning of Joshua in Deut 31. In sermon style the passage follows the formula for the divine installation of a person into public office: a description of the task to be performed, an expression of encouragement, and an assurance of divine assistance. Joshua is presented as the successor to Moses with the command to complete his work.

The task that is given to Joshua is to lead the people into the land that the Lord will give to the Israelites. From the beginning (v. 2) it is made clear that the land is a gift of the Lord to the people; it is not something that they have earned. The granting of this gift is the fulfillment of the promise to Moses (v. 3). The description of the boundaries of the land in verse 4 is the most comprehensive description of the land found anywhere in the Bible. There are three fixed points in this description: the "desert," which refers to the Negeb in the south and the area east of the Jordan River; the "Euphrates," which describes the northeastern boundary; and the "Great Sea," which describes the Mediterranean on the west. As defined here the land included the area of Lebanon to the northwest and almost the whole of present-day and ancient Syria. However, these boundaries were never a reality. The only time Israel even began to have such extensive boundaries was in the time of David and Solomon in the tenth century. Joshua will be able to fulfill the promise because of the Lord's presence with him (v. 5).

Though the land is a gift of the Lord, verses 6-9 insist upon the necessity of Israel being "firm and steadfast," i.e., observing all that is written in the law in order to attain possession of the land. In other words, Israel's disobedience can frustrate the divine promises. All of this is an important message for the exiles, who can hear in this passage both the reason for the loss of the land (their disobedience) and the conditions for regaining the land (obedience to the law, trust in the Lord, and the Lord's promises of presence).

1:10-18 Joshua's orders to the people. Having received the Lord's instructions, Joshua now gives orders that the people are to be instructed to prepare provisions, because in three days they are to march in and take possession of the land that the Lord is giving them (vv. 10-11). Notice how the conquest is described as something peaceful, almost like a cultic procession. It is as if the Lord has already decreed that Israel will possess the land and now the people need only to carry it out.

In verses 12-15 Joshua reminds the tribes who have already settled in the area east of the Jordan River of the command of Moses (see Deut 3:12-20) that all the warriors from these tribes must help their kinspeople to settle in the land across the Jordan before they can return to their own land. The conquest must be seen as a unified undertaking by Israel.

Verses 16-18 present the response of the Transjordanian tribes. They will do all that Joshua commands as long as they are assured of the presence of the Lord with him (vv. 16-17). The main purpose of these verses is to show the acceptance of the transfer of leadership from Moses to Joshua.

2:1-24 Reconnaissance of Jericho. The attentive reader will notice immediately the tension between this chapter and the material in chapters 1 and 3. First of all, the location of the Israelite camp is now said to be at Shittim, which is probably the Abel-shittim mentioned in Num 33:49.

Secondly, the chronology of this chapter is incompatible with that of chapters 1 and 3. Chapter 1 speaks of three days as the interval between Joshua's orders to the people and the actual entrance into the land (see v. 11). However, the present story says that the spies spent three days in the hills before returning to the Israelite camp (2:22), not to mention the time spent going to Jericho and returning. Also, verses 1 and 2 of chapter 3 seem to flow directly after 1:18.

Finally, one encounters a different style in the present story from the style of the material in chapters 1 and 3. All of this means that this present story undoubtedly was a later insertion into the narrative. In fact there are indications that the story of Rahab is quite old and possibly goes back to the time before David. It appears that D has used the story as it was found, with the possible exception of Rahab's profession of faith in verses 9-11. This profession of faith reflects Deuteronomic themes (compare to Deut 26:5b-9 and Josh 24:2b-13).

In its original form the story of Rahab and the spies was probably an etiological tale, i.e., a narrative that explained something by giving the story of its origins. What the story explained was the survival of the Canaanite family of Rahab in the midst of the Israelites after the conquest. In its present context, however, the interest of the author is in Rahab's profession of faith. Through Rahab's profession D is emphasizing that it is the Lord who is responsible for all that is about to take place. The one who is God in heaven above and on earth below has given the land to Israel and with power will now lead them into the land. D is attempting to instill hope in the exiles by reminding them of who their God is. If the Lord could act like this in the past, then that same Lord can act with power on their behalf now.

3:1–5:12 The crossing of the Jordan. Having dealt with the preparations for entering the land, the author narrates the crossing of the Jordan. What is found in this section is a series of events that lack internal unity but are held together by their concern with the crossing and with the ark of the covenant. This is the only place where the ark is mentioned in the conquest narrative. The crossing falls into five scenes: preparations (3:1-13); the crossing (3:14-17); the setting up of memorial stones (4:1-9); the completion of the crossing (4:10-18); and the cultic encampment at Gilgal (4:19–5:12).

3:1-13 Preparations. This narrative, along with the narrative of the crossing, presents the event as a solemn liturgical procession. More than likely the story developed as a cultic reenactment and memorial of the crossing of the Jordan. The author has taken this ancient liturgy and used it as an outline for the story, mainly to show that it was the living God, the Lord of the whole earth, who was responsible for bringing Israel into the land (vv. 10-11). Once again an important message is here for the Israelites, namely, that the Lord is powerful and can bring the exiles back to the land as the Lord once before had brought the people into the land.

The text in verses 1 and 2 follows more from 1:18 than from chapter 2. Verses 2-6 point out that it is Yahweh who leads the people. The ark is a sign of the Lord's presence. The distance that people are to keep from the ark emphasizes the respect that one must show the Lord. The call to holiness in verse 5 flows from the idea that the people are about to experience wonders performed by the Lord, i.e., extraordinary actions. Such a divine intervention requires adequate human preparation. Involved in this sanctification is a series of purification rites and abstinence from all sexual activity and certain foods (see Exod 19:10-15; Num 11:18; Josh 7:13).

Verse 7 presents the purpose of the action to follow: it is to exalt Joshua in the sight of all Israel and to confirm his role as the successor of Moses. What will happen will show the presence of the Lord with Joshua. Joshua's sermon in verses 10-13 states who is responsible for what is about to happen—the living God who is the Lord of the whole earth. It is this Lord who will bring the waters to a halt so that the people can cross over. Verse 10 lists the indigenous population of the land in standard form: the Canaanites are found in the coastal cities; the Hittites in small colonies here and there; the Hivites around Shechem and Gibeon; the Amorites inhabited the hill country; and the Jebusites lived in Jerusalem. It is not clear who the Perizzites and Girgashites were.

3:14-17 The crossing. Everything happens now as foretold. In solemn procession the people follow the priests carrying the ark of the covenant and, when the waters halt, the people cross. The crossing is consciously presented as a parallel to the crossing of the Red Sea, because the entrance into the Promised Land is, in a sense, the conclusion of the Lord's great act of deliverance that began with the Exodus. One sees here how the

Exodus becomes the prism through which all of God's great acts of deliverance are seen. The return from the Exile will also be seen as a new Exodus. To heighten the sense of the miraculous and the greatness of God's activity, it is made clear that it is late winter or early spring, when the Jordan overflows its banks because of melting snow from the mountains to the north. The river halts at "Adam," a city at the junction of the Jabbok and the Jordan Rivers, several miles north of Jericho. The Salt Sea refers to the Dead Sea, and the Arabah is the desert south of the Dead Sea. The people cross over opposite Jericho. There are several known times when the Jordan has been dammed up for a period of hours because its banks collapsed and formed a natural dam. Perhaps such an event stands behind this story.

4:1-9 The memorial stones. The present episode is a secondary insertion into the text. This is clear from the summary statement in 4:10, which refers back to the crossing in 3:14-17, and from the special interest in the twelve stones at Gilgal. Though the actual location of Gilgal is unknown, it is somewhere in the area of Jericho. From a very early period it was an Israelite national shrine. More than likely it was the natural presence of a group of stones at this sanctuary, later linked to the crossing of the Jordan, that gave rise to this episode. The stones were understood to be a physical reminder, a perpetual memorial (v. 7), of how "the waters of the Jordan ceased to flow before the ark of the covenant of the Lord when it crossed the Jordan." The episode, then, originated as an etiological tale, like the story of Rahab in chapter 2. In these verses two traditions are combined: one that explains the presence of the stones at Gilgal (vv. 1-8) and one that explains the presence of stones in the middle of the Jordan River (v. 9). It is unclear where the latter tradition came from and why it is included in verse 9.

In the present context these verses are meant to emphasize that it was the Lord who brought the Israelites across the Jordan. For the exiles this is a message of hope: this same Lord can bring the exiles back into the land. The explanation of the twelve stones in verse 17 is the midpoint of the whole block of material in 3:1–5:12. The inclusion of this episode may also be an attempt at a further assimilation of the crossing of the Jordan to the tradition of the Exodus-Sinai event (compare with the twelve stones for the twelve tribes of Israel commemorating the covenant at Sinai in Exod 24:4).

4:10-18 Completion of the crossing. Though these verses seem jumbled, there is a certain logic to them. The condition of the text here is the result of several editors dealing with various concerns. After the insertion of 4:1-9, verse 10 returns the reader to the main narrative by summarizing 3:14-17. Verse 11 is a summary in advance of the exit of the ark from the river. In this liturgical procession the people, having safely crossed the river, now line up to witness the ark being brought out of the river.

Verses 12-13 are an addition by D, who wishes to emphasize here, as in 1:12ff., that all the tribes of Israel were involved—even those that had been granted land east of the Jordan. The number forty thousand is certainly an exaggeration. Perhaps the solution is that the word that can be translated as "thousand" can also be used as a technical term to indicate a military unit of considerable size.

Verse 14 returns to 3:7 and stresses the major purpose of this miraculous crossing, namely, to exalt Joshua before all Israel. This purpose was accomplished by the great miracle; henceforth, the people respected Joshua as they had Moses. With all the goals of the miracle accomplished, the priests now come up from the river and, as soon as they hit dry ground, the Jordan resumes its course and once again overflows its banks.

4:19–5:12 Cultic encampment at Gilgal. With the crossing of the Jordan, one period in the life of Israel is about to end and another to begin. This section, with its emphasis on various cultic rites at Gilgal, forms the transition from the period of deliverance to the occupation of the land. The section is framed by two cultic events that explicitly refer back to the deliverance from Egypt: the actual setting up of the stones at Gilgal (4:20-24), and the celebration of the Passover (5:10-12). The narrative in 5:1 shows the impact of Israel's entrance into the land on the inhabitants of the area. The circumcision of all males, reported in 5:2-9, is to prepare for the celebration of the Passover.

The scene is set in 4:19. The date is the

tenth day of the first month, known as Nisan. This is the time of the harvest in March–April. The date is important in view of the celebration of the Passover, which is soon to follow. The place where the people camp after crossing the Jordan is explicitly identified for the first time; it is at Gilgal, here located on the eastern limits of Jericho.

In the story of the memorial stones (4:20-24), it is the explanation of the stones that is important. Notice the explicit comparison of the drying up of the waters of the Jordan to the drying up of the Red Sea (see Exod 14:21). The two events provide the beginning and ending points of the period of deliverance. With the entrance into the land, Israel has achieved the goal for which she was delivered from Egypt (see Exod 3:8). The purpose of the Lord's actions is explicit: that all the people of the earth might learn of the might of God, and that the Israelites might fear the Lord. This is an important message for the exiles: in the midst of their pain they must put hope in the power of their God, and give their full allegiance to the Lord who can deliver.

The point of 5:1 is to show that the Lord's purpose has been achieved among the kings in the land of Canaan. They have recognized the might of the Lord in the events of the crossing and have become "disheartened"; literally, "their hearts melted." See the same term used by Rahab (2:10-11) and in Exod 15:13-17, which narrates the results of the Exodus. Once again the author parallels the crossing of the Jordan and the crossing of the Red Sea.

The story of the circumcision in 5:2-9 is placed here more for theological reasons than for historical ones. Exod 12:48 explains that only the circumcised can take part in the celebration of the Passover. For whatever reason (the text gives none), however, the children who were born in the desert during the forty years of wandering since leaving Egypt had not been circumcised. Hence, for a proper celebration of the Passover, circumcision is now necessary. The reference to circumcision taking place for a "second time" (v. 2) intends to show the circumcision and celebration of the Passover at Gilgal as a repetition of the rites surrounding the Exodus (see Exod 12). The site of the ritual is called Gibeath-haaraloth, which means "Hill of the Foreskins," referring to a place near Gilgal where the rite of circumcision was practiced. Notice D's need to explain the reason for the death of all the warriors who had come out of Egypt (see Num 14), probably to explain to the exiles why they had lost their land, namely, because of their disobedience. In verse 9 an attempt is made to explain the name Gilgal. The place is so named because here the Lord "removed," literally, "rolled away" the reproach of Israel. One of the meanings that the root of the word "gilgal" can have is "to roll away." It is not clear what is meant by the "reproach of Egypt."

The section concludes with the celebration of the Passover (vv. 10-12), the festival celebrating the Exodus. The fourteenth day of the first month was the proper date for this celebration (see Exod 12:1-6). As the Exodus began with the celebration of the Passover, so the entrance into the land, which brings this period of deliverance to an end, concludes with the same celebration. The next day the people eat of the produce of the land, and with this event the manna (see Exod 16 and Deut 8:3) ceases, since there is no longer a need for it. It is truly the end of an era.

5:13–12:24 The conquest. These chapters contain the narrative of the conquest: the conquest of the central part of the land (5:13–9:27); the conquest of the southern part (10:1-43); and the conquest of the northern part (11:1-15). The concluding verses (11:16–12:24) present a summary.

5:13–9:27 The conquest of the center of the land. These chapters narrate the capture of Jericho (5:13–6:27), the defeat and victory at Ai (7:1–8:29), the altar on Mount Ebal (8:30-35), and the Gibeonite alliance (9:1-27).

5:13–6:27 The capture of Jericho. The story begins with the apparition of a divine being that recalls Exod 3, the call of Moses. Joshua is to be understood as the new Moses. Though the material in 5:13-15 probably belonged originally to an independent epic, it now forms a unit with 6:1-5, which tells of the Lord's pronouncement of the fall of Jericho and instructions on how the city is to be taken. The presence of the captain of the host of the Lord shows the presence of the Lord in the conquest, right from the beginning. As 6:2 brings out, it is the Lord who is responsible for the fall of Jericho. The trumpets made of rams' horns (6:4) were commonly used in warfare and liturgies.

Archaeological evidence shows that Jericho was already in ruins when the Israelites entered into Canaan. Any habitation of the site of Tell es-Sultan, the site identified as Jericho, was sparse at the time of the conquest. What gave rise to the belief that it had been destroyed in the conquest was the fact that the site had lain in ruins in the period of the Judges and on into the period of the monarchy. Being close to the national sanctuary of Gilgal, the presupposition arose of its destruction under Joshua. Historically, it is not possible to say what lies behind the present narrative.

The narrative in chapter 6 is quite complicated and seems to have gone through various editions. In its final form the story has the characteristics of a religious ritual, a liturgy. D wants to stress to the exiles that it was Yahweh who was responsible for the conquest of the land and that same Yahweh can once again lead them to victory. This first success in Canaan takes on a symbolic value of the power of the Lord. The multiple use of the number seven, a sacred number in Israel, plays up the presence of the Lord in this narrative.

Having received instructions from the Lord on how to go about the conquest of Jericho, Joshua passes them on to the priests and people. These orders are executed and the city falls before the Israelites (6:12-21). The point of the "ban" in verses 17ff. is that since the Lord is the warrior and the victor, the enemy and booty belong to the Lord. Hence, they are sacred and taboo. To approach too close is to approach too close to God. To destroy such is an act of devotion to the Lord.

Verses 22-25, along with the reference to Rahab in verse 17, are probably an addition to help tie the story of the fall of Jericho to the story of Rahab in chapter 2. These verses conclude the etiology begun in chapter 2 that explains the presence of Rahab and her family in the midst of Israel. The mention of the treasury of the house of the Lord in verse 24 is often understood to refer to the temple of Jerusalem, which had not yet been built! More likely, it refers to the sanctuary at Gilgal.

The narrative of the fall of Jericho seems to recall memories of a military conquest on the basis of a ruse (6:1, 20, 21, 25). These may well be ancient memories of the original fall of the city. The curse, which is reported in 6:26, explains why the city was not rebuilt, and finds its fulfillment in 1 Kgs 16:34. (One of these texts depends upon the other, but it is not clear which way the dependency goes.)

7:1–8:29 Defeat and victory at Ai. The material in chapters 7 and 8 is composed of at least two narratives that were combined, probably before the time of D. The main story told of an original defeat of Israel at Ai. To this has been combined an ancient story of the crime and punishment of Achan in order to give an explanation of the defeat. The only difficulty with the combined narrative is that at the time of the Israelite conquest, Ai (today identified as et-Tell) was uninhabited. Archaeological evidence shows that the city was last inhabited at the end of the third millennium and not settled again until the eleventh century. Several theories have been advanced to explain the present narrative. One prominent theory says that the story originally described the fall of Bethel, which is only a couple of miles away, and was later connected with the ruins at et-Tell. The basis for this theory is the archaeological evidence, which shows that Bethel was destroyed toward the end of the thirteenth century. However, it is not clear that this destruction was due to the Israelites. Though the real source of the story is unknown, it is evident that both narratives are quite old. As we shall see, the major thrust of the combined narratives is to show to the exiles that a violation of the covenant leads to defeat and destruction, while faith and obedience lead to victory.

The author begins (v. 1) by explaining that the Lord was angry with Israel because Achan had violated the ban (see 6:18); hence, there should be no surprise at the defeat that is about to take place. Here is introduced the idea of corporate guilt, i.e., how the whole people could suffer because of the sin of one person.

Notice that nothing is said in verses 2-3 of the Lord's involvement. All is being done at the initiative of Israel. Hence, when Israel attacks she is defeated and the confidence of the people melts away (vv. 4-5). The word used here for "thousands" probably refers to a military contingent of some size.

Joshua with the elders now consults the Lord (vv. 6-9). Joshua's real concern is expressed in verse 9, namely, that when the other inhabitants of the land hear of the defeat, they will turn on Israel. The rites described in these verses pertain to the ritual of mourning (see Deut 9:26; Exod 32:11; 2 Sam 12:15-17). The passage recalls Israel's complaints against Moses and the Lord when they were in the desert (see Exod 16:2-8).

In the Lord's response (vv. 10-15) Joshua learns of the reason for the defeat, namely, that Israel has taken goods subject to the ban and so has violated the covenant. Israel is now under the ban and the Lord cannot and will not remain with Israel unless she removes from her midst the one who has incurred the ban. The legal procedure described (v. 14) is that of a trial by sacred lot, though we are given no details of the procedure. The verses express clearly the idea that the whole community can suffer for the sins of one.

Once Achan is identified as the culprit, he and all of his possessions are taken to the valley of Achor and stoned, and the Lord's anger toward Israel relents (vv. 16-26). The final verses present two etiologies as an explanation of the story of Achan. One of them explains a pile of stones in the valley of Achor (v. 26); the other, the name of the valley of Achor (vv. 24 and 26). This latter etiology is developed through a play on the words "Achor" and "Achan" and by the fact that the Hebrew root for "misery" and "afflicted" (see v. 25) is similar in sound to "Achor." More importantly, however, the purpose of the story is to explain to the exiles that the violation of the covenant leads to defeat.

Now that the Lord's anger against Israel has relented, the Lord tells Joshua to prepare to attack Ai. Notice that in contrast to chapter 7 victory is assured (8:1) because it is the Lord who leads Israel into battle. Hence, Israel is not to be afraid; she is only to be obedient and destroy Ai as she destroyed Jericho (v. 2). However, the Israelites are now allowed to take booty, and the Lord sets out the general lines of the conquest—it is to be through an ambush.

Joshua then gives instructions to the warriors who are to carry out the ambush (vv. 3-8), and they leave to take up their positions (v. 9). Notice again the emphasis that the Israelites will be able to take the city because the Lord has delivered it into their power (see 8:1).

Verses 10-23 describe the battle. As the main body of Israelites fled once again in seeming defeat before the king of Ai, all of the soldiers in Ai came out after the Israelites, leaving the city open and unprotected. When Joshua, at the Lord's command, stretches out his javelin towards Ai, the soldiers in ambush rise up and take the city, setting it on fire. By the time the soldiers of Ai realize what is happening, it is too late. They find themselves caught between the two parts of the Israelite army and are cut down to the last person. Only the king of Ai is spared, and he is taken alive and brought to Joshua. Joshua's stretching out of the javelin (v. 18 and v. 26) recalls the action of Moses during the war with Amalek (see Exod 17:8-13). This appears to be another incident in which the life of Joshua is paralleled to the life of Moses.

The story concludes (vv. 24-29) with the report of the slaying of all of the inhabitants of Ai (see Deut 20:16-18), the taking of booty, and the destruction of the city. These final verses contain another double etiology that explains how all was reduced to a mound of ruins, "as it remains today" (an explanation of the name of the city, "the ruin"), and how the pile of stones at the entrance of the city gate came into being—they were used to cover the body of the slain king of Ai.

In contrast to chapter 7, chapter 8 shows how Israel, when she fights under the leadership of the Lord and does the Lord's will, can be victorious. The message for the exiles is clear: while sin leads to disaster, obedience leads to victory.

8:30-35 The altar on Mount Ebal. These verses are an editorial addition, since they interrupt the flow of the story in 8:29 and 9:1. The verses report the fulfillment of the commands of Moses (see Deut 27:1-8, 11-13 and Deut 11:29) concerning what is to happen once the people have entered the land. Notice the often repeated reference to Moses in these verses. We shall see later that these verses are closely related to the material in chapter 24.

Mounts Ebal and Gerizim face one another across a deep ravine in north central Israel, about 20 miles north of Ai. Between them is the city of Shechem, an ancient cultic site. These two mountains flanked the important east-west pass through the central hill country of Israel.

9:1-27 The Gibeonite alliance. The two narratives in verses 1-2 and 3-27 show the possible responses of a people threatened with total destruction: to form a common alliance against the threat, or to enter into an alliance with the threatening party.

The reference (v. 1) to the mountain region, the foothills, and the coast of the Great Sea identifies the three regions (from east to west) of the land of Palestine.

The narrative about the Gibeonites in verses 3-27 reflects a complex literary history. Aside from D's later additions in verses 9-10, 24-25 and 27b, the figure of Joshua appears to have been a secondary insertion into the text, and verses 16-27 appear to be a secondary addition to the original story (one can jump from 9:15 to 10:1 without any sense of a gap). It is also not clear whether one city or four cities (see v. 17) entered into the alliance with Israel; nor is it always clear who was acting for Israel—the "men of Israel" or Joshua.

Like the story of Rahab (see ch. 2) this story is an etiology that has been preserved to explain the presence of the Gibeonites in the midst of Israel, despite the prohibitions of Deut 20:10-18, and their role as slaves (hewers of wood and drawers of water) at an Israelite sanctuary. The story also explains how Israel came into control of the central hill country and serves as background for chapter 10. For the exiles in the sixth century, the purpose of the story would have been to call them to faith in the power and promises of Yahweh (see vv. 9-10 and 24-25). There is little question about the historicity of an alliance between Israel and the Gibeonites (see 2 Sam 21:1-9).

The first part of the narrative (vv. 3-15) reports the deception of the Gibeonites and the conclusion of the alliance. Gibeon is identified with modern el-Jib, a site in the central hill country about seven miles northwest of Jerusalem and situated along an important east-west road from Jericho to the coastal plain. Seemingly, Gibeon belonged to a small four-village alliance (see v. 17). Whatever settlement existed at el-Jib in the time of Joshua, archaeological evidence shows that it was not a large settlement, although it later became an important city.

The Gibeonites come to Israel at Gilgal (v. 6), to which Israel has returned after the covenant ceremony reported in the preceding chapter. Israel's hesitancy regarding the proposed alliance (v. 7) flows from Deut 7:2 and 20:10-18. The alliance would have included peace between the two parties, as well as mutual defense (see 10:1-15). The reason given for seeking this alliance is the fame of the Lord, the God of Israel, and all that this God had done for Israel in Egypt and against Kings Sihon and Og (see Num 21:21-35). Israel, without seeking the advice of the Lord, agrees to the alliance and the parties partake of a covenant meal to seal it (vv. 14-15).

The second part of the narrative (vv. 16-27) reports the discovery of the ruse and Israel's response. The oath was so important that even the discovery of the trickery was not sufficient reason to release Israel from her obligations. However, the Gibeonites must be punished, so it is recommended that they be made "hewers of wood and drawers of water" (vv. 16-21), an expression referring to an inferior form of membership in the community (see Deut 29:10). Joshua confronts the Gibeonites and tells them that they are to carry out their tasks for "the house of my God" (v. 23). It is not clear if the reference here is to Gibeon or Gilgal. In their response (vv. 24-25) the Gibeonites seem to reflect a knowledge of Deut 20:10-18.

10:1-43 The conquest of the south. In a series of related incidents Joshua takes control of the southern part of Israel. The occasion for this conquest is the attack on Gibeon by the five kings from the south.

10:1-27 The Gibeon campaign. When Adonizedek, the king of Jerusalem, hears of how Joshua has dealt with Ai and Jericho and their kings, and that Gibeon has made a covenant with Israel, he becomes frightened and sends for four other kings from the neighborhood to help him attack Gibeon (vv. 1-4). The fear springs from the strength of Gibeon and because Gibeon has gone over to Israel, thus giving Israel an important bridgehead in the central hill country. Thus, the five kings put Gibeon under siege, as a way of stopping Israel's advance into the hill country, and as a punishment. The Gibeon in chapter 10, "large enough for a royal city" (v. 2), contrasts with the Gibeon in chapter 9, so weak that it sought an alliance with Israel. The picture presented in chapter 10 is also at odds with archaeological evidence. When the Gibeonites appeal to their protector, Joshua, he responds immediately and, after an all-night march, takes the five kings by surprise and inflicts a great slaughter on them (vv. 5-10). The march would have covered about eighteen miles along mountainous roads. Note that Joshua is victorious because the Lord has delivered the five kings into his power (v. 8). The hailstones mentioned in verse 11 were, no doubt, the result of an unusually severe midsummer storm that wreaked as much havoc as the army of Israel. Beth-horon was the name of an important pass that was a major point of entry from the west into the hill country.

Verses 12-14 should not be taken too literally. The compiler certainly understood them to be the description of a miraculous prolonging of the day so that Joshua would have enough sunlight to finish off the enemy. However, we should view these verses as a poetic description emphasizing that Yahweh fought for Israel and was responsible for the victory. Much of this story is reported in Judg 1:4-20, where three of the cities listed here are said to have been captured by the tribe of Judah.

Verses 16-27 describe the death of the five kings who had initiated the attack on Gibeon. Makkedah was west of Jerusalem. When the kings are discovered, Joshua does not want to waste time with them. He tells his men, after making sure that the kings cannot escape, to pursue the fleeing soldiers, and to kill them before they escape into their fortified cities (vv. 16-19). The later humiliation of the kings (v. 24) was meant to build up the confidence of Israel and to emphasize the power of the Lord in her midst. The story ends on an etiological note that explains the existence of a pile of stones at the mouth of a cave in Makkedah (v. 27). The point of the story, then, is to build up the confidence of the exiles in the power of their God to overcome their enemies (see vv. 8-14 and 25).

10:28-43 The conquest of the south concluded. Having defeated the coalition of five kings, Joshua follows up this victory with raids against six cities to the west and southwest of Jerusalem (vv. 28-39). The descriptions of these raids follow a definite pattern that reports how the city was captured and its inhabitants put to the sword with no survivors. In this way Joshua fulfilled the doom on each city according to the will of the Lord (Deut 20:10-18). Israel was successful because the Lord had delivered the cities into her power.

It is not possible to harmonize fully the description of the coalition in verses 1-5 with the account of the campaign against the south depicted in these verses. While there is some overlapping of cities, verses 28-39 seem to reflect a tradition different from the one in verses 1-5. What seems to lie behind these verses is a presupposition that Israel's enemies always followed the same route when advancing against Jerusalem at different points in history. It was the route of Sennacherib in 701 B.C.E. (see 2 Kgs 18:13) and of Nebuchadnezzar in 587 B.C.E. (see Jer 34:7) when they advanced on Jerusalem.

The concluding verses (40-43) summarize this part of the conquest. The author's purpose is to show that Israel had conquered all of the territory south of Gibeon under Joshua's leadership. The description is highly exaggerated, the author using the summary to emphasize how Joshua had followed the Lord's commands and had been successful because the Lord fought for Israel. Again, the message for the exiles is clear: they are to be obedient and trust in the power of the Lord.

11:1-15 The conquest of the north. The chapter begins abruptly with no clear connection to the preceding material except that the king of Hazor "learned of this." Originally, this material was probably an independent tradition that is now presented as the northern counterpart to the conquest of the south reported in chapter 10. This tradition may have belonged to one or more northern tribes and was later extended to all Israel. So too, the figure of Joshua has probably been introduced into the story secondarily. However, the tradition seems to rest upon a historical foundation. Notice that this chapter follows the same outline as chapter 10: one king forms a coalition to defeat the Israelites, but Joshua defeats the coalition through a surprise move, and attacks the cities involved.

The narrative begins with Jabin, the king of Hazor, calling together a coalition of northern kings. Notice how the description begins with specific details and then becomes more and more vague. All of the members of the coalition, with their troops, horses, and chariots, now gather together at the waters of Merom, a few miles southwest of Hazor, to launch an attack against Israel (vv. 1-5). The topography of these chapters covers the general area of Galilee, an area that was later assigned to the tribe of Naphtali. Archaeological excavations show that Hazor, located about eight miles north of the Sea of Galilee, was a very impressive city in the thirteenth century B.C.E. and could well have fit the descriptions of it in these verses. Excavations also show that it was destroyed in the mid-thirteenth century, which would coincide with the time of Joshua. The other three cities named here are located south of Hazor. The Arabah is the great rift that contains the Sea of Galilee (here called "Chinnereth"), the Jordan River, and the Dead Sea. The size of the opposing army is no doubt exaggerated here to magnify the victory.

Israel was successful against the coalition because the Lord had delivered the Canaanites into her power and because Joshua had obeyed the Lord by following the tactics laid out for him (vv. 6-9). Notice that nothing is said about where Joshua received the word of the Lord. From the context it would seem that he was still at Gilgal. The crippling of the horses prevented the Canaanites from using their chariots, which were subsequently burned. The Canaanites then had to flee on foot, allowing Israel to defeat them. Since Israel did not begin to use chariots until the time of David and Solomon, it is doubtful that they could have defeated a chariot-equipped army.

The reason for Joshua's actions against Hazor is that Hazor had been the chief of all those kingdoms (vv. 10-12). Behind the remark about Israel not burning any of the other cities "built on raised sites" (v. 13) is a reminder that Israel had neither the strength nor the technical knowledge to defeat the chariot armies of the Canaanites. The extent of the destruction described in these verses is, therefore, probably exaggerated.

This section concludes with a summary regarding the obedience of Joshua: he did all that the Lord had commanded Moses (v. 15). The message to the exiles is reiterated: the need for obedience to the Lord and trust in the power of the Lord. With such trust, victory is possible.

11:16–12:24 Summary of the conquest. The conquest is now summarized in an idealistic fashion by two separate texts. The editorial summary in 11:16-23 was the original summary and conclusion to the narrative. Chapter 12, with its list of conquered kings, was inserted later.

11:16-23 Editorial summary. These verses come from the original compiler of the conquest stories. The basic theme, set out in verses 16 and 23, is that Joshua "captured all this land." Therefore, the Lord has kept all the promises made to Moses (see Josh 1:1-9). The description of the conquered land (vv. 16-17) goes significantly beyond the description in the preceding chapters and also beyond the classical description of "from Dan to Beersheba." Mount Halak, which marks the southern boundary, is at the southern end of the Negeb desert, south of Judah. Baalgad, the northern boundary, refers to a site at the southern end of the Beka valley in Lebanon.

Verse 18 attempts to correct any notion that the conquest was swift. It is pointed out that Israel had to do battle with all these cities because it was the will of the Lord. The Lord had designed it so that all the cities, except Gibeon, would wage war against Israel and so give reason for their extermination (see Deut 20:10-20).

Verses 21-22 are a bit jarring in the context. The Anakim are described elsewhere as "giants" (Num 13:33). The editor wants to show that there were trouble spots where not all the indigenous population had been driven out.

Once more, the conclusion in verse 23 emphasizes that the Lord has kept the promises made to Moses. The same verse forms the transition to the apportioning of the land that begins in chapter 13. The insistence on the Lord's fidelity to the promises made to Moses was an important message for the people in exile.

12:1-24 List of conquered kings. This chapter falls into two parts: a listing of the kings conquered by the Israelites under Moses, east of the Jordan (vv. 1-6), and a listing of those kings whom Israel had conquered under Joshua, west of the Jordan (vv. 7-24). The chapter is an elaboration of 11:23, and is intended to emphasize that the whole country had been conquered by Israel.

The material in verses 1-6 has been developed from Deut 3:8-17 and Josh 13:9-32. Verse 1 points out the northern and southern boundaries of the territory conquered east of the Jordan, namely, Mount Hermon in the north and the River Arnon in the south. The southern half of this area from the River Arnon to the River Jabbok had belonged to Sihon, king of the Amorites, who had his capital in Heshbon (vv. 2-3). The area north of the Jabbok had been under the control of Og, king of Bashan (vv. 4-5). Num 21:21-35 (see Deut 2:26–3:11) recounts the defeat of Sihon and Og. Num 32 reports how Moses had assigned this land to the Reubenites, Gadites, and the half-tribe of Manasseh (v. 6). The Rephaim mentioned in verse 4 were a legendary people of great stature who had inhabited Syria and Palestine in ages past (see Deut 2:11, 3:11; Gen 14:5; 2 Sam 21:16-20).

The listing of the kings conquered west of the Jordan in verses 7-24 is a very important list because verses 13b-24 contain names of cities not previously mentioned. These latter verses are not simply a summary of the preceding stories but represent an independent tradition of the conquest that some scholars say is very ancient, dating from the time of Solomon. Verses 16b-24 are especially interesting, since they list cities found in the territories of Ephraim and Manasseh in central Palestine, where no previous conquests have been mentioned.

The impression given by these lists is that of a total conquest of the land; and that is almost certainly the intention of the author. The interest of the author in these chapters of the conquest (6–11) has not been to give an exact historical account, but rather to show God keeping past promises through great acts on behalf of Israel.

PART II: THE DIVISION OF THE LAND

Josh 13:1–22:34

13–22 The division of the land. These chapters contain elaborate geographical details about how the land was divided among the various tribes, and provide statistical information about persons, places, and tribes. Their purpose is to show how God has given the whole country to Israel as its heritage, just as the Lord had promised Moses (see 11:23). This was an important message for the original audience of this book, the exiles, who had recently lost the land. To these exiles the Book of Joshua is promising above all that the Lord is faithful to the ancient promises made to the patriarchs.

The data found in these chapters are the result of combining various sources. Martin Noth claims that the section is the result of combining two documents: a list of towns of the kingdom of Judah, which dates from the time of King Josiah (d. 621), and a survey of boundaries dating from before the monarchy. Admittedly, the roots of some of this data are quite old, but the chapters reflect the impact of later events. This section may have been composed before the writing of Joshua, and may even be a later insertion into the original narrative of the conquest (compare 13:1b and 23:1b).

While the primary interest of these chapters is with the area west of the Jordan, the section begins with a survey of the allotments of the land east of the Jordan that Moses had made to the tribes of Reuben, Gad, and the half-tribe of Manasseh (13:8-33). It concludes with the narrative of the return of these tribes to their territory in order to take possession of it (22). Chapters 14–21 deal with the allotment to Judah and the Joseph tribes at Gilgal (14–17), the allotment at Shiloh to the remaining seven tribes (18–19), and the setting aside of the cities of asylum (20) and the Levitical cities (21).

In the material that follows, this commentary will not present a detailed analysis of the boundaries and lists of towns given in the biblical text. Readers interested in such detail are referred to the more technical commentaries and atlases. This commentary will limit itself to general remarks.

13:1-33 Introduction to the division of the land. With Joshua far advanced in years, the Lord orders him to apportion the land west of the Jordan among the nine tribes and the half-tribe of Manasseh that still do not have land. This chapter is a D composition in which the author points out that not all of the territory to be allotted had been conquered (v. 1), describes the lands that must still be conquered (vv. 2-6), reminds the reader that the tribes of Reuben, Gad, and the half-tribe of Manasseh had already been allotted territory east of the Jordan by Moses (v. 8), and gives a general (vv. 9-13) and a specific description (vv. 15-31) of this land. Two footnotes have been added to explain why the tribe of Levi had not received an allotment of a block of territory like all the other tribes (v. 14 and v. 33). While the author's purpose seems clear, a certain lack of logic and continuity in these verses is apparent (compare

v. 7 to vv. 1-6 and v. 14 to vv. 8-13). This tells us that there are several layers of material in these chapters.

Verses 1-7 identify the parts of Canaan that Israel had not been able to conquer. That verses 2-6 were added secondarily is apparent from the lack of connection between the description of the land to be conquered and the subsequent order to apportion the land among the nine and a half tribes (v. 7). The area envisioned by verses 2-6 is the area belonging to the empire of David and Solomon.

Verses 8-14 are another addition to the text to explain why Joshua was to apportion land only to nine and a half tribes (v. 8), and to give a general picture of this territory (vv. 9-13). These verses seem to be based on Deut 3.

Verses 15-31 describe the lands allotted to the tribes of Reuben and Gad and the half-tribe of Manasseh. The Reubenites receive the tableland stretching north of the Arnon River to Medeba and Heshbon; the Gadites receive the highlands north of Heshbon; and the half-tribe of Manasseh receives the area of Bashan and a portion of Gilead.

The chapter concludes with another reminder that Moses had apportioned these lands to these tribes when he was in the plains of Moab (v. 32).

14:1–21:42 Allotment of the land west of the Jordan. This is the core section of the second half of the Book of Joshua and falls into five sections: an introduction (14:1-5); the allotment to Judah and Joseph at Gilgal (14:6–17:18); the allotment at Shiloh to the remaining seven tribes (18:1–19:51); a list of the cities of asylum (20:1-9); and a listing of the Levitical cities (21:1-42).

14:1-5 Introduction. These verses present the specific introduction to the allotment of the land west of the Jordan. They stress that Eleazar the priest and Joshua and the heads of the families divided the land (v. 1), and that it was done by lot, in accordance with the instructions that the Lord had given through Moses (vv. 2 and 5; see Num 33:54; 34:13). It is also explained why the land was divided among twelve tribes, even though the tribe of Levi was not given a block of land, namely, because the descendants of Joseph formed two tribes (vv. 3-4).

In the later traditions in the Old Testament Eleazar the priest (v. 1) is presented as a son of Aaron (Exod 6:25; Lev 10:5; Num 3:2). Though the use of the lot is referred to several times in the Old Testament it is not clear from the contexts what was involved. The reason for the need to explain why Joseph's descendants formed two tribes (vv. 3-4) flows from the tradition that Israel was composed of twelve tribes. Not all of the traditions agreed, however, on the identity of the twelve tribes; and some traditions did not even recognize the twelve tribe schema. For example, while one tradition spoke of Joseph as one tribe (17:14-18), another tradition spoke of Joseph's descendants as two tribes. Hence, the editor clarifies from the beginning that the descendants of Joseph formed two tribes: Ephraim and Manasseh.

14:6–15:63 Allotment to the tribe of Judah. This section is composed of four units: the portion given to Caleb (14:6-15); the list of the boundaries of Judah (15:1-12); the gift to Othniel (15:13-19); and the list of the cities of Judah (15:20-63).

14:6-15 Caleb's portion. The story tells how Caleb came into possession of the city of Hebron: it was a reward for his loyalty to the Lord when Moses had sent him to spy out the land many years earlier. Num 13–14 (see Deut 1:20-45) reports how all the spies, except Caleb and Joshua, advised against invasion. As a result God delayed the conquest until that whole generation, except Caleb and Joshua, had died. While a specific promise of land to Caleb is not found in Num 13–14, it is presupposed in Deut 1:36.

In several Old Testament passages, Caleb is identified as a Judahite (e.g., Num 13:6; 34:19), but elsewhere as a Kenizzite (e.g., Num 32:12). The Kenizzites were originally part of the Edomite people (Gen 36:11, 15, 42) who had settled in the southern hill country of Judah and were eventually assimilated into the tribe of Judah. Accordingly, Caleb is presumed to be part of the tribe of Judah. Note that in Judg 1:10 the region shown here as occupied by Caleb was conquered by Judah and Simeon, who defeated the three Anakim chiefs.

Because this passage, as well as 15:13-19, disrupts an otherwise carefully organized presentation of tribal allotments, some claim that they were inserted into the text secondarily. Some also argue that 14:6-15 originally followed 11:21-23 and that 15:13-19 has been drawn from Judg 1:10-20.

15:1-12 Boundaries of Judah. This first of the boundary lists is also the most detailed, indicating that the D editor had more complete records for Judah than for the other tribes. The list, though idealistic, is ancient, and may predate the period of the monarchy. It is certainly older than the list of cities in 15:21-62.

15:13-19 The gift to Othniel. This story, an almost verbatim duplicate of Judg 1:10-15, is an etiology to explain why the Othnielites, who also belonged to the Kenizzite group, had access to pools of water which should have belonged to the Calebites in Hebron. Notice that Caleb is said here to have taken by force the area given him as his heritage in 14:6-15.

15:20-63 Cities of Judah. This list of cities is based on a catalog of twelve provinces that composed the southern kingdom of Judah, probably drawn up for governmental administrative purposes sometime after David. Verse 63 has been added to explain why Jerusalem has not appeared in the city list, namely, because the Judahites could not drive out the Jebusites who lived in the city. It will be David who eventually captures the city (2 Sam 5:6-9).

16:1–17:18 Allotment to the Joseph tribes. This section is made up of four parts: a broad description of the area occupied by the Josephites, in which the Josephites are presented as one tribe (vv. 1-3); a list of the boundaries of the tribe of Ephraim (vv. 4-10); a list of the allotment made to the descendants of Manasseh, other than Machir, who had already obtained land east of the Jordan (17:1-13); and a story of how Joseph's descendants complained that they needed more land (17:14-18).

These lists are in obvious contrast to the detailed Judahite lists in the previous chapters. Fewer details are given and the material is often presented in a very confused way. Notice the concern to explain why Canaanites continued to live in the midst of these tribes (16:10; 17:12), though in both cases it is insisted that the Canaanites were eventually impressed as laborers, even if they were not driven out.

In verses 1-6 we find delineated, by means of a genealogical formulation, the members of the half-tribe of Manasseh, who settled in the area west of the Jordan (see Num 26:28-34). The clan of Machir (v. 1) made up the half-tribe that settled east of the Jordan.

Verses 14-18 consist of two versions (14-15; 16-18) of the same tradition combined into one narrative. The theme of both is a request by Joseph's descendants for more territory, because the hill country they had been given was not large enough to accommodate all of them. In verses 16-18 they also complain that they had been unable to drive out the Canaanites because of their iron chariots. In both versions Joshua responds by telling the Josephites to make better use of their hill country by clearing out some of the forest. In the second version he also encourages them to overcome the Canaanites.

18:1–19:51 Allotment at Shiloh. Having presented the allotment of land to the major tribes of Judah and Joseph, the editor, after an introduction (18:1-10), describes the allotments to the seven remaining tribes: Benjamin (18:11-28); Simeon (19:1-9); Zebulun (19:10-16); Issachar (19:17-23); Asher (19:24-31); Naphtali (19:32-39).

The introduction (18:1-10) describes the procedure of allotting the land: after a representative body (three members from each tribe) surveys and prepares a description of it, the land is divided into seven parts. Joshua assigns the various parts to the seven tribes by casting lots, but it is highly unlikely that the tribes actually received their land in this way. In reality the process was a highly complex one of historical settlement over a period of time. Note that whereas the tribes of Judah and Joseph initiated the procedure for getting their allotment, Joshua is pictured here (v. 3) as admonishing the other seven tribes for not taking more initiative in possessing the subdued land. The reference to Shiloh is probably secondary, since the reference to Judah in the south and Joseph in the north (v. 5) does not make sense if the reference point is Shiloh, which was in the territory of Ephraim. The original tradition supposed Gilgal as the place for this allotment of land. Historically, Shiloh succeeded Gilgal as the national shrine. The reference to the meeting tent (v. 1) is curious, since references to the meeting tent are very rare in the Deuteronomistic sections of the Old Testament (see Deut 31:14-15; 1 Sam 2:22). This reference to the meeting tent is probably due to a later editing of the text.

In general the allotments given to the different tribes are described in terms of ancient boundary lists and city lists drawn up for administrative purposes. Notice that for Simeon (19:1-9) no tribal boundaries are given. The reason is that from a very early period the tribe of Simeon was absorbed into the tribe of Judah and had no territory of its own. Rather, Simeon occupied certain cities within the area belonging to Judah. D justifies this allotment to the Simeonites on the basis that Judah's portion was larger than it needed to be.

Seemingly, the original allotment to Dan was very small. However, the main reason the Danites were forced to migrate north (v. 47) was because they could not conquer the Canaanites in the coastal plain that was part of their original allotment (see Judg 17–18).

That Joshua was granted a specific city as his own is reported only here. Perhaps the passage (vv. 49-50) was added to justify the later statement that Joshua was buried within his own heritage (Josh 24:30; Judg 2:9).

The conclusion to this section is based on 14:1 and 18:1.

20:1-9 The cities of asylum. The right of sanctuary is an ancient tradition that is found in both classical and oriental antiquity and is normally associated with certain sanctuaries. This passage lists those cities where a person who has accidentally killed another could find refuge and asylum. Behind this passage is the fact that in ancient semitic society, in the case of murder, it was the responsibility of the victim's next of kin to avenge the death by taking the life of the murderer. This was true even in the case of an accidental killing. Hence, there was a need to protect a person who accidentally killed another. Cities of asylum have no parallel that we are aware of. The six cities that are listed here show up again in the list of Levitical cities in chapter 21, and Shechem and Hebron housed famous sanctuaries. That a sanctuary also existed at Kadesh (the name means "holy") is also probable. Therefore, it would seem that the right of asylum is connected with these cities because of the sanctuaries located in them.

A difficulty with the picture this chapter presents is that, aside from the laws concerning this custom of asylum in Num 35:9-15 and Deut 19:1-13, no biblical text provides a concrete example of its practice. So, serious questions may be raised about the historicity of what is presented here, and no sufficient evidence is available to give any satisfactory answers.

21:1-42 Levitical cities. D has pointed out several times that the tribe of Levi received no heritage, i.e., no block of territory (13:14, 33; 14:4; 18:7). The Levites received only cities to live in along with their pasture lands (14:4). This chapter lists those cities that were given to the Levites in fulfillment of the Lord's command to Moses (Num 35:1-8).

The major issue regarding the chapter is whether the institution of the Levitical cities is historically true. The list of cities as we have it is artificially arranged, as is apparent in the twelve-tribe scheme imposed upon it. Again, we see nowhere in the Old Testament any concrete example of how this institution functioned. It is not surprising, then, that some see the institution of Levitical cities, and hence this list, as purely theoretical and idealistic. However, there are scholars today who claim that there is a historical reality underlying the story. Specifically they say that the Levitical cities represent "colonies," i.e., places assigned to faithful groups like the Levites in order to bring stability to a given area. Others argue that the list represents an administrative arrangement established by David for governing the frontier areas of his new empire. It is true that Israel controlled the extensive territory presupposed by the list only in the time of David and Solomon, and the majority of the cities listed here are known to have been difficult frontier areas of the empire conquered by David. The Levites were not the only inhabitants of these cities, but they did have certain prerogatives and rights regarding these cities and their pasture lands.

The story of the origin of the Levites as descendants of the three sons of Levi (Kohath, Gershon and Merari) is both late (post-exilic) and an over-simplification of the reality. Notice that the Kohathites are divided into two groups: the descendants of Aaron (the priests) and the other Kohathites.

21:43–22:34 Conclusion. These verses conclude the narrative of the division of the land (21:43–22:9) and provide an appendix regarding the building of a great altar by the Transjordanian tribes on their return to their own lands (22:10-34).

21:43–22:9 Summary and dismissal of the eastern tribes. Verses 43-45 are a summary of the book up to this point. This summary, like the others noted in the book (9:1-2; 10:40-43), goes beyond what has actually been reported in the individual stories that precede it. Despite allusions to the contrary (13:1-6), the editor claims here that Israel has conquered all of the land. What is important, however, is the message that the editor wishes to convey here, namely, that the Lord has been faithful to all the promises made to the patriarchs. As a result Israel has taken possession of all the land and has found peace. As we have noted, this is the major theme of the Book of Joshua and an important message for the people in exile in the sixth century. The exiles can trust this God who is faithful to past promises and who has the power to fulfill them.

The material in 22:1-9 is closely linked to 21:43-45 because it is the "peace" described in 21:45 that permits the dismissal of the eastern tribes reported in 22:1-9. These verses frame the theme developed in 1:12-18. Joshua acknowledges the fidelity of the eastern tribes (vv. 1-3) and, because the tribes west of the Jordan are settled, he dismisses the eastern tribes so that they can return to their own lands (v. 4) with the admonition to remain faithful to the law of Moses (v. 5). He then sends them on their way with his blessing (v. 6). The editor gives special attention to the eastern tribes throughout the book in order to emphasize that the conquest of the land was the work of all Israel. The unity of all of the tribes was quite important to the editor.

22:10-34 Appendix: The construction of the great altar. This story constitutes an appendix to the narrative of the conquest and division of the land. On the surface it tells of how, on their way home, the eastern tribes construct a very large altar in the region of the Jordan River (v. 10). When the other tribes hear of this, they meet to declare war on the eastern tribes (vv. 11-12). The reason for such a strong reaction to the altar is found in the accusation of the delegation sent to get an explanation, namely, the altar is seen as an act of rebellion against the Lord (v. 16). The objecting tribes are fearful of the ramifications of this sin upon all of the tribes (vv. 17-20). What is presupposed here is the belief of the D editor that there can be only one place of worship. The western tribes are mollified when the eastern tribes assure them that the altar is not meant for sacrifices but for a memorial—a reminder to all the tribes that the eastern tribes, though not living in the Promised Land, strictly speaking (see v. 19), did have a right to worship the Lord (vv. 21-29).

Behind the story stands an older narrative that probably dealt with some conflict between the eastern and western tribes over religious practices, and which provided an etiology to describe some great altar. The story has been so thoroughly reworked, that it is impossible to say anything about the original narrative. As it stands, it is a clear warning against illegitimate cultic places, and it stresses the unity of all the tribes. This latter point is found in the concept of corporate guilt expressed in verses 17-20, where the presumed treachery of the eastern tribes is understood to affect all of the tribes, and in the reason given by the eastern tribes for building the altar—as witness to the unity of the eastern and western tribes.

It is not clear from verses 10 and 11 if the altar was built on the western or eastern side of the Jordan. For the story of Peor, see Num 25:6-18. The thrust of the remark in verse 18 would seem to imply that Israel is still offering sacrifices to atone for that sin.

PART III: JOSHUA'S FAREWELL AND DEATH

Josh 23:1–24:33

23–24 Joshua's farewell address. Though these two chapters have separate introductions, they go together in the final edition of the book as the last will and testament of Joshua. Joshua, realizing that his end is near, gathers the people together to remind them of all that has taken place and to encourage them to be faithful to the covenant. He also warns them of the dire consequences of rebellion against the Lord.

Both chapters must be seen against the background of ancient Near Eastern treaties. Scholars are aware of strong parallels between the way the covenant at Sinai is presented in the Old Testament and the form of ancient Near Eastern vassal treaties. These treaties usually contained the following elements: self-introduction by the sovereign; a recounting of history, i.e., what the sovereign has done for the vassal; stipulations that the vassal is to observe as a response to what the sovereign has done for him; blessings and curses for fidelity, or lack thereof, to the treaty; calling upon witnesses; and a demand that the treaty be read periodically before the people. These elements, in different ways, give shape to these two chapters.

23:1-16 Joshua's final plea. This chapter falls into the category of a farewell address. Joshua recalls the past, especially God's actions on behalf of the people, reminds the people of what the Lord asks of them, and of what must still be done. The address has been affected by the style of the Levitical sermon, in which there is much repetition and a mixture of history, stipulation, curses, and blessings. In these latter elements one sees the influence of the ancient vassal treaties.

The chapter is a total creation of the D author, and forms the conclusion to the narrative of the conquest. The purpose of the chapter is to explain to the exiles why they have lost the land, namely, because of their disloyalty to Yahweh, which has brought about the fulfillment of the Lord's threats of destruction. By emphasizing that the Lord has fulfilled all the promises made in the past (vv. 2-11), the author is telling the people that if they again turn to the Lord, they can have their land back; because the Lord is faithful to past promises. Through specific warnings in the text, the author is telling the exiles how they must act in their present situation.

After the Lord has given the Israelites rest from all their enemies, Joshua, in his old age, summons Israel for his farewell address (vv. 1-2). He recalls all that the Lord has done for the people (v. 3), points out that in accord with the promises that have been made, the Lord will drive out the nations before the Israelites from the regions allotted them (vv. 4-5), and calls the people to obedience to the law of Moses (vv. 6-8). The people are to avoid any activity that might even imply the existence of the gods of the foreigners (v. 7). Then the author once again recalls how the Lord drove out the nations before Israel (v. 9) out of fidelity to the promises made in the past (v. 10), and calls Israel to love the Lord (v. 11). Joshua threatens Israel: if she abandons Yahweh and in any way allies herself with the foreign nations (v. 12), then the Lord will no longer drive out the nations before her, but will abandon her to the nations (v. 13). Israel is to acknowledge that every promise of the Lord has been fulfilled (v. 14). Joshua points out that as the Lord has fulfilled all the promises made in the past, so also will the Lord fulfill every threat, namely, to exterminate Israel from the land if she transgresses the covenant (vv. 15-16).

24:1-28 Renewal of the covenant. In contrast to chapter 23 this chapter is based on a tradition that contains authentic memories of ancient covenant renewal ceremonies. The dating of this covenant ceremony to the end of Joshua's life is provided only by the context—not by the report itself. These verses are closely related to the ceremony on Mount Ebal reported in 8:30-35 and, historically, would fit better into that context than at the end of Joshua's life.

While the text may be rooted in some past ceremony, such as a renewal of the Sinai covenant in which the Shechemites were invited to participate, the present text has been influenced by covenant renewal ceremonies that were celebrated periodically in Israel. These ceremonies in turn had been influenced by the form of the ancient Near Eastern vassal treaties.

Joshua gathers together all the tribes of Israel at Shechem in order to address them (v. 1). Shechem, an ancient cultic center, is near the present town of Nablus, about 30 miles north of Jerusalem. No information is available on how Israel came into control of the central hill country where Shechem is located. It was probably a peaceful occupation. Joshua now addresses the people (vv. 2-15). The major part of the address is a recitation of Israel's history from the time of the patriarchs to the period of the conquest (vv. 2-13). Joshua stresses that it was the Lord who was responsible for all that had taken place.

The river referred to in verses 2 and 3 is the Euphrates, and the mountain region of Seir (v. 4) refers to the area south of the Dead Sea. The land of the Amorites (v. 8) is the region east of the Jordan. On Balaam, see Num 22–24. Verse 14 contains the stipulation of the covenant: total commitment to Yahweh because of all that Yahweh had done for them. Verse 15 contains Joshua's challenge to the people: decide whom you will serve! The response of the people (vv. 16-18) is that they, as Joshua's household, will serve the Lord because of all that the Lord has done for them.

In response to the warning of Joshua about

the implications of disloyalty (vv. 19-20), the people reaffirm their commitment (v. 21). Following upon the declaration of witnesses (v. 22), the people solemnly profess their willingness to serve the Lord in response to Joshua's invitation (vv. 23-24). The covenant is then made, a large stone is set up to commemorate the event, and the people are dismissed (vv. 25-28). The function of the stone is not clear. It is possible that the terms of the covenant were written upon it.

In its present context the purpose of this chapter is clear. The author is calling the exiles to total loyalty to the Lord in response to all that the Lord has done for them. As the original Israelites had committed themselves to Yahweh, so now must the Israelites in exile choose whom they will serve. By reporting the renewal of the covenant the editor also makes it clear to the exiles that the covenant can be renewed again if Israel is willing to commit herself completely to Yahweh as her ancestors had done. The threat about the response of the Lord to Israel's infidelity (vv. 19-20) is meant to remind the Israelites once again that the reason they had lost their land was because of their disobedience.

24:29-31 The death of Joshua. After a long life Joshua dies and is buried at Timnath-serah, the Ephraimite town that had been given to him for his services (19:49-50). Verse 31 serves as a transition to the Book of Judges.

24:32-33 Burial traditions. Someone else has added these brief notes about the reburial of the bones of Joseph at Shechem (see Gen 50:25 and 33:19), and the burial of Eleazar, the contemporary of Joshua.

JUDGES

John A. Grindel, C.M.

INTRODUCTION

The Book of Judges tells the story of Israel between the death of Joshua and the rise of Samuel. The core of the book is a collection of stories about several heroes from Israel's past—the judges. Attached to the stories are various traditions concerning the period before the monarchy.

The book is in three sections: a prologue (1:1–2:5); stories of the judges (2:6–16:31); and an appendix dealing with the migration of the tribe of Dan and the civil war against Benjamin (17:1–21:25).

The judges

The book is named for its major protagonists, who are said to have "judged" Israel. The writer distinguishes between the "major" judges and the "minor" judges. The major judges are charismatic military leaders, the subjects of extended narratives. The minor judges are those about whom little information is given beyond their names and the length of their office.

The Hebrew verb that is normally translated as "judge" has two basic meanings: to exercise the function of a judge (in the context of a court or in private judgment) and to rule. None of the judges are ever associated with any function of judgment or arbitration except for Deborah (4:4-5); but this is before she is called by God. Rather, the major judges are shown exercising a specifically military role and sometimes acting as civil rulers. No information is provided on the activity of the minor judges.

Another title that is used for several of the judges is "savior," probably the original title of at least some of the judges. The major judges are presented as charismatics, i.e., people who are raised up by the spirit of the Lord to deliver the people from oppression. Whatever power is given to them is seen as an exceptional measure.

Composition of the book

The book is a series of stories about Israelite heroes who had delivered the people from oppression. The stories originally told of the deliverance of individual tribes and so were limited in their geographical scope. Only later were the heroes made into deliverers of all Israel. These heroic tales from the folklore of the people were meant to entertain and edify, and had been collected together before the Deuteronomistic Historian (D) decided to make use of them. (On the work of the Deuteronomistic Historian, see the introduction to the Book of Joshua, p. 229.)

It was probably D who gave these heroes their pan-Israelite orientation. D also imposed a theological framework on the stories of the major judges. This framework provides an introduction that describes how the people have sinned; how God has allowed them to fall into the hands of their enemies; and how, when the people cried out, the Lord sent a savior to deliver them. Each story ends with a note about how long the land was at peace as a result of the deliverance effected by each savior-judge. D's framework provides the key for interpreting the stories of the judges, i.e., how sin leads to punishment, but repentance leads to deliverance.

The purpose of the Book of Judges

The Book of Judges must be read in the context of the Deuteronomistic History. The author's purpose is to present a basic theology of history: sin leads to punishment, but repentance brings forgiveness and deliverance. This message was meant for the people in exile who had recently lost their land. The author is explaining to them that they had lost the land because of their sinfulness; but if they now repent and turn back to the Lord, the Lord will once again forgive them and deliver them. While a message of hope is present, the book as a whole shows the progressive intensification of the sin of the people. The occasion of this sin is what is presented in the first chapter, namely, that Israel did not drive out of the land the nations with their idolatrous practices. As one goes through the book, the disastrous consequences of this situation become more and more apparent.

Historical accuracy

The basic traditions about the major judges, the material about the conquest in chapter 1, and the reports on the activities of the tribes of Dan and Benjamin in the appendix are quite old. The later Deuteronomistic editors did not significantly rework these stories, but confined themselves to adding comments at the beginning and end of them and inserting connectives between the stories. There is no reason to deny that the stories are based on real events, though each tradition must be studied separately in terms of its historicity. Just because the stories are old does not mean that they can be accepted uncritically as historical.

Later editors modified two aspects of the stories by imposing the "pan-Israel" perspective on them and by adopting an artificial chronology. As we mentioned above, the "pan-Israel" perspective was introduced at a later time on stories that originally spoke of the deliverance of a limited number of tribes. The chronology found in the book is another matter. If one counts up all the years mentioned in the text, then the period of the judges would cover 410 years, obviously much too long, since the evidence available places the period of the judges somewhere between 1200 B.C.E. and 1050 B.C.E., approximately 150 years. A close reading clearly shows that the chronology in the book is stereotyped and artificial. D has imposed the chronology to support the comment in 1 Kgs 6:1 that there were 480 years between the Exodus and the beginning of the construction of the Jerusalem temple. Though the book shows the judges as following one after the other, in reality some of the major judges could have been contemporaries. The sequence chronology is demanded by having each of the judges be a deliverer of all Israel.

COMMENTARY

PART I: THE CONQUEST

Judg 1:1–2:5

This section presents a different view of the conquest of Palestine from the one presented in Josh 1–12. Here there is no acquaintance with the idea of a comprehensive conquest of Palestine by a united army of Israel. Rather, the picture is that of each tribe, alone or with one or two others, struggling to carve out a territory for itself.

The chapter is not a unified literary composition, but has been built up from separate traditions, many of which are quite old, and which come from different sources than the traditions used in Josh 1–12. The material has been arranged to describe the activity of the various tribes on a line from south to north. The Israel presented here is unable to occupy the coastal plains either in the south or in the central part of the country, and is unable to control the plain of Jezreel. As a result, the people are cut off from the great fertile areas of the land. This seems to be more in keeping with the archaeological evidence than the picture presented in Joshua.

However, it is important to see that the editor has not introduced this material either to counter or correct the picture in Joshua, but rather as a report on the activities of the generation after the death of Joshua but during the lifetime of the elders who outlived him. This is clear from the fact that 1:1-3, which come from D, presuppose the singular view of the conquest found in Joshua and the allotment of the land reported in Josh 13–22, and that the material in 2:10 refers to the generation that followed after the elders who survived Joshua. The editor, then, has introduced this prologue to prepare for the negative evaluation of the period that is found in 2:1-5. Chapter 1 is, therefore, intended to provide the basis for the explanation in 2:1-5 of why the Israelites would not be able to clear out the inhabitants of the land from their midst, namely, because they had disobeyed the Lord by making pacts with the inhabitants of the land, and by not pulling down their altars. As a result the Lord will not clear these nations out of Israel's way but will leave them in the land so that they can oppose Israel, and so that their gods will become a snare for Israel (2:3).

As the book opens, the editor seems to presuppose that Israel is still at Gilgal (see 2:1 and Josh 4:19; 10:43; 14:6; and the comments on Josh 18:5). Now that the land has been subdued and apportioned among the tribes (see Joshua), it is necessary for each tribe to lay claim to its territory. They consult the Lord to see who will be the first to attack the Canaanites (1:1). The Lord's response is that Judah shall be first, and Judah invites Simeon to join them (vv. 2-3). This association shows that the tribe of Simeon was absorbed into the tribe of Judah at a very early period, and had no territory of its own (see Josh 19:1-9).

Verses 4-36 present the successes and failures of the various tribes. The fact that Judah is presented first and given such a large amount of space (vv. 4-20) shows that the editor presupposed the preeminence of the tribe of Judah. To a large extent Judah is successful in its encounters with the inhabitants of the land, but not completely (see vv. 18-20). The Perizzites (v. 4) were part of the indigenous population of Palestine (see Josh 17:15 and Gen 34:30). The incident with Adonibezek at Bezek is reminiscent of the story of Adonizedek in Josh 10 and may be related. The location of Bezek is uncertain. Adonibezek's mutilation is intended to humiliate him and render him incapable of war in the future. Verse 8, concerning the capture of Jerusalem, appears to be a later insertion into the text and does not agree with verse 21. The material in verses 10-15 is basically a duplicate of Josh 15:13-19, and is meant to explain why the Othnielites had access to the pools of water that should have belonged to the Calebites in Hebron. The reference to the Kenites in verse 16 explains their presence among the tribes of Judah. Judah is unable to take control of the southern coastal plain because the people there had iron chariots (vv. 18-19). The Benjaminites are mentioned next (v. 21) because of their close association with the tribe of Judah. Jerusalem will not be taken until David personally conquers it.

The editor now presents the attack on the central part of the country by the house of Joseph (vv. 22-29). Note that the house of Joseph is shown capturing Bethel, even though the city has been allotted to Benjamin (Josh 18:22). The story (vv. 22-26) is probably meant to illustrate how Israel made pacts with the inhabitants of the land. Verses 27-29 tell of the tribes being unable to take control of the central coastal plain or the plain of Jezreel. These verses, along with the references to the failures in the north (vv. 30-35), are reported as examples of how Israel sinned by living among the original inhabitants of the land instead of driving them out. Notice that it is not said that they could not drive out the natives but that they did not; rather, they put the natives into forced labor.

In 2:1-5 the editor gives the reason for the survey in chapter 1, namely, to explain why in the stories that follow, Israel will be unable to drive out the native inhabitants of the land: because Yahweh will not be with them, since they have been disobedient (see Josh 23:12-13). These verses, composed by D, are the key to the whole section, and send a clear message to the exiles. D is explaining that they have lost the land because they have been disobedient, and have not lived up to the demands of the reform of Josiah (see 2 Kgs 22:1–23:30). The location of Bochim is unknown. Many surmise that the text here originally read "Bethel" (see 20:18, 26; 21:2). The change to "Bochim" in verse 1 supports the etiology of verse 5, where it is explained that the place came to be called Bochim (weepers) because the people wept there. The angel or "messenger" of the Lord is the envoy of the Lord who can speak in the name of the Lord.

PART II: THE JUDGES

Judg 2:6–16:31

2:6–3:6 Introduction. These verses provide the specific introduction to the stories of the judges. Several hands have shared in the formation of this text, which falls into three sections: the report of the death of Joshua (2:6-9); the specific introduction to the stories of the judges (2:10-23); and a list of the nations that remained in the midst of Israel (3:1-6).

2:6-9 The report of the death of Joshua. These verses parallel Josh 24:28-31, but in a different sequence. The repetition shows that Judg 1:1–2:5 is a later insertion into the text for the reasons already given, and to provide a background for understanding the sinfulness of the people and the Lord's judgment upon them as described in 2:10-23. The report of Joshua's death and burial is repeated here to show that a new era has begun.

2:10-23 The specific introduction to the stories of the judges. This material is not unified. It is highly repetitious with an almost identical content found in verses 11-17; 18-19; 20-23. More than likely verse 10 and verses 20-23 were original, D having inserted verses 11-19 later. Their purpose is to show the tremendous apostasy within Israel during the period of the judges. The gods of the native inhabitants have truly become a snare for Israel (see 2:3). Hence, the need for the "saviors," the judges. The verses make clear that in spite of the deliverance that will be brought by the judges, one should not be misled into thinking that the Israelites truly repented of their sinfulness. Rather, the whole period is described as a time of ever-increasing apostasy (2:19).

The author points out that a new era has begun. There is now a generation that has not experienced the Lord's saving deeds on behalf of Israel nor the law of the covenant (v. 10). Rather they have served the pagan god Baal and the Ashtaroth (plural form for various manifestations of the goddess Astarte), abandoning the God of their ancestors who had led them from Egypt, thus provoking the Lord (vv. 11-12). Baal and Astarte (v. 13) were the embodiment of the idolatrous Canaanite cult. The use of the plural "Baals" and "Ashtaroth" does not indicate many deities bearing these names but rather the various local forms of them.

This abandonment angers the Lord, and so the Lord allows the people to fall into the power of their enemies (vv. 13-15; see Josh 23:11-13). Even when the Lord raises up judges to deliver them, the people do not listen to them or follow their example of obedience, but continue to worship other gods. And when the judge dies the people relapse and do even worse than before (vv. 16-19). Most scholars believe that D introduced verses 11-19 here to serve as an introduction to the stories of the judges, and that the elements of the theological framework for the stories may be found in them, i.e., the sinfulness of the people, the Lord becoming angry with the people and allowing them to fall into the hands of their enemies, the cry of the people, and the Lord's deliverance. Notice, however, that the third element of the framework, the cry of the people, is only mentioned in passing (v. 18). Also notice that the cry of the people is not one of repentance, but only a cry of distress under affliction (but see 10:6-16). The Lord seems moved more by the suffering of the people than by their repentance. What is revealed here is the Lord's love for and dedication to the people.

The people's sinfulness is so great, however, that the Lord must pass judgment on the people; so the Lord swears not to clear away any more of the nations that Joshua left when he died. These nations will test the Israelites and make them prove again their fidelity to the Lord (vv. 20-23).

The message in all of this for the exiles is clear: Israel lost the land because of continuing infidelity to the covenant. However, there is still hope because, as the Lord responded to the cries of distress of the people in the past, so the Lord may do again now. Also, the idea of testing that is emphasized in verse 22 leaves a door open for the exiles—perhaps they can pass the test. The one thing that becomes quite clear from this passage is that God's salvation is a gift; it is not a mechanical response to an action on the part of the people, not even an act of repentance (see 10:10-17).

3:1-6 The nations who remained. These verses give two lists of the nations who remained in the midst of Israel, as well as later reflections on the reason why the Lord left them. The classical listing of the nations who lived in Palestine before the conquest is given in verse 5 (see Josh 3:10). The "five lords of the Philistines" (v. 3) refers to the five cities inhabited by the Philistines (non-Semites who entered Palestine at about the same time as the Israelites) on the southern coastal plain. The added reasons for the Lord leaving the nations in Israel's midst (3:1-2) are intended to be more benevolent than the ones already seen.

3:7-11 Othniel. This report on the first of the judges appears to be constructed by D, and presents an ideal example of D's theology. Because of the generalized nature of the story it is difficult to pin it down to any place or time. Being so short, it helps one to understand clearly the basic elements of D's theology of history.

Israel, forgetting the Lord, serves the Baals and Asherahs (v. 7). This angers the Lord, who delivers the people into the power of Cushan-rishathaim, king of Aram Naharaim. When the people cry out to the Lord, the Lord sends them a savior, Othniel, son of Caleb's younger brother, Kenaz (see Josh 15:17). Here in all their simplicity are seen the introductory formulas of D's framework. The location of Aram Naharaim is unknown. The spirit of the Lord that comes upon the judges in these stories connotes an impersonal power or force that so envelops a person that he or she becomes capable of extraordinary deeds. Verse 11 presents D's normal concluding formula.

3:12-30 Ehud. In the story of Ehud one is able to detect for the first time the existence of an ancient tradition that has been taken up and used by the editor. The story begins with D's framework in which Israel sins, the Lord raises up an oppressor, the people cry out, and the Lord sends a savior (vv. 12-15). The story is filled with humor. The oppressor is "Eglon," which means something like "young bull" or "fat calf" (see v. 17). This king with the ridiculous name is slain by the left-handed Benjaminite (Benjamin literally means "son of the right hand") and the king is so fat that the foot-long dagger gets lost in his belly. The story gloats over how the Israelite hero outsmarts the oppressor and his guards. As a result of the deliverance through Ehud, the land is at rest for eighty years (v. 30).

Moab (v. 12) is situated on the southeastern shore of the Dead Sea. Here the king of Moab is shown in alliance with the people from the north (Amorites) and with southern nomads (Amalekites). The setting for this story, however, is the western shore of the Jordan around Jericho (v. 13), confirmed by the reference to the "cool upper room" (v. 20), appropriate to the desert area around Jericho. The location of Seirah (v. 26) is unknown. Thrown into confusion by the discovery of their dead king, the Moabites attempt to cross the Jordan and return to their home; but the Israelites are ready for them at the fords (vv. 26-29). The story originally dealt only with the tribe of Benjamin in the neighborhood of Jericho (v. 13 "the city of psalms").

3:31 Shamgar. Both the origin and the reason for this reference to Shamgar here in the text is unclear. The reference has no parallel either to the stories of the major judges or to the references to the minor judges. Moreover, it seems to be a late insertion, since 4:1 seems to follow directly on 3:30. The reference to the Philistines as the enemy of Israel is strange here, since they didn't become a problem to Israel until late in the period of the judges. The slaying of the Philistines with an oxgoad recalls the exploits of Samson (15:14-17). Shamgar does not seem to be a Semitic name, and some have surmised that he was really a Canaanite who defeated the Philistines and so delivered Israel.

4:1–5:31 Deborah and Barak. The story of Deborah and Barak is told twice. Chapter 4 is a prose account, while chapter 5 contains a poem celebrating the same victory. Both texts are concerned with a battle between Israel and a strong coalition, perhaps made up of Canaanites and Philistines, near the Wadi Kishon in the valley of Jezreel. Chapter 4 locates this battle on the northern edge of the valley of Jezreel in the neighborhood of Mount Tabor, but chapter 5 locates it more toward the southeastern side of the valley.

4:1-24 The prose narrative. The prose narrative begins with the regular D framework (vv. 1-3). This time the oppressor is the Canaanite king, Jabin, who reigns in Hazor and has a general named Sisera, who lives in Harosheth-ha-goiim. The real actor is Sisera, and the mention of Jabin seems to be secondary, a reference perhaps related to Josh 11:1f. The location of Harosheth-ha-goiim is uncertain, but it would have been in the northern part of Palestine.

Verses 4-10 report the call of Barak through Deborah and his summoning of the tribes of Zebulun and Naphtali for battle. Deborah is described as a prophetess and one to whom people came for judgments (vv. 4-5). She is a judge, then, in the forensic sense. Ramah and Bethel are just a few miles north of Jerusalem. The tribal connections of Deborah are not clear. While she may pass judgments in the mountain regions of Ephraim, she is connected here with the tribes of Zebulun and Naphtali. Barak is from Kedesh, north of Hazor, in the territory of the tribe of Naphtali. The figure of ten thousand men (v. 10) from only two tribes appears to be an exaggeration.

Verse 11 acts as a footnote to prepare for verse 17, explaining how a group of Kenites, who should be located much farther to the south, were to be found in this region.

The battle proper is described in verses 12-16, but there is little detail in the report. God is shown as being responsible for everything that happens. The Lord alone is deserving of glory.

The killing of Sisera (vv. 17-22) is a flagrant violation of the law of hospitality. It also appears that Hazor and the clan of Heber, the Kenite, had an alliance with one another! For whatever reason Jael, wife of Heber, decides to stand with the Israelites. Verses 23-24 are the normal D conclusion, though a partial one. D postpones a final chronological reference until 5:31 so as to present chapters 4 and 5 as a unit.

5:1-31 The Canticle of Deborah. Considered one of the oldest texts in the Bible, this poem, because of its age and the condition of its text, is notoriously difficult. The meaning of many early Hebrew words is uncertain and some verses are nearly incomprehensible. Moreover, the connections with chapter 4 are not always clear. In its present form the poem is a song praising Yahweh, the God of Sinai and the conquest, for what the Lord accomplished through Deborah and Barak.

Originally, verse 1 may have been directly linked to the prayer in verse 31 before the song was inserted. Verse 2 introduces the subject of the song, namely, the chiefs of Israel and the noble deeds of the people, i.e., what was accomplished by Deborah and Barak. Verse 3 is an invitation to listen to this hymn to the God of Israel. Verses 4-5 recall how Yahweh led Israel into Palestine accompanied by a series of cosmic events. Verses 6-8 describe the situation before Deborah: it was not safe to travel the roads, people were worshiping new gods, and Israel was unarmed before foreign armies. Verses 9-11 extend another invitation to sing about the leaders of Israel and about Yahweh. Verses 12-18 describe the muster of the tribes for the battle that is to come. Verse 12 describes the general call to Deborah and Barak to muster the tribes. The gathering of the tribes is described in verse 13, and verses 14-17 describe those tribes that responded positively to the invitation of the Lord and those that did not. Special praise is given to Zebulun and Naphtali in verse 18. Verses 19-22 describe the battle. Behind verses 20-22 there is the idea of a sudden storm that trapped and bogged down Sisera's chariots so that his army was easily defeated.

The events surrounding Sisera's death are reported in verses 23-30. First, the town of Meroz is cursed because, unlike Jael, it did not offer any aid to Israel, perhaps by ignoring the fleeing Sisera. Verses 24-27 gleefully describe the death of Sisera at the hand of Jael. This account is a bit different from what is reported in 4:21. Here Jael appears to hit Sisera as he was drinking the milk. Verses 28-30 report in a mocking way the concern of Sisera's mother over the delay in his return and the response she receives from her wisest princess. Verse 31 summarizes the poem's theology and presents the concluding part of D's framework.

For the exiles the episode of Deborah and Barak is a strong motivation to hope and trust in the Lord, who can destroy Israel's enemies and grant freedom from oppression if Israel will only cry out to the Lord.

6:1–8:28 Gideon. These chapters reiterate the basic cycle of sin, punishment, repentance, and deliverance. This time it is the Midianites who oppress Israel, and the savior sent by the Lord is Gideon. Gideon destroys the altar of Baal at Ophrah, erects an altar to Yahweh in its place, and receives a new name, Jerubbaal. With a few men he wins a great victory over the Midianites, but will not accept the kingship when it is offered to him. While the narrative appears basically clear and consistent there are many tensions within it. First of all, there is the double name for the hero, Gideon and Jerubbaal. Secondly, chapter 6 is obviously made up of a series of different traditions (vv. 11-24; 25-32; 33-35; 36-40). There is significant tension between 6:33-35, where all the tribes are mustered, and 7:3-6 where almost immediately most are sent back home for purely theological reasons. In 8:1-3 Ephraim is angry with Gideon because he had not called them, but this seems directly opposed to what is said in 7:24f. Finally, Gideon is presented not only as a champion of the people, but also as a man set on vindicating the death of brothers. All this suggests that the chapters are a collection of originally independent traditions that have been edited into a continuous whole, but not skillfully enough to rid the stories of all inconsistencies. Many of the stories originally concerned only the family of Abiezer from the tribe of Manasseh, but they were later made to refer to all Israel.

Most scholars accept the historicity of the oppression of the Israelites by the Midianites, a people from the desert region southeast of Palestine. Gen 25:2ff. points out that Midian was a son of Abraham who was sent eastward so as not to interfere with the inheritance of Isaac. It is not clear here if the chapters describe just isolated raids, the movement of a seminomadic people into cultivated areas at certain times of the year, or a full-scale invasion akin to Israel's own invasion of the land. This issue cannot be solved, but what is clear is that the editor was more interested in presenting a theological message to the exiles than in recounting a political and military event.

These chapters fall into four main sections: the call of Gideon (6:1-40); the defeat of the Midianites (7:1–8:3); the pursuit of the kings of the Midianites (8:4-21); and the offer of kingship (8:22-28).

6:1-40 The call of Gideon. The story of Gideon begins with the standard framework for the stories of the judges. The Midianite oppression is described as being very critical and widespread, extending from central and northern Palestine to the southwest. The Midianites, together with other nomadic peoples, the Amalekites and Kedemites, were rapidly and indiscriminately plundering the countryside. The Israelites were forced into hiding, where they established a series of strongholds and invented a way to signal the approach of the Midianites (vv. 2-5). Reduced to utter misery, the Israelites cry out to the Lord (v. 6). A new element now appears: in response to Israel's cry the Lord sends a prophet to remind the people of all that the Lord had done for them and how the Lord had commanded them not to venerate the pagan gods of the Amorites. But Israel disobeyed the Lord and had indeed worshiped the pagan gods. The point of these verses (vv. 7-10) is the indictment that the Israelites had brought on their own suffering through disobedience, an important message for the audience of the book, the exiles.

The call of Gideon is reported in what appears to be two variant traditions in verses 11-24 and verses 25-32. The first is a cultic legend explaining the origins of the sanctuary at Ophrah, and shows Gideon, a farmer, threshing his wheat in a concealed wine press, in order to hide it from the plunderers. An angel of the Lord appears to Gideon and commissions him to save the people (v. 11). The angel here, as in other places in the Old Testament, represents Yahweh and is interchangeable with Yahweh. Gideon, obviously unaware of the prophet's explanation in verses 7-10, challenges the angel's greeting with a sarcastic remark, claiming that rather than being with him, the Lord has abandoned the people (vv. 12-13). Despite Gideon's sarcasm, the Lord appoints him to save Israel (v. 14) and assures him of success because "I will be with you" (vv. 15-16). This interchange reinforces the idea that God alone is responsible for what is about to happen (see ch. 7). Gideon, still not satisfied, asks for a sign, which the Lord gives (vv. 17-21). The sign here is a cultic one in which the deity consumes the offering in a particular way. Consecrated by the fire from the rock, Gideon builds an altar there and calls it "Yahweh-shalom" (vv. 22-24). "Shalom" is a complex word that expresses ideas of peace, cooperation, and agreement between two parties. The idea that seeing Yahweh can be fatal (v. 22) is found several times (e.g., Exod 19:21; 33:18-23).

The story of the destruction of the altar to Baal and the building of a proper altar to Yahweh (vv. 25-32) is a variation of the previous story. The editor has included it here for two reasons: to show that Gideon cannot hope to defeat the enemies of Israel unless he purges out the worship of the foreign gods; and to explain Gideon's other name, his "baal" name, "Jerubbaal," the explanation of which is connected with the people's reaction to Gideon's tearing down the altar of Baal. They want Gideon's father, Joash, to hand him over so they can kill him (vv. 28-30). Joash's response (v. 31) is that if the people act in Baal's place by taking action against Gideon without Baal's authorization, they, too, will be put to death, and if Baal is really a god, he can take care of himself. Gideon's second name is a pun on the Hebrew word which means to "litigate, take action against, sue." Hence, his name means something like "let Baal sue" or "take action."

Verses 33-40 form the transition into the battle with the Midianites described in chapter 7. The Midianites and their allies come across the Jordan from the desert on one of their raids and take control of the valley of Jezreel (v. 33). Originally the story dealt only with the family of Gideon and the family of Abiezer from the tribe of Manasseh, but at some stage in the editing of the material it has become a story about all Israel. Hence, the references here to the tribes of Asher, Zebulun and Naphtali are secondary. Before going into battle Gideon seeks reassurance of divine approval through an oracle (vv. 36-40). Oracles before battle are commonplace in the Old Testament (see e.g., 4:6-7; Josh 6:2-5; 7:10-15; 8:1-2). The use of the fleece may have been an accepted practice. Gideon asks for a second proof, since the first one may have been inconclusive, i.e., because the fleece could have collected dew even though the ground appeared dry.

7:1–8:3 The defeat of the Midianites. Assured of divine approval for entering into battle, Gideon encamps on a hill above the Midianites' camp. Topographical details in verse 1 are not too clear, but it appears that the opposing forces were encamped toward the southeastern end of the valley of Jezreel. Though the Lord said nothing when Gideon first mustered his troops (6:34-35), the Lord now tells him to reduce the size of his army so that the Israelites will not take credit for the forthcoming victory. The point of 7:1-8 is to show that it is the Lord who is responsible for the victory over the Midianites. The original story described the victory of only three hundred Abiezerites over the Midianites. Later, when the victory was attributed to all Israel, the editors took the opportunity to make the point that God had brought about the victory by having Gideon send all but three hundred warriors home. There are two troop reductions (vv. 3-6). The nature of the test in verses 4-6 is unclear. Why pick the soldiers who lap up the water with their tongues like dogs? It may have been an arbitrary test to provide a means by which God can make a selection. Verse 8 explains how the three hundred get enough jars and horns for use in the battle strategy (see vv. 16-22).

Knowing Gideon's need for continued assurances of success, the Lord now takes the initiative and tells him to sneak down to the Midianite camp with his aide and hear what they are saying (vv. 9-11). What is revealed, in contrast to the weakness and fear of Gideon, is the power of the Lord. What Gideon overhears is one man telling another about his dream (vv. 13-14). The point of the loaf of bread symbolizing Israel is to show how small and inadequate the breadloaf is in relation to what it is capable of doing. Once again the point is made that it is the Lord who will be responsible for the victory.

Verses 16-22 describe the attack against the Midianites. Notice that Gideon and his men are not engaged in any fighting; rather, it is the Lord who sets the Midianites against one another (v. 22). Israel divided the night into three watches of four hours apiece. The attack begins at the beginning of the middle watch, about 10:00 p.m. (v. 19). It is hard to imagine how the Israelite soldiers could simultaneously carry out the actions described in verses 19-20. More than likely several different traditions have been combined here. Frightened by the sudden burst of light all around their camp and the noise created by the breaking jars and the horns and the shouts, the Midianites are thrown into disarray and take off toward the east and the Jordan River.

Gideon once again musters the tribes for battle and sends them down to the river fords to intercept the fleeing Midianites as they try to cross the Jordan. Logistically, Gideon's procedure here does not make much sense. He gathers all the tribes and sends all but three hundred home. Then, almost immediately, he turns around and summons the other tribes back. This would have taken time and is not compatible with the speed needed to reach the river fords that is presumed by the text. This tension in the text is the result of making what was originally the victory of one tribe into a victory of all Israel. The summoning of Ephraim in verse 24 does not fit well with the complaint of Ephraim in 8:1-3. Seemingly, the Ephraimites are complaining about the lateness of their summons to battle. The text presupposes that Ephraim was the most important tribe at the time. With good oriental diplomacy Gideon calms down the Ephraimites by quoting a proverb that says how little the family of Abiezer has been able to achieve when compared with what Ephraim has done (vv. 2-3).

8:4-21 The pursuit of the Midianite kings. The focus in this section shifts from the actions of God to the actions of Gideon. Yahweh does not appear in this chapter except for a reference in Gideon's speech (v. 7 and v. 19). The editor may only have wanted to show what became of Gideon. It is not a complimentary picture.

The section begins with a flashback to the situation at 7:22 with Gideon chasing the fleeing Midianites. Both Succoth and Penuel were cities in the Jordan valley, but east of the Jordan River. The reference to the two Midianite kings in verse 5 is surprising, since there has been no previous mention of them. It appears that 8:4-12 may be a variant on 7:22–8:3. The names of the kings are distorted and mean something like "sacrificial victim" and "protection withheld," obvious references to what is going to happen to them. The occupants of Succoth and Penuel are not too convinced that Gideon is going to be victorious and so are not ready to help him, lest they later suffer reprisals from the Midianites (vv. 6-8).

Gideon captures the two kings as they flee from a surprise attack on their camp (vv. 10-12). The location of Karkor is uncertain, but it may have been the central camp from which the Midianites made their periodic raids on Palestine. There is no real proportion in verses 13-17 between the crime and the punishment. Obviously Gideon is attempting to give a message to other people in the area. The "elders of the city" (v. 16) were the governing body when there was no king.

Verses 18-21 come as a real surprise but they explain why Gideon was chasing the two Midianite kings, namely, blood vengeance. They had killed his blood brothers and so now they must be killed. Nothing is known of the incident at Tabor (v. 18) that gave rise to this vendetta.

8:22-28 Offer of kingship. Originally, Gideon (vv. 22-23) would not have been offered kingship by all of Israel as presented here, but by a more limited group or particular city. As a good follower of Yahweh Gideon refuses the offer and states an orthodox Yahwistic principle: the Lord must rule over you. Though Gideon refuses the title of king, it seems clear from 8:24f. and 9:2f. that he accepts power over the people and demands the trappings of a judge. The ephod made from the booty was a cult object used in obtaining oracles (see Exod 28:15-30). This ephod became an object of idolatrous worship, a practice the editor blames for the eventual downfall of Gideon's family (see ch. 9). Notice how the editor stresses that "all" Israel paid idolatrous homage to the ephod (v. 27). The sinfulness of Israel continues.

8:29–9:57 Abimelech. Though there are some tensions in this material, for the most part the story proceeds with a series of clearly defined scenes. Abimelech, one of Gideon's sons, manages to get himself accepted as king over the city of Shechem by killing all of his brothers except one, Jotham, who invokes a curse upon the city and Abimelech. Tension soon develops between Abimelech and the citizens of Shechem and, as a result of a conspiracy headed by a man named Gaal, military conflict breaks out. Abimelech is victorious, but it is an empty victory. In putting down the revolt he destroys the city, wipes out its citizens, and is killed himself. There is no reason to deny the historicity of the story told here. Shechem was on the southern border of the territory of the tribe of Manasseh in the central highlands and had become part of the Israelite confederacy in the twelfth century. Archaeology confirms a significant destruction of the city toward the end of the twelfth century.

The story of Abimelech does not fit the pattern of the other stories of the major judges. First of all, Abimelech is not portrayed as a hero who saves Israel from oppression. Secondly, the D framework is missing, except for the opening statement on the sin of Israel. This passage (8:33-35), along with the conclusion to the story (9:56-57), provides the key for understanding the story. In 8:33-35 Israel is indicted for sinfulness and for being ungrateful to the family of Jerubbaal (Gideon); and in 9:56-57 is found the explanation of the story: it is to show how God requites the evil of Abimelech and the citizens of Shechem who have turned to idolatry and destroyed Gideon's family. In other words, the story is about Israel's sinfulness and punishment. Because it comes immediately after Gideon's refusal of the crown, the story of Abimelech stands out as the tale of the wicked son who accepted the crown—in fact sought it. The story also has a strong anti-monarchy sentiment. The emphasis on sin and punishment is meant especially for the exiles: the reason for the destruction of Jerusalem and the loss of the land in their own time is their sinfulness, especially their following after strange gods.

The all-Israel emphasis in the story is clearly secondary, i.e., added after the fact. Abimelech never ruled over all Israel, but only over the city-state of Shechem and its territories.

The description of Gideon's sons and the note on Gideon's death in 8:29-32 acts as a transition to the story of Abimelech. A concubine (v. 31) is a legitimate wife, but a wife of second rank. The god Baal of Berith (v. 33) was the patron deity of Shechem. By accepting him the people returned to the pre-Israelite form of governance known at Shechem, the monarchy. Rejection of Yahweh is also rejection of a social-political system.

Because Abimelech did not have any right to rule over Shechem, he had to approach the citizens of Shechem through intermediaries, namely, his mother's kinsfolk in Shechem (9:1-3). The "citizens," the prominent people of Shechem who formed a civic assembly, had the power to appoint a person king. Behind the story lies the fact that even though Gideon did not accept kingship, his sons exercised considerable influence after his death and the citizens of Shechem were unhappy with such a situation. They are willing, therefore, to give Abimelech the money to hire the ruffians he needs to kill his brothers (vv. 4-5). The reference to the "one stone" (v. 5) suggests a public execution of all of them at the same place. The number seventy is a round figure for many. For the sacred oak (terebinth) at Shechem see Gen 12:6; Deut 11:30; Josh 24:26.

Jotham's fable (vv. 7-15) has been made to fit here by the addition of verse 15, and reflects a strong rejection of the institution of the monarchy. While the olive, fig, and vine are typical and prized trees in Palestine, the buckthorn, aside from producing beautiful flowers in the spring, seemed worthless to the ancients and a real nuisance because of its thorns. The point of the fable is that only the worst and least qualified are disposed to accept the crown. Jotham's speech (vv. 16-21) is aimed at the citizens of Shechem who have not acted honorably in making Abimelech king, and he utters a curse against both of them. Verses 17-18 are a later addition to the text to explain the statement in verse 16.

After only three years the citizens of Shechem rebel against Abimelech. The author attributes this to the action of God (v. 23) so as to bring on the succession of events that lead to the destruction of Shechem and the death of Abimelech. The civic assembly could depose the king as well as appoint him. What really brings things to a head is the arrival of Gaal, who instigates a full-scale rebellion against Abimelech (vv. 26-29).

When Abimelech hears of these matters from the ruler of the city, he arrives with his army and defeats Gaal (vv. 30-41). Notice that Abimelech does not live in Shechem but at Arumah, a town nearby. Tabbur-Haares means "navel of the world" and Elon-Meonenim means "diviner's oak." They refer to places near Shechem. Once Gaal is defeated Zebul will not allow him to continue to use Shechem as his base of operations, and Gaal disappears. The next day Abimelech returns and ambushes the people of Shechem as they come out to investigate the damage to their crops. Sowing a site with salt (v. 45) is an ancient rite of cursing. From verses 46-49 we learn that Abimelech has destroyed only the lower part of the city. The upper city stood on an artificial platform of earth that supported the ruler's palace and the temple of Baal Berith (also known as Beth-millo; see verses 6 and 20). The remaining citizens take refuge in the "crypt" of the temple of El-Berith. The true meaning of the Hebrew word translated "crypt" here is unknown. Some would translate it by "citadel." The reference is to some part of the fortified temple that Abimelech sets on fire, killing those who had taken refuge there (vv. 46-49).

Abimelech's end comes when he attacks Thebez, a town northeast of Shechem (vv. 50-55). Seemingly, Thebez had taken part in the revolt. Death at the hand of a woman was considered a disgrace (v. 54). With his death the first attempt at initiating the monarchy in Israel fails.

10:1-5 Tola and Jair. These are the first of the "minor" judges. There is a regular pattern followed in the descriptions of these men: name, origin, length of time in office, death, burial, and family. Since the numbers of years of their time in office are not stereotyped, they are probably original to the tradition. Though now they are said to have judged all Israel, their original sphere of influence was probably limited to a particular area. Also, their terms may have been contemporary with other minor judges or even one of the major judges. Their role is unclear. We have already explained in the introduction to this book that the Hebrew word meaning "to judge" can also mean "to rule." It is possible, then, that they were a type of local administrator. Tola is said to have "saved" Israel, perhaps meaning that after the confusion and unrest of the time of Abimelech, Tola brought some stability through his administration.

10:6–12:7 Jephthah. The story of Jephthah is a composite of various traditions to which some later additions have been made. The story proceeds as follows: a prologue (10:6-16); the recall of Jephthah (10:17–11:11); Jephthah's negotiations with the Ammonites (11:12-28); Jephthah's vow and defeat of the Ammonites (11:29-40); and the defeat of the Ephraimites (12:1-7).

10:6-16 Prologue. These verses introduce the story of Jephthah and contain an expanded version of the D framework. What is interesting here is how this framework has been expanded: first by inserting the list of deities in verse 6; then the list of Israel's opponents, past, present, and future in verses 11 and 12; and the discussion between Yahweh and the people regarding Yahweh's response to their cry in verses 10-16. By recapitulating 2:6–3:6 and referring to the past and future enemies (Philistines) of Israel, this section becomes a theological introduction to the second half of the Book of Judges. The point is that there is nothing automatic about Yahweh's response to Israel's cry (see vv. 11-14). More than words admitting guilt are necessary. What eventually moves the Lord to grieve over the misery of the Israelites (v. 16) is that aside from admitting their guilt they also show themselves ready to accept punishment (v. 15) and, most importantly, to cast out the foreign gods from their midst (v. 16). The author is telling the exiles what is expected of them.

The oppressors this time are the Ammonites, who occupied the territory of the Moabites east of the Jordan River. They especially afflicted the Israelites in Bashan, east of the Jordan near the Sea of Galilee, and in the southern part of Gilead, which belonged to the tribe of Gad. At times they crossed over the Jordan and harried the southern tribes of Judah, Benjamin, and Ephraim.

10:17–11:1 Recall of Jephthah. It is obvious from 10:17-18 that none of the princes of Gilead wanted to begin the war against the Ammonites. Hence, attention turns to Jephthah, the chieftain of a group of brigands who plundered the area (vv. 1-3). Because of his illegitimate birth he had been driven out from his own land by the same people who now want him back to lead them in battle. Unlike the stories of the other judges, Jephthah's calling to be a judge does not take place in a single moment; rather, it takes place through negotiation. In negotiations with the elders (vv. 4-10) the elders first offer him only the role of commander (v. 6). When Jephthah does not immediately accept, they raise the ante to being "leader of all of us who dwell in Gilead" (v. 8). This seems to imply that the office of judge included administrative as well as military responsibilities. Verse 11 is about a certain form of investiture.

11:12-28 Negotiations with the Ammonites. Before rushing into battle Jephthah attempts to clarify the reasons for the Ammonite hostility and discovers that the Ammonites want back the land that they claim Israel took from them when they came up from Egypt (vv. 11-13). Jephthah then gives historical and theological justification for Israel's occupation of the disputed land east of the Jordan. The material in verses 13-27 is no doubt a later insertion to justify Israel's possession of the land between the Arnon and Jabbok rivers. The historical argument is that the territory in dispute did not belong to either Ammon or Moab but was part of the former kingdom of Sihon, which Israel had conquered under Moses. The theological argument is that territories belong to those who received them from their particular deity and the Israelite God had given them this territory. The historical survey in verses 15-22 is in basic agreement with Num 20–24.

11:29-40 Jephthah's vow and defeat of the Ammonites. The spirit of the Lord now comes upon Jephthah and he inflicts a severe defeat upon the Ammonites. The center of attention in this scene is Jephthah's vow that if the Lord will deliver the Ammonites into his power, he will offer up to the Lord as a holocaust whoever comes out of his house upon his return (vv. 30-31). The one who comes out is his daughter. There are a number of parallels to this event in comparative folklore. The surprising thing is that the author has not censored this report of human sacrifice! Elsewhere in the Old Testament it is condemned (Lev 18:21; 20:2-5; Deut 12:31; 18:10; Mic 6:7). The fact of human sacrifice here is secondary, however, to the theme of the irrevocability of Jephthah's vow. The vow, once it has been made, must be kept. What complicates the situation is that the story is now used as an etiology for a defunct lamentation festival in Israel (vv. 39-40). Some see the story as a myth passed off as history to explain the festival. Perhaps the story is meant to show the lamentable effects of not trusting in the Lord's willingness to save Israel. There is no need for such pagan practices.

12:1-7 Defeat of the Ephraimites. This story, which preserves memories of frontier conflicts between Gilead and Ephraim, is loosely joined to the rest. As in the story of Gideon (8:1ff.) the Ephraimites are upset because they had not been summoned to help in the battle against the Ammonites. Jephthah claims that they had been invited but had not responded (vv. 1-3). In the dialect spoken by the Ephraimites the initial sibilant of "Shibboleth" could not be pronounced correctly, thus giving them away. The meaning of the taunt in verse 4 is not clear.

The conclusion to the story of Jephthah in 12:7 is from the formula used for the minor judges, leading some to see Jephthah as a later development of one who was originally only one of the minor judges. This idea is supported by the fact that the story of Jephthah stands between the two lists of the minor judges (10:1-5 and 12:8-15).

12:8-15 Ibzan, Elon and Abdon. This is the second and final list of the "minor" judges, following the pattern of the first list (10:1-5).

13:1–16:31 Samson. The Samson stories contain the most extensive cycle of traditions in the Book of Judges. Though there is no reason to deny their historicity, it is clear that these traditions have been deeply colored by legendary, cultic, and folklore elements—possibly even by ancient solar myths. Samson's name is related to the Hebrew word for sun, and he comes from an area not far from Beth-shemesh (temple of the sun).

There are some significant differences between the Samson traditions and the other material in the book. The D framework is reduced to a report on the sin of the people and the Lord's deliverance of them into the power of the Philistines. Nothing is said of a cry to the Lord. Also, Samson never commands an army and he does not liberate Israel either from the Philistines or from any other oppressor. His relations with the Philistines appear to be on the level of a private feud. However, the editor sees these exploits as the beginning of Israel's deliverance from the power of the Philistines.

Each of the various traditions had its own prior independent existence. However, the editor has artfully woven them together into a coherent whole. The material falls into four sections: the birth of Samson (ch. 13); the marriage of Samson (ch. 14); Samson's defeat of the Philistines (ch. 15); and the capture and death of Samson (ch. 16).

13:1-25 The birth of Samson. The chapter begins with a short form of the D framework (v. 1). The Philistines had entered Palestine about fifty years after the Israelites as part of the migration of the sea peoples from the Aegean and Crete. Repulsed by the Egyptians around 1200 B.C.E., they had settled on the southern coast of Palestine.

Verses 2-5 report the angel's announcement of the forthcoming birth of Samson to his unnamed mother. His father is from Zorah, a town in the territory originally allotted to the tribe of Dan and the point of departure for the migration of the Danites to the extreme northern part of Palestine (ch. 18). Barrenness is a common theme in the Old Testament (see Gen 11:30 and 1 Sam 1:2f.) and is used as an occasion for a miraculous divine intervention whereby a child is born to undertake a unique mission. In verses 4 and 5 the nazirite rule (Num 6:1-8) is adapted for the consecration of a person in the womb. Normally nazirites were adults who voluntarily consecrated themselves to the Lord for life or for a particular period. Samson is consecrated from his conception, so the rites before his birth apply also to his mother. The regulations that Samson will live under are: abstaining from wine and strong drink, not shaving his head, and avoiding all contact with the dead. Verse 7 adds that he will be a nazirite until his death.

Because the following chapters do not refer to the nazirite vow that Samson is under, it is possible that this chapter was composed as the introduction to the cycle later on in order to make the story of Samson a narrative of the violation of the nazirite vow. It is this sinful person whom the Lord uses to begin the deliverance of the people from the power of the Philistines (v. 5).

In verses 6-23 Samson's father, Manoah, shows typical Semitic caution about the testimony of a woman and so needs to hear for himself what he and his wife must do for the boy who will be born (vv. 8-14). Manoah, in his conversation with the angel, is looking for a sign, which he receives in the consumption of the holocaust by fire and the ascent of the angel in the flame (v. 19). Only then is he convinced that the messenger is from God. When Manoah asks his name, the angel does not reveal it, saying that it is "mysterious," i.e., incomprehensible, like the works of God (see vv. 18 and 19).

14:1-20 The marriage of Samson. Samson's first exploits take place in the context of his marriage. At Timnah, a Philistine town a few miles from Zorah, Samson falls in love with a Philistine woman and asks his parents to obtain her for his bride (vv. 1-3). Normally, marriage negotiations were carried out by the bridegroom's father. Samson's parents are displeased because she is not an Israelite; a foreign wife was considered dangerous to security. "Uncircumcised" (v. 3) is used only of the Philistines in the Old Testament, pointing to the fact that they were the only ones in the region who did not practice the rite of circumcision. Perhaps the editor did not approve of this marriage either, but in verse 4 he provides the interpretative key for the rest of the chapter: what is about to take place is part of God's plan. Though not explicit, it appears that the editor sees the events here, especially those in verses 19-20, as the way the Lord begins the deliverance of Israel from the Philistines (13:5).

The whole process of Samson's coming and going to Timnah (vv. 5-9, 10) is obscure, and the references to his parents in verses 5 and 10 are awkward. These references might be later additions to show that Solomon's parents went along with him and set up the marriage in spite of their opposition. The important issue, however, is the killing of the lion and later finding the honey in its carcass. It is the spirit of the Lord that gives Samson the strength to deal so easily with the lion (v. 6). Notice that Samson breaks the nazirite vow by eating the honey, which is impure because it has been taken from a corpse.

Samson's riddle (vv. 10-18) is impossible to solve unless one knows about the private actions of the hero. The Philistines are able to answer it only by threatening his new wife (v. 15). This treachery causes Samson to perform one of his feats against the Philistines (v. 19). Ashkelon was a Philistine stronghold on the coast, southwest of Timnah.

15:1-20 Defeat of the Philistines. After his anger subsides Samson goes to visit his wife, taking along the gift of a kid (v. 1). However, he is refused entrance to visit her because her father has already given her to Samson's best man, having interpreted Samson's abrupt withdrawal (14:19) as a repudiation and divorce of her. The father proposes an alternative, but Samson departs in anger (v. 3).

The incident with the foxes is difficult to visualize (vv. 4-5). It is obviously intended to be some sort of guerilla tactic. In all of this Samson seems to be overreacting, since he had been offended by only one family.

The Philistines retaliate swiftly against Samson's wife and her family, and Samson takes revenge against the Philistines (vv. 6-8). Having escaped to Etam in the territory of the tribe of Judah, the Philistines pressure Judah to turn Samson over to them (vv. 9-10). The sites of both Etam and Lehi are unknown. Lehi means "jawbone," its presence here preparing us for the wordplay in verse 17. Men of Judah now go down to capture Samson and, to their surprise, find him ready to surrender (vv. 11-13). That they did not expect such an easy time is reflected in the large number who set out for him (v. 11). When Samson sees the Philistines the spirit of the Lord comes upon him, moving him once again to extraordinary action (vv. 14-16), another deed by which the Lord begins to deliver Israel from the Philistines (see 13:5).

Notice that Samson again violates the law of the nazirite by touching an animal carcass. Verse 17 tells us that the name of the site "Ramath-lehi" (throwing of the jawbone) is explained by Samson's action of discarding the weapon. Verses 18-19 present the etiology of a spring at Lehi called "Enhakkore," that is, "spring of one who called."

The notice about Samson's judgeship in verse 20 probably indicates a conclusion to an early edition of the Samson stories and that chapter 16 was added later (see 16:31).

16:1-31 The capture and death of Samson. This chapter has three separate episodes: Samson and the harlot (vv. 1-3); Samson and Delilah (vv. 4-22); and the death of Samson (vv. 23-31). While the last two episodes are clearly related, the first one appears to be independent. However, because of its emphasis on Samson's strength, it is a good preparation for the question in verse 5.

The episode with the harlot (vv. 1-3) takes place at Gaza, one of the Philistine cities on the southern coast of Palestine. The city gates at that time had a tunnel-like opening that was flanked by guardrooms. Samson was able to escape the ambush at the gate by leaving at an unexpected time when the men were waiting in the guardrooms, since they did not expect Samson to leave until the morning. The distance from Gaza to Hebron is about 38 miles and uphill.

Samson now falls in love with Delilah. This episode (vv. 4-22) is a series of stereotyped scenes in which Samson is shown as so infatuated with Delilah that his behavior is ridiculous and abnormal. A strong element of magic runs through the episode. First of all, the Philistines appear to believe that some magical or supernatural force gives Samson his strength (v. 5). Samson's first three explanations of his strength are also based on magical ideas (vv. 6-14). Bowstrings (v. 7) were made from the tendons of slaughtered animals; hence, once again Samson disregards the nazirite rule by coming into contact with part of a corpse. Finally, the fourth time that Samson gives the explanation for his strength he tells the truth (vv. 15-17). This is the first time that Samson's strength is presented as something permanent and residing in his unshorn hair. In the other stories his strength is given only on specific occasions as a gift of the spirit of the Lord (14:6, 19; 15:14). The story in 16:1-3, however, presumes some kind of permanent strength, as does 15:8. The ominous note in verse 22 prepares for verses 28-30, where Samson's strength is again the result of a gift of the Lord. One can see the tension between the older stories about Samson's extraordinary strength and the later editor's theological explanation of his strength as a gift of the Lord for the deliverance of Israel. Samson is unable to escape after his hair has been cut off (v. 20) because the Lord has left him. The final breaking of the nazirite rule—once too often—occurs with the shaving of Samson's head.

Perhaps the reason that the death episode

(vv. 23-31) was added was to show that though Samson had squandered away his strength out of his own self-interest, in the end he turned to the Lord (v. 28) and died honorably by bringing about God's justice on the Philistines. Dagon (v. 23) was an ancient agricultural deity of the West Semitic world. In the Bible he appears exclusively as a Philistine deity. Dagon means "grain." The number three thousand in verse 27 seems an exaggeration, and was probably the editor's intention in view of the statement in verse 30.

The chapter concludes (v. 31) by repeating the length of time that Samson judged Israel (see 15:20). No reference is made to any peace in the land, since the editor realized that Samson's exploits were only the beginning of the deliverance from the Philistines.

PART III: APPENDIX

Judg 17:1–21:25

The appendix to the Book of Judges contains two episodes that have been placed here because they deal with the period before the monarchy: the migration of Dan to the north (17:1–18:31); and the civil war against Benjamin (19:1–21:25).

The statement, "In those days there was no king in Israel; everyone did what he thought best," appears at the beginning (17:6) and at the end of the appendix (21:25). In both 18:1 and 19:1 there is the reminder that "at that time there was no king in Israel." These are really pro-monarchy statements that the editor has inserted because he did not see the events narrated in these chapters as commendable. They could only have happened because there was no king in the land. The editor saw the monarchy as a necessary stabilizing factor in Israel.

17:1–18:31 The migration of Dan. The purpose of these two chapters is not merely to report on the history of the tribe of Dan, but to give information about the origins and nature of the sanctuary of Dan. This sanctuary had become important in 922 B.C.E., when the northern tribes had broken off from the southern tribes and formed the kingdom of Israel. As a result of this break, the sanctuary at Dan had become the national sanctuary of the northern kingdom along with the sanctuary at Bethel. The priests in Jerusalem frowned upon the Yahweh cult at the sanctuary of Dan. These two chapters argue against this sanctuary by pointing out that its cult there represented a merger of disparate worshipers, and that the silver used for making the sacred object kept there derived from stolen money. The priesthood there, although having a noble lineage, is also shown as having been compromised.

Chapter 17 is a background for the events in chapter 18. Note that the carved idol (vv. 3-4) is an idol of Yahweh, something that is strictly forbidden by the Mosaic law (see Exod 20:4-6). Micah also makes an ephod (see 8:24-27) and household idols, i.e., items used for divining (v. 5). In the beginning he makes one of his sons the priest, i.e., one who took care of the sanctuary and gave oracles.

A young Levite from Bethlehem comes looking for a better situation, and Micah convinces him to be his priest (vv. 7-13). Micah's concern to have a Levite priest suggests that Levites were already known for being more skilled in cultic matters. The title "father" (v. 10) emphasizes the priest's role as cultic diviner and oracle giver.

Chapter 18 begins by stating that the Danites were searching for an area in which to live, since they had received no heritage among the tribes of Israel (v. 1). This statement is difficult to accept in light of Josh 19:40-48. They had been allotted territory to the west of Benjamin and south of Ephraim and north of Judah. However, they were so restricted by the Amorites and Philistines (see 1:34) that they could not control their territory, so they sent out scouts to look for a better district. Zorah and Eshtaol (v. 2) are cities from the old Danite territory that were encountered in the Samson stories. The scouts probably recognized the Levite by his accent as coming from the south (v. 3). One of the primary roles of the priest was to consult God on behalf of the people (v. 5). The priest's favorable response will be used later to justify the conquest of Laish and the slaughter of its inhabitants (v. 10).

Laish (v. 7) was a city at the northern extremity of the land, near the sources of the Jordan River. The place is rich in resources, and the people, quiet and trusting, live in an unwalled city. The statement that the people lived "after the manner of the Sidonians" seems to indicate that the city followed Phoenician customs. The scouts justify their recommendation to attack the city by saying that God has given it into their power (vv. 8-10 and see v. 6). "Mahaneh-dan" (v. 12) means "camp of Dan."

The Danites put their little ones, their livestock, and their goods at the head of the column (v. 21) because they expect to be attacked from the rear as soon as Micah discovers that they have stolen his idols and priest. Micah does chase after them but, when he discovers how strong a force they are, he returns home (vv. 22-26).

The slaughter of the people of Laish (v. 27) is unjustifiable. What sin has led to! The Danites rebuild the city, name it after their ancestor, and set up the carved idol that was Micah's (vv. 28-30). In verse 30 the Levite suddenly has a name, Jonathan, son of Gershom, son of Moses. The "time of the captivity of the land" (v. 30) refers to the year 734 B.C.E., when northern Palestine came under the Assyrians and the temple at Dan was destroyed. Verse 31 mentions that the Danites had preserved their sanctuary at Dan during the same time that the real house of God was at Shiloh (v. 31).

19:1–21:25 Civil war against Benjamin. These three chapters are made up of a number of originally independent narratives that have been skillfully combined into a continuous story. They present another example of how things could go wrong because "in those days there was no king in Israel; everyone did what he thought best" (21:25). A hideous crime is committed, and Israel so overreacts to it that they bring on a full-scale civil war.

These chapters fall into three scenes: the episode with the Levite and his concubine (19:1-30); the assembly of Israel and the resultant war against Benjamin (20:1-48); and the getting of wives for the surviving Benjaminites (21:1-25).

19:1-30 The Levite and his concubine. The story of the Levite who goes to Bethlehem to retrieve his wife, and who then suffers a gross indignity on his return, is told to explain why war breaks out between Benjamin and the other tribes of Israel. The story is full of dramatic irony: the father-in-law's hospitality so delays the Levite's return that he cannot make the trip back home in one day; had he stopped in Jebus, the Canaanite city, he would have avoided the outrage; he is offered hospitality in Gibeah, not by a Benjaminite but by another sojourner.

That the man is a Levite is not important for the purpose of the story. Though the editor identifies "Jebus" as "Jerusalem" (v. 10), Jerusalem, in fact, never bore that name. Perhaps Jebus was a suburb of Jerusalem. At this time Jerusalem was still a Canaanite city. Gibeah was about three miles north of Jerusalem, and Ramah was about two miles further north.

Entering Gibeah, the Levite receives no offers of hospitality from the Benjaminites there, but is taken in by another stranger, an old man who, like the Levite, also came from the mountain region of Ephraim. The old man shows the Levite the same hospitality that his father-in-law had shown him in Bethlehem. The verb "abuse" in verse 22 is an attempt to translate the Hebrew verb that means "to know," a verb used euphemistically in the Old Testament to denote sexual intercourse. It is used here in a deliberately ambiguous way.

The gruesome act of cutting up the dead woman and sending pieces of her to all the tribes serves the purpose of arousing the tribes against Gibeah for the outrage they have committed (see 1 Sam 11:7). The implication is that the tribes must help the Levite take revenge on Gibeah or suffer a like fate.

20:1-48 War against Benjamin. In response to the call of the Levite the Israelites gather at Mizpah, about eight miles north of Jerusalem (vv. 1-2). "Dan to Beer-sheba" is a phrase that represents the northern and southern boundaries of ancient Israel. The Israelites on the eastern side of the Jordan River (land of Gilead) also come to the assembly. The size of the armies (vv. 8-10) is exaggerated. Perhaps the Hebrew word for "thousand" refers to a particular military grouping or contingent, as we saw in the Book of Joshua.

In verse 16 the narrator seems to suggest that one reason why the Benjaminites will endure and be able to inflict great losses on the Israelites is because of the seven hundred sharpshooters. The Israelites go over to Bethel, a few miles away, to consult the Lord on who should attack first. The lot falls to Judah (vv. 17-19).

The first two attacks against Gibeah are repulsed, and the Israelites suffer some significant losses (vv. 20-25). After the second loss the Israelites consult the Lord, they fast, and offer holocausts and peace offerings (vv. 26-27). This time they are told that they will be successful because the Lord will deliver the Benjaminites into their power (v. 28).

Verses 29-43 are two accounts, clumsily combined, of the same event. The account in verses 29-36 describes more the field tactics of the troops, while the account in verses 37-43 describes the victory from the perspective of the successful ambush. Both have a resemblance to the capture of Ai in Josh 8. Notice that in verse 35 it is the Lord who defeats Benjamin. Verses 44-48 give the statistics on the fallen. In the end there remain only six hundred, who escape to the rock Rimmon (v. 47). The location of Rimmon is unknown. Though the tradition of war against Benjamin may be early, the story as we have it here has been revised to make it fit. The original tradition probably dealt with a war between Benjamin and its northern neighbor, Ephraim. It is unlikely that such a near obliteration of a tribe ever occurred.

21:1-25 Wives for the Benjaminites. Having almost wiped out an entire tribe, the Israelites realize that if that tribe is going to survive they must obtain wives for the six hundred male survivors. This chapter presents two accounts of how they obtained wives. The separate accounts have been harmonized by the explanation that each stratagem provided only a partial solution to the problem (v. 14).

The first account (vv. 1-14) states the underlying problem, namely, that at Mizpah the men of Israel had sworn that none of them would give their daughters in marriage to anyone from Benjamin (v. 1). The solution that they eventually hit upon was to see if anyone had not come up for the assembly, since a solemn oath had been taken that anyone who did not come up would be put to death (vv. 2-5). Jabesh-gilead was east of the Jordan.

The second stratagem has parallels in Roman and Greek folklore (vv. 15-23). The elders remember the yearly feast at Shiloh when the girls of Shiloh came out to dance. Each Benjaminite is told to seize one of them for a wife. The elders promise to intercede for the Benjaminites when the fathers or brothers of the girls complain. Because they have been stolen from them, not given to the Benjaminites, the men of Shiloh will not be guilty of breaking their vow not to give their daughters in marriage to a Benjaminite (v. 22). The great assembly, called in 20:1, is now dispersed and the Israelites return to their own heritage (v. 24).

The narrator concludes by saying again that all these sad goings-on took place because "in those days there was no king in Israel; everyone did what he thought best" (v. 25). Israel's history of sin has begun. Eventually that sinfulness will lead to the destruction of the northern kingdom of Israel in the eighth century and the destruction of the southern kingdom of Judah in the sixth century. However, the book has pointed out more than once not only the saving power of the Lord, but also the Lord's will to save the Israelites when they cry out to the Lord.

1 AND 2 SAMUEL

Paula J. Bowes

INTRODUCTION

1 and 2 Samuel were originally one book, as were 1 and 2 Kings and 1 and 2 Chronicles. These were divided into two in the Greek translation of the Hebrew Bible known as the Septuagint, from which early translations into Latin and English were made. The Books of Samuel are the centerpiece of a larger collection of narratives which span Israel's history from their entrance into Canaan in about the twelfth century B.C.E. to the Babylonian Captivity (587–586 B.C.E.). This Deuteronomistic History, so called because the writers based their theology on the teachings of the Book of Deuteronomy, was compiled about the seventh century B.C.E. Its basic message was that God has chosen Israel as a special people and has through Moses redeemed them from slavery in Egypt and made with them a covenant on Mount Sinai. God's word which came to Israel through Moses continues to guide and correct the people as well as their kings through the prophets. If they are faithful to the covenantal laws, they will have prosperity and peace; if they disobey, they can expect punishment through natural disasters, invasion, and even exile. They should therefore, out of loyalty and gratitude, keep the commandments of the Lord who has shown them so much favor and grace. The Books of Samuel, then, are not history in the modern sense but theological history—narrative accounts of God's dealings with the chosen people.

The protagonists

Personalities are important in these books, especially three: Samuel, the prophet of their title; and the first two kings of Israel, Saul and David, whom Samuel anointed as king. The account of the miraculous birth of Samuel, so like other portentous births in the history of Israel, sets the tone for the whole. God has intervened to bring another savior in answer to Israel's need for the Word of God. Like most of Scripture, the Books of Samuel tell of God's care and correction of this special people, and of God's justice and mercy toward them.

Disasters and deliverance

It is noteworthy that the deliverance which comes to Israel at the beginning of Samuel's prophetic mission is accompanied by the ruin of the priestly house of Eli and the loss of Israel's most precious possession, the ark of the covenant, the sign of God's dwelling among them (1 Sam 2–4). Out of this national disaster, it is God who is portrayed as causing the Philistines to return the ark (1 Sam 6). Samuel's covenant with the Lord at Mizpah (ch. 7) would seem to bring satisfaction to the people, but they still fear the Philistines enough to ask for a human king like other nations. In Num 11, God answered the people's demand for meat with quail until they were sick of it. Here God gives them what they want despite the disadvantages of a human king and their rejection of the divine. Over Samuel's objections, God commands the prophet to anoint Saul, with the implicit expectation that the king will always be under prophetic direction and required to obey the Mosaic law.

Israel gets a king

The first king, Saul, although gifted and acceptable to the Israelites, proves to be unacceptable to the Lord, who then determines to try again with a man after God's own heart, David (1 Sam 13:13-14). There now ensues the puzzling situation (for us) of two anointed kings, one of whom is in hot pursuit of the other lest his throne be taken from him. Throughout Saul's persecution of David, the fugitive receives help from various quarters, even from Saul's own children, Jonathan and Michal.

A few years later Saul's career comes to its end in a disastrous battle with the Philistines (1 Sam 31). David is eventually made king, first by the Judahites (2 Sam 2:11) and then, at the death of Saul's last eligible heir, by the Israelites (2 Sam 5). This separate anointing by the two major factions in Israel shows the religious and political division that was to last as long as the monarchy, that is, until 586 B.C.E., when Jerusalem was sacked by the Babylonians.

David's rise

The period from Samuel's first anointing of David (1 Sam 16) until his actual enthronement over both houses of Israel (2 Sam 5) is usually designated as the account of David's rise. Just as Samuel's rise at the beginning of the First Book of Samuel was concomitant with the downfall of the Elides, so David's rise is concurrent with Saul's demise. The Second Book of Samuel contains the accounts of David's accession (ch. 5), his bringing the ark of the covenant to Jerusalem (ch. 6), the promise of a lasting succession (ch. 7), and the engrossing story of David's life as king (chs. 9–20).

The peaceful kingdom and the troubled family

Much like Adam's peaceful life in the Garden of Eden (Gen 2), David finds himself with his enemies subdued on all sides (2 Sam 7:1) and a prosperous and enlarged kingdom (2 Sam 8). As did Adam, David disobeys God's word, bringing unexpected sorrows. True to Nathan's prophecy in 2 Sam 12, a sword will always trouble David's house, for four of his sons will die untimely and violent deaths. These trials chapters 9 to 20 recount for us in dramatic realism. The use of dialogue to portray character and move the action forward provides some of the most fascinating reading in the whole Bible.

Although the unknown author uses techniques of the novel in his writing, these accounts are not products of his imagination. They show, by vivid stories, that God works with human freedom, caring for the people with a love that continually forgives and saves.

OUTLINE OF THE BOOKS OF SAMUEL

1 Sam 1–3	Part I: Samuel and the House of Eli
1 Sam 4–7	Part II: The Ark of the Covenant
1 Sam 8–15	Part III: Saul, the First King
1 Sam 16–31	Part IV: Saul and David
2 Sam 1–8	Part V: The Struggle for the Kingdom
2 Sam 9–20	Part VI: David the King
2 Sam 21–24	Part VII: Appendices

COMMENTARY: 1 SAMUEL

I. SAMUEL AND THE HOUSE OF ELI

1 Sam 1–3

The First Book of Samuel opens with a double need: the longing of Hannah for a son and the counterpart, Israel's spiritual need for the word of God. This word of the Lord, so necessary for Israel's life, is, according to the Deuteronomistic tradition, Israel's greatest blessing, just as the greatest blessing of a woman in Israel is a child. Israel's need is not disclosed until readers have first savored Hannah's suffering. Understanding this will prepare them to appreciate the magnanimity of the Lord in supplying both needs.

1:1-8 Hannah asks for a son. As is true for other birth announcements in the Bible, this one begins with a short genealogy of Hannah's husband Elkanah (compare Manoah's in Judg 13 and Joseph's in Matt 1). None of these is the protagonist; instead their wives carry the action. Here the barren, despised (by all but Elkanah) wife Hannah is set over against her fertile and scornful rival Peninnah. Just so did Hagar gloat over Sarah (Gen 16:4) and Leah struggle with Rachel (Gen 30).

Another characteristic of biblical birth narratives is the portrayal of the particular child's parents as devout and observant of the commandments of the Lord (1 Sam 1:3; Luke 1:5-6). Elkanah's and Hannah's yearly pilgrimages and sacrifice show them to be worthy parents of a specially favored son, Samuel.

Mentioned also in verse 3 are Eli and his sons Hophni and Phinehas, all priests at the shrine in Shiloh, the center for Yahweh worship before the city was taken by the Philistines (see ch. 4). Although Eli's sons do not yet figure in the story, their presence early in the narrative suggests a connection between Hannah and the larger problems of Israel.

While she bears her reproach, not even Elkanah's patient, loving attempts to comfort Hannah can stop her from weeping and being unable to eat. From these depths, the action can only rise, in hope of change and relief.

1:9-19a Hannah prays for the Lord's gift. The biblical author has described what happens in this family year after year. Now he narrows to a particular day in Shiloh. Eli, from his seat by the door of the temple, observes the distraught Hannah at prayer. She bargains: if she is given a son, she will consecrate him to the Lord as a nazirite. Such a vow entailed abstinence from wine, strong drink, the cutting of the hair and contact with a dead body (see Num 6; Amos 2:11-12). Samson (Judg 13–16) was under this vow, but in his case the angel announcing his birth, not his mother, required it. Hannah offers this condition of her own accord, showing considerable renunciation, since the child would be with her only three years.

It is ironic that abstinence from drink is what Hannah offers, while it is drunkenness that Eli suspects from her movements. Once Hannah is able to satisfy Eli that such is not the case, Eli endorses her request. Since he has not heard any words, he does not know that, in effect, he asks for the one who will replace him in the priesthood. After the prayers of Eli and Hannah, there is a noticeable change in the latter. Now she no longer weeps but can eat and drink (v. 18)!

1:19b-28 Samuel is born. When Hannah bears her son, she names him Samuel, explaining that she had asked him of the Lord. The name Samuel however means "he who is from God" and not "asked." The name Saul would be closer to that. This kind of ambivalence is not unusual for biblical names.

Elkanah is characteristically kind in excusing Hannah from the next three pilgrimages until Samuel is weaned. The parents' concern for the worship of the Lord is underlined by its prominence in the story and in the generous details of offerings and customs at that time (eleventh century B.C.E.).

When she at last brings Samuel to the temple, it is natural for Hannah to let Eli know that her prayer has been answered, since he had supported it (see Judg 13 and Matt 1). The key words: "ask," "give," and "pray," repeated in 1 Sam 1:17-28; 2:1, give evidence of divine answer to persistent prayer. Hannah little suspects that the boy Samuel will supply not only her need to be a mother but also Israel's need for a prophet to bring the people the word of the Lord.

2:1-10 Hannah's song. The canticle the biblical author has put into Hannah's mouth finds a counterpart in the New Testament in Mary's Magnificat (Luke 1:46-55). Both hymns express joy at the birth of a special child; both praise God's power, holiness, and salvation. In both the proud rich are cast down and the humble poor are raised up. Hannah's poem reminds of God's justice; Mary's of God's mercy. The Magnificat only hints at enemies, but Hannah's song begins and ends with their discomfiture and derision (vv. 1,10).

In this poem the Lord is seen as holy, omnipotent, omniscient, and in control of all the life events of all creatures. There are strong contrasts between the hungry and the well-fed, the barren and the fertile, the faithful and the wicked. The theme of the Lord's protection of the people, including the foreshadowed king and anointed one of verse 10, pervades the section.

2:11-21 The sins of Eli's sons and the blessings of Samuel. In these verses the approved service of Samuel, even from childhood, is contrasted with the profligacy of Eli's sons. They are characterized as worthless fellows (literally "sons of Belial"), the same designation Hannah hoped Eli would not level against her in 1:16. The summary indictment against Hophni and Phinehas is that they did not know the Lord, a knowledge which meant experience of and obedience to God.

Normally, Israelite priests were allotted portions of the sacrificial animal, in particular the breast and right leg (Lev 7:29-36). But Eli's sons demanded their share before the ritual burning of the fat had taken place, and even before the meat had been cooked—hardly the dignified control one would expect of priests.

The story of their cultic irreverence is immediately followed by the idyllic picture of the boy Samuel wearing the ephod, a foreshadowing of his future role. Eli's grateful blessing to Samuel's parents results in the birth of five more children, God's most welcome gift to the Israelite (see Gen 18:13-14; 21:5-8; Ruth 4:11-15).

2:22-26 Eli rebukes his sons. In remonstrating with his sons, Eli asks the question David will fail to ask his son Adonijah when the latter declares himself king in his father's lifetime: "Why have you done these things?" (1 Kgs 1:6). Intercession can be made for their fornications, but their sins against the Lord, those connected with the sacred sacrifice, have no mediator. Eli warns to no avail, but Hophni and Phinehas cannot cry ignorance. Because they refused to obey their father, the author lets us know they deserved their punishment, since the Lord had decided on their death. Verse 26 underlines again the contrast between Eli's unfaithful sons and Samuel, who as he grows earns the approval of both the people and the Lord (see Luke 2:52).

2:27-36 The prophecy against Eli's house. The accusation by the man of God begins in the traditional prophetic pattern of recalling the Lord's former benefits to the accused, listing their duties, their transgression, and finally their punishment. Eli is implicated along with his sons in verse 29 for enjoying the spoils which they had seized. The heart of the matter is that he had preferred his sons to the Lord. Therefore, their office as priests is for the most part cancelled, and those who do minister will have a miserable existence, begging for some employment which will bring them a stipend.

Nathan's encounter with David (2 Sam 12) after his adultery with Bathsheba and the murder of Uriah, has several parallels here. For both Eli and David, the punishment will be worked out within their families. Like Hophni and Phinehas, David's son by Bathsheba will die (2 Sam 12:19; 1 Sam 2:34), but, unlike Eli, David is forgiven and allowed to continue as king (2 Sam 12:13). The key to the different treatments of Eli and David may lie in 2:25, which states that sins against the Lord have no intercessor. While David's sin was against Uriah, Eli's sons have sinned directly against the Lord by profaning divine worship. Therefore David's kingship remains, but the priesthood of the Elides is replaced. The new priest, who will do what is in God's heart and mind, will have a sure house and will minister before the Lord's anointed (1 Sam 2:35). The prophecy is fluid enough to include as the faithful priest (the same adjective in Hebrew as that for "sure" house) Samuel, the anointed king Saul, Zadok, David or even the Messiah, whose name means "the anointed one."

3:1-18 Samuel's call. The prophecy which removed Eli and his house from the priesthood is not immediately implemented. Samuel was in training and not yet aware of his future role. Although at this time direct word from the Lord was rare, Israel longed for her God as much as Hannah longed for a son. The Lord now moves to remedy this just as Hannah's barrenness was reversed, both through the instrumentality of Samuel.

The picture of Eli asleep and practically blind describes Israel's state in relation to the Lord. The lamp of God, that is, God's word, is almost extinguished through the unworthiness of the officiating priests. The Lord ignores Eli and calls directly to the boy Samuel to receive this divine word. There is humor in Samuel's naive running to Eli three times before the old priest realizes that it is the Lord calling. The fourth call brings Samuel's willing response, "Here I am," the same made by Abraham when the Lord called him to sacrifice Isaac (Gen 22:1-2). Samuel's readiness contrasts with the priests' unwillingness to hear (1 Sam 2:25). Samuel is the faithful, chosen priest who will soon replace the unfaithful and rejected house of Eli. Later a similar drama will be played out between the rejected first king of Israel, Saul, and the chosen king David.

The chapter begins with the notice that visions from the Lord were few and ends with Samuel receiving frequent revelations at Shiloh. In between, Eli and Samuel speak to each other twice (vv. 4-9, 16-18). The center of the chapter is given to the Lord's words to Samuel alone (vv. 10-14). The Lord says nothing about Samuel's future but concentrates on the condemnation of Eli's house, adding that there is no chance for expiation. Eli's resignation under this sentence is an exemplary acknowledgment of the divine sovereignty and justice.

When Samuel opens the doors of the temple in the morning light, he enacts the bursting forth of the word of the Lord to the people after a long silence. For Israel as for Samuel, it is to be a new day.

II. THE ARK OF THE COVENANT

1 Sam 4–7

Ever since their journeyings in the desert of Sinai, the Israelites were accompanied by the ark of the covenant, the tangible symbol of the Lord's presence dwelling among them (Exod 37:1-9). This was a gold-plated wooden box said to contain the tablets of the law given to Moses on Mount Sinai (Exod 19–20). The traditions of chapters 4–7 bridge the gap between the ministry of the Elides and the formal inauguration of Samuel as prophet. During this time leadership of Israel is centered in the ark, for despite the silence of the word, the Lord remained with Israel. Even when captured the ark works against the enemy for the good of Israel. This section of the narrative shows the Israelites, greatly disadvantaged before their Philistine enemy and attempting to use the presence of the Lord to bring them victory.

4:1-11 Israel brings the ark into battle. After their disastrous defeat at Aphek (vv. 1-2), the people of Israel look for a more efficacious defense against their most dangerous enemy, the Philistines. These "Sea Peoples" had entered Canaan from the west and had settled along the coastal plain about 1200 B.C.E. They were non-Semitic, worshipers of the grain god Dagon, and were militarily and culturally superior to the Israelites.

The usual battle strategy having failed, the Israelites send for the ark of the Lord. The Lord is described (v. 4) as seated upon cherubim, representations of winged mythological beasts which guarded pagan temples. These cherubim were positioned on the cover of the ark as emblems of God's ministering spirits. The ark's presence in the Israelite camp disappoints the Philistines but induces them to fight with extraordinary bravery out of fear that they might become slaves of Israel. Not only were thirty thousand Israelites slain (v. 10), but the ark itself is captured—an event that causes all ears to tingle when they hear of it (3:11).

4:12-22 The glory of Israel departs. With the capture of the ark, the ministry of the house of Eli comes to an end in the death of Hophni, Phinehas, and their father. The shock of loss is such that Phinehas' wife dies giving birth (v. 19). Her son, whom she names symbolically Ichabod, meaning "Where is the glory?," lives and is mentioned in 1 Sam 14:3 as the uncle of Ahijah, a priest in Saul's camp. (Giving a name from the circumstances of a child's birth is common in the Bible. Sarah's son Isaac bears such a name [Gen 21:3-6], as do the sons of Jacob [Gen 30:6-24; 35:18]. It is particularly applicable in the case of Rachel who, like Eli's daughter-in-law, dies in the distress of childbirth.)

5:1-5 The humiliation of Dagon. As a relief from the sad events of chapter 4, this account introduces a lighter note. The Israelite audience is assured that though the ark was lost, the Lord whose presence it represented has not lost divine power. Here the Philistine god Dagon is disdained in two increasingly demeaning episodes. In the first he seems to be worshipping before the ark which had been moved into his temple. In the second he is dismembered before it. We are not told if he was ever able to be mended. Such is the fate, says the story, of gods made by human hands.

5:6-12 The ark afflicts the Philistine cities. In the previous section the ark had made trouble for the god Dagon in his temple at Ashdod, one of the five principal Philistine cities. Now it makes trouble for the Philistines themselves. There is a plague of mice in Ashdod, hemorrhoids in Gath, and death in Ekron. Four times (vv. 6, 7, 9, 11) we are told that this happens because the hand of the Lord is heavy upon the Philistines. With the same repetition, this time of the Hebrew verb "to go around," the biblical author emphasizes that the ark was sent around from one city to another (vv. 8, 9, 10). In each city the suffering is escalated, as was the indignity of Dagon. There was a similar escalation during the ten plagues in Exodus 7–12 and in the pressures brought on the captors of Sarah and Rebecca before their release (Gen 12, 20, and 26). We may smile with the Israelite hearers that the Philistines were thus bested, but also that their cry of pain went up, not to Dagon, but to the God of Israel in the heavens.

6:1-9 The Philistines plan to send back the ark. In this theological narrative, the Philistines implement their desire to send back the ark. After consulting their advisors, they let the direction taken by the calfless cows point to the originator of their plagues. The normal response would be for the cows to return to their calves. But if they head toward the Israelite border, it would mean that it was the Lord who had brought their troubles upon them.

The Philistines know enough Israelite history to see a parallel between this event and the plagues brought on the Egyptians before the Exodus, and they are determined not to repeat the Pharaoh's stubbornness nor its consequences. In a kind of sympathetic magic, they shape their conciliatory gifts of gold into five hemorrhoids and five mice, one for each of their cities. With the departure of the symbols of their plagues, they hope to eliminate them from their land.

6:10-18 The ark returns; some unexpected consequences. The cows hitched to the ark perform in exemplary manner as if leading a procession to Beth-shemesh, probably the Israelite town nearest to Ekron, where the ark was last kept. The Israelites rejoice to see it and celebrate by offering a sacrifice, much as Elisha will sacrifice his oxen, using the plowing equipment for the fire (1 Kgs 19:19-21). As often happens, a large stone marks the place of the sacrifice and of the divine intervention.

6:19-21 Trouble for Israel. The ark's homecoming is marred by the death of seventy who failed to greet it and thereby committed a sin of irreverence (compare Uzzah's plight in 2 Sam 6:6-8). The Lord's power and holiness represented in the ark become as frightening to the Israelites as they had been to the Philistines. Without divulging their reason, the people of Beth-shemesh send word to the inhabitants of Kiriath-jearim, about eight miles north of Jerusalem, to come for the ark. The chapter ends as it began with the ark, unwelcome to both Philistines and the Lord's own people.

7:1-6 Samuel begins his ministry. Except for the ark's transfer to Jerusalem in 2 Sam 6, the story of the ark concludes with verse 2. Despite its doubtful welcome and the absence of a fitting shrine as had existed in Shiloh, the Israelites are satisfied that it is at least in their own land once more. Its stay in Kiriath-jearim has positive results, for verse 3 tells of the people's desire to return to the Lord. Twenty years later, they are willing to affirm this publicly before Samuel at Mizpah, probably the site north of Jerusalem. (The scene is reminiscent of Jacob at Bethel [Gen 35:1-7] where the Lord asked him to make an altar. There as here the putting away of all foreign gods was required.) Samuel explicitly mentions Baals and Ashtaroth, fertility objects used in idolatrous worship.

The Israelites express their submission in a ceremony of atonement, which involved the pouring of water, fasting, and the confession of sin. Samuel's leadership in this inaugurates his active ministry in Israel. Hophni and Phinehas were priests who had no knowledge of the Lord (2:12). Now Samuel comes in their place as priest and judge, in that knowledge, and through him Israel receives blessing and victory.

7:7-17 Samuel's leadership. The gathering of Israel at Mizpah was for religious purposes, but the Philistines use it for a military confrontation. Once again Samuel intercedes, and before it is necessary to fight, the Philistines are routed by their own fear of thunder. Israel seizes the opportunity to pursue. The victory is credited to the Lord and duly marked by Samuel with a stone. This "stone of help" (Ebenezer) is not the same as in 4:1, though both show the Lord as helping Israel, the one through the ark, the other through Samuel's intercession.

The presence of Samuel now replaces that of the ark. While among the Philistines, the ark went around their cities; now it is Samuel who goes around judging in the four cities mentioned.

For now, the Philistines are no longer a threat to Israel. David will have to fight them later (chs. 17, 23 and 2 Sam 5:17-25), but at this point the cities which the ark had visited come under Israelite control.

In building an altar to the Lord, Samuel is in the tradition of Noah (Gen 8:20), Abraham (Gen 12:7; 22:9), Isaac (Gen 26:25), Jacob (Gen 35:7), Moses (Exod 17:15; 24:4), Aaron (Exod 32:5), and Joshua (Josh 8:30). Samuel is a prophet like Moses, and like Joshua, is both priest and judge. He is the only biblical figure who is priest, prophet, and judge. After him the priestly and prophetic callings begin to separate. However, even Samuel, with the fullness of authority and charism, does not satisfy the people, who long to be like other nations led by a king.

III. SAUL, THE FIRST KING

1 Sam 8–15

These chapters recount the turbulent change from the rule of leaders like Samuel to that of a king. With the loss of the ark and the ever-present threat of the Philistines as background, the Israelites increasingly see a solution to their weakness in the establishment of the monarchy. Samuel resists at first, but at the Lord's command, he anoints Saul (8:22). After being chosen by lot (10:21) and defeating the Ammonites, Saul is officially inaugurated at Gilgal (11:15). In a negative vein, Samuel warns the people of a king's prerogatives (ch. 12). Monarchy may bring advantages, but they must be ready for side effects.

Samuel's warning finds a certain fulfillment in the Lord's later rejection of Israel's first anointed king. Saul fails, the text indicates, because he disobeyed the word of the Lord mediated to him through the prophet Samuel (chs. 13 and 15). Neither extenuating circumstances nor zeal for the worship of the Lord can overrule this crucial test of obedience to the word, for the king as well as every Israelite.

8:1-5 The people demand a king. The Hebrew text uses the noun or verb for the making of a king a dozen times in this chapter, with the word "judge" a close second. Kingship is about to replace the old system of governing in Israel. Up to this time, charismatic heroes sent by the Lord had led the people in battle against their enemies. Now, instead of praying for a new judge, the people ask Samuel to appoint a king.

8:6-22 The price of kingship. Hardly flattered by this request, Samuel is angry on behalf of the Lord whom he recognizes as the true and only king of Israel. In the revealing conversation between Samuel and the Lord, Samuel is faced with the reality of a people who have been continuously disloyal despite great favors. Verse 8 is encapsuled in a double command to Samuel to obey the people. After Samuel outlines for them what their king will do, the command of verses 7 and 9 is repeated a third time in verse 22. If the sons of Samuel *took* bribes, the king will *take* everything they value including their liberty (vv. 11, 13, 14-17).

The warning is not heeded despite the reminder that there is no way back (v. 18), for once the king is installed, it will be useless to complain. Sometimes God gives us that for which we ask before we know whether or not we really want it.

Verses 11-17 may have been written in hindsight, after the Israelites had learned all too well what it meant to have a king. The description is of a well-established, flourishing kingdom, hardly comparable to Saul's early and simple reign.

9:1-2 Saul is introduced. Twice we are told that Saul is a Benjaminite from the north in contrast to David whose origins are in Judah in the south. This distinction will mean more as the story unfolds. Saul's entrance into it is auspicious. He is handsome, taller than most, and the son of a man of substance. "Handsome" and "stalwart" are also used to describe David (16:18), whose ancestor Boaz was also a man of substance (Ruth 2:1). In the Books of Samuel there are a number of beautiful or handsome people: David, Bathsheba, Amnon, Absalom and Adonijah, but more often than not they come to an unhappy end (see 2 Sam 11, 13; 1 Kgs 1–2). The author seems to warn that such external gifts do not necessarily indicate divine approval and that they can be a source of pride and disobedience to the law. It is not the externals that God approves, but what is in the heart (16:7).

9:3-10 The unsuccessful search. Here we see Saul in action. He is an obedient son, diligently seeking his father's lost asses. Saul and his servant go through four different regions in their wide-ranging but fruitless search. Just as they are ready to give it up, the servant's suggestion leads them to the man of God in Zuph. It is not revealed until verse 14 that the man of God is Samuel. In the discussion whether and how to go to the man of God and what gift to bring for the advice about the asses (vv. 3-10), the verb "go" is used in Hebrew eleven times. The action verbs convey the intensity of the search.

9:11-13 Samuel presides over the sacrifice. Now the verbs change from going to going up, showing that Saul and his servant must not only climb to reach the city but, once within it, they will go up again to the high place where the seer was to officiate at the sacrifice. The high place here is a place of worship of the Lord, but later such places were condemned for idolatrous worship (Jer 2:20; 3:6).

Instead of "man of God," they ask for the seer, that is, one who sees more perceptively either the present or the future. The narrator interjects the information that at his time of writing the proper epithet for both was "prophet" (v. 9).

Verse 13 is important for not only does it include all the action words of the chapter: go, go up, find, eat (three times) and call or invite, but it contains the carefully stated prohibition against eating until Samuel comes and blesses the sacrifice. Knowing this will help the reader understand the significance of Saul's failure to wait for Samuel's arrival in chapter 13. Also, the mention of invited guests implies that the sacrifice was not a public ceremony but by invitation only. The girls who give directions do not seem to be participants.

9:14-25 Samuel and Saul meet. In the revelation in which the Lord prepares Samuel for the arrival of Saul, the word "king" is never used. Saul is to be a military commander who will rescue Israel from the Philistines. Though this had not been the practice with the judges, Samuel is instructed to anoint Saul. This anointing and the special portion Saul is given to eat (vv. 23-24) are indications of the religious character of the newly instituted monarchy.

Without knowing what is ahead of him and before he is anointed, Saul finds himself the guest of honor at Samuel's banquet. Saul objects humbly to Samuel's praise, insisting, as had Gideon, that his family is the least of his tribe (Judg 6:15). Samuel promises to tell all that is in Saul's heart. With this prophetic backing, Saul begins a process of self-discovery as the Lord makes his will known to Samuel. In view of the previous revelation to Samuel that Israel had rejected the Lord in favor of a king (8:7), it is pure irony for Samuel to describe Saul as one ardently desired by Israel (9:20). Both Samuel and Saul in their different roles answer a need of Israel, one for a prophet and the other for a king. Which one will be the real leader of Israel?

9:26-27 After the feast. It is a surprise that the anointing is not public. If all Israel awaited a king, why this secrecy? It may be a way of reminding the people that the Lord works in his own time and in his own hidden way.

10:1-8 The signs of Saul's anointing. Samuel provides Saul with three signs to confirm his anointing as Israel's commander. Each occurs in a different place and each answers a future need of Saul. The first is at Zelzah, a name derived from the Hebrew verb "to rush upon." The verb appears twice in this chapter and refers to the spirit's rushing upon Saul (vv. 6, 10). This sign points to the location of the asses and to Saul's life-work as well. The second sign, the provision of kids, bread and wine, supplies the sustenance for his task. Because the gifts are consecrated as offerings to God, they indicate divine approval. The third sign connects Saul's kingship with the gift of the spirit and the ability to prophesy. The existence of a Philistine garrison (v. 5) at Gibeath-elohim recalls Samuel's prediction (9:16) that Saul will save Israel from this troublesome enemy.

Despite the positive signs, that is, Saul's change into another man and Samuel's promise that the Lord is with him (vv. 6-7), Saul is to undergo an immediate test: he must wait for Samuel for seven days in Gilgal, and then the prophet will tell him what to do. From the beginning Saul is "another man," but he is not his own man.

10:9-13 Saul as prophet. It is easy to see that Saul's prophetic abilities do not win him the respect accorded to Samuel. At this time prophecy was a more common phenomenon in Israel than would be the case later. The early prophets traveled in bands headed by their "father" (v. 12) and were given to ecstatic states often brought on by music (v. 5). (Elijah and Elisha [1 Kgs 17–21; 2 Kgs 1–9] were of this sort.) Saul's experience here foreshadows a similar event in 1 Sam 19:22-24.

10:14-16 Saul's silence. Was it natural modesty that caused Saul to omit the news of his anointing when his uncle questioned him? Or was it that Saul needed the ratification of his kingship by the people before it could be made public? In any case ratification does take place later at Mizpah (vv. 20-24). Much the same will happen in the case of David who will be anointed by Samuel (16:1-13) long before he becomes king over Judah (2 Sam 2:4). A future king of Israel, Jehu, will also be anointed years before he ascends the throne (2 Kgs 9–10). Saul did not in fact become king until after he had proven himself victorious over the Philistines.

10:17-27 Saul is chosen by lot. As happened in 7:5, Samuel once again calls all Israel together at Mizpah for the formal selection of the new king by lot. The Lord's message begins like a treaty between a lord and his vassal, recalling the good the Lord had done for the people in the past. Although the Lord had delivered them from oppressors, the people have rejected the divine king in favor of a human king. Samuel's tone is one of rebuke and chastisement rather than rejoicing over an awaited gift. The choice of Saul proceeds in the manner of an inquisition. Again and again little embarrassments cloud the accession of Saul, hinting that all was not well with his kingship from the start.

In answer to the people's cries in the desert, God had given both quail and manna (Num 17). Eating the quail answered the people's desire for meat but brought them death. Manna was God's answer to their need for food; they soon tired of it, but it kept them alive. In like manner, Saul was what the people wanted but he failed as king. The worthless fellows' question whether Saul could save them will be answered by Saul's deliverance of the men of Jabesh (11:9).

11:1-11 The challenge of the Ammonites. These were ancient and troublesome neighbors of Israel who settled along the northeastern shore of the Dead Sea. Nahash's answer to the request for a treaty with Jabesh is cruel, especially to modern ears. While it terrifies all who hear it, Saul's response would be equally abhorrent today. What is interesting is that Saul, anointed king, has no knowledge of the event because he has been plowing (!) and must be informed by the people. Only then does the spirit rush upon him and impel him to military action.

Saul's gory call to arms carries with it a terrifying threat of punishment, bringing thousands out for battle. A similar dismemberment and sending of parts to all the tribes of Israel is told in Judg 19–20, this time to punish an Israelite atrocity.

Beyond Saul's charismatic leadership, there is no special sign of divine intervention in the battle with the Ammonites (v. 11). The Jabeshites had lulled the Ammonites into expecting surrender (v. 9), a successful trick which the Israelite hearers must have reveled in. Saul's zeal brings the victory which confirms his kingship.

11:12-15 Renewal of Saul's kingship. Although the people ask Samuel to produce the men who challenged Saul's rule, it is Saul who makes the decision to pardon them. However, Samuel's initiative brings about the renewal of the kingship at Gilgal. Samuel retains his role as religious leader and kingmaker, but Saul has emerged as a triumphant military hero worthy to be king.

12:1-5 Samuel asks for an accounting. As Samuel's life comes to a close, he demands an evaluation of his ministry, an unusual event in biblical history. His list of possible infractions would make a fitting examination for any politician's career. Samuel is completely exonerated from fault. He has taken nothing, in contrast to the king who, as predicted in 8:11-18, will take everything the people value. The rule of a prophet, Samuel implies, is just, compared with that of a king.

12:6-12 A history of Israelite infidelity. His own record cleared, Samuel launches into Israel's continued ingratitude to the God who brought their ancestors out of Egypt and saved them from their enemies. Previously Israel had been given a judge in time of oppression, but now the fear of Nahash the Ammonite is great enough to make them demand the permanent rule of a king. Although Saul is now that king, Samuel still smarts under the people's rejection of the Lord as the true king of Israel. Verse 10 explicitly mentions Israel's perennial temptation: the trusting in and worship of other gods.

12:13-18 A sign of the Lord's displeasure. If the people think they can rest easily as far as obedience and worship of the Lord is concerned, they are wrong. Samuel warns them again that the Lord their God is the Lord of history with or without a human king. The king is not above the divine law. The sign of the divine sovereignty comes with Samuel's request for thunder and rain during a season when these almost never occur. The harvest is ruined; in anger the Lord has done the people's will.

12:19-25 Samuel intercedes for the people. While the people admit they have sinned in asking for a king, they cannot undo their act. When they ask Samuel to intercede with the Lord, he gives them support and encouragement but warns against idolatry. Such will be the typical message of later prophets, despite the people's infidelity. They will be punished if they do evil, but, like Samuel, the Lord will never abandon them. For their part they must fear and worship the Lord or else they will be swept away.

13:1-7 Jonathan's victory over the Philistines. After the Ammonite victory (11:11), Saul faces a far superior enemy in the Philistines. Without chariotry and cavalry his three thousand are pitifully outnumbered. The only cheerful note is Jonathan's successful attack on the Philistine garrison in Gibeah (v. 3). After it, Saul claims the victory (v. 4), causing the Philistines to renew the fight. The frightened soldiers desert in large numbers (vv. 6-7) while Saul, holding on to those who are left, awaits Samuel to preside over the sacrifice which will prepare them for the battle.

13:8-18 Saul's test. With his scattered troops deserting, there was enormous pressure on Saul to keep his army from disintegrating. Samuel's failure to arrive on time is puzzling, since delay was demoralizing the soldiers. The point has been made that the people were required to wait for the priest to sacrifice (9:13). It is then disobedience for Saul to usurp Samuel's role and offer the sacrifice himself. Saul's trust was in the "magic" of the offerings—and perhaps the strength the food would give—more than the God to whom the offerings were made and who would decide the outcome of the battle.

This was a test that the impulsive Saul failed, and the failure resulted in the loss of his kingship. Saul is a tragic figure whose story has several portents of an unhappy end. Samuel's rebuke suggests this and points to a new divine choice, a man after the Lord's own heart (v. 14). Samuel departs, leaving Saul with a decimated army to face a threefold attack from the Philistines.

13:19-23 The Philistine advantage. The Philistines controlled not only the price of sharpening tools but the manufacture of iron. The Israelites had to be content with bronze plowshares and weapons which could only be sharpened by the Philistines. If Saul and Jonathan, the only ones who possessed weapons, would attempt battle under such disadvantages, it is because victory in war was seen as belonging to the Lord. If Israel lost, the reason was that the Lord had departed from the people in anger. If they won, the Lord was with them. An important aspect of Israelite warfare in Samuel's time was the ban, which required that all the spoil taken in victory be devoted to the Lord, that is, be completely destroyed as a holocaust or sacrifice. This question of destruction of a conquered people provides a second test for Saul in chapter 15.

14:1-15 Jonathan causes a Philistine panic. The presence of Ahijah (v. 3) associates Saul's efforts with the rejected Elide priesthood. Jonathan, who dominates this chapter, is an exception to this rejection, for, in contrast to his father, nothing adverse is ever reported about him. Jonathan's faith is behind his attribution of his success to the

Lord (v. 6). The armor-bearer's loyalty recalls the loyalty the Lord had expected and not received from Saul. In this awareness of the Lord, Jonathan is like David, who will regularly inquire of the Lord before going into battle (see 23:2, 4; 30:8; 2 Sam 2:1). In Jonathan's exploit, the Philistine panic and the ensuing earthquake are clearly acts by the Lord. Jonathan's trust is a foil for the misjudgment and impulsiveness of Saul.

14:16-23 Saul leads the rout. The unnatural confusion in the Philistine camp caused by Jonathan's raid has two results advantageous for Israel: the formerly fearless Philistines begin to slay one another; and the Israelite deserters return to Saul, who again capitalizes on Jonathan's success (see 13:4). The author attributes the victory to the Lord (v. 23).

14:24-30 The rash oath. Saul's ill-considered oath forbidding his weary soldiers to eat is obeyed by all except his son, who had not been informed. Both the soldier who tells Jonathan of it and Jonathan himself are openly critical of the wisdom of Saul's command (vv. 28-30). The soldier points to the weakness of the people; Jonathan tells of his own revival at having eaten a bit of honey, describing his father's action as troublesome to the people and therefore counterproductive (compare Judg 11:29-31).

14:31-36 Saul corrects ritual disobedience. Saul again shows poor judgment when the over-hungry people fail to let the blood drain from the meat before eating, as they were required to do (Lev 3:17). Saul shows himself piously concerned for the proper ritual and, to his credit, quickly makes appropriate arrangements. Although he wants to do the will of the Lord, he is a bungler who puts more faith in ceremony than in the Lord. Even the altar he builds out of devotion seems unnecessary and extra.

14:37-46 Jonathan freed by the people. After Saul, who had to be reminded to consult the Lord (v. 36), receives no answer from the Lord, he concludes that the cause is someone's sin. Even the life of his son is not too small a price to pay to remove the Lord's silence. Failure to know God's will dogs Saul's reign and will herald his death (see chs. 28 and 31). When the people rescue Jonathan from his father's fanaticism, Saul's sanity is put in question.

14:47-54 Saul's wars and genealogy. Despite the above, Saul seems to have overcome militarily his neighboring enemies (v. 47). The chapter concludes with a list of Saul's sons, wives, and generals. This is standard biblical treatment at the end of a reign. Perhaps it also signals the end of Saul's kingship.

15:1-9 Saul "reinterprets" his orders. Samuel's words make it plain that the Lord is supreme and that since he made Saul king, the king must obey the Lord. Saul's sparing of Agag thwarts the divine decree of punishment, which was to recompense Israel for Amalek's cruelty (Exod 17:8-16; Deut 25:17-19) and flouts the ban (see comment on 13:19-23).

15:10-23 Saul's second rejection. When Saul disobeys by sparing Agag and the best of the Amalekite spoil, the Lord repents of having made him king. Saul's rule now takes a noticeably downward course. Samuel, seeking to rebuke Saul, finds that he has gone to Carmel to erect a monument for himself. When they meet, Saul says confidently, "I have kept the commandment of the Lord." These incidents point to Saul's vanity and failure to know the Lord.

Their meeting is both humorous and ironic. The bleating and lowing which Samuel hears, he should not be hearing; the disobedience Samuel comes to castigate is denied by the one who is guilty. Samuel's poetic oracle (vv. 22-23) puts in perspective external sacrifice as related to an interior attitude of obedience. It also connects Israelite practices of divination and idolatry to sin and presumption. In overrating ritual, Saul has fatally confused his values (see 13:11-13; 14:33-35).

15:24-31 Saul repents. Saul admits his guilt, blaming the people, but Samuel neither accepts the explanation nor acknowledges that Saul may have acted in good faith. Saul finds the rejection impossible to bear and begs Samuel to accompany him to the sacrifice. Samuel agrees, but not before another symbolic rejection is enacted: the tearing of Samuel's cloak stands for the tearing away of Saul's kingship.

15:32-35 Samuel does Saul's job. Samuel's sentence on Agag is a restatement of the *lex talionis* which prescribes that punishment should fit the crime (Lev 24:17-21). Just as Agag rendered women childless by his sword, so shall his mother be made childless. It is a terse, incontestable sentence from the Lord (v. 33), who uses human events to accomplish his inscrutable will.

Today's reader may be astonished at the cold-bloodedness of the prophet as he completes the ban with the slaying of Agag, but biblical prophets are not known to shrink from death (compare Exod 32:25-28; 1 Kgs 18:40). There can be no sentimentality in obeying a God who "puts to death and gives life" (2:6).

IV. SAUL AND DAVID

1 Sam 16–31

Just as the Elide priesthood was cut off and replaced by Samuel, so here Saul is rejected and replaced by David. The Elides sinned against the Lord's worship; Saul sinned by not imposing the ban against Amalek and by usurping Samuel's role as priest in offering the sacrifice. Both infractions touch the worship of the Lord and both incurred the destruction of the respective houses.

As Eli functioned as priest after his rejection (1 Sam 2–3), so Saul continues as king though the Lord is no longer with him. Directed by the Lord, Samuel anoints a new king, David, who proves to be an able soldier and successful in all he does. In these chapters Saul pursues David in jealousy over this success, but David handily escapes each time. Saul at last falls victim to the very enemy he was made king to defeat (9:16; 10:1).

David has all the desired characteristics of a biblical hero: pleasing appearance, speech, and musical ability as well. Compared to Saul, David is superior from his first introduction. More important is that the Lord is with him, something said only once about Saul (10:7) and several times about David (16:18; 17:37; 18:12, 14, 28; 20:13).

16:1-13 David's anointing. Samuel's grief at Saul's rejection suggests not only that he had entertained hope for Saul's success as king but was personally attached to him (see 15:11). The brusque intervention of the Lord precludes further mourning: the Lord is determined to choose another king.

We are surprised that Samuel fears Saul will kill him (v. 2), for it negates the impression that Samuel held authority over Saul. The Lord encourages Samuel by a subterfuge. The new anointing is to be done under the cloak of a sacrifice at the home of Jesse in Bethlehem. The people's question (v. 4), "Is your visit peaceful?" warns that the prophetic word could bring both good and evil (see 1 Kgs 1:9-16; 2:23-24).

Samuel anoints David at a private banquet with little fanfare (compare Saul's in 9:22-27; 10:1). This is Samuel's last recorded prophetic act before his death (25:1; 28:3).

16:14-23 David the future king. In another sign of rejection, the spirit of the Lord now departs from Saul to be replaced by a spirit of melancholy. But Saul is not left without some relief. It can hardly be coincidence that David is the means of banishing the evil spirit, at least temporarily.

David's relationship to Saul has a happy beginning. Saul is immediately attracted to David and gives him the office of armor-bearer, which amounts to on-the-job training for kingship. But this very closeness will soon cause problems.

17:1-11 Goliath taunts Israel's army. The challenger who comes out of the Philistine camp is so powerful and magnificently armed that he terrifies Saul and his army that is encamped on the opposite hill. They seem to have forgotten that it is the God of Israel who determines the victory (14:6; 17:47).

17:12-37 David the hero and savior. Without mentioning his previous anointing by Samuel, the author reintroduces David as a younger son sent by his father with provisions for his brothers in the Israelite camp. This inconsistency has been assigned by some commentators to another tradition which has here been interwoven into the text. However, what we today see as contradiction was often not a problem for the Israelite. David's fearless acceptance of Goliath's challenge shines out against the abject terror of the Israelites (v. 11).

The reward Saul has promised to Israel's defender calls to mind fairy tales wherein the hero is promised wealth and the hand of the king's daughter in marriage. A more realistic advantage comes in the form of tax exemption for the hero's family. From this we see how Saul's army and government were funded and that Samuel's warning about the rights of a king was being realized (8:10-17).

Saul's offer to make David his son-in-law gives him a strong claim to succeed to the throne. Jonathan's later prediction that David would become king may reflect this custom (20:12-16; 23:17).

Now a domestic mini-drama takes place in the angry reception David receives from his oldest brother Eliab (v. 28). David's role here is comparable to that of Joseph, who was sent out to his brothers by his father while they guarded the flocks (Gen 37). In both cases a younger brother of extraordinary promise is the object of jealousy and contempt.

17:38-54 The decisive encounter. When David cannot use Saul's armor to fight the Philistine, he resorts to other skills and puts his trust in the Lord. These along with stones and a sling were the simple means of bringing down Goliath. The theology of the event is summed up by David's statement that "it is not by sword or spear that the Lord saves" (v. 47).

There is an obvious anachronism in verse 54, since Jerusalem was not an Israelite city until after David had become king (2 Sam 5). The mention of Jerusalem and of David's tent is a later addition.

17:55-58 Saul meets David for the first time. It is puzzling that Saul, who had made David his armor-bearer and harp player in 16:21-23, knows nothing of the new hero, nor does his general Abner. Commentators suspect that an alternative account may have been superimposed here.

18:1-4 The covenant of friends. Father and son are immediately attracted to David as a result of his victory over Goliath. Saul makes him part of his household and Jonathan strips himself of his royal garments and weapons to clothe David with them. The gift is tantamount to abdication of the throne in favor of David. Theirs is an unsparingly generous friendship, lasting their lifetime, while Saul's less disinterested love of David soon grows sour.

18:5-30 Saul turns against David. When David's popularity grows with his victories so that the women sing of him to Saul's disadvantage (v. 7), Saul in a fit of jealousy attempts to pin David to the wall as he plays his harp. The king's fear increases when David escapes, and he realizes that the spirit of the Lord had departed from him and rested on David (vv. 12, 15). This transfer of the spirit was the biblical explanation of David's continued success against the Philistines (vv. 5, 30).

Saul, who had cause to be grateful to David, three times acts with duplicity against him. First, he offers his older daughter Merob in marriage, only to give her to another man (vv. 17, 19); second, he sends David into battle with the hope he will be killed by Philistines (v. 17), a tactic David himself will use against Bathsheba's husband in 2 Sam 11–12; third, he offers David the status of son-in-law on delivery of one hundred Philistine foreskins, hoping the danger of the undertaking will bring David death instead (v. 25). Although David demurs at becoming son-in-law out of modesty (vv. 18, 23), he is pleased and seems unaware of Saul's animosity (v. 26). On delivery of double the number of foreskins, Saul gives his younger daughter Michal to David in marriage.

David seems already to have surpassed Jonathan militarily, for no other victory beyond that of chapter 14 is reported of him. Jonathan decreases while David increases (compare John 3:30).

19:1-17 Jonathan and Michal help David. In defense of his friend, Jonathan extracts an oath from his father that he will not kill David (v. 6). However, when the evil spirit returns to incite Saul again to spear David, Michal joins Jonathan in protecting David. After convincing him of the danger from Saul (v. 11), and letting him down from a window to safety, she shows inventiveness in deceiving her father's soldiers (vv. 13-16) and courage in facing his rebuke (v. 17). The unhappy Saul thus finds himself alienated from both his children because of his behavior toward David. The fact that Michal's household contained an idol suggests that the worship of the Lord was not as pure in practice as the biblical ideal demanded (compare Gen 31).

19:18-24 Saul joins the prophets. The spirit of the Lord works to frustrate Saul in his attempt to seize David. Bystanders must have laughed to see all Saul's messengers and then Saul himself seized by the spirit when they approached the frenzied prophets among whom David had hidden himself. The scene in which Saul, in a highly undignified state, rolls helplessly about, raving along with his messengers, confirms the popular taunt of 10:11-12, "Is Saul also among the prophets?"

Such a portrayal reinforces Saul's inadequacy and rejection and at the same time reflects popular disparagement of early prophecy. The main point is that the Lord is protecting David against Saul, to the king's discomfiture.

20:1-10 Jonathan pledges loyalty to David. With the same words Saul spoke when sparing the malcontents who had formerly opposed his rule (11:13), Jonathan utters what is almost a royal decree that David will not die at the hand of his father (v. 21). In so doing he opposes his father's will and transfers his allegiance from Saul to David. On his side David's trust in Jonathan is so great that he requests Jonathan to kill him, should he be proved guilty (v. 8), rather than Saul (compare 2 Sam 14:32).

Jonathan seems at first to be an obstacle to David's becoming king, since he is Saul's legitimate heir. Instead he is the means by which David's destiny is achieved. This chapter marks the change in Jonathan's role from crown prince to David's subject. Also, in his success against the Philistines in chapter 14 and his subsequent rescue by the people, Jonathan in effect replaces his father as king. When Jonathan gives David all the trappings of royalty, he abdicates the throne (ch. 18). David's kingship, divinely instituted by Samuel's anointing (ch. 16), is thus humanly mediated by Jonathan.

20:11-17 The oath of loyalty. The pact David and Jonathan make holds two premonitions: Jonathan, the expected heir to the throne, will give place to David, and then he will die (vv. 14-16). Both face death; both stand in line for the kingship. Jonathan's blessing for David (v. 13) acknowledges Saul's rejection and points to David's succession.

20:18-34 Jonathan tests his father. Saul desperately tries to hold back the tide that is coming in for David by killing him. When Jonathan makes excuses for David's absence, Saul's reaction comes with a vengeance. In highly abusive words, Saul attacks not only Jonathan but his mother, hinting at an undisclosed defection on her part. Rather than attempt to win Jonathan to his side, Saul enlarges the breach by lunging at his own son with a spear. For the first time Jonathan is angry and stalks from the room.

20:35-42 Jonathan sends David on his way. Jonathan here joins his sister Michal in courageously defending David against the murderous intent of their father. With Jonathan's departure from Saul, the king's isolation increases and with it his madness. When the elaborate charade of shooting arrows is over, David offers Jonathan the triple homage befitting a royal person. By saving his life, Jonathan has helped David to become king. David will later preserve Jonathan's posterity by saving Jonathan's son (2 Sam 9; 21:7).

21:1-10 Ahimelech helps David. With David's unexpected arrival alone at Nob, Ahimelech has a premonition that not all is well. He is afraid that David is a fugitive and that he and his supposed men are not religiously prepared to eat the bread designated for the priests. By representing himself as on a mission of Saul's and under the rubrics of holy war, which required abstinence from women (Lev 15:18; Deut 23:10), David allays his fears and enlists his help. Convinced that everything is in order, Ahimelech takes no pains to conceal from Doeg, Saul's henchman, his having given bread and weapons to David (v. 8). Doeg's presence will have to be reckoned with later. The episode shows that human needs take precedence over cultic regulations, a point also made at the disciples' pulling ears of grain to eat on the sabbath (Matt 12:3-4; Mark 3:25-26; Luke 6:3-4).

21:11-16 David flees to Achish of Gath. The second person David meets on his flight from Saul is Achish of Gath. With Ahimelech he had played the part of one commissioned by Saul; with Achish he pretends madness, since insanity was looked upon as possession by an evil spirit and therefore made him untouchable. Although David, the hunted, looks mad, he is not; it is Saul, the hunter, who is the true madman.

22:1-5 David provides for his parents. David's refuge at Adullam's cave makes possible the formation of a guerilla band. Now no longer hostile, his brothers join him, and along with some outcasts of society, provide him with protection. It is the beginning of a power base that will lead to David's coronation.

In view of Saul's pursuit, David asks permission for his parents to settle temporarily in Moab. David's doubt as to where he should go next is resolved by instructions from the prophet Gad to go back to Judah—and the dangerous ambit of Saul. Through all vicissitudes, the Lord continues to care for David.

22:6-23 Doeg betrays Ahimelech. The scene shifts to Saul's camp where, spear in hand, he is complaining about the disloyalty of his men. Paranoia is enveloping Saul's appreciation of events, so that even those closest to him are suspect. Doeg's revelation of David's encounter with Ahimelech at Nob propels Saul into action. When Ahimelech appears before him, Saul again makes a charge of conspiracy (vv. 8, 13) and refuses to hear his pathetic but valid defense. Ahimelech's punishment is a foregone conclusion, but the reaction to Saul's command to slay the priests is not. When not one man moves to obey the command, Saul presses the Edomite Doeg into the cruel business, assuming that a foreigner would be less squeamish about executing Israelites.

Doeg's slaughter begins with the priests and extends to the rest of the inhabitants and livestock of Nob. What Saul should have done to Agag and the Amalekites, he does here against his own people (15:3). Although the true target of Saul's animosity escapes, one son of Ahimelech, Abiathar, survives to report the massacre to David (vv. 20, 21). With the arrival of Abiathar, the story returns to the fugitives in the forest. Here David accepts responsibility for the slaughter at Nob, offering Abiathar what protection he can.

23:1-6 David consults the Lord. In contrast to Saul, who had to be reminded to consult the Lord and then received no answer (14:36-37), David, when he asks whether to engage in battle with the Philistines, not only receives a positive answer but can ask a second time for the sake of his frightened men. David's victory is predictable because the ephod is in his camp, brought by Abiathar in his flight from Saul. Now the Lord is with David in a concrete way, for the ephod permits him cultic access to the Lord's will.

23:7-13 Saul frustrated again. Saul reads David's presence in Keilah as a God-given chance to seize his enemy. His plan to pursue him, as well as the treachery of the ungrateful citizens of Keilah, are made known to David by two further uses of the ephod. Because of this knowledge, David and his men, now six hundred strong, make their escape. Again the narrative contrasts Saul and David: the latter is seen as devout, God-fearing and obedient; the former is hobbled by his lack of the knowledge of God.

23:14-18 David and Jonathan meet for the last time. The essential details of David and Jonathan's relationship, sketched in 18:1-4, are here amplified. Jonathan openly acknowledges that David will be king and that his father will be unable to capture him (v. 17). Only the prediction of Jonathan's position as second to David remains unfulfilled, since Jonathan does not live long enough to see David made king. Jonathan's words confirm his loyalty to David and the relinquishment of any claim to the throne.

Jonathan's brief visit strengthens David's resolve and attests to the hidden care the Lord has for this favored king. Their covenant renewed, Jonathan departs from David and, except for notice of his death in 31:6-7, from the narrative.

23:19-28 Saul is distracted from the pursuit. When the Ziphites offer to disclose David's hiding place, Saul unaccountably asks for further inquiry. Earlier when he heard that David had been at Nob, he acted immediately (22:11). Now he proposes a wide-ranging search, which will only give David more time to flee.

Twice since his complaint that no one tells him anything (22:7-8), Saul is given information which almost leads to David's capture (vv. 7, 19). Each time he has had to abandon the chase because of unexpected developments, or divine intervention. However, Saul has no insight into this, nor does he give up the chase.

24:1-16 David asks justice from the Lord. This is the third sighting of David by spies loyal to Saul, whose three thousand men (v. 3) vastly outnumber David's six hundred (23:13). Saul, discovered in the cave by David and his men, is in his most humiliating predicament. The king's embarrassment serves as a foil to heighten two characteristics of David: his restraint when the enemy is in his grasp, and his extraordinary care not to harm the anointed of the Lord. Since piety holds back his hand from killing Saul, David looks to the Lord to vindicate him.

David argues with Saul with considerable wit. By disparaging himself as a dead dog or flea, he tries to show the king the futility of his chase.

24:17-23 Saul admits David will be king. David's skillful speech (see 16:18) proves so persuasive that Saul is reduced to tears. Gratitude and contrition are in Saul's response, but the announcement that he *knows* David will be king is prophetic. Like his son Jonathan, Saul also asks David to spare his posterity, forestalling the accepted custom of a new king's eliminating the previous ruling house.

Saul is here no longer a dangerous pursuer but a beaten captive at the mercy of one who refuses to kill him. The situation is so emotionally charged that, forgetting their enmity for a time, each leads his army off to his own place.

25:1 Israel mourns Samuel. With the death of Samuel, the role of judge in Israel passes to the king. Samuel was also a priest and a prophet, both of which offices now take on increasing importance in providing a check on the power of the king.

25:2-11 David seeks provisions from Nabal (the Fool). Between the two encounters between Saul and David (chs. 24, 26), there is here what amounts to a romantic interlude. If we have wondered how David supplied his men in the desert, this story provides an answer. Nabal offers David a different kind of opposition from Saul's, but one which could be equally life-threatening. Nabal refuses to share food with David and his men at a time of traditional hospitality, the sheep-shearing festival (compare Gen 38:13; 2 Sam 13:23ff.).

When David asks for gifts from Nabal's feast, he does so by artfully leading from polite greetings, a hint at Nabal's probable indebtedness, advertence to the feast, and finally to the request for provisions. In reply Nabal first tries to make David a nonentity and then equates him with a run-away slave. David addresses Nabal as brother (v. 6) and father (v. 8), but Nabal dismisses him as an unknown (v. 11). Although David may have had no strict right to a share in the feast, Nabal, for his part, fails to recognize (know) what is in his best interest.

25:12-35 Abigail (the Wise) saves David. After hearing Nabal's repulse, David in silent anger girds on his sword, ordering his men to do likewise. By repeating the girding three times, the author delays the action to heighten suspense and show the grim determination of David and his hungry men.

Meanwhile, Nabal's servants inform their mistress Abigail of what has transpired and attest to the good David and his men have done them (vv. 14-17). Their openness in describing Nabal as "mean" (literally, "a son of Belial"—Hannah's "ne'er do well" of 1:16) indicates not only that she had their confidence but that Nabal's ill-nature was well known.

Unlike her husband, Abigail knows wherein her best interests lie. She hurries off with gifts just in time to deflect David's growing wrath. In a speech as skillful as David's, she first blames Nabal for acting the fool and herself for not seeing David's men when they came. Pointing out that the Lord has saved David from blood guilt (v. 26), she presents her gifts. A proof of her wisdom is her perception that because David is fighting the battles of the Lord and there is no evil in him, the Lord will establish a lasting dynasty for him (v. 28).

Abigail concludes her speech with a blessing for David (v. 29) in which she uses two metaphors: (1) she refers to the "bundle of the living" into which David will be bound as a promise of life, and (2) she asks the Lord to hurl the lives of David's enemies as from the hollow of a sling, recalling David's victory over Goliath with a sling (17:40, 49f.). Abigail's last wish, that David remember her when all she predicts comes to pass, brings an equally gracious response from David who then lets her depart in peace.

25:36-39 Nabal's feast. In three short verses Nabal's life comes to an end, with a drunken orgy followed by a stroke. He had prepared for himself the royal banquet (v. 36) which should have been prepared for the true king, David. David had appealed to him as a servant; instead Nabal's wife presents herself as a servant (vv. 27, 41) while predicting David's kingship. Thus the good which David did (vv. 15, 21) is rewarded (v. 30), and the evil which Nabal dealt David (vv. 17, 21, 26, 39) is punished.

25:40-43 David's wives. In making Abigail his wife, David receives not only a woman of wisdom, skilled in speech, but very likely the control of Nabal's estate in the Calebite territory of Hebron (Josh 14:13-14). This advantage is offset by Saul's giving of Michal to another. The name Ahinoam, later listed as mother of David's first-born, Amnon (2 Sam 3:2), appears as Saul's wife in 14:50. If she was now David's and had been Saul's, it could relate to Saul's vicious outburst that

Jonathan was the son of a rebellious woman (20:30).

26:1-12 David confronts Saul. This chapter introduces Joab's brother Abishai, who is second in command of David's army and a man consistently ready with the sword (2 Sam 3:22ff.; 8:16). When he pleads with David to finish off the sleeping Saul, David refuses, once again honoring the sacredness of an anointed king (24:7). Instead of taking Saul's life, David takes away his means of defense, his spear, and his life provision, his water jug. The entry and seizure take place successfully because of the deep sleep the Lord had sent over the camp (v. 12). It is another example of the divine helps continually accorded David at the expense of Saul (see 19:22ff.).

26:13-20 A double rebuke. Abandoning the diffidence he used in his previous encounter with Saul (ch. 24), David, from a safe distance on an opposite hill, openly accuses Saul's general, Abner, of neglecting his king. When this draws Saul's attention, David leaves Abner to attack the king with words. David is willing to accept Saul's persecution if it comes from the Lord, but if from men (that is, Saul), he will be forced by it to flee to a foreign land, where he will be tempted to worship other gods (v. 19).

26:21-25 Saul repents again. Contrite and thankful, Saul admits he has been a fool (compare Nabal, ch. 25). David, however, makes no pact with him as he did in their previous meeting (ch. 24). Ignoring Saul's promise not to harm him (v. 21), David reminds the king that the only reason he has been spared is because he is anointed. This reflects badly on Saul, who, in pursuing one he knows will be king, has no such qualms of conscience. Although the two part in mutual blessing, Saul has stretched David's patience to the breaking point.

27:1-4 David leaves Israel. David experiences discouragement similar to that of Abraham after repeatedly being promised a son (Gen 15:4). Although both Saul and Jonathan have foretold that he will be king, while Saul pursues him, David has little hope for his life in the future.

27:5-12 Achish gives David Ziklag. In a mutually agreeable arrangement, Achish finds an able soldier in David, and David is able, through Achish, to provide for himself and his men. We may wonder why there is no indication of their previous meeting, in which Achish showed himself reluctant to harbor another madman (21:11-16). With the information we have, there is no conclusive resolution to this incompatibility.

In both meetings with Achish, David never betrays his steadfast loyalty to Israel. The raids David makes, ostensibly in Achish's behalf, are against traditional enemies of both Israel *and* the Philistines. David is careful to kill all the humans lest, if they returned as prisoners, they betray him. This deception, like others in the Bible, goes unreprehended.

28:1-2 Achish trusts David. When Achish says that David realizes (in Hebrew, "knows") he is to go out with the Philistines against Israel, David answers that Achish will learn (in Hebrew, "know") what his servant can do. David's response is a cover for his loyalty which has never turned from Israel and means that he hopes not to have to betray himself before Achish. The matter is taken out of his hands in the next chapter.

28:3-6 The Lord does not answer Saul. We are again told that Samuel has died, a fact which, along with Saul's banishing of fortunetellers (according to Deut 18:10-14), severely limits Saul's knowledge of God's will as he faces his enemy. Seeing himself outnumbered, Saul is afraid, something that is never said of David. David is, however, said to be afraid of Saul (23:15). Again, as in 14:37, Saul is left without divine direction, a disadvantage David never had to contend with.

28:7-14 Saul seeks a medium. The name "fortune-teller" in Hebrew is a form of the verb "to know." In contrast to Achish, who will *know* (v. 2) what David will do, Saul does not *know* what the Lord will do and goes to one who *knows* to find out. Although it means breaking his own regulation, Saul in his great fear, seeks out such a medium. At once she parries his request with the statement that Saul—or anyone in Israel—*knows* that it is a capital offense to practice divination. As soon as she brings up Samuel, she *knows* who her petitioner is. Her scream of recognition has echoed down the ages in music and literature.

28:15-19 Saul finds out what he wants to know. Samuel, showing surprise that Saul has not accepted the departure of the Lord from him, repeats the divine rejection of his kingship. Saul is being punished here for the failure to slay Agag (ch. 15). Israel will fall before the Philistines, as will Saul and his sons. The reluctant answer from Samuel tells Saul all that he would rather not know.

28:20-25 The kindness of the medium. Taking a cue from Samuel's declaration that Saul had disobeyed the word of the Lord in verse 18, the author now begins a play on the word "obey." When the woman sees that Saul has fallen to the ground in weakness, she reminds him that up to now she has obeyed him (v. 21). In turn, he must obey her (v. 22) when she insists on preparing him some food. With his companions urging him, Saul obeys (v. 23) and he is given a feast of a fatted calf (compare Luke 15:23, 27). It is Saul's last banquet before his death in the next day's battle.

29:1-11 Achish reluctantly dismisses David. As they had been when the ark was lost, the Philistines are again encamped at Aphek (4:1), ready to fight against Israel. Achish had ordered David and his men to go out with him in 28:21, showing that his trust in David was firm. However, the other Philistine chiefs remember David's history of slaying thousands of their men (v. 5; 18:6-7; 21:11-12) and realistically assess his presence among them as an opportunity for David to ingratiate himself with Saul by turning on them from the rear.

Achish's speech in which he sends David back is flattering, to the point of calling David an angel of God (compare 2 Sam 14:17; 19:28). When Achish finds nothing wrong with David, he is in the tradition of Potiphar and his jailer, both of whom found nothing wrong with Joseph and who trusted Joseph enough to leave everything in his charge (Gen 39:6, 23). David inspires the same confidence in Achish. It is high praise for both David and Joseph from foreigners. Fellow Israelites were not so easily captivated.

David asks Achish why he cannot go out to fight against "the enemies of my lord the king" (v. 8). His words can refer to Achish or to King Saul (compare 28:2). Here David has again adroitly escaped with his friendship with Achish intact.

30:1-10 The Amalekite raid on Ziklag. Although Saul's devastation of the Amalekites in chapter 15 should have rendered them powerless, they now take their revenge by sacking the city Achish had given David. Instead of being put under the ban, as Saul had been ordered to do, Ziklag's occupants were fortunately taken alive. Before they know this, the narrative builds the sorrow of the returning soldiers to a crescendo with the recounting of their weeping until exhausted, the information that David's two wives were among the captured, and finally the extreme bitterness of the men toward David to the point that they were ready to stone him, a rare sign of popular disenchantment with David. In turning to the Lord, David acknowledges that God is the source of his strength and success.

In obedience to the oracle received through the ephod (v. 8), David pursues Amalek, leaving two hundred of his weariest soldiers guarding the baggage. They will have a significant role in the distribution of the spoil (vv. 21-25).

30:11-16 The abandoned Egyptian. David receives providential help in the person of the sick Egyptian slave left behind by the Amalekites. In return for food, drink, and asylum, the Egyptian brings him to the carousing Amalekites. He joins a lengthening list of David's helpers: Michal, Jonathan, and Ahimelech, all of whom appear at the crucial moment.

30:17-25 David recovers the Ziklag captives. After an untold number of Amalekites are slaughtered, all the captives and possessions from Ziklag are rescued. David immediately faces another challenge from his own men in their unwillingness to share the spoil with those left behind with the baggage (v. 10). The ones who complained are called stingy and worthless (v. 22), but it is of such that David's small army was made (22:2). He must continually encourage them to trust in the Lord (23:1-5) and do good to their fellow soldiers out of gratitude to him (30:23). David's quick, sure decision to share the spoil among all members of his army becomes a precedent for Israel (v. 25).

30:26-31 The division of the spoil. David shows himself an astute politician by sending gifts from the booty to the Judean settlements in the Negeb where David was already known. These gifts could be means of gaining acceptance later when David is considered for the kingship after the death of Saul (2 Sam 2:1-4).

31:1-8 How Saul and Jonathan died. The happy picture of David sharing the spoils of the Amalekite victory gives way to the darker picture of Saul and the Israelite army fleeing and falling wounded before the Philistines. Once again David's fortunes rise as Saul goes into decline, both as king and human being.

Ignoring battle details, the narrative section, which begins and ends on Mount Gilboa (vv. 1-8), repeats its notice of the slaying of Saul's three sons and the finding (hit) of Saul (vv. 2, 3, 8), the coming of the uncircumcised/the Philistine (vv. 4, 7, 8), the fleeing of the Israelites (vv. 1, 7), and the discovery of Saul's death first by the armor-bearer and then by the Israelites (vv. 5, 7). In concentric fashion these events enclose the central message of Saul's death (v. 6). The literary embellishment heightens the pathos and significance of the event.

31:9-13 Mercy for the bodies of the slain. The Philistines desecrate Saul's body in three ways: they cut off his head, knowing that any mutilation of a corpse is a horror to Israelites; they strip him literally and figuratively of his glory as a soldier by taking his armor and putting it in their temple; lastly, they do the unforgivable: they impale his body on the city wall. Trophies of war hung in a house of worship apparently credit the god with victory (compare 5:2; 21:10).

While the burning of the bodies is usually abhorrent, it is here a mercy since no further atrocities can be done with them. Their proper burial (v. 13) means they are in peace.

Saul's body returns to Jabesh, the scene of his first victory after being anointed king (ch. 11). The man who was to save Israel from the Philistines (9:16) has himself fallen into their hands.

COMMENTARY: 2 SAMUEL

V. THE STRUGGLE FOR THE KINGDOM

2 Sam 1–8

After the death of Saul, David does not seize power, but waits for the Lord to give him the kingship. David rejects Saul's crown offered by the Amalekite messenger, but after being anointed by the Judeans (ch. 2) does accept the allegiance of the north brought him by Abner, Saul's former general. Although this plan is frustrated by Abner's death at the hand of Joab, the last obstacle to kingship over a united Israel is removed by events beyond David's control (chs. 4–5). Once king, David consolidates both his religious and political position by bringing back the ark of the covenant to the new capital in Jerusalem. All Israel is then a divine gift to David who, despite temporary setbacks, prospers under God's blessing and protection.

1:1-16 The Amalekite's report to David. "Death" is a word used eight times in this section, beginning with the death of Saul and ending with David's execution of the Amalekite who brought him Saul's crown and armlet as testimony of his death. If the Amalekite expected a reward from a man he supposed ambitious for the kingship, he is gravely mistaken. Instead of gratitude, he earns death for claiming to have slain an anointed king. David is here consistent in his remarkable reverence for anyone the Lord had anointed, as he demonstrated in 1 Sam 24:7 and 26:9.

1:17-27 The fall of the mighty. The Hebrew word for "warrior," which also appears in translation as "valiant" (v. 22) or "stronger" (v. 23), is the key word for David's elegy. The repeated "fallen" and "slain" underline its somber mood, while David's special love for Jonathan is emphasized in verse 26. Instructions to keep the news from the Philistine women who might rejoice over the slain is contrasted in verse 24 with orders for the Israelite women to weep over Saul and remember his kindnesses to them. Dew and rain are summoned to share the mourning by not appearing on the mountains where the slain lie (v. 21). Saul's neglected shield, no longer anointed with oil, symbolizes the rejection of Saul's own anointing.

2:1-7 David's announcement of kingship. Instead of his birthplace, Bethlehem (1 Sam 16:1), the Lord directs David to Hebron from where he includes, in a message of gratitude, the announcement that he has been anointed king over Judah. Since the area around Hebron was part of the traditional Calebite allotment, David may have gained control of property in Hebron through his marriage to Abigail, widow of the Calebite Nabal (Josh 14:13; 1 Sam 25:3).

2:8-11 Israel follows Saul's son Ishbaal. Not the Lord, but Abner, his own general, makes Ishbaal king over all Israel, except for David's territory in Judah. Such political weakness in Ishbaal is portentous for David's future.

2:12-24 The three sons of Zeruiah. A symbolic but indecisive combat between the Israelites under Abner and the Judahites under Joab, David's general, escalates to full battle. After the Israelite defeat, Asahel, brother of Joab and Abishai (v. 18), refuses to give up. Compulsively, he pursues Abner who tries to dissuade him, knowing that if he kills Asahel he will be liable to blood vengeance. When Abner is forced to stop Asahel with his javelin, Joab and Abishai continue the pursuit. The introduction of the three brothers, cousins to David, begins in violence and is associated with it throughout their lives.

2:25-32 Benjamin and Judah count their losses. The story has moved from one bloody confrontation in Gibeon to another in Geba. Although the losses of Benjamin are far greater than those of Judah, both sides are grateful to return to their respective camps.

3:1-6 The house of Saul and the house of David. The house of Saul weakens as the house of David grows stronger, a process marked by the death of Saul's sons in contrast to the fertility of David, whose six wives produced as many children. Only three of these—Amnon, Absalom, and Adonijah—will figure in the biblical narrative.

3:7-11 The matter of Rizpah, the concubine. Abner's relationship with Ishbaal's concubine Rizpah, more than an insult to a superior, could be read as a bid for the throne. However, Abner refrains from a coup, recognizing David as the predicted leader of Israel (vv. 9-10).

3:12-21 Abner and David make a covenant. With Abner's defection, all the tribes of Israel associated with Saul are ready to come under David's rule. But David makes the return of his wife Michal, Saul's daughter, the condition of his agreement. Without any compassion for Paltiel, to say nothing of the feelings of Michal, the painful deed is done, clearing the way for serious negotiations between Abner and David. Abner refers to no known biblical passage when he quotes the Lord as saying David will deliver Israel from the Philistines (v. 18). Rather this was promised of Saul (1 Sam 9:16), had he obeyed the Lord (1 Sam 13:13-14). The narrative underlines that Abner departed in peace (vv. 21-24), but it was not a peace that was to last.

3:22-30 Joab's zeal. Abner's insubordination to Ishbaal (vv. 8-10) is mild compared to Joab's attack on David for making an agreement with Abner. Joab says in effect, "How could you let an obvious enemy get away?" Then, without orders, Joab dispatches Abner in cold blood (v. 27), not the last time Joab will act with violence for the good of the state. Substituting vindictiveness and frustration for actual punishment, David delivers a dire curse on Joab and his posterity (v. 29). Presumably impressed by David's outburst, Joab submits to David's order to mourn Abner publicly.

3:31-39 The burial of Abner. David's distress over Abner's death can be felt in the bitter elegy he composed for the funeral. This and the king's extravagant mourning (v. 32) convince the people that David had not ordered Abner's execution. David's acknowledged weakness before Joab is a persistent puzzle in the narrative (v. 39). It required him to endure a man who was a continual thorn in his side at the same time that David owed Joab much of the success of his wars and his rule.

4:1-4 The successors of Saul. With only the crippled grandson Meribbaal left to the house of Saul, besides the frightened Ishbaal, the Israelites can look for no effective leadership from within the northern tribes. Little seems to stand in the way of David's kingship.

4:5-12 The murder of Ishbaal. With Ishbaal demoralized and security lax, it is easy for the two murderers to enter the royal bedroom. Understandably, they see Ishbaal's rule as effectively ended, but they hardly expect David not to welcome their gift of his head. It is a second example of David's refusal to seize the kingdom through violent means (compare 1:1-16).

The execution of the two men, cruel to us, is done according to the law in Deut 21:22f. As the Philistines treated Saul (1 Sam 31:9), so are the slayers of his son treated.

5:1-5 King of all Israel. When the Israelite (northern) tribes come to anoint David king, they have two motivations. First, they claim him as brother (their bone and flesh), a condition for kingship required to prevent foreign rule (see Deut 17:15). Second, they recall David's military leadership (1 Sam 18:16) and the divine promise that David's throne would be established over both Israel and Judah (3:10). Thus he becomes king over an externally united nation, but one whose internal conflicts are never very far below the surface.

5:6-16 A city and a house for the new king. The account of how David made Jerusalem, previously held by pagan Jebusites, his capital is truncated and confused. Despite Jerusalem's reputation of being impregnable (the blind and the lame could defend it), David is able to take it after Joab courageously climbs the water shaft to gain access to the city. This information comes from 1 Chr 11:6, which adds that David rewarded Joab for his bravery by making him commander of his troops.

David's new capital is, for political purposes, ideally situated, since it is on the border between two chief tribes of his kingdom: Judah and Benjamin. Once settled, David has the leisure and resources to build himself a palace. From his friend Hiram of Tyre, David sends for cedar and workmen, just as his son Solomon will later do for the building of the temple (1 Kgs 7).

5:17-25 The Lord goes before David in battle. Success has not yet gone to David's head, for he continues to consult the Lord before going into battle with the Philistines who now seem to resent David's new power. After the first rout of the enemy, David names the place Baal-perazim (literally, "lord of the breaking through"), a play on words referring to the Lord's breaking through the enemy lines so that both the Philistine soldiers and the gods they left behind are scattered (vv. 20-21; compare Gen 38:29).

At the Philistines' second attack, it is the Lord who directs the defense by ordering a rear attack by Israel and by giving an audible sign (v. 24) that the Lord is leading the march. Saul never had the advantage of such tangible support.

6:1-10 The striking of Uzzah. The transfer of the ark is told in fuller detail in 1 Chr 13 and 15, whence we learn in 13:6 that Baala of Judah is another name for Kiriath-jearim, where the ark was left (1 Sam 7:1-2). The joyful procession of thirty thousand (!) is interrupted by the unexpected death of Uzzah when he touches the ark (v. 6). David, upset by the event, leaves the ark at the home of Obededom, significantly identified as from the Philistine city of Gath. If the ark is to bring destruction to the Israelites, let it stay with the Philistines, David's action seems to say. Although this account makes no attempt to explain Uzzah's death, in 1 Chr 15:13 David attributes the Lord's anger to the absence of the priests and Levites.

6:11-19 David brings the ark to Jerusalem. When the king hears of the blessings to Obededom's house, he ventures another transport. In the festal procession David, clothed only with the linen ephod used by priests at liturgical functions, distinguishes himself by his energetic dancing (v. 14). It is a time for joy, music, and the giving of gifts (v. 19). By the transfer of the ark to Jerusalem, that city is established as the religious and political capital of Israel.

6:20-23 The scorn of Michal. For the third time, the presence of the ark brings trouble (1 Sam 6:19; 2 Sam 6:6-7). The Lord, whose presence is said to dwell in the ark, indicates in this way that he is free to dwell wherever he will and not necessarily at the desire of the king. Now David meets another reversal: the scorn of Michal for what she considers his immodest dancing (v. 20). David's wounding retort reminds her that the Lord has rejected her father's house. Her punishment is to remain childless, in that society a woman's greatest reproach (compare 1 Sam 1).

7:1-17 The house of the Lord and the house of David. In peace with all the nations round about, David has the leisure to turn to internal matters, including the public worship of God. In the ancient world a god was truly established when he had a fitting house. Nathan's immediate approval of David's plan to build the Lord a house is revoked by a nocturnal oracle. That the Lord does not communicate directly with David but through Nathan underlines the continued importance of prophecy in relation to the monarchy.

Pointing with pride to his simple tent-dwelling while Israel sojourned in the desert, the Lord turns David's good intentions around. The Lord himself will build a house for David, a house in the sense of dynasty, one that will rule forever (v. 13). In an elaborate play on the word, "house" means palace (v. 1), a dwelling (vv. 2, 5, 6, 7), royal dynasty (vv. 11, 16), and temple (v. 13). Reminding David of his humble beginnings, the Lord unconditionally promises him a great name (v. 9) and a firmly established throne (vv. 13, 16). The prediction that David's son will build a temple comes to realization under Solomon (1 Kgs 8). For another account of the dynastic promise, see 1 Chr 28:1-10.

This passage has been interpreted as the Lord's personal covenant with David. By it the Lord's direct rule over Israel is replaced with a human king, chosen by God, whose posterity will continue to occupy the throne for all generations. Samuel's previously hostile attitude toward allowing Israel to be like other nations has been changed to divine endorsement of the Davidic kingship as well as the establishment of its sure dynastic succession. This text, along with Ps 89 and 1 Chr 17, is the biblical rationale for the royal theology according to which the king was the Lord's representative in bringing Israel victory and blessings.

7:18-29 David praises the Lord. In grateful response to the Lord's promise, David contrasts his own littleness to the Lord's greatness (vv. 18, 19, 22). The Lord is the only God and Israel is his specially favored people (vv. 22, 23). As the Lord did in verse 6, David also recalls Israel's deliverance from slavery in Egypt (v. 23). Then, in a covenant renewal, David reaffirms Israel as the Lord's people and the Lord as their God (v. 24), closing with a prayer for the Lord's blessing (v. 29).

8:1-14 David's victories. This chapter could be called "David strikes" because the verb, variously translated, "defeat," "attack," and "slay," appears in verses 1, 2, 3, 5, 9, 13. The list of victories begins with the Philistines and continues through the countries bordering Israel. The range of conquests includes Moab, Aram (Syria), and Edom.

That David had use for only one hundred chariot horses shows his army inferior in equipment to those of his enemies. However, the plentiful booty enriched David with shields (v. 7), articles of gold, silver, and bronze (vv. 8, 10), all of which were consecrated to the Lord (v. 11).

8:15-18 The heads of government. Besides being a military leader, David governs and administers justice (compare 15:1-6). Joab commands the army and Benaiah the Cherethites and Pelethites, believed to be Cretans and Philistines (see 15:18). By using foreign mercenaries, ancient kings knew how to protect themselves from palace coups.

VI. DAVID THE KING
2 Sam 9–20

David sits on the throne in Jerusalem at peace with his neighbors. Assured of a lasting dynasty (ch. 7), he seeks to do good with his increasing power and wealth. In a moment of passion David breaks the law, bringing on himself divine punishment which escalates from his family to threaten even his throne. These chapters comprise a narrative unit, called the Court Narrative because it tells the story of David's life as king. It is thought to be a separate tradition from those about Saul and David called the Late Source. There are however narrative links in chapters 9–20 to earlier themes, for example, the influence of Joab on David and the recurrent division between the northern and southern tribes, which speak against complete independence of the sources.

9:1-13 David fulfills his oath. A prosperous David remembers his covenant and friendship with Jonathan by looking for descendants to whom he may show kindness. With such close ties to Saul's house, it is strange that David should have to ask if there were any Saulides alive. However, if the events recorded in chapter 21, where David spared Meribbaal when he handed over two sons and five grandsons to the Gibeonite vengeance, took place before those recorded in chapter 9, we can more easily understand why only Meribbaal was left.

When the crippled son of Jonathan, Saul's grandson, is brought to David's court from the house of Machir (see 17:27), David goes out of his way to make Meribbaal feel welcome. Although he protests he is a dead dog—an expression of political and psychological inferiority—Meribbaal becomes part of David's household and has the honor of eating at his table. Ziba, his servant, is assigned to run the family farm, which would provide for them all, including Ziba's fifteen sons and twenty servants.

In doing this David fulfills his oath and shows that he has little to fear from this Saulide. Twice the narrator mentions that Meribbaal is crippled, saying in effect that he is unqualified for kingship (vv. 3, 13). It is then doubtful that making Meribbaal part of his household was a means of keeping an eye on a possible conspirator to the throne. Against this is the allegation of treason that Ziba implies when David's throne is in jeopardy (16:1-4).

10:1-5 David and the Ammonites. David continues his good works, here extending condolences to the Ammonite king on the death of his father. But things turn out adversely due to the negative advice of the young king's advisors. By shaving the beard and exposing the nakedness of David's emissaries, Nahash delivers the ultimate insult. David is considerate and allows the men to stay in Jericho until their beards grow again.

10:6-12 Joab leads the defense against Ammon. Expecting reprisal, the Ammonites prepare to attack first, with the help of Aramean mercenaries. After skillfully arranging his troops for defense, Joab encourages them to fight bravely and leave the outcome to the Lord. The success of battle will then be the typical biblical combination of human effort and the power of God.

10:13-19 The defeat of the Ammonites and Arameans. When the Arameans flee before Joab, their Ammonite allies do likewise before the rest of the troops under Joab's brother Abishai (v. 10). The victory is only temporary, for the Arameans, having gathered fresh recruits from sympathetic rulers beyond the Euphrates, try again to conquer Israel. David now takes the field himself, wipes out the enemy and makes subjects of the Arameans. This account marks the high point of David's military exploits.

11:1-15 David and Bathsheba. While the army is besieging Rabbah, David has little to do but take naps and walk about on his roof. On one such idle afternoon, he sees the beautiful Bathsheba and sends for her. In an extended play on the word "send," the author has David "send" frequently in chapters 10 and 11, alerting the reader to his full royal powers. However, Bathsheba also sends when she informs David she is pregnant (v. 5), and Joab, too, sends Uriah back from the front lines (v. 6).

Not even the information that Bathsheba was the wife of one of his army officers deters David from possessing her. Once he knows she is pregnant, he begins an elaborate intrigue to cover his paternity. When he asks Uriah the triple question about how are Joab, the people, and the war, it is so much talk masking his real purpose to make Uriah go down to his house to his wife.

This attempt is made for three nights (vv. 8, 10, 13), but Uriah sleeps with the king's servants instead. When David asks why, Uriah's amazing answer painfully contrasts the king's evil designs with the moral uprightness of his loyal soldier. On the third evening, although David has made Uriah drunk, he persists in avoiding his house. The frustrated David then devises a way out of his dilemma by instigating Uriah's death under cloak of battle. The irony is that David sends the instructions to Joab in a letter carried by the victim himself.

11:16-27 David arranges Uriah's death. The instructions David gives Joab are not carried out exactly as given. David had intended for Uriah alone to be slain and for the deed to look like an accident. Joab, understandably concerned for his reputation as military tactician, entices the men of Rabbah to attack, causing some Israelites to be slain, among them Uriah.

Now Joab, anticipating the wrath of David for the deviation, prepares his messenger carefully for a possible angry reaction. What David does say gives not only a look at how wars were then fought but what was going on in Joab's mind. For example, the warning about letting the troops go too near city walls recalls Abimelech's shameful death in similar circumstances at the hand of a woman (v. 21; Judg 9:50-54). Joab may be letting David know how Uriah's death actually took place.

David's response is unexpectedly mild. Things like this happen in war, he says, and the sword devours indiscriminately (v. 25). David will later be very much concerned whom the sword devours when it is a matter of his sons. Here he responds as to a run-of-the-mill war report, with appropriate messages to keep up the siege and be of good courage.

After delaying over the scene between the messenger and David, the narrative regains speed at the telling of Bathsheba's mourning for Uriah, her marriage to David and the birth of their son, all in verses 26-27. The adultery and murder completed, the Lord's judgment comes at last: the thing David did was evil in the Lord's eyes (v. 27). This judgment is the key for what follows.

12:1-7a "You are the man!" Now it is the Lord's turn to send. The power-drunk David is about to be brought to his senses. Nathan, the prophet who brought the promise of David's lasting kingdom (7:16), now conveys the Lord's disapproval. In a parable Nathan tells of a poor man (Uriah) whose beloved lamb (Bathsheba) has been appropriated by a rich man (David). The picture of the lamb's intimate daily life with its master reflects the happy marriage David has usurped in selfishness and cruelty. Although nothing is said in the parable about murder, David breaks in with a decree that the rich man shall die. When he adds that the thief shall make fourfold restitution, he inadvertently foreshadows the loss of his own four sons (12:18; 13:28; 18:15; 1 Kgs 2:24-25).

12:7b-15a The sword over David's house. Nathan, reporting the words of the Lord, recites all the benefits given David: the kingship over both Judah and Israel, the harem of the deceased Saul, a fact not made known before. Was this not enough? The Lord would have added more, had David asked (v. 8), so pleased was the Lord with this divine favorite. David was like a spoiled son for whom not enough can be done. Now he has betrayed the Lord's generosity by despising his word (v. 9).

The punishment Nathan outlines comes in reverse order to the deeds. Because of the murder, the sword will not depart from David's house. Because he took Bathsheba, his friend (identity not disclosed) will lie with the king's wives. As David had done this secretly, the punishment will take place before all. At David's humble admission of sin, Nathan replies that the Lord has already forgiven him. The death David deserved will not be his but that of Bathsheba's yet-to-be-born child.

12:15b-25 David prays for his son's life. Although David adds to his prayer fasting and sleeping on the ground (an ironic touch in view of David's concern for sleeping in chapter 11), the child becomes ill and dies. David in effect has mourned in advance and when death is confirmed, surprises his household by rising, washing, dressing, and eating. From all these an Israelite in mourning ordinarily abstained; by ignoring them David shows his independence of established ritual as well as his acceptance of the child's death (compare 1 Sam 21:1-7).

After David consoles Bathsheba, now his wife, the Lord blesses their union with another son. The divine approval is signaled by the sending of Nathan to add the name Jedidiah, or "beloved," to the name already given him, Solomon. The Lord's love for Solomon will be proved by his accession to the throne after David (1 Kgs 1).

12:26-31 David conquers Rabbah. Rather than take the besieged city of Rabbah himself, Joab sends for David to claim it. Along with the gold crown of the Ammonite deity Milcom, David takes much booty and many captives whom he puts into service. From David's military victories, the story now turns to David the king and father.

13:1-22 The rape of Tamar. Absalom, David's third son, dominates the chapter because of his relationship to Tamar, whom his half-brother Amnon loves. The "love" turns out to be an irrational passion that has made Amnon ill. Taking his cue from this, Amnon's clever advisor Jonadab urges him to use the "illness" as an excuse to bring David to visit him.

David suspects nothing in Amnon's request to have Tamar bake cakes for a sick brother. Once Tamar has the food ready and the room has been cleared (v. 9), Amnon, instead of eating, demands that she lie with him. By using the word "lie" in verses 5, 6, 8, 11, 14, the narrator recalls David's lying with Bathsheba and Uriah's refusal to lie in his own house (ch. 11). The reiteration of "brother" and "sister" stresses the evil that is corroding David's own family.

Tamar makes a poignant and eloquent plea to Amnon not to commit an intolerable crime (literally "folly") in Israel, but Amnon will not listen to her sensible arguments. His passion spent, Amnon's underlying hatred surfaces. Where before he had sent all his servants out (v. 9), now he calls his servant to throw Tamar out (v. 17). Tamar pleads not to be humiliated further; again Amnon refuses. His sending her *away* is the reverse of David's sending *for* Bathsheba (11:4). In grief,

Tamar tears the special garment that marks her a princess and ultimately finds a home with Absalom. David, though very angry when he hears of the deed, makes no move against his first-born. Absalom's silent anger however has an air of foreboding.

13:23-28 Absalom punishes Amnon. Patient but determined, Absalom waits two years to settle the score with the hated Amnon for a crime his father had failed to punish. As Absalom usurps his father's prerogative, David is seen as gradually losing his control over his children.

A false report that all the sons were slain (v. 30) causes David to fear the worst. The strangely knowledgeable Jonadab explains that only Amnon was killed. Here David is typical of many powerful leaders who suffer isolation from their subordinates' plans. As with Amnon (v. 21), David does nothing to Absalom who is allowed to flee unchecked to his paternal grandfather in the non-Israelite region of Geshur (compare Gen 34).

14:1-24 The wise woman of Tekoa. When Joab judges the time is right, he engages a woman skilled in speech and acting to instigate Absalom's return. Like Nathan's parable (12:1-6), her story must bring David to make a judgment on a case close to the king's actual situation but with enough difference to offset suspicion until it is too late. Like David's, the woman's story includes two sons who have quarreled and as a result one has been killed. There are two differences: her son's death was not premeditated murder as was Amnon's, and her family is demanding blood vengeance, as David's is not. Both have the problem of saving the surviving son, in the woman's case because he is the only one to provide posterity, and in David's, Absalom is the heir to the throne.

When David promises to protect her son, she immediately makes a correlation with David's situation. Unaware, the king has judged himself, because what he will do for her son, he will not do for his own (v. 13). The woman presses her point: God does not bring the dead to life but devises ways of returning the banished. If the king would protect her son from death by an avenger, so should he provide a home for Absalom (v. 17).

To win David over, the woman has used disguise (v. 2), homage (v. 4), metaphor (v. 7), and outright flattery (vv. 17, 20). (Compare 1 Sam 29:10; 2 Sam 19:27.) At last David recognizes the hand of Joab in the charade, but he is not angry. Joab's ruse permits him to bring back Absalom for the face-saving reason that the country needs the heir to the throne. However, Absalom returns to Jerusalem not completely reconciled to his father, for David refuses him presence at court.

14:25-27 Absalom's beauty. To fill in the passage of time before David's next contact with Absalom, the narrator concentrates on Absalom's beauty and the weight of his hair. This should alert us to possible trouble, because Bathsheba and Tamar were also beautiful and both had trouble because of it.

14:28-33 Absalom reconciled to David. Once again Absalom bides his time for two years (compare 13:23) before bringing his frustration into the open. We are not told the reasons why Joab who engineered Absalom's return should refuse to come when summoned or why Absalom chose to resort to aggressive means to bring Joab to him. The violence of Absalom's character is apparent in this and in his willingness to have David kill him should the king find him guilty (v. 32).

In Absalom's reunion with his father, there is not a word of welcome or forgiveness, only a kiss. Is it the kiss of one who will betray him (compare Luke 22:48)?

15:1-6 Absalom the politician. Absalom now adopts a high profile with chariots, horses, and men to run before him. By touting himself as a judge for litigants who come to Jerusalem, and by fawning on those from the northern tribes, Absalom works to widen the breach between the North and the South in Israel. The picture is of a person of great vanity and treachery.

15:7-12 David tricked a third time. As he was duped in allowing Tamar to go to Amnon (13:5-7) and Amnon to Absalom (13:26-27), David again lets the sword threaten his house by permitting Absalom to go to Hebron. Absalom's reason for going, the fulfillment of a vow he made in Geshur, is one with which the king can hardly quarrel (v. 8). Why Absalom could not have worshipped in Jerusalem, David never challenges, possibly because Hebron was the place of Absalom's birth (3:2-3) and where David was made king over Israel (5:3). These considerations make Hebron both a logical and ironic place for Absalom to rally his followers. When David's counselor Ahithophel defects to Absalom, the conspiracy is launched.

15:13-18a The loyalty of David's officers. The gravity of Absalom's threat is reflected in David's immediate decision, on hearing of the treason, to flee Jerusalem. All David's officers prepare to depart. By noting that ten concubines are left to guard the house, the narrator anticipates another fulfillment of Nathan's prophecy (12:11). On David's sorrowful journey out of Jerusalem, the party stops first opposite the ascent of the Mount of Olives (the scene of Jesus' *via dolorosa*, compare Luke 22:39). It is the first of seven stations.

15:18b-23 The loyalty of a foreigner. As his people pass before him heading east out of Jerusalem, David stops to urge Ittai of Gath to go back to the king, referring not to himself but to Absalom in Jerusalem. Ittai's loyal determination to stay for life or death (v. 21) counterbalances Absalom's treachery. After this second station, David crosses the Kidron (compare John 18:1).

15:24-31 The arrival of the ark. The sorrowful procession is brought to a halt a third time when the priests Zadok and Abiathar appear with the ark. Perhaps with Shiloh in mind (1 Sam 4:4-11), David sends the ark back in the hope that the Lord will once more let him see it in Jerusalem (v. 25). Resigned though he may be to whatever is in store for him, David does not fail to use the priests and their sons as a source of intelligence about Absalom's activities in Jerusalem.

David continues up the Mount of Olives, weeping and barefoot. The heads of all are covered as a sign of deep sorrow. When the king is told that his advisor has joined Absalom, David for the first time prays publicly for Ahithophel's counsel to be frustrated (v. 31).

15:32-37 Hushai sent on a mission. David and the people have now reached the summit of the Mount of Olives where we are told, significantly, that people used to worship God (v. 32). At this fourth station help comes to David in the form of his friend and confidant Hushai (see 1 Chr 27:33). As with the ark, David does not keep him by his side but sends Hushai to counter Ahithophel's counsel to Absalom.

16:1-4 Ziba brings gifts. The tide of adversity begins to turn for David as he descends from the mountaintop. Stopping for the fifth time, David is met by Meribbaal's servant Ziba (9:2-4; 9-10) with three kinds of provisions: transport, food, and drink. Offering no sign of gratitude, David on inquiring learns that Meribbaal is waiting in Jerusalem to be made king. Without further investigation of this treasonous charge, David impulsively gives all Meribbaal's estate to Ziba. Later Meribbaal will attempt to exonerate himself (19:25-31), but David's touchiness at what may be a resurgence of the house of Saul underlines the persistent threat of secession by the North.

16:5-14 Shimei curses and stones David. The sixth stopping place on David's flight from Jerusalem brings the king into confrontation with another Saulide, also treacherous but more hostile. Shimei of Bahurim brings on David the greatest public humiliation he has yet suffered, but to David none of the cursing and stoning compares with the pain of Absalom's rebellion (v. 11). Shimei rejoices that David's bloody history (referring perhaps to the events of 21:1-14) have brought him the Lord's punishment (v. 8), while David, refusing Abishai's offer to behead Shimei, accepts patiently what the Lord has allowed, hoping his trial will win compensation later (v. 12). Mourning, humiliation, doubt, and betrayal have dogged David's journey since leaving Jerusalem. The support of his people, the loyalty of Ittai, and the promise of help from Hushai and the priests' sons (15:36) are the only bright spots. Exhausted, king and people arrive at the Jordan, the seventh station.

16:15-23 Absalom and his counselors. Back in Jerusalem, Absalom holds a council of war. Hushai joins the enemy camp with cries of "Long live the king!" Absalom's vanity urges him to assume "the king" means himself, but he nevertheless questions Hushai's transfer of loyalty. (For a similar play on misunderstood words, see 1 Sam 28:1-2.)

The devotion Hushai now offers to the one "whom the Lord and all Israel have chosen" (v. 18) is likewise understood by Absalom to mean himself. With these two seeming assurances, it needs only Hushai's pledge to serve Absalom as he did his father to convince Absalom of Hushai's sincerity.

Before Hushai's counsel is sought, Absalom obeys Ahithophel's instructions to take David's concubines. This astute political move to claim the kingship will deal a death blow to any hope of reconciliation between father and son (compare 3:6-11). The tent on the roof recalls David's portentous stroll on the roof of his palace (11:1) and the prophecy that David's neighbor would take his wives in broad daylight (12:11). With tongue in cheek, the narrator comments on the high regard both David and Absalom had for Ahithophel's counsel (v. 23).

17:1-14 Ahithophel and Hushai counsel Absalom. Perceptively analyzing David's situation, Ahithophel advises Absalom to move quickly and silently against the weary king. The discouragement of David's followers will cause panic and flight, leaving the king alone and exposed. With David out of the way, the people can be brought over to Absalom in peace. Ahithophel's apt simile for this, the return of a bride to her husband, is the only flattery for Absalom's swollen ego, but it brings initial agreement for his plan.

As if to show off his new counselor, Absalom asks Hushai to speak as well. Making the most of his chance, Hushai diplomatically suggests that while Ahithophel usually gives good counsel, this time it falls short. Hushai describes effusively David's prowess in war, his tactical skill, the courage of his men, warning that failure on the first attack will discourage Absalom's men. All Israel should therefore be called out and Absalom himself lead the army. Since Ahithophel's plan had not given the prince a role in the pursuit, this alternative must have proved highly attractive to Absalom.

Hushai's elaborate picture of a victory in which all Israel falls upon David and drags the city harboring him into a gorge blinds Absalom and his followers to the unreality of the scheme. The narrator comments that Ahithophel's effective plan was rejected because the Lord planned Absalom's ruin (v. 14).

17:15-22 David crosses the Jordan. Hushai must have feared that Ahithophel's plan could still be adopted, for he urges David not to tarry on this side of the Jordan. The two priests' sons, with the help of a clever woman much like Rahab (see Josh 2), are able to deliver the message in time. David and his people spend the night crossing the Jordan, a move that means both separation and safety.

17:23-29 Help for David. Ahithophel knows that Hushai's plan will bring defeat for Absalom and the rebels. It is not the disappointment of personal rejection that leads him to suicide. Ahithophel is a realist who gambled for high stakes and lost. His is not a shameful death, since he was buried in the family grave. Malefactors earned a pile of stones (compare Josh 7:25-26; 2 Sam 18:17).

Well ahead of Absalom, David reaches Mahanaim (see Gen 32:1-3, 11). Necessary and welcome provisions for David's weary men are brought by the Ammonite prince Shobi, by Machir who had housed Meribbaal before David brought him to Jerusalem (9:4), and by Barzillai, a wealthy adherent of Saul's. This unexpected support from non-Judahites helps restore the strength and courage of the fugitives.

18:1-5 David pleads for Absalom. David's battle preparations include dividing the army into three commands: Joab, Abishai, and the newly arrived Ittai of Gath with his men (15:18-22). Ittai's support may have been decisive because of the large number of soldiers lost to Absalom.

David's bid to lead the soldiers into battle is politely refused, either because they were aware that the king was a target for capture or because they wanted to spare him a confrontation with Absalom. David, who was once praised for slaying tens of thousands (1 Sam 18:7; 29:5), is touchingly told he is worth tens of thousands—behind the lines. Before departing, the soldiers and their commanders hear David's clear request not to harm Absalom.

18:6-18 Absalom defeated. The brief notice of the battle in which David's men are victorious (vv. 6-8) tells of heavy casualties caused by the treacherous forest more than by actual fighting. As with many biblical battles, natural forces—mud, hornets or disease—often bring hostilities to an end. The victory is not to those who fight as much as to the Lord who moves events according to the divine will.

The aftermath is far more dramatic than the battle itself. Absalom is caught by his head in a tree, as the loyal soldier and the disobedient Joab argue about who will kill him (vv. 11-14). The soldier's reminder of David's charge fails to deter Joab, who like a matador places his darts in Absalom and lets his picadors finish him off. As was true with Abner (3:22-27), Joab cannot tolerate a threat to the throne. He is a man of action operating under human counsels; David, more sensitive to the will of God in his life, loves his son more than royal power. Here he is made increasingly aware of the punishing sword that Nathan predicted would never depart from his house (12:10).

With the blowing of the ram's horn (v. 16), the battle for the throne is over. The Israelites flee and Absalom is covered with a mound of stones, a malefactor's burial (compare Josh 7:26). The pillar Absalom built for himself recalls the memorial trophy of Saul (1 Sam 15:12). The notice that Absalom had no son is a direct contradiction to 14:27, which gives him three.

18:19-32 Bringing the news to David. Joab may have had in mind David's execution of the Amalekite who brought news of Saul's death (1:13-15) when he keeps Ahimaaz from running to tell David that Absalom is dead. Although Ahimaaz outruns the Cushite, he is unable on reaching David to relay the bitter truth (v. 29). With distractions about runners sighted and formal greetings (vv. 24-28), the narrative delays tantalizingly for some thirteen verses before the blow of Absalom's death crushes the king.

19:1-5 Joab reproves the grieving David. The simple repeated words "My son, Absalom my son!" convey the depths of David's grief more than any description. As before David had wept and covered his head while ascending the Mount of Olives (15:30) because of Absalom's rebellion, here he weeps with covered head (v. 5) because Absalom is dead. Instead of victory songs and rejoicing, the people have stolen back into the city like a defeated army (v. 4). The use of "stole" recalls that Absalom had stolen the hearts of the people in his attempt to win the throne from his father (15:1-6).

Joab's is the voice of reason, and of the state, in contrast to David's absorption in the death he had so hoped to avoid. Disregarding the king's grief, Joab reminds David that he is insulting the very people who have saved his life. David responds to the threatened loss of support by forcing himself to greet his people. The effects of David's sins here pass beyond his family to touch the throne. He is a beaten man, no longer the self-satisfied monarch of chapters 9 and 10, who enjoyed doing good deeds. Now he is forced to do them.

19:10-15 The return of the northern tribes. The narrative leaves the scene at Mahanaim with its half-hearted victory procession before David to what is left of Absalom's fleeing army. Leaderless and divided in their loyalties, they slowly realize that David was not the failure as king that they had once thought. When David hears they want to restore him (a frequent word in vv. 11-15), he becomes the persuasive politician, reminding them of their common kinship and promising to give Joab's command to Absalom's former general Amasa (17:25). This demotion will rankle the hot-headed Joab until he brings about his own restoration (ch. 20).

19:16-24 The apology of Shimei. This will be the first of three meetings which parallel those of David's descent from the Mount of Olives (16:1-14). The Benjaminite Shimei who had cursed and stoned David hurries to be first in bringing the king across the Jordan. The narrative by repeating the words "cross" and "escort" (the same word in Hebrew) conveys the urgency of the king's crossing.

Ziba comes with Shimei (v. 18), showing that his loyalty was with the Saulides all along. At Shimei's plea for forgiveness, Abishai again offers to take off his head, but David will suffer no vengeance on his day of victory (compare 16:9; 1 Sam 11:13). David refers to Abishai as a satan, or adversary, as Jesus did of Peter (Matt 16:21-23).

19:25-31 Meribbaal explains his absence. Blaming his delay on Ziba's betrayal, the crippled Meribbaal shows his loyalty by appearing as a mourner. Although Meribbaal claims Ziba has slandered him and flatters David by calling him an angel of God (v. 28), David answers him brusquely and reassigns him half the estate he had previously given Ziba (16:1-4). This encounter does not prove Meribbaal's loyalty, but it is telling that Meribbaal is willing to let Ziba have the whole property as long as David is safe (v. 31).

19:32-41a David tries to reward Barzillai. Although he is a Benjaminite, Barzillai has shown his allegiance to David in his gift of supplies at Mahanaim (17:27-29). Although he is a man of substance, like Nabal (1 Sam 25:2), the wise, generous Barzillai is a pleasant opposite to the foolish, stingy Nabal.

From Barzillai's protest that he is too old to enjoy life at court, we learn how ancient kings spent their days.

19:41b-44 The smoldering division. By this time all of Judah and half of Israel are with David. The Israelites, who had been reconsidering their position, accuse the Judahites of stealing David away, perhaps in an attempt to cover their own indecision. The Judahites defend themselves vigorously, despite Israelite protests that they have a greater share in the king (v. 44). David's return to Jerusalem cloaks a deeper division between the two parts of the land which will erupt decisively under David's grandson Rehoboam (1 Kgs 12).

20:1-3 Israel follows Sheba. A new leader for the dissatisfied Israelites who had recently brought David across the Jordan appears in a Benjaminite named Sheba, whom the narrator labels a rebellious individual (literally, a "son of Belial" as in 1 Sam 1:16; 10:27; 25:17; 30:22). With Sheba's cry "Every man to his tent," the men of Israel again desert David (compare 1 Kgs 12:16). Once in Jerusalem, David puts the ten dishonored concubines who had been left behind to guard the house (15:16; 16:21-22) into a guard-house (confinement) for the rest of their lives.

20:4-13 The pursuit of Sheba. David in addressing the new threat from Sheba, assigns Amasa to muster the Judahite army. When Amasa fails, David, bypassing Joab, sends Abishai in pursuit. Suddenly we find (v. 7) Joab and his men marching behind Abishai. For all David's reluctance to deal with him, Joab seems too powerful to be suppressed.

On the way, at Gibeon, Joab interrupts the pursuit to eliminate his rival Amasa with characteristic ruthlessness. By killing Amasa, Joab has rid David of one more political problem; this time we do not hear that David wept. The people standing about the dead soldier wallowing in his blood are dismayed. Only after the body is covered and removed from the highway can the pursuit of Sheba continue.

20:14-22 The wise woman of Abel Beth-maacah. When Joab called on a wise woman before in chapter 14, she was told what she was to do and say. Here a wise woman tells Joab what to do (v. 16). Their conversation is about his planned destruction of a city which is a mother in Israel, that is, a place to which Israelites in trouble can resort for advice. To prevent this, the woman is willing to sacrifice one life for her people. With the bloody murder of Amasa just accomplished, it is high irony for Joab to deny so vehemently that he wants to ruin or destroy anything (v. 20). When the woman delivers Sheba's severed head, Joab can sound the horn for retreat.

20:23-26 Government leaders. Joab is securely in command with the restored government in Jerusalem, but Abishai is strangely missing. With this list of officials, the long narrative segment contained in chapters 9 to 20 ends.

VII. APPENDICES

2 Sam 21–24

These chapters supply information about David which does not fit well into the continuous narrative of 2 Sam 9–20. David's devotion to the Lord is here highlighted so that his loyalty to the divine covenant recalls the Deuteronomistic theme of obedience to the Lord and its attendant blessings. David's life story is concluded in 1 Kgs 1–2 with Solomon's accession to the throne and David's death.

21:1-14 David relieves the famine. These events may have preceded David's taking of Meribbaal into his house (ch. 9). Here after consulting the Lord according to his usual practice (see 1 Sam 23:2, 4, 9-12; 30:7-8; 2 Sam 2:1), David is told that the blood vengeance incurred by Saul in an otherwise unknown attack must be avenged. Saul had apparently violated the covenant which the Gibeonites had tricked the Israelites into making (Josh 9:3-27) by wholesale slaughter. It is not the surviving Gibeonites but the Lord who demands restitution. The Gibeonites, however, decide the means of atonement, for which David chooses two sons of Saul and five grandsons for execution.

With a devotion like that of Antigone to her dead brother, Rizpah guards the bodies of the slain, two of whom are her own sons (v. 8). A death which involved exposure to the birds of the air and beasts of the field was considered a horror in Israel. Report of this kindness to the dead arouses David's sympathy so that he has all seven, as well as the bodies of Saul and Jonathan (1 Sam 31:11-13) buried in the tomb of Saul's father Kish (v. 14).

The account of their deaths includes two foreshadowings of the end of the famine: the barley harvest is about to begin (v. 9) and the rain is about to come (v. 10). The bodies are sacrifices to plead with the Lord for a good harvest by means of expiating past unrepented sins. The incident is an example of the Israelite idea of collective guilt for which the people suffer along with the king when he has offended God.

21:15-22 David and his heroes. There follow four short accounts of battle with Philistine giants who are equipped like Goliath (1 Sam 17:4-7). The story of Abishai's rescue of David (v. 17) shows how necessary to him were the "ruthless" sons of Zeruiah (3:39). The reference to David as the lamp of Israel indicates the soldiers' affectionate regard (compare 18:3-4). The confusion between verse 19, with its attribution of Goliath's slaying to Elhanan, and 1 Sam 17:48-51, where David is the hero, finds resolution in 1 Chr 20:5. There Elhanan is said to slay Goliath's brother, thus giving David and Elhanan one giant each.

22:1-51 David's rock of deliverance. In a majestic poem, a duplicate of Psalm 18, David praises the Lord in humility and gratitude for having saved him from his enemies. The opening verses offer seven synonyms for the Lord as savior: rock, fortress, deliverer, shield, horn, stronghold, refuge. The Lord keeps David from violence (v. 3) and rescues him from the violent man (v. 49). The Lord hears the psalmist's voice (v. 7), but foreigners hear the same voice, now clothed with power to subdue other nations (v. 45).

The Lord's action in David's life is compared to the action of nature: breakers surge and floods overwhelm (v. 5); the earth sways, quakes, trembles, shakes (v. 8); fire, wind, darkness, cloud, lightning, waters appear in tumultuous action to portray the Lord's response to the cry of the persecuted one (vv. 5-17). The Lord's rescue is described in mythological terms: The Most High mounts a cherub and flies, borne on the wind (v. 11; compare 1 Sam 4:4; 2 Sam 6:2; Exod 25:10-22). The reasons for the rescue are the Lord's love (v. 20) and because David was found free of guilt (v. 21), loyal (v. 22), and innocent (v. 25).

In the center of the psalm, the poet addresses the Lord directly. "You are faithful . . . you are wholehearted . . . sincere . . . astute . . . you save . . . you are my lamp . . . you brighten the darkness" (vv. 26-29). The Lord deals with people according to their righteousness. Note the contrasts: the sincere vs. the crooked (v. 27), lowly vs. lofty (v. 28), darkness vs. light (v. 29).

Resuming the third person, God is presented again as rock (v. 32), the poet's way is unerring and his feet are swift (v. 34). Preparing for war, God trains David to use the bow and girds him for battle (vv. 33, 35, 40). With this God-given strength, the poet overcomes his enemies, who flee and are destroyed (v. 41), are forsaken (v. 42), ground to dust and trampled (v. 43), enslaved (v. 44), obedient (v. 45), fawning and cringing (v. 46). The poem ends with praise for the Lord's kindness to the anointed king, "to David and his posterity forever" (v. 51; compare 1 Sam 2:10).

23:1-7 David praises God. These "last words" of David begin in the style of the oracles of Balaam (Num 24:3-4, 15-16; Gen 49; Deut 33). After describing himself as raised up, anointed, and favored by the Mighty One of Israel, the poet attributes his words to the spirit of the Lord (v. 2). A just and God-fearing ruler is compared to the action of morning light playing on wet grass (compare Hos 6:3). David's rule has been established in an eternal covenant (2 Sam 7), for he has seen salvation and the fulfillment of every desire (vv. 5-6). By contrast the wicked are dangerous to the touch and like thorns destined for the fire (compare Ps 118:12).

23:8-39 David's heroes. David has attached to himself a loyal group of outstanding warriors. Three are singled out for strength and bravery (vv. 8-12). Together they risk their lives to draw water for David from a well guarded by the enemy (v. 16). David's pouring out of the water before the Lord links their dedication to him with an act of worship. Of the remaining warriors cited, only Abishai and Benaiah have significant roles in David's story.

24:1-9 David's temptation. Ancient Israelites saw the anger of God in every calamity. Here the pestilence in Israel begins because of David's curiosity to know how great his people were, knowledge evidently reserved for the Lord alone. Joab tries to dissuade David from taking a census but fails (vv. 3-4). His subsequent journey through the land gives an idea of the extent of Israel during David's reign. The kingdom is bordered by the Mediterranean on the west, Gilead on the east, Dan in the north, and Beer-sheba in the south. By counting women, children and the aged, the total population could be as much as five times the one million three hundred thousand listed (v. 9).

24:10-17 David repents. Once again David regrets an impulsive act (compare 1 Sam 24:6). The prophet Gad offers a threefold expiation, all of which contain three time units. Seeing the Lord as more merciful than humans, David chooses the three-day pestilence, the shortest but the most intense.

As the famine of 21:9 ended at the beginning of the barley harvest, so here the plague breaks out at the time of the wheat harvest, both signs of divine mitigation. These, with the Lord's merciful staying of the destroying angel's hand before Jerusalem (v. 16), are lessons of God's love in the midst of trial. David sounds a progressive note in ancient theology when, instead of the accepted collective atonement, he asks the Lord to punish him and his family alone.

24:18-25 The threshing floor of Araunah. The command to build an altar in Jerusalem, with the promises to make a lasting house for David (7:8-16), is the basis for Israel's Zion theology which celebrates God's holy mountain Jerusalem as the focal worship place for all humankind (see Isa 2–4; Psalms 46, 47, 76, 84, 87, 122).

David's need to purchase the threshing floor of Araunah means that he did not own all the land in his capital and that Canaanites shared the land with Israel. As Abraham made his ownership of Sarah's grave in Machpelah legal by buying rather than accepting the site as a gift (Gen 23:10-16), so David refuses Araunah's offer and insists on paying a high price for land that will later become the ground for the temple.

Epilogue

The Lord has satisfied the people with two important needs: a prophet to deliver the divine word and a king to govern them. These are the leaders by whom the Lord guides their history, punishing them or delivering them as required. God exacts obedience, loyalty, and gratitude, but does not abandon the sinner. The lives of all are bathed in God's goodness and love.

1 AND 2 KINGS

Alice L. Laffey, R.S.M.

INTRODUCTION

The two books of Kings are, properly speaking, the final chapters of a larger section of the Old Testament known as the Deuteronomistic History. This history also includes the books of Deuteronomy, Joshua, Judges, and 1 and 2 Samuel.

In Deuteronomy the law is set forth. Fidelity to the law is to be Israel's response to its covenant relationship with Yahweh, its God. The book details the responsibilities of the people once they have entered the land promised by God to their ancestors.

The Book of Joshua describes Israel's successful conquest of the land of Canaan under the capable leadership of Joshua, a conquest easily and speedily accomplished because of the faithfulness of the people to Yahweh.

The Book of Judges gives a more realistic account of the Israelites' entrance into Canaan. Progress was slow and not always totally successful. Because the people were not always faithful to Yahweh and often worshiped idols, the Lord left Canaanites to dwell alongside the Israelites in the land. During this period of approximately 240 years of Israelite history, leadership in the land took the form of judges—military leaders or prudent advisors whose governing role was not hereditary.

The Book of Samuel introduces Samuel, the last of Israel's judges, the prophet who will anoint Israel's first king. Despité some opposition, Saul is named Israel's first monarch. However, his unfaithfulness to Yahweh leads to his downfall, and he is replaced by David, the Lord's servant, on whom God's spirit rests. The Second Book of Samuel continues the account of David's rise to power and records his covenant with Yahweh, in which he is promised a dynasty.

The two books of Kings tell the story of David's dynasty. David's son Solomon succeeds him as king and the dynasty is initiated: the Lord's promise is fulfilled. Moreover, Solomon builds a temple for Yahweh, also in accord with the Lord's promise to David.

The First Book of Kings details Solomon's reign, the building of Yahweh's temple, and Solomon's eventual degeneration into unfaithfulness. Solomon's sin and his son's stupidity lead to the division of the kingdom into north and south—Israel and Judah. Much of the remainder of this first book deals with the northern kingdom, especially its idolatrous leaders; for them there can be no lasting dynasty.

The Second Book of Kings continues to assess Israel's and Judah's monarchies. Judah weaves an intricate pattern among its more or less good and bad kings, in contrast to the consistent pattern of evil found in the northern kingdom. Finally the evil northern kingdom is definitively punished; the Lord sends Assyria to conquer it, and the Israelites are taken into exile. Eventually the southern kingdom follows a similar path. Because of infidelity—most explicitly because of the sins of the evil King Manasseh—the Babylonians destroy the temple and lead the people of Judah into exile. Thus do the Second Book of Kings and the Deuteronomistic History end, except for the hopeful note of Yahweh's continued faithfulness in the final three verses of 2 Kings. There it is recorded that Judah's exiled king, Jehoiachin, is released from prison and receives kindly treatment from Babylon's new king.

As one reads through the History and recognizes this frequently repeated pattern, one wonders if they (we) will ever learn.

The Deuteronomistic editor

Most scholars agree that these seven Old Testament books—Deuteronomy, Joshua, Judges, 1 and 2 Samuel, 1 and 2 Kings—originally existed in fragments written at different times by different people in different places. These sources were combined by one or more editors into a literary and theological unity. Some of the material may be as old as the tenth century B.C.E., dating back to the reign of King Solomon; other material, such as the account of Judah's destruction, cannot be dated before the sixth century B.C.E. A final author, usually named the Deuteronomistic editor or the Deuteronomistic historian and referred to as "Dtr" by scholars, wove together the sources at his disposal into a unified, interpreted account of Israel's past.

The Deuteronomistic theology

A consistent theological thread, the perspective from which the entire Deuteronomistic History is recorded, delineates the basic postures between God and the people. Yahweh initiates good for the people, but they turn from God and worship idols. This evil provokes the Lord's anger, and God's response is to punish the people, for example, by selling them into the hands of their enemies. The oppression the people experience leads them to turn again to their God and to ask for forgiveness and deliverance. The Lord hears the people's prayer and saves them, only to have them soon afterward turn from the Lord once again. The pattern—God's good, Israel's sin, God's anger and punishment, Israel's affliction and prayer, God's forgiveness—repeats itself frequently throughout the History.

This theology surfaces in the books of Kings in the form of blessings for kings' fidelity (for example, Solomon's wealth and honor because he sought wisdom to govern the Lord's people) and punishment for kings' sins (for example, the denial to Jeroboam of a dynasty because he caused Israel to sin). Consistently, fidelity issues in well-being, while unfaithfulness leads inevitably to ruin.

Themes

1. **The Davidic covenant.** 2 Sam 7 introduces a special relationship between the Lord and King David. This special relationship, often called the Davidic covenant, is a further explication of the Lord's covenant with Israel. David is "the Lord's servant," "a man after the Lord's own heart." Because the Lord is with David, he is victorious over the Philistines; the Lord grants him rest and enables him to build for himself a palace of cedar. David sins, but he acknowledges and repents of his sin; though he is punished, he is forgiven, and the Lord neither rejects him nor revokes the covenant. Thus David becomes a model—one who walked in the ways of the Lord.

This theme of the Lord's special love for David, and David's faithful response, continues to appear throughout the books of Kings. The fidelity of Yahweh to Solomon and to Judah's kings is very often explained as a consequence of David's intimate relationship with the Lord; David's was a proven faithfulness from which others benefited. We note, then, that Judah's good kings are "like David" in their obedience to the Lord's commands and the evil kings are "not like David." Solomon and Judah's kings are buried "with their ancestors in the city of David." A special effort is made to show that each successive king of Judah is the son of his father, that is, a direct descendant of David. In fact, the Lord relents of the punishment that his people deserve and postpones the end of the kingdom "for the sake of David, his servant."

2. **The Davidic dynasty.** As a consequence of the Lord's covenant with him, David, unlike Saul, will have a dynasty; his sons will rule after him. This theme underlies much of the books of Kings. The promise is fulfilled when Solomon succeeds David. Again, according to the theology of the Deuteronomistic editor, fidelity leads to blessing, wealth, and prosperity for the king and for the people, while unfaithfulness brings ill. Solomon's fidelity leads to wisdom, wealth, honor, and the temple, but his infidelity leads to the division of the kingdom. Yet David's dynasty

remains intact. One tribe, Judah, remains loyal to David's descendants. For some four hundred years, and until the final chapter of 2 Kings, there is a son of David on the throne of Judah.

3. **The Lord's temple.** David is willing to build the Lord a temple, but the Lord prefers that David's son Solomon build it. Its construction is described in the early chapters of 1 Kings. If Yahweh is important, then the dwelling place of his presence must be grand. Three chapters are devoted to elaborate descriptions of the temple's construction, and finally, in 1 Kgs 8, Solomon dedicates it.

The temple figures prominently in the remainder of the History. The major sin of Jeroboam, Israel's first king, was that he built shrines at Bethel and Dan to prevent the people from going south to Jerusalem to worship. Those kings of Judah judged by the Deuteronomistic editor to be "good in the eyes of the Lord" are those who elaborately adorn the temple, who bring offerings to it, who order its restoration, and who remove the idols brought there by their evil predecessors. When Judean kings form alliances with foreign nations, the temple is pillaged and stripped of its treasures. Inevitably, the destruction of the kingdom of Judah and the demise of Yahweh's temple go hand in hand.

4. **Prophecy and fulfillment.** Throughout the books of Kings we find many examples of the editor's conviction that God is faithful. God's word, spoken through chosen representatives, is effective; it always comes to fulfillment. Because the Deuteronomistic editor viewed Israel's history as the lived-out expression of the Israelites' fidelity or infidelity to their covenant relationship with Yahweh, prophets promise, warn, and threaten. They reveal the future consequences of present attitudes and action. They do not speak the word of the Lord in vain. The power of God will bring that word to pass, and the History records explicitly that it does.

5. **The law.** Leadership's fidelity to Yahweh, or lack thereof, is expressed throughout the Deuteronomistic History, including the books of Kings, in terms of Israel's obedience to Yahweh's law. The Mosaic law and the response of David's descendants are the measurements by which to evaluate the monarchy. The Deuteronomistic editor interprets the events of Israelite history according as the kings and people obey or disobey these laws.

These five themes—covenant, dynasty, temple, prophecy, and law—are interdependent and pervade the History. They are key instruments in the Deuteronomistic editor's exposition of his theology, and central to the unity of the books of Kings.

Women and the books of Kings

Many commentators do not notice the significant roles played by women during the period of Israel's monarchies and how these figures have been incorporated into the books of Kings. It is important not only to recognize the evil leadership of a Jezebel, who even outdid her husband in idolatry, malice, and deceit, but also to note other female characters who significantly affected the course of Israel's history: Bathsheba, the queen of Sheba, Jeroboam's wife, the widow for whom Elisha multiplied oil, the Israelite servant girl and Naaman's wife, who together with Elisha made possible his cure. This commentary will make a special effort to point out the contributions of women.

In a similar vein, one cannot accept unqualifiedly that the Deuteronomist—or the Chronicler either, for that matter—was a man. However, considering the period in which the texts were produced, as well as their content and style, I am inclined to attribute them to male authorship.

Then and now

Though the final editing of the books of Kings took place no later than the late sixth century B.C.E., we, as a believing community, regard their word as sacred and as meaningful to us. It is important that we understand the context in which these books were written—by whom and for whom—and that we seek to understand what they meant to the people to whom they were originally addressed. But we must go further. If these texts are to have meaning for twentieth-century Jews and Christians, we must dialogue with the texts against the socio-political and cultural situations in which we find ourselves. We must together seek to understand what constitutes twentieth-century covenant fidelity and, conversely, what forms our idolatry takes.

COMMENTARY: 1 KINGS

PART I: THE REIGN OF SOLOMON

1 Kgs 1:1–11:43

To better understand many of the allusions given in the introductory chapters of the First Book of Kings, some insight into the life of the Israelites in their land in the first millennium B.C.E. might be helpful. First, let us consider the problem of syncretism (the fusion of different religious practices) and foreign women. The Israelites worshiped Yahweh, the God whose marvelous acts in history on their behalf had brought them out of Egypt and into a land that had become their own. But once in this land, they were frequently tempted to incorporate into Yahwism the fertility cults of their Canaanite neighbors. This can be partly explained by their new dependence on agriculture and by their need to guarantee a fertile land and a prosperous harvest. Yahweh had done wondrous things, but could Yahweh make the crops grow?

The infiltration of pagan fertility practices into the Israelite religion was often occasioned by the marriage of Israelite men to Canaanite and other "foreign" women. These women would retain their belief in fertility gods and goddesses after their marriage to Israelite men and were, consequently, often accused of leading Israel into idolatry. That is why the Deuteronomistic historian warns against intermarriage (for example, Josh 23:12) and why, in the text, marriage to foreign women is frequently a foreshadowing of doom.

One must keep in mind, also, that the text we have as Scripture is theologized history; that is to say, history has been shaped here by a theological perspective. A twentieth-century interpreter of history may expect documents to convey what really happened and may facilely label as untrue the shaping of events (for example, by deliberate omissions, emphases, editorial comments, even literary constructions). Yet, are we really so different when we differentiate between an economic history and a political history (with appropriate emphases and omissions), or easily recognize that a Southern interpretation of the American Civil War may read very differently from one produced in Massachusetts?

Applying this principle to the books of Kings, one can only presume that things may not have actually happened precisely as they are here described. In keeping with the intention of the final editor to show how fidelity to Yahweh led to success and the converse, the characters' actual history—what really happened to them and to Israel during their reigns must be interpreted as the consequence of their fidelity or infidelity to Yahweh. This commentary will look closely at how the text portrays the characters and will suggest, when there is obvious inconsistency, what was probably happening in Israel's history.

The first chapters of 1 Kings connect the previous two Old Testament books, 1 and 2 Samuel, to what follows. The "hero" of 2 Samuel, King David, dies and bestows the kingship on Solomon, the son of his favored wife, Bathsheba, despite the fact that an elder son, Adonijah, is a lively contender for the throne. The chapters that follow emphasize that Solomon's reign is characterized by devotion to the Lord, thereby explaining its political and economic success. Solomon begins by acknowledging his fidelity to the covenant, his reverence for the Lord. It is *for the Lord* and because of the Lord's gift that he will succeed as king. The last chapters (11–12), however, show a shift in Solomon's loyalty. He who had "loved the Lord" now "loves foreign women" (11:1), who lead his heart astray. This judgment accounts for the fact that Solomon, because he oppressed his own people (for example, by taxation and forced labor), lost their support—so much so that the kingdom is split after his death.

1:1-4 David on his deathbed. Most scholars believe that this incident—David, now old and "cold," that is, unable to engage in sexual intercourse—functions as an inclusion. (Inclusion is the technique of framing a literary unit by using the same or a similar word, phrase, or episode at both the beginning and end of it.) David's first sin was his sexual encounter with Bathsheba (2 Sam 11). There he took for himself a woman who already belonged to another. Here, ironically enough, Abishag, a "beautiful girl" legitimately his, is not able to warm and arouse him. In this patriarchal society a woman is understood to be the possession first of her father and then of her husband; yet these women—Abishag and

Bathsheba—significantly affect the life of the king, the well-being of the kingdom, and even the circumstances surrounding the king's death. The verses also point out that David, who had stayed home "in the spring when kings go out to war" (2 Sam 11:1), will not die in battle like his predecessor Saul. The kingdom, by the time of David's death, is well established and at peace.

1:5-10 Ambition of Adonijah. One might expect that David's elder son Adonijah would succeed his father as king. Even before his father's death and, seemingly, with his father's tacit approval, Adonijah prepares to take over. He acquires chariots, drivers, and henchmen, the appropriate possessions of one who will soon "lead in warfare and fight the people's battles" (see 1 Sam 8:20). He rallies support, yet he lacks crucial support from Yahweh's spokesman, the prophet Nathan. This, surely, is an evil omen.

1:11-53 Solomon proclaimed king. Nathan supports Solomon as Israel's future king and plans accordingly. Nathan served as the Lord's spokesman to David at least twice before. It was he who communicated to David the Lord's promise of a dynasty (2 Sam 7), and he who communicated the Lord's judgment of David's sin with Bathsheba (2 Sam 12). David has every reason to take Nathan's word seriously. Now, to convince David that Solomon should reign after him, Nathan arranges a meeting between David and Bathsheba. She is to remind David of his promise to her that her son will succeed to the throne. Nathan assures Bathsheba that he, too, will try to persuade David that Solomon should be king.

Bathsheba and Nathan execute their plan successfully. David names Solomon as his successor, orders Solomon to ride on his mule, to be anointed king, and to sit on his throne. The contender, Adonijah, now has no chance. His only hope is that Solomon will spare his life, which, at least for now, he does.

Was this text written during Solomon's reign, at his court? Is it, in fact, the legitimation of a conspiracy? From a historical perspective, perhaps one must answer in the affirmative; yet, from a theological perspective, the spokesman of Yahweh, supported by David's wife, has indeed revealed Yahweh's will.

2:1-11 David's last instructions and death. David's last advice to his son has to do, first and foremost, with covenant fidelity. Solomon is to revere the Lord as David has done; only thus will Solomon be guaranteed success in his undertakings; only thus can it be guaranteed that a descendant of David will remain on the throne. This is the first time explicit conditions are made regarding the dynasty; its continuance is dependent on faithful response to the covenant.

David's other advice regards specific persons: Joab, Barzillai's sons, and Shimei. Because Joab, David's general, had, without David's knowledge and consent, stabbed Abner (see 2 Sam 3) and Amasa (see 2 Sam 20), David wants Solomon to punish Joab. (One must ask here whether Solomon wants Joab out of the way because he had supported Adonijah, whether this request of David legitimates Solomon's decision to kill a political enemy.)

Barzillai, in contrast, represents loyalty. He had helped David flee from Absalom, and such faithfulness merits reward. Twice elsewhere in the Deuteronomistic History (2 Sam 9:10; 2 Kgs 25:29) eating at table with the king is an explicit sign of favor.

Finally, Shimei should be punished. David has kept his promise and has not put him to death, as his treason deserves (see 2 Sam 19:24). On the other hand, such infidelity cannot be ignored. Solomon's reign must not be thwarted by potential conspirators.

Having spoken his last, David dies. He had reigned seven years in Hebron and thirty-three years in Jerusalem, that is, a total of forty years. Whether these numbers denote historical accuracy or are used symbolically is uncertain. (In many biblical texts, including the Deuteronomistic History, as will become evident, the numbers three, four, seven and twelve [thirty, three hundred, and the like] express totality or completion.) David is laid to rest with his ancestors and buried in the City of David. This assertion is the first of many similar expressions that occur throughout the Deuteronomistic History with reference to the Davidic kings. The Deuteronomistic editor explicitly refers to the place of burial to emphasize the close connection between David and each king of Judah.

2:12-46 The kingdom made secure. David legitimated Solomon's elimination of Joab and Shimei as political opponents. Solomon must now legitimate his removal of

Adonijah, his half-brother, for Adonijah will be a potential threat to the throne as long as he lives. Adonijah asks for Abishag, the woman who had "warmed" the dying David (1:3). Recognizing Bathsheba's influence with Solomon, Adonijah petitions her to intercede for him that he might take Abishag for his wife. Solomon's response is a vehement refusal, for he recognizes such a request as a clear bid for the throne (note again the indirect but very real importance of Abishag; compare 2 Sam 16:22). Solomon is now justified in ordering his brother's death.

Solomon next removes the priest Abiathar from his position of prestige (v. 27). After all, he had supported Adonijah. The text legitimates this decision by a reference to the prophetic denunciation of Eli's house (see 1 Sam 2:30-36). The word of the Lord is thus fulfilled.

Another threat to Solomon's throne is David's general, Joab. Joab deserves death for killing two men without David's knowledge, and David himself had wished it, or so we are to understand. Coincidentally, it just so happens that Joab, too, had been one of Adonijah's supporters! Once Abiathar is out of the way, Solomon replaces him with Zadok; once Joab is out of the way, Solomon replaces him with Benaiah (v. 35). Obviously, both Zadok and Benaiah had been strong supporters of Solomon (see 1 Kgs 1:8).

Finally, some excuse has to be found to make Shimei's death legitimate. David had wanted Shimei to be punished for his disloyalty, and Solomon has only to find a way to eliminate him. Solomon creates circumstances conducive for Shimei to violate a sworn oath, and then Solomon waits. His patience is rewarded, and eventually Shimei is put to death (v. 46).

Having removed all the opposition, Solomon is now secure on the throne. The theological perspective of the text's author has established that Yahweh's will, expressed through the prophet Nathan and through David, has been accomplished. If we are to interpret verse 39 historically, it took three years to make the kingdom fully secure.

3:1-15 Wisdom of Solomon. With political threats removed, political alliances are in order. Solomon wastes no time in securing the "friendship" of Egypt by marrying the daughter of Pharaoh. This removes the possibility of invasion from the south and creates the peaceful climate in which Solomon can build his palace, the Lord's temple, and the walls of Jerusalem. Though he has intermarried, no mention is made of idolatry. In fact, his worshiping at the high places—activity that is later associated with infidelity to Yahweh—is explained by the fact that the temple had not yet been built (v. 2).

The first part of Solomon's reign is characterized by covenant fidelity to the Lord, by love and obedience. He worships at the best shrine and, from the abundance of prosperity with which the Lord has blessed him, he makes generous sacrifices to Yahweh. Often, as here, dreams occasion an encounter with Yahweh (note, for example, Nathan's dream in 2 Sam 7). In the ensuing dialogue, Solomon perceives himself as Yahweh's servant and requests from the Lord an understanding heart by which to govern the people and to distinguish right from wrong.

Yahweh responds generously. Solomon's request will be granted, and, in addition, he will receive the standard blessings of covenant fidelity—riches and glory and a long life. (When these texts were being written, the Israelites did not believe in life after death. Therefore, for the Deuteronomistic historian, reward for covenant fidelity took the form of material prosperity, a long life, and progeny to continue one's life.) Solomon's reverence for the Lord, proven by his altruistic request, would merit him wisdom in addition to the usual covenant blessings. Solomon awakes from his dream and again sacrifices to the Lord (an inclusion).

3:16-28 Solomon's judgment. Solomon immediately begins to make judgments with the understanding heart the Lord has given him. Cleverly, he sets forth the condition that will enable him to determine the real mother of the living child, and his insightful decision wins the awe of the people, that is, the glory that the Lord had promised.

4:1-6 Chief officers of the kingdom. Solomon's cabinet, if we can call it that, was composed of Jehoshaphat, who had supported David (see 2 Sam 8:16; 20:24); Abiathar (the same Abiathar rejected in 1 Kgs 2:27?); Benaiah and Zadok, who had supported Solomon in his bid for the throne (see 1 Kgs 1:8); sons of Solomon's supporters (Azariah, son of Zadok, and two sons of Nathan); and, finally, some unknown men not referred to elsewhere in the Bible.

4:7-5:14 Solomon's royal state. Just as there had been twelve sons of Jacob and twelve tribes of Israel, so now the land is divided into twelve parts. This time each commissary is to contribute one month's supply of provisions to the king's household. This is the first textual evidence that Solomon used the people for his own benefit. What Samuel had warned—that the king would set the people to do his plowing and his harvesting, that he would tithe the crops and vineyards and flocks (see 1 Sam 8:12, 15, 17)—is here acknowledged.

Each commissary has a leader, but the identity of the leader seems to be of no particular interest. Seven men are named, as if to distinguish them from other persons similarly named. Five are identified merely as the son of somebody. None is delineated elsewhere in the History in greater detail. Nevertheless, one may safely conclude that what these men have in common is loyalty to Solomon.

The shrewd organization of Solomon's empire ensures peace and prosperity in the land. For this reason Solomon continues to be characterized by the God-given gifts of wisdom, exceptional understanding, and knowledge. Further, his political savvy is complemented by his literary and musical talents, as well as by his expertise in biology. No wonder he wins international acclaim!

[The editors of the New American Bible have rearranged several verses of the original Hebrew here and elsewhere for the sake of better comprehension. It is for this reason that verse 7 begins chapter 5 and verse 20 follows verse 8.]

5:15-32 Preparations for the temple. Solomon builds alliances wherever he can (see 1 Kgs 3:1), and the one he continues with the Phoenicians stemmed from David's time (see 2 Sam 5:11). Appealing to his father's past history of good relations with Hiram, Solomon obtains Lebanese lumber and workers for the construction of the temple. Solomon's kingship is from the Lord, and the building of the temple will fulfill Nathan's prophecy (see 2 Sam 7:13). In this way the text justifies the consolidation of kingship and religion in Jerusalem.

The first stages of temple-building are marked by cooperation between the two countries. The terms of their agreement or "covenant" are observed by both parties. But is there internal cooperation? Or, to put the question another way, under what conditions and obligations do the Israelites participate in the building project? Do the thirty thousand workmen, in relays of ten (note the numbers!) represent forced labor? Does their resentment cause some of the hostility the dynasty experiences at the end of Solomon's reign (see 1 Kgs 11-12)?

Scholars suggest that there was an anti-temple faction in Israel, just as there had been an anti-monarchy faction (see 1 Sam 8). According to this view, a conservative group—how extensive we do not know—resisted a permanent dwelling for Yahweh's presence in their midst. To join temple and king would be to become even more "like the other nations." The presence of such a conservative element would explain why David had not built a temple. It would also explain a certain resistance to temple-building during Solomon's reign. Moreover, the resistance would have been compounded by inhumane treatment of the temple workers.

6:1-38 Building of the temple. The specific dating we encounter here relates this new and important event to two other major events in Israel's history: the Exodus and Solomon's accession to the throne. This dating pattern is common in the Old Testament, including the books of Kings. Dating is never given by year (for example, 964 B.C.E.), but by relating an event to other significant events.

Next follows a detailed description of the temple. The sacredness of the temple is attested to by the statement that as much work as possible is done at a distance from the building site (v. 7). Its magnificence is asserted by the frequent references to fine woods (olive, fir, and imported cedar), finely carved stone, and an abundance of gold and other decoration. The holy of holies, which would contain the ark of the covenant, is singled out by its elaborate wealth of ornamentation.

Inserted into the account of the building of the temple is a prophetic word that sets conditions for Yahweh's fulfilling his promise to David (the lasting dynasty?), as well as for Yahweh's dwelling in the midst of Israel and not forsaking them: Solomon must observe the Lord's statutes, ordinances, and commands (vv. 11-13). This text is a strong echo of Deuteronomistic theology: obedience will yield good, but the blessings are dependent on fidelity. The chapter ends with the assertion that the temple was completed seven years after it was begun.

7:1-12 Building of the palace. Immediately after saying that it took seven years to complete the Lord's dwelling the text tells us that it took thirteen years to complete the king's dwelling. Are we to conclude that "seven" is meant to be symbolic for the completion of the temple, while "thirteen" is intended as an accurate estimate of the time it took to build Solomon's palace? Or are we to conclude that the king cared more for the grandeur of his own house than he did for the Lord's dwelling? Whereas the Lord's temple measures 60 by 20 by 25 cubits, the palace is larger: 100 by 50 by 30 cubits (a cubit varied from 15 to 22 inches). And, in addition, Solomon builds a tribunal, and separate living quarters for himself and Pharaoh's daughter. Everything is well made; he makes a court and a porch for his own palace similar to those made for the temple.

7:13-51 Furnishing of the temple. These verses form an inclusion—temple, palace, temple. Although the temple itself, including the altar, the table for the showbread, and the lampstands, is heavily laden with gold, many of the articles made for use inside the temple quarters—the columns, the water tank, the stands, basins, pots, shovels, and bowls—are shaped from bronze. Hiram, king of Tyre, had been contracted to provide cedar for the temple; now Hiram, a skilled metalworker and an Israelite whose father had been from Tyre, is contracted to help with the furnishings.

David's act of dedicating offerings to the Lord becomes a precedent for Solomon and future kings (v. 51). Such gifts to God are safeguarded in the temple treasury. Whether this treasury was also the palace treasury is uncertain, but pillaging valuables from the Lord's dwelling would certainly be regarded as a serious offense. When everything is completed, the temple is dedicated.

8:1-21 Dedication of the temple. Verses 1-4 bring together the old and the new: the elders, the tribal leaders, the princes of the ancestral houses, the ark and the tent of meeting, the Levites and the priests, the City of David. Whether the text reflects a combination of sources or a later effort to win all to Solomon and the temple is uncertain. In any case, the past—Israel's former leadership and Yahweh's former dwelling place—comes now to the temple at Jerusalem.

The entire community of Israel, Solomon included, is said to have sacrificed sheep and oxen to the Lord and to have watched the priests march in procession with the ark, bringing it to its resting place in the temple's holy of holies. The reader is explicitly reminded that the ark contains the two stone tablets, which symbolize the Lord's covenant with Israel (v. 9). What better way to connect king and Yahweh, to show Solomon's fidelity to the Lord (compare 1 Kgs 3:4, 15), and to express the approval of the people for what Solomon had built? The cloud that filled the temple is a clear indication of the Lord's approval (compare Exod 16:10; 40:38; Num 9:18; and many similar texts). Again, validation is made for king and temple. The prophetic promises made in 2 Sam 7 that David's son would sit on the throne and that David's son would build a temple for the Lord have now both been fulfilled.

8:22-66 Solomon's prayer. The remainder of this long chapter is constructed as Solomon's prayer to the Lord at the time of the temple's dedication. Verses 22-26 are similar in form to David's prayer in 2 Sam 7:22-29: first the singularity of the Lord is extolled; then Yahweh is thanked for the blessings already bestowed and for future divine promise; finally the Lord is asked to effect the remainder of the promise. Here the specific request is for Solomon's sons and the continuation of the dynasty. Solomon then cleverly brings together pro-temple and anti-temple sentiments. He affirms that no place, not even the highest heavens, can contain Yahweh, yet he also affirms that the temple which he has built is the very place in which Yahweh wants to be honored (vv. 27-30).

Many scholars believe that verses 33-34 and 46-51 are later additions to the original prayer because they suggest a condition of exile. This is quite possible, since the original prayer understands the temple as the appropriate place toward which to petition for forgiveness from sin, sin that results in any of a variety of punishments—defeat, drought, famine, pestilence, blight, and the like. The temple is also understood to be the place of just judgment and the place toward which Israel is to pray for victory in battle (the ark will no longer be taken into battle).

Verses 41-43 and 60 suggest an openness to foreigners, which may originate either in Solomon's policies of imperialism or simply in his foreign diplomacy. These verses may even be an exilic addition dating to a time when nationalism was no longer a possibility.

Israel's election as the Lord's chosen people is explicitly and repeatedly given as the reason why the Lord should listen to Israel's prayer.

Solomon's address to the people (vv. 56-61) repeats the form of the opening of his prayer to Yahweh: he praises Yahweh for fulfilling the divine promises and then petitions for the Lord's continued blessings into the future. Again, the text connects Israel's obedience to the Lord with the Lord's not forsaking the people. The dedication concludes the same way it began, with Solomon and the people sacrificing to the Lord. Only after seven days do the festivities end. The people return home contented with king and temple.

9:1-9 Promise and warning to Solomon. The dialogue continues. Solomon has spoken in prayer to the Lord; now the Lord again speaks to Solomon (compare 1 Kgs 3:10-14). Whereas the Lord had previously required obedience for continuing the divine presence in the temple and to Israel, the Lord now sets forth conditions for the continuation of David's dynasty (compare 1 Kgs 6:12-13). Further, the text explicitly names the sin of idolatry (v. 6). The punishment for Solomon's and his descendants' infidelity will include destruction of the temple, loss of nationhood, and exile. The text here foreshadows what is to come.

9:10-18 Other acts of the king. This text suggests Solomon's additional failings. He conscripted his own people to build the temple (see 1 Kgs 5:27-31), and later he dealt unjustly with Hiram. The twenty Galilean cities that Solomon gave to Hiram amounted to less than adequate payment for the materials he provided for the temple and the palace. Moreover, Solomon forced the non-Israelites living in his dominion to help not only in the building of the temple and the palace, but also in the construction of Jerusalem's walls, several cities, and a fleet. Nevertheless, Solomon, at this time in his reign, is still faithful to Yahweh, as attested by his concern for the temple and by his offerings.

10:1-13 Visit of the queen of Sheba. A wealthy woman submits to Solomon's superior wisdom and is duly impressed by his grand style and by his fidelity to God. The two exchange an abundance of precious gifts. Verses 11 and 12 seem misplaced, belonging rather with 1 Kgs 9:26-28. In any case, they attest to the close cooperation between the fleets of Hiram and Solomon, to Solomon's benefit. The gold from Ophir is now supplemented by precious wood and stones.

10:14-29 Solomon's wealth. Solomon is ostentatious with his wealth; he uses gold everywhere. His drinking vessels and utensils are of gold, and he puts gold shields and gold bucklers on display in his palace. Every three years his ships bring a new cargo of precious metals. Solomon seems to have everything: the Lord's wisdom, peace in his land, abundant wealth, recognition by everyone. Perhaps his fame leads to envy and resentment, since part of his wealth comes from annual tribute. One must also ask whether the text describing Solomon's chariots is a subtle allusion to the condemnation of kingship in 1 Sam 8:11-12.

11:1-43 The sins of Solomon. Solomon has married Pharaoh's daughter and loved the Lord (see 1 Kgs 3:1-3). Now he loves foreign women, and in symbolic abundance (seven hundred and three hundred!). Because marriage to foreign women inevitably led, in the judgment of the Deuteronomist, to the worship of their gods, Solomon merits the Deuteronomist's stereotypical condemnation of idolatry. Solomon's heart, therefore, is no longer like his father David's, fully faithful to the Lord. His disobedience is explicit. The Lord had promised the continuation of the dynasty on the condition that the people worship Yahweh and Yahweh alone. The Lord's response to Solomon's sin can only be anger and punishment. And so the Lord again speaks to Solomon (vv. 11-13). One notes the absence of prophetic mediation here; the Lord personally names the punishment. The kingdom will fall not to Solomon's son but to Solomon's servant; yet, "for the sake of David," this will not happen during Solomon's lifetime, nor will the entire kingdom be taken away.

During the latter part of Solomon's reign, political adversaries abound: Hadad and the Edomites to the southeast; Rezon of Syria to the northeast; and even his own servant Jeroboam from the north of Israel. And the king of Egypt gives refuge to Jeroboam! The text vindicates Jeroboam's rebellion with a prophetic word (vv. 31-39). Ahijah delivers to Jeroboam basically the same message the Lord gave to Solomon: the kingdom will be divided, and part will be given to Solomon's servant. Because of David, this will not happen until after Solomon's death.

If ten tribes are given to Jeroboam and one to David's descendant, what happened to the twelfth tribe? Most scholars conclude that the reference here is symbolic (the numbers ten and one can each represent the whole) rather than historical. By this time certain tribes had been incorporated into others; for example, Simeon and Levi into Judah and perhaps part of the tribe of Benjamin as well (compare 1 Kgs 12:21).

The Deuteronomistic editor, whose words are put in the mouth of the prophet Ahijah, is swift to make conditions for Jeroboam's future reign and dynastic potential; they will depend on fidelity to Yahweh's commands. David has become the model *par excellence.* For his sake his descendants will continue a dynasty; only if Jeroboam is faithful to Yahweh, as David was, can he hope for a lasting dynasty. David's descendants will indeed be punished, but the Deuteronomist sees an end even to that.

The record of Solomon's death (vv. 41-43) is similar to that of most Judean kings. Reference is made to a source, no longer extant, where more information can be found regarding Solomon's reign. Reference is also made to the duration of his reign—in this instance forty years (a generation), the same number of years as his father's reign. Further, Solomon is buried with his ancestors, including David, in his father's city. Finally, the text notes that his son Rehoboam, in dynastic fashion, reigned after him.

PART II: JUDAH AND ISRAEL TO THE TIME OF AHAB

1 Kgs 12:1–16:34

This section chronicles the history of a divided kingdom between approximately 930 B.C.E. and 870 B.C.E. During that time three of David's descendants reigned in the southern kingdom of Judah: Rehoboam, Solomon's son; Abijam, Rehoboam's son; and Asa, Abijam's son. A dynasty could not be sustained in the northern kingdom. The house of Jeroboam endured only until Jeroboam's son Nadab was murdered. The house of Baasha endured only until Baasha's son Elah was murdered. Zimri held the throne only seven days until he himself was murdered. The house of Omri succeeded in maintaining a dynasty of four generations. Because the biblical text deems Ahab the most evil king of the north—the king whose wife, Jezebel, killed the prophets and led Ahab to ruin—the Deuteronomistic historian incorporates into his History an entire section devoted to Ahab's reign and his confrontations with the prophets Elijah, Micaiah, and Elisha.

12:1-25 Secession of Israel. Ahijah's prophecy to Jeroboam (11:31-39) is fulfilled. Had Rehoboam been politically shrewd, he might have avoided the split. As it happened, brash self-confidence led to authoritarianism and ultimately to defeat. Solomon's reign produced a rival, but a leader with few followers. Rehoboam's reign produces the followers and the revolt. The Lord warned Solomon of the division to come; Ahijah prophesied to Jeroboam; now Shemaiah tells Rehoboam and his people the same thing. Three times the kingdom's division is explained by the infidelity of the Davidic kings.

Because Jeroboam lacks a geographical center like the one David and Solomon established at Jerusalem, he moves about during the first years of his reign. From this time onward in the books of Kings, the term "Israel" refers only to the northern segment of what had been David and Solomon's united kingdom. "Judah" now refers to the southern kingdom, that part of the land ruled over by a descendant of David.

12:26-32 Religious rebellion. Could there be a religious solution to Jeroboam's political dilemma? Creating a new king demands a new capital and, so it would seem, a new temple. How else can the political-social-religious unity of the people be maintained? Their very identity as a people and a nation is intricately bound to belief in, and worship of, Yahweh, even if idolatry and syncretism are sometimes practiced. Is Jeroboam really guilty, or is he guilty only in the eyes of the Deuteronomistic historian, for whom all the northern kings, without exception, do evil in the eyes of the Lord?

Whatever the true answer to that historical query may be, Jeroboam, from the perspective of the biblical text's author, does the very things that can only merit condemnation: he makes golden calves for the people to worship (v. 28; compare Exod 32); he builds temples on the high places (v. 31); he ordains non-Levitical priests (compare Exod 28ff.); and he arbitrarily establishes a pilgrimage feast (v. 32).

12:33–13:34 Message of the prophet from Judah. It is no surprise that a prophetic condemnation follows. As Jeroboam is offering sacrifice on the altar at Bethel, he is confronted by a Judean prophet, who condemns not only the altar but also the priests whom Jeroboam has created. Later, during Josiah's reign in Judah, the illegitimate priests of the high places will be sacrificed. (Was the text written during Josiah's reign to legitimize the purge?)

The truth of this prophetic word is confirmed by the fulfillment of another of the prophet's words—the destruction of the altar (see 1 Kgs 13:5). The prophet of God is in touch with the power of God. When Jeroboam begs him to ask the Lord that his outstretched, withered hand might be restored, he does so, and the king recovers (13:6). Yet, in spite of his experiences of the power of God, Jeroboam does not repent.

God's power can work through God's representative even when that agent is not obedient to God. Students often ask why the old prophet tricked (deceived!) God's envoy. Should not prophets be believed and obeyed? Prophets are to be believed and obeyed by those who hear the word of God through them, but prophets are to be obedient to the word of God that they themselves have heard. One must not trust a human being—even God's messenger—when one has heard God. The younger prophet is now confronted with God's condemnation of his disobedience by another prophet: he will not be buried with his ancestors. Again, the text records that the prophetic word is fulfilled. The prophet of God dies and is buried, but he is not buried with his ancestors. Yet, he was a true prophet; the word that he spoke against Bethel will be fulfilled. ("Samaria" is used in verse 32 as a synonym for "Israel.")

14:1-20 Death of Abijah. When in trouble, consult God; when all goes well, do as you please—such would seem to be the philosophy of Jeroboam. The sickness of his son brings him to the same prophet whose promise of kingship to him has been fulfilled (see 1 Kgs 11:30-39). Now Jeroboam seeks out Ahijah to learn the fate of his son. Why doesn't Jeroboam himself go to see Ahijah? Why must Jeroboam's wife disguise herself? Is it because the king does not want his people to know that he needs a prophet's help? Just as the prophets in the previous section remained nameless, so does Jeroboam's wife. Abijah is named once. The text deliberately highlights Jeroboam as the central character—Jeroboam, the unfaithful king.

Jeroboam's son will die—such is the word of the Lord. One could have expected as much (compare 2 Sam 12:14). Moreover, the same prophet through whom God conditionally gave Jeroboam a dynasty now removes it. Of Jeroboam's children, only Abijah will not suffer a violent death. Jeroboam is so evil that even the burial of Abijah has to be justified: there is something in him pleasing to the Lord (v. 13)!

Just as the chronicles of Solomon are no longer extant (see 1 Kgs 14:41), neither are the chronicles of Israel (v. 19) nor, for that matter, the chronicles of Judah (v. 29). The length of Jeroboam's reign, his burial, and his son's accession to the throne tie him to the succeeding Israelite reign.

14:21-31 Reign of Rehoboam. The text alternates its accounts of the reigns of the kings of Judah and those of the kings of Israel. Along with the stereotypical notice of Rehoboam's age when he began to reign and the duration of his kingship, his mother's name, Naamah, is given. This pattern is common for most of the kings of Judah. Because the kings had many wives, it was important to record in which house a new king had been raised. For Rehoboam, the detail that his mother was an Ammonite (v. 21) recalls 1 Kgs 11:1-6, where we are told of Solomon's marrying foreign women and his consequent practice of idolatry.

Verses 22-24 tell how Judah under King Rehoboam succumbs to idolatry. This explains the warfare that Judah experiences with both Egypt and the northern kingdom of Israel. Under Rehoboam's leadership Judah becomes like Israel. The books of Kings here begin to depict a proportionate relationship between the quality of the king and the condition of the temple, a thread woven throughout the remainder of the Deuteronomistic History.

In spite of his evil, Rehoboam is David's descendant; therefore, he is buried with his ancestors, and his son Abijam replaces him on the throne.

15:1-8 Reign of Abijam. The description of Rehoboam's son given here is totally stereotypical: What year of whose reign in the north was it when so-and-so began to reign in the south? How long did he reign? Who was his mother? How is his reign to be evaluated from a covenant perspective and in comparison with David's? If the judgment is that the particular king of Judah was unfaithful to the Lord, then the fact that he endured on the throne is explained by a reference to the Lord's faithfulness to his servant David.

If nothing of particular import occurred during a particular king's reign, from a theological perspective, then a reference is made to the king's death and burial with his ancestors. The name of his successor is given. If one should want further information regarding the king, the reader is referred to the court chronicles.

15:9-24 Reign of Asa. Asa reverses his father's reign. Whereas Abijam reigned for only three years, Asa reigns for forty-one. Whereas his father was not entirely with the Lord like David, Asa, like David, pleases the Lord. Whereas Rehoboam allowed the cult prostitutes (see 1 Kgs 14:24), Asa banishes them. Whereas Abijam made idols, Asa removes them. Whereas Maacah, the queen mother of Abijam's reign, venerated a Canaanite goddess, Asa banishes her. Further, Asa brings to the temple precious offerings, appropriate gifts from himself and even from his father. Asa's reign endures through the reigns of at least five northern kings; he has many accomplishments and has built many cities, blessings of Yahweh for fidelity.

The only shortcoming Asa seems guilty of is letting the high places remain (v. 14). Does this mean he tolerates the idolatry of others within his kingdom? Is this the cause of the continued warfare between the south and the north? On the other hand, is Asa's overwhelming fidelity and resemblance to David the Deuteronomistic historian's explanation of why Asa is able to summon Aram to his defense against Israel (compare 2 Sam 10:19 and 1 Kgs 10:29)? Later the text condemns foreign alliances because they evidence a lack of trust in Yahweh.

15:25-32 Reign of Nadab. The reign of Jeroboam's son, concurrent with the first years of Asa's reign in the south, is similar, from a theological perspective, to his father's. On him and on the entire house of Jeroboam the prophetic word of Ahijah is fulfilled (see 1 Kgs 14:10-16). Verse 32 duplicates verse 16. Scholars usually explain such repetitions as the products of multiple sources. The emphasis that repetition gives is often deliberate.

If the historical reality was constant warfare between the northern and southern kingdoms, then the truth must be acknowledged, in spite of the theological judgment that Baasha was evil and Asa good. History can be shaped by Deuteronomistic theology only so far.

15:33–16:14 Reign of Baasha. The capital of the northern kingdom is not yet Samaria but Tirzah, the city in which Jeroboam eventually settled (compare 1 Kgs 12:25 and especially 1 Kgs 14:12, 17).

The Lord, through his prophet Jehu, condemns Baasha. Baasha's evil, like Jeroboam's, will merit for him the same end: his house will be destroyed; only one son will reign, and that son will meet a violent death. From a historical perspective, written discreetly into the text, one may conclude that Baasha's reign was relatively stable. He survived for twenty-four years on the throne, and his son was able to succeed him. Yet, from a theological perspective, his covenant infidelity made eventual punishment inevitable.

16:8-14 Reign of Elah. The Deuteronomistic historian records only one thing about the reign of Elah: Jehu's prophecy is fulfilled. Elah is murdered and the house of Baasha destroyed. His successor is his servant and murderer, Zimri.

One cannot help but note of the instability of the northern kingdom. The house of Jeroboam reigned for twenty-four years before Nadab was murdered; the house of Baasha reigns for twenty-six years before Elah is murdered. In both instances the murderer becomes king. Neither house reigned a full generation.

16:15-22 Reign of Zimri. Elah's murderer lasts only seven days on the throne before he commits suicide (compare 1 Sam 31:4) and is supplanted by the army general, Omri. Omri apparently has more popular backing than either Tibni, another contender for the throne, or Zimri. The Deuteronomistic historian-theologian blames Zimri's short reign and fate on his sin. No sin is imputed to Tibni, and therefore no explanation is given for his death. In accordance with the violence of the period, a likely historical explanation is that Omri's supporters removed his opposition.

16:23-28 Reign of Omri. Omri moves the capital from Tirzah to Samaria—no small accomplishment in Israel's political history. He dies a natural death and is buried with his ancestors. His son Ahab succeeds him on the throne. Nevertheless, punishment will inevitably come for his idolatry and other sins.

16:29-34 Reign of Ahab. Whereas other kings of the north are compared with Jeroboam and may even have done "more evil" than their predecessors, Ahab is clearly cited as being guilty of evil far beyond that of any of the others. His specific sins are marrying Jezebel and worshiping Baal; he even builds a temple for Baal in the capital.

Moreover, Hiel's rebuilding of Jericho during Ahab's reign merits the fulfillment of the curse in Josh 6:26. He loses his first son when he lays the foundation, and his youngest son when he sets up the gates. Whatever the relative dating of these texts (whether Hiel built Jericho and sacrificed his children—historical events condemned in the later text from Joshua—or whether the passage from Joshua represents an earlier tradition that was inserted into 1 Kings to further document Ahab's evil), there is no doubt that 1 Kgs 16:34 serves as an additional indication of Ahab's sin.

PART III: STORIES OF THE PROPHETS

1 Kgs 17:1–22:54

The remainder of 1 Kings is composed of ancient legends about prophets and their disciples. The content is episodic, inserted into the reign of Ahab in Israel and, indirectly, into the reign of Jehoshaphat in Judah. Throughout the narrative the nature of prophets that has thus far been delineated is further emphasized. The word that God proclaims through a prophet will be fulfilled; more powerful than the king is the prophet.

17:1-6 Drought predicted by Elijah. The word of Elijah to Ahab is a warning of drought and an assertion that Elijah will control its duration. The word of the Lord to Elijah is a promise of protection: food and water and a place of safety. Implicit in the word of the Lord to the prophet is the power of Yahweh; implicit in the word of the prophet is Yahweh's punishment for Ahab's sin.

17:7-24 Elijah and the widow. The miracles of the multiplication of oil and flour and the raising back to life of a widow's only son are the second and third accounts of acts of the Lord's power through Elijah; he has already caused the drought. Ahab's sin brought suffering for the people of Israel; Elijah's fidelity brings nourishment, as does the woman's faith. The power of Yahweh to take away life and to restore it is here demonstrated, as is Elijah's confidence in the Lord.

18:1-46 Elijah and the prophets of Baal. The reader should not be surprised at another miracle, certainly not when an episode is meant to contrast the power of God with the power of no-god. The Lord will bring rain after three years of drought and famine.

Elijah emerges as Yahweh's representative, while Ahab and Jezebel are devotees of the Baals. Obadiah functions as their intermediary. Although he is faithful to the Lord, even to the point of risking his well-being to hide the persecuted prophets, Obadiah nevertheless works for and fears the evil king. However, because Obadiah is faithful to the Lord, he obeys Elijah and occasions the meeting, after three years, of Ahab and Elijah. Each experiences the other as the "troubler of Israel." Who, ultimately, caused the drought—the prophet Elijah or the evil King Ahab?

Mount Carmel becomes the place of confrontation: Elijah, Yahweh's prophet, against

850 false prophets. In a text similar to Deut 30:15-20 and Josh 23:14-16, Elijah exhorts the people to choose Yahweh (v. 21). Next follows a demonstration of the power of Yahweh. One prophet against 850, two bulls prepared for sacrifice, extensive intercession (three pourings of four jars of water over the twelve-stone altar), and a single request. Yahweh's sacrifice catches fire. When Yahweh's supremacy has been securely reestablished, drought gives way to rain (v. 45). The incident is meant to teach Ahab the evil of his ways and to teach the reader the power of Yahweh.

Students often comment on Elijah's killing the Baal prophets. The text is not about killing people; it is about the power of Yahweh. Within that context evil must be removed from the midst of Israel.

19:1-18 Flight to Horeb. Elijah's encounter with God on Mount Horeb has been the subject of much study and reflection. Horeb is another name for Sinai, the mountain of God where the Lord spoke to Moses through a burning bush (see Exod 3) and later gave Moses the Decalogue (see Deut 4–5). The episode is artistically constructed. Before the encounter with the Lord, Elijah is discouraged and almost despairing. The land is evil, the king is evil, the prophets are dead, and Elijah's life has been threatened by Jezebel. He wishes he could die.

But just as Elijah was nourished during the drought and famine, so now he is likewise protected. Twice an angel awakens him to eat, the second time suggesting the journey he is to undertake (v. 7). Just as the Israelites wandered forty years in the desert, so now Elijah takes a journey into the desert for forty days and forty nights. Elijah's complaint to God (v. 10) elicits the Lord's invitation to meet him, an encounter that takes place, not where the power of God is most expected—in heavy winds, an earthquake, a fire—but in a tiny, whispering wind, a noisy silence.

No time now for sulking. Elijah states his plight to Yahweh, but God seemingly ignores his problem and addresses him immediately on another issue. Elijah is a prophet, and as prophet he is commissioned to leave the desert and to anoint three people: Hazael as king of Aram, Jehu as king of Israel, and Elisha as his own successor. These men together will effectively remove all those persons who have been unfaithful to Yahweh. However, a faithful remnant (seven thousand) will be spared.

19:19-21 Call of Elisha. Elijah first calls his successor. The function of the cloak may be symbolic (compare 1 Kgs 11:30-31) or at least an allusion to Elijah's encounter with Yahweh (v. 13). Elisha recognizes the subtle call and follows, symbolically putting an end to his former life.

20:1-43 Ahab's victories over Ben-hadad. That the northern kingdom of Israel was at war with Aram during much of Ahab's reign is certain. There had been hostility and intermittent fighting between the two countries since Baasha's time. But the historical fact is that Israel was victorious over Aram during Ahab's reign. How could the Deuteronomistic theologian account for this? How could Ahab's evil merit victory? Remember the power of Yahweh's prophetic word, especially when a prophet is listened to and obeyed? The first encounter results in an Israelite victory because Ahab seeks the prophet's word and acts accordingly. The second encounter also results in an Israelite victory, this time because the Arameans stupidly believe that Israel's god can be conquered in the plain. The disproportion between the two armies is designed to show the power of Yahweh. Victory is the Lord's.

According to the rules of Israel's "holy war" theology, Yahweh is the warrior who fights for Israel, and, consequently, all spoils belong to Yahweh. Yahweh was victorious over Aram; it was the word of the prophet that directed Ahab's strategy in the first battle; the word of the prophet also warned of a second attack. Yahweh showed great power in achieving Israel's victory over the exceedingly larger forces of Aram. Therefore, Ben-hadad belongs to Yahweh, and Ahab has no right to set him free (v. 34). (The growing power of Assyria in the ancient Near East may be the historical explanation behind the interim peace between Aram and Israel. Shalmaneser's Assyrian Annals refer to an alliance between Aram and Israel toward the end of Ahab's reign [compare 1 Kgs 22:1].)

From a theological perspective, the reference to a prophet's companion who refuses to obey a prophet and is consequently killed (v. 36) is a fitting introduction to the prophetic condemnation of Ahab. Ahab condemns himself in his encounter with the prophet (compare 2 Sam 12). Just as the soldier must bear the penalty for neglecting his charge, Ahab's sparing King Ben-hadad (compare 1 Sam 15:8-9) would lead ultimately to his own death.

21:1-29 Seizure of Naboth's vineyard. To understand why Naboth would not sell or exchange his ancestral heritage, one must refer to such texts as Lev 25 and Josh 13. The interaction of characters shows Ahab accepting traditional values and Naboth's verdict, however unwillingly.

Jezebel, on the other hand, who has appeared in the text only minimally until now—she had killed the prophets and threatened Elijah—does not respect Naboth's decision and ridicules her husband for doing so. She therefore usurps Ahab's power, that is, his name and his seal, and successfully plots Naboth's death. Ahab tacitly cooperates with Jezebel and reaps the benefits. Or so it would seem, until Ahab is again confronted with Elijah! Prophetic condemnation is in order; murder and theft will not go unpunished. Elijah now pronounces a condemnation similar to the ones Jeroboam and Baasha had heard—the violent end of Omri's dynasty. Ahab's body will lie at the very site of his sin. And the evil Jezebel will likewise be destroyed.

Because Ahab hears the word of the prophet for what it is—Yahweh's word of power—he repents. One can expect the prophetic word to be fulfilled, but here as elsewhere (compare 2 Sam 12:13-14) it is mitigated; the punishment owed him is delayed until his son's reign.

22:1-40 Campaign against Ramoth-gilead. Probably at some earlier stage in the text's compilation, notice was given that Jehoshaphat had succeeded Asa on the throne of Judah (see 1 Kgs 22:41-45) before this account of an Israelite-Judean alliance against Aram. Jehoshaphat is here depicted as recognizing the former unity and the potential for unity between Israel and Judah. He therefore seeks to help the northern king regain territory. Though never named in the chapter, that king is Ahab. Perhaps he fades into the background when compared with Jehoshaphat! Whatever happened to Asa's treaty with Aram? Did Aram become greedy and begin to infiltrate southward? Did Jehoshaphat see an alliance with Israel as strategically more important than an alliance with Aram? Israel was, after all, a closer northern neighbor than Aram.

In any event, Jehoshaphat wants the prophets to be consulted (v. 6). The northern king sends for the compromised prophets, those who maintain favor by saying precisely what the king wants to hear. He will go through the motions, but he dare not risk the truth lest the word of the Lord be adverse. Jehoshaphat presses for a more trustworthy prophet, one who will say "whatever the Lord tells" him (v. 14).

Ahab recognizes Micaiah's first sarcastic word to him as untrue (v. 16). The true prophet could only condemn the wicked Ahab. Micaiah's real response is a prediction of Ahab's death in battle: the sheep (see 2 Sam 7:8 and 24:17) will be without a shepherd. Ahab's evil has been so great that the Lord's judgment against him is final. To guarantee that Ahab will not listen to the prophets' prediction of his death and be delivered, Micaiah says that Yahweh has even allowed a lying spirit within the prophets' mouths. Whether Ahab seeks consolation in the deceitful assurance of the false prophets or takes seriously the word of Micaiah, his end will not change. The Lord has decreed evil against him (v. 23).

Micaiah's being sent to prison is not the first reference in the books of Kings to the persecution of a prophet. Jezebel killed many, and Elijah fled for his life from her.

With Ahab's death (v. 35) comes the fulfillment of several prophecies, including Micaiah's. Moreover, Aram has helped to wipe evil out of Israel (compare 1 Kgs 19:17). Ahab is buried, and his son Ahaziah succeeds him (compare 1 Kgs 21:29).

22:41-51 Reign of Jehoshaphat. Jehoshaphat's twenty-five-year reign is relatively uneventful from the perspective of the Deuteronomistic historian. Like his father Asa, he does good in the eyes of the Lord. He continues his father's good practice of removing the cult prostitutes (see 1 Kgs 15:12). Yet, like his father, he also allows the high places to remain active as places of worship (see 1 Kgs 15:14). The reference to Edom and a fleet (vv. 49, 50) implies relative power and prosperity.

22:52-54 Reign of Ahaziah. Like the other kings who end dynasties in the north, Ahaziah reigns for only two years. His evil is compared not only to Jeroboam's and to his father Ahab's, as we might expect, but also to his mother's. We conclude that his mother was the evil Jezebel, especially since his idolatry is specified as Baal worship.

COMMENTARY: 2 KINGS

PART IV: THE KINGDOMS OF ISRAEL AND JUDAH

2 Kgs 1:1–17:41

1:1-8 Ahaziah consults Baalzebub. A new opening and a new king of Israel. Immediately the reader knows what kind of king the Deuteronomistic theologian judges Ahaziah to be—he consults an idol! What follows immediately is prophetic judgment and condemnation.

1:9-12 Death of two captains. For the Deuteronomistic theologian, the power of the prophet far surpasses the king's. No mere soldiers can overpower the power of God. Rather, Elijah pronounces doom on the soldiers sent to capture him, the two groups of fifty and their captains (compare 1 Kgs 18:13). The word of God through Elijah cannot be silenced; it is effective.

1:13-18 Death of the king. The third captain sent by Ahaziah recognizes Elijah's power and pleads for his own safety. He knows what the king has failed to understand: Yahweh, God of power, is with Elijah. When Elijah meets Ahaziah in person, he repeats Ahaziah's fate: the consequence of idolatry is death.

2:1-8 Elijah and Elisha. Elijah's departure is developed literarily with great detail and leads to a climax. Elisha knows of their imminent separation and wants to be with Elijah as long as possible. Elisha follows the prophet southward, from Gilgal to Bethel, to Jericho, and even to the Jordan. Other prophets testify to Elijah's departure and even follow the two as far as the Jordan. The symbolic role of Elijah's cloak as an instrument of power again surfaces when it is used to divide the waters.

2:9-18 Elisha succeeds Elijah. The other side of the Jordan is the place of God's intervention. Elijah is taken up in a flaming chariot drawn by flaming horses. When Elisha sees this, he knows that, according to Elijah's word, prophetic power in good measure will be bestowed upon him. He tears his own cloak in two; he picks up Elijah's and uses it to recross the Jordan, where he meets those who will now become his followers. Elijah is not to be found; the power of God that had been in him is henceforth to be sought in his successor, Elisha.

Many historical-critical scholars have suggested historical and literary confusion between the two men. This is partly because God had told Elijah to anoint Hazael and Jehu (1 Kgs 19:15-16), but the texts later record that Elisha directs the anointing (see 2 Kgs 8:13 and 9:6). It is sometimes conjectured that the miracles now attributed to Elijah were originally ascribed to Elisha and that they have been altered, repeated, and rearranged in order to heighten the literary contrast between Ahab and Elijah.

2:19-22 Healing of the water. Proof of the efficacy of Elisha's prophetic word is recorded immediately. Potentially fertile land needs pure water if the harvest and the people are to be healthy. Therefore, at the request of the people, Elisha throws salt into the water, and it is henceforth considered a source of well-being. The power of the prophet effects good.

2:23-25 The prophet's curse. The power of the prophet can also effect harm, especially for those who do not take the prophet seriously. Such is the common interpretation of this episode: the cursing of small boys, leading to their death. The writer does not intend to depict the prophet's heartlessness but rather the gravity of taking a prophet lightly.

3:1-27 Campaign of Joram against Moab. Ahab's son Joram succeeds his brother to the throne, another "chip off the old block." Though not as evil as his mother (Jezebel) and his father, in the Deuteronomist's judgment, nevertheless, Joram is evil, like all the northern kings.

Continued peace between Judah and Israel during Jehoshaphat's reign occasioned their alliance, this time along with the Edomites, against Moab (compare 1 Kgs 22). Faced with a water shortage, the kings, at the request of the king of Judah, consult a prophet about their dilemma. They approach Elisha. He rejects Joram, who is too much like his father for Elisha's taste, but for the sake of the king of the south he consults the Lord: they will have sufficient water and even be victors over the Moabites (vv. 17-18). Yahweh effects the victory. Through the miraculous misperception of the Moabites, the promise of the prophet is fulfilled.

Defeat in battle causes the Moabite king to seek Syrian aid, and when that recourse fails, he sacrifices his own child in hopes of winning his god's favor over Israel. This horrifies the Israelites, who return to Israel. Perhaps even they fear the power of the Moabite god in his own land!

4:1-7 The widow's oil. Multiplication of a widow's oil—a miracle Elijah had performed (see 1 Kgs 17:14-16)—is performed also by Elisha. Her own husband had been a prophet, and she trusts the prophet's power. Her complaint brings her deliverance.

4:8-37 Elisha and the Shunammite. Yahweh's prophet has power over life and death. Elisha promises the barren Shunammite a child, and later raises that dead child back to life (compare 1 Kgs 17:21-23). The woman had recognized Elisha as a prophet and had volunteered to provide for his needs; he rewarded her with a child. Now she seeks the prophet after her child's death, again showing confidence in God's representative; again she is rewarded. Gehazi, Elisha's servant, is introduced here. He was unable to bring life back into the child (v. 31).

4:38-41 The poisoned stew. A famine (compare 1 Kgs 18:3) occasions Elisha's next miracle. Just as salt had purified contaminated water (2 Kgs 3:19-22), now meal purifies a poisoned stew. In each case the prophet intervenes and effects miraculous good on behalf of his people's health.

4:42-44 Multiplication of loaves. This miracle complements verses 1-7, and together they parallel 1 Kgs 17:14-16. Twenty barley loaves and ears of grain—food for the prophet, yes, but hardly enough to feed a famine-stricken people. Hardly enough, that is, unless the power of Yahweh is with you.

The close literary connection between the miracles performed by Elijah and Elisha, especially the multiplication of food and the raisings from the dead, and similar miracles of Jesus recounted in the synoptic Gospels cannot be ignored. The New Testament writers seem to have selected particular acts of Jesus to assert, especially to their Jewish converts, that the power of God worked through him.

5:1-27 Cure of Naaman. Five persons are introduced in this episode: Naaman's wife; the Israelite servant girl of Naaman's wife; Naaman himself; Naaman's master, the king of Syria; and, finally, the king of Israel. Four are identified by their relation to the leper, and they all support a request that the king of Israel cure him. Israel's king, however, is powerless, as he himself admits. In contrast, Elisha, the prophet of God with the power of God, can heal.

Elisha commands Naaman to wash seven times in the Jordan, but the leper had washed in other rivers before and refuses. He does not yet realize that the word of the prophet contains the power of God. He ignores the word of the prophet but later is persuaded by his servants, who re-echo the prophet's words. He does what Elisha ordered and is cured (v. 14).

Naaman's physical cure becomes the basis of faith in Israel's God. He wishes to repay the prophet, or at least to buy some of Israel's soil, on which he can, in the future, worship Yahweh in Syria. Elisha refuses the gifts but commends Naaman's conversion.

Gehazi, however, is another story. The power of Yahweh had worked through Elisha to effect Naaman's cure, but why not reap personal benefit from Yahweh's power? Such would seem to be Gehazi's motivation in asking Naaman for the silver talents and the festal garments—motivation strong enough to allow Gehazi to lie, first to Naaman, then to Elisha. But God's knowledge and God's power are both present to God's prophet, who denounces Gehazi's deceit and condemns him to Naaman's leprosy. Infidelity can only yield a curse!

6:1-7 Recovery of the lost ax. Elisha performs another miracle, this one on behalf of one of the prophets. The prophet of God has the power of God and the knowledge of God (see 2 Kgs 5:26-27) to effect good for those who are faithful to God.

6:8-13 Aramean ambush. Elisha is here depicted as a prophet of God with extraordinary knowledge, which he puts to good use on Israel's behalf and against the Arameans.

Proof of his power is the fact that the Arameans want to take him captive.

6:14-23 Blinded Aramean soldiers. The prophet of God can overcome any obstacle with the power of God. He can inspire confidence in his otherwise frightened servant; alone against an Aramean army, he can mediate their being blinded; he can himself lead a blinded army into their enemy's capital; he can even persuade an Israelite king to feed and free Arameans. Further, he can so frighten the Arameans that he causes the raids to cease—raids whose effectiveness the knowledge of God is preventing in the first place. Elisha is in control—or so the Deuteronomistic theology of prophecy would have us believe.

6:24–7:2 Siege of Samaria. War with Syria and famine in Israel describe a country under curse, a land far from fidelity to its God. Sometimes idolatry prompted child sacrifice; now the imminence of starvation has prompted even child cannibalism. The Israelite king blames Elisha for the famine and tries to kill him. Elisha's response is to reassert the power of God: the famine will end the following day, yet the king's adjutant who questioned the prophet's word will die.

7:3-13 The lepers at the gate. What great option is there between death by starvation and death by the sword? Such is the thinking of the lepers as they flee to the Aramean camp. Their courage is rewarded. The power of God, this time giving the impression of a large army and causing the enemy to flee, works on behalf of his people.

7:14-20 End of the siege. The flight of the Arameans signals the end of Israel's captivity in Samaria and, in consequence, the end of their hunger. The Arameans' supplies become spoils of war. Moreover, the word of Elisha to the king's adjutant (see 2 Kgs 7:2) is fulfilled; he is trampled at the city's gate.

8:1-6 Prediction of famine. The woman who had been good to Elisha, to whom he had given a child and for whom he had raised her child back to life, again believes the prophet. Elisha warns of a famine and she flees the land. The famine lasts seven years, after which time she returns to claim her property in Israel. The encounter with the king reveals a believing king. Hearing Gehazi's testimony and the woman's own account, the king returns the woman's possessions. Though always unnamed, she is a model of one who takes God and God's word seriously.

8:7-15 Death of Ben-hadad foretold. Aram has to have taken notice of the power of Yahweh's prophets before now. Elisha had thwarted the Aramean raids into Israel (see 2 Kgs 6:12) and had led the Aramean army into Samaria (see 2 Kgs 6:19). Now the king of Aram consults the prophet of Israel about his health (compare Ahaziah's consulting idols in 2 Kgs 1:2). Elisha uses this occasion to prophesy to Hazael that he will replace Ben-hadad as king.

The historical fact is that Ben-hadad was murdered by his servant, Hazael, who usurped the throne of Aram. The historical fact is, also, that Hazael waged war against Israel (see 1 Kgs 18:17). However, the Deuteronomistic theologian does not accuse Elisha of precipitating the murder. Elisha merely names the end result and Hazael chooses the means.

8:16-24 Reign of Jehoram of Judah. Though king of Judah, Jehoram is like Ahab. He is married to Ahab's sister (implied is the fact that she is "a chip off the old block," just as his sons Ahaziah and Joram were). Jehoram's reign, judged on its own terms from a theological perspective, deserves termination, but God preserves the dynasty for the sake of Jehoram's faithful ancestor, David. There are hard times, however, like the war with the Edomites and the loss of Libnah, political difficulties interpreted as religious condemnation. In spite of his sin, Jehoram is buried with his ancestors in the City of David, and his son Ahaziah succeeds him.

8:25-29 Accession of Ahaziah. Ahaziah's mother was Ahab's sister. Knowing only that, one can predict the Deuteronomist's judgment on his reign! He does evil and is like Ahab. The Judah-Israelite alliance against Aram results in Joram's being wounded in battle (1 Kgs 18:17 predicted that Hazael would kill many Israelites). This occasions a visit by Ahaziah to Joram at Jezreel.

9:1-15 Anointing of Jehu. The story line is interrupted to legitimize Jehu as the successor of Joram. The prophetic message, this time delivered for Elisha by a guild prophet, places Jehu, Joram's servant, on the throne of Israel. The prophetic pronouncement against the house of Ahab (1 Kgs 21:21-22) and Jezebel (1 Kgs 21:23) will now be fulfilled. The other army commanders affirm the anointing and form a conspiracy with Jehu against Joram.

9:16-26 Murder of Joram. Drama accompanies Joram's murder. While being comforted by Ahaziah, king of Judah, his own army commander betrays him. But treason is easy, as attested by the fact that Jehu can so easily win over Joram's drivers. The encounter of Jehu and Joram is depicted as the encounter of good and evil. Jehu, having been anointed by Elisha, vindicates the Lord for the evil that the house of Ahab has done. Moreover, Joram's blood is spilled in a place symbolic of Ahab's guilt, the vineyard of Naboth (see 1 Kgs 21:21).

9:27-29 Death of Ahaziah. Ahaziah, whose mother was Athaliah, Ahab's evil sister, must also be removed. Jehu orders his death and it is accomplished. Yet, because he belonged to the line of David, his body is returned to Jerusalem and buried there with his ancestors in the City of David.

9:30-37 Death of Jezebel. Punishment comes, finally, to the evil Jezebel. Just as Jehu won over Joram's drivers, so now he wins over two or three eunuchs, who throw Jezebel out the window to her death. The manner of her death and the decomposition of her body are fitting theological judgments for evil such as hers. The word of the prophet—the power of Yahweh—is thereby executed (see 1 Kgs 21:23).

Jezebel addressed Jehu as Zimri. Zimri was a chariot commander who killed his master, Elah, the king of Israel, thus terminating the house of Baasha (see 1 Kgs 16). Now Jehu has terminated Ahab's house. Yet Jehu is here understood as the Lord's instrument in purging both Israel and Judah of their evil leadership.

10:1-11 Killing of Ahab's descendants. Jehu is not content to have killed Joram, Ahaziah, and Jezebel; he must rid Israel of all the house of Ahab, seventy descendants. Just as the other army commanders joined Jehu in conspiracy (2 Kgs 9:13-14), the drivers joined him (2 Kgs 9:18-20), and the eunuchs supported him (2 Kgs 9:33), so now the leaders in Samaria do his bidding by slaying all Ahab's living relatives. Jehu sees their deaths—and the extermination of all of Ahab's supporters—as the fulfillment of Elijah's prophecy against the house of Ahab (1 Kgs 21:21).

10:12-14 Ahaziah's kinsmen. The termination of Ahab's house and of the evil king of Judah, Ahaziah, is still not enough. Ahaziah was Athaliah's son, and there were other sons; and Athaliah was Ahab's sister. These are still living. The relatives going to visit Ahaziah's family must also be terminated—all of them.

10:15-17 Jehu in Samaria. These verses reemphasize Jehu's gathering of supporters (see 2 Kgs 9:18-19, 32; 10:5), his killing of those who supported the house of Ahab (see v. 11), and the editor's understanding that these deaths were a fulfillment of Elijah's prophecy (see v. 10). Whether in Jezreel or in Samaria or elsewhere in Israel, all who supported the evil machinations of the house of Ahab are destroyed.

10:18-36 Baal's temple destroyed. This is not the first time a character has used trickery to accomplish God's purpose. Remember the prophet who lied (1 Kgs 13)? Jehu must accomplish his mission to rid Israel of the evil that the house of Ahab has perpetrated in Israel, and this he does (see 1 Kgs 19:17). His reward is that his sons will reign on the throne of Israel to the fourth generation.

But Jehu is also guilty of walking in the sin of Jeroboam by tolerating the shrines at Bethel and Dan. The text judges that sin with reference to loss of the eastern segment of Israel's land to Aram.

11:1-20 Rule of Athaliah. Even those who know the books of Kings will fail to take serious note of Athaliah. In a patriarchal period such as this, no woman could legitimately rule. Jezebel may in fact have been stronger than Ahab (see 1 Kgs 21), and Athaliah, Ahab's sister, may in fact have ruled Judah for seven years, but the house of the male, be it Ahab or David, is always credited.

Just as the courage of certain women saved Moses (Exod 2), so now Jehosheba, Ahaziah's sister, saves Joash (the Davidic dynasty) from Athaliah's murderous hand. The place of protection is none other than the temple, and the protector is the priest Jehoiada, who anoints Joash king of Judah. When Athaliah realizes what has happened—that a male descendant of David has been anointed king—she, and those who support her, are powerless. The death she inflicted on Ahaziah's other sons now becomes her own fate.

Restoration of the Davidic line demands

covenant renewal, a recommitment of king and people to the Lord, and a recommitment of the people to the king. Once Baal's temple is destroyed (compare 2 Kgs 10:18-28) the king, having reestablished the appropriate covenant relationship, moves from the Lord's temple to his own palace and throne.

12:1-22 Reign of Joash. Joash was seven when he began to reign, and he reigns for forty years. The Deuteronomist credits the good of his reign to the guidance of Jehoiada.

The account of the temple's repair during Joash's reign describes priests who are not administrators. Apparently Joash's rapport with the priests leads to what he considers a convenient agreement: you keep whatever monies you receive, but you also keep up the temple. For twenty-three years the priests keep the money—period! Called to render an accounting, they beg off responsibility; they will no longer accept the funds, but neither will they be responsible for temple repair. Jehoiada's leadership effects a compromise; he facilitates the collection of the money and its use for temple repair.

Joash's reign has a flaw, however—the high places remain. Usually the high places that the Deuteronomistic historian condemns are associated with Israel. But Athaliah had been Ahab's sister . . . In reality, the continued existence of syncretism in Judah, as well as remaining traces of the idolatry that had existed under Ahaziah, can be presupposed. Furthermore, there may still have been resistance in the countryside, even among Yahwists, to the centralization of worship in Jerusalem. The reader should not be surprised, then, to discover a limited punishment for Judah: Aram poses a threat to their well-being.

The fact that Judah buys off Aram with tribute may be a historical fact, as is Joash's violent death. One may suggest, however, that the juxtaposition of the statements is intended to assert an implicit cause-and-effect relationship, from the theological perspective of the Deuteronomistic historian. Whatever his sins, Joash is David's descendant; he is buried with his ancestors in the City of David, and his son Amaziah succeeds him.

13:1-9 Reign of Jehoahaz of Israel. One might think that this text was lifted from the Book of Judges. Jehoahaz's sin leads to the Lord's anger and oppression by Samaria. However, Jehoahaz entreats the Lord, who sends a deliverer, and the Israelites are liberated from Aram. The pattern, however, will quickly repeat itself (compare Judg 2:11-19). Once back in their land with relative security, the people continue to sin; their fate is lack of prosperity. When Jehoahaz dies, Jehu's descendant continues the line (see 2 Kgs 10:30).

13:10-25 Reign of Joash of Israel. If one were to read these verses logically, one would place verses 22-23 after verse 7; verses 24-25 after verse 19; and verses 12-13 after verse 21. Thus, the Israelites who did evil during Jehoahaz's reign would merit the continued oppression of Aram; yet, the fact that Aram did not totally destroy Israel would also be theologically explained.

Joash's encounter with Elisha again demonstrates the power of the prophet. That Joash takes the prophet seriously is a good sign (though he is desperate) and merits Israel's military successes over Aram; on the other hand, his carrying out of the prophet's word with less than full obedience—thus Elisha interprets the three arrows—accounts for the fact that the victory is limited. The text also hints of conflict between Israel and both Judah (compare 2 Kgs 14:8-14) and Moab.

In spite of Joash's encounter with Elisha, or perhaps because of his less than full success, he receives the traditional Deuteronomistic judgment for a northern king: he is evil, like Jeroboam. Joash is buried in Samaria, and his son succeeds him (see 2 Kgs 10:30).

There is a certain confusion regarding this king's name—Joash or Jehoash; the Hebrew text varies. The accounts recorded here about the king come, most probably, from at least two sources (note, for example, the duplication of verses 12-13 in 2 Kgs 14:15-16).

Elisha, unlike Elijah, dies and leaves no specific successor. Yet, as with Elijah, an aura of the miraculous attends his passing. Because the power of the prophet is in his person—in his life and in his bones—one should not be too surprised that, for the Deuteronomistic historian, even contact with Elisha's bones can restore life. To the end Elisha functions to mediate the power of God.

14:1-22 Amaziah of Judah. Amaziah's mother, Jehoaddin, was from Jerusalem. She, like Joash's mother, Zibia, from Beer-sheba, was of southern origin, which suggests that

Amaziah's may be a more positive reign. He is victorious over the Edomites. Yet, like his father, he allows the high places to remain. He engages in an unsuccessful battle against Israel, which depletes the treasuries of both the temple and the palace. Jehoash's advice to Amaziah—don't fight with me because you'll lose—given as an allegory, recalls Jotham's parable (Judg 9:7-15).

Despite Amaziah's violent death outside Jerusalem, he was of David's line. Amaziah is buried in the City of David with his ancestors, and his son Azariah succeeds him.

14:23-29 Jeroboam II of Israel. Jeroboam II, like his namesake, is an evil northern king. Yet his reign is long and prosperous (we know this from 2 Kings and from the prophets Amos and Hosea). This combination of evil and a long prosperous reign is inconsistent with traditional Deuteronomistic theology, where prosperity is normally a consequence of good, and suffering a consequence of evil. However, the long prosperous reign of an evil king can be explained if it fulfills a prophetic promise: the power of the prophet's word will always be accomplished. An interesting thing about verse 25, however, is that it notes the fulfillment of a prophecy that no preceding text has made. This is the first time in the Deuteronomistic History that Jonah, son of Amittai, is mentioned.

15:1-7 Azariah of Judah. The Deuteronomist's judgment of Azariah's reign, like the reign of his father, is mixed. His mother, Jecholiah, is from Jerusalem. Azariah does good in the Lord's eyes; his reign is long (through the reigns of five northern kings). But the high places remain, and he becomes a leper. Azariah, of David's line, is buried with his ancestors in the City of David and is succeeded by his son Jotham.

15:8-12 Zechariah of Israel. Jeroboam's son stands in contrast to his strong father; he maintains the throne for only six months before falling victim to a conspiracy. The Deuteronomistic historian sees both his reign and its termination as the fulfillment of the Lord's word to Jehu (see 2 Kgs 10:30).

15:13-16 Shallum of Israel. Not much can be said about Shallum's one-month reign. The instability of the throne is obvious. Another conspiracy and another king. Even before the Deuteronomistic theologian can evaluate Menahem, Shallum's murderer and successor, the reader can predict what the judgment will be for a king who cruelly takes revenge on the innocent and on those who had been faithful to their king.

15:17-22 Menahem of Israel. Menahem receives the Deuteronomist's condemnation, as one would expect. He is evil, like Jeroboam. He postpones the potential Assyrian threat and secures his throne by paying tribute to the Assyrian king—tribute he has exacted from his own people.

15:23-26 Pekahiah of Israel. Pekahiah is not spared the Deuteronomistic judgment accorded all northern kings. Menahem's son maintains the throne for two years but is then murdered by his adjutant, Pekah.

15:27-31 Pekah of Israel. Pekah is also evil and is compared to Jeroboam. During his reign Israel continues to be troubled by Assyria. Tribute is no longer sufficient; Assyria takes over some Israelite land. Pekah is not strong enough to withstand Hoshea's conspiracy.

15:32-38 Jotham of Judah. The first thing to note is another confusion in names—Azariah and Uzziah as designations for Jotham's father—probably caused here, too, by the presence of two sources. Jotham, like his father, does good in the eyes of the Lord; he survives a sixteen-year reign and builds one of the gates of the temple. Yet the high places remain; Aram and Israel oppress Judah. When Jotham dies, he is buried with his ancestors in the City of David and is succeeded by his son Ahaz.

16:1-20 Ahaz of Judah. Ahaz merits condemnation of the Deuteronomistic historian for his idolatry and child sacrifice (compare Gen 22). Judah is significantly weakened at this time. The Edomites have recaptured territories, and the Aram-Israelite coalition has attacked Judah, with the intention of removing Ahaz from the throne. Though their plan is unsuccessful, it forces a Judean-Assyrian alliance that, for all practical purposes, makes Judah a vassal of Assyria. The prophet Isaiah warned against such an alliance (Isa 7:1-16). The increase of Assyrian influence means not only the continued presence of syncretism, the high places, and idolatry, as well as the pillaging of the Lord's temple, but also the replacing of Yahweh's altar with an Assyrian one. From the Deuteronomistic theologian's perspective, what greater insult could Yahweh be rendered?

Yet, in spite of everything, Ahaz is David's descendant. Therefore, he is buried with his ancestors in the City of David and is succeeded by his son Hezekiah.

17:1-41 Hoshea of Israel. Assyria destroyed the northern kingdom of Israel once and for all about 721 B.C.E. (see 2 Kgs 18:9-12). It was standard Assyrian policy to take into exile many of the leading citizens of a conquered nation (for example, the priests) and to transplant foreign peoples into the subjugated territory. The aim was to prevent the development of opposition capable of effecting a conspiracy.

The text notes three stages in the development of postexilic syncretism in Israel. Since Yahweh is the God of the land, appropriate worship need be rendered to Yahweh alone. However, since the dominant population, at least in influence, is now non-Israelite, Yahweh is ignored. A compromise is reached when Yahwism is combined with the idolatrous practices of other peoples.

The Deuteronomistic theologian interprets Israel's demise as fitting punishment for all the evil committed against the Lord. Both Israel and Judah have constantly and consistently turned a deaf ear to prophetic warnings. Now Israel, at the hand of Assyria, has paid for its infidelity. Moreover, the future seems ominous for Judah. The dynasty of David remains, but if it has more kings like Ahaz (see 2 Kgs 16), one must ask, "For how long?"

PART V: THE KINGDOM OF JUDAH AFTER 721 B.C.E.

2 Kgs 18:1–25:30

18:1-12 Hezekiah. Hezekiah is very unlike his father; he is even compared to David! Not only is Hezekiah credited with destroying the remnants of Ahaz's idolatry, but he even removes the bronze serpent that Moses made (see Num 21:9). His fidelity is rewarded with a twenty-nine-year reign, prosperity, victory over Philistine cities, and the securing of independence from Assyria in the early stages of his reign, at the very time when Israel is conquered.

18:13-37 Invasion of Sennacherib. Yet, Assyria remains a serious threat. The dialogue recorded here focuses on whom to trust: Hezekiah and his God, or the powerful king of Assyria (compare Isa 36 and 1 Kgs 18). Hezekiah is made to look weak, whereas past Assyrian victories are recounted. By now the reader can predict the Deuteronomist's judgment. Fidelity to the Lord and the covenant will yield success, no matter what the odds. Trust in a foreign power and an idolatrous people, however, can only bring doom.

19:1-19 Hezekiah and Isaiah. Having heard the message of the Assyrian king, Hezekiah proceeds to the temple of the Lord and consults Yahweh's prophet Isaiah. Before Hezekiah has even heard the prophet's consoling word, he imagines a happy outcome: Yahweh angry at Assyrian pride and punishing them accordingly. Isaiah confirms that there is no reason for Hezekiah to fear the Assyrian king. When the king of Assyria repeats his threats, Hezekiah again seeks the Lord (compare Isa 37:1-20).

19:20-37 Punishment of Sennacherib. Isaiah again consoles Hezekiah. "For the sake of David," the Deuteronomistic historian reminds the reader, Assyria will not destroy Jerusalem.

The power of the prophet's word is quickly effected. Yahweh, Israel's warrior, destroys many Assyrian troops, and the survivors flee. Nor does the Assyrian king escape punishment; rather, his own sons kill him. Whereas Yahweh's temple had been a source of deliverance for Hezekiah and Judah, Nisroch's temple becomes the site of Sennacherib's murder (compare Isa 37:21-38).

20:1-21 Hezekiah's illness. Hezekiah's relationship with the Lord is further developed by his cure. Although Isaiah had prophesied that Hezekiah would die from his illness, Hezekiah entreats the Lord, who hears his prayer and adds fifteen years to his life. The sign that the prophet's revised word would be fulfilled is the miraculous movement of a shadow (compare Isa 38:1-8), an immediate indication of the effective power of Yahweh (compare 1 Kgs 13:3-5).

With the emergence of Babylon as a world power, Assyria ceased to be a major threat to the nations of the ancient Near East. Such was the political reality. The Deuteronomistic History, however, uses this opportunity to foreshadow Babylon's eventual victory over Judah with a prophetic proclamation to Hezekiah. Friendliness to Babylon, whether now by Hezekiah or later by Josiah, will not prevent Judah's demise at their hands. Yet, Hezekiah himself will continue to be rewarded for his own fidelity; the doom will come only after his death (compare Isa 39). Hezekiah, of David's line, is buried with his ancestors and is succeeded by his son Manasseh.

21:1-18 Reign of Manasseh. Manasseh's desecration of Jerusalem with innocent blood and his violation of the Lord's temple with every possible expression of idolatry are unforgivable. The promise made to Solomon of the Lord's continued presence in his temple and a Davidic descendant continually on the throne of Israel (see 1 Kgs 9:3-5) was conditioned on the kings' adherence to covenant fidelity. The Deuteronomistic theologian now calls on the word of God, through the prophets, to condemn Manasseh's sin and to predict the dire consequences it will have on Judah. The end is coming.

The Deuteronomistic historian acknowledges the fact that Manasseh survived on the throne of Israel for fifty-five years, the longest recorded reign of any Davidic king, yet he was also judged theologically to be the most evil of them. Perhaps the subtle note that Manasseh was buried "in the palace garden, the garden of Uzza" (v. 18) rather than an explicit statement that he was buried with his ancestors in the City of David is his way of judging Manasseh most harshly. To be buried, first of all, and then to be buried with one's ancestors was of prime importance to the Israelites. In spite of Manasseh's evil, his son succeeded him; a Davidic king remained on the throne as long as the nation of Judah existed.

21:19-26 Reign of Amon. A "chip off the old block," Amon is condemned for doing evil similar to that which his father had done. However, Amon falls more easily into the curses such sin merits: his reign lasts only two years; he is murdered; and he is buried, like his father, in the garden of Uzza. The instability of the people can be seen by the murder of those who murder. In any case, Amon's son Josiah is able to succeed him as king.

22:1-7 Reign of Josiah. Josiah, like Hezekiah, merits comparison to David. Moreover, just as Joash restored the temple after the evil Athaliah's reign, so Josiah sets out to do likewise (compare 2 Kgs 11–12).

22:8–23:30 The book of the law. Josiah is in the process of renovating the temple when the book of the law is found. When he hears its content, he judges his own ancestors by its standards and becomes fearful for Judah's future; the nation merits Yahweh's curses. To further evaluate the book's potential impact on Judah, he sends it to the prophetess Huldah, who will render the Lord's judgment. The word she speaks is twofold: yes, Judah will be punished for its history of sin; however, because of Josiah's distress over the Lord's word, the nation will not be destroyed until after the king's death (compare 1 Kgs 21:29).

The reading of the book of the law in the presence of all the people recalls Moses' command that such a reading be done (Deut 31:9-13). The covenant renewal ceremony recalls both Josh 24:25-27 and 2 Kgs 11:17-20. The covenant ceremony and the proclamation of the law symbolize Israel's recommitment to Yahweh.

Josiah's purification of the temple is as extensive as Manasseh's desecration of it. Specific comment is also made concerning the removal of all the idolatrous remnants left over from the reigns of Solomon, Ahaz, and Manasseh in Judah, and even from that of Jeroboam in Israel. Josiah does, in fact, fulfill the word of the prophet recorded about him in 1 Kgs 13:2. Moreover, the celebration of Passover—a return to the nation's roots—is here reestablished (compare Exod 12; Num 9; Deut 16; Josh 5).

How can the Deuteronomistic theologian accommodate the good that Josiah effected in Judah with the imminent fall of the nation to Babylon? He repeats the prophetic condemnation of Manasseh (see 2 Kgs 21:10-15), reminding the reader of the curses Judah would suffer for its neglect of the covenant (2 Kgs 22:16). And Josiah dies before his nation falls.

Josiah dies at the battle of Meggido (609 B.C.E.). Judah has aligned itself with Babylon against an Egypt-Assyrian coalition; thus the king is killed at the hands of Egypt. This historical truth cannot be denied, in spite of the Deuteronomistic judgment of Josiah's reign. However, Josiah is returned to Jerusalem to be buried and is succeeded by his son Jehoahaz.

Many scholars question whether the book of the law was found in the temple or compiled for the first time, from ancient laws, at this period. They also question whether Josiah established—again, for the first time—or reestablished the Passover. For the purposes of this commentary, it suffices to know that there are good arguments to support both positions.

23:31-35 Reign of Jehoahaz. The Deuteronomistic judgment on Jehoahaz is quite simple: he does evil, for which he is punished. His punishment is a three-month reign, exile to Egypt, and death in exile. His successor, although a Davidic descendant, is not his son but one of the sons of Josiah, his half-brother. Egypt's power over Judah's king is symbolized by the change in name—Eliakim to Jehoiakim; he is not to be understood as a servant of the Davidic covenant and of Yahweh but of Egypt. He does what a vassal should do: he collects tribute from the people to placate Pharaoh Neco.

23:36–24:7 Reign of Jehoiakim. With Babylon's decisive victory over Egypt at the battle of Carchemish (605 B.C.E.), Judah's enemy changed names. The threat that had been Egypt-Assyria was now, decisively, Babylon. In fact, Judah became Babylon's vassal.

Jehoiakim's vain attempt to overthrow the power of Babylon could only yield disaster. The Deuteronomistic historian uses this opportunity to explain Judah's fall as prophetic fulfillment. The Lord has changed sides; God now supports all those nations that are against Judah, and this because of Manasseh's sins (see 2 Kgs 21:10-15). Yet, in spite of Jehoiakim's evil, he is of David's line; he rests with his ancestors and is succeeded by his son Jehoiachin.

24:8-17 Reign of Jehoiachin. Jehoiachin, whose mother, Nehushta, is from Jerusalem, himself does evil in the Lord's eyes. His reign lasts only three months. Isaiah had foretold Jehoiachin's exile to Babylon, along with the exile of others and the confiscation of the temple and palace treasuries (see 2 Kgs 20:17-18). Again, the word of the Lord is effective. When Nebuchadnezzar places Jehoiachin's uncle as puppet king on Judah's throne, he changes his name, the same thing Pharaoh Neco had done to Eliakim and for similar reasons. Mattaniah (Zedekiah) is fully under Babylonian control.

24:18–25:21 Reign of Zedekiah. Zedekiah does evil in the Lord's eyes as his predecessor had done. In fact, he functions as Nebuchadnezzar's puppet for a while, in spite of Babylon's harsh treatment of Judah, but then he rebels. He is not strong enough, however, to rebel, either militarily (from a historical perspective) or by way of fidelity to Yahweh (from a theological perspective). The consequence is, as one might expect, disaster. Zedekiah is captured and blinded, his sons slain. Moreover, Jerusalem is totally devastated: the temple is dismantled and burned, as are the palace and the other large dwellings. The city walls are destroyed, and another wave of people are taken into exile. In addition, the exiles close to the king are killed.

25:22-26 Governorship of Gedaliah. Nebuchadnezzar's delegate, according to this testimony, wants a peaceful situation in Judah and is willing to abide Judah's former army commanders and the citizens who remain in the land. Among these, however, is one Ishmael, who leads a rebellion; a takeover, however, is impossible. As a result, since they have murdered the Babylonian governor, the Judeans are forced to flee to Egypt, for fear of Babylonian retaliation (compare Jer 40–44).

25:27-30 Release of Jehoiachin. The granting of amnesty on the occasion of a new king's inauguration was a relatively common practice in the ancient Near East. For this reason many think that the notation that Jehoiachin was released from prison is historically accurate. But, even so, why should these verses, a duplication of which is found at the end of the book of Jeremiah, end the Deuteronomistic History? Some scholars believe that the History was written to explain why Judah fell. Others hold that the History is a call to future fidelity: learn from the past for the present. Those who prefer this latter interpretation see these final verses as open to a new future. Yes, Judah had been destroyed; yes, the temple had been burned; yes, the Davidic dynasty, as it had been known, was at an end. But . . . the king had not been killed; the Davidic promise had not been totally snuffed out. In fact, Jehoiachin is given a seat above other kings and eats daily at the Babylonian king's table. That this assertion has symbolic significance—whether or not it is historically true—is clear from a similar reference in the Deuteronomistic History (compare 2 Sam 9:7).

If we were to follow the inspired record of Judah's history further, we would see that hope does lie, long after the Exile, in a Davidic successor. The Gospel of Matthew, for instance, is quick to name Jesus as "son of David" (Matt 1:1).

1 AND 2 CHRONICLES

Alice L. Laffey, R.S.M.

INTRODUCTION

Scholars believe that the books of Chronicles are a rewriting of Israel's history from the perspective of postexilic priests. It is commonly agreed that these books were written after the Deuteronomistic History, probably even after the exiles had returned to Judah. Generally speaking, the unique texts and the additions describe matters of particular interest to priests, including sabbath observance, ritual specifications, descriptions of various temple accessories, and the like. Because much of the content of these books is identical to the content of the Deuteronomistic History, and since space is limited in a commentary such as this, only those passages which are unique to the books of Chronicles and which, by the nature of their content, shed light on the Chronicler's particular theological purpose will be commented on here.

Yahweh's temple and Israel's postexilic identity

Yahweh's chosen people, those for whom Yahweh had been warrior and king (see Exod 15:3, 18; compare Zeph 3:15, 17), the recipients of the Lord's promises of land, progeny, and prosperity, are now deprived of national independence. The glorious promises lie in Israel's past; the present is haunted by Persian domination. If there is to be hope for the future, it must be found in Israel's identity as Yahweh's people and, consequently, in conscientious and enthusiastic dedication to the Lord's presence in their midst—thus the importance of Yahweh's temple and Yahweh's priests for postexilic Israel and for the Chronicler. The Chronicler encourages a downtrodden people. All is not lost. They remain the Lord's people, and in that very bond is their future.

The monarchic ideal

Reading through the books of Chronicles, one notes radical differences between the Deuteronomist's and the Chronicler's portrayal of Judah's kings. David and Solomon are idealized by the Chronicler. There is no lust for Bathsheba, no prophetic condemnation, no betrayal by one's son, no potential conspiracy. David emerges as the model monarch. And the same can be said of Solomon. One never learns from the Chronicler of Solomon's seven hundred foreign wives and consequent idolatry. Solomon, like his father, is fully faithful to his God. Pride in one's past is hope for one's future; fidelity is the foundation on which to build the future. The God of David's covenant, the God who continues to give life to postexilic Israel, needs fully faithful followers, and they, in turn, need the memory of model monarchs.

The northern kingdom, condemned by the Deuteronomist from Jeroboam I onward, does not even merit mention in the Chronicler's account. There is no time for their infidelity, no place for memories best forgotten. The Chronicler deemphasizes the two kingdoms of Israel's sinful past in order to highlight the one chosen people of the Lord.

The Deuteronomistic theology

While the Deuteronomist understood well-being and prosperity as God's blessing and reward for covenant fidelity, while curses of one kind or another were God's punishment for infidelity, the Chronicler makes the relationship even more precise. He makes no mention of Hezekiah's possessing any shortcomings. The evil Manasseh receives not only immediate condemnation but also immediate punishment. And for the Chronicler, it is not Manasseh who causes Judah's downfall (compare 2 Kgs 23:26), since he is succeeded by the noble Josiah; rather, Judah's fall is fitting recompense for cumulative evil, and especially for the sinfulness of Judah's last kings.

COMMENTARY: 1 CHRONICLES

PART I: GENEALOGICAL TABLES

1 Chr 1:1–9:34

The first section of Chronicles has no parallel in the Deuteronomistic History. Genealogies are normally associated, however, with the Priestly writer of the Pentateuch. For example, Gen 5:1-28 traces the lineage from Adam to Noah (compare 1 Chr 1:1-4); Gen 11:10-17, 31-32, the lineage from Shem to Abraham (compare 1 Chr 1:10-27, 31-32); and Gen 25:12-17 traces the sons of Ishmael (compare 1 Chr 1:29-31). Moreover, a table of nations compiled by the Priestly writer in Gen 10 indicates where the families in the patriarchal line settled (compare 1 Chr 1:4-23 and 4:1–8:40).

The Priestly writer has a penchant for order. Creation, in his account, takes place in climactic order within six days (Gen 1:1–2:4); there is a census taken of the Israelite tribes before their departure from Sinai (Num 1:1-54; compare 1 Chr 4:1–8:40), and the tribes are arranged for departure (Num 2:1-34); a separate census is taken of the Levites (Num 4:1-49); and, finally, a list of the scouts sent to spy out Canaan is enumerated (Num 13:16).

The line of descent from Jacob to David consists of ten men: Perez, Hezron, Ram, Amminadab, Nahshon, Salmah, Boaz, Obed, Jesse, and David (1 Chr 2:3-25). One notes also how tersely the Davidic line is summarized (1 Chr 3:1-24) with an indication that Judah is carried into captivity in Babylon because of its rebellion (1 Chr 9:1). Those who return, those with whom the Chronicler is most familiar, are lay Israelites, Levites, priests, and temple slaves (1 Chr 9:2).

In postexilic Jerusalem the remnants of the tribes, those originally both from northern Israel and from southern Judah, dwelt together. Yet those most influential in the land were the priests and those associated with them.

PART II: THE HISTORY OF DAVID

1 Chr 9:35–29:29

The remainder of the first book of Chronicles is devoted to David. The text is similar to, yet different from, the books of Samuel. First of all, there is no elaborate description of the pros and cons of kingship; monarchy is a given. King Saul functions here—his genealogy and the account of his death and burial—as no more than a context in which to introduce David. In contrast, the role of priests, sacred objects, and sacred places is emphasized. Though 1 Chr 15 in many ways parallels 2 Sam 6—David's bringing the ark of the covenant up to Jerusalem—the following chapter in Chronicles, an addition, is dedicated to the Levites who minister at the ark and their prayers. Moreover, toward the end of David's reign, he himself begins preparations for the temple (1 Chr 22:2-5).

Similarly, the Chronicler notes that before David's death, he organized the Levites into classes (1 Chr 23): the priests (1 Chr 24); the singers (1 Chr 25); the gatekeepers, the treasurers, and the magistrates (1 Chr 26); the army commanders, the tribal heads, and the overseers (1 Chr 27). These chapters have no counterparts in the books of Samuel.

10:13-14 Judgment of Saul. This small addition to the account of Saul's death in Kings is a good example of how the author of Chronicles makes even more explicit the Deuteronomistic theology. Saul's death is explained as a consequence of his rebellion against the Lord (compare 1 Sam 13:13-14 and 15:22-23) and of his consulting the witch of Endor (1 Sam 28).

11:42–13:5 David's mighty men. Typical of the Chronicler, he lists names in great number. In addition to the military supporters enumerated in 1 Chr 11:10-41 (compare 2 Sam 23:8-39), additional names are here given. Except for this mention, we know nothing of these men.

David's army is described in ideal terms: the bowmen can shoot arrows and sling stones with both hands (12:2); the warriors are experts with shield and spear. Men from all Israel—all the tribes—support David. Everyone recognizes that God helps David (1 Chr 13:18); his great army is like an "army of God." David is anointed king over Israel in Hebron (1 Chr 11:3) and gradually wins support for kingship over all Israel (1 Chr 13:38).

15:1-24 The ark brought to Jerusalem. This is a more extensive version of 2 Sam 6. Again, emphasis is given to the Levites. They alone may transport the ark, and they are to direct the appropriate musical accompaniments for the occasion.

16:37-42 Attendants before the ark. Having brought the ark to Jerusalem and having celebrated its presence there, David commissions certain men to remain with the ark. These will offer appropriate sacrifices and make appropriate thanksgiving, while others will serve as gatekeepers and musicians.

21:26–22:19 The altar, the temple, and Solomon. The text asserts that the site of Ornan's threshing floor became the site of Jerusalem's temple. It was more appropriate than Gibeon because the Lord had heard David's prayer here.

Chapter 22 builds on chapter 17. The promise announced there to David—that his son would build the temple—is here developed. David collects materials and workers for the temple and commissions his son. In contrast with David, who fought wars and shed blood, Solomon is to be a man of peace. Whereas 1 Kgs 3 explains that there was not yet sufficient peace in Israel during David's reign for him to build the temple, the Lord now grants this peace to Solomon. Postexilic Judah longs for peace. *Shalom* means much more than an absence of fighting; the term refers to the fullest possible well-being.

23:1-32 The Levitical classes. In contrast with the account in 2 Kgs 1–2, the Chronicler does not depict Solomon as having any rivals to his throne.

All Levites thirty years old and older (v. 3; but see v. 24) are to serve the Lord's temple, the courts, and the chambers. Whether by their presence at the sacrifices, their care of the sacred vessels, or by prayer, their lives are to be devoted to the temple.

24:1-19 The priestly classes. At the time of David there was no distinction between the Levitical and priestly classes. Here lies an anachronism. These men are also temple officers, whose functions are assigned impartially by lot.

24:20-31 Other Levites. The men whose names are listed in typical priestly fashion also served the temple and, just like Aaron's descendants, they too are assigned temple tasks impartially.

25:1-30 The singers. One notes here a reference to David's musical talent (compare 1 Sam 16:18). The music ministers also cast lots to determine their functions in nonhierarchical fashion: young and old, master and apprentice—twenty-four lots in all.

26:1-19 Classes of gatekeepers. The families of Kore and Merari provide the gatekeepers. Again, lots are cast to determine the watches and the gates. No preference is accorded larger families over smaller ones, or vice versa.

26:20-28 Treasurers. All the temples of the ancient Near East had treasuries, and the temple at Jerusalem was no exception (compare 1 Kgs 14:26). These treasuries contained the valuable offerings from previous kings as well as the treasures of the present ruler.

26:29-32 Magistrates. David also appoints civil officials, judges, and police officers to ensure the efficient and effective administration of his kingdom.

27:1-15 Army commanders. Twelve groups of twenty-four thousand men, with each group having its own commander, form David's standing army.

27:16-24 Tribal heads. There is also a leader for each of Israel's twelve tribes. A census is not permitted, since the Lord had promised that Israel would be numerous beyond counting (compare 2 Sam 24 and 1 Chr 21).

27:25-31 Overseers. David also appoints administrators over his treasury, the storehouses, farm workers, the vineyards and their produce, the olive and sycamore trees and the oil, over the cattle, camels, she-asses, and the flocks.

27:32-34 David's court. Jonathan and Jehiel tutor David's sons. Ahithophel (compare 2 Sam 16:23), Jehoiada, and Abiathar (compare 1 Sam 22:20-23) are counselors; and Hushai is David's confidant (compare 2 Sam 17:1-23). Joab commands the king's army (compare 2 Sam 8:16 and 20:23).

28:1-10 The assembly at Jerusalem. 1 Chr 17 (compare 2 Sam 7) promises David a dynasty; the prophet further proclaims that David's son will build the Lord's temple. 1 Chr 22 gives a further explanation of why David will not build the temple—he has shed too much blood. But Solomon must be careful to observe the precepts and decrees that the Lord gave Moses for Israel (1 Chr 22:13). Now, in chapter 28, David commissions Solomon as his successor and reasserts Solomon's role in establishing David's dynasty and in building the Lord's temple. More explicitly than in the other texts, however, the author warns of the consequences of Solomon's infidelity: if he abandons the Lord, he will be cast off forever (1 Chr 28:9).

28:11-21 Temple plans given to Solomon. In contrast with the account in 1 Kings, in which David is already dead before Solomon initiates the building of the temple, here David does the planning and lays most of the groundwork. By the time of the writing of Chronicles, David is clearly understood to be Israel's ideal king.

29:1-9 Offerings for the temple. The temple, the house of the Lord, deserves the most exquisite adornments. Therefore, as a statement of David's wholehearted commitment to the Lord and his dwelling place, David freely gives his personal treasury to enhance the future temple. In so doing, David becomes a model for all wealthy Israelites.

29:10-22 David's prayer. 2 Sam 22 is a thanksgiving prayer attributed to David and inserted into the Deuteronomistic History. The Chronicler parallels this prayer with a shorter one of his own. Not only do his sentiments include praise, but David here adds typical self-abnegation formulae with appropriate petitions (compare 2 Sam 7:18-19 and 1 Chr 17:16-27).

29:22-25 Solomon anointed. David had named Solomon his successor (1 Chr 23:1). In contrast with the first chapters of 1 Kings, this account presents no struggle; here there are no contenders for David's throne; here no enemies or potential conspirators need be removed. This latter account is, of course, an idealization. Anything needlessly problematic, anything that would show either David or Solomon in less than favorable light has been omitted.

29:26-30 Death of David. The Chronicler accords David a slightly more expanded death notice than that which he receives in 1 Kgs 2:10-11. It resembles those given by the Deuteronomistic historian to the other kings of his line. However, here three sources are named—two of the allusions are probably the creations of the Chronicler—from which one is supposed to be able to secure further information about David's reign. The Book of Samuel is a legitimate source familiar to readers of the Old Testament, but what about the histories of Nathan and of Gad? Did those prophets, like the Chroniclers of Israel and Judah, once compose written records that now are lost? Or is the allusion meant merely to call one's attention to these three men of God who validated David as Yahweh's chosen servant and Israel's king?

COMMENTARY: 2 CHRONICLES

PART I: THE REIGN OF SOLOMON

2 Chr 1:1–9:31

The first nine chapters of 2 Chronicles closely parallel 1 Kgs 3–11 and describe the reign of Solomon. More attention, however, is paid to priestly things, as one might expect. For example, in 2 Chr 1:2-5, the narrator makes a special point of distinguishing between the tent of meeting at Gibeon, where Solomon went to pray and to offer sacrifice, and the ark of God at Jerusalem, in the tent that David had pitched for it. No attempt is made in 1 Kings to explain why, if both the ark and the tent were in Jerusalem (see 2 Sam 7:2), Solomon went to Gibeon to worship (see 1 Kgs 3:4). The Chronicler notices the inconsistency and provides an explanation. Although Gibeon no longer functioned as an appropriate place for David to worship (see 1 Chr 21:28–22:1), the tent of meeting still remained there; thus it was appropriate for Solomon to go there.

In a similar way, Solomon, in appealing to Hiram of Tyre for aid in building the Lord's temple, adds a far more detailed explanation than is found in 1 Kgs 5:1-12 of the functions to be performed in the future temple: the burning of incense and sweet spices (compare Exod 30); the continual offering of the showbread (compare Lev 24:5-9); the burnt offerings—morning and evening, on the sabbaths, on the new moons, and at the appointed feasts. The Israelites who were ordered to help with temple building were "aliens living in the land" (1 Chr 22:2; 2 Chr 2:17-18; but compare 1 Kgs 9:15-22 and 2 Chr 8:7-9).

The Chronicler specifies what the Deuteronomistic historian had only suggested: that the site purchased by David where he had offered sacrifice after the census (see 2 Sam 24:18-25 and 1 Chr 21:16-30) became, in fact, the location of the temple. The only other reference to Moriah in the Old Testament occurs in Gen 22. There it is the mountain on which Abraham almost sacrificed Isaac to the Lord. The Chronicler here connects the fidelity of Abraham and the sacredness of his sacrifice with Israel's new cultic site.

After the temple had been built, the ark was brought into it in procession (compare 1 Kgs 8:1-9). To the Deuteronomist's description the Chronicler adds further detail: the priests present sanctified themselves without regard to divisions (compare 1 Chr 24); all the Levitical singers stood with their cymbals, harps, and lyres alongside the priest trumpeters east of the altar, and they all praised the Lord in unison (compare 1 Chr 25). The words of their song echo Psalms 118 and 136.

7:1-3. After Solomon's prayer dedicating the temple, the Chronicler adds that God's acceptance of it took the form of a fire coming down from heaven and consuming the offerings (compare 1 Chr 21:26; Lev 9:24; and even 1 Kgs 18:38-39). The people responded by rendering adoration to the Lord. The musical instruments made by David for the Lord's praise are used at the dedication (compare 1 Chr 17:41-42).

7:13-15. The Chronicler inserts into the Lord's response to Solomon's prayer an affirmation that Solomon's requests will be granted. After drought, locust plague, and pestilence—the Lord's punishments for Israel's sins—if the people repent and seek the Lord, God will forgive them and restore their health and the well-being of their land. Yet, the same conditions set forth in 1 Kgs 9 are included here: Fidelity to the Lord like David's will ensure the continuation of the dynasty; idolatry, however, will lead to the temple's destruction and to exile.

8:11. Solomon had married Pharaoh's daughter, and, according to the account in 1 Kings, she lived in the City of David until Solomon built her a home. The Chronicler, subtly emphasizing the taint of a foreign woman, acknowledges her role as Solomon's wife, but points out that she does not live in the house of David. The place where the ark of the Lord had been is considered holy; therefore, it is inappropriate for her to dwell there.

8:12-15. The Chronicler establishes Solomon as a model worshiper. According to the duty of each day—the sabbaths, the new moons (compare Num 28:14; 29:6), the three annual feasts (compare Lev 23)—Solomon offers appropriate sacrifices; he also appoints the divisions of the priests (see 1 Chr 24), the Levites (see 1 Chr 23), and the gatekeepers (see 1 Chr 26). The Chronicler idealizes Solomon;

contrary to the Deuteronomist's record, there is no mention of Solomon's infidelity.

9:29. Just as the Chronicler names sources for further information about David and his reign (compare 1 Chr 29:29), so here mention is made of records containing more information about Solomon: the history of Nathan, the prophecy of Ahijah, and the visions of Iddo.

PART II: THE MONARCHY BEFORE HEZEKIAH

2 Chr 10:1–27:9

10:1–12:16 The reign of Rehoboam. The Chronicler adds to the Deuteronomist's account of Rehoboam's reign the building of several fortified cities. He further reports that the priests and Levites who had been in the north came south to Judah and Jerusalem, having been expelled by Jeroboam. In addition, those who sought the Lord also came south to Jerusalem to sacrifice.

The first three years of Rehoboam's reign are secure not only because he administers well but, more importantly, because he is faithful to the Lord (no such testimony is given in Kings!). The Chronicler gives an account, omitted from Kings, of Rehoboam's family: eighteen wives, sixty concubines, twenty-eight sons, and sixty daughters. Rehoboam wants Abijah, the eldest son of his favorite wife, Maacah, to succeed him (in 1 Kgs 1–2 Solomon, the eldest living son of Bathsheba, is David's choice).

The second part of Rehoboam's reign is characterized by infidelity to the Lord. The Chronicler's insertion here is consistent with Deuteronomistic theology: the Lord sends Shishak, king of Egypt, to punish Judah's sin (12:1-2). The Lord, however, sends Shemaiah to Rehoboam to interpret for him what is happening. Rehoboam has abandoned the Lord, so the Lord is abandoning Rehoboam. Repentance leads to a mitigation of the intended and deserved punishment; though Shishak attacks Jerusalem, Judah is not completely destroyed.

More information about Rehoboam can be found in the chronicles of Shemaiah and of Iddo (12:15). Again, we note a priestly alteration of the text of Kings, which says that further information about Rehoboam can be found in the chronicles of the kings of Judah.

13:1-22 The reign of Abijah. Whereas Rehoboam's son Abijah (Abijam in Kings) is dispensed with in a brief eight verses of the Deuteronomistic History, the Chronicler devotes considerably more attention to him and characterizes him very differently. In 1 Kgs 15:3 he walks in the sins of his father, and his heart is not wholly true to God. For the Chronicler, he is a foil for Jeroboam. Abijah, in contrast to Jeroboam, has fallen heir to the covenant of salt (compare Lev 2:13). The two fight, and despite Jeroboam's larger army and shrewder military strategy, Abijah's trust in the Lord is rewarded with victory. The Chronicler also adds a note about his family: fourteen wives, twenty-two sons, and sixteen daughters. More information can be learned about the ways of Abijah by consulting the story of the prophet Iddo (v. 22).

14:1–15:19 The first part of Asa's reign. A mere fifteen verses describe Asa's reign in 1 Kgs 15; in contrast, the Chronicler elaborates for almost three chapters. Though nowhere in the Chronicler's account of the previous kings of Judah does it say that they worshiped idols, the Chronicler, nevertheless, praises Asa for removing the foreign altars, the high places, the pillars, the Asherim, the incense altars. Moreover, the earliest part of Asa's reign is blessed with peace, and when there is war with the Ethiopians, the Lord rewards Judah's faithfulness and brings victory.

The prophet Azariah, introduced as Asa's counselor, warns Asa to be faithful. Again, there is explicit reference to the theology of the Deuteronomist: If you seek the Lord, you will find the Lord; if you forsake the Lord, the Lord will forsake you. The prophet's words spur Asa on to greater fidelity, evidenced by the removal of idols, the repair of the temple, and even a recommitment to covenant fidelity. (Joash and Josiah are the only kings of Judah in the books of Kings who explicitly make a covenant with the Lord [compare 2 Kgs 11:17 and 23:3].)

16:1-14 Asa's infidelity. The latter part of Asa's reign meets with political, personal, and theological disaster. Asa turns from trusting God to trusting human forces; for protection against Israel he makes an alliance with Aram instead of trusting in God. Hanani the seer (missing from the Deuteronomistic History) condemns Asa's sin, suggests the happy outcome that would have accrued to Judah had

Asa not sinned, and names the punishment. Asa does not repent and imprisons Hanani. Later, when the king's feet become diseased, Asa does not seek relief from God but consults physicians. Such lack of fidelity can only lead to trouble. The Chronicler makes explicit Deuteronomistic theology: the latter part of Asa's reign suffers from instability and war.

17:1-21:3 The reign of Jehoshaphat. Just as the Chronicler's accounts of most of the kings of Judah contain more detail than their Deuteronomistic counterparts, so likewise the Chronicler gives a more extensive record of Jehoshaphat's reign. He is introduced as a king zealous for the law (compare 1 Kgs 22:43, 47). But then he makes a marriage alliance with Ahab. Anyone familiar with the books of Kings knows that, in the Deuteronomist's judgment, Ahab is a very evil king of Israel. One waits for further judgment on Jehoshaphat. When Ahab and Jehoshaphat fight against Ramoth-gilead, Jehoshaphat wishes to consult the Lord; he therefore escapes theological condemnation. The Chronicler's account of Ahab's and Jehoshaphat's encounter with the lying prophets and Micaiah is very similar to the narrative of 1 Kgs 22.

Added to the Deuteronomistic account of Jehoshaphat's reign is another narrative about battle, this one with the Moabites and the Ammonites (20:1). Jehoshaphat seeks the Lord and is rewarded; Jahaziel, a Levite, proclaims the assuring word of the Lord. The Lord will fight for Judah, and Judah will be victorious. The Chronicler is consistent with only part of the traditional holy-war theology, however. Yahweh wins the victory, but whereas customary holy-war theology demanded that all the spoils of the battle be sacrificed to Yahweh, here all the enemy soldiers are dead (they have killed each other), but the spoils of war—cattle, clothing, and precious things—are, without any later theological reprimand, seized by the Judean army.

Although Jehoshaphat's first alliance with Israel had not caused theological condemnation, his latter alliance with King Ahaziah does. According to the Chronicler, the two of them built ships together. The prophet Eliezer condemns the alliance and predicts the ships' destruction (20:37).

21:4-20 The reign of Jehoram. Both the Deuteronomist and the Chronicler judge Jehoram to be an evil king. The Chronicler justifies his judgment with further elaboration of Jehoram's wrongdoing. He, the first-born of Jehoshaphat's six sons, has killed his brothers and other princes of Israel. And if that were not enough, he has built high places and has encouraged idolatry. The prophet Elijah is inserted into the Chronicler's account with the kind of condemnation one might expect: the Lord will bring a great plague on Jehoram's family, and he himself will suffer from a severe disease of the bowels. Elijah's prophecy is fulfilled when the Philistines and the Arabs take into exile all Jehoram's possessions, including his family, with the exception of his youngest son. Jehoram himself is stricken with the predicted terminal disease.

A major change made by the Chronicler is to note that Jehoram was buried in the City of David, but not in the tomb of the kings (compare 2 Kgs 8:24).

22:1-9 The reign of Ahaziah (Jehoahaz in 2 Chr 21:17). Ahaziah is an evil king in the judgment of both the Deuteronomist and the Chronicler. He is, after all, related to Ahab through his mother, Athaliah. Consequently, it is appropriate for both the Deuteronomistic historian and the Chronicler to associate Ahaziah's downfall at the hands of Jehu with his visit to the Israelite King Jehoram.

No mention is made of the place where Ahaziah is buried. In fact, the only reason the Chronicler's account buries him at all is that he was Jehoshaphat's grandson!

22:10-23:21 The reign of Athaliah. The Chronicler adds very little to the Deuteronomist's portrayal of Athaliah's reign. Simply put, the priests play a larger role, as one might expect. Jehosheba, the woman who saved Joash from Athaliah, is, in this account, the wife of the priest Jehoiada, in addition to being the daughter of King Jehoram (north) and the sister of King Ahaziah (south). In the Chronicler's account, the captains summon the Levites and elders and make a covenant with the king (Joash) in the temple. The priests and Levites arrange the king's debut to the people; they alone are allowed to enter the temple; "they are holy" (23:6).

After Athaliah's death, one of the first things Joash does is to post watchmen under the direction of the Levites and the priests. They are to see to it that no one who is unclean enters the temple (23:19).

24:1-27 The reign of Joash. The Deuteronomistic historian attributes the good that Joash did to Jehoiada's counsel, and the Chronicler specifies this judgment even further. Joash sets out to repair the damage done to the temple by Athaliah. Under Jehoiada's and the priests' leadership, money is collected from the people, and the restoration is accomplished. Jehoiada was so faithful, from the Chronicler's theological perspective (he had saved Joash and had restored the Lord's dwelling), that he is reported to have been buried with the kings. No similar reference is made regarding any non-king in the Deuteronomistic History.

After Jehoiada's death, Joash is influenced toward evil by the princes of Judah and he succumbs. In spite of prophetic warning, idolatry prevails. The Chronicler inserts another priest who prophesies—this time Jehoiada's son, Zechariah. Zechariah predicts that Joash's rejection of the Lord will have dire consequences, but Joash's response is to silence the bad news; he whose life had been saved by Jehoiada now kills Jehoiada's son. Punishment for such sin is inevitable and comes in the form of Aram. The fact that Judah has a larger army means nothing; Judah has forsaken the Lord. Moreover, Zechariah is avenged: Joash's own servants slay him.

For the Chronicler, such an evil king cannot be buried in the tombs of the kings. This is the first mention of the "midrash of the book of the kings" (24:27). Because the Chronicler omits accounts of the northern kings of Israel, he has no need to distinguish the chronicles of Judah from those of Israel.

25:1-28 The reign of Amaziah. The Deuteronomist accorded Amaziah a mixed judgment, and the Chronicler does likewise. The Chronicler inserts two episodes; one speaks of Amaziah's fidelity, and the other speaks of his infidelity. Amaziah has mustered a large army—so large that it includes Israelite mercenaries. But when a prophet cautions him not to include Israelites in his army—because God's strength is far superior to those men, and God is not with them—Amaziah obeys the prophet, takes the financial loss, and dismisses the Israelites. Amaziah is victorious against the Edomites, although the mercenaries' anger causes them to plunder several Judean cities.

After that victory, however, Amaziah does an about-face, in the Chronicler's judgment. He begins to practice idolatry, worshiping the gods of the people he has conquered. He ignores prophetic wisdom—after all, those no-gods have proved powerless; they are unable to secure victory for their own people. Punishment for his infidelity is inevitable, and it comes in the form of a serious military defeat and the consequent pillaging of Jerusalem.

26:1-23 The reign of Uzziah (Azariah in 2 Kgs 15). Like his father, Uzziah gets a mixed rating from both the Deuteronomist and the Chronicler. For the Chronicler, as long as Uzziah seeks the Lord and listens to Zechariah's counsel, he is faithful and all goes well. His successes are both military (a well-equipped army and victories over the Philistines, the Arabs in Gurbaal, and the Meunites) and domestic (cisterns, and towers in Jerusalem and in the wilderness), and he is very prosperous.

However, the Chronicler condemns Uzziah's pride. He records an episode in which Uzziah attempts to usurp the prerogative of priests by burning incense at the altar of incense in the temple. His punishment is leprosy. The Deuteronomist had indicated Uzziah's leprosy but had not explained, from a theological perspective, its cause.

27:1-9 The reign of Jotham. The Chronicler adds little to the Deuteronomist's account of Jotham's reign. He is like his father, but he does not sin by presuming for himself any priestly function. Consequently, the Chronicler emphasizes a prosperous reign for him "because he lived resolutely in the presence of the Lord, his God." He builds cities, forts, and towers; he is victorious over the Ammonites and, consequently, he receives from them substantial tribute.

PART III: REFORMS OF HEZEKIAH AND JOSIAH

2 Chr 28:1–36:1

28:1-27 The reign of Ahaz. The Chronicler adds to the Deuteronomist's description of Ahaz's reign the fact that he makes molten images for the Baals and burns incense in the valley of the son of Hinnom (vv. 2-3). Additional sin merits additional punishment: the Lord gives him into the hand of the king of

Aram and into the hand of the king of Israel. Further, an Ephraimite kills the king's son, the palace commander, and the king's assistant. Both the Arameans and the Israelites take captives from Judah, and the Arameans retain theirs. The Israelites, warned by the prophet Oded, know that taking the Lord's people captive can only lead to their own punishment. They therefore return the people of Judah to their own land.

Ahaz's sin, from the perspective of the Chronicler, leads to even further punishment. The Edomites, the Philistines, and even the Assyrians, to whom Ahaz pays tribute, pillage Judah. To depict the extent of Ahaz's evil, the Chronicler comments that Ahaz's ill fortune leads, not back to the Lord and to repentance, but to further idolatry. Although he sleeps with his ancestors and is buried in Jerusalem, he is not brought to the tombs of the kings of Israel. (Postexilic Judah is also called Israel.)

29:1-32:33 The reign of Hezekiah. Hezekiah's reign begins with a commission to the Levites and priests to purify the temple. This they complete in seven days. Hezekiah then commands that burnt offerings and sin offerings be made for all Israel: seven bulls, seven rams, seven lambs, and seven he-goats. The burnt offering is made amidst the music of harps, cymbals, and lyres, amidst singing and rejoicing, while both king and people worship. The people add to these offerings more burnt offerings, peace offerings, and thanksgiving offerings.

The Chronicler describes Hezekiah's next reform as the reintroduction of Passover (ch. 30). Hezekiah calls large numbers of the people to Jerusalem for the celebration, and encourages those who have avoided exile to Assyria to return to the Lord; perhaps the Lord will even return the exiles to their homeland. Included in this feast are Israelites from the north, from Ephraim, Manasseh, Issachar, and Zebulun. The Chronicler, as might be expected, emphasizes the priests' and Levites' role, especially their killing of Passover lambs for those who have not sanctified themselves—the northerners and the unclean. The feast lasts seven days, and then another seven days. According to the Chronicler, Hezekiah reestablishes the Passover, a feast that had not been so celebrated in Jerusalem since the reign of Solomon. (The Deuteronomistic historian credits Josiah with reestablishing this feast; it had not been celebrated since the period of the Judges; compare 2 Kgs 23:21-23.)

The Chronicler inserts more information about the priests and Levites (31:2ff.). Hezekiah divides them into classes, according to the service they will perform—offering holocausts and peace offerings, ministering in the gates of the camp of the Lord, and giving thanks and praise. Both king and people contribute generously, so that the priests have more than enough to offer and to eat; there is even an abundant surplus.

When the Assyrians come against him (ch. 32), Hezekiah prepares for combat; he is confident that the Lord is with Judah and will fight for it. Although other gods have not been able to save their people against the superior strength of the Assyrian army, Yahweh can and will save Judah. Thus Hezekiah believes, and his faith is rewarded.

Hezekiah does what is good and right and faithful in the eyes of his God. Everything he does he does with his whole heart, and he becomes very prosperous. Yet the Chronicler alludes to Hezekiah's illness (compare 2 Kgs 20:1-11) and to his insufficient gratitude for the Lord's response to his prayer (32:24-25). This provides an occasion for the Chronicler to refer to Hezekiah's humbling himself and to punishment that will come upon Judah and Jerusalem after Hezekiah's death. A foreshadowing of the form this punishment will take may be seen in the envoys who arrive from Babylon. The Chronicler comments that the Lord will test Hezekiah through them, to see what is in his heart (compare 2 Kgs 20:12-19).

In addition to the book of the kings of Judah and Israel, the Vision of Isaiah has more to say, according to the Chronicler, about the reign of Hezekiah (32:32). He is buried in the ascent of the tombs of the sons of David. Hezekiah merits the note that all Judah and the inhabitants of Jerusalem honor him at his death.

33:1-20 The reign of Manasseh. Contrary to the account of Manasseh's reign as given in the Deuteronomistic History, the Chronicler inserts into Manasseh's reign an account of his being taken into exile to Assyria, his petitioning the Lord for help, his deliverance, and his reformed lifestyle. Perhaps the Chronicler is, with this very unusual addition, trying to account for the fifty-five-year duration of Manasseh's reign. How could such an evil king have reigned so long, unless at some point he had repented? Perhaps the Chronicler is simply explaining why the kingdom of Judah did not fall during or after Manasseh's reign.

The chronicles of the kings of Israel and the chronicles of the seers contain a more detailed account of Manasseh's life (33:18). No mention is made of his burial with the other Judean kings; rather, he is buried in his house, or "in the garden of his house, in the garden of Uzza" (2 Kgs 21:18).

33:21-25 The reign of Amon. The Chronicler adapts the reign of Amon to his purposes. Amon is more evil than his father, Manasseh, had been; he sacrifices to the images his father had made, which suggests that Manasseh's idols remain in place. His father's repentance, also added by the Chronicler, was therefore incomplete. The Chronicler makes no mention of Amon's burial. The Deuteronomistic historian states that he was buried in the same garden as his father (2 Kgs 21:26).

34:1–35:27 The reign of Josiah. An interesting contrast can be drawn between the character of Josiah as depicted in 2 Kgs 22:1–23:30 and in 2 Chr 34–35. Though the events recorded are basically similar, the order of the events is significant. The Deuteronomistic historian portrays Josiah as purging idolatry from Judah *after* the restoration work in the temple had recovered the book of the law, while the Chronicler has the purging of idolatry in Judah and parts of Israel as the first act of Josiah's reign; only after such purification does he commission the Levites and priests to oversee the repair of the temple, and only subsequent to that is the book of the law discovered (34:14). Further, to the Passover account of 2 Kgs 23:21-25 the Chronicler adds copious priestly detail (35:1-19).

In contrast with the account in 2 Kings, the Chronicler makes no mention of Manasseh, nor does he associate the doom to come with delayed punishment for Manasseh's evil reign. For the Chronicler, Manasseh's son Amon was even more evil than his father. While both the Deuteronomist and the Chronicler mention the battle of Meggido, during which Josiah is mortally wounded at the hands of Egypt, only the Chronicler (35:20) mentions Carchemish (605 B.C.E.), where the Babylonians were victorious over Egypt.

Josiah, like Hezekiah before him (2 Chr 32:33), receives honor from the people at his death. The Chronicler even comments that Jeremiah made a lament for him (2 Chr 35:25); no such allusion is found in 2 Kings. Josiah is accorded burial among the tombs of his ancestors (2 Kgs 23:30 notes: "in his own burial place").

PART IV: END OF THE KINGDOM

2 Chr 36:2-23

36:1-4 The reign of Jehoahaz. The reign of Jehoahaz is short. The Egyptians had slain Josiah at Meggido. Now they force Judah to pay tribute, exile the reigning king, and replace him with his brother, Eliakim (Jehoiakim). Whereas the Deuteronomist compares Jehoahaz's evil to the wrongdoing of his ancestors, the Chronicler makes no such comparison. Jehoahaz simply does evil and is exiled.

36:5-8 The reign of Jehoiakim. Jehoiakim lasts for a while as Egypt's vassal. When Egypt is conquered, he becomes Babylon's vassal. The Chronicler adds that, eventually, Jehoiakim is exiled to Babylon. In contrast with the Deuteronomist, the Chronicler does not explain the present evils in Judah as a consequence of Manasseh's sins (compare 2 Kgs 24:2-4).

36:9-10 The reign of Jehoiachin. Jehoiachin, Jehoiakim's son, reigns for only slightly more than three months before he is exiled to Babylon, and before his uncle Zedekiah replaces him on Judah's throne.

36:11-14 The reign of Zedekiah. For the Chronicler, one of Zedekiah's major sins is his refusal to defer to the spokesman of Yahweh. Zedekiah revolts against Babylon, in spite of the fact that Jeremiah has interpreted Nebuchadnezzar as the Lord's servant who is executing God's just judgment on Judah's sin; Jeremiah counsels the people to submit to Babylon (compare Jer 21:7). Zedekiah is also guilty of other infidelities, though the Chronicler omits any description of his fate (compare 2 Kgs 25:4-7).

36:15-21 Dissolution of Judah. Nebuchadnezzar destroys Judah and Jerusalem, sparing neither city walls nor Yahweh's temple. The people are slaughtered or exiled. Yet, unlike the Deuteronomistic historian, the Chronicler does not bring his history to an end until the end of Judah's exile.

36:22-23 Decree of Cyrus. The word of the Lord is effective. The seventy years prophesied by Jeremiah are completed (compare Jer 25:11-12 and 29:10). In the first year of the reign of King Cyrus of Persia, he commissions the Jews to go up to Jerusalem to build a temple to the Lord God of heaven.

CONCLUSION

The Deuteronomistic historian chronicled Israel's history from the perspective of fidelity to Yahweh, to the obligations of the covenant, to the word of the Lord through the prophets. Infidelity meant punishment and, eventually, the destruction of the temple, the loss of the land, and exile. No king is supreme. Yahweh is king, and a human king is faithful only to the extent that he observes the covenant. The rulers are male, except for the brief reign of Athaliah. In contrast, the prophets are no respecters of sex, as Deborah (see Judg 4–5) and Huldah illustrate. Only the king who obeys the words of the prophet—the words of the Lord through the prophet—is faithful.

For the Deuteronomistic historian, the person who does not know history is bound to repeat it. Therefore, he retells Israel's past so that those living in the present and in the future may learn from it. These are "the facts"; this is the "theological interpretation" of the facts. If you do not want a future of condemnation and exile, you must take God seriously. There is no substitute for obedience and covenant fidelity. Many of the historical circumstances have changed since the Deuteronomist wrote, and all interpretation must take this into account; yet, even now, many of his insights remain valid.

The Chronicler, with a different audience, different leadership, and a different historical situation, also recalls Israel's past, this time ending explicitly in a new beginning. If the priests are to lead a postexilic people to fidelity, they must have credentials, and these the Chronicler provides.

The theological purpose of the two interpretations of Israel's history is quite similar: Learn from the past for the present. Leaders and people alike must observe covenant fidelity and listen attentively to Yahweh's word through the prophets.

EZRA AND NEHEMIAH

Rita J. Burns

INTRODUCTION

HISTORICAL BACKGROUND

The setting for the Books of Ezra and Nehemiah is the two-hundred-year period in which God's people were citizens of the Persian Empire. The Persian period began in 539 B.C.E. when Cyrus the Great of Persia (Iran) wrested control of the ancient Near Eastern world from the Babylonians. It ended in 333 B.C.E. when the same area fell into Greek hands under Alexander the Great.

More specifically, events narrated in the Books of Ezra and Nehemiah fall within the first part of the Persian period, from 538 B.C.E. to shortly after 400 B.C.E. For the Jews this was a time of return and restoration. Over the course of several generations, groups of Jewish exiles in Babylonia made their way back to their homeland of Judah in southern Palestine. There they undertook the work of restoration. They began by rebuilding the temple in Jerusalem and reviving its worship. Later, under Nehemiah's leadership, they rebuilt the walls of the city of Jerusalem and repopulated the city. Nehemiah and Ezra also initiated reforms based on the law of Moses and aimed at restoring the identity and integrity of the Jewish people. The return and restoration, then, were gradual, interwoven processes which together pressed toward revitalization. The temple lay at the center. Around it grew the city with protective walls. Within and around Jerusalem a people was fashioned anew through the influence of the law of Moses.

Our knowledge of this period in history is, in some cases, sketchy. From the Bible we rely primarily upon the Books of Ezra and Nehemiah, but we also turn to other works relative to the period, including Isaiah chapters 40–66, the Book of Haggai, and the Book of Zechariah. Some extra-biblical documents from the Persian period supplement our understanding of this period.

The writers of the Books of Ezra and Nehemiah were selective in the events they chose to narrate. They focused upon two periods: (1) the early period (538–515 B.C.E.) when the first exiles returned to Judah under the leadership of Sheshbazzar and rebuilt the temple under the leadership of Zerubbabel and Jeshua, and (2) the period marked by the restoration of the wall of Jerusalem and religious reforms under the leadership of Nehemiah and Ezra (445–c. 398 B.C.E.).

Before reviewing these periods in greater detail, it is fitting to set the scene which gave rise to the return of the Jews to Judah and the need for restoration.

The early years of the sixth century B.C.E. marked the end of a four-hundred-year period in which the religious identity of the people of God was intertwined with their existence as an independent nation. A little over one hundred years after the northern kingdom of Israel had been swept away by the Assyrians, the tiny kingdom of Judah in the southern part of Palestine fell into the power of a major ancient Near Eastern empire centered in Babylonia. The final blow came in the year 587 B.C.E.

when Babylonian armies destroyed the capital city of Jerusalem. Many citizens of the country, including civic and religious leaders, were taken to Babylonia. The temple, which had served as the religious center since the days of Solomon, was demolished, and its precious furnishings were stolen. The broken land was left in the hands of powerless people, the country's poor.

Forty-six years after the fall of Jerusalem the Babylonian Empire itself capitulated to Cyrus the Great, head of an expanding Persian Empire. This turn of events was interpreted by an anonymous poet in Exile as the beginning of a new era for the captives from Judah. In the Book of Isaiah, chapters 40–55, the writer whom we know only as Second Isaiah speaks of Cyrus as the one through whom Yahweh was doing a new thing. With the advent of Cyrus, wrote Second Isaiah, there would be a new Exodus in which the chosen people, like their ancestors of old, would be led out of bondage back to their land (Isa 43:1-7; 44:24-28; 45:1-3, 11-13).

Indeed, it was the policy of Cyrus to allow peoples exiled by the Babylonians to return to their homelands and build new lives by reviving their native customs and religions. In a document dating from this period (the so-called Cyrus Cylinder), the Persian king describes his policy:

> I returned to (these) sacred cities on the other side of the Tigris, the sanctuaries of which have been in ruins for a long time, the images which (used) to live therein and established for them permanent sanctuaries. I (also) gathered all their (former) inhabitants and returned (to them) their habitations.

It has been suggested that the Persians may have gone so far as to allow the freed exiles a limited recovery of national identity as well. Two leaders in the Jewish return and restoration, Sheshbazzar and Zerubbabel, seem to have been descendants of the pre-exilic royal family. No doubt their authority was limited, but it is significant that they were appointed and patronized by Persian rulers. Such treatment of exiled peoples was almost certain to win Persia the trust and loyalty of subjects who, through securing their own welfare, could live as productive and content citizens of the empire.

Return and restoration of the temple (538–515 B.C.E.)

The edict which authorized the return of Jewish exiles to Judah is said to have been issued in the first year of the reign of Cyrus (over Babylonia), that is, 538 B.C.E. Not all of the exiles, however, chose to return. The relative freedom they experienced during their years in Babylonia had afforded them the opportunity to become settled and, in some cases, prosperous. Judah, on the other hand, was still marked by devastation and poverty, so few Jews returned in the initial contingent, although others would follow over the course of the next few generations.

The far-flung empire of Persia was divided into several administrative units called satrapies. Each of these units was governed by a satrap or governor who was responsible for several smaller territorial districts which fell under his jurisdiction. Although the Persian rulers maintained a firm hold on the empire, they seem to have upheld a policy of noninterference in the internal affairs of the satrapies as long as taxes were paid and the governors maintained peace and order within their respective regions.

Within this imperial system, Judah belonged to the satrapy called "West-of-Euphrates," an area extending from the Euphrates River westward to the Mediterranean Sea. Its headquarters were in Samaria. In the Books of Ezra and Nehemiah, Samaritan leadership figured prominently in hardships facing Jews who returned to Judah. Samaritan governors may have feared the political rivalry of a restored Jewish community to the south. In addition to political concerns, religious animosities contributed to the tension between the Jews and Samaritans. Samaria had been the capital of the ten tribes which constituted the kingdom of Israel until it fell to the Assyrians in 721 B.C.E. In accord with Assyrian policy, some of its inhabitants were deported while peoples of other conquered areas were transported into Samaria to settle. Such mixing of populations was aimed at breaking the solidarity of captured peoples. Although the Samaritans continued to claim a place among God's people, leaders in the community of Jews who returned to Judah after the Exile did not consider the Samaritans to be truly Jewish because they had intermarried with foreign peoples. When the people of Samaria offered to help rebuild the temple of Yahweh in Jerusalem, they were rejected by the returning Jews.

Cambyses came to the throne of Persia after the death of Cyrus in 530 B.C.E. During his brief reign he succeeded in bringing Egypt under the umbrella of the Persian Empire. Cambyses, however, is passed over in the Books of Ezra and Nehemiah. It may be that the next two Jewish leaders to figure prominently in the biblical record, Zerubbabel and Jeshua, came to Judah during the reign of Cambyses, but the Bible describes their activities within the context of the reign of Darius I (522–485 B.C.E.). Although the change of power from Cambyses to Darius was marked by turmoil and revolution, the greater part of the reign of Darius saw the Persian Empire at its height.

Exiles who accompanied Zerubbabel (a civic leader) and Jeshua (a priest) to Judah bolstered the numbers and strength of the restoration community. Perhaps because uprisings in other parts of the empire sparked hopes in Jewish circles for political independence, there seems to have been a movement afoot to establish Zerubbabel as king on the throne of his ancestor, David. At least this was the vision of two prophets from this period, Haggai and Zechariah (see Hag 2:20-23 and Zech 6:9-15). Although these prophets' messianic hopes were not realized, the strongly nationalistic spirit fostered by the two prophets together with international unrest must have contributed to the rebuilding of the temple. Darius himself supported the temple project, perhaps because he wanted the allegiance of those who lived on the borders of recently conquered Egypt.

Whatever the reason, the reign of Darius was a time of growth and progress for the Jewish community in Judah. Under the leadership of Zerubbabel and Jeshua, the temple was completed and dedicated in solemn ceremony in the year 515 B.C.E. This second temple served as a center for Jewish life in Judah until its destruction by the Romans in A.D. 70. Its reconstruction was the first major achievement and the foundation stone of the restoration community.

Restoration of the wall of Jerusalem and reforms (445–c. 398 B.C.E.)

The Books of Ezra and Nehemiah are virtually silent about the seventy-year period between the dedication of the temple (515 B.C.E.) and the beginning of the mission of Nehemiah (445 B.C.E.). The successor of Darius, Xerxes (485–465 B.C.E.), is mentioned only in Ezra 4:6 where he is called Ahasuerus. (He is given the same name in the Book of Esther.) Xerxes was followed by Artaxerxes I and his reign (465–425 B.C.E.) was a second period of significant progress for the restoration community.

By the middle of the fifth century B.C.E. the Persian Empire had lost some of the strength it had enjoyed under the leadership of Darius I, and revolts in Egypt may have motivated Artaxerxes to try to insure the strength and loyalty of his subjects in Judah, the region which bordered Egypt. Nehemiah was a high-ranking official in the Persian court, and we are told that in the twentieth year of the reign of Artaxerxes (445 B.C.E.) the emperor sent Nehemiah to Judah to serve as leader in the Jewish community (Neh 2:1). There is little doubt that the biblical witness about the date of Nehemiah's mission is historically accurate. The Book of Nehemiah tells us that Sanballat was leader of the province of Samaria in Nehemiah's day (Neh 2:10, 19; 3:33-34). That Nehemiah and Sanballat were contemporaries is confirmed by papyri from a Jewish colony at Elephantine in Egypt. From this extra-biblical material we learn that Sanballat's two sons were governors of Samaria at the end of the fifth century B.C.E. Moreover, the Jewish high priest at the end of the century was Johanan, a grandson of the high priest Eliashib who served during Nehemiah's time. On the basis of the Elephantine texts, it is reasonable to date the beginning of Nehemiah's mission at 445 B.C.E., the twentieth year of the reign of Artaxerxes I.

During his first term as governor of Judah, Nehemiah oversaw the rebuilding of the wall around Jerusalem in spite of considerable opposition from Sanballat and others. Having completed the project, Nehemiah returned to Persia in 433 B.C.E. A short time later, however, he returned to Judah. During this second period he initiated several reforms designed to strengthen the solidarity of the restoration community, a positive effort not only for the Jews but also for the Persian throne which was eager to bolster the strength of the western edges of its empire.

The place of Ezra in the chronology of the restoration period continues to be a question among scholars. The biblical text presents Ezra before Nehemiah. Moreover, the appearance of Ezra within the Book of Nehemiah (Neh 8) creates the impression that the respective missions of the two overlapped. Ezra 7:7 tells us that Ezra came to Judah from Persia in the seventh year of Artaxerxes. If the reference is to Artaxerxes I (465–425 B.C.E.), then Ezra arrived in Judah in 458 B.C.E. and began his work thirteen years prior to the arrival of Nehemiah.

However, there are difficulties with this understanding of the biblical witness. Ezra 10:6 says that Ezra was a contemporary of the Jewish high priest Johanan. If Johanan, Ezra's contemporary, was the grandson of Eliashib (as discussed above) whom we know to have been a contemporary of Nehemiah (Neh 3:1, 20-21), then it is clear that Ezra did not precede Nehemiah but came two generations after him. Therefore, the emperor named in Ezra 7:7 might be Artaxerxes II (405–359 B.C.E.) in which case Ezra's mission is dated 398 B.C.E., the seventh year of the reign of Artaxerxes II.

A third proposal on the date of Ezra's mission is that it began in 428 B.C.E., the thirty-seventh year of Artaxerxes I. Some scholars have suggested that the text of Ezra 7:7 contains a slight scribal error in which the first number of the year ("thirty") was omitted. According to this view, Ezra came to Jerusalem a few years after the beginning of Nehemiah's second mission in Judah.

Although the exact date of Ezra's mission is still a topic for discussion, most scholars agree that Nehemiah's mission preceded that of Ezra. This helps to explain why the Nehemiah material in the Bible acknowledges no awareness of the reform of Ezra which, if Ezra had come first, would have occurred less than thirteen years before Nehemiah arrived in Judah. It is possible that the persons who were responsible for the composition of the Books of Ezra and Nehemiah were simply in error about historical sequence. It is more probable, however, that the overall arrangement of these two biblical books was designed with theological purposes in mind rather than to serve as an accurate historical chronicle of the period (see below on Theological Interests).

Because we do not know the exact dates of Ezra's activity in Judah, we cannot be certain where to end the timeline of historical events which form the background to the Books of Ezra and Nehemiah. We adopt the widely accepted view that Nehemiah preceded Ezra. For purposes of this commentary, we also follow the scholarly opinion that places Ezra's mission in the initial years of the fourth century B.C.E. We do so, however, with full awareness of the uncertainty which remains on this question.

The historical relationship between Persian rule and Jewish restoration can be seen at a glance in this outline:

Persian Emperors	**Jewish Restoration**
Cyrus the Great (539–530 B.C.E.)	Return to Judah
Cambyses (530–522 B.C.E.)	
Darius I (522–485 B.C.E.)	Rebuilding of temple
Xerxes (485–465 B.C.E.)	
Artaxerxes I (465–425 B.C.E.)	Nehemiah's mission including restoration of wall of Jerusalem and reforms
Darius II (425–405 B.C.E.)	
Artaxerxes II (405–359 B.C.E.)	? Ezra's mission including promulgation of the law and reform

THEOLOGICAL INTERESTS

History and biblical accounts

The Books of Ezra and Nehemiah appear within one of three great blocks of material in Hebrew Scripture which present successive events in Israel's history. The first four books of the Bible (Genesis through Numbers) cover the period from the beginnings of humanity to the time when the children of Israel stood on the borders of the Promised Land ready to inherit that space which God had promised to their ancestors. A second block of material sketches Israel's story from the entrance into the Promised Land through the era of the monarchy to the fall of the nation and the Babylonian Exile (see Deuteronomy through the Second Book of Kings). The First and Second Books of Chronicles and the Books of Ezra and Nehemiah trace the last part of Israel's story from the rise of King David (although this is prefixed in chapters 1–9 of the First Book of Chronicles with genealogies which trace Israel's roots back to Adam) through postexilic reconstruction efforts ending shortly after 400 B.C.E.

All of these writings are actually theological interpretations of events rather than historical annals. Each school of writers sets forth its theological reflections on Israel's experience. Readers of the Books of Ezra and Nehemiah must keep this in mind. While the two books contain historical information about the restoration period, the primary aim of the writers was not to present a disinterested chronological account of events. The writers were theologians who carefully selected and arranged materials in accord with theological interests.

Arrangement of materials

A theological order is evident in the present arrangement of the Ezra-Nehemiah materials:

Part I Ezra 1–6
    Restoration of the temple
Part II Ezra 7–10
    Restoration of the worshiping community
Part III Neh 1–7
    Restoration of the wall of Jerusalem
Part IV Neh 8–13
    Restoration of the community around the law

The foundation of postexilic Judaism in Judah was the temple and its worship. Thus Part I of the Ezra-Nehemiah material centers around the rebuilding of the temple even though neither Ezra nor Nehemiah was involved in this initial phase of restoration. Legitimate temple worship required that the worshipers themselves be pure, a people set apart. Part II describes a reform initiated by Ezra to set Jews apart from foreign influence. The city made holy by God's presence in the temple had to be strong and secure. To this end the city wall was rebuilt under Nehemiah's leadership (Part III). All of these works of restoration prepared for and culminated in the restoration of the Jewish community under the law (Part IV). Since both Ezra and Nehemiah were instrumental in restoring the Jewish community, it is theologically appropriate (although perhaps not chronologically accurate) that both be presented as participants in the culmination of their work.

Theological emphases

Just as theological considerations gave direction to the final arrangement of materials in the Books of Ezra and Nehemiah, so certain theological emphases can be seen in the books.

a. God's work and Persian help. Like writers before them, the theologians who composed the Books of Ezra and Nehemiah presupposed that Yahweh, the God of Israel, directed world history. The fall of the nation and the Exile had been Yahweh's doing. Now the same God was bringing the purged people to new life. In the Books of Ezra and Nehemiah, the Persian rulers' ongoing support for the restoration of the Jewish people is traced to God's hand. Likewise, the Jews call upon God to help them in the work of reconstruction and attribute their success to God's gracious aid.

b. Temple and cult. The Books of Ezra and Nehemiah give much attention to the temple and its worship. They present the restoration of the temple as the primary goal of the return from Exile. Moreover, the writers are eager to show that a full life of worship (including sacred festivals and sacred offerings) was an important part of the restoration movement. The writers also show special concern for cultic personnel, priests and Levites.

c. A people set apart. Prior to the Exile, Israel had a national identity, political independence in a land of its own with a capital in Jerusalem, its own king descended from David, and a temple where they thought God was accessible in a special way. The Exile had destroyed all of that. Without land, independence, temple, or king, the postexilic community searched for a new identity which was one with the Israel of the past and yet appropriate for drastically different circumstances.

Membership in the restoration community was limited to those who had been purified through the experience of Exile and who sought to maintain their purity and uniqueness by setting themselves apart from foreigners. Pure blood lineage was especially important, and marriages with foreigners were regarded as threats to the integrity of the restoration community. The objection to marriages with foreigners rests on an identification of holiness with separation—a physical separation from people and things which were not exclusively dedicated to Yahweh. While this perspective might be jarring to today's ecumenically-minded readers who long to reverse centuries of human intolerance based on religious loyalties, the biblical writers reflect a different world and different concerns. The exclusivist policies of the restoration period must be viewed within the context of a community struggling for self-preservation in the rubble of questions of identity occasioned by the experience of Exile.

d. Continuity. The biblical writers sought to show that postexilic Judaism was an authentic extension of pre-exilic Israel. Members of the restoration community had to prove that their ancestors came from pre-exilic Israel. "All Israel" is frequently symbolized by the number twelve, representing the twelve tribes who constituted ancient Israel. For the most part, those who returned from Exile settled in regions their pre-exilic ancestors had inhabited. The temple was restored on its ancient foundations and Jerusalem's wall was rebuilt from the charred stones of the pre-exilic wall. Leadership in worship was reserved to the descendants of pre-exilic Israel's cultic officials. The worshiping community resumed ancient festivals and offerings. The law which gave direction to the community's life was the ancient law of Moses.

LITERARY CONSIDERATIONS

Author and date of composition

We do not know all of the details about the composition of the Books of Ezra and Nehemiah. Contemporary scholarship is virtually unanimous in attributing a significant part of the composition to the Chronicler, that is, the circle of tradition which is responsible for the First and Second Books of Chronicles. In support of this view, one can see points of continuity in the Books of Chronicles, Ezra, and Nehemiah. First of all, the fact that the opening verses of the Book of Ezra duplicate the final verses of the Second Book of Chronicles reflects a deliberate effort to connect the works. Secondly, some of the thematic concerns which come to the fore in Chronicles recur in the Books of Ezra and Nehemiah. These include the prominence given to the temple, the city of Jerusalem, and the cult together with its leading personnel. The manner in which lists and other sources are used has been cited as additional evidence for connecting the author of Ezra and Nehemiah with that of Chronicles.

Despite this, we must guard against imagining that in one sitting a single author composed the final text of Chronicles, Ezra, and Nehemiah from start to finish. Chapters 1–6 of the Book of Ezra bear the strongest traces of the Chronicler's hand. It might be that the rest of the Ezra-Nehemiah materials (Ezra 7–10; the Book of Nehemiah) was subsequently incorporated into the Chronicler's work, perhaps in separate stages.

Although many of the details elude us, it is safe to say that the Chronicler played a significant part in the composition of the Books of Ezra and Nehemiah although the final text probably includes accretions and editing which came from other hands. Thus, when we speak of the authors/editors of the Books of Ezra and Nehemiah, we shall refer to the Chronicler but we do so with the understanding that other unknown writers also contributed to the work of composition.

The language of the books bears the marks of Persian but not Greek influence which suggests that the Books of Ezra and Nehemiah originated prior to the beginning of the Greek period (333 B.C.E.). The latest Persian emperor to be named is Darius II (425–405 B.C.E.) and the latest high priest included is Johanan who is known to have held that position until at least 410 B.C.E. Johanan's son, Jaddua, also appears in Neh 12:23, but we are not told if he yet exercised the office of high priest. For these reasons, most scholars hold that the bulk of the Books of Ezra and Nehemiah was completed in the early years of the fourth century B.C.E. although some additions to the books may have been made later.

Sources

Like many other biblical works, the Books of Ezra and Nehemiah represent a compilation of materials of diverse origin. Because of this, it is proper to regard the Chronicler as a compiler and editor as well as author of biblical tradition. Since the sources used by the Chronicler are no longer available to us in other biblical or extrabiblical works, in most cases it is difficult to judge their historical authenticity. It is possible that previously existing materials were incorporated into the Books of Ezra and Nehemiah exactly as the Chronicler found them. However, it is also possible that the Chronicler altered the materials, shaping them in ways which would serve the theological purposes of this particular part of the biblical tradition. The Chronicler is thought to have used three types of materials: (a) memoirs of Ezra and Nehemiah, (b) official records and correspondence, and (c) lists.

a. Memoirs. Parts of the Books of Ezra and Nehemiah which contain descriptions of the activities of the two main figures are written in the first person. This has led to the suggestion that those parts represent firsthand reports of the activities of Ezra and Nehemiah. It is uncertain whether these sections should be regarded as memoirs (written by the chief figures themselves) or memorials (written by others about the chief figures). Other inscriptions from the ancient Near Eastern world are similar to the Ezra and Nehemiah memoirs. In these inscriptions the first person is used, and their contents typically recount the accomplishments of an individual. Scholars think that these inscriptions were intended as testimony to a deity about the loyalty of a devoted worshiper.

The memoirs of the two biblical figures constitute the most extensive independent sources utilized by the Chronicler in the composition of the Books of Ezra and Nehemiah. The Ezra memoirs appear in Ezra 7:27–9:15. This section contains two lists (8:1-14 and 26-27) which may have been added to the memoirs from separate sources. Although Ezra's prayer (Ezra 9:6-15) also appears in the first person and so may have belonged to his memoirs, it is possible that this was the composition of another writer, since prayers are known to have been placed on the lips of biblical figures by writers in a later period (see, for example, Dan 3:24-45, 51-90; 9:4-19).

The parts of the Book of Nehemiah which appear in the first person are referred to in many circles as Nehemiah's memoirs. These sections constitute a sizeable portion of the book (Neh 1–7; 12:27–13:31). These texts contain a record of restoration efforts under Nehemiah's leadership. They include two lists which may have been added to the memoirs at some later stage of composition.

b. Aramaic source. For those who read biblical texts in the languages in which they were originally written, the most obvious clue to the diversity of sources in the Book of Ezra is that Ezra 4:8–6:18 and 7:12-26 are in Aramaic while the rest of the Books of Ezra and Nehemiah is written in Hebrew. The bulk of the Aramaic material in Ezra 4:8–6:18 claims to be a record of official correspondence between governors in West-of-Euphrates and two different Persian emperors. It also includes a version of the edict in which the Persian monarch Cyrus authorized the rebuilding of the temple in Jerusalem (6:3-5). The Aramaic section of Ezra 7:12-26 contains a copy of the official papers regarding Ezra's mission authorized by the emperor, Artaxerxes.

It is commonly accepted in scholarly circles that these Aramaic sections represent material from separate sources, perhaps records which were retained in official archives either of the Persian emperors or of Jewish leaders.

c. Lists. A number of lists in the Books of Ezra and Nehemiah probably came from records preserved in Jewish archives. The lists include the names of persons and regions as well as records of temple vessels and community responsibilities.

While it is impossible to know the sources and degree of authenticity of the abovementioned official correspondence and of the numerous lists, it is likely that they represent materials which originated independently of the narratives which now appear in the Books of Ezra and Nehemiah. It is possible that different records were adopted into the Ezra-Nehemiah traditions at different stages in the composition of the biblical books.

SIGNIFICANCE

The Books of Ezra and Nehemiah are important to contemporary readers for several reasons. First, they are our chief source of information about the restoration of the Jewish community following the Exile. Even though some of the historical details in the books are puzzling to contemporary biblical scholars, nevertheless they provide the best data at hand for our understanding of this period.

Second, we see in these books a community's courage in picking up the pieces of a shattered past and arranging them in creative ways, even in the face of considerable opposition. We encounter a community willing to engage the slow, gradual process of rebuilding. The community succeeds through God's protection, its own fierce resolve, properly focused efforts, and good leadership.

Finally, in the figures of Ezra and Nehemiah, contemporary readers see models of piety. Both men depend upon and recognize God's help, but they work without the spectacular interventions which characterize God's gracious presence in much of the rest of the biblical tradition. In their time true piety required human initiative and human effort. Ezra and Nehemiah were marked by devotion to their community, and out of that zeal flowed their commitment to the task of recovery. They saw what situations demanded and devised constructive ways to promote the life of the fragile community. Nehemiah was a model organizer resolute in restoring life to a city in ruins. Ezra founded postexilic Judaism in the law. Jewish tradition would eventually compare him to Moses. Both put their talents and efforts at the service of the tradition that had shaped them. They are models of how to be faithful to one's heritage in creative ways required by new situations.

COMMENTARY: EZRA

PART I: RESTORATION OF THE TEMPLE

Ezra 1:1–6:22

The first six chapters of the Book of Ezra contain an account of events beginning with the return of the exiles from Babylonia (ch. 1) and ending with the completion of the temple (ch. 6). The initial return (during Cyrus' reign) is said to have been led by Sheshbazzar, "the prince of Judah" (1:8). Shortly thereafter Zerubbabel (a royal prince) and Jeshua (a priest), with the support of the Persian king Darius, led the community in completing the reconstruction of the temple.

These chapters seem to be carefully documented. Attention is given to personal and place names, and inventories of goods and offerings, frequent dates, and records of official documents including the edict of Cyrus and correspondence between officers of West-of-Euphrates and Persian emperors.

On the other hand, this is a highly selective account. While it covers events spanning a period of twenty-three years (from the edict of Cyrus in 538 B.C.E. to the dedication of the temple in 515 B.C.E.), it is clear that the writers neglect to mention many aspects of life during the return and restoration. We see a preoccupation with the cult: altar, temple, sacrifices, offerings, temple vessels and utensils, religious feasts, and temple personnel. The writers view the restoration of temple worship as the goal of the return and the foundation of the restoration community.

Special concerns are evident in the writers' portrayal of the Jewish community. There is no hint of poverty or internal tension. According to the account, the only hardship facing the second generation of the restoration movement was the opposition of Samaritan leaders and peoples of the land. We see an idealized community: large in number, great in wealth, single-heartedly dedicated to restoring the life of worship with the help of able leaders of legitimate royal and priestly lineage and the patronage of the Persian throne. Moreover, just as the return is said to have been inspired by God (1:1-5), so the pursuit of a restored cultic life is said to have been carried forward by the community's faithful response to religious traditions begun by Moses and David, as well as to prophetic inspiration of its own day.

1:1-11 The decree of Cyrus. The three opening verses of the Book of Ezra repeat the closing verses of the Second Book of Chronicles. In concluding the record of Israel's life as a nation, with reference to the edict of Cyrus the Persian (2 Chr 36:22-23), the Chronicler testifies that the fall of the nation is not the end of Israel's story. The conclusion to Chronicles then forms a fitting background and introduction to the same writers' view of the period of return from Exile and restoration of the people.

A Jewish perspective pervades this account. The subject of the opening sentence (1:1) is Israel's God. Yahweh is said to have inspired Cyrus to issue the edict of release from Exile. Although the Chronicler does not cite the poet of the Exile, Second Isaiah, their theological perspectives are similar. Second Isaiah regarded Cyrus as Yahweh's "anointed" (Isa 45:1; compare 44:28), the one through whom Yahweh's plan for Israel's release would be realized. Moreover, the biblical writers connect the edict of Cyrus with God's word as spoken through the prophet Jeremiah (Ezra 1:1). This is consistent with what the Chronicler recorded in 2 Chr 36:21. It is a reflection on Jeremiah's earlier prophecy about Israel's release from Babylonian captivity after a period in which God's purpose in allowing the Exile would have been realized (see Jer 25:11-12; 29:10). Although the prophet spoke of this period lasting seventy years, we, like the biblical writers, must understand seventy as a symbolic number suggesting fullness or completion. In calling attention to the fulfillment of God's word, the Chronicler shares with other exilic and postexilic writers (for example, Second Isaiah and the priestly writers) the view that events of salvation history take momentum and direction from God's power-filled word.

A Jewish perspective is also evident in the date which appears in the opening verse. The "first year of Cyrus" refers not to Cyrus' ascent to the throne in Persia (c. 557 B.C.E.), but to his conquest of Babylonia and the beginning of his rule over the Jews. For the biblical writers, the "first year of Cyrus" is 538 B.C.E.

The citation of the edict of Cyrus represents the first of the writers' frequent use of documentation. An Aramaic version of the edict appears in Ezra 6:3-5. Most scholars agree that the edict quoted in Ezra 1:2-4 represents a Jewish version of the Persian document and not a verbatim record. Several details support this view. First, it is extremely unlikely that the Persian emperor would have regarded his power as having come from Yahweh, the God of Israel. In fact, in the record preserved in the Cyrus Cylinder the ruler cites Marduk, the god of the Babylonians, as the one who gave Babylonia into his hand. The record in Ezra 1:2-4 is similar to other Jewish theological perspectives, for example, that of Second Isaiah (see Isa 45:1). Second, it is also unlikely that Cyrus expected the Babylonians to contribute provisions for the travelers as well as free-will offerings for Yahweh. It is possible that the writers of Ezra 1:4 were seeking to parallel this return from Exile with the Exodus from Egypt when the Israelites took with them goods contributed by the Egyptians (see Exod 3:21; 11:2-3; 12:35-36).

While the particular Jewish view of the edict cited in Ezra 1:2-4 should be recognized, it is true that in some ways the biblical testimony is true to the spirit of Cyrus' policies. The Cyrus Cylinder includes the emperor's mandate that the restoration of Babylonian captives on their native soil include the rebuilding of shrines to their local patronal deities. In accord with that policy, Second Isaiah prophesied that Cyrus would authorize the rebuilding of Jerusalem and its temple (Isa 44:28). The writers of Ezra 1:2-4, however, have assigned prime importance to this particular detail of Cyrus' overall policy. In their view, Yahweh commanded Cyrus to rebuild the temple in Jerusalem, and that is why the emperor released the Jewish captives and called upon the support of the Babylonians.

The section which follows (vv. 5-11) is a narrative beginning with preparations for the return to Judah and ending with an abrupt notice about the return itself. Verses 5-6 clearly flow from verses 1-4. We see that as God had inspired Cyrus (v. 1), so God inspired those Jews who chose to return (v. 5). The returnees left Babylonia enriched by the donations of their neighbors who had complied with the directive cited in verse 4. And, in accord with God's plan and Cyrus' edict (v. 2), the exiles' purpose in returning was to rebuild the temple (v. 5). Thus, the writers tell us that it was a wealthy, inspired, temple-oriented community that returned.

The Jews who had been taken into Exile were Judahites along with members of the tribe of Benjamin with whom they were closely associated. Therefore, the returnees belong to these two clans. The Chronicler's interest in worship prompted the specific mention of priests and Levites along with the tribal heads (v. 5). Since the restoration of the temple is said to have been the goal of the return, it is appropriate that this preparation for the return emphasize the collection of temple utensils which had been taken by the Babylonian Nebuchadnezzar as trophies of his victory over Judah (compare 2 Kgs 24:13; 25:13-16; 2 Chr 36:10, 18; Jer 52:17-20). The Chronicler's concern for the continuity of Israel's religious tradition required this note. Vessels for the restored worship were those which had been used in pre-exilic worship.

According to verses 8 and 11, Cyrus entrusted the temple vessels to Sheshbazzar who was leader of the initial return. Very little is known of Sheshbazzar, since he is only mentioned here and in Ezra 5:14-16 where he is credited with having laid the foundations for the temple in Jerusalem. Many scholars link him with Shenazzar who is described in 1 Chr 3:18 as son of Jeconiah (that is, Jehoachin, the last king of Judah) and therefore a member of the royal family during the generation in Exile. In Ezra 1:8 Sheshbazzar is called "prince of Judah" (compare Ezra 5:14). We cannot be certain of the meaning of this title. It may refer to his royal lineage and be used here as nontechnical terminology designating his civic leadership among the returnees.

The biblical writers complete their account of preparations for the return with an inventory of vessels taken back to the land by Sheshbazzar. Readers will note the discrepancy between the tally of individual pieces and the total given in verse 11.

2:1-70 Census of the province. After the brief notice at the end of chapter 1, Sheshbazzar's return to Jerusalem, the scene shifts to the land of Judah where the former exiles settled. Ezra 2 is only one of many examples of the Chronicler's fondness for lists and other official documentation. An introduction (vv. 1-2) is followed by a census of the people by families and towns (vv. 3-35), a listing of special groups within the community (vv. 36-58), those without proof of lineage (vv. 59-63), numerical totals (vv. 64-67), and a concluding description of gifts brought to the temple and of the geographical distribution of the settlers (vv. 68-70). Scholars generally regard the list as a composite of the records of various groups (probably from different time periods) which have been brought together. The numbers are suspiciously large.

The introduction to the census (vv. 1-2) neglects to mention Sheshbazzar, the leader of the earliest return (see ch. 1), and includes instead Zerubbabel and Jeshua who are described in Ezra 3–6 as active in the temple building project around 520 B.C.E. The list of leaders in verse 2 also includes Nehemiah. It may be an anachronism or it may refer to a different person from the one who is the chief figure in the Book of Nehemiah.

In verses 3-35 the census of the laity alternates between listing people by families (vv. 3-19 or 20, 30-32, 35) and by locale (vv. 20 or 21-29, 33-34). In some cases (particularly vv. 19 and 20) it is difficult to know if the name refers to a person or place, though the designation "men of" instead of "sons of" would appear to signal town names (but compare vv. 21 and 33-34 where "sons of" is used for citizens of particular places).

The numbering of members of special groups (vv. 36-58) includes priests, Levites, singers, gatekeepers, temple slaves, and the descendants of the slaves of Solomon. All appear to designate groups of people who exercised functions within the temple, although virtually nothing is known of the group called "descendants of the slaves of Solomon." The special listing of temple personnel witnesses to the cultic orientation of the writers.

Verses 59-63 include the names of lay people who were unable to prove that their lineage was truly Israelite (vv. 59-60) and priests who could not produce records to show that they were legitimate heirs to the rights and privileges of Israel's priestly family (vv. 61-62). We are not told of the resolution of the confusion over the families of lay persons, but verse 63 indicates that the questions surrounding the validity of priests could be settled by casting lots with the Urim and Thummim, two sticks or dice which served as primitive means for consulting the will of

God (see 1 Sam 14:41). Late biblical tradition says they were carried in the breastplate of the high priest (see Exod 28:30; Lev 8:8). We are told that until this judgment was made, "His Excellency" (that is, some civic leader; the same title is applied to Nehemiah in Neh 8:9 and 10:2) prohibited the priests without credentials from sharing consecrated food (see Lev 2:3; 7:28-36), a privilege of the priesthood.

Readers will note that the total number given in verse 64 is greater than the sum of the parts tallied in the preceding verses, a discrepancy which we cannot explain. The total number of slaves and animals (vv. 65-67) is impressive and does not harmonize with the humble beginnings of the restoration community nor with the hardships of the Jews in Nehemiah's day (see Neh 5:1-5).

Just as the newly freed slaves contributed to the construction of the tabernacle when Israel came out of Egypt (Exod 25:1-6; 35:4-9), so verses 68-69 portray a people zealous for the restoration of Israel's cultic life. The closing verse of the second chapter (v. 70) describes the settlement of the returnees. Cultic and civic leaders and others who probably assisted them in their duties naturally settled in the religious and civic center, Jerusalem. Those Jews whose performance of cultic functions rotated and those who had no official duties probably returned to regions which had been their ancestral homes prior to the Exile.

The order in which the Chronicler presents materials is important. The census in Ezra 2 is followed by an account of the restoration of the altar in Jerusalem and a celebration of the feast of Booths (Ezra 3:1-6). A parallel arrangement appears in Nehemiah chapters 7 and 8. The census of Ezra 2 is repeated in Neh 7:6-72a where it is followed by the promulgation of the law (Neh 8:1-12) and the celebration of the feast of Booths (Neh 8:13-18). The restoration of the altar and the promulgation of the law were two very important moments of the restoration period according to the biblical writers. By preceding accounts of the restoration with a census list, the writers sought to emphasize that the groups who took part in these events were truly the people of God, people purified by the experience of Exile whose ancestral roots linked them with earlier generations of Israelites.

3:1-6 Restoration of the altar. The primacy of the cult is clear in this account. It is an idealized picture of the apparent haste and ease with which Israel's elaborate life of worship was restored.

As David had built an altar prior to the construction of the first temple (2 Sam 24:25; 1 Chr 21:26; 22:1), so the returned exiles began by restoring the altar. The entire community worked together, supervised by the families of priestly and civic leaders (vv. 1-2). The writers underscore the importance of continuity with past religious tradition by saying that the altar was rebuilt on its old foundations (v. 3) and by noting that the reestablished cult was in accord with ancient religious practice: they offered holocausts "prescribed in the law of Moses" (v. 2), they celebrated the feast of Booths "in the manner prescribed," and "they offered the daily holocausts in the proper number required for each day" (v. 4; see also v. 5).

The high point of communal worship in the postexilic period was the offering of sacrifice, and this required a legitimate altar. Holocausts (burnt offerings) were sacrifices which were completely burned, a symbolic expression of the totality of the gift. According to Exod 29:38-42 two lambs were offered as holocausts daily, one in the morning and another in the evening. Sacrifices prescribed for other sacred feasts (v. 5) are described in the legislation of Num 28 and 29. Free-will offerings (v. 5) could be brought at any time by worshipers. In verse 4 the writers speak of the restoration of the feast of Booths (Hebrew *sukkot*, "booths" or "huts"; Latin *tabernacula*, "Tabernacles"), a seven-day festival which for much of the biblical period was the most prominent of Israel's religious festivals. From earliest times it marked the harvest of grapes and olives (see Exod 23:16; 34:22) and was characterized by great rejoicing and thanksgiving (Deut 16:14-15; Lev 23:40). In this passage we see that Israel's liturgical calendar also included a special observance to mark the beginning of each month ("new moon", v. 5; see Num 10:10; 28:11-15).

Ezra 3:1-6 raises some chronological questions. First, verse 1 places the efforts to reestablish the life of worship in "the seventh month" although the year is not designated. Most scholars suggest that in both verses 1 and 6 the reference is to the seventh month of the year of the earliest return, that is, 538 B.C.E. If this is the case, however, a second question of chronology arises. Verse 2 attributes leadership in the rebuilding of the altar to Jeshua and Zerubbabel. Their leadership is problematic in light of the fact that chapter 1 names Sheshbazzar as leader in the return of 538 B.C.E. whereas chapters 4–6 connect Zerubbabel and Jeshua with the temple building activity which occurred between 520 and 515 B.C.E. Thus, distinctions in the chronology of Sheshbazzar, Zerubbabel and Jeshua have been blurred.

3:7-13 Founding of the temple. Confusing Sheshbazzar's work with that of Zerubbabel and Jeshua continues in the present section. Here we are told that Zerubbabel and Jeshua oversaw the laying of the foundations of the temple. But Ezra 5:16 attributes the same role to Sheshbazzar. The vagueness of the date in verse 8 does not shed light on the matter. The work is said to have begun in the "year after their coming to the house of God in Jerusalem." The pronoun "their" could refer to Sheshbazzar and the earliest returnees in which case the year was 537 B.C.E. But if "their" refers to Zerubbabel and Jeshua it would have been somewhat later. The former possibility is to be preferred because Ezra 4:5 says that delays in temple reconstruction lasted from the final years of Cyrus until the time of Darius. Since Sheshbazzar was a contemporary of Cyrus (see 1:8-11) and Zerubbabel and Jeshua were contemporaries of Darius (see Ezra 5:1-5 and Hag 1:1), we conclude that it was the earliest returnees who laid the foundations of the temple building. If Sheshbazzar is identified with the Shenazzar who appears in the genealogy of 1 Chr 3:18 (as many scholars suggest), then Sheshbazzar was the uncle of Zerubbabel (see 1 Chr 3:18-19). It is reasonable to view the situation as follows: Sheshbazzar led an initial contingent of Jews back to the land where he began work on the temple building in Jerusalem. His nephew Zerubbabel led a second group to Judah some years later, and he resumed work (perhaps virtually started over) on the temple which his uncle had begun in the earlier period but which had been stopped by Judah's opponents.

Although the description of the laying of the temple foundations and the accompanying celebration narrated in verses 7-13 has the appearance of an eyewitness record of events, a careful examination of the details suggests that, to a large extent, this account was shaped by community tradition. First, the returnees are said to have planned carefully for the building project by securing proper materials and craftspersons (v. 7). The details of their preparation parallel the Chronicler's version of preparatory efforts undertaken by David (1 Chr 22:2, 4, 15) and Solomon (2 Chr 2:1-15) for the construction of the first temple. Second, beginning the work "in the second month" is in chronological accord with the beginning of construction of the first temple in Solomon's day (see 1 Kgs 6:1; 2 Chr 3:2). Finally, the account of the celebration which followed the laying of the temple foundations accords with the Chronicler's tendency to highlight both the cultic and musical, and it is consistent with other cultic occasions narrated in the Books of Chronicles. For example, trumpets are assigned to the priests (v. 10) as in 1 Chr 16:6 while the Levites play the cymbals (v. 10; compare 2:41 where the "sons of Asaph" are singers) as in 1 Chr 25:1, 6 (compare 2 Chr 29:25-26). The refrain of the hymn which is included in verse 11 likewise appears in 1 Chr 16:34 and 2 Chr 5:13 and 7:3 (see also Pss 106:1; 136:1). It is clear that the writers of Ezra 3:7-13 were eager for events in the early period of the reconstruction to appear continuous with Israel's past.

According to these verses those who laid the foundations of the temple were "all who had come from the captivity to Jerusalem" and we are told that the priests and Levites directed the exiles' labors (vv. 8-9). Here again the writers underscore the importance of legitimacy. The core of the restoration community consisted of those who had been purged by the experience of Exile, and their efforts to reestablish the cult were directed by those who held legitimate authority in cultic affairs. The writers' idealized view of matters is probably responsible for the notation that the whole community of returned exiles participated in the founding of the temple.

The writers include a tender scene of the community's mixed response following the laying of the temple foundations. Some of the Jews were sad, some joyful (vv. 12-13). The Chronicler's picture of the sorrow of those who remembered the glory of the first temple has probably been influenced by familiarity with the witness of Hag 2:3 which says that the temple rebuilt during the second year of Darius (that is, in 520 B.C.E.) was a disappointment to the older generation.

4:1-5 Samaritan interference. Chapter 3 ends with the completion of the foundations of the temple presumably during the second year of the return in 537 B.C.E. (see our discussion on 3:7-13). Chapter 5 opens about seventeen years later with resumption of work on the temple building during the reign of Darius. In chapter 4 the biblical writers account for the intervening delay by describing the opposition of the returnees' neighbors, the Samaritans and the "people of the land." Opposition which had only been hinted at in Ezra 3:3 comes into full view in chapter 4.

According to verses 2-3, the controversy began when descendants of the mixed populations of Samaria expressed a desire to be part of the rebuilding project. In offering their help, they refer to the reign of the Assyrian Esarhaddon (681–669 B.C.E.) although 2 Kgs 17:24-41 links the Assyrian mixing of populations in the northern kingdom of Israel with the reign of Shalmaneser V (726–722 B.C.E.) while Assyrian records credit Sargon II (721–705 B.C.E.) with the repopulation of defeated Israel. We do not know where the writers of Ezra 4:1-5 turned for their information; although the population to the north does seem to have been mixed, we know very little of what went on there after its final capitulation to Assyria in 721 B.C.E. The petitioners base their desire to assist in the temple reconstruction on their fidelity to Yahweh. The Judeans, however, thought that they alone were orthodox, and they dismissed the request by referring to the mandate of Cyrus. The Judeans' rebuff of the Samaritans stems from their concern for cultic purity among the Jews, an issue which comes to a head during Ezra's leadership and is narrated in subsequent chapters.

Verse 4 (and 5) traces the hostility to the "people of the land." We cannot be certain whether this refers to Samaritans from the north, to people of mixed blood who had moved from the north into Judah, or simply to residents of Judah who had remained in Judah during the Exile and hence, in the eyes of the returnees, had not undergone the purging required of those who, in their view, constituted the orthodox community. Whatever the case, these opponents intimidated and discouraged the returnees and subverted their progress. The end of verse 5 describes this state of affairs as lasting from the days of Cyrus (539–530 B.C.E.) to the reign of Darius I (522–485 B.C.E.).

4:6-23 Later hostility. Chronological shifts as well as changes in content mark verses 6-23 as a unit which interrupts the flow from 4:5 to 4:24. First of all, with regard to chronology, verse 6 jumps from the reign of Darius (v. 5) to that of his successor, Xerxes (here called Ahashuerus). Verses 7-23 take readers forward another generation into the reign of Artaxerxes I (465–425 B.C.E.). Secondly, although the particular issues over which there is controversy in verses 6 and 7 are unclear, the matter of concern in verses 8-23 is the rebuilding of the wall of the city of Jerusalem. This sets these verses apart from the concern of verses 1-5 and verse 24 where the issue is the rebuilding of the temple. This change in topic along with the chronological shifts in verses 6-23 show us that these verses interrupt the flow of the narrative. Presumably they have been inserted into this account about the rebuilding of the temple as additional examples of the kind of opposition which hampered the restoration efforts of the postexilic community.

Verses 6 and 7 are related to verses 8-23 insofar as they witness to written statements composed by the enemies of the restoration community and designed to obstruct their efforts. The enemies of verse 6 are the anonymous "they." Those named in verse 7 (Mithredath and Tabeel) appear to have some official roles but we know nothing further about them. In verses 8-23 the enemies are clearly designated as the governor and officials in the Persian province of West-of-Euphrates.

Verse 8 is the beginning of the Aramaic section of the Book of Ezra which continues until Ezra 6:18. An editor prepares the reader of the Hebrew text for the shift in verse 7b. The contents of verses 8-23 claim to be a record of official correspondence to (vv. 8-16) and from (vv. 17-22) the Persian king. This demonstrates the writers' characteristic style of documenting their accounts with what appear to be official records. The question of whether or not the correspondence recorded here is, in fact, an authentic record remains open, since we have no extrabiblical evidence with which to verify it.

The letter to Artaxerxes reports the rebuilding of Jerusalem (v. 12) as a threat against the Persian throne (v. 13). In verse 14 the writers declare that their report is an act of loyalty. Partaking of the "salt of the palace" refers to an ancient custom wherein sharing salt with another symbolized alliance (see Num 18:19; Lev 2:13; 2 Chr 13:5). In verse 15 the composers of the letter suggest to the Persian emperor that their accusation against Jerusalem can be substantiated by an investigation of the city's past. Jerusalem, they say, has a history of rebellion which is documented in Persian records and which will lead to Persia's loss of the entire province of West-of-Euphrates if the rebuilding of the city is not stopped (v. 16).

The letter from Artaxerxes (vv. 17-22) shows that the enemies of the restoration community achieved their desired result: the suspicions of the accusers were substantiated, and the Persian emperor ordered that the rebuilding of Jerusalem be stopped. The truth of the matters which the Persian emperor said were documented in his records is difficult to assess. That any foreign king ever ruled the territory from the Euphrates River to the Mediterranean Sea (the area subsequently called West-of-Euphrates) from Jerusalem is especially questionable. Whatever the case, verse 23 narrates that Artaxerxes' orders were carried out and the rebuilding of Jerusalem stopped.

4:24–5:17 Rebuilding of the temple. Verse 24 of chapter 4 is a transitional statement which resumes the narratives of verses 1-5 of the same chapter and leads into the materials contained in chapters 5 and 6. Verse 24 takes readers back to the later years of Cyrus and the first years of Darius when the concern was not the restoration of Jerusalem (as in 4:8-23) but the reconstruction of the temple.

In Ezra 5:1-2 renewed efforts to rebuild the temple are traced to the inspiration of two prophets from the early years of Darius' reign, Haggai and Zechariah. The Books of Haggai and Zechariah tell us that during the period extending from the second to the fourth year of Darius (between 520 and 518 B.C.E.) these two prophets were concerned about the necessity, even urgency, of rebuilding the temple. Haggai and Zechariah corroborate the witness of Ezra 5:1-2 that Zerubbabel and Jeshua were leading figures in the restoration community during this period.

Having briefly reported the resumption of work on the temple, the biblical writers divert our attention to the question of proper authorization for the project, a concern which continues throughout the remainder of chapter 5 and throughout the bulk of chapter 6. Regional officials representing Persian interests came to Jerusalem to conduct an investigation regarding the temple project. The blatant hostility which marked the narrative of chapter 4 is absent from the present inquiry (vv. 3-5) and from the subsequent correspondence with the Persian emperor (vv. 6-17). We are not told what precipitated the investigation; although it may have constituted a subtle form of harassment, the text offers no clear indication that this was its purpose. The officials simply inquire regarding proper authorization for the temple reconstruction and the identity of those involved in the work. Verse 5 reports that, unlike the incident reported in Ezra 4:1-5 and 24, the present investigation did not retard progress on the rebuilding and that this was due to God's protective presence. At this point in the narrative the "elders of the Jews" appear to take the lead in the temple project and in dealings with the Persian officials (see Ezra 5:9; 6:7, 8, 14).

The remainder of chapter 5 and 6:1-12 reflect the Chronicler's fondness for including documentation, this time in the form of official correspondence between officers of the Persian province West-of-Euphrates and the Persian emperor. Verses 7-17 claim to be a copy of the letter sent by the provincial officers to Darius. Their report on the rebuilding in Jerusalem (vv. 7-8) and the nature of their inquiry (vv. 9-10) is in accord with what had been narrated in verses 3-4 except that the report contains additional information about building materials and the spirit and progress which marked the Jews' work (v. 8). Verses 11-16 contain a relatively lengthy response on the part of the Jews (a response which is missing from the incident as narrated in verses 3-5). The Jews address only the question about authorization for the rebuilding of the temple. The names which had been requested are not given. (Some have suggested that the list which now appears in Ezra 2 may originally have served this purpose.)

The Jews' response is set within the context of a brief review of history from the beginnings of the first temple. The language of the historical review makes concessions to the fact that this report was prepared for foreigners. The specific identity of the builder of the first temple would have been of no interest to Persian authorities, so Solomon is referred to simply as "a great king of Israel" (v. 11). For the same reason, the personal name of the God of Israel, Yahweh, does not appear, and instead the Jews refer to their God with a more general designation ("the God of heaven and earth" in verse 11 and the "God of heaven" in verse 12) which would have been more familiar to foreigners. At the same time, a specifically Jewish view of history surfaces in verse 12 where we read that the fall of Israel into Babylonian hands was not simply a human exchange of power but an act of God following upon the sinfulness of the covenanted people. The abbreviated report of the fall of the temple and the captivity agrees with longer witnesses to the same events which appear in 2 Kgs 25:8-21 and 2 Chr 36:17-20.

Persian authorization for the rebuilding of the temple appears in verse 13 where Cyrus the Persian is called "king of Babylon." Verse 13 neglects to mention that Cyrus' decree mandated the return of the Jewish exiles. It limits itself to the part of Cyrus' edict which relates to the matter at hand, that is, the rebuilding of the temple (compare the decree as cited in Ezra 1:2-4). Verses 14-15 extend the discussion to some degree by including Cyrus' decree providing for the recovery of sacred temple vessels which had been confiscated by the Babylonian captors.

When we are told in verse 14 that Cyrus appointed Sheshbazzar "governor," the meaning is unclear. The same word was used to describe Tattenai, the non-Jewish official of West-of-Euphrates who sent the letter (see 5:6; compare Ezra 1:8 where Sheshbazzar is called "prince of Judah" and Hag 1:1 where Zerubbabel is called "governor of Judah").

We have said that verse 16 attributes the laying of the foundations of the temple to Sheshbazzar even though Ezra 3:8-10 (and Zech 4:9) gave credit for its beginning to Zerubbabel (see our discussion on Ezra 3:7-13).

The officials' letter ends with their request that Darius verify Cyrus' authorization of the rebuilding of the temple as the Jews had reported and that Darius tell the officials what he wants them to do about this matter.

6:1-18 The decree of Darius. The opening verses of chapter 6 are a further example of the biblical writers' fondness for including official documentation. The statement by Cyrus which Darius found in Ecbatana, one of the imperial centers of Persia, also underscores Persian patronage of Jewish efforts—a consistent witness throughout the Books of Ezra and Nehemiah except for Ezra 4:8-23. The text confirms that the rebuilding of the temple in Jerusalem was authorized, and as such it serves as a response to the inquiry which was the subject of chapter 5. It is presented as an edict issued by Cyrus in the first year of his reign, so it is an alternate witness to the edict cited in Ezra 1:2-4. Although the exact wording of the edict is not the same in the two texts, the content of 1:2-4 is in essential agreement with that of 6:3-5 with the following exceptions: (a) 1:2-4 includes permission for the exiles to return to their land along with permission to rebuild the temple while 6:3-5 confines itself strictly to the temple restoration; (b) 6:3-5 provides for the return of the temple utensils while the document cited in 1:2-4 does not mention them (compare 1:7 and 5:14-15); (c) 6:3-5 contains specific information about the construction of the temple which does not appear in the copy of the edict in 1:2-4. The building materials specified in verse 4 are the same as those used in Solomon's temple (see 1 Kgs 6:36), but there is a significant discrepancy between the proportions of the temple in verse 3 and the size of Solomon's temple recorded in 1 Kgs 6:2. Scholars, citing Ezra 3:12 and Hag 2:3, are skeptical that the second temple was larger than the one which Solomon built.

Having documented the claims of the Jewish leaders, in verses 6-12 the biblical writers cite Darius' response to the final request of the provincial officials that Darius voice his own directives on the matter under investigation. Darius tells the local officials not to interfere with the rebuilding of the temple. He also orders them to facilitate the work with monies collected through taxation within the province and to provide materials for the daily temple offerings required by the Mosaic law (see Exod 29:38-42). Verse 10 makes clear that the Persian emperor's directives are not without self-interest.

In the face of the long delays which mark the biblical writers' account of the rebuilding of the temple, the brief account of the completion and dedication of the temple and the restoration of cultic service (vv. 13-18) may strike the reader as abrupt. Work on the temple went forward in accord with the promptings of the God of Israel, the Persian emperors (Artaxerxes is a later gloss added to verse 14), and prophets of the period, Haggai and Zechariah. It was completed in the spring of 515 B.C.E. The temple was dedicated by a legitimate community of faith defined in verse 16 as priests, Levites, and other Jews who had been purified by the experience of Exile. The offerings for this occasion are relatively modest compared to the sacrifices at the dedication of Solomon's temple (compare 1 Kgs 8:5, 63) and probably reflect the poverty of the struggling community. Finally, we are told that priestly and Levitical personnel assumed their traditional cultic offices (see Num 3; 1 Chr 23–24). Thus the writers establish continuity between ancient practice and the worship of the postexilic community in Jerusalem.

These verses mark the end of the Aramaic section of the Book of Ezra. The concluding verses of the first section (6:19-22) appear in Hebrew.

If the witness of Ezra 6:15 is correct, that is, if the second temple was dedicated in the month of Adar (the twelfth month), then it is realistic to expect that Passover was celebrated soon after, for according to the legislation of Exod 12 Passover was held on the fourteenth day of the first month (Nisan). In including the account of Passover after a description of the temple dedication, the writers are presenting what appears to be a historically reliable account. At the same time, when we note that the Chronicler presents the feast of Booths (Ezra 3:1-6) following the dedication of the altar and that the celebration of Passover followed the reconsecrations of the temple which were part of the reforms of King Hezekiah (2 Chr 29–30; compare 2 Kgs 18–20) and King Josiah (2 Chr 34–35; compare 2 Kgs 22–23), we wonder if the biblical writers offer more of a theological construct than historical fact in Ezra 6:19-22. Whatever the case, a celebration of Passover is presented as following the rededication of the temple, and Passover observance is linked with the feast of Unleavened Bread as it is in the priestly legislation of Exod 12:1-20. Because the law permitted non-Jews to join in the celebration of Passover (Num 9:14), outsiders are invited to join in the celebration described here. However, the biblical writers' inclusiveness on this occasion is restrained by the repeated reference to members of the legitimate community (those who had been purged by the experience of Exile) and by the qualification that those non-Jews who celebrated Passover had separated themselves from the cultic uncleanness of the "peoples of the land."

The concluding verse of this first section of the Book of Ezra reminds readers of the aim of the entire account of these early years of the restoration. The biblical writers recall that it is Yahweh ("the Lord") who controls history and made the Persian king (certainly this is the intent of the expression "king of Assyria" in verse 22) facilitate the rebuilding of the temple which, according to the view of the writers (see Ezra 1:2), was the primary goal of the return from Exile.

PART II: RESTORATION OF THE WORSHIPING COMMUNITY

Ezra 7:1–10:44

Chapters 7 through 10 of the Book of Ezra constitute the second major part of the Ezra-Nehemiah materials. The chief figure in these chapters (and in chapter 8 of the Book of Nehemiah) is Ezra, a reformer important in the reconstruction, whose name was given to the biblical book. Chapters 7 and 8 introduce Ezra and describe the return from Exile which he led. Chapters 9 and 10 narrate the marriage reform which Ezra is said to have initiated within the restoration community. Much of the material was taken from Ezra's memoirs. Ezra 7–10 and Nehemiah 8 credit Ezra particularly with zealous efforts to establish the law of Moses as the center around which Jewish life was reconstructed. This is the foundation for the postbiblical view of Ezra as a second Moses.

Readers must be aware of the chronological, theological, and literary complexities woven into the Ezra materials. Although the exact time of Ezra's mission is unknown, we accept the scholarly opinion which places Ezra within the reign of Artaxerxes II (405–359 B.C.E.). Thus, a lengthy historical gap separates the materials of Ezra 1–6 (ending with the dedication of the temple in 515 B.C.E.) and the mission of Ezra (about 398 B.C.E.) as described in Ezra 7–10. In the intervening years, Nehemiah led the community in the reconstruction of the wall of Jerusalem and in cultic reforms (see Neh 1–7, 9–13).

The present arrangement of the text is understandable if one recalls the theological interests of the writers (see Introduction, (p. 336). They present community purity, the goal of Ezra's marriage reform, as the second stage of the restoration movement, following the reconstruction of the temple. True worship required not only a legitimate temple with proper rituals and feasts (Ezra 1–6), but also worshipers made cultically pure by their separation from foreigners (Ezra 7–10).

Ezra's proclamation of the law (Neh 7:72b–8:18) is now separate from the biblical writers' account of the rest of Ezra's mission. If one sought to reconstruct an accurate chronology of events, one might read Neh 7:72b to 8:18 between chapters 8 and 9 of the Book of Ezra. However, the present arrangement of the text stresses that the proclamation of the law was the theological culmination of all other works of restoration, the event which marked the full restoration of the Jewish community. Therefore, Ezra's reading of the law is presented in the Book of Nehemiah as part of the fourth and final stage of restoration.

7:1–10 Ezra the scribe. With the simple phrase "after these events," the biblical writers span the years which lay between the dedication of the temple and Ezra's mission. The genealogy of verses 2-5, which in part parallels 1 Chr 5:29-40, is not so much concerned with factual data (it is a historical impossibility that the time period between Aaron and Ezra was only seventeen generations) as with Ezra's priestly legitimacy. He is presented as a descendant of the precursor of all Israel's priests, Aaron. If Seraiah is the same person mentioned in 2 Kgs 25:18, Ezra is also presented as son of the last official high priest before the fall of the temple to the Babylonians (see 1 Chr 5:40; since the fall was in 587 B.C.E., it is clear that Ezra was not, in fact, Seraiah's son). The biblical writers use the genealogy not only to tell us that Ezra was a priest but to underscore the legitimacy of his priestly lineage and to emphasize that his leadership in the restoration community was an authentic extension of priestly leadership in pre-exilic Israel.

Ezra's more significant role was that of scribe, a term which originally designated an expert in writing who exercised a significant role, politically. In later periods scribes were experts in the law. That is the meaning of scribe as it is used here although Ezra's close relationship with King Artaxerxes also suggests that, prior to being sent to Jerusalem, he held a position (secretary for Jewish affairs?) in the royal court of Persia. It is difficult to know with certainty what constituted the "law of Moses" in which Ezra was well-versed. It may have been the Pentateuch as we know it or some portion of the law contained therein.

According to the biblical writers, Ezra had other credentials for his mission: he was favored by God and by the Persian king. This is consistent with Ezra 1–6 where God showed graciousness to the Jews by providing the generous patronage of the Persian kings.

Having introduced the chief figure in the second stage of the restoration, the biblical writers offer an overview of his return from Exile, a journey which will be considered in greater detail in Ezra 8. The writers' concern for worship in the restoration community led them to include references to the cultic officers who accompanied Ezra (v. 7). They also provide dates for the journey. It seems to have taken about four months. It is interesting that Ezra left Babylon during the first month of the year, the same month which the priestly writers assigned to the Exodus journey (Exod 12:2; Num 33:3). It is difficult to know whether or not the biblical writers were suggesting a theological parallel between the two events.

The introductory verses to the second stage of the reconstruction close with a portrait of Ezra as one who not only studied and taught the law but also zealously practiced it (v. 10).

7:11-26 The decree of Artaxerxes. Interested in including official documentation for various parts of the return and restoration, the biblical writers offer what claims to be a statement by the Persian emperor which (a) authorized a return under Ezra's leadership, (b) commissioned Ezra to establish the law as the basis for life in the restoration community in Judah, and (c) put Ezra in charge of monetary and other gifts for the temple in Jerusalem. The fact that the decree (vv. 12-26) appears in Aramaic gives it the appearance of authenticity. Yet some of its details (such as the list of offerings in verse 17 and the list of temple personnel in verse 24) suggest that it was written by someone with considerable knowledge of cultic affairs in the Jewish community. Some scholars have proposed that it was drafted by a Jewish member of Artaxerxes' court, while others think that an authentic letter of appointment was amplified by the biblical writers.

The opening (vv. 11-12) and closing (vv. 25-26) of this section echo the main emphasis which appears in the introduction to Ezra in 7:1-10, Ezra's authority with regard to the law. Following his commission to lead a group of exiles back to Jerusalem (v. 13), Ezra's basic role in the restoration community is to be guardian of the law of God within the Jewish community. This role represents an extension of the authority of the Persian government (v. 14).

The remainder of Artaxerxes' decree orders Ezra to obtain sufficient provisions to establish full worship in the temple in Jerusalem. The king and his officers not only contributed silver and gold for temple worship out of their own treasuries but also authorized Ezra to take to Jerusalem any gifts which he could collect from Jews living in Babylon. In addition, Artaxerxes sent utensils for temple worship with Ezra, just as Cyrus had done when Sheshbazzar led an earlier return (see 1:7-11; 5:14-15). As a further gesture of generosity, Artaxerxes promised to provide from the royal treasury whatever else was needed for proper worship and included explicit instructions for his officers in the province to which Ezra travelled. Finally, he declared all cultic personnel in West-of-Euphrates tax-exempt. In verse 23 we see that Artaxerxes' magnanimity toward the Jews and their worship was not without self-interest: proper worship was to be conducted in order to secure Yahweh's favor for the Persian king.

The conclusion of Artaxerxes' decree (vv. 25-26) returns to Ezra's role as chief caretaker of God's law. Like Moses (see Exod 18), Ezra is authorized to appoint administrators of justice within the restoration community. Ezra's own role is to offer instruction in the law. Finally, the Persian emperor provides for the punishment (even the death) of those who fail to obey "the law of your God and the law of the king."

7:27–8:14 Ezra and his companions. The biblical text returns to Hebrew in verse 27. The same verse marks the beginning of what scholars call "Ezra's memoirs," the first-person account which extends to Ezra 9:15 (see our discussion of sources, p. 338). Verses 27-28a are a blessing placed on the lips of Ezra. Its contents reiterate the notion expressed in 7:6 that the generosity of the Persian officials was ultimately an expression of Yahweh's graciousness to the Jewish community. In the remainder of verse 28 Ezra also connects his own work with the providence of God.

Just as the biblical writers included a list of the names in conjunction with an earlier return to Judah (Ezra 2), so the narrative about Ezra's return is delayed by a similar listing which appears in the initial verses of chapter 8. The list begins (v. 2) with the names of returning descendants of ancient Israel's priestly leaders (Phinehas and Ithamar) and of the royal house of David. Verses 3-14 list the names of the heads of twelve lay families who returned along with the total number of returning males belonging to each group. In naming twelve families the biblical writers suggest that "all Israel" returned, that is, representatives from all the twelve tribes of Israel. Nearly fifteen hundred males returned with Ezra—a sizeable number especially if one adds the women and children who must have returned with them. Family names in this list also appear in the longer list in chapter 2, although in a different order.

8:15-36 The journey to Jerusalem. The account of Ezra's journey to Jerusalem is marked by an order similar to that of a religious service. There is (a) an initial gathering of returnees at a location ("by the river that flows toward Ahava") unknown to modern scholars and a three-day rest which will be repeated when the journey to Jerusalem has been completed (see 8:32), (b) recruiting of cultic personnel (Levites and temple slaves), (c) a fast and prayer for a safe journey, (d) the consignment of temple treasures to cultic personnel, (e) the journey itself which unfolded in accord with the prayer of verses 21-23, (f) the delivery of gifts for the temple which in part repeats verses 24-30, and (g) sacrificial rituals to Yahweh and a visit to local civic officials. The biblical writers devote much attention to preparations for the journey and to activities which occurred upon Ezra's arrival in Jerusalem. Among these, interest is particularly focused on cultic concerns. Events during the long journey are only hinted at in verse 31.

Verses 15b-20 contain a record of Ezra's attempts to include cultic personnel in his return. We do not know why Levites did not originally join his group. Some scholars have suggested that not many Levites had gone into Exile because earlier shifts in their cultic duties at the temple had led to their dispersal among outlying cities and towns prior to the fall of Jerusalem. Others suggest that Levites had gone into Exile but had taken up non-cultic professions while they were there. Whatever the case, the recruiters that Ezra sent to Casiphia (Levites were apparently concentrated in this city the location of which is not known) brought a few Levites and a greater number of temple slaves into the caravan. This, like much else in the present account, is attributed to God's guidance. The emphasis upon divine protection likewise appears in the fast and prayer which preceded the journey (vv. 21-23) and in the notation that the group and its many treasures arrived safely in Jerusalem despite the fact that they had neither requested nor received military protection along the way.

Ezra selected twelve priestly leaders and twelve of the cultic personnel recruited from Casiphia to take care of the temple gifts from Persian officials and from Jews in Babylon. The appointment of cultic leaders for this role is in accord with ancient tradition, since Num 3–4 tells us that priests and Levites were appointed to attend to sacred objects on the journey that Moses led through the Sinai wilderness when ancient Israel journeyed toward the Promised Land after the Exodus. The fact that it was twelve priests and twelve other cultic leaders who were guardians of the sacred offerings and utensils again reflects the biblical writers' propensity for the number which symbolized the ideal, "all Israel." Immediately following a brief summary of the journey (v. 31), the biblical writers tell us that the sacred gifts arrived intact and were delivered to the proper officials as Ezra had directed. Cultic matters were most important to them; this priority given to cult led the biblical writers to suggest that, following the standard three-day rest period, the first activity of the returnees was to offer sacrifices to Yahweh.

9:1-2 Denunciation of mixed marriages. Ezra's work in the restoration community (decrying mixed marriage) is narrated in chapters 9 and 10 of the Book of Ezra and in chapter 8 of the Book of Nehemiah (Ezra's ceremonial reading of the law). Some scholars propose that Neh 8 was originally part of the Ezra materials which appear in the Book of Ezra. Accordingly, they have suggested that Neh 7:72b–8:18 be read between the end of Ezra 8 and the beginning of Ezra 9. While this proposal has merit because of the somewhat nebulous opening of Ezra 9 ("when these matters had been concluded"), for purposes of this commentary we shall follow the text as it has come down to us. In view of the reply that Artaxerxes sent to Ezra, the learned scribe, to "supervise Judah and Jerusalem in respect of the law of your God" (7:14), it is surprising that the first reported incident involving his leadership is the dissolution of mixed marriages and not the reading of the law.

The biblical position on marriages with foreigners is not consistent. While some prominent biblical figures (for example, Joseph, Moses, David) had foreign spouses and the Book of Ruth witnesses to the blessings God bestowed on the Hebrew community through the Moabite woman who married the Hebrew Boaz, the prohibition of mixed marriages which appears in the Book of Ezra has precedents in earlier stages of Israelite tradition (see Exod 34:16; Deut 7:1-4). Marital practices in different ages were shaped by changing social, political, economic, and religious situations. In Ezra's time concern for cultic purity and for securing the identity of the Jewish people required pure blood lines.

The situation is reported to Ezra: laymen and clergymen alike have taken foreign wives, and the worst offenders are community leaders. The "people of the land" with whom they were joined are defined by an editor who had access to the lists of Deut 7:1; Josh 3:10; 24:12. The transgressors are also linked with the "abominations" of their spouses; that is, their marriages had brought them into contact with the worship of other gods.

9:3-15 Ezra's exhortation. Ezra was distressed by the report. In a traditional expression of grief, he tore his clothes and pulled out his hair. As the smoke of the evening offering marked the hour of community worship in the temple, Ezra fell on his knees and stretched out his hands.

Ezra begins praying in the first person singular but changes immediately to the first person plural, which he uses consistently throughout the remainder of the confession of guilt.

Ezra states that Israel's entire history has been characterized by sin which brought on the downfall of the nation and the Babylonian Exile (v. 7). This sinful past provides the perspective within which Ezra interprets Israel's present situation. In the present era the punishment of captivity which was an expression of God's justice has given way to God's mercy. A remnant of the Jewish people was spared and brought once again to Jerusalem. As elsewhere in the Book of Ezra, this mark of divine favor is brought into conjunction with the kindness of the Persian emperors toward the exiles. The end result of these divine and human mercies is that the temple was rebuilt and Jerusalem and Judah were made secure (vv. 8-9). But the present favor is now in jeopardy. The land and its peoples are impure (see Lev 18:24-25), and Israel has transgressed God's commandment by intermarrying with foreigners (Deut 7:1-4). (It is noteworthy that the Deuteronomic tradition cited by Ezra prohibits the marrying of Israelite women to foreign men as well as the marrying of Israelite men to foreign women, a more inclusive view than Ezra's own reform which deals only with marriages which Jewish men had contracted with foreign women.)

While Ezra explicitly addresses his questions to God in verses 13-14, the reader senses he has also aimed them at the Jews assembled for worship in order to call to their attention what was happening in their midst. Have they not learned from experience that punishment follows sin? If God were to punish the present guilt, would not the Jews now living in Israel be completely destroyed? Justice is certain, but mercy is a gift. The fragile remnant of Jews in Jerusalem exists only because of gift. Their sin of marrying foreigners will require that God act justly with them.

10:1-15 The people's response. The dramatic confession of chapter 9 serves as the background for the decisions and actions reported in chapter 10. The use of the third person suggests that the report in chapter 10 did not come from Ezra's memoirs but from another source.

Ezra had attracted a very large crowd of men, women and children. A layman, Shecaniah, was stirred by Ezra's speech to confess the community's guilt ("We have indeed betrayed our God"). To ward off the possibility of total destruction, a punishment of which Ezra had warned, Shecaniah proposed that Jewish men dismiss their foreign wives and their children.

Shecaniah's exclamation, "Let the law be observed!" (v. 3) is something of a puzzle. While Pentateuchal law prohibited marriage with foreigners (see Exod 34:16; Deut 7:1-4), it did not make provision for what to do in cases where mixed marriages already existed. In other words, the law did not require divorce in cases of mixed marriages. It is possible that what we see here is the beginning of a new practice adopted to meet the demands of a situation not addressed by tradition. Whatever the case, Shecaniah's proposal makes clear that Ezra's condemnation of mixed marriages in chapter 9 was accepted by the community and required the dissolution of already-established families. Concerns about religious tradition took precedence over regard for the sacredness of family bonds. At once, action to dissolve mixed marriages begins. Ezra demanded that the priests and people of the community swear to act. All exiles in the country (that is, all legitimate members of the Jewish community) were required to come to Jerusalem within three days under threat of dispossession and excommunication.

Meanwhile Ezra retires to the temple quarters of Johanan (v. 6). This brief note has played an important part in biblical scholars' discussions about the dates of Ezra's mission. Johanan is described here as son of the high priest Eliashib. However, Neh 12:10-11 and 22 are probably more accurate in presenting Johanan as Eliashib's grandson. Now Eliashib is known to have served as high priest during the time of Nehemiah (445–433 B.C.E.; see Neh 3:1, 20-21). Most scholars conclude from this that, contrary to the chronological witness of the present arrangement of the Ezra-Nehemiah materials, Nehemiah preceded Ezra in the work of restoration. The biblical writers do not tell us whether or not Johanan served as high priest in Ezra's day. (Extra-biblical sources indicate that Johanan held the high priestly office near the end of the fifth century B.C.E..) He did, however, have his own quarters in the temple.

When the biblical writers say that "all the men of Judah and Benjamin" appeared as ordered (v. 9), they refer to "all Israel" by naming the two ancient tribes who constituted the southern part of the country during much of its history. The biblical writers describe a scene both grave and comic. It was Israel's rainy season and those who gathered on the temple mount shivered—over the seriousness of the matter at hand and "because it was raining" (v. 9). Apparently oblivious to their pathetic condition, Ezra (now specifically described as priest instead of scribe) began accusing those gathered before him in the rain. Without awaiting response or confession, he gave the order for separation. The assembled community acknowledged that it was their duty to obey Ezra but pointed out that because of their numbers and the rain it was both humanly impossible and uncomfortable to proceed immediately. They suggested that appointed leaders could handle the matter for the whole community, in light of the numbers involved, and establish a more realistic deadline for the dissolution of mixed marriages.

Verse 15 notes some dissenting voices among those gathered, but the subject of their disagreement is left ambiguous. We do not know whether they objected to the decision to divorce foreign women or to the procedures designed for the reform.

10:16-44 The guilty. Verses 16-17 report that the leaders appointed by Ezra judged the legitimacy of marriages of Jews with foreign women. These hearings took three months. Most of the remainder of the chapter is a list of the offenders, beginning with priests and other cultic personnel and concluding with members of the laity named by families. The list has some parallels with those in Ezra 2 and 8, although it is not a duplicate of either. It contains only 111 names, a surprisingly small total in view of the thousands who constituted the community. This may have been only a partial listing of the people involved. An alternate explanation is that if mixed marriages were widespread only a few people responded to the action taken by Ezra.

COMMENTARY: NEHEMIAH

PART III: RESTORATION OF THE WALL OF JERUSALEM

Neh 1:1–7:72a

Drawing heavily upon Nehemiah's memoirs, chapters 1–7 of the Book of Nehemiah narrate events of the two-month period from the beginning of Nehemiah's mission to shortly after the reconstruction of the wall around Jerusalem, the third major achievement during the restoration period. Work on the wall presses on in spite of both continuous opposition from Judah's neighbors and tensions within the Jewish community itself. Throughout the chapters there is an underlying parallel drawn between the welfare of the city and the welfare of the Jewish community. The restoration of the city wall in Part III thus functions as a fitting preparation for the full restoration of the community under the law in Part IV.

In these chapters we find the biblical portrait of Nehemiah. Throughout, he is presented as a pious Jew, prayerful and dependent upon God's help. His initial fears are transformed to fearlessness before all but God, and he counsels the Jewish community not to capitulate through fear to the evil designs of its enemies. Other prominent characteristics of Nehemiah's piety are the initiative and zealous effort which mark his mission. His oneness with the Jewish people sparks his decision to act when he hears of the brokenness of Jerusalem and its people. He gives practical matters his full attention, assessing situations carefully before acting.

Nehemiah's mission to Judah was authorized and patronized by the Persian throne, as were the missions of Sheshbazzar (Part I) and Ezra (Part II). Nehemiah's appointment as governor over the province of Judah put him in a position to deal firmly with rulers of neighboring regions and with leaders in the Jewish community who needed to be called to account for their acts. With the community at large, he was consistently decisive but not coercive. He was attentive to their needs, even to the point of self-sacrifice. His view of community included women as well as men.

1:1-11 Nehemiah's vocation. The opening chapter of the Book of Nehemiah falls into two sections: (a) a report about the Judean Jews and the city of Jerusalem (vv. 1-3) and (b) Nehemiah's response to the report (vv. 4-11). Succinctly the chapter presents the roots out of which the remainder of the book will grow. First of all, we learn that it is 445 B.C.E. (the twentieth year of the reign of Artaxerxes I) and that, even though nearly a century has passed since the Jews returned to Judah from their captivity in Babylon, they continue to live as a broken people, a plight symbolized by the brokenness of the wall around the city which is their center. Secondly, this first chapter introduces us to Nehemiah, a Jewish official in the Persian court ("cupbearer to the king"), who has both a strong sense of identification with the Jews in Judah and a recognition that the brokenness in Judah constitutes a call to action on his part.

As the book opens we find ourselves in the memoirs of this Jewish layman. Nehemiah was in Susa, a winter residence of King Artaxerxes whom he served. He met with a group of men from Judah whose mission is not stated. They could have come to solicit help from the Persian throne or from Nehemiah. Or, they may have been on a routine business trip within the empire and secondarily functioned as part of an informal network of communication between Jews in Judah and those scattered abroad. Whatever the case, the group included Hanani, a "brother" to Nehemiah, that is, either a blood relative or perhaps just a fellow Jew. In answer to Nehemiah's inquiry, Hanani reports both about the Jews and about the city of Jerusalem. The fact that Nehemiah is reported to have asked about both the people and the city signals a perspective which flows through the work of Nehemiah. We shall see that for him the welfare of the two are closely intertwined. For Nehemiah, the restoration of the people and the restoration of the city are somehow two sides of the same concern.

The news from Judah is bad, and it grips the spirit of Nehemiah (v. 4). The disgraceful situation of the Jews in Judah and of the city of Jerusalem becomes his own diminishment. In the prayer of verses 5-11 we see the strong bond between Nehemiah and the Jews: their sin is his sin (vv. 6-7); their need for God's favor is his need (v. 11). Into his confession and petition Nehemiah weaves words pushing God to act. He politely reminds God of exactly who is speaking to whom. He and the sorrowing Jews in Jerusalem—those who beg for a hearing—are, like Moses before them, God's own servants (vv. 6, 7, 8, 10, 11). At the same time, he reminds God that God is the one who chose and bought this people for the divine self (v. 10), who preserves a "covenant of mercy" for faithful servants (v. 5), and who, after all, has promises to keep (vv. 8-9).

The prayer of Nehemiah is shot through with elements firmly rooted in Israel's religious tradition. In verse 10 he refers to the Exodus from Egypt. Nehemiah's restatement of God's promise (vv. 8b-9) is a paraphrase of Deut 30:1-5 which Nehemiah freely interprets not simply as God's commitment to bring the Jews back to the land of Judah but specifically to bring them back to "the place which I have chosen as the dwelling place for my name," a Deuteronomic way of referring to the city of Jerusalem.

Much takes place in this seemingly simple chapter. Nehemiah has moved from his initial inquiry about Jerusalem to grief, prayer, and a decision to act. It is a fitting introduction to Nehemiah, a man of action who identifies deeply with his fellow Jews. He hears a vocational call: the Jews and Jerusalem are in distress and he is in a position to help. Empathy and prayer are not enough. The closing words of the chapter (v. 11b) reflect his decision to help Jerusalem.

2:1-10 Appointment by the king. The memoirs resume four months later when Nehemiah is in a position to do something about the vocational call narrated in chapter 1. While Nehemiah performed his duty as cupbearer, Artaxerxes noticed that something was wrong with his servant. Nehemiah reports (v. 2) that he was "seized with great fear" when Artaxerxes inquired about the reason for his sadness. To understand Nehemiah's fear we must recall the incident described in Ezra 4:8-23. At some time earlier in his reign Artaxerxes had halted Jewish efforts to reconstruct the wall of the city of Jerusalem. He did so out of a conviction that the restoration of Jerusalem was tantamount to rebellion against the Persian throne. Hence, Nehemiah was fearful because, in effect, he had to tell the king that his sadness was due to a decision that the king himself had made.

The exchange between Nehemiah and the king constitutes a masterpiece of diplomacy. Politics is left out of the conversation. The personal concern which started the discussion ("Why do you look sad?" v. 2) carries to its end. Nehemiah avoids the word "Jerusalem" and instead speaks of the devastation of "the city where my ancestors are buried" (vv. 3, 5). Thus, his request to go and rebuild the city is made only on personal grounds. The king does not refer to his earlier decision either, although he must have been aware that he was being asked to reverse his decision regarding the reconstruction of Jerusalem. It may be that doing so now was politically expedient. In the earlier period there had been much unrest in the area of the empire surrounding Judah, and the reconstruction of a fortified city in Judah may have only fed fires of revolt. But by 445 B.C.E. revolts in that part of the empire had died down, and entrusting Nehemiah (whose loyalty the king knew personally) with the task of fortifying Jerusalem might indeed enhance imperial strength and security in the area. If politics motivated Artaxerxes to grant Nehemiah's request, we are never told so. Instead, the permission to return to Jerusalem is cast as a personal favor to one who had endeared himself to the king. The permission, however, constitutes a political appointment. In Neh 5:14 we are told that Nehemiah went to Judah as governor. The length of his appointment is only alluded to in Neh 2:6, but Neh 5:14 shows that Nehemiah left to begin a term of office which would last twelve years.

Neh 2:6 implies that Nehemiah's commission came from both the Persian king and queen. The inclusion of the queen (whose name, Damaspia, we know from extrabiblical documents) is an unusual but interesting detail. Queens exercised considerable influence during some periods of the Persian Empire (see the Book of Esther) and this was especially so during the reign of Artaxerxes. In addition, we shall see that the Book of Nehemiah frequently includes the role of women as well as men (see Neh 3:12; 5:1-5; 8:2-3; 10:31; 12:43).

The account of Nehemiah's appointment by the king is consistent with the first chapter's portrayal of Nehemiah as a pious believer. At the same time that he asks

Artaxerxes for help, he calls upon God's help (vv. 4-5), and the favor of Artaxerxes is interpreted by Nehemiah as an expression of God's favor (v. 8). Nehemiah is a man of decisive action who links his efforts at reconstruction to the generative presence of God in the situation (see also Neh 4:3).

Nehemiah shows himself to be a practical man. He secures an official letter of appointment from Artaxerxes and a letter granting him access to the royal supply of wood which he will need for the work he is undertaking (vv. 7-8). Moreover, he receives a military escort for the journey (v. 9).

Verse 10 is a warning of things to come. Nehemiah's reconstructive efforts will consistently be undermined by Sanballat and Tobiah, two officials who appear here for the first time. Sanballat was governor of the province of Samaria to the north of Judah. Readers will recall that his predecessor, Rehum, had successfully blocked the reconstruction of Jerusalem's city wall in an earlier period (see Ezra 4:8-23). Tobiah appears to have been governor of the province of Ammon in the Transjordan area east of Judah. No doubt they viewed Nehemiah's appointment and the restoration of Jerusalem as threats to their own political power in the area of Judah. It is also possible that there was more at stake than political jurisdiction. Extra-biblical documents from the end of the fifth century B.C.E. suggest that Sanballat may have considered himself a worshiper of the God of the Jews because the names of his sons (Delayah and Shelemyah) contain elements of the divine name Yahweh. Neh 6:17-19 and 13:4-9 show that Tobiah was related to some of Judah's most influential people, and he, too, may have been a Yahwist or considered himself so. Thus, in addition to their political concerns, Sanballat and Tobiah may have claimed that they had a legitimate voice in the religious interests of the Jews in Judah. The Book of Nehemiah is unclear about their motivations. We only see their consistent opposition to Nehemiah.

2:11-16 Circuit of the city. Upon his arrival in Jerusalem, Nehemiah rested for three days (compare Ezra 8:15, 32) and then conducted a firsthand assessment of the actual condition of the city wall. The account from his memoirs bears all the intrigue of a modern mystery novel. He set out in the darkness of night with only a few companions and one animal so as not to attract attention. He told no one of his plans (vv. 12, 16). By his secrecy he delayed the interference of those who were hostile toward the restoration of Jerusalem. Although he was convinced that his mission was prompted by God (v. 12), he was practical enough to want to assess exactly what needed to be done before prematurely presenting a plan to the Jews.

Verses 13-15 form one of three texts in the Book of Nehemiah which offer some description of Jerusalem during this period. Like Neh 12:31-39 the present text contains only a partial description whereas Neh 3:1-32 is more complete. In a general way the information in all three is consistent, and, taken together, the three texts constitute an important resource for study of the city's history. At the same time, the picture offered in these texts is not perfectly clear to modern scholars because the exact locations of the landmarks named by Nehemiah are not certain.

According to Neh 2:13-15 Nehemiah left and re-entered the city through the Valley Gate, so named because it either faced the central valley of the city (the Tyropoeon Valley) or because it opened onto the Valley of Hinnom. Nehemiah's inspection took him past the Dragon Spring, the Dung Gate, the Spring Gate, and the King's Pool, sites which are no longer certainly identifiable. At some point the ruins of the wall were so bad that passage was impossible for the animal on which Nehemiah rode so he proceeded on foot "up the wadi" which is generally identified with the Kidron Valley. No further sites are mentioned so some scholars suggest that Nehemiah soon turned around and retraced his steps to the Valley Gate, while others think he forged ahead until he had completed a circuit which brought him back to his starting point.

2:17-20 Rebuilding Jerusalem's walls. Up to this point Nehemiah has shown himself to be a pious, practical man of action. Now we catch a glimpse of his qualities as a leader.

Some time after Nehemiah inspected the condition of the city wall, he addressed the Jews (presumably those mentioned in v. 16). First he articulated succinctly and clearly what they knew to be true: "You see the evil plight . . . Jerusalem lies in ruins . . ." (v. 17). He then challenges them to correct that situation by doing something about it, but he does so through words of invitation: "Come, let us rebuild . . . ." Finally, he identifies the brokenness of the city with the brokenness of its people when he speaks of the purpose and goal of the work: "so that *we* may no longer be an object of derision" (v. 17 emphasis added). The invitation to rebuild the city is at the same time an invitation to restore themselves as a people deserving respect. Throughout his short speech Nehemiah's use of the first person plural shows his identification with his fellow Jews, a trait demonstrated in the previous chapter as well. Nehemiah invites the Jewish community of Jerusalem to acknowledge the relationship between their city and themselves, to face the situation squarely, and then to undertake bold measures to act in a constructive way. All the while, he speaks as one who is with them in brokenness and in the effort to rise up. He assures them that this effort is indeed a call from God and that it has imperial endorsement as well (v. 18a). The people respond wholeheartedly (v. 18b).

Nehemiah's enemies respond as well. In verses 19-20 Sanballat and Tobiah are joined by Geshem who, some say, headed a group of Arabs controlling the Transjordan region of Edom and the Negeb area to the south and southeast of Judah. The three opponents, then, represent Judah's neighbors to the north, east, and south. They surround Judah and encircle the Jews. Through mockery and ridicule they attempt to undermine the spirit of renewal among the Jews. In charging them with revolt, the enemies no doubt intended to haunt the Jews by recalling the past. In an earlier period, work on the city had been called revolt and that had been enough to halt the effort (see Ezra 4:8-23). In the present situation these enemy leaders probably were well aware that Nehemiah's project was authorized by Artaxerxes, so their charge of revolt was in all probability merely an empty accusation aimed at intimidating the Jews.

Nehemiah stands his ground with them. He ignores their charge and the reference to imperial authority. The work will go on not because of Artaxerxes' patronage but because of God's. Moreover, he defines the position of Sanballat, Tobiah, and Geshem with regard to the project. In effect he tells the three that what the Jews are doing is none of their business. They are not part of the Jewish people. They have no authority over the Jews. They are not part of the Jews' religious community. It is a bold declaration of the Jews' independence from those who seek to keep them under control. They take their stand in God alone.

3:1-32 List of workers. The memoirs of Nehemiah are interrupted by a list which was probably borrowed from the temple archives. It describes the entire circuit of the wall around Jerusalem. The naming of strategic landmarks (gates, towers, barracks, arsenal) reflects a sense of order and orientation. Many of the workers on the wall are identified by name or family while others are described by role (priests, members of professional guilds) or residence (Tekoites, Gibeonites). The text conveys the impression that this was a precisely organized effort: identifiable workers are linked with identifiable sections of the wall. This well-ordered sense is enhanced by frequent repetition of words which describe the work itself (see vv. 1, 3, 6, 13, 14, 15) and which link the workers with one another (see "at their side . . . next to them/him" in verses 2-12 and "after him/them" in verses 17-31). As in chapters one and two of the Book of Nehemiah, the text portrays the relationship between city and people.

This section of the Book of Nehemiah is the Bible's most comprehensive description of the wall of Jerusalem. Although efforts have been made to link the picture presented here with modern archaeological data, extensive correlation between this text and the findings of archaeology eludes us. Some portions of the wall built under Nehemiah's leadership have been recovered. They are about eight feet thick and their rough construction might suggest that the rebuilding of the wall was a hurried effort (compare Neh 6:15). Modern archaeology has also discovered that the city enclosed by the wall in Nehemiah's time was much smaller than once thought. It seems to have comprised only a part of the pre-exilic City of David on the southeastern crest of the hill facing the Kidron Valley, the Ophel area connecting the City of David with the temple area to the north, and the temple area itself. It is generally believed that the wall constructed during Nehemiah's time did not encompass the entire populated area of Jerusalem. Some people probably lived to the west of the rebuilt wall.

The description of the building effort

begins at the Sheep Gate in the temple area (v. 1), proceeds in a counterclockwise direction around the contours of the city, and finally returns to the starting point (v. 32). Most of the landmarks on the north and west sides of the wall are various city gates (vv. 1-16). The remaining sections of the wall (vv. 17-32) are described in terms of both public sites (vv. 19, 24, 25, 26, 28, 31, 32) and private homes (vv. 20, 21, 23, 24, 28, 29, 30). Archaeological evidence suggests that although the pre-exilic City of David extended downward onto the slopes of the city's southeastern hill facing the Kidron Valley, during Nehemiah's time the slopes of the hill were abandoned and the city wall was constructed instead along the top ridge of the hill. Thus, some of the work on the wall was probably new construction while part of it was undoubtedly an effort to reconstruct the ruins of a more ancient wall.

The high priest Eliashib, the grandson of Jeshua (who was high priest during Zerubbabel's time), and other priests were appropriately assigned to work on the part of the wall around the temple area (v. 1). The compiler of the list gives priority to this area by making it the beginning and end of the circuit. All in all, there seems to have been widespread participation in the rebuilding effort, including citizens from nearby towns and villages. The text even notes that one of the workers was assisted by his daughters (v. 12). Only in verse 5 do we encounter a slight hint that not all the citizens of Judah were in total agreement about the project.

3:33–4:17 Opposition from Judah's foes. Nehemiah's memoirs resume with a scene similar to the one which immediately preceded the list of workers in chapter 3. By now the reader detects a regular rhythm in the book: Nehemiah's mission meets with opposition from Judah's neighbors at every step. Nehemiah's arrival in Judah met with displeasure (2:10), the community's decision to rebuild Jerusalem met with ridicule (2:19), and now Judah's enemies meet the workers' progress with anger and contempt. Neh 3:33–4:17 is preoccupied with the dangers posed by enemies. It is a series of three escalating tensions for the Jewish community.

In 3:33-38 we are faced for the third time with Sanballat, the Samaritan instigator of troubles for the Jews, and his Ammonite collaborator, Tobiah (compare 2:10, 19). Sanballat appears to be addressing an official assembly in Samaria, and, as was the case in 2:19, he and Tobiah speak words aimed at undermining the rebuilding effort. Sanballat asks questions. Tobiah gives answers. Both ridicule. Sanballat minimizes the worth both of the Jews themselves ("these miserable Jews") and their work ("Will they recover these stones . . . from the heaps of dust?"). Tobiah limits himself to a verbal attack on the city wall. Ancient city walls were ordinarily penetrated by siege weapons only after considerable effort, but Tobiah sarcastically says that the wall of Jerusalem could not withstand the force of a fox hurling itself against it!

Apparently Nehemiah was aware of what was being said and responded to their hostile words with words of his own (vv. 36-37). As in 2:20 Nehemiah does not dignify the enemies' remarks by correcting what they say. Rather, once again he turns his attention to God. He prays for God's vengeance on these enemies in much the same way other believers had (see Jer 12:3; 17:18; 20:11-12; Ps 137:7-9). It is noteworthy that he identifies their crime not as an insult against the city (compare vv. 34-35) but against the people themselves (v. 37). Once again, the text presupposes a close bond between city and people. In spite of enemy hostility, however, the builders are indomitable. They continue work on the wall and at this point have half completed it.

A second, more threatening stage of opposition is narrated in 4:1-5. The host of Judah's enemies has increased. They now include Samaria to the north, Arabs to the south, Ammonites to the east, and Ashdodites (from what had been Philistine territory along the Mediterranean coast) to the west of Judah. In other words, Judah is now encircled by groups poised to launch a common attack on Jerusalem. Hostile words had not been enough to stop them, for the wall was now half complete. Their enemies prepare to use military might. The Jewish response is consistent with what we have seen in Nehemiah before: in the crisis situation they pray and take action (see Neh 1:11; 2:4-5) by posting a watch. But fatigue and despair have taken hold among the builders. Nehemiah quotes what may have been a chant commonly heard in the community (v. 4). In Hebrew the verse rhymes and flows with the distinctive rhythm of chants used by mourners. Meanwhile the enemies conspire to attack.

According to verses 6-17, a third and final threat shows itself in the fear that had taken hold of the community. The Jews came "from one place after another" (that is, from all directions) and reported "ten times over" (that is, repeatedly) that an enemy attack was imminent. The enemies had succeeded in breaking the spirit of the Jewish community. City and people alike were now very vulnerable and Nehemiah took concrete measures to address both problems. He organized the Jews to defend the city against attack. At the same time he addressed their fear by challenging them to fear only God. Once again we see the two sides of Nehemiah's religious zeal: depend upon God and fight for yourselves. He pointed out that defending the city was indeed defending their own people. Again, the city and its people are one.

The measures taken by Nehemiah met the enemies' challenge, and he interpreted that as God's work (v. 9). Freed from the grip of helplessness, the community again gave itself to the rebuilding of the wall. From now on, however, the work of rebuilding and the work of defense go hand in hand. Half of a special group around Nehemiah (the "able men") worked on the wall while the rest stood ready to defend the city. Those who could work with one hand ("the load carriers") did so and held a weapon in the other. Those whose work required the use of both hands kept swords at their sides. Nehemiah watched over the whole procedure accompanied by a trumpeter who could summon the workers scattered along the circumference of the wall to the place of attack if one should come. Nehemiah took an additional security measure: he directed workers not to return to their homes outside the city at night. No doubt this was intended for the protection of the city and the protection of the commuters as well. The long days of work on the wall continued, and even at night Nehemiah and his company were ready for battle.

5:1-5 Antisocial conduct. Chapter 5 puts aside concerns about the restoration of the city wall and turns instead to the brokenness which exists within the community itself. Men and women alike (one translator says especially the women) call some errant Jews to justice. The charge was exploitation. The times were hard, especially for those who made their living from the soil. Verse 3 mentions a famine but it is also likely that the demands of the restoration project in Jerusalem kept farmers from their work. Certainly this was the case if they remained within the city during work on the wall (see 4:16). The issue raised here, however, was not with the project nor with Nehemiah's directives. Rather, it was with those affluent Jews who used this situation to exploit the needy. The situation is described in verses 2-4. The farmers could not raise their own food which meant they had to buy it. In order to pay for it they had to pawn their own children (v. 2) or mortgage their property (v. 3). Others had to borrow money to pay their taxes (v. 4). Presumably their creditors were other Jews. The charge is levied in verse 5: the standard of the community members' fundamental equality had been broken. Community bonds were supposed to be like family ties (see v. 5 "these are our own kinsmen"). Yet some Jews were victimizing other Jews, and the daughters of the poor suffered the most violent indignities. (One translation says that they were raped.)

Once again there are parallels between the city and its people. Just as opposition threatened efforts to rebuild the wall of Jerusalem, so now injustice threatened the strength and integrity of the community. But in this case the attack does not come from foreigners. It comes from within the community itself.

5:6-13 Nehemiah's action. Nehemiah responds immediately even though as in 2:11-16 he does not take action before carefully assessing the situation (vv. 6-7a). He charges corrupt leaders (the Hebrew root "called . . . to account" has legal overtones) with breaking the law by charging interest to other Jews. This is clearly prohibited in Jewish law (see Exod 22:24-26; Deut 23:20; Lev 25:35-38). The New American Bible continues: "I then rebuked them severely" (v. 7c), but this is better translated: "I brought them before a great (official) assembly." In other words, he first accused the nobles and magistrates privately and then brought them to court. In court Nehemiah addresses the buying and selling of members of the community. He attests that the community had made a concerted effort to redeem those poor Jews who had been sold to foreigners (an effort not mentioned elsewhere in the Book of Nehemiah). The honor of the Jewish community required this. (On the practice of paying a ransom for fellow Jews whose dire circumstances had forced them to sell themselves as slaves see Lev 25:47-55.) Now that honor is even more severely offended by the fact that Jews are enslaving other Jews.

The silence of the accused pronounces their guilt. As he had done in the past, Nehemiah calls them back to the only honorable posture for Jews, to stand right before God (compare 4:8). This travesty within the Jewish community invites ridicule from non-Jews just as the brokenness of Jerusalem had.

Verse 10 is difficult. The New American Bible translation seems to exonerate Nehemiah, and in doing so, it follows the witness of the Latin Vulgate translation. A better textual tradition, however, omits "without charge." In other words, Nehemiah confesses that he himself and his closest associates had also broken the law by exacting interest. This seems to flow more naturally into the exhortation which follows: "Let *us* put an end to this usury!" (emphasis added). He proposed measures of reform which were to be taken at once (v. 11), and these were accepted (v. 12).

Finally, Nehemiah put the whole matter in an explicitly theological context by convening a religious service. Priests were called to administer an oath while Nehemiah ritually acts out, then speaks, a curse upon those who do not uphold their oath: may your pockets be emptied if you are unfaithful to your promise.

As the city wall was being restored out of stones left over from a past age, so Nehemiah laid the foundation for a restored people by rooting them in ancient social and religious law.

5:14-19 Nehemiah's lack of self-interest. In the present text the architect of the restored people embodies an ideal of community which goes beyond the strict requirements of the law. As a government official Nehemiah was entitled to appropriate for his own use a portion of the local taxes collected for the Persian throne. But he testifies that, unlike his predecessors (probably the governors from Samaria whose jurisdiction formerly included Judah), he had not used the allowance due him. Moreover, he had contributed to the work on the wall even though he was not a citizen of Judah and at his own expense had extended hospitality as circumstances warranted. He reports the motivations for his actions: he feared God (v. 15) and he had compassion for his people (v. 18).

In verse 19 Nehemiah prays that God remember his service. This and similar prayers (13:14, 22, 31) echo the contents of ancient memorial inscriptions which presented to a deity the righteous deeds of a faithful believer.

6:1-14 Plots against Nehemiah. For the fourth time the enemies of Judah conspire to subvert the work of restoration. Verbal intimidation, ridicule, and rumors of war had been ineffective; the city wall was nearly finished now. The enemies' final assault was to destroy the Jewish leader or, better yet, to trick him into destroying himself. Through it all, Nehemiah remains intractable. His vision and purpose are fixed on restoration.

By now the conspirators are familiar to us (see 2:10, 19-20; 3:33–4:17). Their initial tactic (vv. 1-4) was to lure Nehemiah out of Judean territory (into the plain of Ono) on the pretext of conferring with them. Whatever their real intent (assassination?), Nehemiah viewed the invitation as a trap though his reply to them reveals nothing of his suspicions. He simply says, "I have more important things to do" and points to the work of restoration. One can hardly imagine a response which would arouse more ire in opponents whose sole aim was to prevent the restoration of the wall of Jerusalem. Repeated invitations got the same reply. Nehemiah refused to divert any energy in their direction.

Lack of success in the first plan precipitated a second one (vv. 5-9). It, too, was an invitation to meet. This invitation, however, is attached to news of a widespread rumor that Nehemiah was spearheading a revolt against the Persian throne. The rumor is a covert accusation and threat. It is the same charge which had been issued against the whole of Jerusalem in 2:19 except that here Nehemiah is singled out as the instigator of the treason. Nehemiah dismisses their words with his reply: "It's a lie, and you have fabricated it." As often happens in cases of harassment, the enemies' designs only gave momentum to Nehemiah's resolve.

The final attempt to do away with Nehemiah (vv. 10-13) is more subtle than the first two. The voices of the familiar foes speak deceptively in the words of a prophet, Shemaiah, who appears to be a member of the Jewish community in Jerusalem. There is no agreement among scholars regarding what lay behind the note that Shemaiah was "unable to go about." Whatever the case, Nehemiah sought out the prophet who said he had Nehemiah's best interests in mind when he counseled the Jewish leader to take refuge from his enemies within the sacred space of the temple. As he had done before (see 2:11-16; 5:7), Nehemiah carefully considered the matter and discerned that this one who pretended to deliver God's word had been bought off by Sanballat and Tobiah. The man counseled not just cowardice (seeking refuge) but also sacrilege, for the temple precincts into which Shemaiah urged Nehemiah were reserved for priests alone. A layman like Nehemiah would have been subject to the death penalty for entering them (see Num 18:1-7), or just as effective in his enemies' eyes, such an abomination would have undermined Nehemiah's credibility within the Jewish community. To follow the prophet's advice would have been to fly in the face of hallowed religious practice. One way or another, Nehemiah was being enticed by Shemaiah to bring his influence to an end. In response to Shemaiah, Nehemiah curtly refused cowardice and sacrilege alike. Once again, we witness his fearlessness and his piety.

In the final verse of this section we see Nehemiah's brief petition that God remember. Like 3:36-37 it asks that God make note of the enemies' work. Tobiah and Sanballat are mentioned by name. Alongside them Nehemiah names prophets whose aim was also to divert his energies from the work of restoration. Of these one might expect that Shemaiah be singled out. Instead the name of a prophetess, Noadiah, appears. The Bible offers no other information about her, but she must have been part of a group within Jerusalem who sought to subvert Nehemiah's efforts. The appearance of her name indicates that women served in religious capacities within Judaism during this restoration period as they had during pre-exilic times (see Exod 15:20; Judg 4:4; Isa 8:3; 2 Kgs 22:14).

6:15–7:3 Conclusion of the work. The announcement of the completion of the city wall of Jerusalem is registered with some solemnity in the memoirs of Nehemiah. The date (both day and month, early October of 445 B.C.E.) is precisely chronicled (compare 1:1 and 2:1). It had been only a few months earlier in Susa that Artaxerxes' cupbearer had heard of the sad state of affairs in Jerusalem and only fifty-two days since the rebuilding project had begun. Such an amazing feat seems incredible, and some scholars accept as more likely the witness of the first-century A.D. Jewish historian Josephus, who reported that the wall was constructed over a period of two years and four months. Others, however, point to the relatively small circumference of the city, the probability that a significant portion of the project simply entailed repair or reconstruction of a damaged wall, and the recent findings of archaeologists that the (only) new section of the wall (that on the eastern ridge of the hill facing the Kidron Valley) was very crudely constructed and conclude that, amazing as it is, the biblical text is probably accurate in saying that the task was completed in fifty-two days.

One is somewhat taken aback that immediately following the notice of completion there are no words of relief or exultation. Instead Nehemiah registers the effect upon Judah's enemies (they "lost much face in the eyes of the nations" v. 16). The completion of the wall is foremost a vindication of the Jews over their enemies. God had indeed been the power within this movement, and now that was clear to all. The enemies' effort to frustrate the work had been there through all stages of Nehemiah's mission (2:10, 19-20; 3:33–4:17; 6:1-14), and the Jewish leader triumphantly attaches a pronouncement of their judgment to his announcement of the Jews' success.

One would expect verses 15-16 to bring to an end the ongoing controversy with the opponents and the text to continue with the contents of 7:1-3 and perhaps the account of the dedication of the city wall (which now appears in 12:27-43). Instead we hear about the enemy Tobiah. Some scholars suggest that verses 17-19 have been misplaced from their original position after verse 14. Whatever the case, we learn that Tobiah was related by marriage (his own and his son's) to very influential Jews in Jerusalem and that in his struggles with Nehemiah, Tobiah had won the support of these Jews so that his subversive influence continued. Viewed together with the witness of 13:28 (that Nehemiah's other enemy, Sanballat, had marital ties with the Jewish high priestly family), Neh 6:17-19 cautions us that even though the Jerusalem wall is complete, the work of the restoration of the Jewish people itself will have to deal with the continuing presence of Nehemiah's opponents.

In 7:1-3 Nehemiah reports that he has arranged for proper leadership and security for the city. Guards were stationed at the city gates. ("Singers and Levites" is very likely a gloss which was mistakenly added to verse 1. They were officials in the temple.) Nehemiah appointed Hanani and Hananiah as administrators over the city of Jerusalem. Both were dependable and apparently not susceptible to the influence of Nehemiah's opponents. It had been Hanani who had first informed Nehemiah of the distress of Jerusalem and the Jews (see 1:2), and Hananiah possessed a quality valued by Nehemiah: the fear of God (see also 4:8; 5:9, 15). Although the Hebrew text of verse 3 is troublesome, it appears that Nehemiah directed that guards carefully watch the city gates and open them only during daylight hours. Nehemiah arranged for another precaution: security guards were stationed at various places within the city. It is clear from these verses that Jerusalem continued to be threatened and that the Jews needed to continue to protect what they had accomplished.

7:4-72a Census of the province. The beginning of this section appears to be a continuation of Nehemiah's memoirs. It describes the Jewish leader's effort to strengthen the city of Jerusalem by addressing the problem of its small population. It was this concern that led Nehemiah (with God's coaxing) to call an assembly in the city. An editor's insertion interrupts the account, however, and Nehemiah does not take up his concern about the smallness of Jerusalem's population again until his memoirs resume in chapter 11.

The contents of verses 4-72a are virtually the same as those in the list of Ezra 2. The few minor discrepancies are probably slight emendations which crept in through the copyists' transmission of the text. As in Ezra 2, we find in the present text an early population listed according to family or places of residence, a listing of liturgical officials and of some who could not trace their ancestry, and a total tally of the people and their belongings as well as a list of gifts contributed by these people. As in Ezra 2 the list concludes with a single sentence about where the citizens took up residence. A careful comparison of Ezra 2:70 with Neh 7:72a shows that the latter text diverges slightly from the former in omitting reference to any settlement in Jerusalem. No doubt this represents a slight editorial change designed to fit the list of Neh 7 into the concern for increasing the population of the city.

The exact purpose of the insertion of the ancient census list is puzzling, especially since it apparently played no role in the repopulation of Jerusalem. What it does, however, is temporarily draw attention away from the city itself to the other effort which was part of Nehemiah's mission, that of rebuilding the Jewish people themselves. The city wall had been rebuilt on the stones of ages past. Now an editor recalls for us those who had pioneered the effort to restore God's people in the land of Judah. Just as the list of Ezra 2 precedes the restoration of the altar as the center of Israel's worship, so now the same list precedes a service in which God's people once again gather to commit themselves to what had from ancient times been the center of their life as a community, the law of Moses.

PART IV: RESTORATION OF THE COMMUNITY AROUND THE LAW

Neh 7:72b–13:31

In this final section of the Books of Ezra and Nehemiah the biblical accounts of the restoration period come to an end. The text begins with Ezra's proclamation of the law (ch. 8). The community acknowledged its dependence upon God's help (ch. 9) and agreed, communally, to abide by the law of Moses (ch. 10). Jerusalem's population is restored, and the completed city wall is dedicated in solemn ceremony (chs. 11–12). Finally, Nehemiah initiated several reforms to maintain the community's fidelity (ch. 13).

This section is something of a patchwork quilt incorporating in its complex design elements which had appeared in earlier sections. Ezra and Nehemiah are both present, Ezra in chapter 8 and Nehemiah in chapters 11 through 13. In an effort to lessen the jarring impact of the sudden appearance of Ezra in the Book of Nehemiah, an editor has added the name of Nehemiah to the Ezra materials in chapter 8. Ezra's name was also appended to the lengthy prayer in chapter 9, and he was added to the account of the dedication of the city wall narrated in chapter 12. Both Ezra and Nehemiah have been editorially inserted at the end of the list of priests and Levites in chapter 12. In all of this we see an effort to bring together two great leaders who were probably separated from one another chronologically but who were alike in their commitment to the restoration of God's people.

As in earlier sections, the cult and its personnel receive much attention. We see religious festivals and prayer as well as concern for offerings, observance of the sabbath, cultic personnel, and the purity of the temple and of the worshiping community.

In these final chapters, we see the Jewish community of the restoration period mooring itself in pre-exilic Israel. The law which brought to completion the restoration of the community is the ancient law of Moses. The terms of the community's pact are founded on that law, as are Nehemiah's reforms. The community's prayer reviews the past relationship between God and Israel and that past relationship is the basis for their present reforms.

The entire community, including women and children, is restored in the law and in its commitment to the law. Near the end of the book the city of Jerusalem, made secure by a sizeable population and sure city walls, is whole. The community is restored through the law of Moses and through its attentiveness to the cult. All of this is celebrated at the temple, the place where the work of restoration began.

It is worth noticing that the Book of Nehemiah ends in reform. The story ends not at the temple nor at the city wall but in the community and its struggle to be faithful. The temple building and the walls of Jerusalem were concrete realities. They were externals around which the religious identity of the Jewish people centered. But true religion is dynamic; it is a continual process which takes place not in stones but in the hearts of people. Perhaps in ending their narrative as they did, the biblical writers were suggesting that the work of restoration is a continuing one.

7:72b–8:12 Ezra reads the law. Concerns about Nehemiah and the wall of Jerusalem give way to a description of a solemn religious service led by the priest-scribe, Ezra. The entire community gathers in a public square in Jerusalem. It is the beginning of the seventh month, the high point of Israel's liturgical year, at least in a late period. (According to Num 29, the religious festivals of the seventh month included the Day of Atonement on the tenth day and the feast of Booths from the fifteenth to the twenty-second days of the month. In addition, there seems to have been a regularly recurring festival on the first day of the seventh month, but the feast is unnamed both in Num 29:1 and Lev 23:23-25.)

Even though Ezra proclaimed the law, several details in the account suggest that the biblical writers sought to emphasize the community-centeredness of this event. First, we are told explicitly (twice) that the assembly consisted of the entire community—men, women, and children (vv. 2-3). Second, the writers pay close attention to the community's role in the service. Members of the community initiated the service by summoning Ezra to proclaim the law (v. 1) and then they "listened attentively" as he read (v. 3). They saw the scroll as he opened it and stood for the reading (v. 5). They accepted the proclamation with their "amens" and performed ritual gestures of raising and lowering their hands and bodies (v. 6). They responded with tears which gave way to festive celebration (vv. 9-12). From beginning to end the rhythm of the service is marked by the community's participation. The biblical writers repeatedly show that the Jewish community knowingly and willingly accepted the law of Moses. We see this in the description of the children present at the reading of the law of Moses. They were those "old enough to understand" (vv. 2-3). We see it also in the stress given to the interpretation of the law. Verse 8 assigns the interpretive role to Ezra, emphatically stating the goal that the community understand the law. An editor supplemented Ezra's interpretive role by adding that he was joined by Levitical assistants (vv. 7, 9; compare 2 Chr 17:7-9 and 35:3; the Hebrew verb in verse 9 is singular, which suggests that originally Ezra was the only subject. Nehemiah's name was also a later addition). Some scholars think that the Levites' task was to translate the Hebrew words of the law into the community's vernacular tongue, Aramaic. Others suggest that the Levites explained the meaning of the law. Whatever the case, verse 12 states that the goal was successful. We see that the community which actively sought the law not only saw and heard it but also understood it.

The law which was solemnly proclaimed was probably taken from what now constitutes the Pentateuch of the Hebrew Scriptures. The present text suggests that the law directed the community's attention to the life of worship. This is signalled by Ezra's words of verse 10 (where "rejoicing in the Lord" probably refers to worship) and by the editorial addition in verse 11 which refers to the holiness of the day. (Moreover, see the restoration of the liturgical feast which follows immediately in 8:13-18.) The reading of the law must have exposed their failures for the community responded with tears. (Compare Josiah's response to the reading of the law and the liturgical reform which follows in 2 Kgs 22:8–23:24.) However, Ezra counseled the community to view the liturgical reading of the law not as a source of condemnation but as a source of life and strength. A full-fledged holiday followed the reading of the law. The people brought out their best food and drink and shared them with the needy. (The practice of sharing on festive occasions also appears in Deut 16:9-12; 26:11; 2 Sam 6:19.)

8:13-18 The feast of Booths. On the day following the proclamation and celebration of the law, the community gathers to study its contents further. Lay leaders, priests, and Levites join Ezra, and together they find legislation for the feast of Booths. (On the feast of Booths see our comment on Ezra 3:1-6.)

To observe the feast of Booths the community dwells in makeshift huts. This ritual may have originated with the custom of harvesters living in temporary quarters of branches and leafy boughs constructed in the orchards and vineyards where grapes and olives were harvested in the fall of the year, the season of the feast of Booths. Lev 23:42-43 assigns religious significance to the practice by comparing it with the time the ancient Israelites lived in makeshift dwellings while they wandered in the wilderness between Egypt and the Promised Land. Verses 16-17a report that the community immediately prepared to observe the feast of Booths as the law prescribed. The notice in verse 17b is probably not to be taken literally, especially in light of the witness of 2 Chr 8:13 and Ezra 3:4, which attest to the continued observance of the feast of Booths. Comparison with 2 Kgs 23:22 and 2 Chr 35:18 indicates that this was a stylized way of relating a current festival to the past. The writers of verse 17b want to convey the idea that a new age of religious observance is beginning, but they stress that the newness is actually a revival of authentic ancient practice. The community once again restores itself in continuity with the practices of their ancient ancestors in faith. Their foundation is in the law, the prescriptions of which are followed exactly (compare vv. 15-16 with Lev 23:39-42; also compare v. 18 with Deut 31:10-13).

9:1-37 Confession of the people. Chapter 9 reports a community penance service (vv. 1-5) and a long prayer that includes a summary of the relationship between God and Israel (vv. 6-37). Although they are adjacent to one another in the present text, there is little direct connection between the contents of the two parts of the chapter. They may have originated independently of one another and been inserted here by an editor.

As in the services described in chapter 8, the law stands at the center of the service in 9:1-5. The penitential character of the service is clear from the traditional gestures of repentance and mourning, which include fasting and the wearing of sackcloth and ashes (v. 1). Public confession of guilt and prostration also occur (vv. 2-3). It is noteworthy that Ezra does not appear here. Leadership in prayer belonged to the Levites whose role included leading the community in antiphonal responses of blessing and praise (v. 5).

We cannot be certain of the particular occasion for this service. Because the authors mention in verse 2 that the Jews separate themselves from foreigners before their confession of guilt, some scholars suggest that this service originally followed the Jews' divorce from foreign wives described in Ezra 10.

The prayer of 9:6-37 is a beautifully woven tapestry of threads of tradition from other parts of the Hebrew Scriptures, especially the Pentateuch. In its historical orientation it is similar to other prayers in the Bible (see Pss 78, 105, 106, 135, 136). It offers an overview of God's longstanding relationship with Israel. The biblical view of a God of both mercy and justice is carefully intertwined with a portrait of an unfaithful Israel.

Ezra's prayer begins with the acknowledgement of God's creative activity in heaven and on earth (v. 6) and ends with the political distress of the writer's own day (vv. 36-37). Within these boundaries Ezra rehearses salvation history. It began when God chose Abraham and was faithful to the promise that Abraham would have many descendants who would inherit the land of Canaan (compare vv. 7-8 with Gen 12 and 15). The prayer recites Israel's bondage in Egypt and God's redeeming activity through the plagues and the rescue at the Red Sea (compare vv. 9-12 with Exod 1–15). God's continuing gifts included the law given to Moses at Mount Sinai (vv. 13-14), sustenance during the wilderness journey, and the invitation to inherit the land which had been promised (v. 15). (These traditions run through the Books of Exodus, Leviticus, Numbers, and Deuteronomy.) Up to verse 15 the recital summarizes God's activity, consistently gracious. Israel's response was unfaithful all along the way, but in spite of that, God was "a God of pardons," merciful (vv. 16-22).

Israel's life in the Promised Land is summarized in verses 23-31. As in the earlier traditions, God continued to give, and Israel continued to be unfaithful. In the face of Israel's response, God executed justice against the chosen people while extending divine mercy toward them as well. (Essentially, this is a capsule form of the Deuteronomic history which appears in the Books of Joshua, Judges, Samuel, and Kings.) Hardly a mention is made of the monarchy and the traditions of God's covenant with David through which the Davidic dynasty was established.

The "Now, therefore . . ." of verse 32 signals a change from a recital of salvation history to petitionary prayer. The writer asks God to take into account the hardships that the Jewish people have suffered for several hundred years. (Although the exact reference is unclear, "from the time of the kings of Assyria" may point to the fall of the northern kingdom into Assyrian hands in 721 B.C.E.) In verses 33-35 the writer acknowledges that God has been just in allowing disasters to befall the chosen people but suggests that now is a time for mercy. God's graciousness in giving Israel the Promised Land is compromised by the fact that its rich gifts flow through their hands into the coffers of foreign rulers. They are slaves once again, not in Egypt but in their very own land.

As in 9:1-5, the particular occasion for the prayer of verses 6-37 is not clear. Verses 36 and 37 describe an oppressive situation although it is unspecified. If Persian authorities are the offenders, this is an unusual witness, since most of the Ezra-Nehemiah materials witness to gracious patronage of the Jewish people by the Persian throne. Some scholars have suggested that the prayer of verses 6-37 originally belonged to the prayer of Ezra reported in Ezra 9. (Specifically, some would have us read Nehemiah 9:6-37 between verses 7 and 8 of Ezra 9.) Ancient Greek tradition connected this prayer with Ezra, for in the Greek translation known as the Septuagint the prayer was attributed to Ezra. Translators of the New American Bible have followed this tradition (see v. 6). However, in the official Hebrew text Ezra's name does not appear with the prayer.

Whatever the origin of this text, the lengthy prayer of verses 6-37 reflects the views of a Jewish community which turned to the past and found insight into the present. As in other parts of the Books of Ezra and Nehemiah it shows us a postexilic Jewish community mooring itself in pre-exilic Israelite religious tradition.

10:1-28 Agreement of the people. The community which stood primarily as receiver of God's gifts and mercy in chapter 9 adopts a different stance in its relationship with God in chapter 10. Now it commits itself to responsibility. It solemnly swears to fashion itself according to the law of God given through Moses. No leader administers the oath. Rather, through mutual consent, members of the community bind one another to the requirements of the law.

The bulk of chapter 10 appears to be official documentation of those who entered into the agreement (especially vv. 2-28) and of the contents of the oath (vv. 31-40). This material may have come from records preserved in the temple archives.

The text opens with a connecting verse probably supplied by an editor (v. 1). The introductory phrase, "In view of all this," is vague and functions as a transition to the record which follows. The editor then summarizes the groups who entered into the agreement to live by the law although the order in verse 1 (princes, Levites, priests) differs slightly from the order of the list itself (civic officials, priests, Levites, community leaders). Nehemiah's name heads the list, and it is accompanied by the name of Zedekiah who may have been the secretary who recorded the names (v. 2). Priests are listed according to family (vv. 3-9) while the Levites appear to be listed as individuals (vv. 10-14). We know some of the leaders of the people (vv. 15-28) from the lists of Ezra 2 and Neh 7, although new names also appear here.

10:29-40 Provisions of the pact. Before recording the obligations of the pact (vv. 31-40), the biblical writer stresses that this was a commitment of the entire community. All, including women and children, assume equal responsibility for community life (compare Neh 8:2-3). The obligations of the pact are taken from Pentateuchal tradition. The restoration community adopts ancient law as its own charter thereby establishing itself as a legitimate continuation of pre-exilic Israel. (A number of the obligations listed here will surface again in chapter 13 as the concerns of Nehemiah's reform.)

Preserving the integrity of the community is the first obligation mentioned. The community agrees to be a people set apart by not contracting marriages with foreigners. (Here, unlike Ezra 9–10, there is no provision for what to do in cases where mixed marriages already exist.) It secures the place of daughters as well as sons in the community (v. 31).

According to verse 32, the community also promised to forgo commercial dealings on the sabbath and holy days in accord with Pentateuchal law (see Exod 20:8-11; Deut 5:12-15). The land, too, shall rest every seven years (see Exod 23:10-11; Lev 25:2-7), and those burdened by debts shall have relief in accord with Mosaic law (Deut 15:1-3).

Earlier, the Persian kings had provided materials necessary for the temple cult. Now the community pledges to maintain supplies for regular worship out of its own resources. These included monetary contributions as well as offerings of bread, grain, and meat which were needed for rituals prescribed for daily temple service and also for special days. (For a list of prescribed offerings, see Num 28–29.) In addition, verse 35 describes the arrangement for provision of the firewood needed for temple sacrifice. According to verses 36-38a, the community promises to continue ancient Israel's practice of recognizing that all things which are given to them for their sustenance and growth come from and ultimately belong to Yahweh. They offer back to Yahweh the first of everything—products of the soil as well as the first-born of animal and human life (see Exod 23:19; 34:26; Deut 26:1-11). The community will contribute tithes for the support of temple personnel (vv. 38b-39). All the cultic pledges are summarized in the final sentence of the chapter: "We will not neglect the house of our God."

11:1-2 Repeopling of Jerusalem. Chapter 11 returns our attention to the city of Jerusalem and specifically to a concern first addressed in the opening verses of Nehemiah chapter 7. The city wall had been completed, Jerusalem's officials appointed, and precautionary measures taken to protect the city in case of enemy attack. Only one point of vulnerability remained: the smallness of the city's population (Neh 7:4). The author says Nehemiah convened a meeting "to examine their family records" (7:5a). Presumably Nehemiah was initiating steps to address the population problem. At that point, however, the text digresses. We see a list of those who first returned from Exile (7:6-72a), Ezra's proclamation of the law (7:72b–8:18), prayer (9:1-5, 6-37), and the community's solemn pact (10:1-40). Finally, chapter 11 returns to the population issue. It is reasonable to assume that, prior to the final editorial arrangement, the present text originally followed Neh 7:4-5a.

To solve Jerusalem's population problem, community leaders settled in Jerusalem as did one family in ten chosen by lot. Those who willingly became this "tithe" of the entire community were endorsed by the rest (v. 2). Just as the rebuilding of the temple and the city wall physically restored Jerusalem, so now the "holy city" (as Jerusalem was frequently called in the postexilic period) restored its population.

11:3-24 The residents of Jerusalem. Those chosen by lot from outlying areas are passed over, and we are given a record of the leaders who took up residence in Jerusalem. The list of verses 4-19 is enveloped by reminders that the rest of the population was settled in cities in the surrounding region of Judah (see verses 3b and 20).

The people living in the region of Judah traced their ancestry to two of the sons of Jacob, Judah and Benjamin, so the list begins with names and totals of Judahites (vv. 4-6) and Benjaminites (vv. 7-9) who moved to Jerusalem. There follows a list of cultic leaders: priests (vv. 10-14), Levites (vv. 15-18), and gatekeepers (v. 19). A comparison of this list of settlers with the list of 1 Chr 9:2-18 shows that, while the two are not identical, they have much in common. It is possible that one was taken from the other or that both were taken from a list preserved in the temple archives. The list of 1 Chr 9 claims to be a record of those who settled in Jerusalem following the return from Exile. Here a somewhat parallel list is said to be a record of those who settled in Jerusalem following the completion of the city wall.

As mentioned above, verse 20 notes that the remainder of the population was scattered throughout Judah and to this was appended the miscellaneous information which appears in verses 21-24. There we learn the names of various officers residing in Jerusalem: leaders of the temple slaves (v. 21) and singers (vv. 22-23) and a Jewish ambassador to the royal court of Persia (v. 24).

11:25-36 The other cities. The closing verses of chapter 11 spell out in greater detail what had been said in summary fashion in 11:3b and 20. They list towns and regions outside Jerusalem where Jews resided. Verses 25-30 name seventeen places (many the same as in Josh 15) as far south of Jerusalem as Beersheba where Judahites lived. Verses 31-36 list sixteen areas (some the same as in Ezra 2 and Neh 7) to the north and west of Jerusalem where Benjaminites lived. The entire area is suspiciously large. Scholars suggest that the list may include some cities which lay beyond the provincial borders of Judah but which nevertheless had sizeable Jewish populations.

12:1-9 Priests and Levites under Zerubbabel. These verses constitute the first of a series of lists of cultic personnel from different periods in the restoration movement. They are a record of the priests (vv. 1-7) and Levites (vv. 8-9) who were part of the earlier return to Judah from Exile when Zerubbabel was civic leader and Jeshua was priestly leader (see Ezra 1–6). Some of the priestly names here also appear in the list of those who signed the community pact (see especially 10:3-9). Likewise, some of the Levites named in 12:8-9 appear in other lists in the Books of Ezra and Nehemiah (see, for example, Neh 7:43 and Ezra 2:40). The Levites are temple singers, and here they seem to be arranged in choirs for antiphonal singing.

12:10-11 High priests. Verses 10-11 are a record of those who served as high priests from around 538 B.C.E. to sometime in the early 300s B.C.E. The high priesthood was an inherited office. Little is known of these men except that Jeshua is clearly from an early stage of the restoration shortly after 538 B.C.E. (see his role in Ezra 1–6) and that his grandson Eliashib was Nehemiah's contemporary and thus held the high priestly office during 445–433 B.C.E. (see Neh 3:1, 20, 21). If Johanan, the high priest listed here as Eliashib's grandson, is identical with the Johanan who appears in Ezra 10:6, then he was in office around 400 B.C.E. and was a contemporary of Ezra.

12:12-26 Priests and Levites under Joiakim. The editor's fondness for archival lists again shows itself. Here we find a list of priests who purportedly served during Joiakim's term as high priest, that is, after the dedication of the second temple (in 515 B.C.E. when Jeshua held the high priestly office) but before Nehemiah came to Judah (in 445 B.C.E. when Eliashib was high priest). There is close similarity between the families listed here and those who purportedly belonged to the previous generation (see the list of Neh 12:1-7) although slight differences in names and spellings have crept in, probably as a result of scribal error. The Levitical names in verses 24-25 are also similar but not identical to the families of Levites said to have been from the previous generation (see Neh 12:8-9; also compare the Levitical lists of Neh 7:43-45; Ezra 2:40-42; and Neh 11:15-19). As in verses 8 and 9, the Levitical singers seem to have been arranged in antiphonal choirs. Other Levites served as gatekeepers.

Verses 22-23 suggest that these records agreed with the temple records. (Verse 23 is in error in describing Johanan as Eliashib's son. Verses 10-11 clearly present him as Eliashib's grandson.) The official register of priests and Levites is referred to as the Book of Chronicles but one must not identify these records with the biblical books which bear the same title.

The parenthetical note which concludes this section (v. 26b) is an editorial addition designed to relate the list of cultic leaders from the time of Joiakim to the chief figures of the two biblical books under consideration. It is not chronologically accurate, for all other evidence firmly presents Nehemiah as a contemporary of the high priest Eliashib (see Neh 3:1, 20, 21).

12:27-43 Dedication of the city wall. This account opens with the gathering of the Levites from surrounding villages into the city of Jerusalem for the solemn dedication of the completed city wall. As such, it bears some connection with the note at the end of chapter 11 (v. 36) which told where the Levites settled.

A more logical progression might juxtapose this account of the dedication of the city wall to Neh 6:15, the notice that work on the wall was complete. In the present arrangement of materials, however, a compiler thought it fitting to address other concerns before describing the solemn dedication of the completed wall. Among these concerns were a city strengthened by security measures (7:1-3) and a larger population (7:4-5a and 11:1-2), and a Jewish community restored through the law (ch. 8), prayer (ch. 9), and commitment (ch. 10). Throughout the Book of Nehemiah we have seen that Jerusalem and its people are inextricably linked. The welfare of one somehow signals the welfare of the other. Therefore, it would have been inappropriate to dedicate the restored city wall before the restoration of the people was complete. With the pact described in chapter 10, the people have been restored in the ancient law of Moses. Now the wall, restored from ancient ruins, can be dedicated.

According to verses 27-29 the Levitical musicians (instrumentalists and singers) came to Jerusalem. The first act in the dedication service was purification both of the community and of the city gates and wall (v. 30). The community then formed a grand procession which moved in opposite directions on top of the city wall toward the temple area. Half moved toward the right. The choir was followed by a civic official, half of the community's family leaders, the priests with trumpets, and Levites with musical instruments. (An editor, eager to coordinate the missions of Ezra and Nehemiah, has added Ezra's name as leader of this group.)

A similar group moved in procession toward the left. Nehemiah was part of this group (vv. 38-39). By verse 40 the two groups have converged in the temple where the ceremony continues. There was singing (some have suggested that Psalm 147 might have been used in this service), elaborate sacrificial rituals, and so much festive noise that it could be heard far off (vv. 40-43; compare the clamor at the service marking the laying of the foundations of the temple in Ezra 3:13). As he has done in other parts of his memoirs, Nehemiah specifically notes the presence of women (and children). It was a community, whole and entire, which now dedicated its own restored wholeness in dedicating the wall.

12:44-47 Offerings for priests and Levites. The community's provisions for cultic personnel has been appended to the account of the dedication of the city wall. Many scholars regard this part as the composition of the Chronicler, for like the Chronicler, it features cultic personnel (especially the Levites) and paints a picture of the ideal workings of the community, especially with regard to the cult and its personnel.

The sections open with information about the storage of goods brought to the temple (v. 44a). These were the "wages" of the temple officials contributed by the community in accord with the law (see Neh 10:36-40a). Then the writer subverts any suspicions that these tithes for the clergy's use were obligations imposed on a reluctant community. Indeed, "Judah rejoiced in its appointed priests and Levites" who had a prestigious tradition of service extending back several hundred years to the original design of King David (vv. 44b-46; compare 1 Chr 23–26). Having described the collection of goods (v. 44a) and their recipients (vv. 44b-46), the writer concludes that the system of providing for the cultic personnel functioned with smooth regularity (v. 47). The original writer attested that this was the case in the early days of the return when Zerubbabel was governor. Another writer added a gloss to bring this information up to date. We are told that it was also the case during the time of Nehemiah.

13:1-3 Separation from aliens. Once again the text calls our attention to the prohibition against mixing with foreigners. The topic comes to the fore at a public reading of the law (vv. 1-2). The prohibition is taken from Deut 23:4-7 which, in turn, has its background in the incident recorded in Num 22–24. Ammonites and Moabites are to be excluded from the "assembly of God," an expression which may be technical terminology referring to the worshipping community or it may, by extension, encompass the whole of the Jewish community. It is unclear whether the law excluded Ammonites and Moabites only from the temple or from all contact with the Jewish community. If verses 1-3 were intended as a basis for the reforms described in verses 4-31, both meanings apply. Nehemiah threw the Ammonite Tobiah out of the temple precincts (vv. 4-9), and he also denounced marriages with Ammonites, Moabites, and other foreigners (vv. 23-27). Whatever the case, the community responded immediately to the demands of the law. It set itself apart from all foreign elements (v. 3).

13:4-14 Reform in the temple. We now return to the memoirs of Nehemiah. His first term as governor of Judah had ended in 433 B.C.E. when he returned to the service of Artaxerxes. The monarch is referred to as "king of Babylon" in verse 6 when, in fact, he ruled the Persian Empire. But, like Cyrus before him (see Ezra 5:13), Artaxerxes adopted the title of the king of the empire which the Persians had conquered.

During Nehemiah's absence from Judah, contaminating influences and lax observance compromised some of the Jewish community's earlier accomplishments. Nehemiah held Jewish leaders responsible for the backsliding. After some time (we are not told how long) Nehemiah returned to Judah and initiated a series of reforms aimed at correcting abuses which threatened the purity and smooth functioning of the temple cult (vv. 4-14), restoring strict sabbath observance (vv. 15-22), and maintaining the purity of the Jewish community by strict separation from foreigners (vv. 23-31).

During Nehemiah's absence Tobiah the Ammonite had made his way into the temple precincts and had his own quarters there. Offerings and utensils for use in the temple worship as well as material goods contributed by the community as payment to cultic officials had been removed from storage areas in the temple, and the space was given over for Tobiah's use. Tobiah had not seized the area. It was given to him by the priest in charge, Eliashib (who is not to be identified with the high priest). Nehemiah immediately ousted Tobiah from the temple chambers. The area was then purified and restored to its proper use (vv. 4-9).

Another problem came to Nehemiah's attention; the Levites had abandoned temple service and Jerusalem itself (vv. 10-14) out of necessity. For some reason the tithes contributed to cult officials by the community in return for their service had ceased, so the Levites were forced to move to the country to make their living by farming. (Note how far this situation is from the ideal described in Neh 12:44-47.) Nehemiah held the leaders responsible for this neglect of temple worship. He called the Levites back to their regular service in the temple and resumed the practice of tithing whereby the people brought offerings of food to provide the Levites and singers with a steady income. He placed trustworthy men in charge of the storage and distribution of these goods.

In verse 14, in a manner similar to that found on ancient Near Eastern memorial stones, Nehemiah asked God to remember this proof of his deep concern for the temple and its services (compare 5:19; 13:22, 31).

13:15-22 Sabbath observance. Strict observance of the rules for sabbath rest was an important feature of postexilic Judaism. The sabbath was a day set apart—holy. Through sabbath rest Jews witnessed that their lives and livelihood ultimately were gifts of God. Just as the sabbath was a day set apart, so sabbath observance set Jews apart from others. It was a distinguishing feature of their identity as a religious people. Profanation of the sabbath was a threat to the distinctiveness and integrity of Jewish life.

When Nehemiah returned to Judah to undertake his second term as governor, he saw Jews conducting business as usual on the sabbath. They made wine and transported their produce to Jerusalem to sell it in the marketplace. There they encountered Phoenician traders selling their imported merchandise. Nehemiah instructed the people to stop trading on the sabbath (v. 15) and issued a weightier accusation against the Jewish officials (v. 17). The prophets Jeremiah and Ezekiel had attributed the fall of Jerusalem and the Babylonian Exile to Jewish profanation of the sabbath (Jer 17:19-27; Ezek 20:12-24). Now Nehemiah tells Jewish officials that their neglect of the sabbath might well have the same result (v. 18).

Nehemiah was a man of action. Not content with warnings and accusations, he had the city gates closed on the sabbath (which began near sundown one day and continued until sundown the following day; see v. 19). When vendors continued to appear at the city gates, perhaps hoping to lure some customers outside, Nehemiah drove them off with threats of violence (vv. 20-21). He appointed Levites to monitor the gates so that the sacred character of the day would be maintained (v. 22a). Once again, he asked that God remember what he had done (v. 22b).

13:23-31 Mixed marriages. Mixed marriages seem to have been a recurring problem in the restoration period, for concern about them appears here for the fourth time in the Books of Ezra and Nehemiah (see Ezra 9–10; Neh 6:18; 10:31 and now 13:23-27). During Nehemiah's absence the practice of marrying foreigners had returned (or perhaps continued). Nehemiah saw the consequences of this transgression in the voices of the community's children: some of them spoke Ashdodite and none of them knew Hebrew. The language of Ashdod (a Philistine area near the Mediterranean coast) was Aramaic, probably not too different from the speech of the Jews at this time. The difference that came to Nehemiah's attention, then, may merely have been particular accents or pronunciations. But Hebrew was the Jews' distinctive religious language, and not understanding it was tantamount to a breakdown of their identity as a people.

Nehemiah's reaction to the situation was violent: he beat the guilty. Unlike Ezra, he did not demand divorce in cases of mixed marriages. He did, however, strictly reiterate the requirement to which the community had already agreed (see Neh 10:31). As was his method in the argument with violators of the sabbath (13:18), he recalled an incident in their history from which they should have learned. King Solomon had contracted marriages with foreigners and this had led to sin (see especially 1 Kgs 11:1-10). Could they not see that they were making the same mistake? Women were an essential part of the Jewish community. Jewish daughters were not to be married off to foreigners and foreign women were not to take their places in the community.

Once again, community leaders were among the worst offenders. The high priestly family itself was now related through marriage to Nehemiah's archenemy, Sanballat the Horonite (see Sanballat's role in Neh 2:10, 19; 3:33-38; 4:1-5; 6:1-14). One of Eliashib's grandsons, the son of Joiada the high priest, had married Sanballat's daughter. If the Jewish high priestly family was on such familiar terms with Sanballat who had opposed Nehemiah's mission from the very first, surely this was a serious threat to Nehemiah's earlier success in strengthening the Jewish community. Enemy influence now lived in the leading house of the religious community. Moreover, according to Lev 21:14, the high priest was forbidden to marry outside the Jewish community. Although Joiada's son was not yet the high priest, he was a potential candidate for the office and that may account for part of Nehemiah's reaction. Whatever the considerations were, Nehemiah ousted the young Jew from the community.

In the final verses of the book (vv. 30-31), Nehemiah once again asks that God remember his efforts. The summary of his works seems modest. Essentially, it is a summary of the terms of the community agreement described in Neh 10:31-40.

Nehemiah does not ask to be remembered for having engineered the rebuilding of the wall of Jerusalem which, ironically, is the accomplishment for which most students of the Bible remember him. In 5:19 he asked God to remember his refusal to impose greater financial hardship on an already burdened people. Here, in 13:30-31 as in 13:14 and 22, he asked God to remember that he had abided by the pact that the community had made (compare 10:31-40). It appears that Nehemiah wanted to be remembered only as a faithful member of the community for which he spent himself.

1 MACCABEES

Alphonse P. Spilly, C.PP.S.

INTRODUCTION

This work, originally written in Hebrew, survives only in a Greek version. It mentions John Hyrcanus' leadership at the end, so the earliest date for the book would be sometime during his reign (129–104 B.C.E.). The friendly attitude toward the Romans would indicate that the book was written prior to Pompey's invasion in 63 B.C.E. Most scholars date the book during the reign of John Hyrcanus or his main successor, Alexander Jannaeus (103–76 B.C.E.).

Hellenization

The book depicts the confrontation between traditional Jewish religion and Hellenistic culture. The latter was a mixture of Greek and Near Eastern culture, and it had a very important impact on the Near East from the death of Alexander the Great in 323 B.C.E. well into the Roman period. After the death of Alexander, his empire in the Near East was divided between the Ptolemies in Egypt and the Seleucids in Syria. Jerusalem was under the influence of the Ptolemaic kingdom until 198 B.C.E. Under the Ptolemies, there was some Hellenistic influence, but Judaism was able to conduct its affairs in relative freedom.

When Jerusalem fell under the rule of the Seleucids, however, there was increasing confrontation with Hellenism. Segments of the Jewish community actively promoted the Hellenization of Judaism, and Seleucid rulers such as Antiochus IV were more aggressive than their predecessors in spreading Hellenistic culture throughout the empire.

Civil war

Events within the Jewish community led to a civil war between the orthodox and the Hellenizers. When the Seleucids threw their weight into the struggle, the balance was clearly in favor of the Hellenizing party. At stake was the very survival of Judaism as it had been known up to that time. The struggle between Judaism and Hellenism is reflected in other Jewish literature of the period. Earlier influence of Hellenism on Jewish culture is reflected in the Book of Sirach, written to persuade Jewish youth of the value of their traditions. When the Hellenization process entered a much more aggressive phase (167–164 B.C.E.), the Book of Daniel was written to encourage faithful Jews to persevere despite the defilement of the temple and religious persecution. Non-canonical Jewish literature also survives from this period and provides further perspective on the confrontation with Hellenistic culture (for example, the Book of Jubilees, the Testament of Moses, and parts of 1 Enoch). The first-century (A.D.) Jewish historian Josephus also chronicles this period of Jewish history, but with a rather sympathetic view toward the Hellenization process.

Seleucid domination

The Seleucid empire gained control over Palestine in 198 B.C.E. after the battle of Panium (Baniyas). At first the Jewish population welcomed Antiochus III, the Seleucid king. He, in turn, showed them great consideration and made some improvements in their lives. Antiochus III was succeeded in 187 B.C.E. by Seleucus IV, who appears in the narrative about Heliodorus in 2 Macc 3. The Heliodorus incident portrays increasing conflict between the Seleucids and at least part of the Jewish populace.

The conflict escalated during the reign of Antiochus IV Epiphanes, who ruled the Seleucid empire from 175–164 B.C.E. His policies seem to have been determined by two major considerations: he needed money to finance his military endeavors, and he needed the people under his rule to be unified for defensive purposes. In 169 B.C.E. he plundered the temple in Jerusalem, returning in 167 B.C.E. to put down a rebellion that had been based on false rumors of his death. He set up a citadel at one corner of the temple precincts and manned it with Hellenist soldiers. He forbade the practice of Judaism and set up an "abomination of desolation" (an altar to Zeus) in the temple itself. These are the events that sparked the Maccabean resistance and rebellion.

The Maccabees

The First Book of Maccabees tells the story of a particular family who decided to rebel against the forced Hellenizing of Judaism, first under the leadership of their father, Mattathias, and then successively under the leadership of three brothers. Unlike the Hasideans who preferred a non-violent resistance, the Maccabean family decided to meet force with force. It is difficult to date the brief activities of Mattathias, but they probably took place in late 167 or early 166 B.C.E. Upon his death, Judas assumed control of the rebellion until his own death in 160.

Judas won a series of victories against the Seleucid generals and was able to purify and rededicate the temple in 164 B.C.E. The narrative first recounts his early successes in primarily defensive campaigns, but a turning point occurred when he began to take the offensive against neighbors who were persecuting the Jewish people. Although he was able to restore a measure of religious freedom for his people, his work was often frustrated by the intrigues of the high priest Alcimus. Judas died in battle and was succeeded by his brother Jonathan (160–142 B.C.E.).

Under Jonathan's leadership, political activity began to supplant military efforts. When Antiochus V (164–162 B.C.E.) died, two rival claimants to the throne emerged—Alexander Balas and Demetrius I. Both courted Jonathan's favor because they needed his support, and he alternated in receiving honors and gifts from both of them. In 152 B.C.E. Alexander Balas appointed Jonathan high priest; he assumed the office on the feast of Tabernacles. Jonathan was able to regain parts of the territory of the old Davidic-Solomonic empire, but, in the end, his involvement in Seleucid politics led to his own death at the hands of a treacherous Seleucid general, Trypho.

The third Maccabean brother, Simon (142–134 B.C.E.), followed closely in the footsteps of Jonathan, not only accepting the high priesthood from Demetrius II, but also involving himself in Seleucid politics. He was relatively successful as a leader and further expanded the territory over which he governed on behalf of the Seleucids. He called his family "Hashmonay," and historians refer to the dynasty he established as the "Hasmoneans." Simon and two of his sons were murdered at a banquet by one of his sons-in-law, the assassin in turn being killed by John Hyrcanus, Simon's second son.

John Hyrcanus I (134–105 B.C.E.) continued the Maccabean/Hasmonean agenda by accepting the high priesthood, distinguishing himself as a military leader, and expanding the territory under his control. In 109 B.C.E. he took Samaria and destroyed the Samaritan temple on Mount Gerizim, attempting to force the Samaritans to worship in Jerusalem. The Hasideans, who were basically supporters of the Maccabees (although reluctant supporters because of Maccabean assumption of the high priesthood), seem to have definitively broken with Hyrcanus over his Samaritan policies. The Sadducees, the priestly aristocracy who often seem to have been favorable toward Hellenization, backed Hyrcanus. Although he did not take the title of king, there seems little doubt that Hyrcanus understood himself as restoring the Davidic-Solomonic empire by his expansionist policies.

John Hyrcanus was succeeded by his eldest son, Aristobulus I, in 104 B.C.E. He was quite friendly to Hellenism but unfriendly to his mother and brothers. He imprisoned them and let his mother starve to death. After taking the title of king, he died suddenly and was succeeded by Alexander Jannaeus (103–76 B.C.E.), the oldest surviving son of John Hyrcanus and an avid promoter of Hellenistic institutions. His very name betrays what had happened to the Maccabean rebellion by this time. We might wonder what Mattathias or Judas Maccabeus would have thought of one of their descendants named Alexander, after the famous Greek who started the Hellenization process! The Pharisees, successors of the Hasideans, openly opposed Jannaeus and his policies. The rebellion had come full circle.

The First Book of Maccabees

1 Maccabees differs from 2 Maccabees in several important regards. Clearly all the Maccabees are featured as heroes in 1 Maccabees, whereas 2 Maccabees recounts the deeds of Judas alone and tends to relegate him to the role of a mere agent of God. From what can be compared with other sources from this era, the author of 1 Maccabees is rather reliable when describing the events that took place, although he clearly does so from a Jewish point of view. He tells of Maccabean successes *and* defeats. With regard to the latter, he tells the story succinctly, not glossing over or altering the facts, but without attempting to develop a theology of defeat.

This book gives the impression of agreeing with the pragmatism of the Maccabees (as opposed to the idealism found in 2 Maccabees). When Judas and his brothers find that military operations are less feasible, they engage in typical Hellenistic political and diplomatic maneuvers to achieve their goals. They take the same pragmatic attitude toward the law; they are very flexible in applying it to various situations. Their attitude toward the sabbath provides a key example of this (they are willing to defend themselves on the sabbath), as is their approach to the high priesthood. They are concerned about the Jewish people perhaps more than about the temple as such (unlike 2 Maccabees, which centers attention consistently on the temple). 1 Maccabees covers a much broader time period than 2 Maccabees, which limits itself to part of the story of events that took place while Judas was still alive and the leader of the rebels.

The theology of 1 Maccabees

The theology of 1 Maccabees might be called covenantal. The people are expected to observe the law, the Torah. When they fail to do this, God punishes them. Those within Judaism who are called breakers of the law or non-observers of the law are the ones considered responsible for the disasters that Judaism experiences during the Seleucid period. They include people within Jerusalem, the priests of the temple, and, at times, the high priest himself. 1 Maccabees clearly condemns them and their activities.

At the same time, the book focuses attention on the aggressive and oppressive policies of the Seleucid regimes. There are repeated invasions of the land and attempts to prevent the Jewish people from observing the law, especially regarding worship in the temple.

One of the most important contributions of the Maccabees was their restoration of the temple, the memory of which is still celebrated by Jewish people as the feast of Hanukkah. The Maccabees are described as observers of the law, although they apply it flexibly to particular situations. The Hasideans, or pietists, are presented in 1 Maccabees as rather naive and simplistic in their rigid adherence to the law, especially by not defending themselves on the sabbath and thereby perishing.

The Hasideans were among those who were at first skeptical about the methods of the Maccabees but supported them for a time, after seeing some of their successes. Later a rift occurred when Jonathan Maccabeus became the high priest. There were serious obstacles to recognizing the legitimacy of his claim to that office: he was a warrior with blood on his hands, and he was not of the high priestly family. Onias IV, the son of the last fully legitimate high priest, was living in exile in Egypt. There were probably some within Judaism who favored bringing him back to Jerusalem to serve as high priest. Jonathan, however, was able to remain in office because he was the leader of the people at the time and had great power. Simon, his brother, and his dynastic successors also became high priests and remained in office for the same reasons.

Although the author of 1 Maccabees shows considerable respect for the Maccabees, at times the reader may get an impression that the author did not approve of everything they did. The narrative is very blunt about the fact that violence leads to further violence. The more the Maccabees engage in political and diplomatic maneuvering, the more they find themselves betrayed. At times it costs them their lives. As the narrative unfolds, each of the brothers comes to a tragic end. The reader may wonder whether the author might not be addressing the then-current Hasmonean ruler, subtly recommending that he learn from the mistakes of his predecessors.

Theologically, the author makes clear that all of the victories and successes in the narrative are due to the help and beneficence of God. He tells the story with frequent allusions to Jewish tradition, often comparing the Maccabees with heroes of old, such as Joshua and the judges, David, and others. This he does especially when the Maccabees engage in a controversial action, such as in 2:23-26, where Mattathias slays a Jew about to offer sacrifice in obedience to a Seleucid command, Mattathias being compared with Phinehas of old (see Num 25:6-14). We can presume that the author was trying to influence those who did not fully support Maccabean actions or their assuming the high priesthood.

Theologically, the Seleucids may be considered to be the instruments of God, who is punishing the people for breaking the covenant. However, the arrogance of some of the Seleucid leaders, whether kings or military commanders, is such that it mocks the power of God. These leaders develop their own plans, which often conflict with the plans of God. The reader may anticipate who wins in such a struggle with the divine.

In the story of Israel, and especially among its prophets, there is an important theme of a remnant who remain faithful to God and to the Torah. The Maccabees are presented as the leaders of those within the community who remain faithful despite persecution and constant threats to survival. In the end, despite the deaths of the Maccabees, the people are relatively free to live in accordance with their ancestral customs and their law. God is once again shown to be faithful to the people.

OUTLINE OF 1 MACCABEES

1:1–2:69	Introduction
3:1–9:22	Part I: Judas Maccabeus
9:23–12:53	Part II: Jonathan Maccabeus
13:1–16:24	Part III: Simon Maccabeus

COMMENTARY

INTRODUCTION

1 Macc 1:1–2:69

The first two chapters of 1 Maccabees set the scene for the rest of the book by describing the events that led up to the Maccabean rebellion.

1:1-9 Alexander and his successors. The book opens with a brief description of the career of Alexander the Great, who seemed determined to impose Greek culture on the peoples of the Near East. The mention of his pride and arrogance (v. 3) is quickly followed by the notice of his impending death. After his death in 323 B.C.E., his generals divided up the empire. The two most important divisions in terms of Jewish history were the Ptolemaic kingdom (with its capital at Alexandria in Egypt) and the Seleucid kingdom (with its capital at Antioch in Syria).

Palestinian Jews found themselves situated between these rival kingdoms, and the history of Judaism during this period is closely interwoven with that of the Ptolemies and the Seleucids. The latter kingdom began to dominate the area of Palestine after 198 B.C.E. A Jewish interpretation of this course of events (v. 9) suggests that the Jews' troubles are to be blamed primarily on the Greeks. The association of the Kittim (v. 1) with the "cause of distress" (v. 9) may be an allusion to Num 24:24.

1:10-15 Antiochus and the lawbreakers. In 175 B.C.E. Antiochus Epiphanes became the Seleucid king and greatly influenced Jewish history. Although 1 Maccabees chronicles historical events, it does so from the viewpoint of Jewish tradition and theology. One of the early themes in these first chapters is the tension between the plans of Antiochus and those of God, a familiar theme in Jewish tradition (see Exod 5–15 for a similar contest between Pharaoh and God).

Antiochus is described in these early chapters as arrogant, a second Alexander. The name he chooses for himself, Epiphanes, may indicate that he thinks of himself as the manifestation of a god, or at least as "illustrious." Arrogance is one of the most serious sins according to Jewish tradition. It seems to be a key to understanding the story of the tower of Babel (Gen 11:1-9) and may be related to the motivation that led the Man and the Woman to sin in the story of the Garden (Gen 2–3). Readers familiar with Jewish tradition, therefore, are forewarned in these early chapters that they can expect Antiochus to fall eventually, just as Alexander the Great did. This must be kept in mind, even though at various points in the narrative Antiochus may appear to be winning in his struggle with God's people.

At the same time, it is clear that not all the problems facing Judaism are originating from outsiders such as the king. There are those within the Jewish community itself, "breakers of the law" (v. 11), who find Hellenistic culture attractive and perhaps also convenient, especially those engaged in trade and commerce with Hellenists. Their seduction consists in making foreign alliances, probably to improve their economic circumstances. However, in Jewish tradition, making foreign alliances or covenants always endangers Israel's covenant with its God (see Deut 7:2, for example). It brings Israel into close association with neighboring peoples, an association which can—and which, in fact, often did—lead to worshiping the gods of their neighbors.

The Hellenistic gymnasium (v. 14) was not only a place of recreation, but a center of Hellenistic culture and ideas; it was a rival, therefore, to the dissemination of Jewish tradition among the young. Exercise was taken in the nude, and this seems to have caused embarrassment for circumcised Jewish youths, who consequently took measures to cover over this sign of God's covenant with the people. (For the implications of such an action, read Gen 17:9-14).

Jewish tradition is clear that all will go well for God's people as long as they remain faithful to the covenant and observe the law. On the other hand, when the law is not kept and the covenant is broken, disaster can be expected to follow. Therefore, readers familiar with Jewish tradition will expect from what is described in verses 10-15 that crises will arise within Judaism because of the lawbreakers.

1:16-40 Punishment of the Jews. We do not have to wait long to encounter such crises, punishments for the sinfulness of some within the community: Jerusalem is despoiled, its walls torn down, the sanctuary defiled, and a citadel housing foreigners and apostates established in one corner of the temple area. There is an implicit irony in the telling of the story. Antiochus invades Egypt in 169 B.C.E. and plunders Jerusalem on his way back to Antioch, possibly to help finance his adventures. One might presume that Antiochus is conducting these activities simply on his own initiative. However, for our author, looking at these events with the eyes of faith, what is really happening is that God is allowing the people to be punished for the sinfulness in their midst. It is not surprising that Antiochus is described like a second Nebuchadnezzar because of his profanation of the sanctuary and of sacred things (see 2 Kgs 25).

Antiochus comes to Jerusalem a second time in 168 B.C.E., perhaps in response to a threat of civil war between the Hellenizing Jews and those who are resisting Hellenization. The building and staffing of the citadel, in effect, give control of the city to the Hellenizing party.

The narratives describing these events are interspersed with two laments (vv. 24-28 and 36-40) resembling those that were sung after the destruction of Jerusalem by the Babylonians in 587 B.C.E. (see the Book of Lamentations). They contain many allusions to Old Testament passages and follow a traditional style.

1:41-61 Hellenizing policies of Antiochus. Conditions deteriorate further for the Jewish community. According to the author's view, Antiochus wants to unite all peoples of his kingdom by having them abandon their particular traditions and religious practices and adopt the king's religion. The remainder of the chapter describes the reactions of two groups of Jews: those who comply with the king's edict (vv. 41-61) and those who do not comply (vv. 62-64).

Those who comply are closely associated with the dismantling of Jewish religion: Jewish religious practices are forbidden, objects associated with Jewish worship are destroyed, the observance of the sabbath and feast days is proscribed, circumcision is forbidden, dietary laws are not to be observed, and Jewish sacred books are burned. The temple itself is defiled and turned into a typical gentile sanctuary, in violation of Jewish law. This crisis, in the author's view, is precipitated by the sins of the apostates and any who tolerate them.

1:62-64 Jewish resistance to Hellenization. Although many Jews cooperated with this dismantling of their religion, some—the heroes and heroines of this book—resolve to maintain their fidelity to the covenant at the risk of their lives. The theme of a remnant of the people remaining faithful to God and to the covenant is a cherished aspect of Jewish tradition. Especially from the time of the Babylonian Exile and its aftermath, keeping themselves separate from other peoples is understood as essential for their survival as God's people.

There is a second classic struggle, therefore, being outlined in this first chapter—the tension between the breakers of the law who adopt Hellenistic ways and those who remain faithful to the covenant and Jewish tradition. Again, for those familiar with the tradition, the outcome of this struggle is already known, but the story is still worth telling. God will win a great victory for the people, accomplishing this through human instruments—the Maccabees. It is time for the author to introduce us to this family of heroes.

2:1-14 Mattathias and his family. Mattathias and his family are of priestly descent. Their initial reaction to the Hellenizing policies of Antiochus and to the Jewish collaboration with the Hellenists is mourning and lament. This first reaction is somewhat passive and is expressed in the traditional language and gesture of lamentation.

2:15-28 Incident at Modein. What happens next, however, is decisive in their adopting an aggressive response of resistance to the Hellenization process. At Modein representatives of the king attempt to force Jews, including Mattathias and his sons, into apostasy. Mattathias is singled out as a person of some prominence in the community and is invited to be the first to obey the king's edict by offering sacrifice (vv. 17-18). Despite flattery and attempts to persuade him with privileges and wealth, Mattathias answers for himself and his family by utterly refusing to comply with a request that would imply abandoning the law and covenant (vv. 19-22). The refusal is in accordance with Jewish tradition and gives evidence of great fidelity to, and zeal for, the tradition.

Not everyone in the crowd, however, is disposed to follow his example by resisting the king's officers and risking death. When someone comes forward to comply, Mattathias kills him (v. 24). The author recalls the example of a priestly predecessor (see Num 25:6-15 for a similar action by Phinehas during the wilderness wandering period of Jewish tradition) and thereby justifies the violent deed. Mattathias and his family now have no alternative but to flee to the wilderness to protect their lives and prepare their defenses. They invite all who intend to remain loyal to the covenant to join them (vv. 27-28).

2:29-41 Early example of Jewish resistance. Evidently not all who go to the wilderness in resistance to the king's policies and edicts immediately join the Maccabees. We are told about some rebels who are destroyed because they refuse to defend themselves on a sabbath. Whereas the Maccabees flee to the mountains, where it is safer, this other group merely goes out into the desert. The Maccabees leave their possessions at home in order to move more quickly, but the others take their families and possessions with them. In addition to these encumbrances and vulnerability, this latter group also interprets the sabbath law in a rather extreme way—all of which leads to their destruction (vv. 37-38).

The Maccabees, by way of contrast with these martyrs, decide to fight even on the sabbath in their resistance to Hellenization. Their realism is not only practical (they see their actions as necessary for the survival of the people) but also theologically based (the law is for the people, not the people for the law).

2:42-48 Organization of Jewish resistance under the Maccabees. Those who are faithful to the covenant join the Maccabees and begin to attack the lawbreakers. The Hasideans are probably members of the scribal class, hence interpreters of the law, but here they are described primarily as mighty warriors. These verses describe in summary fashion and with theological nuance the classic struggle between the faithful and the apostates: faithful Jews are successful over arrogant sinners. We are thus given a preview of the victory that God will eventually win for the people through the agency of the Maccabees.

2:49-69 Farewell discourse of Mattathias. The remainder of the chapter describes the last days of Mattathias, especially his farewell address to his family. Farewell discourses are found elsewhere in Jewish tradition (see Gen 49, for example). The fact that Mattathias is a venerable and faithful patriarch adds weight to his words, but they are even more important because they are his last words before he dies. The words put on his lips are a summary of Maccabean theology, deeply rooted in Jewish tradition and focusing on the importance of remaining faithful to the covenant and the covenant God. Various models of such fidelity are raised up from Jewish history, implying by these references that remaining faithful will result in victory. Those under duress who remain faithful to the law and the covenant will be rewarded. (For a similar list of heroes, see Sir 44–49).

It is significant that military leadership is passed on to one of the brothers, Judas, with the charge to inflict vengeance on the Gentiles (Hellenists) who have caused the people such suffering (vv. 66-68). The farewell discourse ends in a traditional way with a description of Mattathias' death and burial. We are at a transition point in the story.

PART I: JUDAS MACCABEUS
1 Macc 3:1–9:22

Judas is the first of the Maccabean brother-heroes to begin turning the tide against the Hellenists and the Hellenizing Jews. Our author again uses traditional language to sing Judas' praises, often comparing him to the judges and King David—Jewish leaders who were victorious against the enemies of God's people because the spirit of the Lord empowered them in battle (see, for example, Judg 3:9-10).

3:1-9 Introduction to Judas' career. Mattathias' choice of a leader to succeed him is confirmed by his family and their supporters. In song the author summarizes Judas' career, describing him as a giant and as a lion, winning victories on behalf of God's faithful people against their enemies (see Sir 46:1-6 for a similar poem and description of Joshua). The language is as theological as it is military. This may help explain the "joyful" waging of war for the preservation of Judaism and the covenant (v. 2). God's plan is being carried out against the Hellenizing Jews and their Seleucid supporters, and Judas is God's instrument.

3:10-26 Early victories of Judas. Judas' first victory is achieved against Apollonius. After defeating him, Judas takes his sword, just as David took Goliath's (see 1 Sam 17:51).

Seron, a commander of the Seleucid army, is the next one to encounter Judas in battle. Motivated by ambition as well as perhaps by duty, Seron makes plans for battle. The author subtly forewarns the reader that, because Seron's plans are not the plans of God, they are doomed to failure. Seron is joined by many renegade Jews who have suffered from Judas' earlier attacks, but Judas is fearless in this encounter, despite the superior numbers of the enemy. Being so clearly outnumbered by the enemy is an opportunity to show that God is the one who achieves the victory, not the human soldiers or their commander (see Judg 7 for a similar concept). Those who attack Judas and his troops are arrogant and non-observers of the law. The outcome can be predicted easily by a believer.

Judas responds with a similar theological assessment of the situation when he is confronted with the fear of his guerrilla companions, who have been weakened by lack of food. Echoing David's friend Jonathan (see 1 Sam 14:6), Judas encourages his men with the assurance that God will help those who fight on behalf of the law. He then immediately takes the initiative and defeats Seron (v. 23). The enemies who survive the defeat retire to the region known in tradition as Philistia, recalling the enemies of God's people who dwelt there and fought Israel during the days of Saul and David. Judas has told his soldiers not to fear the godless; but now the godless begin to fear Judas because God is on his side (see 1 Chr 14:17 for a similar statement about David, or Exod 15:15-16 and Josh 5:1 for similar statements about Israel as a people).

3:27-37 The reaction of Antiochus. Antiochus is understandably angry at this defeat of his armies. His reaction is swift and predictable: he begins to build up a full-scale army to defeat Judas. As is usually the case, however, this requires a substantial financial outlay. The author of 1 Maccabees explains, perhaps with some amusement, that Antiochus is short of money because of his mismanagement and foolish policies that have disrupted the kingdom (v. 29).

Before he goes to Persia to raise the needed monies, Antiochus places Lysias in charge of his kingdom and his army, with the order to destroy Jerusalem and Judah and to settle colonists in the land (vv. 32-36). Again, even though such threats of annihilation seem particularly ominous for the Jews, a believer will rest secure that somehow God will not allow Lysias to be successful against the covenanted people.

Antiochus relies on collecting sufficient revenue for his armies and making alliances with his neighbors. In what follows, Judas' reliance is primarily upon prayer.

3:38-59 Preparation for war. Lysias moves against Judas and Jerusalem with a large army of infantry and cavalry. Slave traders of the region prepare for the enslavement of the Jews, who, they presume, will lose the war. For the Jews, such an enslavement would be tantamount to negating the Exodus and returning to Egypt. Lysias is joined by people from "the land of the Philistines" (v. 41). The author identifies the region in such a way that his readers' memories are turned to the days of old when it seemed certain to all except God's faithful people that the Philistines would dominate them for all time. In those days God raised up David, who definitively defeated these enemies of God's people. Without having to be explicit, the author once again points to Judas as a kind of new David (there are echoes, in this narrative, of 2 Sam 5:17-25 and 1 Chr 14:8-17).

Judas' preparation seems to be primarily liturgical. He and his forces gather at Mizpah, a site famous in the early history of the judges and Saul, but not mentioned again until this passage (v. 46). When Israel was afraid of the Philistines on a particular occasion, the prophet Samuel gathered Israel at Mizpah and prepared them for battle by fasting and acts of penitence (see 1 Sam 7:5-12). Judas' preparation is similar: prayers, fasting, and acts of penitence. In another place in the tradition, all Israel was summoned to Mizpah to combat an enemy; those who did not come were to be put to death (see Judg 20:1, 3 and 21:1, 5, 8).

While their enemies consult the images of their gods, Judas and his followers seek direction from their sacred writings, which have been outlawed by the king (v. 48). The law reserves the use of priestly vestments, the presentation of tithes and first fruits, and the presentation of nazirites for the temple. However, even though the temple has been defiled, it remains a center of focus in this narrative. The people's prayer of lamentation in the face of such severe danger is accompanied by traditional liturgical preparation for war: blowing trumpets and raising a "loud shout" (see Josh 6, for example).

Judas then organizes his army in a manner similar to that of Moses (see Deut 1:15 and 20:5-8) and reduces the size of his already small force by sending home those who were in the process of building new homes, those who are engaged to be married, and those who were planting vineyards (v. 56). He also dismisses the fainthearted, those who perhaps do not have enough faith in God's power to save them all. Victory will come from God, not from the army.

Judas' final prayer focuses the attention of his troops not only on the nation but on its primary symbol, the temple of the Lord in Jerusalem. The last verse is the key to the whole section: "Whatever Heaven [that is, God] wills, he will do" (v. 60).

4:1-25 Gorgias attacks Judas. The account of the first stage of this battle demonstrates Judas' superior strategy and tactical maneuvers. Despite the treachery of renegade Jews who serve Gorgias as guides, Judas is able to elude his adversary. Later, when Judas' forces encounter Gorgias' army, Judas reassures them by recalling what happened under similar circumstances during the Exodus from Egypt, when the people were trapped and in danger of being enslaved once again (see Exod 14). His further words of encouragement echo such passages as 2 Kgs 19:19 and others that refer to the rescue of Jerusalem on another occasion when the Assyrian general Sennacherib besieged the city—unsuccessfully. Judas also recalls for his troops the Jews' covenantal election.

In the ensuing battle the Gentiles are defeated and lose about half of their troops (vv. 12-15). Judas does not allow his own troops to take time out for plundering what is left of the enemy's camp because he does not want them encumbered with booty. There are still contingents of Gorgias' army in the vicinity. When these see what has happened to the rest of their army, however, they flee once again to the land of the Philistines. After Judas' troops plunder the enemy camp (v. 23), they go away singing hymns of praise (see Ps 136 for a similar song). The preparation for battle was primarily liturgical, and the celebration afterward partakes of the same quality.

4:26-35 Battle with Lysias. Lysias' discouragement at being defeated by Judas prompts him to raise a much larger army and to head it in person. The year is probably 165 B.C.E. Lysias moves toward Jerusalem from the south this time, from Idumea.

Judas, too, has a much larger army but is still outnumbered about seven to one. In the face of such odds, he once again prepares for battle by prayer (vv. 30-33), recalling earlier successes of Israel against the Philistines: David over Goliath (see 1 Sam 17) and Jonathan against the Philistines (see 1 Sam 14:1-15). Drawing on consistent Jewish tradition, Judas asks God to destroy the Jews' enemies, who are presumed to be the enemies of God as well.

The tide of battle once again goes against Lysias (v. 34), who then returns to the capital city, Antioch, to raise an even larger army. A more complicated picture is painted in 2 Maccabees, suggesting that Lysias was persuaded that Judas' increasing support from the Jewish population would dwindle once the pressure of persecution was eased. However, the author of 1 Maccabees omits any details in the story that might reflect poorly on his hero. At any rate, Lysias' withdrawal to Antioch provides an opportunity for Judas and his supporters to take control of the temple in Jerusalem.

4:36-59 Rededication of the temple. Although the text may give the impression that Judas proceeded directly to the purification of the temple after the battle with Lysias, a careful reading shows that this did not happen for nearly a year, not until 164 or even 163 B.C.E. The delay may have been caused by those who were concerned that contemporary apocalyptic writings contained predictions for the near future, and only after the passage of time had shown that these predictions were not accurate could Judas proceed with the purification of the temple.

In the ancient world, people faced issues of order and chaos in a religious way. The Jews understood God's work of creation primarily as making order out of chaos. They thought of the wilderness as the place of chaos farthest removed from order. On the other hand, the city (especially Jerusalem with its temple) was the place of greatest order. When the temple is described as a wilderness (v. 38), it symbolizes the great chaos or undoing of creation that the people were experiencing during the Hellenization process. What is needed is a new creation—setting the temple in proper order, following the guidelines of the law.

When Judas and his supporters arrive at the temple, they find it much like a typical Syrian-Canaanite sanctuary, the kind of worship space condemned in Jewish tradition (see Deut 12:2, for example). Their first response is one of lamentation in word and gesture (vv. 39-40). But before they can proceed with the work of purification, they first have to attack the citadel, staffed with government forces, presumably to neutralize it.

Judas selects blameless priests for the work of purification (v. 42). We know from 2 Maccabees that many of the Jerusalem priesthood had been supporters of the Hellenizers. When the carefully chosen priests begin the task of purification, a dilemma arises regarding the altar. Because it has been used for idol worship, the law commands that it be destroyed (see Deut 12:2-3). However, the same law forbids destruction of the Lord's own altar (Deut 11:4). The priests work out a compromise: they tear down the altar to make room for its replacement, but carefully store the stones of the altar until a prophet indicates what God wants to be done with them (v. 46).

Then, in accordance with the ancient law, they erect a new altar, make new vessels and furnishings, and restore the temple to its status before its defilement by the Hellenists. The rededication probably took place in December 164 B.C.E., three years to the day when the first heathen sacrifice had taken place. This is the origin of the annual feast of Hanukkah, a feast of joy and praise because the "disgrace" (v. 58) was removed from among the people. Order is once more established; they have experienced an act of new creation.

4:60-61 Defensive fortifications. Judas fortifies the temple mount and stations a garrison there to protect the temple from any future incursions by the Hellenists.

5:1-8 Judas on the offensive. In areas outside Maccabean control or influence, the Gentiles grow angry at the turn of events and begin to exterminate the Jews who live in their midst. The theme of gentile opposition to the temple is a familiar one in Judaism (see Ezra 4 and Ps 47). Judas moves first against the Idumeans (identified here in somewhat archaic terms as the "sons of Esau," possibly alluding to Obad 15-21, and seeing Judas' action as fulfilling that prophecy).

Judas next turns his attention to the "sons of Baean," whose identity continues to elude us. The Ammonites lived east of the Jordan River. This is the first time that Judas takes the offensive, but it is in defense of Jewish lives that are being threatened.

5:9-54 Deliverance of Jews in Galilee and Gilead. Although the author describes real events in this section, the narrative develops in such a way that Jewish readers would recall Joshua's rescue of the Gibeonites (see Josh 9) as well as Jephthah's deliverance of Gilead (Judg 12:1-7).

Jews whose lives are threatened in Gilead (the territory east of the Jordan River) and Galilee are unable to defend themselves without help from the Maccabees. Ptolemais is the city of Acre (Acco) in the northwest corner of Israel. Tyre and Sidon are towns along the Phoenician coast just north of the Galilean border.

Judas' brother Simon is sent with troops to aid the Jews in Galilee (v. 21), while Judas himself goes to rescue those in Gilead. Joseph and Azariah are left in charge of Judea. Although Azariah is not mentioned elsewhere, Joseph is mentioned in 2 Macc 10:19-22 in unfortunate circumstances.

Simon's campaign is quite successful, but he cannot guarantee the safety of the Jews in Galilee and therefore evacuates them to Judea. Judas and Jonathan cross the Jordan River into Gilead (v. 24). The Nabateans (v. 25) were an Arab people who played an important role in the life and politics of the region from the fourth century B.C.E. until the Muslim conquest. Although our author says that they were peaceable with Judas, 2 Macc 12:11-12 states that they became peaceable only after being defeated in a violent skirmish. The skirmish was probably unimportant for our author's purposes, so he omits it.

Judas' opponent in these Transjordan battles is Timotheus, who rallies many Gentiles to his cause and hires Arab mercenaries as well. Judas wins the battles through superior tactics, including taking the initiative away from Timotheus. The gentile survivors take refuge in a temple (v. 43), either because they think the Jews will respect it as a place of asylum or because they think their goddess (probably Astarte) will save them. Judas evacuates the Jews from the area, probably for the same reason that Simon evacuated people from Galilee. When they return to Judea, they proceed at once to the temple to offer sacrifice and celebrate the victories that God has given them.

5:55-64 A defeat for the Jews. The author draws attention to something that happened while Simon was in Galilee and Judas and Jonathan were in the Transjordan. Joseph and Azariah, left in charge of Judea and motivated by ambition, attack the Gentiles around them, violating their orders, which were defensive rather than offensive. Making a name for oneself in battle is a familiar theme in the Hellenistic world, but it is not acceptable motivation for action in Jewish tradition. These two are defeated because they did not obey Judas' orders. God's salvation is to come through the Maccabees, and other efforts that are not consonant with theirs will not succeed.

5:65-68 Judas attacks Edom and Philistia. Problems accompany Judas on his next campaign. Some priests seem to have ambition similar to that of Joseph and Azariah, and they too are killed in battle. The headiness of victories won by the Maccabees should not distract them or the reader from the real purpose of the military operations: to bring salvation to God's people, not to provide opportunities for individuals to realize personal ambitions.

6:1-17 Death of Antiochus IV Epiphanes. Our author is taking us back to 4:35, resuming the narrative after the defeat of Lysias. We know from other sources that Antiochus IV Epiphanes died in December, 164 B.C.E., around the time of the rededication of the temple. Our author implies that Antiochus died only after he had heard about the rededication of the temple. 2 Maccabees says that

Antiochus died after unsuccessfully attempting to plunder the temples of Persepolis. The Seleucids had a reputation for robbing temples, and Antiochus was no exception.

The narrative states that Antiochus realizes that his defeat at Elymais and his impending death are the consequences of the way he has treated the Jews (vv. 12-13). The news of Lysias' defeat and the taking of Jerusalem and Beth-zur provide additional support for this assessment. However, what seems to surprise Antiochus is no surprise to the reader, who has been expecting such a fall since 1:10 above. The fact that he is going to die in a foreign land (v. 13) would be seen by the Jews as further evidence of the severity of his punishment.

The narrative may be historically correct when Antiochus is described as saying that he is "kindly and beloved" in his reign (v. 12), because his son is called "Eupator" (someone with a good father). In appointing Philip as regent of his son Eupator, Antiochus IV probably means to demote Lysias. Eupator is only a boy at this time, somewhere between the ages of nine and twelve. Antiochus gives Philip the insignia of royal office—the crown, the purple robe, and the signet ring, with which he seals important documents (v. 15). However, even this plan of Antiochus is not to be fulfilled exactly as he has decided. His son Eupator is with Lysias, who appoints the boy king (Antiochus V Eupator) and assumes the regency himself, thereby becoming Philip's rival.

6:18-63 Campaigns of Antiochus V against Judas. Although we have witnessed Judas' successes against nearly all the enemies of the Jews, the only territory that he actually controls is the temple area and Beth-zur. The garrison in the citadel is still intact, despite the attack just prior to the rededication of the temple. Judas will find it difficult to meet other challenges if the citadel is able to force him to reserve part of his troops for the defense of the temple area. Judas and his supporters are still probably only a militant minority in the country.

Judas, therefore, decides to attack the citadel (v. 20), garrisoned by troops of the king and by some Hellenizing Jews. From what has been related so far in this book, the reader may presume that Judas will be successful; however, that is not the case. What is striking about the rest of this chapter is that it contains no theology of defeat. It tends to accentuate the positive by noting Maccabean courage and bravery. The siege instruments that Judas uses demonstrate that he is now in a position to challenge the government seriously. The siege probably begins in the autumn of 163 B.C.E.

Some of the garrison in the citadel escape (v. 21) and report to Antiochus V what is happening in Jerusalem, apparently exaggerating the situation enough to motivate him to take action against Judas. Although Judas could make a case for attacking Jewish apostates (in view of Jewish law) and of defending Jews who are being persecuted in the neighboring territories, his siege of the citadel and fortification of the temple and Beth-zur are clearly rebellious acts against the kingdom.

The boy-king decides, probably with the guiding hand of Lysias, to raise an enormous army to fight Judas (vv. 28-30). There will be no more underestimation of Judas' military abilities. In the Jewish tradition, Gideon slew one hundred twenty thousand Midianites with a force of only three hundred men (see Judg 7). Lysias' army is similar in size, and our author may be suggesting that Judas' defeat came about because he had too many soldiers! The text focuses attention, however, on the enormous size of the Syrian army and on Maccabean courage.

The Syrians attempt to take Beth-zur before advancing on Jerusalem. Judas has to lift the siege of the citadel to confront the Syrian army. Not to do so would not only endanger Beth-zur but would also involve the risk of eventually being caught between the Syrian army and the citadel garrison.

The exact significance of verse 34 has long been debated. Ancient sources tell of other occasions in which elephants were intoxicated, but this was a dangerous tactic, because they could easily turn on their own troops in such a wild state. Presumably they were given something to rouse them for battle. The phalanx, a distinctively Greek military formation introduced by Philip of Macedon and his son Alexander the Great, was particularly difficult to penetrate and hence successful. This battle is described in more detail than other battles, probably to underline the near invincibility of the Syrian force and to help explain Judas' defeat.

Eleazar (v. 43) is a younger brother of Judas. His act of heroism and courage is remembered with good reason; his success in penetrating the phalanx is itself a remarkable feat (vv. 43-46). His motive in killing the elephant seems to be to kill the king (who because of his age is probably not actually involved in the battle, however). Eleazar gives his life to "save the people and win an everlasting name for himself" (v. 44). This may mean that he gave his life for his people and hence won everlasting renown as a martyr. It is not the same kind of making-a-name-for-oneself encountered in the cases of Joseph and Azariah (see ch. 5).

Judas is defeated. Beth-zur is taken by the Syrians, who station a garrison there. Beth-zur could not withstand a siege because of a food shortage. During a sabbatical year crops were not sown. The campaigns of earlier Syrian generals had probably also disrupted agricultural work and storage in the preceding year. Moreover, we learn in verse 53 that supplies were also short because of the number of refugees that had been brought to Jerusalem from Galilee and the Transjordan. Judas is being defeated by lack of supplies as well as by the strength of the Syrian army.

The Syrians turn their attention to the siege of the temple area. We are told that few Jews remained in the sanctuary (v. 54), while the rest were scattered, some of them going home. Judas, curiously, is not mentioned during this siege. He may have avoided the trap of being cornered in the temple and may have fled to the hills or even back to Modein. The author is silent on the matter. To admit that Judas was not a part of the defense of the sanctuary would have been embarrassing to his hero, but his silence about the matter also obviates any difficulties that might arise when we learn about the negotiations with the Syrians and their subsequent treachery.

Jerusalem had been under such a siege before; in 701 B.C.E. the Assyrian general Sennacherib besieged it and then had to lift the siege in order to put down a rebellion in the eastern part of the empire. Something similar occurs here, but the author does not exploit the similarity. Lysias, who is clearly in charge of the entire military operation, learns of a challenge to his authority by Philip, who had been appointed regent by the dying Antiochus IV. Lysias sues for peace with the Jews (v. 58) so that he can return to Syria and defend his position against Philip. His words, designed to convince his fellow officers of the rightness of this move, tactfully leave out his personal concerns. Seemingly, the sabbath-year shortage of food is affecting the Syrians as well, but taking care of the "affairs of the kingdom" (v. 57) is the primary motive for the withdrawal.

The terms offered the Jews amount to a repeal of the decree outlined above in 1:41-50. We are simply told that the Jews accept. Again, Judas is not specifically mentioned in the account. Lysias treacherously reneges, however, when he enters the temple area and orders that its fortifications be destroyed (v. 62). He also leaves a military garrison behind, although the Jews presumably are free to go to the temple and to conduct their worship according to their own law. We might think that the problems are over for the Jewish faithful, but we will learn that the truce is an uneasy one.

No high priest has been mentioned so far in the narrative. We know from other sources that Menelaus was the high priest up to this point. His Hellenized name gives us a clue as to which side he was on in the civil war. According to 2 Macc 13:3-8, Lysias arranged for his execution. The absence of a high priest at this point in Jewish history is a further complication in the story.

7:1-4 Demetrius I becomes king. Demetrius, a cousin of Antiochus V, had been a hostage in Rome. When a Roman delegation came to Antioch, the head of the delegation was murdered. The Romans retaliated by allowing Demetrius to return home as a rival claimant to the throne with the support of the army, and his rivals were killed. The Maccabean story becomes more complicated from this point on because of the internal struggles within the Seleucid kingdom.

7:5-20 Bacchides is sent to Judea. We do not know much about Alcimus' background, but he was of a priestly family. Menelaus, the previous high priest, and other Jerusalem priests were prominent in the Hellenizing party within Judaism. It is not surprising then to find Alcimus in the company of people who make charges against Judas (v. 6). We know from other sources that Demetrius was preoccupied with the rebellious province of Babylonia, and this explains why he entrusted the Judean matter to someone else. Bacchides seems to have been given wide discretionary powers.

Once again, the Seleucid king does not underestimate Judas' capabilities, and Bacchides is sent to Judea with a large army. This large force belies Bacchides' offers of friendship and peace. Judas and his brothers are evidently strong enough to resist or ignore such offers.

The scribes (v. 12) are probably the same group as the "Hasideans" (v. 13). These scholars of the law are duped by Bacchides and Alcimus, the newly appointed high priest. The Hasideans are caught in some theological dilemmas. On the one hand, Menelaus had not been a member of the high priestly family, but Alcimus was. For the Hasideans, this was something very much in his favor. They also believed, on the basis of their tradition, that a high priest was to be appointed by a legitimate king, so placed by God. Was not Demetrius the lawful ruler of the land, and was not Alcimus his choice for high priest? The Maccabees might argue theologically, on the other hand, that the victories given them by God showed that the period of Israel's subjugation by the Seleucids was over; therefore Demetrius was not the divinely appointed ruler over the Jews.

At any rate, the Hasideans are portrayed as naive in trusting Alcimus and Bacchides. The treachery of Alcimus must have been a rude awakening for many of the people, but not for the Maccabees. The fulfillment of Scripture alluded to in verse 17 is a quote from Psalm 79. After Bacchides makes Alcimus the ruler of Judea and Jerusalem and assigns troops to him, Bacchides returns to Antioch. The problems have multiplied for the Maccabees. The high priest has the authority to regulate temple worship and also has civil authority, with troops to back him up. From the author's viewpoint, this is clearly a low point in the Maccabees' career.

7:21-25 The intrigues of Alcimus. The enemy, at this point in the narrative, becomes the high priest and his supporters, highly placed fellow Jews. Evidently they control Jerusalem, while Judas seems to be strong in the countryside. He begins to retaliate against these enemies, who are worse than the Gentiles (v. 23), while Alcimus seeks his primary support from the Syrian king.

7:26-50 Nicanor battles Judas. Nicanor is an archvillain in 1 Maccabees, described as someone who hates all Jews, including perhaps Alcimus and his allies. A somewhat different portrait is painted in 2 Maccabees, where Nicanor and Judas become friends for a time (see 2 Macc 14:18-28). Nicanor might have come to Judea to work out a reconciliation with Judas rather than commit his troops to the difficult task of subduing a guerrilla force. According to 2 Maccabees, he persuades Judas to settle down and marry. Later the Hellenizing party forces his hand by complaining to the king that Nicanor is not carrying out the task for which he was sent. Judas is warned and refuses to associate with Nicanor any longer. In our narrative these events are telescoped (vv. 28-30).

When Nicanor loses some men in his first skirmish with Judas, he does not defeat or capture Judas, but his attitude toward Jews hardens. The sacrifices being offered in the temple for the king would be supported not only by the Hellenizers but by all Jews who recognized Demetrius' authority as coming from God. Nicanor's behavior is particularly tactless at this point, and his demand that Judas be delivered to him is impossible to carry out. His threat to destroy the temple prompts the priests to sing a lament once again (vv. 37-38). The prayer borrows heavily from Solomon's prayer at the dedication of the temple (see 1 Kgs 8:29, 33-34). We can safely presume that Nicanor will be punished for his blasphemies against the temple.

As both sides prepare for battle, Judas prays, alluding to what happened to Sennacherib when he besieged Jerusalem in 701 B.C.E. (see 2 Kgs 19:32-36 and Isa 37:33-38). The implication is clear: God is asked to do to Nicanor what he did to Sennacherib. Judas' forces are considerably fewer than on earlier occasions. However, when the people of the countryside see that he is being victorious against Nicanor, they seem to realize that God is with the Maccabees, so they come out to help Judas defeat the enemy (v. 46).

The treatment of Nicanor's corpse (v. 47) may offend more sensitive readers, but such gloating over a defeated enemy is commonplace even in our contemporary world. The author sees a fitting irony in Nicanor's severed arm being put on display in Jerusalem near the temple against which he had raised the same arm. The feast commemorating this event was still being celebrated in the first century A.D.

The author concludes this chapter with the notice that for a short time there was peace in the land (v. 50). The battle is probably to be dated in March, 161 B.C.E., and Judas will die in battle nearly a year later. The Maccabees have risen somewhat in the estimation of the people of the countryside, but they are a long way from solving the Hellenization problem.

8:1-16 Reputation of the Romans. Judas attempts to break the stalemate of power among the Jews by engaging the Romans as allies. The description of the Romans is decidedly positive in tone. The author has not yet had direct experience of them. He is at pains to point out how similar the Romans are to the Jews! He especially respects their renowned organization and military power as well as their longstanding opposition to the Greeks.

8:17-32 Embassy of Eupolemus and Jason. The Romans seem to have been disposed to allow the Jews to live according to their own law. No doubt there were Jews among Judas' supporters who were favorably disposed toward Rome. However, there were potential theological problems involved in what Judas was attempting to do. The prophets had often warned the people against making foreign alliances rather than trusting God. We can assume that Judas probably would have made appeal to the foreign alliances contracted by Solomon (see 1 Kgs 3:1) as a way of preserving and expanding his empire and influence.

Rome, on the other hand, was probably willing to support the Maccabees against the Seleucids to keep a balance of power in the area. Demetrius had become king against Rome's wishes. Rome had nothing to lose in this arrangement with Judas, and, to a great extent, neither did he. Although Rome pledged to defend Judas and his supporters, they did not interfere in the affairs of the region until much later, when Aristobulus II invited Pompey into Palestine in 63 B.C.E.

It is interesting that the two ambassadors sent to Rome have Greek names (v. 17). No doubt they are also fluent in Greek, the popular language used in Rome at the time. Judas is shrewd and pragmatic. Although he prays in preparation for battle, he also is willing to use whatever seems necessary to achieve victory.

The brief speech of the ambassadors before the Roman senate is noteworthy because it singles out Judas and his brothers as the leaders of the Jewish people (v. 20). Alcimus and his supporters are no longer considered part of the Jewish people, at least not by our author. The agreement that is made requires Rome and the Jews to come to one another's help should someone attack either of them. The wording is rather loose, however (see v. 30 in particular), and the treaty is made specifically with "the Jewish nation," not with Judas or his brothers. The author refers to a threatening letter allegedly sent by the Roman senate to Demetrius (vv. 31-32). However, the wording of the letter seems to be more Jewish than Roman. At any rate, Demetrius (if he did in fact receive such a letter) does not seem to have been very concerned about such a threat.

9:1-22 The death of Judas. The narrative resumes with events after the defeat of Nicanor (see 7:50 above). Despite the important defeat of Nicanor and even after the return of the ambassadors from Rome, Judas still does not seem to enjoy wide support among the people. In the first part of this chapter morale seems very low. Demetrius sends reliable Bacchides into the land, presumably to reinstate Alcimus as high priest and to destroy Judas.

The situation is precarious. The Syrian army attacks a city in Galilee, far from the influence of Judas, and kills the inhabitants. Judas is not in Jerusalem at this time, so Bacchides does not seem to spend much time there. When the Syrian army does encounter Judas' forces, it is clear that once again he is greatly outnumbered. Desertions leave him with a greatly reduced army (v. 6). It is strange but probably true that Judas did not have more support from the people after his brilliant career and the definitive victory over Nicanor.

What is even stranger is his statement just before the battle is joined (v. 10). So often on earlier occasions he had seemed pleased with the fact that he did not have many troops, because then it would be clear to all that the inevitable victory came from God. His preparation for battle on earlier occasions was primarily prayer. This time he adopts a fatalistic approach and speaks about dying with bravery, sounding more like a Hellenistic warrior than the man of faith we encountered earlier.

As was his usual tactic, Judas takes the initiative, but despite a long-fought battle, he is killed. His brothers bury him, and his supporters mourn his passing. Verse 21 is a brief lament recalling David's words of grief at the death of his close friend Jonathan (see 2 Sam 1:17-27).

PART II: JONATHAN MACCABEUS

1 Macc 9:23–12:53

9:23-27 Aftermath of Judas' death. With Judas no longer a threat, the supporters of Alcimus are given the opportunity to reestablish their control of the country. The agricultural situation probably had been greatly affected by the series of wars. During time of famine the government (under the leadership of Alcimus) probably controlled the distribution of food, so it is not surprising that people desert the remaining Maccabees at this time. Those who do not desert are derided and punished. The country is once more in a crisis, as though all that Judas had fought for now eludes his supporters. At this low ebb in Maccabean fortunes Jonathan's career begins to emerge.

9:28-31 Jonathan takes Judas' place. Maccabean supporters choose Jonathan, the youngest of the brothers, to be "ruler and leader" in terms that are reminiscent of the selection of Jephthah, the judge of long ago (see Judg 11:4-11).

9:32-53 Bacchides opposes Jonathan. Jonathan inherits less power, fewer friends, and more enemies than Judas had. In the eyes of Bacchides, Jonathan is a rebel against a king who has ceased persecution of the Jews. Jonathan has to withdraw from the area that had once been controlled by Judas and retires to a wilderness area southeast of Jerusalem, the same area to which David fled when he was being pursued by Saul (see 1 Sam 21–29).

Verse 34 is omitted in this translation, as in others, because it is merely a repetition of verse 43 and out of place here. The Nabateans (v. 35) could be expected to befriend the Maccabees and oppose the Seleucids. Jonathan, in expectation of a Seleucid attack, does not want to be burdened with too many possessions. The "sons of Jambri" (v. 36) are a tribal group; the author does not identify them as Nabateans. Jonathan and Simon decide to carry out revenge against this tribe, which had stolen their baggage and kidnapped or killed their brother John. The bride's father is identified in a curious way as a prince of Canaan (v. 37). Canaan no longer existed as a political entity, but the identification of such an ancient enemy might help explain the violence that ensues.

Bacchides will not let the attack go unpunished and seeks out Jonathan on a sabbath. Jonathan's rousing cry to his troops is an echo of Josh 3:4. Jonathan, like his father, Mattathias, on a previous occasion, decides that it is more important to survive than to observe the sabbath (v. 44). The punishment spelled out in Deut 28:7 affects, not Jonathan, but Bacchides. Jonathan, like Judas before him, counsels prayers to God for deliverance as preparation for the upcoming battle. However, Jonathan seems to be defeated, although the narrative does not say so directly. Bacchides loses many soldiers, while Jonathan and his men escape. There are echoes in this passage of the exploits of David's general, Joab (see 1 Chr 19:10-15).

Bacchides then sets out to consolidate his control of the country by building fortresses (v. 50). He garrisons them, takes the sons of leading families as hostages against their good behavior, and turns the citadel in Jerusalem into a kind of prison. Jonathan and his supporters are conceded the wilderness and probably considered adequately neutralized.

9:54-69 Death of Alcimus and a plot against Jonathan. In 159 B.C.E. Alcimus decides to tear down a wall in the temple. It is not clear exactly which wall, but it may have been one that kept Gentiles away from the inner courts, thus making it possible for them to enter the previously forbidden area. At any rate, he joins the list of people in the Maccabean books who sin against the temple and suffer punishment accordingly. There is some irony in his loss of speech; he can no longer give orders about the temple. Eventually he dies "in great agony" (v. 56).

Once again there is no high priest, and so the Hellenizing party is without a leader. Bacchides returns to Antioch either because his presence is perhaps no longer needed or merely to get new instructions from the king. A period of relative calm seems to take place at this point.

But the peace is not to last. Some of the Hellenizers develop a conspiracy against Jonathan. Peaceful coexistence is not their way. They persuade Bacchides to return and capture Jonathan. Bacchides prefers to have his allies capture Jonathan even before he arrives, but it is difficult to keep such conspiracies secret. Jonathan learns of the plot and kills the ringleaders (v. 61). Jonathan then prepares for a siege by developing fortifications at Bethbasi in the desert, probably two miles southeast of Bethlehem and eight miles from Jerusalem itself.

Bacchides has no choice but to besiege Jonathan. The latter escapes and annihilates some nomadic tribes that evidently were planning to join Bacchides in the siege. Simon and Jonathan take the initiative, attack Bacchides, and overcome him. By now the Syrian's patience with the Hellenizers has come to an end. The Hellenizers are the ones who invited him to capture Jonathan; so, in a sense, they are responsible for Bacchides' present situation. He has some of them executed and prepares to return to Antioch.

9:70-73 Jonathan makes peace with Bacchides. Jonathan is probably the only Jewish figure of any importance with whom the Syrians could make peace. Despite earlier attempts at peacemaking and subsequent treachery on the part of the Syrians, Jonathan offers to make peace, and Bacchides accepts. The text makes it clear that this time the Syrians prove trustworthy. Jonathan, the guerrilla chieftain, becomes in effect a judge, similar to leaders in the days of old (see the Book of Judges). His "judging" amounts to ruling the people, but it is unclear exactly what his authority was. He receives no specific office from the Syrians at this point and does not live in Jerusalem. The reference in verse 73 may be more theological than political in its intent. Meanwhile, there are still Jewish hostages in the citadel at Jerusalem.

10:1-14 Alexander Balas challenges Demetrius. Jonathan's fortunes change rather dramatically in 152 B.C.E., when a rival claimant to the Syrian throne challenges Demetrius by setting up a throne in Ptolemais, a seaport easily defended. Alexander (known as Balas) claims to be the son of Antiochus IV Epiphanes. He is supported against Demetrius not only by the Roman senate, but also by the kings of Cappadocia, Pergamum, and Egypt. Demetrius' problems are multiplied by his unpopularity with his troops. In the ensuing narrative, both Alexander and Demetrius attempt to acquire Jonathan as an ally. He in turn is able to play them off against each other, accepting the best offer in typically pragmatic Maccabean style.

Demetrius is the first to approach Jonathan, giving him permission to raise an army (v. 6)—as though he needed such authorization! Jonathan does not object to this, but he uses Demetrius' letter to arrange the release of hostages from the citadel in Jerusalem. He then takes up residence there and sees to the restoration of the city and the fortification of the temple area. The Hellenizers realize that Jonathan is no longer vulnerable and they flee, some of them taking up residence at Beth-zur.

10:15-21 Jonathan becomes the high priest. Alexander in turn writes a flattering letter and designates Jonathan high priest. Two factors militate against Jonathan's accepting the appointment: it is made by a king whose legitimacy is still a matter of dispute, and Jonathan is not of the high priestly family. On the other hand, expediency gives way to principle, and Jonathan accepts the high priesthood (as well as membership on Alexander's council), thereby consolidating his power (v. 20).

Throughout their history, theological problems concerning their accession to the high priesthood will continue to plague the Maccabees (or Hasmoneans, as they are later called). At this time, however, Jonathan was the only person with so much power and authority within the Jewish community, and it is not clear whether he was seriously challenged for accepting the high priesthood. However, it may have been this event that led to the establishment of the Essene group at Qumran, a group that became alienated from the temple and its "wicked priest." 1 Maccabees does not raise these theological problems, of course, because the Maccabees are its heroes.

The price to be paid for the honors bestowed on Jonathan is loyalty to Alexander. In October, 162 B.C.E., at the feast of Tabernacles, Jonathan assumes the office of high priest. We are not told how the people receive him.

10:22-47 Demetrius attempts to win back the Jews. In a letter to the Jewish nation, Demetrius, Alexander's rival, pointedly does not mention Jonathan. The two references to the high priest in verses 32 and 38 presumably refer to someone yet to be appointed *by Demetrius.* The letter outlines financial arrangements he is willing to make, arrangements extraordinarily favorable to the Jews. In short, Demetrius seems to be making a very attractive offer to the Jewish people, with the intention of wooing them away from Jonathan. This probably would not have been too difficult; there were those who opposed Jonathan and the Maccabees, and those who did not like his accession to the high priesthood.

Demetrius' opening words (v. 22) seem to imply that he either does not know of Alexander's arrangement with Jonathan (which is very unlikely) or that he is presuming he can count on the nation to respond favorably after the people have heard his terms: exemptions from certain taxes and tithes, special tax status for Jerusalem, turning the citadel over to a high priest, and release of Jews taken into captivity in the various battles. Moreover, he names Jewish feasts as tax-exempt days, makes it possible for Jewish mercenaries to be hired for his armies at favorable conditions, and offers to include Jews in prominent places within his kingdom.

Verses 38-39 are somewhat problematic, for Demetrius offers what he probably cannot deliver. He seems unaware of the centuries of hostility between the Samaritans and the Jews. Because Alexander holds Ptolemais, Demetrius can hardly deliver it for the benefit of the temple. He may be implying that he will take Ptolemais soon and overcome Alexander, but such a prediction is seldom wise.

Demetrius makes provisions for royal revenues to be donated to the temple (v. 41) and seems willing to consider it a place of asylum for those who are in debt to the crown. He is not the first king to make provisions for restoring the temple (Cyrus and Antiochus III had done this earlier [see Ezra 6:3-5 and Josephus, *Antiquities*, XII.3.3]). But it is quite extraordinary for a Seleucid king to be willing to finance the fortification of Jerusalem. These extraordinary measures show to what extent Demetrius is determined to win the support of the Jews, and possibly how desperate his situation is.

Jonathan and his supporters do not accept Demetrius' offer (v. 46). The Hellenizing party is ignored. It is not surprising that Jonathan rejects an offer designed to turn the people away from his support!

10:48-50 Alexander defeats Demetrius. The manuscripts vary in their reading of verse 49, and it seems (from other sources) that the confusion is due to the seesaw nature of the battle, with Demetrius gaining the upper hand at first and later being defeated, falling from power in 150 B.C.E. Alexander then takes measures to develop foreign alliances.

10:51-58 Alliance with Egypt. Alexander's request for an alliance with Egypt, sealed by marriage with the Ptolemaic royal family, is probably motivated by a concern that Egypt not ally itself with Demetrius' family. Demetrius has sent his sons abroad for their safety, and Alexander can expect a later challenge to his rule from them. Ptolemy VI responds somewhat cautiously and requests that the marriage be celebrated in Ptolemais, a city named after an Egyptian king.

10:59-66 Alexander honors Jonathan. The gathering for the royal wedding becomes the occasion for both Hellenistic kings to court Jonathan. Alexander still needs his support, and it is possible that Ptolemy has designs on recovering Palestine as part of his empire. Jonathan, on the other hand, also has reasons for going to Ptolemais with gifts. Onias IV, a rival claimant for the high priesthood, is in Egypt. Jonathan's "friendship" with Ptolemy can neutralize Onias and his supporters.

Jonathan's lavish gifts may well be at the expense of the Hellenizers—booty taken from them. Those who come before Alexander to protest against Jonathan are not heeded. Jonathan is in a position of great power and influence.

If there is any doubt among his enemies about Jonathan's current status, the clothing with royal purple and the invitation to sit at the king's table dispel such notions (vv. 62-63). The Hellenizers, the supporters of Onias, and the Hasideans (who seemingly object to Jonathan's assumption of the high priesthood because he is not of the high priestly family) are all effectively silenced by these actions and the royal proclamation that no one should interfere with Jonathan.

Jonathan returns to Jerusalem not only as high priest but also as military and civil governor. He has reason to be pleased. The civil war seems to be over, with the Maccabees the clear winners. However, there are still garrisons of Syrian troops in parts of Judea, including the Jerusalem citadel. The Jews are not yet an independent nation.

10:67-89 Jonathan is victorious in battle. Nothing is said about the years 150–147 B.C.E., presumably a time of Judea's settling down under the rule of Jonathan. In 147 B.C.E. problems develop with the return of Demetrius II to challenge Alexander's rule. Demetrius II, the son of Demetrius I, is still a teenager. What makes his challenge possible is the ineptitude and unpopularity of Alexander. The Syrians are ready for a new ruler.

Demetrius appoints Apollonius as governor (v. 69). Apollonius realizes that before he can successfully attack Alexander, he will have to deal with Alexander's faithful ally, Jonathan. The letter he allegedly sends is modeled on 1 Kgs 20:23-32, dealing with an earlier Syrian invasion. Apollonius' intention is to lure Jonathan into battle by taunting him. The approach works, and Jonathan sets out with a large army and his brother Simon. Jonathan is bound to defend the southern coastal cities by his alliances with Ptolemy and Alexander.

Jonathan is able to drive a strategic wedge between Apollonius and Demetrius by taking Joppa (v. 78), which might have been Apollonius' main supply port (there are not many harbors along the Palestinian coast). Apollonius' retreat southward might have been a ruse to lure Jonathan into the kind of terrain that would favor Apollonius' cavalry (see his taunt in 10:70-73). The ruse works, and Jonathan soon finds himself surrounded by the cavalry. At the same time, Jonathan's forces outnumber the Syrians. By sheer courage and determination, Jonathan's forces hold their ground and wear down the Syrians. When the cavalry weakens, Simon attacks the infantry successfully. When this happens and the cavalry flee, Jonathan is not able to follow them because he has no cavalry. The Syrian infantry seek refuge in the temple of Dagon (v. 83). Jonathan does not honor its status of asylum but destroys the temple and the men who are in it. The neighbors in Ashkalon decide to honor Jonathan, as does his ally, Alexander. Jonathan's rank is raised still further to "Kinsman" of the king (v. 89), and the rest of "Philistia" is given to him. In short, he survives Apollonius' challenge very well.

11:1-19 Ptolemy VI plots against Alexander. Although ancient sources differ about Ptolemy's motives in the actions that follow, 1 Maccabees remains favorable to Alexander and his son against both Ptolemy and Demetrius. Ptolemy may have been merely acting as though he were a faithful ally, coming to Alexander's rescue against Apollonius and Demetrius II. In reality, he may have been taking advantage of the weakness and unpopular position of his son-in-law and attempting to reestablish Egyptian control over Palestine and perhaps Syria as well.

In 145 B.C.E. Ptolemy VI Philometor begins a march toward Syria, probably moving along the Palestinian coast. The fact that he leaves garrisons in each of the cities along his route gives us a hint at his motivation (v. 3). Although some people try to turn Ptolemy against Jonathan, the king needs his support—or at least he does not want to antagonize such a powerful person. Jonathan's behavior is very correct toward this ally. He tactfully withdraws to Jerusalem, leaving Ptolemy and Alexander (both of whom are his allies) to settle their own disputes.

Ptolemy invites Demetrius to form an alliance with him (v. 9) and offers to give him his daughter, Cleopatra, who is Alexander's wife! Ptolemy's intention is probably not so much to underwrite Demetrius' claim to the throne as to undermine Alexander. Ancient sources make clearer the accusation of attempted assassination (v. 10). According to the Jewish historian Josephus, Ammonius, a minister in Alexander's court, tried unsuccessfully to kill Ptolemy while he was enroute to Antioch. Our author, however, defends Alexander and provides us with Ptolemy's "real" motivations.

While Alexander is out of the capital, Ptolemy arrives and assumes the kingship of "Asia," that is, Syria (v. 13). So much for his support of Demetrius II! Ptolemy, however, for all his boldness, does not make a wise decision because he cannot count on Jonathan's support. Moreover, he can expect the opposition of Demetrius II and the Romans, who had kept Antiochus IV from uniting Syria and Egypt in 168 B.C.E. We are told that Alexander was in Cilicia putting down a rebellion (probably fomented by Demetrius, who seems to have been there at the same time). Alexander's immediate return to Syria leads to direct conflict, which ends in the death of both antagonists (vv. 17-18). The populace, not favorably disposed to the Egyptian occupational forces, eliminate them. The way is now open for Demetrius II to assume the Seleucid throne.

11:20-38 Jonathan and Demetrius II. Jonathan has wisely stayed out of the conflict between Ptolemy and Alexander. Before Demetrius has a chance to consolidate his position, Jonathan moves against the citadel in Jerusalem. Both men will need the support of each other, and Jonathan's move against the citadel probably puts him in a stronger bargaining position with Demetrius. Naturally the Hellenizers, who may have become a minority by now, complain to the new king about Jonathan's actions.

What happens next is a lesson in Maccabean diplomacy. Although Demetrius reacts angrily to Jonathan's move, he proceeds more carefully in dealing with him. Demetrius moves south with a threatening army but requests a conference and the lifting of the siege. Jonathan does not honor the request regarding the siege but approaches Demetrius with important Jewish leaders and gifts (vv. 23-24). This pleases Demetrius, who inherited financial problems brought on by a series of wars and fiscal incompetence.

Demetrius confirms Jonathan in the high priesthood and in his status as a Chief Friend. Nothing is said about the citadel at this point, but we will learn later (v. 41) that the siege was lifted. Presumably in return for this "favor," Demetrius agrees to the same basic financial favors that had been offered by his father (see 10:30, 38). Demetrius' letter (vv. 29-37) is addressed both to Jonathan and to the Jewish people. The letter is basically a copy of what Demetrius had sent to his chief minister, Lasthenes, who as a general had helped Demetrius press his claims to the throne.

The letter in effect gives Judea a favored status and increases its territory with the addition of the three Samaritan districts. Taxes previously sent to Antioch now go to Jerusalem for the support of the temple and its priests. However, Judea remains a Syrian possession, and the Syrian garrison remains in the citadel. Afterward Demetrius makes a serious blunder in demobilizing his troops. We know from other ancient sources that he led a dissipated life, and his minister, Lasthenes, was very corrupt. The peace that Demetrius believes he has brought to his kingdom is not to last.

11:39-56 The revolt of Trypho. The next episode in our narrative seems extraordinary when the reader remembers the earlier struggles of the Maccabees against the Hellenizers and the Hellenists. In this segment of the story, Jonathan sends Jewish troops in an attempt to save Demetrius!

Trypho's career is interesting. He first came to public notice as a soldier of Demetrius I; then he became a governor of Antioch under Alexander; he was, perhaps, one of the two courtiers who crowned Ptolemy VI in Antioch; and later he became one of the "Friends" of Demetrius II. Such shifts in loyalty help explain his next adventure—rebellion against Demetrius II and installation of a new king in the person of Antiochus VI, a mere boy. Antiochus VI would have been well advised not to trust such a person.

Meanwhile Jonathan again requests that Demetrius remove the garrison from the Jerusalem citadel (v. 41). Demetrius I had agreed to such an action but did not implement it. Perhaps Jonathan is aware that Demetrius II could use the additional troops in Antioch to shore up his own faltering position. Demetrius agrees to arrange the move later, but after he is secure once again, he also reneges (see vv. 52-53). But, at this point in the narrative, he requests Jewish troops to help defend him.

Demetrius' unpopularity reaches alarming proportions, and the Jewish mercenaries ruthlessly put down a rebellion of the populace. The reader may be excused for wondering what is happening to the Maccabean religious revolution at this point. Demetrius does not become wiser from this experience. He alienates his sole ally, Jonathan, not only by reneging on his promises but also by causing Jonathan new problems, revoking the provisions of the letter found in verses 29-37.

11:57-62 Antiochus VI and Jonathan. Trypho now returns to Antioch with Antiochus VI, who was probably about four years old. Demetrius' army rebels against him and enthrones the boy-king, who promptly confirms Jonathan in the high priesthood and sends him lavish gifts. The letter alluded to in verse 57 was probably ordered by Trypho and drawn up for the young king by royal secretaries. Jonathan's allegiance is once more being courted by restoring the rank he had held under Alexander (see 10:89).

Simon Maccabeus is made governor of the coastal area from Tyre in the north to somewhere between Gaza and the Nile in the south, including some Hellenistic towns that were not pro-Jewish. Jonathan sets out on a tour, ostensibly to develop support for the new regime, but probably in reality to ensure his own control over the area. He is well received at Ashkalon but rebuffed at Gaza (v. 61). Significantly, after he overcomes the dissidents at Gaza, he takes hostages back to Jerusalem rather than send them to Trypho.

Meanwhile Demetrius II counterattacks by sending a large force to confront Jonathan in Galilee and, presumably, to prevent him from organizing forces loyal to Antiochus. Simon Maccabeus takes Beth-zur, the place of refuge for Hellenists who had escaped from Jerusalem (see 10:14). When Jonathan meets the enemy armies, he is defeated in an ambush (v. 68). His expressions of grief—tearing his clothes and throwing earth on his head—are expressly forbidden activities for a high priest (see Lev 10:6; 21:10). Seemingly, there were exceptions to the rule. Verses 71-74 echo Josh 7:5-9, implying that God has listened to Jonathan's prayers. (See also 1 Sam 14:21-22 for a similar victory by an earlier Jonathan.) Jonathan's troops rally to him, and after decisively defeating the enemy, he returns to Jerusalem.

12:1-23 Alliances with Rome and Sparta. According to 2 Macc 11:34-38, there had been diplomatic activity between the Jews and the Romans in 163 B.C.E., and, as we have read earlier (see 1 Macc 8), Judas had contacted the Romans in 161 B.C.E. It is not surprising, therefore, that Jonathan also makes diplomatic overtures to the Romans. What is less clear is why the Romans or the Spartans would consider embroiling themselves in Jewish matters in the Near East. Perhaps they have no intention of actually doing so. Jonathan may simply be seeking international recognition and status, as well as giving Trypho and Demetrius pause before attacking a people who have become friends of Rome. The Romans seem to receive the Jewish embassy courteously and, presumably, at least renew their friendship with the Jewish people.

Although there may be reasons for questioning the authenticity of Jonathan's letter to the Spartans as presented in verses 5-18, the basic contents of the letter might be authentic. The date of the letter seems to be 144 B.C.E. Sparta had become independent two years earlier when the Romans helped it defeat Corinth and the Achaean League. The Spartans might be expected to understand Jewish nationalism and would provide an example of how an ally of Rome had benefited when attacked by neighbors. Undoubtedly, the example would not be lost on Trypho or Demetrius. In other words, in this chapter we probably have two more examples of Jonathan's political and diplomatic maneuvering that at the same time demonstrate his adaptation to Hellenistic ways. Eventually this approach will cost him his life.

The letter to Sparta is sent by Jonathan, the "senate" (the Sanhedrin), "the priests, and the rest of the Jewish people" (v. 6). The reference to not needing such an alliance or friendship because of the "sacred books" (v. 9) is not very tactful or diplomatic in a letter such as this and raises questions about the authenticity of the letter. Jonathan sends emissaries with Greek names; no doubt they are also fluent in the Greek language.

Although there is clear precedent for approaching Rome, Jonathan and his followers need something to establish bonds with the Spartans. That is why they recount a legend about the common origins of both peoples and quote earlier correspondence between Arius, a Spartan king, and Onias, a Jewish high priest (vv. 19-20). Identifying these people is a problem because there were at least two people each with the names of Arius and Onias during the period in question.

The Hebraic nature of verse 23 provides further complications regarding the authenticity of the letter. There are indications, however, that at times the Greeks were interested in associating themselves with ancient Egypt and the Near East. Perhaps the legend that both the Spartans and the Jews were descended from Abraham would have impressed the Spartans at this point in their history. No response is recorded from Sparta, however, and perhaps the very mention of such an embassy has already achieved the author's purpose of increasing Jonathan's prestige.

12:24-34 Demetrius again attacks Jonathan. Jonathan is currently loyal to Antiochus VI and his general, Trypho. When he learns that Demetrius has prepared a large army against him, Jonathan once again takes the initiative by leaving Jerusalem and crossing the border into Syrian territory (Hamath). When the enemy discover how prepared Jonathan and his troops are, they flee (v. 28). While Jonathan is in the territory, he attacks a group of Arabs. His motive is not clear, but they may have been at least partly responsible for the assassination of Alexander Balas, who had been friendly toward the Maccabees. The reason for Jonathan's march to Damascus (v. 32) is also unclear, but he may have had some dreams about restoring the Davidic empire, which at one time included Damascus (see 2 Sam 8:5-7).

Meanwhile Jonathan's brother Simon moves to the coastal area to prevent any active support of Demetrius among its inhabitants. Once again a threat to Maccabean supremacy has been overcome.

12:35-38 Jonathan builds up Judea's defenses. Jonathan seemingly has control of the Sanhedrin (the assembly of elders) and secures their agreement to build up the defenses of Judea. Part of this program includes the attempt to isolate the citadel in Jerusalem from the rest of the city because it is still held by foreigners. In effect, this initiates another siege.

12:39-53 The deceit of Trypho. The general Trypho decides to realize his ambition to become king. According to the author, Trypho thinks that Jonathan, the faithful ally of King Antiochus, will prevent such a move. That is why he now sets out to destroy Jonathan. We are not told what Jonathan knew of this plot, but he goes out to meet Trypho and his army with a large force of his own (v. 41). Trypho, deceitfully changing tactics, flatters Jonathan and gives him gifts. Jonathan makes the fatal mistake of accepting both, along with the advice to allow all but a few of his troops to return home. In past Maccabean history, a small army and prayer were adequate for defense or victory. Such is not the case at this point in the narrative.

Jonathan is invited to Ptolemais, the place where he had been honored by Ptolemy of Egypt and Alexander of Antioch (see 10:59-66). However, this time there is no Egyptian king to protect him, nor is there a Syrian king who needs his support. The inhabitants of Ptolemais seize Jonathan and kill many of his troops (v. 48). When Trypho attempts to destroy Jonathan's remaining troops in Galilee, he is not successful, and Jonathan's men return to Judea to mourn the loss of Jonathan. We are not told whether he is still alive or not. Perhaps they do not know his fate at this time.

The closing verse of this chapter (v. 53) reminds one of Psalm 2, which describes the temptation of surrounding peoples to rebel and attack the Jewish nation when someone (God's anointed) is assuming a new leadership role in Israel. The full psalm in Jewish tradition, however, assures us that these matters are ultimately in God's hands, and God will take care of the people.

PART III: SIMON MACCABEUS

1 Macc 13:1–16:24

13:1-11 Simon becomes the new leader. When Trypho prepares to invade Judea, Simon delivers an address to the people in Jerusalem, drawing upon such familiar themes of 1 Maccabees as devotion to the law and the temple and also commitment to the nation. The author, of course, does not mention any self-interest on the part of his heroes, the Maccabees. Simon appears to believe that Jonathan is already dead (v. 4). As had happened on previous occasions, the people accept a Maccabee as their leader (see 1 Macc 2:65ff. and 9:29-31). It is noteworthy that the people accept Simon as their leader but not as high priest. Perhaps this is an indication of the popular belief that only the legitimately reigning Seleucid king could appoint a high priest. Simon's first task is to complete the defensive measures begun by Jonathan.

13:12-24 Trypho kills Jonathan. Trypho invades the land of Judah, bringing Jonathan along as a prisoner. The offer he makes Simon involves a clear dilemma. If Simon refuses Trypho's offer, the people will hold him responsible for his brother's death. If he accepts the offer, he is taking a major risk with the deceitful, treacherous, and ambitious

Trypho. In effect, however, he has no choice but to pay the ransom money and deliver Jonathan's children to the Syrian general. True to form, Trypho reneges on his offer (v. 19).

As Trypho marches deeper into the land, ravaging it as he goes along, Simon counters his every move and prevents him from taking a direct approach to Jerusalem itself. Trypho becomes a natural ally of the Syrian garrison in the Jerusalem citadel, who accordingly appeal to him for help. But Trypho is prevented from coming to their aid by a seasonal snowstorm; he turns back to Syria, but first he kills Jonathan and probably his sons as well.

13:25-30 Jonathan is buried at Modein. Jonathan's body is buried in the family tomb at Modein. He does not receive the eulogies that Judas had (see 3:1-9) or that Simon will later receive (see 14:28-47). Jonathan's deeds were more political than military. He seems to have been working toward the independence of the Jewish nation but was captured and killed before he could accomplish this. The stage has been set, however, for Simon to realize that dream.

A careful reading of Simon's burial procedures for his brother reveals an astonishing borrowing from Greek or Hellenistic ways (vv. 27-30). The practice of setting up pyramids is borrowed from the Egyptians (and Hellenistic Ptolemies). The setting up of carved suits of armor (trophies) is a Greek burial custom for victorious warriors. The Greeks also had the practice of setting up victory monuments near the sea in memory of sea battles. Simon adopts the practice, even though the Maccabeans were not seafaring. They had no fleet and had won no naval victories. Perhaps the capture of the port town Joppa may have triggered some Maccabean dreams about the potential of developing a navy. At any rate, we seem to have come some distance from Mattathias' zeal and passion for matters Jewish! On the other hand, this cultural adaptation is often found at some point in revolutions throughout history.

13:31-42 Simon and Demetrius become allies. Predictably, Trypho kills the young Antiochus VI and assumes the royal throne. Simon's response seems limited primarily to further defensive measures in Judea. He was probably fairly independent of Trypho, who had demonstrated his vulnerability earlier (see vv. 12-24).

Although the Maccabees had not been on good terms with Demetrius II, Simon now turns to him in order to form an alliance. Trypho was probably already in trouble with the Syrian populace for assassinating Antiochus VI, and there is some indication that his dictatorial ways had also alienated his army. That is why Demetrius was probably in a position to regain the Seleucid throne. The gifts that Simon sends him imply allegiance.

The response of Demetrius seems gracious enough, but he probably has little choice but to respond positively. He addresses Simon as "high priest" (v. 36). Although it is quite likely that the populace or the Sanhedrin had already chosen Simon as high priest, the author of 1 Maccabees is careful to call him by this designation only after it is at least confirmed by a king with some semblance of legitimacy to his reign. The favors Demetrius bestows on Simon are not all they may appear to be at first reading. He has little choice but to revalidate grants he had made earlier (see 1:24-37), to agree to Simon's retaining control over the fortifications over which he already has control, to pardon any acts of rebellion on the part of the Maccabees, and to exempt the Jews from all taxes. At the same time he is also willing to take Jews into his service.

Although verse 41 implies a kind of independence of gentile "yoke," full political independence will not come until later.

13:43-53 Simon captures Gazara and the citadel. Simon now moves to assure complete military control over all Judea and the coast by capture of the remaining Syrian garrisons there. First he takes Gazara, resettles it with Jews who observe the law, and builds himself a residence there.

Jonathan had begun the siege of the citadel two years earlier (see 1 Macc 12:36), and Simon brings it to a successful end in 141 B.C.E., when the garrison surrenders. The citadel is entered with great jubilation and rejoicing (v. 47). For the first time since 169/168 B.C.E., the temple area is free from the menace of the citadel (see 1 Macc 1:33-37). Verse 53 introduces Simon's son John, who is later known as John Hyrcanus, Simon's successor, who ruled from 134 to 104 B.C.E.

14:1-3 Demetrius is captured. According to the author, Demetrius II marched into Media to get help in his campaign against Trypho. However, it is possible that Trypho was fairly immobilized at this point and that Demetrius turned his attention to Media because of the threatening progress of the Parthian empire there. At any rate, the Parthians capture Demetrius, Simon's ally, and imprison him. Arsaces (v. 2) is probably Mithradates I, who actually treated Demetrius fairly well, even giving him his own daughter in marriage.

14:4-15 Song of praise to Simon. At this point in the narrative, the author inserts some poetry that sums up the praises of Simon in much the same way as he did earlier with the praises of Judas (see 3:3-9). The song recounts some of Simon's important military accomplishments, notably the capture of the port of Joppa and the citadel in Jerusalem. It is interesting that Simon Maccabeus is praised for capturing Joppa (v. 5), the gateway to commerce and communication with the Greek isles. Such contact with Greeks was not where this story started! At the same time Simon is described in language that is reminiscent of the reign of Solomon (see 1 Kgs 5:5, for example).

The second part of this song of praise seems to describe Simon's reign as a kind of messianic age, a familiar theme in intertestamental literature. The poem contains several allusions to Old Testament texts (see Lev 26:4; Zech 8:4, 12; Ezek 34:27; Isa 52:1; 1 Kgs 4:25; Mic 4:4; and Isa 27:5-6). The Jewish apocalyptic movement, especially during the second century B.C.E., looked forward to a period of peace for God's people, a time when they would be ruled by someone who was just, someone who would see to it that everyone, including the poor, had enough to eat—that they could eat their bread in security.

Despite what one might think of the political and religious developments in Judaism during the period of the Maccabees, it must be admitted that, under Simon, the Jewish people in Judea experienced their first quasi-independence since the fall of Jerusalem in 587 B.C.E. We might excuse some people of the time, including our author, who might have thought that the messianic prophecies and apocalyptic predictions were indeed being fulfilled under the Maccabees—especially under Simon.

14:16-24 Rome and Sparta renew alliances with Simon. Rome and Sparta learn of the death of Jonathan and express their interest in renewing alliances with Simon. Numenius, the Jewish emissary who had been sent to Sparta and Rome by Jonathan, figures prominently in this narrative also. The full chronological sequence of events is not clear at this point because of the way the author has schematized and telescoped events. Simon responds to the Romans' offer of friendship by sending a significant gift, a golden shield weighing nearly half a ton—an expensive gift from a small nation struggling to stay alive.

14:25-49 The Jewish people honor the Maccabees. We have heard the author's summary praise of Simon as well as the offers of friendship from Sparta and the important ally, Rome. Now it is time to hear what the people themselves thought of the Maccabees. Setting up a memorial inscription to record the great deeds of leaders was a familiar practice in the Hellenistic world. The inscription in this part of the narrative is dated September, 140 B.C.E.

What is curious is what the inscription does *not* say. Although Mattathias, the father, is mentioned (v. 29), Judas' name does not appear, and Jonathan's role is described cursorily. The majority of the praise, of course, is heaped upon Simon, who is the current ruler. Perhaps it was considered impolitic to praise his brothers while he was ruling. Perhaps also the manners in which Judas and Jonathan came to their deaths was a cause of some embarrassment, and therefore not suited to the author's purpose of praising his heroes.

As a result of all that he had done on behalf of the nation, the people acknowledge Simon as permanent leader, high priest, and governor general, implying military, spiritual, and civil authority. His power is just short of royal, as is his official clothing. In effect, we have here a new constitution that outlines Simon's responsibilities and his acceptance of them, as well as the implied responsibilities of the people who have offered these positions to him.

15:1-9 Antiochus VII and Simon. Antiochus VII, the younger brother of Demetrius II, was called "Sidetes" by the people, because he was born at Side in Pamphylia. When he decided to wrest control of the

Syrian kingdom away from the unpopular Trypho, he sought the friendship of Simon. Although Antiochus probably would not have embarked on such a venture without adequate financial and moral support, Simon was nevertheless someone to be reckoned with.

In his letter to Simon (vv. 3-9), he may be exaggerating the conditions in Syria somewhat to enhance his claim to the throne. Although he seems to grant Simon what had been granted by others (or simply taken by the Maccabees), his concessions or privileges make it clear that he considers Judea to be a Syrian province. The authorization to coin money is a new privilege, however. Presumably the coinage was in bronze, because silver and gold were reserved to the king. Since he withdraws most of these concessions a few months later, it seems probable that Simon did not mint any coins.

15:10-14 Antiochus VII invades Syria and Judea. In the autumn of 139/138 B.C.E., Antiochus invaded Syria, forcing Trypho to flee to Dor, a city south of Mount Carmel. In our narrative Antiochus pursues him and besieges this port city. Since Antiochus has moved south into Judea, we might expect some encounter with Simon. However, the author inserts a notice about renewed friendship between Simon and the Romans before resuming the narrative about Antiochus' relationship with Simon.

15:15-24 Rome renews alliance with the Jews. Numenius, the Jewish legate to Rome, brings a letter addressed to such neighboring kings as Ptolemy and Demetrius. The latter, perhaps, had not yet been captured by the Parthians when the letter was written, or perhaps the Romans simply were not aware of his fate. The renewal of friendship is expressed especially in the acceptance of the large golden shield that Simon had sent to Rome (v. 20). The letter provides for a kind of protection of the Jews from their neighbors and includes provisions for extradition to Jerusalem of all troublemakers who seek refuge in neighboring countries. It is not clear why this letter is included precisely at this point in the narrative, but it does in fact provide a kind of contrast between the way the Romans deal with the Jews and the way the Syrians do. The various kingdoms mentioned in verses 22-23 are primarily independent states of the eastern Mediterranean, an area of increasing interest to the Romans.

15:25-41 Antiochus attacks the Jews. The narrative resumes with the story of Antiochus' pursuit of Trypho. Although Antiochus besieged the city of Dor by land and sea (v. 25), Trypho was able to escape (v. 37); however, he has no further influence on the development of events in this area. Antiochus is already in control as this part of the narrative begins. Simon sends some troops to help Antiochus, presumably as a way of indicating his acceptance of Antiochus' offer (see vv. 3-9).

The situation has changed, however—Antiochus no longer needs Simon's help. He refuses to accept the assistance and reneges on his earlier agreement. Moreover, he demands the return of Joppa, Gazara, and the citadel in Jerusalem, all of which formerly belonged to the Syrian kingdom. Simon, in effect, is being asked to make recompense for the cities taken by force. The substitution of a financial arrangement instead of returning the cities or the citadel demonstrates that the matter is open to some negotiation. Although the sum of money is high, Simon can probably afford it.

Simon receives the Syrian envoy, Athenobius, in full Hellenistic splendor at his court (v. 32). Again, the picture given suggests that we have traveled far from where Mattathias and his family began in the revolt against the Hellenization of Judaism. Instead of impressing the envoy with his wealth, however, Simon unwittingly makes it clear that he can in fact afford the recompense demanded by Antiochus. His refusal to pay can now be taken as an indication of his intransigence and rebellion.

Simon's formal response, however, appeals to Greek international law which provided, for example, for one's right to retake ancestral lands that had fallen into the hands of others. The Jews' claim to their land is based on divine promises to their ancestors. Likewise, Greek international law provided for conquest of territory outside the ancestral land through just wars of retribution. Accordingly, Simon argues that the citizens of Joppa and Gazara were doing harm to the Jews (v. 35), and that is why those cities were taken. His willingness to pay a mere tenth of what Antiochus demands as recompense is perhaps an attempt to show that the Jews are willing to make some concessions in the negotiations. On the other hand, the amount is so small that its offer seems to indicate defiance.

The Syrian response is anger. Antiochus appoints Cendebeus as commanding officer of the coastal region to succeed Simon, thereby in effect removing him from office. Cendebeus is also sent to Judea and Jerusalem to prepare for an attack on the Jewish people, while Antiochus himself continues to pursue Trypho. (Trypho died eventually at Apamea, a Phoenician city.) The situation described in verses 40-41 reminds us of earlier days when the Maccabees fought the Syrians and the Hellenists in the heart of Judea. The peace and security that Simon seemed to have achieved have been short-lived.

16:1-10 John Hyrcanus attacks the Syrians. The narrative is nearing its end. Simon, the last of the Maccabean brothers to rule over the Jewish people, is getting too old to lead the troops into battle. He passes on the Maccabean military leadership to his sons Judas and John (Hyrcanus), while retaining other power and authority (v. 3). John attacks Cendebeus with a large army and with cavalry as well, the first reference to cavalry in the Maccabean narrative. Although Judas is wounded in battle, John is victorious and brings peace to the land once again.

16:11-17 Simon and his two sons are murdered. We are now introduced to Simon's son-in-law, Ptolemy, son of Abubus. Ptolemy's name might be a surprise even among the in-laws of the Maccabees. The name Abubus is a Hellenized form of a Semitic name. We have become familiar with Maccabean behavior, which so closely parallels and resembles Hellenistic leaders' actions—their drinking parties, their mistresses, and their tendency to eliminate rivals. This latter tendency emerges in Ptolemy, who decides to succeed his father-in-law and become an ally of Antiochus VII.

Ptolemy invites Simon, Judas, and Mattathias to his home at Jericho and provides a sumptuous banquet for them. One might expect Jewish hospitality and table fellowship, but instead there is treachery and assassination. Simon's death is described very briefly and without comment (v. 16). He joins his brothers in an ignominious death—dying while drunk at the hand of his own son-in-law. We do not know how many Jewish people supported Simon, but a return to Syrian vassalage and taxation probably would not have been very acceptable to them. This may explain why Ptolemy writes to Antiochus and requests troops to help him in ruling the country.

16:18-24 Conclusion. Ptolemy has a traitor in his own midst. Someone warns John of what has happened to his father and brothers and of Ptolemy's intention to have him murdered as well. John has his would-be assassins killed and returns to Jerusalem before Ptolemy can arrive there. The rest of the story is merely summarized in our narrative. We learn that John also became high priest. The book ends on a note similar to that found so often in the books of Kings, referring the reader to the chronicles of John's pontificate.

The book ends somewhat abruptly. The Maccabees have clearly been considered heroes by the author. However, the way the book is composed may provide a clue as to the author's final verdict. Most of the songs of praise about the brothers come at the beginning of their respective narratives rather than at the end. All three brothers died because of treachery. All three fully and freely engaged in Hellenistic diplomacy and became more and more Hellenistic in their ways. One wonders whether the author is not saying that, although they did great deeds on behalf of the nation and had great potential for leadership, there was a flaw in each of their characters. Most of what they gained was soon lost.

On the other hand, Jewish independence became a reality under John Hyrcanus, who seems to have dreamed of restoring the Davidic-Solomonic empire. Perhaps this is what prompted the author of 1 Maccabees to tell the story of the Maccabees' heroism.

2 MACCABEES

Alphonse P. Spilly, C.PP.S.

INTRODUCTION

This book, originally written in Greek, is said to be a summary of a five-volume work written by Jason of Cyrene (2 Macc 2:23). Although it is difficult to date the work, it may be from the reign of John Hyrcanus (129–104 B.C.E.) or later, but before the arrival of Pompey in 63 B.C.E. The work differs from 1 Maccabees in many ways, but significantly in its not being pro-Maccabean or pro-Hasmonean. Because some of its main tenets were contrary to the policies of John Hyrcanus, some date the book to the early years of his reign, a time when the author might have tried to influence a policy debate. Although it might well have been written in Jerusalem (because of its emphasis and propaganda regarding the temple), some would place its origins in Egypt, and more specifically in Alexandria (in part, because of its occasional confusion of Palestinian geography). It may have been written as a corrective to 1 Maccabees (or vice versa). The two books clearly have different purposes and different points of view and thereby complement each other.

The theology of 2 Maccabees

From the prologue to the epilogue, the book's primary concern is with the temple in Jerusalem. It covers a period of the Hellenistic age when the temple experienced profanation, purification and restoration, and renewed attacks, primarily during the reigns of Antiochus IV and his son. The temple is a symbol of what happens to the nation as a whole: the people suffer persecution, followed by liberation and restoration.

The book's theology is primarily Deuteronomic: sin leads to punishment, repentance leads to salvation. Sin means a failure to observe the law, and it breaks the covenantal relationship between God and the people. One of the limitations of this theology is that it has no explanation for innocent suffering and can lead one to think that all suffering is a punishment for sin.

Unlike 1 Maccabees, this book sees the main problems as beginning within the Jewish community. Individuals, including high priests, introduce Hellenistic ways into Judea, Jerusalem, and even the temple—practices that are considered incompatible with the authentic exercise of Jewish religion. The sins of these few bring God's punishment on the community, symbolized especially in the profanation of the temple and experienced in the proscription of Jewish religion.

The reader encounters martyrs here, those especially singled out as models of perseverance and fidelity to the law and religion. Persecution is God's way of purifying the people because of the sin that has been found in their midst. It is not simply punishment but discipline or correction. Remaining faithful during persecution, even to the point of giving one's life, has important effects on the course of events and hastens the people's restoration.

The Gentiles also play an important role in this book. In a manner well known within the Deuteronomic tradition, they become the instruments of God's punishment. However, as is also the case in that same tradition, they frequently become arrogant and step beyond their role as God's instruments to challenge divine authority and power. This results in their fall. The higher they attempt to raise themselves in their arrogance, the lower they seem to fall.

What underlies the theology of this book is the divine control of events. If the Gentiles are mere instruments of God's punishment, then leaders such as Judas are mere agents of God's salvation. Before each major confrontation, Judas prays with the people for divine protection; victory is always attributed to God. Frequently heavenly manifestations and mysterious figures appear to bring about the victory or at least to guide and encourage the people.

The theological viewpoint of the author controls the unfolding of the narrative. Where this calls for modification of historical events, the author does not hesitate to gloss over unpleasant facts or simply to change the presentation of the facts. Whereas 1 Maccabees at times admits that Judas occasionally lost a battle, he does not lose any ground in 2 Maccabees after the rebellion has begun. Characterization is done, not on the basis of historical facts known about the actors in this drama, but in terms of the demands of the author's theological bias. Enemies are archvillains, and heroes and heroines are also much bigger than life. This gives some of the major episodes in the book their legendary quality.

The relevance of 2 Maccabees

The stark nationalism of the book, its earthiness and violence, its near delight in gory details, and its simplistic theology of retribution may not attract the reader to return often to this narrative for spiritual reading. However, there is something valuable in its theology of martyrdom for a world that experiences so much oppression of individual and religious freedoms. The martyrs provide us with striking examples of courage in the face of immoral coercion and of the willingness to sacrifice even life itself rather than deny something as sacred as human and religious rights.

OUTLINE OF 2 MACCABEES

1:1–2:32	Introduction
3:1-40	Part I: Heliodorus
4:1–10:9	Part II: Profanation and Restoration of the Temple
	A. Profanation and Persecution (4:1–7:42)
	B. Restoration (8:1–10:9)
10:10–15:36	Part III: Defense of the Temple
	A. Events Under Antiochus V (10:10–13:26)
	B. Final Defeat of Nicanor (14:1–15:36)
15:37-39	Epilogue

COMMENTARY

INTRODUCTION

2 Macc 1:1–2:32

The first two chapters of 2 Maccabees provide an introduction to the thought of the book with two letters and the author's own prologue.

1:1-10a Letter of 124 B.C.E. The Jewish people in Palestine are writing to their coreligionists in Egypt, primarily about the observance of the feast of the rededication of the temple (Hanukkah). The dating of the letter (v. 10) is significant in the history of Egyptian Jews because it was in 124 B.C.E. that Ptolemy VIII (Euergetes II) and his sister Cleopatra II agreed to end their civil war. The Jewish populace in Egypt had supported Cleopatra and might have needed some encouragement in the face of possible retaliation by Ptolemy VIII. The reference to a "time of adversity" in verse 5 might refer to this specific historical context.

The first six verses contain a typical greeting and prayer for the welfare of the addressees. Noteworthy are the senders of the letter—no high priest, Sanhedrin (senate), or member of the Maccabean family is mentioned. This may be in keeping with a tendency within the book to downplay leadership (with the exception of Judas Maccabeus) and to highlight the common people, who are the real heroes and heroines of the book.

The religious content of the letter centers on God's covenant with the patriarchs of Israel. God's "remembering" this special relationship with the people is not so much a matter of divine memory as God's continuing commitment on behalf of the people—not only those in Palestine but those in Egypt as well. This divine commitment includes rescuing them in their present distress.

The covenantal relationship also has implications for the people's behavior: they are to observe the Torah, the law, the manifestation of God's will for the people. Even their capacity for observing the law is attributed to God's gift. There may be a subtle hint in verse 5 that the reason for their present distress is their sinfulness, but this is not clear.

The next part of the letter (vv. 7-8) alludes to an earlier letter, sent in 143 B.C.E., which chronicled their problems with Jason, a high priest who bought the office from the Seleucid king. Jason and his associates rebelled and brought violence and destruction to the land, as 2 Maccabees will detail later. Prayer led to God's rescuing the people from these calamities.

The letter ends with an exhortation to celebrate Hanukkah, called here the feast of Booths because of its resemblance to that great feast commemorating the years of wilderness wandering after liberation from the slavery of Egypt and its Pharaoh.

This letter may at first seem a strange introduction to a book, but it outlines themes that will run throughout the ensuing narrative: the attacks against Jerusalem and God's rescue of the people. The festival that is to be celebrated is the rededication of the temple, and the rest of the book will continue to focus our attention on that sanctuary. The theology is, as we have noted, basically Deuteronomic: sin leads to punishment, but repentance to salvation.

1:10b–2:18 Letter of 164 B.C.E. The focus of this second letter is also the temple and the feast of Hanukkah. In this letter both the Sanhedrin (senate) and Judas Maccabeus are included among the senders, but the people themselves retain the first place in the greeting. Aristobulus may be a second-century B.C.E. Jewish philosopher who lived in Alexandria and whose writings have survived as fragments preserved in the writings of early Christian writers. He was at the court of Ptolemy VI and, according to this letter, was a member of the high priestly line.

The allusion to historical events in verses 11-12 is vague, although verses 13-16 refer to the death of Antiochus at the temple of Nanea. The author seems to be referring to Antiochus IV, although it was Antiochus III who died in a raid against a temple. This family, at any rate, was known for its raiding of temples. The pretext for the visit to the temple was the ceremonial marriage of the king with the goddess of fertility, but the real intention, according to this author, was his greed for money. This motif will reappear later in the book. The priests at the temple seemingly were aware of the purpose of the king's visit, and became responsible for his death and that of his associates.

Verse 17 contains the moral of the story: this is how God deals with the wicked, especially those who attack temples. The next part of the letter contains five subdivisions, connected primarily by association of ideas rather than by logical development.

Verses 18-36 demonstrate the continuity between the temple of Nehemiah and that of Solomon through the telling of a legend, according to which the fire used for sacrifices in Solomon's temple was hidden at the time of the temple's destruction in 587 B.C.E. and turned to liquid. Nehemiah directed the priests to find the liquid and, in actions that resemble those of Elijah on Mount Carmel (see 1 Kgs 18:30-39), ignited the sacrifices through the power of the sun enflaming the liquid, identified as naphtha. We know, however, that the temple was rebuilt by Zerubbabel many years before Nehemiah arrived on the scene. The point of the story is less historical accuracy than theological highlighting of the importance of the temple in the eyes of the Lord.

The prayer recited on this occasion is notable for its numerous attributes of God, who is designated as the only king of Israel (v. 24). The prayer asks two things of this beneficent God: acceptance of sacrifice and restoration of the people (that is, liberation from the Gentiles who oppress them). This language is appropriate, given the date of the letter—a year or so after the writing of the Book of Daniel.

The next section (2:1-8) centers attention on Jeremiah, who is reputed to have been the one who told the priests to hide the fire in the first place. Although the letter of Jeremiah to the exiles in Jer 29 does not mention the fire, it does mention the observance of the law and contains warnings against idolatry (as in 2 Macc 2:2). The legend continues with a description of Jeremiah's alleged journey to Mount Sinai, where he hid the tent, the ark, and the altar of incense until such time as the Lord would reveal to the people where they could find these objects. The expectation of the glory of the Lord manifesting itself in the cloud (2:8) would remind the Jewish readers of the Lord's presence in the wilderness and especially at Sinai, and also at the dedication of Solomon's temple.

The mention of Moses and Solomon in 2:8 introduces another section of this letter (2:9-12), comparing the roles of these two leaders. Both prayed and fire is said to have come from the heavens to light the sacrifice, just as happened with Nehemiah. This led to the celebration of a dedicatory feast for a whole week—similar to the feast of Hanukkah.

The mention of celebrating a feast for eight days leads back to the days of Nehemiah, who is said to have collected some of the scriptures just as Judas Maccabeus is alleged to have done (2:13-14). These scriptures are made available to the addressees of the letter (2:15).

The last part of the letter perhaps contains its real purpose: notice of the celebration of Hanukkah, celebrating God's deliverance of the people (presumably through Judas Maccabeus' ability to take control of the temple, to purify it, and to reestablish Jewish worship there). However, Judas is not mentioned as the agent of God here; instead, God alone is said to be the one who has had mercy on the people and brought them back together so that they could worship God in the temple. This is consistent with the theological emphasis of the book. Whereas 1 Maccabees highlighted the human agency of the Maccabean family in achieving independence, 2 Maccabees insists upon the ultimate causality of divine favor and intervention.

2:19-32 Author's preface. The author now presents his own introduction, noting that this is the story of the Maccabees, but also of heavenly manifestations. Emphasis is put on the temple and altar once again. It is clear that God has accomplished all this (2:22). The author also identifies his source, a work by Jason of Cyrene, condensed in the present version.

It is remarkable that a book that is so preoccupied with Jewish matters and opposed to Hellenizing efforts is so consciously written with Hellenistic historiographical principles! The analogies of festive banquets and the adornment of houses are also more Hellenistic than Jewish. There is even what approaches humorous self-consciousness at the end of the preface (2:32). With this we are ready to begin the narrative proper.

PART I: HELIODORUS

2 Macc 3:1-40

The introduction has focused attention on the temple and God's protection on its behalf, and has also promised to tell about heavenly manifestations. The story of Heliodorus is a dramatic narrative that delivers on this promise. Although there is a historical core to the story, it is told with great literary license in order to highlight the theological viewpoint of the author.

Events center on two Jews: Onias III, the high priest, and Simon, a wicked schemer. There are also two Hellenistic characters: the greedy king Antiochus and his minister Heliodorus. The story follows the basic outline of a well-known literary type from this period in which a deity defends his or her temple with whatever means are necessary, and so commentators often refer to this narrative as a blend of historical information and pious legend.

3:1-6 Onias versus Simon. Jerusalem is described as living in "perfect peace" because of two factors: the high priest Onias is pious, and the people observe the Torah. Antiochus III was generous in donating sums of money to temples within his domain, and we have no reason to think that Jerusalem would fare any differently. The money donated by the king was meant to underwrite the temple's expensive sacrificial system. However, this royal donation is not the money which will figure in the story that follows.

Simon, the brother of Menelaus (whom the reader will meet in the next chapter), is an official of some standing in Jerusalem. It is not clear what his quarrel with Onias was (v. 4), but there is some evidence that Onias was pro-Ptolemaic (pro-Egyptian) while Simon was pro-Seleucid (pro-Syrian). The politics of the day may lie behind this narrative, as is the case with so many others in the Maccabean books.

Simon's subsequent actions would be considered treasonous as well as illegal by upright Jews and Gentiles. His approach to the governor may be seen as an attempt to ingratiate himself with the Syrian authorities. Antiochus III needs finances to pay a tribute levied against his kingdom by Rome. Simon alleges that there are excess funds in abundance in the Jerusalem temple (v. 6). He says that not all of the funds are needed for the sacrificial system and that the king could have easy access to them. (Later in the narrative we will learn the nature of these excess funds.) The effect of Simon's treachery will be seen in the subsequent narratives in 2 Maccabees. Whereas 1 Maccabees suggests that the Jews' difficulties were primarily caused by the Hellenists, 2 Maccabees focuses the blame on wicked people among the Jewish populace.

3:7-14 The mission of Heliodorus. The governor reports the financial good news to the king, who immediately sends one of his ministers to appropriate the excess funds for royal use. What follows makes it clear that the major difficulties between Jerusalem and Antioch have not yet developed, and relationships between the two are primarily cordial. Heliodorus' subterfuge (taking an indirect route) may have been designed to prevent any depositors from withdrawing their money before his arrival at the temple.

Heliodorus is direct with the high priest, asking him about the excess revenues in the temple treasury (v. 9). Onias' response is probably accurate: some of the funds have been collected to help care for widows and orphans, as Jewish law prescribes in so many places (see, for example, Deut 16:12-13), and some of the money has been deposited by a certain Hyrcanus, son of Tobias.

During the Hellenistic period, the Tobiads were a powerful and wealthy Jewish family. Their initial holdings were in Transjordan, but they also had residences in Jerusalem and Alexandria. They were pro-Hellenist merchants who were primarily pro-Egyptian. During the course of their history, they were often at odds with the high priestly family of the Oniads, although that does not seem to figure in the present narrative. The Hyrcanus of this narrative had earlier collected taxes for the Ptolemies and had remained pro-Egyptian after the Seleucids had taken control of Palestine (after 198 B.C.E.). During this latter period he had maintained a territory in the Transjordan almost independent of Seleucid rule, and evidently had deposited his earnings and family fortune in the Jerusalem temple for safekeeping. He and Onias III probably shared pro-Egyptian sympathies.

At stake in the Heliodorus incident are some legal questions. Because Hyrcanus is pro-Egyptian, he can be considered a rebel by the Seleucids, and his rights could be considered nil. On the other hand, Onias appeals to both Jewish and Greek law regarding the inviolability of a sanctuary and the safety of any funds deposited there. Heliodorus, rather than trying to sort out the legal moral dilemma, relies instead on his orders from the king (v. 13) and makes preparations to defraud the temple. In the dramatic account that follows, the reader may have recourse not only to law but also to the theology of this book: God will defend the temple. The only question that remains is how it will be done.

3:15-21 The reaction of the faithful Jews. With great dramatic strokes, the author describes the impact Heliodorus' mission and intent have on the Jewish faithful. They are helpless in resisting Heliodorus and his royal mandate, but they turn to God with prayer and gestures of mourning and lament. Can God fail to hear the prayers of a people in so much anguish?

3:22-34 God's response to Heliodorus and the Jews. When Heliodorus approaches the temple with his associates and retinue, God is manifested in such a powerful way that Heliodorus' associates are thrown into panic and fainting. A mysterious rider on a magnificent horse charges Heliodorus, and the rider's two companions whip Heliodorus, who falls to the ground, seemingly unconscious (v. 27). His bold approach to the temple precincts ends dramatically with his being ignominiously carried away on a stretcher, utterly helpless. The Jewish people change their prayer from lament to praise at this mighty manifestation of God's power and protection.

The story is not yet over, however, in accordance with this literary genre. Fearful for his death, Heliodorus' associates intercede with Onias, asking him to pray for Heliodorus to the God who has so awesomely struck him down. Perhaps they are already worrying about what they are going to explain to the king about Heliodorus' condition, presuming the king might be somewhat skeptical if they describe what occurred.

Onias' motives in what follows may be equally pious and political. How will he explain to the king that an important minister on an equally important mission has met with such grief in Jerusalem? While Onias prays on behalf of Heliodorus, the young men appear once again to Heliodorus with a message of salvation (because of Onias' prayer) and a mandate to proclaim God's power and majesty. They disappear as mysteriously as they appeared.

3:35-40 The witness of Heliodorus. Heliodorus' offering of sacrifice is not against temple practice. Although Heliodorus bears witness to the power of the God of the Jews as commanded, the king understandably remains skeptical, for he has not shared Heliodorus' experience. The king, by asking who might be better qualified for such a mission (v. 37), appears to accuse Heliodorus of incompetence. Heliodorus replies with some irony: send your worst enemy or someone who plots against your government and he will be appropriately punished. The irony stems from the fact that later in history Heliodorus *did* plot against Antiochus and brought him to his death. The narrative ends with a suitable summary statement about the "power" that is present in Jerusalem, power that will destroy whatever or whoever tries to harm the temple or the people.

PART II: PROFANATION AND RESTORATION OF THE TEMPLE

2 Macc 4:1–10:9

A. Profanation and Persecution

2 Macc 4:1–7:42

The events described in 4:1–7:42 cover the period from 175 to 167 B.C.E. and tell the story of the assault of evil on the Jewish nation and their religion.

4:1-6 Simon continues to oppose Onias. Simon accuses the high priest Onias of treason, a charge that the author of 2 Maccabees is quick to deny. Onias proceeds to the Syrian court to defend himself, probably in the eyes of both the Seleucid king and his own people. His mission is aborted, however, by the king's death.

4:7-22 Jason purchases the high priesthood. With the accession of Antiochus IV Epiphanes to the Seleucid throne, Onias' own brother, Jason, promises the king money in return for being appointed high priest and introducing Hellenistic practices into Jerusalem. The gymnasium and youth club were basic institutions of Greek education. Enrolling the men of Jerusalem as Antiochene citizens probably meant a shift of power to Jason's supporters. All these actions demonstrated a shift away from Jewish values and practices to a Hellenistic way of life.

At the new gymnasium Jason introduced Jewish youths to Hellenistic training. The Greeks exercised naked, wearing only broad-brimmed hats to shield their heads from the hot sun. The author's lack of esteem for Jason is found in verse 13, where he is described as "outrageous," "wicked," "ungodly," and "pseudo-high priest." The temple priests are themselves caught up in Hellenistic fashions and ways. There will be a price to pay for abandoning Jewish practices, especially worship.

The competitive games played every five years were similar to the Olympiad, and Jason, with his predilection for matters Hellenistic, sends a delegation to Tyre. It is not clear how he understands the offering of sacrifice to Hercules, but the delegation has qualms about this and instead donates the money to the building of Antiochus' fleet.

Later Antiochus himself visits Jerusalem, where he is received with great pomp and celebration. This was quite possible because Onias was in exile and Hyrcanus was dead; hence the pro-Ptolemaic party was powerless.

4:23-29 Menelaus supplants Jason. Jason makes a tactical error by sending Simon's brother Menelaus to deliver the promised money to the king. Menelaus betrays Jason by outbidding him for the office and supplants him as high priest. Jason had not proved himself to be a loyal brother to Onias, but at least he was of the high priestly family. Menelaus is not of the high priestly family and can be expected to encounter opposition among the Jewish populace. Further opposition might also be expected because of the high rate of tribute promised by Menelaus. The date is 172 or 171 B.C.E.

Jason becomes a fugitive in the Transjordan (Onias is presumably still in Syria), and Menelaus cannot make good on the money promised to the king. Accordingly, he is summoned to appear before the king.

4:30-38 Andronicus murders Onias. When some important cities in the northwest part of his kingdom rebel, Antiochus marches to pacify them, leaving Andronicus in charge. This man had assassinated the son of Seleucus IV, making it possible for Antiochus IV to succeed to the throne. This perhaps helps to explain the power he wields in this narrative. Menelaus lives up to his wicked reputation and, after stealing some golden vessels from the temple, gives them to Andronicus (v. 32). He also sells some along the way, but we are not told what he did with the money.

Onias III, still in exile in Syria, denounces Menelaus' actions and implicates Andronicus in the deed—the one who is acting in the place of the king! Onias, realizing the seriousness of his accusations, takes refuge in a sanctuary, albeit a Greek one. (Jerusalem, the nearest Jewish sanctuary, was inaccessible.) Menelaus and Andronicus conspire, and Andronicus treacherously persuades Onias to leave his place of refuge, whereupon he is immediately killed (v. 35). The author is quick to point out that this terrible deed prompts a response of outrage among both Jews and Gentiles. Even Antiochus is said to have been remorseful and angry over this action. At any rate, by executing Andronicus, Antiochus also removes a possible threat to his own throne. The author points out that the punishment fits the crime.

4:39-50 Menelaus plots evil against his fellow Jews. The scene shifts back to Jerusalem, where Lysimachus, with the connivance of Menelaus, further plunders the temple of its golden vessels. The people begin to riot and are opposed with Hellenistic armed force. In the battle that ensues, the people are victorious and kill the perpetrator near the treasury, where he committed the crime.

The people bring charges against Menelaus. He in turn promises a bribe to the new governor, Dorymenes (v. 45), who promptly intercedes with the king on Menelaus' behalf. Menelaus is acquitted and his accusers are punished instead. Menelaus remains in power, but the reader will have to ask how long it will be before he is punished for his wickedness, especially his crimes against the temple.

5:1-10 Jason dies in exile. Antiochus invades Egypt in 169 and again in 168 B.C.E. The appearance of mysterious horsemen in the sky for forty days indicates that an event of special importance is about to happen. The motif is frequently found in Greek and Roman literature. Here it would be interpreted as a portent that God is about to act. Although the people pray, hoping that the omen will prove to be a favorable one, that is not how the narrative unfolds.

It was not unusual in ancient (or modern) times for people to attempt rebellion upon the death of a sovereign. If Antiochus had actually died, Jason's acts would not take on the character of treason, because there would be no legitimate king. If that were true, it would also imply that Menelaus was no longer the high priest until reconfirmed in office by a subsequent king.

However, Jason's assumptions are incorrect, and Antiochus is very much alive. Before he finds that out, Jason attacks Jerusalem to regain the high priesthood (v. 5). We are not informed of the role of the people in the matter, but Menelaus takes refuge in the citadel. Jason slaughters his fellow citizens, but is unsuccessful in the venture and has to flee for his life. For a time he becomes a man without a country. His first place of refuge is the Transjordan, but there he is called to account by Aretas, the king of the Nabateans. He might have expected to find refuge eventually in Egypt because he was anti-Seleucid at this point, but he does not find a home there. Eventually he takes up residence in Sparta, where he eventually dies and is buried as an exile. Again the punishment fits the crime.

5:11-27 Antiochus IV attacks the Jews. Even though it is doubtful that the majority of people in Jerusalem defended Menelaus or sided with Jason, neither do they seem to have accepted Menelaus as their high priest. To Antiochus this means rebellion, and he moves swiftly to put it down. He is described in somewhat exaggerated terms to underline his ruthlessness and his pride.

The depth of Antiochus' arrogance is demonstrated by his decision to enter the temple precincts, something we know from ancient historians as historically accurate (v. 15). The traitor Menelaus, who should be expected to know and enforce the Jewish law regarding foreigners' being forbidden to enter the temple, instead leads the way and serves as a guide! Antiochus dares to lay his impure hands on sacred vessels and to remove them for his own use. The actions remind the reader of the impious activities of Nebuchadnezzar and Belshazzar in the Book of Daniel.

Antiochus is contrasted with Heliodorus (5:18); the latter was merely on an inspection tour when he was flogged by the mysterious horsemen. Antiochus could have expected much worse treatment for his looting of sacred vessels—had it not been for the sins of the people that led to this event. The appearance of the heavenly horsemen at the beginning of this chapter is now clear: they came to show that God is about to punish his people for the sins connected with Hellenization, especially those committed by Jason, Menelaus, and their followers.

This is not a new biblical theme. Earlier the Assyrians and the Babylonians were described as being the instruments of God's punishment because of the people's sins. Nevertheless, the Assyrian and Babylonian kings often thought that they were acting on their own, as does Antiochus, and eventually they were brought down because of their pride and arrogance. The reader can expect the same fate to befall Antiochus, but that will not happen until chapter 9.

The author makes clear why, despite the theme of divine protection of the temple, Antiochus is successful against the temple and the inhabitants of Jerusalem (vv. 17-20). Divine protection of the temple is conditioned by the people's observance of the law and their fidelity to the covenant relationship. When the broken relationship is restored, the temple will return to its former glory.

Antiochus is described as being so high and mighty that he thinks he can sail on land and walk on the sea (v. 21). When he leaves Jerusalem and Judea, he leaves behind tyrants such as Philip, Andronicus, and Menelaus. The reference to Mount Gerizim (v. 23) means the Samaritans. Perhaps the overbearing attitude of a governor like Philip caused the people to rebel once again; otherwise it is not clear why Antiochus sends Apollonius to punish the people further.

Apollonius deals treacherously with the populace, seeming to be peaceable until the sabbath, when he parades his men through the streets; those who leave the relative safety of their homes to view the parade are then massacred. The reader is now introduced to Judas Maccabeus, who escapes to the wilderness with a few companions (v. 27). The date is probably early 167 B.C.E. There is no suggestion in 2 Maccabees that Judas does not observe the sabbath (contrary to what 1 Maccabees states). Here there is only a brief mention of Judas, but the keen reader will remember that Judas is waiting in the wings for his day of vengeance on the Hellenists. For now the deliverance of the people remains in the future. Things will get worse before they get better.

6:1-5 Antiochus profanes the temple. Antiochus III had granted the Jews freedom to worship in their own manner and according to their own law. Antiochus IV in effect now abrogates the earlier decree. Although it is not clear exactly what Antiochus has in mind, it is clear that the Jews are no longer free to worship as they wish. The first change is profaning the temple and dedicating it to Zeus, the head of the Greek pantheon. Introducing prostitution into the temple precincts would recall for the Jews their past history when sacred prostitution, an important part of Canaanite ritual, was introduced into the temple despite the repeated condemnation of the prophets. Because it was considered to be one of the reasons for the downfall of Jerusalem in 587 B.C.E., verses 4-5 would have special meaning for the Jewish people.

6:6-11 Antiochus proscribes Jewish practices. The next changes are prohibitions regarding the celebration of the sabbath and Jewish feasts. Then the Jews are forced to observe Hellenistic customs relating to the monthly celebration of the king's birthday and participation in Dionysiac processions. These decrees are adopted by other cities in the area as well. According to verse 10, circumcision is outlawed, and two women who have circumcised their sons are killed. Those hiding in caves are burned to death because they do not defend themselves on a sabbath.

6:12-17 A theology of persecution. The reader was advised earlier that the reason for the ills that befell Jerusalem and the people was that the people had sinned by engaging in various Hellenizing activities. The author now explains that the punishment was not meant to be destructive but corrective, like a parent disciplining a child. In effect, the author states that God gives other nations enough rope to hang themselves; with Israel, God punishes them before they reach the fullness of their sinfulness so that they can then experience God's mercy. The assertion that God does not abandon the covenanted people is found throughout Jewish tradition.

6:18-31 Eleazar becomes a martyr. The narrative now includes a typical account of a martyr's death. These verses describe Eleazar's joyful acceptance of death rather than doing anything—even something trivial—against God's will, the dialogue between the person and the tormentors, his sufferings, his perseverance to death, and the reactions of the tormentors.

There may be an implied contrast between the Eleazar of 2 Maccabees and the Mattathias of 1 Maccabees. Both are priests, and both assess the persecution for its true intent. But whereas Mattathias defies the king's orders and defends the right to observe Torah, Eleazar refuses to violate the law and instead goes to his death. (There are also interesting parallels between this story of Eleazar and that of Socrates.)

In the course of the narrative, Eleazar seems to believe that judgment or punishment takes place after death (v. 26), but he does not mention a resurrection of the body. Besides keeping his integrity before the Lord, Eleazar hopes that his witness will provide a helpful example to youth. The next episode in the narrative demonstrates youth's response to Eleazar's wish.

7:1-42 Seven youths and their mothers become martyrs. This narrative is skillfully written, with each character providing another element of the theological argument in favor of martyrdom. The number seven, in Jewish tradition, symbolizes perfection; accordingly, the reader may look upon this as a "perfect" family. The story, despite its gruesome details, is meant to edify. It underlines the premise that observance of the law is more important than life itself. The presence of the king adds further import to the story.

Each of the seven sons presents a part of the theological argument: (1) it is better to die than to transgress the law; (2) the king may take their lives, but God will raise them up again; (3) the king may dismember them, but God will restore their limbs; (4) they will be restored to life, but the king will not be restored; (5) God will not forsake the people but will torment the king and his nation; (6) they are suffering because they have sinned as a people.

The mother exhorts her sons to remain faithful by recalling for them God's power to create and to restore life (v. 23). When the king intercedes on behalf of the youngest boy, the mother returns to the theme of God's creation and re-creation, arguing that if God can make the whole universe and humanity out of nothing God can also restore life. The last son then sums up all the preceding arguments, adding a new one at the same time: the martyrs' deaths play a role in bringing to an end the divine discipline that the people are undergoing. Martyrdom makes a difference in the life of the people. In the end the mother also becomes a martyr. Eleazar's example has been followed, and it is time to move on in the narrative to demonstrate the effects of the martyrdoms.

B. Restoration

2 Macc 8:1–10:9

In rapid succession Judas Maccabeus defeats an important adversary, Antiochus IV dies a horrible death, and the people purify the temple and Jerusalem. God brings this about, partly because of the faithful witness of the martyrs. The text moves from the assault of evil to its elimination.

8:1-36 Judas defeats Nicanor. We are at the midpoint of the book. The narrative again is skillfully written; the author does not give many details of the battle in order to highlight his theological emphases: God's help in achieving the victory, the disposal of the booty, and Nicanor's fate.

Judas first gathers associates and prays to God, asking for God's favor on the people, their temple, their city, and the blood of the martyrs (vv. 2-3). Verse 5 makes it clear that the tide has turned—God's anger has changed to mercy. The Gentiles and Hellenizers will be helpless now. Judas attacks cities of the Hellenizers and gains a reputation that attracts the attention of Philip, the commissioner in Jerusalem. He contacts Ptolemy, the son of Dorymenes (4:45) and the governor of the area, requesting assistance. Ptolemy in turn sends Nicanor, a skilled general and trusted official of the royal court, to put down Judas' rebellion.

According to 2 Maccabees, the Seleucids still owe considerable tribute to the Romans, dating from an agreement in 190 B.C.E. (It is possible that the tribute had been paid in full by 173 B.C.E., and that the author of 2 Maccabees is mistaken.) At any rate, Nicanor plans to raise money by selling the Jewish populace into slavery (v. 10). Although in 1 Maccabees the slave-traders take the initiative and follow Nicanor's army like vultures, in this narrative Nicanor invites them because he is presumptuous about a victory over the Jews.

Although some of Judas' troops desert at the advance of the enemy army, the rest prepare for battle. Selling whatever property that is left, they show their determination and make themselves less vulnerable to later reprisals. Judas sums up their theological position before the battle succinctly: the Gentiles trust in weapons and strategy, whereas the Jews simply trust in an all-powerful God (v. 18). He further recalls the famous defeat of Sennacherib (recounted in many places in the Old Testament; see, for example, 2 Kgs 19:35-36) and another battle not known from existing sources—both of which demonstrate what happens when the people trust in God rather than in themselves.

The battle is described in a single verse (v. 24), but the accumulation and distribution of booty receive more attention. First of all, scrupulously observing the sabbath, Judas' men do not pursue the enemy as far as they might have otherwise. After observing the sabbath, they distribute the booty not only to the soldiers who had participated in the battle (as was the custom) but also to the widows, orphans, and those who had been tormented (perhaps referring to the surviving members of the martyrs' families). Taking care of the widows and orphans is a key responsibility in the law.

Those who persecuted the people receive their deserved punishments: those who set fire to the temple gates are themselves destroyed by fire; Nicanor, who sought to enslave the people, flees the country dressed like a runaway slave. Verse 35 describes his defeat with sarcasm: he was "eminently successful"—in destroying his own army! He who had promised to enslave the Jews has to acknowledge them as champions instead—because of their observance of the law. The tide has clearly turned.

9:1-19 God punishes Antiochus IV. This narrative follows the typical story about the death of those who set themselves against God, especially with arrogance. The description of the death of Antiochus IV at this point in the narrative differs somewhat from that in chapter 1, but its development and details enable the author to make the appropriate points that fit the overall theology of the book.

Although there is no way of confirming the story that Antiochus attempted to despoil a temple in Persepolis, such an action would not be out of character for this family. As he heads home in disgrace after his unsuccessful raid on the Persian temple (vv. 1-3), he learns of Nicanor's defeat and plans to achieve a definitive victory against the Jewish people. He drives his chariot with determination, but God's condemnation rides with him (v. 4)! He is struck down with a terrible malady, experiencing great pains in his bowels (again the punishment fits the crime). That does not deter him from his plans against God's people, but then he is thrown from his chariot, suffering racking pain throughout his body. Like Heliodorus, despite his great pride and arrogance, he is ignominiously carried away on a stretcher, helpless. His condition worsens with the onslaught of worms and putrefaction. The turning point is described in verse 11: he begins a personal transformation from arrogance to understanding. From this point of the narrative on, it is difficult to verify the historicity of his deathbed conversion. It fits the author's theme well, however, and may be primarily a theological write-up.

What happens next is ironic: Antiochus makes vows to God and writes a surprisingly cordial letter to the Jewish people. However, God will no longer have mercy on him (v. 13). In the end he remains, in the mind of the author, a "murderer and a blasphemer" (v. 28). It is possible to read verses 14-27 as the feeble attempts of Antiochus IV to reverse the inevitable end he is fast approaching. In turn, he promises to set Jerusalem free (despite earlier threats to turn it into a graveyard); to give the Jews full-citizen status (despite earlier judgments that they are not even worth burying); to donate to the temple and restore what had been stolen (despite earlier thefts); and even to become a Jew himself (v. 17)! Like Heliodorus, he is also willing to proclaim the power of God to all. Again, the judgment that frames this part of the narrative is repeated: his promises do not bring any relief from his suffering (v. 18).

Antiochus then composes a supplicating letter to the Jews (vv. 19-27). Jewish gloating over the hideous details of his suffering perhaps gives way to laughter at the words that are said to come from his hand. He addresses them as "esteemed citizens," sends them "hearty greetings and best wishes." Piously he asserts that his hopes lie in heaven (which the reader knows has already condemned him and which will not relent). He tends to gloss over details of his terrible illness, which the reader already knows is serious and nearly unbearable. He speaks of hope for recovery, but commends his son, who, he suggests, will treat the Jews "with mildness and kindness"! Another possible purpose of the letter is to make clear to the reader that the problems Antiochus faces are of his own making. The Jews are good citizens, reliable people who can be trusted.

Antiochus is trying to ingratiate himself with the Jews, according to the letter, and is also attempting to arrange for his successor. According to 1 Maccabees, his son, Antiochus V, was only a boy at this time. Antiochus designated Philip as regent, but Lysias assumed the regency in opposition to Philip (1 Macc 6:12-17).

Antiochus dies in the mountains on foreign soil, while Judas and his associates celebrate in Jerusalem. The archenemy of the temple has been disposed of.

10:1-9 Purification of temple and city. The purification of the temple becomes a symbol of God's mercy, signaling that the period of God's wrath has clearly come to an end. The purification is possible only because of God's help; the providential nature of the action is also alluded to by the notice that the purification takes place on the very anniversary of its defilement.

After restoring the furniture of the temple (v. 3), Judas and his followers pray to God, asking that any future punishment for their sins come directly from God rather than through the mediation of a foreign enemy. Again, the rededication of the temple is compared with the feast of Booths.

This entire section comes to an end in verse 9 with the notification that "such was the end of Antiochus."

PART III: DEFENSE OF THE TEMPLE

2 Macc 10:10–15:36

A. Events Under Antiochus V

2 Macc 10:10–13:26

10:10-13 Lysias becomes commander-in-chief. Although the narrative states that Antiochus V put Lysias in charge of the government and the military, it would be more accurate to say that Lysias made the boy Antiochus king. The first activity under the new regime consists of accusations of treason against Ptolemy Macron, who had treated the Jews with fairness. This possible ally commits suicide. Thus the first section of this narrative opens on an ominous note. The reader will learn that the problems with Hellenization are not over; the temple needs to be defended by Judas and his associates.

10:14-23 Victory over the Idumeans. The Idumeans are harassing the Jews and welcoming fugitives (Hellenizers) from Jerusalem. Responding to these provocations, Judas and his forces attack the Idumeans successfully. When the survivors withdraw to two large towers, Judas leaves some lieutenants, including at least one of his brothers, in charge of besieging the towers. The author of 2 Maccabees dares to write what would not be found in 1 Maccabees: some of Simon Maccabeus' men accept a bribe and commit treason. Judas returns, puts them to death, and successfully completes the siege of the towers.

10:24-38 Judas defeats Timothy. When Timothy approaches Judea with a large force, Judas and his followers pray, as is their custom, before advancing to meet the enemy. After Timothy's forces are overcome, he flees to a stronghold called Gazara (v. 32), which is promptly besieged by Judas. The defenders blaspheme with impunity because of their reliance on the strength of the fortress. Eventually, however, Judas and his associates overcome their resistance and kill Timothy. (However, a Timothy will reappear [see 12:10-25] and fight Judas once again. Presumably it is a different Timothy.) Judas' troops praise and thank God for the victory.

11:1-12 Judas defeats Lysias. The previous attacks were primarily local skirmishes, but now Judas and the main minister of the kingdom engage in battle. Lysias has three objectives in mind in his expedition against Judas: (1) to make Jerusalem a Hellenistic settlement, (2) to levy a tribute or tax against the temple, and (3) to continue to sell the high priesthood to the highest bidder. Although none of this is new in the Maccabean books, at this point in the narrative it demonstrates that the problems of the faithful are far from being over.

Lysias makes the same mistake as his Seleucid predecessors did: he relies on his military might and does not take God's power into consideration. When he begins to besiege Beth-zur, Judas goes to its defense, after having prayed for an angel to help the Jews. He barely leaves Jerusalem when a mysterious horseman appears at the head of the army (v. 8), encouraging Judas' forces. Needless to say, they are once again victorious, and Lysias escapes in shame.

11:13-38 Peace with the Syrians. There follow four letters that purport to give the terms of the treaty arranged between Lysias and the Jewish people (vv. 17-21; 22-26; 27-33; and 34-38). According to the dates given in the letters, three of them are from the reign of Antiochus IV, and only the second letter is from the time of Antiochus V. All the letters may be authentic. Their order and placement at this point in the narrative fit the author's objectives. Antiochus IV was the archenemy of the temple and of the Jews. Conciliatory correspondence is not to be attributed to him but will fit his son's reign.

The intent of the earlier correspondence may have been to undermine Judas' rebellion. The letters might be addressed to the Hellenizing party and those Jews (probably a majority) who had not yet allied themselves with the Maccabees.

The second letter (vv. 22-26), which may be from Antiochus V, is particularly conciliatory. If it is authentic, the reader will wonder what happened in the meantime to break the truce. Perhaps it was the activities of Judas Maccabeus.

The third letter (vv. 27-33) grants a kind of amnesty to those who had rebelled against the proscription of Jewish practices and the forcing of Hellenistic ways. The letter says they acted out of ignorance; the king is clearly not apologizing for the Hellenization process. The reader may wonder whether the recipients of the letter were reassured by the return of

Menelaus, the high priest who was not of a priestly family and who had purchased the office.

The fourth letter (vv. 34-38) is the earliest evidence we have of relations between the Romans and the Jews.

12:1-37 Renewal of hostilities. Although 2 Maccabees goes to great lengths to insist that the Jews want to live in peace, hostilities between the Syrian government and the Jewish people resume. The problems are said to have been caused by some of the local governors and some of the Jews' neighbors. Some of their neighbors may have been fearful that the Maccabean revolt might spread.

The people of Joppa (near present-day Tel Aviv) deceitfully invite some of the Jews for a boat ride and murder them (vv. 3-4). Judas' response is quick and decisive. Although he does not have access to the city itself during his night attack, he destroys the port and boats that are outside the city walls. The people of Jamnia are reported to be considering a similar stratagem, and Judas deals with them in the same way.

The attack by Arabs (12:10-12) is probably geographically displaced. With the help of God once again, Judas is victorious. The battle against Caspin (vv. 13-16) involves themes encountered elsewhere in the book. The inhabitants, relying on the supposed strength of their fortifications, blaspheme. Judas, with the help of God similar to that experienced by Joshua in the battle for Jericho (see Josh 6), overcomes their resistance. A terrible slaughter follows. From this point on, Judas takes the initiative, moving from a defensive to an offensive strategy.

Judas next marches into the Transjordan in search of a certain Timothy, presumably a Syrian military commander (vv. 17-18), but finds that Timothy has already departed from the area. Two of Judas' commanders attack the garrison that Timothy left behind and successfully overcome it (vv. 19-20). Judas continues his pursuit of Timothy, who is accompanied by a large force, and eventually engages him. Once again, despite their overwhelming numerical superiority, the Syrians encounter a mysterious being ("the All-seeing") and flee. Predictably, Judas follows up the rout with slaughter, but Timothy bargains for his freedom and escapes (v. 24).

Judas next marches against Karnion, Ephron, and Scythopolis. The Jews living in the last city testify to their good relations with the citizens of that town, and Judas spares the town (vv. 26-31).

Judas and his soldiers go to Jerusalem for the feast of Pentecost, or feast of Weeks, as it is called in the Hebrew Bible. Afterward they once again take the initiative and march off in search of Gorgias, the governor of Idumea, to the south of Jerusalem. They encounter Gorgias and his army, and a fierce battle ensues. Gorgias escapes capture through the agency of a Thracian mercenary and flees to an Idumean town, Marisa (v. 35). Judas rallies his troops by raising a Hebrew battle cry, perhaps from one of the psalms, and they put the Syrians to flight. Judas retires to a nearby town not far from Marisa, but far enough not to be surprised by an attack on the sabbath. He and his troops purify themselves there and observe the sabbath.

12:38-46 Atonement for the dead. On the day after the sabbath, Judas and his associates prepare to bury those who fell in battle. However, they find forbidden amulets in the clothes of each who died in battle. Whether they wore the amulets because they believed they had special protective qualities or whether they had simply been part of the booty taken during the battle, either action was against the law. The judgment is made that they died because of their sins. This incident resembles the battle at Ai recorded in Josh 7.

The occasion is used to warn the living to avoid such a sin in the future. Judas and his troops pray that the sinful deed be removed, perhaps so that the community would not suffer any further setbacks. However, he then collects money to underwrite an expiatory sacrifice on behalf of those who died in their sins (v. 43). According to the author, Judas was thinking of the resurrection of the dead. Presumably this means that he was praying so that, released from their sins, they would enjoy the rewards of the resurrection with all those who fought on behalf of the Jewish cause.

13:1-2 The Syrians invade Judea again. In the autumn of 163 B.C.E., not quite a year after the rededication of the temple, Antiochus V and Lysias invaded Judea with a very large, well-equipped army. The king was about twelve years old at this time; presumably the invasion was due to complaints about Judas' attacks on the citadel and other offensive activities (see 1 Macc 6:21-27).

13:3-8 The death of Menelaus. With the rededication of the temple under Judas' leadership, Menelaus probably was excluded from functioning as high priest. On the other hand, it is not clear that Antiochus V confirmed him in the high priesthood after the death of his father, Antiochus IV. At any rate, Menelaus wants to return to Jerusalem and resume the privileges of office. God intervenes, and the young king turns against Menelaus (v. 4). The irony in the story is that Menelaus, a leader among the Hellenizers, is executed by the Hellenistic Syrians.

Lysias may have realized that a military solution or a policy of force was not resolving the problems in Judea. He may also have realized that the populace did not consider Menelaus to be fit for the high priesthood because he was not a member of the high priestly family and because of his high-handed manner of carrying out the office. Antiochus V condemns Menelaus to death by asphyxiation. The author of 2 Maccabees once again points out that the punishment fits the crime.

13:9-26 Judas attacks the invading army. Antiochus V is probably unfairly depicted in this narrative, but the Syrian army poses a serious threat to Judea's security. Judas fights on behalf of the country, the temple, and the law. The people prepare for this important battle with prayer, weeping, fasting, and prostrations, in typical Maccabean fashion. Judas moves his troops north of Jerusalem to block access to the city and pitches his camp near Modein, the Maccabean family home (v. 14).

As is often his strategy, Judas attacks at night and begins to rout the Syrians. At dawn he withdraws, and the Seleucid king counterattacks, attempting to draw Judas into battle in another location. Antiochus attacks Beth-zur unsuccessfully, and Judas provides the garrison there with supplies. (According to 1 Macc 6:31, 49-50, Beth-zur capitulated because it did not have adequate supplies. The author of 2 Maccabees overlooks the problems involved and simply presents Judas as a hero in this incident.)

After a second unsuccessful attack, the king turns his attention directly upon Judas. Verse 23 may refer to Antiochus' attack on the temple (1 Macc 6:51-52). But internal affairs of the kingdom turn the king's attention back to Antioch, where Philip is said to have been left in charge and to be in rebellion. This is probably not true, because Antiochus IV had designated Philip to be regent, but Lysias, who had Antiochus V in his care, usurped the office. Antiochus V would hardly have put Philip in charge while he went off to Judea. Philip is simply in rebellion, and the king must return to Syria to defend his throne.

Before he does so, he reaches a truce with the Jews (v. 23). He appoints Judas as military and civil administrator of the territory between Ptolemais (modern Haifa) and the Egyptian border. Not everyone is pleased with the outcome of this expedition (vv. 25-26), but Lysias defends the treaty. However, the opposition to the treaty and the particular circumstances that brought it about may alert the reader that Judas' troubles are not yet over.

B. The Final Defeat of Nicanor

2 Macc 14:1–15:36

14:1-11 Alcimus is antagonistic toward Judas. In 162 or 161 B.C.E., Demetrius, son of Seleucus IV, arrived in Syria to challenge Antiochus for the throne. A change in government could be expected to prompt new requests from the Hellenizing party in Jerusalem. A possible spokesman for this group is Alcimus, who seems to have been appointed high priest by Antiochus V to succeed Menelaus. Once Antiochus was no longer the king, Alcimus would have to be confirmed in office by Demetrius, the new king. 2 Maccabees accuses Alcimus of willfully incurring defilement at the time of the revolt, but no specifics are given.

Alcimus approaches Demetrius with gifts but keeps silent (v. 4). Later when he is invited to a council meeting by the king, he names the Hasideans, led by Judas, as the ones who consistently foment rebellion. (Elsewhere the Hasideans and Judas do not always agree on goals or strategies.) Alcimus objects that they are the ones who keep him from exercising his high priesthood. His speech to the king covers all the rules of Greek rhetoric, including the explanation that his first concern is for the king's interests, and his second, for his people's interests. He gives the king the opportunity to make an independent evaluation of the situation, but at least some of the people attending the meeting heartily agree with Alcimus' assessment of the Judean problem.

14:12-25 Judas and Nicanor. Nicanor, someone familiar with the Judean scene, is sent to kill Judas and restore Alcimus to the temple. Once again, the author makes clear that the violation of the treaty does not come from Judas but from a sinner within the community, in collusion with Syrian authorities. There will be another attack on the temple and its territory. The Gentiles in Judea rally to Nicanor, while the Jews lament and pray for God's help. Judas takes the initiative and decides to encounter Nicanor, but, after a brief skirmish, Nicanor (perhaps like Lysias on an earlier occasion) opts for a non-military solution to the problem. Working first through emissaries, the two leaders finally meet and agree to a truce.

At this point something curious occurs in the narrative. Nicanor moves to Jerusalem, where he behaves quite appropriately. He develops a fondness for Judas and keeps him in his company (vv. 23-24). Judas even follows Nicanor's suggestions, marries, and settles down. Although 1 Maccabees presents Nicanor as a crafty, untrustworthy foe, 2 Maccabees first describes him as fond of Judas, and only later does he become untrustworthy and dangerous.

14:26-36 Alcimus plots against Judas. Naturally Alcimus is not pleased with the progress of events. Taking a copy of the agreement between Nicanor and Judas, Alcimus goes directly to Demetrius and tries to convince the king that Nicanor and Judas are plotting against the throne. The king is understandably angry, but rather than accuse Nicanor of treason, he simply demands that he capture Judas and transport him to Antioch.

This puts Nicanor in a difficult position, and he wrestles with the dilemma long enough for Judas to realize that something amiss is developing. He gathers some associates and escapes (v. 30). Nicanor becomes very angry that Judas has outwitted him and at the same time put him in a very difficult position with his king. Ignoring the right of sanctuary, Nicanor looks for Judas in the temple precincts and, not finding him there, raises his right hand and his voice against the temple, threatening it with destruction. The reader, remembering the opening chapters of this book and the story line to this point, can readily anticipate the outcome of Nicanor's threats.

14:37-46 The story of Razis. Razis, a man of important standing in the community, becomes Nicanor's next intended victim. Despite his status in the community and his reputation as one who stood up to earlier persecution, the reason why he is singled out is not clear. Perhaps Nicanor suspects that Razis knows where Judas is to be found. Although he sends a sizable force to arrest Razis, the effort fails because Razis commits suicide rather than allowing himself to be taken (v. 4). (He may have done so to avoid revealing under torture where Judas was hiding.) Although suicide was not common in ancient Judaism, neither was it unknown (see 2 Sam 17:23). Seemingly, it was not considered sinful, and in desperate situations might have been thought of as morally allowable. In this narrative, Razis' defiance of Nicanor fits the tenor of these chapters, despite the gruesome details.

15:1-5 Nicanor blasphemes against the sabbath. The reader learns that Judas has escaped to Samaria. Nicanor decides to attack on the sabbath, but some Jews in his party plead with him not to act like a barbarian but to respect this day of rest. His answer is filled with arrogance, implying that the one who decreed the sabbath should keep to heaven while Nicanor is ruler on earth. In effect, Nicanor has challenged the God of Israel. Such arrogance is a prime target for God's punishment.

15:6-16 Onias III and Jeremiah appear to Judas in a dream. Judas, meanwhile, rallies his troops in a way reminiscent of the holy war, while adding the story of a dream he had in which Onias III, a respected former high priest, appeared praying for the Jewish community. When another figure also appeared, Onias introduced him to Judas as the great prophet Jeremiah, who also was praying for the people and Jerusalem. Jeremiah gave Judas a golden sword, in accordance with his frequent threats of sending a sword against Israel or its enemies (see Jer 50:35-37, for example). The sword comes from God, he says, and with it Judas would destroy his enemies. This is a familiar motif in ancient literature; the offer of the special weapons gives divine assurance of ultimate victory.

15:17-35 Defeat of Nicanor. With such backing the Jewish forces decide to attack the enemy, primarily to defend the city, the temple, and its sacred vessels. In reality they are also concerned about the Hellenizing party's gaining control once again over Jerusalem and the temple. In proximate preparation for the decisive battle, Judas prays for divine help, reminding God of the defeat of Sennacherib by Hezekiah (2 Kgs 18:13–19:35; Isa 36–37). Martial music accompanies Nicanor's troops; liturgical prayer accompanies Judah's (vv. 25-26). The Jews fight the enemy with hands and hearts, and they are once again victorious, with God's help. Gloating over the dead Nicanor follows; his head and right arm are displayed opposite the temple, against which he had risen both in defiance and blasphemy.

The narrative ends with the celebration of a festival in honor of Nicanor's defeat, similar to the feast of Purim or Mordecai's Day.

EPILOGUE

2 Macc 15:37-39

The epilogue matches the preface. Despite the subject matter, the author states his intention: to delight the ears of the readers. The author, who consistently has argued that the main problems arose within the Jewish community rather than from the Gentiles, ends his book in fairly typical Hellenistic fashion, demonstrating how far the Hellenization process had developed by the time the book was written.

ISAIAH

John J. Collins

INTRODUCTION

The Book of Isaiah presents in a particularly acute way two problems that confront the Christian interpreter of the Old Testament. The first concerns the discrepancy between the surface impression of the text and modern critical reconstructions of its history and meaning. Christian tradition, like Jewish tradition, long regarded the entire book as the work of a single prophet, Isaiah of Jerusalem. Critical scholarship, however, has taught us to distinguish First Isaiah (chs. 1–39), Second Isaiah (chs. 40–55) and Third Isaiah (chs. 56–66). Second and Third Isaiah are now dated to the late sixth century B.C.E., two hundred years after Isaiah of Jerusalem. Moreover, it now appears that less than half of First Isaiah actually contains words of the prophet himself. The remainder was added by anonymous scribes over several hundred years. Jewish legend had it that the prophet Isaiah met his death by being sawn asunder during the reign of the impious King Manasseh. Some conservative Christians have felt that his book has suffered a like fate at the hands of the critics.

The second problem concerns the Christological interpretation of the Old Testament. The Book of Isaiah has been treasured by Christians because it seems to predict crucial elements in the life of Jesus; the most striking examples are the virgin birth in Isa 7 and the passion and death in Isa 53. The book is cited or alluded to more than three hundred times in the New Testament. Jesus himself claimed to fulfill a text from Isaiah (61:1–2) in his sermon at Nazareth (Luke 4:18). Yet, critical scholarship has insisted that we must first understand the biblical texts in their own historical context. Isaiah had a message for the people of his own time, and this message did not require foreknowledge of events that would happen several hundred years later. The use of Isaiah by the Gospel writers tells us about the faith of the early Christians rather than the prophet's own message.

Critical scholarship, then, has cast doubt on the unity of the Book of Isaiah and on the Christian belief that it predicts Christ. Both these points have been shocking for Christians, although the shock has worn off, except in very conservative circles. Yet, the critical approach to the Bible should not be seen as a negative development. It has enriched our understanding of the Scriptures by showing how "the word of the Lord" is rooted in and speaks to concrete historical situations. The Bible is not a book of dogmatic propositions to be learned and believed, but a moving illustration of the faith of a people in ever-changing circumstances. If we know how an oracle conveyed its message in its original setting, we then have a guide to the way it should be understood in other settings. We cannot fully appreciate Matthew's use of the Immanuel prophecy (Matt 1:23) unless we understand the message Isaiah was delivering to King Ahaz when he originally spoke it (Isa 7:10–17).

For those who have mastered it, historical criticism has been a tremendously liberating force, for it has brought to light many aspects of biblical faith that had been submerged by the dogmatic theology of a later age. We now recognize, however, that a purely historical approach is also limited. In the case of Isaiah, we simply do not know the historical setting of some oracles, or we know it only in a very general way. Besides, the power of some passages lies in the fact that they transcend their original situations; they express fundamental hopes, fears, or insights that are applicable in recurring situations. The great messianic prophecies of Isaiah fall into this category. A passage like Isa 11, which dreams of a day when the wolf will lie down with the lamb, articulates a universal yearning for peace that is not peculiar to any historical situation. In this commentary we will try to do justice both to the historical particularity and to the universality of Isaiah's prophecies.

The composition of the book

Fundamental to the critical understanding of Isaiah is the insight that chapters 40–66 cannot be the work of Isaiah of Jerusalem but come from a much later time. Not only do these chapters *predict* the restoration of Jerusalem after the Babylonian Exile, but they *presuppose* the Exile itself. Second Isaiah *presupposes* that the Exile is already at an end. Third Isaiah (chs. 56–66) *presupposes* that the Jewish community has already returned to Judea. The issue, then, is not whether the prophet Isaiah could have predicted events of a much later time; the fact that the later events are presupposed is a sure indication of the time when these chapters were written.

Even within First Isaiah there is much material that was added later. Chapters 13–23 consist of oracles against various nations. Only a few passages in these chapters (for example, ch. 20) are likely to have come from the time of Isaiah himself. Chapters 24–27 constitute the so-called "Apocalypse of Isaiah." These chapters are no earlier than the Babylonian Exile and may even be later than Third Isaiah. Chapters 34–35 come from the sixth century, about the time of Second Isaiah. Finally, chapters 36–39 are taken, with very little modification, from 2 Kgs 18–20. The original oracles of Isaiah are found primarily in chapters 1–12 and 28–33 (plus a few passages in chapters 13–23). Even these chapters have come to us through the hands of editors who left their mark by the arrangement of the material and by minor insertions. (Most of the editorial work can be placed after the Exile, but some may have been associated with the reform of King Josiah in 621 B.C.E.) The Book of Isaiah, then, is not a monograph by an individual author but the collection of an ongoing tradition that spanned more than two hundred years.

The prophet Isaiah

At the origin of this tradition stands Isaiah of Jerusalem. The superscription in Isa 1:1 tells us that he prophesied "in the days of Uzziah, Jotham, Ahaz and Hezekiah, kings of Judah." The great vision in chapter 6, which is usually thought to mark the beginning of his prophetic activity, is dated to the year of Uzziah's death, probably 742 B.C.E. We know that he was active late in Hezekiah's reign at the time of an Assyrian invasion in 701 B.C.E. (described in Isa 36–38). His career, then, spanned roughly the second half of the eighth century B.C.E. His contemporaries included the prophets Amos, Hosea, and Micah.

Isaiah's career was marked by a series of crises caused by the military encroachment of the great superpower of the East, Assyria. The first great crisis, in the years 735–733 B.C.E., was the Syro-Ephraimite war. Syria joined forces with the northern kingdom of Israel (Ephraim) to form an alliance against the Assyrians. When King Ahaz of Judah refused to join, they mounted a campaign against him with a view to deposing him and installing a more cooperative king. This was the occasion of Isaiah's famous Immanuel prophecy. Ahaz appealed to Assyria for help. In 733 B.C.E. Samaria, the capital of northern Israel, was forced to submit. Ahaz remained king in Jerusalem as a subject of Assyria.

The next great crisis came about a decade later. The northern kingdom of Israel rebelled against Assyria, and in 722 B.C.E. Samaria was destroyed. Its population was deported and foreign settlers were brought in. The northern kingdom of Israel ceased to exist. This catastrophe may be prophesied in Isa 28:1-4.

Judah was again in danger in 713 B.C.E., when the Philistine city of Ashdod rebelled against the Assyrians. Isa 20 records the activity of Isaiah on this occasion.

Finally, in 701 B.C.E., Hezekiah of Judah revolted and provoked the famous campaign of Sennacherib. Most of the southern kingdom was ravaged. The Assyrian king boasted that he shut up Hezekiah in Jerusalem "like a bird in a cage." Yet Jerusalem was not destroyed, and Hezekiah remained on the throne. The prose account in Isa 36–38 attributes the deliverance of Jerusalem to "the angel of the Lord" (37:36).

This succession of crises plays some part in the ordering of the material in First Isaiah. Chapters 6–8, which are widely thought to be a memoir from Isaiah himself (see 8:16), clearly belong to the early period. Some material in chapters 10–23 can be attributed to the middle period, between 722 and 701 B.C.E. The oracles in chapters 28–32 relate to the time of Sennacherib. Some scholars think that the oracles in chapters 2–5, which deal primarily with social abuses, belong to the earliest period of the prophet's activity, before the Syro-Ephraimite war, at a time when Amos was making similar charges in northern Israel, but there is no clear evidence of their date.

The politics of Isaiah

Isaiah's preaching is directly concerned with the events of the day. He denounces the luxury of those who join house to house and field to field and of the women who parade in jewelry. His ideal seems to be the simple way of life in which people can live on curds and honey, the natural produce of the land. He does not see the loss of the vineyards—a source of wealth and luxury—as a great catastrophe. He certainly does not urge his people to fight to defend them; rather, he advocates a quietistic, pacifistic stance in the face of the Assyrian threat.

Isaiah's ideal of social simplicity was not conceived in rustic isolation. He was an urban prophet familiar with the temple (ch. 6). He had access to the king as a kind of political advisor, both in the early days of the Syro-Ephraimite war and in the time of Sennacherib at the end of his career. He was an educated man, as we can see from his mastery of Hebrew verse and from his familiarity with international politics. His social and political vision did not arise from naïveté but from his fundamental theological convictions.

Theological principles

At the heart of Isaiah's prophecy is his vision of God as "the Holy One of Israel," which is presented most vividly in chapter 6. The holiness of God shows up the inherent sinfulness of humanity. The power of the spirit contrasts with the powerless flesh (Isa 31). The emphasis on God's holiness is rooted in the praise of God's glory in the temple cult (compare Psalms 29, 93, 96–99). For Isaiah, the exaltation of God is the corollary of human finitude. Human pretensions to power are pathetic and doomed to failure. Consequently, Isaiah is very critical of the attempts of the Judean kings to play power politics or even to control their own destinies. He is in conflict with the sages, the professional advisers of the king, whose plans are overridden by the "plan of the Holy One of Israel" (5:19).

The central demand of Isaiah is for faith in this God. "Unless your faith is firm," he tells Ahaz, "you shall not be firm!" (7:9). Faith here means trust and reliance on God rather than on one's own resources. The context for this faith is provided by the royal ideology of the Davidic house. The divine charter of the dynasty is provided by the oracle of Nathan to David, recorded in 2 Sam 7. There the Lord promises David:

> I will establish a house for you. . . . I will raise up your heir after you, sprung from your loins, and I will make his kingdom firm. . . . And I will make his royal throne firm forever. I will be a father to him, and he shall be a son to me. And if he does wrong, I will correct him with the rod of men and with human chastisements; but I will not withdraw my favor from him as I withdrew it from your predecessor Saul, whom I removed from my presence. Your house and your kingdom shall endure forever before me; your throne shall stand firm forever (2 Sam 7:11-16).

One of the terms used to express the "firmness" of the dynasty is derived from the same root as the word for "faith."

The promise to David is the basis for a theology of kingship found in the psalms. The essential points are found in Psalm 2. If the kings of the earth rise up against the Lord and "his anointed" (the king), God will laugh at them, for "I myself have set up my king on Zion, my holy mountain" (Ps 2:6). The decree of the Lord is then proclaimed: "You are my son; this day I have begotten you" (Ps 2:7). This special father-son relationship is reaffirmed in Psalm 110, where the king is invited to "Sit at my right hand till I make your enemies your footstool" (Ps 110:1). The king can even be addressed as "God" (Ps 45:7), although he is clearly subordinate to the God who blesses him. The king is hailed as God's representative without reservation.

This glorification of the monarchy presumes certain responsibilities. The king is supposed to act "in the cause of truth and for the sake of justice" (Ps 45:5), to defend the afflicted and crush the oppressor (Ps 72). The whole ideology assumes and demands a very high degree of trust and reverence for the kingship (compare also Pss 89, 132).

Trust in the kingship goes hand in hand with trust in Mount Zion, the site of the temple in Jerusalem, as the dwelling place of God. Later Jewish theology might qualify the idea that God actually lived in the temple (1 Kgs 8:27; compare Isa 66:1; Acts 7:48), but Psalm 46 declares that it is "the holy dwelling of the Most High. God is in its midst; it shall not be disturbed" (Ps 46:5-6). The people of Jerusalem need not fear, "though the earth be shaken," because "the Lord of hosts is with [them]" (Ps 46:3, 8; compare Psalm 48). The worshiper in the temple could hope to see God's power and glory (see Ps 63:3), as indeed Isaiah does (Isa 6). The rhetoric of the temple worship, then, proclaims that the people need fear no adversary, because they have God's presence in their temple and God's support for their king.

This theology of kingship and temple provides the context for Isaiah's faith. (Unlike his contemporaries Amos and Hosea, Isaiah does not draw upon the tradition of the Exodus.) Isaiah demands that king and people alike live by the faith they profess. But this was not so easy when the Assyrian army was at the door. Isaiah is not so naive as to think that God will obligingly protect the people from all harm. He recognizes the extent of the suffering and destruction that will be inflicted, but he insists that life will go on. God will leave the people a remnant.

This theme of Isaiah's message, proclaimed in the name of his son Shear-jashub ("A remnant shall return," 7:3), is at once both good news and bad news. The remnant will ensure the survival of the people, but only after widespread destruction; it will be like the survival of a stump when a tree has been cut down. From this stump will come an ideal ruler in a future time (ch. 11), and Mount Zion will be exalted as a center for all peoples in days to come (ch. 2).

The ideal king and ideal temple are future ideals for Isaiah. They highlight the shortcomings of the present rulers and present cult. Isaiah affirms his faith in the royal theology but prevents it from serving as political propaganda for the kings of his day.

The political theology of Isaiah uses the popular traditions in an ironic way. The irony is best captured in the symbolic name Immanuel. "God is with us" was the professed faith of the Davidic line. For Isaiah, however, this is not a guarantee of easy salvation. The presence of God can be mediated by the sword of the Assyrian, the rod of Yahweh's anger (10:5). Salvation, for Isaiah, is not identical with wealth and prosperity, but with the purified worship of God. The people might, ironically, be better off when reduced to a remnant, stripped of their vineyards and forced to rely on curds and honey like the first Israelites.

Isaiah's quietistic stance goes hand in hand with his social criticism. The people who tried to survive by alliances with Egypt or who relied on horses, the armaments of their day (Isa 31), were the same people who joined house to house and field to field and got drunk on the produce of their vineyards. These were the people who stood to gain from national independence, who had something to fight for. Ironically, Judah and Israel were vulnerable to Assyrian greed because they had a measure of wealth and luxury. If they lived the simpler life, without wealth or power, they would be left in peace. The ideal kingdom sketched in Isa 11 is not a powerful empire, but one of peace and simplicity.

We can appreciate why the early Christians saw correspondences between Isaiah's prophecies and the kingdom proclaimed by Jesus. Two thousand years later Isaiah's political ideals have lost none of their relevance to the issues of international politics and the welfare of society.

Second Isaiah

The prophet we know as Second Isaiah worked in a very different situation. In the early years of the sixth century B.C.E., the kingdom of Judah had finally collapsed. In 586 B.C.E. Jerusalem was destroyed by the Babylonians. King Zedekiah had seen his sons slain before his eyes and was then blinded and taken in fetters to Babylon with the leaders of his people. The Jewish people were decimated, and the survivors humiliated. Some Jews saw this catastrophe as a punishment for their sins, but many must have wondered whether their God enjoyed any control over the course of events at all.

Then hope came from an unexpected quarter. The Persian king Cyrus entered Babylon as conqueror in 539 B.C.E. Within a year he had authorized the Jewish exiles to return home. This decree was consistent with Cyrus' generally tolerant policies toward subject peoples. He presented himself to the Babylonians as a liberator who was granted his triumph by the god of the Babylonians, Marduk. To the Jews he proclaimed that it was the Lord, the God of heaven, who had sent him, and that the Lord had also charged him to rebuild the temple in Jerusalem (so Ezra 1:1-4). Second Isaiah, elated at the unexpected deliverance, gladly proclaimed that Cyrus was the anointed ("messiah") of Yahweh (Isa 45:1).

The oracles of Second Isaiah are written in celebration of this deliverance and attempt to reformulate the faith of Israel in light of it. They consist of short hymnic units. It is not clear whether they have been arranged in a deliberate order. Chapter 40 is certainly an introduction to the collection and establishes several of its main themes. Some scholars find a shift at chapter 49. Chapters 49–55 are somewhat more sober in tone than chapters 40–48. They abandon some characteristic themes of the earlier chapters, such as the polemic against idolatry and disputes with the Babylonians. The later chapters show a strong interest in Zion. The differences, however, do not lead us to suppose that chapters 49–55 have a setting different from that of chapters 40–48. All these oracles were delivered after the rise of Cyrus and before the practical problems of the restoration had become apparent. They were probably written in Babylon.

Four of the short poems that make up Second Isaiah are commonly set apart as the "Servant Songs": Isa 42:1-4; 49:1-6; 50:4-9; 52:13–53:12. These passages are distinguished by their focus on the figure called "the Servant of Yahweh." Scholars of an earlier generation thought that these oracles were the work of a different prophet, but that view is now widely rejected. It is also doubtful whether they even represent a distinct, late stage in the composition of the book, as is sometimes claimed. Rather, they should be seen as an integral part of the collection that makes up Second Isaiah and interpreted in that context.

Theological themes

Second Isaiah, no less than Isaiah of Jerusalem, celebrates the transcendent power of God, before whom all flesh is like grass. He relates this to two distinctive themes.

First, Yahweh, God of Israel, is the Creator of all, the first and last, and there is no God besides Yahweh. Second Isaiah affirms that Yahweh alone is God in a more emphatic manner than any other biblical writer. Earlier biblical writers admit the existence of other gods but forbid the Israelites to worship them. Even Second Isaiah does not deny the existence of Babylonian gods (for example, Bel and Nebo—46:1), but he views them as helpless idols that have no power to save, and so they are in effect "no-gods." The monotheism of Second Isaiah is the basis for his highly sarcastic polemic against the worship of idols. All nations are obligated to serve Yahweh, since Yahweh is Creator of all.

Second, this Creator-God is the redeemer of Israel who buys it back from a state of slavery. This theme is based on the idea that Yahweh is bound to Israel by bonds of kinship. It also goes hand in hand with the prophet's view that the liberation from Babylon is a new Exodus.

The theme of the new Exodus is introduced already in 40:3: "In the desert prepare the way of the Lord!" The prophet is not interested in the Exodus as ancient history but as the myth or paradigm that reveals what God is like in the present. Yahweh is a God who liberates slaves, who overturns the status quo. Yahweh is a hidden God (45:15) whose ways may be obscure for a time but who will then be revealed in unexpected ways.

Undoubtedly the best known theme of Second Isaiah is the portrayal of the figure of the Suffering Servant, especially in the great Servant Song of Isa 53. This passage has attracted much attention because it has traditionally been taken as a prophecy of the passion of Jesus, and indeed it played some part in the early Christian understanding of

Jesus' death. The original significance of this figure for the Jews of the sixth century is still in dispute. The Servant has been identified with a wide range of historical figures from Moses to Zerubbabel (the governor at the time of the restoration and heir to the Davidic throne) or even the prophet himself. More probably, however, the Servant was not a historical individual but an idealized representation of the faithful Jews in exile.

The Servant poems, then, can be read as Second Isaiah's explanation of the Babylonian captivity. The view that the Jews were being punished for their sins is inadequate. They had received double for all their sins (40:2). Rather, their suffering had a positive purpose; they were to serve as a light to the nations. It was the infirmities of the other nations that they bore. Their lives were an offering for the sins of the Gentiles. Second Isaiah believed that the unexpected restoration of the Jews would bring the other nations to their senses and lead them to acknowledge Yahweh as the true God. In this he was disappointed, but the Suffering Servant persisted as a model of piety that has had profound influence on both Jewish and Christian spirituality.

Third Isaiah

Isa 56–66 is closely related to Second Isaiah but comes from a slightly later period, after the exiles had returned to Jerusalem and discovered the harsh realities of the situation. Some of the oracles, especially chapters 60–62, still resound with the enthusiasm of Second Isaiah; other passages, however, attest to deep divisions within the postexilic community and a sense of near desperation on the part of the prophet (chs. 63–66). Yet, out of these circumstances emerged the powerful vision of a new heaven and a new earth (65:17) that would be picked up later by the author of the Book of Revelation in the New Testament. These chapters raise fundamental issues concerning the priorities of a community in difficult times and the nature of true worship.

The so-called "Apocalypse of Isaiah"

The oracles that were inserted into First Isaiah at chapters 24–27 resemble Third Isaiah in their sense of near desperation with the present and desire for a radically different future. They are called "the Apocalypse of Isaiah" because of their heavy reliance on mythological symbols, which is a well-known feature of apocalyptic literature. They are not cast in the particular form of an apocalypse, however, which is a supernatural revelation, usually a vision mediated by an angel (see Dan 7–12). These chapters are prophetic oracles from an unknown prophet. They are often thought to reflect the further deterioration of the postexilic community after the time of Third Isaiah, perhaps about 500 B.C.E. Some scholars put the date much later, even as late as 300 B.C.E.

The difficulty of establishing a firm date for these chapters in itself tells us something about their nature. The heavy reliance on mythical symbols has a generalizing effect. These oracles provide a cluster of metaphors for a recurring type of situation. (This is also true of some of the oracles against the nations in Isa 13–23.) The portrayal of cosmic devastation in Isa 24 is as apt in an age of ecological crisis and nuclear threat as it was at any time in the ancient world. The hope that God "will destroy death forever" and "wipe away the tears from all faces" (25:8) remains the ultimate human aspiration.

Within the Book of Isaiah these chapters form a conclusion to the oracles against the nations by moving away from particular denunciations to more general, cosmic descriptions of judgment and salvation.

The unity of Isaiah

It is easier to show that the various parts of the Book of Isaiah come from different periods than to provide an explanation as to why they were all combined under Isaiah's name. Some scholars are willing to suppose that it was sheer accident, that material copied on a single scroll came to be regarded as a single book. The more plausible suggestion is that the later writers considered themselves part of an Isaianic tradition. Despite the differences between the various sections, there are some basic themes that run throughout. These include:

—the centrality of the holy mountain of Zion;

—a reliance on mythical symbolism to express the hopes (and fears) for the future;

—a yearning for universal peace that involves not only Israel but the right ordering of all nations.

All these themes are related to the cult of the Jerusalem temple. It may be that the continuity of the Isaianic tradition is simply that it is a Jerusalem tradition and that "all the Isaiahs" drew on a tradition of cultic piety. We will find that this is true even when the prophets were sharply critical of current cultic practice, for example in Isa 1 and 66. There are also some indications that later "Isaianic" writers drew motifs and allusions from the earlier Isaianic corpus; for example, the oracle on the vineyard in Isa 27 builds on the "song of the vineyard" in chapter 5. In the "new creation" of Isa 65 the wolf and the lamb will graze together, as in the messianic prophecy of Isa 11.

The fondness for mythical symbolism and ideal representations throughout the Book of Isaiah has lent itself to reinterpretation by subsequent generations. The general character of the messianic prophecies allowed the early Christians to see their fulfillment in Jesus. This classical Christian reinterpretation of Isaiah should not, however, cause us to ignore the fundamental messages of these writings in their historical contexts; nor should it distract us from seeking analogies between the prophet's situation and our own or from asking how his religious ideals can be correlated with our modern problems.

COMMENTARY: FIRST ISAIAH (Isa 1–39)

INTRODUCTORY PROPHECY

Isa 1:1-31

The opening chapter singles out the themes of judgment and salvation, which are characteristic of the whole book. It contains some oracles of the original Isaiah but has been edited as an introduction to the collection of oracles. The editor probably wrote after the fall of Jerusalem in the sixth century B.C.E. His message is simple: Whatever disasters befell Jerusalem are a punishment for infidelity; but if the people repent and are obedient, they will again eat the good things of the land.

1:1 The superscription. The "vision" here refers to the entire revelation of Isaiah, most of which is in verbal form. The prophet's father, Amoz, should not be confused with the prophet Amos, whose career overlapped Isaiah's. The reigns of the kings listed cover most of the second half of the eighth century. If Isaiah's career began in the year of Uzziah's death, the probable dates are 742–701 B.C.E.

1:2-8 Judah devastated. The description of Zion, "left like a hut in a vineyard" (1:8), recalls the boast of the Assyrian king Sennacherib that he had shut up Hezekiah of Judah "like a bird in a cage," and may refer to the same situation in 701 B.C.E. Isaiah, however, does not put the blame on the Assyrians but on the Judeans themselves: "They have forsaken the Lord, spurned the Holy One of Israel" (1:4). The opening line, "Hear, O heavens, and listen, O earth" (1:2), introduces an indictment for breach of covenant in Deut 32:1. In this case, however, there is no appeal to the Sinai covenant or to the Exodus from Egypt. Instead, the prophet appeals to an instinctive natural law: if an ox and ass can know their master, then Israel should know its God and know what is right. The prophet's concern is not merely with the breach of specific laws but with the lack of a proper religious attitude that should inform all of life.

Verse 9 introduces the theme of the remnant. It is a small remnant, ensuring survival, but little more.

1:10-16 An oracle on true worship. This oracle begins with a mention of Sodom and Gomorrah, and is placed here because the same cities are mentioned in verse 9. Sodom and Gomorrah were the cities of the Plain, destroyed by fire from heaven because of their corruption (Gen 19). In verse 9 the analogy was with the total way in which they were destroyed. In verse 10 the Judean leaders are addressed as "princes of Sodom" because they are equally corrupt.

The theme of this oracle is true worship. God professes no pleasure in the constant sacrifice of animals or even with the observance of the new moon and sabbath, because "your hands are full of blood!" (1:15), not only because of the sacrifices but because of the violence of their lives. Isaiah is not opposed to ritual as such. He says they need a ritual of washing to symbolize repentance and purification. Ritual, however, is only as good as the intentions it expresses. What matters is how people treat the widows and orphans, not how often they go to the temple or offer sacrifice. A very similar critique of the cult and plea for justice is found in Amos 5:18-27, also from the eighth century B.C.E.

1:18-20 Call to repentance. This brief insertion has the tone of the law in Deuteronomy and expresses succinctly the message of the editor. Rather than just proclaim judgment or salvation, as the prophet typically does, it sets a goal for repentance and so emphasizes human responsibility. The assumption that obedience ensures prosperity is naive, however, and was sharply criticized in the later biblical tradition, most obviously in the Book of Job but also in Second Isaiah.

1:21-31 Redemption by judgment. The chapter concludes with a threat of punishment for political and social corruption. The main point to note is that the punishment is seen as redemptive, like the refining of metals by fire. Zion will be purified. The experience will be severe, but it is necessary if the cherished claims to justice and faithfulness are to be rendered appropriate.

ORACLES AGAINST JERUSALEM AND JUDAH

Isa 2:1–12:6

These chapters are given a new introduction in 2:1 and gather oracles that are mainly from the early period of Isaiah's activity. We may distinguish the rather general social oracles of chapters 2–5, the memoir of Isaiah in chapters 6–8, the messianic oracles in chapters 9 and 11 (separated by oracles on Samaria and Assyria), and a concluding psalm in chapter 12, which may have marked the conclusion of a distinct collection.

2:2-5 The future of Mount Zion. Verses 2-4 are duplicated almost exactly in Mic 4:1-3. Micah, like Isaiah, was an eighth-century prophet of the southern kingdom. We do not know which prophet, if either, composed this oracle. The prospect of nations streaming to Mount Zion is often related to the pilgrimages of Jewish exiles to Jerusalem in the postexilic period. Even in the pre-exilic period, however, Mount Zion was considered to be a sacred mountain, the center of the earth, and important for the whole world (see Psalms 46–48).

In the lifetime of Isaiah, King Hezekiah is said to have tried to destroy the "high places" where people worshiped outside of Jerusalem and to centralize the cult (2 Kgs 18; 2 Chr 31). Samaria and the northern kingdom had recently been destroyed, and Hezekiah was trying to rally the survivors to Jerusalem. Isa 2:2-5 would make good sense in this context. The "house of Jacob" that is invited to walk in the light of the Lord (v. 5) certainly includes the northern kingdom of Israel.

This vision of the future of Zion already contains the idea that Israel is a light to the nations, a theme we will meet again in Second Isaiah. The Israelites are not told to go out to convert the nations but to attract them by their worship on Zion. In the ideal world of the future time, all nations will come together to the central city of Jerusalem. Recognition of the claims of Jerusalem is the converse of recognition of Yahweh as sovereign. This recognition and the acceptance of Yahweh's instruction are seen as the keys to world peace, when swords will be beaten into ploughshares.

Whatever the origin of this oracle, it introduces themes we will meet repeatedly in the Book of Isaiah and is in harmony with the great messianic prophecy of Isa 11. We should note that the prophet Joel (Joel 4:10) inverts the great vision of peace and bids the nations beat their ploughshares into swords in anticipation of battle on the day of the Lord. Neither prophecy should be taken as a prediction of the future; both are projections of basic human hopes and fears.

2:6-22 The Day of the Lord. This long oracle begins by giving reasons why God has abandoned the people, the house of Jacob (probably the northern kingdom, which was conquered by the Assyrians in 733 B.C.E. and again decisively in 722 B.C.E.). The offenses include idolatry and pursuit of treasures and armaments. All are symptoms of human pride. In response, God will manifest his majesty "on that day" (v. 11). The "Day of the Lord" is known from a famous passage in Amos 5:18-20. There it appears that most people look forward to the Day of the Lord, but Amos says that it will be "darkness and not light." Most probably it was a festival day (perhaps during the fall festival of Tabernacles) when God was supposed to be manifested to the cultic community.

Amos suggests that when God is really manifested, most people will not be able to endure it. Similarly, in Isaiah the "day" takes on the character of a battle day when God will rout any foes. The description of the divine manifestation echoes the cultic celebration of the psalms (for example, Psalms 29 and 97) and is related to the tradition of God's kingship. Isaiah is thinking not only of a theophany in the cult, however, but of an occasion when all will flee to caves from the terror of the Lord. It is possible that the terror will be conveyed through the Assyrian invasion, but Isaiah sees it as the manifestation of God. Humanity will then recognize its puny nature before the overwhelming power of God, and the folly of human ambitions to wealth and power will be exposed.

3:1-12 Anarchy in Jerusalem. "That day" will also have effect in Jerusalem. Isaiah sketches a breakdown of the social order. "Hero and warrior," anyone who could lay claim to power is removed. The people will be ruled by mere boys (v. 4), women, or even a babe in arms (v. 12). That "a little child" should be leader may sound idyllic in Isa 11, but here (v. 5) it is a symptom of chaos. There was no such breakdown of order in Isaiah's time. The prophecy is partly a wish and partly an assertion that such a breakdown *could* happen, and that the pride of the leaders has a shaky foundation.

3:13-15 The accusation. The formal accusation in verses 13-15 focuses on one aspect of that foundation. The political leaders, the elders and princes, have built their wealth by appropriating land and exploiting the poor. A similar theme is characteristic of Amos. We will meet it again in Isa 5.

3:16–4:1 The women of Jerusalem. Isaiah is especially severe on the women. He provides an impressive inventory of their finery. He seems to relish the prospect that their heads would be shaved and they would be led away in sackcloth by the Assyrians (they were not, but it was a distinct possibility). He treats the women as the representatives of the culture of luxury and pride, and therefore especially ripe for a fall. We find a similar attitude in Amos, who called the women of Samaria "cows of Bashan" (Amos 4:1).

4:2-6 The glorious remnant. The final oracle relating to "that day" is probably the work of a later editor. Elsewhere in Isaiah the remnant is not portrayed in such glorious terms. The signs of God's presence—the smoking cloud by day and the flaming fire by night—recall the Exodus tradition, which is also out of character for Isaiah. Yet the passage is developing a genuine theme of Isaiah: Jerusalem must be purged if it is to be holy, but the purge is ultimately the means to salvation.

The "branch of the Lord" here is a general reference to whatever God will cause to grow, synonymous with "the fruit of the earth." The same word is used for a messiah in Jer 23:5; Zech 3:8; 6:12.

5:1-7 The song of the vineyard. This famous poem is a parable, like Nathan's parable in 2 Sam 12 or some of the parables of Jesus. The speaker does not at first disclose his true subject but leads his listeners to pass judgment before they realize that they are condemning themselves. The vineyard involves a double allegory. On the one hand, there is the obvious agricultural sense of the words. On the other hand, the fact that the song is said to be a love song, sung for a friend, suggests that the friend's vineyard is really his wife. There is a hint, then, of marital infidelity as a second level in the allegory. The song is not very explicit about the sins of Israel, except that they involve bloodshed and injustice. The indictment draws its force from the analogy with the unproductive vineyard and the less obvious analogy with marital infidelity. It appears that both kingdoms, Israel and Judah, stand accused.

There is yet another nuance to the allegory. The vineyard was very valuable property that contributed greatly to the life of luxury. It symbolized the wealth of the land. The parable suggests that this wealth has not produced a just society. The threat that the vineyard would be overgrown by thorns and briers was fulfilled rather literally after the Assyrian invasions.

The entire poem may be compared to Hos 2, where God threatens to make the land a wilderness and the analogy with marital infidelity is again present. The vine is a favorite symbol for Israel in the Old Testament: compare Hos 10:1; Jer 2:21; Ezek 15:1-8; 19:10-14. Compare also the parable of the vineyard in the New Testament: Matt 21:33-42; Mark 12:1-10; Luke 20:9-18.

5:8-16 Denunciation of social abuses. These oracles are proclamations of woe and have a dirge-like effect. They do not invite the wicked to repent but are announced as certain and unavoidable. They paint a vivid picture of Israelite society in the eighth century. The large landowners add house to house by foreclosing on debtors or pressuring the smaller farmers off the land (see the story of Naboth's vineyard in 1 Kgs 21). The large estates could then be turned into profitable vineyards, which supported the luxurious (and drunken) lifestyle of the rich rather than supplying the staples of life for the poor. Isaiah insists that those who exalt themselves in this way will be humbled before the majesty of God.

5:17-25 Denunciation of the wise. Isaiah is especially angry at the professional sages, the political advisers of their day. They are skilled in political rhetoric, call evil good and good evil. They indulge in petty corruption, acquitting the guilty for bribes. Besides, being "wise in their own sight" (v. 21), they do not allow for God's control of events or for the ability of a prophet to discern it. Isaiah insists that the "Holy One" has a plan, which will humble human pride. The sages doubt this and challenge God (and Isaiah) to get on with it. They are pragmatic politicians. Isaiah can only retort by proclaiming the wrath of God.

5:26-30 The Assyrian danger. Isaiah's threat that Yahweh would disrupt the plans of the wise was not totally lacking in practical reason. He does not simply envisage a miracle. God would act through a "far-off nation" (5:26). Isaiah was an astute political observer who saw the menace of Assyria and had no illusions that Judean diplomacy would be able to avert disaster. The complacency of the wise and their self-indulgent lifestyle left them vulnerable to a changing political situation.

6:1-13 The call vision of Isaiah. Isaiah's vision, reported in chapter 6, is usually thought to mark the beginning of a memoir (6:1–8:20) that was recorded in the time of the prophet himself. The vision is dated to an early point in his career (742 B.C.E.). Since it involves the commissioning of the prophet, it is usually regarded as his inaugural vision. Hebrew prophets were thought to receive their message in the heavenly council (compare Jer 23:19, which claims that Jeremiah's opponents have not had this experience). Such visions were not necessarily confined to the beginning of a prophet's career. The closest parallel to Isaiah's vision is attributed to a prophet named Micaiah ben Imlah in 1 Kgs 22, and it is not an inaugural vision.

Isaiah makes the astonishing claim that he has seen the Lord. There is some ambiguity in the Bible as to whether a person can see God. In Exod 33:11 we are told that God used to speak to Moses face-to-face, but also that Moses was only allowed to see God's back, since "my face you cannot see, for no man sees me and still lives" (Exod 33:20; compare Isaiah's fear that he is doomed in 6:5). The prophet Ezekiel sums up his own introductory vision as "the vision of the likeness of the glory of the Lord"—a very circumspect claim (Ezek 1:28). Isaiah, by contrast, is perfectly direct: "I saw the Lord" (6:1). The parallel with the vision of Micaiah ben Imlah in 1 Kgs 22 suggests that there was a prophetic tradition that prophets could indeed see God.

Here it must be said that what a prophet sees in a vision is inevitably conditioned by his preconceptions and by the beliefs of his contemporaries. A prophet in the eighth century B.C.E. *could* have a vision of God because it was believed to be possible, and the report would be accepted by a significant number of his contemporaries. God is envisaged as a king because the king was the most powerful and majestic figure in the prophet's experience. (The similarity between the heavenly and earthly courts is more obvious in 1 Kgs 22.) The seraphim in Isaiah's vision are evidently inspired by the cherubim, the hybrid figures in the Jerusalem temple above which Yahweh was supposed to be enthroned.

Isaiah apparently had this vision in the temple, possibly on a cultic occasion when the house was filled with the smoke of incense. Such an experience may not have been unique to prophets. The psalmist speaks of gazing toward God in the temple "to see your power and your glory" (Ps 63:3). It may be that worshipers hoped for such a vision when they attended worship in the temple. In any case, the claim to have seen God lends considerable authority to the prophet's message. If it comes directly from God, it takes precedence over the claims of any human institution.

The cry of the seraphim expresses Isaiah's central affirmation about God: "Holy, holy, holy" (6:3). The significance of God's holiness is shown in the prophet's immediate confession of impurity. Isaiah does not recall a specific sin. The impurity is inherent in his human condition and endangers him in the presence of God. The remedy is a drastic one: his lips are purified with a burning coal. An analogous remedy will be prescribed for the whole people.

The prophet's vision is never an end in itself. He is not practicing a life of contemplation. Instead, he is given a message that bears on the political situation in Jerusalem. This message is not to save the people; on the contrary, it ensures their doom by making their hearts sluggish. The prophet's job here is to announce the coming judgment, not to bring about the conversion, at least not directly. We may compare Exod 7:3, where God hardens Pharaoh's heart, thereby setting him up for further destruction.

It would seem, then, that the judgment on Judea cannot be avoided. The question raised by the prophet is not "whether" but "how long?" The answer involves the familiar theme of the remnant. Israel will be like a tree that has been cut down, so that only a stump remains. The editorial gloss, "Holy offspring is the trunk" (6:13), gives the prophecy an upbeat ending. It also is in keeping with the thought of Isaiah that this remnant does indeed have a future. Yet the emphasis in chapter 6 is overwhelmingly negative. The good news of the remnant is overshadowed by the destruction of the majority. The destruction will presumably purify the remnant, as the burning coals purified the prophet's lips.

7:1-25 The prophecy of Immanuel. The opening verse of chapter 7 refers to the campaign of Syria (Aram) and northern Israel (Ephraim) against Judah in the reign of Ahaz. The campaign in question took place between 735 and 733 B.C.E. (see 2 Kgs 16) and is known as the Syro-Ephraimite war. Syria and Israel had already been paying tribute to Assyria since 738 B.C.E. but had now decided to revolt by withholding payment. Judah had refused to join the alliance. As yet Ahaz had no quarrel with Assyria, and in any case hopes of success were remote. Israel and Syria then attempted to overthrow Ahaz and replace him with a king more amenable to their wishes.

The royal ideology of the Davidic dynasty professed a sublime confidence that God would protect his chosen king and city. Recall Ps 46:1-4:

> God is our refuge and our strength,
> an ever-present help in distress.
> Therefore we fear not, though the earth be shaken
> and mountains plunge into the depths of the sea . . . .
> The Lord of hosts is with us;
> our stronghold is the God of Jacob.

Such a profession is easily made when there is no immediate danger. Faced with an actual invasion, however, "the heart of the king and the heart of the people trembled, as the trees of the forest tremble in the wind" (7:2).

At this juncture Isaiah goes to meet Ahaz, who is apparently checking his water supply in anticipation of a siege. Isaiah is accompanied by his son, whose name, Shear-jashub, means "a remnant shall return." His advice to the king is startling. He does not suggest the course that Ahaz would eventually take, to appeal to Assyria for help (2 Kgs 16:7). Instead, he tells him to "remain tranquil and do not fear" (7:4) because the attack will not succeed and the state of northern Israel will soon come to an end. (The reference to "sixty years and five" (7:9) has puzzled commentators. It is too far away to have immediate relevance for Ahaz, and besides, Israel was effectively terminated in 722 B.C.E. Some scholars suggest that this verse is a gloss added in 671 B.C.E. when further settlers were brought to Samaria by the Assyrian king Esar-haddon [see Ezra 4:2]. Others suggest that the original text read "six years or five" [so the Jerusalem Bible], but there is no textual evidence for this reading.) The divine commitment to make the Davidic line "firm" (2 Sam 7:16) is conditional on the faith of the king. (In Hebrew the words for "firm" and "believe" are derived from the same root.)

The birth of a child. Isaiah then offers Ahaz a sign and proceeds to give it even when the king refuses to ask for it. The sign is that a young woman will bear a son who will be "living on curds and honey by the time he learns to reject the bad and choose the good"

(7:15). The mother is called an *almah* in the Hebrew, that is, a young woman of marriageable age, though not necessarily a virgin. The Greek translation of Isaiah used the word *parthenos*, which means "virgin" unambiguously, and this translation is cited in Matt 1:22-23 and formed the basis of the traditional Christian interpretation of this text as a prophecy of the birth of Christ. The Hebrew, however, does not suggest that the birth in itself was miraculous.

Since the sign was given to Ahaz, we must assume that the young woman in question was known to him. There are two possible identifications. The first is the prophet's wife. We know that the prophet gave symbolic names to his children. The second is the king's wife. The name Immanuel, "God is with us," could serve as a slogan for the Davidic house. While the prophet could predict the name of his own child more confidently, a royal child would be the more effective sign for the king. While either identification is possible, it seems more probable that the woman in question was one of Ahaz's wives.

The child about to be born will be "living on curds and honey by the time he learns to reject the bad and choose the good" (7:15). The translation of this sentence is disputed. It could be that he will live on curds and honey *so that* he may learn (so the Vulgate). The age of moral discrimination is usually put at about twenty years. According to this interpretation, Immanuel would be brought up on a diet of curds and honey in order to form his moral discrimination. Some scholars, however, think that the age in question may be much lower—three to five years of age. The lower figure seems more probable in view of 7:16: "For before the child learns to reject the bad and choose the good, the land of those two kings whom you dread shall be deserted." If this sign has any urgency, the interval can be no more than a few years.

The meaning of the sign. The diet of curds and honey is evidently part of the sign and illustrates the ambiguity inherent in this whole passage. The land of Israel was proverbially "a land flowing with milk and honey" (Exod 3:8; 13:5; Num 13:27; Josh 5:6). Such food would appear abundant to nomads from the wilderness; it would surely seem spartan to a king accustomed to live in luxury. The implications of the diet of curds and honey can be seen in 7:21-25: those who remain in the land will have to live on its natural produce, since cultivation will be impossible. Curds and honey will be the only available food. The phrase "On that day" (7:20, 21) suggests that the coming destruction is "the day of the Lord," but it is clear that the instrument of destruction is "the razor hired from across the River" (7:20)—the Assyrians.

Isaiah not only predicts that Syria and Israel will be destroyed but also that Judah will suffer "days worse than any since Ephraim seceded from Judah" (7:17). It would seem from 7:18-20 that the real menace to Judah is seen to come from the Assyrians rather than from the Syro-Ephraimite coalition.

What, then, is signified by the birth of Immanuel? Evidently the name "God is with us" is *not* a promise that God will shelter the king from all harm if only he has faith; rather, it is an ambiguous sign. The presence of God is not always protective. It can also be destructive, as on the "day of the Lord" (see above, chapter 2). Yet it is not entirely destructive. The birth of a child is perhaps the most universal and enduring symbol of hope for the human race. The newborn child does not contribute to military defense or help resolve the dilemmas of the crisis, but he is nonetheless a sign of hope for a new generation. The prophet predicts that he will reach the age of discernment, however bad the times may be. Even if cultivation becomes impossible, people will survive on curds and honey. Moreover, they can recall a time at the beginning of Israel's history when such a diet was seen as a bountiful gift of God. Isaiah prophesies that the vineyards, worth thousands of pieces of silver, will be overgrown with thorns and briers (see the Song of the Vineyard, Isa 5:6). This would be a loss to the ruling class but not necessarily to the common people. The demise of the vineyards might mark a return to a simpler lifestyle, in which Israel and Judah would be less wealthy, but also less torn by social oppression and less entangled in international politics.

Isaiah's advice to Ahaz, then, is to wait out the crisis, trusting not for miraculous deliverance but for eventual survival. The prophet probably feels that there is no need to fight against Syria and Israel, Assyria will take care of them. Sending for aid to Assyria is probably also unnecessary and would bring Judah directly into subjection. In the meantime Judah might be ravaged and reduced to near wilderness, but life would go on, and the society would be purified in the process.

Ahaz, of course, does not follow Isaiah's advice. He sends gold and silver to the king of Assyria and becomes his vassal. Damascus is destroyed. Samaria survives only because a coup puts a new king on the throne, but even then it survives for a mere decade. The politics of Ahaz seem to work well enough for the present, but Isaiah would surely hold that they do not go to the heart of the matter.

The figure of Immanuel in Isa 7 is not presented as a messianic figure, although he probably was a royal child. Nothing is said of his future reign. Instead, he is a symbol of hope in weakness, of new life in the midst of destruction. When early Christianity read this passage as a prediction of the birth of Jesus, it implied an analogy between the two births. In the Gospels, too, a birth in inauspicious circumstances was nonetheless taken as a sign of the presence of God.

8:1-15 Prophecies concerning Assyria. A series of short oracles in chapter 8 throws some light on Isaiah's stance in the crisis of 735–738 B.C.E.

First, the prophet has another child, who becomes a living sign that the Assyrians will plunder Syria and Israel. Unlike Immanuel, this child is explicitly said to be the prophet's son. His relevance to the prophet's prediction, however, is similar: Damascus and Samaria will be destroyed before he begins to talk. The time period is presumably not much less than was implied in the case of Immanuel.

A second short oracle is found in verses 5-10. The people have rejected the waters of Shiloah (a stream in Jerusalem) by not trusting in the divine promises to David and succumbing to fear. The waters of Shiloah flow gently; they are not mighty or threatening. Because the Judeans have not been content with such a passive role, the great river of Assyria, the Euphrates, will flood them. There is pointed irony in this. Ahaz has appealed to Assyria for protection, but the protection of Assyria is overpowering and oppressive in itself. Isaiah is adamant that anyone who resists will be crushed (as indeed they were). The plans of the counselors are in vain, for "With us is God!" (v. 10). Here again the prophet is playing on the name of Immanuel. God is present in the Assyrian onslaught, not with those who resist it.

A third brief oracle in verses 11-15 dismisses political alliances as futile and says that the fear of the people is misplaced—they should fear the Lord. The point here is not only that they should fear the Assyrians as God's weapon but concerns a basic religious attitude. Isaiah renounces all political intrigue and its goal of international power. Yahweh becomes a stumbling block, frustrating the designs of the counselors in Jerusalem as well as Samaria. Isaiah seems to regard political intrigue as sinful in itself. In the context of the Assyrian crisis, he had, at least, good reason to regard the intrigue of the Israelites as ineffectual.

8:16-20 Conclusion of the memoir. This passage gives a rare glimpse of the formation of a prophetic book. The prophet gives instruction that his words be recorded and preserved by his disciples. The memoir (probably chapters 6–8) is, then, a testimony, a public reminder of the prophet's message, like the symbolic names of Isaiah's children. It will be available for consultation, so that people will not need to resort to mediums and fortunetellers (compare the story of Saul in 1 Sam 28). Such signs are necessary when God is "hiding his face from the house of Jacob" (v. 17). At this juncture God was most obviously hidden from the northern kingdom, but Isaiah apparently thinks of all Israel as one people, subject to the God who dwells in Jerusalem on Mount Zion.

8:23-9:6 A new king. The famous prophecy of the birth of a child is properly called a "messianic" prophecy because it describes an ideal king whose reign is still in the future. There is disagreement as to how the oracle was originally understood. It could refer to the birth of a royal child (compare Vergil's famous *Fourth Eclogue*, which was written to celebrate the birth of the Roman emperor's son). More probably it was a hymn in honor of the enthronement of a new king (compare Ps 2:7, where the king is told the decree of the Lord: "You are my son, this day I have begotten you"). Apparently the king was adopted as "son of God" when he came to the throne. The king in question in Isa 9 is surely Hezekiah, Ahaz's successor, who became king in either 725 or 715 B.C.E. (the evidence is inconsistent). The earlier date would make better sense here.

Isa 8:23 refers to the dismemberment of northern Israel by the Assyrians in 733–732 B.C.E., when three districts were taken away from Samaria and made Assyrian provinces. It is disputed whether the text should be translated as "he has glorified the seaward road" or "he has oppressed" it. If "glorified" is correct, the prophet is anticipating something that has not yet happened. In any case, chapter 9 announces light for those who live in darkness—new hope for the people of northern Israel oppressed by the Assyrians. The prophet says that God has smashed the oppressor "as on the day of Midian" (a battle described in Judg 7). He probably says this in anticipation, because of his confidence in the new king. The hope for northern Israel is found in the arrival of a new Davidic king in Jerusalem and involves the reunification of Israel.

The titles given to the royal "child," especially "God-Hero" (9:5), suggest that he is more than a human being. There can be no doubt, however, that the prophet Isaiah is thinking of an actual king in Jerusalem in the late eighth century B.C.E. The divine titles are part of the royal ideology. Ps 2:7 declares that the king is the begotten son of God, although this is probably understood as a formula of adoption. Ps 45:7 addresses the king as *elohim*, "god." The king is not considered equal to Yahweh, but he is regarded as a superhuman being.

This king is expected to bring about an era of peace. He will be able to do this because God will give him all the empire governed by David. This, of course, did not come about in the time of Hezekiah, nor has it ever come to pass since then. In the context of Isaiah's message, this is a vision of hope. The glory of the king is still in the future—it is a matter of potential and possibility, not of accomplished fact. The oracle has endured because it formulates a goal of universal peace, which is still desired by humanity.

Christianity applied this prophecy to the birth of Jesus. In doing so, it disregarded the real political concern of Isaiah for the land of Israel. It picked up instead the fact that these wonderful attributes were attached to a child, to one who has no real power in this world. As in chapter 7 the birth of a child symbolizes the hope of humanity for a brighter future. The prophecy affirms that the key to this future lies in justice and innocence rather than in military might.

9:7–10:4 Judgment on the northern kingdom. We have seen that Isaiah is concerned with the northern kingdom of Israel as well as with his own state of Judah. This series of oracles announces God's judgment on the north. The time in question is not clear; it may have been as early as the Syro-Ephraimite war (see 9:20). The grounds for the judgment are partly arrogance (9:8), partly the social injustice implied by the pursuit of luxury, and partly the failure of the Israelites to turn to Yahweh, who, in Isaiah's view, dwells in Jerusalem (8:18). Since no conversion follows the early setbacks of Israel, Yahweh's wrath is not turned back, so worse destruction is to come. The series concludes with a woe-oracle on social injustice that is closely related to the woe-oracles in chapter 5. Some scholars think that material has been displaced and that some verses from chapter 5 originally belonged in chapter 9 (compare the formula in 5:25, which corresponds to 9:11, 16, 20, and 10:4).

10:5-34 The role of Assyria. Pagan Assyria is the rod with which Yahweh chastises Israel. Yet, Assyria is not itself exempt from judgment, since its intention is not to serve Yahweh but to wreak destruction. This oracle is somewhat later than the passages in chapters 7–9. It comes from a time when Jerusalem rather than Samaria was being threatened, either in 713 B.C.E. on the occasion of a revolt by Ashdod or in the better-known invasion of Sennacherib in 701 B.C.E.

The pattern of this oracle is a familiar one in the Bible (see Isa 14; Ezek 27–28). The king of Assyria is guilty of excessive pride, or *hybris*: "By my own power I have done it, and by my wisdom, for I am shrewd" (v. 13). In Isaiah's view, human power and wisdom accomplish nothing. Assyria is an unwitting helper in the plan of God. The prophet's conviction that Assyria would be broken appears to be based on the divine commitment to Mount Zion. Zion can be struck with a rod (10:24) and so is not protected from all harm. Yet, the ironic quotation of Assyria's claims in 10:8-11 clearly implies that Jerusalem is not like Samaria or other cities and cannot be completely destroyed. So the threatening advance of the Assyrians in verses 28-32 comes close to Jerusalem but stops short of the city. The final assertion of God's majestic power (vv. 33-34) is ambiguous. It is manifested in the subjection of Judah by the Assyrian advance, but it also casts a shadow on the Assyrian success and suggests that it too will be cut off.

The passage on the remnant in verses 20-21 is inserted here because of the occurrence of the word "remnant" in verse 19. The insert shows the typical ambiguity of the remnant: the survivors will be purified and learn to rely on the Lord, but *only* a remnant will be left. This idea is consistent with the message of Isaiah throughout his career.

11:1-9 The ideal king. The messianic prophecy in chapter 11 refers more obviously to a future time than was the case in chapter 9. It is not apparent that the king in question has even been born. He is described as "a shoot from the stump of Jesse," that is, from the Davidic line (compare Mic 5:1, where the lineage is expressed through a reference to Bethlehem, the home of Jesse). This description does not presuppose that the line had been broken: "stump" is roughly equivalent to "roots" in the parallel line.

The oracle that follows falls into two parts. Verses 2-5 describe the attributes of the king. The spirit of the Lord will be upon him, and he will do all that a righteous king should do. Verses 6-9 describe a transformation of nature in his reign. This description is quite fantastic, as it concerns a transformation of animal nature that no king could achieve. It is like a return to the garden of Eden. The reference to "all my holy mountain" in verse 9 suggests that the whole earth will then partake of the sanctity of Mount Zion.

It should be obvious that this is a poetic passage, a fantasy of an ideal world rather than a prediction of the future. Such friendship between wolf and lamb has never come about, and there is no reason to think that Isaiah expected it would. Rather, the purpose of this passage is twofold. On the one hand, it is a beautiful picture that comforts the reader in the midst of the turmoil of the Assyrian crisis. On the other hand, it paints a picture of what an ideal world would be like. As such, it presents a challenge for any king. Perhaps Isaiah had come to realize that Hezekiah was not an ideal king, despite the hopes expressed in Isa 9. Indeed, what king could possibly measure up to the ideal presented here? Yet the ideal is important. It reminds us of the imperfections of the present and gives us a goal to work toward, even though we may never fully attain it.

The goal expressed in Isa 11:1-9 is perfect peace, without "harm or ruin"(11:9). In such a world "a little child [will] guide them" (11:6). The motif of the child was prominent in chapter 7 and in the imagery of chapter 9 (but see also 3:12). The child as leader is a contradiction of political and military reality. In Isaiah's view, the power and supposed wisdom of human rulers are of little account. What matters is "the knowledge of the Lord" (v. 9) that goes hand in hand with "the fear of the Lord" (v. 2)—single-minded devotion to justice and abandonment of human pretensions and ambitions.

11:10-16 Reunification of Israel. This oracle of restoration comes from a later time when not only Israel but also Judah had been scattered in exile. The point of contact with Isaiah's prophecy lies in the opening reference to the root of Jesse. The image of the "signal" or standard for the nations recalls how the nations are said to stream to Mount Zion in chapter 2, but of course the motif of "a light to the nations" is also prominent in Second Isaiah in the exilic period. Here the restoration is presented as a new Exodus (a motif also repeated by Second Isaiah). By contrast, there are no references to the Exodus in those oracles that are ascribed with any confidence to Isaiah himself. The ideal situation envisaged, however, is quite compatible with the hopes of Isaiah. It looks for a reconciliation of Israel and Judah, and their joint sovereignty over the other nations.

12:1-6 A song of thanksgiving. This short hymn of thanksgiving probably concluded an independent booklet of Isaiah's prophecies. The hymn is the work of an editor, despite the use of the characteristically Isaian phrase "the Holy One of Israel" (12:6). The psalmist looks back on hard times but can now praise God, since the crises are past. The judgment oracles of Isaiah are thus put in perspective, for the editor can view these events with hindsight. The reader, too, is encouraged to put the words of Isaiah, bound as they were to specific situations, in a broader, long-term context.

ORACLES AGAINST VARIOUS NATIONS

Isa 13:1–23:8

The oracles in this section are addressed to various foreign nations but include an oracle against Judah and Jerusalem in 22:1-14 and an oracle against a particular official in 22:15-25. Similar collections of oracles against foreign nations are found in Jer 46–51 and Ezek 25–32 (see also Amos 1:3–2:6; Nahum; Obadiah). The number of such prophecies that have survived shows that it was traditional for prophets to predict doom on other nations (and perhaps thereby bring it about—compare the role of the Moabite seer Balaam, who is called on to curse, or prophesy against, Israel in Num 22–24). Usually the prediction of doom on a nation's enemies carries the implication of blessing for the nation itself.

At least some of these oracles come from a time long after Isaiah (for example, the oracles against Babylon in Isa 13–14). Chapter 20 describes an action in Isaiah's own career, and a few passages may be original oracles of the prophet (for example, 14:24-27; 17:1-11). In several other cases there is no clear evidence of origin. We must allow that Isaiah delivered some oracles against foreign nations, that this collection was expanded, and that much of the present collection may not be from the prophet himself.

The oracles against the nations are of historical interest but offer relatively little religious guidance for the modern reader. Here we will comment only on the more notable passages.

13:1-22 The destruction of Babylon. The occasion envisaged by this prophecy is the fall of Babylon to the Medes and Persians, so it was probably composed about 540 B.C.E. Here the destruction of Babylon is "the day of the Lord," a phrase that can be applied to any manifestation of God in judgment. In verses 10-13 the heavens are darkened and the earth shaken. Yet it is apparent that what the prophet has in mind is a military event, described in gruesomely realistic terms in verse 16. The cosmic effects are metaphorical. They provide vivid images of the collapse, not of the world at large but of the world of the Babylonians. This metaphoric use of cosmic imagery plays an important part in other sections of the book and in later apocalyptic literature.

14:1-22 The king of Babylon. The taunt-song against the king of Babylon is famous for its comparison with "Lucifer, Son of Dawn." The comparison is drawn from an ancient Canaanite myth, where Attar, the Daystar, tries to occupy the throne of Baal. The pattern of the story is a very popular one in the Bible. Whoever tries to rise too high will be cast down lowest of all. In a sense this was already the pattern of the story of Adam and Eve, who were cast out of the garden because they wanted to be like God (see Isa 14:14). The same pattern is found in Ezek 27 and 28. By contrast, the pattern is inverted in the case of Jesus, according to Phil 2. Because he did not deem equality with God something to be grasped at, he received a name above every other name. The model of Lucifer can obviously be applied to many figures in history besides the king of Babylon. (Lucifer in this context is simply the Daystar, a heavenly being, but is not identified as Satan. This model, however, played a part in the popular legend of the fall of Satan from heaven, which was developed by John Milton in *Paradise Lost*.)

One other aspect of these chapters should be noted. The prophet evidently delights in the overthrow of Babylon. There is a certain amount of vengefulness here and considerable resentment toward the overlord—an emotion that superpowers often arouse in less powerful people. This aspect of the prophecies may not be to everyone's taste, although anyone engaged in a struggle for liberation will surely resonate with it. It may not be the ideal attitude toward our enemies, but it is at least realistic. Few people get through life without such sentiments. It is better to express them than to deny them hypocritically. The taunts against Babylon are echoed in the New Testament Book of Revelation (chs. 17–18) to vent the feelings of some early Christians against Rome.

14:24-27 The destruction of Assyria. This brief oracle appears out of context here. It suggests that God will allow the Assyrian to invade Israel and will break him there. It raises the question of how Isaiah envisaged God's overall plan for Israel and Assyria. We will return to this question later (p. 432).

17:1-11 Oracle against Syria and northern Israel. This passage is an authentic oracle of Isaiah from the time of the Syro-Ephraimite war. The prediction is that Syria and northern Israel will be brought low, so that they will come to respect the Holy One of Israel.

17:12-14 The turbulent nations. Chapter 17 concludes with a general statement on the nations, which has many parallels in the psalms (for example, Psalms 2, 48). The viewpoint in these verses is that of the Jerusalem cult, which Isaiah shared only with qualifications. The presupposition is that Yahweh and the nations are in opposition. The conflict is expressed through a metaphor drawn from Canaanite myth. The Canaanites had a story in which the god Baal, the god of fertility, is challenged by the unruly figure of Yamm (the Sea) but proceeds to trounce him with two clubs. Here the nations are like Yamm, turbulent rebels, but the same fate will befall them. God's ability to rebuke the sea is given as testimony to the divine power in the Old Testament (Nah 1:4; Ps 106:9). The same motif is used to show the divinity of Jesus in the New Testament (Matt 8:23-27 and parallels).

19:1-15 Oracles against Egypt. It is uncertain whether any of these oracles actually come from Isaiah. We should note at least that the taunts against the sages of Egypt in verses 11-15 recall Isaiah's quarrel with the sages of Jerusalem (5:18-25). Isaiah's interest in Egypt comes from the fact that Egypt is a potential ally, and Judah might be tempted to rely on Egyptian aid.

19:16-24 The future of Egypt. The short oracles with which the chapter concludes are less likely to come from Isaiah. They fantasize how in the future Egypt will fear Judah and come to worship the Lord. Here we must recognize the desire of the powerless little state to get the upper hand over its powerful neighbor. We know that there were Jewish temples in Egypt at Elephantine (about 400 B.C.E.) and at Leontopolis (about 150 B.C.E.), although this was contrary to the law in Deuteronomy. It is unlikely that the passage in Isaiah had either of these in mind. It is simply indulging in a fantasy about the conversion of the Gentiles. Verses 23-24 add another fantasy—that one day Israel will rank as a third world power with Egypt and Assyria. This fantasy was never realized (at least until modern times!). It is strangely in contradiction to the ideals of Isaiah as we have seen them in chapters 2–11, where he held that Judah would be better off to renounce all ambition in the international arena.

20:1-6 A naked prophet. Symbolic actions were a favorite device of the prophets to dramatize their message. Hosea married a harlot. Ezekiel performed numerous strange acts, including the use of dung to cook his food (Ezek 4). Here we find that Isaiah went naked for three years at the time of the rebellion of Ashdod (713 B.C.E.). This was a sign that Egypt and Ethiopia would fall to Assyria, and the captives would be led away naked.

The symbolic action is a kind of street theatre. It grabs the attention and presents the passerby with a visual image more powerful than any speech. How the people react is, of course, up to them. First they must find out what the sign means, then decide what to do about it. In this case the sign is not performed for the benefit of Egyptians or Ethiopians; rather, it is meant to show the people of Judah and the coastland the folly of relying on Egyptian aid. Egypt was not in fact conquered, but it did not protect the rebels either. Isaiah's warning was justified.

21:1-10 The fall of Babylon. Yet another oracle on the fall of Babylon in the sixth century is inserted here. Two points should be noted. The phrase "Fallen, fallen is Babylon," (21:9) is picked up and applied to Rome in Rev 18:2. The significance of this message for the Jews is underlined in verse 10. Judah has been threshed and winnowed by Babylon—she can hardly fail to delight in the fall of the oppressor.

22:1-14 The fall of Jerusalem. This lone oracle against Jerusalem is included in the oracles against the nations, perhaps to make the point that Judah, too, is subject to judgment (compare the treatment of Israel in Amos 1–2). Much of this oracle presupposes the actual fall of Jerusalem to the Babylonians in 587–586 B.C.E. (so 22:4-11). Some scholars, however, recognize an oracle of Isaiah in verses 1-3 and 12-14, which presuppose that the city did not fall. This oracle may have been delivered on the occasion of Sennacherib's campaign against Jerusalem, which we will examine below in Isa 36–39.

In verses 1-3a the prophet chides the people of Jerusalem for their panic and lack of trust. Then in verses 12-14 he rebukes them because they turned too easily to celebrating instead of taking their narrow escape as an occasion for repentance. The slogan attributed to the revelers, "Eat and drink, for tomorrow we die!" (22:13), is often quoted (see Isa 56:12; Wis 2:6; 1 Cor 15:32). The force of the prophet's criticism may be that the people in Jerusalem did not show enough concern for the sufferings of their fellow Judeans and did not take the lesson of the folly of rebellion to heart.

22:15-25 Rivals at court. The two officials who are the subjects of verses 15-25 are also mentioned in Isa 36 and 2 Kgs 18, where Eliakim is called "master of the palace." The oracle cited here may have been setting a seal of divine approval on a reorganization of the royal cabinet. The wrath of the prophet is aroused by the luxury of Shebna, especially the tomb he has prepared for himself. The prophet sees this as an attempt to control his fate, which will be frustrated by God. He also objects to Shebna's delight in chariots. It is interesting to see the prophet engaging in day-to-day politics and endorsing one official against another. Such participation in political life is necessary for anyone who seriously wants to influence public policy.

THE APOCALYPSE OF ISAIAH

Isa 24:1–27:13

These chapters stand out from their context, as they are much less specific than the oracles against foreign nations which precede them. They are loosely structured and were not necessarily composed as a coherent unit. Attempts to tie them to a specific historical setting have usually focused on allusions to the destruction of a city (24:10-12; 25:1-5; 26:5; 27:10-11). The city in question has been identified with a whole spectrum of cities from Babylon in the sixth century B.C.E. to Samaria in the second. It is not certain, however, that all references are to the same city or that all passages envisage a specific city at all. If the references are to a single city, the most likely referent is Babylon, but the lack of specific detail makes these chapters into a general description of a desolate world and the hope for definitive salvation through the power of God.

24:1-20 The desolation of the earth. This passage reads like a ritual mourning for the land. We may compare Joel 1–2, but there the occasion is quite specific—it is a plague of locusts. In Isa 24 the occasion is not clear at all. It may have been a severe drought or some unspecified historical crisis. Some scholars identify the "city of chaos" in verse 10 as a particular city (for example, Babylon, when it was destroyed by Xerxes of Persia in 482 B.C.E.), but it may also be read as a more general reference. Just as the whole land is turned upside down, cities too are reduced to chaos. Special attention is paid to the lack of wine, which dampens festivity (v. 11). The disorders extend also to social relations. Distinctions in status break down. Servant and master are on equal footing. The prophet is developing themes which we have seen already in Isa 2–3 and which were associated with the "day of the Lord" (see also Joel 1–2). The destruction of the earth and the breakdown of social order are seen as manifestations of the majesty of God and correctives to human pride. Hence the surprising call to give glory to the Lord in verses 14-16 (compare Psalm 29, which takes the thunderstorm as an occasion to give glory to the Lord).

Only two verses give a reason for the desolation of the earth. Verses 5-6 lay the blame on humanity. The offenses are stated in very general terms: they have transgressed laws, broken an everlasting covenant (v. 5). The covenant in question is not necessarily the one made with Moses at Sinai. The phrase "everlasting covenant" (our text reads "ancient covenant") is used in Gen 9:16 for the covenant with Noah, which was a covenant with all peoples, not just Israel. The disruption of the earth, then, may be due to a breach of natural law. The underlying idea is that the order of nature is directly affected by human behavior. This idea was common in ancient Israel, especially in the temple cult. We can appreciate it anew in modern times as we observe the effects of technological progress on the environment or contemplate the threat to nature from the development of nuclear power.

The desolation of the earth redounds to the glory of God, but it is nonetheless a hardship for humanity. Verses 16b-20 evoke the sense of terror for humanity in the manifestation of God's majesty (compare Amos 5:19 on the impossibility of escaping from God's judgment; also, more directly, Jer 48:43-44). Verses 18b-19 describe the destruction of the world. The "windows on high" will let in the floodwaters that have been restrained since creation (compare Jer 4:23-26, where the whole earth is returned to its primeval state and creation is undone). Both in Isa 18–20 and in Jeremiah this total destruction is still in the future. It should not be taken literally as a prediction of the end of the world but as a vivid metaphorical way of conveying a sense of impending desolation.

24:21-23 The final judgment. The last oracle in chapter 24 picks up explicitly the motif of "the day of the Lord." The judgment described, however, has no parallel in the Old Testament, for it includes the punishment of the host of heaven—that is, the stars, which were regarded as angels (see Judg 5:20) or as pagan gods (Deut 4:19; Jer 8:2). The story of rebellious angels who are then punished by God is told in detail in the apocalyptic book of *1 Enoch* in the second century B.C.E. This passage in Isaiah raises the possibility that some mythological notions that first appear in post-biblical Jewish literature had in fact been current at a much earlier time.

The parallel punishment of the host of the heavens and the kings of the earth suggests that the two are closely related. The kings of the earth have their heavenly patrons (compare the notion of guardian angels), who are the real source of their power. This idea was widespread in antiquity. We will meet it again in Isa 36–37.

The culmination of the entire "day of the Lord" is that the Lord of hosts will reign on Mount Zion. The basic concepts in these oracles are drawn from Jerusalem cult traditions. The goal is the veneration of God on Mount Zion. This goal is to be reached through widespread destruction that will bring all peoples, including the Jews, to their knees. It is assumed, however, that life will go on on earth. God is to be glorified in Jerusalem, not in heaven. Christian readers may have difficulty with the prophet's insistence on the particular place, Mount Zion. They can at least appreciate some of the implications. The God of Mount Zion is the God of all the earth, and the frailty of humankind is the converse of the majesty of God.

25:1-5 A hymn of thanksgiving. This short hymn would appear to be written to celebrate the fall of a particular city (the most obvious candidate is Babylon). The lack of specificity, however, makes it possible to reapply it to any other city, or even to take it as a general affirmation of God's ability to upset the status quo (see the song of Hannah in 1 Sam 2).

25:6-8 The final banquet. The image of the great banquet is taken from ancient mythology and has a long history in the folklore of the world. The motif is developed in the "wedding feast of the lamb" in Rev 19 (see also the parable of the great supper in Matt 22:2-14; Luke 14:16-24). The banquet suggests a celebration after the victory is won. In this case the banquet is given "on this mountain," presumably Mount Zion. It is, however, a feast for all peoples, in accordance with the tradition that all the nations would flock to Zion. The feast is described with mouth-watering vividness. This is not the heaven of a disembodied soul but probably reflects the desire of impoverished people for a bountiful meal. The salvation desired goes beyond this, however. God will destroy death forever. In Canaanite mythology, Death (Mot) was the name of a god, the opponent of Baal, god of fertility. The prophet is probably alluding to that myth. The resurrection of those who have already died is *not* implied here. Rather, the point is that God will ultimately remove every threat that hangs over humanity, including the ultimate one. God will also remove all sorrow and the humiliation of the Jewish people during the Exile. The prophet may have hoped for such salvation after the end of the Exile, but the destruction of death remains, inevitably, a distant horizon. Christianity transferred the land without tears to heaven; for Judaism it remains a utopian ideal for life on earth. (For the destruction of death, see Rev 20:14.)

25:9-12 Oracle against Moab. The specific reference to Moab here is usually taken to indicate a date after the Exile when relations were bad between Judea and her neighbors. (The oracle in Isa 24:17-18 is cited as an oracle against Moab in Jer 48:43-44.) Moab was located east of the Dead Sea.

26:1-19 Song of trust. Isa 26 begins as a standard psalm of trust in God, affirming that God vindicates the life of the righteous poor. Verses 11-19 proceed to contrast the other lords who have ruled over Israel with the people of God. The other lords are dead; they cannot rise. The allusion here is probably to Babylon, which was indeed dead as a world power. The Israelites had long labored in vain, failing to achieve salvation. But now, "your dead shall live, their corpses shall rise" (26:19). Some scholars take this verse as the earliest attestation of belief in resurrection in the Hebrew Bible. In view of the context, however, that is unlikely. The point is that Babylonian power is broken and will not be revived. Israelite power, which had been broken, will be revived. The resurrection involved is probably another formulation of the increase of the nation noted in verse 15 (compare Ezekiel's vision of the valley full of dry bones in Ezek 37, which is explicitly interpreted to refer to "the whole house of Israel"). It is the resurrection of a nation through a new generation, not the resuscitation of those who are already dead. Of course, the use of resurrection language to describe the restoration of the Jewish people helped to pave the way for the eventual emergence of a belief in the resurrection of the dead (which is first attested in Judaism in the second century B.C.E.).

26:20-21 Hiding from the wrath. This short oracle suggests that Israel (or perhaps the remnant) is exempt from the wrath of God. The idea that some people can hide from the wrath recalls the Exodus story in which the Lord passes over those houses that have been properly marked (Exod 12). For God going forth to judge the world, the reader should compare the theophanies in Judg 5; Deut 33; Hab 3; also Psalm 98. The prophet also assures the people that the time of God's wrath is a brief moment. If they can wait out the bad time, they will yet be glorified. This idea also plays an important role in Second Isaiah's explanation of the Exile.

27:1 Leviathan. A number of passages in the Bible allude to a battle between God and a monster (variously called a dragon or Rahab; see Isa 51:9; Job 26:12). Usually this battle is in the past. The story of this battle is not told in Genesis or Exodus, and we have only recently come to understand the allusion. The Canaanite myths (which were discovered at Ugarit in northern Syria in 1929) include the story of a battle between the god Baal and the Sea. Associated with the Sea are monsters called Lotan, the dragon, and the crooked serpent. All these are probably the same figure, called by different names. The dragon is a symbol of chaos—all the forces opposed to peace and order. The battle between a god and a dragon was a Canaanite story and symbolized the victory of life and order over chaos. For the Canaanites, Baal was the god who slew the monster and made civilized life possible. When the biblical authors referred to this story, they substituted Yahweh for Baal. For them, it was their God who slew the dragon when the world was created or Israel was led out of Egypt.

Leviathan in Isa 27:1 is the Lotan of Canaanite myth and another name for the sea dragon. This passage, however, suggests that he has not yet been slain. The decisive battle for the welfare and salvation of the world has not yet been won. It remains in the future, to be fought on the "day of the Lord." This expectation of a decisive action by God in the future becomes increasingly prominent in later biblical writings and in the apocalyptic literature. The symbolism of the sea monsters plays a prominent part in Dan 7 and in the Book of Revelation, especially chapters 12 and 13.

The symbol of the monster, Leviathan, is exceptionally powerful. Traditional Christianity would relate this figure to Satan, but the original symbol could be used for any threat to human welfare. "Doing battle with the monster" remains a useful metaphor for our various struggles in life.

27:2-13 The restoration of Israel. This section of Isaiah concludes with a series of oracles introduced by the phrase "On that day." The first picks up the motif of the vineyard from Isa 5. Now Yahweh is no longer angry. Briers and thorns are no longer means of punishment; rather, God will burn them.

The restoration of Israel is conditional, however, on cultic purity—essentially observance of the reform carried out by King Josiah in 621 B.C.E. (see 2 Kgs 22–23), which involved the destruction of altars and places of worship outside of Jerusalem, in accordance with the law of Deut 12.

The "fortified city" (v. 10) and "not an understanding people" (v. 11) would seem to refer to a specific city and people. Many scholars identify the city in this case as Samaria. The allusions to Jacob and Israel, then, should be read as "the northern kingdom," and the implication would be that Israel should find its center in Jerusalem and not in Samaria. The passage is obscure, however. Both its origin and its reference are uncertain.

The last two oracles refer to the gathering in of Jews from the Diaspora. As we have come to expect in the Book of Isaiah, they are to worship on the holy mountain in Jerusalem. Part of the editor's program was apparently to reunite the whole people with Mount Zion as the place of worship for all. In this respect he was probably in continuity with Isaiah of Jerusalem.

POLITICS AND SALVATION

Isa 28:1–33:24

With chapter 28 we return to a cluster of oracles from Isaiah himself. The core of this cluster comes from the time of Hezekiah's decision to revolt against Assyria in 701 B.C.E. A major factor in Hezekiah's decision to revolt was the hope that Egypt would support the various rebel states. Many of Isaiah's prophecies are concerned with the folly of that hope.

These chapters have come to us through the hands of an editor. The oracles are arranged so that judgment and salvation alternate. Many of the oracles of salvation may come from a later time. Nearly all of chapters 32–33 consist of later material. The final editing of this material probably took place after the Babylonian Exile.

28:1-4 The fall of Samaria. The first oracle of this section comes from an earlier period of Isaiah's career, before the fall of Samaria in 722 B.C.E. It is included here partly to ensure that the prophet's word will be seen to address all of Israel and partly because drunkenness is also a theme of the following oracle in verses 7-22. The oracle in verses 1-4 recalls Isaiah's preaching in Isa 5 and that of the prophet Amos. The downfall of Samaria comes from the lifestyle of the upper classes, symbolized by their drunkenness. The "garland" in verse 1 refers to the city of Samaria, perched like a crown on a hill.

28:5-6 The remnant. These verses are the work of an editor who wants to give a positive connotation to the image of a crown. The remnant here has a purely positive meaning. For the prophet Isaiah it was always ambiguous.

28:7-22 Judah's covenant with death. Verses 7-13 refer to Isaiah's dispute with the priests and the other prophets. The heavy drinking may have been in the context of a cultic celebration of Canaanite origin. People drank themselves into a stupor in a celebration of fellowship with the dead. It was an expensive practice that only the rich could afford. Whether Isaiah is referring to this ritual or not, the drunkenness of the priests implies social irresponsibility.

Verse 9 is presumably a quotation of Isaiah's opponents. In verse 10 they mock his preaching as if it were the stammering of a child. (The Hebrew makes no real sense.) Isaiah retorts that his speech sounds strange because they do not listen (see Isa 6:9 and, more directly, Ezek 3:5-9). The word of the Lord becomes nonsense to them, so that they stumble without guidance.

Verses 14-15 are addressed to the rulers of Jerusalem, probably including the religious leaders. They are arrogant because they think they are secure. The "covenant with death" probably refers to an alliance with Egypt. The rulers think that the scourge of Assyria will not touch them because of this alliance. Isaiah, however, sees it as a covenant with death. Death (Mot) was the name of the Canaanite god, enemy of Baal, the god of fertility. Egypt, the traditional enemy of Israel, is called "Death" here, as it is given the name of another Canaanite deity, Rahab, in Isa 30:7. The point is that the attempt to secure life ends in death (see the story of Adam and Eve, and also Hos 13:1, where the Israelites who worship Baal find Mot [Death] instead). Isaiah says that the rulers have made lies their refuge. The lies are the double-talk inherent in diplomacy, but also the hope for Egyptian protection, which was only an illusion.

The cornerstone that God lays in Zion (v. 16) is either God or righteousness and justice. It implies a reference to the Davidic covenant, but the security of Zion depends on its adherence to justice (compare the oracle to Ahaz in Isa 7:9: "Unless your faith is firm you shall not be firm"). Those who trust in anything other than God will be swept away by the flood of Assyria (see Isa 8:8). The saying about the short bed in verse 20 means that there will be no place to rest or hide. The Assyrian invasion is the "strange deed" of God, just as surely as David's victory over the Philistines at Mount Perazim (2 Sam 5:17-25) or Joshua's victory over Gibeon when the sun stood still (Josh 10:1-15). The oracle ends with a definitive assurance that Isaiah has heard of the coming destruction directly from God.

28:23-29 A parable of salvation. The severe proclamation of judgment is followed by a promise of relief. The argument is based on analogy from nature: there is a season for everything, destruction cannot go on forever. Whether Isaiah spoke this oracle is disputed. It accords well with his overall message. He never predicted that Judah would be left without any remnant. It is unlikely that he delivered this oracle together with the preceding one, since it would have undermined the threat, but he may well have spoken it later, when the Assyrian invasion was underway or already past. An editor placed it here to show that the threat of destruction was ultimately modified and should not be taken as final.

29:1-8 Ariel, Ariel. Ariel is evidently a name for Jerusalem. Its meaning and origin are obscure. It may be derived from a word meaning "altar."

Verses 1-5a represent God as attacking Jerusalem (presumably through the Assyrians) just as David did long ago. Verse 1 gives the impression that the festivals are observed in a mindless manner and to no avail. Verse 4 vividly describes how Jerusalem will be brought low, but it stops short of saying that the city will be captured.

The sudden visitation by God in verse 6 is ambiguous here. On the one hand, it completes the humiliation of Jerusalem; on the other hand, it is also a saving act. The enemy will be frustrated at the last moment and will vanish like a dream of the night. This passage strongly resembles the Zion ideology presented in the psalms. According to Ps 48:5-6,

> . . . the kings assemble,
> they come on together;
> They also see, and at once are stunned,
> terrified, routed.

The psalm attests the belief in the inviolability of Zion, a popular belief in Jerusalem that was later sharply criticized by Jeremiah (Jer 7:4). Many scholars question whether Isaiah would have endorsed such a belief. Yet, we have found throughout that Isaiah's message was double-edged. First, Judah would be brought to its knees, but it would not be utterly destroyed. Isaiah modifies the Zion theology by insisting that Jerusalem is not protected from humiliation. The "strange deed" (28:21) of the Lord, then, includes both extensive destruction and ultimate deliverance, and is presumably meant to teach Judah a severe lesson.

29:9-16 Criticism of the "wise." These verses continue the critique of 28:7-22. The blindness of the leaders recalls the prophecy of Isa 6:9-10. The reasons for the criticism are twofold: superficial worship (v. 13; compare Matt 15:8; Mark 7:6) and the attempt of the king's advisers to control their destiny by devious diplomacy. Isaiah's ideal of simple submission to the plan of God would, of course, eliminate Judah's ambitions as a state.

29:17-24 Prophecy of salvation. In some respects, the predominant optimism of this prophecy is closer in spirit to Second Isaiah than to Isaiah of Jerusalem (compare 29:18 with 42:7). Yet, much of what it anticipates concerns the internal reform of Judah, especially the removal of the arrogant rulers. This theme follows well enough on verses 9-16. It may be that an original oracle of Isaiah was recast by the editor to provide a counterpart to the negative oracles of verses 9-16.

30:1-18 Alliance with Egypt. Isaiah again castigates the Judeans for relying on international intrigue and especially on the promise of Egyptian help. The gifts given to Egypt are wasted. Egypt is called "Rahab," a name for the chaos monster (see Job 26:12), but it is a subdued Rahab, not only evil but useless. The prophet is irate at the unwillingness of the people to listen to his own message or to consider the Holy One as a factor in their plans. The king's counselors found prophets useful enough when they spoke flattery and were willing to spread propaganda; the prophet who had an independent point of view was merely a nuisance.

Isaiah's message to Hezekiah was essentially the same as his advice to Ahaz: "By waiting and by calm you shall be saved." First, they should not provoke the Assyrians by revolting. Second, they should not compound the problem by alliances and attempts at resistance. Isaiah makes no allowance for national pride, nor even for the natural instinct to provide for one's own protection. The *trust* is that God will protect them, not indeed from all harm, but from being wiped out. This passive approach might mean accepting much suffering, but Isaiah could validly argue that the alternatives were worse. They could not hope to flee from the Assyrians. Patient trust here becomes the cornerstone (Isa 28:16) of the hope for salvation in Zion. We may compare Isaiah's stance with the ethic of nonresistance attributed to Jesus in the Sermon on the Mount (Matt 5:38-42).

We should emphasize, however, that for Isaiah nonresistance was a political tactic that might lessen the danger of outright destruction.

30:19-26 Salvation for Zion. Verses 19-26, probably the work of an editor, expand on the idea that God is willing to show favor. The concern for the destruction of idols (v. 22) and the transformation of the high places (v. 23) point to the time of King Josiah's reform, when the cultic sites outside Jerusalem were destroyed (2 Kgs 23). Verse 21, "This is the way . . . ," is the fulfillment of the promise of Isa 2:3 that God would "instruct us in his ways."

30:27-33 Judgment on Assyria. This oracle, too, may be a later addition, from the time when Assyria fell to the Babylonians in 612 B.C.E. The idea that Assyria would eventually be destroyed had its precedent in Isa 10. The manifestation of God in the thunderstorm is the image used throughout Isaiah for destruction, whether of Israel or of Assyria. The prophet points out that the oppressors of history eventually fall. Even though the prophets use historical crises as occasions to press for the reform of their own people, it is important that they do not thereby endorse the actions of the superpowers.

31:1-3 Flesh and spirit. Yet another indictment of the alliance with Egypt puts the matter in a new way: the Egyptians are human and not divine, their horses are flesh and not spirit. The contrast here is not between body and soul but between human power and divine power. The Egyptians have only fallible human power; they are not supernatural and can work no miracles to save Judah from Assyria. The point is that Judah overrates Egypt. Similarly the horses, a crucial element in the armaments for the day, are only flesh; they cannot withstand what Isaiah sees as the plan of God. This contrast of flesh, as mere humanity, to the spirit or power of God will play an important role in the theology of St. Paul in the New Testament.

31:4-6 Deliverance of Zion. As in the preceding chapters, an editor has balanced the prophet's indictment with an oracle of salvation. The image of God sheltering Jerusalem like a flock of birds fits well with the popular Zion theology but is far too simple for Isaiah, who preached consistently that only a remnant would survive. The reference to idols in verse 7 again shows the concerns of King Josiah's reform.

31:8 Fall of Assyria. Like the preceding chapter, chapter 31 ends with a prediction of the fall of Assyria, to set the record straight. When Assyria did fall, the sword was wielded by the Babylonians, but a Jewish prophet would still see that event as the work of the Lord.

32:1-8 A just king. Unlike the messianic prophecies in Isa 9 and 11, this passage does not refer explicitly to the Davidic line or the royal ideology; therefore it has been thought to come from a later hand. It does presuppose the existence of the monarchy, however, and so must be preexilic. The contrast of the fool and the noble is typical of the wisdom literature. Verse 3 would seem to deliberately revoke Isa 6:10. The concern of the passage is with justice in the land, with feeding the hungry and giving drink to the thirsty. It implies a criticism of the rulers of the day, who are branded as fools for their neglect of the Lord and for social injustice. The oracle is in continuity with the preaching of Isaiah, but the generalized references to the fool and the trickster lack the specificity of a passage like Isa 5.

32:9-13 Prophecy of impending destruction. This passage picks up motifs from earlier prophecies of Isaiah (see the oracle against the women of Jerusalem in 3:16-26 and the briers and thorns in 5:6; 7:23-24). Here, however, the address is to women of the countryside, in view of the references to fields and harvest. It does not indict them for luxury but wants to alert them to imminent danger. The occasion of this oracle is unknown.

32:14-20 A rustic utopia. The New American Bible has transposed verse 19 and placed it before verse 15, thereby altering the sense of the passage. In the Hebrew the transformation of the desert goes hand in hand with the destruction of the city. When the city is destroyed, the people will live in the quiet countryside, imbued with the spirit of the Lord. This passage does not accord well with either the message of Isaiah or with most of the tradition in this book, all of which had an important place for a purified Jerusalem in any final utopia (see especially 2:1-5, but also 33:17-24). The New American Bible solves the difficulty by moving the last verse and so allowing that the city may share in the restoration. Others suggest a different translation (for example, the "cities shall lie peaceful in the plain"—New English Bible), but even this contrasts with the exaltation of Zion in Isa 2. We may at least see some continuity between Isaiah's disdain for the luxury of the upper classes and the negative attitude toward the city here. The blooming of the desert appears again in 35:1 and 43:19-20.

33:1 Oracle against an enemy. This very brief oracle is addressed to Assyria or Babylon or some other enemy. The logic is the same as in Isa 10 or 30:27-33: the day of the oppressor will come.

33:2-16 Prayer for God's manifestation. This section is made up of smaller units that alternate between distress and hope for the manifestation of God. Verses 2-4 pray for God to be revealed on Zion and terrify all enemies. Verses 7-9 describe the breakdown of the country. Verses 10-13 are an oracle proclaiming the theophany. Verse 14 states the initial human response: who of us can live with the consuming fire? The manifestation of God is terrifying even for God's own people. Verses 15-16 give the answer: the virtuous can stand in the presence of God. This whole passage would seem to be derived from a liturgy in the Jerusalem temple (see Psalm 24).

33:17-24 The restoration of Zion. This passage may well have concluded one edition of the prophecies of Isaiah. The editor promises a full restoration of the monarchy and of Zion, which had been major points of reference in the prophecy of Isaiah. Compare the earlier prophecies in Isa 2, 9, and 11.

POSTEXILIC ORACLES

Isa 34:1–35:10

These two chapters are generally believed to belong together. The deliverance of Jerusalem is the counterpart of the destruction of Edom. There are also similarities of language in the two chapters. The setting is after the Exile, when the Jewish community experienced much tension with all its neighbors. Edom lay immediately south of Judah.

34:1-17 Oracle against Edom. This oracle begins with a call to judgment (see Deut 32:1) against all nations and then moves to the specific case of Edom. The presuppositions of the judgment are drawn from the royal ideology: the Lord is Zion's defender and defeats all nations that oppose it. The passage is notable for two reasons. First, it uses the imagery of cosmic destruction—the heavens will be rolled up like a scroll. This imagery is obviously metaphorical here. It is a poetic evocation of utter desolation, which attests the absolute power of God over the world. In the later apocalyptic literature this imagery is used in a more literal way.

Second, we cannot overlook the fact that this is a rather gory fantasy of vengeance. It is true that the vengeance of the Lord is closely related to the idea of justice. It is a matter of punishing the oppressor and vindicating the oppressed (see Deut 32:34-43). Yet, it is no less true that this oracle expresses the frustration and resentment of the Jewish community in the hard times of the postexilic period. The sentiments expressed are less than admirable, but they are certainly an honest expression of human nature. Religious people have often expected their God to satisfy their desire for vengeance. The expectation, however, is seldom fulfilled.

35:1-10 A triumphal procession. Chapter 35 provides the positive counterpart to chapter 34 by focusing on Israel's liberation. The imagery is closely related to that of Second Isaiah: there will be a highway in the desert (see Isa 40:3), the desert will bloom and burst forth with springs (see Isa 43:19). Verse 10 is repeated directly in Isa 51:11. The liberation involves opening the eyes of the blind and the ears of the deaf (see Isa 42:7). The theme of the procession, which is also fundamental to Second Isaiah, is probably derived from the temple cult. The message is one of comfort and hope. Undoubtedly the author of these chapters saw the destruction of enemies like Edom as a necessary precondition for the transformation. In both cases we must recognize the role of fantasy, but the images of chapter 35 have lasting power to console and encourage those in need of liberation.

STORIES FROM THE TIME OF KING HEZEKIAH

Isa 36:1–39:8

The prose narrative that concludes First Isaiah is paralleled, almost word for word, in 2 Kgs 18:13–20:19. Since the account fits into the ongoing narrative of Kings and is written in the style of that work, we may assume that it was borrowed from there by the editor of Isaiah.

The narrative is made up of three episodes: the invasion of Sennacherib in chapters 36–37, the sickness and recovery of Hezekiah in chapter 38, and the Babylonian delegation in chapter 39. The stories in chapters 38 and 39 qualify the miraculous deliverance in chapter 37. Chapter 38 suggests that Hezekiah is a special king in any case, and chapter 39 warns that the deliverance from the Assyrians will not be repeated when the Babylonians attack.

36:1–37:38 The invasion of Sennacherib. The narrative in Isa 36 differs from that of 2 Kgs 18 in one major respect. It omits 2 Kgs 18:14-16, which says that Hezekiah submitted and paid an exorbitant tribute to the king of Assyria, including even the gold overlay from the panels of the temple. The accuracy of that passage in 2 Kings is confirmed by an Assyrian account, which boasts that Hezekiah was shut up in Jerusalem "like a bird in a cage," his territory reduced, some two hundred thousand of his people taken into slavery, and the tribute increased. The account in Isaiah (like 2 Kgs 18:17–19:37) makes no mention of this humiliation but ends instead with a miraculous deliverance by the angel of the Lord.

There are other difficulties in the narrative. 2 Kgs 18:9 puts the accession of Hezekiah before the fall of Samaria, in 725 B.C.E. His fourteenth year then would be 711 B.C.E., but we know that Sennacherib's campaign took place in 701 B.C.E. The dates have been somehow confused in the transmission of the text. Tirhakah, mentioned in Isa 37:9, did not become king of Egypt until 690/89 B.C.E. He is named here by mistake, by an author who evidently wrote long after the events. Moreover, the narrative is not really one account but two—the first in Isa 36:1–37:9a, the second in Isa 37:9b-36. The second account repeats part of the words of the Assyrian messengers from the first account but gives a slightly different account of the role of Isaiah. The main problem, however, concerns the relation of the incident described here to that in 2 Kgs 18:14-16.

Some scholars resolve this problem (and the mention of Tirhakah) by supposing that there was a second invasion by Sennacherib about 688 B.C.E. There is no extrabiblical evidence for this. It is simpler to suppose that a single invasion was remembered in different ways, as indeed there are differences between the two accounts in Isa 36–37. In that case, we must assume that Hezekiah was forced into submission. The cost to Judah was enormous, but Jerusalem was spared and Hezekiah was allowed to continue on the throne. Even this much must have seemed like a miraculous deliverance to the people of Jerusalem, since they had little hope of withstanding the Assyrian attack.

The reason for Sennacherib's *relative* leniency is not clear. Isa 37:7 suggests that he was eager to return home to forestall conspiracy. Isa 37:9 suggests that he was threatened by an Egyptian advance. There is a report in the Greek historian Herodotus that an Assyrian army was overrun by field mice near the Egyptian border. This report has the appearance of a legend, but some have supposed that it arose from an outbreak of bubonic plague in the Assyrian army, and that this in turn was perceived by the Jews as the work of the angel of the Lord. In any case, Judah had not escaped unscathed. The description of the ravaged land in Isa 1:2-8 probably refers to this time.

36:1–37:9a The first account. The first account is largely taken up with the speech of the Assyrian messengers. The capture of Lachish, southwest of Jerusalem, is known from an Assyrian wall relief and from excavations at the site. The speech of the messengers is probably a creation of the Jewish author, inspired perhaps by Isaiah's oracle against Assyria in Isa 10:5-11. The unreliability of Egypt might indeed be a theme of Assyrian propaganda, as it was of Isaiah's preaching. The suggestion that Hezekiah had alienated Yahweh by tearing down some altars presupposes knowledge of Hezekiah's reform (2 Chr 29:3–31:21). The claim that Yahweh sent the king of Assyria anticipates the propaganda of Cyrus of Persia at a later time. In all, the speech reads like clever propaganda, although it may tell us more about Jewish perceptions than about Assyrian views. The punch line comes in verse 18: "Has any of the gods of the nations ever rescued his land from the hand of the king of Assyria?" The success of a nation is taken to reflect the power or weakness of its God. In

Jewish eyes, the assault on Jerusalem was a direct affront to Yahweh (see Ps 79:10: "Why should the nations say, 'Where is their God?' ").

The response of Isaiah (37:6) in the first account recalls his advice to King Ahaz in Isa 7:4: "Do not fear." The advice to remain calm was not, of course, easy advice in the circumstances, but it was consistent with the prophet's stance throughout his career.

37:9b-36 The second account. The second account elaborates on the role of Isaiah. First, he recites a lengthy psalm, affirming that an attack on Jerusalem is an insult to the Holy One of Israel and is doomed to defeat (see Psalms 2, 48). Some of the wording of the psalm recalls Second Isaiah (37:26; see also 45:21; 46:10), and this contributes to the impression that it does not come from Isaiah himself (also compare 37:29 with Ezek 38:4). In verses 30-32, however, we may well have an authentic prophecy of Isaiah, since it recalls his position in Isa 7. Cultivation will not even be possible for two years. Only a remnant will remain, but it will be the bearer of God's promises to Zion. Here the full cost to Judah is acknowledged.

Isaiah's prophecy of the remnant is overlaid here, however, with pious legend. First, in verses 33-35 Isaiah is said to prophesy that the Assyrians would not even reach Jerusalem. The Assyrian account, by contrast, explicitly claims to have cast up earthworks against the city. Then comes the action of the angel of the Lord. Even if we assume that a large number of Assyrians died in a plague (185,000 is impossibly high), attribution of this to the angel of the Lord requires a leap of faith and is the stuff of legend.

What actually happened is far from clear. Sennacherib must have offered Hezekiah terms that did not require his abdication, and he accepted. Whether Isaiah approved of the surrender is not reported. The occasion can hardly have aroused much rejoicing in Jerusalem. Yet, with the passage of time the humiliation was forgotten, and the fact that Jerusalem was not destroyed was seen as proof of God's protection. In one sense this showed a proper appreciation of the gift of life, which was preserved against all expectations. On the other hand, it surely contributed to the complacent belief that Zion could never fall, a belief that Jeremiah encountered with much frustration a century later.

The violent death of Sennacherib is also reported in nonbiblical stories.

38:1-8 The sickness of Hezekiah. The king's own experience parallels the deliverance of Jerusalem. At first his death seems certain; then he gets a reprieve. The reason is apparently his wholehearted piety. We may infer that this is also why Jerusalem was reprieved. Things might be different under another king. This story, too, has a legendary quality in the supernatural sign of the reversal of the sun. Such stories are meant to arouse wonder, not to report fact. Note that Hezekiah is not criticized for asking for a sign, as Ahaz had been.

38:9-20 Hymn of thanksgiving. Hezekiah recites a psalm of a type that is well-attested in the Psalter (see Psalms 6, 13, 22). It begins by describing the plaintiff's distress and then moves to thanksgiving for the Lord's deliverance. The moral in 38:16 applies also to the experience of Jerusalem in the preceding chapter. Note that this psalm entertains no hope for God's favor beyond death. The finality of death made the plight of Hezekiah and of Jerusalem all the more urgent.

39:1-8 The delegation from Babylon. The story of the delegation from Babylon prepares us for the transition to the Babylonian era. The fall of Jerusalem to the Babylonians is never described in the Book of Isaiah, but it is the presupposition of Isa 40–55. The editor of the book fills the gap by having Isaiah prophesy it here in the story taken from 2 Kgs 20. At the same time, the prophecy corrects the impression that Zion cannot fall, which might be derived from chapters 36–37.

Hezekiah's action in displaying his treasures is typical of ancient diplomacy and was designed to impress his visitors. Babylon at that time was a rising power eager to foster rebellion against Assyria. That such a delegation should have visited Hezekiah is not in itself implausible. Hezekiah's reaction to Isaiah's prediction smacks of Louis XIV's famous dictum *"Après moi le déluge."* The author probably meant only to emphasize that Hezekiah ended his days in peace because of his piety. (Compare the idea that the punishment of King Ahaz was deferred until the time of his son because he repented [1 Kgs 21:29].)

COMMENTARY: SECOND ISAIAH (Isa 40–55)

At Isa 40:1 we move to a new setting at the end of the Babylonian Exile (539 B.C.E.), and the oracles that follow are very different from those of Isa 1–39 in tone. They are often called the "Book of Consolation." Unlike chapters 1-39, all the oracles in these chapters are likely to be the work of a single prophet. They may be divided into two parts: chapters 40–48 deal predominantly with liberation from Babylon; chapters 49–55 with the restoration of Zion. The difference between these parts, however, is a matter of degree of emphasis and cannot be taken to indicate different origins or settings.

LIBERATION FROM BABYLON
Isa 40:1–48:22

The first part of Second Isaiah takes the good news that the Exile is at an end as the occasion to contrast Israel and Babylon and their respective gods.

40:1-11 The proclamation of release. This passage serves as an introduction to all of Second Isaiah by specifying the occasion of the oracles—the release of Israel from the Babylonian Exile. In Ezra 1 this event is attributed to a decree of Cyrus, king of Persia. The prophet, however, claims that there is a more fundamental cause, namely, a decree of Yahweh in the heavenly council. The idea of a heavenly council of gods was widespread in the ancient world and was based on the assumption that God has a royal court like any great king. Vivid biblical illustrations are found in Psalm 82, 1 Kgs 22, and Isa 6. The scene in Isa 40 may be viewed as a counterpoint to that of Isa 6. In the earlier chapter the decree was one of judgment on Israel; here it is one of consolation. (Note that Jerusalem can stand for the people as a whole.)

Verse 2 presupposes the usual view that the Exile was a punishment for Israel's sins, but adds that Israel has received "double for all her sins." The implication is that the suffering is not fully explained as punishment. We will find later that Second Isaiah finds a more positive way to understand the experience of the Exile.

The voice in verse 3 is the voice of an angel implementing the divine decree. The "way" is analogous to the great ritual processions of the Babylonian gods, but also the triumphal procession of Yahweh from Mount Sinai at the time of the Exodus (compare Ps 68:8-9; Deut 33:3). The Exodus motif is made explicit by the location "in the desert." The return from Babylon is seen as a reenactment of the original liberation of Israel out of Egypt. The hope for a new Exodus was found as early as Hosea (ch. 2) in the eighth century, but now Second Isaiah claims that it is actually taking place.

The liberation of Israel is viewed as a revelation of God. In the first Exodus, Israel's God went before the people in a pillar of cloud or a pillar of fire. Now all flesh would see the glory of God. The prophet is told to proclaim the difference between the passing power of humanity and the unshakable word of God. The power of the Babylonians, which had seemed so great, had now faded like the grass of the field.

In verses 9-11 Zion/Jerusalem is told to proclaim the good news to "the cities of Judah." (The familiar translation "O thou who bringest good tidings to Zion" is possible but improbable, since the verbs are feminine in agreement with Zion.) Here again Jerusalem is an ideal figure, representing the community of exiles who would join the prophet in returning to restore the actual city. We should bear in mind that not all the Jews who were in Babylon took the opportunity to return; many decided that they were better off in exile. The prophet is not only proclaiming deliverance but urging the people to accept it. He bases his exhortation on the assurance that God is with them with power, but also with loving care, suggested by the popular image of the shepherd (compare Psalm 23 and John 10).

This passage of Second Isaiah is best known to Christian readers from the citations in Matt 3:3 and John 1:23, where Isa 40:3 is taken to mean "the voice of one crying in the wilderness" and applied to John the Baptist. The citation is not quite accurate and does not give the original meaning of the passage. The application to John was apt enough, however, since he too was proclaiming a new act of salvation like the Exodus, and he set himself to prepare for it.

40:12-31 The incomparable God. The threefold oracle in verses 12-31 follows naturally from the declaration "Here is your God" in verse 9. The first stanza (vv. 12-17) asks a series of rhetorical questions reminiscent of Job 38–41. The implied answer is that it is Yahweh alone who has created the earth. The nations are as nothing before Yahweh, since the whole earth is in this God's grasp.

The second stanza (vv. 18-24) begins with another rhetorical question: To whom can God be likened? Second Isaiah mocks the statue-makers, as he will do at much greater length in chapter 44. (The New American Bible unnecessarily inserts verses 6-7 of chapter 41 here.) The initial question is balanced by another: "Do you not know? Have you not heard?" (40:21). What has been told from the beginning is the sovereign power of Yahweh to bring princes to nought and make rulers as nothing (40:23; compare Psalm 107). Yahweh's ability to overthrow the Babylonians comes from the fact that it was Yahweh who created the earth, as the cult tradition of Jerusalem had long claimed (for example, Psalms 93, 95).

The third stanza (vv. 25-31) closely parallels the second in form. The introductory question, "To whom can you liken me . . . ?" (40:25), is followed by a command to look up at the stars, which were often honored as divine by Babylonians. The prophet shares the common belief that the stars are a heavenly host of supernatural beings but insists that they are subject to Yahweh, who keeps them in order. At this point the prophet directly reproaches the Israelites for their despair in feeling abandoned by their God. The second half of the stanza, "Do you not know, or have you not heard?" (40:28), responds directly to this despair. The Creator is everlasting. Not only does God not grow faint but the Creator is a source of renewed power for those who are attentive to the divine will. Hope did not come easily to the Jews during the Exile. It was only possible for those who deeply believed that their God was indeed the supreme God. Second Isaiah was convinced that his faith was now vindicated by the fall of Babylon. Note that in verse 25 God is called "the Holy One," a title often found in First Isaiah.

41:1–42:9 Judgment and election. Many commentators divide this long passage into several short oracles. In particular, 42:1-4 is commonly set apart as one of the so-called "Servant Songs." The key to understanding the passage, however, is to recognize that there are two parallel and complementary trial scenes in 41:1-20 and 41:21–42:9. In each case there is:

—summons to trial	41:1	41:21
—legal questioning	41:2-4	41:22-29
—election and reassurance of Israel	41:5-20	42:1-9

In the first scene the nations are summoned for judgment. The issue to be decided is: Who raised up Cyrus of Persia, the "champion of justice," who overthrew Babylon? The answer is given unequivocally: Yahweh, first and last, is responsible for all developments in history. Verses 5-7 (verses 6-7 are inserted after 40:20 in our text) parody the reaction of the Gentiles. They have to encourage one another in making their idols, since the idols cannot encourage them. By contrast, Israel is chosen as the Servant of the Lord. However despised Israel may be in the Exile as a "worm" or "maggot" (compare Ps 22:6), there is no reason to fear. Yahweh is the servant's redeemer (41:14), buying his freedom from slavery. This section concludes with a prophecy of the transformation of the desert with water for the needy. The reference to the desert suggests that the Exodus theme is implied here and that the poor and needy are Israel. The transformation, however, is also for the Gentiles, so that they will recognize the work of the Holy One of Israel.

The second section has a long series of questions and constitutes a more coherent trial. The challenge is: Which of the gods had foretold the rise of Cyrus, and, more crucially, had heralded good news for Israel? The answer is a resounding "Not one." The conclusion is that "all of them are nothing" (41:29). Second Isaiah is more emphatic in denying the power of pagan gods than any earlier biblical book. The argument presupposes the prophet's faith that it is Yahweh who is responsible for the collapse of the power of Babylon. Anyone who did not already share that faith would hardly be persuaded.

The so-called Servant Song in 42:1-4 corresponds to 41:8-9 in singling out a chosen Servant. In both passages the Servant is Israel, conceived in terms of its ideal destiny. The mission of the Servant is specified much more fully in chapter 42 than in chapter 41. The spirit of the Lord is upon him, as on the messianic king in Isa 11. He is to bring justice to the nations, but in a nonviolent, nonaggressive way. The role is further elaborated in 42:6-7. The Servant is a covenant of the people, a light to the nations. We may recall the portrayal of Mount Zion as a center for the nations in Isa 2:2-4. The precise understanding of "a covenant of the people" (42:6) is disputed, but the idea seems to be that God makes a covenant with the nations through the mediation of Israel. The Servant is also sent to open the eyes of the blind and liberate the imprisoned. In the following passages the "blind" refers to Israel (42:16) and specifically to the Servant in 42:19! The most obvious "prisoners" in this context are the Jewish exiles in Babylon. Yet, the Servant Israel is being sent to help the blind and imprisoned.

Some scholars have drawn the conclusion that the Servant in this passage is not Israel but an individual, and that the passage comes from a different hand than the surrounding oracles. We will see in Isa 42:18–43:8, however, that there is considerable ambiguity in the idea of the Servant. There is tension between the ideal of what Israel is supposed to be and what the community actually is. It is Israel's destiny to be a light to the nations, but in order to fulfill this, the blind among the people must recover their sight and the exiles must be liberated.

The section concludes with affirmations that God does not give divine glory to idols (compare 41:6-7) and that "the earlier things have come to pass" (42:9; compare 41:22-23, 26). In this way the prophet concludes this long section by referring back to two important themes of chapter 41.

42:10-17 A hymn to Yahweh the warrior. The "new song" (v. 10) is a hymn of praise like Psalms 96 and 98, which begin with the same invitation. The reason for praise is given in verses 13-17: Yahweh the warrior, who has held back for a time, will let loose divine anger. Here again there is reference to the Exodus, when Yahweh was first recognized as a warrior (Exod 15:3). The divine warrior was traditionally supposed to have a destructive effect on nature (Isa 42:15; compare Judg 5:4-5; Hab 3:5-15; Nah 1:2-6). In Exodus 15 God leads the people to their triumphant occupation of the land; here too God will lead the "blind" Jews on their return journey. The confusion of idol worshipers in verse 17 is the corollary of the recognition of Yahweh as the true God.

42:18–43:8 The deaf and the blind. Despite his general euphoria, the prophet has moments of dejection. The address to his people as "blind and deaf" betrays some frustration on his part. The problem is not only that they are despoiled and plundered but they have become indifferent. So the prophet insists that even their humiliation in the Exile was the work of their God and was a punishment for sin. Yet Israel is still the Servant (42:19). The tension between Israel's vocation as Servant and its present reality is most obvious in this passage. Despite the past divine wrath, God has now redeemed Israel and promises to protect it in any ordeal, be it fire or water. The Holy One is identified as the savior of Israel, which is more precious than Egypt or Ethiopia. The implication is that the Persians will be allowed to conquer other countries in return for the release of Israel. The reason given in 43:4 is simply "because I love you" (compare Deut 9, which insists that the original gift of the land was not merited by Israel). The new Exodus is an Exodus of the blind.

There is some vacillation in Second Isaiah's portrayal of Israel. Some passages emphasize the ideal, what Israel is called to be, and minimize the people's sin. This passage is exceptional in its frank criticism of their shortcomings. The apparent inconsistency comes not only from the emotional intensity of the prophet but also from the nature of his program, which was to project an ideal of Yahweh's Servant that was not fully realized in the exilic community.

43:9-12 The Servant as witness. This brief trial scene repeats some of the motifs of the longer unit in 41:1–42:9. Again the issue is who is the true God, and the test is the ability to foretell the future. A new motif is introduced with the idea that the Jewish people are witnesses. They are called "my servant" collectively (the Hebrew reads the singular; the New American Bible changes it to "my servants"). The mission of witnessing is the same as being "a light for the nations" (42:6). Whereas in earlier times the Davidic king was Yahweh's representative on earth, that role has now passed to the people.

Isa 43:10 is exceptionally strong in its denial of the other gods and may be taken to mean that they do not even exist. The prophet is not a philosopher, however. What concerns him is not the existence of the gods as such but the power to save. He is completely unequivocal in his assertion that there is no savior but Yahweh.

43:14–44:5 Exodus and election. The immediate point of reference in this oracle is stated at the outset: the release of the Jews from Babylon. Isa 43:15-21 puts this event in context. Yahweh is the creator of Israel by virtue of the Exodus, yet the Jews are told not to remember the things of the past. The Exodus is not past history! It is something new, something that is happening in the present. The present tense in verse 16 ("opening a way") is quite deliberate. God's saving action, summed up in the Exodus story, is not all past but is repeatable. Exodus is a pattern in history. What matters is not so much whether it happened in the time of Moses but whether it is happening in the present. Second Isaiah thus points the way to using the Exodus story to throw light on a new situation. In our own time the Exodus story has been appropriated in a similar way by the liberation theologians of Latin America.

The original Exodus was followed by failure on Israel's part (see especially the indictment in Deut 32). Second Isaiah acknowledges this and even asserts that the destruction of Jerusalem was a punishment for Israel's sin. (The "first father" in 43:27 is probably Jacob; compare Hos 12:3.) Yet Jacob is also the Servant, formed from the womb (44:2; compare 49:5). The descendants of Israel will fulfill their destiny by the help of the spirit (compare 42:1), which will vitalize them as water brings life to dry ground. Compare the transforming power of the spirit in Ezek 36, where there is also an analogy with water, and in Joel 3. Here again we find a contrast between Israel's sinful history down to the present and its future as the Servant of the Lord.

44:6-23 The futility of idols. The comparison of Yahweh with the other gods begins by touching on some themes that are now familiar. Yahweh alone can predict events, and Israel is Yahweh's witness. The passage continues with a scathing attack on idolatry. The prophet is engaging in polemics. He is not attempting to give a sympathetic or even fair presentation of the idol-makers. The idol is only a piece of wood, such as one burns in the fire. It can have no power to save. Of course, the pagans probably looked on their idols much as Roman Catholics have looked on statues of saints—not as the actual sources of power but as representations that are helpful to the worshiper's imagination. The point of the polemic, however, is that the pagan gods are fittingly represented by pieces of wood, because they have no more power than their idols. The God of Israel, by contrast, is represented by a living people, whose resurgence from the Exile witnesses to God's vitality.

The polemic against the idols, then, culminates in the contrast with Israel, whom God has formed to God's own glory. Israel is not an icon but a Servant, a living representative. The "fashioning" of Israel entails wiping out its sin and redeeming it. The liberation from the Exile, then, is the occasion when Israel is to be remade into an appropriate reflection of the glory of God.

44:24–45:13 The Persian messiah. The central contention of this oracle is that Yahweh is creator of all, and therefore the fall of Babylon and the rise of Persia are God's work. The prophet's primary purpose is not to convince the Gentiles of this but to convince the Jews. So he begins by affirming that Yahweh is the redeemer of Israel and by highlighting the restoration of Jerusalem and Judah. The novelty of this passage, however, is the explicit statement that the decree to rebuild Jerusalem will come through the mouth of Cyrus, who is God's anointed king, or messiah (45:1).

The idea that God's purposes are achieved through pagan kings is not a new one. Isaiah of Jerusalem had said that Assyria was the rod of Yahweh's anger (Isa 10:5). Jeremiah declared the Babylonian king Nebuchadnezzar to be the servant of God (Jer 27:6). Unlike the Assyrian of Isa 10, Cyrus is not accused of pride or arrogance. He fulfills every wish of God. One purpose of his mission is that he himself may come to know that Yahweh is God. The prophet is preaching here a thorough universalism. Pagans may serve Yahweh even though they do not know the God of Israel. Ultimately Yahweh must be known from the rising of the sun to its setting (compare Mal 1:11).

The basis for this universalism is a thorough monotheism, which emerges here more clearly than in any earlier biblical book. There is no God beside Yahweh. Persian religion was dualistic: there was a god of light, responsible for the good, and a god of darkness, responsible for evil. Second Isaiah holds that one God creates both light and darkness, good and evil (45:7). (Compare the rugged insistence of Amos 3:6 that if evil befalls a city, Yahweh must have caused it.) The evil that befell Jerusalem was Yahweh's work; so now it is the rise of Cyrus that brings its restoration.

Not all the Jewish exiles could so readily accept a Persian messiah. The "woes" of verses 9-10 are addressed to those doubters who question whether this can be the work of God. All humankind is created by God and counts as children of God (v. 11). Yet, Second Isaiah has by no means abandoned the special place of Israel. The hand of God can be seen in Cyrus' career because he liberates the Jews and mandates the rebuilding of Jerusalem. It is for the sake of Jacob that Cyrus is called (v. 4). It is in the interest of the Jews themselves to accept the Persian sovereignty as the work of their God.

45:14-25 The hidden God. Nations may serve God without knowing it, but Second Isaiah believed that the time had come for universal recognition. People from the ends of the earth would bring gifts to the temple in Jerusalem. Verses 14-17 formulate a confession for these Gentiles. Verse 15 can also be translated "You are a God who hides yourself." The point is that until now the Gentiles would not have suspected that Yahweh controls all history. What has been hidden, however, is now made manifest. Yet the notion of a hidden God is important. What is going on in history may not always be obvious. We should not jump to conclusions because one party is prospering for a time while another is down; we must wait and see how things come out in the end. The prophet assumes that the humiliation of Israel was temporary and is now over. Its exaltation, which is now beginning, will be lasting and definitive.

The Gentiles say that Yahweh was a hidden God. Yet Yahweh protests that the word of God was not spoken in hiding but in the Jerusalem temple, the sacred space that is the very opposite of an empty waste. The predictions to which Second Isaiah repeatedly refers are the claims traditionally made in the Jerusalem cult that Yahweh is king of all the earth (compare Psalms 93, 96–100). Yahweh has been hidden from the Gentiles only because they have not sought God in the right place. Now, claims the prophet, they are like fugitives from a battle, forced to acknowledge Yahweh by the course of events.

We must observe at this point that the prophet's expectations were not fully realized by the Jewish restoration. Other nations did not feel compelled to acknowledge that Yahweh was responsible for the rise of Persia. Israel would suffer further humiliations in future ages. The aspect of the prophecy that has enduring validity is that Yahweh is a hidden God. Only on rare occasions, like the fall of Babylon, does Yahweh appear to be in control of history. The challenge of Jewish and Christian faith has been to wait for such occasions, to affirm that Yahweh is God even in the depths of the Exile, and to hope that the day of liberation will finally come.

46:1-13 The gods of Babylon. Bel and Nebo are gods of the Babylonians. They are being carried on pack animals in flight from the fallen city. By contrast, Yahweh has carried Israel from its birth. Once again, the release from Babylon is seen as evidence that the God of Israel has power over and above the people of Israel, while the Babylonian gods are no more than their wooden statues.

The warning to the rebels, both Jewish and Gentile, is reminiscent of Psalm 2. God is established on Mount Zion. From there God summons Cyrus from a far land. The "former things" are the events by which Yahweh was first established on Zion (see Exod 15) and which are now being reenacted in the return from the Exile.

47:1-15 A taunt against Babylon. The taunt-song against a fallen enemy was a convention of ancient warfare. In this case the gloating is intensified by the fact that Babylon had humiliated Jerusalem. Two charges are brought against Babylon. First, there is the lack of mercy toward the Jews. The Exile was indeed a punishment designed by God, but Babylon was guilty too. We may compare the indictment of Assyria in Isa 10, even though it was "the rod of Yahweh's anger." Second, Babylon was guilty of hybris, the pride that sets itself equal to God. The boast, "I, and no one else!" (47:8) echoes a claim only Yahweh can make, and is therefore blasphemous. The taunt against Babylon here is similar to Isa 14, where it is called "morning star, son of the dawn," and to the taunts against Tyre in Ezek 27 and 28. Babylon's wisdom led it astray, as the pursuit of wisdom misled Adam and Eve in Gen 2–3. Babylon was famous for astrologers, who claimed they could predict the future by observing the stars, but they have no power to help.

This poem is imbued with a spirit of vengefulness that may be distasteful to modern Westerners. It was fully endorsed, however, in the Christian Book of Revelation, where Babylon is used as a symbol for Rome and is taunted bitterly in Rev 17–18 and contrasted with the new Jerusalem. The vengefulness must be seen in context. It is the outpouring of resentment by the oppressed. It is not love of one's enemy and it is not the noblest human emotion, but it is certainly understandable. The fall of Babylon was a necessary part of the liberation of the Jews. The taunt-song plays a part in rebuilding the self-esteem of a Jewish community that had been humiliated by Babylon. It can still strike a sympathetic cord with any people who are oppressed by an arrogant overlord and whose resentment is too deep to be glossed over by professions of charity.

48:1-22 Rebukes and exhortations. The oracle that concludes the first part of Second Isaiah is exceptional in the severity of its tone. We get the impression that the prophet is exasperated by the people's failure to respond. Many scholars have questioned the unity and authenticity of this chapter. There are indeed problems of coherence and consistency, but the chapter is held together by a number of recurring motifs (for example, the allusions to "stock" and "name" in verse 19 refer back to verse 1).

The prophet begins by establishing the reliability of God's word by referring to the "things of the past" that were foretold long ago. He then proceeds to argue for the need for a prophet, since he is now proclaiming something that has not been previously predicted. The denial that anyone could have heard of these things before is hard to reconcile with a passage like 45:21 ("Who announced this from the beginning. . . . Was it not I, the Lord?"), but compare the emphasis on novelty in 43:19. It may be that only the fall of Babylon is regarded as foretold, while the actual return is absolutely new (as in 43:18-19, "Remember not the events of the past . . .").

Verses 9-11 appear as a digression that affirms God's motive for action: for his own sake. This motivation is well established in the tradition (see already Deut 32:27 and several psalms and prayers). Despite the apparent scorn for Israel here, this passage lays a secure foundation for the restoration, since it does not depend on human merit. Verses 14-15 reaffirm that Cyrus will do God's will against Babylon. Verse 16 makes an unusual assertion of the prophet's own authority. Just as the word of God has been public in the past, so the prophet is sent openly now. Verses 17-19 follow with an appeal for obedience. Finally, in verse 20 we get the climactic command, which is the real "new thing" proclaimed by the prophet—the actual command to flee from Babylon. This command comes as the climax not only of chapter 48 but of the first half of Second Isaiah. It is echoed, appropriately, in Rev 18:4, where flight from another imperial city is demanded of Christians in the time of the end. The flight from Babylon becomes a metaphor for liberation from imperial power in any age.

Despite the severe rebukes of the preceding oracles, the prophet concludes that the Lord has redeemed the Servant. Israel's status as Servant is not something established by its past actions but something that is now being brought about by a new creative act of God. It is an ideal on the verge of realization.

THE RESTORATION OF ZION
Isa 49:1–55:13

49:1-7 The call of the Servant. Here, as in Isa 42, we have a direct reflection on the mission of the Servant. (The unit is often identified as 49:1-6, since a new oracle begins in verse 7, and distinguished as one of the Servant Songs.) The Servant is explicitly identified as Israel in verse 3, yet many commentators have argued that this identification cannot be original, for two reasons: first, the statement "from my mother's womb he gave me my name" strongly suggests that the Servant is an individual; second, in verse 5 the Servant appears to have a mission to Israel, and therefore to be distinct. Some commentators, then, have argued that the Servant in this passage is the prophet himself. The passage is indeed problematic, but there is no warrant for rejecting the clear identification with Israel or for supposing that the Servant here is different from other passages in Second Isaiah.

The statement that the Servant has been called "from the womb" echoes the call of Jeremiah (Jer 1:5: "Before I formed you in the womb I knew you"), and indeed Jeremiah appears in many ways to be a model for understanding the Servant. More broadly, the commissioning of the Servant here follows a traditional pattern already found in the call of Moses in Exod 3:1–4:17. God makes the commission, Moses protests his inadequacy, but God reassures him. The call from the womb is a way of saying that the mission of the Servant is like that of a prophet or Moses.

The apparent distinction between the Servant and Israel in verses 5-6 is more difficult. It is not absolutely certain that it is the Servant who is to raise up the tribes of Jacob; it is possible that God is the subject and that the restoration of Israel coincides with the realization of its mission as Servant. The more common understanding, however, sees the Servant as the subject. In this case we must recognize that the prophet has a special role in the transformation of Israel. He has to live out the role of the Servant and persuade the rest of the people to follow him. He and his followers represent the new Israel, and they still have a mission to their fellow countrymen. Isa 49:4 reflects the discouragement of the prophet, which we have already seen in chapter 48. The reassurance, however, is not only that he will be able to persevere (compare Jer 15:19-21) but that the model of Israel which he represents will prevail.

The mission of the Servant is not only concerned with the restoration of Israel; he must also be "a light to the nations" (v. 6), as in 42:6. Jeremiah, too, was appointed as a prophet to the nations (Jer 1:5). The way in which the mission is to be carried out is clarified in the supplementary oracle in 49:7. The "one despised . . . the slave of rulers" (v. 7) is surely Israel in exile (compare Isa 53:3). When Israel is restored, however, the kings of the earth will be astonished by the transformation and will be led to acknowledge the sovereignty of Yahweh. In this way Israel can be to the nations what the individual prophet was to the Jewish people.

Needless to say, princes did not prostrate themselves as readily as the prophet expected. What is significant, however, is the universal breadth of the mission. Israel remains a chosen people, but salvation must reach to the ends of the earth.

49:8–50:3 Consolation for Zion. This passage has a well-balanced structure. It begins with the triumphal procession back to Israel, as in chapter 40. The central part of the prophecy is a reassurance for Zion. Then the prophet returns to the gathering in of the exiles, viewed this time from the vantage point of Zion (compare Isa 11:10-16). Finally, it concludes with two short oracles affirming Yahweh's power to save.

The most striking lines in this passage are surely those in 49:15: "Can a mother forget her infant . . . ?" Female experience, as well as male, can serve as analogy for God. The analogy of the mother is then transferred to Zion. The abundance of children is indicative of the Hebrew idea of salvation—abundance of life in the land of Israel.

The tenderness toward Israel in this passage is in sharp contrast to the vindictive statement in 49:26: "I will make your oppressors eat their own flesh . . . ." The reference is to cannibalism in a besieged city. Yet, even this atrocious situation has a positive purpose, namely, that all flesh may come to know the Lord. The repetition of the word "flesh" is significant, and it highlights the condition of humanity over against the power of God.

The point of 50:1-3 is that the rejection of Zion was only temporary (for the metaphor of divorce, compare Hos 1–3). It was not that Yahweh was overcome by any other power. How could it be, when Yahweh even overcame the primeval power of the sea? Accordingly, no one should doubt Yahweh's ability to save.

50:4-11 The faithful disciple. This unit is often defined as 50:4-9 and distinguished as a Servant Song (although the word "servant" only occurs in verse 10). The reason it is set apart is that it is written in the first person, like 49:1-6, and appears to describe the sufferings of an individual, as does chapter 53. The "well-trained tongue" of verse 4 is literally "a disciple's tongue." The notion of disciple may be picked up from Isa 8:16, where the prophet's message is entrusted to his disciples.

The portrayal of the disciple here recalls

the confessions of Jeremiah (Jer 11:18-23; 15:10-21; 20:7-18). Jeremiah was "like a trusting lamb led to the slaughter" (Jer 12:19), and his pain was continuous (Jer 15:18), yet God made him "a solid wall of brass" (Jer 15:20; compare also Ezek 3:9, where the comparison with flint is used, as in Isa 50:7). The disciple here, like Jeremiah and Ezekiel, is upheld by God in the face of adversity. Moreover, the disciple appears to accept his afflictions willingly, although 50:10-11 may invoke evil on his adversaries, as Jeremiah also did. (Verses 10-11 are very obscure. "Kindle flames" may refer to a Persian ritual or may be merely a metaphor for trying to provide human solutions rather than wait for God.)

The "servant" mentioned in verse 10 is presumably the speaker in verses 4-9. Here again there is some ambiguity as to whether the reference is to the prophet himself or to the community of Israel. The passage makes good sense as an account of the hardships of the prophet, but it could also speak metaphorically of the mission of Israel to the nations. It may be that the prophet and his disciples represent the true mission of Israel, although they meet resistance even within the Jewish community. The enduring significance of the passage is ultimately independent of the historical reference. It paints a picture of the true disciple as one who perseveres in the face of adversity without concern for self-preservation. Christians have appropriately seen a correspondence between this model and the conduct of Jesus in his passion.

51:1-8 Exhortations to trust. The prophet recalls how Abraham was promised numerous descendants while Sarah was yet barren. During the Exile, Zion was as barren as Sarah, but it too will become fertile. Isa 51:4-5 alludes to the oracle in Isa 2:2-4 ("from Zion shall go forth instruction"—the same Hebrew word, *torah,* is used in both passages). The light to the peoples, associated with the Servant in 42:6 and 49:6, is here the justice of God, manifested from Zion. The permanence of God's justice is then contrasted with the potential transience of the earth and the actual transience of humanity. The power and justice of God cannot be judged on the basis of passing circumstances but only in view of the long-term outcome of events.

51:9–52:12 A rousing call. This long oracle is structured by a triple call of "Awake, awake." The first is addressed to "the arm of the Lord," urging God to repeat the wonderful deeds of old. The Bible has no story of a battle between Yahweh and Rahab or a dragon. The battle with the sea monster was part of Canaanite mythology. It is taken over by the Israelites as a metaphor for the work of creation, when God reduced order to chaos (see Job 26:12). Here it also serves as a metaphor for the Exodus, when God "dried up the sea." The prophet is not interested in verifying the historical facts of the Exodus—"slaying the dragon" and "drying up the sea" are equally appropriate ways of referring to God's ability to overcome any enemy or obstacle. What matters is not what God did in the past but what God is doing in the present.

The second call is addressed to Jerusalem. Ezekiel had said that Jerusalem would drink the cup of her sister Samaria, a cup of grief and destruction (Ezek 23:32-33; Jer 25:15-29 uses the image of a cup for the destruction to come upon the nations). Now Second Isaiah proclaims that the cup has been drunk and is being taken away and given to Jerusalem's enemies. We may note that the image of Jerusalem giving her back to her enemies to walk on resembles the Servant giving his back to the smiters in Isa 50:6.

The final call (52:1) urges Zion to put on strength (like the arm of the Lord in 51:9) and promises redemption. In the future, Jerusalem would be pure—free from the uncircumcised. The apparent exclusion of the uncircumcised here serves as a reminder that the universalism of the prophet is not religious pluralism but requires the conversion of the Gentiles to the religion of Israel.

The concluding oracle of this section develops the theme of the new Exodus in a manner reminiscent of Isa 40. This Exodus will not be in haste, as was the first one. God will go before and after, like the pillars of fire and cloud. The joy of liberation is coupled with the call for those who carry the sacred vessels to purify themselves. The return to Jerusalem has the character of a religious procession from the profane place of Babylon to the sacred area of Jerusalem. There God is proclaimed king, just as in the psalms of the old Jerusalem cult.

52:13–53:12 The Suffering Servant. The so-called fourth or last Servant Song is Second Isaiah's best known contribution to

Judeo-Christian spirituality, and deservedly so. Christianity has traditionally seen here a prophecy of the passion of Jesus. Historical criticism, however, proceeds on the assumption that the prophecy made sense to the people of the prophet's time, whatever further levels of meaning were later found in it. The original meaning is inevitably bound up with the identification of the Servant. Scholars who distinguish the Servant Songs as separate compositions usually identify a historical figure here—often the prophet himself or Sheshbazzar, the heir to the Davidic throne. In the context of Second Isaiah as a whole, however, the Servant must be identified as Israel, although the prophet holds an idealized view of the Servant's role, and not all the exilic community lived up to it.

The significance of this passage goes beyond the historical identification of the Servant. It presents a model of piety which allows that suffering can have a positive purpose. As such it broke with a long biblical tradition that regarded suffering as a punishment for sin. It laid the foundation for one of the basic ideas of Christianity.

Isa 52:13-15 is presented as an utterance of God. It focuses on the coming transformation of the Servant from extreme humiliation to glory. Since this change will be witnessed by kings and nations, we must assume that the Servant is the Israelite nation or someone who represents it.

In 53:1 the speaker changes. Chapter 53 expresses the astonishment of the "kings" and the "nations" mentioned in 52:15. It attributes to them a startling affirmation: "it was our infirmities that he bore, our sufferings that he endured . . ." (53:4). The Servant, we are told, was delivered up to death and was counted with the wicked, although he had done no wrong. His life was given as a sacrifice for the sins of others. The concluding verses in 53:10-12 are apparently spoken by God and confirm this affirmation.

The statement that the Servant had done no wrong appears to contradict other statements in Second Isaiah (for example, Isa 50:1: "It was for your sins that you were sold."). The contradiction is only apparent. Isa 53:1-10 is not giving a factual account of Israel's experience but is presenting a model for understanding it. The guilt of Israel is not important for this model. Relative to the nations, Israel was innocent. As we were told in chapter 40, the punishment exceeded the guilt in any case. Here the prophet is concerned with the excess of punishment.

The model of the Servant is indebted to the precedent of the prophet Jeremiah. Jeremiah was like a lamb led to the slaughter (Jer 12:19); so also was the Servant in 53:7. More generally, the experience of Jeremiah showed that a faithful prophet might have to suffer to fulfill his mission. As Jeremiah was a prophet to Israel, so Israel is to the nations.

The model of the Servant goes beyond Jeremiah insofar as the Servant is apparently put to death (53:8-9) and yet will prolong his days and see his descendants. The people of Israel were said to die in the Exile and rise again at its end in Ezekiel's vision of a valley of dry bones and in Isa 26. That is also the original meaning of chapter 53. It is not difficult, however, to see how Christianity could claim that this model was again exemplified in the death of Jesus of Nazareth.

The key notion in chapter 53 is that the sufferings of the righteous can bear the sin of others. This idea is based on the analogy of sacrifice. The logic of the procedure can be illustrated by the famous ritual of the scapegoat in Lev 16. Aaron confesses the sins of the Israelites over the goat and puts them on its head, and then it carries the sins off to the wilderness. This ritual is evidently a symbolic act. It can have a powerful effect on the people, but only if they participate actively in it. They must understand the symbolism and intend to express their separation from sin. The mere performance of the ritual will not of itself transform the people without their involvement.

The dynamic interaction involved in bearing the sin of others can be seen even more clearly in a symbolic action of the prophet Ezekiel. Ezekiel was famous for his insistence on individual responsibility (Ezek 18:4: "only the one who sins shall die"). He clearly defined the role of the prophet as that of a watchman (Ezek 3:17; 33:1-9). His job is to warn the people. They have to save themselves by their reaction. Yet this prophet is told to lie on one side for 390 days, and on the other for forty days, to bear the sins of northern Israel and Judah respectively (Ezek 4:1-8). In Ezekiel's case, bearing the sin is clearly a symbolic act. The strange posture of the prophet is meant to attract attention, give rise to reflection, and lead people to recognize the gravity of their situation. Only if they do this can they hope to be saved. The suffering of Ezekiel does not automatically prevent the destruction of his people. There is not a set amount of suffering that he can undertake instead of them. His suffering is only a sign to them. Whether they then escape their doom depends on how they heed his warning.

The suffering of the Servant in chapter 53 can be understood most satisfactorily on the model of Ezekiel. The Servant is a light to the nations. The experience of Israel is to catch the attention of the other nations, lead them to reflect on their situation, and realize that they are even more deserving of such punishment. The purpose of the Exile was ultimately to bring about the conversion of the Gentiles. The mission of the Servant, to which the Jews were called, was to accept unmerited suffering in patient fidelity and so to serve as an example for the nations.

The Gentile nations did not react to the Jewish experience in the way the prophet hoped. Yet the model of the Servant has endured. It provides a way of making positive sense of suffering, which is always a challenge to the human spirit. It also suggests a style of evangelizing, not by conquering others but by bearing their burdens and setting an example. For Christians this model was intensified by the example of Jesus, whose suffering and death were also understood as a sacrifice for the sins of others.

54:1-7 A promise to Zion. The prophet resumes the joyful proclamation to Zion that was the theme of Isa 52:1-12. Two motifs are especially important here. First, Zion is the wife of God. The prophet Hosea used this metaphor to great effect and suggested that God was divorcing Israel. Second, Isaiah insists that Zion was only cast off for a moment (compare Isa 50:1 for the motif of divorce). Moreover, the abandoned wife will have more children than one who has a husband. (This is a favorite biblical theme. To illustrate how God can reverse any situation, compare the Song of Hannah in 1 Sam 2.) Underlying the metaphor of marriage is the idea of a covenant, a binding mutual commitment. The language of marriage, however, adds an emotional dimension to the covenant and deepens the commitment by arousing feelings of love.

The second theme is the analogy with the days of Noah. After the flood God guaranteed the future of life on earth: "Never again will I doom the earth because of man . . . . As long as the earth lasts, seedtime and harvest, cold and heat, summer and winter, and day and night shall not cease" (Gen 8:21-22). That promise had been kept since the days of Noah. The promise to Zion is equally sure. Second Isaiah is reaffirming the traditional Zion theology found, for example, in Ps 46:3: "Therefore we fear not, though the earth be shaken . . . ."

Here we cannot fail to observe that Zion was destroyed again. On a literal level the promise would seem to be broken. Yet, both Judaism and Christianity continue to affirm that "my love shall never leave you nor my covenant of peace be shaken" (v. 10). The peace must be understood as an inner peace that can survive not only the shaking of the hills but the destruction of Zion itself. The restoration from the Exile had shown that God was with the people even in the darkness. The moment of clarity enjoyed by Second Isaiah would have to be remembered as a witness again in darker days ahead.

55:1-13 Call to a feast. The invitation to eat and drink resembles the call of Wisdom to her feast in Prov 9. The prophet suggests that wisdom lies in heeding his words and returning to Zion. The feast is identified with the promises of the covenant to David. As the king was a witness to other nations, so now the restored people is to assume that role. The prophet does not anticipate a renewed Davidic dynasty; his messiah is Cyrus of Persia. Yet the Davidic covenant is not broken. It is fulfilled through the restoration of the Jewish people. Such transformations are possible because "my ways are not your ways." Second Isaiah maintains the contrast made by First Isaiah between the power of the Holy One (spirit) and mere human flesh (compare Isa 31:1-3).

Isa 55:10-13 provides a fitting conclusion to Second Isaiah by affirming the effectiveness of the prophetic word. The triumphal procession back to Jerusalem with which the prophet began in chapter 40 is the crowning validation of the reliability of prophecy and the power of the God of Israel.

COMMENTARY: THIRD ISAIAH (Isa 56–66)

Chapters 40–55 were set in Babylon on the eve of the return from the Exile. Chapters 56–66 are slightly later in date and reflect the problems of the Jewish community after the return. It is possible that they are the work of Second Isaiah, at least in part, that is, if we allow that his style of prophecy was altered by the new circumstances. It is more probable, however, that they are the work of his disciples, who emerged as a distinct group in the returned community. These disciples are referred to as the servants of the Lord in chapter 65. Presumably they saw themselves as carrying on the mission of the Servant, which played such a prominent part in Second Isaiah.

56:1-8 Qualifications for admission to the temple. Only two things are necessary for admission to the rebuilt temple—observance of the sabbath and fidelity to the covenant. The prophet does not spell out what the latter requirement entails. The point of the oracle is to insist that two classes of people, eunuchs and foreigners, are not automatically excluded. Eunuchs had been specifically excluded according to Deut 23:1: "No one whose testicles have been crushed or whose penis has been cut off, may be admitted to the community of the Lord." Some high officials at royal courts in the ancient world had to be eunuchs so that they could be trusted with the royal harem. Some people castrated themselves in the worship of pagan gods. At least some of these people could not subsequently be circumcised, and Third Isaiah does not appear to insist on circumcision as a requirement. "To hold fast to my covenant" (v. 4) appears to be a broad moral attitude rather than a matter of specific rituals, except for the case of sabbath observance.

The second class in question is that of foreigners (v. 6). The prophet is speaking here of converts who want to join themselves to the Lord. The point is that people who were not born Israelites can become servants of the Lord. The significance of this oracle can be seen by contrasting it with Ezek 44, which presents a different program for the postexilic temple, according to which "no foreigners, uncircumcised in heart and in flesh, shall ever enter my sanctuary; none of the foreigners who live among the Israelites" (Ezek 44:9).

It is evident that there was disagreement within the Jewish community as to whether foreigners should be allowed to worship in the temple. What is remarkable is that both sides of the debate were preserved in the canon of the Scripture. The authors of Isa 56 and Ezek 44 were both sincerely concerned with the welfare of their community, and both were trying to be faithful to older traditions. The exclusivist viewpoint of Ezek 44 received powerful support from Ezra in the following century and may be credited with strengthening the distinctive identity of Judaism. Christianity has undoubtedly found the inclusive vision of Third Isaiah much more congenial in this matter.

56:9–57:21 Denunciation of abuses. There is no agreement among commentators about the unity, origin, or meaning of this passage. Since it resembles preexilic oracles against idolatry, some scholars think that this material is preexilic too. Others read the whole passage as an attack on the postexilic priestly leaders of the community and think that idolatry here is a metaphor for a style of religion of which the author did not approve. Very likely neither of these extremes is correct. The oracles are evidently directed against religious leaders—compare the use of watchman (as prophet) in Ezek 3:17; 33:1-9; Jer 6:17 and of shepherd (as leader) in Ezek 34. We must assume, however, that the charges are meant literally. The leaders are at best negligent, and there is widespread pagan worship. (Isa 57:9, which speaks of sending ambassadors to the "king," *melek*, even down to the netherworld, probably means that people offered human sacrifice to the Canaanite god *Molech*.) The people who engaged in these practices were certainly not the more exclusive faction whose views are represented in Ezek 44 and with whom Third Isaiah had a different quarrel. Much of the Jewish community after the Exile was quite lax in its religious observance, as we can see from the tirades of the prophets Haggai and Malachi, and from the reforms that were necessary in the time of Ezra and Nehemiah.

The rhetoric in much of this passage is simply abusive. The prophet was unlikely to win over the leaders by calling them "dumb dogs" (56:10) or the like. This is the language of polarization, which presumes that the situation is beyond remedy. Such language can only seldom be justified.

Chapter 57 concludes with a more positive attempt "to revive the spirits of the dejected" (57:15) and seems to hold out the prospect of forgiveness. Even the sinners are souls that God has made. In 57:14 ("prepare the way") the prophet seeks to recapture some of the initial enthusiasm of Second Isaiah. The final verse, however, maybe added by an editor, dampens this spirit of reconciliation by insisting that there is no peace for the wicked.

58:1-14 The value of fasting. After the fall of Jerusalem in 586 B.C.E., it became customary to observe four fast days, in the fourth, fifth, seventh, and tenth months (Zech 8:18; compare Zech 7:5). Third Isaiah denies that this observance has any intrinsic value. He does not object to ritual as such—he complains of inadequate observance of the sabbath. Ritual only has value, however, when it is the expression of a just society. Self-affliction is not a good in itself; feeding the hungry is. Verses 6-7 give a concise summary of the essentials of true religion: free the oppressed, feed the hungry, shelter the homeless, clothe the naked. The prophet anticipates the criteria for the final judgment in Matt 25:31-46, but he is drawing on a long tradition of prophetic criticism (compare Amos 5:18-27, which insists that worship without justice has no value). The problems of injustice were apparently as great in Third Isaiah's time as before the Exile, although we might have expected a more close-knit community after the return (the prophet refers to the poor as "your own" in 58:7).

The postexilic community experienced much difficulty after the return. The prophet Haggai attributed their lack of prosperity to their tardiness in rebuilding the temple. Third Isaiah attributes it to the lack of social justice. In this he was the more typical of the older prophetic tradition.

59:1-21 A promise of divine intervention. Chapter 59 continues the theme of chapter 58. Lack of prosperity is not due to Yahweh's weakness but to human sin. In this case the prophet goes on to predict a divine response. Yahweh would be girded as a warrior, as at the time of the Exodus and the Conquest. Underlying this prediction is the prophet's faith that God has the power to punish the wicked and the hope that God will do so immediately, within the course of human history.

There was no miraculous transformation of Jewish society after the Exile. Later biblical literature would increasingly postpone God's judgment to an end-time or until after death. Belief in an eventual judgment remained vital, however. The hope and concern for justice in this world is an important part of the prophetic legacy and is inseparable from belief in the sovereignty of Yahweh.

We should note that Yahweh is expected to take vengeance on a segment of Jewish society, not on foreign nations. Those who will be redeemed on Zion are "those who turn from sin" (v. 20). We find here a division within the Jewish community and a distinction between the servants of God and the members of the Jewish nation as such.

60:1-22 Restoration of Zion. Chapters 60–62 stand out from the rest of Third Isaiah by their exuberant tone, which is very similar to Second Isaiah. Perhaps these chapters were written shortly after the return, before the problems that dominate the other chapters had developed. Jerusalem is seen as the focal point of the nations. The prospect of caravans coming from such places as Sheba (v. 6) recalls the glory of Solomon. The foreigners and their kings will be subject to the Jews and be their servants, but they will be welcome in Jerusalem and their offerings will be accepted in the temple. The vision of the new Zion is universalistic in this sense, in contrast to the exclusive vision of Ezek 44. The prophet envisages a wonderful transformation—the people will all be just, and Yahweh will give light to the city by means of the divine presence. This vision of the new Jerusalem is echoed in Rev 21:22-27 in the context of a new creation after the end of this world. The idea of a new creation is also found in Third Isaiah (65:17). The prophet knew that such a wonderful state is not the stuff of history or of human experience but represents an ideal goal that can serve as a guide for our values.

61:1-11 Good news for the poor. The opening verses are very similar to the so-called Servant Songs in Isa 42 and 49. The prophet sees himself as realizing the mission of the Servant. The prisoners in question are the Jewish exiles in Babylon. The year of favor is the sabbatical year, traditionally the time for the cancellation of debts and the release of Hebrew slaves (see Deut 15; compare Lev 25). The anointing is probably metaphorical (virtually meaning "appointed"). Prophets were not usually anointed, although Elijah was told to anoint Elisha in 1 Kgs 19:16.

In the context of Third Isaiah, this passage illustrates again the concern of the prophet for the poor, a concern that was prominent in Isa 58 and 59. The importance of the passage transcends its historical context, however. It presents a concise summary of the mission of a servant of God in any age. It is a mission to raise up the lower strata of society. The Gospel of Luke has Jesus read this text, with minor variations, at the outset of his career (Luke 4:17-19).

The prophet is here the bearer of good news, like Zion itself in Isa 40:9. Verses 4-9 repeat the universalistic vision of Isa 60 but add a note of concern for justice in verse 8 and a promise of an everlasting covenant, presumably a renewal of the promise to David, as in Isa 55:3. Now all the people are the beneficiaries of that promise. Further, all the people will be named priests of the Lord (v. 6). The prophet sees the whole Jewish people as priestly mediators between God and the Gentiles. This extension of the priesthood inevitably dilutes the role of the official hierarchy and contrasts very sharply with the program for the restoration in Ezek 44, which assigns a very special role to the Zadokite priests. (Compare the dispute in Num 16, where Korah rebels against Moses and Aaron, contending that the whole people is holy, but is swallowed alive by the earth for his impertinence!) The canon of Scripture has preserved both sides of this debate without resolving it. In the New Testament, Rev 20:6 says that all the martyrs who are raised in the first resurrection will serve God as priests for a thousand years, without distinguishing a special priestly class. This, of course, is resurrected life, but it presents an ultimate ideal for the people of God.

62:1-12 Reminding the Lord. Chapter 62 retains the positive tone of chapters 60–61, but it also reflects some initial disappointment after the return to Jerusalem. It is necessary to "remind the Lord" because God does not appear to be fulfilling earlier promises. The prophet insists that all will yet be well, because the Lord has sworn. The purpose of this oracle is to encourage the returned exiles to plant grain, in confidence that it will not all go in taxes, and to build up the city. We may compare the oracles of Haggai of about the same time, when he promised that all would be well if they built the temple.

The assurance of a divine oath, or promise, is a powerful motivating factor. There is a risk in such rhetoric, however. If the land remains relatively desolate, the discrepancy between the promise and the reality can breed extreme disillusionment. The prophet was attempting to use the power of positive thinking (unlike most other prophets!) to raise the morale of the people, in the hope that their efforts would be blessed. Even if the result fell short of the ideal, the efforts of the prophets may have borne fruit insofar as they inspired people to work at rebuilding their community.

63:1-6 God the warrior. The mood changes abruptly in chapter 63. The warrior imagery picks up from Isa 59 (63:5 corresponds very closely to 59:16), but the imagery is much more violent here. The violence is directed against the Gentiles, specifically against Edom and its capital Bozrah. Edom, Judea's southern neighbor, had become a major enemy during the exilic period. It is possible that this oracle was evoked by some hostile action taken by the Edomites, although many commentators assume that Edom is representative of all hostile nations. We met another violent oracle against Edom in Isa 34.

The image of God as warrior is deeply entrenched in the oldest traditions about the Exodus and the Conquest (for example, Exod 15). The God of Israel was never a pacifist, although the people are often urged to take a submissive stance. The assumption here is that Edom and some other neighboring states were impeding the restoration of Judah. The prophet does not call on the Jews to make war on them, but he hopes that his God will remove the offenders by whatever means are necessary.

63:7–64:11 A plea for God to act. This passage is virtually a psalm and especially resembles the communal laments of the Psalter (for example, Psalm 44). It reflects a traditional pattern, which begins by recalling God's saving deeds in the past (especially the Exodus and the Conquest), acknowledges the sin of Israel, and ends with a plea for mercy (compare Deut 32, which ends with a promise rather than a prayer, and such postexilic prayers as Neh 9 and Dan 9). In part it also resembles the laments for the temple in the period of the Exile (for example, Psalm 79). The prayer that God "rend the heavens and come down" (63:19) has a ring of desperation to it. The main problem in interpreting the passage is to determine why the author was moved to such desperation.

Two verses are especially important for the author's situation. One is 63:18. The first half of that verse is translated in the Revised Standard Version as "Thy holy people possessed thy sanctuary a little while," and this rendering is more probable than that of the New American Bible. Does this mean that the whole duration of Solomon's temple—about 350 years—seems short in retrospect? Or does it mean that one Jewish party occupied the sanctuary for a short time after the return from the Exile and was then ousted by its enemies? (Some scholars think here of Ezek 44, which makes the Levites subordinate to the Zadokite priests, and suggest that chapter 63 was written by Levites.)

The second relevant verse is 63:16: "Were Abraham not to know us . . . you, Lord, are our father." This translation suggests a purely hypothetical situation—compare Isa 49:15: "Can a mother forget her infant . . . ? Even should she forget, I will never forget you." The Hebrew, however, could be translated more naturally as "for Abraham has not known us." This understanding of the text has prompted the view that the author of chapter 63 belonged to a party that was rejected by the official leaders of the community, represented here as Abraham and Israel. The passage, then, can be understood in either of two ways: either it reflects a bitter struggle within the Jewish community after the Exile, or it more simply reflects the initial failure of the returned exiles to rebuild and restore the holy place. In view of the other indications in Third Isaiah (especially in chapters 56 and 66), it seems more probable that the prophet's desperation arose from conflict within the Jewish community.

Whatever the precise origin of this passage, it is clearly a prayer for a time of despair. Two features should especially be emphasized. The first is the frank admission of sinfulness: "all of us have become like unclean men" (64:5). Even if there is a split in the community, no party can claim complete innocence. Second, when no human aid is forthcoming, the prophet appeals directly to God. It was God who brought them out of Egypt (63:9: "It was not a messenger or an angel but he himself" can also be phrased differently and understood to say that "the angel of his presence" saved them. In either case the point is the same: it was no human resource). The plea to rend the heavens forcefully (63:19) expresses the need for help from beyond (compare Isa 59:16 and 63:5: "there was no one"). The plea is based, not on the justice of God, but on God's mercy; he is the Father of all. The idea of God as Father assures the right of even outsiders and castaways to invoke God, irrespective of their standing in the community. The motif is used in a similar way in Mal 2:10 in an argument against divorce. The fatherhood of God was a characteristic motif on the lips of Jesus, who argued that the one Father made the sun shine and rain fall on the just and the unjust (Matt 5:45).

65:1-16 My servants will eat. The division within the postexilic community is more explicit here. The prophet evidently identifies with the "servants" who continue the mission of the Servant of Second Isaiah. This group is at odds with another party, which is accused of a range of idolatrous practices. Yet these people claim to be holy and warn others not to touch them. This puzzling passage reminds us of Ezek 44:19, where the Zadokite priests are told to change their vestments when they leave the altar so that they will not transmit holiness to the people. Some scholars read the grotesque practices of 65:3-4 as a parody of the official cult of the legitimate priests (see the commentary on Isa 66). It is more probable, however, that chapters 65 and 57 show that there was actual idolatry going on. The fact that the idolaters think they are holy only adds to the grotesque character of their abuses.

We must also assume that the idolaters enjoyed the main power in the postexilic community. They have now inherited the land. The "servants" are outsiders, who are powerless for the present. The prophecy in 65:13-16 anticipates the beatitudes of Jesus, especially in the Lukan version: "Blest are you poor; the reign of God is yours. Blest are you who hunger; you shall be filled" (Luke 6:20). A major function of religion has always been to give hope to the hopeless. The prophet merely asserts that fortunes will yet be reversed. He offers no evidence for his claim. Neither does Jesus in the beatitudes. The only evidence for such a claim is faith in the power of a God who will ultimately set things right and the knowledge that all human power and wealth must eventually pass.

65:17-25 A new creation. The prophetic dissatisfaction with the present is even more evident in 65:17, in the oracle about a new creation. The idea that God would do something radically new was familiar from Second Isaiah (compare Isa 43:18-19). The replacement of heaven and earth, however, goes far beyond the earlier concepts. This prophecy is picked up in Rev 21:1 ("Then I saw new heavens and a new earth") and is often thought to be typical of apocalyptic literature. In chapter 65, however, the new creation is remarkably similar to the old one. Life will go on on earth. People will still die, and there is no promise of resurrection or immortality, in sharp contrast to the apocalyptic literature. Rather, the prophet presents his ideal of earthly life: freedom from grief, from premature death, from oppression and exploitation.

The concluding mention of the wolf and the lamb (v. 25) very deliberately recalls the messianic prophecy in Isa 11. Both prophecies are fantasies, although chapter 65 is more restrained in its imagery. Both provide consolation and relief from the distress of the present. The ideal presented must also be taken seriously, however, as a portrayal of the goal toward which we strive, even if we cannot fully attain it.

66:1-6 True and false worship. The interpretation of these verses has been greatly disputed. Some scholars contend that the prophet is rejecting temple worship as such; others hold that the issue is how much importance should be attached to the temple. The second point of view is the more probable. Third Isaiah seems to presuppose a temple in other passages (including 66:6). Even Solomon's prayer at the dedication of the temple (1 Kgs 8:27) had declared: "If the heavens and the highest heavens cannot contain you, how much less this temple which I have built!" The point is that the temple must be seen in perspective. It is not the most important thing in the religion.

Third Isaiah's perspective on the temple here contrasts sharply with that of Haggai, who preached that rebuilding the temple was the primary requirement for prosperity in the postexilic community. Here again, the canon of Scripture has preserved both sides of a heated debate. The temple was very important for the morale of the community, and we can appreciate why a prophet like Haggai insisted on thinking positively about it. On the other hand, Third Isaiah walks in the footsteps of the great prophets, including Isaiah of Jerusalem, when he points out the danger of trusting too completely in an institution and reminds people of the ethical demands of their religion.

The interpretation of 66:3 is even more controversial. The Hebrew juxtaposes four pairs of actions, indicated by participles: "slaughtering an ox, slaying a man," etc. These pairs can be understood in either of two ways: "one who slaughters an ox *is like* one who slays a man" (so the New American Bible and the Revised Standard Version), or "one who slaughters an ox *also* slays a man." The first interpretation empties the sacrificial cult of all value; even a cereal offering is no better than swine's blood. If the second interpretation is correct, the problem is syncretism: those who offer the sacrifices to Yahweh also engage in pagan practices. In either case, there is a division within the community, and the prophet and his followers find themselves rejected. The understanding of this passage depends on our understanding of other passages, such as Isa 57. It seems more probable that pagan worship was the issue. The evidence does not warrant the drastic conclusion that the prophet totally rejected the sacrificial cult.

66:7-24 The Lord's power shall be known. The book concludes with a twofold oracle of judgment. On the positive side, the prophet points out how far the postexilic community has already come. Would God have brought them so far only to abandon them? The prophet cloaks his message in plentiful metaphors of childbirth and mother love. At verse 14, however, the negative side of the judgment appears. Power for the servants of God is wrath for God's enemies. The fiery coming of the Lord resembles the coming of God's messenger in Mal 3:2: "For he is like the refiner's fire."

The conclusion, then, has two aspects.

The exiles will return from all the nations. Some will even serve as priests and Levites. All humankind will worship in Jerusalem. This bright prospect has a dark side too. The corpses of the wicked will burn and be eaten by worms forever, as a spectacle for the rest of humanity. The wicked will not be alive to feel the pain of this punishment. The idea of hell did not emerge in the Jewish tradition until about three hundred years after Third Isaiah, yet this passage is rightly seen as a precedent for hell, because it attempts to describe an unending punishment of the wicked.

The lurid spectacle of 66:24 is a rather unpleasant note on which to close the Book of Isaiah. The idea was surely born of the resentment of the prophet's followers, who were excluded from power in the postexilic community. It expresses their hope for justice, but seems excessive in its prolonged torture of dead bodies. It does, however, provide a powerful closing image for the Book of Isaiah. Much of the book was concerned with salvation on Mount Zion. This theme was repeated in chapters 65–66 and reinforced with the theme of a new creation. The final image does not detract from these themes, but it adds a reminder that salvation cannot be achieved without judgment. The wolf will not lie down with the lamb until human evil is eradicated. The smoldering fire of Gehenna stands as a reminder of the reality of evil and its inevitable unpleasant consequences.

JEREMIAH

Peter F. Ellis

INTRODUCTION

Jeremiah the man

Jeremiah lived in changing times. He grew up in the best of times and died in the worst of times. He grew up during the reign of King Josiah (639–609 B.C.E.), when Judah was at peace and when king, priests, and people were engaged in a revitalization of Mosaic faith and worship. He died around 580, an exile in Egypt in the worst of times, when Judah was no longer a nation, Jerusalem was in ruins, the temple had been burned to the ground, and the Jews had been deported into exile in Babylon. His life spanned the last twenty years of the Assyrian empire (destroyed by the Babylonians between 612 and 605) and the first twenty years of the neo-Babylonian empire (605–539). He was and had to be "a man for all seasons."

Jeremiah was born in Anathoth, a few miles north of Jerusalem, belonged to a priestly family, and was called to the office of prophet at an early age (c. 626). During the forty or so years he served as a prophet (626–580), the kingdom of Judah went through one religious reformation (626–609); three wars (against Egypt, 609; against Babylon, 597 and 587); three exiles (597, 587, and 582); and five Davidic kings (Josiah, 639–609; Jehoahaz, for three months in 609; Jehoiakim, 609–597; Jehoiachin, for three months in 597; and Zedekiah, 597–587). During these years Judah went from one of the brightest periods in its history (under King Josiah from 639–609) to the darkest (609–587) in all the 443 years of the Davidic dynasty (1025–587).

Few people in history have been involved so crucially in the fate of a nation as Jeremiah was. He preached the renewal of the covenant under King Josiah in 621. He lived through the first (597) and the second siege (587) of Jerusalem. He saw the temple destroyed, Jerusalem devastated, and his people marched off into exile in Babylonia. At the end he himself was forced into exile in Egypt. There he died, stoned to death, as the legend goes, at the hands of his own people.

With the exception perhaps of Jesus and St. Paul, we know more about Jeremiah as an individual than about any other person in the whole history of Israel. We know from his own words that he was a quiet, peace-loving mystic sent by God, against his inclinations, to rebuke kings, accuse his fellow Jews of infidelity to the covenant, and draw upon himself in return the scorn, contempt, and homicidal hatred of his enemies.

Jeremiah did not want to be a prophet. The prophetic office guaranteed trouble. Jeremiah wanted peace. He had no peace. His own relatives plotted his death (11:18–12:6). Pashhur, the high priest, had him scourged and thrown into the stocks overnight (20:1-2). He preached against abuses in the temple, was put on trial for his life and barely acquitted (ch. 26). He had to go into hiding during most of the twelve-year reign of King Jehoiakim. When a book of his sermons was read before the king, the king fed the manuscript page by page into a fire (ch. 36). During the siege of 588–587, he was first arrested and thrown in prison. Later he was dropped into a cistern to die. He was rescued only at the last minute by his Ethiopian friend, the eunuch Ebed-melech (ch. 38). When the Babylonians captured Jerusalem, they found Jeremiah in chains with other Jews, awaiting deportation to Babylon (44:1-6). Jeremiah describes his internal sufferings in his famous confessions (11:18–12:6; 15:10-21; 17:12-18; 18:18-23; 20:7-18).

All in all, no one in the history of Israel was more like Jesus than Jeremiah. Jesus taught in parables; so did Jeremiah. Jesus was rejected by his own people; so was Jeremiah. Jesus wept for his people; so did Jeremiah. Jesus was scourged, imprisoned, and put on trial for his life; so was Jeremiah. In the end the tragedy of Jerusalem in the time of Jesus paralleled the tragedy of Jerusalem in the time of Jeremiah. Jesus prophesied the destruction of Jerusalem and the temple by the Romans; Jeremiah prophesied the destruction of Jerusalem and the temple by the Babylonians. In each case the prophecy was fulfilled: in 587 B.C.E. by the Babylonians, in A.D. 70 by the Romans. Jeremiah resembled Jesus in so many ways that the Jews of Jesus' time wondered if Jesus might not be Jeremiah come back from the dead (see Matt 16:14)!

It is perhaps too much to say, as Ernest Renan said, that "without this extraordinary man, the religious history of humanity would have taken another course." It certainly is not too much to say that without Jeremiah the mystical side of human nature and the unfathomable capacity of the human heart for unselfish suffering might have lain hidden until the coming of Jesus. The theology Jeremiah lived, more than the theology he preached, influenced the ages that followed him and produced psalmists and wisdom writers who sounded the depths of Jeremiah's heart. His life more than his teaching was a ferment and a fire that permeated the bones of Israel after the Exile and prepared the way for him who came to cast a similar fire on earth and to see it kindled in the lives of innumerable saints.

Jeremiah's message

Jeremiah's message as a prophet to his people was at the same time the most pessimistic and the most optimistic that could be conceived. When he looked at the abysmal state of Judah's covenant relationship with God, he sank into pessimism. When he looked at the patient and long-suffering God of Israel, he was filled with optimism. His God was a God of hope, of promise, of power, and of an indomitable will to make the people of Israel a holy people.

In typical prophetic fashion, Jeremiah accused his people of sins against the covenant and predicted God's judgment upon them. But he did more than just accuse and condemn. He raised the consciousness of his people. He made them see that crimes against each other were crimes against God. He made them see that God loved them even when he chastised them. Finally, when he saw that destruction was inevitable, that Israel was not responding to God, and that the old covenant was finished, he predicted a new covenant (31:31-34). This was the covenant inaugurated by Jesus on the night before his death (see Luke 22:20 and 1 Cor 11:25).

The Book of Jeremiah

In 604 B.C.E. while in hiding, Jeremiah dictated to his secretary, Baruch, the gist of what he had preached during his past twenty-three years as a prophet (see ch. 36 and 25:1-14). When the king had Jeremiah's manuscript burned (36:21-23), Jeremiah had Baruch compose a new manuscript (36:32). Scholars believe that the greater part of this second manuscript has been preserved in chapters 1–20 and chapter 25 of the present Book of Jeremiah. Verses 1-14 of chapter 25 appear to be the conclusion of the manuscript written in 604. The rest of the book (chs. 26–52) is made up of biographical material about Jeremiah (chs. 26–44), a collection of Jeremiah's prophecies against the pagan nations (chs. 45–51), and a final chapter (ch. 52) taken from 2 Kgs 25.

What confuses the reader of Jeremiah is the lack of chronological sequence in the book. The siege of Jerusalem in 588–587 B.C.E. is first mentioned in chapter 21. In chapter 25, however, the reader is back in the year 604 B.C.E. This happens regularly. What is the explanation? The best explanation is that the editors of the prophetic books had before them several collections of material dealing with the preaching of Jeremiah, stories about him, and historical accounts of the last days of Judah. They had the manuscript dictated in 604, together with collections of prophecies against the kings of Judah (chs. 21–23) and against the false prophets (23:9-40). In addition, they had a collection of prophecies dealing with the new covenant (chs. 30–33), a large collection of biographical material (chs. 24; 26–29; 34–45; 52), and a collection of Jeremiah's prophecies against the pagan nations (chs. 46–51). Instead of placing all this material in chronological order, a task that would have been extremely difficult, they put it together more or less end to end and thematically, so that events mentioned earlier in the book in one collection are sometimes duplicated later in another collection of material. An example of this confusion is Jeremiah's famous temple sermon. Jeremiah gives his version of the sermon in chapters 7 and 8; someone else gives another, abbreviated version in chapter 26.

All this is the fault—if we can call it that—of the third-century editors. Nothing can be done now to change it. The best the reader can do is to try to read each collection of material *as a collection,* asking of each collection what its message as a whole is. This is the way we shall deal with the book in this commentary. It is not the only way, but it is the least confusing way. Reading the book in its present order, we shall comment on its message under the following headings:

Part I Jeremiah's call (1:1-19)

Part II Jeremiah's preaching from 626 to 604 B.C.E. (2:1–20:18)
- A. Jeremiah's earliest sermons (2:1–6:30)
- B. The temple sermon (7:1–8:3)
- C. Accusations and judgments (8:4–10:25)
- D. Deuteronomic sermons, confessions, and parables (11:1–20:18)

Part III Prophecies against the kings and the false prophets (21:1–25:38)
- A. Prophecies against the kings and false prophets (21:1–24:10)
- B. The conclusion of Jeremiah's book (25:1-38)

Part IV Biographical material and the new covenant (26:1–33:26)
- A. The temple sermon (26:1-24)
- B. Jeremiah against the false prophets (27:1–29:32)
- C. Jeremiah and the new covenant (30:1–33:26)

Part V Disobedience and destruction (34:1–39:18)
- A. The broken pact with the slaves (34:1-22)
- B. The Rechabites obey but Israel does not (35:1-19)
- C. Contempt for the word of the Lord (36:1-32)
- D. Contempt for the Lord's prophet (37:1–38:28)
- E. The fall of Jerusalem (39:1-18)

Part VI Disobedience to the end (40:1–45:5)
- A. Jeremiah at Mizpah (40:1–42:22)
- B. Jeremiah in Egypt (43:1–44:30)
- C. A message for Baruch (45:1-5)

Part VII Collected oracles against the nations and conclusion (46:1–52:34)
- A. Oracles against the nations (46:1–51:64)
- B. Conclusion of the book (52:1-34)
- C. The influence of Jeremiah

THE LAST KINGS OF JUDAH

Josiah (639–609)

Jehoahaz (609) Jehoiakim (609–598) Zedekiah (597–587)

Jehoiachin (597)

THE KINGS OF BABYLON
Nabopolassar (626–605)
Nebuchadnezzar (605–562)
Evil-merodach (562–560)
Neriglissar (560–556)
Labashi Marduk (556)
Nabonidus and Belshazzar (556–539)

Reading Jeremiah

Understanding Jeremiah, or for that matter any of the prophets, can sometimes be difficult. Jeremiah frequently repeats the expression "The word of the Lord," then speaks in the first person as if he were God speaking. He accuses Israel of crimes as if he were a prosecuting attorney in a courtroom. He then delivers God's judgment on Israel for its crimes, as if God were a judge in a trial that ends with the condemnation of the accused. Surprisingly, while he claims to speak as God's messenger and supports his claim by describing the vision in which God commissioned him as a messenger, he sometimes speaks in his own name (see Jeremiah's confessions in 12:1-6; 15:10-21; 17:12-18; 18:18-23; 20:7-18). These apparent inconsistencies call for an explanation.

First, the reader should understand that the primary way in which a prophet sees himself (his self-image or job description) is as God's messenger, sent to the covenanted people Israel to announce to them God's judgment on how they have failed to live up to the norms of behavior demanded of them by their covenant relationship with God.

An understanding of the prophet's role as messenger helps to explain why he speaks so often as if he were actually God speaking, and why he describes his experience of a vision in which he was called by God and commissioned as God's messenger. Once the art of writing came into existence between 6000 and 4000 B.C.E., communication over a distance could be accomplished by letter. Before the invention of letters, that is, in the preliterary age, communication over a distance could only be accomplished by means of messengers, who served as "living letters." The messenger memorized the message, physically bridged the distance between the sender and the addressee, and ultimately delivered orally the message he had memorized. In the case of a king's message, for example, the messenger would say: "The king sent me. The word of the king: 'I your king say to you . . . .' " In short, since the prophet was God's messenger, he spoke, as a messenger would, in the first person because he was speaking for God who sent him.

Second, behind the concept of God sending the prophet as messenger and with roots in very ancient mythology lay the scenario of the king's council. The pagan mythmakers imagined the world of the gods to be similar to royal society on earth. Such a scenario posited a world populated with gods, goddesses, and sons and daughters of the gods. In heaven as on earth, one god was high god or king over other gods. When the high god wished to legislate, he gathered round him his council of lesser gods. After the meeting messengers were sent out to bear tidings of the council's decisions to the other gods.

Israel took over this scenario from the mythmakers, kept the lesser gods of the council but demoted them to the status of messengers (angels), and envisioned Yahweh and the divine council in the same way that the pagans envisioned their high god and his council (see 1 Kgs 22:12-23). The plurals of Gen 1:26 ("Let *us* make man in *our* image") and Isa 6:8 ("Whom shall I send? Who will go for *us*?") reflect the scenario of God consulting this divine council. Jeremiah saw himself as one who had "stood in the council of the Lord, to see him and to hear his word" (23:18; see also 23:22). The role of the prophet, as we know it from Israel's history, was born when God sent humans rather than angels to be the messengers from the divine council.

The role of the messenger and the scenario of the king's council also explains why a prophet sometimes describes his inaugural vision. Anyone can *claim* to be God's messenger, but only the messenger sent by God can truly claim to speak God's word. Whoever has not been sent and nevertheless claims to be God's messenger is by definition a false prophet. It is a matter of great importance, therefore, for the truth of a prophet's message that he be able to authenticate his position by testifying to his experience of having been directly commissioned by God as a messenger. Jeremiah so testifies (1:1-10); so also do Isaiah (Isa 6:1-13) and Ezekiel (Ezek 1–3). Without the certainty such an experience provides and without such a positive commission, it is hard to see how Jeremiah, Isaiah, Ezekiel, or any of the other true prophets could have sustained for so long the burden of so unpopular a role. Such an experience is popularly referred to as a prophet's inaugural vision.

Third, the role of messenger explains the first-person form of speaking and the purpose of the prophet's inaugural vision experience. It explains as well why he so frequently uses such words as: "The Lord sent me" and "This is the word of the Lord." What it does not explain is the nature of the message that the prophet brings from God. To understand the prophet's message, the reader needs to advert to the accusations against Israel that make up so much a part of the prophet's message. These accusations and the judgments that follow them are all related to the demands of Israel's covenant relationship with God.

These demands are summed up in the ten commandments of the Sinai covenant, which in turn are summed up in the two great commandments: You will love the Lord your God with all your heart, and you will love your neighbor as yourself.

When Israel fails to fulfill these demands either by turning to the idol worship of the pagans (see Hos 1–3) or by committing crimes against the neighbor (see Amos 2:6-16; 3:9-15; 4–6; 8:4-9 for oppression of the poor by the rich viewed as a crime against the demands of the covenant), God sends a prophet-messenger to announce to them divine judgment of condemnation.

Thus, the major part of the prophetic message has to do with Israel's failure to live up to the demands of the covenant relationship with God. This explains why the prophets so often accuse and condemn. It explains as well why covenant theology constitutes the heart of the prophetic message, just as new-covenant theology constitutes the heart of the gospel message.

Fourth, the reader will understand the prophet's prosecuting attorney role if he or she recalls the well-known scenario of a court trial with its defendant, accusations, indictment, defense and prosecuting attorneys, and judge. God, of course, is not really a judge in our sense of the term, nor are the prophets prosecuting attorneys. But the rhetorical use of such an imaginative confrontation between accused and judge—between Israel and God—serves to dramatize for the prophets' audience the seriousness of their relationship with God and the seriousness of their crimes against the God who so lovingly initiated that relationship. Such an imaginative confrontation is popularly known as a trial or controversy and is reflected in the prophet's language whenever, as so often happens, a prophet accuses and condemns either Israel as a whole or particular individuals (see the frequent accusations in Jer 2:1–4:4 and the judgments, frequently introduced by the word "therefore" in Jer 5–9).

In summary, the reader will understand Jeremiah and any other prophet if he or she sees the prophet as one who saw himself as: (1) one who had been present at meetings of the divine council; (2) one who had been commissioned as God's messenger (inaugural vision); (3) one who accused and condemned Israel for crimes against the covenant God; (4) one who played the role of prosecuting attorney when speaking in the name of God and the role of defense attorney when speaking in his own or in his people's name; and (5) one whose concern, above all other matters, was to bring Israel to appreciate and treasure its unique relationship with God. The prophets, and Jeremiah in particular, had what might be called a passion for God and for God's people: for God, that God be truly loved and praised; for the people, that they be, in God's own words to them, "my people, my renown, my praise, my beauty" (see Jer 13:11).

COMMENTARY

PART I: JEREMIAH'S CALL

Jer 1:1-19

1:1-3 The editor's introduction to the Book of Jeremiah. These verses summarize Jeremiah's career from the time of his call in 626 B.C.E. to the fall of Jerusalem in 587. They constitute as well a heading for the collection of materials put together by an editor to make up the Book of Jeremiah as we have it now. Similar editorial headings occur at the beginning of other prophetic books, for example, Amos 1:1; Hos 1:1; Isa 1:1; and Ezek 1:1-3. The editor's heading for the book helps the reader to situate in history the career of each of the prophets.

1:4-10 The call of Jeremiah. Unless a prophet is truly called by God and sent as God's messenger to the covenanted people, there is no good reason why the people should listen to him. Speaking about false prophets, God says through Jeremiah: "I did not send these prophets, yet they ran; I did not speak to them, yet they prophesied" (23:21). To establish his credentials as a prophet, Jeremiah, along with Amos (Amos 7:14-15), Isaiah (Isa 6:1-13), and Ezekiel (Ezek 1:4-3:15), reminds his readers that he was called directly by God and commissioned to be God's messenger to them, the covenant people. That God "knew," "dedicated," and "appointed" Jeremiah to be "a prophet to the nations" even before he was born is the prophet's symbolic way of declaring that God had a role for him to play not only in the history of Israel but in the history of the gentile nations as well (v. 5).

Jeremiah's excuse, "I know not how to speak; I am too young" (v. 6), recalls Moses' attempt to escape the difficulties of the prophetic office (see Exod 4:10-13). Jeremiah knows that prophets lead a lonely life, are frequently scorned, often persecuted, and with few exceptions rejected during their lives. God, however, commands (v. 7). Jeremiah's only comfort is God's promise, "I am with you to deliver you" (v. 8). It is consoling to observe that God regularly promises to be "with" those who have been commissioned for difficult tasks in his service (see Exod 4:12; Josh 1:5, 9; Judg 6:16; 1 Sam 3:19; 16:13; Matt 28:20).

God's touching of Jeremiah's mouth (v. 9) is the prophet's metaphorical way of expressing that what he preaches to the people is truly the word of God and not any human word (compare Isa 6:6-7; Ezek 3:1-4, 10-11). Verse 10 indicates the scope of Jeremiah's message: he will deal not only with Israel but with other nations as well, and his message will be both negative and positive. He will prophesy the end of the old covenant and the existing dynasty of David, but he will also prophesy a new covenant (see chs. 30-33) and a new David.

1:11-16 Two visions. The visions of the branch of the watching-tree (almond tree) and the boiling cauldron may be later than Jeremiah's inaugural vision. They are placed here because they foreshadow the fulfillment of Jeremiah's prophecies concerning the Babylonian invasion and the destruction of Jerusalem and the kingdom of Judah. Jeremiah may have been out in the field in early February when the almond tree first blossoms, and he appears to be watching the still wintry landscape. God too is "watching"—watching over the divine Word to bring it to fulfillment (vv. 11-12). The boiling cauldron tipped to the north indicates the direction from which the invading Babylonian armies will come (v. 13) when they besiege and destroy Jerusalem (vv. 14-16 and see ch. 39).

1:17-19 God encourages Jeremiah. These verses conclude Jeremiah's call. God reminds him that he is not alone in the face of his enemies (v. 17), that it is divine power that strengthens him (v. 18), and that ultimately he will win out over his enemies because God is with him (v. 19). Jeremiah's need for such divine assurance is borne out by the despairing tone of the prophet's famous "confessions" (see 12:1-6; 15:10-21; 17:14-18; 18:19-23; 20:7-18).

PART II: JEREMIAH'S PREACHING FROM 626 to 604 B.C.E.

Jer 2:1-20:18

In all likelihood the major portion of the material in chapters 2-25 comes from the book dictated by Jeremiah to Baruch in the year 604 B.C.E. (see 36:28-32). Scholars debate about where and when Jeremiah preached what is in these chapters and even whether everything in these chapters comes from Jeremiah himself and not perhaps from the editors of the book. These questions have their place, but the when, the where, and the who are not nearly as important as the what of the prophet's message. It is because God spoke to Judah and to us through the mouth of Jeremiah that the Book of Jeremiah has entered the Bible. What God says, therefore, is the important thing, and it will be the aim of this commentary to concentrate on that divine message.

A. Jeremiah's Earliest Sermons (2:1–6:30)

When Jeremiah dictated to Baruch his book of sermons in 604 B.C.E. (see 36:28-32), he began by summarizing the gist of his message in 2:1–6:30. The message is that Judah has been unfaithful to God and therefore deserves a judgment of condemnation and punishment. Since this judgment is based on crimes against the covenant, Jeremiah, like all the prophets, begins by preaching God's accusations against Judah and concludes by threatening Judah with judgment and punishment. Chapters 2:1–4:4 deal mainly with accusations; chapters 4:5–6:30, with judgment and punishment.

2:1–3:5 Accusations. This collection of accusations begins and ends in the same way with the use of Hosea's marriage analogy for the Sinai covenant (see Hos 1–3), in which God is the bridegroom and Israel the unfaithful bride (compare 2:2 and 3:1-5). In verse 5 the people are accused of infidelity to God, a crime against the first commandment of the covenant. Verses 6-9 accuse them of ingratitude for forgetting the great things God did for them at the time of the Exodus and the conquest of the Promised Land. Verses 10-13 continue the accusations of ingratitude, contrasting the fidelity of the pagans to their gods, who are no gods at all (vv. 10-11), with the infidelity of Israel to the true God. Their crime is twofold. They have abandoned God, "the source of living waters," that is, water that flows naturally from the earth in springs and brooks and can be depended upon, and have chosen instead pagan gods, "broken cisterns, that hold no water," and therefore cannot be depended upon (vv. 12-13).

2:14-19 "Is Israel a slave, a bondman by birth?" Jeremiah demonstrates the evil of forsaking "the living waters" for the "broken cisterns" by reminding his listeners how they were punished by their Egyptian and Assyrian allies—"the waters of the Nile" and "the waters of the Euphrates"—(vv. 14-18) when they forsook God, their source of strength (v. 19).

2:20-28 "Long ago you broke your yoke." Jeremiah utilizes the language of Hosea's marriage analogy again to accuse his people of breaking their "yoke" of marriage to God by giving themselves to harlotry, that is, infidelity (v. 20). In verse 21 he uses the Isaian covenant analogy (see Isa 5:1-7), in which God is the owner of the vineyard and Israel is the vineyard, to again accuse them of infidelity. Verses 22-28 continue the accusations with Hosean language likening Israel's rampant infidelity to the covenant to the sexual ardor of a "frenzied she-camel" (vv. 22-25) and to the shame of a thief caught red-handed in his thievery (vv. 26-28).

2:29-32 "How dare you still plead with me?" Despite medicinal punishment, the way of divine pedogogy, Israel continues to rebel (vv. 29-30) and to act as if God had no interest in her (v. 31). Unlike a bride who never forgets her bridal jewelry, Israel has forgotten God.

2:33-37 "How well you pick your way when seeking love!" The indictment continues with accusations of crimes against the innocent (v. 34) and hypocritical avowals of innocence (v. 35). For such crimes God threatens the shame of subjection to Egyptian and Assyrian conquerors (vv. 36-37).

3:1-5 "If a man sends away his wife." Jeremiah concludes this collection of accusations by returning to the theme with which he began it, namely, the theme of the unfaithful wife (compare 2:2 and 3:1, 5). According to Deut 24:1-4, a divorced and remarried wife was forbidden to return to her original husband. Israel in her infidelity has sinned with many lovers and like a harlot refuses to blush (vv. 1-3). Even more, she hypocritically continues to call upon God as "My father . . . the bridegroom of my youth" (v. 4) and to expect forgiveness, all the while committing all the evil it can (v. 5).

3:6-10 "See now what rebellious Israel has done!" This prose passage both summarizes the accusations of 2:1–3:5 and at the same time takes up and develops the theme of 3:1-5: the return of the divorced wife who has rebelled against her husband—God. The key words "rebel" and "return" recur regularly (see 3:1, 7, 8, 10-14, 22; 4:1). The comparison (to the detriment of Judah) with the rebellious northern kingdom of Israel (vv. 6-10) suggests that this sample of Jeremiah's preaching dates to the reform of King Josiah (2 Kgs 22–23), which began in 626 B.C.E. and ended with Josiah's death in 609 B.C.E.

3:11-18 "Rebel Israel is inwardly more just than traitorous Judah." The theme "inwardly more just," which recurs in 4:3-4, frames 3:6–4:4 and summarizes the purpose of Jeremiah's preaching: guilty Judah, like guilty Israel, is called upon to confess its guilt and return to God not just externally but internally (v. 13). God will richly reward such a return (conversion) by bringing back the exiles of Israel (and Judah, if verses 14-18 do not come from editors during or after the Babylonian Exile) and making Jerusalem the special center for the worship of all the nations (vv. 17-18).

3:19–4:5 "How I should like to treat you as sons." This section begins with God's plaintive pleas for Israel to return (vv. 19-22a), continues with a suggested confession similar to the confession in Hos 14:2-4 (vv. 22b-25), and ends with a conditional absolution (4:1-2) and a final appeal for genuine inward conversion: a circumcision of the heart, that is, an inward rather than just an outward sign of commitment to God (vv. 3-4, and see 3:11, where the theme of "inwardly just" is first mentioned).

4:5–6:30 The judgment against guilty Judah. In this section Jeremiah summarizes God's judgment against Judah, the judgment first mentioned in 1:13-17, namely, that enemies will come from the north and destroy Jerusalem and Judah.

4:5-18 "Proclaim it in Judah." In verses 5-8 Jeremiah dramatizes the reaction of the people when they hear that invaders from the north have come to destroy the nation (vv. 6b-7). Verses 9-13 describe the dismay and desperation of the king, the princes, the priests, and the false prophets (vv. 9-10) when they witness the imminent fulfillment of God's judgment upon them (vv. 5-13). Finally, in verse 14 Jeremiah appeals to Jerusalem to "cleanse [its] heart of evil" in view of the disaster (vv. 15-17) about to take place because of its misdeeds (v. 18).

4:19-31 "My breast! my breast! how I suffer!" Jeremiah's grief as he anticipates the judgment and condemnation of Judah (vv. 19-21) is expressed in his repugnance for what his people have done (v. 22), in his horror at the approaching scourge (vv. 23-29), and in his repugnance for their attempt to prostitute themselves before their conquerors in order to stave off destruction (vv. 30-31).

5:1-31 Universal corruption. Combining accusations with judgment, Jeremiah complains to God that he cannot find even one upright person in Judah (v. 1); that all, from the lowliest to the greatest, are guilty (vv. 2-5); they will be punished (vv. 6-10) because they have openly rebelled (v. 11), denying God, as if God were powerless or nonexistent (v. 12), and rejecting the prophets (v. 13). For all this, God threatens destruction by a nation from afar (vv. 14-15), which will destroy their crops, their children, their flocks, and the "fortified city" (Jerusalem) in which they trust (vv. 16-17). Following a gloss from postexilic times (vv. 18-19), Jeremiah urges his people to pay attention (vv. 20-21) and to fear the all-powerful Lord of nature (v. 22). Verses 23-31 further accuse Judah and prepare the way for the climactic judgment that follows in 6:1-30.

6:1-30 The invaders from the north. Verses 1-5 ring with the cries of the invaded and the invaders, followed by a first series of accusations (vv. 6-10) leading up to God's judgment on young and old (vv. 11-12), small and great, false prophet and priest (vv. 13-15). A second series of accusations begins with an exhortation to remember "the way to good, and walk it," followed by Israel's reply, "We will not walk it" (v. 16), and its refusal to hearken to the warnings of God's "watchmen," that is, the prophets (v. 17). Verses 18-26 continue with further accusations and judgments, mentioning again the people "from the land of the north" (v. 22) and the destruction that the invading armies will bring (vv. 23-26). The section concludes with Jeremiah's evaluation of his ministry as a failure (vv. 27-30). He has been sent as a "tester" of his people (v. 27), and he has found them "silver rejected" (v. 30).

B. The Temple Sermon (7:1–8:3)

The temple sermon is the most memorable of Jeremiah's sermons. It is dated (see 26:1) early in the reign of King Jehoiakim (609–598 B.C.E.) and is written in Deuteronomic style, the style of the Book of Deuteronomy, which was found in the temple in 621 B.C.E. and with which Jeremiah was certainly acquainted. Like the material in chapters 2–6, the temple sermon is filled with accusations and condemnations.

7:1-15 Hear the word of the Lord. Standing near the gate to the temple area (v. 2), Jeremiah excoriates the Jews for their superstitious belief that the presence of God's temple will protect them (see Isa 36–37) from their enemies (v. 4) and calls them to reform their lives (vv. 5-7). In verses 8-11 he accuses them of crimes against the covenant, coupled with the hypocritical conviction that they can turn the temple into "a den of thieves" and still escape punishment. He reminds them that the Shiloh temple was destroyed in the time of Samuel (1050 B.C.E.) and that the same thing can now happen to Solomon's temple in Jerusalem (vv. 12-15). As chapter 26 explains, Jeremiah's threat leads to his trial for blasphemy against the temple, a crime of which he is acquitted only when someone reminds the judges that the prophet Micah made the same threat against the temple in the reign of King Hezekiah (715–687 B.C.E.) and was not condemned.

7:16–8:3 "You, now, do not intercede for this people." The sermon continues with accusations dealing with liturgical abuses (7:16-31) and concludes with a long description of the punishment that will be visited upon the people who have made God's temple a "den of thieves" (7:32–8:3).

C. Accusations and Judgments (8:4–10:25)

This section continues in different ways the accusations and judgments of chapters 2–6.

8:4-7 "Tell them." Here Jeremiah bemoans the unnatural conduct of people who, unlike the "Turtledove, swallow and thrush [which] observe their time of return, . . . do not know the ordinance of the Lord" (v. 7).

8:8-12 "How can you say, 'We are wise . . .'?" There is no true wisdom where the word of the Lord is rejected (vv. 8-9). The judgment introduced as usual by the word "therefore" is a just sentence on priests and prophets who in their greed for gain defraud the people (v. 10) and promise peace when there is no peace (vv. 11-12).

8:13-23 "I will gather them all in." The threat of punishment (v. 13) returns to the theme of invasion (vv. 14-17) and concludes with Jeremiah's soliloquy, in which he expresses his uncontrollable grief over the downfall of his people (vv. 18-23).

9:1-21 "Would that I had in the desert a traveler's lodge!" Jeremiah's soliloquy is followed by God's soliloquy (9:1-5). God would like to depart from this people and live alone in a desert lodge (v. 1), free of their lying, deceptions, and violence (vv. 2-5). The soliloquy is followed by a judgment and threat of punishment (vv. 6-8) and concludes with a long dirge that serves as a funeral song lamenting the destruction of Jerusalem and Judah (vv. 9-10), asking and answering why such calamities have come about (vv. 11-15), and calling upon the wailing women to come and intone a dirge (vv. 16-17) over the devastated land and the corpses of the slain (vv. 18-21). The dirge, which asked the question "Who is so wise . . . . ?" in verse 11, concludes with a definition of true wisdom (v. 22), which consists in knowing God as the only source of "kindness, justice and uprightness on the earth" (v. 23).

9:24–10:16 "See, days are coming, says the Lord." Like the surrounding idol-worshiping nations, the whole house of Israel is circumcised in the flesh, that is, outwardly but not inwardly in the heart, the only place where true commitment to God counts for anything (vv. 24-25). Israel, therefore, is no different from the idolatrous nations. Its idolatry, the prophet declares in language similar to that of Isa 40–66, is pure foolishness (10:1-11), and its gods are not to be compared with the true God (vv. 10-13), whose greatness highlights the inanity of idolatry (vv. 14-15) and who is "the portion of Jacob," that is, the God of Israel (v. 16).

10:17-25 "Lift your bundle and leave the land." Jeremiah concludes this collection of accusations and judgments (8:4–10:25) with a poem that probably dates from 597 B.C.E., when the Babylonian armies first invaded and defeated Judah and Jerusalem. The opening lines (vv. 17-18) advise the people to prepare for deportation. In verses 19-21 Jeremiah puts into the mouth of the nation a brief soliloquy lamenting its defeat (vv. 19-21) and blaming this defeat on the shepherds (the kings) who did not seek the Lord and thus brought about the defeat and deportation of the people (v. 22). The whole section concludes with Jeremiah's prayer of intercession for his wayward people (vv. 23-25).

D. Deuteronomic Sermons, Confessions, and Parables (11:1–20:18)

This section continues Jeremiah's accusations and judgments against Judah. It varies their presentation, however, by dramatizing them in different ways, for example, by introducing more Deuteronomic sermons (chs. 11; 16; 17; 19; 20), a number of parables (chs. 13; 18; 19), and Jeremiah's five famous confessions (12:1-16; 15:10-21; 17:12-18; 18:18-23; 20:7-18).

11:1-18 The covenant sermon. In the year 621 B.C.E., in the course of cleaning and reforming the temple and its cult, the priest Hilkiah discovered a manuscript presumed to be the Book of Deuteronomy and had it read before King Josiah (see 2 Kgs 22:8–23:25). Josiah, who had begun his reform some years earlier, used the book to further his reform by sending preachers to the cities of Judah and even to the cities of the defunct northern kingdom. The reform failed, but presumably 11:1-18 is an example of the kind of sermon Jeremiah preached when he took part in the abortive reform.

12:1-6 The first "confession." The five "confessions" of Jeremiah consist of soliloquies in which Jeremiah carries on intimate conversations with God. He laments his misfortunes, considers giving up his hopeless mission, pleads with God to avenge him against his enemies, and in the end rests his hope in God alone. Few people in the history of religion have exposed with such nakedness their inmost objections to God's way of dealing with them. Jeremiah's complaint in the first confession is the age-old complaint that God appears to reward opponents and to ignore those who are loyal (vv. 1-3a). He begs God, therefore, to show preference for the righteous by punishing the wicked (vv. 3b-4). God's reply (vv. 5-6) provides no comfort: Things will get worse not better (v. 5), and even Jeremiah's own relatives will betray him (v. 6).

11:19-23 "Yet I, like a trusting lamb." These verses fit better here after 12:6 and describe Jeremiah's reaction to his relatives' plot to kill him (v. 19). He entrusts his care to God (v. 20), who promises to punish the inhabitants of Anathoth (vv. 21-23).

12:7-17 "I abandon my house." The oracle declares that just as Jeremiah's relatives have turned on him, so his "heritage" has turned on God (vv. 7-8). For this they are punished, as Jeremiah's relatives were punished (vv. 9-13). Verses 14-17, which refer to the possible conversion of the neighboring kingdoms that turned against Judah at the time of the Babylonian invasions of 598 and 588 B.C.E., echo the universalism of the promise to Abraham (Gen 12:1-3) and the later universalism of Isa 40–55. Some consider these verses to be an exilic gloss.

13:1-11 The parable of the linen loincloth. Parables are extended similies in story form. The important element is the central point of likeness. The details are secondary and pertain only to the fleshing out of the story. Most parables, like those of Jesus, are purely literary, that is, made-up stories; for example, the good Samaritan, the prodigal son, Dives and Lazarus. Some parables are acted out; for example, Jesus' washing of the feet of his disciples at the Last Supper. They are called parables in action. In each parable the reader should search out the nature of the parable—literary or in action—and the covenant themes, usually inherent in the accusations and judgments.

In the parable of the loincloth, the central likeness is the closeness of one's underclothes to one's person as the measure of the closeness intended to exist between God and the people (v. 11). The burial of the loincloth in a cleft of the rock by the Parath (Euphrates), where it rots (vv. 1-7), signifies the punishment of Israel for refusing to obey God and following strange gods instead (vv. 8-11). The nature of the parable is probably that of a parable in action. The Parath (Euphrates) is probably not the great river that runs through Babylon but a stream with the same name not far from Jerusalem, used here as a symbol of Babylon and the Exile there. Watching Jeremiah's parabolic burying of the loincloth in a cleft of rock by the Parath would excite curiosity and the question "Why?" Jeremiah answers by telling the parable (vv. 1-7) and then giving the answer (vv. 8-11).

14:1–15:4 The great drought. In the Middle East, when the winter rains fail for two or three years, drought and famine are sure to follow. The drought described in verses 2-6 caused a national emergency. What follows in 14:8 to 15:4 is Jeremiah's intercessory prayer for the nation (vv. 8-9) and God's command to him not to intercede for these people (vv. 10-12). Jeremiah then blames it all on the false prophets (v. 13). God answers him by condemning both prophets and people to sword and famine (vv. 14-16). In the lament that follows, Jeremiah again attempts to intercede for his people (vv. 17-22) and is again rebuffed (15:1-4). God is watching over the divine word (see 1:12) and is determined to see it fulfilled! It is impossible to date this section, but the frequent references to the "sword" (vv. 12-13, 15-16, 18; 15:2-3) suggest a time of war, perhaps the Babylonian invasion of 598 B.C.E.

15:5-9 "Who will pity you, Jerusalem?" This lament follows naturally upon God's determination to fulfill the word of judgment against Jerusalem in 15:1-4.

15:10-21 Jeremiah's second "confession." The mention of a mother of seven swooning away in 15:9 leads Jeremiah to think of his own mother and his own situation as "a man of strife and contention to all the land" (v. 10). Almost in despair he argues with God to avenge him on his persecutors, reminding God how he, Jeremiah, interceded for his enemies (vv. 11, 15), how he delighted in God's word (v. 16), and how this led to his unbearable loneliness (v. 17). Jeremiah concludes by accusing God of betraying and abandoning him like "a treacherous brook, whose waters do not abide" (v. 18). God's reply is a rebuke and an implied accusation. Jeremiah himself needs to repent (return to God) and weigh well his own response to God (v. 19a). If he does, he will continue to be God's "mouthpiece," and God will be with him against his persecutors (vv. 19b-21 and compare 1:18-19).

16:1-21 Jeremiah's celibacy. God commands Jeremiah to be celibate, not because celibacy is better than marriage but because in the days of thirst, starvation, and destruction that would accompany the siege and destruction of Jerusalem, Jeremiah would be spared the anguish of witnessing the terrible suffering of a beloved wife and children. In addition, like the children of Hosea (see Hos 1:4-9) and Isaiah (see Isa 7:3; 8:1-4), Jeremiah would be a living symbol of the unhappy fate of Judah and Jerusalem (vv. 1-4). He is not to mourn with the mourners (vv. 5-7) nor celebrate with those who sit eating and drinking (vv. 8-9), because Judah and Jerusalem are to be punished for forsaking God and God's covenant law (vv. 10-13). Verses 14-15 do not harmonize with the message of destruction in verses 10-13 and probably represent a postexilic gloss. Verses 16-19 continue the message of doom. Like verses 14-15, verses 19-21 probably also represent a postexilic gloss. They speak of the conversion of the pagan nations and ridicule idolatry, two popular themes of exilic and postexilic literature.

17:1-13 "The sin of Judah is written with an iron stylus." This series of sayings contrasts the true and the false Israelite. Sin begins in the heart, and Judah's guilt is undeniable (v. 1). For its sin it will be punished (vv. 2-4). The wicked trust in human beings and are cursed (vv. 5-6); the just trust in the Lord, and their future is assured by God (v. 8 and see Ps 1:1ff.). Verses 9-10 return to the mysterious workings of the human heart (see v. 1) and avow that only God can probe its incalculable ways (v. 10). An example of such incalculable ways is the one who acquires wealth unjustly (v. 11 and see Luke 12:13-21). Jeremiah's observations on the human heart conclude with a declaration of doom for those who forsake God (vv. 12-13).

17:14-18 Jeremiah's third "confession." This confession should be interpreted in the light of Jeremiah's observations concerning the mysterious workings of the human heart mentioned in 17:1, 5-10. As in his first and second confessions, Jeremiah begs God to heal him (v. 14), to observe the blasphemous scoffing of his enemies (v. 16), and to remember how he did not press for his enemies' total destruction (v. 16). Naturally, he prays that his enemies and not he himself be confounded (vv. 17-18), for only thus will it be seen that God is a just God.

17:19-27 Desecrating the sabbath. Here, as in his Deuteronomic temple sermon (see 7:1–8:3), Jeremiah attacks those who sin against God's covenant commandment of keeping holy the sabbath day. All prophetic accusations and judgments deal in one way or another with crimes against the ten commandments. This sermon is notable in that it deals specifically with only one commandment and shows that although Jeremiah is against the hypocrisy of those who make an outward show of piety (see 7:1ff.), he is not against the temple cult in itself (compare Isa 1:12-17). When commanding "Keep holy the sabbath day," God meant what the words say. As with all the commandments, God promises blessings for those who observe them (vv. 24-26) and curses on those who do not (v. 27).

18:1-12 The parable of the potter. The potter with his wheel—one wheel at the top holding the clay and the other at the bottom rotated by his feet—is master of what he will create (vv. 1-4). So is God the master of Israel's fate (vv. 5-6). But God is not a tyrant and leaves the last word to Israel. The divine blessings are conditional, and so are the threats (vv. 7-10). The message of the parable is clear: all depends on Israel. But, as verses 11-12 make clear, Judah has no intention of repenting, and therefore its fate is certain (v. 12).

18:13-17 Judah's unnatural apostasy. Jeremiah's conviction that Judah will not return to God fills him with horror (v. 13). It should be as natural for Judah to be faithful to God as it is for the snow to remain on the mountains of Lebanon and as it is for the mountain streams to run steadily down (v. 14). Yet Israel has done the unnatural thing: it has forgotten God and turned to idolatrous worship (v. 15). In view of what God the potter declared in 18:10, therefore, Judah's fate is certain (vv. 16-17).

18:18-23 Jeremiah's fourth "confession." As in his earlier confessions, Jeremiah is outraged with his enemies because they have not only persecuted him but now even plot his death (vv. 18-19). He argues with God (v. 20a), reminds God how he, Jeremiah, prayed for his enemies (v. 20b), and then launches into a bitter prayer for the destruction of those enemies (vv. 21-23). Since Jeremiah's enemies are God's enemies, it is not unlikely that Jeremiah prays for their destruction in order that all might see that God is not impotent before apparent foes. Jeremiah had, after all, interceded for them, so he could hardly have hated them.

19:1-20:6 The symbolic earthen flask. This episode cannot be dated, but the references to Babylon in 20:4-6 indicate that it occurred sometime after Babylon came to power in 605 B.C.E. The earthen flask, a clay water jar, symbolizes Judah and Jerusalem (v. 3). Jeremiah takes it with him to the valley of Ben-hinnom, the valley on the southwest side of Jerusalem later turned into a garbage dump and called Gehenna (vv. 1-2). At a Baal fertility-cult temple there in the valley, Jeremiah delivers a bitter sermon against Judah and Jerusalem, accusing it of flagrant idolatry (vv. 3-5) and threatening it with total destruction (vv. 6-9). At the end of the sermon, he hurls the earthen flask to the ground, smashing it to bits, thus indicating by a parable in action the destruction of the city and the nation (vv. 10-15). Baruch, his secretary and biographer, or perhaps Jeremiah himself, then describes what happened. Pashhur, chief officer in the temple, has Jeremiah scourged and then placed in the stocks overnight (20:1-2). The next morning Jeremiah, filled with indignation, predicts a bitter end for Pashhur (vv. 2-4a) and for the whole nation (vv. 4b-6). The prophecy is fulfilled when the Babylonians capture Jerusalem in 587 B.C.E. and deport king and citizens into captivity and exile in Babylon.

20:7-18 Jeremiah's fifth and last "confession." Goaded almost to despair, Jeremiah, in a magnificently passionate soliloquy, accuses God of seducing him into accepting a mission that brings only "derision and reproach all the day" (vv. 7-8). He contemplates abandoning his office of prophet but then, in almost a paroxysm of revulsion, admits that God's word is like a fire in his bones that he can neither hold in nor endure (v. 9). God's word brings him only denunciation, the loss of friends, and the threat of death (v. 10). Despite all this, he knows that God is with him and that his persecutors will not triumph (v. 11). With a burst of confidence, he then calls upon God to avenge him on his enemies (vv. 12-13). Finally, emotionally drained, he despairingly curses the day he was born (vv. 14-18). As many have observed, this confession says more about the nature of inspiration and the hardships of the prophetic mission than a dozen learned treatises.

PART III: PROPHECIES AGAINST THE KINGS AND THE FALSE PROPHETS

Jer 21:1–25:38

In the book that Jeremiah dictated to Baruch in 604 B.C.E. (see ch. 36), it is probable that chapter 20 was followed immediately by chapter 25, a chapter whose content sounds very much like the conclusion to that book (see 25:1-3, 13). Later, when editors put the whole book together in the form in which we have it now, they interpolated between chapter 20 and chapter 25 a collection of Jeremiah's prophecies against the kings and the false prophets. They did so in all probability because the content of these prophecies contains the overall theme of chapters 1–20, namely, accusations against and condemnations of those who have been unfaithful to the covenant.

In chapters 21–24 the editors are concerned more with content than chronology. The collection begins and ends with a prophecy against the last king of Judah, King Zedekiah (597–587 B.C.E.). By repeating the same names, Zedekiah (21:1 and 24:8) and Nebuchadnezzar (21:1 and 24:1), and the expression "sword, famine, and pestilence" (21:7, 9 and 24:10), the editors make the collection begin and end the same way, thus creating a frame or, as it is technically called, an inclusion-conclusion for the whole section.

A. Prophecies Against the Kings and False Prophets (21:1–24:10)

21:1-10 Against King Zedekiah. Following the siege of 598 B.C.E. and the deportation of the reigning king, Jeconiah, to Babylon as hostage royalty, Nebuchadnezzar placed Jeconiah's uncle, Zedekiah, the third son of Josiah (639–609), on the throne of Judah. In return Zedekiah rebelled. Infuriated, Nebuchadnezzar besieged Jerusalem for the last time in 588 B.C.E. King Zedekiah, a believer in Jeremiah, seeks from the prophet a good word from the Lord (vv. 1-2). Jeremiah's response provides little comfort: the city will fall to the Babylonians (vv. 3-7), and only those who surrender will save their lives (vv. 8-10).

21:11–22:9 Against the whole royal dynasty of David. In the section that follows, Jeremiah will deal with each of the kings in chronological order, beginning with Jehoahaz. Here he twice gives warning against the Davidic dynasty as a whole, first in 21:11-14 and a second time in 22:1-9. Each warning begins with a reminder of what God expects of the kings (21:11a and 22:1-4) and ends with a threat of destruction (21:11b-14 and 22:5-9). The whole section breathes disillusionment with the messianic dynasty of David (see 2 Sam 7 for the promise of perpetuity to the dynasty) and leads up to the promise of a future successful Davidic king (the Messiah) in 23:1-8.

The "Valley-site" (v. 13a), another name for Jerusalem, which is surrounded by valleys, is considered impregnable (v. 13b), but God will "kindle a fire in its forest," probably a section of Solomon's palace called "the Forest of Lebanon" (1 Kgs 7:2), and destroy it (v. 14). In 22:1-9 the prophecy of destruction is conditional (vv. 4-6), but with little hope that the condition will be fulfilled (vv. 7-9).

22:10-12 Against Jehoahaz. When his father, King Josiah, died in battle against the Egyptians at Megiddo in 609 B.C.E. (see 2 Kgs 23:28-30), Jehoahaz ascended the throne of Judah. He reigned three months, was deposed by Pharaoh Neco of Egypt, and led into exile, never to return. His throne name was Jehoahaz; his personal name, Shallum (v. 11).

22:13-19 Against Jehoiakim. Enthroned as vassal king by the Egyptians, Jehoiakim paid a heavy tribute to Egypt (see 2 Kgs 23:24ff.). Jeremiah accuses him of engaging in vast building projects and refusing to pay his laborers (vv. 13-15a), and contrasts him for the worse with his pious father, King Josiah (vv. 15b-17). The judgment against him is harsh: no one will mourn him (v. 18), and he will be buried as ignominiously as an ass (v. 19). It should be noted that Jehoiakim murdered prophets (see 26:20-24), forced Jeremiah and Baruch into hiding, and was so contemptuous of Jeremiah that he callously fed into the fire the first of Jeremiah's two manuscripts dictated to Baruch in the year 604 B.C.E. (see 36:20-26). Jeremiah had ample justification for his harsh judgment against Jehoiakim!

22:20-30 Against Jehoiachin. Jeremiah's longest prophecy against a king is leveled at Jehoiachin, also known as Coniah and

Jeconiah (v. 24). He succeeded Jehoiakim in 598 B.C.E., reigned three months, and was then deported to Babylon as hostage royalty along with his family and many of the nobles and priests. He is mentioned as still living in Babylon in 562 B.C.E. (see 2 Kgs 25:27-30). The prophecy against him begins with the accusation that he has from his youth refused to listen to God (vv. 20-21). It continues with the threat of exile (vv. 22-23) and concludes with a long denunciation (vv. 24-30) predicting his defeat by Nebuchadnezzar (it happened in 597 B.C.E.) and exile with no hope of return (vv. 24-27). It concludes with a bitter tirade not only against Jehoiachin but against his descendants as well (vv. 29-30). Verse 30 is important because it shows Jeremiah's complete disillusionment with the Davidic dynasty, a disillusionment that leads up to his prediction in 23:1-6 of a future successful descendant of David whom Israel would look forward to as the Messiah! The prediction that Jehoiachin will be "childless" does not mean that he will have no sons (he had seven) but that none of them will ever reign as king of Judah.

23:1-8 A future son of David who will succeed. The prophecy of a future successful son of David begins with the accusation that the "shepherds," that is, the kings, have been responsible for the exile of the nation (vv. 1-2) and the promise that God will be the Good Shepherd who gathers the dispersed sheep and brings them back to their meadow, a symbolic way of speaking about the return from the Babylonian captivity (vv. 3-4 and compare Ezek 34). This promise is repeated in verses 7-8 and thus forms a frame around the messianic promise in verses 5-6. The future ideal king is described as "a righteous shoot [descendant] to David," who unlike his predecessors will reign and govern wisely (v. 5). He will be the savior of Judah and will be called "the Lord our justice." This prophecy, along with the prophecy of Isaiah about "a shoot [that] shall sprout from the stump of Jesse" (Isa 11:1ff.) fueled the messianic hopes of Israel in the centuries that followed and was fulfilled with the coming of Jesus, "the son of David," five centuries later.

23:9-40 Against the false prophets. Besides true prophets, Israel also had to deal with false prophets, those who falsely claimed to have been sent by God as messengers to the people of Israel (see 29:1-17 for an example of a false prophet who told the people the opposite of what Jeremiah told them). In verses 9-14 Jeremiah describes the depravity of some of the false prophets. In verses 14-24 he repeats many of the charges he had made against the false prophets who opposed him. He then concludes with a long deuteronomically styled diatribe against those prophets and their insolent claims (vv. 25-40).

24:1-10 Against Zedekiah. Jeremiah frames the whole section against the kings and the false prophets (21:24) by ending as he began (see 21:1-10)—with a prophecy against Zedekiah and renewed remarks about Nebuchadnezzar and the scourges he would bring: sword, famine, and pestilence. The prophecy is dated to 598 B.C.E. and deals with the fate of the exiles of 598 B.C.E. (vv. 1-7), whom Jeremiah designates symbolically as "the good figs" (vv. 4-7), and with the fate of King Zedekiah and the remaining Jews in Jerusalem, whom he designates symbolically as "the bad figs" (vv. 8-10). Undoubtedly the editors placed this prophecy last in the collection of prophecies against the kings because it not only serves to frame the whole collection but also introduces and foreshadows what will follow: God's promises for the future for "the good figs" (chs. 29–33) and God's threats of doom for "the bad figs" (chs. 34-39). The passage is doubly important because it contains the first promise of what will constitute the heart of "the new covenant" in the words: "I will give them a heart with which to understand that I am the Lord" (v. 7 and compare 31:31-34).

B. The Conclusion of Jeremiah's Book (25:1-38)

Originally this chapter followed chapters 1–20. It formed the conclusion of the manuscript that Jeremiah dictated to Baruch in 604 B.C.E. (see 36:27-32). In 605 B.C.E. Nebuchadnezzar had made himself master of the Middle East from Mesopotamia to Egypt. Jeremiah now knew that "the wind from the north" that would devastate Judah and Jerusalem (see chs. 1–6) would be the armies of Babylon. Writing in Deuteronomic style, he reminds his readers that what he has written constitutes a summary of twenty-three years of preaching (v. 3), which they have rejected, as they rejected the preaching of all the prophets (vv.

4-7). Since they will not listen, their doom is sealed. God will send "the tribes of the north" (Nebuchadnezzar's armies) to devastate the land (vv. 8-10). The nation will be in exile for seventy years (vv. 11-14).

This is the first reference to the seventy years of the Babylonian captivity, which ended in 539 B.C.E. with the destruction of the Babylonian Empire by Cyrus the Great of Persia. However one counts the seventy years, whether from 604 B.C.E., when Jeremiah first spoke of them, or from 597 B.C.E., when the first group was deported to Babylon, or from 587 B.C.E., when the major deportation took place, it is impossible to get exactly seventy years. The figure is best interpreted as a round number signifying a long time. Although Jeremiah did not know it, it was during those seventy years that his book was read, pondered, and heeded. Too late the exiles realized that Jeremiah's preaching made sense, that his enemies had erred, and that God had justly punished them. But it was not too late to return to God, from whom alone, as Jeremiah had so many times insisted, they could confidently expect forgiveness, security, and a future. Out of the ashes of the Exile came a fire, and Jeremiah's book was the spark that ignited it.

The reference in verse 14a to the nations that would destroy the kingdom of Judah leads Jeremiah in verses 15-38 to predict the future downfall of those same nations. In the Greek text, but not in the Hebrew, there follow here the prophecies against the nations in chapters 46–51. The "cup" (vv. 15ff.) symbolizes destiny. The destiny can be good, as in Ps 23:5 ("my cup overflows"), or bad, as in Matt 26:39 ("My Father, if it is possible, let this cup pass me up"). In this case the "cup" is a cup of wrath for the nations that have oppressed God's people.

PART IV: BIOGRAPHICAL MATERIAL AND THE NEW COVENANT

Jer 26:1–33:26

This section of the book comes from sources that contained biographical material about Jeremiah. Like the following chapters (chs. 34–39), it is long on narrative and short on sermons. The narrative material would seem to come from a biography of Jeremiah by his secretary Baruch. Whatever the original source or sources, it is clear that the editors did not arrange the material in chronological order. Chapter 26 deals with the temple sermon dated to 608 B.C.E. Chapters 27–29 date to 593, and chapter 36 dates to 604 B.C.E. More than likely the editors chose to arrange the material according to theme. Thus chapters 26–29 deal with the truth and efficacy of Jeremiah's prophetic words; chapters 30–33, with Jeremiah's predictions of hope for the future and a new covenant for Israel; and chapters 34–39, with the rejection of both Jeremiah himself and his word by kings and commoners.

A. The Temple Sermon (26:1-24)

The hand of the biographer (Baruch?) is evident here in the dating (609–608 B.C.E.), the beginning (v. 1) of the reign of King Jehoiakim (609–598 B.C.E.), and in the pervasive third-person narrative account. The biographer summarizes Jeremiah's famous sermon (see 7:1-8:3) predicting the destruction of the temple (vv. 2-6) and then goes on to tell what the results were for the courageous prophet. He is accused of blasphemy against the temple and threatened with death (vv. 2-6). Jeremiah responds to the charge (vv. 7-11) by declaring that it was God who sent him to prophesy against the temple and the city, and only their repentance (see ch. 18) can save both city and temple (vv. 12-13). If they execute him, they will bring down upon themselves, their city, and its citizens "innocent blood" (vv. 14-15 and see Matt 27:24-25).

In the informal trial that follows, Jeremiah is defended by some of his friends among the elders (v. 16), who remind Jeremiah's accusers that the prophet Micah a century earlier, in the reign of King Hezekiah (715–687), made the same prediction (Mic 3:12) and was not condemned to death (vv. 17-19). Jeremiah is acquitted, but his biographer highlights the danger to the prophet by telling the story of a less fortunate prophet, Uriah, who fled into Egypt, was brought back to Jerusalem, and there executed and thrown into the common grave (vv. 20-24). By placing these episodes here at the beginning of the biographical section of the book, the editors emphasize the nature of the true prophet—one whose prophecy is fulfilled. The readers know how well Jeremiah's prophecy was fulfilled, and the editors leave no doubt about it in the following chapters, especially chapter 39.

B. Jeremiah Against the False Prophets (27:1–29:32)

As in chapter 26, the editors' concern in chapters 27–29 is to emphasize the truth and fulfillment of Jeremiah's prophecies, despite the opposition of his enemies—in this case the false prophet Hananiah in Jerusalem (see ch. 28) and the false prophets in Babylon (see 29:20-32). The biographer begins by explaining the background of Jeremiah's conflict with Hananiah. In 593 B.C.E., only four years after the first siege and capture of Jerusalem, King Zedekiah of Judah, who had been put on the throne by Nebuchadnezzar, plots against Nebuchadnezzar by calling to Jerusalem the ambassadors of the kings of Edom, Moab, Ammon, Tyre, and Sidon (vv. 1-3). Using an ox yoke as a parable in action, Jeremiah declares to the assembled ambassadors and Zedekiah that it is God's will that they all bend their necks under the yoke of the king of Babylon (vv. 4-8). They must not listen to false prophets who predict a successful revolt (vv. 9-22).

What follows in chapter 28 is a vivid account of the face-to-face meeting of the true prophet and the false prophet. Hananiah predicts success (28:1-4). Jeremiah counters with a declaration that implicitly accuses Hananiah of prophesying falsely (vv. 5-9). Hananiah throws Jeremiah's ox yoke to the ground and repeats his prediction of a successful revolt (vv. 10-11). Finally Jeremiah receives word from the Lord and prophesies Hananiah's death within a year for having prophesied falsely in the name of the Lord (vv. 12-17). Once again as in chapter 26, the editors have highlighted the veracity of the true prophet by chronicling these unique encounters between the true prophet and the false prophet.

Chapter 29 continues the theme of Jeremiah's battle against the false prophets. This time the opposition comes from Babylon, where false prophets are assuring the exiles of 597 B.C.E. that they will soon return to Jerusalem. Jeremiah refutes their claims by sending a letter to the exiles via friends sent on a diplomatic mission to Nebuchadnezzar (vv. 1-3). The letter (vv. 4-23) urges the exiles to expect a long stay in the land of their conquerors, to settle down there (vv. 4-6), to pray for the welfare of Babylon (v. 7), and to pay no heed to the false prophets (vv. 8-9). In verses 10-14 Jeremiah assures them that after seventy years God will reverse their fortunes and bring them back to their own land. The letter continues with a threat against Jerusalem and King Zedekiah (vv. 15-20) and against two false prophets in Babylon (vv. 21-23). It concludes with a threat of death for Shemaiah, who had written from Babylon to the high priest urging him to arrest and silence Jeremiah (vv. 24-32).

The editors placed this letter-writing episode here not only because it continues the theme of Jeremiah's battle with the false prophets but also because it serves as an excellent preamble to the theme of the following chapters—the theme of hope for the future and the promise of a new and successful covenant (chs. 30–33).

C. Jeremiah and the New Covenant (30:1–33:26)

The editors of Jeremiah's prophecies grouped in these chapters material from different sources dealing with the prophet's predictions of hope for Israel and Judah in the future. The prophet who predicted with such certainty the fall and exile of Judah and Jerusalem with equal certainty predicted its return from exile and the inauguration of a new and successful covenant in the future. The prophet whose mission was "to root up and to tear down, to destroy and to demolish, to build and to plant" (see 1:10) here builds and plants. The hopes he plants and the future he begins to build take root during the long years of exile and come to fulfillment at the Last Supper, when Jesus declares, "This cup is the new covenant in my blood, which will be shed for you" (Luke 22:20). The editors wisely placed this collection of prophecies of hope after Jeremiah's encouraging letter to the exiles of 597 B.C.E. (see ch. 29) and before the dismal account of the last days of Judah and Jerusalem (see chs. 34–39).

30:1-24 Prophecies of hope. Chapter 30 begins with a statement of hope for the future (vv. 1-3), the general theme of chapters 30–33. Jeremiah's words are directed to Israel, the defunct northern kingdom, and Judah, the soon-to-be-defunct southern kingdom (v. 4). This statement makes applicable to Judah the prophecies of hope in 30:1–31:14; these originally were directed only toward the defunct northern kingdom, which suffered destruction and deportation under the Assyrians in 722 B.C.E. Jeremiah speaks of Israel, therefore, not so much as a national entity, but as that entity better known as the people of God, a moral entity which no national catastrophe can destroy and which exists today and will always exist despite all the vicissitudes and debacles of history.

The prophecies of hope begin with the cries of dismay and fear (vv. 5-7) that fill all hearts when it becomes obvious that the fearful "day of the Lord," the day when God will fulfill earlier threats of destruction for Judah and Jerusalem, has arrived. Bondage to pagan masters, however, will not last. In the future, Israel will serve God and its messianic king (vv. 8-9). This reversal of fortune will be the work of God (vv. 10-23), a work described in language that will be echoed thirty years later in the soaring poetry of Deutero-Isaiah (see Isa 40–55).

31:1-40 The new covenant. Chapter 31 might well be described as Jeremiah's "Hosean" chapter. It shows Hosea's influence on Jeremiah's theology, language, and style (see chs. 2–3 for earlier examples of Hosean chapters). The linguistic and stylistic similarities are obvious (compare vv. 2-3, 9, 18, 20 with Hos 2:16; 11:1-4; 14:2-8). The theological similarities become evident when the reader compares Jeremiah's and Hosea's emphasis on God's love for Israel, and Jeremiah's prediction of a new and eternal covenant (31:31-34) with Hosea's prediction of a new and eternal marriage (Hos 2:18-25).

Verses 1-6 announce the good news of return from exile, emphasizing God's love for Israel (v. 3: "With age-old love I have loved you"). Verses 7-14 rhapsodize over the joy of the returned exiles. Verses 15-20 call upon Israel to end its mourning. Verse 15 calls poetically upon Rachel, the long-dead matriarch of Israel, to cease her cries of mourning for her exiled children. They will return from exile (vv. 16-17), repentant (vv. 18-19) and assured of God's loving forgiveness (v. 20 and see Hos 14:3-9). In the New Testament, Matthew uses this same poetic allusion to Rachel in his story of Herod's slaughter of the innocents (see Matt 2:18).

In 31:21-22 Jeremiah begins to speak about the new covenant. Calling poetically upon the exiles to set up roadmarkers as they go into exile so that they can follow them on their return (v. 21), he asks dramatically, "How long will you continue to stray, rebellious daughter?" (v. 22a) and then answers his own question with the mysterious statement of verse 22b. Scholars do not agree on the exact meaning here of the verb "encompass," but most agree that the "new thing" that God "has created upon the earth" is a responsive and loving Israel, which, unlike the faithless woman of the Hosean marriage analogy (see Hos 1–3), "will encompass the man [God, in the Hosean analogy] with devotion." This is Jeremiah's indirect way of speaking about the new covenant he will describe in 31:31-34.

Verses 23-30 apply to Judah directly all that Jeremiah said about Israel in 30:1–31:22. Verse 28 repeats what was said about the positive aspect of Jeremiah's mission (see 1:10). Verses 29-30 assure the Israelites that God will judge them according to their own merits and not according to the sins of their ancestors, whose wickedness brought down upon the nation destruction and deportation.

31:31-34 The new covenant. This famous prophecy provides the foundation and the core of the central theological teaching of the New Testament. St. Paul in 2 Cor 3:1–5:21 and the author of Hebrews in Heb 8:6–9:15 explicitly expound this prophecy in relation to Christ. It underlies, but without explicit references, much of the "new life" theology of St. John and is central to the teaching of Jesus in John's Last Supper discourse (John 13–17).

What is "new" about the new covenant is not the God who makes it nor the people with whom it is made—the true Israel—nor the will of God expressed in the Sinai commandments, but the results of the new covenant and the means by which those results are brought about. In contrast to the old Sinai covenant, which failed because Israel did not respond to God's love, the new covenant will be successful. It will be successful because it will be God and God alone who will put into the hearts of the people the power to respond with love. We call this power "grace," and as the books of the New Testament, especially the Pauline letters and John's Gospel, insist, it comes to us along with forgiveness of sins through faith in Jesus who died for love of us.

Although Jeremiah speaks only here of a "new" covenant, he speaks of it implicitly in many other places: in the promise to the exiles of 597 B.C.E. to give them a "new heart" (24:7; see also 32:38-40); in the hope-filled letter to the "good figs" in exile in Babylon (29:5-14); and in the new thing that God will create on earth: "the woman [who will] . . . encompass the man with devotion" (31:22). In the years that follow, Jeremiah's prophecy will be echoed by Ezekiel (see Ezek 16:59-64; 36:25-30) and Deutero-Isaiah (see Isa 55:3; 59:21; 61:8). For Jesus, six hundred years later, the making of the new covenant will become the aim and the focus of his passion, death, and resurrection.

The remainder of the chapter emphasizes the certainty of the promise of God to Israel (vv. 35-37) and of the promise to rebuild Jerusalem (vv. 38-40).

32:1-44 More on the new covenant. This chapter, from a biographical source, was added here by the editors because its theme fits with the theme of chapters 30–31—Israel's return from exile and the new covenant. The episode described took place in the tenth year (587 B.C.E.) of the reign of King Zedekiah, when Nebuchadnezzar's armies were besieging Jerusalem and after Jeremiah had been imprisoned in the quarters of the guard (vv. 1-5 and see 37:21). Ostensibly Jeremiah purchases his cousin Hanamel's field in Anathoth because the Mosaic law demanded that the nearest of kin purchase such property in order to keep it within the clan (vv. 6-9 and see Lev 25:25). Since property during a siege is worth nothing (see vv. 24-25), Jeremiah actually buys the field not as an asset but as another way of professing his faith in God's promise of restoration (vv. 10-15). Thus his purchase of the property amounts to a parable in action. His long prayer in verses 16-44, especially verses 24-25 and 36-44, explains the central point of the parable in action. Verses 38-41 repeat in similar words the substance of what Jeremiah said about the new covenant in 31:31-34 and account for the inclusion of chapter 32 in the collection of Jeremiah's prophecies of hope in chapters 30–33.

33:1-26 More on Israel's hope. Like chapter 32, this chapter contains another prophecy of hope made by Jeremiah during the siege of Jerusalem and at a time when the prophet was imprisoned in the quarters of the guard (vv. 1-13). A second prophecy dealing with the future of the Davidic dynasty follows (vv. 14-18) and presents another version of Jeremiah's prediction of a future Davidic Messiah given more succinctly in 23:5-6. Israel's future rests on firm foundations—a new covenant and a new David (vv. 19-26 and see 31:35-37).

PART V: DISOBEDIENCE AND DESTRUCTION

Jer 34:1–39:18

As in the rest of the book, the editors arranged the material in chapters 34–39 in a thematic rather than chronological order. Chapters 35–36 date to 598 and 604 B.C.E., respectively, in the reign of King Jehoiakim (609–598 B.C.E.) while chapters 34 and 37–39 date to the last years of King Zedekiah (597–587 B.C.E.). The theme of disobedience to God and God's prophet—a disobedience that results in destruction—clearly dominates and unifies the whole section.

A. The Broken Pact with the Slaves (34:1-22)

34:1-7 "This word came to Jeremiah from the Lord." The chapter begins with Jeremiah's announcement during Nebuchadnezzar's siege of Jerusalem (v. 1) that the city will fall and King Zedekiah will be captured (vv. 2-3). A promise is made to Zedekiah that if he *obeys* (the key word in this whole section), he will die in peace (vv. 4-5). He does not obey, however, and does not die in peace (see 39:4-7). Verses 6-7 indicate that the siege is far advanced, since only two of Jerusalem's fortress towns, Lachish and Azekah, remain. Interestingly enough, one of the twenty-nine Lachish letters (messages to the garrison commander at Lachish written on broken pieces of pottery discovered by archeologists when they excavated Lachish) contains the words: "Let my lord know that we are watching for the signals of Lachish . . . for we cannot see [the signals] of Azekah." The message would seem to indicate that Azekah had fallen and only Lachish remained.

34:8-22 "This is the word that came to Jeremiah from the Lord." The episode of the broken covenant with the slaves accounts for the inclusion of this chapter in the section that runs from chapter 34 to chapter 39. During the siege the king and the nobles freed their slaves, in accordance with the provision of the Sinai covenant that slaves were to be freed every seventh year (Exod 19:4-6; Deut 15:12-15). However, later they went back on their word and reenslaved their compatriots (vv. 8-11), probably when an Egyptian army arrived and forced the Babylonian armies to lift the siege temporarily (see vv. 21-22 and 37:4-5). By breaking their covenant with the slaves, they also broke their covenant with God (vv. 12-20). As verse 17 puts it: "You did not obey [the key word in this section] me by proclaiming your neighbors and kinsmen free. I now proclaim you free . . . for the sword, famine, and pestilence." The chapter concludes as it began (see vv. 1-7) with a renewed threat of destruction (vv. 21-22).

B. The Rechabites Obey but Israel Does Not (35:1-19)

The editors included this chapter for the same reason they included the previous chapter: it testifies to Israel's disobedience. Jeremiah contrasts the obedience of the Rechabites to their founder, Jonathan ben Rechab, with the disobedience of the Israelites to their founder, God. Founded in the ninth century (see 2 Kgs 10:15-17), the Rechabites, a reactionary group of Israelites, disdained the settled and luxurious life of their kinsfolk who accepted the way of life of the Canaanites. They insisted on going back to the desert way of life of the time of Moses and the Sinai covenant, electing a nomadic life, living in tents, planting no crops or vineyards, and drinking no wine (a vice of the Canaanites).

35:1-5 "The word came to Jeremiah from the Lord in the days of Jehoiakim." This episode (v. 1) occurred at the end of the reign of King Jehoiakim (609–598 B.C.E.), when the Babylonian invasion of 598 B.C.E. had begun (see v. 11). Using the equivalent of a parable in action, Jeremiah tempts the Rechabites to drink wine in order to demonstrate by their refusal their staunch obedience to their founder (vv. 2-5). In justification of their refusal, the Rechabites dutifully recite the commands of their religious founder (vv. 6-11). The key line is verse 10: "we obediently do everything our father Jonadab commanded." In verses 12-17 Jeremiah draws the moral of his parable, contrasting the obedience of the Rechabites to their father with the disobedience of the Israelites to their Father and repeating four times the key word "obey" (see vv. 13-14, 16-17). The lesson concludes with Jeremiah's promise of a blessing on the Rechabites (vv. 18-19).

C. Contempt for the Word of the Lord (36:1-32)

Continuing with source material demonstrating Israel's disobedience, the editors include an episode from the fourth year (605 B.C.E.) of King Jehoiakim (609–598 B.C.E.). The Israelites not only reject God's covenant (chs. 34–35), but they reject as well the words of God's prophet (ch. 36) and the prophet himself (chs. 37–38).

36:1-4 "In the fourth year of Jehoiakim." Why Jeremiah decided to put his prophecies in writing is not clear. Probably it was because under King Jehoiakim he was forbidden under penalty of death to preach; possibly it was because Babylonian armies were in the area, and he feared the end might come sooner than he had expected. His written words read to the people might still bring them to their senses (v. 3). If he died his words would outlast him (as they did) and might eventually bring about Israel's repentance and return (as they did). Baruch the scribe writes from Jeremiah's dictation and the book is done (v. 4).

36:9-19 "In the ninth month." Jeremiah sends Baruch to read his book publicly in the temple area (vv. 5-10). Some of the nobles hear the reading and call upon Baruch to read the book before the king's assembled counselors (vv. 11-16a). The nobles decide that the king should hear about the book but fear for the author and his scribe, and urge them to go into hiding (vv. 16b-19). When the king hears the words of the book, he shows his contempt for the word of the Lord by cutting it into strips and feeding it into a fire (vv. 20-23) and by ordering the arrest of Baruch and Jeremiah (vv. 24-26). The king, however, cannot so easily destroy the word of God. Jeremiah dictates a second scroll (vv. 27-32) and adds to it a searing condemnation of the contemptuous king (vv. 29-31).

D. Contempt for the Lord's Prophet (37:1–38:28)

Chapters 37 and 38 have much in common and may even be two different versions of the same episodes. This would not have bothered the editors, who were intent on demonstrating that the people of Jerusalem not only scorned the commands of the covenant (chs. 34–35) and the written words of the prophet (ch. 36) but the prophet himself (chs. 37–38). Such contempt for the covenant, the prophetic word, and the prophet himself proved how richly deserved was the destruction of Jerusalem described in chapter 39.

37:1-10 "Coniah, son of Jehoiakim, was succeeded by King Zedekiah." The formal introduction (v. 1) suggests that this section belonged to an independent source before it was taken up by the editors and incorporated into the Book of Jeremiah. The words "Neither he, nor his ministers, nor the people of the land would listen to the words of the Lord spoken by Jeremiah the prophet" (v. 2) more than adequately express the theme of chapter 37 and its counterpart, chapter 38. Weak and irresolute and unwilling to abide by Jeremiah's advice, the king sends again and again to Jeremiah, seeking a good word from the Lord (v. 3). This particular appeal to Jeremiah is made during the break in the siege occasioned by the arrival of an Egyptian army in the spring or summer of 588 B.C.E. (vv. 4-5). Jeremiah's reply is consistent: Jerusalem will fall despite the help of the Egyptians (vv. 6-10).

37:11-21 "When the Chaldean army lifted the siege of Jerusalem." In the time between the raising and the resuming of the siege, Jeremiah attempts to go home to Anathoth but is arrested at the city gate as a deserter (vv. 11-14). He is tried and thrown into a dungeon (vv. 15-16). The king has him brought to the palace, hoping that Jeremiah will have good news for him. Jeremiah's reply gives no hope (vv. 17-18). In obvious pain and anguish, Jeremiah pleads with Zedekiah to be released from the dungeon located in the house of Jonathan the scribe (vv. 18-20). He is subsequently imprisoned in the quarters of the guard, presumably a more benign prison (v. 21).

38:1-13 "Shephatiah, son of Mattan." Presumably Jeremiah has greater freedom in the quarters of the guard (see 32:6-15). Whatever the reason, his advice to the people to flee the city is construed as treason. He is handed over to his enemies, thrown into an empty cistern, and left to die in the mud of starvation and thirst (vv. 1-6). Fortunately Ebed-melech, a friend, is able to persuade the king to have him rescued from the cistern (vv. 7-13). Meeting with Jeremiah, the king again asks for a good word from the Lord (vv. 14-16) and again is rebuffed (vv. 17-27). After the meeting Jeremiah remains in the quarters of the guard until the city falls (v. 28).

E. The Fall of Jerusalem (39:1-18)

The editors append here a succinct account of the fall of Jerusalem. Whether it is from Baruch's biography of Jeremiah or freely composed by the editors, it serves the editors' purpose of showing that despite all the opposition of kings, false prophets, nobles, and common people, the word of Jeremiah has been vindicated. God has watched over the divine word and brought it to fulfillment (see 1:11-19).

39:1-4 "In the tenth month of the ninth year of Zedekiah." The siege that began in January of 588 B.C.E. ends with the fall of the city in July of 587 B.C.E. (vv. 1-3). The king tries to escape by fleeing down the Jericho road toward the Jordan. He is captured in the desert near Jericho, taken to Nebuchadnezzar's headquarters at Riblah in Syria, and condemned (vv. 4-5). Before having his eyes gouged out, he is forced to witness the execution of his sons, thus ensuring that the last event he sees by the light of day is the death of his own children (vv. 6-7). In the days that follow, the Babylonians burn the palace, the temple, and many homes and then deport into slavery and exile the cream of the population (vv. 8-10). Jeremiah, probably because he has so often counseled submission to Babylon, is spared (vv. 11-14). The account ends with Jeremiah's promise to Ebed-melech, the eunuch who saved him from death in the miry cistern (see 38:7-13), that his life will be spared (vv. 15-18).

PART VI: DISOBEDIENCE TO THE END

Jer 40:1–45:5

The editors included this section in the book of Jeremiah for two reasons. First, it continues the theme of Judah's disobedience to God and to God's prophet, the theme that dominated chapters 34–39. Second, it proves conclusively that Jeremiah was right when he called the inhabitants of Jerusalem "the bad figs" and predicted (see 24:1-10) for them only sword, famine, and pestilence (see 29:16-19).

A. Jeremiah at Mizpah (40:1–42:22)

40:1-6 Jeremiah in prison at Ramah. This version of Jeremiah's release from prison differs from the version given in 39:8-14. Either the editors used two different sources, or, as seems more likely, Jeremiah was released twice. After his release in Jerusalem, he could easily have been swept up along with others and sent to Ramah, about five miles north of Jerusalem, to await deportation. There Nebuzaradan gave him the choice of accompanying him to Babylon or staying with Gedaliah in Mizpah (vv. 4-6).

40:7-12 Gedaliah at Mizpah. After the destruction of Jerusalem and the deportation of the most prominent citizens, Nebuchadnezzar appointed Gedaliah governor of the conquered territory. He belonged to an old noble family, and his father, Ahikam, had helped save Jeremiah from execution after he preached his famous temple sermon (see 26:24).

As governor Gedaliah sets himself up at Mizpah, a little town about eight miles north of Jerusalem. Jerusalem after its siege and fall is no doubt uninhabitable. To Mizpah come soldiers and their commanders who have successfully hidden in the hills during the last days as well as the poor of the land, whom the Babylonians did not deport (vv. 7-8). To these Gedaliah promises his intercession with the Babylonians (vv. 9-10). Later on those who hid out in Moab, Ammon, Edom, and other countries come to join the others at Mizpah. Gedaliah and his community offer a glimmer of hope in an otherwise dismal situation. But it is not to last.

40:13–41:3 The assassination of Gedaliah. Johanan, one of the army commanders who joined the group at Mizpah, warns Gedaliah that the Ammonite king Baalis has persuaded Ishmael to assassinate him (vv. 13-14). Ishmael is a royal prince. Why he would join in a plot against his own people is hard to explain. He makes no attempt to take Gedaliah's place, and he must know that killing both his own people and the Babylonians will make him an outlaw in his own land. Johanan's suggestion that he kill Ishmael and forestall the assassination attempt shows that he is well aware of the consequences that will follow upon the assassination of a governor appointed by Nebuchadnezzar (v. 15). Gedaliah's refusal to believe in Ishmael's treachery costs him his life (41:1-3).

41:4-10 More murders. Ishmael's slaughter of the eighty pilgrims to Jerusalem is as difficult to explain as his assassination of Gedaliah (vv. 4-7). His release of the ten men with the hidden store of food assures that the slaughter cannot be kept secret (v. 8); so does his imprisoning of the other people at Mizpah (v. 10). However one looks at Ishmael's actions, they remain an enigma.

41:11-18 Rescue of the prisoners. Fortunately for Ishmael's prisoners, Johanan and other military commanders arrive on the scene before Ishmael gets too far, and they liberate the prisoners (vv. 11-14). Ishmael escapes to Ammon (v. 15), but he leaves Johanan and the others with a major problem. Should they wait at Mizpah and hope that the Babylonians will not avenge the murder of Gedaliah and the Babylonian garrison, or should they escape to Egypt and thus evade Babylonian vengeance? They opt for Egypt, heading south and camping near Bethlehem (vv. 16-18). There they will consult with Jeremiah before going on to Egypt.

42:1-6 Consulting the prophet. Jeremiah's presence at Mizpah at the time of the assassination of Gedaliah (41:1-3), the massacre of the pilgrims from Shechem, Shiloh, and Samaria (41:4-9), and the subsequent rescue by Johanan and the others (41:11-18) is presumed but not proven by his presence among the group led by Johanan and the others. He could have joined them later. The story in chapter 42, like so many of the stories in chapters 34-44, centers on the theme of the Jerusalem inhabitants' continued, and by now habitual, disobedience to God and to God's prophet. Here the biographer emphasizes not only their disobedience but their hypocrisy as well. They approach Jeremiah (vv. 1-4) and swear to abide by his word from the Lord (vv. 5-6), when, as will become abundantly evident (see 43:1-7), they are already determined to flee into Egypt no matter what Jeremiah says.

42:7-9 "Ten days passed." If Johanan and the other commanders were already determined to flee into Egypt, Jeremiah's delay of ten days could only have aggravated them and perhaps even incensed them against him. Possible and even probable Babylonian reprisals for the assassination of Gedaliah and the Babylonian garrison made delay agonizing. What Jeremiah did during the ten days is not explained. He probably prayed and just waited. His waiting tells us something about the nature of prophesying. The prophet cannot turn on prophecy like tap water. It is not a human activity. Only when God speaks can the messenger speak God's word to others.

42:10-12 Jeremiah's word from the Lord: Remain and trust in God. Jeremiah's reply, in language that is by now almost stereotyped (compare 25:3-14; 26:2-6; 27:4-15; 29:16-19), calls upon Johanan and the others to do what they fear in their hearts to do: remain in the land and put their trust in God's promise to build them up (v. 10) and to save them from the reprisals of the Babylonians (vv. 11-12).

42:13-22 "But if you disobey." The rest of Jeremiah's reply to Johanan and his followers emphasizes the necessity of obedience (v. 13), anticipates their by now habitual disobedience and their decision to flee to Egypt (v. 14), and concludes with two long warnings on the dire consequences of their anticipated disobedience (vv. 15-22).

B. Jeremiah in Egypt (43:1–44:30)

43:1-7 As expected, they do not obey. Even the people's disobedience needs a hypocritical defense. Despite their solemn protest that they would abide by Jeremiah's word (see 42:1-6) and the implicit belief in the prophet that such a protestation implies, they now accuse him of lying and, equivalently, of being a false prophet (vv. 1-2). The attack on Baruch, Jeremiah's secretary (see 36:4, 16-19), is probably for the sake of the crowd, in order to take their attention off the commanders' refusal to accept Jeremiah's word (v. 3).

In verses 4-7 the narrator spells out the disobedience of the commanders. Against the word of the prophet, they lead the remainder of the group left in Judah into exile in Egypt. It is impossible to tell how large the group was. It contained the leaders, Jeremiah and Baruch, and some princesses from the royal family (v. 6), all important people, most of whom had much to fear from the Babylonians. The arrival at Tahpanhes (probably modern Tell Daphneh, a city at the eastern edge of the Nile Delta) closes the story and provides a transition to the account of Jeremiah's last days among the exiles in Egypt.

43:8-13 A symbolic act in Egypt. The narrator has almost nothing to say about the situation of the exiles in Egypt. He is intent instead on emphasizing and reemphasizing what has been his constant theme: the persistent and hard-hearted disobedience of the people right down to the end. He begins and ends this section (43:8–44:30) in the same way—with a prediction concerning the defeat of Egypt by Nebuchadnezzar (compare 43:8-13 and 44:29-30). In between he gives an account of Jeremiah's last words to the exiles in Egypt.

The symbolic act consists of building a throne for Nebuchadnezzar at the entrance to the royal building in Taphanhes, which was used as Pharaoh's residence when he visited the city (vv. 8-9). Since it is unlikely that a refugee from Judah would be allowed near the palace, it is quite likely that Jeremiah's act was done in pantomime. The throne, as the explanation that follows in verses 10-13 makes clear, symbolizes the future conquest of Egypt by Nebuchadnezzar. (For similar symbolic language, see 1:15; for the actual setting up of such a throne or judgment seat, see 39:3.) The point of Jeremiah's symbolic act is that flight to Egypt against the word of God will not save the people. The Babylonians will catch up with them in Egypt and there have their vengeance upon them. They cannot flee from God or escape God's word of condemnation upon them.

Nebuchadnezzar's devastation of Egypt is described in stereotyped language based upon the typical destructive acts of conquerors (v. 11). Burning temples and despoiling them of their idols were practices well-known (v. 12). Nabonidus, the last king of Babylon, was a fanatic about burning the temples of conquered peoples and carrying off to Babylon their idols and cultic accoutrements. The reference to the sacred pillars of Beth-shemesh (house of the sun) probably refers to Heliopolis, a city about five miles northeast of modern Cairo, famous for its temple to Ra, the Egyptian sun-god (v. 13). Nebuchadnezzar invaded Egypt in 567 B.C.E. (see Ezek 29:17-20). He did not fulfill Jeremiah's prophecy literally. The fact that he came at all, however, was sufficient to verify the substantial truth of Jeremiah's prediction.

44:1-14 Jeremiah's last words. This section summarizes and closes the preaching of Jeremiah. The setting is someplace in Egypt, probably Tahpanhes; the audience, the exiles living in different cities throughout Egypt (v. 1). The sermon resembles and repeats much that Jeremiah said earlier (see chs. 7 and 25). It begins with warning words from Jeremiah (vv. 2-14), continues with the self-justifying response of his stubborn audience (vv. 15-19), and closes with Jeremiah's final condemnation of those now residing in exile in Egypt.

Jeremiah begins by reminding his audience that Judah and Jerusalem were destroyed because of the sin of idolatry (vv. 2-6). That, however, was not enough—they have continued their idolatry in Egypt (vv. 7-8). They have forgotten the sins of their ancestors that brought about this destruction (vv. 9-10), and therefore they are condemned to suffer in Egypt the same condemnation and destruction as their ancestors suffered in Jerusalem (vv. 11-14). Jeremiah had said that the future of Israel lay with the exiles of 597 B.C.E. and not with those who remained in Jerusalem after that deportation. He had called the exiles of 597 B.C.E. "the good figs," and those who remained in Jerusalem "the bad figs" (see chs. 24 and 29). The exiles in Egypt are from those who remained in Jerusalem. They are "bad figs" to the end.

44:15-19 Stubborn self-justification. Deluded people find it easy to justify themselves. Nevertheless, the exiles' self-justification is both subtle and mischievous. Jeremiah blamed the destruction of Jerusalem and Judah on Judah's idolatrous infidelity to God and to the covenant. The exiles blame it on their "mistake" of not continuing their idolatrous practices! Their argument is based presumably on the history of the last one hundred years of the kingdom of Judah (687–587 B.C.E.). During the long reign of Manasseh (687–640 B.C.E.), they practiced idolatry and, despite the idolatry, lived in peace (vv. 16-17). When, however, they discontinued their idolatrous practices, beginning with the reign of the pious King Josiah (639–609 B.C.E.), disaster followed upon disaster (vv. 18-19), beginning with the conquest of Judah by the Egyptians in 609 B.C.E., continuing with Nebuchadnezzar's invasion of the country in 598 B.C.E., and concluding with the death and exile of the nation in 587 B.C.E. In short, they were better off as idolaters! The argument is plausible; the theology is outrageous.

44:20-23 Jeremiah's response. Jeremiah ignores the deluded logic of the argument and reiterates his contention that idolatry, and idolatry alone, explains the national disasters (vv. 20-23).

44:24-30 The last word. Jeremiah tells the stubborn and self-justified people: "You and your wives have stated your intentions, and kept them in fact" (v. 25). The future will tell who is deluded and who is truly justified, and the future Jeremiah predicts is destruction (vv. 26-28). They have trusted in the protection of Pharaoh, but Pharaoh will be handed over to his enemies. As events turned out, Pharaoh Hophra was supplanted and executed by Amasis, the general of his army, who succeeded him as Pharaoh. In addition, Nebuchadnezzar invaded Egypt. More than that we do not know. But it was enough to verify Jeremiah's word. When Judah became reestablished in Palestine after the defeat of Babylon by Cyrus the Great in 539 B.C.E., it was reestablished by exiles from Babylon. Little is known about the exiles in Egypt. The Elephantine letters testify to their continuance in Egypt in later years and to the half-pagan form of worship they practiced in their temple on the island of Elephantine in upper Egypt. Beyond that nothing more is known about them for certain.

With Jeremiah's last words in Egypt, we come to the end of what we know for certain about this extraordinary prophet. Jewish legend has it that Jeremiah was stoned to death by the exiles in Egypt. That is the legend, and no one would be surprised if it was more fact than legend.

C. A Message for Baruch (45:1-5)

When Baruch the scribe wrote down, at Jeremiah's dictation, the summary of Jeremiah's preaching from the year 626 to 604

B.C.E. (see 36:1-4, 27-32), he evidently shared Jeremiah's own dismay and depression when confronted by the dire future in store for his people, his nation, and himself (vv. 1-3). Jeremiah now has a personal word of comfort for his disheartened friend. God would indeed tear down what had been built and uproot what had been planted (v. 4), but Baruch himself will escape death (v. 5b). He is told not to seek great things for himself—as well he might, since he is a professional scribe and an educated man, and his brother (see 51:59) is an officer of importance in the entourage of King Zedekiah. Whatever great things Baruch might have sought for himself, he certainly had to give them up when he associated himself with the prophet so much opposed by the kings and the nobles of Judah.

It is a matter of speculation just how much Baruch had to do with the source materials of the Book of Jeremiah. The material in chapters 34–44, however, has all the signs of an eyewitness account. It is very specific about dates and names and frequently tells of conversations that could only have been known by one extremely close to Jeremiah. Of all the people mentioned in the book, no one seems to have been closer to the prophet than Baruch. It is not idle supposition, therefore, to credit to Baruch the major part of the material found in chapters 34–45.

Nor is it surprising, if Baruch wrote these chapters, that he should have reserved to the end, almost as his signature, this long-remembered word of comfort from his friend Jeremiah. Some authors insist that this chapter is chronologically out of order, belonging more properly at the end of chapter 36. They may well be correct, but only if Baruch intended his book to be a chronological account of the last years of Jeremiah. If he intended it, however, to constitute a theological testimony to Judah's rejection of both God and God's prophet, then the present thematic rather than chronological order would much more effectively have fulfilled his purpose. In that case he might well have reserved this early word of comfort from Jeremiah and used it, as we have suggested, as the equivalent of an author's signature on his work.

PART VII: COLLECTED ORACLES AGAINST THE NATIONS AND CONCLUSION

Jer 46:1–52:34

A. Oracles Against the Nations (46:1–51:64)

Like chapters 25–32 in the Book of Ezekiel and chapters 13–23 in the Book of Isaiah, chapters 46–51 form a distinct section in the Book of Jeremiah. In the Septuagint (Greek) translation of the book, they are placed after 25:13a and conclude with 25:15-38, and the nations are arranged in the order of their political importance. In the Hebrew they follow a geographical order moving from west to east. These variations indicate that the oracles formed an individual collection that was introduced into the book in different ways according to the tastes of the third-century editors of the prophetic books. With few exceptions, which may come from later oracles mistakenly attributed to Jeremiah, most of the oracles date to the decades immediately before and after the fall of Jerusalem in 587 B.C.E.

The basic theme of the oracles against the nations both here and in the other prophets is that God is the God of all the nations and that their destinies, like Israel's, lie in the hand and design of God. In reading the oracles, the reader should be aware of the fact that Semitic poetic expression revels in the symbolic, indulges in gross exaggerations, and frequently sees things only in black and white, with no regard for fine distinctions and careful qualifications. The universal extent of God's power, majesty, and sovereignty is what the poet strives to impress upon the readers. To this all the language, symbolism, and details are subservient. In short, the oracles against the nations are impressionistic rather than realistic.

46:1-12 Egypt defeated at Carchemish. This oracle is dated to 605 B.C.E., when the Babylonian army under Nebuchadnezzar defeated the Egyptian army under Pharaoh Neco at Carchemish on the Euphrates (vv. 1-2). It was a humiliating defeat for the Egyptians and should have taught the king of Judah and the neighboring kingdoms of Palestine to think twice about allying themselves with Egypt. Shortly after this battle Nabopolassar, the father of Nebuchadnezzar, died, and Nebuchadnezzar hastened back to Babylon to take over the reins of the neo-Babylonian empire. His defeat of Pharaoh Neco avenged the death of King Josiah (639–609 B.C.E.) at Megiddo just four years earlier.

46:13-28 Nebuchadnezzar's conquest of Egypt. After his coronation as king, Nebuchadnezzar led several campaigns against Egypt, this one in 568 B.C.E. The Pharaoh referred to in verse 17 is probably Pharaoh Hophra. He is here given the derogatory name "the noise that let its time go by" because he was noted for promising much to his allies and delivering little. Verses 25-28 represent Jeremiah's final words against Egypt.

47:1-7 Against the Philistines. The land of the Philistines lay on the coast bordering the Mediterranean Sea. Since the coast route was the easiest route from north to south and vice versa, the Philistines had the misfortune of being in the way when Egyptian armies moved north or northern armies moved south. In this case it appears that Babylonian armies were moving south against Egypt and overran the coastal cities and Philistia. The oracle cannot be precisely dated.

48:1-47 Against Moab. Moab was directly east of the Dead Sea. Lack of information about the history of Moab makes it difficult to date this oracle. Moab plotted against Babylon in 593 B.C.E. (see 27:3), escaped disaster in 587, but was eventually punished by Babylon, probably in 582, when Nebuchadnezzar marched for a third punitive raid into Palestine. Later, Arab invaders destroyed Moab completely, bringing to an end the ancient nation so long an enemy of Israel and so closely associated with the history of Israel from the beginning (see Num 22–24).

49:1-6 Against Ammon. Located east of the Jordan and just north of Moab, Ammon, like Moab, was a longtime enemy of Israel (see 2 Sam 10). And like Moab, Ammon was a member of Zedekiah's conspiracy against Babylon (see 27:3). It too escaped disaster in 587 B.C.E. but was overrun first by Nebuchadnezzar's armies in 582 and later by Arab invaders. Like Moab, it ceased to exist as a nation.

49:7-22 Against Edom. Edom lay south and east of the Dead Sea. It was remembered with bitterness by Judah not only for the long-lasting enmity between the two nations beginning at the time of the Exodus (see Num 20:14-21) but for its callous and treacherous treatment of Judah at the time of the Babylonian invasion of 587 B.C.E. It not only refused to help the Jews but collaborated with the Babylonians and cheered the downfall of Judah and Jerusalem (see Ezek 35:12-14; Obad; Ps 137:7). Later, when the Arab invaders arrived, the Edomites moved into southern Judah and occupied territory as far north as Hebron, just thirty miles south of Jerusalem. This occupied territory became known as Idumea. The oracle was probably occasioned by a Babylonian raid on Edom sometime after 587 B.C.E., but it echoes with the remembrance of earlier bitter encounters between the two longtime enemy nations.

49:23-27 Against Damascus. Northeast of the lake of Galilee, Damascus paid tribute to Nebuchadnezzar after the battle of Carchemish in 605 B.C.E. The oracle probably refers to a disaster following this date, but it cannot be dated with assurance.

49:28-33 Against the Arab tribes. In 599 B.C.E., on his way south to attack Judah, Nebuchadnezzar led a punitive raid against the Bedouin tribes in the desert area of eastern Syria. This brief oracle probably dates to that event.

49:34-39 Against Elam. Verse 34 dates this oracle to the year 597 B.C.E., the beginning of the reign of King Zedekiah of Judah. Elam lay east of Babylon in the southern part of modern Iran. Elam clashed with Babylon about this time, and Jeremiah may well have intended the oracle to quash any hopes the exiles of 597 B.C.E. had that Elam would save them from a long exile.

50:1–51:64 Against Babylon. Not surprisingly, the longest of Jeremiah's oracles against the nations is against Babylon. No other nation had such a lasting influence on the kingdom of Judah. Babylon invaded Judah in 605, 598, 588, and 582 B.C.E. As a result of the invasion of 588 B.C.E., the nation ceased to exist, its capital was destroyed, its temple burned to the ground, and its people led off into exile. Babylon was the burial ground of the Israelite nation, and only the resurrection of the nation after 539 B.C.E. kept Babylon from being its perpetual tomb. However much Judah deserved the treatment meted out to it by Babylon, it never ceased to consider Babylon its archenemy.

Since no internal evidence points to the rise of Cyrus, the conqueror of Babylon in 539 B.C.E., and since the description of the fall of

Babylon differs greatly from its actual fall (it fell peacefully from within as a result of treachery), the oracle cannot be dated after 539 B.C.E. How long before that date it was composed is difficult to tell. The oracle deals not only with the fall of Babylon but with the return of the people from exile as well (vv. 4-8 and *passim*). Since the oracle against Babylon terminates the collection of Jeremiah's oracles against the nations, it is not improbable that the editors added to it much that had been said against Babylon by Jeremiah himself as well as oracles against Babylon spoken by others during the long years of the Babylonian captivity.

B. Conclusion of the Book (52:1-34)

This chapter is an appendix. It draws upon 2 Kgs 24:18–25:30, the last chapters of the Deuteronomist's history of Israel's covenant relationship with God, a history that runs from Deuteronomy through Joshua, Judges, 1-2 Samuel, and 1-2 Kings. The history was written after 562 B.C.E., the last date mentioned in 2 Kings. Since this chapter repeats much that was already said in chapter 39, one must ask why the editors added it. The best explanation would be that it was added to reinforce both the negative and the positive messages of Jeremiah. By once more describing the fall of Jerusalem (52:1-30), the editors remind the reader how unerringly Jeremiah's predictions of destruction came to pass. By including the good treatment accorded Jehoiachin, the last king of Judah, by the king of Babylon (52:31-34), the editors remind the reader that Jeremiah predicted not only destruction and exile but return from exile and the rebuilding of the nation. Jehoiachin's release from prison in Babylon was a clear sign of hope for the future.

52:1-16 The fall of Jerusalem. Zedekiah, the third son of Josiah and the uncle of Jehoiachin, who was exiled as hostage royalty in Babylon in 597 B.C.E., is judged by the author of 2 Kings to have done "evil in the eyes of the Lord," as had so many kings of Judah, thus bringing about the end of the kingdom (vv. 1-3). The siege began in January of 588 B.C.E. and ended in July of 587 (vv. 4-6). The escape, capture, and blinding of Zedekiah (vv. 7-11) repeat what was said in 39:5-7. A month after the fall of the city, Nebuzaradan, Nebuchadnezzar's general, arrived to overlook the destruction of the city and to supervise the deportation of the citizens (vv. 12-16).

52:17-23 The looting of the temple. The Babylonians first looted the temple in 597 B.C.E. (see 27:16 and 2 Kgs 24:13). It had been refurbished in the intervening ten years. The looted items are for the most part those bronze, silver, and gold items described in Exod 25–30 and 1 Kgs 6–7. Following the first looting of the temple in 597 B.C.E., Jeremiah warned the people that what was left would be carried off later. After the looting the temple was burned to the ground.

52:24-30 Deportation into exile. Deportation of conquered peoples as the most effective means to prevent further rebellion had long been practiced by the Assyrians (see 2 Kgs 17). Babylon continued the practice, and it would have a long history in the centuries that followed. It did not mean deportation of all the people but only those influential persons, leaders, bureaucrats, and the intellectual elite whose presence might sustain or rekindle the fires of rebellion. Some were executed (v. 27), either as examples or for their known part in the rebellion.

The numbers given in verses 28-30 cover three groups of exiles: those of 597, 587, and 582 B.C.E., respectively. The figure of 3,023 mentioned here (v. 28) differs from the 10,800 mentioned in 2 Kgs 24:14, 16. A possible explanation is that the figure mentioned here represents only the males, while the figure mentioned in 2 Kgs 24 represents the total of men, women, and children. The 745 men of Judah mentioned in verse 30 as deported in the twenty-third year (582 B.C.E.) of King Nebuchadnezzar may be those deported after a punitive raid on Judah following the assassination of Gedaliah and the slaughter of the Babylonian garrison by Ishmael (see 40:13–41:3).

52:31-34 The release of King Jehoiachin from prison. The young king who succeeded his father, Jehoiakim, in 598 B.C.E. and reigned only three months before being deported to Babylon as hostage royalty was released from prison in 561 B.C.E. by Evil-merodach, the successor of Nebuchadnezzar (v. 31). Since many people both in Babylon and back in devastated Judah considered Jehoiachin rather than Zedekiah their legitimate king, his release from prison was a sign of hope for the future.

Receipts for supplies given to the king and his entourage have been found in the Babylonian chronicles. Significantly they refer to him as "Yaukin, *king* of Judah."

The favors accorded Jehoiachin (vv. 32-34) may or may not have amounted to special treatment beyond that given to other hostage royalty. For the editors of the Book of Jeremiah, however, this was surely interpreted as special treatment. It was meant to remind the reader that Jeremiah had predicted an end to the Exile and the return of the exiles to their land (see chs. 25; 29; 32; 33). Thus the concluding chapter records the fulfillment of Jeremiah's predictions of disaster as well as a presage of the fulfillment of his predictions of return and rebuilding.

C. The Influence of Jeremiah

There is no simple measure of the influence of Jeremiah. In time his words, like a two-edged sword, penetrated the marrow of Israel, stirred the heart of the nation in exile, and reverberated through sacred writ even into the books of the New Testament.

Like Moses before and Jesus after him, Jeremiah lived at a turning point in his people's history and bridged the gap between the old and the new. In his inaugural vision he was set "over nations and over kingdoms, to root up and to tear down, to destroy and to demolish, to build and to plant" (1:10). He fulfilled his mission to the letter. He saw Assyria disappear from the stage of history and Babylon take over center stage. He preached the funeral oration for Judah and the Sinai covenant and at the same time foretold the institution of a new covenant. He declared the Davidic kings rejected but heralded the coming of a new David.

Of Jeremiah it can be said: no man did more for his nation and was treated worse. The mystery, however, is not in the prophet's suffering but in the resurrection of the nation that died and was buried in Babylon in fulfillment of his prophecies.

Israel's resurrection from national death in Babylon is one of the wondrous works of God. But God works through human beings, and of all those who worked for Israel's resurrection, none did more than Jeremiah. When he arrived on the scene in 626 B.C.E., there was hardly an Israelite alive who would admit that the city of Jerusalem could be taken and the temple destroyed. In the popular mind, God was bound to Jerusalem and to the Davidic kings, and Jerusalem was inviolable because God had chosen it. The defeat of Sennacherib in the time of Isaiah only confirmed the average Israelite in this false theology. More than anything else, it explains the senseless revolts against Babylon and the childish expectation, even in the last months of the siege, that God would intervene and destroy Nebuchadnezzar, as happened with Sennacherib.

Jeremiah's thankless task was the destruction of this false theology. He reminded the people in his temple address that God was not bound to the temple but could and would destroy it as Shiloh had been destroyed in times past. He insisted repeatedly that Jerusalem would be destroyed, that the kings, though they might be as the signet ring on God's finger, could nevertheless be taken off by God and cast away.

Jeremiah tried to make the Jews understand that the fall of Jerusalem would not be the work of Babylon but the work of God using Babylon as a juggernaut. He was derided, mocked, and scorned. His enemies, the false prophets, carried the day.

But when the Day of Yahweh came for Jerusalem, the nation, and the kings, there were those who remembered. *Then* the parables of the loincloth and the potter and the broken flask were seen in a new light. *Then* the temple address was seen to make sense. The false prophets were proved false, the childish optimism groundless, the popular theology a trap.

If that had been all that the people learned from Jeremiah's preaching, it would have been enough to vindicate the prophet, but at the terrible price of national despair. There was more, however. In exile the people remembered that Jeremiah had spoken of the "good figs" that would one day return to Judah and to whom the Lord had said: "Only after seventy years have elapsed for Babylon will I visit you and fulfill for you my promise to bring you back to this place" (25:10). They remembered his sermons of consolation (chs. 30–31), his buying of property in the last days of the siege, and his promise from God: "Houses and fields and vineyards shall again be bought in this land" (32:15). They remembered most of all his promise of a new covenant for Israel

(31:31-34; 32:40) and his promise of a new David in days to come (33:14-26; 23:5-6).

The downfall of Jerusalem, the temple, and the kings came as Jeremiah had predicted. But when it came, some at least were prepared to understand it as it should have been understood—in the light of the covenant between God and the people of God, according to which the nation's future depended on its loyalty or disloyalty to the stipulations agreed to on Sinai. For these at least, the tragedy was explicable, and explicable in terms of the faith by which Israel lived. Among these, too, faith continued to live, through the dreadful days of siege and destruction and through the long years of exile. That faith was the link that joined the Israel of old to the Israel that arose from the grave of the Exile to become a nation again in 539 B.C.E. And it was Jeremiah who forged the link.

BARUCH

Peter F. Ellis

INTRODUCTION

In the years that followed the catastrophic destruction of Jerusalem in 587 B.C.E., some Jews were deported to Babylonia, others fled into Egypt, still others remained in the devastated homeland. In 539 B.C.E. Cyrus the Persian defeated the Babylonians and established Persian rule over what had been the empire of Babylon. As one of his first acts, Cyrus decreed the return of conquered peoples to their homelands. Thus it came about after 539 B.C.E. that the Exiles were free to return to their homeland.

Many returned, but many more remained in the land of the conquerors. Those who remained formed what came to be called the Diaspora—the Jews of the dispersion or permanent exile who never returned to their homeland but remained in colonies situated for the most part in Mesopotamia and Egypt. While many of them no doubt defected from their ancient faith, many more remained faithful. In the centuries that followed, the Diaspora Jews flourished both spiritually and temporally.

Fortunately for Israel's religious future, many of the exiles came from the influential and intellectual circles of the people—priests, scribes, and prophets. From these the exiles received instruction and encouragement. With the temple and its sacrifices so far away, the cult of the exiles came to be localized in the synagogues and centered upon the inspired writings. Thus in the course of time, they came to be the people of the book. Faithful to Jerusalem and the rebuilt temple of Zerubbabel, completed between 520 and 515 B.C.E., the Diaspora Jews gathered in their synagogues, read and studied the law and the prophets, and in due time produced their own inspired books. Among these were the books of Lamentations, Tobit, Esther, Judith, Wisdom, and Baruch.

Diaspora writings, as might be expected, dealt with Diaspora situations and challenges. This is eminently true of the Book of Baruch. It deals in its successive parts with the exiles' relations with Jerusalem, with hope for the future, and with resistance to the idolatrous worship of the surrounding pagans.

Since the material in the book reflects events late in the Exile and shows some dependence on the writings of Deutero-Isaiah (550–540 B.C.E.), it seems reasonable to believe that editors are responsible for the attribution of the Book to Baruch. Baruch had been Jeremiah's secretary (see Jer 36). He had perhaps accompanied the prophet into exile. In addition, he was well acquainted with Jeremiah's letter to the exiles (see Jer 29) and with Jeremiah's message of hope (see Jer 30–33).

It was customary in ancient times to attribute works by unknown authors to more famous authors of previous centuries. Thus many psalms written by nameless authors were attributed to David, and several wisdom books were attributed to Solomon (for example, Proverbs and the Book of Wisdom). It must have seemed fitting to the third-century editors of the prophetic books to attribute to Baruch, Jeremiah's famous secretary, this collection of writings dealing with the situation and challenges of the exiles.

COMMENTARY

A. Introduction (1:1-14)

1:1-4 Baruch's scroll. This section begins in the style typical of Baruch in the Book of Jeremiah (see the opening verses of Jer 32; 36; 38; 39)—with specific names and dates. It makes a bow toward Jer 36 by attributing this second book to Baruch (vv. 1-2). The "fifth year" (v. 2) is perhaps meant to be the fifth year of the exile (582 B.C.E.). Baruch is pictured reading his scroll before the exiled king, his courtiers, and the exiles in Babylon, somewhat as he had read Jeremiah's scroll in Jer 36:8-19 (vv. 3-4).

1:5-9 Concern for temple worship. The weeping, fasting, and praying, in addition to the taking up of a collection for the temple, provide a program for the readers that will keep their hearts centered on the temple and on their traditional Yahwistic faith (vv. 5-7). Nothing is known about a restoration of the cultic vessels taken from the temple after the Babylonian invasion of 597 B.C.E. (v. 8). That new cultic vessels were made to substitute for the looted vessels can be taken for granted (v. 9). It is mentioned no doubt as a reminder to the reader that supporting temple worship was the duty of every true Israelite. At the time the Book of Baruch was put together, the new temple of Zerubbabel had long been in existence. It was completed in 516 B.C.E. (see Ezra 1–6).

1:10-14 A message for the high priest. The message testifies to the exiles' concern for divine worship (v. 10) and concern for good treatment by their Babylonian overlords (vv. 11-12). The juxtaposition of Nebuchadnezzar, the second king of the Babylonian empire, and Belshazzar, the last king, indicates a late date for the book. Belshazzar was coregent with his father, King Nabonidus, when the armies of Cyrus the Great conquered Babylon in 539 B.C.E. No son of Nebuchadnezzar by the name of Belshazzar is known to history. The last two requests—a request for prayers for the contrite exiles and a request that Baruch's book be read publicly on feast days—emphasize what is central to the purpose of the editors: true contrition and a firm purpose of amendment (vv. 13-14). In one way or another, it will be the purpose of every section of the little book of Baruch to arouse and sustain in its readers these sentiments so critical for the spiritual health and the national survival of Israel.

B. A Penitential Prayer (1:15–3:8)

Penitential prayers such as the one preserved here are typical of exilic literature (see Neh 9:6-37; Dan 9:4-19). What the exiles refused to learn from Jeremiah, they learned from the hardships of the Exile. Prayers such as this were a feature of the synagogue services that originated in exilic times.

1:15-22 "Justice is with the Lord, our God." The prayer begins with an acknowledgment of national guilt that embraces the sins of the author's contemporaries (v. 15) and their ancestors (vv. 16-17). It then traces Israel's guilt back through history to the time of Moses and the Exodus (vv. 18-22). Mention of the curse that the Lord enjoined upon Moses (v. 20) reflects the curses of Deut 28 and prepares the way for the just fulfillment of these curses that the author acknowledges in 2:1-10.

2:1-10 Just retribution. All the evils are summed up in the two most horrible of all: the cannibalism of children in the last days of the siege of Jerusalem (v. 3) and the degradation of the nation as a whole following the fall of Judah and Jerusalem to the Babylonians in 587 B.C.E. (vv. 4-5). That all this has been just retribution for the sins of the nation is honestly acknowledged in verses 6-10.

2:11-15 An appeal for mercy. What has preceded has been preamble to the prayer that properly begins here. Firmly believing that God is just, in the sense that God is ever merciful and faithful to earlier promises to save the covenanted people, the author of the prayer, who has already confessed his people's guilt (1:15-22) and their justly deserved punishment (2:1-10), now enters his plea for mercy (vv. 11-13). He appeals to God's honor to show the whole earth, by merciful treatment of the exiles, that God is Lord of Israel and Lord of all (vv. 14-15).

2:16-18 The nether world. Up to the second century before Christ, Israel had no clear knowledge of the future life. In its prayers, therefore, it believed that praise could be given to God only by the living (vv. 17-18).

Clear revelation concerning the future life begins with Dan 12 and 2 Macc 7.

2:19-35 Hopes based on God's unfailing mercy. This section of the prayer begins with an admission that the punishment Israel suffered was deserved because the people refused to listen to the warnings of the prophets (vv. 19-20), and especially the warnings of Jeremiah (vv. 21-26). Verse 23 combines two typical Jeremian warnings (see Jer 7:34 and 27:12). Verse 25 mentions the stereotyped Jeremian trilogy of sword, famine, and pestilence (see Jer 32:24, 36; 34:17). Verses 27-35 recall the unfailing mercy of God (v. 27), who despite Israel's failure to heed the warnings of Moses (vv. 28-29) will deal mercifully with it in the time of its captivity (vv. 30-32), bring it back to the land promised to its ancestors (vv. 33-34), and establish with it the new covenant (v. 35) promised by Jeremiah (Jer 31:31-34).

3:1-8 A concluding plea for mercy. These verses sum up the heart of the whole long prayer (2:11-3:8), emphasizing again God's mercy (vv. 1-4), God's honor (vv. 5-6), and the gift of fear of the Lord, which enables the people to call upon God in praise, even in the land of their captivity (vv. 7-8). The prayer is long and repetitious but filled with a true spirit of penitence and hope. It represents Israel at its best.

C. A Poem in Praise of Wisdom (3:9–4:4)

Modern readers can understand this poem easily if they recall that for the Jews wisdom is equivalent to fear of the Lord (that is, obedience to the will of God) and that the will of God is found in the revelation of God's will contained in the Scriptures, preeminently in the books of the Pentateuch (the Torah). In brief, only God is the ultimate source of true wisdom, and God has chosen to reveal this in the Torah. As a consequence praise of wisdom is indirectly praise of God. Doing God's will, moreover, is the way of the wise; not doing it is the way of the fool. A prayer for wisdom is a prayer for the grace to do God's will. The reader should note that wisdom is personified in the poem from 3:15 to 4:4, just as it is personified in Prov 8:1-36 and Sir 24:1-31.

3:9 "Hear, O Israel, the commandments of life." This beautiful prayer begins with an exhortation to Israel to hear, that is, to obey God's commandments. It ends in 3:37–4:4 with the declaration that God has given wisdom to Israel (v. 37) and that that wisdom is found in the book of the precepts of God, that is, the Torah-Pentateuch (3:38–4:4). As a result, the whole poem is an appeal to Israel to do God's will and thus to be both wise and blessed (4:4).

3:10-14 The consequences of not hearing. Israel is asked how it came about that it is in exile (vv. 10-11). The answer: The people have forsaken wisdom (vv. 12-13 and see Jer 2:13). The admonition "Learn where prudence [that is, wisdom] is" (v. 14) leads into the question of where wisdom can be found (3:15-36), a question that will be answered in 3:37–4:4 with the declaration that wisdom is found in "the book of the precepts of God" (4:1).

3:15-23 Wisdom is not found among the Gentiles. Since by definition only Israel possesses God's revelation, it is clear that true wisdom cannot be found among the Gentiles. Here the author means the wisdom that comes from God, since wisdom and wisdom literature were well known and cultivated among Judah's neighbors, the Egyptians, the Mesopotamians, and many of the smaller nations of the Middle East. The rulers of old who heaped up wealth have not found wisdom (vv. 17-19), nor have the later generations: the Canaanites (vv. 20-22), the Midianites, the Temanites, the children of Hagar (Arabic tribes descended from Abraham and Hagar), and their pagan wisdom writers (v. 23). Human beings on their own are not able to find true wisdom!

3:24-36 Wisdom is found only with God. In all of God's creation (vv. 24-25), no human being has discovered wisdom or found the way to her (vv. 26-31). Only God, who created and established the earth and to whom no other is to be compared, knows wisdom (vv. 32-35).

3:37–4:4 Wisdom is the law. Only God knows the way to wisdom, and God has given her to Israel (v. 37) in the book of the precepts of the law, the Pentateuch. Let Israel cling to wisdom, "walk by her light" (that is, live according to God's law), and Israel will live and be blessed (vv. 1-4). Israel's "glory," which God gives to Israel and not to pagans, is the law (v. 3).

D. A Poetic Plea for Return from Exile (4:5–5:9)

In this beautiful poetic discourse, very much indebted to the poetry of Deutero-Isaiah (Isa 40–55), the speaker personifies Jerusalem as the mother of the nation, explaining to the nearby nations and to her exiled children the reason for her exile and encouraging the exiles to look for an early return home. The discourse has four parts: introduction (4:5-8); Jerusalem's explanation to the nations (4:9-20); Jerusalem's encouraging discourse to her exiled children (4:21-29); the poet's address to Jerusalem to rejoice in the return of her exiled children (4:30–5:9).

4:5-9 "Fear not, my people." The speaker begins by reminding Israel that it went into exile because of its infidelity. Verse 4 introduces Jerusalem, who will be the personified speaker in 4:9-29, as the grief-stricken mother of Israel and the exiles.

4:9-20 Jerusalem's address to her neighbors. Jerusalem mourns for the captivity of her sons and daughters (vv. 9-11), whose sins have brought upon them punishment (vv. 12-14) by a nation from afar (Babylon), which has exiled them and left their mother, Jerusalem, widowed and solitary (vv. 15-16). The widow symbolism in verses 12 and 17 flows from the Hosean symbolism of the marriage between God and the people Israel (see Hos 1–3). Jerusalem asks herself what she can do for her children. She acknowledges that only God can deliver them from the Exile (vv. 17-19). She herself will pray (v. 20) and call upon her children to pray with her. Verse 20, with the mention of crying out to God, provides a transition to verses 21-29.

4:21-29 Jerusalem trusts in God's mercy. Jerusalem calls upon her children to pray (v. 21) and speaks about her trust in God's mercy (v. 22) and her confident expectation that God will bring her children back to her (vv. 23-24). In verses 25-29 Jerusalem concludes her address. She counsels patience and promises God's vengeance on her persecutors (vv. 25-26). Her last words are a plea for repentance (vv. 27-29)—a repentance that has been a goal of the discourse from the beginning.

4:30–5:9 The poet's address to Jerusalem. Now that mother Jerusalem has finished her discourse (4:9-29), the speaker addresses her in soaring language and bids her prepare for the end of her mourning and the joyful return of her children. She should not fear (v. 30), because God will destroy Babylon, "the city that rejoiced at [her] collapse" (vv. 31-35). She should look to the east and see her sons returning home (vv. 36-37). Babylon was due east of Jerusalem, and the poet envisions God leading the exiles back across the desert, as in Isa 1:4-11. Jerusalem, which had taken off her robe of peace in 4:20 for a robe of mourning, is now told to remove the mourning robe and put on the splendor of God—the manifestation of God's saving action in returning her children from exile (5:1-4). In a final apostrophe (5:5-9), Jerusalem is called to stand upon the heights and watch her exiled children come marching home on the road laid out in the desert (see Isa 1:3-5) and led by none other than God (see Isa 1:9-11).

E. The Letter of Jeremiah (6:1-72)

Chapter 29 of the Book of Jeremiah contains a letter written by the prophet to the exiles carried off to Babylon following Nebuchadnezzar's invasion of Judah and Jerusalem in 597 B.C.E. Sometime in the centuries that followed, an unknown author wrote this long satire against the idol worship of the pagans and attributed it to the great prophet of the last days of Judah. Editors included it at the end of the collection of writings now found in the Book of Baruch. Although it exists only in a Greek translation, it was originally composed in Hebrew. Critics believe it cannot be the work of Jeremiah for several reasons, the strongest being that: (a) the editors of the Book of Jeremiah did not include it in the book; (b) it shows a strong dependence on the satires against idol worship in Isa 40–55; (c) it speaks in verses 27-31 of practices of the Mosaic law that never were of any concern to Jeremiah.

All things considered, the letter constitutes a long sermon attacking the foolishness of idol worship and exhorting the exiles not to be taken in by it. The modern reader may consider such an attack superfluous. Few today believe in idol worship. In the ancient world, however, it was otherwise. Few believed in one God. The overwhelming majority believed in many gods and worshiped them in many forms. They not only worshiped them but they built magnificent temples for them, supported a rich and powerful priesthood to serve them, and celebrated a multitude of feast days with processions, sacrifices, the singing of psalms, and elaborate spectacles.

For the Jewish exiles from a tiny Middle Eastern nation with a small unpretentious temple and a modest priesthood and cult, the power, the wealth, and the magnificence of the pagans' idol worship, especially in such a great metropolis as Babylon, must at times have seemed overwhelming. True believers, of course, would not have been impressed. Many others, however, may well have felt that truth was determined by power, magnificence, and numbers. Deutero-Isaiah as early as 550 B.C.E. feared the attraction of idol worship for lukewarm exiles and lambasted idols and idol worshipers in a series of satirical comparisons between the nature and power of Israel's God and the nature and impotence of the pagan gods (see Isa 40:18-20; 41:21-24; 44:6-20; 46:1-7). The idol-worship religion of the pagans was no mean adversary to the revealed religion of Israel!

The letter of Jeremiah proves that the idol worship attacked by Deutero-Isaiah in the first fifty years of the Exile continued, in the centuries that followed, to have a powerful attraction for the exiles who remained in pagan countries. The letter attacks idol worship with scorn, invective, mockery, and incredulity. Its message is summed up in the recurring refrain: "Thus it is known they are not gods; do not fear them" (see vv. 14, 22, 28, 39, 44, 50, 56, 64, 68, 71).

The letter reads easily, is patent in its satirical intent and requires only a few brief comments. **6:3 you will see borne upon men's shoulders gods of silver . . . :** This is a reference to the great processions that were part of the pagan cult. **6:6 my angel:** Symbolic of God's protective presence, the angel here recalls the angel of Exod 23:20-21. **6:10 the harlots:** Sacred prostitution, that is, intercourse with priestesses in the temple precincts, was a prominent feature of pagan worship and was particularly offensive to Israel because of its prevalence in the Baal fertility cult of the Canaanites (see Deut 23:17-18). **6:12 the house:** This means the pagan temple. **6:19 their hearts are eaten away:** The idols were made of wood covered with gold or silver. The wood frequently rotted away or was eaten by insects. **6:25 displaying their shame:** It could be that the idols were naked figures, or it could be that they displayed their weakness by having to be carried. **6:27-31 Unclean practices.** Jewish law considered menstruating women unclean (see Lev 12:2-3). It was forbidden for priests to bare their heads, shave their beards, or rend their garments (see Lev 21:5-10). **6:42 girt with cords:** This is another reference to sacred prostitution (see v. 10). An unbroken cord signified that the woman had not fulfilled her obligation of sacred prostitution in the temple. **6:72 the better for the just man:** This final verse, following so powerful a denunciation of idolatry, is surely a provocative understatement!

CHRONOLOGICAL CHART*
for
AMOS, HOSEA, MICAH, NAHUM, ZEPHANIAH, HABAKKUK

JUDAH	*ISRAEL*	*ASSYRIA*
Uzziah 783–42	Jeroboam II 786–46	
	AMOS	
	HOSEA	
	Zechariah 746–45	Tiglath-pileser III 745–27
	Shallum 745	
Jotham 742–35	Menshem 745–37	
ISAIAH	Pekahiah 737–36	
Ahaz 735–15	Pekah 736–32	
MICAH	Hoshea 732–24	Shalmaneser V 826–22
	Fall of Samaria 722/1	
		Sargon II 721–05
Hezekiah 715–686		
Manasseh 686–42	*Babylon*	Sennacherib 705–681
		Esarhaddon 680–69
		Ashurbanipal 668–27
Amon 642–40		
Josiah 640–09		
JEREMIAH	Nabopolassar 626–05	Sin-shar-ishkun 629–12
ZEPHANIAH		
NAHUM		
		Fall of Nineveh 612
Jehoahaz 609		
Jehoiakim 609–598		
HABAKKUK	Nebuchadnezzar 605–582	
Jehoiachin 598/7		
EZEKIEL		
Zedekiah 597–87		
Fall of Jerusalem 587		
Exile		

*Dates are dependent upon John Bright, *A History of Israel.* 3rd ed. Westminster Press, 1981.

AMOS

Carroll Stuhlmueller, C.P.

INTRODUCTION

The fierce champion of justice

The prophet Amos spoke plainly to the Israelites, even fiercely so. The Hebrew text, moreover, is well preserved. If some sentences seem vague or confusing, the fault lies at our doorsteps, due to our ignorance of ancient times and the ancient way of life. While Amos' words ring with the crystal tones of a bell, the person of Amos is lost in the echo. A few facts are obvious enough. He was from the village of Tekoa (1:1), some ten miles south of Jerusalem in the tribal portion of Judah. Again according to the opening verse, he prophesied during the long, prosperous reign of King Jeroboam II (786–746 B.C.E.), "two years before the earthquake," therefore around 760. We find his shaggy figure in the capital city of Samaria as well as at the venerable sanctuary of Bethel. At the instigation of the high priest, he was expelled from the northern kingdom of Israel and was sent packing back to Judah (7:12). The name Amos means "burden," and the name Tekoa probably means "to sound the [ram's] horn." His message carried a burden of destruction; it was sounded loud across the northern kingdom and was remembered long afterward at Jerusalem (1:2).

Other information about Amos has to be pieced together from details scattered throughout the book. Some of these fragments are distinct, others remain blurred. Twice Amos is described as a shepherd, yet each time the common Hebrew word for "shepherd" is not employed. Instead, in 1:1 the word is the same one used of a Moabite king in 2 Kgs 3:4; in 7:14 the word refers more to the breeding of cattle (Gen 33:13). This fact, along with Amos' acquaintance with the vocabulary and style of the wisdom literature, associates him with nobility. The prophet, moreover, shows himself an absolute master of the Hebrew language; his writing is characterized by structural unity and momentum toward a climax (1:3–2:16); the blending of irony and seriousness (4:1-5); rhetorical questions (at least thirty—2:11; 3:3-6); haunting sounds that speak a message even without words (2:16); the up-and-down, staircase style of literary chiasm (5:4-6).

Yet, any number of other details point to a person economically poor, with neither clout nor prestige. According to 7:14, Amos was forced to take a second job as a "dresser of sycamore trees" (moonlighting to make ends meet?). He worked in dangerous association with lions, bears, and snakes (3:4, 8, 12; 5:17); he knew the groan of heavily laden wagons (2:13) and was desperate about locust plagues (7:1-2). His caricature of women in 4:1-3 smacks of a rough herdsman; he spits disdain at wealthy men lying on ivory couches in their massage parlors (6:3-6). Therefore, we place Amos in the ranks of the poor. He was born brilliant and was desert-trained to perceive color, sound, grandeur, and wonder in contemplative silence. He quickly absorbed the patterns of temple worship, legal proceedings at the city gate, and the sophisticated ways of the sages.

Historical setting

Amos learned much from the marketplaces of Israel's larger cities. As he sat on the ground with other shepherds, displaying his wool, cheese, and leather goods, he swapped news from Tyre, Damascus, Moab, and Gaza. All the while he angrily detected the flagrant injustices of society: extensive international commerce for the benefit of the wealthy; deceitful business practices not only to cheat the defenseless poor but also to seize their land; the amassing of natural resources for sensual pleasure. Some documentation found amid the ruins of Samaria tells of large shipments of oil and wine for the royal court; these were paid from taxes squeezed from the poor. The country was basking in the military victories of King Jeroboam II, who had successfully completed the military plans of his father, King Joash (2 Kgs 13:24-25; 14:25, 28). Israel's long-time enemy, Damascus, had been leveled to the ground by the Assyrians around 800 B.C.E., leaving Israel free to extend its territory and privileges. Such material blessings, the people thought, proved God's good pleasure with them.

Amos' sermons and oracles were radically destructive, that is, cutting to the *roots* of Israel's life. All God's ancient promises to the Israelites and the divine presence among them would end. Whatever survived would be "like a brand plucked from the fire" (4:11), like the shank bone of a sheep that "the shepherd snatches from the mouth of the lion" (3:12). Yet Amos was addressing that part of the twelve tribes most directly linked with Moses' exodus out of Egypt and Joshua's settlement of the land. The promises of the covenant resided among these people of the northern kingdom.

Typical of prophecy, Amos accepted the reality of historical changes, such as the forthcoming onslaught of the Assyrian army against Israel or the earlier inauguration of the Davidic dynasty at Jerusalem. This latter fact is witnessed to in the conclusion of the book (9:11-15), composed by a disciple of Amos if not by Amos himself. In fact, Amos had politics and international affairs at his finger tips (1:3–2:16). God was mysteriously present, at work within this real world. For this reason Amos ends up far ahead of his Old Testament times, for he glimpsed the role of the nations in God's plans for salvation, especially in the one-liner of the appendix (9:7).

A person of tradition

Amos was radical in another way. His roots (the Latin word is *radix*) were firmly set in Israel's traditional institutions and memories. He spoke positively of prophets and nazirites (2:11-12). He did not condemn liturgy, only the selfish spirit of the devotees (4:5). He based his reflections upon the Exodus (2:11; 3:1; 9:7), Israel's hopes for the future (5:18), and its special election (3:1-2; 5:15), even though he reversed the conclusion against what the people expected from these ancient promises. Wisdom traditions show up rather abundantly: didactical questions; numerical sequence (three plus one); themes of good and evil. His morality reached back into ancient norms of the early clans or tribes.

Most of all, in Amos' eyes Yahweh was the God of the poor, as was the case when Yahweh delivered slaves out of Egypt and gave dispossessed people their own Promised Land.

Literary form

Amos is the first prophet with a book to his name. Earlier prophets, like Elijah and Elisha, Gad and Nathan, strongly influenced Israelite policy but left no books. There is no satisfactory explanation for this radical change, only some guesses. Did written scrolls become popular because of a notable advance in literacy among the people? Or did Amos' announcement of destruction point up the necessity of writing down whatever was to be preserved? Or did the sweeping internationalization of Israel, with its extensive correspondence, stir the prophets to communicate with written documents?

The book is arranged with all the neatness of a good household. After a historical and religious introduction (1:1-2), four major presentations of Amos are to be found: oracles against the nations (1:3–2:16); three judgment speeches, which begin with "Hear this word" (3:1–5:6); three collections of Woe Sayings (5:7-17; 5:18-27; 6:1-14); and four visions (7:1-9; 8:1-3). It is possible that the book ended here at one time, especially when we note that the story of Amos' final day of preaching at Bethel was inserted into the vision narratives (7:10-17), stitched in by the mention of Jeroboam in 7:9 at the end of the third vision and in 7:10 at the beginning of the biographical account of Amos' expulsion from Bethel. Later two longer portions were added—a judgment speech (8:4-14) and a vision story (9:1-4), each somewhat different in style from others in the book. Still later an appendix of four "one-liners," with each verse being a separate entity (9:10-14), was tacked on. Liturgical fragments in the style of a hymn were woven into the text (4:13; 5:8-9; 9:5-6). The final addition came during or after the Babylonian Exile, announcing the revival of the Davidic dynasty at Jerusalem (7:11-15). Typical of biblical prophecy, Amos' book thus ends with an upbeat note.

COMMENTARY

INTRODUCTION

Amos 1:1-2

1:1 Historical introduction. The editor situates Amos during the prosperous, heady days of King Uzziah of the southern kingdom of Judah (783–742 B.C.E.) and King Jeroboam II of the northern kingdom of Israel (786–746 B.C.E.). The historical orientation is from the south, where Amos' preaching was edited and preserved; Uzziah's name is given first. **The words of Amos . . . received in vision:** The words contain a divine message, perceptible only in mysterious moments when one is absorbed in God. **shepherd from Tekoa:** See p. 487. **two years before the earthquake:** This earthquake did severe damage to Israelite cities like Hazor in northeast Galilee; it is dated 760 B.C.E. and was still spoken of several centuries later (see Zech 14:5). Dating Amos' preaching by the earthquake may have this fearful insinuation: Soon after Amos the earth and the foundation of Israel will collapse. The rumbling theme of earthquakes spreads fear throughout the book (4:11; 6:11; 7:7-8; 8:8; 9:1).

1:2 Religious introduction. The orientation is again from Jerusalem or Zion, confessing that God's mysterious providence directed the destruction of the north, even of beautiful Mount Carmel, which juts out on the northern coastline. This "antiphon" is repeated again in Jer 25:30 against foreign nations (after the announcement of Israel's and Judah's deportation) and once more in Joel 4:16 against the foreign nations but also as a word of protection and refuge for Israel. Evidently editors in biblical times felt free to adapt ancient inspired texts to new circumstances. The setting of the preacher added a necessary ingredient to the interpretation of God's word.

ORACLES AGAINST THE NATIONS

Amos 1:3–2:16

This section is composed in a style reminiscent of sanctuary oracles and of the wisdom school. Oracles originated in the sanctuary when a person with serious difficulties came either for a blessing and solution or for protection against an enemy. Oracles designate a communication from God to one or more persons gathered in prayer, frequently at a sanctuary (Gen 26:24; 28:13; Ps 12:6). Prophets adopted this style to indicate their conviction that their words expressed a conscience formed from an immediate experience of God. The schema here of three + one consists of the sacred numbers three, four, and seven, each in some way denoting completion—no more crimes will be tolerated. The arrangement also reflects a practice within the wisdom literature of the Bible (Prov 30:15-16, 18-19; Sir 26:5-6). For Amos, the numerical sequence infers God's patience in putting up with three crimes and God's equal determination to put an end to the crimes; yet even in this last instance God is present in the act of punishment. The Hebrew word for "crimes" occurs only once in the Pentateuch (Exod 22:8), where it recalls pre-Mosaic clan traditions. Amos, therefore, may be reaching into basic human nature to judge right and wrong.

Many of Israel's neighbors, frequently hostile to Israel, are named: Aram or Damascus, to the northeast; Philistia, on the seacoast to the southwest; Tyre, on the northwest coast; Edom, south of the Dead Sea; Ammon, east of the Jordan River; and Moab, east of the Dead Sea. The prophet would have received a roar of applause after each oracle. The compact and well-coordinated style of each oracle locks the people and their enthusiasm still more firmly into the discourse. When Amos comes to the oracle against Israel (2:6-16), the audience cannot escape—they must listen in stunned silence!

Each foreign city is condemned for "crimes against humanity," such as acting as middle-persons in selling captive soldiers into slavery, waging war with excessive cruelty, and profaning the bones of the dead. While each oracle is strikingly vivid, that against Judah (2:4-5) appears dull and colorless, making us suspect its genuineness. It is probably a later addition from someone at Jerusalem not nearly as eloquent as Amos. Israel, too, is condemned for crimes against humanity rather than for violating cultic or refined religious norms.

2:6 sell [into slavery] the just man for silver . . . for a pair of sandals: This refers to the brutal enforcement of laws to pay one's debts—only a small amount for the wealthy but the total possessions of the poor—or to the seizure of ancestral lands for flimsy reasons.

Land was normally marked off by the length of one's sandals (see Deut 25:5-10, which deals with the marriage of a relative's widow in order to preserve the name of the husband and to protect the latter's property for the son bearing his name).

2:7 Son and father go to the same prostitute: This alludes either to the degradation of domestic servants in a wealthy household (the Hebrew does not use the word "prostitute") or else to an insidious, lustful father who interrupts a legitimate romance of the son.

2:8 Upon garments taken in pledge they recline: According to Exod 22:25-26 and Deut 24:11-13, the long, flowing outer cloak taken in pledge of the future payment of a debt was to be restored at each sundown, lest the person have insufficient protection against the cold evening air. In making sure that the poor fulfill their obligations, the wealthy priests break the law themselves and commit further sexual sins under the influence of alcohol.

2:16 shall flee naked on that day, says the Lord: The sound of this phrase in Hebrew is haunting, evoking the desperate, silent agony of people led off captive totally naked, to be sold for whatever purpose along the way until the remnant are resettled in a foreign land. The person's shame becomes the instrument of pleasure for the gloating conquerors. There was no need to mention the dreaded name of Assyria.

JUDGMENT-ADDRESSES AGAINST ISRAEL

Amos 3:1–5:6

This section is addressed exclusively to Israel, frequently in the form of judgment speeches. This style is modeled upon that used in Israel's law courts, presided over by elders at the city gates (Deut 16:18-20; 21:19; 25:7; Amos 5:10). A typical example is 4:1-3, which consists of: summoning of the defendant (v. 1a); listing the crimes of the defendant, who is referred to in the third person (v. 1b); words of the judge as a messenger of Yahweh (v. 2a); verdict and punishment (vv. 2b-3). See also 8:4-8. Amos, as mentioned already, remains in masterful control of style. Other literary forms are found in this section. All are linked together by the introductory formula "Hear this word" (3:1; 4:1; 5:1).

3:1-2 This oracle is rooted in Israel's election as the Lord's chosen people. **You alone have I favored:** The Hebrew verb means literally "to know," not in the sense to know about, but to experience and therefore to know with sensitivity, concern, and intimate love (Gen 4:1; Jer 1:5; Ps 1:6). At this time people would then conclude from Israel's election that God will bring a blessing or a happy conclusion. Amos reverses what is expected by declaring: "I will punish you." Neither blood lineage with those who came out of Egypt nor good theology ensures Israel's well-being. To be truly Israel, the people must continue the liberation of the poor, as God once liberated them from bondage in Egypt. Yet, Israelite priests and nobles are using their privileged positions to enslave other Israelites. Religion has become a veneer for supporting the upper class. By comparing Israel with other nations, here as in the oracles against the nations, Amos arrives at common basic human norms for judgment.

3:3-8 The sequence here mounts to a crescendo of strength: first it is animals against animals (v. 4), then humans against animals (v. 5), and finally humans against humans. Not only is there a purpose in each event, but there is also the insinuation that humans turn up no different from animals in their violent state. Verse 7 is probably a later reflective addition. In verse 8 Amos feels the animal urge to roar against human injustice.

3:9-10 The key word here is "castles," those of foreigners and those of Israel, citadels of extortion and robbery where Israel is no different from any other nation. How can Israel strut around as a chosen people?

3:12 This independent oracle combines a moment of shepherd existence with theology and sarcasm! **A pair of legs or the tip of an ear of his sheep:** These words indicate all that is to be left of Israel, hardly enough to reconstruct a sheep or the people. The few Israelites who escape with their life and are marched into exile, nakedly the butt of jokes and selfish desires (2:16), are pictured with mock pathos as clutching a piece of their ivory couch, a remembrance of their lost opulence (see 3:15; 6:4). It is as though people today, in being driven away from their homes, would treasure most their transistor radios! Implied here is Amos' intuition of the "remnant," which we will discuss at 5:15.

4:1-3 As at the beginning of chapter 3, a new subdivision is introduced with the formula "Hear this word." With brutal, even crude language, Amos likens the opulent ladies of the capital city of Samaria to the large, well-fed cows of Bashan, prized for their quality milk and meat (Deut 32:14). They grazed in the open area between Israel and Damascus, presently called the Golan Heights, then as now bitterly fought over. In this area the cattle roamed freely, munched the luscious, dew-laden grass, and became fiercely temperamental. Amos foresees a long siege, the eventual, angry capture of the capital, then the mopping up process. Amos portrays the bloated corpses of these presently pampered women pitched onto a dung heap outside one of the city gates. **the last of you:** The Hebrew may refer either to the very last corpse or more likely to the posterior part of the anatomy whereby barbed poles inhumanly lift the body from the streets.

4:4-5 Similar to 1 Sam 15:22-23; Ps 50:14; Hos 6:6; and Matt 9:13, these verses are not condemning liturgical worship as such but the unworthy motives of the worshipers. **for so you love to do:** "You get a kick out of it, don't you, folks!" Strange for the Bible but typical of Amos, these sarcastic words are placed within the literary form of a solemn liturgical oracle from God!

4:6-13 A rhetorical momentum sweeps us forward by one type of natural catastrophe after another, with the continuous refrain "you returned not to me," and at the end the fearful climax, "prepare to meet your God." Amos' striking images communicate the taste and smell of disaster. Drought is spoken of as "teeth clean of food" and pestilence as the stench of dead horses!

The transition to a historical recollection in verse 11 seems like an editorial addition; part of the verse is identical with Hos 11:8; Isa 13:14b; and Jer 50:40, a "floater" that can end up almost anywhere! Verse 13 is cast in the form of a hymn with participles that bring the excitement of creation into the present moment: "Your God, O Israel, forming the mountains, creating the wind . . . turning dawn into darkness, striding upon the heights of the earth." This verse belongs to a longer hymn, whose fragments are found as well in 5:8-9 and 9:5-6, similar to others in Jer 12:13, 16; Isa 42:5. These were added to the canonical texts as congregational refrains when the Scripture was proclaimed in synagogue worship. Theologically this section confesses the directive hand of God in nature and history, fulfilling a divine purpose for Israel.

5:1-6 This is the final sermon of Amos in the second major division of his prophecy (3:1–5:6). The editor combines a funeral dirge over dead Israel with an exhortation to "seek the Lord" (v. 6) while there is still time. In the dirge the people are sorrowfully addressed as "virgin Israel," stricken before appreciating the joys and fulfilling the hopes of life (Gen 15:2-3; Judg 11:38). As used by Jeremiah, this title indicates new hope. The sinful, barren people, described as the "adulterous spouse," miraculously return to the condition of the Lord's virgin spouse as at the moment of marriage (Jer 31:4, 21-22; see 1 Sam 1; Isa 54:1).

5:4-6 An excellent example of the literary form of chiasm (the word derives from the Greek letter "chi," written as an "x"). The sequence of words in the downward stroke (a-b-c) is followed in reverse order in the upward stroke (c-b-a), as here:

a—Seek me that you may live	a—seek the Lord that you may live
b—not Bethel	b—Bethel become nought
c—not Gilgal	c—Gilgal shall go into exile
not Beer-sheba	

PROPHETIC WOES

Amos 5:7–6:14

A new major section in the Book of Amos begins here, a series of three speeches whose opening word is "Woe!" (5:7; 5:18; 6:1). (We note that the Hebrew word for "Woe" is present in 5:7 only by amending the text.) In his use of this literary form, Amos is at a major turning point of its evolution; he may even be responsible for this change. Earlier passages consider "Woe!" as a way of mourning the dead at funerals (1 Kgs 13:30). Gradually it became a curse with scorn and bitterness at what ought to be dead or is already morally dead (Isa 33:1; Jer 48:1). Later "Woe!" becomes a taunt over someone's foolishness (Isa 45:9).

5:7-17 This passage condemns blatant social injustices. Small landowners are being taxed into bankruptcy and forced to become serfs on their former family homesteads or even slaves somewhere else (see 2:6). The extension of international trade and the craze for foreign luxuries by the powerful clique of noble people have bled the land of its natural resources, just as foolish military ventures will leave the country heavily in debt to pay indemnities to the conquerors. This enforced payment falls heaviest upon the poor. Even archaeology has disclosed a marked tendency by which palaces became larger as peasant dwellings became smaller! Amos does not condemn liturgy as such but the spirit with which it is performed and its split from the people's daily morality. So, too, Amos is not against politics and commerce but calls down "Woe!" upon "those who turn judgment to [bitter-tasting] wormwood" (compare Deut 29:17; Lam 3:15, 19), upon those who exact levies of grain, build sumptuous houses, and accept bribes.

5:15 remnant of Joseph: For Amos, this phrase may mean simply the few who survive, but it became a technical theological term, prominent in the Book of Isaiah (Isa 7:3; 10:19-22). Even for Amos, "remnant," is not to be interpreted externally, in this case numerically. Rather, "remnant" may designate that fragile, delicate but essential aspect of what it means to be an Israelite and a true follower of Moses, the faithful adherence to godly ideals, the courageous search for the mysterious way of the Lord, the strength to give up everything for "the pearl of great price" (Matt 13:46).

5:18-27 The second "Woe!" discourse repeats a very traditional religious idea, God's promises for the future at the heart of the Mosaic exodus out of Egypt, and then reverses what the people normally conclude from it (see 3:1-2). While the normal answer ought to be light and joy, Amos declares that the "day of the Lord" will mean "darkness and not light" (5:18). **day of the Lord:** This phrase already had a long history in extrabiblical documentation. In the Akkadian literature of southern Mesopotamia (modern Iraq) over a millennium before Amos, the "day of the god" indicated a special feast honoring the god with elaborate liturgical ceremonies. For Israel in Amos' time, "Yahweh's day" was characterized as a glorious celebration of the Lord's presence when ancient redemptive acts were renewed liturgically (see 5:21-25).

Amos, however, announced the opposite. After his time, "day of the Lord" came to mean a day of the Lord's wrath against Israel (Zeph 1:15), or later, during the Exile, against Israel's enemies (Isa 13:6, 9; Jer 46:10, 21); still later there was a return to the ancient idea, a day of salvation for Israel (Joel 3:4), and eventually a day of final judgment (Mal 3:19-23; Matt 24:1). Amos gave this phrase its permanent place. He relied upon a most ancient tradition, creatively challenged its misrepresentation in his own day, and thereby attempted to restore the original thrust of Israel, the liberation of oppressed people and the condemnation of oppressors.

5:25-27 These verses are plagued with textual and interpretive difficulties. Against verse

25, the Bible makes it clear that Israel offered sacrifice to Yahweh at every period up to Amos' time: Abraham (Gen 12:7-8; 15:7-21); Moses (Exod 18:12); Joshua (Josh 5:10-12); Samuel (Judg 13:16). The identity of Sakkuth and Kaiwan is uncertain.

6:1-14 This is the third and last "Woe!" statement. To manifest that the Lord can and will send devastation, Amos ticks off in verse 2 the names of once prosperous cities in north Syria, already severely weakened by Assyria and soon to be completely destroyed. He has only contempt for the soft, effete men and women of Samaria (see 4:1-3), who at times talk grandly of patriotism and religion yet remain blind to the misery of the poor, all the while luxuriating in their "massage parlors."

Verses 9-11 recall a plague in which only a single person survives in an infested house, and even that one leaves us with the haunting sound of "Silence!" (see 8:3). Verse 12 is a typical paradox from the wisdom school: Israel's situation is as unnatural as plowing the sea with oxen. In verses 13-14 Amos deflates the false hopes that surged with Jeroboam II's conquests to the east of the Jordan River and even those further north into Syria. Amos' bleak outlook is deliberately modified, almost reversed, with new but futile hopes in 2 Kgs 14:24-27.

THE VISIONS

Amos 7:1–8:3

This new major section in the Book of Amos consists of four visions, into which a biographical account of Amos' expulsion from the northern kingdom has been inserted. The visions follow a careful pattern, easily observable despite the editorial additions. In the initial two visions Amos speaks first, asking for divine patience, and the Lord relents. In the third and fourth visions the Lord speaks first and thereby settles the matter. The refrain rings out: "I will forgive them no longer" (7:8; 8:1). The Hebrew language is marked with literary devices such as question and answer, onomatopoeia, and paronomasia, so that a slight change of consonants or vowels in the Hebrew produces a new, dramatic meaning ("ripe grapes" or *qais* in Hebrew becomes "the end" or *qes* in 8:1-2).

These visions, therefore, were intended for public communication. Each centers on an object clearly visible to others: locust, fire, plummet, and ripe fruit. The vision also includes a secret or symbolic meaning, communicated individually to Amos. Because a vision or a mystic communication from God frequently occurs in the commissioning of a prophet (1 Sam 3; Isa 6; Jer 1; Ezek 1), it is possible that the vision became a normal literary style to indicate God's choice of a prophet. Thereafter the prophet will speak with the personal strength of having stood in the council of the Lord (Jer 23:18-22). The momentum within the four visions leads up to the certitude that the balloon will burst and prosperous Israel will disintegrate as much from internal decay as from external military invasion.

7:1-3 The first harvesting of a crop belongs to the royal treasury (money did not yet exist). Even the poor will be swept into the consuming mouth of destruction. In this experience of mystical prayer and of compassion for the poor, Amos is commissioned as a prophet.

7:10-17 A biographical account is stitched into the account of the visions by the repetition of the name of the king, Jeroboam, in verses 9 and 10. Such biographical accounts do occur elsewhere in prophecy (Hos 1; Isa 7; Jer 26–29 and 34–45); they were composed to provide religious insights into the prophet's mission or else, as here (and with Jeremiah), to justify its divine origin and eventual fulfillment.

7:10 The sanctuary of Bethel, sixteen miles north of Jerusalem, was one of the most ancient, existing before the patriarchs (Gen 12:8; 13:3); it was closely associated with Jacob's dream of a ladder between heaven and earth (Gen 28:10-22). Jeroboam I, founder of the northern kingdom at the death of Solomon, restored Bethel as a prominent place of assembly and worship (1 Kgs 12:26-33). The priesthood of Bethel derived independently of the Mosaic Levitical priesthood, just as the Zadokites, once pagan priests when the Jebusites controlled Jerusalem, were installed by David to officiate with Levites of Mosaic background (1 Kgs 12:21). Amaziah's worry over a revolt was not unfounded; the very dynasty of Jeroboam II was inaugurated through a bloody coup d'état at the instigation of the prophet Elisha (1 Kgs 9–10).

7:12-13 to the land of Judah! There earn your bread by prophesying: Amaziah is insinuating that Amos prophesies for a living (see 1 Sam 9:7-9; 2 Kgs 5:5, 15, 22-27; Mic 3:5). Amos will retort sarcastically that he is no prophet but works for a living as a shepherd and dresser of sycamores! In verse 13 the narrator, by a play on words, points up the obsequious surrendering of temple and priesthood to royal wishes: "never again prophesy in Beth-el" (literally, "house of God"); "for it is the king's sanctuary and a royal temple" (in Hebrew, *beth mamlakah*).

7:14 I am no prophet, nor a member of a prophetic guild: While some translations favor the past tense or a question ("I was no prophet" or "Was I not a prophet?") in accord with the past tense in verse 15, the present tense (which we prefer) harmonizes with verses 12-13 and also with a similar passage in Zech 13:5. Northern prophecy had sufficiently discredited itself in Amos' eyes that he repudiated any association with it. As in 3:1-2 and 4:4-5, Amos is not totally rejecting the institution but its degenerate form. In fact, in verse 12 he seems to accept the title "visionary" or "seer," a title used in the south, Amos' homeland (2 Sam 24:11; Isa 30:9-10). **shepherd and dresser of sycamore trees:** See p. 487.

7:15 The Lord took me from following the flock: The phrase is drawn almost literally from 2 Sam 7:8 and the story of David's call to kingship, another sign of Amos' roots in tradition, and the word "took" in Hebrew frequently signifies a radical, abrupt transfer into another way of life (Gen 5:24; 2 Kgs 2:3; Ps 49:16). **Go, prophesy:** While Amos rejects the categorization of prophet, or at least Amaziah's concept of prophet, he obeys the Lord's command to reinvigorate and transform the ancient institution of prophecy by doing it.

7:16-17 Even in his final words Amos remains bitterly sarcastic as he enumerates with crescendo the punishments to come upon the high priest: his wife a harlot and his children dead; then, what's worse, loss of family property; and, worst of all for a priest so finicky over ritual, death and burial "in an unclean land," without the proper blessing upon a grave in the Holy Land.

The visions and the biographical account complement and support each other. One provides the origin and the other the end of Amos' career as a prophet; each concludes with an unequivocal announcement of Israel's end in exile and of Amos' vindication as God's spokesman. While Israel collapses into exile and oblivion, Amos' words become a permanent book, remembered today as God's word.

ADDENDA

Amos 8:4–9:10

A prophetic judgment speech and a vision, each somewhat different in style from the earlier speeches in 3:1–5:6 and the visions in 7:1-9 and 8:1-3, are added to the book. Similar themes recur: dishonest commerce by which the poor become poorer, ever more dependent and even reduced to slavery (see 5:7-12); darkness as on the day of the Lord in 5:18; destruction and exile. Verse 9 of chapter 8 may be alluding to an eclipse of the sun on June 15, 763; there was another total eclipse in 784. Verses 11-12 make it clear that Israel does not decide on its own terms when and how to return to the Lord; they may "wander from sea to sea . . . and not find" the word of the Lord. Unless the journey is undertaken at God's prompting, it will lead only further into desert waste and famine.

9:1-6 While the earlier visions simply announced the end, this new vision elaborates on the end of Israel with imagery and style that match the catastrophic dimensions of Israel's collapse. Amos' words sweep through the universe, reach into the nether world, summon the sea and its monsters to undo the work of creation. The text not only alludes to the opening antiphon and its reference to beautiful Mount Carmel (1:2 and 9:3), but it also concludes with a continuation of the fragments of an ancient hymn (4:13; 5:8-9) that perceives God as once again subduing the angry sea and putting boundaries to its waves, extending the heavens and regulating the good order of nature: "I, the Lord by name" (9:6).

APPENDIX OF ONE-LINERS

Amos 9:7-10

These four verses, each seemingly an independent unit, share features of Amos' style (rhetorical questions, catchwords, disputation). Even the ideas are not as divergent from those found elsewhere in Amos' prophecy as some scholars infer: Amos saw hope for a remnant in 5:15 as here in 9:8b, 9. The mini-creed about the Exodus in 2:10 and 3:1 is repeated verbatim in 9:7. Amos is not thoroughly at home with the traditions of the Exodus; after all, he was a southerner from Tekoa, while the Exodus and other Mosaic traditions were more deeply rooted in the northern kingdom. Therefore, these four one-liners circulated separately among his disciples, who may have modified them; after the main part of the book was edited, they were added here as an appendix. Other biblical appendices are found in 2 Sam 21–24; Isa 36–39; Jer 52. Short appendices are added to chapters like Isa 1:27-31.

Verse 7 may be one of the most radical, universalist statements in the entire Hebrew Scriptures, similar to Isa 19:24-25; 66:21. Amos compares Israel's Exodus to the migrations of the other nations: the Arameans swept out of the Syrian-Arabian desert in the twelfth century B.C.E., the Philistines possibly from Crete in the eleventh century B.C.E. Amos' statement implies that Israel is no different from any other people in the external pattern of its origin and history. It was Israel's faith, formed through God's inspired word and through the leadership of faithful servants like Moses and Joshua, that transformed a secular migration into a sacred exodus. Amos is implying that the history of other peoples can also be spirited by faith in Yahweh and can become the external form and symbol for believing in Yahweh and worshiping the Lord.

RESTORATION

Amos 9:11-15

This positive, even glorious conclusion to the negative, destructive oracles of Amos not only conforms to the style of editing prophetical books with an upbeat momentum, but it also presents an important norm for our interpretation of prophetic literature.

The section is divided into two oracles, each with its introductory and concluding formulas: verses 11-12 about the revival of the Davidic empire; verses 13-15 about the abundant re-creation of Israel's cities and farmland. Stylistic and logical links bind this final set of oracles to the Book of Amos: verse 13 picks up phrases from 8:13; verse 14 repeats, only to reverse, 5:11. The Exile, so clearly announced in 2:16; 4:2-3; 5:27, will be turned around in Israel's restoration (v. 14).

The composition of this section belongs after Israel's return to its homeland from Babylonian exile. Comparisons with Joel 4:18-21 tilt toward a common date, around 500 B.C.E.

Surprisingly, this affirming, enthusiastic view of the future never permeated the rest of the book; the editors respected the dire threats and stern sarcasm of Amos, even though they saw the future differently. The future generations of Amos' disciples realized that: (1) sin and punishment could come again, so that Amos' warnings remained valid, even though the distant future will eventually turn out bright; (2) while reading of condemnation and desolation, we ought not to forget God's mercy and fidelity; (3) we need to decide whether threat or promise is more appropriate pastorally and spiritually, for "there is an appointed time for everything, . . . to kill and to heal, . . . to rend and to sew" (Eccl 3:1-8). Jerusalem and the Davidic family were the line of continuity, the inheritors of the Mosaic promises, originally received by the ancestors of the northern kingdom. The future was to be considered more a creation of God, generously given in view of just and compassionate relationships among God's people, than a human achievement at Israel's beck and call (see 8:11-12).

The apostle James, as cited in Acts 15:15-17, draws upon Amos 9:11 when approving Paul's apostolate to the Gentiles. David's empire will extend to the world, not by the sword, but by confessing Jesus as Lord and Savior. At this moment the prescriptions of the Mosaic law will not be a prerequisite for baptism. Even the Mosaic covenant is fulfilled beyond its own dreams, certainly beyond the human works of a law-abiding Jew. Amos' words receive an interpretation still more radical than that of the first disciples and editors. Yet, in quoting from Amos, James declares how necessary and valid the Hebrew Scriptures remain for appreciating faith in the new Son of David.

HOSEA

Carroll Stuhlmueller, C.P.

INTRODUCTION

Hosea was a contemporary of Amos. Both prophesied in the northern kingdom of Israel during the reign of Jeroboam II (2 Kgs 14:23-29), yet Hosea's ministry was not abruptly cut short as was that of Amos' (Amos 7:12-13). Rather, according to the scholarly position followed in this commentary, Hosea's words reflect the chaotic, mad, and finally destructive years after Jeroboam II's death. There are other differences. Hosea was a citizen of the north, stressed far more than Amos the intimate love of God for Israel, continuously inserted his own personal feelings, developed and applied such northern traditions as Exodus and wilderness experiences from Mosaic times, and moved within agricultural rather than desert images.

While Amos goes down in biblical annals as the prophet of divine justice—justice in the strict modern sense of punishment equal to the seriousness of the crime—Hosea is known as the prophet of divine love, love ever willing to suffer in order to win back one's beloved. Yet, no justice is fiercer than tender love that has been betrayed and attacked, and so Hosea ends up far more certain and definitive about the destruction of Israel: "I will attack them like a bear robbed of its young, and tear their hearts from their breasts" (13:8). "Where are your plagues, O death! . . . My eyes are closed to compassion" (13:14).

The chaotic times of Hosea

This agonizing reversal from forgiveness to angry rejection parallels the history of Israel from the prosperous years of Jeroboam II's reign to the chaotic years that followed. Hosea began announcing "the word of the Lord . . . in the days of Jeroboam, son of Joash, king of Israel" (1:1; 2 Kgs 14:23-29). As described in the introduction to the prophecy of Amos (p. 488), these were heady years of success and plenty, hard years of indifference toward the poor, years bloated with sensuality and laziness. Amos' sarcastic, even crude sketch of women fat as Bashan cows (Amos 4:1-3) and of men pampered by the sweet scent and tingling touch of massage parlors (Amos 6:4-6) says it all! While Amos viewed the sickening scene with stern eyes from a distance, Hosea experienced its poignant, cruel thrust into the heart of his marriage. Chapters 1–3 and 4:1–5:7 carry the jagged scars of Hosea's heart against the frolic and degradation of Jeroboam II's years as king.

The death of Jeroboam II in 746 B.C.E. also struck a mournful toll over the prosperous land of Israel. Flowers cut in full bloom quickly lose their lovely petals, so that only the dark stem and malodorous water remain. The succinct record in 2 Kgs 15:8-31 captures the style of newscasting on television—one stroke after another without time to breathe: "Zechariah, son of Jeroboam, . . . was king . . . for six months. . . . Shallum, son of Jabesh, . . . attacked and killed him. . . . Shallum reigned one month, [till] Menahem came up, attacked and killed Shallum. . . . Menahem punished the city of Tappuah, even to ripping open all the pregnant women. . . .

During his reign Pul (Tiglath-pileser III) invaded the land and Menahem gave him a thousand talents of silver." The two-year reign of Menahem's son, Pekahiah, was ended by the insurrection of his adjutant, Pekah. During Pekah's reign a new revolt brought the Assyrian army again; the northern provinces were enveloped in darkness (see Isa 8:23) and lost forever to Israel. Hoshea conspired against Pekah, killed him, and reigned in his stead with Assyria's blessing, only to revolt against Assyria and so bring on the end, absolutely and unconditionally. The ten northern tribes totally disappear to history. Each word of this account in 2 Kings lunges, gasps, and collapses, only to start the dreadful process once more. The details can be outlined this way:

Jeroboam II (786–746)
free and prosperous
Zechariah (746–745)
compromising and ineffective (assassinated)
Shallum (745)
anti-Assyria (assassinated)
Menahem (745–737)
pro-Assyria, paying tribute
Pekahiah (737–736)
pro-Assyria (assassinated)
Pekah (736–732)
anti-Assyria (assassinated)
Hoshea (732–724)
pro-Assyria; then anti-Assyria (captured and executed)

Clearly, the anti-Assyrian policy, to align with Egypt and other smaller states in military revolt against the feared monster to the east, was suicidal. Prophetically, in the evaluation of 2 Kings or in the preaching of Amos and Hosea, destruction was already determined by infidelity and injustice that had corroded the moral fiber. Military adventures were condemned, not simply for their foolish miscalculation, but principally for the smokescreen they provided for condoning social injustices.

The period from the death of Jeroboam II until Hoshea's seizure of the throne is reflected in many ways within 5:8–8:14 in Hosea's prophecy. (*Note:* the prophet Hosea is not to be confused with King Hoshea.) The violent rise and quick demise of dynasties tumble through the lines of 7:5-7: "They are all heated like ovens, and consume their rulers" (see 8:4). The abrupt change of policies—first an alliance with Egypt, then one with Assyria—provokes Hosea's disdain: "Ephraim is like a dove, silly and senseless; they call upon Egypt, they go to Assyria" (7:11; see also 5:13; 8:9). When Assyria pounces upon the prey and rends it mercilessly, God wants no mistake about it: "I carry it away and no one can save it from me" (5:14; also 7:8-9).

Chapters 9–12 reflect the false quiet and deceptive hope for peace and relief shortly before and immediately after the succession of Shalmaneser V to the throne of Assyria in 726 B.C.E. Hosea warns: "Rejoice not, O Israel . . . . For you have been unfaithful to your God, loving a harlot's hire" (9:1). When King Hoshea revolts, Assyria's short fuse of patience ignites and its anger explodes against Israel. After King Hoshea has been captured ("Where now is your king, O Israel?"—13:10) and the fury is roaring south against the capital city of Samaria, Hosea's reaction is recorded in 13:1–14:1. He summons the plagues and the deadly sting of destruction and declares on God's part: "My eyes are closed to compassion" (13:14).

The prophet must have escaped before the capital city was burned to the ground, leaving the charred remains of ivory inlaids for later archeologists to discover, and from Jerusalem he composed the finale (14:2-9). Hope triumphs as he writes: "Return, O Israel, to the Lord, your God, . . . [who] will heal . . . defection, [and] will love . . . freely" (14:2, 5). Most probably it was later disciples who added the editorial allusions to Judah found throughout the book (1:1, 7; 4:14; 5:5; etc.). In 12:3 the name "Israel" was replaced with "Judah," but the word "Israel" is now restored by many translators, as in the New American Bible. Finally, the admonition to "understand these things" in the book of Hosea was inserted at the very end (14:10), probably by someone of the school of wisdom that produced such books as Proverbs.

The passionate character of Hosea

The history of the times and of the text has already provided us with biographical information about the prophet Hosea. The sorrows, frustrations, and renewed hopes of his marriage supplied the major image for chapters 1–3 about the sins and infidelities of Israel, and contributed intense passion to important lines in the rest of the book. Hope and agony, springing from strong emotions, characterize not only the book but the person of Hosea. These rise prominently to the surface, as God cries out impassionately: "I will not give vent to my blazing anger. . . . For I am God, no human person" (11:9). Hopes spilling over with compassion induce Hosea to moderate the punishments of Deuteronomy, a book otherwise close to him in spirit and vocabulary. While Deuteronomy legislates the punishment of death by stoning for a stubborn and unruly son (Deut 21:18-21) and for an adulterous wife (Deut 22:13-24), Hosea pulls back from such harshness.

Comparing Hosea with Amos, we discern a whole new set of images. While Amos draws upon his experience of shepherding a flock in the desert wilderness, Hosea frequently refers to agricultural scenes. These he adduces, whether as peacefully present in their rich produce, indicative of the new espousals of Israel with God (2:23-25), or as painfully absent when "the land mourns and everything that dwells in it languishes" because of Israel's sins. While the wilderness is the haunt of lions and bears for Amos (Amos 3:8, 12; 5:19), for Hosea it can be the idyllic place of Israel's honeymoon with God (9:10; 13:4-5). Hosea's appreciation of fertility in the family, in the farmland, and in the folds of livestock should have been soured, one would think, by his wife's infatuation with fertility rites in the temple (2:4-9); yet his estimate of the dignity before God of life and sexuality won the day. He not only received back his wayward wife but responded with heroic compassion in the end.

The covenant theology of Hosea

What secured this triumph in Hosea's soul and writings can be traced back to the covenant between Yahweh and Israel in the days of Moses. Hosea even stresses the two outstanding qualities of this covenant: *bonding in love* and *sturdy trustworthiness.* These are the two words that Yahweh pronounced with dramatic compassion as Moses stood atop Mount Sinai with the two stone tablets of the law in his arms (Exod 34:6-9). Through the heartrending experience of his broken and healed marriage, Hosea transforms the somewhat legal framework of the Mosaic covenant into the intimately personal and loving contract of marriage. Hosea's remembrance of the covenant shows up in his allusion to the Decalogue in 4:2. While the covenant enables Hosea to suffuse the note of compassion, it also provides a straightforward way to brush aside flimsy excuses and to call sin by its honest name—swearing, lying, murder, stealing, and adultery.

Just as sketching the times and sequence of chapters in the book has already introduced us to the person of Hosea, so the preceding biographical details have led us into the major theological lines of this prophecy. Mosaic traditions are not only present in an impressive way, but ancient customs and inspired attitudes (about five hundred years old by now) were seen as a living, motivating force. Unlike Amos, who talked *about* the Exodus as a point of comparison with the present moment (see Amos 2:9-12; 3:1-2; 9:7), Hosea sees it happening right now. Israel's sins bring the people back to Egypt (8:13; 9:3; 11:5), not geographically, because they either remained in the Holy Land or were taken eastward into exile; nor politically, because Egypt pretended to be a friendly state and a place of asylum; but typologically, because Egypt was a symbol or type of sin and bondage. In this regard we note the frequent use of the word "now" in Hosea's preaching (4:16; 5:3, 7; 7:2; 8:8). This ability to see a contemporaneity in ancient redemptive acts of God was probably inherited from Deuteronomy, another ancient northern tradition (see Deut 5:1-5).

One final aspect of Hosea's theology cannot be passed over. Hosea could not refer to God simply and generally as God; at least forty-five times he uses the sacred name Yahweh (Exod 3:11-15), and if he refers to God as Elohim or El, it is almost always as "*your* God" or "*my* God" (2:25; 3:5; 4:6; 12).

The disturbed text of Hosea

The Hebrew text of Hosea seems very disturbed. Various explanations are offered: it reflects a northern style instead of the more customary Hebrew of Jerusalem; Hosea himself was emotionally disturbed and this fact leaves its scars upon the book; or later scribes handled the text with less than satisfactory care. The following variations are to be noted in the numbers for chapters and verses:

Hebrew; NAB	*Greek; Vulgate; RSV*
1:1-9	1:1-9
2:1-2	1:10-11
2:3-25	2:1-23
chs. 3–10	chs. 3–10
11:1-11	11:1-11
11:12	12:1
12:1-14	12:2-15
13:1-15	13:1-15
13:16	14:1
14:1-9	14:2-10

COMMENTARY

INTRODUCTION

Hos 1:1

The introduction or superscription to the book of Hosea is less elaborate and less informative than that found in the Book of Amos. Although Hosea prophesied in the northern kingdom of Israel, more attention is given here to the kings of the southern kingdom of Judah whose reigns extended beyond that of Jeroboam II. This fact hints at the book's redaction at Jerusalem, capital of the southern kingdom.

The introduction accentuates the theological or inspired quality of Hosea's preaching. While Amos' book begins with "the words of Amos," Hosea's opens with *"the word of the Lord* that came to Hosea." The name Hosea means "the act of saving" or simply "Savior." In Greek, the initial "h" was reduced to a small apostrophe, called a "rough breathing." These were customarily dropped when writing with only capital letters. The final "a" of the Hebrew name would have indicated feminine gender in Greek and so was changed to an "e." From the Greek came the spelling of this prophet's name in the Latin Vulgate and in older Roman Catholic editions of the Bible, namely, Osee.

Hosea was "the son of Beeri." The name Beeri is not otherwise found for a person in the Old Testament, although a village located near Bethel had this name. Beeri means "my fountain" or "O fountain." Only here in the entire book is the prophet's name recorded for us!

YAHWEH, SPOUSE OF ISRAEL

Hos 1:2–3:5

The first three chapters center upon Hosea's marriage, the infidelities of his wife Gomer, the doubtful paternity of the second and third children, and the application of this situation to Israel's covenant with Yahweh. It is important to note at the outset that in real life Hosea was the faithful spouse and Gomer the adulterous sinner, but in the application of this background to Israel, the ones targeted most as unfaithful harlots were the religious and civil leaders (particularly the former), all of the male sex (see 4:4-11; 5:1-3)!

Each of the three chapters tells basically the same thing, yet never as a story for its own sake but as a religious symbol about Israel—and for that matter, about what can happen to any one of us. Many important details are missing for a good story: the name of the paramour (or were there many?), the place of their rendezvous (at the temple for fertility rites? secretly in a private dwelling?). While chapter 1 speaks *about* Hosea and the children, chapter 2 consists mostly of Hosea's speech, and chapter 3 follows in an autobiographical style. Chapter 3 is the most succinct, possibly the oldest. Closest to the domestic tragedy, chapter 3 could not humanly sustain long explanations. Chapter 2 represents an outburst of violent emotion, again very near to the raw memory of what happened; chapter 1, written from a distance by a disciple, can afford to be the most explicit about the meaning of the episode.

1:2-8 A similar style is used to tell about the conception, birth, and naming of all three children. **1:2 the Lord said to Hosea:** The marriage of Hosea was probably arranged in the normal way of the time by the parents, yet, viewed from the faith that God's providence covers especially significant events of human life, the Lord is said to *order* it. **take a harlot wife and harlot's children:** The grammatical form of the noun "harlot" (in Hebrew, masculine plural) indicates a woman of such tendencies. Hosea did not look for a prostitute to marry; his wife may have experienced strong temptations due to her initiation at the sanctuary's fertility rites. **1:3 Gomer:** The proper name of the woman, without any significance for the story of Hosea, argues for a real marriage rather than a piece of fiction or allegory. **conceived and bore him a son:** This is the only time Hosea is clearly said to be the father of the child.

1:4 the name Jezreel: Each of the three children's names has a double meaning, good in itself but also bad for Israel. Jezreel refers to the fertile valley stretching from Mount Carmel in the west to the hills above the Sea of Galilee in the east, literally a breadbasket of nourishment. Jezreel was also the site of many bloody battles beginning with the Book of Judges (Judg 4–5). **1:6 Lo-ruhama:** Hebrew for "No pity," a name that could have indicated a child able to hold her own against injustices; theologically, it negates one of the key qualities of the Mosaic covenant, the Lord's compassion (see p. 498). In the singular the Hebrew word denotes the mother's womb, where a child develops in warm security; derivatives like *ruhama* show the feminine, motherly side of God. Hosea eventually interprets the child's name as an end to the covenant. **1:8 Lo-ammi:** Hebrew for "Not my people," a name that originally alluded to the boy's illegitimacy and to his ability to survive alone in this world despite all odds against him. Religiously, the name announces the end of Israel's special privileges and reduces Israel to the status of all other nations. **1:9 I will not be their God:** The Hebrew refers to the divine name as revealed by God to Moses, "I am who I am." When spoken by Israel, it was read in the third person: "He who is [always there with you]," or Yahweh (Exod 3:14-15). Literally verse 9 reads, "No longer am I 'I am' for you."

2:1-3 These verses are frequently placed after 2:25 or, as in the New American Bible, after 3:1-5. The Revised Standard Version, following the ancient Greek and Vulgate enumeration, lists these verses as 1:10-11 and 2:1.

2:4-25 While the overall impact of these lines is unmistakable, the grammar, the emotions, and the sequence of verses are confusing; the New American Bible adjusts the verses in a new sequence. Some scholars claim that verses 18-25, or at least verses 21-22, are editorial additions. Perhaps the editor responsible for the biographical section in 1:2-8 drew verses 18-25 from a treasury of Hosea's speeches.

At first Hosea speaks *to* the children (vv. 4-5) and then *about* them (vv. 6-7); he explodes with vitriolic disdain (vv. 5-6, 11-12) and peacefully settles with nostalgic memories (v. 10 and the end of v. 15, into vv. 8-9); he is at the point of divorce (v. 4) and reverts to reconciliation (vv. 16-17). While bitterly denouncing Canaanite fertility rites at the sanctuaries, Hosea employs the language of this ritual to appreciate the luscious beauty of the landscape. The Hebrew word for "allure" (v. 16), describing God's way of drawing Israel closely into loving covenant bonds, is also the word for sexual seduction. **2:17 the valley of Achor:** This valley southwest of Jericho was once surrounded with sinister memories of military defeat and deceit in the days of Joshua (Josh 7:24-26); now Israel is invited to reenter the Promised Land through it and take possession of its rich source of life. The days of the Exodus are now gloriously repeated and the covenant is enhanced by comparison with matrimonial bonds, as Israel calls the Lord "my husband." True love (v. 20) is never selfish, and so Hosea sees the good effects of Israel's new espousals with Yahweh spiraling outward, even to protect birds and crawling animals.

2:21-22 These lovely lines need to be unpacked for their theological richness. In this marriage between Yahweh and Israel, the Lord offers the dowry "in right and in justice" ("right": a moral rectitude that brings peace and satisfaction; "justice": a public, authoritative declaration that such is true); "in love and in mercy" ("love": affection between those bonded by blood or treaty; "mercy": see above 1:7); "in fidelity" (sturdy reliability in one's relations). **you shall know the Lord:** The Hebrew word for "know" is the one most frequently used for marital intercourse (Gen 4:1, 17, 25) and stresses the experiential or intuitive aspect.

2:23-25 Again intimate love reaches outward toward a new creation. The bonding between Israel and Yahweh hints at its repercussions upon people everywhere; universal mission is already being signaled from afar. Difficult or seemingly impossible, whether for adulterous Israel or for unsuspecting foreigners, God's love acts miraculously, so that Jezreel is once again a fertile breadbasket, and Lo-ruhama and Lo-ammi are to become the Lord's legitimate children. What is biologically impossible—changing a child's natural parentage—now happens. These lines are applied to the Church's universal mission in 1 Pet 2:9-10; Rom 9:25-26; 11:32.

3:1-5 This passage retells the story of Hosea's reconciliation with Gomer. For the application to Israel's covenant with Yahweh, an application continuously being made by Hosea, it is important that Hosea never divorced Gomer nor is he marrying someone else. Here we note several, very human phases in the return of Gomer. Three times verse 1 uses the Hebrew verb "to love," which denotes normal physical and emotional attachment. After Hosea obeys the Lord and brings Gomer back to his home, he still cannot consummate the marriage. After such a severe estrangement, intercourse would be too much a routine physical act, not a full expression of human love. He says to her: "Many days you shall wait for me . . . I in turn will wait for you" (3:3). Verse 5 applies the lines to the southern kingdom of Judah, probably after the destruction of the north in 721 B.C.E., reaffirms the promises to the Davidic dynasty at Jerusalem, and then extends the promises into "the last days" (3:5), a phrase also found among the southern prophets in speaking of the new Jerusalem of peace (Isa 2:2-5; Mic 4:1-5; Jer 23:5-6, 20; Ezek 38:16).

2:1-3 The New American Bible transfers these verses here; for an explanation, see the commentary on 2:23-25. Hosea seems to reach back behind the Mosaic covenant to the earliest memories of Israel with the ancient patriarchs and their wives, to whom were promised offspring "like the sand of the sea" (Gen 22:7), "children of the living God," born of parents too far advanced in age for conception or else barren for a long period of years. Yahweh is not dead like the false fertility gods of the Canaanites. **2:2 one head:** Hosea avoids the title of king, perhaps out of disdain for the reigning monarchs, perhaps too as a way of uniting Israel with the premonarchic days of Abraham and Moses.

CRIMES OF LEADERSHIP IN JEROBOAM II'S REIGN

Hos 4:1–5:7

As already explained in the introduction, this section belongs to the final years of Jeroboam II's long reign (786–746 B.C.E.) and in that sense is a continuation of chapters 1–3. Although promiscuity was involved in the sanctuary fertility rites, the crime of adultery is attached to all serious offenses against the Lord and the neighbor because of the intimate love of Yahweh, which every sin violates.

4:1-3 This section is composed in the style of a legal proceeding at the city gate (see Deut 25:7; Ruth 4:1) and includes a summons of the defendant (v. 1a), evidence of crimes (vv. 1b-2a), verdict of "Guilty!" (v. 2b, literally "blood upon blood," meaning that the crimes are written across the hands), and the consequent punishment (v. 3). For other examples of this type of judicial speech among the prophets, see: Amos 4:1-3; 8:4-8; Isa 1:2-16. The crimes represent a mini-decalogue (Exod 20:1-17; Deut 5:1-21). They are all crimes against basic relationships and human trust: cursing by ritual language, lying, premeditated murder, kidnapping (the original meaning instead of "stealing"), and adultery. In order to challenge a false trust in later theologies and rituals that developed out of the Mosaic covenant, Hosea goes back to the basic ABC's of humanity as reflected in the Ten Commandments. Prophets condemn covenant religion by appealing to precovenant expectations enfleshed in all men and women, and even in "the beasts of the field" and "the birds of the air," which also suffer the effects of human selfishness. For 4:1b, see 2:21-22.

4:4-19 Here are graphic details about fertility rites, even at such ancient sanctuaries as Gilgal (Josh 4:19–5:15; 1 Sam 15:12-33) and Bethel (= "house of God," which Hosea contemptuously calls *Beth-aven,* or "house of emptiness"; for Bethel, see Gen 28:10-22; 1 Kgs 12:29-33). Verse 4 is a very difficult verse to translate confidently from the Hebrew; in any case the accusation is targeted not so much against the ordinary Israelite but against "you, O priest" (in the singular according to the Hebrew and therefore aimed at the high priest legitimately installed but morally corrupt).**4:6 want of knowledge:** See 2:22. **4:8 feed on the sin:** The ritual law of sin-offerings prescribes a stipend for the livelihood of the priests (see Num 5:8-10). Hosea implies that the priests tolerate sin or sharpen the sense of guilt among the people, who then feel compelled to bring more generous offerings. The word "greedy" implies lust or an unusually strong desire. Verse 9a is a proverb found verbatim in Isa 24:2a; it reads literally: "and it will be like people like priest." The priests imitate the worldliness of people about them, and people shelter themselves under the priests' example.

5:1-7 The reference is to the continuation of the lascivious rituals in such renowned sanctuaries as Mizpah (1 Sam 7:5-14) and Tabor (Judg 4:14). The play on words in verses 1-2 makes the lines difficult to translate into English: "a snare *(pah)* are you at *Mizpah,*" or in English, "a snare are you at Miznare." In verse 3, Ephraim is the name of a son of the patriarch Joseph (Gen 41:52; 48:1). Verse 7 refers to children conceived through the fertility rites.

ASSASSINATIONS, INSTABILITY, LOSS

Hos 5:8–8:14

These chapters rumble and tumble with the assassination of kings and their royal families, pro-Assyrian and anti-Assyrian policies, treaties with Egypt against Assyria, and with Assyria against Egypt, big promises and meager delivery, politics in place of moral reform, and distracting military adventures that lead to heavy losses, which again distract the people to seek remedy in new assassinations. We are living through the period from the death of Jeroboam II in 746 to the seizure of royal power by King Hoshea in 732. The period covers only fourteen years, yet it produced seven kings, five dynasties, a major war from 736 to 732, and the loss of the northeast section of the kingdom to Assyria (2 Kgs 15:27-31; Isa 8:23).

5:8-14 The various allusions are difficult to identify; the whirl of events and the tragedy of malfeasance in leadership disrupt any orderly discussion. At one point Menahem captures the throne in the north and tilts in favor of Assyria; at another time Ahaz, king of Judah, in a panic to save his throne, declares himself a vassal of Assyria, sacrificing the independence of his country and enmeshing it in international turmoil. **5:13 cannot heal you:** One of Hosea's favorite words is introduced into the text here and again in 6:1; 7:1; 11:4; 14:5, generally with the other key word, "return," so that interior return or conversion becomes an absolute condition for healing the injuries of any individual or the nation. Verse 14 states that even though Assyrian armies inflicted the mortal wound, God wants no misunderstanding: "I am like a lion . . . I rend the prey and depart." The Assyrians are following through with God's plan! Implicit in such a seemingly cruel interpretation of divine providence is the consoling fact that moral conversion, not military action, can heal Israel for new life.

5:15–6:7 The centerpiece here is a prayer (6:1-3), lovely in itself, stitched carefully into the context by word play and parallel ideas, and then rejected because of Israel's insincerity. The most beautiful words cannot save an ugly heart. While the words speak of conversion, Israel refuses the consequence of adequate repentance. As one author commented, the transition from conversion to repentance is as crucial as waking up without getting up!

The words "heal" in 5:13, "rend" in 5:14, and "go back" in 5:15 are identical with "return," "rend" and "heal" in 6:1. The phrase "look for" in 5:15 is of the same Hebrew root as "dawn" in 6:3 ("dawn" is the first light that we "look for" in the early morning). As mentioned already, the prayer in 6:1-3 is carefully inserted into place. **6:2 third day:** This is a technical phrase in the Bible, symbolic of the Lord's extraordinary appearance as Savior: in Exod 19:11, 16, when the Lord came down to Mount Sinai; in Gen 42:18, when Joseph said to his brothers, "Do this and you shall live"; in Jonah 2:1, Jonah's deliverance from the belly of the whale (see also Josh 3:2; Ezra 8:15; Isa 16:14; 37:30). This long tradition of "three days" converges gloriously in the New Testament doctrine of Jesus' resurrection and is enshrined in the Church's creed.

In verse 4, as in 11:8-9, we eavesdrop on the compassionate heart of God struggling against the inevitable destruction of Israel. **6:5 smote them through the prophets:** A long series of non-writing prophets have been warning Israel, such as the elders in Num 11:16-30, Samuel in 1 Sam, Elijah and Elisha in 1 Kgs 17–2 Kgs 13:20. A conscience that is stirred and challenged becomes a destructive force for revenge and self-justification if one does not obey it. **6:6 love . . . not sacrifice:** This is a classic text (see 1 Sam 15:22; Ps 50:14; Matt 9:13; 12:7). Ritual acts like sacrifice and holocaust were intended to externalize in a sacred assembly the interior spirit of obedience and adoration before God. Without love and knowledge of God they are a sham, or, in Ezekiel's words, a "whitewash" (Ezek 22:28).

7:3-16 Deceitful and cruel dynasties rise and collapse, as though moral turpitude is remedied by military excitement. Kings, after stirring the passions of the people to revolt in order to capture the throne, are themselves the victims of these overheated ovens as people "consume their rulers" (7:7). **7:8 Ephraim, a hearth cake unturned:** Hosea evokes the image of dough being baked on burning coals, unturned, so that it remains raw and cold on one side, burnt to charcoal and reeking with smoke on the other. Hosea refers to social conditions, with half the people too rich and half too poor; religious conditions, with excessive ritualism but no spirit; political busyness, with no consistency or thoroughness; cultural veneer, pretentious and overdone in contrast to the dirt and hunger of the poor; a country of half-fed people, half-cultured society, half-lived religion, half-hearted policy, half-baked cakes.

8:1-14 This poem is carefully crafted with key words stitching the lines together and with major themes in balanced repetition, and at the center the haunting sound of a proverb (v. 7). While verses 1-6 and 11-14 modulate from frantic misdirection in politics to feverish ritualism in worship, verses 8-10 point to the disastrous effects. Such a frenzied whirl of activity can only foment more intense movement until all disintegrates.

8:1 A trumpet . . . You who watch: The latter phrase remains better in its original Hebrew, "like a vulture": first, because of the repetition of the particle "like" (in Hebrew, an emphatic, dramatic word); second, the vulture signals a field of dead bodies—carcasses of animals for immolation on the altar (?) or the bloated bodies of dead soldiers and of city inhabitants after a long siege. Sacrificial animals, sanctifying the altar in signs of adoration, now contaminate the house of the Lord in their rotten state. **8:2 "O God of Israel, we know you":** Israel rejects and yet calls upon the Lord. **8:5 Cast away your calf:** The golden calves set up by Jeroboam I at the sanctuaries of Bethel and Dan (1 Kgs 12:26-33) were originally considered the pedestal or throne for God's invisible presence like the ark or chest surrounded by cherubim wings at the Jerusalem temple (Exod 25:10-22; 37:1-9). Soon the symbol became an idol so as to divinize human talents and work, and to focus on the calf or bull in its fertility symbolism.

8:7 When they sow the wind, they shall reap the whirlwind: This proverb echoes in every language of the world. The three couplets in Hebrew resound with the same sounds and even rhyme at the end. Not only do the words and ideas fit compactly together, but, once begun, they rush like a whirlwind to their destruction. **8:9 Ephraim bargained for lovers:** No longer attractive and with little to offer any more, Ephraim pays her lovers (foreign nations whose assistance she courts) for their sensuous enjoyment of herself—lines bitterly true of the rape and destruction that accompany military invasion. **8:13 they shall return to Egypt:** see the introduction (p. 497). Although Egypt is actually a friendly nation, coaxing the revolt against Assyria, Hosea views Egypt as a type of oppression since the days of Moses. Israel's sins have reversed the covenant at Sinai and have driven Israel back to pre-Mosaic days. Beneath the surface, however, is the assurance that what God did once can be done again if Israel converts sincerely.

INTERLUDE OF FALSE HOPES

Hos 9:1–13:8

As noted in the introduction, these chapters bring us into the reign of the last king of the north, Hoshea (732–724 B.C.E.). After the

Assyrian army had broken the back of the revolt instigated by King Pekah and lopped off the northern provinces of Israel, Hoshea was placed upon the throne with Assyrian help. This period of time represents Israel's last chance at conversion, healing, and survival. The nation failed to realize the futility of seeking salvation by intrigue, treaties, and military armaments. They paid little or no attention to Hosea's threats and previously to those of Amos. Perhaps they felt that they had suffered enough (or too much) and so could settle down to business as usual in the sanctuary worship and in their social injustices now that King Hoshea was enthroned and peace had returned.

Chapter 9 has more than its share of textual difficulties in a book beset with many disturbed Hebrew readings; there are also a number of puns and like-sounding words, which are always difficult to translate into another language. We spot various allusions to the autumnal feast of Tabernacles, at times simply called "the feast," as in verse 5 (see 1 Kgs 8:2; Ezek 45:25; Neh 8:14). Tabernacles was the final harvest festival, in thanksgiving especially for grapes and olives (see 9:2). Several references to dwelling places in this chapter may allude to the practice of dwelling in tents during the octave of this feast (Lev 23:42). This chapter of Hosea witnesses to the prophet's keen awareness of the Exodus traditions. In his prophecy, accordingly, Hosea is not condemning sanctuary worship in itself, because this was one of the principal means of his learning the Mosaic traditions; like Amos, he is against *that* worship rendered evil by its tolerance or active support of sensuality and social injustices.

9:1-2 The references to threshing floor and wine press, along with other details to follow in this chapter, place us within the eight-day festival of Tabernacles; these phrases are also used in Deut 16:13 in reference to the final harvest and the feast of Tabernacles. Harvest is normally symbolic of life. Yet the carousing and excesses even at Israel's sanctuaries contradict God's holiness and concern for the poor. The feast that celebrates God's tabernacling presence among Israel is driving God out. We are reminded of Jesus' reaction when he drove the money-changers out of the temple (John 2:13-22). Once again Egypt is a type of oppression and sin (v. 3); the people's offenses have transformed their own land into "Egypt" (see 7:16).

9:4 mourners' bread that makes unclean: As in Amos 7:17, the people and priests may be violating social justice and turning the sanctuary into a business, even for the sale of sex, yet they can still be scrupulous over fine points of the law such as unclean food or burial in an unblessed or unclean grave! *Mourners' bread* was unacceptable because of the mourners' contact with a corpse (Deut 16:14); strict rules isolated people mortally or contagiously ill as well as those who cared for them (Num 19:11-22; Lev 21). People of nomadic background, occupying an arid area, develop strict rules concerning contagious diseases. Israel, moreover, with very little understanding of the physical body and with little or no appreciation of the healing profession, evolved a system of health care that combined common sense with strange concoctions (see the rules for the purification of leprosy and skin diseases in Lev 14). Israel's legitimate offerings of wine become unclean like mourners' food because sensuality has reduced Israel to a state of being dead, and its sinfulness is contagious! **9:6 Weeds . . . thorns:** The inhabitable oasis where tents are pitched quickly reverts to wild growth; Israel's sins corrupt the earth (4:3), and the harvest festival is replaced with weeds and thorns.

9:7-9 The play on words and sounds in the Hebrew verses carry the enigmatic touch of prophecy as well as its poetic mystique, yet the sense becomes clear enough when we read from the background of prophecy's history. Already from the start, prophecy could turn into a self-serving business for pay (Num 22:17). Even in the days of Moses prophecy needed correction, in this case because of jealousy (Num 11:26-30; 12:6-8). In a later episode we stand by, scandalized and disillusioned, as prophet argues against prophet in 1 Kgs 22 or Jer 28. Amos, we recall, refused to be associated with the prophetic guilds (Amos 7:14) once honored by the presence of Elijah and Elisha (2 Kgs 2). Hosea resounds with his own "Amen!" in declaring that the professional "prophet is a fool!" Moreover, their craft or employment has become a snare for them so that they are sinking to the sexual degeneracy of "the days of Gibeah," the site of a vicious form of homosexual activity and a hideous type of revenge (Judg 19–21).

9:10-17 These lines dramatize the meaning of the word "Ephraim" in reverse. It means, as we read in Gen 41:52 about Joseph's naming his second son Ephraim, "God *has made me fruitful* in the land of my affliction." Though the second-born son, Ephraim was to receive the first-born's blessing from Jacob (Gen 48:12-20), as specially precious to the Lord (see Jer 2:3). Yet the people of Ephraim (= northern kingdom of Israel) have "consecrated themselves to the Shame" (9:10), as happened when Israel was first initiated into the fertility rites at Baal-peor at the instigation of a prophet named Balaam (Num 25; 31:8, 16). The people Ephraim, whose name declares the fruitfulness of the womb, by their sexual excesses will become "childless" (9:12) through the cruel excesses of the military conqueror Assyria. The final verse begins with the formula of a blessing only to end with a curse. Verse 16 reminds us of the deep weariness of sated lust.

10:1-15 This series of short, disparate oracles may date to the early years of King Hoshea. King Pekah has been assassinated (v. 3). The land is again producing its fruit as it recovers from the disastrous war against Assyria. Yet the hopes for moral reform and for a return to social justice have turned into empty words and false promises (v. 4). The idolatrous rites continue, as indicated by the worship of stone pillars, which are representative of the male god Baal and are usually joined by wooden pillars for the female goddess Astarte (see 3:12-13).

Verses 5-8 anticipate a new and worse invasion by Assyria if Samaria continues in its promiscuous rites. Bethel is singled out, referred to as Beth-aven (v. 5) or just Aven (v. 8); the latter word stands for emptiness or shame, a sarcastic way of alluding to the famous sanctuary (see the commentary on 4:5-6). The new king will endure the same fate as Pekah (v. 7; see 13:10 for the actual event). The destruction will be so cruel and complete that people will "cry out to the mountains, 'Cover us!' " (v. 8), words repeated in Luke 22:30 and Rev 6:16. Verses 11-13a draw upon the image of harvest, as in chapter 9, only to see that Israel "reaped perversity." Israel trusted in the military; it will be destroyed by the military (vv. 13b-15). The records about Salman's ravage of Beth-arbel have been lost; the event cannot be documented. Twice the word "chastise" occurs (v. 10); its Hebrew form indicates disciplinary punishment, suffering that purifies and strengthens and so transforms. An elusive element of hope abides in lines sweeping toward destruction.

11:1-11 This chapter seems like an island around which runs the current of Hosea's preaching from chapter 10 to 12:1. The image of Israel here modulates from the adulterous spouse to the wayward child. While the rest of Hosea increases the momentum toward death, dramatically summarized in 13:14, chapter 11 draws from the intuitive hope deep within the heart of Hosea, like an island whose roots extend beneath the river currents.

Grammatically, chapter 11 is divided between verses 1-7 and 8-11. The opening section refers to Israel in the third person; the other part uses the second person. The first verses reflect Israel's wandering in the Sinaitic wilderness, while verses 8-11 reach forward to Israel's settled life in the land of Canaan. Yahweh speaks throughout in the first person singular. If ever there was an Old Testament discourse wrapping God in the warm flesh of human parenthood, this is it—the supreme revelation of divine love in the Hebrew Scriptures. To compose it, Hosea had to overcome the angry disappointment of illegitimate children from his own wife; he had to cleanse from view the lascivious excesses of Canaanite fertility rites. Reaching into the depth of his own human compassion, he recognized God's presence as the source of such heroic love.

The opening line stresses that God loved the child before Israel knew how to respond (see 1 John 4:7-11). When Matthew sees the fulfillment of this line in Jesus' infancy, Hosea's prophecy enables us to recognize the passover mystery in Jesus: through the Red Sea, across the wilderness, toward new life (Matt 2:15). "Israel [as] my firstborn child" was already revealed to Moses (Exod 4:22-23); here it is reaffirmed with stronger personal bonds. The actions described in verses 3-4 are maternal; here we have one of the most striking feminine images of God in the Hebrew Scriptures. *"Healer"* is one of Hosea's persistent titles for Yahweh (see 5:13). **11:5 return to . . . Egypt:** The typology is evident here. Sin and slavery, even in Assyria, are considered a return to Egypt. According to the Hebrew verse 7 should read: "My people are in suspense about returning to *me*"; the second line of verse 7 is almost unintelligible in the Hebrew and is variously reconstructed.

In verses 8-11 God speaks ever more passionately, convulsing within by the contrasting demands for death as humanly required (Deut 21:18-21), and for forgiveness and another chance to be loved yet again (see 3:1) as divinely expected. In the Hebrew verse 8 begins with a strong phrase like "but on the contrary" (Gen 39:9; 44:34). Admah and Zeboiim are the names used in northern traditions, while southern traditions referred to Sodom and Gomorrah (Gen 19:28; Isa 1:9-10). Both sets of names occur in Deut 29:22. With verse 10 the pattern is broken; this verse refers to the Lord in the third person (otherwise in chapter 11 in the first person); the reference to roaring lions is typical of Amos, not of Hosea (Amos 1:2, 3:4, 8). This verse is usually considered a later addition from an anonymous but inspired source.

12:1–13:8 (RSV: 11:12–13:8) Typical of so much of prophecy, this section of Hosea (a) reverts to an ancient tradition, only to reverse the people's easygoing understanding of it; (b) makes an effective use of wordplay; (c) detects a new appreciation of the present situation; and (d) has undergone later revision and application.

The charge of "lies" and "deceit" against contemporary Ephraim in 12:1 is drawn from the ancient story of the patriarch Jacob, who lied to his blind and aged father Isaac in order to acquire the birthright (Gen 27), and again to his uncle Laban, whom he "hoodwinked by not telling him of his intended flight" (Gen 31:20) after Laban had deceived Jacob about the identity of his wife (Gen 29:23-25). While the traditions in Genesis absorbed these lies and deceit into the larger theology of God's mysterious providence, Hosea lifts them out to be seen for what they were—lies! Hosea states how he himself has been victimized by lies that "surround me."

Verse 1b about Judah is a later adaptation to the southern kingdom. The application to Judah continues in verse 3a. Here where the text reads "Israel" (correctly according to Hosea's original intent), the Hebrew text reads "Judah." In verse 3b Ephraim is clearly identified as a chip off the old block continuing to lie and deceive like his grandfather Jacob!

12:4-7 The references to Jacob are intensified: "In the womb he supplanted his brother" (Gen 25:26; 27:36); the word "supplant" *('akab)* is the origin of Jacob's name. "He contended with God" refers to Jacob's wrestling with the angel at the river Jabbok, where God changed the patriarch's name to Israel (see Gen 32:23-33, especially verse 29, where we read: "You shall no longer be spoken of as Jacob, but as Israel, because you have contended with the divine"). The word *sarah* ("contend") contains the central consonants of the word "Israel." It was at Bethel that God appeared to Jacob atop the ladder on which divine messengers ascended and descended (Gen 28:13). Verse 6 is an addition adapting the passage for a liturgical setting, like Amos 4:13; 5:8-9; 9:6b. In verse 7 Hosea's deeply embedded optimism surfaces again.

12:8-13:8 These lines thrice modulate from difficulties to a divine intervention and back again to worse difficulties (12:8-12; 12:13–13:1; 13:2-8). **12:8 merchant:** The Hebrew word is also the proper name "Canaan"; from its origins Israel has been Canaanite—deceitful, covetous, and sensual. **12:9 fortune:** The Hebrew word is spelled almost the same as the words translated "man" in verse 4 and "falsehood" in verse 12. Ancestor Jacob, kindred Canaanites, present Ephraimites—all are marked by greed and deceit.

Verses 10-11 speak of a new beginning with the Exodus, new reformation with the prophets. "Gilead" is possibly a reference to the pact between Jacob and Laban (Gen 31:46-54), solemnized at Galeed (Gal + ed = "hill of witness"); it is very similar to "Gilgal," the site of an ancient sanctuary whose licentious style of worship now witnesses against Israel. **12:12 heaps of stones:** The phrase possibly recalls the stones of witness set up near Gilgal in Joshua's days (Josh 4). In verse 14 Moses is honored by the title of prophet (or is it vice versa?—see Num 12), yet in this section from 12:1 onward Jacob is criticized much more negatively than the traditions in Genesis.

The third poem in this subsection (13:2-8) again opens with the continuation of sin despite all warnings. For Hosea, the principal offense is idolatry and its sensual rites, prompting the scornful gibe "Men kiss calves," which refers to the golden calves that were considered pedestals for Yahweh at Bethel and Dan (see 8:5). Hosea contrasts Yahweh's shepherding of Israel in the wilderness (vv.

4-5) with the gluttonous banquets at the sanctuaries (v. 6). The divine shepherd turns into the bear or lion now attacking the flock (see Amos 3:12).

THE STING OF DEATH

Hos 13:9–14:1

This final preaching of Hosea begins as abruptly as the message is final: "Your destruction, O Israel!" **13:10 Where now is your king:** King Hoshea has been captured by the Assyrians, who are now proceeding southward toward Samaria to besiege and destroy the capital city and deport whatever population remains after war's fatalities and the Assyrian executions at the captured city gate. "That he may rescue you" is a cruel pun on the name of the last king, Hoshea; in Hebrew, *yoshiah* reads "rescue" or "save." **13:11 I give you a king . . . and I take him away:** There were four kings in the space of two years, 746–745: Jeroboam II, Zechariah, Shallum, and Menahem! Is there another sting of irony in the prophet's summoning the Canaanite god Death to condemn the Israelites for their fertility rites honoring the gods of death and life, Muth and Baal (v. 14)? Beyond a doubt, in Hosea's mind is the certainty of total destruction.

The compassion of chapter 11 is reversed unconditionally only to be reversed again by St. Paul, who combines the passage with Isa 25:8 and reads the words as a question that expects the answer "No!" (1 Cor 15:54-55). In his resurrection, Jesus Christ has overcome the sting and plague of death.

CONVERSION, HEALING, AND NEW LIFE

Hos 14:2-9

If this optimistic conclusion clashes with the absolute doom in the preceding section, such an upbeat ending is typical of prophecy. We noticed a similar finale to the Book of Amos. Whether it be the entire Bible or individual books, the beginning and the conclusion generally center on hope; in between is the superhuman struggle to sustain such ideals within the absorbing challenges of Planet Earth. As a matter of fact, Hosea has frequently hinted at the positive side of a strong faith in God as healer and savior underlying his negative, severe condemnations. He continually recognizes a redeeming quality in the worship of Israel, even in its fertility rites, for he makes abundant use of its themes and vocabulary. All the while he condemns the excesses so painfully experienced in his own marriage (5:15–6:7). Whether it is sin or virtue, each has immediate repercussions across the world of vegetation and livestock (2:20, 23-25; 4:3).

Either Hosea himself or a disciple drew upon earlier preaching to end the prophetic book, possibly at Jerusalem after the fall of Samaria (721 B.C.E.). The opening lines follow the style of a prophetic exhortation (vv. 2-3a) and a prayer composed by the prophet for the people (vv. 3b-4). The following verses (vv. 5-9) present God's reply. Each of the two sections—Hosea's preaching in verses 2-4 and God's response in verses 5-9—opens with a favorite word of Hosea, usually linked closely together: "return" and "heal" (5:13; 6:1; 7:1; 11:4-5). Physical healing depends upon moral conversion.

14:2 Lord, your God: Hosea does not speak about the nature of God from any philosophical background but from a personal experience and a liturgical memory of the Lord's intimate sharing in Israel's life (see the Introduction, p. 498).

14:3 render as offerings: The Hebrew text is somewhat disturbed. The prophet has suffered severely from the sexual aberrations at the sanctuaries on the part of his wife and others, but he still speaks positively of ritual and worship. These are the source of his hope in a God who called the people out of Egypt, taught them to walk, and formed a covenant of love with them in the wilderness (2:18-22; 11).

14:4 the orphan finds compassion: The immediate reference is Israel, yet we wonder if there is not also an allusion to Hosea's own second and third children, probably illegitimate (1:6, 8), whom he sees as fully his own, just as God accepts Israel (2:1-3, 24-25).

14:6 like the dew: Dew is a symbol of the divine gift of life. It appears without rain and is an important source of nourishment for vegetation during the long dry season in a land of cold nights and excessively warm days (see Judg 6:37-40; Pss 110:3; 133:3; Job 38:28). Verse 9 is like a divine soliloquy upon which we eavesdrop, as in 11:8-9.

CONCLUDING RECOMMENDATION

Hos 14:10

A scribal annotation—or perhaps a spontaneous exclamation in a public assembly—is attached to the book. As an accepted part of the Bible, the verse is truly inspired and comes from an anonymous inspired writer. It has the hallmark of the sapiential movement as witnessed to by Psalm 1. As the conclusion of Hosea's preaching, it reminds us that our response, too, is an integral part of the prophetical book of Hosea. The Bible remains incomplete without our listening and reflecting, our adapting and assenting within our life-setting today. Yet the Bible remains the basis and support of this reflection. It is our guide toward a conclusion; we must be true to its message and inspiration, in this case to Hosea.

As we look back over the fourteen chapters of the Book of Hosea, the concluding recommendation in 14:10 seems right at home. In his preaching, the prophet shows many other touches that relate to the sapiential movement: Hosea's high appreciation of the knowledge of the Lord (3:22; 4:1); the disciplinary role of suffering (5:9); the impact of good living across the earth (2:19-20; 4:3; 10:1). These are all important motifs in the books of Proverbs, Job, and Sirach, which are later books, of course, but representative of a movement that existed from the time of Solomon. Our adaptation to life today places us within a centuries-old tradition and shows the blending of many traditions in the Bible, traditions that include the patriarchal narratives, covenant laws, settlement in the land, scribes and wisdom, prophecy and its challenges, liturgy and its symbolic power to unite over the centuries.

MICAH

Carroll Stuhlmueller, C.P.

INTRODUCTION

Micah of Moresheth, especially when compared with Amos and Hosea, turns out to be an elusive prophet. Unlike the prophecy of Amos, the Book of Micah provides no visions about a personal call to be a prophet (see Amos 7:1-9; 8:1-3), nor any episode like Amos' tryst with the high priest Amaziah in defense of his divine summons (see Amos 7:10-17). Micah's preaching does not depend upon any highly charged emotional experience as was the case with Hosea and his tragic marriage with Gomer. The poor condition of the Hebrew text of Micah, moreover, and its successive re-editing over the centuries by a "school" of disciples cloak the prophet in a series of textual and editorial disguises. The frequent plays on words that intrigued and enticed his listeners, as they do modern students of his Hebrew style, wove its own puzzling web around the prophet from Moresheth. In this short introduction, therefore, we approach *the man* Micah gradually through an appreciation of the book, its literary style, and its major religious topics.

The Book of Micah

The book, as canonically accepted in its final form, is simple enough in its subdivisions, with its double sequence of threats and promises: chapters 1–3, a series of threats, and chapters 4–5, promises; 6:1–7:7, again threatening poems, followed by promises in 7:8-20. Our commonsense hunch says that Micah did not speak in such a neatly balanced way. If he had, the elders in Jer 26:18 would never have quoted the menace of 3:12; it would have been canceled out at once by the glorious promise in 4:1-5.

The preaching of Micah was re-edited on several occasions: for instance, the final lines of 1:5 were redirected to Judah and Jerusalem; 2:12-13 come from the Babylonian Exile and announce a new ingathering in the Promised Land; 4:4-5 represent two different applications of the vision of the new Jerusalem where foreign nations gather in the holy temple (see commentary below).

The style of Micah

Micah's style as a preacher is being more and more appreciated. No longer is he put down as a country bumpkin, blushing easily and embarrassed in public. He displays an unusual directness. Who can match his condemnation of animal sacrifice at the cost of overlooking the hunger and sickness of the poor in 3:2-3? Stylistically we detect a shrewd and quick turn of phrase in his frequent plays on words (see the commentary on 1:10; 2:4, 6, 11; 4:14; 5:1). Micah kept his listeners guessing, smiling, and intrigued as he enticed them into a devastating conclusion.

Along with these general stylistic qualities, Micah also displays an unusual versatility. He moves easily among: lamentations (1:8-16); question-and-answer repartee (1:5; 2:7); Torah speech, summarizing the Lord's expectations (6:6-8); personal confessions of faith, introduced by "as for me" (3:8; 7:7); oracles of judgment (2:3; 5:10-15) and of promise

(4:1-4); a longer judgment speech, modeled upon legal procedures at the city gate (ch. 6).

The major topics of Micah's prophecy are to be distinguished according to the stage of preaching or editing already alluded to in this introduction. Before and during his preaching, Micah had witnessed severe, even wantonly cruel suffering on the part of the poor. Their land had been violated in order that the Jerusalem government might build defenses in such outposts as Moresheth overlooking the Mediterranean plains and then embark upon reckless military adventures. Several times, as we shall see, the dark and ominous cloud of the Assyrian army swept through the pass of Megiddo and down the coastal plain against Philistine cities or Egypt or Jerusalem, and earlier against the city of Samaria, whose three-year siege left the army time for savage entertainment and sadistic diversion in neighboring areas like Moresheth. Little wonder that Micah spoke with outrage against the social injustices and religious sham by which the administration at Jerusalem sought to distract the country from the dangers of war and the plight of the poor.

The "original" Micah leveled his criticism principally against religious and civil leaders for tolerating these excesses and then gaining financially from it all (see the commentary on 3:5-8). No hope was left when the defenders of religion and morality were themselves corrupted by pleasure and greed.

Micah's continuous interaction with temple and religious traditions, with social justice and civil leadership, points up a person with keen penetration into present reality and long roots into "ancient times" (5:1). Although he was oriented toward Jerusalem and the Davidic dynasty (4:14–5:4), he draws near at times to the style of the more northern traditions of Deuteronomy and is seriously concerned about the northern kingdom of Israel or Samaria (1:2-7; 6:16). He makes poignant use of the Exodus tradition in 6:1-5, again a more northern motif.

Micah's heirs kept his prophetic words closely in touch with the ever new "present reality," now the Babylonian Exile, a century and a half later. In fact, Babylon, the place of exile, is named in 4:10. One of the two closing psalms offers the discouraged people of postexilic times a prayer for rebuilding the walls of Jerusalem (7:11).

The person of Micah

From the background of the Book of Micah, we have already begun to appreciate his character and person. Micah hails from the village of Moresheth (1:1). This city is also considered in some way a dependent of the Philistine city of Gath. The phrase "Moresheth-gath" (1:14) means "property of Gath." Originally Gath belonged to the Philistine Pentapolis of Gath, Gaza, Ashkelon, Ekron, and Ashdod, all in the southwest coastlands. These cities passed in and out of the control of the Israelites and at this time contained a strong contingent of Israelites. It is not at all impossible that Moresheth was administered through Gath. Moresheth was about twenty miles southwest of Jerusalem, nestled in the foothills overlooking the Mediterranean.

Moresheth influenced the language of Micah. His was not the desert imagery of Amos nor even the strong agricultural or rural setting of Hosea, and certainly not the cosmopolitan sophistication of Isaiah. Micah refers to the fields owned by the villagers (2:2, 4-5), the threshing floors on the hillside (4:12). More attention is given to the greedy plans and rapacious actions of people who come from the larger Jerusalem and who, in the comfort of their rented homes at Moresheth, covet and cheat (6:11) and take possession of whatever they desire (2:1-2; 6:9-11). They take over fields because of unpaid debts (2:2, 4). They strip off the mantle of debtors, which the law prescribed always to be returned at sundown (2:8).

The question is raised whether or not Micah belonged to the class of elders at Moresheth, for it was a group of "elders of the land" who recalled his words in Jer 26:17-18. In this case he would have been one of the judges at the city gate (Deut 17:5; 21:19; Ruth 4:1), responsible as well for defending the rights of the small town against the royal officials from Jerusalem. Another suggestion links Micah with "the people of the land," a group who reached back to the early days of David and always remained loyal to the ancient family. They were suspicious of others who manipulated the throne and its power for their own benefit (2 Kgs 11:18-20; 14:21; 21:24). Micah does not oppose the dynasty but wants to see it restored to its pristine purity and purpose, as when he sees its future no longer in Jerusalem but in ancient Bethlehem (Mic 4:14–5:4).

Micah and Isaiah

Both Micah and his contemporary Isaiah interacted vigorously with the Davidic dynasty but with a number of differences. While Isaiah's interests remained with the capital city of Jerusalem (Isa 1; 2:1-5; 4:2-6; 8:5-10), Micah's sympathies gravitated toward Bethlehem. Isaiah was the aristocrat, firmly attached to Jerusalem and its temple, a brilliant poet, a politician with international perspective; Micah was a countryman, less suave, brutal at times in his language, a poor person suffering with the poor rather than a wealthy person defending their rights. Sin for Isaiah turned out to be the sacrilegious act of polluting the temple (Isa 4:4); for Micah it was the callousness of stripping a man of his mantle and driving "the women of my people . . . from their pleasant homes" (Mic 2:8-9). Isaiah was the herald of a faith that demanded respect for the mysterious holiness of Yahweh; Micah was the prophet of divine justice for the inviolable rights of the poor.

Micah and Isaiah were contemporaries. It seems, however, that Isaiah began the prophetic ministry earlier, for he interacted vigorously with the king's policies at the time of the Syro-Ephraimite crisis (735–732 B.C.E.). Syria (or Damascus) and Ephraim (or Israel) had formed a coalition against Assyria; they marched against Judah when its King Ahaz refused to join (Isa 7:1-2; 22:1-14). Micah does not seem to allude to it. King Ahaz's pro-Assyrian policy was reversed into active revolt by King Hezekiah, much to the dismay of Isaiah. The king's bad politics led to an invasion by Sennacherib around 701 B.C.E. In preparation for this invasion, King Hezekiah had taken over landed property in the foothills to the west of Jerusalem. Was it at this time that many of the people of Moresheth lost their property? In this case Hezekiah may go down in the annals of the books of Kings and Chronicles as a very pious reformer of idolatrous and insincere worship (2 Kgs 18–20; 2 Chr 29–32), yet he would have remained insensitive or blind to the many social injustices left unchecked in the midst of the feverish liturgical reform or later in the all-absorbing preparations for war.

We place Micah at the earliest around 727 B.C.E., certainly before the collapse of Samaria (721 B.C.E.); his ministry would have extended into 701, the time of Sennacherib's invasion of Judah.

COMMENTARY

INTRODUCTION

Mic 1:1-2

1:1 Historical introduction. As in the case of Amos, this book too begins with some historical orientation and then with a religious, melodic opening. The editor lists Micah as prophesying under three kings, from Jotham through the reign of Ahaz into the time of Hezekiah (742–696 B.C.E.). Because the book says little or nothing about the great crisis during the reign of Ahaz, we confine his ministry to the time of Hezekiah. The editor may be thinking of Micah's earlier activity as an elder defending the rights of the dispossessed before his preaching came to the attention of many others.

Clearly enough, Micah's ministry is linked with the flow of history, particularly that of his own time. The Bible points out that God does not create the ideal setting for redemptive activity; God accepts us as we are in our total environment. The prophet's word is the product of its own age. Eternal truths emerge from the prophets, not as generic predictions of the future but rather as ideals and hopes rising from the trials and triumphs of the moment. The editor refers to "the vision he [Micah] received." Prophets peered beneath the surface to the ancient covenant, its laws and hopes, and to the merciful God who made Israel a special people. From this perspective came forth ideals and expectations for the present into the future.

1:2 Religious introduction. This verse seems to have been added somewhat late. It has all the marks of non-Mican authorship: Yahweh as accuser-witness is not found until Mal 3:5, in the postexilic age; "holy temple" is an expression not normally used at this time; "peoples, all of you" is a phrase from later literature like Lam 1:18; Ps 67:4, 6; and the use of *'adonai* or "Lord" as a title for Yahweh does not occur again in the Book of Micah. Other aspects of this opening verse link it with other familiar introductions, such as the canticle of Moses in Deut 32:1 and the prophecy of Isaiah in Isa 1:2. The later editor is adapting Micah's book to a common style. While these pieces of biblical literature are directed rather exclusively to Israel, this opening or formal prelude has a universal ring ("O peoples . . . O earth") and touches everyone with faith in God, regardless of religious differences. **all that fills you:** This refers to the abundant gift of life across the earth, vegetation, animals, birds, fishes, and humanity. **his holy temple:** See the commentary on 1:3-4, below.

THREATS AGAINST SAMARIA AND JUDAH

Mic 1:3–3:12

The principal sermons of Micah against social injustices are gathered in this initial collection. The opening poem rivals some of the best in Isaiah. It comprises a theophany introducing Yahweh the Judge (vv. 3-4); presentation of the evidence (v. 5) and sentencing of the culprit (vv. 6-7); after these judicial procedures, mostly related to the final years of Samaria, a long lamentation is added as the same fate strikes Judah in the Assyrian invasion under Sennacherib in 701 B.C.E. (vv. 8-16).

1:3-4 Micah begins the trial of defendant Israel with a solemn entry of the divine Judge; the language here is that of a theophany (meaning "God's manifestation"). We are reminded of the fragments of hymns in Amos about Yahweh forming the mountains, declaring to people their inmost thoughts, and treading upon the heights of the earth (Amos 4:13; also 5:8-9; 9:5-6). Although the passage infers Yahweh's presence in earthly sanctuaries, the primary residence or throne is located above the waters of the heavens, as any number of biblical passages indicate (see Pss 11:4; 19:2; 29:9; Hos 5:15; Isa 29:21). The trembling and even the melting and collapsing of the earth at the touch of the Lord's presence are literary devices for inculcating the Lord's awesome wonder, mighty power, and transforming force upon human life, as declared at Mount Sinai (Exod 19), at the crossing of the Red Sea and the Jordan River (Psalm 114), at Israel's wandering through the wilderness (Ps 68:8-11), at Yahweh's response to the king (Ps 18:8-20).

1:5 Crimes especially of ritual immorality are brought against the defendant, the northern kingdom of Israel, under the name of its ancestor Jacob. The nation's religious and civil leaders, as we saw also in the Book of Hosea, bear the brunt of the responsibility for tolerating and even encouraging such gross transgressions of Yahweh's holiness. **house of Judah . . . Jerusalem:** After the collapse of the northern kingdom, a later editor, applies the statement to the southerners. The verdict of "Guilty!" leads to the harsh sentencing of total destruction (vv. 6-7); for a similar outcome, see Amos 4:2b-3; Hos 4:3. **1:7 idols:** These include not only the golden calf at Dan and Bethel, originally the pedestal for Yahweh's invisible presence but superstitiously turned into an object of worship (see Hos 8:5; 13:2), but also the symbols of male and female deities of fertility (Hos 9:10-14). **wages:** The term refers to the "gifts" to the prostitutes in fertility rites, what Deut 23:19 calls "a harlot's fee or a dog's price" (also Hos 2:11, 14; 9:1). **shall they return:** What the Assyrian soldiers looted from Israel's temples will be returned to Assyrian sanctuaries as favors for their own sacred prostitutes.

1:8-9 This lament is prompted by the agony experienced by Micah's own country of Judah, which has imitated the sin of Samaria and must therefore suffer the same punishment. Several serious theological issues emerge here:

1) Must God inflict such horrendous pain as a military invasion with plunder, rape, fire, and deportation? While there is no satisfactory answer for what remains a mystery of faith, there are several "fixed spikes" (Eccl 12:11) on which to hang our reflections. Military invasion as "evil [that] has come down from the Lord" (Mic 1:12) results from God's willingness to work out our salvation in the midst of human history. Here God's presence can function quietly within our slow process of reasoning and decision-making, but it can also function within other, more violent forms of human reaction. Secondly, when the reward from God is superhuman, even though accomplished on a human level, the struggle turns out superhuman as well, as we recognize in the cross of Jesus.

2) Another theological issue centers on Micah's participation, already by premonition, in the savage outcome of military invasion: "I go barefoot and naked" (v. 8; see Amos 2:16; 3:12). He imitates the action of the prophet of Jerusalem who around 713 B.C.E. went about "walking naked and barefoot . . . as a sign" (Isa 20:2-3). Why must the innocent suffer? Why must the wicked suffer, as Habakkuk will ask (1:13), when they are still "more just" than their conqueror? The presence of the innocent—in this case a prophet like Micah and the small villages in the way of the Assyrian army—provides the only hope for arriving at peace and human dignity as God wants.

1:10-16 In naming the cities leveled by Sennacherib on his way to Jerusalem in 701 B.C.E. Micah chooses small ones, for the most part clustered around his own village of Moresheth; some are not mentioned elsewhere in the Bible, not even in the listing of cities "in the foothills" (Josh 15:22-47). Often he announces the sorrow to be inflicted on the city by a play on words. Every Hebrew word has a meaning. At times the text has been tampered with and at other times poorly preserved.

1:10 publish it not in Gath: These words were taken from 2 Sam 1:20, part of David's dirge over Jonathan, where he mentions Philistine cities in the area of Moresheth. In Hebrew, "publish" begins with the word "Gath" spelled backward. **weep not at all:** This probably ought to read "weep not at Ko," so that the phrase "at Ko" *(bako)* relates to the Hebrew word for "weep," *bakah*. **In Beth-leaphrah roll in the dust:** the word *aphrah* in the name of the village signifies "dust"; *beth* means "house." The phrase might be read: "In the house of dust roll in the dust." The word for "roll" in Hebrew contains sounds similar to the Hebrew word for "house" and for "Philistine."

1:13 Harness steeds to the chariots, O inhabitants of Lachish: Not only do the words "chariots" and "Lachish" sound alike in Hebrew, but the entire line has a continual interchange of the letters.

1:14 Give parting gifts to Moresheth-gath: Because Moresheth, as already mentioned, denotes gift (received) or dowry, the play on words implies, "Give a gift to the gift of Gath."

2:1-5 Micah loved the pleasant fields of the Shephelah, the name given to the rolling, falling hills between the central mountain range and the Mediterranean coastland (in Hebrew *shephal* means "to fall"). Micah mourned, even cursed their loss. By contrast,

Amos never felt the same attachment to the fierce silence of the desert that Micah did to the Shephelah. Micah detests the way in which the fields were coveted at night and seized in the morning. People were not even ashamed of carrying out their evil dreams in open daylight.

The sacrilegious nature of the action becomes clear from such texts as Lev 25:23-24, in which God declares that "the land shall not be sold in perpetuity; for the land is mine, and you are but aliens who have become my tenants. Therefore . . . [every jubilee year] you must permit the land to be redeemed." Wealthy landowners, perhaps from the powerful city of Jerusalem, confiscated whatever they wished for it "lies within their power," words found identically in a long series of texts: Gen 31:29; Deut 28:32; Neh 5:5; Prov 3:27. The problem existed a long time and was always detestable to the Lord. **2:3 from which you shall not withdraw your neck:** The first words are an alliteration in Hebrew. **2:5 you shall have no one** to redistribute the land to the rightful owner once the exile sets in.

From the literary viewpoint, these verses carefully complement each other: what the people carefully plan and quickly accomplish in verses 1-2, God just as quickly reverses in verses 3-5.

2:6-11 Ancient and modern translators come up with different versions and interpretations. Is verse 6 ridiculing or affirming Micah? Is verse 10a spoken by the greedy despoilers ordering the poor from their ancestral land, or is it a command from foreign soldiers to depart for exile? Yet we may be able to detect a balanced structure: verses 6-7, an accusation against Micah and God, with a short reply from God; verses 8-11, spoken by Micah, recounting the people's sins (vv. 8-9), their punishment (v. 10), and finally a repetition of the accusation against Micah, now turned against the people (v. 11).

2:6 preach: The Hebrew verb can be taken in a derogatory sense suggesting saliva dripping out of the mouth of a prophet stirred into a rabid, ecstatic spasm (consider 1 Sam 10:10-12 and 19:22-24; 1 Kgs 18; Acts 2:13). The people consider themselves pious sanctuary-goers, so how can "the Lord be short of patience" (v. 7a)? God quickly replies that divine words promise good things only to those who act uprightly (v. 7b). Verses 8-9 are an eloquent condemnation of those who keep what the law clearly stipulates is to be returned to the poor man at sundown lest he contract intestinal colds (see Amos 2:8). Women and children are deprived of their inalienable honor and their right to the land. The culprits are ordered into exile because of their cruelty and greed. **2:10 rest:** The word may refer to their once happy and peaceful lodging in the land (Ps 95:11; Deut 12:19). **2:11 futile claim:** The phrase can be translated more literally, as in the Revised Standard Version, as "wind and lies." The people's mockery of Micah during their drunken revelry in the sanctuary (see Amos 2:8) ricochets upon themselves.

2:12-13 This passage is generally considered an exilic or postexilic addition, a minor upbeat note in the midst of Micah's condemnations. Verse 12 refers to the gathering of Israel safely within the sheepfold; verse 13 to Israel's breaking loose into a new freedom toward the Promised Land. In this case the king is Yahweh. According to another explanation, the verses are spoken by the false prophets of verse 11, who make use of liturgical language to reassure Jerusalem that all is well. Verse 11 attributes these false hopes to the euphoric effects of strong drink. Verses 12-13 present a liturgical procession with the solemn opening of the gates of city and temple as the ark is carried through the city back again into the holy of holies (see Psalm 24). A third possibility remains, namely, accepting both interpretations according to different periods when Micah is being read.

Chapter 3 counters the greed of Israel's leaders with some of the most violent language in prophecy. Living during the Assyrian epoch of international history, Micah and his neighbors in the villages of the Shephelah will experience the atrocious cruelty of the Assyrian army. Again the question is raised about Yahweh's interaction in history (see 1:8-9). The chapter is carefully structured: verses 1-4, against civil rulers in the northern kingdom of Israel (spoken between 727 and 721 B.C.E.); verses 5-8, against prophets, seemingly closer at hand in Judah of the southern kingdom; verses 9-12, a conclusion that condemns all categories of leadership but focuses upon Jerusalem and its impending destruction. The literary device of "inclusion" (repetition of key words) binds together verse 1 and verse 9, so that verse 9 and the following three verses bring the poem to a strong ending. They apply emphatically to Jerusalem what verses 1-4 had been directing toward the northern kingdom of Israel, an area that now lay in ruins with its population in exile.

3:1-4 These words are addressed to the "leaders of Jacob . . . the house of Israel." The opening phrase, "And I said," denotes an emphatic reversal—"But on the contrary I say!" This fact endorses the second of the interpretations for 2:12-13 (see above). The word "rulers" shows up in Isa 1:10; 3:6, 7; 22:3 for other incapable and venal leaders.

3:2b-3 The language is graphic, even crude, drawn from the action of preparing an animal for ritual sacrifice (see Lev 1:3-9). In a milder form it appears in Pss 14:4; 53:5, and with agonizing moan in Ps 79:1-4. **3:4 cry to the Lord:** In the Bible civil leaders are responsible both to God and to those they govern (Rom 13:1). These leaders, however, deliberately use their divine origin as a club over the people. **hide his face:** The phrase is repeated in Ps 10:11 by wicked rulers as an excuse to proceed in their wickedness; and in Ps 13:2 by persecuted people appealing to God to make the divine presence felt. Micah invokes the phrase as punishment upon the evil rulers.

3:5-8 Micah is not condemning all divination, only that directed by greed, which included most of it in his day. Again the language is graphic and eloquent: feed them well and they declare *shalom;* fail to be generous to their rapacious appetite and (literally) "they sanctify a war against that one." As in Jer 6:4 and Joel 4:8, the word "holy" or "sanctify" occurs, stirring the whole discussion of what is called a "holy war," well known in the history of religions. **3:7 cover their lips:** This is a sign of mourning (Ezek 24:17-22) and of being contagiously unclean (Lev 13:45). Verse 8 provides the purpose of Micah's ministry and clearly states its credentials. **with the spirit of the Lord:** This translation may not be the best. The Hebrew word for "spirit" was used by Micah in a pejorative sense in 2:11, "wind and lies." The Hebrew word can mean both "wind" and "spirit." Micah was completely disillusioned by the sensual, greedy prophets, who were driven by "wind" (see 1 Sam 10:10-13; 19:22-24).

3:9-12 A conclusion in verse 9 repeats key ideas of verse 1; verse 10 relates to the bloodshed in verses 2-3. Verse 11 condemns all leaders with the single charge of greed, yet they have the audacity to claim that God is on their side as they repeat sacred language found also in Amos 5:14 and Isa 7:14. Verse 12 will be cited by the elders of the land in Jer 26:16-19 to protect Jeremiah from being put to death for declaring that Jerusalem can be destroyed "like Shiloh." Shiloh once housed the ark of the covenant and had been the center of Mosaic religion (1 Sam 1–3), yet it was destroyed by the Philistines who captured the ark (1 Sam 4). Micah is said to have spoken these words "in the days of Hezekiah" (Jer 26:18), a king zealous for the reform of the liturgy (2 Kgs 18–20; 2 Chr 29–32) but evidently blind to other abuses against the poor. Because of Hezekiah's piety, the leaders claimed "the Lord in the midst of us" (Mic 3:11).

As we reflect on chapters 2–3, we ponder the cost in human misery because of greed and sensuality in leadership, first driving the people from their pleasant houses (2:9), finally reducing Jerusalem to rubble (3:12).

GATHERING OF THE POOR AND THE OUTCASTS

Mic 4:1–5:14

During the time of the Babylonian Exile, the material in chapters 4–5 was gathered from a reservoir or treasury of prophetic material, some from the prophet Micah, some attracted to the Micah texts by association of words or themes. The purpose of the editor seems clear enough by comparing 3:12 and its view of Jerusalem "reduced to rubble" with 4:1 and its vision of Jerusalem to which "peoples shall stream." The violent devastation of chapters 1–3 is reversed in a peaceful reconstruction. Although familiar historical names like Assyria and Babylon (4:10; 5:4), Jerusalem and Bethlehem (4:2; 5:1) reappear, they also seem to merge with other legendary names like Nimrod (5:5), are caught up in idyllic vision (4:1-3), or else are placed in perplexing parallel, like Bat-gader and Bethlehem (4:14; 5:1). Enough of Micah's style is preserved to ground us in his legitimate school of prophecy, yet too much of the visionary or symbolic is spread through the chapters for us not to strain our eyes beyond Micah's time into the "messianic" future.

Perhaps Israel's liturgical tradition is the most responsible agent for this blending of antiquity with the messianic future. Liturgy has a knack of extracting the best from historical reality, separating it from its political and military context, and highlighting God's concern—in this case, to create a new Jerusalem. This process was already at work in such pre-exilic psalms as Psalms 46–48, and it reaches sublime prophetic expression in Isa 65:17–66:24. As we will see below, the association of the Isaiah tradition suffused a new hope and grandeur about the text of Micah.

4:1-5 A number of oracles from a large prophetic repertoire reappear here. It is difficult to know who is the author, but it is certainly not Micah, for the passage would have neutralized his angry condemnation of Jerusalem in 3:12. Lines reappear in Isa 2:2-4, Zech 3:10; 1 Kgs 5:5; Joel 4:10, never with exactly the same meaning.

4:1 In days to come: The Greek text and the Aramaic Targum make it read: "at the end of days," that is, in the messianic age. **higher than the mountains:** This is to be understood only religiously, for even the Mount of Olives, just to the east, reaches a higher altitude than Jerusalem. A similar idea occurs in Pss 68:16-19; 89:13; Isa 60:1-3; 66:23. These texts already hint at the universal outreach of verse 2: "many nations . . . shall come and . . . climb the mount of the Lord." A lovely counterpoint is perceived here: while nations stream up the mount, instruction flows down and goes forth.

4:3 He shall judge: The subject is not clear, but it is probably Yahweh. Joel 4:10 quotes from this vision, only to reverse it into a statement of war. Earlier, in Joel 4:1-2, the nations are assembled for judgment in the Valley of Jehoshaphat (the word means "Yahweh judges"). For this reason many Jews, Christians, and Muslims today want to be buried in this valley between Jerusalem and the Mount of Olives.

Verse 5 draws our eyes away from the glorious liturgy on the temple mount to the homey setting of each one's vine and fig tree—a warning against liturgical excesses! Verse 6 was added last, correcting what seemed to be the overenthusiastic "ecumenism" of verses 1-3. This text in Micah at least leaves the pagans at peace with their paganism (see Deut 4:19-20; 29:25; 32:8-9 for a similar reaction). The conversion of the nations and their dignified and equal reunion with Israel waited for St. Paul to argue the case in the letter to the Romans (Rom 9–11).

4:6-8 Someone in the days of exile looks back upon "the former dominion" (v. 8)—either the days of Micah or better the kingdom of David and Solomon—and recognizes the Lord as King (notice the end of the Davidic dynasty) over the remnant of people who are lame, outcasts, and afflicted. This scene of Jerusalem is considerably different from that in 4:1-3. We recognize the influence, or at least the parallels, joining the passage to Isa 35:4-6, 10; 41:17, from the time of the Babylonian Exile or later. **Magdal-eder:** The name means "tower of the flock," and is another name for the temple as a home and refuge for the flock of Israel.

4:9-10 As it stands, this poem seems to reflect best of all the period of the Babylonian Exile. Even if the poem was further refined during the Exile, its original composition may reflect King Hezekiah's agreement with Babylon, through its representative Merodach-baladan, against Assyria; the prophet Isaiah had reacted strongly against the negotiations. The solution to Judah's troubles was closer to home in remedying its social injustices (see 2 Kgs 20:12-19, repeated in Isa 39). **Writhe in pain:** The language of childbirth implies that new life lies hidden beneath the suffering of the people. **the Lord redeem:** The Hebrew word for "redeem" implies a blood bond and its consequent obligations of family love (see Lev 25:23-55).

4:11-13 The language of harvesting is applied to Israel's victory over hostile nations. This short poem may have been composed, possibly by Micah, for a harvest festival. Yet Micah's more persistent attitude of repudiating a military solution in favor of internal moral reform points to another author. The poem was stitched in here by the reference to Israel's enemies at the end of verse 10.

4:14–5:5 The play on words in verse 14 makes it difficult to be certain of the text and of the historical circumstances; the setting is probably the time of the Assyrian siege of Jerusalem under Sennacherib in 701 (see 2 Kgs 18:13–19:37; Isa 36–37). Theologically Micah and Isaiah realize the hopelessness of the current Davidic kings; even pious King Hezekiah proved ineffective in stemming the country's immorality but sought a military solution by revolting against Assyria. Both prophets begin to look to a *future* Davidic king. For his part, Micah indicates this by shifting attention from strong, cosmopolitan, and permissively immoral Jerusalem to small, honest, and God-fearing Bethlehem, where the prophet Samuel went to choose a king (1 Sam 16:1-13). The Lord's favor rested on young David.

4:14 The Hebrew word for "fence yourself in" is the same as *gader* in *Bat-gader;* the word for "rod" sounds very much like that for "ruler." *Bat-gader* harmonizes with *Bethlehem.*

5:1 Ephrathah: This is a place-name for a spot north of Jerusalem near Ramah where Rachel died (1 Sam 10:2; Jer 31:15); it is also the name of a clan, descendants of Ephrathah, the second wife of Caleb (see 1 Chr 2:18-19, 50-55, where reference is made to people called Bethgader and Bethlehem). These people settled around Bethlehem, south of Jerusalem, and also at Jaar, or Kiriath-jearim, west of Jerusalem (Ps 132:6). Later tradition confusedly located Rachel's tomb near Bethlehem (Gen 35:19; Ruth 4:11), where it is venerated today as a popular Israeli shrine. **whose origin is from of old, from ancient times:** The Hebrew text uses the plural, "origins," referring to the long, three-hundred year history of the Davidic dynasty with its accumulated promises and hopes; "ancient" does not necessarily mean eternal, but far away in the very distant past or future (see the final verse in the Book of Micah; also Isa 51:9).

5:2 she who is to give birth: Similar to Isaiah (7:14), Micah highlights the mother of the future Davidic king; in Old Testament times the queen-mother occupied an important place at court (1 Kgs 1:11-37; 2 Kgs 10:13). The silence about the father in this verse is interpreted by early Christian writers as an indication of the virginal conception of the promised Messiah. Verse 3 reflects the aura of mystery and promises surrounding the Davidic dynasty, as in Psalm 72.

5:4 he shall be peace: The New American Bible and the Revised Standard Version connect this line with the preceding description of the new Davidic king from insignificant Bethlehem. The Hebrew text joins the line with the following announcement of future shepherds and leaders whom God will raise up to deliver Israel from Assyrian domination. In this latter case a better translation would be: "this [plan] will be peace." Christian tradition certainly favors the former position. Nimrod, ancestor of Mesopotamian peoples (Gen 10:8-12), surrounds the text with mystery. **seven shepherds, eight men of royal rank:** Although rabbinical sources identify these persons, Micah is probably speaking symbolically, as Amos does in 1:3, 5.

5:6-8 Typically un-Micah in style and ideas, this military solution is from the time of the Exile. **remnant:** By now this is an important prophetical theme (see Amos 3:12, 5:15; Isa 7:3; 10:19-22). **Like dew coming:** The dew appears without rain, almost miraculously, a symbol of God's gift of life (Pss 110:3 [Hebrew text]; 133:3; Job 38:28), mentioned in many blessings (Gen 27:28; Deut 32:2; Isa 45:8).

5:9-14 This section ends with vintage Micah, with the destruction of Israel's military forces (vv. 9-10) and idolatrous sanctuaries (vv. 11-13). The final verse, however, condemns "the nations," so that the final word in chapters 4–5 turns in Israel's favor. "Sacred pillars" and "sacred poles" (vv. 12-13) refer to stone pillars and wooden poles representing the male and female fertility deities (Exod 34:13; Deut 16:21-22).

NEW THREATS

Mic 6:1–7:7

The second major section of threats (6:1–7:7) and promises (7:8-20) repeats the sequence of the first. The threats occupy less space than in the first section, and the Hebrew text is even more disturbed; the promises come from the period of the Exile or still later. Memorable lines occur, to resonate again in the New Testament and in the liturgy.

6:1-8 As the Hebrew word for "plea" in verses 1-2 clearly denotes, these verses follow the sequence of a legal procedure: verses 1-2, summoning the court, particularly the witnesses, and naming the defendant; verses 3-5, cross-questioning the defendant; verses 6-7, the defendant's reply and final statement; verse 8, the judge's verdict—probation—as in Isa 1:16.

The appeal in verses 1-2 to the universe as the courtroom and to the mountains and the earth's foundations as star witnesses follows a biblical pattern already found in Mic 1:2 but also in Deut 32:1; Ps 50:1-6. In the questioning of verses 3-4, not only is there an appeal to the Lord's gracious deeds, but we also glimpse God's personal agony over Israel's apostasy. These lines inspired the *Improperia* sung during the veneration of the cross on Good Friday. The abrupt "Answer me!" puts a limit on God's patience. The text of verse 5 is defective.

Miriam, seldom alluded to in the Bible, is accorded honorable mention with Moses and Aaron. The story of King Balak's summoning of the seer Balaam to curse Israel and his act of blessing Israel instead, is told in Num 22–24. Shittim (the word means "acacia tree") was the final stage of the journey from Egypt to the eastern bank of the Jordan River (Num 33:49); Gilgal was the famous sanctuary on the western banks near Jericho (Amos 4:4). This entire history from the Exodus out of Egypt to the settlement in the Promised Land is encapsulated as "the just deeds of the Lord," that is, God's complete or just fulfillment of every promise (see Josh 23:14).

6:7-8 The people seek shelter in feverish ritual actions as in Hos 6:1-7; 7:8; they even sacrifice their first-born, as was done by King Ahaz (2 Kgs 16:3) and King Manasseh (2 Kgs 21:6). They ritually slaughter their own children, imagining to appease God against their oppression of the poor. God's verdict, nonetheless, allows a second chance: "to do the right," as stipulated in the laws of the covenant; "to love goodness" according to bonds attaching them to one another and to Yahweh in the covenant; and "to walk humbly" by realizing that God's compassion is their only hope. This advice is addressed to "you . . . O man"; the Hebrew word *'adam* includes men and women in a very generic sense, reaching outward to all humankind as in Gen 1–3.

6:9-16 The trial scene continues. In verses 9-12 Israel's crimes of greed and injustice are made public (see 2:1-3; 3:11). Verses 13-16 pronounce sentence against the defendant. Yet, because of the poor condition of the Hebrew text, we cannot be sure. Notice how the New American Bible juggles the verses to make better sense! The statements can easily be from Micah, assembled here somewhat freely as though for an appendix (see Amos 9:7-10). **6:9 cries to the city:** Without doubt the city is Jerusalem. **6:10-11 criminal hoarding . . . meager ephah . . . criminal balances . . . false weights:** The repetition is devastating—how low the wealthy stoop in swindling the poor and illiterate! As a result, they themselves and the entire country are completely out of balance, their delicate bonding with the Lord is upset, and their family life is torn apart (see Mic 7:5-6). **6:13 I will begin to strike you:** Here the New American Bible follows the ancient versions of the Greek and Syriac by slightly modifying the Hebrew from *halah* ("to become sick") to *halal* ("to begin"). The Hebrew reveals God's anguish (as in 6:3 and especially in Hos 11:8-9): "On the contrary *it is I myself,* sickened [by the fact that I] must strike you with devastation . . . ." **6:14 food that will leave you empty:** The meaning is not clear; it is possibly a reference to dysentery, weakness, and shame. Verse 16 is addressed directly to the northern kingdom, where Omri achieved fame by building the new capital city of Samaria (1 Kgs 16:23-28) and Ahab by defeating Damascus (1 Kgs 20), yet both were condemned for their religious indifference and social injustice. In this case verses 9-16 represent the early preaching of Micah; or else Micah applies to Jerusalem, at a later date, the lesson of the northern kingdom, whose magnificence collapsed into ruins as a "reproach of the nations."

7:1-7 This lamentation finds Micah sharing the sorrowful destruction of his own people, caused by their interior disintegration, yet in the end he says, "I look to the Lord" (v. 7). Again the Hebrew text is plagued by less than careful transmission. With a touch of pathos, Micah identifies with the vineyard far more completely and personally than Isaiah in Isa 5:1-5. This section about deception and betrayal in family and nation begins with "Alas!" in verse 1 and with "the faithful" in verse 2, the latter word denoting the blood bond and its normal obligations (see Hos 2:21-22). This passage may have influenced Jesus' cursing the fig tree that failed to provide fruit (Mark 11:12-14) and his statement about division in marriage and family (Matt 10:34-37; Luke 12:52-53). The selfish destroy themselves from within.

REBUILDING FROM ANCIENT PROMISES

Mic 7:8-20

Like other prophetical books, Micah's ends happily. In the final verse Micah reaches into the earliest traditions about the patriarchs to assure us of God's faithfulness in the future. A series of allusions to the time of the Exile help establish the date: a final collapse in darkness (v. 8); admission of guilt in experiencing the wrath of God (v. 9); wishing shame upon the enemy (v. 10); the walls of Jerusalem are still in ruins (v. 11). Verses 11-13 were added in the early postexilic Judah, but before the rebuilding of the walls by Nehemiah in 445 B.C.E. (Neh 2:17-20; 6:15).

7:8-10 An address by Jerusalem, possibly against Edom, which plundered the city, or what was left of it, after its destruction by the Babylonians in 587 B.C.E. Hatred rose to white heat against Edom, as we observe in Isa 63:1-6 and in the entire Book of Obadiah. "Fallen, I will arise" overturns the dire statements of Amos 5:12 over the "house of Israel . . . fallen, to rise no more"; "in darkness, the Lord is my light" reverses Amos 5:18: "day of the Lord . . . darkness and not light." Verse 10 is a filigree of customary formulas: "cover with shame" (Pss 35:26; 44:16; 89:46); "Where is the Lord?" (Pss 42:4, 11; 79:10; Joel 2:17); "trampled underfoot" (Isa 5:5; 7:25; 28:18). When we are numbed by pain and despair, we can only fall back upon customary or memorized prayers in order to discover thereby a new hope from the faith of our ancestors.

7:11-13 Now that the empire of David and Solomon is only a memory, hope transforms it into a new universal kingdom, to be achieved by God's mysterious power "from sea to sea." When the theology and legal system of postexilic Israel tended to become ever more narrow and exclusive, the liturgy drew upon memories to dream what God will do and so prepared for the universal apostolate of Christianity. Verse 12 is an allusion to the theme of the day of the Lord, derived from Amos as a time of overwhelming darkness for Israel (5:18) but in later tradition changed into a day of victory (Isa 11:10-11; 12). **they shall come:** The subject is left vague. Is it foreign countries coming to worship Yahweh? Or to pillage Jerusalem? Does "they" refer to the Diaspora Jews returning to Jerusalem from their homes in foreign countries? **7:13 land shall be a waste:** Possibly this is the devastated appearance of Yehud (or Judah) upon the first return (see Haggai).

7:14-17 This prayer of confidence asks God to bring back the idyllic days "when you came from the land of Egypt." Mount Carmel is to the west, Bashan and Gilead to the east (see Amos 4:1). Nations shall stand or collapse in awe and subjugation, with their hands over their mouths (Judg 18:19; Isa 51:15) or licking the dust (Gen 3:14). This is ecumenism or universalism at its worst!

7:18-20 The opening phrase, literally "Who is God like you," may have inspired the name of this book—Micah. Yet the phrase is somewhat elaborate compared to Micah's short name ("who is like" God). Verse 18 is possibly a renewal of the covenant (Exod 34:1-9). **7:20 faithfulness . . . and grace:** These words repeat the great virtues of the Mosaic covenant (see Hos 2:21-22; 4:1; Ps 89:2-3, 25, 34), which are seen to reach back to the patriarchs. Just as the mention of Miriam in 6:4 is rare in the Old Testament, the name of Abraham appears here in somewhat isolated splendor in the Hebrew Bible. Micah can look hopefully to the future because of his loyalty to tradition.

NAHUM

Carroll Stuhlmueller, C.P.

INTRODUCTION

Historical setting

Nahum, one of the most eloquent orators in the Bible, shouts, sings, and celebrates: "Nineveh is destroyed!," and he adds at once, with a play on his own name (Nahum means "the one consoled"): "Where can one find any to console her?" (3:7). For over three hundred years Assyria had controlled the Near Eastern world; the capital city had been Nineveh for over one hundred years (see the attention given to Nineveh in Gen 10:11-12). Assyria ruled by calculated terror and brutality (see the comments on Amos 2:16; 3:12), exacting heavy tribute, permitting no compromise nor repudiation of treaty, deporting entire populations, as in the case of the kingdom of Israel in 732 and 721 B.C.E., and moving new groups of people into the former territory. With clenched fist and fiery despair, people shouted at the silent skies: "How long, O Lord? Will you hide yourself forever?" (Ps 89:47), words still echoing in the New Testament: "How long will it be, O Master, . . . before you judge our cause and avenge our blood?" (Rev 6:10). Nahum's book is the Hallelujah chorus of triumphant relief. In his final verse he writes of Nineveh's destruction, "All who hear of this news of you clap their hands over you" (3:19). Details about the disintegration of Assyria are provided in the introduction to the Book of Zephaniah (p. 524).

Nineveh (in northern Iraq) was destroyed in 612 B.C.E. by a coalition of Babylonians (in southern Iraq) and Medes and Persians (in present-day Iran), with the help of smaller tribes. The leveling was so complete that when Xenophon passed by the site of Nineveh in 401 B.C.E., he was able to learn from the local inhabitants only that a great people had once occupied the site and had been destroyed (*Anabasis*, Bk. III, ch. IV, 10-12). Nahum composed this rhapsody of excitement and grandeur after 663 B.C.E., when Assyria captured and looted Egypt's sacred city of Thebes (see 3:8), probably after 627 B.C.E., when Babylon successfully revolted and achieved independence, but before the fall of Nineveh in 612 B.C.E.

Nahum writes so vividly that some claim that his native city of Elkosh was near Nineveh (where the Iraqi locate it today), but everyone even in far-off Judah knew about Nineveh, a city of 1800 acres with a population possibly as high as 288,000. A double line of fortifications lay to its east, the Tigris River to its west. The city had a circumference of eight miles, with moats sometimes 150 feet broad and colossal walls, some of whose ruins rise 25 to 60 feet above the surface today. While its armies cannibalized the world, its rulers patronized the arts. Ashurbanipal collected the "ancient classics," which provide entry for us today into the myths, folklore, religion, and legal systems of the area.

Style and theology

Nahum not only writes as an eyewitness of the destruction, but he also pretends to be inside the city in its last hours. In chapter 2 his sound pictures boom, with a two-beat cadence for alarm, a four-beat for marching, and a five-beat for wailing. His rhythm rumbles and rolls, leaps and flashes, like the horsemen and chariots in his poetry. If Nahum had written more, he would surpass Isaiah as the poet laureate of the Hebrew Bible.

His theology is focused upon one consuming topic: God does not tolerate injustice forever! Nahum draws upon the vocabulary of the "holy war," as it is called in Mic 3:5; Jer 6:4; Joel 4:9. Here the traditional oracle against the nations (see Isa 13–23; Jer 46–51; Ezek 25–32; Amos 1:3–2:16), always an exceptionally brilliant piece of writing, reaches white heat.

The book is subdivided as follows: 1:1, introduction; 1:2–2:1 (RSV, 1:2-15), hymn to Yahweh; 2:2-14 (RSV, 2:1-13), siege and capture of Nineveh; chapter 3, funereal epitaph.

COMMENTARY

INTRODUCTION

Nah 1:1

1:1 Unique among the prophets, Nahum's work is called a "book." Typical of other prophetical writings, his work is also designated a "vision" (Amos 7:12; Hab 1:1; Isa 1:1; 2:1; especially 13:1), stressing a unique revelation. Elkosh is a city some twenty miles southwest of Jerusalem.

HYMN TO YAHWEH

Nah 1:2–2:3

This section is textually disturbed; many translations, including the New American Bible, revise the order of verses, generally to systematize the persons addressed as "you" in 1:9–2:1; others seek to reconstruct better the alphabetic or acrostic poem at the beginning. Keeping verses 2-11 together (the New American Bible does not), we are able to arrive at an alphabetic sequence for most of the lines, including *mem* (the letter "M"), in which case the author stopped short of *nun* (the letter "N"), which would stand for Nineveh, a city not to exist any longer.

1:2-3a These verses draw principally upon Exod 34. While this chapter stresses the Lord's compassion, Nahum underlines the other theme, also present in a more muted way in Exod 34—the Lord's jealous revenge upon evildoers. Three times Nahum acclaims the Lord as "avenging"; the Hebrew for this word sounds almost like his own name. To be "jealous," in its etymological sense, means to love dearly and so to tolerate no rivals.

1:3b-8 The prophet refers to terrifying desert storms, particularly the fall sirocco. Nahum weaves into the picture the language of other storms in which Yahweh battles monstrous forces of evil, sometimes called by the names of pagan deities, as in Pss 74:13-14; 89:11-12; Isa 51:9-10. The names Bashan, Carmel, and Lebanon in verse 4 recall violent moments in nature (Amos 1:2; Ps 29:5) or moments of new peace (Mic 7:14; Ps 46). Just as the storm in Psalm 29 circles around the land of Israel to spend itself at Kadesh, Nahum allows a harbor of peace for Israel in verses 7-8.

1:9–2:3 Except for 2:2, these verses can be read more clearly by keeping in mind either the city Nineveh, addressed in verses 9, 10, 11, 14; 2:2, or the city of Jerusalem, described in verses 12-13 and 2:1; 2:3. This sophisticated procedure is forced upon us by the disturbed state of the Hebrew text. Verse 9 picks up the phrase "he . . . will make an end" from verse 8 and applies it specifically to Nineveh and adds a definitive end in verse 9c. In verse 11 "scoundrel" translates the Hebrew word *belial*, which comes from the root "to swallow" into the grave so that no descendants will be seen (v. 14; 2 Sam 22:5).

1:12 Speaking for the first time in his own name, the Lord assures Jerusalem, "I will humble you no more." Would that these words were true, for in 587 B.C.E. Jerusalem was not only to be humbled but even leveled to the ground by the Babylonians! Prophecy needs to be interpreted in its setting, at times according to the enthusiastic rhetoric of the speaker. In verse 13, again speaking to Jerusalem, Yahweh assures the city that the yoke of Assyria will finally be broken after more than a hundred years of oppression. Little wonder for the mighty relief, the prophetic eloquence, the angry jealousy.

2:1 This language will be taken up by Second Isaiah to announce the return from exile by "the bearer of good news" (Isa 40:9; 52:7). **Celebrate your feasts:** Some say the reference is the feast of Tabernacles, which later commemorated Yahweh as King and Creator at the new Jerusalem (Zech 14:16). Perhaps the interchange of speakers and addresses in this section may be explained by a ritual of blessing Judah and cursing the enemy, as we see in other biblical passages such as Num 22–24 and Joel 3–4. "The bearer of good news, announcing peace" in 2:1 ought to assuage our fear of ruthless warfare. The Hebrew for "bearer of good news" lies behind the Greek word for "gospel."

2:3 This verse foresees the restoration of the northern tribes, deported by Assyria in 733 and 721 B.C.E. Like Jer 31:1-22, it is one of the unfulfilled prophecies of the Hebrew Bible.

FALL OF NINEVEH

Nah 2:2, 4-14

These lines of attack (vv. 2, 4-6), conquest and looting (vv. 7-10), and mock lamentation (vv. 11-14) deserve first place in the hall of literary fame of biblical Hebrew. On a par with it are Ezekiel's extended image of shipwreck for the collapse of the seaport city of Tyre (Ezek 27) and Isaiah's hushed silence in Sheol as "Lucifer—the morning star" of Babylon enters "the recesses of the pit" (Isa 14:12-19).

2:2 After losing the battle in the approaches to the city, Nineveh girds itself for the fierce final assault. In quick succession and with abrupt commands the enemy sets up the battering rams and other machinery of war at key spots around the city; inside, the defenders are ordered to take their positions on the walls. For the importance of watchmen on the city walls, see 2 Sam 18:24-27 and Ezek 3:16-21; 33.

2:4-5 These verses describe by anticipation the presence of the enemy troops already within the city, or else the frenzied movement and countermovement within the city as parts of the city walls crumble under attack and emergency signals are sounded hither and thither.

2:7-10 These verses describe the collapse and plundering of the city, one of the wealthiest in the world, filled with the loot of world resources. **The river gates are opened:** This may refer to the river Choser, which entered the city at its northeast corner. The Medes and Babylonians may have dammed its water to empty some of the moats around the city in preparation for the moment when the dam was opened and a deluge of water crashed against the walls, flooding the city. Its muddy waters buried the palace treasuries. **mistress . . . and her handmaids:** These words signify the statue of the goddess Ishtar, "queen" of Nineveh, and the priestesses who serviced her fertility rites.

2:11-14 Wailing and judgment. The Hebrew of the opening lines sounds like the wind howling at night through a graveyard. Verse 12 is a cruel question when its only answer is "Nowhere!" The "lion" Assyria, which plundered the world and tore the flesh of its victims and dragged them away from their homeland for its own selfish pleasure and well-being, is "consumed in smoke." The oracle of judgment in verse 14 is spoken in the name of "the Lord of hosts" who went into battle (Exod 15; Num 10:35; 1 Sam 4:4-6; Ps 24:7-10), through his lieutenants, Cyaxares, king of the Medes, and Nabopolassar, king of Babylon.

ASSYRIA IS DESTROYED! CLAP THE HANDS!

Nah 3:1-19

While reflecting upon the fate of Assyria, this chapter is taut with excitement. It erupts with anger, smirks with pent-up revenge, moves with unbelievable cruelty, and ends with a clap of victory over the dying victim. To express one's fury this artistically, each sound and word had to be carefully crafted. Psychologically, anger has a necessary role in our life; nationally and internationally we badly need a way to release desperation and hatred and to be healed of our torturing scars; spiritually we have the inspired prophecy of Nahum. While not the height of perfection nor the only step leading to this height, it may be a necessary step somewhere along the way.

At best, it is a warning that the "Assyria" of any age and place, or the brutal despot within each of us, will not be tolerated by God. If we combine Nahum with other prophecies like that of Hosea or Jeremiah, the Bible recognizes a disciplinary or purifying power in the suffering that even "Assyria" endures.

This final chapter can be divided as follows: the siege and capture are relived (3:1-3); the guilty are punished (3:4-17); victory is celebrated over the dying tyrant (3:18-19).

3:4 Woe! This is a form of speech already encountered in Amos 5:7, 18; 6:1. Witchcraft was punished by death (Deut 18:9-12; 1 Sam 28:8-25).

3:5-7 Assyria, whose divine patroness, Ishtar, governed war and fertility with cruelty and licentiousness, is treated as a harlot (see Hos 2:4-15; Isa 47:1-3); in Assyrian law, an adulteress, found guilty, was stripped and handed over to anyone's pleasure. **any to console?** reverses Nahum's name, which means "the one consoled." Nineveh is compared to cities like No-Amon (religious name for Thebes), over four hundred miles south of Cairo, and to peoples allied with Egypt, such as the Ethiopians, Put (Somalia?), and the Libyans, conquered by Ashurbanipal and now an example of what is happening to Assyria.

3:11-13 The punishment of war includes accepting a place in enemy brothels just to stay alive.

3:18-19 Instead of ending with a pall of silence over the dying victim, Nahum calls for a final, triumphant clap of hands!

ZEPHANIAH

Carroll Stuhlmueller, C.P.

INTRODUCTION

Historical setting

Zephaniah breaks the prophetic silence that hung over Judah since Isaiah and Micah disappeared toward the end of Hezekiah's reign (715–686 B.C.E.). Hezekiah's son, Manasseh, reversed what seemed to be the hopeless anti-Assyrian policy of his father. Hezekiah and Jerusalem may have survived, but the rest of the countryside had been devastated and the country's resources depleted. Manasseh even introduced fertility rites into the Jerusalem temple (2 Kgs 21:7); "he immolated his son by fire" (2 Kgs 21:6). Rabbinical tradition holds that Isaiah was martyred at this time. Zephaniah may have been the first to speak out against such "abominable practices" (2 Kgs 21:2), early in the reign of Manasseh's grandson, Josiah (640–609 B.C.E.).

Several factors prepared the way: first, a conversion experience late in life for Manasseh (2 Chr 33:12-13); second, a strong movement by the "people of the land," with whom Micah had been associated, to revive ancient loyalties and morality (see introduction to Micah, p. 510). This group rose up to suppress a palace revolt that had assassinated Manasseh's son Amon (2 Kgs 21:24); the "people of the land" not only placed a legitimate heir of the Davidic line on the throne, but they also surrounded him with advisers who would eventually undertake the great "Deuteronomic reform" in 621 B.C.E. (2 Kgs 22:3–23:30). Still another condition not only made possible the revival of prophecy but also provided a setting of cosmic upheaval for Zephaniah's literary style, namely, the imminent collapse of the Assyrian Empire.

Even though the last great king of Assyria, Ashurbanipal (669–627 B.C.E.), had marched south into Egypt, captured its magnificent city Thebes, and profaned its most sacred temple in 663, the empire was heaving under symptoms of serious disease. Babylon revolted twice—the first time in 652, only to be cruelly brought back into line; the second time in 633, successfully. Coincidentally (?) King Josiah was publicly converted to the Lord in 633 B.C.E. In 629/28 Josiah began the purge of idolatrous worship across the land of Israel where Assyrian occupation forces were crumbling.

An eerie foreboding spread a mysterious suspense and a weird nostalgia over the Near East. The new twenty-sixth dynasty in Egypt revived many aspects of the age of pyramids, almost two thousand years earlier. Ashurbanipal had been gathering ancient documents at Nineveh and so made it possible for archeologists to recover them in the nineteenth and twentieth centuries A.D. Babylon began to use the Sumerian language in its official archives, thus reviving the initial dominant culture in southern Mesopotamia around 3000 B.C.E. Zephaniah's terrifying "day of the Lord" was a legitimate offspring of this world of colossal change, unbelievable upheavals, shifts of world power, dark clouds of war and destruction, and surprising rebirths from the ashes.

Zephaniah's announcement "A day of

wrath is that day" (1:15), through Jerome's Latin Vulgate translation, provided the script for the famous composition of Thomas of Celano, *Dies irae, dies illa* (ca. 1250 A.D.), formerly sung or recited at Roman Catholic funeral masses. Zephaniah called for silence as before a solemn ritual (1:7), as princes and even royalty were tried and found guilty (1:8-9), to be driven away like chaff (2:2). Zephaniah's way of handling offenses enabled prophecy to take its first steps toward the apocalyptic style, more evident in such writings as Ezek 38–39 and fully developed in Dan 7–12.

The historical background of Zephaniah's preaching is to be located in the early years of King Josiah (640–609 B.C.E.), before his vigorous "Deuteronomic" reform (621–609 B.C.E.). Scholars once associated Zephaniah with a so-called Scythian raid which, according to the ancient historian Herodotus, swept through the Assyrian empire down into Syria and Israel around 630 B.C.E. Yet there is no corroborating evidence, and the opinion is now generally discounted. Josiah inherited not only the social injustices that Micah denounced but also the open idolatry of Manasseh's reign. Much like the Deuteronomic reform, Zephaniah focused only upon false and sensual worship and paid little attention to social injustices. Unlike Amos, Zephaniah was not a spokesperson for the poor; and unlike Micah, he never belonged to their ranks. The opening verse makes him a second cousin of King Josiah, and in 1:8 he speaks familiarly about "the king's sons." He was at home in Jerusalem (1:4, 10).

Style and structure

Stylistically, Zephaniah appears in a steady line of continuity with prophecy of the south. With Amos and Isaiah, he centers upon the remnant, the day of the Lord, sin and chastisement. Other phrases link him with Amos, for example "seek the Lord" (Amos 5:4-7, 14-15; Zeph 2:3) and the customary form of the curse (Amos 5:11; Zeph 1:13). There is scant evidence of stylistic elegance; the language is clear, correct, and sincere. We detect: little perception of the anguish of God, noticeable in Hosea and Micah (only Zeph 3:7a); no vignettes of the wealthy as in Amos, nor of the poor as in Micah; no echoes of the desert sounds that punctuate Amos' words, nor the agricultural landscape that adorns Hosea's preaching. Not even the sharp, bitter tones of satire are perceived here. Besides sincerity of heart and outrage over idolatry, Zephaniah manifests the booming sound of dissolution in the day of the Lord (see 1:14-16) and a courageous vigor to speak out even against royalty.

The plan of the book is what we will come to recognize as more and more typical of prophecy: oracles against Judah and Jerusalem (1:2–2:3); oracles against foreign nations (2:4-15); statement of hope or renewal (3:1-19).

COMMENTARY

INTRODUCTION

Zeph 1:1

Zephaniah's father is called Cushi, which is an Ethiopian name. Zephaniah refers to Ethiopians negatively in 2:12, but more positively in 3:10. While his father mixed African blood into Zephaniah's Israelite origins, his other ancestors reach back four generations to Hezekiah, very likely the king at Jerusalem. Zephaniah is the only prophet whose pedigree is recorded so extensively (normally only the father's name is provided), perhaps to offset the jealousy caused by his Ethiopian father. The name Zephaniah means "Yah(weh) protects or conceals" and was common enough (see Jer 21:11 and Zech 6:10-14).

SILENCE! THE FEARFUL DAY OF THE LORD

Zeph 1:2–2:3

This section can be subdivided for our better appreciation: a cosmic setting for the charges against Jerusalem (1:2-6); silence before the "liturgy" commences (1:7-13); the fearful day of the Lord (1:14-18); probation, perhaps, for the poor (2:1-3).

1:2-6 The opening verses direct our vista across the earth, as God sweeps away every sign of life; the story of creation in Gen 1–2 is told in reverse. Three times the Hebrew word for "sweep away" occurs, canceling out earlier promises expressed by this same word, as in Gen 8:21 after the great flood: "Never again *will I sweep away* the earth because of humankind." Zephaniah reneges on the benefits of the earth celebrated during the feast of Ingathering (Exod 23:16). Liturgy is no guarantee of happy results unless words and actions come from a sincere heart (see Hos 5:15–6:7).

Verses 4-6 explain why Yahweh, "a jealous God" (Exod 34:12-16), never tolerates what the same passage calls a "wanton worship" with sensual fertility rites and child sacrifice. **the very names of his priests:** The Hebrew text uses a rare word for "priests" (Hos 10:5; 2 Kgs 23:2), common in other Semitic languages; here it has the derogatory sense of "priestling." **host of heaven:** Assyrian deities (Jer 8:1-3; Ezek 8:16-18); **Milcom:** He was the god of the Ammonites, who inhabited Transjordan (1 Kgs 11:5); the Hebrew text refers to him under the name *malcom* ("their king"), poking ridicule at the king who tolerated such worship. Verses 5-6, particularly in the Hebrew, show how the people assuaged their conscience, for they also "adore the Lord"; these two-timers were long ago condemned by the prophet Elijah (1 Kgs 18:21).

1:7-13 This section opens with a call for silence in the final preparations for the liturgy of this "day of the Lord," once a time of light and joy, now a time of darkness and death (see Amos 5:18). The repetition of "day of the Lord" (vv. 7, 8, 9, 10) unites all other observations: "slaughter feast," not the animals for the sacred banquet but the inhabitants and worshipers; "foreign apparel" for the heathen ritual (2 Kgs 10:22); "leap over the threshold" superstitiously to avoid the demons there (1 Sam 5:5), yet acting deceitfully once inside the temple.

Different parts of Jerusalem are cited: "Fish Gate" (on the northwest—Neh 3:3); "New Quarter" (location uncertain); "hills" (reaching north, the area of any attack upon the city); "Mortar" (more to the south, at a "quarry," as the word means); "merchants" (or "Canaanites," if we keep the Hebrew word as a proper name), an area of Jerusalem for foreigners.

1:12 explore Jerusalem with a lamp: Like Diogenes in search of a single just person or of the wicked in their secret haunts of sin. **thicken on their lees:** Like undrawn wine, sweet and syrupy, such people are solicitous only for their bodily comfort. Verse 13 is from Amos 5:11 or from a repertoire of prophetic memories.

1:14-18 This *Dies irae* (see p. 525) receives its best commentary in the terrifying booming and rhythmic sound of the Hebrew words. One must listen to the Gregorian plainchant of the *Dies irae* to appreciate this plaintive but triumphant victory song of the grave.

2:1-3 Zephaniah recognizes a possibility—"perhaps" in verse 3—of shelter in the devastating day of the Lord for "the humble of the earth." Zephaniah inaugurates the long development of the theological meaning of humility, poverty, and lowliness as contained in the Hebrew word *'anawim.* Some religious significance was already attached to the state of being economically poor or socially deprived (Prov 15:33; 18:12). Yet, Zephaniah recognizes these as the only ones to be saved. Military invaders executed the wealthy and powerful. During the Exile, Second Isaiah addresses all the people to be reassembled by God in their own land as poor and lowly (Isa 41:17). In the postexilic age, the promised savior is said to belong to the lowly (Zech 9:9). Still later some Jewish people deliberately embraced poverty as a godly way of life, as in the case of the Pharisees and also the covenanters along the Dead Sea (who were to produce the Dead Sea Scrolls). New Testament saints, like Mary, see in poverty an interior attitude of dependence upon God (Luke 1:48).

ORACLES AGAINST THE NATIONS

Zeph 2:4-15

For the meaning and scope of the oracles against the nations, see the commentary on Amos 1:3–2:16 (p. 489). While prompted more immediately by God's designs for punishing Israel, these sections signal God's control over foreign nations, a control that can eventually embrace their salvation. Zephaniah even states such a wild possibility at the end of verse 11 but seems to take it back in verse 15! Yet, even in verse 11 "ecumenism" is toward captured people (see Mic 7:16-17), different from the more open view in Mic 4:1-3 (yet, see Mic 4:4-5). The citation of nations moves from the western shore of Philistine territory to Moab and Ammon, east of the Jordan River and the Dead Sea, from south of Israel in Egypt, under the control of an Ethiopian dynasty (see 1:1), to the north, the route taken by Assyria to invade Israel.

AFTER REPENTANCE NEW HOPE

Zeph 3:1-20

Typical of Zephaniah's negative disposition, even the characteristically happy ending for prophecy starts with a renewed condemnation of leadership, civil and religious (vv. 1-5) and a reiteration of the destruction of the nations (vv. 6-8). Salvation is promised only to the remnant of the lowly (vv. 9-13); two psalms of rejoicing close the prophecy (vv. 14-18a; 18b-20).

3:1-5 These verses resound with themes and even lines heard elsewhere in prophecy. Verse 2a is found again in Jer 7:28; verse 4b, in Ezek 22:26. Condemnation of leaders, civil and religious, in quick succession was already heard in Mic 3:11 (see Jer 2:26). The object of this *Woe!* is Jerusalem. According to the Hebrew word in verse 2, the suffering is said to be disciplinary and corrective (see Isa 53:5). Verse 5 begins emphatically with "The Lord within her is just," in contrast to the other insolent leaders.

3:6-8 These verses intimate that a serious transition is underway. In a divine soliloquy (v. 7) we hear that Jerusalem will now accept the disciplinary correction repulsed in verse 2. **3:8 wait for me:** Waiting upon the Lord is the prophetic posture for salvation, as in Hab 2:3 and Isa 30:15-18 before the Exile, or in Isa 40:31 during the Exile. **I arise as accuser:** The phrase might also be translated "as a witness." **my decision to gather together:** Here we meet the Hebrew word repeated negatively three times in 1:2-3, with the meaning "to sweep away," but now positively in Jerusalem's favor. **3:11 the earth be consumed:** This should not be taken literally, for Jerusalem must survive! Texts like this one always need interpretation.

3:9-13 A strong transition appears here in the Hebrew text. In verse 9 a promise to "purify the lips," reminiscent of Isaiah at the time of his call (Isa 6:5) intends that the deceit and falsehood, as witnessed by Psalm 12, be removed. To "call upon the name of the Lord" (v. 9) imparts many rights and privileges, just as in the case of a child who can call someone mother or father. In verses 12-13 salvation is promised to "the remnant . . . a people humble and lowly." As mentioned in the commentary on 2:3, the humble are already on the way to being the assembly whom God saves as a special people. The Gospel of Matthew makes use of the Greek version of Zephaniah in recording Jesus' words to disciples to "Learn from me, for I am *gentle and humble of heart*" (Matt 21:29).

3:14-18a This first psalm, a hymn of praise, is ready to be sung "at festivals" (v. 18a). In many ways it reminds us of the many jubilant lines in Isa 40–55, particularly in chapters 40–48. Here we draw attention to a number of phrases that cluster again in Luke's presentation of the annunciation to Mary that she was to become the mother of Jesus: "Be glad," "The Lord is in your midst," "Fear not," "mighty savior" (see Luke 1:26-38). Mary, tabernacling Jesus within herself, is thus presented as the new Jerusalem, the model for the poor and lowly.

3:18b-20 As elsewhere in prophecy, the "lame" and the "outcasts" are assembled (see Mic 4:6-7), the very ones rejected from the temple, even if they were priests, by the legislation of the Torah (Lev 21:16-23). Verse 20 was probably added during the time of the Exile. As Israel is assembled, its salvation will strike the attention of "all the peoples of the earth," a hint that universal salvation is possible.

HABAKKUK

Carroll Stuhlmueller, C.P.

INTRODUCTION

Style

Habakkuk and Jeremiah inaugurate a new attitude in prophecy. Up until now, for the most part, prophecy consisted in delivering the oracle of God to Israel; now the prophet's question to God becomes for us the word of God, in some real yet mysterious way revealing God's word in our own challenge to God! Nothing as fully developed as this questioning style in Habakkuk and Jeremiah ever comes totally new. Here or there prophecy has been interrogating God, but never so extensively as to become the gist of the entire prophecy. Even Moses differed with God (Exod 32:11-14); and further back still, Abraham argued with God about the fate of the five cities (Gen 18:22-33). We find Amos putting a question to God in his first two visions (Amos 7:1-6). This style, however, will almost dominate the prophecy of Jeremiah, particularly in his famous confessions (Jer 12:1-5; 15:10-21; 17:14-18; 18:19-23; 20:7-18). In all these cases the starting point is a strong faith in God's fidelity; and at the end God closes the conversation when and how God wishes. God remains God!

Person

Little if anything is directly known about Habakkuk. The name never occurs again in the Hebrew Bible. The deuterocanonical section of the Book of Daniel refers to him as bringing some bread and boiled stew to Daniel in the lion's den at Babylon; this Habakkuk is carried by an angel, who seizes him by the crown of his head and afterward returns him to his own place (Dan 14:33-39), an episode generally considered a popular story of much later vintage. Some explain the name Habakkuk as the intensive form of a Hebrew word meaning "to embrace." Jewish tradition, other than the one in Dan 14, links the prophet with the childless woman at Shunem, to whom the prophet Elisha promised a child. The word "to embrace" occurs in the story (2 Kgs 14:8-37). Other scholars derive the prophet's name from a bulbous plant, known from an Assyrian root word but not found in the Bible. The Greek Septuagint adds to his name in 1:1, "son of Jesus of the tribe of Levi," an identification prompted, no doubt, by the liturgical poem in chapter 3.

Date

The prophecy is to be dated sometime after the Babylonians became an active threat against Judah but before their destruction of the city of Jerusalem in 587 B.C.E. Habakkuk's serious complaints about violent injustice among the people in Judah suggests sometime in the reign of Jehoiakim (609–597 B.C.E.), a king despised by Jeremiah for his abuse of power at the cost of much suffering by the poor and defenseless. Jeremiah declares that he will be given "the burial of an ass" (Jer 22:13-19; see also 2 Kgs 23:37). Certainly chapter 3 qualifies Habakkuk to be numbered among the "cult prophets," who functioned at the temple; chapters 1–2 may leave us some clues for a liturgical ceremony.

Themes

Several major religious motifs thread their way through the prophecy: God's absolute trustworthiness; God's control of the universe; our inability to understand adequately the mysterious ways of God; our failure to fathom the mysteries of the universe and the colossal struggles of nature and politics; God's determination not to tolerate violence, begotten by pride.

COMMENTARY

CROSS-QUESTIONING GOD

Hab 1:2–2:5a

This section consists of a double series of question and lament (1:2-4 and 12-17), each followed by an oracle or reply from God (1:5-11 and 2:1-5a). Such question-answer style follows a pattern that surfaces in some psalms of lament and supplication (see Pss 12; 45; 79). Doubts arise, however, if King Jehoiakim would have permitted Habakkuk, any more than he did Jeremiah, to speak in the temple against the country (Jer 26). Verses 2-4 of chapter 1 place the theme and two key words of Habakkuk before us: the question *Why*? (vv. 3 and 13b) and the situation of violence (1:2, 3, 9; 2:8, 17). *Why* does a God who "comes forth to save [the] people" (3:13) tolerate violence against the innocent? **1:4 the law (torah) is benumbed:** What the prophecies of Micah and Isaiah see streaming down from the temple mount (Mic 4:1-3; Isa 2:2-4) is silenced by "leaders [who] render judgment for a bribe" (Mic 3:11).

1:5-11 God's reply is: "I am raising up Chaldea," that is, the Babylonians, who will punish Jerusalem's wicked leaders, civil and religious. From the beginning of Israel's occupation of the land of Canaan, god is said to have summoned other nations to punish the people for their sins. This theme preoccupies the Book of Judges, whose introduction offers a theological explanation: the abundance of good things induces Israel to sin; sin brings weakness and military invasion; such sorrow moves Israel to pray to God, who sends a "judge," or military leader, to liberate them; and a new prosperity sets in, almost so that the cycle can repeat itself (Judg 2:6–3:6).

Prophecy gradually recognized a more positive attitude toward the nations: in Amos 1:3–2:16 God cares enough to punish them for their offenses against humanity (they are not judged according to the Torah), and in Isa 10:5-15 they are "my rod in anger," directly called as God's instrument in determining the long-term fate of Israel. Only much later does prophecy consider the nations to have a share in Israel's light and salvation (Isa 49:6). Habakkuk's statement is an important link in this development of an ever more positive regard toward the foreigner.

Verses 8-11 reflect the swift maneuvering and sudden success of the Babylonian forces. In verse 11 we encounter the problem of translating the Hebrew word either as "wind" (NAB) or as "spirit" (see the commentary on Mic 2:11, p. 514). In the latter case the same line could read: "[God's] spirit passed by and so he [King Jehoiakim] passed onward" and continued to reign as king. Even though Jehoiakim was installed by the Egyptians, he was wily enough to win the approval of the Babylonian king Nebuchadnezzar.

1:12-17 God's answer is unacceptable, not because Habakkuk lacks faith, but rather because his faith in God is pure, strong, and elevated. *Why* does a God who is "from eternity . . . holy . . . immortal . . . a Rock . . . pure . . . [compassionate toward] misery . . . gaze on the faithless in silence while the wicked man devours one more just than himself" (vv. 12-13)? The Babylonians are more wicked than the wicked leaders of Jerusalem. **1:12 immortal:** This verse contains a scribal correction. The Hebrew reads literally "you do not die," but since it seemed improper to associate death in any way with Yahweh, the Hebrew text was changed in its written form to "we do not die"!

1:13 devours: The word implies a voracious, even ruthless, appetite. The earth swallowed the Egyptians (Exod 15:12); the fish swallowed Jonah (Jonah 2:1); the Lord "destroys (literally "swallows up") death forever" (Isa 25:7).

1:14-17 Habakkuk strengthens his case against the Chaldeans: they undo God's work of creation by treating human beings like fish and animals (vv. 14-15); they offer up ritual sacrifice to their instruments of war (v. 16).

2:1-5a The Lord's reply is elegantly introduced as awaited from a "guard post" or watchtower (Hos 9:8; Mic 7:7; Isa 21:6-21; Ezek 3:17-21; 33). Already the importance of waiting is stressed. The prophet feels an obligation to find an answer for his troubling questions. He has not only a heritage to guard but a present responsibility to discharge.

The Lord's answer is immediate and clear, so precise that it is to be written down (a rare command for a prophet who at best dictated, as in Jer 36, or confided to disciples, as in Isa 8:16) in letters so large as to be read on the run, and so consoling that one runs with eagerness to report it ("run" is the emphatic word here). Verse 3 stresses the need to wait with patience, for it will come true at the "end"—the Hebrew word here does not mean "fulfillment" (see Dan 8:19; 11:27, 35; 12:4).

2:4 the just man, because of his faith, shall live: The word "just" stresses the fulfillment in oneself of the Lord's promises (see Hos 2:21-22; Zech 9:9); "faith" puts the emphasis upon fidelity, sturdiness (Exod 34:5-8); "lives," while the faithless are reduced to silent inactivity (Isa 14:15-20; 38:18-19). **Wealth . . . is treacherous; the proud, unstable:** These words reverse the idea of faith or sturdiness in the preceding line and link with verse 4a about the rash person without integrity. Verse 4b becomes the keystone in Paul's theology of the justification of *all* people by faith in Jesus, whether they have been initiated into the Mosaic covenant or not (Rom 1:17; Gal 3:11); the letter to the Hebrews links the passage with the need for patience, (Heb 10:37-38). The commentary on Habakkuk found in the Dead Sea Scrolls refers the passage to "those who fulfill the law in the house of Judah, whom God will free at the tribunal of justice on account of their labors and their faith in the Teacher of righteousness [their founder]."

ORACLES OF WOE

Hab 2:5b-20

These five oracles of woe do not name any foreign nation; in many ways they address the evils within Judah at the time of Habakkuk. Yet, because of the familiar way of editing prophetic books (oracles or sermons against Israel or Judah, followed by oracles against nations), and because the crimes in the first and fourth oracle seem to be on an international scale, this section is frequently entitled "Oracles Against the Nations." No clear pattern emerges in the five oracles, except for the format of: (a) Woe! with a statement of offenses; (b) the Hebrew word *ki* at the beginning of verses 8, 11, 14, 17, introducing a punishment. Yet verse 14 is not a punishment, and there are other verses out of step!

Woes such as these already occurred in a major section of Amos (5:7, 18; 6:1) and appear elsewhere in prophetic literature in a series of judgments and condemnation only in Isaiah. The style is more common in the Torah (Deut 27–28) and in sapiential books. The section here is subdivided: introduction (vv. 5b-6a); five woes (vv. 6b-19); conclusion (v. 20).

The introductory verses (vv. 5b-6a) stress the unquenchable appetite of death. The inhabitants in the nether world, the foreign nations, take up a taunt against Judah (or Assyria? or Babylon?) in a way similar to their satire against Babylon in Isa 14. The words "satire" and "epigrams," again in Mic 2:4 and Jer 24:9, indicate a message of general import, worthy of serious study.

Verses 6b-8 attack unjust and greedy ways of lending to others (Ps 15:4-5; Exod 22:25; Amos 2:6-8). Verses 9-11 are directed against proud and heartless wealthy people who construct spacious homes, whose "stone in the wall shall cry out" against them with the groaning of the poor and destitute (see Jer 22:13-19 against King Jehoiakim, who "works his neighbor without pay" as he constructs his "airy rooms" and cedar-paneled walls). Verses 12-14 speak against building "a city by bloodshed" (Mic 3:10 has identical words and even names the city), perhaps a reference to the unnecessary bloodshed in the cities of the Shephelah, or low-lying hills where Micah lived, pillaged by foreign troops because of the reckless and selfish policies of Jerusalem. Verse 14 seems to be a familiar refrain; it occurs also in Isa 11:9. Verses 15-17 might reflect the violent forms of sensuality and war among the Assyrians and their allies whose fertility rites entailed drunkenness and nakedness (see Gen 9:20-25) and who deserved the cup of the

Lord's wrath (see Obad 16; Isa 51:17; Jer 25:15). Verses 18-19 rail against idolatry. Verse 20, the conclusion, prepares for the liturgical prayer by placing us silently in the Lord's holy temple.

CANTICLE

Hab 3:1-19

This final canticle moves with the momentum of Israel's most ancient hymns, like the Song of Moses in Exod 3, of Deborah in Judg 5, again of Moses in Deut 32, or the magnificent Psalm 68. Dramatic moments in Israel's history are told against a background of cosmic upheavals, so fiercely does Yahweh battle for the safety and well-being of the people. Even though quite different in style from chapters 1–2, this canticle could have come from Habakkuk. Yet the links are somewhat fragile. If not only 1:2-5 but also 2:5b-20 were directed against Judah's religious-civil establishment, then it is difficult to accept Habakkuk's authorship of chapter 3 with its friendly reference to the king or "anointed one" in 3:13.

3:1 Similar to many psalms, the canticle is introduced with a "title," with liturgical indications. **Prayer:** The Hebrew word, repeated five times in the psalms, indicates a supplication or lament, which this canticle or hymn of praise is not! Is this word a rubric, adapting the canticle to the more normal style of the prophecy of Habakkuk? **a plaintive tune:** This Hebrew word, often left untranslated, is not found elsewhere in the Bible, but because of a similar Babylonian word, it is considered a plaint or lament.

3:2 This introductory verse reminds us of the opening stanza to Ps 44:2-9, "O God, our ears have heard, our ancestors have declared to us . . . ." God is asked to remember (that is, repeat) the great redemptive acts from Israel's origins. "In the course of the years" indicates Israel's optimistic openness to the future, but also a real ennui with the length of time involved.

3:3-7 The poet's gaze sweeps from Teman and Paran, Cushan and Midian, an area to the far south where the Negeb turns into the Sinai desert; other songs like Judg 5 and Psalm 68 recognize the Lord coming up from here at the head of a victorious people: fear (symbolized by pestilence and plague) and earth-shattering victories accompany the journey into the Promised Land. Similar imagery is used in Psalm 46 to prepare for a temple liturgy at Jerusalem.

3:8-15 Yahweh's victory over world forces is told with imagery from Canaanite mythology as found already in Pss 29; 77:14-20 (introduced also by "remember" in verse 12); 89:6-19. Verse 15 seems to refer to the Lord's triumph at the Red Sea and the Jordan River (Psalm 114). Only in verses 16-20 does the element of lament for a plaintive tune (v. 1) appear. Yet the canticle may be using "fear" more as a literary device, as in verse 2, to communicate a sense of awe at what the Lord will do to "the people who attack" (v. 16). "In the course of the years" Israel must turn to the Lord and live in faith (2:4b), and if victory is delayed, must wait for it (2:3b). In verse 16b "decay" can just as correctly be translated "trembling."

Verses 18-19 begin emphatically in the Hebrew, with the meaning "But I, on the contrary." Verse 19bc is very similar to Ps 18:34, a psalm with which the canticle of Habakkuk shares other stylistic features. The psalmist moves with the swift and victorious step of the Lord. The final line, "For the leader; with stringed instruments," is a liturgical rubric, also found at the beginning of many psalms. That liturgical notes are part of the inspired word of God shows that the way in which a later generation used the canticle in its worship belonged to the essential inspiration of the psalm; the psalm will not release its full meaning until it is relived liturgically, as the opening lines of this canticle pray.

EZEKIEL AND DANIEL

Toni Craven

INTRODUCTION

Outline of contents

The Book of Ezekiel is an orderly five-part collection or anthology of writings by the prophet and his followers. Chapters 1–3 tell of the prophet's call; chapters 4–24 contain prophecies about the fate of Jerusalem before its fall in 587 B.C.E.; chapters 25–32 are prophecies against the foreign nations; chapters 33–39 encourage the hope of restoration after the fall of Jerusalem; and chapters 40–48 present a vision of the new temple and the restoration of the cultic and political life of the people in the land of Israel.

The Book of Daniel is a three-part collection containing short stories written by unknown authors about Daniel and his companions (chs. 1–6; and the deuterocanonical Greek chs. 13–14) and apocalyptic visions written in the first person and fictitiously attributed to Daniel (chs. 7–12).

Kind of literature

Form and content define the literary type or genre of Ezekiel as prophetic literature (with some apocalyptic sections, notably chs. 38–39), and Daniel as both edifying short story and apocalyptic vision.

Prophetic literature

Ezekiel, like the other classical Old Testament prophets, is a passionate, uncompromising spokesperson for God. He announces words of judgment and encouragement to his particular community as it faces a crisis in its religious and political existence. Ezekiel makes the sixth-century Jewish community in Judah and Babylon mindful of its false hope in Jerusalem and its false despair after the fall of the city in 587 B.C.E. In a variety of ways, including visions (see chs. 1–3; 8–11; 37; 40–48), symbolic actions that concretely dramatize the message (see chs. 4–5), allegories (symbolic stories with an interpretation, see ch. 16), and judgment speeches (often introduced by the oracle formula "thus says Yahweh" and closed with the recognition formula "that you may know that I am Yahweh"), Ezekiel calls for individual responsibility, repentance, and submission to the sovereignty of God. He does not predict a timetable for the distant future, though he does give voice to a poetic vision of a community restored, for the sake of the divine name, to a new national identity in a new and restored Israel.

Edifying short story

Like Ruth, Esther, Tobit, and Judith, parts of the Book of Daniel (chs. 1–6; 13–14) are self-contained short stories with distinct beginnings, middles, and endings. The nine narratives in Daniel are tales of biblical heroes who cope successfully with difficulties, survive the terrible oppression, and in the end triumph gloriously. In an entertaining fashion, the stories teach that good prevails over evil and that God rewards faithfulness. Daniel, Shadrach, Meshach, Abednego, and Susanna are portrayed as inspiring models of courage and virtue.

Apocalyptic literature

A kind of literature that flourished from 200 B.C.E. to 100 B.C.E. (see, for example, Isa

24–27; Ezek 38–39; Dan 7–12; Joel 3; 2 Esd; Rev), apocalyptic (Greek for "unveiling," "uncovering," or "revelation") works always contain some revelation of information hidden from ordinary human understanding. Through the medium of angels, visions, and bizarre symbolism, special knowledge is revealed. In the Book of Daniel, the special revelations in chapters 7–12 take the form of a kind of resistance literature that encouraged those experiencing persecution under Antiochus IV to persevere because the end of the time of tribulation was at hand. These apocalyptic predictions about the exact time of God's intervention and the heavenly events accompanying the establishment of the divine kingdom on earth are unique in the Old Testament (compare the New Testament Book of Revelation).

Geographical and historical background

Babylon, which was over 750 miles from Jerusalem, is the presumed geographical setting for Ezekiel and much of Daniel. Both books refer to the Babylonian Exile and the fall of Jerusalem in 587B.C.E. to Nebuchadnezzar. This traumatic event occurred during the lifetime of Ezekiel; for the authors of Daniel it was a remembered event that served as a springboard for their veiled discussions of the repressive rule of Antiochus IV Epiphanes (175–163 B.C.E.).

Four centuries separated the composition of the books of Ezekiel (sixth century B.C.E.) and Daniel (second century B.C.E.). Ezekiel described the Exile prophetically as an occasion that demanded the conversion of a sinful, rebellious people and their acquiring of a "new heart" (Ezek 36:26). Daniel interpreted the Exile retrospectively as a time in which heroes of faith successfully resisted religious and political oppression. In Daniel, the Exile and the subsequent dominion of the Persians and the Greeks were understood apocalyptically as signs of promised reward for those who also resisted oppression and patiently awaited God's dramatic transformation of the course of history.

Historical outline

The major dates, events, and personages associated with the Books of Ezekiel and Daniel are summarized in the following historical outline.

B.C.	EGYPT	PALESTINE	MESOPOTAMIA
		THE BABYLONIAN EMPIRE	BABYLONIA
		Jehoiachin (Jeconiah), 3 mos., 598–597	Nebuchadnezzar, 605–562
		First Deportation to Babylonia, 597	
	Apries (Hophra), 589–570	Zedekiah (Mattaniah), 597–587	
		FALL OF JERUSALEM SECOND DEPORTATION, 587	
		BABYLONIAN EXILE Ezekiel, c. 593–573	
			Nabonidus, 556–539 (his son: Belshazzar)
			RISE OF PERSIA Cyrus II, 550–530
			Defeat of Media, c. 550
600 to 500			Invasion of Lydia, c. 546
		(*Second Isaiah*, c. 540) Edict of Cyrus, 538	FALL OF BABYLON, 539

B.C.	EGYPT	PALESTINE	MESOPOTAMIA
		THE EMPIRE OF PERSIA	
	Conquest by Persia, 525	THE RESTORATION JUDAH Return of exiles Rebuilding of Temple, 520–515 *(Haggai)* *(Zechariah)*	Cambyses, 530–522 Darius I, 522–486
500 to 400	Egypt under Persian rule, 525–401	(*Malachi*, c. 500–450) Ezra's mission, 458(?) Nehemiah arrives, 445 Ezra's mission, c. 428(?)	Persia Xerxes I (Ahasuerus), 486–465 Artaxerxes I (Longimanus), 465–424 Xerxes II, 423 Darius II, 423–404
		Ezra's mission, c. 398(?)	Artaxerxes II (Mnemon), 404–358 Artaxerxes III, 358–338 Arses, 338–336 Darius III, 336–331
		EMPIRE OF ALEXANDER THE GREAT, 336–323	
400 to 300	*Ptolemaic Kingdom* Ptolemy I, 323–285	Egyptian Control	*Seleucid Kingdom* (Mesopotamia and Syria) Seleucus I, 312/11–280
300 to 200	Ptolemy II, 285–246 Ptolemy III, 246–221 Ptolemy IV, 221–203	Egyptian Control	Antiochus I, 280–261 Antiochus II, 261–246 Seleucus II, 246–226 Seleucus III, 226–223 Antiochus III, 223–187
200 to 100	Ptolemy V, 203–181 Ptolemy VI, 181–146 Ptolemy VII, 146–116	Syrian Conquest, 198–200 MACCABEAN REVOLT, 168 (167) Judas, 166–160 Jonathan, 160–143 Simon, 143–134 John Hyrcanus, 134–104 Conquest of Shechem, 128	Seleucus IV, 187–175 Antiochus IV (Epiphanes), 175–163 Antiochus V, 163–162 Demetrius I, 162–150 Alexander Balas, 150–145 Demetrius II, 145–138 Antiochus VI, 145–141 Antiochus VII, 138–129
100 to A.D.	Roman Conquest, 30	Pompey captures Jerusalem, 63	Roman occupation of Syria, 63
		THE EMPIRE OF ROME	

The historical outline above is taken from: Bernhard W. Anderson, *Understanding the Old Testament*, © 1986, pp. 650, 651. Reprinted by permission of Prentice-Hall, Englewood Cliffs, New Jersey.

COMMENTARY: EZEKIEL

PART I: CALL OF THE PROPHET

Ezek 1:1–3:27

The opening chapters ascribe this book to Ezekiel ben-Buzi, who had an extraordinary vision in Babylon in the year 593 B.C.E. According to the sixteen dates attached to the book, he remained active as a prophet at least until 571 B.C.E. (see the last dated oracle in 29:17). We know little about this man except that he was married and that his wife died during the siege of Jerusalem (see 24:15-18).

It is generally assumed that Ezekiel was exiled from Judah to Babylon in the first deportation of 597 B.C.E. Together with other exiles skilled in crafts, commerce, and agriculture who settled in Tel-abib, Nippur, and Babylon itself, Ezekiel took up residence in an alien land. On the banks of a river in Babylon, Ezekiel saw a vision which convinced him that God called him to speak as a prophet to the exiles.

The strange imagery of the opening chapters poetically dramatizes a new vision of God's mobile holiness suitable to the difficult times of the Exile. Ezekiel is called to submit his life to the majesty of God and is commissioned to speak a harsh word of judgment and warning to the rebellious people of Israel. The prophet is commanded to eat a scroll covered with lamentation and woe (2:9-10) and to stand as a watchman or pastor over the house of Israel.

1:1-28 The vision: God on the cherubim. Two superscriptions open the book. In the first (v. 1), Ezekiel recounts his visionary experience by the Babylonian river Chebar. In the second (vv. 2-3), the collector of his words and deeds provides information about the beginning of the prophet's career, his name, family, and position in Israelite society.

The reference in the first superscription (v. 1) to the "thirtieth year" is an enigma. The date cannot refer to either of the kingships that might have influenced Ezekiel. More than thirty years had passed from the beginning of the reign of Nabopolassar of Babylonia in 626 B.C.E., and less than thirty years had passed from the beginning of the reign of Josiah of Jerusalem in 621 B.C.E. (2 Kgs 22:23). Though interpreters have variously taken the "thirtieth year" as a reference (1) to the age of the prophet (according to Num 4:30, the minimum age for ordination was thirty), (2) to the date when Ezekiel first published his work, or (3) to thirty years from the time when the high priest Hilkiah found the book of the law in the temple during the reign of Josiah (2 Kgs 22:8ff.), no satisfactory explanation of this date has been discovered. It is even said that the ancient rabbis forbade persons under thirty to read the opening of this book lest they be led astray by Ezekiel's strange vision.

Also problematic is the incomplete date in the second superscription (v. 2). It refers to the year 593 B.C.E., but it does not specify a particular month. Both the first and the second superscriptions specify the fifth day, but neither contains full reference to a year, a month, and a day.

Verse 3 is a kind of heading found frequently in prophetic books (compare Hos 1:1; Joel 1:1; Mic 1:1; Zeph 1:1; Jer 1:2-3). Although syntactically the word "priest" in verse 3 can refer to either Ezekiel or his father Buzi, the phrase has traditionally been interpreted as an indication that Ezekiel was a priest in Jerusalem before he was called to be a prophet in Babylon. Actually, there is no information in the text about Ezekiel's homeland, although it seems highly probable that he came from Jerusalem with the first exiles deported to Babylon in 597 B.C.E.

The vision of Ezekiel is the most detailed account available to us of the call of a prophet. It is similar in many details to Isaiah's call and commissioning (Isa 6), like Jeremiah's call (Jer 1:9-10) in the one respect of the eating of the scroll, and clearly related to the type of call known from the vision of Micaiah (1 Kgs 22). Ezekiel's call combines an earthly setting with a heavenly vision. Like Isaiah and Micaiah, Ezekiel sees God seated on a throne. Ezekiel is near the river Chebar, a canal along the Euphrates River in the vicinity of Babylon, when the heavens are opened and he sees a strange and dazzling vision of God's maj-

---

Parts of this commentary on the Book of Ezekiel were prepared as a co-authored revision of Walter Harrelson's *Interpreting the Old Testament* (New York: Holt, Rinehart and Winston) and are used with permission.

esty. It is in the land of exile that "the hand of the Lord came upon" the prophet (v. 3).

Ezekiel sees a great cloud with fire flashing about it swept along from the North. Within the cloud a bronze object appears. As the cloud draws nearer, strange living creatures are distinguishable, each with straight, human-like legs and hands, feet like those of calves, four wings, and four faces (one of a human, one of a lion, one of a bull, one of an eagle). With one pair of wings each figure modestly covers its body (compare Isa 6:2). The tips of the other pair of wings join the four figures together, so that they shield the object they carry in their midst. The motion of their wings makes a deafening sound, and flaming torches, burning coals, and fire dart out from behind the creatures. Ezekiel sees four wheels, one beside each of the beings (possibly a later expansion of the vision—1:15-21). And looking upward, he sees a firmament (a kind of platform), upon which is a throne. On the throne is a likeness of a man, although the fire and the gleaming bronze make it impossible for Ezekiel to see this figure clearly. The brilliant colors of the rainbow mark the entire scene, and its splendor overwhelms the prophet.

Ezekiel describes the strange details of his experience with care. In the midst of the cloud he sees something that gleams "like" electrum (v. 4). Within the cloud he sees figures "resembling" four living creatures (v. 5), whose four faces are "like" burning coals of fire (v. 13), and over their heads something "like" a crystal firmament (v. 22). He hears something "like" the sound of water, "like" the voice of the Almighty (v. 24). Above the firmament, on something "like" a sapphire throne, is one who has the "appearance" of a man (v. 26), who gleams from the waist up and looks "like" fire from the waist down (v. 27). Such, says Ezekiel, is the vision of the "likeness" of the glory of Yahweh (v. 28). Though this vision is not easily comprehended, it is clearly a sign that God has not abandoned the people. In the land of exile, where the ruling nation honors other gods, Yahweh comes to call a prophet for the community. The Jerusalem temple is over 750 miles away, but Yahweh's relationship to the covenant people continues.

(Fourteen passages in the Book of Ezekiel have been rearranged in the New American Bible translation. To alert the reader to these changes when they occur, comments like the one that follows will be enclosed in brackets.)

[This first chapter is one of the most difficult to translate in the entire Old Testament. The New American Bible translation deletes verses 14, 21, and 25 and transposes the order of the verses that describe what Ezekiel first sees as the stormwind approaches (notice that the text reads 7, 10, 9, 12, 8, 11, 13). The deletions are made on the grounds that certain verses repeat information already given. The transpositions are seemingly made to keep like descriptions together. In the Hebrew text, mixed gender references to the living creatures complicate translation. In verse 5 the references are grammatically feminine, and the New American Bible sensitively translates "their form was human." In verses 7-8 all the references are masculine. Since the New American Bible inserts verses 10, 9, and 12—in which grammatical vacillations are extreme—between verses 7 and 8, the reference to the faces of the creatures in verse 10 is translated "like . . . the face of a man." The Jerusalem Bible better translates, "As to what they looked like, they had human faces" (1:10a). Similar ambiguities occur in verses 23-25, and again the New American Bible reorders and omits certain verses for the sake of smooth reading.]

2:1–3:15 Eating of the scroll. The Israelites who have been taken into exile are to learn that in the alien land "a prophet has been among them" (2:5). Those who have given up hope in the Lord's guidance and who are ready to make a new life for themselves in the land of exile are reminded that even in an alien land God calls them to fidelity. Those who fix their hopes upon the homeland and expect God's deliverance to come from there are assured that God's purpose for the covenant people can be accomplished wherever the people may be. In short, God's active presence in exile is the fundamental import of Ezekiel's vision. In response to the greatly varied hopes and fears of the exiled community, the chief message of the vision is that the Lord is still with the people. Exile in Babylon does not put them outside the range of either God's mercy or God's judgment.

The words heard by Ezekiel (ch. 2) are strange and vague. He is addressed as "son of man" (2:1), an address that occurs over eighty times in this book and is regularly best translated as "human being" or "man" (compare Ps 8:5, where "man" and "son of man" are synonymous terms). In the Book of Daniel (7:13-14), this phrase refers to a special human figure who receives the heavenly gift of dominion. And in the Gospels "son of man" refers variously to a coming heavenly judge and savior; to sayings about the suffering, death, and resurrection of Jesus; or simply to Jesus himself. But in the Book of Ezekiel, "son of man" is used as an address that contrasts Ezekiel's human frailty with God's divine majesty.

God summons Ezekiel to stand up (2:1) and then commissions him to speak a prophetic word (2:4) to the Israelites. Repeatedly God says that the covenant people are a "rebellious house" (see vv. 3, 5, 6, 7, 8), but God does not explain what wrong the people have done. Ezekiel is not told what he is to say to these rebellious people, only that he must speak what God commands whether they heed or resist the message. The prophet is not to fear the looks or the words of the people (2:8) but is to obediently speak the word that God will put into his mouth (2:9). Then the prophet sees a hand extended from the midst of the fiery throne. In the hand is a scroll with terrible words written upon it, front and back (2:10). He is told to eat the scroll, does so, and finds that the scroll is as sweet as honey (3:1-3). Like Jeremiah (Jer 1:9) and Moses (Deut 18:18), Ezekiel is commanded to speak the words that the Lord has put into his mouth (3:4).

Ezekiel is reminded (as was Jeremiah, ch. 1) that the people are stubborn and will not heed the divine message (3:5-11). He is to persist, however, in speaking, letting nothing deter him from his task. He is to say, "Thus says the Lord God" (3:11), whether or not the people listen to his words. Though commissioned to speak the divine word, Ezekiel delivers no oracle until chapter 6. Instead, in the opening chapters of the book he tells how the Lord, seated upon a throne-chariot, came to him in a resplendent vision, how a hand unrolled before him a scroll with "woes, mourning, and lamentation" written upon it, and how he ate the word that the Lord God brought to him on the banks of the river Chebar in the land of Babylon.

Some interpreters believe that the vision of the throne-chariot and the giving of the scroll are two separate acts on two different occasions. They argue that the vision came to Ezekiel during the Exile in Babylon, while the giving of the scroll occurred when he was still in Jerusalem, prior to the Exile. In the present text, however, the two acts are part of one event. In exile, Ezekiel has seen a powerful vision of God that brings to him a divine word and symbolic authorization to speak God's word to the rebellious house of Israel.

The effect of the experience upon Ezekiel is now reported (3:12-15). Hearing the loud rumblings of the departure of the living creatures and the glory of the Lord behind him, the prophet is transported by the spirit from the site of the vision to Tel-abib, one of the exilic settlements beside the river Chebar. For seven days he sits among the exiles, overwhelmed and unable to speak.

3:17-21 The prophet as watchman. The solemn portrayal of the prophet as a special mediator of God's word for the people (ch. 3) relates to other passages in the book (chs. 14, 18, 33). Ezekiel's charge in 3:17-19 to warn the wicked for both their sake and his own is identical with that in 33:7-9. Chapter 33 marks an important shift of emphasis in Ezekiel's prophecies after the fall of Jerusalem in 587 from words of judgment to words of hope. It is likely that later editors of the Ezekiel tradition inserted this passage about the prophet as watchman in the opening section of the book in order to indicate that from the start Ezekiel was appointed to protect the covenant people, to watch over Israel, to turn the evildoer from evil and to confirm the righteous in righteousness. Implicit in this passage about the prophet as a lookout is a break with the narrow idea that the sins of the people in former times have brought God's judgment upon the present generation.

Especially after the fall of Jerusalem, Ezekiel was concerned with convincing the people that they must not interpret God's actions in this way. Each individual stands before the present claim of the covenant God. The prophet is charged with seeing that the individual who is condemned for faithlessness hears the word of condemnation. Though the faithless person is individually responsible for breaking the covenant, Ezekiel, too, will be punished if that person is not warned. In discharging his prophetic responsibility, Ezekiel will save his own life, and each person who heeds his warnings will also live (v. 21). The treatment of chapter 33 will enable us to see more clearly what the brief oracle in chapter 3 means.

3:22-27 Ezekiel's dumbness. This passage, like the preceding one about the prophet as a lookout, seems to belong to a time later in the prophet's career. The portrayal of the prophet as one unable to speak freely (v. 26) contradicts the sentiment of earlier passages in which Ezekiel is commissioned as God's spokesperson (2:4 and 3:4). Later in the book (24:17-23 and 33:22), a period of symbolic silence is observed by the prophet shortly before the fall of Jerusalem.

The scene portrayed in 3:22-27 (the restraining of the prophet by the people after he returned from his overwhelming encounter with the Lord) may be a symbolic act, or it may be an actual occurrence. If it is a symbolic act, its meaning is that the population in Judah will shortly be invaded, bound, and led captive into exile. Perhaps it did happen that the people restrained the prophet, thinking him to have gone mad, and that Ezekiel interpreted this act as a sign of the people's refusal to hear him and as a sign of the coming captivity of Judah. Most likely, however, 3:17-21 and 3:22-27 were later editorial additions.

PART II: BEFORE THE SIEGE OF JERUSALEM

Ezek 4:1–24:27

Chapters 4–24 record the actions and words of Ezekiel before the fall of Jerusalem in 587 B.C.E. These first six years of Ezekiel's prophetic career, according to the highly edited chronology of the final form of the book, were directed to calling the people who remained in Judah as well as those in Babylon to right knowledge of God. In symbolic acts, allegorical stories, visions, parables, and judgment speeches, Ezekiel describes the imminent, irrevocable doom about to befall the chosen people on account of their idolatrous behavior. They have profaned God's holiness by turning to false gods and false prophets, and there can be no peace for them.

The divine presence has been so badly profaned in Jerusalem that in 592 B.C.E. (see 8:1), five years before the temple is to be destroyed, Ezekiel sees the glory of the Lord abandon the temple, moving first to the main entrance of the temple (10:2-4), then to the east gate (10:18-19), and finally to the Mount of Olives (11:22-23; relocated in the New American Bible to the end of chapter 10). The place of the divine presence becomes a scene of divine judgment. And Ezekiel voices God's indictment of the people for their failure to live according to the ethical requirements of the law. In his attempt to call the people back to God, the prophet speaks out against false prophets, calls for personal responsibility, and retells the disastrous history of Israel, tracing Israel's infidelity back to its very beginning in Egypt (ch. 23:3).

3:16–5:17 Acts symbolic of siege and exile. [The New American Bible text for this section has the following alterations: (1) 3:16a is inserted before 4:1; (2) 4:12-15 is placed after 4:17; (3) 5:13-15 is placed after 5:17. The rearrangements are seemingly made to untangle the text; they do not alter the sense of the passage.]

Four symbolic acts in 4:1–5:17 enact the fate of the Judeans who have not gone into captivity. Ezekiel acts out variously the role of God toward the people of Judah and the circumstances of those who will be punished. In the first symbolic act (4:1-3), the prophet draws upon a brick of the sort used in Babylonia for building purposes a picture of Jerusalem under siege. By unflinchingly "fixing his gaze" (4:3) on what he has sketched, Ezekiel dramatizes God's active power against Jerusalem.

In the second symbolic act (4:4-8), Ezekiel lies for a certain number of days on his left side facing north, then for a shorter number of days on his right side facing south, to indicate the number of years that North Israel and Judah must endure exile. Judah's exile is here fixed at forty years (4:6). The reference to God's binding Ezekiel (4:8) is a metaphor for the oppression experienced by the prophet on behalf of the people.

The third act (4:9-17) illustrates the scanty food rations in Jerusalem during its siege. The prophet is allowed only meager allotments of food and water. He eats carefully weighed-out mixed grains, which he is instructed to cook using human excrement as fuel (4:12). Such an act is so repulsive to Ezekiel that God relents and permits him to use cow dung, the more common fuel for cooking (4:15).

The fourth symbolic act (5:1-17) represents the death and hardships the people will experience at the hands of the enemy. Ezekiel cuts hair from his head and beard, and divides it by weight into three parts. One part is burned in the fire, another part is thrown into the air and scattered by a flashing sword, while the third part is blown away by the wind. Complete disaster will befall the inhabitants of the besieged city. The detailed interpretation of this symbolic act is probably very largely an expansion by the later community. The cannibalism suggested in verse 10 is elsewhere attested in the Old Testament as an expression of God's most severe punishment (see Lev 26:29; 2 Kgs 6:29; Jer 19:9).

Some interpreters have suggested that Ezekiel engages in these symbolic enactments of the divine word while still deprived of the ability to speak following his vision. This interpretation may indeed be correct. The visible acts of a prophet unable to speak would be an impressive way of communicating God's message. Yet, the appearance of the four symbolic acts together in chapters 4–5 and the fact that other prophets performed symbolic acts suggest that this interpretation is not necessarily correct. This collection was most likely made by some of Ezekiel's followers, who editorially grouped the traditions that represented the siege of Jerusalem. These dramatic enactments are reminiscent of the actions of Isaiah, who walked about Jerusalem "naked and barefoot for three years as a sign and portent" that the inhabitants of Jerusalem should not trust Egypt and Ethiopia (Isa 20:2-6); and of Jeremiah, who was instructed to buy a loincloth, wear it for a time and bury it, and then dig it up, rotted and good for nothing, to symbolize the corruption of "the pride of Jerusalem" (Jer 13:1-11). Prophets regularly use actions as well as words, visions, and dreams to symbolically portray the divine intent. In the Book of Ezekiel, this grouping of symbolic actions precedes the prophet's utterance of the divine word.

There is still no direct word or oracle from Ezekiel indicating what sins within the community are prompting God's threatened judgment. The elaboration of the last symbolic act (ch. 5) does refer to Israel's rejection of God's statutes and ordinances (5:6) and to the defiling of the sanctuary (5:11), but it is likely that these references come from the later tradition. It appears, therefore, that Ezekiel has first performed certain grim symbolic acts describing the fate of Jerusalem and Judah without having indicated why God is bringing ruin. Chapters 6–11, however, lay out in vivid detail the corruption of Israelite life and worship which, in Ezekiel's view, is leading God to complete the destruction of the holy city and its surroundings.

6:1-14 Against the mountains of Israel. Two oracles (vv. 1-10 and vv. 11-14) describe God's unrelenting anger at the inhabitants of the Promised Land. The reason for the judgment is no longer left in doubt: Israel has turned to idols, has committed abominations on high places, has forsaken God, and has become proud and arrogant.

Each oracle opens with an instruction that Ezekiel perform a gesture ("turn toward the mountains of Israel," v. 2; "clap your hands, stamp your feet," v. 11) and deliver a message in God's name ("Thus says the Lord God," vv. 3 and 11) that death and desolation will befall the entire countryside. The address to "the mountains of Israel" (6:2, 3) is meant in the Book of Ezekiel as an address to the whole Israelite people (see 19:9; 33:28; 34:13, 14; 35:12; 36:1, 4, 8; 37:22; 38:8; 39:2, 4, 17). Because of the sins committed on high places, where Israel has worshipped other gods, all Israel will experience destruction. Those who are permitted to escape the divine wrath (vv. 8-10) will be scattered in foreign lands, where they will remember their pasts with remorse. From this remnant will come those who understand the discipline of God's destruction as they turn from evil "to know the Lord."

The recognition formula "know that I am the Lord" appears over sixty times in the Book of Ezekiel and functions both as a word of judgment and of consolation. Its four occurrences in this chapter (6:7, 10, 13, 14) are harsh predictions that idol-worshipers will be slain and that those who live will remember the calamity and desolation that befell the land. The entire community will experience severe punishment for forsaking the covenant with God. Through the prophet, God here speaks a merciless word that promises utter destruction. In disaster, "then shall you know that I am the Lord."

7:1-27 The end has come. A revelation formula, "thus the word of the Lord came to me" (v. 1), and the recognition formula "thus they shall know that I am the Lord" (v. 27) set the boundaries of an exquisite poem that describes the disaster soon to befall the Promised Land. Though textually difficult to decipher because of duplications and shifts in voice, this poem sounds an alarm of imminent, irreversible doom for those who dwell in the land (verses 2-4 are repeated in a slightly more elaborate form in verses 5-9).

On "the day of the Lord" (v. 10; compare Amos 5:18), the life of the community will come to an end. The dissolution of the community (vv. 10-27) is described as a time when commerce will cease (vv. 12-13), the people will be under siege (vv. 14-16), and grief will be everywhere apparent (vv. 17-18). Wealth will be useless to those who have made idols (vv. 19-20), as God hands over the land to disaster (vv. 21-24). There shall be no peace when God's judgment comes (vv. 25-27). The community will crumble as individuals, prophets, priests, those who counsel, and those who rule can no longer do their jobs rightly. Anguish will replace peace (*shalom:* personal, economic, social wholeness or well-being) when God comes to punish the people.

8:3, 5-18 Vision of abominations in the temple. [The New American Bible text of chapters 8–11 has been extensively rearranged. In this section on the abominations in the temple, 8:1, 2, and 4 have been omitted. In the next section, "Slaughter of the Idolaters," 9:1-11 is followed by 11:24-25. And in the section "God's Glory Leaves Jerusalem," the text reads: 8:1, 2, 4; 10:1-22 (internally reordered); 11:22-23. These changes affect the meaning of chapters 8–11 in a variety of ways, as illustrated by comparison with translations that preserve the canonical order of the Hebrew text, such as the Jerusalem Bible or the Revised Standard Version. Instead of one transportation from Babylon to Jerusalem (8:1-4) and one return from Jerusalem to Babylon after God's departure from the holy city (11:22-25), the New American Bible suggests two round trips (one in what is basically chapters 8–9, another in what is basically chapters 10–11). Other alterations of meaning will be noted in the discussion.]

Ezekiel has a vision in which the spirit carries him from Babylon to the north gate of the Jerusalem temple (8:3). There the prophet is shown four successive acts of abomination taking place in the temple, each more offensive than the last. In 8:5-6, Ezekiel arrives at the gate of the inner court of the temple and looks out to see an altar set up before the image of a deity (perhaps Asherah, the goddess of love). The holiness of God is defiled by this abomination at the entrance to the sanctuary itself, but still greater evils are to be shown to the prophet. In 8:7-13, Ezekiel is led to a hidden room, where he sees seventy elders, including a certain Jaazaniah, the son of Shaphan (perhaps the Shaphan of 2 Kgs 22, who had been a leader in the reforms of Josiah), presenting incense offerings to loathsome creatures and beasts whose representations are inscribed on the walls of the hidden room. In 8:14-15, Ezekiel goes into the temple court, where he comes upon some women weeping for Tammuz, the Babylonian vegetation god, whose death signaled a dry season of infertility during the summer month that bore his name (June-July) until his sister, the goddess Inanna, brought him back to life in the spring. In the last scene, 8:16-18, Ezekiel is taken to the inner court between the vestibule of the temple and the altar of burnt offering, where he finds the worst blasphemy of all: twenty-five men have turned their backs on the temple where God is enthroned to worship the sun.

For Ezekiel the priest, these four acts represent complete apostasy from God and mean that the entire temple area must be violently cleansed of such abominations.

9:1-11; 11:24-25 Slaughter of the idolaters. In 9:1-11, six executioners and a man dressed in linen (linen is prescribed for priestly garments in Lev 16:4) and carrying a writing case are summoned to destroy the city. The origin of these seven figures from the north is obscure. Their job description is like that of God's destroying angel (Exod 12:23; 2 Sam 24:16-17; 2 Kgs 19:35). Their number is fixed at seven for the first time in the Old Testament in this text (compare the later usage of this number in Tob 12:15; Rev 8:2, 6; especially 15:1, 6-8, where the seven angels are dressed in white linen; 16:1-21). Perhaps the seven are an allusion to the seven Babylonian planet-gods, one of whom served as a heavenly scribe and compiled a Book of

Fate. In this text the man in linen is charged with the responsibility of marking the foreheads of those to be delivered.

Only those who "moan and groan over all the abominations that are practiced" in the city are to be spared (9:4). Without pity or regard for sex or age, all others are to be smitten. As the severe punishment is being carried out, Ezekiel asks God if all Israel must be destroyed (9:8). God answers that the evil deeds of the people cannot go unpunished. Then the man in the linen garment returns (the text does not mention the return of the six executioners) and says that God's commands have been accomplished (9:11). The New American Bible here inserts 11:24-25, which tells of the return of the prophet to Babylon and his report to the exiles about everything he has seen in Jerusalem.

8:1, 2, 4; 10:1-22; 11:22-23 God's glory leaves Jerusalem. [The text of the New American Bible differs here from the Hebrew original. Verses within chapter 10 have been rearranged, and verses from chapters 8 and 11 have been added. The text thus reads: 8:1, 2, 4; 10:20-22, 14-15, 9-13, 16-17, 1-8, 18-19; 11:22-23.]

This section opens with a date (17 September 592) and the notice of a transportation from Babylon to Jerusalem (8:1, 2, 4 transposed). Ezekiel's strange guide on this occasion is described in terms much like those used to describe the mysterious figure that appeared to him by the river Chebar (compare 1:27 and 8:2-4). The prophet is seized by the hair of his head and taken to the court of the temple (compare Habakkuk's mode of travel in Dan 14:36).

Once in the temple precincts (10:20-22), Ezekiel fixes his attention upon the glory of God and the same four-faced, four-winged living creatures he had seen in Babylon (see ch. 1). Beside each of the creatures he sees "a wheel within a wheel" (10:10), rimmed with eyes (10:12; compare 1:18). These wheels, which Ezekiel now learns are called "wheelwork" (10:13), are moved by the locomotion of the living creatures' wings (10:16-17).

Above the cherubim Ezekiel sees a throne-chariot like the one he saw in chapter 1 (the notable difference is that the living creatures of 1:26 are named "cherubim" in 10:1). But this throne-chariot is empty, because the glory of the God of Israel has gone up to the threshold of the temple (10:4). The man in linen is instructed to take fire from within the wheelwork and to scatter it over the city of Jerusalem. But before the city is destroyed, God's glory must leave the temple. Thus it happens that the glory of the Lord leaves the threshold of the temple to rest in the throne-chariot, which the cherubim carry to a mountain east of the city. The divine presence departs from the sanctuary and the city. Jerusalem is now without God's protection.

11:1-13 Judgment of the princes. The prophet is transported in an ecstatic vision to the east gate of the temple, where he pronounces an oracle against Jaazaniah (a man mentioned in 8:11, but with a different father) and Pelatiah. As he prophesies the coming death of these men who are misleading the people, Pelatiah falls dead.

It is difficult to know how this story is to be understood. Presumably the exiles later heard of the death of Pelatiah and fearfully assumed that he died just as Ezekiel related his vision of Yahweh's judgment. The section ends with the prophet's haunting cry, "Alas, Lord God! Will you utterly wipe out what remains of Israel?" Ezekiel grieves over the destruction of the people (11:13), just as he did over the fate of Jerusalem (9:8), but he cannot stem God's vengeance.

11:14-21 Restoration of the exiles. A word of promise closes Ezekiel's vision (11:14-21). The people in Jerusalem say that the Lord has sent the exiles into captivity and thereby turned over the land of promise to those who remain in the land. Not so, says this passage; God will punish those who remain in the land for their abominations, while the exiles will be delivered at a later time. This entire section, including the reference to the giving of a new heart and a new spirit to the restored community (vv. 19-20), seems to belong to the later period of Ezekiel's prophecies of hope (see 36:22-32).

12:1-28 Acts symbolic of the Exile; prophecy ridiculed. Two additional symbolic acts (vv. 1-20) and two independent sayings (vv. 21-28) condemning the people's rejection of the divine word are reported in chapter 12. Though Ezekiel dwells in the midst of a rebellious people who refuse to see or heed his message (12:1), he is instructed to perform symbolic acts reminiscent of those described in chapter 5, in the hope that perhaps the people may yet "see" (12:3) and repent of their rebelliousness.

As part of the first symbolic act (12:1-16), Ezekiel is instructed to prepare an exile's baggage and to leave at night by digging through a wall (12:1-7). Though this act symbolizes the fate of the inhabitants of Jerusalem, the verbal interpretation of it that follows (12:8-16) is directed to the exiles, who are warned not to put their hope in the holy city or in a quick end to the Exile. The event is interpreted as referring to Zedekiah, who left Jerusalem at night by making a breach in the walls of the city and fleeing into the hands of the Babylonians; they captured him and took him to Riblah, where he was blinded and led into captivity (see 2 Kgs 25:4 and Jer 39:4). The explanation of Ezekiel's symbolic act found in 12:8-16 is quite clearly a later reworking of the event.

As part of the second symbolic act (12:17-20), Ezekiel is told to eat his food with quaking and trembling as a sign of the panic that will seize the inhabitants of Jerusalem when their city is surrounded. The two sayings at the close of this chapter (12:21-28) prepare the way for the section against the false prophets (13:1–14:11). Those who think that the words of the prophets have lost their power are condemned (12:22-25), as are those who insist that the words of judgment apply only to a far-off day (12:26-28). The Lord's word is sure, and its fulfillment is even now ready at hand.

[Note that the New American Bible text of the two sayings reads 12:21-23, 25, 24, 26-28, presumably for the sake of smooth reading.

Chapter 13, which in its difficult and clearly layered original contains two sayings against false male prophets (vv. 1-9 and 10-16) and two sayings against false female prophets (vv. 17-21 and 22-23), has been extensively rearranged in the New American Bible. The two sayings against false male prophets are given in 13:1-2, 5, 7-8, 10-16 and 13:3-4, 6, 9, and the two sayings against false female prophets in 13:17, 22-23 and 13:18-21. Such radical reordering results in virtually rewriting the chapter. Unfortunately, there is no explanation in the notes to explain these changes.]

13:1-16 Against the prophets of peace; against false prophets in Chaldea. Thematic unity, an introductory revelation formula (v. 1), and a concluding recognition formula (v. 23, displaced in the New American Bible translation) distinguish chapter 13 (compare 12:26 and 14:2). The chapter opens with a word of denouncement for men who prophesy falsely out of their own thoughts (v. 2) when they have seen nothing (compare the parallel passage in Jer 23:9-32). Their unauthorized words are simply an adornment for the desires and wishes of the people, like whitewash placed upon a wall (vv. 10-12, 14-16). The message of these prophets is worthless. They offer hope that rests upon illusion (vv. 10, 16). God intends judgment, not peace, for the covenant people. Prophets who insist that Jerusalem and Judah will be spared have had false visions and speak lies (vv. 6-9). God's judgment is that these false prophets and their works will be utterly destroyed (vv. 15-16).

13:17-23 Against false prophetesses; against sorceresses. Ezekiel also condemns women who prophesy falsely out of their own thoughts (v. 17). These women undermine the faith of all by capitalizing on the dangers of the times to frighten people into paying for good omens (compare 1 Sam 9:7, where bread is the payment for an oracle). The women are involved with sewing magic bands and making veils for every head (v. 18), though it is unclear whether they or their clients wear these objects. They dishonor God by prophesying for venal motives, determining life or death according to the price paid them (v. 19; compare Mic 3:5). Their lies have disheartened the righteous and encouraged the wicked (v. 22). The judgment is that these false female prophets will no longer see visions or practice divination when God rescues the people from their power (v. 23).

It is sometimes suggested that these women should not be classified as "prophets," a title that the Old Testament uses for only a very few women (Miriam in Exod 15:21; Deborah in Judg 4:4; Huldah in 2 Kgs 22:14 and 2 Chr 34:22; the wife of Isaiah in Isa 8:3; and Noadiah in Neh 6:14). Instead they ought to be thought of as "sorcerers" (so the New American Bible heading) because they engage in strange acts of magic (compare the story of the medium at Endor in 1 Sam 28:7ff.). Since the text does not specify these women by the noun "prophets" but rather by a feminine plural participle—"those who play the role of the prophet" (v. 17)—their name has allowed some ambiguity about their role. But the compositional arrangement of the chapter is not ambiguous. In context, the women are understood as false prophets.

Chapter 13 is a two-part structure in which verses 2-16 are remarkably similar in form to verses 17-23. Internal symmetries and carefully drawn parallels between men (vv. 2-16) and women (vv. 17-23) who have misused their prophetic authority demonstrate an intended equation of the two groups. In each half of chapter 13, Ezekiel is instructed as "son of man" (vv. 2, 17) to deliver God's word (vv. 3, 18). Both the oracle to the men and the oracle to the women open with an unusual cry of dismay (vv. 3, 18; used elsewhere only in 34:2 in an oracle against false shepherds, the Hebrew interjection *hoy* expresses pain, "ah" or "alas," which is to be distinguished from the more regularly used *'oy*, translated "woe"). Both the men and the women are accused of prophesying their own thoughts (vv. 2, 17), of having delusive visions and practicing false divination (vv. 6-9, 23). And both oracles contain two recognition formulas (vv. 9, 14, 21, 23). Through the word of the prophet, males and females are denounced for speaking lies that have dishonored God and disheartened the people.

If practicing acts of magic accounts for understanding the women in chapter 13 as sorcerers, then the men must also be so understood. Both groups are accused of practicing "divination" (the men in verses 6-9; the women in verse 23), an act of magic specifically prohibited in Deut 18:10. More likely Ezekiel used a participial circumlocution to address women "who play the role of the prophet" in order to condemn them for practices as abominable as those of their male counterparts (compare also the women and the men singled out for dishonoring the sanctity of the temple in chapter 8).

14:1-11 Prophecy useless for idolaters. As in 8:1 (which was transposed to chapter 10), so here in 14:1 (and again in 20:1) the elders of Judah exiled in Babylon come to consult Ezekiel. Following the revelation formula (v. 2), God explains to Ezekiel that these men are syncretists who have consulted idols and questions whether such as these should be allowed to seek an oracle of the Lord (v. 3). Through the prophet, God warns that those who consult idols before coming to a prophet will not receive a word of the Lord but rather an answer from God in person (vv. 4-5). Again the prophet is instructed to caution the people not to seek a prophetic word of the Lord while they follow idols (verse 7 is a variant of verse 4) lest they personally encounter God, who will make of them an object lesson for others by excluding them from the community. The recognition formula (v. 8) rounds out this word of warning to syncretists.

There follows a word to the prophet who responds to the requests of idol-worshipers, detailing his offense and punishment (vv. 9-10). The prophet who deludes and those who are deluded by other gods will be equally punished (compare Jer 14:15-16; 27:15). The divine purpose is to educate both the people and the prophet who might stray from an exclusive relationship with God (v. 11). Even though they are in a foreign land where Babylonian gods whose power is manifest in the achievements of Nebuchadnezzar are worshiped, the people are not permitted to give allegiance to any god other than the God of Israel without grave consequences.

14:12-23 Personal responsibility. In the remainder of this chapter and in the following nine chapters (14:12–23:49), Ezekiel's message for Israel is related to various events from its past history. Ezekiel, like Jeremiah and Second Isaiah, recounts the history of God's dealings with the people in order to draw a contrast between past acts of mercy and present experiences of judgment, and also to testify to the graciousness of God.

In a two-part oracle (vv. 12-20, 21-23), the prophet declares that even pious intercessors from Israel's past like Noah, Daniel, and Job could not divert God's wrath against the land (compare the parallel text in Jer 14:19–15:4). Four acts of judgment are about to befall its inhabitants as the sword, famine, wild beasts, and pestilence (v. 21) come upon Jerusalem. The sons and daughters who survive will serve as an object lesson justifying God's destruction of Jerusalem (vv. 22-23). Righteousness will save individuals but not the city. The prophet is insisting here on individuals' responsibility and accountability. Each must choose to act righteously and live, or to act faithlessly and die, a theme more fully developed in chapter 18.

15:1-8 Parable of the vine. In this short

allegory on the wood of the vine, the prophet declares that in God's eyes the inhabitants of Jerusalem have become unproductive and valueless, like a useless vine that no longer produces fruit. Like wood that is good for nothing, the homeland will be thrown into the fire. Later on the prophet will return to this image of Israel as the vine of the Lord (19:10-12).

16:1-63 The faithless spouse. In this the longest chapter of the book, Ezekiel narrates the beginning of Israel in an allegory about Jerusalem as the unfaithful wife of the Lord. Ezekiel is regarded as the Old Testament father of allegory, a literary form in which a story is told and then application is made to the contemporary situation (see also chs. 15, 17, 19, 23, 31, 34). Ezekiel is instructed to recount this figurative story so that Jerusalem will know its abominations (v. 2).

Verses 1-14 describe Jerusalem as an unwanted orphan, born from the union of the Amorites and the Hittites, and cast aside at birth by its parents. Neither midwife nor parents cared for Jerusalem. The child lay beside the road, unloved and untended, when God came by and performed the duties of a midwife. God saw to the needs of the child and then left. When Jerusalem came of age, God returned and betrothed the city, showering presents upon it and taking it as a bride. Jerusalem was "renowned" among the nations for exceeding "beauty," queen-like dignity, and the splendid gifts that God had bestowed upon it (v. 14).

Reversing the terms of adornment that closed verse 14, verse 15 opens a section (vv. 15-34) that describes how the "beauty" and "renown" of the city led it astray. Jerusalem's harlotry was idolatry played out with passers-by (v. 16) and with self-constructed male images (v. 17; compare 23:14). Jerusalem sacrificed her children to these images (vv. 20-22). She spread her legs to all, including Egyptians (v. 26), Assyrians (v. 28), and Babylonians (v. 29). So insatiable was Jerusalem's lust that she scorned payment and even stooped to paying lovers to come to her (vv. 30-34).

Verses 35-43 tell how God sentenced Jerusalem to a violent death. The harlot is summoned (v. 35) to hear an oracle that first restates the cultic sins she has committed by turning to other lovers and idols (v. 36), and then lists the consequences she will suffer on account of these sins: she will be stripped naked by her lovers (v. 37), sentenced by God as an adulterer and murderer (v. 38; see the death penalty prescribed in Deut 22:22 and Lev 20:10), and horribly executed by the assembly (vv. 39-40). While many women (a figure for the other nations) look on, Jerusalem will be punished, so that never again will she give payment to other lovers (v. 41). Then God's wrath will be satisfied (v. 42). Jerusalem will have been justly punished according to her own conduct for forgetting her origins and for adding immorality to her other abominations (v. 43).

Verses 44-58, a diatribe comparing Jerusalem to her sisters, opens with an epigram, "Like mother, like daughter," restates Jerusalem's Amorite and Hittite parentage, and moves quickly to an unfavorable comparison of Jerusalem to her two sisters, Samaria and Sodom (vv. 44-46). Jerusalem, the most wicked of the three, is called to blush for her sins (vv. 47-52). Then follows a sequence (vv. 53-58) describing the restoration of Sodom, Samaria, Jerusalem, and their daughters (neighboring cities), and the enduring sense of shame that Jerusalem will experience in the restoration.

A messenger formula (v. 59) introduces the climactic closing section (vv. 59-63) of chapter 16, which includes a dramatic restatement of all that has preceded and the astonishing declaration of an everlasting covenant (compare v. 60 and 37:26). Verses 60-61 recall the covenant God made with Jerusalem in her youth (compare vv. 3-43) and her relationship to her sisters (compare vv. 44-58). Verses 62-63 promise a reestablished covenant between God and Jerusalem. Reconciliation will bring with it sober shame and right recognition of God for Jerusalem. No longer will the city be oblivious to its abominations (see the charge of v. 2). With exceeding graciousness, God will pardon the iniquity of Jerusalem. This closing section of promise may be from Ezekiel, but the likelihood is that it comes from the hand of an editor. In the later chapters (34–37), where Ezekiel sums up his hope for Israel, he uses different language and imagery.

17:1-24 The eagles and the vine. The allegory of the eagles and the cedar (vv. 1-10) and its interpretation (vv. 11-21) comment upon the political disquiet experienced in the land of Judah. In 597 B.C.E. Nebuchadnezzar ("the great eagle," v. 3) came to Judah and took King Jehoiachin (the "topmost branch" of the cedar, v. 4) and the leading citizens to Babylonia. Zedekiah ("seed of the land," v. 5) was then appointed head of the Judean state by the Babylonians. Yet, in 588 he rebelled against Babylonia by turning to Psammetichus II of Egypt ("another great eagle," v. 7).

Ezekiel's message is that the Egyptians will not be able to save the king or the land of Judah. Like Jeremiah (see Jer 37–38), Ezekiel insists that Zedekiah should have submitted to the rule of Babylonia. Ezekiel even declares that the oath and the covenant between Zedekiah and Nebuchadnezzar were as binding as the oath and covenant between the people and the Lord (see v. 19). Rebellion against Babylonia is actually rebellion against God, who had brought Nebuchadnezzar against Judah.

Like chapter 16, this chapter also closes with a word of promise (vv. 22-24). God will plant a sprig from the high cedar, care for it, and cause it to grow. The future of Israel is entirely in the hands of God, who can make a high tree low and a low tree high (v. 24). These closing words of promise may be an addition, although in this instance they are more in keeping with Ezekiel's own style. Perhaps the prophet added this section about the mystery of God's sovereignty to the prophecy at a subsequent time.

18:1-32 Personal responsibility. Following the revelation formula (v. 1), God questions Ezekiel about the proverb "Fathers have eaten green grapes, thus their children's teeth are on edge" (v. 2). Some of the more cynical exiles may have repeated this proverb in order to blame others or God (vv. 25, 29; compare 33:17, 20) for their sufferings. Ezekiel passionately argues that each generation is responsible for its own actions (vv. 3-20). He declares that the judgment of God falls only upon the sinner. The present generation is in no better or worse position before God on account of the sins of the previous generations. God will not destroy Israel for past sins, only for present ones. Each generation receives life or death according to its own actions (vv. 21-31). If the wicked should now turn from their evil ways, God would forgive them, and the present generation would live (see Deut 30:15-20). The prophet appeals to the people to turn back to God, declaring that God takes no pleasure in anyone's death (see vv. 23 and 32). The chapter closes with God's cry to the house of Israel, "Return and live!" (v. 32).

19:1-14 Allegory of the lions; allegory of the vine branch. The tragic end of the princely offspring of a lioness (vv. 2-9) and of a vine (vv. 10-14) is told in two allegorical lamentations. The subject of the first lament is the exile of two royal lion cubs of Judah—one to Egypt and the other to Babylon. Since only one king contemporary with Ezekiel was taken captive to Egypt, the identity of the first lion cub (vv. 3-4) is unquestionably Jehoahaz, the son of Queen Hamutal and King Josiah. After only a three-month reign in 609 B.C.E., Jehoahaz was taken captive by Pharaoh Neco and deported to Egypt, where he died (see 2 Kgs 23:30-34).

The identity of the second lion cub (vv. 5-9) is more difficult, since two kings contemporary with Ezekiel were taken captive to Babylon. If the same mother lion (v. 2) bore both cubs, then the second king is Queen Hamutal's son Zedekiah (2 Kgs 23:31; 24:18), who was taken captive by Nebuchadnezzar in 587 B.C.E., blinded, and led in chains to Babylon (see 2 Kgs 24:18–25:7). If, however, the mother lion is a metaphor for Judah (compare Gen 49:9), from whom many princes emerged, then the second king might well be Jehoiachin, the son of Queen Nehushta, who after a three-month reign in Jerusalem was led away captive to Babylon in 597 B.C.E. and kept prisoner by Nebuchadnezzar (see 2 Kgs 24:8-15).

The subject of the second lament (vv. 10-14) is the annihilation of Zedekiah (compare chs. 17 and 31) and the mother vine. This allegory tells how the vine and its strongest stem were plucked up, exposed to the weather, and burned (v. 12). Then transplanted to a desert land (taken to Babylon; see Jer 52:1-11), this once stately vine had no branches and no fruit. The strength of the royal vine was destroyed (v. 14).

The fate of Judah's royalty is thus the subject of mourning and lamentation (see vv. 1 and 14c). The two historical allegories in chapter 19 are both dirges in five-beat lament meter. Three beats followed by two give the poems a limping, halting rhythm in Hebrew (compare 2 Sam 1:17-21; Isa 14:4-21; Amos 5:1-3). Form as well as content effectively show that, for Ezekiel, nationalistic hope in the Davidic line was virtually dead.

20:1-44 Israel's history of infidelity. Chapter 20 opens with a specific date (August 591, eleven months after the last date given in 8:1, which was transposed in the New American Bible to chapter 10) and presents a familiar scene of certain elders of Judah gathering at Ezekiel's house (compare 8:1 and 14:1). The exiles come to ask that Ezekiel inquire of the Lord for them. As in chapter 14, so too here, following the revelation formula (v. 2), God questions whether the elders should be permitted to seek an oracle (v. 3). Instead of an oracle, Ezekiel is charged to deliver a jarring historical retrospective (vv. 4-31) that underscores the sinfulness of the chosen people from their very beginning in Egypt (vv. 5-9), through the rebellious first generation (vv. 10-17) and second generation (vv. 18-26) in the wilderness, even to the present generation (vv. 27-31). All have profaned God by going after idols (see vv. 7, 16, 18, 24, 30, 31).

Israel can take no delight in its past. As Ezekiel tells the story, there never was a time of right relationship between God and the people (compare the more usual interpretation that once the people entered the land of Canaan, syncretism caused a strain in their relationship with God; see Hos 2). Ezekiel claims that from the moment of the Exodus onward, there has been disharmony between God and the idolatrous chosen people. For the first time in the book, Ezekiel presents the important theological rationale (further developed in chapters 36 and 39) that God has extended mercy to the people, not for their own sake but for the sake of the holiness of the divine name (vv. 9, 14, 22, 39). Deliverance is inextricably bound to God's holiness, reputation, and character in the world. And now, at the conclusion of the historical account, to be true to the divine identity and presence, God refuses an oracle to the idolatrous elders (v. 31).

In the course of the historical recitation, Ezekiel speaks of statutes given by God that were "not good" (v. 25), laws that contributed to the defilement of those who sacrificed their first-born to God (v. 26; compare Exod 22:28-29). Retribution seemingly takes the form of God's misleading the people. Law, more ordinarily understood as a light of guidance (Ps 119:105), is here a cause for stumbling. God deals perversely with this rebellious people (compare Ps 18:26) as a mysterious, incomprehensible judge.

A disputation (vv. 32-44) following the historical recitation reiterates the charge that the present generation is idolatrous. In its first section (vv. 32-38), God promises harsh treatment for those who serve "wood and stone" (v. 32). As a wrathful king (v. 33), God will assemble the exiles and lead them to the desert in a new exodus (v. 34) for a severe "face to face" judgment (v. 35; compare the "in person" encounter promised to idolaters in 14:4). Like a shepherd, the Lord will use a staff to count out the small number of faithful people from the rebellious ones. The transgressors will never again be permitted to return to the land of Israel (vv. 37-38). Thus God promises that the exiles will know the Lord (see the recognition formula, v. 38).

The dispute then continues with a word to the members of the house of Israel urging them to put away all idols (vv. 39-44). Authentic worship requires complete awareness and renunciation of past evil conduct and actions. Then an unexpected word of genuine hope mitigates the severe judgment: God promises to bring Israel back into the land, to receive the offerings of the people, and to accept their repentance (vv. 40-44). By such means the mystery of God's holy name will be made manifest to the nations. Restoration will bring with it true recognition of the Lord (see the recognition formula repeated in verses 42 and 44).

21:1-10 The sword of the Lord. In chapter 21 Ezekiel's voice grows more strident as he warns that the sword of destruction is unsheathed and ready to strike. First the prophet is instructed to deliver an allegory against the forest of the south stating that God is kindling a fire that will devour all the trees (vv. 2-4). Ezekiel protests that the people mock him when he speaks in parables (v. 5), so he is given an interpretation of the allegory to proclaim (vv. 6-10). God is coming with an unsheathed sword, which will not be sheathed again, to destroy the wicked and the virtuous of Jerusalem.

21:11-12 Act symbolic of the city's fall. As in 6:11; 9:8; and 11:13, the prophet expresses grief over the coming suffering of his people. He is instructed to groan with deep emotional sadness as a sign that the end has come.

21:13-22 Song of the sword. Ezekiel engages in a kind of sword dance. He sings a song about a sharpened, ready sword of destruction (vv. 14-15) and performs a number of symbolic actions (vv. 16-22). He cries aloud and slaps his thigh (v. 17), claps his hands (v. 19), and brandishes the sword to the right and to the left (v. 21). He announces that the sword has been put in the hand of an unidentified slayer (v. 16) and that God approves (v. 22). God, the divine warrior, will execute fierce judgment against the people, not for them.

21:23-32 Nebuchadnezzar at the crossroads. Next Ezekiel is instructed to draw a map indicating two possible paths from Babylon (21:23-28), one leading to Rabbah in Ammon (the modern city of Amman, Jordan) and the other to Jerusalem (compare the symbolic acts in 3:16–5:17). In 587 B.C.E. these two small nations joined in an alliance against the threatening power of the Babylonian empire. In verse 26, by three methods of divination (shaking marked arrows and drawing one by lot; consulting teraphim, which were small images of household gods; and interpreting markings on the entrails of a sacrificed victim), Nebuchadnezzar determines that Jerusalem will be punished first (v. 27). Though the people may wish to dismiss this warning, their fate is marked by the arrow in Nebuchadnezzar's hand (v. 28).

Zedekiah is addressed as a depraved and wicked prince whose end is coming (vv. 29-32). A triple repetition, "twisted, twisted, twisted will I leave it" (v. 32), expresses the utter chaos about to befall the city. The sign is thus made clear that Jerusalem and its ruler are doomed to destruction.

21:33-37 Against the Ammonites. In this difficult passage, which may come from a later period, the Ammonites are depicted as wielding a sword against Israel (vv. 33-34). God stays their hand (v. 35) and declares that these people will themselves be judged and destroyed (v. 36). So complete will be their destruction that they will no longer be remembered (v. 37). No worse punishment than this could be imagined.

22:1-31 Crimes of Jerusalem. Three oracles on the common theme of the defilement of Jerusalem have been grouped together in chapter 22. Verses 1-16 attack the violence and idolatry of the bloody city (notice the sevenfold repetition of the word "blood/bloodshed" in verses 2, 3, 4, 6, 9, 12, 13). Verses 17-22 describe Israel as scrap metal of no value. And verses 23-31 condemn the princes (v. 25), priests (v. 26), nobles (v. 27), prophets (v. 28), and people of the land (v. 29) who have turned to sinful ways. The destruction of Jerusalem is inevitable, given the universal corruption of the city (compare Zeph 3:1-8).

23:1-49 The two sisters. In chapter 23 the prophet concludes his grim picture of Israel's past (see 14:12–23:49), using the coarsest language found in the prophetic literature. God tells Ezekiel an allegory about North Israel and Judah, portraying the two nations as harlots (compare ch. 16) who seek to outdo one another in their sins.

Verses 1-4 introduce the two sisters and tell of their immoral childhood in Egypt. Despite their sins, Oholah (Samaria) and Oholibah (Jerusalem) were taken as brides by the Lord and bore many sons and daughters. The names of the two whores can be translated as "(she who has) her own tent" (Oholah) and "my tent (is) in her" (Oholibah). Since the "tent" was a place of meeting with God in the wilderness (see Exod 33:7), the names may be cultic allusions. Another possibility is that the words are simply sound-alike names with a foreign flavor. Though the meaning of the names is now obscure, the symbolism of the two harlot sister cities wed to God as representatives of Samaria (the capital of Israel) and Jerusalem (the capital of Judah) is clear.

Verses 5-10 describe the depravity and punishment of the older sister, Oholah-Samaria, who offered herself to Assyrian lovers. Verses 11-21 describe the even more vile harlotry of Oholibah-Jerusalem, who made open advances to Assyria and Babylonia. In four divine sayings (vv. 22-35), each introduced by the formula "thus says the Lord God" (vv. 22, 28, 32, 35), God declares that on account of her sins Jerusalem will be punished. Original to the text is the judgment that Jerusalem will be handed over to her lovers, who will now unleash violence against her. They will mutilate her so horribly that she will never again be able to play the harlot (see v. 25: "cutting off your nose and ears," a punishment found in both Egyptian and Assyrian texts). Most likely secondary to the text are verses 28-34, which state that Jerusalem will be handed over to those she hates (vv. 28-30) and that she will be judged by sharing her sister's cup of dismay (vv. 31-34).

Verses 36-49, a later retelling of the allegory of Oholah and Oholibah, summarize the sins of the sisters (vv. 36-44) and describe their punishment (vv. 45-49). The women sin simultaneously and will be punished simultaneously. Added here is a warning to individual women not to imitate the lewdness of the two sisters (v. 48). Finally, the recognition formula appears, signaling that judgment is an experience through which God's sovereignty will be known (v. 49).

24:1-14 Allegory of the pot. The siege of Jerusalem by Nebuchadnezzar, king of Babylon, began on the tenth day of the tenth month in the ninth year of Jehoiachin's captivity (v. 1; see also 2 Kgs 25:1). On this very day, which would fall toward the end of the year 588, Ezekiel, who was in Babylon, was commanded to write down the date and to deliver an allegorical oracle to the rebellious people (vv. 1-2). Ezekiel describes the coming fate of those left behind in the city of Jerusalem as the destruction of an unclean and rusty cooking pot (vv. 3-14). God avenges the crimes of the city and its inhabitants in a fire that consumes not only the contents of the pot but the pot itself. God had wished to spare the city, but now the end has come. No one need hope, for God will not relent.

24:15-21, 24, 22-23 Symbol of the destruction of the temple. [For some unexplained reason, the New American Bible translation places verse 24, which contains a recognition formula, before verse 22. There is no change in meaning with this move, but the regularity of the pattern in which the phrase "thus you shall know that I am the Lord" closes a section is here broken.]

Since the Jerusalem temple fell in the summer of 587B.C.E., God's shocking word to Ezekiel in this passage probably took place sometime after the preceding dated allegory (vv. 1-14). The prophet is told that his wife, who is "the delight of his eyes" (v. 16), will suddenly be taken from him and that he is not to mourn her death publicly (v. 17). Ezekiel proclaims this strange message to the people, and on the evening of the same day (v. 18) his wife dies, just as the Lord had said. The people ask for an explanation of these strange acts from the prophet (v. 19), who proclaims that the death of his wife is a sign of the death of Jerusalem. As he has been commanded not to weep over the loss of his beloved, so too must the people not weep over the destruction of their delight and desire, the sanctuary of Jerusalem (vv. 20-24).

24:25-27 End of Ezekiel's dumbness. It appears that Ezekiel neither laments his wife's death nor speaks at all until word reaches him that the city has fallen. Most likely an editor added these words to relate the preceding passage about the destruction of Jerusalem to 33:21, in which a fugitive from Jerusalem (first mentioned in 24:26) arrives in Babylon to announce that the holy city has been taken. As the text now stands, chapters 25–32 have been inserted between these two significant passages about the fate of Jerusalem (compare 24:26 and 33:21).

PART III: PROPHECIES AGAINST FOREIGN NATIONS

Ezek 25:1–32:32

Chapters 25–32 form a unit clearly distinct from the chapters before the siege of Jerusalem (3–24) and those after the fall of the city (33–39). In some of the most exquisite poetry in the book, Ezekiel declares God's vengeance against neighboring countries that have violated the covenant people. Seven groups of foreign people are singled out for judgment: the Ammonites, the Moabites, the Edomites, the Philistines, the inhabitants of Tyre, the inhabitants of Sidon, and the Egyptians. According to six of the seven dates listed in these chapters (see 26:1; 29:1; 30:20; 31:1; 32:1; 32:17), the oracles were delivered within the space of three years, between 585 and 588 B.C.E. A seventh date (29:17) describes a time fifteen years later. It is likely that Ezekiel himself is the author of these important oracles against the foreign nations. International as well as national concerns occupy the interest of the prophet in these chapters.

25:1-7 Against Ammon. The Ammonites are condemned for having exulted over the fall of Jerusalem and the conquest of the land. The defeat of Ammon at the hands of the people of the East is promised. God will bring destruction upon the Ammonites because they have delighted in the ruin of Israel. They will come "to know the Lord" (vv. 5, 7) in their own destruction.

25:8-11 Against Moab. Moab's fate is to be the same as that of Ammon and for the same reason. Moab, too, is to learn that the Lord alone is God (v. 11) and that the fate of Judah and Jerusalem does not mean that Israel is like all the nations.

25:12-14 Against Edom. Judgment is levied against Edom for having taken part in the destruction of Judah and Jerusalem, apparently by rounding up the fugitives and turning them over to the Babylonians and then infiltrating the land of Judah and claiming ownership (see Obadiah). The fate of Edom is different in that the vengeance of the Lord will be executed by the people of Israel. Chapter 35 expands the details of the devastation of Edom.

25:15-17 Against the Philistines. The oracle against Philistia is similar to that against Edom. The Philistines also appear to have harassed the fugitives and taken advantage of them in their plight. Although there is no indication of the means of God's punishment of Philistia, historically it almost certainly was destroyed at the same time as the campaigns of the Babylonians against Judah and Jerusalem.

26:1–28:19 Against the city of Tyre. The next three chapters are devoted to oracles against the famed commercial center Tyre, the chief city of Phoenicia. This city, located on almost impregnable rock at some distance from the Mediterranean shore, withstood the efforts of Nebuchadnezzar to capture it. In 586 B.C.E. the Babylonians began a thirteen-year siege, which ended inconclusively. Not until the time of Alexander the Great (fourth century) was part of the island itself destroyed.

The four oracles in 26:1-21 are of two types. The first two units (vv. 1-6 and 7-14) are oracles similar to those against the other nations. Because Tyre exulted over the fall of Jerusalem, it too will be punished by Nebuchadnezzar. The second units (vv. 15-18 and 19-21) are laments over the death of Tyre and its descent into the nether world. The fall of Tyre will cause all the princes of the sea to gather trembling on the shore, lamenting the death of Tyre and the threat to their own kingdoms. Tyre will be placed in the underworld, there to remain forever.

In chapter 27 Ezekiel portrays Tyre as a great ship beautifully fitted out and proudly sailing the seas. He relates the extraordinary range and variety of Tyre's trading activities (27:12-25a). Then he details the end of this great commercial city as it is destroyed by God's east wind, which wrecks Tyre's exquisite ship, much to the mourning and consternation of the people on the shore (27:25b-36).

Chapter 28 is a second oracle about the ruin of Tyre (vv. 1-10) and a lamentation over the demise of its king (vv. 11-19). Tyre is cast down for misusing its divine position, wisdom, and wealth. Ezekiel grants that God created the king even wiser than Daniel (compare 14:14) but declares that his pride is the undoing of the city. God will cause it to die at the hands of foreigners (vv. 9, 10).

The lament in 28:11-19, seemingly based on a variant version of the Eden story, is a judgment against the king of Tyre. On the holy mountain of God (v. 14) a city was established which Ezekiel calls Eden, the garden of God (see Gen 2–3). The king, the first human being, was created perfect, wise, and beautiful, and was clothed and adorned with precious stones. A cherub guarded the king (compare Gen 3:24), who was blameless until he spurned his beauty and wisdom by acts of violence and arrogance. For his sin he was cast out of the mountain city by a guardian cherub and humiliated before the nations.

Ezekiel recasts this myth to make it portray the imminent ruin of Tyre. The old story probably related the sin of the first king, leading to his expulsion from the mountain city. The mountain thereafter was the dwelling place of El, the high god, and entrance to it was barred to earthly residents. But for Ezekiel, the historical sins of Tyre constitute the real corruption of the city. God executes judgment upon Tyre by stripping away all its treasures, won through its maritime trading, and humbling the people for their pride and injustice. Ezekiel does not contest the truth of the myth of Tyre's origin; he states it in order to dramatize the reversal of Tyre's fortunes.

28:20-26 Against Sidon. A brief oracle against Sidon (vv. 20-24), the other great city of Phoenicia, and a general promise of restoration for Israel following God's judgment of the foreign nations (vv. 24-26) complete the chapter. The composite nature of this section is indicated by the four recognition formulas in verses 22, 23, 24, 26.

The oracles against Egypt (29:1–32:32) are even longer and richer in mythological imagery than were the oracles against Phoenicia. The pride of Pharaoh, who considers himself a god, constitutes the chief sin of Egypt. Repeatedly this theme recurs in the following seven sections.

29:1-16 Egypt the crocodile. In a composite of several brief oracles (vv. 3-6a; 6b-9a; 9b-12; 13-16), dated January 587 B.C.E. (v. 1), Pharaoh is chastised for thinking himself maker and master of the Nile. On account of his sin, Egypt will be reduced to the most lowly of kingdoms.

29:17-21 The wages of Nebuchadnezzar. An oracle dated April 571 B.C.E. (v. 17; this is the latest dated oracle in Ezekiel) refers to the costly siege of Tyre by Nebuchadnezzar and promises the Babylonian king that he will recoup his spent treasures by the plunder of Egypt. Nebuchadnezzar is named as God's agent, and his wages are listed as the riches of Egypt.

30:1-19 The day of the Lord against Egypt. This section, which is the only undated oracle in the collection against Egypt, is clearly a composite (introduction formulas occur in verses 2, 6, 10, and 13; recognition formulas occur in verses 8 and 19). It elaborates the theme that the day is coming when God will devastate Egypt and its southern neighbor, Ethiopia. Nebuchadnezzar will invade Egypt (v. 10), and God will dry up the Nile (v. 12). These punishments will lead to international recognition of the Lord.

30:20-26 Pharaoh's broken arm. The fourth section against Egypt is dated April 587 B.C.E. (v. 20), just a few months before the fall of Jerusalem. About three months earlier, Pharaoh Hophra had come to the aid of Jerusalem, which was under siege by the Babylonians (see Jer 37:5). In this oracle all hope in Egypt's help is crushed. God declares that the arms of Pharaoh will be irreparably broken (v. 22), while the arms of the king of Babylon will be strengthened (v. 24). God will put a sword of destruction in the hand of Nebuchadnezzar (v. 25) and scatter the Egyptians among the nations (v. 26). Thus will the Egyptians know and recognize God.

31:1-18 Allegory of the cypress. The fifth section, dated June 587 B.C.E. (v. 1), is a three-part prophecy addressed to Pharaoh and his retinue (v. 2). A description of a great tree, more beautiful than any tree in the garden of God (vv. 3-9), opens the poem. Then follows a prose account describing the fall of the great tree on account of its pride (vv. 10-14), and its consignment to the nether world (vv. 15-18).

32:1-16 Dirge over Pharaoh. Dated March 585 B.C.E., this composite section opens with a fragment of a lament (vv. 1-3) over the destruction of Pharaoh, here symbolized as a lion and a sea monster. It continues as an oracle of judgment (vv. 3-8) against Pharaoh, allegorically portrayed as a sea monster that God will catch and throw upon the shore, where the beasts of the earth will devour the carcass. Then follows a series of later expansions that abandon the sea-monster imagery completely. First a prose interpretation of the grief that the nations will feel in seeing God's sword brandished against Egypt (vv. 9-10) is added. Next an oracle about Nebuchadnezzar as God's agent in bringing a sword of destruction against Egypt (vv. 11-14) appears. Then, closing the section is a brief prose subscription (vv. 15-16) which first reiterates the claim that the desolation of Egypt will be a means through which the nations will know the Lord and then concludes with an instruction to the daughters of the nations to take up a lament over Egypt's demise (on the role of women in mourning, see Jer 9:16-19).

32:17-32 Dirge over Egypt. [The New American Bible text reads 32:17-18, 20, 19, 21-32. The transpositions were seemingly made to achieve a smoother reading of this difficult passage.]

This seventh oracle opens with a date that most likely is April 586 B.C.E. (the Hebrew text lacks a month). The prophet is told to wail (v. 18) over the condemnation of Egypt to the underworld. Egypt's comfort will consist in the fact that its descent to Sheol has been preceded by that of other great world powers. Already gone down to the underworld from the Mesopotamian region are Assyria (v. 22), which fell to Babylonia in 612 B.C.E.; Elam (v. 24), a country east of Babylon, which was conquered by the Assyrian Ashurbanipal in 650 B.C.E. (see Jer 49:35-39); and Meshech and Tubal (v. 25), two tribes in Asia Minor that traded slaves with Tyre and terrorized Assyria. From the Palestinian region, Edom (v. 29) and the Sidonians (that is, Phoenicians; v. 30) lie among the slain in the pit with Egypt.

Ezekiel's prophecies against Egypt were probably the most important of all for the inhabitants of Judah and Jerusalem. Several of these oracles are dated prior to the fall of Jerusalem in 587 B.C.E. (see 29:1; 30:20; 31:1). Ezekiel tried to convince the leaders of Jerusalem that Egyptian help was a delusion, but his words, like those of Jeremiah, went unheeded. From this group of seven oracles against Egypt (29:1–32:32), the entire cycle of oracles against Israel's seven neighbors (25:1–32:32) may then have grown as Ezekiel and his followers reflected on the worldwide significance of God's judgment of the covenant people Israel.

PART IV: SALVATION FOR ISRAEL

Ezek 33:1–39:29

The fall of Jerusalem marks the turning point in Ezekiel's message. Following the horror of 587 B.C.E., the prophet turns from dire predictions and condemnations of false hope to a radical revival of the spirit of the people. In chapters 33–39 Ezekiel and his followers counter false despair in a series of sermons that project new and renewed forms of life for the community, which doubts its ability to survive. Significantly, this section on salvation for Israel opens with God's demand for personal responsibility both for Ezekiel as a lookout for the people and for every individual.

33:1-9 The prophet as watchman. Chapter 33 resumes the theme of the prophet as God's lookout within Israel (compare 3:17-21). Ezekiel has the responsibility of declaring to the wicked their sins (vv. 8-9). If he fails to do so, the wicked will receive punishment for their misdeeds, and his own life will also be required. Ezekiel's warnings and judgments are designed to lead Israel to the knowledge that God stands ready to forgive those who have turned from their wicked ways. As the lookout, Ezekiel has assumed an awesome responsibility, greater than that of any other prophet in Israel. His duty to watch and to warn the wicked and the faithful must weigh heavily upon him, especially as the end of Jerusalem draws closer and closer.

33:10-20 Individual retribution. This section, which is a disputation on individual responsibility, also resumes an earlier theme (see ch. 18). The prophet seeks to overcome the despair of those who resign themselves to their just fate and to refute the bitter anger of those who hold that the Lord is punishing Israel unjustly for the sins of previous generations. Ezekiel maintains that God longs to forgive the wicked and awaits their repentance (see vv. 11, 19). The prophet also argues that the virtuous will live (v. 13), though just how Ezekiel supposed God would spare the righteous in the coming devastation is not indicated. Presumably he counted upon the preservation of a righteous remnant in exile, with whom the Lord would make a fresh start.

33:21-22 The fugitive from Jerusalem. This brief section reports the arrival of the fugitive who brings the news that Jerusalem has fallen (compare 24:25-27). The date listed in verse 21 is about eighteen months after the actual fall of Jerusalem. The fugitive arrives "on the fifth day of the tenth month in the twelfth year of exile." According to 2 Kgs 25:2, 8-9, Jerusalem fell on the seventh day of the fifth month in the eleventh year of Zedekiah (compare Jer 52:12, which lists the same year and month but specifies the tenth day of the month). The journey from Jerusalem to Babylon would be expected to take about four months (see Ezra 7:9). Even allowing for exhaustion or a circuitous route, the fugitive's traveling time seems unreasonably long.

The evening before the fugitive arrives, Ezekiel experiences the hand of the Lord upon him (compare his similar experience in his call to be a prophet in 1:3 and 3:14). At the same time, Ezekiel recovers his ability to speak (v. 22; compare 3:22-27). The prophet is freed to new action on behalf of the Lord. He begins a new phase in his prophetic career, and from this point onward in the book, he delivers a more hopeful message to the people.

33:23-29 The survivors in Judah. The judgment against those in the ruined land of Judah who assumed that God would restore the land through them probably belongs to the period just after the fall of Jerusalem. Since those who remain in the land continue to practice the same sins that led to the ruin of Israel, further devastation awaits them. The implication of this oracle is that the Lord's fresh start will be made with the exiles, not with those who remain in the land of Judah. The judgment is therefore an implicit word of hope for the people in exile.

33:30-33 The prophet's false popularity. In this section God speaks directly to Ezekiel about his effectiveness as a prophet. Even though Ezekiel is popular, his message is not heeded (v. 32). To the exiles he is only a clever entertainer (compare Ezekiel's complaint that the exiles regarded him as "one who is forever spinning parables," 21:5). God declares that in the near future the exiles will recognize the accomplishment of the words the prophet has spoken; then they will recognize that a prophet has been among them (compare 2:5). This word is therefore an implicit word of encouragement for Ezekiel. His effectiveness is not to be measured by his present reception in the community.

34:1-16 Parable of the shepherds. In a composite oracle (notice that following the revelation formula in verse 1 there are three introductory formulas in verses 2, 10, 11) against wicked shepherds (= rulers; see Ps 78:71; Isa 44:28; 63:11; Jer 2:8; 10:21; Zech 11:4-17), God declares their end. Because the shepherds of the past have failed in their responsibilities to the sheep (vv. 2-6), God is coming against them to punish them and to rescue the sheep. God will take over the shepherd's responsibilities (vv. 11-16). God will be the good shepherd (compare Gen 48:15; Psalm 23; Jer 31:10; Mark 6:34; John 10:1-18), tending the sheep, rescuing the scattered of the flock, bringing them to rest in good pastures in their own land, where the lost will be sought out and those who stray brought back, where the injured will be bound up and the sick healed.

34:17-31 Separation of the sheep. Sayings related to the shepherd theme are grouped here, though the emphasis shifts from the shepherd who has failed the sheep to judgments against sheep who have misused their power. In verses 17-19, which open with an introductory formula, God addresses the sheep with words of judgment, saying that callous self-interest will be punished. Verses 20-22, which also open with an introductory formula, continue the theme of the strong versus the weak sheep. In verses 23-24 there is an abrupt shift in content from the theme of sheep against sheep to the theme of the appointment of a messianic prince. A human shepherd is promised who will feed the sheep (v. 23; compare vv. 2-10, where God was personally to fulfill this task). David, the great ancestor of the royal house in Jerusalem, is to be the future shepherd/prince, and the Lord will be God.

In verses 25-27, which end with a recognition formula, shepherd imagery is abandoned completely as the passage shifts to an elaboration of the covenant of peace between God and the people. Verses 28-30, which also end with a recognition formula, provide information about the security and prosperity the restored house of Israel will experience. Verse 31 reintroduces the sheep imagery in a closing formula that emphasizes God's desire for the salvation of the people.

The many seams in this section demonstrate the importance of the concept of God's desire for the future salvation of the covenant people to both Ezekiel and his followers.

35:1-15 Against Edom. Continuing the denouncement begun in 25:12-14, Ezekiel here repudiates the hope of the Edomites that they will take over the former land of Israel and Judah. He attacks Edom for its enmity against its neighbor nation Israel at the time of Jerusalem's fall in 587 and for its effort to settle in the land (v. 10). Ezekiel denounces Mount Seir, the high place of Edom, and declares that God will not permit the land of Israel and Judah to pass into the hands of the Edomites. Because Edom has cherished enmity toward Israel, it is to suffer a fate worse than that of Judah: Edom is to become a perpetual desolation. And as the four recognition formulas in verses 4, 9, 12, 15 underscore, thus will Edom know the Lord.

36:1-15 Regeneration of the land. The oracle against Mount Seir of Edom prepares the way for the promise of restoration now delivered to the exiles. The mountains of Israel are told a word that explicitly draws a contrast between the destruction promised the high places of Edom and the future restoration of Israel.

In this complex section, which contains six introductory "thus says the Lord" formulas (vv. 2, 3, 4, 5, 6, 13), a displaced concluding recognition formula (v. 11) before the end of the passage, and two closing "says the Lord" formulas (vv. 14, 15), the mountains of Israel, condemned earlier in chapter 6, are promised regeneration. The promise of restoration that was begun in chapter 34 with the announcement of new leadership (the Davidic Messiah) gains momentum with the promise of a new land. Verses 1-7 promise that the nations which have ridiculed Israel, particularly Edom, will suffer reproach. Verses 8-15 promise prosperity to the mountains of Israel when the exiles return to repopulate the land.

36:16-38 Regeneration of the people. The second half of chapter 36, which develops God's reasons for the repopulation of the land, divides into five subsections defined by formulas and shifts in address. In verses 16-21 God speaks to Ezekiel about the cause of the Exile. In God's sight the defilement of the land by the chosen people was "like the defilement of a menstruous woman" (v. 17; compare Lev 15:19). Personal responsibility, as Ezekiel had earlier said, explicitly required that a virtuous person "not defile his neighbor's wife, nor have relations with a woman in her menstrual period" (18:6; see also 22:10). Because of their reprehensible defilement of the land and their idolatry, the people were scattered. Yet, even in other lands they continued to profane God's holy name (v. 20). Now grief over the preservation of the holiness of the divine name motivates God to tell Ezekiel that the Exile will end (v. 21).

In verses 22-23, which are framed as a subunit by an introductory formula and a recognition formula, God speaks directly to the house of Israel. God rehearses their wicked history and emphasizes that it is not for their sakes that the Exile will end. Zeal for the holiness of the divine name motivates God to return the people to the land. Here, as in chapter 20, the dominant motivation for restoration is concern for the preservation of God's holiness.

Verses 24-32 list a series of individual acts that God will initiate so that the people can live in the kind of obedience that will preserve the holiness of God's name. God will gather the chosen people from their exile and lead them back to their own land (v. 24). Then, in a three-stage purification, God will create a new, radically reordered human harmony. First, God will ritually cleanse the people from their past impurities and idols (v. 25; on washing as a means of purification, see Num 19:9-21; Ps 51:3-4). Second, God will transplant new hearts and spirits into the people (v. 26; compare Jer 31:31-34). And third, God will animate their human hearts with the divine spirit, so that the people will have the inner power to live by God's statutes and decrees (v. 27). Verses 28-32 describe the material prosperity God will give the people when they return to the land, and they close with a sober reminder that these benefits are given, not for the sake of the people, but to set forth God's glory in the world.

Verses 33-36, which open with an introductory formula, promise that when Israel is rebuilt, the neighboring nations will recognize God's power. And verses 37-38, which open with another introductory formula, promise that in the future restoration to the land, Israel will be abundantly repopulated.

37:1-14 Vision of the dry bones. Ezekiel's vision in the valley (or the "plain," which is the same location as that in his call, 3:22) filled with dry bones is perhaps the best known section of the book. It is composed of a dramatic report of a vision (vv. 1-10) and its interpretation (vv. 11-14). The occasion is a time when the exiles have lost all hope in the future. The people who had once hoped falsely in the inviolability of Jerusalem and their past history now despair falsely, saying, "Our bones are dried up, our hope is lost, and we are cut off" (v. 11).

The prophet experiences the hand of the Lord upon him (see our comment at 33:22) and is led to the center of a place filled with numerous dry bones (vv. 1-2). In this place filled with countless signs of death, God puts the question to Ezekiel, "Can these bones come to life?" The prophet surrenders to God the power to make such a decision about life and death, and with reserve replies, "You alone know that" (v. 3).

God then instructs Ezekiel to prophesy to the dead bones so that a new spirit, sinews, flesh, skin, and breath will revive the bones (vv. 4-6). Ezekiel does so and hears a great noise as sinews, flesh, and skin cover the bones, but no spirit comes into them (vv. 7-8). In a second instruction God tells him to call the spirit from the four winds to come and breathe life into the slain (v. 9). Again Ezekiel does as commanded, and the spirit revives a great upright army of live bodies (v. 10).

In the interpretation that follows, God declares that those whose hope has turned to despair will be led from their experience of death to new life in the land of Israel (vv.

11-12). This interpretation of resurrection employs a different picture of the place from which the dead bones are reassembled. Here the bones are raised from proper graves (v. 12), not from a valley strewn with unburied bones. The Lord will burst the bonds of the grave to restore the people to new political existence. Verses 13-14, which contain two recognition formulas, emphasize that the new life that the Lord will grant the people will revive both their understanding of God and their life in the land. The picture in Ezekiel is not that of individual resurrection from the dead. This is a visionary description of a new corporate political beginning for Israel.

37:15-28 The two sticks. A symbolic action (vv. 15-17; compare chs. 4–5; 12; 24:17) and its interpretation (vv. 18-28, to which later materials have been added; see the two introductory formulas in verses 19, 21) portray the reunion of North Israel and Judah. Ezekiel hopes not only for the restoration of the Judean exiles in Babylon, but also for the reassembly of the exiles of Israel who were carried away by the Assyrians in 721 B.C.E. to a location most likely unknown to Ezekiel. Though the exiles from Israel have long since ceased to be a recognizable entity, Ezekiel envisions that in the sovereign purpose of God they are destined to return to the land along with the exiles from Judah. The restored people will be ruled by one prince (v. 22), whose identity (v. 24) is the same as the Davidic shepherd-prince described in chapter 34. God promises to dwell among the people and to make an everlasting covenant with them (vv. 26-27). Thus shall the nations recognize that it is the Lord who makes Israel holy (v. 28).

38:1–39:29 Prophecy against Gog. [The New American Bible divides these chapters into three prophecies against Gog by rearranging the text of chapter 38 to read 38:1-13, 17-23 as a first prophecy against Gog, and 38:14-16 as a second prophecy against Gog. These chapters are complex, yet content and the appearance of only one messenger formula in 38:1 suggest that chapters 38–39 are a unity composed of four subsections: 38:2-13; 38:14-24; 39:1-16; 39:17-29, each of which is marked by an instruction to Ezekiel to speak. The first three subsections have Gog as their subject; the last subsection is directed to birds and wild animals.]

The clue to understanding these strange chapters, which are unlike the other materials in Ezekiel, is in 38:17. The question there occurs as to whether the enemy who comes from the land of Magog is that enemy whom the prophets spoke of in former days. This verse suggests that the chapters originated in later speculation concerning the great enemy from the north referred to in Jer 1:13-16; 4:5-8; 6:1-8, 22-26. The enemy here is called Gog, a name that probably does not refer directly to any world power, just as the land named Magog does not refer to any particular land (this vague enemy from the north is allied to Meshech and Tubal; compare 38:2 and 27:13).

This is an apocalyptic vision, similar to that found in Isa 24–27. It tells of the coming of a massive force against Israel, after Israel's restoration to the homeland (38:12). The enemy comes at the will of God, who is about to display a mighty show of power before all the nations. The Lord will defeat the forces of Gog, scattering the slain over the entire land of Israel. It will take seven months to gather up the bones of the slain and bury them (39:12). This carnage will have the double purpose of causing Israel to know that the Lord is their God (39:22) and of causing the nations to see the saving power of God, who exiled the people for their sins but has now secured their lives from harm (39:23-29).

These chapters may have been produced by Ezekiel (the language of 39:21-29 is quite similar to that found elsewhere in the book). More likely, however, they are the product of some of Ezekiel's disciples. The notion of a massive battle at the last day seems not to have entered Ezekiel's thoughts elsewhere in the book. It may be that some of his disciples had portrayed in veiled language the coming destruction of Babylonia. Yet, the fact that Israel will already have been liberated from exile when the enemy arises would seem to make such a view implausible. Gog seems better considered as a mythical world power invented by the disciples to emphasize God's protection of Israel.

PART V: THE NEW ISRAEL

Ezek 40:1–48:35

The closing section of the Book of Ezekiel contains an architectural sketch of the temple complex in Jerusalem (40:1–42:20), a description of restored worship in the temple (43:1–44:3), laws regarding temple personnel and practices (44:4–47:12), and the boundaries for a reapportionment of the land (47:13–48:35). These chapters are an idealized vision of the restoration of a new Israel to the homeland (compare chs. 34, 36, 37). Renewed life is now rightly centered on the temple. And the name of the new city is appropriately "The Lord is here" (48:35).

The New Temple

40:1-5 The man with a measure. Only one date, April 28, 573 B.C.E. (v. 1), appears in chapters 40–48. On this day Ezekiel is transported (compare 8:3) to a high mountain in the land of Israel, where he sees a divine vision of a city being rebuilt. He observes a celestial man at the gate of the city with two measuring devices in his hand—a linen cord and a measuring rod (six cubits long = about 10½ feet; v. 5). The divine messenger explains that he is Ezekiel's guide and cautions the prophet to pay close attention to all that he is to see. Then the guide proceeds to measure the width and height of a 10½-foot-wide by 10½-foot-high outer wall that surrounds the temple.

40:6-16 The east gate. Beginning at the east gate (which is the gate through which God departed the city in 10:19), the guide climbs its steps (there are most likely seven steps—see 40:22, 26) and measures the gate's threshold, or entrance hall, which is 10½ feet long (v. 6). Then he goes into a long corridor that is flanked on each side by three 10½-foot-square roomlike recesses (v. 7a). At the end of the corridor of the gateway is another threshold, or entrance hall, which is also 10½ feet long (v. 7b). This symmetrical entrance way leads to a roomy vestibule (about 14 by 35 feet), which opens onto the outer court of the temple.

40:17-19a The outer court. Thirty rooms occupy the north, south, and east inside perimeter of the outer wall of the temple. A pavement in front of these rooms connects the three sides of the outer court. Verse 19 fixes the distance between the outer and inner east gates as one hundred cubits (a distance of about 175 feet).

40:19b-23, 24-27 The north gate, the south gate. Built into the north and south outer walls are two gates identical in construction with the east gate (see vv. 6-16). Steps, a threshold, a corridor flanked by three rooms, and another threshold lead out to a vestibule. As decorative features, each of the gate structures has recessed windows, palm-tree reliefs on the jambs, and pilasters (rectangular columns set into the walls as an ornamental motif).

40:28-29, 31-37 Gates of the inner court. [The New American Bible omits verse 30 on the grounds that it duplicates verse 29. It should be noted that the dimensions of the vestibule are altered from 50 by 25 cubits in verse 29 to 25 by 5 cubits in verse 30. Most likely verse 30 is corrupt, since verses 29, 33, and 36 agree on the longer dimensions.]

The guide next takes Ezekiel across the outer courtyard (a distance of about 175 feet, according to verse 19) to measure the south, east, and north gates in an inner wall. These gates are duplicates of the outer gates, except that their vestibules are on the outside of the gate structures, so that they face the vestibules of the outer gates. The only difference in these reversed structures in the inner wall is that they have eight steps, not seven (compare vv. 31, 34, 37 and 22, 26) leading to them.

40:38-47 Side rooms. In verses 38-39 it is not clear exactly which gate contains the described sacrificial equipment. Perhaps the vestibules of all three inner gates are furnished with a room for washing burnt offerings (see the requirement of Lev 1:9, 13) and two tables on each side, upon which are slaughtered sin offerings and guilt offerings (see 45:13-17).

From verse 40 to the end of this section, Ezekiel sees twelve tables, which seem to be described from the perspective of the north gate. According to verse 40, two tables stand on each side of the outside wall of the vestibule of the inner gate, which most likely means that these four tables are in the outer court at the foot of the steps leading up to the north inner gate. According to verse 41, another four tables, which are used for slaughter, stand in the vestibule of the inner gate (also described in verse 39). Verses 42-43 describe four small cut-stone tables, which are intended to hold the instruments of slaughter and are most likely located near the slaughter tables on either side of the vestibule.

Verses 44-46 explain that two rooms occupy the inside of the inner court wall, beside the north and south gateways. These rooms face each other, though it is unclear whether they are located to the right or to the left of the gates. The room by the north gate is for the use of the priests who care for the temple. The room by the south gate is for the priests who sacrifice at the altar (Zadokites, according to 44:15-21).

The inner court is next measured as a perfect square (about 175 feet square), and the altar is described as standing in front of the temple (v. 47).

40:48–41:15a The temple building. From the inner north gate, the guide next takes Ezekiel across the inner court to the vestibule of the temple building. Ten steps lead up to the temple vestibule, which measures about 35 by 21 feet. The exterior of the vestibule area is described as featuring wall pillars (pilasters), two columns beside the jambs (compare 1 Kgs 7:15-22), and a wide doorway (40:48-49). Beyond the doorway is the nave, a room that measures about 35 feet wide by 70 feet deep (41:1-2). Ezekiel remains in this area while the heavenly guide proceeds to measure the holy of holies, a 35-foot-square room (41:3-4).

The architectural details of the measurements taken in chapter 41:5-15 are obscure. The guide first measures the wall of the temple, then ninety rooms built in three stories outside the temple with some kind of stairway connecting them, and finally a large structure behind the temple that is simply called "the building" (41:12).

41:15b-26 Interior of the temple. This section resumes the description of the outer vestibule and inner nave of the temple, where Ezekiel was left standing in 41:1. High windows allow light to enter the nave. Ornamental wood carvings of palm trees and two-faced cherubs, each with a human and a lion face, cover the wood-paneled walls of the nave and the vestibule (vv. 15b-20). A 5-foot 3-inch-high, 3½-foot-square table stands before the entrance to the holy of holies (v. 22; compare 1 Kgs 6:21). And two sets of double doors decorated with the same design as that on the walls separate the vestibule from the nave, and the nave from the holy of holies (vv. 23-25).

42:1-14 Other structures. This section is extremely difficult to interpret. Apparently the guide takes Ezekiel to a square area behind the west end of the temple building, where he measures two building complexes on the south and the north sides of the western square. These buildings serve as sacristies for the priests; here they eat the sacred meals, store cereal, sin, and guilt offerings, and vest for temple activities.

42:15-20 Measuring the outer court. The guide takes Ezekiel from the nave to the outer east gate and there begins the final measurements of the external east, north, south, and west walls. The perimeter of the exterior walls forms a square 500 cubits, or about 875 feet on a side. The purpose of this outer wall is to separate the holy area of the temple complex from its profane surroundings.

Restoration of the Temple

43:1-9 The return of the Lord. When full measurements have been completed, the guide takes Ezekiel to the east gate, where the prophet sees the return of God's glory to the reconstituted temple. God, who departed the temple on the throne-chariot by the east gate as a sign of judgment (11:22-23), now returns through this same gate as a sign of restoration (43:1-5). Ezekiel is overwhelmed and falls to his face (compare 1:28b), but the spirit (not the guide; compare 8:3) takes him to the inner court, where God speaks to the prophet, promising to dwell in the midst of Israel forever (vv. 7-9).

43:10-12 The law of the temple. God instructs Ezekiel to describe the measurements and design of the temple and to teach the house of Israel the law, or *torah* (instruction), of the temple, that the "whole surrounding area on the mountain top shall be most sacred." Ezekiel is charged with the priestly duty of making known to the people the *torah* about God's possession of this high mountain (compare 40:2) and the divine presence which sets this area apart as holy. Israel is to be ashamed of its sins in the face of the majesty of God.

43:13-27 The altar. Ezekiel receives detailed instructions about the dimensions and consecration of the altar. The altar of burnt offering is described as a large structure 18 cubits square at its base, with successive layers 16, 14, and 12 cubits square (vv. 13-17). At each of the four corners of the top layer are horns, vertical protrusions about 20.4 inches high (v. 15; traditionally these were places of utmost sanctity and refuge—see Exod 21:13; 27:2; 29:12; and 1 Kgs 1:50; 2:28). In an elaborate seven-day ritual, the Levitical priests are to consecrate this altar to God by ritually sacrificing young bulls, unblemished he-goats, and rams, and by scattering salt (vv. 18-27).

44:1-3 The closed gate. The heavenly guide takes Ezekiel from the inner court (43:5) to the outer east gate, which has been closed. The guide explains that this gate is to remain perpetually shut as a sign that God returned to the temple through it. Only the prince may sit in the vestibule of this gate structure when he eats his sacrificial meal.

The New Law

44:4-9 Admission to the temple. Next the guide leads Ezekiel to the inner court (v. 4; compare 43:5, where the spirit took him to this same place). The prophet observes God's glory filling the temple and once again falls to his face (compare 43:3). In a manner closely dependent on 40:4, the guide urges Ezekiel to listen closely to all he will hear about the statutes and laws of God's temple (v. 5).

The house of Israel is charged as a "rebellious house" (compare chs. 2; 12; 17:12; 24:3) that has in the past admitted foreigners to service in the sanctuary (vv. 6-8). The first law of the restored temple prohibits foreigners from entering the sanctuary (v. 9).

44:10-14 Levites. The next regulation limits the service of the Levites to that of temple servants and gatekeepers. Their duties include guarding the gates (perhaps they stood in the square, roomlike recesses in the corridors of the gate structures—see 40:10) and slaughtering sacrifices for the people (v. 11). This demotion to menial tasks (once performed by foreigners, according to verse 8) has come about because of the Levites' own sins (v. 12). They are now prohibited from the priestly ministries that involve handling the most sacred things of the temple (v. 13).

44:15-31 Priests. Because of their faithfulness, the Zadokites are elected to full priestly service (vv. 15-16). In a composite section, various regulations about their dress (vv. 17-19), personal conduct (vv. 20-22), duties (vv. 23-24), purification after mourning (vv. 25-27), and benefits (vv. 28-31) have been assembled. Within the sacred precincts priests are required to wear linen garments (v. 17; compare the man dressed in linen in 9:2, 11; 10:2, 7; and the vestry described in 42:14). Priests are required to keep their hair carefully trimmed (v. 20), to refrain from drinking before entering the inner court of the temple (v. 21), and to marry virgins or the widows of other priests (v. 22). Their responsibilities include teaching (v. 23) and juridical decision-making (v. 24). Should a priest become unclean by coming near a dead person, he must be ritually cleansed (see Num 19:11-12) and wait an additional seven days before entering the inner court (vv. 25-27). Priests are to own no land (v. 28; contradicted in 45:4; 48:10-12). Their income is a portion of the sacrifices (vv. 29-31).

45:1-8 The sacred tract of land. These verses detail the dimensions of a three-part division of a square area of land, about 43,750 feet on a side, into east-to-west strips (compare 48:8-22). The northernmost strip is assigned to the Levites, the middle strip to the sanctuary complex and the Zadokites, and the southernmost strip to the city and the people. An area on the east and west fringes of these strips is allotted to the prince. This idealized scheme places the temple at the center of the reapportioned land in an area separate from the city and the royal dwelling.

45:9-12 Weights and measures. Verse 9 is a self-contained oracle with its own introductory and concluding formulas. Addressed to the princes of Israel, it warns against violence and oppression. According to verses 10-12, the princes are to see that correct weights and measures are honestly regulated.

45:13-17 Offerings. Two offering ordinances have been combined detailing the contributions required from the people for the support of the temple (vv. 13-15) and from the people to the prince, who in turn is obliged to provide for the support of the temple (vv. 16-17). The original ordinance is most likely the one according to which the people support the temple directly.

45:18-25 The Passover; the feast of Booths. Three seven-day festivals are listed here. The first is an annual rite of purification of the temple (vv. 18-20). The second is the celebration of the Passover (vv. 21-24). And the third is the celebration of Booths, or the Ingathering of the crops. Passover, traditionally celebrated at the beginning of each year, and Booths, in the middle of the year, become occasions on which the prince offers sacrifices to ensure the purity of the community.

46:1-7 Sabbaths. Though the outer east gate is perpetually closed (44:1-2), the inner east gate may be opened on sabbaths and on new moons (and on other special occasions—see v. 12). The prince is permitted to enter through this gate to take sacrifices to the doorpost of the gate on behalf of the people who remain in the outer court. Listed here are the requirements for sabbath and new-moon sacrifices, which the prince presents to the priests, who alone are allowed to enter the inner court to sacrifice to the Lord (vv. 4-7).

46:8-15 Ritual laws. Ritual requires that the people enter the temple area by either the north or the south gate and that they leave by the gate opposite the one they entered (v. 9). Ritual also prescribes that the prince enter and exit in this same manner on nonfestal days (v. 10) and stipulates the offerings the prince is to take on solemn feasts as freewill offerings and as daily offerings.

46:16-18 The prince and the land. The prince's right to the land is strictly regulated. He can give land as a permanent inheritance to his sons and as a temporary gift to his servants. He is forbidden to seize land from others.

46:19-24 The temple kitchens. Once again resuming Ezekiel's tour of the temple (see chs. 40–42; 44:1-9), the heavenly guide takes the prophet first to the kitchen on the west side of the temple, where the priests eat their portions of the sacred offerings (vv. 19-20; not mentioned in the description of the priests' chambers in 42:1-14). Next they go to see four kitchens, one in each corner of the outer court, where the laity eat their sacrificial meals, which are prepared by the Levites (vv. 21-24; also not mentioned in the description of the outer court in 40:17-19; 42:15-20).

47:1-2 The wonderful stream. Ezekiel and his guide return to the front of the temple, where the prophet notices water trickling from below the south wall of the temple (v. 1). As the guide leads Ezekiel through the north outer gate, the prophet sees that the water has changed course and is flowing beneath the south wall of the temple toward the east (v. 2). The farther east the prophet goes, the greater the flow of water becomes. Four times the guide measures the water, and each time its depth increases dramatically until it has become a torrent (vv. 3-5). Ezekiel sees wonderful trees on both its banks (vv. 6-7). The guide explains that the life-giving waters of this river that springs from the throne of God will make the salt waters of the Dead Sea fresh, and barren places fertile with trees whose fruit is good for food and whose leaves drive sickness away (vv. 8-12).

Thus the measurements of the heavenly guide are finished in this climactic vision of the temple in Jerusalem as the source of a great river that flows out to the east, emptying into the Dead Sea and bringing life wherever it goes. This closing motif derives from the ancient myth of the mountain city from which the rivers of the earth flow (see Gen 2:10-14) and reappears in later apocalyptic literature (see Zech 14:8; Rev 22). It fittingly concludes Ezekiel's vision of revitalized worship in a restored temple.

The New Israel

47:13-20 Boundaries of the land. Inserted between an opening oracular formula (v. 13) and a closing formula (v. 23) is a description of the boundaries of the restored land. These boundaries portray no vast expansion of Israelite territory, but they break the old tribal boundaries by providing land in equal measure to each tribe, with little regard to the territory formerly occupied. The northern boundary is fixed as the frontier of Hamath, the pass between the Lebanon and Hermon mountains, and the southern boundary as Kadesh and the Wadi of Egypt. The Mediterranean provides the western border, and the eastern boundary is the Jordan River and the Dead Sea. The extent of this land is no greater than that held under David.

47:21–48:7 The northern portion. Before the distribution of the land begins, the notice appears that resident aliens, like native Israelites, are to have equal rights of ownership (vv. 22-23). Then, beginning in the north, the land is apportioned in equal east-to-west strips to seven tribes: Dan, Asher, Naphtali, Manasseh, Ephraim, Reuben, and Judah (48:1-8).

48:8-22 The sacred tract. The southern boundary of Judah's territory is the land set apart for the Levites, the temple, the Zadokites, and the prince. The details listed here accord with those specified in 45:1-8.

48:23-29 The southern portions. Below the sacred tract the following five tribes will settle: Benjamin, Simeon, Issachar, Zebulun, and Gad.

48:30-35 The gates of the city. The book closes with a reference to the twelve gates of the city of Jerusalem, one named for each of the tribes (the name of Joseph now appearing in place of Ephraim and Manasseh so as to make room for a Levi gate), to the city's circumference, and to its new name, "The Lord is here."

COMMENTARY: DANIEL

PART I: DANIEL AND THE KINGS OF BABYLON

Dan 1:1–6:29

The first section of the Book of Daniel is a collection of six independent, edifying short stories about Daniel and his companions. According to these chapters, Daniel was taken as a youth into Babylonian exile in 606 B.C.E. (see Dan 1:1), where he lived as a pious and loyal Jew who possessed the power to interpret dreams and visions. Purportedly telling of events that occurred in the court of Babylonia and Medo-Persia during the period of exile in the sixth century B.C.E., these stories are of two types: tests of loyalty (chs. 1, 3, 6) and displays of wisdom (chs. 2, 4, 5). They teach that through obedience to the law the faithful will triumph over adversity and convince foreign powers of the sovereignty of Yahweh.

These chapters raise troublesome issues about the date of composition, unity of authorship, and original language of the Book of Daniel. Most scholars are agreed that the Book of Daniel is the work of more than one author and that it took its present form around the year 165 B.C.E., toward the end of the oppressive reign of the Seleucid king Antiochus IV Epiphanes, who persecuted the Jews of Jerusalem and Judah (175–163 B.C.E.). The opening chapters, however, seem to be earlier compositions. Since the tales in Dan 1–6, with the possible exception of chapter 2, do not contain veiled apocalyptic historical references and do not explicitly refer to the persecution of the second-century community, they are likely from a time earlier than that of Antiochus IV. Their vocabulary, knowledge of Persian and Hellenistic customs, and fundamentally inaccurate descriptions of major sixth-century historical events and personages make it equally unlikely that the chapters come from their purported time of the Babylonian Exile. For instance, the historical Nebuchadnezzar attacked Jerusalem and led Jehoiachin, not Jehoiakim, into exile in 597 B.C.E., not 606 B.C.E., as claimed in 1:1; Belshazzar was the son of Nabonidus, not Nebuchadnezzar, as stated in 5:11; and Babylon was conquered by Cyrus, not Darius the Mede, as credited in 6:1. Chapters 1–6 employ a common folklore plot of the success of the uncompromising wise courtier, and thus contain a message for those who are living in oppression or in times when accommodation to foreign culture is a danger. Though there is room for debate, the chapters seem best to fit the need of the third-century community to resist assimilating too much Greek culture into Judaism.

That our final form of Daniel is written in three languages is an additional complication. The book begins in Hebrew (1:1–2:4a), shifts to Aramaic (2:4b–7:28), and then back to Hebrew for the remainder of the protocanonical chapters (8:1–12:13). Deuterocanonical Greek additions consisting of the "Prayer of Azariah and the Song of the Three Young Men" (inserted into the story of the fiery furnace in chapter 3) and "Susanna," "Bel," and "The Dragon" (appended in chapters 13:1–14:42) further testify to the complex compositional history that lies behind the present text.

The Book of Daniel as a whole is a religious tract written to encourage people faced with difficult choices. The opening chapters were likely told to encourage the Jewish people to stand firm in the midst of alien pressures, as Daniel and his friends had done.

Told first most likely in the third century B.C.E. and then retold in the second century B.C.E. by the redactor/author who gave shape to the final protocanonical text (chs. 1–12), these chapters set the tone for what follows.

1:1-21 The food test. The first short story introduces Daniel and his companions, tells of their training in Nebuchadnezzar's court, and recounts their struggle with the compromises required by life in a foreign culture, particularly the dilemma involved in being required to eat and drink ritually impure food.

Verses 1-2 set the story in Babylon in the year 606 B.C.E., identified here as the year in which Nebuchadnezzar laid seige to Jerusalem and led Jehoiakim to exile in the land of Shinar (an ancient name for Babylonia; see Gen 11:2; Zech 5:11). In actuality, Nebuchadnezzar attacked Jerusalem in 597 B.C.E., when Jehoiachin was on the throne, and it was this king who was led into exile when Zedekiah was appointed to rule Jerusalem (see 2 Kgs 24:10-17). Though historically inaccurate, the opening verses create a time of exile in a foreign setting as the scene of the narrative.

Verses 3-7 define the situation and characters involved in this story. Nebuchadnezzar instructs Ashpenaz, his chief chamberlain (=chief eunuch), to choose some talented, noble young Israelites for probationary training in the king's service. During the three years of their education, the candidates are to be fed from the royal table. Among those chosen by Ashpenaz are four young men from Judah, to whom Babylonian names are assigned: Daniel becomes Belteshazzar; Hananiah becomes Shadrach; Mishael becomes Meshach; Azariah becomes Abednego. In addition to a change of name, another historical source, Josephus, explains that selection for the king's service involves being rendered a eunuch (compare Esth 1:10; Deut 23:2). Without question, the identity and destiny of these four young men are altered by their training.

Verses 8-21 show that Daniel and his companions do not completely assimilate Babylonian ways. Daniel asks the chief chamberlain to allow him to eat food other than that from the royal table (the ritual regulations about meat are found in Lev 11:2-47; Deut 12:23-24; 14:3-21; there are no ritual laws concerning wine, though mention of wine as well as food is made also in Jdt 10:5; 12:1-4; on food as a sign of obedience and separation, see Tob 1:10-11; 1 Macc 1:62-63; 2 Macc 5:27). When Ashpenaz refuses out of fear of royal retribution (v. 10), Daniel makes the same request of the steward, this time asking for a ten-day trial on vegetables and water for himself and his three companions (vv. 11-13). The steward agrees, and when the four young men flourish, he allows them to continue a diet of vegetables (vv. 14-16). God rewards the faithfulness of the four by granting them such success that at the end of their time of training the king finds them ten times more knowledgeable than anyone in Babylonia. They enter the king's service, where Daniel remains until the first year of Cyrus (v. 21; 538 B.C.E.). For these four youths, loyalty to the Lord is rewarded with success in the foreign court.

2:1-49 The king's dream. The second short story is a suspenseful tale of God's disclosure to Daniel of mysteries not known to others in Nebuchadnezzar's service. The three companions figure in only a secondary fashion (see vv. 13, 17-18, 49) in this story, which is primarily a demonstration of Daniel's great wisdom.

A brief introduction (v. 1) sets the date as 603 B.C.E., the second year of Nebuchadnezzar's reign (which contradicts the three years of training required in 1:5), and establishes the situation as Nebuchadnezzar's decree that an interpreter from his kingdom tell him the details of a disturbing dream he had dreamt and explain the meaning of the dream.

In the first episode (vv. 2-13), magicians, enchanters, and sorcerers are summoned before the king, who explains that he wants them to help him understand a terrible dream that has robbed him of rest. The first response of the interpreters (the language of the text shifts from Hebrew to Aramaic for 2:4b–7:28) is that they need only be told the dream and then they will give the king its meaning. Nebuchadnezzar commands that they tell both the dream and its meaning, or they will die (v. 6).

A second time the interpreters ask for the details of the dream (v. 7), and a second time Nebuchadnezzar refuses, claiming that he cannot trust their interpretation if they cannot tell the dream (vv. 8-9). In their third word to the king (vv. 10-11), the interpreters declare that no human being, only a god, can tell a dream. Nebuchadnezzar is so angered that he decrees the death of all the wise interpreters of Babylon (v. 12). The threatening note that Daniel and his companions are sought out as members of this condemned company closes the section (v. 13).

The second episode (vv. 14-24b) involves Daniel and Arioch, the captain of the king's guard, who has been sent to execute the wise interpreters. Though there are inconsistencies in this episode (notably between verse 16, where Daniel goes freely to the king and asks for time to discover the dream's interpretation, and verse 24, where Daniel asks Arioch to arrange an audience with the king) which suggest editorial additions, the basic story line is coherent. Daniel goes to Arioch and asks why the wise interpreters of Babylon have been sentenced to death (v. 15). Then Daniel returns home to tell Hananiah, Mishael, and Azariah about the failure and fate of the interpreters, and the four young men pray for deliverance from the God of heaven (v. 18; compare Tob 10:11; Jdt 5:8; 6:19; 11:17). Their prayer is answered during a nocturnal vision, in which God reveals the mystery of the king's dream to Daniel (v. 19). Daniel blesses the name of his God (vv. 20-23) and returns to Arioch, requesting a stay of execution for the wise interpreters and an audience with Nebuchadnezzar (v. 24a, b).

In the third and final episode (vv. 24c-45), Arioch takes Daniel to Nebuchadnezzar (vv. 24c-26), and Daniel tells the king both the dream and its interpretation. In the dream, Nebuchadnezzar saw a huge, human-like statue made of various metals that crumbled when it was struck at its feet by a mysterious stone (vv. 31-35). The symbolism of the destruction is explained as the demise of four successive empires, beginning with Babylon (vv. 36-45). Since this is the only place in the Old Testament where the ages of human history are described by symbolic metals, the kingdoms have been variously interpreted. Most likely, however, the head of the statue, which was made of gold, represented Babylon; the chest and arms, which were made of silver, represented Media; the belly and thighs, which were made of bronze, represented Persia; the legs, which were made of iron, represented Greece; and the feet, which were made of iron and tile, represented Alexander's divided empire ruled by the Ptolemies in Egypt and the Seleucids in Syria (the dynasty to which the hated Antiochus Epiphanes belonged). Daniel confirms as correct Nebuchadnezzar's revelation that the smashing of the statue by the stone cut by no human hand is a sign of the end of the present age and the coming of an indestructible kingdom that the God of heaven was establishing (vv. 44-45).

In a surprising conclusion (vv. 46-49), Nebuchadnezzar falls at Daniel's feet and worships him, readily acknowledges the superiority of Daniel's God (for other instances of royal conversion, see 3:95-96; 4:31-34; 6:26-28), and rewards Daniel for his great display of wisdom in telling the dream and its interpretation (a feat thus greater than that of Joseph, who interpreted the dream that Pharaoh *told* him—Gen 41) by promoting him to the highest office in the kingdom. The chapter closes with the note that Daniel requests administrative posts in the provinces for Shadrach, Meshach, and Abednego, while he himself remains at the king's court (v. 49).

3:1-97 The fiery furnace. The third short story is a dramatic contest about the identity of the true God, in which Shadrach, Meshach, and Abednego show their willingness to suffer death rather than worship a god other than the God of Israel. Daniel plays no part in the story of the fiery furnace (his brush with martyrdom occurs in the lions' den, ch. 6).

No date opens this story (though the Septuagint specifies "the eighteenth year of the reign of Nebuchadnezzar," 587 B.C.E.; compare Jdt 2:1). Instead, verses 1-7 deftly sketch the cause of the crisis. Nebuchadnezzar has set up a huge golden statue (87.5 feet tall and 8.75 feet wide) in the plain of Dura (an unknown Babylonian location) and has ordered an elaborate dedication ceremony, at which all are required to fall down and worship the golden statue or be cast into a white-hot furnace.

The conflict develops when some of the Babylonians approach Nebuchadnezzar and denounce the provincial administrators, Shadrach, Meshach, and Abednego, for refusing to serve the king's god (vv. 8-13). Enraged, Nebuchadnezzar sends for the three and demands that they worship the statue, saying, "Who is the God that can deliver you out of my hands?" (v. 15). Shadrach, Meshach, and Abednego refuse (to do otherwise would violate the commandments—see Exod 20:3-6), expressing both their hope that their God will deliver them and their willingness to die if necessary (vv. 17-18; compare Jdt 8:15).

The punishment is carried out in verses 19-90b. Nebuchadnezzar orders that the furnace be heated seven times more than usual (seven is used as a symbol of fullness and totality; see also 4:13, 20, 22, 29; 9:25). So hot is the furnace that the men who bound and threw Shadrach, Meshach, and Abednego into the flames are consumed themselves (for others who suffer the penalty they seek to inflict, see Dan 6:25; 13:62; Esth 7:10). But the three walk about in the flames, singing to God and blessing the Lord (v. 24).

Verses 24-90b, found only in the Septuagint, detail what happens while the three are in the furnace. Included here are two prayers (vv. 26-45, 51-90) and a brief connective narrative (vv. 46-50) known in the Apocrypha as the Prayer of Azariah (= Abednego) and the Song of the Three Young Men. Though supplements to the Hebrew Bible, these verses are considered fully authoritative, deuterocanonical portions of the story by Roman Catholics. In the first prayer (vv. 26-45), which makes no mention of the fiery furnace, Abednego praises God's wisdom and justice and confesses the sinfulness of his own nation (his petition for deliverance in verses 34 and 43 for the sake of the divine name is reminiscent of Ezek 20; 36:21; 39:25). While Abednego prays, the king's men continue to stoke the furnace, and its flames devour those nearby (vv. 46-48; compare v. 22). An angel of the Lord comes down to drive the flames from the furnace (vv. 49-50). In response to their miraculous deliverance, the three young men sing a song of praise and thanksgiving to the Lord for saving them from the raging fire (vv. 51-90; compare Ps 148).

Astonished to hear the singing and bewildered at seeing four men in the midst of the flames, Nebuchadnezzar calls Shadrach, Meshach, and Abednego out of the furnace (vv. 90c-97). When the king sees that they are unharmed, he blesses their God for sending them an angel of deliverance and decrees that any persons who blaspheme the God of Shadrach, Meshach, and Abednego will be cut to pieces and their houses destroyed, for "there is no other God who can rescue like this" (v. 96). Following this testimony, Nebuchadnezzar promotes the three, mentioned here for the last time in the Book of Daniel, to higher positions in the province of Babylon. As in chapter 2, faithfulness and loyalty to the Lord are rewarded with professional advancement.

3:98–4:34 Vision of the great tree. The fourth short story is written in the form of a testimonial letter from Nebuchadnezzar to his subjects (see 3:98-100). A dream and experiences of madness and restoration have convinced the king that the God of the Jews governs all human kingdoms and determines who will rule them. In this undated narrative, the king of Babylon recounts a lesson in humility taught him by the King of heaven (see 4:34). Daniel figures only in the portion of the story dealing with the interpretation of the king's dream (see 4:1-24).

The story opens with Nebuchadnezzar's account of his interpreters' failure to explain a frightening dream (vv. 1-4; the situation is similar to that of chapter 2, except that here the king will tell his dream). Daniel comes before the king, who graphically describes his dream (vv. 5-15) of a great, flourishing tree (compare Ezek 31:1-9) and the coming of a heavenly sentinel (a designation found only in Dan 4:10, 14, 20; used as a synonym for "angel" in 1 Enoch 1:5; 20:1; 2 Enoch 7:18; Book of Jubilees 4:15; Testament of Reuben 5:7; Testament of Naphtali 3:5). The heavenly sentinel announced that the tree would be cut down, leaving only its stump bound with a band of iron and bronze, and that a man would be struck with a disease that would make him like an animal for seven years.

With polite reserve, Daniel explains to Nebuchadnezzar that he is the tree that will be cut down and he is the man who will become like an animal if he fails to realize that "the Most High rules over the kingdom of men and gives it to whom he will" (v. 22). The stump will recover when the seven years of punishment have passed, but Daniel appeals to the king to atone for his sins by good deeds and thus avoid punishment (vv. 16-24; compare Sir 3:30).

Twelve months later, according to a narrative note about the king in verses 25-30, Nebuchadnezzar is struck down for pride in thinking that Babylon was built by his own achievements. As predicted, the king goes mad and eats grass like an animal (historically this is most likely a reference to Nabonidus, not Nebuchadnezzar).

In verses 31-34 Nebuchadnezzar, speaking in the first person again, says that at the end of the seven years of punishment his health, sense, and kingdom were restored and he blesses the Most High. He closes his letter to his subjects, not denying the existence of the Babylonian gods, but explaining that he now praises and exalts "the King of heaven, because all his works are right and his ways just; and those who walk in pride he is able to humble" (v. 34). In this story, acknowledgment of the Lord brings health and prosperity to a foreign king.

5:1–6:1 The writing on the wall. The fifth short story is a simple one-scene mystery story about a swiftly punished sacrilege committed by King Belshazzar, here described as Nebuchadnezzar's son (the historical Belshazzar was only a crown prince, since his father, Nabonidus, was the last king of Babylon). At a great royal banquet, under the influence of wine, Belshazzar calls for the sacred gold and silver vessels from the Jerusalem temple and uses them as goblets for himself and his guests to toast the Babylonian gods (vv. 1-4). His desecration is dramatically halted when a human finger, unattached to a body, appears and writes a mysterious message on the wall (vv. 5-6). The terrified king offers a reward to the wise interpreter of Babylon who can read the message, but none can be found (vv. 7-9; compare chs. 2 and 4). Hearing of the king's distress, the queen comes before him and suggests that Daniel be summoned (vv. 10-12).

In verses 13-16 Daniel is brought and offered the same reward as the others if he can interpret the writing (compare vv. 7 and 16). In verses 17-23 Daniel refuses the reward (though see v. 29) but agrees to interpret the message on the wall. First Daniel delivers a brief homily about the lesson of humility the Most High had taught Nebuchadnezzar (vv. 18-21; compare ch. 4). Then he accuses Belshazzar of rebelling against the Lord of heaven by profaning the temple objects that evening (vv. 22-23) and declares that the writing translates as a divine declaration of the end of the Babylonian empire (vv. 24-28). Belshazzar rewards Daniel as promised (v. 29). And later that same night the king is slain (v. 30). So it happens in this story that Daniel's wisdom is displayed and a foreign king is eliminated for failing to respect God's sovereignty. A historically confused note that Darius the Mede succeeded to the throne closes the story (6:1; at issue here is the fact that Cyrus the Persian captured the Babylonian throne of Nabonidus in 539 B.C.E.).

6:2-29 In the lions' den. The sixth short story is a dramatic test of loyalty involving King Darius, Daniel, and officials in the Medo-Persian court (compare ch. 3). Verses 2-10 describe an intrigue in which Daniel, who is one of the three supervisors of the one hundred and twenty provinces of the empire, is entrapped by jealous court rivals, who get the king to issue an immutable, irrevocable decree that for thirty days anyone who petitions a god or a person will be cast into a den of lions. Even though Daniel hears of the prohibition, he continues his customary practices of prayer (v. 11), thus violating the king's decree. Three times a day (see Ps 55:18) Daniel withdraws to an upper chamber in his home (compare 1 Kgs 17:19; Jdt 8:5) to kneel in prayer (see also Ezra 9:5; Ps 95:6; Luke 22:41; Acts 7:60; Jewish prayer postures also included standing with hands lifted toward heaven and prostration). The officials catch Daniel offering his petitions to God (v. 12) and hand him over to King Darius, who reluctantly sentences Daniel to the lions' den (vv. 13-16). Before sealing the den, the king says to Daniel, "May your God, whom you serve so constantly, save you" (vv. 17-18).

After a sleepless night, Darius returns to the den and calls out, "O Daniel, servant of the living God, has the God whom you serve so constantly been able to save you from the lions?" (vv. 19-21). Speaking the only words he utters in the entire story, Daniel replies, "O king, live forever! My God has sent his angel and closed the lions' mouths so that they have not hurt me. For I have been found innocent before him; neither to you have I done any harm, O king!" (vv. 22-23). The king orders Daniel taken out of the den, and his accusers and their families cast in (vv. 24-25).

Then Darius sends an edict (vv. 26-28) throughout his kingdom testifying to the power and sovereignty of the living God of Daniel (compare 3:95-96). A narrative note that Daniel fared well during the remainder of the reign of Darius and the reign of Cyrus (v. 29) closes the story.

PART II: DANIEL'S VISIONS

Dan 7:1–12:13

In this section the genre changes from short stories about Daniel and his three companions to apocalyptic visions (revelations; see the introduction) written in the first person and attributed to Daniel. In this series of four visions concerning the course of world history, Daniel is not the interpreter of mysteries but rather the recipient of secret revelations. Through symbolic visions (chs. 7, 8) and direct revelations (chs. 9, 10–12), Daniel learns of divine actions soon to occur. Through the mediation of angels, it is revealed that in the immediate future God will judge and destroy Antiochus IV Epiphanes. Because the chapters anticipate the death of Antiochus, it is likely that they were composed sometime late in his reign when he had turned to persecuting the Jews (around 168 B.C.E.), before his actual death (163 B.C.E.).

7:1-28 Vision of the four beasts. Still in Aramaic (as is 2:4b–7), this dream tells of a mysterious symbolic vision (vv. 1-14) and its interpretation (vv. 15-28) which were revealed to Daniel in the first year of King Belshazzar of Babylon (v. 1; compare ch. 5; Belshazzar ruled only as a regent for his father, Nabonidus, from 549 to 539 B.C.E.). In the first scene (vv. 2-8), the four winds stir the waters surrounding the earth (compare Gen 7:11), causing four horrible, evil beasts to rise from the chaotic waters: one like a lion with eagle's wings, which has its wings pulled off and is given human-like legs and a human mind (v. 4); a three-fanged animal like a ravenous bear (v. 5); a four-winged, four-headed animal like a leopard (v. 6); and a ten-horned, ravaging beast with great iron teeth and trampling feet, which is too horrible to be likened to any animal on earth (v. 7). As Daniel watches, three of the horns of the fourth beast are torn away by the emergence of a little horn with human-like eyes and a mouth that speaks arrogantly (v. 8).

The second scene of the dream is a heavenly judgment scene (vv. 9-12) in which Daniel sees the Ancient of Days (God, portrayed as an old, white-haired man dressed in white) presiding from a fiery throne with wheels (compare Ezek 1:26; 10:1) over a court of thousands of servants (on the heavenly court, see 1 Kgs 22:19; Job 1:6). When the books are opened (v. 10; compare Isa 65:6, Mal 3:16), the four beasts are brought to trial. The fourth beast is sentenced to death, and its body is cast into the fire (v. 11). The other three beasts lose their power but are permitted to live (v. 12).

In a second event in the part of his dream about the heavenly court (vv. 13-14), Daniel sees "one like a son of man" (see comment at Ezek 2:1) coming on the clouds to the court of the Ancient One. This special human figure (a symbol for the "holy people of the Most High," according to verse 27) receives the heavenly gifts of everlasting dominion, glory, and kingship over the nations.

In his dream Daniel is bewildered by the vision of the trial of the four beasts in the heavenly court and the inheritance of the one like a son of man. He seeks the meaning of his vision from "one of those present," presumably an angel interpreter (vv. 15-28). He is told that the four beasts symbolize the four kingdoms over which the holy people of the Most High will triumphantly rule (vv. 17-18; Babylon, Media, Persia, and Greece; compare ch. 2). The ten horns of the fourth beast represent the divided Greek empire of Alexander the Great, and the blasphemous little horn represents the ruler Antiochus IV Epiphanes, who persecuted the Jews of Jerusalem and Judea (see 1 Macc 1:20-63). The angel assures Daniel that though the little horn wars against the holy ones, its triumph will be brief. Dominion over it will soon be given to the holy ones of Israel (vv. 19-27). The son of man here represents God's own people, to whom victory will be given in the immediate future (v. 27). Daniel records that the dream-vision ended and that he kept what he had seen to himself because he was terrified (v. 28).

8:1-27 Vision of the ram and he-goat. Written in Hebrew, this vision, which is dated two years after chapter 7 (see v. 1), tells of a battle between a two-horned ram (representing the Medo-Persian empire) and a he-goat (Alexander the Great). Using another set of symbols, this vision recapitulates the historical story told in chapter 7. The he-goat easily defeats the two-horned ram (v. 7; reference to Alexander's defeat of Persia in a series of battles between 334 and 331 B.C.E.). Then, at the height of the he-goat's power, its great unicorn is broken off (v. 8; reference to Alexander's early death in 323 B.C.E.) and four horns sprout in its place (v. 8; symbols of the four areas into which Alexander's kingdom was divided: Macedonia, Asia Minor, Syria-Babylonia, and Egypt). One of the horns sprouts its own little horn (v. 9; Antiochus IV Epiphanes). This little horn attacks earthly and heavenly powers, coming into combat with the prince of the host (seemingly God, though possibly the high priest, Onias III, who was assassinated in 170 B.C.E. by Antiochus) and desecrating the temple (vv. 10-12).

For this vision, Daniel (who is awake) is transported (compare Ezek 3:12; 8:3; 40:1) to Susa, the capital of Persia, to the banks of the river Ulai (vv. 1-2). There he meets the angel Gabriel (one of the archangels, according to 1 Enoch), who reveals that the appointed time of God's wrath is drawing near when Antiochus will be overthrown (vv. 15-25). The vision of the two thousand three hundred evenings and mornings that are to pass before the purification of the temple (vv. 13-14; 26) is confirmed as true (these 1150 days equal three years and seventy days, which is remarkably close to the actual time that elapsed between the desecration of the temple by Antiochus in 167 B.C.E. and its reconsecration on the twenty-fifth of Chislev in 164 B.C.E.; see 1 Macc 4:52-59; compare 2 Macc 10:3). Daniel is enjoined to keep secret all that he has seen. The note that he felt weak and ill for some days afterward and that he did not fully comprehend all that he had experienced closes this second vision (v. 27; compare 9:22, where Gabriel gives Daniel understanding).

9:1-27 Gabriel and the seventy weeks. The third vision of the divine mysteries concerning the end of time takes the form of a direct revelation to Daniel through the mediation of the angel Gabriel (see ch. 8). This narrative is set in the first year of the reign of Darius the Mede, the son of Ahasuerus (v. 1; no historical Ahasuerus ever had a son Darius; Darius I of Persia had a son Ahasuerus; Darius the Mede in Daniel is not a historical figure; the year according to the chronology of the book is 538 B.C.E.; compare 5:30–6:1). The chapter divides into two parts: Daniel's prayer (vv. 3-19) and God's answer as delivered by Gabriel (vv. 20-27).

Daniel's prayer is occasioned by his meditation on Jeremiah's prophecy that seventy years would pass while Judah remained desolate and its people captive (v. 2; see Jer 25:11-12; 29:10). As he puzzles over the truth hidden in this prophetic text, Daniel does penance and fasts (v. 3; on fasting as an appropriate way to prepare for a revelation, see 10:2-3; Exod 34:28). Then he offers a prayer that opens with a frank confession of the disobedient sinfulness of the covenant people (vv. 4-14); recalls God's graciousness in leading the people out of Egypt and God's justice in punishing Jerusalem (vv. 15-16); and petitions God to deliver the holy city and the nation that bears God's name (vv. 17-19). A threefold request (often called the Old Testament *Kyrie eleison* = "Lord, have mercy") summarizes and concludes the prayer: "O Lord, hear! O Lord, pardon! O Lord, be attentive and act without delay, for your own sake" (v. 19; compare 3:43).

Gabriel is sent by God to instruct Daniel on the meaning of Jeremiah's prophecy (vv. 20-27; cherubim had two wings—see Exod 25:20; seraphim had six wings—see Isa 6:2; but Gabriel is the first angel to travel by wings in the Old Testament; other angels simply appear). Daniel is given a reinterpretation of Scripture. He is told that not seventy years but seventy weeks of years (= 490 years) must pass before desolation will come to an end. The seventy weeks of years are divided into three segments: seven weeks (49 years) until an anointed leader (v. 25; that is, 587 B.C.E., the second deportation, to 538 B.C.E., the arrival of Cyrus the Persian); sixty-two weeks (434 years) until an anointed shall be cut down (v. 26; from the end of the Exile in 538 to the assassination of the high priest Onias III in 170 B.C.E.; historically not 434 but 368 years, an understandable mistake, since the precise length of the Persian period was not known to later Jewish writers like the author of Daniel); and one week (v. 27; 7 years; 170 to 163 B.C.E.), broken at the half-week when sacrifice will be abolished (presumably Antiochus IV's desecration of the temple in 168 B.C.E.). Thus, the fulfillment of Jeremiah's prophecy is at hand for Daniel.

10:1–12:13 Vision of the Hellenistic wars. The fourth and final vision divides into three parts: a lengthy introduction describing the appearance of God's emissary to Daniel and their conversation (ch. 10); a revelation that rehearses the history of the relationship between the Ptolemies in Egypt and the Seleucids in Syria and ends with the death of Antiochus (11–12:4); and an epilogue that closes with the sealing of God's secrets until the end of time (12:5-13). Chapters 10–12, which are actually a historical retrospective written in the form of prophecy, were most likely composed shortly before the death of Antiochus (163 B.C.E.), since the details of his death are inaccurately predicted (see 11:40-45).

Fictitiously dated 536 B.C.E., the third year of Cyrus, chapter 10 finds Daniel on the banks of the Tigris River (he is physically there, not transported as in 8:2). Following a three-week period of penance and fasting, Daniel is granted a revelation (vv. 2-3; compare ch. 9:3). A heavenly emissary appears to him on the twenty-fourth day of the first month (v. 4; it is unusual that Daniel fasted for much of the first month, since Exod 12:1-20 specifies it as the month during which Passover is celebrated; perhaps the author is alluding to the time when this celebration was suspended in 168 B.C.E. on account of a decree issued by Antiochus IV abolishing Jewish religion). Described in language reminiscent of Ezekiel, the angel-interpreter, a gleaming man dressed in linen with a belt of fine gold around his waist (vv. 5-6; compare Ezek 1:27-28; 9:2-3, 11; 10:2, 6, 7), is seen only by Daniel, who faints at the sight (vv. 7-9). Those who are with Daniel flee in terror.

In verses 9-14 the angel raises Daniel to his knees, addresses him as "beloved" (the title given by Gabriel in 9:23), and urges him to stand up and hear the message the angel has been sent to speak (compare Ezek 2:1). Assuring Daniel that he need not fear (v. 12), the angel explains that he was delayed in answering Daniel's prayer because for three weeks he was involved in a heavenly opposition with the patron angel of Persia, until finally Michael, the patron angel of Israel, came to his aid (v. 13; compare 10:21; 12:1). The angel reveals that he has come to tell Daniel what will happen to Israel in the days to come (v. 14).

Daniel responds by falling forward in stunned silence (v. 15). A second time the angel reaches out to comfort and reassure him. When the angel touches his lips, Daniel recovers his ability to speak (compare Isa 6:7; Jer 1:7) and says that he is seized with pangs of labor (v. 16; so also 1 Sam 4:19). Daniel wonders where he will get the breath to speak to the angel (v. 17). A third time the angel touches Daniel (v. 18), again addressing him as "beloved" and reassuring him that he need not be afraid (v. 19). And this time Daniel is strengthened and ready to hear the truth.

The revelation of what is written in the book of truth (11:2–12:4; compare 7:10) includes a brief account of the historical events from the time of Cyrus the Great to Antiochus IV (vv. 2-20) and a lengthier description of the reign of Antiochus IV (vv. 21-45). Much of the detail here is veiled and difficult to decipher. Perhaps the three kings of Persia (v. 2) are the successors of Cyrus: Cambyses, Darius I, and Xerxes. The great king of Greece (v. 3) is clearly Alexander the Great, whose empire was divided into four kingdoms after his sudden death in 323 B.C.E. (v. 4). The king of the south (v. 5) is Ptolemy, one of Alexander's generals, whose descendants controlled Egypt until 30 B.C.E.

After 248 B.C.E., Ptolemy II gave his daughter, Berenice, in marriage to Antiochus II (the grandson of Seleucus, who was king of the north) on the condition that Antiochus II divorce Laodice and disinherit their two sons. Laodice avenged herself and her disinherited children by poisoning Antiochus II and murdering Berenice and her child (v. 6). In retaliation, Ptolemy III, Berenice's brother, put Laodice to death when he invaded and plundered the Seleucid kingdom (vv. 7-8). Then Seleucus Callinicus invaded Egypt in 240 B.C.E., but he was defeated (v. 9). His sons, Seleucus Ceraunus and Antiochus III, continued the fight with Egypt (v. 10). But in 217 B.C.E. Ptolemy IV soundly defeated Antiochus III at Raphia on the southern border of Palestine, and Egypt gained control over Palestine (vv. 11-12). When Ptolemy V acceded to the throne at age five (203 B.C.E.), Antiochus III again attacked Egypt and recaptured Palestine (vv. 13-16).

In 193 B.C.E., hoping to gain control in Egypt, Antiochus III gave his daughter, Cleopatra, in marriage to Ptolemy V (v. 17). His plan failed because Cleopatra encouraged an alliance between Egypt and Rome. In 197 B.C.E. Antiochus III had invaded Asia Minor; in 192 B.C.E. he invaded Greece. The Romans defeated him in 191 B.C.E. at Thermopylae; and in 190 B.C.E., after the defeat at Magnesia near Smyrna, Rome forced Antiochus III into a treaty of subservience, imposed an enormous indemnity upon him, and took his son (Antiochus IV) as hostage (v. 18). In order to pay the tribute to Rome, Antiochus III tried to plunder the temple of Bel in Elymais, but its inhabitants killed him in 187 B.C.E. (v. 19). His successor, Seleucus IV (187–175 B.C.E.), attempted to plunder the temple treasure in Jerusalem but was murdered in a conspiracy led by Heliodorus, possibly abetted by Seleucus IV's younger brother, Antiochus IV (v. 20; compare 2 Macc 3:1-40).

Shortly before his death, for reasons that are now obscure, Antiochus II negotiated an exchange of hostages with Rome. In place of his younger son, Antiochus IV, he sent his older son, Demetrius. Thus in 175 B.C.E. when Seleucus IV was murdered, Antiochus IV, "a despicable person," usurped the throne from Demetrius and seized control of the Seleucid empire (v. 21). After Antiochus IV came to the throne, various parties in Jerusalem began to compete for appointment as high priest (from this time on, Seleucid and Roman leaders assumed the right to appoint and depose the Jewish high priest). First, in 174 B.C.E. Jason, the brother of the legitimate high priest, Onias III, bribed Antiochus IV for the appointment. Then, in 172 B.C.E. Menelaus offered a bigger bribe and secured the office. Menelaus not only bought the high priesthood but he had the deposed Onias III murdered (170 B.C.E.; vv. 22-23; compare 9:26; 2 Macc 4:32-43).

Details of the two Syrian-Egyptian wars are supplied in verses 24-35. In the first campaign (169 B.C.E.) against Ptolemy VI Philometer (the son of Antiochus's sister Cleopatra), Antiochus IV succeeded in taking captive Ptolemy VI, who had been given very poor strategical advice by his counselors (vv. 25-26; compare 1 Macc 1:16-19). When nobles in Alexandria filled the throne by crowning Ptolemy VII, Antiochus IV pretended to ally himself with his prisoner, Ptolemy VI, against Ptolemy VII (v. 27). If he could not conquer Egypt, Antiochus IV hoped, at least, to keep its royal family divided.

Though not entirely successful in Egypt, Antiochus IV returned home a richer man. But trouble brewed in Jerusalem, where Jason tried to reinstate himself in the office of high priest by murdering many of the supporters of Menelaus. Enraged, Antiochus IV invaded Jerusalem, massacred many Jews, reinstated Menelaus, and looted the Jerusalem temple (v. 28).

When word reached Antiochus IV that Cleopatra had reconciled her two brothers, Ptolemy VI and Ptolemy VII, to reign conjointly, he invaded Egypt a second time (168 B.C.E.; v. 29). But as Antiochus IV marched on Alexandria, he was stopped by a Roman delegation (Kittim = eastern Mediterranean people, here Romans) and was ordered by the legate, Popilius Laenas, to leave Egypt (v. 30a). Frustrated and hearing of further difficulties in Jerusalem, Antiochus IV ordered a bitter and bloody persecution of those who resisted Hellenistic culture and religion in Palestine (168–164 B.C.E.; see vv. 30b-35). In 167 B.C.E. an idol was erected and consecrated to Zeus, and swine were sacrificed on the altar of the Jerusalem temple (this is the "horrible abomination" in verse 31; see also 9:27; 12:11). Antiochus IV behaved blasphemously, even claiming divinity for himself (v. 36; on his coins he added the appellation Epiphanes, meaning "God Manifest"; many in his kingdom, however, called him Epimanes, meaning, "Mad Man"). In turning to Zeus Olympios, Antiochus IV neglected his ancestral god Tammuz (v. 37; compare Ezek 8:14).

The description of Antiochus IV's abominable reign closes with an inaccurate prediction of a successful final campaign against Egypt and an incorrect location of the place of his death as between the Mediterranean Sea and Jerusalem (vv. 40-45). The author of Daniel seems to have been unaware that Antiochus IV died of an undiagnosed disease at Tabae in Persia during an unsuccessful campaign in the fall of 163 B.C.E. (see 1 Macc 6:1-16). On account of this break with accurate historical reporting, critics argue that this apocalypse (chs. 10–12) was composed before Antiochus IV's final eastern campaign and death.

According to the poetic conclusion (12:1-3) to the revelation of what is written in the book of truth (11:2–12:4), the great tribulation of the end times will result in the vindication of the elect of God. Michael, Israel's patron angel, will arise to assist the redemption of Israel (v. 1). Many who sleep in graves will awake to live forever, others to be given to everlasting horror (v. 2). This promise of resurrection for individual reward and punishment is nearly unparalleled in the Old Testament (compare Isa 26:19). The faithful who have stood fast during the times of persecution are promised eternal reward (compare the more widespread Old Testament view that all the dead inhabit Sheol, which, though not a place of retribution, was a place where communion with God was cut off; see Isa 38:18; Ps 88:10-12). The new life described in Daniel exceeds both metaphoric description of political restoration suggested by texts like Ezek 37:1-14; Hos 6:1-2; Pss 80:19-20; 85:7 and hyperbolic expressions about being brought up from Sheol in texts like Pss 30:4; 86:13; 103:4; Isa 38:17.

Verse 4 is an injunction that Daniel keep the revelation secret until the end of time (compare 8:26). Given the fictitious date 536 B.C.E. assigned to the fourth vision in 10:1, the injunction is necessary to complete the narrative's pretended chronology. For the author, application of the revelation belonged to the time after the death of Antiochus, a time that was imagined at hand.

Verses 5-13 are little more than an epilogue that attempts to fix the time of the end. To two angels standing on either bank of the river (v. 5; compare the opening setting in 10:4) the man clothed in linen swears that the time of severe persecution will last for three and a half years (v. 7; compare 7:25; 9:27). Baffled at what he hears, Daniel requests further illumination, but he is denied (vv. 8-10). And in what appear to be two later additions, the time of persecution is extended, first to 1290 days (v. 11), and then to 1335 days (v. 12). In verse 13 Daniel is told to go his way until the end. On this note of imminent relief from persecution, the protocanonical text of Daniel ends.

PART III: APPENDIX

Dan 13:1–14:42

The third section of the Book of Daniel is a collection of three edifying deuterocanonical short stories about Daniel (Susanna, 13:1-64; Bel, 14:1-22; the Dragon, 14:23-42). Found only in the Septuagint, these stories are like those in Dan 1:1–6:29. They, too, teach that faithfulness triumphs over adversity and that foreign powers can be convinced of the sovereignty of the Lord.

13:1-63 Susanna's virtue. In the Greek and Old Latin translations of the Book of Daniel, the story of Susanna is placed before chapter 1, as an introduction (most likely because in verse 45 Daniel is described as a young boy in Babylon). In the Vulgate (the Latin translation of the Bible made by Jerome in about 382 C.E.), the story of Susanna is listed as chapter 13.

This story is different from all others in the Book of Daniel in that the conflict is internal to the Jewish community and the protagonist is a woman. Chapter 13 is a test of Susanna's courage and loyalty to the law in the face of false accusation, as well as a display of Daniel's wisdom and cleverness in solving what is sometimes called one of the earliest detective stories.

Babylon is the setting of the narrative (v. 1; compare chs. 1–5). Verses 1-4 tell that Joakim, a very rich and highly respected Jew, married the very beautiful and God-fearing Susanna (compare Jdt 8:7-8), who had been well trained in the law of Moses by her parents (only her father, Hilkiah, is mentioned by name). Joakim's house and its garden are the scene of the tale (compare the instruction in Jer 29:5 that the exiles build homes and plant gardens in Babylon).

Verses 5-14 introduce the two antagonists and describe the situation that occasions the conflict. Two wicked old men, who are appointed judges of the exiled community, lust for Susanna, who usually came out for a walk in the garden at noon, after the judges had finished trying cases and presumably had left Joakim's garden. Secretly watching her every day, the judges develop a passionate desire to have intercourse with her (v. 11; a variety of Greek expressions for sexual intimacy are used in this narrative: "to be with/have intercourse with," vv. 11, 39; "lay down with," v. 37; "so give in to our desire and be with us," v. 20; and "making love," v. 54). Though both judges pretend to leave for lunch one day, they catch each other spying on Susanna, admit their desire, and agree to watch for an occasion when they might be alone with her.

The dreadful day is described in verses 15-27. On a very hot afternoon, when everyone has supposedly left the garden, Susanna instructs her two maids to shut the garden doors and to prepare a bath for her (v. 17). When the maids have gone, the two elders appear and demand that Susanna lie with them (v. 20), saying that if she refuses, they will testify that they saw a young man with her in the garden (v. 21).

Admitting the dilemma, Susanna chooses to call out for help (see Deut 22:23-27), saying, "It is better for me to fall into your power without guilt than to sin before the Lord" (v. 23). As she calls out, the elders also shout, and one of them runs and opens the garden gate, so as to circumstantially convict her. When those in the house rush out, the elders tell their concocted story about the young man and Susanna. Believing the elders, the servants are very much ashamed of their mistress.

The next day, when the two judges come to hear cases in Joakim's garden, they order Susanna to appear for judgment (vv. 28-41). They are determined that she be put to death. Veiled, Susanna appears with her parents, children, and relatives (her husband is not mentioned until verse 63). The elders order her to show her face, "so as to sate themselves with her beauty" (v. 32), and place their hands on her head (see Lev 24:14) as they make their case against her. Without question, the assembly believes the two respected judges and condemns Susanna (v. 41).

Susanna protests her innocence to the Lord (vv. 42-43), and her prayer is heard (v. 44). God stirs a young boy named Daniel to speak out in her defense (v. 45). Daniel refuses to participate in an execution without clearer evidence (vv. 46-49). The trial is reopened (vv. 52-59), and Daniel examines the judges. He asks each separately under which tree they saw Susanna and her lover. One answers, "Under a mastic tree," and is told he will be "split" in two (v. 55; there is a play on words in the Greek). The other answers, "Under an oak," and is promised he will be "cut" in two (v. 59—another play on words). Though Daniel declares the fate of the two evil judges before both have testified, their own lies seal their fate. According to the law (see Deut 19:16-21), they must suffer the fate they planned for the one falsely accused (vv. 60-62). Susanna's parents, relatives, and husband praise God because Susanna is found innocent (v. 63). And Daniel becomes famous among his people (v. 64).

Though seemingly trapped in a situation in which social convention allowed men of age and rank to determine her fate, Susanna teaches that purity, truthfulness, and the practice of prayer are rewarded by a God who answers a woman's prayer, inspires Daniel to interrogate her accusers, and holds out a future of hope.

14:1-42 Bel and the Dragon. Two very brief detective stories that ridicule idolatry appear in chapter 14 (compare chs. 3, 6). In the first (vv. 1-22), Daniel convinces Cyrus that the Babylonian god Bel (= Marduk) does not consume the sacrifices that are daily offered to him. By putting ashes on the sanctuary floor, Daniel proves to the king that the priests and their families enter through a secret trap door and take the sacrificial food for themselves.

In the second story (vv. 23-42), Daniel convinces the king that the great dragon is a worthless god. By feeding the animal pitch, fat, and hair, Daniel causes it to burst and die. Angered that they have lost their priests, Bel, and now their dragon, the people of Babylon demand that they be allowed to throw Daniel into a den of lions (v. 31; compare ch. 6). Daniel spends six days in the den with seven lions, but he is unharmed because God had an angel transport the prophet Habakkuk by the hair of his head from Judah to Babylon to bring Daniel food (vv. 33-39). On the seventh day the king comes out and finds Daniel in good health, praises the God of Daniel, and orders those who sought Daniel's death to be put into the lions' den. They are quickly devoured (v. 42). Daniel's wisdom is once again proven and rewarded, and a foreign power is convinced of the sovereignty of Yahweh.

JOEL, OBADIAH, HAGGAI, ZECHARIAH, AND MALACHI

Mary Margaret Pazdan, O.P.

INTRODUCTION

A variety of starting points is available for exploring a text of the Bible. The process of selection is similar to how a viewer encounters snapshots in a photo album. One individual focuses sharply on a single image, while another admires the arrangements or qualities of composition. A third person enjoys the sequence and patterning of several pages, whereas a fourth examines an entire album for imaginative contours. If the snapshots or the album captures the attention of the viewer, they may provide opportunities for additional variations by repeated inspection.

The viewer's experiences also inform what is perceived. A family member, relative, or friend is delighted to find memories suddenly revitalized by significant photos that celebrate life (for example, birthdays, anniversaries, summer holidays). Juxtaposed to these photos, however, are others that remind the viewer of circumstances that have modified the moment captured on film (for example, distance, aging, death). Viewers unfamiliar with the photos need explanations from others to give the photo meaning.

The photographer's experiences direct the selection of the subject. Often the photo represents more possibilities to the viewers than the photographer saw in framing the subject. The understanding of the photo deepens when the viewer and the photographer discuss its importance. The reality of the photo is seldom exhausted, because each viewer sees with limited perception.

Like the viewer and photographer, a number of biblical scholars began to dialogue with persons of other academic disciplines. No longer confined to the historical-critical method of the nineteenth century, commentators cautiously applied the distinctive methods of new literary, canonical, and sociological criticism to broaden the possibilities of interpreting prophecy, including the five books treated in this commentary. The interdisciplinary method indicated in scholarly and popular articles for over a decade may provide insights into the meaning of postexilic prophecy, which had been generalized and undervalued.

Why does prophecy from its early development (about 1000 B.C.E.) through the period of the Exile (586–538 B.C.E.) receive more attention in surveys of the Old Testament?

a) The books that record the growth of prophecy are wonderful literature. Nathan, the court prophet, indicts King David (1000–967 B.C.E.) by means of the parable of the ewe lamb (2 Sam 12:1-15). A cycle of narratives about northern Israel (869–815 B.C.E.) records the adventures of Elijah and Elisha: a contest on Mount Carmel with the prophets of Baal, meeting Jezebel, miracles, experiences of God, involvement with political and religious leaders (see 1 Kgs 17–21; 2 Kgs 1–9).

Prophetic books named for individuals follow the *narratives about* prophets. They offer biographical details, dramatic gestures, and bold prophetic oracles to communicate the word of God. Isaiah, Jeremiah, and Ezekiel appear as inspiring, heroic figures in the struggles of Judah (782–586 B.C.E.). The prophets stimulate interest and imagination for scholars. Concurrently, they appeal to children and adults in catechetical and sermon contexts as well as by their association with literature, music, and art.

b) Many events described by the texts are supported by the parallel literature of the ancient Near East. Archeological data confirms the historical and literary perspectives of preexilic and exilic prophecy. Analysis and comparison with extrabiblical materials generate additional study and discovery.

c) The books indicate common political-religious dimensions of kingship and temple. Fidelity of the king and community to the Jerusalem temple is *the* standard by which northern Israel and Judah are judged (see 1 Kgs 12–2 Kgs 25). The prophets exhort the people to be faithful to the covenant stipulations first formed with God on Mount Sinai through Moses. They develop the ethical dimensions of Torah, images of God and future liberation, often evoking images from Exodus.

d) New Testament authors frequently refer to persons and passages from preexilic and exilic prophecy to describe Jesus, the Jews, and early communities of believers.

When earlier scholars compared postexilic prophecy with the characteristics of preexilic and exilic prophecy mentioned above, the former appeared unimportant and secondary in the prophetic corpus. The narratives are limited, lacking in personal detail, and seldom the subject of art or literature. The historical and literary data is sparse; often reconstruction is contradictory. The political, social, and religious conditions after the Exile do not compare favorably with the symbolic unity of kingship and temple. The texts are quoted infrequently by New Testament authors.

Contemporary scholars do not judge postexilic prophecy by earlier prophecy. Prophetic forms and content aligned to king and temple are no longer considered necessarily normative or significant. What, then, is appropriate for interpreting postexilic writings? In this commentary the central focus is the particular contribution of each book as a witness to restoration after the experience of exile. Information about a particular author, dating, and composition, together with an outline of the book, is given just before the commentary on each book. Considerations common to Joel, Obadiah, Haggai, Zechariah, and Malachi are described below.

Location in the Old Testament

The Jewish canon and the Alexandrian canon include the Books of Joel, Obadiah, Haggai, Zechariah, and Malachi among the Twelve Minor Prophets. What does the division imply? The designation "minor" has been interpreted as meaning "inferior" or "less important," because the Twelve Minor Prophets follow the Latter Prophets (Isaiah, Jeremiah, Ezekiel) in the Jewish canon, and the Prophets (Isaiah, Jeremiah, Baruch, Lamentations, Ezekiel, Daniel) in the Alexandrian canon. The term "minor" probably refers to the size of the texts compared with the prophetic books that precede them.

In a manner unlike that of the Major Prophets, the historical factors for ordering and collecting the Twelve Minor Prophets remain obscure. Scholars examine the canons and the books for implications of how the process may have occurred. In comparing the canons, the first and the seventh through the twelfth books are identical (Hosea, Nahum, Habakkuk, Zephaniah, Haggai, Zechariah, Malachi), while the second through the sixth books are in different order: Jewish canon (Joel, Amos, Obadiah, Jonah, Micah); Alexandrian canon (Amos, Micah, Joel, Obadiah, Jonah).

Which list is earlier? What accounts for the change of order? There are three suggestions for the ordering of the books in each canon: (a) chronology; (b) repetition of words and phrases between books, for example Amos 1:2 and Joel 4:16; (c) mechanical considerations, for example the length of a scroll. Today the questions and suggestions are unresolved.

How twelve independent prophetic books became a collection that was considered as one book is a puzzle. Often the fact that the Twelve could be written on one scroll is given as a solution. Historically, the process of collection was completed by 300 B.C.E. Sirach, writing a century later, acknowledges the prophets in his praise of Israel's heroes:

> Then, too, the TWELVE PROPHETS—
> may their bones return to life from their resting place!—

Gave new strength to Jacob
and saved him by their faith and hope.
(Sir 49:10).

Sirach's grandson, translating the Hebrew text into Greek after 132 B.C.E., includes the division of prophets in his foreword: "Many important truths have been handed down to us through the law, the prophets, and the latter authors; and for these the instruction and wisdom of Israel merit praise."

The Minor Prophets were also important to the Qumran community, whose scrolls include a commentary on Micah as well as eight incomplete copies of the Twelve Minor Prophets. In Christian tradition the title "Minor Prophets" is attributed to Augustine (*De civitate Dei*, XVIII, 29). Canonical critics observe that the process of ordering and collecting the Twelve Minor Prophets is less important than the factors involved in shaping each book and the way the final form of each book functioned in a particular community of faith.

Historical background

The ministry and textual tradition of Joel, Obadiah, Haggai, Zechariah, and Malachi extended over two centuries of postexilic Judaism. Although the period is poorly documented, some biblical witness and archeological data are available to reconstruct the historical context for the prophets and their literary records.

2 Kgs 23:36–25:30, 2 Chr 36:9-21, and Jer 32–34; 37–39; 52 interpret the final days of Judah and the deportations to Babylon. In 599 B.C.E. King Jehoiakim refused to pay tribute money to Nebuchadnezzar, ruler of the neo-Babylonian empire. Although the biblical texts are unclear about Jehoiakim's fate, they indicate that his son Jehoiachin had ruled for only three months when Nebuchadnezzar forced him to surrender Jerusalem in the spring of 597 B.C.E. Jehoiachin, the royal household, craftspersons, military officials, and prominent citizens were sent into captivity. The sacred vessels of the temple were also transported to Babylon.

To reduce the possibility of further rebellion, Nebuchadnezzar appointed Jehoiachin's uncle, Zedekiah, as king of Judah. For eleven years he wavered between the patronage of the pro-Egyptian party and the protection of Jeremiah. Having chosen resistance as his brother did, he, too, had to surrender to Nebuchadnezzar, who ordered the palace, the temple, and the city destroyed; the ruler and inhabitants were deported to Babylon in 586 B.C.E.

For the few persons remaining near Jerusalem, Nebuchadnezzar appointed Gedaliah as governor. After he was assassinated by a rebel, the Babylonian policy of deportation and division of the land continued in Judah and other parts of the empire. The Edomites, ancient enemies of Israel, seized some territory in Judah. The Book of Obadiah is directed against their treachery. The Book of Lamentations reflects the anguish and tragedy of this period for the Jews.

After Nebuchadnezzar died in 562 B.C.E., the empire gradually declined and Cyrus the Persian seized the opportunity for twenty years of conquest. His success culminated in the surrender of Babylon in 539 B.C.E. Cyrus' liberal attitude toward subject peoples extended to authorizing their return and financing the restoration of temples and cults. The Cyrus Cylinder, an inscription written on a clay barrel and telling of Cyrus' Babylonian triumph and of his policy of allowing captives to return to their homelands, indicates his intentions: "May all the gods whom I have placed within their sanctuaries address a daily prayer in my favor . . . that my days may be long."

Cyrus also issued a decree to the Babylonian Jews. Under the leadership of Sheshbazzar, prince of Judah, a small group returned bringing donations from their neighbors and the confiscated temple vessels (Ezra 1:2–2:70). Meanwhile, large numbers remained in Babylon, preferring their homes, structures of community life, and loyalty toward the lenient government to an uncertain future in ravaged Judah (compare Jer 29:1-9).

The returnees found a decimated land, inhospitable landowners, intermarriage, and syncretistic worship. Sheshbazzar, appointed governor, initiated attempts to restore the sacrificial altar and the foundations of the temple. The confused chronology and narrative detail of Ezra, the only biblical record for the period, do not indicate what happened to Sheshbazzar.

After Cyrus' death, Cambyses, his son, reigned until 522 B.C.E. At his death widespread rebellion occurred in many areas of the empire. Darius, an officer of Cambyses' army, stabilized the empire after two years of fierce battles. During that time another group of Babylonian Jews returned to Jerusalem, including Zerubbabel, appointed governor, and Joshua, the high priest. During their dual leadership there were renewed efforts to rebuild the temple.

Obstacles, however, continued to impede progress. Within the community, antagonism over property claims continued. Droughts and poor soil added to the burden of harsh living conditions. Opposition to the restoration came from neighboring areas under Persian control as well as from the Samaritans to the north. Darius intervened to settle the disputed authorization for rebuilding the temple. Haggai and Zechariah, too, encouraged the residents to persevere in their efforts.

In the spring of 515, nearly twenty-five years after Cyrus' decree, the community offered sacrifice to God and dedicated the temple (Ezra 3–6). There is no evaluation of Zerubbabel's leadership. He, like Sheshbazzar, disappeared mysteriously from the narrative of Ezra. Joshua and the priestly class associated with the temple presumably became the source of political and religious authority for the community.

There is a gap of fifty years in the biblical record, although the undated text of Malachi offers an assessment of community life just before the arrival of Ezra. The author condemns the irresponsibility of the priests in cultic matters, intermarriages with non-Jews, and social injustice.

Ezra, commissioned by Artaxerxes I, initiated a religious reform in 458 B.C.E. by condemning intermarriage, appointing honest magistrates and judges, and assembling the people for the reading of the law (Ezra 7:1–10:16; Neh 8:1–9:37). Nehemiah, cupbearer to Artaxerxes I, was governor of Judah from 445–433 B.C.E. He protected Jerusalem from its enemies by supervising the rebuilding of the city walls. After a brief absence, Nehemiah returned as governor (430–418 B.C.E.) to enforce religious laws regarding the support of temple officials, marriage, and observance of the sabbath (Neh 1:1–7:5; 11:1–13:31).

The undated Book of Joel is considered a witness to the situation of the community after the reforms of Ezra and Nehemiah. The author exhorts the people to public prayer and penance to avert God's judgment. It is a preparation for "the day of the Lord," the ultimate judgment between Israel and the nations.

There is a gap of nearly a century in the biblical record, during which time the Persian empire declined and the Greek empire developed under the leadership of Alexander the Great (336–323 B.C.E.). Second Zechariah (chs. 9–14) is addressed to the Jewish community during this emergence of a new world empire. The oracles describe a cosmic battle, the Messiah, and the new kingdom of God.

Attitudes and perspectives about reconstruction

The Babylonian Jews who returned to Jerusalem in two stages participated in the multiple tasks of reconstruction. What challenges did they encounter together with the group already well established in Judah during the Exile? In addition to the obstacles mentioned above, both groups were confronted with the complex question of identity.

The province of Judah was one of several provinces included in the satrapy "West of Euphrates" (see Ezra 4:17, 20; 5:6), whose administrator, the satrap, probably resided in Damascus. Judah enjoyed the type of independence granted to members of the nearly two dozen satrapies of the vast Persian empire, including freedom for cultic activity. Judah, with Jerusalem as its center, can be identified as a temple-community like others restored and subsidized by the central government. Jerusalem functioned both as a cultic center for prayer as well as an administrative center for the province.

The officials appointed by the central government mediated their authority as governors—for example, Sheshbazzar, Zerubbabel, Nehemiah. In daily affairs, however, the priests exercised authority over the community. They decided on the status of individuals in the community according to their participation in and support of the cult. Their legislation about the standards of purity necessary for worshipers included the condemnation of those who engaged in syncretistic worship, those who married resident aliens, and those who transacted business with non-Jews.

Both residents and returnees were affected by these criteria. Tension developed among the two groups, including the priestly class. The conflict among the priestly functionaries resulted in a division of responsibility. The Zadokite priests (returnees from Babylon) assumed the major position for cult and administration; the Levites were relegated to minor positions with little authority.

Some scholars suggest that two mainstreams of religious authority developed from this situation and that this accounts for the decline of prophecy. The theocratic group was associated with the Zadokite priests and the rebuilding of the temple and the reconstitution of religious life according to the Torah and the vision of Ezekiel (Ezek 40–48). The apocalyptic group was associated with the Levites and a future transformation of the present situation according to the vision of Deutero-Isaiah (Isa 40–55). This assessment, however, is too sharp. It does not allow for the plurality of religious experience and perspective.

The manner of restoration of the community and its identity is related to the interpretation of God's revelation as understood by the individual prophet. Each responded to the needs of a particular community. Each had a provisional proclamation directed toward encouraging that community to be faithful to God:

a) *Obadiah* implored God to destroy the Edomites and to vindicate Israel from their deceit.

b) *Haggai* and *Zechariah* believed that the restoration of the temple would hasten the advent of God for the purpose of dwelling in Jerusalem forever. Zechariah also considered the relationship of God to other nations. Both prophets encountered the resistance of the Jerusalemites due to shattered dreams and oppressive living conditions, which curtailed enthusiasm and stamina for reconstruction. Neither prophet was certain about the role of the governors and the priestly class. Even after the completion of the temple, the past could not be an appropriate model for the present.

The ministry of these prophets was effective because they provided inspiration for a common identity among the residents, that is, a temple-community and the reestablished locus for cultic activity. After their deaths the dilemma of unfulfilled prophecy and unresolved relationships among their neighbors continued. Uncertainty, confusion, and instability characterized the period.

c) *Malachi* addressed abuses in cultic practices. *Joel* admonished the community about its relationship to God and its symbolic expression in worship. Both prophets desired a renewal of dedicated religious life for persons who would accept their message.

d) The writings of *Second Zechariah* stirred dormant hope and dispelled the apathy of the community through visions of climactic struggle followed by the day of the Lord, a day when a kingdom of peace and blessing would be secured forever.

These five prophets may well be remembered for activity during a bleak period of Israel's history. Each prophet with his literary record witnesses to a particular situation somewhat influenced by imperial Persian and Greek policies, yet transcending them with a religious vision related to the experience of the community to whom the message is addressed. Being convinced of the fidelity of God, they spoke a message calling the community to respond appropriately. They exhorted the community to be faithful to God, the constant reality of their past history and their present experience.

The postexilic prophets in this series cannot be judged by whether or not their message was fulfilled in subsequent history. The mystery of the faithful God and the manner in which the individual and the community respond are the perspectives that these books develop. In addition, the fact that communities of believers preserved and edited these proclamations and considered them to be the authentic revelation of God indicates their significance for developing faith in postexilic communities.

Literary forms

The Books of Joel, Obadiah, Haggai, Zechariah, and Malachi contain poetry and prose. There are visions and oracles attributed to the prophets whose names are the superscriptions for the books as well as editorial insertions to consolidate the material and provide interpretation for later communities. The books refer to earlier Scripture (Torah and Prophets) by allusion to and repetition of events and ideas. Occasionally there are direct quotations from earlier prophets.

The literary structure of each book is developed from the particular context in which the message was first proclaimed. Prophetic formulas common to preexilic and exilic books are sometimes located in the postexilic compositions; occasionally they are combined with new patterns. In particular, scholars often regard sections of these books as indicating a new literary form, viewpoint, and content known as "apocalyptic." Since the literary structure of a particular text is a primary indicator for its religious meaning, it is important to understand the structure in order to interpret the significance of the text. A few literary considerations for each book are presented below according to the chronological order already suggested.

Obadiah, the shortest book in the Old Testament, consists of two sets of oracles received in a vision according to the tradition of Jerusalemite prophets. The first set of oracles describes the destruction of Edom (vv. 2-9) in language similar to that of Jer 49:7-22. This neighbor of Israel is condemned for its betrayal of Jerusalem to Babylon (vv. 10-14). The second set was added later to include the day of the Lord as a judgment for all nations (vv. 15-16). The event culminates in the restoration of Israel and the establishment of the universal kingdom of God (vv. 17-21). Some scholars suggest that the structure of the oracles (vv. 2-17) indicates a community at worship proclaiming God's sovereignty through the proclamation of oracles against its enemies.

The two chapters of *Haggai* also contain oracles interspersed with editorial frameworks to interpret them. The frameworks include: (a) the chronology of Haggai's ministry to the residents of Jerusalem (1:1, 15; 2:1, 10, 20); (b) insertions of traditional prophetic formulas to introduce an oracle, such as "the words of the Lord through the prophet . . ." (1:1, 3; 2:1, 10, 20; compare 1:12, 13); (c) a report about the result of Haggai's preaching to the community (1:12, 14). Although words of comfort are included in the oracles, suggesting the judgment of salvation characteristic of classical prophecy (1:13; 2:4, 5), the oracles add a new development—the disputation. Some indications of this pattern are rhetorical questions (1:4; 2:3, 16) and a question-and-answer format (1:9-11).

Oracles do not function as the major literary form of revelation in *First Zechariah* (chs. 1–8); rather, they are a secondary pattern occurring in a collection (chs. 7–8) and attached to visions, which are the primary pattern of revelation (1:7–6:8). The visions constitute some of the most difficult texts to interpret in biblical literature. Some scholars suggest that the significance of the "night" visions consists in providing an alternative to the oracles and visions of Ezekiel (chs. 40–48) and of Haggai about temple reconstruction. Zechariah constructed a theological perspective for fidelity to God in the new situation of "in betweenness."

In the Book of *Malachi* the question-and-answer format that appeared in Haggai (and First Zechariah) becomes the basic structure of the oracles. This catechetical pattern was suitable for exhorting the community and its cult officials to be responsible for their relationships to God. They were urged to revitalize indifferent cultic practices and to observe the laws of marriage and the prohibitions against divorce (1:2–3:21). The two appendices (3:22-24) conclude with an instruction to be faithful to the law and a description of Elijah, God's messenger who will reconcile family members.

The Book of *Joel* is a collection of oracles with two interrelated themes: devastation and salvation. In the first part (1:1–2:17), the prophet functions as a cult figure. He calls the people to repentance in a communal lamentation liturgy intended to avert a disaster far worse than the locust plague. After introducing the concept of "the day of the Lord," Joel admonishes them about their expectations. In the second part (2:18–4:21), the prophet describes the day of the Lord in more detail. Throughout the oracles there is frequent allusion to, or direct quotations of, sayings found in other prophetic collections; for example, Isa 13:6 and Ezek 30:2-3 (Joel 1:15); Zeph 1:14-15 (Joel 2:1-2); Obad 17 (Joel 3:5).

Second Zechariah (chs. 9–14) is separated from First Zechariah by nearly two centuries of political and religious history. The chapters are divided into two sections. Each section has its own introduction (chs. 9–11 and 12–14). Unlike First Zechariah, the oracular structure is prominent. Within the oracles there is no original revelation; rather, the function of the oracles is to collect the expectations of earlier prophets and to indicate how they may be fulfilled; for example, Zeph 3:14ff. (Zech 9:9); Isa 5:26 (Zech 10:8); Joel 4 (Zech 14). Another major difference is the absence of any mention of the temple builders and officials. In addition, there are no chronological indications nor any coherent "historical" framework. Finally, the chapters of Second Zechariah have been assessed for apocalyptic language and viewpoint.

Relationship to apocalyptic writings

In the past fifteen years there has been renewed interest in the origin, language, structure, content, and interpretation of Jewish apocalyptic writings. Postexilic prophecy has been considered a possible source for apocalyptic, since the phenomenon did not parallel the structure and content of classical prophecy. Some scholars constructed a polarity between the "traditionalists" and the "visionaries" existing in the temple-community. Their conflict of interests resulted in the formation of two distinctive groups. The "traditionalists" reaffirmed the position of supporting the temple and its officials. The "visionaries" expressed their radical hopes for a new identity by the transformation of the present situation. Today interdisciplinary analysis with the social sciences, especially cultural anthropology, appears to support this interpretation.

Intra-group conflict and fluctuating circumstances can be catalysts for the formation of apocalyptic groups. The more difficult question is not why *an* apocalyptic viewpoint and literature emerged but why *this particular form* emerged. The religious diversity apparent in postexilic communities suggests that apocalyptic development was not the inevitable result of particular social circumstances.

Most of the present century of scholarship has considered the related question of the origins of apocalyptic language. Did it emerge from prophecy? Is it an adaptation of Persian dualism? Is wisdom literature the matrix? The search for sources appears to be misdirected, since any apocalyptic text combines allusions from a wide range of sources. The meaning of any text is dependent on the sources as well as on the way the sources are combined through the editorial process.

Current investigations of the structure and content of Jewish apocalyptic writings have indicated that some sections of the postexilic prophetic books may be categorized as proto-apocalyptic, for instance, Second Zechariah, Joel 3–4; Mal 3–4. Sharing a few structural similarities and features of content, however, does not indicate that some postexilic texts can be interpreted according to apocalyptic world views. The decision to investigate the linguistic affinity and structural parallel of postexilic prophecy to apocalyptic literature underscores the reluctance of some scholars to analyze these prophetic texts for their own contributions.

JOEL

Mary Margaret Pazdan, O.P.

INTRODUCTION

Authorship

What is known about the author of this book is limited to 1:1, which names and identifies him: "The word of the Lord which came to Joel, son of Pethuel." The verse uses a traditional prophetic formula, "the word of the Lord came to . . . ." The name Joel means "Yahweh is God." It is recorded by the Chronicler (see 1 Chr 4:35; 5:4; 7:3; 11:38; Ezra 10:43; Neh 11:9), whose texts were compiled in the postexilic period. Pethuel is mentioned nowhere else in the Old Testament. "Joel ben Pethuel" may designate the author of the book.

Other biographical detail is inferred from the text. Many scholars suggest that Joel was a cult prophet attached to the Jerusalem temple-community. His concern for temple worship and his prophecies in liturgical form may indicate that he was a temple official. He never identified himself, however, as a priest.

Dating of the text

The superscription of the book indicates no chronological setting for Joel. Earlier scholars, however, suggested a preexilic period for the book, noting its position in the Jewish canon between Hosea and Amos, and its repetition of words and phrases from Amos (compare Joel 4:18 and Amos 9:13). Although a minority of scholars still favor a preexilic dating, the majority of them locate Joel in the Persian period. The book suggests some literary dependency of Joel on earlier prophetic traditions (see p. 576). Historical allusions (1:9; 4:6), the absence of earlier administrators (kings and governors), and the lack of internal dissension and internal oppression also imply a late postexilic period. The approximate dating of the text is 400–350 B.C.E. (see p. 574).

Composition of the text

For the past century the unity of the text has been debated. Some scholars maintained that it was a work composed of two parts by two different authors. Others modified this position or emphasized its unity. Recent scholars suggest that the book has a literary unity. They refer to thematic connections, such as "the day of the Lord" (1:15; 2:1; 3:4; 4:14) and parallel expressions (2:27 and 4:17). Commentators debate whether the literary unity is the work of one author or of a few authors who edited the chapters for its present canonical shape.

Outline of the book

There are differences in the numbering of the chapters and verses in the second part of the Book of Joel. This commentary is based on the New American Bible, which uses the Hebrew text; other Bibles and commentaries may use the Greek text. The chart compares the two versions:

Hebrew Text	*Greek Text*
3:1-5	2:28-32
4:1-8	3:1-8
4:9-16	3:9-16
4:17-21	3:17-21

In this commentary the numbering of the Greek text is given in brackets:

PART ONE:	The Plague of Locusts and the Community (1:1–2:17)
1:1-4	Plague of Locusts
1:5-20	Call to Lamentation
2:1-11	Great Alarm
2:12-17	Call to Repentance
PART TWO:	The Response of the Lord to Israel and the Nations (2:18–4:21 [2:18–3:21])
2:18-27	Compassion for the Community
3:1-5 [2:28-32]	Blessings for the Community
4:1-17 [3:1-17]	Judgment on the Nations
4:18-21 [3:18-21]	Presence of God in Jerusalem

COMMENTARY

PART ONE: THE PLAGUE OF LOCUSTS AND THE COMMUNITY

Joel 1:1–2:17

Situations of catastrophe prompted special liturgies to respond to a particular disaster within the community (see Judg 20:26; Jer 14:2, 7-9, 12). The Book of Joel is developed according to the structure of a communal lamentation. The components of the ritual were expanded for future generations until they attained the present canonical shape. This process broadened the possibilities for interpretation of the book.

Part One consists of two units (1:1-20 and 2:1-17). Both units indicate the structure of the first part of a lamentation liturgy: (a) a call to communal lamentation; (b) a cry and prayer of lamentation. The prophet calls together the Judeans of the temple-community to reflect on the catastrophe of the locust plague. He exhorts the entire community to mourn its devastated land, to repent, and to cry out to God for assistance. The plague is compared to the day of the Lord.

1:1-4 Plague of locusts. After the superscription of the book (v. 1), the setting is introduced. The prophet initiates a summons and exhortation to the community. The elders, leaders of the community in the post-exilic era, are addressed (see Ezra 5:9; 6:7-8; compare Joel 1:2, 14; 2:17; 3:1). All the members of the community are called to consider whether the present disaster ever happened to their ancestors (v. 2). The rhetorical question is a common teaching tool, especially in the Writings of the Jewish canon, which preserved the accumulated wisdom of the people. Likewise, the prophet exhorts the community to hand down its experience of the plague to future generations (v. 3).

An initial description of the locusts appears as the climax of the setting (v. 4). "Cutter," "swarm," "grasshopper," and "devourer" may indicate stages of development in the life-cycle of locusts. How they destroy crops is suggested by the triple reference to the fact that *what (is) left* at each stage is *eaten* by the next stage. The damage that the locusts cause is attested to in biblical and extrabiblical literature. The last recorded plague in Jerusalem is reported to have been in A.D. 1915.

1:5-20 Call to lamentation. Verses 5-14 address members of the community for whom the results of the plague are overwhelming. Exhortations to particular actions refer to ritual activities associated with the liturgy of lamentation. Four groups of people are highlighted:

1) Imbibers of wine (vv. 5-7) are enjoined to "weep" and "wail" for the loss of sweet, new wine used to celebrate the autumn harvest festival (Exod 23:16). Like an invading army, the locusts have destroyed the vine.

2) The second group is not specified (vv. 8-10). It is probably a call to the entire community to "lament." The analogy of "a virgin girt with sackcloth for the spouse of her youth" (v. 8) refers to the mourning ritual of a woman after the first stage of relationship. The bridal price has been paid and public vows have been declared (see Deut 20:7; 22:23-24). The second stage, bringing the woman to her husband's home, has not occurred.

The image suggests deep, personal mourning. What type of loss could evoke such grief? Temple sacrifices have ceased because locusts ravaged the harvest (v. 9). The ritual ingredients of grain, wine, and oil are in short supply (v. 10). Significantly, the community's relationship with God symbolized in worship is severed.

3) Field workers and vinedressers (vv. 11-12) are told to "be appalled" and "wail." Their toil is futile. Their harvest, too, has failed. The yield is "dried up" and "withered." In particular, the land often interpreted as a sign of God's blessing for Israel has now become a curse. Like the produce, "joy has withered away" in the community.

4) Priests (vv. 13-14) are exhorted to "gird [themselves] . . . weep . . . wail." The instruction repeats the directives given to the other groups, with additional stipulations: (a) They are to spend day and *night* in sackcloth, a custom invoked only in extreme situations (see 2 Sam 12:16; 1 Kgs 21:27). (b) As "ministers of the altar," their ritual activity is located in the "house of your God," the temple, where sacrifice is no longer held (v. 13; compare v. 9). (c) Their office authorizes them to announce a fast, to summon and assemble the leaders and the entire community. The formal liturgy of lamentation is convened in the "house of the Lord, your God" (v. 14).

Verses 2 and 14 comprise an inclusion mentioning the "elders" and "all who dwell in the land." Its function is to draw attention to a literary unit by separating particular verses from the text. Here verses 2-14 describe the members of the community gathered for lamentation.

A cry and a prayer of lamentation follow (vv. 15-20). An exclamation of sorrow is attached to the day of the Lord, which is identified as "near" and as a day of "ruin from the Almighty" (v. 15). The statement was alarming to the community for two reasons. First, according to prophetic oracles, the day of the Lord meant God's judgment against the enemies of Israel, "the nations" (see Isa 13:6; Ezek 30:2-3; Jer 46:10). Later the oracles included the judgment of Israel for disobeying God (see Amos 5:18-20; Lam 2:22; Ezek 34:12). After the destruction of Jerusalem (586 B.C.E.), the threatening oracles appeared to be fulfilled. Second, according to the postexilic community, the day of the Lord was considered a future event limited to the nations.

In addition, the prophet invites the community to consider its present situation with a rhetorical question regarding the scanty food supply and the absence of sacrifices (v. 16; compare v. 2). Both persons and animals starve because the locusts have devoured their sustenance (vv. 17-18). The joy especially characteristic of the community at harvest festivals and worship is banished (v. 16; compare v. 12). The clear parallelism between the day of the Lord and the devastation of the plague suggests that the prophet may be interpreting the plague as a foreshadowing of the day of the Lord for the community.

A prayer (vv. 19-20) concludes the first unit of Part One. It is structured according to many psalms of lamentation: an invocation to God and a statement of complaint (vv. 19b-20; compare Pss 12:1-3; 74:1). "Fire has devoured" is a repeated metaphor to describe the locusts as the source of the complaint (vv. 19a; 20b).

2:1-11 Great alarm. This section and 2:12-17 constitute the second unit of Part One. The relationship of 1:2-20 and 2:1-17 is problematic. A few commentators state that 2:1-17 is a doublet. Some prefer to draw literary and theological parallels. Others emphasize the differences between the two sections. Canonical critics suggest that the parallels and redaction are clues as to how later communities of believers interpreted the book.

The section compared with 1:2-14 indicates parallels and differences. Some elements are nearly identical. Catastrophe is the focus. While 1:2-14 described the *results* of the locust invasion, 2:1-11 describes the *agents* of the catastrophe. The images that alluded to the relationship of the plague to the day of the Lord (1:15-20) are repeated. The proclamation is addressed to members of the temple-community. The time-sequence, however, is different. The locust plague is an event of the *past;* the day of the Lord is *imminent.* A second difference is the addition of metaphors to indicate other characteristics of the event.

The new section indicates a parallel setting (2:1-3; compare 1:2-4). Approaching danger is announced to "all who dwell in the land" with the blast of the "trumpet" (v. 1; compare 1:2, 14). The *shofar,* or ram's horn, sounded an alarm for battle as well as a call for the community to assemble in worship. The day of the Lord is the source of anxiety. The event is also heralded by cosmic signs (compare Zeph 1:14-15) and an unprecedented enemy (v. 2; see 1:6). Like "devouring fire" (see 1:4, 19), the oppressor transforms the "garden of Eden" into a "desert waste" (v. 3; compare 1:20).

A series of metaphors developed according to strength, skill, and terror identifies the day of the Lord in the context of battle (vv. 4-9). The details may resemble a description of the "holy war." Some scholars consider the event as an early stage of the day of the Lord. The metaphors are: running and leaping horses, dragging chariots behind them (vv. 4-5a); a crackling, devouring flame (v. 5b; compare 1:19; 2:3); a mighty people arrayed for battle (v. 5b); warriors and soldiers running and scaling the wall with disciplined routine, assaulting the city and climbing into the houses (vv. 7-9). Two groups are affected. Anguish colors the victims' faces (v. 6; compare Isa 13:8). The cosmic forces (earth, heavens, sun, moon, stars) quake and darken (v. 10).

The image of the holy war continues with the appearance of the Lord as the leader of the army (v. 11a). The section concludes with an inclusion, the day of the Lord (vv. 1a and 11b). The short comment "who can bear it?" appears to be a postscript, another example of the rhetorical question noted above (1:2b, 16b).

2:12-17 Call to repentance. This section is constructed to provide connections with the first part of the unit (2:1-11). It also indicates structural and thematic parallels and differences when compared with 1:5-20. The verses suggest an immediate response to the day of the Lord (2:1-11), just as the plague of locusts in the first unit demanded a response. Both events are followed by an exhortation to communal lamentation.

Verses 12 and 13 indicate an unusual circumstance to alter the awesome day of the Lord. The revelation reverses the poignant more-than-rhetorical-question of section one, to which it is structurally connected (v. 11b). God's proclamation, "Yet even now, says the Lord" (v. 12a), presents a possibility other than imminent gloom and destruction (2:1-11). It offers hope to the community trembling from the locust invasion and fearfully awaiting the worse event.

What is suggested? The invitation is to "return to me with your whole heart, with fasting, and weeping, and mourning" (v. 12b; see Amos 4:6-11; Hos 3:5; 14:2). The language indicates a turning toward God with one's whole being, the complete reorientation of thoughts and decisions toward God. Participation in a communal liturgy of lamentation (fasting, weeping, mourning) is encouraged. The ritual will symbolize the process of the community's commitment to God.

Verse 13b is a reaffirmation of the earlier relationship of God and the community revealed in the covenant at Mount Sinai (compare Exod 34:6-7). God is gracious, merciful, kind, relenting in punishment. The members of the present community are dependent upon a new manifestation of God's mercy. God *may* relent. The community is challenged to "return." Only then will there be the restored blessing of "offerings and libations," symbols of the relationship of God and the community (v. 14; compare 1:9, 12, 16).

The new possibility for the community gives a sense of urgency to the ritual of lamentation (vv. 15-17). The ritual actions to initiate the liturgy repeat earlier directions (v. 15; 1:14; 2:1). Additional components comprise this summons:

a) Children, infants, bride and bridegroom are included in the assembly. The gravity of the situation and the witness of "all who dwell in the land" preclude any exceptions for privileges ordinarily given to a young couple (v. 16; compare Deut 24:5).

b) The location for the officials of the service is indicated: "between the porch and the altar" (v. 17a). It is the traditional place for leading the community in lamentation. The distance may refer to the lack of sacrifices due to the locust invasion as well as the symbolic interpretation of strained relationships between the community and God (compare Ezek 8:16).

The prayer of lamentation (v. 17b) that concludes the section differs from the one recorded in 1:19-20. The priests implore God to spare the community, "your people," and to prevent "your heritage" from becoming "a reproach with the nations ruling over them." The plea is a traditional one (Pss 42:4; 79:10; 115:2). Here the collective experience of Israel mirrors the current situation. A rhetorical question is attributed to the nations. It ironically emphasizes their interpretation of the community's plight: "Where is their God?"

PART TWO: THE RESPONSE OF THE LORD TO ISRAEL AND THE NATIONS

Joel 2:18–4:21 [2:18–3:21]

Part One and Part Two constitute identical literary and topical structures. Each part is constructed with two units. Each unit contains two sections. Each part refers to a particular stage of the communal lamentation liturgy. In addition, the ordering of Part One and Part Two follows a chronology of events (locust invasion and imminent day of the Lord); the order of a lamentation service (stage one and stage two); and a development of prophetic revelation.

Part Two consists of two units: 2:18–3:5 [2:18-32] and 4:1-21 [3:1-21]. Both units indicate the structure of the second part of a communal service: a series of oracles containing divine assurance. The proclamations respond to the plea of the community suffering the results of the locusts and fearing the approaching day of the Lord. They promise a *future* of restoration and *new* blessings to reverse the characteristics of the day of the Lord.

In addition to the consistencies in Part One and Part Two, some commentators have identified a new literary genre in Joel 3:1–4:21 [2:28–3:21], namely, proto-apocalyptic (see p. 577). Characteristics of this genre which describe preliminaries to the day of the Lord include: outpouring of the spirit, cosmic signs, judgment against the nations, and blessings for the community.

2:18-27 Compassion for the community. This section describes a restoration of the community's situation by God. Verse 18 provides the transition from Part One to Part Two. God's concerns are the land and the people. The phrase "stirred to concern" is better translated "became jealous" (Revised Standard Version). It indicates the passionate zeal of God *for* the community (see Ezek 39:25; Zech 1:14; 8:2). God responds to the plight of the community with compassion. Subsequent activity is detailed in the assurances about restored life and freedom from enemies. They are presented in three consecutive oracles:

1) Assurances are introduced (vv. 19-20). God will send supplies needed for sustenance and sacrifice: "grain," "wine," "oil" (v. 19a; compare 1:7, 9-11, 13b, 16-17; 2:14). The community will no longer be "a reproach among the nations" (v. 19b; compare 2:17). Verse 20 describes the "northerner," which may refer to the locusts as well as their symbolic counterpart, the army of invaders (see 2:1-11). Hostile forces often approached from the north (see Jer 1:14, 15; 4:6; Ezek 38:6; 39:2). Here the enemy is destroyed by expulsion to an "arid and waste" land and by drowning in the sea.

2) "Fear not" oracles are addressed to the land and the animals connected with the community (vv. 21-22). Both are assured of verdant and fruitful life (compare 1:10-12).

3) Instruction and promises are announced to the temple-community, "children of Zion" (vv. 23-27; Lam 4:2; Ps 149:2). The group is invited to "rejoice in the Lord, your God!" (v. 23a). The second part of the verse is obscure. The New American Bible has God giving the community a "teacher of justice: he has made the rain come down for you." The Revised Standard Version has God as the giver of "the early rain for your vindication." Both translations point to God who restores a favorable condition for harvest by providing rain at the proper seasons.

This favorable situation, in turn, provides supplies for temple sacrifice. "Justice" and "vindication" suggest the ritual act of worship, which represents the covenant relationship of God and the community. The daily sacrifices at the temple had ceased because of the locust invasion.

The next three verses support the interpretation. God will provide grain, wine, and oil in great abundance as restitution for the destruction of the locusts (vv. 24-25; see 1:4; 2:5-9). Needs for sustenance and for worshiping God will be satisfied (v. 26; compare Ps 126:3).

A recognition formula concludes the section (v. 27). It indicates a new understanding of God for the community. God will be in their midst. No other god is comparable to the God of Israel. The community will "nevermore be put to shame" (compare Exod 20:2-3). The reference may be to the disgrace of the

Exile (v. 26). The revelation of the new relationship is a climax to the section as well as a response to the taunt of the nations: "Where is their God?" (2:17).

3:1-5 [2:28-32] Blessings for the community. These verses are connected thematically to 2:18-27. Both describe the characteristics of future restoration in successive stages. "Then afterward" (3:1) provides the transition to a new time-sequence. It presupposes that the conditions of restoration that God promised (2:18-27) have been fulfilled. It points to an uncertain time in the future when God's new blessings (3:1-5 [2:28-32]) will be realized in the community. The section is structured according to three blessings. Each is outlined in a three-line stanza:

1) Participation in God's spirit (vv. 1-2 [2:28-29]). "All mankind" identifies the members of the temple-community (2:19, 27; compare 4:2, 17, 19-21). The Revised Standard Version translates the Hebrew as "flesh" to emphasize the contrast between human weakness (see Isa 40:6; Ps 56:5) and God's vital power, which will transform their lives. The promise is radical, for Jewish tradition had limited God's spirit to persons with official status: a judge, like Gideon (Judg 6:34); a king, like Saul (1 Sam 16:14); a prophet, like Ezekiel (Ezek 2:2). Although Moses desired a spirit-filled community (Num 11:29), God's spirit had been limited to the seventy elders (Num 11:17, 25).

In these verses God's spirit will empower each member of the community to "prophesy." The activity is further clarified with corresponding terms: "dream dreams" and "see visions." The "prophets" are identified as "your sons and daughters," "your old men," and "your young men" (v. 1b). What is unusual is the mention of "servants" and "handmaids" (v. 2). Although their rights were protected according to the law for the sabbath rest (Exod 20:10) and festivals (Deut 12:12, 18; 16:11, 14), they were not considered members of the community. Participation in God's spirit implies *equal* status for each person in the community.

The author of Luke-Acts quotes and interprets Joel 3:1-5a [2:28-32a] in the account of Peter's discourse at Pentecost (Acts 2:17-21). The risen Lord "received the promise of the holy Spirit from the Father and poured it forth" (Acts 2:33). Greek and Jew alike have access to the Spirit if they believe in Jesus and are baptized (Acts 2:38).

2) Cosmic signs (vv. 3-4 [2:30-31]). The activity of God on behalf of the Israelites during the Exodus (1250 B.C.E.) included wonders with blood (Exod 24:4-8), fire and smoke (Exod 13:21-22; 19:18). These elements (v. 3) and the eclipse of the sun (v. 4a; compare Rev 6:12) also indicate traditional imagery associated with the terrible day of the Lord (see p. 581). The identification of cosmic signs as blessings becomes clear when the verses are considered as portents of the day of the Lord, when something *unexpected* will occur (v. 5).

3) Deliverance (v. 5 [2:32]). Rescue is assured for each person who "calls on the name of the Lord" (v. 5a). The directive includes recognition of God (Exod 33:19) and worship (Isa 12:4; Ps 105:1; compare Zech 13:9) before the nations. Those designated as "the rescued" are further identified in verse 5bc as a "remnant" and "survivors." Their home is located on "Mount Zion" and in "Jerusalem." The descriptions indicate the temple-community of Judah preeminently. Some commentators suggest that the descriptions may include the Jews of the Diaspora (see Isa 27:12-13; 57:19), that is, Jews living outside Israel.

Paul introduces verse 5a in Rom 10:12-13 by interpreting its significance universally: "For there is no distinction between Jew and Greek; the same Lord is Lord of all, enriching all who call upon him" (Rom 10:12). The outpouring of the Spirit at Pentecost is interpreted similarly: ". . . the promise is made to you and to your children and to all those far off, whomever the Lord our God will call" (Acts 2:39).

Recognition of earlier prophetic tradition is acknowledged in the clause "as the Lord has said" (v. 5b). The use of "remnant" terminology interprets Obad 17a: "But on Mount Zion there shall be a portion saved; the mountain shall be holy." The prophet also specified the source of life for the "remnant" by drawing on Ezek 39:29: "No longer will I hide my face from them, for I have poured out my spirit on the house of Israel, says the Lord God."

"Survivors whom the Lord shall call" (v. 5c) is a recognition of the mutual relationship between the Lord and the community that "calls upon the name of the Lord" (v. 5a). In 3:1-5 [2:28-32]there is the recognition that

God's community will continue. A community whose home is in Jerusalem will be given God's spirit to function as prophets.

4:1-17 [3:1-17] Judgment on the nations. This section continues the theme of Part Two: Response of the Lord to Israel and the Nations. The circumstances of the community's suffering at the hands of the nations are reviewed. They prescribe God's action and judgment against Israel's enemies consistent with traditional imagery associated with the day of the Lord. Two later additions occur in the text (vv. 4-8, 18-21).

The introduction for the section (vv. 1-3 [3:1-3]) states the reasons for God's judgment. Verse 1 is a transition linking the theme of restoration for the community (2:17–3:5 [2:17-32]) with the consequences of its enemies (3:2-17 [2:32–3:17]). In verse 1 the community is designated initially as "Judah" and "Jerusalem"; in verses 2 and 3, however, it is described in relation to God: "*my* people" (see 2:17, 27; 4:3); "*my* inheritance" (see 2:17); "*my* land."

God will assemble all the nations for judgment (v. 2a). The "Valley of Jehoshaphat" is probably cited more for its connection to the Hebrew phrase ("Yahweh judges") than for its location as a specific geographical area. In early Christian tradition the historian Eusebius (*Onamastikon*) identified the place as the Kidron Valley. In verse 14b the place is referred to as the "valley of decision."

The nations are indicted for three actions toward the community which occurred during earlier Jewish history and continued through the time of Joel (vv. 2b-3):

1) "Scattered among the nations" refers to the deportations led by Assyria and Babylon from the eighth century through the sixth century. The exilic experience of Judah and Jerusalem, in particular, is recalled here.

2) "And divided my land" describes the immediate accessibility to the land for the conquerors who settled there (see Lam 5:2).

3) "Over my people they have cast lots" indicates how little the victors valued the lives of the deportees (see Obad 11; Nah 3:10). Children, in particular, are described as the victims of their pleasures.

The prose addition (vv. 4-8 [3:4-8]) elaborates the guilt of the nations resulting from their treatment of Israel (vv. 1-3). It suggests a courtroom narrative, with God functioning as accuser, judge, and vindicator of the community. To open the trial, God poses a rhetorical question about taking vengeance and promises swift retribution. Tyre, Sidon, and the regions of Philistia (the addressees) refer to territories of traditional animosity toward Israel. Next, God condemns specific actions against the community: plundering the temple, selling persons as slaves to the Greeks, sending them into exile (vv. 5-6). Finally, God promises exact retaliation for their deeds. For engaging in slave trade (see Amos 1:6-10; Ezek 27:13), they will be sold as slaves to the community. As dealers, the community will exile its former enemies by bartering with the Sabeans. The scene concludes with a statement of divine authority: "Indeed the Lord has spoken" (vv. 7-8).

The third division in the section (vv. 9-16 [3:9-16]) continues the poetic and thematic structure of the introduction (vv. 1-3). The Valley of Jehoshaphat is the site for judgment (v. 12) and for battle (v. 14). Unknown addressees are exhorted to announce war, rouse the soldiers, and assemble the peoples roundabout (vv. 9-11). The dire situation implies additional soldiers. The untrained warriors—farmers and field workers—are urged to respond. The directive is an ironic one that intentionally *reverses* the call to peace declared in earlier prophetic traditions (v. 10; see Isa 2:4; Mic 4:3).

Instructions associated with harvest, "apply the sickle," "come and tread" (v. 13), now identify the ferocious battle waged against the enemies of the community. The event is closely aligned to the imminent day of the Lord (v. 14). Additional cosmic imagery heralds the day (vv. 15-16). The Lord dwelling in Zion "roars" and "raises his voice" (v. 16a; compare 2:11a). The action does not indicate anger but *protection* for the community, for whom the Lord is a "refuge" and "stronghold" (v. 16b; see Pss 31:3-5; 61:4).

The climax to the section is a summary declaration of the oracles of assurance and blessing. The ultimate security for the community is knowing that the Lord is "your God," dwelling among them, providing the source of holiness and protection from all enemies (v. 17 [3:17]).

4:18-21 [3:18-21] Presence of God in Jerusalem. This poetic insertion may be regarded as an appendix to the Book of Joel. It amplifies the major theme of restoration by a series of promises to be fulfilled "on that day":

a) abundant sustenance for the community: wine, milk, water (v. 18; see Amos 9:13b; Ezek 47:1-12);

b) the destruction of Egypt and Edom, enduring political enemies (v. 19; see 1 Kgs 14:25; Obad 8-14);

c) everlasting security for Judah and Jerusalem (v. 20; see 3:5; 4:16);

d) retribution for enemies and the presence of the Lord in Zion (v. 21).

Conclusion

A literary analysis of the Book of Joel suggests the structure of a communal liturgy of lamentation. The format, however, has been expanded and developed by editorial activity. While many commentators recognize the development of the book, there is no consensus about the number of persons involved in this process. Some commentators see no connection between the literary development of the book and its religious meaning. They interpret the book according to a few general perspectives:

a) The book presents a restricted, nationalistic point of view. God's promises of restoration are limited to the Zion community in fulfillment of earlier prophetic traditions. Often Joel is compared unfavorably with the breadth of Isaiah and Micah, who include the participation of the nations in the community of Jerusalem (see Isa 2:2-4; Mic 4:1-3).

b) The importance of the book is virtually dependent on the figure of Jesus. He is the fulfillment of the prophecies by dying for the "nations" and giving the Spirit to all who believed in him.

c) Jews and Christians await a future event that will surpass the expectations of restoration that Joel proclaimed (see Rev 21).

Canonical critics offer a different perspective on the relationship of the literary development of Joel and its religious meaning. *How* the Book of Joel emerged as a canonical text provides clues to its religious significance in future communities.

Sources available for the editorial process included the original prophecy of Joel, presenting the devastation of the locust plague, and images and terms describing the day of the Lord taken from earlier prophetic traditions. In arranging and adding to the sources, the editor(s) shaped the text to provide a message for future communities. References to the new addressees are indicated initially in the introduction to the first part of the book (1:3). The entire second part of the book (2:18–4:21 [2:18–3:21]), with its proclamations about future possibilities, is also fashioned to include them.

The editorial process provided a continuity of religious experience and hope for the original community and for future communities. It shaped the book to declare that God's compassion toward the temple-community of Judah because of their repentance would be possible for any community. Correspondingly, the blessings of restoration would be possible for future communities as well. For both types of community, original and future, neither final judgment nor blessings had definitively occurred.

The perspective of canonical critics appears preferable to the interpretation of other commentators because it assumes that a text can be valuable for its own contribution. Consequently, the methodology does not depend on prophecy-fulfillment in the New Testament or on comparison with other prophetic traditions in the Old Testament to validate the importance of the Book of Joel. Canonical criticism provides a necessary focus on the placement of Joel within the Minor Prophets. It also widens the interpretation of Joel through a different methodology that includes implications for future communities.

OBADIAH

Mary Margaret Pazdan, O.P.

INTRODUCTION

Authorship

What is known about the author of this book is limited to verse 1a, which names and identifies him: "The vision of Obadiah. [Thus says the Lord God:] Of Edom we have heard a message from the Lord." "Vision" is a technical term for prophecy (see Nah 1:1; Mic 1:1), whose contents are described in verses 2-4. "We have heard a message . . . ," however, emphasizes that auditory perception is the source for prophetic inspiration. "[Thus says the Lord God:]" and the repetition of the divine name also indicate traditional prophetic formulas. The name Obadiah means "servant of Yahweh." It occurs twelve times in the Hebrew Scriptures. In the Book of Obadiah the name may be used more for its symbolic sense.

Other biographical detail is inferred from the text. Many scholars suggest that Obadiah was a cult prophet attached to the Jerusalem temple before its destruction (586 B.C.E.). The structure of the prophecies reflects a liturgical service in which the sovereignty of God is affirmed through oracles against the nations. Obadiah's connection with the temple in Jerusalem is strengthened by references to God's kingdom and Mount Zion (vv. 17, 21). Other scholars suggest that an unknown prophet utilized a liturgical structure for the deliverance of oracles.

Dating of the text

The superscription of the book indicates no chronological setting for Obadiah. The position of the book in the canons is not decisive for establishing a date. The Jewish canon lists Obadiah after Amos (preexilic), while the Alexandrian canon locates Obadiah after Joel (postexilic).

While most scholars agree that the oracles against Edom were proclaimed after 586 B.C.E., the dating of the final text is disputed. The present discussion involves a consideration of the relationship between Israel and Edom, oral and written traditions, and the process of editorial activity.

According to Jewish tradition, the relationship between Israel and Edom was one of continuous conflict. It is attributed to the fraternal conflict of two brothers, Jacob and Esau (see Gen 25:19-34; 26:34-35; 27:1-44; 32:4; 33:1-17). The hostility developed for several centuries as the descendants of Jacob (Israelites) and Esau (Edomites) refused one another rights of territorial passage (see Num 20:14-21) and freedom (see 2 Sam 8:13-14; 1 Kgs 11:15-18).

Edom revolted against Judah about 844 B.C.E. The animosity between them continued, however, for nearly 250 additional years, culminating in Edom's alliance with Babylon against Judah (see p. 573). Although the extent of Edomite activity against Judah during this period is unclear, the witness of the anti-Edom oracles (see below) indict Edom for treachery and betrayal. There is even a claim that the Edomites burned the temple (see 1 Esdras 4:45). They probably conspired with the Babylonian empire and settled in Judean territory.

A recent archeological investigation supports this position. It uncovered an inscription contemporary with the last days of Jerusalem. A troop commander in Arad sent for additional soldiers to fortify a position against an imminent Edomite attack: "Behold I have sent to warn you: are not the men with Elisha, lest Edom come thither."

Edom, unlike Judah, was independent but not untroubled for over a hundred years after the fall of Jerusalem. Tribes from Arabia frequently raided the land (see Mal 1:2-4). After 450 B.C.E. the name Edom disappeared from historical records. During the reign of Herod the Great (37–4 B.C.E.), however, the territory designated Edom was named Idumea. *Mekiltha*, a Jewish text of the early Christian period, identified Edom as a code name for oppression.

Commentators suggest that the enmity between Israel and Edom was preserved in oral traditions that were later recorded as anti-Edom oracles. While some fragments are located in the Jacob cycle (see Gen 25:23; 27:39-40), the most extensive witness is located outside the Torah (see Isa 21:11-12; 34:5-7; 63:1-6; Jer 49:7-22; Lam 4:21-22; Ezek 25:12-14; 35:1-5; Amos 1:11-12; Mal 1:3-5; Ps 137:7-9). In these passages Edom is condemned for less dramatic but more continuous harassment than burning the temple.

Part of the complexity involved in dating the Book of Obadiah is the relationship of the anti-Edom oracles (vv. 1-14, 15b) to Jer 49:7-22. Some commentators state that Obadiah represented the prior tradition, while others indicate that Jeremiah was the first witness to the tradition. A third group traces both Obadian and Jeremian oracles to a common earlier tradition. Both prophets incorporated the tradition and additional material after the fall of Jerusalem (586 B.C.E.).

Another question is the chronological relationship of the oracles in Obadiah. While condemnations of Edom predominate (vv. 1-14, 15b), there are oracles describing the day of the Lord (vv. 15a, 16-18) and the restoration of Israel (vv. 19-21). The difference of opinion about the approximate date of the oracles and subsequent editorial activity results in a final composition date from early postexilic (535 B.C.E.) to a century later (435 B.C.E.).

In this commentary Obadiah is identified first *chronologically* because of his proximity to the Edomite conspirators and redaction of earlier anti-Edom oracles. In addition, his position as a transitional figure between exilic and postexilic prophecy indicates a singular contribution among the other Minor Prophets. His contribution includes oracles against Edom after the destruction of Jerusalem as well as later oracles about the day of the Lord. These factors indicate that the date for the final edition of the text is a question of secondary importance.

Composition of the text

Although the Book of Obadiah is the shortest book of the Old Testament, discussion about the final dating of the text and related literary questions continues in the literature. There is no consensus about the priority of Jeremiah, Obadiah, or another common tradition for the anti-Edom oracles. In addition, the text has been analyzed according to two extreme positions: a literary unity or a collection of fragments. Presently, several commentators propose a moderate position. The book contains two sets of oracles and an appendix. Thematically, the unity of the oracles consists in Edom's condemnation and future situation in the day of the Lord. The appendix is related to Israel's restoration in that event.

Outline of the book

PART ONE:	Oracles against Edom (vv. 1-14, 15b)
vv. 1-9	Pride and Destruction of Edom
vv. 10-14	Treachery of Edom toward Judah
v. 15b	Condemnation of Edom
PART TWO:	Oracles about the Day of the Lord (vv. 15a, 16-21)
vv. 15a, 16	Judgment of the Nations
vv. 17-18	Return and Restoration of Israel
vv. 19-21	Appendix: Return and Restoration of Israel

COMMENTARY

PART ONE: ORACLES AGAINST EDOM

Obad 1-14, 15b

Part One is a collection of oracles that expand a common tradition of anti-Edom material. The closest parallel is Jer 49:7-22 (see p. 587). Commentators state that no more bitter diatribe exists against Edom in the whole of the Old Testament than what is recorded here.

Two perspectives are prominent about the interpretation of verses 2-9. The context of verses 1b and 7, in particular, is debated. Some suggest that the destruction of Edom has already occurred. The verses are an additional reflection on the event. Others indicate that the verses designate a future destruction. Attempts to establish the context are directly related to considerations of the dating and the composition of the text.

Proposals that seek to identify a specific historical event, that is, an Arabian conquest of Edom, appear to limit the possibilities for interpretation of the section. Although recent archeological discoveries are providing some limited support for this type of analysis, additional research and data are needed.

1-9 Pride and the destruction of Edom. Verse 1 is a prose introduction to the Book of Obadiah. It states his identity and function. It also links him to earlier prophetic tradition: "we have heard a message from the Lord" (v. 1a; see Jer 49:7).

Verse 1b relates the departure of a messenger to proclaim Edom's destruction among the nations: "Up! Let us go to war against him!" It is difficult to determine whether the statement refers to an *actual event*, that is, the approach of the Arabian enemy against Edom, or whether it is a *prophetic formula* of a war summons to the nations (Jer 49:14; Joel 4:9ff. [3:9ff.]; Mic 4:13).

God announces the destruction of Edom (vv. 2-4; see Jer 49:14-16). The dispositions of the nation's heart are condemned. Pride effects Edom's contemptible position among the nations (v. 2). False security arises from dwelling "in the clefts of the rock" and "in the heights." The "rock" refers to the terrain as well as to the Edomite capital, Sela, a nearly impregnable city.

The arrogant challenge "Who will bring me down to earth?" will prove no obstacle to an enemy (v. 3). Even a position as an eagle with a nest among the stars will not thwart God's action: "I will bring you down" (v. 4; compare Amos 9:2; Isa 14:13-14).

God's power of destruction is compared to the strategy of prowlers invading homes in Edom (vv. 5-9). If "thieves," "robbers," or "vintagers" trespassed, they would leave something behind for the household (v. 5; see Jer 49:9; Lev 19:10; Deut 24:21). The destruction of Edom (Esau), however, will be without mercy. The event is described in a traditional cry of lament (vv. 6-7; see 2 Sam 1:19-27; Jer 38:22; Lam 1:1; 2:1; 4:1). It will be as thorough as the forfeit of Jacob's birthright to Esau (v. 6; see Gen 25:27-34). Those closest to the Edomites, allies and relatives, will participate in the devastation. "There is no understanding in him!" indicates the bewilderment and surprise that the event causes among the Edomites (v. 7).

Verse 7 is as difficult to interpret as verse 1. What are the implications of "allies" and "relatives"? Is it an ironic comment on the real but spurned relationships between Edom and Judah, which were completely severed in the fall of Jerusalem? Do the terms relate to the reversal of Judah's situation in the day of the Lord? (see Part Two). Do the bonds of relationship refer to those who supported Edom after the fall of Jerusalem but who later conquered Edom? The comment "There is no understanding in him" is appropriate for each interpretation.

The divine formula "says the Lord" (v. 4) is repeated to form an inclusion expressing God's judgment against Edom (v. 8a). In a rhetorical question God states the disappearance of the "wise" and "understanding" from Edom (Esau). Their demise is related to verse 7, which also commented on "no understanding" (see Jer 49:7). The inhabitants of Edom and Arabia were traditionally considered wise persons (see 1 Kgs 5:10; 10:1-3; Job 1:1; 2:11; Prov 30:1; 31:1).

Warriors will be destroyed with the wise (v. 9). "Teman," an important city in Edom, refers to the whole territory. Another inclusive term is "Mount Esau" (vv. 8b, 9b).

10-14 Treachery of Edom toward Judah. The indictment against Edom is declared:

"violence to your brother Jacob" (v. 10). Specifically, the condemnation is collaboration by passivity toward Babylon's activity, that is, sacking and dividing up the city of Jerusalem (v. 11). A poignant question implied by the arrangement of verses 10 and 11 is: How can you, the "brother," become "one of them," the "aliens"?

Additional details of Edom's behavior during the destruction of Jerusalem imply active participation. They are presented in a series of present-tense protests for what has already occurred. This literary device highlights the sense of irony for the future situation of Edom (vv. 12-14). Although the injunctions repeat sacking the city (v. 13), the more malicious activities are mocking the calamity of "your brother" (v. 12) and hindering the escape of refugees (v. 14).

15b Condemnation of Edom. This statement, which is derived from the traditional Jewish practice of *lex talionis* (an eye for an eye), is the climax to Part One. It summarizes the judgment of retribution against Edom: "As you have done, so shall it be done to you" (see Exod 21:23-25; Lev 24:17-22).

PART TWO: ORACLES ABOUT THE DAY OF THE LORD

Obad 15a, 16-21

The relationship between Part One and Part Two is parallel to the Book of Joel. The plague of locusts in Part One of that book was a foreshadowing of the day of the Lord in Part Two. Similarly, in Obadiah, the anti-Edom oracles in Part One are a foreshadowing of the day of the Lord in Part Two. In addition, the different consequences of the day of the Lord are identical: punishment for the nations (especially Edom) and restoration for Judah (compare Joel 4:1-21 [3:1-21]; Obad 15a, 16-21).

Was one book the model for the other? Since Joel 4:17 [3:17] quotes Obad 17, he may have used the Obadian model with some editorial activity. It is also possible that both books are dependent on earlier traditions that they modified according to a similar structure. Some commentators consider the structure of a communal lamentation to be another convincing parallel for Joel and Obadiah.

15a, 16 Judgment of the nations. The imminent day of the Lord is announced for "all the nations" (v. 15a). The proclamation connects the previous section (vv. 11-14), where the phrase "on the day" was used ten times to detail the guilt of Edom. The proclamation also introduces the prominent theme of the present section (vv. 15a, 16-21).

Verse 16 indicates how the punishment of the nations is related to God's judgment of Judah and Edom. Again, the *lex talionis* is operative: "As you have drunk . . . so shall all the nations drink continually" (vv. 16a, 15b). The metaphor of drinking refers to the cup of God's judgment and wrath (see Jer 25:15-29). Just as the community experienced the bitterness of God's judgment "upon my holy mountain" (Jerusalem) in 586 B.C.E., so all the nations (including Edom) will drink the cup until they "shall become as though they had not been" (v. 16b; compare Jer 50:25-28; Joel 3:4–4:21 [2:31–3:21]).

17-18 Return and restoration of Israel. The nations' judgment (vv. 15a, 16) is contrasted with Israel's future. Jacob (Judah) and Mount Zion (Jerusalem) are emphasized in restoration images (v. 17) corresponding to Joel's vision (Joel 4:17 [3:17]). A "portion" ("those that escape" in the Revised Standard Version) develops the theme of the "remnant" who would escape God's judgment (see Isa 4:3; 37:32; Zeph 2:7-9). Holiness characterizes the group.

Although confirming the tradition of Judah's restoration, Obadiah inserts a new perspective. The prophet includes the *whole* country by referring to Jacob *and* Joseph, who represent Judah and northern Israel respectively (v. 18a). All will share in the possession of Mount Zion. The fate of Esau (Edom) and the other nations symbolized by Esau is quite different. They will not survive (v. 18; compare Joel 1:4, 19; 2:3, 5). The metaphors of "fire" ("flame") and "stubble" indicate God's judgment against the nations through Israel's agency (see Isa 10:17; 29:5-6; Ezek 25:14). Again, the divine formula confirms the judgment (v. 18b; see vv. 4, 8).

19-21 Appendix: Return and restoration of Israel. The additional verses identify the day of the Lord as a day of great blessings for all the people of Israel. The participation of the nations appears to be limited to loss of land. Verse 21, however, suggests a different role.

The appendix outlines the extensive restoration of the boundaries of Israel. Unlike the small territory to which the Judeans returned in 538 B.C.E., their future homeland implies territorial boundaries greater than the ones achieved by King David (vv. 19-20). Precise geographical locations, however, are difficult to establish, since the Hebrew text is obscure. The major emphasis of verses 19 and 20 is to claim for Israel more land than it had possessed before deportations.

The role of Jacob, who "shall take possession of those that dispossessed them" (v. 17b), parallels "occupy," which occurs five times (vv. 19-20). The verbs suggest, in language reminiscent of covenant promises (see Gen 12:7; Exod 3:8; 2 Sam 7:10), how Israel will be restored.

"They shall occupy the Negeb, the mount of Esau" (v. 19a): The Negeb, an area south of Judah, was occupied by the Edomites during their collaboration with Babylon. It is identified by the name Idumea during the rule of Herod the Great. The area is mentioned twice (vv. 19a; 20b) as an inclusion to highlight Israel's restoration as the reversal of Edomite fortune.

Instead of "They shall occupy . . . the foothills of the Philistines," the Revised Standard Version reads: "those of the Shephelah [shall possess] the land of the Philistines" (v. 19a). The Shephelah is a foothill region west of Judah and east of the Philistine coastland. Repossessing the territory of a traditional enemy, the Philistines, is one characteristic of restoration (see 1 Sam 17; Judg 13–16; 1 Sam 31:8-13; 2 Sam 21:15-22).

Ephraim, with its capital Samaria, is a region north of Jerusalem whose traditions are associated with northern Israel. This land, too, will be reclaimed. Benjamin is a territory north of Jerusalem that extends east to the Jordan River. Its inhabitants will extend borders to Gilead, a region northeast of Ephraim and across the Jordan (v. 19b).

Exiles of Israel were scattered in distant regions. Their identity and the geographical locations mentioned in verse 20 are disputed. The first group mentioned is "the captives of this host," which the Revised Standard Version translates "the exiles in Halah" (v. 20a). They may be deportees of northern Israel who were sent to Halah, a city northwest of Nineveh (see 2 Kgs 17:6). The group will occupy "Canaanite" ("Phoenician" in the Revised Standard Version) land along the Mediterranean coast, including the city of Zarephath near the coast, about ten miles south of Sidon (see 1 Kgs 17:9-24; Luke 4:26).

"The captives of Jerusalem" (v. 20b) parallels "the captives of this host" (v. 20a). Some deportees who did not return to rebuild Jerusalem are living in Sepharad. The identity of this city is disputed. Some suggest Babylon as a parallel to Halah, which is located there; others identify it with Sardis in Asia Minor (see Rev 3:1). Several Jewish commentators identify the term as Spain. Most recently it has been identified as Hesperides on the northern coast of Africa. Whatever the precise designation of Sepharad, the verse indicates that exiles far removed from Jerusalem will return to closer proximity by occupying "the cities of the Negeb."

Verse 21 forms an inclusion with verse 17 by returning attention to Mount Zion. Who will exercise dominion on Mount Zion and the mount of Esau (Edom)? The Hebrew is translated here as "saviors" (v. 21a). The people of Israel will function as *judges* and as God's *viceroys* in the kingdom. Sovereignty belongs to God alone (v. 21b). Other scholars interpret the term as God's restoration of the remnant, that is, the people who are "saved." This distinction offers Israel participation in the universal kingship of God. Other nations, however, may ultimately experience God's saving action.

Conclusion

The meager status of the Book of Obadiah among the Minor Prophets has not been transformed by later generations. The text is not listed in a lectionary for reflection on the mystery of God and human response. It is neither utilized for catechetical or preaching events nor suggested for personal or communal prayer. In addition, the book is not generally recognized in extrabiblical literature or contemporary situations. Why, then, was it preserved in tradition?

Commentaries and articles on Obadiah emphasize questions regarding the dating of the text, archeological data, and literary composition. The religious message appears less important in comparison to these considerations. When the religious dimensions of the text are investigated, the results are similar to the analysis about the Book of Joel (see p. 585):

a) The book presents a widely attested Jewish tradition about the relationship of God and the community. Restoration of the land is a symbol of the restoration of a spiritual relationship. Some reflection about the present state of Israel is occasionally related to the same premise.

b) The function of Israel among the nations is to offer witness and an invitation to future possibilities. God's blessing (restoration) can be a sign that judgment (punishment) may not be the ultimate condition.

c) Confidence in God's sovereignty is indicated through the oracles about Edom's punishment and Israel's restoration.

Obadiah's contribution to postexilic prophecy may appear to be a very limited and localized message. In style, too, its bitter invective against Edom may offend believers (although the verses parallel some of the psalms and oracles against other nations).

Nonetheless, Obadiah can be read *in context* as a passionate plea to the God whose sovereignty assures Israel a future. Recourse to this God demands strong faith. The experience of the Exile and the prospect of return have not restored confidence in God nor in the community's self-image. Where else can the community turn? Only this God will forgive and restore Israel. Even more unexpectedly, this God will bless Jacob's (Israel's) estranged brother, Esau (Edom). An invitation will be extended to participate in the universal kingdom of the sovereign Lord.

HAGGAI

Mary Margaret Pazdan, O.P.

INTRODUCTION

Authorship

For the Books of Joel and Obadiah the author's identification was limited to the superscription of each book (v. 1). Additional biographical information was obtained through inferences in the text. For the Book of Haggai, however, there are more citations. The name Haggai appears eight times (1:1, 3, 13; 2:1, 10, 13, 14, 20).

The superscription (1:1) identifies his function as a prophet and names the addressees to whom he proclaims the oracles. Four verses identify Haggai with the word "prophet" and a traditional prophetic formula, "the word of the Lord came to . . ." (1:1, 3; 2:1, 10). Two verses identify Haggai as a "messenger of the Lord [proclaiming] the message of the Lord" (1:13; 2:20). Two verses mention his name as one who proclaims God's oracles (2:13, 14). The absence of any genealogy may be intended to emphasize Haggai's prophetic authority. Outside the text that bears his name, Haggai is linked with Zechariah as a prophet (see Ezra 5:1, 16; 6:14).

The name Haggai means "festival." Other names in the Old Testament are also derived from the same Hebrew root (see Gen 46:16; Num 26:15; 2 Sam 3:4; 1 Chr 3:2). The name may refer to the day of the prophet's birth, that is, a festival. It may designate Haggai's task of restoring the temple for cultic activities that celebrate festivals. While some identify Haggai as a priest, there is no indication in the text for this designation. It is preferable to associate him with cult prophets in Jerusalem. His position in that group, however, is unclear.

Dating of the text

The Books of Joel and Obadiah are difficult to date for three reasons: (a) their different positions in the Jewish and Alexandrian canons; (b) the absence of chronological data in the superscriptions; (c) minimal contextual clues. The dating process for the Book of Haggai presents an opposite situation: (a) an identical position in the canons; (b) clear chronological data in the superscription; (c) five precisely dated oracles.

The Book of Haggai is listed as the tenth Minor Prophet, between Zephaniah and Zechariah in both canons. The superscription and the chronological data of the text indicate that the ministry of Haggai included five proclamations of the word of the Lord from August through December 520 B.C.E.

The addressees are members of the second group of exiles from Babylon, who returned to Jerusalem about 522 B.C.E. under the leadership of Zerubbabel, the governor, and Joshua, the high priest. These two had been appointed to the positions of leadership during the early reign of Darius I of Persia (1:1; see p. 574).

The duration of Haggai's ministry is unclear. Although he is believed to have been a contemporary of Zechariah, there is no acknowledgment in either book of the other's activity. The recorded oracles indicate Haggai's perspective on how to achieve restoration for the Judean temple-community. The final form of the text indicates additional perspectives by the editor. The final date of the text is considered a question of secondary importance among commentators.

Composition of the text

For more than a century questions about the unity of the Book of Haggai have been discussed. The literary relationship between Haggai and Ezra has also been analyzed. More recently, the process of editorial activity has been examined for additional literary forms as well as for the religious significance of the oracles.

Scholars focus attention on one section of the text (2:10-19) in particular. Rearrangement of chapter 2 has been suggested as a partial solution to the difficulties of the verses. The New English Bible prefers this order: 1:14, 15, 13; 2:15-19, 10-14, 1-9, 20-23. Others, including the New American Bible, suggest that 2:15-19 should go after chapter 1. Revision of 2:18 is indicated by brackets. The editors believe that the date of the month is a gloss or that the date should be changed from the ninth month to the sixth month. None of the proposed rearrangements is confirmed in any text or version.

In general, there is a consensus about the structure, which provides a unity to the text, namely, five oracles introduced by editorial frameworks (see p. 576).

Outline of the book

PART ONE:	Reconstruction of the Temple (1:1-15a)
1:1	Superscription
1:2-11	First Oracle: Exhortation to Rebuild the Temple
1:12-15a	Second Oracle: Response and Assurance
PART TWO:	Future Glory of the Temple (1:15b–2:23)
1:15b–2:9	Third Oracle: Assurance and Promises
2:10-19	Fourth Oracle: Decisions and Future Blessings
2:20-23	Fifth Oracle: Future of Zerubbabel

COMMENTARY

PART ONE: RECONSTRUCTION OF THE TEMPLE

Hag 1:1-15a

Part One offers a historical framework for the activity of Haggai by the insertion of chronological introductions and narrative detail. Another component of the oracles is the use of two traditional prophetic formulas: "Thus says the Lord of hosts" (1:2, 5, 7) and "says the Lord" (1:13). The contrast of prose introductions and poetic oracles is also apparent.

1:1 Superscription. This verse is not an introduction to the entire Book of Haggai but is limited to the first oracle (1:2-11). In addition to mention of the date of August 520 B.C.E., the verse identifies the current Persian ruler, Darius I. Since the position of monarch no longer existed for the Jewish community after the Exile, the superscription accommodated the new situation by substituting the name of the foreign ruler.

Zerubbabel and Joshua, the appointed representatives of Darius' government, are the addressees of the first oracle. Their names are repeated in the second and third oracles. Unlike Haggai, both are identified by function *and genealogy:* "the governor of Judah, Zerubbabel, son of Shealtiel, and the high priest Joshua, son of Jehozadak."

Zerubbabel was the nephew of King Jehoiachin, who had been exiled to Babylon in 597 B.C.E. (see 1 Chr 3:17-19). His civic appointment was probably considered a minor position in the extensive Persian empire. In this early stage of restoration, however, his presence was a reminder of the royal Davidic household that had ruled in Jerusalem. Symbolically, he may have been a catalyst for dreams of rebuilding a new kingdom according to the model of the preexilic monarchy (see Hag 2:20-23).

Joshua is named Jeshua in the Books of Ezra and Nehemiah. He was a grandson of the chief priest in Jerusalem. Joshua and his father had been exiled to Babylon (see 1 Chr 5:40-41). The designation "high priest" occurs here for the first time. As the religious leader of the returned exiles, his position may have been more autonomous. After him priestly authority became more significant (see pp. 574–575).

1:2-11 First oracle: Exhortation to rebuild the temple. The oracle consists of three sections related to the problem of temple restoration (vv. 2-4, 5-6, 7-11). Each is introduced by a traditional prophetic formula.

The first section (vv. 2-4) considers the question of the community's attitude toward rebuilding the temple. The initial statement is presented as a quotation from the community: "Not now has the time come to rebuild the house of the Lord" (v. 2). Next, a rhetorical question offers an opportunity to reflect on experience: "Is it time for you to dwell in your own paneled houses, while this house lies in ruins?" (v. 4).

It is clear that the entire community, not just the civic and religious leadership, is being challenged. The repetition of the word "time" (vv. 2, 4) draws attention to the irony of the situation. Who really decides what is the propitious "time" for rebuilding?

In preexilic tradition an interesting parallel suggests a response to the question. God provides the perspective. Recall the encounter between God and David *before* the first temple was constructed. In that situation David confided his worries to Nathan about a dwelling for God, since he, David, lived in a house of cedar (2 Sam 7:2-3). God replied by promising to build David a house! The metaphor of "house" symbolized an everlasting dynasty and kingdom (2 Sam 7:7-17).

Why was Haggai's community waiting to rebuild the temple (v. 2)? The foundations for the temple had been laid in the spring of 536 B.C.E. by the first group that had returned from Babylon (see Ezra 3:7-13). No additional progress, however, had been achieved. What factors impeded the project? Had the community forgotten the edict of Cyrus for the task of restoration? Were the living conditions enervating? Did they experience opposition inside and outside the community? (See p. 574.) Perhaps they were waiting for the literal fulfillment of Jeremiah's prophecy: "Only after seventy years have elapsed for Babylon will I visit you and fulfill for you my promise to bring you back to this place" (Jer 29:10; 25:11; compare Zech 1:12, 16-17). If so, a few years still remain for the fulfillment. There is no specific reason indicated in the text to account for the community's resistance to rebuilding the temple.

The second section, too, invites the community to reflect on its experience (vv. 5-6). "Consider your ways" (vv. 5b, 7b) introduces a series of comparisons between efforts at reconstituting daily living and the results. Although they have labored for food, drink, clothing, and wages, the results are meager and unsatisfying (v. 6).

The third section consists of a command and a judgment from God (vv. 7-11). It indicates the relationship between God's activity and the present experience of the community. The community must obtain timber to build the house of God (v. 8a). The urgency of the task consists in giving glory to God (v. 8b).

The expectations about restoration cannot be met (v. 9a). Why? God has entered into the situation. Efforts are useless, especially in providing homes for themselves while God's house "lies in ruins" (v. 9b). Stark living conditions are the direct result of God's initiative for the drought. The land and its produce, persons and their livestock are affected (vv. 10-11).

The literary form of verses 9-11 is a question-answer pattern. The didactic style of the verses repeats the plight of the community (vv. 4-6). In addition, it emphasizes the need for immediate response on the part of the community. Clearly, the temple must be rebuilt. However, the physical restoration suggests a metaphorical function.

According to Haggai, to rebuild the temple means to restore the relationship of the community with God (compare the commentary on Joel 1:5-20, p. 579). Restoration of God's house is the primary responsibility of the community. Until the task is completed, the community lives under God's judgment enacted through the Exile and continuing in the harsh conditions of their lives. When the temple is completed, blessing will replace judgment. The Lord will dwell in the temple-community again.

1:12-15a Second oracle: Response and assurance. The ordering of the verses is debated (see p. 593). The dating for the oracle does not follow the pattern of the other oracles, that is, a prose introduction (see 1:1; 1:15b–2:1; 2:10, 18, 20). For some commentators, the dating information at the conclusion of the oracle (v. 15) indicates the need for rearrangement. They suggest that the phrase "on the twenty-fourth day of the sixth month" ought to be shifted to 2:15 to provide a chronology for the third oracle (2:15-19). Rearrangement, however, is not necessary.

The prose reflection of verse 12 indicates the importance of Haggai's position in the temple-community. The editor of the text draws attention to his prophetic credentials (vv. 12b-13; see p. 592). In addition, Haggai's proclamation is obeyed by the entire community. "All the remnant of the people" may be inserted to identify the returned exiles as the ones who will receive the blessings of restoration (v. 12a; 2:2; see Isa 10:20-22; Mic 4:7; Zech 8:6, 11-12). This group "listened to the voice of the Lord" (see Jer 23:3; Deut 6:2-3).

The brief oracle is located in the center of the editorial comment (v. 13). "I am with you" is a traditional proclamation of assurance (see Gen 28:15; Exod 3:12; Jer 1:8; 30:10-11; Isa 41:10; 43:5). Here the word is accompanied by action as the Lord "stirs up" the spirit of Zerubbabel, Joshua, and the community for the task of rebuilding the temple (v. 14). The Hebrew verb from which the word for "spirit" is derived is used to describe God's power to activate Cyrus, who authorized the exiles to return (2 Chr 36:22-23) and to activate the exiles themselves (Ezra 1:5).

The phrase "twenty-fourth day of the sixth month" (v. 15a) does not have to be shifted to another place in the text. The date recalls to the community the process involved in their own call to rebuild the temple. Having listened to the proclamations of Haggai (vv. 2-11), they determined to be obedient. God's subsequent word and action of assurance (vv. 13-14) encouraged their response to be faithful. They began the project of restoring the temple.

PART TWO: FUTURE GLORY OF THE TEMPLE

Hag 1:15b–2:23

Part Two refers to future blessings for the Judean temple-community, blessings that were proclaimed before the Exile. It offers hope in present circumstances, blessings for the future, and a role of prominence to Zerubbabel, the civic leader. Four identical structural components link the two parts of the book: chronological introductions; addressees; question-and-answer pattern; assurances. Promises of future blessings are a development of the Lord's assurances (vv. 6-9, 21-23).

1:15b–2:9 Third oracle: Assurance and promises. The chronological introduction (1:15b–2:1) follows the pattern of the first oracle (1:1). The "twenty-first day of the seventh month" indicates nearly one month of work on rebuilding the temple. The date is also important in the Jewish calendar: it is the final day of a week's celebration of the feast of Booths, during which the community would remember its ancestors' living in tents as they journeyed through the wilderness (see Lev 23:33-36, 39-43; Deut 16:13-15). As one of the three pilgrimage feasts (along with Passover and Pentecost), the feast of Booths would draw crowds to Jerusalem.

The addressees of the third oracle are identical with those of the previous oracle: Zerubbabel, Joshua, and the "remnant of the people" (v. 2). Haggai may have chosen the occasion of the festival because of the presence of the civic and religious leaders and other persons gathered in Jerusalem. The celebration provided an association with the period of the first temple. During Solomon's reign the temple had been dedicated on this festival (see 1 Kgs 8; compare Ezek 45:25; Zech 14:16).

The question-and-answer pattern (1:9-11) continues in the first section of the oracle (2:3-5). A series of three questions (v. 3) invites those assembled to reflect on their memories of the temple before Babylon conquered Jerusalem with the probable assistance of Edom (see the commentary on Obadiah, p. 586). The comparison of the Solomonic temple and the sporadic progress of reconstruction since 538 B.C.E. left no doubt about which was a glorious achievement.

A proclamation of assurances links the third oracle to the second oracle. While recorded briefly in the second oracle (1:13), the declaration occurs in an expanded form (2:4-5). Officials and community members are exhorted to "take courage" (three times), and not to fear (v. 4). The Lord is present; God's spirit dwells in all the members of the community (v. 5b; see 1:14).

The traditional language of assurance is developed by an editor in verse 5a. The reference to God's relationship with Israel provides a continuity of experience for the returned exiles. The specific event, "the pact," is the covenant experience at Mount Sinai. "I am with you, says the Lord of hosts" is assurance to both groups (v. 4b; see Exod 29:45-46).

The second section of the oracle announces future blessings for the community (vv. 6-9). The uncertainty of when they will be fulfilled is indicated by "one moment yet, a little while" (v. 6a). The Revised Standard Version, however, interprets the phrase to mean that God will act again in a similar way: "once again, in a little while."

While cosmic shaking is attributed to God in earlier traditions (see Amos 8:8-9; Isa 2:13-21; 13:13; Ezek 38:20; compare Joel 2:10; 4:16 [3:16]), the proclamation here promises a new reality (vv. 6b-7a). The "nations" and their "treasures" will be shaken, too. There is no indication in this verse of "universalism," that is, universal salvation, as some commentators have suggested. They compare this section to Isa 60:5-11, which presents a different concept.

The future action of God will be directed to filling the new temple with "glory" (v. 7b). "Silver" and "gold" from Babylon and the nations will be used for sacred vessels to worship God in glory (v. 8; compare Zech 6:9-15). The Lord's direct intervention, then, will accomplish what no dedicated human effort could accomplish independently. Greater glory will be in the Lord's second temple than in the period of the first temple (v. 9a). The present situation of the community will be reversed.

The section concludes with a comprehensive promise of blessings, "peace" (*shalom*) in verse 9b (compare Zech 8:12, 19). What constitutes "peace"? Where is it to be located? For whom? The term's multiple interpretation transcends any particular designation. The verse may be intentionally unclear in the Hebrew text. In the Greek text, however, a scribe appended a reflection: "and peace of soul as a possession for all who build, to erect this temple."

2:10-19 Fourth oracle: Decisions and future blessings. This oracle is the most difficult passage to interpret. Commentators debate virtually every perspective: dating indications; the connection between verses 11-14 and 15-19; the placement of the oracle; the addressees (v. 14); the religious significance of the passage. The division of the oracle into two sections (vv. 10-14 and 15-19) is generally agreed upon among scholars.

Verse 10 identifies the date for the oracle (compare v. 18). There are several suggestions about altering the date and the placement of the oracle (see p. 593). Rearrangement, however, is not necessary, since precise dating is not the only factor to be considered for interpretation. The verse indicates that a few months after work had commenced on the temple, Haggai proclaimed another oracle.

In the first section of the oracle, the initial statement in verse 11 exhorts Haggai to consult the "priests" for a "decision" (*torah*). Priests were *the* arbitrators for all circumstances of daily life (see Deut 17:8-13; compare Zech 7:2-3; Mal 2:7). Each decision under their jurisdiction was connected with the primary concern of the community: What constitutes holiness, that is, what is involved in purity and defilement? The verses describe a set of circumstances about ritual purity. The situation is formulated in two question-and-answer patterns (vv. 12-13; see 1:9-11; 2:3-5).

The first question is about "sanctified flesh," or roasted meat that had been blessed for ritual sacrifice (v. 12). If a person were carrying the ritual element, would the element effect holiness for other objects that came into contact with it? The priests respond negatively. Holiness is not transferred by contact with a sacred object (compare Exod 29:37; 30:29; Lev 6:26-27).

Another perspective of the first question follows (v. 13). If a person is defiled because of contact with an unclean object, would the defilement be transferred to other objects with which the person comes into contact (see Lev 6:20-21, 25-28; 11:24-28; 22:4-7)? The priests respond positively. Defilement, unlike holiness, is easily transferable. Contemporary sociological analysis of Jewish purity and defilement codes confirms the extraordinary stratification implicit in groups, religious responsibilities, and possibilities of changing one's status of purity and defilement.

The climax of the section occurs in verse 14. It states the judgment of the Lord following the norms of the priests' decisions. To whom is the judgment directed? To "this people . . . this nation." What is the verdict? "All the works of their hands, and what they offer there is unclean." The identity of the addressees and the judgment of the Lord provide the religious significance of the section.

Earlier scholarship suggested that the addressees were the Samaritans or a group later reinterpreted as the Samaritans. According to Ezra, their offer to collaborate with the returned exiles in the restoration of the temple had been spurned. During the leadership of Zerubbabel and Joshua, the Samaritans retaliated, and progress on the temple was hampered (see Ezra 4:1-5). Although the chronology in Ezra is uncertain, the events are part of a reliable tradition. As enemies of Judah, their history indicted them as "unclean." The offerings of the Samaritans would also be defiled.

Contemporary scholarship, however, does not accept the identification of the Samaritans. It prefers to identify the addressees as the temple-community of Judah because (a) the only group that Haggai addresses throughout the book is the returned exiles; (b) the term "this people" refers to the community (see 1:2a); (c) the terms "this people, this nation" are used in prophetic literature to designate Judah in judgments of reproach (see Jer 6:19, 21; 14:10, 11).

What is the indictment against the temple-community? Commentators do not agree. Six interpretations represent the discussion:

a) The phrase "the works of their hands" refers to the yield from agriculture and animals. No ritual offerings are acceptable, because the altar has not been sanctified. Although it is unclear whether the altar was destroyed in 586 B.C.E. (compare 2 Kgs 25; Ezek 43:13-26), restoration of the temple would include a rededication of the altar. Thus Haggai is exhorting the community to attend to the appropriate cleansing of the altar while the work of restoration continues.

b) A similar interpretation proposes that the temple itself may be identified with "sanctified flesh" (v. 12a). Until the temple is restored, the community remains unclean.

c) A third interpretation suggests that the ritual offerings are a symbol of the community's life. Since the group has failed to live according to God's covenant, the offerings are unclean (compare Isa 57:3-10; 65:3-7). The offerings will be acceptable if the community reforms (see Isa 1:15; compare Isa 33:14ff.; Ezek 18:5ff.).

d) Israel had been chosen to be holy (see Exod 19:6), yet subsequent history indicated that it had become defiled. Only acceptance of God's blessings and repentance will redefine the community's status before God (see 2:19).

e) God's future presence in the temple (2:2-9) will not automatically assure that the community is ritually pure for worship. The temple and its ritual are not a guarantee of holiness. Repentance and integrity of life are necessary to give the ritual its context and meaning. This interpretation is based on an addition of the Greek text: "Because of their early profits, they shall be pained because of their toil, and you have hated those who reprove at the gates" (compare Amos 5:10). The addition is the earliest interpretation of the Hebrew text.

f) There is no indictment. Rather, "the works of their hands" refers to the reconstruction of the temple. It is the effort of the community to prepare for the Lord's coming. When the temple is restored, God's presence will fill the temple with glory and renew the community (see Ezek 36:22-32; 43:1-9).

These various interpretations indicate a tension between God's initiative and human effort. They also present the importance of temple restoration and sacrificial worship as symbols of the condition of the community. Both perspectives link the temple-community with the collective experience of Israel. Both realities will continue in future communities.

Verse 15a provides a connection between the first and second sections of the oracle: "But now, consider from this day forward." The directive appeals to the community to reflect on its situation before the task of rebuilding had begun (vv. 15b-16a). The section repeats the comparison in the first oracle between human efforts and results as well as God's intervention (vv. 16b-17; see 1:5-7, 9-11). One new judgment occurs about the community's response to its stark situation: "you did not return to me" (v. 17b).

Although the section repeats the experience of the community, a new emphasis is apparent. Notice that "consider" occurs three times (vv. 15a, 18 [2 times]). The immediate object of the verb is "this day." It is not a reference to an indefinite day but to a precise day, that is, "the twenty-fourth day of the ninth month" (v. 18a). The significance of the date is specified: "a stone laid upon a stone in the temple of the Lord" (v. 15b) and "the temple of the Lord was founded" (v. 18b).

Some commentators propose that the verses identify the day on which the foundation stone of the temple was laid (compare Ezra 3:10-13; Zech 4:9). A sacred place for worship was restored. The formal ceremony of rededication is not described. Rather, the function of verses 15-19 is to compare the situation of the community before and after the event. Beforehand, the community experienced the judgment of God; afterward, however, God transformed judgment into blessing: "From this day, I will bless!" (v. 19b).

Other commentators suggest that the emphasis on "this day" is not directly related to the laying of the foundation stone. Rather, the oracle proclaimed on "this day" reveals the community's need for repentance. Blessing will follow judgment (see v. 17b) if the community returns to God.

2:20-23 Fifth oracle: Future of Zerubbabel. Verse 20 introduces the oracle with the same date as the previous one, which presented the Lord's judgment and blessing on the temple-community. The addressee is "Zerubbabel, the governor of Judah" (v. 21a). The proclamation contrasts the treatment of the nations—judgment (v. 22)—with that of Zerubbabel and the community—blessing (v. 23).

From 522 to 520 B.C.E. Darius I struggled to achieve stability among the rebelling satrapies of the Persian empire (see p. 574). The situation may have been interpreted as a fortuitous one for Judah to achieve political independence as another dimension of restoration. Zerubbabel as a Davidic descendant would restore the hopes of the returned exiles as well as promote the fulfillment of messianic expectations.

The introduction to God's action repeats the cosmic shaking of the third oracle (v. 21b; compare 2:6b). Verse 22 identifies God's action upon Judah's enemies: "overthrow," "destroy," "go down." The terms are found in the Torah and the Prophets to describe the Sodom and Gomorrah tradition (Gen 19:25, 29; Deut 29:23; Amos 4:11); in oracles against the nations (Isa 13:19; 23:11; Jer 51:20-21); and in the Exodus from Egypt (see Exod 14:23; 15:1, 5). There is no indication in the verse of when God will act on behalf of Judah.

Verse 23 describes God's action toward Zerubbabel "on that day." The verbs and titles identify Zerubbabel with other figures who were particularly chosen by God. The first action and title are presented in verse 23a: "I will take you" indicates a special election (see Exod 6:7; Josh 24:3; 2 Sam 7:8). "My servant" assigns Zerubbabel another responsibility to his position as governor. The role especially identified David (2 Sam 7:5; 1 Kgs 11:32, 36; 1 Chr 17:4; Ps 132:10; Ezek 34:23; 37:24-25), Judah, and Mount Zion (Ps 78:68-70).

"I will set you as a signet ring" is the second promise of God to Zerubbabel (v. 23b; see Sir 49:11). The proclamation is a reversal of the one to Jeconiah (Coniah), Zerubbabel's grandfather, just before the Exile: "As I live, says the Lord, if you, Coniah, son of Jehoiakim, king of Judah, are a signet ring on my right hand, I will snatch you from it" (Jer 22:24).

The signet ring contained the king's seal, which was used to stamp important documents with royal approval. The ring is a metaphor to indicate the relationship of the king to God. The king functioned as God's representative. The final phrase of verse 23 appears to confirm the possibility of Zerubbabel's attaining royal status: "for I have chosen you, says the Lord of hosts."

Conclusion

The Book of Haggai has been analyzed according to the perspective of unfulfilled prophecy. Images of restoration were proclaimed during the Exile to revitalize hope (see Ezek 40–48; Isa 40–55). The experiences of the first groups of returnees from Babylon did not correspond to the prophetic oracles. Haggai's contribution about a restored temple and a reconstituted ruler of Davidic ancestry (2:1-9, 20-23) were realized neither in his own lifetime nor in the lifetimes of future communities.

Perhaps the apparent "failure" of Haggai's proclamations accounts for the minimal value given to his book by several commentators. Some commentators, however, assess the value of the book differently. Canonical critics, in particular, present the contribution of Haggai for succeeding generations. It is important to consider his message for contemporaries and for future believers.

Attending to probable expectations of

both groups, one can analyze Haggai's understanding of God's revelation:

a) Haggai's directives to the community addressed both dimensions of restoration, that is, a restored temple and a reconstituted Davidic ruler. He urged the people forward in the immediate task of rebuilding the temple. The process, in turn, facilitated their identity with God as a temple-community. He also warned them that their identity consisted in integrity of life as well as prescribed ritual sacrifice to confirm their covenant relationship with God.

b) Haggai reminded the community that their efforts at restoration would contribute to the fulfillment of visions proclaimed during the Exile. The community needed the motivation to connect their labor, which was so slow and hampered, to their past history and future possibilities.

c) Haggai did not propose that there was a simple relationship between the initiative of God and the response of the community; rather, he respected the mystery of the faithful God and the struggling community. Haggai was convinced that God would never abandon the community. He believed in the God who consistently enters into the human condition, filling it clearly, at times, with glory and presence.

ZECHARIAH

Mary Margaret Pazdan, O.P.

INTRODUCTION: FIRST ZECHARIAH

Zech 1:1-8:23

The introduction indicates that two centuries of political and religious history divide First Zechariah (chs. 1-8) and Second Zechariah (chs. 9-14). As a preparation for the study of Zechariah, then, it is helpful to review the information about First and Second Zechariah, especially the sections on historical background, attitudes and perspectives about reconstruction, and literary forms (see pp. 574-577). In addition, a comparison of the material on authorship, dating and composition of the text, and an outline of the texts will provide a clearer context for study of each section of Zechariah.

Authorship

Unlike Haggai, whose name was supplemented only by his function (prophet), Zechariah is identified by function and genealogy. The superscription (1:1) and the introduction to the first vision (1:7) describe him as "the prophet Zechariah, son of Berechiah, son of Iddo." His identity as a prophet may be inferred from his name, which means "Yahweh has remembered." It occurs about thirty times in the Old Testament.

Outside the text that bears his name, Zechariah is identified with Haggai as a "prophet" and as the "son of Iddo" (see Ezra 5:1; 6:14). The phrase "son of Berechiah" (Zech 1:1, 7) is occasionally considered a gloss (see the note in the Jerusalem Bible; compare Matt 23:25). The phrase, however, may indicate Zechariah's father.

Iddo, the grandfather of Zechariah, was one of the priestly exiles returning from Babylon with Zerubbabel and Jeshua (Joshua; see Neh 12:4, 16). Consequently, some commentators emphasize Zechariah's priestly origin. Others identify him as a priest because of his concerns for the restoration of the temple and cult as well as the priesthood.

Dating of the text

First Zechariah, like Haggai, provides specific dates for oracles and visions. The book, which is found in the eleventh position in both canons, between Haggai and Malachi, is a postexilic text. Exact chronology is established for the beginning of Zechariah's ministry in the superscription: October-November 520 B.C.E., during the second year of Darius' reign (1:1). Zechariah's ministry began two months after Haggai proclaimed his first oracle (see Hag 1:1).

The second date suggests that Zechariah's ministry concluded two years later: November-December 518 B.C.E., during the fourth year of Darius' reign (7:1). Comparing the dates attributed to Haggai's ministry shows that Zechariah's ministry was eighteen months longer (see p. 592).

The civic and religious leaders of the temple-community mentioned in Haggai appear also in First Zechariah: Zerubbabel (4:6-10; 6:11-14) and Joshua (3:1-10; 6:11-14). The addressees of Haggai and First Zechariah are identical, that is, the second group of returned exiles from Babylon.

Nothing in chapter 8 or in any editorial revisions indicates a later chronology for Zechariah's ministry. The final form of First Zechariah is not considered apart from the dating process of the entire text (fourteen chapters) and its canonical placement (see p. 616).

Composition of the text

Visions constitute the major literary genre of First Zechariah (1:7–6:15). They are interspersed with oracles, which function as responses. A separate collection of oracles (7:1–8:23) is also apparent. Additional material has expanded the visions and the oracles to constitute the final form of the text. The motive ordinarily given for the redactional activity is a changing political context.

Scholars discuss two questions about redaction: Who is responsible for the additions? What sources were used? The questions are part of the complex considerations of the relationship of Zechariah (chs. 1–14) to apocalyptic literature (see p. 577). The relationship of First Zechariah to Second Zechariah regarding the editorial process of the book and the development of religious ideas is discussed below (see pp. 616, 623).

Rearrangement of the text is suggested for chapters 3 and 4. The Jerusalem Bible changes verses *within* the chapters: 3:1, 2, 3, 4a, 5, 4b, 6, 7, 9a, 8, 9b, 10; 4:1, 2, 3, 4, 5, 6a, 10b, 11, 12, 13, 14, 6b, 7, 8, 9, 10a. The New English Bible rearranges chapter 4 as frames around chapter 3 (4:1-3, 11-14; 3:1-10; 4:4-5, 6-10). Note that the New American Bible rearranges only chapter 4 (4:4-10, 1-3, 11-14). Rearrangement is one solution to the difficult task of interpreting First Zechariah.

The three-part structure of the text is recognized by most commentators: (a) introduction (1:1-6); (b) visions (1:7–6:15); (c) oracles about fasting and future days (7:1–8:23). Nonetheless, there is little consensus about the interpretation of the visions and oracles. It is no wonder that several contemporary commentators concur with Jerome in their judgment of Zechariah as the most obscure book of the Bible.

Outline of the book

There are two places in the text of First Zechariah where the numbering of chapters and verses is different. This commentary, based on the New American Bible, represents the Hebrew text, while other Bibles and commentaries may use the Greek text. The chart compares the versions:

Hebrew Text	*Greek Text*
2:1-4	1:18-21
2:5-17	2:1-13

In this commentary the numbering of the Greek text is in brackets.

PART ONE:	Introduction to First Zechariah (1:1-6)
1:1	Superscription
1:2-6	Return to the Lord
PART TWO:	"Night" Visions and Responses (1:7–6:15)
1:7-12	First Vision: Equestrians
1:13-17	Responses
2:1-4[1:18-21]	Second Vision: Four Horns and Four Blacksmiths
2:5-9 [2:1-5]	Third Vision: Measuring Line
2:10-17 [2:6-13]	Responses
3:1-5	Fourth Vision: Joshua the High Priest
3:6-10	Responses
4:1-6a, 10b-14	Fifth Vision: Lampstand
4:6b-10a	Responses
5:1-4	Sixth Vision: Flying Scroll
5:5-11	Seventh Vision: Flying Bushel
6:1-8	Eighth Vision: Four Chariots
6:9-15	Responses and a Crown
PART THREE:	Oracles about Fasting and the Future (7:1–8:23)
7:1-3	Question about Fasting
7:4-7	Responses
7:8-14	Another Collection of Responses
8:1-8	Blessings for Jerusalem
8:9-17	Encouragement and Challenge for Jerusalem
8:18-23	Responses about Fasting and the Future

COMMENTARY: FIRST ZECHARIAH

PART ONE: INTRODUCTION TO FIRST ZECHARIAH

Zech 1:1-6

The introduction establishes a continuity between "your fathers" and the returned exiles. What the Judean prophets had proclaimed about God's imminent judgment had occurred in the destruction of Jerusalem. That experience is a mirror for the next generation who returned to rebuild Jerusalem.

1:1 Superscription. The verse is similar to the superscription of Haggai (see Hag 1:1). It identifies the Persian ruler (Darius I), the year and month, and confirms Zechariah's ministry as prophet.

While the superscription of Haggai emphasizes his prophetic credentials, Zechariah's focuses on a genealogy of a priestly family that survived the Exile. Whereas Haggai's oracle is addressed to the leaders of the temple-community and the returnees from Babylon (see Hag 1:1-2), Zechariah's oracle has no specific addressees (see Zech 1:2ff.); from the context it is inferred that it is addressed to members of the temple-community.

1:2-6 Return to the Lord. Verse 2 is an editorial insertion that interrupts the sequence of the prophetic oracle. The verse links the present generation of returned exiles to their relatives: "The Lord was indeed angry with your fathers. . . ." The connection between the two generations is continued by the repetition of "your fathers" (vv. 4, 5, 6; see Ezek 20:27, 30; Jer 7:25-26).

The divine formulas "Thus says the Lord of hosts" (vv. 3, 4) and "says the Lord" (vv. 3, 4) complete the prophetic formula introduced in verse 1. The title "Lord of hosts," which appears three hundred times in the Old Testament, occurs fifty-three times in Zechariah, fourteen times in Haggai, and twenty-four times in Malachi.

The exhortation of the Lord of hosts is "Return to me" (v. 3a). Specific reasons for returning are not indicated (compare 2 Chr 30:6-9; Isa 44:22; Joel 2:12; Mal 3:7). The community, however, is assured that the Lord will return to them (v. 3b).

The exhortation is strengthened by reference to their ancestors' experience (v. 4a). Previous generations had refused to obey the Lord's warning proclaimed through the prophets (v. 4b). By not listening, the "fathers" refused to turn to the Lord (v. 4c).

The term "former prophets" refers to the preexilic prophets (see Jer 35:15). Later, in the Jewish canon, the term indicates a collection of books describing early prophetic activity in Israel (Josh; Judg; 1-2 Sam; 1-2 Kgs).

Verse 5 consists of two rhetorical questions about the existence of "your fathers" and the "prophets." Their mortality is compared with the eternal power of the Lord's "words and decrees" proclaimed by "my servants the prophets" (v. 6a). It is God's words that "overtake your fathers." The verb "overtake" indicates God's action to impart blessing (see Deut 28:2) or curse (Deut 28:15) on a community. Here the context favors "curse," that is, the destruction of Jerusalem.

The second half of verse 6, an editorial addition, refers to the current situation of Zechariah and the community. They have learned from the past that God is faithful to promises. They have accepted the invitation to return, to restore their relationship to God, to reconstruct the temple.

What does the language of the oracle suggest about Zechariah's function in the community? Zechariah may have used traditional prophetic formulas to strengthen his position in prophetic tradition. The authority of the "former prophets" appears to have nearly canonical status: what they proclaimed was fulfilled in the experience of the Exile. In this perspective Zechariah is continuing an old tradition and contributes nothing new to prophecy.

Zechariah's intent may be to appeal to a collective history and to invite the community to be unlike their ancestors, that is, to return to the Lord and rebuild the covenant relationship. The visions indicate dimensions of that choice. Zechariah builds on the past to create new possibilities for the future. The perspectives are not contradictory. The first represents older scholarship (see p. 572), while the second indicates more recent scholarship.

PART TWO: "NIGHT" VISIONS AND RESPONSES

Zech 1:7–6:15

The "night" visions of First Zechariah are regarded as some of the most difficult passages of the Old Testament. Basic questions that contemporary scholars discuss are: What is the specific function of the visions in regard to the ministry and message of Zechariah? What is the relationship of the visions and the accompanying oracles? What is the literary genre of the visions? Does the literary genre determine the religious message?

Visions are common in prophetic literature (see Isa 6; Ezek 1:1; Jer 1:11-19). The visions of First Zechariah, however, are generally identified with a distinctive literary genre called "apocalyptic." One characteristic of the genre is the presence of a secret revelation of God transmitted through a vision. The images of the vision are not taken literally; rather, each image is a symbol that is interpreted for its own value.

Ordinarily an angel assists in the interpretation of the vision. The Hebrew term for "angel" means "messenger." It is used in connection with many persons in the Old Testament. Even the phrase "messenger of the Lord" does not necessarily designate an angelic being. Prophets are identified with this phrase (see Hag 1:13; 2:20).

Other characteristics of apocalyptic literature are well-defined ideas about God, human beings, good, evil, and the world. Since the visions of First Zechariah are "apocalyptic" in form but not in content, scholars do not situate First Zechariah in that category. Some commentators designate the visions as "proto-apocalyptic."

The visions of First Zechariah may be symbolic representations of what is necessary for the restoration for the temple-community. Each vision generally follows a pattern: introductory statement; description; question about interpretation; the angel's explanation.

1:7-12 First vision: Equestrians. The superscription offers additional chronological data (v. 7). The month Shebat is from the Babylonian calendar adopted by the Jewish community after the Exile. The name that appears here does not occur anywhere else in the Old Testament. That detail and "the second year of Darius" place Zechariah's ministry during the Persian period. The visions occurred about three months after the first oracle addressed to Zechariah.

Verse 8a is an awkward transition between the "word" addressed to Zechariah and written in the traditional third-person prophetic formula (v. 7) and the "vision" proclaimed in the first person. Verse 8a states that Zechariah's vision occurred "during the night." No other time-sequence is indicated in the subsequent seven visions. Although it is possible for all of them to occur in one night, most commentators suggest that they are a succession of "experiences."

The first vision (vv. 7b-13) can be compared to focusing a telescope. One adjustment presents a large picture; additional adjustments reveal more details. Verse 8b depicts a tranquil scene. Evergreen shrubs ("myrtle trees") grow alongside streams. An equestrian stands beside his red horse, and behind him are "red, sorrel, and white horses." An exact location is not specified. The place suggests a garden like Eden, outside Jerusalem or near the entrance to heaven.

Zechariah asks the interpreting angel for an explanation (v. 9a). The angel, however, does not offer one but provides another glance at the scene (v. 9b). The central character *within the scene* identifies the horses: "These are they whom the Lord has sent to patrol the earth" (v. 10). The metaphor could point to the angels of the heavenly council (see Job 1:7; 2:2) as well as to Persian messengers, who provided a thorough communication system in the empire.

A third viewing of the scene follows. The central character ("the driver" in verse 8) becomes the "angel of the Lord" (v. 11a; see the note on "angel" above). Equestrians repeat their function: "We have patrolled the earth" and state their judgment: "see, the whole earth is tranquil and at rest" (v. 11b). Cosmic peace may be a reference to the leadership of Darius, who successfully defeated the rebellious satrapies of the empire.

A fourth glance reveals the climax of the vision. The angel of the Lord petitions the Lord of hosts to relieve the oppression of Jerusalem and Judah (v. 12). The lamentation over the situation of the returned exiles, who "felt your anger these seventy years," is a sharp contrast to the judgment of the equestrians (v. 11). God's intervention is needed if there is to be reconstruction (compare Joel 2:14).

1:13-17 Responses. Responses to the vision function with verse 9 as an inclusion to bracket the visionary scene. Similar to the structure in Joel, a lament (v. 12) is followed by divine assurance (v. 13; see p. 579). Verse 13, however, is a *narrative* comment rather than an oracle of consolation. It serves as a transition to the oracles.

Three oracles of consolation have been appended to the vision. They respond to the lament (v. 12). Each is introduced by traditional prophetic formulas (vv. 14b, 16a, 17a). The interpreting angel exhorts Zechariah to proclaim the first and third oracles (vv. 14-15, 17).

In the first oracle (vv. 14-15), God responds. "I am deeply moved" (v. 14b) is better translated "I am exceedingly jealous" (RSV). As in Joel 2:18, the passionate zeal of God *for* Jerusalem and Zion is clear (compare Zech 8:2-3; 9:9). That zeal takes the form of anger *against* the "complacent nations" (v. 15).

The second oracle proclaims what God's zeal means for the community: "I will turn to Jerusalem in mercy" (v. 16a; compare v. 3b). The temple and the city will be restored through divine initiative (v. 16b; compare the commentary on Hag 1:2-14).

The third oracle describes the care of the Lord of hosts for "my cities" (v. 17a). Goodness, consolation, and election will again be present when God returns to Jerusalem (v. 17b). Two details are absent: the time of God's return and the outcome of the complacent nations (v. 15).

2:1-4 [1:18-21] Second vision: Four horns and four blacksmiths. This succinct vision lacks the details and oracular responses of the first vision. The visionary medium proclaims, "I raised my eyes and looked" (5:1; 6:1) and the first image, "four horns," is seen (v. 1 [1:18]). The interpreting angel is asked for assistance (v. 2a [1:19a]). The horns are identified as those who "scattered Judah and Israel and Jerusalem" (v. 2b [1:19b]).

Verse 3a [1:20a] states that the Lord is the agent who reveals the next image. The prophet asks about the function of the blacksmiths (v. 3b [1:20b]). The Lord responds that they "terrify" and "cast down" the "horns" who "scattered the land of Judah" (v. 4 [1:21]).

In earlier commentaries "horns" was a metaphor for world powers (Mic 4:13). The context would identify them as the enemies of northern Israel and Judah, especially Babylon. In the last decade, however, additional possibilities for interpretation have been suggested: two pairs of animal horns, four horns of the altar, horns in the ground, horn-shaped threshing tools, and horned helmets.

Similarly, "blacksmiths" in earlier commentaries was a metaphor for those who exercise judgment (see Isa 54:16-17), that is, the Persians, who reversed the fortunes of Babylon. In the last decade the term "blacksmiths" has come to identify ploughmen, artisans, constructive or destructive creators.

The thought of earlier commentaries is developed in two ways. Both highlight tasks of reconstruction. One identifies the horns as the horns belonging to animals that have roamed over the ruins of Jerusalem. When the ploughmen guide the animals back to their proper enclosures, there is space to rebuild and reconstitute the community. The other identifies the horns of the altar, which provided sanctuary for those who clung to them. After the Exile, artisans came to rebuild and purify the altar area for sanctuary and cult.

There is no specific oracle that responds to the second vision. Among the three interpretations of the vision, only the earlier one replies to the fate of the "complacent nations," which remained unaddressed in the first vision (1:15).

2:5-9 [2:1-5] Third vision: Measuring line. The third vision is introduced with the same formula as the second vision (v. 5a [v. 1a]). The new image is a man with a measuring line (vv. 5b-6 [1b-2]). This vision develops the image of the measuring device noted in the second oracle of the first vision (see 1:16).

Another new dimension is the introduction of a second angel (v. 7 [v. 3]). This angel exhorts the interpreting angel to give "that young man" (the measurer) a message about how people will live in Jerusalem. They will live "as though in open country." The Revised Standard Version translates this better: "as villages without walls" (v. 8a [v. 4a]). Why "without walls"? "Because of the multitude of men and beasts in her midst" (v. 8b [v. 4b]).

A divine assurance is the climax to the vision. It parallels the oracles in the first vision (see 1:13-17). The Lord promises to be present: "an encircling wall of fire . . . the glory in her midst" (v. 9 [v. 5]).

The third vision is related to the other two visions, functioning as the third adjustment of the telescope. The first focus was cosmic; the second focus was the land of Israel; and the third is the city of Jerusalem. In addition, the third vision specifies how God "will turn to Jerusalem in mercy" (1:16a): God will offer presence and glory (2:9). These gifts suggest "prosperity" (1:17b), that is, all living things will flourish (2:8b).

The third vision is a striking illustration of the use of traditional symbols to proclaim a new reality. The "encircling wall of fire" (v. 9a [v. 5a]), which recalls God's presence as a cloud of fire during the Exodus (see Exod 13:21-22; 14:20; 40:34), is reinterpreted as the protective care of God for Jerusalem. God's initiative in rimming the city offers a perspective to human effort involved in the process of reconstruction.

The rebuilding of the temple in all its complexities is also given a new perspective. The vision of temple restoration that Ezekiel offered to the exiles as hope for the return of God's glory (see Ezek 40–48) is broadened. Zechariah's vision extends God's glory *(kabod)* to all *throughout Jerusalem.*

2:10-17 [2:6-13] Responses. The oracles consist of two sections. The first section (vv. 10-13 [vv. 6-9]) comments on the enemies of Israel mentioned in the first collection of oracles (1:15) and the second and third visions (2:1-4 [1:18-21]; compare 2:9 [2:5]). The second section continues promises of blessings for Jerusalem noted in the first collection of oracles (1:14; 16-17) and the second and third visions (2:4b [1:21b], 7-9 [3-5]). In addition to a thematic division, traditional prophetic formulas separate some of the oracles: "says the Lord" (v. 10ab [v. 6ab]; v. 14b [v. 11b]); "said the Lord of hosts" (v. 12a [v. 8a]).

There is no interpreting angel for the oracles (compare 1:13ff.). Rather, the prophet is clearly indicated as the one commissioned by God (see vv. 12a, 15b [vv. 8a, 11b]). The verses suggest that the fulfillment of God's promises will authenticate the prophet's proclamation.

The first section of oracles contains imperatives for the exiles and warnings for those who conquered them. There is a parallel construction for verses 10 and 11. Those who are living in "the land of the north" (v. 10a [v. 6a]; see Jer 3:18; 16:15; 23:8; 31:8) are identical with the ones "who dwell in daughter Babylon" (v. 11b [v. 7b]).

The exiles are exhorted to "flee" and "escape to Zion" before God "scatters" the inhabitants of Babylon "to the four winds of heaven" (vv. 10-11a [vv. 6-7a]). In these verses the identification of Babylon is probably more extensive than the geographical region designated as exilic territory. It includes all oppressors of Israel.

An ironic punishment is pronounced for the nations that plundered Israel (v. 12a [v. 8a]): "they become plunder for their slaves" (v. 13a [v. 9a]). Why such harsh treatment? "Whoever touches you touches the apple of my eye" (v. 12b [v. 8b]). The metaphor indicates "pupil" or "gate" of the eye, that is, a treasured part or relationship.

The second section, like the third vision (see vv. 8-9 [vv. 4-5]), presents new revelation in traditional terms. Let those in Jerusalem rejoice (see Zeph 3:14-15; Zech 9:9; Pss 9:14; 48:11). The Lord is coming to dwell with the temple-community (v. 14 [v. 10]). The Hebrew of the verse indicates the language of manifestation and abiding presence.

The Lord's dwelling is mentioned in the next verse (v. 15 [v. 11]) with unexpected proclamations. "On that day," referring to the day of the Lord (see the commentary on Joel 2:18–4:21 [2:18–3:21]), the "many nations" shall "join themselves to the Lord . . . and they shall be his people." How the nations will be joined or how Israel and the nations shall become a "people" is not indicated. The concept of the Lord's dwelling among the nations and Israel is remarkable, especially when compared with Zechariah's contemporary Haggai. The latter limited the nations' contributions to their treasures for the temple (see the commentary on Hag 2:7-9).

Covenant language ("choose") is used to indicate the Lord's relationship to Judah and Jerusalem (v. 16 [11]). The designation of Judah as "holy land" appears only here. Everything will be holy because of the Lord's dwelling among the people.

The responses conclude with a fragment of liturgical directive: "Silence . . . in the presence of the Lord!" (v. 17a [v. 13a]; compare Hab 2:20; Zeph 1:7).

3:1-5 Fourth vision: Joshua the high priest. Chapter 3 is presented without any rearrangement of the verses (see p. 601). The vision differs from the first three visions in form. There is no introductory statement, question about interpretation, or explanation by the angel. Some commentators suggest that the unusual form indicates a later vision that was added to an original seven visions.

Verse 1 is an introduction to the vision. The "he" probably refers to the interpreting angel who accompanied the prophet during the first three visions (v. 1a; see 1:9, 14; 2:2, 7 [1:19; 2:3]). Three characters appear in the vision of the heavenly council (v. 1b):

a) "Joshua the high priest" appears for the first time (see p. 593).

b) "The angel of the Lord" who appeared in the first three visions convenes and authorizes the proceedings of the heavenly council (see vv. 2, 4-5).

c) "Satan" is a transliteration of the Hebrew word that means "adversary." It is not a personal name in the Hebrew Bible; rather, it designates a role, that is, accuser (see Job 1:6-12; 2:1-7; Ps 109:6; Rev 12:10).

Verse 2 ironically reverses the roles of Satan and Joshua. Whatever accusations the adversary had spoken against Joshua are abrogated by the double rebukes of the "Lord who has chosen Jerusalem" (see 1:17b; 2:16 [2:12]; compare Hag 2:23). Verse 2 concludes with a rhetorical question: "Is not this man a brand snatched from the fire?" (see Amos 4:11). As Joshua represents the entire community in verse 1, here their communal deliverance from exile is suggested (v. 2b).

The position of Joshua before the angel of the Lord (v. 3a) repeats verse 1a. The "filthy garments" that Joshua wears (v. 3b) are associated with the fire imagery of the Exile experience (v. 2b). The garments could symbolize mourning (see Jer 41:4-5) or the guilt associated with living in Babylon.

The authoritative angel of the Lord directs the angels of the council to reclothe Joshua (vv. 4-5). "Festal garments" and a "clean miter" replace the filthy garments. According to some commentators, the ritual dressing indicates garb of the high priest (see Lev 8:1-9). Others propose a figurative context of acceptance in the court (see Isa 62:3; Job 29:14).

The ritual activity symbolizes the judgment of the angel: "See, I have taken away your guilt" (v. 5b). "Guilt" suggests the association of Joshua with the land of Babylon as well as the transgressions of the temple-community, of which he is the religious leader (see Exod 28:36-38; Num 18:1). To function as high priest, the ritual activity was necessary. The temple ritual for purification is not available.

3:6-10 Responses. A challenge and two oracles of assurance interpret the fourth vision. Each is prefaced by a traditional prophetic formula: "says the Lord of hosts" (vv. 7a, 9b, 10a). Each proclamation is directed to Joshua the high priest by the authoritative angel (v. 6).

The challenge is made in verse 7a: "If you walk in my ways and heed my charge . . . ." The first condition refers to moral integrity (see Deut 8:6), while the second is more ambiguous. The Hebrew term suggests a general obligation or prohibition (see Gen 26:5; Lev 18:30), or a duty (Isa 21:8). It also signifies ritual activity (see Num 3). In this context the faithful cultic service of God is apt.

Acceptance of the challenge results in two areas of responsibility (and blessing) in verse 7b. Each one reflects the situation of a *preexilic monarch.* "Judge my house" indicates judicial functions (see Deut 17:8-13), while "keep my courts" refers to decisions about cultic activity. Both responsibilities are carried out at the temple. The judicial functions *there* are new for a high priest (compare Ezek 44:10-31). "Access among these standing here" describes Joshua's approach to the members of the heavenly council.

The second oracle is an unconditional blessing for Joshua and his associates (v. 8). The identity of the group is unclear. Some commentators suggest additional priests or persons of prominence in the temple-community (see Ezra 2; Neh 7). In what sense are they a "good omen"? They are considered signs of God's blessing (v. 8b; 6:12-13). The "branch" imagery was a traditional one for a just ruler (see Jer 23:5; Isa 11:1). The appearance of a monarch like David is part of the expectation of restoration of the temple-community. Haggai, Zechariah's contemporary, had proclaimed that possibility for Zerubbabel (see Hag 2:23). Verses 7 and 8 suggest some type of shared rule. The high priest (and other priests) functions in the temple, while a Davidic heir functions on the throne.

Verse 9a continues the second oracle with another image: "one stone with seven facets." Attention returns to Joshua (see v. 7) as the one before whom the stone is placed. The stone might be a person; a real stone for temple reconstruction; a stone for ritual purposes; a stone belonging to the garb of high priest.

Verse 9b provides additional details about the stone, which clarify its identity. It probably is the engraved stone that adorned the high priest's turban (see Exod 28:36-38). Its inscription, "Sacred to the Lord" (Exod 28:36), suggests cleansing from guilt (see Exod 28:38).

Something new is revealed. Aaron (and his successors) "*bears* whatever guilt the Israelites may incur" (Exod 28:38a). The Lord of hosts *removes* the "guilt of the land in one day" (v. 9b). This completes the process that the angel of the Lord started by removing Joshua's guilt (v. 5). Now God's initiative cleanses the land.

Verse 10 completes the challenge and oracles of assurance. "On that day" identifies a future possibility wherein the community will be at home and extend hospitality (see 1 Kgs 5:25 [4:25]; Mic 4:4).

4:1-6a, 10b-14 Fifth vision: Lampstand. There is some rearrangement of verses in chapter 4. Note the difference between the New American Bible text and the arrangement of the commentary (see p. 601).

The introductory statement of the fifth vision presents the interpreting angel, who stirs up the prophet (v. 1; compare Joel 4:9 [3:9]). Verse 1 may be a literary device to unify the material between the first vision "at night" (see 1:8) and the present one.

Verse 2a is a departure from the first four visions, where the prophet immediately reports what he sees. This time the interpreting angel asks the question (compare 5:1-4). Zechariah responds with a detailed description of a gold lampstand (vv. 2b-3).

The prophet questions the angel about "these things" (v. 4). The angel responds with another question, implying that the image ought to be clear (v. 5a). After the prophet admits he does not know (v. 5b), the angel explains the scene by first interpreting the lamp (vv. 6a, 10b). The seven "facets" (lights) on the lampstand are "the eyes of the Lord that range over the whole earth."

The prophet inquires again about the "two olive trees at each side of the lampstand" (v. 11). Another question follows: "What are the two olive tufts which freely pour out fresh oil through the two golden channels?" (v. 12). Again, the interpreting angel is surprised that the prophet does not recognize the image (v. 13). When the prophet admits that he does not know (v. 13), the angel explains (v. 14).

How may the major components of the vision be interpreted? A description of the lampstand explains the basic structure of the vision. Within the last century archeological discoveries have classified a number of clay lamps and lampstands conforming to a particular shape. A lampstand is at the base. Resting on the stand is a bowl for oil. On the rim of the bowl are indentations for wicks (usually approximately seven). When the wicks are ignited, they burn because they are draped over the oil.

Although the term for the lampstand is *menorah*, it does not match the description of the seven-branched candelabrum used in ritual contexts (see Exod 25:33). What is unusual in the description of the lampstand in the vision is not its shape but its composition of gold.

What does the lampstand symbolize? The lampstand and lights represent the presence of God, who looks kindly upon all of creation (see 2 Chr 16:9; compare Ezra 5:5). The lampstand and lights parallel and develop two images of earlier visions: the equestrians who patrol the earth (1:10-11) and the encircling wall of fire (2:9).

The olive trees (vv. 3, 11) and the olive tufts (v. 12) are clearly interpreted by the angel as the "two anointed who stand by the Lord of the whole earth" (v. 14). Who are the "anointed"? They are Zerubbabel and Joshua, equal in dignity and importance. Their proposed rule is unexpected because only a monarch like David was anticipated. Nonetheless, for the temple-community there are two who will govern. After Zerubbabel's death the office of high priest grew in prominence (see p. 574).

Many commentators considered Zerubbabel and Joshua as messiah figures because of the "anointed" terminology. The Hebrew phrase translates "sons of oil." In addition, the oil is of the type used for harvest festivals, not for an anointing ceremony. As high priest, Joshua had already been anointed. The two rulers function, however, in a revolutionary role. Although verse 12 is difficult to translate, the imagery suggests that Zerubbabel and Joshua are close to God, who needs their oil for the agency of compassionate presence ("seven facets") for the community. They, in turn, require God's support for leadership. The interdependency is new.

4:6b-10a Collection of responses. If the verses were not rearranged, they would appear between the description of the lampstand and its interpretation. The verses are a poetic insertion consisting of two oracles. Both are introduced by traditional prophetic formulas: "This is the Lord's message" (v. 6b); "This word of the Lord then came to me" (v. 8; see 6:9; 7:4; 8:1, 18). The oracles describe Zerubbabel's leadership in restoring the temple, as an earlier visionary ritual had described Joshua's preparation for the office of high priest (3:1-10).

The first oracle (vv. 6b-7) describes how the work of temple restoration will be accomplished. Neither an "army" (compare 1 Kgs 5:20) nor "might" (see Neh 4:10) is adequate to the task. Divine activity will complete the work (v. 6b).

Since God's spirit is with Zerubbabel, he is the leader in the temple reconstruction. First, Zerubbabel is compared metaphorically to a mountain of obstacles and emerges as the greater one (v. 7a; see Isa 40:4; 41:15). Second, he will bear the "capstone" amid exclamations of the community.

Commentators debate the identity of the capstone. Is it the foundation stone or the final stone on the pinnacle of the temple? Some see the oracles (vv. 6b-10a) and the visionary ritual of Joshua (3:1-10) in the wider context of Mesopotamian services for rededication of the temple. The capstone signifies continuity. It is a stone taken from the earlier temple and positioned in the new one to assure cultic continuity. The "select stone" (v. 10a) refers to another type of ritual—placing an engraved tin tablet into the edifice of the new temple.

Others propose that the capstone is the final piece of the new temple. It is the "select stone" (v. 10a) placed by the hands of Zerubbabel, the civic governor of the temple-community. The Hebrew terms used to describe the stone allow both interpretations. In general, Zechariah was convinced that Zerubbabel's leadership was necessary for the project (see 6:12-13).

The second oracle (vv. 9-10a) connects the activity of Zerubbabel with the credibility of the prophet. The Lord's proclamation assures Zechariah that Zerubbabel, who began the foundation, will finish it (v. 9a). The completion of the temple will be a sign to the community that Zechariah's proclamations are validated (v. 9b; compare 2:9, 11; 6:15).

Verse 10a describes the general attitude of the temple-community toward the task of reconstruction (compare Hag 2:3-5; Ezra 3:12). Even these scoffers "shall rejoice to see the select stone in the hands of Zerubbabel." The four references to Zerubbabel's hands (4:7 [implicit]; 9 [twice]; 10a) may refer to his royal function in the cultic ceremonies of temple restoration. In ancient Near East traditions the king often assisted in temple reconstruction either actually or symbolically.

5:1-4 Sixth vision: Flying scroll. The spatial quality and movement of the vision parallel the seventh vision: the flying bushel (5:5-11). Both visions are directed to the temple-community. What is necessary to cleanse the community for renewed relationship with God? The theme of renewal, addressed to Joshua with regard to cult (3:1-10) and to Zerubbabel with regard to temple reconstruction (4:6b-10a), has specific implications for the community as well.

Verse 1 is the introductory statement and description of the flying scroll. It repeats the literary form of the second and third visions (see 2:1 [1:18]; 2:5 [2:1]). The short formula will be repeated in the eighth vision (see 6:1).

The question of the interpreting angel (v. 2a) appears redundant, since the prophet had already announced his vision (v. 1). The vision is described with additional detail (v. 2b). While a scroll would be a familiar sight (see Jer 36:1-8) and symbol (see Ezek 2:9-10; 3:1-3), the proportions are unusual. A scroll is much longer than it is wide. In addition, although no one is holding the scroll, it is unrolled and flying in the air!

The dimensions of the scroll match the area of Solomon's temple porch (see 1 Kgs 6:3) and are similar to those of the desert sanctuary, which is half the size (see Exod 26:15-28). However, there is no apparent connection between the flying scroll and either area.

The interpreting angel identifies the scroll as a "curse . . . over the whole earth"; it will sweep away "every thief" and expel "every perjurer" (v. 3). The curse refers to consequences for covenant abrogations that were added to the ceremony by oaths (see Deut 28:15ff.; compare Gen 26:28; Ezek 17:13). The thought in verses 3-4 is a fusion of the covenant stipulations and the Decalogue prescriptions. Specifically, the thief represents the laws regarding human conduct (see Exod 20:15-16), and the perjurer represents attitudes toward God (see Exod 20:7).

Verse 4 is a divine oracle that interprets the vision. It tells of the consequences for thief and perjurer. Their houses and inhabitants will be consumed by the curse that God sends forth (compare Ps 147:15; Isa 55:11).

What is the particular situation in the community that draws attention to thievery and perjury? The perpetrators of these crimes are forbidden to enter the temple (see Ps 24:4). Thievery was a particular problem for the temple-community, especially the usurpation of land tracts by those who remained in Judah during the Babylonian Captivity. Litigation occurred. The charge of perjury is probably related to these occasions.

The curse of the flying scroll may also represent the continuity of judgment and values. Even though the community will be administered by a new model of leadership (Joshua and Zerubbabel), the standards will remain the same as before (compare the commentary on 4:6b-10a). Another factor of continuity is the phrase "the whole earth" (v. 3a). Within both Judah and the Diaspora the same obligations for all Jews will be in force.

5:5-11 Seventh vision: Flying bushel. The vision is inaugurated by a command of the interpreting angel to look up and identify the new symbol (v. 5). The familiar question pattern follows (v. 6a), with the angel's response (v. 6b). The vision reveals another character: "a woman sitting inside the bushel" is "Wickedness," whom the angel thrusts inside, "pushing the leaden cover into the opening" (vv. 7-8).

Next the prophet sees additional characters. Two women with ruffled wings like a stork's lift the bushel into the air (v. 9). The prophet seeks assistance from the angel, who explains the women's action. They are taking the bushel to Shinar, where they will deposit it in the temple when the building is completed (vv. 10-11).

The bushel container and the woman are central to the vision. Their relationship is the key to interpretation. The bushel container functions as the "setting" for both parts of the vision. The term in Hebrew means "container" (see Ruth 2:17) and a "measure" or standardized weight (see Amos 8:5; Ezek 45:10). The prophet's question, "What is it?" refers to content as well as measure.

The question of content is immediately clarified by the angel: "their guilt in all the land" (v. 7b). What is the source of guilt? The woman named Wickedness is the symbol of evil surrounded by guilt (v. 8). Like the genie in the bottle and unlike Pandora and her box, Wickedness and guilt can be controlled by the leaden cover that the angel thrusts into the opening of the container.

Many speculate about why the woman personifies wickedness. Some refer to the feminine gender of the Hebrew word for "wickedness." Others associate it with Israel's sin, which is often described by use of the metaphor of harlotry (see Jer 3:8; Hos 1:2; Ezek 16). A few point to the garden event (Gen 3) as the origin of the personification.

Two figures, half-animal (stork wings) and half-human (women), appear as *deae ex machina* to remove the bushel basket. Stork wings suggest flying animals (see Jer 8:7) and unclean animals (see Lev 11:9; Deut 14:18). Soaring in the wind, they carry the container to Shinar, an ancient name for the land of Babylon (see Gen 10:10; 11:2; Dan 1:2; Rev 14:8). There Wickedness and guilt will have a temple in which to reside.

The image of removing evil and guilt is parallel to the image of Joshua's "filthy garments" (3:3). God initiates the removal of extensive evil ("in all the land") of the community and the impurity of the high priest through agents—two women and the angel (3:5). God is not contaminated by impurity or evil.

The bushel container and the woman are considered non-standards for the temple-community that has returned to restore relationship with God. Covenant obligations (5:1-4) and the removal of evil and guilt are dimensions of reconstruction.

6:1-8 Eighth vision: Four chariots. The final vision forms an inclusion with the first vision (1:7-12). The first verse (1:7) and the last verse (8:8) indicate visionary experience. Details of place (glen, mountain pass) and time (night, sunrise) are different. Important images, however, parallel one another: horses, colors, patrolling functions.

Verse 1 is a short introductory statement with an initial description of the vision; details appear in verses 2-3. Four chariots emerge between two "bronze mountains" (v. 1). Each chariot is numbered and described by a colored horse (red, black, white, spotted) that pulls it. All the horses are "strong" (vv. 2-3).

The question of the prophet (v. 4) is readily answered by the interpreting angel (v. 5). The chariots turn in different directions (v. 6). While anticipating their patrolling function, the "strong horses" are commanded directly by God (vv. 6b-7a). While they are patrolling the earth, God issues a second command to the prophet (v. 8).

The final vision reveals personified "winds" patrolling the earth for the Lord, whose abode is protected by two bronze mountains. The chariots are primary, while the number and color of the horses are secondary details (vv. 2-3). They may resemble military forces (see 2 Kgs 23:11; Ps 104:4) that are eager to facilitate conditions so that the Lord's spirit may "rest in the land of the north" (v. 8b).

The first and eighth visions function as opening and closing scenes of the night visions. In the first vision toward nightfall, the report of the equestrians patrolling the earth indicates that "the whole earth is tranquil and at rest" (1:11). Nonetheless, there is a plea for mercy on behalf of the temple-community, which does not experience that "rest" (1:12). The Lord is moved to compassion for the community but is "exceedingly angry with the complacent nations" (1:16).

The intervening visions present the plight of the community, especially the importance of dual leadership, temple restoration, and purgation. In contrast, the situation of the oppressors of Israel is included briefly (see 2:1-4, 12-13). The phrase "the whole earth" and movement patterns characterize the process of the visions.

In the eighth vision there is tranquility because God's spirit is at rest "in the land of the north." The downfall of the oppressors as well as the return of the exiles to Jerusalem signals a new reality. Exact chronology is not a concern in any of the visionary narratives or oracular responses.

6:9-15 Responses and a crown. The structure of the final section of the eighth vision consists of two oracles. The first oracle (vv. 9-11, 14-15) frames the second oracle (vv. 12-13). The first oracle is a private proclamation to the prophet: "This word of the Lord came to me" (v. 9), while the second oracle is a public proclamation: "And say to him: 'Thus says the Lord of hosts' " (v. 12a). Both oracles respond to the visions whose reality will occur when the temple is completed. The oracles in their final, edited form, however, focus on an indefinite future.

After the oracular introduction (v. 9) the prophet is commanded by God to take something from the "returned captives Heldai, Tobijah, Jedaiah" (v. 10a). What the returnees possess becomes clear in verse 11: "silver and gold." The names are not found in Jewish tradition. Their orthodox position in returning to Jerusalem is indicated by their *theophoric* names, that is, the consonants for Yahweh appear in their names. They also represent others in the Diaspora who contribute materials for temple restoration.

The returnees are commanded to go immediately to the "house of Josiah, son of Zephaniah (these had come from Babylon)" (v. 10b). There may be continuity between the two groups of returned exiles if Josiah had been taken into exile. On the other hand, if he had remained in Judah, there would be continuity in the two groups who now lived on the land restoring the temple.

The silver and gold brought back from exile will be fashioned into a "crown" (v. 11a). Other ancient texts read "crowns." Arguments based on subsequent verses are persuasive for both the singular and plural forms of the noun. The discussion about "crown" is the beginning of many difficult textual decisions in the section.

Who will wear the crown? The New American Bible states: "place it on the head of [Joshua, son of Jehozadak, the high priest] Zerubbabel" (v. 11b). The Revised Standard Version and the New English Bible, however, delete the reference to Zerubbabel and the brackets around the Joshua description. Again, there are persuasive arguments for either Joshua or Zerubbabel and the crown.

Those favoring Joshua note that the fate

of Zerubbabel is unclear in the tradition. The final editor probably inserted Joshua's name to clarify what happened historically, that is, the high priest became the source of authority for the temple-community (see p. 574).

Commentators who propose Zerubbabel's name refer to his function as the temple-builder (see 4:9; compare 4:12). He would be the logical one to be crowned in a royal ceremony, since the installation as high priest would be a separate ceremony. Others argue that the coronation had to be symbolic due to the position of the temple-community of Judah within the Persian empire.

One scholar noted that Zerubbabel's role was diminished in the lampstand vision by its position in the middle of the vision. Now, Joshua's role is similarly diminished by its position in the middle of the final oracles.

Finally, since a two-person rule had been a possibility suggested before in visionary material (see 4:1-5, 10b-14), *two* crowns may be apt for Zerubbabel and Joshua.

A public oracle of the Lord follows the description of the crown (vv. 12-13). Its focus is temple reconstruction (see 4:6-10a), in particular an individual who has an important role in the project. The person is identified as "Shoot," a name used to describe a future Davidic figure (see the commentary on 3:8). Zerubbabel is the logical referent drawn from 3:8 as well as from the additional detail at the end of the verse: "he shall build the temple" (v. 12b).

The choice of Zerubbabel is strengthened by the details of verse 13. The first part repeats the function of temple-builder and adds the royal function of ruling from the throne (v. 13a). The priest mentioned in the second part of the verse is probably Joshua. Both reign from the throne area, yet Joshua appears to claim more status. "Friendly understanding" describes their new model of leadership for the temple-community (v. 13b).

The next two verses are the conclusion of the first oracle (vv. 9-11, 14-15). The symbolic function of the crown (see the commentary on v. 11b) is described (v. 14). While memorial offerings on behalf of the community were known (see Exod 30:16), the crown will immortalize several individuals.

A comparison of the names in verses 14 and 10 indicates that two of the four names are different: Heldai and Helem (Hebrew text); Josiah and Hen (Hebrew text). In addition, the function of Joshua changes from one whose house served as a meeting place (v. 10b) to one who will be immortalized with the other three (v. 14b). Some commentators suggest that Helem and Hen are nicknames for Heldai and Josiah.

Verse 15 reiterates themes mentioned in the visions and response oracles. First, there is an acknowledgment of assistance for temple reconstruction from those "who are from afar." Not only will they send materials (see v. 11), but they will actively engage in the process (v. 15a).

Second, the cooperation in rebuilding will be another sign of the prophet's authentication from God (v. 15b). The other signs described a new relationship between the temple-community and God (see the commentary on 2:13 [2:9]) as well as leadership for the temple reconstruction (see the commentary on 4:9b).

Third, the last part of the verse, which is incomplete, presents a challenge that was neglected by ancestors before the Exile. It suggests that obedience to the Lord is adhering to the visions and oracles of Zechariah. The challenge offers the community a new beginning and an opportunity for returning to God as God desires to return to the community. The final words of First Zechariah, then, form an inclusion with the first divine oracle (see 1:3ff.).

PART THREE: ORACLES ABOUT FASTING AND THE FUTURE

Zech 7:1–8:23

Part Three consists of the final two chapters of First Zechariah. It is a collection of oracles arranged from various contexts to form a coherent message. The sections present hortatory material that could be developed in greater detail for preaching occasions. The tone of the oracles is an interweaving of encouragement and warning, with constant reference to past experience as a model for present and future activity. The basic structure of chapter 7 is a question-and-answer format, while chapter 8 is a series of ten proclamations. It is impossible to separate the prophet's oracles from the elaboration of the editor.

7:1-3 Question about fasting. The superscription combines a traditional prophetic formula and a precise chronology (v. 1). It is one year after the visions and two years after the beginning of temple restoration, that is, November-December 518 B.C.E. The chronology also indicates the ninth month of the year (Chislev). The notation of month occurs in one other superscription (1:7). The mention of Darius as king occurs here and in Hag 1:1.

Verse 2 introduces individuals who are new to the temple at Jerusalem. Scholarly discussion suggests that Bethelsarezer was a Jewish official in Babylon who acted on behalf of his community. He sent Regemmelech and his retinue to Jerusalem with a request. The phrase "implore the favor of the Lord" describes a situation needing immediate attention (see Exod 32:11). Note that the phrase is structurally parallel to "ask the priests of the house of the Lord of hosts, and the prophets" (v. 3a).

The "priests of the house of the Lord" and the "prophets" (v. 3a) describe those who functioned with authority in the temple-community after the Exile (compare Mic 3:11). Since the verse implies that temple restoration had been completed, it may be an editorial remark. Nonetheless, the cooperation of both groups is needed to address the community's plight both in Babylon and Jerusalem. Their response would probably affect Jews throughout the Diaspora as well. Ironically, the text indicates only the response of the prophet.

The question before the authorities concerns ritual activities of mourning and abstaining (v. 3b). The temple had been destroyed in the fifth month (2 Kgs 25:8-9). Consequently, rituals were observed to commemorate that event. Ought any community observe them now that reconstruction on the temple was in progress? According to several commentators, a deeper question is implied. Has the promise of the prophets been fulfilled? Are we living in a new age following upon the restoration of the temple? If so, mourning is transformed by rejoicing.

7:4-7 Responses. The replies are two oracles consisting of rhetorical questions from God and one from Zechariah. The divine-oracle formula is found in verse 4, and verse 5a states that "all the people of the land" (compare Hag 2:4), including the priests, will be the addressees of the proclamation. In verse 5b another time for ritual mourning commemorates the assassination of Gedaliah, the Jewish governor of Jerusalem, who had been appointed by Babylon (2 Kgs 25:22-26; see p. 573).

The first question focuses on intentions for fasting and mourning (v. 5b). The second question follows immediately. Wasn't the opposite situation of eating and drinking also "for yourselves"? (v. 6). Self-centeredness is the attitude challenged in both situations (compare Hag 1:4-8, 10; Isa 58:3-7, 13).

Zechariah's rhetorical question is a comment on the Lord's question (v. 7). He draws attention to the tradition of the community before the Exile. The "former prophets" had spoken God's word when Judah was populated and at peace (v. 7b). Their collective proclamation vindicates his message, too. Zechariah had spoken about a meager population in Judah after the Exile (see 2:10 [2:8]; compare 2:8 [2:4]). He may be suggesting that fasting before and after the Exile is problematic; its focus is on the individual, not God.

7:8-14 Another collection of responses. These verses can be divided according to topic. Verses 8-10 interrupt the response about fasting (vv. 4-7). They present a summary of ethical teaching promulgated by the prophets before the Exile. Verses 11-14 return to the response about fasting.

Verses 8-9a introduce a divine oracle with a traditional prophetic formula. The oracle (vv. 9b-10) states the genuine nature of fasting proclaimed in earlier tradition. The first part is a general maxim for social conduct: be honest in judgment; be compassionate toward one another (v. 9b; see Jer 7:5). The maxim is reinforced by specific prohibitions (v. 10; see Jer 7:6; compare 1:4b).

Verses 11-14 provide a picture of the community before the Exile (compare 1:3b-6) as a model for reflection. The admonitory style is similar to the Chronicler's (see 2 Chr 30:6-9; Neh 9:25-31). The instruction issues warnings and provides hope. The section reinforces Zechariah's and the editor's claim to authority.

Earlier communities had refused to listen to the Lord's imperative about true fasting (v. 11a). Metaphors of body language dramatize their stubbornness (vv. 11b-12a). What were they resisting? "The teaching and the message that the Lord of hosts had sent by his spirit through the former prophets" (v. 12b). No one but the prophets was entrusted with God's teaching and message (compare 1:4). A closer relationship between God and the prophets is indicated by the phrase "his spirit." Since the prophets shared in God's spirit, to reject them is virtually to reject God.

God's response to the community's stubbornness was reciprocal: "he would not listen when they called" (v. 13). The concluding verse extends the consequences of the preexilic community through the Exile and the restoration attempts of the current community. God acted by scattering the community "among all the nations that they did not know" (v. 14a). The land, too, suffered: it became desolate (v. 14b).

8:1-8 Blessings for Jerusalem. Two prophetic formulas introduce the first oracle (vv. 2-3). The omission of "to me" indicates that Zechariah is repeating what he had heard before (v. 1). God's "intense jealousy" of, and "wrath" toward, Zion indicates passion and concern for the returned exiles (v. 2). The proclamation functioned initially as a response to the first vision (see 1:14). Verse 2 also initiates promises of blessings (8:2-23) following the oracles of warnings (7:4-17).

Verse 3 states how God will respond to the community. Again the language parallels the response after the first vision (see 1:16). In both sections God "will return to Zion . . . and . . . will dwell within Jerusalem" (v. 3a). God's dwelling recalls how the people and God lived in tents (see Exod 25:8; 29:46). However, there is a new revelation here. God's *presence* initiates a new name for Jerusalem: "faithful" and "holy mountain" (v. 3b; see Joel 4:17 [3:17]; compare Isa 1:21-26; Ezek 48:35).

The second oracle (vv. 4-5) is introduced with a traditional formula (v. 4a). It specifies two groups of persons who will revel in the Lord's presence. "Old men and old women" (v. 4b) and "boys and girls" (v. 5) will fill the streets of the city and enjoy their activities without fear (see Amos 5:16; Lam 2:11-12; Isa 65:20; Ps 127:3-4; Jer 30:18-21). The two groups are described in harmony and sexual equality. They represent those who would have found the journey back from exile quite difficult. The groups also reverse the anxiety about the present depopulation of the temple-community (see 7:14; compare 7:7).

The third oracle (v. 6) is introduced as the first two oracles were (v. 6a). It presents God's rhetorical question about the expectations of the community toward divine activity (v. 6b). Does the reversal of present circumstances, that is, depopulated city, "remnant" group (see Hag 1:12), appear impossible? (Compare Gen 28:14; Jer 32:17, 27.)

God reassures the community in the fourth oracle (vv. 7-8). After the introduction (v. 7a), God promises to repopulate the city by delivering the exiles from captivity (v. 7b). The "land of the rising sun . . . of the setting sun" refers to Babylon and Egypt (compare 2:10 [2:6]; Jer 31:8). The exiles will share God's dwelling in Jerusalem (v. 8).

"They shall be my people, and I will be their God" indicates that the covenant contracted by their ancestors remains a reality for those returning (v. 8b; see Lev 26:12; Jer 31:33). The phrase "with faithfulness and justice" suggests God's response to the covenant as well as the challenge of mutuality for the community in maintaining the covenant.

8:9-17 Encouragement and challenge for Jerusalem. The section is comprised of two parts (vv. 9-13 and 14-17). Each begins with a traditional prophetic formula as an introduction (vv. 9a, 14a). Each presents past tragedy and develops future possibilities of blessing. Both refer to earlier ethical teaching as well as to earlier verses in First Zechariah.

After the introduction (v. 9a), the first exhortation is "let your hands be strong." The addressees are those who had heard Haggai speak about the necessity of temple restoration, especially the "foundation of the house of the Lord." The term "prophets" suggests that the addressees of that prophet had also heard Zechariah, who was Haggai's contemporary (v. 9b; see Hag 1:6-11; 2:15-19).

Verse 10 describes the situation before temple restoration began in earnest. At that time there was no economic security (v. 10a). In addition, hostile forces precluded security. God initiated the circumstances by setting each person against the neighbor (v. 10b).

Verse 11 introduces a new oracle. God's judgment is reversed. God will act differently: "But now I will not deal with the remnant of this people as in former days . . . ." The expression is similar to covenant language. How will the present situation be different for the temple-community? It is described as "the seedtime of peace," that is, vine and land will be productive; the heavens will water the earth (v. 12a; compare Hag 1:10-11).

Another contrast concludes the first part. As Israel and Judah were "a curse among the nations," now they will be a "blessing" through God's saving intervention (v. 13a; see v. 7b). The oracle concludes with two exhortations: "do not fear, but let your hands be strong" (v. 12b; compare Deut 28:1-28). The second exhortation forms an inclusion with verse 9b, formally closing the oracle.

The second part begins with an introduction to another oracle (v. 14a). The construction "as . . . so" provides the structure for comparing past history and present experience (vv. 14b-15; see 1:6; 7:13). It also repeats previous oracles. *As* God had decided to harm the community because of its ancestral history and "did not relent" (v. 14b; see 1:6b; compare Jer 4:28; 51:12; Lam 2:17), *so* God decided "in these days . . . to favor Jerusalem and the house of Judah" (v. 15).

The oracle concludes with a short summary of ethical teaching about truth and honesty in judgments (compare 7:9); exhortations against evil plans for others (compare 7:10b) and against false oaths (compare 5:3-4). God detests these activities (vv. 16-17).

8:18-23 Responses about fasting and the future. Two oracles conclude First Zechariah. The first one (vv. 18-19) responds to the delegation's question about fasting (7:2-3), while the second is a description of the role of Jerusalem for the temple-community and the nations.

A prophetic formula introduces the first oracle (v. 18). The phrase "to me" is added to indicate that the response to the delegation is mediated through Zechariah and not the priests (see 7:3). The decision begins with a listing of traditional times of fasting: "the fourth, the fifth, the seventh and the tenth months" (v. 19a).

Compared with the other notations (see 7:3b, 5b), this listing has two additional months. The significance for these days of the months is identical with the other months' commemoration: the tragic events leading to the destruction of Jerusalem. The fourth month commemorates the Babylonian attack on the walls (see 2 Kgs 25:3-7; Jer 39:2), while the tenth month marks the beginning of the siege of Jerusalem (see 1 Kgs 25:1-2; Jer 39:1).

Verse 19b dramatically reverses the commemorative status of the collective days of the four months. The days previously given to mourning and fasting are designated as "occasions of joy and gladness, cheerful festivals for the house of Judah" (v. 19b). The expressions in Hebrew identify times of celebratory banquets (see Esth 8:16-17); happiness at social festivities (1 Sam 18:6; 1 Kgs 1:40; Isa 9:2); and happy assemblies for cultic activity (Isa 33:20).

The addition "only love faithfulness and peace" (v. 19c; RSV: "truth and peace") stipulates qualities of living. "Truth," in particular, attends to how community members are challenged to interact with one another and how they regard one another (see vv. 16-17). Can the community be commanded to love truth and peace? The oracle states a promise for a better future if the community responds according to this norm (compare Deut 6:4-5; Amos 5:4; 6).

A prophetic formula introduces the second oracle (v. 20a). "Peoples, the inhabitants of many cities" (v. 20b), will approach Jerusalem (compare 2:11; Isa 2:2-4; 66:18-21; Mic 4:1-3). There will be a mutual interaction among them as they invite one another to approach (v. 21a). The same motivations of the delegation to approach Jerusalem (see 7:2-3) characterize the city-dwellers: "Come! let us go to implore the favor of the Lord . . . I, too, will go to seek the Lord" (v. 21b).

Verse 22 reiterates verse 21b by forming a *chiastic* structure, a literary device resembling an *X*. The first clause of verse 21b parallels the last clause of verse 22, forming the left stroke of the *X*. Likewise, the second clause of verse 21b parallels the first clause of verse 22, forming the right stroke of the *X*.

Verse 23 continues the notion of the repopulated city drawn from persons of the Diaspora and the nations. "Ten men of every nationality" refers to a number of completeness and the number needed to constitute a prayer grouping (v. 23a). What is even more remarkable is how these persons of different nationalities and tongues "shall take hold of every Jew by the edge of his garment and say, 'Let us go with you, for we have heard that God is with you' " (v. 23b).

The term "Jew" appears only in verse 23 and Jer 34:9. Some suggest that the role of invitation to approach Jerusalem gives the Diaspora Jews a significant role. Others find the expression a missionary statement. The proclamation "we have heard that God is with you" is the fulfillment of God's promise to the temple-community: "Return to me . . . and I will return to you" (1:3). The role of the community is twofold: to live with integrity and hasten the return of the Lord to Jerusalem; and to invite others to share in the Lord's blessings by approaching and residing in the city where God dwells.

Conclusion

First Zechariah, like Haggai, has been assessed according to the criterion of unfulfilled prophecy. The perspective is deceptive. It limits any contribution of the prophet to his contemporaries and subsequent communities of believers. When one evaluates the text according to literary form, redaction, and closely aligned religious insights, however, the prophet stands as an exemplary source of how to construct and discover meaning in the process of restoration.

Zechariah, like Haggai, had a few common goals. This is to be expected, since they functioned separately but as contemporaries.

a) Both encouraged efforts at temple reconstruction. Bleak conditions challenged their vision of the future importance of the temple. Its completion would symbolize the restoration of the community's relationship with God. God's presence would provide a new community identity.

b) The prophets proclaimed a necessary ethical component for the restoration of relationship with God and the continuance of this relationship. Yet neither prophet proposed a simple cause-effect relationship between human effort and God's response. They lived in the mystery of the faithful God who continued to reveal mercy within the community through "glory (*kabod*)" and "spirit (*ruach*)."

c) Leadership in the community was shared. Zerubbabel was a clear candidate for leadership, since he symbolized the restoration of a Davidic figure and stability to the returned exiles.

First Zechariah also contributes individual insights through the complex "night" visions and interpretive oracles:

a) The visions witness to his broad experience of God, whose presence is not limited to Jerusalem. Interesting characters, angels, and an interpreting assistant interact with him to provide a rich understanding of how and why God continues to be with the temple-community. The oracles added by a final editor bridge the distance between the experience of Zechariah and the interpretation necessary for later communities to understand that experience.

b) The visions are characterized by an indefinite geography, fluidity of movement, and solitary or frequent occurrence through "all the earth." No longer is Israel isolated in its efforts at restoration. The cosmos participates and supports the struggle. This dimension adds mystery and awe to the situation of "in betweenness," that is, a time between promises of a new community proclaimed during the Exile (see Isa 40–55; Ezek 40–48) and fulfillment for the recently returned exiles.

c) The visions are directed to "theological" concerns, that is, God's presence, restored ritual, and purity. God, however, is no longer localized in the temple but is described as "glory" and "a wall of fire" for the community. Restored ritual is dependent upon the purity of the high priest and the integrity of the community.

There is also a close correspondence between these concerns and other factors, including leadership, punishment of evil community members, and the future population of Jerusalem. Leadership is to be equally shared by civic and religious authorities, who assist God in the directives for the new community. "Curses" mete out punishment to those who are irresponsible toward one another. Possibilities of urban dwellers to populate Jerusalem are dependent on the cooperation of the Diaspora Jews.

INTRODUCTION: SECOND ZECHARIAH

Zech 9:1-14:21

The reader is invited to follow the suggestions outlined in the introduction to the Book of Zechariah (see p. 600). Reviewing sections of the introduction and preliminary considerations for First and Second Zechariah will provide a clearer context for the commentary on Second Zechariah.

Authorship

There is no indication of authorship. Although the earliest manuscript of the Minor Prophets from Qumran shows no break between Zech 1-8 and 9-14, modern scholarship does not agree that both parts originated from one author. The history of scholarship from the early 1700's, which includes the linguistic analysis of the past decade, offers the same conclusions.

Three arguments against the unity of authorship are presented:

a) The *content* of First Zechariah, which is concerned with temple reconstruction, historical figures, and dated oracles, contrasts with the material of Second Zechariah, which addresses God's judgments and "eschatological" promises (promises about God's future action). The historical context is obscure.

b) The *style* is considerably different. First Zechariah is a compilation of "night" visions and interpretive oracles written in prose, while Second Zechariah is a series of oracles derived from reference to earlier prophets and written in poetry. First-person references of the prophet are absent.

c) The *vocabulary* is different in introducing oracles. First Zechariah uses traditional prophetic formulas, whereas Second Zechariah uses the phrase "An oracle: The word of the Lord" to introduce the two major sections (9:1; 12:1). The vocabulary of Second Zechariah, like the style, is dependent on earlier prophets.

Dating of the text

There are no verses that contain any specific dates. Possibilities for identifying a historical context are dependent upon internal clues:

a) The use of preexilic and exilic prophecy (Isaiah, Hosea, Jeremiah, Ezekiel, Joel), as well as themes characteristic of Joel, for example "day of the Lord," indicates a postexilic context.

b) Some allusions to events that occur after 333 B.C.E. appear especially in chapter 9 (see the commentary on ch. 9).

c) Apocalyptic style and content, especially in chapter 14, suggest a period later than the early postexilic that characterizes First Zechariah.

The consensus among scholars is to date the text after the conquest of Alexander the Great (333 B.C.E.) and within two decades following his formation of the new empire. The final date for the editorial process of First and Second Zechariah is before 200 B.C.E. There is no agreement, however, about the number of editors, the extent of redaction, and the length of time required for the canonical shaping of Zechariah.

Composition of the text

How the oracles were ordered and edited is unknown. Scholars propose that two units of material, each three chapters long, were arranged with common superscriptions: "An oracle: the word of the Lord" (9:1; 12:1). The same superscription appears in Mal 1:1. The two units of Second Zechariah were appended to First Zechariah because of a perceived relationship. The fourteen chapters became the eleventh Minor Prophet. The one unit of Malachi was added to the other prophetic scrolls, thus constituting the Twelve Minor Prophets (see p. 572).

There are several problem verses in Second Zechariah due to the poetic language. Less rearrangement of Second Zechariah is suggested than for First Zechariah. The New English Bible is the only translation that suggests the following order: 9:1-11:17; 13:7-9; 12:1-14; 13:1-6; 14:1-21.

Outline of the text

PART ONE:	First Oracle: Judgments of God (9:1-11:17)
9:1a	Superscription
9:1b-8	Invasion by the Lord
9:9-10	Coming of the King
9:11-10:1	Victory for the Community

10:2–11:3	Shepherd Oracles
11:4-17	Shepherd Allegory
PART TWO:	Second Oracle: Restoration (12:1–14:21)
12:1	Superscription
12:2-9	Jerusalem and Judah
12:10–13:1	Mourning in Jerusalem
13:2-6	Purification in Jerusalem
13:7-9	Sword and Fire
14:1	Superscription
14:2-5	War and Victory
14:6-11	Transformation of Land
14:12-15	Plague and Tumult
14:16-21	Celebration in Jerusalem

COMMENTARY: SECOND ZECHARIAH

PART ONE: JUDGMENTS OF GOD

Zech 9:1–11:17

Part One is an interweaving of God's judgments: destruction and restoration. All judgments are future-oriented. Unlike the future proposed by First Zechariah, however, this future appears closer and virtually imminent. There is one theme that indicates development among the edited oracles. It is the contrast between the leadership that genuine and false shepherds exercise over the community.

9:1a Superscription. The wording of the superscription, "An oracle: The word of the Lord," has already been noted (see p. 616). The translation is common to most versions. The Hebrew, however, specifies the first word as "burden."

As an introduction to the first and second oracles (9:1–11:17; 11:1–14:21), the superscription suggests that a particular responsibility has been given to the prophet on behalf of God's people. Since the first oracle is equally concerned with God's judgments of destruction and restoration, the unknown prophet might well hesitate to proclaim God's message. Yet God's word must be announced as it was received.

The rest of the superscription directs the Lord's word to "the land of Hadrach, and Damascus is its resting place" (9:1a). Although Hadrach does not occur in the Old Testament, archeological data locates it in Syria north of Hamath (v. 2). Damascus, the capital, is located in central Syria. What is the relationship of God's word to this country? The translation "against the land" suggests God's negative judgment toward Syria, especially Damascus, a traditional enemy (see Amos 1:2).

9:1b-8 Invasion by the Lord. Verse 1b describes additional "cities of Aram" and "all the tribes of Israel" as belonging to the Lord. Verse 1 proclaims God's judgment against northern cities that belong to God just as Israel does. Verses 2 and 3 enumerate additional cities under God's judgment: Hamath (in Syria), Tyre and Sidon (south along the seacoast). Some commentators identify the cities (vv. 1-7) as those conquered by Alexander as he destroyed the Persian empire and promised a new age. Alexander may have raised hopes for the messianic age as he conquered Israel's enemies.

The wisdom and riches connected with Tyre and Sidon (vv. 2b-3) will be useless against the Lord's attack and destruction "by fire" (v. 4). Other southern cities, such as Ashkelon, Gaza, Ekron, will witness the consequences and respond with fear, anguish, and despair. The king will flee, as will the inhabitants, and the "baseborn will occupy Ashdod" (vv. 4b-6a; see Neh 13:24).

A grammatical change to first person singular (v. 6a) heightens the role of the Lord in the invasion. God will intervene to destroy the pride of the Philistines and their abominable sacrifices. Nonetheless, even the Philistines will become part of God's "remnant" and will be "like a family in Judah" (v. 7). The final note promises the Lord's protection for all who will live in Jerusalem, "my house." The designation of the trespassers and the promise of the Lord's watching parallel two passages of First Zechariah (see 7:14 and 4:10b).

9:9-10 Coming of the king. The transformation of God's judgment of destruction to restoration noted in the previous section may be the context for the description of the future king (vv. 9-10). Exhortations to rejoice and shout for joy are addressed to the community named "daughter Zion . . . . daughter Jerusalem" (v. 9a; compare Zech 2:10).

The king will be "a just savior . . . meek, and riding . . . on a colt" (v. 9b; compare

Matt 21:5; John 12:15). Most commentators identify the figure as a messianic king who is "just," one actively involved in all aspects of vindication. He is "meek" in his corresponding role as "servant" (compare Isa 49:4; 50:8; 53:12). Riding on a colt was a custom of officials (see Gen 49:10-11; Judg 5:10; 1 Kgs 1:33).

Again a grammatical change to first person singular (see v. 6a) emphasizes the Lord's role. All implements of war will be banished: chariot, horse, warrior's bow (v. 10a). Reconciliation of the northern (Ephraim) and southern (Jerusalem) kingdoms issues forth in "peace to the nations" and worldwide "dominion" (v. 10b; compare Ps 78:7-8).

9:11–10:1 Victory for the community. The section consists of three oracles joined by word associations. The images of return, "theophany," that is, God's manifestation, and restoration of the community and land are highlighted. Earlier history and references to ideas in Second Isaiah are bases for the development of the section.

The grammatical change to first person indicates a new oracle (vv. 11-13). Israel is addressed directly: "As for you, for the blood of your covenant with me . . ." (v. 11a; see Exod 24:8; compare Mark 14:24). The relationship prompts the Lord to initiate a rescue of prisoners from the dungeon of exile (vv. 11-12a; compare Isa 42:7; 61:1b). The exile experience will be reversed: "This very day I will return you double" (v. 12b; compare Isa 40:2; 61:7).

Those who captured Israel will be judged by the captives. Verse 13, which concludes the section, describes how Judah and Ephraim (the totality of Israel) will be as a bow and arrow (RSV) for God's judgment against their enemies (compare Ps 7:13-14). They will be as a "warrior's sword" against "your sons, O Yavan." Although Yavan occurs in the Old Testament to indicate the Greeks (see Gen 10:2, 4; Isa 66:19; Joel 4:4 [3:3]), it probably was added here during the Maccabean era (ca. 167 B.C.E.) to point to current oppressors of Israel.

The role of the Lord as a victorious warrior (vv. 14-15) is the second oracle of the section. It draws on the concept of the holy war (see the commentary on Joel 2:1-11; compare Pss 18:7-15; 77:16-20). The images of lightning, trumpet, and storm correspond to God's theophany on Mount Sinai (v. 14; compare Exod 24:9-10, 15, 18). God protects the covenanted community as they engage in the battle, overcoming and trampling their enemies (v. 15a; see 2 Sam 22:8-18). The victory is described as a sacrificial ritual (v. 15b; Exod 24:6-8; compare Lev 16:14-15; 17:11).

The victory for the community is described in the third oracle (9:16–10:1). God will save the people, who are "like a flock" and "jewels in a crown raised aloft over his land" (v. 16; compare Zech 6:14). Abundance of grain, new wine, rain, and grassy fields indicates a restored community and land (9:17–10:1; see Joel 2:19, 22-24; compare Hag 1:10-11; 2:19).

10:2–11:3 Shepherd oracles. This section and the following one (11:4-17) provide different images of shepherds. The theme constitutes over fifty percent of the first oracle (9:1–11:17). Again, the oracles are separated by third-person and first-person grammatical changes. Themes of genuine leadership, restoration, and punishment for Israel's enemies are used.

The Lord speaks (vv. 2-5). Verse 2 is a transition connecting the theme of "grassy fields" for "everyone" (v. 1b) to the shepherd and sheep theme (v. 2b). "Diviners" have duped the community, utilizing "teraphim" or household gods (see Judg 17:5; 18:5) for future speculations, which God judges as "nonsense," "false visions," "deceitful dreams," and "empty comfort" (v. 2a; compare Jer 23:32; 27:9). Many commentators think use of the teraphim was limited to the preexilic period and the chaotic condition of the community before the Exile. To some extent, they were also used in the postexilic community (compare Mal 3:5a; Isa 65:3-5; 66:17).

Earlier tradition claims that treacherous leadership led the community astray (see Hos 4:4-9; Mic 3; Jer 2:26). The shepherd as leader had been a personal symbol of Hammurabi (1728–1686 B.C.E.). Later "shepherd" was used to designate God (see Gen 49:24; Ps 23), as was "just king" (see Isa 44:28; Jer 23:2-4; Mic 5:4; Ezek 34:23-24).

"Shepherds" and "leaders" are parallel terms and the objects of God's wrath (v. 3a). The verb states that God "visits" different persons, God's visitation "will punish the leaders," but the visitation of the flock results in making them a "stately war horse" (v. 3b). The flock, identified as the house of Judah, is the context for the development of the victor-warrior in verses 4-5 (see 9:11–10:1).

Verses 4 and 5 list a number of traditional metaphors which indicate the type of leadership that will come forth from Judah ("from him"—v. 4). The Revised Standard Version and the New English Bible render the sense of the Hebrew better than the New American Bible for both verses. In verse 4a three metaphors occur: "cornerstone" (NAB: "leader") indicates stability (see Judg 20:2; 1 Sam 14:38; compare Ps 118:22); "tent peg" (NAB: "chief") suggests endurance (see Isa 22:23); "warrior's bow" (NAB also) suggests fearless courage (see 2 Kgs 13:17; compare Rev 6:2). Verse 5 identifies the leaders as "warriors" who will be victorious: "the Lord is with them . . . ."

The second oracle, a composite of several divine proclamations, develops the theme of restoration (vv. 6-12). Verse 6 concludes the focus on Judah by noting God's activities of strengthening and saving Judah and the "house of Joseph," that is, the northern kingdom (v. 6a). Judah and Joseph will be brought back and treated with mercy (see Jer 33:26; compare Hos 11; Zech 7:13). A wonderful expression describes the new situation: "They shall be as though I had never cast them off . . . ." (v. 6b).

Verses 7-9 reveal the future of Ephraim (the northern kingdom). As "valiant warriors" (RSV; see Judg 7:24-25; 8:1-3) with cheerful hearts, their children will witness them and "be glad . . . and rejoice in the Lord" (v. 7; compare Isa 29:19). The Lord will bring them back from exile with a "whistle," that is, a signal. It is an ironic expression first used to denote God's "signal" to Israel's enemies (compare Isa 5:26-30). Ephraim will experience the past in a new way (v. 8a; compare v. 6b). Although scattered "among the nations," they "remember" the Lord and "rear their children and return" (v. 9).

Verses 10-12 continue the theme of restoration of the exiles. Egypt and Assyria were countries involved in the destruction of the northern and southern kingdoms (see Isa 7:18). Gilead and Lebanon are fertile, rich areas ideal for restoration. In Egypt, the Nile will dry up and the scepter will be taken away. In Assyria, "pride . . . will be cast down" (v. 11). For those returning from exile, however, God's strength will enable them to continue home (v. 12; compare v. 6; Isa 40:31).

The final section is a "taunt song" against the treacherous shepherds (11:1-3). The literary form was used by earlier prophets to proclaim God's judgment on Israel's enemies (see 5:2; Isa 14:4-21; Jer 6:1-5). Here the enemies of Israel are compared to trees, and their leaders are shepherds (compare Isa 10:33-34; Ezek 31). Lebanon and Bashan are particularly singled out for judgment; they were often linked together in earlier prophecy (see Isa 2:13; Jer 22:20; Ezek 27:5-6).

Lebanon is addressed first: cedars and cypress are destroyed, devastating the wealth of the area (vv. 1-2a). Cedar was a symbol of the royal house of Judah (see Ezek 17:3, 4, 12f.). Next Bashan is considered: "the impenetrable forest is cut down!" (v. 2b). The different trees symbolize various nations. Finally the shepherds lament, for "their glory has been ruined" (v. 3a). "The roaring of the young lions" may suggest other leaders whose territory is devastated "in the jungle of the Jordan" (v. 3b; compare Jer 25:34-37; 50:44; Ezek 19:1-9).

11:4-17 Shepherd allegory. This section is prose except for verse 17, which is poetry. While the themes of shepherd and sheep have been noted above (see 9:16; 10:2, 3, 8-9; 11:3), they are most developed here. Oracles in the first person contain three symbolic acts. Most commentators interpret the section as allegory, proposing that the symbolic acts are a written imitation of earlier prophetic tradition. The section is divided into three parts: verses 4-6; 7-14; 15-17.

The superscription of the first oracle (vv. 4-6) is unusual (v. 4a). The phrase "my God," found in many prayers (see Pss 7:2; 18:3; 22:2; 88:2), suggests a separation of the speaker from the hearers (see Joel 1:3; Josh 9:23). The prophet may be initiating controversy both through use of the phrase as well as through his self-identification as the shepherd of the flock (v. 4b).

The prophet uses the image of a market with buyers and sellers of sheep to condemn the leaders with Israel. The buyers—foreign nations that occupied Israel—"slay them with impunity," while the sellers—religious leaders *within* Israel—"do not even feel for them" (v. 5; compare Amos 2:6; Jer 38:8-22; Neh 5:10-13). God's judgment mirrors the conduct of the shepherds. Neither leaders nor people will be delivered by God (v. 6b).

The second oracle (vv. 7-14) contrasts the prophet as leader with previous leaders (vv. 4-6). Verse 7 parallels verse 4b. The Lord's command to "shepherd the flock" (v. 4b) is obeyed by the prophet, who is employed by the sheep merchants (v. 7a). Staffs in hand, the prophet "fed the flock" (v. 7b).

Verse 8a is a gloss whose meaning is unclear. Who are the "three shepherds"? How did they function? At least forty interpretations have been suggested in the past century. Since there is little information about what transpired in the Jewish community between 350–200 B.C.E. (see p. 574), it is believed that the three shepherds may have functioned during that time either as high priests or as temple officials.

Verse 8b resumes the narrative and indicates the mutual dissatisfaction of shepherd (prophet) and flock (undetermined). The prophet's rejection impels him to withhold leadership from the people. He leaves them to their own resources (v. 9).

The next response of the prophet is to "snap asunder" both staffs. Verses 10 and 14 function as an inclusion for verses 11-13. The literary structure is similar to the "vision within the vision" (see the commentary on 4:1-6a; 10b-14; 6b-10a). Verse 10 describes the prophet's action of breaking his first staff, called "Favor," and interprets it as "breaking off the covenant which I had made with all peoples." The implication is that gentile nations as well had contracted a covenant with God. The second staff, called "Union," is also broken, which is interpreted as "breaking off the brotherhood of Judah and Israel" (v. 14), the period of the divided kingdom before and after the Exile.

The second symbolic act is described in verses 11-13. The prophet indicates through his action that in rejecting him, the people have rejected God (compare Matt 27:4-6). In Hebrew, "treasury" is also translated "to the potter." Artisans worked in the temple area to provide clay receptacles for the treasury, which held sacred objects and served as a bank for private holdings (2 Macc 3:10ff.; compare Matt 27:6-9).

The third oracle (vv. 15-17) includes a command of the Lord to the prophet to perform a third symbolic act. Although the description of the act is omitted, its significance is emphasized: "God will raise up" an utterly incompetent shepherd unconcerned that the flock will "perish," "stray," need healing or food (v. 16a). Who is the foolish shepherd? Again, the verse defies a clear historical context. Some commentators suggest the office of high priest (compare Ezek 34:1-6).

The allegory concludes with a poetic "woe" imprecation to the "foolish shepherd who forsakes the flock" (v. 17a). Curses of a useless arm and blind eye will render the shepherd incompetent and unable to lead (v. 17b).

PART TWO: RESTORATION

Zech 12:1–14:21

Part Two is a collection of edited oracles about God's restoration of the temple-community. Future battles, purification, and blessings will occur "on that day" for the community as well as for the nations. The collection may have been added to restore communal hope after Alexander's career did not fulfill messianic expectations. Part Two, especially chapter 14, contains more proto-apocalyptic characteristics than Part One (see p. 577).

12:1 Superscription. "An oracle: the word of the Lord" repeats 9:1 and introduces Part Two (see p. 616). The phrase "concerning Israel" was probably added by an editor, since Israel is not mentioned again. It may, however, refer to all the inhabitants of Israel (see 1 Chr 21:1; 2 Chr 29:24). Verse 1b is a new introduction: "Thus says the Lord." The description that follows identifies the Lord as creator, similar to other hymnic identifications (see Isa 40:22; 42:5; Ps 24:1-2).

12:2-9 Jerusalem and Judah. This section is a series of divine oracles proclaimed in the first person. The creator God promises prominence to Jerusalem and Judah as victorious over the nations. Traditional metaphors are used frequently. The phrase "on that day" occurs in five verses of chapter 12 (sixteen times in chapters 12–14).

The first oracle is constructed in perfect parallelism (vv. 2-3). God will make "Jerusalem . . . a bowl . . . and a weighty stone for all peoples roundabout" (vv. 2a, 3a). Both will thwart enemies: "stupefy . . . injure themselves badly" (vv. 2b, 3b). The bowl is a symbol of God's wrath toward Israel's enemies (see Jer 25:15-16; Ezek 23:31-34; compare Isa 51:17), while the weighty stone indicates an unmovable barrier for the enemy (see Isa 8:14-15; 28:16; compare Zech 3:9). "For all peoples roundabout" is a repetition of Joel 4:11-12 [3:11-12].

The second oracle presents the Lord as the victorious warrior on behalf of Judah and Jerusalem (vv. 4-5). The third oracle describes the "clans of Judah" taking a more active role in the vindication of Jerusalem (v. 6). Jerusalem, however, will remain "on its own site" (v. 6b).

The next two oracles have a grammatical change to the third person, that is, the prophet speaks of the Lord (vv. 7-8). The Lord's preference for Judah is indicated by saving her "tents . . . first" (v. 7a) in order to prevent the exaltation of the "glory of the house of David and . . . inhabitants of Jerusalem" (v. 7b). It is unclear whether the references to Jerusalem mean that the community also needs purification or that the verse describes the humbled condition of the community in an ironic manner. Either interpretation provides the context for the next verse as well.

The Lord's protective care as "shield" will protect the Jerusalemites (v. 8). The verse recalls the prestigious memory of David, whom supplicants addressed as an "angel of God" (see 1 Sam 29:10; 2 Sam 14:17, 20; 19:28). Was David's line still represented in the community? Were there new hopes and dreams of a final age when David's ancestor would reign? The difficulty of dating the oracle prevents a response.

The final oracle (v. 9) is God's proclamation about the enemies of Jerusalem. It is a summary of the section.

12:10–13:1 Mourning in Jerusalem. The abrupt departure from the scene of the liberation of Jerusalem (12:1-9) to that of murder and mourning prompted some editions of the Bible to transpose the section to the end of 11:4-17. Nonetheless, the context of the previous passage (12:1-9) prepares for this section with its challenge for repentance. Verse 10, especially difficult to interpret, appears in Johannine literature (John 19:37; Rev 1:7), in Handel's *Messiah*, and in Christian devotion to the crucified Jesus.

Verse 10a promises God's gift, "a spirit of grace and petition," to the "house of David and . . . the inhabitants of Jerusalem." In addition to military victory (vv. 2-4; 6-9) and recognition of God's strength (v. 5), the community will participate in an interior renewal of heart (compare Ezek 36:26-27; 39:29; Joel 3:1-2 [2:28-29]). The "grace" of repentance appears to be the focus of the conversion. It is linked to a specific event: "They shall look on him whom they have thrust through." Intensive and extensive mourning follow (vv. 10b-14).

Who has been "pierced" (RSV)? Hebrew and Greek manuscripts differ here. Some read "on him," some read "on me." The more difficult reading ("on me") is preferred. The emendation "on him" denies the possibility that it is God who is pierced. Some commentators also question the translation "thrust through." Is it literal? Metaphorical? (see Lam 4:9; Prov 12:18). The same question arises when comparing verse 10 to Isa 53:5, which parallels the verse exactly.

Most commentators propose a literal interpretation for "piercing." The identity of the pierced one varies. Possibilities include a representative of God; a collectivity, such as the martyrs of Judah in the Maccabean era; a historical figure who had been murdered, for example, Josiah, Onias III, or Simon Maccabeus; a charismatic figure cast out by officials; the good shepherd of Zech 11. The identity remains unclear. The only "facts" from the verse are of a man murdered by the inhabitants of Jerusalem. Mourning and repentance occur afterward.

Verse 10b begins the detailed description of the mourning. The loss is especially poignant. The description recalls the Egyptians grieving over their first-born (Exod 4:22) and David's lament over his first-born (2 Sam 12:15-23) and over Absalom (2 Sam 18:33).

Two images note the intensity of grieving (v. 11). The name Hadadrimmon recalls the lamentation rites associated with the fall and spring seasons ritualized by the pagan weather-gods Hadad and Rimmon. Megiddo recalls the historical site at which the beloved King Josiah was killed (609 B.C.E.). National rites of mourning were conducted yearly (see 2 Chr 35:24-25).

The "land" and all its peoples are involved in mourning. First, royal houses are mentioned (v. 12; see 2 Sam 5:14), then priestly houses (v. 13; see Num 3:18), then everyone else (v. 14). The phrase "and their wives" (5 times) suggests the separation of women and men during mourning.

Mourning "on that day" is connected with the opportunity "on that day" for purification "from sin and uncleanness" (13:1), which include all human misconduct, ritual and sexual impurity. There was a ritual cleansing for Zerubbabel and the community (see Zech 3:4, 9) and a similar promise according to Ezekiel (see Ezek 36:25).

In Isa 53:5 the piercing and death of God's messenger are related to forgiveness of sin. Yet in 13:1 Zechariah does not identify the pierced one as "servant." The identity of the fountain, its relationship to the one "thrust through," and the effect on the community are perplexing. The interpretation is difficult for us because Christian tradition has appropriated 12:10 and 13:1 to refer to Jesus.

13:2-6 Purification in Jerusalem. As Jerusalem would be cleansed of bogus leaders (see the commentary on 11:4-17), so idol worship and false prophets would be purged from the land. Ezekiel had specified that rejection of idolatry was part of the purification of the community (see Ezek 36). Some suggest that even worship of the temple may have been a problem.

Idol worship may have been promoted by dishonest prophets who sought to reclaim the glory of the preexilic era for themselves. The "spirit of uncleanness" associated with them impeded the community's relationship with God. The phrase occurs only here in the Old Testament, while it occurs frequently in the Gospels as something over which Jesus had power.

The punishment accorded to false prophets is described in verses 3-6. Parental accusation initiates the process (v. 3a; compare Deut 13:1-9; 18:19-22). If the son continued to prophesy, the parents were to "thrust him through" (v. 3b). The verb is the same used in 12:10.

Verse 4 suggests that the false prophet is somewhat honest by being ashamed to speak about visions or to assume a "hairy mantle" for leadership (see 2 Kgs 1:8). The irony of verse 5, however, contradicts this. There the false prophet mimics Amos, who preferred to till the soil (see Amos 7:14).

The deception is uncovered in verse 6, where the false prophet explains that his wounds are the result of punishment by his parents (v. 4b). Several suggest, however, that the lacerations were part of a ritual enacted for idols (see 1 Kgs 18:28), and the "dear ones" (RSV: "friends") were associates in the idolatrous worship (see Hos 2:7, 10-12; Ezek 23:5-9).

13:7-9 Sword and fire. The poetic section takes up the theme of shepherd and sheep. In contrast to previous sections (10:3; 11:4-17), where the shepherds were guilty of not fulfilling their duties, this shepherd is not condemned. He is described as the one who "is my associate" (v. 7a). The Hebrew word is otherwise limited to Leviticus, where regulations are given about relationships among the Israelites. "Near neighbor" is the translation there (see Lev 6:2; 18:20).

Who is this shepherd? As is the case with the pierced one, there are several interpretations. Some link the shepherd with the one who appeared before (see 11:4, 17; 12:10). Others suggest a good leader not previously mentioned. However uncertain the identification, the text describes the shepherd as the one against whom the sword is raised (13:7). Consequently, the sheep scatter and God turns a hand "against the little ones." Why the shepherd is struck down is not clear. The act precipitates the dispersal of the Lord's community, that is, the sheep.

The consequences are quite extreme. Two thirds "shall be cut off and perish" (v. 8a; compare Ezek 5:1-12). The remaining one third will be judged again. Traditional metaphors for God's cleansing action describe their plight: "into the fire" (compare 3:2; Ezek 5:4; Mal 3:3); refined "as silver is refined"; tested "as gold is tested" (v. 9b). The result is a reconciled relationship: "They shall call upon my name, and I will hear them . . . They are my people . . . The Lord is my God" (v. 9c).

14:1 Superscription. The ominous note that begins the final chapter of Zechariah parallels the "day of the Lord" (see Joel 1:15; 2:1). Two battles are then described in which the Lord will be present as antagonist against and protagonist for Jerusalem (vv. 2-3).

14:2-5 War and victory. In a first-person oracle God announces plans for "gathering all the nations against Jerusalem" (v. 2a). Grim consequences mark the defeat of the city: capture, plundered houses, ravished women, and half the inhabitants sent into exile (v. 2b). The rest of the people will remain in the city (compare Isa 1:9).

A grammatical change to the third person narrates another battle in which the Lord will fight against the nations (v. 3; compare Isa 43:13). Verses 4-5 contain the only mention of the Mount of Olives in the Old Testament (compare 2 Sam 15:30), while the earthquake is compared to the one attributed to Uzziah's seizure of priestly functions (see 2 Chr 26:16-21). No Davidic figure is mentioned; God's presence is primary.

14:6-11 Transformation of the land. The changes in the land noted in verses 4-5 continue in this section. Vegetation, animals, and persons alike will benefit from the favorable conditions (v. 7; compare Rev 21:23, 25).

According to verse 8, the valuable gift of water will be assured (compare Ezek 47:1-2; John 4:18; 7:37-39). The changes in the cosmos are related to the Lord's kingship "over the whole earth" (see Ps 97:1). It will be recognized and proclaimed in credal formula (v. 9; compare Deut 6:4-5).

Jerusalem will be accorded greater prominence (v. 10a). The territory described is from the reign of Josiah, who ruled twenty years before the Exile. Geba is six miles north of Jerusalem, and Rimmon is thirty-five miles southwest of Jerusalem (see 2 Kgs 23:8). Jerusalem, however, "shall remain exalted in its place" (v. 10b). Unfortunately, the places for the area markers of the city (v. 10c) are difficult to locate. Today they indicate four directions.

14:12-15 Plague and tumult. This section is an addition that enlarges upon the description of verse 3. The style is exaggerated, characteristic of apocalyptic writing. Verse 12 describes how the plague will affect "flesh," "eyes," and "tongue" (compare Ezek 28:21-22; 39:17-20; Rev 16:6; 19:17-18). Verse 13 attributes the "great tumult" among neighbors to the Lord. "Judah also shall fight against Jerusalem" (v. 14) ought to be interpreted as "with" or "in" Jerusalem, which the Hebrew also allows. Verse 15 concludes the section by mentioning a similar plague that will affect all the animals.

14:16-21 Celebration in Jerusalem. The final section of Second Zechariah parallels the corresponding section in First Zechariah (8:20-23). The verses indicate that nations that were Jerusalem's enemies will come to worship and celebrate the feast of Booths (v. 16). A curse will be leveled against "any of the families of the earth" who do not come for worship. "Lack of rainfall" will be the punishment (compare v. 8). The feast of Booths occurred just before the autumn rains.

Because of the Nile River, rain shortage will not be a serious problem for the Egyptians who fail to come to Jerusalem. However, the plague is the potential curse for them and for all the nations that fail to celebrate the feast of Booths (vv. 18-19).

The concluding verses suggest the total dedication of Jerusalem and Judah to God. The temple itself is not the source of holiness. Instead, ordinary objects will become holy because of the persons who own them.

The Book of Zechariah has no conclusion. The editor probably wanted to use Malachi as the final message. For this purpose, the beginning of Malachi parallels Part One and Part Two of Second Zechariah (see pp. 616-17).

Conclusion

The two parts of Second Zechariah develop the future judgment of God upon the temple-community and upon the nations. Chapters 9–11 outline battles against the enemy, consolation of the community, and the concept of shepherd and sheep. Chapters 12–14 use proto-apocalyptic language and content to dramatize what mourning and celebration entail. The second part also broadens the concept of the significance of Jerusalem and Judah for the nations.

Are there points of continuity between First Zechariah and Second Zechariah? The editor of the scroll and the persons responsible for the canonical status of Zechariah used literary devices to ensure that all fourteen chapters would be considered as *one* Minor Prophet (see pp. 601, 616).

Beyond literary considerations, there are religious relationships of continuity and development between the chapters.

a) Historically, First and Second Zechariah addressed communities separated by nearly two hundred years. While the political situation was different in the Persian and the Greek empires, the religious struggles were similar. Who will provide civic and religious leadership? What is required? Can an emperor fulfill expectations?

b) In proclaiming a future in which God would initiate victory, both communities heard about their renewed relationship to

God. God as warrior and protective presence would give them comfort and support for their activities. Before this happened, however, the community would suffer the ravages of war and the comprehensive process of purification.

c) Fidelity to God's covenant through faithful living and restored worship would characterize those who lived in Judah. Evil is not denied but recognized. God assured the communities that evil will not be ultimately victorious. Transgressors could repent or be punished.

d) God's relationship to the nations, as well as their own relationship to traditional enemies, was developed in radically new perspectives. "On that day" Israel and the nations would share in God's compassion. They would live together in a land free from war and for holiness. Communal worship would be one symbol of the new reality.

e) The vision of an unexpected future was offered to both communities while the uncertainties of the present weighed heavily in their daily experience. How would the communities prepare for the blessings of "that day"? Attention to God's word spoken in the past and reinterpreted by the minor prophet Zechariah would provide some direction in living during periods of "in betweenness."

MALACHI

Mary Margaret Pazdan, O.P.

INTRODUCTION

Authorship

What is known about the author of the Book of Malachi is derived from 3:1, where the phrase "my messenger" occurs. An editor probably used the Hebrew transliteration (*mal'achi*) "Malachi" for 1:1, where the proper name appears. The name Malachi does not occur anywhere else in the Old Testament. The absence of any precise chronology and genealogy in the superscription (1:1) lends support to the suggestion that the author was an anonymous prophet.

The superscription includes the word "oracle" (the Hebrew means "burden") rather than a personal name. It parallels Zech 9:1; 12:1, where the literary device marks collections of oracles that were added to First Zechariah (see p. 616). While a common superscription unites Second Zechariah and Malachi, the historical background, literary structures, and religious significance of the collected oracles differ greatly.

Dating of the text

According to its canonical position, the Book of Malachi is the twelfth of the Minor Prophets. This location is not conclusive for establishing a chronology of the text. The Book of Malachi describes situations that place the prophet about fifty years after the completion of the temple (515 B.C.E.) and just before the ministry of Ezra (about 460–445 B.C.E.). For an understanding of the historical context, see pp. 573–574.

The book offers some perspective about the challenges the prophet encountered. Although the community was under the office of a governor (see 1:8; Hag 1:1; Neh 5:14), civic authority had declined. The priests had assumed civic and religious authority for the community. The priests, however, were irresponsible leaders, failing to correct several abuses: worship, moral and social problems, and mixed marriages.

The book offers valuable insights into Jewish communities in the mid-fifth century B.C.E. It corresponds to Ezra and Nehemiah and supplements these books. It is a historical witness to how a community may participate in the process of restoration with a population of about twenty thousand living in an area twenty by twenty-five miles square.

Composition of the text

A collection of oracles has been edited and unified by a literary device called the disputation. It is a catechetical structure consisting of three elements: (a) an affirmation of God or the prophet occurs at the beginning of each section; (b) a question arises from the audience, usually a reproach or a complaint; (c) God or the prophet responds often with an argument.

The prophet and the editor depend on Ezekiel and Deuteronomy for ideas and images for the disputation. The Levitical sermons of the Chronicler are similar in structure and content. The two appendices were added to conclude the Book of Malachi and the scroll of the Twelve Minor Prophets. The identification of the precursor of the messianic day links the collection to the New Testament (see the commentary on 3:23-24).

Outline of the book

Like Joel and First Zechariah, where the numbering of chapters and verses are different, the Book of Malachi has one discrepancy in the numbering. This commentary, based on the New American Bible, follows the Hebrew text, while other Bibles and commentaries may use the Greek text. The chart compares the versions.

Hebrew Text	*Greek Text*
3:19-24	4:1-6

In this commentary the numbering of the Greek text is in brackets.

PART ONE:	Oracles (1:2–3:21 [1:2–4:3])
1:1	Superscription
1:2-5	First Oracle: God's Love for Israel
1:6–2:9	Second Oracle: Sins of the Priests
2:10-16	Third Oracle: Sins of the Community
2:17–3:5	Fourth Oracle: God's Justice
3:6-12	Fifth Oracle: Ritual Offenses
3:13-21 [3:13–4:3]	Sixth Oracle: God's Servants
PART TWO:	Appendices (3:22-24 [4:4-6])
3:22 [4:4]	Conclusion of Twelve Minor Prophets
3:23-24 [4:5-6]	Identification of Precursor

COMMENTARY

PART ONE: ORACLES

Mal 1:2–3:21 [1:2–4:3]

The six sections of Part One are addressed exclusively to Israel and concern its covenant relationship with God. A covenant theme is developed in the first oracle, which proclaims God's love for Israel (1:2-5). It forms an inclusion with the first appendix, where the people are enjoined to "remember the laws of Moses . . . the statutes and ordinances for all Israel" (3:22 [4:4]). Abuses within the community are discussed in connection with covenant stipulations.

1:1 Superscription. For discussion of "an oracle" and "Malachi," see above (p. 625). "Israel" refers to the whole nation, not merely the northern kingdom. The phrase introduces the focus of Part One: concern for the Jewish community and the experiences of daily life. There is no discussion about the role of the nations; neither are there any judgments of future orientation.

1:2-5 First oracle: God's love for Israel. The catechetical pattern, the structure for the oracles, uses language suggestive of an intimate relationship between the dialogue partners. The oracle begins with a statement of the Lord: "I have loved you" (v. 2a). Anticipating the listeners' response, the Lord's oracle continues: "but you say, 'How have you loved us?'" (v. 2b).

The disputation concludes with a response from the Lord (vv. 3-5). The Edomite situation is offered as a vivid memory from tradition. The mutual distrust of two brothers (Esau and Jacob) ignited enmity between their families and descendants, an enmity that grew to an irreconcilable impasse when Babylon invaded Jerusalem (586 B.C.E.). Complicity *with* the enemy and *against* Judah was unforgivable to the exiles and their descendants (for the historical development of the tradition, see p. 586 and the commentary on Obad 10-14.

In verse 3a God asks a rhetorical question to situate the response: "Was not Esau Jacob's brother?" Next, the declaration of God's love identifies Jacob as the special one (v. 3b). The Hebrew verb designates the *elective* sense of "love." The specific meaning was used in the covenantal context when God declared love for Israel (see Deut 4:37; 7:7, 8; 10:15) and extended an invitation to Israel to respond in love (see Deut 5:10; 6:5; 11:1, 13).

The choice of Jacob ought to be seen as an election. This is not clear in the English translation. The election of Jacob rather than Esau does not entail "hatred" toward Esau. It is a matter of choice, of the mysterious decision of God. Ironically, although Jacob was chosen, his family experienced the Exile while Esau's did not. Paul uses verses 2-3 to develop the theme of election and predestination in Rom 9:13. In the present context, however, predestination is not the issue.

Another appeal to the community's experience is remembrance of the fate of Edom after the Exile. The Lord ravaged the area, toppling the mountains (where the tribe lived in safety) and ruining the land (v. 3c). Historically, the event corresponds to the raids of Arabian tribes that greatly diminished Edom's influence in the Negeb about a century after the fall of Jerusalem.

The downfall of Edom appears to be permanent. Even if they attempt "to rebuild the ruins . . . I will tear down" (v. 4a). More devastating than the ruined land is the name that Edom will bear forever: "wicked country" (RSV) and the judgment of the Lord: "the people with whom the Lord is angry forever" (v. 4b).

The oracle concludes with a third appeal to experience (v. 5a). The conviction of being chosen by the faithful God will impel the community to praise (v. 5b; compare Zech 9:1-8). The ironic expectation of the prophet is a hope that the community will become observant; look beyond Israel and acknowledge that God's dominion is greater than the "land of Israel."

1:6–2:9 Second oracle: Sins of the priests. Eight oracles have been combined to disclose the two principal sins of the priests: offering polluted sacrifices (1:6-14) and abrogating the roles of teacher and leader (2:1-9). Each oracle is identified by an introductory or concluding prophetic formula: "says the Lord of hosts." The literary structure continues the disputation format. The characteristic elements indicate expansions.

The sin of offering polluted sacrifices is described in two sections (vv. 6-9; 10-14). The first section begins with a comparison of familial and household relationships with covenant relationship (v. 6a). The Lord questions the fidelity of the covenant partners. The tone of the rhetorical questions suggests that the covenant relationship has deteriorated: "Where is the honor due to me? Where is the reverence due to me?" (v. 6b; compare Exod 4:22; Hos 11:1; Isa 1:2).

The prophetic formula follows (v. 6b). What is unusual here is the addition "to you, O priests, who despise his name." The grammatical change from the third person to the second person suggests that the judgment is that of the prophet who has spoken the Lord's word or of an editor. The charge of despising the Lord's name is extremely serious. It is equivalent to despising the very being of God.

The next two topics are concerned with priestly matters (vv. 6c-7: see v. 12). There were very strict standards for suitable sacrificial offerings (see Lev 22:18-25; Deut 15:21; 17:1). Contemporary sociological criticism of biblical texts confirms the complexity of standards in regard to purity (holiness) and pollution (sinfulness).

The phrase "table of the Lord" appears only here in the Old Testament, although the idea appears elsewhere (see Ps 23:5; Ezek 44:16). The tables for slaughtering the sacrifices were located at the gates of the inner court of the temple. A single table was located in the sanctuary, where only the priest was allowed (see Ezek 40:39-43).

The questions about sacrifice are answered by additional rhetorical questions of the Lord appealing to priestly experiences (v. 8; see vv. 3-5). Blind, lame, and sick animals constitute "polluted food" (v. 8a). Such offerings would not be acceptable to the governor nor invite his hospitality (v. 8b). The governor's refusal and attitude are the analogy for God's disposition. An ironic question from the prophet concludes the oracle (v. 9; compare Zech 7:2).

The Lord's response to the polluted offerings is developed in the second section (vv. 10-14). Let there be a cessation of all temple sacrifice (v. 10a; see Ezek 40:39-41). God's preference is for *no* sacrifice: "I take no pleasure in you . . . neither will I accept any sacrifice from your hands" (v. 10b). The statement would cause anxiety among the priests. Their function as well as the efforts of the community to restore the temple for worship were being threatened.

The Lord's response continues a contrast between the priests and people of the covenant community and the "nations." There are various interpretations of verse 11. Some commentators suggest that the verse describes imminent expectations of a messianic age when Gentiles will worship with Jews (compare Isa 66:18-21; Zech 14:21). A few Catholic commentators propose that the verse is a reference to the sacrifice of the Mass. Others relate the verse to the situation of the Diaspora Jews and their synagogue activities (prayer and study), which have replaced or substituted for temple sacrifice. The last argument is most probable. However, whatever the particular interpretation may be, the general context identifies a type of activity that is pleasing to God.

The remaining verses of the section continue the contrast between the priests and the nations by indicting priestly thoughts and behavior.

The concluding oracle of the section issues a curse to the priest who deceives himself and the community by offering a "gelding" and holding back a "male" animal (v. 14a; see Lev 22:18). There is an implied contrast between the covenant community and the "nations." The Lord is a "great King whose name will be feared among the nations" (v. 14b). The repetition of "great" (vv. 5, 11, 14) and "name" (vv. 6, 11, 14) throughout the indictment for polluted sacrifices (vv. 6-14) emphasizes the nature of God and how inadequately the priests respond.

The second indictment condemns the failure of the priests as teachers and leaders because they have abandoned personal integrity (2:1-9). The entire section is the Lord's response in covenantal terminology. The priests will be cursed if they do not heed the Lord's warning (vv. 1-2; see Deut 27:14–28:68). "Shoulder" (v. 3) is interpreted literally as the choice portion of animal sacrifices given to the priests (see Deut 18:3). The Revised Standard Version renders "shoulder" as "offspring," implying that the whole priestly lineage will be cut off with no successors, while the New English Bible translates the term as "arm," suggesting that priests will be prevented from officiating at the altar.

God offers a sign to the priests that the commandment is intended for them. It is the "covenant with Levi," whereby "life and peace" were offered. Levi responded by fearing God and standing in awe of God's name (vv. 4-5). In addition, Levi spoke true doctrine (*torah*) honestly, lived "in integrity and uprightness, and turned many away from evil" (v. 6; compare Deut 31:9-13). While the covenant with Levi (v. 4) is not recorded in the Old Testament, it is presupposed in other texts (see Jer 33:21; compare Num 25:11-13).

The covenant with Levi is the model for the priest, who is to be knowledgeable in the law and is to instruct the community (v. 7a; see Deut 17:9; 33:10). The priest must be faithful to the covenant "because he is the messenger of the Lord of hosts" (v. 7b). This is the one verse in the Old Testament where a priest is given the title "messenger," which traditionally was associated with a prophet. The transfer of title and function from prophet to priest may refer to the historical circumstances of Malachi's experience.

The comprehensive model of the covenant with Levi and the additional role of "messenger of the Lord of hosts" are the basis for the judgment of the priests (vv. 8-9). They have not been faithful to the obligations of the covenant nor to their role as teachers and leaders (v. 8). Since they voided the covenant of Levi, the Lord has stripped them of their status. They have become "contemptible and base before all the people," since they refuse to keep God's covenant and to instruct the community in its stipulations (v. 9).

Some commentators have suggested that the description of the covenant with Levi and its authority may be a reference to the contrast between the Zadokite priests (returnees from Babylon) and the Levites. The latter had been given menial tasks in the service of the temple, while the priests were important functionaries (see p. 575). Malachi may be favoring Levitical rather than Zadokite jurisdiction in the community.

2:10-16 Sins of the community. The community is guilty of breaking covenant with God in different situations. While the section begins with a general admonition (v. 10), the sin that is emphasized is the faithlessness of husbands to wives. Divorce, which Jewish law only permitted husbands to initiate under specific conditions, was becoming troublesome (see Deut 24:1-4; Hos 2:4; compare Ezra 9–10).

The returned exiles were wealthy and may have expected to enhance their position in the community by marrying a local woman. The practice of divorce meant that the community included many single, divorced Jewish women. Intermarriage meant that non-Jewish mothers would be responsible for teaching their children the practices of a religion that was foreign to them. It is not clear from the text what reasons were given for the divorce proceedings.

The prophetic injunction goes beyond earlier Jewish law, which regarded the wife as a possession of the husband (see Exod 20:17). The prophet identifies the relationship between husband and wife as a covenant that affects the partners, the individuals in their relationship to God, their children, and the other members of the community. As in the case of the indictments against the priests, here the covenant is the basis of the indictment against the community.

The prophet poses rhetorical questions that address the reality of the community's experience of common origin to begin a new disputation (v. 10a; compare Deut 32:6; Isa 63:16; 64:8). Referring to a common historical tradition, the prophet points out the "abomination" (RSV) that Judah, Jerusalem, and Israel have committed (v. 11a). "Abomination" is a technical term used to describe idols and the practice of idol worship forbidden by the covenant (see Deut 32:16; Isa 44:19). The present community is guilty of the same offense (v. 11b).

The consequences of the community's action (v. 11b) are interpreted in two ways. Literally, the verse identifies *worship* as unacceptable to the Lord due to the covenant faithlessness of the worshipers. Metaphorically, the "temple," "sanctuary" (RSV), "holiness" (NEB) of the Lord may also identify the *community members*, who are called to belong to God (see Deut 32:9). Whether worship or the members themselves are described, the indictment is the same: members have married "the daughter of a foreign god" (RSV; see 1 Kgs 11:1-8; Neh 13:23-27). Mixed marriages violate the covenant with God *and* the bond that unites the community (see Exod 34:13-16; Deut 7:1-4).

The first section concludes with a threatening curse (v. 12a). The identification of "witness and advocate" is difficult. Most commentators propose a universal meaning, that is, anyone involved in the situation. Exclusion from the community and prohibition to sacrifice in the temple are the closely related civic and religious punishments (v. 12b).

Sacrifices are no longer acceptable (v. 13b; compare 1:10b). Verse 14a is the only occurrence of a community question in the disputation: "Why is it?" The relationship of faithful living to genuine ritual is reiterated for the community as it was for the priests (see the commentary on 1:6b-13; 2:3-9). The prophet responds to the question by identifying the Lord as "witness between you and the wife of your youth" (v. 14a; compare Isa 54:6; Prov 5:18).

The severity of the broken relationship is indicated in verses 15-16. This obscure text may be an addition by scribal editors who disagreed with the prophet's insight. The emphasis is on God who created each person as "one being, with flesh and spirit," who in turn creates "godly offspring." The implication is that according to the model of God who is one, the married partners ought to be faithful to their union as "one" and "not break faith" (v. 15). Synonymous parallelism (vv. 14b, 15b) underscores the importance of fidelity to the marriage covenant.

Verse 16 consists of two divine oracles, which conclude the section. Two situations are hateful to the Lord. The first is divorce. While the English translations concur about the clause "I hate divorce," the Hebrew renders it "if he hates send (her) away" (v. 16a). Perhaps the text was amended by a scribe who desired to bring Malachi's teaching into conformity with earlier permission for divorce (see Deut 24:1). The oracle is attributed to the "Lord, the God of Israel," a phrase used nowhere else in the Old Testament. The title fits the context of continuing covenant relationships.

"Covering one's garments with injustice" is the second object of the Lord's hatred (v. 16b). It is an obscure clause. The "garment" may be a symbol for the divorce partners. The final injunction of the prophet (v. 16c) forms an inclusion with verse 15b, which brackets the Lord's oracles. It is a general exhortation to be faithful in all relationships with others and with God.

2:17–3:5 Fourth oracle: God's justice. Consistent with the focus on Israel, God's justice will be enacted upon that community through a judgment that both eliminates social abuses and purifies the Levites. The section 3:1-21 [3:13–4:6] is characterized as "proto-apocalyptic" because of the imminent judgment of the Lord (see p. 577). Nonetheless, the "nations" are not included in the judgment (compare Joel 3–4 [2:28–3:21] and Second Zechariah).

The disputation begins with a statement from the prophet (2:17a; compare Isa 43:24), followed by a question formulated to anticipate the audience (2:17b). The response identifies two attitudes of the community that are weakening the covenantal relationship. The people assume that evil is pleasing in God's sight (see Jer 12:1; Hab 1:2-4). Their belief in a just God is waning, that is, they are beginning to doubt God's existence (2:17c).

Thus the final verse of chapter 2 provides a transition to the next theme, God's justice. The questions about "wearying God" and the "just God" are repeated (3:13-15) and answered (3:16-18) in the context of the sixth oracle (3:13-21 [3:13–4:3]).

The next section (3:1-5) offers an entirely new focus on the "messenger" who will appear before the Lord's judgment. Verses 1a and 5 are first-person oracles representing God, while verses 2-4 are a third-person narration of the prophet. God announces that "my messenger" will be sent to prepare "the way before me" (v. 1a), while the prophet proclaims the coming of this messenger (v. 1b).

The identity of the messenger of the covenant is unclear. Verses 1b-4 are confusing. Did the editor of the book identify "my messenger" with the prophet Malachi (see p. 625)? Will the "messenger of the covenant" fulfill a Levitical role (see 2:4-8; compare Isa 40:3)? Are "my messenger" and the "messenger of the covenant" different individuals or the same individual? Does the description designate an angelic being? God? Or the imminent presence of God?

The prophet probably envisioned "my messenger" as a Levitical figure. A later editor, however, identified him as Elijah (see 3:23 [4:5]). It is possible that the Levitical figure could also function as the "messenger of the covenant." While commentators are divided about the identity of the messengers in Malachi, the messenger is unanimously identified in the Gospel traditions as John the Baptist (see Mark 1:2-8; Matt 3:1-11; Luke 3:2-16).

Verses 2-4 describe the coming of the Lord as judge in traditional metaphorical language. The double questions about the coming of the Lord refer to battle imagery (v. 2a; see 2 Kgs 10:4; Amos 2:15). "Like a refiner's fire or like the fuller's lye" are consistent images in prophecy (see Isa 1:25; Jer 6:29-30; Ezek 22:17-22). In Malachi the images signify that God will remove all impurities and cleanse the sons of Levi (vv. 2b-3; compare Zech 13:9).

In verse 4 the prophet compares future Levitical sacrifices on behalf of Judah and Jerusalem with the sacrifices that pleased the Lord in the past. The era of Moses is an appropriate identification for that period (see Jer 2:2; Isa 63:9, 11; compare Amos 5:25; Jer 7:22). The purification and acceptance of Levitical sacrifices (vv. 2-4) present a sharp contrast to the concluding verse of the section, which enumerates the evildoers who will be judged (v. 5; see 2:17c).

Verse 5a presents a court context in which the Lord is both witness and judge (see 2:14). With the exception of sorcerers (see Deut 18:10-11; Jer 27:9), all the groups responsible for social evils are indicted: adulterers and perjurers (compare 2:11-16); employers who defraud (see Lev 19:13; Deut 24:14-15); those who oppress widows and orphans (see Zech 7:10) or maltreat the sojourner (v. 5b). The perpetrators of social evils are described as the ones "who do not fear me" (v. 5c).

3:6-12 Fifth oracle: Ritual offenses. Four oracles of the Lord have been combined in the section to address the community about the quality of their ritual activity. Their deeds indict them when they approach the altar, just as the priestly activities and attitudes condemned the priests earlier (1:6–2:9).

The Lord's statement about the covenant bond initiates the disputation (v. 6; compare 1:2; 3:5; Gen 27:36). Next, there is a judgment about how that relationship was defiled throughout history (v. 7a). A plea to return to the Lord concludes the oracle (v. 7b). Malachi, like Zechariah, does not idealize past generations (see Zech 1:2, 4). Both invoke earlier Jewish tradition in pleading with their communities to return to God (see the commentary on Zech 1:3).

The Lord anticipates the question of the community: "How must we return?" (v. 7c) and responds with instructions about tithing. This is an unusual prophetic injunction, for earlier tradition insisted that community gifts were neither needed (see Ps 50:7-15) nor acceptable (see Amos 5:21-23; Isa 43:23).

Tithes represented one-tenth of an individual's produce; this portion was given to the Levites, who in turn gave a tithe to the priests (see Num 18:23-24, 28). According to the law, tithes were given to the Levites and to destitute members of the community every three years (see Deut 14:28-29). Therefore, if tithes were not given, members of the community suffered (compare 3:5). Offerings were portions of sacrifices and voluntary gifts given to the priests (see Exod 29:27-28; 25:2-7). By "robbing" God, the community is judged:

"you are indeed accursed" (v. 9; compare Prov 11:24).

Three oracles describe blessings promised to the community if they return to God by obeying the law about tithes and offerings (vv. 10-12). This is probably the prophet's response to those members who doubted God's existence (see 2:17).

The imperative "try me in this" suggests God's willingness to be tested. God's fidelity to the community will be seen in the blessings they enjoy (v. 10b). However, an obedient response of the community is a pre-condition for God's blessings. Two images of land harvest describe some of God's blessings: no locusts will "destroy your crops; and the vine . . . will not be barren" (v. 11; compare Joel 1:4; Hag 2:16, 19; Zech 8:12).

Abundant harvests will be evident to the nations, which "will call you blessed, for you will be a delightful land" (v. 12). Unlike Zechariah, there is no indication here that the nations will share in God's blessings bestowed on the community (see Zech 14:16-19).

3:13-21 [3:13–4:3] Sixth oracle: God's servants. The priests had been indicted for their actions and words. The same judgment is passed on the community, who had already been indicted for their actions (3:6-12). This section describes why their words nullify the covenant with God. The first part contains the questions of the evildoers. The second part is a contrast between those who fear God and the evildoers.

The attitudes of the community indicate skepticism. Lack of personal gain in observing the covenant requirements contributes to an apathetic spirit. The description of being clothed "in penitential dress" (NAB), "as in mourning" (RSV), "behaving with deference" (NEB) is difficult to interpret. It may identify a particular group of the community, such as the Levites, who had suffered because the tithes were not sufficient. They dressed in repentance but continued to experience hardships (compare Neh 13:10-13). Not only is the community lacking in fervor, but judgment suffers as well (v. 15; compare 2:17; Ps 73:2-14). Although these attitudes are widespread among community members, the situation is not a definitive one.

A shift from the Lord's oracles to prophetic narration and oracles announces the second part of this section. Responding to the disputation (vv. 13-15), some members seek to "return" to God (v. 16; compare 2:1). To preserve a record of those who "fear the Lord and trust in his name," a "book of remembrance" is compiled (v. 16c; compare 2:4-5). The book is a traditional symbol in Jewish tradition (see Exod 32:32-33; Isa 4:3; Ps 69:29; compare Esth 6:1-2). The phrase "book of remembrance," however, occurs only in Malachi.

God promises the people another blessing. They will be "mine . . . my own special possession," thus reaffirming the covenant with the Lord (v. 17a; see Exod 19:5; Deut 14:2; Ps 135:4). Compassion is another blessing from God (v. 17b; see 1:6a; 3:6). The ability to "again see the distinction between the just and the wicked" (v. 18a; compare 2:17b) will definitively challenge: "Every evildoer is good in the sight of the Lord" (v. 2:17c).

The second distinction that will become clear is between the one who serves God and the one who does not serve God (v. 18b). The approaching judgment of God will satisfy the scoffers' question: "Where is the just God?" (2:17c). The apocalyptic image of judgment as fire describes the separation of the community. Unlike the "refining" fire (3:2), the "blazing" quality will reduce "all the proud and all evildoers" (to) "stubble . . . leaving them neither root or branch" (v. 19 [4:1]).

For "you who fear my name, there will arise the sun of justice with its healing rays" (v. 20a [4:2a]; compare 3:16c; Isa 57:18-19; Luke 1:78-79). This is the one verse where the "sun of righteousness" (RSV) occurs in the Old Testament. Most commentators attribute the symbolism to the Egyptian and Mesopotamian sun-god, who is pictured with a winged solar disc on many Near Eastern monuments. The god functioned as judge among the gods of the pantheon.

Experiencing the "sun of righteousness" will rouse the energies of those who fear the Lord: "you shall break loose like calves released from the stall" (v. 20b [4:2]; NEB) and "tread down the wicked" (v. 21a [4:3a]). Consistent with the image of consuming fire (v. 19), the wicked will "become ashes under the soles of your feet on the day I take action" (v. 21b [4:3b]). God will vindicate those who fear the Lord (see Deut 32:35; Prov 20:22). The clause "on the day I take action" (vv. 17b;

23b [4:3b]) is an inclusion bracketing the Lord's future activities.

PART TWO: APPENDICES

Mal 3:22-24 [4:4-6]

The appendices summarize characteristic teaching, identify the messenger of the Lord, and describe the day of the Lord. There is no consensus about when they were combined, edited, and added to Part One of Malachi. Their inclusion indicates the importance of the closing verses of Malachi, the scroll of the Twelve Minor Prophets, and the conclusion of the Old Testament for future generations of communities.

"Remember the law of Moses . . . all Israel" (v. 22 [4:4]) points to the importance of the first five books of the Old Testament. Each phrase of the verse is an exhortation to be committed to Mosaic law. The phrases are taken from Deuteronomy's covenantal descriptions.

The next verse identifies the mysterious messenger of Mal 3:1 as the prophet Elijah (v. 23a [4:5a]). Descriptions of him in 2 Kings and Sirach correspond to the functions of the messenger (see 2 Kgs 2:11; Sir 48:10-12; commentary on Mal 3:1). "Before the day of the Lord comes, the great and terrible day" repeats the traditional imagery of that "day" (v. 23b [4:5b]; see Isa 3:5; Joel 2:11; 3:4 [2:31]).

Verse 3:23b [4:5b] may have been judged an inadequate conclusion of Malachi. For whatever reason, another verse was appended (v. 24a [4:6a]). It continues the thought of the first appendix (3:22a [4:4a]) in a chiastic structure whereby "fathers" is the left stroke of the *X* and "children" is the right stroke of the *X*. The verse offers a comment on the purpose of the covenant law, that is, mutual love among parents and children. The verse concludes with a traditional warning from the Lord: "Lest I come and strike the land with doom" (v. 24b [4:6b]).

The verse that concludes Malachi in the New American Bible is not found in the Hebrew text. Commentators propose that rabbis included it in order to formulate an appropriate conclusion, *not* one of doom. They inserted a repetition of verse 23 [4:5], which associates Elijah with the day of the Lord.

Conclusion

The prophet Malachi ministered to the community of Israel at a "trough" period. The process of rebuilding the temple and reconstituting a religious identity had been completed nearly fifty years beforehand. The glorious visions of Haggai and First Zechariah had not been fulfilled. Expectations of a new age related to the cosmopolitan world-view of Alexander the Great had also been disappointing.

The prophet faced a lethargic priesthood and community in which serious cultic, religious, and social abuses were not examined nor judged adequately. How could he revitalize the situation? He would appeal to the one consistent memory of a faithful God of the covenant! His exhortations would give all concerned a sense of continuity with a faded but glorious tradition. Opportunities to meet the same requirements of faithful living in the present would challenge everyone.

The Book of Malachi emerges as an effective text for rousing the hearts of the disenchanted and disappointed. In an age in which nothing spectacular occurred in religious, social, or political arenas to offer temporary distraction or assistance, Malachi offered a clear critique on the status quo. The prophet presents a creative relationship between the Law and the Prophets that can sustain and carry forth the community. The covenant offers a model of integrity between actions and words that is the basis for worship, leadership, and teaching.

The structure of the book is an effective resource for initial evangelization as well as later situations. The disputation style carefully distinguishes between God's exhortations and comments and the questions of the community. The additional responses offer opportunities for clarification and deeper understanding.

The language combines traditional metaphors and new insights in a clear, direct style. The book is not pedantic, dense, or unappealing. The insights often expressed in ironic phrases, questions, and statements breathe a new spirit into traditional material from the Law and the Prophets.

The Book of Malachi is an appropriate text with which to conclude the Twelve Minor Prophets as well as the Old Testament. It is a witness to the mystery of a faithful God who gives individuals and communities what is needed for the present. It is a perennial call to respond to the God who first loved all of creation and continues to transform the cosmos until the blessings promised "on that day" are no longer expectations.

An Introduction to the Wisdom Literature of Israel

Lawrence E. Boadt, C.S.P.

The nature of a wisdom book

After the Revolutionary War, when the delegates of the thirteen American colonies were writing a constitution, it got to the point where everyone objected to some part of the new document, and it looked as though it might never win approval. During the discussion Benjamin Franklin, the elder statesman of the group, noted that while he also did not agree with all the provisions, he had lived long enough to know that he often changed his mind and would likely do so again. He thought that this probably was not the best document, but it was far from the worst, and he would vote for it. It soon passed overwhelmingly. His good sense, discretion, and prudent judgment gave him the right to the title "Father of American Wisdom."

This same spirit that characterized Franklin also marks the wisdom books of the Old Testament. They are an often neglected part of the Bible but reflect an important insight into Israel's religious ideal, which is certainly not just the same as fidelity to the Mosaic law or obedience to the prophets. The Book of Daniel describes this further dimension of the ideal well when the Babylonian king wants some of the captured Jewish youths brought to his court to study wisdom: "young men without defects, handsome, intelligent and wise, eager to learn, prudent in judgment and competent to serve in the king's palace" (Dan 1:4). Other descriptions of the wise person are found in Gen 39:1-6; 41:8-32 (Joseph), 1 Kgs 4:29-34 (Solomon), and 2 Sam 16:15–17:14 (Ahithophel and Hushai).

The wisdom books are not all alike; they differ in style and content from one another. But certain characteristics do set them off from other biblical books; they show:

1) very little interest in the major traditions of the Pentateuch, such as the law of Sinai, the covenant, the cult, the special call of Israel;

2) little or no concern with the history of Israel as a people;

3) a searching for the meaning of life and the mastery of life as it is known from experience and not from faith alone;

4) an eagerness to explore the unknown and the difficult problems of sickness, suffering, death, the inequality of rich and poor, the seeming arbitrariness of divine blessing on people;

5) a curiosity about the world as a whole and the universal experience of all nations and peoples;

6) a commitment to discovering proper moral behavior, the right way to live.

These concerns invited the wise to be questioning about life while at the same time analyzing and ordering common experience into rules to live by. Wisdom encouraged discipline of thinking, careful reasoning, and the control of passions. "Go not after your lusts, but keep your desires in check. If you satisfy your lustful appetites, they will make you the sport of your enemies," says Sirach (18:30-31). At the same time, the sages were extremely broad-minded about borrowing from other peoples. They were, in short, interested in life in all its dimensions from the very practical viewpoint of "How can I get the best out of it for me and for society as a whole?"

This approach often makes the wisdom writings seem very secular in outlook. Many proverbs are never related to divine law at all. Even a non-believer can heartily agree with the admonition "Consort not with winebibbers, nor with those who eat meat to excess, for the drunkard and glutton come to poverty, and torpor clothes a person in rags" (Prov 23:20-21). The Rabbis of the centuries immediately after Christ argued vehemently whether Qoheleth (Ecclesiastes) was an atheist before they decided that the book had to be canonical because Solomon's name was attached to it. Whether optimistic about the world, as is Proverbs, or pessimistic, as are Job and Qoheleth, wisdom looks at the world from a very worldly point of view. The key example of this is Joseph in the Book of Genesis, who acts with discretion and prudence and does God's will without ever receiving any revelation from God at all.

While such qualities are valued almost everywhere in the Old Testament, only a few books can be called specifically "wisdom books" because they maintain the focus on intellectual reflection about the world from a humanist's standpoint throughout. These are: *Proverbs; Job; Ecclesiastes* (or in Hebrew, *Qoheleth); Ecclesiasticus* (or in Hebrew, *Sirach* or *Jesus ben Sira); The Wisdom of Solomon.* Closely related to these is the *Canticle of Canticles (Song of Songs).* Although the Song is love poetry, it is also a confident affirmation of creation and the human capacity for happiness. A number of the psalms may also be listed as wisdom writings: 1, 32, 34, 37, 49, 73, 111–112, 128 and possibly a few others (19:8-15; 119 and 127). Scholars have also pointed to wisdom influences in the prophets, especially Isaiah and Amos, who both place emphasis on knowing the divine "counsel" or wisdom and frequently make use of wisdom expressions. A few echoes of wisdom thinking occur elsewhere, such as in the story of the Garden of Eden (Gen 2–3), the life of Solomon (1 Kgs 3–11), the story of Joseph (Gen 37–49), and the Book of Daniel (chs. 1–6).

Observations on life were not restricted to Israel. Proverbial statements are nearly universal. In the past, biblical scholars often treated the wisdom material almost entirely in relation to other books of the Bible; but in the past few years, the discoveries of wisdom writings from the Egyptians, Sumerians, and Babylonians have increased enormously, and now the evidence points clearly toward how much Israel was indebted to these nations for its wisdom tradition. This should not surprise us. Wisdom's focus on the common questions of human beings everywhere would naturally lead the Israelites to study famous works from other nations.

Egypt, in particular, was a source of study. It produced many collections of proverbs dating from 2400 B.C.E. down to 500 B.C.E. Often these were in the form of a father's instruction to his son, which may well have been a formal way of talking about teacher and pupil. The earliest of these, the *Instruction of the Vizier Ptah-hotep,* gathered advice on how to succeed in life and resembles the older proverbs in the Book of Proverbs. Compare Ptah-hotep's "If you are sitting at the table of one greater than yourself, accept whatever he gives when it is set before your face" with Prov 23:1, "When you sit down to dine with a ruler, keep in mind who is before you." The much later *Instruction of Amenemope,* written sometime between 1000 and 600 B.C.E., has thirty instructions that match very closely the collection in Prov 22:17–24:22. One example is Prov 23:10: "Remove not the ancient landmark, nor invade the field of orphans." Compare this with Amenemope's "Do not carry off the landmark at the boundaries of the arable land nor disturb the position of the measuring cord." The Israelite sage has modified the saying somewhat to apply to the custom of leaving the gleanings for the poor (Deut 24:19; Ruth 2:1-7). For more detail on the relation of Amenemope to Proverbs, see the commentary below on 22:17–24:22.

Egypt's wisdom schools also produced school texts in praise of scribes (see Sir 39:1-11), name lists and classifications of all kinds of things (see the claim for Solomon in 1 Kgs 5:13), pessimistic reflections on life (see Job and Qoheleth), and even a story of honesty and uprightness threatened by lust (the *Story of Two Brothers*) that became the model for Joseph tempted by Potiphar's wife in Gen 39:1-20.

In Sumeria and Babylonia the wisdom tradition was just as developed as in Egypt. Sumerian proverb collections date before 2000

B.C.E. and many of their sayings sound like counterparts in Israel. "While your glance flits to it [wealth], it is gone! for assuredly it grows wings, like the eagle" (Prov 23:5) is similar in message to the Sumerian adage "Possessions are sparrows in flight that find no place to land." Interestingly, the Sumerian editors collected their proverbs by topic, while it is very difficult to find any order in Israel's collections. Also, the Sumerians favored nature images and offered a minimum of moral judgment. In this, too, they differed from Israel.

Babylon produced a great number of works dealing with questions of human life. The poem *I Will Praise the Lord of Wisdom* (in Babylonian, the *Ludlul bel nemeqi*) grappled with the question of why the gods allowed undeserved suffering. It is sometimes called "the Babylonian Job." Other works explore the question of meaninglessness, and there is even a *Dialogue of Pessimism* between a man and his slave, ending with a hint of suicide. A work popularly known as the "Babylonian Qoheleth" also explores the problems of theodicy (God's treatment of the innocent sufferer).

Whereas Sumerian proverbs had a harsh side to them—the forces of nature can be brutal and indiscriminate, and so can the gods—Babylonian wisdom tried to grapple with the uncertainties of life and to reconcile the contradictions of experience. They accented the need to understand the universe in terms of moral laws that would guide human behavior. Thus they could produce many reflective proverbs that are not unlike those favored by the sages in the Book of Proverbs. "What your eyes have seen bring not forth hastily against an opponent; for what will you do later on when your neighbor puts you to shame?" (Prov 25:8) is not far from the advice of the Babylonian *Counsels of Wisdom*, "Do not frequent a law court . . . . for in the dispute they will have you as a testifier, and you will be made their witness and they will bring you into a lawsuit not your own to affirm."

Egyptian, Mesopotamian, and Israelite wisdom generally agreed that traditional wisdom, passed down from long ago, had a special value that no individual could match by a single lifetime of experience. Almost all known works emphasized the importance of sitting at the feet of a father or teacher and learning from the past. The introduction to the *Wisdom of Shuruppak*, a Sumerian work, is typical:

> (Shuruppak) offered instructions to his son. . . .
>
> Oh, my (son), instruction I offer you, take my instruction. . . .
>
> My instruction do not neglect, my spoken word do not transgress.

Since both Mesopotamian and Egyptian wisdom writings were well established and highly developed long before Israel existed as a nation, we must conclude that their influence on later Israelite thinking was very deep.

Wisdom's two ways

The Greek philosopher Protagoras said that "man is the measure of all things." The ancient wisdom teachers of the East would have agreed that this is the starting point for the analysis of experience. While the sages were not truly philosophers in the modern sense of seeking a systematic explanation of the first principles of reality, they were keen observers of the world in which they lived and attempted to find patterns and predictable events that would help humans cope with that world. We must remember that they knew little about the causes of disease and sickness, about the causes of weather conditions, and about the extent of civilization except what was nearby. This meant that they could do little to prevent disfiguring diseases or to cure them, to stop floods or predict droughts, to understand the strange ways of far-off peoples. The physical world in which they lived was much more uncertain, and therefore more frightening, than ours. But it was just as interesting, and the curiosity of the wisdom teachers constantly sought interlinking connections between things. Despite the uncertainties, they were convinced that the world is orderly and can be understood well enough to allow the formation of norms for moral behavior.

The wise would observe, classify, reflect, make comparisons and analogies, and finally draw conclusions for daily behavior. Wisdom oriented its disciples to the good order of the universe, whether called *maat* in Egypt, *ME* in Babylon, or *sedeqah* in Israel. Common observation usually supported a world of order—the sun rises and sets daily, the seasons are predictable, but human certainty was also tied to faith in the divine order of creation. The cause of this certainty lay in the goodness of the gods and their plan for the universe. Only the gods fully understood such a plan, but humans could learn of it in a limited way and act accordingly. Thus on one level ancient wisdom was extremely confident and positive about life and the human ability to live successfully according to divine order. The use of proverbs—short sayings that capture the essence of right behavior—reflects this attitude.

On the other hand, tension developed between what was deduced as good order and passed on as true, and people's day-to-day experience of failure and uncertainty. In contrast to the confident wisdom of Proverbs and Sirach, a second stream of skeptical and questioning reflection developed. It wrestled with the human pain and suffering that arose from not understanding why life was often inconsistent with the beliefs based on divine good order. The Books of Job and Qoheleth are vehement at times in their challenges to traditional wisdom. They fully question our capacity to know and understand why nature acts the way it does and what God intends for us to do. Both propose solutions that rely more on a personal relationship with God than on an understanding of reality. Of course, both Job and Qoheleth also begin with experience and use its discovered regularity to present their cases; they only deny its ultimate ability to explain the purpose for which God acts.

Israel's wisdom teachers tried to solve the tension by more and more affirming that there are limits to what humans can know. Sir 3:20 advises, "What is too sublime for you, seek not," while 3:21 adds, "what is hidden is not your concern." God always lets us know enough by which to direct our lives, but the ultimate meaning of each life is hidden in the silence of the divine purpose. In this, wisdom rejoins the faith proclamations of the Law and the Prophets.

The cosmic horizon

Experience is both highly personal and often impersonal. When bad or good fortune happens to me alone, I turn to the intimacy of prayer to praise God or to beg help; but many events, such as war, natural disasters, the oddities of strange animals, or the regularity of the seasons, have little to do with me personally and raise larger questions about the universe as a whole. It is not at all surprising that wisdom gave great attention to cosmic origins and the wonder of creation itself.

While Israel's Mosaic faith stressed personal salvation by Yahweh for the people, its wisdom circles based their discoveries on the order to be found in the very plan of creation. Hymns in praise of the divine goodness and majesty of God revealed in creation fill the wisdom tradition. Job 28, Prov 8, Sir 16 and 43, and Wis 7 all identify wisdom with the vast and incomprehensible greatness of creation itself. Passages in other parts of the Old Testament (Gen 1, Ezek 28, Isa 40, Ps 8) also praise creation as a sign of God's greatness, but nowhere does it play such a central role in our approach to God as it does in the wisdom tradition. Indeed, many if not all of these other passages may be influenced by wisdom. Even in the short sayings of Proverbs, the Creator plays a focusing role (Prov 14:31; 17:5; Eccl 12:1).

This emphasis on creation places wisdom in the stream of Ancient Near Eastern religion, especially Mesopotamian, in which cultic practice centered on a return to the right order and perfect goodness of the first creation by the gods. The pagan peoples tried to erase the time in between then and now—the sin and the failure—and to restore the wholeness and vitality of that first moment. To a certain extent, Babylonian religion was an escape from the present time to a timeless, ideal world by means of cult.

Israel's attitude differed profoundly on that point. It was convinced that time moved on and one could never return to what was lost. But God would always act again to heal, rebuild, or re-bless the world, and one could trust God completely because God acts unfailingly out of innate goodness. In Gen 1–3 this conviction is expressed by God's blessing of the first humans, their rejection of the blessing, and the divine re-blessing without completely restoring what they had lost. It is expressed in the faith proclamations of the covenant, where God's fidelity to the promise endures despite Israel's infidelity. And it is expressed in wisdom by appealing to the divine act of creation as a source of understanding the goodness of the world. The beauty of divine order and harmony is revealed to our intelligence by reflecting on creation, and although we cannot fully grasp its meaning, it shows us the basic options before us: the way of goodness or evil, the way of the wise or the fool; the attitudes of humility or human arrogance. These themes are treated more fully in the commentary on the Book of Proverbs that follows.

Late wisdom, reflected in Sirach and the Wisdom of Solomon, brings faith and creation reflections closer together by affirming that God as Creator is only fully known through obedience to the law (see especially Sir 24 and Wis 18–19).

Where does wisdom find its home?

Scholars have argued for several different sources of the wisdom tradition. One that appears frequently behind proverbial sayings is the *family*. Many proverbs are directed explicitly from father to son (Prov 1:8; 2:1; 10:1) or from mother to son (Prov 31:1-2). But more than that, a significant number of maxims are directed to questions of relations between parents and children, moral instruction of the young, and family manners. Prov 19:26 warns, "He who mistreats his father, or drives away his mother, is a worthless and disgraceful son"; and 20:11, "Even by his manners the child betrays whether his conduct is innocent and right."

Although everyone agrees that some education had to take place at home, not all believe that Israelites attended formal schools. But the many references to masters as "fathers" in Proverbs, as well as the widespread existence of schools in Egypt and Mesopotamia, suggest that Israel, too, had programs of education that at least some boys attended over many years. These included learning the alphabet, followed by writing and mastering short proverbs, and finally studying longer works of literature. The foreword to the Book of Sirach, written about 132 B.C.E., gives one account: ". . . my grandfather Jesus [ben Sira], who, having devoted himself for a long time to the diligent study of the law, the prophets, and the rest of the books of our ancestors, and having developed a thorough familiarity with them, was moved to write something himself in the nature of instruction and wisdom . . . ." This formal education was probably aimed at developing a professional class of scribes and bureaucrats who would serve administrative functions in the temple, the royal government, and houses of business. There are many examples of Sumerian and Egyptian essays in praise of the scribal profession as the highest in the land. A similar passage can be found in the Bible in Sir 38:24–39:11, and there are many hints at the importance of the scribe elsewhere (1 Chr 27:32-33; Isa 8:16; Jer 26:1-21).

Above all, wisdom in the Ancient Near East was associated with kings and royal administration. David is called wise in 2 Sam 14:20, and Solomon's wisdom is described in detail throughout 1 Kgs 3–11. Prov 25:2 declares, "God has glory in what he conceals, kings have glory in what they fathom." 1 Kgs 5:9-14 declares of him:

> God gave Solomon wisdom and exceptional understanding and knowledge, as vast as the sand on the seashore. Solomon surpassed all the Cedemites and all the Egyptians in wisdom. He was wiser than all other men—than Ethan the Ezrahite, or Heman, Chalcol, and Darda, the musicians—and his fame spread throughout the neighboring nations. Solomon also uttered three thousand proverbs, and his songs numbered a thousand and five. He discussed plants, from the cedar on Lebanon to the hyssop growing out of the wall, and he spoke about beasts, birds, reptiles, and fishes. Men came to hear Solomon's wisdom from all the nations, sent by all the kings of the earth who had heard of his wisdom.

This tradition attributes encyclopedic knowledge to the king, as well as the ability to rule successfully and to make good judgment (1 Kgs 3). But kings gathered around themselves skilled advisors to assure that they did as well as possible (see 2 Sam 16:15–17:23; 1 Chr 27:32-33; 1 Kgs 12:6-7; Jer 8:8-9; Isa 31:1-3). The Books of Daniel and Esther portray the royal courts of the Babylonians and Persians filled with wise counselors of the kings. Still other passages in the Bible refer to the fame of sages in the courts of the kings of Edom and Assyria (see Ezek 28:3-4; Jer 49:7).

When David created his empire, he brought Israel from local tribal organization to world power overnight. He needed diplomats, administrators, and recordkeepers quickly. This necessitated borrowing the techniques of neighboring kingdoms, especially Egypt. Under his son Solomon this training became well established, and a burst of literary activity took place, including the first writing down of Israel's religious traditions by the Yahwist, the historical accounts of David's own rise to power, and the cultivation of wisdom as an art. Even the titles of Solomon's government officials—"the one over the house," the secretary, and the herald (1 Kgs 4:1-6)—are borrowed from the top offices in Egypt, corresponding to vizier, royal scribe, and royal announcer. In this situation, schools for the gifted would have flourished. An Israelite youth chosen to study would have seconded the enthusiastic cry of an Egyptian scribe, Duauf: "The scribe—every position at court is open to him!"

There is no statement in the Old Testament that actually says someone made a living as a teacher of wisdom, but it is highly probable. Jeremiah mentions the wise on the same footing as the priest and the prophet: "Come," they said, "let us contrive a plot against Jeremiah. It will not mean the loss of instruction from the priests, nor of counsel from the wise, nor of messages from the prophets" (Jer 18:18).

Although it may be hard to show a full profile of the professional wise person functioning outside of a political role in the palace, there are enough hints in the Scriptures to put together a reasonable sketch. The philosophy of life found in the Book of Proverbs often reflects the concerns of the wealthy and those with leisure time for study. The emphasis on good speech, writing skills, proper manners, and money lending describes a ruling elite rather than the farming or laborer class. The conservative bent of proverbial wisdom is sometimes attributed to the "haves," who value political stability above everything. Thus the wisdom teacher ran classes for upper-class youths. One proverb seems to imply that the wealthy families paid the teacher directly: "Of what use in a fool's hands are the means to buy wisdom, since he has no mind for it?" (Prov 17:16).

The methods of the wise

Part of the task of education was to memorize the valuable teachings of the past; another part was to learn to reason and make associations. To achieve these goals, the sages perfected many distinctive literary forms, the chief of which were the proverb and the comparison. Since education was for the most part oral, one can well imagine the teacher asking the students questions, and the students answering according to set keys that aided their memories. In light of this, it is surprising how few riddles and fables are found in Hebrew literature. The wisdom teachings of Mesopotamia favored both as teaching aids, but only one or two fables occur in the Old Testament (Judg 9:8-15; Ezek 19:10-14) and a single complete riddle (Judg 14:12-18). The small collection of numerical sayings in Prov 30:15-33 may originally have been riddles, but they now appear in the text as proverbial observations on life.

The *proverb* was an important element in Israelite wisdom because it distilled the lessons of the past in a clever, practical manner, with a touch of the sermon, and in easily remembered form. The popularity of the proverb in Israel was due to its ability to capture both the most commonplace insight into daily life and the most difficult problem of experience in new and interesting ways. In the same way, the *comparison* forced the hearer to make analogies between what was observed in the animal or plant world and human behavior. Neither proverb nor comparison hoped to explain reality fully, but by collecting insights side by side, a richer and more varied picture would emerge.

This search for the multiple faces of life also helps to explain the other literary genres favored by the wisdom schools. They are mostly non-dogmatic and yet educational. The way of wisdom was persuasion, not command, and so the more important genres include *allegory* (Prov 5:15-23; Eccl 12:1-6); *numerical sayings* (Prov 6:16-19; 30:15-33; Sir 25:7-11); *onomastica* (that is, name lists: Ezek 27:12-25; Sir 24:13-17; *hymns* (Prov 8:22-31; Job 28; Sir 24); *dialogues* (Job); *beatitudes* ("Blessed is the one who . . .": Prov 3:13; 8:32ff.; 14:21; 16:20; Eccl 10:17; Sir 14:1-2); *question and answer* formats, especially *rhetorical questions* (Qoheleth); *confessions of praise* (Sir 33:16-18; 51:13-22); *partial riddles* (Sir 39:3; Wis 8:8); *quotations* used as departure for reflections (Eccl 4:8; 10:18; 11:1; 7:3-4; 10:2); and *philosophical reflections* (Wisdom of Solomon). When not using one of the more clever literary forms, the wisdom writers fell back on the straightforward *instruction*, a form borrowed from the Egyptians (Prov 1–9).

Because the wisdom schools developed such effective methods of educating people, the prophets often borrowed their techniques. The rhetorical question was a favorite of the major prophets, particularly Isaiah, as was the dialogue between God and prophet (see especially the so-called Confessions of Jeremiah in Jer 12, 15, 17, 18 and 20). Some prophets, notably Ezekiel, loved the parable and the metaphor as ways to make a point (see Ezek 16, 17, 19, 23, 29, 30, 31, and 32). Amos used the numerical saying as a dramatic device (Amos 1:3–2:6). But whereas wisdom employed these means to open young minds to the world around them, the prophets used them to challenge people's understanding of the covenant. The introduction to the Book of Proverbs (p. 646) discusses many of these in greater detail.

A brief survey of the wisdom books

Solomon's reputation for wisdom was so great in Israel that he was believed to have been the author of the Books of Proverbs and Qoheleth, the Song of Songs, and the Wisdom of Solomon. An amusing legend in the Talmud tells how the great king had written the Song of Songs in his lusty youth, Proverbs in mature middle age, and Qoheleth in his skeptical old age! Proverbs is treated fully in the following commentary, but a brief overview of the other major wisdom books at this point will help to understand their interrelationships.

—Job. The Book of Job uses an old folk tale about an absolutely righteous man who proves faithful under severe trials (chs. 1–2; 42) as the framework for a great dialogue on the question of human suffering and the problem of the human search for personal knowledge of the transcendent God (chs. 3–41). It has many elements of drama, with the outcome uncertain until the end. The Job of the dialogues is neither the patient sufferer of tradition nor the prayerful accepter of his fate found in the folk tale. Instead, the author (seventh or sixth century B.C.E.) had the courage to move beyond simple acceptance of God's will to ask hard questions of the traditional and sometimes overconfident wisdom presented by proverbs and instructions. If God always cares for the just, why do the wicked seem to prosper? Why do the innocent suffer? What hope does uprightness offer?

The book also explores the deeper question of how one can know God. Many of Job's complaints deal with the *silence* of God before the human search for justice and faithfulness. The divine answer, when it comes, denies us any claim to a relationship with God based on our justice but calls for personal knowledge through obedience and reverent worship. As Job finally admits, "I had heard of you by word of mouth, but now my eye has seen you" (Job 42:5). Job's questions are also well known in Babylonian wisdom literature, but the author of Job situates the answer within Israel's commitment to Yahweh's personal self-revelation to them. Job in many ways resembles the psalms of lament with their threefold structure: (1) a cry of pain and lament; (2) a call to God for help; (3) a promise to praise God forever. Job teaches us that ultimately from the midst of doubt and questioning comes trust.

—Qoheleth. The author of this book is the most skeptical writer in the Bible. Like Job, he challenges the traditional certainties of wisdom, examining the same world of experience. "Vanity of vanities, all is vanity," he begins, and he ends no more convinced. It is not for us to understand the meaning of life or to figure out the divine purpose behind events, especially success and failure, reward and punishment of moral behavior, or finally death itself. Instead the writer highlights the transcendence of God, the need to recognize limits to human wisdom, and the ability to accept life as it comes, bearing its pains and enjoying its pleasures in moderation (Eccl 5:17). Everything has a proper time (Eccl 3:2), but it is known only to God in its fullness. Qoheleth's advice to enjoy life as it is given may not seem very religious, but he tempers it with warnings to "fear God" (Eccl 5:6). The outlook is far more pessimistic than that of the optimistic Book of Proverbs, but it stands clearly in the tradition of searching questions directed to all creation on the problems of human justice, the existence of evil, life and death.

—Sirach. Written in the early second century B.C.E., the Wisdom of Jesus ben Sira most resembles the positive outlook of Proverbs. It gathers advice on all the traditional subjects of wisdom by theme and sets them out as a guidebook for young students who want to obtain wisdom. Although wisdom can be attained by study, it is meant to serve as guidelines for human conduct, not as speculation. Sirach makes a special point of identifying sage advice with the religious practices of Judaism, especially linking wisdom with the law of Moses (ch. 24). Wisdom is thus a divine gift to Israel in a unique way. Even more so than for Proverbs, "fear of the Lord" is the way of wisdom. The achievements of the teachers can only be rightly appreciated in the light of divine revelation. Because of its late date, the Book of Sirach was never accepted into the Hebrew canon, but became a favorite part of the Christian Scriptures—hence the later name, Ecclesiasticus, the "church book."

—Wisdom of Solomon. This may be the latest book in the Old Testament and reflects a reaction to Greek philosophy in Alexandria and its challenges to Jewish faith during the first century B.C.E. Because of its date and the Greek language in which it was written, it never entered the Hebrew canon. The main purpose of the book is to reassure the Jewish community in Egypt that keeping their faith is worthwhile despite the hardships met in a pagan culture. It borrows the language of philosophy to achieve this goal. But it also stands out from earlier wisdom books by its intense concern with (1) *salvation history* as a lesson directed to the wise, and (2) *immortality* as an explanation of God's care for the suffering of the just. While it stands in the optimistic tradition of Proverbs and Sirach, it often makes wisdom so abstract that it obscures any practical value for living (see 7:22-25). But it does manifest the ability of Jewish wisdom to creatively meet the challenge of Hellenistic thinking.

—Song of Songs. It is hard to know where to put the Song of Songs among the biblical books. It is frequently included among the wisdom writings because its message is interpreted as an allegory of Israel's loving relationship to Yahweh. Although most scholars today admit that it began as a collection of down-to-earth love songs composed for weddings, it has had a long history of development before reaching its present form. There may have been a stage of application to royal weddings (see Psalm 45), which would have given the songs a religious setting. In any case, it has always invited reflection on the wonder and beauty of divine creation, the mystery of divine (and human) love, and the ramifications of relationships built on the covenant. It uses the dialogue form, which is one of the techniques preferred by wisdom teachers as a way of challenging students to think. The Song of Songs probably received its final editing after the Exile in circles that knew the wisdom traditions of Job, Qoheleth, and Proverbs well.

—Wisdom Psalms. No two lists agree on how many psalms belong to the category of wisdom. The problem is deciding on the criteria. The most certain criteria are: (1) the reflective contrast between the just and the wicked person, or between the wise and the foolish—Psalms 1, 34, 37, 49, 73, and 112 all qualify on this ground; (2) the use of special wisdom expressions such as "happy is the one who . . ." or the "fear of the Lord," as in Psalms 32, 111, and 128. Many other psalms make use of wisdom themes but put their major emphasis elsewhere.

The achievement of wisdom

Biblical theology usually gives much less attention to wisdom than it does to the prophets, the history of salvation, or the legal material. Yet wisdom was important through all of Israel's history. Before prophecy was born, wisdom had a long tradition behind it. The prophets themselves often borrowed wisdom's insights and expressions; and when prophecy failed, in the period after the Exile, wisdom was just reaching its peak. Its international character allowed it to bring the best of other cultures into Israel's thinking and gave a broader context to the special covenant theology that prevented a too nationalistic and too narrow idea of God's will.

Some of the major contributions of wisdom thinking to Israel's religion were:

1) *Emphasis on cause and effect.* Acts have consequences, and moral decisions can never be made outside the context of social responsibility and the experience of others before us. Often much that is unexplainable can be partially explained by analogies with common experience.

2) *Appreciation of time.* Israel did not strive to erase time and return to origins. Time moved on and God always acted with the present and future in view. This gave Israel a true sense of history and a confidence that God would always act again. At the same time, Israel could not hope to control the cycle

of time by cult or magic as the pagans did; rather, God alone knew the times and controlled the future.

3) *Confidence in order.* Wisdom believed in the empirical search for the hidden order of divine purpose in the world. It could be studied and reflected upon, and could provide guidelines for conduct. While wisdom therefore gave great value to tradition, it also provided Israelite faith with the confidence to make new applications in changed situations throughout its history.

4) *God revealed in creation.* The Mosaic law and the prophets brought Israel an awareness of God as a personal savior, but wisdom opened up the more universal dimension of Yahweh as the Creator and the only God by pointing to the order and beauty of creation and the divine will revealed in it. It also gave emphasis to the positive role of human understanding and management of the world.

5) *Humans as responsible.* Wisdom is often accused of having a theology of God's justice but none of divine mercy until the latest periods (Sirach). This is not entirely true. Whereas the prophets stressed mercy after sin, wisdom stressed the *continuity* of God's creation, so that after misfortune or failure there was another chance. More than that, humans share the creative power of God and must exercise it responsibly and prudently according to wisdom.

6) *Personification of wisdom.* Several passages treat wisdom as though it were an independent being close to God (Prov 1:20-33; 8:22-31; Sir 24:1-31; Wis 9:9-11). This is primarily a literary device to express how the transcendent God becomes present in a personal and immanent way by communicating himself to our intelligence, understanding, and faith. Without this development, Christianity's theology of Jesus as Son of God and Word-made-flesh could not have found such expression.

7) *Wisdom as divine gift.* While wisdom put high value on human reasoning, it more and more refined its understanding of the limits of human knowledge to give greater emphasis to the divine initiative. Knowing God and divine revelation gave light to human understanding, light unattainable by experience of the world alone. Wisdom was always ethical in orientation, but it developed a richer stance in which religious knowledge and ethics worked as one.

8) *The meaning of suffering.* Based on experience and reflection, wisdom wrestled with the challenge of suffering and offered several answers that could guide practical decisions of sufferers. None were very adequate (evil as the result of sin, a testing from God, a disciplinary correction of our faults), but neither are most modern answers. It rejected pagan responses of magical protection or legitimate despair and placed evil firmly in the area of ethics. Whatever the reason for a particular evil, the results are always in the hand of a just and merciful God who listens.

9) *Trust as the basic virtue.* Wisdom recognized its limits and emphasized that trust is the basic virtue of the wise. Experience is often paradoxical and seemingly contradictory; fundamental questions of life and death are beyond our control, and God cannot be made to conform to our expectations. Thus the ultimate wisdom looks ahead confidently and bases reasonable hopes and responsible decisions on a firm commitment to Yahweh for better or for worse.

10) *The value of community.* This may seem a strange claim to give wisdom, which so often highlights the *individual* struggle for growth. But it is deserved in the sense that wisdom's concern with the universal human pool of knowledge led it to value other peoples and their contributions, the power of communication and dialogue through words, listening and respecting other opinions, and the need for justice, honesty, and integrity in human dealings. The vision that combined social interdependence and individual worth is far more highly developed in the wisdom writings than in other parts of Scripture.

Wisdom does not stand opposed, therefore, to the teachings of the Pentateuch or the Prophets but serves to unite the teachings of revelation and the obedience demanded by faith with the practical experience of everyday reality in order to enrich both.

Wisdom's relevance today

Religious faith in the modern world has come under increasing pressure from the expansion of human knowledge. Areas of life that were once considered the inviolable preserve of divine action alone are now open to human investigation and even management.

Travel in space, prolongation of life, the creation of human embryos in test tubes, and even genetic engineering of the individual touch on areas that traditional wisdom reserved to the mystery of divine purpose. These are on top of human victories in understanding the factors of climate and weather, the causes of disease and sickness, and the movement of the heavenly bodies that so baffled the ancient thinkers and led them to suggest prayer where human knowledge failed. Many people in our culture no longer see how God impinges on daily life in any meaningful way; their outlook has been, de facto, totally secularized, even if they still nominally profess to believe in God. Their world is a world of human control, and human decisions are all that matter.

Many others, experiencing the horrors of modern war and aggression or living through a personal tragedy of disease or sudden death in the family, wonder why God is silent when most needed. They question the value of creeds and biblical laws, elaborate religious worship, and the theologies of the churches when God seems so distant from human affairs and so unnecessary to solving our worldly problems.

It is here that wisdom has the most to say to us. On the one hand, it affirms that the order, goodness, and beauty of the universe we have discovered and mastered by our powers are really an unfolding of God's own designs. Humans are created in the image of God and given dominion over the universe to govern it wisely by the powers of understanding, prudence, and verbal skills with which God has endowed them. On the other hand, as our own understanding of the world deepens, the wisdom literature assures us that it is natural and permissible to question and to doubt along the way. Job and Qoheleth proclaim that questioning the hidden God often helps us understand better that even in silence God is present.

Above all, wisdom both encourages us to use our human power of reflection and questioning and warns us that today, just as much as in Old Testament times, we run the risk of human pride claiming too much for itself and foolishly, even arrogantly, rushing us toward the destruction of God's good creation.

PROVERBS

Lawrence E. Boadt, C.S.P.

INTRODUCTION

The structure of the book

Proverbs has nine different divisions of varying length. The shortest is seven verses, the longest, thirteen chapters.

1:1-7	Title and general introduction to the whole book
1:8–9:18	The instruction of a wisdom teacher
10:1–22:16	The collected "Proverbs of Solomon"
22:17–24:22	The "Words of the Wise"
24:23-34	Additional "Words of the Wise"
25:1–29:27	Proverbs of Solomon collected under Hezekiah
30:1-33	The collected Words of Agur
31:1-9	The collected Words of Lemuel
31:10-31	"The ideal woman": an appendix to Lemuel

These divisions in turn may well include smaller collections that once stood by themselves, for example 25:2-27 or the group of numerical sayings in 30:10-33. What strikes us immediately, of course, is that this book is a collection of collections. It is substantially different from most other books of the Bible because of the brevity of its single units. The section from 10:1 to 22:16, for example, contains 375 individual proverbs. Even the longest unit, the poem of Wisdom personified as a woman in chapter 8, seems more a series of separate commands and a litany of titles than a strictly integrated work of art. Sayings often stand side by side with no apparent connection to one another. Thus, "Do you see a man hasty in his words? More can be hoped for from a fool!" in 29:20 is followed by: "If a man pampers his servant from childhood, he will turn out to be stubborn." Both are good advice in different circumstances. One can only wonder what brought them together at this point in the text. As a result, many scholars believe that there is no real order in the Book of Proverbs. They suggest that the separate collections were gathered up over a long period of time and loosely joined together by means of the editorial headings that begin each section.

That is far too negative a view, however. While no one denies that many of the short sayings were originally written down as remembered and not necessarily arranged in a set order, signs of organization are everywhere in the book. The instructions of Lady Wisdom in chapters 1–9 clearly parallel the ideal women of chapter 31. The "Words of the Wise" in 22:17–24:23 are modeled on and match the "Thirty Sayings of Amenemope" from Egyptian wisdom literature. And the introductory preface in 1:1-7 sets a clear course that governs the purpose of the whole book. Proverbs is not a novel with a single, carefully written, very dramatic plot, but, as the comments that follow will show, the editors and collectors of Israel's wisdom certainly intended to present a theology in which the great educational tradition of the wise could be understood.

Literary characteristics of the Book of Proverbs

There are two main types of material in the Book of Proverbs. The first is the *proverb* proper, and the second is the *instruction.* Other literary forms also occur here and there but are quite subordinate to the main two. These less frequent genres include riddles, prophetic urgings, admonitions or warnings, personified self-praise, and extended metaphors or model stories. These are discussed where they occur in the text.

—THE PROVERB. While almost all people recognize a proverbial statement when they hear one, few agree on a definition. The most common characteristics include (1) brevity, (2) cleverness, (3) memorable form, (4) rootedness in experience, (5) universal truth, (6) practical aim, and (7) long use (traditional origin). The first three deal with the form, the last four with the content. Thus the proverb is almost always described as poetic or metrical, with terse, vigorous, forceful, striking imagery. Its style is easy to remember and may have originated in oral societies before writing was common.

The content, on the other hand, is often paradoxical at first sight. Proverbs combine real experience of the concrete with general applications to all times and situations. This makes them partially true and partially false at the same time. What one does at one moment may be all wrong at the next. It is no accident that the Book of Proverbs can place contradictory sayings side by side as in 26:4-5: "Answer not the fool according to his folly, lest you too become like him," and "Answer the fool according to his folly, lest he become wise in his own eyes." No generalization ever captures all the human experience for every occasion. The very nature of a proverb forces the hearer or reader to ask, "How does this so-called truth apply to me?" The better the proverb, the more questions it raises along with its apparent answers.

Some writers distinguish between a *proverb,* which has roots in the common people's usage over many, many years and whose origins are unknown, and an *aphorism,* a clever saying invented by a well-known literary figure.

The Ancient Near East was a much more traditional society than modern society, and proverbs are found in all the ancient civilizations, almost always presented anonymously as the lessons of past generations to the youth of today. Israel shared this view completely, and this fact, together with a common tradition of poetic expression, shared cultural values, and identical experience of coping to survive in similar geography makes Israel's Proverbs appear more like the proverbs of Egypt, Sumeria, or Babylon than many modern Jews and Christians feel comfortable with.

—THE INSTRUCTION. Chapters 1–9; 22:17–24:23; and possibly 31:10-31 can be best compared to the well-known Egyptian wisdom form called "Instruction," which is usually framed as the legacy of a father to his son and includes commands and prohibitions along with the reasons why they should be heeded (the *motivation* for obeying). A number of plain proverbs and warnings are thrown in as well. It usually begins with a call, "Listen, my son . . ." The most notable features of this particular kind of wisdom literature are the absolute authority of the father or teacher and the belief that such wisdom can be learned by hearing and doing it. The instructor does not appeal beyond experience nor expect the student to question the truth of the teaching. At the same time, the teacher shows no doubt whatever that the student can master the lesson by understanding and obeying it. Such teaching was based on the conviction that the world is ordered by *maat,* the concept of divine right order (often a goddess), and that the good person can live according to that order and attain success by proper conduct.

Israel saw much of value in this view and made use of the ideas of (1) instruction or discipline (used often, beginning in Prov 1:2); (2) the contrast in the ways of the righteous and the wicked; (3) the conviction that evil deeds reap retribution; and (4) the belief that self-control is essential to success. But while Egyptian literary works such as Amenemope and Ptah-hotep were written only for the professional training of court scribes, Israel's Proverbs opened up the ideal to every youth. What may have started as an elite school program was broadened to become a religious ideal of wisdom for the nation, parallel to the Law and the Prophets.

The artistic beauty of Proverbs

The word for "proverb" in the title of the book, "The Proverbs of Solomon," comes from *mashal*, the Hebrew word for "likeness" or "comparison." But *mashal* has a much wider meaning in the Bible than merely "proverb." It is used in Ezekiel of allegories and stories (Ezek 17:2; 24:3) as well as of short maxims (18:2; 16:44). In several prophetic passages it refers to a taunt song or mocking image (Isa 14:4; Jer 24:9; Mic 2:4). In each case a lesson is to be learned, and so the best interpretation of the term used as a title for the whole Book of Proverbs might be "paradigms," "models," or "examples," as many authors suggest, but always as a work of art. The *mashal* is the product of the skill of the poet and gains acceptance because of its pleasing use of language and imagery.

The chief artistic device is, of course, the good comparison. Often the images are drawn from nature or family life. The aim is to find just the right metaphor or analogy from ordinary experience to capture the extraordinary lesson in the proverb. Thus, in order to describe the evil charms of an adulteress, the teachers compared them to honey-sweet tidbits that cause terrible stomach aches (Prov 5:3-4). Another well-loved tradition was the contrast between the lazy person and the ant. How demeaning to realize that even an ant is better than that (6:6-11)!

More specifically, most of the actual proverbial sayings and many of the instructions in the book are fashioned according to classical Hebrew poetry, with two parallel parts to each verse. This parallelism, or better, use of balanced lines, is the most easily recognized element in biblical poetry. The major types of parallelism employed make the second half of the line say either the same or the opposite of the first half, or else elaborate a part of the first half. These are called:

1) *synonymous parallelism:*

"Even in laughter the heart may be sad,
and the end of joy may be sorrow."
(Prov 14:13)

2) *antithetic parallelism:*

"The memory of the just will be blessed,
but the name of the wicked will rot." (Prov 10:7)

3) *synthetic parallelism:*

"Entrust your works to the Lord,
and your plans will succeed."
(Prov 16:3)

In this last case, the second part describes the results of the first action, thus extending the scope of the message instead of repeating it. Other variations occur occasionally, such as:

4) *"better than" comparisons:*

"Better a dish of herbs where love is
than a fatted ox and hatred with it."
(Prov 15:17)

5) *comparisons:*

"Like golden apples in silver settings
are words spoken at the proper time." (Prov 25:11)

6) *numerical series:*

"Three things are never satisfied,
four never say, 'Enough!'
The nether world, and the barren womb;
the earth that is never saturated with water,
and fire, that never says 'Enough!' "
(Prov 30:15-16)

In all these examples a balance is created between the first and second half of a thought. Usually it is expressed in a regular three-beat-plus-three-beat meter that gives the poetry both solemnity and weight:

"The-glóry of-yoúng-men is-their-stréngth
And-the dígnity of-óld-men is-grév-hair"
(Prov 20:29).

Other poetic devices are also used for effect: *rhetorical questions* (6:9; 23:29); *hyperbole* (2:18; 5:5); *fables* (6:6-8); *irony* (19:24; 23:27; 26:13-15); *chiasmus* (1:16, 29; 2:16); *alliteration* (13:3, 14); *puns* (13:20; 23:5); and *acrostics* (31:10-31—each line begins with the next letter of the alphabet in order). Naturally the last four poetic techniques only appear in the original Hebrew and do not show up in our English translations. How much richer our appreciation would be if we all read Hebrew!

Purpose of the Book of Proverbs

While the Torah and the Prophets stress faith and obedience, wisdom, especially the Book of Proverbs, stresses understanding and obedience. The two poles within which it moves are clearly the intellectual and the ethical. Since the ancient Israelite considered the heart to be the seat of thinking and reasoning as well as of decision, it is to the heart that the teaching of Proverbs is directed. An Israelite would agree with Socrates' maxim "The unexamined life is not worth living." But unlike the great Greek philosopher who asked about the ultimate meaning and nature of life itself, the Israelite sages sought the practical results. They wanted to know how behavior affected the life a person led. They insisted upon *reflection* as the key to understanding, but theirs was not truly a philosophical outlook in the Greek tradition that asks about the origin and why of things. Instead they examined human experience as a series of many different actions that must be sorted out, classified, and their results evaluated. This could not be done by one generation, but required the cumulative verification of many centuries. Thus, while proverbial wisdom is very particular about life, it often seems somewhat rigid and unbending in its conclusions. What is the *same* about life always appeared more important than what *varied* or did not fit established patterns.

The purpose of proverbial wisdom in Israel can be summed up in one word: *education*. Many proverbs originated in family and tribal education of youth, perhaps long before the nation Israel came into being. One can well imagine the village elders advising young farmers-to-be, "He who tills his own land has food in plenty, but he who follows idle pursuits is a fool" (Prov 12:11). Still other proverbs are the products of formal education, oriented toward professional careers in administrative posts or teaching: "By patience is a ruler persuaded, and a soft tongue will break a bone" (25:15). The chapters belonging to the Instruction genre (1–9 and 22:17–24:22) are almost entirely school lessons, whereas the general collections of proverbs in chapters 10–22 and 25–29 contain many more family or folk proverbs, as well as proverbs that have a general social lesson that may or may not stem from a formal classroom.

The vocabulary of the wise

The subject matter of proverbial wisdom ranges over most of the areas of life also met with in other books of the Bible, except for the cultic or legal aspects of the Pentateuch and the events of Israel's history. Thus we regularly find sentences dealing with poverty and evildoing, with mercy and trustworthiness, themes familiar to us from the prophets and the psalms. But there is a whole body of words that occur again and again in Proverbs (and often in Job or Qoheleth) but are rarely used outside of the wisdom tradition. These will be discussed as they occur in the text, but it is worth listing them here to underline how much wisdom is tied to the intellectual activities of intention, understanding, and thinking.

Wisdom	An overall mastery of life through understanding and successful action.
Discipline	Education with a heavy dose of coercion as well as self-control.
Understanding	
Capacity	
Counsel	Good advice and critical sharpness.
Prudence	Trained cleverness.
Competence	Successful grasp of affairs.
Political expertise	
Resourcefulness	
Intelligence	
Rebuke	

On the negative side, there are special terms for those who reject the learning process or who cannot seem to learn.

Simple	Uneducated and in need of much teaching still.
Fool	Usually lacks self-control and discipline.
Stupid	Intransigently wrong-headed.
Scoffer	One who refuses to listen and reviles the value of wisdom.
Arrogant	Basically conceited and always causing strife.
Godless	No respect for God (found only in 11:9).

Lazy	Lives only for the moment with no thought of tomorrow.
Impious	A stupid person but with a blasphemous attitude.

The theology of Proverbs

The religious teaching of Proverbs reflects a long period of development. Among the lasting values inculcated from the very earliest materials are the ideals of family life and filial obligation, and the absolute place of justice in society. Honesty, truthfulness, and above all integrity are taught in dozens of different ways. Concern for the poor and helpless and the value of hard work are both held up to the reader as good. Self-control and the restraint of desires and passions are a common theme. Also, the contrast between the just person and the wicked is explored again and again. Indeed there is a constant conviction that evil does not go unpunished in the divine order of things, even though in the older wisdom God is not always named as the one who brings justice. In this, Proverbs stands in harmony with the theology of Deuteronomy, which promises blessing for fidelity to Yahweh but curse for infidelity. In many ways this older level of proverbial teaching can be summed up as a guidebook for success in life, where life is seen as divine blessing.

With time the wisdom teachers of Israel drew their lessons ever closer to the specific national traditions of their faith, and much of chapters 1–9 reflects the attempt to identify wisdom with the divine authority of their own God Yahweh. This includes equating wisdom with fear of the Lord (faithful fulfillment of religious duty) in 1:7, 29; 2:5; 9:10; and 31:30; and asserting the divine origin of wisdom before the world began (8:1-36). Many individual proverbs in the great collections of chapters 10–22:16; 22:17–24:22; and 25–29 are directly connected to Yahweh and Yahweh's control of history (see 15:3, 11; 16:1, 4, 9; 19:21; 21:2). All of wisdom is now seen as practical lessons that put us into proper relationship to God as well as to our fellow citizens. The final edition of Proverbs proved to be a great achievement because it united the common wisdom of the Ancient Near East with the special insights of Israel about the God who is really present and caring in the affairs of everyday life.

The final edition

Sumerian proverbs similar to those in the Bible are known in collections as far back as the middle of the third millennium B.C.E. And as discussed in the introduction to wisdom literature, there is good reason to presume that the monarchy of David and Solomon established schools modeled on the wisdom academies in Egypt and to a lesser extent those in Mesopotamia.

Thus we may discern at least three major stages in the formation of the Book of Proverbs. The first is the collection of short proverbs used in traditional teaching of youth, whether in family, village, or tribal settings. Some individual groupings may date back to the time of the Judges or earlier.

A second important stage was the court and temple school founded on Egyptian models in the monarchy period. In this regard, Solomon may indeed have been the original inspiration, although the claim that he authored most of the proverbs in the book is not to be taken at face value. To this period belong the majority of the proverbs and most of the instructions found in chapters 1–9 and 22:17–24:22.

A third stage is represented by the additions and expansions that related these teachings specifically to Yahweh as the single guarantor of world order and justice and as the giver of wisdom to human beings. Not that every mention of Yahweh in individual proverbs is necessarily late. For example, Prov 19:3, "A man's own folly upsets his way, but his heart is resentful against the Lord," is more of an observation on life than a theological attempt to prove that Yahweh is the source of wisdom. But generally proverbs with Yahweh's name (the New American Bible has "the Lord") establish a later context for interpreting the meaning of older wisdom sayings. This level of synthesis and the final editing of the book should be probably dated soon after the Exile, about 500 B.C.E., since the book now conforms well to both the general teaching of Deuteronomy on the right way of life and to the affirmation of the vital creative power of God so evident in the exilic prophet Second Isaiah.

COMMENTARY

PART I: WISDOM'S INSTRUCTIONS

Prov 1:1-9:18

Overall plan

Chapters 1–9 stand apart from the collection of proverbs in chapters 10–22 and 25–30 in several ways. They are first of all written in much longer units than the two-line proverbs that dominate the remaining sections. They are also much more impassioned in tone, more like homilies aimed at persuading young minds of the power of wisdom. And they are not neutral, third-person observations about life and reality as proverbial sayings are, but they frequently address the hearer in the second person and even include long speeches from Wisdom personified as a woman. The arguments and warnings addressed to the seeker after wisdom are bolstered by elaborate motivations and reasons why they should be obeyed and even embraced. These are all characteristics of the international "Instruction" genre of literature (see p. 645). It is aimed at the education of youth, usually for positions as scribes or administrators in government. Chapters 1–9 have broadened this to include all citizens on every corner and in every square of the city (Prov 1:8; 8:1).

There has been much discussion over exactly how many individual instructions can be found in these nine chapters. The structure of the whole is the product of some growth, and clear additions such as 6:1-19 (a group of proverbs) break up and to some extent hide the original plan. Chapters 1–9 certainly were intended as an extended preface to the collected proverbs that follow in 10:1 and the chapters following. The role of wisdom as a speaker in chapters 1 and 8 is essential to the plan, as is the contrast between "Lady Wisdom" and the evil woman who is described sometimes as an adulteress and sometimes as foolishness ("Dame Folly") itself.

Fitting all the instructions into one simple outline has proven a block to all commentators. The number of suggested instructions ranges from seven or eight up to twelve or more. Some scholars have thought that the occurrence of "my son" in direct address marked off the separate passages; but a look at 1:15 will show that some occurrences of this phrase fall in the middle of a speech. The best guide is still the natural sense of when one topic ends and another begins. In this way chapters 1–9 can be divided as follows:

(1:1-7)	(General introduction to the whole book)
1:8-19	First instruction
1:20-33	Wisdom's first speech
2:1-22	Second instruction
3:1-12	Third instruction
3:13-35	Fourth instruction
4:1-9	Fifth instruction
4:10-27	Sixth instruction
5:1-23	Seventh instruction
6:1-19	Proverbial collection (a comment on 5:21-23?)
6:20-35	Eighth instruction
7:1-27	Ninth instruction
8:1-36	Wisdom's second speech
9:1-18	Tenth instruction

As noted in the comments that follow, other structures are also present. Chapter 2 is a theme statement for chapters 3–7, and the first seven instructions together may make up the seven pillars of wisdom's house mentioned in 9:1. But how they developed still remains somewhat of a mystery.

1:1-7 The purpose of the book. What stands out immediately in the search for wisdom is its intellectual quality. It is not vision or smell or skill in a worker's craft that receives praise, but the virtues of studying diligently and developing good judgment. "Discipline" is formal education at the hands of a teacher. It is hard work, requiring lessons and practice. The title announces that what follows are the "proverbs" of the wisest king, Solomon. As pointed out in the introduction (p. 646), the Hebrew sense of *mashal* means more than a saying—it is a lesson or model to be followed. Thus the special wisdom of leadership and judgment proper to kings is being offered to all who submit to disciplined study. Humans can become wise by learning and are capable of growth in understanding, but never simply on their own.

The "simple" in verse 4 are the unlearned, especially the young, but also those who have never had formal education.

The impression that is left when all the nouns about knowledge are piled up together in these few verses matches the intention of the older Egyptian instructions. The teachers want to impress upon open and promising minds that successful careers in public service demand thinking for both decision-making and dealing with people. This is what we might call "old wisdom," a self-confident, positive reliance on human ability to learn and to master the world. Israel shared this view in part, and many sections of Proverbs breathe just such optimism about gaining wisdom through mental ability.

The intellectual aspect is matched by moral conduct. Verse 3 mentions three important qualities of behavior to be seen frequently in the following chapters: it must be right, just, and honest. The ultimate criterion, however, is summed up in verse 7: fear of the Lord, which is both piety and religious fidelity. Without it the search for wisdom becomes folly (see the comments on 9:6). Possibly, too, the editors sum up the entire contents of the book in verse 6: it contains proverbs (chs. 10–22; 25–29); parables (chs. 1–9); words of the wise (chs. 22–24); and riddles (chs. 30–31).

1:8-19 First instruction: A warning against the wicked. As in Egyptian models, the instruction is framed as the address of a father to his son, or since it is really a metaphor, a teacher to the pupil. The most important lesson for the beginner in wisdom is how easily one can be misled by temptation and seductive arguments to do evil. The only protection is a firm adherence to what has been learned about the right way of acting.

The sinners of verse 10 contemplate violence to gain money or wealth. Perhaps verses 10-12 describe a theft in the planning stages, or better, thoughts of a general life of crime and extortion that will prove very rewarding financially. It does not really matter, since a larger lesson is involved here, illustrated by the reference to the nether world. Because Israel had no concept of an afterlife as a place of happiness and vitality, life was for here and now. To destroy the quality of life of the innocent, to harm them, defraud them, or dishonor them was as good as killing them. It was handing them over to the power of death that would destroy a rich and vibrant life. Sin is service to the powers of death. The more people become involved in evil, the farther from *real* life they travel. They themselves will soon be trapped in the meshes of death. (See a similar thought in Isa 59:7.)

The image of verse 17 is not clear. It means that the traps set by the wicked will hardly entice a youth into them if they are seen being prepared. But some scholars think that the image says the opposite: some birds are so naive that they go after seed even in an easily visible trap.

The teacher promises that obedient learning at home and school will lead to honor and respect in society. These are the real marks of success, described by the image of the royal crown on the head (v. 9). The whole passage argues from common sense and not from any divine commandment of the Lord. It is old wisdom at its best.

1:20-33 Wisdom's first speech: an invitation scorned. The previous section argued from reason; now the authors present Wisdom speaking as a prophet. She calls aloud in public places, as did the classical prophets (Jer 11:6; Isa 58:1), to persuade people to convert their hearts to Yahweh. Verse 32 suggests that the people's "turning away" ("self-will" misses the point) will be the reason for their condemnation, as will be their rejection of Yahweh's "spirit." Both ideas are common in the prophets (see Jer 2:19; 8:5; Hos 11:7 for "turning away," and Isa 40:13; 44:3; 61:1; Ezek 11:5; Mic 2:7; Joel 3:1 for the divine spirit).

In many ways Wisdom is modeled here on the prophet Jeremiah, who by and large also experienced rejection of his message. The expression "How long?" (v. 22) is a favorite in his oracles (Jer 4:14, 21; 12:4; 13:27; 23:26; 31:22; 47:5). And, like Wisdom in verses 26-28, Jeremiah was finally driven by God not to answer the people when they did finally seek help during the catastrophe of the Babylonian invasion (Jer 14:11). The combination of rebuke for sins and veiled threat of punishment, which is proper to prophetic preaching, is here employed as the power of the word of wisdom to offer life. Wisdom promises rest and peace free from fear to those who seek counsel and reproof (vv. 25, 30), knowledge and fear of the Lord (v. 29), and spirit and word (v. 23; see also Deut 12:10; Ezek 34:25).

In contrast, the simple (v. 22) see no value in working for wisdom. They love their simplicity (NAB: "inanity"). "In ignorance is bliss" becomes their motto. The NAB omits the second part of verse 22: "(How long) will the scoffers rejoice in their scoffing, and the stupid hate knowledge?" It may be an added comment, for it is in the third person, unlike the rest of the passage. But it illustrates what is finally made clear in verse 30: the choice of ignorance ends up in deliberate folly and self-destruction.

2:1-22 The second instruction: the benefits of wisdom. Here the wisdom teacher waxes eloquently on the blessings that wisdom can bestow. Clearly a receptive student is in mind, the ideal candidate for instruction. The chapter is chiastic in structure, with the opening theme repeated at the end, and the two middle sections parallel to one another in an A-B:B-A pattern. Verses 1-11 describe wisdom's blessings; verses 12-15 warn against the evil man; verses 16-19 warn against the adulteress; and verses 20-22 return to the promise of blessing. The whole forms a theme statement for the fuller treatment of both the evil man and the adulteress in chapters 3–7. If 1:20-33 sounded prophetic, this passage echoes Deuteronomy and the psalms, especially in the contrast between the ways of the just and wicked, and the call to obey God's commands (see Deut 4; 11; Pss 1; 37).

In 2:1-11 the vocabulary of old wisdom that was seen in 1:1-7 reappears, but this time it is explicitly related to Israel's conviction that all knowledge and blessing come from Yahweh alone. Wisdom is a gift of God and not the product of native human intelligence or ability. There is no rejection of human searching and questioning in this, but a subordination of ends. The source of knowledge, understanding, and intelligence that can guide right conduct is knowledge of God's role in the process. It is the exact opposite of what the proverbs often refer to as the attitude of those "wise in their own eyes" (3:7; 26:5, 12, 16; 28:11).

The first warning in verses 12-15 sketches the way of the wicked. Their thinking is crooked and their speech is crooked. They are the opposite of the upright and honest person of verse 9. Evil is so much their way that they could no longer be straight if they wanted to! The second warning is against the adulterous woman. Sexuality is always an area of temptation, but involvement with a seductress who is married can lead to grave social consequences beyond merely personal sin. It is the destruction that is death itself. Like Psalm 1, the passage ends by proposing two ways of life to the youth and calling for a decision in favor of wisdom's way.

3:1-12 The third instruction: the blessing of fidelity to God. Verse 1 mentions the Torah and divine commands in the context of a promise of long life. "Kindness and fidelity" (v. 3) also fit into this pattern, which is very close to Deuteronomy's theological view of the covenant on Mount Sinai. Indeed, many aspects of this short section suggest that it is a deliberate attempt to counteract the older concept of a self-reliant wisdom. It twice condemns those who judge themselves wise (vv. 5, 7) and opposes such self-confidence by proposing an ideal of trusting in and fearing the Lord. Although echoes of traditional wisdom are present (long life is also the goal of Egyptian instructions), it has been reworked away from a sharp emphasis on intellectual achievement toward a more meditative and prayerful attitude. This is seen in verse 6: "In all your ways be mindful of him." Even verses 11-12 conclude with a form of reproof that has little in common with the corrections of the teachers and is closer to an explanation of suffering as a way to God (Deut 8:5).

A look at the direct imperatives in these twelve verses shows that not one of them is clearly directed toward the intellectual pursuit of wisdom. In fact, verses 9-10 are close in spirit to Mal 3:10, "Bring the whole tithe into the storehouse, that there may be food in my house, and try me in this, says the Lord of hosts: Shall I not open for you the floodgates of heaven, to pour down blessing upon you without measure?" Among the prophets, Malachi is the most priestly in tone and combines the outlook of Deuteronomy that blessing comes in return for fidelity with a spirituality centered on worship. Not unexpectedly, the priestly-oriented Letter to the Hebrews in the New Testament directly quotes verses 11-12 in Heb 12:5-6, but applies it naturally to Christian believers.

3:13-35 Fourth instruction: wisdom's value in society. Many commentators break up this unit into two parts: a hymn on the worth of wisdom (vv. 13-24) and a collection of short sayings dealing with other people (vv. 25-35). But neither part stands alone. The instructions for social conduct in the second part follow upon the promise of peace and security in verses 23-24. They place human conduct within the context of the divine command to love one's neighbor (Lev 19:18) and thus reveal the real nature of "life" that wisdom offers to those who grasp her (vv. 16, 18). In many ways this entire instruction continues the message of the preceding one in 3:1-12 on the necessity of bringing wisdom under the revelation proclaimed in the covenant with Yahweh.

Some important ideas are raised in this passage. Verses 13-15 hint that wisdom can be personified as an ideal wife (similar to Prov 31:10), more valuable to a young man for success in life than the most costly gems. Verses 16-18 deepen this claim by comparing wisdom to the tree of life at the center of the Garden of Eden in Gen 2:9. At the time of creation it represented the human hope for eternal life; here it symbolizes medicine or balm that gives pleasant help and life to the soul (v. 22). Wisdom also brings peace (v. 17). The Hebrew word *shalom* means much more than our English word "peace." It is wholeness, blessing, prosperity—a full, successful life.

In verse 19, the claim that creation was given order by wisdom prepares us for the full description found in chapter 8. It also reflects Egyptian wisdom's concept of *maat*, "right order," which is at the heart of mastering wisdom. Here Yahweh, the God of Israel, alone gives good order to all things, and not some abstract principle. In the same way, the list of commands about treatment of others in verses 27-31 reflects the universal wisdom of the Ancient Near East, but it is brought under Yahweh's guidance by verses 32-35. There are two ways: one brings friendship with God, blessing, kindness (divine mercy), and honor; the other, curse, retribution, and shame.

4:1-9 Fifth instruction: the summons to get wisdom. In truly traditional fashion, this instruction calls on the pupil or child to receive education eagerly. The terms "instruction," "understanding," and "teaching" in verses 1-2 refer to the lessons of the wise, either passed down in the family or the schools. Here again wisdom is treated almost as a bride to be loved and treasured above all else in life. The strong stress on the home as the source of this insight is probably due to the author's concern to make the point extremely personal. Wisdom is not just another commodity; it must be loved for its own sake.

There is no mention of the Yahweh of faith in this whole passage. The images and metaphors are borrowed from the remembered joys of a warm and loving childhood, in which education was mixed with affection and concern. Like a deeply devoted parent, wisdom will guard and stand by the individual for life (v. 6); like a friend, she will return favor for favor and honor for honor (v. 8); and like a wife that is herself a jewel, she will give the crowning touch to every aspect of a person's life. Perhaps there is even a hint that wisdom is a queen who bestows royal honors on favored servants and courtiers. But one must first get wisdom, and that requires listening, obeying, and the trusting spirit of a child who heeds the words and commands of the father and teacher (v. 4).

4:10-27 Sixth instruction: the two paths. One of the major themes of wisdom literature is that of the two ways. One leads to light and life, the other to darkness and death. One is straight, the other is crooked and devious. To give the metaphor power, various words for road, path, or highway are used. Each step must be deliberately taken. The passage is very artistically arranged in a chiastic fashion to show how walking is as easy on the one path as on the other, but the decision will lead to major differences. The *way* of wisdom stands opposed to the *path* of the wicked, while the *path* of the just opposes the *way* of the wicked. The A-B:B-A pattern argues against the decision to place verse 18 after verse 19, as in the NAB translation. The contents of the right way or path are the traditional wisdom teachings of the sages. The strong command to shun evil in verse 15 comes from the experience of generations that once a person gets into the grip of temptation to evil, it is harder and harder to free oneself.

Verses 20-27 reinforce this message with a series of warnings against playing the two ways off against one another. It is always a human urge to toy with just a few sinful things or to indulge certain vices no matter what, while trying to keep a basically upright lifestyle. But the masters of wisdom had no use for this indecisiveness or deliberate playing with fire. A choice must be made, and one's whole life must then be directed to attaining wholeness and uprightness.

Above all, speech betrays the real directions of a person's heart. False speech is the chief enemy of wisdom everywhere in Proverbs. The strict command in verse 24 is paralleled by the Egyptian advice of Amenemope: "God hates him who falsifies words; his great abomination is the one contentious of belly" (the belly being the source of speech for the Egyptian as the heart was for the Israelite). An Aramaic work, *The Words of Ahiqar*, reinforces the message: "My son, more than all watchfulness, watch your mouth!" Verses 26-27 return to the two paths with a final warning against any compromise. Heb 12:13 quotes verse 26 as the discipline for Christians.

5:1-23 Seventh instruction: the dangers of the adulteress. If speech can be the greatest internal enemy of a person, the lures of the adulteress are the greatest external enemy. The word for the woman is specifically "foreign woman," and many have thought the entire treatment of this theme in Prov 1–9 is a metaphor for apostasy, expressed by participation in the cults of fertility in honor of goddesses of sexuality such as Ishtar (Babylonian) or Astarte (Canaanite). Given the prophetic condemnations of such cults (Ezek 8; Jer 44), some echo of this may be present in part, especially in chapter 9. But the description in chapter 5 is so vivid and direct that there can be little doubt that real-life marriages are being discussed.

Warnings against violating the wife of another man go back as far as the earliest known wisdom literature. The *Instruction of Ptahhotep* (before 2000 B.C.E.) says, "Beware of approaching women. A thousand men have been led astray from their good; a man is but mocked by their glistening limbs . . . but death is the penalty for enjoying it." The *Wisdom of Ani* (1500–1200 B.C.E.) explicitly warns, "Beware of the woman from abroad . . . a woman whose husband is far away."

This section contains four separate statements that contrast the evil woman with the faithful wife. Verses 1-6 describe her words, which quickly snare the youth's uncontrolled passions and enslave him to death itself. Discretion, that is, prudence, is the only safeguard (v. 2). Verses 7-14 then draw the conclusions of failure. The youth's life and reputation are ruined (v. 9), his position and money are lost (in penalty payments to the wronged husband? or to the wife for her favors?), and his whole body is diseased and beaten in punishment. Actually, the penalty in the law was death by stoning (Deut 22:23-24; Lev 20:10), but in practice, the text suggests, it was often much milder. Too late the youth wishes he had listened to instruction.

In sharp contrast, verses 15-19 draw upon the age-old metaphor of fresh running water to describe a faithful marriage. Verses 20-23 then draw the moral conclusion from this: why go after forbidden and disastrous pleasure that merits death and loss because of its folly when so much can be found in faithful love? On top of this, a hint is made in verse 21 that God will see and judge evil. But otherwise the lesson is drawn from common experience.

6:1-19 Four lessons about wise conduct. This section is entitled "Miscellaneous Proverbs." But "proverbs" is a misleading term, since in fact there are four extended descriptions here, far from simple two-line sayings. In the first case, a person agrees to back up the loan of another, probably a foreigner, as the Hebrew word for "neighbor" suggests. This is considered rash and foolish because the guarantor can easily be stuck in the deal. The solution proposed is to browbeat and pester the moneylender until he lets you out of the deal. It is similar to Jesus' solution in his parable of the unjust judge in Luke 18:1-5.

In the second case, verses 6-11, a scene from nature becomes a moral. The ant is famed for its constant, busy search for food and its highly organized community life, which makes the most out of collective effort. The lazy person, on the other hand, acts as though no plans ever need to be made for the future. Everything will somehow work out. The authors cite what must have been a very popular saying in verses 10-11, since it is found again in 24:33-34. The message is plain: disaster overpowers those who do not plan ahead—they are as helpless as the victims of vicious armed robbers!

The third example, in verses 12-15, deals with the person who cheats and defrauds others. He talks fast and his line is smooth; he puts his arm around the intended victims' shoulders, gives a knowing wink, and soon has gotten hold of their life savings, with a promise of future wealth that will never be realized. This kind of evil person destroys trust in social agreements and contracts, creates bitterness and strife, and in the end always gets caught in his own trap—at least that is the pious hope of the sages!

Finally, the section ends with a numerical proverb in verses 16-19, similar to those that appear in chapter 30. Seven is the symbolic number for completeness and equals the summary of all the vices mentioned in verses 1-15. Artistically, the authors have arranged them as though they were a list of the parts of the body, but each comes from within an evil mind that rejects the lessons of wisdom.

6:20-35 The eighth instruction: a further warning against adultery. This instruction opens with a call to accept the commandments and teaching of one's parents. The language is the language of Deut 6:7-8 and 11:19 with one difference: in Deuteronomy it is the profession of faith in Yahweh that one is bound to, whereas here it is the moral lessons of Israel's wisdom traditions. Ps 119:105 says, "A lamp to my feet is your word, a light to my path." So, too, here it is discipline, traditional instruction, which is the light that guides rather than divine revelation.

Sexual license is condemned because it results from uncontrolled lust; but even more wrong is violation of another's marriage rights out of such lust. It leads only to terrible consequences that hurt all the parties, including the betrayed husband. The folksy images of verses 27-29 make the point clear. If you do *X*, you always get *Y*. Verses 30-35 bring out some of the more practical consequences. A thief who gets caught may be punished or fined until he has nothing left, but at least people will sympathize with the need that led him to steal, and may actually respect him for his desperate solution. But an adulterer is publicly humiliated, and the enraged husband will seek vengeance in every possible way. The young man will never forget this foolish mistake. Beyond the punishments, physical and monetary, he will probably be barred from any hope of obtaining position or respect in the community again.

Akkadian wisdom understood another lesson from such conduct. After the affair, the woman may well let the adulterer take the consequences as she sides with the very husband she has cuckolded: "Do not take a harlot, whose husbands are many, an Ishtar priestess devoted to a god. In your trouble she will not support you, in your conflict she will ridicule you; reverence and humility are not with her!" The youth who gets himself into such trouble is said to be a "fool" in verse 32 (the word actually means "lacking a mind"). Adultery is the shortest-enjoyed and longest-paid-for evil act in the wisdom dictionary.

7:1-27 The ninth instruction: more on the adulteress. That this is an independent instruction is shown by the elaborate introduction in verses 1-5, matching the one in 6:20-24. Both cite Deut 6:4-9 as divine law and urge the readers to make wisdom teaching as much a part of their lives as a sister or close friend would be. The description of the adulteress is much more colorful and detailed than the ones in chapters 5 or 6. Although it seems to stick to the case of a married woman who seduces a young man, several new elements enter the picture. Now the woman acts more like a cult prostitute on the lookout for clients. The young man in turn obviously goes to the area where he knows he will find her waiting as she looks out her window. Shortly after, she suggests a connection between sex and religious duty (vv. 14-15; note also the combination of vow-offerings and peace-offerings in the law of Lev 22:21 and Num 15:8).

Illustrating this scene are the well-known ivory images of the goddess Ishtar at the lattice of a window which have been found at various ancient sites but which all originate in Phoenician (Canaanite) areas. They represent love amulets associated with the temple rites dedicated to the goddess, which often included ritual sexual intercourse between worshipers and priestesses. Deuteronomy itself emphatically warned against the dangers of such cultic infidelity on the part of Israel and promised curse and death for those who fell into it (Deut 11:26-28; 30:15-20). There is good reason to believe that in chapter 7 we are dealing with a warning against cult prostitutes and not just with a wayward wife. But the two images are joined into one, and verses 19-20 return to the explicit image of adultery.

Verses 21-27 describe, in metaphors of dumb animals, the stupidity of the youth who becomes involved. Several times before (2:18; 5:5) the penalty has been described as death. The seductive words of the woman are like the mouth of Sheol itself—a pit or gaping jaws that swallow the guilty alive. It is an image borrowed from Canaan. The Epic of Baal from Ugarit describes the hero-god's descent into the underworld through the mouth of Death, who is said to have "one lip to earth, one lip to heaven, and his tongue to the stars."

8:1-36 Wisdom's second speech: her incomparable value. In sharp contrast to the woman of chapter 7, Wisdom herself now calls for attention and offers a counter-ideal. Again the comparisons to prophecy are strong, especially in the introduction of verses 1-11. Like the prophet Jeremiah, Wisdom opposes her true words to the false and lying words of other prophets (see Jer 2:8; 6:13; 23:13-14). But as in chapter 4, Wisdom does not at first appeal to divine authority but to human reason and the value of wisdom for its own sake (see a similar thought in 3:13-15). Her call lays stress on the power of upright words to help the simple gain sense and competence ("resource" in verse 5).

Wisdom's second claim (vv. 12-16) also comes from the best of old wisdom. She offers the gifts of statesmanship, the skills of public office. Much of the vocabulary of traditional older wisdom is found in verses 12-14. We can note, however, that later passages, such as Job 12:13 and Isa 40:13-14, attribute these qualities only to Yahweh. Here Wisdom claims them for herself, thus suggesting an identity between personified Wisdom and God. The same can be said of the divine power to appoint kings in verses 15-16. Note, too, the titles of Ishtar in Babylonian tradition: "Ishtar, creator and majesty, lady of peoples, goddess of humanity, who gives the sceptre, the throne, the royal insignia to the totality of kings."

Wisdom's third offer is made in verses 17-21: a personal relationship of love. There is no direct mention of God in these verses, but the merely abstract comparisons to gold and wealth hardly do justice to understanding the promise made in verse 17 that Wisdom loves those who love her, and she will be found by all who seek her. Job 28 insisted that for a pious Israelite wisdom cannot be found except when given by God as a gift. In an indirect way, the same view is maintained here, for it is by duty (really "judgment") and by justice that Wisdom is found and in return for which she gives her love. These terms, "judgment" and "justice," are the major terms of the covenant law (see Isa 1:21; Hos 2:21; Pss 72:2; 85:12; 89:15).

Finally, the greatest of Wisdom's claims appears in verses 22-31. She belongs to the divine world far more than to the human world of the older sages. She claims to have been created before all else, before all those natural wonders of the heavens that aroused Israel to acknowledge God's almighty power over human affairs. Verses 22-29 refer specifically to Israel's literary accounts of creation, with elements drawn not only from Gen 1–2 but also from Job 38:4-18 and Ps 104:1-9. The purpose is to show that if Wisdom took part in God's creative action, she has a right to as much acknowledgment from the Israelites for her value as they give to the heavenly bodies as signs of God's goodness. Verse 30 has always been the key verse. The New American Bible has translated the Hebrew word for wisdom's role as "craftsman," which suggests a very active role for Wisdom in the process of creation. Others think that it may mean "darling" or "beloved" and may refer more to the playful aspect described in the rest of the verse. Both, however, emphasize a similar point, namely, that Wisdom was before God's presence as a model on the day of creation.

Many attempts have been made to identify the remains of a Near Eastern myth about Wisdom as a creation goddess in this passage. The closest parallels are Egyptian descriptions of *maat*, the personified goddess of world order: "Even to the gods she is precious, to her forever belongs the sovereignty; in heaven she is treasured up, for the lord of holiness has exalted her" (from *The Words of Ahiqar*, found in a Jewish colony at Elephantine in Egypt). Israel uses similar language to express how Wisdom mirrors the orderly plan of Yahweh revealed in his creation. In Prov 8 the personification does not suggest that Wisdom exists apart from God, but is instead a way of expressing the *purpose* of the divine will as it is made manifest in the world. The passage ends with a peroration in 8:32-36: to find Wisdom is to find life as well as divine favor. In fact, they are the same.

9:1-18 The tenth instruction: a parable of two banquets. To cap the eight chapters arguing for Wisdom's superiority to folly, the author or authors end by describing two banquets—one given by Lady Wisdom, the other by Dame Folly. Both sit by the road and call people in; both appeal especially to the simple and to those lacking sense (vv. 3-4, 14-16); both offer a rich reward (vv. 5, 17). But Wisdom's reward turns out to be life (vv. 6, 11), while Folly's turns out to be a poison that brings death (v. 18). The two may not seem equal, but since Wisdom's banquet requires a long period of learning, the lure of quick pleasure offered by Folly easily captures many.

The chapter is divided into three sections. Wisdom's banquet takes up verses 1-6, Folly's 13-18. In between stands a section with three proverbs from old wisdom contrasting once again the way of the wicked and the way of the wise. It includes a warning that all that has been said about wisdom in chapters 1–9 is summed up in the theme already announced in 1:7: the beginning of wisdom resides in piety and true fidelity to Yahweh (fear of the Lord). This is Wisdom's final word. The emphasis placed on it indicates that verses 7-12 are not accidentally inserted here. They are intended to summarize Wisdom's offer. The accent on fear of the Lord also suggests that the strange reference to a house of seven pillars in 9:1 and to Folly's house high on a hill in 9:14 contrasts different temples. The Jerusalem temple and its worship of Yahweh stresses the blessing of life that comes to those who search it out (see Pss 15; 24). The temples of the cult prostitutes and their sexual rites confer only death on their devotees.

Wisdom's house of seven pillars is made up of her teachings. The seven may refer to a holy place (main room of the temple) that consists of the instructions in chapters 2 to 7. In this case the vestibule would be made up of chapter 1 and the holy of holies of chapter 8, thus forming a spiritual model of the temple of Solomon. In any case, the nine chapters of Part I continually interrelate priestly *torah* and prophetic challenge with Wisdom's advice. This hints that the authors or editors saw these chapters as an argument for wisdom as an equal source next to law and prophecy for Israel's faith. Jer 18:18 already alluded to such a triple parallel: "Instruction shall not be lost from the priests, nor counsel from the wise, nor the word from the prophets."

PART II: THE PROVERBS OF SOLOMON

Prov 10:1–22:16

This first collection of proverbs attributed to Solomon is the longest section in the Book of Proverbs, but there are no internal subdivisions marked in the text. It consists of 375 single proverbs covering just about every aspect of conduct involving social relationships. Sayings on one topic, such as proper speech, are not all grouped together, however, but are scattered throughout the collection. The same is true of other topics. Scholars have long sought the principles by which individual proverbs were grouped, but no one has yet proposed a convincing answer. We know that *Sumerian* proverbs were often collected by topic. In one tablet, sayings on dogs are in one place, followed by those involving wild oxen, and then those using the metaphor of the ass, etc. Perhaps someone will yet find a key to unlock the secret of Hebrew ordering.

A few clues already exist. For example, chapters 10–15 are very heavy with proverbs contrasting the just and the wicked person. Chapters 16–22, on the other hand, deal more with practical advice on how to be successful. Perhaps these originally represented two separate collections. Certain smaller sections seem to follow special themes: thus 11:4-11 stresses the rewards of the just; 16:1-9 is on God's rule of life; 16:10-15 is on the behavior of kings; and most of chapter 18 is on the use of speech. None, however, can be clearly identified as originally a separate unity.

Many scholars do not believe that we will ever be able to identify the original collections of proverbs. Individual sayings would have been reworked often, and it is better to distinguish those sayings that reflect earlier wisdom thinking from those that show a later, more developed faith in Yahweh. Three stages have been suggested. The oldest accents practical rules for success in life and rarely or never mentions God. A second stage shows concern for the effects of social versus antisocial behavior, and a third stage uses the thought and language of a fully working Israelite piety. The second group could easily be absorbed into the first group, which would leave only two major stages of proverb development: an older, more neutral proverb used for educating the young and the apprentice public servant in the mastery of life; and a later stage when these were modified and "corrected" by sayings which emphasize Yahweh's control over success and failure, and which make a close connection between wisdom and faith. A possible middle stage between older and later wisdom would have been a developing awareness that moral attitudes are basic to divine order and that upright behavior is always rewarded.

In any case, most scholars agree that few of the proverbs actually come from Solomon's time. A long history of development has taken place, and it is only in the final reading of the total collection that the message of proverbial wisdom for Israel is fully seen. The message combines keen observation of both practical moral conduct and the consequences of human decisions with trust in God and reliance on the divine ordering of the world.

In order to gain the most out of reading this section, it is important to look over a chapter or a good part of a chapter at a time, reflect on how the individual proverbs relate to one another or how they differ, and then ask: How do these diverse sayings build up a picture of the wise believer? How do they reinforce one another? The differences and the apparent lack of unity will sharpen our looking—an essential purpose of the proverb form itself!

10:1-32. The major topic that runs through chapter 10 is the role of the just person. Again and again the just are related either to the wise or to the wicked. It is a kind of theme statement for the rest of chapters 11–22. Smaller units can be seen in verses 18-21 on the power of speech, and in verses 27-32 on the rewards of just behavior. Almost all the proverbs are in antithetic parallelism, setting the ideal against undesired foolish or evil behavior. Above all, the foolish or stupid person lacks self-control over speech and over appetites, and it is primarily on these that the sayings focus here.

Verses 1-7 give examples of careful stewardship on the part of the wise in contrast to the lack of foresight and short-sighted cravings of the foolish. Verses 8-17 focus on still another aspect distinguishing wisdom from foolishness—intention. What does the fool or evil person want? Strife seems to be one answer; quick gain at someone else's expense seems to be another. Violence is never far from the ways chosen by such people, since they want what they want at any cost. These same verses keep returning to the far different goal of the wise—life. It is long-term (v. 14) and requires careful learning (v. 17), careful speech (v. 11), and careful choice of goals (v. 16).

Verses 18-21 illustrate one aspect of wise calculation—the use of speech. Words can destroy and wound, or they can reveal too much and offend against propriety. But they can also contribute advice or comment of value and support others in need of encouragement and recognition. The training of wisdom teachers gave great attention to speech as the means of communicating and revealing wise decisions. (See more on this in chs. 12 and 18.)

Verse 22 asserts the primacy of God's blessing over human effort in the search for success. The following few sayings strengthen this conviction by showing how the upright outlast the wicked.

Verses 27-32 close the chapter by detailing the rewards of God's blessing: long life, joy, security, peace, as well as skill in speaking and a charming manner. In all ways, being just has the advantage over evil behavior.

11:1-31. The proverbs in this chapter continue the theme of uprightness. Verses 2-8 contrast the *personal* attitudes of the just and the wicked, while verses 9-15 describe the *social* implications of the two ways. The remaining sayings are harder to classify, but they generally keep up the opposition between right behavior and evil conduct.

The most common idea in this chapter is that the just person who has virtue expresses most fully the idea of the ideal order (*maat* of the older Egyptian wisdom). This ideal order forms the perfect unifying link between practical wisdom and religious wisdom, since it expresses both good sense and religious obedience to God's will. Closely associated with this concept is the word translated "upright" in verses 3 and 6, and "righteous" in verse 11. It emphasizes the inner, personal commitment to a living out of the divine ideal. It implies the spirituality of a person totally committed to making justice really work.

We can note that this chapter has a strong urban orientation. Verses 9-15 in particular express the ramifications of justice toward one's neighbors. The social community as a whole benefits or suffers from the choices one makes. The chapter opens with a saying on fair scales that typifies the concern for justice. Law and prophets demand just dealings in buying and selling (Deut 25:15; Lev 19:36; Ezek 45:10; Amos 8:5; Mic 6:11). In this they are one with wisdom. But this is part of a larger concern with the evil attitude that is always out to cheat someone else. The Egyptian Amenemope names both false weights and cheating as "abominations" to the god, as does Proverbs in verse 20. The opposite hope is expressed by verse 26: generosity in goods merits divine blessing.

The New American Bible has filled out verse 16 from the Greek Septuagint. Actually the Hebrew text reads: "A gracious woman holds on to honor, but ruthless men cling to wealth." It does not create a perfect contrast, but it makes sense as it stands and did not require a change.

Another small note can be made on verse 22. Nose rings are still known in Bedouin tribes as a sign of beauty, so the point is that a rebellious spirit seems as inappropriate in a woman as putting a sign of beauty on a pig.

Verse 31 can be considered the moral lesson of the chapter. It is quoted in 1 Pet 4:18 as a comfort to Christians under persecution. Indeed, the author of 1 Peter was a great admirer of this section of Proverbs. 1 Pet 4:8 quotes a saying from Prov 10:12.

12:1-28. The education of the beginner in wisdom continues with further examples of the differences between the just and the wicked. Verses 1-3 set the tone by bringing together the older ideal of wisdom through correction and the development of good habits with obedience to Yahweh's will. In verse 5 it is explicitly asserted that the intentions and considerations of the heart are all-important. Those motivated by justice are "legitimate" (NAB), those of the wicked are "deceitful." The word for "legitimate" in this verse might be better translated "good judgment." The sense is taken from legal usage, where the judge must render a decision on a given case. What is justice in this situation? The religious meaning is that the upright do what is just, and God accepts them as legally guiltless. On the other hand, the wicked only produce fraud and dishonesty. The Hebrew word for "deceitful" is the same as that used for "false scales" in 11:1. Legally, the guilty will be condemned for the concrete acts of fraud that their machinations lead to.

The remainder of the chapter gives various examples of the good habits typical of the just: steady work, prudence, kindliness, and self-control. But the largest emphasis falls on speech and the thoughts that motivate it. Verses 14-15 express it as a mixture of choosing good words that win people over and of listening to others in order to learn rather than speaking before thinking. This is given flesh in the series of sayings in verses 17-23 dealing with thought versus speech. Lying and dishonesty can be destructively powerful uses of the tongue, but their gain is short-lived. Truth endures, and it not only outlasts dishonesty but also brings the benefits of peace, security, and joy to the one who serves it.

Once again the message is drawn from older wisdom but given a specifically Israelite turn in verse 22, where it is God who will demand an answer to the abomination of false speech. Amenemope expressed a similar insight: "God hates the falsifying of words, his great abomination is the one who is sick within." Verse 23 also reflects a saying of Amenemope: "Better is the man whose news stays in his body than the one who speaks it out injuriously." Often in the Old Testament an "abomination" is tied to false worship (Dan 9:27; 11:31; 12:11), but in Proverbs and Amenemope it means a fundamental moral flaw. Further Egyptian influence can be detected in the sayings against anger (v. 16; see ch. 14).

13:1-25. This chapter opens, as does the beginning in 10:1, with a contrast between the wise and foolish son (or pupil). Generally the chapter has two major themes to develop this contrast: the dangers of uncontrolled appetites or desires (vv. 2-12), and the quality of life that results from the choices each person makes (vv. 13-25).

The power of appetites was well known to Israelite teachers. Their instructions concentrated on internal dispositions, however—the longing for what belongs to another, the desire for external show, anger, and above all pride. Verse 10 calls it "insolence," a quality that puffs up one's own importance while seeking to cause embarrassment and shame to others (v. 5). Dishonest and violent behavior is always tempting in order to achieve such goals.

Another area that the sages associated with uncontrolled appetite was money. Wealth can be a sign of divine blessing and success for the good person who follows the path of justice (v. 11), but it also focuses the dreams and hopes of the wicked on acquiring more. With wealth they can receive the external signs of blessing. Verse 8, for example, can make the neutral observation that wealth frees one from many normal worries, while poverty makes instruction almost impossible. A similar thought occurs in 18:23: "The poor man implores, but the rich man answers harshly," and also in 18:11: "The rich man's wealth is his strong city." But the search for wealth as a primary goal of life leads to treachery and fraud, so roundly condemned in the proverbs we have already seen. True wealth is in wisdom (3:14; 8:10; 8:18-19; 16:16); in turn, wise behavior, especially generosity, will lead to wealth (recall 12:24-25). A spiritualized interpretation of this is found in verse 21.

The quality of a life of wisdom is summarized in the choice between life and death. Life is more than mere existence, of course. It is the fullness of blessing now. So it is described as a fountain (v. 14) that brings reward (v. 13), favor (v. 15), healing (v. 17), honor (v. 18), good (v. 21), an inheritance for one's children (v. 22), and a full stomach (v. 25). The sinner, naturally, receives the opposite—misfortune, ruin, poverty, shame, and an empty belly. These belong to the realm of death (v. 14). The fundamental message is to acquire this life quality, best expressed by verse 20. The only way to gain wisdom is to walk with the wise.

14:1-35. The difference between the wise and the foolish continues to occupy center stage in this chapter, especially as the one is prudent and cautious, and the other rash and foolhardy (vv. 3, 6, 7, 16, 24, 33). Discipline is needed (vv. 8, 12, 15, 18) and prudent judgment (vv. 4, 10, 13, 20, 23, 30). All of this fits the tradition of international wisdom, but it is tempered here with two religious convictions proper to Israel. Divine concern for the world means that wicked and foolish behavior can expect punishment (vv. 11, 14, 19, 32), and "fear of the Lord" rules the actions of the just (vv. 2, 26, 27).

This "fear of the Lord" does not imply a frightened obedience in order to avoid punishment. It relates to the awe and reverence one must show before the transcendent power and majesty of God. There is a healthy fear of the consequences of sin, but there is also love and a sense of trust in the divine power that cares for and directs all things in our lives. It can be described as loyalty to Yahweh. It is devotion, fidelity, and obedience at the same time (see Lev 19; Deut 10:12; Ps 34:10-12). In practice, it is piety: the observance of the religious obligations and moral standards of the law. In 2 Kgs 17:25-29 priests had to be sent to Samaria to teach the new settlers how to "fear the Lord," that is, to be good Jews. In the later wisdom tradition, keeping the law was identified with fearing the Lord, which in turn was the same as wisdom (Sir 1:14, 16, 18, 20; 15:1; 19:20; 21:11), and the law is the path to wisdom (Sir 1:26; 9:14-15; 24:22-23; 39:1-3). In Proverbs, fear of the Lord has a strong *ethical* content, whereas in Gen 20:11 and other Pentateuchal passages it seems primarily tied to *cultic* concerns. The development of religious wisdom brought the two into one by the time of Sirach, but in Proverbs the connection to living uprightly is still dominant.

Many of the proverbs echo themes already seen. Lying, arrogance, laziness, refusal to learn from discipline, and rash behavior are all condemned. Resourcefulness, truthfulness, and shrewd planning are all praised. A new theme of anger and quick-tempered behavior appears in verses 17 and 29. It is common elsewhere in Proverbs (12:16; 15:18; 16:32; 17:27-28, etc.). It reflects one of the most frequent topics in Egyptian wisdom: the value of the "cool" versus the "hot" spirit. One Egyptian noble left this epitaph on his tomb in self-praise: "Silent, cool in temperament, calm in expression." It sums up the ideal scribe and statesman for Egypt—indeed, it is exactly the description of Joseph as vizier of Egypt in Gen 37–50! The "hot" man cannot control his speech, his desires, his temper, or his rash decision-making. He expresses everything he feels, and wants all his cravings satisfied. No one is less suited to work with or cooperate with others. Amenemope says of such a person, "Like a storm which arises as fire in the straw is the hot man in his time." A few chapters later, it adds, "Do not make the hot man your companion, and do not hold a conversation with him!"

15:1-33. The proverbs in this chapter typify the conduct of the cool temperament over against the hot spirit. The "ill-tempered man" of verse 18 is literally in Hebrew "a man of heat." The early part of the chapter stresses calm speech, cautious affirmation of "knowledge," and an openness to learning (vv. 1-7). They are themes covered many times before (see 12:1; 13:18, 24; 14:33). Above all, discipline is needed to develop such a cool spirit (vv. 5, 10, 12, 20, 21, 24, 31, 32). "Discipline" and "reproof" are the bases of old wisdom's formula for worldly success. A very intentional effort has been made here to link these to the practice of Israel's faith. Proverbs that name Yahweh as the source of wisdom and judgment are more frequent in this chapter than anywhere else in chapters 10–22 except for chapter 16. In verse 33, "fear of the Lord" is equated with both discipline and wisdom. Verse 8 even mentions the role of worship and prayer, a theme very rare in Proverbs. Verse 9 forms a general conclusion on the mutual roles of worship and wisdom that identifies rejection of Yahweh and evil conduct as equal abominations.

Verse 11 presents the only positive view of the nether world in Proverbs. Usually Sheol is a place cut off from life and from God. Here the saying suggests that God takes a personal concern even for the world of the dead. Verse 12 presents us with the "senseless" person. The characteristic of this type of person is that he or she refuses to change anything. Thus there is no way for wisdom to enter moral decision-making.

The concern of Yahweh for the poor and defenseless is a major proclamation of both the law and the prophets (Deut 10:18; 14:28-29; 24:17-22; Exod 22:21-24; Isa 1:17, 23). It is just as important to the wisdom tradition. Verses 16-17 turn two well-known Egyptian sayings of Amenemope into a statement of faith: "Better is bread when the heart is glad than riches with vexation," and "Better is the poor man in the hands of the god than riches in the storehouse" (see Prov 14:31; 19:17; 22:9; and 29:4). Verse 25 goes on to include the widow among the helpless. This, too, fits the traditional Near Eastern sentiment. An inscription of Pharaoh Amenemhet I says,

> I gave to the poor, I nurtured the orphan,
> No one has been hungry in my years,
> No one has been thirsty.

The *Epic of King Keret* at Ugarit, a Canaanite text of the thirteenth century B.C.E., accuses the king of failing in his duty:

> You do not give the widow her rights . . . .
> You do not overthrow those who oppress the poor.
> The orphans are not fed by you,
> Nor the widows fed behind your back.

Israel has made this a divine obligation placed upon all Israelites and not just upon kings: Pss 72:1-4, 12-13; Jer 7:5-6; 22:2-3; Ezek 22:6-7; Zech 7:10. The wisdom teachers do not extol poverty as a special favor from God, but they acknowledge the priority of faithfulness to Yahweh even in want over material signs of blessing.

16:1-15. These fifteen verses are the center of Solomon's collection in chapters 10–22. Verses 1-9 detail the proper relationship of God to human wisdom, and express mention of Yahweh occurs in eight of the nine sayings! This is followed in verses 10-15 by a mini-guidebook for kings. The two groups belong together, since the king enjoyed a special relationship with God as "son" (Pss 2:7; 72:1) and "shepherd" of the people (Ezek 34:23). Kings, therefore, must embody the divine concern for justice. The thought in these two sections rests squarely on the older wisdom insights, but it has been transformed into a declaration of Yahweh's direct control over every aspect of life and especially over human planning.

Verse 1 affirms that even words, those most intimate expressions of a person's private thought, are directed to effects never dreamed of by the speaker. The Assyrian work *The Words of Ahiqar* (seventh century B.C.E.) likewise declares, "If he were beloved of the gods, they would put something good in his palate to speak." Verses 2-3 extend this insight. Only if God directs human plans will they succeed. Compare the early Egyptian advice of *Merikare:* "If the tongue of a man be the rudder of the boat, the Lord of all is its pilot!" The key attitudes are listed then in verses 5-8: humility rather than pride, kindness, piety, peaceful relations with others, and virtue (that is, uprightness) even in the middle of difficulty. Finally, verse 9 sums up the lesson by repeating the opening insight. Wisdom recognizes its limits. God is beyond human understanding, a mystery not comprehended by the skills of learning, and thus Yahweh ultimately exercises control even over wisdom itself.

Verses 10-15 obviously presume an ideal king. His words share divine authority and uphold the order of both justice and right judgment. But verses 11-12 assert that no kingdom can achieve this unless the people also live by the same qualities as kings. Verses 13-15 concentrate on how to win royal favor. They seem to be directed to the instruction of potential diplomats for the royal service. The advice is purely practical. Success will depend on winning the king's favor, and this is done by catering to his ways. But at least Proverbs keeps such fawning suggestions quite limited in scope. The *Wisdom of Ptah-hotep* (ca. 2450 B.C.E.) and the *Words of Ahiqar* (seventh century B.C.E.) both agree on extensive submissiveness before kings to gain favor. One example from Ahiqar reads: "If a thing is commanded you in the presence of a king, it is a burning fire; hasten to do it!"

16:16-33. The remainder of chapter 16 returns to the general advice on good conduct for everyone. If advancement in the king's service had a certain self-serving pride attached to its practical requirements of bowing and scraping, this should not be carried over as the ideal of every Israelite. They were members of the chosen people who bound themselves in a covenant of worship and obedience to Yahweh alone. These more general sayings, which would have been treasured in Egypt or Babylon as well, extol virtues important to the covenant: prudent speech (vv. 21, 23, 24), respect for elders (v. 31), praise of a cool temper (v. 32), and excoriation of evil words (vv. 27-30). But the spirit of humility before Yahweh and the submission of all human hopes and plans to the divine will are declared the only true road to success.

The combination of healthy respect for the limits of human knowledge with deep trust in the providence of Yahweh is summed up in the final saying of verse 33. Although applied here to the search for knowledge by means of learning, the mention of the lots reminds the reader that all major decisions throughout Israel's history were sought by asking God to indicate the answer through the casting of lots or other divination practices (see examples in Num 26:55; Lev 16:7-10; Josh 7:14; 14:2; 1 Sam 10:20-21; Prov 18:18). Later Egyptian wisdom came to the same realization. Amenemope could say, "One thing are the words men say, another is that which the god does." It is a universal insight—there is even a Malay proverb that goes, "Man's designs and God's decrees differ."

17:1-28. Among the general words of advice in this chapter are a number of sayings on strife (vv. 1, 4, 14, 19, 20) and bribery (vv. 8, 23). The first series underscores the importance of social relationships in the thinking of wisdom. The right relations between parents and children (v. 25), servants and employers (v. 2), business associates (v. 18), and friends (v. 17) are constant themes in the Book of Proverbs. Strife breaks down the proper order that exists and creates the sources of future hatred, violence, and lying. As verse 4 puts it, evil seeks ever more evil, and, like a dam that bursts, it becomes a flood (v. 14). The wise also know that evil ways are very hard to dislodge from our thinking. Verse 13 is an Old Testament version of "Those who live by the sword shall die by the sword." The thought of verse 1 agrees with 15:16-17 and the saying of Amenemope, "It is better to be praised as one who loves men than to have riches in the storehouse."

The attitude toward bribery in Proverbs has two sides. In a non-judgmental way, the wise observe that bribes often obtain results (18:16; 21:14). But more often the sayings take a stand against such perversions of justice, not only in this chapter but also in 28:21. In this regard, wisdom condemns bad judges (17:15, 23; 18:5) and perjury (19:5, 9, 28; 21:28) as well. All of these represent the destruction of society's divine order and of law. In this they agree wholeheartedly with the psalms and the prophets (Pss 15:5; 26:10; Isa 1:23; 5:23; Ezek 22:12; Mic 3:11). Deut 16:19 captures the essence of wisdom's position: "You shall not pervert justice or show partiality; and you shall not take a bribe because a bribe blinds the eyes of the wise and undermines the cause of the just."

The fool figures prominently in these sayings (vv. 10, 12, 16, 21, 24, 25). This is not the ordinary foolish person, but one who has too little ability to learn in school and who therefore acts in just the opposite manner out of spite. There is a hard-headed stubbornness in the fool that really tries to break up the accepted order and established ways of human relationships in society.

18:1-24. Several of the proverbs in chapter 18 return to the topic of good speech. This is not surprising in light of the intellectual tradition of wisdom. Even Babylonian wisdom literature gives its greatest attention to the quality of speech. At least ten separate expressions for sinful speech occur in the major Babylonian texts. These include words that are wicked, seditious, offensive, blasphemous, lying, exaggerated, and slanderous. In Prov 18 we meet still other categories of sinful or foolish speech: quarreling (v. 1), vain and empty self-opinion (v. 2), scorn spoken out of contempt (v. 3), creation of strife (v. 6), talebearing (v. 8), and speaking without thinking (v. 13). This reflects wisdom's message elsewhere in the book: empty chatter is foolish (15:2; 14:23); stirring up strife is evil (10:19; 26:21; 29:22 and most of chapter 17); gossip is destructive (11:13; 20:19; 26:20, 22); seeking scandal is wrong (16:27; 17:4).

At the same time, speech rightly used is a powerful tool for the wise person. Frankness and truth can change people (15:32; 24:26); words can heal (12:18; 13:17; 15:1; 16:24); persuasion can win people over (10:32; 11:9, 11); silence or reticence in speaking protects reputations (17:9; 25:8-9); holding back in speech acts shrewdly (12:23; 13:3; 21:23); and patient speech cools tempers (15:18; 17:27; 20:3).

In general, the wisdom teachers valued reserve and careful consideration in speech. It is true that they also had enough of a sense of humor to depict the foolish and stupid in slightly exaggerated cartoons of themselves. But they had a serious purpose in mind, namely, to steer the student through the pitfalls of the most difficult area of human conduct: the impulse to speak out what pops into the mind. The Letter of James in the New Testament is heir to this understanding in its treatise on the use of the tongue in 3:1-12.

19:1-29. No particular theme dominates chapter 19. It has several sayings on the problems of laziness (vv. 15, 24), royal service (v. 12), control of anger (vv. 11, 19), false witnesses (vv. 9, 28), and the training of children through discipline (vv. 13, 18, 25, 27), similar to those in earlier chapters. The most attention is paid to the dangers of wealth. Riches can lead to crooked behavior, false friends, greedy associates, and eventually to dishonesty (vv. 1, 4, 6, 7, 22). On the other side, there is no sign of God's disfavor in being poor (vv. 1, 17), although it leads to all sorts of undesirable difficulties (v. 7).

Wisdom's attitude on the subject of wealth was always ambivalent. Older wisdom saw a definite connection between material blessing and divine favor, while later wisdom developed a piety of the *'anawim*, the righteous who have no inheritance in this world except the Lord. This latter theology is found mostly in the psalms, but its beginning can be found in verse 17 and in 22:4. God's special concern for the poor (see the comments on chapter 15 above) guarantees that any generous charity to the poor will be like a loan to God—its repayment is assured! Late Babylonian wisdom developed a similar insight, expressed in the *Dialogue of Pessimism:* "The man who sacrifices to his god is satisfied with the bargain; he is making loan upon loan."

Scattered throughout the proverbs of Solomon are a number of sayings about the value of a good wife (12:4; 18:22; 19:14). As far back as the *Instruction of Ptah-hotep* in Old Kingdom Egypt, this had been a staple of wisdom teaching: "If you are a man of standing, you should establish your household and love your wife at home as is fitting. Make her heart glad as long as you live. She is a profitable field for her lord." While a minor theme in chapters 10–22, it is a major element in the final summation of wisdom in Prov 31:10-31.

The value of "counsel" is emphasized in verse 20. It is above all the quality of shrewd political advice. It frequently appears in contexts in which scribes are called on to advise the king: 2 Sam 8:17; 20:25; 2 Kgs 18:18; 22:8. Perhaps the most famous episode occurs in 2 Sam 16, where the two most famous givers of counsel in David's kingdom, Hushai and Ahithophel, duel against each other. Ahithophel gives sounder counsel, but Absalom follows the deceptive words of Hushai and thus loses his opportunity to win his revolt against his father David. Joseph, too, is portrayed as a wise counselor of Pharaoh in Genesis.

In Proverbs, counsel is often directly equated with wisdom (15:22; 19:20; 21:30), as it is also in certain royal passages of Isaiah (11:2; 19:11) and in an oracle of Jeremiah (Jer 49:7). Verse 21 gives a definite religious response to older wisdom's pride in human cleverness by affirming that God's counsel is greater than ours. This agrees with the polemical stance of prophets such as Second Isaiah who mock the pretensions of human counselors who think that they can figure out what course God is likely to take. See Isa 40:13-14 as a good example. God does not act according to human decisions but establishes the order according to which humans must act.

20:1-30. The proverbs in this chapter are of a general nature. In some cases it seems that later wisdom thinkers have actually tried to soften or correct some of the more optimistic claims of older wisdom. Verse 12 attributes all seeing and hearing (that is, learning) to God's foresight and intention, lest people claim that goodness or justice or integrity or their virtuous conduct from childhood onward came from their own moral uprightness (vv. 6-11). This should be related to the question of intention. Verse 5 describes human intentions as coming from the very depth of our being. The word used is also "counsel," and the lesson is the same as in chapter 19. Right intention draws on the counsel of God, who makes the eye and the ear instruments of learning and communicating wisely.

Several of the proverbs echo themes found primarily in chapters 1–9. Verse 4, on the lazy farmer, reflects 6:6-11, while the warning against standing bond for a neighbor's loan in verse 16 is similar to 6:1-5. The bread of deceit that seduces someone resembles the stolen bread and water of folly in 9:17. The proverb on sleep and wakefulness in verse 13 is the ancient counterpart to our modern saying "The early bird catches the worm." And the very realistic scene in verse 14 still takes place regularly in the bazaars of the Near East, where bargaining over items for sale involves an elaborate ritual of feigning how much one is losing in the deal. The warning against gossips (v. 19) echoes many similar cautions in Amenemope and other ancient sources.

The careful advice in verse 18 illustrates perfectly the proverb found in 1 Kgs 20:11: "It is not for the man who is buckling his armor to boast as though he were taking it off" (1 Kgs 20:11). The explicit sayings about Yahweh's guidance and the need to trust in God found together in verses 22-24 balance those in verses 10-12. The saying about just weights seems somewhat out of place in verse 23, but it is repeated in both halves of the verse and must represent the ideal behavior of those who trust in the Lord. All the other proverbs in the chapter must be read in the light of these two Yahweh sayings in verses 22-24.

Finally, in verse 29 we come to another saying in praise of old age. Wisdom and age are closely associated in the proverbial literature, and especially in those who serve as town elders. See 16:31 and 17:6 for like sentiments. Ezek 7:26 associates the gift of "counsel" with the elders. Other biblical passages that link age and wisdom are Ezek 27:8-9; Job 26:3; 32:7-9; Eccl 4:13; Ps 105:22.

21:1-31. This chapter opens with three sayings about Yahweh and closes with two more. In between is a body of traditional old wisdom offering advice on a wide range of subjects. Since it is probable that the five sayings on Yahweh are intended to interpret the context for all the others, we can broadly characterize the chapter theme as divine control of events. "Man proposes but God disposes" would be the modern equivalent of the editors' judgments on these proverbs. They are very practical, and some may even be a little offensive to our modern sensibilities (vv. 9, 14). The three opening proverbs stress the major fields of divine action: the king subject to Yahweh, final judgment at death, and the importance of worship to ethical conduct. These symbolize all of life's major moments that fall under divine supervision.

The saying on God as weigher of hearts may be a Hebrew equivalent to the Egyptian belief that the god of wisdom, Thoth, judged the heart of the deceased. The heart is often shown on a balance scale weighed against the feather of *maat*, "right order." If the heart comes out lighter, the soul deserves punishment. Similar references may be seen in Prov 16:2 and 24:12. Generally, Proverbs shows little interest in the question of an afterlife, and so one must be careful not to make too much of this possible interpretation of verse 2. It could mean no more than that Yahweh rewards the just and punishes the wicked in this life. However, verse 3 also has Egyptian parallels on the greater value of right conduct over sacrifice. *Merikare* says, "Righteousness of the heart is more acceptable to God than the sacrifice of an ox by an unrighteous man."

Other interesting sayings include verse 13, which is an equivalent to the modern boy who cried "Wolf!" once too often; and verse 16, which mentions the "shades" (that is, the spirits of the dead) as though they formed a community in Sheol, the land of the dead. Verse 18 seems strange. It may suggest that God often allows enemies to be defeated so that Israel may benefit from freedom, but it may just as well reflect the thought that God forgives the faults of the just by making the wicked bear the punishment for both. It is a reverse atonement. The only other place where a theology of atonement exists in the Old Testament is in Isa 53, the passage on the suffering servant.

Verse 19 returns to one of the favorite themes in Proverbs, the quarrelsome wife (see 6:14; 6:19; 10:12; 18:18-19; 19:13). Verses 30-31 close the chapter by reaffirming the theology of Second Isaiah discussed above in chapter 19. God's counsel and wisdom far exceed all human efforts, and especially in war; only Yahweh decides the outcome of battles. A particularly effective example to illustrate this is the story of Gideon's battle against the Midianites in Judg 7:1-23.

22:1-16. The final group of proverbs in chapters 10–22 deals with general, practical advice more than with any special summary of what has gone before. Education, wealth, laziness, and adultery all make their return appearance in variations of earlier sayings. Indeed, one of the striking features of these verses is how abruptly they end without any notable attempt to sum up or close out the whole.

Since Israel did not have a belief in an afterlife full of blessing for most of the Old Testament period, a good "name" and reputation were highly valued. One lived on after death in the honor and esteem of generations to come. Thus verse 1 places the value of a name above wealth, just as earlier proverbs placed integrity and justice above wealth (15:16; 19:1). The good name, then, must also include a life of integrity and justice. The theology of verses 2 and 4 brings this point out in reference to Yahweh. God values people, no matter whether rich or poor, and will give reward to those who are humble and reverent. The same can be said of the message of verses 11-12, which emphasize Yahweh's approval of integrity and rejection of dishonest plans and calculations.

The cryptic expression of verse 13 shows the humorous side of proverbs. Even in ancient Israel, one would be hard-pressed to run across a lion in the street very often! Verse 14 recalls the repeated warnings in chapters 1–9 against the adulteress as the jaws of death—see 3:18; 5:5; 7:27; 9:18. Verse 15 links the values of physical discipline and learning. From what we can gather, no one spared the rod in ancient education. Proverbs such as 13:24; 23:13-14; and 29:15 extol the value of using a stick to teach wisdom. Comparison with verse 6 and other passing references indicate that the philosophy behind its use was to knock foolishness out of the student. If he or she made the association between mistaken ways of thinking and the painful consequences, the lesson would last a lifetime. This type of education was probably closely tied to memorizing proverbs for the teacher. Forgetting one could lead to a swift rap on the knuckles.

PART III: THE THIRTY SAYINGS OF THE WISE

Prov 22:17–24:22

For over fifty years scholars have recognized the close connection between 22:17–24:22 and the Egyptian *Teaching of Amenemope.* Both are classical examples of the Instruction genre, in which commands alternate with motives for obeying. Proverbs 1–9 and 30–31 are also largely in this form. But what sets 22:17–24:22 apart are the extremely close parallels in wording to Amenemope (particularly in 22:17–23:11), sometimes appearing in the same order! Moreover, the general introduction to Amenemope has a decided similarity to the introduction to Proverbs in Prov 1:1-7. Both state the same purpose, as can be seen from Amenemope: "The beginning of the teaching of life, the instruction for success. All precepts for conversation with the great, the rules for courtiers, to know how to answer one who speaks, to return a written message to one who sends it, to direct one on the paths of life, to make him prosper on earth . . . ." The major difference between this stated purpose and Prov 1:1-7 is that the Egyptian work certainly directed its teachings to an elite class of trainees and emphasized the practical success that would result. The Israelite work was ordered more to understanding the meaning of life, particularly the relationship of human knowing to the divine will.

The same is true in Prov 22:17–24:22. While it seems to have known and borrowed from Amenemope, it did not simply reproduce the Egyptian theology. It modified many sayings and added others to give a specifically Israelite faith perspective. The closest parallel to the message of this section of Proverbs is found in Psalm 37. The psalm stresses the salvation of the just and the punishment of the wicked, as does Proverbs, but it places more emphasis on Yahweh as the sole hope of salvation.

Amenemope was composed sometime between 1000 and 600 B.C.E. It is divided into thirty chapters and includes both long and short thought units. In selecting from these, the Hebrew authors left aside many sections that applied only to Egypt or Egyptian beliefs. Thus they eliminated chapter 5 of Amenemope and its long description of the Nile, as well as the extended directive on praying to the sun-god in chapter 7. Israel kept the form of thirty sayings by adding new ideas of its own. In asking why Israel valued this foreign work so highly, the reason must be found in the particular sensitivity of Amenemope toward human dependence on the gods—a characteristic not often prominent in early Egyptian wisdom, which seemed so often to be mostly clever advice on how to get ahead by one's own efforts. Israel's sages obviously felt that much of this material would help deepen their own understanding of Yahweh's action in the world.

22:17-21: The general introduction. The New American Bible translation of these verses is quite radical. The traditional translations do not recognize "Amenemope" or "thirty" sayings, which make the connection clear. But the text of the Hebrew at these points is extremely uncertain and even corrupt. Where verse 19 has "the words of Amenemope" in the New American Bible, the Hebrew today literally reads, "I make known to you today, even to you," which makes little sense. And in verse 20, where "Thirty" stands, the Hebrew suggests "formerly," in the sense that "I wrote to you formerly." Since no one can identify when this former time was, even the ancient Jewish scholars marked this as a corrupted passage. The New American Bible has made only the slightest correction of the Hebrew and is almost certainly the most accurate reconstruction of the original presently available. Chapter 1 of Amenemope uses almost the same wording: "Give your ears, hear what is said, give your heart to understand it . . . . Let it abide in your breast so that it may be a key to your heart. When there is a whirlwind of words, it will be a mooring-stake for your tongue." In chapter 30 of Amenemope, the author concludes: "See these thirty chapters—they entertain and instruct. They are the greatest of all books, they give knowledge to the ignorant." The Egyptian work then dedicates them to the education of the scribe, while the Hebrew adapter leaves them open for anyone to study.

The message of verses 17-21 follows the traditional methods of the wise. There is first a call to hear and listen to teachings that have been discovered and treasured already by others (see Prov 1:8; 2:1; 4:1; 5:1). This is not an invitation to go out and discover the world for oneself. There is a treasury that has been stored up and is now offered to the minds and hearts of the listeners so that they may own the entire deposit personally.

Verse 18 goes on to indicate that possession is not enough—the wisdom of these words must be communicated and acted upon. For what purpose? To trust in God. This is the ethical dimension of faith. One could be asked to believe in God through sheer faith, to obey God through the commandments, or to fear God through worship. But the author picks the word "trust," used by the psalmists again and again to express their confidence that God is a refuge, a source of strength and protection for the moment of need (Pss 9:11; 22:5; 25:2; 31:15; 52:10; 56:5; at least thirty times in all). An interesting insight into what this trust meant to ancient Israel occurs in 2 Kgs 18:19-24, where the Assyrian general belittles the citizens of Jerusalem for trusting in Yahweh over the gods of Assyria. Jer 17:5-7 presents another parallel from prophecy; the prophet challenges the people to choose: either trust in themselves and be cursed, or trust in Yahweh and be blessed. This passage breathes the spirit of wisdom!

22:22-23 First saying. Amenemope says, "Guard yourself from robbing the wretched and driving away a weak man." The context presumes a legal attempt to cheat the poor of their rights. Trials were held at the city gates (Pss 69:13; 127:5; Ruth 4), where the elders would gather. Like the widow and the orphan, the poor often had few defenders (see the insights of Prov 19:4, 6, 7). But Yahweh had special concern for the poor and the weak and would fight their cause (see Pss 69:19; 103:4; 119:154).

22:24-25 Second saying. Here, too, there is a closely related saying in Amenemope: "Do not associate with the hot man, and do not approach him to converse." The hotheaded have very little control over their temper or their words. Both are anathema to the ideals of the wisdom schools.

22:26-27 Third saying. A bit of humor has been injected into an otherwise serious warning: Even the bed with you in it could go! Cautions against standing as the guarantor of a loan are frequent in Proverbs (6:1-5; 11:15; 17:18). Apparently defaults were frequent, and many friendships no doubt came to an end over bad debts. It is still a common maxim that friends should never lend one another money.

22:28 Fourth saying. This is similar to 23:10. Amenemope also warns against the practice: "Do not carry off the landmark at the boundaries of the arable land nor disturb the position of the measuring cord." Deut 19:14 and 27:17 doubly reinforce this same law for Israel. In rocky and hilly Palestine, it is an easy matter to push the boundaries around by moving the piles of rocks that serve as fences and landmarks for each family's ancestral claims. It is therefore a serious matter.

22:29 Fifth saying. The point is that a person skilled in the art of wisdom and proper behavior will go far in the royal bureaucracy. Amenemope closes with this saying: "As for the scribe who is experienced in office, he will find himself worthy to be a courtier."

23:1-3 Sixth saying. If one wants the king's favor, it is necessary to act with proper decorum and humility. This is common Egyptian advice. Ptah-hotep insists, "If you sit at the table with one greater than yourself, take what he may give when it is set before you." Amenemope suggests, "Do not eat bread before a noble, nor lay on your mouth at first." See also Sir 31:16.

23:4-5 Seventh saying. Amenemope is the source of this saying: "Cast not your heart in pursuit of wealth. They have made themselves wings like geese and are flown away to the heavens." The Hebrew author changed the unfamiliar goose to a familiar eagle, but otherwise kept the saying as is. The first line means, "while your glance flits *away from* it, it is gone."

23:6-8 Eighth saying. The "grudging man" is, literally, a man "of evil eye." This helps make sense of the saying. The meal is a metaphor for involvement with crooked planners. They are either preparing to cheat you or else you will pay a price that poisons you if you join them. Amenemope is clearer: "The property of a poor man is a block to the throat; it makes the throat vomit. If it is obtained by false oaths, his heart is perverted by his belly."

23:9 Ninth saying. Speaking advice to a fool is wasted effort. Compare Amenemope: "Empty not your belly to everybody, and thus damage the regard for yourself."

23:10-11 Tenth saying. This is similar to 22:28 and its parallel from Amenemope. Another saying of the same sage fits here also: "Guard against disturbing the boundaries of the field lest a terror carry you off." It goes on to proclaim that the god protects the land. In Israelite tradition Yahweh is the "redeemer" of the helpless (Prov 19:17; 21:23; 22:9).

23:12 Eleventh saying. This is the standard introduction to the wisdom Instruction form. It seems out of place in the middle here but may introduce a new source for many of the following sayings: *The Words of Ahiqar.* Prov 22:22–23:11 was closely dependent on Amenemope; the remaining sayings are often similar to Ahiqar, but many are independent. Ahiqar was popular among the Jews—a copy was found in the Jewish colony at Elephantine in Egypt (fifth century B.C.E.).

23:13-14 Twelfth saying. Ahiqar 81-82 is very close: "Withhold not your son from the rod or you cannot keep him from wickedness. If I smite you my son, you will not die, but if I leave you to your own heart, you [will not live]." Ignorance puts one into the grip of death's kingdom, and true life is found only in wisdom, "the fountain of life" (13:14).

23:15-16 Thirteenth saying. Again this saying makes a close link between our interior understanding and our public performance, especially in speaking. The teacher's appeal is both intellectual and emotional. Note the artistic arrangement of the two verses in a chiasm: *your—my:my—your.*

23:17-18 Fourteenth saying. There are two antitheses here: (1) the zeal for sin or the zeal for fear of the Lord; (2) a lasting future or a future without hope. The value of sin is short-lived, while fear of the Lord offers a future of blessing. God's promises of security and life will endure. A Christian can understand a fuller sense of eternal life in this passage based on the New Testament and not seen by the writer of Proverbs.

23:19-21 Fifteenth saying. This brings together a group of related vices: gluttony, drunkenness, and sloth, all of which were considered destructive of making a living. They were grave social offenses—see Deut 21:20 and prophetic denunciations in Isa 5:11-12; 28:7-9; Ezek 23:33; Amos 6:6.

23:22-23 Sixteenth saying. This and the following saying deal with the family as source of wisdom. This is sometimes called "clan wisdom," because it is passed down by parents and elders in the tribe rather than in formal schools. The language is the same as for school wisdom, however: truth, wisdom, instruction, and understanding.

23:24-25 Seventeenth saying. Many scholars would consider this to be part of the preceding saying. It moves beyond the older wisdom ideal to exalt the value of justice above everything. Note that all four lines stress the joy that being just will bring.

23:26-28 Eighteenth saying. This instruction is close in spirit to chapter 7. The theme is prominent in chapters 1–9 as the greatest danger to a young man seeking wisdom (2:16; 5:3-6; 6:24-25; 7:5-27; 9:13-18). The "pit" may be Sheol, as noted earlier (ch. 7; see also Ps 30:4), but there may be a *double entendre* here for the sexual role of the female. Hebrew poets loved puns.

23:29-35 Nineteenth saying. This is the longest of the instructions, and the most free in its format. It makes its point about the evils of alcohol by opening and closing with two vividly described scenes of the effects of heavy drinking. Much of the message is carried in rhetorical questions and answers. In fact, verses 29-30 were perhaps originally a riddle and its answer. The warning comes in verses 31-32: wine is great going down, but its effects afterwards! The image of the biting like serpents suggests its fatal results. The authors end on a note of humor that is sadly all too true. The ancients did not know of alcoholism as a disease, but they knew well its symptoms.

24:1-2 Twentieth saying. This proverb echoes Ps 37:1. It is a standard admonition with a standard reason why. Interestingly, this and the next two sayings begin with succeeding letters of the alphabet: aleph in verse 1, beth (v. 3), and ghimel (v. 5). It fails to continue further, but was there perhaps earlier a collection of twenty-two sayings in which each began with the next letter of the alphabet?

24:3-4 Twenty-first saying. Life itself is the house that is furnished by wisdom. A prosperous house is the same as a life full of honor as well as strength. See 9:1 and 14:1.

24:5-6 Twenty-second saying. Wisdom together with strength is the ideal in Israel. See Dan 1:4; 2:23; Isa 11:2, and especially the picture of David and Solomon together. David is the strong hero, and Solomon the wise ruler. Their united monarchy established the pattern of Israel's royal theology. Yahweh, however, is the model for both (see Isa 31:2; Jer 10:12; 51:15; Dan 2:20; Ps 147:5; Job 26:12). Wisdom, though, is superior to strength alone, for it guides strength toward success (see Prov 20:18). The prophets sometimes must condemn human pride in one's own wisdom and strength (see Isa 10:13; Jer 9:23; 51:57).

24:7 Twenty-third saying. The setting for this saying is the city gate, where justice was administered (see the comments on 22:22 above). The NAB translation is strange and somewhat contradictory. The Hebrew text reads more clearly: "Too high is wisdom for the fool; he is not to speak in the gate."

24:8-9 Twenty-fourth saying. The intrigue that is condemned is calculated evil, carefully planned out. A person who plans this is identified with the worst of wisdom's enemies. A literal translation of verse 9 makes the condemnation clearer: "The intrigue is sinful foolishness, and such a scoffer is an abomination to all people."

24:10-12 Twenty-fifth saying. There is some question whether verse 10 belongs with verses 11-12. But it stands as a call to action, which is given concrete application in verses 11-12 for an extreme case. The situation that the proverb writer has in mind is not absolutely certain, although it must deal with the case of an innocent person condemned. Execution was often immediate, so that if a witness knew the truth, the time to act was right away. The reference to God as the tester of hearts is discussed above (p. 663).

24:13-14 Twenty-sixth saying. Honey has always served as the natural sugar and favorite sweet of the Near East. Even today stores throughout the Arab world are filled with pastries smothered in honey. It is very high praise of wisdom to think of it as the honey of the soul.

24:15-16 Twenty-seventh saying. The two parts are not connected by logic. Verse 15 serves as a warning not to do violence against the just person. The reason given in verse 16 suggests that plotting evil soon trips up the plotter in quick ruin, while the upright bounce back from sin. It probably refers the judgment to God, who will forgive the just many times. Note the Aramaic proverb, "Seven parts for the righteous, one part for the wicked."

24:17-18 Twenty-eighth saying. Lev 19:18 commands Israelites not to bear grudges or seek vengeance against their own people. This proverb can be understood as an extension of that law. Its final line, however, gives an unexpected reason: if we do not rejoice in the enemy's downfall, God will assure that it will take place anyway. The ultimate sense must be that we are to leave retribution in God's good judgment.

24:19-20 Twenty-ninth saying. The message of this saying is similar to that of the preceding one, but it is much clearer. Do not be angered yourself nor seek after vengeance (NAB's "envious"). It is God who controls the future and extinguishes the lamp (=life) of the wicked (13:9; 20:20) or establishes it (1 Kgs 11:36; 15:4; Ps 132:17; 2 Sam 21:17—all said of David).

24:21-22 Thirtieth saying. All ancients knew the power of kings to do as they chose. Ahiqar warns his son, "Soft is the tongue of a king, but it breaks the ribs of a dragon!" An example of royal power perverted in the service of evil is found in the story of King Ahab and Naboth's vineyard in 1 Kgs 21. How much more must one fear the judgment and punishment of God!

24:23-34 An appendix: Further sayings of the wise. These twelve verses have a separate heading, indicating that they were attached to chapters 22–24 as a supplement. There are two themes: justice in the law courts and the ethic of responsible work. No special connection to Yahweh is mentioned, and it is reasonable to assume that these are an older series of proverbs aimed at the student of wisdom in the schools. The two themes are interlocked, so that verses 23-26 deal with false judges, verse 27 with work, verses 28-29 with false witnesses in court, and verses 30-34 with laziness at work.

Society depends on both values—justice and work—for health. The false judge and the lying witness are strongly denounced by citizens because the community's basis of trust is undermined. The kiss on the lips in verse 26 was a sign of trust and friendship. The Gospels confirm how sacred was the symbol when they record that Judas betrayed Jesus with a kiss (Matt 26:48-50; Mark 14:44-45; Luke 22:47-48). Verse 29 cautions against vengeance and gives the same basic advice as verses 20-22: leave the punishment in the hands of God.

The picture of the untilled field is a sharply drawn cartoon of the lazy man. Its theme is much the same as that of 6:9-11, and the technique of education by ridicule is exactly the same as that employed in the instruction on drinking in 23:29-35.

PART IV: HEZEKIAH'S COLLECTION OF OLD PROVERBS

Prov 25:1–29:27

A second Solomonic collection

The title of this section states that officials of King Hezekiah (715–688 B.C.E.) edited and collected proverbs that stemmed from the time of Solomon (or from Solomon himself or from the royal schools founded by him!). Two aspects can be noted from the start. One is that many of the proverbs repeat those in the earlier collection of chapters 10–22. Compare, for example, 25:24 and 21:9; 26:15 and 19:24; 27:12 and 22:3; 28:19 and 12:11; 29:3 and 10:1. The second is that the connection to Yahweh is rarely made. Chapter 25 mentions God once, chapter 28 twice, chapter 29 three times, chapters 26 and 27 not at all. The first three chapters are good examples of older secular wisdom, while the last two provide somewhat more direct reflections on Israelite piety.

25:1-28 An Egyptian-style instruction. It has been shown that this chapter is based on an Egyptian model of instructions for a king and his subjects. It is a mixture of admonitions and practical sayings about life. But it has a clear structure. There is an introduction in verses 2-5 stating the role of the king (vv. 2-3) and then that of the wicked who threaten the king's rule (vv. 4-5). This is followed by an extended section on the king (vv. 6-15) and then on the wicked (vv. 16-26). Each part has six units. A general statement concludes the section (vv. 27-28). The chapter is thought to be a product of the royal schools because of its high regard for the king and for loyal obedience by subjects. It contains very few of the important words that occur regularly in chapters 10–22. This probably indicates that this chapter was edited earlier than chapters 10–22.

This royal instruction opens in verses 2-3 with praise for the special divine favor shown to kings. Kings were invested with greater wisdom than ordinary mortals (see 1 Kgs 3) and were subject only to the vastly greater wisdom of the gods. Ancient kings saw themselves as delegated by the god to govern the divine kingdom on earth. And yet, as verses 4-5 make clear, evil tolerated or allowed to gain power will destroy the blessing from the gods.

The advice in verses 6-15 on how to act before a king and how to speak as a diplomat is generally quite practical if we keep in mind that the student of the scribal school is to master the *art* of speaking well. Verse 6 becomes a parable of Jesus on places of honor at table (Luke 14:7-11). Verse 14 could be summarized as "all talk, no action" in modern idiom. Verse 15 recalls the saying of Ahiqar that a king's speech is soft but is also sharper than a sword and stronger than a club that breaks ribs (see also Prov 15:18).

The more general advice in verses 6-16 concentrates on the contrast between moderation combined with self-control (vv. 16, 17, 21, 22, 25, 27, 28) and the destructive effects of disorder (false witnesses, v. 18; unreliability, v. 19; grief, v. 20; backbiting, v. 23; and weak resolve, v. 26). Verses 21-22 propose treating enemies with kindness as a way of putting them to shame and, by means of the image of coals, to "burn" the lesson into them. It may sound anything but altruistic in spirit, but it is a practical way of reducing the bitter violence that hatred causes. Some scholars would soften the picture a little by translating the first part of verse 22 as "live coals you will *take from* his head."

In verse 28, the New American Bible has "feelings" for the Hebrew *ruah*, "spirit." Someone's spirit is the power of life in "the image and likeness of God" (Gen 1:27; see Ezek 37:1-14). Evil will easily overcome the person whose spirit has not been trained in the moderation and self-control proposed by the wisdom teachers.

26:1-28. There is no specifically religious content in chapter 26. It can be divided into three major topics: the fool (vv. 1-12, using the strong Hebrew sense of the "stupid one"); the lazy person (vv. 13-16); and evil speech (vv. 17-28).

Generally, the wisdom position on the fool can be stated simply: to deal with the fool seriously makes one a fool in turn. Wisdom is perverted by the fool, who does not understand the value of good order, logical thinking, self-control, or self-denial for a larger good. The fool thinks only of what he or she can get right now and interprets everything in that selfish light. The result is a totally unbridled person, badly in need of severe disciplining to get back on the way of social responsibility (v. 3). The opposite advice in verses 4-5 shows the difficulty involved in dialogue with fools. They do not learn, and their speaking endangers all around them. The fool cannot be taught and cannot be corrected, and all who attempt it come to grief themselves (v. 10). Verse 11 illustrates the point graphically and is later quoted by 2 Pet 2:22 in the New Testament.

Verses 13-16 gather together another small section on the lazy. Verse 13 repeats 22:13; verse 15 repeats 19:24; verse 14 is similar in theme to 24:33. Thus these are not a new series of ideas. The attention to laziness was popular among the wise, and there were probably two independent collections that used the same sayings.

The remainder of the chapter deals with the harmful effects of speech wrongly used. It is focused on hypocrisy and deceptive words. A surface seriousness conceals evil intentions in the heart of the speaker. Like glaze on the surface of a pot that has never been fired (and thus is likely to break easily), smooth words conceal much deception that will shortly bring the trusting listener to disaster or loss. Verse 26 suggests that such hidden evil is found out by observing the religious practice of the individual. Verse 27 expresses the traditional Israelite conviction that evil brings evil on itself (the plots of both Daniel and Esther are examples).

27:1-27. The advice covers the full range of wisdom concerns, and the individual sayings are not grouped by themes that can be easily identified. Friendship and neighbors appear the most frequently (vv. 5, 6, 8, 10, 14, 16, 19). Verses 23-27 form a single extended image of agrarian life.

The chapter opens with a saying similar to one in Amenemope, "Man does not know what the morrow is like." A parable of Jesus about the rich man who filled his barns and then died the same night makes the same point (Luke 12:16-21). Verses 3 and 7 both echo imagery used in the words of Ahiqar, "I have lifted sand and carried salt, but there is nothing heavier than debt," and "hunger sweetens what is bitter." While Prov 27 certainly does not use the images identically, it does reflect the influence of international wisdom.

Friendship is extolled when it is frankly honest. Correction and learning can only come from a forthright "telling it like it is" in contrast to the flatterer or liar. The New American Bible translation has lost the analogy of friendship in verse 9 by suggesting the word "grief." The second half of the verse more properly reads, "and the sweetness of friends (is better) than perfumed wood." A friend is valued because he or she is close at hand and presumably concerned enough to give help and support.

Other practical advice warns against anger and jealousy (v. 4), loans to strangers who may leave the country without repaying (v. 13), and excessive curiosity (v. 20), which can be as greedy as death itself, never allowing even one victim to go free from its hold. Finally, verses 23-27 draw for us an ideal farming community that is self-sufficient. Such pastoral imagery occurs occasionally in Proverbs and reflects the predominant occupations of farming and herding. But most of its advice is directed to the urban professional class found in palaces, schools, temples, law courts, and civil government. This reminds us that Israel was also an important trading nation that carried on commerce throughout the Mediterranean world and needed large numbers of experts trained in language and diplomacy, and possessing economic and mathematical skills to work out business transactions. This merchant-orientation of Proverbs also explains the insistence on just weights and honest speech free from any hint of fraud or deceit in negotiations. International trust depended on it.

28:1-28. Although Yahweh is mentioned only in verses 5 and 25, the majority of the proverbs in chapter 28 reflect a very developed piety and morality built around the concepts of care for the poor and obedience to the law. The chapter opens with another saying on the just versus the wicked. Poverty is not extolled as a good, but it is far better to be poor and have integrity than fall prey to the temptations of greed that plague the wealthy, who always seem to crave more.

The major development of this theme is seen in verses 3, 6, 8, 11, 20, 22, 25, 27. Wealth may be a sign of both divine blessing and of industrious behavior (vv. 19-20); it is only greed that runs over others that is condemned. This is not, however, merely a late piety speaking. Care for the poor is the foundation of a king's throne, and a nation without justice will fall. This belief is reflected in all ancient societies around Israel as well. Compare the words of Esarhaddon, king of Assyria (681–669 B.C.E.), explaining why Babylon fell to his armies and was destroyed: "They [the citizens] oppressed the weak and gave him into the power of the strong. Inside the city there was tyranny, the receiving of bribes; each day without fail they plundered each other's goods . . . Marduk, the Enlil of the gods, was angry and devised evil to overwhelm the land and destroy the peoples."

The defense against such rampant injustice, according to the authors of this chapter, is faithfulness to the law (vv. 4, 7, 9). The law of Moses is closely associated with the ideal of justice (see Exod 21; Lev 19; Deut 14–15; Ps 119:142). Thus the common wisdom of ancient nations is given a specifically Israelite framework for putting it into pratice.

Another mark of human wisdom subjected to worship is the concern of verse 13 that everyone needs mercy for sins committed. It can be achieved by an open admission of guilt to God. The Babylonians also recognized the value of confession but were not as confident that it always worked. Verse 26 can be taken as a summary of the Israelite point of view. Humans cannot be truly wise if they trust only in themselves. There are too many evils catalogued in these sayings—fraud (v. 24), greed (vv. 22, 25), flattery (v. 23), and partiality (v. 21)—that will lead them astray. All of them result from pride, and the only safeguard is humble submission to Yahweh (see also 29:23).

29:1-27. Many of the sayings in chapter 29 deal with two themes: the king (vv. 1, 2, 3, 4, 12, 14, 16, 26) and the need for disciplined learning (vv. 15, 17, 19, 21). A subtheme, related to these two, deals with the passion of anger and its subsequent loss of self-control. Much of the wisdom language of Prov 1–9 and 10–22 returns in this chapter: the just, the wicked, the wise, the fool, the upright, and the arrogant, as well as justice, correction, and rebuke. It is the best of old wisdom organized around Yahweh, who gives blessing and life to every individual *equally* (vv. 13, 26).

The proverbs in verses 8-11 center on the wise as peacemakers in the community, and verses 17-22 stress aspects of speaking according to wise training. Verses 13-14 return to the theme of the poor (see chapter 28). Verse 13 in particular reminds one of Jesus' saying, "The sun rises on the evil and the good alike" (Matt 5:45). It is also close to Prov 14:31; 17:5; 22:2. Verse 14 on the responsibility of the king toward the poor is very much like the demands of Psalm 72 and reflects the Israelite ideal of kingship (see the earlier discussion on Prov 15:1-33, p. 660, and the Ugaritic text of *King Keret* quoted there).

Discipline is praised as the means to guide a person on the way of the just. The strong statement on the value of physical beating in verse 15 is based on the need to check our personal urges until we have had a chance to examine and question what we should do. This is the method of the wisdom tradition.

Verse 27 closes this fourth collection of materials with the unmistakable assertion that there can be no compromise between the way of the wicked and the way of uprightness. In this, wisdom is completely equated with moral behavior.

PART V: THE WORDS OF AGUR AND LEMUEL

Prov 30:1–31:31

30:1-9. These nine verses are a single unit attributed to Agur, the son of Jakeh, who is otherwise unknown. If, as the New American Bible translates, he is from Massa, it suggests wisdom from the East beyond Edom. Gen 25:14 identifies Massa as an area in northern Arabia. Edom itself, another north Arabian neighbor, was famed for its wisdom in biblical tradition (see Jer 49:7; Obad 8). However, many scholars doubt that this Massa is meant. The Hebrew word also means "oracle," and is closely followed here by a standard prophetic formula, "The pronouncement (of the Lord)." The second part of verse 1 is also very difficult. It may mean either "I have no God" or "who has no God." Some propose another sense, "one who wearies himself about God." The only translation that is certainly not correct is the traditional literal rendering of the Hebrew, "The man says to Ithiel, to Ithiel and Ucal." Such names are unknown and make no sense in this context.

The meaning of the whole passage, however, is not in doubt. Human knowledge is nothing compared with that of God. It is the same message as Isa 40:12-18, prophetic in spirit, challenging the hearer to learn humility before the mystery of God's transcendence (v. 4). God's word is always to be trusted and stands without need of any help from us. The thought echoes the orthodox defense of the divine word found in Ps 18:30 or Deut 4:2. It concludes in verses 7-9 with a double wish: that God may guard the author both from a lying tongue and from want, so that there will not be any temptation to destroy his or her trust in God's powerful care.

Numerical proverbs in 30:10-33. Most of these verses are in the form of comparisons or riddles. The formula for the riddle is the use of succeeding numbers, "three things and four," or just a set number, "four things there are . . . ." Recall the old English riddle: "Four stiff-standers, four dilly-danders, two lookers, two crookers, and a wig-wag." The answer is a *cow*, and it is gotten by making a relationship between the five descriptive comparisons. Though Proverbs does not ask us to guess the answers, it does force us to figure out what the four given elements have in common in the five examples: vv. 15-17, 18-19, 21-23, 24-28, 29-33. Riddles are fun but also educational, and they help train students in the use of analogy.

30:10-14. The New American Bible places the end of Agur's reflections at verse 6; other scholars see it continuing to verse 10. The answer is according to taste. The slander mentioned in verse 10 may be connected to the lying in verse 8, or else it may introduce the groups named in verses 11-14 who do harm by what they say. Since verses 11-14 belong together as four examples of those who destroy the spirit of trust in a community, verse 10 may be a later addition placed next to verse 11 because it also mentions cursing. Probably the four lines were introduced by a formula similar to the ones that follow: "Three groups, yes, four I disdain" (or something like it). This grouping shows strong overtones of condemnation and is not merely a casual observation of behavior.

30:15-16. An independent saying about the leech introduces this first real numerical proverb. The common element in both this saying and the four examples is an unlimited desire for more—greed. Since the focus in these riddles is on human behavior, the key comparison is not in the images from nature, but the example of the barren womb and what it says about longing for parenthood.

30:17. This short saying returns us to verse 11 and thus rounds out the whole section from verses 10-17. The overall theme has been selfish greed, and its worst form leads to rejection of respect for parents. The law in Exod 21:17 and Lev 20:9 is just as strong!

30:18-20. The key to this comparison is in the mystery of how a thing happens, especially the mystery of love between a man and a woman. Some hold that seduction is the issue, but that would make the comparisons meaningless. Others think it is the attraction of forbidden sex because of verse 20. But that is an addition from later intended as a warning against allowing lust to overcome love.

30:21-23. The four objects of comparison in this riddle are all human stereotypes of arrogance. In a sense they are the standard cast of characters from comedy shows, and more than a little humor is intended here. Each one represents the Peter Principle at its worst—someone who has gone way past ability and makes up for incompetence by being overbearing.

30:24-28. In contrast to the preceding, the images in this saying are all from the animal world. The ant is famed for its industry, the badger for its tenacity, the locust for its disciplined mass migrations, and the lizard for its resourcefulness under any conditions. Naturally, the lesson of how these weak creatures succeed so well is intended for the human audience.

30:29-31. The Hebrew text is difficult in these verses and so translations differ. The combination of three proud beasts and a human king fits the pattern of verses 18-19, so that the translation in the New American Bible is probably correct. The message is not profound, but it represents well the ancient experience of kings and their splendor.

30:32-33. This summarizes the riddle collection. The major theme has been pride and proneness to easy anger when others disagree. The reader is warned against both by the prophetic tone of the chapter.

31:1 The words of Lemuel. The label in 31:1 presents the same problem as 30:1. Does "Massa" mean an Arab place name or does it mean "oracle"? The New American Bible fudges here by translating it both ways, "king of Massa" and "The advice." At least the sense is not lost by preserving both! A second problem is whether this heading covers both verses 1-9 and 10-31. Most scholars would consider the poem on the ideal woman to be a separate piece attached at the end as a kind of conclusion to the whole Book of Proverbs. This is discussed below.

31:1-9. This piece is written in the traditional Instruction genre for royal officials. Probably the person of Lemuel is a fiction to give weight to the advice that follows. Under the cover of the education of the king-to-be, the author presents practical guidelines for a prudent and wise life. The fact that it is called a mother's advice probably underscores that what is taught here was reckoned as traditional family or clan wisdom. On the other hand, it may indicate a Judean origin in the royal schools. From the Book of Kings we know that the queen-mother was an important position in the royal administration of the southern kingdom (1 Kgs 14:21; 15:2; 1 Kgs 11:1-16).

The lesson comes with three commands:

restrain your sexual appetite, do not become the victim of drink, respect the rights of the poor by doing justice. The first probably refers to harem intrigues—many kings have fallen or been assassinated because of strife that began in the jealousies of the palace. Wine, too, undoes all of the self-control and discipline that wisdom teaches (see 23:29-35). Israel itself records a fanatical group, the Rechabites, who opposed all drinking of wine (see 2 Kgs 9 and Jer 35). But the most important teaching is last. The king represents justice in the land and must be the final refuge and appeal of the poor against corrupt officials. See the earlier discussion at 16:10-15; 28:1-28 and 29:1-27.

31:10-33. Proverbs ends with this acrostic poem of twenty-two lines (each line beginning with the next letter of the Hebrew alphabet). This makes it a highly artistic creation, and more impressionistic perhaps than strictly logical in its order of thought. The good wife has been an important theme throughout Proverbs (11:16; 12:4; 18:22; 19:14), and so it is not surprising that the book should end with the example of a woman as the ideal wise person. In some ways the litany of good qualities resembles the traditional marriage song in praise of the bride, an example of which is found in Song of Songs 7:1-10. These marriage songs describe the physical beauty of the woman from head to foot to show that her beauty is complete. Here it is her wisdom and good management that are complete.

In light, however, of the themes found in chapters 1–9 on Lady Wisdom versus the adulterous woman or the foolish woman, it is probably better to see in this passage more than a picture of the perfect wife. She is wisdom in action—the model of self-control, prudence, understanding, and just behavior. Even more particularly, it is the wisdom who called out at the city gates for people to listen (1:21; 8:3), and wisdom that was manifest in fear of the Lord (1:7; 9:10), just as this woman is marked by fear of the Lord and her praises sung in the city gates (31:30-31). The husband can be identified with the young man of chapters 1–9 who heeds wisdom's call. As a result, he is a man of stature and respect in the community.

The poem opens with a stanza describing how much a man depends on a good wife for prosperity (vv. 10-12). The remaining verses then alternate between her ability as a business woman and her prudent care of her own family. It may seem strange that a woman is praised for her commercial dealings, since this is an area reserved to men in the Old Testament (except for the rare case of a queen in power—for example, the queen of Sheba in 1 Kgs 10). But we should understand "commerce" in verses 13, 14, 16, and 24 as a metaphor for wisdom. The international exchange of wisdom throughout the Ancient Near East is aptly portrayed as a commercial transaction. Israel buys only the best of what will fit its own theology. The search, however, often leads to far places.

An Arab proverb states, "A clever woman is never without wool." This ideal woman is prepared; she is the opposite of the fool or lazy person. She "delights" in her primary responsibility to her family, working late at night, creating things by the skills she has mastered, seeing needs ahead of time. Making clothes is the chief metaphor of such practical wisdom. The clothes cover the body and give it shape, protection, and a liveliness in the same way that wisdom forms, guards, and enriches the mind and spirit. Moreover, verses 23 and 25 promise that the reward of a marriage to wisdom will be respect and honor—the same "weight" mentioned in other proverbs (11:16; 21:21; 22:4; 29:23). The reference to the city gates in verse 23 emphasizes the judicial role of the husband in settling disputes.

The woman's teaching consists of wisdom and mercy ("kindly counsel" in verse 26). It excels all other virtues that one can strive to obtain (v. 29), and may well combine the ideals of prophet and wise person into one, since "mercy" is the central concept of the covenant theology of the prophets. If we can push this mere hint that far, chapter 31 would correspond nicely to the mix of teaching and prophetic exhortation found in chapters 1 and 9, so that the beginning and end balance one another. Then the children and the husband of the ideal woman represent the disciples of wisdom, who have accepted as one the teachings of the law, the prophets, and the wisdom books.

Although the passage most certainly has Lady Wisdom in mind, we must not forget that it also gives a real example of womanly ability and achievement. Rather than being just another passage describing the submissive wife in the ancient world, it reveals the remarkably even-handed approach of Proverbs that recognizes wisdom where it is found—in men and women alike.

JOB

Michael D. Guinan, O.F.M.

INTRODUCTION

One of the most basic characteristics of being human is the capacity to sense injustice and to fight against it. We experience something as unfair and are willing to stand up and say so; we put ourselves on the line rather than submit. The biblical Book of Job is an expression of just such a capacity and just such a stand. Throughout the centuries many have found in it an eloquent presentation of their own pains and sufferings as they have struggled to understand the justice of God in the face of their own broken experience. (In scholarly circles, such an undertaking is known as "theodicy.") To study the history of the interpretation of Job is almost as revealing of human experience as to study the book itself.

The problem is, of course, nothing new. Some of the oldest literature we know from the ancient Near East, from Sumer, wrestles with this question of the suffering of the innocent. In addition, several treatises along similar lines have come down to us from both Mesopotamia and Egypt. As beautiful a voice as it is, then, Job's is not a solo voice but soars over a surging chorus.

When the Book of Job joined the chorus is not an easy question. Scholars have generally been inclined to locate it in the context of the Babylonian Exile. Some would see it more in the struggles and confusion leading up to the destruction of Judah and Jerusalem in 587 B.C.E. Others locate it in the search for meaning and soul-searching during the time of the Exile itself. Still others place it after the Exile in the Persian period (after 538 B.C.E.), reflecting back on the trauma and chaos recently survived. While full certainty about the dating may be elusive, we must admit that the book has such a universal quality to it that ultimately the dating question may not be of great importance.

The question of dating is not the only problematic aspect of this book. Its readers and interpreters face difficulties on almost every page. It may be helpful to sort these difficulties into two broad clusters: (1) difficulties arising from the book itself; and (2) difficulties arising from its social and religious background. In short, we face problems of text and context.

Difficulties arising from the text

The first problem is the received Hebrew text itself. It is very corrupt, many passages being practically unintelligible. Compounding this is the vocabulary of the book. As very elevated poetry, it abounds in rich and diverse expressions, rare words, and words occurring only once in the Bible. Some scholars have even suggested that the composer of Job made up words to convey multiple levels of meaning. All of this means that Job is an exceptionally difficult book to translate. Recourse is often had to the related Semitic languages—Aramaic, Arabic and Ugaritic—in an attempt to elucidate obscure passages. A comparison of modern translations would prove interesting in this regard. A glance at ancient translations (for example, the Greek or Aramaic) assures us that they faced the same basic problems that we do today.

When we move to the next level, that of literary history and composition, problems again abound. A prose, narrative prologue and epilogue encase a long poetic dialogue between Job and his friends. Was the prose story originally older and separate? There seem to be three cycles of speeches between Job and the three friends, but the third cycle is in considerable disarray. How is this to be sorted out? Are the wisdom hymn in chapter 28 and the Elihu speeches (chs. 32–37) original or later additions? Scholars dispute these and many other points of detail. We will be concerned primarily with the Book of Job as we have it and with the translation of the New American Bible (NAB). While at times we will have to refer to disputed points, they will not loom large in our commentary.

A third type of problem involves the overall meaning of the book. It does not seem to answer nor deal directly with the questions Job raises. We will defer our discussion of this until the end of our commentary, until after we have read and studied our way through the book.

Difficulties arising from the context

The Book of Job was written about 2500 years ago within the context of Israelite culture and religion. We can well imagine that ancient Israelites, reading or hearing the story, would respond from within that context and would pick up overtones and undertones that escape us as inhabitants of another space, time, and thought world. While we can never expect to carry ourselves back in such a way as to catch all the nuances, we can discern certain broad aspects of the ancient culture and religion that can help us to situate ourselves and to begin to bridge the culture gap. Here we would highlight three elements of both the cultural and the religious contexts of Job.

Cultural

1) Job lives within a *tribal* culture. He is the patriarch of the tribe and is concerned about its needs, namely its growth, in terms of both his own descendants and his land, possessions, and prosperity. Family ties are close, and he can expect to live on (at this time the Israelites did not have any concept of a life after death) in the presence of his descendants and in their memory.

2) The tribal culture is also an *oral* one. Communication and education depend primarily on the spoken word; it is this that ties society together. As the exchange between Job and his friends heats up, the rhetoric will become more bombastic, even insulting. This is consonant with an oral culture in which the important thing is not simply *that* something be said but also *how* it is said. *What* people say looms very, very large as well, and this leads directly to our third trait.

3) The tribal, oral culture is predominately a *shame* culture. In such a context honor and shame are pivotal values, if not *the* pivotal values. A good name or reputation carries weight and makes one honorable (the Hebrew word for "honor," in fact, means basically "to have weight"). That Job seems to be in the wrong, and is called such by his friends, would have been in itself a source of great suffering and affliction. It is important not only to be right and just but to be recognized as such by others. While such a position may seem strange to us, for whom "being honest" and "doing your own thing" are so important, many other parts of our globe, such as the Mediterranean cultures (Spain, Italy, Greece, the Arab countries) and the Asian cultures of the Far East, still largely convey an honor-shame value system.

Religious

1) According to Jer 18:18, three sources of religious leadership and guidance were available to ancient Israel: the law of the priest, the word of the prophet, and the counsel of the wise. It is to this third category that the Book of Job belongs. It speaks from the context of *the wise* and *wisdom theology*. For our purposes, two aspects of wisdom thought may be singled out: (a) Wisdom depends on and speaks from experience. It is in the everyday happenings of our lives and in our reflection on them—expressed most characteristically in proverbial form—that we find wisdom and God's teaching. (b) According to the common teaching of wisdom, wise, righteous living should, generally speaking, bring with it the rewards of fuller life, especially offspring and prosperity. It is precisely Job's experience (a) which seriously calls the doctrine (b) into question.

2) In presenting Job's argument with God, the Book of Job draws heavily on *legal imagery*. If someone had a complaint against another, that person would first try to settle the issue informally. If this failed, the defendant swore an oath of innocence and appealed to a third party, a judge, who would call on the accuser to present evidence. Legal language abounds as Job protests his innocence and calls for some third party to stand with him (for example, 9:33; 16:19; 19:25).

3) In addition to wisdom themes and legal expressions, the Book of Job is situated within the context and language of *lamentation*. In times of distress and affliction, Israel poured out its lament before the Lord. Lamentation is the spontaneous response to the presence of the realm of death, in whatever manifestation of brokenness, in our lives. It is a loud, religious "Ouch!" When we stub our toe, we cry out in pain; when something in our experience stubs our "religious toe," we lament. Lamentation is present throughout the Bible (the Book of Lamentations, Jeremiah, many of the psalms), but it is something we today have lost touch with and may need to rediscover. We will return to this at the end of our study.

These elements of culture and religion obviously overlap and influence each other. Thus, Job suffers the loss of his family and possessions; he seems to be unrighteous, a conclusion his friends quickly draw. In his shame he pours out his lament to God and calls on God for a hearing that will acknowledge his innocence for all to see. At various points in our commentary we will refer back to these issues.

Outline of the book

The following general outline may guide us as we work our way through the Book of Job:

I. *The Prologue (1:1–2:13)*
There is a wager in heaven and the just Job is despoiled of everything. Three friends arrive to console him.

II. *The Poetic Dialogue (3:1–31:40)*
After Job bitterly laments his lot, the three friends rise to God's defense. They argue back and forth through three cycles of speeches until Job ends with a fervent oath of innocence.

III. *The Elihu Speeches (32:1–37:24)*
A brash youth interrupts and manages to say little that is new or helpful.

IV. *The Yahweh Speeches (38:1–42:6)*
Yahweh finally responds in two long speeches and overwhelms Job into silence.

V. *Epilogue (42:7-17)*
Job's fortunes are restored and they all live happily ever after.

COMMENTARY

I. PROLOGUE

Job 1:1–2:13

A prose prologue in five scenes, alternating between earth and heaven, opens the book, sets the stage, and introduces the characters. From a calm and happy beginning, the action moves quickly, ending in suffering, tension, and confusion.

1:1-5 Scene one: Earth. We meet "a man" (the first word in the Hebrew text) whose name is Job. Although the name was not uncommon in the ancient Near East, its precise meaning is uncertain. The best guess—"where is [my] Father [God]?"—is appropriate but almost certainly coincidental. The figure of Job seems rather to be an old legendary hero of faith (see Ezek 14:14, 20). Uz is certainly located in the broad territory east of the Jordan River, but whether it is in the more northerly Aramean region or the more southerly area of Edom is hard to determine. At any rate, Job is presented as a non-Israelite.

More important, this man is a model of upright and virtuous living. His "fear of God" refers not to a servile emotion but to a response of obedient faith (see Deut 10:12). Within the context of wisdom theology, the fear of God is also the beginning and the essence of wisdom (Job 28:28; Prov 1:7; 9:10) and usually brings with it prosperity and a full life (see Prov 3:13-18). Job is thus blessed with seven sons and three daughters, an abundance of livestock, and male and female slaves (better than NAB's "work animals").

Job's righteousness is highlighted even further. On the chance that one of his children, in the midst of their periodic family celebrations, might have sinned and cursed God, Job intercedes for his loved ones and sacrifices whole-burnt offerings on their behalf. This rosy, idyllic situation is about to end.

1:6-12 Scene two: Heaven. Yahweh (NAB: "the Lord"), like an Oriental monarch holding court, is surrounded by the "sons of God." In ancient mythology these were originally lesser divine beings, but in the Bible they are demoted to the status of servants and attendants of Yahweh (see 1 Kgs 22:19-23). To imagine them as angels, in the sense of later Christian theology, is surely an anachronism. Among them is the Satan. This is not a proper name, as in the same later Christian theology, but rather describes an office and a function: "the adversary." He seems to have been God's CIA agent checking up on things around the world. We, the readers, are aware of Job's integrity; now we learn that God is also aware of it, and in fact takes pride in Job (v. 8). The Satan is skeptical and, in front of the whole heavenly court, suggests that Job is virtuous simply because he gets something out of it. If Job were to lose all these blessings, what would he say then? He would flagrantly curse God. In the context of a shame culture, Yahweh's honor is now involved and has a stake in the outcome. The Satan is allowed to put Job to the test, something he hastens to do.

1:13-22 Scene three: Earth. In quick succession, four messengers rush in reporting disaster. Job's blessings of scene one are stripped away—first his livestock, then his slaves, finally his children. Forces of destruction both human (Sabeans and Chaldeans) and natural (lightning and whirlwind) are let loose by Satan, reducing Job's cosmos to chaos. With dramatic gestures typical of lamentation and mourning, Job tears his garments (see, for example, Gen 37:29, 34), shaves his head (see Isa 15:2; Jer 7:29), and casts himself to the earth from which he was taken and to which he will return. The Satan, however, is frustrated in his hopes. When Job opens his lips to speak, he utters what seems almost a religious proverb and blesses God. He does not say anything to bring shame to God.

2:1-6 Scene four: Heaven. The scene quickly changes; the heavenly court is again in session. God, almost chuckling, is enjoying the vindication of both God's servant and God's honor. Verse 3b is important because it further confirms what we already know—and what Job will staunchly maintain throughout the book: there is no connection between Job's virtuous life and his sufferings. The Satan replies with a proverb so terse (three words in both Hebrew and English) that its meaning almost completely eludes us. It seems to suggest some sort of trade-off. Job has blessed God, it would seem, only in order to protect his own life. If Job's person is attacked as well, he will surely curse God. Thus Job falls into the power of the Satan, who rushes out to do his dirty work.

2:7-13 Scene five: Earth. Job is immediately struck with a repulsive disease whose poetic description, both here and elsewhere in the book (7:5; 19:17, 20), will not yield to more precise medical diagnosis. His wife enters the stage, delivers her one line, and then disappears into the wings, thus creating a vacuum that later tradition would fill by giving her both a name (Sitis) and a more prominent place. Job reproves her for speaking "as senseless women do" (v. 10). He is not implying that women as such are foolish; biblical wisdom recognizes and praises wise women (Prov 31:10-31; Judg 5:29; 2 Sam 14:1-20). In this instance, his wife has offered foolish advice. Folly, the opposite of wisdom (Prov 9:1-12, 13-18), describes primarily the behavioral failure to recognize, speak, and do the right thing at the right time. As such, folly contributes to the breakdown of social and cosmic unity and harmony that God, through wisdom, calls all of us to foster and manifest. Job does not yield to the temptation to speak foolishness. As the Hebrew text says, "in all this, he did not sin with his lips" (v. 10).

Three friends (there is no basis for the later belief that they were kings) hear of Job's plight and gather from their distant homelands, which cannot be identified with certainty. Moved by genuine compassion, they come to offer comfort and consolation, but the sight of his condition, so radically changed, moves them too to traditional expressions of lamentation (see 1:20 above; also Josh 7:16; 1 Sam 4:12). They sit with him in the dust and speak perhaps the wisest consolation, their silence.

And so the prologue ends. Job is left, "a man" now literally on the earth, and God, who dwells in heaven, looks down. How will these two, in their two places, relate and interact? The Satan has loomed large, using natural phenomena, marauders, physical disease, and Job's wife to get him to curse God, to "sin with his lips" (1:11, 22; 2:5, 9, 10). With his failure, the Satan too disappears into the wings; in what follows, his work will be furthered by Job's friends, until now silent. We, the readers, and God know that Job is in fact completely innocent. The issue at stake is: What will Job say? The audience, the listeners—God, the friends, the readers—wait in anticipation. We do not have long to wait.

II. JOB'S MONOLOGUE: LAMENTATION

Job 3:1-26

The proverbial "patience of Job" comes to a dramatic end, never to reappear. So far Job's responses to his various afflictions have manifested a dangerous conflict between his actions (grief and mourning) and his words (praise of God). This dichotomy is now resolved: his words and actions agree as he pours out his lamentation, to no one and to everyone.

Lamentation, as we noted above, is the spontaneous cry of pain when our lives are overwhelmed by chaos, brokenness, and confusion. The common ancient Near Eastern mythology dealt with this struggle between order and chaos, life and death. Chaos is there symbolized in two ways: (1) as a sea monster, variously called Sea, Rahab, Leviathan, the twisting serpent. The storm god (in Canaan, Ba'al) defeats Sea, tramples it in victory, and then reigns/rains life and fertility from his palace in heaven until the arrival of his other foe; (2) as death, manifested in the hot, dry summer and the barren wilderness. There is no rain and everything dies. Ba'al dies, only to revive with the coming of the fall rains, which usually bring life and fertility for another year. Since language borrowed from this mythic complex recurs in the Book of Job (7:12; 9:8, 13; 26:12), it would be well to keep this in mind.

3:3-10 Curse the day and night. Job does not curse God but rather the day of his birth and the night of his conception (v. 3b, better translated: "the night when they said, 'A man is conceived!' "). In language which reverses that of the Genesis creation account (Gen 1:1–2:4), he prays that the day become night, and the night be wiped out of the calendar. In his affliction, Jeremiah expressed a similar wish (Jer 20:14-18). The translation and meaning of verse 8 are obscure. Since Leviathan was thought to cause eclipses by swallowing the sun, this would fit the context of Job's prayer for darkness.

3:11-19 Longing for death. The struggle between light and darkness was part of the cosmic struggle between order (life) and chaos (death). Job has prayed for darkness; now he prays for death: "I wish my womb had become my tomb!" Two common features of lamentation appear: (1) the repeated question

"Why?" (see Pss 22:2; 43:10; 43:2). While this implies, "I do not understand," it is a cry of pain rather than a request for theological or scientific explanation; (2) the focus on "I" (see Ps 77:1-6). In the face of intense suffering, it is hard to look outside oneself. Job looks to death, in which all are equal (vv. 14-19), to bring him tranquility and rest.

3:20-26 Deliver me from God! The "bitter in spirit" (v. 20) refers more probably to profuse weeping. The expression in Hebrew is literally "bitter of throat" and reflects the belief that in times of great distress, the intestines put pressure on the liver and heart, breaking them down ("broken-hearted") and turning them to liquid, which passes through the throat, leaving a bitter taste, and then exits the eyes as tears.

The question "Why?" recurs for those "whose path is hidden from them" (v. 23a). Verse 23b shows a strong ironic twist. In 1:10 the Satan had accused God of "surrounding" Job with blessings; here Job uses the same word to describe his being "hemmed in" by God. For ancient Israel, Yahweh was the God who had delivered them from death; here, in a statement of great irony, Job prays for death to deliver him, the servant (v. 19; see 1:8; 2:3), from God, the taskmaster (vv. 18-19).

III. FIRST ROUND OF SPEECHES

Job 4:1–14:22

Shocked by Job's lament and moved to answer his repeated "whys," the friends abandon their wise silence (see 13:5). It is difficult to characterize the chapters that follow. Discussion? Debate? Dialogue? Perhaps "speech" is helpful, if we think of politicians less interested in really responding to arguments point by point and more interested in playing to an audience and scoring points that way. We, the readers/hearers, are the audience.

The speeches are given roughly through three rounds: (1) 4:1–14:22; (2) 15:1–21:34; (3) 22:1–27:21. In the first two, each of the friends speaks, and Job responds, usually at greater length; the third round is in some disarray, perhaps the result of textual confusion.

4:1–5:26 Eliphaz's first speech. Beginning politely enough, Eliphaz suggests that the "instruction" (an important word in Old Testament wisdom circles) Job has offered to others in the past should not be forgotten now when Job is in need (4:2-5). After alluding to Job's general uprightness of life ("piety" and "integrity" in verse 6 reflect the Hebrew words translated "fear of the Lord" and "blamelessness" in 1:1, 8; 2:3), Eliphaz makes his first main point. Based on experience ("Reflect now" . . . "As I see it"), he affirms the doctrine of retribution: the innocent do not perish (4:7). Only those reap mischief who have previously sown it (4:8). In proverbial fashion (see Prov 28:15; also Pss 17:12; 22:14, 21), the wicked, like the lion, may make a big noise, but in the end they are cut down and their families left destitute.

In remarkable fashion, Eliphaz appeals next, not to wisdom experience, but to a special vision; the eerie description might best fit a nightmare. Preceded by fear and shuddering, a wind blows over his face (a better translation than "a spirit passed before me") causing him to shudder (4:15). He peeks out and perceives *ein Etwas*, a vague something. And then a voice that makes Eliphaz's second, fairly platitudinous point: All humans are sinful; none are blameless! The reference to the imperfections of God's servants and messengers in verse 18 has nothing to do with the later theory of good and bad angels. If the members of God's own court are not blameless, how much less blameless are human beings, creatures of clay who perish quickly without ever knowing wisdom! Eliphaz does not pursue the implications of this last phrase for himself and his own theory. The anthropological view of human existence expressed here (4:17-21 and 11:11; 15:14-16; 25:4-6), while similar to that of many a radio and television preacher, seems almost a parody of the higher anthropology of Psalm 8 and Gen 1:26-31.

Eliphaz goes on to taunt Job (5:1-2): "Do not bother calling on any of the lesser beings in Yahweh's court either!" Since some Near Eastern religions held that everyone had a personal god who would speak his or her case in the heavenly council, some polemic may be involved here. In fact, Job will later call for some kind of mediator to stand between himself and God (9:33; 16:19; 19:25). Insinuating that Job is a fool, Eliphaz uses the proverb in 5:2 to argue that the prosperity of fools is only apparent; their way ends in disaster that affects not only themselves but their whole family. Their children will have no one to speak for them or rescue them "at the gate" (5:4), the place where tribal business and legal matters were handled (see Ruth 4:1; Prov 22:22). In verses 6-7 a third point is made: Whatever mischief and trouble we find in our lives is a human product.

Between his contrasting descriptions of the lot of the fool (5:3-7) and that of the righteous (5:17-26), Eliphaz urges Job to do as he, Eliphaz, would do, that is, appeal to God! A hymn-like section follows, describing God as the creator and source of the life-giving rain (verse 9 is omitted in the New American Bible as a duplicate of 9:10); as the all-wise one who ordains things justly (vv. 12-14); and as the protector and defender of the poor and oppressed (vv. 11, 15-16). All these images are commonplace in Old Testament thought.

Beginning with a beatitude—suffering can be God's parental and ultimately healing correction—the description of the rewards of righteousness falls into two parts, verses 18-22 and verses 23-26. Verses 18-22 present the negative side: basically, God saves from oppression and death. In an oral-shame culture, the tongue (v. 21) could indeed be a terrible scourge, as Job is in fact experiencing! Verses 23-26 present the positive side. The life-giving relationship of humans with both the earth and the animals, fractured by sin (Gen 3), is here restored (v. 23). The power of life is manifested further by begetting many offspring (so important in a tribal society) and by living to a ripe old age. Fidelity to God, then, brings abundance of life.

Having made his four basic points—what innocent person perishes? (4:7); can mortals be blameless against their maker? (4:17); humans themselves beget mischief (5:7); happy those whom God reproves (5:17)—Eliphaz concludes his opening remarks (v. 27) with a ringing appeal to experience: "So it is, and what's more, you should know it!" Unfortunately, Job knows no such thing.

6:1–7:21 Job's reply to Eliphaz. Job responds with a strong emotional outburst. His anguish and calamity may be too great to be measured (vv. 1-2), but they can, even must, be spoken (v. 3). The divine hunter pursues him with poisoned arrows (v. 4). As the rhetorical question in verse 5 suggests, Job is not braying without reason. To add insult to injury, Eliphaz's advice is too much for Job to stomach (vv. 6-7). The "white of an egg" in verse 6b is a traditional rendering of a very obscure Hebrew phrase.

Job turns to prayer (vv. 8-12). As in chapter 3, he still longs for death to bring relief and consolation, but, as there and throughout the book, this never brings him to contemplate suicide. Job is not an unfeeling statue of stone or bronze (v. 12) but a human being who is being pushed to the limit.

At last Job clearly acknowledges the presence of his friends. Apparently responding only to Eliphaz, throughout Job addresses "you-all" (plural) and gives an object lesson on the meaning of friendship. A friend owes kindness, loyalty, and fidelity to one in despair, even when—or especially when—that one is moved to abandon religion ("fear of the Almighty," v. 14). A friend in need is a friend indeed! Instead, the friends are like the Palestinian wadis (gullies), which fill quickly with rain but just as quickly run dry. They are totally undependable; they cannot be trusted. An ancient caravan, trusting them, would risk not only frustration but even possible death.

This is what Job's friends are; in a way, they came, took one look and ran (v. 21). He had never imposed on them for anything, but he had a right to expect honest words. Job challenges them to show where he has sinned to deserve this treatment (v. 24). Their fear (v. 21) prevents them from hearing the truth in the "sayings of a desperate man" (v. 26). Job's charge in verse 27 would seem as gratuitous as Eliphaz's suggestion that he has sinned. Job resolutely affirms that right and justice are still on his side (v. 29).

To answer Job's first outcry, Eliphaz had painted a fairly unflattering view of human existence (4:17-21). Here Job would seem to agree. Life is a drudgery, and humans are all slaves. The night drags on forever, while life flies by like the wind (vv. 4, 7). Job will soon be gone, descended to the nether world (v. 9). This is one of several statements (10:21; 14:10-12; 16:22) which show clearly that no hope for resurrection or afterlife appears in the book. After death all alike, with no distinction between rich and poor, wicked and upright, go down to the realm of death. But does Job really agree with Eliphaz? It does not seem so. Eliphaz presented a theological view of the way things are; Job is giving an existential description of his experience, which is not the way things should be. If he agreed, why his constant outcry against it as something unjust?

Job will not keep silent. The purpose of the test proposed by the Satan was to see what Job would say, and now he will have his say. Verse 11 is a very important statement in the context of the whole book. God is treating Job like the mythological monsters Sea and Leviathan. Job's struggles stand in the context of the cosmic battle between order and chaos, life and death. Since God has apparently put Job on the side of chaos, he longs to be with the other mythological figure of chaos and oppression, Death (v. 15).

Psalm 8 asks, "What is man, O God, that you watch over him" and concludes to the exalted nature of human existence. Job clearly parodies this. Yes, God watches over him, but like Big Brother in Orwell's *1984* (vv. 17-18, 20). Why won't God leave him alone, at least long enough to catch his breath (v. 19)? Even if he had sinned, why (again that question!) does God not simply forgive? A chasm separates any possible guilt of Job from his sufferings. Job will soon be dead, and then it will be too late (vv. 20-21).

8:1-22 Bildad's first speech. "When are you going to shut up, you old windbag?" (8:2). Thus the second friend jumps with both feet into the fray and comes immediately to a defense of God's justice. While it was implicit before, this is the first time the issue is stated so clearly (v. 3). With logical consistency that allows no room for uncertainty, the death of Job's children (perhaps discreetly alluded to by Eliphaz in 5:4) is attributed to their own sins (v. 4). Still, if Job will only turn and repent (something Eliphaz had likewise recommended, with himself as model, 5:8), he will be restored to his former prosperity (vv. 5-7). This is quite irrelevant, as Job has consistently longed, not for his old possessions, but for understanding and justice.

In the best wisdom tradition, Bildad appeals to the accumulated wisdom of the ages passed down from the ancestors (vv. 8-10). In their name he cites a proverb with Egyptian coloring. Just as plants need water if they are to grow and blossom, so humans need God if they are to grow and prosper (vv. 11-12). Bildad then develops the example of one who forgets God. Forgetting God is not a simple lapse of memory; it is cutting off our water supply in the middle of the desert! It is a personal amnesia. We forget who we are, where we are from, where we are going, and how we are to live. Such persons might find some prosperity, but it hangs by a thin thread (vv. 14-19).

On the other hand, God does not forsake the upright (vv. 20-22). If only Job will repent, he will again be filled with laughter and rejoicing. Verse 21a recalls Israel's happiness when God returned them from exile (Ps 126:2). In verse 22 Bildad gives an ironic foreshadowing of what in fact is going to happen at the end of the book (42:7-17).

9:1–10:22 Job's reply to Bildad. These chapters are beset with many problems of text and translation, but it is clear that they abound in legal images. At times Job is the plaintiff who wants to haul God off to court (9:3). Unfortunately, since the defendant and the judge are the same, what chance does he have? At other times Job seems to be the defendant who has to answer for his life (9:14). Job's sense of helplessness also keeps coming up, especially in the face of God's awesome creative power. At any rate, it is clear that Job's speech is getting bolder and more outspoken.

The friends had argued, "How can one be justified before God?" meaning "All are sinners" (4:17). Job agrees with the question but with quite a different meaning. One cannot be justified when the judge and defendant are the same and so powerful (vv. 2-3). God can overturn the order of creation (vv. 5-7) just as God first established it. Like a warrior with his victorious foot on the back of the fallen prey, God plants a foot on the back of the defeated Sea (v. 8; see Ps 110:1-2). Later (chs. 38–41) Yahweh will appeal to these same wonders of creation.

Job's utter confusion and helplessness are reflected in verses 11-21. He does not know what to do or say that would make any difference. Verse 13 again alludes to God's defeat of the primal sea monster, this time under the name of Rahab. Throughout these verses a series of "if" questions shows Job turning first one way and then another as he looks for some course of action. There is none. He despises his life (v. 21). Who is there to blame but God (vv. 22-24)?

Job's life is going by swiftly, like a runner, a speedy boat on the Nile, or an eagle.

There is no way that he can win; even should he succeed in cleansing his name, God would just muddy it up again (vv. 25-31). Forsaken by his friends, alone, Job longs (in the first of three such passages; see 16:19; 19:25) for some third party, here a neutral arbiter, who might stand between him and God and work out a fair judgment. But he knows that this is hopeless; again, he loathes his life (vv. 9:32–10:1a).

Job now returns to lamentation. Since he does not know what else to say, he will at least speak his complaint (as in 7:10), "Let me know why . . ." (10:1b-2). Does God get pleasure from afflicting this creature, God's handiwork? Job appeals to God's memory of happier days, namely, when Job was created, and compares God then to a potter, a maker of cheese, and a tailor doing their work with care and skill (vv. 9-12). So why does God pursue Job, hunting him down like a wild animal (v. 16)? As in 3:11 and 7:15, Job once more longs for death. His days are so few; why does God not just leave him alone for a breather (see 7:19) before he goes to the dark land of death, from which there is no return (vv. 18-22)?

11:1-20 Zophar's first speech. Zophar's opening attack on Job makes Bildad's (8:2) seem polite in comparison. Job has indeed been outtalking his companions about two to one, but should the one who talks the most be declared right (v. 2)? Zophar sums up Job's excessive "babbling" in five words in Hebrew! "My doctrine is true; my life is clean." Even though Job has not said this in so many words, it seems a fair inference. In fact, Job has not been trying to communicate doctrine but a sense of his own confusion and pain, something the friends completely fail to hear. You may be missing something, Zophar suggests, namely, the "secrets of God's wisdom," and God knows you are guilty! While rebuking Job for being too sure of himself and not respecting the mystery of wisdom, Zophar is himself quite sure and not aware, apparently, of limits to his own wisdom.

Extended praise of the vastness and immeasurability of God's wisdom follows (vv. 7-12). Zophar shares with his friends their low opinion of human beings as worthless and full of iniquity (v. 11). The proverb in verse 12 is illusive, partly because the Hebrew text is not completely clear. As translated in the New American Bible, it suggests that certain creatures cannot really be changed. Can one make a silk purse out of a sow's ear?

Like the two others (Eliphaz, 5:8; Bildad, 8:5), Zophar gives Job advice on what he should do: get rid of those radical ideas, say your prayers, and shape up (vv. 13-14). If he does, then, in accord with his friends' doctrine of retribution, he will enjoy a prosperous life and will find rest (see 3:13, 17, 26). He will also recover the honor and respect of others, for many will recognize his virtue and come asking for his intercession (v. 19b). This is especially ironic because at the end (42:8-9), the friends *will* have to rely on Job's intercession. The last phrase (v. 20c) makes a final point: it is the wicked who eagerly look forward to death. Job has been doing exactly this (3:11; 10:18-19); just what you would expect from one who is wicked!

12:1–14:22 Job's reply to Zophar. Unfazed by Zophar's accusation of verbosity, Job launches into what is, with the exception of chapters 29–31, his longest speech. Chapter 12 abounds with wisdom terminology and ideas; chapter 13, with legal expressions; and chapter 14, with lamentation.

Taunted by the sarcasm of his friends, Job shows himself able to rise to the occasion (vv. 2-3). "Intelligence" in verse 3 is literally "heart" in Hebrew, the core of the person from which flow thoughts, feelings, and actions. In a shame culture, "what the neighbors say" is very important, and in verses 4-6 Job tells us. His misfortunes have made him a mockery and brought him disgrace.

In 8:8-10 Bildad had appealed to the authority of tradition passed down from the ancients. Here Job parodies this with his own appeal to the dumb animals, all of which know what the friends do not—that misfortune equally comes from God, and it is not always connected with sinful behavior. The proverb in verse 11 makes the point that the traditional wisdom must be tested by experience, just as the mouth tastes food. Job has already said that he finds his friends' advice indigestible (6:6-7). In this light, verse 12 is almost certainly sarcastic.

Eliphaz had earlier (5:10-13) sung a hymn to the God of order and creation. Here Job sings to the God of chaos and uncreation (vv. 13-25). For the people of the Old Testament, the world was all of a piece; nature and human society were closely interconnected (an insight we, with our ecological and social crises, would do well to relearn). God brings on chaos in natural creation (vv. 15, 19-21, 22; the Hebrew phrases echo the flood story of Gen 6–8) and also in human society, where social order (that is, justice) depends on the wise governance of kings, counselors, and judges (vv. 17, 18, 20). Verse 20b supports our reading of verse 12 as sarcastic. Job does not say that all this is haphazard and pointless. God's might and strength go together with wisdom and prudence (vv. 13, 16). The problem is that we cannot figure it out; we grope in the dark and stagger with drunken senselessness (vv. 24-25). Like his friends, Job has heard and seen much; he has had much experience (13:1-2), but he wants more.

Job again wants to take God to court (13:3)! The word translated as "reason with" in verse 3b is the same technical legal term translated as "rebuke" in verses 6 and 10. The sense of verse 4 is that the friends whitewash God with their lies (a theme to recur in vv. 6-10), and their treatment of Job exposes them as quack doctors—not to mention their bedside manner! If they were indeed wise, they would know when to be silent (see Prov 17:28).

In an oral culture like Job's, words were the very fabric of society, and this was nowhere more important than in the most formal situations of religion and law. Thus we find in the Old Testament a great stress on bearing truthful witness (Exod 20:16; Deut 5:20; 19:16-21) and on the necessity of two or three witnesses to establish a charge (Deut 19:15). Job does have three witnesses, but their testimony is false! Do they think that God is served by their falsehoods? Is it for God that they are lying? Or is it perhaps for themselves and for their theology, which brings them such security (vv. 6-8)? Verses 9-11 foreshadow what will happen in 42:7-9.

Job will not be intimidated or silenced by the ashen aphorisms of his friends, but persists in speaking out of the depth of his experience (13:12-13). The expression in verse 14 occurs only here in the Old Testament, but the sense is clearly that Job will speak even at the risk of his life. Job is so sure of his innocence that he says he will argue his case in God's very presence—and survive! This alone will prove him right, because sinners cannot live in God's presence (v. 16).

"Pay careful heed to my speech" (v. 17)—the plural verbs here are addressed to the friends, but also to all of us who hear Job's words. The issue at stake, we recall, is precisely that of Job's speech. In verses 20-27 Job addresses God (something the friends never do!) and realistically prays that if he is to stand a chance with God, there have to be some ground rules: God must promise not to overwhelm Job with divine power ("hand") nor divine "terror," which renders helpless those at whom it is directed (see Exod 23:27; Josh 2:9). Then Job is willing to be either defendant (v. 22a) or plaintiff (v. 22b).

From his almost foolhardy confidence, Job suddenly turns to lamentation. He is caught in a quandary: God is either too far away (v. 24a) or much too close (v. 24b). The Hebrew of verse 24b contains a pun: God is treating Job (*'iyyob*) as an enemy (*'oyeb*). This is a source of recurring pain for Job; no one can hurt a person as close friends can. The image in verse 25 is almost ridiculous. The mighty God (v. 21) is relentlessly chasing Job, a mere leaf in the universe. Job has been accused, sentenced, and punished (the shame of the stocks!), but he does not know why. He does not claim to be completely sinless (v. 26), but whatever he may have done, he does not deserve what he is getting.

In chapter 14 Job's lament returns to the dark side of human existence. Two aspects particularly are highlighted:

1) All human life ("Man" in verse 1 is all humanity) is weak and transitory (vv. 1-6). We fade, wear out, disappear like a flower, a shadow, a leather bottle, a garment (13:28 has been moved to follow 14:3). The text and interpretation of verse 4 is obscure; surely a reference to original sin, which some early Church theologians saw here, is most unlikely.

2) There is no hope for life after death (vv. 7-22). Job's remarks on this move through four stages: (a) A tree does have hope. Even though it has been cut down, all one need do is water it and it will sprout again (vv. 7-9). (b) Human life is not like that at all! When we are gone, we are gone, like evaporated water (again, water imagery). Three times it is affirmed (v. 12): no rising, no waking, no being roused. To say something three times in Hebrew (for example, "Holy, holy, holy, Lord God of hosts," Isa 6:3) gives a superla-

tive emphasis. We are dead and that is it—period! (vv. 10-12). (c) Job wishes that things were otherwise. "Oh, wouldn't it be nice if . . ." God would call, and Job, once again in good graces, would respond, whatever misdeeds he may have committed sealed up and forgotten. (d) There is no "if." This is impossible. Reality imposes itself on the dream. Like water (again, water imagery) wearing away stones, so God erodes human hope. The only survival lies in the continuation of the family, in the next generation. And do they know honor or shame? The dead are oblivious of what transpires. The afflicted one is left only with bodily pain and inner distress (vv. 18-22).

And so, on this dim note, the first round of speeches comes to an end. The issues are squarely on the table. For the friends, God's justice is at stake; for Job, the integrity of his experience. Given the choice, the friends side with God, or better, with their theory about God, which, all too easily for "religious people," replaces God. But Job will not give in. He holds to his experience and, perhaps even worse, refuses to keep quiet.

IV. SECOND ROUND OF SPEECHES

Job 15:1–21:34

15:1-35 Eliphaz's second speech. In his first speech (chs. 4–5), Eliphaz was rather gentle and encouraging, but having sat through three speeches of Job, he now changes his tone. If Job were indeed as wise as he claimed (13:1-2), he would not have replied with so much hot air (vv. 2-3). He has, in fact, uttered folly and not wisdom; his words tear down true religion (v. 4; Hebrew, "fear [of God]"; NAB, "piety"). Job is condemned out of his own mouth, tongue, and lips; all the speech organs get into the picture (vv. 5-6). A better translation of verse 5 might be: "Your mouth instructs wickedness, and your tongue chooses craftiness."

Continuing his attack on Job's wisdom, Eliphaz sarcastically asks Job if he is some mythic, primordial sage (see Ezek 28:11-19), begotten in some special way before creation (v. 7). The same image in almost identical words is applied, in Prov 8:25b, to the personified figure of God's wisdom. Or has Job been privy to the council (better than "counsels") of God (v. 8)? This is especially ironic, because we, the readers, know that it was precisely there, in the divine council, that Job's troubles have their root and cause.

Verse 10 perhaps implies two things: that Eliphaz includes himself among the wise, gray-haired elders; and that Job might not be as old as we often depict him. Since he will later beget and raise another family, he might now be in middle age. The godly consolation and gentle speech in verse 11 probably refer back to Eliphaz's first speech; in case Job has forgotten, some of its highlights are repeated here, but in harsher tones. Since not even the members of the heavenly council are completely clean, how much less the abominable, disgusting, sinful creatures we call humans! (vv. 14-16; see 4:17-19).

Appealing, typically, to ancient tradition (vv. 17-18; see 8:8), Eliphaz offers, not as before (5:17-26) a description of the blessings of the righteous, but a harrowing, admonitory account of the fate of the wicked (vv. 17-35). They live in constant inner torment and anxiety (vv. 20-24); impending death lies particularly heavy (vv. 23b-24). Verse 25 surely contains a barbed reference to Job's behavior, and with it the implication that he deserves all that he has received. Grown fat and lazy (v. 27), the wicked cannot survive adversity. Using a series of botanical comparisons, Eliphaz concludes his description, ending with a proverbial comment (see Ps 7:15; Isa 59:4) on the futility of folly (vv. 30-35).

16:1–17:16 Job's second reply to Eliphaz. Job is getting exasperated with the unimaginative advice of his "comforters," who bring weariness (v. 2b) and not the rest he longs for. If they could change places, it would be easy for Job to give them some of the same medicine (see 13:4). In the context verse 5 is ambiguous. It is either sarcastic, or it means that Job would in fact teach them the proper way to bring consolation, with appropriate speech or appropriate silence. But whether Job speaks or keeps silent, it makes no difference; he cannot escape his pain (v. 6).

In typical lamentation language (see, for example, Ps 22:7-9, 13-14, 17, 22) Job speaks of the assaults of his enemies. At times the thought moves back and forth between God and the friends. They are described as traitors (vv. 8, 11), ferocious beasts (vv. 9-10a), bullies (v. 10b), assault-and-battery muggers (v.

12a), an archer (v. 12c-13a), and a fencer who pierces Job's kidneys (not "sides," v. 13bc). Job has reacted with gestures of grief and mourning (see 1:20); they are not expressions of penance. He continues to affirm his innocence; he has not committed deeds of social injustice (a common meaning of "violence"), and his prayer is sincere (vv. 15-17).

Job feels that he is fast approaching death (16:18–17:2). In the Old Testament the blood of an innocent victim was believed to cry out from the ground asking for justice (for example, the blood of Abel in Gen 4:10; see also Ezek 24:8). Job hopes that even after death has closed his lips, his blood will not be silent. Earlier, forsaken by his friends, Job looked for an arbiter to stand between him and God (9:33-35); then he dreamed of God's restoring him after death (14:13). Here, in the midst of his somber reflections, he hopes for a witness, an intercessor on high (16:19). This has been variously interpreted. Is it God? Or Job's prayer? More likely it is some member of the heavenly council who, unlike the Satan, would speak on Job's behalf. He hopes that God may be moved to justice by his weeping. But, as in the two previous situations (9:35–10:1; 14:18-22), Job knows that his dream is hopeless. He is fast on the road to death (16:22–17:2).

The interpretation of 17:3-10 is difficult because the Hebrew text is far from clear. Job seems to ask God to grant someone to offer a pledge for him (v. 3), a practice common in legal and commercial contexts (see Gen 38:17; Deut 24:6-17). Again, there is no one. Job has become a mockery and byword for all; he is held up to shame. If verses 8-9 are accurate, they should probably be read as being sarcastic: "If there were any upright or righteous people, they should be astonished, but since no one is astonished, I guess there are no upright or righteous ones among you."

Forsaken, alone, and mocked, Job returns to thoughts of death (vv. 11-16). The grave is presented under a series of negative images: the land of the dead (vv. 13, 16), darkness (v. 13), corruption and maggots (v. 14), the dust (v. 16). Some of the poignancy of verse 15 is lost in the translation. In the Hebrew, the word "where" is expressed twice in a row with slightly different words: "Where? Where is my hope?" There is none; all go down to death.

18:1-21 Bildad's second speech. With a few words of rebuke, Bildad begins. When will Job be quiet? Let him stop and think a little first; then we can discuss! In 16:9 Job had accused God of angrily tearing him apart. Bildad turns the words against Job (v. 4): "You tear yourself apart in your anger!" and then he adds sarcastically, "because you are upset, you want the whole order of the universe to be rearranged to suit you" (v. 4bc).

The rest of Bildad's speech is an extended depiction of the fate of the wicked, not unlike that of Eliphaz in 15:20-35. Again, a series of images is used. Those who sin forsake the light, so they dwell in darkness (vv. 5-6). Their own counsels and behavior bring retribution with them; they are ensnared in traps of their own devising. Six different hunting terms are used (net, pitfall, trap, snare, noose, toils [a type of net]); their precise meanings are not always clear, as a comparison of translations will show (vv. 7-10). The terrors of Death (the king of terrors), disaster, and disease (the first-born of Death) haunt the wicked at every turn (vv. 11-14).

The references to the tent being destroyed (vv. 14b-15) and to dying childless (vv. 16-19) probably recall Job's afflictions in chapter 1. In the tribal society of Job's time, people had no belief in an afterlife and therefore survived only in descendants who bore their names and preserved their memories. Without these, it would be as if they had never existed. With no children, grandchildren, or survivors, they were surely "banished out of the world" (v. 18b). No worse fate could be imagined.

The people who are appalled and struck with horror at the fate of the wicked (v. 20) are ambiguous. The Hebrew terms, literally "the after-ones/the before-ones," can refer either to time (younger and older ones, as in the New American Bible) or to space (westerners and easterners; directions were taken facing east). The latter is perhaps more likely. This, then, is the fate of the wicked.

19:1-29 Job's second reply to Bildad. Bildad had just asked "When?" Using the same Hebrew word, Job throws it back, "How long?" The "ten times" in verse 3 is to be taken in the same sense as our "I've told you a thousand times," that is, often and repeatedly (see, for example, Gen 31:7, 41; Num 14:22). While unclear textually, verses 4-5 seem to imply something like "Even if I am at fault, that is my business; and you have no right to gloat over me." For the record, Job affirms again that God has dealt with him in a crooked way (v. 6).

As earlier (16:7-14), Job recounts the ways God has mistreated him. When he cries for help, his screams fall on deaf ears (v. 7); he has been stripped of his honor (v. 9; NAB: "glory"). He repeats his charge (16:9), reversed by Bildad (18:4), that God's wrath is turned against him (v. 11a). Although the Hebrew pun is missing, verse 11b expresses the same idea as 13:24: once friends, Job and God now seem to be enemies.

Not only has God forsaken him, but as a result all Job's friends and relatives do the same (vv. 13-22). Not only is he alone, but his shame is so great that his servants ignore his calls, and young children poke fun at him (vv. 15-16, 18). Those whom we love and with whom we have shared intimately can hurt us more than anyone (v. 19). The whole web of relationships that make life both possible and meaningful is cut; Job is as good as dead. While verse 20 has contributed a phrase to our language (escape by the skin of one's teeth), its exact text and meaning are uncertain. The sense must be something like, "I am reduced to such extremities that I am barely alive." In agony, Job calls for some pity from those who should have offered it unasked (v. 20). Verse 22b is better translated, "Are you not satisfied with my flesh?" This is a common ancient idiom referring to calumny. "Aren't you finished," Job asks, "with telling lies about me?" (see 13:7-8).

Close to death and all alone, Job turns, as so often before, to some last hope of vindication (vv. 23-29). First he wishes that his proclamation of innocence be chiseled in stone to speak for him after he is gone. Certainly no other voice has been found in his defense (vv. 23-24). Next (vv. 25-27) Job looks for a different kind of vindication, but what? And when? These are among the most famous—and most difficult—verses in the book. "Vindicator" was an office within the tribal society with the obligation of protecting and defending the weaker members of the family. Perhaps the closest parallel in our experience might be the Mafia Godfather! While the responsibilities of the vindicator could take various forms (see Lev 25:23-24, 47-55; Deut 25:5-10; Ruth 4:1-6), the basic concern was the preservation of the living unity of the family or tribe. Job has just said that all his friends and kin have forsaken him; now he grasps at a straw. He is innocent, and there must be a kin somewhere who will stand up in court ("stand forth") and deliver him.

Who is this vindicator? Some commentators think it is God, like the arbiter (9:33) and the witness (16:19); others, however, see here some third party who can stand with Job against God (who is, in fact, judge, prosecutor, and executioner!). This second opinion is more convincing. And when will the vindication take place? St. Jerome's translation in the Vulgate and its use in Handel's *Messiah* make belief in a resurrection on the last day very explicit. This is surely too much; such a belief goes against the clear position scattered throughout the rest of the book (for example, 14:10-22). Job seems to be clinging to a hope of some last-minute rescue that he will see while still "in the flesh." He will at last see his vindication before God. Such, at least, is his urgent longing (v. 26b). However, given the confused state of the text (apparent also in the ancient translations), any interpretation must remain somewhat tentative.

Job ends with a final warning (and foreshadowing). Those who persist in blaming him and holding him guilty will ultimately have to face judgment themselves (vv. 28-29; see 42:7-9).

20:1-29 Zophar's second speech. Like Eliphaz (15:17-35) and Bildad (18:5-21) before him, Zophar rushes to give his description of the fate of the wicked. Verse 3 is the only instance of one of the friends admitting that anything Job has said has made any impression at all. To answer Job, Zophar relies, in good wisdom style, on both his own reflection (v. 2) and on tradition handed down from of old (v. 4; see Bildad's remarks in 8:8-10).

The wicked ignore God and God's commands and set themselves up in God's place. Almost by definition, then, the wicked are proud and arrogant (v. 6). But any apparent success is short-lived. The wicked perish forever like their own dung (v. 7; NAB: "like the fuel of his fire"). What is more, the actions of the wicked bring with them their own built-in consequences. What seems sweet and delicious in the eating turns to poison in the stomach (vv. 11-16). One of the major consequences of setting oneself up in God's place is that one soon violates the rights of others.

Social injustice follows upon idolatry. The following verses focus on this issue, which will recur later (22:6-9; 29:12-16; 31:16-23). The greed for riches leads one to oppress the poor and the needy (vv. 17-22).

Enjoyment of ill-gotten gain does not last. God, like a mighty warrior, will assail the wicked with a display of cosmic weaponry (vv. 23-28). Both the opening (v. 23) and closing (v. 28) verses of this section contain references to God's wrath, about which there has already been much discussion (16:9; 18:4; 19:11a). If Job is indeed experiencing, as he himself has said, God's wrath, what does he expect? This is the portion of the wicked (v. 29).

21:1-34 Job's second reply to Zophar. This particular speech of Job is a remarkable one; in a real sense, it is a response to the arguments of the friends. It contains many allusions (too numerous to note here) to their previous remarks and thus approaches genuine dialogue or debate. And it is directed entirely to the friends; unlike any other speech of Job's, it contains no soliloquy or prayer to God.

If the friends cannot offer Job their silence (13:5), they can at least pay attention to what he is saying (v. 2). The import of verses 3-5 is this: "My argument is not about (better than "toward") humanity in general; I'm not interested in abstract philosophy. I am a real, concrete individual in pain. Look at me and stop mouthing your platitudes."

A large part of the friends' argument thus far has focused on the respective fates of the wicked (the brunt of the second round of speeches) and the righteous (more in the first round; see 5:15-27; 8:5-7; 11:13-19). Here Job takes this up and rejects it. The wicked do not suffer; as often as not, they thrive and prosper. Wickedness separates one from God, the giver of life, so sinners belong instead to the realm of death. But look at their ripe old age, at the fertility of their families and flocks (vv. 8-11)! This is all evidence of the power of life. And their growing family life is one continuous party (v. 12).

On the one hand, sinners manifest the outward signs of the power of life; on the other, they experience neither the terrors of death (see 15:20; 18:11-14) nor inner torment, but they die a peaceful death (v. 13b). And what is more, they actually thumb their noses at God! "Who needs you? We have no desire to learn how you want us to live ('your ways,' v. 14). We're doing just fine without you" (vv. 14-15). Does experience tell us that they are wrong? No! God's anger is not their portion (vv. 16-17). Here Job directly refutes Zophar's last words to him (20:28-29).

It was a common belief that the effects of a person's sins flowed out and affected the family and its descendants. This may have its truth, but it is not enough for justice. The one who sins must personally feel the punishment; what happens after death makes no difference (vv. 18-21; see also Jer 31:29-30; Ezek 18:1-4). Job's remarks on death as the great leveler (vv. 23-26; also 3:13-19) resemble those of Qoheleth (for example, 9:2-6).

Job turns on the friends directly. "I know that you think I am guilty. If your experience convinces you that you are right, then you haven't been around very much! Ask any traveler; they can tell you how life really is (vv. 27-29). No, the wicked do not suffer; they prosper and die a peaceful death. That is pretty much the way things are now, have been before, and will be afterward" (v. 33b). The friends' "vain comfort" is "empty wind," "vanity" (a word dear to Qoheleth; see, for example, 1:2 and *passim*); they persist in speaking falsehood (see 13:7-9). So ends the second round of speeches.

V. THIRD ROUND OF SPEECHES

Job 22:1–27:21

Unlike the first two rounds, which proceeded in orderly fashion, the friends speaking in turn and Job responding to each, the third round is considerably confused. Eliphaz speaks, and Job responds; Bildad's speech, five verses long, is surely truncated; Zophar does not speak at all. In addition, part of what Job says seems more appropriate in the mouth of his friends (for example, 26:18-25; 27:13-21). Chapter 28 is generally recognized to be a separate composition. Various scholarly attempts have been made to sort this out and provide a more balanced representation; the New American Bible follows none of these but does signal the problems in Job's speeches with a series of asterisks. Here we will follow the New American Bible text, simply noting that the overall effect of these chapters, starting out normally but degenerating into a chaos, as if everyone were trying to shout at once, might not be an unfitting ending for the "dialogue" about cosmic and moral order.

22:1-30 Eliphaz's third speech. After Job's rebuttal, Eliphaz flies right back with a series of rhetorical questions meant to show how wrong Job's position is. Ironically, as we, the readers, know from the prologue, the answers to verses 2, 3, 4 are "Yes." Eliphaz draws the obvious (for him) conclusion (v. 5).

Eliphaz then accuses Job of a series of serious sins (vv. 6-11) that could easily be committed by the "man of might" and "the privileged" (v. 8) against the poor and the helpless. In the ancient Near East the widow and the orphan were especially helpless because they had no one to defend them at law. Throughout the Old Testament it is the task of those in positions of power to stand with the weak and helpless and to work for the establishment, not the perversion, of justice. The "therefore" in verse 10 is ironic. "Because you have done these things, therefore you are now suffering." Eliphaz's reasoning process is exactly the opposite: "You are now suffering; therefore you must have done these things." Job is also accused of thumbing his nose at God. "God is too far off; God will never see me!" In this he is acting just as the generation swept away by the flood did (see Gen 6-9).

But Eliphaz does not give up on Job. One last time he urges Job to come to terms with God (vv. 21-30). If Job will repent (v. 23; NAB: "return"), he will again enjoy prosperity, peace, and power (v. 28). Apparently Eliphaz cannot conceive of serving God without getting something out of it.

So Eliphaz has said his last. He began (ch. 5) with some sensitivity, deference, and encouragement for Job; he ends making wild, raving accusations for which there is not a shred of evidence. In Eliphaz we see a sad picture of the degeneration of a religious person who has too easily confused his own attempts to understand God with divine revelation itself. It would be naive to consider this only an ancient problem.

23:1–24:25 Job's third reply to Eliphaz. Returning to his former pattern, Job reflects, in soliloquy fashion, on his predicament. God's hand lies so heavily upon him that he longs once again (see 9:13-21; 13:14-27) to take his case to court. These verses (vv. 3-7) abound in technical legal vocabulary. Curiously, here Job does not wish for a mediator (arbiter, witness, or vindicator) but is ready to plead his case in person. He is sure he will be proven innocent.

Things are not so easy, however. God is nowhere to be found (vv. 8-9). Verse 10 is probably better translated, "Indeed, he knows (his) way with me." The problem is that Job does not have a clue. The irony of verse 10b is striking: God is testing Job, and Job does come out vindicated. The next verses (11-14) juxtapose two very important concepts. Job has been completely faithful to God, whose dealings, however, are mysterious. And who knows what other surprises lie ahead (vv. 13-14)? Here we have in focus the pervasive tension between Job's fidelity and God's freedom, which cannot be reduced to the size of our human minds.

It is precisely this tension that underlies Job's confusion and fear (v. 15; the Hebrew word used here is different from that representing "fear of God," religious piety). Job is left in his dark night of the soul. He wonders why God does not have scheduled times for holding court and rendering decisions, presumably scenes such as we saw in 1:6 and 2:1 (24:1).

Picking up the theme of social injustice, Job describes the work of the wicked oppressing the weak and helpless (vv. 2-4), but he then goes on to give us an extended portrait of the plight of these poor as they struggle to survive (vv. 5-12). Again, it would be naive to think that this was only an ancient problem; the scene is repeated daily in our streets. But, inexplicably, God does not interfere; the wicked are not punished nor are the poor rescued (v. 13b). The simple view of justice espoused by the friends simply does not work.

The following unit (vv. 13-17) is a wisdom-like reflection on the two ways, light and darkness, and those who love the darkness. Day and night are symbols for two different ways of life. The murderer, the adulterer, and the thief love the dark to accomplish their evil deeds. For them, the coming of darkness is like morning when they rise to go to work. Their lives thus reverse the natural order of things.

The next few verses are very problematic, the text being both corrupt and obscure. The New American Bible has, in effect, thrown up its hands. Given the situation, not much else can be said. Verse 25 would be an appropriate comment after verse 12.

25:1-6 Bildad's third speech. Bildad begins his final words, not with the customary sarcastic remarks about Job, but with hymnic praise of the creator-God who establishes peace (v. 2b; NAB: "harmony") in heaven. Behind this language lies the familiar myth of cosmic combat in which the warrior-god overcomes Sea, the force of chaos, thus establishing cosmic peace. This heavenly condition is expected to be reflected in our earthly situation as well.

The following verses (vv. 4-6) reprise the oft-repeated anthropology of the friends (see 4:17-21; 11:11; 15:14-16). All human beings are corrupt and filled with iniquity. Job's claim to be innocent is thus impossible; there is no such thing as an innocent human being. If the heavenly bodies are unclean (earlier the other heavenly beings were also called unclean; see 4:18 and 15:15), how much more human beings, who are nothing but maggots and worms.

Some scholars see this very brief speech as merely interrupted by Job's outburst in 26:1-4 but resumed in 26:5-14, where similar creation imagery recurs. This is possible but conjectural. In the text as it stands, the exalted reflections on the human condition are the friends' last recorded words.

26:1–27:21 Job's final reply. The following two chapters are problematic and seem almost to be patched together from fragments. Job begins with a typical taunt of his friends and rebukes them with an abundance of classical wisdom terminology: counsel, wisdom, advice (vv. 2-3). However, by failing to take account of a large block of experience, namely Job's, they have departed from the path of authentic wisdom.

As noted above, the magnificent description of God's creation that follows (vv. 5-14) may be a continuation of Bildad's hymn to the Creator (25:2-6), but as our text now stands, Job, after cutting Bildad off, goes on to finish the hymn for him. As we might anticipate in material of this kind, mythological references abound.

God's power is not limited to the heavenly bodies and the earth, but extends even to the realm of Death, variously called the land of shades, the nether world, and Abaddon (place of destruction) (vv. 5-6). In the ancient mythology, the North was the place where the gods dwelled. As if putting up a tent, God stretches out the North over the primordial chaos (the same Hebrew word as Gen 1:2 used to describe the disorder from which creation, or ordering, began); the earth is then hung over the same primordial "no-thing" (v. 7). It would be anachronistic to see later ideas here, such as creation out of nothing or our view of the world hanging, as it were, in space. The next two verses (vv. 8-9) deal with the clouds, first viewed as cosmic wineskins intended to hold the rain, and then seen as the dark clouds which cover the light of the moon and upon which the storm-god rides out to battle.

God then marks out the horizon of the ocean, which is the place where we see the separation of night and day (v. 10). The cosmic pillars (v. 11) hold up the heavens, that is, the dish-shaped dome (or firmament) that keeps out the "waters above" (see Gen 1:6-8). God's "rebuke" (v. 11) is the storm-god's thunder or war cry, which strikes fear in the heart of God's foes (see Ps 104:7-9). Verses 12-13 name the sea dragon, the mythological figure for chaos: God stirs up Sea (better than NAB, "the sea"), crushes Rahab, and splits open the dragon. And all this is but the outline (Hebrew: "the extremities") of God's ways (v. 14)! In the speeches of Yahweh soon to follow (chs. 38–41), some of the outline will be filled in.

The New American Bible omits the new heading in 27:1, "Job once again took up his discourse." Beginning with a solemn oath, "As God lives," Job goes on to maintain yet again his innocence. It is God who is wronging him; unlike his friends, Job will not serve God with lies and falsehood (v. 4; see 13:7-9). He will not concede anything to his friends' position. That Job maintains "my justice" does not imply that he is or has been completely sinless; rather, his position is correct, that of his friends false (v. 6).

The remaining verses (27:7-21) remind us once more of the fate of the wicked. This was the constant theme of the second round of speeches and was thoroughly refuted by Job in chapter 21. For this reason, these verses have struck scholars as curiously out of place in the mouth of Job. The same scholars have tried to reconstruct from them a lost third speech of Zophar. Be that as it may, the verses are now in the mouth of Job; can we make any sense of the text as it stands?

In ancient Israelite law, one convicted of false witness against an innocent person was subject to the same penalty that the innocent party would have undergone. Job wishes that his enemy (that is, his friends who are bearing false testimony) be as the wicked (v. 7), and then quotes back to them the penalties with which they had previously threatened him (vv. 8-21). The only new element is verse 17, which says that the innocent will possess the riches of the wicked.

VI. POEM ON WISDOM

Job 28:1-28

This chapter stands rather loosely in the book. A general scholarly consensus holds that it was originally an independent composition before being incorporated here. Its present function is to act as a resting place, an interlude, or better, an editorial aside of the narrator. Its theme is set in the refrain found in verses 12 and 20, "Whence can wisdom be obtained, and where is the place of understanding?" The answer is captured in the caption, "The Inaccessibility of Wisdom." The Hebrew text is difficult, and while the rearrangement of verses in the New American Bible is rather extensive, that is what we will follow here.

28:1-6 Wisdom cannot be mined. Beginning rather abruptly, the poem mentions precious metals that are taken from the earth. Humans use their ingenuity, skill, and resourcefulness to find them and mine them: silver, gold, iron, copper, precious stones. The New American Bible has regarded verse 4 as hopeless, and a glance at other translations indicates that it may be right. But in all the search for precious things, where is wisdom to be found? What is the way to understanding (v. 12)?

28:13-18 Nor can it be purchased. That wisdom is more precious than silver and gold is a truism of the wisdom literature (see Prov 3:14-15; 8:10-11, 19; 16:16). Here the same thought is developed as we stroll through the whole literary jewelry store. Ophir (v. 16; see also 22:24) was the source par excellence of gold (see 1 Kgs 9:26-28; 10:11; 22:48), but its location is not known. The two great sources of human achievement, ingenuity and skill on the one hand, and riches on the other, are of no avail in the search for wisdom and understanding.

28:21-22 Nothing in creation knows the way to it. Not only is human effort of no avail but no help can be found anywhere else in creation. The sharp-eyed birds have seen nary a trace; the proud beasts have not come on it either. Nor do the two great mythic symbols of chaos, Sea-Abyss and Death-Abaddon have a clue. The quest for wisdom would seem to be hopeless. But is it?

28:23-28 God knows. In the fullness of knowledge and creative power, God alone knows the way to wisdom. General creative activity is described first (vv. 3, 9-11). The association of wisdom with creation is found throughout the Old Testament wisdom tradition. Prov 3:18-20 and 8:22-31 are especially good examples. Verses 25-26 narrow the focus to God's control of the thunderstorm, perhaps a foreshadowing of God's speaking to Job from the storm in 38:1. Then it was that God saw, appraised, established, and searched out wisdom. Just as human wisdom is manifested in human behavior, so too God's wisdom is manifested in God's activity.

It might seem at this point that the human quest for wisdom is at a dead end. Such is not the case. God has told us that fear of the Lord and keeping from evil are the beginning of wisdom. In other words, the human quest for wisdom begins with getting our relationship with God in right order; then our quest will not violate the limits of creaturehood. Interestingly, these are precisely two of the four terms used to describe the virtuous Job in 1:1, 8.

Chapter 28 does serve an important editorial role at this point in the book. It looks back over the preceding debate and suggests that the search recorded there has been misguided. The friends certainly have not respected their limits and have claimed too much. On the other hand, the chapter looks forward to the Yahweh speeches and the end of the book. There it is affirmed that wisdom is with God, manifested in creation, but beyond human grasp. The focus shifts to Job's relationship to God and away from his understanding of God's ways.

VII. JOB'S MONOLOGUE: HE RESTS HIS CASE

Job 29:1–31:37

Job is left with little recourse. His pleas for arbitration, for an "out of court" settlement, as it were, have fallen on deaf ears. God cannot be found to receive a subpoena; the witnesses are false witnesses who will lie on the stand. These three chapters (29–31) constitute one extended speech presenting Job's review of his case, his final lament, and a ringing reassertion of innocence. Like chapter 3, it is a public outcry addressed to any or all who will listen.

The discussion up to now has been fairly general. With the exception of 22:6-9, the friends have accused Job vaguely of being a sinner; just as vaguely (see 6:29; 27:6), Job has rejected their accusations. Now Job replies with much more detail and specificity. He begins with a description of his past happy relationship with God (ch. 29), proceeds to a painful lament from his present situation (ch. 30), and ends, looking to his future vindication, with a resounding oath of innocence illustrated by a series of very specific moral behaviors.

29:1-25 "Oh, for the good old days!" This nostalgic poem begins by recalling God's closeness in the past and the blessings that flow therefrom. Blessing is, above all, the power of life, and this was manifested first in fertility (the life-force) of family, flocks, and field (vv. 5-6). It is manifested in other ways as well, and chief among these in the ancient Near Eastern culture was the experience of honor. The rest of the chapter develops this. At the city gate, where people gathered for social, business, and legal matters, Job was an honored sage, elder, and counselor (vv. 7-10, 21-25, moved in the New American Bible to follow verse 10). Others honored Job especially by the way they waited for, responded to, and respected his speech (vv. 21-23). In the context of the whole book, this is particularly ironic.

Job's honorable behavior appears clearly in the way he has treated others. Refuting Eliphaz's groundless accusations (22:6-9), Job has dealt justly with the poor, orphans, widows, the blind and lame, the needy, strangers, and those being victimized by the wicked (vv. 12-17). Job, therefore, had every right to expect that he would experience these blessings into his old age. Verse 18 is uncertain: Job will multiply years either "like the phoenix" (a legendary bird thought to rise anew from its own ashes, hence a symbol of immortality), or, more likely, "like sand (on the seashore)." Verse 20 summarizes: Job knows strength and vitality (v. 20b) as well as "glory" (v. 20a; in Hebrew the root means "to be/have weight," here social weight, honor). Job was, alas, mistaken.

30:1-31 "Now the tables are turned." Now the situation is reversed. Instead of honor, Job is held in shame and disgrace. Above all, and most painfully, he is derided by the dregs of society, who deserve the mean situation in which they live ("saltwort" and "roots of the broom plant" in verse 4 both represent bitter foods that only the most destitute would consider eating). They are not only poor and hungry (Job had protected and fed these), but they are people "without a name" (v. 8), that is, with no claim to reputation or honor. The hands of such as these have snatched away Job's dignity and welfare (v. 15; literally, "salvation," but here the reference is to the outward signs of abundance, comfort, and honor).

Job's lament now turns to God (vv. 20-26). As usual, God is deaf to Job's cries of distress. Not only this, it seems God will consign Job to death and the nether world. When others were in a similar situation, Job stood by and helped them. Now that he is in need, who will stand with him (vv. 24-26)?

Job has spoken of his enemies and of God; now he describes his own situation (vv. 16, 17, 27, 28-31). His inner life is flowing away; his bones ache; his inward parts (v. 17; literally, "his intestines") are in constant turmoil. He is forsaken and alone. All along he has cried out for a friend to stand with him. Pathetically, his only friends now are the jackal and the ostrich, both beasts of the wilderness known for their offensive "speech" (v. 29).

This chapter is in many ways a classical lament. It echoes many characteristic phrases and images, and moves through the threefold relationship of the lamenter to enemies, to God, and to self. A comparative reading of Psalms 22, 88, and 102 in this light might prove helpful here. Psalm 88 in particular could almost be a prayer straight from the mouth of Job himself. But Job does not stop here.

31:1-40 "I swear I am innocent!" In the prologue, Job, deprived of all, had prayed, "The Lord gave, and the Lord has taken away" (1:21). Chapter 29 described what the Lord gave; chapter 30, how the Lord took away. But now Job has somewhat more to say. Twice before (13:13-19; 23:2-7) he had called on God directly to stand in court and answer his charges. In the form of a "negative confession" (known elsewhere in the ancient Near East), he now utters a lengthy oath of innocence. This was an especially serious step to take. As we have seen, in the ancient, oral culture, words were of utmost seriousness, and words of blessing (see, for example, Gen 27:31-38) and cursing were among the most solemn. Here Job avers his innocence using a self-curse form: "If I have done *X*, then may *Y* happen to me" (see Ps 7:4-6). If Job is guilty, God should bring the curse to pass; if innocent, the curse will not happen, and Job's name is cleared publicly. This is a move of desperation to force God's hand.

Job first calls on God to weigh him in the scales of justice, that is, with a true balance (v. 6). False scales are frequently condemned in the Old Testament (see Lev 19:36; Prov 11:1; Amos 8:5). The figure of God's judgment as weighing may derive from Egypt, where the heart of the deceased was often pictured being weighed against the feather of Truth. Job then begins his "negative confession": "If you accuse me of *X*, I plead 'Not Guilty!'" He presents a truly exalted and challenging moral summary, but the exact number of areas mentioned is problematic. The text is at times uncertain; the New American Bible makes three changes: verse 1 precedes verse 9; verse 6 follows verse 4; and verses 38-40 follow verse 8. Thus we end up with nine general areas of moral concern.

1. Falsehood and deceit (vv. 5-8).
2. Exploitation of the land (vv. 38-40). In our day of ecological crises, we need not belabor the need to recover a sense of the seriousness of this concern.
3. Lust and adultery (vv. 1, 9-12). Coveting the wife of another (see Exod 20:17; Deut 5:21) is the subject of frequent warning in the wisdom tradition (Prov 2:16; 5:3-6; 6:27-35; 7:6-23). Here the self-curse punishment dramatically and graphically fits the crime.
4. Rights of servants (vv. 13-15). Slaves were usually considered one's property and did not strictly come under justice. This was not adequate for Job; not only did he treat slaves fairly, but men and women were equal before him. The reason for this was simple: our common humanity—we are all creatures of the one Creator. This idea is a commonplace in wisdom literature (see Prov 14:31; 17:5; 22:2; 29:13).
5. Hardheartedness against the poor and needy (vv. 16-23). Concern for the poor and oppressed runs throughout the Old Testament and has already appeared several times in the Book of Job (22:6-9; 24:2-9; 29:12-17).
6. Idolatry (vv. 24-28). Social injustice is the reverse side of idolatry; the two go together and are often intertwined (see, for example, Jer 7:1-11; Ezek 18:5-9). It is very appropriate that here numbers 5 and 6 come back to back. Verses 24-25 depict the idol of wealth and money; verses 26-28 warn against the surrounding pagan religions, which worshiped the sun and moon and other heavenly bodies.
7. Hatred of enemies (vv. 29-30). Calling down curses on one's enemies is not uncommon in the lament psalms (for example, 69:23-29; 109:1-20), but other parts of the Old Testament urge us to help our enemies (Exod 23:4-5) and to repay evil with good (Prov 20:22; 24:17-18; 25:21-22). Job is in line with this more difficult position, which is concerned not only with outward behavior but with inner attitudes as well.
8. Hospitality (vv. 31-32). In ancient society, without a police force or highway patrol for help and protection, a stranger traveling alone was an easy and inviting target. Hospitality toward strangers was an especially sacred social obligation. Attempts to find reference here to sexual abuses are not convincing.
9. Hypocrisy (vv. 33-34). Again Job focuses on attitudes of inner integrity. We can all, I suspect, appreciate Job's honesty; it is not an easy virtue.

Job's review has covered all the types of relationships that run throughout the webs of our lives: to God, to self, to others (friends, enemies, servants, the poor and needy), to the natural environment itself. All these are covered by the biblical concept of justice; Job is clearly just and cries out to be recognized as such. If his accuser would write out the charges, they would be so obviously false that Job could wear them proudly as a badge of honor for all to see (vv. 35-37). This is his final plea. The Hebrew (v. 35b) says, "Behold my tau." Tau is the final letter of the Hebrew alphabet and, in ancient times, was written like our letter *X*. Job is saying, in effect, "I sign on the bottom line; here is my *X*; I have nothing more to say. Now let God answer me!"

VIII. ELIHU'S SPEECHES

Job 32:1–37:24

Job has finished his defense by calling on God to respond. We wait, eagerly anticipating what will happen next. Totally out of the blue, an intruder called Elihu jumps on the stage. Previously unmentioned, he says his piece and disappears into the oblivion from which he came. Scholars discuss whether these speeches were part of the original book and whether they were composed by the same author or added by a later editor. These questions need not detain us as we seek to understand the text before us.

Elihu (the name means "He is my God") is an angry young man who has apparently been following the proceedings closely. Thoroughly dissatisfied with what he has heard, he is bursting to have his say (32:19). He does this in four speeches (32:6–33:33; 34:1-37; 35:1-16; 36:1–37:24), which add little that is new, but he does this with passion, conviction, and long-windedness.

32:6b–33:33 Elihu's first speech. Despite his youth, Elihu will speak. Wisdom does not always or necessarily abide with age; it is a gift of the breath/spirit of God (32:8, 18), and Elihu has as much a right to speak as they who have been unable to answer Job satisfactorily. "We can't do it; let God answer him!" (v. 13). Unlike the friends, Elihu addresses Job by name (33:1, 31). Job need not be afraid; after all, he and Elihu are both creatures of God.

After a long windup (32:6b–33:7), Elihu comes to the point. In his speeches he refers to earlier statements of Job, but the quotations are less *verbatim* and more *ad sensum.* Here (33:9-11) it is recalled that Job has claimed to be innocent, that God is wrongly treating him as an enemy and ignores his cries for help (see 9:20; 10:7; 13:24, 27; 19:11). In this Job is wrong (33:12). God does speak; perhaps Job has missed it. God uses dreams and nightmares on the one hand, and sickness on the other to warn sinners and to get them to return to the path of life (vv. 14-22). Elihu, too, mentions a heavenly mediator, one of the divine court (v. 23) who will help lead the sinner to repentance. Job had longed for such a mediator (16:19-22), but had something else in mind for this mediator to do. The friends had often begun by taunting Job; Elihu here ends in that way.

34:1-37 Elihu's second speech. Elihu now turns his attention directly to the friends, sarcastically called "wise" (v. 1). The ability to adapt proverbs to different situations was a skill of the wise; Elihu quotes a proverb (v. 3) similar to one Job had used in a rather different context (12:11). Again, Job is cited (vv. 5-6), but instead of arguing with him, Elihu mocks him as a blasphemer who wallows in evil company (vv. 7-9). A lengthy defense (vv. 10-29) of the justice and righteousness of God follows. Addressing Job, Elihu rebukes him. "You wouldn't talk to a king or prince that way! And who are they in comparison with God?" (vv. 18-19). God sees all and renders judgment. Those who turn away from God have only themselves to blame (vv. 24, 27). As the friends had done in the first round of speeches, Elihu suggests to Job what he might say to God in repentance (vv. 31-32). The choice is up to Job. The concluding verses (vv. 34-37) are as harsh and cruel (and irrelevant) as anything the friends had said.

35:1-16 Elihu's third speech. Elihu continues to develop the theme of God's transcendence and grandeur. "Look at the skies, the heavens above" (v. 5). Human behavior, for good or ill, affects only other humans; what arrogance to think it somehow affects God (vv. 6-8)! The oppressed (like Job) cry out for deliverance, and God seems not to hear. But God does hear. Perhaps no answer is given because they have been too self-centered and have not sufficiently "trembled before him"

(v. 14). This is a glib answer given all too often and all too casually to protect a pet theory about God.

36:1-37:24 Elihu's fourth speech. The first part of this speech (36:1-21) continues the debate of the previous sections. The fate of the righteous and the wicked is reviewed once again. Suffering can be sent by God to educate and instruct us (v. 15). Verses 16-21 are very corrupt and so are omitted in the New American Bible.

The second part (36:22–37:13) is a hymn in praise of the vastness of the Creator. God's power, wisdom, and knowledge are beyond our ability to understand (v. 26). Elihu focuses on God's gift of rain and draws, as we might expect, on the common Near Eastern language about the storm-god who rides on the dark clouds, gives off a war shout (the voice of God, the thunder; see Psalm 29), and hurls spears (the lightning) to the ground. It is an awesome experience; animals and humans react with fear and wonder.

"Consider, Job, the wondrous works of God" (v. 14). In other parts of the Old Testament, the "wonders" of God refer to the mighty deeds that delivered Israel out of Egypt. In the wisdom tradition, with its more universal creation perspective, God's wonders are the deeds of creation, which all can see and respond to. Elihu hurls a series of questions at Job, to which, of course, Job can only answer "No" (vv. 15-21).

God comes from the North, the mythological home of the gods. We cannot call God to account, however wise we may be. All we can do is "fear" (worship and revere) God, and this is, after all, the beginning of wisdom (28:28).

Elihu is indeed an intruder on the scene, but nonetheless he is a real transition figure. His earlier remarks look back to the speeches of Job and his friends. Some of this is reviewed and attacked for one last time, without much new being added. The latter speeches look ahead, focusing more and more on God and ending with the description of a storm and a series of questions meant to humble Job. Now Yahweh will speak from the storm and with a similar list of questions.

IX. THE YAHWEH SPEECHES

Job 38:1–42:6

The Yahweh of the prologue who has, as Elihu observed (35:13), been hearing and taking notice now speaks, and it is a surprise for all involved. The friends had said, in effect, that it was unnecessary for God to speak—Job's condition could be adequately explained by their theory. They were wrong. Job had called either for a list of charges against him or for a verdict; he gets neither. Yahweh enters the argument as another debater.

Yahweh's replies are given in two speeches (38:1–40:2; 40:6–41:26), to which Job gives brief replies (40:3-5; 42:1-6). None of Job's questions are answered. In fact, Yahweh's remarks are little more than a series of counterquestions. Like a teacher springing a surprise quiz, Yahweh is trying to involve Job in the process of learning and to lead him out (the literal meaning of "educate") of his own small context into the larger world. If the speeches contain no answer *to* Job, do they perhaps contain an answer *for* Job? We will return to this later when we discuss the meaning of the book.

38:1-40:2 Yahweh's first speech. Yahweh speaks out of the storm (v. 1). In the Old Testament, appearances of God are frequently described with storm terminology (see Exod 19:17-20; Ps 18:7-17). In fact, Job had predicted just such an eventuality (9:17). Girding the loins (v. 3) is preparation for a difficult and arduous undertaking (see Exod 12:11; 1 Kgs 18:46). Now it is Yahweh's turn to ask questions and Job's turn to respond. This, too, Job had earlier requested (13:22) but with slightly different expectations.

God interrogates Job about the marvels of creation, which manifest the divine power and wisdom. Does Job understand any of these? Can he do any of these? Job is led back to experience anew the mystery of the cosmos from its beginning. First, the founding of the earth is described as if it were a house being built to architectural specifications. The heavenly council rejoiced; where was Job (vv. 4-7)? Next, God restrained the primordial sea (vv. 8-11). There is no hint of a struggle against a monster, as in the myths. Instead, the sea is born, clothed, and confined to its cosmic playpen with clear parental orders. And what of the morning (vv. 12-15), when dawn colors everything (v. 14) and brings to light the dark deeds of sinners (v. 15)?

Verses 16-18 return to the theme of the primordial chaos, but here sea appears with its destructive partner, death. Does Job's understanding reach that far? Verses 19-20 resume the theme of light, which now appears with its partner, darkness. Does Job know where they dwell? Verse 21 records a touch of divine irony.

Having discussed the primary structures of the cosmos, Yahweh now turns to mysteries within the universe, particularly weather phenomena (vv. 22-30). First come the snow, hail, and wind (vv. 22-24), followed by the rain, which also falls in the wilderness (vv. 26-27). God's concern is larger than Job's humanity-centered preoccupations (vv. 25-28). Finally, what of the ice and hoarfrost? All this manifests God's continuing providence for creation.

For many in the ancient world, human destiny was written in the stars. The heavenly constellations are now cited (vv. 31-33). The reference in verse 32 to "the Mazzaroth" is unclear. Various proposals have been made; it may have something to do with the zodiac. Can Job exercise any control over these? Or can he bring the rain, wrapping himself in a storm cloud (vv. 34-35)? Yahweh has indeed created all with wisdom (see also Prov 3:18-20; 8:22-30).

In the remainder of the speech, attention turns to the animal world (38:39–40:30). Five pairs of wild animals are mentioned: the lion and the raven (38:39-41); the mountain goat and the hind (39:1-4); the wild ass and the wild ox (39:5-12); the ostrich and the warhorse (39:13-25); the hawk and the eagle (39:26-30). Yahweh's knowledge and provident care are highlighted. But perhaps there is more here than meets the eye. This animal parade might not have been chosen at random. Studies in ancient Near Eastern art and iconography have shown that almost all these animals are associated with negative images (demons, wilderness, chaos). They represent a world in opposition to human society. Yahweh is saying not only that these mysterious beasts and their ways are understood but that they are controlled and that this is a boon to human society.

Thus the two parts of Yahweh's first speech answer Job's charge that there is no plan, direction, or providence in the world (Job obscures divine plans, 38:2). First, Yahweh shows who is in charge of the natural cosmos, both in its structure and its regular operation; it will not revert to chaos. Then, as Lord of the threatening wild animals, Yahweh protects human civilization from reverting to the same chaos.

40:1-5 Job's first response. Yahweh pauses to catch a breath and to give Job a chance to respond. In his final speech in chapters 29–31, Job had spoken of his honor (weight) and of how others, in a deferential gesture, had placed their hands over their mouths (29:9). Now Job feels small; he has been "overweighted" by God. His response in verse 4 could be translated literally, "I am a lightweight," and he covers his mouth in respect. Job does not confess any sinfulness. He has, rather, been caught up into the mystery of God and the universe. His stance now is somewhat different from that of his concluding words in chapter 31.

40:6–41:26 Yahweh's second speech. Yahweh renews the challenge for Job to stand up like a warrior and respond (see 38:3). Then, at long last, Yahweh shows that he is aware of Job's challenges (v. 8). Is it really necessary for Job to condemn God in order to affirm his own innocence? Yahweh goes on to ask Job, basically, "Are you as big and strong as I am? If so, let's see you administer justice to the wicked." Job had not in fact claimed or requested superhuman power; his desire to understand had motivated him.

The description of two mighty beasts follows—Behemoth (vv. 15-24) and, at much greater length, Leviathan (40:25–41:26). Scholars have noted resemblances to the hippopotamus and the crocodile, but they are also symbols of primordial chaos, which Yahweh subdues in creating. Thus we probably have a mixing of the zoological and the mythological here. Of both of them Job is asked, "Can you put a rope through their nose? Can you capture them?" (vv. 24-26). They can thrash and strut around, trying to return things to chaos, but they are not in charge. Yahweh is! Yahweh does not demolish them but limits them, gives them some rope. In fact, he looks on them with something like joy and admiration.

Perhaps we can go further. It has been suggested that the two beasts are used by Yahweh not only to rebuke Job but also, and especially, to console him. The two beasts are meant as symbols, even caricatures, of Job himself, who thrashes and struts about saying, "Everything is going back to chaos!" Job does compare himself at birth to Leviathan (3:8) and later to the sea monster (7:12). As Job sat on the dust (2:8), so Leviathan knows no equal "on the dust" (v. 25; NAB: "upon the earth"). By looking at these animals as described by Yahweh, Job may also be instructed and consoled. Not only will God not destroy Job, but, in fact, God actually takes pride and delights in him ("Have you seen my servant Job?" 1:8).

42:1-6 Job's second response. Job's final words recognize God's power and purpose, and admit that these are beyond his ability to understand. The wondrous works (v. 3; 37:14) are too much for him. Previously Job had learned of God from the words of tradition, but now, caught up in his experience of Yahweh, he has a more direct kind of knowledge. Job disowns what he has said and "repents" (v. 6). Has Job finally done what they all (the Satan, his wife, his friends, Elihu) have been trying to get him to do? That is hardly likely. Now, as earlier, God is not served by lies. Job may have overstepped his limits in his search for understanding, but his suffering was not the result of sin. The Hebrew word translated "repent" does not primarily convey a confession of sinfulness or guilty remorse; it means "to change one's mind" or "to be sorry." Even God "repents" (see Gen 6:6). "Dust and ashes" is most likely a reference to Job's new realization of creaturely limitation.

X. EPILOGUE

Job 42:7-17

The book began with a narrative prologue; a narrative epilogue brings the story quickly to an end. Job finds that for which he has so ardently hoped: vindication from God and before the community. The conclusion moves through three stages:

1) Yahweh reprimands Eliphaz and the friends, "You have not spoken rightly of me as Job has done!" (v. 7). This is as ironic as it is important. Job has just said that he had spoken of things he did not understand and "repented" his words. "I spoke wrongly." The first thing God says is, "No, you did not!" And in case we might gloss over the remark, it is repeated in the next verse. Job's speaking has been vindicated. Now, if the friends are to escape more severe punishment, they must approach Job, once again called God's "servant," and ask for his intercession. This he gives, and God accepts it. The friends are spared.

2) In addition to having his speech vindicated, Job has his property restored (vv. 10-11). He himself had never mentioned or asked for this; the friends had promised him this, but only if he confessed his guilt. Job's friends and relatives come now and offer real comfort.

3) Finally, Yahweh blesses Job (vv. 12-17). As we have seen before, blessing is the power of life in its various manifestations. Now Job's livestock are returned, but double the quantity in chapter 1. He begets seven new sons and three new daughters, who receive names symbolic of their attractiveness: Jemimah (dove), Keziah (precious perfume), Keren-happuch (mascara jar). Job dies, full of years and surrounded by his children to the third generation.

XI. THE MEANING OF THE BOOK

Now that we have read, studied, and reflected on the Book of Job, we can return to the question we left open in the Introduction: What is the meaning and the message of the book as a whole? We will look at four aspects of the question.

1) **The problem of the suffering of the innocent.** This is surely the first of the recurring themes that catches our eye; it forms, in fact, the substance of the debate between Job and his friends. Suffering, they affirm, is a punishment for sin (see 4:7-9; 8:20; 11:4-6; 22:4-5). When Job rejects this in his own case, they respond, "Don't give us that! All humans, maggots that they are, are sinners!" (14:1-4; 15:14; 25:4-6). Both these positions of the friends deny that there is any such thing as a sufferer who is innocent.

The situation is, however, more complicated, and other answers appear. Suffering is mysterious, and who are we to understand God's ways (11:7-10; 15:8-9; 28; 42:3)? Suffering is God's way of disciplining us and making us better (5:17-18; 36:15). Suffering is allowed by God to test the virtue of the righteous (chs. 1–2). All these answers allow us to hold on to both human innocence and divine justice. Both Job and his friends, in fact, hold strongly to divine justice. For the friends, it is the basis of their pat, traditional explanation; for Job, it is the basis of his crying out for a hearing and of his certainty of being acquitted.

As pervasive as this theme is, though, it is not likely that it is the main point of the book. On the one hand, we, the readers, know the answer to Job's particular case from the beginning: his suffering is probationary. Will Job serve God without getting any reward for it (1:9)? On the other hand, the problem is not really answered within the context of the debate. Even the Yahweh speeches are not much help; they do not add substantially anything that has not already been said (for example, by Elihu, 37:14-24). If the main point of the book lies here, it must be judged pretty much a failure.

2) **The mystery of suffering and relationship with God.** The first approach views suffering as a problem to be argued on the intellectual level. This second aspect takes us deeper. A problem is something "out there"; we can see all the pieces, all its dimensions. The question is, How do we put it together? A mystery, on the other hand, is a situation in which I, as a unique human being, am so immersed that I can never get far enough away to see it "out there." Love is a mystery; so is death. So is suffering. Problems are solved; mysteries are lived, and lived most fully in relationship with others.

For Job, the greatest pain comes from the confusion about his relationship with God. Previously he and God were friends (ch. 29); then that friend seems to become an enemy (13:24). From this perspective the Yahweh speeches do provide an answer, and the answer derives less from *what* is said (the content) and more from the fact *that* something is said. The mere fact of Yahweh's response shows that Yahweh has been present and listening all the time and reaffirms the relationship. Job is thus enabled, despite his continuing darkness about why he has suffered (he never does learn about the heavenly contest), to live through the struggle because he knows that he is not, and has not really been, alone. The book, then, addresses less a problem of theology (though this is, as it were, all over the surface) and more a mystery of faith, of our relationship with God, which is, indeed, its own reward.

From this perspective we can notice a real change in the protagonists. Job at the end is not the same as Job at the beginning. This change has been described as "the humanization of Job." The Job of the prologue may be very virtuous, but he is certainly not a human being like ourselves. He is just unreal. From his first speech in chapter 3, Job is in the depths of human anguish and rises progressively through the debate until, at the end, he stands strongly—perhaps a bit too much so—and throws his oath of innocence at God (chs. 29–31). After the Yahweh speeches, Job admits that now he knows quite a bit more about being "dust and ashes" (42:2-6). Even though the concluding idyllic scene seems to be a return to the prologue setting, it is not. Job has been profoundly changed.

We must also observe—and frequently this is not noted—that the other half of the relationship, God, has changed too. God at the beginning is not the same as God at the end. In the prologue God speaks of Job as a proud parent might. Then the test begins. God is not a disinterested spectator, but God's honor and God's person are at stake as well as Job's. It is not God on one side and Job on the other (as Job thinks), but God-with-Job on the one side, and the Satan, Job's wife, and the friends on the other. Perhaps it would be true to the dynamism of the story to picture God looking down on the debate, anxiously hanging on every word, cheering Job on, wincing at the friends, and more often than not holding back until Job has had his say. Finally, unable to prolong the restraint after holding it in for thirty-four chapters (chs. 3–37), God bursts out like a whirlwind, enters the debate, ostensibly chiding Job's audaciousness, but behind it all a proud parent once again. The test has been passed in glorious fashion. God and Job ("my servant," 1:8; 2:3; 42:7, 8), wiser for the journey, are seen again to be what they always were—friends.

In describing this journey through the Book of Job, some scholars have spoken of Job as a comedy. In the classical sense, a comedy is a story that goes through three acts:

(1) all's well; (2) all's not well; (3) all's well once again. (Think of any—or every—*I Love Lucy* episode you have seen!) In addition, there are recurring moments of humor and irony. Humor is very hard to capture across the great gap of time and culture that separates us from the people of the Bible, but certain moments of irony have been suggested in the commentary. For our canonical Book of Job, this does seem to be a helpful analogy. This dimension of the book—the mystery of suffering and relationship to God—is a rich one that moves us deeply into the concerns and structure of the book, but is there more that can be said to situate this movement more concretely?

3) **"Job has spoken rightly of me."** This powerful and ironic statement of Yahweh (42:7-8), which contradicts in a way the evaluation Job has just offered (42:2-6), points to another dimension of the book and its concerns of suffering, mystery, and relationship. A key point at issue, often noted in this commentary, is precisely: How will Job speak in adversity? Will he flagrantly blaspheme God, as the Satan twice predicted (1:11; 2:5)? Twice he was wrong (1:22; 2:10): "In all this, Job did not sin with his lips" (2:10). The core of the book is, appropriately enough, discourse—speech follows speech follows speech. Job accuses his friends of speaking falsely for God (13:7-9), while he himself refuses to be silent (7:11; 10:1; 13:13; 27:4) until he is finished (31:35, "Here is my tau!"). Balancing off the two challenges of the Satan in the prologue, Yahweh, in the epilogue, affirms two times that "Job, my servant, has spoken rightly of me" (42:7-8).

How is "rightly" to be understood? Grammatically, the word, can be either an adverb ("in the proper way") or a noun ("right things"). Both meanings would seem to be operating in this text. First, Job has spoken in a proper way. He has lamented; he has argued; he has prayed (something the friends never do); he has challenged. All this can be summed up in a phrase: in all his speaking, Job has strenuously maintained the integrity of his experience. What else did he have left to claim as his own? If he abandoned that, he would indeed be bereft of all. Despite pressures to the contrary, he honestly spoke his pain, his confusion, and his doubt, but he never doubted or betrayed his own integrity. God is not served with lies, no matter how well-intentioned (13:7-9). Job knew instinctively that if any healthy relationship was to be maintained with God, it had to be based on the truth; and Job spoke his truth loud and clear for all to hear. He was not satisfied with the theological explanations of the friends, handed down from "former generations" (8:8). Whatever truth they may have had, they violated the integrity of Job, who will not or cannot let them go unchallenged to the next generation. His cry has echoed to the next generation now for over two and a half millennia.

But, secondly, Job has spoken right things as well. Not bought off by cheap "God-talk" and holding to his own integrity, Job was able to see and affirm the presence of a mystery. "I know the theories as well as you; I also know my own experience. What I do not know is what's going on or how I can explain it!" God and our relationship to God are too deep and too vast to be reduced to or contained in our intellectual propositions. The Yahweh speeches (chs. 38–41) are a strong reminder of that. Furthermore, at the center of the mystery, Job has left room for the freedom of God. The speech of the friends had sold short not only Job but God as well. We see once again how Job and God are basically on one side and suffer the same distortions. It is a perennial danger of overly religious people to get their God too much from the past and thus miss the surprises of the biblical God who calls us forward (not backward!) into newness (see Gen 12:1-3). It was speaking rightly of himself that enabled Job to speak rightly of God. Both of these are profound and courageous acts of faith that lie beyond the reach of the friends and their followers through the ages.

4) **The meaning of friendship.** Closely related to this is our fourth and last dimension of the meaning of the book—the role and function of friendship. Here we are drawn first and obviously to the negative example of "the friends." Moved by genuine sympathy, they gathered and came from afar; when they saw Job, they sat on the ground in grieving (and wise, 13:5) silence. But as soon as Job spoke (ch. 3), his words were so shocking that they had to jump to God's defense. We can legitimately wonder if they were defending God or their own overly tidy construction of God. "A

friend owes kindness to one in despair, though he have forsaken the fear of the Almighty" (6:14). Even in the most extreme conditions, a friend should stand by with loving loyalty. Job bewails his friends' unreliability (6:13-27); they have become simply another pain among many. He begins to hope for and dream of someone who will stand with him and say, "That's all right." First it is an arbiter (9:33); then a mediator (16:19); then a vindicator (19:25); finally, any helping hand will do (30:24). But there is no one. As Job says so pitifully, "Only the jackal is my friend" (30:29). He remains alone and forsaken, or so it seems to him.

This is not the only example of friendship in the book. Job himself represents a positive model. He stands by his children, thinking ahead and offering sacrifices to shield them from harm (1:5). He had been friend repeatedly to the needy and the oppressed (29:12-17) and had wept for the hardships of others (30:24-25). Zophar had told Job, with great irony, as things turned out, that if only he confessed his sin, he would prosper and others would come to him, asking his intercession (11:19b). In the end (42:7-9), the three had to come to Job, seeking his intercession. And, good friend that he was, Job stood by them, interceded for them, and turned away their further punishment.

Job has shown himself a true friend, but does he really have no friend at all in the book? We get caught up so easily in Job's speaking that we sometimes forget what we as readers know and Job does not. Despite appearances, God is Job's friend and has done exactly what the three friends did not do: kept silent and let Job have his say. A study of lamentation in the Bible shows that almost every lament psalm ends, rather unexpectedly, with a sudden turn to praise (for example, Pss 22:23-32; 28:69). Scholars have offered various explanations for this, but from a viewpoint of prayer, the meaning is fairly clear. When we experience brokenness and negativity in our lives, it is only after we face it and speak it in some way, only after we lament, that healing can really begin. We may face this negativity in a positive way (lament suggests that we speak it strongly to God) or in a negative way (denial and repression, which eventually take their toll). A friend should stand by and allow us to lament; this is exactly what God has done for Job. It was only after Job had said, "I am finished!" (31:35) that God would speak in turn. God is and has been on Job's side all along.

There is, finally, one more friend who, in some ways, is most important for us. Because of this friend, the situation for us, the readers, is changed. The Book of Job is a classic because it speaks so eloquently to human experience down through the ages. And we, too, know suffering, doubt, and confusion that push us at times to the breaking point. But we need never find ourselves in Job's position, with only the jackal for our friend (30:29). We do have a friend to stand with us and tell us, "That's all right; speak your pain. Hold on to your integrity with all your might. Respect the mystery and freedom of God. Get it all out, even though it be offensive to the pious ears of so-called orthodoxy. God is not served by lies." This friend is the author of the Book of Job, who is also a model of how we can and should be friends to others who are in need. The voice of this author, speaking in the Book of Job, is now part of our wisdom handed down from "former generations" (8:8). If we yield to the "orthodoxies" of our day and falsify our experience, we will falsify God as well, and God is not served by falsehood (13:6-9). If we betray the integrity of our experience, we may never discover in the depths of a renewed, living relationship that God is indeed with us and has been our friend all along.

WISDOM

John E. Rybolt, C.M.

INTRODUCTION

Title

The title "The Book of the Wisdom of Solomon" tells the reader both the subject of the book and the purported author. This is its most traditional designation. Early Latin texts, on the other hand, often name it simply "The Book of Wisdom," and some early Christian writers referred to it as "Solomon." Due to doubts about its authorship, both ancient and modern writers customarily follow the Latin style.

Author

Solomon never appears in the book as the author; the "I," however, refers clearly to acts of Solomon (see his prayer in chapter 9). Unfortunately, we do not know who the author is who masquerades behind the king's history. Scholars have suggested possible authors, but none of these is accepted today. We can conclude from his words that the writer was a pious Jew, loyal to the law. He had a good education, as can be seen from his large and rich vocabulary, some of which contains his own original terms. He knew poetry and demonstrated acquaintance with Greek philosophy. He may have been a teacher, but he was not strictly a philosopher with a firm system to impart.

Unity and structure

The author has presented his readers with a complex structure, using themes and specific terms to hold the form together. This structure has convinced modern researchers that the work is a unified whole. The possibility remains that portions of the work may have been composed previously, even in Hebrew; if so, these sections (perhaps chapters 1–5) have been greatly retouched. No significant differences in theology, philosophy or vocabulary appear among the various parts. The abrupt ending of the book causes questions as to whether the work is complete as we have it. Despite its abruptness, a good case can be made that it was finished. Granted that the structure is clever and complex, scholars differ on the book's outline and the boundaries of its sections.

Date and place of composition

Questions about the date and the purpose of the book are intertwined; hence a decision on one of these issues affects the outcome of the other. It appears that the book uses the Greek translation of certain biblical passages; this translation was done in the middle of the second century B.C.E. Many scholars believe that the Jewish philosopher Philo of Alexandria, born about 20 B.C.E., knew this book. Conversely, many leading ideas in Philo do not appear in the Book of Wisdom. The New Testament, too, seems to know the Book of Wisdom without quoting it exactly. The result is a date in the middle of the first century, about 50 B.C.E.

All these works, however, share in a larger thought-world, with its vocabulary and themes, and it is difficult to untangle the relationships among them. The place of composition was probably Egypt, judging by the author's intense interest in Egyptian matters. His language reflects the upper-class language of Alexandria in Egypt, the largest center of

Jewish life in that country. An origin in Israel is also possible, since so much Greek thinking and language had infiltrated the land by the first century.

Purpose and audience

If the first century B.C.E. date is correct, then the purpose of the book is to build up the faith of its Jewish readers. Some readers would be pious, and the author encouraged their faith amid the troubles of life. Other readers were probably less convinced of Israel's faith, being captivated by Greek philosophy. For them, the book would support the traditional faith against developments of science and free thinking, reminding them of the nobility of their religion in comparison with that of their pagan neighbors. A few readers had abandoned Judaism in Egypt; the book called them back to God. Finally, some readers must have been Gentiles; the book pointed to the folly of idol worship. In all cases, the audience must have been educated, since the book abounds in figures of speech and subtle constructions accessible only to sophisticated readers.

Background and occasion

As mentioned above, the author had a good education, and he betrays his awareness of Greek lifestyle, art, literature, and philosophy. He either quotes or paraphrases the great writings of the Greeks and uses technical terms. He then weds his Greek education to his Hebrew heritage. He knew the Bible thoroughly and dealt with it as educated rabbis did, following similar lines of thought. A good education in Israel must also have included familiarity with Egypt, Israel's closest great neighbor. The author, at least in his attacks on idol worship, demonstrates this. Scholars have pointed to a possible familiarity with the Book of Qoheleth (Ecclesiastes) and theorized that his work appeared in opposition to Qoheleth. This, too, may have been due to certain common ideas in his period.

Language and style

The Book of Wisdom differs from other wisdom works much as Sirach does, that is, both works avoid simple lists of proverbs and write at some length on their topic. The book was composed in Greek; no Hebrew text exists, unlike Sirach. The Hebrew flavor of the book comes through in the author's use of Hebrew ideas ("heart" for the seat of thinking rather than "mind," as the Greeks taught) and in the poetic style. For his larger purpose, the author has written an exhortatory discourse, designed to move his audience to do something practical based on the reasons he presents. The traditional methods employed are personifications, the supposed speeches of adversaries and their objections (together with the author's answers), ridicule, and invocation of past heroes, whose names are often omitted.

Teaching

Again, like Ben Sira, the author is less a theologian than a preacher, with a passionate attachment to his subject. As a result, his teachings are often not carried out to logical conclusions, and contradictions occur. He teaches that God is everywhere active, knows everything, and loves all creatures. God also punishes and rewards, though the rewards may not be temporal ones. Evil in the world has its source in the envy of the devil. Wisdom is almost the same as God, since it emanates from God and somehow is responsible for doing God's will in the world. The pursuit of wisdom is the highest accomplishment; to attain wisdom is to be close to, even identified with, God.

God's human creatures have immortal souls; after death the just will be with God and the holy ones. The author does not speak of the resurrection of the body, however. Righteousness is the key to this immortality; humans are free in some way to seek God and to reject evil.

It is noteworthy that the author omits mention of sacrifice or Israel's cult. Yet Israel has a central place in God's historical plan. Moses, for the author, is a prophet but not a lawgiver. No personal Messiah appears, yet Israel's destiny speaks to this phase of their thinking.

Importance and authority

Echoes of the Book of Wisdom abound in certain New Testament books, particularly in John and the epistles of Paul; despite that, no New Testament author quotes the book directly. It seems to have influenced the development of New Testament Christology (and even Trinitarian thinking), particularly through the activity of the spirit of God in the world and the personification of wisdom. Christian readers can easily meditate on the pursuit of wisdom, especially when this is understood as an imitation of and even identification with God. Themes of providence in history and the immortality of the soul readily mesh with New Testament thinking.

The rabbis did not include this book as part of Scripture, probably because it was not written in Hebrew and betrayed an origin outside of Israel. Early Christians used it often, though the majority understood it as a work by someone other than Solomon. These hesitations have placed it at the edges of Old Testament thinking, and it thus forms part of the deuterocanonical (apocryphal) books of the Bible.

COMMENTARY

The Book of Wisdom falls into three main sections: wisdom, the reward of justice (1:1–6:21); praise of wisdom by Solomon (6:22–11:1); the providence of God in the Exodus (11:2–19:22). Not all scholars agree on the precise numbering of the verses in each section, but the outline is generally accepted.

Wisdom, the Reward of Justice (1:1–6:21)

The first section of the Book of Wisdom is traditionally divided into several clear parts: an exhortation to justice (1:1-15), the speech of the wicked (1:16–2:24), counsels from God (3:1–4:19), final judgment (4:20–5:23), a closing exhortation (6:1-12). These sections teach the value of wisdom, explore its meaning and results, and offer contrasts between the wise and the foolish.

1:1-15 Exhortation to justice, the key to life. As the entire Book of Wisdom is an exhortation, the author appropriately commences with a thematic exhortation: love justice, for this leads to wisdom. The passage begins with the advice to love, think, and seek—three ways of saying the same thing: the pursuit of God. The judges of the earth (recalling Ps 2:10) are Solomon's equals. In reality this is a figure of speech, giving an exalted tone to an essay addressed to everyone. The lesson of Wisdom applies universally.

In addition, "justice" is not simply legal rectitude. Rather, the term echoes the constant Hebrew notion of God's order imposed on the universe. As one seeks to know and then to live in accord with God's justice, one begins to imitate in personal activity the very life of God.

A series of reasons (vv. 2-11) follows, upholding the author's original invitation. To "test" God (v. 2) implies a basic lack of faith; the Lord does not come to such a person. "Perverse counsels" (v. 3) implies thoughts or plans that seek to go contrary to the manifest will of God. The following verse (v. 4) includes both body and soul, referring to the whole person rather than teaching a profound distinction between the two. The "debt of sin" does not mean that human bodies are by their nature sinful; all creation is good (see 1:14). The expression simply means that a person can freely come under the sway of sin.

Throughout, the author uses different expressions to refer to the same reality, a practice common in poetry. Ultimately even "wisdom" is another way of speaking of God, just as "spirit" is. Even though the reasons are complex, the thought is fundamental: seek God in simple piety, and God will come to you. Without simplicity a person is crooked, devious, deceitful (v. 5), and God is absent. God knows all (v. 6) and judges all evil. The text of verse 6 mentions three parts of the human make-up: inmost self (literally "kidneys," the seat of emotion and instinct), the heart (the seat of thought), and the tongue, which manifests one's life. The author employs a term from Greek philosophy, "all-embracing" (v. 7), to explain that God, by divine creative power, holds all the world in existence.

The text mentions again the act of divine justice (vv. 8-9) to uphold God's universal power: God who created has imposed divine order on reality. Any breach of that will be punished. Even one's words (v. 9) will reach the Lord. This may recall Mal 3:16, where a great heavenly record book is mentioned. Even God's ear (v. 10) finds a place: the Lord is jealous of the right order of creation.

The next three verses (vv. 11-14) advise against any evil utterances (v. 11), since each one must be accounted for. To lie is to violate God's order by freely giving witness to an alternate, ungodly way of life. This can "slay the soul," that is, result in life apart from God. The author does not teach that the soul is immortal—suffering eternal punishment or enjoying eternal bliss with God. The emphasis is more on a condition of temporal living, in which one lives unjustly, thus giving proof of internal death.

To "court death" (v. 12) is an expression taken from ancient initiation rites, implying entering into a relationship with anti-God forces. God's commitment to life is further emphasized by the surprising assertion that God did not create death (v. 13); its author is the devil (see 2:24). The Lord made creation perfect and filled it with life (v. 14). The domain of the netherworld (literally, "the palace of Hades") had no place on earth, apart from human choice of evil.

Verse 15 closes this initial exhortation with an expression called by some the essence of the book. As God is undying, so God's order for the universe is undying. To follow this order in personal living is to open oneself to being possessed by God.

1:16–2:24 The wicked speak. In this section, which both exemplifies the first section and contrasts with the just in 3:1-9, we have the words of the wicked (2:1-20), followed by the author's own reflections (vv. 21-24). The writer, of course, is not quoting a group of people but symbolizing their attitudes in speech. This was a common method of writing in ancient times. Modern writers would doubtless prefer to cite their sources exactly, in order to avoid the charge of biased writing.

The introductory verse (v. 16) states strongly the basis of human evil—individual choice. The "wicked" here might refer to Adam and Eve as those who dallied with the evil one, but more likely the passage is simply a generic assertion about human wickedness. The relationship with evil is direct, involving both deeds ("hands") and words; it deepens into friendship and even lust (implied in the Greek for "pined"), and then into long-lasting commitment (the covenant, recalling Isa 28:15). That the wicked deserve to be in the grip of evil is a result of choices, just as wisdom comes to those who seek God (1:2). This manifests the concept of proportion, a predominant feature of the Book of Wisdom.

The wicked speak of the shortness of life (vv. 1-5) in a way not unlike the words of Job (as in 7:1-4). If they are Israelites, the wicked are doubly wrong, since they also overlook the instances in Israel's history where the dead revive (as in the case of Elijah, 1 Kgs 17:17-24). Their approach to human conception is godless: "haphazard" rather than due to loving creation (v. 2). The author echoes here, although not systematically, teachings of contemporary philosophers on the origin and end of life and reason (vv. 2-3). The insubstantial end of life has a further terror, particularly so for Israelites: no memory remains (v. 4). The author did not set out to give his readers a scientific treatise, whether on life and death or on weather; yet his occasional comments on the activities of nature betray the thoughts of an educated observer ("mist pursued by the sun's rays," v. 4). The closing verse (v. 5) balances the opening (v. 1), in good Greek style: brief life, no escape from dying, no return from death.

The outcome of such reflections might lead to pessimism (as in Eccl 2:1-3) or even suicide. Instead, they lead here to wanton behavior (vv. 6-9). Such actions have a certain truth about them, since God's creation is wise and good (see 1:14), and the Old Testament does not advocate austerity or self-denial as a virtue. Pleasure, like all reality, must have its limits. This is something fools do not understand; only the wise know the proper order of creation (see Eccl 3:1-8). The "tokens of rejoicing" (v. 9) recall the heedless littering of modern times; here they are empty containers for wine and perfume, dead flowers, trampled meadows. The most horrifying part of this wanton behavior is the conviction that the wicked must live this way ("our portion . . . our lot"). The wise, by contrast, will see the falsehood of this assertion and will live according to God's plan.

The degeneracy of the wicked takes an evil turn when they wish to silence the voice of wisdom and justice (vv. 10-20). They set out both to oppose the wise (including the elderly, wise with experience) and to violate divine prescriptions of care for the poor and the widow (see Exod 22:21). To join the term "needy" with "wise" is also to subvert Old Testament promises of God's blessings on the just (or wise). For them, the norm is not God's law but their own bullying strength (v. 11).

The author's deft psychological touch is evident in verses 12-16. Here the style of life of the just, involving speaking out against evil, and even their own self-understanding prick their consciences. Like white corpuscles in the bloodstream rushing to attack a foreign body, the wicked fall on the just, whose ways differ so from theirs (v. 15). The expression "child of the Lord" (v. 13, as well as "God is his Father," v. 16, and "Son of God," v. 18) speaks of the close relationship of the just with the Lord, a theme of the Book of Wisdom.

The wicked then plan to test the just (vv. 17-20) to see whether, like Job (Job 1:6-12), the just would persevere in their conviction. It does not appear, however, that the wicked are open to conversion, so blind are they. There is a terrible irony in their words in verse 20: if God truly protects their victim, then they will be punished. The Hebrew term that may underlie "take care of" can also mean "punish."

The author comments on their words in verses 21-24. They erred, not out of stupidity, but because of a fundamental option taken long before (see 1:16). For them, God's order of the universe is inverted: good appears as evil, and evil as good. This is the ultimate foolishness. They have denied the traditional Old Testament affirmation that virtue will be rewarded (v. 22). Even more fundamentally, they did not perceive that humans are the image of God (Gen 1:27). As God is imperishable, so too in some way are God's human creatures. This would have been the lot of everyone had not death come into the world in the murder of Abel by Cain, at the instigation of the Serpent and due to resentment (see Gen 4:3-10). As is evident in many parts of the Book of Wisdom, the author does not clearly separate physical death from spiritual death. The two are functions of the same reality.

3:1–4:19 Counsels of God. This section comprises three parts: suffering (3:1-12), childlessness (3:13–4:6), and early death (4:7-19). Because of the fluidity of the author's language, however, it is difficult to mark these sections off precisely; thus, scholars differ as to their extent.

Typically, theme statements (vv. 1-3) open the discussion. The purpose of the entire section is to shed light on God's designs for the world. Both "souls of the just" and "hand of God" (v. 1) are poetic expressions: the just are in God's care. The "torment" refers more to the earthly sufferings they underwent previously at the hands of the wicked (2:19, for example). Christians customarily read this passage as an exaltation of heavenly bliss for the righteous. The author, however, is less clear than that.

Even though the godless thought the end of the just to be a punishment (vv. 2-3), this would reverse God's design of reward and punishment, and make virtuous living absurd. The peace of the just recalls Isa 57:1-2; this peace is the absence of torment. Nonetheless, the concept of life with God, begun through the gift of wisdom, must have led pious Jews to reflect on the ancient expression "forever," such as "his mercy endures forever" (Ps 118:1). Coupled with this reflection was consideration of the Greek expression "immortality," a term appearing here for the first time in the Bible (v. 4). The just died in the hope of continuing life, marking them off from the foolish, who expected nothing (2:5).

Chastisement of the just (v. 5) is not denied; its briefness is emphasized, a theme that reappears later to explain the punishment of Israel (see 11:9 and 12:2). Suffering, therefore, is purifying, removing what little dross remains. The finished products then are in a condition that makes them ready to be assimilated in some way to God. This same idea continues in verse 6: even gold can be purified, but purification demands a furnace. Sacrificial offerings, too, are good in themselves but acquire a special significance when dedicated and consumed in some way, mainly through fire.

The image of fire continues in the following verse (v. 7). The exact time or occasion of this visitation remains unspecified here. Christians traditionally refer to it as the final judgment, though the concepts in the Book of Wisdom were not so well developed. "Sparks through stubble" would be a common experience for farmers, who burned off the grain stubble yearly, and would be particularly captivating at night. The exact import is unclear, although the figure appears elsewhere (as in Obad 18). The just, though fire-tried, stand out from the stubble of the wicked, dark and lifeless.

Changing the figure, the author advances his thought in verses 8-9. The poetic basis for the theme of judging nations comes from the ancient mythology of Canaan: the holy ones (or gods) had their own peoples, whom they ruled under the headship of a supreme deity. The author adopts this perspective, rewarding the just with life with God on the model of the "holy ones" of myth. They live with God (v. 9a). This assertion is buttressed by a psalm-like couplet, more Hebrew than Greek in style (v. 9b). (This same passage appears in some versions at 4:15; the New American Bible omits 4:15 entirely.)

The fate of the wicked forms the theme of verses 10-12. The thoughts of the wicked have appeared previously (see 1:9 and 2:21). Here the punishment is proportionate, that is, as the wicked forsook God, so God will now forsake them. The text joins neglect of justice with forsaking God. The two are actually parts of the same reality: God is the author of justice, and to forsake the one is to forsake the other. The same remarks can be made concerning abandonment of wisdom and instruction (v. 11a). Both the works of the wicked (v. 11b) and their families (v. 12) are accursed. The tradition of the curse of futility is imposed on the works and the family: neither will turn out well. Common experience shows this often to be the case, especially as a parent's evil involves the children in the ruin to come.

The lesson on childlessness (3:13–4:6) connects easily with the foregoing verses. Just as suffering can appear otherwise than purification for the just, so lack of children can be a blessing. Here the author makes an advance on traditional biblical concepts (see Gen 30:23, for example). The woman of the verse could be either unmarried or married. The fruitfulness required of creation at its beginning (Gen 1:28) is spiritual rather than physical. At the great judgment (see v. 7) this woman's true glory will be apparent.

The author builds on Isa 56:3-5 in his discussion of the eunuch who has remained undefiled, like the woman of verse 13. His reward will be inclusion in Israel (against the decision of Deut 23:2), more likely a reference to a heavenly temple than the earthly one in Jerusalem. Like the landless Levite, the eunuch's reward is God. The author concludes with a proverbial expression (v. 15), advancing a motive for the above: great struggles bear great fruit because their root (wisdom) never fails.

By contrast, children of adulterers (vv. 16-19) are doomed to childlessness. The teaching here is not that childless couples must either be holy or the offspring of adultery; rather, the focus is the contrast between the two kinds of childlessness. Even if the children of adulterers survive into old age, God's curse will follow them (see vv. 11-12). The great judgment will be a day of sorrow, since punishment follows evil (v. 19). Due proportion in punishment is a mark of God's wise creation.

The text concludes, in 4:1-6, with contrasts between the virtuous and the wicked. The opening statement, beginning "Better," seems like the first half of a typical proverbial statement, such as the following: Better is childlessness with virtue, than many children amid sin. "Virtue" is a Greek philosophical term, familiar to the original audience of the Book of Wisdom but employed by the author as a synonym for justice or even wisdom. The author then asserts that the memory or recollection of virtue lasts forever (v. 2), especially since God takes it into account. To be "crowned in triumph" recalls the victory processions of Greek athletic and military celebrations.

The author turns to comparisons between the wicked and trees. This ancient figure has been used of both the virtuous (as in Psalm 1) and the wicked (Ps 37:35-36). In the latter case the success of the wicked is only apparent and lasts only for a time. The issue is significant, since the wicked apparently prosper, contrary to repeated biblical promises. Here the wicked may have numerous children (v. 3), and their branches may flourish (v. 4), but this is only temporary: "for a time" (v. 4) and "untimely" (v. 5). The author uses the same ideas in reference to the apparent punishment of the just—it is temporary (see 3:5). The curse of futility also appears: even though fruit exists, it is useless (v. 5). The conclusion (v. 6) repeats past assertions (3:12, 16), which, to modern minds, seem unjustified. Beyond any theological concepts, the author's experience shows that in ill-run families the children will turn out badly.

The third of the teachings in the section 3:1–4:19 treats of untimely death, a new idea in the Old Testament (4:7-19). "The good die young" is contrary to the biblical teaching that length of days is a sign of divine favor. A more precise examination of events, apart from this theological perspective, shows that at least in some cases the good do die young. A wisdom teacher should explain this apparent contradiction. Isa 57:1-2 seems to offer some background here. The author of the Book of Wisdom chooses quality of life over quantity of years (v. 8) and draws out the implication that grey hairs do not necessarily signify virtue (see Prov 20:29). Traditional wisdom teaches that things aren't always what they seem.

Another motive is given in verses 10-12: the good person was taken away by God from a nearly overpowering world of sin. The language of verse 12 is unusual; the author, in fact, coined a new word, translated as "whirl of desire," not an easy concept to tie down, one that speaks more to the heart than to the mind. The author does not specify where the just are being taken; the supposition is that they shall be with the Lord (as in 3:6).

A question also left unanswered throughout the Book of Wisdom is whether God loves only those who have become perfect or loves all creatures indiscriminately. Is there any love for those who turn from God? Is a change of heart possible for sinners? In 4:13-14a, the answer appears to be that God loves the just once perfected, either quickly, as here, or after a long life.

The ideas of the wicked conclude this section (vv. 14b-19; v. 15 is omitted). Being wicked, they are by definition foolish, and the author underscores their ignorance (vv. 14b, 17). An implication is that the wise can ponder the realities of life and death, free of earlier theological formulations. The condemnation of the just (v. 16) is a moral condemnation or a sting to conscience rather than an act of heavenly judgment. In verse 17 the author again hints at the afterlife without giving exact details: "what the Lord intended . . . made him secure."

A curse of reversal of fortune appears in verse 18, building upon Ps 2:4 and 37:13, in which the laughter is more than delight or surprise. It is an act involving final punishment. The last verse (v. 19) contains recollections of a large number of biblical passages, listed in the New American Bible footnotes. This verse sounds almost homiletic in the vigor of its denunciation by means of well-known citations. The author's intent, therefore, is not to teach when or how this punishment will take place (hell?) but simply to bring the weight of tradition to bear on the fate of the wicked. To be a "mockery among the dead" recalls an underworld existence in which the once proud dead are mocked for their pretensions (see Isa 14:9-11 for a vivid example).

4:20–5:23 The final judgment. The fourth major section of Part One (1:1–6:21) concentrates on the outcomes of both evil and just living, the result of the quest for wisdom. As previously, we have the speech of the wicked (5:3b-13), followed by a description of the just at the time of judgment (5:15-23).

The author has spoken of the great judgment before (see 3:7, 13, for example). The picture in 4:20 has more of the idea of the great account book filled with the record of misdeeds, truly a book worthy of heaven. When and where this takes place is, as before, not specified. The Old Testament concept of retribution is also evident—one's sins carry their own punishment.

The just one (that is, the wise one), said to judge nations (3:8), here is the accuser in the great courtroom (v. 1). God apparently is the judge, although it may also appear that misdeeds return to convict their author, apart from God's direct intervention. The author's psychological interests are apparent in verses 2-3; the shaking and groaning of the wicked remind the reader of Saul's encounter with the shade of Samuel (1 Sam 28:20-21). Part of their anguish comes from an act of perverted wisdom: they finally had their eyes opened to the reality of their lives. The expression "unlooked-for" (v. 2) is typical of wisdom writing, especially showing divine entry into one's life.

The speech of the wicked, similar to the reflections in 2:1-20, brings the reader into the heart of foolishness. Their thoughts were in error (v. 3), their acts were perverted (v. 6), they ignored the Lord (v. 7). The reflections here parallel those of 2:10-20, but now the wicked come to the reward they deserve. The traditional reversals of fortune occur in a somewhat transposed format: the just was accounted foolish by the wicked, but the wicked are the fools in fact. "Sons of God" (v. 5) is an ancient expression for semi-divine beings, even the gods of the heathens, and came to Israel from the Canaanites. The phrase disappeared in earlier Old Testament writing but reappeared, shorn of its mythological overtones, in later Jewish life. The translation "saints" masks the original concept of "holy ones," another expression for "sons of God" in ancient times. Also, this traditional view allowed Israel to grow in its understanding of life after death as life with God, such as the "holy ones" enjoyed.

The wicked then confront their own condition in a great confession of their sins (vv. 6-7). Repentance is no longer possible, mainly because the tenor of their entire life was anti-God. The "light of justice" seems better rendered as "the light which is justice," or, "the light offered by justice." Heretofore the wicked spent themselves in the pursuit of temporary pleasure (2:6-9); now with eyes opened they call their lives "mischief" and "ruin" (v. 7). Verse 8, a cry of remorse on their lips, recalls "What shall it profit . . ." of the Gospels (Matt 16:26).

In the next few verses (vv. 9-12) the writer's poetic imagination outstrips the importance of the thought. He may, in fact, be imitating some of the pompous but sterile rhetoric of the wicked. Comparisons are made with shadows (v. 9), ships (v. 10), birds (v. 11), and arrows (v. 12). The vanity of misspent lives leaves no memory—a curse in Israel's thinking. The observations on ships, etc., probably came from school questions in the author's day: Why can we find no trace of a ship? How do birds fly, and why do their traces disappear, unlike those of other animals? How, too, does an arrow find its way? The wise, of course, know the answers. These are the questions of adult fools. The truth of their condition appears again in verse 13.

The author's own comments parallel the earlier descriptions: the wicked have hopes, but they are as insubstantial as down, foam, smoke, and the recollection of a one-day guest (v. 14).

The rewards for the just conclude the passage (vv. 15-23). The first verse (v. 15) is complex, raising many questions, such as: What does it mean to live forever? Is it to live on this earth or to live apart from the body, associated with the Lord in some way? In succeeding verses the author adopts expressions from Israel's earlier writings to help explain the reward coming to the just (see Isa 62:3; Ps 17:8; and 57:2).

As before, the poetry of verses 17-20 overpowers the simple issues. To describe a hero and military armor, both in real and in poetic terms, is not an unknown biblical method (see Isa 59:16-18 and Eph 6:11-17). This idea has its roots in pre-biblical literature, where ancient heroes wear magical armor to overcome the powers of evil. As with other ancient figures, this one reappeared in the last days of Israel's writing. God's sword, too (v. 20), appears in Isa 49:2 and Ezek 21:8-10.

The heavens were said to fight for Barak and Deborah in Judg 5:20, one of the most ancient and lively pieces of Hebrew poetry. So too here, in verses 21-23a, the author's exuberance strikes the modern reader. God's bow was placed in the clouds (Gen 9:13), but God continued to use it to hurl lightning arrows (v. 21). The hailstones recall the great plague in Exod 9:23-25 and Joshua's victory aided by hail in Josh 10:11. "Sea" and "rivers" (or "streams") are regarded as the same in ancient Hebrew poetry (as in Ps 80:12). All these elements pile up here to give a sense of solemn divine judgment: the Creator alone will punish evildoers. The Hebrew hearer or reader of these words would experience an enhanced sense of God's purpose.

Verse 23b concludes the passage and seems to mean that evil acts will destroy creation as we know it. God will restore it in some way for the just.

6:1-21 Seek wisdom. The first major section of the Book of Wisdom concludes with another exhortation, in many ways closely related to chapter 1. The introduction (vv. 1-4) repeats the address to the powerful on earth (see 1:1). What they are to hear and to understand is explained in verses 3-4 and again in verse 9: their works are subject to God's scrutiny, so they should be performed wisely/justly.

As God gave authority to David and his line of kings in the past, so the author asserts that God is the source of every king's authority. This view repeats the emphasis of Yahweh as Lord of history so prominent in Deutero-Isaiah and later books (see, for example, Isa 44:24–45:25 in reference to God's power over Cyrus of Persia). The author of the Book of Wisdom adopts this theme to apply to those latter-day Israelites enticed by a complete freedom of thought and expression to hold themselves arrogantly independent of God. To "walk according to the will of God" (v. 4) recalls many expressions in Deuteronomy (see 5:33; 8:6).

Divine punishment is described in verses 5-8. The reason for punishment is, as always, sin. Its quality varies according to the responsibilities each one exercises: the lowly have problems enough—hence God's special care for them (another echo of Deuteronomy's call to care for the "alien, the orphan, the widow"—16:11; 24:19). The implication also exists that the mighty are in some way the cause of the misery of the lowly. A further theme (v. 7b) is God's universal providence ("provides for all alike"), recalling Jesus' teaching about the rain (Matt 5:45).

The writer states his purpose again in verses 9-11. Note the connection between wisdom and justice (v. 9): to learn wisdom is to learn how to live justly, or without sin. In the Book of Sirach, the author connects wisdom with the content of the law of the Bible. A similar connection appears here in verse 10. The "ready response" refers to the courtroom scene at the great judgment. The writer concludes with two exhortations, "desire" and "long for." These seem to have little real effect, since simple desire will not make one wise. Rather, desire or longing put into practice through study, observation, and prayer will lead to the gift of God.

As if to back up the exhortation, the author turns to a laudatory description of wisdom (vv. 12-21), thus concluding the entire first section of the Book of Wisdom. Wisdom has several attributes that make the pursuit of her both enjoyable and easy. In the first place, she is easy to see (v. 12). The implication is that, being so, the foolish/wicked should have chosen her. Instead, they willingly looked away and so are blameworthy. Secondly, wisdom will be there when one begins to seek her (vv. 13-14). The implication here too is that the wicked would have had the same opportunity but chose to ignore wisdom sitting at the gate. Verse 15 adds an explanatory comment: prudent planning will include a search for wisdom.

Wisdom's willingness to come to those who seek her is expressed again in verses 16-17a. The picture of wisdom walking the streets on the lookout for others reflects Prov 8. The worthiness of candidates for wisdom is somewhat unclear, both here and elsewhere in the book, in terms of time sequence. Who makes the first approach? Is one worthy even before God bestows wisdom, or does the bestowal of wisdom make one worthy? The same questions bedevil Christian theological reflection on the meaning of grace and election. A further answer appears in the next few verses.

Scholars point to verses 17-20 as a type of Greek logical thinking (the syllogism called "sorites") in which one part of a preceding statement is picked up in the next statement, all of which lead up to a climactic conclusion. The terms here are "discipline," "desire," "love," "keep laws," "incorruptibility." The conclusion is that the desire for wisdom leads, through the steps outlined, to closeness to God. This is understood (v. 20) as possession of a kingdom. As is clear from previous chapters, this kingdom is a symbol for the state of just or wise living, leading ultimately to a reward of life with God.

The final sentence (v. 21) moves from earthly power (itself a symbol of intellectual power and freedom) to the truest power, lasting "forever." This last term, unfortunately, is obscure. It may reflect the blessing called down on kings, "May my lord, King David, live forever" (1 Kgs 1:31). But it may refer at the same time to life forever with God, alluded to in the first part of the Book of Wisdom.

Praise of Wisdom by Solomon (6:22–11:1)

This second part of the Book of Wisdom is devoted entirely to words in praise of wisdom. After describing wisdom and explaining its workings in relation to the just and the unjust, the writer furthers his plan by praising wisdom in the person of Solomon. Part Two is therefore divided into several smaller sections: introduction (6:22-25); Solomon, only a mortal (7:1-6); Solomon's prayer and wisdom came after prayer (7:7-12); prayer for help to speak of wisdom (7:13-22a); nature and qualities of wisdom (7:22b–8:1); Solomon sought wisdom (8:2-8); Solomon sought a counselor (8:9-16); wisdom, a gift of God (8:17-21); Solomon's prayer (9:1-18); activities of wisdom in history (10:1–11:1). Several scholars see the material from 7:1 to 8:21 as seven sections arranged around a central passage on wisdom (7:22b–8:1).

6:22-25 Introduction. Similar in style to the self-revelation of Ben Sira, this passage repeats the author's initial exhortation. The difference from the Book of Sirach is that the figure of Solomon is a literary fiction, while Ben Sira himself speaks as the author. The character of wisdom is laid out in 7:22b–8:1. The expression "consuming jealousy" personifies jealousy as consuming either "Solomon" or, as some translations have it, being consumed itself. Jealousy cannot be associated with wisdom, since the wisdom teacher must not claim selfish possession of wisdom. It must be shared, or it ceases to be wisdom (v. 23). In the next verse (v. 24), the author presents a proverb and then comments on it (v. 25), using it as an exhortation self-evident to the wise.

7:1-6 "Solomon" is only a mortal. This first section opens with a theme statement (v. 1). All kings, despite their pretensions or the exalted rhetoric used of them by others, are human in origin. Even the great David, on whom the promises of God rested (see 2 Sam 7:8-16), never claimed supernatural origins. The author also follows his normal practice of not naming his heroes: "first man" instead of Adam. These normal origins are spelled out in verse 2. The ten-month pregnancy has been explained in various ways; it seems simply to be a commonplace expression. His birth was also normal (v. 3). To "fall upon the earth" may signify a method of birth but may just as easily be a poetic expression. The earth is "kindred" in the sense that all humans share the same experience. The section concludes by stating that every king (that is, everyone) shares humanity, with both birth and death. The author repeats the word "same" from verse 1, providing a traditional bracket around the passage through repetition of a key term.

7:7-12 Wisdom and riches came after prayer. The meaning of "therefore" (v. 7) is that "Solomon," having no special advantage of birth, chose to turn to God in prayer. The text of the prayer is 9:1-18, which itself is modeled on 1 Kgs 3:6-7 (and 2 Chr 1:8-10). In answer to his prayer, he received "prudence" (another term for wisdom). The sequence of events whereby one is led even to ask for wisdom does not find an exact treatment in this poetic text (as in 6:17-20). Repeating 6:21, "Solomon" rates wisdom (in vv. 8-9). The comparisons of gold/silver with sand/mire (or clay) have a typical Hebrew proverb form. Part of the rewards coming to the real-life Solomon were all the elements he compared with wisdom (v. 11): gold and silver (see 1 Kgs 10:14-17, 27, and other descriptions of the building of the temple, 1 Kgs 6:20-32); health, beauty, and light (his long reign of forty years, 1 Kgs 11:42). Note, too, that the expressions "came to me" and "riches" in verse 11 repeat the same words in verses 7 and 8, bracketing the passage. The king did not realize, as he abandoned earthly desires, that wisdom was also the cause of earthly delights (v. 12). It is clear here that "wisdom" is another expression for "God."

7:13-22a A prayer to speak of wisdom. If this entire second part of the Book of Wisdom can be said to have any inherent suspense, it is surely heightened by another interruption before "Solomon" tells his readers the nature of wisdom. The two opening verses (vv. 13-14) praise wisdom again. Verse 14 also demonstrates a kind of logical progression after the manner of 6:17-20; also here wisdom is seen as something leading to, but not identified with, God.

"Solomon's" first prayer is reported, not quoted, in verses 15-20. The distinction between wisdom and God appears in verse 15b and continues in verses 17-20. God is the source of all the king's knowledge, not exactly wisdom itself. The Greek text is emphatic on this point. The knowledge of "Solomon" begins with prudence and handicrafts (called "wisdom" in Hebrew, as in the case of Hiram, the famous bronze worker in 1 Kgs 7:14, where it is translated "skill"). The other intellectual gifts that "Solomon" enjoys correspond to interests of Hellenistic science. Hebrew thought was enriched by Greek inquiry into elements (v. 17), astronomy (vv. 18-19), zoology and pharmacology (v. 20). The author's interests in human behavior are reflected in several places in the Book of Wisdom, but "thoughts of men" seems out of place between winds and plants.

The conclusion (v. 21) means to refer to

all things, encompassed between "hidden" and "plain" (recall "seen" and "unseen" in the Christian Creed). The term "hidden," in addition, is a repeat from verse 13 ("hide away"). Lastly, in verse 22a the author identifies God, the Creator of all, with wisdom.

7:22b–8:1 Nature and qualities of wisdom. This central passage, around which the sections from 7:1 to 8:21 are built, finally lays out the qualities of wisdom. The author follows Prov 1–9 in personifying wisdom apart from God (see Prov 8:22-31, where wisdom attends creation; also Sir 24). As separate, wisdom even has a spirit (v. 22b).

The qualities are not meant to convey exact descriptions in which each word refers to a distinct reality. Like individual colors in a painting, the descriptions give a final picture of wisdom as holy, all-present, and all-knowing (note that there are twenty-one of these attributes, three times the sacred number seven). Wisdom's separation from God (vv. 25-26) has challenged scholars to find background for the terms "aura," "effusion," "refulgence," "mirror." The result is a picture showing wisdom as identical with God in all but the most subtle senses, somehow distinct, somehow the same. The issue of time sequence appears again in verse 27: Are souls holy before wisdom comes or because wisdom comes? "Souls" refers to the entire human person. "Friends of God" may be a technical term from Greek life. Comparisons in verses 29-30 recall verses 9-10, and they end with a moral comparison: night and wickedness with light and wisdom.

The final verse (8:1) forms a fitting conclusion. Wisdom appears as the order which the wise God put into creation and by which it continues its orderly existence. (Note the many repetitions of the word "all," the universe-wide perspective of Greek philosophy embraced by the writer.)

8:2-8 Solomon sought wisdom. This small section parallels 7:13-22a as a report of the "king's" wishes in prayer. It opens with an introductory theme that recalls the marriage imagery of Hosea and the Song of Solomon. The image emphasizes closeness with wisdom, and is repeated in verse 3: "companionship," a term used of marriage in Greek writing. Wisdom's distinction from God is quite clear in verses 2-4.

In verses 5-8 the author lists motives to acquire wisdom: riches, prudence, justice, learning; these recall the prudence and riches of 7:7-12. The four virtues (v. 7) are the traditional "cardinal virtues," or the main strengths of the human character. These four qualities appear individually elsewhere in the Old Testament, but their mutual association comes from Greek thinking. Wisdom as the source of learning (v. 8) corresponds closely with the knowledge of 7:13-22a. The connection with the historical Solomon is evident in 1 Kgs 5:9-14.

8:9-16 Solomon sought a counselor. These verses parallel 8:7-12 in the "king's" prayer for power. Note the bracketing words "live/living with" in verses 9 and 16. The introductory verse (v. 9) connects with the marriage motif of the previous section. The results (vv. 10-15) recall the glories of Solomon in Israel's past: glory, judgment, respect, awesome power, and even immortality. In this latter case, his immortality parallels everlasting memory (v. 13) rather than life with God on the model of the "sons of God" (see 5:5). The conclusion (v. 16) asserts the absence of pain. Unfortunately this did not match the career of the Solomon of history (see 1 Kgs 11:4-13).

8:17-21 Wisdom a gift from God. This last section matches 7:1-6 in reflecting on "Solomon's" origins and repeats the same advantages enumerated just above: immortality, pleasure, riches, prudence, renown (vv. 17-18). The terms for relationship with wisdom are also varied, but convey the same closeness: kinship, friendship, etc.

Verses 19-20 have occasioned much scholarly debate. It may appear that the author teaches that souls (or personalities) exist before being implanted in bodies. The point is, rather, that the author is speaking poetically, not philosophically. Likewise, "unsullied" does not refer to the absence of original sin but to "Solomon's" noble character and natural endowments.

The concluding verse (v. 21) adds another thought to the issue of time sequence: wisdom comes from God, who bestows it as a response to prayer. Even to pray is a mark of incipient wisdom, called "prudence" here.

9:1-18 Solomon's prayer. The prayer divides into three sections. The first two (vv. 1-6, 7-12) have the same general structure; the third (vv. 13-18) has general reflections.

The first part of the prayer opens, like the prayers of the Book of Sirach, with an address to God, followed by attributes of God (vv. 2-3) as Creator. This creation culminates, in the author's mind, in divine wisdom bestowed on humans, particularly on kings for the sake of a just rule. This hierarchical arrangement, with the king closest to God, is more characteristic of the theology of Judah than of Israel in pre-exilic times. The role of prophet or priest is ambiguous in this design.

In the petition that follows (v. 4), wisdom has a position reminiscent of Prov 8 and Sir 24, but also recalls similar statements in current thinking outside of Israel. It is not clear that withholding wisdom will cause "Solomon's" rejection from among God's children. This petition may refer to the "king's" fear of eventual rejection from the "sons of God," those who live with God (see 5:5).

Motives conclude the first part (vv. 5-6). The reflection on weakness comes from the text of Solomon's prayer in 1 Kgs 3:7. To be perfect (v. 6) doubtless refers to having many natural endowments. This expression may also suggest that condition of the human being which is called "worthiness" elsewhere (see 6:16).

The second part of the prayer (vv. 7-12) has a similar structure: address and attributes (vv. 7-9), petition (v. 10), motives (vv. 11-12). The attributes match the occasions of King Solomon's own life. "King" and "magistrate" are parallel terms, with no difference in meaning here. Likewise "temple" and "altar" (v. 8) refer to the same construction. That the earthly temple is a copy follows from reading 1 Chr 28:11-19. This idea in itself may come from earlier pre-Israelite thinking: when the world was created out of chaos, the victor in the battle between order and chaos built a heavenly temple. All earthly temples were in some way modeled on the heavenly one and represented heavenly order on earth. The idea worked forward in time as well: Christians often refer to the heavenly liturgy, to which we join our voices on earth. Personified wisdom also appears: she is said to be with God (v. 9), present at creation (see v. 4 above). As wisdom was present, she must have a sense of God's laws.

The petition (v. 10) asks that wisdom now be with "Solomon" as she was with God, a very bold statement. Just how wisdom could be God's attendant, the king's attendant, and the attendant of all who seek her is left unanswered here. An answer is found in the qualities listed in 7:22-23: subtle, pervading all spirits. The motives (vv. 11-12) differ from those in the first part (in vv. 5-6): here "Solomon" is closer to his goal and, relying on wisdom's power and glory, will be a wise ruler, and his acts will be deserving of God's blessing (v. 12).

The final section is a set of reflections (vv. 13-18). The answer to the questions in verse 13 is "No one." These questions do not look for information; they are intended to form part of an act of praise (see Jer 9:11 for one among many examples). The author then turns to other motives, one built on the other: the plans of mortals are unsure (v. 14), since they are earthly (v. 15), and even earthly problems are difficult (v. 16). Scholars have avidly discussed whether the author of the Book of Wisdom holds to a duality: the earthly and corruptible body versus the spiritual soul. Such dualism would not be consistent with Old Testament thought, which emphasizes the unity of the human person; yet everyone perceives differences between the lofty thoughts of mind and heart, and bodily passions. The poetry of the verse does not set out to solve this complex theological issue.

Questions appear in verse 17, again expecting the answer "No one" (recalling Isa 40:13). The "holy spirit" is another way of saying "wisdom," but undoubtedly the expression led Christians to reflect on the identity of the Spirit apart from the Father and from Jesus.

When God sent wisdom in times past, Israel's ancestors were saved (v. 18). This verse links "Solomon's" prayer with the chapter to follow, as well as with Part Three of the Book of Wisdom: 11:2–19:22. It is absolutely necessary, in the author's mind, for wisdom to be on earth in order for human beings to live correctly.

10:1–11:1 Wisdom's activities in history. "She" is mentioned numerous times in the emphatic first place in sentences, an indication of the author's wish to concentrate on wisdom. Because of this, the author does not mention by name the heroes of Israel's past, familiar enough to his readers and giving pleasure through recognition.

The seven characters are sometimes listed with their adversaries. First is Adam (vv. 1-2) with Cain (v. 3). It is hard to see what wisdom protected Adam from in the Garden; perhaps the reference is to naming the animals (Gen 2:18-20), an action demanding great wisdom.

Noah, in the author's view, was only the means by which creation was saved through wisdom (v. 4). To credit the Flood to the sin of Cain exaggerated his role, but at least it shows historical connections between the first sin and the depravity of Noah's time. "Frailest wood" is poetic and belies the huge size of the ark (Gen 6:15).

Abraham's connection with wisdom is unclear: which came first—Abraham's goodness or wisdom? No matter, wisdom triumphed even over a father's love (v. 5).

Lot (vv. 6-7) was preserved in the nick of time. The implication is that the wicked were being destroyed because of their sin (as Genesis taught, 19:13). The remnants of the disaster are evident even in the twentieth century: burning bitumen, having floated to the surface of the Dead Sea, and the "Sodom apple," impossible to eat despite its outward appearance. It was not the author's purpose to teach that the soul of Lot's wife was entombed in a pillar of salt; his poetic imagination handled the story loosely (Gen 19:26). General reflections on the end of Sodom and Gomorrah follow (vv. 8-9). Note the reverse time sequence: leave wisdom, then lose knowledge of the right way, and finally become a mockery to all (v. 8). Lot's wisdom is seen probably in his choice of Zoar for his escape (Gen 19:20-22).

Jacob, particularly through his dream of the heavenly stairway at Bethel (Gen 28:12-15), was given the resources to make a new life in Egypt (vv. 10-12). The "kingdom of God" occurs here for the first time in the Old Testament and must refer to God's heavenly dwelling shown to Jacob. Verse 11 recalls Gen 29:1–31:21, the story of Laban. The ambush (v. 12) refers to the struggle at the Jabbok (Gen 32:23-33). The prize for this struggle was long life and a numerous family.

Joseph (vv. 13-15) has an extensive account in Genesis (chs. 38–50), but is here reduced to three verses, intended as a figure on which to meditate. Wisdom in the dungeon (v. 14) revealed the meaning of dreams (Gen 40). Joseph rose to prominence just as he had previously dreamed (Gen 37:5-11), thereby reversing his brother's mockery and cruel treatment.

The designation of Israel as "holy people, blameless race" neglects other data present in the text of Exodus and Numbers: the worship of the golden calf (Exod 32:1-6) and the constant murmuring of Israel (Num 14:2). The theological point of salvation at the Red Sea overshadows other considerations.

Moses (10:16–11:1) receives the lengthiest treatment; the account of the Exodus leads into Part Three of the Book of Wisdom. Wisdom came to Moses (his "soul," following Greek thought; not his heart, as in the Hebrew manner), and the future of Israel was secured (v. 16). The "kings" may refer generically to rulers in Egypt or to the other kings whose lands Israel entered (see Ps 135:9-11). The people, again called holy, passed through the sea ("a wondrous road") and continued through wisdom's guidance. The author has, of course, taken liberties in associating wisdom with the cloud ("shelter") and the pillar of fire. "Red Sea" and "deep waters" are synonyms (v. 18). The picture of what happened to the Egyptian pursuers is unclear in historical texts. Here the homiletic flavor has them sinking to the depths and then floating to the surface (v. 19). In Exod 12:36 Israel despoiled the Egyptians before their departure. Here the Israelites despoil the corpses. The author's intent is not to add a second despoiling but to show the reversal, since formerly the wicked Egyptians despoiled Israel (mainly of children, Exod 1:8-22).

The song of Israel is Exod 15:1-18 (v. 20), in which the formerly speechless (possibly Moses, Exod 4:10-17) and even infants took part (see Ps 8:2, although the psalm does not refer to the Exodus event).

The concluding verse (11:1) could belong just as easily to the opening of the next section. To style Moses a prophet recalls one strand of tradition, coming mainly from the north of Israel, emphasizing divine guidance through prophets rather than through the Davidic kingly family (see Deut 18:15 and Hos 12:14, both northern products). By the time of the Book of Wisdom, this distinction had faded.

The Providence of God in the Exodus (11:2–19:22)

Part Three of the Book of Wisdom can be divided as follows: introduction (11:2-5); first example: water (11:6-14); second example: animals (11:15-16); digression on God's mercy (11:17–12:22); second example again (12:23-27); digression on false worship (13:1–15:17); second example concluded (15:18–16:15); third example: manna (16:16-29); fourth example: darkness and light (17:1–18:4); fifth example: first-born (18:5–19:21); conclusion (19:22). The general purpose of this third part is to demonstrate, by a series of contrasts, how wisdom preserved the people of Israel in the Exodus. The tone is homiletical, and the author takes liberties in explaining the text of the Book of Exodus.

11:2-5 Introduction. The passage reflects on certain aspects of the Exodus without following the historical sequence. The reader finds Israel in the desert after crossing the Sea (see Exod 17:2-6). These few verses (vv. 2-4) recall Ps 107:4-6, although the psalm does not refer directly to the Exodus. "Sheer rock" and "hard stone" are parallel expressions in Hebrew poetic style. Verse 5 sets the theme for this entire part of the Book of Wisdom: Israel benefited by the very things used to punish its foes. This is a new idea in biblical writing, one that borrows from the ancient concept of reversal of fortune occurring often, even in this book. In addition, these realities show the wise teacher at work, looking deeply into events to see hidden order. What is uncovered is a grand design, worthy of the Creator, who has so ordered creation to benefit the people.

11:6-14 First example: water. The first three verses (vv. 6-8) form one sentence both in the original Greek and in English, something virtually impossible in Hebrew. The intricate design of these verses makes the message, and indeed the entire book, more difficult to perceive. The teaching is that God punished Egypt with impure water (Exod 7:17-24) but blessed Israel with pure water (Exod 17:5-7). The author likewise has compressed the events in time, since "instead of a spring" seems to refer to the wells that the Egyptians had to dig laboriously (Exod 7:24); simultaneously, Israel received water without labor. The idea in verse 7, "as a rebuke," does not appear in Exodus and is the author's own homiletic conclusion.

Israel's punishment (thirst in the desert, Exod 17:1-2), was only temporary, and for a purpose (vv. 9-14a). God's punishment is father-like for Israel, but king-like for Egypt (v. 10). (The brief punishment appeared first in 3:5 and is a continuing theme in the Book of Wisdom.) For Israel the punishment was an education, as they were to learn from their sufferings, the lesson being that their punishment was mild in comparison with Egypt's. The question why Israel, God's chosen people, should be punished at all does not form part of the author's commentary, since he was discussing just the existing texts of Exodus.

Psychological observations appear again in verses 12-13. Scholars differ on the meaning of "twofold grief"; it may refer to the Egyptians' own torments (thirst) and the blessings given to their enemies (water to Israel). That Egypt "recognized the Lord" (v. 13) refers to their understanding that God was with Israel (probably Exod 12:31). Among other passages, Num 14:13 shows some conviction that Egypt knew of the events concerning Israel in the desert. In any event, such a conclusion on the author's part is not foreign to his method of writing.

The writer adds a final comment (v. 14) to add a motive for punishment. Moses, once rejected, now is the object of wonder—again, apparently, by the Egyptians. The reversal of fortune—a blessing for Israel, a curse for Egypt—occurs once more. Moses, the instrument of Egypt's thirst, is the instrument of Israel's relief. The thought is obviously densely packed in a few words.

11:15-16 Second example: animals. These two verses begin a long sequence, which is interrupted twice. The message is clearly in verse 16. The Egyptians were senseless or irrational, since they worshiped animals, themselves dumb or irrational. The harmony seen in their punishment is a call for the wise to see in it the hand of the Creator.

11:17–12:22 Digression on God's mercy. This passage parallels another digression (13:1–15:17) and opens with further remarks on God as Creator (vv. 17-22). The phrase "formless matter" (v. 17) recalls Gen 1:2 ("formless wasteland"), but does not mean to say that any matter pre-dated creation. As Creator, God could have sent bears or lions on the Egyptians, as had happened to others (see 2 Kgs 17:26 for one example). God's power could have formed completely new animals (v. 18), which, like the classical head of Medusa, would have frightened them to death (v. 19). God might have tracked them down for instant punishment (v. 20a). Instead the Creator acted wisely, proceeding in order: "measure, number, weight" (a phrase possibly known among the educated, coming from the philosopher Plato). The motive (v. 21) ends with the type of question typical of words of praise. The comparisons in verse 22 recall Isa 40:15: all is nothing in God's sight, save his chosen people.

Yet, God's mercy extends to all, despite their low condition (11:23–12:1). Here the author again expresses his convictions on divine love and punishment: God's creatures are good. Only their choice of sin keeps them from God, who does not punish immediately (v. 23). This also explains the apparent success of the wicked (as in 4:4-5). Nowhere else in the Old Testament is such complete divine love explained with such vigor, and opens up continuing possibilities for reflection on the meaning of Jesus for Christians.

The final motive (12:1) sounds strange to modern readers. Is the author expressing the view that a divine spark exists in all creation, or at least in all humans? If so, this is not a biblical teaching. Yet, from a Hebrew perspective the spirit of God is creative (Ps 104:30), and God's creatures live by this spirit (Gen 2:7, "breath of life").

Verses 2-11 expose God's mercy in a set of examples, while concentrating on the gradual nature of punishment for sin. This theme occurs in verse 2; the purpose is repentance, not vengeance. Evidently sinners are reminded by the type of punishment they receive, which in some way is in harmony with their sin.

Even the ancient Canaanites (vv. 3-8), proverbially wicked, suffered punishment little by little. The author here seems to be following popular legend more than biblical tradition; the charge of cannibalism is not borne out in the historical books (but see Ezek 16:20). The expression "holy land," so popular now, makes its first appearance in Zech 2:12, also a late composition. The divine harmony of creation is evident also in verse 7: "worthy colony," that is, the land's holiness required a people who were holy (see 6:16 for similar teaching).

Verse 8 repeats the theme of "little by little" (v. 2) in recalling the wasps (hornets, Exod 23:28) of the ancient story—a detail still not well understood. The disclaimer in verse 9 reminds one of 11:20, but despite divine mercy, the Canaanites were so evil as to preclude their repentance (vv. 10-11). The author balances the great evil of Canaan against God's delay in exterminating them.

The digression concludes with reflections on God's unchallenged power (vv. 17-22). The very sensitive issue of why innocent people die is broached in verses 12-13. The answer is that God is both their maker and the one who cares for all. Since God's power is complete, it should not be challenged. This is also the teaching of the Book of Job.

In the case of the wicked who perish, God does not hold a judicial court to weigh arguments as a judge (v. 12). There is only one God, supreme over all; hence, questioning the divine decree of death or suffering is sinful. Note the repeated "unworthy," a sign of the writer's sense of divine proportion or harmony. This extends to justice (v. 16), which the wicked held to be a function of brute force (2:11); for God, creative power establishes justice and right, and this will teach others whose faith is weak (v. 17).

Israel, following the model of the disciple in quest of wisdom, should learn from these events (vv. 19-22). The greatest lesson is to imitate God's justice (v. 22). Israel's closeness to God is symbolized as being God's elect with whom God chose to enter into multiple covenants (v. 21). Earlier Hebrew thinking would have concentrated on one or other ancient covenant (particularly the Sinai and Davidic covenants). By the period of the Book of Wisdom, the majority of Israel's experiences were explained in covenant language (see Sir 45:24 for a covenant with Phinehas), hence a multiplicity of covenants.

12:23-27 The second example again. The author's complex language is evident in these few verses, but the issue remains the same: the Egyptians acted like foolish children. By divine proportion or harmony in creation, they deserved to become ridiculous in turn. The harmony was broken, since they attributed godhood to mere animals, "worthless" beasts.

Their punishment was proportionate ("worthy," v. 26). As a result, Egypt, like Israel, came to see God's hand (see Exod 10:16,

Pharaoh's admission of sin). In the case of the Egyptians, further repentance was ruled out, probably since they were sinful to the core, like the Canaanites (12:4, hated by God, a sentiment shared by Ben Sira, Sir 46:6).

13:1–15:17 Digression on false worship. This lengthy section divides into two parts: 13:1-9, on nature worship, and 13:10–15:17, on idol worship. The author's tone in the first part is remarkably peaceful and understanding, at least up to the final verses. The theme is stated in verse 1 and is repeated in verse 9: God's human creatures should be able to see God's power at work in the world (see Rom 1:18-25). "Him who is" conveniently expresses in Greek philosophical terms a traditional explanation of the divine name Yahweh (Exod 3:14). This name—the God who is—contrasts with the final part of the sentence—the God who acts—completing the description of God.

The writer lists (v. 2), not the base animals of the Egyptians, but the heavenly powers (from Mesopotamian religion, which also influenced the early Greeks). Even the author calls the heavenly lights "governors," but only in the sense of Gen 1:16-18: the sun and moon that "rule." Verses 3-4 repeat the same lesson, one that forms part of wisdom training. Wonder or amazement normally forms the basis for attaining wisdom, since it leads to questions and analysis of experience. This experience should lead one to work "by analogy," that is, by comparisons, to reach the beautiful and powerful Creator (v. 5). Note that the emphasis on beauty is not strictly a Hebrew interest but more Greek.

Just why idolaters turned from God is hard to explain, especially in comparison with Canaanites and Egyptians, being completely corrupt. Worshipers of the heavens sought God avidly (vv. 6-7) but were "distracted." What they saw were the externals of creation rather than the deepest level of meaning, the Creator of these marvels. Those gifted with divine wisdom surely perceived the truth. The author, however, does not explain clearly why these individuals are blameworthy. Did they deliberately turn from God? Were they intellectually lazy?

The second part (13:10–15:17) has three major sections (13:11–14:11; 14:12–15:6; 15:7-13), with a reflection on the Egyptians (15:14-17). Following the usual pattern, a theme statement opens the section (v. 10): far worse than nature worship is the worship of human artifacts. God made the heavens, but humans made idols—the ultimate foolishness. These idols, unlike the sun and moon ("governors of the world," v. 2) are useless. To show better the foolishness of idolatry, the writer makes fun of the entire process, following the lead of several previous writers (see Jer 10:1-16; Bar 6; Isa 44:9-20).

Carpenters have God-given skill (vv. 11, 13), but they can use it badly. The author heaps scorn on them by showing that they can even use the most useless part of leftover wood (v. 13) to make an idol, full of blemishes. Once secured in its shrine, its maker calls on it—turning the divine order of creation upside down. The most succinct statements are in verses 17-18: "for vigor he invokes the powerless; for life he entreats the dead." This is the ultimate in folly. Idolmakers should rather rejoice in their skill, given by wisdom (14:2), than in a work to no purpose and powerless to save.

In verses 3-11 the author turns to God in prayer and exasperation. The term "providence" appears here for the first time in the Bible (v. 3), even though the concept is clear enough in other expressions, such as "hand of God" (see Josh 4:24 and 1 Kgs 18:46 for examples). Providence is a quality of God, whose creative power does not cease at the moment of creation. The road in the sea recalls the path through the Red Sea (see Ps 77:20) but refers directly to the right way to reach a destination (see Ps 107:28-32). To make one's way through an apparently trackless sea is a work of wisdom, but even Noah ("one without skill," v. 4) could rely on divine guidance.

Other goods of the earth, products of wisdom, would perish if they could not be shipped elsewhere (v. 5); even commerce is a work of wisdom. "Raft" and "frailest wood," referring to 10:4, are terms chosen deliberately to magnify God's power, even though transport ships were doubtless more than simple rafts. Noah, "hope of the universe," came safely to land again, and thus the human race was preserved by wood (v. 6). The author connects the account of the giants (Gen 6:1-4) with the great flood, a possible reading of the Genesis account but not the normal interpretation.

As a result, the author can pronounce

some wood blessed and other wood cursed (vv. 7-8), and likewise some woodworkers blessed and others cursed (vv. 8-10). A further reason for a curse is for having bestowed the name "god" on a non-god. In Israel's thinking, the name stands for the reality, and God's name is incommunicable (see 14:21). To dare to act otherwise is to become worthy of punishment. Finally, even the idols themselves will be "visited," that is, judged and condemned (v. 11; see Jeremiah's thoughts on the destruction of the idols of Egypt in Jer 43:12-13).

The author's teaching on the origin and evils of idol worship (14:12–15:6) is the centerpiece of the entire section and is remarkable for its sensitive analysis (like that in 13:1-9). The theme (vv. 12-14) lays out the evil of idol worship: besides being folly in itself, it leads to other sin (v. 12). The writer does not specify when the sudden end will take place (v. 14).

Two origins for idol worship are proposed, and both are understandable in their context: the missing child (vv. 15-16) or a distant ruler (vv. 17-20). However innocent the original motives, corruption takes over. The royal father contrives rites to honor his dead son, and these assume the force of law; afterward they degenerate into folly, since the incommunicable name of the living God is given to a dead man (v. 15).

In verses 17-20 the king may be the same as the father of verse 15. Whether he is or not, his subjects begin in earnest to honor him through God-given artistic work (vv. 17-18). Human folly takes over and rites develop. The conclusion (v. 21) repeats the author's conviction about the proper order of the universe, now overturned by worshipers of idols ("stocks [wood] and stones").

The resulting evils are explained in verses 22-31. The language in verse 22 is complex. Idol-worshipers made two mistakes: they were in error about God, and they saw nothing wrong in evil rites. They gave the name of God to objects and gave the name of peace to war. The social results of such folly are given in verses 23-26: three evil rites (v. 23), murder and adultery (v. 24), and a welter of other disorders (vv. 25-26). Without the Creator, humans left to themselves tend to sin—traces of the original sin. Once the sense of shame has vanished, any evil is possible. The rites (v. 23) were practiced at various times, particularly in Israel's past (recall the condemnation of the Canaanites, 12:3-6).

The origin, repeated in verse 27, is idolatry. The results are all folly: "mad with enjoyment" is to lose control of reason; "prophesy lies" is to overturn God's order of truth. Without the true and living God, every kind of evil can take place (v. 29, a key verse in understanding how idol worship leads to wicked living). Punishment will overtake idol-worshipers (vv. 30-31) for both reasons; this is the law of the universe, restated in the final clause: it "ever follows" sin.

A second address to God follows (15:1-6); in it Israel disclaims idol worship. Regrettably these earnest words do not square with some periods of Israel's history; recall the idol worship in the Jerusalem temple (Ezek 8–9). It is true that apart from some superstitious practices characteristic of popular religion, Israel held true to the worship of the one God after the Exile.

Verse 1 is quoted from elsewhere (Ps 86:5, 15, for one example), giving traditional warrant for the author's teaching on forgiveness. The following verse is contradictory both in language and in fact ("if we sin . . . we will not sin"). Israel belongs to God by covenant (12:21). The tone of verse 3 is intellectual: justice and immortality come from the knowledge of God. The doing of justice is lacking here; the omission probably signifies nothing. Idol-making is "fruitless," that is, of no real effect and subject to the curse of futility. Note also the proportion in creation, "worthy of such hopes," that is, idol-makers are wicked and foolish, since they long for wicked and foolish things.

A second satire on idol-makers appears in 15:7-13, similar in many respects to that in 13:11–14:2. The writer holds the potter responsible, since he should have learned something from molding clay—namely, that he too was molded from the earth (Gen 2:7). He should in fact have imitated God in creation, working only for the good. Instead he used his God-given skill wickedly, doing meaningless work, a true mark of folly. He should have known, too, the end of his life, when he returns to dust (vv. 8b-9a). That life is lent to God's creatures is an unusual expression (see v. 16). Reflection on the idea, however, could have led Israel to consider that the spirit is tied to individual humans, and does not lose that connection after death. Hence, even though earthly life is ended, the spirit returns to God for reward or punishment.

In addition to the punishment coming to the potter for his foolishness, he is also blameworthy for greed and for making counterfeits. These latter are either imitations of more expensive work or represent gods that do not even exist (vv. 9-12). Like the carpenter's hopes (14:10), those of the potter are doomed (v. 10). A distinction between soul and spirit (v. 11) should not be easily drawn, since the terms are in a poetic parallel construction, signifying the same thing. Nonetheless, the terms eventually came to signify, along with body/flesh, the parts of human existence (as in Paul, 1 Thess 5:23, for a clear example).

The writer concludes with a set of reflections on the guilt of the Egyptians (vv. 14-17). They are foolish, not wise like Israel (v. 14). The main cause was idol worship, especially since the idols had no life, no power to act. The satirical description of idols basically adapts Ps 115:4-7 and Ps 135:15-18. The last two verses (vv. 16-17) also satirize the idolmaker. Being alive, the maker is infinitely greater than the lifeless object. The last sentence recalls 13:18, contrasting true life with death.

The issue of how idol-worshipers judged their worship remains undiscussed. It is quite likely that they understood the difference between life and death, and used the idol to focus attention and respect on other-worldly ideas.

15:18–16:15 The second example concluded. Resuming the argument left off in 12:27 on the worship of animals, the writer concludes. Mention of the Egyptians resumed in 15:14, though not by name, in the usual fashion. Verses 18-19 are quite harsh in their judgment, beyond even traditional biblical teaching on animals. "Loathsome" animals might include dung beetles (scarabs) and various snakes. The assertion that some of these beasts escaped God's approval is a very surprising affirmation in view of the author's teaching on divine wisdom in creation (especially 1:14). It seems quite likely that the writer's vehemence in denunciation got the better of his theology. Punishment for Egypt resulted in insect plagues (gnats and flies, Exod 9:12-20), loathsome creatures in their own way.

Israel, on the other hand, benefited while Egypt suffered. The "novel dish," quail in the desert, satisfied Israel's hunger; an equally novel occurrence—plagues of frogs, gnats, and flies—failed to satisfy Egypt. Israel may have suffered a little, but this follows the author's theory of retribution seen previously (see 3:5). In verse 4 Egypt, formerly an oppressor, did not itself experience hunger. Tormented by Egypt, Israel now sees how Egypt was tormented in turn. This knowledge was not simple vengeance, but gave the Israelites the opportunity to learn God's goodness toward them.

The author contrasts Egypt and Israel again in verses 5-10. True, Israel was punished (Num 21:4-9) as a result of murmuring; but the punishment was not complete, as it might have been in strict justice. To avoid a charge of idolatry, the author makes it clear that it was God who saved, not the serpent symbol erected by Moses. "Savior of all" (v. 7) must refer, in the Book of Wisdom, to God's power to save rather than actually saving all (v. 7).

In the case of the Egyptians, they suffered both from the knowledge of God's power to save from the serpents (v. 8) and from their plagues (v. 9). "He who delivers from all evil" sounds like a divine title, similar to "savior of all." The standard version does not record the death of the Egyptians due to locusts and flies; possibly the author is taking homiletic liberties, based on Exod 10:17, "deadly pest." Divine proportion affects the punishment coming to the oppressors ("they deserved," v. 9).

A few reflections conclude the section (vv. 11-15). Israel's brief punishment is explained again (v. 11), this time using "forgetfulness," a typically Greek expression. This state is a manifestation of folly, since it keeps persons from seeing and knowing God's hand in their lives.

No particular "word" of God seems intended in verse 12, but probably just a general decree or decision to save. To affirm God's power over both life and death claims universal jurisdiction and denies any supreme evil, an adversary of God. "Lead down . . . lead back" (see Tob 13:2) means to bring death and bring life, but more exactly it refers to bringing back from the gates of death, that is, being near death through illness. In the author's day, however, this ancient thought was used more globally, as seen by the contrast in verse 14 (spirit and soul are synonymous here).

16:16-29 Third example: manna. The examples are meant to show divine protection for Israel, contrasted with proportionate punishment for Egypt. Verses 16-19 deal with Egypt's twofold punishment in hail and fire, and open with the usual thematic sentence. Hail, mixed of course with cold rain, is virtually unknown in Egypt. The wonder of it all for the author is that two opposite forces, water and fire (that is, lightning), existed together in doing God's will, whereas they could not do so naturally (Exod 9:22-26). The explanatory clause beginning "for" in verse 17 stems from Israel's most ancient traditions (as in Judg 5:20).

In the text of Exodus, the plague of hail, which kills the animals, follows other plagues involving animals (Exod 9:1-7). In the present text, however, events are compressed; only some beasts are killed (v. 18) so that others could plague Egypt, which in turn would acknowledge God.

Israel thrived on manna, a food that came down from the heavens, pleasing everyone, even those with differing tastes (v. 19). The author follows the older traditions of Ps 78:25 (and Ps 105:40) regarding manna as food of the heavenly beings. Manna had a moral meaning also as a symbol of divine sweetness—another new idea.

Verses 22-29 examine these events more theoretically. Israel took comfort, as noted often before, in the punishment meted out to Egypt (v. 22). Divine creative power so altered the normal operations of nature that God's will was done. Fire (lightning) continued its work even amid water (snow and ice/hail). The explanatory sentence (v. 24) stands as a universal principle to explain miracles. The purpose of it all was to grow in wisdom: "that your sons . . . might learn" (v. 26). In verse 27 the author has also mixed events into one, seeing the hail of Exod 9 as the hoarfrost of Exod 16:14.

The concluding two verses (vv. 28-29) are somewhat disconnected from the foregoing. Verse 29 is a moralizing comment, adding nothing to the strength of the lesson.

17:1–18:4 Fourth example: darkness and light. Following a brief introductory comment (v. 1), the author writes about the darkness afflicting Egypt (vv. 2-21). This section, too, begins with an introduction which, however, treats night as a moral condition rather than a physical reality (see also 17:21). Israel was not, of course, removed from God's providence; it only seemed so.

Apparitions in the night terrified the Egyptians (vv. 3-6). This concept, elaborated at some length here, does not appear in the accounts of the Book of Exodus. The author has dramatized the relatively tame account of Exod 9:21-23, drawing out implications about ghosts (vv. 3-4), sounds in the night (vv. 4, 9), and sights (vv. 5-6, fires). Psychological torment, as always, is worse than physical ones (vv. 6-9). Magicians (as in Exod 9:11), to whom the terrified Egyptians called in the darkness, could do nothing this time. In the thought typical of the Book of Wisdom, shrewd magicians are themselves turned into objects of mockery by the force they sought to expel (vv. 7-10). "To face the air" is an obscure phrase but may be a psychological comment, namely, that the sorcerers were afraid even of harmless air; the only terrors were in their imagination.

Verses 11-13 comment on the fears that accompany evil. The term "conscience" (v. 11) makes its first appearance here; it will be used extensively in the New Testament. The rest of the comments must draw on abundant experience.

On this psychological basis, the writer then explains events further in verses 14-21. The source of this "night" is unusual: the nether world, where eternal night reigns (as in Job 42:17). Sleep is perhaps a symbol of their condition in the darkness rather than their actual state in this period of three "days" (Exod 10:22-23). It is also called a prison (vv. 16-17), taking in Egyptians everywhere. The seven sounds of their terror (vv. 18-19) are beautifully described, but did not form part of the narration of the Book of Exodus. The exemption of Israel and the rest of the world in verse 20 parallels Exod 10:23b. The closing verse (v. 21) refers to night as symbol, similar to the hope of the wicked (in 16:29).

Comments on light for Israel (18:1-4) conclude the example. The author calls the Israelites "holy ones," a new term (repeated in verse 5) destined to move from a description of heavenly beings (as in 5:5) to temple personnel, and finally to the people and the land (12:3). The text puts Egyptians and Israelites in close proximity, a further cause for terror in the night. Once the plague ceased, the Egyptians begged Israel to go (v. 2). "Instead of this" (v. 3) refers to the darkness over Egypt. The pillar (v. 3) and the cloud (causing a "mild sun") lit the night sky for Israel in the desert (Exod 13:21-22). Proportionate punishment ("deserved to be deprived," v. 4) falls on Egypt in the form of darkness, the comparison calling Israel's slavery darkness (17:2, 21). A completely new idea closes the passage: the law, to be given soon on Sinai, is an imperishable light (as in Ps 119:105).

18:5–19:21 Fifth example: Death of the first-born. This last section speaks first of death for both Egypt (18:5-19) and Israel (18:20-25), and then of the events at the Sea (19:1-21).

Following the author's cast of thought, the Egyptians were to suffer a fate proportionate to the murder of Israel's children (v. 5); also, whereas one child of Israel (Moses) was saved from the Nile, all of Egypt's soldiers perished at the Sea. Their time of punishment was announced to Israel (Exod 11:4) when Israel was to celebrate the first Passover (Exod 12:1-28). This Passover (v. 9) was celebrated by the holy people, sanctified in a particular way at this festival and having experienced the dangers of life in Egypt. The praises of the ancestors are either praises of them or more likely the songs of praise they had sung previously. These may be the Great Hallel ("Praise" in Hebrew), Psalms 113–118, which came to be sung at Passover, and may have been used as such in the author's time.

The wailing of families, both high and low, bereft of their first-born sons (vv. 10-12) contrasts with Israel's songs. The Egyptians should have known what would happen, since Moses predicted the disaster to Pharaoh (Exod 11:4-8). The cause of their disbelief was magic, according to the author, who had little other reason to explain this extraordinary obstinacy. A further reason appears in verse 13: Egypt's sons died, but God's son, Israel, was saved. This is a motive in addition to the more usual one of recompense for the death of Israel's children (v. 5).

The next passage (vv. 14-19) elaborates on the traditional accounts of this most dreadful punishment. In the first place, the author sets the stage carefully: at midnight, in the quiet and darkness, the personified word of God appears. At this coming, the scene changes from peace to mourning, and from darkness to a disturbed mixture of ghostly manifestations. These visions found no place in the text of Exodus, but form part of the writer's psychological tools in making his point. We find that the purpose for these visions is to increase the sting of punishment; also, at the point of their death the first-born moved from ignorance to knowledge of the God of Israel.

1 Chr 21:16, which pictures an angel "standing between earth and heaven," may have provided the impetus for later images of a divine figure of great height, that is, of all-encompassing power, similar to wisdom itself (as 8:24). This figure appears in verse 16 as well as in later Jewish writing.

Israel also suffered thousands of deaths in the wilderness (Num 17:14). The difference, as previously, is that Israel's punishment was brief (v. 20). Aaron the priest put an end to the deaths with his weapon (vv. 21-24). Since God sent the punishment for Israel's sins, it is difficult today to appreciate Aaron's role in mitigating it. His priestly robes (praised in Sir 50 for their beauty) here have a mystical power, symbolizing the beautiful world and the tribes of the chosen people. This destroyer, possibly the same figure as the personified word of verse 15, finally yielded (v. 25).

The events at the Red Sea climax the narrative (19:1-21). Even though the Egyptians suffered the full punishment, they were foolish enough to ignore the clear lesson of God's protection for Israel (v. 1). The Lord knew this beforehand and planned an even greater punishment (vv. 1b-2). Their foolishness reached new heights even in their grief (vv. 3-4), with the result that Israel's deliverance was greater again, and the punishment of the Egyptians even more terrifying (v. 5).

The author in the next few verses (vv. 6-12) shows again how the Creator could refashion creation for the benefit of the people. Verse 6 stands as a theme, and the rest of the section gives examples. The Lord brought dry land out of the sea, as happened in the original creation of the world (Gen 1:9-10). The crossing is painted vividly: a grassy plain filled with people roaming like horses or lambs (vv. 7b-9). As usual, the text of Exodus is less colorful (Exod 14:21-22).

Unlike the forgetful, foolish Egyptians (vv. 3-4), the Israelites knew what was happening and why (vv. 10-12). In contrast to the first creation, the land did not bring forth beneficial living creatures (Gen 1:24) but gnats (Exod 8:17). The quail were new, since they came apparently out of the sea, following Num 11:31.

The author moves to an elaborate comparison between the Egyptians and the inhabitants of Sodom. Egypt suffered due to its foolishness, ignoring warnings and enslaving Israel, originally their guests (v. 13; see Exod 1:8-10). The Sodomites did not receive guests hospitably (v. 13b); the guests in this case were heavenly visitors, "strangers" (v. 15). The punishment was destruction. The Egyptians (v. 16) first received Israel with rejoicing (Gen 45:17-20) but later turned to oppression, and their punishment was even greater than that of Sodom. Both the Egyptians and the people of Sodom were punished with blindness (the darkness in Exod 10:21-23; a blinding light in Gen 19:11).

Reversals in nature, a kind of new creation (see v. 16), conclude the book. Verse 18 states the theme by means of a musical image. The "land creatures" were the animals that accompanied Israel through the Sea (Exod 12:38). The water creatures were the frogs that invaded Egypt (Exod 7:25-29). The fire and water (vv. 20-21) appeared in 16:16-29.

The final verse (v. 22) concludes Part Three (11:2–19:22) but applies to the entire book. Addressed directly to God, it praises God's providential care for the chosen people, with whom God has remained, no matter the occasion. The lesson for the disciple of wisdom is to examine Israel's history intently to perceive God's guidance, and thereby to grow in closeness to wisdom, that is, God.

SIRACH

John E. Rybolt, C.M.

INTRODUCTION

Title

There has never been any question about the title of major biblical books, such as Isaiah, Jeremiah, or the Gospels; but books like Sirach are not as well known, and as a result their titles often vary. This book goes by two names, each having several variations. The first is the Book of Sirach (or the Book of the Wisdom of Sirach); the second is the Latin name Ecclesiasticus, meaning "church [book]." The first takes its name from the author, and the second from the use of it made by the church—possibly because others had doubts about it. This commentary uses the name Ben Sira for the author, and Sirach for the book.

Author

It is unusual for an Old Testament book to bear the name of its author, since the books usually contain the words or deeds of individuals—for example, a book *about* Jonah, not a book *by* Jonah. The foreword calls the author "Jesus"; his more complete name is given in 50:27: "Jesus, son of Eleazar, son of Sirach." Ben ("son of") Sira is the common form of his name.

Even though we know the author's name, we know nothing about him other than what we can deduce from the book. He was a family man, given to study and writing. He taught (51:23), read widely, recommended travel, and doubtless enjoyed a good reputation. His concerns reflect upper-class life, and he probably wrote them down in his later life. He has an extraordinary interest in matters liturgical, but this does not prove that he was a priest. His grandson, who translated the book from Hebrew into Greek, remains completely unknown.

Date and place of composition

Scholars have determined the time of composition as the first part of the second century B.C.E., about the year 180. The high priest Simon (50:1-21) died about 190; Ben Sira speaks of him as having died recently. The foreword speaks of King Euergetes, whose thirty-eighth year was 132 B.C.E. Working backward from grandson to son to father brings us close to 180 B.C.E. Finally, the book does not reflect the revolutionary troubles that broke out in 168 B.C.E.

It is more difficult to ascertain where the book was written. Jerusalem is thought to have been the place of composition, since it was the main center of culture, education, and religious life. The foreword was composed in Egypt; scholars suspect that Alexandria was the place, and for the same reasons: Jewish culture, education, and religion.

Language

The New American Bible took the bold step of using the surviving portions of Sirach in Hebrew as its fundamental text. For centuries Sirach existed only in Greek, together with some quotations in Jewish writings. As the foreword notes, a Hebrew version existed and was translated into Greek. In the years

1896–1900 archeologists uncovered about two-thirds of a Hebrew version, and since that time fragments of other manuscripts have been added. Unfortunately it is not always clear that today's Hebrew version is original or even older than the normal Greek version. In many cases, however, the Hebrew and the Greek are identical, and in some cases the Hebrew makes better sense. The differing versions have led to a differing enumeration of verses, sometimes a very confusing situation for a modern reader.

Authority

The Book of Sirach forms part of the "deuterocanonical" books, or as they are often called today, the "Apocrypha." This designation means that from earliest times Jewish scholars did not include it among the books of Scripture. They did use the book on occasion in worship and for study, but since it was unlike standard Judaism in many respects, it did not take its place in the list of sacred books (or "canon"). Early Christian lists often omitted it or at least questioned its authority, but the church used it extensively, and continues to do so. The foreword is always included with the book but is not regarded as inspired Scripture.

Background

The author's work grew out of the experience of Israel, with its concerns and styles of writing and thinking. However, Greek thought and life had been making an impact on upper-class Jewish life for some time before Ben Sira wrote. His book even quotes or paraphrases pagan Greek texts, and his style as a scholar at leisure is much more characteristic of the Greeks than of the Jews, whose scholars made their living with daily labor. The author also demonstrates his acquaintance with Egypt's thought world and quotes from its literature.

Style

The book appears to be Ben Sira's collected notes put into poetry and arranged for publication. This makes an outline of the book quite difficult, apart from major sections. The poetry abounds in rich images taken from nature and shows wide variety in types of writing. Ben Sira often uses multiple terms for the same idea. Sirach is a work of wisdom literature. Unlike Job and Ecclesiastes, it does not treat of a single theme. It resembles the first part of Proverbs in style but does not contain single proverbs without commentary. It also resembles the Book of Wisdom in its interest in history and theory.

Teachings

Ben Sira himself did not summarize his teachings, but in a book as long and complex as Sirach, a summary seems needed. For him, God is all, the only God, the almighty Creator who brought order to all facets of life, both natural and moral. God, the source of good, acts justly but also forgives sin. God is also active in history and is bound by covenants to a special relationship with Israel. Ben Sira has a worldwide view of God's activity and sees the law as applicable in some way to everyone. For him, life continues in some way after death; but judgment takes place at death, not afterward.

For Ben Sira, fulfilling the law of Moses is great wisdom. The law prescribes the liturgy, a feature of great interest to Ben Sira. His spirituality might be called liturgical in some fashion. Whether humans are completely free or in some way subject to destiny is unclear. It is clear, however, that virtuous living will be rewarded, and wickedness punished. Ben Sira knows reason and its demands; the ethical content of his work is high. For that reason it is hard to say that Sirach is "revealed" in any way.

Particularly disturbing to many is the author's harsh treatment of women. Since the author accommodated Jewish teachings to Greek rational philosophy and did not have much to say about oral traditions, scholars have called him an early Sadducee. This observation is even clearer when one compares his teachings with those of Jesus in the Gospels, where Jesus appears to follow more closely the methods of the Pharisees.

COMMENTARY

The Introduction to Sirach

Foreword

Only the Book of Sirach comes with a prologue of this type. Other biblical books have introductions (for example, Psalm 1 for the Book of Psalms, and Deut 1:1-2 for the rest of that book), but none of them gives such details on the book's composition and translation. In the case of Sirach, the author of the foreword had to refer to the translation from Hebrew (into Greek), since Hebrew was no longer the generally spoken language of Alexandria in Egypt, where a large Jewish community made its home.

In the first paragraph the translator, whose name we do not know, makes mention of the law, the prophets, and the "later authors." Scholars see this as the earliest reference to the division of the books of the Hebrew Bible into their three traditional parts: the law, the prophets, the writings. The last category was not fully developed in Ben Sira's day. Further, the usual order followed in Christian editions is law (Pentateuch), history, writings, and prophets. Israel, however, understood the books of history as one with the prophets and joined the two, leaving the writings till last.

The one mention of Israel's wisdom should be read in the light of a more general attempt on the part of Jewish authors of the period to defend the quality of their wisdom teaching over against that of their pagan neighbors. This defense grew stronger in the next couple of centuries, since it was important for Jews living outside of Israel to realize how valuable their own traditions were. The translator offers his readers the insight that wisdom is not just a matter of learning alone but of proper living, in accordance with the whole Jewish law. His insistence on this is derived from many places in the Book of Sirach.

In the second paragraph the translator comments on the difficulties of translation, from Hebrew in particular. The common understanding of this passage is that he is referring to Greek translations, yet translations into Aramaic, the spoken language of Jews in Israel, were already known in Israel itself. Eventually a number of Greek translations were brought together in Egypt in a version known as the Septuagint (meaning the "Seventy," after an old story about seventy scholars in Alexandria producing this version).

In the final paragraph of the foreword, the word "reproduction" refers most likely to other wisdom literature, probably in Greek translation. The publication that the translator mentions involved preparing a master text to be given to copyists for mass production. These copies were then sent to those "living abroad." This expression probably has Israel as its point of reference, since living abroad for a Jew meant living anywhere else than in Israel, not just outside of Egypt.

A person evidently acquires wisdom by reading and reflecting on texts, a method recommended even today. Ben Sira's grandson concludes by repeating his insistence that a change of life (we might call it "conversion") must accompany growth in wisdom.

IN PRAISE OF WISDOM

Solemn Introduction to Wisdom (1:1-29)

These verses summarize the teaching of the sages on wisdom up to the period of Ben Sira and give the author's own developed thought.

1:1-8 The origin and character of wisdom. The book opens with a thematic statement contrasting somewhat with other statements in the book praising the wisdom of Israel, which, to be sure, has its origin in God. The author's use of examples drawn from nature (vv. 2-3) and their application to human experience are characteristic of all wisdom writing—encouraging students to have a contemplative regard for God's creation. Ben Sira pairs wisdom with understanding (v. 5) in Hebrew fashion, intending no difference between them. Elsewhere in the Old Testament wisdom is associated with skill, common sense, or even accumulated human knowledge; but here wisdom is of a higher quality: hidden in God (v. 5), created by God alone (v. 7). As in Prov 8:22, wisdom is not understood as coeternal with the Lord but is created by God. The "friends" of God (v. 8) are likely the people of Israel.

1:9-18 Wisdom is the fear of the Lord. Fear is traditionally understood as reverence, devotion, or awe in the presence of God. To have this quality is a great blessing, compared here to the gladness of a festive banquet (v. 9). It brings blessings, including a long life, to the one who has it (v. 10)—a conservative view uninfluenced by thoughts of eternal life (v. 11).

Ben Sira then discusses fear of the Lord, opening with a traditional statement, copied often (see Job 28:28; Ps 111:10; Prov 1:7, 9:10). Then he goes beyond this with his own expansion. Often in this work the author's sense of predestination is evident, as in verses 12b-13. He does not clearly develop this position, however. He continues with sensory descriptions (drunk with wisdom, v. 14; taste, v. 15; sight and smell of flowers, vv. 16-17). The tree metaphor (v. 18) is traditional in wisdom writing (see Ps 1). "Knowledge and full understanding" are here the results of wisdom, not its synonyms (as in v. 4).

1:19-29 Marks of wisdom. Verses 19-21 seem out of place here, contrasting as they do with the previous verses. In fact, some manuscripts are disturbed here, showing hesitancy even in the tradition. The teaching on patience for a time (vv. 20-21) is developed further in Sirach: a proper time reflects God's order in creation, to be modeled in wise living. Likewise, the connection between wisdom and justice, or right living according to the law, is a major theme in Ben Sira's writing (vv. 22-24).

The negatives of verses 25-29 are counsels against duplicity, in prophetic style. The public humiliation of the unwise (with no hint of the final judgment) is rooted in the conviction that reliance on self rather than on God is the ultimate blasphemy and a reversal of divine creation.

Lessons on Faithfulness and Humility (2:1–4:10)

2:1-18 Duties to God by enduring trials. The first lesson opens traditionally with "My son," words that often mark new sections in Sirach. By "son" the author means "disciple," a student in Ben Sira's lecture hall. The author treats first the theme of preparation for trials, that is, adversity and misfortune. The basis for these trials is not given, but it is probably a test of faith. Then follow lessons (vv. 4-6), a natural experience and its moral application (v. 5). Just as impurities can be removed even from gold, so the just can be purified. One's true value will thereby be seen.

Verses 7-11 set a different tone, since Ben Sira writes in the plural. These sound like psalm verses, recalling Pss 46:1; 71:5; 103:4-5, and others. To emphasize his point, the Sage counsels the study of history, chiefly the Scripture. But his advice is too simple, for it does not account for the apparently meaningless suffering of some biblical heroes such as Josiah. As a result of his own biblical studies, Ben Sira claims that the main motive (v. 11) for being faithful is that God's mercy is consistent (recalling Exod 34:6-7).

Verses 12-18 enumerate the curses (or woes) on those without hope in God. This theme appears only here and in 41:8. Those condemned should have known of God's mercy and forgiveness in history. The blessed (vv. 15-17) stand in contrast. Note that "fear" and "love" occur as parallel terms in verses 15-16; the author intends them to refer to the same state of heart. The final verse recalls 2 Sam 24:14.

3:1-16 Honoring parents. Ben Sira divides his lesson on the honor owed to parents into positive (vv. 1-9) and negative duties (vv. 10-16). In general for Ben Sira, the father serves as the focus, and the mother just as a poetic contrast (see vv. 2, 3, 6, 9, 11, 16). If this is Ben Sira's commentary on the fourth commandment, it is the earliest one we have.

For the positive duties, the text opens with a statement about a parent's right, together with the motive: life—a clear echo of Exod 20:12. The basis for the command is found in the Lord's doing, with its rewards: atonement for sin, children, prayers answered, life, family harmony. The concept of atonement for sin by honoring a parent is a feature new to biblical teaching. Before Ben Sira's day it was taught that atonement is accomplished by sacrifice. Ben Sira also develops the atoning value of alms (3:20; 28:2; 34:26; 35:3). Atonement, however, is not automatic; repentance is also required.

Verse 9 is probably a popular proverb, known from the introductory "for." The contrast here is not between father and mother but between a parent's blessing and curse.

The negative duties (vv. 10-16) begin with a contrast between shame and honor. These lines might also be rephrased as follows: to show honor for a father is honor in a son; but shame for a mother is shame in her children. The interpretive possibilities of such a brief proverb are probably intended. Such pithy statements can be twisted and examined from many points of view. Those of us who read them should extract all the meaning possible from them.

Verses 12-15 do not necessarily refer to Ben Sira's views on family life. He counsels consideration or human kindness for all children. The motive is divine: God will take such kindness (literally "almsgiving") into account. Verse 15 continues the lesson, alluding possibly to a storehouse (or account book?) for good acts. This may sound too mechanical for Christians. Verse 16 is in standard proverbial style, with roots in Exod 21:17.

3:17-28 Lessons on humility. Recall here the upper-class situation of the Sage and his students. Against such a background lessons on humility are dramatic. In verses 17-18 he introduces his lesson with the motive: loved by others, rewarded by God. Verse 19 adds another: an assertion of divine power and condescension to the lowly. Verses 20-24 are negatives. Ben Sira introduces another concept characteristic of his writing, namely, one's lot in life (here, "what is committed to you"). He stands in contrast with Greek thinking, which emphasized freedom of investigation. For Ben Sira, one's lot in life reflects God's created order. Verse 23 is an argument from personal experience, and verse 24 offers an example from nature, designed to provoke reflection about right living.

In verses 25-27 the author contrasts the stubborn (literally, "heavy heart"), with the humble. The assertion of punishment here is fundamental to Ben Sira's thought: each act has its own reward bound up with it. Results follow inevitably.

The section concludes with a general comment (v. 28). Proverbs such as these are wise sayings, usually memorable and sharp, briefly summing up human experience. They were the stock in trade of wisdom teachers. (See also 6:35; 8:8; 13:25; 20:20; 21:15.)

3:29–4:10 Alms. These verses form the last part of the lesson on fidelity and humility and fall into three parts: theme (3:29-30), negative (4:1-6), and then positive recommendations (4:7-10).

The theme here is astonishing: alms can atone for sins. As noted above, this teaching is characteristic of our author. Note that the form is typical: experience (water and fire) and application (atonement). Nothing is implied, however, as to just how alms atone for sin.

The negatives in the next verses are followed by a final assertion of God's activity (v. 6). One would like to read in these verses a completely charitable approach, that is, to do good simply for its own sake. The lesson here is self-protection: doing good to others will involve a reward, just as not doing good (or doing evil) will lead to punishment. Note also that God is called "his Creator," a commonplace expression for us but a relatively new idea in Old Testament times. This term underscores the oneness of all creatures: God made both the rich and the poor.

The positive recommendations of verses 7-10 change the scene from public life on the streets (implied in verses 1-6) to the assembly, some sort of general gathering that heard cases and gave judgment. Ben Sira presumes here that his students will be in a position to help, given their social status. Verse 7 itself is general and may be a quotation. The results of this charitable activity will be the same as in the previous section—reward from God for oneself. ("Most High" is a title for God used principally in the late Old Testament period.) The motherly tenderness of God is surprising, given the rigidly masculine viewpoint in Sirach.

Pursuit and Marks of Wisdom (4:11–10:5)

4:11-19 Rewards of wisdom. The theme statement in verse 11 is typical: wisdom is a female. (The father of these children is not otherwise specified because of the poetic nature of these teachings.) Various rewards are specified: life, favor, glory (or renown). The connection between wisdom and God ("the Holy One") is very close (v. 14). It has proven difficult in many cases to separate wisdom and God clearly (as in the opening chapters of Proverbs). Such a division is rather the task of theology than of biblical poetry.

Verse 15 ("judges nations") refers to the Gentiles among whom the Jews live. The original Hebrew, however, may mean "judges aright." The difference is due to a possible confusion of terms.

Growth in wisdom comes by trusting her (v. 16). This itself comes through testing by wisdom, possibly by the decision that an official might have to make (reflecting the social status of Ben Sira's students). Small, wise decisions will lead to a conviction that wisdom can be trusted. The secrets of wisdom (v. 18) come only with struggle. To abandon wisdom is an evil, and Ben Sira's treatment of this is normal—a reversal of positions takes place: to abandon wisdom means that wisdom will abandon us, and misery will be our lot. We have only ourselves to blame for this, since that is the way God's creation is ordered.

4:20-6:4 Excess and defect of wisdom. Ben Sira knew public life well enough to realize that balance or proportion is needed in all things, even in humility. His teaching here probably revolves around proportion rather than any specific element. Proportion would be, for example, a feature of well-ordered creation, and an observant or wise creature would seek to imitate it.

Verse 21 is a learned explanation of one word with two meanings. Ben Sira may be citing Hesiod, an ancient Greek author; whether directly or indirectly is not known. This points to the general international character of wisdom teaching.

The issue of proportion is carried through lessons about speech (speaking at the proper time, v. 23) and about being vulnerable (admitting guilt or ignorance, v. 26). The proper proportion (or "truth," v. 28) is ultimately at stake, and God, the guarantor of right order, will uphold it. These lessons about created order contrast to some degree with the sense of right and wrong Christians have traditionally learned from a meditation on the commandments. Ben Sira teaches an alternative form of reflection on God.

One of the defects of wisdom is arrogance (vv. 29-31). These negatives recall the prophetic distinction between words and actions, but the text (particularly verse 30) is obscure. The early church (in the *Didache*) quoted verse 31 as a typically Christian attitude toward life.

The section 5:1-10 treats of self-reliance as a defect of wisdom. The introductory theme (vv. 1-2) is a true religious message, counseling against reliance on two false gods, wealth and power. Although self-reliance can be recognized as a good—and was so by many Greek philosophers—its excess is being considered here.

A series of contrasts follows (vv. 3-7), using prohibitions and assertions proving the point at issue. An exception is verses 5-6, which seem to allude to a psalm. The motive for this prohibition contains another instance of the balance or proportion characteristic of Ben Sira's teaching: God's mercy and anger are both in proportion to the human acts involved.

The conclusion (vv. 8-10) is homiletic in style, which is unusual for Sirach. The summary in verse 10 points to the danger of reliance on apparent power; wealth has no real power in the ultimate issues of life.

The next section, on sincerity in speech (5:11-6:1), marks the first appearance of a common theme in Sirach. The author lays out his general views (vv. 11-16), beginning with a rural proverb and drawing out its implication (vv. 11-12). Since some winds are too strong, the prudent person will choose the proper occasion to winnow or speak. The Epistle of James (1:19) quotes verse 13, although in another setting; verse 15 recalls the lengthy discussion in Jas 3:1-12 on restraining the tongue.

The motives behind the general teaching are shame (v. 17) and disgrace (6:1). In a small and closely knit society, shame would be more evident than in today's large, impersonal cities. Notice that both motives are human conditions rather than eternal punishment for sin. Ben Sira has discussed shame with guilt in 4:21; this passage is an example of that teaching.

A few verses on lust (6:2-4) complete Ben Sira's teaching on excess and defect in wisdom. His principal idea is that the wise person should never be in the grip of anything—in this case lust. The comparison differs in the Greek text, which mentions a bull consuming one's soul; even though the versions differ, the idea is clear enough. Both fire and bull can destroy a strong tree, the traditional picture of the wise (see Ps 1:3).

6:5-17 True friendship. One of the loveliest aspects of Sirach is the author's thoughts on friendship, developed in this book more thoroughly than elsewhere in wisdom literature. His normal caution is evident here and is a good check against multiplying friends; his experience teaches him that one's truest friends are few and far between (v. 6).

In verses 8-13 Ben Sira contrasts false and true friends in a set of assertions and explanations. Inconstant friends (vv. 8-10) are the opposite of wise friends, who are true to their word and selfless. The refrain "be with you" (vv. 8, 10) has deep biblical roots, drawn mainly from the presence of God with the chosen people or with particular heroes as a guarantee of success and blessing. Experience shows that a friend must be present particularly in times of need, even though words or solutions to the problems encountered are not available. A very cautious summary (v. 13) concludes these contrasts coming from a long life and broad experience; scholars have seen here an echo of the words of the Greek author Theognis, possibly known to educated Jews like Ben Sira.

True friends, by contrast, are described and praised (vv. 14-16) in a fashion recalling the virtuous wife of Prov 31:10-31. The concluding motive (v. 17) calls for fear of God (internally), coupled with good behavior (externally).

6:18-37 Attaining wisdom. One of several similar sections, these few verses lay out ways for disciples to grow toward wisdom. In the first place (vv. 18-23), the attainment of wisdom involves toil. Discipline, self-control, and longing are prerequisites for a life of work (v. 18). By contrast, the undisciplined (vv. 21-22) will never attain wisdom. The stone (v. 22) may be a heavy stone cast aside by the fool or perhaps a touchstone used to test genuine metals. The Hebrew text of verse 23 contains a play on words: the same word may mean "discipline" or "bond" or "removed."

Another lesson on the same topic opens solemnly with "my son" (vv. 24-31). This section, on submission, has a schoolroom atmosphere, with emphasis on activities—carry, draw close, search, seek (vv. 26-28). As a result, rest and joy will follow. The purple cord (v. 30) recalls Num 15:38-39 and links the law and wisdom. The burden, therefore, is not that of slaves but of scholars and royalty.

The author closes with a lesson emphasizing the will (vv. 32-33). On this basis he mentions other means (vv. 34-37a), principally the company of the wise and virtuous. The connection of law and wisdom (Torah wisdom) is clearly expressed here in summary (v. 37). The last half-verse parallels 1:1: if a person prepares for wisdom, God will grant it.

7:1–9:16 Advice and counsels. This section forms part of 4:11–10:5, on the pursuit of wisdom, and is further divided into public life (7:1-17), states in life (7:18-36), and relations with others (8:1–9:16).

Ben Sira's advice on public life opens with reversals of fortune (vv. 1-3). These are normally employed in Sirach to show how punishment takes place (evil acts carry with them their own punishment). The wise will want to avoid evil consequences. The verses on leadership (vv. 4-7) carry a double message: do not seek leadership, it leads to evil (v. 7); but if you have native abilities, then it is a good (v. 6). At root here is the conviction that all have their own places given them by God. Favoritism (v. 6) is unjust, since it violates the integrity or proportion to be observed in life's dealings.

In verses 8-10 the message is that each sin is punished; this is the order of the universe. Hence God cannot be bought off (v. 9); rather, true piety consists in both prayers and alms (faith and works, v. 10).

Insensitivity in public life (vv. 11-16) is also a great evil. Ben Sira has offered us a series of prohibitions, with a few reasons or motives, such as verse 13: lying always begets more lying. Verse 15 contrasts with the upper-class ethic seen in other places in Sirach. The author's approach recalls Paul's work as a tentmaker (Acts 18:3), living as a scholar by the work of his hands. The truly humble will have their reward (v. 17) elsewhere than in death, the common lot of all.

The verses on states in life (vv. 18-36) are arranged in groups, beginning with the family (vv. 18-26). Negative and positive recommendations are gathered together here. Noteworthy is the author's treatment of slaves (vv. 20-21): they are human beings, deserving of good treatment and respect. Theirs was generally an economic slavery, not one based on race or origins, nor were slaves regarded generally as a class in society. (For the release of slaves, see Deut 15:12.) Other property receives similar treatment (vv. 22-26): stock, sons, daughters, wife (evidently this is a man's world).

Honor is due parents (vv. 27-28; see 3:1-16) for their gift of life, now returned to them by a dutiful son. Priests likewise are to be honored (vv. 29-31), not for their own worthiness, but for the God whose ministers they are. (The offerings alluded to are not intended to describe precisely the rituals of the temple.) The poor, that is, the neglected and powerless, and even the dead deserve attentive treatment. The results will benefit the wise person, since God has ordered the universe so. The summary (v. 36) may lead to considerations of an afterlife; more likely Ben Sira had in mind the consequences of a good life on one's descendants.

The author's advice on relations with others (8:1–9:16) is divided into lessons on men (8:1-19), women (9:1-9), and friends (9:10-16).

The lessons on men treat first of the rich and powerful (vv. 1-2). History shows that wealth can corrupt (v. 2b). The unruly (vv. 3-4) should be avoided, since they are controlled by their passions and speak unwisely. The comparisons in verses 5-7 demonstrate Ben Sira's psychological sensitivity, a feature encountered several times in the book. The Sage may be speaking of his own experience also in verses 8-9. Training in proverbs (as in 3:28) will stretch one's mental potential to see clearly into reality. Real knowledge, which enables one for princely service, comes from accumulated experience (as in Deut 4:9; 11:19; Pss 44:1; 78:3; Job 8:8; 12:12).

Those to avoid (vv. 10-16) are described in terms of the reversals that come to the unwise disciple: the impious man (v. 11) will turn on you, for example. Financial matters (vv. 12-13) show that power can be abused; the wise should be in command of their own finances. The message of verse 14 recalls that of 7:6, but the perspective differs; Ben Sira offers no advice on handling disputes with judges.

Special advice on handling secrets (vv. 17-19) further demonstrates the author's well-known caution in matters of human relationships and contrasts to some extent with his teaching on trusting one's friends (see 6:5-17).

The experience of a man's world continues in 9:1-9, where Ben Sira, following the custom of other wisdom writers even outside Israel, writes negatively of women (see also 25:13–26:27). To give a woman power over a man (or to allow anything to have this power, such as desire or wealth) is a great evil (v. 2). Consorting with "strange women" likewise involves handing over self-control—in this case, to prostitutes or unmarried women (vv. 3-5). The same lessons are featured in verses 6-8a: it is the mark of a fool to hand over control to another. The punishment is to "go down in blood to the grave" (v. 9). This expression (see Prov 2:18; 7:27) probably refers to the death penalty inflicted on adulterers (see Lev 20:10).

The verses on the choice of friends (vv. 10-16) add to the discussion of 6:5-17. The negatives (vv. 10-13) are filled with sound advice. Ben Sira counsels patience, implicitly, concerning the inevitable punishment of sinners (v. 11). Verse 13 recalls Matt 10:28: Avoid the one who can kill both body and soul. The snares and net are pictures taken from bird-hunting.

The positives (vv. 14-16) connect wisdom with holiness, and counsel good companions as the great road to growth in wisdom—timely advice in any age.

9:17–10:5 Wisdom in rulers. This is the sixth and concluding section on the pursuit of wisdom, begun in 4:11.

Ben Sira here compares good rulers with evil ones (9:17–10:3) and then speaks of God as the source of wisdom (vv. 4-5). In the first section the skill of artisans is a kind of manual wisdom. The rash speech of verse 18 reminds one that rulers whose speech is rash or uncontrolled are not successful. The order of 10:1 reflects God's own order in the universe. The traditional proverbial style of 10:2 recalls other proverbs: Like mother, like daughter, etc. God's majesty or glory (v. 5) is a theme seen later in the book, and manifests divine choice and protection.

Lessons on Pride, Violence, and Wealth (10:6–15:10)

10:6–11:28 Eight discourses on pride. These are divided thus: 10:6-18; 10:19-26; 10:27–11:1; 11:2-6; 11:7-9; 11:10-13; 11:14-19; 11:20-28. The first, on the sin of pride, deals also with the violence that can accompany pride. Apparently Ben Sira believes that to act freely involves acting violently (v. 6). The motives in verses 7-8 are that both God and the chosen people hate arrogance, and that history shows that dominion has been transferred to other states.

"Dust and ashes" is a traditional expression for lowliness and the human condition; this is reinforced in verse 10. (Some translations speak here of disease that mocks the doctor's skill.) The origins of pride (vv. 12-13a) point to a central idea: withdrawal from God into self mocks the divine order of the universe and is therefore the worst sort of idolatry. The punishments are the traditional reversals (vv. 14-16) in plant imagery. Two statements (vv. 17-18) conclude the lesson, the second being the stronger.

The second lesson (vv. 19-26) contrasts with verses 6-18. Here Ben Sira has collected various comments reminiscent of rote lessons. The saying in verse 19 is complex, with the English translation making sense of the Hebrew and Greek texts: "can be" means that the human state can be honorable or dishonorable; "are" refers to the certainty of the state of those who fear God or not. In verses 20-21 Ben Sira teaches that personal honor, despite one's social state, comes from honoring God. Since the "poor" fear God alone, they have great honor (vv. 22-23).

The third discourse (10:27–11:1) opens with a theme and a typical introduction, "my son." The question-and-answer format (vv. 28-30) is common in wisdom literature, recalling the scholastic origin of much of Ben Sira's writing. He concludes by going against the upper-class ethic evident elsewhere in his work: wisdom is common to all classes (11:1).

The fourth lesson treats of deceptive appearances (11:2-6). Reflection on the popular proverb on the bee should cause a student to realize that, despite appearances, the bee is a beneficial creature. Likewise, appearances in human beings can deceive. The wheel of fortune (see also 20:10) is not a biblical expression but a way of understanding human experience. The upper-class comments here are apt for Ben Sira's students.

The fifth lesson, on imprudent speech, is very brief (vv. 7-9) and presents a common-sense approach, contrary to the "shoot first, ask questions later" method. The author's usual insistence on maintaining one's proper place (v. 9) involves a sense of the ancient (non-biblical) rule called the Golden Mean, "Nothing to excess."

The sixth lesson (vv. 10-13) deals with self-made men. The sentences in verse 10 recall the Golden Mean and show that violating it brings a curse of futility. "Seek and find" here recalls the gospel injunction to seek and find God. A series of comparisons (vv. 11-13) shows that the Lord, not fate, is the source of one's success, almost passively so. This is not the whole story for the author, since he also encourages one to pursue wisdom actively.

The seventh discourse (vv. 14-19) treats of wealth and death. In the face of the proverbs here, it is difficult to see the role of human freedom. Ben Sira also teaches that God is in some way the source of all, even evil, death, and poverty. Possibly the author is quoting a popular proverb and contrasting it with verses 15-16. The miserliness of a rich man is ultimately foolish, since this man has not reckoned with God's control of all events (this lesson recalls Luke 12:19).

In the eighth and final discourse (vv. 20-28), Ben Sira speaks of wealth and loss. His basic message is: Do your job, that is, stay at the post assigned you in God's plan, a plan with its own time (v. 21). Ben Sira also speaks to the vexing experience of the (apparent) success of the wicked, a problem faced in all wisdom literature. Ben Sira answers by pointing to the judgment (v. 27) to take place at the end of life. Recall that this judgment does not pertain to life after death.

Warnings Against Exploitation (11:29–13:13)

11:29-34 Exploitation by strangers. The caged bird (v. 30) suggests that this innocent bird is to attract wild birds into a trap. The stain resulting from evil does not describe sin (v. 33) but simply the ruin to come. Ben Sira concludes with a reversal of fortune: if you lodge a stranger, you will become a stranger in turn. The gospel teaches a more open-handed hospitality, but Ben Sira's focus differs here.

12:1-7 Exploitation by the recipient of alms. This passage is simply constructed in terms of opposites, the theme (v. 1) being thoughtful and ordered charity as befits the wise. The rewards are stated as opposites: they come from the Lord (v. 2) and not from the wicked (v. 3). Ben Sira's advice consists in asserting motives for behavior (vv. 5-6): reversal of fortune (arms against you) and double evil. The conclusion is very general, not specific to this brief section.

12:8-18 Exploitation by enemies. This lesson is quite elaborate by contrast, particularly with the symbols (vv. 13-17). The theme (v. 8) can better be understood by reversing its order: in prosperity enemies will remain concealed; in adversity we can know our true friends. The author advises not trusting mere appearances, applying the theme in verse 9 and using an example from daily life: a bronze mirror needs constant care and, once pitted with corrosion, cannot be easily polished. The personal comments (v. 12) are surprising here, bringing us clearly into the classroom.

Lessons about snakes and handlers (vv. 13-17) are applied to the same issues, opening with a rhetorical question, the answer being that either no one or only a fool will pity him.

The applications of the lesson (vv. 14-17) echo the teaching of the prophets to keep one's life virtuous both externally and internally. To plunge one into the abyss (v. 16) means to bring one to death. The conclusion (v. 18) parallels the theme statement about true friends and a true face. The actions (nod, clap, hiss) are intended as signs of derision, mentioned elsewhere in the Old Testament, but not in Sirach.

13:1-7 Exploitation by the rich. The opening statement may conclude the previous lesson but can be understood well enough as a part of this one. The form is traditional: a lesson from nature and its application to daily living. The following verse is similar in style but contains a comparison known to the earlier Greek author Aesop; it is possible that his writings formed part of Ben Sira's education.

A series of examples follows (vv. 3-7), pointing out that riches can cause one to let down personal safeguards and become violent, contrary to the stance proper to the wise. The reversal of the moral order (the poor man must ask forgiveness when he should rather be seeking redress) is an enormous evil, since God's designs are subverted, even temporarily. The gesture of shaking the head is, as in 12:18, one of disrespect or cursing.

13:8-13 Exploitation by the powerful. This lesson recalls Prov 25:6-7 as well as Luke 14:8-11. Ben Sira uses a pattern here similar to previous sections: introduction, examples, results, conclusions. His examples (vv. 9-11a) are basically comments of human wisdom and recall even Egyptian thinking known to us from ancient sources. These may not have been Ben Sira's direct source, but these connections at least reflect the international character of wise teachings. The psychological tone of verses 11b-12 is typical of the author's close observation of human behavior, seen often in his book.

13:14–14:19 Lessons on wealth. Ben Sira is clearly of the upper class, and has had the advantages of broad experience, travel, and other opportunities. This leads him to look at wealth with wise discernment, condemning excesses and approving what is good.

The introductory or thematic statements (13:14-15) in Ben Sira's lesson on equals (vv. 14-19) advise that people should keep to their own station in life. This conservative position comes from his theological conviction that God has given people their lot in life, and to act against this is a mark of folly. The examples (vv. 16-18) are known from other ancient literature. Ben Sira does not counsel class warfare (v. 17) but emphasizes observance of law to avoid the evils inherent in differences of class and outlook. Note the connection he makes between the rich and the proud (v. 19); the two conditions of life are similar.

The three verses here on support for the rich (vv. 20-22) point to the paradoxes of living with differences. Verse 20 is quite pessimistic but may be a common proverb explained and expanded by the two succeeding verses. There is almost a comic tone to the word picture in verse 22.

Ben Sira's teaching on a clear conscience (13:23–14:2) is probably connected to what has preceded, showing some good in wealth. The proverb in verse 23 can, like other proverbs, be taken apart and reassembled to show the inherent paradoxes: wealth is evil by the standard of the just, poverty is good when there is no sin. This method is one of the ways open to wisdom students to delve into the possibilities of proverbs. The final verses (14:1-2), in the form of a beatitude, are only loosely connected to the rest of this section.

The theme of the subsection on the bad use of wealth (14:3-10) basically leads to issues of being generous with self and others, that is, taking one's full place in society (see 39:1-11). The remaining parts of the lesson are examples. Verse 4 recalls Luke 12:16-21, where others inherit piled-up wealth. The old concept of automatic punishment occurs in verse 6: by God's design each evil act carries with it its own punishment. Verses 7-10 are lessons about miserliness. The miser's eye (v. 10) repeats the same expression, translated "opinion" (v. 8). Note the curse of reversal of fortune in verse 9.

In his teaching on the good use of wealth (vv. 11-19), Ben Sira is no Christian ascetic, practicing evangelical poverty. Rather, he acknowledges the wealth and position of his disciples and counsels them on the best way to live in their conditions. First of all, enjoy wealth (v. 11, the theme). The motive, surprisingly, is the approach of death. The "covenant of Hades" (or Sheol, the Hebrew term) is the literal translation of the Hebrew text and refers to the decree of the date of one's death, determined of old by God. The wise will understand that there exists a time for everything. Ben Sira, here as elsewhere, shows his very traditional view of death (v. 16): no joys in any afterlife.

The lesson concludes in traditional ways. The proverb in verse 17 is found in Gen 2:16-17 and elsewhere. The teaching of verse 18, a lesson from nature and its application, is very similar to Homer's text in the *Iliad*. Indeed, Ben Sira may even have borrowed the text, aware of it from his own education. The handiwork that follows (v. 19) refers to one's work, but not to other goods—family, reputation, example. (See also Rev 14:13, where one's goods also follow.)

14:20–15:10 Associating with wisdom. The extended beatitude in 14:20-27 presents a series of verses extolling the pursuit and nearness of virtue, done in a style more Eastern than Western—giving a multiple impression rather than a clearly logical expression. The picture is evidently of a suitor who eventually gains the object of his desire, moving from pursuit (v. 22) to living with (v. 27). The symbols here will be resumed in 51:13-30.

To "meditate" (v. 20) implies not simply quiet prayer but pondering, working through the meanings of teachings, and examining proverbs and human experience in wisdom fashion (see also Psalm 1).

The author's teachings on good and evil men (15:1-10) open with a theme statement (v. 1) that clearly identifies wisdom with the observance of the law (joining 14:20-27 with this section). This identification is quite characteristic of Ben Sira's teaching. Calling wisdom both mother and bride (v. 2) does not convey any opposition but is simply a parallel expression typical of Hebrew poetry. The bread and water (v. 3) simply bespeak the nourishment coming from wisdom: understanding is like bread, and learning like life-giving water. As a result (vv. 4-6), wisdom never fails and gives an eternal reward (literally, "eternal name" or "reputation"). Note that the reward here is not eternal life. "Joy and gladness" recall for some scholars the vocabulary of the Greek Stoic philosophers, with which the author may have been familiar.

By contrast (vv. 7-8), the wicked never attain wisdom. The four terms here—worthless, haughty, impious, liars—are not four categories of sins but are Hebrew parallel expressions. Ben Sira concludes (vv. 9-10) by contrasting the sinner and the wise. Likewise, he identifies the wise with the pious, joining wisdom and true worship. The ability to offer praise is itself a gift from God.

Lessons on Sin and Sorrow (15:11–18:13)

15:11-20 Free will. This important teaching opens with negatives: God is not the source of human sin. This assertion contrasts with others in Sirach about God as the source of both evil and good (see 11:14; 16:26-28). The theme statement (v. 13) sets the tone, both as to the origin of evil and its power to reach the virtuous. Ben Sira's lesson on free will (vv. 14-15) is key for later theological developments. For him free will goes back to the beginning of creation and forms part of human nature. Thus good and evil cannot be forced on us. "Free choice" translates a Hebrew term understood by the rabbis as "inclination," either to good or evil; for the author the term has a neutral meaning (see also 21:11, "impulses").

The text closes with a set of assertions about God's wisdom and power (vv. 18-20). Even though powerful (v. 18), God does not command one to sin, nor does God even give the power to sin (v. 20). That we do have the power to sin is not considered by Ben Sira, nor does he give his readers a complete theology of free will.

16:1-14 Certainty of punishment. Ben Sira opens with examples taken from child-rearing (vv. 1-4). He basically teaches that it is better to have a few (or even no) pious children than many who are sinners. Sinners with many children might say, "Since I have children, I know that God has blessed me." The author denies this implication. In the Hebrew mind, the short life of sinners is their curse; it appears that Ben Sira believes that for some people there is no possibility of conversion. Verse 4, a short summary proverb, reshapes Prov 11:11.

A personal expression such as that in verse 5 is rare for Ben Sira; here it refers to verse 4 (see also 12:12). Also rare is his choice of various examples from the history of Israel (vv. 6-10), unknown in the book except for the historical section beginning in chapter 44. The examples he chooses are more allusions than direct historical commentary: verse 6 on the rebellion of Korah (see Num 16:35); the leaders (v. 7) appear as "giants" in other translations (see Gen 6:4); the Canaanites are the doomed people (v. 9), seemingly denied free will in Ben Sira's mind; and the six hundred thousand are the Israelites who murmured in the desert (see Num 11:21).

Despite his belief that the Canaanites were doomed (v. 9), Ben Sira holds out the possibility of mercy (vv. 11-14). God is completely impartial; the wicked simply refuse to repent (v. 12). Examples (vv. 13-14) conclude the section to prove his point.

16:15-21 Lack of escape. In this third set of reflections, the author follows his normal pattern: introduction, theme, application, conclusion. The "world of spirits," an unusual expression, means the world of living human beings, that is, creatures who live because of the spirit they have. The theme (vv. 16-17) reviews parts of the visible creation: heaven (sky); heaven of heavens (God's realm beyond the sky; see 1 Kgs 8:27); earth (the world as we know it); abyss (the area below the world, including both seas and the abode of the dead). That the mountains shake (v. 17) is typical of the presence of God (see Hab 3:6). For one to say that God does not know about him/her, since God is so great and he/she is so small, is to deny God's omnipotence; this is justly condemned as foolish (vv. 18-20).

16:22–17:12 Divine concern visible in creation. The introduction is in very solemn form, in the first person (vv. 22-23), similar to 39:12-35 and 42:15–43:33. Some scholars see here a major introduction to a much larger section of Sirach, running to 23:27.

The theme (vv. 24-25) is that all creation is ordered and has its place. This shows divine wisdom existing before creation (as in Prov 8:22-31). The examples (vv. 26-28) bring the reader through a catalogue of creation: stars (v. 26), plants (v. 27), animals (v. 28). The animals return to earth eventually (as in Ps 104:29); presumably, for Ben Sira humans have the same end.

A second theme statement (17:1) continues the series in nature, from stars to plants to animals and finally to human beings. This reflects the order of creation as given in Gen 1. "God's own image" (vv. 2-8) is explained in a series of simple explanations. After life we return to the earth (v. 2); there is a hierarchy of power over objects (vv. 3-4); we have the ability to think and the means to do so (v. 5). In verse 6 there is a shift about good and evil: we are given wisdom and can know how to distinguish between good and evil, as in Gen 3:22.

With this wisdom we are shown God's works (v. 7), and the ultimate purpose is praise, the acknowledgment of God's power coming from a contemplation of his works (see Rom 1:20-23, where pagans are condemned for not perceiving God through creation). Ben Sira concludes his review of creation with a reflection on the great gift of the law (vv. 9-11). Through Moses, God revealed his commands to Israel (vv. 10-11). In summary, Ben Sira gives his version of the two great commands of the law (v. 12): Avoid all evil, both toward God and toward fellow creatures.

17:13-19 The certainty of judgment. This small lesson continues the section on sin, judgment, repentance, and God's mercy begun in 15:11. Through his theme Ben Sira enunciates God's knowledge of all people (v. 13), and then follows up with reasons: Israel is the Lord's special portion, and God knows both good and bad actions. Possibly verse 14 is a common saying, since it does not fit the context too well here, but it recalls the apportioning of the nations among the deities (see Deut 32:8 and Dan 10:13 for this ancient theme). Also, Ben Sira rarely mentions Israel, apart from the historical section beginning in chapter 44.

The reward of the good (vv. 17-19) usually happens later; the wicked apparently are often rewarded immediately. Yet God does not act capriciously and has no favorites who are protected from the effects of their sin. For the sinner, however, there is always a way back (v. 19). This final verse may belong with verse

20, but in any case it is a sort of pivot around which the two sections revolve.

17:20–18:13 Sorrow and God's mercy. The theme (v. 20) continues with the exhortation to hate what God hates (that is, sin and unjust living). The dead cannot praise God from their place in the nether world, so praise God now. Ben Sira mentions the nether world, not to give a clear idea of a separate place for the dead, but to say that the individuals are truly dead.

The assurance of forgiveness begins with a psalm of praise in the format characteristic of other psalms. A major theme is God's incomparability (vv. 25-27): God has no peer, and human beings, by comparison, are "dust and ashes" (see Gen 18:27 for Abraham's view of himself).

The psalm continues with an assertion emphasizing the mercy of God, a characteristic of acts of praise. A similar form is the question about comparability: no one or nothing is like God (see 17:25). In the same vein, contrasts with human weakness point up the greatness of God (vv. 6-8). The question "What is man?" (v. 6) recalls Ps 8:5 and Job 7:17; the age of human life contrasts with the figure seventy or eighty of Ps 90:10. The conclusions (vv. 9-13) contain a surprising assertion about the universal mercy of God, mentioned here for the first time in the Old Testament, and contrasting even with a kind of predestination that has appeared previously in Sirach (16:9, for example). Also appearing here for the first time is the teaching that God's mercy is instructive, that is, one can learn of God's love and care through his acts of mercy toward oneself or others.

Counsels About Behavior (18:14–23:27)

18:14-29 Uses of caution. The few verses on charity (vv. 14-17) teach that one's charity should be complete, and exercised without harshness. The lessons (vv. 15-16) come from nature, and the conclusion is in the poetic and elevated style of literary proverbs.

The author then turns to a series of instructions on forethought (vv. 18-29). His practical advice on acting in good time resembles the gospel lesson on the man building a tower (Luke 14:28-30). A specific example of forethought is the question of vows (vv. 22-23; see also Eccl 5:2-6). A theologically important verse (v. 24) deals with the problem of evil in the world. For Ben Sira, God's face is hidden. This is an uncommon expression in Sirach and means that God allows evil to happen while not causing it. (To show one's face means to act with kindness.)

The formal conclusion (vv. 28-29) is that the wise are to make wisdom known and to praise her. This involves making their own gift of wisdom known, not hiding their light under a bushel (see Mark 4:21 and parallels). The wise will dispense proverbs (as in 8:8) for the benefit of others and the praise of God.

18:30–19:16 Self-control. After a theme verse (v. 30), Ben Sira offers traditional thinking on the punishment coming from lack of self-control in sexual matters: what causes pleasure will eventually cause pain. It is not quite clear how momentary pleasure will bring on poverty, other than through extravagant living (v. 32). Self-control in food and drink is urged; the apparent reason is simply the possible loss of control that would result from immoderate living—not a preferred condition for the wise. (The events in the story of the prodigal son, Luke 15:11-32, parallel the development here.)

Wine and women can also cause one to lose self-control (vv. 1-4). The theme in verse 1b is a type of ancient proverb, parallel to Prov 23:20-21. The text of verses 2-4 in the New American Bible places verse 4 before verse 3 to make a better flow. When one is giddy there is no self-control, and the wise person can no longer be thoughtful. Ben Sira appreciates merriment and enjoyment but wants to maintain control. "Contumacious desire" (v. 3), that is, reckless or stubborn desire, is an expression not used elsewhere in Sirach. From Ben Sira's perspective, desire also destroys in a kind of reversal, since desire for something else will eventually consume the one who desires. "Rottenness and worms" (v. 3) possibly refers to venereal diseases coming from sexual indulgence.

Self-control in speech (vv. 5-11) opens with a proverb and application (v. 5), and continues on to various lessons (vv. 6-8). Although Ben Sira values friendship, he knows where to be cautious (vv. 7-8). The comparisons in verses 10-11 both refer to the need to remove quickly what is lodged within.

All the sentences on rash judgment (vv. 12-16) have the same general thrust: if you do admonish, know that the person may be innocent, or if guilty, may take the admonition in good spirits. The exception is verse 15, which appears to be an extended commentary on the series, like a teacher's comment in class. The reference to law in the concluding summary (v. 16b) probably is meant generically, with no specific command in mind.

Making Right Distinctions (19:17–20:30)

19:17-26 True and false wisdom. The distinctive Torah wisdom of the Book of Sirach appears in the theme (v. 17); this may have been linked with verse 16b just above, on fulfillment of the law. If so, the method of using key words or ideas helps students to progress through the material of the book. There is also a false knowledge (vv. 18-21), and the author makes distinctions between knowledge, prudence, shrewdness, and intelligence in the righteous, and those same apparent qualities in sinners. The difference is that the truly wise also fear (that is, believe and worship) the Lord.

The word picture of one man (vv. 22-24) brings to mind the injunction of Isaiah: ". . . honors me with their lips alone, though their hearts are far from me" (Isa 29:13; also Matt 15:8). Common sense tells what a person truly is interiorly, despite appearance. Fools may be deceived, and they may also try to deceive (vv. 25-26). Compare this also with 13:25, where natural signs can tell what one truly is.

20:1-7 Speech and silence. The lessons (vv. 2-3) include a "better" proverb and a memorable simile on eunuchs. This latter probably came from court life, where eunuchs were kept to guard the women's quarters. The simile amuses in a bawdy way and speaks of one's results being frustrated.

The comparisons on silence point to paradoxes in life. They show modern readers more of Ben Sira's psychological sensitivity, mentioned elsewhere. The lesson of verse 6 echoes a general theme in Sirach about right order and the proper time to act. This mirrors God's order of the universe.

20:8-16 Paradoxes of reality. This third collection of sayings on proper distinctions (begun in 19:17) presents general paradoxes (vv. 8-11) and lessons on the wise and the fool (vv. 12-16).

In general, paradoxes by their very nature point to real life: it isn't everything it seems. The wise should learn that life is paradoxical at times and should delve below surface appearances. The concept of "wheel of fortune" is not biblical, but something like it comes through here: one day up, down the next (v. 10). This reflects the incompleteness and tentative nature of human life.

The next few verses present a series of contrasts between the wise and the fool. The two verses on the rogue (vv. 13-14) complete the lesson in verse 9 on gifts. The final verses (vv. 15-16) speak of the realization, known from ancient times, that for both good and evil their present lot in life can be reversed. The curse here comes to the generous fool: the recipients of his ill-gotten goods turn on him. (This lesson recalls 18:14-17.)

20:17-30 Proper and improper speech. The introduction (vv. 17-19) mentions the proverb itself, stock in trade of the wise, who also know when to use it; they have a sense of God's order and the right time to act. The basis for the judgment on lies (vv. 23-25) is that lies bring about their own punishment, entrapping liars in further lies. One's standing in the community is ruined thereby. Similarly, in verses 26-30 appropriate speech will help the wise to advance themselves, and prosperity will be their reward. The fact that doing evil results in shame and doing good results in prosperity points to the wise ordering by God of all reality.

21:1-10 Avoid sin. The religious tone here strikes the modern reader strangely, since it is a feature often absent from other wisdom writings. The theological introduction teaches that forgiveness is possible through prayer and reformation of life. Elsewhere Ben Sira mentions sacrifices and good acts as accomplishing the same end. But the lesson here contrasts with his teaching that the foolish (that is, the wicked) seem destined to live and die in their sins.

Ben Sira does not define or describe sin but only compares its effects on the sinner to the destructive effects of sharp and pointed objects (vv. 2-3). His teaching in verses 5-7 links the poor with those denied justice. As immediately above, the author offers no definition of the poor, yet he is conscious of them and their needs (see 4:1-8; 10:21-26; 13:18-22, for example).

In the comparisons of verses 8-10, the implication is always that unjust activities lead to death. "Tow" (v. 9) is an easily flammable fabric used to give shape to a torch and meant to be burned. The "smooth stones" (v. 10) are also pleasant to the just and may tempt them. Yet, note that Ben Sira also teaches that the end of *both* the just and sinners is the nether world without discrimination (see 14:16). The difference in reward lies either in the miserable end of sinners or in the extinction of their memory.

The Wise and the Fool (21:11–22:18)

21:11-18 Contrasts. The teaching of the theme (v. 11) is the "Torah wisdom" typical of the Book of Sirach: wisdom is not just secular skill or diplomacy. The "impulses" may refer to the Hebrew concept of the inborn tendency to good or evil that we all possess. (The Hebrew text of this chapter is unfortunately lacking, so the reference here cannot be precisely stated; yet the concept is known in late Old Testament and rabbinic writings.)

The comparisons (vv. 12-17) seem to be a series of disconnected proverbs, perhaps original to Ben Sira or his students, on the same subject. The concept of teachability appears here (v. 12) and in the next section (v. 18). Note also the automatic process of evil: evil committed comes down upon the evildoer eventually (vv. 27-28).

22:1-18 The lazy and the foolish. A very vivid comparison sets the theme for the discussion of various types of foolish behaviors (vv. 1-2, recalled in v. 13). Typically the author prescribes very rough treatment for daughters (see also 42:9-14 for a more extended but similar discussion). Women in general have value only as they help and support their father or husband. Verse 6 is a general conclusion, applicable to sons and daughters alike.

The difficulty (or impossibility) of teaching a fool forms the theme of verses 7-15 (as in 21:18-21). The obvious lesson of verses 7-8 is to avoid culpable fools; being with them is a waste of time. This approach contrasts strongly with the gospel teaching of love and care for all; even the ignorant deserve help. The basis for Ben Sira's harsh judgment lies in commonsense observation, not in theology. Verses 9-11 should be read together. The sense is not readily clear, but it need not be in order to engage the student in pondering reality. One conclusion is: Better to be dead than to be a fool.

Verses 14-15 are a riddle, a device rarely used in the Bible but a form of education and entertainment then and now. Here the riddle presents experience in a question form (v. 14) and applies the answers to the lesson. The last sentences (vv. 16-18) are a fitting conclusion and are of the same type: experience (v. 16) and application (v. 17). The comparison is well wrought, like the wall in the proverb. Verse 18 resumes verse 1 as a contrast and concludes verse 17.

22:19-26 Preserving friendship. The friendship here evidently exists between males, but it can be applied equally to females. Ben Sira made several contributions to the literature of friendship (see 6:5-17; 19:12-14; 37:1-6). The opening verses (vv. 19-20) follow the traditional pattern of experience and application; verses 21-22 show that reconciliation is possible. The gospel calls for a higher perfection, beyond mere human forgiveness. In his typical fashion (v. 23) Ben Sira puts forth self-interest as a motive. (Verse 24 seems out of place here.) The final sentences (vv. 25-26) change perspective. Treating friends well summarizes the section.

22:27–23:27 Prayer and teaching on sins of speech and lust. This remarkable section concludes the long series on discretion in behaviors begun in 18:14. The prayers here and elsewhere in the Book of Sirach are unusual, since such passages do not normally appear in wisdom literature; these are very personal and true to life, whereas other wisdom books are generally abstract and impersonal.

The questions in 22:27 and 23:2 come from the traditional language of praise; they expect the answer "God alone." They also imply that personally it is impossible to avoid sin (see also Ps 141:3). There are some echoes of original sin here, in its passions and lack of control. Petitions follow (vv. 1, 4-6), acknowledging a personal relationship with God, not just as an abstraction (the Creator of the universe) but as a personal Deity. Also, Ben Sira appears to be the first writer to address God as "Father." This also contrasts with Old Testament wisdom, which is more about God than addressed to God. (The only other prayer is in Prov 30:7-9.)

The "brazen look" (v. 5) and the lifting up of the eyes are not signs of pride but of lust (as in 26:9, where the woman acts wantonly).

In verses 7-15 we have an extensive instruction on this topic, with the kinds of distinctions students must learn. The theme (v. 8) also shows a sense of punishment for sin as being involved in the act itself. The "Holy Name" (vv. 9-10) is the divine name of God, gradually drawn out of common speech; in Ben Sira's time it was still apparently used by some in oaths.

Verses 11-12 offer similar lessons on the types of words. The motive is simply: it isn't done. The reason is that the wise are also the just, and thus the wise avoid all sins (as in v. 13).

The discussion on sins of lust (vv. 16-27) is impressive, contrasting men with women. The women, true to Ben Sira's form, come out badly. The theme (v. 16) typically compares lust to fire. What is atypical is the numerical form (introduced here for the first time in Sirach). In verses 19-21 Ben Sira deals with punishment. The answer to the question is: "God alone" can see. The one who questions in this way is a fool, and should have known the answer. The "eyes of the Lord" is an unusual figure, but they should be understood as searchlights blazing rather than as receivers of light or windows to the soul.

Women sinners (vv. 22-26) receive greater condemnation than men, since, according to Ben Sira, the first woman broke the law; even her children will suffer. This teaching should be contrasted with that of Jesus in the Gospel according to John, where the adulterous woman is forgiven and her male accusers leave shamefaced (John 8:1-11).

Verse 27 concludes the whole section, perhaps even the first half of the book according to some scholars. Some suggest that Ben Sira originally concluded his work here, emphasizing anew the connection between law and wisdom. One would expect the conclusion "nothing is better than wisdom" rather than "nothing is better than the fear of the Lord."

Attractive and Hateful Things (24:1–36:17)

24:1-31 A treatise on wisdom. After a brief introduction (vv. 1-2), Ben Sira reports an address of wisdom (vv. 3-21) and comments on wisdom and the law (vv. 22-31). Chapter 8 of the Book of Proverbs is a model for this entire section, connected with it in its use of both terms and themes. The introduction (vv. 1-2) opens the discourse speaking about wisdom; and then wisdom herself, in the heavenly council, speaks to her own people, the people of Israel, understood as assembled in Jerusalem.

The main feature of the section is the address of wisdom (vv. 3-21), which speaks of wisdom's origins being rooted in Israel, and offers an elaborate series of comparisons, closing with a summons to partake of wisdom. The origin of wisdom (vv. 3-7) is in God; wisdom is not a being separate in origin from God. The perspective is that wisdom is basically a word or utterance from God. The description of wisdom is poetic and should not be pressed for firm details. After her creation, wisdom scours the universe high (the vault of heaven) and low (the deep abyss), looking for a dwelling. That wisdom is feminine is a natural development from the feminine gender of the Hebrew *hokmah;* but this may also fulfill some need to see a female side to the Deity.

God commands (vv. 8-12) a residence in Israel. The subordination of wisdom to God is quite clear here: wisdom is God's gift to Israel. The comparisons (vv. 13-17) run the range of human senses (touch, sight, taste, smell) and refer to Israel both north (Lebanon) and south (Jericho). The perfumes recall the act of priestly anointing (Exod 30:23-24). Amid all this beauty (vv. 18-21), wisdom calls out, almost as a street vendor would. Verse 20 appears to contradict human experience—those who need to eat should be filled; but the focus here is on the increasing pleasure in partaking of wisdom.

The next section (vv. 22-31) associates wisdom with the law, a most important theme in the Book of Sirach. Verse 22 quotes Deut 33:4, showing that the Torah in particular, but also the rest of Scripture, commanded by God as Israel's inheritance, is true wisdom (see v. 8). Ben Sira is the major figure in Israel to equate law with wisdom and to draw forth its implications. More comparisons follow: of wisdom with rivers—here the seasons change from Pishon (winter) to Tigris (spring) to Jordan (summer) to Gihon (fall). The order of the universe is God's.

In verses 27-31 Ben Sira gives a major first-person account, nearly unique in biblical books (except, possibly, Jeremiah). The symbolism continues the water theme above. Ben

Sira's words are as vast as a sea. His meaning is like the prophecy of old, an interesting connection of wisdom teaching with the prophets. At root, both prophet and wise teacher interpret reality for the people under divine guidance.

25:1-11 Numerical proverbs. The movement in the introductory verse (v. 1) moves concentrically from brethren (probably Israelites) to neighbors (in town) to husband and wife (the family). This section is in the first person, an unusual occurrence. The next verse (v. 2) is not concentric but speaks of the persons who are the opposite of those in verse 1: the proud man disrupts harmony; the dissembler is lying, devious, and disrupts friendship; the lewd man destroys family love. There is also a contrast between being proud and a pauper; this is fundamentally against divine wisdom, since it violates the established order of life. The detail in this one verse demonstrates how these little proverbs could be examined from various viewpoints.

Verses 3-6 expand and explain verse 2; it appears possible that the preceding two verses are traditional, and Ben Sira adds verses 3-6 himself.

The numerical proverbs (vv. 7-10) have the usual form of one number followed by the next greater. Here there are actually ten persons mentioned. This is a mixed group, including both the fortunate (vv. 7b-8a) and the pious (v. 8b). The reference to the unequal animals is an application of Deut 22:10 to married life. There is an important conclusion in the case of the tenth man. Ben Sira places fear of the Lord as greater than wisdom (see v. 11). The teaching somewhat contradicts the praises of the uncreated wisdom of God living in Israel, known elsewhere in the book.

25:12–26:18 Lessons on good and evil women. This section has mixed passages on good and evil, and some scholars prefer to place them together, not separated as the present text shows. Possibly Ben Sira did so, but the oppositions in the passages point up significant contrasts.

In verses 12-25 there is no question that Ben Sira had a very negative view of women. Verses 12-14 offer a series of comparisons, including women as the source of evil for men. In verse 14 there is the typical form of experience (serpent) and application (the spite of women). In the comparisons in verses 15-17, women fare worse. Ben Sira has obviously given close psychological attention to men with family problems.

After an assertion of the greatness of evil in women (v. 18), the author turns to some assorted proverbs (vv. 19-22), probably collected, or at least adapted, by him. In verse 23 we have the first place outside Genesis where sin is ascribed to Eve. Elsewhere the origin of sin was regarded as the result of the cohabitation of evil heavenly beings with human women (Gen 6:1-4). Ben Sira's point of view is picked up by Paul.

The conclusion (vv. 24-25) teaches that a husband is to control his wife and should divorce an evil wife. The expression in Greek for divorce is a very violent one, unknown in other biblical books.

These verses (26:1-4) discuss the good wife in general, but only from the viewpoint of her husband. As in other passages in the book, women are not valued on their own. Numerical proverbs (vv. 5-6) are so framed to show that the jealous wife is worse than the preceding three evils.

Verses 7-12 present some of Ben Sira's most bitter comments. Note that he has no comparable section on evil husbands, though the evils of various classes of men are discussed widely in the book. The "bad wife" and the "drunken wife" are unknown figures elsewhere in the Old Testament. Ben Sira gives advice in verses 10-12 on watching over such a wife. The concluding verse (v. 12) is a surprisingly obscene statement, unique in biblical language (but parallel to the prophetic indictments in Ezek 23, among others).

The good wife appears again in verses 13-18, treated more precisely this time than in verses 1-4. Still, the focus is on the husband. To show the value Ben Sira puts on a smoothly running relationship, he compares a good wife to the temple, a very high blessing indeed; the columns recall the desert tabernacle in Exod 26. (Note that in some manuscripts a passage partly composed of quotations from Proverbs appears here. The exact numbering of the verses and their placement here and elsewhere in Sirach are a cause of confusion to modern readers.)

Sins and Sinners (26:19–28:6)

Verse 19 is a numerical proverb, possibly out of place here but connecting in some way with what follows concerning business dealings.

26:20–27:3 Business dealings. In verse 20 Ben Sira asserts the difficulty of maintaining justice in business transactions. The shopkeeper or merchant is rarely mentioned in the Old Testament; and there is very little in the Bible about fair business dealings, apart from the early prophets, such as Amos, Hosea, and Isaiah. Verses 1-3 continue this brief discussion.

Verses 4-10 constitute a digression of sorts, following up on the suggestion of the last few verses about honest living. These verses speak of testing to find one's real character. An important statement follows (v. 8) on the possibility of attaining justice. Comparisons (vv. 9-10) show the familiar experience-application method of proverbs.

Ben Sira continues with a lesson on sinful speech (vv. 11-15). Here the wise are associated with the pious, a viewpoint typical of Ben Sira. There are problems with the speech of the godless. It comes from a godless and disordered spirit, and is seen from the multiplicity of oaths (that is, offensive cursing). The result is bloodshed. This picture is perhaps taken from a tavern filled with evil men, whose drinking and wild behavior lead to quarrels, bloodshed, and even death.

Secrets and friendship (vv. 16-21) change the scene to relations among friends. Once secrets are betrayed (v. 16), nothing can repair the evil done; the experience of the bird released (v. 19) and the swift desert gazelle is applied here. This section closes with a summary statement (v. 21).

The following section on deceit (vv. 22-29) is nearly a standard model of Ben Sira's method: theme (vv. 22-23)—the deceitful person will ruin you; comparisons (vv. 24-27)—stones, a pit, a snare; conclusion (vv. 28-29). In the last two verses Ben Sira outlines a theory of retribution that undergirds his entire presentation, namely, that evil necessarily brings about its own kind of punishment. God is not the direct source of retribution; rather, the divine order has established the system (shown by the comparisons in verses 24-27).

27:30–28:7 Vengeance. The introductory theme (28:1) should be compared with Lev 19:17-18, which counsels one not to take revenge, basically the same message as Ben Sira's. Verses 1-2 involve a reversal of fortune, a typical form of divine punishment. Here the vengeful will have vengeance shown them (itself a reversal of the beatitudes of the Gospels). The next three verses (vv. 3-5) illustrate reversals. In verses 6-7 Ben Sira uses a form of education common in the Old Testament: remember! To do so, his students need a history of some sort, either personal or national, to reflect on.

28:8-11 Strife. This is an additional section with the usual plan: theme (avoid strife, v. 8a), motives (vv. 8b-9), applications based on experience (vv. 10-11). This lesson probably illustrates a common teaching method of the period.

28:12-26 Slander and an evil tongue. This section represents a development in Old Testament teaching, one not dealt with elsewhere, at least in such eloquent detail. Verses 12-16 speak of slander, and verses 17-26 of the evil tongue. Both sections open with lessons from nature and include observations on proper and improper speech.

Both life and death come from the mouth; the abuse of its power makes one "double-tongued" (v. 13), an expression occurring only in Sirach and once in Proverbs. In verse 15 virtuous women have been cast out (divorced) on account of slander of a "third tongue" (following the Greek text); thus they are cut off from their children and household.

The perspective is reversed in verses 18-23, turning from the one who slanders to the victims of evil speech. This involves a kind of living death, being cut off from one's own community, a state worse than physical death. As elsewhere in Sirach, there is no reference to eternal life here. The fire (vv. 22-23) is more a symbol of the consuming power of death than the fires of punishment. Verses 24-26 conclude with comparisons of the normal type in Sirach, and verse 26 concludes the entire lesson. The foe here is death rather than any human enemy.

Borrowing and Lending (29:1-28)

29:1-7 Lending. This is another model section beginning with a theme: to lend to a neighbor is to fulfill a precept of the law (as in Deut 15:8). The point of verses 2-3 apparently is not that lending itself is a good but that its purpose is to cement friendships. By working to restore the divine order of a world in which all have what they need to live, one participates in the creative act of God.

This generosity is contrasted (vv. 4-6) with borrowers who cannot or will not repay loans. The scenes are very true to life, as much so in ancient times as today. Repayment with curses is condemned partly because it violates God's order.

29:8-13 Generosity. The rationale for generosity to the poor here is "the precept," which probably does not refer to any single verse in the Bible but gives the sense of many passages (such as Lev 19:9-10). Ben Sira urges spending money rather than hoarding it idly; the only hoard should be almsgiving (v. 12). This thought recalls the gospel (Luke 12:32-34).

29:14-20 Surety. To go surety is to offer financial guarantees to someone involved in business transactions. The focus of these verses shifts from one who goes surety to one who benefits. The lesson urges prudence and caution, an attitude typical of Ben Sira and summarized in verse 20. The sinner (v. 19) is by definition unwise and does not know or admit his limits. As a result he fails. Interestingly, Proverbs counsels against surety (Prov 6:1-5 and elsewhere), but changed conditions in Ben Sira's time make it acceptable but risky.

29:21-28 Frugality. This lesson opens with what may already be a proverbial statement of life's basic needs: water, food, clothing, shelter. The following verses (vv. 22-23) expand on the theme but urge moderation with piety. The homeless form the subject of verses 24-27. Far better to have a poor home than be at another's beck and call, as a person would be who regularly ate at the expense of another and performed menial tasks in partial repayment. The last verse is a conclusion of sorts, but its connection with what preceded it is not too clear.

Causes of Joy and Sorrow (30:1–31:11)

The sections on children (30:1-13), health (30:14–31:2), and wealth (31:3-11) can be gathered under one heading, although they do not all contain the same format or lessons.

30:1-13 Children. Despite the term "children," Ben Sira undoubtedly refers only to sons, in view of his bias against women. Good care of children must involve discipline (vv. 1-3); this will give the father cause to rejoice in later years. A person's immortality is guaranteed in some way by survival in offspring; no indication of an afterlife is given. Verse 6 contrasts with strictures against vengeance in 27:30–28:7. What is intended here is probably a legal method of guaranteeing the rights of the deceased.

The results of spoiling children are discussed in verses 7-11. Principally, the son will be undisciplined, causing grief to himself and to his father. The wise man has attained wisdom partly through self-discipline, and should therefore help his children grow in it.

The passage closes with two commands: Start early and be severe. The motives include bringing disgrace on the father, much as the discussion on wives focused on the husband rather than on the wife.

30:14–31:2 Health. Here Ben Sira offers a "better" proverb and other comparisons. The "better" form may be an answer to the implied question, "What is better than a rich man with a wasted frame?" The author may even have used this method in his school. Note in verse 17 another expression to cover the issue of the afterlife, "an unending sleep," a poetic parallel to "death." Literally it reads "going down forever," a new expression in the Bible.

Verses 18-20 offer an object lesson on the evils of ill health. Ben Sira also ridicules the religious practice of tomb or idol offerings, which he either saw in his travels or more likely saw in the Israel of his day. Deut 26:14 condemned the practice, which was seen as idol worship. The verses from 30:21 to 31:2 are a remarkable passage on mental health, a positive mental attitude. Ben Sira recognized the close connection between worry or depression and physical illness.

The last three verses (30:25–31:2) are a bridge passage, linking cheerfulness at meals with a proper approach to making a living. Note that weight loss is regarded as a curse (31:1), not as the blessing it would mean today. (At this point the texts of several editions vary, due to a probable disruption of pages. The order in the Greek is 30:24; 33:16–36:11; then 30:25–33:15; finally, 36:12 and on.)

31:3-11 Wealth. Verses 3-4 are both on the pessimistic side, recalling the approach of Qoheleth: no rest for either the rich or the poor. Verses 5-7 concentrate on the pursuit of gold and all it stands for. At root, gold takes the place of wisdom, justice, or even

God; to pursue it is to go astray. Experience has shown this (v. 6); the wise profit from such lessons, but fools never learn (v. 7). That the pursuit of gold is a curse is seen from the traditional formula, "reversal of fortune"—that is, if you try to snare gold, it will snare you instead (v. 7b).

Verses 8-11 are happier in tone, congratulating the one fortunate enough to pass the test inflicted by gold (literally, "mammon" in Hebrew, a word used in Matt 6:24 and Luke 16:13). Verse 10b should be extended beyond this instance to a general praise of all those who overcome temptation. Verse 11 recounts traditional blessings—prosperity and a good name.

Temperance and Good Manners (31:12–32:13)

31:12-24 Eating. These verses are among the most colorful in Sirach, and at the same time the most secular. Certainly no biblical revelation is involved here; rather, the collected common sense of experience is all important. Recall that Ben Sira's audience was mainly wealthy young men, for whom banqueting was common; in earlier times, such meals were generally restricted to religious affairs or victories.

Verses 12-15 call for order, moderation, and sensitivity to the host. Verses 16-18 call for the same, the lesson being that this sort of meal is not principally designed for nourishment but for the event as a whole. Besides, moderation has other rewards, such as health and sound sleep (vv. 19-21). The reference to emptying the stomach may point to the recently introduced practice of inducing vomiting (v. 21). In any case, it is not mentioned elsewhere in the Bible. A general recommendation closes this section: moderation above all else.

The final two verses serve as an appendix (vv. 23-24), referring to generosity in giving a banquet. In this area moderation is not to be counseled.

31:25-31 Drinking wine. Here Ben Sira has collected various statements on the proper use of wine, opening with a theme (v. 25) and a comparison (v. 26). He acknowledges the joys of wine as a gift of God (v. 27). As expected, he also counsels moderation. The author continues this theme, counseling proper order—the essentially wise decision, imitating divine order (v. 28). Misuse of wine violates this order and brings its own recompense (vv. 29-30). Ben Sira concludes with a separate idea on the proper use of words when others are "merry," that is, light-hearted, but not drunk (v. 31).

32:1-13 Proper behavior at banquets. The preceding sections dealt with attending a banquet given by another; Ben Sira here offers wise counsel for one who hosts his own banquet or who acts as a master of ceremonies—a Greek custom in vogue in his day. His advice follows his usual pattern: be modest with guests (vv. 1-2); be moderate in speech and considerate (vv. 3-4). The types of banquets envisioned in chapters 31–32, together with other of Ben Sira's observations, demonstrate his familiarity with upper-class practices and possessions (carnelian, a semi-precious stone, gold, and emeralds, vv. 5-6).

Ben Sira's comments to the young (presumably his students) counsel modesty and brevity in speech and manner. As previously (vv. 5-6), he closes with a comparison (v. 10). The lesson concludes by shifting the focus from host to guest; evidently the banquet is not for self-indulgence but for socializing. Save self-indulgence for home (vv. 11-12).

The final verse is somewhat unexpected, given the secular tone of the last few lessons (vv. 30-32). Some scholars regard them as a conclusion to the entire section beginning with 24:1.

Stability under Law (32:14–33:6)

The tone changes abruptly here as Ben Sira introduces a solemn discourse on disciplined study and wisdom. He proceeds from a consideration of divine providence (32:14-24) and the trials coming to a fool (33:1-3) to preparations for study (33:4-6).

32:14-24 Providence of God. As before, the author begins with his theme, connecting the pursuit of wisdom with the pursuit of God (vv. 14-15). One of the tasks of the wise is to find divine order even in obscurity—basically to interpret confusing reality; this is the import of verse 16, "to draw forth a plan." Sinners/fools are compared with the wise (vv. 15b, 17, 18).

The wise do not act alone; rather, the pursuit of wisdom demands the help of the wise and the discipline they impose (vv. 18-19). Being on guard is the theme of verses 21-23, where the language recalls Deuteronomy (as in 4:9: be on your guard, keep the commandments, keep the law). Verse 24b recalls various psalm passages (for example, Ps 119:31).

33:1-6 The wise and the fool. These verses are a gathering of apparently independent statements that link the verses together through references to the law and wisdom, and the expected comparisons with natural objects: boat, cartwheel, stallion. Verse 3 refers to a "divine oracle," probably an allusion to the practice of Urim and Thummim (1 Sam 14:41-42) or to words of priestly or prophetic benediction.

33:7-15 Moral order of creation. This extremely important section sets out Ben Sira's views on the divine order undergirding all of reality.

The importance of days comes from divine designation of some of them as feast days—an indication of the author's interest in matters liturgical. The illustration shows a balance between ordinary and special days, and also serves the author's usual method of examples followed by applications to daily life. The examples continue (vv. 10-14) with comments about different kinds of persons: even though man (the Greek text has "Adam") was the first human, yet people differ due to God's free choice. Resuming an old theme, Ben Sira shows that each one has his own function or lot in life as part of God's order—a far cry from the contemporary Western concept of the freedom, progress, and change possible to everyone. The author chooses to examine the realities of life, not their possibilities.

A further example/application is given in verse 14—evil/good, death/life, sinners/just—and this is concluded with Ben Sira's general theory of order. Everything works in pairs, as opposites, with a balance between each one. A person should therefore expect both good and bad out of life. The reason why this must be so is God's choice. In Ben Sira's mind, there is nothing one can do about this—human freedom seems nearly ruled out, apart from the choice to sin. Job struggles against this order but finally abandons himself to divine providence.

33:16-18 Author's note. After the all-encompassing theory presented above, Ben Sira speaks in his own name, acknowledging that he has made some progress (v. 17), not for himself but for all, probably his students (v. 18). This section may have ended the book at one point in its growth.

33:19-22 Duties to property, servants. A solemn introduction (v. 19) opens this section, which first advises a man to be independent or self-sufficient, allowing nothing to have control over him. This freedom is to be the mark of the wise in all aspects of life. Without it, a person's "glory" (v. 23) is diminished, a concept expanded later in the book.

33:25-33 Slaves. A particular example of control is over slaves, which were regarded as human property, much like wives and even children. Two proverbial sentences open the lesson (vv. 25, 27); verse 26 seemed out of place where it was and hence appears after verse 27 in our version. On the other hand, this reality is to be tempered by consideration for the human dignity of the slave (vv. 30-32); this good treatment will even have benefits for the master (v. 33). Ben Sira did not call for the abolition of slaveholding, but at least he made suggestions for the betterment of the condition of slaves.

34:1-17 Grounds for future hope. This section offers two contrasting grounds for hope: dreams (vv. 1-8) offer false grounds, whereas the Lord alone is the true ground (vv. 9-17). This division itself further illustrates the law of opposites (33:7-15).

As usual, a theme statement begins Ben Sira's lesson (v. 1), followed by perhaps a traditional proverb (v. 2). His teaching continues with a series of observations. Verse 4 is in a traditional proverbial question, expecting the answer no. Verse 5 condemns not only reliance on dreams but also their superstitious use in divination and omens. Such use is blameworthy, since it attempts to control the future, which only God can do. The author concludes with the possibility of divine intervention (v. 6), such as happened to Joseph in Egypt (Gen 37:5-10), but cautions that experience shows how wrong reliance on dreams has been (v. 7). His conclusion (v. 8) shows that the written law is the real means of divine revelation, and the wise become so because of their fidelity to this law.

God's providence, on the other hand, offers sure ground for hope (vv. 9-17). Ben Sira's remarks on the advantages of travel for growth in wisdom are not completely apropos here (vv. 9-12) but seem to focus less on travel itself than on its inherent dangers and the consequent need of relying, not on one's own means, but on God. Ben Sira's travels are evident here and there in his book, but remarks on exotic places or practices do not form part of his teaching.

Verses 13-15 extol the happiness of the one who trusts in the Lord. Such a one has courage (v. 13) and never fears (v. 14). The question in verse 15 is unexpected; the answer is clear: the Lord alone. The final two verses are attributes of God, quite reminiscent of certain psalms. Here as elsewhere Ben Sira shows considerable freedom in gathering citations to support his teaching. This was and is a common method in biblical studies, though not recommended, because the shaping context of the words is lost. "Sparkle to the eyes" (v. 17) is an unusual expression but not completely unknown in the Greek Old Testament.

Worship of the Lord (34:18–36:17)

34:18-26 Unacceptable worship. Verse 18 is the theme statement, recalling numerous prophetic oracles (Hos 7:4; 8:13, etc.). The prophets called for worship from the heart, not just with outward forms. Ben Sira, in a very violent and pointed comparison, denounces gifts made at cost to the poor (v. 20). Alms, he continues, are life-giving for those who give them as well as for those who need them (v. 21). To deprive a laborer of wages is murder, apparently to be punished as such (v. 22).

The next three verses contrast senses of "gain" for the virtuous and the wicked. The only gain comes to the virtuous, despite outward or temporary gain (vv. 23-25). In verse 25 the reference is to ritual impurity (Num 19:11). The conclusion (v. 26) is in the same vein and ends with the usual teacher's question, expecting the answer "No one."

35:1-10 Acceptable worship. In these verses Ben Sira unites the concepts of law and worship. The theme verse (v. 1) sets out the argument. "Oblation" and "peace offering" refer to types of Hebrew sacrifices, as do "fine flour" and "sacrifice of praise" in verse 2 and "atonement" in verse 3. The author must have been speaking generically, for this listing of sacrifices does not exhaust the possibilities envisioned elsewhere in the Old Testament, even with the addition of "tithes" in verse 8.

The individual recommendations of verses 4-9 are in general wisdom form and may even be from other sources used by the author. Verse 10 concludes the lesson with the basic motive, given in the "timeless" form of proverbial motives: the Lord repays—an assertion true in the past, present, and future. Here as elsewhere the concept of personal reward for doing good is mentioned—charity for Ben Sira is not simply its own reward.

35:11-24 Divine justice and mercy. The prophetic strain in Sirach continues in this next lesson, begun in verses 11-12 with a theme statement and motive. The motive asserts justice and no favorites for God, possibly because there can be no favorites in a world already ordered by God's justice (that is, God's founding decree, establishing the right).

Against this static position Ben Sira places the compassion of God in the face of human sin and need (v. 13). "Orphan" and "widow" are traditional terms designating the most abandoned and helpless (v. 14). Like the blood of Abel calling for revenge (Gen 4:10) are the tears of widows.

In fact, the prayers of the lowly are heard (vv. 16-18). They pierce the clouds—not just atmospheric clouds but the attendants at God's throne (see Lam 3:44), or perhaps God's chariot (Ps 104:3); at the very least, God dwells far above the visible clouds. Delay in prayer, a perennial theme, does not form part of Ben Sira's teaching, apart from verses 18-23, where the concentration is on what God will do. The worshiper is to realize that it takes time to root out all evils and that God is constantly engaged in this task. Being merciless and proud is a mark of the same individuals for Ben Sira: those who rely on themselves alone are led to violence. God repays like with like but shows mercy to humble people (v. 23). Against whom or in what court God is to defend the people is not spelled out; the expression in verse 23 is traditional.

36:1-17 Prayer for Israel. This section both continues the previous chapter and concludes the section beginning with chapter 24. The prayers in Sirach are a distinctive feature of the book, in contrast particularly with other books of wisdom. It is difficult to be precise about the conditions that led to the composition of this psalm-like prayer. Since many psalms lack specific references, Ben Sira may have followed that style here. Thus this prayer would be applicable to Israel at all times—in the disturbed period of Ben Sira's life or later.

The oneness and universal power of God are strongly expressed in verses 1-4. As the one God, Yahweh exercises power over all the nations. The Israelites, beginning probably in the Babylonian Exile, began to proclaim God's holiness (the Hebrew term implies separation) by practicing holiness themselves; defeat of these enemies in the future will show God's power to Israel (v. 3).

Ben Sira moves from a plea for renewed wonders (v. 5) to more traditional and violent expressions (vv. 6-8). These latter are more marks of the author's depth of feeling than his actual literal curses of enemies. The "time" (v. 7) recalls the sense of order and proper time of Israel's wisdom teachers (as in Eccl 3:1-8).

The specific petitions for Israel look to a restoration of the ancient order. The people's origin in fact goes back to Jacob/Israel. The latter name has the traditional element *el*, meaning "God"; hence Israel is called by God's own name (v. 11). The plea to fill the temple with God's glory (v. 13) recalls the mournful period when the glory of God departed the temple (Ezek 11:23). If the glory returns, the prophets like Ezekiel will be proved true (vv. 14-15).

Ben Sira repeats his plea in conclusion, along with the motive that God is always and forever gracious to Israel (v. 16). If God answers, the result will be greater glory for God, to be acknowledged as eternal God by all the world (v. 17). This verse shows a blossoming interest in Israel's vocation as the prophet of the one God throughout the world, and may have encouraged a missionary outreach of the type that converted Galilee to Judaism shortly before Ben Sira's time.

Making Right Judgments (36:18–42:14)

These chapters comprise a major section dealing with advice on how to judge reality correctly. Social relationships (36:21–39:11) and good and evil things (39:12–42:14) are the two major divisions.

Social Relationships (36:18–39:11)

This division opens with a brief introduction (vv. 18-20) and then continues with the following subsections: choosing a wife (36:21-27), choosing friends (37:1-6), choosing advisors (37:7-15), speech of the wise (37:16-25), temperance (37:26-30), illness and physicians (38:1-15), mourning (38:16-23), craftsmen and the wise (38:14–39:11).

The introductory verses (18-20) are two proverbial statements of different types: experience (v. 18) and its applications (v. 19); and contrasts (v. 20). All deal in some way with the distinctions to follow.

36:21-27 Choosing a wife. This passage opens typically with a theme statement (v. 21) showing again Ben Sira's bias against women. Her good qualities (vv. 22-23) are not valued for themselves but make the husband fortunate. A good wife is a support to her husband and makes a home for him (vv. 24-25). This last observation is underscored with two rhetorical questions; the expected answer is "No one."

37:1-6 Choosing a friend. The lesson on true and false friends opens with a general introductory statement warning against false friends. Some so-called friends become enemies (v. 2). Ben Sira exclaims in lament for such an outcome, the only time this method of writing is employed in the book. (Some scholars see the "companion" of verse 3 as the "evil inclination" mentioned elsewhere in Sirach and rabbinic sources.) After a comparison of false with true (vv. 4-5), the author shifts the focus, summoning the person addressed to care for his friends in return.

37:7-15 Choosing advisors. This lesson parallels the previous one on friends, opening with distinctions between good and bad advisors (v. 7). The next verses recommend caution—a typical wisdom point of view, one characteristic of Ben Sira. The series of recommendations on whom to avoid appears to be traditional advice, perhaps collected in one spot (vv. 10-11). The wise should rely first on the godly (Ben Sira's association of wisdom, law, and piety) and then on their own best instincts (vv. 12-14). "Conscience" (v. 14) is "heart" in Hebrew, the seat not of emotion as with us, but of decision-making. The best advisor of all is God (v. 15), a fitting conclusion to this lesson.

37:16-25 The speech of the wise. Continuing the subject of proper choices, Ben Sira introduces a lesson on the wise and how they speak. The usual introductory statements (vv. 16-18) are of major importance, since Ben Sira places reason (word/thought/mind) at the center of human acts. By contrast, he might have asserted that human beings are under influences from outside (whether good or bad) or inside, such as the "evil influence" cited above, or even that we have no will at all. The emphasis, in fact, is on the tongue, whose baleful influence even over reason is easily understood.

Next comes a set of distinctions on time and counterfeit wisdom (vv. 19-25). Ben Sira teaches that wisdom is a gift for others—a "charism," in the theological language of the New Testament. Verse 23 seems out of place; it is only loosely connected to the preceding verse.

37:26-30 Temperance. In a few verses Ben Sira offers his students lessons about moderation in food and other delights. Discipline, balance (vv. 26-29), and learning from observation of others (v. 30) are all required in the wise.

38:1-15 Illness and physicians. Though perhaps intentionally joined to the previous discussion on food, this lesson has independent status. The author discusses the physician, the source of medical wisdom, and general ways to think about illness.

Ben Sira doubtless had to call his young hearers to respect physicians, whose profession is mentioned rarely in the Old Testament, and then only in the late period. Under the influence of Greek culture, medicine grew in stature, and its practitioners developed from healers to those who would diagnose and treat illness. The physician draws wisdom (that is, skill) from God, and is justly to be esteemed (vv. 1-3).

Medical skill comes from wise use of the gifts of God on earth; the reference to Exod 15:25 is proof enough (vv. 4-5). The physician thus participates in God's own work of establishing (or re-establishing) order (vv. 7-8). Ben Sira counsels a regimen to effect cures: pray quickly (v. 9), repent of evil (v. 10), sacrifice generously (v. 11). Once in the proper disposition, turn to the physician (vv. 12-13). Note that the shift is from sacred to secular, since the source of medical skill is God (vv. 14-15).

38:16-23 Mourning. Ben Sira introduces here a topic almost new to the Old Testament. In earlier times laments for the dead were certainly practiced, but his explanation, cautions, and sensitive psychological tone are distinctive. For Ben Sira, it appears that custom and civility rather than prayer for the dead or even with survivors were uppermost in his mind (vv. 16-17). The period of mourning was generally seven days (Gen 50:10; also Sir 22:12), probably more for close relatives than for friends. Ben Sira advises a brief time and gives a psychological motive (vv. 18-19).

In the rest of this short lesson the author counsels attention to right living and one's own end (vv. 20-22). No hope of afterlife exists for Ben Sira, apart from God's judgment near or at death. Verse 23 summarizes the passage. The term "soul" represents, not our concept of the composite of body and soul, but the Hebrew *nefesh*, a word implying personality or individuality. By the time of Ben Sira, *nefesh* may have begun to acquire a more philosophical sense.

38:24–39:11 Craftsmen and the wise. This section either closes the unit on social relationships (36:21–39:11) or begins a new section, the third added by Ben Sira to his earlier work. If the latter, the author is opening with a general description of his own lifework.

Ben Sira here compares various skilled occupations (vv. 25-34) with that of the scribe (39:1-11). The scribe in question (v. 24) is a legal scholar, not simply a person who knows how to read and write. The farmer (vv. 25-26), engraver (v. 27), blacksmith (v. 28), and potter (vv. 29-30) all have practical wisdom in the sense of skill, with its attention to practical order, balance, and beauty. Their work is important in its own way (vv. 31-32) and a gift of God (v. 34), but the great work of decision-making at the top is in the hands of others (v. 33).

With a rare exclamation, Ben Sira extols the difference between the intellectual work of scholars and the manual labor of the craftsmen (as 38:24). Despite his reverence for the priesthood and the accolades given to other professions, such as physicians, this section (vv. 1-11) places the legal scholar on the highest level. The scribe is a conservator of ancient wisdom, personally wise, knowing the deeper levels of meaning of proverbs (v. 2). As a result, the scribe enjoys a good reputation among the world's great. The sources of wisdom are in experience (travel, v. 5), but most especially in personal holiness—the scribe prays to be emptied of sins, and as a result is filled with divine wisdom (vv. 6-7).

Ben Sira appears to offer his pupils reasons for the difficult pursuit of wisdom in verses 8-11—in this case public renown. Self-interest predominates here: wisdom sought not for its own sake but for an eternal memory. Christians would more likely place their trust in divine providence, rejoicing in the utterance given them and in giving glory to God alone.

Note the repeat of the traditional divisions within the biblical canon: law (v. 1a), prophets (v. 1b), writings (v. 2); this appeared previously in the foreword. Some scholars see a developing interest in oral tradition (v. 2) alongside the written word, though this opinion is hard to sustain.

Good and Evil Things (39:12–42:14)

The author begins a new section here, the second main division of 36:18–42:14 on proper discrimination.

39:12-35 A psalm of praise. The content of this psalm is similar to that of 16:24–17:14, but the form is typical of certain psalms: an invitation to prayer (vv. 13-15), motives (vv. 16-31), conclusion (vv. 32-35). The invitation, addressed to disciples ("children"), employs sense images, a style foreign to traditional psalms (petals of roses, odors of the lily, blossoms, harp music).

A theological assertion gives the basic motive (v. 16): the perfection of God's works and of divine providence. This assertion finds proof in divine acts (creation, v. 17). The truly wise should know how God acts and, like God, find nothing unexpected. The theological picture that Ben Sira paints is simplistic: the good are blessed at the right time by good things, whereas the evil are cursed by things both good and evil. It appears that death-dealing events or objects never afflict the good and that the virtuous never suffer. The lesson learned in Job was not learned by the author.

A subsidiary consideration is the proper time (vv. 29, 34). This ordering of the systems of the universe should be pondered by the wise, for it is at the heart of the revelation of God's orderly justice. This psalm-like section concludes by repeating the opening exhortation to praise, that is, to acknowledge publicly God's goodness. To "bless the name" (v. 35) is a late Hebrew expression meaning to proclaim God as good (as in Pss 96:2; 103:1; 1 Chr 23:13).

40:1-11 Suffering. In these verses Ben Sira expands on the evils coming to the wicked, sketched in 39:28-31. This brief section, like several others, has a simple structure: introduction (v. 1a), examples (vv. 1b-7), applications (vv. 8-11). This simple format models the activity of anyone seeking wisdom: observe the realities in faith and then draw conclusions for right living.

The Sage does not discuss why God should allot anxiety to human life; he only observes its universality. "Sons of men" in Hebrew may be translated as "children of Adam" (v. 1a); this is followed by an ambiguous reference to Eve ("mother of all the living"), based on Gen 3:20. The previous verse in Genesis makes it clear that Mother Earth is intended here.

Ben Sira shows his usual psychological insight in the description he gives of human fears, even internalized into nightmares (vv. 2-5). He also partially answers the complaint that the wicked prosper—as king (v. 3) or even priest (v. 4—the Hebrew refers to the priestly turban); retribution will come to them eventually. They share common human anxieties. Even animals are troubled (v. 8).

The issue of predestination is not far from Ben Sira's discussion here or in 39:25. It appears that the author holds that the evil are simply so, "of earth," with no hope of repentance; the good, too, are virtuous throughout, "from above." In holding this, Ben Sira is close to some strains of Old Testament thinking. Despite that, the possibility of repentance for the wicked, as well as of sin in the just, plays a part in other strains of biblical thinking, in the Old Testament and certainly in the New.

40:12-17 What is enduring and what is passing. The next few verses present mainly some comparisons drawn from nature— the traditional contemplative stance of the wise person. Such a person will learn that the evil will ultimately suffer punishment, and the good will endure. No matter how powerful and intimidating evil seems, God's plan will triumph. The wise should come to learn this. The comparisons in verse 15 recall the gospel parable of the sower (Matt 13:3 and parallels).

40:17b-27 Joys of life. These verses are loosely connected with what precedes. They give us some insight into Ben Sira's classroom. The Sage would present a riddle (following v. 17b): wealth and wages can make life sweet; what is better than either? This would provoke several answers. Those that the author chose here have no inherent similarity among them. They rather demonstrate flashes of insight, emphasizing the unexpected (v. 17) or the ordinary (vv. 21, 22). A particularly brilliant answer is found in verse 24: "charity that rescues," that is, in times of stress having helpers is truly good, but an act of charity that relieves the root causes of the stress is better.

Verses 26b-27 appear to be a type of gloss or commentary on verse 26a. Ben Sira has previously extolled the fear of the Lord; such references characterize the entire book. The "canopy" of verse 27 appears to derive from Isa 4:6 ("his glory will be a shelter"; the Hebrew terms for "shelter" and "canopy" are related).

40:28-30 Begging, an evil in life. A life of beggary is one of the evils of life, though the reason for its position here is unclear. Note the refinement of Ben Sira's psychological insight. Also, he follows in the footsteps of Israel's prophets who counseled that outward appearances (particularly of religion) should match inward realities.

41:1-4 Death. Ben Sira continues to reflect on good and evil, and here addresses death dramatically. Death is bitter for the strong but welcome for the weak. The seeker after wisdom should ponder the one at peace and see not contentment but a shadow cast over him by death. Though bitter, death can be welcome—the wise should see this as well. The wise (vv. 3-4) will know God's decree in Gen 3:19: death comes to all. Life does not exist after death; only Sheol, the abode of the dead, remains (v. 4).

41:5-13 Memorials. The previous discussion leads Ben Sira to consider the only remnants of the good and evil—children and reputation. While it is often true that evil parents can create a situation in which children will develop badly, modern readers have to reject the author's blanket statements. Neither do all wicked parents have evil children, nor do wicked offspring have evil parents. Free will doubtless has a role to play.

The woe in verse 8 occurs only here and in 2:12-14. Ben Sira does not draw out the theological implications of the verse. Is the man sinful because he forsakes the law (an expression of Deuteronomic origin), or is he sinful by nature and thus turns from the law? The author closes with a summary statement, noteworthy for its use of the Hebrew term *tohu,* "nought" or "nothingness," a rare word, used in Gen 1:2 ("wasteland") to describe the nothingness existing before creation.

A good name (vv. 11-13) by contrast endures, apparently forever. One may also conclude that virtuous children attest to the virtue of their parents.

41:14–42:8 True and false shame. This section continues the series of observations on good and evil things begun in 39:12. The author focuses on shame, having mentioned the subject in 4:21. After his introduction (vv. 14-17), the text lists evil acts for which one should truly be ashamed (vv. 18-24), and then good and lawful acts for which one should never be ashamed (42:1-8).

The schoolroom atmosphere of Ben Sira's day comes through clearly in these verses. The riddles of 40:17-26 called for student answers; so too the objects of shame before certain individuals seem to call for wise responses. Ben Sira has treated of nearly all the subjects previously (9:8 on lust; 18:44 on harsh words), and the topics here require no lofty insight to be understood. The teaching of Jesus in the gospels follows similar paths (for example, Luke 6:34 on lending).

The motive (v. 24) comes as a surprise: human respect. Doubtless Ben Sira had in mind observance of God's law, which would ultimately bring esteem of the highest type.

Other biblical versions based on the Greek text will show significant differences in the text of verses 15-17.

Ben Sira holds out another kind of human respect in 42:1, here influencing toward sin. Human esteem has its value in enforcing public morality, but the company of the wicked can work just the opposite. The person of integrity will do what is right, specified in verses 2-8.

The first series of acts (vv. 3-5a) focuses on business dealings. Sensitivity about honest dealing (v. 4) took on a special refinement in Israel; prophets voiced similar concerns (for example, Hos 12:8).

The second series focuses on managing one's household. Again, the advice comes from experience and common sense. The chastisement of the aged (v. 8) refers to sexual impropriety in the elderly; the good (read "wise") manager will hold them accountable for their acts as long as they form part of the household. As before, the motive is recognition by others as being wise, one of the chief characteristics of which is caution and discretion.

42:9-14 Wickedness of women. In these few verses the author gives his most extensive treatment of daughters (see also 7:24-25 and 22:3b-5). Nowhere else in the Old Testament are one's daughters discussed as a topic by itself. As elsewhere in the book, Ben Sira treats women from a man's bias. Daughters are usually compared unfavorably with sons; they are a burden and a source of anxiety and potential shame. Since daughters could be a source of economic benefit, the wise father would guard them (v. 9). Women, judged to be foolish, could not have sense enough to preserve themselves from sexual entanglements, so it fell to the father to provide all needed safeguards (vv. 10-12).

Ben Sira concludes this difficult section with two proverbs, possibly not original with him. Verse 14 is particularly difficult for modern readers. Many translators read the text as: "Better a man's evil than a woman's goodness."

Praise of the Lord in Nature (42:15–43:35)

For many scholars the section 42:15–50:24 marks the last great division of the Book of Sirach. In the outline followed here, 42:15–43:35 forms the ninth major section of the book. The passage is psalm-like, similar to others (1:1-10; 24:1-22). This poem has three clear divisions: introduction (42:15-25), catalogue of wonders (43:1-27), conclusion (43:15-25).

Ben Sira concludes his book with the hymn in this section and follows with a lengthy praise of Israel's heroes (44:1–50:29). The two together form an elaborate doxology to his collection of wise teachings. As such, the section serves an educational purpose similar to his use of proverbs: observe the realities of life and draw conclusions for wise living.

Verse 15a introduces the hymn, and the following verses (15b-22) speak of the origin of God's works and the impossibility of describing them all—not even the "holy ones" (v. 17) can (an ancient expression for God's attendants). "Depths" (v. 18) translates the Hebrew term for the region under the visible world; it and the human heart are symbols of impenetrable realities. The Creator alone can understand them. Verses 23-25 add a series of observations on the goodness and order of creation. Ben Sira does not mean to teach that there will never be an end to the world (v. 24).

43:1-27 Catalogue of wonders. This listing treats the sky and sun (vv. 1-5), heavenly phenomena (vv. 6-12), weather (vv. 13-23), and the sea (vv. 24-26).

The Hebrew text is difficult in the first several verses, and translations differ considerably. The language of praise used here is typical of psalms: exclamations (v. 2), questions expecting a negative answer (v. 3), assertions of greatness (v. 5). Ben Sira's poetic view of the sun drawn across the sky by horses is a commonplace idea in the ancient Near East (v. 5).

The value of the moon, besides its beauty, is that it guarantees the observance of festivals on their proper days; for Israel (and even for many in the modern world) both the feast and its fixed day were of equal value. In verse 8 we have an echo of two Hebrew words, *yerah* (moon/month) and *hodesh* (new moon/month). The poetic view of the relationship between stars and bad weather (v. 10) is clear: the stars must protect against bad weather, since when they appear, weather is good; should they "relax their vigils," bad weather results. God's bow (v. 12) is likewise an ancient poetic view of the rainbow (see 9:13).

Similar to Job 38 is Ben Sira's treatment of weather phenomena (vv. 13-23). The storm serves as an instrument of God's wrath: the arrows from his bow are lightning (v. 13; see Ps 29). The ancient Canaanites viewed the storm as a god; by Ben Sira's day, Israel knew that storms received their power from God (v. 15), at God's command (vv. 16-17).

The images of cold (vv. 18-21) contrast strongly with the heat of verse 22—both phenomena are known in Israel. The dew (v. 23) was regarded as a great blessing in a land of scant rainfall (see Deut 33:28; Ps 133:3; Isa 18:4). Israel's awe in face of the sea is evident in verses 24-26. It is noteworthy that the ancient idea of rivalry between the sea with its creatures and God had disappeared by Ben Sira's time. Here God calms the deep;

God alone is the maker of all its exotic inhabitants.

The final verse (v. 27) appears to conclude this catalogue by asserting that God alone is in control of all the great phenomena, using them to carry out the divine will.

43:28-35 Conclusion. Ben Sira concludes by resuming his former theme of the impossibility of knowing God through and through. "He is all in all" does not express any supposed pantheistic notions, as some scholars have held. It seems rather an expression of praise and wonder at the Creator of all (as in verse 35). The piety of our author is evident: his contemplation of the wonders of creation does not lead him to become a scientist, but instead to give praise. The result of this is the gift of wisdom.

Praise of Israel's Ancestors (44:1–50:29)

Just as the previous section both praises God and shows disciples how to grow in wisdom, so this last section praises God for his greatness toward Israel and leads disciples through a sort of gallery of heroes, holding them up for emulation. We do not have a history here in the sense of a connected series of causes and effects. Consequently, Ben Sira felt free to omit details or even to reshape events for his own purposes.

44:1-15 Introduction. "Let us now praise famous men" is the traditional wording of verse 1. The Hebrew is in the singular and focuses on the piety (Hebrew *hesed*) of Israel's ancestors. "Portion" (v. 2) is a traditional expression recalling the early belief that each deity had his/her own people. Israel was the Lord's portion among all others (see 17:14; also Deut 32:9; Jer 10:16). The twelve types of heroes, probably all Israelites, strangely do not include priests. In verse 4 the "spikes" of the wise makers of epigrams refers to the pointed quality of their words (as in Eccl 12:11), which encourage reflection.

Verse 9 seems to be a general comment on the wicked (as in 10:17). Verses 8 and 10 are joined and repeat Ben Sira's views on the long memory and numerous children of the just.

44:16-23 Early patriarchs. This section begins, not with Adam, but with Enoch. Just why Adam is omitted is not clear. The Enoch verse is enclosed in brackets to show its doubtful place; many say it is an expansion of 49:14. That Enoch did not die but was simply taken up became a source of much speculation in late Old Testament times.

Ben Sira's interest in the preservation of Israel through divine providence is clear in the verses that follow: Noah preserved the race (v. 17), Abraham's (v. 21) and Isaac's (v. 22) descendants. In addition to God's plan, the virtue of the patriarchs was rewarded in the usual way, with numerous offspring. Each of them received signs and had an agreement or covenant with God. A close check of the corresponding passages in Genesis will show the freedom Ben Sira employed in shifting events for the sake of his argument. He also quoted Ps 72:8 in verse 21. The references here to sea and river, at least in the mind of the psalmist, were to the great sea surrounding the land. No specific sea or river (the poetic counterpart of sea) should be looked for, even less a divine promise concerning modern boundaries for the state of Israel.

God's hand in Israel's history is seen in the division of the land and its allotment. That this system no longer existed in Ben Sira's day seems of no concern.

45:1-26 Moses, Aaron, Phinehas. Ben Sira begins this section with Moses, not with Joseph, as one might expect. The omission seems to be corrected in 49:15. Moses is here regarded as a worker of wonders, endowed with divine power. After beholding God face to face, Moses hands on the law, the truest wisdom. Elsewhere Ben Sira has made a close identification of wisdom with the law (see 19:17 and 32:14-16). The basis of God's choice of Moses appears to be his natural but God-given endowments (v. 4).

The treatment of Aaron is surprising in its length (vv. 6-22) and in its detailed descriptions. The attention given by Ben Sira to the priesthood, and to the cult in particular, has been taken as proof of his being a priest. True or not, the author's interest seems to be more in the presence of God to Israel, along with Israel's proper response in worship. The Lord deserves the best and most magnificent worship possible.

Ben Sira points to the single priesthood (v. 7), probably with an eye to the pre-exilic struggles between two priestly branches (Aaron and Zadok). The vestments listed in verses 8-13 are not exactly described (Ben Sira confuses the meaning of ephod); rather, the author gives a poetic evocation of their glory.

The mention of colors (vv. 10-11) is quite rare in this book, indeed throughout the Old Testament.

Similarly, the sacrifices listed in verses 14-17 are only loosely described. Following his usual practice, Ben Sira mentions several covenants (vv. 15 and 24-25). These do not conform exactly to the details of other Old Testament books, where relationships between God and Israel or with individuals are called by various names. Ben Sira has subsumed all these into a single system of covenants—an apt theological construction on his part.

A further element of the ensemble is the focus on permanence: Aaron's priesthood (v. 7), use of vestments (v. 13), Aaronic covenant (v. 15). God's commitment to Israel thus becomes a further motive for his praise. The persistence of the liturgy is a symbol of this commitment.

The zeal of Phinehas (Num 25) had become legendary (see, for example, Ps 106:30-31, where his merit is said to endure forever). Ben Sira, true to his previous thinking, equates Phinehas's act with sacrificial atonement (see 3:3). As a grandson of Aaron, ("third of his line," v. 23), he was already in the priestly line. The author restates the outcome of his zeal—a recommitment to the priesthood (see Num 25:12-13). The office of high priest, however, developed only after the Exile.

The final verse appears to be addressed to the priests of Ben Sira's day, though on what occasion is unclear. His message to them comes from his concern to preserve the cult, guaranteed in a way more wondrous than the covenant with David, which at that time was in fact not being realized, since there was no Davidic king.

46:1-20 Joshua, Caleb, Judges, and Samuel. This brief chapter is clearly divided into accounts of Joshua (vv. 1-6), Caleb (vv. 7-10), the judges (vv. 11-12), and Samuel (vv. 13-20). As previously, Ben Sira has shaped and understood the events of Israel's past from his own perspective: God continues the choice of Israel, the glory given to Israel thereby, manifested in the continuing glory of the cult and in the wisdom given to Israel; lessons for contemporary Israel in the piety of her ancient heroes in the face of foreign oppressors.

Joshua appears here as a prophet, a role not given him elsewhere, since he was chiefly a military leader. As a successor of Moses, he would have to be, in Ben Sira's mind, his successor in all ways, including the prophetic office. Moses, in fact, is styled a prophet only in texts coming from the northern kingdom, where the title of prophet was used more widely than in the south (see Hos 12:14; Deut 34:10).

Joshua as commander of Israel's armies is found in verse 2 (the battle at Ai, Josh 8:18-19) and in verses 4-6 (the battle at Gibeon, Josh 10:12-14). "Most High God" (v. 5) is an ancient designation (*El Elyon*) found here in Sirach for the first time and repeated three times in the rest of the book. In these uses Ben Sira may be consciously adopting a more elevated, liturgical style to correspond to his subject matter.

Joshua and Caleb are linked in the next few verses as the only two spared from the desert wanderings (Num 26:65). The "summits of the land" (v. 9) refers to the hills around Hebron in southern Judah, where the Caleb tribe settled.

In the case of the judges, their record of devotion is not entirely stainless. Possibly Ben Sira refers (v. 11) to Gideon and Samson, not exactly models of piety. "May their memory . . ." becomes a traditional rabbinic expression of regard for the deceased. Verse 12 clearly is not a prayer for the judges themselves to rise from the dead (see his wish for prophets in 49:10); this would run counter to all of Ben Sira's thinking. The prayer is for a renewal of their spirit in the author's age. Despite that, may we not see here a dawning hope of resurrection, prominent in other late Old Testament writings?

Ben Sira includes a quiet wordplay on the name Samuel and the term "dedicated," a feature evident only in the Hebrew. Since Samuel was so complex a figure, later authors see him as prophet, the last of the judges, and a priest. These three roles are developed: judge (v. 14), prophet (vv. 15, 20), priest (v. 16). In addition, Samuel exercised some political power (anointing Saul and David as kings, v. 13b).

Ben Sira's reluctance to paint too dark a picture of parts of Israel's past leads him to mention Saul only indirectly (prince, vv. 13, 19; king, v. 20).

47:1-24a Nathan, David, Solomon. In these verses appear Nathan (v. 1), David (vv.

2-11), and Solomon (vv. 12-24a), the latter two having accounts of the same relative length, but both somewhat sanitized.

The inclusion of Nathan as part of the succession of prophets (Moses, Joshua, Samuel) is a contribution made by Ben Sira to our thinking. The account of David's young life is colored by poetry: parallels between lions and kids, bears and lambs. The account of his military prowess is based on 2 Samuel, and his interest in liturgy on 1 Chronicles. The latter work is notorious for its whitewash of David's career, a decision taken by Ben Sira as well.

"The might of his people" (v. 5) is literally "horn of his people," a traditional expression for power, similar to the power exercised by animals through their horns. Notice also the twofold mention of *El Elyon* ("Most High God" vv. 5, 8). The might of the Philistines (v. 7) had been shattered indeed, but the Roman conquerors of Israel adopted their name for occupied Israel, Palestine.

A possible play on Solomon's name ("man of peace") occurs in verse 13. The peace characteristic of his reign allowed him the leisure to pursue the building of the temple (v. 13), wisdom (vv. 14-17), and commerce (v. 18). He shared a name, "beloved of Yah[weh]" (Jedid-iah) with the whole people of Israel (in Jer 11:15).

The dark cloud that began to overshadow Israel's life in the career of Saul (not mentioned by name, but see 46:19-20) and of David (his sins, 47:11) is quite apparent in Solomon's career (vv. 19-21). His sin, at least in Ben Sira's view, consisted in allowing self-control to slip away in favor of control over him by women. The author has already spoken critically against this (see 9:2; 25:12). Despite sin, God's promise remains—an assertion made here clearly (v. 22). Note also the principle useful for interpreting biblical passages: God does not "permit even one of his promises to fail."

Many translations include both Rehoboam, Solomon's son, and Jeroboam, the first king of the independent northern kingdom. Since the latter should not be remembered (v. 23), some translations omit mention of him. "Expansive in folly" is a wordplay on Rehoboam's name.

47:24b-48:16 Elijah and Elisha. The growth of sin, mentioned previously, continues in ominous counterpoint to the accounts of Israel's heroes. The connection of Elijah with fire (vv. 1, 3, 9) is a brilliant poetic accommodation. This prophet's powers over nature (restricting rain, 1 Kgs 17) reinforces his reputation: because of him the sun scorched the earth and broke the staff on which Israel relied—abundant grain (v. 2). He had powers to raise to life (v. 5) or to cause death (v. 6). So God-like in many ways was he that he did not die a human death but was taken up (like Enoch, 44:16). This event became the source of much speculation in Elijah's case too; Mal 3:23 records it. The allusion here to the text of Malachi shows that that book was known to Ben Sira (see the mention of all the twelve prophets in 49:10).

The author includes some small measure of messianic hope in 48:10: "to re-establish the tribes of Jacob." Despite his interest in the continuation of God's promises, he knew from the facts of daily life that the Davidic monarchy had ceased and that the old tribal organization was long out of use.

If Elijah was a wonderworker, his successor Elisha was even more so. Nonetheless, the wonders worked through him had little effect on righteous living in the northern kingdom. As a result, the people of Israel were destroyed. Ben Sira exaggerates for effect the totality of the destruction and scattering; probably only a small percentage of Israel was taken away and resettled in a few specific locations in the Assyrian domains. Judah's territories were also annexed by Assyria, and what was left to the Davidic kings was tiny indeed (v. 15).

48:17-23 Hezekiah and Isaiah. Ben Sira gives his readers another wordplay in verses 17 and 22: the Hebrew for "to strengthen, hold fast" is at the root of the name Hezekiah. For the people of subsequent centuries as well as for Ben Sira, the salvation of Jerusalem from Sennacherib's attack stood as the most striking proof of God's faithfulness to the Davidic kings. Ben Sira modifies the tradition to include the whole people of Jerusalem at prayer, whereas in 2 Kgs 19 it is Hezekiah alone.

Isaiah appears here mainly on account of his deeds, not his prophetic speeches. Modern scholarship attributes to an unnamed prophet or prophets chapters 40–66 of Isaiah. Ben Sira's view is that prophecy involved foretelling the events of the Exile (vv. 24-25). His reference to these chapters demonstrates that they were known under Isaiah's name in Ben Sira's time.

49:1-10 Josiah and the prophets. Ben Sira gives us abundant proof of his regard for Josiah, appealing to smell (incense), taste (honey), and hearing (music). The reason for Josiah's renown is found in his thoroughgoing piety. Note that the author connects himself and his contemporaries with their ancestors: "our betrayals" rather than "their betrayals" (v. 2). He then turns to a traditional restatement of the causes of Judah's destruction (vv. 4-7): the kings—and the people—turned from God's law. As in other places in the book, we find here the implication "they should have known better." As a result, their foolishness (lack of wisdom and foresight) is proved, and the punishment is a foregone conclusion.

Ben Sira includes Jeremiah, even quoting Jer 1:5, 10, and Ezekiel, whose chariot became a feature of later rabbinic speculation. The reference to Job is customary, as in Jas 5:11; both Ben Sira and the apostle James have neglected the anger and impatience of Job in the main chapters of the book in favor of the conclusion, Job 42:7-9.

The "twelve prophets" (v. 10), Hosea through Malachi, are the minor prophets—those whose names are attached to brief prophetic books, which form almost a fourth major book in company with Isaiah, Jeremiah, and Ezekiel. The role of the minor prophets in the sustenance of Israel has been correctly evaluated by Ben Sira. Yet, through all of these accounts Ben Sira does not mention Babylon—nor Assyria, for that matter—nor the Exile.

49:11-13 Postexilic heroes. The three heroes have one verse each. The concept of the signet (v. 11) may refer to the use God would make of Zerubbabel (see Hag 2:23), as one uses a signet ring to formalize a document or offer proof of authenticity. The obscure Jeshua (the Joshua of Hag 1:12) stood with Zerubbabel and continued the priestly line after the return from exile. To Nehemiah is given the credit for building the city's walls again to shelter the temple. Note, too, the repeated use of "our" (v. 13), joining Israel of the past with Ben Sira's contemporaries.

49:14-16 Heroes before the Flood. There are nearly as many theories to explain the inclusion of Enoch (v. 14), Joseph (v. 15), and Adam and his sons (v. 16) as there are writers on the subject. Whether included deliberately or not, these men close the historical circle begun in 44:1. The splendor or glory so often mentioned in Sirach comes to a fitting climax associated both with Adam as well as the great high priest Simon, whose praise fills the following chapter.

50:1-24 Simon. We do not know of the repairs mentioned in verses 1-2 from other biblical texts, but the historian Josephus confirms them. These are the only acts mentioned for which Simon should receive praise. The next several verses describe in loving detail Simon's appearance in his high priestly vestments and as presiding at temple sacrifice.

The images employed here appeal almost entirely to sight; as such they contrast with 24:13-17, similar in its attention to detail. A close examination of these images will reveal overtones: for example, clouds (v. 6) recall incense; sun on the temple (v. 7), the golden plates that adorned the Jerusalem temple and were brilliant in the sun; the rainbow (v. 7), God's covenant after the Flood; trees of Lebanon (v. 8), which provided material for the temple's construction and for sacrificial wood; olive tree (v. 10), a symbol of eternal life. Above all is the theme of glory, running all through the sections beginning in 42:15.

The liturgy described here was very likely that prescribed for the Day of Atonement. The detail in verse 15 was not fixed exactly in earlier biblical texts; Ben Sira is describing the practice of his day. The mention of the very name of the Lord (v. 20) refers to the custom of reciting the exact name only once yearly on the festival.

Note also the various designations for God: Lord (vv. 13, 20), Most High (vv. 14, 16, 17, 21), Most High God (v. 15), Holy One of Israel (v. 17), Merciful One (v. 19), God (v. 19), God of all (v. 22). These were all familiar to Ben Sira and his contemporaries from their liturgical life.

The little hymn in verses 22-24 is addressed to no one in particular, but seems to arise from Ben Sira's consideration of the liturgy. He recommended the same praise after contemplation of the majesty of nature (see 43:11 for the rainbow). (The popular hymn "Now Thank We All Our God" takes its origin from verse 22.) The actual Hebrew text of verse 24 is a prayer for Simon; the translators of the New American Bible omitted it here, choosing to follow the canonical Greek version.

50:25-26 Fragments. The surprising numerical proverb (see 25:2; 26:5) focuses on the third group of despised peoples, namely, Samaritans. The Edomites on Mount Seir and the Philistines were traditional enemies of Israel but no longer a threat. Particularly galling for Ben Sira must have been the rival Samaritan temple and clergy at Shechem. The woman of Samaria (John 4:19-20) referred to the ancestral rivalry. Their pretension to the true cult must have led Ben Sira to include these verses.

50:27-29 Epilogue. Another surprise is the signature, a feature unknown elsewhere in the Old Testament, though Ben Sira has referred earlier to himself on occasion in the first person. He concludes with a piece of advice to his students, joining together his themes of wisdom, proper living, and divine guidance.

Appendix (51:1-30)

Several Old Testament books have appendix materials, for example 2 Sam 21–24; Isa 36–39; even Lamentations is attached as a sort of appendix to Jeremiah. The purpose of this appendix is unclear, but it may have been intended to preserve (pseudo?) Ben Sira materials still in circulation but not yet a part of Sirach.

The hymn of thanks is a personal composition, referring to events in the life of Ben Sira that are otherwise unknown to us. In any case, the author has mined the treasures of Old Testament prayers to derive a new composition. It follows the traditional form, known from the psalms: introduction addressed to God (v. 1); a narrative offering motives for thanks (vv. 2-6); a prayer for deliverance (vv. 7-11a); God's response (vv. 11b-12). The reference to death and the nether world may simply be a commonplace expression for danger or suffering. Calling the Lord "father" (v. 10) is not original with the New Testament.

The second poem is an acrostic, each succeeding verse beginning with the next letter of the Hebrew alphabet. This acrostic is incomplete; up to half is missing. The author is probably not Ben Sira himself.

The first section speaks of the quest for wisdom (vv. 13-22), often with erotic overtones. The writer began with a search for wisdom, followed the "level path" (of the law, v. 15), and so grew in wisdom—the object of which is the praise of the Lord (v. 22). This approach is consistent with Ben Sira's methods.

In the second section (vv. 23-30) the author turns to his students. The poem has the feel of an advertisement. The "house of instruction" (v. 23) is an expression that appears here for the first time, meaning a school. He urges hard work and promises rewards ("silver and gold," v. 28, which may stand for blessings other than simply material gain).

The Hebrew text ends with "in his own time," an expression consistent with Ben Sira's teaching about the providence of God, who acts according to the wise divine plan.

PSALMS

Richard J. Clifford, S.J.

INTRODUCTION

At the center of every psalm is the presence of Yahweh, the God of Israel, "the Lord" in Jewish and Christian translations. Yahweh is present to the psalmists most often in the temple. Built on Mount Zion in Jerusalem by King Solomon in the tenth century B.C.E. and rebuilt in the late sixth century B.C.E., after the Babylonian Exile, the temple complex was the site of the three great annual festivals: Passover in early spring, Pentecost seven weeks later, and Ingathering (also called the Feast, or Booths) in early fall. In the temple court the people encountered their Lord; they recalled the moment of their creation, the Exodus-Conquest (sometimes depicted in mythic language of victory over the sea) in solemn liturgical remembering.

According to the psalms, the temple was not the only institution through which Yahweh was present to the people. They also encountered God in the king, son of God by adoption, intermediary between God and people, and conduit of divine blessings to the people. Another mode of presence was the divine word to Israel, the law or *torah.* The Christian church sees in Jesus Christ and in the church that embodies him a presence so definitive as to include and fulfill all previous modes of presence.

The 150 psalms express Israel's experience of the Holy One, directly and concretely, with a wide range of feeling. As deep and as true as the psalmists' feelings are, their expression is strongly marked by the ancient Near Eastern tradition of hymnody. Genuine religious feeling, a strong tradition, and literary craft—these made the psalms. To know them, to share their religious feeling, one must be willing to study the tradition and the craft.

The most concise approach to the tradition and craft of the psalms is that perfected by Hermann Gunkel (1862–1932), professor of Bible at Berlin and later at Halle, in his great commentary (1926) and in his introduction (1933). Gunkel, with a romantic's love of the popular feeling and spontaneity of the psalms, and with a scholar's mastery of the relevant literatures and languages, recognized that the thoughts and emotions of the psalms are expressed in extremely traditional ways, "forms" or "genres," customary ways of speaking in the ancient Near East. Largely on the basis of his observations, scholars divide the psalms into a relatively few genres or forms: *laments* (individual or communal), *thanksgivings* (individual or communal), and *hymns.* A few psalms do not come directly under the above categories; these include royal psalms, songs of Zion, songs of trust, and psalms influenced by wisdom literature themes. These are classed according to their subject matter rather than according to their formal structure.

We sketch below the typical features of the main genres of (A) lament, (B) thanksgiving, and (C) hymn. References to this general treatment will be given throughout the commentary.

A. Psalms of **lament** are characterized by:

—a direct, unadorned cry to Yahweh.

—Complaint. A vivid description of the affliction of the community, such as military or agricultural distress, or of the individual, such as sickness, unfair legal process, treachery of former friends, or the consequences of sin. Sometimes there is a protestation of innocence; the punishment is undeserved.

—Expression of trust. Despite the crisis, the psalmist maintains a hope, however modest, that God will act. Such a hope is often introduced by "but" or "nevertheless."

—Petition. The psalmist prays for his own or his people's rescue, and often for the enemies' downfall.

—Words of assurance. A word delivered to the psalmist by a priest in the course of the lament. Only rarely is it transmitted with the text of the psalm, for example, Pss 15:5 and 60:6-8. Apparently, it was considered the priest's part, not the petitioner's.

—Statement of praise. A serene statement at the end of the psalm, in striking contrast to the anxiety of what has gone before. The psalmist states the intention to live the word of assurance delivered by the priest *as the word of the Lord.*

Each lament records a drama with three actors: the psalmist, God, and "the wicked." In the complaint the psalmist dramatizes his plight and protests his innocence so as to move God to action: Will you, just God, allow this innocent poor person to be vanquished by the wicked? In community laments the question is: Will you allow your choosing of Israel to be nullified by another power? The words of assurance, the fifth element in the outline above, function like a judicial verdict, affirming that the Lord does not allow evil to triumph ultimately and will vindicate the poor person. In the vow of praise the psalmist promises to live in the hope that God will act.

B. **Thanksgiving psalms** are closely allied to laments; in essence they are the report of rescue from the hands of the wicked. The term "thanksgiving" is somewhat misleading, for in the Bible to "give thanks" does not mean to say "thank you" but to tell publicly of the rescue that has occurred. The audience then recognizes the hand of Yahweh and gives praise. As a result, Yahweh's glory is acknowledged by human beings.

Most such psalms begin with an expression of thanks and then describe the act of rescue: the psalmist was in distress, even near despair, cried to Yahweh for help, and was saved. The psalmist is conscious of the congregation as he delivers his prayerful report, for the world must acknowledge what Yahweh has done.

C. The **hymn** is simple in its structure: a call to worship, often with the addressees named; for example, "Praise the Lord, all you nations," (Ps 117:1). The main section gives the basis for praise and is introduced by "for." The basis for praise is the activity that displays the Lord's majesty on earth.

The Psalter is an anthology of small collections finally edited into five books, perhaps in imitation of the five books of the Pentateuch: Psalms 1–41, 42–72, 73–89, 90–106, and 107–150. It is sometimes called the hymnbook of the second temple of 515 B.C.E.–A.D. 70, an accurate designation as long as we remember that songs of many periods of Israel's history, including the pre-exilic, are represented in the collection, and that non-liturgical considerations may have influenced the later editing.

A striking feature of the later editing of the Psalter is the superscription, like that written at the beginning of Psalm 51: "A psalm of David, when Nathan the prophet came to him after his sin with Bathsheba" (see 1 Sam 12). Such redactional statements make psalms originally at home in the temple liturgy applicable to any individual, since David was the typical Israelite; what happened to him could happen to each of us.

COMMENTARY

BOOK I: PSALMS 1–41

Psalm 1

This poem is classified as a wisdom psalm because it depicts and contrasts dramatically the "two ways," the two fundamental options for human beings. Hebrew rhetoric often views moral life as action, as choosing, and describes it by mentioning typical actions and their consequences. The psalm divides people into two groups: those obedient to the will of the Lord in verses 1-3, and the wickedly disobedient in verses 4-5. Each group will experience the consequences of their activity: life and prosperity for the obedient, ostracism and unrootedness for the wicked. The psalmist is not self-righteous, disdainfully separating people into righteous and sinners; rather, he celebrates the Lord's world, which is experienced as inherently just, rewarding the righteous and punishing the unrighteous. One places oneself in the community of the righteous or of the unrighteous by one's actions. The psalm therefore invites the person of faith to join those who revere and obey the Lord and to avoid those who rebel against the Lord.

Psalm 2

This royal psalm affirms the Israelite king to be regent of the Lord. In four sections of approximately equal length (vv. 1-3, 4-6, 7-9, 10-11), the Lord's sovereignty over the earth, a sovereignty exercised by the Israelite king, is expressed in a series of actions. In verses 1-3 the kings of the world try to throw off the dominion of the Lord and the Lord's anointed: "Let us break their fetters!" Such a wish is laughable (vv. 4-6). There is but one God in the heavens; the "gods" that the nations believe guide their destinies are not powerful before the one God who chose Israel. In verses 7-8 the narrator pronounces, in the legal adoption language of the day, the divine decree that has made the Israelite king the representative on earth of the one true God. In principle, then, this king is the ruler of the whole world and all its other kings (vv. 8-9). In verses 10-11 the unruly kings are warned: Revere the Lord, revere the king!

Psalm 3

In this lament (A—see p. 754) the psalmist is surrounded by enemies who threaten his life and deny the possibility that the Lord will come to the rescue (vv. 2-3). Against such taunts, the psalmist hopes that the Lord will answer heartfelt prayer, even managing to boast that the Lord will give protection in life's most vulnerable moment—lying down to sleep (vv. 5-7). Verse 8 prays that the Lord, like a warrior, will defang the taunting enemy. Such defeat of the enemy constitutes public vindication of the psalmist. Verse 9 is a peaceful statement of praise uttered after hearing the oracle of salvation promising rescue. The "salvation," or rescue, that the enemies denied will come without fail.

Psalm 4

This lament shows a more vigorous confidence in the Lord's protection of the just than in most instances of the genre; it can be called a song of trust. The psalmist prays to the God whose help was experienced in the past (v. 2). Out of that confidence he lectures the wicked; they, not he, are in danger and should make their peace with the Lord through ritual means. The psalmist's nearness to God enables him to warn those who have distanced themselves to be reconciled (vv. 3-6). That nearness also makes the psalmist a model of the blessings of God (vv. 7-9).

Psalm 5

In this lament (A) the psalmist contrasts the security of the house of the Lord (vv. 8-9 and 12-13) with the danger of the company of the wicked (vv. 5-7 and 10-11). He therefore prays insistently for God to hear him (vv. 2-4). Both worlds—the danger of the wicked and the enjoyment of the righteous—are imagined concretely: verses 8-9 describe admittance to the temple; in verses 12-13 the verbs "be glad," "exult," and "be the joy of" describe the singing and shouting of liturgical procession.

Psalm 6

This lament (A) is one of the Penitential Psalms, a designation that originated in the seventh century A.D. for seven psalms (6, 32, 38, 51, 102, 130, 143), that are especially suitable to express repentance. The psalmist feels burdened with the consequences of his sin—bodily and mental distress (vv. 3, 7-8) and harassment by enemies (vv. 9, 11). The word "sin" in the Bible can denote not only the act of sinning but its consequences as well. Sin brought consequences that had to be borne, consequences such as personal distress and the taunts of enemies. The speaker pleads for forgiveness not only for the past act of sin but also for the consequences of that act. Thus he asks that his bodily self be healed and that his enemies depart. The return of health and the departure of enemies publicly demonstrate divine acceptance. In the last stanza the psalmist shows the effect of hearing the word of assurance—confidence in the Lord's nearness.

Psalm 7

Psalm 7 is a lament (A), specifically the prayer of an accused person who flees to the presence of the Lord in the sanctuary for justice and protection (vv. 2-3). He takes an oath that he is innocent of any crime that would justify his enemies' attack (vv. 4-6). Since in this case he is innocent, having allowed God to scrutinize his inmost heart, the attacks upon him constitute attacks upon the innocent just person. The God of justice must therefore put the enemies down (vv. 7-14). The rout of the enemies by the Lord is at the same time the judicial verdict: the psalmist is declared innocent, and the enemies are declared guilty. The punishment of the wicked comes about by the inherent force of the wicked actions themselves (vv. 15-17). The psalmist dares to put his whole life in God's hands and to rely on God alone for protection against evil and violence.

Psalm 8

The psalm is a hymn (C) in praise of God for having given human beings responsibility and dignity. One should compare Gen 1:1–2:3 and Psalm 104. Verses 4-5 declare that heaven and earth, now arranged in beauty and order, invite praise. The hymnist expresses wonder at the marvelous world crowned by human beings (vv. 6-7). Human beings stand between heaven and earth; the world is made for them.

Psalms 9–10

The two psalms are actually one acrostic poem, that is, each section begins with a successive letter of the twenty-two letter Hebrew alphabet. Like many other acrostic poems, this one appears to be a series of brief, disparate statements given unity by the outer frame of the alphabet. The poem deals with three themes: (1) the rescue of the helpless and poor from their enemies; (2) the Lord's worldwide judgment and rule over the nations; (3) the prosperity of the wicked, which tempts the believer. A clue to the genre may be 9:14-15, where the psalmist offers thanksgiving (B) for being rescued by God. The psalmist, from the experience of personal salvation, points to other instances of divine power.

Psalm 11

Some themes of lament have been made the basis of a song of trust: instead of calling out for rescue from a specific danger, one rests contentedly in the Lord's presence. The psalmist is in danger; friends counsel flight to the hill country, the traditional hideout for people in danger (vv. 1-2). The chaos that, in the Bible, always lurks on the edge of God's creation is closing in on the psalmist; his own innocence appears to offer no help (v. 3). The psalmist chooses not to follow the advice and leave town but to seek the Lord in the temple. He entrusts his plight to the Lord, all-powerful and all-knowing (vv. 4-5). The psalmist's desire for the punishment of the wicked is a desire that God's justice in its totality be done (vv. 6-7).

Psalm 12

In this lament (A) the psalmist is caught in a human jungle, where violent people and liars oppress the just (vv. 2-3). The psalmist prays that the unjust be punished (vv. 4-5), not from a desire for revenge but from a desire to see God's will appear on earth. Verse 6 preserves the words of assurance delivered to the lamenter; usually it is not transmitted with the psalm. Verses 7-9 are statements praising the word of assurance the psalmist is willing to live by.

Psalm 13

In this lament (A) the psalmist prays to be healed lest his death be interpreted by his enemies as divine condemnation. Untimely death and serious sickness could be interpreted as the consequences of sinful conduct. The psalmist is afraid that his enemies will be vindicated. His healing would be a divine verdict in his favor.

Psalm 14

In this lament of the individual (A), duplicated in Psalm 53, the psalmist imagines the world as consisting of two types of people: "the fool" in verses 1-3 and the "just generation" in verses 4-6 (also called "my people" and "the afflicted"). The psalmist complains that the wicked persecute the community of the just (a better translation than "just generation," v. 5), while God watches from heaven. He expresses a firm hope that God will stride forth from the temple, punish the wicked, and uphold the faithful.

Psalm 15

This psalm, like Psalm 24, reflects the ceremony admitting the Israelite to the temple court. The temple was not like a church that one could enter at any time. It was God's house and could be entered only at certain times and under the proper conditions. One had to be admitted by a priest. The visitor had to answer the question of the priest at the gate: "Who may sojourn in 'your tent'?" (a traditional designation for the temple in Jerusalem). The response in verses 2-5 is a list of twelve stipulations, which sum up the covenantal obligations. Without commitment to the covenant, without conversion, one cannot enter the presence of the Lord. The psalm shows that nearness to the Lord is not a matter of external ritual alone; it demands heartfelt commitment as well.

Psalm 16

In this song of trust the psalmist takes refuge in the temple ("for in you I take refuge," v. 1), expressing trust that the Lord, and not the so-called gods of other nations, reigns over the land of Israel. Verses 3-6, despite corruption in verses 3-4, apparently express the psalmist's refusal to honor the local "gods." Only the Lord, who has displaced the Canaanites and their gods by giving the land to Israel, will receive the psalmist's worship (vv. 5-6). Verses 7-11 express how committed the psalmist is to Israel's God, how willing to trust the Lord who has brought the people here.

Psalm 17

This psalm is a lament (A) of one unjustly accused who has taken refuge in the temple to await divine settlement of the case. Verses 1-2 are a prayer for vindication; verses 3-5 are an affirmation of innocence. Verses 6-9 are another prayer, more anxious than the first because of the pressure of the foe in verses 10-12. Verses 13-14 plead that the wicked be broken, and verse 15 is a serene statement of praise. The psalmist seeks a public judgment. He prays for the public punishment of his enemies so that everyone will know that he has been found innocent by the court of last resort, the Lord.

Psalm 18

Psalm 18, duplicated in 2 Sam 22, is a royal thanksgiving (B) for a military victory. The king, in the throes of his suffering, prays in the temple (vv. 5-7), trusting not in his privileges as king but in his loyalty to God (vv. 21-25) and in his membership in God's people (v. 28).

Thanksgivings are in essence reports of divine rescue. The rescue and establishment of the king are told twice, once in mythic language (vv. 5-20) like that used in the narratives of Pss 77:14-21 and 89:10-28, and then in historical language (vv. 36-46). The outline is as follows: (I) hymnic introduction, vv. 2-4; report, vv. 5-20; conclusions regarding why the Lord effected the rescue, vv. 21-25; (II) hymnic introduction (in the second person), vv. 26-35; report, vv. 36-46; proclamation of the Lord's glory to the nations, vv. 47-51.

The king represents Israel, especially to the nations (vv. 44-46, 48, 50); his victory shows to the nations the power of his patron God, Yahweh. The movement of the king from humiliation and suffering (vv. 5-7, 19) to exaltation over the nations (vv. 44-46) makes him a living witness to the Lord's fidelity to the promises made to David and to the Lord's power.

Psalm 19

This unusual poem is a prayer that the law of the Lord, which contains such power to enlighten and enrich the person (vv. 8-11), not be denied to "your servant," the psalmist (vv. 12-15). The serene functioning of the universe expresses the wide scope and precision of the Lord's victory over what once was unbounded sea and primordial darkness, a chaos that had made human society impossible. The picture is the same as that in Psalm 104 and Gen 1.

The "glory of God" that the heavens declare in verse 1 is the power and wisdom that the Lord displays on earth in arranging them. In comparable religious literatures the sun is a judge and lawgiver; hence verses 5b-7 form a transition to the description of the law. The law is the will of the powerful Lord visible to the servants of that Lord; hence the prayer for openness to it (vv. 12-14).

Psalm 20

The psalm is a prayer for the king, who is the representative of the people, before he and his army set out for battle. In the first section (vv. 2-6) the people ask for divine help, and in verses 7-10 they express confidence that such help will be given. A solemn promise of God's help must have been given between the two sections in the liturgy, something like the promise of Pss 12:6 and 21:9-13. The "name" as a surrogate for the Lord occurs frequently in this psalm (vv. 2b, 6b, 8b) and indeed elsewhere in the Psalter (for example, Pss 44:6; 54:8; 118:10-12; 124:8). The idea is that Yahweh dwells in heaven and the name makes Yahweh present on earth. The name is not a magic force but aids those who trust in it alone (vv. 8-9).

Psalm 21

The first part of this prayer for the king is a thanksgiving for benefits given (vv. 2-8), and the second is a promise that the king will triumph over enemies (vv. 9-14). Verse 14 is a brief prayer. The psalm may reflect a temple ceremony that celebrated the Lord's choice of the Davidic king. The king's trust in the Lord (v. 8) and his confident prayer (vv. 3, 5) enable him to receive divine gifts. Vitality and peace are not the only divine gifts visible in the king; through his military prowess the land is kept secure. Hence verses 9-14 portray the warrior-king as helped by the Lord. The heightened language is typical of the Oriental court. When kings ceased in Israel after the sixth century B.C.E., the language came to be used of a future son of David.

Psalm 22

The exceptionally powerful lament (A) freely recasts the lament structure. The complaint is duplicated. The first complaint, verses 2-12, contains two expressions of trust, verses 4-6 and 10-11, with the petition of verse 12 as the climax. The second complaint, verses 13-22, extended by vivid images, climaxes in the petition of verses 20-22. The psalm is unusual in the length of the statement of praise (vv. 23-32), which usually consists of only a verse or two at the end of the lament. The psalmist appears to have had an intense experience of God who saves, and boldly praises God "in the midst of the assembly" (v. 23) for coming to the poor person who hoped for salvation. The psalmist has come to know the Lord in a new way through the divine act and cannot restrain his appreciation and love.

Psalm 23

This, the most beloved psalm in the Psalter, is a song of trust. The Lord is portrayed as a shepherd, a common designation for the god or king in ancient Near Eastern poetry. The title connotes care for the people and, in the case of Israel, leadership in the Exodus-Conquest (compare Pss 78:52-55; 80; Isa 40:11 and Jer 31:10). The psalmist is so confident of the divine shepherd's leadership as to trust even when the path leads through dangerous mountain passes (v. 4a); the shepherd is there (v. 4b). The Exodus-Conquest ended with Israel safe in the Lord's land. That journey is concluded in the psalm with a banquet. The enemies that tried to hinder the journey toward the divine dwelling are shamed as they see God's favor bestowed on the psalmist in the temple.

Psalm 24

Like Psalm 15, this psalm appears to have accompanied the ceremony of admittance to the temple on a solemn occasion (compare v. 3 with Ps 15:1, and vv. 4-6 with Ps 15:2-5). One had to affirm commitment to the covenant in order to appear before the Lord. Verses 1-2 and 7-10 reflect the ceremony. In the first verses the Lord's sovereignty over the created world is celebrated. People of that time imagined that the earth was suspended over vast waters, supported by great pillars. Verses 7-10 describe the procession of the Lord approaching the temple in triumph. Two choirs, singing antiphonally, identify the approaching Lord (perhaps represented by the ark carried by priests). The psalm invites worshipers to commit themselves anew to their Creator-Lord as they join in the triumphant procession.

Psalm 25

The psalm is an acrostic poem, each verse beginning with a successive letter of the Hebrew alphabet. Acrostic psalms are often a series of unconnected statements; poetic unity is supplied by the extrinsic device of the successive letters. Despite the looseness, the psalm is a lament (A) containing complaints mixed with pleas to be delivered from enemies (vv. 1-2, 16-22). The psalmist is acutely conscious of having sinned; there is no claim of innocence as in some other psalms. The psalmist's fragility leads to reiterated prayer to be led along the path taken by the friends of God, where one is safe from one's enemies.

Psalm 26

Psalm 26 is often classified as a lament, but the enemies here do not attack, as in laments. Probably the song was sung by the priests who ritually washed before they offered sacrifice. Exod 30:20-21 states: ". . . when they approach the altar in their ministry, to offer an oblation to the Lord, they must wash their hands and feet, lest they die." The psalm was suitable for use by all who sought God's protection as they entered the temple. Verses 1-3, echoed in verses 11-12, remind God of past sincerity while asking for further purification. Verses 4-5, matched in verses 9-10, make a sharp distinction between the wicked and the just; the psalmist prays to be of the company of the righteous. Verses 6-8 are the central panel and the center of the poem. The psalmist expresses the inner meaning of the ritual: joy before the transcendent God who draws near.

Psalm 27

Tradition has handed down the two sections of the psalm, verses 1-6 and verses 7-14, as one psalm, though each part could be understood as complete in itself. The first section is a song of trust, and the second a lament (A). A common theme unites the poem: those who seek the Lord in the temple are protected (see vv. 4-6 and v. 9). Verses 1-3 remind one of another song of trust, Psalm 23, in which the psalmist's conviction of the Lord's protecting presence is intense. Verses 4-6 refer to the temple and the delight and safety to be found there in the midst of a broken and dangerous world. In the liturgy the living, victorious God appears. Verses 7-13 are an anxious prayer that the saving presence not be withheld from the psalmist, who is in danger from enemies. Verse 14 is the statement of praise that customarily ends such psalms.

Psalm 28

In this lament (A) the statement of praise (vv. 6-8), uttered after the priest's words of assurance (not transmitted in this or in most psalms), is exceptionally lengthy and vigorous. The psalmist turns toward the temple, the unshakable center of an otherwise dangerous universe (vv. 1-2). "Those going down into the pit" in verse 1b is a stereotyped expression for those overcome by death and descending to Sheol, the shadowy nether world. Verses 3-5 are a petition that God judge publicly. The psalmist knows that evildoers are heading toward annihilation as a result of their actions; by praying for their destruction he is lining himself up with the just and is thus able to claim God's promised protection of the just. The last verses express the psalmist's acceptance of the word of assurance as effective divine words. The psalmist does not neglect to pray for the people also (v. 9).

Psalm 29

The hymn (C—see p. 755) invites the members of the heavenly court to join in giving glory to Yahweh, the sole God (vv. 1-2). The "glory and strength [rather than praise]" that they give is their recognition that Yahweh alone is king (v. 10), who alone has shaped the world by means of victory. The weapons in that victory are those of the storm-god—thunder ("the voice of the Lord," in verses 3-9), lightning, and wind. With these the Lord has vanquished the forces hostile to civilization and has made them part of the world of men and women. Verse 11 prays that the Lord will impart the power that shaped the universe to the king of Israel and, through that king, to the people. Thus the hymn celebrates the power of the Lord and the sharing of that creative power with the people of God.

Psalm 30

In this thanksgiving (B—see p. 755) praise is given to God for rescue from near fatal illness. Verses 2-4 describe the divine mercy, the snatching of the sick person from the annihilating power of death. As often in thanksgivings, the one rescued is so relieved and delighted that he teaches and exhorts the assembly to trust the saving Lord (vv. 5-6). The assembly learns about the psalmist's inner journey, from his unthinking self-confidence (vv. 7-8a) to his panicky pleas and bargaining when illness struck (vv. 8b-11). Verses 12-13 express the delight of one who has experienced God's favor and forgiveness.

Psalm 31

The psalm is primarily a lament (A), with elements of a thanksgiving (the rescue seems to have already taken place according to verses 8-9 and 20-21) and a song of trust (vv. 4, 6, and 15-16). Moreover, the psalm seems to unfold in two narrative phrases, verses 2-9 and 10-25, probably an instance of the parallelism characteristic of Semitic poetry.

As usual in laments, the affliction is couched in general terms. The psalmist is in danger of being overwhelmed by evil people. In all these pains the psalmist turns to the "faithful God" (v. 6), whose being is described in verses 20-21.

Psalm 32

This thanksgiving (B) is the second of the seven Penitential Psalms of church tradition (see p. 756). The psalmist reports the Lord's rescue: sin once reigned over him, body and soul. Sin here, as often in the Bible, is not only the personal act of rebellion against God but also the consequences of that act—the waning of vitality and frustration.

Burdened with the consequences of personal folly, the psalmist declares everyone blessed who has been forgiven by God (vv. 1-2). Verses 3-4 describe his past refusal to open himself up to the Lord, and verses 5-7, the happy result of letting God be the forgiving God. In verses 8-11 the psalmist becomes a teacher, sharing with the assembly the fruits of personal experience: the wicked (v. 10), who do not open themselves to the forgiving Lord, are unhappy, but those who trust in the merciful God are filled with gladness.

Psalm 33

In this wonderfully complex hymn (C) the just are called to praise God, who made the world by a mere word (vv. 4 and 9). The world is portrayed as three-tiered: the heavenly tier and its inhabitants, the cosmic waters that surround the universe, the earthly tier and its inhabitants (vv. 6-9). The words and plans of human beings, in contrast to God's word, effect nothing (vv. 10-11).

Of all the wonders created by the word of the Lord, human beings are special because they are free to plan and to revere the Lord (vv. 8, 10-11). Verses 12-19 sketch how a people and its king are to conduct themselves on the earth God created. Their greatness consists in God's choice of them and God's clear vision into their hearts (vv. 12-15), in their leader's acknowledgment of the Lord (vv. 16-17). The psalmist directs the people to trust in the One who makes the people great (vv. 20-22).

Psalm 34

This thanksgiving (B) is in acrostic form, each line beginning with a successive letter of the Hebrew alphabet. In this psalm one letter is missing and two are in reverse order. The psalmist, fresh from the experience of being saved by the Lord from danger (vv. 5, 7), calls on all the "lowly" (vv. 3b-4) to praise the Lord, who saves the poor who trust. The "lowly" are the defenseless, who have only the Lord to turn to. If the defenseless person prays, the Lord will hear and that person will become powerful (vv. 7-11). In the second part of the poem, the psalmist, taught true wisdom by his suffering, now teaches the assembly (vv. 12-23). Anyone who is wise will, by right conduct, join the company of the righteous and thus enjoy God's favor.

Psalm 35

In this lament (A) a person unjustly accused by former friends takes refuge in the court of last resort, coming before the divine judge (v. 1) and all-seeing witness (v. 22). Verses 1-8 are a prayer for justice, asking that the evildoers be publicly exposed as such by their punishment. Verses 9-10 are a kind of anticipatory thanksgiving, praising God in advance of the rescue. Verses 11-16 extend the complaint of verse 7: friends have done it! Verses 17-21 press for speedy assistance, and verses 22-26, like verses 1-8, pray for the destruction of the psalmist's unjust persecutors. The modern reader, offended perhaps by the vindictive tone of the psalm, should remember that the psalmist asks for *public* redress of a *public* injustice and leaves in God's own hands the carrying out of the work of justice.

Psalm 36

This lament (A) is the prayer of one who feels threatened by "evildoers," people who attack the just (v. 13). The psalmist depicts the wicked in all their arrogance and moral obtuseness (vv. 2-5), and then comes before the just and merciful God, who punishes such evildoers and draws near in tenderness to the beleaguered just (vv. 6-10). Verses 8-10 show the closeness of the saving Lord in the temple service. "The shadow of your wings" refers to the cherubim in the holy of holies. "They have their fill of the prime gifts of your house" reads literally, "they are sated with the fat [of the temple sacrifices]."

Psalm 37

A wise teacher speaks to disciples troubled by the prosperity of the unjust and the hiddenness of God. The psalm is an acrostic; its statements are unified by the extrinsic device of beginning the verses with successive letters of the Hebrew alphabet. In the culture of the time, lore was handed down orally, its authority being based upon the stature and experience of the teacher. Priests, kings, royal officials, and parents were expected to hand on what they had received.

To people troubled by the fact that the unjust victimize the just without being punished, the wise teacher asserts that the disturbing situation is only temporary; the Lord will punish the wicked in the future. In the view of the psalm, people place themselves in the ranks of the unjust by their actions and attitudes. Each path of life, or "way," has its own inherent dynamism—eventual frustration for the wicked, eventual reward for the just. Good things, especially symbolized by the land, lie in the future for the just, a theme with echoes in the New Testament beatitudes. Let the just wait for the Lord!

Psalm 38

In this psalm of lament (A), one of the Penitential Psalms (see p. 756), the psalmist is afflicted with deadly sickness, commonly a sign of divine disfavor. People believed that actions brought consequences of themselves: health, reputation, and prosperity came from good actions; illness, loss of face and poverty followed from evil actions. The psalmist is gravely ill (vv. 4, 6-9) and recognizes that his own actions are the cause (vv. 4-5, 19) of physical and mental suffering and ostracism. There is no one to turn to for help; only the Lord can destroy the cause-and-effect chain of past folly and present misery.

Psalm 39

A mortally ill person, keenly aware of the imminent end of life, prays this individual lament (A). In verses 2-4 the psalmist resolves to remain silent, lest he speak against the God from whom all things come. The psalmist's strategy of reverent silence and submission before the all-knowing and all-effecting God has not, however, brought the hoped for healing and peace. Verses 5-7, uttered with a keen sense of the fleetingness of life, ask how long the psalmist has to live. Verses 8-10 are in tension with verses 5-7; they are a hopeful prayer for rescue after the acceptance of death. Verse 9 should read "Deliver me from all those who rise up against me," on the basis of the parallel verse. "Those who rise up" are the ones who have concluded that the illness is a punishment from God for sinful behavior and are ostracizing the psalmist. People judge the sick person to be punished by God and are hurling insults.

Verse 10, recalling the resolve of silent submission of verses 2-4, is key. The psalmist, recognizing that God is the author of all, including the mortal illness, can only lay out the whole situation before God: "it was your doing." Verses 11-12 again reveal the tension between acceptance (v. 12) and change (v. 11), as do verses 13-14 by the reference to Israel as guests in the Lord's land who have no claim on the life to be found there yet have hope.

Psalm 40

Verses 2-13 are a thanksgiving (B). A distinct psalm, a lament, comprising verses 14-18 has been appended, probably because it reprises some of the vocabulary of verses 2-13. (Verses 14-18 appear also in Psalm 70 and will be treated there.)

The psalmist describes God's rescue in spatial terms, as the pulling out of someone trapped in a bog onto dry land. Even in adversity he hoped. Verse 4 states that rendering thanks is not simply a gift one makes to the Lord in return for rescue but is itself a gift of God. It makes visible to one's neighbors the divine act of mercy (v. 4b). The next verse associates the individual salvation with the great acts of salvation of Israel's past.

Verses 7-9 have suffered some displacement but the gist is clear: the rescued person was expected to offer sacrifice but declares that God desires obedience instead. The verse recalls the memorable words of Samuel to Saul in 1 Sam 15:22: "Obedience is better than sacrifice, and submission than the fat of rams." The mysterious "Behold I come" in verse 8 may reflect a scene like that of Ps 118:19, "Open to me the gates of justice; I will enter them and give thanks to the Lord." The psalmist, then, would enter the temple precincts to give thanks, not with the sacrifice of animals, but with a new song and a devotion to "your law." The final verses emphasize the unrestrained, open-hearted proclamation that characterizes one who has experienced the saving mercy of God.

Psalm 41

This psalm of thanksgiving (B) recounts God's rescue of a sick individual (vv. 4, 5, and 9). The psalmist begins by declaring blessed, that is, regarded favorably by God, those who behave well toward the poor (v. 2). Other psalms use the same formula for those who have been placed in a right relation to God (Pss 32:1-2; 34:9; 40:5; 65:5), but here the right relation is toward the special friends of the Lord.

The psalmist has apparently become part of that privileged group who have experienced the Lord's protection (vv. 3-4), sometimes called "the poor" in the Bible. The narrative of the rescue, essential to a thanksgiving, is done in this psalm by quoting the psalmist's lament before rescue (vv. 5-11). Verse 5 is the beginning of the prayer, "Once I said . . . ." The misery of the past contrasts with present safety. The quoted prayer shows that the chief pain was not physical but emotional—betrayal by enemies, among whom were friends. They wanted all memory of the sufferer erased (a horrible fate for the Hebrew) because they judged the affliction to be the fruit of sin. By their talk they encouraged the separation of the sufferer from the community of God.

Verse 11, the petition for health to requite the enemies, is disturbing to modern readers; the point is that the healing itself is an act of judgment through which God decides for the defendant and against the false friends. The judicial tone carries over to verses 12-13: recovery from illness is a mark of favor showing God's love for this individual. The integrity of which the psalmist boasts is his innocence in the present situation, not for the totality of his life. The blessing in verse 14 is not part of the psalm; it marks the end of Book I, the so-called collection of David's psalms.

BOOK II: PSALMS 42–72

Psalms 42–43

The refrain "Why are you so downcast, O my soul," repeated in 42:6, 12, and 43:5, shows that Psalms 42–43 are a single poem; the traditional separation into two psalms is wrong. It is a lament (A) of an individual who lives beyond Israel's borders in the north and who longs to join the community of God worshiping in the temple in Jerusalem. In the Hebrew scriptures Yahweh is the God of all the world but is revealed only in Jerusalem. What distresses the psalmist is the absence of God, the feeling of deep hunger without the ability to satisfy it because of distance from Jerusalem and the hindrance of enemies. Their taunt, "Where is your God?" (vv. 4, 11), intensifies the pain.

Verses 7-8 show that the psalmist is in the north; Mount Mizar is generally thought to be a mountain in the region of Mount Hermon. In verse 9 the psalmist is caught like Jonah (Jonah 2:3-4) in the deep, a metaphor for the place where Yahweh will not be found. In the last of the three stanzas, Ps 43:1-5, the psalmist prays that Yahweh decide against the enemies who say that Yahweh cannot bring the psalmist to Jerusalem.

Psalm 44

Community laments (A) are often built on the contrast between God's gracious creation of Israel through the Exodus-Conquest and the present distress that seems to negate that creation. The Lord expelled the nations in order to give Israel its land (vv. 2-9), but now the nations expel Israel from that land (vv. 10-17), undoing God's work. Verses 2-9 emphasize the divine initiative in the grant of the land. Israel does nothing—everything is done because of God's own gracious will. But the Lord is now silent as the people are despoiled, even though they are not conscious of any sin against the covenant (vv. 18-23). Here the community struggles with being the Lord's special people and witness while the Lord remains silent before their real pain. Keenly aware of the divine favor that gave them the land in the past, they wait for God's return. The last three verses are a spirited prayer for help, showing that the people do not lose hope.

Psalm 45

This poem is perhaps the most specific in the Psalter; it was sung at the king's marriage to a princess of Phoenicia. Retained in the collection when there was no reigning king, it came to be applied to the anointed king who was to come, the Messiah.

The court poet, conscious of the power of his song (vv. 2, 18), sings first of the Lord's choice of the king over others (vv. 3, 8bc) and of his privilege of establishing the Lord's purpose (vv. 4-8). In verse 9 the poet depicts the ceremony in which the bride, in a majestic procession, is led to the king. The princess is to forget the royal house she came from ("your father's house" of verse 11) and be wife to the king, the viceroy of the Lord of all the earth. Verse 17 is addressed to the king; with his new wife the ancient Davidic (and Abrahamic) promise of progeny and power will come true.

Psalm 46

In this song of Zion, Yahweh is hymned for making the holy city a sure refuge to worshipers, who are terrified by the prospect of a collapsing world. There are three stanzas (vv. 2-4, vv. 5-8, vv. 9-12); the last two are ended by the refrain of verses 8 and 12.

God created the world by subduing the disorderly primal forces that made human life impossible, and established Zion as the glorious divine dwelling. Because God is present at the ordered world's center, the psalmist is confident that there will be no unleashing of those once unruly forces (vv. 2-4), especially in the Lord's own space. The city and temple of the Lord are the place where the memory of God's creation victory is most vivid. That creation can be celebrated in the Lord's shrine, even though the nations, unruly like the primal forces, rage outside (vv. 5-8). The very buildings of the city make visible to the chosen community how powerful the Lord is over all that is chaotic and anti-human. Verse 11 majestically commands all hateful and hurtful powers to submit to the Lord.

Psalm 47

This enthronement psalm celebrates the kingship of Yahweh over all the beings of heaven and earth. The Lord, invisibly enthroned upon the ark is carried in procession into the temple.

The psalm is divided into two parts of equal length, verses 2-6 and 7-10, each beginning with a call to praise. The thought expressed in each stanza is the same: Yahweh is the king, victorious over the powers of heaven and earth (the powers of earth are emphasized in this psalm), and selects Israel as a special people (vv. 5 and 10). The choice of Israel is part of the establishment of the world. Verse 6 probably refers to the trumpet blasts and shouts that accompanied the entry of the ark into the temple, the entry signifying Yahweh's taking possession of the temple as king.

Psalm 48

This psalm praises Zion, the city where Yahweh's world-establishing victory is remembered. The splendid buildings, especially the temple, bespeak Yahweh's power to protect the people from all attack. So suffused with Yahweh's presence is the site of the holy mountain that the psalmist declares the mountain to be higher and more beautiful than any other and to be impregnable to all enemies.

Verses 2-3 praise the mountain where God graciously encounters human beings. The next section, verses 4-9, describes the great deed that proved the Lord's presence on the mountain: the easy defeat of the enemy kings by means of God's storm wind. Verses 10-12 describe the festivities of triumph, resounding far and wide in celebration of the victory that establishes the world. "We ponder" (v. 10) means "we recite" (the stories of Yahweh's victories). The final part, verses 13-15, sees in the solid structures of the temple and city such clear evidence of divine might and loving protection that one need only walk through them to feel secure and loved.

Psalm 49

Though often called a "wisdom psalm" because it contains reflections about the human condition, Psalm 49 is really a confession of trust in God like Ps 27:1-6, except that here there is a more confident tone (note the assurance of vv. 2-5). Also, the enemy is seen in greater profundity—it is death itself.

The opening verses, like Ps 78:1-4, boldly make a new statement about human life before God. In verses 6-10 the psalmist refuses to fear the wealthy who are wicked; their wealth cannot protect them from the ultimate enemy, death. Experience shows that death takes all, the wise (=the righteous) and the wicked. The wealth that once emboldened the wicked to do violence will be scattered. A refrain stating that death levels all closes the first part in verse 13, as it will the second part in verse 21. Verses 14-15 emphasize the theme of the first part: those who live by wealth and violence somehow have death as their shepherd. In contrast, the innocent afflicted person who refuses to fear (v. 6) has as shepherd Yahweh, who will in a mysterious way protect that trusting person from death. The perhaps deliberately enigmatic "by receiving me" recalls God's taking of Enoch in Gen 5:24 (compare 2 Kgs 2:11-12). The Hebrew of verse 16 sounds like and plays on verse 9: a human cannot ransom or save another human but God can save "me," the trusting or persecuted person. In verses 17-21 the psalmist exhorts from the conviction that human beings are not to be feared—they will all die. Only God is the ultimate ransomer.

Psalm 50

Psalm 50 is the record of a ceremony in which the Lord judges the people gathered on Mount Zion. Have they been faithful to the covenant, positively by worshiping and calling upon the Lord alone (as opposed to false gods, vv. 14-15), negatively by avoiding violations of the Ten Commandments (vv. 16-20)? Only a selection of the basic commandments are listed in the psalm. The liturgy reenacts the great encounter of the Lord and Israel at Sinai (Exod 19–24). In liturgical time Mount Zion stands for Mount Sinai as each generation of Israel faces the Lord.

Verses 1-6 describe the manifestation of the Lord on Mount Zion, mediated, in all probability, through trumpet blasts and smoke and fire. In verse 6 the heavens are summoned as witnesses to the people's conduct; heaven and earth (and other cosmic pairs) were often invoked in antiquity as witnesses at the sealing of covenants. Verses 7-15 are divine speech, mediated by the voice of the priest; the Lord does not need the food of animal sacrifice as do the gods of the ancient world (vv. 8-17) but desires the freely given response of the people (vv. 14-15). In verses 16-21 that same divine voice judges the wicked, that is, those who violate the fundamental covenant relationship. Such people are to repent, change. Verses 22-23, despite their vigor, are a positive conclusion to the liturgical encounter: the Lord seeks the free response of the people.

Psalm 51

One of the great laments (A) in the Psalter, this Penitential Psalm (see p. 756) is primarily a plea for the removal of the personal and social distress that sins have caused. The poem is divided into two parts of approximately equal length: verses 3-10 and 11-19, with a coda in vv. 20-21. The two parts are carefully interlocked by repetition of significant words: "blot (wipe) out" in the first verse of each section (vv. 3 and 11); "wash me" in the verse just after the first verse of the first section (v. 4) and just before the last verse (v. 9) of the first section; the repetition of "heart," "God," and "spirit" in verses 12 and 19.

In the first section the psalmist, relying entirely on God's gracious fidelity, prays to be delivered from sin. Verse 10 suggests that the psalmist is sick, and attributes the sickness to sin. Sin is depicted with intense realism, not just a past act against God but its emotional, physical, and social consequences. The psalmist experiences the destructive results of sin (v. 5) and knows that this suffering is self-inflicted and deserved. Before the all-holy God a human being can plead no self-righteousness (v. 7) but can only ask for God's purifying favor (vv. 8-10).

Verse 11 begins the second part by repeating the prayer for forgiveness. Something more profound than the wiping clean of sin is the theme of verses 12-19, namely, a state of nearness to God, a living by the spirit or power of God (vv. 12-13). Such nearness brings joy (v. 14) and enables the forgiven sinner to speak from personal experience to all who are estranged from God (vv. 15-16). That proclamation is the response that God desires, even more than sacrifice in the temple (vv. 17-19). The last two verses make precise the situation: the experience of sin is the exilic absence of God from the temple and its ceremonies.

Psalm 52

Though often classed as a lament, this psalm is unique. The psalmist pronounces judgment upon the wealthy and self-sufficient violent person whose prosperity is a temptation to "the godly," that is, those loyal to God in all things. One can compare Isa 22:15-18, in which the prophet denounces Shebna, a royal official, for his arrogance.

Verses 3-6 resemble a prophetic accusation against the arrogant. The speaker is one of the righteous: in the psalms they often are the victims of "champions of infamy." Lies, violence, and exploitation are their way of life; their prosperity tempts those who believe that God rewards only the righteous. The cry for judgment in verse 7 comes from the troubled heart of a righteous person who believes that the Lord will not allow the godless to triumph. The removal of the godless from the land of the living assures the righteous that the just God is active in their regard; the divine act makes them rejoice (vv. 8-9). Rejoicing over a fallen enemy is distasteful to modern readers, as are the neat categories "the righteous" and "the worker of treachery." The psalmist, however, is not speaking of permanent categories of being but only of the present unfair situation. The psalmist presumably would not deny that a righteous person could join the ranks of the wicked tomorrow, or vice versa.

The last verses are full of confidence. Nearness to God is the ultimate answer to the experience of injustice. Olive trees grow in the sacred precincts of the Dome of the Rock in Jerusalem even today, their fertility testifying to God's presence in the shrine. The last verses thank God for upholding justice; the godly can rejoice in divine protection.

Psalm 53

Psalm 53 is a duplicate of Psalm 14 (see p. 758 for commentary). As in Psalm 14, the psalmist sees two kinds of people: the fool (v. 2) and the just (called "my people" in verse 5).

Psalm 54

The psalm is almost a textbook lament (A). The troubled person, attacked by the wicked, calls upon Yahweh directly for help (vv. 3-5). The psalmist refuses to despair and hopes in God, who is active in human history and is just (vv. 6-7). Verses 8-9 render thanks with a certitude that suggests that a priest has in the meantime spoken a reassuring oracle (not transmitted) and the psalmist has accepted it as the word of the God who has promised protection to the poor.

Psalm 55

The psalmist, betrayed by those who were once intimate friends (vv. 14-15 and 21-22), prays that God punish those oath breakers and thus be recognized as the protector of the wronged. The customary structure of the lament (A) is verified here: the unadorned address to God (v. 2); the prayer for deliverance and punishment of the enemy (vv. 3, 10, 16); the vivid dramatization of the oppressive situation so as to appeal to God's sense of honor (vv. 4-9, 11-15, 21-22). The malice of the personal enemy is seen by the psalmist as an instance of the mysterious residual evil in the world, an evil that is palpable in the streets of the city (vv. 11-12). It frightens and discourages those who trust in the Lord. As in other laments, the psalmist trusts so strongly in the salvation of God that he can exhort others (v. 23) and live calmly in the expectation of salvation (v. 24).

Psalm 56

The lament (A) of a person whose enemies threaten death (v. 14) but cannot ultimately keep him from uttering a prayer of trust is enclosed by a refrain (vv. 4-5 and 11-12). The psalmist is glad to be one of the poor, the *'anawim*, who by their vulnerability to the attacks of the powerful and wicked invite the special protection of the just and merciful Lord (vv. 2-3). So sure is the hope of the poor that they need not fear even at the height of danger (vv. 4-5 and 11-12). At the moment of danger, which the psalmist does not minimize (vv. 2-8), they can be certain that God tenderly regards their tears (v. 9). No enemy can stand in the way of their joyous duty to give thanks publicly, by vows and offerings, for the life that God has given back to them.

Psalm 57

A lament (A) in which the victim of hostile actions by enemies (vv. 4, 5, 7) prays that God be a refuge and a protection. The drama of the lament, featuring the victim, the wicked, and God, is here especially vivid. The enemies are lions with teeth like swords to devour the just (v. 5); they dig a trap (v. 7). The psalmist expresses with deep feeling his fragility and his confidence in God's protecting presence. "The shadow of your wings" (v. 2) probably refers to the wings of the cherubim (powerful winged animals) whose wings spread over the ark, the throne of the invisible Lord, in the inner chamber of the temple (see 1 Kgs 6:23-28). The refrain "Be exalted . . . O God," is repeated boldly in verses 6 and 12. The psalmist's confession, "My heart is steadfast, O God" (vv. 8-11), is exceptionally vibrant and joyous. The whole psalm is the record of a sensitive yet exuberantly trustful person.

Psalm 58

In this lament (A) the psalmist expresses great trust in the Lord's power to dethrone all that stands in the way of the divine governance of the world. The first verses condemn "the gods," the demonic forces that were popularly imagined to control human destinies (vv. 2-3), and "the wicked," the human instruments of these forces (vv. 4-6). Verses 7-12 pray that God take away their ability to harm the just (vv. 7-10). Such divine vengeance will make the righteous glad; they will see that their Lord is not indifferent to their suffering and has in fact upheld them.

Psalm 59

A lament (A) in which a person endangered by the lying tongues of those who seek to separate him from his God (vv. 7-8, 13, 15) prays that God will uphold him and punish them, and hence be seen as the just God of Israel. Verses 2-8 alternate prayer (vv. 2-3, 5b-6) and depictions of the wicked rampaging against the innocent psalmist (vv. 4-5a, 7-8). The psalmist vividly expresses confidence in the God who is just and loving (vv. 9-11). The near curse upon the enemies in verses 12-13 is not a crude desire for blood vengeance but a wish that the supremacy of Yahweh, about to break into human history, be recognized as such by all people (v. 14b). The God who rules the world (vv. 9, 14b) is also the God who rules the psalmist's life (vv. 17-18).

Psalm 60

In this community lament (A) the people dramatize their situation as defeated and deprived of their God-given land. Informing their complaint before God is their conviction that they are "[God's] people," "those who fear [God]," "[God's] loved ones" (plural; vv. 5-7). They claim the protection of their God Yahweh, who is the Lord of all the nations of the earth. Yahweh has permitted their present plight and hence can reverse it.

The prayer of verse 7 is for an oracle of salvation; "answer us" is a special term for the seeking of the divine word of assurance in crises of war (see, for example, 1 Sam 14:37; 28:6, 15). The oracle of verses 8-10 is the divine response to the prayer, spoken by a priest in the temple. The Divine Warrior, through the priest, declares ownership of the land; the invasion of other nations is not permanent and will ultimately be reversed.

The territories mentioned in verses 8-9 were all part of the God-given territory. Whenever any were taken by an enemy, the people could hold God to that ancient oracle of grant. Verse 11 is the community's faith-response: "The land is ours; let's take it!" Verses 12-14 continue the opening lament, but now, in the light of the favorable divine promise, the words are uttered with a new confidence in the Lord and with a sober awareness of the limits of unaided human power.

Psalm 61

This psalmist, using elements of the lament (A) and thanksgiving form (B), prays in a place far distant from God's saving presence ("from the earth's end," v. 3) to be led to the security of God's presence. The language for security with God is traditional: rock, refuge, tower (vv. 3-5); to dwell forever in the Lord's tent (see Pss 15:1; 27:4); beneath the outstretched wings of the cherubim.

In the second half of the poem the psalmist confesses that God has come to the rescue and given "the heritage [the land] of those who fear [God's] name" to the one who trusted (v. 6). The holy land has a king; prayer is offered that the king reflect adequately the divine vitality (vv. 7-8). The one rescued is happy to sing praises to the name.

Psalm 62

This song of trust takes from the lament a sense of the fragility and danger of life, and from the thanksgiving a serenity arising from the experience of God's power. The serenity appears in the two refrains, verses 2-3 and 6-7, with verse 8 expanding the theme; the anguish is in the angry taunt against the rampaging wicked in verses 4-5. In verses 9-10 the psalmist steps forward as teacher to the community, so vivid has been his experience of God's power. That experience can be Israel's. Verse 12 reveals the astonishing source of the psalmist's contagious trust and inner poise: not the removal of danger but the word of God received as such, which relativizes all other powers.

Psalm 63

Like Psalm 61, this psalm also has elements of a lament (vv. 3-4 and 10-11), of a thanksgiving (vv. 4-6), and of a song of trust (vv. 7-9). The psalmist's situation explains the unusual juxtaposition of diverse genres: the psalmist, beset by liars and enemies (vv. 10, 12b), seeks God (v. 2) in the temple as an asylum in danger (vv. 3 and 8). He may even be spending the night in the sanctuary (vv. 7-8), intending to provoke a dream of reassurance. The one endangered then goes to the place of God's holy presence, the temple, in whose protective power he may be safe and where he can pray that justice be meted out to the wicked.

Psalm 64

This lament (A) is uttered by a person who feels overwhelmed by the malice of the wicked, the enemies of the righteous in the psalms (vv. 2-7). They seek to cut off the individual from the holy people. Hence the prayer to destroy the evildoers' plan is vehement—that God turn against them the very arrows they had aimed against God's friends. The world will then see who is the true ruler of the world (vv. 8-10). Verse 11 is a vow of praise expressing the lively hope that God will bring about a just world.

Psalm 65

There are hymnic elements in this community thanksgiving (B), recited, most probably, at the festival when Israel enjoyed the fruits of the land. The festival could have been Pentecost, when wheat was harvested, or the feast of Ingathering of fruits, grapes, and olives in early autumn, when the rains resumed after the summer dry spell (vv. 10-14).

The Lord is given praise for three mercies: for making Zion a place of encounter and reconciliation for the holy people (vv. 2-5); for overcoming the primordial unbounded waters that once covered the earth and prevented human life from appearing (vv. 6-9); and for making those same waters fertilize the earth to bear fruit (vv. 10-14).

Psalm 66

In genre, this liturgical poem resembles a hymn (C) in verses 1-12 and an individual thanksgiving (B) in verses 13-20; it is now a unified liturgy. Verses 1-2 contain an invitatory exhorting the world to acknowledge Israel's God as uniquely powerful. The greatest proof of this power is the way Yahweh broke the sea's power to keep Israel from its land; let the nations revere this just God (vv. 5-7). Israel's history, the story of its humiliation and exaltation (probably the Babylonian Exile and the restoration), witnesses to God's justice and fidelity—justice, because God punished Israel's sins; fidelity, because God did not abandon the people forever (vv. 8-12).

Any member of this sinful yet rescued people may acknowledge the merciful God through appropriate sacrifice (vv. 13-16). As often in thanksgiving, the one who has experienced God's mercy steps forward as teacher; God is ready to be merciful to all who repent (vv. 16-20).

Psalm 67

The psalm reflects a temple liturgy in which the congregation echoes a part of the famous benediction of Aaron (Num 6:24-26). The people affirm the priestly blessing (v. 2), conscious that their God-given prosperity witnesses to the mercy and power of their God (v. 3). The first of two refrains, inviting the nations to acknowledge Yahweh (v. 4), serves as preface to the statement that Yahweh guides the nations; the second refrain (v. 6) serves as preface to the statement that Yahweh makes the earth bountiful.

Psalm 68

About no other psalm are there so many and such radically different interpretations. The text is disturbed. Some scholars believe that the psalm is simply a collection of short fragments. This commentary sees the psalm as reflecting a liturgical ceremony, a procession to the temple; it is like Pss 24; 106:19-29; and 2 Sam 6.

In verses 2-7 the procession begins, the people following the ark of the covenant, the throne upon which Yahweh is invisibly enthroned. The movement of so powerful a Deity frightens any possible foes but gladdens friends. In verses 8-21 the procession of the ark symbolizes the great battle between Yahweh and Yahweh's enemies, Sea or Death. The evil powers were defeated, and a shrine to the victory was prepared (vv. 16-19). The psalmist acknowledges that the victory of Yahweh over the forces of chaos creates a just world in which the righteous will be safe from the attacks of the wicked (vv. 20-24). The procession includes all the tribes of Israel, rejoicing in their unity (vv. 25-28). The psalm ends with a warning to the nations: recognize the one God and honor God's people.

Psalm 69

The psalm is a lament (A), unusual by its length and by the sufferer's keen sense of suffering for the Lord (vv. 8, 11-12). The depiction of suffering is both metaphorical (vv. 2-3; 15-16: the waters characterize chaos before God creates) and realistic (vv. 4, 5, 9, 11-13: exhaustion, alienation from family and community, misunderstanding of religious acts). Especially in the second part of the psalm is there fervent prayer that the enemies be punished (vv. 23-29). God's punishment of the psalmist's enemies is public vindication of the psalmist. As in other laments, the psalmist expresses hope in God and makes a vow of praise at the end (vv. 31-37); the vow recognizes that God is more pleased with praise than with sacrifice. The sufferer fasts and laments, conscious of the need for purification before the all-holy God, who is no longer encountered in the destroyed temple. These gestures are misinterpreted by his enemies, who judge him to be guilty and rightly afflicted by God. The psalmist's situation of suffering for the Lord and his hope of vindication by an attentive and faithful God applies to all servants of the Lord (vv. 18, 36-37).

Psalm 70

In this lament (A) one of the "afflicted and poor" (v. 6), a group which recognizes that they have no other resource than Yahweh, cries out to be saved from the enemy, "who seek my life" (v. 3). May the group of righteous, to which the psalmist belongs, be upheld with the divine presence that brings joy to the heart (vv. 5-6)!

Psalm 71

This lament (A) is uttered by an old person (v. 9) who seeks asylum in the temple. Persecuted by enemies, who interpret the afflictions of old age as divine judgment (v. 11), the psalmist turns to the God of righteousness whose praise he has sung from his youth. Verses 1-4 are an impassioned cry to God, the immovable rock of refuge. Verses 5-9 express a hope learned from a lifetime of praising God. Verses 10-13 dramatize the menace of the enemies and pray for their downfall. Verses 14-21 develop a prayer for deliverance. The psalmist has sung of God's wonders all these years. Will God allow that voice of praise to grow silent under the attack of enemies? Verses 22-24 are a vow of praise; the psalmist, in the light of the reassuring oracle given by the priest in the temple, will continue the song of praise begun in his youth.

Psalm 72

This royal psalm presents the king as the vicar of Yahweh. He represents to Israel and to the world the justice and peace with which the world was created. The king, however, is a human being who gives only what he has been given; intercession must be made for him. Intercession is the purpose of the psalm.

In verses 1-4, echoed in verses 12-14, the king is the "lengthened arm of Yahweh," exercising divine judgment. Justice here—and generally in the Bible—is not impartial deciding but vigorous upholding of the oppressed party. Verses 12-14 state that the king redeems the life of the poor; he is the agent of Yahweh's rescue of the people. The king embodies not only divine justice but also divinely intended peace and fertility; in verses 5-7 and 16 he embodies health and fertility for the whole land. Yahweh, the sole Deity in heaven and on earth, has a sole vicar, the Israelite king. To that king, therefore, all the nations of the earth come, bringing gifts that acknowledge the just and life-giving divine presence manifest in him (vv. 17-19).

BOOK III: PSALMS 73–89

Psalm 73

This unique probing of the just power of God fits no single genre but comes closest to the thanksgiving psalm (B—see p. 755). The psalmist tells of his rescue from near despair by an experience of God in the temple (vv. 16-20, 21-26).

The opening verse, "How good God is to the upright," is the conclusion. The painful experience behind that faith-inspired affirmation is the matter of the rest of the poem. What scandalized the psalmist was the prosperity of the wicked (vv. 2-14). Israel imagined life as two paths—the path of the wicked that leads to destruction and the path of the righteous that leads to prosperity (see Psalm 1). The prosperity of the wicked makes a mockery of God's governance of the world. To seek a solution to this temptation, the psalmist goes to the temple and there realizes that the end of the wicked shows that God does indeed rule the world with justice (vv. 15-20). Their sudden destruction shows their impermanence.

In the temple the psalmist receives a special sense of God's care: "Yet with you I shall always be" (v. 23). Verse 24, "and in the end you will receive me in glory," has traditionally been understood as a mysterious rescue by God, like the taking up of Enoch in Gen 5:24. The experience of being near God allows the sufferer to affirm God's justice (vv. 1, 27-28).

Psalm 74

This communal lament (A—see p. 754) could appropriately be sung whenever an enemy overran the temple of Yahweh. The destruction of Jerusalem and the temple by the Babylonians in 587 B.C.E. was surely such an occasion. Verses 1-11 directly summon Yahweh to look upon the ruined sanctuary and to remember the very congregation that Yahweh has created (better than "built up") and redeemed (v. 2). Zion and Israel, Yahweh's shrine and people, are inextricably bound together; an attack on the temple is an attack on the project Yahweh has initiated. "How long?" (v. 10) is a real question; ancients often looked for oracles that would tell them how long a disaster would last.

To persuade Yahweh to act, the community remembers liturgically the deed that established their world. As often in the Bible, creation is portrayed as conflict; first unbounded water is tamed and then unbounded darkness (vv. 13-17). Will the one who led Israel to dwell in Zion (vv. 1-2) allow the enemy to scoff (vv. 18-23)? "Your dove," "the humble," "the afflicted and the poor" (vv. 19-21)—these are the terms the faithful use of themselves; they prefer to wait for their God Yahweh to defend them rather than take matters into their own hands as if there were no promise.

Psalm 75

The psalm is a national thanksgiving (B). There had been threats against the people from their enemies, the people cried out, and God judged for them, that is, upheld them and put down their enemies. Verses 3-4 state that in crises threatening the very existence of the world, God alone determines the time of an intervention. That intervention is an act of judgment, which is not an impartial judicial decree but an act in favor of the wronged party (vv. 5-6). That judgment comes from no other source than Israel's God (vv. 7-9). The cup of the Lord that the enemies must drink is a common biblical metaphor for the unopposed power of the Lord over all nations. The community rejoices in the peace brought by the just God (vv. 10-11).

Psalm 76

Psalm 76 is a song of Zion that glorifies the holy mountain as the place where Yahweh is revealed as the creator by vanquishing forces hostile to human community. Verses 2-4 state that Zion is the place where God is acknowledged as sole God because it is the site of the world-establishing victory. Yahweh is the God of all but is uniquely revealed in Jerusalem/Zion. Verses 5-7 and 8-11 describe the victory of the Lord; at the divine rebuke all enemies lay stunned. The afflicted of the earth in verse 10 are all those who wait for Yahweh to save them from the arrogant ones of the world. The final two verses urge those who recognize that the Lord is present in Zion to hasten there with tokens of homage.

Psalm 77

In this community lament (A), someone speaking for the community ("I") describes the intense anguish of Israel when its Lord does nothing for the people. "Will his kindness utterly cease?" (v. 9) is the root question. Has Yahweh forgotten the loving commitment meant to ensure the people's peaceful existence? The assurance had been given time and again in the past to the patriarchs and to the people at Sinai. Verses 12-21, the second half of the poem, recite the divine deed that brought Israel into existence; it is retold in liturgical context ("remember," "meditate," and "ponder" in verses 12-13 really mean "recite") so as to awaken the community's faith that Yahweh will not let that initiating act become null and void. The "works" of the Lord (v. 13) are the victory over the sea that enabled Israel to cross over to Canaan and live as a community under Moses and Aaron, as God intended. The psalm prays that God will be faithful to this original intent.

Psalm 78

This long retelling of Israel's traditions of the Exodus-Conquest makes important changes in the ancient story, changes that would be immediately perceived by the sensitive Israelite. The speaker promises, in the tripartite introduction (vv. 1-4, 5-7, 8-11, each section ending with "the wonderful deeds of Yahweh" or a similar phrase), to draw a new meaning from the ancient story. That story contains a lesson: the present generation ought not defy the new act of God as did their ancestors.

The rest of the psalm consists of two parallel recitals of approximately the same length; they illuminate each other.

First Recital

Wilderness events, vv. 12-32
- Gracious act, vv. 12-16
- Rebellion, vv. 17-20
- Divine anger and punishment (manna and quail), vv. 21-31
- Sequel, vv. 32-39

Second Recital

From Egypt to Canaan, vv. 40-64
- Gracious act, vv. 40-55
- Rebellion, vv. 56-58
- Divine anger and punishment (destruction of Shiloh), vv. 59-64
- Sequel, vv. 65-72

The first recital arranges the old narrative so that the crossing of the Red Sea and the water in the wilderness constitute one great miracle of water, making all the more inexcusable the consequent rebellion—"Can he also give bread, or provide meat for his people?" (v. 20). In punishment, God does not hesitate to make use of the gracious gift of manna and quail to smite them. In the sequel the people fail to recognize the true significance of what has happened.

The second recital concerns Israel's movement from Egypt (whom Yahweh defeats in seven attacks) to the holy mountain shrine of Shiloh. The people's infidelity again provokes divine wrath and punishment, the destruction of Shiloh (the gracious gift). The sequel is the choice of a successor to the rejected Shiloh—Zion and David. Will Israel now fail to see the significance of the divine pattern of gift, sin, punishment, new gift? Will the people recognize that the southern kingdom of Judah is the heir to the destroyed northern kingdom? God has not left the people without a shrine and shepherd. But they must come to both in faith.

Psalm 79

This communal lament (A) complains to God that the nations have defiled the temple and murdered the holy people, leaving their corpses unburied (vv. 1-4). The situation is apparently that which existed after the destruction of the temple by the Babylonians in 587 B.C.E. The people ask "how long" the withdrawal of divine favor will last (v. 5). They acknowledge that their sins have brought the suffering upon them (vv. 8-9). In their plea for divine intervention, the people complain that nations that do not acknowledge Yahweh as God are running rampant (v. 6); that Yahweh's honor is compromised (vv. 1, 10, 12); that Israel, Yahweh's servants, suffer (vv. 2-4, 11). The last verse is a vow of praise, a statement of faith in the Lord who saves.

Psalm 80

In this communal lament (A) the people, defeated in war, appeal to the Lord of all heavenly powers ("O Lord of hosts," v. 5). By reciting the story of their founding, they appeal to God's honor: Will God allow the nations to ravage the chosen vine that was taken from Egypt and planted in Canaan? The magnificence of the vine once proclaimed God's greatness; its despoliation now insults God's honor. The people's hope is in God, not themselves; they promise repentance so that God will never again turn away (v. 19).

After the opening two verses call upon the shepherd of Israel to intervene, the usual lament elements of plea, recital of history, and complaint are punctuated by the refrains of verses 4, 7, and 20. The Davidic king in verse 18 represents the people; his restoration means favor again for everyone.

Psalm 81

The psalm seems to be a record of a liturgy celebrated at one of the three great festivals—Passover, Pentecost, or Harvest. The community is summoned before God in verses 2-4, the gathering being commanded by the law (vv. 5-6). A speaker then recites to the community the great act of liberation that made Israel into a people: the Exodus from Egypt (vv. 6b-8). In Egypt the people had been unwilling servants of Pharaoh, but at Sinai they became willing servants of Yahweh, freely agreeing to obey the commandments, the first of which is repeated in verses 10-11. The speaker rebukes the people for violating the commandment that makes them God's people (vv. 12-13). But there is still time to obey, to "hear" the great commandment; to obey will bring divine protection and nurture (vv. 14-17). The psalms bring the people before their God, who seeks from them a free and loving response.

Psalm 82

The psalmist paints a vivid picture of the heavenly assembly, where Yahweh declares that no other divine being controls human history. In the ancient Near East, people commonly assumed there were many gods who controlled human destinies. Yahweh accuses these "gods" of injustice, of not upholding the cause of the defenseless (vv. 2-4), and proclaims judgment in earthshaking thunder (v. 5). Verses 6-7 strip power from such beings. Because Yahweh is now the sole judge (=ruler), the faithful are to direct their pleas for justice to this God alone (v. 8).

Psalm 83

The community laments (A) the attacks of the nations against Zion. Yahweh's shrine on earth is inviolable (Psalms 2, 46, 48, 76). When enemies overrun it, Yahweh's claim to be the sole Deity comes into question.

After the unadorned cry to God in verse 2, the complaint in verses 3-9 portrays all the enemies who have plagued Israel through the ages as conspiring to wipe out Israel's name. The name (vv. 5, 17, 19) is the means by which one is known. Verses 10-13 pray that Yahweh destroy the current crop of enemies as the enemies of old were destroyed. The children of Lot are Moab and Edom (Gen 19:36-38 and Deut 2:9). The victory of Gideon at Midian is told in Judg 6–8; the defeat of Sisera and Jabin, in Judg 4–5; of Oreb and Zeeb, in Judg 7:25; of Zebah and Zalmunna, in Judg 8:21. Verses 14-19 extend the prayer: Yahweh is to storm against the foes so that they will learn that the sanctuary is indeed a secure place for the people.

Psalm 84

How joyfully the Israelite fulfills the obligation of the law to go up to Jerusalem three times a year (Deut 16:1-17) is vividly portrayed in this psalm. All living things are safe from threat in the presence of the Lord (vv. 3-4). The pilgrim forgets the difficulties of the journey (vv. 5-8). The king is the representative of Yahweh, and prayer is offered by him at the feasts (vv. 9-10). The Lord's presence is not just a matter of space; only those who walk uprightly and who trust enjoy the blessings of divine nearness (vv. 11-13).

Psalm 85

In this national lament (A) Israel recalls how their God in the past has forgiven their sins and restored their land and fortunes (vv. 2-4). To Yahweh, their forgiving and restoring God, they pray in their distress: Once more show yourself a healing God (vv. 5-8). The people, because of their sins, do not demand restoration; they wait in faith for God: "I will hear what God proclaims." God's favor is neither automatic nor indiscriminate;

only those among the people who fear the Lord can hope to enjoy salvation (vv. 9-10). The divine answer comes in verses 11-14. God's attributes, "kindness and truth . . . justice and peace," will once again work in the land, making a place fit for God to dwell. The psalm was probably composed during the sixth-century Exile, when Israel was tempted to believe that God had left forever.

Psalm 86

In this individual lament (A), which draws many of its expressions from other psalms, the singer describes himself as "afflicted and poor" (v. 1); "devoted" (v. 2); "your servant" (vv. 2, 4, 16); "rescued from the depths of the nether world" (v. 13); attacked by the haughty (v. 14). These are the self-designations of one who confesses that there is no other protection from life's dangers than the graciously bestowed protection of Yahweh. All the elements of a lament are here—the unadorned cry for help, the complaint, the prayer, the expression of hope. But in this psalm the distress of the psalmist seems less particular; the servant does not seem to be overly frightened by threats, for somehow they bring him closer to the Lord. In that attitude the servants find their identity.

Psalm 87

This poem, unfortunately textually damaged, is a song of Zion, like Psalms 46, 48, 76, and 132. The situation seems to be the Exile or its aftermath, when Zion's citizens were scattered over Babylon and Egypt. To be a citizen of Zion is protection enough for anyone, for it is the city of the only powerful God.

Psalm 88

In few laments (A) is the fear of death so vividly portrayed. A land of darkness and oblivion far below the earth (vv. 4-8), of separation from friends and human society (vv. 9, 19) is the way the psalmist imagines Sheol in the era before there was any thought of resurrection from the dead. Nonetheless, the frightened and afflicted person continues to cry out to the God of life; prayers punctuate the psalm (vv. 2-3, 10, 14). The psalmist's strategy is clever: he reminds God that only the living remember and celebrate the wonderful divine mercies (vv. 11-13). The life that the psalmist seeks is life with God and with one's community. What is terrifying in death is the loss of others.

Psalm 89

The community laments (A) the defeat of the king, who represents Yahweh's mastery of the world and its inhabitants. That mastery was shown by God's creation victory. The defeat of Yahweh's lieutenant on earth, the king, raises the question of whether Yahweh is truly the powerful God. Verses 2-5 hymn the God who made secure in one creative act the heavens and the Davidic dynasty. Like other communal laments, verses 6-38 narrate the original event that brought Israel into existence—in this psalm, the conquest of primordial sea, the making of the earth through orderly pairs of elements, and the leading of the people to the land (vv. 9-19). Part of that world-establishing victory is the installation of the Davidic king, with whom Yahweh shares the fruit of this universal victory in a solemn promise (vv. 20-38). But now in our day, complains the community, our king is not protected; enemies break through at will (vv. 39-52). The community, despite its grief, has faith enough to hold Yahweh to the original promise.

BOOK IV: PSALMS 90–106

Psalm 90

In most community laments (A) Israel recalls the founding event, the divine act that brought them into existence—the Exodus-Conquest, the act of creation. The people's plea is that God not allow the present danger to wipe out the community that has been graciously established. In this psalm the danger is not external, for example a foreign nation, but the evil intent of the people themselves. Humans and God are incommensurate—their life, plans, and power (vv. 3-11). The psalmist remembers the eternity of God; even before the world was made, God was (vv. 1-2). Hence the prayer in verses 12-17 that God teach the people to know themselves before God, to let them experience the special joy of servants, of those who see the power of God and see their own plans affirmed by grace. The poem is not simply a meditation on human frailty; it speaks from the experience of God's just punishment of sin and from confidence in God's forgiveness.

Psalm 91

This song of trust comes from a person who has experienced the asylum of the temple. From that spot, safe under the wings of the Most High (vv. 1-2; see 1 Kgs 6:23-28), the psalmist assures those laboring under the dangers always besetting the just that God will overcome all. Verses 3-13 are a series of promises that the salvation of the Lord, so palpable in the temple, will be available in all areas if one makes the Lord one's refuge. In verses 14-16 the Lord speaks directly to all who maintain their trust in the face of the danger and bitterness of life. Adapted from the promise of salvation in the lament (A), it invites those in danger to the ultimate protection and loving relationship.

Psalm 92

The song is a hymn (C), in that it states how appropriate it is to praise God for the work of just and gracious governance, and a thanksgiving (B), in that it tells how the psalmist was rescued from personal enemies (vv. 10-11). Because of the triumph of the wicked, the psalmist must have been tempted by the kind of doubts about God's justice that are vividly described in Psalms 37, 49, and 73. Profound rejoicing in the just and merciful God mark this psalm. Verse 9, "while you, O Lord, are the Most High forever," is the exact center of the poem. Also, the same Hebrew verb is repeated at the beginning and end (translated "to proclaim" in verse 2 and "declaring" in verse 16).

Verses 2-5 emphasize how beautiful and fitting it is to praise God for showing justice. Verses 6-12 describe the experience of one who has just seen that merciful justice in action. That supremacy can be seen, however, only by those who are themselves just. "How very deep are your thoughts!" (v. 6) means "your intentions are hidden." The person who waits for the Lord, like this psalmist, will experience rescue. The last section (vv. 13-16) describes what life in the presence of the only God consists in. The trees in the great court of the temple symbolize the life offered to those who are just. The security and happiness of the just will declare the Lord's mercy and fidelity.

Preface to Psalms 93, 95–100

These psalms all elaborate the kingship of Yahweh in a similar way. In all of them "Yahweh reigns." In the ancient Near East, polytheistic except for Israel, a god was acclaimed powerful over the other gods because of a specific act of power. The greatest act was creation, bringing the world of men and women into existence. In the Bible creation is frequently the creation of Israel as a people securely dwelling before Yahweh in the sanctuary. This could be expressed either in the language of the Exodus-Conquest or in the language of cosmogony, the overcoming of forces hostile to human community. The latter language was already centuries old when borrowed by Israel. Yahweh proves to be supreme among the gods by conquering the annihilating power of sea (less frequently, the power of primordial night). Yahweh then arranges the elements to support human community and brings the people to dwell securely in the sanctuary, the temple. The temple and its ceremonies figure prominently in these psalms. The jubilant people are admitted into the court, where they acknowledge Yahweh's great victory that has made them God's people. Whether Israel annually celebrated Yahweh's kingship is a matter that is still unsettled.

Psalm 93

(Read the preface to Psalm 93 above.) This hymn (C) celebrates the kingship of Yahweh, who created the world (vv. 1-2) by defeating sea (vv. 3-4). Sea completely covered the land, making human life impossible. Sea in the psalm, as customary elsewhere in the Bible, is endowed with will; it roars in wrath against the power of Yahweh. The decrees of verse 5 are the designs that the Lord imposes upon the newly ordered world, designs also found in Israel's law. Verses 1ab and 5 thus frame the poem; a gloriously garbed Yahweh utters those words that structure the world.

Psalm 94

This lament (A) complains to God that the wicked and the arrogant have the upper hand and that those who are faithful, "the righteous," are their victims. It is more a personal than a national lament (the psalmist speaks of personal distress in verses 16-19), yet there is concern for the people as well (vv. 5-7, 20-21). It is probably placed among the psalms of Yahweh's kingship (Psalms 93 and 95–100) because of its expectation that Yahweh will judge the earth.

Verses 1-2, a cry to Yahweh, contain the striking epithet "God of vengeance." "Vengeance" here means the intent to right an unfair situation by punishing the wicked. "How long" introduces the complaint of verses 3-7: For what length of time must the psalmist suffer the silence of God in the face of rampant injustice against the poor? Verses 8-11 and 12-15 are declarations of faith. The first bravely tells the evildoers that their statement that the Lord does not see (v. 7) is false and that their plans (rather than "thoughts," v. 11a) are doomed; the second assures the persecuted that their sufferings have meaning and are only temporary. In verses 16-19 the psalmist teaches the people from personal experience that the Lord does indeed console, even in the midst of trials like these. The last section (vv. 20-23) boldly affirms, on the basis of God's justice and the psalmist's experience, that the Lord will indeed rectify the present intolerable situation.

Psalm 95

(Read the preface to Psalms 95–100, p. 774). Verses 1-5 and 6-7 are parallel (ten lines in the first section, five in the second). Each invites the people to come to the temple, the sole place where Yahweh's power is manifested in building and ritual. In verses 3-5 Yahweh's supremacy over all powers in the heavens is shown through the easy arrangement of the paired elements that make up the world: the depths of the earth and the mountains, the sea and the land. After the second invitation in verse 6, the second step in creation is mentioned—the creation of Israel as Yahweh's special flock (v. 7). In verses 7c-11 the flock is abruptly confronted: Will they be obedient as befits Yahweh's flock? People had to be admitted in a gate ceremony like those portrayed in Psalms 15 and 24. "Does your behavior really say you are God's people?" they were asked. This psalm ends with such a scrutiny. The question is not simply a convention; Israel's first generation was never admitted to the holy land because of its apostasy. Yahweh's people must live by Yahweh's word.

Psalm 96

(Read the preface to Psalms 95–100, p. 774.) The theme of the sole kingship of Yahweh is again elaborated in this hymn (C), but with a special call to the nations (vv. 7-10)—indeed all creation, animate and inanimate (vv. 11-12)—to join the chorus of welcome. The first section (vv. 1-6) calls for a new song, that is, a song appropriate to the renewal of the earth through creation. The very proclamation of the act of creation, ("his salvation," "his glory," "his wondrous deeds," vv. 2-3), is itself a denial of other gods, for they had nothing to do with the making of the world (vv. 4-5). The temple, the last great deed in Yahweh's creating, embodies divine glory in a special way (v. 6).

The second invitation, that the nations bring their gifts to Yahweh in the temple (vv. 7-10), flows logically from the first section. Verses 1-6 state that Yahweh, by virtue of creation, is supreme over "the gods," the patrons of the nations, and that this work of creation is specially visible in the temple. The final section (vv. 11-13) exhorts nature to greet the Creator-God who comes to judge, that is, to see that the newly created world operates according to the divine intent.

Psalm 97

(Read the preface to Psalms 95–100, p. 774.) This hymn (C) extols the reign of Yahweh, portraying in its two sections the manifestation of that reign to the world at large (vv. 1-7) and then, in a special way, to Zion and its cities (vv. 8-12). The sections are demarcated by the repetition of the verbs "rejoice" and "be glad" in verses 1 and 8 and the polar opposites of worshipers of images and worshipers of Yahweh in verses 7 and 12. In the first section the kingship of Yahweh is manifested dynamically in the weapons of thunder and lightning that overcame all opposition; other so-called gods and their worshipers are shamed. In the second section Zion welcomes its victorious Creator-Lord. The righteous are those who worship aright; they are the ones who are vindicated when their Lord comes in power.

Psalm 98

(Read the preface to Psalms 95–100, p. 774.) In this hymn (C) the community celebrates the victory of Yahweh, which brings joy to the world and establishes Yahweh as judge over all (v. 9). The victory of which verse 2 speaks (the "wondrous deeds" of verse 1 and the "justice" of verse 2) is specific: the conquest of all threats to the peaceful existence of Israel. The threats are depicted in the psalms in various guises—cosmic forces such as sea, nations bent on Israel's destruction, evildoers seemingly triumphant. Yet all are reductively one: those who condemn Yahweh's will for a just universe in which Israel dwells secure. God's judging can only cause exultation to all peoples, for evil forces will be destroyed (vv. 7-9). God's judging is not an impartial settlement of claims but the vigorous upholding of the wrong and oppressed; such protection was promised to Israel of old (v. 3). The hymn is structured by a threefold invitation (vv. 1, 4, and 7).

Psalm 99

(Read the preface to Psalms 95–100, p. 774.) The emphasis in this hymn (C) to the supreme King is upon Zion, the place where that supremacy is visible, and upon Israel, the people who have transmitted God's royal decrees. Yahweh is, to be sure, the sole God of all the world, but Yahweh is revealed in Zion by means of the people Israel. The poem is structured by the threefold statement that God is holy (vv. 3, 5, and 9) and by the twice-repeated command to extol Yahweh (vv. 5 and 9). Verses 6-8 single out Israel as the sole nation in dialogue with Yahweh by mentioning its most famous spokespersons—Moses, Aaron, and Samuel. They heard the authentic word of Yahweh and handed it on. Yahweh's help, given when "he answered them" (vv. 6, 8), is a sure sign of the validity of that word. All nations are to respond to Yahweh, God of the world, by serving this God in Zion of Israel.

Psalm 100

(Read the preface to Psalms 95–100, p. 774.) Though this hymn (C) does not mention kingship explicitly, it presumes the same thought-world as the other psalms of kingship—the invitations to the world to rejoice and to do so in the court of the temple. Much is condensed in this brief poem. The world is to rejoice and to come to the temple because Yahweh is God. It must be assumed that God's supremacy here is manifested through the same act as in Psalms 93, 95–99: the creation victory over hostile forces, a victory that makes the world and Israel. It is appropriate, then, to enter and give thanks.

Psalm 101

In this royal psalm the Davidic king liturgically affirms his task of overseeing the justice of God in the kingdom. The first verse is the leitmotif: kindness and judgment describe God's gracious choice of the king, and, through the king, of Israel. The king here, as in Psalms 72 and 89, is the agent of God's holiness and justice in the world of men and women. He cleanses his house of evildoers (vv. 3b-5, 7-8), his "house" (vv. 2, 7) meaning his family and palace. He is the model Israelite (vv. 2-3a) and champions all who are faithful by putting them in positions of responsibility (v. 6). The psalm is a vow in the sight of God; before the people the king promises to avoid Oriental despotism and to be the servant of the just God.

Psalm 102

In this lament (A), a Penitential Psalm, the psalmist's experience of bodily and psychic disintegration (vv. 4-12) impels a cry to God (vv. 2-3), whose "fury and wrath" (v. 11) have caused the suffering. The psalmist attributes whatever happens to God; hence the present affliction must be due to God's "fury and wrath."

Psalms of individual lament include a statement of hope in the midst of the complaint. In verses 13-23 the distressed person, standing in the temple, the very place where Yahweh has promised to be present, hopes that help will be given. In verses 17-18 the Lord has built Zion, and so it is a refuge from every danger. Verses 19-23 are the motto of Zion: In this spot the Lord protects the people; and this protective care is revealed in the sight of the whole world. Verses 24-29 restate the original complaint and prayer for salvation (vv. 24-25) and add an act of faith in the God who will always guard the faithful servants. The psalmist, by going to the temple and being one of the Lord's servants, finds security in the midst of suffering.

Psalm 103

In this hymn (C) the speaker praises the God whose graciousness has been shown in all moments of personal life—in actions of forgiveness and protection from life-threatening forces (vv. 1-5). This is the same Lord who ever acts on behalf of the needy, having acted for Israel through the mediation of Moses. Verses 6-18 characterize the God of Israel as just, yet never allowing justice to circumvent a merciful choice. Human sin cannot destroy God's favor (vv. 11-13), nor can frailty and insignificance (when measured against God's eternity). Those who are faithful to the covenant become members of that company with whom God has promised to remain (vv. 17-18). The praise of the Lord is not the task of Israel alone; the beings of the heavenly world are to join in the praise (vv. 19-22).

Psalm 104

This hymn (C) praises God, who with ease and skill has made primordial night and rampaging waters into a world everywhere vibrant with life. The conception of the psalm is the same as Gen 1, where a dark and watery chaos (Gen 1:1-2) receives light on the first day and dry land on the second day. The two forces, night and waters, that had made human community impossible are not annihilated; they are made into an integral part of creation.

In verses 1-4 the speaker acknowledges that the Lord's palace, entourage, and very self by their splendor reflect God's mastery over the heavenly world. In verses 5-18 the divine mastery extends to the waters; the waters that once completely covered the earth flee to their proper place at the divine rebuke (vv. 5-9). Water now is tamed for the service of people, nourishing life in rivers (vv. 10-12) and in rain (vv. 13-15), and even fertilizing the fabled mountain of Lebanon (vv. 16-17). Verses 19-23 show the mastery over darkness; it is now part of the sequence of night and day, necessary and helpful to humans and animals (vv. 19-23). In the face of such wisdom and power, the psalmist exclaims in awe (v. 24). Even the vast sea, the mysterious fringe of the known world, is under God. There, too, God has placed a living being, Leviathan, that it might enjoy life, (vv. 25-26). God's world is not the clock of the Deist philosophers, wound and left to run mechanically; at every moment each creature looks to God for its being. God's spirit, or breath, is necessary for life, as it is in Gen 2–3 and Ezek 37:1-14 (vv. 27-30).

Control over the elemental forces on earth shows the glory of the Lord, the theme of religious song (vv. 31-34). The only thing that can obscure God's glory is human sin. The psalmist prays that sinners no longer deface the handiwork of the Lord (v. 35).

Psalm 105

This is a hymn (C) to the Lord who has promised the land of Canaan to the people, the Lord who can be sought in all places and at all times, whose word of promise is everywhere effective. In verses 1-6 Israel, descendant of the patriarchs Abraham and Jacob, is invited to praise and seek the Lord's presence. Verses 7-11 identify God as the Lord of the whole world and as the one who remembers the promise of land to the patriarchs. Verses 12-45 retell the mighty deeds of the past that are relevant to the present situation:

vv. 12-15	the ancestors in the land of Canaan
vv. 16-22	Joseph in the land of Egypt
vv. 23-38	Israel in the land of Egypt
vv. 39-45	Israel in the desert on the way to Canaan

In each of the four episodes there are three elements: (1) a servant(s) through whom appears (2) the ancestral word of promise of (3) the land of Canaan. Yahweh has always been faithful to the promise to give Israel the land of Canaan. The psalm seems to be a song of Israel in the sixth-century Exile, when it did not actually possess the land. It invites praise of the Lord who will act to bring the people home.

Psalm 106

This community lament (A) retells incidents from Israel's national story, the Exodus-Conquest, to show that God's mercy has been as evident as God's justice. The speaker's "I" in verses 4-5 includes all Israelites, whose plea for mercy rests completely in the God whose work has never been destroyed by sin.

The opening five verses praise God and God's great deed of fashioning a people. May the speaker and the congregation always be among those whom God favors! Verses 6-12 portray the first of the eight incidents in the psalm in which the people responded to God's gracious act by rebellion. At the Red Sea (Exod 14–15), the Lord saved the people despite their rebellion. The same will to save is depicted in the scenes of divine deed, rebellion, and punishment of verses 13-15 (see Num 11); vv. 16-18 (see Num 16); vv. 19-23 (see Exod 32–34); vv. 24-27 (see Num 13–14); vv. 28-31 (see Num 25:1-15); vv. 32-33 (see Num 20:1-13); vv. 34-39 (see Judg 3:3-6). Verses 40-46 describe the same general rhythm of apostasy, punishment and rescue that characterized Israel during the period of the judges (see Judg 2:6–3:6). Israel's history shows that God has punished justly but has never let destruction be the last word. Therefore, in verses 47-48 the people pray that God bring them back from the just punishment of their exile so that they might again give praise.

BOOK V: PSALMS 107–150

Psalm 107

This hymn (C) invites all Israelites to praise the Lord, who has brought them into being as a single people, redeeming them from every danger, bringing them from the four corners of the earth (vv. 1-3). In verses 4-32 four archetypal divine rescues of perishing people are described: rescue from the sterile desert in verses 4-9, from the bonds of primordial night in vv. 10-16, from mortal illness in verses 17-22, and from the angry sea in verses 23-32. God's power on behalf of the endangered and needy invites them to praise (vv. 8, 15, 21, 31). The number four in ancient Near Eastern literature often suggests totality, as in the phrase "the four corners of the earth"; the four cases, therefore, represent all cases of extreme need.

The same redeeming activity of the Lord is shown in Israel's story in verses 33-41. Yahweh destroyed Sodom and Gomorrah in Gen 18–19, which this psalm sees as a type of the destruction of the wicked inhabitants of Canaan in order to clear the land for Israel (vv. 33-34). The Lord led Israel in the desert, settling them in the land and giving increase to crop and herd (vv. 35-38). Whenever the people are endangered, as in the four cases of verses 4-32, the Lord rescues them (vv. 39-41). Israel thus becomes a showcase of this Lord's power and mercy to the entire world. Verses 42-43 invite all to see that Israel witnesses to the Lord's graciousness; in the daily life of the people graciousness of the Lord appears.

Psalm 108

This poem is a composite of old pieces. Verses 2-6 are the same as Ps 57:8-12, and verses 7-14 are the same as Ps 60:7-14. Probably it is a prayer for victory. Verses 2-7 are a bold song of confidence and of petition to God for victory. Verses 8-11 are an oracle of salvation, uttered most probably by the priest in the temple during war; they promise that God the Warrior will defend the land. Verses 12-14 take up and develop the petition of verses 6-7.

Psalm 109

This lament (A) is noteworthy for length and vehemence of its prayer against the evildoer (vv. 6-20). The cry to God in verse 1 and the complaint of verses 2-5 and 22-25 are brief in comparison. The psalmist apparently is the victim of a campaign of slander, which could be devastating in a society where reputation and honor are paramount. In the dramatic perspective of the psalm, there are only two types of people: the wicked and their poor victims. The psalmist is one of the poor (vv. 22, 31), one of the friends of God who are enemies of the wicked. The poor person asks vindication not because of personal virtue but because God has promised to be the friend of the poor.

Psalm 110

In this royal psalm, which resembles Psalm 89 and especially Psalm 2, a court singer delivers three oracles concerning the king (vv. 1, 2, 4). They promise, respectively, a place of honor with God, who achieves victory over evil, divine sonship, and priesthood or mediation between God and people. The three oracles are expanded in verses 5-6; the king, as ruler for Yahweh, will exercise divine sovereignty over the whole world. Verse 3 is corrupt; the translation is a guess. The poem is most probably from the coronation of the Davidic king. The last verse about drinking from the brook may refer to a rite at Gihon brook, like that implied in 1 Kgs 1:38-40.

Psalm 111

Like Psalms 9-10, 25, 34, 37, and 112, this poem is acrostic, each verse beginning with a successive letter of the twenty-two-letter Hebrew alphabet. Verse 1 gives the situation: a temple singer praises the Lord by reciting the Lord's actions in Israel's history. The singer is a teacher as well as a leader in song. Verses 2-10 teach that the Lord is revealed in historical act. In the recital, precept and gracious act are both divine gift; to remember and to obey are simply two modes of responding to God's initiative.

Psalm 112

Like Psalm 111 and other psalms, this poem is acrostic, each line beginning with a successive letter of the Hebrew alphabet. Like Psalm 1, it assures life to the person who remains close to the Lord by willingly obeying the divine will. In the psalm life consists of abundant progeny (v. 2), wealth that enables one to be magnanimous (vv. 3, 5, 9), and virtue that enables one to support other people in the community (v. 4). The words "forever" or "everlasting" occur three times, spaced evenly throughout the poem (vv. 3, 6, 9), showing how rooted and stable is the person near the Lord. The just person is an affront to the wicked, whose life wastes away in envy and frustration (v. 10). The psalm draws upon the tradition of the two ways of life; the ways are starkly set before every person so as to elicit a choice.

Psalm 113

This hymn (C) exhorts the servants or worshipers of the Lord to praise the divine name, that is, the way in which God is presented to the world. The name is especially manifest in the celebrations of the temple (v. 1), but, since God is over all things, praise cannot be confined to a particular time or place (vv. 2-3). Yahweh, Israel's God, acts in the heavens above and on the earth below. The last three verses celebrate Yahweh acting as judge. In the Bible, to judge is not to render an impartial verdict from afar but to right wrongs and relieve the poor.

Psalm 114

This hymn (C), lacking the usual invitation for others to join in, celebrates the Exodus-Conquest, the act by which Israel came into being as a people. In the concentrated perspective of the poem, the people move directly from Egypt to Israel/Judah, the sacred land of Yahweh (vv. 1-2). Sea/Jordan, which stands between the people and their land as an obstacle, is personified. Like a panic-stricken soldier, it flees before the mighty Yahweh, who fights at the head of the people. The earth quakes at the cosmic battle and victory (v. 4). The natural elements are then taunted, as one would taunt a defeated enemy (vv. 5-6). As Yahweh heads the procession of the rescued people into the safety of the holy land, the natural elements are commanded to greet their new master, Yahweh.

Psalm 115

The psalm probably records a liturgy performed by Israel at a time when its misery and small numbers provoked its neighbors to taunt, "Where is your God?" The community answers with a prayer to Yahweh to uphold the divine name (vv. 1-3) and with a countertaunt that the neighbor's gods are as impotent as the statues that represent them in the splendid rituals (vv. 4-8). Israel has no images of its God, Yahweh; it is itself the image of Yahweh, testifying to God's glory by its actions. Verses 9-11 describe the Israelite community as constituted by its trust in Yahweh, its sole support. And that hope is answered by the blessing in verses 12-18. Blessing means enhancement of life and increase of progeny. Israel is confident that its own blessed existence on earth redounds to God's glory, showing that Yahweh is a living God (vv. 14-16). This psalm and Psalm 135 make use of ideas about Israel as the image of God found in Second Isaiah. The psalms are probably postexilic.

Psalm 116

In this loosely knit thanksgiving (B), the speaker responds to God's rescue of him from the clutches of death (vv. 3-4) and from near despair (vv. 10-11) with vows and sacrifice in the temple (vv. 13-14, 17-19). The chief praise, however, is expressed in the vivid description of the divine mercy and the public proclamation of the Lord's attentiveness to the cry of the poor. Grievous indeed in the Lord's sight is the death of the faithful ones (v. 17). It is the experience of the saving Lord that enables one to say, "I am your servant" (v. 16).

Psalm 117

In this shortest of all hymns (C), the nations are called to acknowledge Yahweh's sovereignty because of God's never-ending fidelity to Israel. Israel's secure existence, owed entirely to Yahweh's grace, is the proof to the world that only Yahweh is God.

Psalm 118

A thanksgiving (B) after a victory, this psalm accompanies a procession into the temple precincts. Solemn entry into the temple by king and people and their partaking of a banquet were ways of celebrating the Exodus-Conquest, when Yahweh led the people from the domain of Pharaoh to Yahweh's own domain. Verses 1-4 call upon the ranks of worshipers to praise the Lord, for the Lord is faithful. In verses 5-18 the speaker tells of the divine mercy shown by Yahweh's rescue of the people from their enemies. The citation of the old poem about the Exodus-Conquest in Exod 15 (v. 14 = Exod 15:2; vv. 15-16 = Exod 15:6; v. 28 = Exod 15:2) suggests that today's victory is an extension of the original victory that made Israel a people.

Verses 19-29 echo the cries of the procession as it enters the great court of the temple. Only the just, those whom God has chosen, may enter; victory today has shown the people that they are chosen and thus may enter. Verse 22 is a proverb; what is insignificant has become great through divine election. The reference may be to the foundation stone of the temple. The psalm orchestrates the people's movement and shouts a hymn to the Lord of victory.

Psalm 119

Psalm 119 is the longest psalm in the Psalter. The 176 verses of the poem are arranged acrostically, according to the order of the Hebrew alphabet; there are twenty-two sections of eight verses. In its great length and in its utilization of many psalmic genres—the blessing, the individual lament, the song of trust, the individual thanksgiving, the hymn—it is unparalleled in the Bible. It is an anthology of poems praising the law. There are eight words for law in the psalm: way, law, decrees, precepts, statutes, commands, ordinances, words. The poem expresses faith in the word of God delivered to the people in various situations, such as the inexperience of youth (vv. 9-16), pain (vv. 25-32), contentment (vv. 97-104), but mostly the situations of ordinary life. The singer stands for us all—people conscious of life's limits and wise enough to ask for the illuminating and strengthening hand of the Lord.

Psalm 120

This thanksgiving (B) was sung in the temple by a person who, like the author of Psalms 42-43, sojourned in a foreign land away from Yahweh's presence, the victim of liars and violent people (vv. 5-7). Verse 1 reports the rescue, verse 2 cites the psalmist's prayer in the grim time before salvation, and verses 3-4 cite the psalmist's wish that the wicked be punished by the Lord. Verses 5-7 further recall sentiments from the past. The verbs of verses 5-7 should be in the past tense. The speaker suffered from being among a people that did not observe the Lord's precepts. Violence prevailed. It is not certain whether Meshech, a region in the far north (Gen 10:2), and Kedar, a tribe of the north Arabian desert (Gen 25:13), are meant literally as places where the speaker actually resided as an alien or metaphorically as typical places far distant from the temple.

Psalm 121

This blessing assures those embarking on a dangerous journey of the Lord's protection. It may well be the priest's dismissal of pilgrims who have come to the temple and have experienced, in common with their fellow Israelites, the presence of the Lord in the services. About to return home from Jerusalem, the people look anxiously at the wooded hills; danger lies along those roads. Will the Lord of the temple protect them on their journey (v. 1)? In their moment of anxiety the priest declares that the Lord is not confined to a place or a time (v. 2), that every step is guarded (vv. 3-4); night and day (vv. 5-6) the Lord guards their return and their dwelling (vv. 7-8).

Psalm 122

The song is sung by pilgrims arriving at the gates of Jerusalem in obedience to the command of the Lord to gather in worship three times a year. The singer can scarcely contain his joy as he waits to join the procession into the court: "We will go up to the house of the Lord" (v. 1). The splendor of the city is not simply its great buildings. Jerusalem is the place of encounter. Here the people praise the Lord (v. 4) and hear God's authoritative words to them (v. 5). The very buildings bespeak the power of Yahweh (see Ps 48:13-15). The last four verses turn into prayer. May the grace and peace experienced here transform the people at all times!

Psalm 123

In this communal lament (A) a speaker for a people taunted by its neighbors for its weakness and poverty cries out to God for salvation. The speaker makes a gesture for the whole community, lifting up his eyes to the powerful God who dwells in heaven, a gesture of obedience and of hope (vv. 1-2). Verses 3-4 contain the plea and the motive for divine action: Take pity for we are scorned. The speaker does not cite the righteousness of the people as the motive. The very poverty of the people is motive enough for the Lord to act on behalf of those who have been chosen.

Psalm 124

In this thanksgiving (B) the singer teaches Israel to attribute its very existence to the Lord who rescues it. Israel's enemies are compared to a mythic dragon (vv. 2b-3a; see Jer 51:34) and to the Flood (vv. 3b-5; see Isa 51:9-10). Sometimes the Bible, in order to express the full malice of historical enemies, portrays them with the traits of the primordial enemies of creation. Verses 6-8 praise the saving God directly and with touching simplicity: Israel is a bird freed from the trapper's snare. Israel is ever a freed people—freed originally from the clutches of Pharaoh and now from the clutches of the current enemy.

Psalm 125

The poem is a song of trust that the righteous, those who are faithful to the Lord and delight in God's law, will inherit the land and live safely in Zion. It is a response to postexilic anxieties about whether God would honor the ancient promises of restoration. Will Israel again possess the land? Will Zion be rebuilt? What about promises like Isa 57:13: "The one who takes refuge in me shall inherit the land, and possess my holy mountain"? The answer is that those who trust are like Mount Zion, surrounded by God like the high mountains that surround Jerusalem (vv. 1-2). Verse 3 cites perhaps an ancient promise that the just will not be contaminated by the wicked. Verses 4-5 are a prayer recognizing that the inheritors are righteous by the Lord's grace, not by their virtue. To live on Zion is a gift.

Psalm 126

This communal lament (A) was most probably sung shortly after Israel's return from exile in Babylon. Verses 1-3 express the intense joy of being in the holy city. Mere presence in Zion, however, is not enough; the people must pray for the divine intervention that will give fertility to the land (v. 4). Verses 5-6 are an oracle of promise: the painful labor of sowing will be crowned with life by the Lord who has brought them back.

Psalm 127

The psalm puts together two proverbs (vv. 1-2 and 3-5), both concerned with Yahweh establishing families, in order to affirm that all life is a divine gift. "House" in verse 1 means the family or household. In biblical times a household often consisted of several families under the authority of the oldest married man. The prosperity and protection of this group are not the work of humans; God has chosen to provide for them (v. 2). Verses 3-5 expand the affirmation with a proverb. "Gift" in verse 3 is the word that traditionally describes the holy land; like the land, children are pure gift, evidence of the Lord's favor.

Psalm 128

The poem is a statement of faith that the ever reliable and just God will always bless those who show reverence. "Fear of the Lord" does not mean craven fear or mere obedience to a set of commandments but a way of life (v. 1b) that sets God above all. As Psalm 1 shows, the Bible often dramatizes human life as two ways, the way of the just and the way of the wicked; each person must choose which of the two paths to walk. Verses 2-4 portray the consequences of the way of the Lord: enhanced life in the family. The perspective is that of the adult male, ordinarily the ruler of the household in the biblical world. In verses 5-6 the speaker, possibly a priest on the temple staff, extends the blessing on the household to the whole people of Israel for generations to come.

Psalm 129

The song resembles a thanksgiving (B) in which the speaker narrates a specific rescue by the Lord. Here, however, Israel looks back, not on one rescue, but on a whole series of divine acts since its "youth." Israel's history has been a series of trials, but the Lord has always given freedom, like the freedom of a beast when its harness is removed (v. 4). Israel's oppressors have been the wicked; in oppressing Israel they have opposed Yahweh. Hence the prayer in verses 5-8 is that Yahweh will continue to uphold Israel and cut off the life of the wicked. Like the stray blades of grass on the roof sod that shoot up and die quickly, may the wicked never know the joy of harvest.

Psalm 130

This poem, one of the Penitential Psalms, seems to be an individual lament (A). As in Psalms 12 and 60, the priestly assurance of salvation (vv. 7-8), given in response to the psalmist's plea, is included; ordinarily the assurance is not transmitted in the lament. The petitioner cries out from the depths, the abyss of the underworld. The pain and alienation make the psalmist feel "like those who go down into the pit" (Ps 143:7). Yet even here one can cry out to the God who does not keep books and whose last word is a word of forgiveness (vv. 3-4). Though the trial is severe, the sufferer still hopes (v. 5). Perhaps the psalmist is keeping vigil in the temple during the night and sees help coming with the dawn (v. 6). The priest's answer to the psalmist is that God's steadfast loyalty to the covenant will be available to each Israelite, as it has always been available to Israel.

Psalm 131

This is a song of trust, like Psalms 16, 23, and others, in which the psalmist lays aside all self-sufficiency in order to be completely open before the God who saves. The psalm is a song of the poor, the *'anawim,* who renounce power in order to stand more surely under the divine protection. The image of a child, quiet with its mother, unselfconsciously trusting, memorably sums up the inner attitude.

Psalm 132

This psalm accompanied a liturgical ceremony in which the Lord, invisibly present on the ark-throne, was carried in procession to the temple. The Israelite king, "son of God" by adoption, played a central role in the rites. The blessings of God include preeminently the king and his dynasty (vv. 11-12). 1 Sam 4:1–7:1 and 2 Sam 6–7 tell the story of the movement of the ark from the town of Kiriath-jearim ("the fields of Jaar," v. 6) to the temple in the time of David (tenth century B.C.E.). The psalmist reminds God of David's fidelity, in particular his care to build a suitable house for his Lord (vv. 1-5). Verses 6-10 record the shouts of the marchers, who begin their procession in Kiriath-jearim, a few miles north of Jerusalem, and end it at the temple. After having taken possession of the temple, the Lord now founds David's "house," the dynasty. If his sons will be loyal vassals like David today, the dynasty will have no end (vv. 11-12). And the place that the Lord has chosen, Zion, will become a place of blessing—abundant life, joy, and security for all those who rely on God present in the temple and in the Davidic king (vv. 13-18).

Psalm 133

Though often termed a "wisdom psalm," Psalm 133 does not teach but declares a particular situation blessed by God. The situation was a common one in ancient Israel whenever the property of the (extended) family, held in trust as Yahweh's gift, became the eldest son's upon the death of the father. The younger brothers' families then came under the headship of the eldest brother. Would peace still reign among family members? The psalm utters a blessing over the fragile family in crisis. Brothers and sisters living in peace are like the refreshing oil poured out in hospitable greeting, like dew watering the crops in the rainless summer. Both metaphors hint at the key role of the oldest brother, the source of blessings to his siblings. In a peaceful house the Lord's blessings unfold.

Psalm 134

In this brief liturgy a priest exhorts the other temple singers to "bless" (that is, acknowledge publicly) the great deeds of the Lord. The clergy are ministers in the sanctuary during a night service (see Isa 30:29). In verse 3 the priest utters a blessing of the Lord in response to the other priests' blessing, a blessing from the Creator enhancing the life already bestowed. Mount Zion is the place where God dwells and where the fruitful encounter between God and creature takes place.

Psalm 135

This hymn (C) begins and ends with an invitation to Israel to praise the Lord (vv. 1-3, 19-20) who has created Israel, an act demonstrating that the Lord is the only God. Only the Lord creates. The song is appropriately sung in the Jerusalem temple, for it is the gathering place for the people the Lord has created.

In the first verses the people are invited to praise the Lord, to tell God's story to the world. That story is summed up in verse 4, the choosing of Israel as a special possession. Verses 5-14 narrate a single event. Creation in verses 5-7 should not be distinguished too sharply from redemption in verses 8-14, since both describe the emergence of an ordered and secure human society. Verses 6-7 allude to Yahweh's easy mastery over chaos by means of the weapons of wind and lightning. The power that mastered chaos in verses 6-7 also destroys the enemies of Israel in verses 8-14. God liberates Israel from Egyptian bondage, defeating Pharaoh and the kings who stand in the way of Israel's entry into Canaan.

Yahweh's defeat of hostile powers means that images representing those powers are worthless; the inertness of the images shows that what they represent is without power. Verses 15-18 also appear in Ps 115:4-8.

Psalm 136

The hymn (C) praises Yahweh, the only powerful God ("the God of gods" in verse 2), who has created the world in which Israel lives. The refrain "for his mercy endures forever" occurs after every line, suggesting that a speaker and chorus sang the psalm antiphonally. "Mercy" is God's fidelity to the oath to Israel, God's *noblesse oblige.* To "give thanks" (vv. 1-3 and 26) is to tell publicly what God has done. Verses 4-25 ought not be divided into deeds of "creation" in verses 4-9 and deeds of "redemption" in verses 10-22, as is commonly done; rather, the actions constitute a single process. God makes the environment for human community by arranging heaven and earth, and makes the community itself by freeing the people from Pharaoh and giving them their land. Verses 23-25 are intimately related to the previous verses. The Lord who made Israel a people by giving it this land continues to make it a people by ever rescuing it from its foes and giving it the produce of the land.

Psalm 137

This lament (A) was sung by the community in Babylon during the exile of the sixth century. In verses 1-3 Israel is engaged in a liturgical rite of lament. The lyres for joyful song hang unused nearby. The captors' question, "Sing for us the songs of Zion," are like other taunting questions in the Bible, such as "Where now is your God?" How can Israel sing songs of Zion, such as Psalms 46, 48, and 76, which speak of Zion as impregnable and its inhabitants as happy and safe? In verses 4-6 the singer swears never to lose hope in Zion; the Zion songs will ever be sung. Verse 7 wishes annihilation upon Edom, a country to the east of Judah that raided Jerusalem during the Exile. In verses 8-9, appalling to the modern reader, Babylon, the archetypal enemy of God, is to be eradicated; its children, therefore, are to be killed.

Psalm 138

The psalmist gives thanks (B), telling in the temple how Yahweh heard his cry and came to the rescue. Not because of the psalmist's virtues did Yahweh act but because of Yahweh's own merciful fidelity (vv. 1-3). The deed is not simply a private transaction between an individual Israelite and Yahweh; it is great enough to provoke the nations of the world to praise God's grandeur and God's care for the people (vv. 4-6). Rescued, the psalmist trusts that Yahweh will always be there in moments of danger, continuing the earlier protection (vv. 7-8).

Psalm 139

This famous psalm resembles a thanksgiving (B) in that it narrates God's merciful care in the past (vv. 1-18), and an individual lament (A) in that it prays that sinners be punished (vv. 19-24). The drama is simple: the psalmist is keenly aware of the Lord's penetrating gaze (vv. 1-6), of God's guidance in every part of the universe (vv. 7-12), and of God's control over the psalmist's very self

(vv. 13-14). Verses 17-18 are an expression of wonder summing up verses 1-16. There is only one thing that can keep God and psalmist apart—sin. The psalm speaks of sin in verses 19-24.

The Bible frequently imagines the world as divided into two communities—the wicked and the righteous. The psalmist prays to be reckoned in the number of the righteous, that is to be separated from the wicked. He opens his being to God; if there is any evil, let it be cleansed (vv. 23-24).

Psalm 140

In this individual lament (A) the psalmist, beset by liars and attackers (vv. 2-6), makes a statement of trust in God in the temple (vv. 7-8). The psalmist prays that the wicked people's plans fall back upon their own heads (vv. 9-12). Verses 13-14 presumably are the statement of praise that the psalmist utters after receiving an assurance of salvation from the priest (not transmitted in psalms of lament). The psalmist expects the Lord to exercise judgment in a public way by punishing the liars and attackers and by upholding him, one of "the afflicted," "the poor," "the just," "the upright," that is, a member of the group that God has promised to uphold.

Psalm 141

This individual lament (A) is uttered by a person who is aware that only the righteous can properly worship God and who, consequently, is fearful of becoming one of the unrighteous through personal sin. In the perspective of this and other psalms of the "two ways," there are two groups of people: the righteous, pleasing to God, whose works perdure; and the unrighteous, hostile to God, rootless and doomed. The psalmist prays to be among the just, whose prayer is acceptable (vv. 1-2). God must, therefore, guard the person against being drawn into the plots and feasts of the wicked.

Verses 3-5 may be compared to Ps 85:11. The gist: Better to be reproved by the righteous than to be feted by the unrighteous. Verses 6-7 are corrupt; the translation is a guess. In verses 8-10 the psalmist prays to be saved from the corrupting fellowship of the wicked. Only God can admit one to the company of the just.

Psalm 142

The persecuted speaker of this lament (A) feels utterly alone (v. 5), exhausted (v. 7), and may actually be imprisoned (v. 8) prior to undergoing an ordeal to prove guilt or innocence (see Lev 24:12 and Num 15:34). Prison is possibly a metaphor for general distress. In the temple the psalmist lays out the complaint: attacks by the wicked with no one to give protection (vv. 2-5). Nonetheless, the psalmist still hopes that the just God will rectify the unjust situation ("you know my path," v. 4). The opening cry for help is repeated in verse 6, with a more vivid expression of hope and a more vivid complaint and prayer in verses 7-8ab. The last two verses of the poem are the vow of praise the psalmist makes after receiving an assurance from the priest: the Lord always protects the just, among whom is the psalmist.

Psalm 143

In this lament (A), ranked among the church's Penitential Psalms, the psalmist prays to be freed from death-dealing enemies. Verses 1-2 contain a straightforward address to God, made with a keen sense that there is no equality between God and humans; salvation is utterly gracious. Verses 3-4 contain the complaint: the psalmist is the victim of evil people. Verse 5 is much more vivid than most translations suggest; the verbs mean "to recite aloud." The psalmist recites the old stories of God's rescues of the poor from the power of evil, and the recitation encourages him to pray for personal salvation now (vv. 6-9). Mere rescue from the present danger is not enough, however. The psalmist goes on to pray that God's life-giving breath inspire the psalmist's life and give protection from enemies (vv. 10-12).

Psalm 144

The psalm seems to reflect a ceremony at which the king, the leader of Israel's armies, asked God's help in national crises (vv. 1-8). The tone of the poem shifts abruptly in verse 9 from pleading to thanksgiving, and then (verse 11 apart) it shifts again to prayer for the well-being of the people.

Verses 1-4 acknowledge that all the king's military prowess is from the Lord; the king, like any human being, is fragile and undeserving of God's help. May the Divine Warrior fight for Israel with the storm weapons of thunder and lightning (vv. 5-7). Perhaps in response to an oracle assuring divine assistance to Israel (not transmitted), the king vows to praise God for the expected victory. The victory is given in virtue of the divine promise to be with "David, your servant," not because of the king's military skill (vv. 9-11). The psalm concludes with the king, representing the people before God, praying for *shalom*, peace in its fullness.

Psalm 145

The hymn (C) is acrostic, that is, each verse begins with a successive letter of the Hebrew alphabet. The poem, like most acrostics, states several themes without developing them much. In verses 1-3 and 21 the singer invites "all flesh" to bless the name of the Lord. The "works of the Lord," God's activity in the world, make God present and invite the praise of all. According to verses 4-7, unending generations give thanks to the Lord, their thanksgiving climaxing in the confession of verses 8-9. Verses 10-20 urge all to acknowledge and acclaim the kingship of Yahweh, which directs all human activity in justice and love. The kingship of Yahweh will become a major theme of Jewish and Christian literature.

Psalm 146

The singer of this hymn (C) urges the hearers to praise and rely upon the Lord who rules all, and at the same time warns against relying upon mere mortals, no matter how powerful they seem. Verses 1-2 and 10 constitute the invitatory; the psalmist's exhortation to self is a model to all. The psalmist's concept of praising implies reliance upon God alone—hence the exhortation not to rely on human beings in the place of God (vv. 3-4). Israel's happiness is assured if it relies upon its God, "the God of Jacob," who created all things. Part of creation is the governance of the people. God's powerful care makes an environment fit for humans and maintains society in justice and peace (vv. 5-9). God's kingship is expressed in the favor shown to the oppressed and to those who rely upon God's help alone (v. 10).

Psalm 147

The hymn (C) is divided into three sections by separate commands to praise (vv. 1-6, 7-11, and 12-20). In the first section people are to acclaim God, who has built Jerusalem by bringing back the exiles. Verse 4 shows Yahweh's power over the divine beings who were thought to be in the stars, controlling the fate of human beings. Yahweh's control of even them means that nothing can hinder the people's return.

The second section hymns the God who makes the earth bring forth vegetation for animals and humans; from the latter a free and loving response is called for.

The third and climactic section exhorts the holy city to recognize that it has been recreated and that it is the privileged place of divine disclosure. From there Yahweh sends forth the word to Israel alone of all the nations, a word that is as life-giving as water.

Psalm 148

This hymn (C) invites the beings of heaven (vv. 1-6) and of earth (vv. 7-14) to praise the Lord. The singer does not distinguish between inanimate and animate (and rational) nature. Since every being hangs upon the divine decree (a better translation than "duty" in verse 6), it is oriented by that fact toward God (vv. 5-6). The motive for earth's praise in verse 13 is noteworthy: because "his name alone is exalted; his majesty is above earth and heaven." The name is what makes one present to another. Only Yahweh among all the "gods" is truly present on earth, and hence only Yahweh deserves acclaim. Verse 14 is the climax, which may be paraphrased in this way: Of all the peoples on earth, God has chosen Israel ("lift up the horn" = "to strengthen," "to favor") to render special thanks and praise to God.

Psalm 149

The hymn (C) is sung by "the lowly" (v. 4), who have sought asylum from danger in the temple on Zion. The hymn resembles songs of Zion (Psalms 2, 46, 48, 76): Zion is Yahweh's inviolable dwelling, where impious kings are defeated. Verses 1-3 invite Israel, gathered in Zion, to shout joyfully to its Creator. The reason is given in verse 4: the Lord loves Israel and protects "the lowly," those who have made the Lord their refuge. Verses 5-9 describe the equipping of the people who have sought protection. In the power of their Lord they attack and defeat the kings assaulting the holy city. At this critical hour the people are the means whereby the Lord's glory is displayed to the nations.

Psalm 150

A fitting end to the Psalter, this hymn (C) calls upon all in the temple and under the sky, "all flesh," to give due honor to God. A variety of musical instruments underline and unify the human voices. The reason for the praise is scarcely developed amid all the imperatives to sing and play. Verse 2 explains that praise is due because of Yahweh's mastery of nature and history.

SONG OF SONGS, RUTH, LAMENTATIONS, ECCLESIASTES, ESTHER

James A. Fischer, C.M.

INTRODUCTION

This commentary contains an explanation of five books of the Old Testament called Megilloth ("scrolls") by the Jews. They are gathered together for convenience, since the Jews read them on feast days in the synagogue. The tradition, however, is not constant and unanimous, and it is certainly not as old as the books.

The Song of Songs comes first because it was read during Passover. There are passages in the Song that speak of winter being over, so it is appropriate for the spring. The Exodus seems to be suggested by the reference to Pharaoh's steeds (Song 1:9). Most of all, the Song speaks of youth and love, and that is certainly the theme of Passover.

The Book of Ruth was read for the feast of Shavvoth, an early harvest festival, or what Christians call Pentecost. The story of Ruth takes place during the harvest season. There was also an ancient tradition that King David was born on Shavvoth.

The Book of Lamentations was read on the ninth of Ab, which is in July or August. This is the traditional date for the destruction of the temple by the Roman emperor Titus in A.D. 70. It was, therefore, a day of mourning.

The Book of Ecclesiastes was read on Succoth, the most popular of the three major feasts. Succoth was celebrated in the fall as a farmers' festival for gathering in the grape and olive harvests. The theme of aging, either of the year or of people, fits both the festival and the book. Some traditions said that the Song of Songs remembered Solomon in his youth, and Ecclesiastes in his old age, since both books refer to Solomon. However, using Ecclesiastes for synagogue reading is the least consistent part of the tradition and a rather late development. Some groups do not use it at all.

The Book of Esther contains the story that is the basis for the celebration of the feast of Purim, a kind of Jewish Mardi Gras. This tradition began in Persia and only later spread to Western Judaism. It apparently was an attempt to counteract pagan New Year's celebrations.

The Greek translation of the Bible known as the Septuagint, which was completed by at least 100 B.C.E., has a different order for these five books. The Book of Ruth is put right after the Book of Judges. The New American Bible follows the Greek in the order of books.

The curious grouping here offers an opportunity for a word about the kind of commentary given for these books. There is no common theme or approach in the books themselves. Ruth and Esther are stories, but of very different kinds; the Song of Songs is love poetry, and Lamentations is sad poetry; Ecclesiastes is an essay on human life. Since they are all so different, they cannot all be interpreted in the same way. The conclusions to be reached will depend on the method one adopts to interpret them.

If the principal concern is to discover what the original Hebrew text said, then we must study differences that have occurred in copying the manuscripts and alternate ways of understanding the text. This is called *textual* and *grammatical criticism*. The commentary will occasionally refer to such verbal problems. If we want to find out what actually happened, we need *historical criticism* to get at "the facts," as much as possible. There are no serious historical problems in our books. If we want to know how the original units were composed according to standard forms of writing, we need *form-criticism*. This will concern us often. If we want to know how these units were put together to form a book, we use *redaction criticism*. If we ask what role this book plays within the whole body of the canonical Scripture, we need *canonical criticism*. And if we ask how this story or poetry or essay works as literature and how good it is, we need *literary* or *rhetorical criticism*.

Each of these methods can only tell us something about the text; none of them is immediately the key to interpretation. All of them are important, but they do not get at what the ordinary reader of the Bible wants to know, namely, how does it help my faith or spiritual understanding? To make the step to a spiritual meaning for ourselves, we must appropriate the reading into our own experience. This commentary is written largely from the viewpoint of rhetorical criticism, in the hope that that will give us the quickest and closest approach to experience.

SONG OF SONGS

James A. Fischer, C.M.

INTRODUCTION

The problem with the Song of Songs is to find some honest reason why it should be in the Bible. Unlike most other books of the Old Testament, it has nothing to do with the sacred history, the law, the covenant, or the prophets. In fact, it does not even mention God. It seems to be a somewhat disjointed collection of popular love songs. We do not know when it was written or by whom; we do not know for what purpose it was written or for what it was used.

The Jews themselves had misgivings about including this book in their list of sacred writings. At the final determination made by the teachers of Judaism about A.D. 90, much discussion took place. The matter was finally settled when Rabbi Akiba, one of the leaders, was won over to the interpretation of the Song of Songs as reflecting the marriage of Yahweh to the chosen people. It was finally appointed for reading in the synagogue during the feast of Passover. Christians accepted the book as sacred without dispute, but its use in the liturgy was rather restricted. In later times various passages were applied to the Virgin Mary on her feasts.

Literary form

At first reading the Song seems to be a jumble of poetry in which various parties are speaking. Unfortunately, they keep shifting, and whatever plot there may be keeps disappearing. The New American Bible translation helps by identifying in the margin who is speaking. A girl lover (designated *B* for bride) can be identified as expressing her longing; a shepherd and/or king (designated *G* for bridegroom) is also actively involved. These identifications have a long history; they were first noted in Greek manuscripts made about A.D. 400. A vague "we" and some "daughters of Jerusalem" (designated *D*) also appear. Solomon and brothers of the bride complete the cast (these are not designated by any letter in the text). None of this is particularly consistent; as soon as the poetry begins to concentrate on one person or theme, it dissolves and another scene unfolds.

Discerning some structure in these eight chapters is a frustrating quest. Efforts have been made to read the Song as a story, but there is too little plot, except for a general feeling that the lovers are finally united despite the efforts of antagonists such as the brothers and perhaps the king to keep them separate. Since much of the poetry is couched in direct speech, attempts have been made to cast the Song as a drama or a dramatic reading. No agreement has been reached, however, as to how the parts should be played or by whom. More important, we have no evidence that dramatic presentations, whether in the temple or elsewhere, were ever a part of Jewish life.

This leads to a theory that the Song of Songs is simply an unstructured collection. The use of direct speech in love poetry can be illustrated from other ancient cultures, particularly Egyptian. Different parts of the discourse can be classified on the basis of themes and forms. Thus we have titles assigned by scholars, such as: song of admiration, self-description, the tease, song of yearning, description of a love-related experience, descriptive song, boasting song, and so on. The meanings are usually self-evident, and the forms do show some consistency in the elements used to compose them. Unfortunately, they do not shed a great deal of light on how one should interpret the passages. How these poems functioned is still unknown. Were they simply notes written between lovers? Recited? Used at weddings? Some sort of popular music of which we know nothing? All of this eludes us.

The explanation that the Song is simply a collection of about twenty-five love poems or sayings has its own difficulty by way of being too little. There is something of a story line in the Song. A girl loves a shepherd boy. She desires to be with him and sometimes fantasizes about him as a king and herself as a queen. But something keeps them apart. Verbs of coming and going, which are characteristics of storytelling, abound. And there is tension: at the end something—a lattice, a gate, a departure, watchmen—prevents them from the final touch.

This much of a story line clearly exists: there are characters with a definite form, movement, tension, and a resolution. The outline of it is faint and overlaid with a kaleidoscope of love imagery, which keeps intruding. The pictures are mostly from the rustic life of those who live closely with nature. The girl is a dove, sweet-scented, like a lily of the valley, beautiful, adorned with gems, enclosed in a garden. The boy is a gazelle, fleet, gentle as a lily, glitteringly beautiful as ivory or gold. He is neither warrior nor hunter, but perfumed and handsome. King Solomon enters either as competitor or fantasy. The images of him are always of opulence, and he is rejected. The imagery as well as the story line sets up a tension here.

The mood is one of "love conquers all"—but not yet. Love is celebrated in all its physical joy. Lips are made to be kissed and savored like good wine, breasts to be admired, hair to be caressed, the wedding couch to be enjoyed. The invitation is to meet beneath the apple tree where your mother conceived. The mood of love is unrestrained by prudery, but not by prudence.

> Do not arouse, do not stir up love,
> before its own time (8:4).

The mood may be destroyed by our own reaction to some of the imagery. Who could love a girl whose nose is like a tower of Lebanon and whose hair is like a flock of goats, or a boy whose hair is like palm fronds? Our own love imagery may appear as odd to others. At any rate, these comparisons do seem to come from a fairly conventional vocabulary of love.

The meaning of the book

Over the centuries both Jews and Christians have tended to give the Song a symbolic meaning and have thus avoided the plain references to physical love and its ecstatic emotions. The marriage of Yahweh to Israel or of Christ to the Church has dominated. Sometimes, as in the Christian liturgy, the girl has become the Virgin Mary. In the writings of the mystics the individual soul has often been the soul's yearning for her lover, Christ.

How this identification is made determines much of the interpretation. If the interpretation is allegorical, then every verse and every detail has a secret meaning in which this equals that. Obviously this has spiritual value; equally, it may become silly if it is carried too far. Some commentators have opted for parable, that is, it is the story line, not the details, that parallels the spiritual meaning in our own lives, either communal or individual. This avoids difficulties and has much to commend it, but since the story line is so tenuous, it leaves much of the text without meaning.

Completely different is the wisdom interpretation. In this view the Song is indeed composed of popular love songs joined only by a whisper of a plot. Human love is good. It need not be justified by esoteric spiritual reasonings. The sages taught that God's order and goodness pervade all; there is no such thing as the secular. The love of boy and girl is one of God's beauties. Even so, it went far beyond emotion. One was aware of a secret, mysterious force, an uncontrollable power that might overwhelm. So we have the only explanation of the refrain which links together the various songs:

> Set me as a seal on your heart,
> as a seal on your arm;
> For stern as death is love,
> relentless as the nether world is devotion;
> its flames are a blazing fire.

Deep waters cannot quench love,
nor floods sweep it away.
Were one to offer all he owns to purchase love,
he would be roundly mocked (8:6-7).

If one adopts this viewpoint, then the Song turns back the corner of the page of human love to reveal a deeper reality. The overall interpretation adopted in this commentary is that the Song originated as somewhat isolated love songs, was arranged in the order in which it now stands to give a faint story line, which built up to the climax expressed in the wisdom saying in 8:6: "For stern as death is love."

COMMENTARY

1:1 The title. The title "Song of Songs" is not part of the canonical text but was added later. "Song of Songs" is simply a Hebrew superlative: "The best song." "By Solomon" simply says that the tradition associated the Song with Solomon in some way. As it stands, it has a whole gamut of possible meanings: Solomon as author, Solomon as inspirer of all song and wisdom, Solomon as king of marriage, etc.

1:2-4 Invitation to a wedding. This first song seems to be an invitation to a wedding. The bride is looking forward to wedding kisses. The invited "we" are presumably the bride's party ("daughters of Jerusalem"); the king is the bridegroom, either in fantasy or as a title in wedding festivities. Some sort of exchange of voices in the song is indicated by the switch of speakers from "me" to "we" and by the marginal notations. This song introduces us to the setting of joy and praise for the bride and groom.

1:5-6 Praise of the bride. The second song is a song praising the bride herself. She is a sunburned girl, perhaps in contrast to the city daughters of Jerusalem. Yet she is not a naive country girl, but a coquette, as her brothers had found out. She had not taken care of her own "vineyard" (a biblical stand-in word for one's self), perhaps by dalliance with her lover, so they put her to work taking care of real vineyards.

1:7-8 A duet of love. This duet sings of the search for love. The girl wants to know where her shepherd-lover is so that she will not be annoyed along her way by falling in with other shepherds. His reply implies that she knows well enough where they are accustomed to meet.

1:9-11 The girl's beauty. Comparing the girl to a horse may seem ungracious to us. This is a special kind of horse, however—one of Pharaoh's chariot steeds. The text seems to suggest sexual appeal as the point of the comparison. This horse is a mare, and mares were not used in war; in fact, they were kept far from the stallions lest they distract them. The rest of the song describes the attractiveness of the bride. Perhaps it is another way of looking back to those shepherds in verse 7, who would have been glad to have had the girl wandering among them.

1:12-17 A wedding duet. This last duet in chapter 1 is an exchange of anticipations about the wedding feast. The girl can only describe the coming delights in terms of perfumes; then the bride and groom exchange professions of the beauty they see in each other. Oddly, the girl's eyes are said to be like doves. Just what is intended is not clear—perhaps "sparkling" if the dove's iridescence is the point, or "gentle and loving," as some of the ancients believed. The final wish is for the bridal chamber, pictured here as a magnificent hall made of cedar and cypress.

2:1-7 A love duet. This unit consists of a duet between the girl and her lover, followed by a description of the arousal of love, and ending with the refrain in verse 7. It seems to be separate from the springtime song which follows and which is less passionate. The refrain (see also 3:5 and 8:4) always occurs at the climax of the love scenes. The action here proceeds from the introduction of the girl as a lily of the valley (beautiful) and the boy as an apple tree (a symbol of sexual desirability in some way) to the bridal chamber and a desire for sexual union, but it ends with an admonition not to go too fast.

2:4 "His emblem over me is love" seems to be the obvious reading of the Hebrew text. The "emblem" seems to be some sort of military insignia. As such, it does not make much sense, and we do not know to what it might refer.

2:5 Raisin cakes were foods considered to be an aid to love, but we know nothing more specific. Cookies in the form or symbol of love goddesses were used in the banqueting of some fertility rites, but the connection with Israelite courting customs is not at all clear.

2:7 The refrain begins solemnly with an adjuration that interrupts the passionate wishes of the girl. The appeal to gazelles and hinds may be to animals that were thought to be amorous, or the phrase in Hebrew may be a stand-in for the similar-sounding "by the Lord of hosts," just as our old-fashioned "Jiminy Crickets" is really a substitute for "Jesus Christ."

"Do not arouse, do not stir up love before its own time" is not exactly what the Hebrew text says. The word "time" is not used in Hebrew; it is only implied in the conjunction "until," that is, "until it is satiated or eager." Whatever the exact sense, it is clear that some brake is being applied to the runaway love-making previously described, since we have a solemn oath and an admonition of some sort. More will be said about this at 8:6.

2:8-17 The springtime song of love. This delightful love song has left its traces in our own literature from "In the spring a young man's fancy" to "The voice of the turtle dove is heard in the land." It is a self-contained song as defined by the theme and the use of "gazelle" at the beginning and end. This is an ancient way of marking off a unit, much as we use paragraphs.

This song begins with a gentle longing, a considerable cooling off of the passionate phrases in the preceding verses. The young girl seems to be confined at home behind a wall, windows, and lattices. Yet she keeps hearing her lover's invitation: winter is over, the time for love is here. She will not go to him, but she can tease him with hints that others may be vying for her favors.

2:9-10 The lover is pictured as coming from afar to visit his beloved. Something keeps them apart, and he can only rush around, gazing through windows, peering through lattices. Why she does not come out to meet him or invite him in is not revealed, but the poem centers on longing that cannot be satisfied. And yet it should be.

2:11-13 All this delightful imagery, including the dove, which is a sure sign of spring, hints at a proper time for love, as 2:7 had hinted and as Qoheleth will later express in his song about a time for everything (see Eccl 3:8).

2:15 "Catch us the foxes" is apparently a line from a well-known song. Its connection is not entirely clear. The girl is the vineyard; foxes are predators, and the intimation is that this girl has a lot of them watching her and needs protection. This is called a tease song.

3:1-11 A wedding dream. Although this chapter can be divided between a song of seeking and finding (vv. 1-5) and a description of a wedding procession (vv. 6-11), the two need to be connected to account for the second half. The poem begins with a dream wish by the girl and ends with a picture of the king on the day of his marriage. That is what the dream is all about, and the wedding procession is a fantasy creation.

We left the girl in chapter 2 still confined to her home. Now in her dream she is wandering the streets of the city looking for her lover. The watchmen cannot tell her where he is, but love can. She finds him and holds him fast, but then the dream is restrained by the refrain and the admonition not to arouse love before its time. This is followed by another dream fantasy of a wedding procession in which her lover is King Solomon coming to his wedding couch in splendor.

3:3 Among the many shifts of scene in the song we have this change from countryside to city. The watchmen, of course, are the police.

3:4 In the preceding song the girl knew where her lover was but could not or would not go out to him. Now she does not know where he is and must look for him. She intends to bring him to her mother's house (v. 4). We do not know why she would not have brought him there before, or what cultic or mythological background there may be for such a statement. Numerous solutions have been offered.

3:5 Whatever the situation implied in verse 4 may be, it is quite clear that the girl wanted to seal her marriage at home. But just before the final act, the refrain is once more introduced to delay the consuming expression of love.

3:6-11 The description given here is certainly of a royal procession connected with a marriage, but it does not fit the facts we know about Solomon. It is part of a dream sequence like the preceding; the girl is dreaming of her lover as King Solomon and fantasizing her wedding day. The physical descriptions given here, the column of smoke, the perfumes, the sixty valiant soldiers, the dangers in the watches of the night, the wood of Lebanon, the columns and roofs and ivory, etc., are all mentioned in connection with something pertinent to kings and gods and weddings in the Old Testament, but never together. We can only assume that this is a product of imagination.

4:1–5:1 A song of longing. Verses 1-7 are a song in praise of the physical beauty of the girl. It is a well-known type of hymn from Hebrew and Arabic styles. Assigning it a name does not help very much to interpret what it means, but it does take away some of the strangeness of the details describing the girl's beauty. This leads to an admiration song (vv. 8-11) that is more symbolic. It begins with an invitation to a celebration, and then speaks of the girl in terms of a garden (v. 12). This is common biblical imagery for one's beloved. The garden is fragrant, fruitful, and full of delights. Then the beloved is called "a fountain sealed." The fountain of flowing water is a symbol of life. What is being spoken of, therefore, is a faithful and fruitful marriage. This part of the song ends with an invitation to the friends of the bridegroom to eat and drink of the wine of love.

4:1 In content all this verse says is that the girl has long hair, but the image is one of richness and constantly changing shades.

4:2 Once again the physical fact is simply praise for the girl's white and regular teeth, which are as extraordinary as ewes having twins.

4:3 The girl has firm and rosy cheeks. The pomegranate is something like an orange, reddish in color.

4:4 We do not know what David's tower was, but that would not help very much anyway. Apparently the picture is of a lady, stately and erect, who is wearing tiers of necklaces, which suggests the battlements, bucklers, and shields of which the poet speaks.

4:5 The picture is one of softness and perfection. The gazelle is the boy, and he is a lotus-eater. This last image conjures up some idea of a drug-like ecstasy. All these physical images are probably foreign to our tastes.

4:8 Lebanon is far to the north. The other places mentioned—Amana, Senir and Hermon—are also remote, sometimes unknown. The poet intends to create a feeling that a great distance separates the lovers. To complete the image, he mentions the haunt of lions and the leopard's mountains.

Consistently in this song (vv. 9, 10, 12, and 5:1) the girl is described as "my sister, my bride." Considering the broad usage of "sister" in the Bible, this is not surprising. Love's relationship is reinforced by a reference to family ties, whether real or conferred.

4:12 The Hebrew text has a stronger expression: "sealed garden." The reference is to a signet ring that can be used only by the owner. The enclosure is to keep away those who do not have a right to be present.

4:15 The fountain suggests life, as does the following description: "flowing fresh from Lebanon." Prov 5:15-20 has a beautiful use of the same imagery, with a strong emphasis on the husband's obligation to be faithful to his own fountain: "Let your fountain be yours alone."

5:1 The bridegroom has arrived and shares his gladness by inviting his friends to the wedding banquet.

5:2–6:3 A dream sequence. This is the longest continuous passage in the Song, but it is probably a secondary addition. Basically it is a dream sequence in which the girl loses and finds her lover. As in a dream, the action is disjointed and illogical. However, there is motion as the girl hears her lover trying to get in the gate, but then being too late when she finally gets up to admit him. She pursues him through the city at night but cannot find him. The watchmen beat her, and she has to appeal to the daughters of Jerusalem to help her find him. At the end she finds him in her garden. The search sequence is interrupted by a praise song for the boy, which leads up to a final song of yearning and fulfillment.

5:4 From the later reference to a lock (v. 5), it would appear that the boy was reaching through the keyhole to open the door. Ancient keys and locking devices were huge, often made of wood. Apparently by the time the girl had beautified herself ("With my fingers dripping choice myrrh"), he had already gone.

5:7 In this dream the girl is now roaming the streets at night. The watchmen naturally consider her an intruder or a prostitute.

5:8 It is quite unrealistic for the daughters of Jerusalem to appear so suddenly at night, but this is a dream. The dialogue between them is only hinted at. After the girl explains her search, they ask: "What shall we tell him?" As the next section demands, they also ask what he looks like.

5:11 It is probable that "palm fronds" simply means "curled" or "luxuriant."

5:12 Previously the girl's eyes were described as dovelike, but here there is added "beside running waters." Possibly the bridegroom has dark pupils, as suggested by doves, and sparkling irises, as suggested by running water.

5:14 That the lover's arms should be described as gold is understandable; in the next verse his legs are columns of marble. But the word "rods" is strangely inappropriate, although it is an accurate translation.

6:3 The final statement of the girl is that she, and she alone, claims her lover. "Browsing among the lilies" probably has sexual connotations. The refrain that urges restraint is not used at this point, although the adjuration was mentioned in 5:8. As noted at the beginning, this section seems to be a secondary addition.

6:4-12 A description and a meeting. Most of chapter 6 seems to be a song of admiration for the girl, leading first to a rejection of the royal beauties and then a choice of the girl alone, and ending in an enigmatic description of some meeting between the two. As we will see, the chapter ends in an unintelligible statement where we would expect some decisive development in the love affair.

6:4 Tirzah was the capital of the northern kingdom of Israel between 930 and 880 B.C.E. On this basis some commentators have dated the whole Song of Songs. The text is quite clear about the name of the city, but we have no information as to why Tirzah was considered beautiful or how the girl was like it. Oddly enough, the very ancient Greek translation and the Jewish paraphrases read: "You are beautiful and pleasing," but we do not know how they got this wording.

The phrase "as awe-inspiring as bannered troops" recurs in verse 10. It is the only harsh image used of the girl, and one wonders why it is used. If the text is accepted, some reference must be made to the usual mythology of the goddess of love who is also the goddess of war. If the text is emended, it will probably read: "as awe-inspiring as these great sights."

6:8 Previously the girl had fantasized about her lover as though he were King Solomon; here the boy seems to be daydreaming about his girl as a queen whom he would choose in preference to innumerable royal ladies. The "sixty . . . eighty . . . without number" progression is probably an escalating superlative built up from twenty times three, four, and *x*. At any rate, as the next verse says: "One alone is my dove," and she is better than all.

6:11 The last part of this poem is spoken by the boy, who wants to see if the girl is ready to receive him. Clearly, she is the garden. Here the garden is described as a nut garden, specifically a walnut garden. The word occurs only here in the Bible and we have no idea what its significance might be.

6:12 This must be the decisive verse in chapter 6 because chapter 7 will treat a quite different topic. Unfortunately we have no clear idea what the Hebrew text means. English translations differ widely. The New Jewish Version has: "Before I knew it, my desire set me amid the chariots of Ammi-nadib," and the Anchor Bible reads: "Unawares I was set in the chariot with the prince." In effect, we do not know what happened in the walnut garden.

7:1–8:4 A song of yearning and restraint. It might be well to consider this section together, however disparate and disconnected the individual units. Here we begin with a dance that displays the girl's charms (7:1-6); sexual closeness under the image of climbing a palm tree (7:7-11); a yearning for love under the image of springtime awakening (7:12-14); and finally a fervid desire for union, ending in the refrain that counsels the proper moment (8:1-4). The shifts in scene and speakers (sometimes enigmatic, as in 7:10) suggest that these songs were originally independent and so do not fit neatly together. Yet, they are all full of motion, and the action does seem to be going somewhere—hence the importance of the conception of a story line, however faintly hinted at. All this depends, of course, on what one has read consistently into the refrain.

7:1 We really do not know what the term "Shulammite" implies. It may be the feminine form of Solomon (like the name Salome in the New Testament), or it may be derived from a town in Esdraelon noted for its beautiful women, or it may have a hint of "the peaceful one." None of these meanings, however, helps us to understand the significance better. Neither do we know what kind of dance is referred to here. Suggestions have been made of a sword dance, a special dance before a wedding, or a war dance. However out of place the last-mentioned may be, it does have something to do with the description.

7:5 Whether this is a special, well-known tower, or whether Mount Lebanon looks like a tower is unclear. In any event, it probably does not increase our aesthetic response.

7:8 The palm tree is a symbol of richness and fertility. Its figs hang in clusters by the hundreds.

7:10 As indicated in the New American Bible text, the speaker shifts suddenly from the groom to the bride in the middle of the sentence. We suspect that two poems have been run together here, and not very skillfully. The imagery also shifts suddenly from the palm tree to a springtime scene in the country.

7:11 Previously the girl had said: "My lover belongs to me and I to him" (6:3). There is a different emphasis here. She is committed to him and recognizes that he must be drawn to her. The phrase "for me he yearns" is reminiscent of Gen 3:16: "your urge shall be for your husband." These are the only times in the Bible that the expression is used. Something more than physical passion is hinted at.

7:14 Mandrakes are underground tubers related to the potato and reputed to have aphrodisiac powers. This verse again brings out the intensity of physical love.

8:1 Although this is a separate song of yearning, it goes naturally with the preceding. Indeed, there would be no climax to chapter 7 without this. Something still keeps the lovers apart. The girl wishes that her lover were her brother so that she could freely consort with him.

8:4 The poetic climax is reached with the repetition of the refrain just at the moment of most intense feeling. The Hebrew wording of the text is somewhat different here than previously. The appeal to the gazelles and hinds is dropped; after "I adjure you" we have not a request but a prohibition. In other words, the reading is shorter but stronger.

The New American Bible translation ends the sentence with "Do not arouse, do not stir up love, before its own time." This implies that the time is not yet here. Various other translations and commentators understand that the time has come to reach the conclusion of the longing. Such an interpretation depends upon an understanding of the total Song of Songs as culminating in the fulfillment of love's desires. Then one needs to explain from a literary, aesthetic viewpoint why this happens three times in the Song and yet the poem continues. The more normal and traditional understanding of the refrain would imply that every time love reaches its climax, something hinders the final consummation. What this is will depend upon the interpretation given to the following section.

8:5-14 Finale. The finale of the Song of Songs is a series of disjointed and perhaps fragmentary pieces. It begins with verse 5, which, according to the New American Bible text, is a jerky dialogue between the daughters of Jerusalem and the groom. The bride is coming to meet her lover. As she approaches, he points out the apple tree under which he was conceived. This is followed by what appears to be a completely incongruous reference to love being as stern as death. Then there is some sort of dialogue between the brothers, who do not want their little sister to get married yet, but she is determined to go ahead. It ends with a final song of the bride that she prefers her lover to all of Solomon's wealth and desires only him.

It is agreed by all that verses 6-7 are decisive for the meaning of the Song of Songs. It is also clear on purely poetic grounds that the songs turn much more serious at this point. The playful celebration of falling in love is replaced by serious thoughts of childbearing. The allusion to the apple tree under which one of them was conceived sounds a new note. The love they have been enjoying is recognized as being as relentless as death. Once committed, they cannot escape. The girl's response is a deliberate and free choice of total fidelity. The final choice of her lover instead of Solomon's wealth also sets her future unchangeably. The insight of the Song, therefore, seems to be that however delightful falling in love may be, its flames have an unquenchable power that cannot be extinguished.

8:5 A problem exists here as to who is speaking. The Hebrew text indicates that it was the boy's mother who conceived and that the speaker is the girl. The whole of verse 5 seems to be rather fragmentary. What is decisive for our understanding is that the question of children is introduced for the first time.

8:6 "Stern" is "relentless." That is the common description of death in many passages of the Old Testament. Death is a hunter that cannot be eluded. The parallel line reinforces the idea: "relentless as the nether world is devotion," and this in turn is further strengthened by "its flames are a blazing fire." It is possible to translate the final word as "a flame of God," but that is unusual both as translation and within the context of the Song.

8:7 The metaphor is not of putting out a fire, but of death as a raging torrent that cannot be held back. The picture is used consistently in the Old Testament. The only power stronger than death is love, but the point of the comparison is the enormous strength of both. The final saying here, "Were one to offer all he owns to purchase love, he would be roundly mocked," is not in poetic form and seems to be an inserted wise saying.

8:8 The brothers object that their sister is too young for marriage and childbearing. The following description about building up a wall and protecting a door describes their strategy in military terms. They do not seem to be cruel in their plans but want to overwhelm the girl with gifts. She rejects this by asserting that she is ready for marriage.

8:11 The sudden shift seems to have nothing to do with Solomon as such. The girl is simply saying that even if she were offered the wealth of Solomon, she would still choose her lover. In verse 12 she asserts her own independence: "My vineyard is at my own disposal."

8:13 The conclusion begins with an appeal by the boy to learn what his lover's final choice will be. Her response is, "Be swift, my lover." We have come to a decisive conclusion. However, it will be noted from the remarks above on this last section that the final choice is not of the pleasure of love-making but of the acceptance of love as a power that demands total commitment.

RUTH

James A. Fischer, C.M.

INTRODUCTION

The story

The best way to read the Book of Ruth is simply as a good story. It really is a short story, one of the best that has come down from antiquity. In four brief chapters the author has created unforgettable characters and a plot that involves us in our own solution.

The actions can be briefly described in scenes:

Act One—*Prelude: Naomi the Loser* (1:1-22)

Naomi, a pleasant and capable Jewish girl, follows her husband into the frontier land of Moab during a famine, raises a family, loses her husband and her children, and is forced by another famine to return to Bethlehem. There she curses God for having taken everything from her.

Act Two—*The Harvest and the Matchmaking* (2:1–3:18)

In Bethlehem, Naomi sends her daughter-in-law Ruth to glean in the fields. Ruth meets Boaz, a rich bachelor, and is encouraged by Naomi to court him. Ruth and Boaz fall in love.

Act Three—*The Marriage Contract Concluded* (4:1-12)

Boaz must first clear up some legal problems connected with a field that Naomi wants to sell. The terms include an obligation to marry Ruth. Boaz settles the matter fairly and openly, and then takes Ruth as his wife.

Act Four—*Conclusion: Naomi the Winner?* (4:13-16)

In due course a child is born to Ruth, but it is hailed by the local women as Naomi's. A curious genealogy (4:17-22) attributes the child to Boaz and traces the succeeding generations to David.

The history of the book

The setting of the story is during the days of the judges (approximately 1200–1050 B.C.E.), probably toward the end. There are no specific references in the text that would enable us to check more exactly the date or the historical accuracy. Although the Hebrew Bible placed Ruth among the Megilloth, the pre-Christian Greek translation known as the Septuagint put it after the Book of Judges. The least we can say is that there was an ancient tradition that the story belonged to the time of the judges. The picture it paints of early Israelite village life conforms to what we know of the era. Things such as the meeting place at the city gate, the words used for weights and measures, the names, the techniques of harvesting, and so on, all fit into our data.

The story was written at a later time. The first words, "Once in the time of the judges," indicate a distance between the writer and the events. In 4:7 the author explains a forgotten custom about handing over a sandal as a way of concluding an agreement. The book concludes with a genealogy that traces the descendants of Boaz down to the time of David (1004–965 B.C.E.). Most likely the story was written sometime shortly after David. Similar forms of storytelling, such as the story of Joseph in Egypt and the story of David, seem to come from about the same time.

The only alternate date of writing proposed is in postexilic times, more specifically in the fifth century B.C.E. Apart from a few late expressions, the argument for postexilic dating depends upon interpreting the book as a protest against the rather harsh marriage laws of Ezra and Nehemiah. However, this is to base the dating upon a very questionable interpretation of the story as story, as we shall see later.

Interpretation

One type of interpretation would center on the details concerning marriage regulations. The point of the story would be that from ancient times pagan girls were legitimately taken as wives, and entered into the stream of Israel's history. The problem with such explanations is that they do depend upon details, especially the concluding genealogy. That may or may not be an addition to the original text. In any case, it is clear that the story was not told simply to explain the genealogy.

Another set of interpretations centers on the example of the virtuous life illustrated by Ruth and Boaz. The word *hesed* (1:8; 2:10; 3:10), variously translated as "kind," "merciful," "loyal," is a key term in the story. Ruth is a gracious girl who sacrifices everything to embrace the God of Israel. Boaz is a magnanimous and kindly kinsman who rescues a family in distress. Concern for the poor is one of the major obligations of the chosen people. Loyalty to God and kinsfolk ranks high. This is undoubtedly an important impression created by the storyteller. Unfortunately, it has little to do with Acts One and Four of the story. Neglecting the beginning and ending of this story is like tearing out the first and last pages of a detective story.

The approach in this commentary is to consider the story first of all simply as story. As a rule of thumb, all storytelling is either hero story, tragedy, or comedy. The hero story leads the principal character through various perils to victory. It has a rather rigid chain of cause and effect. In the Bible there are very few hero stories, and God alone is the hero. If we interpret the Book of Ruth as an exemplar story of virtuous living, we have made it into a hero story. By and large, that neglects the character of Naomi and certainly downplays the role of God, who appears only in oblique references.

If we interpret the story as a protest against overly harsh marriage laws, then the Book of Ruth is a tragedy of sorts. A tragedy is a story that inevitably results in the destruction of the principal character. It is clear that this is not the plot of this story. The only tragedy may have been that the protest went unheard.

Comedy is the most difficult literary style. To be successful, a comedy must link together actions that have a certain fittingness and yet whose conclusion defies rational expectation. Most of the stories of the Bible are comedies in this sense. God's actions cannot be confined to normal human ways of acting. Obviously, we are not talking about comedy as fun or frivolity.

To get at the literary character of the Book of Ruth, we have to reflect on it as we do on other stories. First of all, it is a self-contained story, and we do not need to worry about where it begins and ends. Secondly, we instinctively develop our own pictures of the characters, and these are finely drawn in Ruth.

NAOMI is pictured at the beginning as an earlier Ruth—pious, practical, and loyal. But when she returns to Bethlehem, she changes into an embittered woman who blames God for all her troubles and demands an accounting from God. In the following chapters Naomi is pictured as a scheming woman who manipulates people to accomplish what God would not.

RUTH is a loving and loyal girl. She has a strange mixture of initiative and submissiveness.

BOAZ is pictured in regal dress. He is rich, magnanimous, discreet, and protective. He talks in a rather formal manner. At the end, however, he simply vanishes from the action.

YAHWEH has no speaking part, but the story is always aware of Yahweh's presence.

A good story needs tension or conflict. There is no tension between Ruth and Boaz or between Naomi and Ruth; the tension is between Naomi and God. It begins at the end of the first chapter when Naomi curses God. At the end the scheming woman has achieved her purpose of having an heir who assures her future. And yet the village women sing: "Blessed is the Lord who has not failed to provide you today with an heir" (4:14). Who won? The comic conclusion leaps from the page, but the author leaves us to handle it ourselves.

COMMENTARY

NAOMI IN MOAB

Ruth 1:1-22

The first chapter sets the scene for the main action of the story. Here the action rushes along in breathless fashion. The famine triggers the migration to Moab. The characters are introduced briefly: Elimelech, Naomi, Mahlon, and Chilion. The husband dies; the two sons are married to Moabite women, Orpah and Ruth. Then the two sons die, and Naomi makes ready to go back to Bethlehem, since she has heard that the famine there has abated. It will be noticed that no adjectives are used; the story is bare-bone fact, but the facts are arranged in dry-eyed fashion to elicit our sympathy.

Then the pace slows to record Naomi's conversations with her daughters-in-law. This is a loving family that Naomi has presided over; the "Go back!" that is wrenched from her (1:8, 11, 12, 15) is mingled with tears. But Naomi is ever a realist, even when she is fantasizing about her own childless future. She accepts her fate as due to the hand of the Lord. Ruth refuses to leave her: "Wherever you go I will go, wherever you lodge I will lodge, your people shall be my people, and your God my God" (1:16). Ruth's dedication is first to Naomi and then to Yahweh.

So the two women go back to Bethlehem, and there in familiar surroundings Naomi's character suddenly changes. "Do not call me Naomi. Call me Mara, for the Almighty has made it very bitter for me" (1:20). The "amiable one" has become the "bitter one." The challenge to Yahweh has been laid down unequivocally and publicly. We are now fully informed as to what the point of the story will be.

1:1 The narrator indicates clearly that this is a story; no interest is shown in citing specifics of time or place that could be tied to historical facts.

1:2 We do not know the exact significance of Ephrathites. The tribe of Ephraim lived far to the north, so the reference cannot be to them. Perhaps it was a clan name for one of the Caleb families of the tribe of Judah. At any rate, they belonged to the village of Bethlehem and, as emerges later (4:3), Naomi owned property there. Naomi belongs and yet she doesn't; she is always one who is different.

Moab is across the Jordan in an area the Israelites had never fully conquered. Sometimes relations with Moab were hostile and sometimes friendly. The story implies that the Judean family had no problems in being allowed to settle on this high and windy land.

1:3-4 The storyteller makes no comment at all about these mixed marriages, which seem to have been forbidden to the Israelites (see Deut 23:3), although this is not entirely clear. At any rate, the story treats the marriages as well as the sojourning in a foreign land as matters of practicality that need no justification.

1:8 The repetition of the advice to return has already been noted in the preliminary comments. The "mother's house" is odd and of uncertain implication. What is clear is that Naomi is always the practical one. Three widows are now the problem; women know best how to handle such matters and to arrange marriages. It is not the time to grieve but to do something.

1:16 The prose of the Book of Ruth has a lilt to it and can easily pass over into poetic form, as this balanced speech certainly does. Later on Boaz will know about Ruth's conversion. We know this passage as a popular song; perhaps it was so originally. It is also somewhat ironic: Naomi's first defeat in arranging things comes from the girl who loves her most.

1:20 Naomi means "lively," "delightful"; Mara means "bitter." These are authentic-sounding names from ancient times. Whatever may be the connection of such names with God, the storyteller is obviously contrasting personal qualities, perhaps nicknames. The admirable girl who had left Bethlehem in her youth has returned as a quite different character. The change in Naomi's character is essential for the story to work.

1:21 Naomi is exaggerating, for they had to go away because there was a famine. She seems to have enjoyed the good life in Moab, and that was an expected result for being a good Israelite. The problem posed is the eternal one: Why did this happen to me? It is presumed that God is in control. Naomi, like Job, blames God when that control seems irrational. The "Almighty" (Shaddai) is a name given to God particularly as judge.

"The Lord has pronounced against me": These are quasi-legal terms taken from a court setting. As in Job, the conflict between Naomi and Yahweh is open and absolute. At the same time, Naomi, as a practical woman, takes it for granted that nothing can be done about the situation.

THE MEETING

Ruth 2:1-23

Chapter 2 is a self-contained scene. It begins with the storyteller's note that Naomi has a kinsman named Boaz. It ends with Naomi recognizing him as the one in whose field Ruth has been gleaning. The description of Boaz befriending Ruth creates vivid pictures of both the girl and the man. Ruth is energetic in setting out to provide for her mother-in-law and in bringing home both provisions and news. She is also portrayed as highly submissive and deferential toward both Naomi and Boaz. Boaz, on the other hand, is more than generous in safeguarding the rights of the poor and the alien, in protecting Ruth and providing for her convenience. He speaks in formalized language, which sets him above Ruth. He is and acts like a prominent man (2:1). It is precisely these qualities that Naomi recognizes at the end (2:20). The point of chapter 2 is to show how Ruth comes under his protection and how Naomi recognizes it as a good thing.

2:1 The kinsman was not just a relative, but someone bound by custom to take the side of those who were in trouble. It was later used to mean "redeemer." Boaz is honoring an obligation as well as being magnanimous.

2:2 The obligation of allowing the poor and the alien to glean was recognized by law (see Lev 19:9; Deut 14:19-22). Ruth is both poor and alien. There is really no need for her to ask permission of Naomi or even Boaz.

2:8 Boaz is rather peremptory about deciding what Ruth shall do. Still and all, there is a pragmatic understanding that however pleased the young men are at having Ruth working in the fields with them, there is some danger that demands the protection of Boaz (2:9).

2:11 Boaz is not only prominent, but well-informed. However, he makes no allusion to being a kinsman. His initial kindness to Ruth is based simply on the report.

2:14 Boaz is here going beyond the demands of the law in allowing Ruth to glean in his fields. He gives instruction to the harvesters to let her get in with them and even to drop some handfuls of grain for her. All this emphasizes his graciousness.

2:19 The story is very realistic about this at-home talk between the two women. Naomi knows that Ruth has been successful, for she has brought home a bag of barley.

2:20 As readers, we already know of the relationship from 2:1. As a story, however, the identification implies more. Naomi sees in it not happenstance but opportunity.

2:22 Naomi's advice is prudent, especially in the Hebrew text, where the language is considerably more explicit than "insulted." Yet, in the light of Naomi's character, there is already a hint of advantages to be gained by staying close to the prominent kinsman.

NAOMI THE MATCHMAKER

Ruth 3:1-18

Chapter 3 is a model of artistic suspense that will lead up to chapter 4. All the actors think that they know where they are going. Naomi has just identified Boaz as their kinsman (2:20). It was not idle chitchat. Naomi knows that the kinsman-redeemer must provide for the widows. But she must draw him closer.

Nothing further happened during the harvest season. Now it is time for winnowing the grain, a happy time when Boaz will be in the right mood. Naomi makes the bold move of sending Ruth out in her best finery for a night meeting. She does not know exactly what will happen, but she realizes that she must push Boaz.

Ruth has her own mind. She does not wait for Boaz to begin the courting but creeps under his blanket. She reminds him that he is her kinsman, not to justify her bold conduct but to inform him that she has ties to him.

Boaz himself has plans. He wants to marry Ruth, but he is a prominent and honorable man. The setting and the wording clearly imply a tension that night: will they or will they not? Boaz knows what Ruth and Naomi do not: he cannot honorably marry Ruth because a closer relative has a prior claim.

And so the night scene ends inconclusively with nothing happening. It is all kept very quiet. But when Ruth tells Naomi what happened, the old lady knows what she must do. At the end of chapter 1 Naomi lost her faith that God would provide; at the end of this scene she tells Ruth to wait. Naomi already knows why Boaz will settle the matter today. She has her own way.

3:1 Ordinarily it was the duty of the menfolk to provide for widows. Already in 1:9 Naomi expressed her concern about providing for her two daughters-in-law. Yet she is not entirely disinterested. Ruth's security is a guarantee for herself.

3:3 "So bathe and anoint yourself; then put on your best attire and go down to the threshing floor." This is a nicely balanced chain of words in Hebrew; it was meant to go together. There were no highly restrictive customs keeping girls away from boys. However, this is pushing events a bit. Boaz himself is later aware (3:14) of what the neighbors will say.

3:4 Without advising deliberate seduction, Naomi is well aware of what might happen when Ruth lies at the feet of Boaz. The Hebrew words have a certain suggestiveness. The tension is deliberate on the part of the storyteller.

3:9 "Spread the corner of your cloak over me": literally, "spread your wing over me." The words are intended to call to mind the protecting wing of Yahweh. Ruth's intentions are more than amorous; the most important thing she wants to remind Boaz of is that by custom he is her protector. But she makes a mistake in thinking that Boaz is her closest kin.

3:12 Obviously Boaz has done his homework. The protector was not just any relative; there was a definite line of priority, although we do not know precisely how it worked. The point of the story is that Boaz does. In spite of his enthusiasm, however, and his promise to resolve the matter tomorrow, Boaz does not know how to bring this about. The storyteller has caught all of his characters at loose ends.

3:18 Naomi seems very confident, but we are not told why. There is a gap in the story here. In 4:3 we are told for the first time that Naomi is putting up a piece of property for sale. At the end of chapter 3 we are simply left wondering: What will happen now? Quite clearly, Naomi has been busy making sure of what will happen.

BOAZ MARRIES RUTH

Ruth 4:1-12

The marriage negotiations are described with considerable haste. We do not know what some of the customs were about, but the general tenor is clear enough. Boaz knows two things that the other characters do not: there is a nearer kinsman, and Naomi is putting up a piece of property for sale.

The kinsman and the elders are conveniently present when Boaz needs them. As a good trader, he holds out the most attractive prospect first. Naomi's field is available, and in fairness he offers the first bid to the kinsman. Only then does he put in the hook—he must also buy Ruth. The redemption of the widow involves her support, Naomi's support, and that of possible children.

At this the nearer relative cedes the right to buy the field. Boaz is obviously waiting in the wings to take over. And so, in a curious ceremony the arrangement is legally closed. The people at the gate witness to the transaction and pronounce a blessing upon Boaz and his house to come.

At this point it looks as though everybody has won. Naomi has provided for Ruth and for herself. In all likelihood she has also preserved her family line. Boaz has his girl and his field. Ruth has the man who has been so kind and faithful to her. But there is more to come.

4:1 The description of the proceedings corresponds to what we know of biblical times, but there are specific difficulties because we do not know enough. Each town had some sort of governing body of elders. A quorum of these members—ten in this case—sufficed for public hearings and decisions. General principles of law drawn from the Mosaic legislation governed the proceedings, but all citizens were not equally informed about legal niceties, nor are we.

Two general laws were involved in this case. Property was to remain in the hands of members of the same tribe or family. If it was lost, the relative-protector had to help get it back. Secondly, if a husband died before he had a son, then a brother-in-law or some other relative was to marry the widow and have a son in the name of the deceased. This is called a "levirate marriage" from the Latin word *levir*, meaning "brother-in-law." In such cases the brother-in-law or near relative recognized his obligation to continue the family line. Implicitly, this was a way of providing social security for the widow. In this case, it is not quite clear why the two widows are involved.

"He called to him by name, 'Come and sit beside me!' " From the beginning Boaz is totally in charge and dominates the whole scene. The closer relative is never named in the story. Perhaps the storyteller did not want to complicate matters by naming another character at this late point.

4:3 The conditions under which women could own land are somewhat obscure, but they certainly could do so. Just how Naomi came to sell the property at this time or how Boaz knew about it is not made clear in the story.

4:4 Boaz is being fair. At the same time, he lets it be known that he wants to buy the land. He takes it for granted that it would be an attractive purchase.

4:5 First the good news, then the bad. The closer relative had an advantage by his prior claim on the property; now he is told that he also has a stronger obligation to take care of the widow. The widow in question should be Naomi, but it seems taken for granted that she can no longer have children and that Ruth will have to be the bride.

4:6 With so many more mouths to feed and the need to leave an inheritance, the closer relative recognizes that he will be hurting his present family. No criticism is leveled against him in the story. The obligations fell upon the whole relationship, and it is evident that Boaz is willing to assume them.

4:7 We do not know who took off whose sandal, and we have no references elsewhere in the Bible to this curious custom.

4:10 This is the last time that Mahlon is mentioned. Boaz is always called the father, despite the levirate law, which was intended to preserve the name of the first husband.

4:11 Rachel and Leah were the wives of Jacob. In the next verse the blessing is: "May your house become like the house of Perez, whom Tamar bore to Judah." Jacob was the hero of the northern tribes; Judah, of the southern tribes. Both are mentioned apparently in reference to David, who was king of both north and south. Tamar was the widowed daughter-in-law for whom Judah neglected to provide a husband. By disguising herself as a prostitute, she managed to have a son by Judah himself (Gen 38).

THE BIRTH OF OBED

Ruth 4:13-17

The final scene centers on Naomi. It balances the prologue in chapter 1. Naomi had been the faithful wife who had everything taken away from her by Yahweh. It was Yahweh whom Naomi fingered as the villain. Through the rest of the story Naomi tried to take life into her own hands and to make provision for her old age and for the continuance of her family. Apparently she succeeded, although her manipulations did not always come out as she planned. But now she has a rich son-in-law and a successor. Did she win? As Naomi sits there with her grandson in her lap, the village women once more greet her. They had nothing to say when Naomi bitterly denounced Yahweh at the end of chapter 1. Now they sing: "Blessed is the Lord who has not failed to provide you today with an heir!" The storyteller does not spell out what this means. But it is dramatic.

4:13 Everything happens rapidly at the end. Ruth had been barren for the ten years of her marriage to Mahlon, but now she conceives quickly.

4:14 We cannot miss the point that it is Naomi, not Ruth, who is on stage. We do not know what customs may have been involved, but it is clear that this is deliberate as a storytelling technique. We are brought back to chapter 1, where the village women last appeared.

4:15 Ruth's worth is based on two claims: she loves Naomi and she has provided an heir. This may sound rather self-serving, but Naomi's complaint was precisely that Yahweh did not take care of her, although Yahweh has just now taken care of Ruth. The conflict between Yahweh and Naomi has been resolved, but not by Naomi's craftiness.

4:16 No more seems intended than that Naomi has become a good grandmother to the boy. The glad cry "A son is born to Naomi" need not have any legal implications of adoption.

4:17 It is too legalistic to ask why the neighbor women name the boy. The context indicates that they are celebrating this glorious birth and congratulating Naomi by using the boy's name, Obed. Obed is a name to remember. He will be the grandfather of King David.

THE GENEALOGY OF DAVID

Ruth 4:18-22

The story ends with a genealogy: Perez, Hezron, Ram, Amminadab, Nahshon, Salmon, Boaz, Obed, Jesse, David. There is no question that the genealogy is authentic within the traditional way of citing such lists. Despite all that was said in the story about raising up a son for Elimelech or Mahlon, neither is mentioned in the genealogy. Whether the genealogy was an afterthought of the author or a later addition to the text cannot be determined. It fits in well enough with the storyteller's chorus of village women crying "May he become famous in Israel." In that sense it would simply round off the story without being the central point.

On the other hand, it is rather odd that the author should conclude his story of Ruth with a genealogy that does not even mention her. Nor is she mentioned in the corresponding list in 1 Chr 2. Yet the tradition was preserved. Matt 1:5 does mention Ruth. Three women are remembered in Matthew's genealogy: Rahab the harlot, Ruth the Moabitess, and Bathsheba (although she is mentioned only discreetly in connection with Solomon, "whose mother had been the wife of Uriah"). Even in the final genealogy there are surprises.

LAMENTATIONS

James A. Fischer, C.M.

INTRODUCTION

Traditionally the Book of Lamentations has been pictured as the writing of Jeremiah the prophet as he saw the destruction of Jerusalem in 587 B.C.E. This certainly gives visual expression to much of the thought. The prophet was watching the smoke rise from the destroyed city. He heard the wailing of women as they found their dead ones or sought those long lost. Soldiers milled about, driving victims before them and setting fire to the ruins. It was the prophet's city and his people. Often had he preached in it, imploring his compatriots to turn back from folly. Now the terrible word of the Lord had come. It was too much. God had been right, but who could live with such a ruthless God? Prayer to God had been as useless as preaching to the people. God had made a mockery of former glorious promises and deeds.

Such is the literary setting of the five poems (chapters) that comprise the Book of Lamentations. They are incandescent with emotions of desolation, grief, incomprehension, and indignation. Sin has been revealed in its raw evilness. Nothing of nobility survived except a bleeding memory.

The form of the book

Yet the book is a rigidly controlled outpouring. As poetry it is spontaneous, heartfelt, torn from exacerbated feelings and yet elaborately planned and precisely executed. Three of the poems are acrostics, each verse beginning with a succeeding letter of the Hebrew alphabet; the other two are also built on the pattern of twenty-two. Such a numerical pattern gives a feeling of inescapable completion. In each poem a break occurs just slightly before the middle, setting the two parts against each other. The middle poem (chapter 3) is totally different in mood, as we shall see. All five poems must be read to grasp the overall feeling and meaning; that is the aim of the poet.

Some of the poems are written in the rhythm of a funeral dirge. Some verses have the form of taunt songs. The meter is still disputed; reconstructions and explanations based on it do not seem to get us very far.

Out of the controlled literary form comes a theological insight. God can be faced and prayed to in all the divine anger and stony silence. Grief and bitterness can be surmounted to arrive at repentance and acceptance. When history has become unendurable, faith still endures.

The history of the book

The picture given of Jeremiah at the beginning will not stand up to historical analysis. Although he could have composed the lamentations, it appears more probable that they were written over a period of years after him. Perhaps, indeed, many such laments were written for memorial services in the ruined city or elsewhere and our collection represents a selection by an editor. The first and second poems seem to be eyewitness compositions; the rest are clearly from a later time. All are heavily flavored by the expressions and thoughts of the prophet Jeremiah and so have been traditionally associated with him.

Certainly the book as we know it was completed by 538 B.C.E. It is possible, but not provable, that the poems were sung in some liturgical setting. We know that much later they were used in synagogues for the celebration of the ninth day of Ab in late summer to remember the destruction of Jerusalem.

COMMENTARY

JERUSALEM ABANDONED AND DISGRACED

Lam 1:1-22

The first poem (chapter 1) or dirge is an acrostic, that is, a poem whose lines begin with succeeding letters of the Hebrew alphabet. It is divided into two parts. Each begins with a cry:

How lonely she is now,
the once crowded city! (1:1)
Look, O Lord, and see
how worthless I have become! (1:11)

The first section describes the utter loneliness of the daughter of Jerusalem, now a widow. It is a funeral dirge over Jerusalem itself. The precise rhythm of the dirge song is used. The widow weeps. Her friends have betrayed her, and she has no peace. There are no more pilgrims coming to her; her priests groan, her foes triumph, her little ones have gone away, her glory is vanished, she has no home, her foes gloat over her. And added to all this, she is aware that it is her own sins that have brought it about. This first section winds down to a piteous plea:

Astounding is her downfall,
with no one to console her.
Look, O Lord, upon her misery,
for the enemy has triumphed! (1:9)

The second section begins with a confession of guilt and yet a plea for others to understand her misery:

"Come, all you who pass by the way,
look and see
Whether there is any suffering like
my suffering,
which has been dealt me . . ." (1:12).

Images are heaped up: blazing wrath, fire, sins plaited together and tied around her neck, brought to her knees, young men crushed, trodden into the winepress. There is no one to console her: Jerusalem has become a thing unclean. This section also finally emerges into a prayer, but a prayer for vengeance:

"Let all their evil come before you;
deal with them
As you have dealt with me
for all my sins;
My groans are many,
and I am sick at heart" (1:22).

It is a dark mood that has come upon the poet. Loneliness is the most dreaded evil; there is no one, not even God, to offer any consolation. There is no denying that God has been just in punishing; yet God seems to be playing favorites by not punishing the more sinful invader. Repentance comes down to a need for some immediate vindication against the foe: "deal with them as you have dealt with me for all my sins."

1:1 The note of loneliness is struck from the beginning. Jerusalem never had a large population, but during the festival days it was overflowing with Jews from all over Palestine and foreign countries.

The city is "she." Such was the ancient way of referring to cities. Wealth, education, and power flowed from cities. Capital cities were referred to as "queens." In the Bible "daughter of Zion" or "mother Jerusalem" are the ordinary designations. The metaphor gets mixed up here, for although the dirge is for the female whose funeral song is sung, it is the widow who pronounces it over herself.

1:3 The text is not clear. It seems to refer to Judah in exile, but that has not yet happened and the Hebrew text supports the usual picture of pre-exilic Judah as living among the nations as their savior. If so, the pity is that Judah has failed to bring "rest" or peace to the nations.

1:5 As elsewhere in the Old Testament, there are no explanations about the sociological or political forces at work. The Lord is fingered from the first as the cause of disaster. So also in verse 12: "the Lord afflicted me."

1:8 Although Jews were not at all squeamish about sex, they did abhor nakedness. There is some dispute about the actual meaning in Hebrew; perhaps the picture does rely on a known punishment for treaty violations, namely, the political leaders were stripped naked so that they should be shamed before their own people. The same punishment also seems to have been used sometimes for prostitutes.

1:10 The Babylonians carried off the sacred vessels of the temple. What hurt the most was not the loss of money but the desecration of such treasures. The Book of Daniel (Dan 5:2) knows of this tradition (see 2 Kgs 25:13-17).

Deut 23:4 has a most severe rule against any Moabite or Ammonite ever being accepted into the community. The tradition persisted with uneven application for centuries. Actually, there do not seem to have been any Moabite or Ammonite soldiers among the Babylonian conquerors. For the poet this is immaterial; the picture is of utter desecration of the sacred.

1:12 The second section begins with an appeal for help against the Lord. Presumably those who pass by the way are uninvolved people who could make an unbiased judgment. The suffering of widowed Jerusalem is not just another normal tragedy of war; it is unprecedented, since it comes directly from the Lord.

1:14 The poet knows that sin is not a bit of dirt to be brushed off. It is "plaited," woven together into an entangling and heavy burden that cannot be shaken off.

1:17 Jacob is another name used generically for all Israel or for parts of it, such as Judah. Once more the lament is against the Lord directly. The physical terrors of war must be borne; the spiritual terrors of God as the enemy are less perceptible but are the cause of real grief.

1:19 The lovers seem to have been nations such as Egypt and Assyria, with which Judah had attempted to make alliances to stave off Babylonia. The verse also suggests a trifling with paganism. Unfaithful Jerusalem is often called a temple prostitute, a woman willing to abandon her husband to consort with the gods.

1:20 The poet knows that Jerusalem has been unfaithful and that she knows it. The pain lies not so much in the external suffering as in the loss of integrity. "My heart recoils within me from my monstrous rebellion." So the problem is posed in its most excruciating form: Jerusalem knows that the Lord is just (see v. 18), but accepting this is just too painful.

1:21 The ungracious ending begins quite openly. The "Day of the Lord" was a familiar theme—a time when God would defeat the nations and usher in God's glorious reign. The prophets had warned that the Day of the Lord was a two-edged sword; it could be directed against the chosen people also. So it had happened. But the Day had not fallen on the oppressors. If there is vengeance here, it is at least based on the belief that the Lord alone could do it. At this point acceptance is very slight; it is inescapable but narrow-minded.

THE LORD'S WRATH AGAINST ZION

Lam 2:1-22

The second poem is a wild outpouring of grief over destroyed Zion, but the wildness is controlled both by the literary artist and by the believer, as is signified by the same use of the alphabetical arrangement. This poem, too, divides into two parts. The problem is first raised:

How the Lord in his wrath
has detested daughter Zion! (2:1)

The Lord has been ruthless in punishing, even self-distrustful, as the poet implies: "unmindful of his footstool." The Lord has dishonored everything in the land: dwellings, fortress Zion, king, princes. Then follows a poetic reverie: "his hand has brought ruin, yet he did not relent" (v. 8). The images heap up into an overwhelming picture of awesome destruction.

Then the poet turns to his own reverie:

Worn out from weeping are my eyes,
within me all is in ferment (2:11).

Like King Jehoiakim, who saw his children slaughtered and then had his own eyes put out, the poet can see and feel the final scenes:

As child and infant faint away
in the open spaces of the town.

They ask their mothers,
"Where is the cereal?"—in vain,
As they faint away like the wounded
in the streets of the city,
And breathe their last
in their mothers' arms (2:11b-12).

There is no recourse but a cry to God, a cry bound to fall on deaf ears. It is unmerciful and unparalleled in history:

Look, O Lord, and consider:
whom have you ever treated thus?
Must women eat their offspring,
their well-formed children?
Are priest and prophet slain
in the sanctuary of the Lord? (2:20)

No hope pervades these dreary thoughts. The day of wrath continues to the end.

The problem is the total disregard of God for mercy. Rather than deny it or cover it over with pious words of promise, the poet flings it in God's face. It is God's own self-interest that is badly served. What will the enemies think of such a God?

2:1 Each of the first eight verses describes the Lord as an enemy; the Lord detests, consumes in anger, blazes up, shoots, scorns, and so on. What is left unspoken is the implicit paradox: it is the Lord's chosen that is detested.

Zion is sacred soil because it is there that the Lord's feet have touched the earth and consecrated it. It is this sacred touch that the Lord now seems to forget.

2:3 The horn as a symbol of strength is a common Old Testament figure; see Ps 75:11 for an example.

2:6 The exact meaning is unclear. Perhaps the reference is to the shelters that were erected in the vineyards during the growing season so that the owner could mount a guard. They could be easily demolished. Israel is God's vineyard; God should have protected it.

2:8 The image is of an architect measuring a building. He knows precisely the size and shape that he wants. So the Lord has decreed destruction of Zion's wall not haphazardly but with precise planning.

2:9 The reference is to the bars that were put up to lock the gates of the city after they were closed.

Among all the calamities, the worst were the losses of spiritual things, such as the instruction in the law given by the priests. Religious education had come to a halt.

2:10 The esteemed elders are sitting on the ground either humiliated or as a sign of mourning. At any rate, the education by the wise has ceased. Usually the daughters of Jerusalem are pictured as dancing; now they are mourning.

2:11 The first part of the poem has concentrated on what God the enemy has done. Now the thought turns back to the personal dismay of daughter Jerusalem (see 1:20 for the same phrasing).

2:12 Nothing more vivid could be added to this picture of starving children. It is just a few words, but it is the detail that says immense amounts. In verse 20 the poet will allude to women eating their offspring. It was one of the terrors of sieges amply attested by the Old Testament and by other ancient Near Eastern texts.

2:14 The Hebrew text is more vivid: "Your prophets saw visions that were mere whitewash." The reality was horrendous and the prophets knew it; they whitewashed it by crying "Peace!" when they knew that there was no peace of the Lord in the land.

2:15 Obviously the passersby are not clapping in approval as we do. Clapping of the hands is a fairly frequent sign of derision in the Old Testament.

2:20 The paradox here is brought near the surface. The enemies of Israel were obviously the sinners and deservedly suffered defeat, famine, pillage, and siege. But nothing like this had ever happened to the chosen ones. It is a reproach to the justice of God that God has punished the chosen people without mercy.

2:22 The poem ends on a note of total disgust and reproach; God doesn't even have manners, and God's feast day is a grisly banquet of death. There is nothing more to be said than "if that is the kind of God you are, we don't want you." It is notable that it is not said. The twenty-two-verse pattern ends precisely before it, and nothing more can be added.

SUFFERINGS OF THE PROPHET AND HIS PEOPLE

Lam 3:1-66

The third poem is completely different. It is not the agonized outpouring of an eyewitness over Jerusalem in its death throes. It is a personal meditation or reverie:

I am a man who knows affliction
from the rod of his anger (3:1).

How can such a man live with his God? The problem of affliction is described in rather traditional images having only a vague reference to the destruction of Jerusalem. But in any affliction, mysterious as it may be, the sages can still assert that God is good.

The favors of the Lord are not exhausted,
his mercies are not spent;
They are renewed each morning,
so great is his faithfulness.
My portion is the Lord, says my soul;
therefore I will hope in him (3:22-24).

Affliction is seen to have a medicinal effect:

Why should any living man complain,
any mortal, in the face of his sins?
Let us search and examine our ways
that we may return to the Lord! (3:39-40)

At this point the meditation turns from the personal "I" to the collective "we." The rest of the poem is a somewhat conventional lament that confesses sin, complains that the enemy is still triumphant, expresses confidence that God will hear, and ends with a prayer for vindication against enemies.

It is a soothing prayer. The imagery is much less violent than in the preceding two poems. The alphabetic form has been used, but now the poem has stretched out from twenty-two to sixty-six verses to heighten the understanding that not only has all been said, but it has been fully said. The poet often reaches back for hallowed phrases traditionally sung in the temple; some ten verses are very close to psalm quotations. Often the vocabulary and style parallel the wisdom writers' techniques, and so give a calming effect. God is viewed as the Creator, the Most High, the Lord from heaven. Despite the harsh note of vindictiveness at the end, the poem carries the gentler spirit of the sages of Israel. God is hidden in these harsh facts of life, but God is still there, and still there as a good God.

Seen against the background of the first two poems, this lengthy meditation begins to investigate a livable solution. It is a mysterious solution, since, as the sages realized, no one can understand God. But if the question is raised of how Israelites can live with their God, as it was in the preceding poems and in the beginning of this one, then the ancient faith in a good God who eventually uses power both to chastise and to vindicate must be added. It does not solve the problem. This poet has managed to quiet the raw emotions of loneliness and incomprehensibility into something more peaceful where the thought that things may not be what they seem to be can begin to emerge.

3:2 The sharp contrasts between light and darkness, life and death, good and evil in this poem are characteristic of the sages' techniques.

3:6 The Jews of this period did not speculate about what happened in the afterlife, although they believed that life continued for them. The experience of death was that a body was placed in a grave and stayed there. As far as anyone could see, such a life was useless. So death was darkness and a nonentity.

3:8 We are so accustomed to saying that God always hears prayer that we ignore our own experience. The Hebrews felt more comfortable admitting that God did not need to hear anything and that their efforts to reach God often seemed to be ignored. Thus verse 44 says: "You wrapped yourself in a cloud which prayer could not pierce."

3:10 For the next six verses the poet pursues the picture that God is the enemy. The Jews had no theories to explain evil in the world. It simply existed, and in some way it was due to God (see vv. 37-38). The experience of life often seemed to make God the enemy.

3:20 Here again the experience of life dominates. We keep mulling over our problems and the broken-record process gets in the way of our ever seeing more in our situation.

3:22 Note the sudden inbreaking of light here. This is a standard feature of the lament psalms and is called a "certainty of a hearing." No lament is complete without it. Here it introduces a new section.

3:24 "My portion is the Lord": Ps 16:5 and 73:26 use the same metaphor. It was the conviction of all that God has given each person a place in life and a work to do. This might become specific, as in the allotting of portions of the land to the various tribes. There was a portion for all, and it was given not haphazardly but because the Lord decreed it.

3:25 "Good is the Lord to one who waits for him": This is part of the faith statement. It is also put in the form of a wisdom admonition. It will be noted that verses 25, 26, and 27 all have the same form: "It is good . . ."

3:29 The metaphor expresses surrender and is probably taken from a scene of political subjugation.

3:31 We are getting into an insight of how evil actually operates in the world. Experience taught that the Lord always came to rescue Israel, although this might take time. The worst thought was that God simply did not care about what went on here on earth. Verses 34 to 36 are a repudiation of that idea. The same occurs in the Book of Job (see Job 35).

3:37 Here we have, not a philosophical explanation of the problem of evil, but a simple statement of observed fact and faith. Good and evil do come; unless one is prepared to say that there is another god of evil, one can only say that both good and evil come from God in some way. What that way may be is subject to endless philosophizing, but the assertion here bears on the fact that there is only one God who controls everything.

3:39 Whatever turns the notion of disaster and sin took, it seemed reasonable to the Jews to concede that all human beings were sinful, and if they were not punished for one thing, they deserved it for another.

3:40 This is another wisdom admonition, and, typically, it makes practical use of the reflections that have preceded it. Suffering has a medicinal value if only we will search for it.

3:48 This is the first reference to the destruction of Jerusalem, and apart from verses 48-51 there is no other allusion to it in this poem.

3:54 Water as a symbol of trouble is common in the Old Testament.

3:65 There is no doubt about the vindictiveness of this prayer. But it should at least be conceded that the poet was thinking in spiritual terms. The worst evil he could wish was a spiritual one—hardness of heart. From that there was no escape, as he himself knew from his own experience.

MISERIES OF THE BESIEGED CITY

Lam 4:1-22

After the reflective mood of the third poem, the fourth chapter can take a more reasonable approach to lament. Past and present jostle for sorrowful consideration at the beginning.

> How tarnished is the gold,
> how changed the noble metal! (4:1)

The glory of Zion past is compared with the present ignominy, the prosperity of yesteryears with the starvation of today. The poet will not flinch from even the worst:

> The hands of the compassionate women
> boiled their own children,
> To serve them as mourners' food
> in the downfall of the daughter of
> my people (4:10).

Then the mood changes to one of honest admission that all this punishment has come upon them because of their sins. Prophets, priests, elders, even the anointed (king) have proven false and have been dispersed. The last hope is gone with the king in prison:

> He in whose shadow we thought
> we could live on among the nations (4:20).

And the simple fact is admitted: the Lord himself has dispersed us (v. 16). There is one last outburst of resentment—this time against Edom, the traditional enemy. However, it is clear that the poet has made progress in elevating his thought. God is the punisher, and yet punishment is justifiable.

4:3 The starving mothers of Jerusalem know that even wild animals can feed their young; they cannot. "The daughter of my people has become as cruel as the ostrich in the desert." There was a widespread belief that ostriches abandoned their eggs after laying them and allowed them to be trampled on.

4:12 The belief was that of the Israelites; we have no evidence that any others held it. Still and all, Jerusalem remained unconquered from the time of David to the Exile, some four hundred years.

4:13 No specific sin is mentioned, and the Hebrew text is somewhat uncertain. However,

Jeremiah himself was unjustly imprisoned and accused of treason by the priests and the prophet Hananiah (see Jer 26). So also Christ refers to a tradition of bloodshed in Jerusalem caused by the officials (see Matt 23:35). It should also be noted that the Old Testament does not distinguish, in using the title "prophet," between false prophets and true ones, as present-day scholars are accustomed to do. Among those called prophets there were many political sycophants and downright liars.

4:20 The reference is to King Zedekiah, who was captured trying to escape from Jerusalem during the last siege (see 2 Kgs 25:3-6). The king is called "our breath of life," a very ancient Canaanite title for a king. There is no reason to suspect irony.

4:21 "Daughter Edom" is, of course, the country across the Jordan. A somewhat vagrant tradition says that Esau, the brother of Jacob, was their progenitor. Actually, they seem to have been a mixed people among whom the Jews mingled and did business. For some reason that is not entirely clear from the Bible, they are usually singled out by the prophets for the fiercest of denunciations.

4:22 This is about the happiest thing said in the Book of Lamentations. In contrast to Edom, whose punishment is in the future, Zion is on the upswing.

THE PROPHET'S LAMENT AND SUPPLICATION

Lam 5:1-22

The last poem must be seen against the backdrop of the preceding chapters. The poems began with an untrammeled lament over the destroyed city and a questioning of how God could do this. The third poem introduced a reflective mood: God is still the good God, and suffering has its curative value. The fourth poem spoke much about a true confession of faith. Now the poet is ready to put this horrendous experience in the light of Israel's historical traditions.

> Remember, O Lord, what has befallen us,
> look, and see our disgrace:
> Our inherited lands have been turned over to strangers,
> our homes to foreigners (5:1-2).

The exiles are the foreigners now, worked to death and begging for water. The facts cannot be belied. Sin has worked its havoc according to the ancient law that children are to be punished for the crimes of their parents. So be it.

But there is more to remembering than that. The destruction of Jerusalem is in the past for these exiles. And it was not simply the sins of the parents that had brought it about.

> Woe to us, for we have sinned! (5:16)

Yet Israel's God has always been a king, unchanging in both goodness and power. Such a king cannot forget his own.

> You, O Lord, are enthroned forever;
> your throne stands from age to age.
> Why, then, should you forget us,
> abandon us so long a time?
> Lead us back to you, O Lord, that we may be restored:
> give us anew such days as we had of old (5:19-21).

On this humbly supplicant note the Lamentations end. The poet has come to the peace of confession and of waiting for God to remember without any bitterness against God who inflicted the punishment and without resentment against the enemy who did it. There is an opening into a new understanding of the tragedy of the destruction of Jerusalem. As if to indicate this by the literary form used, the poet has dropped the acrostic formula and has not employed the funereal meter of lament. The future is open. It is a simple theological statement of hope.

Title: Some Greek manuscripts have a title prefixed to this chapter: "A prayer." So it is. The tone of this chapter is prayerful and calming. Although it has twenty-two verses, this poem is not alphabetical (an acrostic) like the others. It is in the form of a national lament with all the expression of confidence that such a song demands.

5:6 Although the Exodus from Egypt and the events leading up to it were hundreds of years in the past, it continued to be the central experience and measuring stick for most later reflections on the ways of God. The Hebrew text is not as harsh as the translation: "We shook hands with Egypt . . ."

5:7 The idea that the sins of parents are visited on their children is common in the Old

Testament. It is also common sense from a historical perspective. The poet accepts such guilt, or at least such punishment, as just. He also allows space for the guilt of the present generation.

5:8 The Hebrew word is used as a slur on government officials, especially the lower ones, who were often corrupt.

5:11-14 These verses picture a society in which all the norms of accepted social behavior are overturned. Wives and maidens are no longer respected and protected; princes are executed; elders are not honored; young men have no job opportunities; the elders who govern prudently do not even bother to gather at the city gates, and the young do not have fun.

5:18 The more terrible prophetic threats predicted the destruction of Jerusalem and pictured wild animals as the only inhabitants. That Jerusalem as the center of worship, and so of all religion, should be abandoned was unthinkable. The rallying cry for the preservation of Judaism in exile centered on the unquenchable desire to return to the Holy City.

5:19 The enthronement of Yahweh as King was both a theological conviction and a liturgical celebration of great importance in pre-exilic Judaism. Essentially, the statement expressed the faith that God alone ruled all things and would eventually win. It is noteworthy that the Exile brought out some of the strongest expressions of this faith in Old Testament history. It was a time when the Old Testament was largely edited, and the events of the past reinterpreted in dynamic fashion.

5:21 The New American Bible translation catches the right meaning of the words: "help us to repent!" That repentance was still possible is taken for granted. In synagogue reading the Jews repeat this verse after the end of the chapter, so that the whole of Lamentations ends on a hopeful note that God will grant repentance. Thus was the book conceived. It is not a pious book of idealistic sayings that tell us how we ought to be. It is a human as well as a divine document that witnesses to the power of God to save even when we are in the depths of despair and resentment. It is salvation achieved, but at a great price.

ECCLESIASTES

James A. Fischer, C.M.

INTRODUCTION

The Book of Ecclesiastes is the most damnable book in the Bible and yet the most satisfying for those who have learned to live comfortably with doubt. That it is damnable seems clear; it has been denounced many times as cynical, pessimistic, worldly, and downright heretical. That it is in the Bible at all and provides great comfort for those who are willing to face life honestly is also a fact. Ecclesiastes—or to give him the Hebrew name by which he is often known, Qoheleth—destroys most of the accepted clichés on which the superficially pious live.

> Because the sentence against evildoers is not promptly executed, therefore the hearts of men are filled with the desire to commit evil—because the sinner does evil a hundred times and survives (8:11-12).
>
> Consider the work of God. Who can make straight what he has made crooked? (7:13)
>
> A good name is better than good ointment,

and then Qoheleth adds:

> and the day of death than the day of birth (7:1). One man out of a thousand have I come upon, but a woman among them all I have not found (7:28).

That may be the unkindest cut of all. On the other hand, Qoheleth's favorite slogan is "Eat, drink and be merry" (Eccl 2:24; 3:13; 5:17; 9:7-10). Somewhere among all this one must begin to wonder what Qoheleth believed in, if anything. And then there is the greater problem that a whole people accepted this as the word of God. The Book of Ecclesiastes is one of the great books of the Bible and of ancient times. It is not an easy book to deal with. But neither is life, and that is what Qoheleth ventured to examine.

We do not know much about the author. The name "Ecclesiastes" is a title made up from the Greek word for "church" or "synagogue." It is roughly a translation of the Hebrew "Qoheleth," but neither is a very happy title for somebody who apparently was much more a professor in an academy than a churchman. He must remain forever unknown.

From the contents of the book we can create a somewhat imaginative but largely responsible picture. Qoheleth lived sometime between 300 and 200 B.C.E. The quality of his diction betrays that. Apparently he was a teacher in Jerusalem. We know too little about the educational system of that time, but we can reasonably suspect that Jewish education was a cut above the average in the ancient world, and that there was a well-organized system from the grades to the college level in Jerusalem. Qoheleth appears to have been one of the more honored members of that academic community. He also appears to have been wealthy, and that certainly was not due to his academic pursuits. Apparently he was happily married, at least in his youth. Children do not figure in his admonitions; "son" is always a conventional term for "student."

After many years in the classroom, Qoheleth was compelled by the usual demon of professors to set down his best discoveries in life. Many young men had sat before him and gone out into the world. They came back occasionally to consult their old teacher. They were successful, full of importance, with a formula for "making it." The old man looked at them and wondered if he had overaccomplished his task. They still had not learned, and beneath the veneer of achievement he detected a great doubt and fear. So he asked the question for them: Is it all worthwhile? He himself had been through it. He realized that he first had to impress them with the impossible question so that they would admit their need. Only then could he give them the answer that life is worth living, not just for the sheer joy of living to the hilt, but for the deeper reason that this is what God had appointed them to do when creating them as caretakers on earth. But that took a good deal of explaining.

The book was originally written in Hebrew. The style is excellent, as is also the somewhat free Greek translation that was made very early on. It is hard to determine for whom it was written. It certainly was not written for church reading, whatever that word may mean. It was an essay to be distributed and cherished among students. But somehow it came to be read in synagogues. Today it is read for the feast of Succoth to add a somber note to the ending of the year. This is not entirely compelling; there is really nothing in the book to suggest fall, and some Jews do not read it at all.

How the book got into the Bible is also something of a mystery. The title, "The words of David's son, Qoheleth, king in Jerusalem," is probably a later addition. It gives some justification for including the work in the sacred Scriptures by placing it within the wisdom tradition, which was always connected with Solomon. Especially in later times, when the title was taken more literally, this seems to have been a powerful argument among the rabbis. The last verses of the book (Eccl 12:9-14) were added by an editor, as is clear from the text itself. Someone else, therefore, published the book.

Between publication and acceptance as a sacred book, however, there is a large gap. This book did not have the backing of priests, prophets, synagogue officials, or other authorities. It had to be accepted because of its own excellence and then transformed from being an insightful essay into being a word of God. There were arguments among the Jewish rabbis of a later date as to whether it should be accepted in the list of sacred writings, but when it was accepted, it was accepted without further argument. Perhaps the ascription to "David's son" did carry the day. If so, the book is in the Bible for the wrong reason—which would please Qoheleth no end. The Christians found no problem whatever in embracing it, although it is obviously no inspiring Sermon on the Mount.

Form of the book

Unlike the Books of Ruth or Lamentations, this book has no intricate or tightly controlled form. For purposes of reading, it may be just as well to simply note the following divisions:

First section—1:1–3:15 is a fairly well organized series of reflections on life as a pursuit of objectives that always end up being unsatisfying. It begins with a poignant poem on the inevitability of the constant round of activity in this world and ends with another poem about a time for everything, followed by a reflection that we do not know why this should be.

Middle section—3:16–11:8 seems to be a jumble of occasional remarks on various topics that Qoheleth found particularly enigmatic. Included here are mostly proverbs—sometimes proverbs that stand traditional proverbs on their heads; occasionally a parable; sometimes that refrain about "Eat, drink and be merry"; and, toward the end, a tendency to indulge in poetry.

Final section—11:9–12:8 strikes a different note, as if the author were aware that he might leave his readers with a dissonant sound reverberating in their ears. So he goes back to his job of giving hope to the young. Live life to the full, he advises. Old age comes too quickly. But what are we walking into? The darkness of a deserted village? The grave? That is only for the dust that we are. What of the life-breath? Where does it go?

Editor's footnote—As indicated above, the final verses are from an editor. It is not your conventional dust-jacket blurb. This editor tells us that Qoheleth taught the people proverbs and true sayings with precision. Yet even here he recognizes that "of the making of many books there is no end." So he published another one. Qoheleth would have liked that.

Theological insight

This is obviously a problem book, and the first need is to define the problem. It seems from the middle section of the book that the young Qoheleth had high ideals of justice and honesty in human affairs. He was perhaps a brilliant and competent student, and had access to the inner chambers of government. Despite the "perhaps," it is clear that he was disillusioned. His first thought in the middle section is of the intractability of injustice in the world.

> And still under the sun in the judgment place
> I saw wickedness, and in the seat of justice,
> iniquity (3:16).

The higher one went, the worse it got. The petty graft of tax-collectors and civil servants was nothing compared with that of judges and administrators.

> If you see oppression of the poor, and violation of rights and justice in the realm, do not be shocked by the fact, for the high official has another higher than he watching him and above these are others higher still (5:7).

And there the author leaves it, although he adds somewhat bitterly that people still say: "Yet an advantage for a country in every respect is a king for the arable land" (5:8).

But Qoheleth was no prophet who could go to his death denouncing injustice in the land. He was a party man who succumbed to the wisdom that one cannot fight City Hall. So he could only fold his hands while protesting:

> I have seen all manner of things in my vain days: a just man perishing in his justice, and a wicked one surviving in his wickedness. Be not just to excess, and be not overwise, lest you be ruined (7:15-16).

On the other hand, he never gave up protesting the dishonesty he saw in his society. Much of his concern about justice was simply that politicians will not call a spade a spade. But then he found out that this was true among his academic friends as well. They peddled knowledge as the cure-all. But it was not true, as Qoheleth knew from personal experience.

> When I applied my heart to know wisdom and to observe what is done on earth, I recognized that man is unable to find out all God's work that is done under the sun, even though neither by day nor by night do his eyes find rest in sleep. However much man toils in searching, he does not find it out; and even if the wise man says that he knows, he is unable to find it out (8:17).

It was simply dishonest to fool people by repeating the popular wisdom that had been handed down without question through the centuries. Good and evil constantly happened, but no one could say exactly why. The law and the prophets were powerless. Although people did not say so explicitly, they expected that virtuous living would be rewarded with prosperity, peace, family, and happiness; on the other hand, the wicked always perished. Qoheleth knew that it was not true. The older wisdom had extolled the values of hard work, moderate pleasure, and the discipline of wisdom. Indeed, this had become almost a stained-glass picture of a sage. Job had railed against it by using the story of the good man who was afflicted in every way and then demanded to know why.

Qoheleth had suffered the opposite fate. He had everything that the traditional wisdom said that a sage should have. And he found it nothing but a vapor, a puff of smoke, the greatest "vanity" of all. So his essay begins with a rather slashing attack on wisdom, pleasure, and toil as means of attaining any understanding that was worthwhile. The truth was that life kept flowing in the same channel no matter what a person did or was. Life and death, war and peace, love and hatred—these things happened, they were not caused. They were all the inevitabilities of time. What was behind them? The central problem is that we admit they have meaning, but we cannot in any way find the meaning.

> I have considered the task which God has appointed for men to be busied about. He has made everything appropriate to its time, and has put the timeless into their hearts, without men's ever discovering, from beginning to end, the work which God has done (3:9-11).

That is the problem. Without a religious code, there is no problem with the craziness of the world. It is only when a person like Qoheleth really believes, that the incomprehensibility of it all becomes unendurable. The best of human resources fail where they must succeed.

Something of balm comes from the recognition that life itself is good. Qoheleth was one of those normally happy persons who could not doubt the glory of sunshine in the morning.

> Indeed, for any among the living there is hope; a live dog is better off than a dead lion (9:4).

We are alive and we can enjoy. So Qoheleth has his comforting refrain (2:24-36; 3:12-13; 3:22; 5:17-19; 7:13-14; 8:15; 9:7-10; 11:7-10):

> Go, eat your bread with joy and drink your wine with a merry heart, because it is now that God favors your works (9:7).

> Anything you can turn your hand to, do with what power you have (9:10).

Life blossoms in doing something; don't just sit there and die. Even in acquiring knowledge Qoheleth knew that there is a difference between the wise person and the fool even when there was no pay-off.

> I went on to the consideration of wisdom, madness and folly. And I saw that wisdom has the advantage over folly as much as light has the advantage over darkness. The wise man has eyes in his head, but the fool walks in darkness (2:12-14).

The sheer exuberance of living is some consolation and validation of life. In all of this there is a usually implied but sometimes expressed understanding that everything good is a gift of God. It cannot really be merited; it is simply there, and sometimes there in surprising places, such as among the unjust. But as long as one has one's own measure, that can be borne. So the goodness of God is also a partial reason for accepting life as it is. That God wants to be good to others may be inexplicable, but not unacceptable.

Yet there was a deeper problem. If the sages had the advantage of having eyes in their heads, they ended up in the same grave as the fools. If the just and the unjust both seemed to enjoy life, the grave swallowed them both. If the wise could save a city by wisdom (Eccl 9:13-16; see 2 Sam 20:14-22), they could also be forgotten along with the fools who started the war. The inexplicability could not simply be accepted; it had to be understood.

And so Qoheleth pursued his way toward his own solution. It was not all that much of a solution, for it too leads to the grave. In the last great and haunting bit of poetry in the book, he pictures himself, an old man now, walking slowly through a devastated village. The strong men stand bent; the mourners inside shroud their heads as he passes; the birds stop singing. He finally comes to the village well, which had been the source of life. As he watches, the waiting pitcher topples and breaks, and the pulley falls into the deep pit.

> And the dust returns to the earth as it
> once was,
> and the life breath returns to God
> who gave it.
> Vanity of vanities, says Qoheleth,
> all things are vanity! (12:7-8)

What happened after that no one knows. But Qoheleth had gotten them as far as he could. The new revelation awaited the Son of God.

COMMENTARY

THE FIRST SECTION
Eccl 1:1–3:15

Chapter 1

1:1 Despite the apparent meaning, the author is not Solomon but Qoheleth. Forging authorship was not a practice among the Jews. Rather, the need was for one to remain unknown while indicating the kind of writing that one intended. Later the author will dress up his own experience as a well-to-do bon-vivant and businessman in terms more suitable for King Solomon. This was accepted practice.

1:2-8 The introductory poem is matched by the concluding one in 3:1-8. Both concern the relentless succession of events, and both are well-known because of their elegant style. The images conjure up the feeling of endless sameness; the balanced phrases are measured to lull us into acceptance. Here one generation succeeds another endlessly; the sun rises and sets each day; the wind keeps blowing, now from one direction and then from another; the rivers keep running down to the sea but never fill it; we keep explaining, but we never really say anything; we keep seeing and hearing, but we never learn what it is all about. The whole enterprise is the greatest puff of vapor imaginable, "vanity," for that is what "vanity of vanities" means.

1:11 The one thing that is thought to have permanence is a family name. People live on in that endless remembering that is so much a part of their religious heritage. Qoheleth denies it.

1:12-18 Qoheleth's first attempt to solve the riddle is by wisdom. Those with wisdom are the observers, sometimes the natural scientists of their day. Qoheleth sees it all and concludes that it is all made up of crooked lines and leads nowhere—"a chase after the wind." All that work for nothing! He can only reach the opposite conclusion that the sages before him reached: "For in much wisdom there is much sorrow" (1:18). Disillusionment, not contentment, is the fruit of learning.

Chapter 2

2:1-12 This section recounts Qoheleth's attempt to find an answer in frantic pleasure. It is not the heady flower-children escapism in which the Greeks were tempted to indulge (see Wis 2:1-9). This is the more substantial Jewish way of displaying power by banquets and sumptuous building projects—in short, becoming a patron of the arts. "Nothing that my eyes desired did I deny them, nor did I deprive myself of any joy, but my heart rejoiced in the fruit of all my toil" (v. 10). But who will keep it all up when he is gone? "For what will the man do who is to come after the king? What men have already done!" (v. 12).

2:12b-17 An aside is inserted here to reflect on the vanity of it all. Qoheleth might just as well be a fool, one who simply spurns the ethics of Jewish righteousness and lives selfishly as though there were no God; such is the meaning of "fool." Even though those with wisdom have eyes in their head, they come to the same end as the fool; all will be forgotten. And so he loathes a life that has no real meaning whatever one does.

2:18-26 Next Qoheleth buries himself in work. From the beginning he knows how vain this is. He knows not whether he will leave it all to a fool or a wise person. Meanwhile he must worry about it, so that "even at night his mind is not at rest" (v. 23). Still and all, working at play is about the best one can do. "There is nothing better for man than to eat and drink and provide himself with good things by his labors" (v. 24). It was not exactly escapism which Qoheleth embraced, but thankfulness. Hard work did not produce results; it did make one aware that everything good came from the hand of God.

Chapter 3

3:1-8 This famous poem, which we have made into a popular song, celebrates the inevitability of life. "There is an appointed time for everything under heaven." It is not a moral judgment of which times are good and which are bad, but the much worse judgment that they are simply inevitable. Birth and death, sowing and harvesting, killing and healing go on no matter what we do. And so it comes down to those alternatives on which we all take sides: a time to love and a time to hate; a time of war and a time of peace. It will not do to say that we opt for love, not hate; or peace, not war. That is immaterial—they simply happen.

3:9-15 So the poem leads to a meditation on what we are all thinking of: Why? Merely working for peace or love does not seem to affect the outcome very much, despite all the glorious stories of how one person changed the world. Somehow God has placed us all here in these intractable situations that keep us busy without ever bringing us closer to a conclusion or even revealing what it is all about. All we know is hustling time that will not let us rest with the good things we want.

Yet the tradition of the sages said that there is an appropriate time for all things. Nothing happens haphazardly or outside its time. But we do not know what or why the appropriate time is.

> He has made everything appropriate to its time, and has put the timeless into their hearts, without men's ever discovering from beginning to end, the work which God has done (v. 11).

This is the crux of the problem. Unfortunately, the Hebrew is not quite clear about the word we translate as "timeless." It is an adverb, and the translation might be: "he has put the love of the world into their hearts." If so, the final problem is that all are earthbound. The final poem (see Eccl 12:7) seems to persuade acceptance of our translation. At any rate, Qoheleth returns to his refrain about eating and drinking. Now, however, his thought goes further than thanks. All things happen because God has done them; that remains, and nothing can be added to it or taken away from it. God alone can put things back in their proper place: "God restores what would otherwise be displaced" (v. 15). The exact meaning is somewhat obscure.

THE MIDDLE SECTION

Eccl 3:16–11:8

As noted above, the middle section has no real order to it. It seems to be a collection of various proverbial sayings and reflections on almost all aspects of Israel's wisdom. Some of them Qoheleth accepts, others he modifies, and many of them he rejects outright and ridicules. However, it is possible to see a concentration on matters of justice and honesty. Our commentary will simply investigate the sayings that seem more striking or obscure.

3:16-18 Qoheleth begins his collection with a bitter saying about injustice at the highest government levels. He has a traditional confidence that God will eventually judge all, but meanwhile nothing more can be done than to accept that God is testing us.

3:21 Qoheleth is apparently referring to some popular saying that there is a happy future in store for good people. He challenges them to produce the evidence. Both the good and the wicked return to the dust.

Chapter 4

4:4 It was accepted that Jews should be hard-working, not lazy. But Qoheleth doubts the validity of such high-flown reasons as are given. In the end competition, not spiritual motives, prevails.

4:9 Again Qoheleth is citing a popular saying that teamwork is better than working alone. He continues a similar thought in verse 11 that marriage is better than being single. Then he laughs it to scorn by saying that there is nothing more in it than that a team makes more money and that a married partner is a good bed-warmer.

4:13-16 This section of reflections on the political community might be connected with "court wisdom," as it is called, except that the sentiment expressed would never be taught to young persons aspiring to government office. There is no end to the bootlickers at court, but the one whose boots are licked isn't worth remembering. There are a fair number of such reflections on the lifestyle of government officials; perhaps Qoheleth had had some role in this himself.

4:17 This is one of Qoheleth's few references to temple worship. It is respectful of God and scornful of the hypocrisy that Qoheleth observed.

Chapter 5

This chapter begins by continuing the theme of religious practice mentioned above. Then it shifts to a consideration of the folly of riches and ends with the refrain "Eat, drink and be merry."

5:4 The sentiment was traditional; Deut 23:22 and Sir 18:21 both say the same thing. In Qoheleth, however, it has a sharper tone, perhaps a repudiation of those scribes who were mostly interested in finding a way around fulfilling vows.

5:9-11 The vanity of riches is a consistent theme in both the Old and New Testaments. Qoheleth expresses it in pragmatic terms: "Where there are great riches, there are also many to devour them."

Chapter 6

Chapter 6 is mostly a series of reflections on the canker of wealth. Riches beget a desire for riches; even the approach of death does not seem to assuage it. "All man's toil is for his mouth, yet his desire is not fulfilled" (v. 7). Why people should react like this cannot be explained; that is the way God made them, and they might as well desist from arguing with One mightier than themselves. And yet, is that a tolerable explanation? That is Qoheleth's problem, as it was Job's. "Who is there to tell a man what will come after him under the sun?" (v. 12).

6:1 "There is another evil . . .": In effect, it is the same evil with which chapter 4 ended. The rich are never satisfied. If the rich man has a hundred children, he worries about the money that slips out of his grasp and whether he will be buried with suitable pomp. "The child born dead is more fortunate than he" (v. 3).

6:9 Apparently this is a quote from a common proverb. For once Qoheleth agrees.

6:10 ". . . he cannot contend in judgment with one who is stronger than he": The "one" refers to God. No one can demand that God give a reason for what God does. And if God won't, nobody else can.

Chapter 7

Chapter 7 is particularly unorganized. It begins with a litany of proverbs, some of which Qoheleth accepts and some of which he ridicules. Then it turns to considering a mean that is not a Golden Mean but a livable compromise. Toward the end Qoheleth confesses that he is in over his head as a sage and then compounds it by some scathing words about women in general. Apparently Qoheleth found trouble himself observing his admonition to avoid excess.

7:1 "A good name is better than good ointment, and the day of death than the day of birth": This is usually cited as the typical example of Qoheleth's technique. He has taken a proverb that is exceedingly common and turned it on its head by adding a comment that ridicules it. Verses 2, 3, and 4 use a similar approach but are less biting, since they do not trap us but warn us from the beginning that the author's views are unconventional.

7:13 The cliché is that God writes straight with crooked lines. Qoheleth will not suffer clichés. He turns the saying around. Experience has taught him about the crooked things in life and his inability to do much about them. All one can do is accept (see v. 14).

7:16-18 The New American Bible puts these words in quotation marks to indicate the translator's opinion that they are common sayings that Qoheleth knows but repudiates. Qoheleth was no martyr, willing to die uselessly for a justice he could not achieve. Nor did he think that he himself could lead a blameless life. He could not be self-righteous, nor could he be ruthless. Yet life constantly caught him in such dilemmas. His wisdom did not give him a way out. There was some truth in both sayings, but not enough in either. He went back to the traditional saying that the fear of the Lord is the beginning of wisdom. It arrived, but it was only the beginning. So he would counsel simply trying to stand in awe of the great God and letting things take their course. "He who fears God will win through at all events" (v. 18).

7:23 The personal note gives punch to the traditional view that wisdom, like everything else, is a gift, not a reward for work. The wisdom to unravel the enigma that has just been discussed is beyond Qoheleth.

7:26-29 This section on the human race is characteristic of Qoheleth. It is partly tongue-in-cheek and partly serious. It begins with "the woman who is a hunter's trap." The reference is probably to Egypt or some such symbol of paganism that led Israel astray. Escape from her is due solely to God. Yet there is a more personal note to the section. From experience Qoheleth does not have much faith in the men he knows; he accuses them of being unjust and dishonest. He would say even less of women. It may be a social prejudice or a deliberate slur intended to provoke dissent and proof to the contrary. That, too, would be like Qoheleth.

7:29 The Hebrew text is not quite clear, especially as to who is doing the calculating—the men or the women. Most likely Qoheleth means that the whole race has engaged in spoiling the work that God created good. That would be a normal wisdom viewpoint.

Chapter 8

Chapter 8 begins with some conventional sayings taken from the court wisdom, that is, instructions to students on how to act in the service of the king. Loyalty is stressed, especially sticking by the administration when injustices seem to have been done: "while one man tyrannizes over another to his hurt" (v. 9). The wise man knows that there is a proper time and judgment for all things; he does not know when the proper time or judgment is.

The second half (8:10-17) almost seems to deny the wisdom of the above as Qoheleth reflects on the lack of any apparent consistency in retribution. The wicked are not punished, and so society is tempted to lawlessness. However, he clings to his religious belief that reverence toward God finally pays off, but he does not know when. The wicked still prosper, and the wise can simply try to enjoy life as best they can. This reflection continues into the next chapter (9:1-3). The most perplexing thing about life is the apparent lack of any different result between being good or bad: "Among all the things that happen under the sun, this is the worst, that things turn out the same for all" (9:3).

Chapter 9

This section seems to run from 9:4 to 10:2, as the translation indicates. It begins with the sunshine of seeing the joy of living. Here Qoheleth has put his longest statement of the refrain into almost poetic form. Not only can one find satisfaction in good food and drink; fine clothes and perfumes help. Enjoy life with the wife whom you love. Give all you got in everything you do. Then comes the somber note: death is on the way. Life is a game of chance; victory does not go to the best, and we do not know when uncontrollable accidents will wipe out all we are trying to do.

In Eccl 9:13-16 occurs one of the finest uses of parable in the Bible. A parable is not a simplistic story telling us to do in like manner; it is a thought-provoking story that traps us with simple pictures and then stings. It is conventional to say that wisdom pays off and the wise are respected. Qoheleth says that it does not happen if you are wise but poor. His sage saved a city—and was promptly forgotten. A single fly falling by chance into the ointment can spoil it all.

9:5 "For the living know that they are to die, but the dead no longer know anything." So also in verse 10 Qoheleth concludes that "there will be no work, nor reason, nor knowledge, nor wisdom in the nether world where you are going." Such was the traditional attitude. Israel had been chosen to be God's worshiper on earth. Very little was said to them about the afterlife. In Qoheleth's time the view was beginning to change. A hundred years later there was not only a full-blown belief in a judgment in a world beyond, but also the clearest statement about the doctrine of purgatory, as we call it. But Qoheleth was a theological conservative; he lived on what had been handed down, even when he challenged it.

Chapter 10

Chapter 10 probably runs from 10:3 to 11:2. It is a grab bag of wise sayings from conventional wisdom.

10:2 The right hand is used as a symbol of skill for biblical authors; the left is used to express foolishness.

10:11 Snake charming was (and is) a realistic feat in the Near East. The proverb is cautionary, like the modern proverb that says: "It's no use locking the barn door after the horse has been stolen."

10:19 This is somewhat cynical but observable. Money does seem to "provide" for all our merrymaking.

10:20 We may well think that this is fanciful, but so is the spy system that gets word back to the king of what one says secretly, and that is the meaning of the admonition.

11:1 The meaning of this familiar quotation is to make doubly sure that one has plenty of everything so as not to be caught short.

Chapter 11

Only verses 3 to 6 are considered here. These are prudential remarks on providing abundantly, since we do not know what the future will bring. The rain falls just so much and that is that; the tree falls and stays there. Too much caution gets in the way. We do not know how babies are fashioned, and we do not know what God is doing in the world, so we should work hard and provide doubly. The words are conventional wisdom that Qoheleth does not contradict, but he centers them on the thought that we do not know what God is doing.

THE FINAL SECTION

Eccl 11:9–12:8

The final hymn is to life. This is one of the most hauntingly beautiful poems in all of literature. The impact is achieved by a careful conjuring up of images and balancing of structure.

We can see the sun shining, the clouds gathering, the dawn and the sunset, the birds in the trees, the village well. Yet these images are also carefully balanced against opposites. Light and darkness, the nothingness of death and the life breath jostle one another. The strong stand but they are bent; the mill still grinds, but slowly; the birds sit in the trees, but do not sing; the well is full of water, but no one is around, and as one looks, the rope breaks and the bucket falls into the depths.

So also the addresses to the youth and the aged are contrasted. Qoheleth gives four verses to youth and then multiplies this to eight verses for those his own age. It is this careful structuring of image against image, age against age, that gives an internal rhythm to the thought and produces the right mood.

The thought can then emerge. Qoheleth first addresses the young men before him. He is consistent with his previous teaching: life is good; live it to the full.

> Rejoice, O young man, while you are young,
> and let your heart be glad in the days
> of your youth.
> Follow the ways of your heart,
> the vision of your eyes;
> Yet understand that as regards all this
> God will bring you to judgment (11:9).

"Judgment" sounds a discordant note, and we wish it meant something else. Apparently it does. Qoheleth knew nothing of judgment as the Last Judgment in our sense, nor does he ever mention any examination of merit and punishment. Judgment is revelation. His consistent cry has been that life is inexplicable; good and bad seem so haphazard; success and failure do not belong to us; justice and injustice mix in such strange ways. He has concluded that only God knows, and God is not talking. Yet somehow, sometime, God will reveal it all. Qoheleth does not admonish youth to live a good life lest they be punished, but not to presume to know more about life than they really do, lest they transgress God's secret border.

Yet, youth is fleeting, and Qoheleth stands at the end of the road. He is like an old man wandering into a silenced village. The sun has gone behind the clouds, the menservants stand bent over, the women waiting at the mill are few, the ladies in the house only occasionally peek out of the windows. The doors of houses are closed; the birds do not sing; the old man totters along precariously as though on a precipice, fearing a mugging; the trees blossom but do no more. And as he passes through this silent village, he arrives finally at the well, the center of town. But no one is trading news at the well. As he looks at this source of life—for good water is called living water—he sees the whole apparatus of pulley, bucket, and counterbalance fall into the pit as the rope breaks. Need anything more be said?

> And the dust returns to the earth as it once was,
> and the life breath returns to God who gave it.
> (12:7)

Qoheleth shrieks for some greater knowledge. Faith says that life is safe in the hands of the Life-giver. But how? And why?

12:1 The tradition of the sages was strong on God the Creator. In spite of everything pessimistic that he says, Qoheleth always believes in a good Creator behind the universe. That conviction of goodness is central to wisdom thinking. It is not God the Judge that youth needs to think of, but God the Creator; and then they must strive to be creators themselves.

12:3 The older Jewish rabbis were accustomed to interpret each of these images as referring to some part of the body. Later scholars thought they saw only a smorgasbord of varied images that had no connection with one another. However, the impression and central theme seem to relate to a silent village or estate. These are the usual employees who are now idle.

12:4 A catastrophe of some sort, such as a plague, has idled all these people.

12:5 This is an old man who is being pictured. He totters as though he were on a high place. He also fears the young who roam the streets.

"When the almond tree blooms": This is not clear. One meaning may be that the trees bloom, but do not bear. The caper berry was reputed to restore sexual powers, but even that does not work anymore.

"Because man goes to his lasting home": It is lasting because it is the grave; it is not much of a home. Meanwhile, he can see the mourners already assembling for his funeral.

12:6 Apparently the rope is old and white. The pitcher is the bucket, and the golden ball is some sort of counterbalance.

12:7 "And the dust returns to the earth": The phrase undoubtedly reflects the well-known saying: "Dust thou art and unto dust thou shalt return." On the other hand, the word used for "life breath" is more normally used for a word of God or a spirit from God. It is not the equivalent of our word for "soul."

THE EPILOGUE

Eccl 12:9-14

The epilogue speaks of Qoheleth in the third person, so we presume that it was written by someone else. He is described as holding some sort of official position as a teacher. He was also something of a research scholar, collecting the traditions of the past. Here the editor makes his own comment, perhaps to apologize that Qoheleth's research did not uncover many comforting proverbs. His were like "fixed spikes." Then he seems to presume that many books of this sort have been published, although we know of only a few. One should appreciate authors; they spend much time doing the writing. And, being a much more conventional man himself, he adds the theme-saying of all wisdom writers: "Fear God and keep his commandments." He is not laying down a law; he is expressing the conviction that the only wise way to live is to be in awe of the incomprehensible God who lives behind the appearances of things and to try to be holy as God is holy. One day God will reveal what this is all about.

> Because God will bring to judgment every work, with all its hidden qualities, whether good or bad (12:14).

ESTHER

James A. Fischer, C.M.

INTRODUCTION

The Hebrew Book of Esther is a melodrama. When the story was read in the synagogue during the feast of Purim, the men stomped their feet, banged the tables, hissed the villain, and cheered the hero. It was a riotous celebration with much drinking; "too much" was when one could not tell the difference between "Bless Mordecai" and "Curse Haman," said some rabbis. In medieval times Purim became a kind of carnival celebration with dramatizations of the story spinning off from the biblical tale.

The ancient tradition should be respected for its insight. The story was heard as a hero tale in which the Jews triumphed over their enemies by better intrigue. The hero, Mordecai, was cast in the role of the trickster, as Jacob and Joseph before him had been in more discreet ways. The justification for the celebration was simply that the Jews of Persia had been given relief from persecution and had thus been able to care for their poorer neighbors. Such were the reasons given by Queen Esther in her official decree establishing the feast. Some such justification is also given by many modern Jewish scholars. The story itself does not mention God; it has no pious lesson, nor does it raise any disturbing questions in the text. It was just fun to recall one triumphant moment of salvation for one's people.

The acceptance of the Book of Esther has always been a problem of more or less concern in Jewish circles. Esther has not been found among the Qumram documents (which is unusual), and even after its acceptance as Scripture by the Jewish scholars at Jamnia around A.D. 90, it was still denounced by some rabbis as unworthy of honor as sacred Scripture. Present-day Jewish scholars tend to vindicate the book on the basis that whatever preserves the Jewish community must be part of God's plan. God is not mentioned in the Hebrew text, but Jewish spirituality rests on the conviction that God is present in the most mundane affairs, even when not seen. There is much to be said for this viewpoint.

The Hebrew and the Greek versions

The hero story is the one preserved in Judaism and in most non-Catholic Bibles. The Greek translation, which Catholics use, introduced a more somber note. The moral problem raised by the slaying of so many pagans was addressed by a dream sequence added to the beginning and the end. The pious need was met by interspersing various prayers to God and confessions of guilt.

The history of the Book of Esther

Since the Hebrew story of Esther is so obviously a tale to be enjoyed, there seems to be little reason to delay over questions of historical accuracy. That there was a King Ahasuerus, otherwise known in Persian chronicles as Xerxes I, who ruled from 486 to 465 B.C.E., is indisputable. In many places, the book reflects authentic information about the Persian period. On the other hand, there is nothing known about a Queen Vashti or a

Queen Esther or a Haman or a pogrom against the Jews. Some of this seems unlikely. The most prudent supposition seems to be that some master storyteller welded together several stories that may have arisen from local events and produced a story of intrigue that was credible and exciting without being an attempt to chronicle actual facts.

We do not even know whether the story produced the feast of Purim or whether a preexisting feast attracted the story to itself. The feast was called Purim ("lots") from the mention of the lots that were cast before the king to determine the date for the extermination of the Jews (3:7). It was celebrated in the spring of the year on the fourteenth and fifteenth of the month of Adar. The story and the feast originated among Persian Jews sometime between 465 and 167 B.C.E. and spread westward to the rest of Judaism.

The story

The Hebrew story (designated in our text by the usual chapter numbers from 1 to 10) tells of how Mordecai, a Jew at the court of King Ahasuerus, revealed a plot to kill the king, but was left unrewarded. The king had to choose a new queen, and Mordecai was able to have his cousin Esther selected. She became the favorite and learned of a plot to destroy all Jews. This was the work of Haman, the prime minister, who personally hated Jews, and Mordecai in particular. One night the king suddenly remembered that Mordecai had saved his life and summoned Haman to tell him how to honor a man to whom the king was indebted. Haman thought that he was the man and heaped up the honors. He planned to execute Mordecai on a huge scaffold in his yard. But then he discovered that Mordecai was to be the honoree. Moreover, Esther revealed to the king that Haman had already issued a decree that all Jews be killed. Haman knew that he was undone and went to plead before Queen Esther and threw himself before her. The king entered the room and thought he was attacking the queen, and ordered him hanged on his own scaffold. Then Esther got another royal decree that the Jews would be allowed to defend themselves. So they did, and that day was proclaimed by both Mordecai and Esther as a great festival day for the Jews.

Such is the Hebrew story. To it the Greek translators added the chapters that are designated in the text by the letters A to F. The first and last chapters are dream sequences reminiscent of a kind of literature called apocalyptic. They have two dragons, a saving river, and a cosmic battle. The other chapters are prayers of confession and petition or official documents. Only one piece of additional narrative is supplied; chapter D tells how God made Esther appear even more beautiful and so averted the king's anger.

The touch is light, but the implications for the story are enormous. In the initial dream Mordecai sees two dragons threatening every nation. In the final explanation of the dream, Mordecai identifies the two dragons as Haman—and himself. The story had raised disturbing moral questions about the Jewish role in the pogrom. The Greek editors had fingered their own people as equal culprits. The dream sequence is a common enough way for an author to add editorial comment, but the apocalyptic technique did elevate the problem to one of the cosmic struggle of good and evil. God enters the story. Mordecai's character gets changed around at the end. He is no longer the trickster but the honest man who must face his own lack of integrity in victory. God alone is the hero; the story has passed from straight fun to irony.

COMMENTARY

INTRODUCTION

Esth A:1-17

A:1 Ahasuerus is very probably Xerxes I (485–464 B.C.E.), known to European history as the villain who attacked Greece. He was, however, an enlightened ruler. Mordecai is unknown to secular history, although we know of a Marduka, an imperial accountant from the capital of Susa under Darius and Xerxes. Mordecai is described as a prominent man, and later on we learn from the Hebrew text that he was a minor official at court.

"Mordecai had a dream . . .": This is a storyteller's technique for indicating that the author already knows what the story means. It is used frequently in the Bible in such narratives as those of Joseph in Egypt, Gideon, and Daniel, and in Matthew's infancy narrative (see v. 11).

A:4 Mordecai's dream includes a cosmic battle, darkness, confusion among all nations, dragons, and a saving river. This is common stock-in-trade for writers of apocalypse (Ezek 47; Dan 12:5-7; Rev 12 have similar elements). All this introduces us to a world in which good and evil fight on a cosmic level.

A:12-16 The plot against the king's life is also narrated in the Hebrew text (2:21-23). However, the Greek editor has combined the apocalyptic dream sequence and a political awareness of some future pay-off to capture the bi-level approach of apocalyptic, which deals with both heaven and earth.

A ROYAL BANQUET

Esth 1:1-22

1:3 No occasion is given for the feast. It will be noted that most of the action in the story takes place during banquets. This motif ties the story together and serves as an appropriate connection with the feast of Purim.

1:10-22 It is difficult to judge whether the author admired Queen Vashti for refusing to perform for the king or whether he agreed with the decree that women should be kept in a proper place. In either case, he is simply telling a story, and he certainly sets up a contrast between the strong-willed Vashti and Queen Esther, who does what she is told to do. Evidently Esther is not so much a heroine as a pawn.

1:19 The royal decree is irrevocable. This odd provision of Persian law is referred to also in the story of Daniel in the lion's den (compare Dan 6:8), but it is not known from any other source.

ESTHER MADE QUEEN

Esth 2:1-23

2:2 The theme of the contest to choose a new queen is fairly common in literature, most notably in the Arabian tale *A Thousand and One Nights.* A historical difficulty exists here, since Esther was a Jewess and the Persian queens were always selected from the seven dominant Persian families. Xerxes' queen was named Amestris. The name Esther seems to be a take-off on the Babylonian name for the goddess Ishtar, but that does not seem to have any significance in the story.

HAMAN'S PLOT AGAINST THE JEWS

Esth 3:1-15

3:1 Haman the Agagite is unknown to history. Obviously he is intended to be a Persian, but his genealogy is traced back to Agag, the king of the Amalekites whom Saul slew (see 1 Sam 15:7ff.). Mordecai's ancestry is traced back to Saul. This looks suspiciously contrived but explains that the antagonism between the two men is irrevocably rooted in the past.

3:6 In the story there is no Persian prejudice against the Jews. This seems to be factual. Mordecai the Jew was accepted as a royal official without comment. The same is also implied in the story of Daniel. As the storyteller had it, the sole cause of hatred for the Jews was the personal animosity of Haman.

HAMAN'S LETTER

Esth B:1-7

This letter was composed by the Greek editor as a propaganda piece, specifying the racial prejudice of the nations against the Jews who lived outside Palestine. It probably reflects Alexandrian social situations more than those of Persia.

ESTHER'S PROBLEM

Esth 4:1-16

Now that Esther has become queen, she begins to use some of her power to protect Mordecai. However, it will be evident to the end of the story that Mordecai is the principal actor throughout, both as a Persian official and as the family advisor of Esther.

4:9 Verses 8-9, which refer to invoking the Lord, are not in the Hebrew text. They have been imported into the English translation from the Greek.

PRAYERS OF MORDECAI AND ESTHER

Esth C:1-30

C:1-11 Mordecai's prayer is a rather traditional lament recalling God's past favors to the Israelites.

C:12-30 Esther's prayer is a traditional complaint against paganism and a confession of righteousness. The Greek interpretation, which makes Esther some sort of savior of her people, describes her far more piously than the incidents of the story warrant.

ESTHER RECEIVED BY THE KING

Esth D:1-16

This is the only Greek addition to the narrative itself. It quite clearly shifts Esther's success from her beauty and cunning to the initiative of God, who makes all things happen rightly.

ESTHER'S PLOT

Esth 5:1-14

5:1-8 The banquet motif is here expanded to introduce an essential tension to the plot. The first banquet is apparently useless except as an invitation to a second banquet. However, this allows time for Haman to act.

5:9-14 Haman thinks that he is to be exceptionally honored by the second banquet. Full of confidence in his own success, he anticipates his victory by building a mammoth scaffold, fifty cubits high, on which to hang Mordecai. For vanquishing a superior foe no ordinary gibbet would do.

HAMAN'S DOWNFALL

Esth 6:1-14

Haman is now firmly set on the road to tragedy. In the classical understanding of tragedy, the final destruction must necessarily occur because of some essential weakness in a noble character. Haman has been portrayed as a quite successful prime minister. His flaw is his own hatred and pride. Esther is merely the catalyst that sets the tragedy in motion. So in verse 13 the inevitable tragedy is predicted by Haman's wife and friends. Nothing can prevent it from occurring. Later in the story (see 9:1, 24-26) the word *pur*, "lot," will be interpreted as fate.

THE PUNISHMENT OF HAMAN

Esth 7:1-10

7:1-6 Esther's appeal to the king to cancel the pogrom against the Jews is based on his own self-interest. She cites the harm that will be done to the king by the destruction of the Jewish community. That does not seem to convince him. It is only then that she reveals that Haman is behind the plot. Obviously the king has not been paying much attention to business.

7:7-8 The king, who is already angered, re-enters the room and finds Haman on the couch with his wife, pleading his case. He makes the natural conclusion and executes Haman, not for any official policy decision, but for the personal insult.

7:9-10 The theme of reversal is again stressed in the ironic execution of Haman on the grandiose scaffold he himself has erected.

THE DECREE REVERSED

Esth 8:1-17

8:2 The king's signet ring is given to Mordecai, and that virtually makes him prime minister. It is noteworthy that it is Mordecai and not Esther who is given the regal power.

8:3-17 King Ahasuerus once again shows his little interest in the pogrom against the Jews by simply commissioning Esther to write anything she wants. In her letter she instructs all the officials to ignore Haman's letter. According to the previous reference to the laws of the Persians, which cannot be changed, this is impossible, so she adds a separate protocol that allows the Jews to defend themselves on the thirteenth of Adar. She also encourages them to celebrate.

8:11 "To kill, destroy, wipe out, along with their wives and children, every armed group of any nation or province which shall attack them, and to seize their goods as spoil": This bloodthirsty decree is actually required to reverse the earlier edict of Haman, which was put in the same terms (see 3:13).

THE ATTACK

Esth 9:1-32

9:5 The text records that five hundred Persians were killed in Susa, in addition to the ten sons of Haman. More were killed on the second day. In the provinces, the Hebrew text says, seventy-five thousand were killed; the Greek version mentions fifteen thousand. Numbers, especially round numbers, in Old Testament texts are subject to considerable doubt. Since this is a story, the author's intention was simply to say that there was a great victory for the Jews. The decree had authorized the killing of any who attacked the Jews. The numbers are limited to indicate restraint. So also the text in three places (9:10, 15, 16) emphasizes that the Jews took no booty, although they were commissioned to do so.

9:21-22 It is noteworthy that it is Mordecai who writes the first and decisive letter authorizing the feast of Purim. Although the slaughter of the Jews was set for the thirteenth day of Adar, the feast is celebrated on the fourteenth, when the riots took place in the provinces, and on the fifteenth, when the mopping up was completed in Susa. Even with this explanation the chronology of the feast of Purim does not work out exactly. It is to be noted that Mordecai stresses that the feast commemorates the "rest" that was granted to the Jews on this occasion. Rest is a gift of God. He also specifies that Purim is to be a time of feasting and gladness, with the sending of food to one another and of giving gifts to the poor. The victory concept is considerably played down.

9:24-26 A curious summary of the whole plot is given here. However, it brings in the essential concept of tragedy. In the original story of Saul and Agag (see 1 Sam 15), Saul failed to put Agag the Amalekite to death as God had commanded. That led inevitably to Saul's destruction. The text here mentions Mordecai as the descendant of Saul, and Haman as the descendant of Agag. In this case, it is inevitable that Mordecai should destroy Haman. In our text the word pur, "lot," is taken in its Akkadian sense of "fate." Purim does symbolize the inevitable destruction of God's enemies.

THE DREAM EXPLAINED

Esth F:1-10

F:1 The dream will now explain how God, who was not mentioned in the Hebrew text, nevertheless was working behind the scenes. That there is an order in the world is the general supposition of wisdom literature, and the Greek Book of Esther is certainly related to wisdom.

F:2-6 The identifications are clearly made. The saving river is Esther; the nations are the persecutors of the Jews, who are in turn saved by the Lord. The surprising identification is: "The two dragons are myself and Haman." Dragons are biblical symbols for the enemies of the just. The Hebrew story had developed a series of reversals: Mordecai the oppressed became Mordecai the victor; Haman the Jew-hater was executed on his own gibbet; the day of slaughter became a day of rest for the Jews. The Greek editor simply carried the motif to its final step; Mordecai the hero became Mordecai the villain. His hands were as bloody as Haman's.

F:7 To continue the tragic or saving theme, the author once more has recourse to the doctrine of fate. God arranged two lots—one for the people of God, the second for all other nations. The lot for God's people is the joy and happiness of the feast of Purim (see v. 10). Nothing is said about the nations' lot.

JONAH, TOBIT, JUDITH

Irene Nowell, O.S.B.

INTRODUCTION

It has been said that we use stories to tell ourselves the truths we cannot explain. Biblical authors used many types of literature to convey the word of God. Besides historical accounts, parables, hymns, and love songs, they also used stories, fictional tales crafted to carry truths more profound than a simple recital of everyday facts could bear.

The Books of Jonah, Tobit, and Judith are among the best examples of such fiction in all of biblical narrative. The authors of these three books took essential elements of biblical faith and used all the techniques of their literary skill to weave stories that illustrate the dynamic effectiveness of traditional beliefs in the situation of their audience. They constructed plots that show the workings of God in ordinary human activities and events. They drew characters who, through stubborn resistance and courageous obedience, would be witnesses to the ongoing relationship between God and believers. They used irony and humor to attract their audience and to fix the message in their memory. In short, the authors of these three books were master storytellers. Their message was vital for the audience of their time, and it remains vital for us: the word of God is living, effective, and demanding in every age, including the present one.

The authors of these three little books do not directly answer the questions put to them; rather, they tell stories. To a fifth-century audience bent on separating itself from the rest of the world, one author tells the story of an eighth-century prophet who fled from God's call to bring the good news to the rest of the world (Jonah). To a second-century audience wondering if God is still active in their lives, another author tells the story of a seventh-century family who find God's healing power hidden in their obedience and care for one another (Tobit). To a mid-second-century audience despairing of God's deliverance from horrible persecution, a third author tells the story of God's victory through the hand of a woman (Judith). Each author used the power and beauty of literary skill to bring the word of God to life in the stress and need of the contemporary situation.

The basic truths about God and the people who strive to be faithful to God can be found throughout the Bible. The application of these truths to the specific audience of their own time was the mission and service of the authors of the Books of Jonah, Tobit, and Judith. It is our task to discover what these three books have to tell us about the dynamic presence and insistent demands of God in our own time.

JONAH

Irene Nowell, O.S.B.

INTRODUCTION

The Book of Jonah was written in Palestine around the fifth century B.C.E., when the Jews were still recovering from the Babylonian Exile, a serious threat to their existence. Throughout the ninth and eighth centuries B.C.E., major foreign powers had nibbled away at the territory once controlled by David and Solomon. In 722 B.C.E. Assyria had conquered the northern kingdom of Israel, taken its leading citizens captive, and settled groups of people of other nationalities in northern Palestine. The little kingdom of Judah hung on through another century, survived a change of power in Mesopotamia from Assyria to Babylon, but could not escape indefinitely. In 587 B.C.E. Nebuchadnezzar and the Babylonian army destroyed Jerusalem and led the blinded king and much of the population into exile in Babylon. Fifty years later, in 538 B.C.E., the Persian king Cyrus, having defeated Babylon, issued a decree permitting the Jews to return to Jerusalem and to rebuild the temple there. The struggles between the returning exiles and those who had remained behind, along with grinding poverty and the incessant labor necessary to rebuild a land left desolate and destroyed, provide the background for the Book of Jonah.

The returning Jews were convinced that they had suffered exile because of their infidelity to God. As a result, they developed an attitude of exclusivity and rigorous observance of the law. They avoided anything that might lead them away from God, such as foreign customs or even foreign wives (see Ezra 9:1-3; 10:10-15; Neh 13:23-30). Even the people of the former northern kingdom of Israel, called Samaritans because their capital city had been Samaria, were scorned because they had become a mixed race after the Assyrian invasion (see Ezra 4:1-5).

The author of the Book of Jonah sets his story in opposition to the attitude of exclusivity. In the story, God calls Jonah to prophesy, not to his own people, but to the people of Nineveh, the hated capital of Assyria. Not only must Jonah associate with the idolatrous Gentiles of that city, but he is called to be the instrument through which God's mercy is brought to them. Jonah makes a desperate attempt to flee from God's call. As he complains in chapter 4, he knows what God is like. "I knew," he says to God, "that you are a gracious and merciful God, slow to anger, rich in clemency, loathe to punish" (Jonah 4:2). Jonah knows what effect his message might have. Because he knows that God is merciful, Jonah fears that Nineveh will be converted. Jonah would prefer a god who would destroy Nineveh to one who would forgive it. The author told this story to an audience that desired to avoid other peoples in order to be faithful to God. The story of Jonah presents the shocking truth that "other nations" may also be dear to the heart of God. It is a hard truth, conveyed through a powerful story.

COMMENTARY

CONFRONTATION BETWEEN JONAH AND YAHWEH

Jonah 1:1-16

The Book of Jonah opens with a title announcing the word of the Lord to Jonah, son of Amittai. Jonah, son of Amittai, was the name of an eighth-century prophet who prophesied the restoration of Israel's boundaries by Jeroboam II (see 2 Kgs 14:25). The Book of Jonah, however, was written much later, probably in the fifth century B.C.E. The author wanted to establish his main character as a prophet and so chose the relatively unknown Jonah to fill the role.

The call of Jonah is an exaggerated version of the call-narrative pattern, which consists of the following parts: (1) divine confrontation; (2) introductory words of God; (3) commission of the prophet by God; (4) objection by the prophet; (5) reassurance by God: "I am with you"; (6) promise of a sign. There are some noteworthy correspondences between this pattern and the events in the Book of Jonah. Jonah is confronted by the word of the Lord (1:1) and commissioned to go to Nineveh to preach against it (1:2). Jonah not only objects to this task but flees from it (1:3). The Lord does not simply reassure him but goes after him and brings him back by force (1:4–2:10). Then the call narrative begins again: "The word of the Lord came to Jonah a second time . . ." (3:1).

The city of Nineveh to which God sent Jonah was hated by the Israelites. It was the capital of Assyria, the major power in Mesopotamia in the eighth century. The Assyrians conquered Israel, the northern kingdom, in 722 B.C.E. and took its most powerful citizens into captivity. Israel's hatred of the Assyrians is powerfully described by the prophet Nahum. Jonah is reluctant to go to Nineveh, not so much because he wants to avoid the prophetic call, but because he is unwilling to bring the word of the Lord to such a hated enemy.

The story of Jonah's flight is a masterpiece of irony. According to the narrator, it is Jonah's purpose "to flee away from the Lord" (1:3), so he boards a boat sailing for Tarshish. A storm arises. The sailors pray to their gods to no avail until, by casting lots, they determine that it is Jonah's God who is angry. When the sailors wake Jonah to question him, he tells them, "I worship [fear] the Lord, the God of heaven, who made the sea and the dry land" (1:9). (If he believes this, why does Jonah think that Tarshish is far enough away to escape the Lord?) When the storm begins, the sailors have enough wisdom to pray to their gods while the prophet sleeps. When Jonah tells the sailors that he is running away from God, they are wise enough to be afraid, while the self-proclaimed God-fearer Jonah seems untouched by fear. The word "fear" is repeated in 1:16, after the men have thrown Jonah into the sea. The sailors themselves become God-fearers: "Struck with great fear of the Lord, the men offered sacrifice and made vows to him" (1:16).

Jonah describes Yahweh as the one "who made the sea and the dry land" (1:9). Yahweh controls the sea and its creatures. Yahweh sends the wind to stir up a great storm, stills the storm as soon as Jonah is stopped in his flight by being cast from the ship, and commands a great sea creature to bring Jonah back to his starting point. The sea and the sea monsters are mythological images of creation (see Pss 74:12-14; 89:10-11; 104:25-26; Isa 27:1; Job 40:25). Yahweh created the world by defeating the sea monster, set limits for the sea that it might not pass (Ps 104:9), and made the sea monsters to play in it (Ps 104:26). The image of Yahweh in chapter 1 of Jonah is the image of the all-powerful Creator who commissions the prophet and pursues him until he accepts.

JONAH'S PRAYER

Jonah 2:1-11

Chapter 2 consists of a psalm probably inserted into the narrative from another source. It is set in context by putting the prayer in Jonah's mouth as he rides home in the belly of the docile sea monster.

The prayer belongs to the genre of lament. It is constructed of standard phrases of lamentation and begins and ends in the pattern of laments. The psalmist opens by calling upon God (2:2) and moves immediately to a description of his distress. The end of the prayer is an expression of confidence and thanksgiving to God by the psalmist, who, with unwavering trust, believes in God's salvation.

Many of the phrases in this prayer are common to the psalms; for example:

2:3a—Pss 86:6-7; 120:1;
compare Pss 34:7; 81:8
2:3b—Pss 18:6-7; 116:3-4
2:4b—Ps 42:8
2:5a—Ps 31:23
2:6a—Pss 18:5; 69:2-3;
compare Pss 88:17-18; 116:3
2:7b—Pss 16:10; 30:4
2:8a—Ps 42:7
2:8b—Ps 18:7; compare Ps 88:3
2:10a—Pss 50:14; 116:17
2:10b—Pss 22:26; 50:14; 66:13-14;
116:14, 18; 3:9; 37:39

There seems to be a special correspondence between the lament of Jonah and Psalms 18 and 116.

The psalm lends itself well to Jonah's situation. He is certainly in lamentable straits and needs to turn to Yahweh in confidence. The references to the nether world (vv. 3, 7), however, indicate that the psalm describes general distress. Water, a symbol of primeval chaos, is only one of the images used, but it fits Jonah's situation well. The psalm is well placed, but probably not original to the context.

JONAH IN NINEVEH

Jonah 3:1-10

Chapter 3 begins with Yahweh's second call to Jonah. This time Jonah makes no objection. Jonah surrenders to God's call far more readily than Moses did. Moses objected to Yahweh's call five times before he surrendered (Exod 3:11, 13; 4:1, 10, 13). His last objection is the most poignant: "If you please, Lord, send someone else!" (Exod 4:13). Jonah's compliance with the Lord's second call is only outward, however; his inner feelings will become obvious in chapter 4.

Jonah goes to Nineveh, the ancient city on the left bank of the Tigris River across from modern Mosul. In the nineteenth century, two tells (mounds covering ancient ruins) were identified as Nineveh. Archeologists found many historical treasures in the ruins, among them relief sculptures from the palaces of Sennacherib, Esarhaddon, and Ashur-bani-pal and an extensive library of Ashur-bani-pal. The city itself was occupied from the fourth millennium B.C.E. to 612 B.C.E., when it fell to the Babylonians and Medes. The inner wall, which encloses a space of less than three square miles, is about seven and one-half miles long. One day's walk would have put Jonah well beyond its center.

The description of Nineveh as an "enormously large city" that required three days simply to go through it, illustrates a key technique in the whole book—exaggeration. "Great" or "large" is one of this author's favorite words; it occurs fourteen times in the book. Nineveh is a "great" city (1:2; 3:2; 3:3; 4:11). Yahweh sends a "great" wind upon the sea, and the tempest that results is "great" (1:4 [twice], 12). The sailors fear with a "great" fear (1:10, 16). After the sailors throw Jonah into the sea, Yahweh sends a "great" fish to swallow him (2:1). The repentance of the people of Nineveh extends from the "great" to the small (3:5), and it is proclaimed throughout Nineveh by decree of the king and his nobles (his "great" ones, 3:7). When God shows mercy toward Nineveh, Jonah's displeasure is "great" (4:1), but his delight in the gourd plant is also "great" (4:6).

The frequent use of the word "great" emphasizes the exaggeration in the content. Everything is larger than life-size. Nineveh is not only great, it is exceedingly great (literally, "great even for God," 3:3). The fast that is proclaimed is worthy of such a great city. It extends from king to beasts and is a total fast even from water (3:7). Jonah's objection to his call is excessive; Yahweh's pursuit of him is equally excessive. In this story there is no moderation.

The numbering of days has a significant balance. Jonah spends three days in the belly of the fish and is then returned to his responsibility to Yahweh. Three days, however, are not enough to bring about a real change of heart in Jonah. The city to which Jonah is sent is reported to be a city so large that it requires a three-day journey to go through it. Yet the city does not need even three days for its repentance; one day is sufficient. Yahweh's mercy, however, does not limit Nineveh to three days. Yahweh allows "forty days," a very large number of days, before the city will be destroyed (3:4).

The message of Jonah proclaims destruction. The response of the Ninevites contains a key word of conversion, "turn." The king proclaims that everyone should "turn" from evil ways; then perhaps Yahweh might "turn" and "repent" of retaliating against Nineveh. Indeed the Ninevites "turn"; indeed Yahweh "repents" (3:8-10). The word "turn" is a key word in the writings of the prophets. It is developed particularly by Jeremiah, and forms the basis of his call to the people. The word "repent" is used primarily of Yahweh in the prophets. If the people "turn," Yahweh "repents" (see Joel 2:12-14). These two words merge into the concept of *metanoia,* or repentance, which, in the New Testament, is demanded of those who would belong to the kingdom of God (see Mark 1:15 and parallels).

RESPONSE TO NINEVEH'S CONVERSION

Jonah 4:1-11

The final chapter contrasts God's merciful response to Nineveh's conversion with Jonah's anger. The chapter is a modified palistrophe (mirror):

A. Jonah's anger (4:1).
- B. Jonah knows God's mercy (4:2).
  - C. Double refrain: Let me die (4:3). Do you have a right to be angry (4:4)?
    - D. God's mercy on Jonah (4:5-8; note "appoints" 3 times).
  - C'. Double refrain: Let me die (4:8b). Do you have a right to be angry (4:9)?
- B'. God knows Jonah's anger and lack of mercy (4:10).

A'. God's mercy (4:11).

Both the irony and the theology reach a peak in this chapter. First of all, we discover Jonah's reason for fleeing in chapter 1. He dreads the conversion of Nineveh. Because he "knows" that God is "a gracious and merciful God, slow to anger, rich in clemency, loathe to punish (4:2; compare Exod 34:6; Num 14:18-19; Joel 2:14), Jonah fears that he will be a successful prophet and convert the Ninevites. He is angry because he knows that God is not a judge who exacts retribution equal to the crime but rather a merciful God who repents of anger.

God, on the other hand, is merciful because God knows who Jonah is. Instead of punishing Jonah for his flight, for his half-hearted prophesying, for his lack of mercy, God works with Jonah as if he were a child who "cannot distinguish his right hand from his left." God teaches Jonah a lesson. Near his hut God provides a gourd plant that gives Jonah joy and shade. The next day God allows a worm to destroy the plant; this angers Jonah. Then God sends an east wind so hot that Jonah desires death. This is the heart of the chapter and the center of the palistrophe. Divine mercy knows no bounds. God is even merciful to the recalcitrant prophet.

The book ends with a question that challenges the audience of the author's time and all its future readers. God asks: "Should I not, may I not, be merciful even to Nineveh?" Is God free? Or must God act, as Jonah thinks, according to the narrow limitations of human justice?

TOBIT

Irene Nowell, O.S.B.

INTRODUCTION

Not all canonical lists of biblical books include the Book of Tobit. There are seven books which, for various historical reasons, are found in the Roman Catholic canon and not in Jewish or Protestant canons of the Bible. They are: Judith, Tobit, Wisdom, Sirach, Baruch, and 1 and 2 Maccabees, along with additions to the Books of Daniel and Esther. These books are referred to as "deuterocanonical" by Roman Catholics and "apocryphal" by others. They are universally recognized as good books. The primary distinction in modern times is in their use in the liturgy. They are used liturgically by Roman Catholics, but not by Jews or Protestants. They are sometimes found in a separate section in some editions of the Bible.

The Book of Tobit was written around the beginning of the second century B.C.E. Alexander the Great's powerful sweep through the Near East had brought Palestine under his domination in 332 B.C.E. Alexander's death in 323 resulted in a division of his territory, with Syria falling to the Seleucids and Egypt to the Ptolemies. Palestine, a buffer zone between these major powers, was controlled first by the Ptolemies and then, after 198 B.C.E., by the Seleucids. This period was marked by growing Hellenization. Greek customs were adopted, the Greek language became common, and Greek cities were built with gymnasia and hippodromes.

Jewish response to Hellenization was mixed. Zealous Jews resisted every trace of Greek influence, while others found ways to adapt Greek philosophy and language to the service of Judaism. The question of whether to adapt to Greek culture became crucial under the Seleucids, who began to force what had been a rather peaceful progress of Hellenization. The author of Tobit wrote for Jews who were concerned about being faithful to God and who were questioning God's fidelity to them in the midst of this cultural turmoil.

The author uses several old folk tales—the Grateful Dead, the Monster in the Bridal Chamber, and the Story of Ahiqar—as the framework for his story about two ordinary believers, Tobit and Sarah. From the beginning Tobit declares that he has "walked all the days of [his] life on the paths of truth and righteousness" (Tob 1:3). Sarah can say to God, "I have never defiled my own name or my father's name" (Tob 3:15). Each of these faithful people is struck by disaster. Tobit is blinded by bird droppings; Sarah is grieved and humiliated by the sudden deaths of seven successive bridegrooms on the wedding night. The question raised by these crises plagued the faithful Jews under the domination of the Ptolemies and Seleucids: How can we be virtuous if the only result is increasing darkness and disaster?

The author proposes an answer to the question through a story that demonstrates the fidelity of God and the courage of believers. Tobit and Sarah each turn to prayer in their grief. The author informs the readers that their prayer is answered; an angel has been sent to bring them healing. The characters, however, do not know the end of the story, and their continued fidelity bears witness to their courage. Their healing comes about and their fidelity is demonstrated in the midst of the joys and sorrows of family life. The characters trust in a God who is both merciful and just. They in turn act in mercy and justice toward God and one another by rigorous observance of the law, hospitality, almsgiving, and loving respect within the family. Through their fidelity to one another, and specifically through the courage and obedience of Tobit's son Tobiah, who becomes Sarah's husband, both Tobit and Sarah are healed and the power of God's love in their lives is revealed. The story shows that, although God's fidelity may be hidden, human beings are ministers of God's providence, and ordinary human events are the setting for God's faithful care.

COMMENTARY

THE DISTRESS OF TOBIT AND SARAH

Tob 1:1–3:17

1:1-2 Title. The Book of Tobit opens with the common introduction to a historical work: "The book of the words of . . ." In the Septuagint (Greek version) and in English Bibles where it is included, this book is put with the historical works. It cannot, however, be considered a historical work. First of all, there are many historical inaccuracies, which indicate that the author had no intention of producing strict history. The story is set in the reigns of the Assyrian rulers Shalmaneser V (726–722 B.C.E.), Sennacherib (704–681 B.C.E.), and Esarhaddon (680–669 B.C.E.). Sargon II, who should be listed between Shalmaneser and Sennacherib, is missing. It seems that the author of Tobit used 2 Kgs 17:1-6 and 18:9-13 for his list of kings. In that account Sargon is not mentioned. Thus the author of Tobit may have presumed that Sennacherib was the immediate successor of Shalmaneser.

The style of the book also indicates that the author did not intend to produce a historical account. The prayers and monologues could not possibly have been known to a recorder of facts. Parallel events occur simultaneously in such a striking fashion that they indicate an author's manipulation of facts rather than a strict account of happenings. The interests of the book also indicate a period much later than the seventh century B.C.E. in which it is set.

The use of historical information, however, conveys an important theological point in the book. The chronicle of public events, which situates the story in the context of world history, occurs only in the first and last chapters. In the first chapter we find the succession of Assyrian kings—Shalmaneser, Sennacherib, and Esarhaddon. A few notes about Tobit's life indicate what life was like under each of these kings. Under Shalmaneser there was civil order, and exiles like Tobit could hold positions of importance and acquire reasonable sums of money. Under Sennacherib travel was unsafe, and the exiles were persecuted. Restoration of order occurred under Esarhaddon (2:1). There is no mention of public events from the last mention of Esarhaddon in 2:1 until the discussion of the fall of Nineveh to Cyaxares, king of Media, in chapter 14. The fall of Nineveh is mentioned twice in the last chapter. Tobit predicts its fall, and Tobiah rejoices over it.

By setting his story within the context of Assyrian history, the author has made a subtle commentary on the main events of Tobit's life. The Assyrian kings mentioned in chapter 1 are wicked. Shalmaneser takes the Israelites into exile; Sennacherib persecutes them. In chapter 14 Assyria is punished. In contrast, Tobit is righteous all the days of his life, and in chapter 14 he and his family are rewarded. The contrast is subtle but effective.

1:3-22 Tobit's life. After the title (1:1-2) chapter 1 continues with the exposition. Three main sequences are set in motion: (1) Tobit walks in the way of truth and righteousness; (2) Tobit marries Anna; (3) Tobit deposits money in Media. These three sequences open the plot and prepare the way for the questions that will finally be answered in the resolution.

The exposition opens with Tobit speaking in the first person: "I, Tobit, have walked all the days of my life on the paths of truth and righteousness." Three key words in 1:3 are repeated in 14:9 to form an inclusion. The book is a story of "truth," "righteousness," and "almsgiving/mercy." Chapter 1 portrays Tobit's life as an example of truth, righteousness, and almsgiving or charitable works. His righteousness during his youth is illustrated by his fidelity to worship in Jerusalem and his strict keeping of tithes. He follows the rigorous interpretation of tithing common in the second century. It was believed that Num 18:21-24, Deut 14:22-26, and Deut 14:28-29 referred, not to different ways of distributing the one tithe, but to three different tithes. Josephus, a Jewish historian, interprets the texts in this fashion: "In addition to the two tithes which I have already directed you to pay each year, the one for the Levites and the other for the banquets, you should devote a third every third year to the distribution of such things as are lacking to widowed women and orphan children."

Almsgiving is another example of Tobit's fidelity. During Shalmaneser's reign, Tobit reports, he fed the hungry, clothed the naked, and buried the dead (1:16-17). Burying the dead put Tobit in danger of death during the reign of Sennacherib (1:18-20). He flees Nineveh, returning only during the reign of Esarhaddon, when he again begins to invite the poor to dinner and to bury the dead (2:1-7). Tobit's active charity is his most evident characteristic.

In chapter 1 Tobit says that he has been faithful to Jewish law and custom. He has observed the dietary laws of Judaism and has married a woman from his own lineage and family (1:9).

Tobit's marriage to Anna introduces the second sequence of the plot. His marriage is not only an example of his fidelity to Jewish law and custom, but it also introduces two other main characters: Anna, Tobit's wife, and Tobiah, his son. Tobiah becomes the major instrument of God's providence in the rest of the story. Marriage, with its joys and sorrows, is a major theme of the book. The relationships in marriage manifest the working of God.

The third sequence of the plot opens with Tobit's trip to Media to do business for Shalmaneser (1:12-14). On one of his trips, Tobit deposits a large sum of money with a kinsman, Gabael, who lives in Media. The central section of the plot revolves around Tobiah's journey to Media to regain the money. He is guided on his trip by an angel, Raphael, and he becomes the instrument of healing in both families.

Two questions are raised by these three sequences. Tobit is a model of fidelity. What will be his reward? In Media there is money that belongs to Tobit. How will he regain it? The marriage sequence does not raise an immediate question. The solution to the questions from sequences one and three, however, will be found in sequence two.

2:1–3:6 The affliction and prayer of Tobit. We must read chapters 2 and 3 as panels of two different events happening simultaneously. The first scene is set at Tobit's home in Nineveh, the second at Sarah's home in Media. The first scene (2:1-8) opens with Tobit the almsgiver telling Tobiah to find a poor kinsman with whom he can share his Pentecost dinner. Tobiah finds a dead man in the square instead. Tobit immediately buries the dead man, a practice that had previously won for him exile and poverty. The neighbors mock his folly, and the reader wonders what his reward will be for such selfless righteousness.

That night Tobit, weary after the burial, sleeps in the courtyard of his house and is blinded by droppings from birds nesting above him. His reward for righteousness seems to be suffering rather than blessing. The blindness gradually becomes total. Tobit is left dependent on his wife Anna, who goes to work weaving cloth. In an incident that illustrates the tension in the household, Tobit accuses his wife of stealing a goat that was given to her as a bonus. Her retort cuts to the heart of the matter. Since the righteous should be rewarded and Tobit is being punished instead, Anna taunts: "Where are your charitable deeds now? Where are your virtuous acts? See! Your true character is finally showing itself!" (2:14). Tobit is grief-stricken and prays to God for death (3:1-6).

3:7-15 The affliction and prayer of Sarah. Simultaneity is a key technique in this chapter. "On the same day" that Tobit quarrels with Anna and prays for death, Raguel's daughter Sarah is taunted by one of her father's maids and also turns to prayer. Sarah is troubled by a demon who has killed her seven bridegrooms on the wedding night. There is no other near kinsman for her to marry (3:15). She is driven to despair and considers suicide. She reconsiders, however, for love of her father and turns instead to God in prayer. Her prayer is similar to that of Tobit. She, however, gives God a choice: she prays either for death (3:13) or for another solution to her problem (3:15).

Sarah's story picks up the important theme of marriage. She recognizes the significance of marriage and is willing to comply with her father's wishes and the prevailing Jewish custom by marrying a close relative. But the demon, who loves her and wants her for himself, keeps killing off her intended bridegrooms. Her situation has become unbearable.

The two prayers in chapter 3 also demonstrate the importance of prayer in this book. Both a man and a woman turn to prayer in desperate situations. Their prayers are equally significant for the plot. Both pray with phrases familiar from other biblical prayers. Tobit asks to die. He thinks that death is the only solution to his problems. Sarah puts herself completely in God's hands. She illustrates the proper way to pray: she spreads out her hands and turns to face Jerusalem.

3:16-17 The answer to prayer. The conclusion to the chapter emphasizes both the importance of prayer and the technique of simultaneity. The prayers of Tobit and Sarah are heard simultaneously, and God sends the angel Raphael to answer both prayers for help. Raphael's task is to heal both of them. He is to restore Tobit's sight and to free Sarah from the demon. While Raphael is God's messenger to both Tobit and Sarah, the instrument of both healings will be Tobit's son Tobiah. "At that very moment" both Tobit and Sarah return from prayer to their families. Now both lives are linked, both prayers are linked. The reader now knows that both of their prayers will be answered. Only the characters in the story must continue in the darkness of faith. The exposition of the story's plot ends here, but the reader is left with three questions: How will Tobit be healed? How will Sarah be delivered from the demon? How will the lives of these two families continue to be linked?

THE JOURNEY

Tob 4:1-6:18

4:1-21 Preparation for the journey: a father's speech. Chapter 4 belongs to the genre of farewell discourse. In biblical literature this genre has several distinct parts. Some of the parts found in the farewell discourse in the Book of Tobit are: (1) the speaker announces his departure; (2) the speaker recalls the past, either of the people or himself; (3) the speaker exhorts the hearers to keep God's commandments; (4) the speaker exhorts the hearers to unity of spirit; (5) the speaker predicts the future of his children; (6) the speaker wishes peace and joy to his children; (7) the speaker promises his children that God will be with them. Examples of this genre in the Old Testament are the farewell of Jacob (Gen 47:29–49:33); Joshua's farewell (Josh 22–24); David's farewell (1 Chr 28–29); and the whole book of Deuteronomy, which is cast as Moses' farewell discourse. In the Book of Tobit there are three farewell discourses: two of Tobit (4:3-21 and 14:3-11) and one of Raphael (12:6-10).

Tobit instructs Tobiah in the three virtues characteristic of his own life: truth (fidelity), righteousness, and almsgiving. The instruction to almsgiving is the most lengthy. Tobit tells Tobiah to care for Tobit's burial just as his father has cared for the burial of others (4:3; compare 4:17). He instructs Tobiah to pay servants' wages immediately (4:14), to feed the hungry and to clothe the naked (4:16), and to give alms in proportion to what he has (4:7-8, 16). Almsgiving will be for him a protection from death and will be a worthy offering, a worthy worship, to God (4:9-11; compare Sir 35:1-9).

Tobit also instructs Tobiah in the basic theory of retribution: if you are righteous, you will be blessed; if you are evil, you will be cursed (see Deut 28). Even though Tobit's own situation seems to belie the theory—he seems to be cursed even though he has been righteous—he tells Tobiah that doing good works "will bring success" to him and to all who live in righteousness (4:6, 21). Even as he recites the theory, however, Tobit leaves God free to choose how to execute retribution. He tells Tobiah that "if the Lord chooses, he raises a man up; but if he should decide otherwise, he casts him down to the deepest recesses of the nether world" (4:19). Whatever happens comes from God. Tobiah is to trust that God, too, is faithful, righteous, and merciful.

Marriage is the third major subject of Tobit's instruction. In the last centuries of the Old Testament period, the custom had arisen for Jews to marry within close kinship. The Book of Nehemiah reports the harsh requirement that returning exiles who had married non-Jewish women had to put away their foreign wives and marry Jewish wives (Neh 10:31; 13:1-3, 23-30) if they wanted to remain in the Jewish faith. Tobit cites the example of the patriarchs marrying close relatives: Abraham (Gen 20:12), Isaac (Gen 24:3-4), and Jacob (Gen 27:46–28:5). The tradition that Noah married a relative is not found in the Pentateuch but in the Book of Jubilees (4:33). The practice of marriage not only with Jews but within close family ties is probably based on the story of the daughters of Zelophehad (Num 27:5-11; compare Num 36:2-10), who had no brothers to inherit Zelophehad's property. In their case, they were to marry within their clan so that their father's property might remain within the clan. Sarah's situation, since she has no brothers, is the same as that of the daughters of Zelophehad. There is no evidence, however, that for her to marry outside her relationship would be "a capital crime," as Raphael says in 6:13.

The plot is advanced through this section by comments before and after Tobit's speech. The reason given for his farewell discourse is twofold: he has prayed for death and therefore expects it. He remembers the money that he deposited with Gabael and decides to send his son Tobiah to Media to get it (4:1-2). Tobit tells Tobiah about the money and, characteristically, connects it with the theory of retribution: "Do not be discouraged, my child, because of our poverty. You will be a rich man if you fear God, avoid all sin, and do what is right before the Lord your God" (4:21).

5:1–6:1 Preparation for the journey: a guide. Chapter 5 begins immediately with the practical preparations for the journey. Tobiah, although willing to obey his father's wishes, brings up two difficulties: since he does not know Gabael, he will need a sign to give him so that Gabael will give him the money. Also, he does not know the way to Media.

The answer to the first difficulty is simple. Tobit informs his son that when he deposited the money with Gabael, they exchanged signatures on a document written in duplicate. One copy was put with the money. It is implied that Tobit kept the other copy.

Finding a guide to Media occupies the rest of the chapter. Tobit instructs his son to look for a trustworthy man who knows the way. Raphael's immediate appearance answers the question left at the end of chapter 3: How will Raphael function?

The narration of the hiring of Raphael as guide is a masterpiece of irony. With the exception of Raphael, the audience knows more about what is happening than any of the characters involved. As soon as Tobiah finds Raphael, the narrator informs the audience that he is an angel but that Tobiah does not know it (5:4-5). Raphael ("God heals") tells Tobiah that his name is Azariah ("Yahweh is my help"). From this point on, all the characters will call the angel Azariah. The narrator, however, will continue to refer to him as "the angel Raphael," "Raphael," or simply "the angel" (see 5:8, 10, 12, 13, 16; 6:2).

Raphael's disguise makes his conversation with Tobit and Tobiah another element of the irony. When Tobiah asks Raphael who he is, Raphael replies that he is a kinsman who has come to find work (5:5). Indeed he has. He was commissioned in 3:17. When Tobit greets Raphael, the angel replies that there is healing in store for Tobit (5:10). He surrounds his assurance of healing with words that appear in all the healings: "Take courage" (5:10; compare 7:17; 11:11). Tobit ignores the promise of healing and moves on to the business at hand, but the readers know that Raphael's assurance is true.

Tobit, who is careful about his son's associations, quizzes Raphael regarding his identity. He is interested not only in his ability as a guide but also in his tribe and family. After turning the question aside once (5:12), Raphael finally answers: "I am Azariah ['Yahweh is my help'], son of Hananiah ['Yahweh is merciful']." Tobit adds the information that Hananiah is the son of Shemaiah ("Yahweh hears"). It is true that Raphael is there because Yahweh is merciful and Yahweh hears, but not true in the way that Tobit understands it. Raphael's statement inspires Tobit to exclaim, ". . . you are a kinsman, and from a noble and good line!" (5:14). That statement is far truer than Tobit realizes!

The chapter ends with a final twist of irony. Anna, Tobiah's mother, worries in typical motherly fashion. Tobit, equally worried, as we will learn later (see 10:1-3), reassures her by telling her what he has also prayed in blessing over his son: "A good angel will go with him, his journey will be successful, and he will return unharmed" (5:22; compare 5:17).

The relationship between Tobit and Anna and their parental concern for their son are carefully drawn in this chapter. Anna's attention throughout the book is concentrated on her son. The narrator identifies her as "his [Tobiah's] mother." She complains to Tobit: "Why have *you* decided to send *my* child away?" (5:18, emphasis added). After a single mention of "our child" (5:19), she refers to Tobiah as "*my* child" from this point until his return (10:4, 7). Only when she sees him coming down the road does she turn and tell Tobit, "*Your* son is coming" (11:6, emphasis added). In her relationship with Tobit, Anna tends to be sharp-tongued and quick (compare 2:14). In this chapter she turns the conversation to an attack on Tobit, accusing him of preferring money to the life of "her" son (5:19).

Tobit is also devoted to his son, who is the center of his life (see 11:14). He is careful to instruct him in the ways of righteousness (ch. 4). He, too, worries about Tobiah's journey (see 10:1-3). He characteristically puts aside his worry, however, to reassure Anna (5:21-22; compare 10:4-6), who, for the moment, stops weeping (6:1).

6:2-18 The journey. Tobiah's journey is outlined by the few statements that make up the itinerary. On the first night the travelers make camp beside the Tigris River (6:2). "Afterward they traveled on together till they were near Media" (6:7). They enter Media, and finally, in 7:1, they arrive at Ecbatana, which seems to be the goal of their journey. This is a surprise to the reader, who thinks that the two set off for Rages to get Tobit's money from Gabael (see 4:1, 20; 5:3). Raphael's instructions to Tobiah, however, indicate the real goal of the journey: the healing of Sarah and her marriage to Tobiah.

The angel's instructions to Tobiah form most of the material written concerning the journey. They consist of three parts, each one occurring in a different segment of the journey: instruction concerning how to prepare the fish (6:4-6); information about the healing properties of the fish's heart, liver, and gall; and detailed instructions concerning Tobiah's marriage to Sarah and her healing (6:10-18).

The fish represents a common element in romantic quests in folklore. The hero on a romantic quest conquers a dragon or a water monster such as Leviathan. This sea monster then becomes the source of life for the hero and for other characters in the story. Water as a source of both life and death is a common biblical image (see Gen 1:2; 2:5-6, 10-14; Job 38:8-11; 40:25–41:26; Pss 74:13-15; 89:10-11). The fish in the story of Tobit attempts to swallow Tobiah's foot (or to swallow Tobiah in the shorter Greek text!), but when Tobiah follows Raphael's instruction, seizes the fish, and saves its gall, heart, and liver, it becomes a source of healing.

The struggle with the fish occurs on the first night of the journey. Night is a common image for death. The alternation of the words "night" and "day" in the Book of Tobit reveals an important progression in the plot. There is a concentration of references to "night" in the chapters referring to Tobiah's journey and the healing of Sarah. Between 6:2 and 8:18, "night" occurs ten times (6:2, 11, 13 [twice], 14, 16; 7:10, 11 [twice]; 8:9). It occurs only twice more: once in 2:9 when Tobit is afflicted with blindness, and once in 10:7 when Anna weeps all night. "Day," on the other hand, is concentrated toward the beginning and end of the book: fourteen times in the first five chapters (1:2, 3, 16, 18, 21; 3:7, 10; 4:1, 3, 5 [twice], 9; 5:6, 21); eighteen times in chapters 8 through 14 (8:20; 9:4 [twice], 10:1 [4 times], 7 [twice], 12 [twice], 13; 11:17, 18). The movement of the plot goes from apparent light and life for both Tobit and Sarah, to darkness with Tobit's blindness and Sarah's affliction on her wedding nights, back into light with the return of Tobit's sight and the transformation of Sarah's wedding night into joy. The skillful use of these two words symbolizes the direction of the plot.

Raphael begins to fulfill his commission from 3:17 when he gives instructions regarding the healing of Tobit and Sarah. In the first instruction (6:7-9), Raphael informs Tobiah that the heart and liver of the fish are useful in removing an evil spirit from a man *or a woman,* and the gall is useful in curing blindness *in a man.* The reader, of course, knows that it is a woman who is afflicted by a demon and a man who is blind. Tobiah, instructed by Raphael and supplied with the parts of the fish, will be the means of their healing.

Raphael's detailed instructions concerning Tobiah's marriage to Sarah and her healing point forward and backward in the plot. Raphael reminds Tobiah that he has been instructed by his father to marry someone from his own kindred (6:16; compare 4:12-13). The reader also knows that Tobit himself married a wife from his own lineage (1:9) and that Sarah expects to marry either a relative or no one (3:15). It is not only the reader who knows that marriage to Sarah is a dangerous enterprise. Tobiah also knows that she has had seven husbands who have already dropped dead on the wedding night and that it is a demon who killed them (6:14-15). However, Tobiah also knows from Raphael that burning the heart and liver of the fish can drive off demons. Once the demon is banished, Tobiah is to begin his marriage in the spirit of prayer, and that prayer, joined to his willing obedience to his father and the great love he already feels toward Sarah, will seal the marriage that was determined "before the world existed" (6:18).

THE HEALING OF SARAH AND TOBIT

Tob 7:1–11:18

7:1–8:18 The wedding. When the travelers arrive in Ecbatana, they are immediately greeted by Raguel and introduced to his family. The greetings lead to a discussion of Tobit after Raguel recognizes Tobiah's likeness to him. The dialogue is well structured. Edna, like her counterpart Anna, is a strong woman who emerges as the moving force in the questioning of Tobiah. Two emotions characterize the meeting: joy at seeing Tobit's son and grief over Tobit's blindness.

The narrative moves immediately to a banquet scene that sets the stage for the wedding of Tobiah and Sarah. The scene fits a common pattern for betrothals in the Old Testament, for example, that of Isaac (Gen 24:1-67) and that of Jacob (Gen 29:1-30). The structure of Isaac's betrothal scene is much like that of Tobiah's. The father commands his son to take a journey to find a bride among his own kindred. (This is the obvious motive in Gen 24:3-4; in Tobit the motive is disguised by the matter of the money.) The travelers are given a meal (Gen 24:33; Tob 7:9) but refuse to eat until the betrothal is arranged (Gen 24:33; Tob 7:11). The host yields, recognizing that the marriage has been decided by the Lord (Gen 24:50; Tob 7:11). There are other similarities to the betrothal scene of Jacob. After an opening conversation, which in Tobit is cited directly from Genesis (Gen 29:4-6; Tob 7:3-4), the traveler is greeted warmly when he makes himself known as a relative (Gen 29:12-13; Tob 7:6). The father of the bride is reluctant to agree to the marriage (Gen 29:23-27; Tob 7:10-11). By using the common pattern of the betrothal scenes of the patriarchs, the author of the Book of Tobit is linking the marriage of Tobiah and Sarah to the patriarchal marriages, a connection already made by Tobit (4:12).

The wedding scene reveals much about the characters. Raguel, who is modeled after Abraham, is a man of hospitality. His favorite words are "Eat and drink" (7:10, 11; compare 8:20). He loves his daughter and is reluctant to see her suffer an eighth attempt to marry. Tobiah, who has been in the shadow of Tobit and Raphael until now, emerges in this scene as a man in his own right. When the travelers arrived in Ecbatana, Tobiah instructed Raphael to take him straight to Raguel's house (7:1). In the banquet scene, he refuses to eat until the marriage is determined (7:11). He has taken hold of the instructions given him by Raphael, and he will carry them out.

The wedding itself follows the pattern of a marriage contract found among the fifth century B.C.E. papyri discovered at Elephantine in Egypt. The marriage contract of Mibtahiah reads: "She is my wife and I am her husband from this day for ever" (compare Tob 7:11).

The phrase "Be brave" introduces the healing of Sarah (7:17; compare 5:10; 11:11) as Edna prepares her daughter for her eighth wedding night. When he is led into Sarah's bedroom, Tobiah remembers Raphael's instructions and performs the necessary ritual of burning the fish's heart and liver (8:2). This is the third description of the manner of Sarah's healing (see 6:8, 17-18). Each of the healings is described three times.

Sarah's healing, however, is not accomplished by means of the fish's heart and liver alone. They are only the physical symbols. Raphael pursues the demon after he flees and binds him (8:3). Even more significantly, Tobiah and Sarah turn to prayer, in accord with Raphael's instructions (8:4-9; compare 6:18). Prayer is an important activity throughout the book. At every crucial moment the main characters turn to prayer (see 3:2-6; 3:11-15; 11:14-15; 13:1-18). It is this turning to God in prayer that finally delivers Sarah from the demon Asmodeus.

In his prayer Tobiah links their marriage, not only to the patriarchs, but to creation and Adam and Eve. It is in this spirit of unity with the people of God that Tobiah and Sarah are united in marriage. Sarah joins Tobiah in the "Amen," the only word she speaks in the presence of another human being in the whole book.

Sarah is healed; the marriage is consummated. The irony of the book, however, continues. Raguel has given his daughter in marriage for the eighth time because he has no choice (see 6:13; 7:11), but he is not convinced that the end will be other than tragic. Protecting himself, he has a grave dug so that Tobiah can be buried "without anyone's knowing about it" (8:12). Had Tobiah died, one wonders whether Raphael would simply have gone home alone. Would Anna and Tobit have inquired about their son? Raguel, however, is worried about the neighbors. After the grave has been dug, he asks Edna to send a maid to see if Tobiah is dead. The maid becomes the messenger of the good news: "He is alive!" Raguel immediately turns to prayer and then instructs his servants to fill in the grave before the new day dawns. All signs of death will be wiped away from the new day (8:18).

8:19–10:7 The delay. As soon as day comes, Raguel prepares a feast (compare 7:9). In his great joy he doubles the length of the normal seven-day wedding celebration. He puts Tobiah under oath to stay the full fourteen days and bring joy to Sarah. The resulting delay in Tobiah's journey has two consequences.

First of all, Tobiah, who cannot leave Ecbatana, sends Raphael to Rages for Tobit's money, the original goal of the journey. Raphael is also instructed to bring Gabael back with him to the wedding feast. The journey to Rages and back seems to take very little time. This corresponds to Raphael's statement in 5:6 that Rages is only two days away from Ecbatana. As a matter of fact, it took Alexander's army eleven days of forced march to cover the same distance, approximately three hundred kilometers. We can draw two conclusions from this discrepancy. For one thing, the author is not interested in geographical details, nor is he intending to present a historical account. Also, the aura of speed and haste that seems to surround Raphael is not inconsistent with his angelic character (compare 5:8; 8:3; 11:4).

The second consequence of the delay is the effect on Tobiah's worried parents. Both parents act in typical fashion. Tobit, "day by day, was counting the days," and when the appointed day arrives and Tobiah has not returned, he begins to worry and to imagine all sorts of alternatives. Anna, who was already worried on the day Tobiah left, is convinced that her son is dead. She is not so convinced, however, that she does not go out every day to watch the road by which he will return. Just as he reassured his wife and concealed his own worry at Tobiah's departure (5:21-22), Tobit attempts now to console Anna. This time he is unsuccessful. She refuses to eat, and she weeps all night. She and Tobit are still in the dark, even though the day has dawned in Ecbatana.

10:7–11:18 Vision. The next section picks up the thread of the story after the fourteen-day delay. The scene in which Tobiah and Sarah prepare to leave Ecbatana and return to Nineveh illustrates several of the ideas concerning marriage in the book. First of all, marriage is seen to link families. Raguel instructs Sarah to honor Tobiah's parents, since, as he says, "they are as much your parents as the ones who brought you into the world" (10:12). Both Raguel and Edna refer to Tobiah as their son (10:11, 13). Edna tells Tobiah directly that she is his mother and that Sarah is his sister (10:13; compare Raguel's speech in 8:21). ("Sister" as a term for "beloved" is used throughout the book [7:11-12; 8:21; 10:12]. The same term is used in the Song of Songs [4:9-12; 5:1-2; compare also Prov 7:4].) Joy is an expected outcome of marriage (10:13; compare 8:20). Children are expected and are considered a blessing (10:11, 13; compare 4:12).

After being blessed by both Raguel and Edna, Tobiah begins the journey back to Nineveh in a spirit of prayer (10:14). The journey itself is summarized in one verse (11:1). The arrival, which is masterfully set up in a series of scenes alternating between the travelers and the parents as they approach each other (Raphael and Tobiah, 11:1-4, 7-8; Tobit and Anna, 11:5-6, 9-10), is a character study of all concerned. Raphael is hurrying again (11:3) and functioning in his angelic role as giver of information (11:4, 7-8). Tobiah, obedient to Raphael's instructions, is on his way to be the instrument of healing. Anna is still watching the road for *her* son, who she is sure is dead (compare 10:4-7). When she sees him coming, however, her true love for Tobit emerges. She turns "to *his* father, and exclaims, 'Tobit, *your* son is coming' " (11:6; emphasis added). In response, the blind Tobit gets up and stumbles toward the son whom he cannot see (11:10).

Tobiah begins the process of healing his father with the words that are characteristic of all the healings, "Take courage" (compare 7:17). The description of his actions is the third description of the method by which his father's blindness is to be healed (see 6:9; 11:8). Tobit's first words after vision returns are an exclamation of joy at seeing his son, the light of his eyes (11:14). Then he immediately turns to prayer.

Tobit prays in praise of God, whom he sees both as a source of affliction and as a source of healing (11:15; compare 13:2-5; 1 Sam 2:6; Wis 16:13). He thus declares one of the major theological principles of the book: God is free, and God's actions are beyond human understanding. Tobit, although he believes that God rewards obedience and punishes wickedness (see 1:12-13; 4:6, 21), accepts his blindness as coming from God (see 3:5). Throughout his affliction he never turns away from God and never ceases praying. His prayer as his sight is restored is a striking manifestation of his own extraordinary faith.

The joyful scene concludes with the greeting of Sarah, who has just arrived at the gate of Nineveh. Tobit continues the insistence that marriage has linked the two families. He refers to Sarah as "daughter" four times in his effusive welcoming speech (11:17).

Another seven-day celebration is begun, with Ahiqar (see 1:21-22; 2:10; 14:10) and his nephew Nadab in attendance (11:18). The Story of Ahiqar is one of the major sources of the Book of Tobit. Knowledge of the story is presumed in 11:18. The story probably originated as an Assyrian tale, and was written down in Aramaic around 500 B.C.E. It circulated widely in many languages, and several late versions are still in existence. The outline of the plot concerns a man named Ahiqar, who was a royal official under Sennacherib and Esarhaddon. He adopted his nephew Nadab and trained him to succeed to his royal position. Nadab, however, accused Ahiqar of treason, and Ahiqar was condemned to death. The executioner spared his life and hid him because of a kind deed Ahiqar had done for him earlier. When the king began to wish for Ahiqar back again, the executioner produced him, and Ahiqar was restored to his former honor. Meanwhile, Nadab was imprisoned and died. Thus the story, like that of Tobit, concerns a man who suffers unjustly but who, in the end, is rewarded for his virtue.

DENOUEMENT

Tob 12:1–14:15

12:1-22 The angel. The final chapters of the Book of Tobit reiterate the main themes and conclude the remaining details of the plot. The first detail to be settled is the matter of Raphael's wages. Tobit had assured Tobiah that his guide would be paid well (5:3), and Tobiah repeated the assurance to Raphael (5:7). In Tobit's conversation with Raphael he promised him a bonus as well (5:15-16). The journey has been completed with far more success than either Tobit or his son anticipated. Thus the two decide not only to give Raphael a bonus but to pay him half of the money that was brought back from Gabael (12:1-2). This motif belongs to a folk tale widely known in the Near East and in Eastern Europe called The Grateful Dead. This folk tale is one of the sources for the plot of

Tobit. In the folk tale a dead man, whom the hero has buried at great difficulty to himself, returns to act as a guide for him in his quest for a bride. The grateful dead man saves the hero from the demons that afflict the bride and kill her bridegrooms. As a reward, the hero offers the grateful dead man half of all the treasure he has acquired. At that point, the grateful dead man reveals his identity and disappears.

Raphael, following the model of the grateful dead man, refuses the wages and reveals his identity. This is the occasion for the second farewell discourse of the book (see 4:3-21; 14:3-11). Raphael's speech reiterates the major themes of the book. He exhorts Tobit and Tobiah to pray, to give thanks to God, and to praise God before all the living (12:6-7, 17-20). He also exhorts them to give alms, one of Tobit's characteristic virtues, in which he has also instructed his son (12:8-10; see 1:3, 16-18; 4:7-11, 16-17).

The major content of Raphael's speech is the revelation of his identity: "I am Raphael, one of the seven angels who enter and serve before the Glory of the Lord" (12:15). The developed figure of the angel is a primary contribution of the Book of Tobit to Old Testament theology. Four functions of angels, all of which derive from the identity of angels as messengers (the word *angelos* in Greek means "messenger"), can be seen in the character of Raphael. The angel is guide and protector, instructor, mediator, and tester.

The function of guide and protector is the primary function of the angel in this book. Raphael emerges as a main character only in the scenes that involve the journey (5:1–6:18; 11:1-8) and in the farewell speech (12:6-22). It is in those scenes that the narrator continually reminds us that Raphael is an angel (5:4; 6:2, 4, 7). After the opening scene with Tobiah, the first dialogue in which he participates is the discussion with Tobit concerning his qualifications as guide (5:10-17); his first activity is the journey (6:2–7:1). It is he who travels to Rages to get Tobit's money in order to complete the initial task of the journey (9:1-6). In answer to the initial question, Raphael will function primarily as guide and protector.

Raphael also functions as instructor and conveyor of information. He has two major conversations with Tobiah in which he functions in this role. In 5:5-9 Raphael is a channel of information concerning the trip to Rages and Ecbatana. The second exchange is far more important (6:7-18). He is the conveyor of information concerning the three major events of the plot: the marriage and the two healings. Raphael performs few actions, but he consistently instructs other characters how to act. He tells Tobiah how to gain mastery over the fish (6:4) and how to use its parts for the healings (6:5, 8-9, 16-18; 11:4, 7-8). He instructs him to marry Sarah (6:10-13). In his farewell discourse he instructs Tobit and Tobiah to pray and praise God (12:6-7, 17-20).

Raphael is a mediator of prayer. He comes in answer to prayer (3:16-17). He instructs Tobiah to pray on his wedding night (6:18). In this chapter he exhorts Tobit and Tobiah to pray in thanksgiving (12:6-7, 17-20). He identifies himself as one who presents prayers before the Glory of the Lord (12:12).

Finally, Raphael is a tester. He tells Tobit that he was sent to put him to the test (12:14). There is no indication of what his function in the test is. Does he bring the blindness? Is his hidden identity part of the test? He certainly tests Tobiah's obedience (6:4-5, 11-18). Beyond those implications, we have only Raphael's own statement concerning his function as a tester.

The angel in this book is a messenger. He mediates between God and the believers. The primary agents of God's providence are the human beings. Throughout the book, Tobiah is the instrument of healing. The primary actor is God. It is God who heals, as Raphael's name ("God heals") asserts; it is God who deserves thanks and praise (see 12:17-20).

13:1-18 Praise and thanksgiving. Raphael's exhortation to Tobit and Tobiah in chapter 12 to praise God is followed in chapter 13 by Tobit's song of praise. The prayer falls into two major sections: God's freedom and mercy (vv. 1-8); Jerusalem's distress and glory (vv. 9-18).

The first section is cast in the form of a hymn, with several calls to praise (13:1, 3, 4b, 6cd) alternating with the reasons for praise (13:2, 3b-4, 5-6). It ends with Tobit's presenting himself as an example to his kindred (13:7-8). The message of the first section reflects several themes of Deuteronomy. God is one who both scourges and has mercy (see

Deut 32:39; compare 1 Sam 2:6). Although the people have been scattered, God will again gather them (see Deut 30:1-5). The condition for their restoration is their turning back to God, an idea common to both Deuteronomy and Jeremiah (see Deut 4:29-31; 30:1-10; Jer 3:12, 14, 22; 4:1).

The second section, also a hymn, is addressed to the city of Jerusalem. After an introductory section that links the situation of Jerusalem, scourged and raised up, to the situation of the exiles, scourged and raised up (see 13:2, 5), the poem moves into a modified ring structure. A description of Jerusalem as a bright light drawing all nations (13:11) parallels a description of Jerusalem built of precious metals and jewels (13:16b-18). These descriptions of Jerusalem surround a set of curses and beatitudes:

Cursed are those who harm Jerusalem (13:12).
Happy are those who bless the Lord of the ages in Jerusalem (13:13).
Happy are those who love Jerusalem and rejoice in its prosperity (13:14).
Happy are those who grieve over Jerusalem's distress; they shall rejoice (13:15).
Happy is Tobit if a remnant of his offspring survives to rejoice in Jerusalem (13:16).

The second section is dependent on the imagery of the prophets. The vision of Jerusalem built with precious stones is found in Isa 54:11-12. Jerusalem as the source of great light to which many nations will come is the image of Isa 60:1-14 (see also Mic 4:2; Zech 8:22). Those who love Jerusalem will rejoice (Isa 66:10, 14) while those who do not serve Jerusalem will be destroyed (see Isa 60:12). Tobit believes in the word of the prophets (see 14:4), and the description of Jerusalem in his prayer is dependent on the prophets' vision.

The prayer of Tobit reflects the story of his own life. In his prayer he makes himself an example for his people. He exhorts them to praise God (13:1, 3, 4, 6, 8) as he does (13:7) and to trust God in adversity as well as joy (13:2-3, 5). In the second section he makes the same call to praise (13:10) and to trust God both in sorrow and in joy (13:9). He concludes the prayer with a hymn of joy over Jerusalem's future glory (13:16-18).

Joy is a primary characteristic of Tobit in the last part of the book (see 14:7). The prayer he composes is described as "joyful" (13:1), and "joy" is its constant refrain. Tobit himself rejoices (13:7). He prays that God's tent be rebuilt in Jerusalem with joy (13:10), that all the former captives be made glad (13:10), and all generations give joyful praise in Jerusalem (13:11). He exhorts Jerusalem to rejoice over the children of the righteous (13:13). He declares happy those who love Jerusalem, who rejoice with it, and who grieve over its distress. They shall rejoice in it as they behold its joy forever (13:14). Even the gates of Jerusalem shall sing hymns of gladness (13:18).

Tobit sees his own distress as a model of the distress of Jerusalem during the Exile. Just as God had mercy on him (see 11:15), so God will have mercy on Jerusalem. The return of Tobit's sight parallels Jerusalem's return to glory. Just as he praises God, so Jerusalem shall praise. His prayer makes it clear that the author understands the story of Tobit as a paradigm for the Exile and the restoration of the people.

14:1-15 Farewell. The third and final farewell discourse is found in 14:3-11 (compare 4:3-21; 12:6-10). It is introduced by the information that Tobit was indeed rewarded with the Deuteronomic blessings for righteousness: long life, joy and prosperity, and many descendants (14:1-3; compare Deut 4:1, 40; 5:32-33; 12:7, 12, 18; 30:15-20; 32:46-47).

Just as Tobit had called his son Tobiah to him in order to instruct him after Tobit had prayed for death (4:2-3), once again Tobit calls his son and his seven grandsons to him (14:3). First he tells them to trust the word of the prophets (14:3-4, 8). The prophet Nahum's dire prophecies concerning Nineveh will surely come to pass. In fact, the word of all the prophets shall come to pass in the proper time; therefore, it will be safer for Tobiah and his family to flee Nineveh and to take up residence in Media.

The second prophetic word to be proved true concerns the Exile and the destruction of Jerusalem (14:4-7). Just as the prophets announced the fall of Jerusalem, however, they also announced its restoration. The key word in the first section of this exhortation is "desolate," which is repeated three times. The country of Israel will be "desolate"; the capitals,

Samaria and Jerusalem, will be "desolate"; God's temple will be "desolate." The key word in the second section is "rebuild." They will "rebuild" the temple; they will "rebuild" Jerusalem; within Jerusalem the temple will be "rebuilt"; the temple will be "rebuilt" for all generations to come, just as the prophets said. Finally, as the prophets said, all nations will "turn" and fear God. All true Israelites will remember God and will be gathered in Jerusalem. The land in which they will dwell is the land of promise, promised generations ago to Abraham with a promise that has never been taken back.

Tobit ends his discourse with an exhortation to his descendants to live as he has lived. He walked all the days of his life "on the paths of truth and righteousness" and "performed many charitable works" (1:3). He exhorts his children to "serve God in truth," "to do what is right," and "to give alms" (14:9). As he has remembered God and constantly turned to God in prayer (see 3:2-6; 5:17; 11:14-15; 13:1-18), so his descendants are to do (14:9). As he is instructing them (see also 4:3-21), they are also to instruct their children (14:9). Tobit concludes with the story of Ahiqar, which illustrates the reward for almsgiving, just as his own life illustrates the reward for almsgiving (14:10). His final sentence summarizes the message of the book: Almsgiving gives life; wickedness brings death.

After Tobit's death, Tobiah proves himself a worthy son of his father. As his father had concern for the honorable burial of others, so Tobiah buries his parents and his wife's parents (compare 1:16-20; 2:1-7; 4:3-4, 17). He obediently leaves Nineveh and lives to see his father's faith in the prophets vindicated by Nineveh's destruction (14:15). Like his father, Tobiah is rewarded with prosperity and a long life (14:14).

JUDITH

Irene Nowell, O.S.B.

INTRODUCTION

The Book of Judith was written in the second century, somewhat later than the Book of Tobit. This book was a response to a new crisis that arose to threaten Jewish believers in Palestine. In 175 B.C.E. the Seleucid ruler Antiochus IV Epiphanes came to power in Syria and Palestine. He soon embarked on a policy to force the Jews not only to adopt Greek ways of thinking and worshiping but also to abandon traditional Jewish practices such as circumcision and special dietary laws. Stories of the horrible persecution that ensued can be found in the Books of the Maccabees.

At the height of the persecution (167 B.C.E.) a courageous Jew named Mattathias, forced to offer sacrifice on a pagan altar, killed the king's messenger and fled to the hills with his five sons. Soon other faithful Jews joined Mattathias and his sons and began what came to be known as the Maccabean revolt. (The name "Maccabean" comes from the nickname of Mattathias' son Judas, who was called Maccabee, which probably means "hammer.") The Maccabees reclaimed the temple and rededicated it in 164 B.C.E. After a long period of guerrilla warfare and intrigue, the Jews finally achieved a period of relative independence under Hasmonean rulers who were descendants of Mattathias and his sons.

The Book of Judith was written during the period of the Maccabean revolt. Its setting is in an earlier period, but many details reveal the author's interest in his own time rather than that of the seventh century B.C.E. In the story, an Israelite town is besieged by Holofernes, commander-in-chief of the Assyrian army. The town leaders despair of help from God and declare that if deliverance does not come within five days, they will surrender. A beautiful widow—an observant Jew—upon hearing the decision of the elders, scolds them for their lack of faith. She prays, placing herself in the hands of God. Finally, she prepares her weapon—beauty. Because God works through her beauty, she beheads Holofernes and delivers her people.

The message of the book is that victory comes not from human might but through the power of God. God can deliver the faithful people at whatever time and in whatever way God wishes. Even though the way of deliverance may look like folly from a human point of view, the story of Judith demonstrates that the real fools are those who place their trust in human power and weapons. The whole army of Holofernes is defenseless against God's weapon—the beauty of a faithful woman.

COMMENTARY

THE ASSYRIAN THREAT

Jdt 1:1–3:10

1:1-16 Nebuchadnezzar's war against Arphaxad. The opening chapter of the Book of Judith sets the stage for the conflict that is to follow and presents Nebuchadnezzar, one of the main protagonists. The date and names given in the first verse signal immediately that the intention of the author is not the presentation of historical material since they are not accurate. The story opens in the twelfth year of the reign of Nebuchadnezzar, 593 B.C.E. Nebuchadnezzar is identified as one of the Assyrian kings who ruled in Nineveh. Actually, Nebuchadnezzar reigned as king of the Babylonians from 604 to 562 B.C.E.; his capital was the city of Babylon. Nineveh, the capital of Assyria, was destroyed in 612 B.C.E. by Nabopolassar, the father of Nebuchadnezzar, during the Babylonian rise to power.

Other historical inconsistencies abound throughout the book. In the first chapter, Nebuchadnezzar's enemy is Arphaxad, king of the Medes (1:1). The ruler Arphaxad is unknown. The name is found in Gen 10:22 in the list of descendants of Shem. The city named as his capital, Ecbatana, was fortified around 700 B.C.E. by Deioces. The kingdom of the Medes, founded by Phraortes (675–653 B.C.E.), lasted until 550 B.C.E., when Cyrus, not Nebuchadnezzar, conquered Astyages, not Arphaxad (see 1:13-16).

The geographical information is equally inconsistent. The list of peoples summoned to assist Nebuchadnezzar in his battle against Arphaxad (1:7-10) includes regions moving from Mesopotamia in a counterclockwise fashion to the northwest and down the Mediterranean as far as Egypt. The places mentioned are in the right general area, but many are out of sequence. For example, Anti-Lebanon belongs between Damascus and Lebanon, the plain of Esdraelon between Carmel and Gilead. The cities of Egypt (1:9-10) also seem to be in no particular order.

Nebuchadnezzar, the protagonist in this drama, is, like everything else in the work, painted larger than life. He expects the inhabitants of most of the known world to come to his aid. The peoples of the West, however, are not impressed. They see him as one lone mortal (1:11) and not only refuse to assist in his battle but even turn away his messengers. Nebuchadnezzar's impression of himself is that of a divine being rather than a mortal. At the refusal of the western peoples to assist him, he falls into a violent rage and swears, not by a god but by himself, to destroy all the nations as far as the two seas (the Mediterranean to the Persian Gulf). Before he can begin that terrible expedition, however, he must destroy Arphaxad, king of the Medes. He achieves this victory in the seventeenth year of his reign (588 B.C.E.). The chapter ends with Nebuchadnezzar feasting for 120 days in celebration with his army. The stage is set for the campaign against the West.

2:1-28 The war against the West. The second chapter begins with another date, the eighteenth year of Nebuchadnezzar, the twenty-second day of the first month (Nisan). Both the year and the month are significant. The eighteenth year of Nebuchadnezzar was 587 B.C.E., the year in which his siege of Jerusalem succeeded and he took its citizens captive (see Jer 52:29; but compare Jer 52:12). The twenty-second of Nisan is the day after the Passover celebration ends (see Exod 12:2, 18). The author, by means of one date, is reminding the readers both of Israel's most terrible defeat (587 B.C.E.) and Israel's greatest deliverance by God, the Exodus, which is memorialized in the Passover.

Nebuchadnezzar's divine pretensions are clearer in the second chapter than in the first. He declares his intention of taking revenge on "the whole world" in verse 1. His vengeance will be nothing less than total destruction. The language he uses in summoning Holofernes is language that ordinarily belongs to Yahweh in biblical literature. For example, he begins, "Thus says the great king" (see Exod 4:22; Jer 11:3; Amos 1:3), "the lord of all the earth" (see Josh 3:11; Zech 6:5). Other phrases include: "to the very ends of the earth" (see 1 Sam 2:10; Ps 59:14; Isa 41:5); "what I have spoken I will accomplish by my power" (literally, "my hand will accomplish"; see Deut 32:39; Isa 43:13; compare Isa 10:12-15). He swears with a formula proper to divinity: "as I live" (see Isa 49:18; Jer 22:24; Ezek 5:11). Nebuchadnezzar, the first major character, has set himself up as a god, thereby opposing

Yahweh. In this opposition, the Book of Judith is similar to the Exodus event in which the opponents are Pharaoh, considered to be divine, and Yahweh (see Exod 4:22-23; 15:3-4).

Each of the divine figures is represented in the action by a mortal figure. Nebuchadnezzar is represented by his general in chief, Holofernes; Yahweh is represented by the holy woman Judith. Holofernes is introduced in chapter 2. The name Holofernes is found among the generals of Artaxerxes III Ochos (359–338 B.C.E.). The name Bagoas (see Jdt 12:11) is also found in lists of his retinue. For this reason some scholars have thought that the Book of Judith originated in the fourth century, either with regard to the events it narrates or to the period of its writing.

When Holofernes is summoned by Nebuchadnezzar, he is identified as "general in chief of his forces, second to himself in command" (2:4). From this point on, as soon as Nebuchadnezzar finishes his speech of instruction, Holofernes is in the foreground, and we see Nebuchadnezzar only through him. Nebuchadnezzar's punishment of the West, his challenge to Judea, and his ultimate defeat are acted out in the person of Holofernes. The power of Nebuchadnezzar comes to an end as Bagoas cries out: "A single Hebrew woman has brought disgrace on the house of King Nebuchadnezzar. Here is Holofernes headless on the ground!" (14:18).

Holofernes begins the campaign with an army consisting of 120,000 select troops and 12,000 cavalry (2:15-16). He gathers abundant provisions and much money for the support of his army. He sets out with this regular army and its provisions, along with a huge irregular force, "like locusts or the dust of the earth" to "cover all the western region" (2:19-20). This mammoth war effort will be matched against Bethulia, a tiny Israelite village whose main hero is a woman. The battle is between gods. Each god summons the best in human power in order to defeat the other. Nebuchadnezzar trusts in human force, Yahweh in human virtue.

The geographical notations continue to be confusing. The general direction again seems to be toward the northwest, then sweeping down along the Mediterranean. Bectileth, the camping place reached by the army after a three-day march, is unknown. Upper Cilicia, the next camping place, is, however, at least three hundred miles from Nineveh, an impossible distance for such a short march. Put and Lud are mentioned in Gen 10 (compare Nah 3:9); they are generally understood as African and Semitic peoples. Lud, however, is also identified as a place in Asia Minor (see Isa 66:19), maybe the same as Lydia. In any case, if the two names are taken together, they cannot be taken literally as part of the progress of Holofernes' army. Many of the other locations are unknown, such as Rassis and Japheth. Some identify not places but nomadic tribes, such as the Ishmaelites and the Midianites. Many of the names come from the table of nations in Gen 10, for example, Japheth, Put, and Lud. The effect of the geographical notations is to create a list of peoples long enough and disparate enough to indicate that Nebuchadnezzar, through Holofernes, is well on his way to conquering the whole world. Fear of him has indeed spread to the ends of the earth.

3:1-10 Surrender of the West. Holofernes expects that the result of his sweep through the lands west of Mesopotamia will be the surrender of all peoples to him. Chapter 3 seems to confirm that expectation. The author says that "they," presumably all the peoples listed in the last ten verses of chapter 2, "sent messengers . . . to sue for peace" (3:1), offering total surrender: "Do with us as you will." Wherever Holofernes and his troops arrive, they are welcomed with feasting and dancing.

Holofernes, however, responds to the welcome by devastating the territory and destroying all the shrines to local gods. "He has been commissioned to destroy *all the gods of the earth*, so that every nation might worship Nebuchadnezzar alone, and every people and tribe invoke him as a god" (3:8, emphasis added).

It would seem that Holofernes' victory is complete and that no one stands in the way of Nebuchadnezzar's being declared god of all the earth. At this point Holofernes stops in the plain of Esdraelon to rest and refurbish his army before attacking the Israelites. Now, the territory of Esdraelon is familiar to the biblical reader who knows that this is not the first time that Yahweh has appeared to be defeated here. More than once here the people of God have had defeat turn to victory in the most surprising circumstances. In the time of the judges, when the Israelites were oppressed by the Canaanite king Jabin and his general Sisera, Yahweh won a great victory for his people at the Wadi Kishon in the valley of Esdraelon. Even the stars fought for the people of God (Judg 5:20). The army of Sisera was defeated by the Naphtalite Barak. The final victory, however, belonged to Yahweh, who worked through two women. The prophetess Deborah, judge of Israel, instructed Barak, telling him that God had delivered the enemy into Israel's power (Judg 4:4-7). Jael, wife of the Kenite Heber, killed the enemy general, Sisera, with a tent peg (Judg 4:17-22; 5:24-27). For this victory Jael was declared "blessed among women" (Judg 5:24).

The people of God would also remember that the valley of Esdraelon had received the blood of their own kings. Saul was defeated there and died on Mount Gilboa with his son Jonathan (1 Sam 31). Josiah, "before [whom] there had been no king who turned to the Lord as he did, . . . nor could any after him compare with him" (2 Kgs 23:25), was killed there defending the pass at Megiddo against Pharaoh Neco in 609 B.C.E. (2 Kgs 23:29-30).

It would seem that nothing stands in the way of Holofernes' victory and Nebuchadnezzar's pretensions to divinity. But the army of the enemy rests in the valley of Esdraelon, the valley of defeat and victory, and the people await the action of Yahweh.

SIEGE OF BETHULIA

Jdt 4:1–7:32

4:1-15 Resistance of Israel. Just as all the peoples to the north and west of them feared Holofernes' army, so all the Israelites who lived in Judea were afraid when they heard of Holofernes' exploits. The Israelites' reaction to invasion differs from their neighbors in two respects: the nature of their fear and their response. Their fear is not only for themselves but primarily for Jerusalem and the temple of the Lord (4:2). The temple is the center of their lives and the sign of God's presence among them. They had, the narrator reports, only lately returned to their own land from exile. Only lately had the temple been purified from profanation (4:3). The people fear another profanation of the temple and perhaps even another exile.

The historical inaccuracies are a manifestation of high irony. The profanation of the temple and the deportation of the people to Babylon did indeed take place under Nebuchadnezzar in 587 B.C.E. The exile from which it seems the people have only lately returned was the Babylonian Exile (587–538 B.C.E.). Thus Nebuchadnezzar functions as a symbol for the worst that could possibly happen. With regard to the second century, the author's own time, the most recent profanation of the temple was that which took place under the Seleucid ruler Antiochus IV Epiphanes during the Maccabean war. The temple was restored and purified in December of 164 B.C.E., after the victory of Judas Maccabeus. (The yearly celebration of this rededication forms the basis of the feast of Hanukkah.) Thus the author, by claiming that the people have only lately returned from exile (538 B.C.E.), that the temple has only lately been purified (164 B.C.E.), and that the threat comes from Nebuchadnezzar (587 B.C.E.), has layered three events one on top of the other: the major disaster of the past, the major restoration of the past, and the crisis of his own time. Nebuchadnezzar may have brought the greatest disaster, but even that disaster was turned to victory within forty years. The crisis of the second century, it is implied, will also be reversed.

The second way in which the Israelites differ from their neighbors is in their response to invasion. Their neighbors surrendered and welcomed Holofernes with joy, but the tiny country of Judea prepares to defend its most precious possession, Jerusalem with the temple, against Holofernes' advance. Their preparation takes two forms. First of all, there is material preparation. The Israelites in Judea notify the whole region. The people post guards and store up provisions from the newly gathered harvest. Those living near the Esdraelon valley prepare to hold the mountain passes that give the only access from that region through the Carmel range to the country in the south.

The people's most important preparation for siege, however, is spiritual. They pray and fast, practices that will later become two of the three pillars of Pharisaism. They act like the people of Nineveh in the Book of Jonah. Not only the men, women, and children but even the domestic animals join in penance

(4:9-10; compare Jonah 3:8). Their efforts, like those of the people of Nineveh, are rewarded: "The Lord heard their cry and had regard for their distress" (Jdt 4:13). Thus the narrator informs the reader of the eventual outcome of the story. The people of Judea, however, will face many days of distress before *they* know the answer of the Lord.

A key word in this chapter is "cry." During the oppression in Egypt the people seemed to be doomed. God appeared to be absent and is only mentioned twice between Exod 1:1 and 2:22, and then only with regard to the Egyptian midwives. Yet when the people "cried" out to God, "he heard their groaning and remembered his covenant with Abraham, Isaac and Jacob" (Exod 2:24). Their cry was the beginning of their deliverance. In the Book of Judges this pattern is repeated consistently: (1) Israel abandons Yahweh; (2) Yahweh is angry with them and gives them over to their enemies; (3) they "cry" out to Yahweh, and (4) Yahweh sends a judge to deliver them (see Judg 3:2-11). In Judith, the people "cry" to Yahweh three times in seven verses (4:9, 12, 15), and Yahweh hears their "cry" (4:13).

5:1–6:21 Holofernes' response. Holofernes reacts to Israel's resistance in two ways. He summons the leaders of the lands surrounding Israel, indicating that he has the military power to squeeze the little nation to death. Then he asks two key questions: (1) Who are these people? Why are they different? Why has every other nation of the West surrendered and this tiny country refused? (2) Who is their king? What is their power? In the answers to these questions the reader finds the central message of the book.

Achior, leader of the Ammonites, answers Holofernes' first question, and the dialogue between the two men forms the basis of this section. Achior functions as the reporter for Israel, and the author indicates that through him the truth will be told (5:5). Achior begins by reciting the history of the people of God. He starts with Abraham and continues through the patriarchs, the sojourn in Egypt, the Exodus, and the conquest. He ends with the story of the Exile and the return. His historical survey is reminiscent of Joshua's speech during the covenant renewal that took place at Shechem after Israel had gained a foothold in the land of Canaan (Josh 24; see also Deut 26:5-10; Neh 9:6-31).

The historical recital answers the question "Who are these people?" Achior turns next to the second question: "What is their power?" He repeats the basic principles of the Deuteronomic theory of retribution: If Israel is obedient to God, the people will be blessed; if Israel is disobedient, they will be cursed. This theory finds its clearest expression in Deut 28. It is one of the basic principles illustrated in the Deuteronomic history (Joshua–2 Kings), and in the Book of Judith, Achior incorporates it into his advice to Holofernes. "If these people are at fault, and are sinning against their God, . . . then we shall be able to go up and conquer them. But if they are not a guilty nation, . . . their Lord and God will shield them" (5:20-21). The power of this people comes from their God.

The question Holofernes should ask, according to Achior, is whether or not the people of God are faithful. If they are, then God will fight for them and they cannot be defeated. If they are not, then Holofernes will be able to conquer them. The implication of Achior's speech is unavoidable: Even if Holofernes wins, it will not be because of his own power but because God has sold the Israelites into the hands of their enemies on account of their infidelity (see Judg 3:7-8; 4:1-2). Holofernes has finally met a power stronger than his own.

Holofernes, however, misunderstands the real question. Neither he nor his attendants can envision a power greater than the material power of arms. His advisers tell him that the Israelites are a powerless people, incapable of a strong defense. "Let us therefore attack them; your great army, Lord Holofernes, will swallow them up" (5:23-24). This misunderstanding of true power will prove to be a fatal error for Holofernes.

Holofernes ignores the advice of Achior and follows the advice of those who counsel attack. However, before the attack he makes a three-point response to Achior's recommendations. First of all, he recognizes that Achior's function is that of prophet (6:2), even though he condemns Achior for delivering the message of the God of Israel. Holofernes' analysis of Achior's role is accurate. A prophet is "one who speaks for," one who delivers a message for another. Achior is delivering to Holofernes God's message concerning Israel: If they are faithful, you cannot defeat them. Achior is also delivering God's message concerning Israel to the people of the second century: If you remain faithful, you will not be defeated in this time of distress. Achior the Ammonite functions as a prophet of the God of Israel, a role recognized although repudiated by Holofernes the Assyrian.

Secondly, Holofernes proposes a course of action directly opposed to the advice of Achior. He refuses to accept Achior's message because he does not recognize the God from whom the message comes. He recognizes no god but Nebuchadnezzar (6:2); therefore Holofernes thinks that the God of Israel is powerless to save the people. Holofernes thinks that he himself will be the instrument by which the power of Nebuchadnezzar, "lord of all the earth," will be unleashed. No other god exists to withstand him. The words of Nebuchadnezzar "shall not remain unfulfilled" (6:4). Holofernes, in the name of Nebuchadnezzar, has declared war on Yahweh, God of Israel.

Thirdly, Holofernes condemns Achior to share the fate of the Israelites (6:5-9). He instructs his servants to hand Achior over to the people of Bethulia. Because the Israelites hurl stones down at them, Holofernes' men leave Achior bound at the foot of the mountain below Bethulia. When the Israelites untie him and bring him into the city, Achior again functions in the role of messenger-prophet. All the people gather to hear his report concerning Holofernes' declaration of war, and the Israelites' response is in direct contrast to that of the Assyrians. The Israelites understand the question about the source of their power. They *know* that their only power, their only hope is in God, and they call upon God to witness the arrogance of the enemy and their own lowliness.

7:1-32 Siege of Bethulia. The siege of Bethulia is described by a series of scenes that alternate between the Assyrian army and the Israelites. The two opening scenes are brief. Holofernes initiates a threefold action against the Israelites: to move against Bethulia, to seize the mountain passes, and to engage them in battle (7:1). Holofernes completes the first maneuver immediately, and his army lies spread out before the eyes of the Israelites at the spring that waters their city (7:3). The Israelite response is mixed (7:4-5). They are terrified by the size of the army that opposes them, yet they continue to keep watch and to maintain communication with the surrounding towns by means of fire signals. There is a reference to the use of such fire signals in one of the letters found at Lachish describing the siege of the city in 589 B.C.E.

The two remaining scenes (7:6-18, 19-32) portray the siege in greater detail. Holofernes seals off the approaches to the city and seizes the water sources. Traditional enemies of Israel—the Ammonites, the Edomites, and the leaders of the seacoast—advise him not to attack but to wait. The siege, in midsummer, will soon render the inhabitants of Bethulia helpless from thirst. In one respect, the time of year proves to be an advantage to the Israelites because the harvest has already been gathered (see 4:5); however, they cannot expect any rain until October. Thirst will be the Assyrians' weapon.

The Israelites, meanwhile, begin to suffer the effects of the siege (7:19-32). They suffer thirst. Water is rationed, and people begin to collapse from dehydration and weakness. The physical effects, however, are far less serious than the spiritual ones. The people become disheartened and begin to lose faith—first of all in God. Perhaps God has sold them into the power of the enemy as in the days of the judges (Jdt 7:25; compare Judg 3:8; 4:2; 10:7). They begin to murmur as the Israelites did in the wilderness: It would be better to fall into the hands of the enemy and live than to continue resisting them and die (7:26-27; compare Exod 16:3; Num 14:2-4). They also lose faith in themselves. The Deuteronomic theory of retribution says that suffering comes as a result of sin; therefore, they must be suffering because of their own sins and those of their ancestors (7:28). In either case the only solution is to surrender to the enemy.

Uzziah, whose name means "Yahweh is my strength," exhorts the people to have courage; however, he demands that God act within five days. If not, the people of Yahweh will abandon themselves to the army of Holofernes, and Nebuchadnezzar will declare himself god of all the earth (see 3:8; 6:2-4).

The five days stipulated by Uzziah (7:30), added to the thirty-four days of the siege (7:20), make a total of thirty-nine days. Deliverance will come on the night between the fourth and fifth days of Uzziah's limit (see

12:10). Thus within forty days, the traditional length of affliction (Moses' forty days of fast on Sinai, forty years in the wilderness, forty years of exile, Judith's forty months of mourning [see 8:4]), Yahweh will indeed send help to the people.

JUDITH, INSTRUMENT OF YAHWEH

Jdt 8:1–10:10

8:1-8 Judith, Yahweh's representative. War has been declared between Yahweh and Nebuchadnezzar, God against god. Each divinity has an acting human representative. The reader has been introduced to Holofernes, who functions as the representative of Nebuchadnezzar. In this chapter the reader meets the representative of Yahweh, the widow Judith.

Judith's introduction is one of the most lengthy genealogies in the Old Testament. It extends back sixteen generations. This alone declares the importance of this woman. It also indicates that her name, "Jewess" or "Judahite," is a true indication of her identity. In exilic and postexilic times the ability to trace one's ancestry back to the patriarchs, to know oneself to be a true descendant of Abraham and thus heir of the blessing, was of great importance. The Priestly tradition in the Pentateuch, which developed in the exilic period, lays great stress on genealogies. The people of God, when they regather in the land, need also to rediscover their roots. Judith's genealogy indicates that she is indeed a true Judahite, a true exemplar of her people.

Judith is a model of Jewish observance. She had, according to custom, married within her own tribe and clan (see the commentary on Tob 4:12-13). She lived piously—fasting, wearing widow's weeds and sackcloth, and fearing God. She was beautiful, a clear indication in biblical literature of virtue as well (see Gen 29:17; 39:6; 1 Sam 16:12; Esth 2:7; Dan 1:4-15). She is not only a model for her people because she is a true descendant of the patriarchs; she is also a model for their behavior.

Judith is a widow. Widows are significant in biblical stories. They are, first of all, objects of special concern, especially in Deuteronomy (see Deut 10:18; 14:29; 16:11, 14; 24:17, 19, 20, 21; 26:12-13; 27:19). Care for them is required because God cares for them (Deut 10:17-19; compare 24:18, 22). They are among those people who know that they have no help except in God; therefore, they are under God's special protection.

In addition to their special status as a group, there are several individual widows who have affected the history of the people of God. In the patriarchal narrative, Tamar, widow of Judah's son Er, continues to insist on the right of levirate marriage even after she is left a widow a second time by Judah's second son, Onan. Her determination finally leads her to take matters into her own hands and pose as a prostitute so that her husbands' father might give her a child to raise up in the name of her husbands (Gen 38). Judah himself claims that Tamar is more righteous than he (Gen 38:26). Because of her courage, the line of Judah continues. Twins, Perez and Zerah, were born to Tamar. A second widow who took matters into her own hands married into the line of Perez. Ruth, the Moabite woman who left her homeland to follow her mother-in-law back to Bethlehem, married Boaz, descendant of Perez, in another levirate marriage. A son named Obed was born to Ruth and Boaz. Obed became the father of Jesse, who was the father of David (see Ruth 4:18-22). Thus the genealogy of Israel's greatest king was shaped by the lives of two courageous widows. In the Book of Judith, another courageous widow becomes the instrument by which God delivers the people.

8:9-36 Judith and the elders. When the holy woman Judith hears that the people, in their despair, have challenged the elders' judgment (see 7:23-32), she sends her maid to ask the elders to visit her. She talks to the elders about the two major doubts of the people—their lack of faith in God and their lack of faith in themselves. She concludes her speech with an exhortation to action and a statement of the basic theological principle in question.

The first doubt that Judith treats is the people's lack of faith in God's fidelity to them (see 7:25). She scolds the elders for limiting God to the human understanding of the Deuteronomic theory of retribution. They have allowed themselves to be convinced that if God is just, God must reward all virtue and punish all disobedience according to human understanding of reward and punishment. They can see only the immediate distress;

therefore, if God is just and they are virtuous, God must relieve their thirst within five days. Judith corrects this misunderstanding by declaring the basic principle that God is free, that God's ways are not human ways (8:12-16; compare Isa 55:8-9; Tob 4:19). The proper thing to do is to wait for God's salvation and trust in God's good pleasure (8:17).

The second doubt that Judith treats is the people's lack of faith in their own fidelity to God (see 7:28). They think that if God is just and yet they are suffering, then they must have been unfaithful. They have made the theory of retribution into an equation that is automatic and interchangeable. If disobedience brings suffering, then all suffering must be the result of disobedience. But the relationship between God and the people is personal rather than mathematical. Just as God is free to send blessing when it is undeserved, so also is God free to send suffering for purposes other than punishment. The people must not abandon hope in God. They have reason for hope because they have been faithful. They have not worshiped other gods; they *know* no other god but Yahweh (8:18-20, emphasis added). They have need for hope because if they despair and abandon God, the sanctuary will be profaned, the people will be slaughtered, and the land will be devastated. They will then bear the responsibility for this destruction because they have failed in hope. As a result, they will be enslaved and become the mockery of all (8:21-23).

Having treated the two problems of the people, Judith concludes with an exhortation to action and a restatement of the basic theological principle involved. Her call for action has three parts. The people of Bethulia must set an example because the fate of the land, the temple, and the people depends on them. They must be grateful to God, even in the midst of distress and even on account of their distress, because their affliction is a proof of God's love for them (see Prov 3:12). Finally, they must remember God's dealings with their ancestors so that they will understand God's fidelity and the meaning of their own suffering. The theological principle upon which Judith bases her argument is the freedom of God: God can send blessing even if it is undeserved; God may send suffering, not as punishment but as a test (see Deut 8:2-5, 16; Judg 2:22-23; Tob 12:14; Job 5:17-18).

Uzziah responds to Judith by confirming her wisdom but excusing the weakness of the elders for succumbing to the demands of the people (8:28-31). Even though he recognizes the rightness of Judith's words, he is caught in a dilemma. The elders have sworn an oath that they cannot take back (see Gen 27:33). The two different solutions to the dilemma, proposed by Uzziah and Judith, emphasize the contrast between Uzziah's small hope and Judith's great courage. Rain is the only solution he can imagine to relieve the immediate distress (8:31). Judith, on the other hand, envisions a total liberation to rank with the Exodus, a liberation that "will go down from generation to generation among the descendants" of Israel (8:32).

Judith does not tell Uzziah her plans. Both he and the readers are left in suspense, wondering how God will rescue Israel through her. The readers, however, have an advantage over Uzziah: they have been told by the narrator that God *will* deliver Israel (4:13). What they do not know is how.

9:1-14 Judith prepares for war: prayer. Judith makes two preparations for her war of liberation. The first preparation is prayer. Her prayer is important, first of all, as a model of how to pray. Judith prays during the time when the incense is being offered in the temple in Jerusalem, thus joining her prayer to the official prayer of her people (9:1). Her prayer posture is the classic posture of radical humility—prostration. Her attire is symbolic of penitence—sackcloth and ashes. She prays in traditional fashion, first reminding God of the mighty deeds performed for her ancestors (9:2-4; we may disagree with her evaluation of the slaughter of Shechem by Simeon and Levi), and then calling upon God to exercise divine power in her behalf (9:5-11). She concludes by reminding God of the benefits that will come from aiding her (9:12-14). Her prayer mirrors the exhortation she has given to her people to call upon God in hope (see 8:17).

The content of her prayer illustrates three basic principles of Holy War. The first principle has to do with trust. Those who trust in horses and chariots will be defeated; those who trust in Yahweh will be victorious. It is not possible to trust in both (see Ps 20:8-9). Trust in armaments is the same as trust in another god. It is idolatry (see Mic 5:9-12). The

Assyrians' folly is that they trust in weapons of war, horses, and chariots. They do not know that Yahweh crushes warfare (Jdt 9:7-8; see Exod 15:3; Ps 76:4-7).

The second principle has to do with power. Those who trust in armaments trust in human power, those who trust in Yahweh trust in divine power. A key biblical word for power is "hand." Divine power is exercised for the people by Yahweh's mighty hand (see Exod 3:19-20; 6:1; 13:9). Frequently the power of Yahweh comes through the hand of a chosen instrument such as Moses (see Exod 9:22-23; 10:21-22; 17:11-12), the judges (see Judg 3:15, 21, 28; 6:36-37), or David (see 2 Sam 3:18). Yahweh's chosen instrument is sometimes weak, for example Jael (Judg 4:9, 21; 5:26) or the reduced army of Gideon (Judg 7:2, 7, 14-15). The weapons of Yahweh are not the same as human weapons. Judith, trusting in the power of Yahweh, asks for a strong hand so that by the hand of a woman the pride of the Assyrians might be crushed (9:9-10).

The third basic principle of Holy War has to do with victory. Victory belongs to the lowly and the vulnerable. The lowly, the oppressed, the weak, and the forsaken are not tempted to trust in human power; they have none. They know that they have no hope except in the power of God (Jdt 9:11; compare 1 Sam 2:4; Zeph 2:3).

On the basis of these three principles, Judith makes her plea to God. She does not trust in horses and chariots. She does not trust in human power. She knows that she has no hope except in the power of God; therefore she calls upon Yahweh to win the victory (9:12-14).

10:1-10 Judith prepares for war: beauty. Judith's second preparation for war is the enhancement of her beauty. After bathing, she uses all the human arts available to her to make herself both beautiful and captivating: perfumed ointment, a fancy hairstyle, festive clothing, and jewelry (10:1-4).

Judith understands the goodness of her body. She knows that her physical beauty is good and that it comes from God. She also knows that the power of her beauty comes from within her, from her holiness, from her faithfulness to God. Since both her exterior and interior beauty come from God, her beauty must be devoted to the service of God. God intends to use her beauty as a weapon to liberate the people. She will wield the weapon to the best of her ability.

The response of others to this second preparation of hers testifies to its effectiveness. The men of her own city are astounded at her beauty (10:7). After she arrives at the enemy camp, the guards of Holofernes gaze at her face in awe because of its wondrous beauty (10:14). The crowd that gathers within the camp at her arrival marvels at her beauty. They say to one another: "Who can despise this people that has such women among them? It is not wise to leave one man of them alive, for if any were to be spared they could beguile the whole world" (10:19).

Judith's preparation is now complete. She gathers provisions (kosher food) and departs with her maid for the enemy camp. Let Holofernes beware!

JUDITH GOES OUT TO WAR

Jdt 10:11–13:20

10:11-19 Judith in the enemy camp. In her words to the elders, Judith advised her people to trust in God and to call upon God to help them (8:17). She has already been an example of calling on God in prayer (9:1-14). Now she demonstrates her trust in God. With great courage, alone except for her maid, she leaves her city at night and walks to the Assyrian camp. She has proclaimed in her prayer that God protects the powerless (9:11). Now she puts that word to the test.

Her trust in God is not misplaced. As soon as she meets the guards of the enemy camp, they are overcome by the weapon of God, her beauty (10:14-17). The same victory is won when she meets the crowd of soldiers within the camp (10:18-19).

Judith's words are a masterpiece of irony. She treads lightly through deceit and guile (a true Israelite, indeed!—see Gen 27:36; 30:25-43; 32:28-29). In her prayer, she had already announced her intention to deceive (9:10, 13). An element of truth is consistently present in what she says but cleverly masked throughout. She tells the guard truthfully that she is a daughter of the Hebrews (10:12). She announces that she is fleeing, which is false, but the reason for her flight seems true to everyone but her: the Israelites are about to be delivered up to the Assyrians as prey (10:12). She announces truthfully that she has come to see Holofernes, and the message that she has for him is indeed trustworthy. Those who will be saved from loss of life, however, are not Holofernes' men but her own people (10:13).

The statements of the soldiers are also high irony. They do not know the implication of their words when they tell Judith that by coming to see Holofernes she has saved her life (10:15). She has indeed saved her life, but Holofernes has lost his. The soldiers unwittingly recognize Judith's power. They proclaim that the power of Israel is in women such as she. Women like Judith, they declare, could beguile the whole world (10:19). They are soon to discover how right they are.

10:20–11:23 Judith meets Holofernes. The encounter between Judith, servant of Yahweh, and Holofernes, servant of Nebuchadnezzar, opens with Holofernes reclining on his bed. The scene of Judith's victory over Holofernes will be that same bed. As soon as Holofernes sees Judith, it is evident that she will be successful against him because her beauty strikes Holofernes with amazement.

Their encounter proceeds with two speeches. Holofernes makes the initial statement. At the beginning and end of it, he exhorts Judith to take courage (compare Tob 5:10; 7:17; 11:11) because he presumes she serves Nebuchadnezzar, the king (Jdt 11:1, 3-4). In actual fact, she has already taken courage because she serves the Lord. Holofernes has missed the key point. Judith is courageous and her life is spared because she is a servant of Yahweh, the true king of all the earth (compare 11:1).

Judith's answer to Holofernes, like her speech in chapter 10, is a cunning mixture of truth and deceit. She weaves her message through three topics: the destiny of Holofernes, the message of Achior and its effect on the Israelites, and the deed that she herself will accomplish. She says to Holofernes that if he follows her advice, "God will do the deed perfectly" with him (11:6). *Her* Lord will not fail in any undertaking (11:6). Holofernes presumes that this means *he* will be victorious. Precisely the opposite interpretation—that Yahweh will be victorious—is also possible. Judith continues to deceive him when she refers to "the power of him who has sent you to set all creatures aright" (11:7). Holofernes again presumes wrongly that she refers to Nebuchadnezzar.

Judith concludes her treatment of Holofernes' destiny with words of great flattery and turns to the subject of Achior's speech and its effect on the Israelites (11:9-15). Again she begins by telling the truth. She confirms Achior's message that if Israel is guilty (which she knows is not true), then Israel will be punished; then she turns to deceit by reporting the imagined guilt of her people (11:11-15). Her description of their guilt provides a list of the most significant practices of Judaism in the second century: dietary laws, laws regarding first fruits and tithes, laws regarding the sanctuary (see commentary on Tob 1:3-22).

She concludes her speech by declaring her own intentions. It is true, as she says, that God has sent her "to perform with [Holofernes] such deeds that people throughout the world will be astonished on hearing of them" (11:16). She is indeed a God-fearing woman. It is also true that she will set up the judgment seat of Holofernes (11:19), but it is he who will be judged and found worthy of condemnation. She deceives by her report of the truth.

Holofernes and his servants respond to her speech in wonder. Previously they had marveled at her beauty; now they marvel at her wisdom. Holofernes ends the encounter with a speech worthy of Judith. Even though he does not understand the truth, there is truth woven through his words. "God has done well in sending you ahead of your people. . . . You are fair to behold, and your words are well spoken. . . . You shall be renowned throughout the earth" (11:22-23). The battle lines have been drawn.

12:1–13:10 Battle and victory. The conflict between Judith and Holofernes is introduced by the narrator with a series of incidents that demonstrate Judith's piety, even while in the enemy camp (12:1-9). She continues to keep the dietary laws. Holofernes offers her food, but she insists that her mission will be accomplished before her own provisions run out. She continues to depend upon prayer. Every morning before dawn she leaves the camp to beseech God to "direct her way for the triumph of his people" (12:8). She keeps ritual purification. Along with her daily prayer, she bathes in the spring of the camp.

The primary function of these incidents is to demonstrate Judith's piety. They serve two other functions, however. First of all, they further the plot by establishing a regular routine for Judith. When the crucial morning comes, she will need to leave the camp before dawn to avoid being questioned. Her ordinary daily practices provide the means of her escape after Holofernes' death. The second function served by these daily incidents is the creation of suspense. For three days, long enough to establish the routine, Judith bides her time and follows a regular daily schedule. The reader knows that her time is short. On the fifth day Uzziah is bound by oath to surrender the city. The crucial encounter does not come until the last possible day. Trust in Yahweh is pushed to the limit before relief comes.

On the fourth day Holofernes invites Judith to a banquet. The excuse he gives to Bagoas is that Judith will laugh them to scorn if they do not entice her (12:12). Judith's response continues the impression that she is eager to be enticed. She sends the messenger back with the response that the evening's activities will be a joy for her until the day of her death (12:14). As she begins her preparations, however, it soon becomes evident who is enticing whom. She prepares her weapon, her beauty, with care and sallies forth to battle.

The power of her beauty is immediately evident. Holofernes is overcome with desire for her, and because of her charm he drinks a greater quantity of wine than he has ever drunk in a single day in his life. As a result, by the end of the banquet he lies drunk on his bed. The stage is set for the victory. All the other guests have departed. Holofernes and Judith are left alone. Judith is armed; Holofernes is helpless.

Judith begins by turning to God, the source of her power, her hope for victory (13:4-5). She reminds God that she acts for the sake of God's people and God's sanctuary in Jerusalem. She draws Holofernes' own sword, prays for strength, and with all the power that God gives her, she beheads him (13:8). Judith, widow of Israel, servant of Yahweh, has vanquished Holofernes, general in chief of the Assyrian army, servant of Nebuchadnezzar. The Assyrian advance is stopped; the Assyrian victory has been reversed. Nebuchadnezzar, who claimed to be king of all the earth, has been defeated by Yahweh, true Lord of all the earth.

Judith then returns to her normal routine. After she wraps up the head of Holofernes and gives it to her maid, who has been waiting for her, the maid puts the head in the food pouch, and the two go out of the camp together "as they were accustomed to do for prayer" (13:10).

Judith's words throughout this section continue to be ironic. When Holofernes asks her if she has enough food, she replies, "As surely as you, my lord, live, your handmaid will not use up her supplies till the Lord accomplishes by my hand what he has determined" (12:4). As surely as Holofernes lives, this is true. As soon as the Lord accomplishes the victory through her, Holofernes will no longer be alive. There can be no more than five days to wait. When Judith is invited to the banquet, she replies, "Who am I to refuse my lord? Whatever is pleasing to him I will promptly do. This will be a joy for me till the day of my death" (12:14). The misunderstanding turns on the meaning of "my lord." The servant undoubtedly understands her to mean Holofernes; the reader knows that she means Yahweh. Her action will please Yahweh because it will bring about the downfall of Holofernes. It is that action which will be her joy. At the banquet itself, Judith tells Holofernes that she has never enjoyed life as much as on that day. That day will bring victory to her, death to Holofernes.

13:10-20 Liberation proclaimed. Before dawn on the fifth day, Judith announces their liberation to the people of Bethulia. This whole section is built around proclamation and prayer. Judith calls out the news in three statements, each one more specific than the one preceding it. Her statements are answered by two blessings, one by all the people and the second by Uzziah, to which the people answer, "Amen! Amen!"

The parallel structure and the repeated words in Judith's statements and in the responding blessings indicate an underlying poetic base in the original Hebrew. Her first two statements begin with repeated words (vv. 11 and 14; compare Ps 24:7). All three of her statements are rich with parallel structure (vv. 11 and 15). If the blessings by the people and by Uzziah are taken together, they form a threefold beatitude (vv. 17-18). The poetic style is significant. At the moment of victory, both the savior and those saved break forth into praise of God, by whose power they have been victorious. Prose has been sufficient to announce their distress; their deliverance calls for poetic praise of God.

VICTORY

Jdt 14:1–16:25

14:1–15:11 Response to the news of Holofernes' death. After the initial liturgy of rejoicing when Judith proclaims the news of Holofernes' death, several clean-up activities remain to be done. The story of the response to Holofernes' death is set in three scenes: (1) in Bethulia, (2) in the Assyrian camp, and (3) throughout Israel.

In Bethulia, Judith acts as general of the army and leader of the people. She has won the victory by assassinating the enemy's general. What remains is to consolidate the winnings. She gives orders, first of all, to the Jewish men to hang the head of Holofernes on the city wall and then to fake an attack on the Assyrian camp (compare Gideon in Judg 7:16-22). This action will rouse the enemy camp and will bring about the demoralizing discovery of the death of Holofernes.

Secondly, Judith summons Achior the Ammonite, whom Holofernes had sent to share the fate of the Israelites (see 6:10-14). Achior had understood the source of the Israelites' power (see 5:17-21). He had recognized that their victory would be through God alone (5:21). Now, when he sees the head of Holofernes in the hand of one of the Jewish men, he recognizes the manifestation of the power of God. He responds in threefold fashion. Recognizing the presence of God in the victory, he faints (see Gen 32:31; Judg 6:22-23). Recognizing in Judith the instrument of God's power, he falls at her feet in homage and blesses her. Recognizing God's fidelity to the Jews in Judith's account of her visit to the Assyrian camp, he believes in God and joins the house of Israel through faith and circumcision (14:6-10).

Meanwhile, the Assyrian camp responds to the fake attack of the Israelites as Judith had predicted. Observing protocol, the enemy soldiers notify all the proper authorities until the news comes to the tent of Holofernes (14:11-13). Bagoas attempts to rouse Holofernes discreetly, but getting no response, he enters Holofernes' tent, only to find him headless and Judith absent (14:14-17; compare Eglon in Judg 3:24-25). Bagoas proclaims the news to the troops: "A single Hebrew woman has brought disgrace on the house of King Nebuchadnezzar!" The announcement causes complete disarray among the Assyrian troops (14:19–15:3). "*No one* kept ranks any longer" (15:2, emphasis added). Judith's action has completely ruined the army of Nebuchadnezzar.

Throughout Israel messengers arrive to report the good news and to summon the Israelites to pursue the fleeing Assyrians. From Jerusalem in the south to Damascus in the north and Gilead in the east, the Israelites pursue and eradicate the enemy. The victory is complete; the quantity of booty is enormous (15:4-7).

The high priest Joakim and the elders arrive from Jerusalem to recognize the victory officially. They come to "see for themselves the good things that the Lord had done for Israel and to meet and congratulate Judith" (15:8). They officially recognize God, the source of the victory, and Judith, the instrument of God. They sing another hymn of blessing (15:9-10), to which all the people respond "Amen!"

Their hymn points out succinctly what has been evident throughout the story. Judith, "the Judahite," is a type of the whole people. Her fidelity to God is symbolic of the fidelity of the Jewish people as a whole. Her victory, by her own hand, is the victory of the whole people. God is pleased with her, as with the whole people, and God's blessing is called down upon them all forever. The message for the people of the author's time, the second century, is evident. God will win their deliverance from oppression. What they must do, together and individually, is remain faithful. God may choose the weakest hand among them, even that of a woman, to bring about the victory. But even though the whole people is weak, the victory is not impossible for God.

15:12–16:17 Judith's prayer. Judith's prayer of praise and thanksgiving is set within the victory celebration of the whole people (15:11-12; 16:18-20). Before and after the prayer there is a report of the physical results of victory. Before the prayer the Israelites plunder the Assyrian camp and Judith is given the choicest booty, Holofernes' tent and furnishings. After the prayer all the people go to Jerusalem to worship God and to offer holocausts and gifts. Judith offers God all Holofernes' things that she possesses. The booty hardly passed through her hands. No sooner had she received it than she loaded it on wagons to take to Jerusalem (15:11). This is not a war for personal gain; it is a war for the liberation of God's people. After offering their gifts to God in thanksgiving at the temple, Judith and the people remain in Jerusalem to celebrate for three more months.

The material gains from victory are turned back to God. The spiritual results, the people's joy and exultation, are also returned to God in celebration. The celebration begins in Bethulia with a dance by the women in honor of Judith. Then Judith joins the dance as leader. Finally, the men, dressed in their armor, join the procession singing hymns.

The celebration is reminiscent of other victory celebrations in Israel. When Saul and David returned after David's victory over Goliath, a victory in which God acted through a youth with a slingshot who seemed powerless, the women came out to meet them, singing and dancing, with tambourines and joyful songs (1 Sam 18:6-7). The model for every deliverance, however, and for every victory celebration, is the Exodus. After Israel marched through the sea, a victory over the pursuing Egyptians in which Israel was powerless, "the prophetess Miriam took a tambourine in her hand, while all the women went out after her, dancing with tambourines, and she led all Israel in the victory song" (Exod 15:20-21). Judith's victory over Holofernes is a victory to be compared to that of David over Goliath; the deliverance of her people is comparable to the Israelites' deliverance from slavery in Egypt.

The song of Judith is a hymn built according to the basic structure of that genre. The song opens with a call to praise (16:1) and continues with the reasons for praise (16:2-12). There is a new beginning in verse 13, which is followed by additional reasons for praise (16:13b-16) and a concluding remark on the fate of the wicked (16:17).

The theme of the book is stated in verse 2: "The Lord is God; he crushes warfare" (see 9:8). The statement is a quotation from the Septuagint of Exod 15:3, the victory hymn of Miriam. Judith's song, as well as her victory, is comparable to the corresponding section in the Book of Exodus. After the announcement of a song to the Lord (Jdt 16:1; compare Exod 15:1; Jdt 16:13) and the declaration of Yahweh's power (Jdt 16:2; Exod 15:2-3), each song continues with a description of the powerful enemy and his boasting (Jdt 16:3-4; Exod 15:4-5, 9). In Exodus (15:6, 12), the right hand of the Lord shatters the enemy; in Judith, the Lord confounds the enemy by a woman's hand (16:5). Foreign nations are dismayed at the story (Exod 15:14-16; Jdt 16:10). Each song refers to the power of Yahweh's breath/wind/spirit (Exod 15:8, 10; Jdt 16:14). In the Exodus, the deliverance of the Israelite people by Yahweh when they were utterly helpless is celebrated by a hymn to Yahweh's power. Judith personifies the powerlessness of the people in the face of the Assyrian threat (Jdt 16:5-6, 11-12). The victory that Yahweh accomplishes through her is also celebrated by a hymn to Yahweh's power.

Judith's hymn may also be compared to Deborah's victory song in Judg 5. The situation is similar. In Judg 4 the hero who exhorts the people to have hope is a woman, Deborah; the deliverer who conquers the enemy by cunning is also a woman, Jael. The announcement of a new hymn to be sung to the Lord is found in both (Judg 5:3). The mountains tremble at the power of Yahweh (Judg 5:5; Jdt 16:15). In the midst of each hymn is a song of praise for the woman whose hand Yahweh used to bring deliverance (Judg 5:24-27; Jdt 16:5-9). Each song concludes by contrasting the fate of Yahweh's friends with that of Yahweh's enemies (Judg 5:31; Jdt 16:15b-17). The Book of Judges is built on the premise that Yahweh sends heroes to deliver the people when they cry out for help. The victory of Judith confirms that premise.

The hymn of Judith is called a "new song" (16:1, 13). That phrase is common in the psalms of Yahweh's kingship (see, for example, Psalms 96; 98). Those psalms share a common imagery connected to the autumn feast of Sukkoth (Booths). The references to fire, heat, earthquake, and wind suggest the fall weather pattern of the sirocco (see Pss 97:2-5; 99:1; Jdt 16:14-15, 17; compare also Isa 66:15; Joel 4:15-16). These psalms also describe the great eschatological battle of the nations (see Pss 48:5-8; 98:2; 99:1-3; Joel 4:1-2, 11-12; Isa 66:16, 24; Jdt 16:17). Yahweh has won victory, and will bring the new creation (see Pss 96:11-13; 98:7-9; Isa 66:22-23; Jdt 16:14). The people will rejoice and sing a new song to the name of Yahweh (see Pss 96:1; 98:1; Jdt 16:1, 13). Much of the imagery throughout the Book of Judith reflects the Exodus event and the feast of Passover. The Passover celebration is also suggested by the reference to Nisan (Jdt 2:1). But the siege begins after the end of the harvest (4:5; compare 2:27), a time closer to the feast of Weeks, or Pentecost. The thirty-nine days of siege (7:20, 30) and the thirty days of plundering (15:11) suggest a time for the celebration close to Sukkoth. Judith's victory would then be symbolic of Yahweh's final victory over evil, the preservation of the sanctuary, and the deliverance of the people. Later exegesis, which saw in Judith's beheading of Holofernes a symbolic defeat of the devil, would support this interpretation.

The Vulgate adds a note at the end of the chapter (16:25) concerning the feast day on which Judith's victory is celebrated. There is no such celebration known in the Jewish calendar. In Jewish folklore, however, the story of Judith has been connected with the feast of Hanukkah, the celebration of the purification of the temple at the time of the Maccabees, the time in which the book was written. Thus the Book of Judith has connections to the whole Jewish liturgical year, to Passover, Weeks, Sukkoth, and Hanukkah.

15:12–16:17 Conclusion. The rest of Judith's life is a confirmation of the Deuteronomic theory of retribution. Judith remains faithful beyond the demands of the law, both in life and in death. She honors the memory of her husband Manasseh, although taking a husband would have been acceptable. At her death she frees the maid who shared in her daring exploit and distributes her wealth to her own and her husband's relatives. In reward for her obedience to God in crisis and her fidelity throughout her life, she is prosperous, renowned, and lives to a ripe old age.

The book ends with a statement similar to the ending found in the stories of the judges: During her life and after her death, no one disturbed the Israelites (see Judg 3:11, 30; 5:31; 8:28). This section of the book is clearly reminiscent of Judges. Bagoas' discovery of Holofernes' body is like the discovery of Eglon (see Judg 3:23-25); the Israelites' faked attack is like the action of Gideon (see Judg 7:16-22). Judith herself is modeled in part on Deborah and Jael (Judg 4–5). The message of the Book of Judith is like the pattern of the stories in Judges: (1) the people are in distress; (2) they cry out to Yahweh; (3) Yahweh sends a judge to deliver them; (4) they have peace throughout the lifetime of the judge.

The people of the author's time, who suffered under Seleucid persecution, needed to hear the message of the Book of Judith. The message remains pertinent for us, who face powers of evil beyond our strength. The story of Judith teaches us that the power of God can bring victory even through the most vulnerable. Judith's example exhorts God's people to persevere in hope. Uzziah proclaims: "Blessed are you, Judith, by the Most High God, above all the women on earth . . . . Your deed of hope will never be forgotten by those who tell of the might of God." And all the people answer "Amen! Amen!"

THE
NEW TESTAMENT

MATTHEW

Daniel J. Harrington, S.J.

INTRODUCTION

Tradition and newness in tension

Matthew's Gospel has a strongly Jewish flavor. Its special concerns are to place Jesus of Nazareth within the traditions of God's chosen people and to show how this same Jesus burst the bonds of those traditions and brought them to fulfillment. From beginning to end, there is a tension between tradition and newness. Neither pole of the tension is rejected. The interplay between the two generates life and fresh insights.

Matthew takes pains to point out how this or that event in Jesus' life fulfills the prophecies of the Old Testament. All through the account of the passion and death, he assures us that those terrible events conform to God's will as expressed in the Old Testament. Nevertheless, at certain points (see 5:21-48) Jesus seems to contradict or abolish some precepts of the law. He can do so because, as the Son of God, he is the authoritative interpreter of the Jewish tradition.

The identity of Jesus is expressed in terms that have rich Old Testament backgrounds. Jesus is the Son of David, the Messiah or Christ, Wisdom, and so forth. All these titles express aspects of Jesus' identity, but no one of them alone is an adequate description of him. The two most prominent terms are Son of Man and Son of God. The former title reflects Jesus' way of referring to himself and probably has some connection with the heavenly figure of Dan 7. The latter title could be used in the Old Testament with reference to the king (see Pss 2 and 110). When applied to Jesus, however, these titles take on new meaning and go far beyond whatever content may be attributed to them in the Old Testament.

The identity of God's people is also worked out in the tension between tradition and newness. Matthew has no doubt that Israel is God's people, and so a major thrust of his Gospel is to show the continuity between Israel of old and the new thing that God has done in Christ. But after the coming of Jesus, who are God's people and who inherits the kingdom of God? Matthew's answer is simple and straightforward: Those who follow Jesus are God's people. Attachment to Jesus the Jew makes membership in God's people possible even for those who are not Jewish by birth (see 21:41, 43). Those Jews who do not accept this new definition of God's people are said to belong to "their synagogues" (see 4:23; 9:35; 10:17; 12:9; 13:54), which are also called the synagogues of the hypocrites (6:2; 23:6, 34).

Sources and structure

When the person whom we call Matthew determined to write about Jesus, he decided to write a Gospel—a literary form something like a biography. Though surely not a biography in the nineteenth- or twentieth-century use of the term, Matthew's Gospel does follow the story of Jesus of Nazareth from his birth, through his public activity as a preacher and a healer, up to his death and resurrection. Matthew could have written a long letter or a poem or a chronological report of the events in Jesus' life; instead, he chose to write a narrative about Jesus. His Gospel is a collection of stories that portray Jesus as a powerful and living person. By means of these vivid stories we are invited to become part of the story of Jesus, the Son of Man and the Son of God.

Matthew did not compose the Gospel entirely out of his own imagination and experience. He appears to have had at his disposal several written sources. In chapters 3–4 and 12–28 he drew heavily on Mark's Gospel. Mark wrote before Matthew did, and so it is fair to call Matthew's Gospel a revised and greatly expanded version of Mark's Gospel. Furthermore, in about two hundred verses Matthew and Luke are so much alike that it is reasonable to assume that both evangelists made independent use of a common source. This source was a collection of Jesus' sayings that circulated in Greek in the fifties of the first century A.D. This source used by Matthew and Luke is usually designated by the letter Q (from the German word for "source," *Quelle*). Finally, Matthew had access to sayings and stories that no other evangelist had. This material peculiar to Matthew's Gospel is often designated by the letter M.

The fact that Matthew depended very much on existing material indicates that his story of Jesus is deliberately traditional. But in addition to handing on the traditions about Jesus, Matthew also interpreted these traditions in order to bring out certain aspects and to speak to certain problems that the Christian community of his time faced. Perhaps his most original literary contribution was the general structure that he imposed on the story of Jesus. Since Matthew was telling the story of Jesus, he was clearly obligated to follow the pattern provided by the life of Jesus. Since he had access to Mark's Gospel, he could not disregard entirely the outline of Jesus' life provided by it. Q was simply a collection of sayings, and so the evangelist had more freedom in using it.

What structure does Matthew's story of Jesus take? The most obvious features are the beginning and end of the Gospel. Mark's story of Jesus began with Jesus' adult years, but Matthew in chapters 1–2 goes back to his birth and infancy. Mark's story ends with the death of Jesus and the discovery of the empty tomb in Jerusalem. Matthew in chapters 26–28 follows Mark very closely, but he adds the story of Jesus' appearance to the eleven disciples in Galilee (28:16-20). Between chapters 1–2 and 26–28, Matthew presents five major speeches by Jesus: the Sermon on the Mount (chs. 5–7), the missionary discourse (ch. 10), the parables discourse (ch. 13), the advice to a divided community (ch. 18), and the eschatological discourse (chs. 24–25). We must not assume that these five speeches are exact transcriptions of sermons given by Jesus on five occasions; rather, everything about them indicates that Matthew has constructed the speeches out of traditional materials and imposed upon them their present literary structures. Matthew was obviously very interested in Jesus' teaching and went to great lengths to highlight it.

The five speeches of Jesus are an important structural principle in the Gospel, and they are separated from one another by large blocks of narrative material. When we look at the Gospel as a whole, the following general outline emerges:

1:1–2:23	The genealogy and itinerary of Jesus
3:1–4:25	The beginning of Jesus' ministry
5:1–7:29	The Sermon on the Mount
8:1–9:38	The powerful deeds of Jesus
10:1–42	The missionary discourse
11:1–12:50	The importance of Jesus and the rejection of him
13:1-53	The parables concerning the kingdom of God
13:54–16:4	Miracles and controversies
16:5–17:27	The way to the cross
18:1-35	Advice to a divided community
19:1–23:39	Growing opposition to Jesus
24:1–25:46	The coming of the kingdom
26:1–28:20	The death and resurrection of Jesus

Authorship and historical setting

Originality of authorship was not an important value in the culture in which the Gospel of Matthew was written. The title "According to Matthew" was most likely not part of the first edition of the text, and no explicit claim is made in the Gospel that its author was an eyewitness to the events described in it. The Gospel is basically an anonymous composition. But calling the Gospel "anonymous" does not mean that we know nothing about the author. The evangelist was a Christian who was well versed in Jewish methods of teaching, living in Syria or some other area in which Jewish influence was strong, around A.D. 85. He sought to show that those who acknowledge Jesus as the Messiah will inherit the kingdom of God.

The traditional ascription of the Gospel to Matthew the tax collector (see 9:9) who became an apostle (see 10:3) generates more problems than it solves. Why is the same tax collector named Levi, the son of Alphaeus, in Mark 2:14? How did a tax collector, living on the fringes of Jewish religious life, produce such a religiously sophisticated Gospel? Why did an eyewitness depend on written sources like Mark and Q, and never put forward the claim that he saw this or that take place? Perhaps the church for which the Gospel was written took the apostle Matthew as its "patron saint." Or perhaps the apostle Matthew was responsible for some of the special material (M) in the Gospel.

The tradition of the existence of an Aramaic or Hebrew version of Matthew also generates more problems than it solves. The church historian Eusebius quotes the early Christian writer Papias to the effect that Matthew collected the "oracles" in the Hebrew languages and then others translated or interpreted them. Does this statement refer to the completed Gospel, or to the Old Testament quotations used in it, or to the sayings of Jesus? Why does Papias say Hebrew, when Jesus spoke Aramaic? Did Papias have any special reasons for placing Matthew's Gospel before Mark's? All these questions indicate that the ascription to Matthew the apostle and the tradition of an Aramaic or Hebrew version of Matthew involve too many problems for us to place much reliance on them in interpreting the Gospel.

Matthew's Gospel was put into final form around A.D. 85, perhaps in Antioch of Syria. That means that the Christian community had existed for about fifty years since Jesus' death, and about fifteen years since the Jerusalem temple had been destroyed in A.D. 70. This dating is based to a large extent on what appears to be a partial description of the events of A.D. 70 in 22:7: "The king was enraged and sent his troops, destroyed those murderers, and burned their city." Other possible allusions to the destruction of Jerusalem occur in 21:41 and 27:25.

The Matthean community was a mixed group, but the majority apparently were Jewish Christians. By A.D. 85 it had become clear that not all Israel was going to accept Jesus as the Messiah of Jewish expectations and that non-Jews represented a very promising missionary field (see 28:19). Matthew was encouraging a largely Jewish-Christian community to recognize itself as the legitimate heir of God's promises to Israel. He also wished them to broaden their missionary horizons to include the Gentiles. Antioch in Syria would have been an appropriate location, but there is no absolute certainty on this matter.

This commentary

The following commentary on the Gospel of Matthew aims to explain clearly and simply what the evangelist whom we call Matthew was trying to say to his first readers. It pays particular attention to the literary structures and the theological concerns of the passages. Since the readers of this commentary live in a world that differs greatly from that of the original readers of the Gospel, historical information and explanations about cultural presuppositions are also supplied. The goal of the expositions is to allow twentieth-century readers to share more deeply in the excitement that the Gospel of Matthew must have inspired among its first readers.

COMMENTARY

I. THE GENEALOGY AND ITINERARY OF JESUS

Matt 1:1–2:23

1:1-17 The genealogy of Jesus the Messiah (see Luke 3:23-38). The genealogy at the beginning of the Gospel establishes Jesus' place within the Jewish tradition. Jesus is the son of Abraham and of David as well as the continuation of David's line after the exile of 587 B.C.E. The names in the genealogy up to Abiud in verse 13 are found in the Old Testament, and here they are arranged in three sets of fourteen names each (v. 17). Israel's history is traced from its beginning with Abraham (v. 2), through its high point with King David (v. 6) and its low point in the Babylonian Exile (v. 11), to its fulfillment in Jesus the Messiah (v. 16). Luke emphasizes Jesus' universal significance by tracing his lineage back from Joseph to Adam (see Luke 3:23-38), but Matthew is concerned with rooting Jesus of Nazareth in the heritage of God's chosen people, Israel.

The literary flow of the genealogy is disturbed by the inclusion of the names of four women. Not only is the occurrence of women's names in a Jewish genealogy unusual, but what is known about them from the Old Testament makes their appearance all the more surprising. Tamar (v. 3) disguised herself as a prostitute and conceived her sons by Judah, her father-in-law (see Gen 38). Rahab (v. 5) was a prostitute of Jericho whose life was spared on account of her collaboration with Joshua's spies (see Josh 2; 6). The tradition that she was the mother of Boaz is found only in Matthew's Gospel. Ruth (v. 5) was a Moabite who joined herself to Israel through her husband's family (see Ruth). The "wife of Uriah" (v. 6) was Bathsheba; King David shamefully arranged her husband's death in battle and took her as a wife (2 Sam 11).

The appearance of these four unusual women in the genealogy of the Messiah prepares for the surprising birth of Jesus in verses 18-25. Just as their inclusion breaks the genealogical pattern of "A became the father of B" and just as what is known about them from the Scriptures indicates some kind of irregularity, so the birth of Jesus breaks the traditional pattern (v. 16) and is highly irregular. Thus, the genealogy of Jesus in Matt 1:1-17 goes in two directions: It stresses the continuity of Jesus with the great figures of God's people ("son of Abraham . . . son of David"), and it also prepares for the very irregular and indeed unique birth narrated in the following passage.

1:18-25 The birth of Jesus (see Luke 2:1-7). The story of Jesus' birth is really an extension of the genealogy. Its primary concern is Jesus' right to a place in the messianic genealogy through Joseph, and its climax comes in Joseph's resolve to make Jesus a Davidic child by assuming the legal obligations of paternity. The tension between continuity with the Jewish tradition (legal paternity through Joseph) and the sharp break with tradition (the miraculous conception of Jesus) develops the basic theme already raised in the genealogy.

Engagement or betrothal in Jewish society of Jesus' time involved a much stronger commitment than it does in modern Western society. The description of Joseph's embarrassment and his plans in verses 18-19 may presume his suspicion that Mary had been raped or seduced. As a devout observer of the Old Testament law, Joseph could not take Mary as his wife (see Deut 22:23-27). Not wishing to subject Mary to the shameful trial of the woman suspected of adultery (Num 5:11-31), he decided to forgo the public procedure and took upon himself the responsibility for the divorce. Divorce proceedings were carried out, not in a law court, but rather on the initiative of the male (see Deut 24:1).

Joseph's plans are interrupted in verses 20-23 by the appearance of a messenger from God in a dream—a device familiar from the Old Testament account of the birth of Samson (Judg 13). The angel's message assumes the virginal conception of Jesus by the Holy Spirit and concentrates on the names of the Messiah. As the legal son of Joseph, Jesus will be named the "Son of David" (v. 20). His given name is Jesus, which is related to the Hebrew verb for "save." This name is entirely appropriate because, in Matthew's perspective and in the faith of all the early Christians, Jesus saved the people of God from their sins. The third name applied to Jesus appears in the citation from Isa 7:14: "and they shall name him Emmanuel." As a sign to King Ahaz and his royal court, the prophet Isaiah had announced that a certain woman would bear a son. The early Christians took the Greek translation of "young woman" as "virgin" to confirm their belief in the virginal conception of Jesus. But Matthew may have been more interested in the child's name "Emmanuel." In Hebrew, "Emmanuel" means "God with us," and this expresses the significance of Jesus for Matthew and the early church. A similar note is struck in the final verse of the Gospel: "And behold, I am with you always, until the end of the age" (28:20).

The dream allayed Joseph's fears. Not only had Mary not been raped or seduced, but this child has been conceived by the Holy Spirit and deserves the names Son of David, Jesus, and Emmanuel. Joseph acts in accordance with the divine communication and takes Mary to be his wife (v. 24). The statement in verse 25 that he did not have sexual relations with her before the birth of Jesus neither affirms nor denies the perpetual virginity of Mary.

The whole of Matt 1:1-25 serves both to situate Jesus firmly within God's people and to call attention to his extraordinary status. On the one hand, he is the descendant of Abraham and David and the fulfillment of the promises and hopes attached to those great Old Testament figures. On the other hand, the mode of his birth is highly unusual, and the names given to him—Jesus and Emmanuel—suggest that he far surpasses any of his ancestors.

2:1-12 Wise men worship Jesus at Bethlehem. Each of the four episodes in chapter 2 revolves around a place name: Bethlehem, Egypt, Ramah, and Nazareth. Jesus was known as a Galilean (see John 7:41-42) from the town of Nazareth. The four scenes in the chapter explain how Jesus the Son of David was born in Bethlehem, how he was taken to Egypt in order to avoid the threat of death, why he did not return to Bethlehem, and how Nazareth came to be his home. Each episode includes an Old Testament quotation that contains the name of a place. This appeal to the Old Testament indicates that the Messiah's itinerary was guided by the will of God.

After situating the place of Jesus' birth in Bethlehem and its date late in the reign of King Herod the Great (37–4 B.C.E.), the first episode introduces wise men from the East who possess astronomical and astrological knowledge. The "star" that they observed may have been the conjunction of the planets Jupiter and Saturn. There may also be a reference to speculations based on Num 24:17 ("A star shall advance from Jacob") that connected the Messiah's birth with the appearance of a star.

Efforts at identifying the star should not divert attention from the more central concerns of the passage. The threefold occurrence of "do him homage" in verses 2, 8, 11 expresses the basic theme, and the contrast between the Magi and Herod (and those on his side) is developed in the course of the story.

In response to the imperfect revelation given in the star, the Gentile wise men come to worship Jesus. But they need to learn from the Jewish Scriptures that the Messiah is to be born in Bethlehem (vv. 5-6). They proceed to Bethlehem and worship the infant Messiah. From the three kinds of gifts listed in verse 11, the tradition of *three* wise men developed in the fifth century; in the eighth century the three were given names.

The faith of the Gentile wise men stands in contrast to the cynical cunning of Herod. As an Idumean whose Judaism was suspect, Herod would naturally fear all Jewish messianic movements as threats to his political power. Even though he had access to the Scriptures and could see plainly what the prophet Micah (see Mic 5:1; 2 Sam 5:2) had said about the place of the Messiah's birth, Herod was not willing to worship the newborn king. The episode of the wise men reflects the early church's experience of the Gentiles' readiness to accept the gospel and the disappointing slowness of all Israel to receive it. It also prepares for the recognition of Jesus as King of the Jews (Matt 27:11, 29, 37) and for the universal mission of the disciples (Matt 8:11-12; 28:18-20).

2:13-15 The flight into Egypt. The structure of the story of the flight into Egypt is similar to that of the birth story in 1:18-25. It consists of the angel's appearance to Joseph in a dream, a command and the reason for the command, Joseph's determination to carry out the command, and a quotation from the Old Testament.

Egypt was a common place of refuge for Jews of this time, and only after the death of Herod in 4 B.C.E. was it safe for Jesus to return to Palestine. The quotation from Hos 11:1 ("Out of Egypt I called my son") places this part of the Messiah's itinerary within the framework of God's will. It not only identifies Jesus as the Son of God, but it also suggests that he is the personification of the people of God. Just as God called Israel of old out of Egypt in order to create a special people for himself, so he calls Jesus out of Egypt into the land of Israel in order to create a new people (see Matt 21:41, 43). The principle of continuity between the old people and the new people is Jesus the Jew.

2:16-18 The slaughter of children in Judea. Although the slaughter of innocent male children two years and under is consistent with Herod's ruthlessness in defending his throne during the last years of his reign, there is no record of this event in any ancient source outside of Matthew's Gospel. The quotation from Jer 31:15 focuses on Ramah, a place about five miles north of Jerusalem. Ramah was the place where Rachel, the wife of Jacob, died; it was also the place where the Jews in the sixth century B.C.E. gathered for their march into the Babylonian exile.

Herod's savage action is a repetition of Pharaoh's slaughter of the Israelite children in Egypt (Exod 1:15-22). Indeed, this episode and the preceding ones seem to suppose a reversal of the Exodus story: Jesus is taken to Egypt for his own safety, and the king of Jerusalem represents unbelief and hardness of heart. Herod acts as the enemy of God's people represented by the newborn Messiah. The Old Testament passage explains Herod's action as consistent with God's will but does not condone or justify it.

2:19-23 Jesus' arrival in Nazareth. After Herod's death in 4 B.C.E., his kingdom was divided among his sons. Archelaus ruled Judea, Samaria, and Idumea from 4 B.C.E. to A.D. 6. The story of how Jesus got to Nazareth follows a now familiar pattern: the angel's appearance to Joseph in a dream, a command and the reason for it (see Exod 4:19), Joseph's determination to carry out the command, and a quotation from the Old Testament. The precise source of the quotation is not certain; the texts most often cited as possible sources are Judg 13:5, 7 and Isa 11:1. At any rate, the episode explains why Jesus was connected with Nazareth and why he began his public ministry in Galilee.

The tension between the continuity with the Jewish tradition and the new act of God in Jesus that was so prominent in Matt 1:1-25 also emerges in chapter 2. Each point in the Messiah's itinerary is grounded in a quotation from the Old Testament, and the individual episodes contain phrases and characters reminiscent of certain biblical passages. On the other hand, the Gentile wise men come to worship the newborn king of the Jews while Herod does everything in his power to destroy him. The future of the people of God seems to rest with Jesus of Nazareth—the Son of God who has been called from Egypt to live and work and die in the land of God's own people.

II. THE BEGINNING OF JESUS' MINISTRY

Matt 3:1–4:25

3:1-12 John's preparation for Jesus (see Mark 1:2-8; Luke 3:1-18; John 1:19-28). In the summary of the preaching of John the Baptist, material from the Markan and the Q sources has been used. Matthew's most important contribution comes at the very beginning (v. 2), where John's preaching is summarized in exactly the same words as Jesus' preaching is summarized in 4:17: "Repent, for the kingdom of heaven is at hand." Both preachers demand a radical conversion of the whole person to God, and both urge it as preparation for the new age when the God of Israel will be acknowledged as the Lord by all creation. That time is very close at hand.

The first part of the material about John the Baptist (vv. 1-6) makes John's activity a part of the momentous and eventful time of Jesus ("in those days") and locates him in the wilderness of Judea—the area in which the community that has given us the Dead Sea scrolls had its center. The relation of John to Jesus is explained by the quotation from Isa 40:3: John's preaching in the wilderness prepares the way for Jesus. The description of John's haircloth and belt in verse 4 reminds the reader of the prophet Elijah's clothing as described in 2 Kgs 1:8. John cultivates the prophet's lifestyle and can be aptly described as the new Elijah (see Matt 11:14; 17:11-13). The Jewish historian Josephus (*Antiquities* 18:116-119) confirms that John drew large crowds for his exhortations to justice and piety. He describes John's ritual of baptism as a symbolic action signifying that conversion of heart had taken place.

In verses 7-10 John's preaching is directed to members of two Jewish groups ("the Pharisees and Sadducees") that will furnish unbelieving opposition to Jesus throughout the Gospel. They are warned to reform their lives as a preparation for the decisive intervention of God ("the coming wrath"). They are warned not to rely on their Jewish descent ("Abraham as our father") to protect them. The references to "children" and "stones" probably reflect a play on two very similar Aramaic (or Hebrew) words. Finally, they are warned that the time is short ("the ax lies at the root"). In the coming time of judgment prior to the fullness of God's kingdom, it is the fruit of good deeds that will count. John's stress on repentance, action now, and "bearing fruit" in good deeds foreshadows Jesus' instructions to his own disciples.

The second sample of John's preaching (vv. 11-12) subordinates John to Jesus. In this context "the one who is coming after me" must be Jesus. In verse 11 John protests that he is not even worthy to act as the slave of Jesus by carrying his sandals, and he contrasts his own symbolic water-baptism with the immersion in the Holy Spirit and the refining fire of judgment that will complete Jesus' proclamation of God's kingdom. The traditional image of the last judgment as a harvest is used in verse 12. The judgment will separate the good ("wheat") from the bad ("chaff"); it is very near.

Whatever the historical relationship may have been between John the Baptist and Jesus (and their followers), Matthew and the other New Testament writers took care to draw John into the circle of Jesus' influence and to subordinate him to Jesus. Far from contradicting Jesus, John preaches precisely the same things: conversion of heart, the coming of God's kingdom, and bearing fruit in good deeds. Far from engaging in a rivalry with Jesus, John makes it clear from the start how much the person and baptism of Jesus surpassed him and his baptism. John the Baptist emerges as a faithful "Christian" preacher! His warnings have relevance not only to the Pharisees and Sadducees but also to Christians.

3:13-17 The baptism of Jesus (see Mark 1:9-11; Luke 3:21-22). That Jesus was baptized by John is undoubtedly a historical fact. According to the Gospel accounts, Jesus received from John a baptism connected with the forgiveness of sins. It is inconceivable that the early Christians, who held Jesus in such high esteem, would have invented a story in which Jesus received something from John and that this reception would involve the baptism of repentance (see Matt 3:2, 6, 8, 11).

Indeed, the early church's embarrassment at Jesus' having been baptized by John is reflected in the dialogue found only in Matt 3:14-15. John demonstrates his humility and reveals his prophetic insight that Jesus is the "one to come." Jesus' first words in the Gospel are a request that he be baptized by John because this is in accord with God's will; it must be done in order to fulfill the divine plan. Thus Matthew explains how Jesus the sinless one could have received a baptism of repentance.

Jesus' emergence from the waters of the Jordan (vv. 16-17) is accompanied by several extraordinary, supernatural phenomena with long and rich Old Testament backgrounds. With the opening of the sky, the separation between heaven and earth is broken through (see Ezek 1:1; Isa 64:1). The descent of the Holy Spirit "like a dove" recalls the activity of the Spirit of God in the creation (see Gen 1:2). The voice from heaven describes Jesus in phrases taken from various Old Testament passages (Gen 22:2; Ps 2:7; Isa 42:1). The story reaches its climax in the identification of Jesus as the Son of God.

The theories that the events following the baptism occurred as a private vision granted to Jesus and that only then did Jesus become conscious of his divine sonship have no foundation in Matthew's account. The public character of the signs in verses 16-17 and the message referring to Jesus in the third person ("This is . . .") leave no doubt that, for Matthew, these events could have been experienced by onlookers. Matthew's primary concern is to show that at the very beginning of Jesus' public ministry he is publicly acknowledged as the Son of God. This in turn makes clear the significance of everything that Jesus will do in the course of that ministry. His is the ministry of God's own Son. A new age under the power of God has begun, and in it all the plans of God will be fulfilled.

4:1-11 The testing of God's Son (see Mark 1:12-13; Luke 4:1-13). The theme of Jesus as the Son of God that is so prominent in the baptism account is developed in the story of the temptation. The passage is best entitled the "testing of God's Son," because the first two tests are introduced by the phrase "if you are the Son of God." The tests and Jesus' responses to them show what kind of Messiah and Son of God he really is. The setting in the desert (v. 1) and the use of the number "forty" (v. 2) suggest a contrast between ancient Israel and Jesus. During its wandering in the wilderness after the escape from Egypt, ancient Israel was tested and found wanting. Where ancient Israel failed, Jesus now triumphs.

Mark's narrative of the testing of Jesus (Mark 1:12-13) contains only two verses, but Matt 4:1-11 and Luke 4:1-13 provide a lengthy debate in which the devil presents three tests and Jesus answers with three quotations from the Book of Deuteronomy. After forty days and nights of fasting, Jesus would be very hungry. So the first test (vv. 3-4) is the temptation to change stones into bread in order to feed himself. Jesus takes his reply from Deut 8:3: The Son of God is fed by the word of God, not by bread alone.

The second test (vv. 5-7) involves Jesus' being taken up to the highest point on the wall surrounding the Jerusalem temple. There he is tempted to throw himself down and call on God for aid, thus fulfilling Ps 91:11-12. Jesus takes his reply this time from Deut 6:16: The Son of God does not put his Father to such foolish and magical tests.

The third test (vv. 7-10) promises all the kingdoms of the world to Jesus if he will offer worship to the devil. Jesus' reply is taken from Deut 6:13: The Son of God offers worship only to his heavenly Father.

What kind of a Son of God is Jesus? His conduct during the three tests makes it clear that he does not seek to satisfy his own material needs, to make a miraculous display of his status and power, or to enter into partnership with the devil for the sake of political authority. Jesus emerges as totally obedient to the will of his Father, especially as that will is expressed in the words of the Old Testament Scriptures. His attitude provides a model for Christians who may be tempted to pay too much attention to material goods, to provoke God, or to seek influence and wealth without regard for justice and morality. Having personally withstood the assaults of Satan on these matters, Jesus is able to free others from their tyranny.

4:12-17 Preaching God's kingdom (see Mark 1:14-15; Luke 4:14-15). After being identified publicly as the Son of God in the baptism account (3:13-17) and after proving what kind of Son of God he is (4:1-11), Jesus journeys from Judea to Galilee in order to begin his public ministry (4:12-17). Unlike Mark (see Mark 1:14-15), Matthew feels obligated to explain in some detail why the Messiah should exercise his ministry in Galilee rather than in Jerusalem and Judea. John's arrest by Herod Antipas (a son of Herod the Great) and the danger that spelled for Jesus were not sufficient reasons for this move. As was the case in Matt 2:1-23, geography is explained in light of the Scriptures: Jesus' Galilean ministry is in accord with the words of Isa 9:1-2, and thus in accord with God's will.

The substance of Jesus' preaching is summarized in Matt 4:17: "Repent, for the kingdom of heaven is at hand." The same message was attributed to John the Baptist in 3:2. The first part of the message contains the command calling for a complete conversion and reorientation of life. The second part supplies the reason for the command: The definitive display of God's power and judgment and the establishment of his rule over all creation are near. In fact, as we will see, the ultimate victory of God is being inaugurated in the ministry of his Son.

4:18-22 The call of four fishermen (see Mark 1:16-20; Luke 5:1-11). Matthew's story of the call of the first disciples is very similar to Mark 1:16-20. In the overall plan of Matthew's Gospel, it introduces three of the disciples who will form Jesus' inner circle among the Twelve: Peter, James, and John. It also prepares for the presence of the disciples at the Sermon on the Mount (5:1) and for the promise to Peter (16:17-19). Jewish teachers did not usually call their own disciples; rather, prospective disciples sought out a teacher with a good reputation for learning and holiness. This account emphasizes the extraordinary attractiveness and magnetism of Jesus.

The first disciples encountered Jesus in their everyday occupation of fishing in the Sea of Galilee—then as now, an important and profitable business in Israel's economy. Without any preparation and with little or no deliberation, they leave behind their business and their families in order to follow Jesus. Discipleship is first and foremost being with Jesus, and the quick response of the first disciples ("at once" according to verses 20, 22) suggests how appealing the invitation to be with Jesus must have been. But discipleship also involves sharing in the mission of Jesus ("fishers of men" according to verse 19), and that dimension too is stressed from the very beginning.

4:23-25 A summary of Jesus' activities (see Mark 1:39; Luke 4:44). Almost every word in the summary of Jesus' preaching, teaching, and healing activities is found in some passage in Mark (see Mark 1:39; 1:28; 3:10; 3:7-8). Although Jesus' activity is confined to the region of Galilee, word of it spreads to the whole province of Syria. The outward movement of Jesus' reputation as a teacher and healer results in the movement of many people toward him. People suffering from all kinds of diseases are brought to him, and they are cured (v. 24). People from every region of Israel except Samaria join the crowds that follow him (v. 25). Such people, along with the disciples, form the audience for the Sermon on the Mount (see 5:1; 7:28).

By way of preparation for the Sermon on the Mount, Matthew has established Jesus' superiority to John the Baptist (3:1-12), recounted the divine acknowledgement of Jesus as the Son of God (3:13-17), and shown what kind of Son of God Jesus is (4:1-11). He has also explained why Jesus taught and healed in Galilee (4:12-17) and how he attracted an inner circle of disciples (4:18-22) and a larger circle of interested followers (4:23-25). The Sermon on the Mount (5:1–7:29) will reveal what a powerful teacher Jesus is.

III. THE SERMON ON THE MOUNT

Matt 5:1–7:29

The Sermon on the Mount is the first of Jesus' five major speeches in the Gospel. It is obviously related to the Sermon on the Plain in Luke 6:20-49 but is more than three times as long. Matthew has gathered together traditional sayings and shaped them into an epitome of Jesus' teaching. The basic thesis of the Sermon is stated in 5:20: "Unless your righteousness surpasses that of the scribes and Pharisees, you will not enter into the kingdom of God."

The introductory section (5:1-20) describes those who are blessed (5:3-12), the role of the disciples (5:13-16), and the role of Jesus (5:17-19). The second major section (5:21-48) contrasts the holiness or righteousness of the experts in the interpretation of the Old Testament law ("the scribes") and the better holiness or righteousness taught by Jesus. The third section (6:1-18) warns against the purely external holiness cultivated by groups like the Pharisees, and the fourth section (6:19–7:29) furnishes more advice for Christians in their pursuit of holiness.

The teachings contained in the Sermon on the Mount have been interpreted in many different ways: principles of Christian ethics, counsels of perfection, ideals that are impossible to practice, and so forth. For Matthew, these teachings are the directives of Jesus the Messiah and Son of God, whose authority far surpasses that of every other teacher (see 7:29). They are presented as a sample of Jesus' basic demands made on his disciples and as an expression of Christian values. They presuppose the personal experience of Jesus and the good news of God's coming kingdom, and thus they offer practical advice on how to respond to Jesus and his preaching.

5:1-2 The setting. The site for the Sermon is a mountainside, presumably in Galilee. In the Bible and in other religious literatures, the mountain is frequently a privileged place for revelations of or from God. The fact that Jesus' first extensive block of teaching is set on a mountainside gives it special importance. The audience for the Sermon has already been introduced. It certainly contains the disciples chosen by Jesus (4:18-22). It also includes some of the crowd (4:23-25), as both the beginning (5:1) and the end (7:28) of the Sermon indicate. The Sermon is intended for a wider audience than the inner circle of Jesus' followers.

5:3-12 The beatitudes (see Luke 6:20-23). The beatitudes declare "blessed" or "happy" some surprising people. The beatitude is a literary form common in the Old Testament book of Psalms. There persons or groups are declared to be blessed or happy (see Pss 1:1; 32:1-2; 41:1; 65:4; 84:4-5; 106:3; 112:1;

128:1), and sometimes the reason for the declaration is supplied. The Matthean beatitudes differ from the Old Testament models in their references to the coming kingdom of God and to the reversal of human values that accompanies it. The four beatitudes in Luke 6:20-23 are commonly thought to reflect the form ("Blessed are you . . .") and the content (blessings on the poor, the hungry, the weeping, and the persecuted) of Jesus' preaching more closely than the Matthean beatitudes do. Matthew's version tends to spiritualize ("poor in spirit" . . . "hunger and thirst for righteousness") and contains further beatitudes that do not add appreciably to the content of Luke's version.

The first set of beatitudes (vv. 3-6) proclaims as happy the poor in spirit (those whose condition demands total trust in God), the sorrowing (see Isa 61:2-3), the meek (see Ps 37:11), and those who hunger and thirst for righteousness (those whose central task in life is the fulfillment of God's will). Their happiness is largely future, but it also extends into the present time. By living out the values of the kingdom of heaven here and now, they anticipate and share the happiness that a fuller form of life with God will bring. God is the source of all their happiness.

The second set of beatitudes (vv. 7-10) also climaxes with a reference to righteousness, just as the first set did (see v. 6). Here a blessing is pronounced upon the merciful, the honest (see Ps 24:3-4), the agents of peace, and those who suffer on account of their search for righteousness. They too are promised future happiness from God. The final beatitude in verses 11-12 (see Luke 6:22-23) develops the theme of persecution for the sake of Jesus and relates this to the persecution suffered by certain Old Testament prophets.

5:13-16 The role of the disciples (see Mark 9:50; Luke 14:34-35). The role of the followers of Jesus is expressed by the images of salt and light. In Jesus' time, salt was used not only to improve the taste of food but also to preserve meat and fish. When Jesus compares his followers to salt (v. 13), he says that they improve the quality of human existence and preserve it from destruction. In Jesus' time, the only lamps available were small dish-like devices in which oil was burned. By our standards these lamps did not give off much light, but in the time before electricity their light must have seemed very bright. When Jesus calls his disciples the light of the world (vv. 14-15), he says that their actions serve as a beacon of light in a dark world. The disciples are challenged to let their light shine (v. 16) as a witness to their fidelity to Jesus and his heavenly Father.

5:17-20 The role of Jesus. The role of Jesus is treated with reference to the Old Testament, or rather, the Old Testament is treated with reference to Jesus. Jesus came to reveal the true meaning of the Old Testament, to express what the law and the prophets wished to say, and thus to bring it to fulfillment (v. 17). The saying in verse 18 appeals to the Jewish idea that the law is eternal, or at least that it remains in force "until all things have taken place" (the fullness of God's kingdom, or perhaps the death and resurrection of Jesus). In its context in the Sermon on the Mount, "these commandments" in the third saying (v. 19) may refer to Jesus' own instructions rather than to the precepts of the Old Testament. Jesus appears as the authoritative interpreter of the Jewish tradition, the one who is able to bring to light its most profound aspects. The final saying (v. 20) demands that Jesus' disciples surpass the scribes and Pharisees in seeking righteousness; otherwise they cannot enter God's kingdom. This saying states the basic thesis of the entire Sermon and gives structure to the various sayings contained in the three remaining sections.

5:21-26 Murder and anger. The second part of the Sermon (5:21-48) contrasts the scribes' ideal of holiness based on the literal reading of Scripture and Jesus' more radical and demanding teaching. This contrast is carried out by means of six antitheses in which the words of the Old Testament ("You have heard") are placed beside the sayings of Jesus ("But I say to you"). The antitheses illustrate how Jesus came to "fulfill" the law and the prophets by explaining the meaning of the Old Testament commandments at their deepest levels. In some cases, the biblical precept is extended in order to get at the root disposition beneath the forbidden action. In other cases, the precept itself is pushed so far as to be effectively repealed or superseded. Sayings on topics having some connection with the subject matter of the six antitheses are also included.

The first antithesis (vv. 21-26) concerns the prohibition against murder (Exod 20:13; Deut 5:17). Jesus' followers cannot be satisfied with merely avoiding the act of murder but must also curb the anger and the insults that lead to murder. The three courts or places of judgment mentioned in verse 22 (judgment or the local court, the Sanhedrin, the fiery Gehenna) would normally be connected with trying a case of murder, but here they are related to anger. The point is that anger should be taken as seriously as murder is. Two illustrations of putting away anger and being reconciled to others are provided in verses 23-26. The first instance (vv. 23-24) suggests that reconciliation may even take precedence over participating in worship at the temple, and the second instance (vv. 25-26) warns against letting a dispute go so far as to end up in court, where the judgment could go against one.

5:27-30 Adultery and lust. The second antithesis demands that lust as the root cause of adultery (Exod 20:14; Deut 5:18) be avoided. The mention of the lustful look in verse 28 is developed by means of the sayings about the right eye (v. 29) and the right hand (v. 30) being occasions of sin (see Matt 18:8-9). The salvation of the whole person is of more value than the preservation of any one part that may lead to sin.

5:31-32 Divorce. The antithesis concerning divorce seems to repeal or reject the permission and procedure found in Deut 24:1. According to Jesus, divorce is not allowed (see Luke 16:18; 1 Cor 7:10-11; Mark 10:2-12; Matt 19:3-12). The Matthean versions of Jesus' teachings on divorce include some kind of exception: "unless the marriage is unlawful" (5:32; 19:9). The Greek word is *porneia,* which refers to some sort of sexual misconduct or irregularity. In Acts 15:20, 29 *porneia* has to do with marriages contracted within the degrees of kinship forbidden by Lev 18:6-18, and thus technically incestuous unions. These exceptive clauses were probably intended to deal with members of the Matthean community who were already in such irregular marriages before they became Christians.

5:33-37 Oaths. The antithesis regarding oaths also seems to go so far beyond the Old Testament prohibition against swearing falsely (Lev 19:12; Num 30:2; Deut 23:21) as to do away with it entirely. At a time when oaths and vows were proliferating in Judaism, Jesus recommends that his disciples simply be honest and straightforward in their speech. No human being has control or ownership of the heavens, the earth, or Jerusalem. Only God does. We cannot even control our own bodies completely. Therefore, no one has the right to make an oath based on such things as witnesses.

5:38-42 Retaliation (see Luke 6:29-30). In the fifth antithesis the Old Testament law of retaliation (Exod 21:23-24; Lev 24:19-20; Deut 19:21) is also pushed to the point of abrogation. The law of retaliation ("an eye for an eye and a tooth for a tooth") was intended to restrict vengeance and to keep violence within limits. Jesus urges his followers to forgo even the limited retaliation allowed by the Old Testament and thus to interrupt the whole cycle of revenge. The disciples must not adopt the attitudes and actions of their enemies, and four practical examples of non-retaliation in the face of evil are provided in verses 39-42 (see Luke 6:29-30). Each example challenges accepted, instinctive human behavior patterns.

5:43-48 Love of enemies (see Luke 6:27-28, 32-36). The final antithesis demands that Jesus' followers love not only the members of their own national or religious group (Lev 19:18) but even their enemies. This new demand is based, not on human nature, but on the example of God. It is human nature (represented by the tax collectors and pagans) to love those who love you and to greet only members of one's own family. But God makes the sun rise on good and bad alike, and rain falls on both the just and the unjust. When God's love and care for all people are taken as the standard, the disciples of Jesus cannot limit their love to their own group or their own nation. The disciples' perfection reflects and is measured by God's perfection.

6:1-4 Almsgiving. Three religious practices that would have been especially important for the Pharisees are treated in the third major part of the Sermon (6:1-18). After stating the general principle that religious acts should be done to honor God and not simply to better one's own reputation (v. 1), the passage considers almsgiving (vv. 2-4), prayer (vv. 5-15), and fasting (vv. 16-18). Each section contains a description of behavior that should be avoided, an instruction on the proper attitude, and the promise of a reward from God. Pious self-display is criticized, not the pious actions in themselves.

In a society without a highly organized welfare system, the obligation to offer charity (vv. 2-4) to the poor, the defenseless, and the sick was taken very seriously by religious people. In verse 2 Jesus criticizes those who make a great display of their charity by means of the image of blowing a horn. He calls such people "hypocrites," a term that originally referred to actors on a stage but here carries the sense of "phonies." The charge of hypocrisy is also leveled against the scribes and Pharisees in chapter 23. Jesus' disciples are instructed to be so free from religious showiness that they do not even seek the self-satisfaction of knowing what they are giving (6:3). Both verses 2 and 3 rely on obvious exaggerations in order to contrast self-seeking and selflessness in religion. The God who sees acts hidden from human sight will surely reward charity given without fanfare (v. 4).

6:5-15 Prayer (see Luke 11:2-4). The section on prayer begins the same way as the preceding section did. Here the behavior to be avoided is making a public spectacle of oneself in prayer (v. 5). The only fitting reward for such prayer is the public notoriety that it attracts. Indeed, prayer offered to win human praise is not prayer at all. Jesus' disciples are instructed to avoid making a public display of themselves in prayer (v. 6). That public prayer should be condemned outright was unthinkable for Jews like Jesus and Matthew, and it is not condemned here. Rather, another exaggerated statement is used in order to underline the warning against religious showiness. God will reward only genuine prayer offered in sincerity to him.

Attached to this teaching are sayings on prayer (vv. 7-8), a sample prayer (vv. 9-13), and sayings on forgiveness (vv. 14-15). In Jewish piety the prayer of petition was very important, and Jesus' disciples are warned not to confuse quantity with quality (v. 7). God as a loving Father knows the needs of his children even before they make their requests, but he wants them to ask in confidence and trust (v. 8). In petition, we do not so much inform God of some situation as express our dependence and faith.

The so-called Lord's Prayer or Our Father (vv. 9-13) is offered as a sample. Most of its phrases have close parallels in Jewish prayers of the time. The shorter and perhaps more primitive version in Luke 11:2-4 addresses God simply as "Father" and lacks petitions found in Matt 6:10, 13. The Matthean version begins with a typically Jewish form of invocation in prayer: "Our Father in heaven." The three "you-petitions" are addressed directly to God (vv. 9b-10) and pray for the coming of God's kingdom. They ask that God let the time come when he will be recognized as the Holy One by all creation, that the fullness of his kingship be revealed to all creation, and that the perfection with which his will is done in heaven should extend to earth also. The three "we-petitions" (vv. 11-13) ask for physical and spiritual well-being in the difficult period before the fullness of God's kingdom. They ask that God provide the bread we need today, that the forgiveness we receive from God may lead us to forgive those who have wronged us ("debts" is a metaphor for sins), and that in the time of testing accompanying the coming of God's kingdom we may not fall prey to the Evil One.

The saying on forgiveness (vv. 14-15) is joined to the Lord's Prayer because it concerns the same issue that the second of the "we-petitions" (6:12) treats. It makes our willingness to forgive one another the necessary condition for God's willingness to forgive us our sins.

6:16-18 Fasting. The section on fasting follows the pattern set in the sections on almsgiving and prayer. There were special days designated for fasting in the Jewish calendar, and pious Pharisees fasted two days a week. Not the act of fasting itself, but rather making a public display of one's fast, is criticized in verse 16. Jesus' disciples are instructed to disguise their fasting by looking as if they are preparing for a holiday (v. 17). God will know that they are fasting and will reward them accordingly (v. 18).

6:19-34 Trust in God (see Luke 12:33-34; 11:34-36; 16:13; 12:22-34). The final section of the Sermon (6:19–7:29) gives advice regarding the Christian pursuit of holiness. The basic theme is the decision for or against God. The major topics bear some relation to the "we-petitions" in the Lord's Prayer: trust in God to provide food and clothing ("Give us today our daily bread"), avoiding the condemnation of others ("as we forgive our debtors"), approaching God as Father with our requests

("Our Father in heaven"), and traveling the narrow and hard way ("deliver us").

The material in the first part (vv. 19-34) concerns various aspects of the choice between God and earthly wealth. The sayings on true riches in verses 19-21 (see Luke 12:33-34) contrast the fragile nature of earthly treasures and eternal treasure with God, who rewards those who give alms, pray, and fast in secret (vv. 1-18). The following saying (vv. 22-23) assumes that the eyes are the conduits for the entire body. In this context (see Luke 11:34-36), it refers to the need for sound spiritual vision if the person is to act properly. Those whose vision is not focused on obedience to God will plunge their whole selves into darkness. The decision for or against God carries over into all dimensions of the person's life. The choice between God and earthly wealth is made explicit in verse 24 (see Luke 16:13), where the latter is personified as Mammon ("that in which one puts trust or faith").

The sayings on care and anxiety in verses 25-34 (see Luke 12:22-34) seek to free the followers of Jesus from excessive concern about food and clothing (see v. 31) by means of several considerations. They are urged to reflect on God's care as shown in nature (the birds and the wild flowers) and to realize that human beings are even more important in God's sight. They are asked to admit that worrying does not really solve anything (v. 27) and to recognize that if their heart is set on serving God alone, these matters will take care of themselves (v. 33). The God whom they address in prayer as Father knows all that they need.

7:1-6 Avoiding condemnation (see Luke 6:37-38, 41-42). The followers of Jesus are warned to avoid condemning other people ("stop judging"). This is the prerogative of God on the day of judgment. The way in which they deal with others in this matter will determine in large part the way that others and God himself will deal with them (vv. 1-2). This does not rule out the practice of correction within the community (see 18:15-18), but such correction must be carried out with an awareness of one's own failings and prejudices (vv. 3-5). It also does not rule out discernment and discretion in dealing with hostile outsiders or even with apostate and unrepentant Christians (v. 6).

7:7-11 Approaching God in prayer (see Luke 11:9-13). In prayer, God is to be approached with boldness and confidence. The importance of the prayer of petition is underlined ("ask . . . seek . . . knock"), and the efficacy of such prayers is assumed (vv. 7-8). The way that a human father cares for his children and gives them good gifts when they ask him is used in verses 9-11 to illustrate the way that the heavenly Father answers petitions in prayer.

7:12 The golden rule (see Luke 6:31). The so-called golden rule of verse 12 about treating others as you would wish them to treat you is not original or unique to Jesus. Matthew's primary interest was the use of it as a summary of the Old Testament tradition. The Jewish teacher Hillel offered a similar teaching ("What you do not like, do not do to your neighbor") and asserted that the rest of the law and the prophets is a commentary on this (see Tob 4:15).

7:13-27 Decision for or against God (see Luke 13:24; 6:43-44; 13:25-27; 6:47-49). The Sermon concludes with a series of contrasts regarding the decision for or against God. The image of the two ways in verses 13-14 (see Luke 13:24) is common in the Old Testament and was developed in the Dead Sea scrolls and in the early Christian writing called the *Didache.* The idea that the gate is narrow and the way is constricted is noteworthy in Matthew. The false prophets of verses 15-20 (see Luke 6:43-44) are to be judged in accordance with Deut 13:1-5 and 18:20-22. Does the prophet's word come true? Does the prophet lead the people astray? The results (or fruits) show the prophet's character (the tree).

The sayings in verses 21-23 (see Luke 13:25-27) also focus on the relationship between word and action: It is not enough merely to say "Lord, Lord," for only doing God's will gives entry to his kingdom. The firm foundation mentioned in verses 24-27 (see Luke 6:47-49) includes both word and deed.

7:28-29 Conclusion. The Sermon on the Mount ends as the four other major speeches of Jesus in the Gospel do (see 11:1; 13:53; 19:1; 26:1): "Jesus finished these words." The contrast between the authority displayed by Jesus and the lack of authority on the part of the scribes (see Mark 1:22) was important to Matthew and his community as they experienced the split between the church and the synagogue ("their scribes").

IV. THE POWERFUL DEEDS OF JESUS

Matt 8:1–9:38

Having illustrated the power of Jesus as a teacher by the Sermon on the Mount, Matthew now gives examples of his power as a healer and a wonder-worker in chapters 8–9. Jesus is powerful in both word and deed. Nine acts of power are arranged in three groups of three (8:1-17; 8:23–9:8; 9:18-34). The groups are divided from one another by non-miraculous materials (8:18-22; 9:9-17; 9:35-38) in which the theme of discipleship is prominent. Both the Sermon and the mighty acts of Jesus are set in the framework of his ministry in Galilee (see 4:23; 9:35).

8:1-4 Power over leprosy (see Mark 1:40-45; Luke 5:12-16). The first cycle of Jesus' mighty deeds (8:1-17) presents demonstrations of his power over leprosy, paralysis, fever, and demonic possession. He shows mercy to the marginal people of Jewish society: lepers, Gentiles, servants, women, and the possessed.

Matthew's version of the healing of the leper (vv. 1-4) contains a transitional sentence (v. 1), the leper's request for healing (v. 2), Jesus' response and the miraculous healing (v. 3), and the final instruction that the healed man show himself to the priest in the temple (v. 4). The key words are "make clean" or "cure," which appear in the request for healing (v. 2), in Jesus' response (v. 3a), and in the narrator's description of what took place (v. 3b).

The Matthean account is simpler than Mark 1:40-45. The references to Jesus' emotions in Mark 1:41, 43, as well as the report about the public impact of the healing in Mark 1:45, are absent. In Matt 8:2, Jesus is addressed as "Lord," which not only heightens his dignity but also places the miracle in the framework of praying faith. The simpler structure also helps to highlight Jesus' concern that the Old Testament law regarding lepers who had been cleansed (Lev 14:2-9) be fulfilled exactly. The authority of Jesus as Messiah and Son of God, how he should be approached in prayer, and his fulfillment of the Old Testament emerge as the central themes in Matthew's account.

8:5-13 Power over paralysis (see Luke 7:1-10; John 4:43-54). The themes of Jesus' authority and power are carried on in the healing of the centurion's servant. But here special attention is given to a non-Jew's act of faith in Jesus' power. The centurion was a Gentile soldier (probably a Syrian) who was stationed at the military garrison in Capernaum. Whereas Luke's account portrays him as communicating with Jesus through intermediaries (the elders of the Jews and friends), Matthew pictures him in a dialogue of faith directly with Jesus. His request in verse 6 is prefaced with the title "Lord," and his response to Jesus' willingness to cure his paralyzed servant highlights the power of Jesus' word (v. 8). As a military man, he knows the force of a verbal command in a well-run army, and so he believes that the word of Jesus is powerful enough to cure his servant (vv. 8-9).

The Gentile centurion's faith is praised as surpassing anything that Jesus has encountered among God's chosen people (v. 10). It is seen as anticipating the situation after Jesus' death and resurrection when the Gentiles will find a place among God's people at the heavenly banquet (and in the church) and many Jews by birth will be excluded for their unbelief in Jesus (vv. 11-12). As a response to the centurion's display of faith, Jesus carries out the act of healing (v. 13).

8:14-17 Power over fever and demons (see Mark 1:29-34; Luke 4:38-41). In 8:14-17, Matthew compresses Mark's accounts of the healings of Peter's mother-in-law and of the many sick at Capernaum. Besides omitting the Markan context, Matthew also omits the mention of Simon (Peter), Andrew, James, and John. Jesus miraculously heals the woman, and as proof of the healing she serves him (not them, as in Mark 1:31). In the account of the general healing (vv. 16-17), Matthew leaves out what he regards as extraneous details as well as Jesus' refusal to let the demons speak. On the other hand, in verse 17 he adds the notice that in this healing activity Jesus brings to fulfillment the prophecy of Isa 53:4. This quotation not only carries on the theme of Jesus as fulfilling the Old Testament but also serves to identify Jesus as the Suffering Servant of God.

8:18-22 The demands of discipleship (see Luke 9:57-60). The first and second triads of Jesus' acts of power (8:1-17; 8:23–9:8) are separated by sayings on the radical demands of discipleship. In the first instance a scribe addresses Jesus as "Teacher" and offers to follow him anywhere, only to be warned that Jesus the Son of Man gives no guarantee of security. In the second instance a "disciple" requests permission to attend to the burial of his father (see 1 Kgs 19:20), but the Lord demands that he choose between discipleship and family obligation. This is an extreme way of making the point that the call to follow Jesus supersedes all other obligations and that it may even involve cutting family ties. Such sayings are designed to force us to reflect on the seriousness and significance of discipleship. Their extreme character creates a tension that can only be resolved by accepting the call.

8:23-27 Power over the sea (see Mark 4:35-41; Luke 8:22-25). The second cycle of Jesus' mighty acts (8:23–9:8) reveals his power over the sea, the demons, and sin. Matthew's account of the stilling of the storm (vv. 23-27) drops some details found in Mark 4:35-41 and makes more explicit the themes of discipleship and faith. In verse 23, Jesus takes the initiative, and the disciples "follow" him (a technical term for discipleship). Thus the material on discipleship in verses 18-22 is connected with Jesus' power over the sea.

It is possible that Matthew's readers were sensitive to one or more of the following symbolic equivalencies: the sea as the forces of chaos allied against God, the storm as the eschatological earthquake, and the boat as the church. Their request in verse 25 takes the form of a prayer: "Lord, save us! We are perishing!" Jesus' response to their prayer takes over Mark's theme of the disciples' obtuseness and describes it under the term "little faith." Although they have some faith, the disciples still have a long way to go before they reach perfect faith. Under Matthew's careful editorship, the theme of Jesus' power is complemented by the themes of discipleship and faith made concrete in prayer to Jesus as Lord.

8:28-34 Power over demons (see Mark 5:1-20; Luke 8:26-39). The second act of power in this series is located by Matthew at Gadara, which was much closer to the shore of the Sea of Galilee than Gerasa is (see Mark 5:1). It concerns two men possessed by demons rather than one man as in Mark 5:2, perhaps because Matthew has combined Mark 1:21-28 and 5:1-20 into a single, short account. The demoniacs fade from the scene and give way to the demons, who address Jesus as the Son of God and complain that they should not be disturbed until the coming of the kingdom (v. 29). Then the demons request that Jesus send them into a herd of swine (unclean animals for Jews), and their "prayer" is granted by Jesus (vv. 31-32). The focus of the Matthean account is the dialogue between Jesus and the demons and his display of power over them.

9:1-8 Power over sin (see Mark 2:1-12; Luke 5:17-26). Matthew's story of the healing of the paralytic and the forgiveness of his sins omits Mark's descriptions of the crowd and the difficulty that the friends encounter in bringing the sick man to Jesus. The effect of this compression is to keep the theme of the forgiveness of sins in the spotlight. The faith of the friends is noted (v. 2), and the conversation between the scribes and Jesus serves to establish his authority both to forgive sins and to bring about physical healing. The healing itself (vv. 6-7) is offered as a visible proof of the Son of Man's power to work wonders even in the realm of the invisible or the spiritual (the forgiveness of sins). The statement in verse 8 that the crowd praised God for giving such authority to human beings suggests that in Matthew's community Jesus' authority to forgive sins was viewed as having been transmitted to members of the church (see 18:15-20).

9:9-17 The defense of the disciples (see Mark 2:13-22; Luke 5:27-39). The section that separates the second and third triads of Jesus' acts of power (8:23–9:8; 9:18-34) begins with the call of the tax collector Matthew in 9:9. In Mark 2:14 and Luke 5:27 he is named "Levi." His name may have been changed in our Gospel to make him one of the Twelve (see 10:3) and/or because the community in which the Gospel was written retained a traditional attachment to the apostle Matthew. There is no reason to suppose that the tax collector-turned-disciple had two names. Tax collectors were suspect to pious Jews on the grounds of their collaboration with the Roman officials and their practice of extorting more than was owed to the government. Jesus' willingness to accept such a person as a disciple prepared the way for the acceptance of all kinds of people into the church.

Jesus' practice of dining with tax collectors (v. 9) and sinners (vv. 10-11) scandalized the Pharisees, for whom ritual purity and table fellowship were important religious practices. They ask Jesus' disciples why he does this. In verses 12-13, Jesus himself supplies three explanations: (1) the spiritually sick need him most; (2) Hosea 6:6 bears witness to the greatness of God's mercy; (3) Jesus came to call sinners to conversion of heart. Then in verse 14 disciples of John the Baptist, for whom ascetic practices like fasting would have been important, ask why Jesus' disciples do not fast. They are told that the time of Jesus the bridegroom is not a fitting one for fasting (v. 15); when he is taken away from them, there will be ample time for fasting. The radical newness of Jesus and the incompatibility between his message and the old forms of piety are brought out in verses 16-17 by means of the images of the new cloth and the new wine.

9:18-26 Power over death (see Mark 5:21-43; Luke 8:40-56). The third cycle of Jesus' mighty acts (9:18-34) reveals his power over death and chronic illness, blindness, and speechlessness. The stories of the revival of the synagogue leader's daughter and the healing of the woman with the hemorrhage had already been intertwined in Mark 5:21-43. In verses 18-26, Matthew has greatly simplified the Markan narrative in order to make the theme of faith stand out even more sharply. According to verse 18, the ruler knew that the girl was already dead but still believed that Jesus could restore her to life. The way in which the girl's restoration to life is described in verse 25 ("arose") connects this miracle to Jesus' own resurrection. In verses 20-22 every detail not relevant to the theme of faith in Jesus' power is omitted. The words that are translated as "cured" and "saved" are part of the New Testament vocabulary of salvation.

9:27-31 Power over blindness. The second incident in the third cycle was probably designed to combine the two stories found in Mark 8:22-26 and 10:46-52 (see also Matt 20:29-34). The Matthean account revolves around Jesus' question in verse 28 ("Do you believe that I can do this?") and the affirmative response by the two blind men. The healing is worked because of their faith (v. 29).

9:32-34 Power over speechlessness. The third section recounts in the briefest possible way the healing of a man who could not speak, and then contrasts two possible reactions: the amazement of the crowds at the unprecedented acts performed by Jesus, and the Pharisees' ascription of Jesus' power to Satan. The third cycle as a whole concerns the necessity of faith in Jesus' power and ends by noting that some people could witness the miracles and still refuse to believe that Jesus was sent from God.

9:35-38 The mission of the disciples. The final block of material on discipleship begins by repeating the description of Jesus' ministry that appeared in 4:23. Then the idea that discipleship involves mission is brought out by means of two images: the people are like sheep without a shepherd and like a harvest that needs workers to bring in the crops. God is the ultimate shepherd and harvest master, but he needs the cooperation of those who accept Jesus' invitation to discipleship. The three sections on discipleship in chapters 8–9 emphasize the radical demands that it can involve (8:18-22), the fact that all kinds of people can be called to it and the radical newness that it represents (9:9-17), and its missionary dimension (9:35-38).

V. THE MISSIONARY DISCOURSE

Matt 10:1-42

The idea that discipleship involves mission sets the stage for the second major speech by Jesus—the so-called missionary discourse in chapter 10. The sayings that make up this discourse have been gathered from various traditional sources and woven by the evangelist into a lengthy instruction on how the disciples of Jesus are to act (10:5-15) and what they can expect (10:16-42). The basic theme is stated in 10:24-25: "No disciple is above his teacher, no slave above his master. It is enough for the disciple that he become like his teacher, for the slave that he become like his master." Just as the disciples share in Jesus' power, so they must share his lifestyle and his sufferings.

10:1-5a Introduction (see Mark 3:13-19; Luke 6:12-16). After demonstrating his great powers as a healer in chapters 8–9, Jesus in 10:1 passes on to his twelve disciples the authority over demons and diseases that he had received from the Father. In his list of the Twelve (see Mark 3:16-19; Luke 6:13-16; Acts 1:13), Matthew stresses the primacy of Simon Peter ("first, Simon") and identifies Matthew as the tax collector of 9:9. The only significant disagreement among the various lists of apostles involves Thaddaeus, who in Luke 6:16 and Acts 1:13 is called Judas the son of James and in some manuscripts of Matthew and Mark is named Lebbaeus.

10:5b-15 What the disciples are to do (see Mark 6:7-13; Luke 9:1-6). The disciples' mission is limited to the people of Israel (vv. 5b-6), and they are to avoid entering the cities of non-Jews and Samaritans (whose Judaism was suspect in the eyes of Judeans and Galileans). Only after the death and resurrection of Jesus does the mission to the latter groups begin (see 28:19). The disciples' mission (vv. 7-8) replicates and extends the mission of Jesus in preaching the coming of God's kingdom and in healing the sick (see 4:23). As discipleship has been offered to them as a gift, so they are to offer it to others.

Wandering preachers representing various philosophies and religions were a common sight in the world of Jesus' time. Jesus' disciples are instructed not to be anxious about money or baggage or lodging, but rather to depend on the charity of their hearers (vv. 9-13). Their lack of concern for money, clothing, and lodging allows them to carry out the mission in a more single-minded way. It also bears witness to their trust in God's care for them and to their conviction that what has been freely received should be freely given. When the preachers are rejected in a place (vv. 14-15), they are to react without violence and only symbolically ("shake the dust from your feet"). They are to remain faithful to their task and trust that God will settle these matters in the final judgment. According to Gen 19, Sodom and Gomorrah were examples of extreme wickedness, especially with regard to hospitality.

10:16-25 Hostility (see Mark 13:9-13; Luke 21:12-17). The remainder of the missionary discourse tells the disciples what they are to expect. They can expect the same treatment that Jesus himself receives. Far from promising a mission free from conflict or opposition, Jesus prepares his disciples for hostility. They are sent as defenseless creatures ("sheep") among predators ("wolves"), and so they are urged to be shrewd while retaining their guilelessness (v. 16). In being tried and punished (vv. 17-18) by Jewish religious leaders ("their synagogues") and by Roman governmental officials ("governors and kings"), they share in Jesus' own passion (see 26:57-68; 27:11-26). Among the terrors awaiting the disciples are the anxiety connected with speaking at a public trial (v. 19), divisions within families and subsequent acts of betrayal (v. 21), hatred (v. 22), and persecution (v. 23). These terrors are outweighed by confidence in the Spirit (v. 20) and in their ultimate vindication when God's kingdom comes (v. 22).

In verse 23b the "towns of Israel" refers to the Jewish regions of Palestine, and "before the Son of Man comes" represents the coming of God's kingdom. According to Matthew's perspective, the coming of the Son of Man began with the death and resurrection and will terminate only at the end of time. The mission to Israel (10:5b-6) occupies the disciples until they receive the broader commission (28:19) that lasts until the end of this world. The sayings in verses 24-25 summarize the themes of the entire discourse and establish a link between the treatment accorded to Jesus by unbelievers and what the disciples of Jesus can expect.

10:26-33 Do not fear! (see Luke 12:2-9). Whatever the original contexts of the sayings in verses 26-33 may have been, here they serve to encourage the disciples to fearless confession in the face of opposition. Each saying is introduced by "Do not be afraid" (vv. 26, 28, 31) and attacks the fears that could cause the disciples to abandon their mission. The first saying (vv. 26-27) appeals to the inevitability of the coming of God's kingdom and Jesus' witness to it. Then the hypocrisy of the disciples' opponents will be revealed. The second saying (vv. 28-30) appeals to God's care for Jesus' disciples. Their opponents can destroy the body but not the soul. The third saying (vv. 31-33) appeals to the final judgment before God, which will be based on the disciples' faithfulness to Jesus during the conflicts that are part of their mission.

10:34-39 Family conflicts (see Luke 12:51-53; 14:26-27). Jesus does not guarantee the absence of conflict. In Jewish society of his time, family ties were far stronger than they are in the modern societies of the West.

But faithfulness to Jesus may involve the rupture even of these bonds. The passage is not an attack on family life as such, but it does insist that the disciples have a greater loyalty to Jesus than to the members of their families. In the extreme cases of having to choose between Jesus and one's family, Jesus demands absolute loyalty to himself. The sayings about the cross (v. 38) and losing one's life (v. 39) foreshadow Jesus' own fate and continue the theme of the disciples' identification with Jesus.

10:40-42 Receiving disciples of Jesus (see Mark 9:41). The concluding section of the missionary discourse reiterates the basic point of the discourse. The disciples are the representatives of Jesus. To receive them is to receive not only Jesus but also his heavenly Father (v. 40). Fitting rewards will be given to those who receive Christian prophets and holy men or even simpler Christians, because they all represent Christ and his heavenly Father.

VI. THE IMPORTANCE OF JESUS AND THE REJECTION OF HIM

Matt 11:1–12:50

The missionary discourse ends in 11:1, but nothing is said about the disciples' actual mission or their return. The spotlight remains on Jesus as he continues his work. The themes of unbelief and rejection that were so prominent in the missionary discourse are developed further in chapters 11–12, and we are given more information about Jesus' identity as the Messiah (11:1-6), the Wisdom of God (11:25-30), and the Servant of God (12:15-21).

11:1-6 Jesus as "the one who is to come" (see Luke 7:18-23). John's imprisonment had been mentioned in 4:12. The question in 11:3 regarding Jesus concerns his identity as "the one who is to come," which appears to have been a messianic title (see 3:11; 21:9; 23:39) derived from Ps 118:26 and Mal 3:1. Jesus' answer to John proves his messianic identity by listing the Messiah's deeds in terms of Isa 35:5-6 and 61:1. These deeds were described in chapters 8–9, and the list climaxes with the mention of the gospel having been preached to the poor (v. 5). The final saying (v. 6) declares "blessed" (see 5:3-12) those who do not find Jesus to be a scandal or a stumbling block. Though this beatitude may imply some misgivings on John's part concerning Jesus, it more likely prepares for the following incidents in which many people do find Jesus to be a stumbling block.

11:7-15 John the Baptist as Elijah (see Luke 7:24-30). The departure of John's messengers furnishes the occasion for Jesus' words about John's identity and the meaning of his rejection. John preached and baptized in the wilderness of Judah and lived very differently from the courtiers of Herod Antipas. Herod had John put in prison for questioning the propriety of his marriage to Herodias (see 14:1-12). In verses 9-10, 13, Jesus identifies John as a prophet but goes further by proclaiming him to be the fulfillment of Mal 3:1 (see Exod 23:20)—the prophet who will precede the coming of God's kingdom. This identification is made even more explicit in verse 14, when John is called Elijah. According to Mal 4:5, God would send Elijah the prophet from heaven before the great and terrible day of the Lord comes. But for all John's greatness, he has not yet inaugurated the decisive new age that the coming of God's kingdom will represent (v. 11). Nevertheless, John's imprisonment constitutes a violent attack against the coming kingdom (v. 12), an attack that will be repeated in the case of Jesus. Those who oppose the preaching of John and Jesus about the kingdom oppose the kingdom itself.

11:16-19 John and Jesus are rejected (see Luke 7:31-35). The austere and ascetic John was dismissed as having a demon (v. 18), and the joyful and expansive Jesus is rejected for keeping bad company (v. 19). Despite rejection by those who consider themselves wise, divine Wisdom will win out and confirm the actions of both John and Jesus. The beginning of the passage (vv. 16-17) compares the unbelievers to sullen children who refuse to play either the happy game of Jesus or the sad game of John.

11:20-24 Warnings to Galilean cities (see Luke 10:12-15). The Galilean cities in which Jesus had done his mighty deeds are given stern warnings. There are two pronouncements. Each contains a judgment ("woe"), an explanation and a comparison, and a prediction concerning the final judgment. First Chorazin and Bethsaida are threatened with "woe," because they have not repented in response to the deeds of Jesus. Their final judgment will be worse than that of the pagan cities of Tyre and Sidon (vv. 21-22). Then Capernaum (vv. 23-24) is threatened with woe, and its delusions of grandeur are compared to those of the king of Babylon as described in Isa 14:13-15. Capernaum too had refused to respond adequately to Jesus' deeds, and its final fate will be even worse than that of the wicked city of Sodom (see Gen 19:24-28). Both sayings of judgment assume the decisive importance of Jesus in human history.

11:25-30 Jesus as the Wisdom of God (see Luke 10:21-22). The themes of the decisive importance of Jesus and the rejection of him are linked in verses 25-30. Matthew has put together traditional sayings according to the following outline: the praise of the Father (vv. 25-26), the identity of Jesus (v. 27), and the invitation to come (vv. 28-30). Beginning with typically Jewish formulas of prayer, Jesus praises God for revealing to the simple and uneducated people, who were most receptive to Jesus, what has been hidden from the scholars and religious experts. Then in verse 27 Jesus asserts that God has granted him the revelation of himself as completely as a father discloses himself to a son. The relation between God and Jesus is so close that the only adequate terms for it are Father and Son. Therefore, only Jesus can pass on to others real knowledge of God. The language of verse 27 is very similar to many passages in John's Gospel (see John 3:35; 7:29; 10:14-15; 17:1-3).

In verses 28-30, Jesus expresses his invitation to discipleship in terms employed by Jesus ben Sira in Sir 51:23-27. Using the traditional image of the law as a "yoke," Jesus, the authoritative interpreter of the law (see 5:21-48), promises refreshment and rest in his wisdom school. All genuine searchers for wisdom are invited to come to Jesus. In Jesus, God's own wisdom dwells and can be learned.

12:1-8 Work on the sabbath (see Mark 2:23-28; Luke 6:1-5). Jesus' status as the authoritative interpreter of the law is exemplified in the incident of the disciples' plucking and eating grain on the sabbath. The disciples' actions would be considered the equivalent of reaping on the sabbath and therefore forbidden labor (see Exod 20:8-11; Deut 5:12-15). The Pharisees, who appear as the leaders of the opposition to Jesus and to his followers during most of the Gospel, protest against this unlawful act.

Jesus gives them four answers: (1) The disciples' act is compared to that of David and his followers in 1 Sam 21:1-6. In both cases a commandment was broken out of the need to satisfy physical hunger. Matthew has omitted the name of Abiathar the high priest from Mark 2:26, because in fact the high priest of the Old Testament story was Ahimelech. Thus the disciples of the Son of David had a good precedent in David himself. (2) In verses 5-6, Matthew cites an argument that is not present in Mark's account. The priests are allowed to perform acts of work in the Jerusalem temple on the sabbath on the principle that laws pertaining to the temple take precedence over laws pertaining to the sabbath. Perhaps the claim that Jesus is greater than the temple is implied here. (3) The quotation from Hos 6:6 ("I desire mercy, not sacrifice") is used to criticize the Pharisees' faulty scale of values. (4) Jesus as the Son of Man has the ultimate authority over the sabbath and even more right than David or the priests in the temple to overrule the Old Testament legislation regarding the sabbath.

In Matthew's community this passage would serve as a source of defenses against Jewish criticisms about early Christian laxity in observing the sabbath. The early Christians based their practice on the example and the authority of Jesus the Son of Man.

12:9-14 Healing on the sabbath (see Mark 3:1-6; Luke 6:6-11). The question of sabbath observance arises with respect to Jesus himself and takes the form of a debate. The place of the debate is "their synagogue"—an expression that suggests a sharp division between the Pharisees and the followers of Jesus. The question concerns the propriety of healing on the sabbath (v. 10), and Jesus' response involves a counter-question (v. 11) regarding the case of rescuing an animal on the sabbath (see Deut 22:4). If it is right to save an animal, how much the more is it right to save a human being (v. 12)!

As an illustration of good deeds done on the sabbath, Jesus restores to health the withered hand of a man in the synagogue. Why the good deed could not wait until after the sabbath or to what extent the man was in danger of death is not considered. Just as God desires mercy more than sacrifice, so good deeds override the sabbath regulations. Rather than convincing the Pharisees, Jesus' teaching and action only increase their opposition, to the point that they begin the plot to kill him (v. 14).

12:15-21 Jesus as the Servant of the Lord. In the midst of the rising opposition to Jesus from the Pharisees, Matthew pauses and places Jesus' response in the context of the Old Testament Servant of the Lord. Jesus was fully aware of the rising opposition (v. 15) but continued his healing activity and avoided publicity (vv. 15-16). His modesty and gentleness in the face of hostility are viewed as the fulfillment of Isa 42:1-4. By refusing to use violence against the Pharisees or to reveal himself openly, Jesus did not "contend or cry out." But other features in the Old Testament passage are also significant: Jesus' identity as the Servant of the Lord (see 3:17; 17:5), Jesus as especially endowed with the Holy Spirit, and his role in God's plan of salvation for the Gentiles. Matthew's identification of Jesus as the Servant of the Lord sets the stage for the debate with the Pharisees regarding the source of Jesus' powers. The thrust of their attack is that Jesus is in league with Satan. But Matthew's readers know that he is really the Servant of the Lord.

12:22-37 The source of Jesus' power (see Mark 3:19-30; Luke 11:14-23; 12:10; 6:43-45). The healing of a possessed man who was blind and mute provides the occasion for exploring the source of Jesus' power. The healing (v. 22) produces two reactions: wonder on the part of the crowds whether Jesus is the Son of David or Messiah (v. 23), and hostility from the Pharisees, who are convinced that he is the instrument of Satan (v. 24).

In response to the Pharisees, Jesus offers three arguments: (1) If Jesus' power over the demons were from Satan, Satan would be setting his own agents against themselves and thus destroying Satan's kingdom (vv. 25-26). (2) Jesus' exorcisms should be interpreted as good actions inspired by the Holy Spirit, just as the exorcisms performed by other Jewish exorcists are (vv. 27-28). (3) Jesus could not cast out demons unless he had some power over the chief demon (v. 29). The saying in verse 28, linking Jesus' exorcisms to the coming of God's kingdom, is very important for understanding all of Jesus' miracles: They are signs that, in Jesus, God's kingdom is breaking into the world and will reach its fullness in due time.

Having met the objections of the Pharisees, Jesus takes the offensive with three warnings: (1) Closeness to Jesus is absolutely essential, and the Pharisees must recognize it or run the risk of being on the wrong side when God's kingdom comes (v. 30). (2) The only unforgivable sin is attributing the work of the Holy Spirit to an evil spirit, as the Pharisees were doing in the case of Jesus. Failure to recognize the Son of Man for what he is may be understandable and even pardonable, but failure to recognize the source of his power is inexcusable (vv. 31-32). (3) The Pharisees' opposition to Jesus stems from their wickedness, and in the final judgment they will be judged with regard to their willingness or unwillingness to confess that Jesus is empowered by the Holy Spirit (vv. 33-37).

12:38-42 The sign of Jonah (see Luke 11:29-32). Despite all the miracles that Jesus had already worked, the scribes and Pharisees ask for more signs. The exasperated Jesus promises them only the sign of Jonah. The basic meaning of the sign of Jonah seems to involve the preaching of repentance to non-Jews and its acceptance by them. When the Old Testament prophet Jonah preached conversion of heart to the people of Nineveh, they acted on Jonah's preaching and repented (v. 41). The queen of Sheba came to Jerusalem to hear the wisdom of Solomon (see 1 Kgs 10:1-6), and she was duly impressed by him (v. 42). Jesus surpasses Jonah and Solomon, and so the scribes and Pharisees have good reason to repent. In verse 40, Matthew has given a second interpretation of the sign of Jonah: The three days spent by the prophet inside the fish (see Jonah 2) were a type or a foreshadowing of the three days between Jesus' death and his resurrection.

12:43-45 The evil spirit's return (see Luke 11:24-26). The passage about the evil spirit's return is joined to the sign of Jonah by its reference to "this evil generation" (vv. 39, 45), and to the entire section beginning at 12:22 by its concern with evil spirits. The activity of Jesus has made an impact on the evil spirits, but their power is far from broken. Matthew and his community probably viewed the Romans' destruction of Jerusalem in A.D. 70 as the fulfillment of Jesus' warnings.

12:46-50 The true family of Jesus (see

Mark 3:31-35; Luke 8:19-21). The long treatment of unbelief and rejection that began in the missionary discourse of chapter 10 and continued in the incidents of chapters 11–12 concludes with the definition of the true family of Jesus as those who do God's will. Matthew's account contains no explicit criticism of Jesus' relatives; they serve merely as a foil to emphasize the point that those who obey God constitute the real family of Jesus. In a society that placed a very high value on blood relationship, Jesus' teaching about his disciples forming a spiritual family would be quite challenging.

VII. PARABLES CONCERNING THE KINGDOM OF GOD

Matt 13:1-53

Jesus' parables about the kingdom form the third major discourse in the Gospel. A parable is a simile or metaphor drawn from everyday life or from nature. Its vividness or strangeness gains the hearer's attention but demands further reflection regarding the precise meaning. The kingdom of God refers to God's future display of power and judgment in which he establishes his rule over all creation. Its coming is basically God's work, though the cooperation of people in the present time is demanded. In Jesus' teaching, the kingdom has both present and future dimensions.

13:1-9 The seeds (see Mark 4:1-9; Luke 8:4-8). The first part of the parables discourse (13:1-35) envisions Jesus as sitting in a boat, with the crowds standing along the shore (vv. 1-3). The crowds are the mass of people. They are the object of Jesus' mission and are not yet totally incorrigible in their unbelief, like the scribes and Pharisees. The parable of the seeds (vv. 4-9) contrasts three kinds of wasted seeds with one kind of fruitful seed. The seeds were wasted because they landed on bad soils: a footpath (v. 4), rocky ground (v. 5), and among thorns (v. 7). But the seed that fell on good soil (v. 8) yielded great results. The parable uses repetition in order to build up a pattern of expectations and at the end changes the pattern in order to emphasize the real point of the story. It explains why Jesus' preaching of the kingdom of God has not been universally accepted and encourages those who have accepted it to keep on bearing fruit in good works. The seed growing in the good soil will achieve enormous results.

13:10-17 Why Jesus used parables (see Mark 4:10-12; Luke 8:9-10). The contrast between the fruitful seed and the wasted seeds continues in the explanation of why Jesus used parables as a teaching device. The disciples want to know why he teaches in parables when he could use simple and direct speech (v. 10). In response to their question, Jesus asserts that the gift of understanding is given to the disciples but not to others (vv. 11-12) and that the disciples are blessed with special sight and hearing (vv. 16-17). Because the others fail to see and hear Jesus' plain teachings about the kingdom, he is forced to use the mysterious speech of the parables (v. 13). The general lack of understanding of Jesus' teaching is explained in verses 14-15 as the fulfillment of Isa 6:9-10. The spiritual dispositions of the disciples (the fruitful soil) render them capable of seeing and understanding, while the others remain incapable of seeing and understanding at all because their spiritual dispositions are not capable of allowing the seed to bear fruit.

13:18-23 The explanation of the seeds (see Mark 4:13-20; Luke 8:11-15). The hearers of the parable of the seeds were clearly expected to draw some equivalencies: the seed is Jesus' preaching of the kingdom; the good soil is proper dispositions; the bad soils are improper dispositions; the fruitful seeds are the disciples; the wasted seeds are the unbelievers. But the explanation of the parable given in verses 18-23 goes beyond these obvious correspondences and focuses on the reasons why the seeds failed or prospered. Whether this explanation goes back to Jesus or was worked out in the early church is a point of debate.

According to the explanation, the bad soils are lack of understanding (v. 19), superficiality (v. 21), and division within oneself (v. 22). The corresponding obstacles to belief are the "evil one" (v. 19), tribulation or persecution (v. 21), and worldly cares and the desire for wealth (v. 22). In the good soil, however, the message of Jesus is taken in and yields remarkable results (v. 23).

13:24-30 The grain and the weeds. The parable of the grain and the weeds uses another agricultural comparison to explain the lack of universal acceptance of Jesus' preaching. Jesus sowed good seed, but the evil one has sown a kind of weed that is difficult to distinguish from the grain in the early stages of growth. The parable concerns the proper attitude toward the mixed reception accorded to Jesus. The harvest (v. 30) was a common Old Testament and Jewish symbol for the final judgment, and so the advice is tolerance and patience until God renders his definitive decision. In verses 28-29 the disciples are restrained from any attempt at forcibly rooting out the unbelievers among their fellow Jews. This separation will accompany the final appearance of the kingdom.

13:31-35 The mustard seed and the leaven (see Mark 4:30-32; Luke 13:18-21). The parables of the mustard seed and the leaven use everyday things to illustrate the dynamic of the kingdom of God. The activity of God in the ministry of Jesus seems as small as a mustard seed or as a little yeast, but its result in the fullness of God's rule will be very great. These comparisons suggest that in Jesus' preaching, the kingdom already has a present dimension and that the process moving toward its fullness has in some way been inaugurated. The part of Jesus' discourse that was addressed to the crowds ends (vv. 34-35) by explaining that he used parables in order to fulfill Ps 78:2. The quotation also calls attention to Jesus' exalted status as the one who can reveal the mysteries of the universe.

13:36-43 The explanation of the grain and the weeds. At this point Jesus turns away from the crowds and concentrates on his disciples. To their request for an explanation of the parable of the grain and the weeds, he first responds in verses 37-39 with a catalogue of equivalencies that serves to decode the parable, though according to verses 10-17 the disciples should not need such aids. Then in verses 40-43 he provides a scenario for the events surrounding the last judgment. The latter feature has the effect of shifting the focus from patient tolerance in the present (as in verses 24-30) to the spectacular events that will constitute the end of the world. Again there is a debate regarding the origin of this explanation of the parable. Did it come from Jesus, the early church, or the evangelist?

13:44-50 The treasure, the pearl, and the net. The parables of the treasure and the pearl in verses 44-46 illustrate the zeal with which the kingdom should be pursued. They express the great value of the kingdom, the joy that it brings, and the total commitment that it deserves. The parable of the fish net in verses 47-50 reminds us that the coming of the kingdom will include a final judgment in which good and bad will be separated and receive their fitting rewards and punishments.

13:51-53 Conclusion. The parables discourse ends with a saying that expresses well the ideal to which the evangelist aspired: the ability to see the radically new act of God in Christ in the light of the Old Testament tradition. Such a person understands the relation between the new (Christ) and the old (Jewish tradition). The discourse closes in the customary way (see 7:28; 11:1; 19:1; 26:1).

VIII. MIRACLES AND CONTROVERSIES

Matt 13:54–16:4

13:54-58 Rejection at Nazareth (see Mark 6:1-6; Luke 4:16-30). The themes of unbelief and rejection continue in the incidents about Jesus at Nazareth (vv. 54-58) and the death of John the Baptist (14:1-12). The reference to Jesus as teaching in "their synagogue" (v. 54) suggests a separation between Jesus' followers and other Jews, and probably reflects the situation that existed when Matthew's Gospel was written. The description of Jesus as the "carpenter's son" (v. 55) shows that the people of Nazareth do not know what the readers of the Gospel know from 1:18-25. Their admiration quickly turns to disbelief—a fact explained in verse 57 by what seems to have been a proverb about the prophet's lack of acceptance in his home territory. Lack of faith on the people's part is presented in verse 58 as the explanation for Jesus' refusal to perform miracles there (see Mark 6:5-6).

14:1-12 John's death (see Mark 6:14-29; Luke 9:7-9). The tradition about the reaction of Herod Antipas (the son of Herod the Great) to Jesus is tied to the account of Jesus' activity in and around Nazareth. As the official in charge of governing Galilee from 4 B.C.E. to A.D. 39, Herod showed curiosity toward Jesus and wondered whether he might be John the Baptist restored to life (vv. 1-2). This provides the occasion for Matthew to tell the grisly story of John's execution and to connect the rejection of Jesus to the rejection of John (see

11:2-19). The description of Herod's marriage in verse 3 (see Mark 6:17) is not exactly correct, since Herodias had been married to another Herod, who was Herod Antipas' half-brother. In any case, the account in verses 3-12 develops the parallel between the tragic fate of John and what awaits Jesus. Both were regarded by the people as prophets, arrested on very flimsy grounds, executed on account of the weakness of a government official, buried by their disciples, and thought to have been raised from the dead.

14:13-21 The feeding of five thousand (see Mark 6:30-44; Luke 9:10-17; John 6:1-14). Matthew's concentration on the rejection of Jesus is interrupted by three miracle stories of varying length and content. Jesus' suspicion about Herod's interest in him leads him to depart to a deserted place, but the crowds continue to follow him. After curing some of the sick, Jesus provides enough food for five thousand men, plus women and children (vv. 15-21). Matthew's account is similar to Mark's, except that it is more concise and places the disciples in a better light. Matthew 14:16-18, when compared with Mark 6:37-38, softens the disciples' lack of understanding. The disciples appear as partners in the discussion and share in feeding the crowds. The language of Matt 14:19, when compared with that of Matt 26:26, suggests that the feeding was viewed as an anticipation or preview of the Last Supper and thus of the church's celebration of the Eucharist. The fish (v. 19) and the twelve baskets of leftovers may point beyond the Last Supper to the banquet of the Messiah at the final coming of the kingdom.

14:22-33 Walking on the water (see Mark 6:45-52; John 6:15-21). The transitional passage in verses 22-23 situates the disciples at sea and Jesus alone in prayer on the mountain. The disciples are on their own, and they are faring badly. The boat may well be a symbol of the church (see 8:23). In the disciples' time of need, Jesus comes to rescue them and appears as the lord over the powers of nature (vv. 24-27). Into this episode Matthew has inserted the story of Peter's attempt to walk on the water and his subsequent failure on account of his little faith (vv. 28-31). Peter represents the disciples (and all Christians) in his enthusiastic love and insufficient faith. In his fright he addresses Jesus with a prayer ("Lord, save me"), and he receives a criticism about the smallness of his faith. The story climaxes with the adoring confession from the disciples that Jesus truly is the Son of God (vv. 32-33).

14:34-36 Healings at Gennesaret (see Mark 6:53-56). The healings at Gennesaret constitute the third member in this series of miracle stories and repeat the theme of the great impression made by Jesus on the general public. The very favorable reaction to Jesus stands in contrast to the rejection at Nazareth in 13:54-58 and the hostility shown to him by the scribes and Pharisees in 15:1-20.

15:1-20 The controversy about ritual purity (see Mark 7:1-23). Jesus' three acts of power are followed by a controversy with the Pharisees and scribes. The specific issue for debate is the disciples' failure to observe the rules of ritual purity as exactly as the Pharisees did (v. 2). The Pharisees had built up a body of tradition designed to ensure the observance of the written law. They also wished to extend to all Israelites the rules that originally applied only to members of priestly families on the grounds that Israel is a priestly people. Thus they expected Jesus and his followers to observe the rules of priestly purity spelled out in Lev 22:1-16.

The first part of Jesus' response (vv. 3-9) attacks the Pharisees' idea of tradition. Jesus argues that sometimes their tradition leads to breaking the clear commands of the law (vv. 3-6). The commandment about honoring one's parents is stated in the law both positively (Exod 20:12; Deut 5:16) and negatively (Exod 21:17). But the Pharisees' tradition, according to Jesus, allows a person to place property under sacred vow as a means of preventing the parents from having access to it. Thus a pious fiction provides the excuse for disregarding and getting around a sacred obligation encouraged by the law. The words of Isa 29:13 are used to brand such behavior as hypocrisy. The tradition that claims to protect the law actually violates it.

The second part of Jesus' response (vv. 10-20) concentrates on the specific issue of ritual purity. The statement in verse 11 to the effect that there is only moral uncleanness is very radical, since large parts of the Old Testament law concern ritual uncleanness contracted by touching and by eating certain foods. Only a firm faith in Jesus as the authoritative interpreter of the law could allow Matthew and his community to accept such a revolutionary teaching.

To the basic statement in verse 11 are joined a very harsh judgment on the Pharisees (vv. 12-14) and an explanation for the disciples of Jesus (vv. 15-20). When informed about the Pharisees' offense at his teaching, Jesus denies their spiritual roots (v. 13) and condemns them as blind guides leading others to destruction (v. 14). Peter's request for an explanation of Jesus' teaching in verse 15 assumes that "parable" means "mystery" or "riddle." Jesus' explanation in verses 17-20 merely expands and makes concrete the radical statement in verse 11. Moral purity alone is important, and the evil designs of the mind make a person morally impure and issue in the kinds of action forbidden by the Old Testament. The complaint raised against Jesus' disciples in verse 2 has no validity, because the whole tradition of ritual impurity and purity has no validity.

15:21-28 The healing of the non-Jewish woman's daughter (see Mark 7:24-30). The pattern of three miracles and a controversy story found in 14:13–15:20 is repeated in 15:21–16:4. The first healing takes place in the area surrounding the southern Phoenician cities of Tyre and Sidon, and involves the possessed daughter of a non-Jewish woman. In fact, the healing is simply the occasion for a dialogue of faith between the Gentile woman and Jesus. In verse 22 she tries to initiate the dialogue with a prayer and addresses Jesus as Lord and Son of David, but is rebuffed by Jesus on the ground that his mission during his ministry prior to his death is confined to the Jews (v. 24). When the woman persists in her prayer ("Lord, help me"), Jesus again rebuffs her with a sharp saying that equates non-Jews with dogs, and Jews with sons and daughters of God (v. 26). The woman has the presence of mind and the cleverness to point out that even dogs are given crumbs and scraps from their masters' tables (v. 27). This display of faith so impresses Jesus that he grants her request that her daughter be healed. This story of salvation being offered to Gentiles through faith in Jesus would have encouraged the church's mission to the Gentiles after Jesus' death and resurrection. In God's plan of salvation, pride of place belongs to the Jews ("the children"). But Jesus himself praised and respected the remarkable faith of non-Jews (see also 8:5-13).

15:29-31 The healing of many people. The second miracle story in this series summarizes Jesus' many acts of healing (see 12:15-21; 14:34-36). After the geographical introduction in verse 29, words and phrases from Isa 35:5-6 and 29:18-19 are used to describe the kinds of physical maladies (v. 30) and the remarkable changes brought about by Jesus the healer. At the center of the account is the person of Jesus (v. 30). The sick are brought to him and he cures them.

15:32-39 The feeding of four thousand (see Mark 8:1-10). The third miracle story involves the feeding of another large crowd of people. It has many features in common with the feeding of the five thousand in 14:13-21. The two accounts differ chiefly in the numbers: loaves (five versus seven), baskets of leftovers (twelve versus seven), and the number of men (five thousand versus four thousand). Jesus' compassion for the crowds (v. 32) leads him to supply their physical needs, and the language in which the multiplication is described (v. 36) again suggests Eucharistic overtones (see 14:19; 26:26). There is no good reason to view this miracle as the "Gentile feeding" as opposed to the "Jewish feeding" of 14:13-21. The two passages may represent independent accounts of a single event.

16:1-4 The controversy about signs (see Mark 8:11-13; Luke 12:54-56). Just as the preceding series of miracle stories in 14:13-36 ended with a controversy story in 15:1-20, so the second series of miracle stories in 15:21-39 ends with a controversy in 16:1-4. Despite all the miracles that Jesus has worked, the Pharisees and Sadducees want some further sign that he is from God. Although the Pharisees and Sadducees opposed each other on many points, here they appear to be united in opposing Jesus.

The reply in verses 2-3 does not occur in some important manuscripts of the Greek text. Whether it belonged in the original Gospel text or not, its basic point is that Jesus' miracles are signs of God's coming kingdom. The opponents know enough to predict the weather from the color of the sky, but they are blind to the real nature of Jesus' miracles. The sign of Jonah could be the offer of salvation to the Gentiles (see 8:5-13; 15:21-28), but in light of 12:40 the evangelist probably understood it to be the death and resurrection of Jesus.

IX. THE WAY TO THE CROSS

Matt 16:5–17:27

16:5-12 The leaven of the Pharisees and Sadducees (see Mark 8:14-21). With the so-called discourse on the leaven, Jesus turns to his disciples and instructs them throughout the rest of the chapter. His instructions concern the teaching of the Pharisees and Sadducees (16:5-12), the identity of Jesus and Peter (16:13-20), the cross and resurrection (16:21-23), and the discipleship of the cross (16:24-28).

In the discourse on the leaven (vv. 5-12), the disciples' failure to bring bread along for their journey is joined to Jesus' puzzling warning against the leaven of the Pharisees and Sadducees (v. 6). The leaven apparently refers to a corrupting influence. By substituting "Sadducees" for Mark's "Herod" or "Herodians" (see Mark 8:15), Matthew prepares for the concluding explanation (v. 12) that the leaven describes the corrupting teaching of the Pharisees and Sadducees.

Jesus' response to the disciples' misunderstanding takes the form of five questions in verses 8-11. Allusion is made to the feedings of the five thousand (14:13-21) and the four thousand (15:32-39), with the implication that the disciples should know by now that Jesus is capable of caring for their physical needs. The disciples again show weakness of faith—a characteristic way of describing the imperfect condition of Jesus' closest followers in Matthew (see 6:30; 8:26; 14:31). Though Jesus' rebuke of the disciples seems quite sharp, it is not nearly as cutting as the series of questions in Mark 8:17-21. At any rate, the disciples' slowness to understand shows how much they need to be instructed about Jesus and about what it means to follow him.

16:13-20 The identity of Jesus and Peter (see Mark 8:27-30; Luke 9:18-21). Peter's confession of faith begins as a dialogue between Jesus and the disciples. It takes place near Caesarea Philippi in northern Palestine and marks the initial step of the journey that will issue in Jesus' passion and death in Jerusalem. When Jesus asks concerning popular speculations regarding his identity, the disciples list some current opinions (v. 14). According to 14:2, Herod Antipas thought that Jesus was John the Baptist restored to life. The return of Elijah was expected to accompany the coming of God's kingdom (see Mal 4:5-6). The reference to Jeremiah is found only in Matt 16:14 (see Mark 8:28; Luke 9:19), and it may indicate that the similarities between the prophet Jeremiah and Jesus were recognized (see Matt 2:17; 27:9).

In the second stage of the dialogue (vv. 15-16), Jesus asks not for popular speculations but rather for the disciples' own assessment. As is often the case in this section of Matthew (see 15:15; 16:22; 17:24; 18:21), Peter appears as the spokesman for the group and proclaims Jesus to be the Messiah. (*Messiah* is a Hebrew word that means "anointed one"; its Greek translation is *Christos.*) Peter's confession of Jesus as the Messiah reflects the disciples' hope that Jesus would deliver Israel from its enemies and establish God's kingdom on earth.

Up to verse 16b, the account closely parallels Mark 8:27-29. But to Mark's narrative Matthew adds in verse 16b a further specification of Jesus' identity ("the Son of the living God") and Jesus' promise to Peter in verses 17-19. This addition changes the flow of the story in Peter's favor. Whereas in Mark 8:27-33 the confession of faith is passed over and gives way to a misunderstanding on Peter's part, in Matthew the confession brings a solemn blessing on Peter.

The phrase "Son of the living God" in verse 16b corrects and transcends any false implications present in the title "Messiah." The blessing in verse 17 declares that Peter's confession was a revelation from God, and verse 18 promises that Peter is the rock on which the Christian community will be built after Jesus' death and resurrection. No power opposed to God will be able to destroy that community. Finally, in verse 19 Peter is portrayed as the "major-domo" or prime minister in the kingdom proclaimed by Jesus (see Isa 22:15-25). His exercise of the power to bind and loose (see 18:18) will be confirmed by God. The content of that power is not completely clear. It may involve laying down rules and giving exemptions, imposing or lifting excommunications, forgiving or not forgiving sins, or even performing exorcisms.

The language of the passage is very Semitic, and clearly verses 16b-19 transmit an early tradition. There is a debate about whether this blessing was uttered by Jesus during his earthly ministry or after his resurrection (see 1 Cor 15:5; Luke 24:34). Other scholars trace its origins to the church at Antioch in Syria. Whatever its origin, the passage praises Peter as the recipient of a divine revelation (v. 17), declares him to be the foundation of the community (v. 18), and gives him special authority (v. 19). With the command to silence in verse 20, Matthew rejoins Mark's account.

16:21-23 The first prediction of the passion (see Mark 8:31-33; Luke 9:22). The first prediction of the passion removes any doubts about what kind of Messiah Jesus is. In verse 21 Jesus proclaims unambiguously that his earthly future will involve suffering and death in accord with his Father's plan ("he must go to Jerusalem"). The content of the passion prediction closely parallels the events of Matt 26–28. Despite his confession of faith and the blessing in response to it, Peter in verse 22 rejects the possibility that Jesus' messiahship could involve suffering. In verse 23 Peter's attitude is rebuked sharply as coming from Satan, as a stumbling block in Jesus' way, and as purely human thinking.

16:24-28 The discipleship of the cross (see Mark 8:34–9:1; Luke 9:23-27). Sayings on the cost and reward of discipleship follow the first prediction of the passion. The saying about taking up the cross in verse 24 (see 10:38) connects the fate of the disciples with Jesus' own fate. Whereas in 10:1 the disciples were given a share in Jesus' power displayed in chapters 8–9, here they are warned that discipleship also involves a share in the cross. The sayings in verses 25-26 revolve around the theme of life and suggest that only in letting go of self and letting God do the guiding can we ever find freedom and happiness. In verse 27 the typically Jewish belief in rewards and punishments as being determined at the coming of God's kingdom in the judgment is given a Christian interpretation: Jesus the Son of Man will be in charge. Whatever verse 28 may have originally referred to (the imminent coming of the kingdom, the death and resurrection, Pentecost), here it serves as an introduction to the transfiguration in 17:1-8. In that event the disciples receive a preview of the Son of Man's glorious coming in the kingdom.

17:1-8 The transfiguration (see Mark 9:2-8; Luke 9:28-36). The story of the transfiguration of Jesus is a preview of the Son of Man's coming in his kingship (see 16:28). Some interpreters have argued that the account originally told of an appearance of the risen Lord and has been put back into the earthly ministry of Jesus. But the narrative has very little in common with the resurrection appearances in the Gospels. The transfiguration seems to have been a historical experience of a visionary character. The reference to "six days later" in verse 1 is puzzling, though the traditional significance of the mountain as a privileged place of divine revelation suggests an allusion to God's appearance to Moses on Sinai (see Exod 24:16). Here as elsewhere in the Gospels there is an inner circle of disciples constituted by Peter, James, and John. The word "transfigured" used in verse 2 to describe what happened to Jesus indicates a change of form or shape. The disciples experience a glimpse of Jesus' lordship as it will be fully manifest at the coming of the kingdom. The order of the names of Moses and Elijah in verse 3 makes it clear that they represent the law and the prophets of the Old Testament.

Matthew's primary interest in the account of the transfiguration is the disciples' reactions to the event. In verse 4 Peter addresses Jesus as "Lord" and asks his permission to erect the three booths. Apparently he hoped that all of them would remain in this glorious atmosphere until the kingdom came. The disciples' hopes are raised still higher in verse 5 with the voice from the cloud (a Jewish image of God's presence) that affirms Jesus' special status in exactly the same terms as at the baptism (see 3:17). The awesome character of the experience frightens the disciples (v. 6), but Jesus acts as a comforter and encourages them not to be afraid (v. 7).

17:9-13 The sequel to the transfiguration (see Mark 9:9-13). The sequel to the transfiguration connects the preview of Jesus' glory with his suffering, death, and resurrection. In verse 9 the transfiguration is characterized as a vision, and the disciples are warned not to talk about it until after the resurrection. In contrast to the disciples in Mark 9:10, they apparently understand what rising from the dead means. Their question about Elijah in verse 10 refers to the tradition based on Mal 4:5-6 that the prophet Elijah would return from heaven before God's kingdom would come. Jesus' reply in verses 11-12 accepts this tradition as valid but asserts that Elijah had already come in the person of John the Baptist (see 11:14). Just as John was not recognized but rather underwent suffering and death, so Jesus as the Son of Man will be misunderstood and put to death (see 14:1-12). In case there were any doubts about the identification of John the Baptist as Elijah, Matthew adds that the disciples then realized that Jesus had been speaking about John the Baptist (v. 13).

17:14-20 The healing of the possessed boy (see Mark 9:14-29; Luke 9:37-43). Matthew's account of the healing of the possessed boy is much shorter than Mark's. Indeed, the issue is not so much Jesus' power to heal, as it is in Mark, but rather the disciple's failure to heal as due to their "little faith" (v. 20). The lengthy description of the boy's condition in Mark 9:17-18, 20-22, 25-26 is condensed considerably, and he is simply described as being affected by the phases of the moon ("a lunatic"). The boy's father in verses 14-15 approaches Jesus in a prayerful way ("knelt down before him . . . 'Lord, have pity'"). Given the way that Matthew tells this story, the stern rebuke in verse 17 seems to be directed at the disciples; this is confirmed in verse 20, where they are criticized for their "little faith."

The mention of little faith is the occasion for using the saying on faith the size of the mustard seed. The mustard seed is tiny (see 13:31), and the point of the saying is that even a small amount of faith can have dramatic effects. The connection between the story in verses 14-19, whose point is the ineffectiveness of the disciples' faith, and the saying in verse 20, whose point is the great power of even a little faith, is purely formal. In other words, the two units have been joined only because they deal with "little faith" and despite the fact that the meaning in each unit is quite different. Some manuscripts include as verse 21 the saying found in Mark 9:29. Yet, if the passage were originally part of Matthew, there would be no good reason why it should be omitted in the other ancient manuscripts. It most likely was added to Matthew's text in the process of copying.

17:22-23 The second prediction of the passion (see Mark 9:30-32; Luke 9:43-45). The second prediction of the passion reminds us that the fate of suffering and death awaits Jesus in Jerusalem. The term "handed over" in verse 22 suggests that these events will take place with God's permission and in accord with his plan. Unlike the disciples in Mark 9:32, who do not understand the prophecy and are afraid to ask about it, the disciples in Matt 17:23 understand it very clearly.

17:24-27 The temple tax. When questioned about whether Jesus paid the tax for the upkeep of the Jerusalem temple and the sacrifices offered there (see Exod 30:11-16; Neh 10:32-33), Peter, as the spokesman for Jesus, answers affirmatively (vv. 24-25a). But the story goes on to make it clear that Jesus had no real obligation to do so. The illustration used in verses 25b-26 is based on Jesus' identity as the Son of God. Just as kings gather taxes from foreigners but not from their own sons, so God (whose house the Jerusalem temple is) demands taxes from people in general but not from his Son Jesus. The story ends in verse 27 with the miraculous provision of the money for paying the tax.

Although Jesus was under no obligation to pay the temple tax, he did pay it in order to avoid giving scandal to anyone. After A.D. 70, when the Jerusalem temple had been destroyed and the Jewish temple tax was diverted to provide for the upkeep of the pagan temple of Jupiter Capitolinus in Rome, this story would have furnished advice for the Jewish members of Matthew's community. As free children of God through Jesus, they are not obliged to pay the tax but should do so in order to avoid further problems (see Rom 13:1-7; 1 Pet 2:13-17).

X. ADVICE TO A DIVIDED COMMUNITY

Matt 18:1-35

The fourth of the five major discourses of Jesus (see chs. 5–7; 10; 13; 24–25) has been aptly described as Matthew's advice to a divided community. The evangelist has taken sayings from various sources and arranged them to supply guidance for Christian communities as they try to deal with status-seeking, scandal, lapses, reconciliation, and forgiveness. The two major parts of this discourse concern the care of the "little ones" (18:1-14) and the proper attitude toward community members who have sinned (18:15-35).

18:1-4 Greatness in God's kingdom (see Mark 9:33-37; Luke 9:46-48). The occasion for the discourse is provided by the disciples' question about who is the greatest in God's kingdom (v. 1). Their question had a context in Jewish society of the time, since there was a good deal of speculation about position and status in the coming kingdom. The community that gave us the Dead Sea scrolls even arranged the communal meals according to rank within the group. The meals were supposed to mirror what would happen when God's kingdom comes.

As an answer to the disciples' question, Jesus points to a child (v. 2) and urges the disciples to become like children (v. 3). In ancient society the child had no legal rights or standing and was entirely dependent on the parents. The child necessarily received everything as a gift. Likewise, no one through rank or status has a real claim on God's kingdom; only those who recognize this fact and receive the kingdom as a gift will enter it (v. 4). The child is presented as a symbol of those without legal right or claim to the kingdom, not as a model of innocence or humility. All speculations about rank in the coming kingdom and about the present as a mirror of the future are dismissed as a tragic misunderstanding of God and his kingdom.

18:5-10 Scandalizing little ones (see Mark 9:42-48; Luke 17:1-2). In this section the word "child" takes on a different meaning. In the preceding passage it referred to one without legal status, but here it describes a simple and good-hearted member of the community who can be led astray. The saying about receiving a child in Jesus' name in verse 5 expresses an identity between the little ones and Jesus. He dwells in them in a special way. Those who would lead them astray are given three sharp warnings: (1) It is better to be dead than to cause one of these little ones to stumble on the path of discipleship (v. 6). (2) Personal responsibility for scandal cannot be dismissed on the ground that scandal is inevitable (v. 7). (3) Anything—even going without a foot or a hand or an eye—is better than giving scandal within the community (vv. 8-9). This third warning may presuppose the image of the community as the body of Christ, from which offending members are to be cut off or excommunicated. The passage closes in verse 10, as it began in verse 5, with a reference to God's special care and concern for the "little ones."

18:12-14 Little ones who stray (see Luke 15:3-7). What happens if one of the little ones does go astray? This passage compares God to a shepherd who searches out those sheep that stray. The search is not automatically successful ("And if he finds it," v. 13), but the return of the "strays" gives great pleasure to God. God wishes that none of the little ones should ever perish or be damned (v. 14). Note that a distinction is drawn between those who stray and those who perish.

18:15-17 Reconciling a sinner. The second major part of Jesus' fourth discourse (18:15-35) concerns attitudes toward community members who have sinned. The first section (18:15-17) outlines the various steps to be taken when one Christian sins against another. At each stage (personal discussion, discussion before witnesses, discussion before the whole community), the aim is to win the erring Christian back to the community. Even the drastic step of excommunication probably was intended to shock the offender into reconciliation. Similar procedures were employed by the Dead Sea community, on the basis of Deut 19:15. The designation of the excommunicated member as a Gentile or a tax collector in verse 17 is odd in view of Jesus' openness to both groups. Here the terms simply describe people who were excluded from the mainstream of Jewish religious life.

18:18-20 Binding and loosing. In their present context within Jesus' advice to a divided community, the sayings about binding and loosing (v. 18) and the two or three gathered in Jesus' name (vv. 19-20) probably refer to the community's power to exclude erring members as a last resort. In verse 18 the disciples (see 16:19, where Peter alone receives the power) are promised that God will stand behind their decisions on earth. In verses 19-20 the agreement of the community joined in prayer will be accepted by God as binding, because he is present in the community's prayer in a special way. The momentous and painful character of cutting off one who has ignored the community is balanced to some extent by the community's confidence that God approves its decisions.

18:21-35 Forgiveness. Having dealt with the extreme case of the totally incorrigible member and the extreme punishment of excommunication, the discourse turns to the more ordinary experience of forgiveness and reconciliation within the community. The situation is the same as that of 18:15: "If your brother sins against you . . . ." In this case, however, the erring person listens to the offended party or to the several witnesses or to the community as a whole. How many times should such a person be forgiven? Once again Peter serves as the spokesman for the group and gives what he imagines to be a very generous answer to his own question. Seven times (v. 21). Jesus corrects Peter and answers: Seventy-seven times. The new number is not to be taken literally. The point is that Christians have no right to place any limit on forgiveness.

Why Christians may not set limits to forgiveness is illustrated by the parable of the merciless steward (vv. 23-25). This parable puts in story form the second "we-petition" of the Lord's Prayer: "And forgive us our debts, as we forgive our debtors" (6:12). In other words, God's willingness to forgive us depends on our willingness to forgive others (see 6:14-15). The actions of the king in the parable indicate that he is to be identified with God. He demands a reckoning (v. 23), is approached as lord (v. 26), and shows great mercy in writing off the huge debt (v. 27). Yet the merciless servant failed to learn from the example of the king, and his cruelty toward the other servant results in the revocation of his own forgiveness (vv. 28-34). The story warns us that the forgiveness granted to us by God will be revoked unless we are willing to forgive others (v. 35). The unforgiving are excluded from God's mercy. Those who wish to receive God's mercy must show mercy toward others.

XI. GROWING OPPOSITION TO JESUS

Matt 19:1–23:39

19:1-12 Marriage and divorce (see Mark 10:1-12). The fourth discourse ends in the usual manner ("When Jesus finished"), and Jesus enters Judean territory (19:1). For Matthew (as for Mark), Galilee is the place of revelation (see 4:12-17) and Judea is the place of rejection and death. Jesus continues to attract great crowds and to heal the sick (v. 2).

As a way of testing Jesus, the Pharisees question him about marriage and divorce. The phrasing of their inquiry in verse 3 ("for any cause") places Jesus' teaching in the context of the Jewish debate about the grounds for divorce. According to Deut 24:1, the husband wrote out the terms of the divorce, presented it to the wife, and thus ended the marriage. The grounds for divorce in Deut 24:1 ("because he finds in her something indecent") are vague. In Jesus' time, one school restricted divorce to the case of adultery on the woman's part, and another school was far more free in its interpretation, to the extent that a woman could be divorced if she was a bad cook or not beautiful. It was assumed that divorced men and women could marry again, though the Temple Scroll from Qumran casts doubt on this for members of some Jewish circles at least.

Matthew's presentation of Jesus' teaching on marriage and divorce in verses 4-9 first cites Gen 1:27 (v. 4) and Gen 2:24 (v. 5) to the effect that in God's original plan of creation marriage was indissoluble and no human agent could end such a union (v. 6). In the Old Testament (see Deut 24:1-4) divorce was allowed only as a concession to human weakness. This was not God's original intention (vv. 7-8). Once again Jesus assumes the role of the authoritative interpreter of the law, and in verse 9 he forbids divorce and remarriage absolutely, except for the case of *porneia*—most likely a marriage contracted within the degrees of kinship forbidden by Lev 18:6-18 (see the commentary on Matt 5:32). There is little doubt that Jesus regarded marriage as indissoluble (see Mark 10:11-12; Luke 16:18; 1 Cor 7:10-11). But it is not easy to know whether in this case Jesus was stating an ideal or laying down a command.

The radical nature of Jesus' teaching on this topic (it does away with Deut 24:1-4) leads the disciples in verse 10 to question whether it is advisable to marry at all. In 19:11 Jesus clearly states that celibacy is a gift from God and is not for all (v. 11). According to verse 12, Christian celibacy is a response to the experience of God's kingdom as made present in the teaching and example of Jesus. It is not based on male suspicion of women, cultic purity, or the demands of community life. The Dead Sea community also seems to have had both married and celibate members.

19:13-15 Children and the kingdom (see Mark 10:13-16; Luke 18:15-17). As someone with a reputation for holiness, Jesus' blessing was much sought for children (v. 13). The assumption was that the power of holiness somehow went forth from him and communicated itself to others. The occasion is used to teach about receiving God's kingdom. As was the case in 18:1-4, the child represents those without legal claims or rights, those who must necessarily receive everything as a gift. The kingdom is for those without pretensions to status and superiority, for those who recognize that it is a gift.

19:16-30 Wealth and the kingdom (see Mark 10:17-31; Luke 18:18-30). The theme of wealth as a possible obstacle to perfect discipleship is raised in the story of Jesus' encounter with the rich young man. When asked what is necessary to have eternal life, Jesus invites the young man ("If you wish") to enter eternal life by observing the Ten Commandments and the command to love one's neighbor as oneself (vv. 16-20). When he replies that he has already been observing these commandments, Jesus invites him to a new stage ("If you wish to be perfect") in verse 21. For this person, perfection as a disciple of Jesus involves distributing his wealth to the poor and sharing in the insecurity and the trust that were characteristic of the earthly Jesus and his first followers. The young man was unable to accept Jesus' invitation to the new stage of perfection beyond the observance of the law (v. 22).

The rich young man's inability to accept Jesus' challenge sets the scene for general teachings on wealth as an obstacle to discipleship in verses 23-26. Not only is it difficult for the rich to enter God's kingdom (v. 23); it is practically impossible, as the saying about the "eye of a needle" in verse 24 makes clear. The disciples' amazement in verse 25 stems from their assumption that wealth is a sign of divine favor. In verse 26 Jesus teaches that no one can enter the kingdom because of his or her own possessions or achievements; the kingdom is God's gift.

As the spokesman once again, Peter asks about the rewards for accepting Jesus' challenge to radical poverty (vv. 27-30). Peter had left his fishing business in Galilee (see 4:18-22) and his family (see 8:14-15). The risks and sacrifices of Jesus' first followers should not be minimized. In the "new age" of the kingdom, they will share in the glory of the Son of Man (v. 28) and will be rewarded with an even better social and religious community (v. 29). The odd saying about the reversal of positions between the first and the last in verse 30 is illustrated in the following parable.

20:1-16 The parable of the good employer. By bracketing the parable in 20:1-15 with the sayings about the first and the last in 19:30 and 20:16 and by placing it in the context of the rewards for the disciples (19:27), the evangelist makes it illustrate Jesus' promise that the disciples, now considered the last, will be the first in receiving rewards (see 20:8). In the context of Jesus' ministry, the parable was probably addressed to his opponents who criticized him for preaching the good news of the kingdom to tax collectors and sinners. In that setting, the parable is best entitled "the good employer." The employer is God as revealed in Jesus as his representative.

The good employer hires workmen at dawn for the usual daily wage of one denarius and sends them off to work in his vineyard (vv. 1-2). Other workmen in verses 3-7 are hired at various times during the day (midmorning, noon, midafternoon, late afternoon), but their wages are not specified ("whatever is just"). In verse 8 the employer commands that the workers be paid in the reverse order of their hiring and that all receive the same wage (v.11). To the complaints of those who had worked all day (vv. 11-12), the employer answers that he has been just in paying the agreed wage to them (vv. 13-14); they have no right to complain if he wants to be generous to others (v. 15). God's own justice and generosity are used to explain why Jesus preached the kingdom to both the already pious and the lost sheep of Israel (see 10:6). If they accept his preaching, both groups will be granted an equal share in God's kingdom.

20:17-19 The third prediction of the passion (see Mark 10:32-34; Luke 18:31-34). The third prediction of the passion occurs on the road leading up to Jerusalem, which is located in a mountainous region. This prediction is more detailed than the two previous ones (16:21; 17:22-23) and mentions explicitly the Jewish and Gentile tormentors of Jesus. Matthew's version specifies crucifixion as the mode of Jesus' death.

20:20-28 Places of prominence in the kingdom (see Mark 10:35-45). The question of status in the coming kingdom (see 18:1-4) appears again with the request by the mother of James and John that her sons should have places of special prominence in the kingdom. In Mark 10:35-37 the two disciples make the request on their own. Jesus replies in verses 22-23 that (1) in order to share in his kingdom, the disciples must share his cup of suffering, and (2) it is not his prerogative to assign positions of prominence in the kingdom. The indignation of the other disciples in verse 24 furnishes the occasion for Jesus to teach about service to others as the way of leadership in his community. Then leadership as power according to Gentile patterns ("lord it over them") is contrasted with leadership after the pattern of Jesus, the servant and slave of all (vv. 25-27). This style of leadership as service to others is grounded in the example of Christ's sacrificial death as a "ransom for many" (v. 28).

20:29-34 The healing of two blind men (see Mark 10:46-52; Luke 18:35-43). The story of the healing of the two blind men at Jericho parallels the healing of Bartimaeus in Mark 10:46-52, but there are many differences. In Matthew's account there are two blind men (for a similar phenomenon, see 8:28), and more attention is paid to their faith in Jesus' power than to the process of the healing. They address Jesus in verses 30, 31, and 33 in the language of prayer. They call him "Lord" and "Son of David." The irony is that those who are blind physically have the spiritual insight to recognize Jesus for who he really is. Jesus the merciful healer then gives them physical sight (v. 34), and they join the band of his disciples.

21:1-11 The Messiah's entrance (see Mark 11:1-11; Luke 19:28-38; John 12:12-19). Jesus' entry into Jerusalem is made from the east, from the Mount of Olives, which was connected with the "day of the Lord" in Zech 14:4. Matthew understood the event as the fulfillment of Isa 62:11 and Zech 9:9 (Matt 21:5). Isa 62:11 ("Say to daughter Zion") is fulfilled by the enthusiastic reception given to Jesus by the crowds (v. 8) and the greeting given to him as the Son of David in the words of Ps 118:25-26 (v. 9). The whole city is interested in Jesus, and he is identified as the prophet from Galilee (vv. 10-11). Zech 9:9 is fulfilled in the humble manner in which Jesus enters the city. The two beasts of burden ("the ass and the colt") in verses 2, 7 fulfill in an overly literal way the double mention of the animal in the Old Testament passage. Jesus' entrance into Jerusalem was the entrance of the Messiah and so conformed fully to Old Testament prophecy and Jewish expectations. However, it was also the entrance of a humble person, not that of a military conqueror.

21:12-17 The Messiah's temple (see Mark 11:15-19; Luke 19:45-48; John 2:13-22). The Messiah's first actions in the holy city involve the temple of Jerusalem. His action in overturning the commercial enterprises in the outer court of the temple (v. 12) is also presented as fulfilling Old Testament prophecies. According to Isa 56:7, the temple should be a house of prayer; according to Jer 7:11, those businessmen have turned it into a den of thieves.

Besides this symbolic protest against the commercialization of the temple, Jesus also cures the blind and the lame. The presence of the blind and the lame in the temple area was probably not welcomed by the temple officials (see 2 Sam 5:8). Up to this point, the Pharisees had been the chief opponents of Jesus, but now and throughout the rest of the Gospel the chief priests and elders emerge as the major enemies. Angered by Jesus' demonstration, the healings in the temple area, and the popular enthusiasm for Jesus, the opponents ask for an explanation in verse 16. The explanation that Jesus offers is that the children's enthusiasm is simply the fulfillment of Ps 8:3. With that, Jesus departs for Bethany, a village east of Jerusalem, and spends the night there.

21:18-22 The cursing of the fig tree (see Mark 11:12-14, 20-24). The cursing of the fig tree is the only miraculous action of Jesus that does any harm or works destruction. In fact, it is best seen as a symbolic or prophetic action: When the Messiah came to search for the fruits of righteousness in the holy city, he found nothing there. The action prefigures the fall of Jerusalem and the destruction of the temple in A.D. 70. Matthew's emphasis on the miraculous character of the action ("immediately the fig tree withered") in verses 19, 20 sets the stage for the sayings in verses 21-22 on the extraordinary power of prayer offered in faith. The disciples can share in the power of Jesus if they have faith like his. As is customary in Matthew's Gospel (see especially chs. 8–9), the display of Jesus' miraculous power dissolves into a teaching on the dynamics of prayer and faith.

21:23-27 Jesus' authority (see Mark 11:27-33; Luke 20:1-8). The debate about Jesus' authority in verses 23-27 is the first in a series of controversies between Jesus and his opponents. The series is interrupted by three parables in 21:28–22:14 and rejoined in 22:15-46. In the first controversy the opponents are the chief priests and elders of the people. This group will be instrumental in getting Jesus put to death. The point of controversy is the authority (v. 23) on which Jesus had entered the city, cleansed the temple, healed the lame and the blind, and taught.

Jesus' response takes the form of a question to his questioners (vv. 24-25). He promises to answer their question if they will first state publicly whether John's baptism was from God or purely human. Jesus' question puts his opponents on the defensive: If they say "from God," they admit their stupidity and lack of spiritual insight in not taking up John's cause. If they say "purely human," they risk the anger of the many people who regarded John as a prophet sent from God. Jesus' counter-question reduces his opponents to silence ("We do not know"). They have been put to shame, and Jesus has come away from the debate with honor (v. 27). The controversy also continues the parallel between John the Baptist and Jesus. Matthew's readers know that God was the source of the authority for both John and Jesus.

21:28-32 The two sons. The controversies are interrupted by three parables dealing with the culpability of Jesus' opponents (vv. 28-32), the punishment allotted to them (vv. 33-43), and the carrying out of that punishment (22:1-14). The parable of the two sons (vv. 28-32) assumes that Jesus' preaching of God's kingdom is a pivotal moment in Israel's religious history. Just as the second son initially refused the father's command but later repented and obeyed (v. 30), so the tax collectors and prostitutes (v. 31) are now reforming their lives in response to Jesus and are entering the kingdom. Just as the first son promised to obey but did nothing (v. 29), so the professedly and publicly religious opponents of Jesus fail to act upon Jesus' message of the kingdom. The opponents' culpability consists in their refusal of Jesus' preaching and stands in sharp contrast to the openness and resolve of those whom they despise. In verse 32 the parallel between John and Jesus continues: The dynamic of the parable of the two sons was present in John's ministry also. The conversion of the tax collectors and sinners to the way of righteousness should inspire Jesus' opponents to accept his preaching, and not to regard him with suspicion and hostility.

21:33-46 The tenants (see Mark 12:1-12; Luke 20:9-19). The parable of the tenants concerns the punishment allotted to the religious and political leaders of Israel. The parable obviously alludes to the description of Israel as God's vineyard in Isa 5:1-7, and many of the phrases in verse 33 are taken directly from that Old Testament passage.

God is the owner of the vineyard; he has leased out his property to the religious and political leaders. Many servants (prophets) were sent to the vineyard, but they all met the same bad fate (vv. 34-36). The owner expects that at least his son (Jesus) will be received with respect. In fact, he receives even worse treatment, to the point of being killed outside the vineyard (vv. 37-39). When the owner himself comes, he will punish the tenants by destroying them (v. 41) and taking away their claim to preeminence in God's kingdom (v. 43). The vineyard will be leased to others (the church), and the people of God in Christ will yield an abundant harvest. The opponents' rejection of Jesus ("the stone") is the reason for their punishment. This brings to fulfillment Ps 118:22 (v. 42). Matthew's community would find in this parable an explanation for the destruction of Jerusalem by the Romans in A.D. 70 and a justification for its claim to be the true people of God.

The saying about the stone in verse 44 is absent from many early manuscripts and may have been added in other manuscripts from Luke 20:18 because of the thematic connection with Matt 21:42. The major enemies of Jesus—the chief priests and the Pharisees—recognize that these parables concern them (v. 45) but fear to arrest Jesus because the crowds consider him to be a prophet (see 21:11, 26).

22:1-14 The royal marriage feast (see

Luke 14:15-24). The parable of the royal marriage feast concerns the punishment of Jesus' opponents (especially vv. 5-7) and has many features in common with the parable of the tenants in 21:33-46. The marriage feast or banquet was a popular way of imagining what life in the coming kingdom would be like. The king and his son clearly represent God the Father and Jesus respectively. The invitation offered by the first group of servants (prophets) is refused (v. 3), but the invitation given by the second group of servants (perhaps John the Baptist and Jesus) encounters not only indifference (v. 5) but also hostility, to the point that those servants are executed (v. 6). The vivid description in verse 7 of how the king's army destroyed those murderers and their city surely brought to the minds of Matthew's first readers the Roman conquest of Jerusalem in A.D. 70. Because the professedly and publicly religious people of Israel refused the invitation to the kingdom of God, a general invitation has been made (vv. 8-10) to all kinds of people, including tax collectors and prostitutes (and perhaps even non-Jews).

Mere acceptance of the invitation, however, does not guarantee participation in the banquet, as the incident in verses 11-13 makes clear. Guests at a wedding banquet would be expected to appear in clean and neat clothing. When the king (God the Father) sees a man who is not dressed properly, he questions him in a cool manner ("My friend") and has him ejected from the banquet hall. Being a tax collector or prostitute is no more a guarantee of salvation than being a Pharisee or chief priest is; rather, one must receive Jesus' invitation to the kingdom and act upon it so that when the banquet actually begins, one will be properly prepared to participate. In this context the saying in verse 14 suggests that the invitation to the kingdom has been offered to all kinds of people, but only a few of them act upon it in such a way as to be allowed to participate in the banquet of the kingdom.

22:15-22 Taxes to Caesar (see Mark 12:13-17; Luke 20:20-26). After the three parables directed at Jesus' opponents, the series of controversies is rejoined. The second controversy concerns paying taxes to the emperor. The opponents are the Pharisees, who as religious people resented paying taxes to a foreign government, and the Herodians, who may have administered the system of taxation in Palestine. The two groups join forces to trap Jesus. If he affirms that taxes should be paid, he loses the esteem of the religious nationalists. If he denies that taxes should be paid, he is subject to arrest as a political revolutionary.

The Pharisees and Herodians approach Jesus in a flattering but hypocritical manner (v. 16), and then spring their question about whether it is lawful to pay taxes to the emperor (v. 17). Recognizing their hypocrisy (v. 18), Jesus eludes their trap by asking them to show him a coin bearing the image and the name of the emperor. The very fact that both the Pharisees and the Herodians use the emperor's coin implies that they should pay taxes to the emperor (v. 21). Jesus, however, moves the debate to another level by challenging his opponents to be as observant in paying their debts to God as they are in paying their debts to the emperor. The opponents are revealed as hypocritical and not really religious, and Jesus gains honor for having recognized their character and having eluded their trap.

22:23-33 Resurrection (see Mark 12:18-27; Luke 20:27-40). The third controversy in the series focuses on belief in the resurrection of the dead. The conservative, priestly party of Sadducees denied the resurrection of the dead on the grounds that it appears in Old Testament books other than the Pentateuch. The Sadducees accepted as authoritative only the first five books of the Bible. The references to belief in resurrection appear in Isa 25:8; 26:19; Ps 73:24-25; and Dan 12:2.

The objection of the Sadducees in verses 24-28 uses the practice of levirate marriage described in Deut 25:5-10 (the obligation of a man to marry the wife of his dead brother) in order to reduce belief in the resurrection to absurdity. Instead of unraveling their argument, Jesus charges that they understand neither the Scriptures nor the power of God (v. 29). They fail to understand God's power (v. 30), because the resurrected life will be entirely different from the present life. Since there will be no marriage then, the Sadducees' argument on the basis of levirate marriage is groundless. They also fail to understand the Scriptures (vv. 31-32), because Exod 3:6 ("I am the God of Abraham, the God of Isaac, and the God of Jacob") presupposes that the patriarchs of Israel were still alive in Moses' time. Therefore, the resurrection of the dead is taught in the Pentateuch.

22:34-40 The greatest commandment (see Mark 12:28-34; Luke 10:25-28). The fourth controversy revolves around the greatest commandment in the Old Testament. The questioners are the Pharisees in the person of a lawyer (vv. 34-35). Jewish teachers of Jesus' time were frequently asked to summarize the law in a brief statement. For example, Hillel summarized the law in a way that is much like the so-called golden rule of Jesus (see 7:12): "What you hate for yourself, do not do to your neighbor. This is the whole law; the rest is commentary. Go and learn." Jesus' summary of the law consists of two commandments that encourage love of God (Deut 6:5) and love of neighbor (Lev 19:18). These two commandments are the threads on which the entire law hangs. With this answer, Jesus proves his fidelity to the Jewish tradition and his commitment to a spirituality that emphasizes the essentials.

22:41-46 The Messiah (see Mark 12:35-37; Luke 20:41-44). In the fifth controversy in the series, Jesus asks the Pharisees about the Messiah. They respond correctly that the Messiah is David's Son (v. 42). Jesus' further question in verses 43-44 assumes (as Jews of his time did) that David was the principal author of the Book of Psalms and that the Scriptures, under the Spirit's inspiration, contained prophetic statements about the future. In Ps 110:1, David refers to the Messiah as "my lord." Therefore, the Messiah must be superior to David, and "Son of David" is not an adequate title for the Messiah. A more sufficient title is "Lord." This controversy and the two preceding ones illustrate the superior ability of Jesus in interpreting the Scriptures. Those opponents who claimed great knowledge of the Scriptures are reduced to silence (v. 46).

23:1-12 Warnings against the scribes and Pharisees (see Mark 12:38-40; Luke 20:45-47). The controversies with, and the parables against, Jesus' opponents culminate in a stinging attack in 23:1-39. The passage contains a severe warning to avoid the religious style of the scribes and Pharisees (vv. 1-12), seven woes against the scribes and Pharisees (vv. 13-36), and a final lament over Jerusalem (vv. 37-39). The seven woes have led some interpreters to view chapter 23 as the introduction to the fifth major speech, with the woes corresponding to the beatitudes of chapter 5. But the abrupt changes of audience and the subject matter of chapter 24 indicate that chapter 23 is best taken with the preceding material about Jesus' opponents.

The audience for Jesus' attack on the scribes and Pharisees consists of his disciples and the crowds (v. 1). The scribes were religious intellectuals, skilled in interpreting the Old Testament and in applying it to everyday life. The Pharisees belonged to a religious fraternity that expressed its fellowship in communal meals and prided itself on the exact observance of the law. Not every scribe was a Pharisee, nor was every Pharisee a scribe. A modern Christian equivalent to the phrase "scribes and Pharisees" would be something like "theologians and Jesuits." The scribes and Pharisees in verses 2-3 are said to occupy the chair of Moses, which was the way of describing the seat of honor in the synagogue from which the teacher delivered his teaching. The audience is urged to follow their teachings but to avoid their hypocrisy. It is difficult to square verse 3 with the many other statements in chapter 23 and elsewhere in the Gospel that criticize the teachings, and not merely the practices, of the scribes and Pharisees. Their imposition of the priestly regulations on lay people contrasts with the easy yoke and light burden of Jesus (see 11:28-30).

The opponents' love of self-display and desire for honorific titles are criticized in verses 5-10. Among their showy practices are enlarging the small scroll boxes (phylacteries) worn during prayer (see Exod 13:9; Deut 6:8; 11:18); lengthening the tassels worn at the four corners of the cloak (see Num 15:38-39; Deut 22:12); competing for the places of honor at social and religious gatherings; and seeking after prestigious titles like "rabbi," "father," and "master." These titles are rejected in verses 8-10 on the grounds that only God deserves the title "father" and only Jesus merits the title "master." Religious showiness is rejected in verses 11-12 in light of the Christian ideal of leadership as service to the community (see 20:25-28) and the dynamic of humility and exaltation.

23:13-36 Woes against the scribes and Pharisees (see Luke 11:37-52). Pronouncing a "woe" on someone or some group expresses grief at their sorry state and warning of the very bad consequences to follow. The first of the seven woes against the scribes and Pharisees (v. 13) accuses them of hindering people from entering God's kingdom, perhaps by their opposition to Jesus and his disciples. The second woe (v. 15) accuses them of making great missionary efforts in gaining converts but actually doing harm to the converts' spiritual lives. The third woe (vv. 16-22) refers to the Pharisees' attempts at discouraging oaths sworn by the most sacred things (the temple, the altar, God) and shifting the oaths to less important things (the gold of the temple, the gift on the altar, heaven). Jesus rejects this campaign as ridiculous casuistry.

The fourth woe (vv. 23-24) criticizes the opponents for neglecting the most important concerns of the law (justice, mercy, and fidelity) on account of their obsession with calculating the religious taxes to be paid on vegetables and spices. This overwhelming interest in trivia (the gnat) leads them to overlook the big things (the camel). The fifth woe (vv. 25-26) and the sixth woe (vv. 27-28) both contrast a pure exterior with a rotten interior. The opponents' concern with the ritual purity of cups and dishes used at meals is not matched by their efforts at moral purity. So wide is the gap between external appearance and internal reality that the opponents may be described as "whitewashed tombs" (v. 27).

The seventh woe (vv. 29-36) reflects the widespread building of tombs and shrines for martyred prophets around Jerusalem. Jesus accuses the scribes and Pharisees of being the physical and spiritual descendants of the people who were originally responsible for these martyrdoms. Proof of this charge is the hostility shown to Jesus and his followers in the present and in the future (v. 34). The retribution promised against "this generation" (vv. 35-36) would have been interpreted in Matthew's community as the destruction of Jerusalem by the Romans in A.D. 70. Abel (see Gen 4:1-16) was the first righteous person to be killed, and Zechariah (see 2 Chr 24:20-22) is presented as the last canonical prophet to have been martyred.

23:37-39 Concluding lament (see Luke 13:34-35). Jesus' final lamentation over Jerusalem characterizes the city as murderer of the prophets and opponent of the Messiah (v. 37). Therefore God will cease to dwell in the temple (v. 38), and Jesus the Messiah will not be seen there until he returns as judge with the coming of the kingdom of God. Jesus speaks as God's prophet decrying Israel's apostasy and as the Messiah who is to come again in glory.

XII. THE COMING OF THE KINGDOM

Matt 24:1–25:46

The fifth and final discourse concerns the events surrounding the future coming of God's kingdom. Since the kingdom will mark the end of history as we know it, the discourse is often called the "eschatological discourse" (from *eschaton*, the Greek word for "end"). The first part (24:1-36) relies heavily on Mark 13:1-37 and describes the events that must happen before the end will come. The second part (24:37–25:30) contains parables and other traditional materials that encourage an attitude of watchfulness. A picture of the last judgment (25:31-46) concludes the discourse.

24:1-3 The setting (see Mark 13:1-4; Luke 21:5-7). The scene of the discourse is set in verses 1-3. Jesus had entered the temple area in 21:23 and foretold that God would desert the temple in 23:38. His prediction of the temple's destruction in 24:2 would represent an accomplished fact for Matthew's community after A.D. 70. Seated on a place with traditional connections to the coming of the kingdom (see Zech 14:4; Matt 21:1), Jesus talks with the full circle of disciples. They ask him when (1) the temple will be destroyed, and (2) he will come as the Son of Man, and the world as we know it will end. In his reply Jesus is careful to make a distinction between these two happenings.

24:4-14 The early stages (see Mark 13:5-13; Luke 21:8-19). Jews of Jesus' time believed that great sufferings would accompany the coming of God's kingdom. The first section of Jesus' answer to the disciples' questions warns against mistaking the early stages of those sufferings (v. 8) for the final stage. Among the events in the first stage are the appearance of false messiahs (see Acts 5:33-39) or even persons claiming to be Jesus returned from heaven (v. 5); wars between nations (vv. 6-7a); and various natural disasters (v. 7b).

The Christian community will not be immune from the "labor pangs" of the kingdom.

It will experience persecution and hatred from outside (vv. 9-10a) as well as apostasy, false prophets, and widespread tepidity within the community (vv. 10b-12). The only appropriate attitude for loyal Christians is patience (v. 13). They are assured that the end will not come until the gospel has been preached throughout the world. Matthew's community had already seen some of the religious, political, and natural disasters mentioned in verses 5-8. It had probably also experienced first-hand the problems proper to the church (vv. 9-13). An important motive for writing the Gospel was to encourage the community to preach the good news of Jesus the Messiah to all the people of the world (see 28:19).

24:15-22 The great tribulation (see Mark 13:14-20; Luke 21:20-24). The time of the great tribulation will begin with the so-called abomination of desolation (v. 15). That phrase originally referred to the attempt of the Syrian king Antiochus IV Epiphanes to set up an altar to Baal Shamen in the Jerusalem temple in 167 B.C.E. (see Dan 9:27; 11:31; 12:11). It was probably used again with reference to the emperor Caligula's plan to have a statue of himself erected in the temple in A.D. 40. Perhaps Matthew identified it with the Roman profanation and destruction of the temple in A.D. 70 or with some still future event.

In either case, Jesus presents instructions in verses 16-18 on how to avoid the great tribulation by fleeing to safe refuges in the mountains, by coming down from the roof by the outside staircase and not bothering to try to rescue anything inside the house, and by not bothering to pick up one's coat left by the side of the field. The point is clear: Get out of the way, and be quick about it! In verses 19-20, he takes pity on pregnant women and nursing mothers (who could not move quickly) and hopes that the great tribulation will not occur during the cold, rainy season or on the sabbath (when travel would be either very difficult or contrary to the Jewish law).

This tribulation will be the greatest that the world has ever seen or ever will see (v. 21). But on account of the patient members of the Christian community (see v. 13), God has shortened this period of tribulation. If he had not done so, no human being could survive at all. Whatever connections may have been made between the advance of the Roman army in A.D. 70 and the great tribulation, the language used to describe the tribulation far outdistances those historical happenings. The tribulation signals the end of the world as we know it.

24:23-36 The coming of the Son of Man (see Mark 13:21-32; Luke 21:25-33). The graphic description of the coming of the Son of Man (vv. 29-31) is sandwiched between two warnings not to be deceived about when he is to come (vv. 23-28, 32-36). The disciples (and Matthew's readers) should not be misled by false messiahs and false prophets even if they can work miracles, or by rumors about the Messiah being in the desert or in hiding (vv. 23-26). The actual coming of the Son of Man will be sudden and public, like a lightning bolt (v. 27). Its signs will be unmistakable and unambiguous, just as the vultures signify the presence of a carcass (v. 28).

Nearly every phrase in the description of the Son of Man's coming (vv. 29-31) can be found in the Old Testament passages concerning the coming of God's kingdom. After great cosmic disturbances (see Isa 13:10; Ezek 32:7; Amos 8:9; Joel 2:10, 31; 3:15; Isa 34:4; Hag 2:6, 21), the Son of Man will come on the clouds of heaven (see Dan 7:13-14). The tribes of the earth will beat their breasts (see Zech 12:10), and the trumpet blast will begin the last judgment (see Isa 27:13). The judgment will vindicate the chosen ones of the Son of Man, who is pictured here as a superhuman figure with divine authority. Early Christian tradition identified him with Jesus, the humble and suffering Son of Man.

The fig tree (vv. 32-33) is one of the few trees in Palestine that sheds its leaves annually. Thus it allows the intelligent observer to tell the time of year from its stages of growth. Likewise, when all the signs listed in verses 3-22 have come to pass, then people will know that the Son of Man is near (v. 33). The prophecy that all these events will take place in the present generation (v. 34) is balanced by the insistence that only the Father knows exactly when the Son of Man will come (v. 36). It is not possible to identify "all these things" (v. 34) with the death and resurrection of Jesus. A second, glorious arrival of Jesus is clearly intended. The passage makes clear that not even the Son himself knew the precise moment.

24:37-44 Pictures of the Son of Man's coming (see Mark 13:32-37; Luke 17:26-30, 34-36). The second part of the eschatological discourse (24:37–25:30) consists of parables about the coming of the Son of Man and related traditions. In the parables there is frequently a division of people into two groups. The coming of some figure (the Son of Man) is uncertain or delayed, but suddenly it happens. Rewards and punishments (the last judgment) are handed out. The lesson is watchfulness in the present. Watchfulness is responsible service of God shown in the careful fulfillment of one's duties until the Son of Man comes.

The first section (vv. 37-44) combines several pictures in order to describe the arrival of the Son of Man (v. 37). The Noah parable (vv. 37-39) contrasts Noah and the other people of his generation. The flood came upon them suddenly and had dire consequences for many. The pictures of the two men in the field (v. 40) and the two women grinding meal (v. 41) emphasize the suddenness of the coming and the separation that it will bring. Since the exact hour of the coming is unknown, the only appropriate attitude is constant watchfulness (v. 42). This attitude is encouraged further by the story of the homeowner (v. 43). If a homeowner knows when a thief is coming, he exercises watchfulness at that time. But since the time of the Son of Man's coming remains unknown, the watchfulness must be constant (v. 44).

24:45-51 The two servants (see Luke 12:41-48). The parable of the two servants contrasts watchfulness and lack of vigilance. The faithful and wise servant (vv. 45-47) does his duty. When the master returns and discovers him at work, he is abundantly rewarded. The wicked servant (vv. 48-51) takes advantage of the master's prolonged absence by mistreating the other servants and wasting time in foolish pleasures. The master will certainly return sometime. When he does, the wicked servant will be punished. The lesson is that constant watchfulness will be rewarded and lack of vigilance will be punished when the Son of Man comes.

25:1-13 The ten bridesmaids. The parable of the ten bridesmaids contains many features already familiar from the preceding parables. The ten bridesmaids are divided into two groups: the foolish and the wise. The foolish ones have made no provisions for lighting their torches, while the wise ones have. The story assumes the Palestinian custom of the bridegroom's going to the bride's house in order to make the marital agreement with his father-in-law. When the bridegroom returns with the bride to his own home, the wedding feast can begin. The bridesmaids are expected to meet the bridegroom and the bride as they approach the house. The foolish bridesmaids are sure that the bridegroom will not arrive at night, but the wise ones recognize that he can arrive at any time (vv. 2-4). The bridegroom is delayed (v. 5), but he finally arrives at a most unexpected time (v. 6). The foolish bridesmaids are caught by surprise and are unable to obtain oil in time for the beginning of the wedding feast (vv. 7-10). The door is locked, and they are refused entrance (vv. 11-12). Once more, the lesson is constant watchfulness (v. 13).

25:14-30 The talents (see Luke 19:11-27). The parable of the talents has many elements found in the preceding passage, but it concentrates on the judgment scene (vv. 19-30). The master (the Son of Man) goes away and distributes various sums of money to three servants. The Greek word that describes these sums is "talents." The parable is the source of the English term "talent" as the description of a natural ability that can be improved by diligent practice. Though there are three servants in the parable, they really constitute two groups: the two who invest and double the amount, and the one who buries the money. The master is away for a long time, and suddenly he returns and demands an accounting (v. 19). The accounting is clearly the last judgment. It involves rewards for the two servants who doubled the sums given to them (vv. 20-23) and punishment for the servant who did nothing (vv. 24-30). Constant watchfulness demands fruitful action and even boldness.

25:31-46 The judgment of the nations. The eschatological discourse reaches its climax and conclusion with the scene of the last judgment. Even though the story compares the Son of Man to a shepherd, it probably should not be classed as a parable, since the judgment is presented in a direct and straightforward way. When the Son of Man comes in his glory (see 24:29-31), he will divide "all the nations" into two groups (vv. 31-33). Those who have done good deeds for one of "these least brothers of mine" (v. 40) will be blessed (vv. 34-40), but those who have failed to do these deeds for one of "these least ones" (v. 45) will be condemned (vv. 41-46). The good deeds are feeding the hungry, offering hospitality to the homeless, clothing the naked, comforting the sick, and visiting the imprisoned. These deeds deserve a reward at the last judgment because of the relationship of identity between the Son of Man and "the least" (vv. 40, 45).

Who are "all the nations" (v. 32), and who are "the least" (vv. 40, 45)? The usual interpretation understands "all the nations" as including all humanity, and "the least" as including people in distress of some kind. Therefore, at the final judgment all humanity is to be judged according to acts of kindness done to poor and suffering people. But is this what Matthew and his community understood by the story? In Matthew's Gospel, "nations" and "all the nations" usually refer to people other than Israel (see 4:15; 6:32; 10:5, 18; 12:18, 21; 20:19, 25; 21:43; 24:7, 9, 14; 28:19). In several passages (see 10:40-42; 18:6, 14), the "least brothers" seem to be Christians. If these terms have the same meaning in 25:31-46 that they have elsewhere in the Gospel, "all the nations" are the Gentiles who have not explicitly accepted either Judaism or Christianity, and "the least" are Christians with whom the Gentiles have had some contact. According to this interpretation, the Gentiles will be judged according to acts of kindness done to Christians (see 10:40-42).

XIII. THE DEATH AND RESURRECTION OF JESUS

Matt 26:1–28:20

Almost eighty percent of Matthew's passion account is identical in vocabulary and content with Mark's account. Matthew adds some materials that tend to develop themes already present in Mark 14-16. Jesus is even more obviously in command of the events, and everything proceeds according to God's will as revealed in the Old Testament.

26:1-5 The plot (see Mark 14:1-2; Luke 22:1-2; John 11:45-53). The introductory scene sets the major figures on stage. Jesus tells his disciples plainly that at Passover time he will be arrested and crucified (vv. 1-2). Passover is the spring festival commemorating ancient Israel's release from slavery in the land of Egypt. The major opponents of Jesus are not the scribes and Pharisees, but rather the chief priests and elders gathered around the high priest Caiaphas (vv. 3-5). Passover was a pilgrimage feast that attracted large crowds to Jerusalem, and so the opponents wish to avoid setting off a revolution by arresting a popular religious teacher from Galilee during that time.

26:6-16 The anointing (see Mark 14:3-11; Luke 22:3-6; John 12:1-8). At a house not far from Jerusalem, a woman shows Jesus the signs of respect and hospitality by anointing his head with some expensive ointment. The disciples' complaint that the ointment could have been sold and the proceeds given to the poor (vv. 8-9) furnishes the occasion for Jesus to interpret the woman's action. The first interpretation (vv. 10-11) concerns the extraordinary status of Jesus and the special privilege connected with the time of his earthly presence. The second interpretation (vv. 12-13) suggests that the anointing is a preparation for Jesus' burial. The Hebrew word *Messiah* means "anointed," and from the very start the passion of Jesus is the story of the Messiah's suffering and death. The woman's beautiful deed stands in sharp contrast to Judas' plans to betray Jesus (vv. 14-16). Matthew suggests that Judas' motive was greed (v. 15) and that the thirty pieces of silver promised to him fulfilled Zech 11:12.

26:17-25 The meal at Passover time (see Mark 14:12-21; Luke 22:7-14, 21-23; John 13:21-30). Matthew's account of the preparations for the Passover meal (vv. 17-19) focuses on Jesus' command in directing the course of events. Jesus is very much in charge. Although Matthew follows Mark in interpreting the meal as marking the actual beginning of the Passover festival, the reference in John 18:28 and the supposed activities of the chief priests and elders during these days indicate that it more likely took place on the evening before the first day of Passover. At the meal, Jesus predicts that one of the Twelve will betray him (vv. 20-25). In verse 25, Matthew makes it clear that Jesus knew that his betrayer was Judas. The other disciples' addressing Jesus as "Lord" (v. 22) contrasts with Judas' "Rabbi" (v. 25). The enormity of the betrayal is brought out by the fact that the one sharing the meal with Jesus would hand him over. The fact that God's plan is being fulfilled (v. 24) does not absolve Judas of responsibility for Jesus' death.

26:26-29 The Eucharist (see Mark 14:22-26; Luke 22:15-20). Jesus' actions and words with the bread and the wine anticipate and interpret his impending death. What happens to the bread in verse 26 will happen to Jesus' body, and what happens to the cup of wine in verse 27 will happen to his blood. Sharing in the bread and wine means sharing in Jesus' death. The "blood of the covenant" (v. 28) alludes to Exod 24:8, where Moses seals the old covenant by sprinkling the people with blood, and "on behalf of many" suggests some connection with the atoning suffering of the Servant of the Lord in Isa 53:12. The expiatory or atoning value of Jesus' death is underlined by "for the forgiveness of sins." According to verse 29, Jesus' meal with the disciples anticipates the heavenly banquet that will be part of God's kingdom. This account of the Last Supper brings together many aspects of the church's Eucharistic celebration: Passover meal, memorial of Jesus' death, covenant, sacrifice, and preview of the kingdom.

26:30-35 Peter's denial foretold (see Mark 14:27-31; Luke 22:31-34; John 13:36-38). The discussion between the disciples and Jesus on the Mount of Olives is further evidence that Jesus knew what awaited him and that all these events were proceeding according to God's will as expressed in the Old Testament. He tells them that their faith in him will be shaken this very night, and that his arrest and their scattering will fulfill Zech 13:7 (v. 31). He also commands them to go to Galilee, which is the place of revelation (see 4:13-17) and the site of the climactic resurrection appearance (see 28:16-20). Jesus even knows that Peter will deny him three times before dawn (v. 34). Peter's self-confident boast (vv. 33, 35) sets the scene for the dramatic story of his denial in 26:69-75.

26:36-46 Prayer in Gethsemane (see Mark 14:32-42; Luke 22:39-46). The account of Jesus' prayer in Gethsemane presents him as the obedient Son of God who accepts God's will that he suffer and die (vv. 39, 42, 45-46) and the disciples as needing instruction on how to remain on guard in times of trial (vv. 40-41, 43, 45-46). Gethsemane (v. 36) was a small olive garden on the Mount of Olives, and once again the inner circle of disciples consists of Peter, James, and John (v. 37). The wording of Jesus' statement to the disciples in verse 38 reflects phrases found in Pss 42:5, 11; 43:5. Jesus prays three times, and returns three times to find the disciples asleep. The content of the prayers (vv. 39, 42) indicates that Jesus had to school himself to accept the suffering that awaited him. His final summons to the disciples (vv. 45-46) shows perfect submission to the Father's plan and confidence that the power of his evil opponents is only temporary.

26:47-56 The arrest (see Mark 14:43-50; Luke 22:47-53; John 18:3-12). The story of Jesus' arrest first describes how Judas arranged to betray Jesus to the chief priests and elders (vv. 47-50). In the crowded and excitable conditions of Jerusalem during the Passover pilgrimage, careful planning was needed if a riot was to be avoided. Judas determined on the typical signs by which a disciple would greet his teacher—the embrace (vv. 48-49) and the greeting "Rabbi" (v. 49). Jesus' response is the cool greeting "Friend" (see 20:13; 22:12), and with that he is arrested.

The incident of the cutting off of the ear of the high priest's servant (v. 51) provides the occasion for Jesus to repeat that these events are taking place in accord with God's will and the Old Testament Scriptures (vv. 52-54). Jesus' parting words to the crowds (vv. 55-56) emphasize his political innocence and harmlessness as well as his recognition that the disciples' desertion was the fulfillment of Zech 13:7 (see 26:31).

26:57-68 The trial before the Sanhedrin (see Mark 14:53-65; Luke 22:54-55, 63-71; John 18:13-14, 19-24). The trial of Jesus before the Sanhedrin is located at the high priest's house (v. 58) and involves the chief priests, scribes, and elders. After fruitless efforts at developing a case against Jesus (vv. 59-60), two charges are made: He threatened to destroy the temple (v. 61), and he claimed to be the Messiah (v. 63). The charge about threatening to destroy the temple probably reflects Jesus' preaching that the coming of the kingdom would demand a new kind of worship (see Mark 14:58; John 2:19-21; Acts 6:14) or may have a connection with his prophetic cleansing of the temple (see 21:12-17). The charge about his messiahship suggests that the

Jewish and Roman authorities viewed Jesus as one more in the series of political-religious agitators so common in Palestine during this period.

Instead of meeting these charges directly, Jesus in verse 64 speaks about the coming Son of Man (see Dan 7:13-14). The reaction is swift and furious. The high priest calls it blasphemy (v. 65). The council sentences him to death (v. 66). Others mock him and challenge him to play the prophet (vv. 67-68). Even though both Mark and Matthew understood this proceeding at the high priest's house to have been a legal trial, the Fourth Gospel's understanding of it as an investigation something like our grand-jury proceeding (see John 18:13-14, 19-24) is more likely on historical grounds.

26:69-75 Peter's denial (see Mark 14:66-72; Luke 22:56-62; John 18:15-18, 25-27). Peter's denial of Jesus is highly dramatic. His partner in conversation progresses from simply a maid (26:69), to a maid plus the bystanders (v. 71), to the crowd of bystanders (v. 73). His denials advance from a plea of ignorance (v. 70), to a denial accompanied by an oath (v. 72), to cursing and swearing followed by an outright denial that he knew Jesus (v. 74). The crowing of the cock at dawn (vv. 74-75) brings the shock of recognition that Jesus' prediction in verse 34 has come to pass. Peter's cowardice under pressure stands in sharp contrast to Jesus' faithfulness unto death.

27:1-2 The delivery of Jesus to Pilate (see Mark 15:1; Luke 23:1-2; John 18:28-32). The story of the handing over of Jesus to Pilate assumes that the Jewish leaders held a second legal proceeding at daybreak and passed the death sentence on Jesus. Pilate was the military governor of Judea from A.D. 26 to 36. His headquarters were at Caesarea on the Mediterranean shore, and he came to Jerusalem during the Passover pilgrimage to keep order.

27:3-10 The death of Judas. Matthew's story of Judas' death continues the theme of Old Testament fulfillment, since the goal and climax of the passage is the quotation presented in verses 9-10. That quotation, though attributed to Jeremiah (v. 9), actually joins phrases from Zech 11:12-13 and Jer 18:2-3; 19:1-2; 32:6-15. The story also proves that Jesus, who knew beforehand what Judas was plotting, was correct in his judgment about the terrible fate of his betrayer (see 26:24). Matthew describes Judas' death as a suicide by hanging (v. 5). A somewhat different account appears in Acts 1:16-20. A third concern of the passage is the responsibility of the Jewish leaders for Jesus' death. They have condemned Jesus to death (v. 3). They do not deny his innocence (v. 4). Their scruple about adding blood money to the temple treasury leads them unwittingly to fulfill the Old Testament text (vv. 6-8).

27:11-26 The trial and sentencing of Jesus (see Mark 15:2-15; Luke 23:3-5, 13-25; John 18:33–19:16). The account of Jesus' questioning and sentencing by Pilate places the responsibility for Jesus' death on the Jewish leaders. The chief priests and elders manipulate the Roman governor (v. 12). The portrayal of Pilate as weak and indecisive contrasts with other ancient characterizations of him as inflexible, merciless, and obstinate. His question to Jesus in verse 11 probably carried a political nuance. Although Jesus was in fact the Messiah and thus the genuine King of the Jews, his only response to Pilate is silence (v. 14), perhaps in accord with Isa 53:7 and Ps 38:12-14. Pilate could not have understood the spiritual nature of his messiahship.

The practice of giving amnesty to a prisoner at Passover time is known only from the Gospels. Given the choice of Jesus or Barabbas, the chief priests and elders manipulate the crowd to have Pilate free Barabbas and crucify Jesus (vv. 15-18, 20-23). Jesus' innocence is confirmed by the report of a dream experienced by Pilate's wife (v. 19), and the Jewish leaders are charged with acting out of jealousy at Jesus' popularity (v. 18). When asked what crime Jesus had committed, the crowd gives no answer (v. 23).

By offering the crowd a choice between Jesus and Barabbas, Pilate had apparently hoped to release Jesus. The plan backfired. Seeing that a riot was developing (and he had come to Jerusalem to prevent a riot), Pilate declares Jesus to be innocent and places the responsibility on the crowd for the death of Jesus (vv. 24-25). The crowd accepts the responsibility. The scourging was intended to weaken Jesus so as to shorten the time of crucifixion (v. 26). The episode as a whole (vv. 11-26) stresses that the Roman governor allowed Jesus to be crucified, not because he was guilty of a crime, but rather because the crowd, incited by the chief priests, forced him into it.

27:27-31 The mockery (see Mark 15:16-20; John 19:2-3). The account of the mockery of Jesus contains two features that run through the entire account of Jesus' death in verses 27-50: (1) The way in which the soldiers are described in verse 27 is reminiscent of Ps 22:16: "A company of evildoers encircles me." Psalm 22 is the psalm of the righteous sufferer, and Matthew, following Mark and other early Christians, saw in that psalm an explanation of Jesus' death. The crucifixion was part of God's plan for the Messiah. (2) "Messiah" is preeminently a royal title in the Jewish tradition, and Jesus is mocked as a king. He is given a mock robe, crown, and sceptre. The soldiers kneel before him and address him as "King of the Jews." Right from the start and with exquisite irony, Matthew emphasizes that Jesus suffered as the King of the Jews in accordance with Psalm 22.

27:32-44 The crucifixion (see Mark 15:21-32; Luke 23:26-43; John 19:17-27). The crucifixion story begins when Simon of Cyrene, a Jew from North Africa, is forced to carry Jesus' cross (v. 32). Golgotha (v. 33) was a small hill just outside the wall of Jerusalem at that time; criminals could not be executed within the walls of the holy city. The offer of wine mixed with gall (v. 34; see also v. 48) fulfills Ps 69:21. The two major themes of the crucifixion account appear in verses 35-37: The division of Jesus' garments fulfills Ps 22:18, and the charge on which Jesus was crucified involves his identity as King of the Jews.

Three groups insult the crucified Jesus in verses 38-44: the passers-by (vv. 39-40); the chief priests, elders, and scribes (vv. 41-43); and the robbers crucified along with Jesus (v. 44). They unwittingly fulfill Ps 22:7-8. The content of their mockery reflects the two charges raised against Jesus at his trial before the council in 26:57-68: the threat to destroy the temple and the claim to be the Son of God or Messiah. The opponents are correct in calling Jesus the King of the Jews (v. 37), even though they do not realize the truth of their statement.

27:45-54 The death of Jesus (see Mark 15:33-39; Luke 23:44-48; John 19:28-30). Even in death, Jesus remains the righteous sufferer of Psalm 22. His last words (v. 46) are a direct quotation from Ps 22:1. The darkness over the land of Judea (v. 45) may have been an eclipse or a sandstorm that fulfilled Amos 8:9 or Exod 10:22. Jesus' use of Psalm 22 on the cross (v. 46) does not preclude an experience of intense suffering. In fact, the words of the psalm express most appropriately his feelings of abandonment and his subsequent reaffirmation of his total trust in the Father. The confusion about Elijah (vv. 47-49) probably reflects Jewish traditions about the prophet's roles as forerunner of the Messiah and helper of people in distress. The description of Jesus' death in verse 50 is simple and even understated.

Jesus' death is accompanied by several signs (vv. 51-54) that help Matthew's readers to understand its significance. First, the curtain in the Jerusalem temple is torn (v. 51a). This signifies either the end of the barrier between God and humanity or the end of the old covenant. Then in verses 51b-53 (and only in Matthew) the signs that were expected to accompany the coming of God's kingdom occur. Those signs are described in terms found in Ezek 37 and indicate that Jesus' death inaugurates a new stage in history that will culminate in the resurrection of the dead. Finally, in verse 54 the centurion and his men, who were surely non-Jews, confess that Jesus was truly the Son of God. Their confession provides a model for all non-Jews who accept Jesus as the Son of God.

27:55-61 The burial of Jesus (see Mark 15:40-47; Luke 23:49-56; John 19:38-42). The account of Jesus' burial establishes that he was really dead and that on Easter Sunday morning the women did not go to the wrong place. Matthew describes Joseph of Arimathea as a rich disciple of Jesus and thus avoids the possible inference from Mark 15:43 that Joseph had shared in the Sanhedrin's condemnation of Jesus. Unless Jesus had really died, Pilate would not have allowed the release of the corpse (v. 58) and Joseph would not have placed the corpse in the burial cave (vv. 59-60). The women, who had known Jesus for a long time (v. 55), saw him die and also saw the tomb in which the corpse of Jesus had been placed (v. 61).

27:62-66 The guard at the tomb. The same points made in the preceding account are emphasized in the story of the guarding of Jesus' tomb, a passage found only in Matthew's Gospel. For the first time in the passion narrative, the Pharisees appear along with the chief priests (v. 62) and demand that Pilate establish a guard around Jesus' tomb. Their suspicion that Jesus' disciples might steal his corpse probably reflects the Pharisees' response to the early Christian preaching about the resurrection of Jesus. According to Matthew, Pilate refused their request. So the opponents established their own guard at the tomb, thus affirming that Jesus really died and that they too knew where he was buried.

28:1-10 The empty tomb (see Mark 16:1-8; Luke 24:1-12; John 20:1-10). No one witnessed the resurrection of Jesus, nor does Matthew suggest that anyone did. He and the other evangelists tell only about the empty tomb and the appearances of the risen Lord. The explanation for the emptiness of the tomb is that Jesus had been raised from the dead (v. 6). The women, who had seen Jesus die and knew exactly where he had been buried on Friday afternoon, return to the tomb early on Easter Sunday morning (v. 1). They encounter an angel who had rolled back the large round, flat rock fitted into the groove at the entrance of the tomb and who had terrified the guards dispatched by the chief priests and Pharisees (vv. 2-4). The angel explains the emptiness of the tomb in verses 6-7 with reference to Jesus' three passion predictions (see 16:21; 17:23; 20:19). The women, inspired by both joy and fear, hasten to tell the disciples (v. 8). On the way they encounter the risen Lord and do him homage (v. 9). He instructs them in verse 10 to tell the disciples to leave Jerusalem (the place where Jesus was rejected) and to go to Galilee (the place of revelation). After his resurrection, he too goes to Galilee (see 26:32).

28:11-15 The report of the guards. The story of the guards and the chief priests explains why the guards assigned by the chief priests and Pharisees (see 27:65-66) and present at the angel's appearance (see 28:4) did not come forward and make public what they had experienced. According to this account (only in Matthew's Gospel), the guards were bribed by the chief priests and elders to say that the disciples stole Jesus' body from the tomb. The opponents do not deny that Jesus died and was buried, but they do reject the resurrection of Jesus as the explanation of the empty tomb. Instead, they circulate the false story that Jesus' body was stolen.

28:16-20 The great commission. The appearance of the risen Jesus on the mountain in Galilee is a very important scene in the overall plan of Matthew's Gospel. The mountain (see 5:1; 17:1) and Galilee (see 4:12-16) are preeminent places of revelation. The eleven disciples are the Twelve minus Judas. Their doubts (v. 17) may involve the possibility of having such an experience at all or the propriety of worshiping Jesus. In either case, their doubts vanish quickly. They, like the women in verse 9, worship Jesus (see 2:1-12).

The so-called great commission of verses 18b-20 consists in the statement about Jesus' authority (v. 18b), the command to make disciples (vv. 19-20a), and the promise of Christ's abiding presence until the fullness of God's kingdom comes (v. 20b). Thus it summarizes the three major themes of Matthew's Gospel: (1) Supreme and universal authority has been given to Jesus by his heavenly Father. Therefore he far surpasses every other human being and deserves all the exalted titles given to him. (2) The disciples are to share their discipleship with all people (not simply their fellow Jews) and to hand on Jesus' teaching to them. The largely Jewish community for which Matthew wrote his Gospel probably needed some encouragement to share their faith with non-Jews, and the statement in verse 19a was most likely understood as a reference to the Gentile mission. The wording of the command to baptize (v. 19b) undoubtedly reflects a baptismal formula used in the Matthean community. (3) The promise of Jesus' continuing presence with the disciples and their successors brings to fulfillment the name "Emmanuel" ("God is with us") given to Jesus at conception (see 1:23), in accordance with Isa 7:14. The promise assumes a "time of the church" between the inauguration of God's kingdom through Jesus and its fullness at the end of the world. The spirit of the risen Jesus will guide and protect the church during this time.

MARK

Philip Van Linden, C.M.

INTRODUCTION

Mark's Gospel: one of four portraits of Jesus

It is commonly accepted by the majority of contemporary New Testament scholars that Mark's Gospel was the first to be written and that it was a source used by Matthew and Luke in the composition of their Gospels. (The Gospel of John, it seems, developed out of a tradition that did not know of the other three Gospels.) God's purpose in inspiring *four* evangelists was not primarily to "preserve the facts" about Jesus' life on earth but to meet the many different needs of the people in the newly formed first-century Christian community. God chose several believers to communicate the "good news" about Jesus in such a way that the various spiritual needs of the early church community could be met.

The Christian community today is also made up of people with a great variety of spiritual needs, and its faith can be nourished by the four inspired "Jesus portraits" of Mark, Matthew, Luke, and John. When Christians choose to encounter Mark's Jesus, they meet with that side of Jesus that is the simplest of the four, and very demanding! They discover that Mark's version of Jesus' life centers on his death and on the meaning of suffering. When they open themselves to involvement with Jesus as Mark presents him, they realize that they too are invited to discover the meaning of life and death as he did, namely, by radical trust in God and by loving service to others' needs.

A glimpse at the whole of Mark's Gospel

The overall plan and framework of Mark's Gospel is simple and involving. As his drama unfolds, his readers will be involved in the mystery of who Jesus is and what it means to be his follower. The Gospel develops gradually in three stages. In the *first stage* (chs. 1–8), Mark's readers are drawn into a relationship with the powerful healer and preacher, Jesus of Nazareth. During this first stage no one seems to understand Jesus' true identity, not even his disciples. Suddenly, in the encounter at Caesarea Philippi, what had been hinted at earlier (e.g., 3:6: "they took counsel . . . against him . . . to put him to death") becomes clear: "The Son of Man must suffer greatly . . . be killed, and rise after three days" (8:31). In this first climax of his Gospel, Mark's readers also learn that the way of Christ is the way of the Christian (8:34: "Whoever wishes to come after me . . ."). Theirs too is the way of the cross!

The *second stage* of Mark's Gospel (chs. 9–15) gradually reveals to its readers the concrete means of true Christian discipleship. This is summed up best in 10:45, where Jesus says: "The Son of Man did not come to be served but to serve and to give his life as a ransom for many." And that is precisely what happens in the second climax of the Gospel, as Jesus dies for his people (chs. 14–15).

Jesus' death, however, is not the end. For the *third stage* of the Gospel of Mark begins with the proclamation of Jesus' resurrection and with his going to Galilee ahead of his disciples (16:6-7). It is at the empty tomb that Mark's readers take the place of Jesus' first followers and become the major characters in his Gospel drama (16:8). It is as his Gospel ends that Mark challenges his readers most dramatically to respond to Jesus in their lives with trust, and not with the trembling and bewilderment of the women at the tomb! The third stage of Mark's Gospel continues in the life of the church, until the risen Lord comes again.

The characters and themes in Mark's Gospel

Mark's narrative account of Jesus' ministry, death, and resurrection emphasizes certain themes that were of great importance in the early church. It is also important for the Christian community of the twentieth century to meditate upon them: (1) the *humanity* of Jesus; (2) *trust* as the heart of discipleship; and (3) *service to others* as the daily way of taking up Jesus' cup and cross.

1) Of the four Gospel portraits of Jesus, Mark's is by far the one that best reveals *the human side of Jesus*. While Mark's Jesus spends most of his time performing incredible acts of mercy, which reveal that he is God's Son, he is also depicted as a most human Lord. Only Mark preserves those details that bring out how sharp (1:25), deeply grieved and angry (3:5), or indignant (10:14) Jesus could be with those around him. Mark alone adds the touching detail to the story of Jesus' raising of the little girl from her deathbed: "she should be given something to eat" (5:43). Only Mark's Jesus looks at the rich man and *loves him* (10:21) before he challenges him to give up all to follow him. Mark's Jesus is often discouraged by his inability to get his own disciples to understand him and his mission (e.g., 4:13; 8:14-21). Mark reveals a Jesus who is at once the powerful Son of God and a most human person. Mark's readers will sense that the Jesus of this Gospel is very approachable, because he has experienced life as they have, with all its disappointments and its loves, with all its joy and sadness.

2) Mark believes that the truest sign of being Jesus' disciple is *trust*. He challenges his readers to a radical trust in the risen Lord in a most provocative way by portraying Jesus' first disciples as slow-witted, even blind. Mark's Jesus looks for *trust in who he is*, but the disciples respond with *amazement and fear to what he does*! They see who Jesus is on one level (their Messiah-Savior, who gives them bread, in 6:34-44 and 8:1-10). But they are blind to him on another level (their Messiah-Suffering Servant, who gives them life through his death, in 10:35-45). The Jesus who could give sight to the physically blind (8:22-26; 10:46-52) could not give insight and understanding to his most intimate followers!

The blindness of Jesus' disciples is one of the tragic threads of Mark's narrative. In presenting them in this way, however, Mark hopes that his Christian readers will *see* better than Jesus' first disciples did. He hopes that they will trust in Jesus, not as the "instant cure-all Messiah," but as the one whose death gives meaning to the life and suffering they experience.

3) A final cluster of Markan images is closely related to Mark's presentation of the human Jesus and the blind disciples. Jesus' challenge to trust in him leads to *the cup and the cross*. And in concrete daily life, Jesus' cup and cross take the form of being "the slave of all" and serving others rather than being served by them (10:44f.). Although Mark's Gospel does not give long lists of "how to" serve God and others, its readers cannot avoid the model of Mark's Jesus as the suffering servant of all. They know that they must seize every opportunity to serve others in charity if they want to be his followers.

It is in the garden of Gethsemane that the major themes of Mark's Gospel seem to come together. In his agony there, the human heart of Jesus is "troubled and distressed" (14:33). The one who has challenged his disciples to trust in God alone comes close to giving up himself: "Father . . . take this cup away from me." However, as his disciples sleep, Jesus continues his prayer in faith: "but not what I will but what you will" (14:36). Anyone searching for the meaning of Christian life and discipleship in Mark's Gospel can turn to the Gethsemane passage (14:32-42) and hear it all summed up: "Give yourself to the suffering Messiah. Trust as he did, even though he would rather not have trusted. Join him in serving the needs of your brothers and sisters, even unto death."

The Gospel of Mark in the liturgy

For centuries most of the readings at Sunday Eucharists were chosen from the Gospel according to Matthew. With the renewal of the liturgy after the Second Vatican Council, there came a major restructuring of the Gospels to be proclaimed on Sundays. Mark's Gospel became the "Cycle B Gospel," read on most Sundays from January to November every third year (1988, 1991, 1994, etc.). Weekday Eucharists feature Mark's Gospel even more regularly, daily during the eight weeks that precede the Lenten season. Consequently, by being open to the Liturgy of the Word, Christians can now experience the person and message of Mark's Gospel on a regular basis, in union with all those who share in the church's liturgy. With all of God's people, they are invited to follow Mark's Jesus from his baptism and first preaching (1:7-11 and 1:14-20: Third Sunday in Ordinary Time) to his last days before entering upon his passion (13:24-32: Thirty-third Sunday in Ordinary Time). The liturgical experience of Mark's Gospel can thus be very formative of the church's relationship with Jesus. It can also serve as a weekly, even daily, rallying call to deeper involvement in service to others, which is the hallmark of the Markan Christian.

The author and his times: A matter of urgency

According to some fathers of the early church (e.g., Papias, A.D. 135; Irenaeus, A.D. 200; and Origen, A.D. 250), the "Gospel according to Mark" was the work of an associate and interpreter of Peter. The Acts of the Apostles links a certain "John Mark" with Peter (Acts 12:12), and the First Letter of Peter concludes with encouragement from Peter and greetings from "Mark my son" (1 Pet 5:13). Most scholars today feel that the tradition of Peter's influence on Mark's Gospel was more practical than historical, that is, such a tradition assured this Gospel of apostolic authority ("It came to the church through Mark from Peter!"), which was so important in the formative years of the church. From the Gospel itself, it is possible only to identify its author as a zealous member (pastor?) of the second-generation church, who seems to be writing around the time of the destruction of Jerusalem by the Roman army in A.D. 70 (see especially 13:1-23 for indications of this time-frame).

It also becomes evident as one reads Mark's Gospel that his message is a most urgent one. It seems that Mark and his community belonged to that part of the early Christian community which believed that Jesus was going to return very soon, *as he said* (9:1; 13:30-31). In order to be on guard and ready for his glorious return as "Son of Man coming in the clouds . . . to gather his elect" (13:26-27), Mark urges his Christians to learn from his Jesus the meaning of radical, here-and-now discipleship, as if there is no tomorrow.

And so it begins, "the gospel of Jesus Christ, the Son of God," according to Mark.

COMMENTARY

"AND SO IT BEGINS"

Mark 1:1-45

The Gospel of Mark begins with a powerful title sentence. In his theme verse, Mark announces his belief that *Jesus of Nazareth,* who had lived among the people of Palestine for some thirty years, healing their sick and teaching them the goodness of God, and who had been put to death among thieves, *is indeed alive as the risen Christ, the Son of God.*

Mark, unlike Matthew and Luke, does not relate anything about the infancy of Jesus; instead, he immediately introduces his readers to the adult Jesus through his forerunner, John the Baptist. Mark's readers are quickly drawn into the drama of Jesus' active ministry. They witness Jesus' miraculous power and the ensuing conflicts with those who fail to understand his life's mission. The drama that begins here in chapter 1 will eventually unfold in the final mystery of conflict and power, the death and resurrection of Jesus. It is in the crucified and risen Jesus that Mark and his Christian readers find their source of hope and strength for living as Jesus did.

1:1 The Son of God. Mark's first verse is more power-packed than a casual reading would suggest. It is more than a title verse, announcing the Gospel's central character: Jesus Christ, the Son of God. It also provides the key to understanding the succeeding sixteen chapters. That is because in only one other place in the Gospel does a human being proclaim that Jesus is Son of God (the centurion who put Jesus to death, in 15:39). This prepares Mark's readers to question their own faith-convictions about Jesus of Nazareth. According to Mark, no one else would recognize Jesus' true identity while living with him and witnessing his powerful teaching and healing. In his first verse, Mark gives his readers the clue to the end and purpose of his whole Gospel: to know Jesus as the Son of God is to believe that he is their suffering Messiah, who died on the cross and who now lives as their risen Lord. Mark's Jesus asks his disciples to follow him to life on his way—the way of loving service, even unto death.

1:2-8 John points to Jesus. John the Baptist has only one function in the Gospel of Mark: he is the one who points to Jesus as the Messiah. His call for conversion to God through baptism and the forgiveness of sins, as well as his clothes and food, makes him the new Elijah (see 2 Kgs 1:8) sent by God "to prepare the way of the Lord." John recognizes that one more powerful is soon to come after him. Although Jesus will be baptized by John, it is clear that even John knows his subordinate role in the Jesus drama. As Mark's narrative unfolds, he will present John the Baptist again, in 6:14-29. There, by his death at the hands of King Herod, John will fulfill the role of pointing to Jesus' death, just as here his baptism with water points to Jesus' baptism "with the Holy Spirit." John's whole courageous life and death point to Jesus of Nazareth. He is a model of total witness to Christ for Mark's readers.

1:9-11 God confirms John's preaching. What John's preaching points to, God himself confirms. Although Jesus comes from Nazareth to be baptized by John in the Jordan River (Matthew, Luke, and John diminish John's role in Jesus' baptism), Mark makes it very clear that it is God himself who blesses Jesus. It is God who rends the heavens, sends his Spirit upon Jesus in the form of a dove, and says: "You are my beloved Son. With you I am well pleased." God likewise has descended upon Christians in their baptism, making them favored sons and daughters of God. As Mark's readers follow *the* Son, they learn how to be like him. They see how he let the Spirit of his baptism lead him to drink the cup of suffering at the end of his life of service and interpret his impending death as a second "baptism" which his disciples would share (10:35-45).

1:12-15 Jesus' journey begins. Mark's version of the temptation in the desert is much shorter than Matthew's or Luke's. Its brevity, however, makes its significance more direct. The Spirit leads Jesus into the desert. Tempted and tested there by Satan for forty days, as the people of Israel were tested before him, Jesus is protected by God through his angels. Mark's two verses state simply that Jesus has withstood the test and is ready for his brief but saving life of service to God and humanity. Experiences of temptation and weakness were not unknown to the Son of God. Mark thus tells his readers that the protecting spirit of Jesus is with them in their weakness just as God was with him in his desert experience.

With John's arrest (v. 14), Jesus' work begins. Mark's "gospel of Jesus Christ, the Son of God" began at verse 1. Now the "good news of God" begins, as Jesus' first words are heard: "This is the time of fulfillment" (v. 15). Yes, says Mark, God's reign of power has begun in Jesus, who is God's good news in person. Jesus' announcement would have exhilarated the faithful Israelites of his day. However, he immediately links the good news with an equally important call for radical response: "Therefore, repent and put all your trust in the gospel of God that I bear!" In these brief inaugural words of Jesus' ministry, Mark summarizes the gospel message that Jesus preached: the very power of God is available to those who open themselves to Jesus and to his gospel way of loving service.

1:16-20 The call of the first four followers. Jesus, who has just begun preaching about the kingdom of God and conversion, effects what he preaches. Immediately after Jesus says "Come after me" to the brothers Simon and Andrew, James and John, they turn from family and lifework as fishermen to follow him. In this brief but very striking scene, Mark shows how powerful and direct Jesus' call to share in his mission can be. He also holds up as a model for his readers the immediate and total response of the four. But if Mark's readers are to gain the full impact of this passage, it is vital that they be aware of how Simon (named Peter by Jesus in 3:16), James, and John will respond elsewhere in the Gospel. (Andrew is mentioned only three other times: when Simon's mother-in-law is cured, 1:29; when Jesus names him among the Twelve, 3:18; and when he is with Peter, James, and John again, talking with Jesus about the end of the temple, 13:3.)

This first involvement of Peter, James, and John with Jesus is only the beginning of an exciting yet tension-filled journey. These three will be the only ones whom Jesus permits to share in four experiences in which he most clearly reveals the power and purpose of his life (healing and giving life, in 1:29-31 and 5:37-43; the glory-filled transfiguration, in 9:2-13; the message about the future times, in 13:1-37). At the same time, they will be the ones who will most seriously misunderstand their Lord and fail him at crucial points of their intimacy with him (Peter at Caesarea Philippi, in 8:27-33; James and John seeking "to be first," in 10:35-45; all three of them in the garden of Gethsemane, 14:32-42; Peter's denial, in 15:66-72).

The eager and total response of the disciples here, once seen in Mark's overall drama, draws the readers of the Gospel into a tension that will be experienced over and over as the journey with Jesus unfolds. For Mark, to "come after" Jesus and to join in his mission means to walk a journey of life-giving exhilaration and draining confusion, of overwhelming power and powerlessness. It is an invitation to respond, "Yes, I leave all and follow you," not only in one radical conversion experience but continuously until the end.

1:21-28 Spellbound and amazed by his teaching and power. Mark's readers do not learn *what* Jesus teaches in the Capernaum synagogue, but they do learn *how* he teaches ("with authority," vv. 22 and 27), and *what effect* his powerful teaching has (people are "astonished" and "amazed," vv. 22 and 27; the unclean spirit is overwhelmed, v. 26). The repetition of the phrase "with authority" (found twice, at v. 22 and v. 27) indicates that Mark wants the events of Jesus' first teaching and first powerful action to be seen as intimately related. He not only speaks with authority—he also acts with power!

It is important to know that for Mark and his first-century Christians the "unclean spirit" (v. 23) and other "demons" (see 1:32; 3:11, 15, 22; 5:2, etc.) represented evil, mysterious powers who were hostile to God, health, and goodness. These demons were thought to be so perceptive that they could know who was a representative of God's power. Here, the "unclean spirit" reveals Jesus as "the holy One of God" (v. 24) and cunningly tries to thwart his mission for goodness. Jesus' two commands are sharper and more forceful than the challenges of the unclean spirit. For *Jesus' word effects what it says:* the unclean spirit leaves the man, shrieking one last time as he goes down in defeat (v. 26). The "amazed" bystanders acknowledge the teacher's authority, yet they still have to ask: "What is this?" (v. 27).

Mark's intention here is to make his readers confident in their Lord as teacher and healer. However, the allusion to the people's amazement (v. 27), which caused Jesus' reputation to spread throughout Galilee (v. 28), also has another purpose. It is precisely the people's response of being *amazed* (1:27 and 5:20), or *astounded* (2:12 and 5:42) that will eventually bring other hostile forces to seek to destroy Jesus (see 6:14-29, where Herod is threatened by Jesus' reputation and ends up beheading John the Baptist). Mark wants more from his readers than amazement; he wants them to be alert when Jesus reveals himself in less appealing ways. "Will you also be amazed when Jesus begins to teach that the Son of Man has to suffer much, be rejected by the chief priests, be put to death, and rise three days later (8:31)? Will you recognize him for who he is when he hangs on the cross, abandoned by most of his followers who were amazed by his first signs of power?"

The followers of Mark's Jesus can have much confidence in Jesus as wonderworker. However, those who want to follow the "amazing one" must also go the way he goes. They must deny themselves, take up their cross, and follow after him (8:34).

1:29-31 Simon's mother-in-law. In verse 29, Mark has Jesus move immediately from his first powerful miracle to another. The visit to Simon's mother-in-law turns into a second sign that God's kingdom of wholeness is present in him. In 1:25 Jesus cured with a word; here he cures sickness by a touch (1:31). His touch saves as surely as his word. The fact that the woman's cure is immediate and total is made clear by Mark's emphasis on how she resumes her duties of hospitality, waiting on her guests in verse 31.

1:32-34 The Messiah and his secret. Jesus' first day of ministry does not end with sundown. That evening "the whole town" gathers around him with their sick and possessed. His first day of preaching and healing has given them hope that God is at work among them. After Jesus has cured many, Mark's readers first hear the curious phrase "not permitting them (the demons) to speak, because they knew him" (v. 34). This reminds Mark's readers of the "Quiet!" of 1:25 and prepares them for what they will hear repeatedly in Mark's Gospel (1:44; 3:12; 5:43; 7:36; 8:26; 8:30; 9:9). Mark presents Jesus as being very reserved about letting his reputation as miracle-worker spread. This reticence is called the "messianic secret." By emphasizing such secrecy regarding Jesus' identity as Messiah, Mark hopes that his Christian readers will accept Jesus' true identity, on his terms, in the context of his entire life and mission. Mark's Jesus will reveal himself as Messiah by being powerless on the cross. Christians are free to proclaim Jesus as their Messiah and Lord only when they accept his way of suffering messiahship along with his miraculous works.

1:35-39 The good news spreads. Jesus rises early and withdraws to a desert place to pray alone (v. 35), because he knows that the people are seeking him out *only* because of his miraculous powers. They have misunderstood him, and so he must move on to neighboring villages and continue his ministry of preaching and healing throughout all of Galilee (v. 39). Not even Simon can hold him back, for not even Simon understands where Jesus' way leads. Perhaps Mark's readers, who already know the end of the journey, will profit much from their own desert experiences of prayer with "the misunderstood Messiah."

1:40-45 The leper is healed and misunderstands. The healing of the leper is a remarkable scene, full of marked contrasts. It is a fitting conclusion to Mark's first chapter. The powerful but misunderstood Messiah is approached directly by a person who is normally denied any contact with healthy people. This outcast's trust in Jesus is met by the pity and power of his touch and word. However, the leper's exhilaration at his cure is dampened by a stern repetition of Jesus' prohibitive messianic secret: "Tell no one anything!" (v. 44). (Only the priest is to know, because only his word can allow the outcast to re-enter the society from which his sickness has kept him.)

Instead of following Jesus' word, the cured man tells everyone! And Jesus' mission is thwarted as soon as it begins: "It was impossible for Jesus to enter a town openly" (v. 45). Through this concluding story of chapter 1, Mark asks all Christian followers to take Jesus at his word. He asks them to take Jesus seriously, as he is, at his pace on the journey, and in his time. To be a Christian is to respond to Jesus' word with fidelity, whether that word is "Be made clean" or "Tell no one anything!"

JESUS IN CONFLICT

Mark 2:1–3:6

In Mark's first chapter, Jesus' appearance as teacher and healer had drawn the sick, possessed, and needy to him "from everywhere" (1:45). Now, in this section of five closely related scenes (2:1–3:6), Jesus' activity on behalf of those in need will draw the scrutinizing attention and threatening ire of the scribes and Pharisees, who make their first appearance in the Gospel.

The Markan drama continues to portray a powerful Jesus, whose "teaching with authority" (1:27) still issues forth in miraculous cures of the sick. But now there is more. Now it becomes evident that Jesus' claims to forgive sins (2:5) and to be "lord of the sabbath" (2:28) are the cause of open conflict with the religious leaders of his day.

As Mark's readers journey with Jesus from the cure of the paralytic (2:1-12) to the cure of the man with the withered hand (3:1-6), they will sense an increasing tension. They will be lifted up with joy by Jesus' powerful but gentle love of the needy and outcast. They will swell with pride at their Lord's wise teaching, which will eventually bring his wise antagonists to silence (3:4). At the same time, they will sense the dark place where all these "successful encounters" lead. They will sense that the Son of Man already stands in the shadow of the cross, even before Mark makes it clear at 3:6, when he concludes this section: "The Pharisees went out and immediately took counsel with the Herodians against him to put him to death." How well Mark prepares his Christian followers for the ultimate conflict of Jesus' life!

2:1-12 "My son, you are forgiven/healed." Back in Capernaum, Jesus is surrounded by great numbers of people again (v. 2; see 1:33). As he preaches to the crowd, four friends of a paralyzed man lower him on his mat through the roof so that he can be close enough for Jesus to see him and cure him (vv. 3-4). (Such extraordinary means to get close to Jesus emphasized the faith of these friends as well as the overwhelming size of the crowd Jesus attracted.) Jesus responds to this act of faith, not by healing the man immediately, but by touching off the first of a series of controversial dialogues with the onlooking scribes and Pharisees. When Jesus says, "Child, your sins are forgiven" (v. 5), he is as much as saying, "It is God whom you approach." (In the Old Testament, only God is capable of forgiving sins; and it was expected that he would do so only at the end of time.) It thus becomes clear why the scribes murmur "he is blaspheming" (v. 7) and why Jesus brings it all out in the open. His claim to be able to forgive sins better reveals his identity as Son of God than do the miracles he performs.

Aware of the silent censure his forgiving word has caused in the crowd, Jesus proceeds to prove that "the Son of Man has authority to forgive sins on earth" by commanding the man to rise and walk in the sight of everyone (vv. 8-11). In concluding this miracle, Mark asks his readers to praise God for his presence in their midst as the forgiver-healer, just as the crowd did (v. 12), even in the face of those who do not believe.

It is significant that Mark has chosen to present this miracle and teaching about Jesus' power to forgive sins so early in his Gospel drama. It shows that the need for the experience of God's forgiveness was as important to first-century Christians as it is today. Mark's readers praise God for saying clearly, even today, "My sons, my daughters, I absolve you from your sins."

2:13-22 Jesus and Levi; eating and fasting. After the conflict with the Pharisees over his dealing with the paralytic, Jesus continues to teach the crowds and to gather his first band of disciples (v. 13). He calls a tax collector, Levi, who immediately leaves his work to follow him (v. 14). It is significant that Jesus chooses his followers from among those with simple or even despicable occupations (e.g., Levi would be held in contempt by his fellow Jews because he cooperated with the Romans in exacting taxes for the emperor. His profession would place him among the recognized sinners of the Jewish people).

Even more significant is the fact that Jesus goes to Levi's house to associate with other "sinners" (v. 15). This provokes the scribes, who object, "Why does he eat with tax collectors and sinners?" (v. 16). This Jewish teacher, in contrast to the Pharisees, seeks out sinners to follow him. He even eats with them! The entire scene ends with a general statement from Jesus: "Those who are well do not need a physician, but the sick do" (v. 17).

By relating this second conflict situation, Mark encourages his readers to understand that to follow Jesus means that their meals, especially their Eucharistic meals, must include people who are aware of their weakness and of their need of healing. This stands in contrast to anyone who might think that only those who are "righteous" may participate in the meal. Indeed, the meal at which Jesus is present as *the* righteous one is the meal at which the sick and the sinner are most welcome. Paradoxically, then, the Christian Eucharist is for those who seem "not to belong," but really do!

If Jesus' eating habits challenged the life style of the Jewish leaders, so also did his disciples' style of fasting (vv. 18-22). When confronted by the question why his disciples do not fast (v. 18), Jesus responds with his own question: "Why fast while the groom is at the wedding?" Drawing on Old Testament imagery (wedding imagery often referred to God's presence with his people, and fasting was seen as preparation for God's coming), Mark's Jesus is as much as saying that God's kingdom is now present in his person. Indeed, he goes on, once the groom is "taken away" (a reference to his death), the guests will fast until he returns in his glory (v. 20). As Mark's readers await that final coming of Jesus, they fast with a certain hope and joy in him.

Mark's readers today can live with the same joyful hope that Mark held out for his first readers. They too can understand the meaning of the two parables (the unshrunken cloth sewn on an old cloak, v. 21; and the new wine in old wineskins, v. 22), which are meant to teach that a true follower of Jesus does not fast for the wrong reasons. The kingdom of God has already been established. When Christians choose to fast, Mark implies, it is to heighten their anticipation of the full joy of the heavenly banquet they will share in. At the Eucharist, Christians already celebrate the groom's presence with them in sacrament. When they fast, they proclaim their hope in the fullness of union with him to come.

2:23-28 The lord of the sabbath. Mark next relates a peculiar incident about Jesus' disciples picking grain as they walk along with him on a sabbath. Again, the actions of Jesus and his followers cause a furor among the Pharisees. In response to their protest, Jesus argues from Scripture that even David took exception to the law for the sake of his hungry followers (1 Sam 21:2-7). Mark's Jesus goes on to proclaim that God created the sabbath for human beings, and not vice versa. Those who follow Jesus are to interpret the whole Jewish law by living according to God's spirit of the law, namely, loving kindness. Later in his Gospel, Mark will make it clear that all laws are summed up in the one law of Christ, his dual commandment of love. When a Christian chooses "to love God and one's neighbor as oneself," that one will be approved by the Lord (12:28-34).

The importance of this sabbath incident in Mark's Gospel lies in the summary character of its last verse. When Jesus says that the "Son of Man is lord even of the sabbath," he is summing up his own authority. Mark's readers will remember that this entire section began with Jesus' telling the crowd at Capernaum that "the Son of Man has authority to forgive sins on earth" (2:10). What happens next, on the same sabbath (3:1-6), will show how this claim of Mark's Jesus channels the flow of the whole Gospel. The Pharisees will stop arguing and begin plotting against the Son of Man. The die is cast!

(A note on the title "Son of Man": Jesus never refers to himself as the Son of God in Mark's Gospel. He often calls himself the Son of Man. This title, from Dan 7:13, came to be understood as referring to the future redeemer of the Israelite nation. Mark's use of the "Son of Man" title points rather to *the means* that the Redeemer would use to save his people, namely, his suffering and death on the cross. Mark's intention becomes even clearer when the reader notes that the next time the "Son of Man" title is used is in 8:31, in the first explicit prediction of Jesus' suffering and death.)

3:1-6 The withered hand and the plot. Jesus' mercy toward the man with the withered hand is the climax of the section that began with Jesus' cure of the paralyzed man (2:1-12). Its climactic nature becomes evident when one notices three things. First, Mark places this synagogue cure on the sabbath, immediately after the statement that Jesus is lord of the sabbath. The cure is concrete proof of his claim to lordship. Secondly, a dramatic change of rhythm in the narrative becomes evident when one reads the withered-hand passage in connection with the four preceding ones. Here it is Jesus who asks the provocative question ("Is it lawful to do good on the sabbath . . . ?," v. 4), not the Pharisees, as they do in 2:7, 16, 18, 24. Here Jesus is angry with them (v. 5), instead of them being upset with him. In fact, now the complainers have nothing to say (v. 5)! Thirdly, after Jesus shows his merciful power by perfectly restoring the man's hand, the Pharisees withdraw to plot how they might destroy Jesus (v. 6).

Mark concludes this series of five "conflict stories" on a sobering note. His readers cannot help but see that Jesus' way of life is leading to his death (v. 6). They also realize that Mark will suggest that the same is true for those who follow the "Son of Man" (8:31-38). Nevertheless, no matter what tension Mark's readers will experience while trying to live the Christian life, Jesus will be there on their behalf. Mark has assured his readers that Jesus will respond generously to their faith in him (2:5), because he has come for the needy (2:17) as a merciful Lord of the sabbath (2:27 and 3:4-5).

REFLECTING ON THE MEANING OF DISCIPLESHIP

Mark 3:7-35

Good storytellers involve their listeners in their stories by the use of various techniques, such as character development, comparison and contrast, vivid detail, pacing, etc. In his first two chapters Mark has already shown that he is a good storyteller. He has begun to reveal the human side of Jesus' character by certain details that Matthew and Luke leave out of their accounts (for example, only Mark describes Jesus' grief and anger during the cure of the man with the withered hand, 3:5). He has already established a mounting tension in his drama by placing the five conflict stories of 2:1–3:6 (they "took counsel against him to put him to death," 3:6) after the "success story" of chapter 1 ("people kept coming to him from everywhere!" 1:45).

Mark the storyteller also has a message he wants to convey by his Jesus story, and so he wants to give his readers time for reflection. That is why he presents a brief summary passage here (3:7-12). It not only sums up Jesus' overwhelming appeal to the crowds (vv. 7-10), but it also reminds his readers that Jesus did not want his identity as God's Son to be proclaimed for the wrong reasons (vv. 11-12; see the comment on "secret" in 1:32-34). Mark hopes that this pause for reflection will prepare his readers for the rest of their journey with Jesus. Their walk with him will often be confused by "great crowds and multitudes" in search of only a part of what Jesus and Christians come to give (vv. 7-8). It will be complicated by forces bent on obstructing the path that leads to the fulfillment of the Lord's mission (vv. 11-12). Therefore, Mark rounds off this part of his Jesus story with two passages (the choice of the Twelve, vv. 13-19, and the conflict about Beelzebul, vv. 20-35) which help his readers to understand the true meaning of Christian discipleship.

3:13-19 Called by name to be with Jesus. By the time Mark wrote his Gospel in A.D. 70, most of those who had been Jesus' first disciples were no longer present to lead the Christian community. In this passage, in which Jesus' choice of the first twelve disciples is described, Mark emphasizes for the Christians of his day two important elements of discipleship: "being with Jesus" and "being named" by him.

The first ingredient of Christian discipleship emphasized here is being a "companion" of the Lord (v. 14). To be Jesus' "disciple" is to be a "learner," and to learn from him it is necessary to be with him. From this point on in the Gospel narrative, Jesus will keep his Twelve close to him. They will learn from him the mysteries of the kingdom (in parables, 4:1-34). They will also discover the difficulties of his way (chs. 8–16, in which Jesus details his way of the cross and the cost of following him). The fact that Mark has Jesus choose his Twelve on the mountain (v. 13) not only indicates the solemnity of the moment but also points to other scenes of the Gospel when the disciples will be with Jesus on other mountaintops, for example, to witness the transfiguration in 9:2-10 and to see him in agony on the Mount of Olives in 14:26-42. Mark's readers are asked to be with Jesus and to learn from him in experiences of mysterious glory and painful agony.

A second element of Christian discipleship is located in the meaning of "being named" by Jesus. In Genesis, because God had "named" the heavens and the earth and all creatures, they became God's own possession (Gen 1:3-10). When God gave Adam the command to name the animals, Adam shared God's own power over them (Gen 2:20). To be "named" by Jesus means to be possessed by him, to be under his control. It also means that those named by him will share in his power (vv. 14-15). In this brief passage, Mark's readers, baptized "in the name of Jesus," hear the invitation to be companions with the risen Lord and to learn from him how to share in his mission and power.

3:20-35 Possessed by God and doing God's will. Once Jesus has come down from the mountain with his twelve companions, many people crowd around him, so much so that he and his disciples cannot even manage to eat (v. 20). Mark's readers will notice various reactions to Jesus and to his ministry among the people. His family is "standing outside." They have come to protect him from doing too much. They think he is "out of his mind" (v. 21). Important scribes have come from Jerusalem to see why Jesus is so popular. They claim that he is "possessed by Beelzebul" and that he expels demons with Satan's help (v. 22). After Jesus has cleverly and forcefully responded to these accusations (vv. 23-30), Mark's readers learn what the proper reaction to Jesus is. They learn that, of all those who crowd around Jesus, the only ones who can really be considered his brothers and sisters are those "who do the will of God" (vv. 32-34). Jesus expects his followers to have the same single-minded dedication to God's will as he does. Such dedication may lead to conflicts with people like the Jerusalem scribes. It may seem "crazy" or "overdone" to others, even to members of one's own family! But this is what it means to be "family" with Jesus.

Jesus' response to the accusation that he is possessed by the devil is brief and pointed. In two parables about divided kingdoms and divided houses (vv. 24-27), he shows how self-defeating it would be if he, who drives evil spirits out of people (3:11), were an agent of Satan! Jesus also points out that the only unforgivable sin belongs to his accusers, who refuse to accept the power of God's Holy Spirit at work in him (vv. 28-30). Jesus is possessed by *God's* spirit, and so are all those who choose to do God's will.

THE MYSTERY OF THE KINGDOM; THE POWER OF JESUS

Mark 4:1-35

Chapter 4 begins and ends with Jesus in a boat. Mark's readers will hear him teaching the crowds "in parables" about the kingdom of God. This preaching will be followed by Jesus' revelation of his power over the raging sea. Jesus not only preaches about the power of the kingdom, but he also practices what he preaches!

4:1-20 Teaching in parables. C. H. Dodd, a renowned British Scripture scholar, describes what a parable is and how it was meant to function in the time of Jesus. "At its simplest, the parable is a metaphor or simile drawn from nature or common life, arresting the hearer by its vividness or strangeness, and leaving the mind in sufficient doubt about its precise application to tease it into active thought." Here in chapter 4, Mark puts his readers in touch with the first-century world of parables. They will hear how Jesus used the familiar in a new way, inviting his listeners to new thought about God and God's kingdom. In effect, Jesus' parables say that God's ways may not be our ways. They call for conversion.

In Jesus' first parable (vv. 3-8), Mark's readers hear that something small, like a seed (or like the small Christian community of A.D. 70), could grow (or not grow) and yield (or not yield) much grain, depending on whether the soil was good (or thorny or rocky or hardened like the footpath). A good parable, by its nature, is open-ended and gives the hearer the choice to respond on various levels. Mark's hope in relating this parable is that his Christians would respond: "Let *us* be good soil! Let *us* be full of hope, even in the fragile times of our beginnings as a small community! *We* want God's seed to produce one hundredfold *in us,* as Jesus promised it would!"

The private discussion between Jesus and his disciples (vv. 10-12) sounds as though Jesus is giving the crowd ("those outside," v. 11) no chance to understand him or become his followers. This is very strange, considering that parables were meant to stimulate their hearers to conversion. What is going on in the harsh verse 12 (taken from Isa 6:9-10) is this: The early church knew that certain people had heard Jesus' word and had rejected him; they also knew that others ("you" disciples, in v. 11) had believed in him. Mark therefore shows that Jesus, like Isaiah before him, brought a message that truly caused people to take a stance, either for him or against him. Jesus' parables, says Mark, were intended to bring all people to God's kingdom, but some chose to remain "outside." Mark's readers are asked to be open to God's word in their day. They are challenged to let his word draw them "inside," into a deeper faith-relationship with their risen Lord.

Although Jesus' first parable was originally an open-ended invitation to radical involvement with him, the explanation that follows it (in vv. 13-20) becomes a practical, point-by-point application of the parable's details to the life of Mark's Christians. Listening carefully to this explanation, they could respond: "Yes, we understand the parable for our time (v. 13). We know that the seed is God's word (v. 14). But we also can see how the various types of seed stand for those people who respond to the word differently (vv. 13-20). Some of us have let Satan lead us away from the faith (v. 15). Some of our number let pressure and persecution wear us down (vv. 16-17). Others of us are struggling with cravings for money and other things of this world that draw us away (vv. 18-19). Nevertheless, we want to hear the word, take it to heart, and be true followers of Jesus' way" (v. 20).

4:21-34 Hearing the word in parables. After the parable of the seed and its explanation, Mark records five other parables that are meant to enable his audience to take Jesus' word to heart more personally and more profoundly. By the parable of the lamp (v. 21), Mark suggests that his readers will have to ponder the meaning of Jesus' life and message much more thoroughly for themselves before they can share it fully with others (vv. 22-23). The parable-like saying about getting back "in the measure you give" (v. 24) is much like the preceding parable about the lamp. Mark's readers must continuously grow in their understanding of Jesus for themselves, or they will lose what they think they possess. The parable of the sleeping farmer (vv. 26-29) shatters the illusions of those who think that they can control the coming of God's kingdom. Indeed, says Mark, "God's ways are not our ways! We must be patient and let God be God!" The last parable of chapter 4 is also about a seed, the smallest of all seeds, the mustard seed (vv. 30-32). Even though the early Christian community was small in number, this parable assures Mark's readers that all their efforts will be fruitful in the growing kingdom of God—if they will just understand (see vv. 33-34).

Mark summarizes how the people "heard" Jesus' parables: some attentive ones "were able to understand" them (v. 33), while the disciples understood them perfectly because "he explained everything in private" to them (v. 34). With such special tutoring, Jesus' disciples would seem ready to prove their enlightened discipleship. The following scene on the sea is proof that they were *not* ready!

4:35-41 Jesus stills the storm and calls for faith. In this first storm scene (see 6:45-52 for a similar account), Mark's Jesus gives his disciples an opportunity to show that they have come to know him for who he really is. They have shared in the secrets of the kingdom (4:1-34), and they have been with him as he healed all sickness and drove out demons (chs. 1–3). Now they are with him on the raging sea, and he sleeps! (v. 38). They think that he does not care for them (v. 38), after all they have seen him do on behalf of those in need. After quieting the violent storm with a word, "Quiet! Be still!" (v. 39), Jesus turns to his disciples (and Mark's readers) and asks: "Why are you so terrified? Do you not yet have faith?" (v. 40). The first disciples' only response is: "Who then is this?" (v. 41). Mark wants his Christians, with their knowledge of Jesus' entire life, death, and resurrection, to be assured of his protection in their times of stress and confusion. He asks for more than "great awe" (v. 41) at Jesus' stilling of the storm. He asks for deep here-and-now faith from all who struggle to understand the meaning of Jesus' life, death, and resurrection in their own daily experience of Christian living.

THE MIRACLES GO ON

Mark 5:1-43

The disciples, the Jewish leaders, and the Jewish crowds have all seen Jesus calm devils and the sea. They have heard him preach about conversion and the kingdom of God.

After all this, the disciples still ask, "Who then is this?" (4:41). With the first miracle of chapter 5, Mark has Jesus reach out beyond Jewish boundaries to see if non-Jews will recognize him for who he really is (in 5:1-20, the cure of the demon-crazed man takes place in Gerasene-Gentile territory, east of the Jordan River). When Jesus returns home from this amazing encounter with non-Jews, he meets with increasingly more profound faith in him (from a Jewish synagogue official, Jairus, in 5:21-24 and 35-43, and from a simple, suffering woman in the crowd, in 5:25-34). It would seem that after these three miraculous events Jesus' disciples would understand his purpose and mission better. However, because the chapter ends with yet another reference to "the secret" ("He gave strict orders that no one should know this," 5:43), Mark's readers realize that Jesus still wants his followers to see more in him than a powerful worker of miracles.

5:1-20 Jesus reaches out to non-Jews: The Gerasene demoniac. Mark's vivid description of the possessed man, who violently roars around the tombs and hillsides of Gerasene territory (vv. 1-5), sets the stage for Jesus' encounter with him (vv. 6-10). Even before Jesus drives the devils from the man (strangely, the devils within the man *ask* Jesus to send them into a herd of swine, which he does, vv. 11-13), the possessed man comes to Jesus, pays him the homage due to God alone, and recognizes him as God's Son (vv. 6-7). Like other possessed persons before him (see 1:24; 1:34; and 3:11), this man sees and proclaims what the disciples and the Jewish crowds do not: Jesus is God's Son!

When the people of the village come out to see if the swineherds' incredible story is true, they find their well-known wild man "sitting there clothed and in his right mind" (vv. 14-15). They also presumably see two thousand pigs afloat in the sea. Naturally, they are filled with fear. They cannot fathom the power of Jesus and ask him to leave their land before he shocks them any more. It was obviously easier for them to cope with a violent possessed man than it was to deal with the one who had the power to cure him (vv. 16-17). The healed man, so long tormented and isolated from society, asks if he can stay with Jesus (v. 18). Although Jesus does not let him come along with him, he does not tell him to keep quiet about the cure, as he has so often done after his miracles. The consequence is that the non-Jews throughout the region of the Ten Cities hear what God's mercy has done for him through Jesus (vv. 19-20). By this remarkable miracle, Mark not only displays Jesus' loving concern for one outcast but also sets the stage for Jesus' mission to all non-Jews.

Mark's community of Jewish *and* Gentile Christians would be very alert as Jesus enters the foreign land of Gerasa (v. 1). They would be anxious to see how the keepers of swine (obviously Gentiles, since this was an occupation prohibited to Jews) might react to Jesus (vv. 11-17). They would recognize in this event Mark's way of describing the initial step in Christianity's spread to the Gentiles. Indeed, the Christian faith of Mark's day, which was adhered to by Jew and non-Jew alike, was rooted in Jesus' own loving outreach. Christianity had no limiting boundaries of race or nationality. Jesus' saving word and power were intended for all of God's people.

5:21-43 Jesus and women: life and trust. In Mark's Gospel Jesus is closely involved with women nine times. Here in verses 21-43, Mark's readers enter into two of Jesus' more moving encounters with women (Jairus' daughter and the woman with the hemorrhage). Both stories begin with someone seeking out Jesus, the healer. Both stories end in the cure of a person who had been hopelessly sick. Even the way Mark intertwines the two stories (the story of Jairus' daughter begins, the account of the hemorrhaging woman is related in full, and the Jairus story is then completed) shows that Mark wants his readers to hear one important message common to both: "Do not be afraid; just have faith" (v. 36)! The father of the little girl trusts Jesus even after hearing the report that she is dead (vv. 35-40). He is invited to witness Jesus' healing touch and word, and then sees his little girl walking around alive (vv. 41-42). The woman shows her trust by touching Jesus (v. 27) and by coming forward in spite of her fear (v. 33). She learns that her faith is rewarded by peace and lasting health (v. 34). Like Jairus and the woman, Christians of every age are urged by Mark to approach Jesus confidently with earnest appeals on behalf of the sick and dying.

Even as he reports Jesus' miraculous power, Mark preserves the human side of Jesus. For example, the one who has more healing power than the physicians of his day (he cured the woman who had spent all her money and twelve years of time in going to doctors, who failed to help her, v. 26) did not know who touched him (v. 30). Likewise, the one who raises the little girl from her deathbed (v. 41) is also sensitive to her need for something to eat (v. 43). Such details make Mark's Jesus very approachable. He was not a perfect human (for example, he did not know everything), but he was perfectly human (he was full of compassion). Mark's readers can trust him now as those in need did when he walked on this earth. He is sensitive to the needs of those who seek him out.

It is important that Mark's readers notice the details in this passage that point to the climax of the Gospel. Such hints reveal Mark's desire to keep his readers moving with Jesus to the place where his journey leads. For example, Peter, James, and John, who witness the raising of the dead girl here, will soon question what "to rise from the dead" means (9:10). Likewise, the fearful, trembling woman with a hemorrhage points to the three women who will leave the empty tomb "seized with trembling and bewilderment," so afraid that they say nothing to anyone (16:8). There is almost no section of Mark's Gospel that does not draw his readers to its conclusion. Mark asks his readers, women and men, to stay with Jesus to the end. Even when life's confusion and tragedies get them down, Mark's readers are reminded: "Fear is useless. What is needed is trust in God, who brings life, even from death."

OF BREAD AND BLINDNESS

Mark 6:1–8:26

In chapters 1 to 5 Mark has highlighted Jesus' miracles and power over cosmic forces: over demons, over raging seas and winds, over sickness and death. He has also let his readers know that the proper Christian response to Jesus' power is faith in him, not terror or fear (4:40 and 5:36). In chapters 6 to 8 Mark will continue his picture of the powerful Jesus. However, he will emphasize even more how blind Jesus' disciples are to the meaning of Jesus' power (6:52 and 8:14-21).

Mark's readers will also notice a new emphasis in these chapters, namely, the breads. In chapters 6 to 8 Mark will repeatedly connect bread with the disciples' lack of understanding of Jesus. It gradually becomes clear that Mark is suggesting to his Christians that they will recognize the true meaning of Jesus for themselves only when they realize what their Eucharistic sharing of the bread really means. (The Eucharist commemorates their union with the risen Lord, who came to his glory through his suffering and death.) It is by "bread and blindness" that Mark's Jesus leads his followers to the halfway point and first climax of the Gospel, that is, to the revelation by Jesus to Peter and the disciples that the road to his final glory (and theirs) is by way of much suffering and death (8:27-38).

6:1-6 He was too much for them in Nazareth . . . and they for him! Jesus' disciples are with him as he teaches a large synagogue crowd in his hometown, Nazareth. While many of Mark's readers are interested in this passage because of its reference to Jesus' "brothers and sisters" (v. 3), Mark's own interest lay elsewhere. (Because of the Catholic church's teaching on the virginity of Mary, this mention of Jesus' brothers and sisters causes questions to be asked. However, neither this section nor 3:31-35, where his brothers and sisters are mentioned again, says anything definitive about Mary's virginity or Jesus' blood family, because in Mark's day "brothers and sisters" could refer to cousins, stepbrothers or stepsisters, or members of the extended family, as well as to blood sisters or brothers.) Mark passes on the account of the hometown folks' rejection of Jesus for a special reason: to provide an important transition and surprising contrasts at this point of his drama. The passage is transitional, for it bridges the greatest of Jesus' miracles (raising the girl from death) with the sharing of his healing power with the disciples (6:7-13). The surprising contrasts lie not so much in his town's rejection of him ("A prophet is not without honor . . .," v. 4) as in his discouragement and ineffectiveness in their midst: "So he was not able to perform any mighty deed there, apart from curing a few. . . . He was amazed at their lack of faith" (v. 5). Up to this point people have always been amazed and fearful in Jesus' presence. Here Jesus is amazed at them and at the lack of faith he finds in Nazareth. Mark's readers, no matter how familiar they are with Jesus, might well evaluate the depth of their faith in him in order to allow him to be as effective as he wants to be in their midst.

6:7-13 The apostles are sent to preach and to expel demons. Rejected by his own, Jesus preaches elsewhere and sends his twelve disciples out with special instructions and powers. The reader will remember that Mark has carefully prepared for this important moment when Jesus sends the apostles out. First, he had Jesus call them personally (1:16-20). Then he selected twelve special ones to accompany him (3:13-19). The Twelve, tutored by Jesus and present with him as he healed many from sickness and evil (chs. 3–5), are now ready to become "ones sent out" (the Greek word for "apostle" means "one sent out"). The specific order to expel unclean spirits (v. 7) is accompanied by further details regarding clothing, what to bring, where to stay, and what to do when they are rejected (vv. 8-11). These detailed directions were indications for the early church of the need to move quickly and to be dependent on God's care. Were Mark's Christians in A.D. 70 as trusting in God as Jesus called his Twelve to be? What are the specific apostolic mission orders for today's apostles who read Mark's Gospel? One thing seems clear: Mark is asking all his readers to consider prayerfully how to balance their eager action in building up God's kingdom with their trust in God's own loving involvement in their lives.

6:14-29 King Herod, John the Baptizer, and Jesus. This rather long account of the death of John seemingly interrupts the flow of Mark's story about Jesus. However, it is likely that Mark presents this account here in order to prepare his readers for Jesus' death, much in the same way that John's first appearance in the Gospel prepared for Jesus' coming on the scene (1:2-11). A careful reading will indicate how John's death was truly a foretelling of Jesus' own death. Consider the clues. Although Herod was wrong about John being "raised up" (v. 16), Jesus will indeed be raised up (16:6-8). Like Herodias (v. 19), the chief priests want to kill Jesus but have to go about it by devious means because of what the people might do (11:18 and 14:1-2). Like Herod (v. 20), Pilate will have Jesus put to death even though he does not know what crime Jesus has committed (15:14). Finally, like John's disciples (v. 29), a follower of Jesus will get his dead body and "lay it in a tomb" (15:46). Such clues show that Mark wants his readers to see the fate of their Lord in the fate of his forerunner John. Mark also wants his readers to be so much like John, preparing others for the experience of Jesus in their lives and in death, that people will confuse them with Jesus too. Herod thought that Jesus was John come back to life. Will others think that Jesus has come back to life when they witness the life of Mark's Christian community, then and now?

6:30-52 Crowds, breads, and the walk on the water. The short passage in 6:30-33 serves to "round off" the missioning of the Twelve (in 6:7-13). It also prepares Mark's readers for the rest of chapter 6, which features two closely related and marvelous manifestations of Jesus' identity as their Lord: first, as the one who feeds his people abundantly (with bread, 6:34-44); secondly, as the one who is with them in the most serious conflicts of their lives (on the raging sea, 6:45-52).

Although the apostles need time alone with Jesus (v. 31), he responds first to the greater need of the crowd that has found his place of refuge (v. 33). The first miracle of the breads (6:34-44) reveals for Mark and the early church that Jesus is as powerful and as loving as the God of Exodus 16, who provided manna for his wandering people in the desert. When Jesus pities them, "for they were like sheep without a shepherd" (v. 34), he becomes for Mark's readers the Good Shepherd of Ezekiel 34, tending his needy flock and teaching them at great length (v. 34). These allusions to the Old Testament remind Mark's readers of God's providence in the past. When, however, Mark has Jesus take the loaves, raise his eyes to heaven, pronounce a blessing, break the loaves, and give them to the disciples to distribute (v. 41), Mark's Christians become conscious of their present experience of the Lord in the Eucharist. The details of Jesus' *past* care for his hungry people are experienced in the *present* when his needy followers come to him for nourishment. Mark's readers share in the abundance of leftovers (v. 43)! God cares for God's people in Eucharist!

Immediately after the multiplication of the loaves, Mark presents a second scene in which

Jesus calms a wind-swept sea on behalf of his fearful disciples (6:45-52; recall 4:35-41). As the wind begins to toss the boat around, Jesus comes walking toward them on the water (v. 48; in 4:38 Jesus was in the boat with them, but he slept). Jesus' calming of the sea *and* the disciples (vv. 50-51) would be further signs for Mark and his readers that Jesus was their Lord of creation. Only God had such mastery over the sea (e.g., Gen 1:1-10). Only "I AM" had the power to divide the Red Sea for the Hebrew people (Exod 3:14 and 14:21). Even the strange phrase "He meant to pass by them" (v. 48) would point to Jesus' identity as Lord. (In Exod 33:22, God set Moses in the hollow of the rock and covered him with his hand until *he had passed by*. This was to protect Moses from seeing God's face, which meant death in Old Testament times.) Although Jesus intended to "pass by them," he reveals a new way of God's protecting the chosen people: he comes to be with those who are afraid. He assures them with his word: "IT IS I!"

The back-to-back miracles of the breads and the walk on the water would seem to be enough to convince anyone that God was once more among the people in the person of Jesus. However, when Mark says that the hearts of Jesus' disciples were hardened (v. 52), it seems that he is looking for something more from his readers. He hopes that they will question their own degree of intimacy with their risen Lord. In their own wind-tossed times, some forty years after Jesus' death and resurrection, would the reassuring words of Jesus ("Do not be afraid!") be enough for them? Or was the fear of the first disciples still present in the Christian community? Mark hopes that his readers will come to understand the meaning of *all* the events, including Jesus' humiliating death, as they understand more about the loaves. He hopes that their fears will be resolved when, at the Eucharist, they come to understand their own suffering in the light of Jesus' sacrifice for them and for all his people.

6:53-56 The touch that heals. Chapter 6 ends with the summary statement that "as many as touched the tassle on his cloak were healed" (v. 56). What a contrast! The crowds (of vv. 53-56) ran to Jesus wherever he put in an appearance. His disciples, however, the ones closest to him, "were completely astounded . . . their hearts were hardened" (vv. 51-52). The enthusiastic crowds also stand in sharp contrast to the antagonistic Pharisees who gather around and against Jesus in chapter 7. This brief passage helps Mark's readers, who wish to be intimate disciples of Jesus, to focus their faith on the only one whose touch can heal them of the brokenness and lack of meaning in their lives.

7:1-23 Conflict over eating bread and serving God. After Mark has shown how successful Jesus' mission of healing among the crowds has been (6:53-56), he reminds his readers of the heavy cloud that hangs over his entire Gospel drama. He now reports the detailed and sharp conflict between Jesus and the Pharisees over the issue of what and how to eat properly. It was conflicts like this one (and those already recorded in 2:1–3:6) that would bring to completion the Pharisees' plot, how they might "put him to death" (3:6).

What Jesus teaches in this passage is as important for Mark's readers today as it was in A.D. 70. Jesus, presented here by Mark as the clever Jewish rabbi, turns the Pharisees' challenge about the manner in which his disciples prepared to eat bread (it is unlike their traditional rites of purification, vv. 2-5) into a wide-sweeping exposure of their "lip service" interpretation of God's law (quoting Isa 29:13 in vv. 6-7). He continues with a second example of their false piety, the *qorban* tradition, which would deny parents the care due them by their children (vv. 9-13). (Scholars are hard pressed to find such a lack of filial piety in Jewish rabbinic tradition, which indicates that this *qorban* tradition was probably some extreme and isolated circumstance of Jesus' or Mark's day.)

Finally, Mark's Jesus expresses the timeless principle that it is not what or how one eats that makes a person clean or unclean. It is what comes from inside the depths of the person that makes one pure or impure (v. 15). Then, as if Jesus' stance were not clear enough, Mark has Jesus explain his powerful one-liner to his disciples. External things, like the food one eats, do not make a person evil. It is one's actions, inspired from within, that show when a person is not living according to God's commands (see the list in vv. 17-23). Mark hopes that his readers will look to the various ways they are living in relationship with others to see if they are responding to

God "from within" (with their whole being) or merely with "lip service" (with superficial nods to tradition).

Why Mark presents this heavy conflict passage here is just as important as the message it contains. This conflict section interrupts a chain of six miracle stories (it comes after the feeding of the multitude, the walk on the water, and the healing of the crowds; it is followed by the healing of the Canaanite child, the cure of the deaf-mute, and the second feeding of the multitude). Mark seems to have at least two reasons for doing this. First, this heightens the tension of his drama, suggesting that anyone who chooses to follow Jesus as healer will be involved in many conflicts for the sake of the gospel, perhaps even with religious leaders and structures. Secondly, the conflict passage builds on his theme of the slow-witted disciples, because they need special tutoring again (here in v. 17), as they did earlier (in 4:10, 34). Thus Mark challenges Christian leaders within his audience to reevaluate the way they understand and pass on the Christian tradition entrusted to them.

7:24-37 Non-Jewish women and men are healed and spread the news. The two miracle stories that conclude chapter 7 are linked by the now familiar Markan theme of Jesus' desire for secrecy (see the comment on 1:32-34). Before healing the Syro-Phoenician's daughter, "he entered a house and wanted no one to know about it" (v. 24). After curing the deaf-mute, "he ordered them not to tell anyone" (v. 36). Of course, people *did* recognize him. They *did* spread the news of his healing power (vv. 24, 36-37). But even as Mark faithfully and readily records the marvels that Jesus performed, his secrecy theme does not allow his readers to forget that the true glory and identity of their Lord were only fully revealed in the death he underwent on their behalf.

The Syro-Phoenician woman who asked Jesus to heal her possessed daughter would seem to have had two counts against her from the start. Being a woman and a non-Jew, it is no wonder that she crouched at the feet of this male Jewish preacher, begging him for help (vv. 25-26)! The first-century readers of Mark's Gospel would not be overly surprised at Jesus' harsh-sounding refusal to give to Gentiles (the dogs) what rightfully belonged to the Jews (the children of the household). They would be surprised, though, that Jesus would allow a Gentile woman to persist in her pleading and even play off his own words to get what she wanted: "Lord, even the dogs under the table eat the children's scraps!" (vv. 27-28). Her persistence forces Jesus to make an exception to the rule (i.e., take care of your own people first, then go to others, v. 27). He cures her possessed daughter by a word as a reward for her mother's staying power and faith in him (v. 29).

Mark's readers would hear in this passage several invitations to action: first, to imitate the persistence of the woman, even when things seem hopeless; second, to imitate Jesus' "breaking the rules" on behalf of an "outsider"; and third, to examine their openness to those of other faiths, especially the Jews, the first "sons and daughters of the household."

The story of the deaf-mute is like a gate swinging back and forth. It swings back to the story of the Syro-Phoenician woman, because the deaf-mute also comes from a non-Jewish part of Palestine (v. 31). It swings forward to the next chapter, to the story of the blind man (8:22-26), which closely parallels this cure. Both the deaf-mute and the blind man are brought to Jesus by others (v. 32; 8:22). Both times Jesus takes the men away from the crowd (v. 33; 8:23) and touches them, using spittle to heal them (vv. 33-35 and 8:23, 25).

These obvious parallels make it clear that Mark wants the two cures to be read side by side. In this way, Mark's readers will hardly be able to miss that Jesus is the Messiah promised by Isaiah long before when he said: "Then will the eyes of the blind be opened, the ears of the deaf be cleared" (Isa 35:5-6; see Mark 7:37). However, with the final parallel element in the two stories (Jesus' request for secrecy in 7:37 and 8:26), Mark asks his readers to remember another Isaian passage that Jesus has fulfilled by his life and life-giving death: "Who would believe what we have heard? . . . He was spurned and avoided by all, a man of suffering, accustomed to infirmity . . . . pierced for our offenses, crushed for our sins. Upon him was the chastisement that makes us whole, by his stripes we were healed" (Isa 53:1-5).

Jesus, for Mark, was the perfect fulfillment of all Isaiah's prophecies. He was the promised Messiah who healed the deaf, the mute, and the blind. He was also the innocent one who suffered on behalf of his people. For Mark and his readers, Jesus is the one who says: "Follow me on my way. Care for my people, until there are no longer any sick or hurting people on this earth. But know that in your healing service of others you will experience the same pain that I experienced in making you whole. Stay with me. I will provide the nourishment you need" (see 8:1-10, which follows).

8:1-10 Jesus feeds the crowd again. The second time that Mark's compassionate Jesus feeds the hungry crowds (8:1-9; recall 6:34-44) is another foreshadowing of the Eucharist (14:22-26), so important to Mark and to his community. Some readers think that this is the report of an actual second feeding incident (noting that there are many *differences* from the first feeding, e.g., the numbers of people and loaves, the different geographical locale, etc.). Others wonder if this might be a second written version of one and the same feeding event, pointing out the *similarities* in the two accounts, e.g., the pity Jesus feels, the similar words and gestures he uses, the same basic marvelous deed performed, etc. They also point to the disciples' question in 8:4 and believe that it makes no sense if the disciples have just seen Jesus feed five thousand people with five loaves in chapter 6.

Whatever the solution to this debate, it is fairly clear that Mark has included this second feeding account to make sure that the Gentile members of his community know they are welcomed to the Eucharist from the very beginning. (Notice that Jesus is still in Gentile territory at this point, 7:24, 31, and 8:10. Notice also the phrase in verse 3, "Some of them have come a great distance," i.e., "from afar," which is a well-known early Christian way of referring to Gentile converts.) Mark thus claims that Jesus is the giver of bread, ready to satisfy hungry followers of whatever background. He also suggests that the Christian Eucharist is the place for true Christian community to form, where people of diverse backgrounds become one in the Lord who gives bread to all in great abundance.

Was Mark's first audience in need of hearing that the Eucharist was meant to gather various segments of that community together? Are the readers of Mark's Gospel today in need of the same message, as people of the various Christian churches struggle to become one again in worship as well as in mission? Perhaps Mark wants all his readers to hear Jesus say: "Today my heart is moved with pity *for you*. You hunger for unity. I want you to 'become one body, one spirit' in me" (Eucharistic Prayer III).

8:11-13 This age seeks a sign. This brief encounter with the Pharisees is little more than a transition passage. It links the second feeding (8:1-10) with the scene of Jesus in the boat with his disciples, asking them *eight* times to try to understand who he really is (8:14-21). Yet, this small transitional passage serves the purpose of heightening even more the severely strained relationship between Jesus and the Pharisees. It is wrought with emotion and tension. In Matthew's version (Matt 12:38-42), Jesus gives a clear, self-possessed answer to the Pharisees' demand for a sign: they shall be given the sign of "the prophet Jonah," signifying Jesus' three days in the tomb before his resurrection. Here in Mark's version, Jesus only "sighs from the depths of his spirit" (v. 12). He leaves them, without satisfying their desire for any words or actions concerning a "heavenly sign."

In this way, Mark portrays a Jesus who is so human, so much like his readers, that they could identify with him in his frustration with the religious leaders of his day, just as they have identified with him in his pity for the hungry crowd in the preceding passage. Mark's Jesus is one like them in all things. They will be like him in all things, even in frustrating conflicts with the unbelieving religious leaders of their day.

8:14-21 Jesus seeks recognition and understanding. In two previous episodes on the sea (4:35-41 and 6:45-52), Jesus has revealed himself as Lord over the sea, and in both cases his disciples' "hearts were hardened" (6:52). Once again on the lake with them, Jesus wants them to see who he is. This time he instructs them to keep their eyes open and not to be like the bad "leaven of the Pharisees and the leaven of Herod" (v. 15). (The latter saw Jesus as a popular wonder-worker who threatened their authority as religious and political leaders of the people.) Since the disciples "had forgotten to bring bread along," they missed Jesus' point about the leaven of the Pharisees (vv. 14 and 16). Consequently, with a barrage of eight questions, Jesus makes his followers realize that they misunderstand him as much as the Pharisees do (v. 17). They who were with him as he healed the deaf-mute (7:31-37) have ears but are not hearing (v. 18). They who were witnesses of his feeding the multitudes with bread (chs. 6 and 8) "still do not understand" that he alone is enough nourishment for them (v. 21).

When Jesus asks how much bread is left over (v. 20), it marks the seventeenth time that the breads have been mentioned in chapters 6 to 8 and the last time bread occurs until the Last Supper scene at 14:22. As the end of the "Bread and Blindness" section of his Gospel draws near, Mark hopes that his readers will examine their appreciation of the Christian community's celebration of the Eucharist. He also invites them to see, to hear, and to understand the many ways that their Lord (the "one loaf" of v. 14?) wants to be involved in their lives.

8:22-26 A blind man sees perfectly, gradually. By now, the fact that Jesus heals yet another person is nothing special to the readers of Mark's Gospel. However, to anyone following the developing threads of the Gospel drama to this point, this is a very special cure. That is because this is the first blind person to be healed. He is also healed "in stages," just before the passage in which Peter and the disciples begin to get a glimpse of the way Jesus must go (vv. 27-38). These special details lead Mark's readers to the realization that the blind man of chapter 8 is much more than an individual whom Jesus cured in A.D. 30. He is the symbol of the first disciples and of all disciples of Jesus, ever in need of his enlightening touch. Mark's readers have begun to see more clearly. Are they ready to go forward with Jesus on his way?

THE WAY OF JESUS BECOMES CLEARER

Mark 8:27–10:52

In the first eight chapters of his Gospel, Mark has portrayed the people around Jesus, both friend and foe, as people blind to the true meaning of his miraculous works (nineteen miraculous events conclude with 8:21: "Do you still not understand?"). What follows are two and a half tightly knit chapters, bound together by the blind-man story just concluded (8:22-26) and a second blind-man story that will end with the cured man following Jesus "on the way" to Jerusalem, the goal of his journey and the end of his way (10:52 and 11:1). Between these two "book-end" blind-man passages, Mark has placed three clear predictions of Jesus' passion, each followed by his disciples' continued lack of comprehension.

As these chapters unfold, so unfolds Jesus' revelation of himself as the one who will rise from the dead (in each of the predictions and in 9:2-9). But of course the disciples do not understand this either (9:10)! Perhaps the most important thing to happen in these chapters is the way in which Mark turns the various miracle stories and dialogues into opportunities for explicit "teaching moments" about the meaning of the Christian life and its radical demands. Thus, the miracles in the first half of the Gospel are replaced by hard teachings in the second half.

If there is any general call that the readers of these chapters will hear, it will be the call to be as trusting as little children in the service of others. (The word-fields of "little child" and "servant" dominate these chapters as "the breads" and "blindness" dominated chapters 6–8). Perhaps by the account of the second blind man's cure (end of ch. 10), those who *hear* Jesus' message and teachings will finally *see* that the person they follow and the mission they share is radical but simple, tiring but transforming, impossible for them alone but not for God. His is a way of service and self-giving that gives life to others and preserves one's own.

8:27–9:1 Revelation of the way of the Messiah and his followers. As Mark's readers approach Caesarea Philippi with Jesus and his disciples (v. 27), they arrive at the first major climax of Mark's Gospel drama. (The second climax is the passion account, chs. 15–16). Until now, Mark has been revealing who Jesus is in the mighty deeds he has done. Along with this revelation, Mark has also reported Jesus' reluctance to have people believe in him only because of those wondrous deeds. (Recall the "secret" of 8:26; 7:36; 5:43, etc.) This Caesarea Philippi passage is the heart of the matter. Jesus now says explicitly that his way is a way of suffering. The way of the Messiah is the way of the cross.

Mark, Matthew, and Luke all record this important passage. However, whereas Peter's confession of faith gets rewarded with "the keys to the kingdom of heaven" in Matthew's Gospel (Matt 16:19), Mark only reports that Peter is told not to tell anyone that Jesus is the Messiah (v. 30). Mark knew what Peter meant by "Messiah," namely, "the powerful deliverer of God." Mark also knew that Jesus understood that title differently, i.e., that it signified that he was "the Son of Man, [who] must suffer greatly and be rejected . . . be killed, and rise after three days" (v. 31).

The account goes on to show that Peter and the disciples were not ready for this. They wanted a leader who would deliver them from pain, not one who would experience pain and death himself! Consequently, Peter rebukes Jesus (v. 32), angering Jesus to the point of sending Peter away as if he were the devil himself (v. 33). Indeed, when Mark shifts the focus of the scene from Peter to the crowd and the disciples (v. 34), his readers find out that they also must share the disciples' struggle with the hard, cold reality that Jesus is not the "instant cure-all" person they would like him to be. They can hear him speak directly to them, saying: "Whoever wishes to come after me, must deny himself, take up the cross, and follow in my steps!" (v. 34).

Even today's reader finds it hard to swallow the absolute and radical statements that follow: "For whoever wishes to save her/his life will lose it . . . ." (v. 35); "What could one give in exchange for one's life!" (v. 37). Yes, says Mark, all who call themselves followers of Jesus must lose their lives for Jesus' sake and the sake of the gospel (v. 35). Mark thus pushes his readers to the edge. Either they give themselves in total trust to the suffering Messiah they follow, or they open themselves up to the awful prospect of hearing an unfavorable judgment: "The Son of Man will be ashamed of them when he comes in his Father's glory with the holy angels" (v.38).

Although Mark's readers in A.D. 70 were not among those standing there in A.D. 30 (9:1), his urgent challenge was still theirs, because "the kingdom of God coming in power" could be upon them at any time. Likewise, although twentieth-century readers of Mark's Gospel might not share his expectations of an imminent return of Jesus in glory and judgment, the urgency of this whole section of his Gospel does provoke profound questions for individual Christians and for the whole church. If Mark's readers are to take his Jesus seriously, how can they begin today to live the Christian life more radically? What are the times and circumstances in which they can be people of gospel values in the midst of their world today? Mark's Jesus will respond to these questions with some concrete means in chapters 9 and 10. For now, Mark allows his readers to sit back and respond to these questions before he takes them up a high mountain with Peter, James, and John (9:2-8).

9:2-13 Revelation of glory (and suffering). It almost seems that Mark knows his readers will be exhausted after the encounter at Caesarea Philippi, because he follows it six days later with one of the most refreshing and consoling events of his Gospel—the transfiguration. Jesus takes Peter, James, and John up the mountain with him, the same three whom he had brought with him when he restored the little girl to life (v. 2; recall 5:37-40). The three have a glimpse of Jesus in his dazzling glory (v. 3). When they see him conversing with Elijah and Moses, they are awe-struck at the realization that Jesus is the fulfillment of the prophets (Elijah) and of all the law (Moses).

Peter wants to capture the consoling moment and keep Jesus, Moses, and Elijah there with them (v. 5). However, Mark does not allow his readers to linger on the mountaintop any longer than Peter, James, and John do. Instead, God's voice from the cloud repeats what it had said earlier at Jesus' baptism: "This is my beloved Son" (1:11). Then the voice adds: "Listen to him!" (v. 7). Mark's readers do not have to think hard to remember what Jesus has spoken for them to hear (8:34–9:1). Their refreshing pause on the mountain is over. Glimpses of glory that Christians receive from God are real, but according to Mark, they are given so that Christians can move on with him, and with him alone (v. 8).

Any enlightenment that Peter, James, and John received on the mountain seems dulled as Mark reports the conversation they have with Jesus on the way down (vv. 9-13). Jesus knew, says Mark, that they would have difficulty accepting the fact that he would have to suffer and die before rising from the dead. Consequently, he tells them not to get themselves or others excited about the glory of the transfiguration event until after he has risen from the dead (v. 9). They ask about the role Elijah is to play in the restoration of God's people, to which Jesus responds with a question of his own about the suffering role of the Son of Man (v. 12). Then he answers their question, saying that Elijah has already come and fulfilled his role (1 Kgs 19:2-10; likewise, Mark's Jesus is referring to John the Baptizer as "Elijah, his forerunner"). Thus, as this section ends, Peter, James, and John, as well as Mark's readers, are left to respond to Jesus' unanswered question (v. 12): "Why does Scripture say of the Son of Man that he must suffer greatly and be treated with contempt?"

9:14-29 "I do believe! Help my unbelief!" The healing of the possessed boy is one of the longest miracle stories in Mark's Gospel (only the expulsion of the demons in 5:1-20 is longer). It is also one of the more detailed stories, becoming a bit complicated in the repetition of some of those details (e.g., in v. 22 the father of the boy tells Jesus what he has *already* told him in v. 18; the crowd gathers twice within the same story in vv. 15 and 25). Despite its length and detail, there is a very clear and simple message that Mark wishes to convey: Anything is possible to one who trusts (v. 23), and trust is deepened by prayer (v. 29)!

Although Jesus is the one who heals the boy (vv. 25-27), it is the father's profession of faith that Mark holds up for his readers to imitate. Even in the most desperate moments, when prayer and trust seem useless, Jesus invites his followers to go one step further and pray like the boy's father: "I do believe! Help my unbelief!" (v. 24). Perhaps the alert reader of the Gospel will hear the echoes of Jesus' message all along (e.g., "Do not be afraid; just have faith" in 5:36; "Please, Lord, even the dogs under the table eat the children's scraps" in 7:28), calling for a persistent and ever more radical trust in him. The same theme will carry over into the following passages, in which the total trust of little children becomes the model of what is needed to take part in the kingdom of God (9:35-37 and 10:13-16).

9:30-32 The second (of three) predictions of death and resurrection. Jesus' disciples were not able to expel the demon from the young boy (9:18) because of the lack of belief among the people (9:19) and because of their own lack of prayerfulness (9:29). Is it surprising, then, that the disciples will fail to understand the meaning of Jesus' second prediction of his death and resurrection (vv. 31-32)? Mark's note that "they were afraid to question him" about this prediction (v. 32) might help his readers to deal with the fact that the Twelve abandoned Jesus in his passion and death. It might also encourage his readers to pause, take stock of their own fears, and confidently express them in prayer with their Lord.

9:33-50 Some radical demands of discipleship. Each evangelist records those teachings of Jesus that meet the needs of his readers. Here we notice some concerns that Mark hopes his community will face: (1) ambition among themselves (vv. 33-37); (2) envy and intolerance of others (vv. 38-41); and (3) scandalizing others (vv. 42-48).

The first concern, the evil of ambition, is a major one for Mark as pastor of his community. (This becomes even clearer in chapter 10 when the third passion prediction is followed by another warning against ambition, 10:35-45). How ambitious Jesus' disciples are! They argue about who is the most important among them (9:33-34) instead of trying to understand the meaning of their leader's passion prediction (9:32)! The response of Jesus (and Mark) is direct and simple: to be "important" among Jesus' followers means to be a humble servant, not a proud "first" (v. 35). In verses 36-37 Mark's Jesus presents himself and the child as models of openness to others: "Whoever receives one child such as this in my name receives me." What a contrast this is to the disciples' interests (in v. 34)! How different from their closed attitudes toward others (in vv. 38-42)!

Mark's second concern, the pettiness of arrogance and envy, is exposed when John and other disciples try to exclude a "non-member" from doing ministry in the name of Jesus (v. 38). Jesus (and Mark) challenge the disciples to be tolerant and open to others of good will: Working in Jesus' name brings its reward to anyone who "is not against us!" (vv. 40-41).

A third concern, the danger of causing scandal to others (v. 42), is met by Jesus' (and Mark's) harsh, traditional imagery of the unquenchable fires of Gehenna (vv. 43-48). In order to avoid those fires, Jesus' followers must be extremely cautious of giving bad example to anyone. Indeed, it would be better to cut off an arm or leg and enter heaven maimed than to give scandal to others and be thrown into hell!

Mark concludes this demanding section of his Gospel with a confusing but powerful mixed metaphor. Jesus claims that his followers will be cleansed ("salted" by the fire of v. 49) so that they can be at peace within and with others (the useful, tasty salt of v. 50). He thus presents a highly seasoned mixture of challenges to his own disciples and readers in A.D. 70 and today. His readers must reflect upon the liveliness of their gospel spirit. They must also root out the evils of ambition, envy, and scandal wherever they exist in their midst.

10:1-12 The Pharisees ask about divorce; Jesus responds. Journeying south from Capernaum (see 9:33), Jesus finally comes to Judea (10:1), on his way up to Jerusalem (10:32). In Judea, Jesus continues to preach his demanding message (begun in 8:34-38 and 9:33-50). However, in chapter 10 there seems to be an intentional attempt on Mark's part to establish a certain pattern and rhythm that gradually build up to the climax of his Gospel. The Markan arrangement consists of three passages in which Jesus meets with individual characters (the Pharisees of v. 2; the young man of v. 17; and James and John in v. 35). Then Mark's Jesus uses the encounters to teach his Twelve privately (v. 10, v. 23, and v. 41). These three similar passages are rhythmically balanced by three interspersed "models" for the Christian disciple to imitate (the child of vv. 13-16; Jesus himself in vv. 32-34; and the blind man in vv. 46-52).

The first encounter of chapter 10 has to do with the ever important issue of the fidelity of spouses in the marriage relationship (vv. 1-12). The early church was careful to preserve Jesus' attitudes concerning significant matters of daily living. Here Mark passes on the earliest tradition of Jesus' attitude toward marriage and divorce (vv. 6-9). While other teachers allowed men to divorce their wives in certain circumstances, Jesus taught that it was not permissible "to separate what God has joined together," using Gen 1:27 and 2:24 as authority for his interpretation. In other words, the Jesus tradition made it clear that it was not permissible for a man to divorce his wife. After Jesus talks privately with the Twelve (v. 10), Mark passes on what had come to be the earliest adaptation of Jesus' words for the Christian community, namely, if a man or a woman should have to divorce his or her spouse, he or she could not remarry without being considered an adulterer (vv. 11-12).

In these few verses, today's readers of Mark's Gospel can see the early church's struggle with one of the most painful areas of concern in the contemporary church and society—the meaning of fidelity in marriage relationships. At the core of Mark's Gospel message is Jesus' challenge to spouses to live in faithful and perpetual union until death. At the same time, recognizing the hard reality of life, even this early Gospel seems to allow for the separation (without remarriage, however) of spouses who can no longer love one another as husband or wife. (Matthew's Gospel, at 19:9, adds another "exception clause," which shows how this vital issue was dealt with in Matthew's community.) Thus, there are some whom Mark's Jesus will challenge to continue to be faithful forever. There are others whom he will challenge to adapt, as the early church did, to the needs and feelings of those who no longer can live with their spouses.

10:13-16 The model of the child: total trust. Perhaps Jesus' teaching concerning fidelity in marriage inspired Mark to follow that passage (10:1-12) with the image of the child (vv. 13-16). Mark claims in these verses that only a childlike trust will enable his Christians to live up to Jesus' demands in the concrete day-to-day relationships they have, in the family and elsewhere. Once more the disciples seem to want to avoid hearing the truth. They scold the people for bringing children to Jesus (v. 13). In turn, Jesus' human compassion is aroused to passionate indignation with them. Only Mark records Jesus' anger with the disciples and his tender touching of the children (vv. 14 and 16).

When Jesus says that it is only to those who are as needy and receptive as children that the kingdom of God belongs (vv. 14-15), he invites his readers to delve more deeply into the realization of their own human helplessness. Only thus can the power of their God and Father live in them. The positive acceptance of one's own powerlessness and God's power draws Mark's readers very close to the experience of having the kingdom of God established in their hearts. As Jesus will say in the next section of the Gospel, "For human beings it is impossible but not for God. All things are possible for God" (10:27).

10:17-31 The rich man asks about everlasting life; Jesus looks at him with love. In Matthew's version of this encounter, Jesus tells the rich man: "If you wish to be perfect, go, sell what you have, and give to the poor" (Matt 19:21). In Mark's account there is no "if" clause. The one who wants to follow Mark's Jesus must give up all he or she has, give the proceeds to the poor, and then follow him (v. 21). What a demanding person Mark's Jesus is! Here is an eager, prospective disciple, who has kept all the commandments since his childhood (v. 20). He wants everlasting life (v. 17). Jesus looks on him with love, but then challenges him beyond his capacities (see v. 22: "He went away sad . . .").

Mark's Jesus turns to his disciples and makes it clear to them that having many possessions is an almost insurmountable deterrent to possession of the kingdom of God (vv. 23-25). This overwhelmed Jesus' disciples (v. 26) and probably overwhelmed Mark's first readers as thoroughly as it challenges his readers today. Mark calls for the trust of the child in its parents: "All things are possible for God" (v. 27; recall the model of the child in 10:13-16). However, that challenging response did not satisfy Peter, just as it probably did not satisfy Mark's Christians, who had already left so much to follow Jesus (v. 28). In verses 29-31, Mark assures his readers that anyone who is detached from everything and everyone, so that he or she can follow after Jesus, will receive a hundredfold of family members and possessions in this life, while inheriting everlasting life in the age to come. (Mark's readers will note that those who leave all for Jesus will also receive "persecutions," v. 30. Even when he assures his Christians of their reward, Mark's Jesus reminds them that they stand in the shadow of the cross.)

In the world of today, just as in the time of Jesus and Mark, security in possessions and in money can pull people away from depending on God as the true source of their life, here and hereafter. Like the man in the Gospel story, all of Mark's Christians are called to radical discipleship. To follow Jesus still means to go and sell what one has. To be for Jesus still means to be for the poor. The man in the Gospel story wanted everlasting life. The Christian way to everlasting life is to be poor. Jesus' way is to rely solely on God, for whom all things are possible!

10:32-34 The "Suffering Servant" predicts his fate for the third time. Mark records Jesus' third and final prediction of his death and resurrection, with some details that were missing in the previous two predictions: it would happen in Jerusalem; and the Gentiles would mock him, spit at him, and flog him before killing him (vv. 33-34). As the end of Jesus' way draws closer, the more explicitly he identifies himself with the suffering servant of Isaiah, who would heal his people by the very stripes, chastisement, and harsh treatment he would endure for their sakes (Isa 53:1-7).

The manner in which Mark sets the scene for this third prediction is significant: "They were on the way, going up to Jerusalem, and Jesus went ahead of them" (v. 32). Jesus knows where they are headed and what awaits him in Jerusalem. But the disciples follow, "amazed," and the crowd trails along in fear. By this time the reader must wonder what effect such predictions had on the first disciples, especially when two of the Twelve (James and John) show that they have completely misunderstood what he has said (see next passage, 10:35-45). Mark hopes that his unfolding Gospel drama will have a more lasting effect on his Christian readers. He hopes that they will consciously choose to model their lives on Jesus, the Suffering Servant, who walks ahead of them.

10:35-45 James and John ask about glory; Jesus gives them the cross. The request of James and John to sit at Jesus' right and left in glory makes up the next to last scene before Jesus arrives in Jerusalem, the place of his death. It seems almost impossible that these two disciples could ask such an ambitious and inappropriate question after Mark's Jesus has been describing his way of suffering so clearly, since 8:31! (Matthew casts James and John in a better light, having their mother pose the request, Matt 20:20.)

Jesus responds to their request with a challenging question of his own: "Can you drink the cup I shall drink or be baptized with the baptism with which I am baptized?" (v. 38). Since "the cup" and "baptism" language is symbolic for Mark of Jesus' agony and death to come, it is obvious that Jesus is challenging James and John to take very seriously what it means to follow him to glory. Then, in response to their eager "We can" of

v. 39, Jesus divides the issue: You shall share in my cup, in my baptism, in my death. But it is up to someone else, my Father, to give out the seats of glory! (v. 40).

Jesus thus concludes the dialogue in such a way that James and John get a profound (and unwanted?) answer to their ambitious request. The answer is not a simple "yes" or "no," but a challenge: "Perhaps the Father will reserve the seats for you, *if* you willingly take on my cross, my cup, my baptism." Who among Mark's readers in A.D. 70 or today is eager to go "all the way" with Jesus?

Verse 41 is the transition verse by which Mark draws his own Christian readers more explicitly into the dialogue. Today's reader of the incident might become indignant with James and John, like the other ten disciples did, and say, "How selfish they are!" However, Mark's Jesus calls *all* of his followers together and says: "It is not only in this one incident that Christians manifest selfish, unchristian attitudes. Whoever wants to follow the Son of Man must take an uncompromising stance against such non-gospel values as 'lording it over others' " (v. 42). To be a Christian is to be a servant, as Jesus was (v. 45). To be first and greatest is to serve the needs of all, as Jesus did (v. 44). That is the way to glory for a disciple of Mark's Jesus!

Because this scene features James and John, two of Jesus' most intimate disciples (remember that they were with him at the transfiguration, 9:2-9, and that they will be with him in the garden of his agony, 14:32-42), Mark's message here is especially relevant to anyone in a leadership position in the church. It is a "servant leadership" that Mark calls for. The church's leaders are meant to be the first to "drink the cup," daily serving the needs of their brothers and sisters, whatever those needs are, whenever they are perceived. If this call seems too radical and even impossible to fulfill, Mark next offers his readers the example of someone else—the blind beggar Bartimaeus of verses 46-52—who probably thought his situation was hopeless.

10:46-52 The model of the blind man: "I want to see!" The cure of blind Bartimaeus concludes this demanding section of Mark's Gospel drama, just as the cure of the other blind man (8:22-26) concluded the "Bread and Blindness" chapters (6–8). In contrast to the first blind man, who was brought to Jesus by others (8:22), Bartimaeus cries out on his own initiative: "Jesus, Son of David, have pity on me!" (v. 47). The title he gives Jesus, "Son of David," indicates that he, a *blind* beggar, actually *sees who Jesus is* more clearly than the disciples and crowd who have been with him all along! Although some people try to quiet the man (v. 48), his persistence wins out. Jesus has his disciples call him closer (v. 49). Bartimaeus responds with great enthusiasm and comes to Jesus. He becomes the one and only person in Mark's Gospel who calls Jesus "Master." (This particular way of addressing Jesus appears in the New Testament only here and at John 20:16, when Mary Magdalene meets the risen Jesus near the empty tomb.)

In the Gospel of Matthew, the parallel story has two blind men call for Jesus' help; and Jesus, moved with compassion, *touched their eyes* (Matt 20:33-34). Here in Mark's version of the incident, Jesus need not touch Bartimaeus. He does not even have to say "Your faith has saved you" (as Luke has it, in 18:42), because Bartimaeus' cry and actions reveal his deep faith. Jesus is his master! It is just such profound trust in Jesus that Mark wants to elicit from the Christian recipients of his Gospel.

When the blind man immediately received his sight and started to follow Jesus "on the way" (v. 52), Mark offers a smooth transition to the next section of the Gospel (i.e., the *end* of the road, Jerusalem and Calvary, chs. 11–15). More important, however, he offers his community the hope and encouraging example of this early disciple of Jesus (the phrase "to follow him on the way," was a familiar designation for discipleship in the early church). Consequently, after Mark presents the very difficult teachings of Jesus about the Christian attitude toward divorce, riches, and ambition (earlier in ch. 10), this miracle-discipleship story becomes Mark's rallying call to his Christian readers in their own situation, on their own way of the cross: "You have nothing to fear from him! Get up! He is calling you!"

ON TO JERUSALEM

Mark 11:1–13:37

This major section of Mark's Gospel begins with Jesus' entry into Jerusalem

(11:1-11) and ends with his long discourse about the Jerusalem temple and the "days of tribulation" (13:1-37). Throughout these three chapters, Mark's readers will find themselves involved with Jesus in a series of foreboding incidents that build up to his betrayal, passion, and death in Jerusalem (chs. 14–15). Almost all of the scenes in chapters 11 to 13 are conflict-ridden, showing Jesus in confrontation with the religious leaders of Jerusalem over the issues of prayer and piety (11:12-25 and 12:28-44); life after death (12:18-27); tribute due to Caesar (12:13-17); and Jesus' authority in all such matters (11:27-33). This series of conflict stories will remind Mark's readers of earlier conflicts (2:1–3:6), which ended with the Pharisees' plotting with the Herodians how they might destroy Jesus (3:6). This time the plotting leads to his arrest and death (14:43-52 and 15:21-26).

By his choice of the various scenes for these three critical chapters, Mark leaves no doubt in his readers' minds about what the basis of their Christian discipleship is: they are to put their trust in God (11:22), and they must put that trust into action by loving their neighbor as themselves (12:31). Their models will be two: (1) the sincere scribe of 12:28-34 and (2) the poor widow, whose generous trust in God urged her to give "from her poverty, all she had, her whole livelihood" (12:44).

11:1-11 Jesus' entry into Jerusalem. Mark's account of Jesus' triumphal entry into Jerusalem functions much as the transfiguration event did earlier (9:2-8). It is another exhilarating moment on the otherwise long and arduous "way" of Jesus to his saving passion and death. Because Jerusalem was the holy city of God, and because the details of Jesus' arrival there (vv. 7-10) point to the coming of Israel's Prophet-Savior (e.g., "See, your king shall come . . . riding on an ass, on a colt, the foal of an ass," Zech 9:9), Mark's first readers would not be able to miss the obvious connection: *Jesus was the longed-for Savior of Israel!* They could join the crowds and shout: "Hosanna! The reign of God and of our father David has begun with Jesus' coming!"

However, because Jerusalem was also the city of Jesus' death, Mark is quick to play down the enthusiasm surrounding Jesus' entry. (This nuance in Mark's Gospel becomes evident when his account is compared with Matthew's version, which has "the very large crowd spread their cloaks on the road," Matt 21:8, and "the whole city was shaken" at his entry, Matt 21:10.) Consequently, the way Mark presents this episode allows his readers to rejoice in the risen Lord's kingship over them while not allowing them to forget the cost of being his disciples, namely, that they must deny their very selves, take up their cross, and follow in his steps (8:34).

The exhilarating moment of the entry into Jerusalem has come and gone. After a night's rest at Bethany with the Twelve, Jesus returns to the city for the final days and the final act of the Gospel drama (11:11-12).

11:12-25 The cursed fig tree and the cleansing of the temple. At first reading, the story of Jesus and the fig tree (vv. 12-14 and 20-21) is one of the strangest in the Gospels. It is uncharacteristic enough of Jesus to curse a fig tree for not having fruit on it. But when Mark includes the detail that "it was not the time for figs" (v. 13), Jesus appears even more unreasonable, and the incident becomes more difficult to understand.

Two keys are needed to unlock the meaning of this strange passage. First, Mark's readers may recall that the fig tree was a common Old Testament image for Israel (e.g., Hos 9:10). Therefore, Jesus' cursing of the tree would symbolically stand for his anger with the Jewish people. But why does Mark's Jesus curse Israel at this point of the Gospel drama? (Remember that the people have just welcomed him triumphantly into Jerusalem!) A second key to understanding this passage is its immediate context, which reveals an angry Jesus driving the buyers and sellers from the sacred temple area. They have turned what was meant to be "a house of prayer for all peoples" into a "den of thieves" (v. 17, quoting Isa 56:7). Consequently, Mark's readers can see why he wove the fig-tree passage together with the cleansing of the temple. The withered fig tree (v. 21) is meant to symbolize the fruitless side of Jewish temple piety in Jesus' time.

This passage might well challenge Mark's Christian readers to evaluate the depth of their own faith. In contrast to the superficial ceremony of the old temple, Mark hopes that they will have the type of profound trust in God that can move mountains (vv. 22-23). In verses 23-24, Mark's Jesus uses very bold, even exaggerated, language to say that by faith and prayer his people will be able to do what seems impossible, as well as receive *whatever* they ask for in prayer. (Remember the similarly strong "image with a point" in 10:25: "It is easier for a camel to pass through the eye of a needle than for one who is rich to enter the kingdom of God.")

Jesus and the early church believed in the infinite power of prayer. It seems that the only thing Mark's readers cannot hope to receive in prayer is an escape from their share in the suffering way of the Lord. For example: "Amen, I say to you, there is no one who has given up house or brothers or sisters or mother or father or children or lands for my sake and for the sake of the gospel who will not receive a hundred times more now in this present age: houses and brothers and sisters and mothers and children and lands, *with persecutions*, and eternal life in the age to come (10:29ff.).

Mark concludes his description of Jesus' type of true piety by saying that anyone who prays with forgiveness for those who have offended them shall be forgiven in turn by the Father in heaven (v. 25). Although Mark does not relate the Our Father in his Gospel, as Matthew and Luke do, this little section brings out the attitudes of radical trust and forgiveness that are expected of children in their lives and in their prayer.

11:27-33 The lines of authority are drawn: conflict! The chief priests and scribes, who were looking for a way to destroy Jesus after he had cleansed the temple (11:18), question him "by what authority" he teaches and acts as he does (v. 28). This is not a simple question put by one teacher to another. It is a most serious challenge, the first in the final series of challenges that Jesus will face from the religious leaders of his day (11:27–12:44).

Mark's readers will notice how each conflict ends with a victorious Jesus silencing his opponents, the experts in Jewish law and scriptures. Here, for example, in verses 29-33, Jesus takes their question about his authority and turns it into his own clever question about the authority of John the Baptizer (v. 30). Since the scribes feared what others, friends or foes of John, might think of their response (vv. 31-32), they are forced to admit: "We do not know" (v. 33). What began as a threat to Jesus' authority ends as an example of how little authority (and courage) his antagonists had! Mark wants his readers to take pride in the confounding wisdom of their teacher, Jesus. He also might be cleverly questioning his readers as to how they use the authority they possess in the church or how courageously they challenge the way others use the authority vested in them.

12:1-12 The parable of the vineyard: the rejected stone (son) is the cornerstone. For the first time since chapter 4, Mark has Jesus "speak to them in parables" (v. 1), namely, in the parable of the vineyard and the evil tenants (vv. 3-8). This is the last parable Mark records, and what a perfect last parable it is! By it, Mark anticipates the final act of his whole Gospel drama, since the rejection of the owner's son (v. 8) looks to the crucifixion of Jesus, and the reaction of the owner (vv. 9-11) points to the resurrection, when God vindicates Jesus' death.

Mark's Christian readers would understand the various elements and the deeper message of this parable as clearly as the scribes and chief priests to whom it was addressed ("They realized that he had addressed the parable to them," v. 12). The care of the vineyard (the people of Israel) had been entrusted by God to the leaders of the Jewish people (the "tenant farmers"). They treated the son (Jesus) as ruthlessly (vv. 6-8) as they had treated the Old Testament prophets before him (vv. 2-5). Because they did so, they no longer have any authority with God's new people. Rather, that authority now rests with the leaders of the early church (v. 9).

Mark conveys the same message when he has Jesus quote Psalm 118. Only the key image changes, namely, the "son" becomes the cornerstone (vv. 10-11). As Mark prepares his readers for their encounter with Jesus' death, he makes it clear where the blame for the Son's death lay—with the Jewish leaders. He also challenges Christian leaders to examine the relationship they have with Christ, "the cornerstone." For them, this parable is food for serious thought about how they are caring for the church entrusted into their hands by the risen Lord.

12:13-27 Of tribute due to Caesar and to the living God. Mark moves from his last parable to two more of Jesus' conflict encounters with Jewish leadership. The first concerns the tax due to the emperor (vv. 13-17), and the second has to do with belief in resurrection and life after death (vv. 18-27). Mark's readers will discern a similar pattern in both encounters. First, the leaders approach Jesus with trick questions, obviously trying to "ensnare him in his speech" (v. 13). The Pharisees and Herodians ask if a good Jew should pay taxes to the Roman emperor or if that is against the law of Moses (v. 14). Then the Sadducees, who were known for not believing in the resurrection, ask a legalistic and cynical question about marriage relationships in the risen life (v. 23).

In response to their questions, Jesus shows a cunning wisdom that unveils their intent to trip him up. He exposes their hypocrisy in one case (v. 15) and shows their shallow understanding of their own Scriptures in the other (v. 24). Good Jews (and good Christians in Mark's audience) are expected to pay "tax tribute" to lawful civil leaders and "praise and true allegiance tribute" to God (vv. 15-17). Jews (and Christians) who really understand their sacred Scriptures should also know that "the God of Abraham, the God of Isaac, the God of Jacob" (and of the risen Jesus) is "not God of the dead but of the living" (vv. 24-27).

The cumulative result of these two encounters is that Mark's readers, like those first involved with Jesus, might be "amazed" at Jesus' wisdom (v. 17) and at his dedication to his Father, the God of life. But Mark wants more than amazement—he wants his Christians to imitate their Lord by being courageous apostles of truth and life themselves. How they are to be such apostles is up to them in their own circumstances. However, the following passage will give them a concrete model to follow.

12:28-34 The scribe who was close to the reign of God. After all the scheming and malicious questioning from the elders and scribes, for Jesus to claim that a scribe is "not far from the kingdom of God" (v. 34) is quite remarkable. Yet, upon examining this dialogue over which is the "first of all the commandments" (v. 28), Mark's readers can readily approve of the scribe's sincerity and honest attempt to understand the underlying basis of Jesus' way. Jesus responds to his question with the traditional *Shema* prayer, which every Israelite prays twice daily: "Hear, O Israel! The Lord our God is Lord alone!" (v. 29). Since the Lord is one, Jesus and the *Shema* continue, one's whole being (heart, soul, mind, and strength) should love God (v. 30). Jesus then adds a second command: "You shall love your neighbor as yourself." In effect, he makes the first of all the commandments into one dual commandment ("There is no greater commandment than *these,*" v. 31).

The scribe appreciates Jesus' response. He sees how Jesus has combined two commands given to Israel by Moses (Deut 6:2 and Lev 19:18). He also hears in Jesus' response more than Jesus has said! He hears in it the echo of the prophet who declared that love, not sacrifice, is what God desires of all people (v. 33, quoting Hos 6:6).

Mark's readers know how correct the scribe was, because they knew that Jesus practiced what he taught. He had loved God and his neighbor unto death. His sacrifice was love! As they leave the crowds, who no longer "dared to ask him any more questions" (v. 34), Mark's readers might well ask themselves how their love of God is verified by their love of neighbor. They might ask how their sacrifice and liturgical worship of God are made manifest in their sacrifices for others. Mark's report of this encounter thus challenges his Christians to be like Jesus and also like this singular scribe, who had such insight into the ways of the kingdom. It also prepares them for the last two episodes of chapter 12, which will contrast the generous piety of the widow with the empty prayer of certain scribes (12:38-44).

12:35-37 Jesus is David's Lord and God's Son. Up to this point in chapter 12, the scribes have been asking Jesus challenging questions. He now asks them one: "How do [you] claim that the Messiah is the son of David" (v. 35), when David himself (in Ps 110:1) refers to the Messiah as "my Lord" (v. 36)? Mark's readers know that Jesus is their Messiah. They also know that he was of Davidic descent. However, Mark wants his readers to acknowledge even more, namely, that Jesus is the Son of God. Some people put Jesus to death because he claimed to be "the Son of the Blessed One" (14:61-64). How will Mark's readers renew their commitment to their Lord, who is also David's Lord and God's Son?

12:38-44 The poor widow shows the scribes the meaning of religion. The last time Mark presents Jesus in the temple is one of the most dramatic moments of his whole Gospel. Jesus first warns people to beware of the scribes, who pray long and loud in order to be seen and respected as "the holy ones" (vv. 38-39). At the same time, because they "devour the houses of widows" (v. 40), they show how empty their prayer is. (They also disobey a special commandment given to their ancestors by Moses: "You shall not wrong any widow or orphan or stranger," Exod 22:21.)

To this story of hypocrisy Mark has added the touching picture-example of the poor widow (vv. 41-44). Look at her, says Mark's Jesus. She puts much less money in the box than the wealthy ones (v. 41), but she, from her poverty, has contributed all she had, her whole livelihood" (v. 44). Her offering is a sign of what total dependence on God really means. The widow thus becomes a model of faith for Mark's readers. If they imitate her generous and trusting faith, they will also be imitating Jesus, who likewise gave up his very life for the many (chs. 14–15)!

13:1-4 The end of the temple and the end of "all these things." As Jesus and the disciples leave the temple area, Mark has Jesus predict that "there will not be one stone [of these great buildings] left upon another" (v. 2). They respond to Jesus' remarkable statement with an important related question: "Tell us, when will this happen? And what sign will there be when all these things [i.e., the world as we know it] are about to come to an end?" Mark's readers today might not see how the disciples' question about the end of the world follows logically from Jesus' prediction about the end of the temple. They will understand the connection, however, if two significant facts are made clear: (1) the early church saw the destruction of Jerusalem as a pre-eminent sign of the soon-to-come end of the world; and (2) the early Christians for whom Mark was writing had *already* witnessed that destruction of Jerusalem (in A.D. 70 by the Roman army). Such historical background will help today's readers of Mark's Gospel understand this important chapter.

It is also helpful for Mark's readers to realize the special type of literature they will be involved with for the rest of chapter 13. All of Jesus' talk about "the end" and the signs that will accompany it belongs to the type of first-century writing known as "apocalyptic." In the early church, apocalyptic writing was used to communicate hope to fearful people by revealing how God would definitively save his faithful ones from any and all evil forces at the end of time. Apocalyptic literature made up a small (in content) but very significant (in meaning) part of Christianity's first gospel message. (Such writing was rather common in certain Old Testament communities, which were longing for the coming of their Messiah to deliver them from foreign, pagan rulers. See, for example, the Book of Daniel, chapters 7–12, written about 150 B.C., which describes the coming of the Son of Man in terms very similar to those found here in Mark's Gospel. See also New Testament writings like Matt 24–25, Luke 21, 1 Thess 4–5, and the Book of Revelation, which reflect the early church's keen consciousness of the Lord's absence and its expectations of his imminent return in glory.) It is in chapter 13 that Mark passes on to his community the early church's hopeful preoccupation with Jesus' return. It is here that Mark describes the attitudes to be adopted by his readers in the time between Jesus' resurrection and that return.

13:5-23 Christian alertness and endurance in "the end times." Mark begins Jesus' apocalyptic speech with a section (vv. 5-23) that exemplifies very well two ways in which apocalyptic language is meant to move its readers to response and action. First, the catch phrase that begins and ends this section ("See that no one deceives you" at v. 5, and "Be watchful" at v. 23) signals his readers to be very alert to their response to certain misleading preachers in their midst ("who come in my name," v. 6, and "false messiahs and prophets," v. 22) who say the end is already here because of certain signs (for example, wars, v. 7; earthquakes, v. 8; persecution, vv. 9-13). The proper Christian response, says Mark, is not to panic (v. 7) but to persevere. Mark encourages his readers to view their perseverance in times of tension as a positive sign of God's protecting Holy Spirit with them until the end (vv. 9 and 11). Even more important, Mark demands that his readers be alert to means of spreading the good news about Jesus "to all nations" (v. 10), because only when that missionary effort is concluded can the end really come.

A second characteristic of apocalyptic speech is that some events that have already begun to happen (in the past and present) are cast as a part of the future scheme of things. This mode of writing was meant to assure the readers of the reliability of those parts of the message that really do pertain to the future. For example, Mark's readers can say, "Yes, some families already have broken up and have been divided because some of their members chose to follow Jesus" (vv. 12-13). They can also say, "Yes, 'the desolating abomination' of Roman idols already stands in Jerusalem, where the holy temple once stood" (v. 14). At the same time, what is most important is that they realize that the Lord *will* protect his faithful ones when the end really comes, even shortening the days of distress for the sake of those he has chosen (v. 20). In fact, reports Mark, the most reliable sign of the end of time is yet to come, namely, the glorious return of the Son of Man (to be described in vv. 24-27).

By being in touch with the nature of apocalyptic writing, the readers of chapter 13 can experience the urgency of the early church's waiting and watching for the return of their absent Lord (vv. 15-19). They can also hear Mark's invitation to put aside useless and fearful calculation of deadlines regarding the end of the world, in order to live courageously in the present as discerning and alert missionaries of Jesus' gospel.

13:24-27 The consoling coming of the Son of Man. While apocalyptic writing is recognized by its scary and dark imagery of trials, tribulations, and turmoil in the heavens (vv. 24-25), there is also the consoling light at the heart of it all, which overcomes the darkness. Here that consolation takes the form of the glorious Son of Man, Jesus, coming on the clouds to gather his chosen and faithful ones from all over the earth (vv. 26-27). Mark borrows this encouraging picture of God's deliverance from the promises of the Old Testament prophet Daniel (Dan 7:13-14). Mark's readers today, as well as his first readers, might well be lifted up by this promise of God's final victory over whatever difficulties or darkness envelop them and their world. Encouraged by this hopeful vision, they can accept more readily their responsibilities to be a consoling light for those who may not yet have experienced the hopeful side of the gospel promises.

13:28-37 "We do not know when, but it is near, so persevere!" Just as surely as Jesus' other predictions have come to pass (his death and resurrection, the fall of Jerusalem, the trials his followers would endure), so also will he come again in glory to save his chosen ones. This encouraging message of 13:3-27 concludes with the final call of Jesus to his faithful followers: "The end is near and will happen soon. You will see the signs of the end (vv. 29-31) just as clearly as you see the coming of summer by the new leaves on the fig tree (vv. 28-29)." "*But,*" underlines Mark's Jesus, "since no one knows the day or the hour when the end will come, be watchful and be alert (vv. 32-33). Look around you like the gatekeeper (v. 35). Do not be found sleeping (v. 36), but 'watch!' (v. 37)."

The apocalyptic chapter 13 ends with Mark's sharp challenge for all his readers (not only for Peter, James, John, and Andrew of v. 3). He asks them to persevere in their faith, even in dark days of suffering on behalf of the gospel. It should be clear to Mark's readers that it is their duty to be alert missionaries of that gospel in the present, since the Son of Man entrusted it into their hands until his return in glory.

THE SON OF MAN WILL BE PUT TO DEATH AND WILL RISE THREE DAYS LATER

Mark 14:1–16:8

The very familiar account of the death and resurrection of Jesus is the climax of Mark's involving drama. Everything has been leading to these three chapters, and Mark tells the passion story in such a way that many of the key themes of his Gospel are now drawn together. For example, *the disciples* still fail to have any clear sight or faithful confidence in the Lord they follow. Indeed, they all scatter in the garden when one of them betrays Jesus to his killers with a kiss (14:43-52). Likewise, the alert reader will see how the important images of *bread* and *cup* (developed through chs. 6–8 and 10) come together in the Eucharistic passage that precedes Jesus' agony in the garden (14:22-26). A third developing theme of the earlier chapters, namely, Jesus' identification of himself as the *suffering Son of Man,* finds its climax at the foot of the cross, when the Roman centurion declares at Jesus' death: "Truly this man was the Son of God!" (15:39).

By now, Mark's readers expect some of the developments that occur in these closing chapters. Yet, Mark's passion account also surprises his readers with a very abrupt ending (16:8). When the women leave the tomb and say nothing to anyone because they were afraid (16:8), Mark's readers are left to complete the story with their own careful reflection and response. Why did Mark end the Gospel in this strange way? When did the women overcome their trembling and bewilderment and carry out the mission given to them by the young man at the tomb (16:7)? What about the readers' own hesitation to be courageous proclaimers of Jesus' message? While Mark's readers know that most of Jesus' predictions have come true, two are left unfulfilled. First, did Jesus ever appear to the disciples in Galilee, as he had promised (14:28)? (The reader knows that he did, but *not* from Mark's account.) Second, will Jesus keep his promise to return "in the clouds with great power and glory . . . and gather his elect . . . from the end of the earth to the end of the sky," as he had promised (13:26-27)? This certainly has not happened yet!

The ending of Mark's Gospel is, therefore, more like the beginning of something else. It is as if Mark is saying that the Gospel is not over yet. In fact, Mark's ending leaves his readers with the startling realization that they have to conclude the Gospel by living out its values. What seemingly began as Mark's account of the *past* life of "Jesus Christ, the Son of God" (1:1) ends with the dramatic invitation that all his readers be faithful imitators of Jesus, the servant Son of Man (10:45), *in the present*, until he comes again to establish the reign of God in power (8:38 and 9:1)!

14:1-11 The preparations for Jesus' death and burial. The first verses of the passion narrative set the scene and the emotional tone for all that is to follow. While the chief priests are afraid to arrest Jesus because "there may be a riot among the people" (v. 2), one of the Twelve makes it easy for them by arranging to hand him over, thereby changing their fear into jubilant anticipation (vv. 10-11). In the midst of the plotting and planning for Jesus' death, Mark places the story of the woman at Bethany (vv. 3-9), whose bold act of reverence for Jesus "will be told in her memory wherever the good news is proclaimed throughout the world."

Typically, those with Jesus do not understand what is going on around them. They fail to see that the woman's act of anointing is the anticipation of Jesus' burial (v. 8). Their intentions are good (the money could be given to the poor, v. 5), but their infuriation with the woman (vv. 4-5) shows that they missed the point of her symbolic action. It should have reminded them of the reality of Jesus' suffering way! Mark does not want *his* readers to miss the point. To care for the poor is a key part of following Jesus (recall the challenge to the rich man in 10:21). But Jesus' followers must also choose *all* that is involved in being his disciples, even to the extent of giving their lives in service of the needs of all, in imitation of the suffering Son of Man (10:44-45).

14:12-26 Jesus makes his own preparations: the Passover Eucharist. Jesus' triumphal entry into Jerusalem (11:8-11) had been preceded by his remarkable prediction that the disciples would find a "colt on which no one has ever sat" (11:2-7). A similarly remarkable prediction precedes the Passover supper that Jesus will celebrate with his disciples (see 14:12-16). Such amazing circumstances prepare Mark's readers for a very special part of the Jesus story.

The Passover meal of the Hebrews celebrated their deliverance from Egypt. ("The Lord will go by, striking down the Egyptians. Seeing the *blood* . . . on the doorposts, the Lord will *pass over* that door and not let the destroyer come into your houses to strike you down," Exod 12:23). As Jesus' Passover meal with his disciples begins, an unnamed (for now) and pitiable disciple is symbolically singled out as the one who will bring about Jesus' betrayal and, ironically, the new deliverance of God's people (vv. 17-21).

Such dramatic preparation leads to Mark's account of the first Eucharistic meal (vv. 22-25), which was as central to his Christian community's life then as it is today. Certainly Mark was faithful in passing on the early church's tradition that the Christian Eucharist is the *new Passover*. Jesus' saving death and resurrection was God's new and perfect way of delivering all people. Mark's Christians shared in the new covenant of Christ's body and blood when they shared the Eucharistic bread and cup! At the same time, Mark uses the occasion of the first Eucharist to round off a special theme he has been developing in regard to the disciples' blindness. (*Bread* has not been mentioned since chapters 6–8, where the disciples did not see the deeper meaning of Jesus' miracles, especially with "the breads"; *the cup* has not been mentioned since 10:35-45, when Jesus made clear its intimate connection with his death.) Consequently, Mark is telling his readers that those who wish to share in Jesus' Eucharistic cup (now and at the heavenly banquet, v. 25) must first choose to share fully in Jesus' way of suffering service (10:45a: "The Son of Man did not come to be served but to serve"). They must participate actively in Jesus' mission on earth, which involves pouring out their lives "for *many*" (v. 24), always in imitation of him (10:45b: "The Son of Man has come . . . to give his life as ransom *for many*").

14:27-31 "The sheep will be dispersed." After Jesus and his disciples arrive at the Mount of Olives (vv. 26-27), he makes three more predictions: (1) the sheep (his disciples) will be scattered at his death (v. 27); (2) once risen, Jesus will go to Galilee before them (v. 28); and (3) Peter will deny him three times "before the cock crows twice" (v. 30). Despite the protests of Peter and the others, Mark's readers know that two of these predictions will shortly (and sadly) be fulfilled. The disciples will all desert Jesus and flee (v. 50), and Peter will deny him (vv. 66-72). However, the prediction about seeing him in Galilee will be left unfulfilled, even when Mark's Gospel ends (16:8). Mark challenges his readers to ponder the meaning of this unfulfilled prediction as they enter the garden with Jesus, Peter, James, and John (v. 32).

14:32-42 The garden experience: model of radical trust. Mark's account of Jesus' agony in the garden is actually two moving scenes in one. In the first (vv. 33-36), Mark's readers are privileged to witness Jesus' profound humanity, as he is overwhelmed by fear and sadness at the prospect of his imminent death (i.e., the cup of v. 36). They also recognize in his final acceptance of his Father's will the ultimate act of his loving humanity, i.e., his choice to give up his life for the Father and for all people.

The second scene (vv. 37-42) focuses the readers' attention on the disciples who fall asleep as Jesus struggles in prayer. Mark hopes that his readers will face life and choose to be human like Jesus, not like the disciples. The profundity of Jesus' choice to take the cup can be grasped, ironically, only by certain readers of Mark's Gospel—that is, only those who have come as close to despair as Jesus did in the garden can really identify with him. Mark hopes that Jesus will be for them a realistic (truly human) model of trust and love in their painful "hour" (v. 41) of Christian and human life!

14:43-52 It all starts to fall into place: the betrayal and arrest. Once Jesus has made the decision to give himself up to his Father's will (v. 36), the other pieces of the passion account quickly fall into place. Immediately after Jesus is betrayed by the kiss of Judas (vv. 44-45), he is arrested and led off as if he were a common robber (v. 48). Mark makes it clear, in verse 49, that the arrest of the innocent Jesus, like the rest of his passion experience, is in accord with Old Testament prophecies about the way the Messiah of Israel would be treated by his own people.

Three other details in the passage bring out how oblivious Jesus' companions are to what is really happening. One of them thinks he can stop violence with violence (v. 47). All the rest leave him alone (v. 50). And even the young man who does follow, "wearing nothing but a linen cloth," runs away as soon as Jesus' enemies try to seize him (vv. 51-52). These details of Mark's passion account serve not only to recall for his readers "the way it all happened" but also to stimulate them to ask themselves how far they would go in staying with Jesus and his gospel values in their own difficult life situations.

14:53-65 The trial and the verdict and the sentence: Death! The so-called trial of Jesus is full of false and trumped-up charges against him. In response to such testimony, Jesus "was silent and answered nothing" (v. 61). The high priest's verdict of guilty (v. 64) comes only when the "silent one" does acknowledge that he is "the Messiah, the Son of the Blessed One," who will sit with God ("the Power") in the heavens, and who will "come with the clouds of heaven" as judge in the last days (v. 62). It is ironic that none of the *false* testimony can disprove Jesus' innocence (v. 55). It is only when he speaks *the truth* about himself that he is condemned to death (v. 62)! Certainly Mark's readers would be proud of their Lord's perseverance in the face of this humiliating trial and the mocking taunts and spittle that accompany it (v. 65). But will they be any more faithful to him than Peter was (see the next passage) when their faith is severely tested?

14:66-72 Peter denies Jesus three times. As Jesus had predicted (14:27), all his disciples deserted him in the garden and fled (14:50). As he had predicted (14:30), even Peter denies him, not once but three times (vv. 66-72). Peter's tears (v. 72) indicate his remorse, however, and his sorrow could be encouraging to any of Mark's readers who may at times have been unfaithful followers of Jesus. For they know that the one who denied his Lord three times would go on to experience the mercy of a forgiving God and become the early church's greatest apostle among the Jews (Gal 2:8) after the resurrection. Through the tears of Peter, Mark offers a great deal of hope to any of his Christian readers who lack courage and trust. It is never too late for them to say with contrite hearts: "Yes, *I am with* the Nazarene, Jesus!"

15:1-15 The chief priests and Pilate hand over "the king of the Jews." It is clear from the start of this passage (15:1: "As soon as morning came") how anxious the Jewish priests are to get the cooperation of the Roman official, Pilate, in putting Jesus away. Earlier the high priest had asked Jesus, in Jewish terms, if he was "the Messiah, the Son of the Blessed One." The Roman now asks, in terms that have political meaning for him, if Jesus is "the king of the Jews" (15:2). Jesus accepts the title given him by Pilate (15:3), which is the equivalent of saying "guilty" to the charge of high treason. (There is no king in Roman territory but Caesar!) Even so, Pilate sees through the charges made against Jesus (15:10: "He knew, of course, that it was out of envy that the chief priests had handed him over"). He tries to release Jesus instead of Barabbas, but the priests influence the crowd to ask for Barabbas (v. 11). Pilate ends up "wishing to satisfy the crowd," which calls for Jesus' death: "Crucify him!" (vv. 11-15). In so doing, Pilate plays out his cowardly role in the Gospel drama. Though convinced of Jesus' innocence, he still yields to pressure and hands him over to be scourged and crucified. And Jesus begins to drink deeply from "the cup."

15:20-32 The climax: they mocked and crucified him. Once again, after the intrigue of "the trials" that shows how innocent Jesus really is, the horrible events of the passion quickly unfold. After Jesus is scourged (v. 15), he is dressed "in purple" and "crowned" with thorns by the Roman soldiers, who mockingly call him "King of the Jews" (vv. 16-20). Through all the spitting and the beating he receives, Jesus remains silent. Mark's readers would certainly recognize in this the fulfillment of the Isaian prophecy concerning the Messiah: "I gave my back to those who beat me. . . . My face I did not shield from buffets and spitting" (Isa 50:6).

The climax of the Markan drama comes in Jesus' crucifixion. The readers of Mark's Gospel will notice that some familiar details are missing as they read Mark's account of the way of the cross. For example, the lamenting women of Jerusalem (Luke 23:27-31) do not meet him on the way. Likewise, *both* of the men who are crucified with Jesus join the passers-by in taunting Jesus (vv. 27-32), unlike what is recorded by Luke in the memorable exchange between Jesus and the "good thief" (Luke 23:40-43). Consequently, Mark's readers are left with the starkest of pictures. Their Lord hangs alone on the cross, exposed to the mockery of the people he came to save.

One of the last cries of mockery (v. 32: "Let the Messiah, 'the King of Israel,' come down now from the cross that we may see and believe") becomes for Mark a profound challenge to his readers' faith. Will they believe in Jesus precisely because he did *not* come down from the cross? Will they be able to see meaning in their own inexplicable suffering in the light of the absurd suffering of their Messiah and King? Will they be able to see the positive, saving value of their suffering as St. Paul did: "In my flesh I am filling up what is lacking in the afflictions of Christ on behalf of his body, the church" (Col 1:24)?

15:33-41 In his death Jesus is seen as the Son of God. Mark's readers have now come with Jesus to *the* moment that all his life has prepared for. Along with Jesus' "blind" disciples, they have walked with Jesus as he has shared life and healing power with others (chs. 1–8). They have learned what is necessary to be enlightened and true Christian disciples (chs. 9–13). All that is needed now is for them to stay with him to the end!

It is in the dark hour of Jesus' death (v. 33) that Mark's readers see the light. It is there, at the foot of the cross, that they hear their

Lord's cry, "My God, my God, why have you forsaken me?" (v. 34). Mark does not want his Christians to mistake Jesus' cry for what it is not (as did the bystanders, who thought it was simply a desperate appeal for Elijah's help, vv. 35-36). Rather, he wants them to recognize in Jesus' last words and death the ultimate act of self-giving and trust. Like the Psalmist who first uttered this cry (Ps 22:2), Mark's Jesus believes that God will hear him (Ps 22:25) and will give him life, precisely because he suffered and died out of love and obedience! Who would ever believe that life could come from death? Yet Mark wants his readers to believe that this *is* true, not only for Jesus but also for anyone who will follow in his steps. Who would expect a Gentile centurion to be the first to declare that Jesus is "the Son of God"? Yet Mark asks his readers to see the *living* Son of God most clearly in his humble and loving *death*, just as the pagan centurion did.

15:42-47 Jesus is buried by Joseph of Arimathea. Near the end of Jesus' ministry in Jerusalem, he had met with a scribe who was "not far from the kingdom of God" (12:28-34). For Mark's readers, that scribe's sincere response to Jesus was more authentic than the response of Jesus' own disciples. Once again, in the burial scene, it is not Jesus' disciples who respond properly, but Joseph of Arimathea, "a distinguished member of the council" (15:43). He was bold enough to take reverent care of Jesus' burial (vv. 43-46). Thus, even as he relates the account of Jesus' burial, Mark prods his readers to have more faith than Jesus' first disciples. Pilate's inquiry as to whether Jesus was already dead (v. 44) also becomes an important detail for Mark. Such insistence on finality prepares Mark's readers for the most striking reversal of the entire Gospel, namely, the proclamation of the young man at the tomb: "Do not be amazed! You seek Jesus of Nazareth, the crucified. He *has been raised;* he is not here. Behold the place where they laid him" (16:6).

16:1-8 The end is the beginning! Go now and tell that he is risen! "They said nothing to anyone, for they were afraid" (16:8). This is how the women respond to the wonderful news of Jesus' resurrection. This is also how Mark ends his Gospel. (It is generally agreed that verses 9-20 were added to Mark's Gospel later by those who could not believe that Mark would end it as he did!) By ending it this way, Mark actually invites his readers to step in and take the place of the women at the empty tomb. The women failed to carry out the mission orders they received from God's messenger (the young man "clothed in a white robe," v. 5). Mark wants his disciples, men and women, to spread the good news that God has brought life from death by raising Jesus from the dead (vv. 6-7). He wants them to do so without the fear, bewilderment, or trembling of the three women at the tomb (v. 8).

Mark's readers might well ask how they could be any better as disciples than the women and men who were with Jesus during his life, at his death, and at the empty tomb. Mark would probably answer this way: "It is for you that this Gospel has been written! Persevere as faithful followers of the Jesus I have presented to you. His resurrection is not the end! He has gone ahead of you as the servant Messiah. Now you must care for the needs of those most in need, until he comes again. He has given meaning to suffering and has brought life from death. Trust in him and give his life to those who have no hope. Whatever you do, let others know by your courageous words and your lives of service that you have heard the Lord's call and that you have chosen to follow his lead until you see him, as he has promised."

THE THREE "OTHER ENDINGS" OF THE GOSPEL

16:9-20 +

Although virtually all of today's scholars of the Bible believe that Mark had a purpose in ending his Gospel abruptly at 16:8, this was not always the case. Some first- or second-century Christians tried to "complete" his Gospel drama by adding scenes that they thought Mark should have added himself.

The first extra ending, the so-called *Longer Ending* (vv. 9-20), includes appearances of the risen Jesus to Mary Magdalene and to the disciples. These visions were meant to inspire the early missionary church to "go into the whole world and proclaim the gospel to every creature" (v. 15). The church's missionaries had nothing to fear, because the ascended Lord

(v. 19) was with them in their preaching (v. 20) and would confirm their message with special signs of his protection and power (vv. 17-18). Alert readers will notice some themes in these verses that are unlike anything they have seen before in Mark's Gospel. They may also recognize in them echoes of familiar scenes from the other Gospels, gathered together to round off Mark's abrupt ending (for example, Mary Magdalene meets with Jesus alone in John's Gospel, 20:11-18; the appearance to the two disciples is reminiscent of Luke's Emmaus appearance, 24:13-35; and the commission to "go into the whole world to preach" sounds like the ending of Matthew's Gospel, 28:16-20).

The so-called *Shorter Ending*, when read immediately after 16:8, was another attempt of the early church to end Mark's Gospel more smoothly. It reverses the fear and silence of the women at the tomb and shows how the message of the resurrection came to be proclaimed through "Peter's companions."

The *Freer Ending*, preserved in the Freer Gallery in Washington, D.C., is a fifth-century addition to the Longer Ending. Appearing between verses 14 and 15, it excuses the disbelief and stubbornness of the disciples found at 16:14.

Although the church has recognized these "added endings" as worthy of inclusion in the inspired text, none of them is as inspiring and involving as Mark's own. Mark's abrupt ending leaves it up to his readers to "complete" his Gospel in their lives.

LUKE

Jerome Kodell, O.S.B.

INTRODUCTION

The Gospel of Luke is the first half of a two-part work that tells the story of the origins of Christianity from the infancy of Jesus until the arrival of Paul, the foremost preacher, in Rome around A.D. 60. Just the length of the Gospel and of its companion volume, the Acts of the Apostles (more extensive than the contribution of any other individual New Testament writer), would have made its author a prominent influence on Christian theology and spirituality. But he is in addition a gifted writer, organizing his materials creatively and telling his story with clarity and artistic coloring. Dante called Luke the "scribe of Christ's gentleness" because of his emphasis on Jesus' mercy to sinners and outcasts. Some of the most memorable Gospel stories of divine mercy are found only in Luke (the widow of Naim, the prodigal son, Zacchaeus).

The author and his audience

At the beginning of his Gospel, Luke recognizes the work of those who have gone before. He is not trying to replace the earlier Gospel of Mark, but he sees the need for a new account for a new generation in different circumstances. Luke is a Greek-speaking Christian, possibly a convert of Paul, writing in Antioch (Syria) or Asia Minor (modern Turkey) late in the first century—probably in the eighties. The Christian church is quickly becoming more Gentile than Jewish in composition; it is no longer confined to Palestine but is a configuration of communities scattered throughout the Roman Empire. Its language is not Aramaic but Greek. Luke wants to show the continuity of this modern Greek church with Jesus and the early Hebrew community. He finds that he can trace these roots best by adding a sequel to the story of Jesus, connecting the two parts thematically while preserving the historical distinctions. He uses the Gospel of Mark, editing it according to his own needs, and other written and oral sources besides, some from traditions used also by the evangelist Matthew.

To Luke's readership, the geography, language, and religious and political conditions of Palestine were foreign and remote. Most were unfamiliar with the Jewish writings that the preachers often referred to in explaining the story of Jesus. The Christians of Asia Minor and Europe were concerned to be good citizens of the Roman Empire, a government that had been treated as an intruder by many of Jesus' contemporaries in Palestine. Many of the new generation of Christians were not poor but well-to-do, more urban than rural. The question arose, either spontaneously or with help from their pagan neighbors: Why are we Greeks following a religion with so much of a Hebrew core? How did the news about Jesus get here? Were our missionaries reliable? Are we by now independent of happenings in Jerusalem?

These Christian citizens of the Roman Empire would have heard, of course, of the destruction of Jerusalem by the Roman army, a catastrophe foretold by Jesus and interpreted as punishment for sin. Did this indicate that they should cut their Jewish roots? How could Jesus' words to a Hebrew audience a half century earlier be appropriate to a modern Greek audience? All this would have been heightened by their neighbors' pervasive hostility to Christianity and by subtle persecution in many forms, particularly social and economic.

Issues like these swirled about Luke as he conceived his two-part work. He addressed these and more, directly and indirectly. He wanted his readers to know that they had been included in God's plan of salvation from the beginning, even though historically the Jews were the first to hear the message as the channel for all others. The story of salvation unraveled according to the exact plan of God, just as was promised in the Old Testament. It is a journey to the kingdom under the guidance of the Holy Spirit. The Gospel portrays the beginnings of the Christian story, from the first announcement of the fulfillment of salvation until its achievement in the death and resurrection of Jesus. The Acts of the Apostles tells of the rise and development of the church, pointing out the major decisions and turning points as the leaders were guided by God into the Gentile mission. Once the church's decision to evangelize all people, not only Jews, is made definitively (Acts 15), the story follows the apostle Paul as he carries the gospel across the Empire, into Europe and eventually to the center of the contemporary world, Rome.

Themes

Every preacher of the gospel delivers the fundamental proclamation of salvation in Jesus Christ. But each one develops the insights into the mystery that come from personal reflection and experience and that are needed by a particular audience. There are four written Gospels; there might have been many more. They tell us the same basic story about Jesus and interpret its meaning. Their approach to the subject is like that of four painters assigned to produce portraits of the same person. Each evangelist brings to the task a personal relationship to Jesus, individual talents, a particular experience of Christian life in a certain place or places, a wealth of material learned in the community or researched in other ways. Some of Luke's prominent themes are the following.

1. Salvation for all. The realization that God wants to save all people goes back to the earliest times in Israel's life as a people (Gen 13:2). All the communities of the earth would find blessing through the Hebrews. The early Jewish Christians knew this well, but they had to struggle with the question: Does God mean to open up salvation in Jesus to everyone directly, or should we bring converts in through Judaism? The decision had already been made in favor of universal salvation by the time any of the Gospels were written, so this theme is present beginning with the earliest, the Gospel of Mark. But reflection on this truth proceeded in various directions. Luke seems to have the most thoroughgoing message of universal salvation. Matthew's Gospel, for example, has the mandate to preach to all nations (Matt 28:19), but Jewish rejection of Jesus still smolders (Matt 27:25). Luke is not affected by this kind of anguish, and he stresses that Jesus is still available for Jews who turn to him (Acts 3:17-20).

2. Mercy and forgiveness. This theme has already been pointed out as distinctive of Luke's portrait of Jesus. In this Gospel, Jesus is constantly concerned to help the poor, the sinner, the outcast. Shepherds instead of Magi come to his crib (2:8-18); he welcomes the sinful but penitent woman at a Pharisee's meal (7:36-50); he speaks well of Samaritans (10:30-37); he seeks hospitality from a tax collector (19:1-10). The place of women in Luke's Gospel is also noteworthy in this regard. Women were second-class, often mistreated citizens of the world at that time. Jesus befriended women (10:38-42) and accepted their help (8:1-3); they did not weaken in faithfulness at the time of his passion and death (23:49; 24:1; Acts 1:14).

3. Joy. Luke's Gospel radiates the joy of salvation. The joy flows from a confidence in God's love and mercy as demonstrated in the teaching and action of Jesus described in the previous section. The births of John the Baptist and Jesus are announced as causes of great joy (1:14; 2:10). The repentance of a sinner is a source of great joy in heaven (15:7-10). The Gospel ends with the disciples returning to Jerusalem full of joy after Jesus' ascension (24:52).

4. The journey. All three synoptic Gospels (Matthew, Mark, Luke) begin the account of Jesus' public ministry with John's preaching from Isaiah: "Make ready the way of the Lord, clear him a straight path" (Isa 40:3). The mission of Jesus is presented as the continuation and culmination of the "way of the Lord" that began when Abraham left his homeland, and continued with the Exodus from Egypt led by Moses and, later, the return from the Babylonian captivity. Luke capitalizes on the journey theme to organize the central section of his Gospel (9:51–19:44) around the final journey of Jesus from Galilee to Jerusalem.

The Father's guidance of Jesus and the church brings to the fore emphases on the role of the Holy Spirit and the place of prayer. Luke is occasionally referred to as the "Evangelist of the Holy Spirit" or the "Evangelist of Prayer." The role of the Spirit begins before Jesus' birth (1:35, 67). Jesus is led by the Spirit into the desert (4:1) and on returning announces that he is the one foretold on whom the Spirit rests (4:18). This theme continues even more strongly in the Acts of the Apostles as the Spirit empowers the disciples to preach the gospel (Acts 2:1-17). The Spirit guides the emerging church in deciding how to expand the mission (15:28) and leads the missionaries on their journeys (16:6-7). Prayer is the context for the opening announcement of salvation (Luke 1:10). Jesus prays before choosing the Twelve (6:12); he is praying as he is about to be transfigured (9:29) and when the disciples ask him to teach them to pray (11:1). Prayer characterizes the community in Acts (Acts 1:24; 2:42; 3:1).

5. Modern Christian living. Luke is determined to make the teaching of Jesus applicable to his readers living a middle-class life in a cosmopolitan society. He indicates that good citizenship is compatible (and expected) with Christianity. This is more evident in Acts than in Luke's Gospel. Paul's Roman citizenship is carefully noted (Acts 16:37-40; 22:26), and his honorable civic conduct is insisted on (18:14-16). But already in the Gospel, Jesus is presented as an observant citizen maligned by false charges (Luke 20:25; 23:2). His death was at the hands of the Roman magistrate, true, but one who was too weak to free Jesus as he was convinced he should (23:1-25). If these good citizens were persecuted—the implication might further be—don't be alarmed at your own mistreatment in the cause of Christ.

The question of possessions is treated often. In Luke, Jesus' beatitudes are harsh and stark: "Blest are you poor . . . . Woe to you rich" (6:20, 24), but overall there is no simplistic message of personal despoilment. The point is rather that one must not be enslaved by attachment to possessions (12:13-43; 14:25-33); they must be expended on others (18:22). Renunciation extends even to one's personal relationships. Not even one's own family must come between the disciple and Jesus (14:26).

6. Fulfillment of prophecy. Jesus' mission of salvation had been prepared from ages past. Luke incorporates a surprising amount of Old Testament teaching for his Greek readers, though not as much as Matthew does. One of Luke's favorite usages is "it must happen"—"it had to happen" (2:49; 4:43; 9:22). The cross, the way of suffering, was a puzzle to his Greek readers—how revolting that the Savior, Son of God and King, should be treated so shamefully. Luke repeats again and again that the suffering had to be: it is the way to glory (18:31-33; 24:26).

7. Ascension. Luke sees the goal of Jesus' mission as "to be taken (up) from this world" (9:51; 24:51). The ascension comes in the event of the resurrection; it is the act of glorification whereby Jesus takes his place at the right hand of the Father. The ascension is crucial to Jesus' saving work, because it is through this glorification that the Spirit is released on the church (Acts 2:33) and salvation is made available for all people.

OUTLINE OF THE GOSPEL

1:1-4	Preface
1:5–2:52	Part I: Beginnings
3:1–4:13	Part II: The Messiah Is Prepared
4:14–9:50	Part III: The Ministry in Galilee
9:51–19:44	Part IV: The Journey to Jerusalem
19:45–24:53	Part V: Suffering and Victory

COMMENTARY

PREFACE

Luke 1:1-4

Luke's preface is like a memo clipped to a book manuscript, describing the book's contents and explaining why it has been written. The book in this case is not only his Gospel but also the companion volume, the Acts of the Apostles. Acts has its own preface as well, also addressed to Theophilus (presumably a prominent Christian convert), describing its connection with the Gospel (Acts 1:1-3).

While introducing his book and giving his reasons for writing, Luke also tells us a fair amount about himself and the readers he is trying to reach. He admits that he is not one of the original eyewitnesses of the deeds and words of Jesus; he is a "second-generation" Christian like his readers. The classical Greek style of his preface indicates that he is an educated convert writing for others like himself scattered throughout the Roman Empire. The gospel story has already had wide circulation through traveling preachers and through the teaching of established Christian communities; it has even been circulated in written form by this time. Only one product from these "many" earlier gospel-writers, however, has come down to us in complete form—the Gospel of Mark, which Luke uses as a source.

Since the story of Jesus is already familiar to Luke's audience, what is to be gained in going over the same territory? Does this writer have a better interpretation, more information, new stories? Luke does not try to lure his readers with flashy promises; his whole emphasis is on establishing the reliability of the information they have already received. He has made his own painstaking investigation into the gospel and intends to set it out in an orderly fashion so that any doubts may be laid to rest. Skepticism had naturally arisen concerning the authenticity of a Jewish religion in a Greek world, and as the years went on, the far-flung Christian communities had tended to become disconnected from their Palestinian origins. Luke wants to help his non-Jewish brothers and sisters in the Lord to trace their roots back to the historical Jesus (Gospel) and to follow the growth of Christianity as the early church spread from Jerusalem to Asia Minor to Rome (Acts).

PART I: BEGINNINGS

Luke 1:5–2:52

Luke's account of the conception, birth, and infancy of Jesus is one of his finest creations. There was nothing in Mark's Gospel to guide him. Matthew has an infancy narrative, but there is every indication that Luke and Matthew had no knowledge of each other's work. Rather, they composed their accounts separately at a time when the church was reflecting back beyond Jesus' public ministry to his earthly beginnings.

The traditional preaching outline began with Jesus' baptism (as is evident in the sermons of Peter and Paul in Acts, and in the structure of Mark's Gospel). The infancy stories were added to the front of that outline to serve as a prologue to the main narrative. A prologue announces the themes to be pursued in the body of the work. Both Luke and Matthew proclaim the good news in advance in a kind of mini-gospel based on the birth and infancy of Jesus. If Luke's infancy narrative had been lost before his Gospel began to circulate, we wouldn't know it had existed, because there are no clear references back to these chapters in the later account of the public ministry. But the reverse is not true—there are many references forward to the later developments. What we know about the infant Jesus comes from the teaching of the adult Jesus and the early church's reflection on his life, death, and resurrection. Who is this child? He is Messiah and Lord (Acts 2:36). What does his coming mean? He will save his people from their sins (Luke 24:47). A reader's understanding of the prologue depends on his or her understanding of the rest of the book. It means much more when read a second or third time after the entire book has been read. The infancy narrative grows in meaning the more the life, death, and resurrection of Jesus resound in the faith of the reader.

Both Luke and Matthew stress the fulfillment of Old Testament promises in the story of Jesus' beginnings. Matthew does this by explicit "formula quotation" (Matt 1:22-23; 2:15, 17-18), but Luke prefers to indicate the fulfillment through hints and allusions. Luke also puts his stamp on the material by subtle structural organization, especially by paralleling the origins of John and Jesus. Both births are announced by the angel Gabriel and come as a resounding surprise to all, including their parents. They are circumcised on the eighth day according to Jewish law, but their names are assigned by the angel. A parent interprets each child's coming in a canticle. In comparing the two boys, however, Luke carefully demonstrates Jesus' superiority. Luke's craftsmanship is also noticeable in the construction of the annunciation scenes, which are based on a standard birth-announcement pattern from the Old Testament (Isaac: Gen 17; Samson: Judg 13):

1. An angel appears (or the Lord himself).
2. There is apprehension and fear.
3. The angel reassures the recipient, then announces the birth.
4. An objection is raised.
5. The angel gives a sign.

1:5-25 Announcement of John's birth. Luke begins his story of Jesus and the Christian church with the introduction of the parents of John the Baptist. We should notice the very Jewish beginning of this Gospel for the Greeks. Zechariah and Elizabeth come out of the heart of Judaism. They are both of a priestly tribe, blameless in their observance of the Mosaic law. Further, Luke subtly relates them to the ancient Hebrew parents Abraham and Sarah, who were also advanced in years and childless, but able to believe in a divine surprise (Gen 17:1-20).

The scene is set in the temple in Jerusalem, where the hopes of the people of God were always centered. Luke's Gospel will likewise end in the temple (24:53). The angel allays Zechariah's fear and announces the promise: "Your wife Elizabeth will bear you a son." He is described as an ascetic Nazirite (Num 6:1-21) and compared to Elijah the prophet. Zechariah's objection is answered with his loss of speech. Perhaps the harshness of this sign is due to the fact that he asked for proof and not simply for information, as Mary did (1:34).

By the time Zechariah returns home, there is an aura of expectancy among the people. Dramatic events of salvation are underway. The conception of John takes place as foretold, unknown to the world at large. At this point, it is still only an elderly Jewish couple who know that God has begun another important intervention, the most important of all, in the history of their people.

1:26-38 Announcement of Jesus' birth. If continuity with Hebrew history and hopes was stressed in the announcement of John's birth, the radical newness of God's saving action is the focus of the announcement of the birth of Jesus. The scene shifts from Judea, center of Jewish life and worship, to Galilee, a province scorned as a secondary outpost in Judaism. This location for the momentous proclamation is only a minor surprise compared with the announcement itself. This child will not only be "great in the sight of [the] Lord" like John (1:15); he will be called "Son of the Most High." John's birth was made possible by natural means through the healing of sterility; Jesus will be born of a virgin. John will be filled with the Holy Spirit while in the womb; Jesus is conceived by the power of the Spirit. John will be a prophet; Jesus will be the final and eternal King of Israel.

Mary is mystified by the angel's greeting. How is she the highly favored one, blessed among women? It is not because of something she has done, but because of God's choice of her for a special role in his salvation. She responds with the classic words: "I am the handmaid of the Lord." Mary is the model Christian disciple from the beginning. Her physical motherhood was a unique grace, but her motherhood on the spiritual plane is one shared by all who make the same faithful response she did (8:21). The larger implications of Mary's response to the angel were summarized succinctly at Vatican Council II: "At the message of the angel, the Virgin Mary received the word of God in her heart and in her body, and gave life to the world" *(Constitution on the Church,* 53).

1:39-56 Visit to Elizabeth. Zechariah had been promised that his son would be filled with the Holy Spirit (1:15). Once Jesus is conceived by the power of the Holy Spirit, the Spirit can become active in others. John receives the Spirit in the presence of Jesus; the Spirit fills Elizabeth, and later Zechariah and Simeon. This foreshadows the future glorification of Jesus, which will release the Spirit on all (Acts 2:33). Elizabeth's question, "And how does this happen to me, that the mother of my Lord should come to me?" recalls the words of King David when the ark of the covenant was being brought back to Jerusalem after having been captured by the Philistines: "How can the ark of the Lord come to me?" (2 Sam 6:9). The ark symbolized the presence of Yahweh, the God of Israel. Mary's visit to Elizabeth sanctifies her home with the presence of the Lord.

Mary's canticle, traditionally called the *Magnificat* because of its first word in Latin translation, is a mosaic of Old Testament quotations and allusions interpreting the coming of Jesus. The hymn is strongly influenced by the canticle sung by Hannah, the mother of Samuel the prophet, after the birth of her son through divine intervention (1 Sam 2:1-10). Both canticles see these actions of God as part of a longstanding process of overthrowing proud human expectations and exalting the lowly. Mary's word for it is "mercy."

1:57-80 The birth of John. John's father, mute till now, regains his power of speech as soon as the name designated by the angel is confirmed. The people are filled with fear—not terror, but awesome reverence in the face of God's wonderful deeds. They are not simply shocked but show their awareness of deeper meaning in the events.

Zechariah's canticle (the *Benedictus*), like that of Mary, weaves traditional Hebrew quotations and themes into a hymn of praise. His hymn is described as a "prophecy" under the inspiration of the Holy Spirit. Prophecy in this fundamental biblical sense does not mean primarily a foretelling of the future, as in modern parlance, but a divinely enlightened proclamation of the meaning of events. Zechariah sees in the birth of his son God's remembrance of his covenant promises to David (2 Sam 7:8-16) and the definitive salvation for all the people. In the first part of the canticle, the salvation hoped for sounds roughly like the overthrow of national enemies (a concept of Messiah that would plague Jesus during his ministry), but in later verses salvation is understood more profoundly as freedom from sin (see Acts 2:38).

Luke's way of ending this story of John's birth is a good indication of his technique in keeping the reader's attention on one episode at a time, even though several events are interlocked. Verse 80 has John growing up from infancy to manhood and taking his place in the desert even before Jesus' birth is described. He is stationed there for his next appearance in the story thirty years later (3:1-3).

2:1-7 The birth of Jesus. The scene shifts again, now from the lonely Judean wilderness and from small villages in the hills of Galilee and Judea to the vast arena of the Roman Empire. The mysterious events recounted in chapter 1, still hidden and local, will have significance for the whole world. Emperor Augustus orders that a census be taken. Joseph and Mary, law-abiding citizens, make the journey to Joseph's ancestral city.

The census under Quirinius has caused much debate. Quirinius did not become governor in Syria until A.D. 6; shortly afterward he conducted the census in Judea that provoked the rebellion of Judas the Galilean (Acts 5:37). If Jesus' birth is situated during the reign of Herod the Great (Luke 1:5), it cannot have taken place during this census several years later. Among the various solutions proposed, the most satisfactory views Luke as associating a number of loosely related historical events around the time of Jesus' birth in order to fix its context in the minds of his readers, without intending ironclad accuracy. The precise dating of these remote Judean events cannot have been too important to Greeks of the Empire seventy or eighty years later. But the realization that Palestine was part of the Syrian province at the time of Jesus' birth might bring those events closer to Luke's readers in Antioch, the center of the church's missionary thrust in his time.

Mary gives birth to her "first-born son." This does not mean, as the Fathers of the church commented from earliest times, that she had other children later. "First-born son" is a legal designation for the one who has special privileges and position under the Mosaic law (Deut 21:15-17). Christian faith understands Jesus to be the "first-born of many brothers" in a spiritual sense (Rom 8:29). The swaddling clothes and the manger illustrate the poverty and humility of Jesus' birth, but the wrappings are also a subtle reminder of his royalty. Hidden here is a parallel with the birth of King Solomon: "In swaddling clothes and with constant care I was nurtured. For no king has any different origin or birth" (Wis 7:4-5).

2:8-20 The shepherds hear the good news. The humble King's birth is proclaimed first to the lowly. The shepherds were generally poor and to some extent outcasts, considered by the "respectable" to be ignorant, dirty, and lawless. Like the hated tax collectors, these outcasts are ready for the gospel. The appearance of God's messenger lights up the sky (Deut 33:2); there is fear and reassurance as at the annunciation to Mary. It is through these lowly ones that the message of salvation comes to the whole people of Israel. The titles "Messiah" and "Lord" will be the theme of the early preaching (Acts 2:36); though mentioned here in the prologue, these titles cannot be fully understood until the resurrection and the outpouring of the Spirit.

The angels announce peace as a gift of God's favor. Augustus was revered for having established peace in the Empire in 29 B.C.E. after a century of civil strife. But the Pax Romana is an exterior calm enforced by military power. True peace will come through Jesus (John 14:27). The shepherds go "in haste" to Bethlehem, eager (as Mary was: Luke 1:39) to respond to the news of salvation. Their telling of the events provokes the astonishment that will later accompany the work of Jesus and the early gospel preachers (5:26; 8:56; Acts 8:13). Sometimes this surprise and wonder lead nowhere, but those who listen to the shepherds respond by glorifying and praising God, while Mary, the ideal recipient of God's word and the model (after Jesus) of Christian prayer (8:21; 11:27-28), reflects on God's words and deeds in her heart.

2:21-40 Jesus comes to the temple. Jesus' parents obeyed imperial law at the time of his birth; now they are portrayed as observant Jews, fulfilling the prescriptions of the religious law concerning circumcision and the presentation of the first-born to the Lord. The scene at the temple is slightly confused because Luke has entwined two separate ceremonies. The Book of Exodus required the presentation and redemption of the first-born son because the first-born sons "belong" to the Lord who saved them when the Egyptian first-born were destroyed at the Passover (Exod 13:15). Leviticus described the ceremony for the ritual purification of the mother forty days after giving birth (Lev 12:1-8). On this occasion she was to offer a lamb and a pigeon or a turtledove, but a poor couple was permitted to bring only two pigeons or doves.

The emphasis is less on the purification of Mary than on the presentation of Jesus in the temple, where he will receive a more official recognition as the promised Savior of Israel. The temple symbolizes for Luke the continuity between Judaism and Christianity. The first announcement of the definitive act of salvation takes place in the temple (1:11), Jesus teaches in the temple (19:47), and the disciples continue to worship in the temple well into the new age (24:53; Acts 3:1).

Simeon and Anna are faithful, humble Israelites waiting in the temple for the revelation of God's salvation. Just and pious (see 1:6), they are open to the Holy Spirit's inspiration. Simeon recognizes Jesus as the Anointed of the Lord and in his *Nunc Dimittis* (2:29-32) further prophesies that Jesus will be a "light for revelation to the Gentiles." In blessing the parents, he warns that this child will be a sign opposed and that Mary will be pierced with a sword. With these two utterances of Simeon, we are given a foreshadowing of the universal salvation that will be proclaimed in Jesus and of the necessity of suffering in the mission of this Messiah. The shadow of the cross falls across the Holy Family. The later followers of Jesus are not to be surprised that suffering is encountered in their pursuit of a gospel life. Even families and friendships will be broken up as "the thoughts of many hearts" are laid bare, because the peace Jesus brings will not be a counterfeit covering secret divisions (12:51-53).

2:41-52 Jesus in his Father's house. Verse 40 sounds like a conclusion setting the stage for Jesus' adult career. The story of Jesus' origins seems to be complete with the family's return to their hometown after his birth and the fulfillment of the law's prescriptions. But a unique story has been added. It serves to illustrate the wisdom and grace with which this boy is said to be endowed and makes even more evident his special mission and destiny. Like many childhood stories of famous people, this one is recalled because it shows glimmers in Jesus' boyhood of the qualities that will emerge in a superior way in his manhood.

Jesus and his parents journey to Jerusalem for the feast of Passover. The next time Luke portrays Jesus on his way to Jerusalem it will be for the Passover again; it will be his final trip to Jerusalem, and the Jewish feast will coincide with his own Passover. Jesus is also "lost" then for three days before he reappears as the victorious risen Lord.

At his presentation, Jesus was unable to speak for himself; others interpreted his identity and mission for him. Now he proclaims the meaning of his life. He states the priority of God's claim in his mission. His life has a meaning that transcends the relationships of his human family. Thus he confirms the sword prophecy of Simeon. The astonishment of Jesus' parents is difficult to reconcile with the revelations surrounding their child's birth. This is a sign that some of the infancy stories were originally passed along independently of one another. It also underlines the fact that the full understanding of Jesus' identity and mission awaits the resurrection.

PART II: THE MESSIAH IS PREPARED

Luke 3:1–4:13

3:1-6 John the forerunner. Luke took pains to describe the historical context of the birth of Jesus. He is even more thorough in setting the scene for the beginning of John's ministry. The majestic first sentence reflects the ancient tradition that began the gospel story with John's Jordan ministry (Mark 1:1-4; Acts 10:37). There is also a change in Greek style at this point. Luke has already shown his mastery of classical Greek (1:1-4) and given an example of Hebrew-flavored Greek in the infancy stories; now for the rest of the Gospel he writes in the Greek style of the Septuagint, the Old Testament translation familiar to his readers.

After the death of Herod the Great, his kingdom had been divided among his children as a tetrarchy (four provinces). By the time of the events recorded here, a Roman procurator had been placed in charge of Judea, because Herod's son Archelaus had made such a mess of his rule there. The Herod mentioned here is another son, Antipas, about whom Luke has information not found elsewhere (23:7-12; Acts 13:1). There was only one ruling high priest at any particular time; in this case it was Caiaphas, but Annas is mentioned because he retained the title and exercised important influence in retirement (see Acts 4:6).

The call of John is patterned on that of Old Testament prophets (see Jer 1:2). He is the last of the old dispensation, serving as a bridge to the new. He prepares the way of the Lord that led from Egypt to Israel and now, through Jesus, leads into the messianic kingdom. John's baptism was a ritual act expressing the willingness of individual Hebrews to join the movement of renewal. It counted on an interior disposition of repentance without which there could be no forgiveness.

Luke extends the Isaiah quotation further than Mark or Matthew (vv. 5-6) in order to incorporate the promise of universal salvation that is so important to him and his Gentile readers. The confirmation of this promise given here at the beginning of Luke's writing (see also 2:32) comes at the end of his two-part work in Paul's announcement that salvation has indeed come to the Gentiles (Acts 28:28).

3:7-20 John the prophet. Through a series of questions (as in Acts 2:37), this new prophet is given the opportunity to explain what repentance means. Words or titles are not enough. A child of Abraham must demonstrate his or her heritage in deeds. This is done especially in sharing with the poor and in social justice. John's message is consistent in this with the doctrine of his prophet-predecessors.

John is approached by two groups whose professions were considered questionable by the Pharisees: the tax collectors, who customarily made handsome profits by overcharging their compatriots; and the Jewish soldiers who belonged to the Roman peacekeeping force. John does not require that they give up their jobs, but that they perform them fairly and honestly.

John's activity gave rise to speculation about the Messiah. Expectation had been high for decades; several pseudo-prophets and pseudo-messiahs had already appeared (Acts 5:36-37), leaving disappointment but only adding to the expectancy. John gives an official answer to "all" in Israel: "One mightier than I is coming." In comparison with the Messiah, John considers himself lower than the lowest slave: only a non-Jewish slave could be required to loosen his master's sandal strap, and John will not even venture that.

John contrasts his baptism with that of Jesus. The point is not that one baptism is with water, the other in the Holy Spirit and fire (the early church also baptized in water from the beginning), but that John's baptism is *only* in water, that is, a ritual sign expressing outwardly what the person must express inwardly. The baptism of Jesus will be definitive: it will be an act of God bringing salvation (Holy Spirit) and judgment (fire). The image of fire is expanded by reference to the process of separating wheat from chaff. A "winnowing fan" or shovel tosses the mixture into the air; the heavier kernels of wheat fall to the floor, while the chaff blows away for later burning (Isa 21:10).

John the prophet challenges Herod to repentance for his marriage to Herodias, the wife of Philip. Luke does not repeat the details of Herod's marriage nor of his crime against John. Here he simply mentions the imprisonment. Later there will be a reference to the martyrdom of John, but obliquely after the fact (9:9). The vivid details had obviously had wide circulation by this time, thanks to Mark's account; Luke did not think it necessary to repeat the story.

3:21-38 Son of God, Son of Man. Jesus joins the pilgrimage to the Jordan to be baptized by John. In his case, however, the baptism is the occasion for his special anointing as the Messiah (Acts 10:38). Luke presents him as the last one to be baptized by John, the climax of John's baptismal ministry. Immediately after this, a new era begins. The heavens are opened, signaling a visitation of God with a new revelation for the people (Isa 63:19). The Holy Spirit comes on Jesus to reside with him "bodily" (Greek text). The voice from heaven identifies Jesus as the long-awaited Anointed One with the words of messianic Psalm 2: "You are my son" (v. 7) in combination with an allusion to Isa 42:1, where God's servant is described as "my chosen one with whom I am pleased." Jesus is announced as the expected messianic king, but his kingship will not be exercised in pomp and power; it will be a mission of humble self-sacrifice.

Luke waits till this point in his narrative to insert Jesus' family tree (unlike Matthew, who uses the genealogy to start his book). Perhaps he does this to emphasize the dramatic importance of the anointing by the Spirit at the Jordan as the inauguration of Jesus' public ministry.

There are many differences between the lists of Luke and Matthew. Some of the differences have received plausible explanation; others remain a source of debate. Matthew traces Jesus' ancestry beginning with Abraham; Luke takes it all the way back to Adam. These decisions fit well with the purposes of the evangelists: Matthew is interested in Jesus' Jewish credentials for the sake of his Hebrew Christian readers; Luke, writing for Gentiles, wants to show from the beginning that Jesus brings salvation for all the children of Adam. Mary is not mentioned, though the fact of her virginal motherhood is recalled (v. 23). Both genealogies trace the descent through Joseph, the legal father of Jesus. The vague reference in verse 23—"about thirty"—is one of the New Testament's rare clues to Jesus' age during his ministry (see John 2:20). Much of the kind of biographical detail that catches our eye, in fact, was irrelevant to the gospel preachers and writers, who were presenting the meaning of Jesus rather than a collection of facts about him.

4:1-13 Testing in the wilderness. Before he launches out into his preaching and healing ministry, Jesus is led by the Spirit to the wilderness of Judea for a forty-day period of preparation. The Palestinian desert is not the sandy waste of the Sahara. The parts around the Dead Sea are utterly barren, but most of the Palestinian desert is semi-arid, with some vegetation, particularly in the winter. It was a dangerous place, uncharted, inhabited by wild animals and bandits. The wilderness was believed to be the haunt of demons (Isa 13:21; 34:14); it is no surprise that Jesus met the devil there. But Jesus' forty days in the desert is meant to trigger an association with Israel's forty years of wandering in the desert after the Exodus. Stephen's speech in Acts describes these as years of testing and failure for the people of God (Acts 7:39-43). Jesus is also tested in the desert but remains faithful.

The account in Mark says only that Jesus was tested, but Matthew and Luke describe three temptations. These are typical of the temptations Jesus faced throughout his life and typical as well of the testing his followers will undergo. In the first and third temptations, the devil addresses Jesus as Son of God but tries to make him deviate from the path of filial obedience to the Father. Jesus is tempted to turn stones into bread, that is, to use his power for his own ends rather than to be the Messiah planned by his Father; and he is taunted to test the Father's word rather than go forward on his mission in faith. The second temptation is an attempt to make Jesus give to someone else the allegiance that belongs to God. The devil claims that the power and glory are at his disposal; he is a liar and not to be trusted, but many before and after Jesus have fallen for this temptation.

Jesus answers all three temptations with the scriptural word of God, quoting from the Book of Deuteronomy, which described Israel's apostasy in the desert (Deut 8:3; 6:13-16). The devil even tries to use Scripture himself (vv. 10-11), but Jesus is quick to turn aside the challenge to his Father's fidelity. Scripture is no more authoritative than any other word if it is wrongly interpreted. The second and third temptations are transposed in Luke and Matthew, though it is apparent they are both working from the same written source. It was probably Luke who changed the order of the scenes in order to place the climax of the series in Jerusalem, which he highlights as the focus and pivot of Jesus' saving work and the life of the early church (Luke 9:51; Acts 1:4). The story breaks off with the devil departing "for a time." The reader will be alerted to the devil's heightened activity at the beginning of the passion account (22:3).

PART III: THE MINISTRY IN GALILEE

Luke 4:14–9:50

Jesus returns to Galilee fresh from his victory over the devil. This section shows Jesus in the early days of his mission, preaching and healing in his native area before he makes the decisive turn toward Jerusalem (9:51) and his passion, death, and resurrection.

4:14-30 Acclaim and rejection. The account of Jesus' return to his hometown embodies the gospel story in miniature. Jesus is met initially with praise and acclaim, but this response sours through jealousy and suspicion until his own people are seeking his life. As an observant Jew, Jesus customarily worshiped in the synagogue. In the sabbath service there were two readings, one from the Pentateuch (the first five books of the Bible) and a second from the prophets. Jesus took this second lesson, probably by prearrangement, opening the scroll to Isaiah (61:1-2) and reading a promise of the restoration of Israel. The original context is the anointing of a prophet, but the figure of the promised Messiah, the kingly Anointed One, is also implied in Jesus' usage of the text. He is the spirit-bearer foretold by Isaiah (Isa 11:2), the Prophet and Messiah who will usher in a new age of freedom and divine favor.

There is an air of expectancy (as before the baptism in 3:15) as Jesus sits to interpret the reading (a synagogue teacher might either sit or stand). He announces that the day of fulfillment has come. The "today" he speaks of is the inaugural day of the "year acceptable to the Lord." That day continued to unfold until the goal of Jesus' glorification (ascension), when it became the eternal day of salvation. The listeners were impressed by his preaching, but just at this point a jarring note is heard: "Isn't this the son of Joseph?" In Mark's account of this Nazareth visit, the cloud of suspicion is described more thoroughly (Mark 6:2-3). Luke has modified Mark's chronology by moving this story earlier in the Galilean ministry. As a result, the mention of deeds done in Capernaum (actually deeds still to be done) is awkward.

Jesus compares himself to two great prophets of ancient Israel, noting that they served non-Israelites because their own people were not open to their ministries. The implication is that he, too, a prophet not accepted by his own people, will take his message to outsiders. This prospect threatens his listeners, arousing murderous thoughts. The same judgment on Israel will be made by Paul with similar results (Acts 22:21). The hostility does not overcome Jesus for the time being; he still has a mission to accomplish in fulfillment of God's plan. In the decisive act of rejection that results in his death, Jesus will seem to be destroyed but will emerge victorious (Luke 24:26).

4:31-44 A day at Capernaum. Jesus moves on to Capernaum, a city on the north shore of the Lake of Galilee, which becomes his headquarters during the period of the Galilean ministry. Following the Gospel of Mark, Luke presents a typical day in the life of Jesus, a sabbath in Capernaum. Jesus appears in the local synagogue as God's authoritative preacher and representative, bringing an official attack on the power of Satan. The unclean spirit recognizes the kind of challenge that has been issued: "Have you come to destroy us?" Jesus does not permit the demon to speak, probably to demonstrate his authority over the spirit world, but possibly also Luke has in mind here the "messianic secret," a theme developed by Mark (Mark 5:43). Jesus does not want his identity known before he is able to invest the title Messiah with its true meaning. Again the people are struck with awe at his words and deeds redolent of divine authority. But amazement does not necessarily lead to faith (Luke 4:22; 5:26).

From the synagogue Jesus goes to Simon's house for the main sabbath meal. Simon Peter is so well known in the Christian tradition by this time that Luke does not introduce him to the readers. Jesus finds Simon's mother-in-law with a fever, which he "rebukes" as he had the demon. Jesus has come to free the people from whatever binds them, whether demons or diseases or other handicaps that keep them in bondage. Verses 40-41 indicate that Jesus' merciful ministry to the demoniac and to Simon's mother-in-law were simply dramatic examples taken from his general practice. The evidence piles up until the demons no longer have to guess at Jesus' identity; he still requires their silence.

Jesus' reception at Capernaum is the opposite of that at Nazareth. The people try to keep him in their midst. But even this is a way of holding him bound, and Jesus escapes from these friends just as he had from his enemies. He is not tied down to one group or one place—he has been sent to all the people. In mentioning the "synagogues of *Judea,*" Luke is using Judea in the broader sense of all Palestine without specifying which part of the country, even though at this period Jesus' mission has been limited to Galilee in the north. He is implicitly offering salvation to the whole nation.

5:1-11 Jesus calls the fishermen. Jesus continues his ministry in the territory around the Lake, here called Gennesaret after the fertile plain on its northwest shore. Jesus' preaching is called "the word of God" for the first time. He will describe the word as a life-giving source for those who receive it in faith (8:21; 11:28); the ministry of this word will continue in the church (Acts 4:31; 6:2). The introduction of this term at the beginning of the episode signals that the calling of the fishermen and their response is an occasion of the effective proclamation of the word of God.

In Mark's version of the call of the first disciples (Mark 1:16-20), the scene is shared by two sets of brothers. Here the spotlight is on Simon, with his partners in the background (Andrew is not even mentioned by name). Jesus seems familiar with this group and they know him (see 4:38; John 1:35-42). While the fishermen are doing their morning cleaning of the nets and hanging them to dry, Jesus uses Simon's boat to distance himself from the crowd a little in order to preach. The water would have helped his voice carry. With verse 4, the crowd is suddenly gone, and the rest of the scene is interaction and dialogue between Jesus and Simon.

Simon is called to obedience based on faith. It was certainly not reason that provoked this fisherman to cast his nets back into the water at the instigation of this carpenter from the inland hills. Fishing was best at night; if nothing had been caught then, daytime fishing was useless. But Simon placed his trust in Jesus: "But at your command, I will lower the nets." The result is a marvelous catch of fish.

Now Simon is called Peter for the first time, "the Rock," the name he will later have as the leader of the church. His eyes are opened through his act of faith, and he falls before Jesus. Peter is the first person in the public ministry to call Jesus "Lord" (no longer only "Master": v. 5). Suddenly we realize that the story has been more than the initial calling of the fishermen disciples. From earliest times the church has seen herself as the "bark of Peter" in which faith in Jesus is tested (Mark 4:35-41; Matt 8:23-27). Jesus chooses Simon's boat, sending him into deep water and calling for a decision based solely on personal faith. The faith of Simon's response is what makes him the rock on which the church is built (Matt 16:18).

Simon Peter is aware of the distance between himself, a sinner, and the Lord. His natural reaction is to plead unworthiness. The divine holiness is too much for a human to bear (Exod 20:19). But Jesus has not come to drive sinners from his presence. He rather associates sinful people with himself in his ministry, if they will put their trust in him. They must leave *everything* (a Lukan stress: 5:28) and follow him. The three stories following this one show Jesus "catching men" (5:11), involving himself with the outcasts and sinners.

5:12-16 A leper comes to Jesus. Lepers were thoroughly ostracized at the time of Jesus. They were considered a menace to society. Jesus shows his ability to break through the social prohibitions to help these outcasts. "Leprosy" was a term used to cover any number of skin diseases, not only Hansen's disease. It was considered particularly difficult to cure; therefore, the man's request indicates the strength of his faith in Jesus. Whenever a skin disease of this sort seemed cured, the afflicted person reported to the priests, who were the examiners appointed to protect society's interests. This disease was also connected with ability to participate in public worship. Rules for examination and purification rituals ("what Moses prescribed") are given in the Book of Leviticus (chs. 13 and 14).

Jesus does not stand at a distance like one fearing contamination. He touches the afflicted man. The use of touch in healing was shown earlier to be characteristic of his healing ministry (4:40). Despite his instruction to keep his work secret, his reputation continues to spread. Crowds come, as people always must, to hear the word of God and to be healed. Jesus does not let his busy mission interfere with his communion with his Father. He takes time to get away from the crowds to pray. Perhaps his notoriety kept before him the temptation to personal goals (4:1-12), and he felt the need of prayer to keep his ministry in proper focus.

5:17-26 The healing of a paralyzed man. The question of the nature and source of Jesus' authority has arisen before (4:22, 32, 36). Here Jesus displays his authority before leaders of Judaism from all over the country. This is the first of four conflict stories leading up to the laying of a desperate plot (6:11). Some men (four, according to Mark 2:3) have heard about Jesus' healing power and want to bring their paralyzed friend to take advantage of the opportunity. The strength of their concern for their friend and of their faith in Jesus is evident from the lengths they are willing to go. They make the awkward ascent to the roof (probably by an outside stairs), carrying the man on his mat. The roofs of Palestinian houses were made of tiles or of mud and thatch. The man is lowered into the presence of Jesus, surely amid much complaining by the crowd. Both Mark and Luke mention that it was the faith of the man's friends that evoked Jesus' statement of forgiveness. The action of faith has been decisive in the two preceding stories. Here, for the only time in the Gospels, an adult is healed because of the faith of someone else—a strong testimony to the bonds that faith forms among Jesus' followers.

The paralyzed man and his bearers were probably surprised by Jesus' statement of forgiveness rather than physical healing. This also stuns the scribes and Pharisees, who complain, correctly, that forgiveness of sins is in the hands of God. Jesus has come with an offer of thoroughgoing salvation, not one that stops at the surface. He has performed the more difficult inner healing and now will cure the limbs of the man. But he uses the occasion to demonstrate his power to forgive sins as well as to heal bodily ailments, and to identify the source of his authority. He is the "Son of Man": this title has its primary reference in the Book of Daniel, where the Son of Man receives dominion and kingship. Jesus uses this title to describe his authority now and at the time of judgment (6:5; 9:26; 12:8). The reaction to this event is astonishment, but this time also praise of God, both by the healed man and by the onlookers.

5:27-32 A tax collector is called. Jesus' attitude toward sinners was glimpsed in the exchange with Simon Peter (vv. 8-11). Now, after the healing of a sinner, Jesus' attitude toward sinners is given more explicitly. Tax collectors were classed as sinners because of the dishonesty and injustice associated with their profession. Jesus does not talk to Levi privately but calls him in the midst of his business, and goes to a public banquet where a "large crowd" of tax collectors and other friends of Levi are present. The Pharisees emphasize the impropriety of sharing a meal with these people, who, besides being sinners, would have had contact with Gentiles and thus been ritually unclean. Jesus uses a proverb to explain his stance: he has come to help those in need and will go out to them. Those who will not recognize their own need are not ready for the doctor.

This story may have been recalled to give a norm for relations in the early church. The question of preaching to Gentiles and eating with them looms large in the Acts of the Apostles (10:28; 11:3). Jesus' example gave warrant for transcending the traditional boundaries of ministry. The story showed that even an unclean public sinner could respond to the preaching with the same total self-gift as the first disciples did (5:11, 28).

5:33-39 The old and the new. These verses deal with questions arising from Christian differences from Judaism, beginning with practices during Jesus' own lifetime. The Pharisees fasted on Monday and Thursday (see 18:12) as well as for the regular Jewish observances, and John the Baptist encouraged fasting as well. The challenge to Jesus here is more an introduction to the statement about the bridegroom than an emphasis on a Christian posture against fasting (and prayers). Jesus was apparently much freer on such questions (see 7:34) but did not undervalue fasting (Matt 6:16-18). Acts shows the early Christians regularly praying and fasting (Acts 2:42; 13:3; 14:23).

Jesus compares the present time of his ministry to a wedding, implying that this is a foretaste of the messianic banquet. Fasting as a sign of mourning is inappropriate. There is a veiled reference to the passion in the mention of the removal of the groom. The followers of Jesus did mourn at that time (24:17-38) before they became aware of the resurrection and Jesus' continuous presence in their midst (24:52). In Acts, fasting is part of praying for the Holy Spirit's guidance rather than an expression of mourning.

A different kind of answer to the question about fasting is given in the two sayings about the coats and the wineskins. The gospel life proclaimed by Jesus is something entirely new. It was born in the matrix of Judaism, but it must be allowed to develop on its own, adapting in ritual, in religious observances, in social practices, in doctrine, according to its own principles. If Christianity is fettered to Judaism, it will be ruined. The sayings have wider application in terms of any kind of clinging to past ways for their own sake.

6:1-11 Jesus and the sabbath. The final two conflict stories in this series deal with Jesus' attitude toward the sabbath. Judging from the number of such stories in the Gospels (see 13:10-17; 14:1-6), confrontations about the sabbath must have been frequent during his ministry. In the first incident, Jesus' disciples are doing what would have been allowable by the Mosaic law (Deut 23:26), but on the sabbath this could technically be described as a forbidden work of "harvesting" in the Pharisaic interpretation.

In Mark, the Pharisees question Jesus about his disciples, but Luke has them address the disciples directly so that Jesus can intervene on their behalf as their master and defender. He uses an incident from the Old Testament to defend their actions. When David was hiding from Saul with a band of followers, he went to a local shrine to ask for food. The only food available was the holy showbread, which no one but priests consumed. The priest in charge allowed the bread to be eaten, because the disciplinary restrictions of the law gave way before human need (1 Sam 21:2-7). In the application here, if David's authority to interpret the law is accepted, how much more ought one accept the authority of the Son of Man as "Lord of the sabbath."

Immediately Jesus demonstrates his lordship by an act of healing. The sequence is the same as in the healing of the paralyzed man (5:21-25). In the case of the man with the withered hand, the scribes and Pharisees are no longer just responding to problematic actions of his ministry, but are actively scrutinizing him to find difficulties. Jesus knows by now that it is useless to try to keep his acts of power secret. He does not avoid the confrontation with his enemies on this occasion, but provokes it in order to make another statement about the sabbath and to expose to the scribes and Pharisees their own false motives.

The Pharisaic interpretation of the law allowed medical intervention on the sabbath for birth, circumcision, and mortal illness. Jesus doesn't ask merely whether it is lawful to heal on the sabbath, but asks about the purpose of the sabbath: If the sabbath was given by God to his people for their good, shouldn't an observant Jew do good instead of evil on the sabbath? In posing the question this way, Jesus implies that in this case, not to do the good that can be done is an act of evil—letting a person suffer needlessly. His enemies cannot hear what he is saying; their minds are already made up.

6:12-16 The Twelve Apostles. Luke places the choice of the Twelve just before the "Great Discourse" so that it can take on the character of an official instruction for the whole church assembled under its leaders. The importance of Jesus' decision in selecting the Twelve is underscored by mention of his all-night vigil. He calls all the disciples together, choosing the core group from among them.

Three of these we have met before and will meet again (Peter, James, and John), one other will have a large role later (Judas Iscariot); but the rest are mentioned only here by Luke's Gospel (see also Acts 1:13). The fact that there are Twelve is itself important, because these Christian leaders are to rule over the renewed Israel in place of the patriarchs of old (Luke 22:29-30).

The Twelve are called "apostles," from the Greek word *apostello,* meaning "to send out." Andrew is now mentioned along with Simon Peter, his brother, then the Zebedee brothers. Philip and Thomas are known from John's Gospel (John 1:43-48; 20:24-29). Of Bartholomew and James son of Alphaeus we know nothing more from the New Testament. Matthew is called a "tax collector" in Matt 10:3. The second Simon is called the "Zealot," a title that aligns him with the Jewish nationalists plotting the expulsion of Rome. Judas son of James is mentioned also in John's Gospel (John 14:22), but otherwise only in Luke's writings (Acts 1:13), where he takes the place of Thaddaeus in the traditional list (Mark 3:18; Matt 10:3). Probably these are two names for the same person. The meaning of "Iscariot" is a matter of speculation; it may mean "man of Kerioth" (a village in Judea).

6:17-49 The sermon on the plain. At this point in his narrative, Luke incorporates part of the material Matthew had included in the Sermon on the Mount (Matt 5–7). But instead of staying on the mountain to deliver his discourse, Jesus comes down from the mountain like Moses descending to deliver the law to the people (Exod 34:15). As before, people crowd around him to hear the word of God and to be healed (5:1, 15).

6:20-26 The blessings and the woes. The differences between this passage and the eight beatitudes in Matthew are striking. The best explanation is that the two evangelists received a common core of material from the preaching tradition, some of which had already been adapted by various Christian communities, and further edited it for the needs of their own readers. Luke's beatitudes correspond to the first, fourth, second, and eighth in Matthew's list, but with significant variations.

The point has been made that Matthew's beatitudes suggest what Jesus' disciples ought to be, whereas Luke's describe what they actually are. This should not be carried too far. Luke's own readership included wealthy and middle-class citizens of the Empire. To be "poor" involves a state of dependence, which is what both sets of beatitudes are aiming for. The fourth Lukan beatitude holds the key. It is not good simply to be poor or hungry or persecuted, but one is fortunate to be dispossessed or mistreated for the sake of the Son of Man. The prophets of old were treated shamefully though they were God's spokesmen (Jer 15:15; Amos 7:10-12). More pertinently, so was Jesus (Luke 13:33).

The reason for the woes to the rich and well-fed is not given here but may be sought in other parts of the Gospel. The rich did not use their wealth to help the needy (16:19-31), hoarding it rather for themselves (12:21). They did not recognize the source of their gifts (21:3-4) or were trapped by them (18:24-25). Riches kept such persons from trusting God (12:22-34). They are compared to the false prophets who always found friends because of their falsely optimistic statements (Jer 5:31; Mic 2:11).

6:27-35 Love of enemies. The radical love of Jesus and his heavenly Father, the love that must be the mark of the Christian, is presented clearly and emphatically in these verses. The test of discipleship is the love of enemies, which makes sense by no earthly standard and must be based on faith. Three times the sequence "love, do good, give" is repeated (vv. 27-30, 32-34, 35) to bind the admonition into mnemonic phrases. If you love, do good and lend to your friends—that is merely good politics or good business. To be a child of the Most High more is required. Even the Golden Rule in the middle of these verses (v. 31) seems tinny against such a dazzling standard.

6:36-42 Relationships. It is in the call for compassion that Jesus calls God "Father" for the first time in his public ministry (see 2:49), though he has implied this relationship in verse 35. To be like the Father is to be compassionate, which means, as the subsequent sentences unfold, not to judge or condemn, but to forgive offenses and to give without counting the cost, as God himself has done. He will not be outdone in repaying the generosity.

Luke uses the saying about the blind leading the blind in a different context than Matthew does. There it is a stricture against the Pharisees; here it is a warning against false teachers in the Christian community. The true Christian teacher will always remain a disciple of the Master, not changing or "surpassing" his instruction. The famous image of the splinter and the beam drives home the point about judging others (v. 37). The passage says nothing about fraternal correction that is an action generated by love; the hypocrite, blinded by his own sin, is interested only in exposing another's weakness.

6:43-49 A tree and its fruit. Jesus uses two different fruit-tree images to make the point about the source of a person's actions: in verse 43, the fruit tells whether or not the tree is healthy; in verse 44, the fruit verifies the variety of tree. Those who call upon Jesus as Lord must demonstrate the reality and the quality of the relationship. They will be able to do this if they hear his words and put them into practice (8:15, 21).

Both Luke and Matthew end the discourse with the comparison of the two builders. The example has been adapted to different audiences. Matthew's story seems to reflect the Palestinian situation, where a house could easily be built on exposed rock without digging; Luke's good builder has to dig to reach rock (more likely in Asia Minor). Matthew's foolish builder builds on sand, which Luke does not mention; his vulnerable house is one that is built on top of the ground. Matthew's house is destroyed as much by wind as by water on the exposed Palestinian plain; Luke's house seems to be in a city, protected from wind but vulnerable to a flood that would wash away a house built on the surface.

7:1-10 The centurion and his servant. Stories like this one from Jesus' ministry were crucial during the debate of the early church concerning the mission to the Gentiles. The nationality of the centurion is not given, but he was not a Jew (v. 5). He would have been a member of Herod's peacekeeping force (see 3:14) rather than a member of the imperial army, which had no forces in Galilee at this date. In Luke, this incident foreshadows the various statements in Acts that God knows no partiality; rather, "The man of any nation who fears God and acts uprightly is acceptable to him" (Acts 10:34-35; see 15:9). If even the observant Jews of Jesus' own time brought a non-Jew to Jesus, and if Jesus went to him without quibble—the church's argument must have run—why shouldn't Jewish Christians accept Gentiles?

The centurion is introduced as a compassionate man seeking the compassion of Jesus. His Jewish friends argue in his favor that he has been generous to their people. In the light of what Jesus has just said about selfless generosity, this would not have been the compelling motive of his action. The centurion surprises him with his humility and his faith. Possibly the officer's thoughtfulness is implied here, too: he would have known that entering the house of a Gentile rendered a Jew ritually unfit for worship. But it is the centurion's faith, not the good works that captivated the man's Jewish friends, that Jesus wants to impress on his listeners. The healing is mentioned almost as an afterthought.

7:11-17 The widow and her son. Another demonstration of Jesus' compassion follows in the Galilean village of Naim. The comparison of Jesus to the prophetic figures of Israel's past underlies the narrative. His action of revivifying the son of a widow along with the expression "he gave him to his mother" alludes to the earlier act of power by Elijah (1 Kgs 17:23). When the people see what has happened, their reaction is to recognize a "great prophet." Jesus' compassion for the woman draws him to the scene. As in the previous story, there is a possibility of ritual uncleanness (by touching a corpse: Num 19:11). The response of the people is first fear, but ultimately the praise of God, as in the healing of the paralyzed man (Luke 5:26). Faith is not mentioned preliminary to the deed as in the healing of the centurion's servant; but the action elicits faith in the form of divine praise.

7:18-35 Jesus and John. John has been confined in prison (3:20), but his disciples have kept him abreast of Jesus' ministry. Now he sends two of them to ask Jesus point-blank whether he is "the one who is to come," using an expression for the expected Messiah originating in the prophecy of Malachi (Mal 3:1). There might also be an overtone of expectancy for the awaited prophet-like-Moses (Deut 18:15) with whom both John and Jesus are connected in popular estimation (John 1:21; 6:14). Why did John doubt that Jesus was the one expected? Probably in the stories of Jesus' compassion and in his message of love of enemies and forgiveness John did not see the exercise of eschatological judgment he had predicted for the one to come who is "mightier than I" (Luke 3:16-17). Luke's own faith is unmistakable in the statement that John "sent them to the *Lord* to ask . . . ."

The disciples arrive at a time when they can observe Jesus' healing ministry. Jesus responds to John's question by interpreting his action through texts from Isaiah that envision the days of messianic deliverance: the blind seeing, cripples walking (Isa 29:18-19; 35:5-6). The two disciples are told to relate to their teacher "what you have seen and heard." This will be the mission of the early church; the apostles will carry it out even at the risk of persecution and death (Acts 4:20). Jesus understands his work as the unraveling of the program he had proclaimed in his inaugural sermon at Nazareth, "glad tidings to the poor . . . a year acceptable to the Lord" (Luke 4:18-19). John is warned that even he may block God's plan if he is not ready to adapt himself to divine surprise. The statement of verse 23 is, of course, addressed not only to John but to people of any age: Jesus as he was and is has frequently been found a stumbling block; his true image has suffered many distortions.

This encounter is followed by Jesus' glowing description of John. He is not a reed wavering in the wind, but a staunch prophet of the Lord whose unyielding fidelity lands him in prison. He is even more than a prophet—he is the one selected to be the forerunner of the Messiah, the messenger who comes in the spirit of Elijah (Mal 3:23; Luke 1:17). No one born of woman is greater than he, but even the least born into the kingdom is greater. This is a paradoxical way of stating the importance of being in the kingdom, no matter what one's human credentials. There is no notion here that John was excluded from the kingdom (see 13:28).

Those who had benefited by John's ministry praise God when they hear Jesus' testimony about him. Luke sees in the Jewish leaders' refusal to receive John's baptism a sign that they are closed to God's plan for them. The evangelist contrasts this attitude with Jesus' commitment to fulfill God's designs (18:31). The "people of this generation" are not willing to open themselves to God's action in Jesus and will not cooperate any more than obstinate children do. They find excuses to reject John, and then opposite excuses to reject Jesus. God's plan (his "wisdom"), however, will prove its validity in the lives of those who embrace it.

7:36-50 The loving woman. Though Jesus is willing to dine with outcasts (5:29), he does not reject invitations from the well-to-do (11:37; 14:1). A "sinful woman" approaches him in Simon the Pharisee's house in the presence of the other invited guests. It is a moment of embarrassment for Simon and for the woman as well, whose courage is shown by her action; but shown more importantly is her faith in Jesus and her trust that he will receive her with compassion. The guests were reclining, so Jesus' feet were exposed behind him.

Simon judges that Jesus cannot be a prophet because he allows a sinner to touch him. Simon overlooks his own sinfulness and misunderstands Jesus' prophetic ministry. At an earlier meal with "sinners," Jesus had compared himself to a doctor (5:31). Jesus does know who the woman is, but Simon does not even "see" her until challenged by Jesus (v. 44). To open his eyes, Jesus tells the parable of the money-lender. Simon is forced to admit that the one forgiven the larger debt is more grateful. But he does so hesitantly, perhaps even sneeringly—"I suppose"—wary of being caught in a trap by the clever carpenter.

But with the admission the Pharisee is already caught. Jesus draws out the comparison of gratitudes point by point: you provided no water, she washed with her tears; you gave me no kiss, she kissed my feet; you did not anoint my head, she anointed my feet. The climax of Jesus' pronouncement and of the story comes in verse 47, which may be translated two different ways with vastly different meanings. The New American Bible's original version of the Greek is defensible—"her many sins are forgiven because of her great love"—but the revised translation of 1986 is more consistent with the parable in verses 41-42: "her many sins have been forgiven; hence, she has shown great love."

Jesus says that the woman has already been forgiven her sins; that is evident because of her love. She would not be able to show such love unless she had first accepted love (forgiveness, acceptance). The forgiveness has set her free to love. When Jesus says "Your sins are forgiven," he is confirming what is already true in her; in the different context of the healing of the paralyzed man, Jesus forgave the sins at the moment of declaration (5:20). It is not that her love has earned forgiveness. By faith she accepted Jesus' (God's) loving forgiveness that saved her (see 1:77) and is now able to love.

Jesus' pronouncement in verse 47 interprets the parable of the money-lender. The woman has received "five hundred days' wages" worth of forgiveness, or a great amount. We do not know about Simon, but the implication is that he has been forgiven a lesser amount and is less able to show gratitude and love. This does not mean that one has to be a great sinner to love greatly. We all need "five hundred days' wages worth" of forgiveness, but we may be blind to our sinfulness or too fearful or proud to ask that our debt be written off. And then we are chained to our guilt, which keeps us from the freedom of love.

8:1-3 Jesus' women companions. Jesus now undertakes a systematic preaching tour of the local towns and villages, accompanied by the Twelve and by several women and others who helped provide for their needs. These women had been healed by Jesus and were expressing their gratitude in this way. It would have been exceptional for a traveling preacher to associate women with himself, so this is another sign of Jesus' openness and concern for all and his ability to transcend prejudice and custom. Two of these women, Mary Magdalene and Joanna, will be named among the first witnesses of the resurrection (24:10); perhaps they and others of this group are implied among those waiting with the Twelve for the outpouring of the Spirit after the ascension (Acts 1:14).

8:4-21 Listening to the word of God. This section on response to the gospel message contains two parables with commentaries; it climaxes with a pronouncement of Jesus on the basis of the proper relationship of his disciples to him. The parable of the sower (or more properly, of the *sowing*) appears in all three Synoptics (Mark 4:3-8; Matt 13:4-8). The parable itself (vv.5-8) is open to more than one interpretation, but the commentary (vv. 11-15) describes what must have been the most common interpretation in the early church. The seed is the word of God, which will bear fruit in a receptive heart (fertile ground), but which may be ineffective in other soils for any number of reasons: the birds = the devil; no moisture = buckling under to persecution; thorns = cares, riches, and pleasures. In verses 13-15, the listener is compared to the seed rather than to the soil. Characteristic of Luke is the emphasis on perseverance (v. 15; see 21:19; Acts 11:23).

After telling the parable, Jesus calls for attention to the deeper meaning of his preaching (v. 8), something he must have done often to shake his hearers into listening more carefully (see 14:35). When the disciples ask him to explain the meaning of the parable privately, he assures them that the "mysteries" (hidden designs) of God's reign are revealed to them, and then utters the puzzling statement that parables are meant to keep others from understanding. Jesus obviously does not want his listeners, whoever they are, to be prevented from understanding (the reverse of the admonitions in verses 8 and 18 and of the parable of the lamp in verse 16). He uses the quotation from Isa 6:9 to describe the case that, in fact, some will see but not perceive, hear but not understand, because of hardness of heart. The phrasing is a form of Hebrew overstatement that translates awkwardly. It is even harsher in Mark's version (Mark 4:12), which both Luke and Matthew (Matt 13:13-15) have softened.

The parable of the lamp is applied here to the revelation of the "mysteries of the kingdom of God" mentioned in verse 10. God means for the proclamation of Jesus, now somewhat limited in its scope and even necessarily secret, to go out into the world. This will be the mission of the apostles (Acts 1:18). Jesus urges his listeners again to "take care how you hear," for those who are open to the word of God will become richer and richer in the life it engenders and nourishes (see v. 8), but those who do not listen will find that the spiritual life that seems to have germinated will wither away (see v. 6). The section concludes with the visit of Jesus' family, which gives him the opportunity to assert for his followers that the fundamental relationship to him is not through blood ties or other earthly connections but through hearing and acting on the word of God.

8:22-25 The storm on the lake. The identity of Jesus has been a recurring issue during the Galilean ministry (4:22, 34, 41; 7:16). Now for the third time the question is asked point-blank: "Who is this?" (v. 25; see 5:21; 7:49). Still once more will it arise (9:9) before Peter makes his profession of faith in Jesus as the Messiah (9:20). This time it is the disciples themselves who raise the question as they experience his power while they are alone with him on the lake. The early Christian community saw this story as a call to faith in Jesus who is present in the church during stormy times.

8:26-39 The Gerasene disciple. After exhibiting his power over the storm, Jesus demonstrates his authority over the demons in Gentile territory. Further, he works a dramatic transformation in a human life. The man is said to be "possessed" by demons. This English term is too strong. The Greek in verse 27 says he "had" demons, in verse 36 that he was "demonized" (see Mark 1:32), but the modern notion of possession, leading even to replacing the ego, is foreign to the New Testament. The unclean spirit turns out to be a regiment ("legion" was an imperial army term), which recognizes Jesus as did other demons.

The man's condition is dangerous to himself and to others, and has persisted over a long time. This is no ordinary exorcism. Its lasting effects could be doubted, which is probably why Jesus agrees to send the demons into the swine—for visible proof that the demons have left the man. They ask not to be sent to "the abyss." The word used could mean Sheol, the underworld of the dead (see Rom 10:7), but here it means the prison of evil spirits (2 Pet 2:4; Rev 9:1-11). Jews, for whom pork was unclean, would have thought it appropriate that the demons were sent into the swine.

The local people are terrified by what has taken place. Their fear does not lead to praise of God (5:26) but to the rejection of Jesus. Luke's favorable treatment of Gentiles does not blind him to the possibility of their failure. The loss of the swine impresses them more than the transformation of the man, who, when the people arrive, is sitting at Jesus' feet in the attitude of a disciple listening to his word (see 10:39). The man wants to follow Jesus (like the women who had been healed: 8:1-3), but his vocation is to share what has happened to him with his own people.

8:40-56 Jesus and the two daughters. The demonstration of Jesus' power over disease and death completes a cycle of four miracle stories. Luke links the raising of the girl with the earlier incident at Naim by adding to the account in Mark that she was an only daughter. Several touches in the synoptic narrative tradition link the stories of the little girl and the woman. Both are called daughter; the father and the woman fall at Jesus' feet; the girl's age and the duration of the woman's condition coincide; they are both affected "immediately" by contact with Jesus; and the centrality of faith is highlighted in both events. Luke adds that the girl is "saved" (v. 50: rather than "spared"), the same word used to describe the healing of the woman (v. 48).

The woman with the hemorrhage touches the tassel of Jesus' cloak and is healed in a way that is almost magical. To remove this overtone of superstition (which Luke himself detests: Acts 8:9-11; 19:19), the tradition emphasizes that Jesus' power has gone out in response to faith, and that the healing has been more than physical. The trust in Jesus that prompted her to come forward is like that of the woman known to be a sinner (7:37-38), and Jesus' final word to both of them is exactly the same: "Your faith has saved you; go in peace" (7:50; 8:48). Peter does not call Jesus "Lord" but "Master" in verse 45, as he did on an earlier occasion when he was uncertain about the extent of Jesus' power and knowledge (5:5).

Jesus' care for the woman seems to have delayed him just long enough to prevent his saving the girl's life. Jesus reassures Jairus, "Do not be afraid; just have faith." Fear had ruined his visit to the Gerasenes (8:37). Jesus takes his three closest disciples with him. Luke changes the traditional order of the names of James and John (see 5:10) to prepare for the teamwork of Peter and John in Acts (Acts 3:1, 11; 4:1; 8:14). The mourners at Jairus' house are not ready for the surprise Jesus brings (see 7:23); they laugh at him, remaining closed to God's action.

9:1-9 The apostolic mission. The ministry in Galilee is coming to an end. The material in the first part of this chapter shows Jesus preparing his closest disciples for accompanying him on the journey to Jerusalem and continuing his work later. He shares with them his own power and authority, gives them a vision of his glory, and makes it clear that his mission and theirs will involve humiliation and suffering. The Twelve are "sent" (*apostello*) with instructions to imitate the Master in taking nothing along. Christ's disciples must concentrate on the mission, not on their own needs, depending on the good will of the people to whom they bring the gospel. Thus there must be no special concern for accommodations, and certainly no idea of making a profit from the task. The Jews would shake pagan dirt from their sandals when leaving Gentile territory. Here the practice is a warning that people closed to the gospel proclamation are cutting themselves off from salvation (see Acts 13:51).

This expansion of Jesus' mission draws the attention of more people, including Herod Antipas, the tetrarch of Galilee, who will be curious (v. 9) and even alarmed about Jesus until his death (13:31-33; 23:6-12). We are informed of John's death through the allusions in verses 7 and 9. Jesus' preaching and mighty works remind people of prophetic figures of the past, especially Elijah. But his identity remains a matter of debate.

9:10-17 The feeding of the people. Jesus takes the apostles away for a time, probably to rest and to discuss their experiences. Luke specifies the place as Bethsaida, the hometown of some of the Twelve (John 1:44). When interrupted by the needs of the crowds, Jesus again preaches and heals. The implication may be that though the disciples have been given a share in his ministry, they cannot take Jesus' place; this will be even more evident in their inability to take care of the hungry crowd without his help. The feeding of the five thousand had a meaning for the early church in the responsibility of the leaders to feed the flock, particularly with preaching and the Eucharist. The wording of verse 16 draws our attention to the Last Supper and to the Eucharist, a source of superabundant nourishment to those who receive Jesus' word and his healing.

9:18-27 The Messiah of God. Jesus' absorption in prayer signals the approach of a decisive moment (see 3:21; 6:12). He is ready to confront his followers with the question that has been tantalizing audiences since the beginning of his ministry: "Who is this?" (8:25). They give the standard response about public opinion: John, Elijah, a prophet (vv. 7-8). When he asks for their own conclusion, Peter speaks up for the rest: "The Messiah of God." This answer is correct, as we know from the preview during Jesus' infancy, but it may be misunderstood (23:35), so Jesus imposes silence until he has a chance to instruct them in the true meaning of his Messiahship. Peter's leadership role is highlighted as he answers this crucial question in the name of the other disciples (see Acts 2:14).

Immediately Jesus gives the first of three predictions of his passion (see Luke 9:44; 18:31-33), using the title "Son of Man," which he preferred and which in this context seems interchangeable with "Messiah." There should be no mistaken identity: Jesus will not be the Messiah of popular expectation, capitalizing on national patriotism to remove the yoke of Rome and restore Davidic rule. He will suffer, be rejected by the leaders God's people, and be killed. Only then will he be vindicated. His followers must follow in his steps, taking up the cross (the Lukan version adds "daily"). To deny one's very self and to lose one's life does not mean an ego-suppression that would be psychologically harmful; it means giving up control over one's destiny and opening oneself to true self-knowledge by laying aside the image constructed from worldly illusions about the meaning of life. The stakes are high: one's response now will determine the outcome of the great judgment (v. 26). Jesus' remark that some of his companions will not die till they have seen the reign of God refers, in its Marcan setting, primarily to the experience of the transfiguration; Luke's usage expands this to the experience of the resurrection and the gift of the Holy Spirit (Acts 2:32-36).

9:28-36 The glory of God's Son. The transfiguration is a dazzling contrast to the message of suffering and humiliation. The two extremes need to be held together, as always in the gospel tradition, in order to accept Jesus as he is—Son of Man and Son of God. Several details recall the Sinai experience of God: Moses, the mountaintop, the cloud (Exod 24:9-18). Jesus is seen as God's Son in his heavenly glory. He is "changed in appearance" (v. 29), as he will be in his glorified resurrection body (Mark 16:12). Appearing with him are two key Old Testament figures, Moses the Lawgiver and Elijah the Prophet. They are a sign that Jesus will fulfill the expectations of the Hebrew people. In fact, they speak with him about his own *exodus*—his death, resurrection, and, in Luke's theology, especially his ascension—which he will "accomplish" in Jerusalem.

The three intimate disciples behave disappointingly. They fall asleep, as they will later at a crucial moment (22:45). Peter, confronted with divine glory, fails to call Jesus by the title "Lord," which adequately identifies him as the Savior, and babbles incoherently about building earthly tents for the heavenly beings. The revelation climaxes with the voice from the clouds as at Jesus' baptism. He is God's Son, his Chosen One (Ps 2:7; Isa 42:1). The admonition "listen to him" underscores the importance of what Jesus has been saying about his own mission and the nature of discipleship.

9:37-50 Jesus returns from the mountain. Jesus' mission is not an aloof solitude on the mountain but a ministry to the children of God. On his return, he immediately becomes involved with human need, a beloved and chosen Son (2:22; 9:35) serving another beloved son, an only child (a Lukan detail). The disciples had begun their mission with the power to overcome "all demons" (9:1), but they are unable to cast this spirit out. This experience, added to that of the loaves (9:13) and the transfiguration, puts their power in perspective as a participation in the messianic authority of Jesus. They still need his help; further, their ministry is not magical, but dependent on faith. Jesus shakes them out of their awe by repeating the prediction of his passion. They do not understand. Luke's phraseology stresses that their inability to penetrate this mystery was according to the divine plan. Full understanding must await the resurrection with the gift of the Spirit. But the disciples may have refrained from inquiring further because of uneasiness about the harsh conclusions for their own lives that had followed from the first prediction (9:23-24).

Elsewhere Jesus says that the disciples must become like little children (18:17; Matt 18:3-4). This point emerges from his saying here, but in an oblique way. He emphasizes the seeming unimportance or insignificance of the little child in a world with selfish interests. The child and others who are helpless and "least" in the world's eyes are the greatest in the kingdom. A true disciple recognizes Jesus in them. Whoever serves these least ones shares in their worldly insignificance and is great in the kingdom. The incident of the strange exorcist, originally independent of the foregoing, is added here as an example of the kind of openness to others just commented on. The disciple of Jesus does not sit in judgment (6:37) but waits for the fruit to emerge (6:43-44) and is ready to accept the action of God in unexpected people and places.

PART IV: THE JOURNEY TO JERUSALEM

Luke 9:51–19:44

Jesus now makes the decisive turn toward Jerusalem and the accomplishment of his *exodus* (v. 31). The theme of the final journey is already in Mark (Mark 10:1, 32), but Luke has developed it to show Jesus' commitment to the Father's plan (9:62; 13:33). He keeps the reader alert to the journey theme (13:22; 17:11) and lengthens this section by inserting a sizable addition to Mark's narrative (Luke 9:51–18:14), containing several stories and sayings he received from independent sources. Besides knitting the separate episodes together under the journey motif, Luke binds the section together thematically by inserting it between two children episodes in Mark (Mark 9:36-37; 10:13-16). The journey of Christian discipleship is characterized by the lowliness of a child, characterized by availability for God's action and dependence on God.

9:51-62 The beginning of the journey. Jesus' journey to Jerusalem is a march toward exaltation ("to be taken up") in fulfillment of God's plan. The earthly journey of Jesus serves also as the framework for the progress of the church in the time after the ascension. We find ourselves on the way toward Jerusalem with the Lord. But the march to glory, as Jesus has already warned, is a path through suffering. The disciples must expect to be treated no better than the Master. The cost of Christian discipleship is clearly stated as the journey gets underway.

The hostility of the Samaritans is not the personal hatred Jesus will meet in Jerusalem. It is evidence of the national or racial prejudice between Samaritans and Jews. Jesus' disciples cannot expect to be free from this treatment, but the answer is not retaliation. James and John must learn to avoid useless clashes and to look for new places to spread the kingdom.

Illusions are dispelled for would-be disciples. The person who offered himself with absolute availability (v. 57) is told the cost: you will be less secure than the foxes and the birds. Another responds to Jesus' call with the request that he be allowed to take care of one of the most sacred duties under the law, the burial of a parent. The urgency of the gospel supersedes this claim. Jesus' saying means that those who do not respond to the gospel call will be spiritually dead; they will have time to bury the physically dead. Elijah gave permission to his disciple Elisha to bid good-bye to his family (1 Kgs 19:19-21), but the call of the reign of God is more urgent than that.

10:1-20 The mission of the seventy-two. Only Luke among the evangelists tells of this second mission of disciples. He probably means it to have special significance for the missionary activity of the church after the departure of Jesus. According to rabbinic teaching, there were seventy-two nations in the world (based on the reading of Gen 10 in the Greek Septuagint). The disciples are to go "ahead of him," therefore not announcing themselves or their own message, but preparing the way for Jesus. This is the continuing charge of Christian preachers. The missionaries are sent in twos in order to give a witness that can be considered formal testimony about Jesus and the reign of God (see Matt 18:16). Jesus urges prayer for more harvest workers. The Lord of the harvest is concerned about its progress, of course, but he has made his own response to the need somehow dependent on the active concern of those sent into the mission.

Again, there is no room for illusion. The disciples will be lambs among wolves, defenseless, completely dependent on the Lord of the harvest for whatever is needed. Several of the admonitions to these disciples repeat the instructions to the Twelve (9:1-5). The admonition to greet no one is another emphasis on the urgency of the gospel task. The peace they offer seems like a tangible gift or even a living reality with a mind of its own. This notion of peace rests on the biblical concept of the word of God as being not only a message but somehow an embodiment of God's own personality and power (Isa 55:10-11; Jer 20:8-9). The peace-wish of the Christian missionary is more than an expression of good will—it is the offer of a gift from God of which they are privileged to be the ministers and heralds (see 1:2; Acts 6:4). Those who bring spiritual gifts can expect their physical needs to be taken care of by the beneficiaries (v. 7; see Gal 6:6).

Because the proclamation of the gospel is the word of God, it is not to be treated as a merely human message—"take it or leave it." There are harsh consequences for closing ears and hearts to the news of God's reign. Jesus makes drastic comparisons for the obstinate cities of Galilee where he centered much of his ministry. Chorazin and Bethsaida will be no better off than Sodom. And proud Capernaum, Jesus' "headquarters" in Galilee, has learned nothing from the Jewish heritage that was preparing for the coming of the Messiah. Tyre and Sidon, Gentile cities, would have been able to read the signs that Capernaum overlooked. The conclusion of the instruction is a reminder of the deeper dimension of the mission: the disciples are bringing Jesus and the Father to their listeners.

On their return, the seventy-two are amazed at the power that has been given them through the name of Jesus. They have driven out demons, furthering Jesus' attack on Satan's dominion in this world. Jesus envisions Satan falling from the sky through their ministry, another way of saying that the eschatological or final battle between good and evil is taking place now; the victory is being won in Jesus' name (John 12:31; Rom 16:20). But the disciples must not lose their perspective. The prize is not human glory through feats of power but heavenly glory through following Jesus to Jerusalem, to Calvary. The divine registry is a theme in Jewish literature (Exod 32:32; Dan 12:1).

10:21-24 Jesus the revealer. This passage gives a rare glimpse into the personal prayer of Jesus. In Luke's arrangement (differing from Matthew's by the insertion of the return of the missionaries: see Matt 11:20-27), the prayer is an exuberant outcry provoked by the disciples' happy report on the success of their mission. Jesus speaks intimately to God as "Father," praising him for letting these "little ones" understand what is really going on in the world: not an endless round of superficial activity, but a decisive battle between good and evil. The humble disciple is able to see and hear what prophets and kings looked forward to, a truth which, because of its simplicity, is often hidden from the worldly great and worldly wise. The revelation of the meaning of existence is under God's full control; it cannot be bought, nor can it be deduced by human cleverness.

Jesus is the revealer of the Father. The phraseology here is very similar to that of John's Gospel (John 1:18; 6:46). The Son mediates knowledge of the Father as he wishes: he can share with others his special relationship to the Father. Very shortly Jesus will give the disciples a share in his intimate prayer (11:1-4).

10:25-37 The Good Samaritan. This story and the following one together give a complete picture of Christian discipleship in terms of love of neighbor (active service) and love of Jesus (prayer). They combine to illustrate the way to everlasting life given in the lawyer's answer (v. 27). When he responds with the statement about love of God and love of neighbor, the lawyer is quoting from the ancient Hebrew prayer, the *Shema* (Deut 6:4-5), linking it to a saying from Lev 19:18. This combination was evidently original with Jesus (Mark 12:29-31) and known to the lawyer, who used it when Jesus turned the question back to him. To "justify himself" (because Jesus has made the lawyer's question seem easy), he raises the disputed question about the identity of the neighbor. In the Leviticus text, the neighbor is one's fellow Israelite.

As a parable, the story of the Good Samaritan is intended to challenge a wrong but accepted pattern of thought so that values of the kingdom can break into a sealed system. This it does by showing a Samaritan, a member of the people despised and ridiculed by Jews, performing a loving service avoided by Jewish religious leaders. This would have been shocking and, for many Jews, unbelievable and unacceptable. The impact in Luke's Gospel is heightened in view of the Samaritan inhospitality of 9:52-53.

This story, once accepted, also gives a vivid example of the fulfillment of the love commandment. The lawyer's question implies that someone is not my neighbor. Jesus' story replies that there is no one who is not my neighbor. "Neighbor" is not a matter of blood bonds or nationality or religious communion; it is determined by the attitude a person has toward others. The priest and the Levite were well-versed in the demands of God's law and, like the lawyer, would surely have been able to interpret it for others. But they missed its deepest purpose, while the Samaritan, by practicing love, showed that he understood the law.

10:38-42 Martha and Mary. To judge from the story of the Samaritan, Martha should have been praised for her practical service to Jesus. Her action, in fact, is neither praised nor condemned, but she is challenged to consider her priorities. The whole gospel is not contained in loving service to others, no matter how important that is. Christian discipleship is first and foremost personal adherence to Jesus. There must be time to listen to his "word" (v. 39: singular in Greek); devotion to Jesus is the "one thing required." This relationship shows itself in loving service, but without prayer, care for others' needs may not be love.

The Good Samaritan parable and the story of Martha and Mary, then, serve to illustrate the double commandment (10:27) in reverse order: the action of the Samaritan emphasizes love of neighbor; the action of Mary emphasizes love of God.

11:1-13 Jesus teaches his disciples to pray. The disciples realize that the right relationship to the Father (and to Jesus) is sought in prayer. Jesus, like John the Baptist, must have a distinctive insight into prayer flowing from his mission. In response to the disciples' question, he reveals the Lord's Prayer. Here the setting is a time of prayer; in Matthew's Gospel, the Lord's Prayer is part of the Sermon on the Mount (Matt 6:9-13).

Comparison of the two forms of the Lord's Prayer reveals that the structure and content are basically the same, reflecting the original instruction of Jesus. They were shaped by different community traditions at a very early stage. Matthew's text, an adaptation for liturgical use, has been used in worship down to our day; the briefer text of Luke, though less familiar, is probably closer to the original phrasing of Jesus. Both begin with Jesus' distinctive address for God, "Father" (Hebrew: *Abba*), and pray first for the glorification of God's name on earth and the full establishment of his kingdom. Then they turn to the disciples' needs: God's continual protection day by day and his sustaining support in the face of the "final test" at the end of time. In slightly different wording, both formulas relate God's forgiveness of us to our forgiveness of others.

The story of the midnight visitor and the sayings following it are a strong admonition to perseverance in prayer. God always responds to our prayer in ways that are best for us, though not perhaps in ways that we would expect or like. The extravagant examples of the sleeping friend and the father who would give snakes and scorpions to his children drive home the absurdity of thinking of the heavenly Father as harsh or cruel. God wants the best for us—which ultimately is the Holy Spirit, the gift of the age to come (see Acts 2:17). "Ask. . . seek . . . knock" are three different descriptions of petitionary prayer; but "seek" also implies the search for the kingdom of God and union with the Father.

11:14-28 Jesus and Beelzebul. The words and deeds of Jesus often provoke amazement in the witnesses, with varying reactions: praise of God (5:26), questions (4:36), wonder (9:43). The crowd viewing the casting out of the mute demon is closed to the meaning of the event. Some put the worst possible interpretation on Jesus' act of power, others demand even further signs before they will believe. This is the kind of hardness of heart that even ten plagues would not penetrate (Exod 7–11).

"Beelzebul" was a popular name for the master of demons. Jesus points out the absurdity of the accusation. If he is working for Beelzebul, Beelzebul is destroying his own kingdom. Other Jewish exorcists fall under the same suspicion. No, Jesus' routing of the demons is a sign that a stronger power is manifesting itself, a power that can only be from God and a sign of the inbreaking of the kingdom. Jesus compares himself to a victorious warrior carrying away the very arms Satan has been relying on. He warns his critics that there is no middle ground: if you do not side with Jesus, you are in the army of Satan. The point is pressed with the example of the wandering unclean spirit. If the place vacated by the demon is not incorporated into God's reign, it still virtually belongs to the kingdom of Beelzebul; and false security will make it even more susceptible to Satan's domination.

A woman in the crowd cries out in admiration for Jesus' deed and his wisdom in answering the critics. Her comment takes the form of praise of the mother who had brought him into the world, with the implication that this achievement and the physical relationship with such a son must make her completely happy. Jesus responds that true happiness consists in hearing the word of God and keeping it. Earlier he had said that physical motherhood is subordinate to this spiritual relationship open to all (8:21; see 6:47-48), not excluding Mary, of course, but intimating where her real excellence lies (see 2:19, 51).

11:29-36 The sign of Jonah. Jesus takes up the remarks of those asking him for a further sign of his spiritual authority (v. 16). He himself is sign enough for the present generation. He compares himself to Jonah, at whose coming the Ninevites reformed their lives (Jonah 3:5). Jesus, too, has a message of salvation, if the people will only heed it. The queen of Sheba had come to investigate the rumors of Solomon's wisdom and wealth (1 Kgs 10:1-13). At the judgment, all these Gentiles, like the inhabitants of Tyre and Sidon (Luke 10:13-14), will be recognized as more open to God's will than these chosen people of his.

The saying about the lamp, used earlier in the context of listening to the word of God (8:16), is repeated here in a similar context. Jesus and the gospel proclaimed by him are the light (lamp) God offers to his people. To refuse this light (for example, by seeking signs) is to prefer darkness in one's life. The lamp of the gospel is always burning, but it is not necessarily burning for you (v. 36). A secondary application of the lamp image is to one's eyes, understood as the window that can be fogged or shaded and thus keep the light from entering the person.

11:37-54 Woes to the Pharisees and the lawyers. The host is surprised that Jesus does not perform the ritual ablutions, though this custom was only a Pharisaic practice not required by the law. His puzzlement provokes a reply that was more than he bargained for, not an answer to the specific question of ritual washing but a full-scale condemnation of a general religious attitude associated with the Pharisees. The speech is preserved in a considerably different order in Matt 23.

Jesus accuses the Pharisees of emphasizing externals in religion while overlooking in their own conduct the breach of essentials. He mentions the absurdity of religiously cleaning the outside of a cup while one's own inside is full of evil. The antidote to greed, he says, is to give away one's money in alms. Luke records several sayings of Jesus about the need to be poor (6:20; 14:33; 12:21), but he also shows that riches are not condemned as long as they serve the needs of others and do not make one a slave (12:15; 19:8; 16:13). The tithes that the Pharisees were paying should have led in this direction, but instead had become a decoy covering the neglect of justice and charity (v. 42; see 17:12). Their blindness had made them a danger to those they were supposed to lead.

This speech offends one of the lawyers at table. These lawyers or experts in the teaching of Moses are otherwise called "scribes" (v. 53), but Luke has adopted here a term that would be more understandable to his Greek readers (see 10:25). The scribes did not necessarily belong to any particular Jewish group, but most of them were in fact Pharisees. Jesus accuses them of using the law as a rod to punish the people instead of interpreting it for them as a gift from God. They have taken away the "key of knowledge," the means for true understanding of God and salvation, and by misusing the law have been themselves misled.

The criticism of the scribes and Pharisees leads to a condemnation of the practices of their ancestors, an especially stinging rebuke. Stephen would be stoned for accusing Israel of murdering its prophets (Acts 7:52-54). Jesus calls the present generation to account for the blood of God's messengers, from Abel, the son of Adam and Eve (Gen 4), to Zechariah, the son of Jehoida, the chief priest during the reign of King Joash of Judah (837–800 B.C.E.), who was killed in the temple when he tried to call the nation back to true worship (2 Chr 24:17-22). As a result of this outburst, the animosity of the Jewish leaders is no longer subtle. They manifest their hostility and set traps for Jesus.

12:1-12 Fearless discipleship. The size of the swelling crowd is in contrast to the attitude of the religious leaders. Jesus continues to use the way to Jerusalem as a school for his disciples. Note, he says, the hypocrisy of the Pharisees. They think that their surface respectability will keep what is underneath from being discovered. A saying used earlier about the revelation of God's word is now used to teach that all personal secrets will be revealed on the day of judgment. The point is enforced with the images of exposure to daylight and an announcement from the rooftops.

All this leads to an admonition to the disciples (called "friends" here for the only time in the Synoptic Gospels; see John 15:13-15) to be open and aboveboard in their adherence to Jesus and his gospel. They should not let human fear keep them from openly living their faith. Humans can only kill the body. The only one to fear (in the sense of realistic reverence because of his authority over our destiny) is God, who decides life and death, reward and punishment. But this fear is not the cowering of a slave before a cruel master; God is Father. He cares even for the dime-a-dozen sparrows. Therefore one of his own children should know nothing of enslaving fear. "You are worth more than many sparrows." This could not have been said with a straight face. Jesus dispels fear with a smile in the midst of harsh language (see v. 24).

In the Acts of the Apostles, the fearlessness of gospel proclamation is a sign of the presence of the Holy Spirit (Acts 4:29-31). Jesus will treat his disciples as they have treated him. Their fidelity or their inconstancy will not remain hidden. The saying in verse 10 promises, though, that there is always the possibility of repentance for denying the Son of Man. "Blaspheming against the Holy Spirit" means the denial of God's desire or ability to save. This attitude, as long as it exists, makes forgiveness impossible.

12:13-21 The poor rich man. Jesus is interrupted in his instruction of the disciples by a man who wants help in acquiring his rightful share of the family inheritance. Besides being rude, the interruption betrays an insensitivity to what Jesus has just said about matters of essential importance. Rabbis were often asked to arbitrate in family disputes. Jesus certainly has the authority to do this (even more as the Son of Man), but he sees behind the question the very greed he warned the Pharisees about (11:39-42). He uses the opportunity to tell a parable about the trap of possessions.

The rich man would be the envy of most people—so wealthy that he does not have room to store his goods. But he is a fool because in the midst of his good fortune he has lost the sense of what is really important. He imagines that he can control his life. Possessions create this kind of illusion. The rich man is really poor in the sight of God. He does not even think about the possibility of sharing what he has with others. The implications of this story will be carried further in the tale of another rich man (16:19-31).

12:22-34 The care of a loving Father. The discussion of possessions leads to one of Jesus' most radical statements about the life of faith. What he says here about the conduct of life goes directly against the normal human approach: striving to get life under control by arranging for all immediate needs and wants and by covering all contingencies. Jesus says that worry about such things is a sign of lack of faith (v. 28) and a misunderstanding of our God. What is condemned here is not foresight and industry but an anxious approach to life that subconsciously denies that God is a loving Father who has everything carefully under his control.

In the desert, Jesus had won his own battle with this temptation by declaring that there is more to life than food (4:4). And no matter how protective and solicitous one is for health and safety, the length of life is completely under God's control. God takes care of the birds. He adorns the flowers and gives sunshine and moisture to the grass, which will soon perish. You are meant to live in his kingdom forever: will he not take care of you? Freedom from frantic anxiety is a sign of faith. The primary concern is the establishment of God's kingdom (Lord's Prayer: 11:2), not one's own. It is absurd to let life be consumed in the building of a vanishing kingdom when the Father wants to give you his own eternal kingdom.

Finally Jesus comes back to the admonition to give alms (11:41). Parting with what one depends on is the best way to learn the freedom of the kingdom. The attitude toward earthly goods is not an indifferent or innocent question; it is the barometer of what is really important in a person's life.

12:35-48 Waiting for the Master's return. The mention of the kingdom, the thief, and the treasure prompts Luke to add here some sayings of Jesus about the coming of the Son of Man at the end of the world (*parousia*) and the judgment. Central to the test of faith is the challenge of constant readiness for the Master's return. In several ways Jesus emphasizes that the time of the return will be a surprise (17:20; Mark 13:33). Comparisons are made to the return of a master from a wedding, when the coming is certain but the timing is not, and to the coming of a thief, when not even the coming is certain. These sayings have been adapted to the situation of the early church as it experienced the delay of the coming, especially the instructions about the leaders of the community (vv. 41-48). But authentic sayings from Jesus are at the root of the discourse; for example, no disciple would have originated the comparison of the Son of Man to a thief (vv. 39-40).

The fastening of the belt recalls the preparations for the Exodus (Exod 12:11). The Hebrew people were to be ready to move immediately when the call of the Lord came. The disciples of Jesus are to be ready to open to the Master "immediately when he comes." The answer to Peter's question (v. 41) directs the discourse toward the Christian leaders especially. The care of what has been entrusted foreshadows the parable of the sums of money (19:11-27). The sayings on the distribution of responsibilities or gifts in the concluding verse of the section are clearly pertinent for those in authority, but they have a wider application for all on whom spiritual and temporal gifts have been bestowed.

12:49-59 The urgency of the kingdom. Jesus has given his disciples a glimpse of the culmination of his mission in the return of the Son of Man at the time of judgment. He is already engaged in the task of lighting a fire on the earth. Judgment is taking place as people decide for or against him. Fire is a symbol for the Holy Spirit as well (Acts 2:3-4); the fire of the Holy Spirit will be cast on the earth through the fulfillment of the events for which Jesus is heading toward Jerusalem. Jesus means by his "baptism" the plunge into this saving mission, a prospect that produces mixed emotions because of the suffering connected with it (see Mark 10:38-39). Some of his teaching on forgiveness and peace may have given the impression that he was spreading a soft gospel; John the Baptist seems to have worried about that (7:18-23). Jesus assures his listeners that Christian discipleship is costly, even causing division in the family (see Mic 7:6). The Gospels give us glimpses of differences of opinion about Jesus among his own kin (Mark 3:21; John 7:5).

The gospel challenge is clear. Anyone who can see the clouds or feel the wind can certainly see the signs of the times. It is hypocrisy to blind oneself to the evident signs of the coming of the kingdom. In trying to fool others, a hypocrite fools himself. There is still time for decision, warns Jesus, but do not put it off. When judgment comes, you will wish you had settled out of court.

13:1-9 Reform while there is time. Jesus continues his call for decision and reform by referring to contemporary disasters and telling a parable. Pilate was notorious for his harsh rule and his insensitivity to Jewish religious feelings. The first of these otherwise unknown incidents refers to the killing of some Galileans while they were offering sacrifice (probably in the Jerusalem temple at Passover). The second example involves what was probably a construction accident at the Siloam reservoir at Jerusalem. Popular wisdom associated disaster with punishment for sin (Job 4:7-9; John 9:2). Jesus says that in the present age good fortune and disaster are no indication of a person's spiritual state (see Matt 5:45). But in the judgment to come, those who have been evil will certainly experience disaster. Now is the time to produce evidence of a life dedicated to the kingdom (see 6:43-44). The time may even be extended for us as for the fig tree. But ultimately the judgment will come.

13:10-17 Healing and hypocrisy. Two sabbath incidents have already been presented (6:1-11). This sabbath cure is inserted here as an example of the hypocritical blindness Jesus has been describing (12:54-57). The synagogue official cannot see what is happening right before his eyes—the inbreaking of the kingdom in the freeing of this crippled woman from eighteen years of suffering. He has become too hobbled by the letter of the law to recognize its spirit. The Pharisees allowed animals to be taken care of on the sabbath (see 14:5); why begrudge this woman an extraordinary gift of God? The official's reaction is predictable: rather than confront the miracle-worker, he vents his ire on the people. The action produces division; the judgment is already taking place.

13:18-21 Two parables of the reign of God. These two parables stress the great results that can grow out of tiny beginnings. The small mustard seed becomes a shrub that may reach nine feet in height. A small lump of yeast helps the dough expand to several times its original size. Jesus uses these daily examples to give insight into the kingdom. The reign of God cannot be thoroughly described or explained in human language, but the world is full of signs of this reign. Parables give us flashes of understanding. From these two parables we learn primarily that we must expect the beginnings of the kingdom in the smallest happenings and (in the world's eyes) the most insignificant people. A crippled woman, for example, is a sign of the reign of God in the preceding narrative.

Though a parable usually has one principal focus, often an insight into the meaning of existence that upsets comfortable prejudices, it can be used for further applications. The early church saw a further meaning in the large mustard shrub and the birds as the gospel preaching spread and Gentiles found a home in the Christian community (v. 29). And the idea of yeast would lead naturally to the comparison with Christian influence in the world.

13:22-30 The narrow door. This section contains several references to the seriousness of the proclamation of God's reign and to the need for a sober decision to undertake the journey to Jerusalem with Jesus, a journey that will end in suffering and death (9:22-23). Luke reminds us that Jesus is still on the journey to Jerusalem according to God's plan. The question along the way offers him the opportunity to mention once again the difficulties involved in following him. He does not answer the question whether few will be saved, but he does say that many will not be. There is specific mention of the sad case of those who had been under the illusion that they were following Jesus but had maintained only a loose relationship with him. They ate and drank with him, indeed, but with no intimate fellowship; they heard his teaching but did not accept it as the word of God to be put into practice (8:21). Jesus' harsh words to "you evildoers" are meant as a challenge to the readers of Luke's Gospel to redirect their steps toward Jerusalem with Jesus while there is still time.

The patriarchs and prophets of Israel are waiting to share the banquet of the kingdom with those who are now on the way. Many of those who ate and drank with Jesus will not be there, but there will be others who never knew him while he was ministering in Israel. The gospel will be offered to the Gentiles; they will come into the kingdom from all over the world. Luke's Gentile audience would listen eagerly to these words, but they would also be challenged not to take for granted themselves their eating and drinking with Jesus at the Eucharist. The pronouncement closing this speech guards against both presumption and despair; as long as the journey is underway, some may fall away and others may still join.

13:31-35 The way of the prophet. The attitude of the Pharisees who bring the warning about Herod is not described, but their intervention is probably meant to be understood as hostility rather than helpfulness (see 11:53-54). Herod could have expressed a desire to get the troublemaker out of Galilee. Jesus' reference to "that fox" may be a way of recognizing the cunning in the threat that urges him on to the place where prophets traditionally met their fate. Twice Jesus describes his mission in terms of three days, surely meant here by Luke as a foreshadowing of the resurrection: ". . . on the third day I accomplish my purpose." The theme of the divinely appointed task is very strong. No matter what human rulers may want, Jesus has to follow the established pattern. Implied too is a warning that God will permit no interference in this plan, though kings will be permitted to cooperate in the execution of it (Acts 4:27). The confrontation between the prophets and their enemies often took place at Jerusalem or even in the temple (11:51; see Jer 26:20-24). Though historically the murders did not take place in Jerusalem exclusively (1 Kgs 18:4), Jerusalem stands for the heart of the land and its people, and symbolizes the stubbornness that counteracted the prophets (Acts 7:51-52).

Reminded of this tragic hostility of Jerusalem to the messengers of God, Jesus laments over the city, seeing himself as the last in the line of the prophets to meet destruction there. He foretells the abandonment of the "house," which should probably be interpreted as the whole city. Jesus will not be seen in Jerusalem before the allotted time. He still has to make the stages of the journey as it unfolds according to plan. But eventually he will come in the midst of cries of praise (19:38), which will only deepen the irony of his rejection.

14:1-6 Another sabbath cure. For the third time Luke presents a scene with Jesus in the house of a Pharisee (7:36; 11:37). The man with dropsy, a disease in which the body swells up with excess fluid, was presumably one of the guests. The possibility of a friend's cure might have provoked the host and his guests at least to discuss the propriety of this healing on the sabbath, but all are silent. Jesus then heals the man. He tries to open the minds of his hearers by showing the absurdity of denying healing on the basis of a law of the sabbath, the day given as a gift by God to refresh his people; the argument is similar to the one used in the synagogue (13:15).

14:7-14 Worldly honor and praise. Jesus addresses a parable to the guests and gives advice to his host. In both speeches he appeals to what would seem to be base motives. Guests are urged not to seek the first places at table, not because this sort of self-promotion and pride is wrong, but in order that they may later be honored. Honored guests, of course, were notorious for the ploy of coming late precisely to be noticed by the assembly as they went to their prominent seats. The point could be interpreted as a suggestion not to seek worldly honor openly but to employ false humility as a subterfuge. Dickens's Uriah Heep comes to mind. Jesus is using the worldly image, though, only because it is so familiar. His point is made in the pronouncement: "Everyone who exalts himself shall be humbled and he who humbles himself shall be exalted." Self-exaltation must not be sought either openly or secretly. Earlier Jesus had reprimanded his disciples for vying for rank (9:46-48).

A similar unworthy motive appears superficially in Jesus' words to the host. The impression is that an invitation to dinner is given for the sake of some reciprocal reward, whether only a return invitation or, in the case of serving the poor, the prize of resurrection with all the just. The point, though, is that in doing good we should serve freely, without regard for our own prospects, leaving the recompense to God. This is the way Jesus went about doing good, emptying himself for others without counting the cost. There is Semitic exaggeration in the statement that one should not invite friends, relatives, and neighbors. The kingdom is for everyone, and our hospitality is to embrace all, especially those who are overlooked by people with only selfish motives.

14:15-24 The great banquet. The mention of the resurrection prompts one of those at table to repeat a favorite maxim or beatitude: Happy are those who share the great banquet in the kingdom of God. This would not ordinarily evoke a response, but Jesus discerns a complacent attitude among the Pharisees and the lawyers toward their share in salvation. They feel protected by observing religious rules, even allowing observances to shut out new possibilities of good (vv. 1-6). He tells a parable about those who take a banquet invitation too lightly and because of their casual attitude lose their own right to a share at the table and are replaced by others. The original meaning concerned observant Jews complacent in their religion who might be surpassed by those they considered outcasts; the early church made the obvious comparison with Israel's rejection and the Gentiles' acceptance of the gospel.

The host in this story has typically invited his friends and relatives first (see v. 12), before turning to the poor and handicapped. It was customary in the social circles of the time to send a personal summons at the time of the dinner, even though an invitation had been sent earlier. It was also typical of Semites to refuse the summons politely so that the host's messengers could urge the invitation more strongly. This is the sense of "make them come in" in verse 23. By the time the summons comes, these invitees have had a change of plans. Perhaps the excuses were legitimate. A man could be released from military service to care for a new house or vineyard, or if recently betrothed or married (Deut 20:5-7; 24:5). But the guests have been too inconsiderate or careless to inform the host of their change of plans. They have not taken his hospitality seriously, and this makes him furious.

An invitation to the salvation banquet is not something to be taken lightly. Jesus implies that some at table with him do not appreciate the urgency of the situation. The host sent his servant out "quickly" to fill up the places. God's desire to fill his house is urgent; he wants as many as possible to partake of the messianic banquet. The final statement (v. 24) is directed to the gathering in the Pharisee's house ("you" is plural): If you take the happiness of sharing God's table in the kingdom too much for granted (v. 15), you may miss the urgent opportunities to respond to his summons by doing the good that he presents.

14:25-35 The cost of discipleship. Jesus moves on toward Jerusalem. The story of the carelessness of those invited to the banquet has been linked by the evangelist to other sayings spelling out the seriousness of discipleship. The call to follow Christ cannot be taken up half-heartedly (v. 35); such an attitude is a tragic miscalculation. These verses reestablish the tone set at the beginning of the journey toward Jerusalem (9:57-62).

Jesus returns to the theme of family division that might come because of the gospel (see 12:51-53). Jesus says his disciples must *hate* father and mother and family. This is another Semitic exaggeration to stress that anyone who stands in the way of thorough commitment to Jesus, even one's closest relations, must be renounced. "Hate" in this sense means "prefer less." This is the radical message of the cross (see 9:23).

Discipleship is thus an all-consuming vocation. It must be accepted with mature deliberation. Jesus uses two examples: a wise builder would not begin a project without assessing his ability to complete it; only a madman would go into a battle without considering the odds. The punch line for the Christian disciple is that renunciation is the salt of discipleship. When a follower of Jesus begins to hold anything back, discipleship becomes a charade. The salt parable has various applications. In Matthew's Gospel it is connected with the light image and used in terms of good example (Matt 5:13); in Mark, salt is the source of peace in the community (Mark 9:50).

15:1-10 Lost and found. This chapter is bound together by the theme of joy over the recovery of what was lost. All three parables apply to the return of the repentant sinner; the story of the prodigal son develops the theme of God's love and adds the contrast of the older brother's hostility. Jesus is surrounded by "tax collectors and sinners," causing murmuring among the scribes and Pharisees (see 7:39).

Jesus addresses his listeners directly: "What man among you . . . ?" What he suggests all will do in going after the one lost sheep is actually *not* what many of us would do, but the attractiveness of this extravagant individual concern makes the listener want to agree. In a split second we are drawn into God's world, seeing and acting as he would. The shepherd's joy is like God's joy; his dedication to the individual sheep, carrying it back to the flock, is a reflection of God's love. Francis Thompson's *Hound of Heaven* might be a commentary on this parable. The joy in heaven is over the change of heart (*metanoia:* see 3:3; 5:32) of the sinner. "No need of repentance" is ironic and tragic (see 5:32; 7:47).

A different image is used in a second parable to the same effect. The woman has lost one of her ten *drachmas,* Greek silver coins. She turns her house upside down in search of this one coin in ten. Perhaps it was part of her dowry and thus had added sentimental value. Her joy is like the joy in heaven over one repentant sinner. It needs to be shared. It is too great for one person. She and the shepherd invite their friends and neighbors for the thanksgiving party. What about the other nine silver pieces and the ninety-nine sheep—are they not important, too? Surely, but the joy of the kingdom breaks out of the ordinary categories of reason and good business. What was given up as lost has been found. It is like a new life, a resurrection, and must be celebrated.

15:11-32 The prodigal son. This story is probably the most famous of Jesus' parables. Besides being a classic of spiritual insight, it is a literary jewel. Through this story Jesus illustrates the earth-shattering acceptance available in the kingdom of God. The traditional title is too well entrenched to be changed, but it is a misnomer. The story is about a father and two sons, and its pivot is the father's prodigality in love to both of his sons rather than the younger son's wastefulness of worldly goods.

Under Jewish law, the first-born son received a double share of the inheritance (Deut 21:17). The younger son in this case was entitled to a third of the estate. The division of property ordinarily awaited the death of the father, and there were provisions in traditional law for penalties when the share was withdrawn ahead of time. This is not important here. By demanding his share and leaving, the younger son is cutting his ties with his family, with no regrets. He takes everything with him; there is no reasonable hope that he will be back. His departure with a substantial share of the family estate also means a loss to his father and brother, adding to the latter's animosity.

Imagination can fill in the familiar story line that is compressed with great economy: the extravagant spending, the attraction of freeloading friends, the crash. For the Hebrew, caring for pigs evoked the idea of apostasy and the loss of everything that once identified the younger son as a member of his family and of God's people. He is even lower than the swine—they have access to the husks, but he does not.

Calamity finally brings him to his senses. He will return to his home as a hired servant. He carefully rehearses his speech, expecting to be treated with cold reserve and suspicion. But his father still loves him. He has been keeping vigil and sees his son coming "a long way off." Anything but coolly reserved, he runs to meet his son, hugging and kissing him. The son cannot get through his rehearsed speech. This reunion is almost identical to Esau's meeting with Jacob (Gen 33:4). Jacob remembers his crime against his brother and fears for his life. But Esau, like the father in this story, is interested only in reconciliation. The father cannot act quickly enough. He arranges for the finest robe, a ring and shoes, all of which classify the young man as a son of the household rather than a servant. There is no thought of recrimination, no policy of making the young man prove himself worthy. The only important thing is that he is alive. The son himself is more important than anything he has done.

The story would be complete as it stands with the return of the prodigal son and the father's open-armed acceptance. But another story interlocks with this one. The elder son's anger and self-righteousness make him resentful; not even the return of his brother will make him share the family celebration. Again the pivot is the father's love. He goes out to the elder son as he went out to the younger. He wants both of them to be happy. The elder son cannot see beyond propriety and is trapped in his own righteousness. The father does not deny the faithfulness of his elder son. He implies that all that is beside the point at this special moment. Something far more important is going on: a son and brother has returned from the dead. Everything else fades before that fact: "We had to celebrate and rejoice!" The Jacob story comes to mind again. At a later stage he has discovered, like Esau, the importance of reunion. When he discovers that his son Joseph is alive, he forgets recriminations and simply rejoices: "It is enough. My son Joseph is still alive!" (Gen 45:28).

A parable is not an allegory (in other words, there does not have to be an application for each part of the story), but besides experiencing the heavenly joy and the thorough acceptance of the younger son, we can see the father as God and put ourselves into the story. Am I like the father? Or like the elder or younger son? Do I have parts of all three in me? A parable this rich blossoms out with new meaning for each reader, and at each reading.

16:1-13 The right use of money. Jesus returns to the theme of use of wealth (see 12:13-34). The chapter begins and ends with parables. The story of the wily steward has been a problem for interpreters. Does Jesus encourage dishonesty? As verse 8 shows, he is rather contrasting the clever industry of the this-worldly with the lethargy of children of the kingdom. Whether the steward is moral or immoral in his actions is not the point of the comparison.

The steward has been careless in managing his employer's estate. Faced with expulsion, he knows that he will get no recommendation for a similar job. He is not physically capable of day labor, and begging would be too humiliating. While there is time, he uses his position to make friends for the bleak future. He reduces the debt of each of his master's debtors (only the first two instances are described), hoping they will remember. It appears that the steward has played fast and loose with his master's property. The charge against him was not dishonesty, however, but wastefulness and mismanagement; and in his preparations for the future he may not have been dishonest either. Stewards were often paid from the interest charged on loans. In the present case, the amounts he deducted from the individual debts may have been the (exorbitant) interest originally coming to him. Usury was against the law (Exod 22:24). By erasing this extra charge, the steward might have been seen as reforming his life and performing an act of justice!

Jesus' teaching, however, is an appeal for the "children of light" to be as enterprising in their pursuit of the kingdom as this steward was in trying to make a place for himself in this world. He follows this with a corollary on the use of worldly wealth in preparing for eternity. The crafty steward used his money to prepare an earthly dwelling, but earthly wealth, though it may be associated with evil (it is called literally "mammon of wickedness" in v. 9), can be put to good use for God's kingdom. It can be given as alms to the poor and lowly so that their benefactor may share with them a place in the kingdom (see 11:41; 12:21). This admonition looks ahead to the story at the end of the chapter.

A conclusion about stewardship is drawn for the followers of Jesus. As in this world, so in the kingdom: trustworthiness in small things leads to a greater trust. This refers to spiritual realities but is also concerned with physical stewardship (v. 13). The community of Jesus will have to deal with problems of spiritual and material stewardship (12:41-47; Matt 18:1-18). There is always the danger of subordinating the spiritual to the material without realizing that a new master has taken over.

16:14-18 The law, the prophets, and the kingdom. Jesus' statement that a person cannot serve both God and money triggers dispute and derision from Pharisees in the audience. They are described as "loving money" and obviously felt that they could combine worship of God and pursuit of riches. Jesus accused them of trying to prove their justice in the eyes of men, perhaps by almsgiving (see 21:1-4). They hold Jesus in contempt because his teaching on this matter is too rigorous and "unrealistic"; Jesus counters that their scale of values is contemptible to God.

The following three verses seem to break the flow of the chapter. They are sayings on the law collected from various places in Luke's sources (Mark 10:11-12; Matt 11:12-13; 5:18-32; 19:9). Why did the evangelist insert these sayings here before returning to the topic of wealth? The connection is to be found in the challenge to Jesus' whole moral teaching implied in the sneering reaction of the Pharisees. The law of Moses is the norm; Jesus has no business introducing his own law. Jesus replies that the law and the prophets have indeed been the norm, and even now that he is proclaiming the kingdom of God their validity does not cease. But the teaching of the kingdom brings into the open implications of the traditional teaching that were unrecognized.

John the Baptist is the turning point. He is the last of the Old Testament prophets, but, as the herald of Jesus, he belongs also to the preachers of the gospel. He is the bridge between old and new. From his time on, "everyone who enters does so with violence." The kingdom of God is open to every kind of person (3:10-14; 13:29), many of whom will still have to take aggressive action to find their way in. Luke will illustrate this later with the story of Cornelius, the first Gentile convert (Acts 10).

The way into the kingdom is open for the Pharisees, too, but it will not be the escape from observance implied by their derision. The law has abiding validity, but Jesus has the authority to interpret it correctly. His statement on divorce is an example of his interpretation (the most original form of the saying is found here and in Mark 10:11). In case the Pharisees think that Jesus' teaching waters down the law, they should note that his teaching on this point is stricter than that preached by their rabbis. They permitted a husband to divorce his wife on the basis of Deut 24:1. Jesus says divorce and remarriage is adultery.

16:19-31 The rich man and Lazarus. Jesus' teaching on the proper use of wealth is now illustrated by the story of two reversals of fortune. The rich man was oblivious to the needs of the beggar at his gate. He did not realize the seriousness of the present opportunity in preparing for the eternal future (vv. 8-9). It was not his wealth that kept him from Abraham's bosom, but his untrustworthy stewardship. The lives of the two men were quite different, and so were their deaths. Lazarus is carried away by angels, but the rich man is simply buried; it is the end for him, but the beginning for Lazarus.

The rich man is in the "netherworld," or Sheol, or Hades (as the Greek has it). It is a place hopelessly separated from the place of happiness with Abraham, though not synonymous with our "hell." The rich man can see Lazarus there (which probably increases his own torment). The rich man still thinks of Lazarus as his errand boy, first asking that he bring a drop of water to cool his tongue, then that he go to warn his brothers. Lazarus is probably surprised that the rich man knows his name. Abraham explains to the rich man why things have turned out this way. Though the man addresses Abraham as his father, he is Abraham's son only by blood relationship, not by the true spiritual relationship that effects salvation.

That the rich man wants Lazarus to go to his father's house is the first sign we have that he is concerned about others. But it is too late, and the action would be useless and inappropriate. They have Moses and the prophets. The word of God proclaimed through centuries in Israel should be enough. This statement harks back to Jesus' words about the law and the prophets in the center of the chapter (vv. 16-17). Jesus is still speaking to the Pharisees and still warning them that lip service to the law and superficial correctness in observance do not really mean listening to the word of God. Abraham closes with a statement that was probably embellished by the church in its transmission of the parable. Even resurrection will not convince those who are not disposed to listen attentively to the law and the prophets. This sentence adds an ironic twist and broadens the intended audience to all who read the story.

17:1-10 Four sayings on discipleship. As he makes his way to Jerusalem, Jesus continues to teach his disciples by sayings, stories, and his own example. It is inevitable, he says, that there will be stumbling blocks to faith and to the living of Christian discipleship because of Satan's interference and because of human misuse of freedom. The one who blocks another's way has a heavy responsibility to answer for. With the graphic image of the millstone, Jesus says it would be better to die than to become the source of another's failure.

Then, looking at the other side of the relationship (vv. 3-4), Jesus describes the proper attitude of the disciple who has been offended or "scandalized." It is an act of love to correct the brother who is a stumbling block for others. There is a false tolerance that permits a fellow disciple to continue down the wayward path. Jesus encourages correction and forgiveness. "Seven times" (v. 4) is a symbolic way of saying "every time."

The apostles ask for an increase of faith.

Jesus casts doubt on their possession of any faith. Maybe they are too self-assured because they are accompanying him to Jerusalem. He describes the power that comes through faith, using an exaggerated image for a memorable effect. The example of the treatment of a servant probably goes with Jesus' demurral about the apostles' faith. Servants of the Lord must beware of thinking that they deserve or can earn a special reward because of their service. Jesus may be alluding also to an attitude among Jewish religious leaders that correct observance deserves God's reward (see 18:9-12). The listeners would easily understand the example of master and servant relations. If good work is expected of the servant as an ordinary part of his duties, why should the disciple of Jesus think faithful service is not a basic requirement of following the master?

17:11-19 The grateful leper. The condition of lepers in the time of Jesus has been described (see 5:12-16). The group that meets him is composed of both Jews (Galileans) and Samaritans. The companionship of these usually bitter enemies indicates the desperation of their condition, which led them to depend on one another. Because they were required to avoid contact with non-lepers (Lev 13:45-46) but had to depend on their charity for survival, lepers haunted the outskirts of towns. This group shouted at Jesus from the proper distance; they had heard about his compassion and his healing power. Jesus simply gives a command, as Elisha did to the leper Naaman (2 Kgs 5:10-12), which could also be a test of their faith and obedience. They are to show themselves to the priests, whose responsibility it was to judge whether a leper was permitted to return to society (Lev 14:2). They obey his instruction, going to report their healing while they are as yet unhealed.

Only one of the group returns to express gratitude. He attributes the healing to God, openly singing his praises. The ingratitude of the others is a jarring note, but possibly the fact that the one grateful returnee was a Samaritan was more shocking at the time (vv. 16, 18). Jesus' final words to him are the message he gave to the woman in the Pharisee's house (7:50) and the woman cured of the hemorrhage (8:48). The faith of all the lepers led to their physical healing; perhaps it was more than this for the others as well, but for the Samaritan at least, this healing brought "salvation," thorough wholeness and a proper relationship to God.

17:20-37 The coming of the reign of God. When Jesus sent the seventy-two disciples on their preaching mission at the beginning of his journey toward Jerusalem, he told them to proclaim the nearness of the reign of God (10:11). Earlier he had sent the Twelve to announce his reign (9:2). As he proceeds toward Jerusalem, the question arises, when will the reign of God come? Jesus answers first that the reign is already present (vv. 20-21) and then speaks of the definitive establishment of the kingdom at the end of the world (vv. 22-37).

The establishment of God's reign was expected with the coming of the Messiah (see 3:15). This would be the day of the Lord, a time of judgment and reward (Joel 2:1-2; 3:4-5). Jesus tells the Pharisees that knowledge of the time of the day of the Lord is not important. What is crucial is to recognize the presence of God's reign already in their midst. Jesus' ministry is the clear sign that God's reign has begun. No matter how clearly Jesus stated that the end cannot be calculated (v. 20; Mark 13:32-33) and that its timing is not a question to be concerned with (Acts 1:6-8), the question continued to arise as he went toward Jerusalem (19:11) and afterward in the church. Today it is still a major concern for many Christians, and the concern is still misplaced. Jesus' teaching on the question could not be clearer. Don't waste your time looking for signs and listening to clever calculations. Be aware that the reign of God is already in your midst; unless you give his present reign your full attention now, you will not be ready for the return of the Son of Man when it does occur. And no one can know when that will happen.

After calling attention to the present reality of God's reign, Jesus turns to his disciples to explain what is still to come. The presence of God's reign does not mean that the trials are over; there is still much suffering in store for Jesus (v. 25) and for his followers (v. 22). The disciples will be desperate for the coming of the Son of Man, and this will lead them to follow false prophets and misleading theories about his appearance. But when it happens, the appearance of the Son of Man will not be subtle or mysterious. Everyone will know. It will be as vivid as lightning across the sky. The contrast of the Son of Man's glory with the suffering that must precede will make his coming even more evident.

No matter when it happens, people will be unprepared. Worldly pursuits will captivate them, as they captivated those who lived in the days of Noah before the flood and the inhabitants of Sodom right up to the day of its destruction. That is why Jesus emphasizes the importance of recognizing the presence now of God's reign. It must govern our lives now, not just at the end; otherwise we will not be prepared to leave when the sudden call comes. One who is concerned about his possessions (14:33) will try to save them and be lost himself. Lot's wife is remembered as a person who was too attached to refrain from looking back (Gen 19:17, 26; see Luke 9:62).

The examples of the two men and the two women illustrate the suddenness of the coming of Christ and the readiness or unreadiness he will find. This has nothing to do with the "Rapture," a modern perversion of the scriptural teaching, which interprets these and the corresponding texts elsewhere (see Matt 24:37-41) as a description of the separation of good and evil people before the final coming. Verse 36 is omitted in most versions because it is a scribal insertion taken from Matt 24:40, adding the example of two men in the field to Luke's text. The proverb about the carcass and the vultures corresponds to the image of the lightning (v. 24). Jesus closes the instruction with a final stress on the dominant theme: the coming of the day of the Son of Man will be unmistakable. Meanwhile, do not devote your time and energy to signs and calculations but to living in readiness.

18:1-8 The corrupt judge and the widow. This parable on persistence in prayer shares many similarities with the parable of the man waking his neighbor at midnight (11:5-8). The context here is comfort and encouragement for the disciples as they await the coming of the Son of Man. Keep praying, don't lose heart.

The judge is completely unscrupulous, guided by neither divine nor human law. The widow is asking only for her rights; by Jewish law she was one of the special helpless ones who should be given priority (Deut 24:17-22). The judge's refusal to act may have been due to laziness, fear of her adversary, or her lack of importance in his eyes. He is finally moved to do her justice by fear of the consequences to himself if she persists in her request. Jesus contrasts the judge's insensitivity with God's care for his elect. If the unjust judge will act after persistent requests, will not God? But delay of an answer to prayer, and especially here the delay of the coming of the Son of Man, may cause followers of Jesus to give up. When the Master does come, some will have lost faith.

18:9-14 The Pharisee and the tax collector. Jesus was constantly combating the self-righteousness that he found such a sinister enemy of spiritual progress (5:32; 15:7). This parable is addressed directly to the self-righteous. The Pharisee and the tax collector are stereotypes of the good and the sinful person. The Pharisee prays with straightforward gratitude for his healthy spiritual state. There is no sign that he is trying to deceive. Pharisees did fast severely twice a week, on Mondays and Thursdays, for the good of the whole nation. And there is no reason to doubt that he tithed. The tragedy is that he does not understand the flawed nature of this prayer. He is deceiving himself. He does not look upon himself as God's servant but as one who deserves good of God for a job well done. Besides this pride, he is guilty of contempt for the tax collector.

The tax collector is conscious of his sinfulness. He knows that he does not deserve consideration because of anything he has done. The prayer he utters is one of the sources of the ancient Jesus Prayer: "Lord Jesus Christ, Son of God, have mercy on me, a sinner." It is this helplessness and dependence that opens one to God's grace; it is the spirit of the child. Earlier Jesus commended one who would say, after doing good work that was a duty, "We are unprofitable servants" (17:10). The debate over faith and works is already engaged here (see Rom 3:27–4:5). Jesus himself draws the shocking conclusion from the parable: the observant Pharisee goes home unjustified, the sinful tax collector is justified. The reversal maxim concludes the story (see 14:11).

18:15-17 Jesus and the children. At the beginning of his narrative of the journey to Jerusalem (9:51), Luke departed from the outline of Mark and began introducing material from sources either personal or common to Matthew and himself. At this point Luke begins to follow Mark again. In Mark, the episode of the children (Mark 10:13-16) is preceded by Jesus' statement on divorce and remarriage. But Luke uses it along with the story of the rich man, to which it is connected in Mark, as an illustrative sequel to the parable of the Pharisee and the tax collector. The tax collector has the attitude of a child, defenseless and expectant, while the Pharisee is like the rich man (vv. 18-25), not yet ready to give up control over himself.

The disciples are infected with the attitudes of the Pharisee and the rich man. They have no tolerance for children and what they stand for. In their view, Jesus is wasting his time on these children who are unable to comprehend the great work he is about. He startles them by saying that the reign of God belongs precisely to such as these children. This narrative later supported those in the developing church who argued for infant baptism.

18:18-25 Jesus and the rich man. Whether the official is a Pharisee or not, his self-righteous attitude (v. 21) is the same as that criticized by Jesus earlier (v. 11). Jesus contests the use of "good" in the address, not because he doubts his own goodness, but because this was an unusual way of addressing a rabbi and was probably meant in flattery. Jesus' perception was proved accurate when the man did not obey the instruction of the "good" teacher. Maybe this insight into his character explains the mention only of the "social" commandments of the Decalogue. The commandments dealing with love and service of God are much more subject to illusion.

Jesus does not draw the man into closer relationship immediately. But when he hears a wish to go further, Jesus offers him his own way of life (see 9:57-58). The ruler cannot take the step because of his wealth, so often a threat to life in the kingdom (14:33; 16:13). He seems to know deep down that Jesus has spoken the word he needs to hear, but he is too enslaved by his possessions to follow it through. This provokes Jesus' memorable remark about the camel and the needle's eye. Semitic exaggeration is used, not to deny the possibility of salvation for the rich (see v. 27), but to imprint indelibly in his hearers' minds the sinister influence that riches can be even on those sincerely desiring the reign of God.

18:26-34 The demands of discipleship. Jesus' listeners are shocked by his warning to the wealthy. They would have thought that prosperity was a sign of God's blessing because of a person's goodness (Prov 10:3, 22). Jesus does not retract the harshness (see 6:24) but enunciates the important principle that God is willing and able to save all who call out to him. Peter notes that the disciples have done what the rich ruler could not do, and asks rather crassly about the reward. Jesus promises an "overabundant return," without specifying his meaning (in Mark's version he adds "with persecutions": Mark 10:30), and speaks again of the priority of kingdom over family (see 14:26). Then to the Twelve Jesus makes the third prediction of his passion and resurrection, adding this time that these things will happen in fulfillment of prophecy. The meaning of his words is lost on them.

18:35-43 The blind man at Jericho. The approach to Jericho signals the final stage of Jesus' journey to Jerusalem. Here, as in the incident of the children, the disciples try to keep an "insignificant" person from bothering the Master. The evangelist continues on another level to present the life of the church as a journey with Jesus on the way of the Lord. The note that it is "the people walking in front" who reprimand the beggar is a subtle warning to church leaders who might overlook the needs of the powerless (see Acts 6:1). But it is for these lowly who express their need for salvation that Jesus has come. The present chapter is a gallery of such people: the widow, the tax collector, the children, now the blind beggar.

The beggar's name is given in Mark as Bartimaeus (Mark 10:46). Blind as he is, he cries out with inspired insight, calling Jesus by the messianic title "Son of David." When questioned, he goes further to identify Jesus as "Lord." In response to this faith, he receives the message of deliverance that by now is a stereotyped phrase: "Your faith has saved you" (7:50; 8:48; 17:19). Both the beggar and the witnesses see the ultimate meaning of this act of power and glorify God.

19:1-10 Jesus and Zacchaeus. The story of Zacchaeus is unique to Luke's Gospel. It serves to synthesize dramatically some key themes of discipleship as Jesus nears Jerusalem. First of all, Zacchaeus is a wealthy man—probably very wealthy as the "district supervisor" of the tax collectors. As a result, he would be seen by Jewish leaders as the "chief of sinners," bearing the responsibility for the dishonesty connected with the activity of all his field workers. The question of the proper use of wealth is thus addressed again, and also the issue of eating with sinners. There is the usual murmuring (see 5:30; 15:2). But the breach of decorum is even worse this time, because Jesus does not wait to be invited to the tax collector's house. He invites himself; the shepherd seeking the one lost sheep (v. 10; 15:4-7).

Zacchaeus, in spite of his reputation, is an attractive person. In our brief meeting, qualities akin to those of Peter emerge. Zacchaeus is spontaneous and impetuous, given to extravagant statements. But there is a deep genuineness. Though he is a person of some importance, his position does not prevent him from climbing the sycamore tree nor from publicly admitting his guilt and professing his repentance. Jesus takes the initiative in this conversion story (contrast the blind beggar: 18:38-43), but Zacchaeus had to be ready for the saving word or it would not have been effective (see 8:11-15). Jesus says this is a son of Abraham, even if he is a tax collector. He should not be ostracized because of his failings but helped to find his way back to the flock. Zacchaeus's gratitude is an illustration of the parable of the money-lender and the debtors (7:41-43). Jesus' love of him has awakened new possibilities of love and service.

19:11-27 The parable of the investments. Matthew has another version of this parable (Matt 25:14-30), involving only three servants and different sums of money (his "talents" are also much larger than Luke's *mnas,* translated here as "gold coins"). Luke has added the kingly coronation theme because of the popular anticipation of God's reign (19:11). In its present form the parable answers questions from the time of the early church about the return of Jesus and what to do in his absence. The additions have allegorized the parable, that is, made the individual elements more easily applicable to the story of Jesus.

After the resurrection Luke's readers saw in the reference to a faraway country Jesus' ascension to heaven, where he received the Father's glory and awaited the time when he would return as judge. The servants are not to sit around idle meanwhile nor simply preserve the *status quo,* but are to continue his work while he is away (Acts 1:8-11). The mention of the deputation hostile to his kingship is an allusion to the accession of Archelaus on the death of his father, King Herod the Great, about thirty years earlier. Archelaus had gone to Rome to seek imperial appointment as his father's successor, but a Jewish deputation to Caesar Augustus had managed to restrict Archelaus's rule to only part of the original kingdom. Subsequent cruelty and mismanagement led to Archelaus's early banishment by Rome.

Only three of the ten servants are mentioned in the king's review of accounts. The result of the review is the same as in Matthew's version. The enterprising servants are rewarded with more trust. The servant who played it safe out of fear is condemned for his conduct and loses his sum of money to the one with ten. This provokes criticism from those who dislike the king's largesse. They prefer wages gauged to work, like the vineyard workers in another parable (Matt 20:1-16). The saying in verse 26 appeared in a variant form in 8:18. Openness to God's action in Jesus continues to intensify one's share in the kingdom, but a closed or fearful heart is incapable of sharing these riches.

19:28-44 Arrival at Jerusalem. Jesus' long journey to Jerusalem reaches its goal as he enters from the east through the small villages of Bethphage and Bethany. Luke follows Mark closely here but adds material in verses 39-40 with faint similarities to Matthew's additions (Mark 11:1-10; Matt 21:1-9). Verses 41-44 are unique. In all three accounts this event marks the public acclamation of Jesus as the Davidic Messiah. Earlier he had silenced such acclaim (4:41; 5:14); now he defends the disciples (vv. 39-40) and the children (Matt 21:16) against the criticism of the leaders.

Behind this event and the narratives is the prophetic oracle of Zechariah:

"Rejoice heartily, O daughter Zion,
shout for joy, O daughter Jerusalem!
See, your king shall come to you;
a just savior is he,
Meek, and riding on an ass" (Zech 9:9).

Only Matthew makes specific reference to it (Matt 21:5). This background explains the mention of peace in Luke's account (vv. 38, 42). Riding on an ass was not so much an emphasis on humility as on peacefulness. Kings rode horses when they came in war (Jer 8:6); entering Jerusalem on an ass indicates the kind of kingship Jesus is exercising. The two disciples are sent to find an animal that has never been ridden before. Animals for certain types of ritual use had to be previously unused, like the cows chosen to pull the ark of the covenant (1 Sam 6:7; see Num 19:2). The Greek Septuagint version of Zech 9:9 speaks of a "new" colt.

To judge from the space devoted to it, the disciples' errand is considered very special. Perhaps Jesus' foreknowledge or messianic authority is implied in the mysterious instructions about getting the ass. When the disciples return they take an active part in the procedure, laying their cloaks on the colt and on the roadway, and helping Jesus to mount. Their cry of praise in Luke's account emphasizes that Jesus comes as king. Their words are similar to the words of the angelic chorus at Jesus' birth (2:14) to signal the fulfillment of the prophecy made then. The Pharisees think that Jesus' disciples have gone too far, making claims for him that he would not dare make. But Jesus replies that the time for proclamation of his full identity and mission has come. God's plan must be revealed now, even if the stones must be called into service.

Like Jeremiah at an earlier time (Jer 8:18-23), Jesus laments the blindness of Jerusalem to the evidence of God's plan for her. She will not accept the true peace he offers by his entry. Jesus foresees the days of Jerusalem's destruction by Rome in A.D. 70. Destruction came once when the city would not listen to Jeremiah and the other prophets; this time it will be because of failure to accept the Messiah.

PART V: SUFFERING AND VICTORY

Luke 19:45–24:53

Now that Jesus has arrived at Jerusalem, the drama will move quickly toward its divinely planned climax. Jesus goes to "take possession" of the temple as its legitimate teacher. In this setting the conflict with the Jewish leaders will heighten (chapter 20). He will speak of the last days of Jerusalem and of the world (chapter 21). Then will come the days of his Passover (chapters 22–23) and the victory of God in his new exodus (chapter 24).

19:45-48 Jesus comes to the temple. Luke's account of the cleansing of the temple is the shortest among the Gospels. It is one of the few episodes recounted by the Synoptics that also appears in John, where it occurs at the beginning of Jesus' ministry rather than at the end (John 2:13-17). Luke has played down the violence and gives no description of the activities Jesus objects to, letting the quotations from Isa 56:7 and Jer 7:11 be reason enough for expelling "those who were selling things."

Luke is more interested in showing the reason for the cleansing as the preparation for the true teacher to take his seat in the place designed for him. From now on Jesus makes the temple the center of his Jerusalem ministry. In the verses that conclude this section of temple teaching (21:37-38), Jesus is described as teaching daily in the temple, while spending his nights on the Mount of Olives, by implication in communion with his Father as the days of fulfillment draw near.

20:1-8 Teaching in the temple. Jesus has taken his place as the authoritative teacher in the temple. Chapter 20 begins with a general challenge to his authority by the religious leaders; then the remainder of this chapter and all the following give examples of Jesus' teaching activity amid the continuing attacks of his adversaries.

The group that comes to question Jesus first is an official delegation of the Sanhedrin, the supreme council, representing the three classes that comprised it: the high priests (former high priests and leaders of the four high priestly families), Pharisees (scribes of the Pharisee sect), and elders (leaders of the chief Jewish families). They ask for an explanation of "these things": Jesus' cleansing of the temple and assuming an official teaching role. Jesus counters with his own question about John the Baptist, whose baptism some or all of them had refused to accept (7:30). This throws them into the dilemma described in the text. They cannot answer, which is proof to Jesus (as it should be to them) that they have no right to be standing in judgment over Jesus' authority.

20:9-19 The parable of the tenant farmers. In their hearing, Jesus tells the people a parable in which the leaders recognize themselves (v. 19). The parable of the tenant farmers is clearly a description of the response of the Jewish leaders to Jesus, God's beloved Son. It is variously allegorized in the versions of Luke, Mark (Mark 11:27-33), and Matthew (Matt 21:23-27) to draw out the comparisons to the history of Israel and the sending of the prophets. Israel as a vineyard is a traditional theme (Isa 5:1-7; Ps 80). The sending of the beloved son is something new. The details of what happened to Jesus have affected the telling of the story; for example, the fact that the son is killed outside the vineyard in Luke and Matthew might reflect Jesus' crucifixion outside the city (see Heb 13:12).

When the audience hears that the tenants will be destroyed and that the vineyard will be given to others (the Gentiles), they cry out in disbelief. Can it be possible that the land of the promise, the kingdom given to David as a permanent inheritance, will pass to others? Jesus quotes Ps 118:22 on the irony of the rejected stone that becomes the keystone and then adds a saying of his own: the stone will crush its opponents. Jesus is the keystone of the spiritual building in which all his followers are "living stones" (1 Pet 2:4-8). The episode ends with the recurring theme of the hostility of the leaders and the openness of the people. Because of the readiness of the people to hear the gospel in spite of their leaders, the vineyard of the renewed Israel will contain sturdy Jewish roots in addition to the new Gentile growth (see Rom 11:17-18).

20:20-26 Caesar's taxes. In two successive episodes Jesus' teaching and authority are challenged by groups who are themselves at odds: first by the scribes and high priests (still smarting from the parable of the tenant farmers) and then by the Sadducees. The first group is described as waiting in the wings for an opportune moment to trap him through spies who would not be as immediately recognizable as the leaders themselves. The leaders expect Jesus to speak unfavorably of the Empire, which will give them grounds for handing him over to Pontius Pilate. When the time comes, they will accuse Jesus of opposing the payment of taxes in spite of his response here (23:2).

The spokesmen try to cajole Jesus into giving an answer defiant of the Empire. They describe him flatteringly as "showing no partiality," therefore able to utter the truth even if it should be critical of the emperor. He teaches the "way of God" and is courageous and truthful enough to answer in God's favor even when it means that he must counteract worldly powers. They ask if it is right to pay taxes to the emperor. This is not a question about the justice of taxation, but whether a theocracy, a state under God's leadership, should pay taxes to an intruding pagan overlord.

The coin Jesus asked for was a denarius, the Roman coin that would have been used in paying taxes. Practically all of the imperial coins by this time would have carried the image of Tiberius Caesar, who had been ruling for at least fifteen years (see 3:1). Jesus avoids later quibbles by having his questioners identify the coin as Caesar's. His pronouncement on what is Caesar's and what is God's does not separate the world into two realms—one of the emperor and the other of God. God is Lord of all; when there is a conflict of interests, God's demand must be honored over any others. But the coin is proof of Caesar's political domain; like it or not, the citizens of Israel must give him what is his due (without, of course, denying the Lordship that belongs to God).

20:27-40 The Sadducees and resurrection. Jesus is challenged from another side by the Sadducees, who appear here in Luke for the only time (though they will be frequently on the scene in Acts [4:1-2; 5:17; 23:7-8]). The Sadducees were the aristocratic leaders who scorned the Pharisees and their "modern" beliefs and interpretations of the law. They were the conservatives, accepting only the first five books of the Bible (the Pentateuch) and not allowing the Pharisaic beliefs in the bodily resurrection of the just and the existence of spirits. Like the spies in the preceding incident, the Sadducees try to dispose Jesus for the answer favorable to their cause, in this instance by showing the absurdity of the doctrine of the resurrection.

By the law of levirate marriage (Deut 25:5-6; Ruth 3:9–4:12), a brother was supposed to raise up an heir for his childless dead brother so that the property would not leave the family and that his brother's name would continue in his posterity. The Sadducees pose a case that they think will force Jesus either to renounce the resurrection or to allow polyandry, which was considered immoral. Jesus replies that the succession of husbands is a problem for the Sadducees only because they have not thoroughly comprehended the meaning of the resurrection: resurrection life and current existence are two completely different things. In heaven the marriage relationship will be transcended by a new kind of relationship that will not involve procreation.

All three Synoptics record words of Jesus about the age to come (that is, after the final resurrection: Mark 12:25; Matt 22:30), but Jesus' phraseology in Luke (vv. 34-36) implies also that the age of the resurrection has already begun and that marriage has already lost its role as an absolute in human life (see Gen 1:28). Here is a hint that the state of celibacy (the state adopted by Jesus) has validity as a sign of the kingdom present and to come (see Matt 19:12). Those "judged worthy of a place in the age to come" are already children of the resurrection and no longer liable to death. They can imitate the angels in their complete absorption in God. Celibacy sacramentalizes this attitude of all Christians.

After saying this, Jesus takes up again the issue of the teaching of Moses with which the questioning began (v. 28). He shows that even Moses believed in a resurrection life when he spoke of God as the God of Abraham, Isaac and Jacob, who are still alive before him. Jesus' rebuttal of the Sadducees arouses the admiration of some of the scribes (probably Pharisees), but this was surely more of a political applause than a real adherence to the teaching of Jesus. As before (v. 26), Jesus' answer to their question has reduced his opponents to silence.

20:41-47 The Lordship of the Messiah. Jesus raises a question without giving the answer at the present time: if David (in Ps 110:1) calls the Messiah "lord," how can the Messiah be his son? Jesus was introduced as the son of David when his genealogy was given (3:33), and he has been correctly identified as the Messiah (9:20). The answer will come in the resurrection whereby Jesus, son of David and Messiah, will be exalted to God's right hand as the Lord (Acts 2:33-36). The criticism of the Pharisees made on the way to Jerusalem (11:41-43) is now made of the scribes (generally the same group) in the Jerusalem temple.

21:1-4 The widow's mite. Pursuing the theme of wealth and stewardship, Jesus draws the contrast between the temple contributions of the rich and a humble widow. He makes it clear that it is not what a person gives that expresses his or her generosity, but what one keeps. The beatitudes and the woes for the poor and rich are recalled (6:20, 24), as is the teaching on trust in providence (12:13-34). The scribes have just been condemned for going through the savings of people like the poor widow (20:47); earlier there was the charge of rapaciousness and laying impossible burdens on such people (11:39, 46). This reference to the evil conduct of the religious leaders forms a backdrop for the prediction of the destruction of the temple.

21:5-19 Prediction of the end. In Mark's version of this episode, Jesus comes out of the temple, allowing the disciples to get the impressive view that prompts their statement about the temple's beauty. Luke presents Jesus as teaching within the temple; this will be his last appearance in the temple, his final statement announcing its destruction. The destruction of the temple was connected in the popular mind with the end of the world. This had been true when Solomon's temple still stood: the Israelites felt that they were secure because of God's promise of an eternal heritage to David, and the temple was a symbol of divine protection. Jeremiah pointed out the illusion of relying on the earthly temple (Jer 7:4). Herod's temple was a glorious sight, too. Its adherents tended to base all their hopes on its sturdy security. Only the cataclysm of the end could shake it.

This connection of the fall of the temple with the end of the world leads Jesus to involve both ideas in answering their question "When will this happen?" First he speaks of the end of the world. This sermon on the end (*eschaton* in Greek) is commonly called the eschatological discourse. Fear and expectation will make people vulnerable to false messages and fake messiahs. They will point to apocalyptic signs (wars, earthquakes, plagues, signs in the heavens) to show that the end is near. Jesus has already said that the attempt to calculate the end is a waste of time (17:20-21). The signs he mentions can be observed in every age. They indicate that the end is indeed coming, but they are no help in determining the day or the hour.

The core of the discourse goes back to Jesus himself, but it has been affected by the experience of the early church in witnessing the fall of Jerusalem and the persecution of the first martyrs. Readers of the Gospel would be able to think of concrete examples of the persecution foretold by Jesus. In the mention of "kings and governors" they would see the faces of Herod and Pilate, and probably Agrippa I and Agrippa II, Felix and Festus (Acts 12; 24–26). Jesus' disciples are not to become frantic and anxious about the coming persecution. It will give them the opportunity to bear witness (Acts 3:15; 4:20). They must not worry about what to say in the time of trial; they will speak with a divine wisdom that no one can contradict (Acts 4:13). Family ties will not protect the disciple (Luke 12:51-53). Jesus' followers are to carry the cross all the way to Calvary, as he did. The promise that no harm will come to even one hair seems strange in the prediction of persecution. It is simply a graphic statement of the ultimate spiritual protection of all those who endure the persecution for the sake of Jesus.

21:20-24 The fall of Jerusalem. Jesus shortens the range of his vision from the end of the world to the destruction of Jerusalem. Luke modifies Mark's account, leaving no mention of the mysterious "abomination of desolation" or of the tempering of the disaster. He adds a description of the siege from post-factum information. The people in the Judean hills and countryside are warned not to flee into the city, where destruction is sure to descend. The mention of retribution and fulfillment brings prophetic judgment into the description of Jerusalem's fate. Writing for Gentiles, Luke highlights their role in Jerusalem's downfall. The enigmatic "times of the Gentiles" refers to the era of the Gentile mission, the beginning of which is recorded in the Acts of the Apostles.

21:25-38 The coming of the Son of Man. The "times of the Gentiles" will last until the end; their fulfillment (v. 24) brings Jesus back to the topic of the end of the world. The shaking of the cosmic forces will herald the coming of the end. Then the Son of Man, the risen Lord to whom judgment and authority have been given, will come in God's glory. It will be reason for panic for God's enemies, but the disciples should stand erect, expectant and ready like the people of the Exodus for God's deliverance (Exod 12:11).

The image of the fig tree is expanded by the addition of other trees for environments where figs might not be known. Spring budding is always a sign that summer is coming. The statement about the present generation (v. 32) seems difficult. It does not mean that the end of the world will come before the generation of Jesus passes (that generation had already passed at the time this was written). The emphasis of the statement is on the certainty of the events foretold by Jesus, and probably this means that the first of the events leading to the end of the world (the fall of Jerusalem) will happen within the experience of the present generation. The word of God, brought in the words of Jesus, bears witness to this prophecy (v. 33).

After describing the days of the coming of the Son of Man, Jesus urges on his listeners the proper conduct for awaiting his return. His warning is especially against the pleasures and cares represented by the "thorns" in the parable of the sower (8:14). These pressures of daily life lull people into false security. The exhortation to watch and pray foreshadows the same appeal during Jesus' agony in the garden (22:46). The section closes with a summary of Jesus' typical activity during these final days in Jerusalem (see 19:47). He taught in the temple during the day and spent the night in prayer on the Mount of Olives. Though the leaders were trying to put an end to him, the common people continued to be eager to listen to him.

22:1-6 The plotters and the betrayer. With the setting of the trap by the plotters and the betrayer, the story of the passion begins. Luke presents Jesus as the righteous man suffering martyrdom. He proceeds step by step according to the Father's plan. Jesus' pain is not diminished, but he endures it with an inner peace and is able to go out to others from the midst of his own agony (23:28, 34, 43).

The feasts of the Unleavened Bread and the Passover were originally two separate celebrations—the one an agricultural festival at the beginning of the barley harvest, the other a nomadic feast in which the first-born of the flock was sacrificed. Early in Israelite history the feasts were joined to commemorate the deliverance of Israel from Egypt. The Passover was observed on the first of the seven days of Unleavened Bread (v. 7). Jesus' enemies in the Sanhedrin hope for an opportunity to put him to death under the cover of the crowds thronging Jerusalem. The assistance of the temple guards would be needed should Jesus be arrested in the temple area.

After the temptations in the desert, Luke had remarked that the devil left Jesus to await another time. The opportune time has come (in John's Gospel, "the hour": John 13:1), and Satan enters Judas (see John 13:2, 27). The church realized that the enormity of the passion was beyond mere human agency. The evangelists note the tragic irony that the betrayer was one of the Twelve.

22:7-20 The Passover meal. Luke, like Mark and Matthew, presents the Last Supper as a Passover meal. In John's Gospel, the supper takes place the night before, and the death of Jesus occurs at the time of the sacrifice of the Passover lamb. Peter and John are sent to make the arrangements: the place, the food and its preparation, and needed attendants. Possibly Jesus did not specify the place clearly to avoid premature arrest in case Judas should overhear. Their signal is to be a man carrying a water jar: women usually carried jars and pitchers, men leather bottles.

Jesus realizes that the climax of his mission is approaching. His action dramatizes his own self-offering as the new Paschal Lamb. He will not eat the Passover supper again until it is fulfilled in the kingdom. The church understands this of the Eucharist, which he institutes in the following words, and of the eternal banquet of heaven (v. 30). Some modern translations omit verses 19b and 20 because they are missing in certain ancient sources, but the most recent critical texts (both Catholic and Protestant) contain them as authentic. At the Passover meal, the various dishes and cups were shared ritually with accompanying prayers and narratives. Jesus interrupts the customary flow of the ritual to offer himself to his disciples in the form of bread and wine. This signifies the making of a new covenant. In the old covenant the union of God and the people was symbolized by the sprinkling of the blood of an animal (Exod 24:5-8); now the union is perfect in the blood of one who is God and man. Jesus' followers are told to do what he has done in his remembrance. This refers both to the ritual action and to the self-gift it sacramentalizes.

The Eucharistic institution accounts come to us in two traditions, that of Mark and Matthew and that of Luke and Paul (1 Cor 11:23-25). Luke does not seem to be directly dependent on Paul, however, and is the only writer to mention two cups (the Passover meal called for four cups of wine).

22:21-38 Division at table. Luke's arrangement of the material makes the harshest contrast between the covenant action of Jesus and the action of the betrayer at the same table. Even presence at the Lord's table, Luke is saying to his readers, is no guarantee of fidelity to Jesus. The betrayal goes according to God's plan, but the one who carries it out still bears personal responsibility. The callousness of the whole group of the Twelve is revealed as their argument about which of them could be guilty of betrayal evolves into a dispute about their greatness. This dispute occurs at a different place in the other Synoptics (Mark 10:42-45; Matt 20:25-28). Jesus tells them that the kingdom has completely different categories of greatness than the world has. He notes ironically that those who tyrannize over their subjects are called "Benefactors": this was the case in Rome, Egypt, and other Gentile territories. The one who is great in the kingdom of God will be the one who serves in imitation of the Master himself. The Twelve will be given authority, however; they have shared the journey with Jesus (which is not yet finished), suffering the onslaughts of his enemies. They will become the new patriarchs of the renewed Israel of God.

Jesus addresses the leader of the new patriarchs by his Hebrew name. He says that Satan has asked to test the Twelve; the implication is that God's special permission is needed to interfere with the Twelve. Jesus' powerful intercession will help the leader. Jesus refers to the coming apostasy of Peter, from which he will return to strengthen his brothers. Peter does not accept the hint of his weakness and protests his allegiance and fidelity. Jesus then utters the prediction of his betrayal with unequivocal clarity. Peter must get over thinking that his special role among the Twelve was earned by his own strength. Jesus' promise of intercession is not idle.

In a parting message to all, Jesus asks them to recall the instructions they were given for the preaching mission (9:3). They had been told to rely on God's providence for the things they would need. Now, because of the impending crisis of Jesus' passion and death, and in view of the persecution sure to come on the early church, Jesus tells them to prepare themselves well for the struggle, even to taking up arms. He is speaking figuratively to alert them to the seriousness of the struggle, but they take him literally, producing two swords. "It is enough!" puts an end to a conversation that has been over their heads.

22:39-53 The agony and the arrest. Luke has streamlined and simplified Mark's account of the agony in the garden. Jesus does not select three disciples out of the group to accompany him; as a result, his admonition to pray so as not to be overcome by temptation is addressed to all the Twelve (and the readers) as a main theme (vv. 40, 46). Jesus himself is tested by his desire to avoid the cup, but he accepts the will of the Father. This is the climax of the struggle with Satan (see 4:1-13); an angel comes to his aid, so that he is able to pray with greater intensity. His sweat is not bloody but falls from him like drops of blood. Meanwhile the disciples, still unaware of the significance of what is going on in their midst, have fallen asleep. In the warning to them, we hear Jesus admonishing us to strengthen ourselves by fervent prayer for the persecution that will surely come to his followers.

The betrayer is again identified with tragic irony as one of the Twelve (v. 47). Still misinterpreting Jesus' words and their role as his disciples, his followers strike with the sword. Only in Luke's version does Jesus heal the servant's ear. He upbraids the arresting party for seeking him in an out-of-the-way place under cover of darkness, indicating that their deed cannot bear the light of day. What they are doing is indeed a sign of the "power of darkness" (v. 53). Jesus refers to the time of his passion as the "hour"; but the tone is not positive as in John's Gospel, where the hour is the time fulfilling the Father's plan (John 13:1; 17:1). Here it is "your hour" of darkness.

22:54-65 Peter denies Jesus. Unlike Mark and Matthew, Luke has no arraignment before the Jewish authorities before the morning session. At this point he focuses on Peter's denials, forgetting Jesus for the moment. Peter does not move about as in the other Synoptics, remaining rather in the courtyard, where he will be visible to Jesus after the cock crows. A woman and two men accuse Peter over a period of an hour or more. Luke probably means to show the endurance of Peter, who remains in the same place where he is in constant danger of identification, as a sign of his willingness, though half-hearted, to stand by Jesus. When Jesus looks at him, he is not hopelessly crushed by remorse but is able to return as Jesus prayed he would (v. 32). The taunting punishment of Jesus is envisioned as taking place in the courtyard at the hands of the temple guard. His role as God's true prophet is mocked, which Luke regards as blasphemy against God (Greek text of v. 65). Luke does not mention the treatment of the Roman soldiers (Mark 14:65; Matt 26:67-68).

22:66-71 The Sanhedrin's decision. Luke's description of a single meeting of the Sanhedrin, taking place at daybreak, is more likely than that of Mark and Matthew, who describe a night meeting followed by a morning session to carry out the decision. A night meeting of the Sanhedrin is otherwise unknown. Jesus is unwilling to identify himself as the kind of Messiah popularly expected; rather, he speaks of himself as authoritative judge in his role as the Son of Man (Dan 7:13-14). They interpret this answer (correctly) as an affirmation of a special divine status; they can only view this as blasphemy, sufficient reason to condemn him to death (see Mark 14:62-64). The Sanhedrin is not empowered to impose the death sentence; they must submit their accusation to the judgment of the Roman authority.

23:1-12 Pilate and Herod. Pontius Pilate had been procurator, or Roman governor, of Judea for about five years (see 3:1). His seat of government was at the seacoast town of Caesarea, but he was in Jerusalem because of the large gathering of Jews for the feast of Passover. Luke follows Mark's outline but makes several additions to throw into relief Jesus' innocence. The Herod episode is also proper to Luke.

One of the charges is clearly false—the opposition to Roman taxes (see 20:20-25). Jesus has not spoken clearly to the Sanhedrin about being the Messiah (22:66), but he has not denied it; his entry into Jerusalem implied it (19:28-40). Luke has added the explanatory "a king" for the sake of his Greek readers. After Jesus' noncommittal reply, Pilate pronounces him innocent. No reason is given, because in abbreviating the account Luke has taken the arguments for granted. The charges are repeated, this time in terms that encompass Jesus' whole ministry as traditionally described, beginning in Galilee and eventually affecting the whole land (Acts 10:37).

The mention of Galilee gives Pilate the opportunity to divert the case to the tetrarch of Galilee, Herod Antipas, who was also in Jerusalem for the feast. Herod's curiosity about Jesus was mentioned earlier (9:9). Jesus does not respond to the request for a sign nor to the ill-motivated questions, as he never does in the Gospels. Herod's mocking treatment of Jesus ironically heals an enmity with Pilate (whose conduct cited in 13:1 may have been one of the causes). The cooperation of the two is later seen as the fulfillment of prophecy (Ps 2:1-2; Acts 4:25-28).

23:13-25 The death sentence. The second scene before Pilate is a threefold crescendo of Jesus' innocence, the crowd's hostility, and Pilate's weakness. Pilate tries various routes to convince the people of Jesus' innocence. But he is not strong or free enough to do what he knows is right. The people call for the release of the prisoner Barabbas under terms of what must have been a local custom authorized by the Judean procurators. Barabbas was a revolutionary and murderer who really would have constituted a danger to the stability of Roman rule. Verse 17 is omitted because it was an insertion from Mark 15:6.

Crucifixion is suddenly mentioned for the first time in verse 21. Luke does not explain why the crowds have become so violent (see Mark 15:11). Crucifixion was a cruel and humiliating punishment that the Romans inflicted only on slaves and non-Romans guilty of the worst crimes. Jews saw in this treatment the sign of a curse (Deut 21:23; Gal 3:13). Pilate tries to appease the crowd with a promise to have Jesus scourged—an absurdity if Jesus is innocent. Finally he cannot withstand the pressure. Jesus is delivered to the will of the crowd; their will is allowed to prevail, perverse as it is, because it coincides with the will of the Father (22:42).

23:26-31 The way of the cross. That the man pressed into service to Jesus was a Cyrenian would have been significant to the early Cyrenian converts (Acts 6:9; 11:20; 13:1). Simon is given the crossbeam, which had become too heavy for Jesus in his weakened condition. This would later be fastened to the upright that remained fixed in the ground at the site of execution. Luke adds to Mark's account the detail that Simon walked "behind Jesus" to make him a symbol of the ideal disciple (14:27).

Jesus is being led to his death according to the Father's will, powerless now in the hands of his executioners. But he is the Lord, and on his way he makes another prophetic statement about Jerusalem (see 19:42-44). The women of Jerusalem who customarily solaced condemned prisoners are recipients of the divine pronouncement for the city as well as for themselves. They will wish to be hidden from the catastrophe soon coming upon Jerusalem (see Hos 10:8). Unlike the woman who rejoiced that Mary had borne and nursed Jesus (11:27), these women will rejoice if they have no children to suffer through the time of siege. Jesus leaves them with a proverb: Dry wood burns better than green. If the innocent Jesus has to suffer so much, what will be the fate of guilty Jerusalem?

23:32-49 Crucifixion and death. Luke does not use the Aramaic name "Golgotha" as the other evangelists do, but simply refers to the place of execution as "The Skull," a name that described the rock formation at Calvary. Jesus is crucified between two criminals (see 22:37; Isa 53:12). He utters the words of forgiveness that will become the hallmark of the innocent Christian sufferer, words echoed by Stephen, the first martyr (Acts 7:60). The dividing of the garments reflects the words of Ps 22:19. Though Luke does not exonerate the Jewish people completely from complicity in the death of Jesus, he continues to show that it was caused mainly by the hostility and jealousy of their leaders (v. 35). Luke has the scoffers refer to Jesus as the "chosen one" (as at the transfiguration: 9:35) rather than as the "king of Israel" (Mark 15:32; Matt 27:42), a title less striking to non-Jewish readers. The soldiers offer him their own cheap drink, which might be considered an act of kindness, but it is mockery to offer such a drink to a king.

The incident of the good thief is unique to Luke. The criminal who mocks Jesus is said to be blaspheming, a conclusion of Christian faith regarding Jesus' true identity. The other criminal asks Jesus to remember him when he begins his reign. He means the definitive messianic kingdom that Jews expected at the end of the present age, but in Luke's theology it also refers to the time of Jesus' exaltation through resurrection and ascension. Jesus promises him a place in "Paradise" *today*, because the death of Jesus is beginning the exodus (9:31) that will open a new way to salvation. "Paradise" goes back to the Persian term for an enclosed park and was used in the Greek Old Testament for the Garden of Eden in Genesis. Late Hebrew writings considered paradise an intermediate state of happiness of the righteous before the final judgment (4 Ezra 4:7; 2 Enoch 42:3). This intermediate state seems to have been the meaning of paradise here.

The triumph of darkness (22:53) now seems complete as Jesus nears death. Luke does not speak technically of an eclipse of the sun but of the failure of its light. The tearing of the curtain between the Holy Place and the Holy of Holies in the temple symbolizes that in Jesus a new access has been gained to God's presence and that a new dispensation has replaced the old. Jesus dies with a prayer of acceptance of the Father's will taken from Ps 31:6. The pagan centurion gives the verdict of innocent in climaxing a long build-up (rather than "Son of God" as in Mark 15:39; Matt 27:54). The crowd now beat their breasts—probably a combination of grief for the death of a man now recognized as innocent and of repentance for the wrongdoing in which they have participated. Luke did not report the desertion of the disciples in the Garden (see Mark 14:50; Matt 26:56). He implies that they have been helplessly and fearfully watching the events of the passion from a distance.

23:50-56 The burial of Jesus. Joseph of Arimathea (a town north of Jerusalem) is described in the same terms as Zechariah and Elizabeth (1:6) and Simeon (2:25). Like Simeon and Anna (2:38), he is awaiting the reign of God. The details of Jesus' burial in a new tomb bring Luke and the other Synoptics into rare coincidence with John's description (John 19:40-42). They do not, however, record an anointing of the body at this time.

The women from Galilee are still faithfully near to Jesus (see 8:1-3; Acts 1:14). The remark that they saw the tomb and the body (v. 55) is probably meant to counteract later rumors that the resurrection story was concocted when the women went back to the wrong (empty) tomb on Easter morning. Luke does not say when the spices were prepared—before or after the sabbath. Such preparations for burial were not contrary to the sabbath observance, but Luke is taking extra pains to avoid the impression that anything was done without regard for the law of Moses.

24:1-12 Discovery of the resurrection. Luke's account of the discovery of the empty tomb follows Mark but adds the story of Peter's visit to the tomb (known in a different form by John: John 20:3-8). The Gospel stories of the resurrection surprise us by their disagreements: Was there one man or angel, or two? Did Peter go alone to the tomb or was John with him? Did Jesus appear to the disciples in Galilee or only in Jerusalem? These discrepancies have arisen because of word-of-mouth transmission. The fact that they have not been ironed out into a smooth story testifies to the authenticity of the experience behind them. The witnesses were convinced of what they had seen and heard and felt, and had no concern for editing the proclamation.

Jesus is referred to by the official title "Lord Jesus" (v. 3), which belongs to him because of the resurrection. The question to the women contains an implicit proclamation of faith and is addressed with many-layered meaning to the readers of the story as well: "Why do you seek the living one among the dead?" Jesus' resurrection has come about as foretold by himself and in fulfillment of the Father's will. What has happened to him is described in both passive and active forms: "he has been raised" (v. 6); he will "rise" (v. 7). Both of these usages are correct and are found elsewhere in the New Testament. The passive form is more frequent, expressing the truth that the whole work of salvation, including the resurrection of the Son of God, originates in God the Father.

The names of the women vary in the lists, but the name of Mary Magdalene is in all of them. Joanna was one of those mentioned as accompanying Jesus during his ministry (8:3). The third woman is called simply "Mary of James" in the Greek text; comparison with Mark 15:40 identifies her as James's mother rather than his wife.

24:13-35 An Easter walk to Emmaus. Two of the disciples who had been with the Eleven on Sunday morning (v. 9) leave for Emmaus after having heard the report of the women and of Peter. This story, another unique offering of Luke, has pattern similarities with the story of the baptism of the Ethiopian eunuch by Philip later on: a journey, the interpretation of Scripture, a significant action, and a mysterious disappearance (Acts 8:26-40). In the Greek text, the village of Emmaus is said to be "sixty stadia" from Jerusalem. A *stadion* was about six hundred feet, making the distance around seven miles.

Jesus is taken for another pilgrim returning home from the Jerusalem festival. The two disciples do not recognize him. Their eyes are "held back," an expression for spiritual blindness. Various appearance stories say that Jesus looked "different" (Mark 16:12; John 20:14; 21:4). His body has definitely been transformed by the resurrection, but the point in these descriptions seems to be that it takes faith, a gift of new eyes, to recognize the risen Lord. Readers are helped by knowing that some of Jesus' friends did eventually recognize him and testified to the reality of his resurrection, but even more by realizing that recognition of the Lord does not depend on his natural visibility.

The disciples are distressed by the death of Jesus and cannot believe that the event that has shaken their world is not known by another pilgrim. Cleopas is named, but not the other; perhaps Cleopas later exercised an important role in the Christian community. They describe Jesus as a mighty prophet, the long-awaited prophet-like-Moses (Deut 18:15; Acts 7:22). They had hoped he would be not only a prophet but the messianic deliverer of Israel (see 1:68). Again there is emphasis on the role of the leaders in Jesus' crucifixion (v. 20). The "third day" is probably remembered as part of a mysterious promise of Jesus (18:33). Even the accounts of the empty tomb did not lead them necessarily to conclude that he had risen, because the resurrection expected by the Jews was the general victory of all the just at the end. It was obvious to them that the end and the establishment of a new order had not come. They did not expect an individual resurrection in the midst of history.

Jesus upbraids them for their blindness. They have read the prophets all their lives but not recognized the fulfillment in the *necessary* suffering and death of Jesus (according to God's plan). The cross preceded the glory. This will be the pattern for his disciples (Acts 14:22). The disciples are struck by what Jesus has said and ask him to *stay* with them. The word "stay" or "abide" here may have richer overtones, as in John's Gospel (John 14:17; 15:4-10). Jesus shares a meal with them, which is described so as to recall the multiplication of the loaves (9:16) and the Last Supper (22:19). In this "breaking of the bread" (an early name for the Eucharist: Acts 2:42, 46) they recognize him; immediately he disappears from their physical sight. They remember that their hearts were "burning" without their knowing why when he was explaining the Scriptures to them. Now they know that it was his risen presence they were experiencing. Luke's readers know that the same experience is available in the church in the Eucharist and in the reading of the Scriptures.

The experience of the risen Lord cannot be held in. It must be shared, proclaimed (Acts 4:20). By the time they return to Jerusalem, the good news is already known. Jesus has appeared meanwhile to Simon Peter, the leader of the Twelve; this appearance is not described in the Gospels. Luke closes his narration of the story with a reminder for his readers of its special significance for them: recognition came in "the breaking of bread."

24:36-49 Jesus appears to the community. If the reality of Jesus' spiritual presence in the church was emphasized in the preceding narrative, the physical reality of his resurrection body is emphasized here. From the earliest times in the church, there was a danger of docetism, the heretical belief that Jesus was God behind a thin veneer of humanity: thus his suffering was only playacting, and his resurrection was simply a return to a completely spiritual existence with no bodily effect. The Letters of John combated this error (1 John 4:2-3; 2 John 7). The present narrative stresses that Jesus' resurrection body is real. The disciples touch him; the marks of the passion are visible in his hands and feet; he eats with the disciples.

Their panic is not surprising, even though they have already heard about the earlier appearance. They are still excited and tense with the unfamiliarity of it all, and Jesus suddenly appears in their midst. His question to them is rhetorical, a way of introducing the Scriptural instruction that will help them to assimilate the truth of this marvelous event. The Old Testament is referred to in a traditional way by naming its three collections: law, prophets, and psalms (usually "writings"). His words commissioning them as witnesses of his resurrection foreshadow the Acts of the Apostles. The "promise" of the Father is the Holy Spirit who will be given to empower them to fulfill their mission (Acts 1:8).

24:50-53 The ascension. Luke's Gospel ends with the fulfillment of the journey begun in 9:51 (see Acts 1:2). It is surprising to find two contradictory accounts of the ascension by the same author. Here the ascension takes place on the day of resurrection; in Acts, it takes place forty days later (Acts 1:3, 9). The ascension as the exaltation of Jesus as the risen Lord at the right hand of the Father took place immediately as part of the resurrection triumph, but his visible leave-taking of the community happened at some later time. The accounts vary because Luke treats the same event from two points of view: in the Gospel the ascension is the climax of Jesus' work; in Acts it is the prelude to the church's mission.

Bethany is on the far side of the Mount of Olives, which lies east of Jerusalem (Acts 1:12). Jesus' blessing indicates his handing on of the mission to the disciples and his promise of assistance as they carry it out. The whole scene is reminiscent of the blessing by the priest in Sir 50:20-21 (see also John 20:21-23). The Greek word for "homage" or "worship" (v. 52) is used for the first time in the Gospel for reverence toward Jesus (earlier it was given to God the Father: 4:7-8). The resurrection has revealed his divinity.

The Gospel ends in the temple, where it began. Christianity at this point is still understood as the fulfillment of Jewish promises within Israel, not something radically separate from Judaism. The first Christians are faithful Jews. Their mission is still within Judaism (Acts 1–7) until they are led beyond under the Spirit's guidance. The disciples are not despondent at the departure of Jesus (compare John 14:1). They are full of joy, understanding the fulfillment of Jesus' mission and awaiting the gift he has promised.

JOHN

Neal M. Flanagan, O.S.M.

INTRODUCTION

This introduction is not intended to be an initial, preparatory summation of John's theology nor a presentation—with solutions—of the various problems regarding the author of the Gospel and the nature of his community. I prefer that the readers first have the opportunity to study through the Fourth Gospel as a journey of discovery. Only at the end, after they have assimilated much of what John himself has to say, will I attempt to pull elements together into a résumé.

The commentary is not a verse-by-verse study, though of course numerous individual verses will be considered. Insistence will be placed, rather, on the illumination of the successive Johannine themes as our author offers them to us.

Scholars are by no means in agreement as to the literary divisions intended by the author. My own strong preference is for those of C. H. Dodd, who divides the material into two main sections: the Book of Signs (chs. 2–12) and the Book of Glory (chs. 13–20). The Book of Signs is subsequently divided into seven thematic episodes. It is this division that I will follow here.

With sincere thanks I admit my debt to a long list of previous and contemporary scholars, but especially to C. H. Dodd, B. Lindars, R. E. Brown, J. L. Martyn, and O. Cullmann.

COMMENTARY

A. THE INTRODUCTION

John 1:1-51

The first chapter of John serves as an introduction to the whole Gospel, introducing the reader both to John's theology—what he believes about God and Jesus—and to Jesus' ministry. It contains a prologue and a series of testimonies.

a) 1:1-18 Prologue. The prologue serves somewhat like an overture to a formal musical composition. It may well have been written after the main body of the Gospel. (This is true of most prologues.) In its short span of eighteen verses, it states briefly what the whole of the Gospel will spell out over twenty-one chapters. It has both structure and content. The *structure* has been partially determined by the presentation of "wisdom personified" in the Old Testament books. There, as in Wis 9:9-12 or Prov 8:22-36, wisdom is first with God, then shares in creation, will come to earth, and there gift humankind. This same progression is found in our prologue. The other factor that has determined the structure is the Hebrew fondness for parallelism—notions being repeated in order—and for inverse parallelism, that is, repeated in inverse order. Visually, John's poetic prologue unfolds as follows.

1. The Word with God (vv. 1-2)
2. Role in creation (v. 3)
3. Gift to humankind (vv. 4-5)
4. Testimony of John (vv. 6-8)
5. The Word enters the world (vv. 9-11)
6. Through the Word we become children of God (vv. 12-13)
5. The incarnation (v. 14)
4. Testimony of John (v. 15)
3. Gift to humankind (v. 16)
2. Role in re-creation (v. 17)
1. The Son at the Father's side (v. 18)

The movement of the prologue swings like the arm of a mighty pendulum, each point of which on the left side will be matched by an equivalent on the right.

In *content,* these eighteen verses speak of God's revelation, of how he has explained himself to us. It is this that accounts for the extraordinary title that our author uses—"the Word." Its best equivalent is "revelation." As we humans reveal ourselves through what we say and, even more, by what we do (our body language), so God through the centuries has offered his own self-revelation through act and speech. The prologue details this. God revealed himself through creation (vv. 2-5), but also through his Old Testament word (vv. 10-13), that is, through his covenants, the Mosaic writings, the prophets, and the wisdom literature. Those who opened their eyes and believed in this ancient revelation became "children of God . . . born . . . of God (vv. 12-13). Finally God has revealed himself to the utmost through the incarnation of the Word, in whom God's glory, his presence, stands revealed as a sign of his enduring love (v. 14). (The Greek text tells us that the Word "pitched his tent" among us, a striking reference to God's Old Testament presence in the tent-tabernacle during Moses' wanderings with Israel in the desert.) To this incarnate Word John the Baptist has given testimony, a testimony that initiated the historical manifestation of Jesus, in whom the Father stands completely revealed and in whose fullness we, the Christian community, have all shared. The prologue ends with the upstroke of the pendulum arm to the right, in parallel to the very beginning of the poem. The Word, whose name is Jesus Christ (v. 17), is the Son, the only Son, who is "at the Father's side" (v. 18) and reveals him to those open to light and truth.

As you may have noticed, this explanation of the content of the prologue has ignored verses 6-8, the initial statement about John the Baptist, and in so doing has been able to interpret verses 9-13 as pre-incarnational, that is, as referring to the Old Testament revelation rather than to the historical presence of Jesus in the world. In our opinion, verses 6-8 occur where they do simply to balance the statement about the Baptist on the right side of the pendulum swing (v. 15). They are where they are, not for theological sequence, but for purely artistic reasons.

Consequently, verses 1-18 are an artistically fashioned poem summarizing the main point of John's theology: Jesus of Nazareth is God's supreme revelation, God's interpreter, his exegete. Being God himself (vv. 1, 18), he not only mediates God to us, he *immediates* him. He is God's wisdom speaking God's ultimate word about himself.

b) 1:19-51 Testimonies. This second section of chapter 1 contains a whole list of witnesses to Jesus who, one by one, identify Jesus for John's audience. Like the audience at a play, who by means of the printed program receive advance information about the actors, so these verses in John put the readers/hearers in a position of special knowledge as the drama of Jesus' life-story is played out. From the very beginning they are told who and what Jesus is. The testimonies flow as follows:

First day (vv. 19-28).

Witness: John the Baptist to priests and Levites.

Testimony: John is not Christ, nor the expected Elijah of Mal 3:23 (4:5 in some versions), nor the prophet of Deut 18:15, 18, but "the voice of one crying out in the desert," himself unworthy to untie the sandal strap of the one coming after him.

Second day ("next day" of vv. 29-34).

Witness: John the Baptist at sight of Jesus.

Testimony: Jesus is "the Lamb of God who takes away the sin of the world"; he who ranks before John; he on whom the Spirit descended and who baptizes with the Spirit; God's chosen One.

Third day ("next day" of vv. 35-39).

Witness: John the Baptist to two of his disciples, who go to Jesus about 4 p.m. and stay.

Testimony: "Behold, the Lamb of God." (This would be a reference to the paschal lamb and/or to the suffering servant of Isa 53:7, silent before its shearers.)

Fourth day(?) (vv. 40-42).
Witness: Andrew to Simon.
Testimony: "We have found the Messiah."

Fifth day ("next day" of vv. 43-51).
Witness: Philip to Nathaniel.
Testimony: "the one about whom Moses wrote in the law, and also the prophets."

Witness: Nathaniel.
Testimony: "You are the Son of God; you are the King of Israel."

Seventh day ("On the third day" of 2:1-11).
Witness: Jesus' Cana miracle.
Testimony: ". . . and so revealed his glory, and his disciples began to believe in him" (2:11).

Our author seems to be laying out an artistic first week in the good news of Christian re-creation to recall the first week of the creation story in the Book of Genesis. Both Genesis and John's Gospel begin with the identical phrase, "In the beginning." This is probably intentional. The succession of days in John are clearly marked except for the fourth, where the otherwise unnecessary reference to the two disciples going to Jesus about 4 p.m. and staying with him (v. 39) intends to say that they stayed overnight. Why else would John mention 4 p.m.? This first week of re-creation will conclude with the Cana miracle and the first manifestation that in Jesus is God's residing glory, his divine presence. "On the third day" of 2:1 should also remind us of *the* future supreme manifestation of God's glory, the resurrection.

This series of testimonies can be a source of confusion and difficulty for anyone who has read Mark's Gospel, in which the disciples come to their faith-knowledge of Jesus only hesitantly, timidly, and imperfectly—and that over a lengthy period of time. John seems to contradict Mark's picture. By the end of chapter 1 the Johannine disciples seem to know everything there is to know about Jesus, even his divinity. I think we must say that John is not attempting here to give a historical presentation of the first disciples' advance in faith. He has a different purpose in mind. He wishes to impress these christological statements on the minds of his audience at the very start of his dramatic presentation; therefore his actors appear in a succession of brief scenes to pass along the required information. The testimonies indicate that the Gospel's main interest is Christology. John may also wish to indicate through this procedure the way in which his own community advanced to its knowledge of Jesus: by moving from the circle of John the Baptist to the greater personage of Jesus, who was gradually recognized as the Lamb of God, God's chosen One, the Messiah, Son of God, and King of Israel. Jesus was the fulfillment of all the Old Testament hopes.

There is another purpose that John, a man of rich creative genius, may have intended. His list of characters in this first act/period of seven days seems to typify the basic personal elements of the Christian community. In order there appear: (1) John the Baptist, precursor to the new creation, whose sole function is to witness; (2) the Savior; (3) disciples who hear, follow, look for, and stay; (4) Peter, the rock; (5) missionaries like Andrew and Philip who spread the good news; (6) Nathaniel, the true Israelite in whom there is no guile, who, as some Jewish traditions expressed it, studied law under a fig tree and was rewarded. With this, the founding elements of the community are assembled. Let the drama begin!

The unexpected and ambiguous reference in verse 51 to a future vision of angels "ascending and descending on the Son of Man" insinuates the unifying function of Jesus. Like the angels on Jacob's ladder (Gen 28:12), he will join through himself the above and the below, the heavenly and the earthly.

B. THE BOOK OF SIGNS

John 2:1–12:50

Our author begins at this point what is aptly called "The Book of Signs." It moves by way of narrative and discourse through seven distinguishable episodes, or themes, and through seven sign-miracles. John's terminology regarding these sign-miracles is very distinct: they are "signs" pointing to some deeper theological truth. What the deeper truth is will frequently, but not always, be identified in the discourse. The material in these eleven chapters appears to be organized into theme clusters, which we will call "episodes."

2:1–4:42 Episode I: New Beginnings

In this section John will provide four different accounts—Cana, the temple, Nicodemus, the Samaritan woman—each of which will emphasize the newness that Jesus has brought into the world. The basic message throughout will be the same as that of Paul in 2 Cor 5:17: "The old things have passed away; behold, new things have come." John's Gospel is in many ways a Christian Genesis, a story of re-creation.

1. The Cana sign (2:1-12). With this account, located in the small town of Cana, north in Galilee, John begins his sign theology: "Jesus did this as the beginning of his signs" (v. 11). The question, as always in John, is: What does the sign mean? In this instance the meaning is multiple, but it is centered on one basic point: the arrival through Jesus of the new messianic age. What is changed in this incident is not simply water, but water for Old Testament ceremonial washings. It is changed not simply into wine, but into wine of highest quality and of surprising quantity (six jars, each holding fifteen to twenty-five gallons). Such a superabundance of wine was a frequent prophetic figure of speech for the dawning of the messianic age (Amos 9:13-14; Joel 3:18). The symbol was current also at the time of Jesus, as we read in the almost contemporary 2 Baruch 29: ". . . on each vine there shall be a thousand branches, and each branch shall bear a thousand clusters, and each cluster produce a thousand grapes, and each grape produce a cor [about 120 gallons] of wine . . . because these are they who have come to the consummation of time."

Changing Old Testament water into messianic wine, consequently, signifies, or signs, for John the passing of the old into the new. The messianic era has arrived. The feast symbolizes the messianic banquet. And the messianic bridegroom, he who supplies the wine, is Jesus himself (3:29). The allusion to the hour of Jesus' death in verse 4 may even mean that John wants his audience to think also of *the* messianic wine that will be the result and Eucharistic sacrament of Jesus' death.

Verse 4, "Woman, how does your concern affect me? My hour has not yet come," is extremely difficult to explain. Cancel the verse out and the story flows with ease. Leave it in, as the text itself demands, and we have the mother asking, Jesus responding negatively, yet the sign-miracle taking place. Leave it in, and we must ask: Why does Jesus call his mother "Woman"? Why is his verbal response negative but his action positive? Of what "hour" does Jesus speak? Explanations of all this are multiple and extremely divergent. One of the most probable is that verse 4 was not in the original pre-Gospel account, which presented a straightforward story of the incident in which the mother's request was answered by the son's positive response. The evangelist, however, who wished to use the story for his theme of new beginnings, inserted verse 4 to affirm, as do the other Gospels, that during Jesus' public life, until his hour came, his work was determined solely by the Father's will. It is this which is stated by the negative tone of the response and by the use of the impersonal "Woman."

John has also used this story to initiate his theology of glory. ". . . and so revealed his glory" (v. 11). This is the beginning of a magnificent Johannine conception of glory as being *God's manifested presence.* God glorifies us when he manifests himself in us; we glorify him when we manifest him to the world. In this instance at Cana, God's presence is manifested in his Son, his Revealer.

2. The temple purification (2:13-25). This is another newness or transformation story. The temple itself will be replaced. Destroyed in A.D. 70 by the soldiers of Titus' Roman army, its place as the center of worship and sacrifice, the site of God's presence and the visible symbol of his fidelity, will be taken by the risen body of Christ. The physical destruction of the temple was a spirit-crushing disaster for Israel. The loss was softened for Jewish Christians by this Johannine theology of the Christ-temple, which, indeed, Paul had already expanded into a doctrine of the Christian-temple (1 Cor 6:19).

This physical purification of the temple might remind us of the type of symbolic deeds acted out by the prophets; and, indeed, Jesus' approach to the temple on this occasion resembles that of Jeremiah (Jer 7). The action, though not a miracle, is a sign, a double sign. The temple, soon to be destroyed, stood in need of purification. And its function would be replaced by the risen body of Christ.

Jesus goes up to Jerusalem at Passover time

(v. 13) at the beginning of his ministry. This stands in contrast to the other Gospels, in which Jesus goes to Jerusalem but once, and then at the very end of his ministry. With regard to multiple visits, John is probably more correct historically. Our author has considerably more interest in Jerusalem than the other evangelists, an indication that his roots are more oriented in Jerusalem than in Galilee. The temple purification, however, probably occurred toward the end of Jesus' life, as the Synoptists (Matthew, Mark, Luke) indicate, serving as a final straw leading to Jesus' condemnation. John may well have transferred the story to this initial phase in Jesus' life because it fits so well into his "newness" theme and because he intends that Lazarus' resurrection (ch. 11) be the incident leading to the crucifixion (11:53; 12:10).

The mention of "forty-six years" in verse 20 is one of the clearest chronological indications given in the Gospels (see Luke 3:1 for another). This temple, which was finished in the early sixties, was begun by Herod in 20–19 B.C.E. The addition of John's forty-six years would date this scene to about A.D. 28.

Finally, there are four Johannine peculiarities that make their first appearance in this incident:

a) "The Jews" appear (v. 18) as the primary antagonists of Jesus. Certainly Jesus the Jew and his Jewish disciples had their share of difficulties with their Jewish contemporaries; but the marked distinction between Jesus and Jews must echo the later and sharper antagonism between Jews and Christians during the period of John's own community.

b) We find in verses 19-21 the first appearance of a dramatic technique by which the author makes his point through a progression from ambiguity to misunderstanding to comprehension. The ambiguity of verse 19 leads to the misunderstanding of verse 20 and to the final clarification of verse 21. This technique will occur frequently in the Gospel.

c) Verse 22 tells us that many of Jesus' words and acts were not understood during his lifetime but became intelligible only through the light of his resurrection. It is from this perspective that our evangelist writes.

d) Finally, in verse 23, John speaks of the many who believed because they could see the signs Jesus performed. We must be cautious here. John is not speaking of a deep and viable faith in this and the following verses; he is speaking of the initial faith of those who simply see the signs. It is not those who see that become the true disciples but those who understand. In the incident that follows we shall see a man attracted by signs (3:2) but with little understanding of what they mean.

3. Nicodemus (3:1-36). As a further development of the theme of "newness," John brings Nicodemus onto the scene, but in the night darkness that symbolizes lack of faith-light. Nicodemus has been attracted by Jesus' signs, an attraction not to be despised, yet at a distance from true faith. He has a role to play in the drama, for he is both a Jewish leader (v. 1) and a teacher of Israel (v. 10), a representative of so many interested Jews over the decades after Christ who have shown initial interest in Jesus. A dialogue ensues, animated once more by ambiguity and misunderstanding. Entrance into the "kingdom" (this expression is limited to vv. 3-5 in John, who prefers rather to speak of "life" or "eternal life") depends on being reborn through water and Spirit. Verse 3 speaks of birth "from above." The original Greek at this point can mean either "from above" or "again." John is quite capable of meaning both, though his future statement in verse 31 should incline us to put the greater emphasis on "from above." The "wind" of verse 8 might seem to introduce a jarring notion, but the Greek for "wind" and "spirit" is the same, *pneuma;* and our text is saying that the origin and movement of both wind and spirit is a divine mystery.

What begins as a dialogue in verses 1-10 turns into a monologue in verses 11-12 as Nicodemus disappears momentarily into the darkness from which he came. (He will reappear in better light in 7:50-52 and for a courageous action of discipleship in 19:39-42.) This pattern of dialogue turning to monologue is frequent in the Fourth Gospel, where minor characters are at times introduced simply to help develop an important theme. The Greek original is interesting at this juncture as singulars change to plurals, and Jesus addresses not simply Nicodemus but a world of Nicodemuses as well as John's readers and hearers. Thus verses 11-12 read in Greek: "Amen, amen, I say to you (singular) . . . but you (plural) do not accept our testimony. If I tell you (plural) about earthly things and you (plural) do not believe, how will you (plural) believe if I tell you (plural) about heavenly things?"

Verse 14 contains both an allusion to an Old Testament incident and the introduction of important Johannine theology. The elevated serpent in the desert refers to a fairly confusing incident in Num 21:9 in which a bronze serpent raised on a pole by Moses was a source of salvation (Wis 16:6). To this reference John adds that the Son of Man, too, "must be lifted up." This phrasing will be repeated three more times (8:28; 12:32, 34), and its theology of crucifixion-exaltation will be clarified as the Gospel proceeds.

Extremely important for Johannine and Christian theology is the conviction that God's love (v. 16) is the dynamic principle for world salvation. Jesus' God, John's God, our God is a God motivated by love so great that he has gifted the world with his own Son, not to condemn but to save.

John uses the word "world" (v. 17) in different senses. Here its use is neutral. The whole of creation, and in particular its human inhabitants, is the object of God's saving love. More frequently, as we shall see, "the world" will become symbolic for those who refuse to believe. It is mainly of these that verses 18-21 speak. Though Jesus has come to save and not to condemn, human actions play their own part in determining salvation and condemnation. Salvation is belief in Jesus (v. 18) accompanied by deeds done in God (v. 21). Condemnation is a from-within process, consisting in non-belief in the light that is Jesus, accompanied by the evil works done in the darkness. The light-darkness opposition should remind us of the same theme in the prologue (1:4-5).

Verses 22-30 present the Baptist's final witness to Jesus. They constitute such an obvious break between the preceding verses and those that follow (vv. 31-36) that many scholars believe they are out of place here. This need not be. John may have wanted to reintroduce the Baptist here to clarify through baptismal references what was meant by "born of *water and Spirit*" in verse 5. This reintroduction is admittedly awkward, but it might well serve this purpose. John's baptism (the site of Aenon near Salim in verse 23 is uncertain) leads into Jesus' form of baptism, the type suggested by verse 5. John's last testimony is given in verses 27-30. Here, as in 1:19-36, the Baptist stresses Jesus' superiority. (This stressing may flow from the fact that John's own community had opposition from descendants of the Baptist's original followers who claimed that the Baptist, not Jesus, was the real Messiah.) "He must increase, while I must decrease," says the Baptist (v. 30). And with these apt words he disappears personally from the Gospel.

What follows in verses 31-36 seems to be a continuation of verse 21, interrupted by the paragraph concerning the Baptist. There is a sharp distinction in this Gospel between above and below, light and darkness, belief and unbelief—and all of this centers upon the person of Jesus who comes from above (v. 31) and testifies to what he has seen (v. 32) as the One whom God has sent (v. 34). To believe in Jesus is to accept the Father and the Father's love, to have and live eternal life. The content of the final verse, "Whoever believes in the Son has eternal life," both summarizes the whole of the chapter and ties the chapter's ending to identical statements in its centrally located verses 15-16. The "wrath of God" (v. 36) is the loss of life, the death and darkness that are willful unbelief.

4. The Samaritan woman (4:1-42). The evangelist has already presented us with various aspects of the "newness" that Jesus brings. It is the messianic wine of Cana, abundant and exquisite; the renovated temple of God; a rebirth in water and Spirit. In this next attempt to describe God's gift in Christ, John pictures it as *a spring of water,* life-giving, welling up into eternal life; as *a worship suitable to God who is Spirit,* a worship therefore in the Spirit of truth. He insists, moreover, that Jesus' food is the accomplishment of his Father's will. Part of that will is the missionary work in fields ripe for harvest.

This chapter is surely one of the most dramatically constructed in the Gospel. Divide it into its various speaking parts—(1) a narrator; (2) Jesus; (3) the Samaritan woman; (4) the disciples; (5) the townsfolk—and you have instant theater. Another element in the account that lends itself to dramatic presentation is the way the stage is cleared for dialogue with the woman by the disciples' departure (v. 8), and for dialogue with the disciples by the woman's exit (v. 28). Her jar, left behind in verse 28, acts like a stage prop to advise the audience that she will return. There is even dramatic progression in the faith-knowledge of the woman and her townsfolk. From simple knowledge that Jesus is a Jew (v. 9), the characters move to belief in him as prophet (v. 19), Christ (vv. 25-26, 29) and, finally, Savior of the world (v. 42).

The chapter, additionally, is excellently structured, focusing on the two central dialogues—the first with the woman, the second with the disciples. The structure is built like this:

Introduction (vv. 1-6), in which Jesus leaves Judea for Galilee to the north. Enroute he passes through Samaria, where, at Shechem, he rests at noon next to Jacob's well (still in useful existence today).

FIRST DIALOGUE (vv. 7-26), between Jesus and the Samaritan woman concerning:

a) *living water* (vv. 7-15). The water of Jacob's well is surpassed by the water that Jesus will give, "a spring of water welling up to eternal life" (v. 14).

Transition: Jesus' knowledge of the woman's past moves her toward faith: "Sir, I can see that you are a prophet" (v. 19).

b) *worship in Spirit and truth* (vv. 20-26). "Yet the hour is coming, and is now here, when true worshipers will worship the Father in Spirit and truth" (v. 23).

The woman begins to think in terms of the Messiah. Jesus states that it is he.

SECOND DIALOGUE (vv. 31-38), between Jesus and the disciples concerning:

a) *Jesus' food* (vv. 31-34). "To do the will of the one who sent me and to finish his work" (v. 34).

b) *the harvest* (vv. 35-38). "Look up and see the fields ripe for the harvest" (v. 35).

Conclusion (vv. 39-42). Belief of the Samaritans: ". . . we know that this is truly the savior of the world" (v. 42).

A few additional comments seem necessary to clarify even further the content of this moving chapter.

1. Jewish relationship with the Samaritans lodged between Galilee to the north and Judea to the south was bad, deep, and historically conditioned. About the year 722 B.C.E. the Assyrian army descended upon northern Israel with force, took its populace into an exile from which it never returned, and colonized its land with foreigners who partially adopted Israel's religion over the centuries but were always viewed by the Jews as hated, semi-pagan invaders. (2 Kgs 17:23-41 gives a brief summary of the story.) The woman, therefore, was justly surprised when the Jew Jesus spoke to her and indicated that he was even willing to drink from her water jar.

2. Jesus is described in very human terms in verse 6, sitting at the well, exhausted from his journey. John usually paints his portrait of Jesus in colors more definitely divine. The woman, too, is very human. Her appearance at the well about noon (v. 6), long after the village women would have replenished their water supply for the day, may indicate her isolated position in the town's society. Sexually immoral, she was left to herself and her merry-go-round retinue of men friends. Yet it is she who, rebounding from Jesus' healing words, becomes a missionary to her people. The Lord's word moves her from isolation to faith to mission.

3. The account, as happens frequently in John, may be telescoping different periods of time. It seems to reflect strongly the Church's post-resurrection mission to Samaria, such as is described in the work of Philip, Peter, and John in Acts 8:4-25. It may even be indicative of the life-story of John's community, which would then have included, and been influenced by, Samaritan converts. What I am proposing here is that John's literary technique has rather amazing depths and turns. He specializes in bi-level presentations. There are *theological bi-levels* when, as one out of many examples, the water changed into wine (ch. 2) really speaks of the old covenant giving way to the new. Both levels are present in the Cana story; both are intended by the author. And, in a way unexpected by us twentieth-century readers, there are also *historical bi-levels.* Events in Jesus' lifetime are interpenetrated by later events happening in the life of John's community. In this chapter, water symbolizes the eternal life given by the Spirit of truth, the theological bi-level. On the other hand, the encounter with the Samaritan woman is influenced by the later, post-resurrection outreach to the Samaritans, the historical bi-level.

4. Finally, it is important to note that the conversion of the Samaritans is effected, not

by any miraculous sign, but by *the force of Jesus' word:* "Many more began to believe in him because of his word. . . . We have *heard* for ourselves, and we know that this is truly the savior of the world" (vv. 41-42). It is to this theme of the life-giving word of Jesus that John will turn in the following episode.

4:43–5:47 Episode II: Jesus' Life-Giving Word

This second thematic episode consists of three sections:

1. narrative healing of the official's son;
2. narrative healing of the infirm man at the pool;
3. discourse.

All three will emphasize the life-giving quality of Jesus' word.

1. Healing of the official's son (4:43-54). This account is prefaced by verses 43-45, which tie this incident to the preceding. Verse 44, ". . . a prophet has no honor in his native place" is a bit strange. It is probably the author's way of saying that the people of Jesus' own Galilee were overenchanted by miracles, and that the only proper response to Jesus at this point will be offered by a pagan official.

The story itself is strikingly similar to the Capernaum cure reported in both Matt 8:5-13 and Luke 7:1-10, but with the kinds of differences expected as the story was passed along in oral form. The sign-meaning of this "long-distance cure" is very clear. It is uniquely Jesus' word—he does nothing but speak—that gives life to this child "near death" (v. 47). *That* Jesus spoke is noted three times (vv. 50, 53); *what* he spoke is also mentioned three times (vv. 50, 51, 53). That is the insistence. Jesus' word gives life—to those who believe (vv. 50, 53).

The evangelist has couched Jesus' words in verse 48 in the plural: "Unless you (plural) people see signs and wonders, you (plural) will not believe." In so doing, he makes Jesus speak, not mainly to the quite admirable official, but to men and women of John's own day and ours. Thus, though the evangelist is willing to mention the signs (and this is now the second of them, says verse 54) and, perhaps, even to use an existing collection of them in his Gospel (2:11; 4:54; 20:30), he does not overestimate their efficacy. They are important if their deeper meaning is understood. What is more important is to stand open and receptive to the life-giving power of Jesus' word.

2. Healing of the infirm man at the pool (5:1-18). This incident takes place in Jerusalem at a Jewish feast that John does not identify. What is important for him, and for us, is that it occurs on a sabbath (vv. 9-10, 16, 18). The pool has been located by modern archaeologists next to the Crusader Church of St. Anne. The excavations have shown that the pool was enclosed rectangularly by four porticoes, with a fifth running across the pool and dividing it into two sections. (John's knowledge of Jerusalem is good.)

Our text lacks a fourth verse, which speaks of an angel descending to move the water. This verse is missing in our oldest and best Greek manuscripts dating back to the second and fourth centuries, and was probably added by someone who wished to attribute the moving of the water in verse 7 to a direct heavenly intervention. The original text says simply that the water bubbled up on occasion and that healing power was attributed to it.

This sign-miracle follows the preceding one in rapid succession because it has the same theological bi-level, and John wants the two together to reinforce his teaching at this point. Again, it is Jesus' word—and only that—which gives life to a man whose body has been devitalized for thirty-eight years. And again, *what* Jesus spoke, "Take up your mat, and walk," is mentioned in almost identical terms three times (vv. 8, 11, 12).

One instructive yet sad part of the story is that the cured man, though he has directly seen and benefited from the sign, has not understood it. To him the sign has not revealed its meaning. He heads off to inform the adversaries that it was Jesus who had healed him and for whom they were looking (v. 15).

Verses 16-18 lead us from the narrative into the discourse, in which the theological meaning of the two cures will be spelled out in full. The early mention of the sabbath (v. 9) becomes important. To carry around a sleeping mat on the sabbath was contrary to the law. Yet Jesus authorized the action. In initial response to his critics (v. 17), Jesus compares himself to his Father. Since the Father works on the sabbath, as on all days, so can Jesus. This response is dangerous, since it places Jesus and the Father on a similar (equal?) plane. And so the dramatic plot thickens. Who is this Jesus who treats both God and the sabbath as his own family possessions?

Here again we are caught up, I believe, in a historical bi-level. The questions arising in verses 16-18 (sabbath rest and Jesus' divinity) are precisely those that John's own community faced in its dialogue with the Jews of its own neighborhood. Was Jesus really divine? What did the sabbath mean and enjoin for Christian Jews? The following discourse will treat the specific question of Jesus' relationship to his Father at greater depth.

3. The discourse (5:19-47). The main reason for considering units 1–3, the two cures and this discourse, as one literary unit is that all sections sound the one theme: the life-giving power of Jesus' word. He has just healed the official's son by saying, "You may go; your son will live" (4:50), and the infirm man with the words, "Take up your mat, and walk" (5:8). And now the discourse will underscore the theological depth of this same truth. Note how the words of Jesus keep coming back to this teaching:

> "For just as the Father raises the dead and gives life, so also does *the Son give life* to whomever he wishes" (v. 21).
>
> "Amen, amen, I say to you, whoever *hears my word* and believes in the one who sent me *has eternal life. . . . and has passed from death to life*" (v. 24).
>
> "Amen, amen, I say to you, the hour is coming, and is now here, when the dead will *hear the voice of the Son of God,* and those who hear *will live.* For just as the Father has life in himself, so also he gave to his Son the possession of life in himself" (vv. 25-26).
>
> ". . . because the hour is coming in which all who are in the tombs [like Lazarus in chapter 11] *will hear his voice and will come out*" (vv. 28-29a).

What has happened in John's construction is that Jesus' right to work on the sabbath because his Father works has developed into a consideration of the relationship between Father and Son on a more elevated and more general level. Notwithstanding the Jewish commandment of sabbath rest, it was always recognized that God's two primary activities did not, and could not, cease on the sabbath: these were the divine acts of life-giving and of judgment. Both formed a constant part of God's life: babies were born and people did die on the sabbath. Our present discourse insists that what God does, the Son also does. The Father gives life, and so too does the Son, by his word. And a new point enters into consideration. As the Father judges, so too does the Son (vv. 22, 27, 30). In the Fourth Gospel, however, this judgment is not projected for the future. It occurs right now, depending on one's attitude toward Jesus. Whoever hears and accepts him receives eternal life and does not come under judgment (v. 24), since he or she thus hears and accepts the Father. Whoever responds negatively judges himself or herself by that very fact.

Now all of this—and one can justly imagine our author arguing the various points with his neighboring non-Christian Jews—leads to the impossible, incredible question: If this is all true, is not Jesus God, which, since the Father is certainly God, makes for two Gods? The language of the discourse becomes very circumspect at this point. Our author is certain of two facts—the divinity of Jesus and the oneness of God—which neither he nor the whole of Christian tradition has been able to reconcile completely, though believing in them ardently. The best John can do is to insist on the divinity of Jesus, while insisting equally on his dependence and obedience. And so here, as elsewhere when Jesus' divinity is stated, the discourse is also intent upon noting that "a Son cannot do anything on his own" (v. 19); that the Father shows the Son "everything that he himself does" (v. 20); that the Father "has given all judgment to the Son" (v. 22); that the Father "gave to his Son the possession of life in himself" and "gave him power to exercise judgment" (vv. 26-27). In a word, and a strong word it is, "I cannot do anything on my own" (v. 30). Our author's predicament is clear, and we too are involved in it. Jesus, divine as he is, is not the Father; and the Father is God. Little wonder that Jewish Christians of the first century had difficulty explaining Jesus to their fellow Jews.

The final section of the discourse details the various witnesses that testify to Jesus. Above all, there is the Father himself who renders testimony (vv. 31-32). And there is John the Baptist for those who have been impressed by him (vv. 33-36). Then there are the works that Jesus has done through his Father's power, works that are visible words revealing both Father and Son (vv. 36-37). Finally—and this argument is aimed peculiarly at the Jewish community—there are the words of Scripture and Moses himself that testify to Jesus (vv. 39-47). "If you had believed Moses, you would have believed me, because he wrote about me" (v. 46). In the episode that follows, we shall see an example of how this Old Testament scripture could be utilized to evolve and describe a further theological characteristic of Jesus: his power to nourish as the bread of life.

6:1-71 Episode III: Jesus as the Bread of Life

This chapter will center on the one theme of Jesus as the bread of life. It has four clear divisions: (1) the multiplication of the loaves; (2) walking on the water; (3) the discourse; and (4) an epilogue of reactions.

Before speaking at all of the loaves miracle, it might be well to notice what has often been presented as a real difficulty in the order of John's Gospel and a possible proof that somehow, in its earliest history, its pages got mixed up. At the end of chapter 4, Jesus is found in Galilee. In 5:1 he goes up to Jerusalem. But in 6:1 he is again in Galilee. Geographically this is strange, to say the least, so that some commentators have suggested that chapter 6 be placed before chapter 5. None of the Greek manuscripts has this suggested reordering, and there are many good reasons for keeping the present disposition, while realizing that John need not be nearly so much interested in historical-geographical order as in organizing themes. Chapter 6, I believe, belongs where it is as a demonstration of the statement in 5:46-47 that Moses and Scripture refer to Jesus. This, as we shall see, is precisely what the discourse in chapter 6 will expound. I believe, too, that the reference to the sick in 6:2 points *back* to the identical Greek phrasing in 5:3. Finally, leaving chapters 5 and 6 in their present order gives us a combination of word and bread, the essential elements and order of Christian Eucharist, a combination that need not have escaped John's attention.

1. The multiplication of the loaves (6:1-15). The Jewish Passover (v. 4) was an unleavened bread feast, so the reference prepares us for the bread miracle that is about to take place. *This miracle is the only one narrated by all four evangelists:* by Mark twice, in 6:31-44 and 8:1-10; by Matthew twice, in 14:13-21 and 15:32-38; by Luke in 9:10-17. It must be that the primitive Christian Eucharist made the prefiguring loaves miracle common property in all the Christian communities. And, indeed, what Jesus does with the bread sounds like the rubrics for what the Christian minister continually did in the celebration of the Eucharist. In the accounts of Mark, Matthew, and Luke, Jesus *took* the bread and *blessed* and *broke* and *gave.* So would the Christian minister. John's description is equally ceremonial, but with one even more Christian peculiarity. In 6:11, Jesus took, *gave thanks,* and distributed. The Greek for "give thanks" is *eucharisteō,* which gives us our word for Christian Eucharist. It occurs again in 6:23. This same Eucharistic overtone is heard again in verses 12-13, where the fish have disappeared from the discussion, which speaks exclusively of the bread and the care to be taken of the remaining fragments. The ultimate *sign* (v. 14) of this miracle points to Jesus as the bread of life, particularly in the Eucharist.

The reaction in verse 14, "This is truly the Prophet, the one who is to come into the world," refers again (as in 1:21, 24) to the prophet like Moses (Deut 18:15, 18) who was expected in the final days. Jesus has just fed the people with bread; Moses did the same with the desert manna.

One final note of interest is that the two disciples who function in this manifestation of Jesus to the crowd are Philip and Andrew, the same two who in 1:41, 45 acted as apostles to Nathaniel and Simon Peter, and who will later be apostles to the Greeks (12:20-22). Their role in the Fourth Gospel is to reach out.

2. Walking on the water (6:16-24). It is striking that John's sequence—the loaves miracle followed by that on the Sea of Galilee—is identical to that of Mark 6:34-51 and Matthew 14:13-33. The tradition of this ordering must be very old. In all three accounts Jesus calms his disciples with the identical majestic phrase: "It is I. Do not be afraid" (John 6:20; Mark 6:50; Matt 14:27). As we shall see later, this phrasing, which in the Greek has no predicate and simply reads *egō* *eimi* = *I am*, has strong overtones of divinity, echoing the name for Yahweh found in Isa 43:10, 13, 25. Jesus is the divine presence; the disciples need have no fear.

There is a question as to why the water miracle should be situated at this point in a chapter that otherwise speaks exclusively of bread. What is it a sign of? No answer is completely satisfactory, but the following have been offered. (a) The Old Testament Passover miracles were manna bread plus the crossing of the Reed Sea, and water springing from the rock. Exod 14–16 ties together in tight sequence the account of the Reed Sea crossing and the gift of the desert manna. This traditional Exodus coupling of water and bread, found also in Ps 78:13-25, may have encouraged the first Jewish Christians to attach the Christian water-sign to that of the bread. They are so found in Mark 6, Matt 14, and now in John 6. (b) John is simply extending his theme of life-giving word by presenting Jesus as life-giver in time of famine and of storm. (c) The storm scene is intended as a sign of Jesus' divine status (the "It is I" of verse 19 masks the profound I AM of the original Greek) and his ever-helping presence, "do not be afraid" (v. 20).

The account closes (vv. 21-24) with the boat suddenly coming to land (this is seemingly miraculous too) and the crowd, or part of it, transferring itself to Capernaum to find Jesus. This will provide the audience for the discourse that now follows.

3. The discourse (6:26-59). The best way to understand this discourse is to recognize that it is a homily based on Jesus' teaching but elaborated extensively by a Christian preacher aided by Jesus' Spirit. In this sense, the whole discourse comes from the Lord. It centers on one biblical text, "He gave them bread from heaven to eat" (v. 31), and is therefore a conscious demonstration of the truth of 5:39, 46-47 that the Scriptures elucidate the person of Jesus. The pivotal text is a loose, by-memory combination of several possible Old Testament quotations:

Exod 16:4: "I will now rain down *bread from heaven* for you";

Neh 9:15: *"Food from heaven you gave* them in their hunger";

Ps 78:24: "He rained manna upon them for food and *gave* them *heavenly bread*";

Ps 105:40: ". . . and with *bread from heaven* he satisfied them."

All or some of these associated texts have been combined by the preacher into the one amalgam of verse 31. The homily is broken by the short interruptions of verses 30-31, 34, 41-43, 52, which, by introducing live dialogue, help to keep the audience's interest while at the same time pointing out the precise difficulties felt by both the Jews of Jesus' time and of John's own later period.

This homily on a biblical text—what the Jews would call a *midrash*—follows a phrase-by-phrase order. It will treat in order: *He gave; bread from heaven; to eat.* Let's observe this happen.

a) *He gave* (vv. 26-34). In this first section, the emphasis lies on the giving. Jesus will give (vv. 27, 34), not as Moses gave (v. 32) a perishable manna food of mortality, but as the Father, source of eternal life, gives (v. 32). Thus far, Jesus appears as the giver of bread and therefore as the new and superior Moses.

b) *Bread from heaven* (vv. 35-47). The insistence now shifts to the bread from heaven that Jesus not only gives but actually is (vv. 35, 38, 41, 42). It is important to note here that the operative verb is "believe." Jesus as bread from heaven is accepted and consumed through the belief required in verses 35, 36, 40, 47. What this means is that this is a faith nourishment. Jesus is bread from heaven, feeding all believers, in the same sense that Old Testament wisdom nourished all who accepted it (Prov 9:1-5). We might call this type of feeding "sapiential."

c) *To eat* (vv. 48-59). In this final section, the vocabulary changes radically. The significant words are "flesh," "blood," "*eat*," "drink." Note the constant repetition of "eat" in verses 49, 50, 51, 52, 53, 54, 58. "Feed on" (an even more physical verb in the Greek than "eat") occurs in v. 57 of this translation. These verbs become overwhelmingly insistent, as does the constant reference to flesh and blood, food and drink. The meaning of the discourse has changed. Where in the preceding section Jesus nourished through wisdom-revelation those who believed, the verb "believe" has now completely disappeared and is replaced by "eat," "feed on." Our homilist is clearly speaking now of *sacramental* nourishment, of the food and drink that one eats and feeds upon, of the Eucharistic nourishment provided by the flesh and blood of the Son of Man (v. 53). The "Son of Man" phraseology tells us that this is not the physical flesh and blood of the earthly Jesus and that we are asked to eat and drink but the spiritual, Spirit-filled flesh and blood of the heavenly Son of Man. Verse 58 ties the homily together by referring back to the central phrase of verse 31.

What this homily has done, therefore, is to deliver a rich and multi-faceted exposition of the Jesus-as-Bread-of-Life theme. Jesus is first of all the *giver* of the bread, a new Moses. He is also the *bread of wisdom and revelation* who nourishes all who come to him in faith. He is, finally, the *Eucharistic* source of eternal life for all who eat and drink the flesh and blood of the heavenly and glorified Son of Man. Because John uses this Eucharistic material in this Bread of Life homily, it will not be too surprising—yet surprising enough—that the Eucharist will not be mentioned at the Last Supper. Its material has been transferred to this incident. John has also succeeded, with this transfer, to unite in this one chapter the essentials of Christian Eucharist, the word and the bread—the revealing word of verses 35-47 and the sacramental bread of verses 48-59.

4. Epilogue of various reactions (6:60-71). These final verses resume the murmuring criticisms of verses 41-43, 52 to describe a mounting crisis of faith for Jesus' disciples. "This saying is hard; who can accept it?" (v. 60). At this point in the text, our historical bi-levels (Jesus' time and John's later period) reappear. If these verses refer to Jesus' Galilean ministry, in which he hardly would have spoken of the Last Supper Eucharist, the critical reactions refer solely to the material of verses 26-47, and are a negative response to his presentation of himself as object of faith, as bread-wisdom giving life to those who believe in him. But the passage as a whole certainly reflects also the crisis (present for all Christian centuries) of John's own community, the difficulty involved in accepting Jesus as the sacramental bread of life. To this difficulty will be added the scandal of the ascent of the Son of Man "to where he was before" (v. 62). The first step of that ascent will be Jesus' elevation onto a cross on top of a hill.

The chapter concludes (vv. 66-71) with a presentation of two models. Peter is one. He takes the risk, opening himself to the Word whose revealing words give eternal life. "Master, to whom shall we go? You have the words of eternal life. We have come to believe and we are convinced that you are the Holy One of God" (vv. 68-69). The other model is Judas. He will remain in the group, living a divided existence, but already moving into darkness and into the demonic power which that darkness symbolizes (13:26-30). His appearance here as future betrayer (v. 71) lends further proof to the belief that John is using Last Supper material in this latter part of the discourse to complete his total presentation of Jesus as the bread of life for the Christian community.

One final observation before leaving this rich chapter: verses 67, 70-71 speak of "the Twelve." Only here and in 20:24 (Thomas) does John use this terminology. He speaks, rather, and so very often, of "the disciples," his favorite description of Jesus' followers. John leans much more toward the equality of discipleship than the grading of hierarchy.

7:1-8:59 Episode IV: Identity Crisis

These two chapters, in which Jesus is both manifested and rejected as the prophet, Christ, the unique Son of the Father, and the divine I AM (*egō eimi*) are among the most difficult to synthesize in the Gospel. There is such an overwhelming richness of movement and content that the chapters are strongly resistant to external ordering by a commentator. Yet, elements of structural and theological order can be found.

1. Introduction (7:1-14). (a) The background of these chapters is the Jewish feast of Booths (or Tents or Tabernacles)—*Sukkoth* in Hebrew—an annual autumn feast of thanksgiving for the yearly harvest and for the historic Exodus miracles of the water and pillar of fire. The feast, similar to our Thanksgiving, was the most joyous and popular of the Jewish calendar; and during it the celebrants lived in branched huts reminiscent of those used during the harvest time and the desert wandering.

Two distinctive features of this week-long ceremony in September–October have made an impression on the text. Water was brought daily from the pool of Siloam to the temple, where it was poured over the altar as prayers were recited for the all-important winter rain. And the lights in the women's court flamed so brightly that the city was lit up by them. Water and light play a fairly important part in these two chapters.

b) The brothers (7:3-10) fare poorly in this episode. They see and cannot deny the works that Jesus is doing; yet their suggestion that Jesus should go public in Jerusalem, the heart and capital of the country, is banal and incorrect. Verse 5 reads literally: "neither did his brothers believe in him." This agrees with the picture of Jesus' family given in Mark 3:21, 31-35; 6:4. Happily, the brothers do form part of the post-resurrection church in Acts 1:14. They, too, had to struggle through failure into the Christian faith.

c) In general, chapters 7 and 8 report a hectic clash of dialogues and controversies as the Gospel turns toward the passion. Deep within the rapid disagreements lie the theological disputes that brought Jesus to the cross and, years later, forced John's community out of the synagogue.

d) The two chapters are linked together by their content, which repeats again and again the issues under discussion, and also by what is commonly called "literary inclusion," a statement toward the beginning that will be balanced, like two bookends, by a similar expression at the end. In this instance, the "in secret" (vv. 4, 10)—*en kryptō* in the original Greek text—is counterbalanced by the use of the same Greek root *ekrybē*, "hid," in 8:59. These bookends show that the author intends that these two chapters form a unit.

2. Parallel structure of 7:14-53. It is clear that this long section has been arranged into direct parallels, with the initial division of 7:14-36 neatly balanced by its equivalent in 7:37-52. At issue are the initial questions as to whether Jesus is the Christ and the prophet of Deut 18:15, 18.

a) *Jesus' teaching* (7:14-24). His doctrine is not his own but comes from God who sent him. Jesus speaks this doctrine faithfully. They, on the contrary, do not keep the law of Moses, which they profess. Why is it that they can circumcise on the sabbath but become so irate when Jesus cures a man on the sabbath? (5:1-10).

a') *Jesus' teaching* (7:37-39). On the last day of the week-long feast, Jesus invites all who thirst to come to him. Either from Jesus himself (the Greek text here is uncertain) or from those who believe in him will flow the rivers of living water, the Spirit. But the Spirit has not yet been given, nor will be given, until Jesus is glorified through the cross and resurrection.

b) *Discussion about Jesus* (7:25-31). The question here is whether or not Jesus is the Messiah (vv. 26-27, 31).

b') *Discussion about Jesus* (7:40-44). The discussion continues as to whether Jesus is the Messiah (vv. 41-42) and expands to ask whether he is the Prophet of Deut 18:15, 18. (John's admittance that the Messiah should be born in Bethlehem [v. 42] is strong proof that he himself believed that Jesus was born there.)

c) *Temple officers* (7:32-36) are sent by the chief priests and Pharisees to arrest Jesus. He responds that he will be with them for just a little while. Will he go to the Diaspora (v. 35), to the lands outside of Palestine to which, in fact, Christianity spread after Jesus' death?

c') *Temple officers* (7:45-52) report back to the priests and Pharisees that Jesus speaks as did no one previously, but their report is treated with authoritarian scorn. Nicodemus, passing from the night of 3:2 into considerably more light, defends Jesus, but to no avail.

3. Intense disputes (8:12-59). The clear and simple paralleling in the previous chapter disappears with our present material, in which there is a steady alternating of statements and responses on the part of Jesus and his opponents—the chief priests and Pharisees from verses 13-19, and the Jews from verses 22-57. The ball passes from one side to the other, with only occasional editorial comments (vv. 20, 27, 30, 59) to slow up the game. Whereas chapter 7 disputed the titles of "Messiah" and "the Prophet" as applicable to Jesus, chapter 8 discusses with passion two different issues. What is Jesus' relationship to the Father? Is it something so completely different, so unique, that God is his Father in a way that God is Father to no other human being? This controversy ranges through the whole of the chapter. Read for a moment 8:16, 18, 19, 26-27, 28-29, 38, 42, 49, 54. The issue refuses to stay down or go away. The negative side to it is that if Jesus is the unique Son of God, what do they become who refuse to believe in him? They themselves plead that Abraham is their father (vv. 33, 39) and that through him they are related to God. Jesus' answer is that, though they are from Abraham's stock (v. 37), they actually deny their family origin by refusing to do what Abraham did—*believe.* They turn thereby from the truth to be believed over to its opposite, a lie engendered by the devil (v. 44). If actions indicate parentage, theirs show the devil as their source, their father.

As if this issue were not powerful enough, another raises its head, and this an even more dangerous and troublesome one. Into the chapter comes the majestic designation of the divinity—the awesome, powerful I AM, the *egō eimi.* Used all alone, with neither noun nor adjective to accompany it, as it would be in "I am the good *shepherd*"; "I am *meek* and *humble,*" it echoes the divine name found in Isa 41:4; 43:10, 13, 25; 48:12.

In this chapter the form I AM appears three times, in ever increasing clarity:

> 8:24: "For if you do not believe that I AM, you will die in your sins."
>
> 8:28: "When you lift up the Son of Man, you will realize that I AM . . . ."

If these two texts leave some slight doubt about the divine content of the phrase, the final incidence does not:

> 8:58: "Amen, amen, I say to you, before Abraham came to be, I AM."

Little wonder that "they picked up stones to throw at him, but Jesus hid and went out of the temple area" (8:59).

4. Theological questions and their historical bi-levels. This brief study of chapters 7 and 8 brings to the surface four questions regarding Jesus that were the object of intense and emotional controversy, first during Jesus' lifetime and later during the life of John's Christian community. During the time of Jesus—and later as well, but beginning with Jesus himself—there began the discussion as to whether he was indeed the awaited (a) *Messiah, the Christ,* as also (b) the *prophet like Moses* of whom Deut 18:15, 18 had written. It is this Jesus-level dispute that is apparent in chapter 7—but not in chapter 8. In this latter chapter the questions change, a sign probably that its contents are chronologically later than those of chapter 7. Now the controversy heats up as the issues become even more important. Was, and is, Jesus the (c) *completely unique Son of the Father,* with a relationship so close that he and the Father become identical in will and work and word? Pushing this a step further, can and should Jesus be referred to as (d) *the divine I AM?* Is he God? These two—unique Son and I AM—are the awesome issues of chapter 8 (not of chapter 7). These are also questions, I believe, that originated only after the resurrection of Jesus—questions, then, of John's later community, whose affirmative answers put it in direct and powerful opposition to the Jewish synagogue, within which it had originated.

5. Further comments. This treatment of chapters 7 and 8 is already lengthy, but a few more comments seem required.

a) The reader may have noticed how often Jesus calls himself the one "sent"—sent by the Father, from above, from heaven. Just checking through chapters 7 and 8 brings to evidence ten occurrences: 7:16, 18, 28, 29, 33; 8:16, 18, 26, 29, 42. This word, while implying Jesus' divine origin, also indicates his obedience and subservience to the Father. It will assume a subtle importance in the following chapter.

b) ". . . no one laid a hand upon him for *his hour* had not yet come" (7:30). Jesus' "hour" in John is a very specific period of time. At Cana (2:4), as here in 7:30, Jesus' hour is still in the future. We find in 7:39 that the Spirit had not yet been given, "because Jesus had not yet been glorified." The notions all coalesce. The Spirit will be given when Jesus' hour arrives, which is the hour of his glorification, of his elevation. In an instance of Johannine punning, this hour of glorification-elevation begins with the elevation onto a cross. At that precise moment, as the Son of Man is lifted up, will the divine I AM be manifested (8:27).

c) We have noted that the special adversaries of Jesus in 8:22-59 are "the Jews." It is very important for Christians reading, teaching, or especially preaching from the Fourth Gospel to realize that it can be used to promote anti-Semitism—and we all have had far too much of that over the centuries and particularly in our own. There are two points to be made here. One is that "the Jews" can be contrasted in our Gospel to a whole other segment of the population that is equally Jewish.

Take, for example, 7:13: "Still no one spoke openly about him, because they were afraid of *the Jews.*" In this context, all the "no ones" are Jewish people. Who, then, are "the Jews"? As adversaries of Jesus and as contrasted to the people of Jerusalem (7:25-26), they seem to be clearly identified with the Pharisees of 7:32, 47; with the chief priests and Pharisees of 7:45; and with the Sanhedrin and Pharisees of 7:48. Yet even here there are exceptions, as we see in the person of Nicodemus (7:50-51). In John, consequently, the unfortunate title "the Jews" represents the authorities, yet not all of them, who by choice and office opposed Jesus and his teaching. This would be but a small fraction of Jews in Jerusalem, to say nothing at all of the far greater majority of Jews living away from the capital city.

The second point is that by the time John is writing this Gospel, a change has occurred. Christians have come into existence. The majority would now be Gentile, but even Jewish Christians will have assumed their own Christian identity and been separated from their previous Jewish society. Contact between Jewish Christians and non-Christians has moved from tolerance to discussion to controversy to angry separation and excommunication. In this sorry evolution, the term "the Jews," which in Jesus' day represented just a small body of in-family adversaries, can be used to represent the Jews as a whole, resistant to Christian belief. This was a pitiable development, perhaps inevitable; but the ill feelings of John's time will be thoroughly immoral if perpetuated in our own century. The long and heavy legacy of hate and murder that has piled up over the centuries must be attacked with a peculiarly Johannine weapon —that of love.

d) Critical readers will have already noticed that nothing has been said thus far about 8:1-11, the account of the woman taken in adultery. In modern editions of the Fourth Gospel, this passage is ordinarily either dropped into the footnotes or placed within brackets to indicate that it is not part of John's original text. It is missing from our oldest and best Greek manuscripts and seems to have been unknown to the early Greek Fathers, since they did not comment on it. In various old manuscripts it is found either at 8:1, as in our text, or after 7:36, or at the end of the Gospel, or after Luke 21:38. The earliest certain reference to the story is found in a third-century writing on church discipline called the *Didascalia.* In a word, it did not form part of the original Gospel of John.

Notwithstanding the mystery of the story's transmission, and of its insertion into John (because of 8:15?), it contains one of the most striking portrayals of Jesus' mercy and is a strong plea for its own authenticity. It possesses all the signs of historical truth. It must be a story dating back to Jesus that was passed along by oral tradition and used, perhaps, to solve the problem of forgiveness of sin for baptized Christians. It sounds incredibly like a Lukan narrative, dealing as it does with mercy, sin, and a woman.

One of the questions always asked about this beautiful passage is what Jesus was writing on the ground. Two reasonably plausible suggestions are that the doodling indicated lack of interest or that John wished to refer to the Greek text of Jer 17:13: ". . . may those who turn away from thee *be written on the earth,* for they have forsaken the fountain of life, the Lord."

e) The light and water aspects of the Jewish feast of Booths manifest themselves in the significant reference to the living water of the Spirit in 7:37–39, and to Jesus as light of the world in 8:12. It is to that last notion that John will turn his attention in the following chapter.

9:1–10:42 Episode V: Light of the World, Sight and Blindness

This fifth episode focuses on light, on Jesus as the light of the world (prepared for in 8:12), which light can bring sight to those previously blind as well as blindness to those who, confident in their own sight, turn away from the light. The episode does not stop with chapter 9 but continues on into and through chapter 10. It includes three sections: the man born blind (ch. 9); the good shepherd (10:1-21); the feast of Hanukkah (10:22-42). The sections are linked together. Verse 10:21 connects the good shepherd segment to the man born blind, and 10:26-28 connects the Hanukkah segment to that of the good shepherd.

1. The man born blind (9:1-41). We have spoken already of dramatic elements in John: of the technique of ambiguity, misunderstanding, clarification; of dramatic progression of knowledge in the case of the Samaritan woman; of characters, historical though they be, who also have dramatic roles to play, like the "missionary figures" of Andrew and Philip. Chapter 9 is undoubtedly the most dramatic of John's Gospel, and we would like to demonstrate this to an extent by laying it out, word for word from the text, but with the verses divided among various readers as it might be on the stage. Pass out the parts, and *voilà*, instant theater!

[SCENE 1]

Disciples: [1]As he passed by he saw a man blind from birth. [2]His disciples asked him, "Rabbi, who sinned, this man or his parents, that he was born blind?"

Jesus: [3]Jesus answered, "Neither he nor his parents sinned; it is so that the works of God might be made visible through him. [4]We have to do the works of the one who sent me while it is day. Night is coming when no one can work. [5]While I am in the world, I am the light of the world."

[6]When he had said this, he spat on the ground and made clay with the saliva, and smeared the clay on his eyes, [7]and said to him, "Go wash in the Pool of Siloam" (which means Sent).

Blind Man: So he went and washed, and came back able to see.

[SCENE 2]

Neighbor 1: [8]His neighbors and those who had seen him earlier as a beggar said, "Isn't this the one who used to sit and beg?"

Neighbor 2: [9]Some said, "It is,"

Neighbor 3: but others said, "No, he just looks like him."

Blind Man: He said, "I am."

Neighbor 1: [10]So they said to him,

Neighbors 1-2-3: "[So] how were your eyes opened?"

Blind Man: [11]He replied, "The man called Jesus made clay and anointed my eyes and told me, 'Go to Siloam and wash.' So I went there and washed and was able to see."

Neighbors 1-2-3: [12]And they said to him,

Neighbor 1: "Where is he?"

Blind Man: He said, "I don't know."

[SCENE 3]

Pharisee 1: [13]They brought the one who was once blind to the Pharisees. [14]Now Jesus had made clay and opened his eyes on a sabbath. [15]So then the Pharisees also asked him how he was able to see.

Blind Man: He said to them, "He put clay on my eyes and I washed, and now I can see."

Pharisee 2: [16]So some of the Pharisees said, "This man is not from God, because he does not keep the sabbath."

Pharisee 3: [But] others said, "How can a sinful man do such signs?"

Pharisee 1: And there was a division among them. [17]So they said to the blind man again,

Pharisees 1-2-3: "What do you have to say about him, since he opened your eyes?"

Blind Man: He said, "He is a prophet."

[SCENE 4]

Authorities 1: [18]Now the Jews did not believe that he had been blind and gained his sight until they summoned the parents of the one who had gained his sight.

Authorities 2: [19]They asked them, "Is this your son, who you say was born blind? How does he now see?"

Parent 1: [20]His parents answered and said,

Parent 2: "We know that this is our son and that he was born blind. [21]We do not know how he sees now, nor do we know who opened his eyes. Ask him, he is of age; he can speak for himself."

Parent 1: [22]His parents said this because they were afraid of the Jews, for the Jews had already agreed that if anyone acknowledged him as the Messiah, he would be expelled from the synagogue. [23]For this reason his parents said,

Parent 2: "He is of age; question him."

[SCENE 5]

Authorities 1: [24]So a second time they called the man who had been blind and said to him, "Give God the praise! We know that this man is a sinner."

Blind Man: [25]He replied, "If he is a sinner, I do not know. One thing I do know is that I was blind and now I see."

Authorities 2: [26]So they said to him, "What did he do to you? How did he open your eyes?"

Blind Man: [27]He answered them, "I told you already and you did not listen. Why do you want to hear it again? Do you want to become his disciples, too?"

Authorities 3: [28]They ridiculed him and said,"You are that man's disciple; we are disciples of Moses! [29]We know that God spoke to Moses, but we do not know where this one is from."

Blind Man: [30]The man answered and said to them, "This is what is so amazing, that you do not know where he is from, yet he opened my eyes. [31]We know that God does not listen to sinners, but if one is devout and does his will, he listens to him. [32]It is unheard of that anyone ever opened the eyes of a person born blind. [33]If this man were not from God, he would not be able to do anything."

Authorities 1: [34]They answered and said to him,

Authorities 2: "You were born totally in sin, and are you trying to teach us?"

Authorities 1-2-3: Then they threw him out.

[SCENE 6]

Jesus: [35]When Jesus heard that they had thrown him out, he found him and said, "Do you believe in the Son of Man?"

Blind Man: [36]He answered and said, "Who is he, sir, that I may believe in him?"

Jesus: [37]Jesus said to him, "You have seen him and the one speaking with you is he."

Blind Man: [38]He said,"I do believe, Lord," and he worshiped him.

Jesus: [39]Then Jesus said: "I came into this world for judgment, so that those who do not see might see, and those who do see might become blind."

Pharisee 1: [40]Some of the Pharisees who were with him heard this and said to him,

Pharisees 1-2-3: "Surely we are not also blind, are we?"

Jesus: [41]Jesus said to them, "If you were blind, you would have no sin; but now you are saying, 'We see,' so your sin remains."

The preceding lay-out makes the dramatic pattern of the chapter clear. There are six logically successive scenes; brilliant dialogue; characters that are, in turn, merciful, confused, strong, bullying, weak, and self-interested. Playing the major role—even upstaging Jesus—is the intriguing figure of the blind man, courageous and intelligent, counterpunching with success every blow thrown his way. And the play closes with a fine line (v. 41) that gives the gist of the whole story.

The account demands little or no explanation of small details. What is all-important is to capture the deep, underlying truths that our evangelical dramatist has written into it.

a) The story has undoubtedly been used for baptismal instruction. The reader will have noted the happy coincidence of the *blind* man *washing* in a *pool* called *Siloam*, which means *sent*. Having already noted (Episode IV, 5 [a]) that "sent" is a veritable nickname for Jesus in the Fourth Gospel, we can be certain that John is writing of the physical cure in such a way that it reflects and calls to mind the cure of spiritual blindness—from birth—granted to those who wash sacramentally in the pool that is truly Jesus, the "sent one." (It is not hard to imagine that the effect of baptism was explained to catechumens as the immersion in Christ that would provide the insight of reality to which they had been blind from birth.)

Speaking in the same vein, the blind man's progressive enlightenment parallels the progress in knowledge that the catechumens would have followed as they were instructed in the faith. From first knowledge of the fact that there was a man called Jesus (v. 11), they would have advanced to deeper insights into his character as prophet (v. 17), as man from God (v. 33), as the heavenly Son of Man (v. 35), culminating in the final act of worship of Jesus as Lord (v. 38). This progression reflects not only the steps of the catechumen toward complete faith but also an enlivening dramatic technique on the part of the evangelist.

b) The passage is rich in irony, another dramatic touch. The reality of things is just the opposite of what it seems to be. Those who are sure they can see are, in truth, blind, and are so by their own choosing (vv. 40-41). He who starts out blind takes a risk at Jesus' invitation (v. 6) and ends up seeing. He passes from blindness to sight to insight. He is a striking example of the deep theology of which his cure is a *sign*. Jesus is indeed the LIGHT OF THE WORLD (v. 5). The sad foils to this man cured of both blindness and ignorance are the neighbors, who remain in ignorance (vv. 8-12); the parents, who refuse to take a risk—"He is of age; question him" (v. 23); the Pharisees, who cannot make up their collective minds (vv. 13-17); and the authorities and Pharisees, who refuse to believe what their eyes see (vv. 24, 40). No one is so blind as the person who refuses to see. "If you were blind, you would have no sin; but now you are saying, 'We see,' so your sin remains" (v. 41).

c) We find in this chapter the most outstanding example in John of the use of historical bi-levels. The Jesus-level of the cure of the blind has been subtly interpenetrated by the later historical level of John's own community experience. The revealing element in this compenetration is the statement in verse 22 that "if anyone acknowledged him as the Messiah, he would be expelled from the synagogue." And, of course, the cured man was thrown out (v. 34). Such excommunication from the synagogue because of belief in Jesus was not a feature of Jesus' lifetime, nor even of Paul's, whose final trip to Jerusalem found him worshiping in the temple (Acts 21:26). But the relationship between Jewish Christians and the synagogue soured over the decades, and especially with the increasing Christian insight that Jesus was truly God, truly the I AM. Eventually the synagogue prayer was enlarged to include a curse of such heretics as the Christians. No Jewish Christian could, of course, share such a prayer, and that resulted effectively in the excommunication of Jewish Christians.

This whole Gospel, and chapter 9 in particular, reflects this historical crisis. John and his fellow Jewish Christians are angry. They have been thrown out (v. 34). Part of the reason for including this chapter in the Gospel was to strengthen those who had undergone this trauma. Expelled from synagogue, family, and friends as heretics, they were encouraged by this account to fall at the feet of the Lord to worship him (v. 38).

2. The good shepherd (10:1-21). The first question to tackle here is why this section is in this position. Why does it follow the story of the man born blind? There appears to be no connection between 9:41 and 10:1; rather, 10:1 introduces abruptly the shepherd theme, which is totally unexpected after the material of chapter 9. This difficulty has again led some scholars to move chapter 10 to another place in the Gospel. It is, they say, a displacement. Yet it need not be and probably is not. The reference to the cure of the blind in verse 21 ties this segment to the preceding chapter. More to the point, the discussion about the sheep and the shepherd is probably being used by John as a statement regarding the miserable shepherding being effected by such authorities as appear in the case of the man born blind. Blind guides themselves, they not only fail to recognize the leading light that is Jesus but cast out of the synagogue the one man who does accept the light. Verse 6 insists that they still just do not understand.

Crucial to the identification of the author's purpose at this point is the necessary realization that he is writing about Jesus with the text of Ezek 34 in clear view. In that passage, Ezekiel, speaking God's word, excoriates the authorities of his own time. They had become irresponsible and thieving shepherds, feeding themselves rather than their flock. So God would take away their maladministration and become the shepherd himself. Finally he would appoint another shepherd after the figure of David. John sees all of this coming true in Jesus. God has become the shepherd in Jesus, himself Messiah and Son of David. Jesus' fidelity to his sheep, his sacrifice for them, stands out in contrast to the failure of the stumbling, blinded, bullying authorities in chapter 9.

Metaphors come fast and often in these verses. There are the sheep—easily identified as the flock that Jesus intends to lead into good pasture (v. 9), those whom he knows by name and who recognize his voice (vv. 3-4, 14), those whom he intends to defend against thieves and robbers (vv. 1, 8, 10) and whom he wishes to join together with all others who, listening to his voice, will come into the one fold (v. 16). Jesus will effect all this because he is the GOOD SHEPHERD (vv. 11, 14), loved by the Father because *he will lay down his life for the sheep.* It is this act of total, loving self-sacrifice that is mentioned again and again as the central motif. Appearing first in verse 11 as the good shepherd title is introduced, it occurs again in verses 15, 17, and twice in verse 18. Though the shepherd-sheep metaphor was well known in the Old Testament Scriptures (as in Ezek 34), this laying down of the shepherd's life is something new. It is the characteristic function of Jesus. He is the good shepherd especially because of his willing self-sacrifice.

A final metaphor is that of the gate (vv. 7, 9), also applied to Jesus. He it is who provides safety for the flock by prohibiting entrance to marauders and who provides food by opening out onto good pasture lands. That the two metaphors of shepherd and sheepgate do not co-exist easily may be a sign that they originated separately but have been brought together here for this chapter.

In these verses we have seen two more of John's I AM—plus a following noun—statements. Jesus, who has identified himself as "I am the bread of life" (6:35, 41, 51) and "I am the light of the world" (8:12; 9:5), now says, "I am the gate for the sheep . . . the gate" (vv. 7, 9) and "I am the good shepherd" (vv. 11, 14). And since Jesus is the incarnate-Word revelation of the Father, we recognize in these personal characteristics of the Lord the same loving features of the Father.

Such revelation, as always, is followed by a crisis of faith. Is Jesus a possessed madman or just the opposite? Whose power is it that opens the eyes of the blind (vv. 19-21)?

3. The feast of Hanukkah. This feast celebrated the reconsecration of the temple by Judas the Maccabean (164 B.C.) after its profanation three years earlier by the Syrian Antiochus IV Epiphanes (1 Macc 4:36-59; 2 Macc 10:1-8). This yearly celebration lasted nine days, was a "lights" ceremony like the feast of Tabernacles (7:2), and was celebrated in mid-December. "It was winter" (v. 22). The scene for the present incident in John is set "in Solomon's Portico," a colonnade on the east side of the temple overlooking the Kidron Valley. It was a favorite rendezvous for Christians in Acts 3:11–4:4; 5:12, where it also appears as a place of controversy between Jewish Christians and some of their fellow Jews. Material from such a subsequent argument may well have entered into these verses.

The substance of the dialogue (vv. 24-38) is quite similar to that of chapters 7–8. One question at issue is whether Jesus is the Messiah (v. 24), a possible editorial link to the David figure of Ezek 34, which stood in the background of the preceding section. The other question is whether Jesus is the unique Son of God, whether God is in a very unique way *his Father.* In this brief section, "Father" appears nine times (vv. 25, 29 [twice], 30, 32, 36, 37, 38 [twice]); and "God's Son" is Jesus' claim in verse 36. What more can he offer as proof than his works done through the Father, works that are themselves the Father's revealing words? But Jesus' adversaries will not believe, as Jesus' divine works indicate, that he and the Father are one (v. 30), that the Father is in him and he in the Father (v. 38).

At one point Jesus almost plays with his opponents over the unique-Son-of-God issue. If Ps 82:6 calls judges "gods" because they share in the divine work of judgment, why should people object if Jesus is called "Son of God," since the Father has consecrated him and sent him into the world (vv. 34-36)? To this do the works testify. The incident ends on a sad note: "They tried again to arrest him; but he escaped from their power" (v. 39).

The final verses (40-42) are a brief presentation of the other side of Jesus' mission. Many came to him, accepted the witness of his signs and of John's testimony (a final reference to the Baptist), and came to believe in him. This paragraph also begins to position Jesus for his move to Bethany (ch. 11) and, in triumph, to Jerusalem (12:12).

John may well have intended a linkage between Jesus as the one "whom the Father has *consecrated* and sent into the world" (10:36) and the feast of the Dedication (v. 22), a memorial of the temple's *consecration* after Syrian profanation. If so, this is another in a line of attempts by John to show how Jesus had replaced the Jewish institutions. We have seen (1) how Jesus replaced *the temple* (2:13-22); (2) how he is a veritable *Lord of the sabbath,* working as does his Father (5:16-18); (3) how at *Passover* (ch. 6) he gives and becomes the manna bread and saves from the water; (4) how in chapters 7–8 at *Tabernacles* he is the living water and the light of the world. And now (5) Jesus replaces *Hanukkah.* He is the consecrated one. As John writes, the temple has disappeared, and Jewish Christians have been expelled from the synagogues. Fear not, says John, Jesus himself is sufficient to replace all these lost and precious treasures.

11:1-54 Episode VI: Life over Death

Jesus is both resurrection and life (11:25), and the restoration of Lazarus is the sign. John has already introduced us to the "life theme" when speaking in Episode I of rebirth (Nicodemus) and living water (Samaritan woman); in Episode II's life-giving word; in Episode III's life-giving bread; in Episode IV's "light of life" (8:12); in Episode V's "I have come that they might have life and have it to the full" (10:10).

Our present episode concentrates on this theme in one well-organized presentation, again one that adapts easily to theater. Pass out the roles—the sisters, Jesus, the disciples and Thomas, Jews/authorities and Caiaphas, a narrator—and the stage is set. It is drama with constant motion. The message of distress goes *from Bethany near Jerusalem* (v. 18) *to Jesus,* a message so simple and trusting that it might well become ours when friends are ill: "Master, the one you love is ill" (v. 3). Jesus and his disciples move *toward Bethany.* Martha and Mary move *to Jesus.* All move *to the tomb.* Lazarus moves *out of the tomb.* Informers move *to the Pharisees.* Jesus and his company move *to Ephraim* in northern Judea.

Mary and her sister Martha are known to us also from the Martha and Mary story in Luke 10:38-42. The personality characterizations are similar in both Luke and John. Martha comes through as the more dominant and active. It is she who is so busy in Luke 10:40 and who moves rapidly at first notice to meet Jesus here in John 11:20. Mary sat at home and later fell at Jesus' feet (John 11:20, 32); in Luke 10:39 she also sat at the Lord's feet to listen to his words. Surprisingly, Luke says nothing about a brother Lazarus, though he does present a parable regarding Lazarus, the poor man who ends up in Abraham's bosom. The Lukan story ends with the provocative conclusion: "If they will not listen to Moses and the prophets, neither will they be persuaded if someone should rise from the dead" (Luke 16:31). This is not meant to insinuate that John has turned the Lazarus of the parable into the brother of Mary and Martha. His characters are real people, and his knowledge of Jerusalem and its environs—which includes Bethany—is trustworthy.

What is truly touching about this incident is the author's insistence on the deep love that Jesus felt for this small family group, within which he must have felt so much at home. This love is evident in verses 5, 11, 35-36. Since Lazarus is the only male disciple of whom Jesus' love is predicated in the Gospel, some commentators have suggested that he is the beloved disciple who will become prominent in our later chapters. This is not probable, since the evangelist goes out of his way to preserve the anonymity of this central character.

There is some evidence that this Lazarus story was a second-edition addend to John's Gospel. This would explain the otherwise odd reference in verse 2 to the anointing by Mary, which will occur only in the following chapter. The oddness would disappear if the author had already included chapter 12 in his first edition and could thus allude to it when adding on what was to become chapter 11.

Our story is rich in the theology it unfolds.

1) Verses 25-26 are the theological center of the whole chapter. Jesus is both the resurrection and the life for all who, like Martha, believe that he is "the Messiah, the Son of God" (v. 27, the same profession that will be found in 20:31). One who has faith, even after death, shall live; one who has faith and is alive will never really die. Of this the restoration of Lazarus is the sign.

2) We find here a stunning example of Jesus' *life-giving word* and are reminded of the sayings in Episode II: "Amen, amen, I say to you, the hour is coming and is now here when the dead will hear the voice of the Son of God, and those who hear will live. . . . the hour is coming in which all who are in the tombs will hear his voice and will come out . . . ." (John 5:25, 28-29).

3) John's salvation theology is voiced in the unintentional prophecy of Caiaphas. "Jesus was going to die for the nation, and not only for the nation, but to gather into one the dispersed children of God" (vv. 51-52).

4) Deeply hidden in the episode is a further truth: that Jesus' gift of life to Lazarus involves his own death, the offering of his own life. To love Lazarus and give him life, Jesus must be willing to risk and lose his own. This trip to Bethany is shadowed by the approaching cross (vv. 7-8, 16, 50-53).

It is remarkable how the account of Lazarus' resurrection parallels that of Jesus himself in chapter 20. Both accounts speak of:

—a mourning Mary at the tomb (11:31 and 20:11);

—a cave tomb closed with a stone (11:38, 41 and 20:1);

—grave clothes plus a face cloth (11:44 and 20:6-7);

—a special role given to Thomas (11:16 and 20:24-28).

John has written the story of Lazarus in such a way as to prefigure Jesus' resurrection. Chapter 11 is meant to prepare the reader for chapter 20.

We conclude this chapter with a few minor observations. We must be struck by the unexpected delay on the part of Jesus in verses 4-7. Why didn't Jesus prevent the death rather than wait to overcome it? Our author looks at the event from the divine viewpoint rather than the human, and it is this that is promoted by Jesus' words in verses 4, 9, and 15. John, *looking back at the incident*, can now see, and have Jesus proclaim, that it was all for the better. The miracle sign has evidenced God's glory, his presence, and in the person of the Son of God. The miracle was an epiphany. The God of healing love is revealed through the work of his Son. And it is through walking with this Son, himself the light of this world (v. 9), that we are assured of not stumbling.

Caiaphas, whose words unintentionally become so theological in the final verses, was high priest for some nineteen years, from about A.D. 18–37. He was the son-in-law of Annas.

The final verses of the episode (53-54) position Jesus in Ephraim near the desert. From there he will ascend a last time to Bethany and Jerusalem.

11:55–12:50 Episode VII: Life Through Death

This final episode in the Book of Signs will teach not only that Jesus overcomes death (as in the Lazarus story) but that he will give life precisely through death. The text is divided into six clearly distinct but interconnected segments: the introduction; the anointing; the triumphal entry; Jesus' hour; the evangelist's evaluation; Jesus' summary proclamation.

1. Introduction (11:55-57). Our initial verse is almost identical to 6:4, which also introduces Passover material. The double mention of the Passover (v. 55) will lead us naturally into 12:1. The scene is being set as people wonder aloud whether or not Jesus is coming. Meanwhile (v. 57), the trap, too, is being set.

2. The anointing (12:1-11). As we move into material concerning the passion, we find that John's Gospel becomes much more similar to the other three. This story of the anointing, for example, resembles closely that of Mark 14:1-11 and Matt 26:1-16. (Luke 7:36-50 also has an anointing incident, but its time frame and purpose are quite different.) Although Martha, Mary, and Lazarus are prominent, the text definitely avoids saying that the meal was given at their home. Mark and Matthew place it in the home of Simon the leper. John does not disagree.

It is interesting to read, and it seems so correct, that "Martha served" while Mary "anointed the feet of Jesus" (vv. 2-3). The protest by Judas Iscariot allows the evangelist to put at center stage for just a moment this disciple who will be the tragic figure in the drama beginning to unfold. He steals from the poor; eventually he will lose his all. The key expression in this narrative, however, is that of Jesus in verse 7: "Let her keep this for the day of my *burial.*" The ointment is not simply cosmetic perfume; it is not simply preparation for death; it is burial ointment and fills the house with fragrance just as the scent of funeral oils pervades a tomb. This burial motif will surface again shortly.

With verse 9 the "large crowd" moves onto the scene. It will remain throughout, and for a purpose that will appear in just a moment. But for now Lazarus is featured. The authorities plan to have him, like so many later disciples, share Jesus' fate. His very existence is too strong a proof of Jesus' life-giving word.

3. The triumphal entry (12:12-19). The crowd takes over this scene (vv. 12, 17, 18) as Jesus enters Jerusalem one last time. He comes as king (vv. 13, 15), a motif that will become very strong in the passion account. The exultant prayer of verse 13 originates from Ps 118:25-26, a psalm used regularly by pilgrims entering the Holy City. To it is joined a post-resurrection application (v. 15) of Zech 9:9. Zechariah's king, like John's, is humble. Though victorious, he rides, not the stallion of war, but the donkey of service. The crowds that introduce the scene (v. 12) are in strong evidence at its conclusion (vv. 17, 18), where their presence provokes the Pharisees' reaction. Jesus' gift of life to Lazarus is going to demand a frightening exchange: Jesus' life for that of his friend. This segment concludes with the important phrasing: "Look, the whole world has gone after him" (v. 19). Part of this world is the Jewish crowd that we have observed repeatedly.

4. Jesus' hour (12:20-36). This section—a combination of narrative, monologue, and dialogue—is the key to the whole chapter. It follows one narrative (#2) that emphasized *burial* and another (#3) that repeatedly introduced the *crowd*. And now, in unexpected fashion, onto the stage come "some Greeks" (v. 20), who start a move toward Jesus through the aid of our *typical* missionaries (1:41, 45; 6:5-10), Philip and Andrew. Those following Jesus now include both Jews and Greeks, the latter peculiarly illustrative of "the whole world going after him" (v. 19).

In the verses that follow, John begins to pull the whole chapter together—the burial ointment, the large crowd, the Greeks, the whole world. The narratives will now be interpreted by Jesus' words. The HOUR has come (v. 23) in which Jesus will be glorified, that is, in which God will manifest to the utmost his presence in his Son. But this hour entails death: the grain of wheat must fall into the ground if it is to produce fruit (v. 24). Jesus will enter the ground (the burial ointment of verse 7 is an advance statement of that), and his dying will produce much fruit. We have begun to see the whole world going after him—the Jewish crowds of verses 9, 12, 17, 18, 29, 34 as well as the first fruits of the Gentile harvest (vv. 20-22). It is this same teaching, but in different words, that Jesus proclaims in verse 32: "And when I am lifted up from the earth, I will draw everyone to myself." The beginning of this being lifted up will be Jesus' crucifixion.

What Jesus is insisting upon in this episode is that life will be offered to the world *through* his death. If he is buried like the seed, if he is lifted onto the cross, then much fruit will come; then he will draw all to himself. The crowd and the Greeks are simply the initial harvest. And, in a remarkable way, this being buried, this being raised on a cross, is also Jesus' glorification (vv. 23, 28), the manifestation in him of his Father's presence, nowhere more evident than in Jesus' act of self-sacrificing love. (So, too, does Isaiah's servant song join to the death of the servant his glorification and elevation. John's theology flows from Isa 52:13: "See, my servant shall prosper, he shall be *raised high* and greatly *exalted* [glorified].")

As Jesus mentions his own self-giving (vv. 23-24), he joins to it that of his disciples. They are called to identical servant roles (vv. 25-26).

Verses 27-30 are strangely reminiscent of the agony in the garden—missing in the Fourth Gospel, for which it may present a too human Jesus. Yet at this point, as in the garden scene, Jesus' soul is troubled, and he is tempted to pray for the hour's passing—yet he doesn't (v. 37). Rather, reinforcement comes from the Father, who has glorified (manifested) himself through the signs and will glorify himself even further through Jesus' resurrection (v. 38). Lines are being drawn, since the manifestation of God's loving presence at the moment of crucifixion will demand reaction, and the reaction will determine individual judgment (v. 37). The world's prince of darkness will be driven out by the light that is Jesus. The present moment, however, is the hour of Jesus' sunset. "The light will be among you only a little while. Walk while you have the light . . . ." (v. 35). As Jesus leaves the scene (v. 36) and the ministry of the signs ends, some are still stumbling in the darkness: "Then how can you say that the Son of Man must be lifted up? Who is this Son of Man?" (v. 34).

5. The evangelist's evaluation (12:37-43). The signs' ministry has been no great success, neither in Jesus' lifetime nor in the later preaching of them by Jesus' disciples. It is as though Isa 53:1 had been written for this occasion: "Lord, who has believed what has reached our ears?" Paul would have the same feeling with regard to his own preaching ministry (Rom 10:16). It is as though Isa 6:10, too, had been written for Jesus' times. The sad comment of verse 40 was well known and often used in the early church (Mark 4:12; Matt 13:15; Luke 8:10; Rom 11:8; Acts 28:26). It is not a proclamation of predestination. Any blinding and hardening that occur are always seen as a penance that follows personal guilt. Isaiah's text was meant to inform the prophet—and numerous preachers after him—that the comparative failure of his mission entered somehow into God's plan and should not discourage him.

Verse 41 could be clearer for us poor readers in the twentieth century. In what way did Isaiah, living centuries before Jesus, see his glory? This must refer back to the contexts of the quotes from Isa 53 and 6. In the first, Isaiah speaks of the servant; in the second, of his inaugural glorious vision of God as King and Lord of hosts. In God's glory, he has seen that of Jesus, for the Father shares it with him;

and it is with the same glory that the servant has been exalted.

Verses 42-43 introduce us to a fringe group of disciples, crypto-Christians, who hid their feeble faith in Jesus lest, like the man born blind in chapter 9, they be expelled from the synagogue. John is writing now about such Christians of his own generation.

6. Jesus' summary proclamation (12:44-50). There is no attempt here to indicate an occasion or audience for these verses. What we have, rather, is a résumé of the salient points of Jesus' teaching, in his own words, located here by John as a recapitulation before starting the account of Jesus' passion-glorification. Reappearing in summary fashion is the statement of (a) the union of Father and Son (vv. 44-45); (b) Jesus as light of the world, come not to condemn but to save (vv. 46-47); (c) the inevitable judgment that depends on personal reaction (v. 48); (d) the identification of Jesus' word with that of the Father and of the eternal life that it gives (vv. 49-50). These themes have been constantly cycled through these first twelve chapters.

As we come to the conclusion of this first half of John's Gospel, it might be of help to review very briefly what the sign theology has involved. By means of signs—seven of them are miracles—the evangelist has attempted to tell us who Jesus is and what he has effected, so that by knowing Jesus we might know the Father. The seven miracle-signs have taught us that the new era of messianic wine has arrived (Cana); that Jesus' word is life-giving (the official's son, the infirm man at the pool); that Jesus is the bread of life and the saving presence of God (ch. 6); and that he is, finally, both the light (ch. 9) and the life (ch. 11) of the world. If this is who Jesus is and what Jesus does, it is perforce who God is and what God does; for Jesus, by word and action, reveals the Father. Thus far can the signs take us. But if we really want to advance from this position to know Jesus and the Father in the very heart of their being, we must take a further step. Jesus' passion will reveal both him and his Father in their heart of hearts.

C. THE BOOK OF GLORY

John 13:1–20:31

With chapter 13, we turn from Jesus' public ministry and its revelatory signs to Jesus' last days, to the period of his glorification, that is, his death and resurrection, in which God's glory, God's presence, will be manifested. For this reason, this second half of the Gospel is frequently entitled "The Book of Glory." It includes the farewell discourses (chs. 13–17), the passion narrative (chs. 18–19), the resurrection (ch. 20), and the epilogue (ch. 21).

13:1–17:26 The Farewell Discourses

These five chapters veer sharply from the previous presentation of Jesus' ministerial signs to an insistence on the Christian's actual, realized life in Jesus. The emphasis is not on the future but on the present. We hear the voice of Jesus, as though already risen and glorified, speaking to his disciples of present life, of indwelling, of love, of effected judgment, of the Spirit Paraclete who is at once both advocate and revealer. Jesus leaves to go to the Father and, in a little while, to return. The central stress is on union: the union of Father and Son; the gift and indwelling presence of their Spirit; the union of Son and disciples; the union of disciples with one another. The dynamism of all this is *love*, a word that now begins to take over John's good news. If we really want to know who and what Jesus is, so that we might know who and what God is, LOVE is the answer.

1. The opening scene: foot-washing (13:1-30). Again we approach Passover season (v. 1). But this time it will be Jesus' own passover from this world to the Father (vv. 1, 3). In this dramatic scene, Jesus, servant of the Father, becomes the servant of humankind. His hour has come, and he loves his friends "to the end" (v. 1), a Johannine double-entendre that includes both time and measure. Jesus does the servant task (cf. Luke 22:27); so, too, must his disciples serve one another. We are all called to wash one another's feet. All this is clear, and it is enunciated precisely by Jesus to remove any possible doubt (vv. 12-17).

Verses 6-10, however, are confusing. They seem to have a different thrust. What Jesus does cannot be understood till later (v. 7). Peter objects, as he did to Jesus' servant *death* in Mark 8:32; the washing, or rather, the being washed, is so important that without it the disciples can have no part in Jesus (v. 8). This reads like more than a simple example of Christian service and has tempted many commentators to believe that this *servant foot-washing* is also symbolic of Jesus' *servant death*. Moreover, the absolutely essential washing of verse 8 is reminiscent of baptismal teaching.

These clues suggest that the theology here is particularly rich, even though obscure. (a) Jesus' servant foot-washing is symbolic of his servant death. (b) Participation in this salvific death is through baptism, without which "you will have no inheritance with me" (v. 8) and through which we are "clean all over" and need not be washed again (v. 10). The line runs from symbolized salvific death to sacramental participation. (c) All this, in turn, leads to the ethical servant role that we must live with regard to one another (vv. 12-17). Baptized into Jesus' salvific death, we must lead his servant life. "I have given you a model to follow, so that as I have done for you, you should also do" (v. 15). This is a prophetic-action description of the role of all Christians, but especially of authority (like Peter) in the church. This must be exercised on one's knees before the people of God. Peter's difficulty with Christ's servant role—a difficulty felt a million times over by church authorities and ordinary Christians down through the centuries—reminds us of his similar difficulty in Mark 8:32-33.

One disciple is not clean. At this "hour," at this initiation of final conflict, he denies his share with Jesus, he refuses belief in the I AM (v. 19). He too passes over, but into the power of Satan (vv. 2, 27). Judas Iscariot, table companion of the Lord (v. 18, citing Ps 41:9), will now desert the light of the world. As he passes from light to darkness, the evangelist notes significantly and sadly, "It was night" (v. 30).

This insistence on Judas underlines a problem felt by the first Christians and, perhaps, tossed up at them in controversies. What did Judas' act of betrayal say about Jesus' wisdom and knowledge? Could the true Messiah have made so unfitting and fatal a choice? These questions were felt so strongly in the early church that Judas receives special attention in all four Gospels, as well as in Acts 1:15-26. John insists that Jesus knew of the betrayal and that it fit into God's saving plan.

Verse 23 speaks for the first time of the disciple, "the one whom Jesus loved." No name is given, but his function is significant. Close to Jesus' side—as was the Word to the Father's side in 1:18—he mediates between Jesus and Peter; his subsequent appearances will almost invariably be related to Peter.

2. Jesus' departure and return (13:31–14:31). Once Judas has left the light, Jesus begins to speak to his own, his dearest friends. Various disciples—Peter, Thomas, Philip, Judas—carry the discussion forward by the questions they pose. This enables us to break down the whole, hopefully to see it more clearly, by dividing it according to the characters who ask the leading questions.

a) The first section (13:31-35) is simply an introduction. Judas' departure has set in motion the events of the passion. Jesus will be glorified, God will be glorified, since God's presence as infinite love is about to be manifested in Jesus. Jesus will leave, and that absence (or is it presence?) is the problem underlying this whole section. As he leaves, he leaves behind his one essential commandment: "Love one another" (v. 34). It is a *new* commandment because this mutual love must be modeled on something new—on the love that Jesus shows for his disciples. Mutual love must be the sign, the indispensable sign, of their discipleship.

b) *Peter* (13:36–14:4) moves the discussion further: "Master, where are you going?" (13:36). This appearance of Peter permits the evangelist to present a bit of tradition shared, seemingly, by the whole church, that Jesus predicted Peter's denial (13:37-38). Yet, though Peter would deny his Lord, he would also follow him in death (v. 36).

In the subsequent verses (14:1-4), the basic problems that control the rest of the chapter are touched upon. The disciples are troubled (v. 1, as also v. 27)—and so later will be John's own community—because of Jesus' departure. In response, Jesus insists on the necessity of faith, stating that he goes to prepare a place for them and will return to take them with him (v. 3). This sounds very much like a promise of Jesus' future return as visible Lord of the world (the technical term for this is the *parousia* = coming). The early church awaited this with fervent hope (1 Thess 4:16-18). But John's Gospel will now reinterpret such a futuristic approach. Jesus has not passed over a bridge that was subsequently blown up; there is a *way* to him, and they already know it (v. 4).

c) So *Thomas* (14:5-7) asks, "How can we know the way?" Jesus' answer states that Christian hope is not in a method, not in a procedure, but in a person. Jesus himself is "the way and the truth and the life" (v. 6). Through and in Jesus, one *comes to* the Father, *knows* the Father, *sees* the Father.

d) *Philip* (14:8-21) seizes on that final phrase to ask: "Master, show us the Father . . . ." (v. 8). One can hear the sigh of weariness, almost of failure, in Jesus' voice: "Have I been with you for so long a time and you still do not know me, Philip? Whoever has seen me has seen the Father" (v. 9). And the discussion continues, pointing to the perfect union of Jesus with the Father: both his words and his works are the Father's (vv. 10-11). With this, Jesus turns his attention to the disciples. They, too, will do the works that Jesus has done because he will respond according to their petitions, so that God will be manifested in the Son. The disciples' love will bring from the Father another Paraclete, the Spirit of truth, to remain with them always (v. 16). In this sense, Jesus will come back; they will not be left orphans (v. 18).

At this point, the reader's head should be spinning a bit. What is going on? What seemed to be a statement of Jesus' future return to take his disciples to places prepared for them (14:3), a movement carrying believers into some future and unknown paradise, has subtly turned around like a boomerang targeting in on the place from which it was originally launched. Jesus goes, but he returns; and the dwelling places he prepares, which seemed to be located out there somewhere (v. 2), will be found, rather, within the believers themselves (vv. 20-21). In some way, this return is connected with another Paraclete (cf. 1 John 2:1, where Jesus is called the first one) who takes Jesus' place as both advocate and revealer.

It is this boomerang movement—Jesus' departure and consequent return through the Paraclete—that explains the "little while" in verse 19. Just as the disciples see Jesus now, so they will soon know of his union with the Father, which union he will share with them. The disciples who love will be loved by both the Father and Son, who (through the Paraclete?) will reveal himself to them (v. 21). All they could have hoped for in the future will soon be now.

e) This provokes the *Judas* (not Iscariot) sequence (14:22-31). How strange that Jesus should speak of all this Spirit return, indwelling, union with Father and disciples, when what Judas and the others were expecting was a visible return in majesty accompanied by a fearsome display of celestial fireworks. "Master, [then] what happened that you will reveal yourself to us and not to the world?" (v. 22). Jesus' answer almost avoids the question as it merely insists on what has already been proclaimed. He and the Father will come to those who love and will dwell with them (vv. 23-24). (This, for John, is the all-important coming, *parousia*, of the Lord.) This coming is directly related to the Paraclete whom the Father will send to instruct and to remind. John's community is clearly a Paraclete community, confident that the Spirit, Jesus' Spirit, is with them still, reminding them of, and interpreting, Jesus' words, instructing them with the words and wisdom of the Lord. Surely this Gospel is filled with Paraclete reminders and instruction.

The fear and distress of people awaiting a delayed future return (vv. 1, 27) must give way in John's community to the peace that is Christ's gift, to the joy that is theirs at the knowledge that Jesus has returned to the Father who is his origin, "greater than I" (v. 28).

This discussion, says Jesus, is long enough; now it is time to face the conflict with the Prince of this world (v. 30). The Father has commanded total love, and the world will soon know that this is what the Son will give. "Get up, let us go" (v. 31).

3. Discourse on Jesus and his community (15:1–16:33). There are two major difficulties with this material. The *first* is that it is completely unexpected. Seemingly 14:31 has just set Jesus and his disciples in motion: "Let us go." What would follow naturally after this is 18:1, "When he had said this, Jesus went out with his disciples across the Kidron valley." But between 14:31 and 18:1 we have all the material, almost all discourse, of chapters 15–17.

A *second* difficulty is that chapters 15–16 repeat much of what has already been said in chapter 14. Jesus talks again of indwelling, of the Paraclete, of departure and return, of love, of the "little while." These facts have led numerous students of John to detect here an addition, some kind of parallel to, or alternative version of, chapter 14. This is highly probable. Yet, if chapters 15–16 are an addition, they are surely not an intrusion; they are not a detour, but a circling around the same center. The motifs of chapter 14 appear, disappear, reappear. Not new knowledge, but reinforcement of the already given, seems to be the purpose of these two chapters. They divide themselves into one long monologue, followed by a combination of dialogue plus monologue.

a) *The long monologue* (15:1–16:16)

This is the longest monologue in the Fourth Gospel. It begins with:

i) The allegory of the vine (15:1-17)

The ancient Old Testament allegory of Israel as Yahweh's vine (Ps 80:9-20 is one example among many) becomes deeply Christianized at this point. Jesus is the true vine (vv. 1, 5) of which the Father takes personal care, pruning the barren branches, trimming clean the fruitful. These latter are the disciples who have accepted Jesus' life-giving word (vv. 3, 7). They are invited, encouraged to live on, to abide in Jesus. (The Greek word for "remain," *menō*, occurs eleven times in these few verses, a repeated insistence on the return of Jesus by indwelling. It is, however, translated in various ways in our English text.) The other all-important word here is "love." Just as "remain" is the essential word of verses 1-8, so "love" becomes essential in verses 9-17, while both bring this minor section to its conclusion in the "remain" and "love one another" of verses 16-17. The central teaching of this allegory is clear. *Remaining in Jesus through love* is what this little homily is all about. If this happens, when it happens, the disciple will produce fruit (vv. 5, 8). When it does not happen, the disciple is no disciple at all, but good for nothing but fuel (v. 6).

The love of which Jesus speaks is one, but many. It begins with the Father's love for Christ (v. 9), moves on to Jesus' love for his friends (vv. 9, 12-13), is reciprocated in the disciples' loving obedience to Christ (vv. 10, 14), and radiates out through their love for one another (vv. 12, 17). It is this love that will be the source of their joy (v. 11) and the essential condition of their intimate friendship with the Lord (vv. 14-15). The model of love for all true discipleship is extreme, limitless; for it is Jesus himself who lays down his life for his friends (v. 13), as does the good shepherd of 10:11, 15, 17, 18. Yet it is precisely for love like this that Jesus has chosen them. They will bring forth enduring fruit, their prayers will be answered, to the extent that they love one another (vv. 16-17).

ii) Hatred from a hostile world (15:18–16:4a)

The words of the text are clear, as is the logical progression. The disciples are warned that the price of discipleship will be high. Just as Jesus was hated, as he was persecuted (v. 20), as his words were not accepted, so will it be for his followers—hated, persecuted, unaccepted by the world (vv. 18-20). Such will be the *fact*, a fact seemingly well known in the experience of John's community. The deep-down *crime* is that the adversaries have seen the evidence yet refuse to believe. Jesus has spoken to them (v. 22), he has performed works never done before (v. 24); yet they really know nothing about the Father who sent Jesus (v. 21), and in hating him, they hate the Father also (vv. 23-24). In the words of Ps 69:4, "They hated me without cause." *Witnesses* to the crime will be both the Paraclete and the disciples, who, having seen from the beginning, can bear witness to all (vv. 26-27). The *reason* why this subject comes up at all is that excommunication and even death await the disciples (16:2-3). May their faith not be shattered in such periods of terror (16:1, 4)!

Our text here has been paraphrased easily. Two issues, however, need explanation. The *first* is Jesus' use of the word "world" (vv. 18-19). In the present context, "world" has a strong negative content, quite different certainly from its beautiful appearance in chapter 3: "For God so loved the world that he gave his only Son, so that everyone who believes in him might not perish but might have eternal life. For God did not send his Son into the world to condemn the world, but that the world might be saved through him" (3:16-17). This world that God loves with infinite love, that he saves and does not condemn, seems oceans apart from the hating and persecuting world of chapters 15–16. One identical word is being used in completely different fashions. This is a difficulty in John's Gospel that we must keep before our eyes. The "world" can be the work of God's hands (1:2-4), the object of his love (3:16-17)—that is God's world. But there is another world, too, what we in the twentieth century might call the epitome of worldliness, in which reign darkness and hatred, untruth and death. Of this world, better entitled "anti-world," Satan is prince (14:30; 16:11). John's community has already encountered it.

This brings us to the *second* issue. We find once more a historical bi-level. Expulsion from the synagogue (9:22; 12:42), even death, has touched the Johannine Christians; and this they see as the lot of those who follow the Master (15:18-21). Seemingly, persecution and disbelief have widened in their experience, being found not only in non-Christian Judaism but also among the Gentiles. In this sense, a whole segment of God's world has been transformed for them into a force of disbelief and hatred.

iii) The Paraclete (16:4b-16)

The Paraclete was barely mentioned in the final verses of chapter 15, but will now be the center of discussion. Jesus' departure, followed by persecution, was not a necessary subject of discourse at the beginning of the ministry, since it was not yet imminent (v. 4b). Not surprisingly, to speak of it now brings grief to the disciples. (To record that no one asks, "Where are you going?" [v. 5] ignores that very question raised by Peter in 13:36 and alluded to by Thomas in 14:5, an indication that chapter 16 is of different origin.) Jesus insists that grief is improper, for only his departure will assure the coming of the Paraclete. Into the Jesus-vacuum will come the Paraclete-presence. This divine presence, effectively experienced by John's community, will be proof positive that disbelief was sin, that justice was accomplished through Jesus' passage to the Father, that the prince of evil has been condemned to defeat (vv. 8-11).

The Paraclete will do even more. As the Spirit of truth, he will be the constant guide of the disciples, speaking to them (through inspired preachers and writers like the evangelist) what he *hears* from Jesus, who, in turn, receives from the Father. The verbal form "he *hears*" (v. 13) is important. It places the Paraclete's function simultaneously in God's eternity and the reader's now. Through the Paraclete, what Jesus says in his Father's realm is *now* transmitted to the disciples. Jesus who once spoke in the flesh now speaks through the Spirit. Much of this present discourse, surely, comes from Jesus speaking through his Spirit to the community. In this sense, Jesus' earthly departure is a gain, for it enables the glorified Jesus to be present. The disciples will lose him in earthly form within a short time but will soon receive him back again in Spirit (v. 16).

b) *From dialogue into monologue into dialogue* (16:17-33)

The long monologue has ended, but there is still more to be recounted in a sort of dialogue between disciples and Master. Jesus' statement about the short time, the little while, brings the disciples back into view. What is meant by this "little while" (vv. 17-19)? Jesus does not answer the question directly but explains instead how grief will be turned into joy (see 20:20 for the actualization of this), like that of a mother once her child is born into the world (vv. 20-22). On that day of birth, to continue the simile, the time of veiled language will be over (vv. 23a, 25), and the time of direct and effective petition to the loving Father will have begun (vv. 23b-24, 26-27) for those who have loved Jesus and believed in his divine origin (vv. 27-28). When the disciples affirm their belief (v. 30b), Jesus gives a final warning. During his hour they will be scattered, leaving him abandoned by all but his Father (v. 32). They will suffer, yet only in Jesus is peace to be found. "Take courage," he says to the disciples of then and now. The glorified Jesus has already overcome the world (v. 33).

4. Jesus' prayer (17:1-26). These chapters of farewell discourse (chs. 13–17), with a precedent in the formal and final addresses of Moses (Deut 29–34), of Jacob (Gen 49), and of Paul (Acts 20:17-38), are brought to a fitting conclusion by Jesus' prayer in chapter 17. This whole chapter is one long prayer directed by Jesus to the Father, his own solemn expansion, one might say, of the simple "Our Father" he taught his disciples in Matt 6 and Luke 11. Positioned between heaven and earth, between his Father and his disciples, Jesus prays for believers present and future. The prayer is often called Jesus' "Priestly Prayer." The title can be justified only if one believes that intercession is priestly, that the union for which Jesus prays is priestly work, that the consecration spoken of in verse 19 deals with sacrifice. Better, surely, to call it simply Christ's prayer for union.

a) *Division and content*

i) Father and Son (vv. 1-5)

In these five verses, Jesus speaks directly to his Father. The hour has come; the manifestation of the divine presence (glorification) is the task. Eternal life will consist in recognizing this divine presence. As the evangelist puts it in verse 3—and this is his whole Logos, or word theology—"Now this is eternal life, that they should know you, the only true God, and the one whom you sent, Jesus Christ." To know God in the Son whom he has sent is eternal life. Jesus has manifested that presence on earth (v. 4) and will now return to that presence at the Father's side (v. 5). He has finished the work given him to perform (v. 4). The true nature of God, which is love, is about to be manifested in Jesus' self-sacrificing death.

ii) Son and disciples (vv. 6-19)

Jesus' conversation with the Father now turns to the subject of the disciples. To them has Jesus made known the Father's name (presumably the I AM that the Father has shared with the Son), and they have accepted the word (v. 6) and the message (v. 8), believing that what Jesus has comes from him who sent him (vv. 7-8). In a word, they have believed in Jesus' divine origin and divine union.

It is for these disciples that Jesus prays at this moment of departure in verses 9-19. He prays specifically:

—"keep them in your name that you have given me" (v. 11);
—"that they may be one just as we are one" (v. 11);
—"that they may share my joy completely" (v. 13);
—that the Father "keep them from the evil one" (v. 15);
—that he "consecrate them in the truth" (v. 17).

In paraphrase, what Jesus asks for his disciples is that they be protected by the immense power of the I AM (which will be demonstrated graphically in 18:6); that their unity resemble, and be based on, the intimate union of Father and Son; that their sorrow be changed into the divine joy that the Son reflects from his Father; that they be guarded from the prince of this world; that they be truly consecrated—as is Jesus—in complete dedication to God's service, which will be a mission to the world (vv. 18-19).

iii) Son and future disciples (vv. 20-26)

For future disciples, Jesus prays for one central gift—unity: "that they may all be one, as you, Father, are in me and I in you . . . that they also may be one in us . . . that they may be one, as we are one, I in them and you in me, that they may be brought to perfection as one" (vv. 21-23). It will be only through this evidence of loving unity that the mission to the world (v. 18) can be effective; for only if the loving union of disciples is apparent can the world believe (v. 21), can the world know (v. 23) that the Father has sent Jesus and that the Father's love can be found in the disciples as it can be found in Jesus himself (v. 23). Where this loving unity of disciples is found, there too will be found the company of Jesus (v. 24), the divine presence (v. 24), the power of the divine name, and the living love of both Father and Son (v. 26).

b) *Recurring themes*

i) One cannot fail to note the frequent recurrence of "Father," a total of six times (vv. 1, 5, 11, 21, 24, 25). This reflects Jesus' own unique use of the Aramaic *Abba* ("loving Father"), with which he customarily began his prayer. Perfectly joined to the Father in oneness, he remains at all times the obedient and loving Son.

ii) The central motif of the prayer is that of unity—unity of present and future disciples, a unity modeled on that of Father and Son, a union that takes root from the love of Father and Son that is gifted to all disciples (v. 26).

iii) There is strong insistence on love: the Father's love for the disciples (v. 23), the Father's love for Jesus (vv. 23-24), the Father's love for Jesus and the disciples (v. 26). The

Father's love is the supreme revelation of the Gospel. Jesus, the incarnate Word, speaks the Father in one word—LOVE. Throughout this whole prayer, it is clear that the church is meant to be a community of love, the living sign or sacrament of the mutual love of Father and Son.

iv) The "world" is mentioned seventeen times in these verses. It is the world of anti-world, the center of disbelief and hatred and unlove, the contrast and contradiction to what Christian living should be. Judas (v. 12) is an example of one to whom all was offered and rejected, one who experienced light and life but left it for darkness and death. While this world is not here the object of Jesus' prayer, yet it is not a world for which Jesus has no hope or feeling. While the strong emphasis lies on prayer for Jesus' actual and future disciples, verses 21 and 23 do pray that, through Christian unity, the world may *believe* and *know* that Jesus has been sent by a loving Father.

c) *Echoes of the Our Father*

Though the customary "Our Father" is not found in the Fourth Gospel, there are tiny echoes of it that, fittingly enough, appear in this uniquely Johannine prayer. "Father," as we have seen, is found six times as Jesus' prayerful address. Reference to God's name—similar to "Hallowed be thy name"—occurs in verses 6, 11, 12, and 26. Reference to glorification in verses 1, 5, and 24 brings into view the divine presence, the hope of "Thy kingdom come." And the request (v. 15) that the disciples be guarded from the evil one echoes the similar and final request of the "Our Father" in Matt 6:13.

d) *Eucharistic material*

Concluding chapters 13–17, the reader must have noticed the lack of any mention of Eucharistic institution. Seemingly, the evangelist has chosen to locate his Eucharistic material at the end of chapter 6, where it brings the homily on the bread from heaven to a powerful conclusion. The vine allegory of chapter 15, however, may reveal an original Eucharistic setting, especially since its "remain in me" language parallels closely the "remains in me and I in him" of 6:56.

18:1–19:42 The Passion Narrative

We now turn from discourses—at least four whole chapters worth—to narrative. Our feet come back to the ground after a head-and-heart trip through the world above where the Father and Son live in eternal unity and from which they will send the enlivening Paraclete. Here we find the earthly Jesus enroute to the passion and to that elevation on the cross that is the glorification of divine love. It is at this point in the Gospel that John presents material that, in both content and sequence, is quite similar to that of the other three Gospels.

1. The arrest (18:1-11). Jesus and his disciples exit through the city walls, moving eastward a short distance down and across the Kidron Valley to a garden. The name of the garden, Gethsemani, is not given (Mark 14:32; Matt 26:36), nor does John mention the agony found in the other Gospels. John's portrait of Jesus tends to omit characteristics that are, in his judgment, overly human. He must know of the agony, however, since echoes of it do appear, though with changed emphasis and context, in 12:27: "I am troubled now. Yet what should I say? 'Father, save me from this hour'?" and in 18:11: "Shall I not drink the cup that the Father gave me?"

That "Jesus had often met there with his disciples" (v. 2) explains how Judas knows where to find him and agrees with the Johannine insistence on multiple visits to Jerusalem during Jesus' ministry. So it is here that Judas comes with forces from the Romans, "a band of soldiers," and from the Jewish authorities (v. 3). The lanterns and torches provide a stage of light and darkness on which this dramatic scene will be played out. Jesus, armed with divine knowledge (v. 4), confronts his adversaries, including Judas (v. 5), the Satan figure of 6:70-71; 13:2, 27, with the question: "Whom are you looking for?" To their reply, "Jesus the Nazorean," Jesus answers with the majestic and awesome response, I AM—*egō eimi.* In the presence of the I AM, "they [Satan and his assistants] turned away and fell to the ground" (v. 6) in compulsory adoration. Jesus, the one "sent" by the Father, is very much in control of his own destiny. He is in charge, also, of the destiny of his own sheep: "Let these men go" (v. 8). Jesus will not lose any of those whom his Father has given him (v. 9, and see 6:39; 10:28; 17:12).

The violent reaction of Peter's sword is paralleled in Mark 14:47, Matt 25:51, and Luke 22:50, though only John names Peter as the slasher and Malchus as the victim. (Oddly, both John and Luke agree that it was the *right* ear that was affected.) Jesus puts an immediate end to the violence. His food is to do his Father's will (4:34); his drink will be whatever the Father offers.

2. Before Annas and Caiaphas: Peter's denials (18:12-27). From the garden, Jesus is led to Annas, father-in-law of the high priest Caiaphas (whose unintended prophecy of Jesus' salvific death was noted in 11:50). Annas had an extraordinary career in the Jewish hierarchy. High priest himself from A.D. 7–14, he was succeeded in later years by five sons as well as by Caiaphas, a son-in-law. Not surprisingly, he remained a person of substantial power in Jerusalem, even though no longer high priest himself. In these verses the evangelist, as though utilizing a double stage, focuses the spotlight in turn on the Annas-Jesus discussion and then on the nearby encounters of Peter with his accusers.

Peter's first difficulty is at the very gate of the courtyard. Another disciple (the Beloved Disciple?) known to the high priest has used his influence to obtain entrance for Peter also. Peter is a mixture of courage—he is there following Jesus (v. 15)—and intense fear. At the challenge of a servant girl, he capitulates. "You are not one of this man's disciples, are you?" "I am not" (v. 17). The violence of Peter's sword has been transformed into the lying timidity of his tongue. Peter moves to the "charcoal fire" (v. 18). A chill has fallen on both body and spirit.

On the stage of a room apart (vv. 19-24), Peter's fear is being contrasted with Jesus' courage. Jesus' teaching has been "spoken publicly to the world." Why, then, is he questioned as though he were a conniving malefactor? A blow to the face is his answer. Annas, unable to gratify what seems to be cheap curiosity, sends Jesus, bound, to his son-in-law, Caiaphas.

Meanwhile, back at the fire (vv. 25-27), Peter is slipping from bad to worse. Confronted by other bystanders and by a relative of the injured Malchus (v. 26), Peter, so courageous at the supper table (13:37), surrenders completely. "You are not one of his disciples, are you?" "I am not" (v. 25). With the third denial, Peter strikes out—and a cock began to crow.

The details of Jesus' trials vary somewhat in the four Gospels. The arrest in a secluded place outside the city walls is a constant, but there is a variation regarding what happened after that. Where Mark 14:53-65 and Matt 26:57-68 speak of a formal night trial before the Sanhedrin, the religious governance in Jerusalem, Luke 22:54, 63-64 and John describe a less formal meeting that evening at the high priest's house, according to Luke, and with Annas, according to John. These discrepancies are the kind that would naturally arise as the accounts were passed along orally over the years. All four agree on some type of inquisition the following morning and on the definitive appearance before Pilate.

3. Pilate: Condemnation (18:28–19:16). Pilate, as a historical character, is fairly well known. He ruled as Roman procurator of Judea, subordinate to the governor of Syria, for ten years (A.D. 26–36), during which time his chief duty was to administer finances and collect taxes for the imperial treasury. His treatment of the Jews was insensitive, frequently cruel. When his troops marched into Jerusalem with insignia bearing the image of Caesar, the Jews were incensed and persuaded him to have them removed only after a courageous and dangerous confrontation with the procurator in Caesarea, where his official residence was located. He also sequestered money from the temple funds with which he financed an aqueduct for Jerusalem. This caused another protest that terminated with violence as the protesting Jews were scattered by the clubs of Pilate's soldiers. His cruelty to the Samaritans resulted in their appeal to the Syrian governor, the legate Vitellus, who dismissed Pilate and sent him back to Rome to answer complaints before the emperor Tiberius. Tiberius, however, died before Pilate's arrival; and at that time Pilate disappears from history. The date of his death is unknown. (The early church historian Eusebius believed that he committed suicide.) A man of no great talent, he has entered history almost entirely because of his role in the death of Jesus.

Numerous commentators have noted that this trial before Pilate has been organized using the double-stage technique (*outside* with the crowd, *inside* with Jesus) and in the order of inverse parallelism (as was the case with the prologue). Schematically, we find the following seven scenes:

Outside (a) 18:28-32: Jewish authorities demand from Pilate the death of Jesus.

Inside (b) 18:33-38a: First dialogue between Pilate and Jesus.

Outside (c) 18:38b-40: Pilate wishes to release Jesus, since he finds him guilty of no crime.

Inside (d) 19:1-3: Flagellation and crowning with thorns: Jesus as king.

Outside (c′) 19:4-8: Pilate finds Jesus guilty of no crime (twice).

Inside (b′) 19:9-11: Second dialogue between Pilate and Jesus.

Outside (a′) 19:12-16: Jewish authorities obtain from Pilate the sentence of death.

Clearly, and remarkably, (a), (b) and (c) are matched by (a′), (b′) and (c′). Section (d) climactically stresses the kingship of Jesus. It is this ordering that we will follow as we study this section.

Outside (a) 18:28-32. John tells us nothing about Jesus' appearance before Caiaphas apart from the fact (18:24, 28). The praetorium (v. 28) was the official tribunal of the procurator while in Jerusalem. It is disputed as to whether it was located at the northwest corner of the temple area (the Antonia) or at Herod's palace on the western hill of the city. Mention of the avoidance of ritual impurity in order that they might eat the Passover supper (v. 28) informs us that John does *not* present the Last Supper as the paschal meal (13:1; 19:14, 31). The other three Gospels do. Commentators are far from agreeing upon any solution to this famous difficulty. The dialogue between Pilate and the authorities makes evident the intent of the latter to do away with Jesus, and it is Pilate who forces this admission (v. 31). The evangelist sees in this a fulfillment of the divine necessity that Jesus be lifted up (3:14; 8:28; 12:32-34) on the cross, a Roman punishment. What evidence we have lends credence to the statement in verse 31 that the Jerusalem Sanhedrin did not have authority to impose capital punishment, and especially while Pilate himself was in the city.

Inside (b) 18:33-38a. Pilate's question, "Are you the King of the Jews?" (v. 33), constitutes the first words of Pilate to Jesus also in Mark 15:2, Matt 27:11, and Luke 23:3. This supposes and constitutes strong proof that such an anti-Roman claim to kingship was the official accusation made against Jesus by the chief priests. Pilate's question was dangerous—an imprudent answer could bring condemnation as a revolutionary. Jesus' first response, consequently, is indirect, an appeal to Pilate's conscience (v. 34). But verses 36-37 are direct and to the point. Jesus is a king, but of a strikingly different type. His kingdom is not of this world (v. 36), not of earthly origin. In response to Pilate's following question, "Then you are a king?," Jesus answers that his whole mission is to witness to the truth. All who are committed to the truth hear his voice. The question up for judgment, insists Jesus, is whether or not one accepts him, truth incarnate (v. 37). Pilate stands in the shadow. He does not even understand the terms of the question (v. 38).

Outside (c) 18:38b-40. Out Pilate goes again, hoping this time that the choice of the crowd would free him from a decision he fears to make. Surely they will prefer to liberate Jesus rather than the criminal Barabbas (and, in so doing, liberate Pilate as well). But Pilate will not be let off the hook so lightly. "They cried out again, 'Not this one but Barabbas!' " (v. 40). Barabbas, says the Greek text, was a *lēistēs*, probably a political insurrectionist, although the term can also apply to an ordinary robber or bandit. The ball moves back into Pilate's court.

Inside (d) 19:1-3. John stresses here the elements of mockery that echo kingship—a kingship that Jesus truly possesses, but on a different level. Thus come the crown, the cloak of royal purple, the salutation as king. Ironically, notes John, he who was so thoroughly and diversely mocked as a king was truly king. It is this truth, stressed here in irony, that constitutes the theological and structural center of the trial before Pilate.

Outside (c′) 19:4-8. This section parallels (c), Pilate's declaration of Jesus' innocence. In this instance Pilate states his opinion twice: "I find no guilt in him" (vv. 4, 6). Verse 6's "Take him yourselves and crucify him" is neither a condemnation nor a permission granted the accusers. A paraphrase might be: "Go ahead. Do it on your own and under your own responsibility, but don't expect me to be responsible for it." The answer to this reveals in all clarity the real reason for the antagonism of the local authorities: ". . . according to that law he ought to die because he made himself *the Son of God*" (v. 7). The Romans became involved because of a false accusation of kingship rivaling Caesar's; the Jewish accusation was that Jesus acted as the unique Son of God.

Inside (b') 19:9-11, the second dialogue. Pilate's reaction to this talk about Jesus' divine sonship is one of increasing fear and wonder. This is further increased, first by Jesus' silence (v. 9) and then by verse 11, the answer of a man confident of his own innocence and destiny.

Outside (a') 19:12-16. The condemnation is finally forced from Pilate by a return to the political accusation: "Everyone who makes himself a king opposes Caesar" (v. 12). This accusation carries the day. The final scene shifts outside before the public, onto the stone pavement called Gabbatha. (An enormous pavement of huge worked stone lies evident today in the excavation of the Antonia at the corner of the old temple area.) The dialogue between Pilate and the crowd is kingly and ironic by Johannine intent. "Behold, your king! . . . Shall I crucify your king?" (vv. 14-15). Back comes the dreadful confession of the chief priests: "We have no king but Caesar" (v. 15). This was blasphemy, for it was religious dogma that Yahweh and only Yahweh was king. John is telling us that those rejecting Jesus cannot have his Father as king. Pilate yields to political pressure and hands Jesus over. "It was Preparation Day for Passover, and it was about noon" (v. 14). As the Lamb of God (1:29, 36) is sentenced to death, the Passover lambs are being readied for sacrifice. Mutually responsible for Jesus' death are Judas, a disciple; Pilate, a Roman; and the Jewish authorities of Jerusalem.

4. Crucifixion (19:16b-22). Jesus himself carries the cross (v. 17). John is not denying the assistance given by Simon of Cyrene—if, indeed, he knows of it—but is emphasizing the control of Jesus over his own life and death. He accepts his own death; he carries his own cross. He is crucified at the Place of the Skull (in Hebrew *Golgotha* and in Latin *Calvaria*, whence our "Calvary").

The inscription on the cross is mentioned, always with slight variations, by all four evangelists, but only John, who insists so much on Jesus' kingship, tells us of the three languages. Greek was the tongue of the Mediterranean world; Latin, that of the Roman empire. John is saying that Jesus' kingship is universal, proclaimed from the cross to the whole world. Pilate's stubborn insistence on letting the inscription stand as written is his own bit of revenge against those who pressured him to condemn the innocent. Now let them squirm a little at a title that insults them.

5. Christ's clothing (19:23-24). This is the first of a series of incidents in which John sees the fulfillment of some Old Testament prophecy. The pitiful booty of Jesus' clothing is referred back to Ps 22:19, a psalm much used by the early church as a pre-shadowing of Jesus' passion. The reference to the seamless tunic *may* be a conscious parallel between Jesus and the high priest, whose robe was also seamless, but such a possibility is disputed by scholars. John speaks of Jesus, not as priest, but as king.

6. Jesus' mother and the Beloved Disciple (19:25-27). This scene, placed at the most important moment in the Gospel, must have more than simple filial significance, that is, the care of Jesus for his mother at the hour of his death. The only question is: What does this incident symbolize? Suggestions are numerous. Since this paragraph is set in the context of Jesus' delivering over his spirit (v. 30) and of the blood and water flowing from his pierced side (v. 34), I suggest that we find in these few verses John's symbolic picture of the birth of the Christian community. It is the hour of Jesus' glorification—his being lifted up—and as he dies, he hands over his Spirit. Beneath him stand a woman and a disciple, both unnamed as if to emphasize their symbolic character. The woman may well signify mother church, and the Beloved Disciple all disciples called to follow the loving obedience of their Lord. When to the mother-church woman and the Beloved Disciple figure are added the Spirit, which Jesus gives (v. 30) now that he has been glorified (7:39), and the blood and water, signs of the Eucharist and baptism, the Christian community stands revealed. This suggestion, though not certain, is not exaggerated, especially when working with an evangelist so theologically bi-leveled as John.

There may even be a subtle reference to the woman of Gen 3:15 and the enmity between her offspring and that of the Satan-serpent. John shows interest in the Book of

Genesis. Starting his Gospel with the same initial phrase and a reference to creation, he presents a conflict between Satan and Jesus (12:31-33; 14:30), and speaks of Satan's offspring (Judas and the adversaries of 8:44). If the "woman" of 19:26 is, indeed, a reference to the woman of Gen 3:15, then John has reassembled all the elements of the Genesis story for a re-creation event: the serpent, the serpent's seed, the woman, the woman's seed and, perhaps, even the garden locale for "in the place where he had been crucified there was a garden" (19:41). Indeed, the crucifixion account not only ends in a garden (19:41) but also begins in one (18:1); and it is only John among the four evangelists who so locates it.

The Fourth Gospel may be presenting Mary beneath the cross in a double role:

a) *as feminine symbol of mother church*, caring for, and placed in the care of, Jesus' disciples, who become her children and, consequently, Jesus' brothers and sisters. Relation to Jesus is not merely individual; it includes a community, a family of brothers and sisters;

b) *as woman of the victory*, emphasizing the feminine contribution to salvation. The negative biblical portrait of Eva has been replaced by that of the life-giving Ave.

7. Death (19:28-30). For John, Jesus dies when he is ready to die, at the proper time, when Scripture has been fulfilled. The Scripture "I thirst" may refer to either Ps 69:21 or Ps 22:15. Both psalms are used often in the New Testament. The wine (v. 29) was the thin, bitter drink of the soldiers. The hyssop plant (v. 29) could hardly hold a sponge soaked with wine. It may enter here to recall to John's Jewish readers the plant that sprinkled Israelite doors with the saving blood of the Passover lamb in Exod 12:22. If so, it is intimately connected with what follows. "It is finished" (v. 30)—accomplished is the work Jesus had to do, the will of his Father, the Scriptures, the salvation of humankind. "And bowing his head, he *handed over* the spirit" (v. 30). This wording is unique, proper to the Fourth Gospel. Jesus' death-glorification has released the Spirit into the world (7:39; 19:34; 20:22).

8. The lance (19:31-37). The urgency apparent in verse 31 arises from the fact that it is Friday afternoon, with the Sabbath (also Passover for John) beginning at sundown. There were but a few hours left for what would necessarily be done to the bodies. The legs of the other two, consequently, were broken to hasten their death, but this was useless for Jesus, already dead. Instead, his side was pierced, releasing a mixture of blood and water, to which the evangelist, or his source of information, bears testimony as an eyewitness. Verse 35 emphasizes this fact. Many of the church fathers have seen in the blood and water signs of the Eucharist and baptism, the life sources of the church, the new Eve, coming forth from the side of the new Adam. John refers again to fulfillment of Old Testament passages. "Not a bone of it will be broken" is a fusion of Exod 12:46, which concerns the paschal lamb, and Ps 34:21, which describes God's protection of the just man. "They will look upon him whom they have pierced" refers to Zech 12:10, where the piercing is joined to God's pouring out on the inhabitants of Jerusalem a spirit of grace and petition. The piercing of Jesus does even more.

9. The burial (19:38-42). All four evangelists mention the participation of Joseph of Arimathea in Jesus' burial (Matt 27:57-60; Mark 16:43-46; Luke 23:50-53). Only Matt 27:60, however, explains how it was that the new tomb was available for use—it belonged to Joseph. And only John introduces Nicodemus. For John, both men were crypto-Christians breaking free from the darkness of their fear. Their courageous act is a verification of John 12:32: ". . . And when I am lifted up from the earth, I will draw everyone to myself."

The huge amount of myrrh and aloes (v. 39) used for the burial may be one final Johannine reference to Jesus' kingship. He receives a regal burial.

20:1-31 The Resurrection

Here, as in chapter 9, the text is arranged in dramatic form, as it might be if performed by actors and actresses. The number of participants could be reduced by having only one angel (A) and one disciple (D). The surprising and challenging fact is that John's text lends itself so naturally to such dramatic arrangement.

[ACT I: The Tomb
Scene 1: *Sunday morning.* Mary Magdalene *(MM),* Peter *(P),* Beloved Disciple *(BD),* Narrator *(N)*]

N: [1]On the first day of the week,

MM: Mary of Magdala came to the tomb early in the morning, while it was still dark, and saw the stone removed from the tomb.
[2]So she ran and went to Simon Peter and to the other disciple

N: whom Jesus loved,

MM: and told them, "They have taken the Lord from the tomb, and we don't know where they put him."

P: [3]So Peter

N: and the other disciple

P and BD: went out and came to the tomb.

N: [4]They both ran,

BD: but the other disciple ran faster than Peter and arrived at the tomb first; [5]he bent down and saw the burial cloths there, but did not go in.

P: [6]When Simon Peter arrived after him, he went into the tomb and saw the burial cloths there, [7]and the cloth that had covered his head, not with the burial cloths but rolled up in a separate place.

BD: [8]Then the other disciple also went in, the one who had arrived at the tomb first, and he saw and believed.

N: [9]For they did not yet understand the scripture that he had to rise from the dead.

P and BD: [10]Then the disciples returned home.

[Scene 2: *The same Sunday morning.* Mary Magdalene *(MM),* Angels *(AA),* Jesus *(J),* Disciples, Narrator *(N)*]

N: [11]But Mary stayed outside the tomb weeping.

MM: And as she wept, she bent over into the tomb [12]and saw two angels in white sitting there,

A-1: one at the head

A-2: and one at the feet where the body of Jesus had been.

AA: [13]And they said to her, "Woman, why are you weeping?"

MM: She said to them, "They have taken my Lord, and I don't know where they laid him."

N: [14]When she had said this,

MM: she turned around and saw Jesus there,

N: but did not know it was Jesus.

J: [15]Jesus said to her, "Woman, why are you weeping? Whom are you looking for?"

MM: She thought it was the gardener and said to him, "Sir, if you carried him away, tell me where you laid him, and I will take him."

J: [16]Jesus said to her, "Mary!"

MM: She turned and said to him in Hebrew, "Rabbouni,"

N: which means Teacher.

J: [17]Jesus said to her, "Stop holding on to me, for I have not yet ascended to the Father. But go to my brothers and tell them, 'I am going to my Father and your Father, to my God and your God.' "

MM: [18]Mary of Magdala went and announced to the disciples, "I have seen the Lord," and what he told her.

[ACT II: The Upper Room
Scene 1: *That Sunday evening.* Disciples *(DD),* Jesus *(J),* Thomas *(Th),* Narrator *(N)*]

N: [19]On the evening of the first day of the week,

D-1: when the doors were locked, where the disciples were,

D-2: for fear of the Jews,

J: Jesus came and stood in their midst and said to them, "Peace be with you." [20]When he had said this, he showed them his hands and his side.

DD: The disciples rejoiced when they saw the Lord.

J: [21][Jesus] said to them again, "Peace be with you. As the Father has sent me, so I send you."

N: [22]And when he had said this, he breathed on them and said to them,

J: "Receive the holy Spirit. [23]Whose sins you forgive are forgiven them, and whose sins you retain are retained."

Th: [24]Thomas,

N: called Didymus, one of the Twelve,

Th: was not with them when Jesus came.

DD: [25]So the other disciples said to him, "We have seen the Lord."

Th: But he said to them, "Unless I see the mark of the nails in his hands and put my finger into the nailmarks and put my hand into his side, I will not believe."

[**Scene 2:** *One week later.* Disciples *(DD),* Jesus *(J),* Thomas *(Th),* Narrator *(N)*]

N: [26]Now a week later

DD: his disciples were again inside

Th: and Thomas was with them.

J: Jesus came,

N: although the doors were locked,

J: and stood in their midst and said, "Peace be with you." [27]Then he said to Thomas: "Put your finger here and see my hands, and bring your hand and put it into my side, and do not be unbelieving, but believe."

Th: [28]Thomas answered and said to him, "My Lord and my God!"

J: [29]Jesus said to him: "Have you come to believe because you have seen me? Blessed are those who have not seen and have believed."

N: [30]Now Jesus did many other signs in the presence of [his] disciples that are not written in this book. [31]But these are written that you may [come to] believe that

All: JESUS IS THE MESSIAH, THE SON OF GOD,

N: and that through this belief you may have life in his name.

1. Literary arrangement. John has composed this chapter with artistic care. Act I is located at the tomb, where the two different incidents (scenes) occur. Act II takes place in the upper room, the two scenes occurring one week apart. Each scene has two main characters: Peter and the Beloved Disciple; Mary Magdalene and Jesus; Jesus and the disciples; Jesus and Thomas. As we advance through the four scenes, a minor character in one (Mary, then the disciples, finally Thomas) becomes a major one in the following. All is tightly coordinated, neatly orchestrated. In schematic form, with the italicized names being the main characters in the scene, we find:

ACT I—Tomb

Scene 1 (Sunday A.M.)
Mary M., *Peter, Beloved Disciple*

Scene 2 (Same Sunday A.M.)
Mary M., two angels, *Jesus,* disciples

ACT II—Upper Room

Scene 1 (Same Sunday P.M.)
Jesus, disciples, Thomas

Scene 2 (Sunday one week later)
Jesus, Thomas, disciples

2. Theological intent. John's theology becomes evident through observing the reactions of the participants. How do they arrive at belief in the risen Lord? In the opening scene, Mary, a minor character, sees the stone moved from the tomb. Her reaction is the natural one: "They have taken the Lord from the tomb" (v. 2). She does not yet believe.

Peter and the Beloved Disciple, the central actors, proceed to the tomb with haste (and hope). They see the burial clothes and head wrapping. Peter remains perplexed, but the response of the Beloved Disciple is one of faith. "He saw and believed" (v. 8). This loved and loving disciple saw only the minimum yet believed.

In the following scene (vv. 11-18), Mary now becomes a major character. She still holds the natural explanation (vv. 13, 15 repeat the substance of v. 2). She comes to faith only when she has heard (v. 16) and seen the Lord (v. 18). Jesus' sheep recognize his voice (10:4).

The disciples, introduced in Scene 2, become central in the scene that follows (vv. 19-25). Beginning in a state of fear, they pass from fear to joy "when they saw the Lord" (v. 20). For them, too, faith comes through seeing.

Thomas, a minor character in verses 19-25, becomes central in the final scene. His stance is one of extreme incredulity. He will not believe unless he sees and touches (v. 25). And so Jesus invites him to faith through sight and touch (v. 27).

The evangelist is reviewing all these varying reactions and possibilities *for people of his own time.* What will be their reaction, continued reaction, to the resurrection? Will it be the perplexity of Peter? Will it be that of the Beloved Disciple, who, united so intimately with his Lord in love, believed immediately with minimum evidence? Will it be that of Mary Magdalene and the other disciples, who believed only when they saw and heard? Will they be like Thomas, who refused to believe unless he saw and touched, unless placed in a position in which unbelief became impossible? The evangelist is saying to his own fellow Christians: "Those first disciples were by no means exemplary, nor was their situation so fortunate. Faith was almost forced upon them. That is not something to be envied. Our own situation can be more positive, more profitable, more Christian. Let us follow the example of the Beloved Disciple, who believed with such little evidence. We can be gifted with the ninth beatitude: 'Blest are they who have not seen and have believed' (v. 29). And indeed, blest are we who, without seeing, *believe in the risen Jesus, our Lord and our God.*"

3. Specific verses. *Verse 2:* "They have taken the Lord from the tomb!" John knows this natural explanation, probably from controversies with non-Christians (Matt 28:13-15). He also denies it. The burial clothes were found, and in order (vv. 6-7), which would hardly be the case if someone had taken the body. These clothes were intentionally similar to those of Lazarus (ch. 11), who, however, came forth still wrapped in his. Resurrection is different.

Verse 8: "He saw and believed." The singular "He" limits this to the Beloved Disciple. Intensity of love leads to instant belief. It is this same love that will enable him to recognize the Lord in 21:4, 7 when the others do not.

Verse 9: This verse alludes again to the process by which the post-resurrection disciples interpreted Jesus' life by means of the Old Testament Scripture (John 2:17, 22; 12:16).

Verse 14: "But [she] did not know it was Jesus." The various resurrection accounts accent this phenomenon, that the risen Lord was truly Jesus of Nazareth, *the same but different.* He passes through locked doors (20:19, 26) and is unrecognized by personal friends (by Mary here, by the disciples in 21:4, by the Emmaus pair in Luke 24:16). The Lord *is* recognized, however, by the sound of his voice (Mary in v. 16); by love (the Beloved Disciple in 20:8 and 21:7); in the breaking of bread (Luke 24:30-31); and in the power of God's written word (Luke 24:32). All these elements are integral to community liturgy.

Verse 16: "Jesus said to her, 'Mary!' " This should remind us of 10:4. Jesus' sheep recognize his voice.

Verse 17: "Stop holding on to me, for I have not yet ascended to the Father." The meaning is difficult to ascertain. Is it that Jesus is at that moment enroute to the Father and Mary is seen to delay the passage? Or that she clings to his feet *in worship* (as in Matt 28:9), whereas Jesus' humanity will become the glorified center of worship (the new temple) only after his ascension, with its fulfillment of his glorification?

". . . to my Father and your Father, to my God and your God" could stress the difference between Jesus' relationship to the Father and ours. But it can also do just the opposite, indicating that Jesus' Father is truly ours, that his God is our God also.

Verse 20: "The disciples rejoiced when they saw the Lord." In the context of the "little while—short time" passage of 16:22, the disciples were told: "So you also are now in anguish. But I will see you again, and your hearts *will rejoice* . . . ." Our present verse, 20:20, is the fulfillment. Jesus has returned, already returned, through his resurrection and through his gift of the Spirit in verse 22.

Verses 21-22 are a key passage in Johannine theology. The disciples receive the Holy Spirit at this second coming of Jesus: the *eschaton,* the final era, is now; future is present. In 7:39, the Spirit had not yet been given, since Jesus was not yet glorified. On the cross, Jesus, manifesting the nature of God, which is love, delivers over the Spirit (19:30), symbolized immediately afterward by the flow of the sacramental symbols of blood and water. And now, at his first encounter with the believing community, he breathes the Spirit again as he celebrates the re-creation of God's people. Simultaneously, he sends out these disciples just as the Father had sent him (v. 21). His mission becomes theirs; his work is placed in their hands. And that mission, that work, is to manifest God who is love in their words and deeds. Through them now, enlivened by the Spirit, will the presence of God become known and seen and felt in the world. If in truth Jesus is God's sacrament, God's exegete, we in turn through the Spirit become Jesus' sacraments, his living exegetes.

Verses 22-23, which speak clearly of the community's share in Jesus' power to forgive sins, can be simply a reference to baptism, the traditional sacrament of forgiveness, or to the church's continuous preaching of forgiveness of sins in Jesus. But this reference to sharing in Jesus' power probably intends more than that. Through the ever-present Spirit, the Christian community can offer a restored union with Father and Son, a divine indwelling that creates peace (v. 21) with God and neighbor. Over the centuries, Christian communities have developed different means by which this unifying power is put into effect.

Verse 24: Only in the Fourth Gospel does Thomas receive any emphasis (11:16; 14:5; 20:24-28; 21:2). A historical character, he also functions in this Gospel as a character type. He is a combination of seeming courage (11:16) and ignorance (14:5), but especially is he a stubborn seeker of manifest resurrection credentials. Surely he calls to mind and reflects, for the evangelist, fellow Christians in the community who, beneath a courageous exterior, manifest both ignorance and lack of deep faith. To all such, Jesus and John say: "Do not be unbelieving, but believe" (v. 27).

Verse 28: "My Lord and my God!" There is no doubt that John intends this powerful phrasing (Ps 35:23-24) as a, or better *the,* Christian profession of faith. For the Johannine disciple, Jesus is both Lord and God. With this profession, John creates his own inclusion to the Gospel, the corresponding covers to his book of good news; for "My Lord and my God" at the conclusion corresponds to the opening ". . . and the Word was God" (1:1). The two statements are intentionally parallel.

Verses 30-31 are quite clearly a conclusion, the ending to the original edition of the Gospel. What the evangelist has written—which is not all that he could have written—is meant to urge and strengthen belief in Jesus as the Christ—and as the Son of God. John has already given us this profession in 11:27 on the lips of Martha in the context of another raising from the dead. To live, to really live, is to believe this: that Jesus of Nazareth is indeed the Messiah. And more, he is truly God's Son, dependent on the Father and obedient to him, yet himself divine. He is the Christian's Lord; he is the Christian's God.

D. EPILOGUE: APPEARANCE IN GALILEE

John 21:1-25

This final chapter is an addition to an original Gospel version that concluded with the magnificent statement of 20:31. It is found, however, in every ancient manuscript of the Gospel that we possess and must have been appended almost with the original publication of the work. Added by an expert in John's thought—surely by one of his disciples, and by one thoroughly conversant with the Gospel material—it is a genuine part of the canonical Gospel.

Chapter 21 has been tied to the previous chapters by a host of literary and theological links. Johannine characteristics found in this chapter are the Sea of Tiberias in verse 1; the names of Simon Peter, Thomas the Twin, Nathanael from Cana in verse 2; the night-day contrast of verses 3-4; the lack of recognition in verse 4; the Beloved Disciple of verse 7, who relates to Peter and who first recognizes the Lord; the charcoal fire of verse 9, together with the image of Jesus as servant and giver of bread to the disciples; the reference in verse 14 to two previous appearances (in ch. 20); Peter's triple profession (vv. 15-17) to counterbalance the triple denial and to reintroduce the shepherd theme (ch. 10); the glorifying aspect of Peter's death in verse 19; the reference to the Beloved Disciple's position next to Jesus at the Last Supper in verse 20. If this chapter is an addition—and it is—it is nonetheless a beautiful addition, and the Christian community would be considerably poorer without it.

1. The catch of fish (21:1-14). This story may well be the same as that recounted in Luke 5:4-10. Luke purposely limits Christ's resurrection activities to the area of Jerusalem, so he placed this Galilee story in chapter 5 of his Gospel for its rich homiletic advantage. Called to be fishers of men and women, the disciples can catch nothing without the assistance of the Lord. And indeed, Peter's confession in Luke 5:8, "Depart from me, Lord, for I am a sinful man," makes more sense if this was originally a post-resurrection story following Peter's denials.

The Sea of Tiberias (v. 1) is a Johannine locale (6:22-23), and the fishing companions are, in general, already known to us, with the exception of "Zebedee's sons," who here make their only appearance in the Fourth Gospel. Among the "two other disciples," seemingly, is the Beloved Disciple, who appears unexpectedly in verse 7. The lack of success during the night, followed by enormous success with the daylight presence of Jesus (vv. 3-6), is a practical application of John's frequent comments about night and day, light and darkness. The disciples' failure to recognize Jesus reminds us of a similar failure on the part of Mary (20:14), and we are hardly surprised when the Beloved Disciple is the first to recognize the Lord (v. 7).

The charcoal fire (v. 9) serves a double purpose. It sets the scene for Jesus' servant role as he becomes giver of bread (and fish) to the disciples and also serves as a stage prop for Peter's profession of love, recalling the previous charcoal fire (18:18), next to which Peter had denied the Lord.

The mention of precisely 153 fish (v. 11) has led to symbolic interpretations of all kinds. And indeed, there must be symbolism involved. John hardly means that the disciples took time out to make a count that then became part of Christian tradition. Saint Jerome believed that the zoology of his time taught that there were 153 different kinds of fish; and the number, as a result, reflected universality. Jerome was probably incorrect about the zoologists of his own day, but his suspicion of some universal symbolism was probably correct. Others have arrived at the same kind of symbolism by pointing out, for what it is worth, that 153 is a "universal" number, the sum of a triangle of increasing lines of dots whose tip is one and whose base is seventeen.

Another symbolic possibility at this point is drawn from the fact that the disciples bring the catch (humankind) to the meal (Eucharist) prepared by the risen Lord.

This appearance is Jesus' third (v. 14), when added to the two "room" appearances of chapter 20.

2. Peter (21:15-19). This encounter of Peter with his risen Lord is filled with beautiful material. Jesus offers Peter a public opportunity to profess repentance through love, surely a striking example of what it is that reestablishes our relationship with the Lord after sin. Peter's threefold denial is balanced by this threefold profession of love (the charcoal fire is the visible stage link). With this, he and his Lord are "at-oned."

This incident is also a continuation of the shepherd theme of chapter 10. There seems to be no real difference between Jesus' three commands:

"*Feed* my lambs";

"Tend my *sheep,*" to which is added the composite

"*Feed* my *sheep.*"

The function of Yahweh-shepherd in Ezek 34 passes to Jesus-shepherd in John 10 to Peter-shepherd in John 21. It is important to note how Peter's shepherd role is tied to love (vv. 15-17) and to a willingness (like the good shepherd of 10:11-18) to lay down his life (vv. 18-19). Note, too, how Peter's laying down his life glorified God, as did that of Jesus. Love, love to the limit, selfless, life-giving love manifests (glorifies) God because that is God's nature. An act of selfless, life-giving love is God's name published before the world.

When this chapter was written, Peter's death was already an accomplished fact. Like his Lord (note the "You follow me" of v. 22), he had already stretched out his hands (v. 18) to die on Vatican hill. The tying fast (v. 18) would be the fastening to the cross, always accomplished in part by ropes.

3. The Beloved Disciple (20:20-23). This final incident centers, fittingly, on the Beloved Disciple. The question is: What about him? (v. 21). Verse 23 makes sense only if a belief that the Beloved Disciple would live to see Jesus' final coming had been shattered by his unexpected death. As his followers—among whom was the author of this chapter—looked back to recall the source of their misguided belief, they could discover only an ambiguous statement of Jesus upon which this erroneous concept had been based: "What if I want him to remain until I come? What concern is it of yours?" (v. 22). The mystery of the Beloved Disciple's life and death was not theirs to comprehend. His hour, like the Lord's, had come, leaving them behind. The important thing for the moment, says verse 24, is that this disciple remains on as the eyewitness testimony on which the written Gospel is based. It was he who wrote—or caused to be written, like Pilate in 19:22—this version of the good news. The "*we* know" indicates that this chapter itself has been written by others, that it is a God-sent addition.

Verse 25 concludes the chapter with a brief statement that cannot match in content the magnificent original conclusion of 20:30-31. The reader should be encouraged to re-read that beautiful finale as one finishes the reading and studying and praying of this impressive presentation of the Good News that is Jesus, God's revelation, God's love manifested in self-sacrifice, and for us the sole way and truth and life.

Having studied chapter 21, we can now hazard a guess as to why it was added to the original Gospel. There are two centers of attention in the chapter. The first is Peter, who is successively reconciled through his profession of love, then constituted the shepherd, and finally described as a martyr whose death glorified God. The second is the Beloved Disciple, whose death has deeply disturbed the community, but whose eyewitness testimony remains the secure foundation of its faith. This chapter has taken origin from these two concerns: to paint a portrait of Peter as the reconciled, loving, and martyred community shepherd, and to base the faith of the community in the Beloved Disciple on firmer footing. All-important for the Christians is not the Beloved Disciple's visible presence but his life-giving word. And this is enclosed forever in this Gospel.

CONCLUSIONS TO OUR STUDY OF JOHN'S GOSPEL

Now that we have finished our study of John's Gospel, it might be of help to attempt a brief résumé of some of the more important issues regarding the theology, literary origin, and community background of the Gospel.

1. Revelation. John's central theological teaching concerns revelation: God's revelation of himself in his completely unique Son, Jesus of Nazareth, one with the Father, the living and incarnate Word, who in himself bespeaks, proclaims, identifies, immediates the Father. To know Jesus is to know God. And so, too, John gives us the Book of Glory, which climaxes in the ultimate revelation of the Son as self-sacrificing love. It is on the cross that Jesus glorifies/manifests the Father. God the Father, therefore, is love. This will be the final, simple, concise definition of 1 John 4:16, "God is love, and whoever remains in love remains in God, and God in him."

2. Mission. To reveal the Father is Jesus' mission; it is for this that he has been sent. This mission is, in turn, passed to us who believe in him. Our Christian mission is to reveal both the Father and the Son within us. God who is love, the Son who lays down his life, will be known only through us, through our lives of self-sacrificing love. The baton of the Word-made-flesh has been passed to us, who are now called to reveal the Word through our flesh. Only in this way will the world come to know and to believe. Since all Christians are called equally to share in this mission, John ceaselessly speaks of "disciples—*mathētai.*" John's Christianity is very egalitarian: his challenge is a question to us all. Do we, or do we not, reveal the God who is love?

3. Paraclete. In this mission we are not alone. To us has been given the Paraclete, both to enliven and to enlighten us. As Jesus is God-with-us (Matthew's Emmanuel), so the Spirit is Christ-with-us. He appears as Jesus leaves. He is delivered over as Jesus dies on the cross, breathed upon the disciples at Jesus' first resurrection appearance to them, sent from above as Jesus returns to his Father's side. Every step in Jesus' exaltation is accompanied by a gift to us of his Spirit.

4. The Beloved Disciple. If it is the Paraclete's function to enlighten and enliven the disciples, the community of the Fourth Gospel has experienced this in a particular way through the effect of the Spirit on the Beloved Disciple. It is he who, as eyewitness, provides the firm basis for the belief of the community. As the Word can reveal the Father, since he is at the Father's bosom (1:18), so the Beloved Disciple can reveal the Son, since he rested at the Son's bosom (13:25).

Appearing possibly in 1:35-40 as the anonymous of the two disciples, the Beloved Disciple makes frequent appearances starting with the passion material: at the Last Supper in 13:23-25; very probably in the high priest's courtyard as the other disciple of 18:15-16; at the foot of the cross as Jesus is glorified and the Christian community comes into being (19:25-27); at the tomb (20:1-10); and, finally, during the fishing trip of 21:7, 20-24.

The Beloved Disciple seems to be a Jerusalem disciple with connections to the high priest. His presentation of Jesus—on the solid presumption that he either authored the Fourth Gospel or was extremely instrumental in shaping its literary form (19:35; 21:24)—is so different from that of the other three Gospels that he was hardly one of the Twelve, a title he rarely uses (only in 6:67-71 and 20:24). He is coupled with Peter, over whom he has a certain kind of spiritual precedence. Peter asks Jesus through him (13:24); Peter knows Jesus through him (21:7); Peter believes after him (20:8).

At this present moment of scholarship, it seems best to accept the Beloved Disciple as anonymous, yet as a true disciple and eyewitness of the Lord, connected with Jerusalem, not one of the Twelve, whose different background and different Christian experience led him to produce, directly or indirectly, a version of the Good News strikingly different from that of Mark, Matthew, and Luke.

Historical as he is, the Beloved Disciple is also presented to us as an ideal, a model of what we should be as disciples ourselves—loved and loving.

5. John's community. One very striking facet of the Fourth Gospel is the manner in which the life of John's own community interpenetrates that of Jesus. Since Jesus lives on through and in his Spirit, the Paraclete, the life and history of John's community continue to be the life and history of the risen Lord. What happens to the community happens to Jesus. What is spoken by the Paraclete-enlivened disciples is spoken by Jesus, for the Paraclete transmits what he hears Jesus saying (16:13). Jewish controversies with John's group become controversies with Jesus, and what Jesus says is the community's response. This is Gospel writing and, clearly, not modern history. Let us note three of the most obvious instances. At the end of chapter 6, the sharp discussion regarding the consumption of Jesus' flesh and blood is a later Johannine controversy. In chapter 8, the controversy between Jesus and the Pharisees concerning his unique Sonship and identification as the I AM is, historically speaking, a controversy between the later Pharisees and John's community. A third is apparent in chapter 9, where the blind man excommunicated from the synagogue represents Johannine Jewish Christians of the eighties–nineties, for whom profession of faith in Jesus means radical excommunication from religion, family, and friends. The Jesus of the Fourth Gospel speaks differently than the Jesus of the first three Gospels because his voice is so frequently transmitted through the lips of the Paraclete-inspired community.

If it is true that the Gospel reflects John's own community, we can identify this community as a group that includes (1) true Israelites, such as Nathanael (1:47) and previous followers of the Baptist (1:35) and the man born blind (ch. 9), all of whom have become disciples out of Judaism; (2) Greeks, such as those of 12:20-22; (3) Samaritans who, white for the harvest, have recognized Jesus as Savior (4:42).

This community is in uneasy relationship with the unbelieving world; with the Pharisees, who reject Jesus' claims (chs. 7–8); even with other Christians who are deficient in their Eucharistic belief (6:66) or who remain crypto-Christians out of fear of expulsion from the synagogue and Judaism (12:42-43).

It is also a community that, while recognizing the importance of the Twelve in general (6:67-70) and of Peter in particular (1:42; 6:68-69; 21:15-19), places its main emphasis on discipleship and the presence of the Paraclete.

6. Dramatic elements. This combination of Beloved Disciple, community, and Paraclete has, for some as yet unexplained reasons, given us a Gospel that is amazingly rich in dramatic techniques. Chapters such as 4, 9, 11, and 20 can be given instant staging. Peter, Thomas, Philip, and Judas (chs. 13–14) are present simply to ask leading questions that help to carry the discussion forward. Other characters, historical as they are, model roles. Nathanael (1:47) is what all true Israelites should be. Andrew and Philip (1:41, 45; 6:5-9; 12:20-22) perform like real missionaries. Nicodemus portrays a person who passes gradually, though with fear, from darkness into light (3:1-10; 7:50-52; 19:39). The Samaritan woman (ch. 4) clarifies the possibility, for a woman as for a man, to move from sin and ignorance into faith and mission. Jesus' mother models Mother Church. The Beloved Disciple portrays what all disciples should be.

The Gospel is filled with other dramatic elements, too: with frequent irony as the obviously untrue turns out to be eminently true—Jesus *will* die for the whole world (11:52) and he really is king (19:19-22); with the use of ambiguity, misunderstanding, clarification to capture the interest of the hearers; with an almost pre-play program description of Jesus in chapter 1; with the stage props of the bucket of the Samaritan woman (4:28) and Peter's charcoal fire (18:18; 21:9).

All of this helps to make this Gospel so rich that a lifetime of study cannot plumb its depths. As Christians of the past twenty centuries have written about the Fourth Gospel without coming close to exhausting its riches, so, it seems certain, will Christians of the next twenty as well.

1 JOHN

Neal M. Flanagan, O.S.M.

COMMENTARY

Tucked far away from the Fourth Gospel in our Bible lie the three writings called the Epistles of John. It is to these that our attention must now turn. As was done with the Gospel, we shall postpone a consideration of what are usually treated as introductory questions (author, occasion, date, community, theological content, interrelationship of the three epistles) until we have actually encountered the material that provides what answers there are to such problems. The only introductory issue we want to face here is that of the possible division of the First Epistle of John. This is a difficult and confusing question, since the epistle is repetitious and circular—like a spiral, suggest some authors, which goes round and round but with a definite, even if not too distinguishable, progression. Though commentators differ in their breakdown of the material, there is sufficient consensus to propose the following division as workable. Though admittedly very general, it will help the reader both to distinguish diverse elements and to synthesize them into an overall unity.

PROLOGUE:

1:1-4	The historical reality of the Christian message
1:5–2:2	Walking in the light: the question of sin
2:3-17	Keeping the commandments (accent on love)
2:18-27	Warning against false teachers, the antichrists (accent on faith)
2:28–3:24	Children of God, children of the devil, love versus hatred
4:1-6	The two spirits
4:7-21	God's love inspires ours
5:1-13	Faith: conclusion

EPILOGUE:

5:14-21	Prayer for sinners, summary

PROLOGUE: 1:1-4 The historical reality of the Christian message

Summary: First John, like the Gospel, begins with a prologue. The entire emphasis is upon the historical reality of what our author and his fellow Christians have experienced. This is the Word of life (v. 1), the message that has been heard and is now to be proclaimed. The message, however, has been incarnated in a human being, the Son, Jesus Christ (v. 3), who was actually heard and seen and touched. In him eternal life became visible so that both he and it might be shared with us (vv. 2-3). This is a fellowship *(koinōnia)* with both Father and Son, and the very act of describing it in writing is, for the author, a source of consummate joy (v. 4).

Comments: This short section is not written with smooth articulation—thus the breaks in continuity, usually indicated in English translations by a dash or parentheses or both. It is almost as though the author were speaking extemporaneously, with the natural breaks in thought that occur away from the discipline of pen and ink. Notable are the phrases reminiscent of the Fourth Gospel, though their content has slight differences from the Gospel meaning. The "from the beginning" of verse 1 is not a reference to eternity (John 1:1), but to the inception of the gospel preaching. The "Word of life" (v. 1) is not exclusively that word which became flesh (John 1:14), but the *gospel message* that became audible, visible, and tangible in the human Jesus.

Does the insistence upon hearing, seeing, and touching demand that the author be an eyewitness to the words and works of the historical Jesus? That, surely, is the most obvious meaning. Yet the words also permit the solid possibility that the author is simply, but forcefully, uniting himself to the actual eyewitnesses from whom he has derived his version of the good news. Through them—and he can summon them up in his memory—he has truly experienced the Lord and his word of life.

1:5–2:2 Walking in the light: the question of sin

Summary: Part of the message for Christians is that there is a sphere of life and righteousness that can be called "light." It is God's sphere, for "God is light" (v. 5). But there is another sphere, too, which is that of darkness, of untruth, and there are those who walk in it. To have fellowship with both God (v. 6) and one another (v. 7), we must walk in the light, cleansed from sin by the blood of God's Son (v. 7). This cleansing demands from us a personal acknowledgement of our sin, which will be answered by the cleansing that comes from God. To pretend that we have never sinned is, in itself, a lie that would continue to bind us to the sphere of darkness (vv. 8-10). Such admission of sin is by no means a suggestion that sin makes little difference in Christian life. Our author's purpose in writing is to keep Christians from sin (2:1). Yet, though living in the light, he is not blinded by it: he can see that Christians can and, on occasion, still do sin. Christ, however, remains effective, both as intercessor (Paraclete) and as sin-offering, and not for us only but for the whole world (2:1-2).

Comments: There are a number of peculiarities in this section. "God is light," says verse 5, a statement that is not too strange after our study of the Fourth Gospel, but yet is a bit different. In the Gospel the emphasis falls on *Jesus* as the light of the world (John 8:12; 9:5).

A second peculiarity is the description of Jesus as a sin-offering (2:2) whose blood not only cleanses *us* from all sin (v. 7) but is effective for the whole world (2:2). This, too, is an emphasis not seen in the Fourth Gospel, for which Jesus' death is not nearly so much expiatory—perhaps only and barely in the Lamb of God statement (John 1:29)—as revelatory of God's love.

The "children" of 2:1 is a third novelty. In John's Gospel the author's posture is egalitarian: the followers of Christ are simply disciples (*mathētai*), and there is little, if any, hierarchy evident. First John makes extensive use of "children" and, in so doing, gives a picture of a person of special responsibility addressing Christians whom he fully expects to listen to his advice and pleading.

Finally, it comes as a surprise for those reading 2:2 in the Greek, or from a literal translation, to find Jesus called "Advocate" (intercessor). John's Gospel reserves that name for the Spirit, though John 14:16 does call the Spirit "another Advocate," thus leaving room for Jesus, too, to fulfill that function.

2:3-17 Keeping the commandments

Summary: Christianity is not simply a "head trip," a question only of knowledge. It demands a life consonant with the God of love we claim to know and experience. Fortunately, we have a human exemplar to follow and thus are challenged (v. 6) to conduct ourselves just as Jesus did.

And this means a challenge to love (vv. 7-11). In a sense, this is now an old commandment, one that Christians have heard from the beginning of their instruction (v. 7). On the other hand, it is still new, for Jesus has given us the abiding newness of his own example, which we renew in ourselves (v. 8). We must live in one of two polarities: in the light that is the sphere of reciprocal love (v. 10) or in the darkness of hatred (v. 11), where one can only stumble blindly in darkness (vv. 9, 11).

Encouragement flows out to the inhabitants of the light: to "the children" (vv. 12, 14), who, though spiritually immature, have, through personal experience of the Father, been freed from sin; to the "fathers" (vv. 13-14), the spiritually mature, whose knowledge of the Father is secure and unmovable; to the "young men" (vv. 13-14), the spiritually proficient, whose strength, rising from the abiding word of God, has conquered the evil one.

All of these Christians are now advised to treat the ungodly world with cautious discernment (vv. 15-17). Passions, greed, wealth and its trappings (v. 16) leave no place for the Father's love to dwell (v. 15). Whereas all things are transitory, the one who does God's will abides forever (v. 17).

Comments: The material in this section has a loose unity, held together by the obedience to the commandments of the initial verses (3-8) and by the doing of God's will (an identical concept) in the final verse (17). The emphasis throughout falls on love. It would be possible to interpret "just as he did" (v. 6) of God the Father, but this expression is uniformly used in 1 John of Jesus. Our author has no difficulty in passing imperceptibly from the Father to the Son, as he does here.

The precise meaning of "children," "fathers," "young men" of verses 12-14 is much disputed. The designations could refer to age groups. Or the "fathers . . . young men" could be officials (like presbyters and deacons) in the community, the membership of which would be referred to in general as the "children." We suggest that these names loosely differentiate states of spiritual maturity. Emphasis—by final position and length of description—falls on the "young men," those advanced in spirituality yet not completely mature, who bear the brunt of the crisis that has occasioned this writing. No one explanation of this terminology has been accepted by all scholars.

Verses 15-17 are surely a pessimistic summation of Christian relationship to the world. As was true in the Gospel, this is largely a question of language. The world of which these verses speak is not God's world, not the "whole world" for which Jesus is an offering for sin (2:2), but the sphere of anti-God, that is, of unlove and untruth. It will be personified in the antichrists of the following verses.

2:18-27 Warning against false teachers, the antichrists

Summary: The appearance of antichrists tolls the final hour (v. 18). Sad to report, they are "of our number" (v. 19), and it is they who now "would deceive you" (v. 26). Protection comes from the divine anointing that provides knowledge (v. 20), that teaches all truth, so that, free from any lie, "you do not need anyone to teach you" (v. 27).

Comments: The "last hour" (v. 18) is a common motif throughout the other New Testament writings, though certainly not central to the theology of John's Gospel, where Jesus' future coming is very secondary to his already experienced presence. The term "antichrists" is found only in this epistle and 2 John among the whole of the New Testament literature. It is similar, however, to the "false christs" of Mark 13:22—they, too, are signs of an impending judgment. Cardinal John Henry Newman suggested that the movement of salvation history went along on a straight line up to the brink of the end time, where it changed direction ninety degrees to follow along on the edge of the precipice. Our Christian lives, in this description, would be lived on the brink, just a step away from the plunge into the beyond.

Verse 19 indicates the crisis that has occasioned this epistle. Members have left the Johannine community, members whose very exit proved their insincerity. Like Judas (John 13:30), whom our author may consider as their model, they went out into the darkness. The insistence on knowledge and truth apparent in the following verses (20-27) makes it evident that those who left were faulty in their teaching. Verse 22 is to the point: "Who is the liar? Whoever denies that Jesus is the Christ. Whoever denies the Father and the Son, this is the antichrist." This appears to be an out-and-out denial that Jesus was the Christ, a denial, then, of the central theology of John's Gospel: ". . . that you may [come to] believe that Jesus is the Messiah, the Son of God, and that through this belief you may have life in his name" (20:31). Further passages in 1 John will give us more evidence about the content of this disbelief. The accent in this passage is on faith.

Defense against errant teaching will be provided by the divine anointing (vv. 20, 27) that we have all received, our Christing ("anointing" is *chrisma* in Greek) in baptism with the teaching (vv. 20, 27) provided at that time (v. 24) and our subsequent dwelling in both the Son and the Father (v. 24). This is eternal life, and the promise of an even greater sharing in it (v. 25).

2:28–3:24 Children of God, children of the devil, love versus hatred

Summary: If we but remain in God, our future is without fear, since the holiness of our lives will prove that we are God's children (2:28-29). And indeed, this is precisely what we are now by God's love (v. 1). And we shall become even more intimate children as, seeing him as he is, we meld into his likeness (v. 2). If only we remain pure as he is (v. 3), holy as the Son is holy (v. 7).

The other option is to exist and act in the sphere of sin and lawlessness (v. 4), which is to become a child of the devil, one whose actions are unholy, specifically one who does not love (v. 10).

That we love one another was our first instruction (v. 11), and in this love we have passed from death to life (v. 14). The opposite is to become the devil's child like Cain (Gen 4), who killed his brother in jealous rage, just as the anti-God world now rages against us (v. 13). Not to love is death, the condition of both the murderer and the hater (vv. 14-15). Our call, on the contrary, is to lay down our lives for one another as Christ sacrificed his for us (v. 16). This means, at least, to share what we have with the needy (vv. 17-18). If we do, even though we may be imperfect (v. 20), the magnanimous God will be with us (vv. 20-21), and with him, his peace (v. 19). But all depends on this double commandment: that we *believe* in his Son, Jesus Christ, and *love* one another (v. 23). If we do, God remains in us, evident by his gift of the Spirit (v. 24).

Comments: Verse 2:28 speaks again of Jesus' coming, the final hour of 2:18. As we noted, this is a minor issue in John's Gospel.

The repeated reference to the "children of God" (vv. 1, 2, 10) employs the language and distinction of the Gospel. Christians are God's children, the *tekna Theou;* only Jesus is God's Son, the *huios Theou.* As our author describes the "begotten by God" (v. 9), he slips into strongly figurative language. The Greek of verse 9 speaks of God's seed remaining in his children. John 3:1 has already insisted that this is what we really are—God's children!

The imagery of verse 2 is fascinating. Looking at God as though into a mirror, our own visage is reflected, but with divine configuration. As God's children we will, says the author, bear an amazing family likeness.

Verse 3 is ambiguous. Are we to keep ourselves pure as God is pure or as Jesus is pure? Probably the latter, since in subsequent verses it is Christ who is sinless (v. 5) and the Son who is holy (v. 7).

Verse 4 seems simplistic in stating that sin is lawlessness, but our author wants to insist that there are definitely things that we *should do* and others that we *should not do.* Disobedience is sin, the pattern of the devil (v. 8), who from the beginning fostered disobedience unto death (Gen 3:4-5). John 8:44 concludes in a similar fashion that the devil was a liar and murderer from the beginning. His followers are his children (John 8:44), and for 1 John the murderer Cain is an example (v. 12).

The double reference to the laying down of life in verse 16 recalls the repeated statement in John 10:11-18 that Jesus, as good shepherd, would lay down his life for his sheep.

Verse 23 provides in miniature the theological heart of 1 John: we must *believe* in God's Son, Jesus the Christ, and *love* one another. Belief and love—basically 1 John speaks of nothing else. Where these obtain, the divine indwelling is an accomplished fact, to which the presence of the Spirit testifies. This first mention of the Spirit in 1 John leads us into the following section.

4:1-6 The two spirits

Summary: Be not immediately impressed by a powerful spiritual presence, however, for it may indicate the spirit of antichrist (v. 3), that of the many false prophets who have gone out (from us) into the world (v. 1). The spirits must be tested, and the test is crucial: Do they, or do they not, believe that Jesus Christ has come in the flesh? (v. 2). It is this which we believe and by which we, with the strength of God, have won the victory (v. 4). Those who do not believe belong to the anti-God world that listens to them (v. 5). Theirs is the spirit of deception, ours the spirit of truth (v. 6).

Comments: This question of discernment of spirits comes down to a single practical test: What do the prophets—true or false—believe? What do they teach about Jesus? If they acknowledge Jesus Christ come in the flesh, they are genuine Christians; if they do not, they are false prophets and belong to the world. This test is a clarification of the doctrinal difficulty first expressed in 2:22: "Who is the liar? Whoever denies that Jesus is the Christ." The faith statement "Jesus is the Christ" is nuanced now in verse 2 to insist that Jesus Christ has come in the flesh. *The emphasis falls on the humanity of Jesus.* He in whom we believe, he whose name we bear as Christians, is Son of God, is the Christ, is intimately united with the Father, and is also, and of his essence, *a human being.* It is about this last phrase that the controversy rages, a controversy that, for the author, is absolutely critical for Christian faith.

That the world listens to the opponents (v. 5), to the false prophets (v. 1) with the spirit of antichrist (v. 3), indicates that the opposition is having considerable success. Is our author's group in danger of becoming a minority among what had been a united Johannine community?

4:7-21 God's love inspires ours

Summary: God is love (vv. 8, 16), and he has first loved us (vv. 10, 16, 19). He evidenced this love through the gift of his Son (v. 9), sent as Savior (v. 14). Because God has so loved us, we too must become lovers (v. 9), lovers of one another (vv. 7, 11, 12, 20, 21). Only if we love the visible neighbor can we love the invisible God (vv. 12, 20).

God's love for us and our love for him and for one another should afford us fearless confidence (v. 18), for we have overcome the world just as Christ has (v. 17). It is in him as Savior of the world and as Son of God that we profess our faith through the Spirit (vv. 13-14). On the other hand, sadly and simply, the man without love has known nothing of God (v. 8); his profession of love for God without love for neighbor is a disastrous lie (v. 20).

Comments: This section is a tight unity concentrating without distraction on the one point that God's love generates ours. The verses are linked together by numerous connections: 8//16; 10//16//19; 10//14; 12//20; 20//21, with the whole converging on the central truth that if God has loved us we must have similar love for one another (v. 11). That "God is love" (vv. 8, 16) is now the second description of God given in this epistle; we have already seen that "God is light" (1:5). God is not love in the abstract but in all his activity. He creates lovingly, he saves lovingly, he judges lovingly. Our God is a God of love.

Reference to the Spirit (v. 13) returns us for a moment to the context of 4:1-6. It is the Spirit, as in 4:2, who enables us to affirm the truth—the truth that Jesus is Savior of the world, that he is Son of God (4:14-15). The basic creedal affirmations of this Johannine community are assuming a more definite shape. For the Johannine Christian, Jesus is the Christ (2:22) come in the flesh (4:2); Jesus is Savior (3:16; 4:14), an offering for the sins of the world (1:7; 2:2; 4:10); Jesus is Son of God (3:23; 4:15).

5:1-13 Faith: conclusion

Summary: All who believe that Jesus is the Christ (v. 1), the Son of God (v. 5), are themselves children of God, to be loved as is their Father (v. 1). In fact, this reciprocal love is the Father's unburdensome command (v. 3), originating from the Christian faith that has conquered the world (vv. 4-5).

Faith is belief in Jesus Christ, who came in essential humanity, in a human ministry stretching from baptism till human death, both testified to by the Spirit (v. 6). Not only does the Spirit testify, but so too do the present-day water and blood (v. 8)—the sacraments of baptism and Eucharist—which bespeak the presence of Christ himself and the eternal life he brings (vv. 11-12). Spirit, water, and blood are part of God's testimony. To deny them is to reject God's own witness and to affirm that he is a liar (v. 10). And, indeed, the purpose of this whole epistle is to help all to realize that they actually possess eternal life—if, that is, they believe in the Son of God (v. 13).

Comments: To the preceding section on love (4:7-21), recalled briefly in 5:1-3, is now added a section on faith. The creedal statement proposed here is that Jesus is the Son of God (vv. 5, 10, 12)—but a Son of God who is also thoroughly human, both at the baptism (at which the Spirit testified in John 1:33-34) that initiated the ministry and in the bloody death that terminated it. Son of God, yes—but a Son of God whose humanity was essential. This is the insistence of verse 6. In verses 7-8 a shift is made. To the Spirit as witness are added both the water and blood. The historical incidents of verse 6 are replaced by the sacraments. The Spirit still testifies to Jesus, and so do the sacraments of baptism and Eucharist. All three give their testimony in the Christian assembly: the Spirit through those speakers who are his inspired mouthpiece; baptism and Eucharist as signs of the eternal life that God gives us in his Son (vv. 11-12), as occasions during which faith in Jesus is solemnly affirmed and strengthened.

Verse 13 looks very much like a conclusion and, indeed, bears striking resemblance to John 20:31, the original conclusion to the Fourth Gospel. Apparently to this conclusion to the epistle have been added the final verses 14-21.

5:14-21 Prayer for sinners, summary

Summary: Our prayer should be made in complete confidence: what we ask for is already ours (vv. 14-15). One specific thing we should request is the conversion of the sinner, except in the case of one sinning in deadly fashion—there is doubt about that (vv. 16-17). We who are begotten by God, however, will not sin, shielded as we are by Christ, part of God's sphere and not of the devil's, to whom belongs the anti-God world (vv. 18-19). Actually we indwell both the Father and the Son, true God and eternal life. One final word—guard yourselves from the idols.

Comments: This short section touches on four different points. The first (vv. 14-15) is simple: Ask and you shall receive (Matt 7:7-8; Luke 11:9-10). God's door is always open. The second (vv. 16-17) is considerably more complicated. We are encouraged to pray for Christian sinners with the promise that this prayer, too, will be answered. But the author expresses serious doubt about the value and efficacy of prayer for those Christians sinning in deadly fashion. He does not say not to pray for them and cautions: "There is such a thing as deadly sin, about which I do not say that you should pray" (v. 16). He must view those whose sin is deadly as ex-Christians who have, with fatal deliberation, moved out into the darkness. Unfortunately for us readers, the deadly sin is not described. Some commentators have suggested murder and adultery, but it seems more in accord with the whole of 1 John to identify the sin as deliberate apostasy—the choice of darkness over light, of death over life, of hatred over love.

The third point (vv. 18-20) presents a rather black-and-white world view. On the one side are ranged the children of God, protected by divine power, dwelling in both Father and Son, graced by divine life; on the other side are the evil one and his anti-God world. For twentieth-century readers the contrast is too strong, too definite. The modern world in which we live specializes in shadows.

The epistle concludes with a terse warning against the idols. These are, in all probability, not false images but false doctrines, especially those that peek out between the lines of this letter—a faulty appreciation of Jesus' humanity and of its saving power.

CONCLUSIONS TO OUR STUDY OF 1 JOHN

This first, and principal, of the three Johannine epistles is elusive. It says nothing about its author, little about his community and about the crisis that occasioned the writing of this epistle. Even the doctrinal elements lack sharp definition. Yet some conclusions can be drawn regarding all of these elements.

1. Occasion. The clearest evidence can be found in 2:19, where we are told that the opponents, the "antichrists," are people who *exited from the author's own community.* They are described as deceivers (2:26) against whom the epistle hopes that the Spirit and instruction received in baptism will provide protection (2:20, 24-27). They are false prophets (4:1) whose spirit is one of deception (4:6). It is their teaching, surely, that constitutes the idols, the false doctrines, of the epistle's final verse. The author has clearly been shocked and offended by this terrible split in the community. He hesitates even to hope that something can be done to repair it (5:16). Whereas the Johannine community of the Gospel has been excommunicated from the synagogue, the community of 1 John has been abandoned by Christians (1 John would hardly call them that) who no longer wish to share belief and life.

2. Theology. (a) The nature and work of *Jesus Christ* is the central issue. The epistle insists, as we have seen, that Jesus is the Christ (2:22; 5:1), come in the flesh (4:2); that Jesus is Savior (3:16; 4:14), an offering for the sins of the world (1:7; 2:2; 4:10); that Jesus is the Son of God (3:23; 4:15; 5:5, 10, 11-13); that

Jesus came through both water and blood (5:6). Although these elements still do not allow us to paint a completely clear picture of what 1 John is arguing for and against, it must be that the opponents are challenging Jesus' humanity and its salvific function. A little later in the history of the church, Cerinthus would teach that the supernatural Christ descended upon the man Jesus at baptism, revealing God during Jesus' ministry, and departed from Jesus before his death. This presented an antiseptic Christ, hardly touched by Jesus' humanity, and not touched at all by his death. If the opponents of 1 John have not quite arrived at the position of Cerinthus, they are well on the way. For them Jesus' humanity was not of salvific importance. And so 1 John insists on the flesh, on the death, on the salvific function, on the offering for the sins of the world. For 1 John, Jesus—the man Jesus—was truly Son of God, but in this unique Sonship the truth and value of his humanity were never diminished. This same insistence on Jesus' humanity may explain why 1 John is considerably more God-centered than the Fourth Gospel. The more emphasis placed on Jesus come in the flesh, the sharper the contrast between him and the eternal Father.

b) The epistle's *moral teaching* is almost too simple. Two verbs describe it all: *believe* and *love.* The author is anguished by those whose belief has been corrupted, by those whose love stands denounced by the very fact of their departure. And so the epistle insists that we believe what was taught from the beginning (1:1; 2:7, 24; 3:11) and that we can only love God if we unfailingly love one another. The core of 1 John's ethics is given clearly in 3:23: "We are to believe in the name of his Son, Jesus Christ, and are to love one another."

c) The position of the *Advocate* in 1 John is subdued in comparison to the importance of this figure in the Fourth Gospel. Actually, the word occurs only once, in 1 John 2:1, where, surprisingly, it is applied to Jesus, who intercedes for us in the presence of his Father. The entire function of the Spirit gets only brief attention. The references to the anointing in 2:20-27 may refer to the Spirit, but without specification, and the first clear reference is in 3:24, which leads immediately into a warning about testing the spirits (4:1-6). We find other references to the Spirit only in 4:13 and 5:6-7. A scholarly guess is that the opponents have argued so strongly from the supposed presence of the Spirit in bolstering their own positions that the author of 1 John has backed off a bit from a strong Advocate theology, lest he play into their hands.

3. Author and community. The epistle leaves its author unnamed, without even references such as those to the Beloved Disciple that indicate either authorship or original testimony in the Fourth Gospel. The epistle resembles the Gospel in vocabulary and in theological emphases, though these latter show nuanced differences from those of the Gospel. The epistle also seems to be from a later period when the opponents are no longer outsiders, as in the Fourth Gospel, but fellow Christians who have broken unity with the group. These characteristics point with some firmness to a writer different from the evangelist but thoroughly imbued with his theology, writing some years—not necessarily many—after the Gospel was published. About A.D. 100 is a good guess. Some scholars believe that he may have been the writer who re-edited the Gospel by adding on material such as chapter 21. That is possible but not certain, though 3 John 12 must be editorially related to John 21:24. His community is Johannine, related closely in mentality to the Fourth Gospel, with a theology differing from, but not contradictory to, that of the other Gospels. It is a community with little evidence of structured authority, more egalitarian than hierarchical. And it is a community which, perhaps because of that very non-hierarchical structure, has suffered a devastating schism. Unity has been broken. Our author has taken up pen and ink to encourage faithfulness, to protect the truth, to inspire mutual love.

2 JOHN

Neal M. Flanagan, O.S.M.

COMMENTARY

Structure: The Second Epistle of John is a short letter, just long enough to fill one papyrus sheet. It contains the ordinary letter divisions of the time: the introduction (vv. 1-3); the note of happiness or thanksgiving (v. 4); the body of the letter (vv. 5-11); the conclusion (vv. 12-13).

Occasion and contents: The letter fits well into the picture of the Johannine community sketched out at the end of 1 John. Visitors to the author, who now terms himself "the Presbyter" (v. 1), have shown themselves faithful to the truth as he sees it (v. 4). So he writes with joy to the Johannine church (the "Lady" of vv. 1, 5) from which they have come to express his happiness and to tender his advice. The advice, not surprisingly, concerns *love* and *belief*. They are to love one another (vv. 5-6). Equally, they must beware of those who have broken unity, the antichrists who deny that Jesus Christ has come in the flesh (vv. 7-9). They should not even offer them welcome, lest their homes become the pulpits of the evil one (vv. 10-11).

The note concludes with hope for an impending visit and greetings from the members of the author's own church, the children of their chosen sister (v. 13).

1 and 2 John were most probably authored by the same person who in 2 John warns a different Johannine community of the dangers spelled out at length in the first epistle. The two epistles are, consequently, closely related, written because of the same crisis, by the same author, and most probably about the same time, close to A.D. 100.

Comments: (a) Verses 1 and 13, the beginning and the end, use identical terminology. The letter is addressed to the *chosen* Lady and her *children* and encloses final greetings from the *children* of her *chosen* sister. It is ecclesiastical language that is being used. The chosen Lady and her chosen sister are sister churches, of which the children are the members. The "Presbyter" of verse 1 is an ambiguous term. It means more than "older man," since the author calls himself "*the* Presbyter" and addresses the church with some degree of authority. The most probable meaning of the designation is that the author is a second-generation Christian who has known the eyewitnesses of primitive Christianity and can, therefore, testify to what was seen and taught from the beginning.

b) The Johannine polarity between believers and deceivers is strongly phrased. There are those who know the truth, in whom it abides, and who walk in the truth with love (vv. 1-6). And there are the others, antichrists, who do not confess Jesus Christ coming in the flesh (v. 7). The theological framework is clearly that of 1 John. Verse 9 deals with the radical "progressives" who abandoned the traditional truth for novelty. The author has a real fear, reflected in verse 8, that his sister Johannine community might succumb to such novelty. It is that fear which moves him to bar house churches and their pulpits to such false teachers (vv. 10-11).

c) Verse 12 is an affirmation that personal encounter is of more value than literary correspondence.

3 JOHN

Neal M. Flanagan, O.S.M.

COMMENTARY

Structure: The Third Epistle of John is another brief note, slightly shorter than 2 John, and with similar divisions: the introduction (v. 1); the note of happiness (vv. 2-4); the body (vv. 5-12), which centers successively on Gaius, Diotrephes, and Demetrius; the conclusion (vv. 13-15).

Occasion and contents: This letter is addressed to an individual, Gaius, a member of another Johannine church, of whom visitors to the author have spoken well (vv. 3, 6). The purpose of the letter is to congratulate Gaius (vv. 2-4) while encouraging his continued support for Johannine missionaries (vv. 5-8), such as Demetrius, who probably has been sent by the author himself (v. 12) and is the bearer of this letter. The author also wishes to warn Gaius against Diotrephes, who has taken leadership in one of the Johannine groups and refuses to afford hospitality to the missionaries. Even worse, he expels from the church those Christians who do help them.

The epistle, consequently, centers on hospitality and authority, not on the Christological and soteriological problems evident in 1 and 2 John. Yet the same author seems to have written all three, and at approximately the same time. We have already seen how 2 John is linked to 1 John. 3 John, on its part, is linked to 2 John both by the designation of the author as "the Presbyter" and by the close similarity of 3 John 13-14 to 2 John 12. There is a further fascinating similarity between 3 John 12b: ". . . and you know our testimony is true," and the Gospel of John 21:24: ". . . and we know that his testimony is true," which provides argument for those who believe that the Johannine epistles were written by the redactor of the Fourth Gospel, whose hand is seen most clearly in John 21.

Comments: (a) About Gaius (v. 1) absolutely nothing is known except what is told us in this letter. That he is one of the author's "children" (v. 4) has suggested to some commentators that he owed his conversion to the author, but "children" is used so often in these epistles that it need not carry such specific meaning.

b) Verses 5-8 give us a picture of early Christian missionaries, whose subsistence depends completely on the hospitality provided by fellow Christians. Those who give such aid should be considered co-workers (v. 8).

c) Most of the scholarly conjecture regarding 3 John concerns Diotrephes. Of him nothing is known except the few particulars given in verses 9-10. His precise position vis-à-vis the elder is uncertain, though there is no lack of suggestions on the part of scholars.

i) Some believe that he had assumed a position of authoritative leadership, much like that of a bishop, and was firmly opposed to the itinerant missionaries deriving their authority from "the Presbyter."

ii) Others suggest that the difficulty concerned doctrine, and that Diotrephes was an innovator and a heretical teacher. In that case, however, it is surprising that the author makes no specific mention of false teaching.

iii) Still others believe that the shoe should be put on the other foot and that the author himself was the innovator.

All that is known for certain, however, is contained in our text: Diotrephes did not acknowledge the Presbyter's authority, claiming precedence for himself; he refused to welcome the missionaries and expelled those who did; he appears to be opposed by Gaius and the others (vv. 5-8, 10, 15) who have welcomed the missionaries. These particulars lead us to support the opinion (i) that Diotrephes had become overly authoritative, challenging the position of even "the Presbyter."

d) Demetrius is evidently one of the Johannine missionaries sent out by the author and probably carrying along this letter.

e) Verses 13-14 are almost identical to 2 John 12, an indication of the same authorship.

f) Verse 15 gives us a view of one Johannine community saluting another. On both sides, the church members are the beloved, the friends, *hoi philoi.* The author has written to keep these friends united and their church intact.

THE ACTS OF THE APOSTLES

William S. Kurz, S.J.

INTRODUCTION

WHAT IS ACTS AND BY WHOM?

1. Importance

Acts is the only book in the New Testament which continues the story of Jesus into the early church. If it were not for Acts, we would have only isolated pieces of information about the beginnings of the church. We would have to dig these bits and pieces out of the New Testament letters, but would have no framework into which to put them. Acts has provided a framework for understanding not only the information it contains but facts gleaned from Paul's letters and other New Testament books.

But Acts means more than this for Christians today. As part of Scripture, we believe it is God's inspired word to us, and therefore it does not just concern the past. As is true of all biblical narratives, the stories in Acts act as models and examples of how God deals with his people. They give Christians of all ages something to imitate and exemplify how God acts in our lives.

Luke wrote Acts to be read in this way. Out of many possible events he could have described, he picked out those which were most important or most able to exemplify Christian living. He concentrated on a few stories and described them in depth. He tied these stories and the speeches that explain them together by means of summarizing passages and travel notices.

Readers today might at first be surprised at such freedom in putting Acts together. But if we put ourselves in the place of the writer, we realize it had to be this way. In both his Gospel and Acts, Luke had many stories from different sources that he had to join together into one continuous narrative. He had to choose which stories he could use and figure out in which order to put them.

Luke is writing not as some kind of "pure historian," but as a pastoral leader to provide his Christian readers with models to follow. His account is a faith account, full of belief in God's action within the events he narrates. It tries to edify or build up the readers' faith as well. In fact, one could describe Acts as a presentation of the Christian way of following Jesus, as seen in the lives of the earliest Christians.

2. Who wrote Luke and Acts?

The author of Acts never gives his own name. Since few historical books of the Bible give the author's name, this is not surprising. Acts is addressed to Theophilus, who obviously knew the author's identity. But today we are not sure who either the author or Theophilus was. Though Theophilus means "lover of God," he is probably a specific person. He seems to have been a Christian leader or a man wealthy enough to have the Gospel and Acts copied and distributed, i.e., the "publisher" or "patron."

There is much debate about who wrote this Gospel and Acts. Traditions from the early church identify him as Luke, which is why we use that name for the Gospel. They say he was a companion of Paul and tend to identify him with the Luke mentioned in some of Paul's letters (e.g., Phlm 24, Col 4:14, 2 Tim 4:11). Since Colossians calls Luke "the physician," he is often called that in tradition.

Many scholars today doubt these traditions. They see too many differences between Luke's and Paul's descriptions of the same events. They wonder why Acts never mentions Paul's letters and consider his theology to be too different from Paul's for him to have been Paul's disciple. For example, the "Paul" in Acts makes little direct reference to Paul's major themes of salvation by faith and being "in Christ." Acts has toned down the clash over whether Gentiles first had to become Jews before becoming Christians.

Others, including myself, do not consider these problems insuperable. Luke and Acts were written in the eighties or nineties, some twenty to thirty years after Paul's death. The controversies that are fresh in Paul's letters are "ancient history" in Acts. So it is not surprising that the tone and outlook are different. It seems historically plausible that the writer was Paul's companion on some of his later journeys, as the narrative use of "we" claims. The writer is less familiar with Paul's early life and controversies, and does not mention Paul's letters that refer to them. His theology is somewhat different from Paul's, as mentioned above, because his situation, audience and purposes are different.

3. Reliability of Acts

Many scholars distrust much of the historical information in Acts. They argue that if the Acts picture of Paul is so different from that in Paul's own letters, then other information is probably also slanted. They consider Acts a glorified picture of the early church that downplays the tensions it had.

Much of this criticism seems extreme, and there is a growing reaction against it. Studies in biblical and Hellenistic historiography have shown that Acts is comparable to the best ancient historical writings, such as the biblical Samuel-Kings and 1-2 Maccabees and histories contemporary with Acts by Josephus and his model, Dionysius of Halicarnassus. All histories had to appeal to a popular audience by rhetorical devices like speeches, vivid episodes, and proofs from prophecy. Luke-Acts continues the biblical history up to Paul's ministry in Rome, using familiar Hellenistic motifs, as Maccabees had.

Another reason some scholars are skeptical over Acts is its stress on the miraculous. In its extreme forms, rejection of the miraculous exemplifies the pervasive modern prejudice against miracles. Yet since the 1970s there is a widespread awareness of phenomena that defy natural explanations, such as healings through prayer and widely attested phenomena that accompany some alleged apparitions.

Other scholars object to measuring Luke's worth by Paul's theology. The Protestant Reformation sometimes tended to make Paul the standard of genuine Christianity. Acts is often labled a corrupt "early Catholicism," in which the genuine Paul has been "watered down" to be more acceptable to the "early-Catholic" church. Even that negative term betrays anti-Catholic bias.

Biblical studies are undergoing an important shift from exaggerated historical criticism to more holistic and literary approaches. "Canonical criticism" reads Acts in the context of the whole Christian Bible as it has been appropriated by the church. "Narrative criticism" approaches Luke-Acts with literary questions.

4. Narrative approaches to Acts

Analysis of how Acts is constructed as a narrative considers both the author and readers that the narrative implies, plotting and deliberate gaps to be filled in by readers, and the narrators of the story with their points of view from which it is told. Narrative studies have relativized the dogmatism of some historical-critical conjectures. For example, instead of "seams" and dichotomies between sources, literary critics often find sophisticated "gaps" to engage the reader's imagination. Rather than trying to locate the precise author and historical community for which Luke-Acts was intended, narrative critics investigate what the author reveals about himself in the text (the *implied* author) and the kinds of readers implied by the information that is included in or left out of the text.

Thus: the author implied by Luke-Acts is a Christian follower of Paul, active towards the end of Paul's ministry, who writes in Greek and is aware both of methods of

Hellenistic history and of motifs of the Greek Old Testament. The readers implied by Luke-Acts are familiar with the Greek Old Testament, Judaism, and Christianity. Acts usually has the narrator speaking in the third person ("he," "she," "they") from the common biblical "omniscient" point of view that tells what characters are thinking, in ways that go beyond what an immediate observer could discover. But after Acts 16:10 a "we" narrator describes some events from the perspective of a minor participant. This narrative device claims that the implied author is present at those events and thus sometimes a companion of Paul. Plotting is not purely chronological, but tends to finish treating one character before moving on (e.g., Herod's death in Acts 12). Plotting also illustrates how events fulfill older prophecies. By not stating what happened after the two years of Paul's Roman captivity (28:30-31), the ending of Acts leaves a deliberate gap to be filled by the readers. Mention of "for two full years" implies that the situation changed after that fixed time and that the narrator knows what the change was.

5. The revised New Testament translation of the New American Bible

Revision of the New American Bible New Testament translation on which the Collegeville Bible Commentary is based was one occasion for the revision of this commentary. After comparing the old and new translations of Acts, I find the revised version a significant improvement for liturgical proclamation and for reading and study. Far less idiosyncratic, it has a more traditional "biblical" style and tone.

I have one major objection to the revised NAB translation: it has stopped capitalizing "holy" in "Holy Spirit." I find this uncapitalized "holy Spirit" an uncanonical historicism inappropriate for the Christian Bible. It is true that the Holy Spirit was not defined as one person of the Trinity until well after the New Testament was written. But in the context of the Christian Bible and tradition, as well as in the Western literary tradition, the term "Holy Spirit" in the New Testament has consistently been understood as the Trinitarian Holy Spirit and capitalized. In reading Acts, contemporary Christians encounter the capitalized Holy Spirit of their tradition and experience.

PURPOSE OF ACTS

The preface for Luke and Acts: Luke 1:1-4

Prefaces to a book often state its purpose. The preface in Luke 1:1-4 has stereotyped technical language used in Greek prefaces. Readers expected to find statements about the writer's care and accuracy at the beginning of Greek books, just as readers today expect a "Dear Mr. Smith" at the beginning of a letter. This is true even if the writer hates Mr. Smith and is about to fire him from his job. Despite the conventional style of Luke's preface, however, it does indicate his real purpose. He wrote "so that you may realize the certainty of the teachings you have received" (Luke 1:4).

By "certainty," Luke is not referring merely to how accurate his facts are. He is also showing why these events and developments are legitimate answers to the hopes and promises of Israel. He explains what happens, even the horrible death of Jesus, as according to God's saving plan. In Acts he shows how Peter, Paul, and other Christian missonaries carried on the work of Jesus according to this plan. He demonstrates continuity between what happened to Jesus and the apostles and what the Old Testament had foretold. He also establishes that the traditions he uses are genuine. They go back to eyewitnesses, not mere hearsay, and have been carefully handed down in the church. He shows how God, especially through his Holy Spirit, was active in these events. Thus Luke is not writing the same kind of history as Josephus, a contemporary Jewish historian. Josephus wrote two major histories during the seventies to nineties of the first century, the same time as Luke. Both made more use of Greek conventions than Luke-Acts and had the secular purpose of winning the Romans' respect for Jewish culture and history, despite the Jewish rebellion against Rome in 66–70. Luke, however, writes to build his readers' faith.

A major problem Luke dealt with was the identity question of early Christians. If their founder was the Jewish Messiah, and they were supposed to be receiving the promises made to the Jewish patriarchs in the Jewish Scriptures (Old Testament), why are so many Gentiles and so few Jews members of the church in Luke's time? At the time of Jesus there were several Jewish parties or sects. At first both Jews and Christians considered Jesus' followers to be another such group within Judaism.

Confusion began when this subgroup of Jews, the Christians, started to admit non-Jews as fully equal Christians, without making them first become Jews. Imagine the confusion today if a Catholic parish began a prayer group for its parishioners, and soon admitted so many non-Catholics into the group that the parishioners were outnumbered. Would the group still belong to the Catholic parish? And imagine the trauma if either the parish expelled the prayer group or the group left the parish to begin its own "non-denominational church." Bitterness on both sides would most likely be deep. Certainly people would question how this new non-denominational church could claim to be a continuation of the Catholic parish from which it began. These kinds of questions also were asked about the relationship of the new subgroup from its parent Judaism, especially after it became an independent group. Luke's Gospel and Acts tried to answer some of these questions. He showed how what happened to Jesus and the early church was according to God's plan in the Old Testament. God willed both the restoration of Israel and the blessing of all nations through Christ. Acts 1–6 demonstrate especially the restoration of Israel, through the thousands of Jews who accepted the good news about Jesus and became Christians. The later parts of Acts show how the good news blessed the Gentiles.

HOW ACTS IS CONSTRUCTED

1. Use of the Greek Old Testament

Luke used the Greek translation of the Old Testament, rather than the Hebrew original, as he wrote his Gospel and Acts in Greek. An even more important difference from the rabbis of the first Christian centuries is seen in how Luke used the Greek Bible. Whereas the rabbis tended to treat all of their Bible as law, Luke and other Christians tended to see the Jewish Bible primarily as prophecy. The law approach mined the Old Testament for guidelines and rules of how to live in the daily aspects of one's life. Christians, however, searched the Jewish Scriptures for prophecies of the Messiah and end times of fulfillment.

Thus, Luke viewed Moses not as "The Lawgiver" but as "The Prophet." Moses was the type and model for other prophets. And since Moses was considered the author of the Pentateuch (the first five books of the Bible, from Genesis to Deuteronomy), these books also could be treated as prophecy. For example, Luke stressed the Genesis promises to Abraham as prophecies fulfilled in Jesus and the church.

2. Speeches and letters

Speeches make up a large part of Acts. Where did they come from? No one had tape recorders when speeches were made. Nor is it likely anyone was taking notes, which Luke then obtained and copied. It is possible that Luke did have some speeches in the material he collected. But we know that even when speeches were available to a writer, Greek training in how to write histories insisted that the author of the history rewrite all speeches in his own words. This would insure that the whole book would have a consistent style. Most scholars think Luke followed this convention. Therefore Luke either composed the speeches in Acts according to what he thought would have been said on that occasion, or he heavily rewrote speeches which he inherited. This is why the speech of Peter in Acts 2 sounds so much like Paul's speech in Acts 13.

The three most important kinds of speeches in Acts are missionary speeches to convert Jews or Gentiles, defense speeches in the trials of Paul, and the farewell speech in Acts 20. Most speeches explain some event which has taken place and give the author Luke a chance to tell his readers the real meaning of that event. Thus the speech in Acts 2 explains the Pentecost event and, in turn, leads to the conversion of thousands. The speech in Acts 3 gives the meaning of the healing of the lame man and leads to further conversions. The defense speeches, as in Acts 22, answer objections Jews had made to Paul and his ministry. The farewell speech in Acts 20 gives insight into what was most important in Paul's ministry and what later concerns would have been most important to him.

Several of the speeches seem to be interrupted, and yet it is clear that Luke has included as much as he wanted. Thus, the speech to the Greek philosophers in Athens in Acts 17 is interrupted after mention of the resurrection, and the Acts 22 defense to Jews is broken up after mention of Paul's mission to non-Jews. This writing technique enables Luke to stop reporting the speech at the most important point and provides dramatic underlining of that main point. In Acts 17 it is resurrection that annoys the Greeks, and the mention of non-Jews in Acts 22 angers the Jewish listeners. This enables Luke to show clearly that Paul's witness to Jesus' resurrection and his mission to the Gentiles were the main reasons he met so much opposition.

3. Repetitions in the story

Readers of Acts may be surprised to find some stories repeated up to three times. Paul's call is described in Acts 9, 22, and 26, for example. Luke repeats some of the key events in Acts to signal their special importance for understanding the rise and spread of Christianity. He tells about the conversion of the Gentile Cornelius three times. This makes clear how it was God's will to baptize non-Jews without making them become Jews first through circumcision. And it was Peter, not Paul, who first endorsed this principle.

The Apostolic Decree from Acts 15 is also repeated, as the compromise that enabled Gentile and Jewish Christians to share table fellowship (and therefore Eucharist) without forcing Gentiles to become Jews. The three versions of Paul's call by the risen Jesus reinforce the fact that Paul saw the risen Jesus and received his mission to the Gentiles directly from him. And three times Luke shows Paul telling Jews that he took the good news first to them, but since they rejected it, he would take it to the more receptive Gentiles.

All these repetitions are especially helpful for explaining how Luke's predominantly Gentile church can legitimately claim to be heirs of the Jewish promises through the Jewish Messiah. They show why and how the shifts from Jew to Gentile were made.

4. Parallelism between Jesus and Christians in Acts

Luke goes out of his way to point out parallels between Jesus and Peter and Paul. All three raised dead people to life, healed, preached, and suffered rejection. Luke often waits until Acts to mention things about Jesus found in the other Gospels. For example, he does not mention false witnesses charging that Jesus preached against the temple in the Gospel, but he does refer back to this charge during Stephen's trial in Acts 6. And he mentions a slap in the face at Paul's trial before the high priest, but not at Jesus' trial. By stressing parallels Luke shows how Paul and others were following the example and instructions of Jesus. Thus he also defends them against criticism like that in Acts 21:21-24, which seems still to have been current in Luke's time.

5. Humor in Acts

These serious concerns in Acts should not make us overlook how much fun Luke has telling the story. He loves to bring out the humor in incidents. Thus the pagans in Lystra look absurd as they bring bulls to sacrifice to Barnabas and Paul in Acts 14, or those in Ephesus as they keep chanting for two hours, "Long live Artemis of Ephesus," in Acts 19. Such humor reflects Luke's confidence in Christianity and sometimes mocks its rivals.

OUTLINE OF ACTS

1:12–8:3	Birth and growth of the church in Jerusalem through the Spirit
8:4–9:31	Persecution and expansion in Judea and Samaria
9:32–15:35	Gentiles: Peter and Cornelius, Barnabas and Saul, the Council of Jerusalem
15:36–18:23	Paul's mission to the Gentiles: The second journey
18:24–21:14	Paul's destiny in Jerusalem: The third journey
21:15–26:32	Paul as prisoner witnesses to the resurrection
27:1–28:31	"You shall bear witness at Rome."

THEMES IN ACTS

Acts should be studied as a narrative, but several theological motifs continually reappear. They include:

1. The fulfillment of God's saving plan

God's enthronement of the risen Jesus as Messiah in heaven and his outpouring of the

Holy Spirit were the unexpected fulfillment of all Jewish longings for salvation and God's kingdom. The Spirit is the ultimate realization of the promises to Abraham. It would anoint leaders for God's people and empower Christians to preach, heal, cast out evil spirits, and witness even unto death. Thus it would restore Israel and bless all nations by cleansing and incorporating them into God's people without circumcision.

2. The risen Jesus acts through his Spirit-filled disciples

After his ascension into heaven, Jesus continues to act on earth through his disciples by giving them his Holy Spirit and enabling them to preach and heal in his name. Especially through Paul, he will "proclaim light both to our people and to the Gentiles" (26:23). Those who reject his disciples in Acts reject Jesus and are excommunicated from his people (3:23).

3. Continuity amid change: God keeps his promises to his people

Acts reassures Christians facing unexpected changes in God's people. Just as today many Christians are bewildered and dismayed by rapid changes in the church, so it was in Luke's time. Acts shows how God himself initiated the great changes in his people from the Jewish disciples of Jesus to the mostly Gentile church throughout the Roman Empire, as when he had Peter and Paul convert Gentiles without circumcising them.

Other principles of continuity are the Twelve and the many Jews who became Christians. These were the "missing link" between the primarily Gentile church of Luke's day and its Jewish origins. The Twelve were the transitional leaders between Jesus and later leaders like Paul. The Jewish Christians were the restored Israel who continue the people of God's promises (in contrast to Matt 21:43, where Israel is replaced by a new people of God).

4. Healing and restoration of God's people

Acts treats healing as a sign of restoration and salvation. In Acts 3 the healing of the cripple (who was unclean) cleanses and enables him to enter the temple, and symbolizes the restoration of Israel to be able to pray worthily (Luke 1:75). In Luke's Gospel, Jesus often says, "Your faith has saved you." In Acts 4:9-10 Peter uses "saved" for the cripple's healing. Luke carefully distinguishes healing from magic (Acts 8 and 19).

5. Triumph of Christianity despite all obstacles

Frequently Acts remarks that "the word of God continued to spread" (6:7), no matter what persecutions got in the way.

6. God's guidance of the Christian way

All through Acts God guides Christians; they may not go wherever they choose. He refuses to let Paul go into Asia but directs him to Macedonia and Greece instead (Acts 16). God's guidance through the Holy Spirit, appearances, visions, dreams, angels, and prophecies demonstrates for Luke that the decisions and actions of the early church were not human ideas but responses to God's direction.

7. Apologetic for Christianity, especially for Paul

Acts defends Paul and other Jewish Christians from the charge of being Jewish apostates by stressing their fidelity to Jewish law and insisting that the decision to admit Gentiles without circumcision came from God.

Acts also has an apology for Paul's innocence before Roman law like the one Luke's Gospel had for Jesus. The verdicts of "innocent" by Roman judges in Paul's trials in Acts 22-26 show that Christians are no threat to the order of the state.

COMMENTARY

INTRODUCTION

Acts 1:1-11

1:1-5 Foreword. To understand Acts, we must remember that it is volume 2 of Luke-Acts—a continuation, by the same author, of the Gospel of Luke. The way New Testaments are printed obscures this fact because the Gospel of John intervenes between volume 1, Luke, and volume 2, Acts.

Acts tells how Jesus' disciples received his Holy Spirit and continued his work after he ascended into heaven. Much of Acts is a travelog, following the Christian missionaries, especially Paul, as they spread God's word. Similarly, Luke's Gospel had put a unique stress on Jesus' journey to Jerusalem from Luke 9:51 to the end of the book.

Luke begins Acts as he began his Gospel, with a foreword to his patron Theophilus.

Jesus had prepared his apostles for their mission by instructing them during his lifetime. He also appeared to them some forty days after his death and resurrection. The forty days seem the same kind of round number as Jesus' forty days and Moses' forty years in the desert (Luke 4:1-2 and Exodus). The difference between the ending of Luke's Gospel and the beginning of Acts does not seem to have bothered Luke. The Gospel treated the ascension as the last event on Easter Day. Acts dates it forty days later.

The disagreements imply that Luke was less concerned with the date of the ascension than with its importance as the event that closed the series of Jesus' resurrection appearances (except the extraordinary appearance to Paul; compare 1 Cor 15:5-9). Each passage has its own theological message. The Gospel ends with Jesus' priestly blessing as he ascends (Luke 24:51). Acts compares the ascension to Jesus' return from heaven (1:11).

Luke also stresses that the risen Jesus gave the apostles convincing signs that he was alive after his death. He appeared several times and continued teaching them what God's kingdom meant. Since they both saw and heard Jesus risen from the dead, they could be genuine witnesses to his resurrection. Others had only hearsay knowledge about Jesus (e.g., Herod in Luke 9:7-9). Throughout his Gospel and Acts, Luke emphasizes how important it is to both see and hear Jesus. See how Luke contrasts Paul with his companions in Acts 9:3-7.

Luke also underscores how Jesus gave new insights to his disciples after his resurrection. The risen Jesus would give the same kind of instruction to Paul in Acts 9.

The same Holy Spirit who was with Jesus when he chose and instructed the apostles would now be given to them. Both Luke's Gospel and Acts emphasize that being "baptized by the Holy Spirit" is the way God's power is given to humans. The Spirit came upon Jesus and thus began Jesus' mission of preaching and healing (Luke 3:21-22). At Pentecost the same Spirit would be given to the apostles to begin their preaching and healing in Acts. Receiving God's powerful Spirit far surpasses the effects of John's baptism, which had merely used water as a sign of repentance (Acts 11:15-17).

Usually in Acts people receive the Spirit when they are baptized as Christians, like the followers of John the Baptist in Acts 19:1-7. But at the very beginning of Christianity, God gave his Spirit to the apostles at Pentecost and to the Gentiles in Acts 10–11 before anyone could give them Christian baptism with water and the Spirit.

These accounts are meant to show how Christianity began by God's free action, independent of any human cooperation or ritual. The church is not just some human sect, but comes directly from God. The gift of the Spirit which began the church fulfills the Father's promises in the Old Testament, as Jesus had explained them.

1:6-11 Jesus taken up into heaven. In Luke 17:20-37 and 21:7-9 Jesus had to tell people not to listen to those who said the end was near. Nor should they try to estimate when or where the end of the world would come. The same prohibition is repeated in Acts 1:6-7 (see also Luke 12:35-46).

The question about restoring the rule to Israel in 1:6 also shows continued misunderstanding about what the kingdom of God meant. Acts 2:3 will show that God's promise was about the coming of the Holy Spirit, not some earthly kingdom. The prohibition against trying to compute the times of the end is meant to discourage Luke's readers from guessing what cannot be known. Rather, they should focus on the power of the Spirit as the sign of living in the promised final days. Luke says Christians are to use this power during whatever time is left to witness to Jesus to the ends of the earth. They should not waste time (as Christians are still tempted to do) trying to figure out when the end of the world will be.

Verse 1:8 provides a "table of contents" for Acts. The witness "in Jerusalem" is Acts 2 to 7. "Throughout Judea and Samaria" is from chapters 8 to 12, and to "the ends of the earth" from Acts 13 to 28. "The ends of the earth" is an echo of Isa 49:6. Both Acts and the Psalms of Solomon, a slightly earlier Jewish writing, apply the phrase "the ends of the earth" to Rome. Acts ends in Rome. And Pss Sol 8:15 calls the Roman general Pompey "him that is from the end of the earth."

Acts 1:9 mentions that the disciples saw Jesus actually being taken up to heaven to remind readers of 2 Kgs 2:4-15. There, the prophet Elijah told his disciple Elisha that only if he saw Elijah being taken up to heaven would he receive double Elijah's portion of the Holy Spirit. Elisha did see the flaming chariot take up Elijah and therefore received the same Spirit as Elijah. So in Acts 1:9, the disciples saw Jesus being taken up in a cloud and received Jesus' Holy Spirit at Pentecost. The two men in white garments are angels, as in Luke 24:4. Their statement in 1:11, that Jesus will return the same way they saw him leave, refers to his coming on the cloud at the end of the world, as predicted in Luke 21:27.

BIRTH AND GROWTH OF THE CHURCH IN JERUSALEM THROUGH THE SPIRIT

Acts 1:12–8:3

1:12-26 Matthias chosen to restore the twelve apostles. The names of the eleven apostles left after Judas' betrayal come in a different order than in Luke 6:14-16. The Gospel list seems to follow the order in the list as Luke received it. However, Acts adjusts the list in order of importance. It names Peter first, then John (his partner in Acts 3–5), then James, and fourth Andrew. Luke 6:14 had "Peter and Andrew, James and John."

There were at least three important men called James. The brother of John, one of the Twelve, was with Jesus at the transfiguration and agony in the garden and was killed in Acts 12:2. He is often known as "James the Great." The son of Alphaeus also belonged to the Twelve. Tradition calls him "James the Less." And there is the brother or relative of Jesus who had become leader of the Jerusalem church (see Acts 12:17, Acts 15 and 21.)

Little is known about most of the Twelve aside from lists of their names. Most do not appear elsewhere in the New Testament. They are less important as individual personalities than as members of the Twelve. Jesus promised that the twelve tribes of Israel would be restored and that the Twelve would rule them in God's kingdom (Luke 22:28-29). To have twelve rulers, Judas had to be replaced. Acts 1:15-36 shows that all twelve are in place by Pentecost, when the Holy Spirit empowered them to become the new leaders of God's people in Jesus' name.

Acts 1:14 also makes it clear that the Twelve were not the only ones waiting for the Spirit. They were part of a complete community that included both men and women. Acts 2:17-18 shows this fulfills the Joel prophecy that the Holy Spirit will be poured out on "all flesh" in the final days, and both "sons and daughters" will prophesy. Acts 1:14 also stresses the unity in constant prayer of this Christian community. Prayer is a major theme in Luke. For example, of the four Gospels, only Luke 3:21-22 explicitly says that Jesus was praying when the Spirit came upon him.

Luke probably had several reasons for singling out Jesus' mother Mary and his brothers in Acts 1:14. One is the saying in Luke 8:19-21 that Jesus' mother and brothers are those who hear and keep God's word. Another is to draw a parallel between Mary's role in Jesus' birth and her presence at the church's birth on Pentecost, when the Spirit came upon her in a new way. Related to this is Luke's narrative claim that Mary was the ultimate source of information in the infancy narratives ("Mary kept all these things, reflecting on them in her heart," Luke 2:19 [cf. 2:51]) and was present in the Jerusalem church, whose members could pass on to the author traditions about the events in Luke 1–2 (Luke 1:2-3). Another reason is probably the importance of "James the brother of Jesus" in Acts 15 and 21. It is certain the "brothers of Jesus" were considered his blood relatives. Mary's perpetual virginity is church dogma. From New Testament evidence and later church tradition, their exact relationship to Jesus and to Mary is unclear and debated.

Peter continues in Acts 1:15-22 to exercise the leadership role of strengthening his brethren that Jesus had promised at the Last Supper (Luke 22:32). It had begun in Luke 24:34, when he was the first to report that the risen Jesus appeared to him. The round number of "about 120" (12 x 10) is symbolic. It probably alludes to the restored twelve tribes of Israel under the soon-to-be twelve apostles. The community of 120 will be the core of the Spirit-filled Israel at Pentecost.

This is Peter's first speech in Acts. It argues that Judas' betrayal had to happen to fulfill the prophecies in Ps 69:26 and 109:8. Like most of his contemporaries, Luke considered all the psalms as written by David under the inspiration of the Spirit (see also Acts 2:30). Luke usually explains shocking events like Jesus' death and his betrayal by one of his closest followers this way: they are necessary to fulfill God's scriptural plan of salvation (e.g., Luke 24:25-27, 44-47). Even when God seems to be absent, Luke insists he is always in control of events.

One aspect of God's control is his punishing extraordinary sinners like Judas here, and Herod in 12:21-23. God's punishment of the wicked is a common theme in both the Old Testament and in Greek histories. The punishments of Judas and Herod are similar to that of Emperor Antiochus IV, a notorious enemy of the Jews. His death is described in 2 Macc 9:4-10. In the first century both Jews and pagan Greeks and Romans felt that some stress on God's punishment of the wicked was needed to defend God's justice and power. If the wicked got off scot-free, God would seem either unjust or unable to maintain law and order in the world.

The rules for Judas' replacement in 1:21-22 make plain what Luke means by an apostle and witness to Jesus' resurrection. Only someone who knew Jesus before his death could witness that the risen Jesus is the same one who died. According to this strict sense, Luke does not treat Paul as an apostolic witness to Jesus' resurrection. (Acts 14:14, however, calls Paul and Barnabas "apostles," extending the term's meaning.) Thus, Acts 13:30-31 cites Paul as saying the first witnesses to Jesus' resurrection were the Galileans who came with Jesus to Jerusalem. Paul's own letters were much more insistent that Paul was a genuine apostle and witness to Jesus' resurrection, though not one of the Twelve (e.g., 1 Cor 15:1-11).

Luke distinguishes apostles from Paul because he wants to trace the links from Jesus' earthly ministry, through the twelve apostles, to later missionaries like Paul and Barnabas who did not follow Jesus before his death. Even Paul admits in 1 Cor 15:3-7 that he received from earlier witnesses the message he was passing on.

The community found two men who fulfilled all requirements for joining the Twelve. They left the final choice to God. After praying that God would pick the one he wanted, they drew lots between the two. The one selected by lot was considered God's choice.

2:1-13 Coming of the Holy Spirit at Pentecost. Finally the long-awaited day for the fulfillment of the Father's promise has arrived (see 1:4-5, 8). The community is together, presumably in prayer (1:14), on the Jewish feast of Pentecost. Jewish pilgrims came to Jerusalem on that feast to celebrate God's establishing his people by giving them the law on Mount Sinai. Since early in the Old Testament, Jews had associated wind with Spirit. Both fire and the Spirit were prophesied by John the Baptist in Luke 3:16 (referred to in Acts 1:5 and 11:16). A mightier one than he would "baptize you with the Holy Spirit and fire." There is a strong pattern in Luke and Acts of showing how a prophecy made earlier in the account has come true.

When all were filled with the Holy Spirit, they spoke in the tongues or languages the Spirit gave them (as in 10:46 and 19:6). Both the expression "as the Spirit enabled them to proclaim" (2:4) and the explanation in Acts 2:16-18 seem to envisage a prophetic gift with a missionary aspect. How helpful it would be if missionaries were simply given the ability to speak God's word in many languages! Luke does not seem to be thinking so much of the kind of "gift of tongues" mentioned in 1 Cor 12–14 and common today in charismatic prayer groups.

Paul had described tongues not as human language but as a way to pray to God without words or mental understanding (1 Cor 14:2, 9, 14-19). He said outsiders might think the community was insane if they overheard it (1 Cor 14:23), presumably because tongues at Corinth sounded like incoherent babbling. Even in Acts 2:12-15, the objection that the apostles were drunk seems to indicate they appeared to be babbling. Perhaps the original description of Pentecost that Luke heard treated their speech as babbling. In any case, Luke's version in Acts 2 symbolizes the reversing of the punishment at the Tower of Babel. In Gen 11:1-9, people at Babel who spoke one language became unable to understand one another. At Pentecost, even people of many languages understood the apostles.

There is no need to deny *a priori* that the apostles could have given such a public speech without immediate reprisal from the same authorities who had had Jesus killed. Those authorities later interrupted Peter's temple speech (Acts 4:1-3), but they would not have been prepared for this one. The early church simply could not have spread as fast as it did without some such public preaching.

2:14-21 Explanation of the Pentecost events. In Acts 2:14, Peter acts as spokesman for the Twelve, explaining the sign the people had just seen and heard. For Luke, miraculous events need to be explained, as the empty tomb in Luke 24 and the healing of the lame man in Acts 3. As he demonstrates, miracles in themselves are usually open to either believing or unbelieving interpretations. God does not force people to believe when he provides a miracle. This is why Luke calls them not miracles but signs—signs of God's power and goodness which invite belief but do not force it.

In the beginning of his speech, Peter explains that the apostles' behavior is not drunkenness, but fulfills Joel's prophecy that in the last days God will pour out his Spirit on all flesh. In the Old Testament, the Spirit's coming upon someone was often overwhelming and caused quite different or unusual behavior (e.g., Saul's in 1 Sam 10:5-13).

Luke seems to have added words to the Joel quotation to show more clearly how Pentecost fulfills the prophecy. He changed Joel 3:1, "then afterward," to "in the last days" (Acts 2:17). Acts 2:18 added "and they shall prophesy." Joel 3:3 had "wonders in the heavens" and Acts 2:19 has "wonders in the heavens above and signs on the earth below." This could hint at the wind and fire from heaven and the languages below. But Luke is probably also trying to echo more closely the "signs and wonders" by which God performed the Exodus of his people from Egypt.

The Joel quotation shows how Christians can be living "in the last days" (Acts 2:17) and yet have to wait for "the great and splendid day of the Lord" (2:20), the final day of judgment. On judgment day, all who call on the name of the Lord (identified as Jesus in 2:36) will be saved (2:21).

2:22-36 Proof that Jesus is Messiah. Messiah and Christ both mean "anointed." Messiah is Hebrew and Christ is Greek. The term originally referred to the king of Israel as God's anointed. When the kingdom was destroyed, Jews hoped God would restore it through a descendant or "Son of David" who would be anointed by God's Spirit as David was. This is how hope for a Messiah began.

Verses 22-36 use resurrection as the identifying sign of the Christ or Messiah. Through an intricate argument, they relate scriptural prophecies to the life of Jesus. The argument is the kind a lawyer in those days would use in court. The speech proves that Jesus, not David, is both the Lord who will rule in heaven and the Messiah sent to save Israel.

The argument in verse 22 begins from "mighty deeds, wonders, and signs" (note the "wonders and signs" in the quotation in 2:19). Those signs showed God's approval of Jesus, as the people themselves witnessed. Yet they rejected the one God approved. Many wondered how Jesus could be the Jewish Messiah if rejected by the Jews themselves. The speech answers that God knew and willed it all beforehand. The sign that God had permitted Jesus' death was his raising him from the dead, fulfilling Ps 16:8-11. The psalm says, "I set the Lord ever before me . . . my body, too, abides in confidence." This might be why Luke's Gospel omits the cry of Jesus in Mark and Matthew, "My God, my God, why have you forsaken me?" (Compare Luke 23:44-49 with Mark 15:33-41 and Matt 27:45-56.) The reason for Jesus' hope is that he knew he would not be abandoned in the nether world, nor would his body corrupt (Ps 16:10 in Acts 2:27).

Verses 29-34 and 36 explain how these psalm verses apply to Jesus. Most people thought David wrote the psalms, so when a psalm says "I" they assumed it meant David. But Luke argues that the prophecy about not corrupting in the grave cannot apply to David himself. For his body never left his well-known tomb in Jerusalem. The argument can only work if Jesus' body, by contrast, is no longer in its tomb. Luke would violently disagree with those who say it would not matter to faith if Jesus' body were still in the tomb. Jesus' empty tomb is the key to Luke's argument. In itself the empty tomb cannot prove that Jesus has been raised (see Luke 24:9-12, 21-27). But if the tomb were not empty, as David's was never emptied, that would end any talk by Luke about Jesus being raised from the dead.

The prophecy that "you will not abandon my soul to the lower world nor let your faithful one see corruption" cannot therefore apply to David as the "my" seems to indicate. When David said "my soul" or "my flesh," he was speaking for the Messiah descended from him. The speech explains that David was prophesying the resurrection of his descendant the Messiah (2:30-31).

David relies on God's promise, given in 2 Sam 7:12-14, in which Nathan prophesies that the throne of David's descendant would stand forever. This promise, repeated in Pss 132:11 and 89:4, became the source of many hopes for the Messiah.

Verses 33-36 use a similar argument from Ps 110:1. The signs that people saw and heard at Pentecost were caused by Jesus, now exalted at God's right hand, pouring out the Holy Spirit. "Sit at my right hand" in Ps 110:1 foretells that David's Lord would exercise the Father's own authority. Since David did not ascend into heaven, this too refers to his descendant Jesus. The conclusion of the whole speech is 2:36: "Therefore let the whole house of Israel know for certain that God has made him both Lord and Messiah, this Jesus whom you crucified."

2:37-41 Response and baptism of three thousand. That the crowd addressed their question to "Peter and the other apostles" indicates that Peter was speaking for them all, as the pope often speaks for the college of bishops today. The reaction to Peter's speech parallels the response to John the Baptist's speech in Luke 3:10-18. Both crowds ask what they should do, both are told to repent, and both are baptized. But John's baptism is only a prophetic sign of the baptism received at Pentecost: "I am baptizing you with water, but one mightier than I is coming. . . . He will baptize you with the Holy Spirit and fire" (Luke 3:16). The promise of the Holy Spirit was given "to you and to your children" (Acts 2:39)—namely, to Jews from all over the world gathered for the feast and to later generations. "All those far off whomever the Lord our God will call" (2:39) foreshadows the outreach to Gentiles later in Acts. The hearers are to be saved "from this corrupt generation" (2:40). This phrase is from biblical passages about punishment (like Deut 32:5). Luke applies it to the generation that rejected Jesus (Luke 11:29-32, 47-51).

Acts 2:41 mentions the number three thousand to show that a substantial portion of the Jewish people did believe in their Messiah and thus continued as the people of God's promises. This also indicates that salvation has both individual and communitarian dimensions. Each person has to accept his or her salvation, but this is not merely a private matter between the individual and Jesus. One is baptized into God's people and saved as a member of the church.

2:42-47 The Spirit bears fruit in community. Luke gives an idealized picture of the first community, but his message still holds for today. When a Christian community seriously repents of sin and opens itself to the power of the Spirit, this dramatically changes the way Christians live and attracts others to Christianity. The elements of community life Luke highlights are teaching by the apostles, sharing their lives with one another, "breaking of the bread" (Eucharist), and prayer together. They felt the power of the Spirit in many "wonders and signs" (Joel 3:3 in Acts 2:19) through the apostles. This is the first of several summary passages Luke composed to show that the individual stories he reports exemplify more general patterns of behavior.

In 2:44, unanimity and considering all things as common express the ideal of friendship at that time. The point is that all community members had their needs met, and no one hoarded selfishly while others were in want. Luke often stresses another major fruit of the Spirit: the joy and praise of the community. As Jews, the community maintained its links with its Jewish traditions. The first Christians remained faithful to Judaism, were respected by other Jews, and continued winning new Jewish members. Luke emphasizes that people are saved both as individuals and as part of a saved community: "the Lord added to their number those who were being saved" (2:47).

3:1-16 Healing in the name of the Lord Jesus. Peter's speech in Acts 2 foreshadows later events in Acts, as Jesus' speech at Nazareth in Luke 4:16-30 previewed his healings, teachings, and rejection in the Gospel. Thus the cure of the lame man in Acts 3 illustrates the "signs on the earth below" (2:19) that God works through the Spirit's outpouring. It also exemplifies how everyone "who calls on the name of the Lord" will be saved (2:21).

Chapters 3–5 call Peter and John partners, but Peter does most of the acting and talking. Luke seems to be going out of his way to mention John, even when John adds nothing to the action. One reason may be to show that there were two witnesses to the events, since at least two witnesses were needed in some Jewish law cases. Another reason might be Jesus' instruction in Luke 10:1 to go out in pairs. A third might be to bring out the parallel with Paul and Barnabas working as a pair in Acts 13 to 15.

Often Luke shows crowds naturally reacting to miracles by focusing on the human healers, which is still a temptation regarding faith healers today. Both Peter and John in 3:12 and Paul and Barnabas in 14:14-18 corrected the people and told them not to focus on human individuals. The man was not healed because of Peter and John's power or piety but because of faith in the name of the Jesus "you put to death" but God raised. To heal someone by faith does not require power or holiness in the human who prays for healing. It can be done by any Christian who prays in Jesus' name with faith. Today we are witnessing a resurgence of many healings through prayers of ordinary Christians, such as parents praying with their sick children. Sometimes we also hear of faith healers who themselves fall into sin, even though God uses their faith to heal the sick. So in Acts the focus is on God who heals, not on those who pray for healing.

Thus faith healings in Acts are the opposite of magic. They are not a manipulation of power, in which the healer is in control. Faith healing is a form of prayer, as when Peter prayed over the body of Tabitha (Dorcas) before raising her to life (Acts 9). Healing through prayer and faith, both in Acts and today, is a request of God to heal. It does not force God to heal, but can receive either a yes or no answer according to God's will.

The healing in Acts 3 shows God's vindication of his Servant, Jesus, whom his people had rejected. By healing the cripple when Peter addressed him in Jesus' name, God was showing he had raised Jesus from the dead and was honoring his name (3:13-16).

3:17-26 "Obey the prophet like Moses, that you may be blessed." The speech does not condemn those who rejected Christ. It convicts them of wrongdoing and offers them a chance to repent. Acts 3:17 makes an important distinction between wrongs done to Jesus in his lifetime and rejection of him and his apostles after he was raised. On the cross Jesus had asked his Father to "forgive them; they know not what they do," according to Luke 23:34. Two later speeches differentiate a preresurrection time of ignorance when there was an excuse for not accepting Jesus (17:30 and 13:27). But after God has cleared his Servant's name by raising him from the dead, ignorance is no excuse. Those who reject Jesus a second time after his resurrection deserve to be cut off from God's people (3:22-26). The result for Luke is that Jews who disbelieved that God raised Jesus were "excommunicated" from the chosen people. Therefore only Christian Jews inherited the blessings God had promised his people since the time of Abraham.

The argument in 3:18-21 is similar to those in Acts 2. It claims that God foretold the death of his Messiah in "all the prophets" and used the ignorance of Jews who rejected him to fulfill the prophecies. They can be forgiven if they repent and now accept Jesus as their Messiah (3:19). Repentance can also hasten the long-awaited times of messianic blessings when God will send Jesus back in his second coming. Although the resurrection confirmed Jesus as Messiah, only at the end of the world will his enemies and unbelievers recognize him as Messiah (Luke 21:27). Now he is in heaven from his ascension in Acts 1:9-11 until the final restoration.

The same Greek word can be used both for resurrection and raising up or calling a prophet. Luke puns on "raise up" in Moses' prophecy, "A prophet like me will the Lord, your God, raise up for you from among your own kinsmen" (a loose citation of Deut 18:15 in Acts 3:22). He interprets "raising up" as "resurrecting" the prophet like Moses—that is, Jesus.

Acts 2:23 continues Deut 18:15 with a threat: "Everyone who does not listen to that prophet will be cut off from the people." This verse from "Moses" paraphrases and joins two Old Testament passages, Deut 18:19a, "If any man will not listen to my words which he speaks in my name," and Lev 23:29b, "shall be cut off from his people." It shows how Luke's paraphrasing of Scripture from memory can occasionally make a biblical "point," but in his own wording.

Notice that Luke treats Moses as the first and greatest of the prophets and Jesus as the prophet like Moses. Whoever does not heed the resurrected prophet Jesus (speaking through his apostles) will be cut off from the people (3:23). Acts 3:23 is thus the key to how Luke solves the problem of Jews who do not accept Jesus and how Christianity relates to God's people. Whereas Matthew talks of Christians as a new people replacing the old Israel (Matt 21:43), Luke stresses the continuity in God's people through Jews who accepted Jesus. Thus Acts 2:24-26 announces that Peter's Jewish listeners are parties to the covenant by which all nations will be blessed in Abraham's seed (Gen 22:18). By resurrecting and sending Jesus, God is blessing the Jews as each of them repents.

The introduction mentioned how Acts has a pattern of interruptions that end speeches, but only after everything has been said that Luke wanted mentioned. Those who interrupt Peter in 4:1-3 are Jews who do not believe our bodies will be raised. Acts frequently juxtaposes Jews who believe in resurrection (Pharisees, including Paul) from those who do not (especially the Sadducees, as in 23:6-10). Such unbelievers, who sounded so much like Epicurean philosophers who denied life after death, could hardly be considered good Jews, Luke implies. It is no surprise they did not believe in Jesus' resurrection.

In Acts 4:2, "proclaiming in Jesus the resurrection of the dead" is thematic (see Acts 23:6-8 and 11). Preaching about Jesus as resurrected exemplifies the Jewish belief in resurrection. Though this approach may seem artificial, it is another way that Luke shows the continuity of Christian preaching with true Judaism.

Luke also links Jewish religious leaders with the unbelieving group of Sadducees. Acts 4–5 will show how the apostles take over leadership of God's people from these former leaders.

4:1-22 The apostles obey God, not Jewish religious authorities. Acts 4 focuses especially on the conflict between the old and new leaders of the Jewish people. Luke shows from this incident that the old religious leaders forfeited their claims by rejecting the Messiah God gave them. Since they were disobeying God, the apostles no longer had to obey them but God alone. The apostles replaced them as the new leaders of God's people, in the name of the Jewish Messiah Jesus, who had appointed them (Luke 22:29-30).

The Sanhedrin was the Jewish supreme court and ruling body. The Sanhedrin leaders challenge Peter and John's authority, asking "by what power or in whose name" they have acted (4:7). For this formal charge in a Jewish court, John is needed as a second witness. The confrontation between Peter and John against Jewish leaders who refuse to believe a miracle recalls that between Moses and Aaron against Pharaoh and his magicians in Exod 7–11.

Acts 4:8 mentions Peter received the Holy Spirit for his reply. This fulfills Jesus' prophecy in Luke 12:11-12 that when disciples are dragged before authorities, the Spirit will teach them what to say (see also Luke 21:12-15).

Acts 4:8-12 repeats that the cripple was healed in the name of Jesus, who is "the stone rejected by you the builders which has become the cornerstone" (4:11), as Ps 118:22 had foretold. Salvation comes only through Jesus.

The Jewish leaders were amazed at the boldness of such uneducated and common men (4:13-14). Luke had attributed Peter's boldness to the Holy Spirit (4:8). This boldness is the mark of Jesus' witnesses in Acts (of Peter here and at Pentecost, 2:29; of the community in answer to its prayer in 4:29 and 32; and of Paul at the climactic end of Acts, 28:31). In the helplessness of the Sanhedrin to answer Peter and John, Luke is underlining the bankruptcy of its leadership. Like Pharaoh, the Jewish leaders cannot deny the healing, yet refuse to obey God's will clearly shown in it.

Instead they try to prevent the apostles from spreading the word about Jesus. Peter cannot therefore be considered a rebel when he tells the Sanhedrin he must obey God rather than them. The saying recalls *Antigone,* a play well known in Luke's time, and a similar Old Testament situation in 2 Macc 7:2. The Sanhedrin is helpless to stop the apostles because of the people. In Acts 2–6, "the people" (*ho laos)* is the technical term for God's chosen Jewish people who see the apostolic signs, are impressed with the community, and listen to the sermons, and over whom a contest of leadership is being waged. The Sanhedrin cannot stop the apostles; thus Luke indicates their loss to the apostles of real leadership over "the people."

4:23-31 The community celebrates God's victory through them. The community thanks God for Peter and John's victory, as Moses and the Israelites did after escaping from Pharaoh at the sea (Exod 15). Their prayer celebrates the fulfillment of Ps 2:1-2. According to the Christians' midrashic interpretation, the psalm predicted that kings and rulers, Jews and Gentiles would be helpless against the Lord God and his anointed Messiah. So King Herod and the Jews, and the ruler Pilate with his Gentile Romans, were unable to stop Jesus the Messiah, even though they killed him. In fighting God they fulfilled what God had planned all along (4:24-28).

God's victory even in his Messiah's death reassured the community as they faced new threats from the Sanhedrin. They prayed that as Peter and John had just overcome the Sanhedrin, they could overcome all future threats through God's continued healing, "signs and wonders." God's servant Moses had overcome the Pharaoh by signs and wonders. They pray that new signs and wonders might be done in the name of God's new Servant, Jesus. The community's prayer resulted in a "second Pentecost." The place shook, all were filled with the Spirit, and they spoke God's word with boldness, as Peter had at Pentecost. This was God's stamp of approval on the community despite harassment from Jewish religious leaders. Christians were now as free from the Sanhedrin's leadership as the Israelites had been from the Egyptian Pharaoh.

4:32–5:11 Unity under the apostles, fostered and threatened. The apostles' newly confirmed leadership bears fruit in a community marked by unity of mind and heart and expressed by Christians' putting their possessions at the apostles' disposal. The plot against unity by Ananias and Sapphira is as threatening to their God-given leadership as the revolt of Korah, Dathan, and Abiram had been to Moses' leadership in the desert (Num 16). The death punishment for both groups shows how seriously offensive to God are such threats to community and his appointed leaders. Judas' fate had already illustrated this. As Luke 22:3 says that Satan entered into Judas, so Acts 5:3 asks Ananias, "Why have you let Satan fill your heart . . . ?" Judas bought a field with the money from betraying Jesus and died gruesomely on it (1:18). Ananias cheated on money from the sale of a field and fell dead (5:1-5).

Many find this passage shocking, but Luke would certainly disagree with efforts today to explain away hell or God's punishment. He insists that outrageous and deliberate rebellion against God will be severely punished. God is not mocked. Though this same Luke is known for his stress on God's forgiveness of repentant sinners, we should not overlook his balancing emphasis on a prudent fear of God's power to punish when faced with unrepented sin and rebellion. God will go to any lengths to save sinners who are willing to return to him (Luke 15). But those who refuse to admit their sin and ask forgiveness will suffer the consequences of their separation from God.

In Acts 4:36–5:11, Luke provides contrasting positive and negative examples of surrender of goods to the apostles: Barnabas, and Ananias and Sapphira. Acts 4:36 is the first mention of Barnabas, who later introduces Paul to the apostles (9:26-28). Both the new name he receives from the apostles and his surrendering his money to them signify Barnabas' submission to their leadership. Acts 5:1-11 contrasts Ananias and Sapphira with Barnabas: like him they sold property and ostensibly put the money at the apostles' disposal for the community, but by secretly keeping part for themselves they maintain a hidden independence from the community. In effect, they refused to share fully with them or to submit completely to the apostles' authority. Whether or not unneeded real estate was supposed to be sold for the sake of the community, or goods were to be surrendered before the person's full incorporation, as at Qumran, Ananias and Sapphira did not have to imitate Barnabas' complete submission to the apostles (5:4). By their hypocritical deceit, they "lied not to human beings but to God" (5:4). They sinned against the Holy Spirit (Luke 12:10) in the apostles.

Ananias and Sapphira were in fact challenging the presence of Spirit in the community's midst. Their deaths indicated for Luke that, yes, the Spirit was truly present in the community, and it upheld the apostles' authority. The result was great fear upon "the whole church," the first time this expression is used in Acts.

5:12-16 Third summary: Signs and wonders through the apostles. This is Acts' third summary and linking passage that generalizes from particular incidents to general practices. It brings the apostles' authority to a climax of almost unlimited healing power, like Paul's in 19:11-12. Writing in ways familiar to his Hellenistic readers but sounding a lot like magic, Luke says even Peter's shadow or handkerchiefs that touched Paul's body healed the sick. But 19:13-19 immediately distinguishes Paul's power in verses 11-12 from magic. Likewise, in 5:12-16 Luke expects his readers to remember his careful explanation in 3:12-16 that Peter's healing power was from God in Jesus' name.

Solomon's Portico, where the Christians met, is where Peter had explained the cripple's healing in Acts 3. Some Jews were afraid to join the meetings because they were in direct defiance of the Sanhedrin's order in Acts 4 not to speak further about Jesus. But 5:13-14 stresses that many Jews, both women and men (2:17-18), believed, and that the Jewish people held the community in great respect.

5:17-42 Second confrontation with the Sanhedrin; Gamaliel. The conflict between the old and new leaders of the Jewish people comes to its final head when the high priest and his Sadducee followers arrest the apostles out of envy (5:17-18). Luke shows that God confirms the apostles' leadership by miraculously freeing them from prison and sending them back to the temple to preach to "the people" (5:19-21). Verses 22-26 further mock the helplessness of the Sanhedrin. Its members fear being stoned by the people if they publicly abuse the apostles. When the high priest complains of their disobedience in continuing to preach Jesus, Peter repeats that they must obey not men but God (5:28-29), who had freed and commanded them to keep preaching about this life (5:20).

Verses 30-32 summarize the Christian witness to God's vindication of the man the Jews had crucified. The words "hanging him on a tree" allude to the curse in Deut 21:22-23 against anyone hanged on a tree. Jews considered that Jesus' crucifixion put him under this scriptural curse and asked how God's Messiah could possibly be cursed by God. In Gal 3:10-14 Paul had had to answer this objection directly. Here in Acts 5:30-32 the response is only indirect, since the curse is not explicitly mentioned. The answer is simply that God raised and exalted the man so disgracefully killed to be Ruler and Savior of Israel. Even though the Old Testament considered people who were crucified as cursed, God willed that his Messiah die this death and then be resurrected. The witnesses for this bold claim are the apostles and the power of the Spirit seen in Jesus' followers.

The high priest and Sadducees, who did not believe in resurrection (4:1-2), are again distinguished from a Pharisee who did, Gamaliel. In 22:3 he is said to be Paul's teacher. The speech portrays Gamaliel as speaking historical wisdom and moderation. It is also an ironic prophecy that opponents of Christianity would be fighting God himself (5:35-39—compare 2 Macc 7:19). Because Luke believes this, he stresses throughout Acts how the Christian cause triumphs no matter what the obstacles. For example, the persecution after Stephen's death in Acts 7 resulted in hastening Christianity's spread in Acts 8. This speech also contrasts Christianity to other messianic movements of the time, which the historian Josephus also mentions, but in a different historical order. The false movements died out with the death of their leaders, but the true one continues to grow because its plan and activity (5:38) are from God.

Luke portrays Gamaliel's advice as an ironic commentary on history, not as advice to be followed by Christian authorities in evaluating spiritual events like apparitions. Gamaliel's principle of having "nothing to do with these men" until their movement either dies out or is confirmed is not a Christian position but that of an unbelieving outsider. One cannot just "wait and see" whether God is acting in or speaking to our time, but must test the fruits and heed those words that correspond to the gospel and church teaching. For example, if God, through apparitions of Mary, is urgently calling Christians to repentance (as many believe he is), a disengaged "wait and see" approach is in effect a negative response to the call. This could be true even though "private revelations" are not binding, as the public revelation of Scripture and tradition is. Genuine private revelations are usually exhortations to live the public revelation more urgently.

The Sanhedrin accepts Gamaliel's "wait and see" advice. They beat the apostles, warn them not to teach, and release them. The apostles' joy at suffering for Jesus is an example for Christians (5:39-41). Obeying God, not the Sanhedrin, they return unhindered to teaching about Jesus the Messiah (5:42). This section of Acts ends with the helplessness of the old leaders of God's people, the Sanhedrin, and the unstoppable preaching of the new, the apostles.

6:1-7 The community needs additional authorities. The apostles have displaced the Sanhedrin as rightful leaders of God's people, but they soon have to expand the leadership. Because of the community's rapid growth, the apostles had to appoint more leaders to help them, as Moses had to do in the desert (Exod 18:17-23). At the same time Luke is showing how church leadership was passed on to a new kind of leader. Like Jesus, the Twelve had all been from Galilee and spoke Hebrew (actually the closely related Aramaic). Jews from all over the world gathered in Jerusalem. Many new Christian Jews were more comfortable with Greek, the international language of that time. The term "Hellenistic" describes people who had Greek language and culture. Jews who used Greek were "Hellenistic Jews," and "Hellenistic Jewish Christians" describes Greek-speaking Jews who became Christians. Just as language group differences have caused friction in French and English Canada, so did they between Aramaic-speaking and Greek-speaking Jews in the Jerusalem Christian community.

The apostles' leadership had been symbolized by their control over the community purse. So this friction is exemplified by charges of unfair distribution of community food between the poor of the two language groups. Although the Twelve speak of praying and preaching while the Seven would wait on tables, that is not in fact what Luke later reports the Seven doing. Stephen has the same gifts of the Holy Spirit, worked similar "signs and wonders," and debated and preached as much as the Twelve (6:8-11 and 7:1-53). Actually, handling the community's goods again symbolizes authority over the community.

The church has added a new set of authorities, Greek-speaking Jews. As the number twelve symbolized the twelve tribes of Israel, the number seven signified universality, since it was considered a "perfect number." The Twelve rooted the church in Israel. The Seven were a sign of the church's outreach to the whole world through those who spoke the world language, Greek. They derive their authority from Jesus' original apostles because they were ordained by them.

Luke ends this account with another summary. Once the church's authority structure has been made more universal, "the word of God continued to spread" and the Jerusalem church "increased greatly" (6:7), beyond the last-mentioned five thousand (in 4:4). Even many priests, who had earlier opposed the Christians (4:1-2), came to believe. On the eve of the church's outreach beyond Jerusalem in Acts 8, Luke pictures the huge Jerusalem community as the restored Israel which was promised in Scripture. It was living the ideal life that Jews since Isaiah had been longing for.

6:8-15 Stephen brought to trial. The new leader, Stephen, soon found himself in conflict with Greek-speaking Jews who did not believe in Christ (6:8-9). They were no match for Stephen's wisdom and Spirit (6:10), as Jesus had promised in Luke 21:15. They falsely accused Stephen of attacking the sacred Jewish institutions of temple and law, and stirred up the people, the elders, and scribes against him (6:11-13). Compare the challenge to Jesus by chief priests, scribes, and elders as he taught the people in the temple (Luke 20:1). Stephen was hauled before the Sanhedrin, as Jesus had been in his passion. The account of Jesus' trial in Luke 22:66-71 had omitted a major incident stressed in Mark 14:55-61 and Matt 25:59-63. It was the false charge by lying witnesses that Jesus had said he could destroy the temple. Now Acts 6:14

mentions that charge against Jesus during Stephen's trial. the temple charge leads into Stephen's speech in 7:1-53.

7:1-53 Stephen's speech to the Sanhedrin. This speech is a major turning point in Acts. The Jewish Sanhedrin rejected and killed the Spirit-filled Stephen, as they had earlier rejected and handed over Jesus. Thus they were rejecting their Messiah a second time, as their ancestors had twice rejected Moses. Stephen's speech presupposes Peter's in Acts 3. Both treat Jesus as "the prophet like Moses" and mention the penalty for rejecting that prophet (Acts 3:23 and 7:39-43). In turn, the Old Testament events mentioned in Stephen's speech are complemented by those in Paul's Acts 13 speech. All this, plus the similar style, structure, and use of the Old Testament, are evidence of Luke's hand in these speeches.

The Old Testament survey pivots around two points. The first is the promise to Abraham that his descendants will be saved from Egypt and receive the land of Israel where they can worship God freely (7:5-7). It is fulfilled in the Moses events (7:17). The second key point is Moses' prophecy, also mentioned in 3:22, that "God will raise up for you from among your kinsmen a prophet like me" (Deut 18:15 in Acts 7:37).

The speech indirectly shows how Jesus is like Moses. It parallels Moses' life to the way Luke's Gospel had described Jesus' life, from their births on. Both grow in wisdom (Acts 7:22 and Luke 2:52) to become "powerful in word and deed" (Acts 7:22 and Luke 24:19). Both Moses and Jesus were disappointed that their own people did not recognize that God wanted to use them as their saviors (Acts 7:25, Luke 13:34-35, and 19:41-44). After Moses was rejected and fled Egypt, God reconfirmed him and sent him back to save them with "wonders and signs" (7:27-36). Acts 7:37 makes explicit the comparison to Jesus' resurrection. After Jesus' rejection and death, God reconfirmed him as Savior. He raised him from the dead and sent him again to save the people from their sins, through preaching, "wonders and signs" (6:8) of Christians like Peter and Stephen, who are filled with Jesus' Spirit and act in his name.

The last part of Stephen's speech recalls the charge in 6:13-14 that he and Jesus were against the temple. It quotes the Old Testament to say that God does not dwell in temples made by hands (Isa 66:1-2 in Acts 7:48-49). It ends by accusing them of being a stiff-necked people (Exod 32:9) who always resisted the Holy Spirit (Isa 63:10). This is what they were doing in resisting the Spirit-filled Stephen. As their ancestors had killed the prophets (Luke 11:47-51), they, the Sanhedrin, had handed Jesus over to be killed (Acts 7:51-52).

These accusations are actually based on the way the Old Testament describes the relationship between God and his people. It emphasizes the people's disobedience, God's long-suffering mercy, warnings through prophets, and the people's refusal to listen (resisting the Holy Spirit, Zech 7:12). Thus it explained why God allowed the chosen people to be exiled. In Acts 7 the accusations explain why many Jewish leaders did not believe in Christ and why they were therefore replaced by the new Christian leaders of God's people.

7:54–8:3 Stephen's martyrdom and the spread of the church. Filled with the Spirit, Stephen witnesses that he saw the resurrected Jesus with God in glory (7:55-56). The reference to the heavens opening indicates a vision, as for Jesus in Luke 3:21-22 and Peter in Acts 10:11. Stephen's reference to the Son of Man at God's right hand (7:56) is the only use of "Son of Man" in the New Testament that is not on Jesus' lips. Casting Stephen out of the city and killing him parallel the casting of Jesus out of Nazareth in Luke 4:29 and his crucifixion outside Jerusalem. Luke draws many other parallels also. Stephen's "Lord Jesus, receive my spirit" (Acts 7:59) is like Jesus' "Father, into your hands I commend my spirit" (Luke 23:46). Both forgive those who kill them: "Father, forgive them; they do not know what they are doing" (Jesus in Luke 23:34), and "Lord, do not hold this sin against them" (Stephen in Acts 7:60). Notice also how Stephen prays to Jesus as Jesus had prayed to his Father.

These prayers of forgiveness are very important for Luke. He links Jesus' prayer for forgiveness to the second chance offered to the Jerusalem Jews in Acts 2 and 3. And Luke implies that Stephen's prayer was responsible for Saul (later called Paul) being forgiven and chosen to preach Christ (9:4-6). That is why he mentions Saul right after Stephen's prayer in 7:60.

It is also one reason he mentions here the resulting persecution that scattered the church throughout Judea and Samaria (as Jesus had predicted in 1:8). The persecution did not force the apostles out of Jerusalem. It only expelled Stephen's fellow Greek-speaking leaders, such as Philip (8:4-5). Saul was also involved in this scattering of the church, but still on the persecuting side (8:3). Thus ends the Jerusalem phase of Luke's account of the growth and spread of Christianity.

PERSECUTION AND EXPANSION IN JUDEA AND SAMARIA

Acts 8:4–9:31

8:4-8 Philip in Samaria. Paragraphs like Acts 8:1-3 are transitional. They both sum up the preceding section and introduce the next one. This notice that persecution scattered preachers throughout Judea and Samaria both concludes the Jerusalem phase of Acts and prepares for Philip's travels to Samaria. At this point Saul (Paul) plays an ironic part as persecutor in the spread of Christianity.

For persecution could not stop the word from spreading. The expulsion of Philip, one of the Seven (Acts 6:3-6), caused him to move on to the city of Samaria. Samaritans were descendants of Israelites and foreigners living in Israel after most of the people were exiled. In Samaria Philip proclaimed the Messiah to that despised "mixed race." He drew crowds by what he said and by signs, especially exorcisms and healings of cripples.

8:9-25: Simon the magician misunderstands miracles. These healings led to the comparison and meeting between Philip and Simon, a practitioner of occult magic. Simon is infamous in later Christian tradition as the head of a sect that combined Christian and pagan elements and became a rival to Christianity. This is the first of several confrontations in Acts between occult magic and Christian healings (also 13:4-12 and 19:11-19).

First-century magicians differed from those today who perform magic shows by sleight of hand and clever tricks. Magicians tried to manipulate life by occult power so as to accomplish whatever they wanted. The magicians themselves were in control, and effects were ascribed to their power. Thus Simon focused attention on himself and not on God.

In comparing Philip and Simon Magus, Luke emphasizes how much more impressed the crowds were by the Spirit-filled Philip's deeds. Even Simon was awed. It is not clear how this account relates to later traditions about Simon as an archheretic. They seem to presuppose some Christian elements in Simon's sect. So this identification of Simon as at least a temporary Christian could account for those Christian aspects. Contemporary cults have a similar mixture of Christian with occult and non-Christian elements.

Acts 8:16 distinguishes the coming of the Spirit from Christian baptism in the name of the Lord Jesus. This has caused much confusion among interpreters and theologians. Usually Luke and the rest of the New Testament (e.g., John 3:5 and Titus 3:5-7) link receiving the Spirit with being baptized as a Christian (Acts 2:38 and 9:17-18). But Luke also mentions receiving the Spirit before baptism (Acts 10:44-48 and 11:15-17) and after (here and in Acts 19:1-7). In these cases Luke is making some other point besides the meaning or practice of baptism. The point in Acts 8:16 is to show confirmation by God and by the apostles of Philip's unexpected outreach to despised Samaritans (see 10:44 and 19:6).

This story cannot be used to prove that a second step of receiving the Holy Spirit must follow Christian baptism before one can become a complete Christian. Nor can it prove the separate sacrament of confirmation, since the church and the rest of Acts and the New Testament teach that Christians receive the Spirit in baptism. Such uses would fail to respect Luke's limited intent. He would not want these stories used to solve problems of baptism, since his only concern was to show that God ratified the church's outreach to the Samaritans and non-Jews.

Though Acts 8:17-19 says only that the Samaritans received the Spirit when the apostles imposed hands on them, Simon the magician wanted to buy this power. The story implies that the manifestations of receiving the Spirit were awesome to Simon. He was even more impressed by what happened through Peter than by the healings through Philip.

The account shows the difference between manifestations of the Spirit and magic and that the Spirit's power is God's free gift for the sake of those who are helped by it. It cannot be bought, controlled, or manipulated as in magic occult arts. Simon the magician becomes an example for Luke's readers (even today) of how we cannot mix Christianity with pagan or occult practices and attitudes. Once that point is made, Luke does not even bother to tell us what later happened to Simon.

8:26-40 Philip and the Ethiopian eunuch. The story of Philip and the African eunuch makes extensive use of Luke's vocabulary for journeying and the imagery of "the Way" to imply the spread of the word and to locate Philip in Caesarea where he next appears in Acts 21:8. Luke uses this story to foreshadow the full-scale turning to pagans in Acts 10–11 and 15. Though 8:26-40 also relates a pagan's conversion, Luke does not stress this event as much as he did the "pagan Pentecost" for Cornelius' household in Acts 10.

As often in Acts, God takes the initiative by directing Philip through an angel (compare Acts 12:7), or a dream or vision (Acts 16:9-10), or the Holy Spirit (8:39). Luke wants to show clearly that God, not mere human decisions, guided the spread of Christianity.

Not only was the Ethiopian a pagan, but he had been castrated. This was an added block to his fitness to enter the assembly of God (Deut 23:1-2). He is another example of the outcasts to which Jesus and his followers reach out in Luke-Acts. As a vision later told Peter (Acts 10:15), "What God has purified you are not to call unclean," that is, unfit to associate with.

Because the Ethiopian was reading from Isaiah, Luke probably considered him a pagan Godfearer (as Cornelius in Acts 10). Godfearers were unable or unwilling to become full Jews, but were attracted by Jewish belief in one God and by their high morality.

Luke also insists repeatedly that the Scriptures need explanation. Private interpretation is not always sufficient. The groups of disciples on the road to Emmaus and at Jerusalem both needed the risen Jesus to interpret the Scriptures for them (Luke 24:25-32 and 44-47). Acts 13:27 says the Jews in Jerusalem and their rulers failed to understand the prophets they read every sabbath. So here Philip has to explain to the eunuch that Isa 53:7-8 referred not to Isaiah but to Jesus (as Acts 2 had explained that Pss 16 and 110 referred not to David but to Jesus) and prophesied his self-sacrificing death (Acts 8:31-35).

The way Philip taught the Ethiopian is undoubtedly the way Christians taught all their converts, including pagans. Even pagans in the first century put great value on fulfillment of predictions as signs that a religion was true. Beginning from this Scripture, Christians "proclaimed Jesus to" their converts (8:35).

Luke relates the snatching of Philip away after baptizing the eunuch as a further sign that the baptism was God's will.

9:1-9 Saul is called by the risen Jesus. We have said that Luke repeats major events up to three times in Acts, usually with minor variations. He will retell this conversion of Saul (9:1-29) in speeches in Acts 22:3-21 and 26:9-20. He thus underlines its importance and highlights several meanings in it. When we compare the three versions of Paul's call in Acts 9, 22, and 26, the unchanged core has these events. The high priest commissioned Saul to imprison men and women of "the Way," which seems to have been the first name Christians had. On his journey to Damascus he was thrown to the ground, surrounded by a light, and heard a voice saying, "Saul, Saul, why do you persecute me?" Only Paul saw the light and heard the voice. This is similar to modern apparitions: at Fatima, Lourdes, and the reputed apparitions of Medjugorje only the visionaries see and hear the apparition even when others are present. In Acts 9:7 Paul's companions only heard the voice, and in 22:9 and 26:13-14 they only saw the light. (Luke does not seem bothered by this inconsistency.)

All three versions emphasize that Paul is to witness especially to the Gentiles.

Christ's message, "Saul, Saul, why do you persecute me?", clearly shows that Christ is identified with Christians (compare Matt 25:31-46). What is done to them is done to him. Luke mentions this three times, showing how important it is to Acts. This evidence is often overlooked by those who say Luke lacks Paul's teaching that Christ lives in Christians.

The Lord called and appeared to Paul directly. Yet he required his baptism and reception into the Christian community. God overruled Ananias' objections and insisted he go to Saul, just as God would overrule Peter's objections about going to the Gentile Cornelius in Acts 10.

As Luke so often stresses, God's action took place as Ananias, Saul, Cornelius, and

Peter were praying. Even today, Luke-Acts can teach Christians how important it is to let God show us his priorities as we listen to him in private prayer. Often in prayer we will find our own priorities and projects changed by God's different plans for us.

The translation in 9:18, "things like scales fell from his eyes," misses the way the Greek noun for what is peeled off Paul's eyes echoes the verb for peeling off the blinded Tobit's cataracts (Tob 3:17 and 11:13).

9:10-31 Paul switches to the Christian side. It is not easy to harmonize the dates and information about where Paul went after his call that are given in Acts 9 and Gal 1:11-24. Nor are Acts 15 and Gal 2 easy to reconcile regarding the Jerusalem Council. Luke's information cannot be simply dismissed, even when it does not agree with what Paul himself says, for two reasons. First, Gal 1–2 are obviously written in a state of passion and defensiveness. Paul, not Luke, may be going out of his way to prove a point, namely, his independence from and equality with the Jerusalem apostles. Second, it is not always clear how the information given in Galatians corresponds to that in Acts. Nor is it even clear to what extent the same or multiple occasions are meant.

At any rate, Acts 9 focuses on Saul's immediate reversal from persecutor of Christians (see Gal 1:13, 23; Phil 3:6; 1 Cor 15:9) to preacher to the Jews at Damascus about the Christ. What Paul had persecuted the Christians for teaching, he himself now preaches. Luke stresses everyone's amazement at this turnabout. In response to Paul's aggressive witness and arguing that Jesus is the Son of God and the Messiah, the Jews naturally plot against him. 2 Cor 11:33 also mentions Paul's escape over the wall in a basket.

Luke reminds his readers how the Jerusalem Christians realistically feared Paul at first, not believing he was really one of them. Barnabas is the link between Paul and the Twelve. In Acts 4 he had submitted to the apostles. Now he introduces Paul to them and explains Paul's call and his witness to Jesus in Damascus. Because of Barnabas, they accept Paul, who confronts the Hellenistic Jews in Jerusalem as he had in Damascus. The Christians therefore have to save Paul from Jewish plots in Jerusalem also. They send him home to Tarsus.

Usually Acts uses "church" for individual communities, but 9:31 refers to "the church throughout all Judea, Galilee and Samaria." This is another Lukan summary and transition, and describes the church as at peace, "walking [or journeying] in the fear of the Lord," and growing through the Spirit.

TO THE GENTILES: PETER AND CORNELIUS, BARNABAS AND SAUL; THE JERUSALEM COUNCIL

Acts 9:32–15:35

9:32-43 A healing and raising through Peter in Lydda and Joppa. These healing accounts have two main functions in this part of Acts. First, they show how signs helped spread Christianity in Judea and along the Mediterranean coast. Second, they account for Peter's presence in the seacoast town of Joppa when Cornelius in Caesarea (up the coast) sends for him. Thus they set the stage for the pivotal Acts 10–11 report that legitimates the Gentile mission.

Both healing stories use the same command in Greek, "rise" (translated by the NAB as "get up" at 9:34, and "rise up" at 9:40) which recalls Jesus' resurrection. The healing of Aeneas is told simply, according to the basic form of healing narratives. Luke gives the name, sickness, and length of time Aeneas was paralyzed. Jesus had healed paralytics on his own authority (Luke 5:24-25), but Peter tells Aeneas that Jesus Christ heals him and commands him to rise and make his bed. The result is immediate. Whereas Jesus' healings often led to wonder but not to full belief in him, Aeneas' cure resulted in many conversions to "the Lord" (Jesus).

The story of the raising of Tabitha (Dorcas) uses language from Elisha's raising of the widow's son in 2 Kgs 4:32-37. In Kings, the prophet Elisha was alone with the dead person, as Peter was. Each prayed. 2 Kings and Acts 9 both mentioned the dead person opening his or her eyes. But whereas Elisha laid himself on the boy, Peter simply commanded the widow to get up. The resuscitation in Kings was gradual and took two tries by the prophet. Tabitha simply opened her eyes and sat up (as the widow's son did in Luke 7:15). Both Elisha and Peter presented the resuscitated person to the loved ones.

Luke-Acts frequently alludes to the Elijah-Elisha stories. They provide a good model for wonder-working prophets and their disciples that can be applied to Jesus and his followers. And, as Sir 48:15 says, despite two such prophets "the people did not repent . . . until they were rooted out of their land and scattered all over the earth." Luke 21:24 predicts something similar with the destruction of Jerusalem.

Acts 9:36–10:48 thus parallels Luke 7:1-17 in having back-to-back stories about a centurion and raising a widow or her son.

10:1-8 The vision of Cornelius. Acts 10–11 and 15 are major turning points in Acts. They legitimize the Gentile Christian church by grounding it in the approval of Peter and the Twelve. More radically still, Acts 10–11 show that God himself clearly was dispensing pagans from having to become circumcised Jews first before joining his people. The very difficulty Peter had accepting this brings home the fact that it was God's idea. God had made the law that every male of his people must become circumcised (Gen 17:10-14). Now God was repealing that requirement because the final days of fulfillment have come. The expected Holy Spirit is now poured out upon all flesh (Acts 2:17-18 and 10:44-47). This makes the entrance rite of circumcision superfluous, since the Spirit purifies even unclean pagans (see Acts 10:15).

Cornelius' vision is the first of two complementary visions that laid the groundwork for Peter's preaching to him. God takes all the initiative. Luke is defending the church from the charge of human tampering with God's law by letting pagans remain uncircumcised.

Cornelius is like the centurion Jesus helps in Luke 7. He both prays to God and helps the Jewish people (Acts 10:2). Both Cornelius and Peter are praying when this epoch-turning event takes place. Luke again impresses on his readers the importance of prayer. It readies humans for the major events in his Gospel and Acts. Luke implies that if we too are to be able to hear God's call and receive his gifts, we must pray.

10:9-23 The corresponding vision of Peter. The next day Peter is praying and thinking of food. Going into a trance, he has a vision of food that is symbolic. Seeing animals that the Old Testament calls unclean and forbids Jews to eat (e.g., Lev 11), Peter is told to kill and eat. He protests, like the prophet Ezekiel (Ezek 4:14), that he has never eaten unclean food. The heavenly voice's answer shocks Jewish sensibilities, including Peter's. He should not call unclean what God has made clean. Luke stresses Peter's consternation over the meaning of this enigmatic vision. God had to repeat it three times to get through to Peter. Acts 10:28 shows that the vision refers to admitting "unclean" pagans or Gentiles. "What God has made clean" (10:15) must allude to the Spirit's transforming action upon Gentiles as well as on Jews (10:44-47 and 11:15-17).

10:24-33 Peter goes to Caesarea. This account reminds Luke's readers how hard it was for the original Jewish-Christian church leaders to relate to non-Jews. It gives precedents in Peter's life for Paul's interactions with Gentiles.

Thus Peter rejects the pagan's prostration to him. He tells him he is also human (10:25-26), just as Barnabas and Paul reject the pagans' treatment of them as gods with the words, "We are of the same nature as you, human beings" (14:11-15).

The second apologetic point is in Acts 10:28. It shows Peter's awareness how improper and against all custom it was for Jews to associate closely with non-Jews (the same problem as in Gal 2:12). But the triple vision of "unclean" food had shown Peter not to call any human being unfit for sacred things. Even though Gentiles sullied themselves with idol worship, the Spirit purified them, so that they, as well as Jews, could approach God. Consequently, there was no reason to exclude Gentiles, once they had been made fit to approach God.

This theme of clean and unclean runs throughout Luke and Acts and is hard for us moderns to appreciate. It recalls a more primitive sense of what is sacred and profane than is common today. Recall the former Catholic prohibition against touching the sacred host by hands other than the priest's. Only consecrated hands should touch the consecrated host, it was felt.

In the first century many people were considered profane and unfit to partake in Jewish temple worship and assemblies. They included those who did not keep the purity laws of washing and foods, who were lepers or mutilated or eunuchs, Samaritans or

Roman tax collectors or notorious sinners (like prostitutes), those possessed by unclean spirits, or Gentile idol worshipers. All these people are the focus of cleansing by Jesus in Luke and the Spirit in Acts. They are all invited to God, but first they are cleansed from what makes them unfit to approach God. Luke is famous for his compassion for sinners and outcasts. But neither Luke nor Jesus himself is soft on the presence of sin or on involvement with pagan or immoral practices or the occult. Levi had to leave his tax collecting, the sinful woman her sinning. The possessed were exorcised. Gentiles had to give up both their associations with paganism and their sexual immorality. (That was a major charge both Jews and Christians made against pagans.)

Cornelius recognizes the need to change when he tells Peter that he and his pagan household are ready to obey whatever commands God has for them through Peter (10:33).

10:34-43 Peter's speech to Cornelius' household. The theological core of Peter's speech is from the Old Testament: "God shows no partiality" (as judge—Deut 10:17). As Paul does in Rom 2:11 and Gal 2:6, Luke applies this statement to God's accepting not only Jews but Gentiles who act rightly. Acts 10:34-35 is close to Rom 2:10-16. God is not an unjust judge. He will not favor an unjust Jew over a just Gentile, but in every nation the one who fears God and acts uprightly is acceptable to God (10:35).

Acts 10:36-43 summarizes Christian preaching about Christ to Gentiles. God gave the good news of peace through Jesus Christ (10:36, notice the use of Christ as Jesus' second name). He is "Lord of all" (both Jews and Gentiles, 10:36). Next come Jesus' ministry, death, resurrection, and commissioning of the apostles (10:37-42). Finally the speech recalls the witness of the Old Testament prophets that all who believe in him (Jews or Gentiles) will receive forgiveness through his name (10:43). As the speech began with the Pauline kind of teaching found in Rom 2:10-16, it ends echoing Paul's forgiveness or salvation by faith in Jesus.

Acts 10:39 shows Luke's special focus on the apostles as witnesses. Verse 40 is another allusion to Deut 21:22-23, the curse on him who hangs on a tree (see Acts 5:30). The gospel message continues in 10:40-42 to include not just the resurrection (where Mark ended) but the command to apostles to witness that God has established the risen Jesus as "judge of the living and the dead" (10:42). Acts 17:31 and 2 Tim 4:1 confirm that preaching to pagans stressed Jesus as ultimate judge of everyone's actions.

10:44–11:18 "Pentecost" for the pagans. The Acts 10 outpouring of the Spirit on the Gentiles strictly parallels the first Pentecost in Acts 2. The Jews with Peter are amazed that Gentiles received the same gift of the Spirit as they. The pagans also speak in tongues and tell of God's wonders, as the apostles had. The difference is that the first Pentecost for the 120 mentioned no water baptism. Everyone after the 120 who received the Spirit were also baptized with water as a reception into the church (10:47-48). God, however, had again taken the initiative. No one baptized uncircumcised pagans until God showed by the visible sign of tongues that he had already given them the Holy Spirit.

The falling of the Spirit on Gentiles is like what happened on Pentecost "at the beginning" (11:15). It also fulfills Jesus' prophecy in Acts 1:5 that "you will be baptized with the Holy Spirit."

11:19-30 Outreach to Antioch and return of help to Jerusalem. After the principle of admitting Gentiles into the church is established, Acts 11:19-30 provides a narrative link back to 8:4 and mentions again the geographical spread of the church that resulted from the persecution after Stephen's death. Whereas Acts 1–8 had concentrated on the Jerusalem church and its missionaries, Acts 11 focuses on the second great missionary church, Antioch in northern Syria on the Mediterranean Sea. The first missionaries to Antioch spoke only to Jews, but Christians from the island of Cyprus and from Cyrene in African Libya won over many Greeks as well. The Jewish mother church in Jerusalem sent Barnabas, who also came from Cyprus, to investigate this unexpected development. Once Barnabas confirmed this new kind of church which included Gentiles, he got Paul to help with it. Antioch is where the name "Christian" was first used, presumably because the influx of Gentiles distinguished that church from Jewish communities.

When Christian prophets warned of coming famine, the Antioch church returned help to the churches of Judea. Thus they showed their gratitude for the missionaries sent to them.

The use of "presbyters" (or "elders") in 11:30 is the first time this term is applied to Christian leaders. Acts 4–6 and 23–25 use it for Jewish leaders, usually members of the Sanhedrin. In the Acts 15 Jerusalem Council, "presbyters" and "apostles" are paired. Here and in Acts 16–21 "presbyters" refers to Christian leaders with no mention of apostles. Luke's only use of "bishop" or "overseer" for Christian leaders is in Acts 20:28 as a synonym for the elders Paul set up in Ephesus. It took until the second century for our standard "bishops, presbyters, and deacons" to become established as fixed leadership terms.

12:1-19 Herod kills James and imprisons Peter. Stephen is the first martyr in Acts 6. James, the brother of John, is the first of the Twelve to be martyred. Herod who killed him also arrested Peter. (This is a different Herod from the one who killed John the Baptist and tried Jesus. That was Herod Antipas; this is Herod Agrippa, the brother of Herodias who married Herod Antipas and caused the Baptist's beheading in Mark 6:14-29.) The portrayal of "the Jews" as hostile in 12:3 is relatively new in Luke-Acts. "The people" in 12:4 and "the Jewish people" in 12:11 are also described as enemies, in contrast to "the church" whose fervent prayers for Peter's escape triumph over Herod's plans and prison and Jewish hostility. The first negative mention of "the Jews" was their attempt to kill the newly converted Paul in 9:23, and "the Jews" will be hostile for much of Paul's career (Acts 14, 17–26, 28). Like Jesus, Peter is arrested around Passover time. God frees Peter as he will later free Paul and Silas (16:25-34).

We see Luke's humor in the spectacle of Peter left knocking at the door while believers inside argue whether Rhoda was hallucinating or seeing an angel. The comic touch emphasizes how unexpected Peter's deliverance was.

James is probably head of the Jerusalem church by now, for Peter says to report his release to James. Herod's execution of Peter's guards underlines his cruelty and prepares for the fear of Paul's Philippian jailer when he thought Paul had escaped in 16:27.

12:20-23 Herod is punished by a gruesome death. Though Herod died later, Luke mentions his death here to show how God punished this persecutor, before Acts turns from Peter to Barnabas and Saul. Luke associates Herod's death with the blasphemy of the people calling him a god and not man. For not giving the glory to God, Herod died of worms. In the Bible worms were the fate of blasphemers and persecutors like Antiochus (2 Macc 9:9). Luke's contemporary Josephus gives a more detailed version of Herod Agrippa's death (*Antiquities* 19:343-50). He too mentions how the people flattered Herod as a god and how he died of stomach pain. Verse 24 is another summary verse and contrasts Herod's death with the continued spread of the word of God.

Acts 12:25 is unclear and the text is uncertain. Perhaps the best translation is to read "to Jerusalem" with the following phrase about completing their mission, instead of according to the more normal word order after "they returned," thus: "After Barnabas and Saul completed their relief mission to Jerusalem, they returned [to Antioch], taking with them John, who is called Mark." For Barnabas and Saul were mentioned in Jerusalem in 11:30; John Mark's mother lives in Jerusalem (12:12); and immediately after this verse, in 13:1, Barnabas and Saul appear in Antioch, from where their first missionary journey began (13:2-4) with John Mark as assistant (13:5).

13:1-12 The Spirit chooses missionaries and punishes a false prophet. When Acts 13:4 says Barnabas and Saul were "sent forth by the Holy Spirit," this does not mean according to their private inspirations. The Spirit worked through the leaders of the community fasting and praying together for guidance. Through a prophecy to these five leaders, the Spirit chose Barnabas and Saul. The leaders then commissioned them, which implies that they were accountable to these leaders for the mission. Their report to the Antioch church on their return confirms this (Acts 14:26-27).

Luke here provides a model for how church leaders should make decisions through fasting and prayer together and be accountable to one another. Thus they will get their decisions from God and not merely human planning. Being answerable to other leaders ensures that a person is really hearing God and not being deceived. A few parishes today have tried to follow Luke's model and have found extraordinary fruit.

On the island of Cyprus, Barnabas and Saul encountered the Jewish magician and false prophet Bar-Jesus (which means "son of Jesus," the Greek equivalent of the common Jewish name Joshua). The magician tried to turn the proconsul away from "the faith." (This is a post-Pauline expression referring to the Christian religion rather than the act of faith, as in Paul's writings; see Acts 6:7 and 14:22). Saul used a punishing sign against him as Peter had against Ananias and Sapphira in Acts 5. Luke mentions that Saul was "filled with the Holy Spirit" and the magician was temporarily blinded. This sign converted the governor. Somewhat surprisingly, Acts 13:12 calls this sign "the teaching about the Lord" (compare Mark 1:27). Teaching involves more than just words. Powerful signs confirm its truth.

This is the first use of the name Paul in Acts. Verse 9 is the transition from the Jewish name Saul to the better-known Roman name Paul: "Saul, also known as Paul."

13:13-43 Paul's first major sermon: Antioch in Pisidia. At the beginning of the first journey, Barnabas is named before Saul, implying he was leader. Already in 13:13, Luke focuses on Paul, merely including Barnabas among "his companions." The John who abandoned them (13:13) is also called Mark (12:12). Mark was his Roman name, John his Jewish (compare the Roman "Paul" and the Jewish "Saul"). Mark, traditionally known as the author of the Gospel of Mark, was Barnabas' cousin (Col 4:10). Barnabas and Paul split up over Mark in 15:36-41, but in Phlm 24, Paul refers to Mark as his fellow worker. Acts 12:12 and 1 Pet 5:14 are evidence that Mark also knew Peter.

Antioch in Pisidia is part of the Roman province of Galatia in Asia Minor. It should not be confused with Antioch in Syria, where the church commissioned Barnabas and Saul. Several Hellenistic cities were named Antioch after the Greek emperor Antiochus. Going first to the synagogue and being invited to preach on the sabbath is Paul's basic approach in Acts, as it was Jesus' in the Gospel (Luke 4:16-21).

As Paul's "inaugural address," this speech is similar to Peter's at Pentecost in Acts 2. It summarizes the main Christian preaching to Jews, which was based on scriptural precedents and arguments. Both Acts 13 and 2 use the same Ps 16:10 text, "You will not suffer your faithful one to undergo corruption" (13:35). They argue that the promises are fulfilled in Jesus who was resurrected, not in David who did see corruption. This further exemplifies how Luke parallels Paul and Peter.

Paul's summary of Jesus' mission begins with John the Baptist (13:23-25) and emphasizes Jesus' passion. It stresses the failure of the people and their leaders in Jerusalem to recognize him, thus unknowingly fulfilling the prophets they read every sabbath. It names as primary witnesses those who came with Jesus from Galilee to Jerusalem as ensuring continuity with Jesus' mission (see 1:22).

Acts 13:38-39 hints at Paul's teaching on justification by faith. Through Jesus, forgiveness of sins is being proclaimed "to you." Everyone who believes in him will be justified from all those things from which "you" could not be justified through the law of Moses. The speech ends with a warning against cynical unbelief, quoting Hab 1:5 (Acts 13:40-41).

The first reaction is positive. Many were converted and the whole city turned out to hear Paul on the next sabbath.

13:44-52 Jewish persecution and Gentile acceptance. But other Jews were jealous and caused trouble. Paul and Barnabas (notice Paul is mentioned first) say they will turn to the Gentiles because of Jewish rejection. Acts reports three such statements, the other two in 18:6 and in the finale at 28:25-28. Repetition indicates emphasis, as we have seen.

Acts 13:47 applies Isa 49:6 to Paul: "I will make you as a light to the nations." Simeon had used this same passage for Jesus in Luke 2:32. Similarly, Acts 26:23 says that the Christ after rising must "proclaim light to our people and to the Gentiles." Christians like Paul and ourselves share in Christ's mission of being God's servant and light to the Gentiles.

This news causes Gentile rejoicing and conversions and the spread of God's word. Some Jews cause Paul and Barnabas to be expelled from the territory. Their gesture of shaking the dust from their feet recalls Jesus' instructions in Luke 10:10-12. The episode ends on the high note of being full of joy and the Spirit (13:52).

14:1-7: Success and persecution in Iconium. In Iconium, about eighty miles from Pisidian Antioch, we find a similar pattern. Through bold preaching, signs and wonders, Paul and Barnabas win large numbers of Jews and Greeks in the synagogue. The unpersuaded Jews then incite the pagans against them. The city divides between those siding with the Jews and those with the "apostles." Some plot to kill them. Luke often stresses how the Gospel divides people into those who accept and those who reject it. Conversion is a totally free response, he thus implies. Persecution again results in spreading the word, this time to Lystra and Derbe, each twenty-five to thirty miles distance. Note also how Acts 14:4 and 14:14 describe Paul and Barnabas as "apostles," a term Luke usually reserves for the Twelve. He may have had the word "apostle" in his source and not thought of changing it.

14:8-18 Healing of a lame man and preaching in Lystra. Paul and Barnabas worked many "signs and wonders" (14:3). Luke focuses on this healing of a lame man to parallel Peter's first healing in Acts 3. Both involved looking closely, faith to be saved, an order to stand, jumping up and walking. Both times the crowds focus on the two "healers," Peter and John or Paul and Barnabas. Both Peter and Paul tell the crowds not to focus on them but on God. The difference is that Jews tended to concentrate on Peter's and John's piety or power, whereas pagans ignorantly treat Paul and Barnabas as gods. Luke again highlights comic aspects of the scene, mocking pagan ignorance and worship of divine men.

The Lystra speech is a good example of typical preaching to pagans by both Jews and Christians. It stresses the folly of worshiping humans or many gods. It emphasizes the one living God who created all things and revealed himself through creation (a kind of "natural theology"). In fact, Jews could have given this speech, since it does not mention Jesus or Christianity. This illustrates how New Testament religion flows from the Old Testament and Judaism. Both have the same basic beliefs about God and creation and prayer and morality. They differ over Jesus as Christ and Savior.

14:19-28 End of first mission and return to Antioch in Syria. With incredible fickleness the crowds turn from worshiping Paul to stoning him. After the Jews incited them to stone Paul, they drag him out of town (cf. Stephen in Acts 7). Stoning is usually fatal. Lest anyone dismiss this as pious legend, 2 Cor 11:25 confirms that Paul was stoned. It also mentions three shipwrecks, which were usually as fatal as plane crashes today.

Paul and Barnabas exemplify remarkable courage by going right back to where they had been beaten. Nor were they irresponsible wandering evangelists. In each town they taught and built up church communities and installed leaders called presbyters or elders. They solidify conversions by teaching and by a community with authority structures that enable it to carry on after the preachers have left. Luke has thus given his readers an example of how evangelism should be done.

Finally, the missionaries return to their home church and report on their mission. This shows that Paul and Barnabas are accountable to the Antioch church. It also puts the prestige of that major missionary center behind Paul's work in Asia.

15:1-21 The Gentile controversy and the Council of Jerusalem. As the mission in Asia Minor was accountable to the Antioch church, it in turn was accountable to the mother church in Jerusalem. Some converted Judean Pharisees objected to the Antioch practice of baptizing uncircumcised pagans. Acts 15 portrays the debate as a question of salvation—no salvation without circumcision. Luke does not cover over disagreements as he is often accused of doing. He shows Paul and Barnabas in violent dissension from this position.

The so-called Council of Jerusalem opens with a report of the fruits of the Antioch practice. The Pharisees insist on circumcision and the law for Gentile Christians. After much argument, Peter recounts (for the third time) how God gave the Spirit to the Gentiles through his ministry, having cleansed their hearts by faith. Therefore they are no longer unclean or unworthy to enter God's presence in worship, as some Jews felt. Peter sounds a lot like Paul: "On the contrary, we believe that we are saved through the grace of the Lord Jesus, in the same way as they" (15:11).

Building on Peter's theological principle, Barnabas and Paul relate their experience. God worked signs and wonders through them among the Gentiles, as he had through Moses in the Exodus. Experience shows this approach bears good fruit.

James gives the clinching argument. He is the brother of Jesus and the leader of the Jerusalem church by this time. He was known as an exemplary Jewish leader. If Luke can show that James approved of Gentile Christianity, he can take the sting out of charges against Paul. For Gal 2:12 proves that people from James' community were the ones who objected to Antioch practices toward Gentile Christians.

Scripture justifies the Antioch practice, according to the James argument. "The words of the prophets agree with this" (15:15). It uses the Greek translation of Amos 9:11-12 to claim that Scripture foretold both the restoration of Israel and then the conversion of the rest of the human race to the Lord Jesus. In other words, Scripture had predicted the events described in Acts 1–6 (Israel's restoration) and 11–15 (Gentile conversions). All are according to God's plan.

Therefore Christians should not put obstacles to Gentile conversions. They should ask only the compromises needed to enable Christian Jews to associate in table fellowship with non-Jewish Christians. Three concern kosher regulations and avoiding meat sacrificed to idols. The fourth has to do with illicit sex (*porneia* in Greek); its import is not totally clear. It probably refers to marriage within degrees of kinship forbidden to Jews, hence "unlawful marriage," as the New American Bible translates it. But others see a reference to ordinary sexual immorality, for which pagans were often criticized by Jews. New Testament letters frequently charge pagan converts to change their sexual ways. Chief among practices condemned were fornication, adultery, prostitution, and homosexual practices, which all undermined the family. New Testament morality was just as countercultural in the first century as it is to popular morality today. But the stipulations asked converts to change only what threatened Christian community or its basic unit, the family.

If the meeting in Acts 15 refers to the same meeting that Paul mentions in Gal 2:1-10, then this compromise (to facilitate table fellowship and community between Christian Jews and Gentiles in mixed churches) may refer to a later problem and meeting. Perhaps it refers to the one about eating with Gentile Christians mentioned in Gal 2:11-16 (whose solution is not stated), which gets linked with the first meeting in this one account. Though Paul makes no mention of it in his letters, the "Apostolic Decree" was in effect when Luke wrote Acts and into the second century.

The reference in 15:21 to Moses read throughout the civilized world probably implies that these basic requirements for pagans who associate with Jews were nothing new. They were probably already accepted by such pagans throughout the empire. Therefore, they would be no obstacle to Gentile conversions.

15:22-35 Letters and delegation to Antioch. Silas is first introduced as a leader and prophet whom the Jerusalem church chose to accompany Paul and Barnabas and to bring the "Apostolic Decree" to Antioch. Only a few maverick manuscripts have verse 15:34, "But Silas decided to remain there," or the like. Later copyists were apparently trying to account for Silas' presence in Antioch in 15:40 when Paul takes him as his new partner from Antioch.

The letter is in the standard Greek style of the time, including its beginning and ending. It does not have the expanded Christianized greetings and endings found in letters that are books of the New Testament. (Many of the expressions are characteristic of Luke's style, e.g., "it seemed good to us having become of one mind," [v. 25 in the NAB: "we have with one accord decided"].) We have mentioned how it was customary for a writer of his time either to reword letters he had into his own style or to compose what he thought would have been written.

The letter recommends Paul and Barnabas, Judas and Silas. They in turn guaranteed that the letter was authentic and explained its meaning. This was necessary because letters were hand delivered. There was no postal system Christians could use.

Acts 15:32 mentions Judas and Silas as Christian prophets. Acts 13:1 had named Barnabas and Paul among the prophets at Antioch. Since little is known about what Christian prophets did or how they spoke, Acts 15:32 is important. It indicates that a major function of prophets in Christian churches was to encourage and strengthen the community (see also 1 Cor 14). Paul and Barnabas belonged to the Antioch community. Judas and Silas remained part of the Jerusalem church and returned there after helping the daughter church at Antioch. The passage provides pastoral wisdom for how an older community can aid a younger one by sending helpers.

PAUL'S MISSION TO THE GENTILES: THE SECOND JOURNEY

Acts 15:36–18:23

15:36-41 Paul and Barnabas separate. Here is another case of sharp dissension among leaders in the early church that Luke is not afraid to report. Acts relates the dispute to the pastoral choice of a helper for their next missionary journey, but the argument over table fellowship with converted pagans reported in Gal 2:11-13 might also have contributed to the rift. Acts reports that Paul objected to Barnabas' selection of John Mark because Mark had deserted them on their first journey. The argument got so heated that Paul and Barnabas parted ways. Barnabas took John Mark with him to his native Cyprus, and Paul took Silas to his home province of Syria and Cilicia (in modern Turkey).

Luke implies that God works even through tragic separations like this. Paul no longer needed Barnabas' guidance as he had at first. Now there were two teams: Barnabas and Mark, Paul and Silas. As an important leader in the Jerusalem church, Silas was Paul's link to that church. Since a respected leader of the Jerusalem church worked with Paul, he could hardly be as disobedient to the mother church as some charged.

Nor was Paul's antagonism toward Barnabas and Mark permanent. Though Gal 2:9 (no later than A.D. 54–55) refers to Paul and Barnabas as co-leaders to the Gentiles, followed by their disagreement in 2:13 over eating with converted Gentiles, 1 Cor 9:6 (about A.D. 56–57) shows Paul appealing to the example of Barnabas as well as of himself, where their common practice differed from Peter's. And in Phlm 24 Paul later refers to Mark as one of his co-workers.

16:1-5 Paul recruits Timothy in Lystra. Because of Paul's statements in Galatians against circumcising Christians, many scholars wonder about the account of Paul's circumcising Timothy in Lystra in the province of Galatia, now in Turkey. But others point out that Paul circumcised Timothy not because he needed it for salvation but only "on account of the Jews of that region" (16:3). An uncircumcised son of a mixed marriage between a Jewish mother and Greek father would be a stumbling block to winning Jews. Paul himself cited the principle of submitting to the law to win over those under the law (1 Cor 9:20). Paul did not circumcise Titus, who had no Jewish blood, but did circumcise Timothy as a special case to render him acceptable as a missionary to Jews as well as Gentiles.

Acts also notes that Paul promulgated the decisions of the Council of Jerusalem in the province of Galatia in Asia Minor, and not just to the churches in Syria and Cilicia to whom they were originally addressed. This is the last mention of the original twelve apostles in Acts. From now on, Luke traces the spread of the word through Paul. Even his visit to Jerusalem in Acts 21 mentions only James the brother of Jesus and the elders there, but not the original apostles.

16:6-10 The Spirit directs Paul's course toward Europe. Twice Luke says the Spirit prevented Paul from going one direction, but steered him in another. He does not say how the Spirit acted, through prayer or prophecy, for example. He does tell us that it was a dream in the port city of Troas that directed Paul to sail to Macedonia, the province above Greece. In Acts, God's Spirit uses many means to guide Christians. Luke most frequently mentions prayer, visions (including appearances of angels), prophecies, and dreams, and also attributes the church's Jerusalem decision in Acts 15 to the Spirit. The reference in 16:7 to "the Spirit of Jesus" shows the close relationship in Acts between the action of the risen Jesus and of the Holy Spirit (see 2:33).

Acts 16:10 is the first of several passages that use "we," the first person, instead of "he" or "they," the third person. Scholars have noted a convention in ancient Greek histories and fiction, namely, using the first-person "we" when narrating sea voyages to convey the vividness of an eyewitness's account. Therefore some scholars explain the "we" passages in Acts as mere convention and not a serious claim that the author was actually present on Paul's voyages.

However, one must consider not only the presence of a convention but variations in the uses to which it is put. Variations in the use of "we" and "they" in several Acts passages imply that whatever convention may be present is subordinated to the writer's purposes. For example, none of Paul's sea trips in Acts 13-14 have the convention, nor does 18:18-19. Also, the "we" in 20:5-6 distinguishes some companions of Paul from others, and in 20:13-14 "we" refers to his companions but not to Paul. In Luke 1:1-4 the author clearly shows his intention to write what took place, not fiction. This evidence leads me to believe that the author's use of "we" in Acts is meant to imply to his readers that he was present on those sea journeys where "we" is used, and not on other voyages like Acts 18:18-19 where it is not.

16:11-15 Conversion of Lydia's household at Philippi. The first city in Europe that Paul evangelized was Philippi in Macedonia. We know from his Letter to the Philippians that this church remained his favorite. Luke's description of Paul's procedure gives us glimpses of how Christianity spread. Note that Christians did not usually begin from scratch trying to convert pagans who never heard of God. In Athens, Paul began with pagans. But even there he presupposed some knowledge of the one God from popular philosophers, and he had little success.

Usually Christians went where Jews had paved the way before them, to people whom Jews had already instructed about God and morality, but who had remained uncircumcised. Thus, most early Christian churches were in places where there was a significant Jewish population, in cities, not the countryside. Often missionaries began in synagogues.

Here in Philippi they went on the sabbath to a "place of prayer" by the river. "Place of prayer" could be another word for synagogue, but it is curious that only women were there. In any case, the text implies that the women were Jews or "God-fearing" Gentiles. God-fearers were pagans attracted to the monotheism and morality of Judaism but unwilling to become full Jews.

Lydia is the most prominent Christian in this account, but she is not mentioned in Paul's Letter to the Philippians. She seems to have been a wealthy businesswoman and head of a household where a Christian community in Philippi met (see 16:40). Before churches were built, Christians met in larger households, which also provided hospitality to traveling missionaries.

Lydia was probably a widow. Her whole household followed her lead and was baptized, as were the households of Cornelius, of the jailer at Philippi (16:33), and of Crispus in Corinth (18:8). Often whole households were converted together, which provided a solid community base for the local church. We cannot be sure whether the baptized household included children and babies, but many scholars see this pattern as evidence for the beginning of infant baptism. If the church imitated Judaism in this as in so many other aspects of its life, it seems likely that Christians baptized and raised their children as Christians, as Jews circumcised and raised their children to be Jews.

16:16-24 Exorcism and imprisonment at Philippi. At the beginning of Jesus' ministry in Luke's Gospel, demon-filled men named Jesus' identity as Christ and Son of God until he silenced them (4:33-35, 41). Similarly, the Philippian girl with the occult spirit identified Paul and the missionaries as "servants of the Most High God." What she says is true. They are servants of God who teach a way of salvation. As in Luke's Gospel, Acts presents truth in the mouths of evil spirits, who perform for readers of Luke-Acts some of the same functions that the chorus of all-knowing gods have in a Greek play of Luke's time. They state truths that readers know but people in the narrative would not.

Acts clearly shows that the charge against Paul and Silas was false. They were not disturbing the peace or Greco-Roman customs, but had angered the owners of the slave girl by taking away their source of income.

The magistrates had ordered Paul and Silas to be stripped and beaten with rods, which Paul suffered three times (2 Cor 11:25). 1 Thess 2:2 might be referring to this incident as "the humiliation we had suffered at Philippi."

16:25-40 God rescues his servants and converts their jailer. Luke stresses how irrepressible Paul and Silas were. Despite their wounds, they prayed and sang in prison. Luke's humor may be evident in this picture of criminals listening to prayer and singing at midnight.

The earthquake and opened doors and chains are commonly mentioned in other stories of Luke's day. Luke is also paralleling Paul's release from prison with Peter's. Herod had executed Peter's jailers. Fear of execution prompted Paul's jailer to contemplate suicide, but Paul converted him with his whole household. The jailer becomes Paul and Silas' host, cleaning their wounds and feeding them in his home. But they are back in jail the next morning before the magistrates order them to be released. Luke delights in showing Paul insisting on his rights as a Roman citizen, and even rulers quaking before the Christian missionaries. He stresses that Paul and Silas strengthened the church at Lydia's house before they left the city as requested.

17:1-9 Preaching and persecution at Thessalonica. Paul's actions directly parallel those of Jesus coming to Nazareth in Luke 4:16. He journeys, arrives at a city, and teaches at a synagogue on the sabbath "following his usual custom." Jesus had taught that the Scriptures which foretold the Messiah were speaking about him. So Paul gives a two-part proof from Scripture that the Messiah was supposed to suffer and rise from the dead, similarly proving that Jesus was that Messiah.

In all the New Testament only Luke's Gospel and Acts give proof in argument form that Jesus is the Christ. Usually the New Testament merely states that Jesus fulfills prophecies or that the Christ who died for our sins was raised on the third day. In argument form Luke's premise is that the Christ was supposed to suffer and rise from the dead. He implies a second premise that Jesus did so die and rise. The conclusion is that Jesus is therefore the Christ or Messiah.

Luke is using Greek persuasion from his culture to prove and not merely claim that Jesus is the Christ. Eventually this will become a standard argument in Christian apologetics, which is the rational explanation of Christian faith in the face of opposition. Luke certainly sees no contradiction between faith and reason. Nor is he afraid to use reason to explain and defend his faith.

The results of the argument are mixed. Some of Paul's listeners are persuaded. Many God-fearing but uncircumcised Greeks and several influential women join the few Jews whom Paul persuaded.

Such mixed response is a common pattern in Paul's mission. So is the Jewish resentment and stirring up a mob against Paul (for example, Acts 13:45). It corresponds to the different responses by the prodigal and older sons in Luke 15:11-32. The older son in 15:28-29 resents the reception for the sinner, since he, the elder, had always remained home doing the father's will. So Acts shows resentment by Jews, who had always tried to do God's will, against newly converted pagans, whom Jews considered godless and immoral.

17:10-15 Paul in Beroea. Persecution in one city again leads to spreading Christianity to the next. Paul and Silas go to Beroea, about fifty miles southwest of Thessalonica (in modern Greece). The narrator's ideological point of view appears in the aside, "These Jews were more fair-minded than those in Thessalonica, for they received the word with all willingness and examined the Scriptures daily to determine whether these things were so" (17:11). Paul's letters to the Thessalonians confirm that the church there was able to endure without Paul. Another pattern in Acts is how Jewish hostility was so deep that Jews followed Paul long distances (here fifty miles) to cause him trouble in the next city. The hostility seems focused on Paul. Silas and Timothy remain behind to minister to the church before rejoining Paul.

17:16-34 Confrontation with Greek philosophers at Athens. At Athens Paul worked on two fronts: in the synagogues with Jews and God-fearing Gentiles and in the marketplace with pagan passersby. Paul's approach in the market was similar to that of popular philosophers, who preached to whomever they met. Luke tends to parallel Epicureans with Sadducees, Stoics with Pharisees, as does his Jewish contemporary Josephus. Epicureans urged people to ignore the Greek myths about vindictive gods and torments in the afterlife. Stoics, on the contrary, did believe in the providence of the gods and in natural law by which humans are to live.

In the first-century Roman Empire, many new religions and cults were spreading, especially from the East. Paul might well seem to be promoting another Eastern cult, preaching new gods called Jesus and Anastasis (the Greek word for resurrection, which sounds like the name of a goddess). The narrator reveals a negative point of view toward the

Athenians, repeating the stereotype that they have "itching ears" for novelties.

Paul's speech in the Areopagus, the academic meeting place in Athens, sounds quite different from speeches to Jews, which argued from Scripture. Addressed to Greek philosophers, it sounds more philosophical. Nevertheless, it too is steeped in Scripture, but sticks to the parts that sound like philosophy. It is a good sample of the way both Jews and Christians tried to convert pagans by appealing to "natural theology," that is, evidence from nature for the God who created it. Since there are many natural theology passages in the Old Testament, neither Jews nor Christians saw any contradiction between philosophical natural theology and revealed truths about God in Scripture.

Although Acts 17:16 mentioned Paul's annoyance over the many idols in Athens, here Paul praises the Athenians for being so religious! Having gone in their door, he comes out his own immediately by identifying the "unknown god" as the God he preaches. Scholars have found literary references to "unknown gods" but no Athenian inscription to an "unknown god." In any case, such a phrase implied many gods, but both Jews and Christians would reinterpret it as referring to the one God.

The image of all nations groping for God (as a person in darkness) expresses both that all humans are able to know God and how much better off are Jews and Christians to whom he has revealed himself. As in Rom 1:19-20, humans can know God through both nature and revelation. But the resurrection of Jesus is the complete revelation. The ages before the resurrection are the "times of ignorance" when failure to know God could be excused. Revelation brings also the responsibility to repent and believe (Acts 17:30; see also 3:17, 13:27 and Luke 23:34).

Just as the Pharisees and Sadducees listen only until the mention of resurrection in Acts 23:6-8, the Greek philosophers "interrupt" the speech at the same point. Some were intrigued (presumably the Stoics here, the Pharisees in Acts 23). Others mocked and rejected the claim of resurrection (the Epicureans probably, and Sadducees).

18:1-11 Paul founds the church in Corinth. Paul meets Aquila and his wife Priscilla in Corinth. These important co-workers are mentioned in Rom 16:3-5, 1 Cor 16:19, and 2 Tim 4:19. The emperor had expelled them and all Jews from Rome. Acts often demonstrates how Rome did not distinguish between Jews and Jewish Christians. Aquila and Priscilla shared Paul's trade of tentmaker, some kind of skilled craft practiced in cities. Frequently in his letters, and in Acts 20:33-35, Paul stresses how he supported himself and did not drain the church to which he ministered. Scholars also suggest that philosophers used workplaces to teach bystanders and customers, and perhaps Paul also taught while working. But Acts mentions only his teaching on the sabbath in the synagogue, perhaps to accent Paul's similarities to Jesus.

The arrival of Paul's helpers Silas and Timothy from Macedonia changed this (Acts 18:5). It freed him to devote his whole time to preaching. 2 Cor 11:8-9 tells the Corinthians that Paul was supported by churches in Macedonia, which confirms Acts 18:5. It also explains how his helpers coming from Macedonia freed him for full-time ministry, through the money they brought.

Paul's reference to Jews' responsibility for their refusal to believe ("Your blood be on your heads!"—18:6) alludes to Ezek 33:4, and is in turn echoed in Paul's farewell in 20:26. Acts 18:6 is the second of three statements by Paul that since Jews reject the gospel, he will take it to the Gentiles (also in 13:51 and 28:25-28). Yet, though Paul moved from the synagogue to the neighboring house of Titus Justus, a God-fearing Gentile, he did convert Crispus, the ruler of the synagogue, with his whole household (1 Cor 1:14). Thus Jews continued to be an important part of the church at Corinth.

Jesus appears to Paul in Acts 18:9-10 and tells him, "I have many people in this city." This fulfills the prophecy in Acts 15:14-17 that God will acquire "from among the Gentiles a people for his name."

18:12-17 Gallio refuses to judge between Paul and the Jews. Because we know Gallio's term of office at Corinth, A.D. 51–52, we can estimate other dates of Paul's career. The main point of this account is that Roman magistrates found nothing in Christianity to condemn, despite Jewish complaints against Christians. Their differences seemed merely intramural religious squabbling. The story ends with the humorous beating of Sosthenes, implying that the Jews turned on their own leader in frustration.

18:18-23 Return to Antioch and beginning the third journey. Acts 18:18-22 describes Paul's sea voyage from Corinth hundreds of miles back to Antioch in Syria without the use of "we," which disproves any automatic or merely conventional use of "we" for sea voyages.

Acts takes every opportunity to show that Paul remained a practicing Jew. It mentions him shaving his head because of an unspecified vow. This might refer to the ending of a temporary nazirite vow not to cut one's hair, but the details are unclear. The regulations for nazirite vows appear in Num 6:1-21. Also note the expired nazirite vows in 1 Macc 3:49.

That Aquila and Priscilla remained in Ephesus is confirmed in 1 Cor 16:19.

The passage glides almost imperceptibly from the second to the third journey of Paul from his home base in Antioch, back through Galatia to Ephesus (18:23).

PAUL'S DESTINY IN JERUSALEM: THE THIRD JOURNEY

Acts 18:24–21:14

18:24–19:7 Apollos, Priscilla and Aquila, and Paul in Ephesus. These stories raise a lot of questions. How can Apollos teach accurately about Jesus and know only John's baptism? Why do Priscilla and Aquila merely instruct Apollos, with no mention of his baptism and receiving the Spirit? How does this incident relate to Paul's teaching the twelve disciples in Ephesus about the Spirit, then baptizing them so they receive the Spirit?

The story of the twelve Baptist disciples seems to have colored the Apollos account. Luke may have known that Priscilla and Aquila instructed Apollos, but not the content of the teaching. Perhaps Luke added the reason for Apollos' further instruction from the account about the followers of John the Baptist at Ephesus—that is, not knowing about being baptized with the Spirit. The main point is clear: to show that Paul's followers corrected the teaching of Apollos, whom the Ephesian church then recommended by letter to the church at Corinth.

Notice the similarities between Acts 19:1-7 and 8:14-17, where Peter and John confirm and extend Philip's work by laying hands on the Samaritans so they would receive the Spirit. In 19:1-7 Paul brings non-Christian followers of the Baptist into the church. The Spirit leads them, as it led the original apostles, to speak in tongues and prophesy (19:6). "About twelve" recalls the Twelve at Pentecost—otherwise why use "about"?

19:8-20 God's power vs. magic. Paul's arguments with the Jews concerned the meaning of the "kingdom of God." For Paul, it referred to the Messiah's reign from heaven, whereas Jewish concerns were more nationalistic. When Paul could no longer function in the synagogue, he moved his disciples to a lecture hall. This new base was like that of wandering philosophers. Luke continues to stress that Paul and the church fulfilled its obligation to tell Jews of the fulfillment of their promises before offering it to the Gentiles.

The extraordinary miracles through Paul in Acts 19:11-12 parallel those of Peter in 5:12-16. Contemporary experience of some Christians with famous ministries of healing is similar. Such persons, including priests, are not infrequently mobbed. People try to touch them or grab some article of their clothing, despite all their efforts to get people to focus on God and not on them.

Using cloth that touched Paul to heal the sick can look like magic. But Luke stresses its difference from magical practices. He juxtaposes this incident with that of the Jewish exorcists who tried to use Jesus' name magically. He again uses humor to mock these exorcists. The spirit stripping and beating the seven exorcists reads like slapstick comedy. But the crowd's reaction shows Luke's serious purpose. Their awe and reverence for Jesus' name increased. And they repented of their magical practices and burned their magic books (for which Ephesus was well known). The Jewish exorcists failed because they tried to use Jesus' name as magic power, without being personally submitted to Jesus' authority as Paul was. Magic books that survive from Luke's time often try to name as many gods as possible in exorcism formulas, even including Jewish names for God.

19:21-22 Pastoral planning and teamwork. Paul habitually sent disciples ahead or had them stay behind to prepare or finish his work. This might be why only Luke mentions Jesus sending two disciples ahead to Samaria

(Luke 9:51-52). It shows another similarity between how Jesus and Paul used disciples to help in their missions.

19:23-40 Riot of the idolmakers and silversmiths. The statement by the silversmith that Paul had misled many people (19:26) illustrates how every narrative is filtered through a point of view, in this case an ideology hostile to a hero of Acts. Implied readers are to take account of the unreliability of this silversmith as narrator. Luke's humor appears again in the senseless riot and comic two-hour chant, "Great is Artemis of the Ephesians!" The idolmakers' fear of financial loss caused the riot, just as monetary loss angered the owners of the slave girl who prophesied in 16:18-21. Christians are often left alone until they threaten someone's profits. This is why the rich often persecute the church today when it backs land distribution to the destitute in some Latin American countries.

Paul's Macedonian co-worker Gaius is mentioned in Rom 16:23 and 1 Cor 1:14. Paul tells the Corinthians that Gaius and Crispus (converted synagogue leader in Acts 18:8) were the only two besides the household of Stephanus whom he baptized in Corinth. Aristarchus never appears in Paul's letters.

The riot was senseless: most of the crowd did not even know why they were there (19:32), and the two-hour chanting was absurd. The town clerk's decision to break up the meeting provides another example of Roman officials as guardians of order. When Jews had accused Paul, a governor had refused to try to settle that intramural religious fight. Now when pagans riot for religious reasons, the town clerk refuses to get involved in such issues.

20:1-6 Paul's travels in Greece and to Troas. The riot was Paul's signal to leave Ephesus, but first he strengthened the church he would leave behind. His mission in Macedonia was to strengthen churches already founded.

The list of Paul's companions in 20:4 illustrates how Paul attracted followers from most of the churches he founded—from Beroea, Thessalonica, Derbe, and other places in the province of Asia.

20:7-12 Raising of Eutychus to life. Luke is not afraid to use humor even about Paul. In Troas (Turkey) he portrays Paul talking all night long because he had to leave the next day. A young listener fell asleep and toppled off the windowsill to his death. Paul restored him to life, ate, and resumed talking until morning. Thus Paul too raised a dead person, as Jesus and Peter (and Elijah and Elisha) had. This is also the first mention of Sunday rather than the Jewish sabbath (Saturday) as the day for Christian worship (see Rev 1:10).

20:13-16 Paul and "we" journey to Miletus. This time the "we" travel by boat and await Paul coming overland to Assos, a seaport not far from Troas along the shore of the province of Asia (now Turkey). Mitylene is a seaport on the island of Lesbos. Notice how sea voyages were often short hops from port to port. At Miletus, Paul met with presbyters (often translated "elders") who led the church at Ephesus.

20:17-38 Paul's "farewell address" to the Ephesian elders. Luke gives us two farewell speeches—Jesus' at the Last Supper in Luke 22:15-38 and Paul's in Acts 20:17-38. His method was probably to gather information about Jesus and Paul, which he then edited into a farewell address, a kind of writing prevalent in his day.

These elements of Paul's speech in Acts 20 are typical of farewell addresses: (1) he summons the elders, (2) points to his own mission and example, (3) testifies he did not fail in his duty, (4) alludes to his imminent death, (5) exhorts them regarding future problems, (6) prophesies apostasy and false teachers after his death, (7) blesses his followers, (8) prays with them, and (9) exchanges farewell gestures.

The main use of farewell addresses was to lift up a founder as a model to imitate. So Luke 22 does with Jesus, as he tells the Twelve to "do this as a remembrance of me," and Acts 20 with Paul. Paul is Luke's chief model for what a Christian bishop or presbyter should be like. (The word in 20:28 translated "overseers" can also be translated "bishops.") He should serve God and the flock by self-sacrificing labor, authentic teaching, and careful pastoring. He should not look for gain and should be courageous against attacks from both without and within.

The speech also defends Paul. It is not his fault if the church at Ephesus later falls away from what he had tried so hard to teach them. It implies that only after Paul's death did heresy grow as widespread as in Luke's time.

By showing how the presbyters take up where Paul left off, the speech also demonstrates continuity in the church through changes in epochs, such as the passing of the first apostles.

People commonly cherish the last words of someone as stating his or her most urgent concerns. Thus, Jesus' farewell speech in Luke 22 gives us the Eucharist, the leadership of the Twelve over the church, and the true meaning of Christian leadership as service, not domination. Paul's farewell in Acts 20 stresses generous pastoring, care for the poor and weak, courage in facing persecution and apostasy, and the central importance of preserving the true message of Jesus in the face of widespread heresy. Luke presents these to his readers as Jesus' and Paul's chief concerns.

The speech ends with a clear prophecy of Paul's impending death.

21:1-14 Further voyages to Caesarea in Palestine. Paul's sea route went from the port of Miletus to the island of Cos, then the island of Rhodes, next the port of Patara in Lycia in southernmost Asia Minor. The cargo ship they boarded in Patara headed past the island of Cyprus without stopping, straight to the port of Tyre in Palestine.

There were Christian communities at all the port cities of Tyre, Ptolemais, and Caesarea. During the week with the Christians in Tyre, some of them gave him prophetic warnings against going to Jerusalem. The farewell scene highlights the Christians' affection for Paul and his party.

At Caesarea, Paul stays with Philip. He was one of the Seven who were scattered by Paul and other persecutors when Stephen died. Acts 21 calls him "the evangelist" and makes special reference to his four virgin daughters who were prophets. Luke probably mentions them to illustrate the fulfillment of the Joel 3 prophecy quoted in Acts 2, that "your sons and daughters" shall prophesy.

Agabus, the Jewish Christian prophet from Judea (Acts 11:28), performed a prophetic sign of binding his feet and hands, as Jeremiah had worn a wooden yoke to illustrate the slavery he was prophesying (Jer 27:1-15). Agabus' binding of his hands and feet illustrated his prophecy of Paul's arrest. The "we" group joins the Christians of Caesarea in trying to dissuade Paul from going to Jerusalem.

PAUL AS PRISONER WITNESSES TO THE RESURRECTION

Acts 21:15–26:32

21:15-26 James persuades Paul to prove his fidelity to Judaism. The "we" style continues all the way to Jerusalem. Luke wants to imply that his party accompanied Paul all the way to Paul's destined suffering at Jerusalem, as his Gospel had shown the Twelve accompanying Jesus to his capture in Jerusalem. But as the Twelve were not with Jesus in his imprisonment, trials, and suffering, which he bore alone, so the "we" group were not with Paul in his imprisonment and trials in Jerusalem and Caesarea (Acts 21–26) or Rome (28:16-31), though they also accompanied him on the journey to Rome (27:1–28:16).

At this time James is the Christian leader in Jerusalem. The Twelve are not mentioned as even being there anymore. "Many thousands" is an indefinite number. It indicates that a considerable number of Jews believed in Jesus and thus constituted the restored Israel promised by the prophets.

James lists the charges that were frequently made against Paul. This passage answers those charges for Luke's generation also. Rumor had it that Paul taught Jews apostasy from Moses, telling them not to circumcise their children or keep the law. The rumor confused what Paul said to non-Jews with his instructions to Jews. Paul told non-Jews they did not have to be circumcised or keep the law. But Luke here shows that Paul did not turn Christian Jews away from obligations they had taken on as Jews.

The Introduction mentions what a traumatic identity question it was for early Jewish Christians when so many Gentiles joined them. Against that background Paul shares the Jewish ritual with four Christian Jews, laying to rest charges that he forsook the Jewish law.

James distinguished between obligations of Jewish and non-Jewish Christians. The four stipulations from Acts 15:20 and 15:29 recall the obligations of Gentile Christians who share community and meals with Jewish Christians.

For the ritual itself, compare 18:18 and the remarks there.

21:27-40 Jewish rioting against Paul in the temple. Jews and Christians had surprising mobility in the first century. The "Roman peace" (or "law and order") made that possible. Asian Jews (who had caused Paul so much trouble in Ephesus) may have come to Jerusalem on pilgrimage, as did Paul. They charge Paul with the same things James had mentioned (21:21), adding that Paul opposed the temple as well as the people and law. The accusation that Paul polluted the temple by bringing in unclean pagans is a rash judgment. They had seen Paul in the city with the pagan Trophimus (20:4), whom they had recognized from Ephesus.

The charge of profaning the temple stirred up a riot among the Jerusalem Jews. Luke shows that Jewish mob would have killed Paul if the Roman army had not intervened. The mob's cry, "Away with him" (or "Kill him"), is the same as the cry against Jesus when Pilate held him (Luke 23:18).

Acts 21:37 and 21:40–22:2 show that Paul was fluent both in Greek, the international language, and in Hebrew, actually the related Aramaic then spoken in Palestine. Luke may be combining several uprisings in this account, but his main point is clear: Roman officials recognized that Paul and the Christians were not rebels against Rome.

22:1-21 Paul's defense speech to the crowd. This is the first of several apologetic or defense speeches for Paul (Acts 22, 23, 24, 25, 26). Luke rewrote the apologetic speeches, just as he had rewritten earlier missionary speeches in Acts 2, 3, 13, and 17. The beginning is stereotyped: motioning the people to silence, the address "brothers and fathers," the appeal to listen to his defense. (Compare "Friends, Romans, and countrymen, lend me your ears" in Shakespeare's *Julius Caesar.*)

Many commentators doubt that Paul was brought up in Jerusalem under the great rabbi Gamaliel, as Acts 22:3 claims. They cite Gal 1:22, "And I was unknown personally to the churches of Judea that are in Christ," to argue that Paul could not have spent much time in Jerusalem. But that fails to explain the next line: "they only kept hearing that 'the one who once was persecuting us is now preaching the faith he once tried to destroy'" (Gal 1:23). The fact that Paul persecuted Christians in and around Jerusalem makes it likely that he was well respected among Jerusalem Jews. Also, the son of Paul's sister apparently lived in Jerusalem (Acts 23:16). The reasons for doubting Acts about Gamaliel and Paul seem unconvincing. In its context, all that the Greek of Gal 1:22 states is that *as a Christian*, Paul did not *personally* visit most of the churches in Judea.

Luke's point is clear, regardless. Paul was thoroughly grounded in Judaism, so zealous that he persecuted the Christian sect. This second of three versions of Paul's conversion accentuates Paul's Jewishness, as expected in a speech to Jews.

22:22-29 Paul is imprisoned. This is another apparent interruption that dramatizes the end of a speech and highlights the statement which "causes" the interruption. In 22:21-22 the Jewish mob interrupts when Paul says Jesus will send him to the Gentiles. Likewise, in Luke 4:25-28 the people of Nazareth first erupted against Jesus when he referred to prophets helping Gentiles rather than Jews. Luke-Acts emphasizes Jewish anger at ministry to Gentiles as an explanation why so many Jews opposed Paul.

22:30–23:11 Paul's defense before the Sanhedrin. The incident where Ananias the high priest has Paul struck during his trial is similar to the blow to Jesus before Annas in John 18:19-24. "Whitewashed wall" brings to mind Jesus' expression "whitewashed sepulchers" (Matt 23:27). Has Luke heard of those incidents or sayings and instead of reporting them in Jesus' ministry and trial, as Matthew and John do, alluded to them through similar incidents in Paul's trial? Luke 1:1-4 presupposes that his readers knew other Gospels. He may be trying to describe the trials of Stephen and Paul in ways that remind them of Jesus' trials, referring to details which his implied readers would be expected to know but which were left out from his telling of Jesus' passion.

Luke probably does not interpret Paul's remark in 23:5 against insulting God's legitimate high priest as sarcasm. Even under great provocation, he implies, Paul is careful not to undermine legitimate Jewish authority.

Whatever Sadducees actually believed, the aside in Acts 23:8 reports a widespread stereotype about their unbelief in resurrection, angels, or spirits. Luke treated only Pharisees as Jews with true beliefs. Sadducees were really heretics all along, even though in good standing before the destruction of Jerusalem in A.D. 70. Luke portrays Paul as a true Jewish believer, supported by other Pharisees and persecuted by heretical Sadducees for witnessing to the resurrection.

In the dream, Jesus mentions Paul's witness in Jerusalem. How did Paul do this, since the Acts 23 speech does not even mention Jesus' name? The answer lies in the way Luke equates witness to the risen Jesus with witness to belief in the resurrection held by Pharisees.

23:12-35 Plot against Paul and his transfer to Caesarea. At Jerusalem the son of Paul's sister overhears and rescues Paul from a plot by some forty Jews to kill him. The Romans protect Paul by escorting him out at night with 200 soldiers, 70 horsemen, and 200 light-armed men—quite an expense for one Roman citizen!

Lysias' letter, which is in standard letter form with the ending omitted, states Paul's innocence of anything deserving punishment. He was sent to Felix, the Roman governor of Palestine, to get away from plots against his life.

24:1-21 Paul's trial before Felix. The trial scene gives glimpses into how trials were run in the first century. For the Roman trial Ananias hired a lawyer named Tertullus to argue his case against Paul. After the lawyer's accusation comes the defense by Paul, acting as his own lawyer. First-century lawyers were actually called "rhetoricians." Their training was less in the legal technicalities of modern law schools than in oratorical techniques on how to persuade a judge. Both Paul's and Tertullus' speeches use these techniques.

Tertullus' speech puts heavy emphasis on winning the judge's good graces. It then charges Paul with offenses against the empire. He was a troublemaker stirring up sedition among Jews as leader of the sect of the Nazoreans. Note the parallel false charge against Jesus to Pilate: that he incites revolt, opposes tribute to Caesar, and claims to be king (Luke 23:2). "Nazoreans" was an early Jewish name for Christians. The speech calls Paul, rather than Peter or James, the most influential leader of this worldwide sect. It falsely accuses Paul of trying to defile the temple. The Jewish high priest and leaders supported their spokesman's presentation by vouching for its facts.

Paul also begins his defense by appealing to the judge before refuting the accusations. The only charge Paul admits is that he worships the ancestral God "according to the Way," the name for Christians that even Felix knew. Though the Jews considered the Way a sect, Paul insists that he believes everything in the Jewish law and prophets (= Scripture). He too believes in a resurrection of the just and unjust, as in Dan 12:2.

The speech in fact describes Christianity to outsiders. Christianity is seen as a form of Jewish worship and expectation of resurrection. Jewish presentations to Gentiles usually stressed judgment after death based on how one lived. And Paul's witness to Jesus' resurrection comes under the general theme of resurrection of the dead.

Paul ends by explaining that he was in the temple "to bring alms for my nation" (24:17), which may be an indirect reference to Paul's collection for the Jerusalem church, which Paul's letters emphasize more.

24:22-27 Captivity in Caesarea. The writer Josephus tells us that Felix had stolen his wife Drusilla from her first husband. That probably explains why Felix became afraid when Paul preached to him about sexual morality. The situation reminds one of John the Baptist's rebuke of Herod for his adulterous marriage. Christian preaching to pagans in the first and second century often focused on righteousness, self-control, and the coming judgment, as in Acts 24:25.

Luke has to explain why Felix did not free Paul if he was innocent. He notes that Felix was expecting a bribe, for which he was notorious, and that he wanted to please the Jews. Paul has to suffer years of imprisonment because he would not give a bribe. He is an example for Christians of suffering for refusing to perform an unjust practice, even one that "everyone does."

25:1-12 Trial before Festus and appeal to the emperor. Luke frequently parallels Paul's trials with Jesus'. Only his Gospel mentions all the following: Jesus before the crowd that captured him, the Sanhedrin, the Roman governor (Pilate) *twice*, and the Jewish king Herod (Luke 22–23). Likewise, Paul addresses the mob that seized him, the Sanhedrin, two Roman governors (Felix and Festus), and the Jewish Herodian king Agrippa (Acts 21–26).

With the new governor the Jews again try to have Paul brought to Jerusalem so they can kill him en route. Festus declines to move Paul, but he invites them to accuse Paul at Caesarea. The trial repeats the one before Felix. The Jews "brought many serious charges against him, which they were unable to prove" (Acts 25:7). This echoes Luke 23:10, where the chief priests and scribes accused Jesus vehemently before Herod. Paul repeats the defense he used before Felix. He has done nothing against the law or the temple or Caesar.

Like Felix before him (24:27), Festus curries favor with the Jews by refusing to free Paul. Paul does not acknowledge any authority of the Jerusalem Sanhedrin over him (see 4:18-21; 5:27-29, 40-42). He could not hope for a fair hearing in Palestine, so he appeals as a Roman citizen for trial before the emperor in Rome.

Acts does not focus on Paul's frustration in prison but on how God used these injustices to get Paul to Rome. There he would give the Jews their last chance to accept the message.

25:13-27 Festus invites Agrippa to hear Paul. Only Luke 23:6-12 mentions Pilate inviting Herod Antipas to try Jesus. Luke may mention that as a parallel to Festus' invitation to a later member of the Herod dynasty, Agrippa II, to try Paul. The New Testament tells of four different rulers in the Herod family: (1) Herod the Great (Matt 2, Luke 1:5), (2) Herod the Tetrarch (= Herod Antipas) who killed John the Baptist and appeared in Jesus' passion in Luke 23, (3) Herod in Acts 12 (= Herod Agrippa I) who killed James, and (4) Agrippa (= Agrippa II), son of the Herod from Acts 12 and judge at Paul's hearing in Caesarea in Acts 25–26.

Paul follows closely in the suffering footsteps of Jesus. Pilate in Luke 23:15, 22 repeatedly declared Jesus innocent of charges against him. So Festus and many others assert Paul's innocence in Acts. Festus considers these charges mere intra-Jewish squabbles, "about a certain Jesus who had died but who Paul claimed was alive" (25:19).

26:1-32 Paul's defense before Agrippa and Festus. Acts 26 has been called "the christological climax of Paul's defense" (see Robet O'Toole's book by that name). Christology describes the meaning and identity of Jesus as Christ and Son of God. All the trials from Acts 22–26 culminate in the hearing before Agrippa and Festus, with its verdict of not guilty (26:32). The speech in Acts 26 is interrupted at its climax, according to the pattern seen in Acts 17 and 22. Its final statement is its christological climax. Paul preaches only what the prophets and Moses had foretold. The Christ would suffer, and as first to be raised from the dead, he would proclaim light to both God's people and the Gentiles (26:22-23). All of Acts 22–26 leads up to this suffering witness to Christ's resurrection.

The resurrection hope as God's promise to Israel unites the parts of the speech. The discourse places more emphasis than earlier speeches on how strongly Paul persecuted the church, even unto death. Therefore his about-face when the Christ he rejected called him by name is more striking. Instead of mentioning Paul's blindness, as in 9:8-9 and 22:11, the speech describes Paul's mission as opening eyes and bringing others from darkness to light. Blindness and turning from darkness to light are common themes in both Jewish and Christian preaching to convert pagans.

This is the third time Acts describes Paul's conversion, which puts great emphasis on it. Luke portrays Paul as the model witness to Jesus' resurrection and as fulfilling Jesus' predictions in Luke 21:12-19 and 12:11-12 that Christians would witness before kings and governors.

Acts 26:24-28 contrasts the Roman governor who sees the talk as madness with King Agrippa who understands Jewish controversies and finds it compelling. Luke may also imply that Paul's speech is prophetic. To unbelievers tongues and prophecy can appear madness or drunkenness (Acts 2:13), but they come from the power of the Holy Spirit. Here the power of Paul's speech is almost enough to convert Agrippa!

Acts 26:31-32 ends all Paul's trials saying that Paul was innocent and could have been freed if he had not appealed to Caesar.

"YOU SHALL BEAR WITNESS AT ROME"

Acts 27:1–28:31

27:1-44 Shipwreck on the voyage to Rome. The "we" narrative resumes with Paul's voyage and shipwreck, and is introduced abruptly, without it being clear in what capacity "we" were to sail to Italy with Paul (27:1) or were put on board by the centurion (27:6). This chapter should be read with a map of Paul's journey to Rome and with an appreciation of how risky sea travel was. Boats were unable to tack against the wind, and so were more at the mercy of a fierce storm than sailboats today. In both pagan literature and the Old Testament, the motif of sailing in a storm was quite popular. Acts 27 is as graphic as any such stories.

Paul's effect on his ship contrasts with Jonah's. Whereas Jonah because of his sinfulness polluted the ship and caused its distress, Paul was the salvation of his vessel. Both were prophets. Paul's prophecy that he would stand trial in Rome and his shipmates be saved gave hope to the 276 on board. Paul's prophecy that "not one of you shall lose a hair of his head" echoed Jesus' words in Luke 12:7 and 21:18.

The narrator's point of view, which confidently trusts Paul's opinion over that of the pilot and owner in 27:11, contrasts with normal expectations. The narrator shifts between "we" in 27:15 and "they" in verse 17, and distinguishes between "they . . . took some food" and "two hundred seventy-six of us on the ship" (vv. 36-37). The narrator shows the persuasive power of Paul's example of eating to encourage the others to eat (vv. 35-36).

Paul's breaking bread and giving thanks to God sound Eucharistic, though with pagans this was obviously not an actual Eucharist. As Luke relates the incident, he adds symbolic reminders of Jesus' promise and the Eucharist. When Christians flounder in the storms of life, we should recall Jesus' assurance of protection. And the Eucharist gives new courage in our trials.

28:1-10 Miracles on Malta. The "natives" of the island of Malta are yet another kind of people who respond to Paul. Luke calls them in Greek *barbaroi*, from which "barbarian" comes. The term originally meant non-Greeks. Acts had shown the reactions of Jews, Greeks, and Romans to Paul. Acts 28 and 14 showed how "natives" of Malta (in the Mediterranean) and Lycaonia in Asia Minor (Turkey) responded to him. Both of the latter groups showed much more primitive and superstitious reactions than had Jews, Greeks, or Romans. This could explain why during the Dark Ages, after Rome's fall to primitive western tribes, Christianity became more affected by superstition than during the Roman Empire.

Luke's humor again comes to the fore. In Lycaonia the crowds had comically treated Barnabas and Paul as gods. In Malta the natives wait for Paul to puff up and keel over. Then they decide he is a god. Notice also the popular first-century view of avenging Justice killing a murderer by a snake after he had escaped the sea.

Luke continues the "we" style until Paul's arrival in Rome. In fact, the revised New American Bible translation of Acts 28:16 is misleading: the Greek says "When *we* entered Rome," not "When *he* entered Rome." Luke does not report any preaching by Paul during the three winter months on Malta. But Paul's healing of his host's father led many islanders to bring their sick for healing. The way to win simple people like the Maltese begins with healing. Christians with healing ministries find the same true in travels to less industrialized countries today. In sophisticated countries they report that healings are less common. Among simple peoples they find more openness and cures.

28:11-16 Christians greet Paul and escort him to Rome. Luke reports "brothers," that is, communities of Christians, in the port of Puteoli (near Naples). Other Christians from Rome travel south the forty miles to the Forum of Appius or the thirty-some miles to Three Taverns to greet Paul. Luke is emphasizing that Paul was in very high standing with the church of Rome for Christians to go to such trouble to welcome him.

Some commentators think Luke is trying to downplay the fact that there was a church at Rome that Paul did not found or even to imply that Paul founded the Roman church. But this is not the point of Acts 28. Luke makes clear there were already Christians at Rome who greeted Paul. Christianity is not arriving at Rome for the first time with Paul, nor is his mission to found the church there. In Paul, Christianity is to make one last major appeal and offer of the good news to the *Jews* of Rome. By ending with Paul's conference with leading Roman Jews, Acts makes clear he was not a Jewish apostate. He spoke to the main centers of Jews, even though he was known as "the apostles to the Gentiles."

28:17-28 Paul's appeal to Roman Jews. Paul insists to the Jews of Rome that he had not betrayed the Jewish people or customs, even though it was Jews who handed him over to Rome for punishment. This is Luke's last apology or defense for Paul from the charge of Jewish apostasy. All day Paul witnessed that the kingdom Jews were expecting was becoming a reality. He tried to persuade them from their Scriptures that their promises were fulfilled in Jesus. As often in Acts, some believed and some did not.

The finale of Acts is the third repetition of the theme that Jews rejected the good news, so Paul turned to more receptive Gentiles. We have seen how Acts uses triple repetition to put major emphasis on an event (e.g., Paul's conversion, Cornelius, the Apostolic Decree). The repetition combines with the powerful scriptural quotation in the climactic final position in the book as strong evidence that this is one of the most important themes in Acts. Luke wants to explain how the church of his day is so predominantly Gentile if it is the fulfillment of Jewish promises through the Jewish Messiah. Luke's church is Gentile not because Paul failed to honor God's promises to the Jews. It is so because the majority of Jews, especially those living away from Palestine, rejected Paul's offer.

28:30-31 Through Paul the word is preached without hindrance. Many have wondered why Acts ends without mentioning the result of Paul's two-year Roman imprisonment. Some say Acts was written before Paul died. But most find certain references in Luke to the destruction of Jerusalem in A.D. 70, after Paul's death. Others suggest Luke intended to write a third volume, or that he wrote the pastoral Epistles (to Titus and Timothy). I think Luke ended here because he wanted to end on a high note, as most narratives of his time were expected to. More importantly, he had made the points he wanted to make about how the church came to be as it was in his time. He had kept his promise to Theophilus in Luke 1:1-4. He had shown how the things "handed down to us" have fulfilled God's saving plan found in Scripture. All but one of the prophecies from Scripture, Jesus, and Christian prophets have come true. The church is now living in the final epoch, the "last days" when the Spirit has been poured out as Joel 3 expected. The church is now in the "times of the Gentiles" (Luke 21:24). It is enduring the times after Paul's death when false teachers will arise (Acts 20:29-30). All that must yet be accomplished are cosmic catastrophe and the Final Day when the Son of Man returns as judge.

GALATIANS

John J. Pilch

INTRODUCTION

About ten years ago I wrote my doctoral dissertation on Paul's use of the Greek word *apokalypsis*—usually translated "revelation" —in the first two chapters of Galatians (1:12; 2:2; the verb in 1:16). In the defense of the dissertation, I justified my conclusions by responding with convincing answers to the questions of five examiners.

Now, ten years later, there are some areas about which we know much more than we did then, but there are other areas of biblical study about which we are still undecided. For example, scholars do not agree upon the specific identity of the Galatians, the people to whom Paul wrote this letter. Looking at a map of antiquity doesn't help because the map changed often. Initially, the name Galatia described a north central section of Asia Minor which contained the cities of Ancyra (modern name Ankara, Turkey), Pessinus, and Tavium. In 25 B.C.E. Rome combined this section with southern territories into one province named Galatia, though these latter territories preferred to keep their names. To whom then is Paul writing? Many believe he is writing to inhabitants of the South in places like Lystra and Derbe mentioned in Acts, but others argue for the North. No definite conclusion is yet possible.

The same uncertainty characterizes opinion on the date (sometime between A.D. 49 and 55) and the place from which the letter was written. If I were writing my dissertation today on the same topic, I would still be unable to resolve these uncertainties.

For our purposes, however, the letter itself provides enough information for an adequate understanding of the message. The recipients of the letter are converts to Christianity from paganism (see Gal 4:8; 5:2-3; 6:12-13). Paul converted them, but not too long after he departed Judaizing Christians came along and argued that in order to be a good Christian one had first to be a good Jew by being circumcised and by observing other prescriptions of the Torah.

This, of course, struck at the heart of Paul's conviction that the Torah was no longer binding as law, but continued to be Scripture, that is, story telling how Israel arrived at its present situation. News of the wavering faith of his converts prompted Paul to write this very polemic letter.

Moreover, the contents of the letter and the force with which it is written clearly demonstrate that the letter does not stem from that period (the forties) during which Paul was an apostle "dependent" upon Antioch like Barnabas, but rather from that period (the fifties) when Paul was an "independent" apostle. This is very clear especially in the first two chapters of Galatians.

These aspects of our knowledge about Paul's Epistle to the Galatians have remained basically the same over the last ten years. On the other hand, my rather unusual position as a trained biblical scholar engaged for the most part in medical and health-care settings has made me sensitive to certain new developments in biblical study over the last ten years.

One such development is the increasing application of insights from sociology and cultural anthropology to biblical texts with refreshing results.

For instance, the fine literary and theological analysis of Paul's "conversion" told three times by Luke in the Acts of the Apostles (9; 22; 26) can now be *supplemented* with interesting and plausible conjectures from the modern medical understanding of temporary blindness. In addition, the social and cultural meaning or interpretation of blindness, sight, darkness, and light highlighted by sociology and cultural anthropology suggests still other ways of reading those three accounts. If I were writing my dissertation on the same topic today, I would definitely include these new data.

The present commentary therefore blends some of these innovative insights with the traditional and time-tested interpretations of Paul. In addition to gaining a basic understanding of his Epistle to the Galatians, the reader will also learn some fundamental principles of the exciting and ground-breaking social science approach to interpreting Scripture. One precious result of such a combination of the old and the new is a better grasp of Paul's original meaning. Such knowledge will make it a little easier to uncover the contemporary relevance of our ancient texts.

OUTLINE OF GALATIANS

1:1-10	Greetings and Introduction
1:11–2:21	Paul, His Gospel, and Peter
3:1–4:31	A New-Old Way to Please God
5:1–6:10	Practical Exhortations
6:11-18	Conclusion

COMMENTARY

GREETINGS AND INTRODUCTION

Gal 1:1-10

1:1-5 Paul greets the Christians in Galatia. When I attended Mass as a youngster in Brooklyn, New York, the priest who read the Scriptures to the congregation in the vernacular (Polish) would always begin with the excerpt from the epistle with the phrase "Dearly beloved (*Najmilsi*)." Until I began reading the Bible myself, I believed that Paul began every letter with this same simple phrase.

The introductions to Paul's letters are, of course, more complex than "dearly beloved." They more or less follow the basic format of letter introductions in antiquity, identifying the sender and the recipients and including expressions of greetings. Yet each letter's introduction is different.

Paul begins Galatians with an uncharacteristically strong declaration of his apostolic authority—an authority not so much due to human appointment or commission, but rather to Jesus Christ and God his Father. Since Paul himself founded these churches (perhaps together with the brothers or fellow believers who are with him), the specific aspect of authority he uses in his letter is an appeal to the Galatians' loyalty, an appeal hoping to reactivate their previous commitment. He plays on their emotionally anchored sense of duty to God's activity in Christ (v. 1) as well as to the gospel Paul preached to them (v. 9).

The special description of what God accomplished in Jesus tips off the thrust of the letter to follow: Jesus died for our sins to free, deliver, and rescue us from the present evil age, that is, Jesus' redemptive death has made it possible for believers to pursue a different life-style than that of some other people in this present age.

1:6-10 Paul defends his doctrine and authority. Just where Paul ordinarily writes a prayer of thanksgiving (see 1 Thess 1:2-10), he launches straightway into the body of his letter with a resounding criticism of the Galatians calculated to "shame" them, shame (not guilt) being the core emotion among his readers. The first words, "I am amazed," express intense disbelief that the Galatian Christians are willfully forsaking previous loyalty and commitment to God and choosing some other good news. But no other news is good news!

As a matter of fact, Paul has specific culprits in mind whom he holds responsible for confusing, troubling, and unsettling the minds of the recently (about five years ago) converted Galatians. His shocking statement against the very thought of an "angel from heaven" (v. 8) attempting to preach a different gospel suggests that the troublemakers are Judaizers, that is, Christians who believe and insist that converts to Christianity should also (or continue to) observe certain Jewish ritual practices as well, for instance, circumcision and dietary restrictions.

Paul is quite blunt. Those who are presently daring to present a gospel different from the one Paul preached on his first and founding visit to these churches deserve to be abandoned, indeed, condemned by God.

PAUL, HIS GOSPEL, AND PETER

Gal 1:11–2:21

1:11-17 How Paul learned the good news. Though he is quite serious and perhaps even angry, Paul nevertheless begins his comments with an affectionate address of fellowship, "Brothers" (which would also include sisters). The term is an appeal to their emotion-laden loyalty and again illustrates the style of authority Paul exercises in this letter. He reminds his readers of his thoroughly Jewish background, his way of life prior to his category-shattering experience on the road to Damascus. He was both an ardent student of Judaism and a persistent and thorough persecutor of Christians. Indeed, he was recognized by fellow Jews as far advanced among his peers in practice as well as in zeal.

But just as God did to Jeremiah (1:5) and Isaiah (42:1), he chose Paul for a special task, called him, and then revealed to him who the Son really is so that he might tell this good news about him to the non-Jewish world.

Paul's response could well shame a modern believer: it was immediate, unquestioning, and intense. He went immediately to Arabia, that is, the region west and south of Judea known as the Nabatean Kingdom and began preaching at once.

The repeated declaration of independence by Paul from all other apostles or teachers (v. 12) is as puzzling as it is strong. How can he insist that he did not receive his gospel from any person (v. 12) when in 1 Cor 15:3 he admits: "I handed on to you first of all what I myself received," using Greek words that are technical vocabulary for receiving and handing on tradition in a reliable and trustworthy fashion? It seems best to interpret the Galatian statement as saying that Paul received his understanding of the good news "not so much" from any human person or schooling, *"as rather"* through God's gracious revelation about who Jesus really is.

1:18-24 First meeting with Peter. The remainder of chapter 1 and most of chapter 2 describe three meetings with Peter. Having just boldly announced his independence of people (teachers, authorities), Paul now vigorously strives to associate himself with Peter (and the "pillars" with him) in a relationship of equality!

The underlying dynamic is different from what the ordinary, natural born citizen of the United States might expect. Our strong sense of individualism ("rugged" at times), unsurpassed in the history of humanity, as well as our readiness to offer introspectively generated explanations for the behavior of *others*, tempt us to interpret Paul as a highly stubborn, strong-willed individualist. Yet Paul's statement reflecting conformity to tradition in 1 Cor 15:3 would challenge our projection of such American individualism on that Mediterranean person.

Like nearly all the people who populate the pages of Scripture, Paul is not an individualist in our understanding of that word. He is rather a "dyadic personality." Dyadic comes from the Greek word meaning "pair," and it describes the kind of person whose self-awareness, self-esteem, and self-fulfillment depend entirely upon relationships with other people and upon what other people—especially a group—think. Our culture would call such people "other-directed." Let's use that word instead of dyadic in this commentary.

In Galatia the struggle took place between groups. The churches or believers of Galatia as a group forged their identity according to the gospel Paul preached to them, a gospel presumed to faithfully reflect the beliefs and practices of the *Jerusalem church group*. The *Judaizer group* which is disturbing the Galatians claimed that Paul's preaching was incomplete and urged the Galatian churches to mold their identity rather according to the Judaizing concept of the good news, which they insisted was a more accurate reflection of the faith of the Jerusalem church group. Thus, in such a culture, Paul can justify or defend himself only by proving his embeddedness in the right group. He will proceed to do this by asserting a position of equality as apostle with Peter as apostle.

Some three years after his 180-degree turn from Pharisaic Judaism to preaching Jesus as Messiah, Paul went to Jerusalem to "get to know" Kephas. The Greek word for "get to know" could also be translated "gather information from." Because of Paul's emphatic insistence that God alone revealed Jesus to him, translators have preferred "get to know." Yet Jewish tradition says that when two Jewish teachers meet in a Jewish context, the word of Torah was between them, that is, they exchanged information about doctrinal statements from their teachers and predecessors. Or in other terms, they "checked each other out" as is the custom among other-directed personalities.

As such an other-directed personality, Peter knew his self-identity in terms of the Jerusalem community, and very shortly in this letter we'll see how much he experienced and yielded to pressures of that group. In his turn as an other-directed personality, Paul's major task is to persuade Peter that his conversion is genuine, that he has really changed group loyalty from Pharisee-persecutor of Christians, to Jewish-Christian preacher of Jesus as Messiah. Paul's group reference point now is Jerusalem.

Paul's successful change of membership and loyalty from one group to another as just described is evidenced in the concluding verse of chapter 1: "He who was formerly persecuting us is now preaching the faith he tried to destroy." The reality of that conviction is reflected in the glory given to God on Paul's account.

2:1-10 Second meeting with Peter. God prompted Paul to visit Kephas and the Jerusalem church leaders again some fourteen years after his first visit. He took along Barnabas and the Gentile Titus, and in a private conference with Peter and the leaders Paul explained the good news which he habitually and customarily had been preaching to the Gentiles all this time. Paul expresses a note of apprehension when he admits that he called this conference "to make sure the course I was pursuing, or had pursued, was not useless." He had no doubts about his teaching. He was worried about what his converts would do if he could not win support from Peter and the leaders. They would probably be lost to the Judaizers, and the gospel Paul preached would be perverted.

Paul's apprehension was solidly founded. Some sham Christians (literally false brothers, a shocking counterphrase to the emotion-charged title by which he's been addressing the Galatians) spied on Paul and his followers. They hoped to gather enough evidence to show how unfaithful Paul and his kind were to the Jewish law and then to force them once again to submit to the system of Jewish ritual. But Paul resisted that effort to distort—indeed to reject and make null and void—the gospel. Further, the fact that the leaders did not order Titus to submit to Jewish ritual circumcision as a requirement for continuing in Christian belief was living proof of the legitimacy and validity of Paul's work.

The incident is either part of or very close in time to the so-called Jerusalem Council. Acts 15:6-12 is probably a description of the same meeting Paul relates in Gal 2:1-10. The basic decision by Kephas/Peter and the leaders is not to impose any part of the Jewish law on Gentile converts to Christianity, as with Titus.

There is, however, a significant difference in the two accounts just mentioned. In Galatians, Paul creates the impression that independently and on his own initiative (even if prompted by God) he has gone to visit with the Jerusalem leaders. Acts, on the other hand, says that he is *sent* from Antioch to Jerusalem. The truth most likely is that at that stage of his career Paul was not yet an independent missionary but rather indeed an emissary from Antioch. His perspective at the time of writing this letter about five or more years later seems to color his recollections.

The result of Paul's second meeting with Peter is not only that nothing was added to the gospel Paul habitually and customarily preached, but they also decided on a territorial division of labor. Paul would henceforth preach mainly in the dispersion, that is, to both Jews and Gentiles living outside of Palestine. Kephas/Peter and his co-workers would continue to focus their evangelizing activity in Palestine (Jerusalem).

Notice once again how careful Paul has

been to present himself as an apostle completely "equal" with Peter. The fact that the leaders extended the right handshake of fellowship can be interpreted to mean that they accepted Paul as an apostolic partner on equal footing with themselves. The one proviso to which Paul readily agreed was to remember the "poor," that is, God's spiritually privileged (not necessarily economically destitute) followers in the churches of Judea.

The understanding of Scripture personalities culturally as other-directed personalities helps us grasp yet another aspect of Paul's outlooks reflected in these verses. He describes the Jerusalem leaders as "those who were regarded as important" (2:6, 9) and notes that "it makes no difference to me how prominent they were—God plays no favorites" (2:6).

Some readers have considered these statements as a sign of Paul's arrogant independence. That judgment is technically known as eisegesis, that is, reading into a text something that isn't there. These statements of Paul's further mark him as a man of his culture and time, an other-directed personality. The only way other-directed people get to know one another is externally, by appearances, by one's "face." Thus when Paul says the leaders "were regarded as important," he recognizes and admits the cultural limitations. By all outward appearances, these people seem to be important.

The literal statement behind "God plays no favorites" is that "God does not accept or lift up the face of a person." The dictionary says the Greek phrase means to show partiality or preference. That is correct, but God is not an other-directed (dyadic) personality. He can see within a person, beyond the face, and he and he alone can know everything inside and out.

Paul's point is simply this. Both I and my opponents judge by externals; that's a fact. But the leaders agreed with me and we reached a mutual understanding. So we believe God's on our side. Since we are restricted to externals, what more can we do?

2:11-21 Third meeting with Peter. Some time after meeting in Jerusalem (that is, after A.D. 50), but before the writing of this letter (around A.D. 55), Peter came to Antioch and mingled freely with all believers, converts from paganism as well as from Judaism. But when a (Judaizer?) group arrived from Jerusalem, Peter began to withdraw from fellowship and meal sharing.

See once more the strength of group pressure on other-directed individuals in these scenarios. Peter did indeed know and remember his very own decision not to impose Jewish observances on converts to Christianity from paganism. But old allegiances die hard, group pressures continue strong. It seems that Peter's "category shattering experience" of Jesus was not as thorough as Paul's. Peter knew full well that a Christian is made right with God through faith in Jesus and not through accomplishing works prescribed by the Jewish law. But Peter's former group-identity as a Torah-abiding Jew apparently resumed a prominent and directive place in his consciousness when the Jerusalem representatives came. To avoid displeasing them, he acted externally in a way that contradicted what he taught, said, and even practiced when it wasn't uncomfortable.

Perhaps if it were only Peter who changed course, Paul might have been more tolerant and patient. But when the rest of the Jewish Christians and even Barnabas began to follow Peter's example, Paul faced him as an apostolic equal and rebuked him publicly.

Verses 15-21 conclude these first two chapters of Galatians and introduce the next two. Paul now sums up what he has described in the meetings with Peter: we are made right with God by faith (v. 16) and not by legal observances (or in another translation, "deeds of the law"). In order to be fair to Paul, it is critically important to try to understand his use of the word "law" and our common understanding of the word.

When he uses the word translated in English as "law" in Galatians, Paul (with the obvious exception of Gal 3:21 and 5:23) has the Torah in mind. The Hebrew word *torah* means instruction or directive. It is the name given to the first five books of the Hebrew Bible (Genesis, Exodus, Leviticus, Numbers, and Deuteronomy) because they contain instruction and directives given by God to facilitate the achievement of the basic and core value of the chosen people, namely, *shalom* or peace, that dynamic state in which one continues to become and to be what one should be: a limited, finite, free human being.

When the Hebrew Bible was translated into Greek (the version we call the Septuagint), the word *nomos* was used consistently to translate *torah*. Paul, too, used *nomos* in his letters when he referred to the Torah. But *nomos* literally should be translated into English by the words "rule" (*explicit* instruction or directive) or "norm" (*implicit* instruction or directive). It is the historical and literary context that helps decide when *nomos* should be translated into English as "standard" (rules or norms between two individuals), "custom" (rules or norms in society's institutions), or "law" (rules or norms taken from these institutions and raised to the political or legal order).

Thus, *torah* (or *nomos*) can be translated "law" when it pertains to the period of the Jewish monarchy or the restoration after the Babylonian Exile (587–537 B.C.E.). In this period, law should be understood in its strict sense as a body of binding rights and obligations that have been "twice institutionalized" —once in custom, and then once again in the legal or political realm. So when Israel possessed self-rule, autonomy, Torah was law strictly speaking.

But in the Hellenistic period (300 to 6 B.C.E.) and in the Roman period (6 B.C.E. onward into Paul's time), when Israel lived under the law of its victors, Torah was reduced to custom legitimated by God. These various customs were embedded in the basic institutions of society: family, government, economics, education, and religion. They governed life within each institution because they were recognized as binding, legitimated by the Divine Will.

Here in Galatians, Paul says that in his own lifetime (Roman period) he was once a Torah-observing Pharisee, that is, he studied and lived the Torah. He perceived and understood it to be normative Jewish custom legitimated by God. But when he realized that Jesus is Messiah, that God raised Jesus from the dead (Gal 1:1), he also realized that the normative Jewish customs enshrined in Torah lost divine approval.

For Paul, Torah now became a normative story, the Sacred Scripture, telling readers how they arrived at the present, but offering nothing more since God abrogated it as normative custom. We are therefore made right with God by faith and no longer by legal observances. In Gal 3–4 Paul will present Jewish scriptural arguments to buttress his point.

A NEW-OLD WAY TO PLEASE GOD

Gal 3:1–4:31

3:1-5 Faith, not legal observances. The next major section of Galatians begins as Paul asks his pagan converts to reflect upon their experience of the Spirit (v. 4): has that experience come from legal observances or from faith? The only way Paul can understand how they could turn against their own experience is that someone must have momentarily cast a spell on them after the pattern of an evil-eye strategy.

Mention of the evil eye is not just a tolerant nod toward some pagan practice but is actually part of the everyday first-century Semitic understanding of the whole person. Each person is viewed on the basis of "externals," of parts of the body used as metaphors. Thus, a person has a heart for thinking along with eyes that bring data to the heart. The mouth is for speaking while the ears take in the speech of others. Hands and feet are for activity, for "doing." Another way of saying this is that in the Bible, each person is viewed holistically, but in terms of three kinds of interactions with the external world: eyes-heart representing emotion-fused thought, mouth-ears representing self-expressive speech, and hands-feet representing purposeful and effective action.

Notice the complete and total human experience described by John when he mentions each zone explicitly:

> This is what we proclaim to you:
> what was from the beginning,
> what we have heard,
> what we have seen with our eyes,
> what we have looked upon
> and our hands have touched—
> we speak of the word of life. . . .
> What we have seen and heard
> we proclaim in turn to you
> so that you may share life with us.
> (1 John 1:1-3)

Observe also how the third section of the Sermon on the Mount (Matt 6:19–7:27) concerning the righteousness of the disciples covers the three zones: the first part of the material deals with eyes-heart (Matt 6:19–7:6), the second with mouth-ears (Matt 7:7-11), and the last section with hands-feet (Matt 7:13-27).

The cluster of words in Gal 3:1: "stupid," "bewitched," "eyes," "publicly portrayed" all pertain to the zone of emotion-fused thought. So, like every other-directed person in his culture, Paul doesn't try to guess at internal motivations, but rather lists these external aspects of human existence as one possible explanation for the Galatian turnabout. Moreover, the fact that this cluster of words relates to *emotion*-fused thought demonstrates once again that this letter is Paul's attempt to reactivate the Galatians' emotionally anchored commitment to the gospel he preached to them.

3:6-14 Abraham, model of faith: midrashic homily number 1. If Paul is writing to his pagan converts to Christianity, why does he now proceed to present arguments rooted in and requiring more than a passing knowledge of Jewish interpretation of Scripture? Perhaps because the Galatians needed persuasive arguments to use against the convincing suggestions of the Judaizers.

The modern reader will probably experience difficulty following the logic of these two chapters and may be overwhelmed with the stream of Scripture references drawn from all over the Jewish Bible. The technique is known as stringing pearls and was a common feature of one kind of Jewish homily in Paul's day. Some scholars have even suggested that the early Christians—perhaps even Paul himself—gathered together especially appropriate strings of Scripture references that could be used in preaching and teaching about Jesus.

Thus, this first midrashic (the word "midrash" means explanation) homily strings together Gen 15:6 (see Gal 3:6), Gen 18:18 or 12:3 (Gal 3:8), Deut 27:26 (Gal 3:10), Hab 2:4 (Gal 3:11), Lev 18:5 (Gal 3:12), and Deut 21:23 (Gal 3:13) to demonstrate that Scripture testifies that Abraham was made right with God by faith and not by legal observances. If a person chooses legal observances, then ALL rules must be obeyed. Anything short of that results in curse. But Christ became just such a curse for us by dying a death accursed by the law. Yet God raised Jesus, indicating that he no longer approves the law, but rather the way of faith in Christ Jesus. We ought to be like Abraham.

3:15-18 Midrashic homily number 2. Continuing his reflections on Abraham, Paul notes that God made his promise to Abraham and his offspring about 430 years before he gave the law to Moses. The promise which preceded the law has been fulfilled in Jesus, the offspring of Abraham (see Matt 1:1).

The contemporary reader might find these verses rather confusing, perhaps even nitpicking, and not very enlightening or convincing. Paul's listeners or readers would note at least two things. One, the Hebrew Bible does not speak unambiguously of a 430-year period between Abraham and the law (see Exod 12:40 and Gen 15:13), but the number does appear in a Targum, that is, a paraphrase of Scripture heard in synagogue services at the time of Paul. "But the number of 430 years had passed away since the Lord spoke to Abraham . . . until the day they went out of Egypt" (Palestinian Targum on Exod 12:40).

Two, Paul's insistence on "descendant" (singular) rather than "descendants" (plural) is clear and obvious in the Hebrew Bible. It would strike the modern reader as preacher's overkill. But in the Targums wherever this word "descendant" appears (Gen 12:7; 13:15; 17:7; 22:18; 24:7), the rendition is always plural: descendants, making it impossible to apply the text to a single individual like Jesus.

What is the point? Paul bases himself NOT so much on what his readers (or their antagonists) might have *read* in the Scriptures, but rather on what they would have *heard* in the Targums, the paraphrases, at synagogue services. In one instance Paul agrees with the Targums, in another he disagrees. Ever the masterful pastoral minister, Paul moves from the known to the unknown, but he always respects the experience and abilities of his people.

3:19-28 Why then the Torah? The answer is simple. The Torah was to be like the pedagogue in ancient times (NAB: "disciplinarian"), whose task it was to take children to school, make sure they paid attention, to discipline them when necessary, and to see to their moral and physical safety. The monitor insured discipline and restraint in the young person's life until that individual reached the age or gained the skill of self-discipline and self-restraint. Like the monitor, the Torah provided discipline and restraint until Christ came and made authentic self-restraint and self-control possible.

The direct address in verse 26, "You are all children of God," makes the remarks personal and is also still another appeal to the emotional anchorage these converts used to have to the gospel Paul preached. According to this good news, "You are all one in Christ Jesus" (v. 28). Differences are not important, so don't bother about them. (See 1 Cor 7:17-28 for a repetition of these contrasting pairs with Paul's comments on not bothering about the differences.)

3:29–4:7 Midrashic homily number 3. The word "heir" appears in 3:29 and 4:7, indicating that all these verses constitute a unity and that inheritance is their theme. Indeed, verse 29 boldly and clearly announces that one who believes in Christ is an heir of Abraham (not Moses) and inherits the fulfillment of the promises made to Abraham.

Now, according to Palestinian custom, a father would appoint a guardian for his son in his will who in the event of the father's death would administer the son's inheritance until he came of age. From this perspective, the son, even if entitled to enormous wealth, is no better than a slave.

In the same way, argues Paul, before believers came "of age," that is, before Christ came to take up his earthly mission, they too were no better than slaves. Specifically, the slavery was bondage to the "elemental powers of the world" (vv. 3 and 9). Scholars are divided on the interpretation of this phrase. One very plausible interpretation relates the phrases to astrology and the heavenly bodies which fascinated the ancients. They believed that the heavenly bodies controlled the physical elements of the world and guided human destiny. Modern individuals who check the newspaper daily to determine whether their horoscope is favorable or not are in a bondage similar to the one Paul describes. Evidence of the thorough permeation of astrological beliefs in ancient Judaism can be found in the mosaic on the floor of the sixth-century Beth Alpha synagogue just south of Galilee. The design contains the twelve signs of the zodiac, but substitutes the twelve tribes of Israel for the expected designations.

Christ, who was born under the law, delivered believers from the law as well as from bondage to astrological determinism. He offers the possibility of being daughters and sons, not slaves. And God himself confirms one's status as his child by sending the spirit of his Son who empowers the believer to speak intimately to God as Father, "Daddy."

4:8-20 A personal plea. In this section Paul intensifies his personal and emotional appeal to his readers. Playing on the Semitic understanding of "know" as descriptive of the most intimate possible relationship between people (as when Adam "knew" Eve and she conceived), he asks how they could ever turn away from such a relationship with God to something less.

Why in the world would the Galatian converts want to embrace ceremonial observance of "days and months, seasons and years"? Paul probably has in mind such days as the sabbath, seasons like Passover, months like the "new moon," and years like the sabbatical year (see Lev 25:5). Granted, these Jewish practices are not in the same category as pagan star worship, but Paul's point is almost hidden in verse 9: "Now that you have come to be known by God." In other words, since it is God's initiative that counts, why do you revert to reliance upon human observances, human calculations? That attitude is equivalent to worshiping those "elemental powers."

"I implore you, brothers," pleads Paul pulling out all the emotional stops, "be as I am because I have also become as you are." By this he means: "Adopt my attitude toward the Torah: as law, it is abrogated; we are free!" His plea echoes similar statements in 1 Cor 11:1; 1 Thess 1:6; Phil 3:17, where he offers himself as an example worth imitating.

Finally, Paul resorts to a feminine image (quite surprising for an alleged misogynist!) of labor pains (v. 19) to describe his loving concern for the Galatians. (See also 1 Thess 2:7 where Paul presents himself as a nursing mother.) His point is that he, not the Judaizers, is the more tenderly caring and genuinely concerned for their spiritual welfare.

4:21-31 Midrashic homily number 4. Mention of labor pains may have prompted this final homiletic snippet on Abraham's wives, the mothers, and their children Ishmael and Isaac. Paul identifies this section as "allegory," that is, a creative reinterpretation of scriptural events and personalities as foreshadowing future truths and events. Clearly everything is hindsight in this interpretation and not at all literally in the text.

The point is that "you, brothers" are free children, "children of the promise" (v. 28). You are children of Sarah who can be interpreted as representing the Abraham Covenant, a context entirely free from the Torah's legal prescriptions. You are not slave children, like Ishmael, son of Hagar, who can represent Mount Sinai and all the legal prescriptions of the Torah.

We can almost hear Paul laughing derisively as he writes: "Do you really want to be subject to the Torah?" Then do what the story says: "Drive out the slave woman and her son . . ." (v. 30 citing Gen 21:10). Cast out those Judaizers and you will really be obeying the Torah!

Paul has developed these reflections on the basis of Gen 16, 17, and 21, but nowhere in these or any Hebrew texts is there mention of Ishmael persecuting Isaac (see Gal 4:29). Very likely Paul once again draws on a rabbinic interpretation familiar in his day. The Hebrew text of Gen 21:9 states simply that Ishmael was playing with Isaac. But in the rabbinic commentary Genesis Rabbah, the Hebrew word translated as "playing, joking, laughing" is taken in a bad sense. The tradition then says this: "And Ishmael took a bow and arrows and started shooting them in the direction of Isaac, making it appear as if he was joking." Paul applies this tradition to the experience of the Galatians from the Judaizers.

Is this farfetched? Not really. The Palestinian Targum on Gen 22, that is, the interpretation that might well have been heard in synagogue services, situated the "persecution" notion just mentioned in the context of a discussion on circumcision. "Ishmael . . . said: I am more righteous than you [Isaac], because I was circumcised at thirteen years of age. At that age, if I didn't want to be circumcised, no one could have forced me. But you, Isaac, were circumcised as a child of eight days. Who knows? If you had been older, perhaps you would have resisted circumcision." Isaac, of course, denies this hypothesis and says that now (at age thirty-six in this situation), he'd give all his members to be cut off if that's what the Holy One were to require. Once again, then, Paul uses traditions familiar to his people from the synagogue.

PRACTICAL EXHORTATIONS

Gal 5:1–6:10

5:1-12 Remain free. Having completed his scriptural argumentation in chapters 3 and 4, Paul now draws practical conclusions in the final chapters. He urges those who have yielded to pressure and adopted circumcision (v. 4 "are separated from Christ" and v. 7 "hindered" both describe accomplished facts) to dig in, to stand firm, to yield no more!

The absolute and uncompromising stance Paul takes in this letter against circumcision may have been a development in his own thinking. True, in Gal 2:3 he is pleased that Titus, at the Jerusalem meeting around A.D. 49, was not forced to accept circumcision. Yet Acts 16:3 (describing a time frame very soon after the Jerusalem meeting) indicates that Paul had Timothy circumcised in order that he might gain increased legitimacy and credibility in his ministry among the Jews. Timothy came from mixed parentage (Jewish mother and Gentile father), and it seems clear that Paul had him circumcised NOT that he might be saved, but rather that his chances of being accepted by Jewish audiences be improved. But this present letter, from a slightly later time frame, shows no willingness to allow even this consideration. We have been freed from the demands of the Torah; we ought to remain free.

5:13-25 True freedom. Earlier (2:4) Paul mentioned the "freedom that we have in Christ Jesus." Now, addressing the Galatians affectionately ("brothers"), he offers a further explanation. Freedom is not unfettered self-indulgence. "Serve one another through love" (v. 13), says Paul. The Greek verb should literally be translated "render slave-service" to one another. That would accurately reflect Paul's Judaism-conditioned understanding that the human person is never absolutely free, subject to no one. Even in the Exodus, the Jews were freed only to be able to serve God more faithfully.

Paul's point is that formerly, that is, before the advent of Christ, we all were slaves to the elements of the world or to all the legal demands of the Torah (see Gal 4:21-31). But when Jesus died the death cursed by the Torah and was raised from the dead by God, it became obvious that Jesus was the individual who pleased God most entirely; he was the perfectly obedient person. By raising Jesus, God abrogated Torah, and in Christ we have a new freedom, a freedom for a new kind of service. In Christ, differences are not important; what really counts is "faith working through love" (*agápē* in Greek, v. 6), through slave-service to other Christians.

How can a believer render this service concretely? Paul summons two favorite images: "flesh" and "spirit" to explain. We must serve believers by fruit of the spirit and not by deeds of flesh. "Flesh" describes the human being as entirely self-reliant, weak, earthbound, unredeemed. "Spirit" describes the knowing and willing core of the individual, that part of a person most suitable for receiving and responding to the Spirit of God. The present tense of the Greek verb "serve" or "render slave-service" to one another describes an enduring line of conduct, a way of life, not just an individual, isolated act.

This is, in fact, Paul's way of life! He likes to describe himself as slave (1 Cor 9:19) or servant for Jesus' sake (2 Cor 4:5). In context, it is Paul's service to other believers that proves that he is slave or servant.

Specifically for the Galatians, Paul lists actions to be avoided (5:19-21) and actions to be done (5:22-23). The deeds to be avoided, that is, the deeds of a way of life rooted in the "flesh" (self-reliance, selfishness) can be clustered into four groups: sexual aberrations (the first three items), heathen worship (the next two), social evils (seven items, many in the plural indicating numerous and repeated occurrences), and intemperance (the last three items). Notice that these are all failures against justice and love. This cannot and should not be the life-style of those who have accepted the rule of God in their lives.

In contrast, Paul proposes for imitation the fruit of the spirit which is love (*agápē*), together with nine other representative desirable qualities that should characterize a believer's relationships with other believers (5:22-23).

Such lists were very common in antiquity. Ezek 18:5-9 is one example in Jewish Scripture; pagan philosophers, like Aristotle, had their own similar lists. But the pagan Plutarch criticizes the virtue list drawn up by Chrisippus as a "creation of a beehive of virtue neither customarily practiced nor well known from experience." What is noteworthy about Paul is that his lists are shorter, and they appear very rarely in his authentic letters. (The Gospels have no such lists at all!)

Paul is not interested in setting up new laws. Throughout his letters he offers a variety of suggestions for appropriate behaviors: sometimes he presents his own life-style (Gal 4:12); at other times he proposes the general notion of freedom that includes slave-service to believers (Gal 5:1-15). The present listing of deeds of flesh and fruit of the spirit (Gal 5:19-26) suggests how believers ought to behave and not behave toward other believers. There is no indication of how the recipients of these deeds should respond. On the other hand, 1 Cor 9:1-14 is an example of a list of reciprocal rights and duties between and among believers. Behind all these Pauline suggestions is Paul's hope that Christians will "be transformed by the renewal of your mind, that you may discern what is the will of God, what is good and pleasing and perfect" (Rom 12:2).

The final verses (5:24-26) of this section sum up Paul's feelings very pointedly. Those who have accepted Christ have definitively, once and for always put aside the way of the flesh and should live, walk, and be led by the spirit.

6:1-10 Final exhortations. Though some have yielded to Judaizing pressures (5:4), there still remain among the Galatians those who live by the spirit. Paul addresses these individuals and urges them to fulfill the law of Christ by gently helping one another bear any problems that may occur. The apparent contradiction in verse 5 ("each will bear his own load") disappears when it is viewed as a natural sequence to verse 4, encouraging personal responsibility for individual conduct.

Verse 6 stands apart from the context because it seems entirely unconnected with what precedes and what follows. Yet the comment is eminently practical. Even in Paul's day, there was no such thing as a free lunch. The verse is addressed to those under instruction (catechumens, to use a later word) and urges that such an individual share all she or he has with the instructor, that is, make a financial or other contribution to the support of the teacher.

The remaining verses exhort the readers once more to be faithful to a spirit-guided life-style rather than to a flesh-directed one. The general instruction to do good to all people but especially to fellow believers squares well with the specific suggestions in 5:21-23, all of which are one-sided directives. These instructions do not describe what one can expect in return for such behavior. This is quite normal in the context of the household. Paul's generalization sums it up well here.

CONCLUSION

Gal 6:11-18

6:11-18 Personal concluding comments. As in other letters (1 Cor 16:21), Paul now adds personal comments in his own handwriting. For a final time he repeats his criticism of the Judaizers who continue to pressure the Galatians to be circumcised for failing themselves to obey the entire Torah. They are interested solely in personal satisfaction and in gaining an accomplishment about which they might boast far and wide.

Paul's boast and pride is in the redemption wrought by the passion and death of Jesus. United to this event and embracing its significance, Paul has rejected a way of life measured by external observances of the law and has been created afresh. That's what really counts. Those who accept this kind of life-style as a meaningful way of life are the really chosen people of God, the Israel of God, the authentic Christian community. To them Paul sends wishes of peace (total well-being) and mercy (God's kindness).

His final lines are as terse as the salutation of this letter. His body already shows the physical effects of his labors and sufferings in the ministry (2 Cor 11:23-25). He pleads with the Galatians not to add any more by troubling him. The concluding blessing is unusually brief and formal, though warmed ever so slightly with his affectionate address, "Brothers." Even in closing Paul makes one final attempt to reactivate their emotional anchorage to the gospel he preached.

ROMANS

John J. Pilch

INTRODUCTION

At the beginning of his third missionary trip, Paul wrote his Epistle to the Galatians. Now at the end of this same period of activity, during a three-month stay in the province of Achaia (Greece), he wrote this letter from the city of Corinth to the Christians in Rome. The date is probably very late in A.D. 56, or early in 58, during the winter.

Paul, of course, did not found the Roman church as he did the Galatian churches. It seems that it was established by members of the Jewish-Christian community in Jerusalem who had traveled to Rome. But about A.D. 49 Emperor Claudius ordered the Jews expelled. After Claudius died around year 54, Jewish Christians who returned to Rome were surprised to meet a large number of Gentile Christians. Converts had multiplied. The Roman Christian church, then, to whom Paul sent this letter was predominantly Gentile-Christian.

Now during his missionary activity, Paul encouraged the Gentile churches to take up a collection which he would personally deliver to the poor in Jerusalem (Rom 15:25-27). His plan was to visit Jerusalem briefly and then to set out for Spain and the West with an intervening visit to Rome (15:28).

Paul may well have had some concerns or even apprehension about visiting Jerusalem. Perhaps he even feared for his safety. Yet he hoped that delivering the collection in person would defuse any still-smoldering anger or hostility concerning his preaching. The circumstances surrounding the Jerusalem visit make it quite plausible that Paul wrote this letter to the Romans to achieve a number of purposes.

First, the letter provided an opportunity to introduce himself to a community which for the most part did not know him personally. Second, he could marshal, evaluate, and summarize the arguments he might have to present in Jerusalem if his preaching were still being challenged. Third, he may well have had the Jewish-Christian minority in Rome uppermost in mind when he composed this letter. The section on the Jews (Rom 9–11) and the chapters on living in mutual harmony (especially Rom 14–15) could have been calculated to win the affection of this minority. If Paul were successful, he would have powerful support from them for his anticipated difficulties in Jerusalem.

History records that Paul's fears were realized. He was arrested in Jerusalem, imprisoned in Caesarea for two years, and finally arrived in Rome around A.D. 60 or 61, some three or four years after his letter had arrived.

Has the biblical God of surprises ever acted differently with his people? The old proverb expresses it well: the creature proposes but God disposes!

Yet this same proverb or outlook raises a question about God's fair play. This epistle, and especially chapters 9–11, could create the impression that God is unjust. How can he have made such great promises to Israel, but grant their fulfillment to the Gentiles instead? To understand Paul, remember that he views God's word as promise and gospel or good news. But God's word can trigger two possible responses: belief or unbelief. God is always faithful; he never leaves his creatures without his address or promise. Experience shows, however, that some hear him and believe while others hear him and take offense. Paul believes that some of Israel is in the latter category.

Rom 9–11 stands at the heart of contemporary Jewish-Christian dialogue. It is important for the reader to understand Paul, his sociocultural context (for example, his post-conversion attitude toward the Torah), and his attempt to analyze and explain the actions of both God and his creatures. But it is equally important to strive to grasp the Jewish perception of Paul, the Jewish evaluation of and response to Jesus, and the healthy and thriving pluralism in Jewish belief and practice. We are still far from possessing totally satisfying answers to all our questions, but each new effort—like this commentary—is another sure step in the right direction.

OUTLINE OF ROMANS

1:1-17	Greetings and Introduction
1:18–11:36	I. SUMMARY OF PAUL'S GOSPEL
1:18–3:20	The Human Condition Without Christ
3:21–4:25	Salvation Through Faith in Christ
5:1–8:39	The Christian Life
9:1–11:36	Israel's Hope
12:1–15:13	II. EXHORTATION TO HARMONIOUS LIVING
15:14-33	Conclusion
16:1-23	Phoebe Commended
16:25-27	Concluding Doxology

COMMENTARY

GREETINGS AND INTRODUCTION

Rom 1:1-17

1:1-7 Paul greets the Christians at Rome. In this longest of all greetings in Paul's letters, he adds to the customary wishes of grace and peace six verses that describe the good news he preaches everywhere. This good news concerns Jesus who is both a descendant of David and God's Son as is evident from God's having raised Jesus from the dead.

This last statement is crucial for understanding Paul's Epistle to the Romans because it is central to his new attitude toward the Torah or the Law. After Jesus died a very shameful and dishonorable death—accursed by the Torah itself (Deut 21:23)—he was believed by some Jews to have been raised by the God of Israel. If God so blessed such an individual, then he must have abrogated the Torah. In other words, in Paul's understanding the Torah was no longer "law," no longer normative or obligatory. Instead, Torah became a guiding story, a Sacred Scripture that tells how we all got to the present, but it no longer has any binding rules for the future (see Rom 3:20).

Then, by way of introducing himself to this community which he did not personally establish, Paul declares that God appointed him to preach this good news—even at Rome—so that all people might become completely obedient to God as a result of accepting and believing in Jesus.

1:8-15 A prayer of thanksgiving. Continuing the customary letter-writing format of his day, Paul thanks God for the world-acknowledged progress that the Roman Christians are making in their faith. There is an interesting dynamic underlying this thanksgiving prayer. At least four times in this paragraph, Paul mentions his longstanding eagerness to visit the Romans. The purpose of this thanksgiving and its repeated mention of the desire to visit is that Paul eagerly strives to initiate a personal relationship with people for the most part still strangers to him.

Thus, whereas with the Galatians Paul could reasonably presume to (re)activate commitment to himself, here with the Romans he will have to rely on his powers of persuasion. Note an immediate example in verse 11, where Paul promises to share with his Roman hosts in the future some spiritual gift, perhaps one or more of those mentioned later in Rom 12:6-8.

1:16-17 The letter's chief idea. The theme is announced briefly and pointedly. The gospel itself contains God's power to save. Faith is central: everything starts and ends with it. As Habakkuk (2:4) told his compatriots, the righteous individual lives out personal destiny by faith. It is precisely this human faith which makes it possible for God to exercise his power to the fullest.

I. SUMMARY OF PAUL'S GOSPEL

Rom 1:18–11:36

The Human Condition Without Christ

Rom 1:18–3:20

First, Paul paints a rather gloomy picture of existence without Christ. Neither paganism (1:18-32) nor Judaism (2:1-29) is able to deliver what Jesus can. Throughout this section (as well as the entire letter) Paul uses his ethnocentric Jewish perspective to prove his point. While addressing this letter to a church that was predominantly Gentile-Christian, Paul nevertheless felt very sensitive to the disillusioned Jewish-Christian minority in Rome, and he concludes this section (3:1-20) with the recognition of some special advantage to being a Jew. Nevertheless, in the eyes of God, without Christ no one is innocent.

1:18-32 Paganism without Christ. Here Paul is particularly concerned about the irreligious or ungodly people who do not behave according to God's plan, which is plain as day to everybody in the orderliness of creation.

Paul's perspective is rooted in the concept of God as holy and its logical consequences: all God's creation should be holy too (throughout Leviticus, for example, 11:45). Holiness means wholeness, wellness, personal integrity. Now these irreligious people certainly know what wholeness, wellness, and integrity in human life mean, but they have chosen the opposite. They have substituted parts of God's creation for God himself; this disregards the wholeness and completeness of God.

Further evidence of this distortion is to be found in their sexual conduct. As is clear in the Leviticus (11–15) rules regarding purity, holiness, wholeness, the human body is a symbol of the social religious body or community. These rules seek to protect body boundaries. Notice the high degree of concern about orifices or body openings, both ordinary (like the mouth, genitals) and unusual (like leprosy = skin eruptions). Thus Paul's remarks about "unnatural relations" (vv. 26 and 27) should be understood in the context of his concern for order, for wholeness, and for bodily integrity, which is supposed to mirror the order and integrity of society and the cosmos, viewed, of course, from a Jewish perspective. Hence "natural" and "unnatural" should be more accurately translated "culturally approved" and "culturally disapproved."

Another way of illustrating these irreligious people's disregard for appropriate wholeness, wellness, and integrity in creation is to list their sins, as in verses 29-31. Scholars generally admit that the list is rhetorical, haphazard, and reflective of popular outlooks. Recent research, however, suggests that the list does have a logic of its own.

Throughout the Bible the human person is viewed in terms of three zones of personal activity clustered around heart-eyes, mouth-ears, and hands-feet. These zones describe and symbolize the entire person. When all three zones are mentioned and not criticized, all is well. The person is considered totally good, integral, whole, holy. But when any zone is omitted or criticized, the person is perceived to be incomplete, unwhole, suffering lack of integrity. Here in these verses all zones are mentioned: greed = heart-eyes; murder = hands-feet; deceit = mouth-ears. But the total picture is faulty, undesirable, unwholesome, indicating that the irreligious or ungodly non-Jewish outlook and life-style are thoroughly and completely perverse, fragmented, and incomplete. Well, what else would you expect without Jesus?

2:1-11 Religious alternatives in living. The basic principle which guides Paul's thinking here is expressed in verse 11: "There is no partiality with God" (recall the discussion at Gal 2:1-10 above). Lest anyone feel especially privileged or exempt from God's judgment, Paul reminds the readers that each person will reap the consequences of individual deeds. Those who pursue the life-style described by the list in Rom 1:29-31 will earn God's wrath and fury. Those who seek glory, honor, and immortality by patiently and persistently doing the right thing will gain eternal life. It makes no difference whether one is Jew or Greek!

2:12-16 The Torah is not a privilege. Pagans who of course do not possess the Torah are nevertheless guided by their experience of the transcendent claim of God's will. Their own interior reflections debate the propriety or impropriety of what they seek to do. If they do good, it will be to their credit. If not, it will redound to their judgment. And the same is true for the Jews! It is not mere possession of the Torah that is important and salvific. It is rather obeying or transgressing the Torah that counts. And it is Jesus who will do the judging at the final reckoning. This is part of Paul's good news.

2:17-24 Jews fail to live up to the Torah. Here for the first time Paul's imaginary debating partner since Rom 2:1 is identified: one known as "Jew," the common name by which members of God's chosen people were designated by non-Jews. In a masterpiece of rhetoric, Paul first lists five legitimate claims (verbs) deriving from being a Jew (vv. 17-18); he then switches to four nouns (vv. 19-20) identifying key roles Jews could fulfill for non-Jews.

But in verses 21-22, Paul raises four embarrassing and indicting questions that each point out a discrepancy between claim and performance. The preachers simply don't live according to what they preach!

This segment of the debate is brought to a close with a reinterpreted citation from the Greek version of Isa 52:5: "Because of you (my unfaithful Jewish people), I am continually blasphemed among the Gentiles." It is a stinging rebuke to the imaginary Jewish debating partner who could well be imagined applauding Paul's earlier indictment of the pagans at the end of chapter 1.

2:25-29 Circumcise the heart, not the body. To drive the barb even deeper, Paul criticizes circumcision interpreted as an automatically effective ritual. Quite the contrary, argues the Apostle. What really counts is not a mark on the body, but a changed heart. The true Jew is not one that carries a visible physical credential, but rather one whose inner core, whose heart, has been affected by the Spirit. In a play on words rooted in Hebrew, the true Jew (*Yᵉhûdî*) is the one praised (*hôdāh*) by God, not by other human beings.

3:1-8 Paul responds to objections. Continuing the diatribe, Paul anticipates the obvious objection: is there any advantage to being a Jew if the Gentiles can be so well off? Though his argumentation may suggest a resounding no, Paul says quite definitely yes! Chief among the privileges of Judaism is that God shared his word, the entire Jewish Scripture, with these people.

But the questioner persists: what if some of them (Jews) have proved unfaithful? Will God then break his part of the covenant, renege on his promises? Not at all, replied Paul. God will definitely be vindicated in the final analysis, even though human beings—perhaps every single one—will fall short. Paul cites Ps 51:6 to bolster his point.

Pressing still further, the questioner wonders: if our sole purpose is to make God look good, isn't he unjust in punishing us for our wrongdoing? Again Paul answers firmly in the negative. To support his contention he recalls the very basic Jewish belief that God is indeed the judge of all the world—Jews as well as non-Jews (see Isa 66:16).

Verse 8 appears to suggest that Paul's teaching was misunderstood and considered blasphemous. Some had pushed his views to unwarranted conclusions that individuals should sin freely in order to let God do good things. Paul identifies the charge as a slanderous presentation of his teaching and concludes the verse with "their penalty is what they deserve."

3:9-20 All human beings are under the power of sin. In these concluding verses to the opening section of this letter, Paul continues the line of reasoning he has been pursuing and asks whether Jews might consider themselves in some way superior to all others. His answer is direct and forceful: no, all people are under the power of sin.

Notice that phrase "domination of sin." Literally, the Greek reads "under sin," yet the addition of domination (or power) is a correct and proper interpretation. Paul understands sin as a negative and hostile power permeating society. It is a coercive power that dominates groups (see Rom 6:12, 14). It is also a lawgiver subjecting human beings to itself (see Rom 7:23, 25).

Sin's power is very much like that of a slave dealer (Rom 6:16-19) or like that of sickness, specifically the first-century sickness known as demonic possession (Rom 7:8-24). Thus, three well-known "power" experiences in Paul's social world (empire, slavery, demon possession) provided him with imagery to describe the power of the evil (sin) permeating his groups. Individual sinful actions are merely symptomatic of sin.

Then, following his custom, Paul turns once again to Scripture to support his arguments. Verses 10b-18 string together assorted citations from the Greek translation of the Jewish Scriptures: Ps 14:1-3, or 53:2-4; Pss 5:10; 140:4; 10:7; and Isa 59:7-8. The citations are comprehensive, colorful, and quite varied in detail.

Modern readers are understandably awed by this sweeping knowledge of Scripture. Yet the frequent repetition of certain passages and the regular linkage of certain texts have led scholars to conclude that Paul and other Christian preachers gathered favorite passages into collections of testimonies or "proof texts." As a preacher found a passage which might be applied to Jesus, it was recorded and added to other such passages. These testimonies then served as the basis for reflective and creative meditations on the Scriptures in the light of Jesus. Similar clusters of texts or testimonies are found in Rom 9:25-33; 10:15-21; 11:8-10, 26, 34-35; and 15:9-12.

In the present passage notice that the various citations seem to be linked to one another by references to parts of the body. Superimposing the Jewish understanding of the human body as noted earlier, we observe this concentric arrangement: *a* (v. 11) heart-eyes; *b* (v. 12) hands-feet; *c* (vv. 13-14) mouth-ears; *b'* (vv. 15-16) hands-feet; and *a'* (vv. 17-18) heart-eyes.

This deliberate arrangement draws attention to the centerpiece *c*, which emphasizes mouth-ears. All these verses together describe a totally, comprehensively unrighteous person, but mouth-ears stands out. How cleverly appropriate then is Paul's closing comment that "every mouth may be silenced," and the whole world without exception is totally convicted.

This tissue of texts is identified as pre-Pauline, that is, it was very likely compiled prior to Paul's usage of it. Its obvious purpose is to describe the human being as totally, comprehensively unrighteous. The opening sentence (v. 11) affirms that everyone without exception—non-Jews as well as Jews—falls under this description. Paul may have made the concentric rearrangement, but he clearly has added the pointed conclusion (vv. 19-20).

Actually, the concluding verses of this section summarize the point of the entire discussion since chapter 1. In the presence of God, no one is innocent. Paul's curious reference to what the *law* says in verse 19, following the list of citations from the psalms and a prophet, makes it quite clear that Paul uses law here in a wider sense than Torah/Pentateuch. He means the entire Jewish Scripture. His concluding implicit citation is from Ps 143:2 which he emends by adding "by observing the law." The law is thus a moral informer, that is, it gives a reflective person a real and deep religious awareness and recognition of moral disorder.

SALVATION THROUGH FAITH IN CHRIST

Rom 3:21–4:25

Having painted a gloomy picture of hopelessness for human existence apart from Christ, Paul now shares with his readers the exhilarating and liberating insight that God has a much simpler way of putting people right with himself: namely, through faith in Christ Jesus.

3:21-31 Here's how God does it. Yet another statement of Paul's basic thesis is expressed in verse 28: a person enters into a right relationship with God by faith and not by seeking to observe all the detailed requirements of the Jewish Torah. One must believe rather than achieve. And this thesis does not contradict or nullify Jewish Scripture (v. 31, notice that "law" really refers to all of Scripture). On the contrary, it supports and confirms the basic message of Scripture.

The rabbinic tradition records this opinion: "I am God over all that comes into the world, but I have joined my name only with you. I am not called the God of the Gentiles, but the God of Israel" (Exodus Rabbah 29, Rabbi Simon ben Yohai). Wrong, Paul would say! The one God (an echo of the Jewish prayer "Hear, O Israel") is God of all—Jews and Gentiles.

All human beings have failed God, have not measured up to their potential glory through their individual, personal misdeeds. But God quite freely has made it possible for all people to regain a right relationship with him through a believing acceptance of the redemptive death of Christ.

This, in fact, is the meaning of the phrase "the righteousness of God" in this passage. The words describe not so much an attribute of God as his activity. It is none other than God himself who justifies or renders upright each person on the basis of faith (v. 30).

4:1-25 Abraham, a model for the Christian believer. In the first century there was a popular Jewish opinion that Abraham knew and obeyed the Jewish Torah, even though he lived long before it was revealed to Moses. Paul challenges this opinion on the basis of Scripture itself. He cites two passages in support of his challenge: Gen 15:6 (in vv. 3, 9, and 22) and Ps 32:1-2.

In Genesis it is reported that Abraham believed God and it was credited to him as justice. The key word is "credited" (or "reckoned" in some translations). It is a bookkeeping term applied figuratively in Scripture to the conduct of a person. Here, in Rom 4:3-6, 8, Paul's use of the word means more than that. His point is that Abraham's faith was recognized by God for exactly what it was: namely, a sign of his uprightness, his good standing with God.

Paul quotes Ps 32:1-2 to repeat the idea: truly fortunate is the person to whom God credits or reckons justice or uprightness, apart from the performance of deeds listed by the Jewish Torah.

Arguing according to Jewish rules, Paul has cited two witnesses to support his view: Abraham (Genesis) and David (Psalms). Deut 19:15 required two witnesses in order that any testimony might be considered valid and convincing. But if Paul was truly convinced that the Torah was no longer binding (see commentary on Rom 1:1-7 above), why would he himself try to obey Deut 19:15? Even though the death and resurrection of Jesus have given him a totally new interpretation of the Jewish Scripture, Paul remains in the last analysis a Pharisaic Jew (Phil 3:5) and is best understood as continuing to reason and argue within that cultural mindset.

But Paul's imaginary Jewish opponent is still not satisfied because it would seem as if the psalm declares happiness for the Jew and not for the Gentile. Again Paul looks to Abraham to illustrate his answer. About twenty-nine years after God declared Abraham upright (see Gen 15), Abraham was circumcised (see Gen 17). Clearly then Abraham was reckoned as upright before circumcision, and the psalm's declaration of happiness therefore applies to anyone who like Abraham strives to believe rather than to achieve. In Abraham's case circumcision was a sign or seal that testified to the uprightness gained by faith long prior to the actual circumcision. Thus Abraham is truly the father of all believers whether circumcised (Jews) or not (non-Jews).

In addition, God promised Abraham an heir and a huge posterity (Gen 15:4; 22:16-18), also independently of observing the Jewish Torah. Verses 17-25 play on the word "dead." Abraham was positively convinced that God could realize his promise from the reproductively "dead" bodies of himself and his wife Sarah. Indeed, Abraham is a father of many nations, a father of us all. Three times in this chapter Paul repeats the Scripture that affirms that Abraham's faith was reckoned or credited to him as uprightness, driving home the importance of this fact for his Roman readers, both the predominant Gentile Christians as well as the Jewish-Christian minority.

Both we and Abraham believe in God who can bring life out of death. For Abraham, God brought life out of Sarah's dead womb; for Christians, God raised Jesus from death and thereby restored them to life through the resulting justification.

THE CHRISTIAN LIFE

Rom 5:1–8:39

In chapter 5 a new emphasis emerges. God's love comes to the fore while justification and righteousness recede to the background. Specifically, Paul describes the Christian experience of new life at peace with God.

5:1-11 How it feels to be right with God. Nearly everyone at one time or another has experienced the relief that follows the resolution of a doubt or the solution of a problem. That feeling of relief is very much like the three effects Paul identifies which result when one has a right relationship with God: peace (v. 1), confidence (v. 2), and a present share in the risen life of Christ himself (v. 10).

These effects are all the more impressive when one recognizes that Jesus died for us when we were at our worst! As difficult to believe or accept as that might be, we have the proof of it in our hearts where God's love has placed the Holy Spirit to guide us in the new life.

Small wonder then that Paul "boasts" three times in these few verses. Boasting, in its biblical meaning, is a way of acknowledging one's personal lord and master. The unredeemed person boasts through self-praise, but the person who acknowledges redemption through Jesus boasts in God himself (v. 11; see Jer 9:23) and in the certainty of sharing in God's glory (v. 2).

This understanding explains how in addition to boasting about his hope (v. 2) and God (v. 11), he can also boast about his afflictions (v. 3). Paul is not a masochist. Rather, he describes his newly discovered ability to resist the challenges and risks of *thlipseis* (Greek for "afflictions") that results from following Jesus. The risk they entail is that they could possibly cause an individual to give up on God. Patiently endured, however, these hardships serve to highlight a God-pleasing attitude of openness to the future characterized by great freedom from death and sin (5:12-21), from self (6:1-23), and from the Torah as law (7).

5:12-21 Freedom from sin and death. This passage has stimulated centuries of debate and caused deep divisions among Christians. Catholics have some guidance in the debate from the Council of Trent (1545), which declared that Paul's words in these verses do indeed teach some form of original sin.

Of course, neither Trent nor Paul used that exact phrase, and readers should be careful not to read into these verses of the epistle the fuller understanding which they have gained from modern religious instruction. Trent affirms that Paul declares the reality of the sin and its universal terrible impact upon all creation. The sin is transmitted (or inherited), but Paul does not indicate how.

In reading verses 12-21 it is important to recognize that "sin" and "death" are personifications of forces. Sin in Paul is an active force within and among all human beings. It has been present since the very beginnings of the human race (as this passage asserts) and expresses itself chiefly through the "flesh." Flesh is not a synonym for body. Rather, flesh describes a person from the perspective of unredeemed weakness. Death is also a personified, cosmic (Rom 8:38) force, which not only destroys the human body but causes definitive separation from God as well.

Paul's main interest is not to talk about sin or death, but rather to draw a contrasting picture of Adam and Christ, prominent figures of the beginning and the end time respectively. Adam is a "type" or "prototype" of the person to come, namely, Jesus, who would far surpass what Adam did. The world was changed by both of these individuals.

Adam unleashed an active hostile force into the world (sin), which had the power to cause definitive alienation (death) from God, the source of all life, inasmuch as or because all individuals have sinned through personal, actual deeds (v. 12). Thus death has two causes in human existence: Adam's sin and personal ratification of that deed by individuals who sin. This was Adam's effect on the world.

In contrast, Christ's effect is starkly different. Through the gracious gift, namely, the redemptive death of Jesus Christ uprightness and life superabound for all individuals who accept him.

The far-reaching perverse consequences of Adam's disobedience is reported in rabbinic terms which divided time into three periods: Adam to Moses, two thousand years of chaos; Moses to the Messiah, two thousand years of law; from the Messiah onward there would be two thousand years of blessing. In the first period, Adam to Moses, there was no law to disobey (v. 14), yet definitive separation from God (spiritual death) held sway, so pervasive was the effect of Adam's misdeed.

Jesus changed this dreary situation through his obedience. The contrast between Adam and Jesus not only highlights the tragedy of Adam's failure but also the magnificent plenitude of Christ's redemption.

In the final verses (20-21) law is personified as a force and identified as the cause of sin and its companion death. But law as force has been overcome by grace which now rules through uprightness, which grants a share in the very life of God himself through Christ our Lord.

6:1-11 Freedom from self. Whereas in Rom 3:5-8 Paul explained why a Jew should not continue sinning so that God could "star," here he answers the same question for the Christian. Baptism, he explains, has worked a very real change in the life of a believer. Through baptism, a believer is united very intimately with Christ and his destiny. As Christ has died so too the Christian truly dies or is truly liberated from the hostile force known as sin which alienates a person from God. As Christ was raised by the Father and thereby enjoys a new relationship with his Father, so too the believer now has a very real share in this new way of life, this new principle of vitality. The power of the resurrection already rules in us. How then can anybody deny this reality and return to a former sinful way of life? It's simply unthinkable!

The "sinful body" mentioned by Paul in verse 6 is an instance of a part representing a whole. The body represents the entire person insofar as it is dominated by an almost unavoidable proneness to sin. But this "old self" truly died with Jesus. The sinful inclination has been destroyed. The tyranny of death has been broken. In fact, death has brought a new status. Verse 11 sums up the thrust of this passage with an exhortation to the Christian: consider yourself snatched away from the power of the sinful force and incorporated instead into new life for God "in Christ Jesus." This latter phrase is a special term in Paul's writings that describes the intimate association of a believer with the life and destiny of Christ.

6:12-23 Free to serve. The high number of imperatives in this section characterizes it as a fervent exhortation that flows as a natural conclusion from the truth described in the first eleven verses. Notice how Paul's efforts at persuasion can easily take the form of a command if the premise is clear and convincing.

Don't let that alienating force (sin) govern your living (v. 12). Don't yield to the powerful cravings, desires, and intentions of your natural self which will only pit you against God. Once and for always give yourself over completely to God, literally to slave service of God (v. 22), so he might use you to do what is right. Don't let the force of sin have power over you. You live now under grace and not the canceled Jewish law.

What does this mean? What kind of freedom is a freedom for rendering "slave service"? It is a freedom quite unlike that which mainstream citizens of the United States are familiar with. They understand freedom in terms of freedom from external obstacles or restraints in order to choose and pursue an individualistically determined goal.

For Paul, it is impossible to live a human life in total independence in the sense of being subject to no one. In these verses he clearly argues that the freedom from the power or force of sin worked by Jesus' death and resurrection does not mean total and complete human independence, but rather acceptance of another master, namely, God (v. 22). This is why the baptized person (slave of God in Christ) cannot continue to sin (be a slave of the power of sin).

7:1-25 Freedom from the law. Having discussed union with Christ (Rom 5) and the resulting freedom from sin and death (Rom 6), Paul now completes his discussion of Christian freedom with still another explanation of how believers are freed from the Jewish Torah understood as law.

In the first six verses Paul organizes his thoughts around the notion of death, suggested by the reflection on baptism immediately preceding. His example drawn from marriage is weak and unfinished, but the general idea is clear: death terminates obligations. When a woman's husband dies, she is free to remarry. Similarly through baptism we have been united to Christ's death which freed us from bondage to the Jewish law so as to be able to belong to Jesus and be productive in the service of God.

As verses 5-6 point out, the "law" here stands for a religious observance as a way of salvation. It involves a legalistic approach to Torah or any other objective norm of good and evil that does not at the same time give an individual the ability to fulfill it. Rather, a person's social and individual attempt to fulfill the law normally ends in nonfulfillment, thus revealing the presence of this powerful force (sin) actively promoting alienation from God. Paul insists that we died to this. Now we can serve God through a dynamic principle of new life (Spirit), whereas before all we had was a dead letter of the Mosaic law as guide.

Now Paul must take up a very painful consideration. The problem is: how is it that something which is good, just, and holy—indeed given by God (namely the Jewish

Torah) failed to bear good fruit but only fostered sin itself?

Paul's answer is that it was not the law that brought permanent alienation from God (death), but rather the power known as sin working through it. The reader must not be misled by Paul's use of "I" in these verses. In the light of his bold affirmation that "I was above reproach when it came to justice based on the law" (Phil 3:6), the "I" cannot be understood in an autobiographical sense. Paul is not talking about himself personally in Rom 7:7ff. Scholars rather identify the use of this personal pronoun as a rhetorical device in order to describe common human experience, an experience with which the readers could certainly identify.

Without the law, a person leads a relative or neutral existence: not in union with God, nor in rebellion either. But when the law was made known, it stimulated and unmasked sin, that pernicious power hostile to God. Upon close examination, we see that Paul is retelling the story of Adam as typifying the common lot of humankind. Though Adam lived long before the Jewish law was given, that first parent did receive a command from God. But sin, that latent force capable of diverting people from obeying God, did just that to Adam. Sin first deceived Adam, and then through the disobedience brought about death, that is, alienation from God. But the law itself is not synonymous with or equivalent to sin; it was rather intended to make people holy and just and good.

Verses 14-20 now describe what goes on inside a pious person, but from a Jewish perspective. Jewish tradition taught that there are two urges or drives in each person: a good one and a bad one. They are constantly at war with one another. The Jewish law derives from God's sphere, the "spiritual," and causes reverberations in the good drive or urge in each person. But experience shows that more often than not "weak flesh" prevails, that is, the natural self, that aspect of human existence that reverberates with the bad drives or urges. It is a natural playground for the force of sin. Hence the internal strife between the urges with embarrassing and discouraging outcomes. Sin as force is the culprit, not the law (v. 20). Our modern focus on sin as a deed or act makes it difficult to appreciate sin as force.

The final verses (21-23) move the picture to a broader horizon and describe every person. Here Paul's use of the word "law" is correctly translated as principles or recurrent patterns of personal experience. Paul says each person has an internal part which desires what God desires. He calls this the "inner self" or "mind" even in the unredeemed person. But there are also negative forces, and the internal struggle that takes place between the two is a frustrating and weakening process. No wonder Paul cries out for relief: "Who will deliver me from this mortal body?" The answer will come in the next chapter of Romans. In anticipation Paul sings a brief statement of praise.

8:1-39 Christian life in the Spirit. Rom 8 is the climax of the epistle to this point. Specifically it answers the question in 7:24: "Who will deliver me . . . ?" The liberator is the Spirit (the word, which until now has appeared only five times, occurs twenty-nine times in this chapter alone), which is nothing else but the power or force of the risen Jesus present upon earth. The believer comes into contact with this force by living in union with Christ Jesus, a union already begun in baptism. This Spirit brings a vitality that the Mosaic law never could.

The contrast spirit-flesh introduced in verse 4 is further developed in verses 5-13. The terms represent competing fields of force or spheres of power. Flesh describes the earthbound person left to unaided individual ability. Spirit describes the earthbound person guided by the life-giving force or Spirit of Jesus. The self-centered all-sufficient person leads a life that can only lead to death, that is, definitive alienation from God. Such a person doesn't need God, doesn't submit to God's law in general, can't obey and can't please God.

On the other hand, the person guided by the life-giving Spirit finds both life and peace. Paul uses various descriptions of the Spirit: Spirit of God, Spirit of Christ, Christ—all to express the multifaceted reality of the Christian experience of a share in divine life.

In the final analysis the indwelling Spirit of God who raised Jesus will also raise us in the resurrection. So the inescapable conclusion is that we are in debt to the Spirit. We have an obligation to put to death the deeds, actions, pursuits of a person dominated by the flesh and live instead by the Spirit.

A very important result of being subject to the Spirit is that one becomes a true child of God. This is the first time the concept appears in Romans (8:14-17). The Spirit or force we have received is not one that would cast us back into fear, even a reverential fear. Rather this Spirit says we are dear to God, we are his very own children. Further, not only does the Spirit make this child relationship with God possible, but the same Spirit gives each of us the power to recognize it, that is, to say "Abba, father." Yet, lest anyone get too carried away with all this good news, Paul reminds the readers with two special compound verbs in Greek that we must suffer with Christ in order to be glorified with him.

Suffering, of course, simply can't compare with the glory or intimate share in God's life which is the destiny of each believer. Three things persuade us of the greatness of this glory: the testimony of creation (vv. 19-22), of believers (23-25), and of the Spirit (26-30).

God subjected creation to futility, that is, an inability to reach its goal. But he also left a spark of hope, and for this reason all creation is groaning as it waits for the final removal of chaos and the restoration to wholeness and integrity. We believers also are awaiting final and definitive redemption of our whole selves (our bodies) in confident hope with patient endurance.

Finally, the Spirit is the third witness to our glorious destiny. But the statement "we do not know how to pray as we ought" (v. 26) appears to contradict the one in verse 15 where the Spirit prompts the confident prayer "Abba, father." Perhaps Paul is offering a corrective to enthusiasm, an excessive emphasis on the gifts of the Spirit. The Greek of verse 26 literally says that the Spirit "intercedes over and above" our own intercessions "with ineffable groanings." It is possible that these groanings refer to the "words which cannot be uttered" heard by Paul in the third heaven (2 Cor 12:4).

Observe the plurals in verses 28-30. The statements refer to Christians as a group and not to individual believers. Paul underlines assurance about salvation. God is in control of everything. His will is that we be conformed to the image of Christ by a progressive share (v. 30—predestined, called, set right, given a share in glory) in the risen life of Christ himself. The ultimate goal is to become like the God who revealed himself in Jesus Christ.

The concluding verses (31-39) are a hymnlike celebration of the reality of the victory, the reality of being in the Spirit. The chief message is that God is for us, and the verses describe what "God-for-us" looks like. In a series of five questions, Paul explores how secure we really are, how certain we ought to be. That, of course, does not mean that life is a bed of roses. Verse 35 lists seven dangers or troubles that might separate us from the love Christ has for us. The list is not purely imaginary; it sums up the varied and potentially fatal attacks to which followers of Christ are commonly subject. The citation in verse 36 from Ps 44:23 was used often by the rabbis to describe the martyrdom of the pious. Yet the bottom line is positive, firm, and confidently secure. No other forces or powers (vv. 38-39), not even the personified power of the stars (height . . . depth), can separate us from the love of God that comes to us in Christ Jesus our Lord.

ISRAEL'S HOPE

Rom 9:1–11:36

Throughout this letter Paul has insisted that the Jewish Torah no longer binds as law, is no longer valid except as sacred story to tell how we reached this point in history. Now the time has come for Paul to draw from this story an explanation of how his spiritual and cultural kin have come to a moment of apparent rejection by God in the history of salvation.

9:1-29 God's free choice. The first five verses are quite an emotional statement. They reflect Paul's deep sensitivity in regard to his sisters and brothers, the Israelites (using their God-given title, see Gen 32:38). Proudly he enumerates seven privileges granted by God to the Jews: adoption as children; God's intimate presence; the covenants; the law; beautiful liturgy; the promises; and the patriarchs, from whom descended the greatest gift of all, the Messiah "who is God over all, blessed for ever" (RSV).

But what good is all of this if it proves to be of no benefit to Israel in the long run? Wouldn't we have to admit that God didn't keep his word? Of course not, Paul insists. Yet he will have to do some fancy scriptural footwork to explain his position convincingly to the Jews. Scriptural deftness, however, is no problem for Paul.

Gen 18:10 (or 18:14, or both combined) identifies Isaac as the child of promise (Rom 9:9). And the true children of God or children of the promise are the descendants of Isaac (Gen 21:12). It is faith that counts, not ethnicity. All of this is clear in the Scripture just cited.

Then Paul moves the argument even further to highlight God's free choices, his freedom to make choices. Just as God chose between two mothers, Sarah and Hagar, to find a recipient for his promise, so too does he choose between the two sons of a single mother, Rebekah: Esau and Jacob. Indeed, the choice of Jacob took place while the twins were still in the womb, before they were at all capable of doing anything toward merit or demerit. The scriptural proof is from the Torah and the prophets: Gen 25:23, "The older shall serve the younger," and Mal 1:2-3, "I loved Jacob, but hated Esau." God is entirely free to do what he wills and to choose whom he wills. The obvious application to Paul's discussion of Jews and Gentiles in his day raises a new objection: God is unjust!

Paul vigorously denies any charge that God is unjust. Again he returns to his arsenal of biblical texts to defend God's behavior. Moses and Pharaoh serve to illustrate the point. In Exod 33:19 God declares his free will to Moses. He can show mercy and pity to whomever he wills. Human intentions or activities are not the prime consideration. And Pharaoh illustrates how God can even use an enemy to achieve his will. Pharaoh hardened his own heart, that is, became stubborn and obdurate. God recognized the situation, affirmed and accepted it. In the process he gained salvation/redemption for the Israelites.

The reader can almost anticipate the next objection: if this be the case, how can God blame anybody? How can anyone be held responsible if no one can resist the will of God? Paul never really answers this question in the text. His actual answer is a diplomatically stated "shut up." The tradition of clay and the potter, or moulder of clay in the Scripture (Isa 29:16; Jer 18:6; Wis 15:7), provides the images for his reply. It's unheard of that any creature ever questioned its maker.

Actually God is quite patient. He has tolerated creatures who deserve his wrath in order that he might demonstrate the wealth of his glory to both Jews and Gentiles. This statement helps Paul finally describe quite clearly the present situation. He uses a tissue of texts that once again seem to have preexisted the composition of this letter.

Beginning with a text patched together from Hos 2:25 and 1:9 and originally applied to the ten unfaithful northern tribes, Paul applies them to the Gentiles: a nation not God's people would become his people; a nation formerly unloved would now be loved by God.

Then turning to Isa 10:22-23 Paul finds a bright spark of hope for his cultural and spiritual kin: "A remnant will be saved." Thus, God's promise continues to be valid, continues to tend toward final fulfillment. Without such a remnant Israel would be no better off than Sodom and Gomorrah. But there is hope. Even though God's ways appear arbitrary, he faithfully keeps his promises. Scripture, says Paul, bears witness to that.

9:30-33 Israel's failure is its own fault. Rom 9:30-33 both conclude chapter 9 and introduce chapter 10. The concluding Scripture citation is a combination of two texts. In their original context Isa 28:17 describes the Messiah as a foundation stone, and Isa 8:14-15 marks God as the stumbling stone. Paul's combination of these texts asserts that the Messiah who was intended to be a "stepping stone" for the Israelites became for them instead a "stumbling stone."

10:1-4 Christ is the end of the law. The truth of the matter for Paul is that with the coming of Christ, the time of the Messiah has arrived. The old order exists no more. In this sense Christ is the end of the period in which the Torah was operative and normative as law (review the commentary on Gal 2:11-21). Paul fervently prays for and earnestly desires the salvation of his compatriot Israelites. He knows firsthand that they have a keen zeal for God. But their zeal is not based on true knowledge. They sincerely believe that they can put themselves right with God. That is what they pursue. The authentic righteous relationship with God, of course, comes through faith.

10:5-13 Salvation is for all and is easy. As he often does, Paul adduces scriptural proof for what he has just said in verse 4. This string of texts again appears to be linked on the basis of the tripartite view of person in the Bible: hands-feet, mouth-ears, and heart-eyes. Lev 18:5 refers to hands-feet: the one who observes Torah will live as a consequence. The emphasis is on doing and achieving.

The righteousness that counts, however, is faith. Faith reflects the zone of heart-eyes. Indeed, that is what Deut 30:11-14 reflects as Paul adapts it to his purposes. Though the text originally applied to the Torah, Paul applies it to Jesus. No one need go up to heaven (hands-feet) to bring him down, for Christ came to earth in human form. Nor need anyone go to bring him back from the dead (hands-feet), because he has already been raised. God's salvation is available in Jesus Christ.

The word is on your lips (mouth-ears) and in your heart (heart-eyes). Observe how Paul draws on the two constituent zones of activity that contrast with doing (hands-feet). The emphatic conclusion is that no one who puts faith in Jesus will be confounded or gypped. All will be saved in the same way: Jew and Gentile alike.

The concluding citations (vv. 11 and 13) confirm the Deuteronomy passage in the same pattern of emphasis. Isa 28:16 is a heart-eyes passage: no one who believes in him will be shamed. Joel 3:5 is a mouth-ears passage: everyone who calls on the name of the Lord will be saved. The important thing is to recognize and declare Jesus as Lord, a phrase very likely borrowed from early church worship.

10:14-21 Israel has refused the Messiah. To wind up this discussion, Paul proposes four objections that could remove blame from Israel. The style is that of chain-argumentation. Each question retraces part of the previous one: (1) Perhaps no one preached the new understanding to Israel. No, preachers did come; Paul was one. He very definitely spoke about Jesus-Messiah and concentrated his efforts outside Palestine. This can't be an excuse. (2) Only very few believed (v. 16). True, says Paul, but already Isa 53:1 foresaw that kind of a situation. (3) Maybe the Jews didn't hear the preaching. Paul counters with a resounding "they most certainly did." And he cites Ps 19:5, saying creation itself has proclaimed the glory of God. (4) Finally, perhaps having heard the message about Christ, they didn't really understand it. Paul denies that. Again he turns to Scripture (Deut 32:21) to show that even this ancient text predicted that Israel will be humiliated. Isa 65:1-2 wraps up the entire discussion, but Paul divides the verses and applies verse 1 to the Gentiles (they found God though they did not seek him), and verse 2 to the Jews (God patiently tried to reveal himself to an unbelieving people).

11:1-10 Israel's disbelief is partial, not total. Paul returns still once more to the nagging question: Has God rejected Israel? Again he denies it most emphatically and points to himself as an example. He is perhaps the most Jewish of all Jews, holding mint-Jewish credentials: he is an Israelite, descended from Abraham, and tracing lineage from the tribe of Benjamin. This was the first tribe to cross the Reed Sea, and it includes among its worthy members both Saul and Jeremiah.

But is Paul alone the "remnant"? No, he's like Elijah. In 1 Kgs 19:9-18 Elijah felt very much alone, but he had about seven thousand compatriots who were faithful to God just as he was. So too Paul is not alone among Jews who believe in Jesus as Messiah. This group of Jewish Christians is a remnant (see Rom 9:27) selected by God not because of anything they have done, but simply because of God's benevolence. Israel as a whole was unable to find what it had sought. Only a remnant succeeded. The rest were hardened as a result of their resistance to the good news.

What's the problem? Paul cites three passages from Jewish Scripture, all linked by the word "eyes." Deut 29:3, Isa 29:10, and Ps 69:23-24 are drawn each from a different section of the Jewish Scripture: the Torah, the Prophets, the Writings. The indictment is severe: the entire Scripture proves that Israel failed to respond appropriately to God's earlier interventions. They also failed to respond appropriately now to the Messiah. God simply seals the situation.

11:11-24 Israel's fall is temporary, not definitive. Israel's stumbling is not definitive or irremediable. Deut 32:21 remains in the back of Paul's mind as he explains how Israel's fall made it possible for the Gentiles to accept Jesus and thereby stir Israel to envy. If the failure of Israel brought such a blessing, imagine the result when they all accept Jesus!

Addressing himself to the Gentiles, Paul describes his own ministry among them as one that is precisely calculated to make his own people jealous. When they finally do accept Christ, the result for them will be nothing less spectacular than a change in status as if from death to life. The influence of the foundation (Judaism) is strong indeed. Since the root is holy (patriarchs), the tree will also be holy (see Jer 11:16-17). If the first lump (the remnant) is consecrated, so too will the entire loaf be (see Num 15:18-21).

A word of caution, however, is directed to the Gentile Christians lest they begin to boast. They have been grafted like a wild olive branch onto a cultivated root. As Israel was lopped off because of disbelief, the Gentiles were grafted on because of faith. If they lose faith, they too can be lopped off.

Paul takes the opportunity to build an even stronger case for hope for his beloved Israel. If they should turn away from their unbelief, it will be even easier for God to reattach them, the natural branch, to the cultivated root, than it was to attach the wild branch, the Gentiles. Clearly then the rejection of Israel is not definitive or final, but only temporary.

11:25-32 God shows mercy to all. At last Paul speaks plainly because he does not want his Jewish readers to be misguided, misled, or "wise in their own way of thinking" (see Prov 3:7). A partial insensibility has come over Israel until the number of Gentiles determined by God will be saved. Then all Israel will be saved. This concern for numbers is an apocalyptic idea especially familiar from the Book of Revelation. Paul reflects that mentality, though he generally tends to simplify rather than complexify apocalyptic traditions. Notice that he doesn't even guess at a specific number.

To this point having cited their Scripture against them, it is interesting to see Paul quote from Isa 59:20-21 and 27:9 in their favor. While the Jews have ruptured the right relationship with God by rejecting the good news, they are still loved by him because the election of Israel is irrevocable. The promises or covenants with the patriarchs still stand firm. God simply doesn't vacillate about those whom he blesses and chooses. In point of fact, all groups have been disobedient to God at one time or another. This is what allows God to have mercy on all (see Mark 2:17).

11:33-36 Final doxology. Having now completed to his satisfaction an exploration of how Israel fits into God's plans for salvation and redemption, Paul concludes with a brief but marvelous hymn of praise to the all-merciful God. The Apostle has no doubt that God has complete control over history and human life, that is, that he knows its design, purpose, and fulfillment. And who can understand or explain this? After all, no one has advised him (Isa 40:13), nor is he in debt to anyone (see Job 41:3 or 41:11). He is indeed the creator, sustainer, and goal of the universe (characteristically Stoic ideas accepted by Hellenistic Judaism and absorbed by Paul in his education and travels) responsible for its origin, course, and end. To him be glory forever. Amen.

II. EXHORTATION TO HARMONIOUS LIVING

Rom 12:1–15:13

Following the pattern of all his letters, Paul turns his attention in these remaining chapters to practical exhortation. His discussion presumes that the Torah is no longer a norm for conduct. There are, of course, new demands for believers, but these are based on love and not law. These new demands develop in individual instances and are thus by definition standards. A standard is a value applied to a generally recurring interaction between two individuals (review commentary on Gal 2:11-21).

It is Paul's hope that sooner or later these standards might evolve into custom. A custom is an institutionalized set of standards; that means customs inhere in institutions. In Paul's world there were only two formal, or distinct, institutions: government and family. The additional formal, or distinct, institutions known to us, namely, economics, religion and education, were embedded in the two formal institutions. Thus Paul repeatedly calls these believers "brothers [and sisters]" not because he wants them to consider him especially sensitive, but rather because family—even fictive kinship, or extended family—is the arena in which the standards of individuals can become customs of the community. Until this takes place, primitive Christian exhortation often deals with the challenges of daily life more by way of example than by way of precept or command. This is very common in the letters of Paul.

Rom 12–13 spell out general exhortations, while 14–15 speak of a more specific situation centering on the relationship of people who are "weak" in faith with those who are "strong" in faith. The general idea is that Christian freedom should promote life in peace and harmony among all believers. Individuals should mutually strengthen one another. Rom 15 brings the specific example of Jesus to bear on the problems posed by the relationship between weak and strong.

12:1-8 Proper use of spiritual gifts (charismata). The first two verses of chapter 12 open with three appeals to the Roman Christians: (1) they ought to offer themselves in living sacrifice to God; (2) they ought not reflect their culture (rather they should shape it); (3) they ought to let God transform them through his Spirit. The appeals are made on the basis of what has been shared in the letter to this point: namely, a history of God's "mercies" (the Greek is plural reflecting many acts of graciousness) towards his creatures.

How is this done in concrete daily life? Paul's suggestion needs to be understood in terms of his basic cultural values: honor and shame. No one is to increase or augment his or her honor (think more highly of self) at the expense of the honor (or to the shame) of others. Honor and shame are almost understood as concrete quantities which are limited. If one increases honor, someone must have been deprived. That's simply unacceptable.

Applied to the discussion of gifts (v. 6, charismata), honor and shame set limits. Each one must remain in the limit and recognize the complementarity of other gifts. Charisms, of course, are never intended for personal gain or individual benefit. They are by definition concretions or individuations of the Spirit (this means individual people receive them as individual gifts) intended solely for the service and upbuilding of the community.

Jesus is the guiding norm or criterion for how to use the gifts, for we are all one moral body in union with Christ (vv. 4-5). Thus individual members are incorporated into but do not constitute the body. Therefore there is a need for all to cooperate for the common good.

Paul lists seven gifts and suggests how each one should be used for the good (or for the honor) of the community. Notice once again how the list reflects the tripartite view of the individual person: mouth-ears, hands-feet, heart-eyes. The one who preaches should be faithful to the basic body of tradition. The one who serves ought to faithfully administer material aid and distribution of alms. The one who teaches is to be guided by the subject matter. The one who exhorts should encourage all who need it. Those who share personal wealth with the needy or distribute community alms should do so with generous simplicity. Leaders (note the position in this list of gifts!) ought to fill that position with sensitive care. And those who aid the sick and abandoned ought to do so cheerfully.

Both Rome and Corinth were port cities which had many neglected widows and orphans, had a constant stream of proletarians to their harbors, and many poor and sick. Hence the practical relevance of Paul's advice. Moreover, since the enumeration reflects all three parts or zones of the person, Paul has described how to deliver holistic care to the entire person. His statement looks like yet another effort to curb enthusiasm, that excessive reliance upon the gifts of the Spirit. Clearly Paul urges a sober analysis of personal gifts and an appropriate holistic response.

12:9-21 Love among other-directed persons. These verses appear to be a random collection of maxims, roughly rooted in the notion of disinterested love, *agápē*. Verses 9-10 actually speak of two distinct kinds of love: *agápē* (v. 9) and *philadelphia* (v. 10). The first love is wider in scope than the other one, rather familiar as "brotherly love," but perhaps preferably translated "sibling love." Thus some scholars believe that the verses explain or suggest particular ways of practicing love in general.

A sharper focus might be gained by remembering the discussion in Galatians about dyadic or other-directed personalities as the dominant personality type in the Mediterranean world. Such individuals always need the opinions of others to ascertain self-identity, self-esteem, and indeed, honor and shame! A literal rendition of Rom 12:10b identifies honor and shame as the context of Paul's exhortation: "Outdo one another in showing honor."

Honor is a claim to worth PLUS public acknowledgment of that worth. Hence, the claim to honor is always a communal or public affair, since it relies on the judgment of the public. Honor has to be granted. Shame is an attitude of sensitivity about one's honor, a concern about what others think, say, and do relative to oneself. Thus, shame includes an all-pervading interest in and a desire for a grant of reputation on the part of others.

Paul's remarks all support honorable living. Above all, he says, serve the Lord; do the honorable thing. Have confidence reaching out for your future (rejoice in hope). Don't just suffer your troubles passively (be patient), and remain open to God (persevere in prayer). Remain honorable: meet the needs of all believers (be conscious of their need for honor), both those you know (widows, orphans, prisoners, and needy in your city), as well as those you don't know (traveling Christians need your help).

Do not shame your persecutors by cursing them. Have the same attitude toward all; don't slight the honor of anyone. If you have been shamed (injured), don't repay that shame with an affront to the honor of your opponent (similar to Jesus' advice to turn the other cheek). See that your conduct is honorable to and in the eyes of all.

For the one who believes in God, God will see to the redress of balance in honor and shame. God's wrath is a description of how God restores his honor when it is affronted or shamed by a challenge of one or another kind.

Advice for treating one's enemy is borrowed from Prov 25:21-22. Heaping burning coals on his head appears most likely to derive from an Egyptian penitential ritual in which the penitent carried on his head a dish of burning charcoal to express repentance. So, by returning "honorable" deeds for an opponent's "shaming" deeds, one embarrasses the opponent into repentance before God. In other and final words, don't be shamed into shaming activity; rather, shame evil by your honorable response.

13:1-7 Duties toward civil authority. These verses seem to be a further development of Rom 12:3, which cautioned that no one think more highly of self than is fitting. Paul may have been worried about yet another form of enthusiasm. Some Christians believed they were already citizens of another world, had gained new freedom in Christ, and therefore did not have to obey civil authority. Paul feared the anarchy that would result from such an outlook and therefore felt obliged to discourage it.

It is quite incorrect to think Paul intends to spell out a general theory of church-state relationships. He seems to have a specific kind of situation in mind. His Greek vocabulary (for instance, *diakonos* in v. 4 and *leitourgous* in v. 6) is the vocabulary of Hellenistic civil administration. The word translated by the New American Bible as "servant" in verse 4 and "ministers" in verse 6 describes the bearers of civil power with whom the common, ordinary person comes into daily contact. Behind these stand the regional or central administration. His argument is that God ordered all of creation and expects order in the political community as well. Thus his imperative "Do what is good . . . right" means be sure your political conduct is right, proper, fit. The assumption, of course, is that rulers are working for the common good of the subjects (v. 4). To highlight the assumption, three times in the passage Paul highlights the delegated nature of political, civil authority (13:1, 4, 6).

There are two reasons for obeying: to avoid punishment and for the sake of conscience. But Paul's understanding of conscience is not an interior voice independently telling us what is right and wrong, good and bad. The Greek word literally means a knowledge with others, that is, individualized common knowledge and common sense. In first-century Palestine, the word describes a person's sensitivity to his public ego-image and the determination to align personal behavior and self-assessment with that public ego-image. His or her conscience is a sort of interiorization of what others say, do, and think about the person, since these others play the role of witness and judge. Their verdicts supply the grants of honor necessary for a meaningful, human existence.

Notice how on the one hand Paul tells us that he rejects the opinions of others (1 Cor 4:1-4), yet at other times he seeks approval from his significant others for what he does (1 Cor 9:1). Jesus, too, is a man of honor not acting "out of human respect" (Mark 12:14), yet nevertheless concerned about "who do you [people] say that I am" (Mark 8:27). Paul's advice is that one should obey the civil authorities because it's expected. What will the others say? The command to pay taxes merely specifies the general obligation: don't shame anyone to whom honor is due.

13:8-14 Duties to one another. The word "owe" (translated "due" in v. 7) links this passage with the preceding comments. The one thing we owe one another is love. This fulfills the Torah, no matter which of the 613 commandments deriving therefrom appeal to us. Paul sums them all up in the citation from Lev 19:17 about love of neighbor. It was very common among the rabbis as well as in the New Testament, but there is a significant difference, too. In Jewish understanding "neighbor" meant compatriot, kin. In the Jesus tradition neighbor has a much wider scope. Thus, if Jesus is the end of the period of the law (10:4), and his motive for redeeming us was love (8:35), this kind of love now becomes the norm for Christian conduct, and it replaces the Torah.

Finally, Paul concludes these reflections by drawing a notion from apocalyptic outlooks: *kairos,* time. With the death and resurrection of Christ, the *kairos,* the critical moment has arrived. The present moment has a pressing challenge. True to form, Paul phrases the challenge in honor and shame terms, urging, of course, the honorable path. The images of day and night, light and darkness, symbolize good and evil and reflect honor and shame.

Concretely, Paul presents a list of six shameful life-styles to be avoided. Again, they reflect the three zones of the biblical person: eating and drinking excesses (mouth-ears); sexual excess and lust (heart-eyes in the planning, hands-feet in the execution); quarrels and jealousy (mouth-ears and eyes-heart). The point is that each individual person must avoid, completely and entirely, every shameful life-style (as listed), but seek instead total and comprehensive honor, just like the honorable Jesus. Don't give in to unredeemed and misdirected living (flesh), but rather imitate the quality and direction of the life of Jesus.

14:1-12 Accept one another. Though some scholars have proposed that Paul is addressing his comments here to as many as five distinct and specific parties, factions, or groups in the Roman church, it seems more plausible to assume that Paul continues to keep uppermost in mind the Jewish-Christian minority in the Roman community (see introduction to Romans). Paul draws from his general missionary experience to address a recurrent pattern of behavior between various group-types. Perhaps he witnessed it most recently in Corinth (party strife, exclusive allegiance to Paul, Kephas, Apollos), from where he is writing this letter.

The group-types are described as strong in faith and weak in faith. The strong in faith believed themselves to have enlightened consciences, to be progressive. They threw around the slogan "Everything is lawful for me" (1 Cor 6:12) and may have been one of the specific targets of Paul's comment in Rom 12:3. They felt so liberated in Christ that they believed that everything goes. No restraints are necessary or desirable.

The weak in faith were scrupulous in particular observances, conservative, and still troubled with concepts of "clean" and "unclean." Paul mentions three particular concerns: they are vegetarians (vv. 2, 21); they drink no wine (v. 21); and they consider certain days important, perhaps lucky or unlucky from an astrological perspective (v. 6). No one has been able to identify this group with certitude. They do not seem to be Jews. Perhaps these practices and beliefs were retained from some kind of pre-Christian experience and background.

No matter. Paul has only one solution: mutual respect and acceptance. Give room for growth. Arguments, ridicule, judgment over these matters are forbidden.

God has accepted each person. Can we do less? Each individual acts in order to honor the Lord. We are each of us the Lord's and responsible to him. Since we all must be accountable to the Lord's judgment, how dare anyone anticipate that judgment now?

14:13-23 Peace and joy for everyone. It is important to realize that the main thrust of this passage is Paul's wish for all to enjoy justice, peace, and joy. No one should hinder or destroy that. If this point is lost sight of, the passage seems to contradict Paul's preaching.

No one should destroy the joy of another. Paul uses himself as an example. His firm conviction, rooted in nothing less than the authority of the Lord Jesus, is that nothing in itself is unclean. But there are individuals who cluster into groups which hold the opposite opinion. Paul says it would be wrong to impose his views on this group and ruin their peace. It may often be necessary—out of love, which replaced Torah for Christians—to relinquish one's legitimate claim of freedom for the sake of an individual or group that is weak in faith.

Paul's opinion is typical of other-directed (dyadic) personalities. In verse 20 he points out that it is wrong for a person to eat something if it specifically offends his conscience. Conscience, as explained before, is comparable to group pressure. And since Paul's hope is mutual peace, anything that disrupts that peace is wrong.

Accepting God's rule has little to do with eating and drinking, food and beverage. Rather the rule of God should cause all believers to live together in righteousness, in peaceful openness to all, and in joy that comes from standing in a posture of openhandedness in the presence of God. Whoever served Christ in this way wins friends and pleases God.

The Greek aorist tense in verse 21 suggests that the believer needs to make a fresh judgment on each occasion whether or not to live openly with the conviction personally held (whether to eat or drink this or that). The next verse urges the strong in faith to keep that clear conviction between self and God. The rule of peace, however, may require that a person forego that freedom in certain social contexts. The concluding beatitude sums it up well: Happy the one—whether strong or weak in faith—who has no misgivings about personal choices.

15:1-6 Follow the example of Christ. For the first time Paul now openly includes himself in his remarks to the strong in faith. He continues his call for forbearance, but adds a significant twist. The word translated "put up with" literally means "carry or help carry" the burdens of the weak. It is a call to the strong to be willing to experience self-denial for the sake of weak believers.

The challenge to the strong in faith is that they ought to build the community and its members up rather than tear it all down. Look to the example of the Messiah. Christ's sacrifice was motivated by love, and that should become an effective motive for all believers. The citation from Ps 69:10 about bearing the reproaches intended for God is addressed to the strong in faith, perhaps the Gentile-Christian majority at Rome, that they strive to put up with persecution or misunderstanding just as the persecuted psalmist did.

The doxology (perhaps the letter was read publicly at worship?) prays that God cause the recipients to become patient and not to be discouraged. May they learn to live together in harmony, to seek a common viewpoint by following the example of Jesus so that all may give glory to God together.

15:7-13 Final appeal for unity. With one more statement Paul urges mutual acceptance, perhaps acceptance of the majority Gentile Christians by the Jewish-Christian minority. Again Jesus the Messiah is the example for such a minority. Jesus became a servant for the Jews in order to show them that God is faithful to the promises he made to the patriarchs. If such a minority follows this example, they will give glory to God. The Gentiles give glory to God because of the mercy he showed them, a "no-people," a people not deserving mercy (see Rom 9:25).

Then summoning his rabbinical skills one more time, Paul strings pearls from the Torah (Deut 32:43), the Prophets (Isa 11:10), and the Writings (Ps 18:50 or 2 Sam 22:50, as well as Ps 117:1) to emphasize that the entire Jewish Scripture foretold that the Gentiles would become part of God's plan and join his chosen people. The concluding prayer repeats the hope for joy and peace for all (whether strong or weak in faith) and urges the Holy Spirit to give them hope that will continue to grow.

CONCLUSION

Rom 15:14-33

These concluding verses seem to reveal Paul's actual life situation while writing this letter. Perhaps his real motive emerges as well. He opens the section with diplomatic flattery (serving the technique of persuasion suggested in the introduction). Paul confesses his abiding conviction that the Romans are full of goodness (uprightness expressing itself in mutual openmindedness). He also recognizes that they are filled with complete knowledge, that is, insights into the meaning of salvation history. Therefore, they are perfectly capable of giving advice, correction, admonition to one another—as other-directed (dyadic) personalities are accustomed to doing.

But Paul has decided to write boldly in order to remind them of a tradition, taking courage for his boldness from the fact that God has graced him with the office of Apostle to the Gentiles. He sees his ministry as that of serving like a priest of the Messiah in preparing the Gentiles as a worthy offering to God. He has replaced slaughtered animals with a repentant people. And to the extent that he has done this in union with Christ, he is proud of this service for God and freely and openly boasts of it.

Indeed, he has been traveling and preaching from Jerusalem in territories around it, even to Illyria, working mighty deeds in virtue of the Spirit's power at work among those he meets. He remained in these regions because there were always new paths to cut, new lands to visit, and his guiding principle was never to build on the foundation laid by another. He personally preferred to lay fresh foundations for the faith.

But now that there are no more opportunities in the East, Paul turns his attention to the West. It will be possible for him to visit the Roman church on his way to Spain. He hopes that they will be able to spend some time together, and then he will be able to get to know them better personally. By saying that he trusts they will be able to send him on his way to Spain, Paul subtly hints that they might want to provide him with food, perhaps traveling companions familiar with the roads, some means of travel, and other necessities.

Before he can do that, however, there is a pressing matter to attend to. Paul must take a collection to the poor in Jerusalem. He did promise not to forget them (Gal 2:10). Indeed, just as the Jews have shared with Gentiles the fullness of spiritual blessing which had been promised and delivered to them, now the Gentiles ought to share in return a little of the material blessings in recompense. The exchange is not extraordinary. It is a normal transaction in the culture following the rule of balanced reciprocity.

Still Paul is uneasy about the trip. He describes it and its goal as a "struggle" (v. 30) and asks for prayers that he be "delivered from the disobedient in Judea," that is, either non-Christian Jews or Jews who oppose the gospel. Clearly, Paul was still not out of the woods in Jerusalem. So for the sake of the unity of the church, which was a major concern for him, Paul hopes to accomplish two things with this letter: (1) to rehearse the presentation he would make in Jerusalem and (2) to win to his support the Jewish-Christian minority in the Roman church. The very recent experience of this minority could help them appreciate Paul's plight.

In A.D. 49, Claudius, emperor of Rome, banned and exiled the Jews (and quite likely Jewish Christians) from Rome. When Claudius died five years later, some deportees returned to Rome, not only as a result of his death but also because his decree slipped into insignificance. Yet upon their return, they found themselves a minority in a predominantly Gentile-Christian church.

Writing this letter to the Romans not too long after the return of the deportees, Paul hopes that his pleas for unity, mutual tolerance, peace, and harmony would persuade the Jewish Christians there of the wisdom of such peaceful coexistence. He further hoped it would inspire them to urge their friends back in Jerusalem to give Paul a kind reception when he arrived with the collection.

Paul could not omit delivering the collection because he promised it. If he sent an intermediary, he could not be certain that the collection would not be attributed to another source. At the same time, he couldn't help wonder if his visit would only antagonize hostility in Jerusalem and jeopardize his own future plans. Perhaps he'd even meet his own death because of the still unsettled situation. Jewish-Christian support from Rome would be so helpful.

One can almost hear the sigh of relief with which Paul wrote the final part of his prayer: God willing, after I drop off the collection, I can come to see you with joy. Your company would refresh my spirit. And with one last tug at their help: May the God of *peace* be with you all. So be it.

PHOEBE COMMENDED

Rom 16:1-23

After reading more than one apparent conclusion in the last two chapters (for example, 15:30-33; 15:13; 15:6), it is probably not too surprising that the letter continues. Yet the tone of chapter 16 has raised questions among readers throughout history. Not many have ever doubted that Paul actually wrote these verses. The real question is: were they written to the Romans? Personal greetings to such a large number of people familiar to Paul in a church he neither founded nor yet visited prompts reasonable skepticism. True, these friends and acquaintances could well have moved to Rome. Some of these names, however, are more familiar in the context of the Ephesian church, suggesting that Paul wrote this letter to introduce Phoebe to the church at Ephesus. (One very early manuscript does not include this chapter, but rather has Rom 16:25-27 following immediately after Rom 15:33.) Current scholarship, however, accepts 16:1-23 as an integral and original part of Paul's letter to the Romans.

In antiquity, when communication was rather slow, and travel was difficult and dangerous, letters of recommendation were quite necessary as a person left a familiar place to visit an unfamiliar territory and people. This was especially true for women travelers.

Phoebe is identified as a "sister," another instance in which Paul continues to build extended-family relationships in the early church. She carries her own letter of recommendation (some scholars believe she carried the entire letter to the Romans to that community). Paul also identifies her as a minister (deaconess or auxiliary in the generic sense as in 2 Cor 3:6) in the church at Cenchrae, the eastern seaport of Corinth. The Apostle writes these lines on her behalf and urges that she be welcomed because she belongs to the Lord and because she has been of very special help to him and many of the church members.

Verses 3-16 send greetings to no less than twenty-eight acquaintances, each of whom most probably regularly gathers a group of believers in meeting. Thus, the circle of people to whom Paul actually introduces and recommends Phoebe is very wide indeed.

The first-mentioned couple is very well known and mentioned more than once in the New Testament. Prisca and Aquila were among the leading early missionaries in the Dispersion, that is, outside Palestine. Both had accepted Christianity prior to Paul's conversion. They began their missionary activity independently of Paul, but later consented to work in association with him.

Prisca and Aquila were Jewish Christians who moved to Corinth when Emperor Claudius banished their kind from Rome. At Corinth they engaged in tentmaking and extended hospitality to Paul when he first arrived (Acts 18:1-3).

In time they traveled with him to Ephesus where among others they instructed Apollos (Acts 18:26). To judge from 1 Cor 16:18, which Paul wrote from Ephesus, Prisca and Aquila led a group of Christians in a house-church, for this group sends greetings to the Corinthian church. Paul's greetings in Rom 16:5 to the house church of Prisca and Aquila seem to suggest they were still in Ephesus.

As a missionary couple, Prisca and Aquila seemed quite effective in the early days of Christianity. The wife in such a situation did not simply accompany her husband for moral support (consider the implication of 1 Cor 9:5), but had access to the women's quarters (a special word in Greek), which would not generally be accessible to men. This role played by Christian women in the formation of the first churches has rarely been paid sufficient attention.

Epaenetus, who is mentioned next, was the first convert in western Asia (with its gubernatorial seat at Ephesus). Paul honors him by affirming that through his conversion he consecrated the rest of Asia to Christ.

Andronicus and Junia (the second-named individual could be a woman) were early Jewish-Christian converts who either designated themselves as apostles or were deputized by some community. In any case they were recognized by Paul as eminent apostles, Christians who accepted the faith before Paul did.

The remaining names in verses 8-16 appear to be chiefly slave names. Yet the concluding comment is that all greet one another affectionately with a holy kiss. Paul's added observation that all the churches send greetings is again not only a statement of fact but also a further cementing of the bonds of fictive kinship Paul is eager to strengthen.

Verses 17-20 mark a sharp shift in tone that strongly contrasts with the rest of Romans. Paul warns against those who would destroy the unity of the community. Good teaching (mouth-ears) aligns well with the entire person (hands-feet and heart-eyes). But their teaching (smooth and flattering speech) serves rather their bellies (a distortion of the three zones or possibly a sarcastic reference to dietary narrowness). The God of peace will crush all disorder and dissension in the community (personified by Satan).

The writer of this letter, Tertius, adds his greetings to those of others—unknown to us except for Timothy. Erastus may have been the co-worker of Paul mentioned in Acts 19:22.

Some English translations (like the new NAB) omit a twenty-fourth verse. This is done because our most trustworthy and reliable ancient Greek texts do not contain the sentence "May the grace of our Lord Jesus Christ be with you all, amen," which was very likely added later by a scribe who was copying an original.

One might wonder why all this fuss over a sentence which is relatively harmless. It is neither blasphemous nor theologically inaccurate. The church, however, and its biblical scholars are very interested in determining as accurately as possible the "original" form of the Scripture as accepted and used by the early church, or perhaps even as written by the original author. Our problems are compounded enough by the fact that most of us have to rely on translations. Each translation is in some sense an interpretation. So we need all the help we can get. A reliable text is definitely the first requirement for serious reading and study of Scripture.

CONCLUDING DOXOLOGY

Rom 16:25-27

The final doxology is a glorious hymn of praise to God who alone can make believers firm and immovable in living out the good news Paul preaches. Whether authentically written by Paul or not (a matter of dispute), this doxology is a fitting conclusion to Romans.

1 CORINTHIANS

Mary Ann Getty

INTRODUCTION

If Paul can be compared to a maker of films, his average reader today is like the moviegoer who views only one or a couple of frames at a time. Sometimes we gather at liturgies or classes or study groups and review a passage or section from Paul to the Corinthians. We often feel inspired (for example, read 1 Cor 1:1-13), impressed (2 Cor 12:1-10), challenged (2 Cor 5:11-21), or perplexed and rebuffed (1 Cor 11:2-16; 14:34-35; 15:33-34). Such is the result of viewing the frames separately. Even the fact that each passage can speak to us so powerfully threatens to blur the whole picture which Paul and the Corinthians create. The more we can discover about the Apostle and the Corinthians, the better we can understand the message's relevance for us today who believe that somehow this correspondence contains God's revelation. We are fortunate, for no other New Testament document reveals so much about the writer and his addressees as Paul's correspondence with the Corinthians. We need to know at least a little about the city, the Apostle's experience at Corinth, the church there, and the purpose and occasion of these letters.

The city of Corinth

At the time Paul wrote these letters (about 56–58 C.E.), Corinth was probably the leading Greek city, its rival, Athens, having declined in political and economic importance. Situated on the narrow isthmus joining the Greek mainland to the Peloponnesus, Corinth was a gateway between the East and the West. This city played a significant role in Greek history and in the whole Mediterranean world of the first century. Paul went to Corinth around 51 C.E. during the course of his second missionary journey. There it was that Paul seems to have realized the implications of concentrating on the Greeks in order to win the Jews. Corinth was a remarkably apt testing ground to establish the validity of this mission.

Corinth, the capital of the Roman province Achaia, exhibited all the tough features of an important city of commerce whose population was mixed and mobile. Jews came there from east and west to find a home. Some were displaced by the Emperor Claudius' punitive expulsion of all Jews from Rome because there had been riots among them over a certain "Chrestus," which is probably a mistaken reference for Christ (see Acts 18:1-3). Many Jews had gone to Corinth from Palestine, some no doubt as slaves, others in search of a livelihood, attracted by the commercial possibilities of the city.

As a leading Greek city reestablished by the Romans under Julius Caesar in 49 B.C.E. Corinth had all the best and the worst of a vital, throbbing pagan capital. The high ideals of Greek civilization challenged citizens of Corinth to a certain spirituality, asceticism, and cultivation of the aesthetic. The worst in pagan vices was nourished by the Greeks' scorn of the physical, a scorn that had given birth to such apparent opposite extremes as hedonism and stoicism. Economic and political growth did not necessarily promote ethical development. The Corinthians' reputation for licentiousness was well known. Religious syncretism provided the melting pot for Jewish, Roman, and Greek practices that tended to boil down the precious and leave a residue of counterfeit alloys.

The Apostle at Corinth

Paul is reported to have stayed in Corinth longer (eighteen months according to Luke in Acts 18:11) than in any other place he evangelized. His relationship to the Corinthians was as an artisan-preacher rather than an itinerant. Simply put, he lived and worked among the Corinthians and his whole apostolic relationship as reflected in the correspondence with them is characterized by all the features of a day-in, day-out rapport, shared experiences such as require time, complete with intimacies, strains, disappointments.

According to Luke, Paul in Corinth first tried to evangelize the Jewish population, teaching in the synagogue and enjoying a modicum of success (Acts 18:1-4). He lived and worked with Aquila and Priscilla, his Jewish-Christian friends who were part of his missionary team there. After being continually assaulted by the Jews (Acts 18:5-6, 12-17), Paul reviewed his priorities. He stopped concentrating on the Jews and focused on the Gentile mission for which he was affirmed by a vision of the Lord (18:7-10). Later Apollos himself preached in Corinth. Apollos' eloquence (18:24) contrasted with Paul's having come to the Corinthians "in weakness and fear, and with much trepidation" (1 Cor 2:3). The Corinthians, impressed by this eloquence, became disaffected with Paul. If perhaps there existed a certain amount of human rivalry between Paul and Apollos, there certainly was some overt competition among their followers. And then some of the disciples of the other apostles joined in, so that it was hard to see the unity of the Corinthians for the disparate groups who clustered around the various apostles.

Paul's reaction to such rivalry is characteristically strong. Even if he were not an apostle to anyone else, he is indisputably the apostle to the Corinthians (9:2), and none of their false notions about the superiority of others can alter this fact (see 9:1-18; 2 Cor 10:1–13:21). His authority lies in the very fact of the existence of the Corinthian community. He knows these people. They are entitled to their opinions about him, but he insists on their unity. He is firm and forceful. Yet he is also kind and pastoral. He certainly has his own opinion about how they should live, but he will not impose arbitrary regulations on them. He will only call them to the unity mandated by the gospel.

About this unity, Paul is adamant. It is not hard to guess reasons for the urgency in his tone. Undoubtedly he was not the only one interested in monitoring the success of the Corinthian mission. Those who had been sent by James to authenticate the Galatian mission, for example, would have found the Corinthian disorders much more potentially damaging to Paul (see Gal 2:12; also 2:4).

The church at Corinth

A Christian group existed in Corinth before Paul came to share their life. Aquila and Prisca were prominent members of that community and already exercised some leadership (Acts 18:2-3). It was this couple who completed the instruction of Apollos after Paul had left for Ephesus (18:24-28).

The church at Corinth seems to have been composed of Christians of both Jewish and Greek origin. Paul frequently uses scriptural references in such a way that familiarity with the texts is taken for granted (see, for example, 1 Cor 10:1-10). Roots in Judaism probably contributed to the scandal that resulted in the eating of idol-meats by some and the controversy over whether women could conduct liturgical service and the appropriate dress and conduct at the liturgy (11:2-34). The influence of paganism, on the other hand, is evident in almost every issue. Paul, who had a hard enough time convincing the Jewish authorities that the mission of the Gentiles was valid and that the Gentiles received and lived the same gospel as the Jews, would have been understandably concerned about the impact of the Corinthian situation not only on his other missions but also on his reputation and credibility among the Jewish Christians. Consistently he preaches unity, but rarely is Paul's message so threatened by misunderstanding and division as it is in Corinth.

For such a complex church, summary is always dangerous. But if we were to risk the danger, we might characterize the Corinthian Christians as "enthusiasts." Although they were zealous, they lacked depth. They were so drawn to certain ministers that they felt justified in outdoing each other to prove their allegiance. They believed so strongly in the spiritual life that they underestimated even their own physical needs or the vulnerability of their young community. They were so zealous for the sacraments and for the spiritual gifts which they admired that they overlooked the most spiritual of all, charity, the one they all received, which could heal their divisions. Vaguely they were aware that their beliefs should be reflected in practice, but they practiced the wrong things, fluctuating between the extremes of asceticism on the one hand and indifference to the seductions of the world on the other. Their misguided zeal had to be tempered and rechanneled, but not abolished. They had to learn the primacy of charity in their relationships with each other and the consequent subordination of what they ate, what they put on at liturgies, or what gifts they possessed. They had to be encouraged to contribute to the support of the saints of Jerusalem, who were suffering a famine, and this support takes on a great symbolic value as Paul links it to the success and acceptance of the entire Gentile mission (Rom 15:25-27).

The letters to Corinth

There is something many people find generally very fascinating about letters. Even though they may represent only one side of a dialogue, many levels of disclosure can be found in letters between people, leaving much that appeals to the imagination. There is, of course, the self-disclosure of the author. In Corinthians we learn more about Paul from Paul than in any other New Testament work. In Corinthians we can even hear how Paul feels. This implies that by the process of identification we can, from studying Corinthians, learn something also about ourselves as we reflect on Paul's example of what it means to be a preacher and minister of the gospel. We also learn much about the lovable and difficult Corinthians whose experience of Christianity is so pertinent to our own. Theirs, like ours, was no simple reading of the gospel. How they seem to have needed to refine their understanding so that their intellectualizing would not inhibit their incarnating the gospel's message! Paul's tone is firm but compassionate, intimate and challenging, authoritative but not dogmatic. Whether admonishing or cajoling, defending or persuading or correcting, he shows himself as warm and caring toward a community he understands very well.

Paul wrote to the Corinthians from Ephesus. Taken together, the letters we have give a movie-like glimpse into the never dull life of the Paul-Corinthian relationship. The whole is more than the sum of the parts we have to study. At times the strong tone of the letters gives hope that the picture will eventually become very clear. The sequence of the frames, however, threatens to jeopardize the impact of the whole story. We seem to have two letters, but clearly there must have been more. And the order of those we have is jumbled. Finally, never one for oversystematization, even in the most objective of circumstances, Paul seems to invent his own "structure" as he writes this running dialogue with the Corinthians. We need to consider briefly the tone, the number, and the literary characteristics of the overall correspondence of Paul with the Corinthians.

Internal evidence indicates that there were more than two letters to the Corinthians. There must have been a letter before our extant 1 Corinthians. Paul refers to this "precanonical," now lost letter in 1 Cor 5:9-13; this seems to have been Paul's first written response to the Corinthians' questions about how to survive as Christians in an alien environment. Later, "Chloe's people" (1:11) brought the Apostle news of some disquieting disorders among the Corinthians. Perhaps these messengers also brought to Paul a letter (see 7:1) from the Corinthians with some questions about life within the community. Yet no part of 1 Corinthians, however strong, seems to fit the description of the "tearful letter" Paul alludes to in 2 Cor 2:1-4, which he said he previously wrote. This could refer to 2 Cor 10–13 or yet another letter which is also lost. Many interpreters note the detachable character of 2 Cor 10:1–13:9 and the two conclusions in 9:15 and 13:1-13. Further still, 2 Cor 8 and 2 Cor 9 appear as repetitious exhortations about the collection for Jerusalem, as if these reminders were originally self-contained, independent notes on this topic. In other words, what appear as two letters in our Bibles are the remnants of an ongoing dialogue contained in several letters between Paul and the Corinthians. The fact that these were preserved by the community means that they were valued, and probably read and reflected upon frequently whenever the Corinthians met to deepen their faith and their community life.

Our appetite for appreciating Paul is whetted. We are encouraged to lay aside any inhibiting preconceptions to permit ourselves to see a pastor and his people at work integrating the gospel in their lives. We need not be put off by the fact that the originators of these works lived thousands of years ago. Here are sincere people like ourselves in many ways, struggling to live Christian lives with integrity in a complex world. Far from being the egocentric chauvinist he is sometimes portrayed as being, Paul presents himself as vulnerable, compassionate, caring, strong, convincing. Taken seriously, his invitation to "imitate me as I imitate Christ" (1 Cor 11:1) shows truly remarkable transparency which arrogant people are not usually capable of. And considered to be literally true, his reminder that these things "have been written as a warning to us, upon whom the end of the ages has come" (1 Cor 10:11), is challenge, encouragement, and cause for gratitude to both Paul and the Corinthians who go before us. They give us a model—not pat answers to our twentieth-century problems, but a kind of living legacy witnessing to our common call to be true to the gospel.

The occasion, message, and characteristics of First Corinthians

The city before Paul's preaching presents no simple profile. Worldly, successful, sophisticated, Corinth has all the accoutrements of the best and the worst of worlds. Any religion would have had a hard time being taken seriously there. This is especially true of Christianity as preached by a suspect Jewish convert who felt called to the Gentiles, and who hoped, as a result of this mission, that his fellow Jews would become jealous and themselves accept the gospel of Jesus Christ (see Rom 11:25-32). Already impeded by the hardness of the Corinthian shell, Paul seemed weak in appearance (see 2 Cor 10:10) and eloquence (1 Cor 2:1-5), preaching the good news which had as its sole recommendation the message of the cross, its only wisdom (1 Cor 1:17–2:16). Smitten by Greek philosophical trends, the more spiritually minded Corinthians might have found the tension between the flesh and the spirit which was part of Paul's preaching intellectually acceptable, but for the wrong reasons. Raised on a body-soul dichotomy that was part of the Greek world view, the Corinthians had great difficulty understanding Paul's Semitic perspective. That perspective treated the entire human person from the viewpoint of the body or from the viewpoint of the spirit; either could express the whole person who could not be divided into only one or the other, body *or* spirit. But the Greek viewpoint that influenced the Corinthians was more dualistic. It tended to separate the body and the spirit, claiming superiority for the latter while neglecting the physical. This provided a basis for the Corinthians to create and tolerate a dichotomy between their beliefs and their conduct (for example, 1 Cor 5:1-11). Paul is eager to refute such a gross misunderstanding of his gospel.

This misinterpretation was part of the root cause of the divisions within the Corinthian community. It reinforced the elitist-separatist tendencies that spawned factions based on allegiance to different ministers (1:10-17; 3:1–4:21), on celibate versus married lifestyles (7:1-40), on the dietary practices of the weak contrasted with those of the strong (8:1-13; 10:23-30), the ostracizing of the poor (11:17-34), or on competition for popularly coveted gifts (12:1-31; 14:1-40). Scorn for the body and all things physical likewise produced misunderstanding and even mockery of belief in the resurrection of the body (15:1-58), and, on the other hand, a smug acceptance of certain extremely basic taboos, including incest (5:1-11). Paul has to show the Corinthians that such disorders as suing other Christians (6:1-11), judging the authority of apostles on the basis of externals (9:1-27), downplaying sexual differences (11:2-16) or complacency in possession of the sacraments (10:1-22; 11:17-34), are inconsistent with the real understanding of the gospel message, which has the cross at its center and limitless mutual charity as its measure of authentic expression.

The eighteen months Paul spent living among the Corinthian Christians seems to have done little to alleviate the fear and trepidation (1 Cor 2:3) he experienced when he first came to them. The disquieting if not alarming reports he received from Chloe's people (see 1:11) and the fundamental questions of the Corinthians themselves betrayed insidious divisions and confusions and probably confirmed Paul's fears. Writing First Corinthians from Ephesus during his third missionary journey (ca. 56–57), Paul seems to alternate between pleading and indignation as he tries to introduce some sanity and balance into the contorted Corinthian version of Christianity.

The structure of First Corinthians, compared to Second Corinthians, is relatively simple. In the first part Paul responds forcefully to the reports he has about the divisions in Corinth (1:10–6:20). For him the most absurd divisions are those based on exclusive devotion to the various leaders, devotion that pits one apostle against another, creating chaos of the divided leadership and misplaced fellowship. Paul could hardly be more adamant in his rejection of this abuse, which he sees as a form of idolatry that confuses ministers with the one Lord (1:10–4:21). The immaturity of the Corinthians' faith is evident in the wedge they have driven between their faith and their behavior (5:1–6:20). Paul cites the most blatant examples of their lack of moral authority (5:1-13), their inability to settle disputes among themselves (6:1-11), and their succumbing to the temptation to return to pagan ways (6:12-20; see 10:14-22). Paul's reaction to these reports is stern and demanding.

The second part of this letter consists of Paul's responses to the Corinthians' questions relayed to him by messengers. Paul does not abandon his adamant tone. The questions are related to the Corinthians' struggle to live a credible Christianity. They include issues regarding social status (7:1-40), problems that arise from trying to live as a Christian with integrity within a pagan environment (8:1–11:1), and internal conflicts related to liturgical celebrations (11:2–14:40). It is not certain whether questions concerning the resurrection were actually addressed to Paul by the Corinthians or if the Apostle identified this as the basic misunderstanding that seems to have spawned all their other difficulties. In any case, since the Corinthians display in their many problems a fundamental lack of appreciation for the body, Paul concludes this letter with a presentation of the resurrection as the basis of faith (see 15:1-58).

These two main parts of the letter are enveloped by the customary introductory and concluding sections. Three further elements, characteristic of Paul's style generally, help to clarify the structure and development of the Corinthian correspondence. These three elements are the indicative-imperative method of presenting content, the so-called ABA' schema Paul frequently uses to develop his thoughts, and Paul's adoption of his addressees' own positions in order to correct and admonish them.

One of Paul's most used pedagogical tools is the indicative-imperative schema which underlies his message. This means that Paul's reaction to the disorders and his responses to the Corinthians' questions proceed from certain basic premises. These premises are based on Paul's understanding of the nature of Christian life which itself flows from Christ's action on the cross. For Paul, the gospel is the fundamental reality which provides the measurement for all other reality. Factions in Corinth, for example, should not exist because in Christ all are one. Unity, signified in baptism and in the Eucharist, enables Christians to overcome all their differences. Paul approached the question of how the Corinthians should act by means of his description of the new creation they have become in Christ (see 2 Cor 5:17-20).

A second general remark about the structure of the correspondence with the Corinthians can help us to thread together the sequential frames of Paul's movie. Throughout, Paul uses the ABA' schema, whereby he introduces a subject (A), interrupts discussion of it with another topic (B), and then returns to the initial subject (A'). While this may seem confusing at times, awareness of its purpose and frequency helps us become less distracted by Paul's method and more able to grasp the implications of his whole perspective. So, for instance, in the middle of a discussion of the relationship between the weak and the strong (1 Cor 8:7-13 and 10:23-30), Paul defends his apostleship, pointing out that his own example shows how the Corinthians must be all things to all people (9:1-27). Similarly, he describes the way of love "which surpasses all the others" (1 Cor 13) to make his point about the destructiveness of competition for spiritual gifts (12:1-30; 14:1-40). Especially First Corinthians is full of examples of this ABA' schema at work. We will make specific reference to how it affects and enhances Paul's development as we work through these letters.

In a variety of ways Paul demonstrates the truth of his statement, "To the Jews I became like a Jew to win over Jews . . . . To those outside the law I became like one outside the law . . . . I have become all things to all, to save at least some" (1 Cor 9:20-22). In both 1 and 2 Corinthians Paul frequently quotes the Corinthians themselves (for example, in 1 Cor 8:1: "All of us have knowledge") as if anticipating their challenges based on his real knowledge of them and of the ways they think. These "quotes" help Paul move the argument forward even while he eliminates his addressees' objections. They also provide a way for Paul to identify with the Corinthians without agreeing with their conclusions and while trying to correct or modify their positions. Similarly Paul sometimes betrays his own agreement with the strong, his own ability to speak in tongues, his own preference for celibacy. Paul likewise regularly draws on Old Testament and Jewish images, linking his religious experience and tradition to that of the Corinthians. Yet Paul also draws on athletic imagery and other experiences more at home in a non-Jewish milieu. Thus he is able to describe the church as a body with many members, and Christians together as a new creation, a society never before known but now visible and active in the real world and developing a rich common tradition.

OUTLINE OF FIRST CORINTHIANS

1:1-9	I. INTRODUCTION: ADDRESS
1:1-3	Greeting
1:4-9	Thanksgiving
1:10-6:20	II. REPORTED DISORDERS IN THE CORINTHIAN COMMUNITY
1:10-4:21	A. Divisions in the Church
1:10-17	Groups and slogans
1:18-2:5	The message of the gospel
1:18-25	The paradox of the cross
1:26-31	The experience of the Corinthians
2:1-5	The illustration of Paul's preaching
2:6-4:21	True and false wisdom
2:6-16	True wisdom as spiritual maturity
3:1-4	The immaturity of the Corinthians
3:5-4:5	The role of the apostle
4:6-21	The true evaluation of an apostle
5:1-6:20	B. Other Examples of the Corinthians' Immaturity: Moral Disorders
5:1-13	A case of incest
6:1-11	Lawsuits before unbelievers
6:12-20	The idolatry of sexual sins
7:1-11:1	III. ANSWERS TO THE CORINTHIANS' QUESTIONS
7:1-40	A. Questions Concerning Social Status
7:1-16	Advice concerning marriage
7:17-24	Against change in believers' social status
7:25-40	On virgins, widows, married life
8:1-11:1	B. Struggles Within a Pagan Environment
8:1-13	The idolatry of knowledge
9:1-10:22	Principles of Christian behavior
9:1-27	The example of Paul
9:1-18	Paul's rights
9:19-23	Paul's freedom to serve all
9:24-27	Zeal for the gospel and renunciation
10:1-22	Caution against complacency
10:1-13	The lesson of Israel
10:14-22	Participation at sacrificial banquets
10:23-11:1	Seek the good of others
11:2-14:40	IV. PROBLEMS IN LITURGICAL ASSEMBLIES
11:2-16	A. Liturgical Dress and Behavior
11:17-34	B. Celebration of the Lord's Supper
11:17-22	Reported abuses
11:23-27	Tradition of the institution
11:28-34	Practical recommendations for healing the body
12:1-14:40	C. Spiritual Gifts and the Community
12:1-11	The Spirit's gifts
12:12-31	The analogy of the body
13:1-13	Love, the more excellent way
14:1-5	Prophecy, a most desirable gift
14:6-19	A comparison of gifts
14:20-25	Another measure of the Corinthians' immaturity
14:26-40	Some rules for order
15:1-58	V. THE RESURRECTION
15:1-11	A. The Resurrection of Christ
15:12-34	B. The Resurrection of the Dead
15:12-19	The absurdity of the Corinthians' denial

15:20-28 Paul's alternative
15:29-34 The Corinthians' ignorance attacked
15:35-58 C. The Manner of the Resurrection
15:35-49 The reality of the resurrection
15:50-58 The resurrection as a mystery of faith
16:1-24 VI. Conclusion
16:1-4 The collection
16:5-12 Paul's plans
16:13-24 Directions and greetings

COMMENTARY

I. INTRODUCTION

1 Cor 1:1-9

1:1-3 Greeting. According to the ancient form of letters, authors begin by identifying themselves. Paul follows this custom, naming himself and Sosthenes as the senders of this letter to the Corinthians. Paul's description of himself is brief. He is called by God's will (see Gal 1:15-16). He is an apostle, that is, "one who is sent." As such, Paul represents the One who sends him. Although his authority is challenged, Paul adamantly defends it. It is Paul, rather than one of the Twelve or any of the eyewitnesses to Jesus' life, who first coined the word "apostle" and fashioned it for Christian use.

Paul's vocation is also a mission that is far from being merely an interior, purely personal, individual call. His response is lived in active service of Jesus Christ whose slave he has become (see Rom 1:1; Gal 1:10). Paul's use of "slave" gives that term a kind of honor it did not ordinarily connote. Jesus Christ is almost synonymous with the gospel Paul preaches. Paul has been "grasped" by Christ (Phil 3:12). He pledges absolute, total commitment to Jesus, who changed his life and now not only influences him strongly but becomes Paul's point of identification.

Sosthenes, a "brother," joins Paul in greeting the church at Corinth. A Sosthenes, described as a leader of the synagogue in Corinth, was beaten before the proconsul by the Jews who had first accused Paul and had not been given satisfaction (Acts 18:12-17). It is not certain from Acts whether this man became a Christian or if his punishment had any direct relationship to the accusations brought against Paul. In any case, this was a common name, and Paul's lack of further description implies that he was well known to the Corinthians. The Sosthenes of 1 Cor 1:1 was, of course, a Christian, a "brother," since Christians become kin to one another, sharing through faith a fellowship that compares in depth with family ties.

Paul greets the "church of God . . . in Corinth" (1:2). Drawing on some Old Testament images, Paul suggests already in these opening verses two ideas which will undergird his instructions to the Corinthians throughout this lengthy epistle: their holiness is based on their common call and their unity under the same Lord. Like Israel, the church is a holy people (Exod 19:6). Consecrated in Christ Jesus, the Corinthians rank with "all those everywhere" who call on the Lord (see Joel 3:5), that is, with all the baptized. The fact that they recognize the same Lord means that Christians everywhere are indebted to one another. (See Paul's self-description in Rom 1:14-15; his description of the debt which links the pagans and the Jerusalem Christians is in Rom 15:26-27.)

Characteristically, Paul bids his readers grace and peace (Rom 1:7; 2 Cor 1:2; Gal 1:3; Phil 1:2; 1 Thess 1:1; 2 Thess 1:2; Phlm 3). These gifts summarize the messianic blessings bestowed in Christ. Paul brings together the usual greeting among the Greeks, *charis* (i.e., grace) and that used by the Jews, *shalom,* reflecting the unity of all those who profess to believe in the one Father and in the one Lord. By addressing such a difficult community in this positive way, Paul exemplifies the manner in which the preacher must challenge Christians to possess their legitimate inheritance.

1:4-9 Thanksgiving. The greeting leads Paul to express thanks. Some form of initial thanksgiving is another trace of the ancient custom Paul follows. Yet, normally authors of letters begin by expressing thanks for their own health or well-being, using the occasion, perhaps, to inform readers about their latest accomplishments. Paul, however, gives thanks not for himself but for the Corinthians and for the grace they have received. Paul acknowledges that the Corinthians have been "enriched in every way." But this letter, written in answer to their questions and because of reports Paul has heard, makes it painfully clear that the very gifts they have received, especially the gifts of "all discourse and all knowledge," which they prize so much, are the basis of the divisions that trouble them. Paul reminds the Corinthians that all gifts come from the same Lord (see 12:5).

The community is the credential of Paul's apostolate, living evidence that the gospel has been preached and heard by them (see 9:2). It is not gifts that are lacking. But the gifts' misuse by the Corinthians does not indicate the proper attitude of those waiting for "the revelation of our Lord Jesus Christ." At his coming, the Corinthians will be called to account for how their gifts have nourished love among them.

Paul's prayers are "eucharistic" (that is, a thanksgiving) because they are based on confidence in God, who will assuredly finish the good work already begun. God is steadfast and trustworthy. This is why Paul offers such effusive thanks, despite his realistic outlook on the very serious nature of the church's problems at Corinth. Paul's own testimony to God's fidelity has been received by the Corinthians. They have experienced the grace of the gospel as promise that God will not abandon them. Despite their problems, Paul expresses grateful confidence that they will be strengthened and ultimately judged victorious.

II. REPORTED DISORDERS IN THE CORINTHIAN COMMUNITY

1 Cor 1:10–6:20

The divisions among the Corinthians are the main threat to the gospel. Apparently the Corinthians had their own set of questions they wished Paul to answer (see 7:1). But first the Apostle gives his reaction to the gross disorders reported to him. He attacks the rival groups who oppose one leader to another (1:10–4:21). He shows how these factions betray the Corinthians' grasp of true wisdom. Then he proceeds to list other examples of the Corinthians' spiritual immaturity (5:1–6:20).

A. Divisions in the Church (1:10–4:21)

Christian life is based on the message of the cross. This message is contained in the gospel Paul preaches, which is the only true wisdom. There is only one gospel and its wisdom must unite rather than divide. Its acceptance is signified by baptism. The very fact that there is dissension among the Corinthians surrounding the very symbol of unity betrays the Corinthians' immaturity. Paul cannot be indifferent to such divisions, since they threaten the basis of the gospel he preaches. He deplores the dissensions (1:10-17), presents the paradox of the cross as true wisdom (1:18–2:5), and then distinguishes the lesson of the cross from the false wisdom of the Corinthians (2:6–4:21).

1:10-17 Groups and slogans. The divisions among the Christians at Corinth belie the purpose of their common baptism. "I urge that all of you agree . . . ," Paul begins his instruction in this letter. Using many examples, he will not really say anything more important or complex than this. Paraphrased, he insists that since they are one in baptism, diversity among them must be an expression of community which signifies the action of the Spirit among them.

Paul launches into his main concern, which centers on the news he heard from "Chloe's people" (1:11) about the dissension among the Corinthians. Nothing is known about this woman herself, but she is obviously a leader of the church, well acquainted with the Corinthians, with unquestionable reliability. The early Christian groups often took their name from the heads of the households in which they met. Chloe might well have been engaged in commerce with associates who traveled between Corinth and Ephesus, where Paul was when he wrote Corinthians. Reports from her to Paul described cliques among the Corinthians. Some identified themselves as followers of Paul; others favored the more dazzling eloquence of Apollos. Then there were some who championed Kephas (as Paul prefers to call Peter; but see Gal 2:7-8). And, finally, there seem to have been those who outdid all the rest in their claims of simply being for Christ. But all, through baptism, become members of one body (12:12-30). To Paul it is inconceivable that Christians be divided, least of all on the basis of who baptized them. Some not only asserted the superiority of the one who baptized them but even seemed to assess their own importance in relation to this alleged superiority.

Yet in Christ, in whom they were baptized, Christians have more than a model. More than just giving them an example to be followed, Christ empowers Christians to be "of the same mind, with the same love, united in heart, thinking one thing" (see Phil 2:1-2). It is not the one who baptizes but Christ who, in being crucified for all, unifies all.

The role of the apostle, as Paul describes it, is to create, form, and maintain community in dynamic relationship with Christians everywhere. It is not part of Paul's call as an apostle that he baptize, and for this he is grateful (1 Cor 1:14, 17). But Paul recommends the example of one he did baptize, Stephanas, who heads a house-church and is probably one of those who had brought messages to Paul from the Corinthians (see 16:14, 17). With a tone of urgency, Paul admonishes the Corinthians to repair the damage to the community caused by such dissension and conflict. Baptism is the outcome of the preaching of the gospel which brings all into the community of the sanctified. He begs the Corinthians to come to their senses, to embrace the wisdom of the gospel, lest the union the cross signifies be emptied of its meaning.

The message of the gospel (1:18–2:5)

God's power, which is stronger than any human power, teaches the wisdom of the gospel. This, Paul shows, is the message of the cross (1:18-25), verified in the experience of the Corinthians (1:26-31) and illustrated in their acceptance of Paul's own preaching to them (2:1-5).

1:18-25 The paradox of the cross. The gospel Paul preaches is the power of God (see 1:18; Rom 1:16-17). The gospel is not like any other truth human wisdom can discover. Indeed, human wisdom can obscure the truth of the cross of Christ. The cross *is* the gospel.

The cross divides humankind into two parts, into those who reject it, who are on their way to perdition, and those who accept its message and are experiencing the power of God. In this sense, the cross is the judgment of God. The cross is also the fulfillment of Isaiah's warning that God reverses the wisdom of the world (Isa 29:14).

Suffering, the message of the cross, is certainly one of the greatest human mysteries. This mystery, expressed in Jesus' passion, is at the center of the gospel preaching. Such preaching rejects two obvious "answers" which make suffering comprehensible, and therefore somewhat acceptable, to human wisdom. These options are either that suffering is punishment for sin or that, in its absurdity, innocent suffering reveals an unjust God. These are the options of the unjust. Both of these possibilities are defied by the mystery of the cross whereby Jesus, the innocent Just One, did not break faith with God.

Since the cross does not follow human reason, it is an obstacle, a scandal, a stumbling block for both the Jews who expect signs and for the Greeks who look for wisdom. Such expectations blind them so that they cannot see what comes to them, but stumble instead against the "scandal" in their path (see Rom 10:1-2). Conventional wisdom, in the light of the gospel, becomes foolishness: "Whoever would save his life will lose it" (Mark 8:35). And the folly of the cross that confounds the wise, empowers the foolish for salvation. Paul describes himself and those who are in Christ as "fools" and "weak" on Christ's account, and for the sake of the community (1 Cor 4:10).

But belief in Jesus is regarded by the gospel Paul preaches as the greatest wisdom. God's folly is wiser than all human wisdom. Not only is the "weakness" of God more powerful than all human strength, but God's strength supplies for all human weakness. (Paul uses a metaphor here because, of course, God is in no sense "weak.") Paul had experienced the truth of this in his own flesh when he begged God to remove from him the thorn that afflicted him and learned the lesson: "My grace is enough for you, for in weakness power reaches perfection" (2 Cor 12:9). Jesus' disciples learned this lesson when they, despairing of being able to achieve salvation, heard Jesus' word: "For human beings this is impossible; but for God all things are possible" (Matt 19:26).

1:26-31 The experience of the Corinthians. Paul returns to the subject of the divisions he described in 1:10-17, excluding competition and divisions on the grounds of the Corinthians' own experience of the gospel. If only the worldly wise and the worldly powerful were to be the receivers of wisdom, Paul argues, you yourselves would never be included. Paul's point is not simply to insult the Corinthians or to make them humble (see 4:14-17). He tries, rather, to show that the Jewish and the Greek conclusions are erroneous because their premise and their boasts before God are absurd (1:28-29).

Paul challenges the members of the Corinthian community to reflect on their own history. Their world exalts the wise, the influential, the highborn. But the Corinthians do not number among these. Indeed, they were called by God, but not because they had anything to recommend them. As a matter of fact, they were mocked by the world, considered unworthy and insincere by religious people, probably even by the more mature and rooted Jewish Christians. They were suspect even by many Christian authorities. Some of them were even considered "weak" by members of their own Christian community (see 8:7-13; 10:23-30). Paul implies that they may be tempted to aspire to acceptance by the world and by other, more settled communities. Yet, he reminds his kin in the faith, God has already begun in them the good work of confounding the strong in order to reveal the foolishness of boastful pride before God. In giving us life, wisdom, justice, sanctification, redemption, God willed that these become ours in Christ Jesus, who eliminates all individual and divisive boasts.

2:1-5 The illustration of Paul's preaching. Paul personally exemplifies the idea of 1:17: "Christ [sent me] . . . to preach the gospel—not with the wisdom of human eloquence . . . ." Paul's own weakness is evidence that what he preaches is the power of God. From the perspective of worldly standards, Paul's mission should be a failure. He cannot rely on what the world values or commends. He is plagued by illness (2 Cor 12:7), his appearance is unimpressive (2 Cor 10:10), his personal delivery weak (1 Cor 2:5). Yet the very existence of the community at Corinth is a powerful argument for the presence of the Spirit, since only the Spirit can create community (see 9:2; 12:1-3). Thus, Paul continues to draw gospel conclusions that defy the human limitations of his own or the Corinthians' experience. A clear result is that faith is built not on the merits of either members or minister, but on the power of God.

True and false wisdom (2:6–4:21)

The gospel shows the difference between worldly or false standards of wisdom and the true wisdom that measures spiritual maturity (2:6-16). The Corinthians, in their immaturity (3:1-4), fail to recognize the true role of the apostle (3:5–4:5) or to employ tools adequate to the true evaluation of an apostle (4:6-21).

2:6-16 True wisdom as spiritual maturity. Paul does not deny that the gospel is wisdom, but he argues that it is a different kind of wisdom than the world understands, one which the world does not recognize. The Gentile Christians at Corinth were tempted by many forms of worldly wisdom. It is difficult to identify precisely which expression or form Paul opposes in 2:6-16 to the real wisdom he describes in 3:1-4. It was probably some form of logic such as was taught by Philo, the Alexandrian philosopher (died ca. 50 C.E.) who attempted to translate Jewish teachings into philosophical categories. Greek philosophy generally held that the spiritual was superior in every way to the physical (see p. 1103). All that pertained to the body could and perhaps even should be ignored. The material is irrelevant. Ethics was often ignored, while what one could grasp with the mind was considered to be of sole importance. Paul is against spiritual elitism because it moves away from everyday Christian life led in the body. Paul warns that such "wisdom," which he characterizes as of this world, breeds division, jealousy, competition. The Corinthians pursued a kind of enlightenment that would give them superiority over those who were considered merely infants. The "rulers of this age" used such ideas to maintain power over others, and even to put Jesus to death (2:8; see Luke 22:25).

But, says Paul, only the Spirit of God can plumb the depths of God and only the truly spiritual person can receive the revelation of God. God's is a revelation summed up in the wisdom of the cross. This is a revelation that changes the criteria for judgment, enabling us to put on the mind of Christ (2:16; see Phil 2:5).

3:1-4 The immaturity of the Corinthians. After describing what God's wisdom is not (2:6-16), Paul goes on to say what it is in 3:1-4. Yet, from the perspective of true spiritual wisdom, the Corinthians, especially those who use worldly standards as a measurement of worth, are themselves "infants." The barriers they erect and justify convict them of spiritual immaturity. Although they are in Christ, they have not yet been able to absorb anything beyond food appropriate for infants. Their behavior shows that they have not yet understood the wisdom of the cross. Such conceits are absolute foolishness before God (3:19).

3:5–4:5 The role of the apostle. In the light of God's wisdom, factions based on the alleged superiority of one minister over another or of one group over the other are absurd. All are servants of the one Lord, fulfilling the roles assigned for the nurturing of the community. God does not need human help (Acts 17:25), but has chosen ministers according to the divine purpose. God's purpose will not be frustrated.

Using the imagery of farming in 3:5-9, Paul emphasizes the unity and cooperation that characterizes the task and common goals of the ministers. The Corinthians are working against the very plan of God when they oppose their ministers to one another. Since the ministers work toward a common end, their followers must not sabotage this work by competing against one another.

Whereas unity is the point of 3:5-9, the complementarity of roles is explained by Paul using construction imagery in 3:6-23. Jesus Christ is the one foundation upon which the new temple of God is built. There are several examples in Judaism where the dual images of farming and construction are associated (Jer 1:10; 12:14-16; 24:6; Ezek 17:1-8) in a manner similar to Paul's association here.

Paul underscores the contribution not only of such ministers as himself and Apollos but of all the members of the Corinthian community. His emphasis is on the Christians' corporate identity as the temple of God. As Christians mature spiritually, they contribute to the upbuilding of God's temple (see 1 Cor 12:4-26). God lives in a temple not built by human hands (see Acts 17:24). The God of the Old Testament is reluctant to allow the Israelites to build a temple because they could then mistakenly conclude that God is more present in one place than in another (see 1 Chr 17:3-10). Proportionate to the people's failure to remember that God dwells among them is their insistence that they should build God a house. Paul echoes a prophetic warning to his readers: If anyone destroys God's temple (that is, the unity of the community), God will destroy that person (see John 2:19). If in 1 Cor 3:5-9 Paul seems to subordinate his role as teacher and leader of the community, he emphasizes its importance here. The early church, and especially the Corinthians, seemed to have been plagued with false teachers who compounded the sin of their own disbelief by leading others astray. This was the ultimate scandal in a struggling community, that leaders would misrepresent the gospel. Better, Jesus warned, that these tie a millstone around their necks than that they be the cause of the downfall of one of the "little ones" (see Matt 18:6; Mark 9:42).

Jesus as Judge is one of the oldest christological images. The image is linked with the Old Testament concept of the Day of Yahweh (see 3:13; Amos 5:15, 18), a day of hope for the remnant, but a day of judgment against God's enemies. Paul transfers the title "Lord" and the judgment role of God to Jesus. One of Christ's main roles as Paul describes it for the Corinthians is the subjection of all creation under himself and the return of all to God (see 1 Cor 15:24-28; 2 Cor 5:17-20). This is the work of salvation or reconciliation. In carrying out this work of the reconciliation of the whole world, Jesus reevaluates all creation, determining what will be saved. All is therefore judged in view of Jesus' action on the cross. Paul reiterates his conviction that the cross of Christ brings to an end and destroys all human wisdom.

Paul attests that his conscience is clear. Nevertheless, he continues, this is not enough to convict or acquit him. His conscience is subject to the higher authority of the Lord who judges the hearts of all. Thus, even his own spiritual maturity, his role as leader in the community does not give him the right to judge. He is not merely imposing his own convictions on the Corinthians. Nor is he subject to any other judgment than God's own.

4:6-21 The true evaluation of an apostle. When Paul uses himself as an example to be followed, he could be misinterpreted as displaying the epitome of pride. But Paul avoids all boasting, cogently showing that Christians have nothing that they have not received. His transparence as an apostle fixes him always under the scrutiny of others. He renounces the right to a private, unexamined life. His apparent arrogance is, in reality, a marvelous humility and integrity that allows others to observe all his actions, his words, his very life, and thus learn what it means to imitate Christ (see 11:1). Paul has effectively shown the absurdity of claiming self-importance over others. Now he proceeds to contrast such attitudes with the role of the apostles which causes them to be considered foolish on account of Christ (4:10).

Still Paul does only what he invites the Corinthians to do. He suggests that they consider their own experience, the gifts they have received. Without cost to them, he argues, they have, as believers, been called to reign over the world. This authority they have received from God's mercy.

B. Other Examples of the Corinthians' Immaturity: Moral Disorders (5:1–6:20)

5:1-13 A case of incest. Pride has tempted the Corinthians to take an "enlightened" view of a very basic disorder, namely, incest. They are "inflated with pride," no doubt thinking themselves possessed of a knowledge that transcends ethical norms (see 8:1-2; also 4:6-18). They consider themselves above the ordinary taboos related to marriage and family, taboos which characterize even the most primitive civilizations. The Corinthians rejoice in their own broadmindedness. Paul forcefully admonishes that the man guilty of incest must be excluded from the community and thus "delivered to Satan." Impressed that they are already living a supernatural life that frees them from sin, they seem to delight in the sophistication that suggests that they cannot be harmed by the desires of the flesh. Behavior to the Corinthians does not seem important; only spiritual enlightenment matters.

Paul is undoubtedly reacting against the Corinthians' blatant rejection of common moral standards. He upbraids them for their lack of moral authority and courageous leadership (see Gal 6:1). Yet it is the context which betrays Paul's even deeper concern. The fledgling Corinthian community is not capable of discerning conduct consistent with commitment to Christ. Nor do the Corinthians even seem to think that it is necessary to bring behavior into line with beliefs. Paul has already stated in the preceding chapters that the Corinthians are spiritually immature and have failed to grasp true wisdom. Such failure is evidenced in this separation of beliefs and practice. Their obligation to the offender is to separate him from the community and thus, hopefully, be a means of his coming to repentance.

Paul's own preaching may have inadvertently contributed to the Corinthians' misunderstanding. The Apostle ascribed to the view of humankind that saw people as being under some force, either for good or for evil. In order to emphasize the difference, Paul often speaks of the dichotomy between the spirit and the flesh (see, for example, Rom 8:1-13). He also insists that in Christ we are dead to the law (Rom 7:1-6) and to sin (Rom 6:1-14). Enthusiasts already, the Corinthians would have easily fallen prey to one extreme of this thinking which would suggest that since they have been saved, they are no longer subject to the flesh with its taboos. Paul the realist, however, knows how susceptible this community could be to eliminating all standards. Although he does not explicitly include here the problem of scandal in his instructions to the Corinthians, the fact that they were ignoring ordinary taboos recognized by both Jews and pagans would have provoked negative criticism from Paul. The Corinthian community had enough problem being accepted by the Jerusalem authorities and by the other, more exemplary communities. But Paul is reacting against anything which would cause sufficient scandal to inhibit others, and especially other Gentiles, from accepting the gospel. For this is his mandate—to make the gospel accessible to all the Gentiles.

The image of the leaven, borrowed from the Passover liturgy, reveals Paul's real emphasis as he proceeds to address the immorality which plagues the Corinthian community. This emphasis is twofold: first, conduct must be consistent with Christian commitment and, second, an individual's behavior has implications for others. Just as the Jews rid their homes of all leaven to celebrate the Passover, so Christians must rid the community of the corruption and wickedness that contaminates it, guarding their consecration and call (see 1:2) with the leaven of "sincerity and truth" (5:8).

Besides ignoring the universally recognized laws of decency, some of the Corinthians are guilty of another extreme. Taking literally Paul's instructions in a letter now lost (see 5:9) about not associating with sinners, they were becoming judgmental and elitist. Corinthian extremists were all too ready to escape from the world by rejecting it. Paul tries to help them live with the tensions of the world. Paul's comments here and in the next chapter about different life-styles are primarily intended as a corrective against this kind of extremism. Paul reminds the Corinthians of their missionary obligations to the pagans. They are not to judge the outsiders, but leave them to God. But they are to correct the erring within the community (see Gal 6:1-5). Their responsibility is to develop faith and to reflect this faith in their conduct as members of the community of the justified. Paul concludes the chapter with another reference to the incestuous man, quoting the law (Deut 13:6) to reinforce the order to expel him from the community.

6:1-11 Lawsuits before unbelievers. Paul's reference to judgment in 5:12-13 provokes him to set aside the issue of immorality for the moment and consider another abuse in Corinth that has been reported to him. Christians are betraying their own members by bringing their disputes before pagan courts. Paul reminds them that the world itself, indeed, even the angels, are to be judged by those who believe in the gospel. Christians recognize a morality more binding than that which characterizes pagan courts which, at best, may claim to arbitrate right and wrong. Christians recognize the law of love which qualifies all other judgments. Is it not then absurd, a scandal even, that petty quarrels among believers be brought before pagan courts? When such quarrels occur, Paul insists, they must be settled within the community (6:1-6). Yet the Apostle, before he returns to the issue of sexual immorality in 6:12-20, denounces the fact that disputes even arise (6:7-11).

It is to the Corinthians' shame that they do not acknowledge one among them who is wise enough to give sound judgment in these everyday matters. At the close of this epistle (16:15-18), Paul will recommend the leadership of Stephanas, Fortunatus, Achaicus, who could have been the very bearers of the reports of this abuse. The Corinthians dispute among themselves even about leadership roles while failing to recognize in their leaders the authority to help them reconcile their differences.

Paul denounces the fact of lawsuits among the Corinthians as no less than tragic. The power of the gospel mandate is that Christians would willingly allow themselves to be cheated rather than retaliate (see Matt 5:21-26, 38-42; Rom 12:14, 19-21). God's grace attained through baptism enables Christians to act toward each other in the same gracious way that God acts toward them (see Matt 5:45). If, however, Christians merely repay evil for evil and thereby cheat their own, they will be judged by their own baptism and fail to inherit the kingdom of God. Paul lists the vices that characterized their pre-baptismal, pagan existence. But *now*, having been baptized, Christians already have begun to share in the blessings of God's kingdom, made accessible through Jesus (see Rom 5:1-11; 8:1). Formerly pagan sinners, they now have a new identity, having been washed, consecrated, justified.

6:12-20 The idolatry of sexual sins. Paul tries to be especially careful when speaking to the Corinthians, who seem to be so quick to misinterpret his words. In 6:10-11, Paul contrasted the former life of paganism with the "now" of the Christian who has been justified through baptism. Paul's own teaching insists that the baptized are free from this former sinful condition. But Paul's anthropology also suggests that, freed from one master, we are made subject to another. If, in freedom, we do not live for God, we risk falling back into the slavery of sin.

Paul's teaching on freedom had been abused to legitimize the sexual licentiousness of the Corinthians. The same extremism that prompted their complacency regarding incest in their midst is used to justify their sexual conduct. They seem to argue that since sex is natural, it is necessary. Paul, who develops his theology of the resurrection in more detail in chapter 15, now grounds his comments on the dignity of sexuality in the resurrection and in his introduction of the image of the body to describe the union between Christ and the faithful (see 12:12-30).

Through baptism we have become members of Christ's body. The image of marriage is used to express how perfect then is the union between Christ and the baptized. Sin prompts us to prostitute ourselves, giving ourselves over to the false gods of pleasure and promiscuity. Drawing on a long Old Testament tradition, Paul identifies idolatry and adultery. He refers not only to sexual sins but to any pact with evil which desecrates the Christian committed to God (see 10:21). Any return to paganism is a form of prostitution, since by baptism we belong to God.

Finally, Paul caps the chapter by returning to the image of the temple of God. Fornication defiles the one who has, through baptism, become the sacred dwelling of the Spirit. This Spirit, given to us by God, is the pledge of our inheritance (see Eph 1:14). Therefore, we no longer belong to ourselves or to sin. We have been purchased at the great price of the death of Christ who reconciled us to God (Eph 2:4-10; Col 1:19-20).

Paul thus concludes his reactions to reports he has heard about the Corinthians. Continuing his straightforward, blunt approach, he now addresses the questions the community has posed to him (1 Cor 7:1–11:1).

III. ANSWERS TO THE CORINTHIANS' QUESTIONS

1 Cor 7:1–11:1

The young Corinthian church posed several questions to their pastor. Paul's responses to these questions comprise most of the next major part of the epistle (1 Cor 7:1–11:1). To these responses Paul adds his reactions about other problems in Corinth: appropriate behavior at the liturgy (11:2–14:40) and a true understanding of the fact and manner of the resurrection (15:1-58). So important is this last doctrine and so central to all comprehension of the gospel, Paul implies from this structure, that all the other misunderstandings and problems of the Corinthian community hinge on the fact that they do not grasp the resurrection and its implications.

Paul sorts out the questions posed to him by the emissaries of the Corinthians. They fall, the Apostle suggests in his response, into two general categories: questions concerning social status such as marriage and slavery (7:1-40), and the survival and identity struggles experienced by the minority Christian mixed community within a hostile pagan environment (8:1–11:1). Probably nowhere in Paul are both the complexity and the simplicity of the Christian message more evident than in this section of 1 Corinthians. Clearly Paul had opinions on how the community was to act, but never does he impose his own style of conclusions on his churches. Rather, he calls them to a new level of awareness of the implications of doing whatever they do with love, for the glory of God (see 10:31; 16:14).

A. Questions Concerning Social Status (7:1-40)

Some of the Corinthians' questions arose from debates on the relative significance for the life to come of one's social status in this world. The Corinthians' spirituality caused them to disdain human institutions, including marriage. On the other hand, however, the institution of slavery, prevalent in Paul's day, seemed to validate discrimination against the slaves. Paul's emphasis on freedom could have been understood to support the Corinthians' disregard of the obligations incurred by human institutions. At a time when wives and slaves were expected to follow the religion of their husbands and masters, Christianity could have been considered dangerously subversive by outsiders and as an opportunity to avoid responsibility by insiders. Paul first addresses the question of marriage and obligations to one's spouse (7:1-16) and then returns to basically sexual issues in 7:25-40. He inserts within this discussion some comments on other social issues, especially slavery. This is an example of his use of the ABA' schema where he teaches the implications of a guiding principle (usually expressed in "B") by introducing an example, enunciating the principle, and then returning to his initial example. In this case, Paul's basic argument is that no change in status should be sought in view of the imminence of the parousia (see 7:17-25).

7:1-16 Advice concerning marriage. Paul begins his reactions to their questions by quoting the position of the Corinthians themselves that it is well for a man not to touch a woman. This quotation tactic occurs rather frequently in First Corinthians (for example, 10:23; 14:34-35). Concerning celibacy, the Corinthians' position is basically one which Paul can identify with. But while he himself admits his preference for celibacy, he also recognizes the serious errors involved in trying to legislate this as the life-style for everyone. The Corinthians view celibacy as a preferred state. Some seem to be even using their baptism as an excuse to escape commitments already made. Just as they had tried to escape reality in shunning all sinners (see 5:10-11), now they wish to use baptism as an escape from the burdens of married life, under the pretext of asceticism. They seem to have devalued marriage on the assumption that it has no place in the eschatological kingdom of God (see Matt 22:30; Mark 12:25; Luke 20:35). Further, the degraded status of women in the society of Paul's day provided good reason, especially for women, to look for excuses to escape the oppression of marital responsibilities. Christian converts in Corinth argued that since they already lived in Christ, they were exempt from their pre-baptismal commitments, including marriage, which they saw as only concerned with life in the flesh. Considering the spiritual to be higher and therefore better, they denied their own sexuality as expressed in marriage.

The realist, Paul, corrects this tendency and invokes reasoning similar to that which he uses to resolve the conflict between the weak and the strong (see 1 Cor 8:1–10:33). One's choice for abstinence, although admirable, cannot be unilateral or absolute. Christians live out their baptism in this world, respecting their commitments, subjecting their decisions to the demands of mutual love. Christians consider Jesus' new law of love not only one command among many but primary. Nor is it merely an external demand, but empowerment for fidelity. Paul reminds the Corinthians to honor commitments already contracted. Marital relations are a "duty" owed to one who has authority over the other's body mutually. This dutiful view may at first appear negative and legalistic, and it has been interpreted historically as such. Actually, however, in comparison to the Corinthians' view, Paul's is quite positive.

Paul goes on to justify marriage by reasoning that marital fidelity is better than sexual promiscuity (7:9). One's choice of life-style is based on faith in the Lord and the coming of the kingdom. Those who choose celibacy must be faithful and vigilant. Likewise, those who choose marriage are to be faithful to and respectful of one another.

Jesus' approach to this question as recorded in the Gospels should be compared to Paul's (see Matt 19:1-12; Mark 10:1-12; Luke 18:15-17). In answer to a question about divorce, Jesus pronounced on the indissolubility of marriage. This is his instruction, by which believers are expected to be able to make lasting promises. When his disciples learn how seriously Jesus views the marriage contract, they reply that it might be better not to make such promises (Matt 19:10). Jesus' response is that celibacy is a gift not given to all (Matt 19:11-12).

Husbands and wives belong to one another (1 Cor 7:4). Such union reflects the order of creation (Matt 19:4-6). In the positive perspective, then, marriage thus provides a model for the kind of union attainable for Christians. Paul often exhorts Christians to obey one another, carry one another's burdens, support, love, challenge one another. Christian love requires that all selfish ambitions be subordinated to love.

Thus, even though there may be a legitimate personal desire for periodic sexual abstinence to enhance prayer, such a decision ought to be mutual and limited. All the decisions of a Christian are based on mutual love and responsibility, so that whether a believer chooses to marry or not to marry, to abstain or not to abstain, there is no superior rule, no other absolute than charity.

Jewish law made no provision for a woman's divorcing her husband, since only men were responsible for the marriage contract. In a sense, then, Paul's reflections on marriage represent progress regarding the mutual obligations of both wife and husband for fidelity in marriage. Paul recognizes a woman's obligation regarding marriage and insists that baptism does not provide an excuse for women to evade such responsibility.

The Corinthians' situation also involved questions concerning their obligations to unbelievers, especially in marriage. Customs in the society required that wives and slaves adhere to the religion of their husbands and masters and that all citizens fulfill the religious obligations dictated by the state. This requirement put believing wives of unbelievers in a particularly vulnerable position, and Paul responds to the Corinthians' questions regarding this vulnerability. 1 Cor 7:15 has been interpreted as the basis for the so-called Pauline privilege to provide for the necessity of divorce under certain circumstances. But originally Paul addressed the particular needs of married believers living in tension with unbelieving spouses. As long as the unbeliever tolerated the faith of the believing spouse, the marital union existed. But since the commitments of baptism were primary and could not be jeopardized, if the unbeliever was not willing to live with a believer, the couple must separate. It is God's will that a couple live in peace.

7:17-24 Against change in believers' social status. Paul's ideas on the desirability of marriage reflect the general rule of 7:17 about Christians continuing in the state in which they were called. Paul undoubtedly believed that the parousia was imminent. His letters therefore address problems as they arise, providing solutions to questions within the context of living in the "in-between" times, which are shortened and which will be ended with the sudden coming of the Lord (see 1 Thess 5:1-11; Rom 13:11-14). Thus, Paul's personal preference for celibacy is reinforced by his conviction that the end times relativize the value of all human institutions, including marriage, circumcision, and slavery.

Believing that the time before the parousia is short, Paul says that each should continue in the state he or she was at baptism (7:17, 20, 24). The Apostle has just addressed the issue of sexual differences in marriage. Now he reflects on two other divisions that threaten Christian unity—the differences between Jews and Gentiles, slave and free (see Gal 3:28). Although baptism does not overlook these differences, it renders them impotent to divide people. It is not necessary, then, or even desirable that one's state of life be changed after baptism. Christians must only live their baptismal commitment in an exemplary way. This means that because of the union established among believers through baptism, there can be no discrimination or inequality due to sexual, religious, or social differences.

While Paul denies that any social change should be sought on principle, he does consider that changes may be necessary to accommodate weakness. And, if they are necessary, they are acceptable. This applies not only to changes in marital status but to any social or legal change, including whether one is circumcized or not or whether one is slave or free. God's call is gratuitous. It is independent of a person's standing in the eyes of the world. By the same token, a convert cannot argue that this call demands an upgrading or change in status. Paul is less interested in the revolutionizing of the institutions of the world than in challenging Christians to live out their Christian commitment in the particular situation in which they were called. If, for example, the nonbelieving master frees the believing slave, this change may be acceptable. But, in view of the imminent parousia, this change should not be sought by the believer.

Neither circumcision nor non-circumcision counts before God. Apparently some tried to reverse the operation of circumcision. Nor does God regard one's status as free or slave. Paul could have stated his own preference here as he does in the case of marriage. In his letter to Philemon, for example, he argues that Philemon may not exercise the ordinary recourse that would be followed by a wronged head of household toward a runaway slave. Yet Paul himself refrains from commanding Philemon, with one result that it remains unclear what exactly Paul was asking of Philemon. An authoritarian, doctrinaire statement, however tempting to Paul or to us, would have been a contradiction of all Paul is trying to teach about the relative value of any principle except love. Paul concludes his advice concerning social status with the admonition not to return to the slavish ways of thinking merely in human categories. All are subject only to the one Lord who is soon to come.

7:25-40 On virgins, widows, married life. Paul now considers the relative freedom of the unmarried (7:17-35). He regards virginity as preferable since the "time is short" and marriage tends to scatter one's energies. Paul's thinking is shaped by his conviction that the Christian has already begun to live a heavenly existence and therefore should not become more ensconced in this world. In heaven there is no marriage, so marriage is not necessary for Christians. It is irrelevant to inheriting the kingdom of God (see 15:50).

The Corinthians, in their enthusiastic extremism, seemed to even suspect that marriage is sinful (see 1 Tim 4:1-5). On the contrary,

Paul responds, marriage is the chosen life-style of the majority and its obligations cannot be avoided on the pretext that now one is Christian. Marriage is not sinful. Indeed, it is better to marry than to ignore the needs of the flesh. Since Paul's society considered women the property of men, the Apostle addresses men when he advocates marriage rather than irresponsible and promiscuous sexual behavior.

Paul is against change in marital status, not only for virgins but also for widows. This represents another departure from Jewish tradition which advocated remarriage after the death of a spouse. Paul reinforces this opinion by expressing the belief that he is guided in this by the Spirit of God.

B. Struggles Within a Pagan Environment (8:1–11:1)

8:1–11:1 forms a unit manifesting Paul's typical method of dealing with the everyday problems that arose in the Corinthian community as a church struggling within a pagan environment. The ABA' schema is operative. In 8:1-13, Paul deals with the question of food offered to idols (A). Then, in 9:1–10:22 (B), Paul turns to some of the underlying principles which must influence the Christian judgment of behavior. Finally, Paul returns in 10:23–11:1 (A') to the issue of idol-meats, stressing charity as the motivating power behind any decision about which foods to eat.

8:1-13 The idolatry of knowledge. Among the issues that threatened to divide the Corinthians was the issue of food offered to pagan idols. Just as the community was divided on the basis of ministers (1–4), and life-style (7), so the advanced "knowledge" of some (that is, the strong) separated them from others whom they considered to be weak and unenlightened. The language of love which upbuilds (13:4) is exactly the opposite of knowledge which inflates the ego (8:1; see 4:6, 18; 5:2). Those who consider themselves enlightened presume superiority over those who are scandalized by the eating of meat offered to idols. The enlightened ones argue that since idols do not exist, there can be no harm in eating meat which had been offered to them and which was often served at public banquets. Since these gatherings had religious meaning for most participants, many Corinthians shunned them and were shocked at the participation of the strong. The gist of Paul's response is that although the enlightened are actually objectively correct, they are not therefore justified in wounding the consciences of the weak. What Paul says here is actually very startling. In effect, he asserts that even the profession of faith that there is one God who is Father and one Lord, Jesus, is not enough. This faith has consequences in one's acceptance of the sensitivities of others. No believer may give offense to others and exclude them without sin (see Rom 14:23). There are many "gods" and "lords"; some people even deify certain practices which they claim lead to self-righteousness. But the one true God who is Father calls us to subordinate all things, including knowledge, to the reign of Christ which is love.

There are many who do not possess knowledge of certain things, and so responsibility in the one Lord is to act out of love. The actions of a believer are not merely private as if salvation depended on the enlightenment of individuals. Paul reminds the Corinthians that many of them have so recently converted from the worship of idols that their consciences are weak and immature. Subordinate your knowledge to love of the weak and to the whole community, he admonishes.

Principles of Christian behavior (9:1–10:22)

Paul is no stranger to the difficulties involved in the Corinthians' struggle for integrity within a hostile environment. He draws principles for Christians, not *a priori* but from his own apostolic vocation and from the example of Israel as recorded in the Scriptures. In 9:1-27, Paul gives some reflections on being an apostle, suggesting that his own life can serve as a model for the strong to study in reconciling themselves with the weak. In 10:1-22, Paul warns the Corinthians, and especially the strong, to learn from the Israelites not to become complacent.

The example of Paul (9:1-27)

Paul's call from God gave him an authority he does not hesitate to defend. It is clear that especially in Corinth he must defend it. With their propensity to misunderstand, at least some in Corinth, noting that Paul did not exercise the same rights as the other apostles, argued that he must not have these rights, that he is an inferior apostle (see 2 Cor 12:11). There are two main issues Paul introduces in 9:1 which he will develop in this chapter—his freedom and his rights as an apostle. He will defend these in reverse order, beginning with his rights (9:1-18) and then explaining the terms of his freedom (9:19-27).

9:1-18 Paul's rights. Paul's response to his detractors is more than a justification of his own life. It is significant that his defense occurs in a context of admonishing the strong to consider the needs of the weak (see 8:7–10:33). Paul defends his apostleship because it is the authority upon which his gospel preaching is based. This apostleship carries rights and privileges that Paul clearly recognizes. Yet he renounces certain of these for the sake of the community. In other words, he himself provides a model for the strong to follow in subordinating their course of action to the needs of the weak.

Paul is an apostle no less than any others because he has seen the risen Lord (see 15:3-5). This is the fundamental criterion for being an apostle. Yet even if he cannot prove that he has seen the Lord, the very existence of the Corinthian community is ample testimony that Paul is indeed an apostle. His poignant statement that even if he is not an apostle for others, he is certainly one for the Corinthians, indicates how deeply Paul is affected by the criticism he hears from the community. Yet his defense goes beyond personal hurt or self-justification, revealing how fundamental is his conviction that his apostleship must be recognized. It is imperative that the questions of rights and their use not inhibit the spread of the gospel.

The other apostles accepted support from the community. This included food and drink, not only for the apostles but for their families. The reference to marriage might seem strangely out of place, except that it appeared as a problem in chapter 7. The fact that the apostles married might have given further authority to Paul's attempt to curb the Corinthians' disdain for marriage. Paul might also have been inspired by the threefold proverbial connection made by the unjust whose motto is to eat, drink, and be merry, for tomorrow we die (see 10:7). The last, of course, is a euphemism for enjoying the pleasures of the flesh. Thus, Paul includes this in the list of the rights of an apostle, a right, he has already indicated, that he renounces. The Corinthians who may have been sympathetic to his decision not to marry, then, should not criticize his apostleship for that very reason. Nor is it legitimate to criticize him for not exercising the rights generally recognized as belonging to an apostle.

Four arguments to justify the support of the preacher by the community are furnished by Paul in 9:6-14. First, in 9:6-7, Paul argues from common sense, citing examples from ordinary life, like that of the soldier, the farmer, the shepherd, all of whom are supported by their trade. Second, these examples from common experience are supplemented by the teaching of the law (9:8-9): Moses prescribed even the care of animals. Paul's readers are not to surmise that this example is farfetched. There is a parable in this, a lesson in the respect due to all creatures.

Paul draws the third argument (9:10-11) from a Greek philosophical tradition which influenced the Corinthians' thinking. The Corinthians recognize the superiority of the spirit over the flesh. Paul uses this spirit-flesh tension to his advantage. Since he has shared spiritual blessings with the Corinthians, he is clearly entitled to expect from them the less significant blessings represented by their material support of him (see the commentary on 2 Cor 8:1–9:15 for Paul's description of the collection as a "debt"). Paul's apostolic service has directly benefited the Corinthians. The other apostles have had a less direct impact on them. If these others are supported by the Corinthians, how much greater are Paul's rights! So far, apostle and community agree.

Yet Paul interrupts the chain of arguments to remind the Corinthians that he has not used these rights among them. They can recall the months he stayed with them, working at his tentmaking trade, preaching to them while he worked with his hands. The Apostle says repeatedly, "Imitate me" (for example, 11:1; 2 Thess 3:7). He has renounced his right to support precisely so that his life-style will not be an obstacle to the message he preaches. This decision has meant that he has endured every manner of hardship and sacrifice. Just such a model is now needed by this very community that criticizes him. Paul himself dredges up the very criticism that has so pained him as an example of how the strong must act. The Apostle incarnates the primacy of love to provide an example of how the Corinthians are to address the issues which threaten to divide them.

The fourth argument (9:13) in favor of the support of the preacher by the community is well rooted in both Jewish and pagan religious practice. Moreover, the Lord himself ordered that all who preach the gospel should live by it (see Matt 10:14). This last argument seems to be so conclusive that Paul's unwillingness to be ruled by it is all the more surprising and calls his position into question. He reasons that even the Lord's command can be set aside for the sake of the community. With similar freedom and conviction, the Apostle had justified his exception to the commands of the Lord regarding divorce while he defended, on the other hand, his own decision not to marry despite having no command from the Lord. In other words, for the Apostle, even the sayings of Jesus himself cannot be applied in any literal, legalistic way, disregarding the discerning role of the community. Such an application would effectively relativize or nullify the only absolute command, which is love. All of the commands, even the sayings of the Lord, are summed up in this, for love alone cannot hurt another (see Rom 13:8-10).

Paul's mission as Apostle to the Gentiles revealed that the gospel has no limits. He has made a rule for himself not to limit the gospel by preaching only to the communities which support him. Thus he opts to preach while supporting himself, not only to avoid scandal but to insure that the gospel be independent of a community's wealth. This has been his practice since the beginning, although he does accept financial aid from communities after he has left them. This practice gives him the freedom needed to speak prophetic, challenging words without either jeopardizing his livelihood or incurring a financial obligation to certain people.

The reasons Paul gives in 9:15-18 for renouncing his rights bridge the preceding consideration of an apostle's rights and his description of freedom in 9:19-27. Paul lives by his convictions and would rather die than be deprived of his role as an apostle who preaches without condition. Yet he does not boast because he preaches the gospel. This he is compelled to do because Christ has grasped him (see Phil 3:12). If Paul preaches willingly, that is his recompense. If he is unwilling, the obligation nevertheless remains. Since he accepts this commission, he exemplifies freedom all the more in not accepting material support.

Freedom is never an absolute for Paul. It is always described as freedom from something (sin, death) for other service (to God, to Christ). For the sake of the gospel, Paul becomes free for the service of all. He is not limited to serving either Jews or Greeks. Once more he is describing his own experience by way of example to challenge both the strong and the weak. Although he is not bound by anyone, he serves everyone so as to bring the salvation of the gospel to as many as possible (9:19-23). At the same time, Paul runs the race as if to win, and his zeal for the goal involves renunciation (9:24-27).

9:19-23 Paul's freedom to serve all. Paul respects the traditions of the Jews. He himself lives according to these traditions when he is among the Jews. Although he knows he is not bound by the law, he imitates, for their sakes, those who think they are. Likewise he acts with those who are not bound by the law, not assuming erroneously that mere knowledge will free them or change them. In this reference to "those not subject to the law," Paul includes both Jews and Gentile Christians, whom he previously designated with the title "the strong." Paul also identifies with the weak, lest his freedom regarding the law be an obstacle to them. By making himself "all things to all," Paul diminishes the possibility of being one by whom the least are scandalized and fall (see 8:11-13).

9:24-27 Zeal for the gospel and renunciation. The Greeks were renowned for their games. His readers' familiarity with sports makes Paul's athletic illustrations appropriate for suggesting the proper motivation to inspire a healthy Christian self-discipline, sacrifice, and renunciation. The Corinthians had a special need for balance, being too prone to become extremists, either in overindulgence or in asceticism. Paul uses images from two of the more popular sports, running and boxing.

Paul compares Christian life to the disciplined runner who keeps focused on the goal and thus subordinates all other desires to the attainment of the prize. To the winner the Greeks awarded crowns which symbolized victory and supremacy. Paul's argumentation implies that if single-mindedness and self-renunciation are necessary to gain a perishable reward, how much more important these are in the pursuit of the imperishable crown. Paul "fights" in like manner. The contest is real and often the enemy is within. Paul alludes to the Greek boxing practice of completely vanquishing and humiliating the opponent. Paul's own experience showed him the need to deal the decisive blow to give him mastery over himself. Occasionally in this correspondence (see 2 Cor 4:8-10; 6:4-10; 11:23-29), he rehearses the sufferings he himself has endured for the sake of the gospel. Predictably and for the sake of balance, Paul situates his self-discipline, his asceticism and willingness to suffer, in the context of service for others. He not only accepts hardship but even seeks it in order to provide a more credible witness to the gospel and to transform his own life into the kind of Christian witness others can imitate (see 11:1).

Caution against complacency (10:1-22)

Paul continues to reflect on the principles of Christian behavior which will help to reconcile the weak and the strong. Having reflected on his own experience as an apostle, he widens his circle of examples, appealing to the lesson of Israel and the circumstances of the Corinthians before he returns in 10:23–11:1 to the question of idol-meats and his warning against scandal, which is a fundamental threat to the community (see 8:1-13). The Israelites, Paul reminds the Corinthians, became complacent and were punished (10:1-13). Paul warns against likewise incurring the wrath of a jealous God by the idolatry of participating at sacrificial banquets while also assisting at the Eucharist (10:14-22). He contrasts such recklessness with the love and mutual respect characteristic of the Christian who does all out of love for the glory of God (10:23–11:1).

10:1-13 The lesson of Israel. The reality of grace, which is an expression of God's mercy, is an antidote to complacency. Having invoked athletic imagery to emphasize the necessity of self-discipline and vigilance, Paul warns his fellow Christians against pride, using the example of Israel. The Old Testament is full of examples of prophetic utterances against the infidelity of God's people. Israel is the spiritual ancestor of the Christians. Paul presupposes that his audience is very familiar with the story of the Exodus. He uses events from that story in the same order in which they appear in the Old Testament—the cloud, the sea, the manna, water from the rock. All the Israelites, Paul reminds the Corinthians, as a warning, were under the cloud that represented the presence of God. All of them passed through the sea that symbolized for them God's mighty deeds.

Paul continues to draw parallels he hopes his readers will identify with. He helps them to this end by presenting the passage through the sea as being "baptized into Moses." There is no direct Jewish precedent for this phrase. Paul may have coined it himself and used it to evoke a parallel between the Israelites' perception of the Exodus and the Christians' perception of it. Baptism literally means "immersion" and signifies belonging to the one in whom they are baptized.

Instead of referring explicitly to the manna and the water, Paul alludes to the spiritual food and spiritual drink. This allusion could allow his readers to relate not only to baptism but to the Eucharist. A Jewish tradition, popular in Paul's time, was that a stream of water accompanied the Jews through the desert. Another tradition was that a well from which they drank followed them. Paul's point is that even these signs did not insure the Israelites against God's wrath or envelop them in a protective covering. They displeased God and their rebellion was punished.

The Scriptures were written for our instruction (10:6; 11; Rom 15:4; 2 Tim 3:16). Our ancestors became idolaters, erroneously assuming that these signs were gods who would protect them. They had no concern for the context in which the meaning of these signs would be made clear.

10:14-22 Participation at sacrificial banquets. Paul reminds the Corinthians of his love as if to indicate that this is basic to understanding what he is about to say. Avoidance of idol worship is fundamental to true faith. The cup of blessing makes all Christians sharers in the blood of Christ. The bread they share binds them to Christ and to one another. As the body of Christ they are nourished by this sharing. This is no empty symbol.

"Israel according to the flesh" represents the community's link with the history of Israel and serves as a lesson for us (see Rom 9:6; Gal 6:16). All those who participate at one altar share in the eating of what is sacrificed. Paul, like the strong, denies the existence of the idols whom the Gentiles honor by their sacrifices. But this denial does not bring with it license for idolatry. Once converted, Christians must guard against any return to paganism. All actions must proceed from faith in the one Lord. One cannot serve God and mammon (see Matt 6:24), nor can we assist at the altar of Christ while simultaneously condoning divisive practices. The unity represented by the Lord's Supper is desecrated by the idolatry of ideas and practices that scandalize and divide. It is not possible to eat at the Lord's table and to disregard the consciences of some Christians. If one eats at a sacrificial banquet, one is united in some way to the god in whose honor the sacrifice is offered and to those who honor this god. When Christians do this, they risk the anger of a jealous God whose will it is to bring all to unity and fellowship with one another in Christ.

10:23–11:1 Seek the good of others. Paul accepts the slogan of the strong that "all things are lawful" in Christ. But this does not imply that all things are good or constructive to community, which is the one "law" or goal binding all Christians. Whereas public ritual banquets are excluded on the basis of the scandal and division they might provoke, Paul grounds the Christian's freedom to eat anything that is served at private meals in the love command. Christ put an end to the law (see Rom 10:4) that distinguishes between clean and unclean foods. Love alone is the absolute enabling the believer to eat of the fullness of creation. Food is irrelevant. Just as charity gives the believer the freedom to eat anything, it may also, in some instances, require abstinence. Charity links and rules Christian consciences.

Christians submit to each other's consciences in charity, as to the Lord. The only sufficient motivation for Christian action is charity which is neither self-seeking nor slavish scrupulosity. Love is sincerely interested in the welfare and the edification of others (see 1 Cor 13). Freedom in Christ enables Christians to be subject to one another in faith. Thus, like Paul, who himself imitates Jesus, all seek the salvation of the many (see 9:19-23). This is why Christ came to give his life (see Mark 10:45; 14:24).

IV. PROBLEMS IN LITURGICAL ASSEMBLIES (11:2–14:40)

Paul has been told of some of the disorders in the Corinthian community's celebration of the liturgy. He has heard that there is confusion about liturgical dress, a topic he addresses in 11:2-16. More serious are the abuses against communal charity, which deny the very meaning of the Lord's Supper (11:17-34). Likewise, Corinthian Christians are competitive and divisive about the place and the importance of some of the more dazzling spiritual gifts such as speaking in tongues, and this attitude of superiority leads to violations of charity (12:1–14:40). Since all these disorders occur in liturgical celebrations, Paul considers them together despite the disparity of their importance.

A. Liturgical Dress and Behavior

11:2-16 Liturgical dress. This is a topic that, according to all evidence, almost had to have been introduced by the Corinthians themselves rather than by Paul. Paul, who chided his readers for being divided on the basis of what ministry itself means and who their valid ministers are, would apparently have considered liturgical dress a relatively insignificant matter. This section is sometimes mistakenly described as addressing the issue of *women's* attire and appearance at liturgies. This is misleading in that Paul comments on the appropriate appearance of both men and women who both pray and prophesy (11:4-5). It is clear that Paul recognized the possibility of liturgical leadership roles for both men and women.

Many problems among the Corinthian Christians arose because of their disregard for the physical and for legitimate mores. Paul characteristically argues for a correct appreciation of sexual differences, depicting failure to honor these differences as foolish, a sinful rejection of the order that God intended in creating male and female (see Rom 1:24-27). His comments to the Corinthians regarding liturgical dress are in this vein. Failure to respect the wisdom of common practice regarding dress could lead to more serious abuses of authority and Christian freedom, and undermine the real purpose of coming together in liturgical assembly to worship. Just as Paul argues for peace and harmony in the regulation of spiritual gifts (1 Cor 14:1-40), he similarly instructs both men and women in the appropriate decorum and attire at liturgical celebrations for the sake of offering fitting worship to the God of peace.

First, he praises the Corinthians for holding fast to the traditions he has taught them, thereby cleverly reminding them of his own authority and supporting the instinct which moved them to submit this issue to him for comment. Despite the apparent insignificance of the issue of attire, Paul commends the Corinthians. But for the more gross and more threatening violations of charity even at the Lord's Supper, he does not commend them (11:17).

The subordinationist view some interpreters see in 11:3 is excluded by Paul's reasoning in 11:11-12. Paul's opinion, supported, he says, by the order of creation and by common sense, reflected in the practice of all thinking people and all the churches, is that there should be a difference between men and women. This difference is not in role, for he talks about their both having the same role, that is, to pray and prophesy. The point of 11:3 is that all comes from God, who is the source (= head) of all life. This implies recognition of the order of creation (see Rom 1:20-32), which imposes responsibility for the mutuality of men and women. Although deutero-Pauline writings sometimes do *appear* to support the subordination of wives to their husbands (for example, Eph 5:22-24; Col 3:18–4:1), this is clearly not the point of our passage, which makes no reference to relationships between married people, but speaks of the dress and appearance of both men and women while they perform identical liturgical roles. Further, it would be a mistake to propose that "headship," an image used to describe unity in Christ, could be interpreted to support a subordinationist-domination mentality, especially when it is precisely just such misinterpretations that Paul attacks.

Paul argues from creation in 11:3-9. Christ is the first-born of all creation (Col 1:15). Man is the image of God and reflects God's glory. It would not be appropriate, then, for man to pray with his head covered, Paul contends, lest this glory be concealed. Paul argues that the custom of the day for men to wear their hair short is authoritative. Women, however, wear their hair long and cover their heads as a sign of God's authority over them as mediated by men. For women, then, as for men, Paul accepts the custom of the day as authoritative, reflected also, Paul suggests, in the order of creation of the sexes. Women without veils implied availability. The whole of 1 Cor 11:2-16 represents Paul's elaborate way of warning the Corinthians against divisions and competition that may arise at other gatherings, but which are intolerable for the Christian community in a liturgical context.

The veil is to be worn by women because of the angels (1 Cor 11:10), who were considered the guardians of the liturgy. This could be a scriptural reference to Gen 6:1-4, which describes the desecration of the design of human creation, when the sons of God lusted after the daughters of men and produced a race of giants. This atrocity prompted God to regret having created the world and to vow to destroy it with the flood. Thus, Paul reasons, in preserving the customary "sign of authority on her head," women assume their rightful place in the liturgy, subordinate to the angels who guard its order. In this way there is no danger of women's being a distraction to either men or angels. Since a woman's long hair is her glory, it would be her shame if she would have to have her head shaved. The long length is perhaps in contrast to the practice of prostitutes and lesbians to wear hair cropped short. Shaving a woman's head could refer to a punishment sometimes mandated for prostitutes. But a woman cannot use the liturgy for her own glorification, so she must cover her hair lest she provide a distraction at the liturgy. However unconvincingly, Paul is trying to give scriptural and authoritative reinforcement for customs that prescribe differences between the sexes while also maintaining women's right to "pray and prophesy" at the assemblies. In short, appearance must be conventional so that decency is respected and the liturgy does not occasion perversions.

Also, the element of scandal is to be avoided. Women played major roles in the rites of pagan religions, but only men presided at the Jewish liturgies. Paul advocates that the freedom of men and women alike to celebrate in Christian communities composed of both former Jews and Greeks should not be a cause of scandal to either the former Jews of Corinth or to the Jewish-Christian authorities, who would have been shocked had they themselves heard the reports Paul had received. As is the case throughout the epistle, the spirit of charity governs even the freedom won through Christ.

B. Celebration of the Lord's Supper (11:17-34)

Paul begins this section emphasizing that he cannot commend the Corinthians for the very serious abuses he now addresses. Paul is unambiguous. Proceeding according to his typical ABA' pattern, he outlines the abuses in Corinth, focusing on the way social and economic differences are allowed to inhibit appropriate celebration of the Lord's Supper. First he details these abuses and these differences (11:17-22). Then he focuses attention on the memory of Jesus' action and command in the institution account (11:23-27). Finally, he returns to the abuses and recommendation for healing the Body (11:28-34).

11:17-22 Reported abuses. Perhaps the Corinthians had implied in their letter to Paul that although they experienced some conflicts, such as what is appropriate liturgical dress (see 11:2-16), they nevertheless prided themselves on dutifully and regularly meeting to celebrate the Lord's Supper. Paul is not impressed. Such meetings as are described to him are not profitable but harmful. The really faithful tried and true, those interested in deepening their faith, are challenged to "stand out clearly," distinguishing themselves from the factious members.

The Corinthians are not assembling for the Lord's Supper. They have ulterior, destructive motives. Two meanings are suggested. First, it is not their *intention*, when they get together, to celebrate in remembrance of the Lord (11:24-25), and second, in fact, this is not the *result* of the Corinthians' gathering. In other words, from what Paul says, it is clear that the intention of many Corinthians is more divisive than reflective of the Lord's command, with the result that they do not carry out this command in their meetings.

Reports allege that the many divisions among the Corinthians are allowed to be part of the Eucharistic celebrations. Violations of charity, directly opposed to Jesus' command, are flagrant. Some are gluttonous, eating their own food, unmindful of the needs of others. On the other side, "one person goes hungry," even in the midst of the assembled community whose obligation it is to provide for the needs of all, especially the poor (see Gal 2:10). Some people become drunk, dramatizing the inability of the self-centered to contribute to building community. If it is only for eating and drinking that they assemble, the Corinthians would do better not to risk the judgment of God by assembling without a willingness for conversion, as if the Eucharist were magic. The Corinthian temptation to be overconfident seems to need correction once more (see 1 Cor 10:1-12). Their coming together, when not motivated by charity, shows contempt for the community. By embarrassing them rather than showing hospitality to those who have nothing, some members test God and court judgment against themselves (11:29).

Paul cannot avoid his pastoral responsibility to condemn the disorder rather than overlook it. Paul will not condone the Corinthians' gross misinterpretation of the real meaning of the liturgy. Apparently they mistakenly assumed that it was sufficient to come together regularly, and they seemed to have prided themselves on observing a ritual which brought together people of every walk of life or social standing. Nothing commendable in this, Paul says. In fact, such hypocrisy, while failing to reconcile the differences among them or make charity really practical, is, in fact, testimony against them. Even though in other parts of this letter Paul betrays a deep sensitivity to his fragile popularity in Corinth, he is not willing to soft-pedal his reaction to these abuses.

11:23-27 Tradition of the institution. Without suggesting that they have neglected the literal practice of the Lord's Supper, Paul inserts in his general instruction on the liturgy an account of the institution of the Eucharist. For emphasis, Paul enhances this account with a repetition over the cup as over the bread of the words "do this in remembrance of me." The memory of Jesus, who offered himself and whose death Christians proclaim in their liturgy, is the antidote to the factions in Corinth. Jesus' life and death is more than a memory. It effects unity among all those who recognize him as Lord.

Paul begins his institution account using technical language of receiving and handing on the Christian tradition (see 15:1-3). The phrase "from the Lord" does not necessarily mean that this tradition was part of the revelation of Paul's initial vision of Jesus which Luke describes as occurring on the way to Damascus. The tradition was an essential part of the gospel which Paul identifies with Christ. Even if the account was mediated by the Christian community, its authority, like the word prohibiting divorce (see 7:10), was the Lord's.

Paul rarely refers to the earthly life of Jesus. But this account of the action of Jesus, specified as happening the night before he died, is particularly significant because of its uniqueness. The aspect of betrayal on the part of Jesus' followers, which is part of the synoptic account (see Mark 14:17-31 and parallels), is accentuated in Paul's account, too. Betrayal and human weakness provide the context for the Eucharistic institution account (see 11:17-22 and 27-32), wherein Paul describes the abuses surrounding the memorial celebration in Corinth. Similarly, the gospel reports the betrayal and denial of the disciples at the Last Supper. Luke, in particular, stresses the constant misunderstanding of the disciples who, even at the moment of the Eucharist, argued among themselves over which one was the greatest in the kingdom of heaven (see Luke 22:24-30).

Jesus took ordinary bread and gave thanks for it. After it was broken, he identified it with his body. In contrast to the more original account of Mark, Paul has the words "which is for you." This addition emphasizes at once the timeless but very real significance of the Eucharistic celebration. Whenever believers share this bread and this cup, they recall the Lord's command to do this in memory of him. In so doing, they recall his death as they await his coming in glory. Three stages of time, the past (the original Last Supper and Jesus' death), the present (the community's celebration), and the future (the parousia) are brought together in this action. Anyone who performs this action unworthily, that is, separating one of these aspects from the other, sins in not fulfilling the Lord's command.

11:28-34 Practical recommendations for healing the body. To avoid this sin, one must examine oneself, recollecting, in the literal sense, the necessary faith to transcend all that would prohibit a realization of the implications of eating and drinking as a disciple of the Lord. Such a self-examination allows one to recognize oneself as a member of the body. Anyone who eats and drinks without this recognition sins against the body and blood of the Lord, thus calling a judgment down upon oneself. This accounts, Paul says, for the suffering so many of the Corinthians experienced through sickness and death. These are the punishments of the Corinthians' disbelief, most of all in the body, which is the church. Like the Israelites, who were chastised in the desert (10:5-12) for their complacency, the Corinthians are witnessing God's displeasure.

Nevertheless, there is still hope that they will be converted and saved if they consider these chastisements as a warning. For Paul, Christ's judgment is salvation for all who believe, but it is condemnation for disbelief (see 1:18). Paul's stern words, then, are actually a loving admonition urging the Corinthians to show that they are different from the nonbelieving world. This difference can be expressed in very significant, concrete ways that will demonstrate for all to see that participants recognize the real meaning of the Lord's Supper. When Christians assemble, they are to be considerate, waiting for one another. The hungry are to eat at home so that it is clearly not for selfish reasons that they gather. Since they will not be gathering merely to obtain food, there will be no danger of selfish motives prohibiting the genuine communal celebration.

The community must have raised other questions about the celebrations of the Lord's Supper, but Paul defers instruction in these matters until he comes. This is the essential. The rest can afford to wait (see 4:19; 16:5-9).

C. Spiritual Gifts and the Community (12:1–14:40)

The Corinthians' lack of appreciation for the body affected more than their liturgical celebrations. It permeated their understanding of all things Christian, including the basic profession of faith. Paul's attempt to correct this continues in 12:1–14:40, where he shows how the use of even the most spiritual of gifts is meant for the edification of the "body," the church (see 12:12-31). For example, the elementary saying "Jesus is Lord" (12:3) is a confession of faith in the bodily resurrection of Jesus (see Rom 10:9). The opposite, which says "Cursed be Jesus," attacks and weakens the body and is therefore a grave sin against the Spirit. All gifts with which the community is richly endowed (see 1 Cor 1:5), must be valued in proportion to their role in the building up of the body. Paul now turns to a discussion of the relative importance of such gifts in 12:1–14:40.

Yet there are still some pressing liturgical matters that Paul must address at this time. Again we find him using the ABA′ schema in the next three chapters, which discuss the spiritual gifts and their use in the community. This discussion is highlighted by his main idea, which is a development of the notion of charity (12:31–13:13) (= B). Charity must become practical by effecting unity and enabling those with gifts to serve the whole body, the church. There was much confusion in Corinth, particularly over the apparent superiority of the gift of tongues, and this led to dangerous competition (chapter 12) (= A) and even to chaos (chapter 14) (= A′).

Paul acknowledges that no spiritual gift is lacking in this community (see 1:5, 7). He readily admits that speaking in tongues, so coveted by the Corinthians, is among the spiritual gifts they possess. Indeed Paul himself exercised this gift (see 14:18-19) and may have introduced it into the community (14:6-14). Paul discusses the relative significance of various gifts, warning against ignorance of the purpose of all spiritual gifts. Clearly knowledge is especially cherished by the Corinthians. The Apostle would have their appreciation of spiritual gifts based on Christian wisdom, which has unity as its goal.

12:1-11 The Spirit's gifts. When they were pagans, the Corinthians were easily led by all kinds of false ideas. Driven by compulsion, they did not hear God's revelation but were led by mute idols. Paul refers to the powerful idols such as Elijah opposed (see 1 Kgs 18:21-40). Again he takes for granted his readers' acquaintance with the Old Testament Scriptures (see 1 Cor 10:1-13).

Apparently the Corinthians tended to consider any persuasive speaker or collective impulse as evidence of the possession of the Spirit. Perhaps this explains why Paul's own lack of eloquence in comparison, for example, to the silver-tongued Apollos caused some in Corinth to disregard Paul while exalting Apollos (see 1 Cor 2:1; 3:5; 4:6; 2 Cor 10:1-2, 9-10; Acts 18:24). The point of all Christian speech, Paul maintains, however, is not eloquence, but the proclamation of the lordship of Christ. No one who "curses Jesus" can be moved by the Spirit. Paul may be referring to those who tear down the community by nurturing divisions. The Apostle might also envision the more flagrant apostasy of those who failed to sustain their faith in Christ and actually returned to Judaism or paganism. At a time of increasing antagonism with Judaism, for example, some Christians continued to worship in the synagogue, where gradually phrases condemning Jesus and his followers were introduced and became more bitter. This was obviously intolerable to the early Christians who considered themselves rooted in Judaism. Paul emphasizes that the proclamation of Jesus as Lord can only be made through the Spirit, and that this proclamation cannot be divisive. The same Spirit who gives the gift of faith distributes all other gifts. The Spirit brings the variety of gifts into a marvelous unity. Experience shows that even gifts can be divisive if faith, not only in Christ but also in the church, is not strong. Gifts can result in envy, pride, arrogance, exclusiveness. The Spirit is required for the church to use gifts to effect unity.

Similarly, the talents of ministers who provide needed services sometimes induce people to make them lords. Yet since all Christians acknowledge the same Lord, they recognize all ministries as subordinate to one Lord over all. All are brought into unity and harmony by the same God, source and goal of all that is. Each manifestation of the Spirit is designed not for the promotion of the one who administers the gift but for the good of all. The idea of the "common good" described in 12:7 is a prelude to Paul's description of the community as a body (12:12-31). This draws on the analogy of the Stoic politic as a commonwealth.

Paul proceeds in 12:8-10 to give several examples of the variety of the gifts before reiterating in 12:11 that all gifts are manifestations of the same Spirit. The list is not exhaustive. Similar, but not identical, lists occur elsewhere (12:28-30; Rom 12:6-8; Eph 4:11). One may be a great rhetorician, another a great scientist or teacher. Clearly Paul does not mean that faith is necessary only for some. All who are justified share a common faith. Yet, in some, this faith is a visible evidence of things unseen (see Heb 11:1). In others, the predominant sign is their ability to heal physical and spiritual ills. Some even have the ability to perform miraculous deeds. The list is not intended to be a comment on the respective value of each of these gifts. Prophecy, which elsewhere Paul describes as having greater value than tongues (14:1-3), is simply listed as one of the manifestations of the same Spirit. Each gift is distributed, not according to individual merit, but according to the will of the Spirit.

12:12-31 The analogy of the body. The Corinthians exalted spiritual gifts and did not sufficiently respect the body. As part of his corrective, Paul describes the Spirit as the unifying power making all one. He uses the analogy of the body to teach this lesson. According to Paul, all reality is reevaluated in the light of Christ. Thus, even the "inferior" body (see 12:24-25) provides the most appropriate image to describe the work of the Spirit. Paul borrows the image of the body from the Stoic philosophy popular in his day. The Stoics presented the state as a commonwealth, a body with many members. This image was forcefully suggested by Paul's application of the meaning of the Eucharist for the Corinthian community (see 11:17-34). The body represents the unity and the diversity of the community. The body needs the diversity of many members, just as each member depends on the cooperation of the other members to function as part of the body. The interrelationship is symbiotic.

So it is with Christ. Paul nowhere says explicitly that the church is the body of Christ. But he does apply this image to the communities he addresses. Through baptism, believers participate with Christ in his dying and rising. Through the Eucharist they are joined to one another in his body. Thus, all natural distinctions which may have tended to divide people are eliminated through these sacraments. The Spirit enables us to transcend racial or national (Jewish or Greek) or social (slave or free) differences. Gal 3:28 adds to these the unity of the sexes. The discussion of 1 Cor 11:2-16 already spoke of this relationship (see 7:17-40).

The body is not identified with any one member, but needs many members cooperating as one. Each believer is a member of the body of Christ; the believer's body is also called a temple of the Holy Spirit (see 1 Cor 6:19). The body, the church, gathers the members and all belong to one. All the parts contribute essentially to the building up of the body. The differences of the members contribute to their unity. One cannot become the other, nor can one inhibit the function of the other. If one member suffers, every other member suffers, and all other members instinctively supply for the hurt member. Similarly, if one member is given special recognition, all members are more animated because they share in this honor.

The Corinthians naturally valued the things of the mind and of the spirit more than the physical. Yet they realized that the mind had influence on the body and vice versa. Regarding the whole person, then, the "less important" or less "honorable" members are given propriety by the more honorable members. In other words, just as our minds govern our passions so that there is no contradiction in ourselves, so, too, the Spirit brings together in harmony the less and the more honorable members of the body. Thus, too, for example, the "weak" and the "strong" can be reconciled (see 1 Cor 8:7-13; 10:23-30).

So it is with the body of Christ, the church. Each Christian finds a new identity in relationship to other Christians of the same body. The gifts of God bestowed upon the church range from apostleship to the gift of tongues. The apostles here seem to be ranked first, yet they are considered the "last of all" (1 Cor 4:9). They qualify as apostles by accepting the wisdom of God, which makes them appear foolish to the world (4:10). Their function, as Paul describes it, derives from the vision of the risen Lord (9:1; 15:8-10). The apostle's task is to preach the gospel, form communities (9:2), maintain the local churches in harmony with the greater church, notably the authorities in Jerusalem (see Gal 2:1-10). The apostles are not synonymous with the Twelve. Nor does Paul, who fashioned the term "apostle" for Christian use, describe apostles as followers of Jesus during his earthly life. Their mission is from God and not necessarily subject to the qualifications the community might wish to impose.

After the apostles come the prophets. Paul defers his description of the function of the prophets to 14:1-5. Then come the teachers who explain the gospel's implications and thus strengthen faith. It is not clear that for Paul there existed a real hierarchy. Yet, as a corrective for the Corinthians, who believed that speaking in tongues was of utmost importance, Paul mentions this gift last. His emphasis is that there are many ministries to be performed, and so there should not be competition. While each one has a gift, not all have the same gift. The greater gifts are not necessarily the most dazzling. The greater gifts are those which best serve the needs of the community. So, Paul concludes, set your hearts on the greater gifts, and the greatest of these is charity.

13:1-13 Love, the more excellent way. In understanding this very famous passage, we need to bear in mind Paul's description of charity as the gift of the community. It is the more excellent way, which is also the more fundamental way, the way for all. The "love of God," Paul says, "has been poured out into our hearts through the holy Spirit that has been given to us" (Rom 5:5). Any gift without love is really nothing. It is allusion. Paul's audience at Corinth would understand this as an absolute statement of futility. The Apostle has just finished discussing the variety of spiritual gifts. Now he considers three of the more extolled. And without love, they amount to zero.

Paul considers first the gift the Corinthians favored, eloquent speech, the ability to express oneself in human or even superhuman tongues. Without love, this is a senseless void. In fact, lovelessness, according to Paul, makes *me* nothing. In 14:7-8, Paul uses a musical example. In 13:1, he seems to anticipate this analogy. A gong or a cymbal, while capable of enhancing the harmony of other instruments, are mere loud noises themselves. So it is with eloquence devoid of love.

Even prophecy, which Paul himself exalts above tongues (14:1-5), is nothing without love. So also with faith. Too often faith seems to pertain exclusively to one's relationship to God. For Paul, however, without faith in the community, nourished by love, there is nothing. Even almsgiving and martyrdom are nothing without love.

The characteristics of love are the opposite of the self-seeking, competitive characteristics of knowledge. The Corinthians' hierarchy of values fostered factiousness. But this is opposed to Christian community. Unlike the strong who anathematize the weak, love is patient. Unlike the weak who condemn the strong, love is kind. The enlightened or the celibate may put on airs or expect certain honors, but this is not the way of love. The poor, the outcast, or the neglected may brood over their injuries, but love will teach them to forgive without limit and hope without condition. It cannot be love that prompts the Corinthians to rejoice over wrong, as in the case of the incestuous man, for example (see 5:1-13). Perhaps Paul did not really intend his description of love to be applied to each of the matters brought before him by the Corinthians. But clearly the Apostle stresses that the divisions in Corinth would not exist if the community had been mindful of the primacy of love.

Love does not run out. Prophecies, tongues, knowledge, have limits, but love does not. The chapter begins and ends with a list of these three gifts that are reduced in 13:9 to two (prophecy and knowledge). Paul will compare prophecy and tongues in chapter 14 to show the superiority of prophecy. Thus, he concentrates for the moment on the remaining gift, knowledge, which decreases in importance in proportion to love.

The perfect eliminates the imperfect, which it fulfills. Love perfects knowledge, which is imperfect. The Corinthians strive for knowledge, but Paul tells them that this is symptomatic of their immaturity. Even the clearest knowledge is like a shadow compared to love, which sees face to face. The Corinthians reason like children. As they grow in Christian wisdom, they will learn to put aside childish ways and pursue love as the greatest wisdom. They despise what they do not love, but when they become mature, they will see that only love lasts. Of the three realities which endure, the greatest is love.

There are other spiritual gifts, but love is the one essential gift that characterizes the community worthy of the name Christian. Love is the criterion for judging the relative value of all other gifts, since all gifts are given for the sake of building up the community (14:1-5). Paul then develops this understanding, using the example of sound without intelligibility being like tongues without love (14:6-19). Admissible evidence for the presence of love in the community is the impact and witness value of that community upon the non-believer (14:20-25). Paul proceeds, then, to prescribe concrete rules for order which will help the community make love practical in the building up of the community (14:26-40).

14:1-5 Prophecy, a most desirable gift. True wisdom seeks love, realizing that if the community possesses this greatest gift, all the rest can have meaning. Paul considers prophecy next to love. In this section he contrasts this gift with the gift of tongues preferred by the Corinthians. One who speaks in tongues communicates with God, but not with others, whereas the prophet speaks for the sake of others. Rather surprisingly, perhaps, communication with God alone is not better than communication with others. On the contrary. Because the prophet's words are for the community, the gift supersedes the gift of tongues.

Influenced by pagan mystery religions, perhaps, the Corinthians erroneously considered the gift of tongues to be superior. Paul shows the extent and the implications of his preference for love. Tongues can separate one from the community and may be used to promote oneself. Whatever builds up the church is the greater gift. Paul recognizes tongues as a spiritual gift, but the criterion for evaluating all gifts is the edification of the community. This is the same criterion by which, Paul has insisted, all actions of the Christian, such as the judgment of personal life-style (7:1-40), of conscience (8:7-13), of whether one has the right to eat meat offered to idols (e.g., 10:23-30), or conduct at liturgies (11:17-34) must be made.

14:6-19 A comparison of gifts. Paul continues to develop the topic of the importance and function of the gift of tongues and of prophecy. Clearly appealing to the Corinthians' practical sense, Paul asks what good he would be to them if he were to come to them speaking a foreign language they did not understand. Perhaps, Paul reasons, the Corinthians would understand his point if they considered themselves as the outsiders, those who would be frustrated by his use of tongues rather than as ones who possessed this gift. Tongues without revelation, knowledge, prophecy, or instruction are useless.

Next Paul borrows an image from the world of music. The arrangement of different notes gives meaning to the sounds produced by a flute or a harp. If the notes are indistinguishable, the instrument is useless. Similarly, the bugle has to produce the expected sequence to call an army to battle. Otherwise, not only confusion, but even disaster, could result.

So it is with speaking in tongues. As long as these remain unintelligible sounds without the essential complement of interpretation, they are useless. It is absurd for the Corinthians to be impressed with futility and nothingness. Even the laws governing human languages teach us this. Unless we can interpret the sounds of others' languages, they remain strangers to us, outside the possibility of our communicating with them. But languages are designed to be a means of communication, making possible bonds among people. Language needs intelligibility, however, to become the communication it was meant to be. Tongues without interpretation are not what they are meant to be. If the Corinthians are serious about spiritual gifts, they should enrich themselves with those gifts that edify the church.

And so, the one who speaks in tongues, recognizing that this gift needs its complement, should pray for the gift of interpretation. The Greeks made a distinction not only between the body and the spirit but also between the spirit and the mind. The mind grasps intelligible things. Although with the gift of tongues we may pray with the spirit, the gift of interpretation helps us also to pray with the mind.

The mind (*nous* in Greek) or intelligibility and harmony can control even the spirit. Paul challenges the Corinthian view that speaking in tongues is more excellent because it withdraws one from the body and *nous*. Rather, Paul argues that the more excellent way is charity by which all gifts, including those of both body and spirit, work in harmony for the building up of the church and the glory of God who is peace (see 12:31–13:13).

The traditional response of the community to the words of the leaders in prayer is "Amen," which means to accept something as steadfast, to proclaim faith that what is said is true (see 2 Cor 1:20). For this "Amen" to mean anything, the members of the community must understand the reality they accept. If tongues only praise God but fail to speak to other people, then the community need not answer "Amen." Such praise could be given to God in private. Unless the community understands, its "Amen" does not signify a common prayer of the church. Paul's last comment is *ad hominem:* he gives thanks that he excels any of the Corinthians in the gift of tongues. But he far prefers the gift of instruction which serves the community.

14:20-25 Another measure of the Corinthians' immaturity. The Corinthians are childish in their conceit. With a touch of irony Paul admonishes them to be childish so far as evil is concerned, but to grow up mentally and spiritually. Such instruction echoes Jesus' words: "Be shrewd as serpents and simple as doves" (Matt 10:16). The Corinthians' competition for spiritual gifts shows how immature they are (see 3:1-4; 13:11).

Once again Paul assumes a certain knowledge of the Old Testament when he quotes Isa 28:11-12, implicitly threatening the proud Corinthians with the punishment of unbelievers. Paul seems to want to penetrate their complacency and to shock them into looking closely at how similar they are to unbelieving Israel, which did not heed God. Then Paul plays on the idea of unbelief. The nonbeliever may be attracted or impressed with the gift of tongues, just as the Corinthians were. Thus, in a sense, tongues is a gift for unbelievers. It dazzles and attracts them. But if they enter a whole assembly speaking in tongues, the nonbeliever could become indignant and judge that the whole community was out of its mind. If, however, an unbeliever enters where believers are prophesying and speaking for the upbuilding, encouragement, and consolidation of all (14:3), he or she will be confronted with the truth and given an example of love in practice. They will be led to worship God and to acknowledge that God lives among people. Thus the church functions as a prophet bringing God to the world.

14:26-40 Some rules order. Paul now lays down some rules of order in the use of the variety of spiritual gifts by the community. Having shown the propensity on the part of the Corinthians for abusing even the spiritual gifts, Paul makes some practical suggestions that could help the Corinthians avoid further confusion and make love effective in strengthening the community. Having already acknowledged that all have some spiritual gifts, Paul says that now the point is to use these for a constructive purpose.

Since the gift of tongues seems to be the most troublesome, Paul begins there. This gift must be controlled in a variety of ways—by the number of those permitted to speak, by the order in which they speak, and by requiring them to be interpreted. If there is no one with the gift of interpretation, there should be silence, since God does not require that the word be externalized and spoken. At most two or three should speak and then two or three interpret. Part of the problem of the Corinthian assembly is that the extravagant length of the services contributes to disorder and competition. The services would be limited to a reasonable length of time. Even the number of prophecies spoken are limited. The "two or three" may have reflected the promise of Jesus: "Where two or three are gathered in my name, there am I in their midst" (Matt 18:20), and "If two of you join your voices on earth to pray for anything whatever, it shall be granted you by my Father in heaven" (Matt 18:19).

It is for the assembly to decide upon the impact of the prophets' words. If one who had not even prepared to speak should receive a revelation, this one should take precedence and those who had planned to speak should listen to that one. Eventually all the prophets may speak, but only one at a time. Even the prophets themselves need to be advised and encouraged. Therefore, they must listen to the others.

The idea of control of the spirit was probably repugnant to the rambunctious Corinthians. But Paul's reasoning leaves no room for rebuttal. God is a God of peace, not of chaos. God does not inspire disorder and dissatisfaction, competition and empty rhetoric.

1 Cor 14:34-35 expresses a viewpoint which apparently contradicts what Paul had said earlier about women's prominent role in worship (see 11:5, 11-12). Moreover, Paul's use of the law to support the submission of women is contrary not only to what he says elsewhere on the subject of women (see Gal 3:28) but also to the legitimate role of the law for Christians (see Gal 4:10; Rom 10:4). Two ways of reconciling the contradiction between 1 Cor 11:5, 11-12 and 14:34-35 have been proposed.

According to one view, 14:34-35 represents an interpolation dating from the end of the first Christian century and expressing a heretical view such as the one challenged in 1 Tim 2:11-15. A problem in the early church was that women, particularly vulnerable and susceptible because of their general lack of education, fell prey to heretical teaching about sexuality and marriage. Given the propensity in Greek cultures to deemphasize the body, teachers easily went one step further, asserting that marriage was evil and abstinence better. Women themselves began to perpetuate this by believing and teaching it to other women and to their children. The author of 1 Timothy responds that women must not teach but listen, and that, far from being sinful, childbearing is for the salvation of woman (1 Tim 2:11, 14).

The second solution to the contradiction between 1 Cor 11:5, 11-12 and 14:34-35 is this. Paul is quoting the slogans of the Corinthian male elitists in 14:34-35; 14:36 is his rebuttal to this viewpoint. His sarcastic tone can almost be heard: "Did the preaching of God's word originate with you? Are you [that is, males] the only ones to whom it has come?" In a similar way he quoted and then corrected the negative view of some of the Corinthian males on marriage: "A man is better off having no relations with a woman" (7:1). Such quotations of the Corinthians' positions which Paul challenges punctuate this letter (see also 8:1; 10:23). Having discussed the appropriate way for both men and women to pray and prophesy in 11:2-16, Paul could not now be denying this liturgical or some other leadership role to women in the church. Especially at the close of this section (12:1–14:40), where Paul argues for peace and harmony in the exercise of divinely inspired gifts, it is not possible or reasonable to assume that Paul is now siding with the elitists, excluding women and alleging male superiority.

First Corinthians represents Paul's attempt to reconcile rather than aggravate factions in Corinth. 1 Cor 14:34-36 must be interpreted in the light of the reconciliation Paul tried to effect, and any interpretation of these verses has to consider the overall conciliatory tone of the entire epistle.

V. The Resurrection (1 Cor 15:1-58)

By adding his instruction on the resurrection, Paul implies that the Christians in Corinth would not have experienced so many problems and conflicts if they had understood—or better, if they had really accepted—the ramifications of the resurrection of the body. Almost all the Corinthians' misunderstandings were related to their failure to correctly appreciate the physical. All Christian faith depends upon acceptance of the reality of the resurrection (see 15:17). Paul concludes and summarizes his entire message to the Corinthians with a review of the foundations and the implications of this basic teaching. First, he presents the basic traditional elements of belief in the resurrection of Christ (15:1-11). He then addresses the Corinthian hypothesis that there is no resurrection, but dismisses this as hopeless nonsense (15:12-24). Paul goes on to try to explain the manner of the resurrection (15:35-58), concluding that this mystery can only be grasped through faith.

A. The Resurrection of Christ (15:1-11)

Paul reminds those who have become family through baptism and the gospel they have heard preached to them, which they have received, that the gospel is not mere catechetics or doctrine; it is the power to save (see Rom 1:16). And it is even now saving the Corinthians if they remain committed to what they have learned from Paul. If they do not persevere in the same gospel, they will have been converted in vain.

Again employing technical language for tradition ("I handed on to you . . . what I also received"), as he did when he spoke of the Eucharist (1 Cor 15:3; see 11:23), Paul bases the gospel on the firm ground of the tradition reaching back to Jesus' life on earth. At the center of Christian teaching is Jesus' death and resurrection. For this tradition, Paul borrows from an existing creed, which he quotes in 15:3b-5. The creed professes four elements: Christ died, he was buried, he was raised, he appeared. The Old Testament Scriptures had promised one who would save us from our sins. This is what Christ's death accomplished.

Christ's burial emphasizes the reality of his dying. In Jewish thought, burial is the final stage of death. The three days in the tomb signify the reality of that death and burial. Jesus is not presented by Paul as the agent of his resurrection. God is the judge of the living and the dead. Christ was raised by God, Paul says (see Rom 10:9). Christ truly lives. Then Christ appeared to many leaders of the church. They had no hallucinations. The Christians expressed their own consciousness that what happened was something objective, namely, Christ appeared, rather than merely "was seen." These appearances ground the Christian faith.

Paul proceeds to list some of the resurrection appearances that are important to his development here because they are foundations of the church. Some of the appearances Paul mentions are not in the Gospel accounts (for example, to the five hundred). On the other hand, all four Gospels record appearances first to women, which Paul overlooks. Paul's selectivity here betrays his motive for appealing to the resurrection appearances. Paul is reinforcing his own apostolic authority and referring to the resurrection appearances as the basis of the faith he shares with the Corinthians. Paul's own vision concludes the list. His point is that an appearance of the risen Lord gives his apostolic work its authority. Although he is the least of the apostles (Paul's name means "least"), he has been called not because of his own merit but because of God's grace in him. This grace has produced fruit, a reference to Paul's missionary activity. By the grace of God Paul preached, and by grace the Corinthians believed.

B. The Resurrection of the Dead (15:12-34)

15:12-19 The absurdity of the Corinthians' denial. In this section Paul entertains, for the sake of argument, the Corinthian hypothesis which leads to absurdity. The Corinthians who have already demonstrated certain false assumptions about the significance of the body, deny the resurrection of the dead and, with it, Christ's resurrection. Paul asks: Then why has Christ been preached as raised from the dead? Is this a lie? Is faith in vain? The resurrection of believers hinges on the resurrection of Christ. If those who have died do not have hope, believers are the most pitiable of all people, because they would be the most disillusioned. Paul's Corinthian audience would appreciate the hopelessness of such a fundamental ignorance. And without hope, what do we have? If we have this life only, we are doomed to despair and absurdity. The Corinthian hypothesis leads to no solution at all. It is a dead end.

15:20-28 Paul's alternative. Paul dismisses the Corinthian hypothesis as false, since it is based on the falsehood that Christ is not raised. Paul proceeds to review his own conviction. Christ is now already raised. His resurrection is a promise for all those who die, which, of course, includes everyone. His resurrection already has an effect on our lives of faith. As the first fruits, Christ represents the promise that all others will become as he is. This is so because Christ is the antitype of Adam, whose sin brought death to the world. How much more effect for life does Christ's resurrection have!

Paul's anthropology here is christological. The universal consequences of Adam's sin implied a universal need for salvation. Sin brought death to all. Christ's resurrection, which saves all from the reign of death, brings life to all. As the first fruits, Christ's resurrection in the past is a promise for the future.

In the end Christ will have subjected all things, spiritual and physical, to himself. His role is to destroy all disbelief and then to hand over all who are under his lordship to God the Father. The final enemy is death. Death has been vanquished in Christ, but not yet in all creatures everywhere. Paul invokes the Old Testament Scriptures to validate his point. The word of God says that all things will be placed under his feet. Christ's death began the process of overcoming the enemy powers of sin and hostility. But Christ's death is not fully accomplished even in the believer. Similarly, the author of Colossians says, "In my own flesh I fill up what is lacking in the sufferings of Christ for the sake of his body, the church" (1:24). In Christ, God has given us a part of the work of reconciling the world to himself (2 Cor 5:17-20; Col 1:20). Christ is the pledge of our inheritance, the first payment against the full redemption of a people God has made his own.

By his resurrection Christ became Lord. He was exempted from the subjection of all things, since all was to be subjected to him. He obediently subjects himself to the Father, emptying himself, taking on the form of a slave. Therefore he is exalted, and given a name above all other names (see Phil 2:9), so that always and everywhere, God is all in all.

15:29-34 The Corinthians' ignorance attacked. Having shown the absurdity of the Corinthian hypothesis in contrast to the obvious validity of his own convictions, Paul resorts to *ad hominem* arguments. He begins by asking what would be the point of some of the practices of the Corinthians themselves if Christ is not raised. He ends this section, begging them to return to reason, concluding by saying that they are ignorant.

If the dead are not raised, the custom, apparently popular in Corinth, of being baptized on behalf of the dead is absurd. Some interpreters have taken reference to this practice as evidence that the Christian community in Corinth might have modeled itself along the lines of a burial society, a voluntary association common in Paul's day that had as its goal the burial and memorial of its members.

Paul continues with an example from his own life. Continually he puts himself in danger, facing death. What wisdom could explain his being so willing to face the "beasts at Ephesus," a probable reference to the strong hostility he encountered there (see 16:8; Acts 18:19-21; 19:1-12).

If death is the last word, then the only wisdom is that of the unrighteous who preach, "Let us eat and drink, for tomorrow we die" (1 Cor 15:32; see Wis 2:6-9). This motto summarizes the selfish, unethical, purposeless existence of those without hope. Paul has already implied that some Corinthians have fallen prey to such a philosophy. The real bait of his argument is that they who are so zealous for wisdom are, in fact, ignorant of God. Because of this lack of faith in the resurrection, they are being counted with the unbelievers whom they despise.

C. The Manner of the Resurrection (15:35-58)

15:35-49 The reality of the resurrection. The skeptics among the Corinthians, because they could not describe the manner of the resurrection or the appearance of the body at the resurrection, challenged the very idea that there is a resurrection. Again Paul deals critically with these opponents. What nonsense! They pose the wrong questions. An ordinary example from agriculture demonstrates their error. The seed must die to produce the full-blown plant. The mystery of the resurrection is an everyday occurrence, and yet humans could not predict this or make it happen.

God gives to each the body he pleases, but even this cannot be fully understood. The terms "flesh," "body," and "glory" have several meanings. Simply put, Paul suggests that the term "body" after the resurrection could have a meaning we do not yet know. The body that is put in the earth is corrupted; the body that rises is incorruptible. The Corinthians certainly believe that the present body is inglorious; what rises is glorious. Many Greeks considered the body as the weaker element; what rises is strong. The physical body pulls downward, but the risen (spiritual) body ascends.

Even more sure than the existence of the "natural body" is the existence of the "spiritual body." This phrase is not intended to detract from the real aspect of the risen body. Rather, for the Corinthians with Greek philosophical tendencies, the spiritual is more real than the physical. Thus Paul cloaks his arguments in terms that those with a Greek philosophical bias will appreciate.

Next Paul introduces the Jewish conception of the two Adams made pouplar by Philo. The first man was created alive, even though he was to bring sin and death into the world. The last Adam, Paul argues, is so fully alive, so fully spiritual, that he passes on life. As the archetype of all humans, even the first Adam is the image of God. As the originator (rather than the goal) of human life, Adam was formed from dust. Earthly people are like this Adam. But spiritual people become more and more like the image of God. As we all resemble the earthly Adam, so we shall resemble the spiritual Adam (Christ). But this will require a transformation such as Paul describes in the concluding section of this chapter.

15:50-58 The resurrection as a mystery of faith. What is most clear about the resurrection is that it is based on a faith conviction rather than empirical data. We experience the body as corruptible. This universal experience demonstrates the necessity of the resurrection. The body requires a transformation before it can inherit the kingdom of God. By "flesh and blood," Paul refers not to the body per se, but to the as yet unredeemed part of our humanity. The whole argument of this chapter has been that indeed there is a resurrection of the body. Thus, it is not possible that Paul could deny the body's inheritance of the kingdom of God. Now Paul merely wants to emphasize that this is based on grace rather than on any merits inherent in the human condition.

All of this is a mystery. Paul seems only to begin to realize that there might be an extended time before the return of Christ. Many may die before this return, but not all, he thinks. Nevertheless, by the power of God, all of us will be changed. Paul uses conventional apocalyptic signs—quickly, at the sound of a trumpet (1 Thess 4:16), the dead will be changed to incorruptibility and so will those who are alive. This new incorruptible body will be necessary in the new life we will lead.

VI. CONCLUSION

1 Cor 16:1-24

Paul concludes this letter somewhat abruptly, probably because he intends to visit the church soon (16:5-7). He refers briefly to the collection (16:1-4) which he considers in much greater detail in 2 Corinthians (see 8:1–9:15). He presents his own and his companions' plans for the immediate future (1 Cor 16:5-12). He then closes with remarks about union and charity and with personal greetings (16:13-24).

16:1-4 The collection. An essential part of the gospel is the effort to relieve the needs of the poor (see Gal 2:10; Luke 4:18-19). As Apostle to the Gentiles, Paul was particularly sensitive to the possibility of making the Corinthian collection to help the starving in Jerusalem a symbol of the unity of the whole church. For Paul the collection came to represent the "debt" which the Gentile Christians owed their Jewish-Christian brethren because they reaped the benefits of the more important spiritual inheritance (see Rom 15:27). To Paul the collection also came to represent the full acceptance of the Gentiles into the church by the Jerusalem church authorities (see Rom 15:31).

Nevertheless, Paul is careful especially with the Corinthians to be completely above board and obviously free of any possible criticism about his own interest in the collection. Like the discussion on the resurrection, the collection is probably part of Paul's own agenda. The Corinthians are to follow the instructions Paul must have already issued to the Galatians, but which are not known to us. The Corinthians are to set aside whatever they can afford "on the first day of the week." This could indicate the incipient custom of Christians' gathering on Sundays, although this is not self-evident.

Paul asks that the collection be taken up before he arrives, either to avoid the time-consuming work of gathering it, which anyone could have done, or to anticipate any criticism about any particular method of collecting. Paul suggests that if the community wishes to choose its own emissaries without his personally accompanying the money, he will provide the necessary letters of introduction (see 2 Cor 8:16-24). The issue is expedited quickly, as if lingering on the details could become too painful.

16:5-12 Paul's plans. Paul speaks of his own and of some of the others' plans. He desires to visit Corinth. He thinks his business in Macedonia will not require much time, yet he needs to pass through that region before visiting the Corinthians.

Then he speaks of the others, Timothy and Apollos. He is uncertain whether to send Timothy, whom the hard-to-please Corinthians may disdain. In Paul's name the author of the Pastorals admonishes Timothy himself not to allow anyone to look down on him because of his youth (1 Tim 4:12). Apparently Paul had sent a message which he feared the younger man had not received. He wanted Timothy to return to him in Ephesus via Corinth. In any case Paul reminds the Corinthians to be instruments of peace. He concludes this section with a telling reference to Apollos, whom the Corinthians did revere. Paul heads off any suggestion that he himself may have prevented Apollos from visiting them, as if motivated by rivalry. It was Apollos' idea not to go, Paul says, despite Paul's own strong urging. No reasons are given for this disappointment. But Paul adds a promise that they will see Apollos when circumstances favor a visit.

16:13-24 Directions and greetings. Finally, typical of Paul's style and following the ancient letter form, the epistle concludes with directions and greetings. Again he warns: "Be on your guard, stand firm . . . ." This is a gospel watchword, and one Paul repeats (see Mark 13:32-37; Rom 13:11-12; 1 Thess 5:4-8). Be courageous. Be strong. Do all out of love. These sentences summarize the whole epistle.

Paul reminds the community that there are some exemplary Christians among them. He likewise calls on Stephanas, Fortunatus, and Achaicus to be models of service to the community. Perhaps these were the bearers of the Corinthians' letter and questions to Paul (see 7:1). The enthusiasm with which Paul wrote this letter suggests that he might have sent them back with many spoken and unspoken messages which a mere written response could not contain. Their example will be their most eloquent statement.

Part of Paul's mission is to maintain communication among the churches. Thus he includes greetings from the believers in Asia. Aquila and Prisca had lived with Paul in Corinth where they met and shared his means of livelihood after the couple had been expelled from Rome (Acts 18:1-3). Now they are presented as leaders of the church at Ephesus from where Paul writes.

Paul instructs that the letter be read during the liturgy and that Christians make the kiss of peace the sign of acceptance of the contents and the lessons. Paul seals the letter with a postscript in his own handwriting. The Old Testament idea of a choice of ways, one leading to life and the other to death, lies behind Paul's curse of all who do not love the Lord. The Lord's favor and Paul's are one. He ends with a profession of his own great love for the Corinthians.

2 CORINTHIANS

Mary Ann Getty

INTRODUCTION

Nowhere else in Paul's writings is the passionate human character of this great apostle more evident than in Second Corinthians. Here we have the personal testimony of Paul, his ardent reactions when distrusted and accused and concerned about a community he loves deeply. There in broad strokes Paul paints his own profile and, at the same time, gives us a look inside himself, at his vulnerability and strong feelings for others. Second Corinthians conjures up that part of Paul which most attracts us—his depth, his affection. Second Corinthians also provides the focus on what readers most dislike and suspect in Paul and what they are most likely to misunderstand and reject. Some of the outstanding qualities of this letter are related to three focal points on very sensitive issues: Paul's apologia and self-defense, his stress on suffering, and his insistence on the importance of the collection.

In a sense, this appears as a very harsh letter, punctuated with solemnity and oaths (for example, 1:3-5, 23), issuing corrections and warnings (see 2:9-11, 17; 11:18-23), spotted with threats of severity, self-justification, and complaints (for example, 10:3; 13:2). The frequent appearance of the term "boasting" suggests that the charge of egoism often levied against Paul is well-founded (see especially 10:1–13:10). Paul is hardly mild in his reaction to the challenge that he is not a true but an inferior apostle, and he turns sarcastic in his references to the "super-apostles" (see 11:5; 12:11). The Corinthians, for their part, seem to be incorrigible in their need to measure and control love as they demand proof that they are loved by the Apostle (see 12:15-16). Paul counters their skepticism and competitiveness with reminders about the only evidence admissible to the only court he recognizes as valid. Before God and before the tribunal of Christ, the faith of the Corinthians provides the irrefutable witness of the Apostle's authority and integrity.

In Second Corinthians Paul stresses the value of suffering as a witness to the truth of the gospel, the power of God (especially 10:1–13:10). So powerful is this witness that suffering is transformed from an evil into the most eloquent testimony of faith. In First Corinthians, Paul presented the cross as the decisive truth, folly for those who were perishing, but salvation to those with faith (1 Cor 1:18). In Second Corinthians, Paul describes his own suffering as indisputable evidence of his call as an apostle, of his authority to make all things subject to God in Christ, of his mission to share the ministry of reconciliation with others. An experience of suffering and of receiving God's healing mercy qualifies the minister of the new covenant (see 2 Cor 2:16; 4:1, 7-15). This is a ministry Paul shares with the recalcitrant Corinthians (5:17-20).

Finally, in Second Corinthians, Paul gives a theoretical, theological basis for the very practical collection (8:1–9:15). Although he himself rejects financial support and downplays the value of this support as a sign of his apostolate, he insists on the importance of the Corinthians' generous giving as a symbol that they accept kinship with the starving saints in Jerusalem. Although he himself is criticized precisely because he refuses personal support, he warns the Corinthians that their willingness to contribute liberally is essential, not secondary, to their full participation in the spiritual benefits of the gospel.

Second Corinthians contains many unique allusions to events we cannot corroborate with any other New Testament writing. This observation underscores another reason tradition has so highly valued this letter. Further, there are in 2 Corinthians sporadic changes of mood, sudden shifts of emphasis, changes of subject, disruptions and resumption of topics already presumed to be settled. These may tempt us to despair of ever trying to fit together the pieces of the puzzle which would elucidate the reasons Paul wrote and give us a clear picture of the unity of this letter. Most scholars concur that this canonical letter is a composite of possibly as many as four separate letters or fragments of letters. The most readily separable parts are 2 Cor 6:14–7:1; 9:1-15; and 10:1–13:10, each of which we can briefly introduce in anticipation of our commentary.

The warning against pagan contacts (2 Cor 6:14–7:1) appears suddenly and intrusively within the context of Paul's personal appeal to the Corinthians to widen their hearts (7:2) as he has done in their regard (see 6:11-13). This suggests that 6:14–7:1 is an interpolation or a digression. The hypothesis that this is a fragmentary interpolation representing what remains of a pre-canonical letter referred to in 1 Cor 5:9 is attractive, but it lacks sufficient hard evidence. Since Paul is completely capable of whimsical digressions whenever he happens to think of a topic, the more reliable possibility is that, while speaking "frankly" (2 Cor 6:11), he could have digressed to the topic of the undivided devotion required of the true believer (6:14–7:1). Paul's language and ideas in this digression are not only foreign to this context but even unique in Paul's writings. On the other hand, they are familiar in Qumran literature, and Paul could have drawn on this contemporary source to give another dimension to his notion of the community as the temple of God.

2 Cor 9:1-15 is a kind of doublet compared with chapter 8 but with another perspective and reasoning. Both deal with the collection for the poor. The introductory statement (9:1) about how it would be superfluous to mention the collection is particularly strange in view of the preceding chapter. Possibly chapter 9 was originally a separate letter to the churches in Achaia. It might have been written as a letter of introduction for the delegates, who would use it as credentials for their mission of actually taking up the collection. The early church, which would have wanted to make sure that it was not lost, probably inserted it here because of the congruity of content with chapter 8.

Finally, 2 Cor 10:1–13:10 does not seem to be part of the original unity of this epistle. Again, there is an abrupt, unexpected change of tone and return to some issues already presumed to be settled in the preceding chapters, especially compared to the first seven chapters (for example, the charge of Paul's recommending himself, of his not accepting support for his mission from the Corinthians, of his credentials compared with the "super-apostles," etc.) Further, it seems surprising that Paul would relegate to the end of this epistle these important reflections on how he authenticates his apostleship through sufferings. The apparent self-contained, detachable qualities of these chapters make it questionable that they originally belonged precisely here, at the end of Paul's highly charged letter.

OUTLINE OF SECOND CORINTHIANS

1:1-11	I. Introduction: Address
1:1-2	Greeting
1:3-11	Paul's hardship and blessing
1:12–7:16	II. The Crisis Between Paul and the Corinthians
1:12–2:13	A. Past Relationships
1:12-14	Paul's sincerity
1:15-24	Paul justifies his change of plans
2:1-4	The tearful letter
2:5-11	The offender is forgiven
2:12-13	Paul's anxiety and relief
2:14–7:4	B. Paul's Ministry
2:14–3:3	Ministers of the new covenant
3:4-18	The contrast between the new and old covenants
4:1-15	Paul's versus his detractors' ministry
4:16–5:10	Suffering as the credential of the Apostle

5:11-21	The ministry of reconciliation
6:1-10	A description of Paul's apostleship
6:11-13	A personal plea to the Corinthians
6:14–7:1	A digression: You are the temple of God
7:2-4	Paul resumes his plea
7:5-16	C. Resolution of the Crisis Good news from Titus
8:1–8:15	III. THE COLLECTION FOR JERUSALEM
8:1-24	A. Appeal to the Corinthians' Generosity
8:1-5	Example of the Macedonians
8:6-24	Titus' role and motives for generous giving
9:1-15	B. A Second Appeal Addressed to Achaia
9:1-4	Exhortation to promptness
9:5-15	The blessings of liberality
10:1–13:10	IV. PAUL'S DEFENSE OF HIS MINISTRY
10:1-18	A. Paul Refutes His Enemies
11:1–13:10	B. Paul's Cause for Confident Boasting
11:1-15	Paul versus the super-apostles
11:16-33	Paul's experience of mercy and healing
12:1-10	Ecstasies and humility
12:11-21	Paul's apprehension regarding the Corinthians
13:1-10	C. Final warnings
13:11-13	V. CONCLUSION

COMMENTARY

I. INTRODUCTION

2 Cor 1:1-11

Paul's introduction to Second Corinthians is brief, as if superfluous. The Apostle begins with the customary self-introduction and greeting (1:1-2), which is markedly abbreviated. The usual thanksgiving is replaced with a benediction for the blessings Paul has received, especially for the hardships he has been able to endure (1:3-11).

1:1-2 Greeting. Characteristically Paul identifies himself as an apostle, one sent by Jesus Christ, called by God's will. On that call his authority as an apostle rests. He is joined in sending greetings by Timothy, a Christian whose brotherhood also is recognized both by Paul and by the Corinthians. Timothy, trusted by both, acts as mediary, facilitating the difficult relationship between the Apostle and this troublesome community (see 1 Cor 4:17; 16:10; 2 Cor 1:19; Acts 18:5; 19:22). The Corinthians, regardless of how quarrelsome and sinful, are identified as "holy ones." Paul greets the church of Corinth, capital of the Roman province of Achaia. Recognition of the mixed character of the church is implied in Paul's joining of the Greek "grace" to the Jewish "peace."

1:3-11 Paul's hardship and blessing. The usual thanksgiving found in all Paul's letters, except in 2 Corinthians and Galatians, is replaced by a benediction calling for praise of God, Father of our Lord, of mercies, and of consolation. According to the ancient custom, letter writers begin with thanks for their own good health. Paul's implication is that his recent suffering and hardship that even threatened death (1:8-9) do not nullify his thanksgiving but cause him to offer praise to God. The suffering of a believer can actually contribute the dimension of conviction and credibility to ministry. The strengthening of having suffered that God communicates to a disciple through afflictions is not merely a selfish, interior thing. It is passed on to others. Sharing the suffering of Christ means having the hope and consolation he brings through his victory over suffering and death.

The Apostle sees in his own experiences an opportunity for encouragement of others. Indeed, this can be the salvation of others, who see his patience as a testimony against despair. Thus Paul fulfills the role of the prophet (see 1 Cor 14:3). Paul, the consummate optimist, holds on to his belief in the fidelity of God. Jesus' own death experience, although it threatened to break the thread of hope that bound him to a faithful God, only served to provide the source of life for all believers after him. Similarly, Paul acknowledges to the Philippians that even the great suffering of his imprisonment is turned into the good of encouragement for the sake of other believers (Phil 1:12-14). Paul himself provides a model of a believer for whom there is no comparison between the sufferings of this world and the glory as yet to be revealed, but all things work together unto good (see Rom 8:18, 28).

The Corinthians are Paul's kin because of their common faith. He shares with them his hardships so that they will be strengthened. This encouragement will come not because they will either understand suffering better or somehow be pleased to know Paul's recent struggle has been so excruciating. Nor is Paul merely wanting to rehearse his trials to impress the Corinthians. It is not certain exactly what suffering Paul refers to here, but clearly it was some adversity that went so far as to confront him with death. The experience of suffering, so threatening to faith, deepens in Paul not only his own faith convictions but his credibility as a minister of the gospel which has the cross at its center. Having faced even the possibility of death, the Apostle now manifests a new dimension of compassion, a new appreciation of life, a new level of confidence. Having been rescued from death, the Apostle recognizes how God continually sustains him in life. His hope having thus been strengthened, Paul asks for the aid of the Corinthians' prayers. These prayers express Paul's and the Corinthians' thanks to God, who is recognized not only as the originator of life but as a sustainer and consoler in trials.

II. THE CRISIS BETWEEN PAUL AND THE CORINTHIANS

2 Cor 1:12–7:16

The charges of the Corinthians draw from Paul a self-defense poignant in the depth of human feeling it betrays while it is balanced by Paul's confidence in ultimate reconciliation. Paul defends his sincerity when it is attacked by the Corinthians, whose confidence has been strained by the Apostle's change of plans (1:12–2:13). He then presents his ministry of the new covenant and his own suffering as qualifying credentials (2:14–7:4). Finally, Paul returns to the strained relationship between himself and the community, expressing the basic conviction that they will be reconciled (7:5-16).

This structure is determined by the general ABA' schema characteristic of Paul's style. According to this schema, Paul typically introduces a topic, suddenly abandons it for another idea, and then returns to the original subject. Often his emphasis is expressed through the middle or "B" section (in this case, 2:14–7:4), where Paul states principles and gives further illustrations of their implications. Thus, Paul's divinely inspired ministry is the basis on which he defends his sincerity (1:12–2:13) and expresses confidence in eventual reconciliation with the Corinthians (7:5-16).

A. Past Relationships (1:12–2:13)

Paul undertakes a self-defense, noting his sincerity and trustworthiness (1:12-14), despite his change of plans (1:15-24). He then refers to a previous letter written with many tears (2:1-4). He does not specify why he had to thus justify himself and his change of plans, and this section of the letter was apparently written before he received good news from Titus regarding the compliance of the Corinthians (see 7:6-7).

1:12-14 Paul's sincerity. Paul calls on his own conscience and, later, on God (1:23), as witness to the truth he speaks. He is absolutely sincere. His behavior is motivated by the call and authority he has from God. Holiness as described here by Paul is relational, given by God and certified in the actions of a legitimate apostle. Such Paul is. His is a true channel for God's holiness to be read and understood by God's people, the Corinthians. Paul refers to their past experience together. His comparatively long stay with them means the Corinthians are acquainted with him. A better knowledge will bear out the truthful sincerity of Paul's words.

Paul's boast before God and the indisputable evidence of his apostleship (see 1 Cor 4:15; 9:2) are the Corinthians themselves, who in the flesh of the life of their community, are writing a letter of recommendation to God on Paul's behalf (2 Cor 3:3, 6). The judgment which will vindicate the truth of this will come on the day of our Lord Jesus when the only legitimate boasts will be the works done in the service of the Lord (see 1 Cor 1:31). These alone lead to salvation.

1:15-24 Paul justifies his change of plans. Apparently Paul's detractors have undermined the Corinthians' confidence in him, so that he must justify why he has delayed so long in visiting them. It appears that a promised visit never occurred. Paul reviews his plans so that they will understand why some changes were made rather than accuse him of insincerity in raising their expectations for that postponed visit. Originally Paul had hoped to go to Corinth twice, once in passing on the way to Macedonia, and then to stay longer on his return (see 1 Cor 16:6-7), before he would travel on to Judea. The implication of insincerity pains him deeply. He pauses in his review of what unexpectedly intervened to emphasize how fundamental he considers the trust which is threatened by the Corinthians' charge.

Paul is true to his word. Jesus' injunction against oath-taking might have inspired Paul's insistence that there is no need among believers to be more emphatic than a simple yes and no. Nevertheless, to reinforce his point, Paul implicitly makes reference to the law which demands at least two witnesses for the admission of valid testimony. He then calls on the witness of his co-workers Silvanus and Timothy who, together with Paul, preached Jesus as the faithful Son who fulfilled God's trustworthy word. The faith of the Corinthians rests on this same preaching. Thus the Corinthians must believe Paul.

Both the Corinthians and Paul express their Amen to Jesus in worship (see 1 Cor 14:16). Paul's solemnity is extreme because of the seriousness of the charge against him. His testimony rests on God's word which, above all, established the relationship between the Corinthians and their apostle. God anointed Paul an apostle, and the Corinthian ministry sealed this apostleship (see 1 Cor 9:2). The love of God poured into human hearts by the Holy Spirit (Rom 5:5) will enable the Corinthians to accept Paul. The Spirit is the first fruits, the payment or pledge of our final inheritance (see Eph 1:13-14).

Paul's word can be trusted. But it was out of love for the Corinthians that Paul's plans were changed. The Apostle is convinced that love is the only thing that cannot hurt another (see Rom 13:8-10). Thus, charity is the only thing that offers adequate explanation of Paul's change of plans. Charity qualifies and relativizes even the most cherished projects such as Paul's ardent desire to see the Corinthians. When Paul decided that a visit to them would suggest that he was trying to dominate the Corinthians' faith, he abandoned his plans for the time being. His physical presence with them was relatively unimportant; the only essential was that they stood firm in their faith. Paul abrogates the role of domination for himself, preferring to work side by side in equal and reciprocal partnership with his communities (see Phil 1:3-8). His goal is their happiness. As long as their faith is firm, he is willing to forego his own projects.

2:1-4 The tearful letter. Paul returns to the fact that, indeed, he decided not to visit them "again" (see 1:23) under painful circumstances. On a former visit, he had to admonish and punish them. He resolved not to further undermine their relationship with him by appearing again in this role he now repudiates. He adds that just as he is capable of making them sad, so is he affected by them. And he can only be made glad again by the repentance of those he had to punish. Paul explains that his letter was intended to provoke the conversion upon which both the Corinthians' and his own happiness depends. Formerly he chided them for their failure to correct an erring member (see 1 Cor 5:1-11). Now he shows his willingness to follow his own advice while recognizing how dearly he pays for chastising those he loves. His copious tears testify to the great love he bears for the Corinthians. He is not indifferent to them. That they are saddened must be transformed into gratitude for the love that binds apostle and community.

2:5-11 The offender is forgiven. The community could not smugly overlook blatant offenses. It had a responsibility to promote justice. Paul had instructed the community to judge and punish the offender, as in the case of the incestuous man. It is possible but not certain that this is the same person whom Paul now advises the community to readmit lest he be crushed by his sorrow. It is futile to try to identify the person in question on the grounds of the offense he has committed. Paul's point is that he himself takes no pleasure in that man's punishment. Nor is Paul's issue that he himself was personally offended, so that restitution has to be made to him. The offense injured the community, which explains why the community who punished him could and should now be reconciled to him. Jesus entrusted the power to bind and to loose to his disciples (see Matt 18:15-18), who are contrasted with the scribes and the Pharisees who bind but do not loose (see Matt 23:4). The community's authority is exercised in healing and reconciling. Its goal (i.e., the repentance of the sinner) has been achieved. Now the community must show itself capable of integrating the offender within the unlimited boundaries of forgiveness.

Just as the community had shown itself faithful to Paul in punishing the offender, now it must believe that reconciliation is possible. Paul's instruction serves also as evidence of the Corinthians' loyalty to him. His own forgiveness of the offender represents an example for their sakes. This he also swears before Christ. One of the functions of forgiveness is that it is a weapon against Satan, who tries to divide and overcome the community. The incestuous man had been expelled from the community and delivered over to Satan only so that his spirit would be saved (1 Cor 5:5). Such exclusion must be temporary and ultimately replaced by reconciliation, so that evil will not triumph.

2:12-13 Paul's anxiety and relief. Paul's change of plans involved skipping Corinth and traveling on to Troas where there was ample need and opportunity to preach. But his concern for the Corinthians impeded him so that he continued on to Macedonia, where he encountered Titus fresh from Corinth. Titus' news included the report of the Corinthians' passing the "test" Paul administered. The Apostle, heartened by the fact that they had obeyed his instruction and punished the offender, now implies his confidence in their forgiving his own change of plans and acceptance of his loving motives.

God's ways are mysterious, but the believer does not let sorrow, incomprehension, or despair darken the heart. No pain endured or length of time passed without understanding should cause a believer to lose faith. There seems to be a complete break between the poignant pain expressed in 2:13 and the mood expressed in the hymn of praise that erupts in 2:14. But this is not atypical of Paul (see Rom 7:24 and 25; 8:35-39 and 9:1-5). The experience of the cross strengthens Paul's faith in the provident wisdom of God to whom he offers thanks.

B. Paul's Ministry (2:14–7:4)

Having been assured by Titus' reports about the Corinthians, Paul embarks on a series of reflections on his apostolate (2:14–7:4), testifying that his mission is an extension of Christ's own. As he did in 1 Cor 1:18, Paul identifies the two divisions among people that are effected by the judgment which the cross of Christ represents. There are those who are being saved and those who are headed for destruction. The distinction is made by faith (2:14-17).

Paul continues his defense of his ministry of the new covenant (3:1-18). He identifies the divine origin and power of his ministry (4:1-15) and looks to the everlasting recompense for his fidelity (4:16–5:10). He goes on to describe the ministry of reconciliation which excludes no one, but includes all who are in Christ (5:11–6:10).

2:14–3:3 Ministers of a new covenant. No mere human qualifications can prepare a person for such a mission as this. Paul's authority and motivation come from God. As an apostle, Paul represents the One who "sent" him, for this is the meaning of his apostolate. His very lack of human credentials testifies to this authority. No one will accuse him of gaining personally from preaching the word.

Paul refutes a double charge of the Corinthians. First, they accuse him of arrogance and boasting. In addition, they point out that he bears no letters of recommendation such as were customary to expect from a messenger. These might have testified to Paul's credentials, his gifts, the authorities' approval of him. The Corinthians valued such things. Paul's rhetorical question suggests incredulity and sarcasm. Others might need such letters. But the Corinthians themselves are all Paul needs to recommend him. Even if he were not an apostle to anyone else, he is to them (see 1 Cor 9:2). They are his letter, written by Christ. The whole world can read this recommendation. The letter is written on the Corinthians' hearts.

The letter is not written in mere ink but by the spirit of God. Paul combines the allusion to the stone tablets of Exod 31:18 to the new covenant written on human hearts of Jer 31:33, and to the spirit God promises, who will change hearts of stone into hearts of flesh (Ezek 11:19; 36:26). This combination prepares the stage for Paul's contrast between the "new covenant" (3:6) and the "old covenant" (3:14), which the rest of the chapter develops.

3:4-18 The contrast between the new and old covenants. Continuing his response to the charge of arrogance, Paul describes the basis of the confidence of the minister of the Lord (3:4, 12). The only legitimate boast is in the Lord (see 1 Cor 1:31). Interested in external, superficial qualifications, the Corinthians continually erect false standards for judging the apostles. Paul resists the claim of entitlement. The same God who called him when he was a persecutor of the church (see Phil 3:3-7) is faithful. Although no one could conceivably be qualified for this mission (see 2 Cor 2:16), the God who created and who made the covenant written in stone, now recreates and qualifies ministers for the new covenant. The purpose of the law was to define sin which kills. But the spirit of God gives life.

Paul's argumentation in 3:7-8 should not minimize the power of his contrast between the old and the new. Not only the former Jews among his readers would affirm the first "conditional" clause. Indeed, the entire early Christian community, which adapted the titles originally claimed by Israel for itself, recognized the glory that went with Israel's being chosen as God's people. Indeed, Exod 34:29-35 describes how Moses had to cover his face with a veil when he descended the mountain to talk to the people after speaking with God, so great was even the mere reflection of God's glory on Moses' countenance. If such be the force of glory that fades, of a covenant that condemns and that had the knowledge of sin (see Gal 3:19), how much greater will be the glory of the spirit and of the ministry which gives life? The former covenant is characterized by a fading glory, limited and condemning. In comparison to the new covenant, the former glory is no glory at all.

The glory of the new covenant, which far surpasses and relativizes the glory of the old, gives Paul full confidence. In the following chapter he will describe the trials he has endured (2 Cor 4:8-12); here Paul reveals the reason for his boldness and assurance. "We are not like Moses." Whereas Moses hid his face and the glory that shone on it, Paul announces the unveiling of the covenant of the Lord.

The metaphor of the veil becomes confused in the transfer from Moses' face to the minds of the Israelites. Paul alludes to the blindness that prevents them from recognizing the true meaning of the law (Rom 10:1-3), namely, its passing nature. The law has been both abrogated and fulfilled in Christ who is its end and in whom there is justification for all who believe (Rom 10:4). A quotation that originally referred to Moses and God is applied by Paul to the Christian who recognizes Jesus as Lord.

In Paul we can trace only the faint beginnings of a Trinitarian conception. Here he equates the Lord (usually a reference to Jesus) with the Spirit. In the Lord we are given the spirit of freedom. This freedom makes us children of God, capable of saying, "Abba, Father" (see Rom 8:15; Gal 4:6). In freedom, believers are transformed into the image of God. All are thus transformed, growing in likeness to the Lord through the Spirit. Just as Paul's confidence develops from great (2 Cor 3:4) to "full" (3:12), so Paul expands his consideration from his own ministry to that of all believers.

4:1-15 Paul's versus his detractors' ministry. Paul continues to contrast his view of the gospel and his mission with the views of his opponents. He is undaunted, not because he is indifferent to the charges made against him but because his confidence is firmly rooted in God's mercy, which never changes (see Gal 1:15-17). This experience of mercy qualifies Paul as a minister (see 2 Cor 2:16-17). Because his ministry is based in God rather than in his own merits, he is enabled to repudiate every falsehood and to proclaim the truth with disarming boldness.

Paul's detractors accuse him of exercising cunning and of not being trustworthy (see 1:17-18; 12:16). They add that he does not show the recognizable signs of a true apostle (see 11:13; 12:11-16; 1 Cor 9:3-18), signs they themselves have deemed necessary, such as letters of recommendation (see 2 Cor 3:1-3). Paul's disclaimer is that since his ministry is based on an experience of God's gratuitous predilection and mercy, he has nothing to hide. Indeed, with startling transparency, he continually invites his readers to scrutinize all of his actions and words and his entire life and to imitate him (see 1 Cor 11:1; Phil 1:27-30; 4:9). Paul shows little interest in the external criteria of "true apostleship" invented and recognized by the Corinthians. He adamantly denies that he falsifies the gospel message, although he accuses his opponents of doing just that (see 2 Cor 2:17), probably because they make it dependent on other things besides God. He has repeatedly taught that there is only one gospel, and even if he himself tried to change it, he would be anathema (see Gal 1:8; 2 Cor 11:4). Yet the truth persists.

Paul concedes that he does commend himself. This for several reasons. Certainly he needs no other recommendation than that he introduced the Corinthians to the gospel. He completely identifies himself by the gospel he preaches and places himself at the service of those to whom he preaches (see 1 Cor 9:19-23). He is, then, in a sense, the gospel link between Jesus Christ and the Corinthians. This is the truth, plainly revealed and recognized by all except those on their way to perdition.

Continuing his use of the image of the veil, Paul also tentatively and provisionally concedes that there is, for some, a veil over the truth he preaches, but this is due to their unbelief rather than to his cunning. Paul has no false humility which would obscure the gospel. Those headed for destruction ally themselves with the god of this age. Possibly Paul refers to Satan who, for a time, appears to dominate the world. Or Paul could be adapting the traditional Jewish teaching of the successive aeons of the world: chaos, which reigned before the law; the period of the law, which previously separated the just from the unjust; and finally the coming of the messianic age, when the observance of justice would be perfect and universal. The relationship of this messianic age to the present time was disputed by the rabbis. Paul presents Jesus as ushering in the final, decisive time and thus makes the gospel the new basis, replacing the law, for distinguishing between the saved and those who are not.

The exact charge of Paul's detractors is unclear, but the context suggests that they refer to Paul's personal weaknesses (see 10:10) as disqualifying him from the apostolate. Paul himself recites the history of his suffering, not as a detraction but as proof that his ministry is rooted in God's own power. Such a ministry reflects the witness of Jesus as the image of God manifest in his sufferings on the cross (see Gal 3:1). Paul uses the reference to the image of God in Gen 1:26-27 to complement his very powerful paradoxical image of the treasure carried in earthen vessels. Jesus is the image of God and, through the cross, Jesus revealed the power and the wisdom of God. This is scandal for those who do not believe, but salvation for those who do (1 Cor 1:18). By referring to Christ as the image of God, Paul implies his preeminence (see Col 1:15-20) and his obedience to the point of death on the cross (Phil 2:6-11).

Just as Jesus' own ministry is reflected in Paul's life, Paul's ministry is bearing fruit in the believing Corinthians. The contagious character of the Christian mystery teaches that life comes through death and the sharing of faith. This mystery begins with the power of the resurrection already taking place among believers. The power of grace is that through faith God is glorified, and thankful praise is offered by the many who believe.

4:16–5:10 Suffering as the credential of the Apostle. The sting of suffering is the severe strain it puts on faith. It tests belief both in a just God and in the efficacy of redemption. Paul reiterates his own faith while at the same time inviting others ("we") to dispel discouragement. Even while his body is being spent in ministry, his inner being is being daily renewed. Paul adapts a Greek philosophical idea about the tension between the body and the spirit. This section employs several images (the inner being, a house, clothing, exile) to describe Paul's apparently just dawning realization that the in-between times, that is, the lapse between Jesus' promise to return and the final judgment (see 5:10), may be prolonged. Even the most firm belief in the resurrection does not detract from the poignancy of the sufferings of this life. Paul describes salvation generally in terms of fixing our gaze, not on the here and now, but on what is unseen and hoped for.

This hope is a form of firm knowledge. We live as in a tent, preparing for the eternal dwelling God is providing for us. No believer is really at home in the world. Attempts at comprehending the relationship between this life and that which is to come constitute mere groanings of the spirit, such as the Israelites in Egypt uttered even before they knew the name by which they could call upon God (see Exod 2:23-25). Nakedness is a symbol of shame and depravity in the Old Testament (see Gen 3:10; Isa 33:11; Ezek 16:7, 37-39). Christian life clothes us with armor to guard us against such evil (see Rom 13:12-14; 1 Thess 5:8). Yet so helpless and overburdened is the human condition that we depend completely on what is immortal to save and envelop us. Paul's language reflects his resurrection teachings: "This corruptible body must be clothed with incorruptibility" (1 Cor 15:53). The mortal must be absorbed and transformed by the immortal, death is transformed by life. What we see only leads us to hope, since despair renders all absurd. God has fashioned us for life and God does not repent of his creation. The pledge of this life is the Spirit who has been given to us.

In the Spirit is our confidence. While we are still in the earthly body, we groan awaiting the full redemption of the children of God (see Rom 8:14-27). Faith is not a static condition but a dynamic life in which we walk. Faith tells us to be full of confidence as we acknowledge our desire to be already with the Lord. This desire makes life in this body seem like an exile, while we long to be at home. Yet we subordinate personal desire to the will of the Lord. Imprisoned and frustrated, Paul himself felt this same tension and he wrote to the Philippians: "To me, 'life' means Christ; hence dying is so much gain" (Phil 1:21). The purpose of the life of faith is not to completely understand God's will but to acknowledge that such a will exists, that it is provident, and that it includes a ministry for all believers. All of this can be fully revealed only at the tribunal of Christ. Christ is perceived as a judge (1 Thess 1:7-10) whose gospel reevaluates all things, giving a new basis for distinguishing between good and evil.

5:11-21 The ministry of reconciliation. Placing himself constantly before the tribunal of Christ (see 5:10), the sole arbiter of his sincerity, Paul continues his self-defense (see 1 Cor 4:1-5). At the same time, he continues to demolish the false standards by which the Corinthians judge their ministers. Paul's accountability is to the Lord, but he wishes that his integrity would also be recognized by the Corinthians. He refers again to the charge of recommending himself (see 2 Cor 3:1). Vowing that he will not repeat this offer, Paul now invites the Corinthians to revise their negative judgment and, on the basis of the qualifications Paul has described, not only to accept him and his ministry, but to take pride in him. This will enable them to respond to those who falsely pride themselves on externals.

Paul's own life is a parable of the way God works, which reverses human standards. Paul seems to alternate between mystical or ecstatic experiences and the very down-to-earth experiences of his weakness. And this is also because he is a minister of the new covenant—on the one hand knowledgeable in the ways of God, and on the other a servant to all people. It is God's own charity that impels him. Grace *(charis)* provides the guiding conviction of Paul's life, which says that since Christ died, all have died—to sin, to self-seeking, to any need for self-aggrandizement. Christ's death for our sins was also a promise that with him, all will truly be raised up.

The resurrection provides a new perspective, a godly vision that restores all things. If, before the conversion effected by the resurrection, we judged Christ and others from human standards such as the Corinthians counted important, now we see everything differently. All is new in Christ. Priorities have changed. All that matters is that one is created anew (see Gal 6:15). The same God who created out of nothing is certainly capable of recreating and of making us, however poor, unpromising, and undeserving, sharers of his work. God reconciled the world to himself in Christ. Further, in Christ, God overcame the obstacle of our transgressions so that we are enabled to become partners in the ministry of reconciliation. And not only the apostles, but all who are in Christ, have been sent out into the world with a single message: Be reconciled! This is both imperative and empowerment. For our sakes God made the sinless one sin so that redemption could penetrate the darkest, most forbidding, isolated, and inhuman part of our human experience. This was so that God, in Christ, could bring us to holiness.

6:1-10 A description of Paul's apostleship. Paul describes the ministry of all believers. Paul identifies the Corinthians as his co-workers, detaching himself in his role as apostle from any claim to power or domination over others. The optimism of Isaiah's promise is already fulfilled today, Paul insists. Paul calls us to the now moment. His primary motivation is the spread of the gospel. He wishes to do nothing that would impede that ministry. He does not wish to be an obstacle so he struggles to liberate the gospel from any binding circumstances of his own life and actions. He reflects Jesus' beatitude: "Blessed is the one who takes no offense in me" (see Luke 7:23).

Paul proceeds to give a description of that ministry which already in his life has manifested itself as "much endurance" through every kind of adverse condition—afflicted by nature and accidents, maligned by others and subjected to self-imposed discipline. The mettle of his sincerity has been tested by fire. He is not a victim of circumstances but a warrior who sharpens his "weapons of righteousness." While the war imagery is decidedly objectionable to many Christians today, Paul's use here underscores the realism and vigilance required of the minister of reconciliation who struggles for serenity and integrity, not only when honored but when dishonored, not only when assailed by outside opponents but also when experiencing inner conflicts and fears, not only in favorable but in unfavorable circumstances, too. The "gospel" has effected a reversal of values. The most blatant dichotomy exists between how the apostles were viewed and the real meaning and experiences of being an ambassador of reconciliation (see 1 Cor 4:9-13). Accounted as fools, having nothing, the ministers of the gospel are rich and wise in the only reality that matters.

6:11-13 A personal plea to the Corinthians. Paul pours out his heart. He makes an appeal to all the sympathy that characterizes the relationship between apostle and community. Having spoken personally (see 4:8-15; 6:4-10), he now reminds the Corinthians of the grandeur of their calling in God and then urgently, passionately exhorts them to manifest this identity in their relationship and acceptance of him.

Paul has defended his sincerity and he invites the Corinthians to witness the openness of his heart. He refers to himself as a parent to the Corinthians, to whom he has given birth in Christ. With disarming tenderness, he begs them to reciprocate his sincerity. He does not ask of them more than he has already done by way of example (see 1 Cor 11:1).

6:14–7:1 A digression: You are the temple of God. It is entirely possible that this apparent digression was originally part of another letter, perhaps the pre-canonical, now lost letter written in tears (see 1 Cor 5:9-11; 2 Cor 2:3-4; or 7:8-9 or a combination of these). But even though it appears abruptly, without transition, with ideas and vocabulary somewhat foreign to Paul, this section serves as an appropriate reminder to the difficult Corinthians of their real identity in God and their need to reevaluate all things in relationship to this identity.

The Corinthians were continually in danger of succumbing to the pagan environment in which they lived. There was a traditional religious connection based on the Old Testament between idolatry and adultery, and Paul uses this to form a graphic link between the Corinthians' well-known reputation and their tendency to be easily misled. Although he does not allude to the questions of false credentials or to the Corinthians' charge of recommending himself in this passage, Paul's warning about a mismatching between God and idols does qualify this section as a particularly apt illustration of the dangers of misinterpreting the real purpose of ministry and failure to recognize the true ministers. Several antitheses serve Paul's point. Light has nothing to do with darkness (see John 3:19-21; 11:10), just as righteousness is opposed to lawlessness. Christ opposes all that is evil, personified as Belial, as the evil one or Satan is called in some Jewish writings. Faith is the valid criterion for salvation. There is no common ground for worship of idols alongside worship of the one true God (see also 1 Cor 10:21-22). The God of Israel is a jealous God, as the Old Testament teaches.

Paul identifies the community as the temple of the living God, drawing on a collection of references from the Scriptures (see Lev 26:12; Ezek 37:27; Isa 52:11; Jer 31:9). Whereas in 1 Cor 6:19 Paul presented the individual Christian as the temple of God, his meaning here is collective, depicting the bonds between believers as sons and daughters of God which distinguish them from those who follow idols. Paul's inference is that the Corinthians risk falling back into paganism when they erect false criteria by which to judge true apostleship. Paul concludes this section with a reminder of the promises which define the goal of all believers. "Fear of God" does not reduce the believer to abject servility. It describes the virtue of singleminded awe that recognizes only God's own judgment as operative in our decisions (see 2 Cor 5:10-11).

7:2-4 Paul resumes his plea. Paul reiterates his sincerity and openness, dispelling any notions of either blame or guilt. He has harmed no one, another way of saying that he has acted out of love. Nor does he condemn anyone. He emphasizes the positive. He speaks openly and honestly, joyful that he still can, as before, so completely trust in the Corinthians, his boast in the Lord (see 1 Cor 1:31). He is full of confidence that his trust will be vindicated (see 2 Cor 7:14-16). Paul's joy is disproportionate to his afflictions (see Rom 8:18). Indeed, because it is based in God rather than in human limitations, Paul's joy knows no bounds (see Rom 15:13; Phil 1:18-21).

C. Resolution of the Crisis

Having treated the apostolic ministry in an objective way (2:14–6:10), Paul returns to a description of the strained personal relationships he has with the Corinthians (6:11–7:4). He inserts a reference to them as the temple of God (6:14–7:1), within his personal appeal to them to open their hearts to him as he has to them (6:11-13; 7:2-4). Paul concludes these reflections on their rocky relationship with a confident, almost exultant celebration of the good news Titus bore and the hope it inspires in his apostolic heart (7:5-16).

7:5-16 Good news from Titus. The good news of Titus' report on the Corinthians is part of Paul's gospel. It refreshes his spirit and removes the shackle of sorrow, timidity, and fear. This is a particularly sensitive section that shows Paul's reaching for some ways of expressing the care he has for the Corinthians and the boundless joy he feels from hearing of their loyalty. He is like a parent who forgets her own pain and apprehension at the successful achievement of her child. The story line, interrupted since 2:13, refers to the occurrences after Paul's departure from Troas, as he awaited word from Titus.

Paul's description of his exhausted depression echoes the plight of Elijah who complained, even after his victory over the false prophets of Jezebel, that the loneliness of the true prophet was intolerable (1 Kgs 19:1-13). Even if it is possible to accept suffering for the sake of a just person, as Paul says of Christ in Romans (5:7), it is particularly painful to persevere when one is opposed by others and fearful within. Yet God, who does not test us beyond our strength, consoled the hearts of both Elijah and Paul in the form of tangible ordinary human signs that revealed his presence and providence.

Titus' report included the affirmation Paul needed. Paul refers to the kind of reaction that must have endeared the Corinthians to him all along. He hears of their longing, their remorse, their concern for Paul, and he is heartened. Although he regrets the grief his letter reportedly caused them, he happily acknowledges the affection that this grief betrays. If grief can produce such zeal as Titus describes, he is more than comforted. His letter was not inspired by pettiness nor a desire for vengeance. It verifies before God, whose judgment alone is significant, the loyal devotion between Paul and the Corinthians.

Paul's personal consolation, and the evident zeal of the Corinthians, are the fruits of this strained time between them, but not the only fruits. Because of this Titus has experienced an invaluable lesson in apostolic ministry. Common faith does not exclude nor even, perhaps, erase the strain among Christians or the pain they might experience individually. But faith makes tensions relative and subordinate to the common bonds of love. Faith ultimately transforms misunderstandings and doubts into manifestations of the fidelity of God for all. Paul's faith in the Corinthians is vindicated. Not only has he saved face but, indeed, God is shown at work reconciling all, and this grounds Paul's faith.

II. THE COLLECTION FOR JERUSALEM

2 Cor 8:1–9:15

Once reconciled with the Corinthians, Paul presses on to the topic of the collection which, in the context of his whole perspective on the gospel, is of singular importance as a manifestation of faith. While remaining sensitive to the fragility and intricacies of his relationship to the Corinthians, Paul makes no apology for the significance he assigns to generosity in the giving of alms. The collection becomes for him an essential element of the gospel as evidence that it has been completely accepted. Thus, Paul considers worthwhile the risk of instructing even the skittish Corinthians on this delicate issue as if to suggest that it cannot be avoided simply because the matter is so sensitive.

A. Appeal to the Corinthians' Generosity (8:1-24)

After setting the Macedonians up as an example of liberality for the Corinthians (8:1-5), Paul explains the spiritual motivation for almsgiving and then recommends the delegates who will actually pick up the collection (8:6-24).

8:1-5 Example of the Macedonians. Paul presents the Macedonians, who provided hospitality for him while he wrote to the Corinthians, as an example of extreme generosity. They gave not only out of their abundance but out of their poverty. They were not responding merely to a concept of justice that could be considered natural. Nor were they motivated merely by so lofty an ideal even as the equitable distribution of resources to all. They had a deeper source of motivation and power. Grace combined their own deep poverty with overflowing joy to enable them to perform a service that would be a sign to all. Beyond all hopes, the Macedonians actively searched for the opportunity to reach into their own experience of poverty in order to testify to their dependence on God and their joy in being Christian. Their surrender in faith was expressed in astonishing liberality.

8:6-24 Titus' role and motives for generous giving. Paul reintroduces Titus, already known as bearer of good tidings about the Corinthians. In addition Paul identifies Titus' role as initiator and delegate in taking up the collection. This is a work of grace which binds rich and poor, making them one.

Paul had testified that the Corinthians are rich in every conceivable blessing (see 1 Cor 1:5, 7). For him this is a sure sign of their "debt" (Rom 15:27; see 1:14-15) to those with whom and because of whom they share in the blessings of salvation. The intended beneficiaries of the collection are the starving saints in Jerusalem, who were suffering the effects of persecution and deprivation (see Rom 15:25-27; also 1 Cor 16:1-4).

Paul reasons that since the Corinthians are rich in spiritual benefits because they are identified as heirs to the promises originally made only to the Jews, they owe the Jewish-Christians a share in their abundance. Paul capitalizes on the Greek notion that spiritual benefits have priority over the material, so that the Corinthians' own integrity would make them see how generous they should be in sharing their material goods.

One of the real effects of the gospel is that faith makes believers responsible to one another. If the gospel is really preached and really believed, it has practical effects for the betterment of all. The same faith that eliminated the spiritual barriers between Jew and Gentile now acts as an equalizer, expressing itself in acts of justice and mercy toward the poor. The collection, for Paul, represents acceptance of mutual responsibility. The Israelites' confidence in God was similarly tested when Moses required that they collect only as much manna as was needed for one day. This was to prevent them from letting greed cause divisions among them and to allow their dependence and equality before the Lord to be manifest in their daily actions.

Paul recommends Titus as his trusted coworker and as someone as zealous for the good of the Corinthians as he himself is. Paul is grateful to God that he did not have to convince Titus to undertake this mission but that Titus freely accepted it. Like the Macedonians, he seeks to do more, not less (see 2 Cor 8:2-4). Titus is Paul's delegate; two other delegates are chosen by the faithful, but their exact identity is not known. Tradition presumes one to be Luke, but positive identification is impossible.

Paul seems exceptionally prudent with regard to this collection, unlike his sentiments in Romans where he sees his role as one of those who will actually make the delivery in Jerusalem as essential (see Rom 15:28-33). The issue of money is at best delicate, but probably even more so with regard to the Corinthians who are still prone to suspicion. Paul relinquishes his own role in making the collection so that there can be no criticism of him. Whereas he is sure of his own motives and does not require the approval of others (see Gal 1:7-10; 1 Cor 4:1-5), he is sensitive to the need for complete trust between himself and the Corinthians and does not wish that anything, least of all money, interfere with that. He seeks, then, on this one issue, their good esteem as well as God's approval. This admission underscores the importance of the collection as a symbol for Paul.

B. A Second Appeal Addressed to the Churches of Achaia (9:1-15)

Chapter 9 is a doublet that seems to have originally been composed as a separate note to serve as an introduction to the collectors. As capital of Achaia, Corinth might have been included in the wider appeal Paul extended to all the churches of the province. Paul's motivation and language are a little different in this second appeal where he concentrates on the need for promptness (9:1-4) and then enumerates the blessings of liberality (9:5-15).

9:1-4 Exhortation to promptness. The first sentence, protesting that it is superfluous to write about the collection, suggests that this chapter was probably a separate missive originally sent as a letter of introduction to the delegates to the churches of Achaia. Paul admits that he uses the Corinthians as a model for the Macedonians, just as he portrayed the Macedonians as generous to the extreme for the edification of the Corinthians (see 2 Cor 8:1-5). Paul supports this challenge with a reminder of his confidence and his boasting because of the Corinthians. His reputation and theirs are at stake.

9:5-15 The blessings of liberality. Paul's reputation is all the more important because acceptance of the gospel itself hangs in the balance. Although Paul is not explicit here, the urgency of the collection as evidence of the sincerity and good will of the Corinthians was probably heightened by a certain amount of understandable skepticism on the part of Jewish-Christian authorities, and especially those in Jerusalem. Paul has had to confront certain of these authorities on the issue of the Gentile Christians' equality in the church (see Gal 2:11-21). The flagrant abuses in the Corinthian church might have threatened Paul's position and made his mission there vulnerable. Apparently Paul hoped a generous response from the Corinthians to his appeal about the collection would have appeased these Jewish-Christian critics.

In 9:5-15 Paul provides a theological and scriptural basis for his financial appeal. Generosity is its own reward. Anyone who gives liberally will benefit from this same gift. Paul reflects the teachings of Jesus on the use of talents and on the measure with which a believer is asked to share. God is infinite in gifts, so that there is no need to covet or hoard those entrusted to us. The role of the believer is to reflect the richness of God in concern for the poor while acting as God's steward. This form of justice requires faith in the unlimited resources of God. All of this sharing is motivated by a desire to proclaim God's name and to render the thanks which is God's due.

The practical outcome is that the Jewish Christians will be helped in their need. But this is not all. They will also be prompted to give thanks in recognizing that the same God is working now through the Gentile believers who have the gospel preached to them. The gospel leads to the obedience of faith of both Jew and Gentile in Christ through whom all are reconciled (see Rom 1:5; 16:26). Thus all join in a common prayer of gratitude and praise not only for the gifts accorded each one personally but for the community of believers. This grateful community is evidence of the surpassing grace, the indescribable gift.

III. PAUL'S DEFENSE OF HIS MINISTRY

2 Cor 10:1–13:10

These chapters probably comprised a separate letter. The abrupt change of tone and the return to the defensive topic suggest that Paul did not originally intend these to follow chapter 9, or chapter 7, which showed how Paul resolved similar questions and seemed to have cooled his emotions. With chapter 10 the Apostle strongly refutes the charges made against him by his detractors at Corinth (10:1-18). Then he indulges in some boasting, allowing us an intimate look at his feelings, vulnerability, and strength (11:1–12:21). Paul ends the epistle with a solemn warning (13:1-10) and farewell (13:11-13).

A. Paul Refutes His Enemies (10:1-18)

The Corinthians deride Paul by saying that he is forceful with words on paper, in letters, but not so impressive in the flesh. This particular charge of weakness Paul refutes with a warning to his detractors not to push him to show just how severe he can be when he is with them (see 1 Cor 4:21). Rather, Paul urges, may they be inspired by the meekness and kindness of Christ himself to relinquish such foolish standards for judging his power.

Paul insists that he does have power. He evokes his familiar battle imagery to express its nature and uses. While he admits ordinary human frailty, he identifies his weaponry as spiritual, possessing God's own power. Although his enemies are spiritual, too, they are mere creations—sophistries, pretensions, thoughts. However strong they may seem, they are nothing compared to the power of God, who in the process of reconciling the world is subjecting all to Christ. As minister of the gospel which proclaims this truth, Paul has and will use the power to destroy all that is an obstacle to the knowledge of God. Once these obstacles are overcome, all will recognize God's wisdom in the cross of Christ. The Apostle expresses confidence in the Corinthians' ultimate submission while he declares war on all that threatens to prevent their obedience.

The Apostle blames their susceptibility to false teaching and their false standards on their own superficial perspective. Believers must judge themselves as well as their ministers in Christ. This will bring about unity among them. If Paul needs to, he can make further claims about his power. He has been restrained thus far so that the Corinthians would not be intimidated. There is no real dichotomy between his letters and his actions. Forced to, he will act more severely.

Sarcastically, the Apostle pokes at the opponents he will face head-on shortly (see 11:1-15). These, he says, futilely erect the standards by which they compete and judge themselves and one another. Their ignorance is abysmal. He will not fall prey to the temptation to imitate them by comparing himself to them.

Rather, he stays "within the bounds" of the same God who led him to the Corinthians in the first place. His apostolate with them is the only limit he will accept. His boasts about the Corinthians are justified, since they are his work in the Lord (see 1 Cor 1:31; 2 Cor 10:17). Further, his evangelization of the Corinthians provides a legitimate basis for boasting because he is respecting his own personal vow not to build on another's foundation (see Rom 15:20). This was also the agreement of the church, that he go to the Gentiles while the others concentrate on the Jewish mission (see Gal 2:9). As the Corinthians grow strong in their faith, Paul can relax a little his need to nurture and sustain them. Paul hopes that his influence on them will overflow to others. He probably refers not only to the hope that he will be able to give his energies elsewhere but that the Corinthians themselves will be able to help in the work of evangelization. The closing line of this section contains a warning that the ultimate judge is the Lord whose verdict or recommendation alone counts.

B. Paul's Cause for Confident Boasting (11:1–12:21)

The Corinthians are impressed with ostentatious qualifications. Paul challenges them to review some of his own credentials. Paul contrasts himself to the "super-apostles" (11:1-15). Then he reminds the Corinthians of the suffering that gives him the right to speak (11:16-33). Finally Paul speaks of his ecstasies and visions (12:1-4, 7) before concluding with an impassionate testimony of his concern for the Corinthian church (12:11-21).

11:1-15 Paul versus the super-apostles. Since the Corinthians appear only too willing to listen to the credentials of others, Paul invites them to tolerate his own "folly," by which he means his comparing "degrees" in the school of Christ's apostleship. He is prompted to do this by God's own jealousy. Paul's apostolic role is to present the church as a chaste bride for her husband only. His fear is that the too impressionable Corinthians will be seduced by the same evil one who seduced and corrupted Eve.

Paul interprets the image of Eve in a traditional way, that is, as the more susceptible, weaker element of humanity in comparison with Adam. This traditional male-biased interpretation is elaborated upon in other New Testament writings (for example, 1 Tim 2:13-14; see 1 Pet 3:7). Here Paul simply uses Eve to explain his concern for the Corinthians, whom he sees as easily seduced by errant teachers, and to warn them to be cautious in their evaluation of the gospel and its true ministers.

Jealousy is an attribute of the unique relationship of one God with the chosen people. The one gospel Paul preaches is authorized by God. A single gospel was endorsed by the church (see Gal 2:1-10). Paul's apostleship, no less than that of his antagonists, sarcastically called "super" here and "false" in 11:13, is based on the call of God and a vision of the risen Christ. He may be lacking in eloquence compared to the others, but he is equal in the authority based on his knowledge of Christ crucified. This is evident in his relationship with the Corinthians. His frustration with their challenge is hardly veiled in 11:6.

Paul refers to the old charge that he must be inferior, since he does not accept financial support. Whether they brought up the charge again or whether some simply remained unconvinced is not clear. With impressive simplicity, Paul indicates the absurdity of the charge. Are the Corinthians so senseless as to use his independence in their regard as an accusation against their minister? Paul testifies that he does not believe in being a burden to the communities he evangelized. He only accepts support for communities after he has worked among them. So, for example, he refers with gratitude to the support he received from the Macedonians (2 Cor 11:9; see Phil 4:10-20). But he does not want to allow money to in any way inhibit his work of evangelization. He struggles to free himself and to be self-supporting so that he will not be restricted by or dependent on only those churches capable of financing his mission. This would limit the gospel and Paul's role in its spread. Paul also seeks to be above suspicion personally and especially in his use of money so as to incur as little legitimate criticism as possible. Thus he chides the Corinthians' insincerity in suggesting that such independence implies his inferiority to the other apostles.

Paul goes so far as to say that not only is this not reprehensible, but he swears in Christ's name that he will continue to be able to boast about this fact. Not that he does not love the Corinthians enough to become indebted to them. They and God witness his love. He only wishes to forestall any possible reason for maligning and criticizing his ministry. And the Corinthians have given Paul adequate reason to be this prudent. Paul's anger is provoked against those who disturb the precarious balance of the community's faith. Satan disguised himself as Lucifer, an angel of light. It follows, then, that Satan's ministers claim to serve the justice of God. The ominous threat of Paul's last line should haunt his detractors. Their end will correspond to their deeds.

11:16-33 Paul's experience of mercy and healing. Paul and the Corinthians had two different ideas of foolishness. Paul bases his in the wisdom of God and reckons anything wise by worldly standards as vain, futile. Such, for example, are the Corinthians' criteria for an apostle. But since the Corinthians respond to such foolishness, Paul indulges in boasting of his own qualifications. He is impelled to do this not by values the Lord recognizes, but by the ways of the foolish Corinthians. They even, he says, tolerate those who exploit them and impose upon them and those who use brutality and force to show their strength. If these are what is necessary to convince the Corinthians, Paul confesses that he is indeed weak. Yet he will have his say.

Are qualities of birth and religion admitted? Paul has these no less than his opponents. Ethically and religiously he is credentialed (see Rom 11:1; Phil 3:3-7). Whereas Paul's Jewish past was privileged, he is a minister of Christ only by his sufferings. There are no other New Testament parallels for many of the hardships Paul mentions. His point is that if others gain recognition because of their witness in suffering for the gospel, their trials would seem insignificant in comparison to Paul's own.

Luke tells us some of the hardships of Paul's litany. According to Luke, Paul was scourged once at Philippi and stoned once at Lystra (see Acts 16:22-23; 14:19). Luke records that in the course of his three missionary journeys Paul faced opposition and trials from accidents and nature, from both Jews and Greeks, and from rivals within the church. Further, Paul endured the physical hardships of his labors and his voluntary act of self-discipline. But without furnishing the details, Paul recites the continual adversity he suffered from five times enduring the maximum number of lashes the Jews permitted within their law and the three times he was beaten by the Romans. He adds the shipwrecks and the horror of being adrift in the open sea. He recounts the explicit opposition and the inner doubts, tensions, and fears. He cannot refrain from adding his anxiety over the churches he has founded, suggesting not too subtly that the Corinthians will be able to appreciate that point.

There is left no weakness Paul cannot identify with. Surely no one can be scandalized by the mounting indignation of his tone on needing to remind his own churches of this painful history. He qualifies himself as one who has experienced weakness, mercy, and healing. When he mentions God as his witness, he cannot help but add a prayer of praise. Finally Paul concludes his litany of sufferings with an incident that might seem surprising in its detail, but which actually shows better than any other that the mighty providence of God protects Paul from all the powerful forces that militate against him.

12:1-10 Ecstasies and humility. The charges of Paul's detractors and the Corinthians' susceptibility have combined to compel him to be so foolish as to imitate them on their own terms. If they are impressed by visions and revelations, he says, then he can add these to his credit. He refers to a revelation he received in about 42–45 C.E. that transported him to paradise. He speaks of himself in the third person as if to emphasize more strongly the gift quality of this experience which was completely undeserved. Paul gives a classic description of an ecstatic, mystical experience. He was so caught up in the divine that he lost consciousness of himself and of his body. He was absorbed in God.

Until driven to this extreme by the Corinthians, he had refrained from speaking about this experience, which is not recorded elsewhere. His witness to the gospel requires only the truth of what others can see and hear of his life. Yet, in order to prevent him from becoming proud, he was gifted, too, with a "thorn in the flesh" (see Phil 1:29). Exactly what Paul means is uncertain, but the function of this affliction is clearly to humble Paul. It serves as a weapon of Paul's perennial enemy, Satan, and reminds Paul that he is vulnerable. Paul's temptation is to not accept this, and he persistently asks that it be removed. His threefold request reflects Jesus' prayer in the Garden (Matt 26:39, 42, 44).

Paul's answer reveals the truth that divine power is made more evident in human frailty. When Paul is most empty of all human cause for boasting, he is able to identify and testify to the source of his power and strength. This amazing reversal of all earthly wisdom transforms weakness, distress, and mistreatment into powerful evidence of God's presence.

Stepping back, Paul appears to be almost shocked to find that he has been driven to the epitome of foolishness in recounting God's favors to him. Yet the good he draws from this foolishness, as he reminds the Corinthians, is the consciousness that since all apostleship comes from God rather than from himself, he is not in any way inferior to any other apostles who, if they are sincere, claim the same source of their apostleship. These others Paul labels the "super-apostles." And if apostolic signs are the only credentials the Corinthians recognize, then they should be commending Paul, for he has worked signs and wonders among them. But, less foolishly, the real "signs" of Paul's apostleship are the very existence of the Corinthians' faith and Paul's willing endurance of sufferings and hardships for the faith.

12:13-21 Paul's apprehension regarding the Corinthians. Two recurrent, apparently related charges remain to be answered. The fact that Paul did not accept support for his apostolic work prompted the Corinthians to accuse him of deceit. Paul has already responded to these charges, but a residue of distrust remains. The Corinthians' competitive spirit even goes so far as to charge that Paul is in some way rejecting them in not accepting their support. They mistakenly search for reasons to explain Paul's gratuitous faithful love for them. No wonder he refers to the consummate patience he has had to manifest in working with them. Perhaps the Corinthians are even beginning to imagine that Paul considers them inferior to the other churches. Paul stands firm in his decision not to burden them financially. His frequent and prolonged visits are the most telling evidence of his love for them. If they must rely on external signs to reassure themselves of Paul's love, they need look no further than his willingness to be spent for their sakes. His is a parent's love which is provident and generous in its concern for the children. His love is no less strong because it is not self-seeking. Because it is a gift, his love should not be considered undeserving of love in return. There is no craftiness or guile in this. He has no ulterior motive. He has never deceived or taken advantage of them, either personally or through his envoys.

Paul swears that he had done everything possible and necessary for the edification of the Corinthians he finally addresses with a note of endearment. He expresses his apprehension about their imminent meeting and the petty obstacles that threaten to make it disastrous for the community. Paul fears this. The Corinthians need to be fortified and encouraged, yet he fears that, finding them divided and not really corrected from their former pagan ways, he will have to act severely with them and increase the tension among them. Paul's apprehension makes him ambivalent about the visit he desires so much.

C. Final Warnings (13:1-10)

Paul will come a third time. By quoting Deut 19:15 he ominously warns the Corinthians of the significance of a third visit being as painful as the first two. If he again finds the Corinthians guilty, that would constitute a third and therefore complete testimony against them. His actions will follow his own counsel. The unrepentant must be judged and punished by the community. If the Corinthians want proof that Christ is working and speaking through Paul, they can expect a powerful manifestation in Paul's dealing with sin in the community.

He returns to the paradox he first raised in the beginning of First Corinthians. God's wisdom is in what is humanly regarded as weakness and folly. In his crucifixion Jesus appeared to be weak, but God showed his power in him by raising him from the dead. Paul compares the Corinthians to himself. They, like him, experience this paradox of their weakness being the manifestation of God's power in them.

Paul, then, warns: Test yourselves. They know the criteria for judgment. It shall not come as a surprise. They must realize that Jesus Christ works in them, unless, of course, they have not surrendered themselves to him in faith. Without faith, they would fail the challenge. But Paul has not failed.

Paul's prayer is that the Corinthians do no evil. He has no ulterior motive for this, such as his own approval. Rather, doing no evil, they will only do what is true and good. This is its own reward. The Apostle is not self-seeking, nor is he jealous if they seem strong while he is weak. He neither fears their mistakes because they redound on him, nor does he look for credit. His prayer is that they will be strengthened by the finding of what God has begun in them.

V. CONCLUSION
2 Cor 13:11-13

Paul writes as he does so that his visit will not bring unexpected and unwanted severity. The Lord has bestowed on him the authority to build up the community, and he hopes that will not involve destroying any of the confidence that links him to them. He abruptly brings the letter to a close, repeating his hope that they will mend their ways. He admonishes them to live in peace and love. He expects the letter to be read at the liturgy and encourages the Christians to let the kiss of peace signify their acceptance of the difficult and the easy suggestions he makes. He includes the greetings of all the Macedonian Christians who are called to the same holiness as the Corinthians are. Paul's blessing is unusually solemn. The Trinitarian formula is odd in Paul, who usually ends with some reference to Christ and then to God, but who does not suggest such a developed understanding of the three Persons. Yet this solemn formula is particularly apt for the Corinthians. Paul includes them all in his heartfelt prayer that their divisions and misunderstandings will be healed by the grace of our Lord, the love of God, and the fellowship of the Holy Spirit.

1 THESSALONIANS

Ivan Havener, O.S.B.

INTRODUCTION

Until fairly recently Paul's First Letter to the Thessalonians was largely neglected by biblical scholars, but that is no longer the case. Two key factors are responsible for this change. The first is the recognition that this is the earliest writing in the New Testament and, therefore, the oldest extant document of Christianity. The second factor is a better understanding of the Book of Acts that views it less as a series of objective historical accounts about the beginnings of Christianity and more as a theological interpretation of those beginnings.

In the past 1 Thessalonians had been interpreted in the light of what Acts had to say about Paul's missionary involvement at Thessalonica. But since 1 Thessalonians is a first-hand document written by the apostle who was himself present and since Acts was written thirty to thirty-five years later and after Paul's death and is primarily a theological rather than a historical work, it has become increasingly clear that 1 Thessalonians should not be read in the light of Acts but just the opposite. This is especially important in the case of this letter, for the account of the founding of the Thessalonian church as given in Acts 17 is quite different from the information we receive from the letter itself. It is questionable, therefore, whether the two accounts can be or should be harmonized.

With 1 Thessalonians freed from the interpretation of Acts, the way has become clear to study the letter on its own merits. This has led to a rigorous investigation of the letter's form and content, a study yielding new insights into the development of the Christian letter form and into Paul's early ministry among the Gentiles.

When Paul wrote 1 Thessalonians, his letter-writing style was not yet fixed. He was in the process of breaking with some literary conventions of his time and forging a new means of communication, the Christian letter. Therefore, the form of this letter is somewhat different than the Letter to Philemon, which is more typical of Paul's later letter form, as this comparison shows:

1 Thessalonians	**Philemon**
Introduction 1:1	Introduction, verses 1-3
Sender	Sender
Recipient	Recipient
Greeting	Greeting
Thanksgiving 1:2-3:13	Thanksgiving, verses 4-7
Instructions 4:1-5:22	Body, verses 8-21
Conclusion 5:23-28	Conclusion, verses 22-25
Prayer	Announcement
Greeting	Greeting
Blessing	Blessing

In 1 Thessalonians the thanksgiving section is the largest part of the letter, whereas it usually consists of only a few verses in Paul's later letters, and the instructions are often found to be only one small section of the body of later letters rather than a large section by itself. The remarks Paul makes about the senders and recipients in the introductions and the form of the initial greeting break with the usual pattern found in Graeco-Roman letters of the time and with Aramaic letters, too. Likewise, the concluding blessing is an innovation. In a sense, then, we may speak of

1 Thessalonians as an experiment in Christian letter writing. Its form is refined in later letters.

The content of 1 Thessalonians reveals a Paul more closely associated to other Jewish-Christian missionaries to the Gentiles and to a more Jewish-Christian theology than in his later writings. For instance, the place of God (the Father) is more prominent in this letter than is the naming of Jesus (the Lord). Even what Paul says about Jesus here has a different emphasis than in his other letters. Thus while Paul stresses the significance of the death and resurrection of Jesus in his later writings, here the primary saving event is seen as the coming of the Lord at the end time. This may seem strange to us because that truth, while still present, is not at the center of contemporary Christian thought. For the Thessalonians, however, it was a major concern because they expected that event to occur yet in their lifetime.

Paul gently encourages this congregation to have confidence as the day of the Lord approaches and that they should go about their everyday lives in a calm, responsible, and loving manner. This is advice valid for all times, and in this regard Paul points out the importance of Christian example. How one lives one's Christian life affects others, Christians and non-Christians alike. For Christians, it is a means of strengthening one another in faith and in our common commitment to serving God as we await that final glory promised to us. For non-Christians, our example bears witness to the radicality of our commitment to a God who wills that we live as God's children, that we owe allegiance to something beyond ourselves which is one, true, and living.

Paul worked for his keep while he proclaimed the gospel to the Thessalonians, but the primary motivation for this work may have been for another reason than the poverty of the congregation, rather, to distinguish himself from other traveling preachers (usually non-Christian philosophers) who often had a bad reputation for preaching for personal gain and also to give an example for the Thessalonians to follow, so that they not cause scandal to their non-Christian neighbors and therefore place barriers to the spread of the gospel. The congregation is located in the port city of Thessalonica in Macedonia, the modern city of Thessalonike in northern Greece, and it appears to be primarily, if not entirely, a Gentile congregation. Most likely the letter was sent from Athens or Corinth about the year A.D. 51.

COMMENTARY

INTRODUCTION AND GREETING

1 Thess 1:1

The senders of this letter are Paul and two of his fellow workers, Silvanus and Timothy, who are mentioned together also in 2 Cor 1:19 and 2 Thess 1:1. While all three preached "Jesus Christ as Son of God" among the Corinthians (2 Cor 1:19), we never hear anything else specifically about Silvanus in Paul's letters, whereas Timothy appears very frequently with Paul and is his righthand assistant. While all three have sent the letter, Paul himself is responsible for its writing (3:5a; 5:27), though he often speaks in the plural and thereby usually includes his helpers in his thoughts (1:2; 2:1). In contrast to his other letter introductions, this one is unique for its simplicity. Paul uses no title as "apostle" (Gal 1:1) nor any other designation such as "slave" (Phil 1:1) or "prisoner" (Phlm 1) to describe himself.

The letter is addressed "to the church of the Thessalonians"; it is meant to be read before the assembly of the Christians at Thessalonica, who probably gathered in homes for worship, since there were no church buildings at this early time.

The community is greeted more simply here than in Paul's other letters. Paul probably abbreviated the usual liturgical formula (see Phil 1:2), since he has already mentioned God the Father and the Lord Jesus Christ in the previous sentence.

THANKFUL REMEMBRANCE—PART I

The Gospel Comes to Thessalonica

1 Thess 1:2-10

1:2-3 Thanksgiving for an active faith. As Paul and his helpers give thanks to God for all the members of this community, they remember them in their prayers for the way they are showing themselves to be people of faith, hope, and love, the Pauline triad of Christian virtues (1 Cor 13:13). Their manner of life bears witness to their Christian calling and points to the power of example.

1:4-5 The gospel takes root. Paul looks back upon his initial preaching at Thessalonica to account for the fact that the Thessalonians have become God's chosen people in Christ. The word of the gospel that he proclaimed to them was not just ordinary speech, but was filled with the power of the Holy Spirit and was, therefore, convincing to the hearers. The word of God was effective because the Holy Spirit was operative in it. The other factor in the success of the gospel among them was the example given by Paul and his companions in their actions on behalf of the community.

1:6-8 The Thessalonians as imitators and models. Upon hearing the preaching of the gospel and experiencing the example of Paul and his fellow workers, the Thessalonians became imitators of them and of the Lord, whose example Paul was following. To follow this example was no easy task for the Thessalonians who had to endure suffering and persecution, when they accepted that word which Paul preached, but they received it anyway, filled with the joy coming from the Holy Spirit. This all-pervasive joy, this divine power, gave them peace in the midst of opposition.

As imitators of Paul and of the Lord, the Thessalonians themselves have become models to believers in their own and neighboring regions. In fact, their example of faith has become renowned even beyond these areas, so clearly has the word of the Lord reverberated from them.

1:9-10 Content of the gospel. What exactly it is that others in Macedonia and Achaia have found so praiseworthy in the Thessalonian example is now spelled out. First is the reception that they gave to Paul and his fellow missionaries. Evidently, unlike some others, the Thessalonians welcomed Paul and readily listened to him. Second is their turning to God and away from idols. Apparently the Thessalonians have been able to make a clean break with their former pagan past, whereas their neighbors are having more difficulty doing that, as reflected also in Paul's comment to the Corinthians (1 Cor 10:14).

Then quoting from a catechetical formula used by Paul and by other missionaries before and alongside him, Paul repeats the gospel message given to the Thessalonians. According to this formula conversion to

Christianity involves two simultaneous processes: (1) a service of worship and obedience to the living and true God, instead of the dead and false gods of paganism, and (2) an awaiting of the arrival of God's Son from heaven, who will effect salvation by delivering us from condemnation at the last judgment. The mention of Jesus' resurrection in this context, the first time it appears in extant Christian literature, serves the purpose of showing why the historical person of Jesus can be expected to come as God's Son from heaven—because God raised him from among the dead.

How and when Jesus will come as Savior in the end time and what effect it will have on believers dead and alive is a key theme of 1 Thessalonians, as indicated by the numerous references to his coming: 1:10; 2:19; 3:13; 4:15; 5:23.

THANKFUL REMEMBRANCE—PART II

Paul's Stay in Thessalonica Explained and Defended

1 Thess 2:1-12

2:1-2 The favorable reception. Referring back to the good reception which the Thessalonians had given him (1:9), Paul notes that his presence among them was not in vain, a welcome change from the stormy reception he had received in Philippi, where he had suffered and been maltreated. In Thessalonica, however, God had given him courage to proclaim the gospel with good results despite the strain he was under from others in the city who were not so receptive (see 1:6).

2:3-7a Paul's defense against assumed accusations. Drawing upon the language of contemporary wandering Greek philosopher preachers, Paul makes a defense of his ministry among the Thessalonians. There is no evidence here that he has been personally attacked for the issues he raises, but he is aware of the general mistrust that local people often had against such outside preachers because so many of them were, in fact, charlatans. Paul wants to distinguish himself from them and therefore takes up the accusations usually leveled against these preachers. His motives for preaching are not for any other reason than to do what God has entrusted him to do, namely, to preach the gospel. In doing this he has sought to please God, not his audience, and he is confident that God will rightly judge his motives, for it is God himself who has commissioned him.

Calling upon the knowledge of the Thessalonians themselves, as well as God as his witness, Paul also denies that he has been guilty of certain other charges often raised against wandering preachers: flattery, greed, and seeking of praise. On the contrary, he and his missionary helpers have not even claimed what they could rightly expect as apostles of Christ. This use of the word "apostles" is unusual in 1 Thessalonians because it is the only time in this letter that Paul refers to himself as an apostle and because Paul includes his companions among the apostles. In other letters he frequently refers to his apostleship, but does not give that title to his fellow workers. There seems to be a narrowing of the meaning of "apostle" as the New Testament writings are composed one after another.

2:7b-12 Paul's presence among the Thessalonians. After countering the charges that might be leveled against him, Paul summarizes what his presence among the Thessalonians was like in order to underscore the groundlessness of any such accusations. He does this by means of two parental images.

First, he describes himself and his companions as displaying the gentleness of a nursing mother caring for her children. These apostles are so full of love for the Thessalonians that they not only want to share the gospel message with them but also to give of themselves for the sake of the community. Paul cites the example of their working for their keep. In this way they encouraged the Thessalonians to do the same, but at the same time showed that they proclaimed the gospel free of charge and did not want to become a financial burden to the congregation. (Actually, it may not have worked out as ideally as it sounds, for in Phil 4:16 Paul thanks that community for the financial aid he twice received from them during his stay at Thessalonica.) Paul probably worked as a tentmaker (see Acts 18:3) from sunrise to sunset (= during the "night and day"; see 3:10 where Paul also prays "night and day") and may have preached even while he was employed in his workshop. The reference to individual attention in verse 11 easily fits into this workshop setting. Again both the Thessalonians and God are named as witnesses to Paul's integrity with regard to his conduct among the community (see 2:5).

Second, he describes the apostolic trio, as exhorting in the manner of a father concerned about each of his children. Therefore, the Thessalonians were encouraged and pleaded with to lead lives acceptable to the God who has called them into God's kingdom and glory.

Thus Paul and his fellow missionaries have been both mother and father to the Thessalonians, not only in begetting this church through the preaching of the gospel but also by expressing their love and concern for their "children," bringing them up in the Faith. It would be a misapplication of Paul's intention, however, to see in this family-life imagery a model for family life today, in which mothers are to be warm and loving, whereas fathers are to be stern disciplinarians. Paul is merely describing his concern for the Thessalonians using two aspects of family life, both of which are applied to himself.

A NON-PAULINE ADDITION

1 Thess 2:13-16

At this point, the flow of Paul's letter is surprisingly interrupted by a second thanksgiving that disturbs both the continuity of what precedes and follows it. The authenticity of this second thanksgiving is frequently questioned because the content of the passage conflicts with what we know about Paul and the historical circumstances in which he lived. It appears to be an interpolation or an addition to Paul's original letter; and its non-Pauline use of Pauline language suggests that an editor is trying to copy Paul in order to have the Apostle address himself to issues that are a matter of concern to the editor in a period after the Apostle's death.

Borrowing terminology especially from 1 Thess 1:2, 5, the editor writes a second thanksgiving section of the letter. Convinced by what Paul and his fellow workers had to say and by their example among them, the Thessalonians have accepted their message not as human words but as the word of God. This word has become operative among these Thessalonian believers, and because of this, Paul constantly gives thanks to God.

The Thessalonians are said to have become imitators of God's churches in Judea (see 1:6 where the Thessalonians are "imitators" of Paul and his helpers). These Judean churches are described as being "in Christ Jesus." (The Greek text of 1:1 speaks of "the church of the Thessalonians in God the Father and the Lord Jesus Christ.") The Thessalonians have suffered at the hands of their pagan neighbors like the Judean Christians suffered at the hands of the Jews. These Jews are charged with having done three things: they killed the Lord Jesus, they killed the prophets, and they persecuted "us" (= Paul and his fellow workers?). Furthermore, they are said to be displeasing to God, hostile to all people, and trying to prevent the preaching of salvation to the Gentiles. By doing such things and having such attitudes, the author says they are meeting their limit of sin and, therefore, wrath has already come down upon them.

This anti-Semitic sentiment can hardly be attributed to Paul, who even in his last letter still proudly speaks of himself as an Israelite (Rom 11:1). He never attributes Jesus' death to the Jews but only to "the rulers of this age" (1 Cor 2:8). Far from being despised by God, the Jews have not been abandoned by him, for "all Israel will be saved" (Rom 11:26), and according to 1 Thess 1:10 the wrath of God is still to come; it is not something that has already shown itself.

How then do we account for this addition to 1 Thessalonians? Most likely, the editor is reflecting on the fall of Jerusalem in A.D. 70, which is interpreted as God's wrath that has descended on the Jews. The editor is living at a time after that event, when Jews and Christians are in conflict, with the Christians being expelled from the synagogues. Therefore, the editor writes in a polemical spirit against the Jews because he or she has personally tasted the hostility of this persecution. To counteract it, the editor projects the situation of the present back into the time of Paul and states his or her own observations and comments through the mouth of the Apostle, thus giving them apostolic authority.

In making use of this text today, it is important that we keep in mind the stressful situation which gave rise to its composition and to its author's polemical generalizations. In highly emotional situations, such as this, overstatement and lack of proper perspectives often go hand in hand. Therefore, the claims of this passage must be tested in the light of historical evidence. According to the gospel passion narratives, *some* Jews conspired with Roman officials to put Jesus to death, but Jesus died directly at the hands of the Romans. *Some* Jews were responsible for the death of *some* prophets, a tradition common to Christians and Jews alike. We have no record from Paul's early missionary experience that he was persecuted in Judea. If the "us" in verse 15 refers to Christians in general, rather than specifically to Paul and his companions, it is possible that *some* Jews may have persecuted Christians, like Paul himself had done (Phil 3:6), but there is no evidence of a widespread, systematic persecution of Christians in Judea before the fall of Jerusalem. In any case, it would be wrong to condemn all Jews because of the actions of some. There is no place for anti-Semitism in Christian teaching.

THANKFUL REMEMBRANCE—PART III

Paul's Current Situation

1 Thess 2:17–3:13

2:17-18 Paul is orphaned. Paul turns now to the present situation in which he is physically but not spiritually separated from the community. Continuing to speak in familial terms, he describes that separation as temporarily being bereft, that is, "orphaned." This orphaned condition has led to an intense longing to be reunited with the community. Although all three missionaries have tried to visit, and Paul himself has tried more than once, these attempts have always failed because Satan has prevented it. What exactly the situation is that Paul attributes to Satan's activity is unknown to us, though it may refer to some problem that has arisen in Thessalonica itself (3:5). The reason for Paul's longing to be with the community is due to his deep love for them. It will be the Thessalonians who will give him cause to exult before the Lord at his coming. He later says very similar things to the Philippians whom he describes as his "joy and crown" (Phil 4:1) and who give him cause to boast on the day of Christ (Phil 2:16).

3:1-8 Timothy's mission to Thessalonica. Because of the Thessalonians' special place in Paul's heart and his genuine concern for their welfare, Paul could wait no longer to hear about them, so he decided to send Timothy to them while he remained behind in Athens by himself. It is not clear whether Silvanus was still with Paul, since the "[we] sent Timothy" in verse 2 becomes "I sent" in verse 5. This may indicate that Paul is merely using the convention of the epistolary plural, that is, he is speaking in the plural when it is really only himself who is meant. Certainly, Timothy was already known to the community, so what appears to be a misplaced introduction here is really an explanation of why Paul has sent Timothy as his representative. Paul considered him to be eminently qualified for this role, for he is "our brother" in Christ and preaches the gospel of Christ as a worker through whom God is operative. As God's fellow worker he is sent by Paul to strengthen and encourage the Thessalonians with regard to their faith, so that they would stand firm in the persecution they are currently undergoing. Such persecution should have come as no surprise to them, however, since Paul had told them, while he was still with them, that this was a common fate for believers. Now Paul's words have been proven true, and the Thessalonians are experiencing that bitter reality. Paul was anxious to know how their faith was bearing up under this pressure, and when he could no longer endure the suspense, he decided to send Timothy to find out. Paul's concern derives, in part, from his own experience during persecution; he is aware of the danger to faith, and for this reason he expresses some fear that the tempter may have tried them beyond their endurance, with the result that all his work among them may have been in vain.

Happily, Paul's fear was not very well grounded, for Timothy's report upon his return from Thessalonica was the good news that the Thessalonians had remained steadfast in faith and love and that they were constantly thinking well of Paul and wanted to see him as much as he wanted to see them. Their faith is so consoling to Paul in the midst of his own distress and tribulation that he will flourish despite those troubles, and this will continue to be the case as long as they remain firm in the Lord. Thus a mutual strengthening in faith is one effect of Christian example.

3:9-13 Thanks and prayer. Paul concludes this section of the letter with a prayerful reflection. It begins with a rhetorical question which indicates that it is virtually impossible to adequately thank God for the joy that Paul has received in God's presence because of the Thessalonians. He prays constantly—night and day—that he will be able to see them personally and to supply them with whatever is still lacking in their faith. In this gentle way he lets them know that Timothy's report included some areas of Christian life and understanding that need work and development. Since he cannot yet visit the Thessalonians in person, this letter will have to serve as his apostolic presence among them and be the means for addressing the faith issues he has just alluded to.

The prayer itself consists of two parts. In the first petition Paul asks God the Father and the Lord Jesus that he may be able to visit the congregation without further delay. This invocation of Jesus, together with God, the first to be recorded in Christian literature, shows the intimate relationship of Jesus to the Father, for he shares in God's ability to answer prayer.

The second petition goes a step further, when Jesus alone is addressed in prayer, another first in Christian literature. Paul prays that the Lord may increase the Thessalonians' capacity to love and that they may overflow with that love not only for one another but for everyone, like the example of Paul's love for them. Paul prays, in effect, that they become imitators of himself (1:6). The purpose of this petition is that the Lord may also strengthen their hearts so that they are spotlessly pure in the presence of God the Father on judgment day, when the Lord Jesus comes with all his holy ones (see 1:10). The meaning of "holy ones" is uncertain. Paul usually means "Christians" when he uses the term (Phil 1:1), and thus he may be anticipating his discussion about the dead being raised on the day of the Lord (4:13-18), or the "holy ones" may refer to the angels who accompany the Son of Man at judgment (Matt 24:30-31). The awkwardness of the Greek text of verses 12-13 suggests that Paul is taking over a traditional expression which he had not coined and which may, therefore, have used the term "holy ones" in a way different than Paul uses it himself.

INSTRUCTIONS

1 Thess 4:1–5:22

4:1-2 Introductory exhortation. Paul begins the second part of the letter with a general introductory exhortation, given "in the Lord Jesus," that is, he speaks as the Lord's representative to them. He admonishes the Thessalonians to continue to conduct themselves in a manner pleasing to the Lord. When Paul was with them, he and his companions had taught them to do this; the Thessalonians are, in fact, doing it, but Paul encourages them to make even greater progress. They should act confidently, for they know what instructions had been given to them.

4:3-8 Negative admonitions. Instead of speaking directly to problem issues at Thessalonica, Paul draws upon a traditional catalog of vices as the basis of his instruction with regard to sexuality. Perhaps Timothy has reported that such a general reminder would be in order and helpful. These are things the Thessalonians are to avoid: sexual immorality, passion, desire, greed, and impurity (this is exactly the same list of sins as in Col 3:5, except that "idol worship" is not mentioned in 1 Thess 4).

Growth in holiness, which is God's will, requires abstention from sexual immorality. This means honorably acquiring a spouse with pure motives and actions and not living like the Gentiles, who do not know God and who give their bodies up to their passions and desires. It also means not overstepping oneself into sin and greedily taking advantage of one another in this matter, because the Lord punishes all such actions. Again, this is not new information, for Paul had already given it to the Thessalonians. The goal of God's call is holiness, not impurity; therefore, God has given the Holy Spirit to us that we may grow in holiness, and to reject what Paul has instructed is not merely to reject him but God, whose word Paul makes known.

4:9-12 Positive admonitions. After this general reminder of what to avoid in sexual matters, Paul exhorts the Thessalonians, once again in a general way, to make greater progress in the expression of mutual love. They certainly know that they are to love one another. God himself has taught them this through Paul, who has proclaimed God's word among them, and they have, in fact, responded by their love for their fellow Christians in Macedonia (see 1:7-10). Such a love should also be reflected in a quiet life and the minding of one's own business instead of meddling in the affairs of others. As Paul had directed before, they should continue to work despite the nearness of the Lord's coming and thereby take care of their material needs and at the same time be an example to their non-Christian neighbors. The power of Christian example is not only important, then, for inter-Christian growth and strengthening but is important also for non-Christians to see and experience.

4:13-18 Day of the Lord as a consolation with regard to the faithful departed. At this point Paul introduces into his creation of a Christian letter an element not found in typical pagan letters of the time, namely, teaching concerning the end time. Since Paul treats this subject in the context of general exhortations, it may be that he is not presenting something new nor taking up an issue that was especially troubling to the Thessalonians, but was merely repeating for them a part of his teaching from the beginning. In this section he reviews for the congregation what will happen to those members whose deaths have occurred before the coming of the Lord. Paul assures his readers that these dead Christians have not missed out on the deliverance which the Lord is to effect when he comes. Therefore, Christian grief over one who has died in the faith is not the same as that of those who have no hope.

To show why Christians are hopeful, even when saddened by the death of fellow believers, Paul draws upon a creed that was familiar to the congregation: "We believe that Jesus died and rose." This belief is important because what happened to Jesus will analogously happen also to those who die believing in Jesus. God will take them up from among the dead even as God raised Jesus.

Paul also makes use of an early Christian prophecy, through which the risen Lord has spoken. According to this prophecy, those who are alive at the Lord's coming, and Paul seems to include himself among them, will not be any better off than those believers who have died. This is clear from the prophecy's description of what will happen to believers on the day of the Lord. It is told in vivid apocalyptic imagery, as we find in Mark 13, 1 Cor 15:24-28, and throughout the Book of Revelation. With spectacular sound and glory the Lord will come down from heaven (see 1:10), and those who have died will rise up to meet him first; then the living will be swept up, too, and all believers will meet the Lord in the clouds to begin an external existence with him in glory. Less important to us is how this is done than the fact that all believers, dead and alive, will share in the glorious presence of the Lord forever.

While Christians certainly grieve when their fellow believers die, their grief is tempered by the hope of the resurrection and eternal life. Therefore, Paul exhorts the Thessalonians to console one another with the message of hope.

5:1-11 Day of the Lord as a consolation to the living. Because the day of the Lord is the primary saving event according to this letter, those Christians who are still alive at its arrival have no need to fear either in regard to how or when it takes place. The Thessalonians already know that the Lord will come at a time when he is least expected, like a thief in the night (Matt 24:42-44), and that no one will be able to escape the judgment that will take place at that event. For some it will be a day of God's wrath, a time when they will experience sudden ruin and destruction, but for Christians it will be a time of deliverance and salvation (see 1:10).

Even though the Lord is described as coming like a thief in the night, Christians do not fear this darkness, for they are children of light and day. Through baptism, which seems to be alluded to here, they have become illumined and have no part with darkness or night. Thus they are not like their non-Christian neighbors who sleep at night unprepared for the coming of the Lord or who waste their time carousing around in the same unsuspecting darkness. Instead, Christians must be alert by their very nature, clothed in the triad of faith, hope, and love (1:3), which is the armor of salvation (see Eph 6:11, 14-17). The reason for this Christian optimism is God's saving activity; God has not destined Christians to wrath but for that future salvation that comes on the day of the Lord. Despite that future notion, however, salvation has already begun through the agency of the Lord Jesus Christ, "who died for us." This is a short creed, appearing frequently in Paul's writings (Rom 5:6; 8:3; 14:15 etc.), but given here for the first time in Christian literature. Through baptism this saving death takes its effect among Christians, who then become children of light. Therefore, whether Christians are physically awake or asleep at the Lord's coming, or even dead or alive, they will live with him.

With this complete confidence in their salvation, the Thessalonians are to encourage and console one another, even as they have been doing.

5:12-22 General admonitions on Christian conduct. In a final series of instructions, Paul gives another table of Christian duties that are so general that the list could be used for almost any community of his.

With regard to church order, it appears that some provision has been made for the administration of the community. Therefore, the Thessalonians are asked to respect and honor those in the community who have the job of exercising authority and admonishing. Harmony among the members is to be maintained.

Four brief exhortations then follow, all of them addressed once again to the whole community: to admonish the insubordinate, to cheer the discouraged, to support the weak, and to show patience to all. Vengeance is to be avoided, and the good of all, whether Christian or not, is to be sought.

Paul calls on the Thessalonians to do what he has done—to rejoice (3:9), pray, and give thanks (1:2-3) always and constantly. He asks them to do this because that is God's will in Christ Jesus.

Finally, since the Spirit manifests itself in many ways (1 Cor 12:4-11), care should be taken that its gifts are properly used and acknowledged. Prophecies are singled out for special attention and respect. But everything is to be tested whether it is of the Spirit or not. That which is of the Spirit, that is, the good, is to be retained. On the other hand, evil is to be avoided in all its forms because it is devoid of the Spirit.

CONCLUDING PRAYER AND BLESSING

1 Thess 5:23-28

Paul's concluding prayer underscores the reality of the Thessalonians' Christian existence. They can be exhorted to do all the things mentioned in the whole letter because through Jesus Christ, God has made it possible for them to do so. For this reason Paul addresses his prayer to God and asks that they may be made perfect in holiness. Earlier Paul had stated that it was God's will that they grow in holiness (4:3, 7) and that they dwell in peace (5:13). Only this God of peace can bring them to perfection, for it is God who preserves their total being (spirit, soul, and body) blameless at the Lord's coming (3:13). It is God who calls them (2:12) and is trustworthy (5:9) and will complete their salvation.

Paul also asks the congregation to continue to pray for him and his companions and to greet one another with a holy kiss, a ritual sign of Christian fellowship. Then speaking in the singular, he asks them to swear by the Lord that his letter be read to all in the congregation. This request may indicate that there was more than one house church in Thessalonica at which the letter was to be read. The letter concludes with a liturgical blessing that the grace mediated by the Lord Jesus Christ be with them all.

PHILIPPIANS

Ivan Havener, O.S.B.

INTRODUCTION

The Letter to the Philippians shows Paul at his pastoral best—at one moment he is praising the community, then teaching, then encouraging, then admonishing, then warning, but always clearly loving the members of this community as he gives it advice and direction. He speaks to this community of Philippians with the pride of a founding father and frequently associates the words "joy" and "rejoicing" with it.

There is a complex set of circumstances in which the community is living. On one hand it is struggling against hostile neighbors, and on the other it is troubled by visiting missionaries who, in one case, say things differently than Paul does, but still preach the gospel and yet, in another case, directly contradict Paul's presentation of the Christian message. Besides this, and perhaps also because of it, the community itself is beset with disharmony and bickering, the sort of troubles that have plagued Christian communities throughout the centuries.

At the time that Paul was writing to this community, Philippi was a Roman city located in Macedonia (part of northern Greece today) along a major Roman military and trade road, the Via Egnatia, and only nine miles from the port town of Neapolis. Despite its Roman background, the city had a mixed population, as the names given in the letter indicate. For example, "Clement" is a Roman name whereas "Epaphroditus" and "Syntyche" are Greek names. While Acts 16:11-40 records the initial visit of Paul to Philippi, almost none of this bears upon the information provided in the Letter to the Philippians itself. According to Acts, this was Paul's first mission foundation on European soil.

Although the Letter to the Philippians looks like one document, a closer inspection of the text shows that three originally separate letters of Paul have been welded together to form our present text. While we cannot be sure why this was done, it may simply have been a more adequate means of preserving these apostolic writings, especially when they were passed on to other Christian communities for their edification. Since two of these three letters were written on a single sheet of papyrus apiece (or on a part of one sheet), less space was taken up and some of the repetition removed, like the introductions and thanksgivings, when all three letters were combined together. The editor placed two truncated letters into the framework of a larger letter, where he or she thought they fit best. Since the editor was reluctant to change any of the material, the seams of the editorial work are relatively easy to find. Most likely this editing was done at Philippi itself, where the community's high regard for Paul, inspired by his love for them, found expression in the desire to preserve and pass on his writings.

By looking at each of these letters separately and noting how they relate to one another, we are better able to understand what was going on at Philippi and what the situation of Paul was on three different occasions.

Letter A (4:10-20) is a fragment of a thank-you note to the Philippians for the monetary aid which the community had twice given to Paul when he was at Thessalonica (4:16) but especially now for their aid when Paul is suffering from distress (4:14). The "distress" probably refers to his imprisonment, a situation which continues and is spoken of at greater length in Letter B. The gift for which Paul gives thanks has been brought personally by Epaphroditus, a member of the Philippian community who has also been given a charge to stay with Paul and help him (2:25). The place of Paul's distress is not mentioned, though it is probably not far from Philippi, as Epaphroditus' travel suggests. Perhaps the place of imprisonment was Ephesus, where we know that Paul spent a lengthy period of time.

Letter B (1:1–3:1a; 4:4-7, 21-23) is a lengthier letter to which the other two letters were added. Paul has been in prison for some time, but expects to know soon what the outcome of his trial will be. Although he is anxious about the result, he has come to find a deep joy in the Lord which he can share with the Philippians and which he encourages them to share with one another. He has time to reflect on the news he receives about the Philippian community, and he speaks concretely to them about their situation, as he also reflects on his own. He is concerned about the advent of other Christian missionaries among the Philippians, but is not upset. He gently encourages the community to unity, especially in the face of the enmity of their neighbors. His cheerful attitude is seen even in his admonitions, where he cites a hymn about Christ (2:6-11) as an example for the community. Epaphroditus had fallen ill during his stay with Paul and nearly died, but now he is well enough to be sent home and look after Paul's concerns for the Philippians till Timothy comes and, perhaps, even Paul himself.

Letter C (3:1b–4:3, 8-9) is written after Paul's imprisonment has come to an end—at least, he makes no further mention of it. In this letter he is responding to two immediate needs: to counter the infiltration of the community by false teachers and to settle a particularly destructive quarrel between two leading women in the community. Evidently, the good news which Paul expected to receive from Timothy was not so good after all. The teachers he spoke of in Letter B (1:15-18) were more disturbing to him after he learned more about them, and his previous calls to unity were not heeded, a situation especially grievous to Paul, since the quarreling women were his helpers in the gospel. This letter fragment is especially treasured for its autobiographical material in 3:4-11 and its short summary of Paul's attitude toward the keeping of Jewish law by Gentile Christians, along with his understanding of what salvation is.

All three letters were written close together. If Ephesus was the place of imprisonment, they can be dated somewhere between A.D. 55 and 57.

In the following commentary the three letters will be presented in the order in which they apparently were originally written.

COMMENTARY

LETTER A: A THANK-YOU NOTE

Phil 4:10-20

When this letter was edited into the present text of Philippians, it lost at least its introduction. What remains is the body of a short letter, together with its conclusion. It was written early in Paul's imprisonment, perhaps, the same trouble he refers to in 2 Cor 1:8.

4:10-14 Joy in the midst of distress. The first phrase preserved for us in the Philippian correspondence speaks of "rejoicing," the term so characteristic for Paul's attitude toward the Philippians. Paul rejoices in the Lord because they have now been able to express their concern for him, a situation which had not been possible before this and the absence of which had made life more difficult for him. But Paul does not complain, for experience has taught him to be content both in good and bad circumstances, in times of poverty and abundance, in facing plenty and hunger, wealth and want. The secret for his success in these situations is the strength he receives from the Lord (4:10). Nonetheless, he is grateful for the kindness of the community for sharing in his troubles.

4:15-19 The generosity of the Philippians. What exactly the Philippians had done for Paul becomes clearer in the following verses. Paul reminds them how they alone among those churches which had received the gospel from its introduction into Macedonia had shared in giving and receiving. In fact, the Philippians after receiving the gospel had twice sent monetary aid to Paul while he was staying in Thessalonica and had need of their help, despite his attempt to earn his own way there (1 Thess 2:9). In his thankfulness Paul does not seek more of this gift; rather, he hopes for the result of this generosity which redounds to them. He has been so richly paid back that he abounds with the gift that he has received from Epaphroditus, who has personally brought it from the community. Paul describes this gift in worship terminology, as a fragrant sacrifice, pleasing and acceptable to God. Even as they have been generous, so also God will fulfill their every need according to God's glorious riches, which are found "in Christ Jesus."

4:20 Concluding doxology. This letter fragment concludes with a liturgical doxology, glorifying God the Father unto the ages of ages, together with the acclamatory "Amen!" which means "So be it!"

LETTER B: THOUGHTS FROM PRISON

Phil 1:1–3:1a; 4:4-7, 21-23

This is the only letter of the three which comprise our present text of Philippians which has come down to us in its complete form. Since it is the longest and most important of the three, the other two were incorporated into it.

INTRODUCTION AND GREETING

Phil 1:1-2

1:1 The senders and recipients. Paul and his fellow worker Timothy are the senders of the letter. They are slaves of Christ Jesus, for he is their Lord and master. This slavery leads to life (Rom 6:22-23) and requires obedience. The Christians at Philippi, together with their overseers and ministers (the respective terms for bishops and deacons), are addressed. The mention of bishops and deacons is striking, since Paul never speaks of them elsewhere in his genuine letters, though he does mention the woman deacon Phoebe in Rom 16:1-2. It is, perhaps, a sign that he is concerned that his community have administrators in his absence and that he is coming to grips with the possibility that Christ will not return during his own lifetime (see the contrast with 1 Thess 4:17); the bishops and deacons will continue to lead the community after Paul is gone.

1:2 The greeting. The community is greeted with a stereotyped liturgical formula frequently used by Paul (Phlm 3), which is more elaborate than greetings found in ordinary Greek letters of the time (for example, Acts 23:26). It incorporates both Greek and Hebrew elements, but becomes specifically Christian with the naming of the Lord Jesus Christ.

THANKSGIVING AND INTERCESSION

Phil 1:3-11

1:3-8 Joyful thanks. Though Timothy was mentioned as one of the senders of the letter (1:1), it is clear that Paul has actually written it himself, when he writes, "I give thanks . . . ." He begins his thanksgiving to God in this generally cheerful letter with an emphasis on completeness: "*every* remembrance," "praying *always*," "in my *every* prayer." While he certainly means what he is saying, he enjoys this play on words, and in this lighthearted mood he first speaks of "joy," a theme occurring more frequently in the Philippian correspondence than for any other community. Paul is thankful, in part, due to the Philippians' openness in sharing the gospel—something begun when Paul founded the community and something they have continued to do up to the present. He is also thankful that the God who worked through him in the establishment of the community and in its mission of sharing the gospel will bring that good work to completion on the day when Christ Jesus returns, that day which brings final deliverance (1 Thess 1:10). A third reason for giving thanks is the mutual affection between Paul and the community; he has them in his heart, and they are partners in God's grace. While he is imprisoned, they share in the task of defending and establishing the gospel. Paul's warmth and depth of feeling for this community is underscored when he names God as witness to his longing for everyone of them with the affection of Christ Jesus.

1:9-11 Intercession. From thanksgiving Paul moves into intercessory prayer, asking that the Philippians' rich love might continue to increase in knowledge and experience for the discernment of that which is truly valuable. He asks this so that they arrive at the day of Christ pure and blameless, filling themselves up with the fruit of righteousness which comes through Jesus Christ and redounds to the glory and praise of God.

SPREAD OF THE GOSPEL DESPITE OPPOSITION AND RIVALRY

Phil 1:12-18a

1:12-14 Imprisonment aids gospel. Paul begins the body of this letter by pointing out to the Philippians that the circumstance of his imprisonment has actually been advantageous for the spread of the gospel, and this is clear in two ways. First, Paul's imprisonment has been made known "in Christ," probably through testimony at his trial, to the whole household of the political officials in charge and to "all the rest." Second, Paul's imprisonment has also been a source of encouragement for the majority of his fellow Christians to proclaim the gospel further without fear, but he does not explain why. Perhaps his fearless testimony in the midst of oppression has influenced other Christians to do the same.

1:15-18a Rivals preach Christ. This mention of Christian witness reminds Paul of some inter-Christian difficulties with regard to the preaching of the gospel. As elsewhere in his letters, Paul speaks here of Christians who are his rivals and, perhaps, even opponents. While admitting that they proclaim Christ, Paul questions their motives, claiming that they do so out of envy and contention. He is probably referring to how they seem to react to him and his influence on the Christian mission; there is an obvious disagreement. On the other hand, some proclaim Christ from good will, their motive being love; such as these are in agreement with Paul and see the value of Paul's role in the defense of the gospel. In Paul's view, however, his rivals proclaim Christ out of selfish ambition and from impure motives, even hoping to add affliction to Paul's imprisonment. In fact, they may see his imprisonment as a sign of weakness. While this clearly disturbs him, nonetheless, he remains in a cheerful mood and rejoices, because no matter how it is done and whatever the motives, the main thing is that Christ is preached. He has, of course, already pointed out that his imprisonment, far from being a sign of weakness, has been a means for proclaiming the gospel (see 1:12-14).

PERSONAL FATE OF THE APOSTLE

Phil 1:18b-26

Looking on the bright side, Paul says that he will continue to rejoice, for what he is doing and undergoing will lead him to deliverance, in the sense of release from prison but, perhaps, also in a broader sense of salvation as well. This will occur through the intercessory prayer of the Philippians and the support of the Spirit of Jesus Christ, that is, with Christ's dynamic presence as an aid. Therefore, Paul rejoices in this eager expectation and hope that the Spirit will not let him be disgraced and that Christ will in all boldness be publicly praised now and always in Paul's body, whether through his life or through his death. He cannot lose in either case, for Christ is associated both with life and death. But if he continues to live in the flesh, that is fruitful work for him. What he will prefer he does not make known, since the choice is so difficult: he has a longing to depart from life and to be with Christ, for that is a much better situation; yet other considerations are in order. For the sake of the Philippians, it is more necessary at this time for Paul to continue in the flesh. Confident in this greater necessity, he knows that he will remain and go on living with all of the Philippians so that they might progress and have joy in their faith. This will result in their abundant boasting in Paul's presence again with them, but all Christian boasting is done "in Christ Jesus" (1 Cor 1:31).

CHRISTIAN LIFE AS IMITATION OF CHRIST

Phil 1:27–2:18

1:27-30 United in Suffering. Paul reminds the congregation that while they bear witness to the gospel of Christ, they should also lead lives worthy of it. He mentions this because of some inter-Christian squabbles in the community about how Christianity is to be expressed. They must not only proclaim the gospel but also live according to it. If they do this, then it makes no difference whether Paul visits them or only hears about them in his absence, which in this case is his imprisonment. He will learn of their firm stance in the one Spirit as they bear their struggle with one mind in the faith that is called forth by the gospel. Given this threefold unity of Spirit, mind, and resolve to lead lives worthy of the gospel, they will not be intimidated in any way by their non-Christian opponents. They will form a united front. All of this is an omen of destruction to the gospel's opponents, but for the community it is a sign of their salvation which comes from Christ, even as he was their source of boasting in verse 26. Paradoxically, however, this life for Christ which has been granted the Philippians to lead involves not only belief in Christ but also suffering because of him and undergoing themselves the same kind of struggle which they have seen in Paul's example before and what they are currently hearing about. Christian life means suffering, the taking up of one's cross (Mark 8:34-35).

2:1-5 Christian characteristics. Again addressing the unity of the congregation, Paul lists a number of characteristics that he thinks are part and parcel of being a Christian. The Christian should have consolation in Christ, encouragement in love, sharing of spirit, compassion and mercy. If the Philippians have these characteristics, Paul wants them to manifest these qualities and thereby complete his joy, for then they will be of one mind with Paul and one another and possess the same love. As a result they will treat one another not selfishly and with haughtiness but with humility, considering others to be better than themselves and looking after the concerns of others rather than their own. The supreme example of this way of life is Christ Jesus himself, and Paul exhorts the community to be disposed to this example, which Paul explicates by quoting an early Christian hymn about Christ.

2:6-11 Christ's example in a hymn. The first part of the hymn (vv. 6-8) deals more directly with some of Paul's immediate concerns with regard to the Philippians, for we find a portrayal of Christ who did not selfishly cling to his exalted position of being "in the form of God." A contrast seems intended here between Jesus and Adam who was made in the likeness of God (Gen 1:26-27), but tragically succumbed to the temptation to grasp at equality with God. (In Gen 3:5 the serpent says, "You will be like gods.") Rejecting Adam's sin, Jesus freely emptied himself from his exalted position and took on Adam's condition of slavery to sin and corruption; he accepted "the form of a slave." Then being found in this corrupt, human-like condition, which we all have a share in, Christ completed the way of Adam by humbling himself even further in obedience to God by undergoing death. Paul probably selected this hymn because of the emphases of selflessness and humility which ultimately meant death itself. These are precisely the matters he has been instructing the Philippians about. Paul may have added that this death was "on a cross," since the earliest credal formulas and hymns, otherwise, generally avoid mention of the cross. For Paul, however, the cross is not a symbol of shame but of glory (1 Cor 1:18).

Although Paul may have been more specifically interested in the first part of the hymn, nonetheless, the second part (vv. 9-11) is also significant, for what has happened to Christ Jesus, who humbled himself and died, is important as an example of what will also happen to the Philippians, who humble themselves and, perhaps, even undergo death in bearing witness to the gospel. As God exalted Jesus, the second Adam, so Christians who suffer and die for the faith may expect to be raised to new life when the exalted Lord returns (1 Thess 4:13-18). The remainder of the hymn discusses the exaltation of Jesus and his uniqueness: he has been given a name which is above every name, so that when it is pronounced the whole cosmos responds by kneeling and glorifying God the Father by confessing and praying, "Lord Jesus Christ!" It is both an invocation of the name of Jesus and a profession of who he is.

Thus this hymn that emphasizes the uniqueness and importance of Jesus also provides Paul with the example he wishes the Philippians to follow.

2:12-18 More admonitions to Christian conduct. Continuing in his own words, Paul refers back to the Christ hymn by taking up the concept of obedience, recognizing that his beloved Philippians have been ever obedient, not only as in the case when Paul is himself present but even now that he is imprisoned and is, therefore, absent from them. Their obedience is to Christ who, in turn, was obedient to God, even unto death. With this obedience he urges them to play an active role in the working out of their salvation in awe before God, not in the sense that they can add to the salvation won by Christ, but they can make that salvation come to effectiveness among themselves as a community, because God in his good will is at work among them producing both their desire and action.

Once again referring to some dissension in the community, Paul admonishes them to do everything without grumbling and questioning so that united in the midst of their non-Christian neighbors, whom Paul describes as a crooked, perverse generation, the Philippian Christians will become blameless and innocent, unblemished children of God radiating like stars of the universe among those neighbors and clinging to the word of life. They will become a reason for Paul to boast on the day of Christ's coming and at the same time prove that he has run an effective race and his difficult labor has been vindicated by the results. Then moving abruptly from these images to cultic imagery, Paul says that even if he is offered as a libation on the sacrifice and worship service of their faith (that is, if his death is required in behalf of their faith), that is reason for him to rejoice, indeed, to rejoice together with them all, and vice-versa, they also should rejoice and especially rejoice with Paul. Togetherness in witness and Christian community means rejoicing, even in the face of death.

ARRIVAL OF TWO FELLOW WORKERS

Phil 2:19-30

2:19-24 Paul hopes to send Timothy. Still cheerful despite his imprisonment, Paul continues to hope in the Lord Jesus. This hope has two aspects in this context—first, that after a short while Timothy will be sent to the Philippians as Paul's representative and, second, that Timothy will report good news concerning the community when he returns to Paul. Timothy is praised by Paul for his trustworthiness and his genuine concern for the Philippians, attributes not found among all whom Paul could also send but does not, because they are more concerned about their own interests than for those of Jesus Christ. The Philippians, too, know Timothy's value when he served with Paul like a child with a father for the sake of the gospel among them. As "father" Paul is the leader, the one in charge. He it is who sends others and who hopes to send Timothy, as soon as he finds out what the outcome of his trial will be. Paul expresses some confidence that even he himself may be able to come soon.

2:25-30 Epaphroditus returns home. In trying to decide when to send Timothy, Paul has found it necessary to send Epaphroditus on ahead, probably as the bearer of this letter. He is described as Paul's brother, co-worker and fellow soldier, ministering to Paul's need, especially acute while he is in prison. Besides this, he is the Philippians' apostle who was sent by the community to help Paul. Therefore, he is not only known to them but was one of them (4:18). They have heard of his near fatal illness, and Epaphroditus is eager to return home and put their distress over him to rest. God was merciful both in restoring him to health and in not adding the death of a fellow worker to Paul's present sorrows. Epaphroditus' arrival in Philippi should, of course, be a source of rejoicing to the community, even as it is a source of relief to Paul, that his anxiety over them will be alleviated. Therefore, Paul asks the Philippians to receive Epaphroditus with joy, honoring people of his sort, who are willing to give all, even to die for the work of Christ. Epaphroditus has risked his life in carrying out the community's commission to serve Paul in his mission work.

ADMONITION TO JOY

Phil 3:1a

3:1a Call to rejoice. Paul admonishes the community one last time to rejoice "in the Lord," even as he hopes "in the Lord" (2:19). At this point the text is abruptly interrupted with a fragment of another of Paul's letters (3:1b–4:3), but Letter B continues again in 4:4 where the admonition to rejoice is taken up again and emphasized.

FINAL ADMONITION AND ASSURANCE

Phil 4:4-7 = Letter B

At this point Letter B resumes, repeating the call to rejoice that was begun in 3:1a. The community is also encouraged to reveal its considerateness to all, even as it has done so to Paul. Since the Lord is not far away but is nearby, the community need not be anxious about anything, for it can turn to God in prayer with petitions and thanksgiving and be assured of his care.

4:7 Assurance of God's peace. The main body of Letter B ends with Paul's final assurance that God's peace, which is beyond all human understanding, will preserve their hearts and minds "in Christ Jesus." Once again Letter B is interrupted by fragments from other letters (4:8-9 = conclusion of Letter C; 4:10-20 = Letter A).

CONCLUSION OF LETTER B

Phil 4:21-23

4:21-22 Greetings. Picking up on the phrase "in Christ Jesus" from 4:7, Paul sends his greetings to each of them "in Christ Jesus" (they are members of the church because Christ has made them holy, setting them apart, and because they are one with him). Those with Paul also send greetings, as do all the brothers and sisters in Christ, especially those who are in the service of the government, probably in Ephesus.

4:23 Final blessing. Letter B concludes with an abbreviated liturgical blessing upon the entire community, the phrase "with your spirit" virtually interchangeable with the phrase "with you" (cf. Gal 6:18; Phlm 25 with 1 Thess 5:28).

LETTER C: AN APOSTOLIC SALVO

Phil 3:1b–4:3, 8-9

This letter fragment says nothing of Paul's imprisonment and contrasts in tone with his otherwise cheerful disposition in the previous two letters. The major portion of Letter C clearly intrudes between what is said in 3:1a and what is said in 4:4; therefore, it appears to be another letter of Paul altogether and is addressed in more forceful and sharper terms than we find in Letters A and B.

POLEMIC AGAINST FALSE TEACHERS

Phil 3:1b–4:1

3:1b-2 Speaking out against false teachers. This letter no longer contains an introduction and thanksgiving, but begins with a statement about Paul's fearlessness to speak out on an issue which he finds very troubling. The primary purpose of his writing is to protect the Philippians against an assault on the gospel which he has proclaimed to them.

Paul launches into a frontal attack on the false teachers who have infiltrated the community, telling it to be on the watch for them. His choice of unflattering names for these false teachers suggests that he is arguing against a Jewish-Christian group. "Dogs" is a term that Jews used for Gentiles; thus Paul is especially insulting to his opponents by using this term to designate them. "Evil-workers" is just the opposite of what the opponents claim for themselves as they demand others to keep Jewish law. "Mutilation" is the unflattering term Paul uses to describe circumcision when they require that of Gentile Christians.

3:3-11 The value of gaining Christ. In contrast to these false teachers, Paul points out that the Philippians are already a chosen people, the spiritual circumcision, for they worship in the Spirit of God and boast in Christ Jesus and, therefore, do not need to place confidence in the marks of a physical circumcision in order to gain entry to God. Then Paul digresses into some autobiographical material, noting that if anyone has reason for confidence in the marks of this physical rite, he certainly has and even more so than others. He proceeds to list his Jewish pedigree, which shows that he was completely a Jew, faithful in religious observance, a Pharisee so zealous that he persecuted the church and kept the law blamelessly. Yet as good as all this was, in comparison to having gained Christ, it can only be seen as a loss for Paul. Indeed, everything else must be seen as loss in view of gaining Christ; everything else must be seen as so much garbage which can be thrown out.

Paul's understanding of Christ has changed his whole value system. Because righteousness comes from God through Christ, it is faith in Christ which saves—not a self-gained righteousness by the keeping of the law. And this salvation means a participation in the power of Christ's resurrection, even as it also means sharing in his sufferings and becoming like him in death. It is an imitation of Christ which Paul hopes will be completed by his resurrection from the dead, even as Christ also was raised.

3:12-16 The goal of perfection. Now Paul's argument takes a new twist; he points out that he has not yet reached his goal, that is, he has not yet been raised and is not yet perfect—the same kind of issues he needed to deal with in 1 Cor 2–4, 15. Resurrection and perfection are goals which are pursued, not that which we already have. The Philippians are urged to pursue these goals to make them their own, even as Christ has made the Philippians his own, but Paul relates this in the first person, giving himself as the example (see v. 17). This goal becomes so all-consuming an ambition that all else recedes into the background and lies forgotten, as in an athletic contest the runners strain forward to attain the prize, not concerned with what they have passed by. The prize of which Paul speaks is "God's upward calling in Christ Jesus," that is, knowing and experiencing Christ (v. 10). Those who are really perfect should think the way Paul has just suggested, but if not, God will still reveal it to them anyway. But in the light of the current missionizing by Paul's opponents, it is at least necessary to hold firm to what has already been attained.

3:17-21 Citizenship in heaven. The Philippians are not left to drift along on their own, however, for Paul calls them to imitate himself and others in the community who live like him. These examples of Christian life are important, especially when, as Paul claims in tears, there are others present who live as enemies of the cross of Christ, who downplay the significance and embarrassment of that instrument of torture and death, who are wrapped up in their dietary laws, making a god of rules and thereby showing concern only for the things of this earth, whereas the true Christian citizenship is in heaven. It is from there that Christians await the coming of the Lord Jesus Christ as Savior. At this future coming, this Savior will transform our bodies to be like his glorious body with his all-encompassing power (see 1 Thess 4:16-17). Paul's view is not that this world is evil, rather, that there is more to Christian life than this world offers, a point which he feels that his opponents are not taking sufficient stock in.

4:1 Appeal to stand firm. Paul concludes this section of Letter C with an appeal to the Philippians, his fellow Christians, loved and longed for by him, his joy and crown, that they not give way to his opponents but stand firm "in the Lord."

EXHORTATION TO HARMONY

Phil 4:2-3

With his major task of Letter C behind him, Paul now intervenes in a dispute between two women at Philippi, namely, Euodia and Syntyche. He exhorts them to harmony "in the Lord" and asks a third person, designated as "my true yokemate" and who is otherwise unknown to us, to help them. It is not clear whether this person is meant to be a mediator in the dispute or is being asked to assist them in their work in behalf of the gospel, work which they have done together with Paul and with Clement and the rest of Paul's fellow workers. In any case, Paul is concerned that discord in the community is a hindrance to the proclamation of the gospel.

CONCLUSION OF LETTER C

Phil 4:8-9

4:8-9a Practicing virtues. With a rhetorical flourish, Paul closes Letter C with a catalog of virtues that the Philippians should reflect upon, and in addition to this they should also continue to follow Paul's example (see 3:17) by putting into practice what they have learned, received, heard, and seen.

4:9b Assurance of God's peace. Paul assures the community that "the God of peace" will be with them, a fitting conclusion to Letter C where peace has so often not been apparent.

PHILEMON

Ivan Havener, O.S.B.

INTRODUCTION

Paul's Letter to Philemon is the shortest complete letter of the Apostle which has come down to us. It provides us with a good example of how Paul could bring his apostolic authority to bear upon a member of one of his communities in order to encourage him to act in a responsible, Christian way. It is a masterpiece of persuasion, a kind of letter writing which was frequently done in the Graeco-Roman world of Paul's time.

While we may admire and even enjoy Paul's power to persuade, the timelessness of the letter lies in its primary message of how we treat our fellow Christians. That ultimately has some implications for how Christians view the social system of slavery, but Paul was not addressing himself to the issue of slavery, even though it provided part of the context out of which he wrote. Paul's concern is simply that conversion to Christianity places Christians in a new relationship to one another. They are brothers and sisters in Christ or partners, as it were, in the Lord, and this relationship transcends all other relationships, such as master and slave. This Christian existence does not, however, automatically do away with other relationships, though in the course of time it should certainly affect them. Paul does not deal with this latter concern, because in his excitement to proclaim the gospel before the coming of Christ or his own death, he has not worked out the social implication of the message. That has been left to us.

The letter itself does not indicate when it was written nor where Paul was imprisoned nor where Philemon's home was. If we accept as historically accurate the information from Colossians, it is likely that Philemon's home was in Colossae, a small town in the southwestern part of what is today modern Turkey, and that Paul's imprisonment was not far away, perhaps, in Ephesus. Since Paul expected to be released from prison soon, the letter may have been written around the same time as the Philippian Letter B (1:1-3a; 4:4-7, 21-23) or shortly thereafter, if, indeed, the same imprisonment is being referred to as in Philippians. In that case the date of composition was close to the year A.D. 56.

COMMENTARY

INTRODUCTION AND GREETING

Phlm 1-3

1a The senders. Both Paul and his assistant Timothy are senders of this letter, though Paul himself has actually written it (see v. 19). Because Paul likes to play on words, his self-designation in the Greek text as "a prisoner of Christ Jesus" probably refers not only to his physical confinement but also to his commitment to Jesus. He is Christ's prisoner, even as he describes himself elsewhere as Christ's slave or servant (Phil 1:1).

1b-3 The recipients and greeting. The primary recipient of the letter is Philemon, whom Paul addresses in glowing terms—the first step in the process of encouraging Philemon so that he will eventually meet his Christian responsibilities as Paul will point them out. Instead of sending this letter privately to Philemon, as he could have done, Paul chooses to send it to the whole community which meets at Philemon's home; thus he also addresses two other members by name, Apphia and Archippus, about whom we know nothing. (At this early date, the Christian communities were often quite small, perhaps no more than thirty people, and they were not yet worshiping in church buildings but in private homes.) The whole community, in whose presence the letter is to be read, is greeted with a blessing which may have been a liturgical formula, since it appears so frequently in Paul's writings with exactly the same wording (Phil 1:2). The remainder of the letter, with only a couple of exceptions, is addressed to Philemon alone. This is a brilliant ploy on Paul's part, for by writing to Philemon via the community, Paul has made it difficult for Philemon to turn down his request without public embarrassment to Philemon. Paul has also given the community a chance to plead his cause should Philemon hesitate to fulfill Paul's request.

THANKSGIVING AND PRAYER

Phlm 4-7

4-5 Thanks to God for Philemon's example. After Paul tells Philemon that he is continually remembered in his prayers, he mentions why Philemon is the object of thanksgiving to God: Paul has heard of Philemon's love and faith for the Lord and his fellow Christians. Thus by letting Philemon know that he considers him to be a model Christian, Paul has set the stage for this good Christian person to listen to the request of an apostle, and this becomes obvious when he reveals the contents of his prayers on Philemon's behalf.

6-7 Paul's prayer for Philemon. Paul prays that Philemon's sharing of faith will be effective when it is accompanied by the knowledge of the good which Paul and Timothy have for Christ's sake. Before Paul tells Philemon how to share his faith more completely, he expresses his joy and comfort in the way Philemon is willing to be of service to his fellow Christians. The path has now been paved for Paul to make his request.

THE APOSTOLIC REQUEST

Phlm 8-21

8-12 Paul appeals for his child out of love. Paul reminds Philemon of his apostolic right to command Philemon to do what he wants, but says that he prefers, instead, to make his request out of love. Although Paul is no doubt sincere in making this claim, he has, in effect, really underscored the impact of his apostolic authority by the mere fact of bringing it up.

As an old man and a prisoner of Christ Jesus (see v. 1), Paul invites Philemon's sympathy, while he makes his request on Onesimus' behalf. Paul speaks of the runaway slave Onesimus as his child, whom he has "fathered" into Christianity. Before Onesimus' conversion to Christianity, Paul notes that the slave was, in fact, useless to Philemon (was he disloyal or slothful or a thief?), but now he is useful both to Philemon and Paul. Paul makes a word play on the literal meaning of Onesimus ("useful"), but in what way Onesimus is useful is explained later. At this point Paul acknowledges his reluctance to send Onesimus back to Philemon, since the relationship between the slave and Paul has become so close that Paul considers Onesimus a part of himself.

13-14 Philemon owes Paul a debt. Paul takes the argument one step further and expresses the desire he has to keep Onesimus to serve him in Philemon's place, especially while he is in prison for the sake of the gospel. Paul implies that Philemon owes him something, but he is not asking for Onesimus' freedom from slavery, rather, suggesting that Philemon may possibly place his slave at Paul's disposal. Paul would not take it upon himself to do this without first asking Philemon; otherwise he might appear to be forcing Philemon to do "the good" when Paul prefers that Philemon would make that decision of his own free will. For Philemon not to do what Paul wants, however, would be the opposite of "the good," something not worthy of a model Christian.

15-17 Paul's specific request. Paul suggests that Onesimus' separation from Philemon for a time may have taken place so that Philemon will receive him back forever, not merely as the slave he used to be (and still is) but also as a beloved fellow Christian, a state much more important. In this capacity Onesimus is especially beloved by Paul, but Philemon is twice blessed because he will be receiving Onesimus back both in the flesh as his slave and also as a brother in Christ.

The letter reaches its climax with a deceptively simple request that Philemon receive Onesimus back, as if the slave were Paul himself. But Paul is once again subtly persuasive, since he assumes that this will follow naturally, if indeed Paul and Philemon are partners, something Philemon would be loath to deny. Paul is not asking for Onesimus' freedom from slavery, but that Philemon accept this slave back without meting out the harsh punishment or penalties usually imposed on runaway slaves.

18-21 Philemon asked to be useful. Paul offers to correct any wrongs or pay any bills which Onesimus may have been responsible for, and his concern is highlighted by the fact that he has written this letter himself and repeats his offer to pay any damages. This is a generous offer, in Paul's view, since Philemon himself owes his very Christian existence to Paul. Therefore, Paul feels justified in asking that Philemon now be of some profit, that is, "useful" (another reference to the meaning of Onesimus) to him and do this favor in the Lord. In this way Paul's anxious heart can be put to rest in Christ.

All suspicions that Paul is hardly giving Philemon a free choice in this matter are proven correct when Paul says that he has written to Philemon trusting in his compliance (literally "obedience") and in his willingness to do even more than Paul says. Paul has let his apostolic authority weigh heavily on Philemon, but not for mere manipulation. He has sought to show Philemon the necessity of responding in a Christian manner to a matter having serious social consequences. How one receives a brother or sister in Christ cannot be a matter of indifference, but requires action that may go beyond secular conventions and laws, because life "in Christ" is of a new order. This is the abiding message of Philemon for every generation of Christians.

CONCLUSION

Phlm 22-25

22-24 Announcement and greetings. Having finished his major reason for writing, Paul asks Philemon to prepare a room for him and then announces to the whole community that he hopes that through their prayers he will be able to come to them, evidently expecting his prison term to come to an end soon.

Greetings are sent to Philemon from Epaphras, who is a prisoner with Paul, as well as from other fellow workers: Mark, Aristarchos, Demas, and Luke. This is the only time Paul himself names these persons, though later traditions mention all of them again, as in Col 4:10-14, or some of them, as within scattered references in Acts.

25 Blessing. The letter concludes with the same liturgical blessing upon the entire congregation that we find in Phil 4:23.

2 THESSALONIANS

Ivan Havener, O.S.B.

INTRODUCTION

Second Thessalonians is a pastoral letter which addresses a number of problems that have arisen in a Christian community jolted by the claim that the "day of the Lord" has come upon them. Some in this community have reacted in terror, quit work, and are making a general nuisance of themselves to others within the community as they await the full effect of the Lord's coming.

The author seeks first of all to comfort the agitated and disturbed with the message that the day of the Lord is not yet here, for certain events have to take place yet before that happens. Meanwhile, the community is to continue going about its everyday existence as usual, calmly exercising its Christian responsibilities and earning its own keep. The author is concerned that the faith itself, as well as individual members of the community, may come into disrepute and disbelief if fanatical doomsday preachers are listened to. Therefore,the author suggests an appropriate sanction against those who are unwilling to follow this teaching.

Who is this author? What is the community that is being addressed? Which circumstances have led to the claims that the author attacks? In one sense we do not know the answers to any of these questions, but an explanation for this state of affairs is necessary because of the claims of the letter itself.

The author claims to be Paul and is writing to the Thessalonians, but there are a number of indications in the letter which suggest that the author of 2 Thessalonians is actually writing under Paul's name but is not Paul and that the letter has nothing to do at all with the Christian community at Thessalonica but to an unknown community or communities which know about Paul and respect his place in the early church. In other words, the author wants Paul to speak authoritatively on the crisis that the author's community is currently facing, so he or she writes fictively as the Apostle to the Thessalonians. The author may have chosen "the Thessalonians" because in 1 Thessalonians the coming of the Lord was also an important issue. Also the author is very familiar with 1 Thessalonians, frequently borrowing phrases, terms, and ideas from that letter but ingeniously using them in a new context. Therefore, while the vocabulary of 2 Thessalonians is heavily Pauline, the author often uses that vocabulary in a non-Pauline manner both with regard to the combination of ideas and sentence structure.

A comparison of the arrangement of the two Thessalonian letters reveals some similarities that cannot be overlooked. While the parts of 2 Thessalonians are more distinctly separate units than their counterparts in 1 Thessalonians, there is a clear literary dependence of 2 Thessalonians on the first letter (minus the later addition of 1 Thess 2:13-16, which 2 Thessalonians shows no clear signs of knowing):

1 Thessalonians	2 Thessalonians	
Introduction and Greeting 1:1	Introduction and Greeting 1:1-2	
Thanksgiving Section 1:2–3:13 a. Thanksgiving and Prayer 1:2-4	Thanksgiving 1:3-4 Comment 1:5-10 Prayer 1:11-12	Thanksgiving Section I 1:3-12
b. Past and Present Mission (main issue) 1:5–3:8	Lord's Coming (main issue) 2:1-12	
c. Thanksgiving and Prayer 3:9-13	Thanksgiving 2:13-14 Comment (admonition) 2:15 Prayer 2:16-17	Thanksgiving Section II 2:13-17
Instructions 4:1–5:22	Instructions 3:1-16 Admonition 3:1-4 Prayer 3:5 Admonition 3:6-15 Prayer 3:16	
Conclusion 5:23-28 Prayer 5:23-24 Admonitions and Greetings 5:25-27 Blessing 5:28	Conclusion 3:17-18 Greetings 3:17 Blessing 3:18	

While the precise situation which gave rise to the claim that the day of the Lord has come upon the author's community cannot be found in the letter, the references to "persecutions and the afflictions" (2 Thess 1:4) may indicate that a major pogrom was underway within the Roman Empire. The intensity of such persecutions as well as their widespread nature may have been interpreted by some Christians as a sure sign that the world was coming to an end and that judgment day had fallen upon them. The dating of the letter could fall anywhere then between A.D. 70 (the fall of Jerusalem) and the early years of the second century. Two widespread persecutions took place in this period: A.D. 81–96 under Domitian and A.D. 98–117 under Trajan. Since the effectiveness of a writing written under Paul's name would be questionable in areas where Paul's genuine letters were well known, the author's community is probably to be found in Asia Minor instead of Macedonia or Achaia and almost certainly not in Thessalonica itself.

Although 2 Thessalonians hardly stands in the forefront of our theological interests today, its message (despite the strange apocalyptic imagery) has a peculiarly contemporary cast in the light of numerous modern doomsday preachers. No doubt, dire predictions of the end time will be stated even more frequently and stridently as the end of the twentieth century approaches. Thus 2 Thessalonians may speak even more directly to us in the near future, as it spoke to those living near the end of the first century.

COMMENTARY

INTRODUCTION AND GREETING

2 Thess 1:1-2

The naming of the senders and recipients of this letter is given in almost exactly the same wording as 1 Thess 1:1, the only difference being "God *our* Father" instead of "God the Father." This is already a sign that the author of 2 Thessalonians is copying from 1 Thessalonians, since Paul does not elsewhere use such fixed wording in his introductions. Unlike the greeting of 1 Thess 1:1, however, the greeting of 2 Thess 1:2 is not abbreviated, but it presents the full liturgical blessing which Paul often does repeat with exactly the same wording (Phil 1:2; 1 Cor 1:3; Phlm 3). This indicates that the author of this letter is familiar with Paul's writings beyond 1 Thessalonians, especially (but perhaps only) with 1 Corinthians.

THANKSGIVING AND PRAYER

2 Thess 1:3-12

1:3-4 Thanksgiving. The thanksgiving is introduced with a somewhat impersonal tone, "We ought to thank," suggesting that the author is following a literary rule, already a traditional convention, rather than Paul's more spontaneous and personal thanksgivings (see 2 Thess 2:13 where a second thanksgiving is introduced in a similar manner). The author, writing fictively in Paul's name, gives thanks to God unceasingly for the Thessalonians (1 Thess 1:2) because they are growing in faith (1 Thess 1:3) and their love for one another is increasing (1 Thess 1:3; 3:12; 4:9-10), but the author omits any specific mention of "hope" (1 Thess 1:3). This faith and love of the Thessalonians is reason for Paul and his companions to boast of them—not before the Lord Jesus Christ at his coming as in 1 Thess 2:19-20—but "in the churches of God" (1 Thess 2:14; 1 Cor 11:16, 22), so exemplary is their steadfastness (1 Thess 1:3) and their faith during persecutions and afflictions (1 Thess 1:6-8; 3:3-5).

1:5-10 Judgment and the Lord's coming. Sandwiched between the thanksgiving and prayer is a short excursus on judgment and the Lord's coming, which are really the key concerns of the author. What the Thessalonians have had to endure at the hands of others points to God's just judgment in the future when the wrongs done to them will be rectified; they suffer in order to worthily share in God's reign (Phil 1:28-29; Acts 14:22; 1 Thess 2:12). Justice seems to require also that their persecutors be paid back by God in such a way that these persecutors will become the persecuted. The relief that is promised to all believers is seen as a future event; it will be provided by God first at the revelation of the Lord Jesus from heaven together with his mighty angels (1 Thess 1:10; 3:13; 4:16). This revelation of the Lord Jesus (1 Cor 1:7) which is the same as his "coming" or "presence" (2 Thess 2:1, 8) is described in 2 Thessalonians not only in terms of what will happen to believers, the primary concern in 1 Thess 4:13-18, but also what will happen to those who do not acknowledge God (1 Thess 4:5) nor listen to the gospel of the Lord Jesus. 1 Thess 1:10 mentioned this latter aspect only briefly as God's wrath, but in 2 Thessalonians we receive a more detailed account, steeped once again in apocalyptic imagery. Those who have rejected God and God's message will suffer the punishment of eternal ruin (not annihilation!), separated from the Lord's presence and the glory of his power, when he comes to judge in flaming fire (1 Cor 3:13, 15). At the same time, that day will include the glorification of the Lord among his holy ones and adoration by all who, like the Thessalonians, have believed in the message of Paul and his companions. The "holy ones" and "all who have believed" may mean the same group, or the "holy ones" may refer to the angels who have accompanied the Lord (2 Thess 1:7; see comment on 2 Thess 3:13), so that we have here a scene of cosmic worship (Phil 2:10-11) on the day of the Lord.

1:11-12 Prayer. The single Greek sentence which began with verse 3 is now concluded with a prayer that borrows a number of words and ideas from the long thanksgiving section of 1 Thessalonians but in the same impersonal tone as in 2 Thess 1:3 (see the same phenomenon in the prayers of 2:16-17; 3:16). The author, writing as Paul and his companions, says that they "always pray for you" (1 Thess

1:2), that the Thessalonians be made worthy of God's call (1 Thess 2:12), and that with God's power (1 Thess 1:5) they fulfill every good purpose (Phil 1:15) and effort of faith (1 Thess 1:3), that is, that they live upright lives. The result of such Christian living is, first, the present glorification (in contrast to the future glorification spoken of in v. 10) of "the name of our Lord Jesus" (Phil 2:9-11; cf. Rom 15:6) and, second, their glorification by him (Rom 8:17) according to the grace of God (1 Cor 9:13-14) and of the Lord Jesus Christ. God's initiative is preserved throughout this prayer, for it is God who empowers believers to conduct their lives according to God's will.

THE COMING OF THE LORD JESUS CHRIST

2 Thess 2:1-17

2:1-2 Admonition to remain calm. The author returns to the topic of the Lord's coming, also described here as the assembling of believers together with him (1 Thess 4:17), in regard to a different concern. The author begs (the same term as in 1 Thess 5:12) the Thessalonians not to be easily shaken in their understanding of that coming nor to be intimidated by a claim that the day of the Lord has even now come upon them, a claim that they may have heard attributed to the Spirit, or to a saying (1 Thess 4:15 refers to a saying of the Lord and 1 Thess 4:18 refers to sayings [NAB: "words"] taught by the Apostle), or to a letter supposedly from Paul and his companions. Prophecies said to be uttered under the influence of the Spirit, sayings ascribed to the Lord or to other important figures, and letter forgeries were common problems to early Christians; they had to try as best as they could to determine what was authentic and accurate information. The development of the New Testament itself was, in part, an attempt to fulfill this need for a rule, a canon, by which the reliability of claims could be measured. There is some irony in the mentioning of forgeries, since the author of 2 Thessalonians claims to write as Paul himself. While the author may believe himself or herself to be doing this honestly, others who say things differently than the author does may also believe themselves to be mouthpieces for the Apostle in a new age. Therefore, the problem of deciding who was right was a real one for these early Christians.

2:3-4 Signs of the Lord's coming. The author warns the community not to be taken in by the claim that the day of the Lord is already taking place; the author seeks to allay their terror at the thought of it by pointing out that certain events must occur before the Lord comes. To do this, apocalyptic traditions that were probably first formulated around 167 B.C.E. when the Syrian ruler Antiochus IV Epiphanes imposed Greek culture and customs on the Jews and rededicated the Jewish temple in Jerusalem to Zeus Olympius are drawn upon. Reacting violently to this blasphemy and the apostasy of some of their fellow Jews (2 Macc 5:8), the Maccabean revolt broke out, in which the Jews gained control of Palestine and saved the integrity of their religion. (The story is related in rich apocalyptic language in the Book of Daniel.) Before that "time of salvation," terrible events took place, so now before the day of the Lord, there will first be a mass apostasy. It is not clear whether the author is referring specifically to Christian apostasy in a time of persecution (see 1:4) or just to wretched circumstances in general, that are interpreted as rebellion against God. A massive Christian apostasy hardly fits the time of Paul's ministry, since there were only a few Christians then. It does fit, however, a later period when widespread persecution was taking place and when Christians were rapidly growing in numbers. Second, "the lawless one" will be revealed before that day. This mysterious figure is also described as "the one doomed to perdition" and as an "opponent" who is self-exalted above other false gods, seating itself in God's temple and proclaiming itself to be a god. This figure is the embodiment of evil but is a human and not a demon or Satan (see v. 9). Since mention of the temple belongs to the tradition which is cited, it cannot be used as evidence that the temple was still standing in Jerusalem at the time 2 Thessalonians was written.

2:5-7 Author's commentary. At this point the author interrupts his telling of the apocalyptic tradition about the lawless one to address the community directly, using the first person singular (also in 3:17). The author reminds them that they were told (oral tradition) about these things when the author was still with them, but this still does not resolve the conflict between this information and what Paul says in 1 Thess 5:1-12, where he repeats what he had told them before, namely, that no one knows when the day of the Lord will come and that the Lord will come like a thief in the night. Having reminded the community of the past message given to them, the author of 2 Thessalonians adds what they also have learned since then: they know what is preventing the appearance of the lawless one. Unfortunately, the author does not identify this positive power for us, though it provides a helpful function of restraining the lawless one until the proper time. Perhaps the delay of the Lord's coming itself, as part of God's plan, is meant, so that ultimately it is God who is restraining the lawless one. It is God who can remove the delay which restrains this evil character. Even though the lawless one is currently restrained, nonetheless, the mystery of lawlessness is at work, a mystery which is revealed completely only at the release of the lawless one. With the assurance that God is still in control, however, the author seeks to calm the fears of the readers or audience.

2:8-10a The lawless one overcome. Returning to the apocalyptic tradition of verses 3-4, the author states again that the lawless one will be revealed, but only after the restraining power is removed. The author comforts the community by announcing that this evil revelation will be countered by the presence of the Lord Jesus, who at his manifestation will utterly destroy the lawless one "with the breath of his mouth" (Isa 11:4b). The lawless one will appear as a tool of Satan, having power to do signs and wonders which lead to deception and to exercise every manner of wicked seduction.

2:10b-12 Condemnation of those who reject the truth. Those who give in to the seduction of the lawless one are destined to ruin because they have not accepted the love of truth, which is the way of salvation. This rejection does not first occur when the lawless one appears but in the present when the mystery of lawlessness is at work (v. 7). Since they have chosen the way of falsehood instead of truth, God sends a deluding influence to lead them further into falsehood, the final result being condemnation on the day of the Lord. This harsh statement concerning God's activity preserves the integrity of God's sovereignty as also in Rom 1:24, 26, 28.

2:13-14 Thanksgiving for those chosen for salvation. Having discussed the condemnatory side of the Lord's coming, the author turns attention to the saving side of that event. Using almost the same wording as in 1:3, the author gives thanks a second time, even as Paul does in 1 Thess 3:9. This thanksgiving draws heavily upon Pauline language scattered throughout 1 Thessalonians; therefore, the author addresses the "brothers loved by the Lord" ("brothers loved by God" in 1 Thess 1:4) in giving thanks to God, because God chose them as the first fruits for salvation through sanctification by the Spirit (1 Thess 3:2, 4, 7) and belief in truth (see vv. 10-11). Then the author paraphrases what Paul said in 1 Thess 5:9, that God has called them "through our gospel" (Paul says "through our Lord Jesus Christ") unto the possession of the glory of our Lord Jesus Christ (Paul says "to gain salvation").

While at first glance it might look like God predestines some to destruction (2:11-12) and others to glory (2:13-14), it is clear from 2:10 that the destiny to ruin is not God's will but the choice of those who did not believe in God's truth when it was offered to them. God wills the salvation of all people, but does not force anyone to accept it.

2:15-17 Concluding admonition and prayer. In language reminiscent of 1 Cor 11:2, 23; 15:1-3, the author exhorts the readers or audience to stand firm (1 Thess 3:8) and to hold fast to the traditions they were taught by word of mouth or by letter (see 2:2). These traditions are not necessarily different in one form or the other, nor is the intention of the author to present a two-source theory of revelation.

This portion of the letter concludes with a prayer patterned after 1 Thess 3:11-13. The author prays that both the Lord Jesus Christ and God the Father will encourage and strengthen their hearts (1 Thess 3:13) for every good deed and word. While this prayer begins structurally in a manner very similar to that in 1 Thess 3:11-13, the naming of Jesus and God the Father are reversed. God is described also as the one "who has loved us" (1 Thess 1:4) and "given us everlasting encouragement" ("who [also] gives his holy Spirit" in 1 Thess 4:8) and good hope through grace.

With this prayer the major concern of the author is brought to a conclusion. The day of the Lord is not yet breaking in upon the community, and the author has consoled them in their time of persecution that other events must first take place and that as long as they love and believe in the truth, they need not fear the events that will occur on that day.

INSTRUCTIONS

2 Thess 3:1-15

3:1-5 Admonition to prayer. The set of instructions which makes up the last major section of the letter begins with a request for prayers which repeats the wording of 1 Thess 5:25 but, in this case, names specific petitions. The first petition asks for the success of the mission preaching of Paul and his companions, that the word of the Lord may be effective and glorified by others, even as it has been so received by the Thessalonians (1 Thess 1:8-9). The "word of the Lord" presents the Lord himself who is effective and, therefore, he is glorified by those who willingly receive him; a similar idea was expressed in 1:12, where a prayer is made that the "name of our Lord Jesus" might be glorified, that is, that the Lord himself be glorified. The second petition asks that the Apostle and his companions be saved from wicked and evil opponents because faith does not belong to everyone. Since these petitions are directed fictively to the Thessalonians, they are not addressed to a concrete situation and thus they speak in imprecise and general terms. (Who are these opponents? What are they doing?) Though some people are without faith, the Lord is faithful nonetheless, and the author assures the readers or audience that the Lord will strengthen them (1 Thess 3:2, 13) and protect them from the evil one. The "evil one" is probably Satan (2:9), but in this context could also refer to the lawless one who is being restrained (2:6-7). "Confident of you in the Lord"—terminology frequently found in Paul (Phil 1:14; 2:24; Rom 14:14; Gal 5:10) but not in 1 Thessalonians—the author is assured of the community's obedience in continuing to do what is asked of them (Phlm 21; 1 Thess 4:11), and he prays now for them that the Lord will direct their hearts (in 1 Thess 3:11 the Lord directs "our way") into God's love (1 Thess 3:12-13; Rom 5:5; 8:39) and into Christ's endurance (1 Thess 1:3 speaks of "endurance in hope").

3:6-16 Admonitions to proper conduct while waiting for the Lord. The author commands (1 Thess 4:11) the community to avoid a fellow Christian who goes astray and departs from the apostolic traditions that have been given to them (1 Cor 5:9-13). This matter is taken up again in verses 14-15 after the author has shown what the proper conduct should be based on Paul's example and Paul's rule in this regard and after the author has admonished the readers or audience to do what is right.

The author underscores the community's knowledge of what it takes to be imitators of Paul and his companions (1 Thess 1:6; 4:1) and repeats several facts from 1 Thessalonians which are worthy of imitation: Paul and his fellow workers lived orderly lives among them (1 Thess 2:10), worked for their own keep, so as not to be a burden (1 Thess 2:9). They did not exercise their apostolic rights (1 Thess 2:7) because they were more interested in providing a good example to be imitated. (Specific commands to imitate Paul, however, are found, for instance in 1 Cor 4:16; 11:1 but not in 1 Thessalonians.)

This example of the orderly, hard worker is based not only on Paul's own activity but also on a rule he laid down "in the Lord Jesus" (1 Thess 4:1). According to this rule, which has become the basis for the so-called work ethic, no one should eat who has not worked. This rule is not stated in 1 Thessalonians, though Paul encouraged the Thessalonians to work with their hands and thereby give an example to outsiders and at the same time provide themselves with their own material necessities (1 Thess 4:11-12). In 2 Thessalonians the author speaks of some different reasons for working. If the Thessalonians are working quietly, they are keeping themselves busy in a useful way. They are avoiding rowdy behavior and keeping themselves from being a nuisance to others. The author seems to be counteracting those who were so upset at hearing of the Lord's coming: they stopped working and became busybodies, running about in their frenzy and also sponging off others for their food.

In view of these "judgment jitters," the author feels compelled to state that proper conduct continues on and is not to be set aside; those who do so are to be considered wayward fellow Christians (v. 6) and are to be marked out for separation from the community. This exclusion is meant to make the wayward ashamed of their faulty behavior, but this punishment is to be carried out in the consciousness that fellow Christians are being dealt with rather than enemies (1 Cor 5:9-13; 2 Cor 2:5-8; Rom 16:17-18).

Like the sets of instructions preceding it (2:15-17 and 3:1-5), this set also concludes with a prayer. The author asks that "the Lord of peace" (1 Thess 5:23 has "the God of peace") bestow peace on the community in *every* way through *every* time and that the Lord be with *each* of them.

GREETING AND FINAL BLESSING

2 Thess 3:17-18

While Paul does write his own greeting in some letters (Phlm 19; Gal 6:11; 1 Cor 16:21), he does not say that he does so in Romans, 2 Corinthians, Philippians, or 1 Thessalonians. Therefore, it is an exaggeration by the author of 2 Thessalonians to claim that Paul does so in "*every* letter" he writes. This raises the suspicion that the author "protesteth too much" about the authenticity of this letter (2 Thess 2:2) in the attempt to secure apostolicity for this message.

The concluding blessing is the same liturgical formula that is found in 1 Thess 5:28, except that the word "all" (that is, "*every* one of") has been added to 2 Thessalonians. The author has consciously used the word "every/each/all" several times in verses 16-18 for emphasis and for rhetorical effect as the letter comes to a close.

COLOSSIANS

Ivan Havener, O.S.B.

INTRODUCTION

In many ways the Letter to the Colossians is a mysterious document. We do not know precisely who the author is, nor do we have a clear picture of the doctrines of the false teachers that the author is arguing against, nor do we even know if the letter is actually written to the Christians living in Colossae, a small town in the southwestern area of modern Turkey near the neighboring towns of Laodicea and Hierapolis. Despite these uncertainties, however, the overall theological message of the letter stands out clearly enough, with its striking presentation of Jesus as the cosmic Christ and what it means for us as Christians to be free to serve him alone.

While the author claims to be Paul (1:1; 4:18), he or she is in reality someone unknown to us but clearly standing within the Pauline tradition. The author is familiar with a number of Paul's writings, especially Philemon, and with some important Pauline concepts, such as the body of Christ (3:15), the formula "in Christ" (1:2, 4, 28), dying with Christ in baptism (2:12), the triad of faith, hope, and love (1:4-5). But how the author makes use of these concepts and terms often moves in a new direction and away from Paul's understanding. In this respect the author of Colossians is a more theologically creative disciple of Paul than is the author of 2 Thessalonians, who ingeniously reuses Pauline terminology, but does not provide any significant theological developments beyond Paul.

That Paul is not the author of Colossians is supported also by the style of the letter. How sentences are formulated and the use of rhetorical devices and words, like conjunctions and prepositions, clearly breaks with Paul's style, despite the presence of many Pauline phrases and words and allowing for incorporation of blocks of traditional liturgical material.

But even more telling is the fact that Colossians simply does not fit into what we know of the biography of the Apostle. The letter purports to be written in the same situation as Philemon—Paul is imprisoned, probably at Ephesus, and sends greetings from the same large number of people. This means that Paul would have written Colossians some time before his Letter to the Romans, creating the difficulty that Romans often betrays less development than Colossians with regard to some key concepts such as "body of Christ," the relation of baptism to resurrection, and emphasis on Christ's future coming.

Because Colossians is probably not written by Paul, the question arises whether the letter is meant to specifically address the Christian community in Colossae or whether the author indirectly addresses his or her own community, which is completely unknown to us, through the fiction of a letter supposedly sent to the Colossians. This latter possibility seems more likely because the omission of Philemon's name in the greetings, when he is clearly a key figure in the Colossian congregation (Phlm 2), is unthinkable if the author is truly writing to that community. If the author is only writing fictively, then specific names are not so important. Since the author is familiar with almost all of Paul's letters, including Romans, it is clear that Paul's letters have already been collected together, a fact attested also in the last of the New Testament documents to have been written (2 Pet 3:15-16). Allowing for some time to have elapsed while these letters were being gathered together, it is probable that Colossians was written after the Apostle's death, which reduces the possibility that it was actually written to the Colossians.

When was Colossians written? There is a broad range of possibility, for if the author is dependent upon Paul's letters, there is no reason at all to assume that the author must be temporally close to the historical Paul. Therefore, the letter was written somewhere between A.D. 63 and 90.

We are never directly told who the author's opponents are; yet, most of the author's theological thought is developed in argumentation against them. Terminology dealing with "wisdom" and "knowledge" plays a significant part in the presentation. While this kind of language was common to Jewish literature of the time, it was part of Gentile modes of thought as well. The author tries to show against the rivals, who apparently have combined elements from Judaism, Christianity, and paganism, that wisdom and knowledge can only be interpreted properly when they refer to Christ. His unique position as the agent and Lord of creation, the conqueror of the elements and cosmic powers, is to be acknowledged. Through him alone comes redemption, the forgiveness of sins. Christians, as members of his body, the church, are freed by their baptism from any sort of submission to regulations and ascetical acts which are meant to serve these inferior elements and powers. Anyone who tries to impose such restraints on the Christian's freedom to serve Christ alone must not be listened to; such teaching falls outside the apostolic tradition. Therefore, the author by writing in Paul's name underscores for the author's own community the apostolic teaching—what Paul would say if he were addressing the same situation himself.

This freedom attained by Christ must, in turn, be exercised in his service. Freedom in Christ brings with it certain responsibilities. Therefore, the letter includes several instructions on what to avoid or what to strive for and specific instructions for Christian households. The whole manner in which Christian life is lived is characterized by the author as "giving thanks."

COMMENTARY

INTRODUCTION

Col 1:1-2

The senders of this letter and the words that describe them are found with exactly the same order and wording in 2 Cor 1:1a (see similarly 1 Cor 1:1). Paul is singled out for special honor as an "apostle," whereas Timothy is given a secondary position with his designation as "our brother." This distinction between Paul and Timothy was not so marked in 1 Thessalonians, where titles were avoided in the introduction (1 Thess 1:1) and where Timothy is included, later, among the apostles (1 Thess 2:7). As Paul's understanding of the nature of his apostleship deepened, he seems to be responsible himself for this distinction. The author of Colossians, writing in Paul's name, preserves this heightened understanding of Paul's apostleship. Paul is the "one who is sent" by Christ Jesus in fulfillment of God's will. As such, he plays a leading role in the early Christian mission to the Gentiles.

The letter is addressed to Christians in the town of Colossae. They are described as "the holy ones" (typical Pauline expression) and "faithful brothers [not found elsewhere in Paul] in Christ." The "in Christ" phrase is an important Pauline concept, used here to reflect the grounding of the community's life in the saving activity of Christ. The greeting appears in an abbreviated form, with the concluding words "and the Lord Jesus Christ" being omitted. This expression has been left out due to the mention of "Christ Jesus" and "in Christ" in the preceding verses; therefore, the present text does not reflect an earlier Jewish or Jewish-Christian formula to which mention of Jesus Christ was later added on.

THANKSGIVING AND PRAYER

Col 1:3-20

1:3-8 Giving thanks. Despite some unusual features, like the complicated Greek style, this thanksgiving section begins in a typical Pauline fashion. The author gives thanks (in plural, as in 1 Thess 1:2) to God who is described as "the Father of our Lord Jesus Christ" (2 Cor 1:3; Rom 15:6). The prayer on behalf of the community and the giving of thanks to God are simultaneous actions, and the author is engaged in this unceasing practice, having heard of two things—their faith in Christ Jesus and their love for all the holy ones (Phlm 4-5). The reason for their faith and love is the hope stored up for them in heaven. In this way the Pauline triad of faith, hope, and love, first stated in 1 Thess 1:3; 5:8, again comes to expression, but hope is the guiding principle in Colossians, whereas love is singled out in 1 Cor 13:13, and the relationship of faith to hope is different than in Rom 5:1-5. This hope was heard through the preaching of the gospel, which is the word of truth that had come to them. Even as that gospel has borne fruit and grown among them (see the parable of the mustard seed, Mark 4:30-32) from the day they first heard it and came to know God's grace in truth, so also this same phenomenon has been taking place in the whole world—something of an exaggeration, even for this post-Paul author, but a hyperbole which expresses the exuberance of the author's own hope. The Colossians learned this message from a certain Epaphras, who is called "our beloved fellow slave," a faithful minister of Christ on their behalf. He—not Paul—has first preached the gospel to this community, but his reporting of the results back to Paul indicates that his ministry has Pauline approval, that he is subservient to the Apostle and has probably been given the commission to preach as Paul's representative. Through this legitimation of his ministry by Paul, Epaphras comes to stand within a line of apostolic succession, a matter of increasing concern toward the end of the first century and throughout the second. The language of "hearing," "learning," "coming to know" suggests a community familiar with the terminology of a nascent Gnosticism, whose teachers are combatted in chapter 2 through "apostolic" teaching.

1:9-14 Prayer. This summary of the content of the author's prayer concludes the thanksgiving section of the letter. It consists of another very long, complicated Greek sentence, which begins with verse 9 and continues on through verse 20. Due to the special nature of the material in verses 15-20, however, we will treat that part separately.

In response to Epaphras' report, Paul continues to pray and intercede for the community (see v. 3). He takes up language familiar to this community, giving the terms an apostolic interpretation and thereby also countering some who interpret them differently. He prays that the Colossians "be filled" with "knowledge" of God's will in "all spiritual wisdom" and "understanding." The real meaning of these terms becomes obvious by the community members' manner of life, when they lead a life worthy of the Lord completely pleasing to him, shown by "every" good work, bearing fruit and growing in "knowledge" of God (see v. 6), empowered by "every" power according to the strength of his glory unto "all" endurance and patience with joy. By emphasizing the "all/every," the author makes clear what a total commitment Christianity demands of its members and what a complete "knowledge" entails.

All of this includes giving thanks to the Father, because it is God and not themselves who empowers the community to share in the inheritance of the holy ones in light (1 Thess 5:5). Then the author continues to speak of God's saving activity in hymnic language; the shift from "you" in verse 12 to "us" in verses 13-14 also indicates that traditional liturgical material is being employed here. Because the Father has delivered us from the power of darkness, it is clear that salvation is already present; God has already brought us into the kingdom of God's beloved Son. (The "beloved Son" phrase occurs in the accounts of Jesus' baptism and transfiguration, as well as in the parable of the wicked tenants; see Mark 1:11; 9:7; 12:6.) Paul himself, drawing upon traditional apocalyptic, also speaks of the kingdom of the Son, but this contrasts with the usage in Colossians, where the kingdom is present and where no emphasis is placed on the future. By the saving action of God's Son, we already have redemption, which is described here as "the forgiveness of sins."

1:15-20 The Christ hymn. At this point in the discussion of Christ's role in God's plan of salvation, the author adds a whole block of hymnic material concerning Christ. Because the style of this material is different from that in verses 13-14, it is a hymn which the author takes up and quotes more fully, probably adding some of the author's own comments and interpretations as he or she does so. Like the Christ hymn of Phil 2:6-11, this hymn is one of the most important theological statements about the person of Christ in the New Testament.

Christ is praised as the icon or image of the invisible God, that is, he manifests God's presence in his person. He is called the first-born of all creation because everything else was created through his mediation. Therefore, he existed before all creation and is preeminent among all creatures. The author of Colossians adds some phrases to show what the full scope of creation is. The author begins with the antitheses—heaven and earth, visible and invisible—and continues with synonyms for power and might, especially with regard to spiritual beings—thrones or dominions, principalities or powers. All of this was not only created in him and through him but also for him. (This kind of terminology, borrowed indirectly from Stoicism, appears in other liturgical formulations: see Rom 11:36; Eph 4:6; 1 Cor 8:6.) Everything is subject to him, and it is through his continuing creative power that creation itself continues on. Nothing is left to chance, all is in Christ's control.

That Christ is also head of his body, the church, is a development of the body of Christ concept which goes beyond Paul's notion, for Paul himself never distinguishes between head and body in this regard. The mention of the church here, without elaboration and without close connection with what precedes and succeeds it, suggests that the author has added it to the hymnic material because the author wants to discuss the matter later (see 2:9-19). The author's understanding of "church" here, as in 1:24, is a universal entity, whereas for Paul "church" usually refers to the local community. ("Church" in 4:14-16 means "local community.") In the original hymn, "head" probably referred to Christ's role as leader of the universe.

The second major portion of this hymnic material speaks of Christ as the beginning—he is the starting point of redemption. He is the first to experience the resurrection life and is, therefore, the first-born from among the dead. Once again he is preeminent in "all things" even as "all the fullness" of God's presence was pleased to dwell in him, to reconcile "all things" through him and for him. By the frequent use of the word "all," the cosmic dimensions of Christ's power and effect are emphasized. The reconciliation which he brings about is the peace-making accomplished by the shedding of his blood on the cross, and this, too, has cosmic proportions, for this reconciliation applies to everything, whether on earth or in heaven.

APOSTOLIC MINISTRY TO THE CHURCH

Col 1:21–2:3

1:21-23 Gospel of the Apostle. The author underscores the significance of the Christ hymn by reminding the community of their own pre-Christian, pagan past. They were once alienated from Christ and were hostile in attitude, reflected by their evil works. But this former existence has given way now to a new one through Christ's action in reconciling them by his death "in his fleshly body" (literally "in the body of his flesh"). This last phrase is peculiar to Colossians (see 2:11), not being found elsewhere in Pauline literature. "Body" is a broader term than "flesh," which in this case means the physical, mortal flesh; therefore, the church can be described as his body (v. 24). The purpose and effect of Christ's reconciliation is to present the community's members to God holy, without reproach and blameless (1 Thess 3:13), but the future concern with judgment so apparent in 1 Thessalonians has almost completely receded into the background in Colossians. Instead, stress is laid on the present state of holiness and blamelessness in view of Christ's past action of reconciling and on the preservation of this new state. Therefore, the community is admonished to hold fast to "the faith" (see 1 Cor 15:1-2), which is here almost synonymous with the gospel itself, and to remain unshaken in the gospel hope they heard, when the gospel was preached in all of creation under heaven. This is the gospel whose minister the Apostle is.

1:24–2:3 Apostolic revelation of a mystery. The author of Colossians, speaking as Paul, tells of the nature, content, and perils of the ministry of the gospel. The author presents an idealized picture, vaguely placed within the historical setting of Paul's ministry. Thus, ministers who suffer for the Christian community do so with joy, following Paul's example (Phil 1:18; 2:17). They continue to experience in the flesh the tribulations which Christ experienced before his resurrection, for these tribulations did not end with his death. Therefore, it can be said his ministers fill up what was missing yet in Christ's suffering. As with Christ, so their suffering is undertaken for the sake of his body, the church (see v. 18a). Ministers of this universal church, steeped in the apostolic tradition—the very reason for writing under Paul's name—are given the commission by God to make known the fullness of God's word. (Paul could hardly say he was commissioned to preach "for you" if, as he claims in 2:1, they have never seen him!) This word of God is called a "mystery" that is revealed now to the holy ones (see v. 2) but formerly was hidden. More specifically, the mystery is Christ himself who through the preaching becomes present among the hearers, the Gentiles, according to God's plan. God wanted to make known the wealth of glory, the hope for glory, which is Christ. This is the same Christ whom the ministers proclaim, and this is done by admonishing and teaching "every" person in "all" wisdom, so that "every" person is made perfect. (Similar terminology is used in vv. 9-11.) Perfection comes only "in Christ," that is, within his body and not apart from him (Phil 3:12-15a). Perfection in Christ is the goal of ministry, which itself is both work and a struggle, but which must be done under the powerful force of Christ's energy that is operative within his ministers.

After this generalized picture of apostolic ministry, the author briefly touches ground historically by referring directly to the Colossians, Laodiceans, and many others who have never met Paul in person (1:7-8). The impersonal tone reappears almost immediately, however, when the author wishes "their" (instead of "your") hearts to be strengthened and that this strengthening be accompanied with their unification in love and entrance into "all" wealth of assured understanding. Ultimately this is knowledge of the mystery of God which is Christ, for it is in him that "all" treasures of wisdom and knowledge are hidden.

THE PROBLEM OF FALSE TEACHING

Col 2:4-23

2:4-8 Remaining faithful to apostolic teaching. Addressing the community directly again, we are told why the author has spoken of the things he has mentioned so far. The author is trying to prevent the community from being deceived by false teaching. At the same time, the author is encouraged by their good order and the steadfastness of their faith in Christ. While the reference to "absent in the flesh . . . am with you in spirit" (1 Cor 5:3) is a return to the literary fiction of the author, it also points to the unity of Christians in the body of Christ, the church.

The author's community is admonished to lead lives in accord with the Lord Jesus Christ whom they have come to know through apostolic teaching. They should have their roots in him, building on the apostolic foundation, growing stronger in faith just as it was taught to them, and abounding in thanksgiving (cf. 1:9-12). They are told to be on their guard against anyone who seeks to captivate them by a false wisdom and empty deceit proceeding from human tradition, a wisdom based on cosmic elements instead of on Christ.

2:9-15 The preeminence of Christ. Returning to some earlier statements, and especially developing some of the themes mentioned in the Christ hymn of 1:15-20, the author once again speaks of Christ's saving role. The author states in even clearer terms than did the hymn, that the "fullness" of deity dwells bodily in Christ (see 1:19); Christ is the head (1:18) of every principality and power (1:16), and all of this has consequences for the author's community. They "share in this fullness" in Christ (1:9) because they are his body. Even as circumcision is a sign of God's covenant with the Jews, so in baptism Gentile Christians have become a covenant people. Baptism for Gentiles is, then, a type of non-physical circumcision in which they are so identified with Christ that they share in his circumcision and the baptism of his death, having been buried with him and also having shared in his resurrection (Rom 6:3-5). Here baptism and the credal formula that "God raised Jesus from the dead" (1 Thess 1:10) are closely associated with one another, even as the present rite of baptism includes a profession of faith in Jesus' resurrection.

In this discussion of baptism, two significant differences between Paul and the author of Colossians become apparent. In Galatians and Romans Paul argues so strenuously against the need for Gentiles to be circumcised that it is unlikely that he would use the rite of circumcision as a positive parallel to baptism, as the author of Colossians has done. Second, there is a greatly reduced tension between the present and future in Colossians in comparison to Paul. Both authors say that Christians have been buried with Christ, but for Paul the resurrection remains a future reality, even though baptism leads to a new life now (Rom 6:4-5). In Colossians, however, we have already been raised in baptism with Christ, and Paul's future concern is virtually missing here.

God's role in the redemption by Christ is shown in that while the community was still pagan—spiritually dead and uncircumcised—God brought them to life together with Christ, pardoning all their spiritual debts (and letting them share in Christ's circumcision—2:11). God has done away with this bill of debts by nailing it to the redemptive cross together with Christ. In this way the armor of the cosmic principalities and powers was stripped off, and these cosmic forces were publicly ridiculed as they were paraded as captives in the triumphal procession of the victorious Christ. The imagery here is typical of the triumphal return of a military victor publicly humiliating the conquered foes by having them march in the conqueror's victory parade.

2:16-23 Freedom in Christ. As members of the body of Christ, the author's community is not subject to regulations concerning food, drink, festivals, new moons, and sabbaths which are associated with cosmic powers and astrological signs. Therefore, they cannot be condemned for not following such rules, despite the claims of some false teachers. In fact, the community must not let itself be robbed of its freedom in Christ by becoming subject to lesser, angelic powers and worship of them. Those who teach differently than the author are the victims of their own self-deception and pride because they have not maintained contact with Christ who is head of his body, the head from which the whole body with all its parts is given growth by God.

If the community has died together with Christ and has thereby shared in Christ's victory over the cosmic elements, then it makes no sense for them to follow regulations which serve these elements and to live as though Christ has not conquered. That would be giving up the freedom of Christ to become servile to merely human prescriptions and teachings. These rules and doctrines may appear to have the trappings of wisdom, but are really only a show. Pious religiosity, humility, and bodily asceticism are expressions of human pride, when Christ, the source of true wisdom, is not accepted for who he really is.

INSTRUCTIONS

Col 3:1–4:6

3:1-4 General admonition. Since the community has been raised with Christ and freed by baptism from serving cosmic powers, this new-found freedom requires responsibility in its exercise. Therefore, the author provides several admonitions, beginning with one to seek out those matters which pertain to spiritual life, where Christ has the place of honor next to God. Their concern should not be over matters pertaining to a worldly, nonspiritual life because they have died to that in baptism. Now their life is hidden in God together with Christ. When Christ, their life, becomes manifest at judgment, then, they also will be manifested in glory with him. This is the only specific reference in the letter to the hope of Christ's future coming; it is important, however, because we see that this expectation remains part of Christian belief, even though it is no longer given the emphasis it had in Paul's genuine letters.

3:5-11 Negative admonitions. Those matters which pertain to worldly life and which are to be put to death are now specified in a catalog of vices—the same list as in 1 Thess 4:3-8 but with the addition of "idolatry" here. The author has merely taken over this traditional listing without defining the terms; the only comment of the author is that these are sins which provoke God's wrath (1 Thess 1:10). These sins were part of the community's everyday life in their pagan past, but since they are now Christian, these sins are to remain in the past. Instead of immediately countering these vices with a catalog of virtues, the author adds yet another catalog of vices to be avoided. As with the first set, these are sins which were set aside when they became Christian, when they put on a new person who is renewed in knowledge according to the image of the Creator. They have put on Christ, the new Adam. This new existence is not dependent upon one's former religious background or ethnic origins or social status, for what is important in each, what is, in fact, everything in each is Christ himself.

3:12-17 Positive admonitions. God's chosen ones are those who are in Christ, holy and beloved, even as he is, and this requires putting on the clothes of virtue. The author cites a catalog of virtues which should be the dress of Christian life. In addition to this, the author names specific admonitions to patience and forgiveness, singling out love as the highest virtue, uniting and perfecting the rest (1 Cor 13:13; 1 Pet 4:8). Peace is the calling of Christians as members of Christ's body, the church. As such, its understanding cannot be limited only to a private spiritual state; it has communal implications, too. Finally, the community is urged to be givers of thanks (3:15b), a theme mentioned again with greater precision in 3:17b. What is mentioned between these verses, however, are ways in which thanksgiving is to be done: letting Christ's word dwell in them richly, teaching with all wisdom according to apostolic understanding, admonishing one another, worshiping and singing to God from the heart in gratitude, doing everything in word and deed in the name of the Lord Jesus. Seen in this light, thanksgiving to God the Father through Christ becomes a whole way of life. Christian life is eucharist, that is, it is thanksgiving.

3:18–4:1 Household duties. Writing at a time when Christian communities were beginning to settle down in the world and Christ's coming was seen as an event in the more distant future than was true for Paul, the author of Colossians wants the community to make a favorable impression on its pagan neighbors so that no unnecessary stumbling blocks stand in the way of the gospel's proclamation. Therefore, the author admonishes the community to follow the conventions of that society with regard to family relationships. In a patriarchal society it was the duty of wives to be obedient to their husbands, so the author admonishes the community to do the same, as their duty in the Lord. In our society, however, where the patriarchal system is breaking down and where other social practices based on Christ's teaching have taken on greater importance, equality in the Lord needs to be more seriously incorporated into the husband–wife relationship; we do better to speak of mutual obedience today, as well as mutual love and mutual avoidance of bitterness. Also, both mother and father should not nag their children, even as children should obey both parents.

Similarly, what is said here about slaves and masters must be interpreted in view of the circumstances of the time in which it was written, for once again the author is speaking to a social setting different from ours. Instead of arguing against the system of slavery, the author encourages slaves to be good slaves and masters to be good masters. At this point in time, the radical social implications of Christ's teaching, which would eventually lead to condemnation of slavery, had not yet been noted and acted upon. Nonetheless, the individual admonitions of how to serve one another—whether those addressed to slaves or to masters—are valid for all Christians also today: mutual justice and fairness, all being slaves of the Lord, reverently serving him as they carry out their various activities.

The teaching concerning reward for the good which is done and punishment for the evil, while found in Paul (1 Cor 3:8, 14-15), is not emphasized by him, especially in view of his teaching on justification by faith.

4:2-6 Final admonitions. Prayer is a key term in these closing admonitions: the community is encouraged to persevere in it, to be attentive in it with thanksgiving (see 3:15b-17), praying together in behalf of the apostolic ministers, that God open the way for them to speak the mystery of Christ, to make it known, even as these ministers are under compulsion to proclaim it (1:24-29). The reference to imprisonment is probably to be understood in two ways: Paul is writing from prison (part of the author's literary fiction), and he is a prisoner to revealing the mystery of Christ, that is, he is not free to do otherwise (Phlm 1a).

The concern for not offending outsiders, implicit in the formulation of household duties in 3:18–4:1, is stated explicitly in the admonition to be prudent in dealing with them, in making the most of each situation, and even by their manner of speech and their response to anyone who speaks with them.

CONCLUSION

Col 4:7-18

4:7-9 Announcement of the arrival of Tychicus and Onesimus. The conclusion of the letter shows that the author is familiar with the names of several of Paul's companions and friends. The author names Tychicus first (Acts 20:4), describing him warmly in three ways: "beloved brother," "trustworthy minister," and "fellow slave in the Lord." He is being sent to tell the community about Paul and thus put their anxiety over him to rest. He is accompanied by Onesimus (Phlm 11), a "trustworthy and beloved brother" from Colossae. Together they will fill the community in on events concerning Paul.

4:10-14 Greetings from Paul's fellow workers. The Apostle also sends greetings from his fellow workers. This is an attempt on the part of the author of Colossians to give this letter the appearance of authenticity, whereas in reality the author has merely taken over a list of names from Philemon, especially verses 23-24, and fleshed them out with brief comments. Also, the author knows some names of Paul's companions who appear in Acts. Aristarchus, Mark, and Justus are the only circumcised among those working with Paul for "the kingdom of God" (see 1:13, which speaks, instead, of "the kingdom of his beloved Son"). As earlier in the letter (1:7-8), Epaphras is given special attention here, as well. He is a Colossian himself and a slave of Christ Jesus, whose pastoral concern for the community is apparent by his solicitude and continual prayer on their behalf, that they stand firm as "perfect ones" (1:28) who "are filled up" with every desire of God (1:9). Epaphras' activity as Paul's representative extends beyond Colossae to the neighboring towns of Laodicea and Hierapolis. Luke, who is described here as a doctor, and Demas, who is simply mentioned by name, are both named also in Phlm 24.

4:15-18 Final comments and blessing. The Christians in Laodicea who meet at Nympha's house church (see Phlm 2) are also greeted, and this letter is meant for reading at their worship assembly as well. A textual problem in the Greek manuscripts makes it difficult to know whether the owner of the house in which the Laodicean community met was a woman (Nympha) or a man (Nymphas). The exchange of letters between communities reflects the common practice of early Christians and helps to explain how some writings in the course of time became well known over a wide geographical area. Finally, Archippus (Phlm 2) is asked to carry out the ministry the Lord has commissioned him to do.

The letter concludes with a reference to Paul's own signature (Phlm 19; see comment on 2 Thess 3:17) and a request that he be remembered in his imprisonment—a point not explicitly asked in Philemon but made obvious there by Paul's numerous references to his imprisoned state. The concluding blessing is an abbreviation of the liturgical formula: "The grace of our Lord Jesus Christ be with you all." Only in Colossians is mention of the "Lord Jesus" omitted entirely in this formula, though it is probably understood even without it being stated.

EPHESIANS

Ivan Havener, O.S.B.

INTRODUCTION

While the Letter to the Ephesians shares an interest with Colossians in the portrayal of the cosmic Christ, Ephesians is unique among New Testament writings for its description of the church as one, holy, catholic, and apostolic. It is this teaching on the nature of the church that is the key contribution of Ephesians.

The understanding of the church which Ephesians sets forth has developed out of and built upon the Pauline tradition and, therefore, goes beyond Paul's own teaching. Paul tended to speak of "church" primarily in terms of the local community, whereas the author of Ephesians, writing at a later period, has seen the churches develop into an institution which he calls "the church." For the author of Ephesians, the church is the cosmic (that is, the catholic or universal) body of Christ, with Christ himself being its head.

Although Paul made no distinction between the head and body when he spoke of the "body of Christ," he did stress the unity of the whole, while noting the diversity of the parts. The author of Ephesians applies these insights to the concept of the cosmic church, but the emphasis clearly falls on unity. The author stresses, in particular, the oneness of Jewish and Gentile Christians in the body of Christ, the church. They are united through the reconciling peace of Christ which has been attained by the redemptive shedding of his blood on the cross.

Cleansed by this redemptive action of Christ and sharing in that redemption through the washing of baptism, the church has been made holy, blameless, spotless, and without wrinkle. This has already happened, so the notion of the imminent end of the world has receded into the background and is of little concern in this letter.

Finally, the church is also apostolic. The author looks back with reverence to the time of the "holy apostles." Using building imagery, the author speaks of their role as the foundation upon which the church is built, with Christ as its capstone. At the time that the author is writing, toward the end of the first century A.D., it was important to stress continuity with the apostolic tradition and origins of the faith in the face of some esoteric, revelatory forms of Christianity which departed at key points from traditional teaching. By writing in Paul's name, the author clearly wanted to anchor his or her own teaching in the apostolic tradition.

In the light of the subsequent history of the church, it is significant that the author of Ephesians saw no conflict between the existence of an institutional church and the work of the Holy Spirit. In fact, the Spirit is mentioned more frequently in Ephesians than in many other writings within the Pauline tradition. Even as there is one body, the church, so there is one Spirit. Despite this frequency of the Spirit's presence in Ephesians, however, the author has not yet developed a systematic understanding of what the Spirit is and what its role is.

Much of Ephesians is based directly on material borrowed from Colossians, though the author has frequently given a new or expanded interpretation of that material. The two letters even show many points of similarity in structure, as the following comparison indicates:

Colossians	Ephesians
Greeting 1:1-2	Greeting 1:1-2
	Benediction 1:3-14
Thanksgiving 1:3-14	Thanksgiving 1:15-23
Hymn 1:15-20	
Gospel of the Apostle 1:21-23	God's Plan for Gentile Christians 2:1-10
Apostolic Revelation of a Mystery 1:24-2:3	Role of the Apostle 3:1-13
The Problem of False Teaching 2:4-23	
	Apostolic Prayer 3:14-21
	Unity of Body and Diversity of Gifts 4:1-16
Various Admonitions Based on Catalogs of Vices and Virtues 3:1-17	Various Admonitions Based on Catalogs of Vices and Virtues 4:17–5:20
Household Duties 3:18-4:1	Household Duties 5:21–6:9
	Preparation for Battle with Cosmic Forces 6:10-17
Prayer 4:2-6	Prayer 6:18-20
Announcement of the Arrival of Tychicus and Onesimus 4:7-9	Announcement of the Arrival of Tychicus 6:21-22
Greetings from Paul's Fellow Workers 4:10-14	
Concluding Comments and Blessing 4:15-18	Final Prayer and Blessing 6:23-24

Sometimes Ephesians quotes verbatim from Colossians as in 6:21-22 (= Col 4:7-8) but more frequently uses blocks of material, like the catalog of vices and virtues and the table of household duties, from Colossians and expands upon them.

The tone of the letter is, for the most part, quite impersonal. If the formal letter structures of the document were to be stripped off, the remaining material has all the characteristics of a theological treatise, eminently suited for widespread circulation. Almost certainly the letter was not intended for the sole use of the Christian community at Ephesus, a major seaport on the southwestern coast of Asia Minor (present-day Turkey). In fact, in some of the earliest extant Greek manuscripts of this letter, the city of Ephesus is not mentioned at all. This fact lends support to the possibility that the document was meant from the beginning to be a circular letter, or, more precisely, a theological treatise in a circular-letter form. It was written by an unknown author standing within the Pauline tradition.

COMMENTARY

INTRODUCTION AND GREETING

Eph 1:1-2

Paul, the sole sender of this letter, is described in exactly the same wording and word order as in Col 1:1; only the reference to Timothy has been omitted. This omission heightens the importance of Paul even more, with emphasis falling on his apostleship—a matter of significance in this letter. The recipients of the letter are, likewise, designated by some of the same terms as in Col 1:2: "to the holy ones . . . in Christ." The modifications in the phrasing show that the author of Ephesians is familiar with other writings of Paul, where Paul, for instance, also uses the phrase "in Christ Jesus" in a similar way (1 Cor 1:2; Phil 1:1b). The phrase "at Ephesus" is printed in brackets in our text because it is missing from several important manuscripts and may not, therefore, belong to the original letter. This is significant, since no other letter of the Pauline tradition is addressed so vaguely. The author intends the letter to be imprecise, for it is destined to be read in several communities—not really to the specific community at Ephesus. The reference to Ephesus was added at a later time to give the letter the appearance of greater authenticity and was possibly added under the influence of someone from Ephesus. The greeting repeats the usual liturgical formula but without abbreviation (unlike Col 1:2b).

BLESSING GOD

Eph 1:3-14

1:3-12 A Jewish-Christian benediction. Even as the author of Colossians incorporated a hymn into the thanksgiving section of that letter (Col 1:15-20), so the author of Ephesians places a benediction, written in highly poetic style, at this point in this letter. This material comes completely before the thanksgiving section, however, and is independent of it; the opening words have a precedent in 2 Cor 1:3 which begins similarly, "Praised be God, the Father of our Lord Jesus Christ . . . ."

This poetic material differs from that in Colossians in that it emphasizes God's action in Christ and speaks of the role of the Holy Spirit as well but always for the praise of God's glory (vv. 6, 12, 14). Thus God is "blessed" for having "blessed" us with every spiritual "blessing" in the heavens. This is a Jewish-Christian manner of speaking, a "benediction," which names God first and is addressed directly to God. Christ Jesus is the agent of God's plan of salvation to such a degree that despite the cosmic proportions of this plan, all is done "in Christ."

God's saving plan began before creation itself, when God chose us "in Christ" to be holy and without blemish in love before him. Therefore, what 1 Thess 3:13 envisioned as preparation for judgment at Christ's coming and what Col 1:22; 2:12 saw as happening already in baptism by dying with Christ is here seen in the mind of God before the world began. Already then we were destined to be God's children through Jesus Christ in accord with God's will, so that the gloriousness of God, manifested by this free gift of our adoption through God's beloved (Col 1:13), might be praised. This tremendously generous gift from God is defined as "redemption," that is, a release through the blood of Christ and the forgiveness of trespasses. (Similar terminology appears in Col 1:14, 20 and Rom 3:24-25.)

God, the source of all wisdom and understanding, has taken the initiative in making the mystery of the divine will known to us. Wisdom, understanding, and knowledge (similar concerns in Colossians) are seen in proper perspective only when seen in the light of God's role. God wanted the divine plan, this mystery, to be carried out in Christ at that grand climax of history when all things whether in heaven or on earth (Col 1:15) are united under the headship of Christ. It is in Christ that we were called to be partakers in God's plan, so that in Christ we might be the first to hope (similar to "first-born" in Col 1:15, 18) unto the praise of God's gloriousness.

1:13-14 Inclusion of the Gentile Christians. There is a shift at this point from the confessional "us" to the direct address of the readers as "you." What was professed in the Jewish-Christian benediction applies also to the author's Gentile-Christian audience. In Christ, the readers have also heard the word of truth (Col 1:5), which is here defined as the gospel of salvation. Having believed in Christ they were sealed by the promised Holy Spirit, probably a reference to baptism. This Spirit is the guarantor of the inheritance God had planned for them, the attainment of their redemption—all to the praise of God's gloriousness.

THANKSGIVING

Eph 1:15-23

1:15-19a Thanks and intercession. The author, writing as Paul and evidently considering Colossians to be a genuine letter of the Apostle, continues to draw heavily upon the wording and ideas of Colossians. In verses 15-16 there are only a few minor variations from Col 1:3-4; for instance, Ephesians uses the phrase "in the 'Lord' Jesus," whereas Colossians has "in 'Christ' Jesus." (The "Lord" title appears twice as often in Ephesians as in Colossians.) God is named in two ways—as "the God of our Lord Jesus Christ" (similar to Col 1:3) and as "Father of glory," an expression unique to Ephesians. The purpose of the prayer is that the baptismal event referred to in the benediction will take effect in the lives of the readers. Therefore, the author prays that they be given the Spirit of wisdom and of revelation which are to be found in God's knowledge (see Col 1:9, 26-28), the Spirit proceeding from the Father as in the language of the Hebrew Bible (Isa 11:2). The "revelation" suggests the "mystery" of verse 9 which needs to be revealed. Given this Spirit, the author prays that they will be illumined (see 1 Thess 5:4-5), so that they will know three things: what the hope of their calling is (1 Thess 5:8-9), what wealth of gloriousness God's inheritance among the holy ones is, and what the immeasurable greatness of God's power is for us who believe, according to the effect of his great strength.

1:19b-23 Confessional formulation. Drawing upon traditional credal and hymnic formulations, the author concludes the thanksgiving section with a brief summary of Christian belief. The greatness of God's power is shown by the effect of God's strength exercised "in Christ," when God raised Jesus from among the dead (Col 2:12; 1 Thess 1:10) and seated him at God's right side in heaven (Col 3:1; Rom 8:34). There Christ reigns over all the cosmic forces (Col 1:16) and has a name exalted above all others (Phil 2:9-11). God has placed all things in Christ's control and has made him the head of the church, which, as his body (Col 1:18), completes his being; he it is who fills all that exists, the whole cosmos (Col 1:19).

GOD'S PLAN FOR GENTILE CHRISTIANS

Eph 2:1-10

2:1-3 Present and past. The author reminds the readers of their present Christian way of life by contrasting it with their pagan past. Now they are dead to their trespasses (1:7) and sins, which characterized their former way of life. At that time they were under the influence of worldly existence and the satanic ruler (Col 2:10, 15; 1 Cor 2:6, 8) of the air, who is also described as the spirit who is now active among the children of disobedience. (This contrasts with the adoption spoken of in 1:5.) The author says that "all of us" lived at that time according to (physical) passion, giving in to the desires of the flesh and evil thoughts and, like the rest, were by nature children of wrath, that is, were deserving of God's wrath (1 Thess 1:10). While the author's inclusion of himself or herself among sinners of this sort is usually interpreted to mean that Jews and Gentiles alike were under the domination of sin (Rom 3:9), it is not likely that Paul would have spoken in quite this way because the sins named here are those specifically associated with paganism and hardly fit the situation of Jews in general nor of Paul in particular; Paul even boasted of how well he kept the Jewish law (Phil 3:3-6). Therefore, the "all of us" may be a slip of the tongue which betrays the real author's distance from the historical Paul.

2:4-10 God's mercy in Christ Jesus. Because God is rich in mercy, God did not leave the Gentiles to suffer divine wrath. God's great love for them was manifested, when God quickened them from their death in trespasses (2:1) to live with Christ, to be saved with Christ by God's favor, to be raised with him and to be seated with him in the heavens (1:20). As a result of this merciful action in Christ Jesus, the immeasurable wealth (cf. 1:19) of God's free gift will also be manifest to the ages to come. (The author clearly does not expect Christ's coming in the near future.) This saving action is a gift from God which comes through faith and is not something that can be attained on one's own. Good works, therefore, do not in and of themselves save, so that no one can boast of attaining salvation through self-effort. On the other hand, as the product of God's creative hand, we have been made "in Christ Jesus" for good works. The doing of good works was planned out by God before creation and is an integral part of Christian life.

ONE CHURCH IN CHRIST

Eph 2:11-22

2:11-13 Gentile Christians belong to the promise. Without polemic and arguing rather matter of factly, the author begins the discussion of the relationship of Gentiles and Jews in Christ. Before they were Christians, the readers, who were Gentiles by birth, were derisively given the epithet "foreskin" by the Jews who had entered God's covenant with Israel through the rite of circumcision. Because of their lack of circumcision, these Gentiles were excluded from the community of Israel, had no part in that covenant relationship with God, and so did not share in the promises associated with that covenant. Their existence in the world was without hope, without God, and at that time also without Christ. But now in Christ, this has all been reversed—they who were so far away from hope have been brought near through the shedding of Christ's blood.

2:14-18 Jews and Gentiles united in Christ. In elevated language and perhaps drawing upon hymnic material, the author takes up the theme of peace (2:14, 15, 17a, b) in order to show the unity of the relationship of Gentiles and Jews in Christ. Christ who is our peace has also effected peace by uniting Jew and Gentile. He did this by breaking down the barrier wall of enmity separating them, that is, through his death he abolished the law with its commands and prescriptions as a divisive factor. The purpose for doing so was to create one new being in himself from the two groups, Jews and Gentiles. In this way, through the cross, he reconciled both to God in one body, having put the enmity between them to death. The one body is a pregnant term referring both to Christ's physical body which was put to death and to his body, the church, which consists of Jews and Gentiles. Therefore, through his coming and by his action, he proclaimed peace to both—to the Jews who were near and to the Gentiles who were far away (2:13). As a result, both have access to the Father in one Spirit (4:4); the Spirit is at work in the body of Christ, is active in the church.

2:19-22 Place of Gentile Christians in the church. Because of the reconciling action of Christ, the author's Gentile readers are no longer outsiders (2:12) but are fellow citizens of the church with Jewish Christians, having equal rights with them, and they are fully members of God's family. Abruptly switching imagery, the author notes that they have been built up into the church on the foundation of the apostles (Rev 21:14) and prophets. This departs from Paul's statement that Jesus Christ is the foundation (1 Cor 3:11) and reflects the concern of Christian writers toward the end of the first century and into the second to show a continuity with apostolic tradition in order to stand up against false teachers, some of whom claimed special revelations from Jesus himself. The "apostles" spoken of here are certainly not limited to the Twelve, for Paul, who was not a member of that group, was still an apostle (1:1). The "prophets" do not refer to the Old Testament figures but to a specialized group of Christians whose ministry is still attested in Christian literature long after all the apostles had died (*Didache* 10:7; 14:1-3). Paul speaks of the gift of prophecy as one of the manifestations of the Spirit (1 Cor 12, 14).

For the author of Ephesians, Christ is not the cornerstone on which the church is built but the church's capstone, its crowning glory. Yet, despite this somewhat static image of the church as a building already built, an enclosed entity, the author still speaks of its "growth," thus combining "body of Christ" imagery with building construction. The whole structure, having been fit together in Christ, grows into a holy temple. In Christ, these Gentile readers are built into this temple, too, the place where God dwells in the Spirit (2:18).

APOSTOLIC MINISTRY TO THE GENTILES

Eph 3:1-21

3:1-13 Role of the Apostle. By placing emphasis on the figure of Paul, the author shows how the message preached to the Gentile readers is based on apostolic tradition. As a prisoner of Christ, Paul's incarceration is an example for these readers, a notion more fully explained in 3:13, but as a prisoner of Christ, he is also in Christ's captivity for their sake in that this captivity includes a stewardship of making known to them God's mystery which had been revealed to him. They stand in continuity with apostolic tradition, for they have already heard this message before when it was preached by the Apostle, and they will recognize it again when they read this letter. The Apostle Paul, as the representative of apostolic tradition, has become himself a part of the catechetical teaching.

The mystery, of which the author speaks, is no longer hidden as it was in the past (Col 1:26), but has been made known because of the activity of the Spirit working through the holy apostles and prophets, who are the foundation of the church (2:20). The word "holy" in this context (3:5) is evidence of an aura of piety and reverence that is already surrounding the apostles and prophets, as figures in a past that is now becoming legendary. The content of the mystery revealed by the apostles and prophets is different from the meaning given to the term in Rom 11:25 and Col 1:26-28; in Ephesians, "mystery" refers back to 2:11-22, where "in Christ Jesus" the Gentiles share in the inheritance that God has promised the Jews. They are all part of the same body, that is, Christ's body, the church. This mystery has been revealed through the preaching of the gospel, but "gospel" and "mystery" are not clearly differentiated here.

Again, reverence for the person of the Apostle is coupled with the importance of his apostolic mission. God's gracious gift was given to Paul so that he might minister. God's exercise of power, in this regard, is virtually synonymous with the phrase "in the Spirit" (2:22). That God chose Paul to preach to the Gentiles, despite his earlier persecution of the church, was a paradox to Paul himself, who said that he was the "least of the apostles" (1 Cor 15:9; see 2 Cor 12:11); in Ephesians, however, he is described in even more lowly terms as "the very least of all the holy ones." (This may also be a word play on the name "Paul" which in Latin means "little.") This heightened contrast enhances the portrayal of Paul's humility, but it also underscores the astounding magnanimity of God's grace which the Gentiles are heir to through that apostolic ministry of his.

This ministry is described in terminology similar to that in Rom 11:25-36 and Col 1:25-28, as proclaiming the gospel of the inscrutable riches of Christ and enlightening of all with God's mystery. Here "mystery" and "riches of Christ" are one and the same. In continuity with this ministry of the Apostle, the ministry of the present (therefore, in the time after Paul) is being carried out "through the church." It is the church which continues the apostolic ministry, making God's wisdom known to the cosmic powers in accord with God's eternal plan. Thus, "in Christ," the church has taken on Christ's cosmic role! It is in him and by faith in him that we can confidently and freely have access to God (2:17-18).

This section concludes with a reference back to Paul's imprisonment in 3:1. The Apostle's tribulations are for the sake of the readers of this letter; these tribulations are their glory and not reason for being disheartened. Suffering (and martyrdom) have apostolic approval and example (Phil 1:29) and their own peculiar power of proclamation.

3:14-21 Apostolic prayer. In a profound posture of worship, the Apostle kneels (Phil 2:10; Rom 14:11) before the Father of the cosmos and prays for his readers. From the Father, every family of heavenly and earthly beings has received its name, and from the Father with his wealth of glory, the Apostle prays that his readers will be strengthened inwardly in power through the Father's Spirit. As in the case of 2:22 and 3:7, power and Spirit are closely related. Second, he prays that Christ dwell in their hearts through faith, faith being the means for this indwelling. This second petition makes precise what was meant in the first. Then he asks that they, being rooted and grounded in love, may fully understand with all the holy ones (that is, also with Jewish Christians) what the full dimensions of Christ's love are. But to know the love of Christ is paradoxically to know a love which surpasses knowledge itself. Finally, the prayer comes to a climax in the petition that they themselves be filled with all the fullness of God, the same which is attributed to Christ in Col 1:19.

The prayer concludes with a doxology, a liturgical formula in praise of God. In this case, the Father, whose ability to act far exceeds anything we are able to ask for or even think of and who lets his power operate in us, is to be glorified forever in the church and in Christ. The church and Christ are intimately related, as the author of Ephesians has sought to point out from the beginning.

INSTRUCTIONS

Eph 4:1–6:20

4:1-6 Unity of the body. The author exhorts the readers to lead lives worthy of their Christian calling (1 Thess 2:12; Col 1:10) and names a catalog of virtues borrowed from Col 3:12-15 which they should practice. Unity of the Spirit, however, is unique to Ephesians and reflects the author's greater interest in the role of the Spirit. A whole series of "one formulas" are introduced to further describe the components of the Christian calling: one body, one Spirit, one hope, one Lord, one faith, one baptism, and one God. Since the sole ritual action in this list is baptism and because eucharist is not mentioned, it is possible that such "one formulas" were used as liturgical shouts during the baptismal rite itself. The formula which speaks of "one God" appears to be a unit in itself, a Jewish formulation which has been incorporated into Christian teaching. It consists of the additional designation of God as the "Father of all," plus the three prepositional phrases—over, through, and in all. This is a Stoic manner of speaking, taken up and transformed by Greek-speaking Jews and Christians. See the "one formula" of 1 Cor 8:6 and the similar use of prepositions there.

4:7-16 Diversity of gifts. Each individual in the one body of Christ has been given grace according to the measure of Christ's gift. While Paul speaks of similar subject matter in 1 Cor 12 and Rom 12:4-6, he refers to "charisms" (gifts) instead of "grace," and these charisms come from the "Spirit," instead of "Christ." Both Paul and the author of Ephesians emphasize, however, the diversity of gifts within the one body.

Ps 68:19 is quoted directly by the author as scriptural support that Christ has given gifts, but this passage also enabled the author to take up the notion that the cosmic powers have been taken captive in the person of Christ (Col 2:15). By arguing that "ascent" requires a previous "descent," the author seeks to show that the passage really refers to someone other than Moses. The descent into the lower regions of the earth probably refers to Christ's victory over the realm of the dead (1 Pet 3:19-20), which prepared the way for his ascent high above the heavens as the cosmic conqueror to fill all. Thus, he is the source of gifts.

It is Christ who has given the leaders of the church. This list of leaders is similar to that given by Paul (1 Cor 12:28), but the Pauline triad of apostles, prophets, and teachers is interrupted here by the addition of evangelists (2 Tim 4:5) and pastors (1 Pet 5:2-4), roles that took on greater importance as the apostles died. These are not just random examples but roles essential to the life of the church; those who exercise them are responsible for equipping the holy ones for ministry, that is, for service, and thus for the upbuilding of Christ's body (2:20-22). The goal is the future unity of us all in faith and knowledge of the Son of God (this is the only time in this letter that Christ is given the Son of God title), the formation of a perfect, mature person, completely grown in the fullness of Christ.

Since the goal is perfect adulthood in Christ, the author exhorts the readers not to act then like children, when false teaching is being bandied about. Because Christ has bestowed on them church leaders steeped in the apostolic tradition, they need only heed that message alone, that is, to profess that truth in love which has already been taught them and thus continue the process of growth toward maturity in Christ, the head. It is through Christ that the body grows. With all the members working together, doing their proper function, it builds itself up in love. There is unity in the attempt to attain unity in Christ.

4:17-24 Discontinuity with the past. Solemnly invoking the apostolic role "in the Lord," the author declares that the readers must no longer live as pagans. As in 2:13, the author describes again the worthlessness of paganism: pagans have purposeless dispositions and darkened understanding; they are separated from the life of God (2:12; Col 1:21) on account of the ignorance and hardness of their hearts, and they have given themselves over to immorality (Col 3:5). This manner of life contrasts starkly with what had been taught to them when they learned about Christ, for in Jesus they heard and were taught truth itself. Therefore, they were taught to set aside that former manner of life, that old person corrupted by seductive passions and to be renewed, instead, in the spirits of their disposition, putting on a new person, that second Adam who, like the first, was created in God's image. This new person's attributes are justice and holiness, which come from Christ who is truth.

4:25–5:7 Community rules. Since Christians are members one of another in Christ's body, there are certain vices which need to be avoided and certain virtues which need to be practiced for the body to function properly. Therefore, lying is to be supplanted by speaking the truth to one's neighbor; the sun should not set on a sinful anger; the devil should be given no opportunity to act; stealing is to be replaced by honest labor, so that what is obtained from it can be shared with the needy. Evil talk should give way to constructive talk that builds up and imparts grace on the hearers. The readers should not trouble God's Holy Spirit in whom they were sealed (1:13) for the sake of their redemption on the last day. In 4:31, the author cites a whole catalog of vices (Col 3:8) which should be removed from them. Then follows a catalog of virtues as a replacement. Among these virtues, forgiveness is singled out, in view of God's forgiveness of them in Christ (Col 3:12-13).

As Paul asked his readers to be imitators of him (Phil 3:17) and as he himself was an imitator of Christ (1 Cor 11:1), so now the author of Ephesians asks his readers to be imitators of God. As God's beloved children, they should conduct their lives in love, like Christ did for "us" when he offered himself up as a sweet-smelling sacrifice to God. (The change from "you" to "us" suggests that a traditional confessional formula has been taken up here.) This way of love excludes a whole series of vices which are incompatible with the life of the "holy ones." Their life should be characterized, instead, by thanksgiving, for the practitioners of the vices listed here do not have an inheritance in the kingdom of Christ (Col 1:13) and of God (Col 4:11). It is important, therefore, not to be led astray by teaching to the contrary and not to participate in such vices, because these sins bring the anger of God upon the children of disobedience (Col 3:6).

5:8-20 Living in the light. The readers of this letter were once Gentiles without Christ and were darkness itself, but now as Gentiles in the Lord, they have become light. Their new identity as children of light requires that they live in a different way. The fruit produced by this light-life is all goodness, righteousness, and truth, considering what is pleasing to the Lord. Therefore, instead of participating in the unproductive works of darkness, they should condemn such deeds. It is even shameful to speak of the deeds done in secret by the children of darkness. Such deeds condemned, however, are illumined by light, and everything so illumined becomes light. To underscore the point, the author quotes a passage from an unknown source, probably a fragment of a baptismal hymn. It challenges the one to be baptized to wake up from the sleep of a spiritual death and to arise from among the spiritually dead. Resurrection is conceived here as entry into newness of life, permeated by the light of Christ.

Those who have been so enlightened are also "wise" and should take care to live accordingly—not as the foolish do. They should make the most of the opportunity (Col 4:5) during these evil days, being alert to discerning what the will of God is—not unthinking. Drunkenness with wine is to be avoided because it hinders that discernment process and is yet another indication of base, pagan life. In contrast to being filled up with wine, they should be filled up with the Spirit. This Spirit-life is expressed in community by psalm and song to the Lord which proceeds from the heart and also is manifested in giving thanks constantly to God the Father in the name of our Lord Jesus Christ (Col 4:17).

5:21-33 Household duties—wives and husbands. Another manifestation of being filled in the Spirit is mutual obedience out of reverence for Christ who is himself the prime example of one who is obedient. By incorporating and explaining the household duties of Col 3:18–4:1, the author develops this concept of mutual obedience.

While the author takes up the same exhortation as Col 3:18, that wives should be obedient to their husbands, the statement is modified to the effect that such obedience should be like that given to the Lord. The author's explanation for this follows this line of argumentation: as Christ (masculine) is head of the church (a feminine word in Greek), so the husband (masculine) is head of his wife (feminine), and as his body, the church (feminine), is obedient to Christ (masculine), so wives (feminine) should be completely obedient to their husbands (masculine).

This interpretation, sexist by our standards today, is balanced in part, however, both by the call to mutual obedience in 5:21 and by what husbands are admonished to do in verses 25-33. Care must be taken, therefore, not to lift verses 22-24 out of context, as though it were meant to be a put-down of women; that would be a clear distortion of the author's purpose.

As in Col 3:19, husbands are exhorted to love their wives, but unlike Colossians this is explained in Ephesians in terms of the church. As Christ (masculine) loved the church (feminine) and gave himself up for it, so completely should husbands (masculine) love their wives (feminine).

The line of thought is interrupted by a brief explanation of the ecclesiastical significance of Christ's self-sacrifice. Christ acted in this way in order to make his church holy, purifying it with the baptismal washing and the proclamation of the word, and thus to present "to himself" (1 Thess 3:13 has "before our God and Father") a glorified church, holy and spotless. With this description of the church as "holy," the author of Ephesians completes the naming of the four characteristics of the church, summarized later in the Nicene Creed: one, holy, catholic, and apostolic church.

Returning to his discussion about husbands, the author continues to argue in a similar vein: like Christ loved his body, the church, and as husbands love their own bodies, so they should also love their wives. When they love their wives, they are, in fact, loving themselves. The author cites a common proverb about not hating oneself, which is thought to lend support to the author's argument. Love of self (a positive virtue here) is shown by our concern to feed and care for our bodies, something which Christ does for his church and which we experience as members of his body. (The feeding may be a reference to the Eucharist, which is not otherwise spoken of in this letter.) The author adds scriptural support by quoting Gen 2:24 to show the unity of husbands and wives in the one body of Christ which is his church. Therefore, every husband is exhorted to love his wife, and the wife is admonished to revere her husband.

6:1-4 Household duties—children and parents. Exhorting children to obey their parents (Col 3:20), the author of Ephesians quotes another passage from the Hebrew Bible (Exod 20:12) and notes the unique promise of long life associated with that commandment. This command is to be carried out "in the Lord" for the simple reason that it is the right thing to do, whereas Col 3:20 says, with a slightly different emphasis, that "this is pleasing to the Lord."

Fathers are admonished not to anger their children, but no explanation of this is given here. In Col 3:21, however, they are warned not to nag their children "so they may not become discouraged." Instead of this explanation, the author of Ephesians adds another admonition to fathers: that they rear their children in Christian discipline and instruction. This is yet another indication that the imminent end of the world has receded from consciousness.

6:5-9 Household duties—slaves and masters. Slaves are exhorted to obey their earthly masters with reverence and awe (Phil 2:12), as if they were obeying Christ himself. (Similarly, Col 3:22 notes that when slaves obey their masters, they are by that very fact showing reverence to the Lord.) These "slaves of Christ" (see commentary on Phil 1:1) do the will of God when they carry out their duties responsibly and willingly, doing them to please the Lord rather than their earthly masters and, perhaps, even in spite of them. Unlike Col 3:25, Ephesians speaks of a positive reward: everyone will be rewarded by the Lord for the good that is done. It is meant to be a message of comfort to slaves.

Some of the material used to address slaves in Colossians is employed with better effect by the author of Ephesians in applying it to masters. Both master and slave have one and the same Lord who shows no favoritism due to one's higher (or lower) rank in society. Masters are to act with the same knowledge as their slaves, namely, that they also have the Lord over them, and they must serve him. They have the specific obligation not to threaten their slaves. What is revolutionary in this teaching is that masters not only have rights but also have obligations with regard to their slaves.

6:10-20 Preparation for battle with cosmic forces. Although Christ has already triumphed over every cosmic principality, authority, power, and domination (1:21), and even though believers are freed from bondage to the ruler of the power of the air (2:2), nonetheless, these cosmic forces still maintain a threatening influence. The author of Ephesians, therefore, takes up military imagery to describe how Christians should stand firm against these powers. They are exhorted to be strengthened "in the Lord" (NAB: "from the Lord") and in the power of his strength as they prepare to do battle. They are to put on the armor of God in order to stand firm against the devil's own military strategy. This armor of God is necessary because the battle is not with mere flesh and blood (2 Cor 10:4) but with cosmic forces; this armor will enable them to stand their ground on the evil day and consists of truth as a belt, righteousness as a breastplate, gospel of peace as footgear, faith as a shield, salvation as a helmet (1 Thess 5:8), and the Spirit (described as the word of God) as a sword.

Thus armed, the readers are to keep a persevering watch, praying and interceding at all times in the Spirit on behalf of all the holy ones. The author, writing as Paul, adds the more personal note that they should also pray for him that he will be able to speak the word, to make known with courage that gospel mystery for which he is now Christ's imprisoned envoy.

CONCLUSION

Eph 6:21-24

6:21-22 Announcement of the arrival of Tychicus. The letter concludes with an announcement of the sending of Tychicus to the community to tell them how Paul is and what he is doing and thus put their anxiety over him to rest. This seemingly personal announcement has, in fact, been quoted directly from Col 4:7-8. Of the thirty-four Greek words in the Colossian passage, thirty-two have been repeated here verbatim and in exactly the same order. This is the clearest sign of a direct literary dependence of Ephesians on Colossians.

6:23-24 Final prayer and blessing. Both the final prayer and blessing have an impersonal tone, the readers being referred to in the third person. This indicates that a wider audience is meant than a single community. In the prayer, "peace," a major theme in this letter (2:14-18; 4:3; 6:15), has replaced "hope" in the Pauline triad of faith, hope, and love. The blessing is addressed generally to "all who love our Lord Jesus Christ in immortality." It is unclear whether the phrase "in immortality" belongs with "love," or belongs with "grace," or refers to Jesus Christ who reigns in immortal glory, or refers to those who love the Lord and, therefore, have a share now in immortality. All of these are grammatically possible.

THE PASTORAL EPISTLES

Jerome H. Neyrey, S.J.

INTRODUCTION

Author

Modern biblical criticism has seriously challenged the claim that Paul wrote the so-called pastoral Epistles—1 Timothy, 2 Timothy, and Titus. The vocabulary in the Pastorals differs from that in the undisputed Pauline letters. The bold themes in Paul's letters are only formulae here, but above all the view of the church is significantly different from that found in Paul's letters. The question of authentic authorship, while important for historical studies, is distracting here. The letters are not less valuable for faith because Paul probably did not write them, nor more valuable if authentic. Their value for us as Christians comes from the fact that they are inspired by God and important for the church's self-understanding. It was common, moreover, in the Old Testament to attribute later psalms, prophecies, and bits of wisdom to earlier noted authorities, such as David or Solomon. The same procedure was common also in many New Testament writings. Since it is unlikely that Paul wrote the Pastorals, an early date for their composition is unwarranted. It is generally agreed that they stem from the last decades of the first century.

If the historical Paul did not actually compose these letters, they were, nevertheless, intended by their genuine author to be taken as Pauline statements, in accord with Pauline traditions. And I will regularly point out the many similarities between Paul's undisputed letters and these pastoral Epistles.

Form and function

In many ways these letters, at least 1 Timothy and Titus, seem to be extended codes of "household duties," a common form of exhortation in pagan, Jewish, and Christian literature. The Pastorals are, moreover, collections of very traditional moral materials, echoing not only gospel sources but Pauline advice to his churches and Petrine materials as well. Most importantly, in all three letters we find a formal written document which certifies the present status of Timothy and Titus as church leaders and which subsequently authenticates their successors. These letters, then, stress church order and morality and so function as official constitutions for their respective churches.

Changes in the early churches

Comparing the view of the church in the Pauline letters with that in the Pastorals, we note many significant changes which are characteristic of "early catholicism." This concept is a useful historical label for indicating just the shift in the church's profile mentioned above: (1) *Leadership*—no longer does Jesus commission apostles, nor is leadership designated by God's Spirit, but volunteers arise and are validated by the church. (2) *Doctrine*—the great, dynamic themes of faith, righteousness, and grace are now reduced to slogans and formulae; more stress is placed on correctness of doctrine than on the dynamics of conversion and allegiance to Jesus. (3) *Church*—the freely elected group of Christians enflamed with charismatic gifts and waiting for the parousia has quieted down to a group of second-generation believers who are urged to be exemplary citizens and to live long and full lives. (4) *Equality*—the freedom and equality of men and women, so strong in the Pauline churches, is moderated here; conformity to local cultural norms is urged.

"Early catholicism" is a useful historical tag for pointing to this clear shift in the early churches, but it is open to considerable misunderstanding. For some, this shift is interpreted as a corruption of the Pauline genius and as an indication of the smothering institutionalization of the church; still others find in the shift a quasi-warrant for later authoritarian and doctrinal controls. Here is the crux—we should neither overly depreciate the shift nor unduly celebrate it. It is not true that the church went to ruin after Paul due to compromises within it, nor is it accurate to champion later developments as divinely ordained evolutions, necessarily good.

The pastoral churches were seriously adapting the gospel to their unique situations. As they grew from small groups into large urban churches, they suffered the stresses and pains of any growing religious group. And herein lies their importance for us, the warrant to adapt and develop in the face of new cultures and situations. It would surely be a mistake to expect our church to look and feel like the Pastorals; we must preach the gospel to our own world, not simply cling to old traditions and formulations which suited a world long since passed.

Conservatism and tradition

How frequently the Pastorals speak of the "deposit of faith," of "sound teaching," of the gospel of truth. How often Paul tells Timothy to adhere to the gospel and resist false teachers. This sounds conservative and traditionalistic, but the needs of these churches were such that they had to clarify many important things: (1) the orderly succession of leaders, especially where there are competing claims; (2) the orthodoxy of teachers, especially when there are radical differences of opinion; and (3) the central tenets of the gospel faith, clearly expressed and without excesses. These problems were especially acute as the older leaders of the young church died and the church spread and matured socially. The crisis called for firm decision-making, for saying: "This is the gospel! That is heresy!" and "Here is our leader, not that one!"

The stress on tradition does not mean that all new ideas or developments are corrupt; this would be naive and clearly wrong. The Pastorals do not formally address the issue of valid development of gospel teaching, for they merely identify certain erroneous teachings about the law, ascetical practices, and the resurrection. To read them as a charter for freezing church teaching and becoming doctrinally conservative, afraid of change or development, is a misinterpretation of them. They are "pastoral" in the rich sense that they squarely address problems troubling the life of their churches and offer novel solutions and solid advice to the developing churches. For all their formalism, they are vitally alive with the love for God's church and with a keen sense of the total conversion to which the gospel calls us. They are "pastoral" in the way they call upon their foundational traditions about Jesus and how these theological ideas intimately structure and enrich the way we live. They are "pastoral" in the demand they make on the church to become acculturated in pagan society and yet to be distinctly faithful to the gospel. They are "pastoral" in the practical development of church offices to ensure stable succession, fidelity to the gospel, and fresh leadership in a church in transition.

1 TIMOTHY

Jerome H. Neyrey, S.J.

COMMENTARY

1:1-2 Letter opening. All ancient letters begin with a notice of sender, recipient, plus a short greeting. The author typically begins by stating that he is an official "apostle" of God and Jesus Christ, thus underscoring his authority, as is the case here. He calls Timothy his "true child in faith," just as he spoke of himself to Christians as their "father" (1 Cor 4:15; 1 Thess 2:11). This way of speaking illustrates the church's understanding of itself as a genuinely new family, especially reflecting warmth to those who may have sacrificed natural family ties for Christ (see Matt 10:34-39). The greeting here expands the typical Pauline greeting ("grace and peace") to three items ("grace, *mercy*, and peace"), perhaps to signal the stress on "mercy" shown to Paul in 1:13.

1:3-7 Defender of the faith. Verse 3 alludes to the command that Timothy take his place in Ephesus and become an "overseer" of that church. Ephesus was a church particularly important to Paul. He spent two years there (Acts 19:1-10), where he met both great success and hostility (Acts 19:11-20; 1 Cor 15:32). The great Alexandrian preacher Apollos became a convert there (Acts 18:24), and Paul summoned the elders of Ephesus to himself for a farewell speech (Acts 20:16-35). This was obviously an influential church, for we have one long letter addressed to it (Eph) and a shorter one as well (Rev 2:1-7).

Timothy's commission was to guard the faith, which means here to charge other would-be teachers to cease from propagating deviant doctrines. It is impossible to know just what these "myths and genealogies" were, but we know what was wrong about them: they did not promote integrity of faith and life. Here we touch the heart of the author's concern for these churches, that their lives be worthy of their calling. He sees that true doctrine leads to good morals and to a religiously integrated life. The would-be teachers promote only mere speculation but not "training" in faith, that is, ordering of lives in the wholeness of faith. In contrast, Timothy's task is an active one—practical love which comes only from what is pure, good, and sincere. In this concern for the inner relationship of faith and life, the author echoes the gospel charge that "by their fruits you shall know them" (Matt 7:16). The inner person, totally caught up in the gospel, will express itself richly in a morally upright life, but the inner self must be formed in truth. So Timothy stands confronting would-be teachers of religion, not only in their conclusions about the validity of the law but especially in the emptiness of their understanding of the relationship of faith to life.

1:8-11 The value and function of the law. It is not clear just what the would-be teachers of the law are proposing: either abolition of all law (libertinism) or imposition of esoteric laws (Jewish gnosticism). Either way the author will have none of this excess. He rather asserts the essential worth of the law, just as he did in Rom 7:12, 16; after all, God revealed it and his word is true (see 2 Tim 3:16). In his genuine letters Paul claimed that the law had various functions: (1) to increase trespasses (Rom 5:20), (2) to act as guardian or educator (Gal 3:23-24), and (3) to restrain wickedness (Gal 3:19). Here in verse 9 the last reason is stressed; obviously not all "need" a law if they are truly led by the Spirit and have been totally converted to God. Because of sin and error, some need to have the implications of Christian faith spelled out for them, hence the list in 1:9-10. It is a common feature of popular moral preaching that teachers would remind their audiences of typical moral virtues and vices by citing lists of such, which Paul regularly did (Gal 5:19-21; 1 Cor 6:9-10). The list here is special, for it is based on the core of the Old Testament covenant law, the Ten Commandments, much the same way that the list of virtues cited in Matt 15:19 is also based on the Ten Commandments. Despite Christian arguments that Jewish law was no longer binding, the Ten Commandments always remained a central part of Christian moral teaching, probably because they are the essential covenant law which spells out the implications of our covenant faith. The great love command of Jesus (Matt 22:36-40) is in fact the covenant code found in the Ten Commandments; this is what covenant love means (see Matt 19:18-19). The law is intended to restrain whatever is contrary to "sound" teaching, a common phrase in these letters which suggests that the author's doctrine is both healthy (accurate) and health-giving (1 Tim 6:3; 2 Tim 1:13). After all, good theology leads to good morals. The measure of what is "sound" is determined by what is in accord with tradition, i.e., the gospel entrusted to Paul and the church, which is another indirect polemic on the would-be teachers with their speculation on myths (1:3-7).

1:12-17 Prayer of thanksgiving. It is typical of Pauline letters to contain a thanksgiving prayer at the beginning of the letter, usually in gratitude for God's gifts to the church addressed (see Rom 1:8-10; 1 Cor 1:4-9). Here the author gives thanks for the grace shown him, which he does in characteristic fashion. He notes his former sins (see 1 Cor 15:9; Acts 8:3) and his call to repentance and ministry (Gal 1:13-16; Eph 3:8). Stories about Peter always seem to remind us of his weakness or his denial of Jesus, just as accounts of Paul's commission retain the fact that he formerly persecuted the church. The point of this is to underscore the kernel of our faith, which is confessed clearly in verse 15, "Christ Jesus came into the world to save sinners" (see Mark 2:10; Luke 15). So Paul's total conversion from sin to ministry becomes the moral example for Timothy and for all of us (v. 16)—leaders were not always perfect when called, but they are expected to be totally converted to God, a theme developed in chapter 3 where the rules for bishops and deacons appear. It is characteristic of Paul to tell the church: "Be imitators of me" (1 Cor 4:16; 11:1). This pastoral repetition of Paul's election is climaxed with a typical Jewish blessing or act of praise to God (see Rom 16:27); another beautiful prayer will close the letter in 6:15-16.

1:18-20 Timothy's difficult duties. Timothy's general task, which was described earlier (1:3-7), is repeated in specific terms. Like Paul, he was entrusted with a mission by the church's prophets (Acts 13:1-3), a mission "to wage warfare" on error in the church; this is a common metaphor for popular preachers and one that will be repeated again and again in these letters (6:12; 2 Tim 4:7). Even Paul saw his task occasionally as warfare (2 Cor 10:3-5). The weapons are "faith and good conscience," which apply equally to orthodox teaching and to constancy in faith. Two deviants are cited as examples of those who have turned away from the truth: Alexander, who is said to have harmed the author (see 2 Tim 4:14), and Hymenaeus, who distorted the meaning of the resurrection (see 2 Tim 2:17-18). These two, like the incestuous man in 1 Cor 5:1-5, have been temporarily expelled from the group for lives that are radically incompatible with the ideal of sound faith/good morals. A similar procedure is reported in Titus 3:10-11. This excommunication is not punitive, but educative, as it should lead to a reconversion (1:20). This process is not taken lightly, and it indicates that the church is *not* unsure of itself but vigorously witnesses to the gospel even at the cost of causing separations from the group.

2:1-7 Christians and the secular world. Here begins a long exhortation to the church, spelling out "household duties." In earlier Christian writings, these duties are restricted to those of husband/wife, parent/child, and master/slave (Col 3:18–4:1), but here the whole church is addressed (see 3:15, what kind of conduct befits a member of God's *household,* "the church of God").

A typical assembly is envisioned in which "supplications, prayers, petitions, and thanksgivings" (2:1) are made. Paul regularly enjoined his churches to pray for civic rulers; here the aim of prayer is religious toleration for the new religious group. This presupposes, however, that the church will live "quiet and tranquil lives" in full accord with the gospel, "in perfect piety and dignity" (v. 2). Implicit in this advice is the call to be exemplary citizens, as well as complete Christians. This appeal has a missionary edge to it; prayer for the civic rulers pleases the Christian God who is thoroughly ecumenical in his plan of salvation and "wills everyone to be saved and come to knowledge of the truth" (v. 4). Hence the traditional confessional formula cited in verse 5 (God is One! Jesus ransoms all!) suggests that the church is praying as well for the rulers to share its faith. These few verses suggest a view of this church that is clearly not sectarian or world-denying but ecumenically open to all and which sees Christian life as fully compatible with good citizenship in the empire.

2:8-15 Husbands and wives. The exhortation then addresses the family unit, in particular husbands and wives; such advice is common in Christian moral teaching (see Eph 5:21-33). Men (husbands) should lift holy hands in prayer—again a community meeting is envisioned which is *not* filled with factions and quarreling, as were many of the Pauline communities (see 1 Cor 1:11-12). The oneness of God (2:5) should be reflected in the oneness of the church.

Comparably, women (wives) are instructed to appear in the assemblies clothed not in wealth and fashion but in "good deeds" (see 1 Pet 3:1-6), advice which was common fare even in pagan exhortations. The instruction that women should keep silent is very problematic: (1) In the Pauline churches there are women prophets (1 Cor 11:1-13) and deaconesses (see Phoebe, Rom 16:1). (2) Paul's churches experienced a remarkable degree of equality among men and women (Gal 3:28), equality based on the gospel that Christ has redeemed *all* people and that God has called *all* to grace. Here, however, we see a community which professes the same equality of call from God (2:5), but the social structure is considerably more restrictive and the implications of the gospel in this regard are muted. The reasons for women's silence in 2:11-14 are based on bizarre exegesis of Genesis: (1) Because Eve was created *after* Adam she should listen to him (yet both accounts of Eve's creation indicate her equality with Adam: Gen 1:27; 2:18, 23). (2) Because Eve seduced Adam she should not advise her husband ever again (yet biblical theology clearly speaks of *Adam's* sin, not Eve's: see Rom 5:12-19). The church here seems to be mirroring the typical social patterns of the world around it in restricting the role of women in the church assemblies. But evidently in its desire to accommodate itself to the local culture an important aspect of the gospel message is forgotten, an ironic feature of a letter which defends the old traditions so carefully. There is, however, a sense in these letters that women are especially prey to the would-be teachers who are disturbing the churches (5:13; 2 Tim 3:65; Titus 1:11). Hence, the concern for women probably represents a genuine pastoral concern which was unfortunately smothering and unenlightened. Would that Timothy had been more traditional in this regard!

One final note: the concern in chapter 2 seems to be with the visible side of the church, the public, assembled community; for the advice in 2:1-7 concerns public prayer, as does the exhortation to husbands in 2:8; and women's silence makes sense primarily in the context of the assembled church. This concern for the orderly face of the church has its missionary side. Paul can even enjoin silence on prophets and those who speak in tongues for the sake of its mission (1 Cor 14:23-25).

3:1-7 Qualifications for bishops. The list of household duties is extended with a list of qualifications for bishops and deacons in 3:1-13. Although there is no clear job description here, we are told of the qualifications for this position. The list of 3:2-7 is typical of pagan as well as Jewish lists of qualifications for office; in fact, there is hardly a hint of anything distinctively Christian about this list. A good leader is typically without reproach, respectably married, temperate. He should be noted for hospitality—for as Christians traveled more widely, it was necessary to welcome them (see the notice of travelers in Rom 16) as well as traveling prophets and missionaries

(3 John 5; Rom 12:13; 1 Pet 4:9). Besides being a figure of good personal character, the bishop should be a unifying social force. His motive for service should not be mercenary, like the false teachers (6:5; Titus 1:11). In the world view of the pastoral Epistles, proper order is most important, hence the bishop's right ordering of his family according to recognizable standards will qualify him to order the church. As in Paul's case, a suitable apprenticeship is fitting after conversion (see Gal 1:17). And the bishop, because he is a public figure, should be a person of character and respectability in relationship to the secular world.

So many questions are raised by this passage for which there are no clear answers: (1) What is the role of the bishop? Economic assistance? Yes, and probably clear teaching of the tradition as well (see Titus 1:9). (2) How does one become a bishop? Timothy was prophetically designated (1:18), but the figures here seem to be volunteers. (3) What is the nature of their authority? The very fact that we have letters confirming Timothy's position suggests that legitimation of bishops was becoming increasingly important. Even Timothy is seen here as authorizing other bishops and successors. (4) What is the status of the office? We have no clear sense that "bishops" here are different from "elders"; both are mentioned interchangeably here and elsewhere (see Jas 5:14; 1 Pet 5:1); they are surely not the monarchical bishops, such as Ignatius of Antioch. This new office is still developing and adapting to the pastoral needs of the church members.

3:8-13 Qualifications for deacons. In Phil 1:1 Paul addressed "bishops and deacons," and it is hard to distinguish them clearly at this early stage of the church. Deacons served the poor (Acts 6:1-6) but they preached as well (e.g., Philip in Acts 8:4-8, as well as Stephen's great speech in Acts 7). It is simply unclear in 1 Timothy what ministry deacons performed, although we are probably safe in seeing them as performing broad and varied tasks such as in the Pauline churches. For example, there are people who do teaching, helping, and administering (1 Cor 12:28); Rom 12:7 speaks of those who do serving, teaching, and helping.

The list of qualifications is similar to that of the bishop: the deacon is a person of good character and standing, but he is noted in verse 9 as singularly orthodox—he holds fast to "the faith with a clear conscience," which implies that he is somehow responsible for correct teaching. Does verse 11 refer to deaconesses? We know of Phoebe the deaconess from Cenchreae (Rom 16:1). But most probably verse 11 speaks to the wives of the deacons.

3:14-16 The church of God. Brief mention is made of the author's travel plans and the possibility of his delay, a common theme in his letters (1 Cor 4:19). In the event of his inability to visit, the letter will function as a type of church constitution (v. 14). All of the preceding and subsequent lists of household duties serve one purpose—to inform the community how to behave as a Christian church (3:15). The images of the community here are an important clue to how we should understand "church" in these letters. It is "the household of God which is the church of the living God." The last image stresses the free yet universal call of God to all people (see 2:4-6), while the first image touches on the orderly structure of the new temple, the community of God. Neither image implies that the church is set against the world or is exclusivist or world-negating.

One of the distinguishing characteristics of this church is its possession of truth, the "mystery of devotion" (v. 16). What this means is immediately demonstrated in the hymn to Christ in verse 16; the pastoral Epistles are full of such fragments of hymns and confessions (see 2 Tim 2:11-13; 4:1). Two questions need to be answered: (1) What does the hymn refer to? (2) How is it functioning in 1 Tim 3? As regards its meaning, it is best to compare it with a similar hymn in 1 Pet 3:18-19, 22. (For a full discussion of its meaning, see the commentary under that passage.) It is sufficient to note here that "manifested in the flesh" probably refers to Jesus' public crucifixion, not his incarnation. Indeed this hymn encapsules various aspects of Jesus' paschal mystery. As regards its function in 1 Tim 3, inasmuch as Jesus is heralded as the one "mediator between God and the human race" and as the "ransom for all" (2:5-6), the Jesus of this hymn is also the universal Jesus "proclaimed to the Gentiles . . . believed in throughout the world." The universality of Jesus' role is stressed in his resurrection visitation to angels as well as to humans and in his enthronement as Lord of the church. A catholic church has a catholic Savior.

It is often said that the Pastorals reflect a time when Christian faith was becoming frozen in dogmatic propositions. It is true that "the faith" of this church is remarkably clear and can be stated in brisk formulae, but this was true even of the Pauline churches, which knew of hymns (Phil 2:6-11) and confessional touchstones (Rom 10:9). The Pastorals evidently are concerned with false teachers and deviant doctrines, and so it is pastorally appropriate to point to the clear core of Christian faith. The traditions about Jesus' paschal mystery are the central aspects of the church's faith in him: he died for all, was vindicated by God, was enthroned as Lord of the church, and will come to judge the living and the dead.

4:1-5 Errors in the church. The mention of explicit errors in the church is prefaced by a "prophecy" about heretics arising in the community. This is a very conventional phrase, found especially in literature which purports to leave the "last will and testament" of an apostolic figure. Hence Paul predicted heretics attacking the church like wolves (Acts 20:29), just as Peter did (2 Pet 3:3). Yet differences of opinion existed even in the earliest Christian groups, so heresy is not a late event in the history of the church. It might be said that doctrinal pluralism has been with us from the beginning. False teachers will arise, possibly the same figures mentioned in 1:3-7. Here they are said to forbid marriage and impose dietary restrictions. Paul encountered similar problems at Corinth about marriage (1 Cor 7:1) and food (1 Cor 8, 10); rigorous dietary rules are noted in Rom 14 and Col 2:16-23. Although we know there are would-be teachers of the law expounding on the Old Testament, the situation here requires further clarification. There are strains of Judaizing concern for law observance which may be linked with claims that the resurrection has already occurred in the lives of authentic believers (see 2 Tim 2:18). This would imply that we are already "spiritual" and should abstain from physical pursuits such as sex, marriage, and food. Some claim that even this early we find the roots of a later heresy, gnosticism, which took a negative stance toward the world (see the mention of "gnosis"/knowledge in 6:20). Those most affected by this radical error seem to have been certain women in the church who are described as easily deceived (5:13; 2 Tim 3:6). It is not surprising, then, that we find considerable favorable attention given to marriage: the urging of young widows to remarry (5:14) and instructions about married women (2:11-14; Titus 2:4).

The response to the errors is straightforward: all God made is good and for our use, which was also Paul's answer in 1 Cor 8:6 and 10:26. There is certainly nothing world-negating in this posture, and it accords with the view of God calling all people into this catholic church. A word of thanksgiving before meals reminds us of God's creative word and how all was made good and good for us (Gen 1:29-31). Like the prayers mentioned in 2:1, 8, this word of thanksgiving may well be a public blessing before a community meal (see 1 Cor 10:30-31).

4:6-10 False vs. true teachers. Ostensibly we have an exhortation to Timothy, but the content and context suggest that Timothy is contrasted with the false teachers of 4:1-5. A set of contrasts seems to structure the passage: false teachers busy themselves with myths and tales (4:7; see 1:4); true teachers are concerned with "the words of the faith and of sound teaching" (4:6). False teachers promote eccentric asceticism (4:3); true teachers admit the need of genuine spiritual discipline (gymnasia), but without excess. False teachers boast that they are already experiencing the resurrection (see 2 Tim 2:18); true teachers admit that future life is still a promise (4:8, 10). This last item, the promise of future life, is called in the Greek "a word of faith"; it represents a central item of early Christian belief, a clear tenet of faith touching on our relationship with God and Christ.

4:11-16 Timothy's duties. When bishops were discussed in 3:1-7, no specific duties were mentioned. Now we are told of Bishop Timothy's duties, which may conveniently serve as the job description for typical bishops in these churches. This is one more example of the list of "household duties" which extends from 2:1–6:2. Although young, Timothy is not to be overlooked in deference to "elders" in the group. He is to be a living example of full Christian faith—in the way he behaves, in what he believes, and in whom he loves. The advice in 4:12 is remarkable in its sense of how Christian faith should touch every aspect of our lives, moral and social as well. His specific task is to read the Scriptures accurately, unlike the false teachers of the law (1:7). Preaching and teaching indicate that his work is not simply missionary but full care of the church as it grows in time. Verse 4:14 speaks about Timothy's vocation in such a way as to undergird the authority he has in the church; God's grace to minister was given him through prophetic recognition (see Paul's calling in Acts 13:1-3); and this very letter serves as confirmation of this. Finally, Timothy is strongly encouraged to be constant in faith and labor, to persevere. The duties of bishops are, then, twofold: they are the church's authorized teachers and guardians of the faith, but they are also the living witnesses of their faith both in the integrity of their lives and in the perseverance in their tasks.

5:1-2 Respect for elders. Two more instructions are given to Bishop Timothy that are very appropriate for ancient cultures. As well as the Ten Commandments prescribe care for aged parents (see Sir 3:3-16), there is in the ancient world a deep respect for the elderly, which is reflected in the advice that Timothy deal gently with older men and women. Those more equal in age are treated as equals, as brothers and sisters in Christ. Although for conversion's sake one may be asked to "hate" parents (Luke 14:26), Christianity reinforced family social structures.

5:3-16 Rules for widows. Still more parts of the church's list of household duties are mentioned, this time rules concerning widows in the church. The first and most noteworthy rule is that Christian families should support widows—a point so important that it is mentioned three times (5:4-5, 8, 16). Popular biblical tradition speaks of God defending widows (Ps 146:9) and commanding their protection (Exod 22:22; Deut 16:14), and it may be that certain Christians expected God to provide miraculously for their own widows. But like Jas 1:27, true religion shows practical covenant love in care for the aged. In 5:5-6, true widows are contrasted with false ones; a true widow is first of all a religious woman who depends actively and totally on God, whereas a false widow is self-indulgent. Verses 9-10 lay down specific qualifications for true widows, qualifications not unlike those for bishops and deacons: age minimum, marital stability, a tested character, ability to manage one's own family, and hospitality. The key test is her life of service, a life which she will continue to exercise much like a deaconess, although she is called "widow" instead.

In contrast to rules for including true widows, Paul gives rules for excluding others (vv. 11-13). Young women especially are urged to remarry, which probably should be seen in connection with the false teachers' attack on marriage in 4:3 (see also 2:15). The great danger of early widowhood is the time it gives for idleness and curiosity which Timothy sees as the soil sought out by the heretics (5:15). Far from rejecting God's gifts of family and marriage like the heretics, the author supports them and sees them as an important public witness to the church's world-endorsing attitude.

What is important in this archaic list of rules? Pauline churches celebrated the liberation and equality of women in Christ (see the discussion on 2:11-14), a thrust which appears to be muted in these very letters. The rank of widow may well be the last vestige of the public ministries which women were allowed to perform and of their free and independent lives in the church. There is no question here of eliminating this tradition, but one senses a move toward limiting the role of women in the public life of the church, both in scope of their actions and in the number of women who will perform these tasks.

5:17-22 Church elders. Chapter 5 began with concern for how Timothy should treat older men and women (vv. 1-2) and continued with questions of support for older women/widows (vv. 4-5, 8, 16). Now rules for dealing with the "elders" of the church are stated, another item in the list of household duties. Like the widows, the elders seem to be an important group in this church; they are probably to be distinguished from the bishops, although they too share the duty of preaching and teaching. They also are responsible for authorizing bishops, such as Timothy (4:14). There is no doubt that Bishop Timothy is the leader of this church, but his ministry seems to be in collaboration with a variety of elders, bishops, deacons, and widows. The first item in the rules for overseeing elders is their remuneration. Obviously "preaching and teaching" are the most important tasks in this group, a point made evident in the special double payment for this service (v. 17).

Although some Christian traditions speak of "giving freely" of what the preacher has freely received (Matt 10:8), yet as verse 18 states, there is biblical warrant for support. The text almost insists too much, for it cites the Old Testament (Deut 25:4) as well as the Christian tradition (Luke 10:7). Paul has attacked the false teachers as being money hungry, so one is surprised to find this seeming over-insistence on financial matters here.

Correct procedures are established for processing complaints and accusations against an elder. According to biblical tradition (see Deut 19:15; Matt 18:16), unless an accusation can be substantiated, it must be discounted. In Matthew, a church council rebuked an erring member (5:22; 18:17), a procedure also found in 1 Cor 5:1-5. Since an elder is a public figure and his sin is scandalous to the church, a public reprimand is in place. This is obviously a task as necessary as it is unpleasant, for the author practically requires a special oath on Timothy's part to carry this out (v. 21). The sense of holiness as well as fairness in the church demands no less. Finally, Timothy is warned not to be hasty in laying hands on any elder, implying that a period of testing is appropriate; the same advice is given in regard to deacons (3:10) and widows (5:10). This may stem from the confusing situation of the church with so much divergent teaching.

5:23-25 Miscellaneous remarks. Inasmuch as a strange form of diet and asceticism was wrongly urged in 4:3, the encouragement to drink wine is probably a further counter to that false teaching. Verses 24-25 present a typical exhortatory contrast between bad and good deeds. Some evil deeds are so flagrant that they call for present judgment (see the judgment of the elders in 5:19-21), and others will be revealed at God's judgment (see 2 Tim 4:1). Likewise some good deeds shine like lamps (see Matt 5:16) while others will be revealed later. Although this is reminiscent of the warning in Matt 10:26 that God's judgment will prevail, it seems to stress the importance of good deeds to promote the church's standing and the harm which evil deeds do to its mission (see 1 Pet 2:12). This should be linked with the concern for the public face of the church, which was treated earlier in regard to 2:1, 8 and 3:1-7.

6:1-2 Advice to slaves. Typical of Christian lists of household duties is advice to slaves and masters (1 Pet 2:18), but oddly only slaves' duties are mentioned here, although some of their masters are Christians. The early church proclaimed "freedom" in Christ, a bold proclamation which evidently led to considerable misunderstanding about the social status of slaves even in the Pauline churches. Most of the early churches did not see themselves as radically countercultural groups and thus did not promote slave liberation (1 Cor 7:20-22) or the abolition of all cultural customs (see the problem of women's veils in 1 Cor 11). Surely in the Pastorals the issue is: Can a Christian be a good citizen? In its struggle for toleration in ancient society, the church did not regularly see the world as an evil to be avoided or condemned. It urged its members on to civil obedience and civic responsibility as well as to moral excellence. The motive in 6:1-2 for slaves' behavior accords with this; failure to be responsible brings abuse upon the name of the Christian God and upon the Christian faith. Remember that bishops, who represent the church publicly to the world, should have a good public reputation (3:7). Christian slaves, especially those of Christian masters, should be responsible persons. Their tasks are not just menial for their "good works" are virtuous acts as well (the Greek *euergesias* implies an "act of kindness").

6:2-10 The evils of false teaching exposed. Verses 2-16 contrast two kinds of teachers: false teachers (2-10) and good teachers (11-16). In this first part the root causes and the final results of evil teachers are exposed. By definition a false teacher is one who does not adhere to the sound teaching proper to religion; he is rather inclined to speculation, polemics, and controversy (see 1:3-4). And since by their fruits you shall know them, they are shown to be false from the list of vices to which false teaching traditionally leads. The vices are just those which fracture a community, not unlike the problems which Paul confronted in 1 Corinthians. The sense of morality here is fully in keeping with the large sense of the church and its role in the world as light, example, and truth. The author imputes mercenary motives to the false teachers, a traditional charge in such debates (see 2 Pet 2:3). Once on the topic, the author contrasts the avaricious false teachers and anyone else lusting after money with the correct Christian appreciation for moderation and sufficiency; this contrast sounds similar to the gospel warning that we cannot serve two masters (Matt 6:24). The polemical attacks on the false teachers are rather traditional and stereotyped, but they serve to point out how false teaching is totally wrong—wrong in its motives, sources, and consequences.

6:11-16 Good teachers and their accountability. We now come to the last of the household duties mentioned in this letter. In contrast to the false teachers is Timothy, a man of God. Instead of seeking money, he should seek after virtue, especially virtues which build up the church, such as piety, faith, loving service, perseverance, and gentleness (see 1 Cor 13:4-7). True teaching does not fracture communities and lead to factions and arrogance. Timothy's task is faithful witness to Christ and the gospel, just as Jesus bore faithful witness before Pilate (see Luke 21:12-13). So difficult a task has a special reward, everlasting life (see 2 Tim 2:11).

Timothy is charged with keeping the "commandment," which may be the general covenant law required of all (see 1:8-11) or his own special commission from God. At any rate, he is called to be blameless and irreproachable, code words in this letter for faithful, persevering, and wholehearted service. Like Paul, the exercise of his commission is linked with the coming of Jesus and the divine scrutiny of human lives, especially those of leaders (1 Cor 4:1-5; 1 Thess 2:4). The solemn injunction to Timothy is closed by a typical benediction, calling upon the Christian God and acknowledging his uniqueness and sovereignty (6:15-16). The function of invoking God's judgment in regard to one's commission is common in the Pastorals (see 5:21 and 2 Tim 4:1). And the substance of the benediction is typical of the monotheistic doctrine of God characteristically preached here as well (see 1:17; 2:4-5). The benediction underscores the importance of the task entrusted to Timothy. And so ends the extended exposition of the household duties of the church.

6:17-19 A last word to the wealthy. A few last remarks are addressed to wealthy church members to be generous in their use of wealth and not to be proud of it nor trust in it. This advice is typical of the exhortations found in Luke that Gentiles who had no previous traditions of almsgiving and covenant charity should see that wealth is good only when generously used in service. Treasure in heaven has nothing to do with treasure laid up on earth (Luke 12:32-34).

6:20-21 Final advice to Timothy. This letter curiously closes without any mention of travel plans, greetings, etc., so typical of other letters. It ends, rather, on an anxious note. Final reminders are given to Timothy to guard the deposit of faith and to shun the useless speculations and myths of his rival teachers which pass as "gnosis"/knowledge. This is virtually the same advice given Timothy throughout the letter, but its repetition here seems urgent, suggesting that the crisis in the church is rather inflamed.

2 TIMOTHY

Jerome H. Neyrey, S.J.

INTRODUCTION

The basic introduction to 2 Timothy is well covered in the earlier general introduction to the pastoral Epistles. But certain important features of 2 Timothy deserve to be highlighted for they will help us to read the letter more sympathetically. Compared to 1 Timothy, the second letter is quite personal: The author complains of loneliness and abandonment; he relishes the kindness of fellow Christians (1:15-18; 4:9-13). Whereas 1 Timothy contains an extensive list of household duties for the diverse members of that church, the second letter addresses Timothy personally as a distinct individual, sympathizes with his difficult job, and encourages him in many touching ways to persevere. The list of greetings at the letter's close also points to a more familiar and personal ambiance for the letter.

The letter frankly acknowledges the plight of Timothy and his church. The bloom is surely off the rose in this church; day-to-day problems plague Timothy; unpleasantness (see "persecutions" in 3:12) besets him. His is not a glamorous job, hardly one to be ambitioned, for it is a thankless job of patient correction and guidance.

Some changes are noticeable in the theological contents of 1 and 2 Timothy. 1 Timothy was enormously rich in christological hymns and confessions, celebrating Christ's death and resurrection, his ransom of all people (1:15-16; 2:5-6; 3:16; 6:13-14). The second letter confesses Jesus primarily as Judge of the church, who rewards fidelity and faithful service and requites evil and error (1:18; 4:1, 8, 14). In 2 Timothy, Christ is still the pattern to be followed: endurance with him means that we shall reign with him (2:11-12). The christological teaching of 1 Timothy was functionally integrated into the exhortation of that letter, which is also the case in the second letter, although the stress on Jesus as Judge is intended to support Timothy in hard times with promises of reward and success (see 4:6-8). The doctrine about the Christian God was so much fuller in the first letter than in 2 Timothy. Rich benedictions (1:17; 6:15-16), assertions of God's oneness and his universal salvific will (2:4-5), appeals to God's creative goodness (4:3), all point to a conscious reminder to pagan converts of the excellence of their faith in the God of Jesus Christ. This thrust is muted in the second letter, where there is only casual and passing mention of God as the one who chooses and commissions the church's leaders (1:6-8, 9; 2:10). God is likewise witness to the ministry of Paul and Timothy and will reward them accordingly. The shift obviously is a pastoral concern to call attention to Timothy's authority and the seriousness of his task.

So much attention is given to Timothy's role as protector of the faith that one might feel that only conservatism befits church leaders. Timothy's church surely faced serious and pressing problems with the orderly succession of its leaders, a problem commonly experienced by all religions. Its solution was to see succession validated in a living chain of witnesses from Paul to Timothy to others (see 2:2). Paul's sense of his impending death motivates him to confirm Timothy and to authorize him to appoint successors. The Spirit is less the designator of new leaders in the church than the abiding strength and support of the church (1:6-7) and the source of its fidelity to the gospel (1:14).

If the conservation duties of Timothy are so heavily stressed, this should be seen in the light of the churches of that period. They were beset with serious doctrinal problems which threatened the gospel (2:18); some of its leaders had quit the ministry (4:10); others seem to be advocating unacceptable doctrines (2:23; 3:6). Love seems to have grown cold (4:16). The leadership is disbursed (4:9-12). This was a time to strengthen the internal character of the church, to solicit and confirm new leaders, to clarify the faith of the developing church, and to keep firmly rooted in the tradition. Less exciting than a letter to a new church full of charismatic converts, 2 Timothy is a window into a church in an age of transition, in a confusingly pluralistic society.

COMMENTARY

1:1-2 Letter opening. Like typical letters, the opening of 2 Timothy indicates the sender (Paul), the addressee (Timothy), and a greeting. Although 1 Timothy suggested that the author's vocation comes from Jesus (1:12), here it is God who "wills" Paul to be an apostle, a theme repeated in 1:9. The purpose of the author's calling is unusual here: it is to proclaim the promise of life, which is explained more fully in 1:10.

1:3-8 Thanksgiving. Typically Pauline letters contain thanksgiving prayers right after the letter opening (see 1 Cor 1:4-9), and these thanksgivings typically function as summaries of the main themes and issues of the letter. Such is the case here also. The thematic items are introduced in verse 4 where Timothy's "sincere faith" (v. 5) is prayed over; this faith was evidently handed on from grandmother Lois to mother Eunice to son Timothy, a living and faithful chain of believers, which is just how Paul sees his relation to Timothy and to Timothy's successor bishops (see 2:2). Second, "faith," the central theme of the letter, has many meanings; it is helpful to distinguish them early in the letter. "Faith" may mean: (1) *fidelity* to duty or tradition (2:22; 3:10; 4:7), or (2) *orthodoxy* of belief (1:13; 4:7; negatively expressed in 2:18-19; 3:8), or (3) *personal bond* with Jesus (3:15). Third, Timothy's vocation is celebrated in such a way as to evoke faithfulness in him, a theme continually recurring in the letter (2:1-2; 4:2-5). Whereas, according to 1 Tim 4:14, the elders laid hands on Timothy, Paul claims that distinction here, perhaps to stress the clear chain of authority and correct teaching from Paul to Timothy and to his successors. Timothy is indeed charismatic in his vocation, for he has God's Spirit; but the function of the Spirit here is more structured as the guardian and support of God's chosen members than as the source of their appointment. The Spirit here gives "strength," evidently a code word for perseverance and fortitude in a difficult job rather than a power for charismatic signs and miracles (see 1 Cor 12:9-10). In fact, the fourth theme in the thanksgiving points to the hardships which Paul, Timothy, and their successors must endure in their jobs, a theme developed in 1:11-12; 2:2-7, 8-10; 3:12; 4:3-5. So the thanksgiving prayer calls immediate attention to the themes of the letter: vocation, fidelity, orthodoxy, and hardships.

1:9-14 The Pauline model of vocation. Paul regularly tells communities to imitate him (1 Cor 4:16; 1 Thess 1:6), and here the author says the same to Timothy (v. 13). Paul recalls that his vocation was a gift of God's grace (v. 9; see 1 Cor 15:10). This grace was already active "before time began," which is a typical Jewish statement about pre-existence which stresses how holy or important something is. In Eph 1:4 the church is said to be already chosen in Christ for redemption before creation. Paul himself saw his vocation as naturally linked to the appearance of Jesus, his Savior (see Acts 9:4-6; 1 Cor 9:1). Both 1 and 2 Timothy interchangeably designate God and Jesus as "Savior" (1 Tim 1:1; 2:3-4), which title in verses 9-10 speaks of Jesus' achievement as the vanquisher of death and the bringer of life and immortality. Typical Jewish-Christian references to our eschatological future speak of resurrection, but here a Greek phrase is used, "immortality" (of the soul), which may be just one more of the pastoral adaptations of the gospel message characteristic of these letters; after all, Paul used this language also with the Corinthians (1 Cor 15:42, 50-54). The pastoral thrust of this advice is centered in verses 12-14, where Timothy is commanded again to "guard this rich trust." The role of Timothy, then, is seen as custodian of the tradition, as one who faithfully hands on the gospel (see 2:2; 4:3). He does this with the strengthening power of God's Spirit who dwells in the church (1:7). It is not uncommon for Paul to speak of the Spirit in the church as a spirit of holiness (1 Cor 3:16-17) or as the holiness in individual Christians (1 Cor 6:19). Here the Spirit has a more structural role as the preserver of the gospel's integrity, very much the way we tend to understand the promise of infallibility to the church in contemporary theology.

1:15-18 False and faithful friends. Twice in the letter the author laments that church members appear to have failed in charity to him, first in Asia (1:15) and then in Rome (4:16). He contrasts these false friends with Onesiphorus, who literally fulfilled Jesus' command to visit those in prison (Matt 25:36); hence he prays for his reward on the day of judgment. The "Lord" spoken of here is surely the Lord Jesus, who is characteristically described as overseer of his church, who rewards the good and faithful servant at his return (see 4:1, 8, 14; Matt 24:45-47).

2:1-7 The hardships of ministry. The topic of this exhortation is summed up in 2:1, "Be strong in grace." As we have seen, Timothy's "strength" comes from God's Spirit who supports him daily in his difficult tasks. The prime task of his ministry is to "hand on" what he received, which is a technical formula in Jewish writings for indicating both that the material handed on is of prime importance and that its accurate transmission is a sacred enterprise. Paul prefaced his "handing on" of both the Eucharist and the resurrection traditions with just this tag (1 Cor 11:23; 15:3). This official handing on parallels the domestic handing on of faith from Lois to Eunice to Timothy (1:5). And this verse may be especially important as a clue to the function of this whole letter. As Paul laid hands on Timothy and confirmed his authority, so Timothy is empowered to do the same. This letter, then, serves as a source of authority both for the post-Pauline churches and beyond, for the chain of valid ministry is established through a correct "handing on" of the gospel and authority. The ministry of Timothy seems quite unenviable, for it will entail hardships (v. 3), singleness of life (v. 4), rigorous athletic training (v. 5) and simple hard work (v. 6).

2:8-13 Endurance and victory with Christ. The high point of this exhortation is the hymnic passage in 2:11-13 which invites us to conform to Jesus' paschal mystery and so to share his victory. This presumably is a popular hymn in Timothy's church and the appeal to it reflects the pastoral sensitivity of the author to explain his exhortation in terms meaningful to his hearers. Although addressed to Timothy, the invitation is open to all Christians. In substance, those who suffer hardships with Christ and for him, who die (v. 11) and who hold out to the end with him (v. 12) will live and reign with him. This clearly should be linked with the mention of "Jesus . . . raised from the dead" in 2:8 (1:10) and the suffering which Paul and Timothy experience for the gospel (2:9). Fidelity with Christ means victory with the Lord, a theme repeatedly stressed in the letter, especially in terms of the reward for faithful service (1:15-18; 4:1, 8, 17-18). But there is a problem in verses 12b-13. One verse says that denial of Jesus will be met with denial by Jesus, a common gospel warning (Matt 10:32-33). But verse 13 contradicts that and says that *even "if* we are unfaithful, he remains faithful." God's faithfulness is constantly noted in Paul's letters (1 Cor 1:9; 10:13; 1 Thess 5:24), in regard to God's promise of election and justification by faith, but not in regard to God's indifference to human sinfulness. This letter, however, which stresses the rewards and punishments for service and failure, would seem to suggest that verse 13 is somehow an addition to the text and that the theological stress is on verses 11-12—the appeal to conformity to Jesus as the source of life.

2:14-19 Why the job is so hard. Preaching the gospel of Jesus would be a serious enough task, but Timothy's job is complicated by the fact that his church seems to be beset with conflicting teaching on very crucial points. He, of course, should follow the straight course in preaching the truth (v. 15), which echoes the earlier command to "hand on" the truth (2:2) and to "take as your norm the sound words that you have heard" (1:13). Others in the group are seen to be engaged in disputes over words (v. 14), disputes which spread like a plague through the church (v. 17). One such error is pointed out: Philetus and Hymenaeus claim that the resurrection has already taken place, probably an overstatement of the proclamation that in baptism we die and rise with Christ (see Rom 6:3-5). It seems that certain charismatics in Paul's Corinthian church began to say the same thing (see 1 Cor 4:7), which led them to despise flesh and body in favor of "spiritual" existence, to feel superior to all authority, and to reject all rules in the name of resurrected freedom (1 Cor 6:12). Even this letter implies that we are to share with the risen Jesus "life and immortality" (1:10), and if we die with him we shall live with him (2:11-12). But the author never meant such confessional language to be taken so literally, for he constantly preaches in this letter the future scrutiny of all, even of heavenly appointed apostles (see 4:1, 8). He surely implies that we are indeed already justified and saved in Christ, but he equally insists that we will render an account to the Lord of how we have lived a life worthy of our calling (see Rom 14:10, 12). Because literalist and fundamentalistic interpretations can be very distorting of the truth, the church needs learned and authorized teaching.

2:20-26 A pure life of service. In contrast to false teachers, Timothy and other bishops must cooperate with God's calling and so cleanse themselves of evil things, to be fit and faithful ministers of the gospel. The differences in gold, silver, wood, and clay realistically point to people in the church variously gifted, similar to Paul's body metaphor in regard to diverse gifts in the church (1 Cor 12). What counts is not the material of the vessel but its holiness, its being set aside exclusively for the Lord's work. The contaminations to be avoided are twofold: (1) youthful passions, and (2) senseless disputations. But what positively consecrates a minister is the pursuit of the Christian virtues of righteousness, loving service, peace, and faithfulness. After all, the object of ministry is "every good work" in the service of the gospel. Likewise, a minister must guard the rich deposit of faith (1:14) and teach with clarity and charity, "correcting opponents with kindness" (v. 25). In short, he is the shepherd of God's flock (see Matt 18:12-14).

3:1-9 False teaching in the church. This passage follows up the exposé of the false teachers in 2:14-19, giving not so much a refutation of their doctrinal errors as the inevitable consequences of wrong teaching. A prediction is made by Paul that in the future ("the last days") false teachers would arise; this is a common convention in New Testament writings; e.g., in 1 Tim 4:1 the Spirit says that "in later times some will turn away from the faith," whereas in Acts 20:29-30 Paul predicted the same in his farewell address to the church of Ephesus. The function of this convention is to take the horror out of finding God's holy church split into factions and gangrenous with heresy; to lessen that shock the future horrors are artificially predicted. The danger to this church, nevertheless, is genuine, and the harm to it no less real. No specific identification of the false teachers is given, again a convention, for it does not make sense to give false ideas free publicity (yet see 2:18). Rather, the pattern here is to argue that false doctrines must be wrong, to judge by their evil results. Bad theology leads to bad morals. So we have a brief and stereotyped list of vices. Vice lists are a common feature of New Testament moral exhortations (1 Cor 6:9-10; Gal 5:19-21); Paul even used one in Rom 1 to show how wrong theology leads to base morality, the same point made here. The converse of this tactic is also true: good teaching leads to good morality. In 2:21-25 the good vessel, full of truth and gospel, is also full of virtue.

It is noted that these false teachers prey on women in the church (v. 6), which should not automatically be dismissed as an anti-feminist remark. After all, Lois and Eunice are noble evangelists (1:5) of their families; widows are virtuous and exemplary (1 Tim 5). But it would seem that Christianity was as vulnerable as the rest of the Graeco-Roman world to novelty in religion, a novelty especially attractive to women. Hence the Pastorals are quite sensitive to groups of women who do not find an ordered place in church and family (see 1 Tim 2:10-15; 5:12-15). Like the parable of the wise and foolish virgins (Matt 25:1-13), there are obviously two classes of women in these churches: the wise, faithful, upright and the foolish, unstable gadabouts. Although no specific identification of the false teachers is given, they are described as contentious people, constantly quarreling with the church's leadership. They oppose the truth (v. 8), like the two magicians of legend who argued against Moses when he tried to lead Israel out of Egypt (see Exod 7:11). This brands them as the ultimate opponents of the church's freedom in Christ.

3:10-17 The author's example as teacher. In contrast to the false teachers who oppose the truth, Timothy is praised as one who has "followed my teaching" (v. 10; see 2:2). The emphasis here is squarely on the fidelity needed in a burdensome job. Timothy is explicitly told that his task is not simply to guard the rich deposit (1:14), but gently to correct his "opponents" (2:25) and to correct, reprove, appeal "through all patience" (4:2). The firm but patient exercise of authority by the bishop entails hardships, which is why Timothy is reminded of Paul's conduct as well as his teaching (v. 10). Persecutions come with the job—not political harrassment from state officials but hostility from within the church. Hence the prized virtues are those which support one in such difficulties: "purpose, faith, patience . . . endurance" (v. 10). The foundation of this good behavior is adherence to the truth, so Timothy is urged to be faithful to the belief of the church, to the authentic chain of its teaching (1:5; 2:2).

Special mention is made of Timothy's acceptance of the Scriptures—surely the Hebrew Bible, which is read in the light of faith in Jesus. The Scriptures alluded to here may well be the Pentateuch, the way of covenant living; for the author notes that these Scriptures lead to salvation those who believe in Christ. Hence, they do not prophetically point so much to Jesus himself but to how Christians live. We know of a debate in 1 Timothy over interpretations of the Old Testament law (1:7) and erroneous attitudes to marriage, diet, and other ascetical practices. The author indicated there (1:8-11) that the Ten Commandments are the covenant code of the Christian church, suggesting a Christian insistence, not on Old Testament laws and legalism but on the expressions of the law of love as found in the essential covenant code.

The early church was beset on both sides by erroneous attitudes to the law. Some would throw out all laws and live as libertines and antinomians, freed from all authority and order; they based this stand on the radical freedom they experienced in sharing Christ's resurrection and in the possession of God's Spirit (see 1 Cor 6:12); this line of thinking may be reflected in 2 Tim 2:18. Others would reimpose Judaism on Christianity and demand strict observance of the law (Acts 15:1, 5; Gal 5:1-2); they based their arguments on the lasting importance of God's revealed word as Scripture. The early churches saw dangerous excesses in both directions and tried to insist both on the essential end of the law in Christ and freedom in the Lord, yet freedom which was understood as complete obedience to the Lord Jesus and the living of a life worthy of one's calling. In 3:15-16, the lasting value of Scripture is maintained. It is, after all, the inspired Word of God. Unlike Marcion and other early heretics who would completely dispense with the Hebrew Bible, this author insists that the Jewish Scriptures remain the Bible of the church. Nor were they merely spiritualized, as a collection of prophecies about Jesus. For as verse 16 shows, they are useful for "teaching—for refutation, correction, and training in righteousness." Yet for all this concern for the permanent validity of the Old Testament, there is relatively little of it explicitly cited in the Pastorals (see 1 Tim 5:18; 2 Tim 2:19), although these letters are incredibly rich in allusions to the Scriptures and to the traditional moral teaching of late Judaism.

4:1-5 Timothy's solemn commission. The author invokes a most solemn setting to confirm Timothy's commission. God is called to witness that Timothy is duly commissioned with this office, as is Jesus who is the Lord of this church and its Judge. A similar formula was used in 1 Tim 5:21 to undergird Timothy's teaching of church order. Here the solemn appeal not only confirms Timothy's commission but reminds him of the importance of his task, one which Christ will evaluate at the church's judgment, a familiar theme in the synoptic Gospels (see Matt 24:42-51). Paul frequently invoked the final judgment in his letters as an appeal to the churches to cease judging him and to let God's true judgment prevail (1 Cor 4:1-5), but here the appeal is made for another purpose, to underscore the importance of this job.

The tasks of this office are many and varied: Timothy is evangelist (4:5), teacher (2:24), and guardian of the deposit of faith (1:14). But his job has many unpleasant aspects as well, for his leadership will entail correction (2:25) and rebuke (4:2). The author never ceases to warn of the hardships of this job (1:12; 2:3; 3:11-12); to be forewarned is to be forearmed (see 2:2-7). Obviously Timothy's greatest trial is dealing with the opponents described in 2:18 and 3:7-8, some of whom are seen as rejecting all law and order in the church while others seem to be bent on binding the church with rigorous laws and customs. They are the ones preoccupied with myths and speculations (4:4; see 1 Tim 1:4; 4:7; Titus 1:14). They will not tolerate "sound doctrine," which is a favorite phrase in these letters, "soundness" being a quality of *teaching* (1 Tim 1:10; 2 Tim 4:3; Titus 1:9), *words* (1 Tim 6:3; 2 Tim 1:13), *preaching* (Titus 2:8), and *faith* (Titus 1:13). Soundness reflects both on accuracy of teaching and the correct morality to which it leads. Evidently the church is struggling to find some accepted mechanism within the group to solve doctrinal problems and so avoid schisms and heresies. This effort put great burdens on Timothy and his successors, as well as it demanded great loyalty from church membership.

4:6-8 Farewell. Often in his letters Paul warned that he was about dead in Christ's service (Phil 1:21-23; 2 Cor 5:2), a topic which seems to be more seriously treated here. In fact, this letter is often cited as an example of Paul's farewell address, his last will and testament, which was a common enough convention in the early church. We have Jesus' farewell addresses in John 13–17 and Luke 22:14-38, Peter's in 2 Pet 1:12-15, even Paul's in Acts 20. Typical of such literary forms are: (1) acknowledgment that death is near, (2) warnings about the coming of false teachers, (3) the appointment of successors to carry on the tradition, and (4) correct interpretation of disputed points. The language here is typical of Paul's farewells; he is a libation already poured out (Phil 2:17); he has fought the good fight (1 Tim 6:12), run the race (2 Tim 2:5; 1 Cor 9:24). His crowning achievement is: "I have kept the faith" (v. 7), which means both his careful handing on of the gospel to his successors (2:2) and his faithfulness in his office as evangelist and teacher. Like Paul in 1 Cor 4:1-5, he looks forward to God's judgment to prove him worthy and to reward him with the traditional crown of success. Crowns of laurel go to athletic champions (1 Cor 9:25), to church leaders (1 Pet 5:4), and to typical Christians (Rev 2:10). Here the phrase stresses the crown of life, the immortality which Jesus won for us (see 1:10). The letter, moreover, emphasizes that death endured with Jesus will result in life with him (2:11-12). This stress on eschatological reward (4:1, 8) is not accidental, especially in light of those who would deny a future reckoning with Jesus in their insistence that the eschatological event has *already* come, since they are *already* sharing in Jesus' resurrection (2:18). In this modest way, the letter reinforces a disputed aspect of the gospel tradition about Jesus by affirming him as Judge and Lord of the church.

4:9-13 Loneliness in ministry. Just as the author complained of loneliness in 1:15-18, he again gives us a very personal statement. But this passage is equally remarkable for the window it gives us on the geographical spread of the early church: Thessalonika, Dalmatia, Galatia, Troas, and Rome. Travel was relatively easy; journeys were frequent, and Christianity moved easily and quickly in this mobile society.

The list of persons mentioned is difficult to evaluate. The names themselves are very common in the ancient world, and they may be related to known figures of the Pauline communities. Demas, Luke, and Mark all send greetings with Paul to Philemon (v. 24) and to the Colossian church (4:14). Luke may be the traveling companion of Paul in Acts 16 and 20–21; Mark may be the co-worker of Paul in Acts 15:37-39; and Tychicus of Acts 20:4 may be the same faithful figure whom Paul regularly sends as his personal emissary (Col 4:7; Eph 6:21; Titus 3:12).

4:14-18 Trials and rescues. Faithful and false friends were contrasted earlier in 1:15-18, and as Onesiphorus was commended to God's blessing judgment for visiting the author in prison, now Alexander is commended to God's severe judgment for harming him. His harm, however, is compounded by his having "resisted our preaching," which makes us think of Alexander in 1 Tim 1:20 who made a shipwreck of his faith. The notice of escape from the lion's jaw need not imply his imprisonment under Nero and the threat of execution in the arena; after all, Daniel suffered for God's word and was likewise rescued from the lion's jaws. Paul once stated that he "fought those beasts at Ephesus" (1 Cor 15:32), not necessarily with animals at all, but with Epicurean philosophers, who were popularly called "animals" in the ancient world. Even Peter warns the church of a roaring lion stalking the church, not a real beast but the present danger of evil (1 Pet 5:8). Verses 17-18, then, probably speak of Paul's heightened sense of divine protection for his continued mission.

4:19-22 Letter closing. Like typical New Testament letters, a series of greetings concludes the letter. Aquila and Prisca were Paul's most frequent companions and co-workers, who themselves traveled from Pontus (on the Black Sea) to Rome, to Corinth, and then to Ephesus (Acts 18:2; Rom 16:3; 1 Cor 16:19). They are warmly remembered as is the family of Onesiphorus, who took such good care of the author in prison (1:16-17). To judge from the list of greetings in Rom 16, the Roman church was very well known, probably due to the intense missionary traveling of the early church, and the Roman church sends greetings to the eastern churches (v. 21). The letter quietly closes with a typical Christian farewell: "The Lord be with your spirit."

TITUS

Jerome H. Neyrey, S.J.

COMMENTARY

1:1-4 Letter opening. The letter opening contains the typical note about the sender (Paul), addressee (Titus), and a greeting ("grace and peace"). The author is both an apostle and "slave of God," which was a common biblical description of one commissioned by God (see 2 Sam 7:5), a description used by James (1:1) and 2 Pet (1:1). What is unusual about this letter opening is the lengthy remark about the purpose of the author's commissioning. It is not only to bring pagans to faith but to promote "the recognition of religious truth," suggesting a more long-term, settled role than the picture of Paul in Acts and his letters, dashing from city to city, making converts, and moving on. Obviously for pastoral reasons the author is calling attention to his new role as one who teaches the fine points of the gospel faith, with special attention to the proper understanding of Jesus' resurrection and second coming and the Christian's relationship to these.

1:5-9 Qualifications of presbyters and bishops. Structurally 1:5-9 balances 1:10-16, contrasting good leaders with bad teachers in the church. Here we find a list of qualifications for the good teachers, the bishops, which list probably tells us about the prime purpose of the letter: the authorization of both Titus and his successors. And in its list of qualifications, Titus shows greater affinity to 1 Timothy than to the second letter; not only do they have a list of qualifications, but the items in both lists are almost identical.

The qualifications of church leaders do not seem to differ from those one would expect of a reputable city official: a person of good character, experience, probity, whose upright life is an excellent argument in support of his good advice. In short, he must be a responsible public figure. The duties and tasks of bishops, however, are only mentioned in passing in verse 9, where they are expected to be orthodox in preaching, both to encourage and to rebuke. The virtues of bishops are the same as those expected of all church members. But what makes this list important for contemporary readers is the window it gives us on the church at that time and place, a church realizing that its leaders are as important as witnesses to the secular world of Christianity's excellence as they are internal guides and models of the power of the gospel to permeate and shape full, responsible life.

1:10-16 In contrast, false teachers. Titus is warned about false teachers, especially converts from Judaism. Now Paul and the early church were beset with a similar and persistent problem, whereby new converts were required to be circumcised and otherwise made to live like Jews (Gal 5:1-2; Phil 3:19). Evidently this erroneous movement in the early church lived on, for it is addressed harshly in 1 Timothy where some would reimpose on converts the Old Testament law (1:7) and Jewish dietary restrictions (4:3-4). Here it is a threat to the church at Crete, imposing on converts "rules invented by men" (see Mark 7:7-8, 13), especially dietary laws. The statement in verse 15, "to the clean all things are clean," is similar to Paul's argument against clean/unclean foods in Rom 14:20, a function which it has here as well. The fuller response, of course, is found in 1 Tim 4:4, where God's creative goodness touches all creatures and so there can be no unclean (or "bad") creature, especially in the new creation begun in Christ's resurrection. The Judaizing dietary observances are evidently based on bad theology, or "Jewish myths," as they are called in the Pastorals (1:14; 1 Tim 4:7, and 2 Tim 4:4).

Asceticism and a strict moral life are *not* the issues here. Titus is hardly liberalizing the life of this church. These Judaizing problems threaten the core of the church's life and so must be taken seriously. If successful, the Judaizing threat from the right would reduce Christianity from a religion open to all (see 2:11; 1 Tim 2:4-6) to a mere splinter Jewish sect. If the strict keeping of Jewish customs was *necessary* for being a Christian, then this challenges the absolute redemption effected in Christ's death (see Gal 2:21). Either we are saved entirely by Christ or we save ourselves by observing laws and customs. When the issue is put this starkly, the church has always maintained that redemption is a gift of grace from Christ, not our own doing. While resisting these Judaizing tendencies, the author is no less emphatic that true Christian faith must subsequently flower in a life of uprightness and integrity. Morality is no less important for him than it was for the Judaizers, but the understanding of its place in relationship to Jesus' saving death is radically different.

2:1-10 The church and social structures. Like the list of domestic duties urged upon the church in 1 Tim 5:1-16 and 6:1-2, we find a similar list here. Unlike 1 Timothy, there is no concern for widows in Titus' church, nor is he instructed how to deal with older Christians. The focus is typically on the responsibilities of recognizable social groups, a pattern of exhortation found in many New Testament writings (Col 3:18–4:1; Eph 5:21–6:9; 1 Pet 2:18–3:8). In a chiastic form, older men (A), older women (B), young women (B′), and young men (A′) are addressed. They are all called upon to be good family examples, self-controlled, steadfast, and loving. The importance of these exhortations lies not in the list of virtues or vices, which are rather obvious, but in the sense of the public face the new religion must have. Could Christians be good parents and raise honorable families? Would Christianity so liberate people from former ties and structures that the social fabric would be destroyed (see Mark 10:29 and 1 Cor 7:10-15)? Would Christians be loyal and upright citizens? Verse 5 clearly tells us of the church's public concern: If families are authentically Christian, then "the word of God may not be discredited." This same concern stands behind Titus' own charge that he be sound in faith and practice; if he does, "the opponent will be put to shame without anything bad to say about us" (v. 8). Likewise, by honest lives slaves will "adorn . . . the doctrine of God our savior" (v. 10). Thus there is a strong evangelizing thrust to this teaching. The best apology the church had for its new doctrine was the probity of the lives of its converts and the result of this good theology in exemplary moral lives. By their fruits you shall know them.

2:11-15 Faith and moral living. We noted above that good theology leads to good morals, which axiom serves as the link between the previous list of duties and the present passage. "Grace" is proclaimed (v. 11), which if authentic "trains us to reject godless ways and . . . live temperately" (v. 12). But what is the faith of the church? In verses 11, 13-14 we are reminded of the basic kerygma in crisp, clear terms. God has appeared in our history to save all people (v. 11), which plan was realized in Jesus who redeemed us by his sacrifice (v. 14). Already justified, we wait for our sanctifying confirmation at "the appearance of the glory of the great God and of our savior Jesus Christ" (v. 13). The gospel kerygma is not at all theoretical, for it is told in a way that stresses how it is the pastoral foundation of the church's ethical exhortation. We were redeemed from "lawlessness" and cleansed from sin and made eager to do what is right. Our redemption was both a radical change of life from sin to grace and also an instruction and empowerment by God's Spirit in integrity (see "training," v. 12). If this conversion of mind and life is authentic, then we will stand confidently on the day of God's scrutiny.

3:1-2 Citizenship and Christianity. These are the final bits of exhortation in the church's list of "household duties." It is not uncommon in Christian exhortations to encourage prayer for the emperor (1 Tim 2:1-3); here obedience to legitimate civil authority is praised as a

Christian virtue, as was the case in Rom 13:1-7 and 1 Pet 2:13-17. The church does not see itself as a sect opposing the state or the world but indicates that Christians belong to that world and should be exemplary citizens. Part of that citizenship is "to be open to every good enterprise" (v. 1). The text literally says "ready for every good," which may refer equally to virtue as to employment. Perhaps "employment" is valid, for in 3:14 the church membership is encouraged to live lives of "good works to supply urgent needs." And in 2 Thess 3:6-11, we find a lengthy exhortation to avoid idleness and pursue an honest day's work, climaxing in the famous saying that "anyone who would not work should not eat" (3:10). Since Christian citizenship is the topic in 3:1-2, it is probably safe to interpret verse 1 as urging Christians to a full civic life—respect for government, full employment, and a neighborly avoidance of quarrels and slander.

3:3-8 The difference Christianity makes. This paragraph tries to spell out the difference Christianity should make in the lives of believers by contrasting former lives of sin with new lives in faith; the same pattern may be found in Eph 2:3-10 and 1 Pet 4:1-3. The argument is one we have already seen in the letter: good (i.e., Christian) theology leads to good morality. Hence good citizenship is not only compatible with Christianity but enhanced by it. Former pagan lives were typically characterized by slavery to passions—malice, envy, hatred of self—hardly a commendation for good citizenship.

The contrast between former pagan lives of vice and present Christian lives of virtue rests not on a strenuous moral effort on the part of Christians but on God's action of grace. And given the tendency of the Judaizing members of this church to exaggerate the meaning and importance of law observance (1:14-15), the theological foundation of the Christian's new life is explained. Excellent is the Christian God, a God of kindness and philanthropy (v. 4); God's excellence is not abstract but historical; it has "appeared" (see 2:11) in time and history; and it is active—it saved us. Salvation, however, does not come from the Judaizing perfection of law obedience but rather from God's mercy (v. 5). This is vintage Pauline teaching, which occurs also in Eph 2:8-9 and in 2 Tim 1:9. We saw earlier in 2:14 that God's salvation was realized in Jesus' sacrificial death, and Christians personally participate in that salvation when they receive the cleansing of a new birth and the gift of God's Spirit.

Both of these items are standard elements in Christian preaching: conversion is often described as a new birth (see John 3:5; 1 Pet 1:3, 23; 2:2), a baptism of cleansing (Eph 5:26), and as a gift of a new spirit (Gal 4:6). Just as God gave a spirit of life to Adam's lifeless clay body and made him alive, and as God put a new and holy spirit in Christ's body at the resurrection and made him alive (Rom 1:4), so in our sharing in Christ's death and resurrection God made us alive by putting a new and holy Spirit in us, a Spirit which allows us to love and acknowledge God as "Abba" and to walk blamelessly in our new lives (Gal 4:6; Rom 8:14-17). Far from being God's enemies, we become God's children, even heirs (Gal 4:7; Rom 8:17). Our life does not end in death, as pagans believed, but we have in God a hope of eternal life (see 1:2; 2:13 and 2 Tim 2:10). So Christians are radically changed because God has entered their lives, and to the pagan world the Christian God is proved to be true Lord and Savior of all. Faith in this God, far from corrupting us, perfects us for a full and responsible life.

3:8-11 Final directives to Titus. Timothy certainly had ample instruction concerning his duties (see 2 Tim 4:2-6), but only here does Titus receive a brief set of "dos and don'ts." Titus should "insist" on what has been said (v. 8), that is, both the truth about the free gift of salvation from our God and the new moral lives to which our faith leads us. This is not only true but is a selling point for Christianity in the religious marketplace (v. 8b). Titus is *not* to be like the false teachers who were exposed in 1:10-16. He must shun arguments like theirs over "genealogies" and abstain from controversies, especially quarrels over the law (see 1:14-15). This point has been adequately thrashed out in the early church, and there can be no going back on the issue of law vs. grace. It is useful ("advantageous") to insist on the truth (v. 8), but Judaizing insistence is definitely not useful (v. 9).

Like Timothy, Titus is to rebuke and correct the wrong-thinking members of the church (v. 10; see 2 Tim 2:25; 4:2). Two warnings, in fact, are given, which in some way resemble the gradual process of correction in

Matt 18:15-17. If the warnings fail, then the "heretic" would appear to be censured with some form of social correction, seemingly a form of excommunication (see 1 Tim 1:20). The severity of the action is in proportion to the danger perceived. Not only was this false doctrine a contradiction of the cross of Christ, its proponents were apparently avid proselytizers (see 1 Tim 5:15; 2 Tim 3:6), and so were becoming like gangrene in the church (see 2 Tim 2:17-19).

3:12-15 Final directives. The mobile state of the first-century church is well reflected in these final directives. Messengers are to be sent, presumably from Rome or the western Mediterranean eastward to Nicopolis. Tychicus must do a lot of traveling for the author claims to be sending him to Ephesus in 2 Tim 4:12. And missionaries, it would seem, are also being dispatched: Apollos, who may be the famous Alexandrian scholar known from Acts 18 and 1 Cor 1–4, and Zenas, who is otherwise unknown. It is interesting to note that Zenas is a "lawyer," not a Jewish scribe but a jurist; he is evidently a figure of considerable education and social standing, like Erastus, the city treasurer mentioned in Rom 16:23. They are to be equipped for their journey by the host community, a procedure typical of Paul's own missionary practice (see 2 Cor 11:8-9; Phil 4:14-16). Verse 14 is a general summary exhortation to the church to be good citizens, taking care of their own needs and not being idle or lazy (see 3:1 and 1 Tim 5:8). The letter concludes with a typical epistolary greeting and farewell.

JAMES

Jerome H. Neyrey, S.J.

INTRODUCTION

Author

There is considerable scholarly debate over the authorship of this letter. If James is truly the author, then he could be "James, son of Alphaeus" (Matt 10:3) or more probably "James, the brother of the Lord" (Gal 1:19; see also Mark 6:3). This James, moreover, was a major figure in the early church; the risen Jesus appeared to him (1 Cor 15:7); he became second head of the Jerusalem church (Acts 12:17), and he was a leading figure in opening the church to Gentile membership, both in his guidance of the Jerusalem conference in Acts 15 and in his confirmation of Paul's ministry to the Gentiles (Gal 2:9). He is the figure Paul visited on his last trip to Jerusalem (Acts 21:17-18). But as is the case with the pastoral and catholic Epistles, there is a solid argument that the letter is pseudonymous, only attributed to James. The material in James is very common hortatory material and does not demand an eyewitness either for its source or value. The vision of the church is that of a more developed group than the apostolic churches. The debate over authorship eventually is irrelevant to a pastoral understanding of the text, for the letter is transparently rich with traditional New Testament materials. It does not need genuine authorship to secure its authority or the worth of its contents. To judge from the pseudonymous character of the letter and its developed view of the church, the date of James' composition is judged to stem from the late first century.

Genre and thrust of James

Although it is loosely put in a letter form, the genre of James is more accurately that of exhortation or popular moral teaching, which was common in Jewish wisdom literature, in the Sermon on the Mount (and 1 Pet), and in Graeco-Roman writings as well. Characteristically there is a frequent use of imperatives and a persistent urging to excellence. The exhortation typically consists of a chain of smaller items, sometimes connected (especially by catchwords), but often haphazardly strung together. The main topics typically include concerns for perseverance, proper speech, prayer, practical charity, avarice, pleasure, etc.—all standard items in exhortatory literature. The exhortation is laced with vivid metaphors and pointed citations from the Scriptures.

The author delights in sharp contrasts between good/evil and alive/dead to highlight his point. One must insist on the very traditional character of all of James' material, for he serves as an excellent window on the preaching of the church to converts on the need for perseverance and for a thorough conversion of their lives to God. James represents the pastoral concern of the early church to lead the flock of God into greater and greater possession of its gift of salvation. Far from overturning the advances in Pauline theology, as some have contended, James' concern for the moral life of the church really takes seriously Paul's basic exhortation "to live a life worthy of the calling you have received" (Eph 4:1; see also 1 Thess 2:12; Phil 1:27; Col 1:10).

Major themes

While there is surprisingly little material about Jesus (1:1 and 2:1), there are extensive reminders about the Christian preaching about God. After all, pagans were regularly converted to faith in the one true God (see 1 Thess 1:9-10) as well as to faith in Jesus. The rich portrait of God in James is, of course, traditional and is based on biblical sources: God is "compassionate and merciful" (5:11), Lawgiver and Judge (4:12); God is one (2:19), creator (1:18), constant and unchanging (1:17).

James' main concerns are for perseverance in conversion to God and growth in the living of gospel morality. He sees the intimate relationship between faith in God and love of neighbor, for both are characteristic of covenant faith. The integrity of the moral life is maintained: one cannot pick and choose among God's covenant laws (2:10-11). James never tires of pointing out the roots of disorder in our lives and urging us to control them lest they devour us like a forest fire. James' sense of church constantly dominates his writing to remind us that religion is not a private affair between us and God but a covenant relationship between God and his covenant people; hence love of neighbor (2:8) as well as the foregoing of judgment are persistent themes. One cannot but be impressed by James' pastoral sense of the wholeness of Christian life, the maturity to which the gospel must grow in believers, and the active relation between religion and life. No part-time Christians in James' churches!

COMMENTARY

1:1 Letter opening. The work begins with the most unexciting of letter openings. The sender is identified as James, "slave of God" (see introduction). The addressees are the "twelve tribes in the dispersion," which probably means the church at large in the pagan world. The fact that the twelve tribes are addressed suggests the catholicity of James, that it was written not just to one church (e.g., Corinth), or to seven churches (Rev 1–3), or to the regional churches of Pontus, Asia, and Galatia (1 Pet 1:1), but to Christian churches everywhere.

1:2-4 Perseverance. Where typical letters start with "thanksgiving prayers," James begins with an exhortation to persevere. Instead of being depressed by difficulties or thinking that trials give a lie to the Christian proclamation of Jesus' victory, we are to count trials as "all joy." In 1 Pet 1:6-7 trials are deemed valuable because they test the gold of faith in fire; here they are acceptable because they lead to worthwhile ends: endurance, perfection, and maturity (v. 4). The chain effect of one virtue leading to another is a common feature in this type of literature (see Rom 5:3-5 and 2 Pet 1:5-7). Obviously this is addressed to people who have been justified in Christ and for whom sanctification (i.e., endurance and growth toward maturity) is now the dominant task.

1:5-8 Prayer and faith. The catchword linking verses 4 and 5 is "lacking": the perfect Christians lack nothing, but if anyone lacks something, let them pray. So the new topic is introduced. Perseverance will lead to maturity in which we lack nothing, but a shortcut to supply what is lacking is prayer. Typical of this author is the use of contrasts in describing what is right/wrong. Here we find contrasting "pray-ers": true believers ask in faith (Mark 11:24) but false pray-ers are doubters or "split persons" (see v. 8). The advice is less a word on how to pray than it is another call to completeness and maturity as Christians. And for the first time we find one of the vivid images used by James: a doubting pray-er is like surf tossed by the wind.

1:9-11 Rich and poor. We are introduced briefly to a theme which James will develop more at length later. This terse word only stresses the contrast between right and wrong behavior: the poor of the community are correct to boast in their exaltation which eventually comes from God; the rich are wrong to boast for they are as fragile and short-lived as flowers which the sun scorches. This image reminds us of God's fiery and discerning judgment (see Matt 3:11-12). It is assumed that the rich are somehow split persons (see v. 8) for they are described as "fading away" because they are involved "in the midst of pursuits" (v. 11) besides God and the gospel.

1:12-16 Temptation. James returns to the theme with which he began the letter in 1:2-4; temptations befall converts to Jesus. But blessed is the one who endures such temptations, a phrase resembling the beatitudes in the Sermon on the Mount (Matt 5:3-11). Many themes and terms return for fuller consideration: temptation, endurance, testing (1:2-3, 12). Whereas endurance led to maturity, now we are told that it leads to a crown of life, which is a traditional statement of God's saving judgment (see 1 Cor 9:25 and 2 Tim 4:8). The source of temptations remains a problem; the author insists that God does not bring them upon us but that we are tempted by our own lusts and desires. But all of us, nevertheless, are subject to testing. The speculative aspects of this problem are less important than the pastoral contrast between two possible results: the one who endures temptation is blessed (v. 12) but others when tempted give birth to a chain of evils leading to death (v. 15).

1:17-18 God and God's gift. James returns to God's giving (see 1:5-7), but now to remind the converts about the God whom Christians worship. God gives good gifts (1:5, 17) impartially to all. God rewards (v. 12) and punishes (v. 11); God does not tempt us (v. 13), nor is God changeable or fickle (v. 17). What this means is that God is a moral God. He purposefully made the world and chose us (v. 18), and his moral purpose pervades the universe of his chosen ones. Hence, those who commit themselves to a moral God must be moral as well. As God is steadfast, so should we be.

1:19-25 True vs. false believers. Two different contrasting pieces of advice are contained here: we are to be swift to listen (v. 19) but woe betide the listener who is slow to act (v. 22). The first advice contrasts patient with quick-tempered people (vv. 19-21); the second comment contrasts believers who only listen with believers who act on their faith (vv. 22-25). The term "word" is the catchword linking verses 18, 21, and 22-23: God's word created us, resides in us to save us, but must be acted upon. The emphasis here is on verses 22-25; what one does and how one lives out the faith is the moral concern of this author. Typically he uses a contrast to get his point across about what the true Christian is like. The false Christian only glances at the mirror and has no perseverance, no memory, no moral response to the gospel. The true Christian looks, sees, remembers, and acts. The seed of faith is alive and active (see the parable of the seeds again, Mark 4:14-20). According to verse 25, the true Christian is not lawless but shoulders the yoke of Christ (Rom 6:18, 22) and so the law is a law of freedom from evil, a perfect law which does not enslave. James labels this person with the traditional tag for success, "such a one shall be blessed" (v. 25). Some commentators see here an attack by James on Paul's "works vs. grace" principle, but that is unjustified by the text. What we have is a contrast between two types of believers, between true and false believers. For while all are freely justified by God through faith, our sanctification demands that we live a life worthy of our calling.

1:26-27 True vs. false religion. In still another contrast, James tells us what is true/false religion. False piety, like faith without action in 1:22-23, is religion which has no ramifications in the life of a believer. Anyone who professes love of God yet whose tongue is abusive of the neighbor is empty and misguided (see Matt 5:22)—the theme of correct speech is both a common topic in this type of literature (Sir 28:12-16) and a topic which will be developed later in 2:16; 3:1-12; 4:11 and 5:13. True religion acknowledges the bridge between covenant faith and covenant love, for it manifests itself in concern for "orphans and widows," the traditional people in the community most in need of covenant support (see Deut 27:19; Ezek 22:7 and Acts 6:1; 1 Tim 5:3-16). True religion also abstains from worldly self-seeking and self-assertion (see 4:2) and so is unstained and purehearted before God.

Chapter 1, then, presents a wide sample of small bits of exhortation. In general, James addresses the developing life of Christians, reminding them of the moral God who redeems them and calls them to a wholehearted and faithful life. His favorite technique is to describe right and wrong in vivid images (waves, burning sun, mirrors) and by means of sharp contrasts between good and evil, true and false.

2:1-7 Favoritism in the church. A community meeting is described where two clients come to the elders for a judgment (see 1 Cor 6:1-6). James attacks the favoritism that is naturally shown to successful and influential people, arguing that such is wrong. In a different context Paul insisted on God's lack of favoritism, both in judgment (Rom 2:11) and in election (Rom 3:22; 10:12); this impartiality destroyed the privileged position of the Jews as God's favorites and led to a radical sense of egalitarianism in the Pauline churches (see Gal 3:28). This is probably the basis for James' attack on favoritism here: God's impartiality to us and our equal status in the church. The attack again centers on the way Christians evaluate rich and poor; in the Old Testament literature, wealth is seen as a sign of God's blessing and favor (Ps 128), but not so in the Christian tradition which calls the poor "blessed" (Matt 5:3) and sees them as God's favorites (Luke 1:50-53). So James argues in verse 5 that God's election is to the poor as well, to make them rich (and equal) in faith (see 1:9). The church is called to witness to its faith: as God is impartial, calls all to life, and even favors the poor, orphans, and widows, so the church must mirror God's actions in its structures, lest it be like the person of shallow faith without works (see 1:22-25).

2:8-11 Love as the key to faith. In contrast to the favoritism condemned in 2:1-7, true religion is described in verses 8-11. One acts rightly if one keeps the law of the kingdom, to love one another. Ordinarily in the New Testament this command occurs alongside the command to love God with all one's heart (Matt 22:37-39), but here it is presumed that one is a believer in (and lover of) God. The problem is: How does faith/love of God show itself practically in our lives? Hence, the stress in 2:8-11 is on love of neighbor as the demonstration of the one who hears and acts (1:22-24) and of the one whose faith is alive (2:14-17).

Covenant love excludes favoritism (v. 9) as well as aggression against a community member. The argument insists that we are to keep the whole law, probably the Ten Commandments as covenant law (see Matt 15:19; 19:18-19). To fail in covenant love in one area is to fail completely. This demand for completeness in the Christian moral life is quite characteristic of James, who repeatedly calls upon us to be mature and perfect (1:4), faultless (3:2), and spotless (1:27). Religion, then, is not a part-time, selective, compartmentalized activity. This exhortation ends with the call to expect moral scrutiny from God for our lives. Merciless people, who show favoritism or neglect widows and orphans, will find little mercy with God (see Matt 7:2; 25:33-46); but in typical Christian fashion, mercy will cover many sins (see 1 Pet 4:8). Typical also is the idea found even in the Our Father that what we do to others will be done to us (see Matt 6:14-15).

2:14-17 Dead and live faith. In another series of contrasts, James juxtaposes active faith with verbal faith, live faith with dead faith. The passage begins and ends with the same phrase, "faith that does nothing in practice" (vv. 14, 17), which controls the discussion and highlights the central theme. The focus is on how one shows covenant faith to a community member; if one sees a naked, hungry person and only *says:* "Keep warm and well fed," then one does not "love your neighbor as yourself" (v. 8), and so faith in God cannot save (v. 13). This sounds similar to the parable of the sheep and the goats in Matt 25:31-46. The concern for practical faith here simply continues the stream of arguments in 1:22-25, 26-28, and 2:1-8 on how Christian faith, if real, permeates one's life. In 2:14-17 James makes a bold demand which requires some theoretical justification, which follows in 2:18-26.

2:18-26 Two kinds of faith. The echoes of Paul's teaching on "works vs. faith" are strong, but it is not correct to argue, as many do, that James is attacking Paul or radically disagreeing with him. They are discussing two different issues (see the discussion above of 1:19-25). Paul opposed Jewish claims that the principle of salvation is the keeping of the law. By evangelizing Gentiles he came to realize that God was impartial in selecting all to salvation—all who believed in God and Jesus Christ. So, as regards basic justification before God, Paul saw that not just a few law observers were justified, but all who believed God's promises were invited to life. Hence, *law vs. faith.* James is dealing with a different problem; he presupposes justification through faith and treats of two kinds of faith: *active vs. dead faith.* He is consistently trying to show that true religion is not just a right confession of words, which a convert makes initially and forgets later. But true religion is covenant faith in God and covenant love of neighbor which lasts, which realizes itself in deeds of love, and which is alive and active.

In 2:19 James repeats the traditional Jewish-Christian formula about God which was the foundation of the new faith of converts from polytheism: God is One. Demons acknowledge this principle of faith, but do not act on it; hence, adherence to an idea is not itself salvific, no matter how important it is. Professing the right creed is not the same thing as living one's faith. Abraham is cited because he is the traditional witness Christians summon in their arguments on these matters (Rom 4; Heb 11). Whereas Paul contrasted Abraham's naked belief in God's promise of a son with Moses' doing of the law, James shows that Abraham's faith has a history—it was tested and showed itself as genuine covenant obedience in the episode where Abraham was commanded to sacrifice Isaac. The contrast is not between works and faith but between enduring, active faith and transient, verbal faith. Abraham's faith was "perfected" only when he acted upon it (2:22). The example of Rahab proves a different point, namely, that covenant faith, if real, must lead to covenant love. Rahab showed hospitality to strangers, giving food, shelter, and clothing (v. 25). She exemplifies the one who acts in love toward widows and orphans (1:27-28), who acts to feed, warm, and clothe the needy (2:16). Together, Abraham and Rahab complement one another and show that genuine faith is faith that has a persevering and active history, faith which is faithful when tested, faith which is not just verbal but active, faith which is obedient and loving. And so, James shows that religion either deeply penetrates our lives or it is not true religion.

3:1-12 Control of the tongue. This lengthy passage on control of the tongue begins with a command that there be few teachers in the group. Teachers are mentioned as officials in the early churches (Acts 13:1; 1 Cor 12:28; Eph 4:11). Different from prophets, teachers may be thought of as people who give new insights into old materials, as people who guard and reinterpret the tradition. James surely functions as a teacher himself in his reinterpretation of the law (2:8, 10), in his reapplication of the Scriptures (1:10; 2:23), and in his reuse of Jesus' teachings (1:5, 17; 4:3). It is not clear why there should be few teachers (3:1), for this group does not seem to be particularly threatened by false teachers. James only says that teachers face a stricter judgment, a theme he has repeatedly stressed (see 2:12-13).

Concern for teaching is only the preface to the major discourse on controlling one's tongue (vv. 2-12). Although we are warned that we must perfectly keep *all* the commandments (2:9-11), here it is admitted that we are all still sinners, failing in one or another thing. Yet the one who controls the tongue is a "perfect" person, perfection being the completeness or totality of one's growth in faith, not simply sinlessness. "Perseverance" brings perfection (1:4); the hearer who practices faith is likewise perfect (1:25); Abraham's faith was perfected by his faithful actions (2:22). Again we have the ideal set before us: a great value put on careful speech. Now control of the tongue is a standard topic in traditional moral exhortations (see Sir 14:1), which tradition James echoes not only in his advice but also in the metaphors used to dramatize its importance. As a bit can control a powerful horse, so guarding the tongue serves to control the whole person (see Ps 32:9). Likewise a huge ship is controlled and guided by a small rudder, just as we are by our mouths (see the Egyptian counterpart of this by Amen-em-Opet: "Steer not with thy tongue alone; if the tongue of a man be the rudder of a boat, the All-Lord is its pilot"). Still a third example is used to stress the importance of this virtue: a spark can set a forest ablaze, so a small tongue can wield great destructive power.

In 3:6 the importance of control of the tongue is repeated, in terms used earlier in verse 2. The whole person and the whole body depend on this one organ for their integrity. This idea resembles the gospel description of the eye which is evil darkening the whole body and vice versa (Matt 6:22-23). The danger of an unbridled tongue is perhaps exaggerated when James calls it a "world of malice" which is always endangering us from birth (3:6), but this is probably traditional language used to describe the importance of this. Surely charity (2:8) is more important to

James. As dangerous and as extensive as is the damage which an unbridled tongue can bring, it is also uncontrollable (v. 8) and demands constant attention. James' concern for the tongue pervades the exhortation: on the one hand he is worried about faith which is only verbal, without action (2:15); he warns against oath-taking (5:13); he warns that speaking ill of one another brings judgment (4:11); and here he stresses the constant need to control an organ which potentially can set forests ablaze and kill with poison. Obviously the early church prized charity and brotherhood, and was fiercely on guard against anger and factionalism. Lest anyone think they are keeping the law by avoiding murder, Jesus told them that name-calling and slander come under that prohibition as well (Matt 5:22).

In a final argument, James maintains that as judgment belongs to God (see 4:11-12), our speech should never be cursing but only blessing. And he employs once more his vivid metaphors: blessing and cursing are as incompatible in one mouth as finding fresh and foul water in the same spring, as gathering grapes and figs from the same plant.

3:13-18 True and false wisdom. Verse 13, the introduction to this presentation of true and false wisdom, is James' typical demand for a living and practical faith which shows itself actively in deeds. An appeal is made for humility, which links verses 13-18 to verses 1-10, for the control of speech will mean a nonaggressive behavior which avoids bitter jealousy and selfish ambition. The community focus of this advice is clear in the appeal for unity of heart and speech, which clearly is prized over against arrogant and false claims to individualism. Typically James contrasts true with false wisdom, wisdom from above with earthbound wisdom. Earthly wisdom promotes the self (see v. 14); it is concerned with earthly matters, such as riches, power, and prestige; it is not spiritual but material; it is devilish, just as was the unbridled tongue (see 3:6). In 1 Corinthians, Paul also found a community split into factions, seeking self-interest, full of strife and jealousy (see 1:11; 3:3), just as James describes here. In general, James is showing how false theology (false wisdom) leads to false morals, a typical argument in the ancient world for showing the evils of heresy: it leads surely to division and immorality.

In contrast to false wisdom is wisdom from above. It is pure and spotless, James' favorite concepts (see 1:27; 3:6). True wisdom is community-building: it makes peace (Matt 5:9), is forebearing and willing to give in to teachers and group leaders. Typical of James, it is full of mercy (2:13) and good works (2:18-26), it shows no favoritism (2:9), nor is it pretentious (2:2-3). In short, "wisdom" for James is not esoteric knowledge or gnostic secrets but the traditional Jewish notion of correct behavior and moral uprightness. Again James shows his hand in exalting the living out of the Christian faith over merely knowing its tenets or simply confessing its creed. Wisdom, like faith, is practical, active, and community-oriented. In listing the contrasting results of this prime value, James mirrors Paul's similar list of typical vices and virtues which stem from true freedom in Christ (see Gal 5:16-26). He concludes his exhortation here with another typical saying: As you sow, so you reap (see Gal 6:7). Here he stresses again the moral character of the Christian universe, just as he did earlier in 2:13. Our actions have consequences and the harvest is the judgment time of God when we will reap what we have sown.

4:1-3 The arch-vice and its cure. This passage is structured in three parts: the prime vice is identified (4:1-3), its incompatibility with God is described (vv. 4-7), and the cure of the vice is indicated (vv. 7-10). As regards the identity of the vice, moralists in the ancient world traditionally reduced wickedness to four prime vices (desire, pleasure, fear, and grief). James already identified "desire" as the root of temptation in 1:14-15 (the translation here is "covet," but the meaning is "desire," one of the four cardinal sins), and in 4:1-3 he returns to that theme. Where there is a lack of heavenly wisdom, conflicts abound (3:14, 16) and these conflicts James says stem from "desire," which cannot yield anything good: "You covet but do not possess. You kill and envy but you cannot obtain." It is, of course, a popular saying even in the Bible that "money (desire) is the root of all evil" (see 1 Tim 6:10).

James keeps insisting that the roots of evil and sin are within us. Temptation comes, not from God but from deceiving hearts and passions (1:14-15); anger and hostility, which reside in the passion with which we were born, flame out in an unbridled tongue (3:6). Despite conversion and baptism, Christians are not perfect yet and must strive to let God's grace rule their hearts progressively in every way. Here James is content to show the wickedness of "desire" by dramatizing its evil results: desire and envy lead to murder and quarreling, just as an uncontrolled tongue leads to a blazing rage (3:5-6). Vices, moreover, are interrelated: "desire" leads to other vices, such as "passion." Just as "covet" means "desire," so "passions" mean "pleasure," the second of the four cardinal sins. People covet goods for the sake of pleasure (4:3) and not for the sake of sharing them with others (see 2:14-17).

4:4-6 God vs. world. Christians still under the dominance of "desire" and "pleasure" are friends of the world and so enemies of God (4:4); they have broken the covenant and so are "adulterers." Typical of James is the contrast between friends of the world and enemies of God. As the gospel says, one cannot serve two masters (Matt 6:24), and James indicates in 4:5 that God is a jealous God. Another contrast is stated between proud and lowly: as Scripture says, God resists the proud (the desirous) and gives grace to the lowly—a very traditional principle in the Bible (see Job 22:29; Prov 3:34; 1 Pet 5:5). "Proud" and "humble" are surely code words for desirous pleasure-seekers and for total Christians.

4:7-10 The cure of the vices. The antidote to these cardinal vices is to wage war on sin, a traditional metaphor in moral exhortations (1 Pet 2:11; Rom 7:21-23). The sides are clearly drawn: God versus the devil. James has already called earthly wisdom "demonic" (3:15), and he stated that an angry tongue was kindled from hell (3:6). Yet the reader knows as well that evil and vice are not simply the devil's doing but reside in human hearts (see 4:1). The cure of vice is metaphorically described as a battle, but James clarifies that by saying the real cure is to "draw near to God" (v. 8), to let God be Lord of our hearts and lives (see Matt 22:37; Rom 6:22). The reconversion of our hearts is described in the Old Testament language of repentance which does not mean that Christians are gloomy or guilt-ridden (see Jer 4:8; Joel 2:12-14); along with that is the advice to "cleanse your hands . . . purify your hearts"—spotlessness, which in James refers to the completeness of Christian conversion. And "those of two minds" in 4:8 are the double-minded people who pray falsely in 1:7-8 (the Greek term is the same in both cases); they are people who have two Lords and hedge their bets. Hence a *total conversion of heart and life* is the remedy for vice which James urges. His exhortation concludes with the traditional appeal for a complete change of mind, heart, and action: Be humble and God will raise you up. This is a popular saying found in Matt 23:12; Luke 14:11 and 18:14. Here it refers less to humility than to the complete reversal of direction of our lives from vice to God and to the comprehensiveness of our conversion to the Lord.

4:11-12 Do not judge. These verses continue the earlier themes of correct speech (3:1-12) and the warnings about conflicts and fights (3:14-15; 4:1-3). In essence they proscribe slander as well as private judgment of a community member (group judgment, reflected in the courtroom setting of 2:1-7, is approved). This is typical of moral exhortations and is found even in the Sermon on the Mount (Matt 7:1); it reflects the principle behind the gloss on the Our Father in Matt 6:14-15 to forgive and so be forgiven. Slander and judgment are contrary to "the law," that is, the royal law of love mentioned in 2:8. They are condemned for good reason: all judgment belongs to God, a traditional belief which is found also in Paul's exhortations (Rom 12:19). The simple mention of judge and judgment are essential elements in the religious world of James: God is a moral God and our lives must be moral as well. This requires a clear sense of what is enjoined and what is proscribed, which is the whole point of James' letter. This also implies that the moral God will scrutinize the moral lives of his creatures, and so James reminds us periodically in the letter about judgment. Our actions count (2:12-13); God both rewards and requites (4:11-12); the Judge is genuine and his coming is imminent (5:9). Let no one take God's role!

4:13-17 Total trust in God. This advice, while it sounds as if it is addressed to merchants, is really a statement of a general Christian principle. It calls for a radical reorientation of the whole of our lives in the light of conversion to the one true God. Hence, our lives, whether we live one or a hundred years, whether or not we succeed in our undertaking, are all under God's providence and not our own control. Again James stresses that Christianity requires a sweeping and pervasive change in our lives which are totally caught up in God. The contrast is clear: God is Lord, not we. This extends the polemic against radical self-assertion, which is condemned throughout the letter (see 1:11; 4:1-3). The point is not quietism or passivity but completeness of our conversion to God with our whole heart, mind, and strength.

5:1-6 Woe to the unjust rich. A vigorous condemnation of the rich occurs here which echoes New Testament attacks on unjust wealth and Old Testament prophetic charges as well. Like Matt 6:19-20, the unjust wealth is shown to be ultimately profitless, for it is rotted, moth-eaten, and rusted. No lasting gain there! It is, moreover, lethal to be its owner for it bears testimony against its possessor, probably in the sense that it was not spent on orphans, widows, or the needy as was urged in 1:27; 2:14-16 (see Sir 29:10). It witnesses rather to the vice "desire" (see 4:1-2). Fiery punishment is a common biblical description of judgment (see Matt 18:8-9); and it is common in New Testament eschatological discussions to speak of wrath "treasured up" in heaven (see 2 Pet 3:7). The rich are not condemned simply for being rich (see Luke 6:24) but for their injustice. The stated cause of condemnation in James is the withholding of wages from workers, a thing proscribed by the law (Lev 19:13). Remember how the owner of the vineyard in Matt 20:8 paid his workers promptly at the end of the day! This crime is considered so serious that it cries to God for redress (Deut 24:15), as did Abel's blood (Gen 4:10), and the sin of Sodom (Gen 19:13). Again James calls attention to the role of God as judge, to remind the church of God's moral lordship over all people (5:4). Like the rich man in Luke 16:19-31, the rich in James are accused of using wealth only for their pleasure, a major vice (see 4:1, 3). Using another vivid metaphor, James describes how these sinners bring ruin upon themselves as though they were cattle fattened for slaughter through constant feeding on injustice and pleasure. It is unlikely that the rich are seen as murderers in verse 6; rather, the extreme extent of self-seeking is projected, showing how evil self-centered vices are. The rich, nevertheless, are said to harass the poor (see 2:6-7).

5:7-11 A persevering life. As in 1:2-4, James again puts great stress on a full and faithful Christian life. Difficulties will surely beset Christian converts (see 1 Pet 4:4), so they are urged to be faithful and patient. In another vivid comparison, Christians are to be like farmers waiting for the early and late rains. Genuine Christians are not afraid of God's coming; they long for it and even hasten it (see 2 Pet 3:12). In the meantime they are not to grumble, presumably against those hostile to them (4:11-12), but to leave justice in God's hands, for he is the judge at the gate (see Matt 24:33). As models they take the prophets who suffered for God's word, which bears close resemblance to one of the traditional beatitudes (Matt 5:11-12). "Blessed" are they (5:11), a cry of praise reserved in 1:12 for the one "who perseveres in temptation." As James would say, this one is a mature, complete Christian. In support of this advice, another biblical precedent is cited: Job, who was a paragon of patient endurance and an example of God's generous rewarding (Job 42:10-17). Although James has stressed God's judgment to the wicked, the moral God of Christians is especially a God of mercy and compassion (v. 11), the very self-description given by God to Moses (Exod 34:6). God truly is judge, who both saves and requites (4:12).

5:12 Oaths and speech. As well as Christians avoid judgmental speech (4:11), and angry speech (3:5-6), they are to avoid swearing, just as the Sermon on the Mount indicated (Matt 5:37). The only proper speech is blessing (3:10) and praise—speech which builds up the community.

5:13-18 Prayer, healing, and forgiveness. The common thread holding verses 13-18 together is the concern for prayer which appears in every verse. The structure, however, is complex, for we move from the injunction to pray always (v. 13) to what to do when a community member is ill (vv. 14-16) to the example of Elijah, the model of powerful and persistent prayer (vv. 17-18). In verse 13 James again expresses his sense of the completeness of faith permeating our lives; whether things are going well or ill, we should "draw near to God" in prayer—a good general principle (4:8). A more specific situation is next envisioned, the illness of a member of the community. Obviously misfortune and illness are *not* signs of divine displeasure, and so the leaders of the group are urged to show charity and to pray over and anoint the sick with oil (see 2:14-17). This procedure seems to presuppose gifts of prayer and healing in the group, not unlike Paul's Corinthian church (1 Cor 12:9, 28). It was common Jewish practice as well to ask that holy figures of the synagogue officially pray for the needy. As we were instructed in 1:6, the prayer must be made wholeheartedly and this prayer of faith will not only restore bodily health but lead to forgiveness of sins. Again James stresses the influence of grace on the whole person.

The introduction of "forgiveness" in verse 15 leads James to further general advice to the church in verse 16 that in its common meeting it develop a procedure of confession, prayer, and forgiveness. It was expected of Christians that they break with their former sinful lives through baptism. Ever the realist, James addresses throughout the letter the unfortunate fact that even believers fail and sin, and so the church must take that into account. The procedure James suggests is hardly an inquisition or a courtroom scene, but a structural way of living out the Our Father, which calls upon us to forgive one another. His letter has stressed this over and over (see 2:13; 4:11). It is passages like verses 14-16 that suggest the roots of later Christian practices such as the anointing of the sick. In his final remarks on prayer, James cites Elijah's persistent prayer: "He prayed . . . and prayed again" (vv. 17-18). And in accord with God's will, this prayer was powerful for it could mean drought or life for the people.

5:19-20 More on community prayer. The final verses of the letter continue the theme developed in 5:13-18; now the sick person is the one who has strayed away from the group. Lack of perseverance is the worst thing James can think of. This one deserves the same attention as the physically sick person in 5:14; the community should act vigorously to save him. This is what James means when he speaks of love of neighbor (2:8) and of doing something concrete for the needy (2:14-17). And the healing this produces will "save his soul" from death, from the moral judgment of God. James echoes popular tradition when he notes that such kindness "covers a multitude of sins" (see 1 Pet 4:8). Thus the errant sister or brother, as well as the shepherd who goes in search of the lost, will find favor with God (see Matt 18:12-14).

1 PETER

Jerome H. Neyrey, S.J.

INTRODUCTION

Author

An uncritical reading of 1 Peter would innocently say that Peter the apostle wrote this letter on the occasion of his martyrdom at Rome under Nero, exhorting other churches to prepare for the great Roman persecutions. But martyrdom is not the topic of the letter, although there is much language about suffering; no formal persecution of Christians occurred until the last decade of the first century. Although we cannot prove who did or did not write the letter, the church addressed looks very much like the churches of the pastoral Epistles and Ephesians and Colossians—late first-century churches concerned with household duties and with the church's relationship to the pagan world. The letter is no less valuable for faith if Peter did not write it, nor more precious for faith if he did. It speaks for itself.

There is no solid reason to date this letter to the sixties if it does not speak of Nero's persecution. Rather, scholars tend to date it late in the first century, probably in the nineties.

Occasion

It was once fashionable to see 1 Peter as a martyrdom exhortation, a trend which has prudently faded. Nor is it a Passover baptismal liturgy, although there is much baptismal material in it. Rather, it is very similar to typical Christian exhortations with its stress on traditional morality, lists of household duties, concern for the public face of the church in relation to pagan society, and appeals to recognizable traditions. The audience is very general and broad: Christians in Asia Minor who live as "sojourners" among their pagan neighbors. Included in the audience is a spectrum of social classes: slaves, families, leaders. Great concern is given to the issue of how a Christian can also be a good citizen. While a certain emphasis is put on conversion and the new status of converts, the letter addresses a variety of people on a wide range of topics. Less dramatic than martyrdom, perhaps, but more practical and easier to identify with!

Major themes

The letter develops two major ideas: (a) church, and (b) God and his Christ. As regards church, the letter reminds Christians of their free election by God, their conversion, and their noble and rich life in Christ. Great stress is put on the wonderful character of the church and how superior life in Christ is to pagan religion. Whence the church came about, how God founded it, its structure, its dignity, its call to holiness, its relations with pagan society—these are all treated carefully in the letter. The character and history of the church, then, are major themes.

Alternatively, the church is reminded of its new Christian God. He cares for them, chooses them, exalts them, and judges them. The Christian God is so far superior to their former pagan gods! Correspondingly, God's actions on Jesus are retold, how Jesus was vindicated from his sufferings and became a living spirit. The retelling of Christ's paschal career serves a very pastoral purpose in 1 Peter, for Christian experience is interpreted in the light of that pattern. As we shall see in regard to chapter 2, the career of Jesus is the career of the church, with special emphasis put on suffering and vindication. As God raised up the suffering Jesus, so God will sustain and vindicate all converts who suffer for their new faith in God and Jesus.

A pastoral letter

1 Peter is a very pastoral letter, for it aims precisely at encouraging Christians in the face of real problems and crises which beset their daily lives. The letter is pastoral in the choice of exhortation materials, nothing less than the kerygma of faith. Since that faith is called into question by the crises of life, the author tries to show how Jesus is the sure pastoral pattern of life, how God is involved in the daily lives of Christians, and how God saves us precisely insofar as we are like Christ, sufferings included. The letter does not ignore problems or minimize them, but calls us to see our lives more clearly in the light of the truth about a redeeming God and Jesus, the proof of God's power and plan.

COMMENTARY

1:1-2 Letter opening. Like typical ancient letters, 1 Peter begins with the formula "X to Y, greeting!" The sender identifies himself as "Peter, an apostle of Jesus Christ," and his audience as "sojourners of the dispersion." The greeting ("grace and peace be yours in abundance") is likewise typical (see Rom 1:7; 1 Cor 1:3). The address highlights the free gift of grace to these Gentile communities, for they were "chosen . . . in the foreknowledge of God the Father," a phrase suited to stress the full inclusion and equal status of Gentiles in the early church (see Eph 1:3-5); in fact, their divine election will be stressed throughout the letter (see 2:4, 6, 9), for one of the purposes of this letter is to celebrate God's gift of grace to them. Although the recipients are strangers of the Diaspora, they are not from the Jewish dispersion, for this phrase stresses their separation from their pagan neighbors which conversion to Christ has caused (see "sojourners" in 1:17; 2:11). This separation, in fact, has occasioned suspicion and hostility, which may account for the letter's stressing how Christians are now different from their pagan pasts (see 2:11-12; 4:2-4, 16). By identifying the church as the Diaspora, there may be an implied remark that the church is the new Israel (see Gal 6:16; Phil 3:3; Jas 1:1), scattered as was the old Israel.

In the popular mind it is generally thought that the twelve apostles went out on missionary journeys all over the world, but oddly, we have little literary evidence for this, and only fragments of Peter's journeys to Lydda and Joppa (Acts 9:32ff.), Antioch (Gal 2:11-14), Corinth (1 Cor 1:12; 9:5), and finally Rome (see "Babylon" in 1 Pet 5:13). His preaching to these churches is otherwise not known.

Although God, the Spirit, and Jesus are mentioned in verse 2, we should not rush to identify this text as a dogmatic Trinitarian formula. It is typical of other places in the New Testament where God acts on the world by the power of his Spirit to create a new Israel in Christ (see Rom 8:11). This letter focuses on God's activity first on the church (1:3-5, 13-21), then on Christ (2:20-24). After all, pagans were converted from their many gods to the one true Christian God (see 1 Thess 1:9-10), and this is surely stressed even in 1 Peter where God is judge (1:17) and midwife (1:23). The "obedience" to Christ is the obedience of faith, the taking of a new Lord whose rule is so much better than service to old pagan gods which led to decadent morality (see Rom 1:22-32). The call to obedience (1:14, 22) is a call to holiness and responsibility, which will be treated in detail later in the long list of household duties (chs. 2–4). The letter greeting, therefore, sounds the two dominant themes of the letter when it identifies the awkward situation of the pagan converts and the grace of God calling them to a new and consecrated life.

1:3-5 Thanksgiving. Typical of ancient letters, a thanksgiving prayer follows the greeting. This one is unusual for it praises God rather than "thanks" God, which may indicate a more Jewish form of greeting (see 2 Cor 1:3; Eph 1:3). Typical New Testament thanksgivings tend to serve as a summary of the main themes of the letter, which seems to be the case here: (1) God gave us a *new birth* (see 1:22–2:3), (2) this birth leads to a *hope* (1:8, 21; 3:15), (3) which is based on Jesus' *resurrection* from the dead (3:18–4:6), and (4) Christians have a heavenly *inheritance* which is incapable of fading (1:7-8). Our new birth is through faith in the gospel (3:18-22). New birth and faith correspond to the conversion experience of this group; the future hope and inheritance to be revealed at the last day surely urge perseverance in one's conversion.

1:6-12 Grace and yet suffering. The letter immediately addresses a real issue for this church. How great and exhilarating was their conversion, but how odd and incomprehensible are the difficulties and suffering which accompany it. The author often speaks of the dislocation that conversion has caused in the lives of these pagan converts (2:12; 4:4, 16), which might call in question the value of the new faith. So repeated attention is given to this theme, at least to show that it is appreciated and what it might mean. The best possible interpretation is given in 1:6-9: the new faith is more precious than gold, but like gold it is put in a furnace and proven true only after much testing. This view attempts to make sense of their experience and to evoke sentiments of perseverance and hope. Like Christ's suffering, their conversion dislocation leads to glory (1:11).

Another way of shoring up the new faith is to stress its antiquity and uniqueness. No, Christian faith in God and Christ is not a recent invention, a fad. It is found in the Old Testament where prophets foretold its unfolding; hence, it is an ancient faith whose antiquity gives great respectability to it in the eyes of the pagans. But it is also new and precious, for those prophets did not know the riches which the converts now know, nor were the angels in the know either. How wonderful, then, that the converts possess this knowledge of God and Christ. Christian faith, then, is more precious than gold, ancient, and specially revealed—all of which support the value of the new convert's faith.

1:13–2:3 Response of faith. But it is not enough simply to have converted; so great a faith requires a special response. So converts are urged to live a life worthy of their faith: "Live soberly . . . like obedient children, do not act in compliance with desires . . ." (1:13-14). Ideally they are to be like God, holy as "I am holy" (1:16). This passage also reminds the converts that as great as was their conversion, they must persevere; so "set your hopes completely on the grace to be brought to you at the revelation of Jesus Christ" (v. 13). And the gracious God whose foreknowledge chose them will judge them impartially (v. 17). Hence, their conversion faith must be supplemented by hope in God who will raise the dead and judge them.

Delivered by God from the futile ways of their ancestors, they are expected to be out of step with their former pagan culture; so they are exhorted: "Conduct yourselves with reverence during the time of your sojourning" (v. 17). Purchased by the priceless blood of Christ, they are to live like that, spotless and unblemished. In this way the author acknowledges their experience and pastorally addresses them with a word of encouragement, reminding them of their grace-filled past, and with a word of exhortation, calling them to responsibility.

Several postscripts are added to this long celebration of their new faith. By conversion, they may have suffered the loss of kin and clan (see Mark 10:29-30), for they seem alienated from their former culture and are now sojourners and exiles among their former neighbors. But Christians gain a new family by their conversion, new brothers and sisters (v. 22), and the church becomes a new family in which genuine love is shown (see 3:8-9). And so their conversion is celebrated as a new birth into a new family, and it entails a new way of living. Finally, the author touches on a sensitive point: If Christianity is so new, might it be just a fad? Might God be fickle? Is this for real? Most emphatically the converts are told that their rebirth comes from an imperishable seed, that is, through God's word which is living and trustworthy. To support that encouraging idea, the author cites Isa 40:6-8, which contrasts human frailty and mortality with the word of the Lord which "endures *forever*." Hence, their faith, as ancient as the prophets, will endure forever, for God is forever faithful.

2:4-10 Christ and church: Precious to God. This passage is very rich with Old Testament texts which bear on our confession of Jesus and our knowledge of the church. The key to these riches is to remember that this is the last and most glorious reflection on the church, which is meant to serve as a foundation stone for the exhortation which follows. So, all the rich images here serve two purposes: they tell the story of a holy church and conclude to a holy way of life worthy of that identity. The passage is structured around two Old Testament images, "stone" and "people," both of which are interpreted in terms of the church. "Stone" is the catchword common to verses 6-8; those verses, moreover, speak about Jesus, "the stone": he is "the stone" which God laid in Zion, a cornerstone, chosen and precious (see Isa 28:16); he is "the stone" rejected by some but important to God (see Ps 118:22); finally, he is "the stone" which is an obstacle and scandal to some (see Isa 8:14). This Christ-stone is the pattern for the church; like Jesus, we are chosen and precious to God; we are also rejected by pagans and unbelievers. But as Christ is the cornerstone, so we are being made into a household, a holy body of priests. Hence the stone image does two things: it first explains our situation in the world, how we share the pattern of Christ (suffering/election) and then how we join Christ in becoming a new and holy dwelling place of the holy God.

"People" is the catchword linking verses 9-10. The church is a "people of his own," and so it is a chosen race, a royal dwelling place, a holy nation (see Exod 19:3-6); the church has gone from being "not my people" to being "my people," from "not having received mercy" to "having received mercy" (see Hos 1:6, 9; 2:1). Both the "stone" and "people" images speak, then, of our election by God and of our holiness. And they point to what this means in our lives: as a household of priests we offer "spiritual sacrifices," that is, a holy way of life characterized by faithfulness and obedience (2:5). And as a holy nation we tell the story of the holy God and his saving deeds (2:9). So our "priesthood" is a way of being called to a holy status before a holy God and an exhortation to do holy things like acting holy and speaking about the holy God. These images, then, do not reject formal worship in the church, nor do they argue against liturgical leadership for this group; their sole purpose is to tell the church of its exalted status as "chosen" and "holy."

2:11-12 The Christian way of life. These verses begin the extended exhortation to the various constituencies of this church. As general as these initial remarks are, they are thematic. Christians have left paganism and its vices, so they are spiritual exiles and strangers (v. 11; see 1:1). Hardship will surely follow conversion, for pagans will view Christians with uneasiness, even hostility. Because they are truly different in so many ways, Christians will be perceived as troublemakers (v. 12). So the best apology for this suspicion and hostility is a blameless life which will convince the neighbors of the church of its rightness and so lead to praise of God.

2:13-17 General civic duties. The list of community duties begins with a general exhortation to all Christians to be good citizens, which advice is made concrete in the exhortation to respect civil government. Emperor, governors, and officials of the city, state, and empire legitimately command Christian obedience (vv. 13-14). This advice makes concrete the statement in verse 12 that an obedient Christian life is the best apology for hostility to the church (v. 15). Christians by baptism are made free in Christ; among Christians there is no slave or free, no Jew or Gentile (Gal 3:27); nevertheless, Christian freedom is hardly lawlessness or opposition to responsible living in society. So, Christians are encouraged to have a positive attitude toward society, i.e., love of the brethren as well as respect for the emperor (v. 17). Even if strangers in exile, Christians are called to responsible civic life.

2:18-25 Christian advice to slaves. The specific constituencies of the community begin to be addressed here, the first being Christians who are slaves. There is a typical form of exhortation in Christian moral teaching called a code of household duties, which addresses the mutual responsibilities of husband/wife, master/slave, and parent/child (see Col 3:18–4:1 and Eph 5:21–6:9). This standard form is evidently being used here, but in an adapted way. Carrying Christian civil responsibility one step further (2:13-17), slaves are called to obey masters "with all reverence" (v. 18). The focus of this exhortation differs from typical advice to slaves, for here the difficult plight of the slaves is fully recognized and their suffering is the center of the exhortation. Suffering, especially for those of the slave class, is a bitter fact of life, but the letter attempts to interpret that experience in the light of the Christian kerygma about Jesus: he too suffered, albeit unjustly. Slaves, like all Christians, are called to moral excellence, and thus Christians will eliminate suffering from their lives as a just retribution for irresponsible behavior. And so slaves will come to be more like Christ, whose example is presented through the reference to Isaiah's Suffering Servant in verses 21-24 (Isa 53:1-12). Christ was truly innocent, no deceit was found in his mouth; and when he suffered, he did not counter with threats. So Christian slaves are called to imitate Christ, living out the pattern of their baptismal likeness to Christ in a special way. And it is implied that as Christ by suffering won healing for us, the slaves by their honest suffering might also win converts to Christ or at least end hostility (see 2:12, 15). Oddly, this part of the code of household duties addresses only the faithfulness of slaves and strangely omits any mention of the duties of masters.

3:1-7 Advice to husbands and wives. The bulk of the advice is to wives, especially wives of pagan husbands, and their excellent behavior is seen as a strong missionary ploy (3:1). Hence, Christian wives are called to be different from pagan wives in not being fashion-crazy; they are to shun the extravagant ornamentation, clothing, and hair-styling which seemed to be the passion of that day. Their beauty is in the purity of their "chaste behavior" (v. 2), an interior beauty of the heart and a gentle disposition (v. 4). Typical also of household codes is the repeated exhortation to wives to be obedient to their husbands (3:1, 5-6). This obedience is probably to be understood as part of the Christian apology that church members are not lawless citizens, destructive of their cultures in their claims to freedom in Christ. Probably 1 Cor 7:12-16 reflects a comparable fear that some new Christians are abandoning former marriages and corrupting the social fabric under the guise of the new freedom they have gained in Christ.

The duties of the husbands reflect the cultural bias of their time, for they are to recognize woman as the weaker sex; yet the Christian note of equality in Christ is also struck: they are "joint heirs of the gift of life" (v. 7), an idea commonly tied to the understanding of baptism ("in Christ there is no male or female"; see Gal 3:28). This advice would seem to have a definite propaganda bias: such good behavior will put an end to suspicion and hostility about Christians being free and irresponsible vis-à-vis civic institutions.

3:8-12 General advice to the whole church. Where typical codes of household duties next treat the reciprocal duties of parents and children, this letter departs from the tradition and gives advice to the whole church. The community is called to a great ideal: not friction but rather sympathy and love for one another (v. 8). Especially are they called to bear up well under suspicion and hostility from their neighbors. They are to bear insults and evils, and to give blessing in return (v. 9; see Matt 5:38-48; Rom 12:14-21). Moreover, Christians are once again called to an excellence befitting their Christian call (vv. 10-11). As the psalmist says: "Keep your tongue from evil and your lips from speaking guile; turn from evil and do good; seek peace . . ." (Ps 34:14-15).

3:13-27 Christian realism: Election yet suffering. The difficulties which beset Christian converts are pastorally dealt with once more. By living exemplary lives, Christians will not be persecuted for doing what is wrong. But even virtue has its costly price, hence this intensified exhortation on how to interpret suffering and how to see it in the light of one's baptismal conversion.

Christians will evidently be the focus of public controversy, but that is no cause for fear (v. 14). When questioned or accused, Christians should readily witness to the truth and proclaim their faith (see Mark 13:9-11; Matt 10:16-21). But the best witness is an honest life which refutes defamation and libel by its evident goodness (v. 16; see 2:12; 3:2). The sufferings of converts are real, but the author repeatedly calls Christians to suffer for their good deeds, like Jesus (v. 17; see 2:19-23), and not for their sins.

3:18-22 The example of Jesus. The warrant for the advice to suffer nobly has been the example of Jesus, known through the church's preaching and ritualized in the baptismal catechesis of the converts. At this point in the letter, the author appeals to another source of the Jesus tradition to ground the exhortation, in this case a creedal formula, a confession which is quite similar to that in 1 Tim 3:16:

1 Pet 3:18, 22

put to death in the flesh
made alive in the Spirit
to the spirits in prison he preached
at the right hand of God
having gone to heaven
angels, authorities and powers subject to him

1 Tim 3:16

manifested in the flesh
vindicated in the Spirit
seen by angels
preached among the nations
believed on in the world
taken up in glory

The pastoral use of this confession of baptismal faith goes in several directions: (1) Christ's death (v. 18) is life-producing, just as Christian suffering can be. (2) Baptism, which is our spiritual coming to life, is our way of ritually participating in Jesus' death. (3) As Christ died in the flesh and was made alive in the spirit, so converts likewise put off fleshly sins in baptism and live irreproachable lives through Jesus' resurrection (v. 21). So 1 Peter is emphasizing the baptismal situation of these new converts, reminding them of the gift of liberation which baptism was to the few—to Noah and his seven companions and to the few Christians as well. Baptism, likewise, is a sharing in Jesus' paschal mystery: we share his new life, but we share also his suffering. So Christians are reminded of the roots of their moral newness of life in Christ's passover through the catechesis of their baptism.

4:1-6 Conversion and alienation. A further appeal is made to Christ's paschal transition, once more to his suffering. "Christ suffered in the flesh." This is literally applied to converts who, because of conversion to Christianity, will suffer after baptism. But this suffering is proof that converts have in fact "broken with sin" (v. 1). There can be no thought of lapsing from Christian holiness back into vice; enough time was spent on vice in former pagan lives; Christianity means a death to that old way, a radical break with the past. But such a break brings down suspicion and hostility (v. 4) from former comrades who do not understand the excellence of the new religion. Christians have passed through judgment into life by baptism; not so their pagan comrades who will be judged according to their deeds (v. 5; see 1:17). Christians once were dead in their sinful flesh, but through baptism they are made alive in the Spirit, like Jesus (v. 6; see 3:18). Converts, we are reminded, have radically broken with the past and are conformed in baptism to Jesus, dead in the flesh, alive in the Spirit.

4:7-11 More general advice. The code of household duties is evident again in this general community exhortation. God's judgment was mentioned in 4:5 and now becomes the background to this part of the letter ("the end of all things is at hand," v. 7). Living in the final age of God's grace, Christians are called to display distinctive virtues: constant love (v. 8), hospitality, and generosity, especially to those who suffer economic hardship because of conversion (vv. 9-10). Christian duties within the church are singled out for special emphasis: speakers in the assembly and servers of the group are exhorted to fidelity and generous service (v. 11; see 5:1-7).

4:12-19 Our trials and Christian future. Ever the realist, the author returns to the theme of suffering and the difficulties which befall the convert. Faith, baptism, and conversion do not mean that Christians are somehow "out of this world," immune to flesh, suffering, and sin. So it is necessary to identify and interpret correctly the disturbing areas of Christian life. Suffering is unfortunately a fact of life. But what does it mean? Verse 12 speaks of a general trial of the church which the author interprets as a test, much like the testing of gold in a furnace (see 1:6-7). Gold will survive! Hope-filled optimism is part of Christian faith; so we can rejoice in the measure in which we share in Christ's sufferings. Happy are we, for as Christ was made alive in the spirit by God's Spirit (Rom 1:4), we who are conformed to Christ are given the same gift of Spirit. But as we were told earlier and often, Christian suffering must be in innocence, not as a just punishment for an immoral life (v. 15). The tone of the exhortation shifts in verse 17. Optimism is tempered; because the church is the elite, the testing of God will begin with it. And how difficult it will be for the church to survive. This somber note serves to underscore the importance of fidelity to baptismal ideals. But we are reminded here of how our lives are totally caught up in God's providence: our suffering is mysteriously part of God's will and we should, like Jesus, totally entrust our lives to our faithful God (v. 19; see Luke 23:46).

5:1-5 Advice to church leaders. The code of household duties now explicitly extends to the mutual duties of leaders and members of the church. The elders of the church are addressed first, and their dealings with the church are clarified: their ministry should be done with eager service; their motives should be noble, not mercenary; their exercise of leadership should be supportive, not authoritarian. In this typical advice 1 Peter reflects the common tradition in the New Testament about the quality of leadership, which is prized in the church: the Gospels give us Jesus' advice to be servants of one another (Mark 10:42-45); the duties of a bishop in 1 Tim 3:3 warn against avarice as a motive for ministry; Eph 4:11-16 likewise instructs us that leaders are indeed called to special tasks, but ones which do not negate Christian equality in baptism. Evidently the early church was sensitive to the shambles which authoritarian leadership could make of its baptismal catechesis of the freedom, dignity, and equality of all Christians (Gal 3:28). Leadership was and is no easy charge in the church, and so special mention is made of the concerns of the chief shepherd for his flock. Faithful service will be recognized by a special recognition (v. 4; see 2 Tim 4:1; Matt 19:28 and 24:45-47).

Church rank and file are alternately reminded to have respect for the tasks and authority of their shepherds (v. 6), otherwise their ministry of leadership would be impossible. Although we are all free and equal in Christ, it behooves us to show how as a free people we serve God in orderly and responsible lives (see Rom 6:16-18). Thus our freedom leads us to humility and to close bonds with the church. The call to obedience and humility echoes the tradition of Jesus' words to would-be masters in Matt 23:12. This appeal to order and obedience should be seen in conjunction with advice given throughout the letter: how Christians are to be good citizens of the state, good members of family households, and responsible members of the Christian church. A certain propaganda appeal is made in this exhortation to upright and orderly living, implying that Christians make very good and unselfish members of every part of society.

5:6-11 Faith in God. As the letter draws to a close, the church is called once more to faith, this time to know their God more clearly. Unlike impotent pagan gods, the God of Jesus is truly powerful and genuinely faithful. We remember the great emphasis put on the right knowledge of God in this letter: in chapters 1–2 we were reminded of God's free and generous call, even of pagans; God's exaltation and vindication of Jesus was stressed in chapter 3. Now the letter emphasizes how we are to place our total trust in God; we do this safely because God "cares for you" (v. 7). No adversary can withstand our God—not sin, nor death, nor Satan (vv. 8-9). The "God of all grace" wants us to be happy and he will vindicate us from suffering, just as he raised up his son, Jesus (v. 10). Our God is loving, powerful, trustworthy, and faithful. And to him we give dominion forever and ever (v. 11).

5:12-14 Letter closing. The author indicates that he is using a secretary to write this letter, an important point for our understanding of early Christian literature. It does *not* mean that the author is illiterate. It was typically the task of educated slaves to act as secretaries, for they were trained in formal correspondence, which fact accounts for the good Greek style of the letter. See Paul's use of secretaries in 1 Cor 16:21 and Gal 6:11. Typical of Christian letters, we find a formal greeting at the end of the letter: the churches of the East are greeted by the church of the West (Rome; see "Babylon," v. 13). East-West, Jew-Gentile—all people are freely and equally chosen by God. "Mark" also sends greetings, a figure often said to be Mark the evangelist, who was reputed to have edited Peter's recollections of Jesus. But "Mark" is such a common name, and this link between Peter and Mark's Gospel is very doubtful. Despite the great social diversity of the early church, it functioned as a close family, for members greeted one another with the sign of intimacy, the holy kiss (v. 14), a gesture common in the ancient churches (see Rom 16:16; 1 Cor 16:20; 2 Cor 13:12).

2 PETER

Jerome H. Neyrey, S.J.

INTRODUCTION

Author

Despite the claims of the letter (1:1, 12-15; 3:1), modern scholarship considers 2 Peter a pseudonymous letter, not written by Peter but attributed to him. The evidence for this judgment includes the following: (1) 2 Peter virtually incorporates the letter of Jude, which casts doubts on the authenticity of 2 Peter itself. (2) It alludes to several of Paul's letters, which further argues for its lateness, since these were scarcely known that early nor collected until the end of the first century. The appeal to Peter, then, reflects the growing tradition in the early church of ascribing theological as well as missionary and administrative leadership to Peter.

Topics

The figure of Peter is important as a spokesman for the traditions which the letter defends. Opponents are attacking the parousia (Jesus' return to judge), prophecy of the parousia, and theodicy (God's providence to reward and punish)—all traditional topics which need support from people who had firsthand experience of Jesus and his words. The author's testimony is intended to ground these issues at a much later time. Probably 2 Peter was written about the year 100, long after the deaths of Peter and Paul. It looks back on the church's early days from a much later time (see 3:1-2) and is concerned with orthodoxy in the church.

Church

The church of 2 Peter reflects a mixture of Jewish-Christian and pagan converts; all of the biblical examples cited in chapters 2–3 have close parallels in pagan literature as well as in the Bible. For example, Noah's flood is mirrored in the pagan accounts of Deucalion; the fall of the heavenly angels (Gen 6) is reflected in the casting of the Titans into Tartarus (2:4). This pastoral concern to make the traditions of eschatology equally understandable to Jew and Gentile alike suggests an urban church setting, of mixed ethnic and religious backgrounds, in dialogue with the surrounding pagan culture and very reflective of the church's long heritage. This letter is unusual in the number of biblical authors it acknowledges: it claims to know 1 Peter (3:1-2), gospel traditions about the transfiguration (1:16) and the parousia, some of Paul's letters (3:15-16), Jude's letter, as well as an extensive knowledge of biblical traditions. We would say that the author is a sophisticated churchman who argues against heresy in ways which reflect the best of Jewish-Christian and pagan culture.

COMMENTARY

1:1-2 Letter opening. Like typical New Testament letters, 2 Peter opens with a greeting: (1) The sender is Symeon Peter. (2) The addressees are "those who have received a faith of equal value to ours" (oddly, no place designation is given). (3) To the typical wish ("grace and peace") is added here the desire for correct acknowledgment of God and Jesus, the Lord, which is probably a clue about the central problem of the letter, the denial of God's judgment. So the letter is addressed to orthodox Christians who have a correct confession of God. When Peter calls himself "slave," he is echoing a common title in Jewish and Christian literature for designating an official person (see "Moses, the slave of the Lord," Deut 34:5; and "James, a slave of God and of the Lord," Jas 1:1).

1:3-4 Main theme introduced. At this point letters typically have a thanksgiving prayer, which is absent here. Substituting for this is the statement about God's power which providentially bestows life and piety on the church through the correct acknowledgment of God. Moreover, God has given the church great and precious promises, promises which 2 Peter will defend against heretics and scoffers, promises about the parousia (3:3-4), a new creation (3:10-12), and even a share in God's own nature to those who flee the corruption of this world (1:4). The correct acknowledgment of God and God's promises, then, is the focus of the letter. The hopeful promise is fulfilled by Christians who act in accord with it: they see the moral implications of the prospect of a future with God and so act honorably on earth in accord with that future, thus showing the close link between doctrine and life.

1:5-11 Religion and life. We find here a typical list of virtues (see Rom 5:1-5) which illustrates the goodness of the promises by showing how this correct doctrine leads to correct moral life. But whoever disregards this teaching on God and God's promises is blind and myopic (v. 9). In contrast, Christians will hasten to confirm their vocations by proper thought and behavior and so richly secure their entrance into Christ's kingdom. The dominant theme of 1:1-11, then, stresses three points: (1) There *is* a future, (2) which is the everlasting kingdom of Christ, our Savior and Lord, (3) where the ultimate promise is a share in God's own nature. God's promises, power, and providence are the key topics which are being attacked by heretics but which are likewise vigorously defended by 2 Peter.

1:12-15 Last will and testament. Peter tells us of a revelation from Jesus that he would die soon (see John 21:18-19), which prompts him to give us his last will and testament. There is a common tradition in biblical literature that patriarchs and leaders on the occasion of their death gave special teaching and even prophecies of the future to their disciples, a convention found in John 13–17 and Acts 20. Our author uses this convention to give us the definitive word about the church's eschatological tradition. He consciously intends to set down for all time the authentic memory of the promises and prophecies which he alluded to earlier (see 1:4, 11). But before he can do this, he needs to attend to a pressing problem—his reliability to give authentic heavenly teaching.

1:16-21 Defense of the parousia prophecy. This is the first explicit mention of problems in this church. Heretics are maligning the traditional teachings about Jesus' parousia by claiming that these teachings are not heavenly revelations but only human concoctions, made up to control naive Christians. In reply, 2 Peter denies this charge and cites his eyewitness experience of Jesus' transfiguration as an event which foreshadowed the parousia. Jesus' honor and glory, then, were prophetic of his status when he would return in glory to judge the living and the dead. The author did not make up the transfiguration event, nor does he pass on secondhand material, for he was an eyewitness there: he heard God's voice (1:17-18). Hence, the future coming of Jesus at the parousia (which the transfiguration foreshadows) is grounded on God's own word.

The appeal to the transfiguration, then, serves several apologetic purposes in response to the slander in 1:16: (1) The parousia prophecy is *not* humanly concocted, for it has God as its author, and (2) Peter has firsthand experience of it, and so the tradition about the parousia is not a rumor or an unverified event. In verse 19 the author can then claim that the "prophetic message" about the parousia has a very firm foundation, which phrase refers to the transfiguration-as-parousia prophecy in 1:16-18. Such an authentic prophecy is a lamp shining in Christian hearts until Christ, the daystar, dawns and the fulfillment of the prophecy is wonderfully realized. But even 2 Peter's interpretation of the transfiguration is open to dispute by the heretics. They argue that his interpretation is farfetched and fantastic—a point he denies in 1:20. He argues that just as humans do not originate prophecies on their own (see 1:16), so they do not interpret prophecy on their own, in esoteric ways. *God* gives prophecy to prophets (see God's voice at the transfiguration in verses 17-18); and *God's* Spirit inspires correct interpretation of those prophecies as well.

Peter, we will recall, is often cited in the New Testament as a recipient of special revelations (Matt 16:17; 17:26-27; 28:16-20) and special prophecies (Mark 13:1-3; 14:27-31; John 21:18-19). So at the end of chapter 1, Peter has laid the foundation for his defense of the eschatological tradition of the church. He defends the prophecy of the parousia in its formal aspect as prophecy: God is its author, not Peter; he is its authentic recipient and he is its inspired interpreter. Now that the groundwork of Peter's knowledge of the parousia is laid, he can get on with his plan in 1:12-15 to leave a solid and lasting exposition of the eschatological tradition.

2:1-3 Exposure of the false teachers. Whereas Peter claimed to write this letter on the eve of his death (1:12-15), that was only a literary convention, a convenient occasion to stress the importance of the topic at hand and to lay out the truth of the matter. The real occasion of 2 Peter is the presence of heretics and scoffers in the church. We saw earlier that they rejected the parousia prophecy as a human concoction (1:16), and they will further scoff at the parousia in 3:3-4, 9. In 2:1 they come in for criticism as false teachers. They are compared with the "false prophets" of the Old Testament, who were called false precisely because they preached peace and security when God's prophets preached judgment and imminent ruin (see Jer 4:10; 5:12; 6:14; 14:13-14). This is an important clue, for by comparing his own false teachers with false prophets, Peter alerts us to their opposition to God's judgmental action on the world, especially as this is developed in the church's eschatological traditions about the parousia. When he claims that they deny the Master (2:1), this means that they are practical atheists—they do not deny that there is a God, but they deny that God notices or cares about us: *God does not judge us.* The psalms often tell us about sinners who say "there is no God" (see Pss 10:11, 13; 14:1, 73:11) and because they fear no judgment, they live sinful lives. So the opponents of 2 Peter are false prophets who deny the Lord's judgment. But like the false prophets, they will meet ruin, for God's judgment does not sleep *nor* is it idle (2:3).

2:4-9 Proof of God's judgment. To prove that God acts with judgment on the world, the author cites three examples. While this material is borrowed from Jude 5-7, 2 Peter has changed the examples to tell a new message:

Jude 5-7

desert generation
angels
Sodom and Gomorrah

2 Peter 2:4-8

angels
Noah
Lot and Sodom and Gomorrah

Whereas in the examples of the desert generation and the holy angels Jude warned of the danger of lapsing from faith and salvation into destruction, 2 Peter argues more simply that God knows how to rescue the devout and to guard the wicked in punishment (2:9). 2 Peter rearranged Jude's list (substituting Noah for the desert generation); his list is more clearly following the events of Genesis. The reason for these changes is the purpose of 2 Peter to support the fact of God's judgment (rescue of the godly, ruin for sinners); the changes also stress how God has already acted on the world by water and by fire, a point he will return to in 3:7. And the focus is clearly theological, for as 2:4, 9 state, God does act in judgment! And so he answers the false prophets who "deny the Master," proving that our sacred traditions prove that God acts in the world, with judgment and power. The heretics are surely wrong.

2:10-16 Immoral consequences of wrong doctrine. After this theoretical argument in support of God's judgment, the author begins to point out other disturbing aspects of the scoffers, again showing how bad doctrine leads to bad morality. He warns that God especially judges those who are at home in a corrupt world, who live lustful lives and who show contempt for lordship (especially God's). In 2:10-11 the author points out that the scoffers even deny that God's angels participate in the judgment of the world, which is contrary to the tradition of the early church (see Matt 13:41-42). Their rejection of judgment is total—neither God, nor Jesus, nor even the angels exercise judgment.

Such heretics are like brute animals, born for capture and destruction; what they do not understand they scoff at (see 3:3-4). But these denials bring ruin (2:12); and they will receive an appropriate reward for their wickedness (2:13). It is typical of aggressive writers to see opponents in the worst possible light, envisioning the ultimate consequences of their errors (see Rom 1:29-31); 2 Peter sees the heresy of the scoffers as leading to sexual depravity (2:13-14), a typical polemical charge against heretics. Another typical vice credited to heretics is greed (1 Tim 6:5; Titus 1:11), of which 2 Peter accuses his opponents in 2:3, 14.

Borrowing the example of Balaam from Jude 11, this author finds in Balaam not only an example of greed repaid but, more to his point, an example of a false prophet who wandered away from the way of truth, who was rebuked by his donkey, and who ultimately received a terrible recompense for his wickedness in a violent death. Balaam, then, is another example of a wicked person who met judgment, and so he stands as a rebuke to the heretics who by denying judgment bring ruin on themselves.

2:17-22 From grace to slavery. Borrowing again from Jude 12, 2 Peter charges his opponents with being empty and directionless like waterless springs and mists whipped by the wind. Worse than that, they corrupt new Christians, leading them right back to the immorality from which they fled at conversion. As in 2:10, 13-14, the charge of sexual immorality is probably a stock accusation against heretics, showing the ultimate depravity to which false teaching inevitably leads. Just as the scoffers mock Christians about unfulfilled prophecies of the parousia (3:3-4), the author accuses them of unfulfilled promises: They promise them freedom, not only from restricting laws (1 Cor 6:12; 10:23); but especially from fear and judgment. Hence, the heretics are accused of denying the Lord (2:1), i.e., denying divine judgment as well as the moral laws of the group. Their promise of freedom from judgment ironically leads to slavery, just as their denial of punishment leads to swift ruin. Far from liberating their converts, the heretics lead them to a worse state than their previous paganism, for now they know the truth about God but spurn it for false doctrine. The author compares them to a sow, after being washed, returning to wallow in mire, and to a dog going back to its vomit (2:21-22).

All of chapter 2, therefore, is a polemical portrait of 2 Peter's opponents: (1) He accuses them of teaching evil practices and charges them with traditional vices; (2) their doctrine is evil; (3) they are mercenary; (4) they corrupt God's church. Their doctrine is wrong in itself and in its effects, for it leads to immorality and ruin. The author has said the worst he could about them. The fact that so much of chapter 2 is borrowed directly from Jude's letter and that so many of the charges against the heretics are standard polemical materials suggests that 2 Pet 2 is not a vivid historical portrait of these opponents. Rather, it is a stereotypical attack on the enemy, using easily recognizable and traditional accusations to point up the error of the false doctrine. What is distinctive, however, about chapter 2 is the careful identification of the false teaching: the denial of judgment, the rejection of all judgmental agents, even angels, and the freedom from fear and punishment.

3:1-2 Foundations of the doctrine of judgment. The author begins the main part of his letter by linking this work to a previous letter, presumably 1 Peter. As he said in 1:12-15, his task is to remind the community and to give them the correct interpretation of the tradition. (Perhaps *eilikrinē dianoian* in 3:1 might better be translated as "correct interpretation" than as "sincere disposition.") The tradition he is interpreting is nothing less than the teaching of the holy prophets and of Jesus. In 1:16 his opponents accused Peter of fabricating the prophecies of the parousia; but as he did there, he also insists here that the source of his teaching is God's and Christ's word. *His* teaching is authentic! His constant "reminding" the church of the truth (3:1-2 and

1:12-15) is in stark contrast to the willful forgetting of the same by the opponents (see 3:5, 8).

3:3-7 Opponents scoff at the tradition. When the author alerted us to his impending death in 1:12-15, he invoked the last-will-and-testament convention, a typical element of which is the prediction of future false teachers. The future heretics (3:3) will scoff at the church's traditions about the parousia: "Where is the promise of his coming?" (3:4). When biblical texts cite questions which begin with "Where is . . .?" they imply ridicule and skepticism on the part of the questioner (see Judg 6:13; 2 Kgs 18:34; Isa 36:19); hence, these scoffers are calling into question the truth of the parousia prophecies. The ground for their skepticism is the apparent permanence of the world; from time immemorial the world has remained and so it will always be. But this argument implies several things: (1) The scoffers doubt that God has ever been actively involved in the world, so why should God suddenly become active? (2) The concern about the parousia here is narrowly focused on cosmology, the destruction-renewal of the world. For the time being the questioning of God's judgment is put aside and the brunt of the attack is on the predictions of the end of the world (see Mark 13:24-25).

The author's response to this scoffing meets the criticism head-on in support of (1) God's *constant* activity in the world, (2) the *reliability* of God's word/predictions, and (3) the *judgment* of God which awaits the wicked. Inasmuch as the author's task is "reminding," he accuses his opponents of willfully forgetting ("they deliberately ignore," 3:5) their biblical history. By God's word the heavens and earth were fashioned out of water (v. 5), by God's word the world was judged and destroyed by water (v. 6), and by God's word the heavens and earth are reserved for fire and judgment (v. 7). This response parallels the argument in 2:4-6 where we were told of Noah and Lot, whose worlds were destroyed by water and fire respectively; those stories proved that God knows how to rescue and requite (2:9). So in 3:5-7, God's judgmental activity in the world is defended and the reliability of his word is assured, even the promises of the parousia. The scoffers are wrong, then, when they question God's prophetic word about divine involvement in the world and about the parousia. Biblical history is proof against their objections.

3:8-14 Defense of God's delay in judging. The author continues his defense of the parousia traditions here. For a second time he accuses the scoffers of willfully overlooking biblical truths (v. 8); so, apropos of the delay of Christ's coming, he reminds them of the scriptural saying that one day with the Lord is like a thousand years (Ps 90:4). Since God's timetable is mysterious to us and virtually incalculable, the scoffers are erroneous in harping on the delay of the parousia. It was common knowledge that God told Adam that "the moment you eat from it [this fruit] you are surely doomed to die" (Gen 2:17), but still Adam lived on for many hundreds of years after his sin; this "delay" was interpreted as a gift of grace to Adam to allow time for repentance before judgment. In 3:9, when the heretics accuse God of being slow about his promise, they imply that slowness to them is evidence that God has no intention of judging. According to them, God has never acted previously to judge the world, and every day is further proof that God will not. This fact of delay is disturbing, to be sure. But the author treats it positively in a traditional fashion as a sign of God's forbearance in giving sinners time to repent before judgment comes (see Rom 2:4-5).

The author draws out the moral implications of the doctrine he has defended. Since God will judge the world at the end of the age, we should live godly lives of holiness (3:11) and be found without spot or blemish (3:14; see 2:13). Our goodness is the logical consequence of our correct theology. This world is corrupt and passing away; so believers are invited to a pure future life, even a sharing in God's nature (see 1:4). Those who accept God's promises of the parousia live accordingly and so flee immorality and prepare for the end of this age. Their destiny is a new heaven and a new earth where righteousness resides. Not so the heretics; they think that this world is all and everything. They are at home in this world's corruption and expect nothing further from God. Making no preparation for the future, they are headed for genuine and permanent ruin.

3:15-18 Even Paul agrees with Peter. When the author appeals to Paul, he shows acquaintance with some of Paul's letters, which for him are inspired. Paul's teaching on God's universal judgment is found in Rom 2 and 14:10-12. The delay of judgment as a gift of time for repentance is found in Rom 2:4-5, and the depiction of Jesus' coming as a thief in the night is treated in 1 Thess 5:1-7. Paul was divinely inspired in these teachings (3:15) just as the present author claims to be (see 1:12-15, 16-21). So the teaching is authentic, even if it is hard to understand. Implicit in this is an appeal to the church to accept the normative teaching on the parousia as genuinely "traditional" in the sense that God is the ultimate source and Christian teachers like Peter and Paul are divinely authorized to teach it; thus it was always taught everywhere in the church. Let the scoffers realize how out of step they are with God's Scripture and God's authorized tradition.

As ancient letters do, this one ends with a typical letter closing (3:18). There is a special note in this closing, however, which seems to sum up the letter: the author wishes the church to grow "in the knowledge of our Lord and savior," and the insistence on "knowledge" echoes the wish he made at the letter's beginning for the same (1:2). This suggests how dominant in the letter is the concern for true teaching and orthodox knowledge of Jesus, especially in regard to Christ's parousia and the eschatological tradition of the church.

JUDE

Jerome H. Neyrey, S.J.

INTRODUCTION

Author

The stated author is "Jude . . . brother of James." It is probably not the case that Jude is the same figure as the Apostle Jude/Thaddeus (Mark 3:18; Luke 6:16; Acts 1:13). He claims blood ties with James, who was himself "the brother of the Lord" (Gal 1:19) and leader of the Jerusalem church (Acts 15:13-21). Such ties, if authentic, would serve as excellent credentials, placing Jude in the mainstream of early Christian orthodoxy. But modern scholarship is critical of this for several reasons: (1) the seemingly late date of the letter (e.g., verse 17 speaks of "the apostles of our Lord" as figures of the distant past); (2) the sense of "the faith, delivered once for all" as representative of thinking in the late first century; (3) the typical convention of validating later orthodox teaching by linking it with known earlier authorities. For internal reasons, the letter of Jude is judged to come from the late first century and is pseudonymously attributed to Jude.

Occasion and contents

The church addressed is disturbed by conflicting teachings, and appeal is made for fidelity to "the faith, delivered once for all," which is somehow under attack by members of the church. The nature of the doctrinal disagreement is extremely difficult to describe, for there are no firm clues, only hints and suspicions recorded. The very silence about the heretics is itself typical of anti-heretical literature, where the author avoids giving more free publicity to the errors under attack by not mentioning them further. The charges of moral libertinism are not so much descriptions of the heretics' actual positions but the author's interpretation of the direction in which their errors will lead. What we are certain of is a wrenching internal conflict, as much over the leadership of the church as over traditional issues.

Unusual features

Jude quotes several ancient writings which were not admitted to the Christian canon: 1 Enoch in verses 14-15 and the Assumption of Moses in verse 9. He surely saw great value in citing them as authoritative arguments on his side and that may be the point: they do reinforce and echo traditional statements about God's judgment and Christ's coming. The use of these unusual writings may indicate the scope of the theological discussion in this church when the group is sifting out the main points of its faith, "delivered once for all," and the foundations of that faith. Use of these unusual writings, as well as extensive use of the Old Testament and popular Jewish traditions, may indicate the author's sense of the truth of Christian faith, supported by such diverse and respected sources. It has long been recognized that most of Jude's letter reappears in 2 Pet 2. And it is generally accepted that 2 Peter borrowed from Jude and reworked that material to fit his situation.

Pastoral importance

The relevance of Jude does not seem to lie in its moral exposé of the heretics or in its simple demand to fight for the faith. Although Jude pleads with his church to remain faithful to its tradition, it would be unfair to the letter to translate this advice into a modern plea to hold on to our tradition without further ado. This would be traditionalism of the worst sort and unfaithful to the gospel which must be preached anew to every culture in every generation. The pastoral importance of Jude is the window it offers on the church struggling to recognize its roots, traditions, and faith, but not in a fearful or defensive way. Differences of opinion *within* this church go back to its very beginning, and addressing new peoples with different cultures has challenged the church from the days of the apostles. Jude's church is not unlike ours: a church with a rich tradition, but one sailing through a pluralistic sea of many different religions and even indifference to religion. The pastoral importance lies in the image of a church trying both to recover the roots of its faith and yet attempting to speak to a different culture.

COMMENTARY

1-2 Address to the church. Jude opens the letter with a typical letter greeting. The sender is Jude, "slave of the Lord" (see Jas 1:1; Titus 1:1). Since this Jude seems to be relatively unknown to this audience, he is further identified as "brother of James," presumably "the brother of the Lord" (Gal 1:19). This type of identification serves as Jude's credentials to represent the orthodox tradition of the church. The addressees are not said to belong to any specific church (such as Corinth, Thessalonika), but are general members of the church, hence Jude's "catholic" or universal character. These Christians are said to be "kept safe," but this is perhaps a bit ambiguous. The verb used here (*tereō*) can mean "kept safely" as in verse 1, but it likewise means "kept locked up" as in a prison—the meaning it has in regard to the sinful angels (v. 6) and the deviant heretics (v. 13). So the church is guarded by God in the truth, which ironically contrasts it with the heretics who will be locked up in judgment. The greeting ("mercy, peace and love") is a typical letter greeting (see 1 Tim 1:2 and 2 Tim 1:2).

3-4 Occasion: The arrival of heretics. The letter lacks the typical prayer of thanksgiving found in Paul's letters or the typical commendation of the recipients. Instead, there is an immediate note of urgency: the author claims that his eagerness to write about their "catholic," or common, faith was supplanted by an urgent sense of crisis. Rather than merely discussing their common faith with them, Jude exhorts them to fight for the faith, which was handed on accurately once for all. The fight is necessary because heretics have entered the church, heretics whose coming was predicted (v. 18) and whose judgment is likewise noted (v. 4).

Who are they? What was their heresy? As was noted in the introduction, these are difficult questions to answer because the language in verse 4 is quite general and could apply to any person the church considered deviant: (a) They pervert grace (freedom?) to licentiousness, and (b) they deny the Lord and Master Jesus. These two comments probably reflect the typical view of heretics as people whose doctrine is so perverse that it leads to the worst type of sexual immorality. Their "denial" is the author's perception that the heretics dispute some important items of faith and so are seen as rejecting Jesus' teaching (see Matt 10:33). This type of general language would make sense in a church which was cruelly split over doctrinal matters, for the hearers would surely know who the enemy is. Moreover, it is typical of attacks on heretics *not* to keep mentioning their errors as a way of denying them further publicity for their false teaching.

5-8 Warnings from the past. A series of biblical examples is immediately brought forward as a "reminder" to the church. The common thread running through the three examples is the warning that ancient figures who experienced God's grace/favor fell from that position and were destroyed in their sin. Baptism and initial conversion do not automatically protect a Christian, for living in faith and truth is essential to life. So we are told of the Exodus generation, once sacred, but which fell from grace and truth and was destroyed (v. 5). Some angels fell from heavenly grace and are kept for judgment (v. 6). Sodom and Gomorrah are included because their sin was "unnatural"; literally, they were after "other flesh," thus abandoning former grace and bringing upon themselves ruin. Three examples of falling from grace into judgment are sobering indeed!

The three biblical examples are brought to bear on the heretics who are charged with polluting flesh, spurning dominion, and reviling angelic beings (v. 8). The Exodus generation broke God's covenant and so proved adulterous (Num 14:35); the angels refused to serve God and were cast down. And Sodom and Gomorrah defiled the angels sent to warn Lot and his family (Gen 19:1-11). The heretics are said to be doing the same thing and so are inviting a comparable judgment.

9 Judgment pronounced. An obscure writing (The Assumption of Moses) is cited here. As the heavenly angel Michael did not dispute with Satan but left all judgment to God ("May the Lord rebuke you," v. 9), so Jude will not wage war on the heretics but leave their judgment in God's hands (see vv. 14-15). The obscure writing is probably cited because it is seen to endorse traditional statements of God's judgment of sinners.

10-13 General description of the opponents. More general errors of the heretics are pointed out. Of course, it is assumed that the heretics are ignorant, a point stressed in verse 10 where they are said to revile what they do not understand. But even what they know is only the passion of brute animals which is leading them to ruin. Like verses 5-7, three more biblical examples of sinners who were requited are cited in verse 11: Cain, Balaam, and Korah. In Jewish traditions these three are characterized as figures who reject God's judgment, act contrary to divine directives, and rise in rebellion against God's established leaders. They are even commonly linked together as people who lead rebellions or who lead Israel into error ("The following have no share in the world to come: Cain, Korah, Balaam . . . ," *The Sayings of Rabbi Nathan*, 41).

More polemical charges are leveled against them which are typical of this type of literature. The doctrinal errors of these heretics lead them into immorality; hence, they soil and pollute some solemn Christian assemblies. Is this a hint that they should be expelled? (see 1 Cor 5). Their errors are easy to spot: they have no direction or substance—they are like moistureless clouds blown this way and that; they are fruitless trees which should be uprooted (see Matt 3:10; 7:19; 21:19); like wild waves they splash their immoral foam everywhere; like stars without direction they will never see light. So will the heretics of this church fare: they will be locked in the gloom prepared for them.

14-15 Another warning of judgment. Another esoteric writing (Enoch) is cited by Jude to the same purpose as the earlier one (v. 9). The Lord will come with his holy ones (see Matt 16:27; 25:31) to judge sinners, especially ungodly sinners who rebel against God. This echoes the charges in verse 4 that the heretics deny the Lord and in verse 8 that they deny authority. This citation of Enoch probably serves to emphasize the traditional character of divine judgment rather than to identify the heretics more fully.

16 More charges. This string of charges interprets the behavior of the heretics in the worst possible light, pointing out how they have always been mavericks in regard to doctrine, following passion rather than truth, prone to boastful claims, and with an eye to the profit such behavior might bring. These charges are general in character and do not help us identify the heretics with any greater precision.

17-18 Prophetic warnings. The author appeals to well-known traditions that on their deathbeds prophets and apostles predicted the future for their followers, a common element of which was the warning about heretics entering the group (Acts 20:29; Matt 24:11-12; 2 Pet 3:2-3). This warning serves to defuse the shock of finding division in the church. It was expected! predicted! But the same warning serves to identify false parties: the traditional faith, given once for all (v. 3), is authentic; not so the errors introduced later.

19-21 Who has God's Spirit? The heretics are called "sensualists," which means that they are living in the flesh as opposed to a spirit-filled life (see Gal 5:16-25). Their morality is fleshly because bad doctrine leads to nonspiritual or fleshly morality. Their doctrine is also wrong because they are not led by God's Spirit but by error and deceit. The heretics, of course, probably claimed divine inspiration for their ideas, so discerning God's Spirit became important in the early churches as a test of truth. Certain statements can never be inspired by God's Spirit, such as "Cursed be Jesus" (1 Cor 12:3) or "Christ did not come in the flesh" (see 1 John 4:1-3). Paul claimed that genuinely spiritual people do not cause divisions (1 Cor 3:1-4), which is the same charge here. The church, on the other hand, is characterized by union and love, upbuilding in shared faith, and prayer in the Spirit. In this way the church will "keep itself" (i.e., continue) in God's love (v. 21); we recall here that they were called in love and urged to persevere in that love (v. 1). Their steadfastness in love contrasts the church with the heretics who wander in lust and turn aside into error (vv. 12-13). So their future is one of eternal mercy and salvation, whereas the wandering heretics face eternal ruin.

22-23 A saving hand extended. The church must do more than guard itself against heresy. Like a physician, it should act to save those being led astray by the heretics. This means trying to convince some who are wavering (v. 22) and snatching others from ruin, even some of the most depraved who soil in lust their baptismal garment of grace. This is not unlike the advice to Timothy and Titus to argue the church's case with conviction and charity (see 1 Tim 4:1-2, 11-13; 2 Tim 4:2-4).

24-25 Farewell and conclusion. The letter closes with a characteristic farewell greeting. God is named as the one who keeps the church upright and pure, because right theology leads to right morality. And uprightness in faith and morals leads to joy and glory. A formal benediction ends the letter in which God is acclaimed by the church for his glory, power, and authority—items which Jude insists that heretics deny (vv. 4, 8).

HEBREWS

George W. MacRae, S.J.

INTRODUCTION

This eloquent document, one of the best written works of early Christianity, has its origin shrouded in mystery. In antiquity as well as in modern times, there has been a great deal of inconclusive speculation about its author, place of writing, and destination. Traditionally it has come down to us in the New Testament as "The Letter of Paul to the Hebrews." But this title does not belong to the original writing. All the elements of it are suspect, and modern scholars agree that the work is not a letter, it is not by St. Paul, and it is not addressed to "Hebrews." Such a negative conclusion should not leave the reader with a negative impression of Hebrews, however. On the contrary, this is a magnificent work, treasured for centuries in the life of the church and well worth our effort to read and study it carefully.

A literary sermon

Hebrews is clearly not a letter, even in the rather broad category of New Testament letters. It has no letter greeting and is not directed to any particular church or individual. Its conclusion contains some elements typical of early Christian letters (see especially 13:18-25), but these seem to be added merely because the writing was circulated. They testify to the authority of letters as a means of communication among early Christians. Instead Hebrews is a written sermon, and it is important as one of the very earliest Christian sermons on record. It combines theological explanation, most of it based on interpretation of the Bible, the Old Testament, with exhortation to persevere in hope and faith. The passages of exhortation are scattered throughout the sermon, and it becomes clear to the reader that these are the main focus of the work as in any good sermon. This commentary will highlight these passages.

The fact that Hebrews is a sermon may help us to understand one of its classical problems for the interpreter. It is the problem of the thought world of the document. Two different, and somewhat conflicting, views are present in it. One is the common expectation that the world is about to come to an end. God will resolve human history by intervening in it to send Christ again and establish his kingdom. This kind of thought, which we call apocalyptic, is oriented to the future and has a certain urgency about it. With many variations of detail it is characteristic of much of Judaism in the time of the early Christians and also of much of early Christianity itself. The other view is one that is much more concentrated on the present than on the future. It makes a distinction between the heavenly world of true reality and the earthly world of copies. It has its roots in popular Greek thought as interpreted by such thinkers as the Jew Philo of Alexandria of the early first century A.D. In this view God's promises are already realized in heaven. The saving work of Christ has already taken place there, and faith is insight into its reality.

Both of these views are prominent in Hebrews, and modern interpreters have tended to stress one or the other as the dominant view of the author. The situation may be more complex, however. The preacher does not always have the very same presuppositions as his hearers, but he does not always want to do away with them either. Hebrews makes the best sense if we suppose that the hearers are oriented toward traditional apocalyptic thought, and the author seeks to reinforce that orientation with the assurance that the future hope is already grounded in the present. We shall see the interaction of these two perspectives as we read Hebrews carefully.

Authorship

Like many other New Testament writings, Hebrews is anonymous, and all attempts to identify the author are ultimately guesswork. Before Hebrews was accepted widely as part of the canonical Scriptures, in the second to the fourth century, the Christian church in the East was convinced that Paul was the author, and this view finally won out. But it was clear then to many Christians that in style, vocabulary, and theology, this sermon was not written by Paul. The great theologian Origen, early in the third century, discussed the question and concluded, "Who really wrote the letter, God knows." Ancient speculation tended to concentrate on Luke, or Barnabas, the missionary companion of Paul according to the Acts of the Apostles, or Clement of Rome. Later writers, starting with Martin Luther in the sixteenth century, suggested the name of Apollos, another associate of Paul (see Acts 18:24-28 and 1 Corinthians *passim*). Apollos has won a wide following since, and if any known Christian leader was the author, he would be the best candidate.

To Hebrews?

It is by no means clear to whom this sermon was addressed. It makes various references to the lives of the Christians it speaks to, but these are all of a rather general kind and do not permit us to draw a very specific portrait. The ancient designation "Hebrews" is itself not very clear, but it probably refers to Christians of Jewish background. Because Hebrews uses the Old Testament so extensively, it was thought in antiquity, as well as by many modern interpreters, to be addressed to former Jews who were in danger of losing their hope in Christ and slipping back into Judaism. Such a situation is possible, of course, but not easy to demonstrate. We must remember that intense familiarity with the Old Testament, which was readily available in its Greek translation, was common among all Christians, whether Jew or Gentile in background (see, for example, Paul's letter to the Gentile Christians of Galatia). And there is nothing in Hebrews that clearly suggests the danger of a relapse into Judaism. It is therefore probably best to assume that the sermon is addressed to Christians in general and not merely to former Jews. It would be interesting to know where they were, but we could only guess.

It is more interesting to speculate where the sermon was written. Because of the similarity of its thought to that of Alexandrian Judaism, people have thought of Alexandria as its origin. That is possible but not essential, since philosophical thought of the Alexandrian type was fairly widespread over the ancient Mediterranean world. Hebrews has some ideas in common with the First Letter of Peter, which purports to come from Rome. Even more significantly, it is related closely to the non-biblical First Letter of Clement, the reputed bishop of Rome near the end of the first century. These contacts suggest that Hebrews shared a kind of Roman theology and was most likely written from Rome.

Date

The question of when Hebrews was written is also controversial. The sermon itself hints that it was written some time after the first generation of Christian preaching (see 2:3 and 13:7). Some interpreters have understood it to refer to contemporary Jewish temple worship, since it uses the present tense to describe Jewish sacrifices. But they fail to recognize that Hebrews is essentially biblical commentary, using the accounts in the Pentateuch of ancient Israelite worship in the wilderness tabernacle or tent to interpret the supreme sacrifice of Christ. Because the author believes that the biblical word of God is still "living and effective" (4:12), it is appropriate to use the present tense. In fact, Hebrews never mentions the Herodian temple or its ritual. That temple was destroyed by the Roman army in A.D. 70, and there is no evidence on this ground that Hebrews was written before or after the destruction.

The First Letter of Clement of Rome, generally thought to have been written in the nineties of the first century, contains several passages that seem to quote or allude to Hebrews. This would suggest that Hebrews was circulating at that time. Yet Clement does not indicate that he is quoting, as he does for example with 1 Corinthians or the Old Testament. The similarity to Hebrews may mean only that he shares with it some common ideas and formulations of Christian thought in Rome. In this case Hebrews itself might be dated late in the first century.

The issue of Hebrews' dependence on the text of the Old Testament has broader significance than merely the question of date, however. It reminds us that the theology of this work is primarily a matter of interpretation of the Bible. That means that the reader of Hebrews should first look to Old Testament passages to understand the author's reasoning. The argument is sometimes complicated, but almost always it can best be understood as interpretation of the word of God expressed in the early Christians' Bible.

Structure

It is always useful to discuss the literary structure of a work in order to understand it better. With Hebrews this is difficult, not because it is badly structured, but because it is so carefully crafted with the techniques of ancient rhetoric. Key words and phrases are used to sum up themes and to introduce new ones, sometimes with interlocking references that make outlining the work very complex. For example, one can note how the subject of angels is introduced in 1:4, to be discussed in 1:5-14, and how the whole passage is held together by the use of the word "inherit" in 1:4 and 1:14. In a brief commentary such as this one, it is not possible to point out the many structural elements, but the careful reader will notice them in the text.

The main body of the sermon (chapters 1–12) may be understood best as making three points, which constitute the major divisions of the work. Since this is a sermon, these divisions should be understood as exhortations, even though the bulk of the text is devoted to theological explanation. The first section, 1:1–4:13, deals with the word of God spoken in his Son and exhorts the hearers to pay attention to this word more carefully than to God's word communicated through angels or through Moses, that is, the word of the Mosaic law. The second, and the principal, section, 4:14–10:31, interprets the saving death of Jesus against the background of the Israelite priesthood. Jesus is the eternal high priest whose sacrifice does away with sin once and for all and establishes a new covenant relationship between God and humanity. Christians therefore have grounds to persevere in their hope. The third section, 10:32–12:29, seeks to bolster this hope by the concept of faith as insight into the heavenly world of reality where Jesus' work has already been accomplished. The work concludes (chapter 13) with some practical instructions and some letter features.

The importance of Hebrews

This New Testament document is important in more than one way. First, it is a completely self-contained theology of salvation in Christ. It is somewhat surprising in the fact that it does not lay emphasis on the resurrection of Jesus or on the liturgical side of Christian life. Indeed, one might have expected some attention to be given to the Eucharist in such a sermon. But Hebrews shows us a dimension of early Christianity that is entirely centered on the death of Jesus as the saving act. Second, the sermon is important because it shows us more clearly than any other New Testament writing the extent to which the interpretation of the Old Testament played a role in the development of early Christian thought. Such a role can be seen in most New Testament books, and it is important for the Christian belief in the continuity of salvation history from creation to redemption, but Hebrews illustrates it in a special way.

We might sum up the theology of Hebrews in a threefold statement of the function of Christ, corresponding to the three main divisions of the sermon. First, Christ is seen as the new word of God, the communication of God to humanity in a new idiom that is personal. It is a word spoken in the life and death of a human being who is also God's Son. Second, Christ functions as the unique, eternal high priest whose self-sacrifice in death finally atones for sin, inaugurates a new covenant, and provides a new and open access to God.

And third, Christ's own insight into the heavenly world of God is the model of faith that Christians need to persevere in their hope. This is a remarkable sweep of Christian faith focused on the person and role of Christ himself.

How to study Hebrews

The sermon to the Hebrews is so carefully written that it deserves to be studied carefully. Some suggestions may be helpful toward that end. To begin, it would be useful to read the whole sermon quickly in order to have an overview of its message and its structure. In such a reading one should note the main divisions of the book, for in detailed reading it is easy to lose sight of the forest while examining the trees. Then, when reading the text slowly along with the commentary, one would do well to have a copy of the whole Bible at hand in order to look up the many Old Testament and occasional New Testament passages referred to. Studying Hebrews this way is a good method of integrating the Old Testament with understanding Christ's saving work. The reader should be aware that Old Testament passages in our modern Bibles will not always make the point that Hebrews wants to stress. This is because modern Bibles usually translate the original Hebrew and Aramaic of the Old Testament. The author of Hebrews used the Bible in its ancient Greek translation, which sometimes differed from the Hebrew.

COMMENTARY

THE WORD OF GOD SPOKEN IN HIS SON

Heb 1:1–4:13

1:1-4 Prologue: God has spoken. Hebrews shares with the Gospel of John and the First Epistle of John the fact that it begins with a prologue focusing on the idea of word (John 1:1-18; 1 John 1:1-4). As we shall see, the term "word" is applied rather differently in these three New Testament books, but in all its meanings it is important to the beginnings of Christian thought.

Prologues are a kind of introduction to literary works, and Hebrews is one of the most literary pieces in the New Testament. This prologue serves two functions. First, it introduces the first major division of the sermon, which has to do with the appropriate response of the hearers to the new mode of God's speaking in a Son. After showing the superiority of this kind of divine word, the author will sum up his statement in 4:12-13, thus indicating one of the structural principles of his rhetorical style, namely, enclosing units of thought within clearly related statements. Second, the Hebrews' prologue functions like a kind of "text" on which the preacher-author bases his sermon. In content these few verses range from a brief interpretation of the word of God in the Old Testament to a summary of what has been accomplished in the event of Jesus Christ.

The underlying idea is that of "word" as God's revelation to humanity. In the Gospel of John, "Word" is a personification of Jesus himself; in the First Epistle of John it is the gospel message preached in the author's church. Here it suggests the broader concept of all God's dealings with humanity, starting with the Bible and extending to the significance of the divine Son. The theme that permeates the whole sermon is how to hear and respond to God's revelation. Of old, God spoke variously in the Bible; now, in the "last days," he has given a new message in his Son Jesus. But it is the same God who has spoken, and therefore the Old Testament may be used to interpret the person and work of Jesus.

The style and content of verses 2-3 remind us of the hymns of early Christianity, of which we have examples in Phil 2:6-11, Col 1:15-20, and elsewhere. These tend to emphasize the divine closeness of the Son to God the Father, even his preexistence and role in creation. Such a series of statements was made possible by applying to Christ features of the personified figure of God's "wisdom." For a good parallel to our passage, one should read Wisdom of Solomon 7:25–8:1, where even the Alexandrian Jewish vocabulary is similar.

The second half of verse 3 refers to the saving activity of the Son, his sacrifice of himself for sins and his exaltation into heaven, which will be the subject of the second major division of Hebrews. Verse 4 both announces the theme of the section to follow and concludes the preceding statement (it is part of the one Greek sentence formed by verses 1–4). The name that Christ has inherited is that of Son, and the superiority of that name to the name of angel is yet to be shown.

1:5-14 Jesus, superior to angels. Even given the transitional statement of verse 4, one cannot help asking, Why the comparison with angels? It has often been thought that the author wanted to argue against a view, seen in some strands of second-century Christianity, that Jesus was an angel, not a real human being. But there is little evidence of polemic in these verses. Instead there are two considerations to bear in mind. First, the angels were thought in some sense to be the mediators of God's word in the law of Israel (see 2:2; Acts 7:53; Gal 3:19), which was superseded by the Christian gospel. Second, the scene introduced already in verse 3 is that of the heavenly enthronement of the Son (see Ps 110:1) beside God in heaven, reminiscent of frequent Old Testament conceptions of God and reflected in the imagery of the Israelite king enthroned in the psalms. The one who is enthroned is clearly superior to the angels who are in attendance before the throne.

This passage is a very important introduction to how Hebrews interprets the Old Testament, and three points need to be clearly understood. First, the Old Testament is taken to be God's word. This is a clear doctrine of inspiration, shared by all of early Christianity, and it matters little whether God, the Holy Spirit, or even Christ is understood as speaking the words of Moses or David or others. Second, passages are used in isolation, without any necessary regard for their context, though the author can sometimes allude to more words of them than he actually quotes. Third, and most important, the Old Testament can be seen as speaking about or to the divine Son Jesus. This last point is significant, for it reveals one of the most important constitutive elements of early Christian theology, namely, the reinterpretation of the Scriptures of Israel as a way of understanding the person and meaning of Jesus.

It is possible that at this point the author was not simply combing the Old Testament for suitable passages, but that he had a collection of passages used for messianic preaching. That such collections existed is no longer a mere conjecture; we have Jewish examples among the famous Dead Sea Scrolls.

Despite the lack of emphasis on original context, the reader would do well to refer to the passages cited in their own Old Testament settings. There is a pattern in the seven citations in these verses, referring to son-son-angels, angels-son-son, son-angels (the last statement without a citation, v. 14). The general point is to suggest that the angels are subordinate and impermanent, while the Son is exalted and enduring. In chapter 2 we shall see a much more radical statement, that the angels are subordinate to human beings as such (already hinted at in verse 14).

The citations of biblical texts are often familiar to readers of the New Testament because some of them are used elsewhere pertaining to Christ. Verse 5 cites Ps 2:7 and 2 Sam 7:14, well-known messianic passages. Verse 6 is problematic; it cites something like Deut 32:43, but the introductory formula, "And again when he leads the first-born into the world," might refer to the second coming of Christ (see 9:28). By a slight twist of interpretation, verse 7 makes Ps 104:4 refer to the impermanence of the messengers (angels), and verses 8-9 refer to Christ (Ps 45:7-8). Verses 10-12 (Ps 102:26-28) contrast the permanence of the Son with the impermanence of the heavens, which are perhaps a category of angels or at least the place where they dwell. Verse 13 refers to Ps 110:1, which is an important proof text both in Hebrews and elsewhere in the New Testament.

2:1-18 The humanity of Jesus. Chapter 2 begins with the first of the many exhortations of the preacher to his congregation. The danger they face is called that of "drifting away." We are not yet told exactly what this means, but we shall see that it involves abandoning faith and especially hope, in effect ceasing to be true Christians. This exhortation draws the conclusion from the first chapter: since the Son is superior to the angels, the message of salvation he brought is even more to be obeyed than the law of Moses, which came through angels. Verse 3 clearly implies that Hebrews is being written in a second- or third-generation church, but one which has experienced miracles and gifts of the Holy Spirit as evidence confirming the message (v. 4).

The author again takes up the argument

that Christ is superior to the angels, but from a new angle. In chapter 1 Christ was superior as the Son of God; here he is superior because he is a human being. The argument again is based on Scripture as verses 6-8 quote Ps 8:5-7, but this time the author explicitly interprets the text he quotes. Two features of his interpretation are important. First, he understands the passage as referring not to humanity in general but to Jesus the man. And second, he reverses the meaning of the original psalm, which had said that God created human beings "a little lower than the angels." For Hebrews, Jesus the man is superior to the angels but was made "for a little while lower" than them in that he suffered death (v. 9). The subjection of all things to Christ still belongs to the future, but the process has begun with Jesus' exaltation to heaven after his death.

What is of most interest to the author in declaring the true humanity of Jesus is the fact that he shares that humanity with all human beings, who in verse 10 are called God's "children." In order that Jesus' death might be *for all* a liberation from slavery to the power of death (vv. 14-15), Jesus had to share their human nature fully. Verses 12-13 quote Ps 22:23 and Isa 8:17-18 with the supposition that Christ is speaking the inspired words. He is a brother to human beings, and like them he praises and puts his trust in the Father. Jesus' solidarity with humanity is also brought out in their common origin in the Father (v. 11), their sharing in flesh and blood (v. 14), and above all their sharing in death itself.

The last verses of the chapter perform the typical Hebrews' function of announcing new themes to be taken up. Jesus must share fully in humanity because he is to take on the role of high priest offering himself for the sins of his fellow human beings (v. 17). In particular he is a merciful and faithful high priest. His merciful character, suggested already in verse 18, will be spelled out further in chapter 5; his faithfulness is the subject of the next paragraph.

3:1-6 Jesus, superior to Moses. The paragraph begins with an exhortation to reflect on Jesus the faithful one. The readers or hearers are addressed in a lofty manner: they are holy because they have been consecrated by Jesus' sacrificial death (see 2:11), and they share in a "heavenly calling" to follow him into heaven. Only here is Jesus called an apostle, that is, one who is sent on a mission. There is no reference to the way the New Testament customarily uses the word to identify various Christian leaders. It is normal to think of a "confession" of faith (3:1), but we shall see that Hebrews is distinctive in referring to our "confession that gives us hope" (10:23). Moreover, the context here is one of hope, not of faith (v. 6).

Why the comparison with Moses? For one thing, Moses was the model of faithfulness and thus a good Old Testament foil for Jesus. But, in addition, Hebrews seems to be concerned with showing Jesus' superiority to various figures who functioned as intermediaries of God's word (such as the angels), and Moses, who received the law, was such an intermediary (see v. 5).

Most of the arguments of Hebrews are based on the interpretation of Scripture, and this one is no exception. Only this time the passage is not formally quoted but merely alluded to. It is Num 12:7-8 in its Greek version: "Not so with my servant Moses. He is faithful in all my house. With him I shall speak mouth to mouth . . . ." Two elements of the passage are contrasted with Jesus. Moses is only a servant in God's "house," the people of God; Jesus is God's own Son, not *in* the house but *over* it. In addition, the Son ranks with the founder of the house in the sense that Jesus establishes a new "house" of God, namely the Christian community, which must cling to its hope in order to remain God's house.

3:7–4:11 Entering God's rest. All of chapter 3 and most of chapter 4 are dominated by the theme of faithfulness: first the faithfulness of Jesus the Son compared with Moses (3:1-6), then the unfaithfulness of the Israelites in their desert wanderings (3:7-19), then the faithfulness required of Christians (4:1-11), and implicitly God's faithfulness to his word in Scripture.

What we find in this section is an extended commentary on Ps 95:8-11, quoted, with some slight modifications, in Heb 3:7-11. It is a preacher's use of the text—not merely an exegesis of it but an application to the lives of the hearers. Thus it shows us yet another facet of Hebrews' varied scriptural interpretation. Underlying the whole passage there is a carefully structured argument which supports the exhortation summed up in 4:11. With some simplifying we can restate the argument this way. As Psalm 95 shows, God created a "rest" for his faithful followers to enter (3:11). But the Israelites, who were repeatedly unfaithful in their Exodus journey, were excluded from entering it (3:16-19). Yet that rest was a part of God's creation, and it remains for those who are faithful to him to enter it (4:1-6). God reminds us of the continuing openness of this promise by saying through the psalmist David, centuries after the Exodus, "Oh, that today you would hear his voice" (4:7-10). Therefore Christians have the opportunity to enter God's rest and must strive to do so by being faithful.

The failure of the Israelites to enter the Promised Land, the rest after their journey, hinges on a particular passage of the Bible, Num 14, which is clearly alluded to in 3:16-19. According to this version of the Exodus story, only Joshua (see 4:8) and Caleb, and presumably their extended families as well as the women and youth of Israel, actually entered the land of Canaan.

The emphasis on the presentness of the word "today" is important to the argument (3:13; 4:7), for it shows how the word of God in Scripture is regarded as effective in the present (see 4:12-13 below), speaking to the reader now and not just then.

It is also worth noting how the author blends three different notions of God's "rest" in this passage. The first is the rest of the Promised Land, rest at the end of the desert wanderings of Israel, as implied by the literal meaning of Psalm 95. The second is God's own sabbath rest from his labors in the creation story; Heb 4:4 quotes Gen 2:2 (and see Heb 4:10 in particular). The third, and most fundamental for the purposes of Hebrews, understands God's rest as the ultimate destiny of his faithful followers in heaven. The idea of entering God's rest as the goal of Christian life implies an image of that life as both labor and a pilgrimage or journey toward a heavenly homeland, a metaphor which will be picked up again in Hebrews (for example, in chapters 11–12).

What is the danger of unfaithfulness for the Christians? We learn a little more about their situation from this passage, in which exhortation dominates. The danger is one of succumbing to "the deceit of sin" (3:13) in such an extreme way as to "forsake the living God" (3:12). It is the risk of apostasy, of so losing faith and hope in God as to abandon him and the promises he made—by implication to cease to hear the word of his revelation in Scripture or in his Son. Deep-rooted discouragement might motivate such an attitude, and that would be consistent with the emphasis in Hebrews on clinging to hope and confidence (see 3:6). In this light, perhaps one should translate the second part of 4:1 in more directly personal terms: "we ought to be fearful lest any one of you think he has missed his chance of entering."

4:12-13 The living word of God. The first major division of the sermon began with a very rhetorical, almost poetic, statement about the modes of God's speaking in the Bible and in his Son, and it continued with emphasis on both the Old Testament and the salvation announced by Jesus. It is appropriate that the section should end with another carefully composed, again almost poetic, statement about the power of God's word. In its immediate context this statement sums up the argument based on Psalm 95, but it also extends to the broader concept of God's word as revelation introduced in 1:1-3. Thus, typically of Hebrews, this statement looks backward to the scriptural arguments and forward to the interpretation of Jesus as high priest.

The language of this short passage is in fact rather conventional, particularly in Alexandrian Judaism or Christianity. One can find some close parallels in the writings of the Jewish philosopher and biblical interpreter Philo, though he personifies God's word in a way that Hebrews does not. The author's intellectual background nevertheless is reflected in passages like this.

According to verse 12, God's word is alive (v. 7: "Oh, that *today* you would hear his voice") and so effective that it penetrates to the innermost parts of a person, forcing one to come to grips with what really matters. Verse 13 is less than completely clear in the original Greek and has been translated in many different ways. As an alternative to the New American Bible translation, we might suppose that it refers not to God but still to God's word, and that it makes a transition to the main division of the sermon that is about to begin. In Greek this short paragraph begins with "God's word" and ends with "our word."

So we might translate the verse: "Nothing is concealed from it (God's word); all lies bare and exposed to the eyes of that (word) toward which our word (or message) is directed."

HOPE IN THE SACRIFICE OF JESUS

Heb 4:14–10:31

4:14-16 Confidence in our high priest. The theme of the second major section of Hebrews is the role and activity of Christ as unique high priest whose once-for-all sacrifice of himself for the sins of humanity accomplished what the elaborate sacrificial ritual of the ancient Israelites could not do. Consequently, the sacrifice of Christ inaugurates a new covenant and replaces the entire old order described in the Old Testament. Yet the Old Testament is still the word of God, and therefore it will still be used to interpret the meaning of Jesus' death in this section.

Just as the first major section of the sermon was enclosed between two passages on the word of God, so the second is bounded by two passages of exhortation (4:14-16 and 10:19-31) that have many similarities, even verbal ones (see especially 10:19-23). We shall note some of them in discussing chapter 10 below.

Jesus had been introduced as high priest for the first time in 2:17, where he was called merciful and faithful. Having discussed his faithfulness in chapter 3, the author turns now to his quality of mercy, first in the transition passage 4:14-16 and then further in 5:1-10. His mercy is rooted in his sharing of human nature, to the point of being tempted in every way that all humans are, yet without yielding to sin (v. 15).

Jesus' passage "through the heavens" (v. 14) perhaps reflects the common Jewish view of a series of heavens above the earth, in the highest of which God dwells. His successful entry into God's presence grounds the hope and confidence of his followers, as will be repeatedly stated in the sermon. The reference to "our confession of faith" in verse 14 leads us to the same caution made in the commentary on 3:1. The text literally says only "let us hold fast to the confession." As the parallel verse 10:23 will show, it is a confession of hope, not faith.

This short passage introduces us to an important shift in the imagery of exhortation in Hebrews. It is the shift from holding fast to hope and confidence, or the confession (see 3:6, 14; 4:14), to moving forward: "approach the throne of grace" (4:16). The imagery of forward movement was already anticipated in 4:11 and will be prominent from now on. It has three dimensions, which we shall note as they occur: continuing on the journey toward God's rest, approaching God as worshipers approached the altar of sacrifice, and growing up in one's understanding of Christianity.

5:1-10 Christ as high priest. By this point the author has identified Jesus as high priest several times (2:17; 3:1; 4:14-15), but he has not explained or justified this notion. Now he does so in a classic rhetorical way by defining what a high priest is and showing how the definition fits Jesus. For these ten verses it is important to recognize the structure used by the author. He first defines a high priest by stating three qualifications, which he derives from interpretation of the passages relevant to Israelite worship in the Pentateuch. The high priest is the descendant of Levi described there, and though historically Jesus does not qualify (see 7:13-14), nevertheless he fulfills the proper conditions. The qualifications are stated in verses 1-4: (1) the high priest is chosen from human beings and represents them in the sacrifice he offers; (2) he can perform his representative function because he shares in human weakness; and (3) he is called to this office by God and not by his own choice.

Verses 5-10 show how Christ meets these qualifications, but in reverse order. In addition, they introduce a new element of comparison, the priesthood of the shadowy figure Melchizedek, who will be dealt with formally in chapter 7. First, Christ did not assume the office of high priest, but he received it from God, as the Scripture attests, understanding Pss 2:7 and 110:4 as addressed to him. One should note that the latter passage speaks only of a priest, not a high priest. Melchizedek will be "elevated" to the high priestly status starting with verse 10 because this status is important for the author's argument. Verses 7-9 demonstrate the solidarity of Christ with human beings in weakness, but the argument is a subtle one because Jesus has been declared to be sinless (4:15) and thus cannot offer "sin offerings for himself as well as for the people" (v. 3). This nuance will continue to be a delicate issue.

Verse 7 in particular has long been a focus of interest. Traditionally it has been taken to be a reference to the prayer of Jesus in the Garden of Gethsemane, as reported in Mark 14:32-42 and parallels. But two factors make one hesitate to understand it in this way: it has nothing in common with the Gethsemane story from a language point of view, and also this would be the only reference in Hebrews to a specific Gospel passage. The alternative is to suppose that the verse is a depiction of the typical Jewish hero, such as Abraham or Moses, who prays demonstratively to God, and the language used has notable parallels in Philo's description of such persons. If there is any reference to the Gospel story, it is very indirect.

Verses 9-10 clearly illustrate the role of Christ as the representative of the people for whom as high priest he offers sacrifice. His intercession was so effective that he became a source of salvation for others. The transition from a priest like Melchizedek to a *high priest* like Melchizedek takes place quietly, but the reader will have to wait until chapter 7 before perceiving its significance.

5:11–6:20 Exhortation to hope. This rather long section, dominated by exhortation, seems to interrupt the author's flow of thought. Instead of going on to explain what it means for Jesus to be a high priest like Melchizedek, the author both reproaches his hearers for sluggishness and encourages them to hope. But the passage looks much less like an interruption if we bear in mind that Hebrews is a sermon, not a treatise. Here especially the art of the preacher comes through skillfully. Before entering into a rather detailed and complicated explanation, he pauses to motivate the hearers to follow it. Again, the underlying theme is that of moving forward, growing in mature understanding of Christian life (6:1) and in hope following Jesus the forerunner (6:18-20).

The preacher begins by using a metaphor that must have been familiar to his congregation, that of milk and solid food, little children and grownups (5:11-14). St. Paul uses the same metaphor in a very similar way in 1 Cor 3:1-2, and there are examples of it in such more or less contemporary Jewish writers as Philo of Alexandria. The problem is that the hearers are refusing to grow up in their understanding of Christianity. They are stuck at the level of the ABCs; the Greek word translated "basic elements" means exactly that. We must pause for a moment over the word "mature" or "adult." In Greek it is the same word that is often translated "perfect" in Hebrews, and it is an important theme of the sermon as a whole. In Greek, "perfect" does not mean not having any defects, as we often use the word, but it means being complete, being all that one is supposed to be. Repeatedly Hebrews says that Jesus was made perfect in this sense through his suffering and death (2:10; 5:9), thus becoming a source of salvation for others. Christians too must share in this salvation; they must become complete and mature and eventually partakers of the same heavenly destiny as Jesus.

Chapter 6 begins with a list of the "foundations," elementary Christian teachings that one must go beyond in order to grow up. They are not of course to be abandoned, but the Christian cannot stay at that level. To use our language, Hebrews is a work of adult education. Nothing in the list directly concerns Christ, and most of the rest of Hebrews does. We can conclude, therefore, that for Hebrews adult Christian education focuses on understanding the person and saving work of Christ the high priest. The modern reader cannot be certain of the exact meaning of each item in the list given in 6:1-2. For example, "baptisms" probably does not refer to Christian baptism as such but to some kind of ritual washings which Christians inherited from their Jewish background. "Laying on of hands" might mean commissioning members of a community to perform certain functions—what we would call ordination.

The danger for those who refuse to advance toward maturity is that of losing hope, of turning away from God (see 3:12). In 6:4-8 the author sternly warns his hearers of the consequences. One who has become a Christian, been enlightened, shared in the Holy Spirit, tasted God's word, and yet has rejected it all can even be said to participate in responsibility for the death of Jesus. Hebrews is often said to take a hard line on the matter of penitence and forgiveness (see also 10:26-31), but note that the author is careful not to say that God does not forgive, but only that personal repentance is beyond the reach of one who definitively rejects the Son of God. Verses 7-8 make use of a biblical metaphor that is quite clear in its application here. The language is partly drawn from Gen 3:17-18, but there is no allusion to the Genesis context here.

The good preacher does not leave his hearers with a strongly worded warning ringing in their ears, but goes on to encourage them. The remainder of chapter 6 is a reassuring exhortation to hope marked by the decided change of tone in verse 9 and the commendation of the hearers' love and service to one another (v. 10). As a basis for perseverance and progress in hope, the author refers to God's oath and promise to Abraham that he would bless Abraham's descendants (6:13-18; see Gen 22:16-18). The argument supposes that the promise made to Abraham applies to all Christians and therefore gives them confidence. The famous example of Abraham is often used in a similar way in the New Testament. Verse 15 may mean only that Abraham obtained the promise; what was promised was to come later, only with the saving work of Christ.

Verses 18-20 perform several functions, as most transitional passages in Hebrews do. They summarize the theme of hope; reintroduce the next topic, a priest like Melchizedek; and give advance warning of a new topic, which reaches "beyond the veil." That phrase refers to the Israelite high priest's entry into the inner shrine of the tabernacle, the Holy of Holies.

7:1-28 A priest like Melchizedek. Chapter 7 deals in reality with three priesthoods, and it is helpful for the reader to keep them distinct. First, there is the priesthood of Melchizedek, an ancient and somewhat mysterious figure from the time of Abraham. Second, there is the high priesthood of the Israelite tribe of Levi, legislated for in Num 18. And third, there is the priesthood of Christ himself, which resembles that of Melchizedek in its perpetuity and also has the function of that of Levi.

The author has built up to the comparison of Christ and Melchizedek by referring three times to Ps 110:4: "You are a priest forever, according to the order of Melchizedek" (5:6, 10; 6:20). We know of no *order* of Melchizedekian priests, and we should probably understand this expression to mean simply "a priest *like* Melchizedek" (see v. 15). But how is Christ like him? Indeed, why the comparison with Melchizedek at all? Several answers are possible. For one thing, Christ is an eternal priest, not a merely mortal one like the levitical priests, and Melchizedek is a priest forever. And as we have already seen more than once, passages from the psalms such as this one are often understood as speaking about or to Christ. In addition, there is some evidence that in Judaism even earlier than Hebrews, namely, in the Dead Sea Scrolls, there was some speculation about Melchizedek as a heavenly figure, perhaps even a saving figure. It may have been natural to compare the exalted, heavenly Christ with him.

In this chapter we have another excellent example of the biblical interpretation and exegetical reasoning of the author. The reader needs to be reminded that Hebrews has no interest in Melchizedek as a historical figure; the entire argument is an interpretation of Old Testament passages. Besides Ps 110:4, only one other Old Testament passage mentions Melchizedek—the brief and somewhat obscure story found in Gen 14:17-20. It would be useful to read that story in its context when reading Heb 7, since the author uses it to interpret Ps 110:4. His interpretation of it may seem fanciful to us, but it is typical of his own day.

Popular explanations of Melchizedek's name and kingdom enable the author to associate justice and peace with him and, by inference, with Christ (v. 2). Since the Genesis text says nothing of Melchizedek's personal background or even his birth and death, the inference is that he is a priest forever (v. 3). The two elements of the story that are most important are the facts that Melchizedek blessed Abraham and that Abraham gave a tenth of his spoils of war, a "tithe," to Melchizedek. Both of these demonstrate Melchizedek's superiority, and since Levi and all the levitical priests to come were to be descended from Abraham, they too are placed in a position subordinate to Melchizedek (vv. 4-10). The conclusion will be spelled out further: a priest like Melchizedek is superior to the Israelite priests.

The argument of verses 11-17 becomes clearer if we understand the "law" in question as the law of Moses regarding the levitical priests, their right of inheritance, their right to tithes, and other matters, found in Num 18. We should then translate the parenthesis in verse 11: "concerning which the people received a law." The argument runs as follows. If the priesthood of the law were not inherently deficient, there would have been no need for God to appoint a priest like Melchizedek (v. 11). But Christ could not have been a levitical priest because he was of the tribe of Judah, not of Levi (vv. 13-14). And he was appointed as an eternal priest like Melchizedek, not by a law of physical descent (Num 18), but by the living word of God addressed to him in Ps 110:4 (vv. 15-17).

One should note how the theme of perfection, including the sense of completeness, pervades this discussion (vv. 11, 19, 28). The law has been incapable of bringing the priesthood to perfection. But the appointment of Jesus as high priest was in Ps 110:4 accompanied by a divine oath, "the Lord has sworn," and thus was made more sure (vv. 20-21; compare 6:13-18). The basic reason why the Israelite priesthood was deficient was that it resided in mortals whose death terminated their priestly activity (vv. 23-24). This point will be spelled out further, as well as the relationship between priesthood and covenant. As an eternal priest, Christ offered a once-for-all sacrifice which did away with sin forever (v. 27). Having established the eternal character of Christ's priesthood, the author can leave Melchizedek behind and not mention him again.

8:1-6 Old and new ministry. Chapter 7 introduced the theme of contrast between the priesthood of the Old Testament and that of Christ. The next three chapters will extend that contrast to the priestly ministry, the covenant which it implies, the sanctuary where the priest functions, and the sacrifice which he performs. We begin with a short passage on priestly ministry, and the main thrust of the preacher is his assertion in verse 1 that Christians *have* such an eternal high priest as he has described, namely Christ, who has been exalted into heaven, as Heb 1:3 had already declared. There he exercises his unique priestly ministry, which takes place only in heaven, since on earth Jesus, not being a Levite, would not be a priest. Verses 4-5 do not really imply that the Jewish sacrificial ritual is still going on, that is, that the temple has not yet been destroyed in the war with Rome, for the basis for the argument is the text of the Bible, not observation of current practice.

Underlying this paragraph is a principle of the author's thought that will remain important for the next few chapters of the sermon. It hinges on the notion that the superiority of Christ's priestly work lies in the fact that it is performed (eternally) in heaven. Verse 5 quotes Exod 25:40, recalling that Moses was instructed to build the wilderness tabernacle according to a divine plan or pattern revealed to him. The preacher to the Hebrews has his background in the popular philosophical ideas of the day, which held that the true realities were in the heavenly world of God, and the earthly ones were merely copies or shadows of them. Thus the divine plan for the tabernacle has become the "true tabernacle" (v. 2) in heaven as opposed to the shadowy imitation on earth. Christ's ministry is superior because it is exercised in the world of true reality. Verse 6 summarizes this point while at the same time introducing the next comparison.

For centuries Christian theological interpretation of Hebrews has been fascinated with the question of whether Christ's sacrificial act took place on earth, on the cross, or takes place in heaven, in his entrance into the sanctuary of the true tabernacle. The question may be impossible to answer, and perhaps unnecessary to ask, since the author shows no awareness of it. For him the sacrificial death of Jesus *was* his entry into the sanctuary of God, and the transition between the historical and the eternal was instantaneous. We shall see later that Hebrews does not simply assume that the present world is not the real arena of human salvation. It is indeed, and almost despite the interest of the author in the heavenly realities above, it is on earth that human beings associate themselves with the suffering and death of Jesus.

8:7-13 Old and new covenant. This section of Hebrews merits little comment, for it consists mostly of a rather long Old Testament quotation, the majestic passage from Jer 31:31-34, which will be commented on more thoroughly in 9:15-22 and especially 10:9-18. This unique announcement of a *new* covenant in the Old Testament itself obviously invites comparison with the old covenant, which is here limited to the covenant with Moses on

Mount Sinai. It also suggests a rationale for the new relationship between humanity and God inaugurated by Christ. The minimal comment of the author (v. 13) emphasizes the theme of replacement.

The idea of covenant dominates much of the Old Testament. Set against the background of treaties between kings or kingdoms in the ancient Near East, the biblical idea of covenant suggests a kind of legal agreement between God and his people setting forth the duties and responsibilities of each party. Basically the people of Israel must obey God's will, and he will in turn be their protector. Jeremiah's vision of a new covenant in the future portrays a somewhat less legalistic and more personal relationship between God and his people. It is hardly surprising that the Christians should have seen this prophecy fulfilled by the mediation of Christ.

The link between priesthood and covenant, or priestly sacrifice and covenant, is important for the thought of Hebrews. According to Exod 24:3-8, Moses had ratified the Sinai covenant with the blood of sacrifice, a passage which will be referred to in 9:19-22. The hint is already present in our passage that the sacrificial blood of Jesus will be the ratification of a new covenant. The most important feature of the new covenant, as we shall see, is that God will forgive the sins of his people (v. 12).

9:1-10 The old sanctuary. In preparation for describing Jesus' death as a sacrifice for sin, the author first gives a very concise and stylized description of the wilderness tabernacle of Exod 25–26 and other passages, as well as of the ritual that went on in it. Again it should be noted that there is no allusion to current practice in the temple of Jerusalem, which probably no longer existed when Hebrews was written. The basis of the description is biblical interpretation, even if we cannot verify all the details in our texts of the Pentateuch. It is possible here that the author was familiar with some Jewish tradition about the furnishings of the tabernacle. He refers to the tabernacle furnishings and ritual as regulations of the first covenant, since the prescriptions for worship were part of the law given at Mount Sinai. Verses 2-5 describe very concisely the two divisions of the tabernacle—the essential structure of ancient Near Eastern temples—and what was in them. The golden splendor of the Holy of Holies contrasts vividly with the fairly austere outer tent.

Verses 6-7 describe the ritual, highlighting the once-a-year entrance of the high priest alone into the Holy of Holies. This is the ritual of Yom Kippur, the Day of Atonement, and since it was a blood sacrifice, it serves the author's purposes as the model for the sacrificial death of Jesus. There is, as we shall see presently, a spatial imagery here: Jesus enters heaven (or the innermost sanctuary of heaven) as the high priest enters the Holy of Holies. But verses 8-10 also introduce a temporal dimension which complicates the picture. Perhaps we can make the best sense of the complication by taking "the present time" (v. 9) to refer to the time contemporaneous with the sacrificial ritual of Israel described in the Old Testament. The ritual of this time does not get to the heart of the matter, the conscience of the worshipers. But when the time of "the new order" has come, that is, the time spoken of in verse 11, sacrifice has a wholly new significance.

9:11-28 The sacrifice of Jesus. After setting up the Old Testament contexts of priestly ministry, covenant, and sanctuary ritual, the author finally turns to an application of these categories to the saving death of Christ. It may be helpful to the reading of this and the following section to realize how the author envisions the heavenly temple or tabernacle, which is the scene of Christ's sacrifice. He draws on two somewhat different pictures, both of them known in contemporary Jewish thought, without always clearly distinguishing them. One is the picture of a complete tabernacle in heaven with its outer court and its inner sanctuary beyond the veil where God dwells. This seems to be the picture presupposed in verse 11. The other sees the universe itself structured like a tabernacle in which the earth is the outer court and heaven itself is the inner sanctuary. Entering heaven, by death, is passing through the veil into God's presence; this imagery seems to underlie verse 24.

The important point of this passage is that the death of Christ is interpreted as the one really effective sacrifice that atones for the sins of humanity (vv. 14, 26, 28). The principal underlying image is the ritual of the Day of Atonement as described in Lev 16. But the author blends with it two other pictures. Verse 13 refers to the sacrifice of the red heifer, a sin offering, described in Num 19. The ashes of the heifer had the power of making holy again persons who had incurred various forms of ritual defilement. Thirdly, verses 19-22 refer to the sacrificial ratification of the Sinai covenant described in Exod 24:3-8. What all three of these rituals have in common is that they involve the shedding of blood and thus can be applied symbolically to the death of Jesus. Sacrificial blood is a powerful and pervasive theme in ancient Israelite worship. It could be used as a petition for the forgiveness of sin, as a means of purification, and as a way of sealing a covenant with Yahweh. In all these respects the one effective sacrifice of Christ replaces the old ritual. To understand the details of this passage better, the reader should look up all three Old Testament passages.

Verse 15 begins the author's commentary on the new covenant prophesied by Jeremiah. What is essential is that it involves the definitive forgiveness of sin. Since Christ has accomplished that in his sacrificial death, he is the mediator of the new covenant. The following verses 16-18 are puzzling until one realizes that in Greek the words "covenant" and "testament" (in the sense of last will and testament) are the same. By a play on the two meanings, the preacher finds another way of showing how the covenant involves death. A will is executed only after the one who made it has died. St. Paul uses the same play on the word in Gal 3:15-18.

The main force of the contrast between the sacrificial death of Christ and the Day of Atonement sacrifices of the Israelite high priest is brought out explicitly in verses 25-28. The latter sacrifices were inadequate to take away sin in a definitive way because they had to be repeated every year. Sin continued to be a part of peoples' lives. But Christ's death was a once-for-all sacrifice that took away sin for good. To understand Christ's saving work this way means for the Christian to renounce sin completely. The terms "once" and "once for all" are important for the theology of Hebrews and are used frequently.

The passage ends with a rather clear reference to the second coming of Christ which is not wholly consistent with the author's own viewpoint in other passages. Through his once-for-all sacrifice Christ has effectively made salvation available already (compare the language of verse 11). It may be that the preacher mentions the second coming because he knows that it is part of the belief of his hearers.

10:1-18 Old and new sacrifice. The author concludes the argument of the main section of the sermon with a summary comparison of Christ's sacrifice with those of Israelite ritual, to be followed by further exhortation. Verses 1-18 contain a certain amount of repetition because the passage is a summary, but they also contain some new ideas. The picture they portray of the levitical priests and their sacrifices is sad (for example, v. 11), but we need to be reminded that Hebrews is not making an anti-Jewish statement. The superiority of Christ's sacrifice, and consequently of Christianity itself, is not being established at the expense of the author's Jewish contemporaries. He does not speak of current or recent Jewish practices, but only of the ancient Israelite tabernacle ritual as it is described in the Pentateuch. It is God's word in the Bible that indicates the limitations of this ritual and at the same time points toward the meaning of his word spoken in the Son.

The passage begins with several contrasts between the sacrifices in question. First, there is the inherent imperfection of the law of Moses, which is described as being at two removes from the divine reality (v. 1). The background is that of popular philosophical thought, which distinguished between reality which is spiritual, the visible image of that reality, and the shadow cast by the image. Since the law pointed toward the future, it was only in the realm of shadow. Verses 2-3 make explicit the argument we have already seen that repeated sacrifices for sin are ineffectual precisely because they have to be repeated. But verse 4 introduces a new idea, that it is impossible for animal sacrifices to take away sin. The proof lies in the quotation of Ps 40:7-8 (in its Greek translation), in which, as often is the case, the speaker is understood to be Christ. There God is said to reject animal sacrifices. The author then interprets the psalm as a displacement of the law, the old covenant, by the sacrifice of the body of Christ, which was God's will for his Son (vv. 9-10). Verses 11-14 repeat the contrast between multiple sacrifices and the once-for-all sacrifice of Christ, emphasizing the eternal effects of the latter. Verses 12-13 refer again to

Ps 110:1, which has been used several times from 1:3 on.

Some final comments on the new covenant passage of Jer 31 round off the argument (vv. 15-18). This time the Holy Spirit is said to be the speaker of God's word, but the quotations are in fact the author's paraphrases of the text. The conclusion is that since the new covenant mediated by Christ has achieved the forgiveness of sins, on the authority of the word of God himself, all other sacrifices for sin have come to an end.

10:19-31 Confidence and judgment. The final passage of exhortation in the second major division of the sermon, which, as mentioned above, counterbalances the opening one (4:14-16), contains both encouragement (vv. 19-25) and dire warning (vv. 26-31). But warning is not the last word, since the exhortation continues to the end of chapter 10. The resemblance of verses 19-23 in particular to 4:14-16 is striking, and one should at this point read again the earlier passage. In the discussion of that passage, it was pointed out that many of the hortatory passages of Hebrews take the form of "holding fast" and "moving forward." Both appear here also: "let us approach" (v. 22) and "let us hold unwaveringly" (v. 23). The former is the language of approaching God in worship as in 4:16. The latter finally identifies the Christian confession as a confession of hope ("our confession that gives us hope" is literally "the confession of hope"). It is hope that really defines the basic Christian attitude for Hebrews, hope in God's promises of salvation through Christ. Unlike many other New Testament writings, Hebrews makes faith subordinate to hope in the sense that faith provides the grounds for hope. We shall see this more clearly in chapter 11. Here verse 22 expresses the idea in that "the fullness of faith" (the literal translation of the words "absolute trust" in the New American Bible) is not the goal but a necessary condition for reaching it. Note that our passage also mentions love in verse 24, thus taking up and using in its own way the familiar Christian grouping of faith, hope, and love.

Verse 20 contains a famous difficulty of translation from Greek that has occasioned much discussion. Literally it speaks of "the new and living way he opened up for us through the veil, that is, his flesh." The New American Bible understands the veil, the curtain that separated the Holy of Holies from the outer sanctuary in the tabernacle, as symbolic of Jesus' physical existence, and it has translated the verse accordingly. It is equally possible, however, to read the verse in such a way that the path of access to God is symbolic of the physical existence of Jesus. This would mean that the sacrifice of the body of Jesus (see 10:10) is the way to God that is now open to Christians. It would imply that Jesus' "flesh" was not an obstacle to approaching God but the very means of doing so. The important point in any case is that followers of Christ now have access to God himself in the heavenly sanctuary, thanks to the sacrifice of Christ. One is reminded of John 14:6: "I am the way . . . no one comes to the Father except through me."

It is often the case that the Greek of Hebrews lends itself to more than one translation. Verse 25 affords another example. In the New American Bible translation the issue is that some of the congregation addressed have been neglecting to attend community gatherings, perhaps as a symptom of their abandoning hope in God's promises. This may well be the case, for the preceding verse seems to deal with practical matters also. But the word for "assembly" in verse 25 is unusual in the New Testament, and in its only other use there, 2 Thess 2:1, it clearly refers to the gathering of Christians about the Lord at his second coming, on the "day of the Lord." In this sense verse 25 would be a warning against giving up on the idea of a future gathering with the Lord, that is, a warning against abandoning hope.

Verse 26 begins a very solemn warning about deliberate sin—turning away from God, as we have seen—by referring back to 10:18. If one turns his or her back on the atoning sacrifice of Christ, there is no other sacrifice for sin to appeal to. The warning is made sharper by comparison in verse 28 with the fate of the Israelites who turned away from the law of God (see Deut 17:6 and especially its context). Such persons were subject to death by stoning. What will be the fate of those who reject the salvation that comes in God's Son (recall the similar argument in 2:2-3)? Verse 30 is a reminder that judgment by God is inescapable; the evidence is from Deut 32:35-36.

THE POWER OF FAITH

Heb 10:32–12:29

10:32-39 Living by faith. The third major division of the sermon begins with a continuation of the preacher's exhortation to his hearers, again softening the rigor of his warning with a reassuring note. Yet this is an appropriate place to see a new section beginning because the passage is a typical transition in Hebrews, shifting the focus from hope and confidence (vv. 35-36) to faith (vv. 38-39).

Verses 32-34 seem at first glance to tell us something concrete about the background of the congregation to which Hebrews is addressed. They are people who, having become Christians, have suffered for their Christian identity and willingly sympathized with other Christians who suffered even more. The passage mentions public exposure to insults, imprisonment, the confiscation of property. But all of these things are expressed in very general terms, and there is no way to draw from them specific conclusions regarding the history of a particular early Christian church. They sound like the typical things various early Christian communities may have had to confront, and that may be precisely the author's intention—to be universal rather than particular. The main point is implicit in verses 35-36: you have made a heavy personal investment in following Christ; much is at stake for you. To give it all up now is an alarming prospect.

What do such people need to sustain their hope? The author finds the answer in the text of Hab 2:3-4 (mainly in its Greek form): it is by faith that the just one shall live. St. Paul quotes this famous line of the passage (Rom 1:17; Gal 3:11), but in a different way. The faith that he has in mind is faith in the person and work of Christ. As we shall see, that is not what Hebrews understands by faith. But it is those who have faith who are able to maintain their confidence and hope (v. 39).

11:1–12:2 A cloud of witnesses to faith. The main component of the third major section of Hebrews, and by far the best-known passage in the work, is the long list of examples of Old Testament models of faith, culminating in the example of Jesus, the new and supreme model, in 12:1-2. The literary form of this passage is well known. Lists of figures from the Old Testament whose lives illustrate some virtue or quality are not uncommon, in the Jewish wisdom literature especially. One can find good examples in Sir 44–50 or Wis 10.

The passage begins with something like a definition of faith that deserves careful attention. For centuries there has been a tradition of interpretation of verse 1 that emphasizes faith as a subjective attitude on the part of the one who has it. This is often reflected in the translation of the verse that is made to speak of "confident assurance" and "conviction." (It is interesting that the older Catholic translations from the Latin of St. Jerome were more objectively oriented, translating the words as "substance" and "evidence.") In fact the Greek text uses very objective language and should be translated more literally: "Now faith is the reality of things hoped for, the evidence of things not seen." Of course faith is personally appropriated, but it is first of all an objective quality. We might well describe it in modern terms as insight into the reality of the invisible divine world. It is related to hope, to be sure, but as a motivation that sustains hope when the goals hoped for are not visible. Since such faith is characteristic of the heroes of the Old Testament (v. 2), it is obviously not oriented toward Christ but toward God and his promises. Verse 6, speaking of Enoch, gives a kind of minimal description of the object of faith: belief that God exists and that he rewards those who follow him. The faith of the Christian will be informed by the word of God spoken in his Son, but it is not really qualitatively different from the faith of the biblical heroes. Perhaps we could preserve a little of the objective character of faith if we substituted the phrase "in faith" for the translation "by faith" in each of the examples to follow.

Verse 3 surprises us. Expecting examples of the "men of old," we first meet a statement in which "By faith we understand that the universe was ordered." If the author wishes to begin at the beginning with creation (Gen 1), there were no witnesses to respond in faith. But perhaps he wants to suggest that there is in fact a continuity between the faith of the ancients and that of his contemporary Christians, for whom faith in God's creation is fundamental to everything else. The examples to follow are not museum pieces, but are illustrative of the same faith demanded of and implicit in the very existence of Christians.

Ideally it would be good to have the space to comment fully on each of the Old Testament examples in this long litany of people who acted in faith. To appreciate the chapter properly, and to enjoy reading it, the reader should be sure he or she has a fresh memory of each story referred to. That involves more "homework" than can be done here. Instead we shall point out some individual instances of exactly what actions were performed in faith, and marginal references in most modern Bibles will provide information about the relevant Old Testament passages to look up.

The story of Cain and Abel (v. 4; Gen 4:1-16) naturally highlights Abel as the example of faith. The fact that Abel "still speaks" may be a reference to his blood crying out to God from the soil (Gen 4:10; see Heb 12:24) or a general reference to the example of Abel still speaking in the Scripture. The faith in which Enoch lived (vv. 5-6; Gen 5:21-24) is deduced from the fact that he was pleasing to God (the Greek version of Genesis) and therefore did not suffer death. Contemporary Jewish literature was fascinated with the idea that Enoch, like Elijah long after him, was "taken up" without experiencing death. The example of Noah (v. 7; Gen 6–9) is clear. Abraham (vv. 8-12; Gen 12–25) was a prime example of faith even for New Testament writers such as St. Paul (see Rom 4:13-25). Verse 11 is notoriously hard to translate. In the Revised Standard Version, Sarah, taken as the subject, tends to interrupt the example of Abraham and is in conflict with a key word of the passage referring to male begetting. Another translation is possible and perhaps preferable: "In faith—though Sarah herself was sterile—he received power to beget even when he was past the age, since he thought that the One who had made the promise was worthy of trust."

The eloquent verses 13-16 sum up the examples of the wandering patriarchs by recalling the theme of pilgrimage in search of a permanent home, thus linking the faith of the patriarchs to that of the Christians. The extended example of Abraham ends with reference to the so-called sacrifice, or "binding," of his son Isaac (vv. 17-19; Gen 22:1-18). This is the supreme example of Abraham's insight into the invisible world of hope. Confronted with the promise that he would have descendants through his only son Isaac and with the paradoxical command to sacrifice Isaac, Abraham could only act with the insight that God could raise from the dead.

Isaac (v. 20; Gen 27) acted in faith when he gave his blessing to Jacob instead of to the older son Esau; subsequent events justified his action (see also Heb 12:16-17). Jacob (v. 21; Gen 48) also reversed the blessing of the sons of Joseph and was vindicated by the history of Ephraim. Joseph (v. 22; Gen 50:24-26) in faith foresaw the Exodus from Egypt when he asked to be buried in the land of promise.

The story of Moses and the Exodus (vv. 23-29; Exod 2–14), given its prominence in the tradition of Israel, naturally provides another extended list of examples of faith. Most of them are clear if one refers to the Book of Exodus, but two details may be mentioned here. In verse 26 God's "Anointed" might be a reference to the Messiah (Christ), which means "the anointed one," but it may equally well refer to Ps 89:52, where "the anointed" means the people of God. Second, Moses' departure from Egypt (v. 27) could refer to his flight to Midian (Exod 2:15), which is more likely, or to the Exodus itself, as many interpreters understand it. The occupation of the land of Canaan is represented by only two allusions: the fall of Jericho (literally "By faith the walls of Jericho fell"; v. 30; Josh 6) and the incident involving Rahab (v. 31; Josh 2:1-24; 6:22-25).

In good rhetorical style the author concludes this long list with a series of summary statements without identifying specific persons with specific events (vv. 32-38). With some detective work one can recognize the Judges, Daniel, the Maccabees, the fate of the prophets (for example, legend had it that Isaiah was sawed in two, v. 37). Appreciation of the passage depends in part on one's knowledge of the biblical and also non-biblical traditions about more recent heroes, but the thrust of the paragraph as a general summary of examples of faith does not depend solely on such knowledge. The main point of the whole list is in verses 39-40: though all the above are valid examples of faith, God deferred the content of his promises until the present time when the Christians respond in faith to the saving work of Jesus Christ.

Although 12:1-2 changes in style to exhortation, it nevertheless functions as the climax to the list of examples of faith and therefore may be included in the same section. Jesus is seen as the supreme example of faith—in the particular sense of Hebrews, in which faith does not have Jesus as its object—with which his followers can identify. Verse 2 speaks of him as what one could call "the leader and perfecter of faith." Christ is thus not only the high priest whose sacrifice finally achieves salvation, but he is also the supreme model of the faith that enables his followers to sustain their hope in the promises of God.

12:3-17 Divine discipline. The long passage of exhortation that follows actually is begun in 12:1-2, and these two verses, besides forming a climactic ending to the list of examples of faith, are the transition to exhortation. The whole passage makes use of an elaborate set of metaphors, some of them developed at length. The first is an athletic one, "running the race that lies ahead" (v. 1), and it is picked up again in verses 12-13. Second is the metaphor of the father disciplining his children (vv. 5-11), and third, that of the "bitter root" (v. 15).

Verses 3-4 continue the metaphor of the Christian life as an athletic contest. The example of Jesus' suffering as a man of faith can help to sustain the Christian in the ongoing struggle. The struggle is against sin, and human suffering is interpreted as the price one must pay to avoid sin. It is not certain whether persecution of Christians is hinted at here, or even martyrdom, though 10:32-34 clearly implied opposition to Christians from outside their own circles. Resisting "to the point of shedding blood" might be a vivid description of the athlete's exertions, perhaps those of a wrestler rather than a runner.

Verses 5-6 quote a well-known passage from Prov 3:11-12, and verses 7-11 are the preacher's homiletic interpretation of it. Among the many ways he understands the word of God in Scripture—the Holy Spirit speaking, Jesus speaking, God speaking to or about his Son, and the like—we meet a new one here. This time the word addresses the Christian hearers directly as sons of the Father (compare the direct address in Psalm 95; Heb 3:7). The designation of Christians as sons or children of God is not frequent in Hebrews (recall 2:10), but it is important. Because they share in the saving work of the divine Son, they share in his sonship also. The application of the metaphor of discipline is clearly presented. This time human suffering is interpreted as evidence that God is disciplining the children he loves to bring them to maturity. Like the divine Son, they too must learn from their suffering (see 5:8). Verses 12-13 return to the image of a runner who, weary and sore, is tempted to give up the race.

The next exhortation is of a somewhat different kind, resembling more what we will find in chapter 13. But the author turns it to a familiar theme in verse 17. There is in verses 14-16 a concern for what we might call the integrity of the Christian community: peace with all, holiness, the absence of any notorious sinners who might lead others astray. The "bitter root" in verse 15 refers to Deut 29:18, a warning against the harmful effect on the Israelite community of people who turn to the worship of idols. Gen 25:27-34 tells the story of how Esau gave up his rights as the elder son of Isaac in exchange for a meal. In later Jewish interpretation Esau was accused of many kinds of evil, and that is probably why Hebrews makes him an example of a fornicator and a godless person. Verse 17 has caused difficulties for interpreters. It refers to the story in Gen 27 of how Esau's younger brother Jacob received the blessing of his father Isaac instead of Esau himself (see 11:20). Esau becomes an example of a person who renounced his salvation (by selling his birthright) and was unable to repent afterwards. The example is, of course, a warning to the Christian community not to abandon their salvation, a warning familiar to us from such passages as 6:4-6.

12:18-29 The unshakable kingdom. There seems to be an abrupt change of thought as we begin to read verse 18, but actually this is not the case. The verse begins with "for." The example of Esau was a warning, but it was not really a threat. Christians do not have to live in fear of imitating the failures of certain figures in the history of salvation, real as the danger is, for they have advantages which the ancients did not have. In a truly eloquent passage the preacher contrasts the ancient Israelite's approach to Mount Sinai, the place of the law and the old covenant, with the Christians' approach to the heavenly Jerusalem on Mount Zion, the "place" of the new covenant mediated by Christ (v. 24). At issue are two fundamental theological questions. First is that of access to God. The

Israelites' access, according to the Exodus story, was at best indirect and at worst reluctant. They experienced it in an atmosphere of fear and trembling (v. 21). The Christians by contrast, thanks to the saving sacrifice of Christ, approach God in confidence and splendor. The second theological question has to do with time. The Christians' access to God has been made possible by Christ's entrance into the heavenly sanctuary, but for individual Christians this entrance, following the forerunner, is still in the future. We encounter here the poles of the "already" and the "not yet," which also characterize the thought of other New Testament writers such as St. Paul.

The picture of the Israelites at Mount Sinai in verses 18-21 is drawn with details derived from Exod 19 and other Old Testament passages. It is obviously selective, designed to emphasize the gloomy and fearful aspects of the old covenant experience in contrast to the picture of Mount Zion (vv. 22-24). In the latter we again find a scene of God enthroned in heaven, with the angels in attendance. The groups mentioned in verse 23 have been interpreted in different ways. Perhaps the "assembly of the firstborn" refers to Christians of an earlier generation, and the "spirits of the just made perfect" to the Old Testament heroes of faith, who now have access to God along with the Christians (see 11:39-40). The "sprinkled blood" of verse 24 connotes the death of Jesus interpreted as a covenant sacrifice (see 9:15-22). Speaking from heaven, it is contrasted with the blood of Abel already alluded to in 11:4 (see Gen 4:10), which cries out from the earth.

Verse 25 repeats a now familiar argument (see 10:26-31) warning that Christians who do not listen to God speaking through the sacrifice of Christ in heaven risk an even greater punishment than the Israelites, who refused to obey God speaking on Mount Sinai. The importance of heeding God's word recalls the beginning of the sermon. God's voice was accompanied by an earthquake (v. 26) at Mount Sinai (according to Ps 68:9). He has promised in Hag 2:6 to shake the world once more in the time to come, and there will remain only an eternal, unshakable kingdom for those who are faithful to him. Because Christ has already made access to God possible, the preacher can reassure his hearers that they are in the process of receiving that kingdom. The main part of the sermon ends (v. 29) with a quotation from Deut 4:24, an eloquent reminder that God's justice should motivate the Christian's faithfulness.

FINAL INSTRUCTIONS AND CONCLUSION

Heb 13:1-25

13:1-17 Various instructions. The sermon to the Hebrews seems to conclude at the end of chapter 12. If that is the case, chapter 13 is a kind of appendix which provides a variety of practical instructions and exhortations (vv. 1-17) and a number of features typical of the endings of letters (vv. 18-25). There is every reason to think the chapter was written by the author of the whole document: the style of writing is the same, and especially the use made of the Old Testament is similar. In addition there is no evidence that chapter 13 was added at some later time. We have already seen, for example in chapter 10 and elsewhere, how closely the preacher-author links practical matters of Christian living to his theological explanations, and in effect he continues the process in chapter 13. The point is an important one: as in the letters of St. Paul and other New Testament letters, practical Christian conduct is not a matter of indifference. It flows from one's understanding of the person and saving work of Christ.

The first six verses form a list of disparate instructions concerning brotherly love, hospitality, concern for prisoners and the suffering, fidelity in marriage, and avoiding love of money. The list may be rather conventional, but it is meant seriously. Christian conduct is not always distinctively different, but it is always distinctively motivated. In support of dependence on God and not on money, verses 5-6 quote Deut 31:6 and Ps 117:6 (in its Greek form).

Both verses 7 and 17 refer to "your leaders," using a term that is very general and not very common in the New Testament (see also v. 24). One cannot deduce from it what might have been the official leadership, if any, of the church in question. But the two verses refer to different leaders. The first are the former leaders who proclaimed God's word (message) to the community in the past. One is reminded of the people mentioned in 2:3.

They have passed away, but their lives remain as examples of faith, of insight into the invisible realm of God. In this context verse 8, perhaps the most memorable line in Hebrews, has an application. The statement that "Jesus Christ is the same yesterday, today, and forever" may well have an independent origin as a formula used in worship. Here it suggests that generations of church leaders may come and go, but the content of their proclamation, Jesus Christ, remains (a priest) forever. The leaders of verse 17 are contemporaries, whose function seems to be mainly to protect the community from harm. It is possible that verses 7 and 17 enclose the warning against "strange teaching" (vv. 9-16), with the implication that following the leaders would obviate the danger. But the passage is less than fully clear.

It is very difficult to be certain what situation is envisaged in verses 9-16, or even what the author is recommending. The "strange teaching" has to do with foods, but whether the context is Jewish food laws or some non-Jewish practice is unclear. Compare the somewhat similar warnings in Col 2:16, 20-23. The Old Testament background of the passage is Lev 16:27, which stipulates that some of the animals sacrificed on the Day of Atonement are killed outside the Israelites' encampment and burned there. Likewise, Jesus died outside the gate of Jerusalem as was traditionally believed (see John 19:17). The sanctuary and "outside the camp" are clearly understood in a symbolic way here, but there is little agreement on how, and interpreters offer even contradictory explanations. One possibility is that the author is warning against living the Christian life as though it were a sanctuary. One must go out into the everyday world to experience suffering where Jesus himself suffered. Since there is only one true sacrifice, the once-for-all sacrifice of Christ in the heavenly sanctuary, Christians can offer only analogous sacrifices of prayer, good deeds, and generosity (vv. 15-16).

13:18-25 Conclusion. The final verses remind us very much of the conclusion of a letter. They include a request for prayers for the author (18-19), a rather elaborate blessing or prayer (20-21), reference to what has been written (22), news of Timothy and mention of a planned visit (23), greetings (24), and a final blessing (25). Several of these features can be paralleled, for example, in 1 Thess 5:23-28, where we find a long blessing or prayer, a request for prayers for the author, greetings, and a final blessing. 1 Thessalonians is also a letter in which Timothy figures prominently (see 1:1; 3:2, 6). The author of Hebrews uses these letter features because he is sending his sermon in writing. Note that verse 22 refers to writing, not a letter, but a "message of encouragement" (or exhortation), that is, a sermon. In its only other New Testament usage, in Acts 13:15, this expression refers to a synagogue sermon of Paul.

The very beautiful blessing of verses 20-21 is often thought to have its origin in the worship of the Christian community. That may be so, but in its reference to "the blood of the eternal covenant"—a brief summary of the argument of chapters 8–10—and its use of Old Testament language, it may also have been composed by the preacher as a solemn conclusion to his sermon, which is mentioned in the next verse. It is not certain that the final phrase, in Greek "to whom be glory forever," points to Christ. That is possible in such passages (for example, 2 Pet 3:18), but it would be more usual for it to refer to God (for example, 1 Pet 5:10-11). The biblical background of the opening statement is Isa 63:11, which refers to God's having raised up from the sea the shepherd of the sheep, that is, he saved Moses and the Israelites from the Red Sea during the Exodus. There is no clear reference to the resurrection of Jesus here. The word "brought up" is not a resurrection word in the New Testament. Instead, the passage refers to bringing Christ from the dead up into heaven, which has been the basic picture throughout the sermon ever since 1:3. Though one must assume that the author knew about the resurrection of Jesus, it is not a central part of his theology.

What ought to be concrete hints about the origin of Hebrews in the final verses actually gives us little help. Timothy (v. 23) was a well-known figure in the early church, as is shown in the letters of Paul, the letters to Timothy, and the Acts of the Apostles. But how he relates to the author is not stated ("our brother" means merely our fellow-Christian). The second part of verse 24, which says literally, "Those from Italy greet you," does not help us locate the document since it could mean writing from Italy itself (probably Rome) or from somewhere where there are Christian visitors from Italy. The final blessing is identical with that of the letter to Titus. Paul himself prefers the phrase "the grace of our Lord Jesus Christ," while letters imitating him usually just say "grace."

REVELATION

Pheme Perkins

INTRODUCTION

A book for troubled times

The past ten years have seen an explosion of interest in the Book of Revelation at all levels, from that of the biblical scholar down to the casual Bible reader. From one end of the globe to the other, people are asking questions about Revelation. Why the attraction of this complex, often bizarre writing, which seems as far as one could get from our modern world of science and technology? Of course, most of the questions are based on a misunderstanding of Revelation, which assumes that it is a symbolic code predicting the exact persons and events that are leading to the end of the world. This type of understanding has existed in heretical Christian circles since the second century A.D. A group of Montanists even went off into the Phrygian wilderness to see the heavenly Jerusalem descend out of heaven. Like such prophets ever since, they were disappointed in their expectations. The church did not end Sacred Scripture with this book in order to provide glorified predictions of future events.

Anyone who expects predictions of that sort misses the spiritual message of Revelation. It is this spiritual truth that should compel present interest in the book. Despite scientific progress, despite communications media which give us greater and greater access to information and events, despite national and international efforts to relieve human suffering, the world seems more out of joint than ever. Senseless brutality, war, oppression, starvation—wherever we look civilized societies seem to be coming apart at the seams.

Perhaps the best index of our distress is in our movies. The popular movies *Star Wars* and *The Empire Strikes Back* picture a future in which most of the universe has been subjected to evil forces. The "high-tech" background of these movies also mirrors our society. The power of good, "the force," seems reduced to its last card in young, inexperienced, and spiritually undisciplined Luke Skywalker. These movies are not like the old Westerns to which they are often compared. There we always know that the "good guys" will win. They are bigger, better looking, smarter, have better horses, etc. The *Star Wars* movies, on the other hand, no longer provide the good with such an overwhelming advantage. *The Empire Strikes Back* ends with the hint that Luke's own father may have deserted the force to head the empire. Thus, these movies give a striking portrayal of the uncertainty of technological progress and of its futility in the face of evil and spiritual confusion. At the same time, they evoke hope for a time of spiritual renewal.

The Book of Revelation is like such a movie of its time. We find cosmic distances between earth and heaven; the good represented by a small, persecuted group of humans on earth; heavenly aid and inspiration to sustain them; strange, symbolic animals, and cosmic warfare between the forces of good and evil. So, we might ask ourselves what this Christian prophet from the end of the first century has to say to the end of the twentieth. What letters would he be writing to our churches? What would he say about the spiritual disorientation of Christians today? The growing interest in the Book of Revelation shows that people have an instinctual feeling for its message. They are looking for a vision of the struggle between good and evil which does not leave inspiration to modern filmmakers or, for that matter, to simplistic prophets of doom.

Revelation as an apocalypse

A person who has never seen the *Star Wars* movies will not understand the comparison in the previous section as well as one who has. Most twentieth-century readers are in a similar position with regard to Revelation. It is full of images that have a long history, stretching from ancient Near Eastern myth through the Old Testament prophets to Jewish apocalypses like the Book of Daniel. These images were also being used and reused in Jewish writings from New Testament times. Some images in Revelation might also evoke Greek mythology, which would be familiar to its readers from the consistent use of such themes in the decorative arts.

Apocalypse is the Greek word for "revelation." From Daniel at the end of the Old Testament to Revelation at the end of the New, and even beyond the time of Revelation, we have a wide variety of such visionary writings from Jewish and Christian circles. They were a form of expression that the audience was familiar with, just as people today are familiar with the *Star Wars* type of film, even if they have not seen the above examples. Read Dan 7–12. Much of the imagery in Revelation derives from Daniel and from the imagery of Old Testament prophets. These chapters of Daniel contain a series of visions of the course of world history. The cycles of visions overlap and provide alternate pictures of the same events. Revelation uses cycles of visions in the same way. Daniel and Revelation are both addressed to a community suffering persecution. When Daniel was written, the Syrian ruler of Palestine had been trying to force people to renounce Judaism. Many who refused were put to death. Reflection on the significance of their martyrdom led to a theology of martyrdom. The blood of these martyrs was seen as expiation for the sins of those Jews who had not remained faithful to their religion.

That theology of martyrdom played an important part in early Christian understanding of the death of Jesus. His blood was seen as an expiation for the sins of the whole world. Revelation presents us with this picture of Jesus as the faithful martyr. He can use the Danielic picture of the faithful martyrs to encourage Christians who face persecution. Just as Antiochus failed to wipe out Judaism, so the new imperial beast, Rome, will fail to destroy the Christian faithful. Notice the image of "one like a Son of Man" ascending to God's throne in Dan 7. Originally, the "Son of Man" who receives dominion over the world referred to the martyrs of Israel. Once again, Revelation is able to apply that image to Christ. Jesus is revealed as the heavenly Son of Man in the opening verses of the book.

The Jewish apocalypses 4 Ezra and 2 Baruch, which were written about the same time as Revelation, address the suffering and spiritual disorientation felt by the Jews after the Romans had destroyed Jerusalem and burnt down the temple. Like Revelation, 2 Baruch includes letters to those who are to receive the revelation. All three apocalypses are concerned with the question of why God does not step in and send the messianic age by destroying evil—especially the Satanic embodiment of evil in the Roman Empire. All three answer with symbolic visions of world history unrolling according to a plan that God has measured out. They promise the faithful that they are much closer to the end of history than to its beginning. They reassure the suffering with the certainty of divine judgment on those who do evil and happiness for those who have endured. Those who have suffered and died out of faithfulness to God are not forgotten. They are enjoying happiness and peace. Though the images and themes of Revelation seem strange to us, these parallel examples show that they were well known at the time the book was written.

All of these apocalypses come from people oppressed by imperial powers. That situation is another reason that they use highly symbolic language, which only people familiar with the tradition of interpreting such images could understand. Criticism of political rulers could be dangerous business. Some ancient philosophers criticized tyrannical political power, but they would often wait until a particular emperor had been assassinated and was out of popular favor before making critical remarks. The Jewish writers use an additional device both to protect themselves and to lend authority to their visions. They present their writings as the secret, recently discovered revelation of a famous person from an earlier time of persecution. Daniel was a wise man at the court of the Babylonian king three centuries earlier. Baruch was a scribe at the time of the Babylonian Exile and an associate of the prophet Jeremiah. Ezra was a scribe who brought some people back to Palestine from the Exile when the Persians came to power almost a century later. These sages of Israel are claimed to have left symbolic revelations of the future sufferings that had now come upon Israel.

The reader of Revelation will immediately notice a difference. The author does use the tradition of symbolic language and has the evils of Babylon stand for the evils of the Roman Empire, but he does not hide behind a pseudonym. He tells us who he is and where he is: a Christian prophet named John, on the island of Patmos. On the artistic plane, there is an immediacy and sweep to his revelation that is different from his Jewish contemporaries. They engage the revealing angel in extensive dialogues about evil and divine justice. Their visions are said to take place over a lengthy period, often punctuated by periods of fasting and isolation. John's vision does not include such theological dialogue. It appears to happen all at once, so that the reader is swept through scene after scene. Like an epic movie, these scenes are linked together with a dramatic sound track—the chaos and disorder of battle, the thunder of horses, the sound of trumpets, and the beautiful pauses in heaven when the heavenly hosts sing praises to God and to Christ. The onrush does not stop until we find ourselves in the peace of the new Jerusalem.

In this study of Revelation, we will break up the book and trace the background of its symbolic visions. Such a process, however, ruins its dramatic sweep. Try reading the whole through without stopping. It is best to read it through aloud, since most people only came to know Revelation as they heard it read—probably during a liturgical assembly. The details of this study should contribute to that vision of Revelation as a whole.

The author and his situation

People often assume that Revelation was written by the same person who wrote the Fourth Gospel. However, the author does not identify himself as the evangelist. In fact, he even refers to the apostles as a separate group from the past (18:20; 21:14). Even in ancient times people recognized that the two books could not have been written by the same person, since they do not have the same style. But the use of Revelation by heretical groups had led many Christians to be suspicious of it. By treating the John of Revelation as though he were John the evangelist, it was possible to win recognition for Revelation among Christians who might otherwise have rejected it. Today we do not require such a fiction about the author. We recognize that the church has included this writing in Scripture because it does contain an authentic and important vision of Christian faith.

Revelation opens with seven very stylized letters to churches in cities in Asia Minor. However, the author clearly expects that the whole book will be read. That means that all seven letters are intended to instruct all Christians, not just those in the particular churches. Doubtless, Christians living in Asia Minor at the end of the first century were able to understand the symbolic allusions to people and events better than we can today. However, some general problems emerge clearly enough. Some Christians are becoming lax. They seem to have lost interest in testifying to their faith. Others are being led astray by false Christian teachers and prophets, both men and women. It is harder to tell what the references to the "synagogue of Satan" and to "those who claim to be Jews but are not" mean. Some scholars think that the Jewish population of the cities mentioned was responsible for the persecution of Christians. Others suggest that Christians were trying to avoid suspicion and persecution by claiming to be Jewish.

The visions show us faithful Christians who are liable to persecution, and sometimes martyrdom, for failure to worship the emperor. There is no evidence for a formal decree enforcing such veneration throughout the empire. The persecution referred to in Revelation must have been a local phenomenon. Perhaps it was even instigated by local officials or other citizens who wanted to demonstrate their own loyalty to Roman imperial rule. Tradition associates Revelation with the period of the emperor Domitian (assassinated A.D. 96). He emphasized the monarchic side of imperial office and ruthlessly executed those in his own circles whom he suspected of disloyalty. Though he sometimes tried to gain favor in the provinces by removing a particularly unpopular local official and though his rule was a time of prosperity in Asia Minor, he was not universally loved. His assassination was greeted with outbursts of violence against his statues. Clearly, Christians were not the only Roman subjects who were discontented.

People often find it hard to understand "emperor worship." They think that it meant putting the emperor in the place that we reserve for God. Revelation agrees, but most people would have been puzzled by that attitude. Remember, the ancients had many gods. They also believed that some humans were exalted to dwell with the gods after death. Roman art depicts the soul of the emperor being carried up into such heavenly company from the time of Julius Caesar on. Veneration of living emperors began with his successor, Augustus. Often it simply meant using the same language about the emperor and the benefits he bestowed on humanity as was used about the gods in prayers and hymns. Private citizens or individual towns might honor the emperor by establishing holidays and offering sacrifices and holding festal games in his name. They might send an emissary to the emperor's court to inform him of those honors. They hoped, of course, that the emperor would respond by showering his divine favor on their city—perhaps granting relief from some form of taxation. Towns would also vie with their neighbors to see who could come up with the most lavish honors. These practices, then, involved a large measure of civic pride and even local political maneuvering. All this activity was in the hope of gaining some advantage from this distant figure whose statues and images were everywhere, who was felt to control the whole world, and yet whom most people would never see.

Such civic occasions were not the only ones on which a person who refused to venerate the emperor could be exposed to ridicule or suspicion. Elements of emperor worship formed part of everyday life. Slaves and people who had suffered losses in court suits might flee to a statue of the emperor in hopes of obtaining mercy from this distant person who represented "all-seeing" justice. Of course, such hopes were rarely fulfilled, but the mere fact that people had heard stories of people being so helped kept the hope alive. Most formal business and legal transactions were sealed with oaths sworn to the gods and the emperor. People might be asked to swear such an oath when receiving a loan or paying taxes. Local trade guilds might have banquets at which toasts were spoken in honor of the emperor. Perhaps the meal would begin with a libation being poured out in his honor. Even in private homes such libations might be offered at the beginning of the meal.

Jews avoided such situations by avoiding business and social contact with non-Jews. They were well known among non-Jews for their refusal to participate in the various manifestations of civic pride and solidarity. Consequently, they had the reputation of being "haters of humanity." Christians were in a different position. Most belonged to that larger non-Jewish community. Further, they could not carry out the task of witnessing to their faith if they withdrew from contact with the larger world. However, we can see as early as 1 Corinthians that Christians had problems in their social contact with non-Christians. 1 Cor 8 and 10 discuss the various sorts of banquets that a Christian might attend. St. Paul told Christians that they did not have to isolate themselves. They did not even have to avoid meat that had been used in sacrifice to a pagan god and then sold in the market, but they had to avoid compromising their faith in two ways. They could not accept an invitation to a banquet held in a temple honoring a pagan god (1 Cor 10:14-22). While they could accept invitations to the homes of pagan friends and eat whatever was served, they had to refuse to eat meat if someone made a point of telling them that it had been used in a sacrifice to an idol (10:27-32).

St. Paul also tried to deal with the question of Christian loyalty to the political order in Rom 13:1-7. Even though Christians know that all authority is based in God and that Jesus' return will soon bring human authorities to an end, they should still obey those in power, since their role is to see that good is promoted and evil punished. 1 Pet 2:12-17 echoes the same sentiments. Christians are even instructed to "honor the emperor." Since this benign view of poitical power was widely held in early Christianity, we can presume that it may have contributed to the confusion felt by Christians in Asia Minor. Should they avoid persecution, giving offense, by going along with local customs and demands? What was the difference between not asking questions about the meat and, perhaps, pouring a little libation in honor of the gods? If authorities are to be obeyed, then shouldn't one just swear the oaths required? Considering the social context of emperor worship, how easy it might be for Christians to come to such a conclusion. Perhaps some of the false teachers mentioned in the letters taught Christians that they could make such accommodations. John wants to make it clear that there is a big difference: Using language about the emperor as though he were a god or participating in rituals that honored him as such was equivalent to denying that one is a Christian. That is equivalent to joining forces with Satanic power.

The theology of Revelation

Revelation addressses serious questions about how Christians are to live in a larger, often hostile society. We may not know people today who are compelled to such veneration of political power, but we do not have to look far in the morning paper to read of the harassment or even murder of those who oppose governmental oppression in the name of Christian love and concern for the poor. The most perplexing cases are those in which governments of so-called Christian countries seem to promote policies of oppression that run directly counter to the ethical teaching of Christianity. Revelation speaks about such experiences. It warns us against the temptation to be silent or look the other way in the presence of evil and injustice.

There are also the smaller situations of daily life in which Christians prefer to remain silent and apathetic. Some would require us to act as a group, a church, or group of churches to oppose wrongs in the local community. Others, like the situation of the Christian at a friend's banquet, are more individual. Perhaps we allow people to slander or make fun of what we believe in rather than speak up. We would rather avoid controversy than question opinions, attitudes, and practices that we think are wrong. Of course, sometimes people remain silent because they do not know how to speak in defense of what they believe. People often want to defend their beliefs but lack the words with which to do so. We need to do everything we can to help one another become more articulate believers. After all, as Revelation so often insists, no Christian is immune from the obligation to bear witness.

Finally, the grand sweep of Revelation should lead us to resist the kind of pessimism that looks at the vastness of evil in the world and decides that any effort to change things would be a waste of time. Such judgments are false because Christians are not to measure what is true or right by statistics. Such judgments are arrogant because God is the only one who can determine "what's worth it." Such judgments are demonic because they only contribute to the hold that evil and pessimism have over human lives. Revelation is not a book aimed at scaring Christians into being good. It is a book to encourage them in the face of the most awful shape that evil can assume: when it takes on all the trappings of divine, imperial power; when it also has the force of local opinion behind it; when even some religious leaders are lined up against the few who would resist. Yet, it is the faithful few who share the victory that Christ's death has won over evil.

Structure of Revelation

Revelation has a complex structure. Many scholars think that the author put together vision accounts that were originally separate. While this subject of source analysis is beyond the scope of this commentary, please note that the author announces the next cycle of visions before he is finished with the cycle he is recounting. Such passages are similar to the flashes forward and backward in movies. The broad skeleton of the book seems to be built on the series of seven used to organize the vision cycles. In addition, the visions are presented as the contents of two scrolls: one, opened by the Lamb, dominates chapters 5–10; the other, eaten by the prophet, covers chapters 11–22. The second half of the book also has a dualistic axis embodied in the struggle between God and Satan, which is presented as the contrast between two cities—Babylon (= Rome) and Jerusalem.

OUTLINE OF THE BOOK OF REVELATION

1:1-8	a. Prologue Preface (vv. 1-3) Prescript and Sayings (vv. 4-8)
1:9–3:22	b. Seven Letters
4:1–8:5	c. Seven Seals
8:2–11:19	d. Seven Trumpets
12:1–15:4	e. Unnumbered Visions
15:5–16:21	f. Seven Bowls Babylon Interlude (17:1–19:10)
19:11–21:8	g. Unnumbered Visions Jerusalem Interlude (21:9–22:5)
22:6-20	h. Epilogue Sayings (vv. 6-20) Benediction (v. 21)

COMMENTARY

PROLOGUE

Rev 1:1-18

The prologue has two parts. The first is a titular introduction to the Book of Revelation as a whole (vv. 1-3). The second is an introduction to the first section, the letters to the seven churches (vv. 4-8).

1:1-3 Heed this revelation. The opening words of the book are: "The revelation of Jesus Christ." The word "revelation" has a special meaning here, just as it does elsewhere in the New Testament. It does not refer to any sort of divine inspiration. Rather, it means knowledge of how the world will stand under God's judgment when history comes to an end. Such knowledge does not require detailed predictions about the events or timing of the end of the world, the sort of false interpretation often given of Revelation; what it requires is an understanding of the conditions for salvation, whenever that final judgment comes. We have already suggested in the Introduction that Revelation seeks to correct Christians who are confused about what is required for salvation.

The opening sentence is awkward, since everyone responsible for this revelation is included. The message in Revelation is both a messsage from Jesus to his churches and from God about the coming judgment. The seven letters are tied to a vision of Jesus as the heavenly Son of Man. The visions which follow the letters introduce angelic mediators, who interpret what John sees. Such angels are a common feature of Jewish apocalypses. As we have already seen, this apocalypse is unusual in being attributed to a living prophet rather than to a famous figure of the past.

Several expressions in this section are used to conclude the book. The promise to show "what must happen soon" (v. 1) reappears at 22:6. In 22:16, Jesus is the one who sends the angel. Similar promises to reveal "what will happen in the last days" appear in Dan 2:28f., 45. There "what is to happen" refers to the destruction of human empires and the establishment of the eternal rule of God. The same structure informs the visions that are to come in Revelation.

Some scholars think that "servants" in verse 1 only refers to a school of Christian prophets who were seeking such visions; however, we agree with those who feel that it refers to all Christians. The next verse pronounces a blessing on all who read, hear, and heed the message. It suggests that Revelation is to be read aloud in the liturgical assembly and is addressed to all. A similar beatitude appears in the conclusion (22:7). The solemn announcement of beatitude in a liturgical assembly carries a note of warning. Those who do not heed the revelation will not find themselves included in salvation. These beatitudes may reflect Luke 11:28, "blest are they who hear the word of God and keep it." Revelation contains the only beatitudes outside the Gospels. In keeping with the number symbolism of the book, there are seven (1:3; 14:13; 16:15; 19:9; 20:6; 22:7, 14). The others refer to the blessings of salvation.

Verse 2 introduces important words in the vocabulary of Revelation, "testimony/witness." The same Greek word underlies both English words. The parallel phrases "word of God" and "testimony of Jesus Christ" suggest that Revelation uses "witness" in a wider sense than that of a martyr who dies for the faith. In verse 9 (RSV) we learn that John was exiled to Patmos "on account of the word of God and the testimony of Jesus" (the New American Bible has interpreted this sentence by adding words that are not in the Greek). Here in verse 2, John places the whole revelation in the category of "word of God and testimony of Jesus." Since he can use the same expression in both contexts, we should presume that the content of this revelation is not a complete surprise. He already holds to the principles that are expressed in these visions. He has already opposed the "beast" in some way. Perhaps he was also worried by the laxity that he saw growing up among Christians. The revelation will bring together and clarify those experiences and concerns. The prophet can say for sure that Christians must not be taken in either by false teachers or the desire to avoid hardship and embarrassment. Instead, they must heed this vision of God as the sovereign ruler of the world.

1:4-8 A message to the churches. This section begins with the standard opening for a letter. Once again, multiple testimony is behind the message in the coming letters. John is the mouthpiece for God and Jesus. "Grace and peace" was a common early Christian greeting for the opening of a letter. The last verse will come back to this letter introduction with the concluding benediction: "The grace of the Lord Jesus be with all" (22:21). The greeting ends with verse 5a. It is followed by a doxology (vv. 5b-6) and two prophetic oracles.

Balancing lists of titles set off the names of the senders of the letter, God and Jesus. Instead of the standard expression for the divine "is, was, and always will be," God is described as the One "who is and who was and who is to come." The standard formula might be misunderstood. It might suggest that God will not do anything about manifesting his sovereignty over evil. The seven spirits before the throne use Jewish liturgical images. They can have a number of interpretations: seven archangels; the seven eyes of God (so Zech 4:10); seven lights (as in the Jewish apocalypse *2 Enoch* 6, 11). The three parts to the name of Jesus parallel the name of God. "Faithful witness" may refer to all of Jesus' testimony and not simply his death, since Revelation often uses "witness" in a more general sense. "First-born of the dead" refers to Jesus' resurrection. It appears in a hymnic passage celebrating Jesus' cosmic rule in Col 1:18. Finally, "ruler of the kings of the earth" begins to introduce the political overtones of the message. Jesus already rules those who are using their power to harass his followers. The doxology which follows upon verse 5a calls Christians to give glory to Jesus for the salvation that they have received. Doxologies and hymns of praise are an important part of the prophetic insight of Revelation. They teach Christians that they already owe God thanks for his victory and salvation. They do not have to wait until the final destruction of evil for victory.

Two prophetic sayings conclude this section. The first is a combination of Dan 7:13 and Zech 12:10. Early Christians used this saying as a judgment oracle against those who reject Jesus (Matt 24:30; John 19:37). Oracles of judgment such as this one have a dual perspective, since they also point to the salvation promised the faithful. Revelation itself is to be read from this perspective. Judgment against evil and its forces represents the salvation of those who are faithful.

The final saying reminds the hearer that this revelation comes from the one who is truly God. Revelation uses "Alpha and the Omega," the first and last letters of the Greek alphabet, for both God and Christ (1:17; 2:8; 21:6; 22:13). "The almighty" *(pantokratōr)* is a divine title (4:8; 11:17; 15:3; 16:7, 14; 19:6, 15; 21:22). It sets God off as king against the power claimed by the empire in the later visions. The liturgical imagery of this section makes it clear from the beginning that this revelation comes with all the authority of God.

LETTERS TO THE CHURCHES

Rev 1:9–3:22

1:9-20 Prophetic call vision. The first vision of Jesus in Revelation commissions the prophet to write to the churches in Asia Minor. Though addressed to specific communities, these messages introduce a revelation addressed to the whole Christian community.

The problems in those churches were probably typical of those faced by Christians elsewhere. John's prophetic call is somewhat different from the Old Testament call stories. The Christian prophet is primarily a witness to the message from the risen Jesus. Jesus, not the prophet, is pictured as the one standing over against a wayward people with the words of judgment or consoling the faithful with those of promise.

The prophet makes it clear that he is a member of the community to which this revelation is addressed. "Distress," "the kingdom," and "endurance" present the conditions for Christian salvation. "Endurance" is a special term in the New Testament. It means more than just putting up with hardship. It is the virtue which enables people to remain faithful right through to the end, even though the final days of the world would be characterized by terrible distress and affliction for the righteous. Usually, people think of kingly rule as something that they will share with Jesus only in the future. However, John means more than that. He has already shown that Jesus is ruler of the kings of the earth. Therefore, he can speak of the Christian who endures the sufferings of the last days as already sharing in that rule.

Patmos was a small, poor island with no city on it. John makes it clear that his witness has led to his banishment there. He does not explain the situation further, since the Christians in Asia Minor were probably familiar with the circumstances. Early Christians substituted celebration of the "Lord's Day" for the Jewish sabbath, since it was the day on which Christ rose (see *Barnabas* 15,9; Ignatius, *Magnesians* 9). It was the day on which they met to celebrate the Eucharist (*Didache* 14). Thus, the author sets his visions at the most solemn liturgical time in the Christian week. The voice of God appears as a trumpet in the Old Testament (Ezek 3:12; Exod 19:16). A trumpet call was to signal the end of the world (1 Thess 4:16).

The number seven, which is the primary numerological symbol in Revelation, has many different associations. Some ancient authors would see the seven as the seven planets. The Roman emperor could be portrayed as holding seven stars (= the planets) as symbols of his universal dominion. Consequently, the image of Jesus holding seven stars provides a symbolic challenge to that claim of authority. He is the ruler of the cosmos. In the immediate context of the book, seven refers to the churches to which the letters are addressed (v. 20).

The description of Jesus is not intended as the representation of a visual image. Rather, the seer has brought together a number of images from the Old Testament to express the divine nature and authority of Jesus. The basic image combines the Son of Man who takes the throne in Dan 7:13-14 with the image of God, the Ancient of Days, who gives him that throne (Dan 7:9-10). Other elements in the description come from a vision Daniel has of a revealing angel in 10:5-6. Read those passages. A person familiar with Daniel would immediately recognize that Jesus is presented as an angelic, heavenly being who is both the source of revelation and the one who has dominion over the world. The sword in the mouth of the figure probably refers to the sword of the word of God (cf. Isa 49:2).

The initial reaction of fear at the appearance of the angelic or divine revealer is common in such visions (Isa 6:5; Ezek 1:28; Dan 8:18; 10:9-11). It is followed by reassurance (Dan 10:12). The description of Jesus had given him some divine attributes. Now he receives the titles of God: "first and last," "the one who lives." He merits these titles because of his death and resurrection.

One theme continuing throughout Revelation is the paradox of death and life. Jesus died and now lives. Those who are not faithful may live now, but they will die later when they are condemned at the judgment. If Christians can remain convinced that Jesus' death/resurrection has reversed the poles of life and death, that there is life far more important than anxious concern for our mortal bodies, then they will not be subject to fear and intimidation. Revelation tries to deal with that fear throughout its visions with vivid, almost grotesque portrayals of the reality of earthly life in contrast to the peace and glory of heaven. We make many decisions that are unconsciously motivated by our fear of dying—either actual death or symbolic death in the loss of something that we love or think we cannot live without. Thus, even if we are not faced with the threat of martyrdom, we still need to examine our own conviction about life/death. Is it really changed, reversed even, by our belief that Christ died and now lives? Or is it the same anxious concern with present self and security that motivates those who have no faith?

Some interpreters try to argue that the "angels of the churches" refers to the bishops of those communities. However, the letters never suggest that they are directed toward specific church leaders. Therefore, we would agree with those who assume that Revelation is thinking of the angelic guardians of those churches along the lines of Jewish speculation of the time which held that angels had been assigned to the different nations of the earth. This perspective also fits in with another feature of Revelation: The truth of external earthly events is found in the action in heaven which initiates them.

The letter pattern

The letter section provides prophetic evaluation, critique and encouragement to the churches mentioned. Each letter follows a pattern:

1. Command to write.
2. Prophetic messenger formula with a description of Jesus as the sender.
3. "I know" section.
   It includes some of the following elements: (a) "I know that" + description of the situation; (b) "But I have it against you" (censure); (c) command to repent; (d) "Look" + prophetic saying; (e) promise: the Lord is coming soon; (f) exhortation to hold fast.
4. Call to hear.
5. Promise of reward to those who are victorious.

These letters do not give us much information about the problems in the churches of Asia Minor. They speak in a cryptic way about situations that were familiar to the original audience. Their message is a prophetic warning that Christians must take care lest they lose the salvation that Christ has won for them.

Ignatius, the bishop of Antioch, wrote letters to churches in the same area about two decades later (ca. A.D. 110). They show that some of the same problems mentioned in these letters continued to plague the churches in that area. Ignatius mentions heretical teachers. He says that they were denying that Christ was really human. They were also challenging the authority of the local church leaders. Other Christians are continuing to follow Jewish customs. They refuse to believe any teaching which is not contained in the Old Testament. The opposition in Ignatius' time seems to be more doctrinally oriented and better organized than that in the letters in Revelation. However, that strong opposition may have been the continuation of trends that are beginning as Revelation is written. If so, John's stern warnings against the false teachers is certainly justified. They would continue to plague the church.

2:1-7 To Ephesus. The city of Ephesus had undergone a great revival during the Roman period. That renewal would have given the populace reason to be enthusiastic about the empire. Consequently, we are hardly surprised to find this civic pride manifested in devotion to the emperor. At the same time, this city was also an important Christian center, since it had been part of the Pauline mission in Asia Minor.

The description of Jesus reminds the reader of 1:13, 16. The letter opens by praising this community for its endurance and its resistance to false teachers who claim to be apostles. Revelation usually limits the term "apostle" to the Twelve (so 18:20; 21:14). Presumably, people claiming to be apostles were using the term as it had been used during the time of Paul in reference to traveling missionaries (see Rom 16:7). Perhaps these traveling missionaries had been preaching the doctrines of the Nicolaitan sect mentioned in verse 6.

Though not in danger from false teachers, the Ephesian community has to be recalled to its former enthusiasm. The image of a fall from its former heights may have been based on the image of the fallen star in Isa 14:12a. The lampstand image recalls the single lampstand with seven lamps in Zech 4:2, which is in the divine presence. Revelation threatens Ephesus with removal of its lampstand.

The call to hear which forms a set part of the conclusion to the letters is a common prophetic warning. (It also appears in Rev 13:9; 21:7; 22:2.) The promise, eating from the tree of life, appears in first-century Jewish apocalypses as well. It shows that salvation reverses the curse of Adam. Revelation has already shown its audience that lost immortality is regained through Jesus.

2:8-11 To Smyrna. Smyrna was a fairly

new city north of Ephesus. It had a sizable Jewish population. When its bishop, Polycarp, was martyred in A.D. 155, conflicts between Christians and Jews were blamed. This letter leads off with the theme of life through death to encourage the suffering community. However, we cannot be sure whether Jews were the ones responsible for that suffering. It is possible that some Christians were trying to escape persecution by keeping to Jewish customs. (Compare the reference to those who will not admit to believing in Jesus because they prefer human glory in John 12:42-43.) Revelation must encourage this church to endure because more suffering awaits it. The "crown of life" image may be a combination of the crown of precious stones placed on the head of the righteous (Ps 21:4) and Yahweh as crown of hope (Isa 28:5). The audience might also have imagined it as similar to the crown given to victorious athletes.

Verse 11 explains the death that Christians really should fear: condemnation in the judgment or "the second death." They can avoid that death only by remaining faithful in their present suffering.

2:12-17 To Pergamum. Pergamum was an important city in Asia Minor. Its famous temple to Caesar was placed on a high, terraced hill. The city was known for its devotion to the cult of Augustus Caesar and the goddess Roma. This reputation for devotion to the emperor cult has earned the city the epithet "throne of Satan" in the eyes of the prophet. Perhaps refusal to participate in some form of that civic cult led to the death of the famous martyr Antipas.

The church is chided for following the teachings of the Nicolaitans. They are compared to the Israelites when they were misled by the false prophet Balaam (Num 25:1; 31:6). Some interpreters suggest that this sect might have taught that Christians could engage in ceremonial acknowledgements honoring the emperor. The condemnation of their eating "food sacrificed to idols" might indicate participation in ceremonial banquets, for instance. Ostensible paticipation would win such Christians freedom from persecution. They may have felt that such rites were not worship, since they did not believe that the emperor was divine. Revelation reverses their evaluation. Any form of participation in imperial cult is worship of Satan.

The promises of salvation pick up the two themes for which some are being condemned. Christians saw the "manna" as a prefiguration of the Eucharist, which in turn prefigures the final messianic banquet with Christ in heaven. The victors are also promised a new name. In Phil 2:6-11, Jesus receives the new name "Lord" when he is exalted in heaven. The new names received by the faithful are part of their share in the victory of Christ when they will eat the heavenly banquet. For the time being, both the manna and the new names remain hidden in heaven, but that should not cause Christians to abandon their glorious salvation.

2:18-29 To Thyatira. This city was less important than the previous three. Its citizens had lost their bid to have the emperor's temple built there instead of in Pergamum.

The church in this city appears to have been severely divided. The author encourages those members of the community who are remaining faithful. He castigates others who are following the teachings of a woman prophet. He calls her "Jezebel," after King Ahab's pagan wife, who caused her husband to worship the pagan god Baal (1 Kgs 16:31). He threatens her and her followers (= children; perhaps even disciples as prophets, just as in the Old Testament a disciple of a prophet might be a "son of a prophet"—see Amos 7:14). Jewish traditions frequently link sexual immorality with idolatry. Consequently, the combination does not provide us with any specific information about her group. We are told that they claim to know the "deep things" (RSV) of Satan, according to the author of Revelation. They must have claimed to know the deep things of God. Such an expression in a Jewish apocalypse of the period would most naturally express the claim to know the secrets surrounding the end of the world and the judgment. Perhaps their visions also legitimated participation in pagan cult. John's revelation will provide the true Christian knowledge of such deep things. The followers of this false prophecy are reminded that they must repent; nothing can be hidden from God who knows all (Jer 17:10). The violence of the punishments against the woman and her followers corresponds to the seriousness of their sin, perverting the true gift of prophecy. However, those in the community who do continue to resist Jezebel and her children will share not only the victory celebration but also the actual rule of Christ over the nations.

3:1-6 To Sardis. Rebuilt after it had been leveled by an earthquake in 17 B.C.E., this city was a famous port for the reshipment of woolens. The promise that the victors will go clothed in white (v. 5) may be an allusion to the city's wool trade. We cannot be sure what had given this city the reputation of "being alive" although it is really dead. Perhaps the Christians there were known for enthusiasm or spiritual gifts. The letter warns that they could lose everything if they do not pay attention to the commandments. Their deeds are not those of Christians. Since the author does not mention any specific faults or false teachers, the problem with this church may simply be a waning of their initial devotion. Each of the promises to the faithful contains a warning to those who are not faithful. They might find their names erased from the book of life. The author reminds them of two judgment sayings attributed to Jesus. He will deny those who deny him (Matt 10:32). They must watch out for the thief in the night (Matt 24:42-44; also as a warning of impending judgment in 1 Thess 5:2).

3:7-13 To Philadelphia. This small city lay in the earthquake zone to the southeast of Sardis. The church is not censured, but it is warned to hold out against those who claim to be Jews but are not. We cannot tell if this controversy was between Christians and Jews over who were the real people of God, the true Israel, or an internal conflict between those to whom Revelation is addressed and a group of Jewish Christians. Just as the author spoke of Pergamum as "Satan's throne" because of the emperor cult, so the Jewish problem here leads him to speak of their gathering as "Satan's assembly" or synagogue. Apocalypses of this type frequently designate opponents of God with Satan epithets. The use of Satan in both letters does not mean that the problem here is the same as in Smyrna.

Revelation alludes to several messianic prophecies to prove that Jesus is the true successor to David. Isa 22:22-25 seems to be the closest to this prophecy, since it refers to the key and the open door: "I will place the key of the House of David on his shoulder; when he opens, no one shall shut, when he shuts, no one shall open." Since the door is still open before this community, they still have the possibility of salvation if they continue to hold out. The letter even promises that the truth of their belief will be demonstrated when some of those who claim to be Jews are converted. Like the calls for repentance in other letters, this promise reminds us that the letters in Revelation are not proclaiming a fate that is already sealed. It is not too late for those being censured to repent. Those who are faithful must be encouraged to continue.

The concluding promises look forward to the coming of the new Jerusalem, which will conclude the visionary section of Revelation. Isa 22:23 makes the messianic steward a sure peg on which the whole weight of his father's house can hang. Again, the victors are promised a new name. Here we learn that the name is that of the victorious Jesus.

3:14-22 To Laodicea. Also in the earthquake belt, Laodicea lies east of Ephesus. We have completed our circle of cities. There had been a church in this area from the time of Paul (Col 4:13). This final letter is most often quoted for its imagery of "lukewarmness." Laodicea's water supply came from hot springs and arrived in the city lukewarm. The prosperity of the city and its trade form the basis for other images used by the prophet. It was known for its clothing industry, as a banking center, and for its medical school, which specialized in eye diseases. The problems of the church in this city are tied to the material prosperity in which Christians here live. They are neither poor nor suffering, but their prosperity is endangering their spiritual well-being.

The prophetic warnings draw on several images from the Old Testament. Only they can obtain gold who will pass the test of divine fire from Jesus. The Lord promises to separate the bad from the good among his people by refining them like precious metal in Zech 13:9. The promise of garments of salvation to cover the shameful nakedness of the people refers not only to the clothing industry of the city but also to the reversal of a prophetic curse: God will strip his enemies and expose their shameful nakedness. Isa 47:1-3 connects this curse with an image of the people as "bride." We will see that that imagery returns at the conclusion of the vision section. The new Jerusalem will be the true bride of the Lamb. Ezek 16:8-14 describes Israel as a young bride decked out for her wedding to the Lord. The bridal imagery appears in this passage because the first promise is a share in the divine wedding feast. The culmination of all promises of salvation in Revelation is a share in the victory which the lamb has won. Here the victors are promised a seat on the throne of Jesus and his Father at the festal celebration. Though the letters have been addressed to specific cities, both their warnings and their promises of salvation can apply to all Christians.

SEVEN SEALS

Rev 4:1–8:5

A new vision introduces the next section of the book. Some interpreters think that the letters and the visionary cycles were originally independent and were only combined when the book of visions we know as Revelation was put together. Even if they were originally independent, the imagery of the two sections fits together. The letters presuppose the visions of salvation that are coming in order to make their promises and warnings clear. We would not know that the concern with idolatry and with the throne of Satan refers to the emperor cult without the account of the beast in chapter 13, for example.

The various cycles of visions which make up the rest of Revelation overlap. The trumpets are introduced before the seals are concluded, and almost two chapters stand between the sixth and seventh trumpet. Apocalypses commonly included repetitious cycles of visions, which went over the same ground from a different perspective. The interlocking of the various cycles in Revelation suggests that its visions do the same.

Apocalypses also wish to show their audience that they are nearer to the end of the world than to its beginning. Symbolically, they make this point by having visions that encompass the past history of Israel. These past events may be from the salvation history of the Old Testament and/or from the recent experiences of the people under the Babylonian and Persian Empires such as we find in the visions of Daniel. In that way the audience can see the divine truth behind those past events and can be reassured that the future is no less subject to divine rule, however chaotic and confusing it may seem.

Revelation follows the same process. While reading through the visions carefully, notice that most of them have already been fulfilled from the standpoint of the author and his audience. One should never pay any attention to an interpretation of Revelation that applies to contemporary people and events the images which the author claims apply to the past. Revelation wants us to understand that the same divine judgment and guidance that were manifest in those past events are at work today, not that those past events have to be repeated in some way. When apocalypses come to describe the future events of judgment/salvation, they often move away from any connection to historical events and speak in the language of mythological symbols and metaphors. Revelation does the same. This shift in language reminds us that the seer is having a vision of the divine or symbolic truth that is to be worked out in the course of history. He is not trying to predict a sequence of historical events as they might be recorded in a history book or a newspaper.

It would also be a mistake to think that the imagery of wrath and punishment is the real foundation of Revelation. Both the letters and the visions make it clear that they seek to encourage Christians to remain faithful in a difficult and confusing time. Remember, John even has to contend with other Christian prophets who claim that they know the "deep things" of God. Revelation does not seek to teach Christians to glory in the expectation that others will suffer a terrible fate while they rest in the bliss of heaven. John sees that the victory that has been won in Christ is the beginning of a divine process of redemption that is to take in all of creation. Throughout the book hymns of rejoicing and celebration invite Christians to celebrate their salvation.

4:1-6a The divine throne. The Old Testament contains several visions of the heavenly throne and its surroundings. They introduce the mission of a prophet whose experience in the heavenly court gives him the authority to speak God's word to the people (1 Kgs 22:19; Isa 6:1-13; Ezek 1:4-26; Dan 7:9-10). Read the Ezekiel passage. It shows how familiar the scene in Revelation would be to a person who knew the earlier images. Not only is the vision of God's throne room a customary beginning for a prophetic revelation, but it also reminds the audience of this book of one of its major themes: God, not Caesar, is the ruler of the cosmos. The final letter promised that Jesus and his faithful ones would even share the divine throne at that final victory banquet. The next vision will show us the victorious enthronement of the lamb.

Visions of heaven often begin with the invitation to enter or to look through the open door into heaven (Ezek 1:1; Matt 3:16; Acts 7:56). Though the visions follow the letters, the author does not imply that everything in the letters has to happen before the events described in the visions will begin. The promise to show "what must take place in time to come" is the customary introduction to an apocalypse. As we have noted, such apocalypses may still contain visions that begin in the past, describe persons and events known at present to the audience, and then look to the future.

The seer has been commissioned in the visions which opened the book. After this first cycle of visions is over, he will be commissioned again. Now he provides a vision of the divine throne room. The scene combines images of the temple of Solomon in the Old Testament (see 2 Chr 3–5), throne of cherubim, brazen sea, incense, singing, and altar of sacrifice, with the scroll image of the synagogue, its elders and hymns, and the imagery of the heavenly court assembled in judgment (as in Dan 7:9-14). The crowns and white robes suggest that the twenty-four elders represent human rather than angelic figures. Some commentators think that they may represent the prophets of Israel.

The author has combined images of heavenly liturgy with those of the heavenly court assembled in judgment. When the lamb opens the scroll in the next scene, we see that judgment has begun to unroll. The piling up of images makes it clear where power and authority lie. Between the throne and the elders the image of the divine is manifest in a great storm. The seven torches are the seven spirits of God which ovesee the whole cosmos (Rev 5:6; see Zech 4:2). The bronze sea reflects that which stood before the temple of Solomon. It symbolizes the creative power of God, which is victorious over the sea of chaos. The cosmological mythology of the sea as the home of a great monster of chaos, which must be defeated by the divine storm god before the world can be created, becomes even more explicit later in Revelation. The empire is embodied in the beast which comes from the sea. God as creator imposes order by defeating the sea monster.

4:6b-8 The four heavenly creatures. In Ezek 1:4-20 the prophet first sees a great storm wind. Within it he finds the throne chariot of God being drawn by four creatures. Ezekiel supposes that each creature has four faces: man, lion, ox and eagle. Revelation has assigned one face to each of the four throne bearers. The images may have been taken from Babylonian signs of the zodiac. The ox, Taurus, is an earth sign; the lion, Leo, a fire sign; the third, with the face of a man, may be Scorpio, since the scorpion was often drawn with a human face, and is a water sign. The eagle provides a sign for the fourth element, air. It also provides another sign of divine sovereignty over the Roman Empire. Thus the four creatures not only serve to identify the divine throne chariot but also proclaim divine rule over the four elements of the cosmos and over the signs of the zodiac. The final verse brings in the vision of the throne room in Isa 6:1-2. The creatures merge with the cherubim and seraphim of that scene. Later Christians gave each of the four evangelists one of the creatures as a symbol.

4:8b-11 The heavenly praises. The transition to the Isaiah vision is continued with the singing of the threefold "holy." God is glorified by all in heaven as the sovereign creator. This praise makes the implications of the symbolism clear: God is the creator and Lord of all that exists. Several writings from Jewish groups in the New Testament period contain descriptions of the divine throne and of the praises of angels in heaven. The liturgical setting suggests that the acclamations offered by worshipers on earth are an image of the real worship of God which takes place in heaven.

5:1-7 The Lamb receives the scroll. We now turn from praising the divine creator to the plan of redemption. In Ezek 2:9-10, the seer is shown a scroll, which was "covered with writing front and back, and written on it was: Lamentation . . . and woe." That scroll was unrolled before the seer so that he could see what was written on it. Revelation has introduced a slightly different image. The scroll is sealed. That image reflects the revelation of Daniel. There the visionary is told to seal up his revelation: "As for you, Daniel, keep secret the message and seal the book until the end time; many shall fall away and evil shall increase" (12:4). John's question about who can unlock the scroll really is addressed to such apocalyptic visions. It rejects the possibility that any apocalypse, any revelation except the Christian one, could unlock the secrets of God's plan for the end of the world. Thus, he makes it clear that as the successor to the prophets Ezekiel and Daniel, he is also the last. The hidden book is now to be opened by the Lamb and the unfolding of the final stages in the history of salvation can begin. The angel issues the summons to the whole cosmos to witness the opening of the book, a feat that cannot be performed by any creature in the cosmos.

The messianic prophecy of the Lion of Judah answers the call. The messiah is now present and worthy to open the book. 4 Ezra 11:36-46 has the Lion emerge and speak the sentence of doom against the fourth imperial beast, the Roman eagle. Here the opening of the scroll by the victorious Lion will begin the visions that spell the end of imperial power. Revelation combines other images with that of the Lion of Judah, the sprout of David from Isa 11:1-10, and the more general messianic image of victory. The Christian audience knows that the victory won by Christ was in his death and resurrection. This fact is symbolized in the vision of the messianic lion as the slaughtered lamb. Several images have been combined. Early Christian traditions identified Jesus with the passover lamb and with the defenseless servant of Isa 53:7, 10-12. In another Jewish apocalypse, *1 Enoch*, the seer sees the Lamb of David grow into a great horned sheep, which defeats the hostile beasts that attack the people of God (89, 45-46; 90, 9-16). The Lion of Judah/Lamb in this vision also appears with the horns of a victorious ram. He has the flaming eyes of the seven spirits before the throne (1:4; 3:1; 4:5).

5:8-14 Praises for the Lamb. Once again, we hear the heavenly chorus sing praises. "New song" often appears in the call to worship in the psalms. Here it has the added significance of offering praise to the victorious Lord, enthroned in heaven. He has created a new people of God from all those on earth. Thus, the universality of God's cosmic rule is echoed in the univesal redemption won by the atoning death of the lamb.

As we hear the praises, the author widens the angle of vision so that we see the myriads of heavenly beings and then all creatures at the various levels of the cosmos praising the Lamb. Their praise is confirmed with the answering AMEN of the four throne creatures and the worship of the elders. The vision of the praise offered by all creation forms a high point in the book. It is the heavenly basis for the confidence that Christians are to have in the truth of the visions of divine victory that are to follow. The Lamb has already been enthroned victorious in heaven because he has won a new kingdom of priests. The Christian is shown that the whole cosmos praises God and the Lamb for their saving power.

6:1-8 The four horsemen. Revelation uses images which flow into one another. We have seen this process at work in the earlier descriptions of the divine. When the author now turns to describe the inner reality of earthly events, he blends together the mythic symbols, the prophetic allusions, and the hints at the historical events to which they correspond. The four horsemen allude to a very concrete set of experiences of people living in a war-torn area, the disasters wrought by wars and invading armies. The white horse and the bow were favorite weapons of Rome's hated enemy along the eastern frontier, the Parthians. Later, the Parthians are summoned by the voice of God to come from beyond the Euphrates and initiate the downfall of Rome (9:13-21). The vision predicts that Parthian attacks would bring the downfall of Rome. That expectation was a reasonable one, since Rome had suffered defeat at the hands of Parthia in A.D. 62. Parthia would not be the nation to sack Rome, but Rome would eventually fall through war with an enemy on her borders.

The images of a company of horsemen also evoke the prophets. Zech 1:8-15; 6:1-8 pictures riders on different colored horses sent to range the earth and to punish those who oppress the people of God. The terrors of war in these first visions all fit the periods of conflict in the region. The eruption of Vesuvius (A.D. 79) was followed by a devastating fire and plague in the city of Rome and by famine in Asia Minor.

The prophets also picture the horrors of war, famine, plague, and wild beasts as chastisement from God. Ezek 5:12-17 has God utter a terrible curse, which is the basis for this section. In Ezekiel the destruction will kill a third of the people by plague and hunger; a third by war; and the remaining third will be scattered in exile. Perhaps because there are so many more plagues to come, Revelation has its version of the Ezekiel curse carry off a quarter of the earth. The third horseman images the disorienting economic effects of war that might lead some to starvation. The fourth horseman represents death by plague. All of the evils brought by the horsemen referred directly to common experiences in the life of the region through its combination of prophetic images.

6:9-11 The fifth seal. This scene forms an interlude between the plagues of war and the destructive earthquakes of the next scene. It also introduces the theme of the martyr. Those who have suffered call out for vengeance. This cry is not a manifestation of personal animus or spite as some people often think. It is also a common feature of the apocalypse genre: the righteous make a call for God to give some definitive manifestation of his justice and truth. This manifestation would counter the appearances of a world which seems able to ignore God's justice without any ill effects, a world which can persecute or simply ignore those who speak out for God. The plagues brought by the four horsemen serve to remind the audience that the world is not as peaceful or prosperous as it might be.

The position of those calling out for vengeance reflects that of the Old Testament "just ones" between the temple and the altar in Matt 23:35. The prayer to God to come and avenge the blood of the righteous alludes to Ps 79:5-6, 10. That psalm was a prayer to the Lord not to continue being angry with his people but to avenge them against the enemies that had laid waste the nation. The words are those of a nation laid waste by war and its devastation; it can only call out to God for help. Here the martyrs are asking God to pronounce sentence on the rightness of their cause and to execute judgment. The visions in Revelation that began with the opening of the scroll make it clear that God has pronounced his sentence against the wicked. But he does not promise immediate execution of judgment. More is yet to come. People often object to the tone of this passage, which seems to make God something of a sadist, unwilling to act until enough righteous blood has been shed. The New American Bible translation contributes to that impression by rendering the Greek "they are fulfilled" as "until the number was filled." The passage is not really about a quota. Apocalypses are concerned with the problem of righteous people who seem to suffer and die needlessly in God's cause. They often reassure their audience that such suffering is not endless, not going to go on forever, by imagining that there is a fixed time period or a set sequence of events that must transpire. Neither the righteous nor the wicked can force the events of history out of that pattern. It is part of the mystery of the divine plan. Revelation does not relish suffering. The book is built around the image of the Messiah as the sacrificed Lamb. Those who suffer for the sake of righteousness are assured that God is attending to their cause; their sufferings and struggles are acknowledged in heaven.

6:12-17 The sixth seal. This vision of cosmic catastrophe piles up all the metaphors that the author can find for the horrors of the final day of judgment. Compare the vision of the judgment in Mark 13:4-19. Several Old Testament prophecies are behind this passage. It begins with the earthquake as the sign of divine theophany (see 1 Kgs 19:11; Isa 29:6). This sign would be familiar to many of the audience, since several of the cities addressed were in an earthquake zone. There are to be signs in the stars and the moon (Joel 3:4); darkness (Isa 50:3); falling stars (Isa 34:4). The terrible cry of people for the hills to fall and cover them also appears in the prophetic traditions (Hos 10:8 ties it to the earthquake; Isa 2:10, 19; Jer 4:29). The "great day" of verse 17 appears in Isa 2:10, 19 (also Zeph 1:14). The question posed by this terrible vision, "Who can withstand it?" (see Nah 1:6; Mal 3:2) will be answered by the sealing of the righteous in the next chapter. Thus, the author has piled together all the horrors of the judgment as they were known from the biblical tradition. Those horrors form a prelude to the sealing, which assures the righteous that they can withstand, just as they have withstood persecution in the world.

7:1-8 Seal the 144,000 from the tribes of Israel. Normally, the announcement of the terrible day of judgment would be followed by the vision of the divine theophany, God coming forth in judgment. Revelation breaks into that pattern to answer the question of who can withstand by describing the sealing of two groups. Interpreters are divided over the identity of the 144,000. Some think that they represent the righteous of Israel. Others argue that they represent Christians, who could also speak of themselves as the "twelve tribes" (as in Jas 1:1). Such a Jewish Christian tradition may underlie this passage in Revelation.

Several passages in the Old Testament use the imagery of sealing to indicate that a person belongs to the people of God. Exod 28:11, 21 associates that sign with deliverance from the disaster of the final plague. The Egyptian plagues will appear later in the visions. Isa 44:5 describes a sealing of the Lord's chosen ones as writing the names "I am the Lord's," "Jacob," and "the Lord's" on the hand. We have seen that in the letters Revelation promises the victorious that they will be given a new name which is that of God, of the new Jerusalem, and of Jesus' own "new name" (3:12). Ezek 9:4 instructs one of those who are to scourge the city of idolaters to pass through first and mark the foreheads of all those who lament the abominations being practiced there with an "X" so that they will not be touched in the coming disasters. In addition to all of these Old Testament examples of sealing and salvation, the Christian audience would also remember their own tradition, which spoke of baptism as "sealing."

God is holding back the four angels who are about to let loose the divine storm winds. They will come from the four corners of the earth as signs of divine wrath (see 1 Kgs 19:11; Jer 49:36; Ezek 37:9; Zech 6:5).

7:9-12 The elect praise the Lamb. On the basis of the Ezekiel parallel, we might expect the new vision of doom to follow immediately. Remember we are still waiting for the seventh seal to bring this first vision cycle to a conclusion. However, Revelation is not simply a prediction of disaster. It also shows the heaveny basis of salvation and Christian hope. Consequently, we are shown a new vision. Just as in the previous vision of cosmic praise, the angle of vision widens until we see multitudes from all the earth praising the Lamb. All of the elect are singing praises and waving palms, a sign of victory (1 Macc 13:37, 51; John 12:13). As in the earlier glimpse of the heavenly liturgy, the hymn is antiphonal. The praises of the elect are answered by heavenly beings who say "Amen" and then offer their own song to God and to the Lamb.

7:13-17 Interpretation of the vision. Interpretation of the seer's vision by an angel is common in apocalypses (compare Ezek 37:3). This passage combines allusions to Ezekiel and Daniel. The tribulation through which these people have passed may be that of the judgment (Dan 12:1), which has just been announced. Verses 15-17 are somewhat problematic, since they seem to narrow the focus of the vision from all the elect to just those who have died for their faith. However, the author may be thinking of all as having a share in martyrdom, since they have been redeemed by the blood of the Lamb.

Several images of salvation from the Old Testament describe what awaits the elect. The righteous will not hunger and thirst (Isa 49:10; Ps 121:6). The sheep will have their shepherd (Ezek 34:23; Ps 23). God will wipe away the tears of the elect (Isa 25:8). Now that we have seen the salvation won for all the elect by the death of Jesus, we are ready for the opening of the final seal.

8:1-5 The seventh seal. The account of the seventh seal includes a verse which introduces the next cycle, the trumpets (v. 2). This interlocking is typical of the style of Revelation. We expect a grand, perhaps terrifying, vision of the divine warrior to follow the announced judgment. Trumpets belong to the announcement of the beginning of judgment (as in 1 Thess 4:16). They announce the appearance of the Lord. Thunder and lightning are also signs of divine presence. However, we do not have the terrifying epiphany of the Lord; instead, there is a half-hour silence followed by further prayers. The silence may reflect the "small voice" of the appearance to Elijah (1 Kgs 19:11-12; 2 Chr 2:17; Hab 2:20). Amos 9:1 pictures the Lord standing beside the altar as he announces to the prophet the judgment he is to bring against his people. Here an angel is offering up the prayers of God's people. Since that offering is followed by his hurling the burning coals down on the earth, we assume that the prayers are the same as those of the martyrs in the earlier chapter. God's people have asked for salvation; the symbolic response shows that their prayer is to be answered.

THE SEVEN TRUMPETS

Rev 8:6–11:19

This cycle is structured like the previous one. Four trumpets herald plagues to come upon the earth. The movement toward the culmination in which Satan is cast out of heaven is interrupted. First we see two faithful witnesses and their fate. Then the prophet is again commissioned by an angel and so prepared for the revelations which form the second half of the book. As in the previous series, the first four trumpets are a short, unified group, while the last three are longer and more diverse. This series is modeled on the plagues of Egypt. It teaches a sobering lesson. The plagues and disasters do not lead to repentance. Instead, the humans who survive continue in their idolatrous ways. This cycle is more intense than the previous one; a third rather than a quarter of the earth is to be affected.

8:6-13 The first four trumpets. The humans who survive this succession of plagues do not realize that they are suffering divine punishment. This series, like the earlier one, presents disasters which are not those of the final judgment. The vision combines images from various Old Testament prophecies with the plagues of Egypt. Ps 18:13 ties the appearance of God to save his people with casting fire and coals on the earth. Blood recalls the plague in Exod 9:24. The second trumpet announces the destruction of the fish in the sea (see Exod 7:18). The image of disaster created by a burning mountain falling into the sea has both historical and prophetic overtones. For the audience at the time, it might evoke the eruption of Vesuvius in A.D. 79, with its rivers of molten lava flowing into the sea and destroying everything in their wake. A burning mountain also appears in Jer 51:25. The Lord will send a destroying mountain against the empire of Babylon.

Allusions to the overthrow of Babylon continue in the next trumpet. The falling star recalls the taunting of the king of Babylon in Isa 14:12. In Jeremiah (23:15; 8:14; 9:14), the Lord threatens to give poisoned water, wormwood, to his people because they have abandoned his ways and gone astray into idolatry. The darkness of the final trumpet in this group recalls the darkness over the land of Egypt (Exod 10:21-29). The prophets frequently refer to the darkness of the day of judgment (Amos 8:9; Isa 13:10; 50:3; Joel 2:3, 10; Ezek 32:7-8). However, this darkness does not represent that of the final day; only a third of the heavenly bodies lose their light.

The first cycle of disasters recalled the trials of international wars. This cycle, disasters in nature, might be called forth by divine command. Verse 13 brings it to a culmination with the ominous vision of the eagle flying across midheaven and crying out three "woes" against the inhabitants of earth (compare the "woe" introduction to prophetic oracles of doom as in Amos 5:7-27, a prophetic announcement of three woes). The vision of the eagle in midheaven may also recall the comparison of the coming of the Son of Man in judgment to eagles/vultures gathering above a corpse in Matt 24:28. The woes announce the next three trumpets. Two will be described immediately; the third will be delayed as in the previous cycle.

9:1-12 The fifth trumpet. With the fifth trumpet we move out of the realm of earthly disasters into that of the mythological. Mythological beasts come forth to attack the inhabitants of the earth. As though we were watching a horror movie, these creatures come out of the earth to torture humanity. Though the fifth trumpet recalls the plague of locusts (Exod 10:13-15), these locusts are not the ordinary sort of grasshopper that sweeps across fields destroying crops. A great star falling from heaven, possibly Satan, has the keys to let these creatures out of the underworld. They do not harm nature, the grass, at all. Instead, they are sent to torment humanity. They are really scorpion-like creatures. Scorpions were known as "fiery dragons" (Deut 8:15; Num 21:6; Isa 14:29). The prophetic pattern for this vision can be found in Joel 1:4, where the locusts and grasshoppers are sent against humanity. However, Revelation has moved out of the realm of that prophecy, which describes a possible natural disaster, into the realm of the mythological and demonic. Their sting torments but does not kill. The intensity of human suffering at this plague leads to a repetition of the cry of the sixth seal: people wish to die and cannot.

(Compare Jer 8:3; Job 3:21; the most horrible suffering leads people to seek death, which they cannot find.)

Some of the features in the description of the locusts come from Joel: teeth, flight, warrior's attire and comparison with war horses (1:6, 2:4-5). The human face was part of the traditional iconography of the scorpion. Perhaps the woman's hair was also derived from astral symbolism. The golden crown will appear later in the crown of the beast. The leader of these creatures is probably the same angel/demon whose fall brought their release from Hades. They torment humanity for five months. Another cry of woe and warning brings this vision to its close.

9:13-21 The sixth trumpet. A new contingent of demonic creatures appears. These terrible horsemen do not signal earthly disasters; they attack and kill a third of humanity. The angelic voice from the altar announces the time for the release of these destroying angels. Such an angelic cry is associated with the trumpet announcing the day of judgment in 1 Thess 4:16. The association between the voice and the altar also reminds the readers of the plagues as answer to the prayers of the righteous. But this woe is not the end of the world, either. Only a third of the inhabitants of the earth are killed. These terrible riders are deliberately more lethal than the previous group. They slay with the fiery breath of their mouths and with the venom of their serpent-like tails.

In these two visions Revelation has moved beyond the metaphors of the Old Testament prophets and beyond metaphorical description of the horrors that might accompany natural disasters or human wars. The author has now moved into the realm of the mythological, of the demonic and of the terrifying. That move makes the conclusion of this series even more sobering. Even attack by such mythic beasts does not change humanity. The conclusion remains much the same as it had been throughout the Old Testament: those who are hardened against the word of God do not repent, no matter what happens to them. Suffering does not convert them. Terror does not convert them. Those who live through such times continue in idolatry and sin. More signs must occur before a terrified humanity recognizes that God is at work (11:13).

10:1-7 The small scroll. Once again we must wait for the final woe, the seventh trumpet. The seer will be commissioned once again, and those who are to be witnesses to God's actions in the last days will be established. God will not commence those final events without further prophetic testimony. This vision brings us back to the prophet Ezekiel. The cloud and the rainbow are signs of divine presence (Ezek 1:28). The angel's face shines with the glory of God. All the demonic images that we have just seen are erased in this new vision of the divine. The scroll scene will rework the scene in which the prophet eats a scroll in Ezek 2:8–3:3. Cries of thunder and the lion's roar both appear as signs that the day of judgment is beginning in the prophets (Amos 1:2; 3:8; Joel 4:16). The seven thunders also remind us of the seven spirits of God.

But the end is not yet. The prophet is not allowed to reveal what is said by the thunders. Daniel seals up the mysteries of his revelation (12:4) because they are for the generation that will live in the last days, not for the people at the time in which the book is said to have been written, several hundred years before the events to which it alludes. John, however, was not such a fictional work. It begins as a revelation to a Christian prophet well known to the audience, not as the words of a wise man long dead. The sealing up of what John hears suggests that it is not yet the end time. Lest the audience become alarmed by that new sign of delay, the angel swears an oath by God that the time of the end, the time of the seventh trumpet, is not far off. When that time comes, everything that God has announced to the prophets will come to pass.

10:8–11:12 Commissioning the prophet. The section in which John is commissioned again for the visions ahead recalls two actions from Ezekiel: eating a scroll and measuring the temple. Like Ezekiel, John is instructed to eat a scroll which tastes like honey (Ezek 2:8–3:3). The bitterness [NAB: "sour"] in the stomach recalls the bitterness of having to announce the day of the Lord (Zeph 1:14). Verse 11 is awkward: "they" [NAB: "someone"] tell the prophet that he must prophesy again. He is set over against nations and kings (as in Jer 1:10). Yet, we have not yet seen the prophet fulfill the first commission. The verse may simply be an awkward transition between the two different allusions to the prophet's vocation as being like that of Ezekiel.

Measuring the temple of God appears in Ezek 40:3. The prophet measures the temple in view of the fact that it is to be restored. Here the prophet's measuring represents preservation of part of the temple in the period leading up to the end time. The three and a half years during which the outer court is under Gentile dominion is roughly the 1290 days during which the temple was profaned in Dan 12:11. Dan 7:25 has three and a half years as the time during which the fourth and final beast will dominate the saints of God. In Dan 12:7, the revealing angel swears an oath by the Most High (compare the oath of the angel at 10:5-6), that the period of domination by this final empire will be three and a half years. Thus, the audience of Revelation would know that the vision is invoking that earlier tradition. Preservation of part of the temple from domination symbolizes preservation of a remnant, the holy ones of God. The saying in verse 2 may reflect an older Jewish oracle about the destruction of the temple, just as we find an oracle about the "times of the Gentiles" in Luke 21:24. As they hear these prophecies, both author and audience know that the Roman imperial armies had completely leveled the temple in Jerusalem almost a quarter century earlier. They were not looking for precise predictions about the time of domination, or they would not have preserved the Danielic three and a half years. They could see this prophecy as one of those historical allusions to the past which show that the events described and the expectations for the future all belong to the times in which they live.

11:3-14 Sign of the two witnesses. The dominion of the Gentiles is matched by the sign of the two witnesses. Two probably refers to the number of witnesses required by law. It is difficult to determine who the two witnesses are. Ezekiel has to prophesy against two false advisors to the city in 11:1-4. The witnesses to God might be an antitype to such false advisors. Other interpreters suggest that the two represent the two eschatological prophets Moses and Elijah. The signs that they perform recall Moses' sending the plagues on Egypt and Elijah's closing the heavens (1 Kgs 17:1). Verse 4 identifies the witnesses with the lampstand and olive trees that the prophet Zechariah saw next to the Lord (Zech 4:3, 11, 14). No human enemy can attack these witnesses, but they meet their death at the hands of a mythical beast. He is the beast from the sea who fights against God's holy ones in Dan 7:3-7, 19, 21. Here we have another example of Revelation's fondness for interlocking cycles of visions. This beast will be back in chapters 13 and 17. He is embodied in Roman imperial power and its deadly conflict with the truth of God's sovereignty.

Further allusions to Ezekiel structure the rest of the section. In the midst of Ezekiel's prophecy against the two false teachers, they die (11:13). The image of the corpses of the two prophets lying in the street recalls Ezek 11:6. The symbolic naming of Jerusalem as "Sodom and Egypt" reflects oracles against Sodom and Egypt in Ezek 16:26, 48, 53, 56. We have seen that an early Christian prophecy against the temple may be behind Rev 11:2. This section may also draw on such a tradition. Matt 23:29-30 calls the graves of the prophets to witness against Jesus' contemporaries.

The nations that are trampling the holy city are also the ones that will witness the exaltation/resurrection of the two dead prophets. This section preserves a traditional Jewish story pattern: the wicked kill and mock the righteous; the righteous are exalted/resurrected; the wicked see the exaltation of those whom they had despised and cry out lamenting their own condemnation. As with many of the passages in which the author moves toward the mythical, Revelation intensifies the grotesque and terrifying in its presentation. Refusal to bury a corpse was the worst punishment antiquity could imagine. An unburied corpse would render the whole city polluted. Yet Revelation shows us people staring at and even celebrating around the two corpses in the street. All the world is involved. The corpses lie there unburied for the symbolic period of three and a half days.

After that period, God acts. The bodies arise as in the dry bones vision of Ezek 37:10 and are carried to heaven like Elijah (2 Kgs 2:11). The earthquake associated with the end of the world was transferred to the crucifixion and resurrection of Christ in Matthew (27:52). The terror of the people watching the sign recalls another Old Testament prophecy which early Christians used for the reaction of the nations when they say the crucified return in glory, Zech 12:10. It is important to remember that in this "exaltation of the righteous" pattern, the wicked acknowledge their sinfulness at the end when they see the righteous person exalted. But that acknowledgment is too late. They are not saved by it. Thus, the nations worship, but they do so out of fear. They are admitting their sinful neglect of the prophetic word. The resurrection/exaltation stands over against the wicked as a sign of their own condemnation.

Verse 14 ties this long section back to the second woe, from which it departed. However, the traditions in these two sections seem to have had an origin in prophecies that were not originally part of the trumpet cycle. We are warned that the final trumpet is about to sound.

11:15-19 The seventh trumpet. We shift back into the focus of the earlier cycles with a vision of the victorious ascent of the Lamb to his throne. Perhaps the early Christian prophecies of resurrection/exaltation and vindication that are related to the images of the previous section help tie that vision to this one. We are lifted out of the terrors of the previous vision to the heavenly splendor of a new king assuming the throne. The angelic herald announces the beginning of his rule. We are somewhat removed from the woe associated with the seventh trumpet, since the ascent of the Lamb to his throne does not immediately provide the occasion for further destruction on earth.

This vision resumes the earlier vision of the Lamb in chapter 5. That vision concluded with a hymn which proclaims the Lamb worthy to rule (5:9, 12). This one moves beyond that acclamation. The elders are singing a hymn of thanksgiving to the Lamb for having assumed his rule over the nations. That hymn envisages the Lord's rule over the raging nations (Ps 99:1). It proclaims the judgment of those who are hostile to God's people as having occurred. Their sentence has been passed with the enthronement of the Lamb, even though it is clear that the Lord has not yet destroyed such powers from the face of the earth. Jewish legend held that the ark, lost in the destruction of Solomon's temple, would be returned in the messianic age. Here we see it resting within the heavenly temple. The violent storm surrounding the ark is a sign of divine presence.

This vision proclaims the present sovereignty of the Lamb. It provides a heavenly prologue to the horrors of the beast that are to come, much as the visions in chapters 4 and 5 provided a prologue to the first two vision cycles. We are about to move into events which affect the author and his audience. The beast, like the fourth beast from the sea in Daniel, represents the empire under which they live and the imperial ideology against which they must struggle.

UNNUMBERED VISIONS

Rev 12:1–15:4

A new series of visions contrasts the followers of the beast with the followers of the Lamb. Many interpreters think that the dragon's attack on the woman and her offspring is the third woe. They point to the woe in 12:12: "Woe to you, earth and sea, for the Devil has come down to you in great fury!" The author may also have thought of this section as divided into seven visions. However, he does not provide a numbered cycle for them, and there is no agreement among commentators as to how the section should be divided. All of the literary devices introduced in the first half of the book continue. Horrors on earth alternate with visions of heaven. Symbols loaded with mythological allusions collapse into one another. Present realities and future predictions overlap. We cannot always tell where one begins and another leaves off. The author takes traditional imagery for evil and intensifies it in the direction of the grotesque. However strange these visions may be, we must always remember that they are interpretations of the world that Christians are experiencing. They seek to point out the real truth about the powers at work in that world.

12:1-6 "A woman clothed with the sun." The story of the woman and the dragon draws upon a wealth of symbolism from the myths of the ancient Near East, from Jewish and Greek sources. Many parallels can be brought to the events in this section. We will be content with sketching a few of the major images in order to indicate how deeply rooted the symbol is in the mythic consciousness of humanity. An important function of the woman in Revelation is to provide an antitype to the image of Babylon as whore.

The "woman clothed with the sun" would easily remind the audience of the Roman use of the story of the sun god, Apollo. Roma, the queen of heaven, was worshiped as mother. The emperor Augustus claimed that he had brought about the golden age of kingship associated with Apollo, the sun god. The emperor Nero, who will play a large role in the beast visions to come, went even further. He claimed that as an infant he had been rescued from a serpent's attack just as the infant Apollo had been. The Apollo myth said that Python was seeking to kill Leto, who was pregnant with Apollo, Zeus' son. Zeus has the north wind rescue Leto by carrying her off to an island. Poseidon, the sea god, then contributes to rescuing the woman by covering the island with waves.

The similarities with the story in Revelation are obvious. The woman clothed with the sun is being pursued by a dragon. She is carried off to safety by an eagle. Then the earth contributes to the rescue by swallowing the dragon's water. Other mythological traditions also tell stories of the goddess-mother who must ward off attack from a serpent being. None of the stories is exactly identical to any of the others, any more than the story in Revelation is the story of Apollo. They all reflect an archetypal symbol of the heavenly mother and her divine child, who are attacked by the evil monster from the waters of chaos. The mother and child must be rescued from the forces of evil.

For the audience of Revelation, which has just seen the enthronement of the Lamb, this scene is a flashback to the primordial story of the birth/rescue of the divine child. It will provide a mythic explanation for the hostility between the followers of the beast and those of the Lamb. It is easy to see why later Christians identified the woman with Mary. However, Revelation stays with the archetypal meaning of the symbol. It does not descend to the level of identification with a single person. All of the images of "the woman" in these chapters are to be read on that transpersonal level. The children of the persecuted woman will also be described as those who must struggle with the dragon on earth. Thus, the sign of the woman in heaven becomes the mythic prototype of the earthly realities that are faced by the audience.

We have already seen that John never takes his images from a single source. The woman also evokes traditions from the Old Testament. Being clothed with the sun recalls the glory with which God, the creator, is clothed in Ps 104:1-2. The twelve stars in her crown have astral symbolism, standing for the twelve signs of the zodiac, but they can also stand for the twelve tribes of Israel (compare the moon and the eleven stars of Joseph's dream in Gen 37:9). Isa 7:14 pointed to the child about to be born as a messianic sign. The woman's labor pains reflect those of the daughter of Zion (Mic 4:10; Isa 26:17). Her cry is reminiscent of the voice calling out from the temple just before Zion gives birth to the Messiah in Isa 66:6-8. The imagery makes it clear that the child born to the woman is the Messiah. He shepherds the nation with a rod of iron (Isa 66:8; 7:14).

However, we find another of those delays that permeate the images of Revelation. In Isa 66, the woman's birth pangs are followed by the messianic age of salvation. Here they bring on an attack of the dragon, which is still not yet the final showdown between good and evil. The dragon is a mythological representation of the opponent of God. In ancient Near Eastern creation myths, the warrior storm god must conquer the dragon of the watery chaos before the world can be created. In Jewish apocalypses conquest of the beast signals the final destruction of the world and the beginning of the new creation. This beast represents an intensified image of the beast from the sea in Daniel. His color and the destruction of the stars link him with the agents of destruction in the first half of the book. As in Daniel, the beast has many heads to symbolize the many kingdoms (7:7). Stars are swept from the heavens (8:10). As in the trumpet visions, the destruction of the stars is limited to a third.

The dragon is the last of the heavenly signs. The rest of the mythic creatures will emerge from the seas or will be associated with the earth. The symbolic protection of the woman for three and a half years returns at the end of the chapter after the dragon is cast out of heaven. Her flight into the desert recalls the Elijah story (1 Kgs 17:1-7). Presumably, angels care for her in the desert (1 Kgs 19:5-7).

12:7-12 Victory in heaven. We have seen that Revelation consistently shows victories that remain to be won on earth as completed in heaven. The story of Satan's fall from heaven now emerges as a preliminary battle between Michael and Satan. It will show that the persecution and hostility experienced by Christians have their source in this ancient conflict. The myth of the fallen angels has been combined with the imagery of the god's victory over the monster of chaos. The story in Revelation maintains the timeless quality of its mythic symbols. The story of the myth was repeated annually in the cults of the ancient world. It had the quality of being an eternally valid expression of the divine victory over the sources of evil and disorder. Something of those overtones must attach to the heavenly representations of victory in Revelation. Like the myths of old, they would reassure the persecuted of the fundamental victory of order over chaos. Michael is traditionally the guardian of the people of God and the opponent of Satan (see Dan 10:13, 21; 12:1). The heavenly victory symbolizes his permanent dominion over Satanic forces.

Verse 8 recalls Dan 2:35; verse 9, Isa 14:12. The tradition that Satan's fall from heaven is linked with the messianic age also appears in sayings of Jesus (Luke 10:18; John 12:31). Verse 9 reminds the reader that the dragon being defeated is Satan. The hymn of victory in verses 10-12 sounds an ominous note. On the one hand, it celebrates Michael's victory over Satan and shows that victory to be realized in the victory of God's faithful people. On the other hand, it sounds a note of warning to those on earth.

Casting out of Satan, the heavenly accuser, belongs to the image of the victorious ascent of the Messiah. Satan's attempts to accuse the saints before God have been defeated by their fidelity and by the sacrifice of the Lamb. The jubilation of the hymn reflects Ps 96:10-13 and the rejoicing of the cosmos in Isa 44:23; 49:13. The previous hymns might lead us to expect this hymn to end on that note. Instead, a warning is given. The defeated, angry dragon will be even more severe in his persecution of the woman and her children on earth. Michael's victory has shown that his rule is coming to an end. What follows is a description of the messianic suffering of the faithful.

12:13-18 The woman's flight. The story of the woman's flight, first exhibited in heaven, is now repeated on earth. Eagle's wings as a sign of divine protection appear in the Old Testament (Exod 19:4; Deut 32:11; Isa 40:31). She is cared for again for the symbolic three and a half years. Associated with the waters (see Isa 29:3; Job 40:23), the dragon tries to use his element, raging flood waters, against the woman, but she escapes (Ps 32:6; 69:16). Rescue from raging waters emphasizes the image of the woman as people of God, rescued from the sea and the raging hostility of Pharaoh (Num 16:32; Deut 11:6; Isa 29:3-5, 10; 30:12).

Verse 17 makes it clear that the woman stands for the people of God. The dragon goes off to find her offspring. The specification of the righteous as those who "give witness to Jesus" makes the hostility against the Christians the expression of the dragon's anger. However, the author's references to those experiences are indirect, since he continues the practice of imaginative intensification of mythological symbols in this section. Prophetic predictions of salvation, stories of Israel's formation as a people of God, and archaic mythological symbols all blend together in the visions of conflict and salvation that are about to unfold. We have already seen that the letters suggest that many in the audience would not have seen their experience of Roman imperial power as Satanic. Some have probably worked out compromises with the surrounding environment.

13:1-10 The beast from the sea. The dragon's authority comes to rest in two beasts, one from the sea and one from the earth. The beasts symbolize the antichrist and false prophet of the end time in Jewish apocalyptic visions at the same time as they are the final embodiment of imperial power opposed to the rule of God, the final beast of Daniel's visions. We have seen that 4 Ezra pictured Rome as a great eagle emerging from the sea (11, 1). The sea indicates that the beast in question embodies the watery chaos monster of ancient Near Eastern mythology, the primordial source of all evil. The author identifies the beast for his audience by reminding them of a piece of esoteric numerology that would apparently have been well known to Christians in such circumstances: the number of the beast is 666 (13:18). This number is not a prediction of the future. All interpretations of Revelation that claim to attach the number to a present-day figure should be dismissed. This code is one which the author and his audience share. The best solution to the identity of the beast remains "Nero Caesar," since the Hebrew letters for that title add up to 666.

Several other features of Revelation suit the Nero legend and add to our conviction that Nero is the person to whom the author is referring. A legend circulated among the subject peoples of the eastern part of the empire that Nero had not died. He would return leading a revolt against Rome. Remember the Parthians of the first horseman? The legend held that Nero had fled to live among the Parthians. The period between A.D. 69 and 88 is punctuated by a series of revolts led by those who claimed to be Nero redivivus. We have a collection of Jewish prophecies from this period known as the Jewish Sibylline Oracles. The earlier oracles, from the period after the destruction of the Jerusalem temple by the Romans, picture Nero as leading a great victory of Asian forces over Rome.

In other words, the legend functioned for the Jews at the time much as it did for other conquered peoples in the East: it was a symbol of anti-Roman feeling and hopes for a revolt that would bring freedom and wealth to Asia. Later oracles in the fifth book continue to suggest that Nero is alive somewhere in the East, but they switch their view of Nero to one more like that in Revelation. Nero is identified as the mythological opponent of God in the last days. They make fun of his claims to divine birth. They seem to conceive of Nero as still living and fighting a terrible war against the king sent by God. Other passages both in the Jewish Sibyllines and in a Christian edition of a Jewish apocalypse from the first century, the Ascension of Isaiah, clearly identify Nero with Satan. They speak of him as performing cosmic signs, as claiming to be God, as setting up his image in all the cities and demanding worship from the peoples of the earth. Since Revelation appears to be earlier than all but the oracles in the fourth book of the Jewish Sibyllines, its image of the Satanic Nero may well be the earliest example of the perception that Nero would not return as savior of the eastern peoples but would embody the final outbreak of evil against God and his people.

Remember, most people seem to have thought that Nero was still alive, even though he was said to have died. That was not difficult to believe, since he had only been about thirty-one at the time of his death. Verse 3 describes a mortal wound on the head of the beast, which nonetheless lives. The story of Nero's coming from the East with Parthian troops seems to be referred to in 17:8-10, when the author speaks of the amazement of the peoples who see the beast who once existed, now does not exist, and will exist again. We have already seen that the image of the woman with the sun in chapter 12 serves as an antithesis to the imperial propaganda which pictured Nero in terms of the Apollo legend. Finally, the emperor who appears to have been on the throne at the time Revelation was composed also tried to appropriate the positive side of the Nero image. He used "Nero Caesar" as one of his official titles.

Considering the positive expectations of Nero in the populace at large, it was necessary to speak in a symbolic and guarded way. Criticism of Roman rule was dangerous to begin with. Revelation adds to that critique the presentation of Nero, a symbol of reversal for many opposed to that rule, that makes him the epitome of Rome's demonic power. At the same time, symbolic words about and allusions to Nero and the political affairs of the region were a common way of speaking. Both Jews and Christians would understand the type of writing embodied in the prophecies of Revelation. The author has not tried to conceal his meaning from those who are accustomed to such a way of speaking.

The two beasts, sea and land, have their counterparts in Behemoth and Leviathan of Job 40:15-27. They also reflect the beast of the final empire in Dan 7:3. Daniel divides world history into four empires, each represented by a beast and each hostile to God. Revelation is following a tactic that it used before when it compresses the four beasts into one and intensifies the grotesque nature of the beast by adding heads. The audience would have no trouble recognizing that the beast represented the empire of their experience, the Roman Empire. They would see the challenge to the Roman Empire's claim to enjoy the favor of the gods and even be ruled by a "divine" emperor in the picture of the beast as the embodiment of Satan. In addition to Jewish and Christian apocalypses, there is some evidence for "apocalyptic" thought among the conquered peoples of Egypt and Babylonia. Though the mortal conflict between the sovereignty of a "Satan" and the true God is not necessarily part of pagan apocalypses, they show a longing for national liberation, return to tradition, and to former glory that is much like the desires of their Jewish counterparts. The general development of eschatological expectations among peoples of the East after the conquests of Alexander the Great has been understood by some political philosophers as evidence of the "underside" of imperial conquest. The self-glorifying and even self-divinizing inscriptions and proclamations of the imperial rulers presented the empire as beneficent. So does the literature written by those who benefited from the opportunities given by imperial expansion. We have seen that those local, civic authorities who sought favor with the empire joined the proclamation of the benefits of the empire through the various cultic activities in honor of the emperor. Clearly, the local citizenry did not have a universally agreed upon assessment of the empire.

Indeed, Revelation portrays most of the world as awed by the beast. None could imagine that its power would be overthrown. Just as the beast is a double parody of both the emperor and the false messiah, the antichrist, so following the beast is not just a sign of loyalty to the empire. It is also a parody of true Christian discipleship. The wound which heals not only refers to the legends about Nero. It also parodies the true healing of mortality in the resurrection, Christ, who died and now lives. The two witnesses lifted up into heaven in chapter 11 can also be seen as the antitype of another imperial symbol, the apotheosis of the emperor. Art works represent the deceased emperor being carried up to the heavens to be with the gods. Some people even claimed to have seen the souls of deceased emperors ascending into heaven from their funeral pyres. Such false claims of imperial divinity contribute to the veneration of the emperor. Revelation has already shown its audience that the true exaltation is Christ's ascent to the throne from which he now rules. The acclamation which the peoples give the beast are a parody of the true hymns of praise that are sung in heaven to the Lamb. Verse 4 even parodies the celebration of God's triumph over his enemies in Exod 15:11. The audience already knows from the previous battle in heaven that Michael, the heavenly angels, and even God's faithful ones can triumph over this beast which the world holds in such awe. The audience knows the answer to that rhetorical question, "Who can compare with the beast or who can come forward to fight against it?"

Verses 5-8 intensify the conflict imagery. The symbolic forty-two-month period represents the time of authority given any hostile power. Some interpreters suggest that the blasphemy referred to in verse 6 belongs to the titles of Domitian, the ruling emperor. He was called "dominus et deus," lord and god. These verses make it clear that the world itself is divided in two between the followers of the beast and the followers of the Lamb. Only those who belong to the Lamb will hold out against the dominion of the beast.

The story of the first beast ends with a prophetic oracle. The familiar call to hear suggests that it is directed to the followers of the Lamb and is not a woe oracle against the followers of the beast. The first part reflects Jer 15:2. The oracle may also be related to Matt 26:5. The oracle clearly warns the faithful of a period of suffering. Perhaps it also intends to instruct them that no human revolt will stop its blasphemy. Some interpreters point to the Jewish rebellion under Trajan about twenty years later as evidence that such warnings were in order. Revelation may also have an earlier Christian oracle from the time of the Jewish revolt in A.D. 66–70 in mind.

13:11-18 The beast from the land. The authority of the first beast is passed to a second. However, both beasts clearly represent the empire. Verse 12 suggests that the second beast represents the power of the empire as it was exercised by local authorities. We have already seen that the spread of the emperor cult in the East was due to the initiatives of local governments and private citizens. They usually thought to gain some imperial favor or recognition for their city. Verse 12 describes such a process at the same time that it hints once again that the beast is Nero. We have seen that the signs and wonders could belong to the Nero legend. However, they are also typical of the false prophets of the end time (see Matt 24:24). Calling down fire from heaven was considered a particularly impressive sign of divine power (see 1 Kgs 18:21-23 and the disciples' request of Jesus in Luke 9:51-56). Cities and temples might also claim signs and miracles as a way of gaining support for local shrines. The cultic imagery continues in verse 14 when the people are instructed to erect a cult statue. Failure to worship will carry a death penalty (compare Dan 3:2-3). We have no evidence for any attempt to enforce such veneration throughout the empire. Pliny's correspondence with Trajan two decades later shows that the Romans had no specific crime with which to charge those denounced as Christians. Pliny and Trajan are willing to dismiss those accused of being Christians if they will acknowledge imperial power by offering incense before a statue of the emperor. They also refuse to accept anonymous accusations against people. Should the accused comply with the imperial directive, the person who brought the charge would have to pay a penalty. Should the accused resist, he or she would be executed as a potential danger to the state. We do not know how such cases were handled in Asia Minor at the time of Revelation. Perhaps such problems are only beginning and John is warning Christians that the beast will eventually expand its demands.

We have no direct evidence for a practice of marking people on the forehead such as we find mentioned in verse 16. John may have created that image as an antitype to the sealing of Christian baptism. The "sign" which a person wears identifies him or her as a member of either the followers of the beast or the followers of the Lamb. There is no grey area in between. Verse 17 rapidly brings us back to the sober reality of refusing to comply with demands to venerate the emperor. Christians seem to be excluded from or at a disadvantage in commerce, an important activity in cities like Laodicea. The letter to that city certainly hints that Christians were as much involved in its commercial prosperity as any of the other citizens. Some interpreters think that the disadvantage came from a refusal to use coins, which often carried images of the emperor as divine on one side. However, even if Christians did use such coins, they might still face problems. They might refuse to swear oaths that accompanied many transactions if they mentioned the emperor as divine. Thus it would appear difficult for Christians to engage in commercial transactions with non-Christians without being willing to go along with customs which appeared to acknowledge the divinity and authority of the beast.

14:1-5 The followers of the Lamb. The scene now shifts back to the 144,000, those who bear the mark of the Lamb. Condemnation of imperial power will resume in chapter 17. Mount Zion was often pictured as the place where the Messiah would appear prior to his final battle with the forces of evil. Here the Lamb appears with his faithful ones. This image consolidates the opposition between the two groups, the followers of the beast and the followers of the Lamb. This group is described as the "first fruit" of the people of God. Verse 16:14 will show the gathering together of the nations at the end time.

The opening of this scene recalls prophetic announcements of the day of Yahweh (see Joel 2:27; 3:3-5). However, this gathering is not the end. Instead, we are given the antitype to the worship paid to the beast. The 144,000 learn the "new hymn" to be sung before the Lamb. Revelation sees the prophetic promises that the remnant of Israel will be purified and will dwell without sin on God's holy mountain as fulfilled in this group (Zeph 3:8-13; Isa 53:9). Perfection and holiness are characteristics of the true people of God redeemed by the Lamb. Since Christians are being warned against the idolatry of worshiping the beast, we find the customary assertions of sexual purity in the assertion that the followers of the Lamb "were not defiled with women." This verse does not mean that Christians were expected to be ascetics. Jewish prophetic language often spoke of idolatry as sexual immorality. Revelation will come back to this combination in the pictures of the whore of Babylon in chapter 17. The angel is about to announce the destruction of Babylon (14:8).

14:6-13 Announcements of judgment. Remember the three cries of woe from the eagle in midheaven (8:13)? Now an angelic herald flies across midheaven calling out oracles of divine judgment. These oracles warn against following the beast. At the same time as the announcement of divine judgment means woe for those who follow the beast, it represents salvation for the faithful. It summons them to repentance and endurance. Consequently, the first angel is pictured as proclaiming the "gospel," the eternal good news, to all the people on earth. The gospel message given by the angel is that the time of salvation is at hand; the creator of heaven and earth has assumed his throne. Thus, the hymns in other parts of Revelation which celebrate the victory of the Lamb are also announcements of the gospel according to Revelation. The announcement recalls the celebration of the victory of the Lord on his holy mountain in Isa 25:9-10. The angel in Revelation is summoning the whole world to pay homage to its victorious creator.

The second angel brings an oracle of woe against Babylon which combines Isa 21:9 and Jer 59:7. Jewish apocalypses always identify the ruling empire with the Babylonian Empire, so that in Daniel, Babylon is the Syrian Empire of Alexander's successors. Revelation, of course, identifies Rome and Babylon. Once again, drinking the "wine of her lewdness" refers to homage and idolatry. These images will be expanded in the vision of Babylon, the great.

The third angel concludes with a stern warning against worshiping the beast. The punishments combine a number of prophetic themes. Sinners drink the cup of divine wrath (Isa 51:17, 22; Jer 25:15). They experience the sulphur sent on Sodom and find themselves in everlasting torment (Isa 66:24; 34:9f.). The godless have no rest (Ps 95:11). Their torment contrasts with the peace which awaits the faithful (Isa 57:2, 10).

Verses 12 and 13 apply these oracles to the followers of the Lamb. They are encouraged to persevere. They are promised that their fate will not be like the death of those who worship the beast. Remember, all these cries of woe are not invitations for Christians to gloat over the eventual fate of their enemies. They are reassurance for those who might be tempted to give up, who might think that the "gospel" of God's rule over the world just couldn't be true, who might be in awe of the greatness and power of the beast themselves. Revelation uses all the symbolic resources at its disposal to show that God's salvation is the truth about power and dominion for all the nations of the world, that it really does matter whether or not one resists the power of the beast.

14:14-20 The eschatological harvest. This image of the angelic harvest of the earth combines two Old Testament passages, Dan 7:13 and Joel 4:13-16. The harvest takes place in two stages: first wheat, then grapes. The image of the Son of Man on the clouds is taken from Dan 7:13. Although early Christians usually applied the Son of Man image to the second coming of Jesus, the Son of Man here is an angel. He is subject to the command of another angelic voice from the temple. We have seen that pattern frequently in the earlier scenes of angelic workers of destruction. The first harvest recalls the saying about the lord of the harvest in Mark 4:29 and the angelic reapers of Matt 13:39. Opinion on the significance of the first harvest is divided. Some scholars see it as the destruction of the pagan nations that come to attack the Messiah on his holy mountain in the last days. Others point to the positive images of the wheat harvest elsewhere in the New Testament. They suggest that the first act of harvesting gathers the righteous prior to the judgment of the wicked. We favor the first opinion. Joel 4:13-16 gives the basic elements of this vision. The call to harvest with sickle and winepress is negative. After the harvest oracle, the prophet proclaims the holiness and salvation of the Lord's people on Mount Zion. Revelation has presented us with the elements of this prophecy in reverse order. We have seen the vision of the holy ones on Mount Zion (14:1-5). They have been promised that the Lord is coming in judgment (14:7). Now that harvest begins.

There is no question about the negative imagery attached to the grape harvest in the second half of the passage. The angel at the incense altar ties this vision back to the earlier visions of the trumpets. Before the trumpets began, he brought the prayers of the holy ones to God and then cast the coals from the censer down on the earth (8:3-4). Then he commanded the angel of the sixth trumpet to release the deadly horsemen from the banks of the Euphrates to kill a third of humanity (9:13). Now we find a third grim reminder of the deadly consequences of that angel's voice as he unleashes the trampling of the grapes of wrath. Verse 18 recalls Jer 25:30. Trampling the enemies of God in a great winepress was traditional (see Isa 63:1-6). The enemies of God are turned into a great sea of blood.

15:1-4 The song of Moses. Once again, just as we feel the narrative coming close to the great day of divine wrath and judgment, Revelation turns away. Verse 1 announces the final plagues, but they are interrupted by the song of the victors. Many interpreters think that the final woe, announced by the trumpets and then delayed, is represented in the vision of destruction that comes with the last cycle of seven—the seven bowls. In the interlude, we return once again to the heavenly temple. The images of the sea of the beast and the sea of blood are reversed in this image of a sea of glass and fire on which the victors over the beast stand to sing their hymn. The "song of Moses" and "of the Lamb" praises God and promises that all the nations of the earth will come to worship the Lord when they see his mighty deeds. It appears to be a collage of Old Testament passages (see Pss 111:2; 139:14; Amos 4:13; Jer 10:7; Pss 145:17; 86:9; Hos 6:5). This song looks forward to the universal recognition of God's rule which has been the theme emphasized again and again by the scenes of heavenly praise.

THE SEVEN BOWLS

Rev 15:5–16:21

This cycle brings to a conclusion the series of plagues on earth. Each of the cycles has repeated the theme of the coming judgment from a different perspective. Each has been more intense than the previous one. Each opens with a series of short plagues and concludes with more elaborate and mythological ones at the end. Like the trumpet cycle, the bowl plagues include allusions to the Exodus plagues. The image of the bowl combines two elements from the Old Testament traditions that have already been presented in the course of Revelation. Exod 27:3 describes the bronze basins used by the priest to carry out the ashes and fat from the sacrifices. Rev 8:3-5 has the angel at the altar of incense empty the censer of coals on the earth. Here, angels come out of the temple carrying bowls filled with the plagues. The second image, introduced in the vision of the winepress, is that of the cup of wine, which represents the wrath of God (Ps 75:8; Isa 51:17, 22). Also, like the previous plagues, these plagues do not bring people to worship God or to repent. They only continue to blaspheme the Lord, thus sealing their own doom.

15:5-8 The angels carry out bowls of wrath. Chapters 9 and 10 of Ezekiel provide the model for this section. In that section of Ezekiel, the scribe and six angels make up the needed seven. They are summoned to execute the guilty ones in the city of God. The scribe goes before the angels and marks the righteous to spare them from destruction. Revelation does not need such a process, since the righteous and the wicked already bear the seal of the one whom they follow. The description of the angels combines Dan 10:5-6 and Ezek 28:5. Ezek 10:4 describes the cloud of divine glory which fills the temple when the Lord is present. Here the smoke symbolic of his presence prohibits anyone from entering the temple until the plagues are carried out. In Ezek 10:6-8 the angels cast fire on the earth from the divine throne chariot. Here one of the chariot creatures gives the bowls to the angels.

16:1-11 The first five plagues. The first five plagues strike humans and water creatures with sores, blood, fire, and darkness. The voice which calls out from the temple may be that of God (see Isa 66:6), since no one can enter there, or that of the revealing angel (see Ezek 9:1). The intensification of these plagues is indicated by the affliction which hits the whole earth, not just a part of it. The third plague, which destroys all fresh drinking water, is accompanied by an antiphonal proclamation of the justice of God's judgment against those who have shed the blood of the righteous (see Pss 119:137; 145:17; 79:3; Isa 49:26). The fourth plague combines the apocalyptic sign in the sun with the casting of fire on the earth. Instead of darkening, as in other apocalyptic visions like the third trumpet, the sun flares up and burns people with its fire. The darkness of the final plague resembles the darkness over Egypt. It also recalls the destruction of the light of the heavenly bodies in the earlier plagues. Human suffering comes from the affliction with boils, as in the first plague of this series.

The fourth and fifth plagues are also linked to the earlier trumpet series in their emphasis on humanity's failure to repent. Instead of turning from wickedness, humans blaspheme God all the more as the cause of their suffering. This intensification of their hostility to God prepares the way for the summoning of destruction from the East. In Isa 46:11-13, Yahweh answers the hard of heart by summoning his man from the East. That summons is the prelude to salvation: the beautiful daughter of Babylon is reduced from luxury to slavery in Isa 47. Revelation will follow a similar pattern. We are about to see the luxurious daughter of Babylon and then to witness her fall. However, two more plagues intervene before we come to that vision.

16:12-16 Armies assemble in the East. We have already seen that people expected destruction from the Parthians in the East. We have also seen that Revelation turns to more grotesque and mythological images for the concluding plagues of a series. The sixth plague presents us with a ghastly image of the armies drawing up for battle. In a mockery of "preparing the way of the Lord," the river Euphrates is dried up to provide a way for the demonic armies. Like the Egyptian frogs (Exod 7:6-11; Pss 7:45; 105:30), they come forth. They work signs and assemble all the kings of the earth for battle. This assembling provides a demonic antitype for the assembling of the righteous with the Lamb in chapter 14. It translates into the macabre imagery of Revelation—the prophetic vision of the armies coming against Jeruslem in Zech 14:2-5. Zechariah shows us the Lord going forth against his enemies from Zion. When he stands on the Mount of Olives, it splits in two; the valley fills and a great earthquake ensues. Later in the same vision, the Lord strikes his enemies with a plague that causes their flesh to rot (Zech 14:12).

Verse 15 interrupts these predictions of disaster with warnings to the righteous to be on their guard. Related sayings about the second coming are common in the New Testament (see Matt 24:43; Luke 12:39; 1 Thess 5:2, 4; 2 Pet 3:10).

16:17-21 The seventh bowl. We have seen that the violent earthquake, lightning flashes, and announcement of judgment with "it is done" all belong to the scenario for the appearance of God at the end of the world. That theophany should, as in Zech 14, bring the final destruction of the wicked. Once again we will be put off. The description of Babylon and her destruction is being held off until the next section.

The final plague is ordered from the throne in the sanctuary and is accompanied by all the signs of a theophany. The division of the great city and its fall may have been derived from the image of the quake on the Mount of Olives. Revelation is recapitulating the woe of 14:3-16 and looking forward to the vision of the fall of the "great city" Babylon which is to come in the next section of the work. Flight of the islands and mountains is a sign of the divine appearance (see Isa 41:5). Even the destruction of a multitude of cities and great hailstones do nothing to change the ways of humanity. As they have done in response to the earlier plagues, they continue to blaspheme. The evil of the last days is intensified by the punishments which God has sent against humanity.

BABYLON THE GREAT

Rev 17:1–19:10

All the delay and expectation, all the hints of the fall of Babylon will come to a head in this section. Her fall was announced in 14:8. Chapter 18 will finally show us her demise. First, a description of her appearance reminds the reader that Babylon represents the Satanic power of imperial Rome.

17:1-6 The great whore of Babylon. One of the bowl angels takes the seer to witness the destruction of Babylon. The seventh bowl identified Jerusalem as city of destruction with Babylon. The epithet "harlot" recalls the prophetic oracles against a faithless Jerusalem as well as against other cities (see Isa 1:21; 23:15-18; Ezek 16:15-35; 23:3-49). The drunkenness of the kings of the earth appears in Jer 25:15-29. There it is the cup of wrath from the hand of the Lord which is given to the nations.

There is no direct Old Testament image for the harlot riding on the beast. However, John may have created the image out of chapter 13 and pagan cultic imagery. The color of the beast reminds us of all the plagues of blood and fire that have been shed on the earth throughout the book. The interpretation in the second half of the chapter makes it clear that this vision is a variant of the earlier vision of the beast. The description of the woman combines several Old Testament images from Isa 3:16-24 against the finery of the daughters of Zion; Ezek 28:11-16 against the wealth and ostentation of Tyre; and Jer 51:7 against Babylon. In Jer 51:7, Babylon is the golden cup in the hand of the Lord which makes the nations drunk. Here they are drunk with the lewdness of the harlot (=idolatry) just as the beast was leading the world into idolatry in chapter 13.

The symbolic name on the forehead of the harlot recalls the other names which the faithful, whose blood she drinks, have received; the mark of the beast on the forehead of its followers, points to the seal on the foreheads of those who follow the Lamb (9:2). She is drunk with the blood of those faithful ones (16:16; 18:24; cf. the image of the land drunk with blood in Isa 34:7). The faithful martyrs reappear at the end of this section.

17:7-18 Interpretation of the vision of the whore. Like the earlier picture of the beast, this one is a symbolic expansion of traditional imagery. Like most symbolic accounts of history, the number of heads does not match a strictly historical account of the Roman emperors. It seems to best represent a rough sketch of the emperors up to the time of Domitian. Clearly, the beast that returns as the eighth, but is one of the seven, refers to Nero. The eagle vision of the Roman Empire in 4 Ezra has wings which may intend to represent all the emperors, but it only selects three to represent the heads: Vespasian, Titus, Domitian (11:29-32; 12:22-28). The best suggestion is that the emperors indicated represent those particularly hated. Since Revelation is close to contemporary Jewish apocalypses in its anti-Roman sentiment, we may use those sources to suggest a possible identification.

Caligula was the first emperor to cause opposition among the Jews when he demanded that his statue be set up in the temple. (Remember, the beast is accused of doing that in Rev 13:15.) Beginning with Caligula, the heads would represent Caligula, Claudius, Nero, Vespasian, and Titus. Domitian, "the one who is," is sixth. One further emperor is needed to fill out the number seven. As in many apocalypses, the author feels that he is almost but not quite in the last days. The rule of the seventh emperor is to be very short.

No one can miss the parallel between the beast and Rome, since the woman is enthroned on the seven hills of that city. Verse 11 associates the coming of the eschatological age with Nero's return from the East. The ten horns are taken from the vision in Dan 7:7, 27. They appear to represent allies of Rome, who suddenly bring the destruction of the harlot by turning viciously against her. Although Revelation uses more archaic and bizarre imagery than the Old Testament prophets, the author shares their conviction that the nations of the world finally do the Lord's bidding. He can turn the nations from friendship to hatred when that is necessary to the plan of salvation. Though the horns hint at the destruction of the harlot by the victorious Lamb and the revolt of her own allies, the full description of her fall awaits the next scene. Verse 16 alludes to a number of prophetic texts (Hos 2:4; Ezek 23:29; Jer 41:42; Mic 3:3).

This interpretation of the harlot vision repeats much of what the audience has already heard. The whole world is taken in by the beast except the followers of the Lamb. They have the insight and wisdom to know the truth about the times in which they live. They can identify the harlot as Rome and know the fate which awaits her. They are not taken in by her pretensions to divinity. The title of the beast, "existed once but exists no longer, and yet it will come again" (v. 8), may even be a parody of the title of God, "who is and who was and who is to come," from the opening of Revelation (1:4). They are certain of their salvation, since their names are recorded in the book of life (see Dan 12:1).

18:1-8 Fallen, fallen is Babylon. Rev 14:8 announced the fall of Babylon. Now a great angel from heaven announces that the condemnation passed by the heavenly court is upon her. This angel is more glorious than all the others we have seen (compare Ezek 43:2). Dan 4:27 provides the epithet "Babylon the great." Several Old Testament prophetic oracles against great cities are recalled in this passage (see Isa 13:21; 34:11, 14; Jer 50:39; 51:8). This passage comes closest to the condemnation of Tyre in Ezek 27:12-18. Nah 3:3-4 describes Babylon as a city of prostitution and drunkenness. Isa 23:17 refers to the drunkenness of the pagan nations. However, the oracles against Tyre bring out the theme of a city whose luxuries are due to trade and whose fall is not prevented by that great wealth.

The two angelic voices present the grounds for the condemnation of Babylon. When she is sentenced for her crimes, God will repay her double for all the evil she has done. The righteous are warned to flee Babylon, lest they become entangled in her sins. Similar warnings occur in the oracles against Babylon in Jer 50 and 51. Other passages from Jeremiah and Isaiah provide the pattern for the rest of the second announcement. Verse 5 is modeled on

Jer 51:9; verse 6, on Jer 51:15, 29 (also Isa 40:2). Verses 7-8 reflect Isa 47:1-9. But while Isaiah tells the boastful daughter of Babylon that she will suffer both loss of husband and loss of children in a single day, Revelation tells her that she will suffer all the plagues, death, mourning, famine, being consumed by fire, at once. The punishment of this Babylon will epitomize all the plagues described in the book at one time.

18:9-10 The kings of the earth lament. Those who had profited by the prosperity and sinfulness of the city now lament her fate. The inspiration for this whole sequence of laments is found in Ezek 26 and 27. The kings' lament alludes to Ezek 26:16. They see the city being destroyed by fire.

18:11-17a The merchants' lament. Like the kings of the earth, the merchants lament the overthrow of the great city. The description of her markets would suit any of the great trading ports of the Mediterranean. Her conquests in the East had made Rome famous as a center into which all the wealth and luxuries from those provinces flowed, even spices from faraway India. This great catalog of wares recalls that in Ezek 27. According to Ezek 27:13, Hellas demanded slaves.

Although no change of speaker is indicated, verse 14 appears out of place in the lament of the merchants. It probably represents an angelic condemnation like the longer one in verses 21-23.

Like the kings, the merchants draw back. They do not wish to share the fate of the city. They weep for all the great wealth that has been destroyed along with her.

18:17b-19 The seamen's lament. The final group to bewail the fate of the city are those whose ships bring her the wealth of the world. Each lament has followed the same pattern:

1. Introduction: "Alas, alas, great city . . ."
2. Statement of the relevant loss: kings—power; merchants—goods; shipowners—profit from trade.
3. Formal conclusion: "In one hour," destruction. The seamen's lament has a parallel in Ezek 27:29.

These laments paint a striking picture of the fall of a great trading center. Those who had benefited from her glory stand at a distance and watch her burn to the ground. Situated between two angelic proclamations of her judgment, they provide a strikingly human touch in the midst of an intense drama of divine and mythic symbols.

18:20-24 Rejoice! Babylon perishes! The call to rejoice contrasts with the laments of the previous section. It is the antitype of the rejoicing of the people in the city (=Jerusalem) over the death of the two witnesses in 11:8, and it contrasts with the call to rejoicing in 12:12. There the heavens could rejoice at the destruction of the beast, but those on earth had to expect woe. This call is the answer to the prayers of the saints. All who have suffered at the hands of the city are called to rejoice. The model for this summons appears in Deut 32:42; the nations are called to praise God for avenging the blood of her servants. Jer 51:48-49 summons the heavens and the earth to sing for joy over the destruction of Babylon. The legal grounds for the divine sentence, the "slain of Israel . . . the slain of all the earth" (Jer 51:49), is the same one that is found at the end of this passage. The city falls because of the blood of the prophets and saints.

The summons to rejoice and the legal sentence frame a final angelic cry as the destroying angel hurls a great millstone into the sea. The angel is enacting the conclusion to the great prophecy against Babylon in Jer 51:63-64. The prophet was told to bind the words of his prophecy against Babylon to a stone. As he cast the stone into the Euphrates, he was to say, "Thus shall Babylon sink. Never shall she rise, because of the evil I am bringing upon her." Rev 18:21 echoes those words, "With such force will Babylon the great city be thrown down, and will never be found again." The angel goes on to catalog the signs that she will never again rise as a city. That catalog continues to echo Ezek 27 with echoes from similar prophecies (see Isa 23:8, 27; Jer 25:15-17; 49:38). This city will never rise from the ashes of its destruction.

Even the announced destruction of the great city does not bring the story to its conclusion. The story of Revelation is about more than the fall of Roman power. It is about the conflict between God and those faithful to him and the forces of evil. The city embodies the beast, but the beast itself must be destroyed. It is the activities of the beast which underlie all the empires that are opposed to God. Before that story is told, we have another interlude in heaven to give thanks for the divine act of salvation that has just been described.

19:1-10 Hymn of divine victory. The heavenly assembly sings another victory song. God's judgment and justice are praised. It is important to recognize the theological perspective of such a hymn. The avenging of the martyrs represents more than the personal desire to see a wrong punished. It represents proof that God and his justice do rule the world. His judgments of the glory and power of Rome are the right ones. Thus, such victory hymns celebrate a world in which divine justice will win out in the affairs of humanity and nations, however much the evidence appears to go against that truth.

Verse 4 returns us to the divine throne room. One of the creatures of the throne calls to all the servants of God, all in the cosmos, to praise him (see Ps 135:1). That call is answered with a psalm of rejoicing by the great assembly (see Ps 118:24). Just as the earlier hymns had given us a glimpse of the future victory of God, so this hymn gives us a glimpse of the salvation which is about to come, at the wedding feast of the Lamb. The bride is the antitype to the prostitute Babylon. That contrast will be made more explicit when the heavenly Jerusalem is revealed. Here the bride's dress is interpreted as the virtuous deeds of the righteous. They are to share in the salvation of the Lamb at that great wedding banquet. This scene also evokes another part of the ancient myth of the defeat of the monster of chaos, which is about to be played out. The victorious young god would celebrate a banquet on the divine mountain. Since fertility and new creation followed from the divine victory over the forces of chaos, some forms of the myth celebrate a sacred marriage as part of the manifestation of the new divine rule.

Verse 10 is somewhat awkward. Verse 9 would provide a suitable conclusion to the section with its beatitude on those who will partake of that feast. Suddenly the seer worships the angel. While such a response might occur at the first appearance of an angel to make a revelation, it hardly makes sense here. Certainly the seer knows that God and the Lamb are the objects of heavenly worship. Perhaps this verse represents an independent piece about the truth of Christian prophecy—every true spirit testifies to Jesus—that the author has included to authenticate his Christian vision of the victory of God over his enemies.

UNNUMBERED VISIONS

Rev 19:11–21:8

It indeed seems that "delay is the stuff of which Revelation is made." We find another series of visions before we see the bride at the wedding feast. These visions also reflect the mythic patterns of divine victory. God has yet to overthrow the monster and establish his divine presence on earth. The wedding feast can only take place as part of this final cycle, which brings the mythic allusions in the book to their completion. The mythic pattern of new creation also includes the building of a new temple to the god. Here the theme will be somewhat altered, since the new Jerusalem will be the dwelling place of the Lord. The basic elements of the pattern of divine combat and victory celebration can be found in the concluding sections of Revelation. They have been expanded by the addition of other materials, as is common in all the visions of Revelation. We actually have a double victory over the beast. Such a victory appears in some versions of the myth when the god must conquer chaos and death in separate battles. The basic elements in the pattern are:

1. Divine warrior appears (19:11-16)
2. Threat to divine sovereignty (19:19; 20:8-9a)
3. Combat and victory (19:20–20:3; 20:9b-10)
4. Victory shout (19:17-18)
5. Manifestation of divine kingship (20:4)
6. Salvation (20:5-6; 21:4; 22:1-5)
7. Renewal of creation/ sacred marriage/ building of temple (21:1-3, 9-27)

The victory shout actually comes before the divine victory rather than afterwards, as it would in the mythic stories. We have seen many examples of the "anticipation" of salvation, even the enthronement and kingship of the Lamb, in Revelation. Such anticipation forms part of the author's concern with assuring the audience of the present certainty of salvation.

When the author structures his story in accord with an archaic, mythic pattern as he has done here, we see that much more is involved than a simple prediction of historical events. The eternal realities imaged in that myth are shown to be fulfilled in the Christian story. The psychological power of those symbols to assure people of the order of the cosmos is evoked through the narrative. We no longer view the world in the dimensions of profane time or ordinary history. We view it from the perspective of divine time.

If the author is imaging Christian salvation as the fulillment of the most archaic, mythic hopes for salvation, then he has moved quite beyond the level of historical predictions. He has even moved beyond the level of social critique. The condemnation of Rome ended in chapter 18. Now, even the struggle with Rome is but an episode in the greater struggle with the primordial forces of evil and chaos for control of the world. Revelation was right about the Roman Empire, which had seemed both divine and immortal to many of its contemporaries. That empire, like all such empires, did collapse. Revelation is right: even the worst disasters will not turn those who do not have prophetic insight into God's view of truth and justice to the Lord. Humanity can continue to ignore, or worse, to blaspheme God, even in the face of unspeakable horrors. When Revelation keeps asserting that the rule of God is victorious over evil, it does not do so out of a naïve optimism about humans and their behavior; rather, it claims that the only source of confidence in salvation can be the victory of God.

Now we come to the final movement in our journey, the final intensification of the images of salvation. Revelation shows us that all human hopes for salvation must be realized in the rule of God and the Lamb. The mythic patterns are taken up because, like the Old Testament prophecies, they are fulfilled in the Christian story of divine victory.

19:11-16 The messianic warrior. Christ wins the real victory in his death. Consequently, Revelation places much less emphasis on description of the messiah-warrior and his battle with the foes of the Lord than we might expect. Unlike other apocalypses of the period, the righteous do not participate in an earthly war paralleling the conflict of the divine warrior and Satan. All elements of conquest in this book are on the divine level. Human armies are not involved. This approach is quite different from the War Scroll that was found among the writings of the Essenes at the Dead Sea. That Jewish sect had a scroll which claimed to give instructions as to how the army of the righteous was to draw up for the wars that would be part of the messianic victory. It gave instructions about what was to be written on the trumpets and standards of the assembled hosts, and it included the hymns of victory that the army of the Lord would sing after defeating its enemies.

The Messiah finally appears for battle. Like the armies in the War Scroll, names are inscribed on his person and his equipment. But he comes only at the head of divine armies, not human ones. The names designate this rider as the source of divine salvation; he is not the earlier horseman of destruction (6:1-2). The description of the rider contains a string of his divine names: Faithful and True, Justice, unknown name, Word of God, and, finally, the divine acclamation, King of Kings, Lord of Lords. The unknown name may refer to the "new name" God gives Jerusalem when he bestows salvation on her in Isa 62:2. All these names signify divine sovereignty and salvation.

The flaming eyes of Dan 10:6 are familiar from Rev 1:14 and 2:18. The messianic crown evokes the Psalms (Pss 21:4; 132:18), the title "King of Kings," and, of course, the many crowns worn by the beast. The rider goes forth to battle in blood-stained garments much as God does in Isa 63:1-3. The sword in the mouth recalls Isa 11:4 and 49:2; the rod, Ps 2:9. We are already familiar with the divine winepress from Rev 14:10 and 17:6 (see Isa 63:2; Joel 4:13). The combination of names, images and symbols attached to the divine warrior makes it clear that no one will escape this judgment. God is taking the field against the embodiment of evil.

19:17-21 The vultures' feast. As in the other mythic sections, this battle between the divine warrior and the beast is hardly described. Instead, ominous birds once more appear in midheaven. They are gathering to feast on the enemies of God (see Num 16:30; Isa 63:1-6). The curse against Gog in Ezek 39:4 warns that he will fall on the mountains of Israel and be given to the birds as food. So many will be killed that God will summon the birds and the wild beasts to come to a great sacrificial feast, to dine on the bodies of the fallen warriors and their horses (Ezek 39:17-20). So here the birds are summoned to feast on all who had followed the beast. Some interpreters suggest that this feast is a gruesome parody of the heavenly victory feast that follows the defeat of the beast in the mythic cycle. Once again, a delay; the inhuman enemies of the divine warrior, the beast, and the false prophet are not slain but imprisoned in Hades.

20:1-6 A thousand-year reign. This section has combined several apocalyptic themes. Speculation about a thousand-year reign of the Messiah is uncommon. However, the section of Ezekiel on which the author has been drawing does contain a doubling of the end-time images of salvation: the Messiah rules; Gog and Magog are defeated; the new Jerusalem is described (Ezek 37–43). This passage in Revelation pictures a rule by the Messiah prior to the defeat of Gog and Magog. Before that reign can occur, an angel imprisons the dragon in the abyss. He resembles the star-like angel with the keys to the abyss in Rev 9:1. The descent into Hades continues the imagery of Satan's fall from 12:9.

The significance of the throne imagery in this passage is not clear. At the end of the last letter, the victors are promised that they will share the throne of God/Jesus (3:21). Traditionally, the righteous or some group of them ascended thrones to judge the wicked (see Dan 7:9, the beast; Matt 19:28-30, the nations; also 1 Cor 6:2). Though Revelation has those sitting on thrones empowered to pass judgment, it is not clear whom they would be judging, since the messianic kingdom is established on earth, and the final judgment is yet to be described.

This section also seems to have mixed traditions about the resurrection. Images of resurrection in the first century vary between a general resurrection for a judgment, which separates righteous from wicked people, and resurrection as the reward for the righteous. The awkward distinctions in verses 4 and 5 may represent a combination of both traditions. The faithful witnesses are rewarded with an early resurrection and share the thousand-year reign. Verse 6 makes it clear that that resurrection is a definitive sign of salvation. Others will be resurrected at the judgment.

20:7-10 Against Gog and Magog. As in the previous battle scene, there is little description of the actual battle. In the tradition upon which Revelation draws (Ezek 38:22, 39), the armies are made up of people from among the nations. Either Revelation assumes that some have survived the previous destruction, since the dragon is said to be prevented from leading the nations astray, or one must assume that this army is made up of the dead/resurrected. The traditional image has the nations draw up against the people of God who are with the Messiah in Jerusalem (= the beloved city). That seems to be the tradition behind this battle. Revelation does not specify the nature of the opposition any further. What is significant is the final and eternal imprisonment of the devil, the beast, and the false prophet.

20:11-15 Judgment of the dead. God appears on his throne to execute judgment (compare Dan 7:9). This image of judgment presupposes a universal judgment of all those who are dead, wherever they may be. All that is hostile to God is cast into the fire of judgment, the second—and real—death. This punishment includes the destruction of both death as enemy and the underworld (see Isa 25:8; 1 Cor 15:26).

21:1-5a New heaven and earth. This section closes with the vision of a new heaven and earth that replaces the old creation, which has finally passed away (see Isa 65:17). The author is not interested in the implications of the image of a new creation which he has taken from Isaiah. Consequently, we cannot push this verse for information about the renewal of the natural world, as some interpreters concerned with ecology have tried to do. The real centerpiece of the new creation is the new Jerusalem (see Isa 52:1-3). The holy city will be the true dwelling place of God and also of the bride in the final section of the work. The throne voice announces that the promises of divine presence are fulfilled in this city (see Ezek 37:27; Zech 2:14; Jer 38:33). This city of divine presence and peace forms a striking contrast to the fallen Babylon (see Isa 25:8; 35:10; 65:19). In Isa 43:18-19 the Lord tells Israel not to remember the old things, since he is doing "a new thing." Revelation proclaims that that promise is finally fulfilled. God is making all things new.

21:5b-8 Second conclusion. These last chapters anticipate the conclusion of the whole with injunctions to the seer to record the trustworthy vision which he has received (see 19:9). The following section resumes the vision of the bride of the Lamb with an introduction that is parallel to the vision of the whore of Babylon (compare 21:9 and 17:1). This interruption also provides Revelation the opportunity to anticipate the bridal scene and the marriage feast (already anticipated once in the hymn of 19:7-8). The command to write and the divine name Alpha and Omega also bring us back to the beginning of the book (1:11, 19). The exhortations in this section are reminders of the exhortations in the opening letters, as are the promises to the victors (largely derived from the prophetic sayings in Isa 55:1-6). The passage seems to recapitulate the warnings of those letters. Verse 8 warns against various vices and idolatry. Thus, the section reminds the audience that the lessons of the book are to be applied to their own situation. They must heed the revelation and repent, lest they find themselves excluded from the final salvation. Now we find one final image of that final salvation, the new Jerusalem.

THE NEW JERUSALEM

Rev 21:9–22:5

We finally see the new Jerusalem in all her glory. This vision of the city in which God truly dwells rounds out the condemnation of all the false claims of the beast and Babylon in the previous chapters. It also represents the final gathering of the community which belongs to the Lamb.

21:9-21 The bride of the Lamb. The introduction to the vision of the bride deliberately recalls the introduction to the vision of the whore of Babylon. The two cities are antitypes of one another. Much of the imagery of the city also derives from Ezekiel: the city on the mount from 40:2; the city full of the glory of God from 43:2-4. The description of the walls primarily draws upon Ezek 40:5; 48:31-35, though other prophetic descriptions of the walls of Jerusalem might also lie behind this passage (see Jer 30:18; Isa 26:1; 60:10, 18; 62:6). Angelic watchers appear in Ezek 49:12 (also Isa 62:6, 10). Ezekiel's gates represent the twelve tribes (43:31-34). For Revelation, the Twelve are the apostles. The use of Ezekiel imagery has switched from description of the woman as bride to the architectural features that define the city.

The next actions continue that image. Like Ezekiel (ch. 40), the seer measures the city. The measurements emphasize the perfection and size of the city. The stones in the walls seem to be based on Exod 28:17-20 (also 39:10-13; 36:17-20). Some interpreters try to give astrological interpretations of the various stones. If the author was acquainted with such traditions, he does not give any indication that he is exploiting that symbolism in the description about the city.

21:22-27 Divine presence in the city. This city is introduced as quite different from its prototype in Ezekiel when we learn that there is no temple there. The presence of God and of the Lamb makes the whole city a temple. Metaphors derived from Isaiah are used to describe the divine presence in the city; the basic passage is 60:1-20. Most of the elements of this passage can be found there. The glory of the Lord fills Jerusalem, so that she has no need of heavenly bodies to provide light (60:19-20; also Isa 24:33). The kings of the earth come bringing their wealth (60:3, 11). The city gates are always open (60:11a). The city is one of holiness. Nothing profane enters. Only the righteous live in this city (60:21; also Isa 35:8; 52:1; Ezek 44:9). Revelation has taken the vision of Isaiah and made appropriate additions to suit the images of the Lamb and the book of life. In so doing, it has proclaimed that vision fulfilled. The glory of divine presence is shared between God and the Lamb. The righteous who dwell in the city are faithful Christians.

22:1-5 The water and the trees of life. The vision of the new Jerusalem concludes with an image of the blessedness and immortality of those who inhabit it. The life-giving water flowing from the thrones of God and the Lamb recall the image of the streams of water flowing from the temple mount in Joel 4:18 and Ezek 47 (also Jer 2:13; Pss 46:5; 36:10). The tree of life from Gen 2:9 has been combined with the trees by the stream from Ezek 47:12 to provide twelve fruit-bearing trees. They provide the healing predicted for the pagan nations in Joel 1:14; 2:15. Just as nothing profane can enter the city, so nothing cursed can dwell in the grove near the stream (see Zech 14:11). These final verses bring Revelation to a fitting close by summarizing the promises that have been made to the elect throughout the work. Those promises are all fulfilled in the heavenly city.

EPILOGUE

Rev 22:6-21

Revelation concludes with a collection of separate prophetic oracles. They testify to the authenticity of the revelation contained in the book. The speaker shifts from oracle to oracle. We hear words of the revealing angel, of Jesus, of the Spirit, and of the prophet. Three themes are reiterated throughout: heed the revelation; the end is near; the righteous are rewarded. The "I am coming soon" of the opening exhortations ties this conclusion back to the initial revelation (1:1; 2:16; 3:11; 22:6b, 7, 12, 20).

The nearness of the Lord's coming is often tied to exhortations to remain faithful. That combination suggests that the phrase was part of the regular ethical exhortation of the churches addressed. It was not primarily directed at calculating exactly when the end would be; rather, the phrase assures the audience of the Lord's coming so that they will continue to be faithful. In Rev 2:16 it belongs to the exhortation against the Nicolaitan heresy. In Rev 3:11 it encourages perseverance.

As in the conclusion to Daniel (12:5), the author signs his name to the revelation to attest to its authenticity. Unlike Daniel (12:10), the words of the revelation are not sealed. For the second time the seer is rebuked for worshiping the revealing angel (also 19:10). Both the angels and the faithful stand together in praising God, as we have seen throughout the book in the scenes of the heavenly liturgy.

The oracle confirming the division between righteous and wicked in the last days also confirms a phenomenon to which the visions have given us dramatic testimony. The various plagues did not bring humanity to repentance. The prophecy does not convert the wicked from their ways (compare Ezek 3:27; Dan 12:10).

Jesus speaks with his divine authority, Alpha and Omega, to affirm the reward that is to be given to each. The beatitude (v. 14) is a variant of 7:14, which now includes the new visions of the holy city, in which nothing profane dwells with the tree of life. Verse 15 cites a catalog of vices to indicate the evils that cannot be allowed to enter the new city (see Joel 3:22–4:17; Rev 21:7-8).

Verse 16 has Jesus authenticate the angel of 1:1 as his messenger. The messianic titles given Jesus come from the Old Testament: root of Jesse (Isa 11:10); star of Jacob (Num 24:17); morning star (Isa 9:1; 60:1).

The summons to "come" in verse 17 allude to the liturgical practice of summoning the righteous to the Eucharist. Here we find an antiphonal summons to come and receive the promised reward. Another part of the same liturgy was the prayer to the Lord to come. Paul indicates that it was spoken in Aramaic, *Marana tha*, "Lord, come!" (1 Cor 16:22). It was also connected with the pronouncement of a formula excluding all nonbelievers and all who are not holy. The catalog of vices in verse 15 could function as such a formula for Revelation. Thus, the audience is reminded that the summons into the liturgical assembly is an image of that final summons to the gathering of the holy ones of God. We are also reminded that Revelation was read in such a community gathering.

The final verses provide further testimony to the truth of the prophecy. The curse against those who tamper with the words of such a revelation derives from Deut 4:2. Such curses also appear in Jewish apocryphal writings from New Testament times. Jesus' own testimony to the truth of the revelation is answered by the liturgical prayer for his coming. A common conclusion in Pauline letters ends Revelation. It reminds us, as much of the epilogue has, that the revelation is given to the audience which has also heard the warnings and promises in the letters. They must apply these visions to their situation. Those who are praised should continue, confident in the salvation that they have been promised. Those who are called to repent should heed the warning, lest they be found among the hardened and blasphemous who will not listen to any of the words of the Lord.

The message of Revelation does not depend upon calculations about the time of the second coming of the Lord. People must be convinced about the "nearness of the Lord" and the certainty of the Christian vision of salvation if they are to heed the warnings in the book. Many of the questions raised by Revelation continue to create problems for Christians. They must question false claims of political and economic systems when they destroy values that Christians are committed to. They must question the nature of human compliance with evil and injustice. Christians must also face the dangers of sectarian groups which pervert the gospel by claiming to have esoteric wisdom not available to others, "to know the depths of God." They must also ask whether they really believe in God's rule over the cosmos, which Revelation presents as real and active. Or, perhaps, Christians really feel that God is "far off' and not really concerned with the problems of our day beyond some record-keeping of individual transgressions. Perhaps the justice demanded in the prophets to whom Revelation is constantly alluding does not seem to count for much in the complexities of the modern world. Revelation would never tolerate such an attitude among Christians. It has used all the mythic and symbolic resources at its disposal to show Christians the dangers of a false estimate of the powers of this world. Christians live on the edge of times. They take their values from the gospel and from the way God sees things. They should always expect that "the Lord is coming soon!"

LIST OF MAPS

1. Table of Nations
2. Culture and Commerce in the Ancient Near East
3. Ancient Near East in the Second Millennium B.C.
4. Palace at Mari
5. The Near East in the First Millennium B.C.
6. Babylon
7. The Land of Canaan
8. The Walls of Jericho
9. The Coming of the Israelites
10. The Exodus
11. The Kingdom of David and Solomon
12. Megiddo—Chariot City
13. The Kingdoms of Judah and Israel
14. Jerusalem of the Old Testament
15. The World of the Greeks
16. Empire of Alexander the Great
17. The Roman Empire
18. Rome
19. Palestine in Graeco-Roman Times
20. Jerusalem of the Hasmoneans
21. Jesus in His Land
22. Jerusalem of the New Testament
23. Jesus in Galilee
24. The Journeys of the Apostles
25. Antioch
26. Caesarea Maritima
27. The Spread of the Early Church
28. Paul's Missions
29. The Growth of Christianity
30. Palestine in the Time of the Old Testament
31. Palestine in the Time of the New Testament
32. The Near East, Physical
33. The Holy Land Today

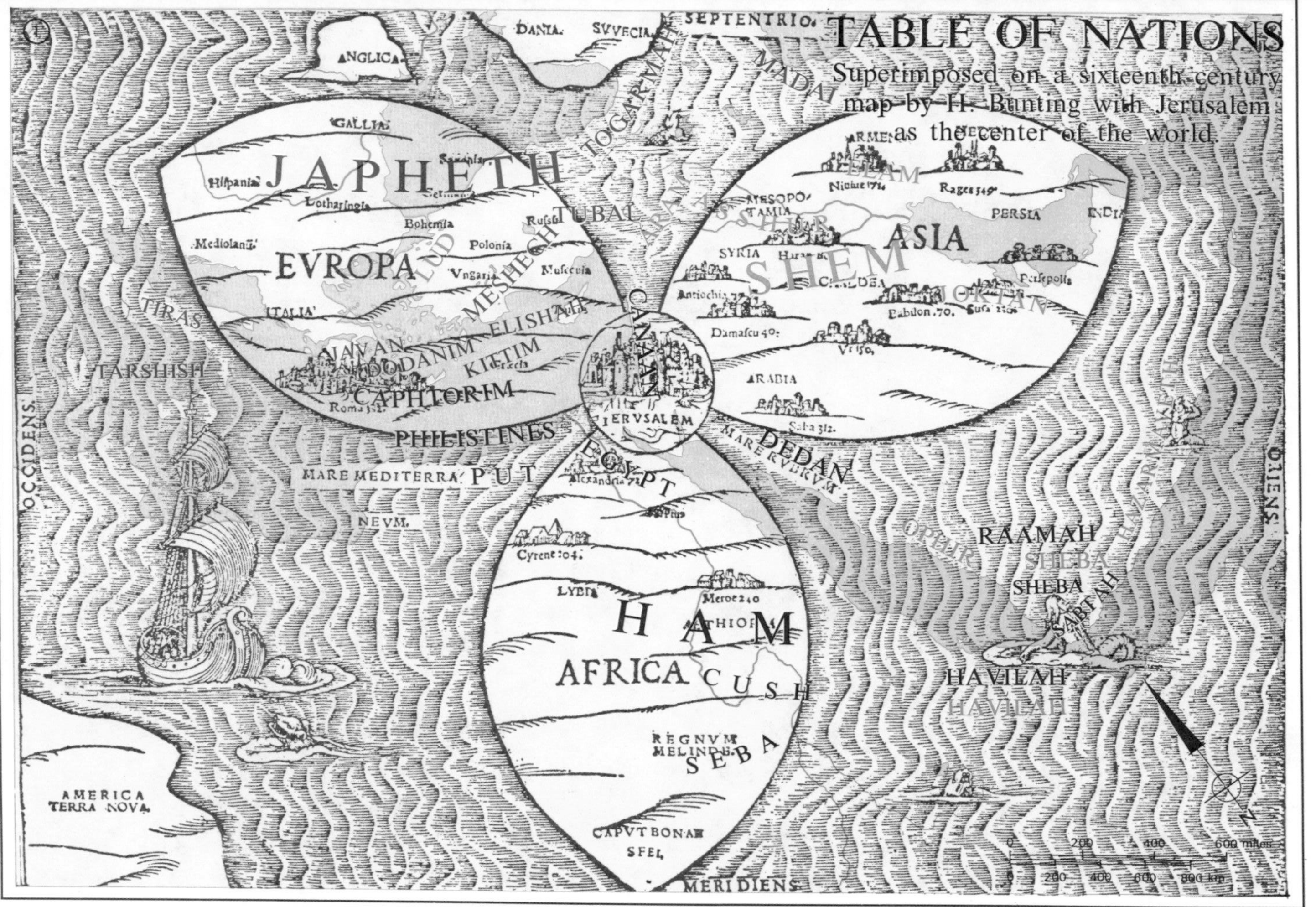
TABLE OF NATIONS
Superimposed on a sixteenth century map by H. Bunting with Jerusalem as the center of the world.
SEPTENTRIO
OCCIDENS
ORIENS
MERIDIENS
DANIA
SVVECIA
ANGLICA
GALLIA
Hispania
Lotharingia
Bohemia
Polonia
Vngaria
Muscovia
Mediolanu
ITALIA
Roma
JAPHETH
EVROPA
TUBAL
MESHECH
LUD
TIRAS
TARSHISH
JAVAN
DODANIM
ELISHAH
KITTIM
CAPHTORIM
PHILISTINES
MADAI
TOGARMAH
CANAAN
IERVSALEM
ARMENIA
ELAM
Niniue 171
Rages 349
MESOPOTAMIA
PERSIA
INDIA
ASIA
SYRIA
SHEM
CHALDEA
Antiochia
Persepolis
JOKTAN
Babilon 70
Susa
Damascu 40
Vr 150
ARABIA
Saba 312
DEDAN
MARE RVBRVM
MARE MEDITERRA
PUT
NEVM
EGYPT
Alexandria
Cyrene 104
LYBIA
Meroe 240
HAM
AETHIOPIA
AFRICA
CUSH
REGNVM MELINDE
SEBA
CAPVT BONAE SPEI
OPHIR
RAAMAH
SHEBA
SHEBA
SABTAH
HAVILAH
HAVILAH
HAZARMAVETH
AMERICA TERRA NOVA
0 200 400 600 miles
0 200 400 600 800 km
N

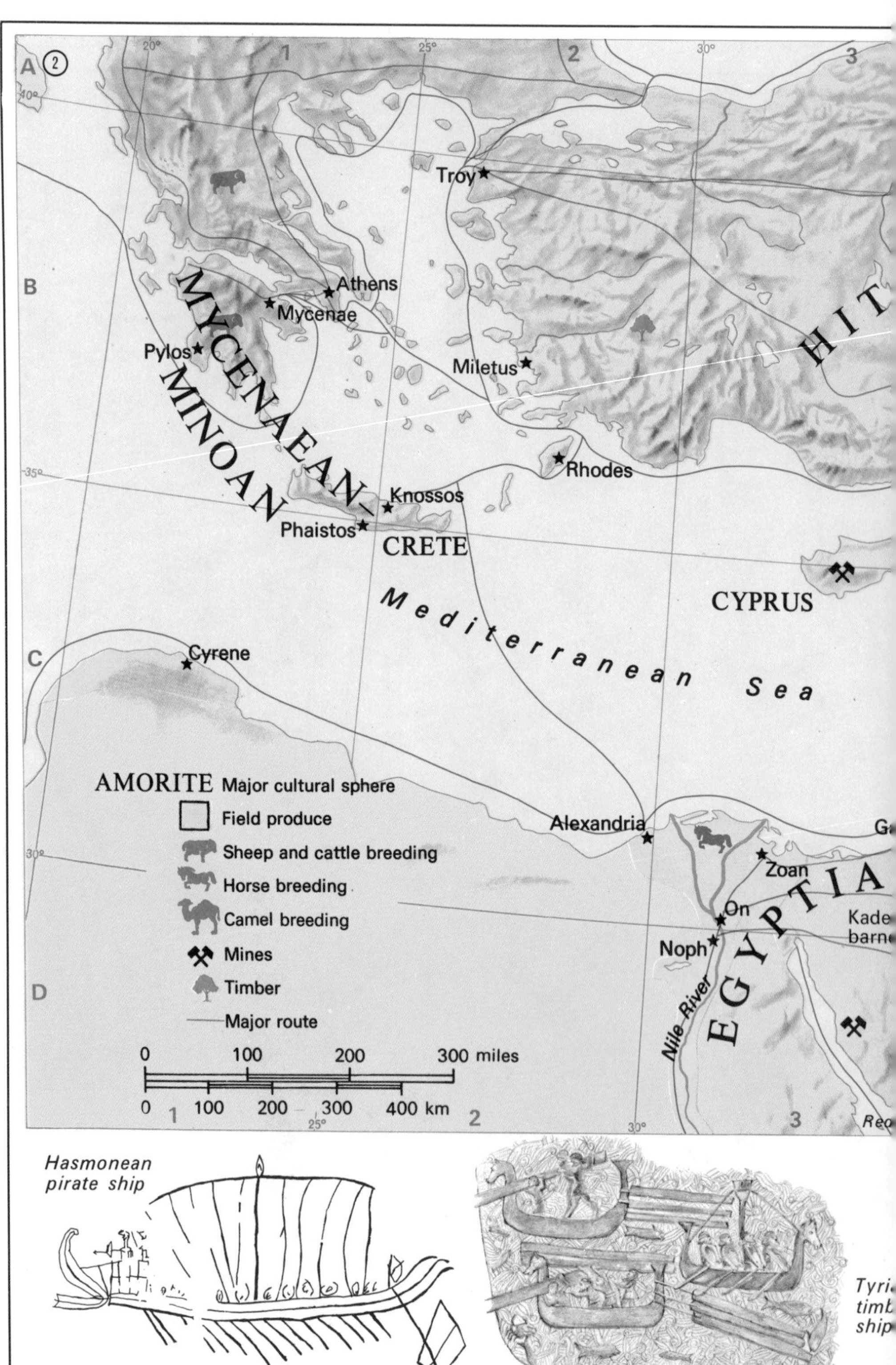
A
2
1
2
3
B
C
D
20°
25°
30°
40°
35°
30°
Troy
Athens
Mycenae
Pylos
Miletus
Rhodes
Knossos
Phaistos
CRETE
MYCENAEAN–MINOAN
HIT
CYPRUS
Mediterranean Sea
Cyrene
Alexandria
Zoan
On
Noph
Nile River
EGYPTIA
AMORITE Major cultural sphere
Field produce
Sheep and cattle breeding
Horse breeding
Camel breeding
Mines
Timber
Major route
0 100 200 300 miles
0 100 200 300 400 km
Hasmonean pirate ship

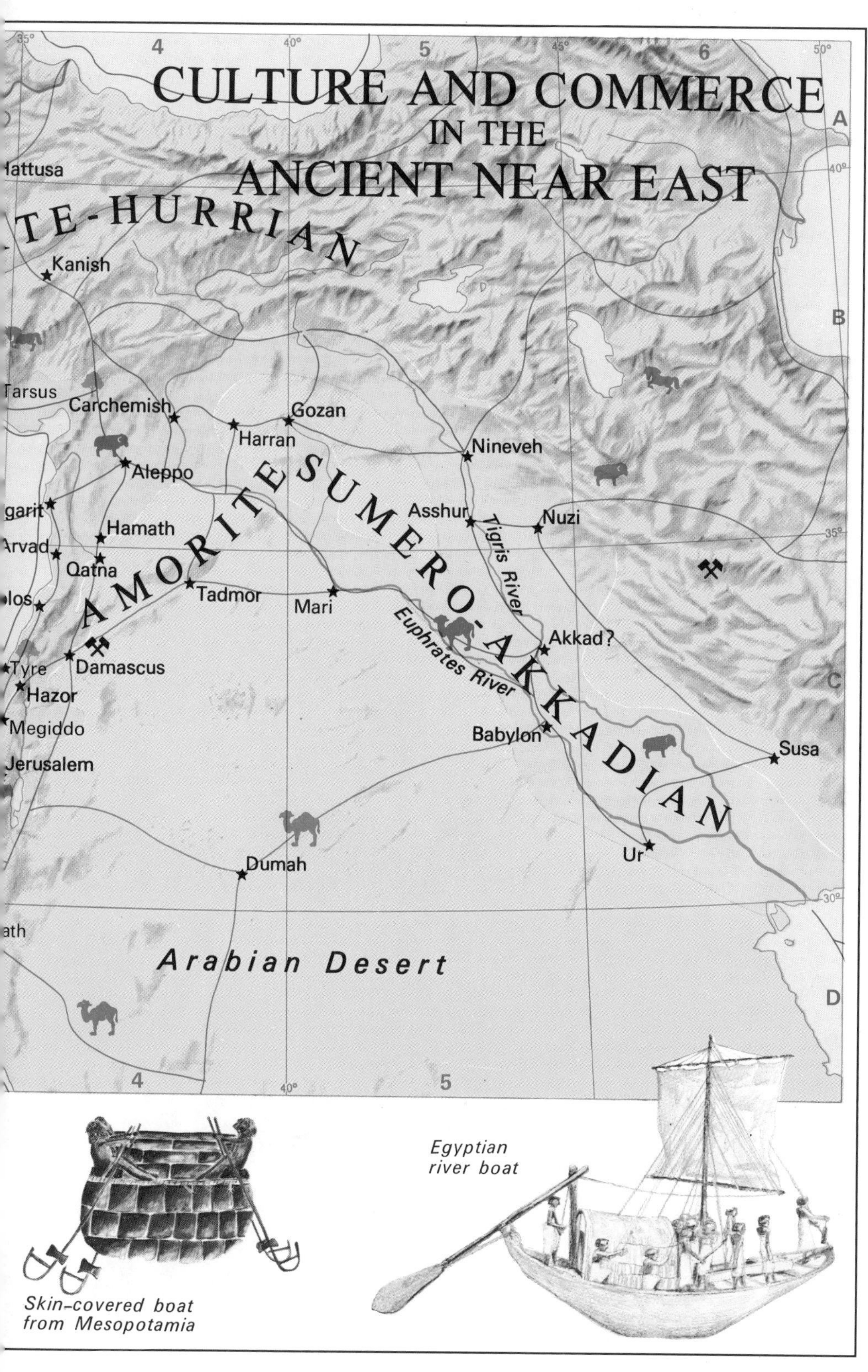

Egyptian river boat

Skin-covered boat from Mesopotamia

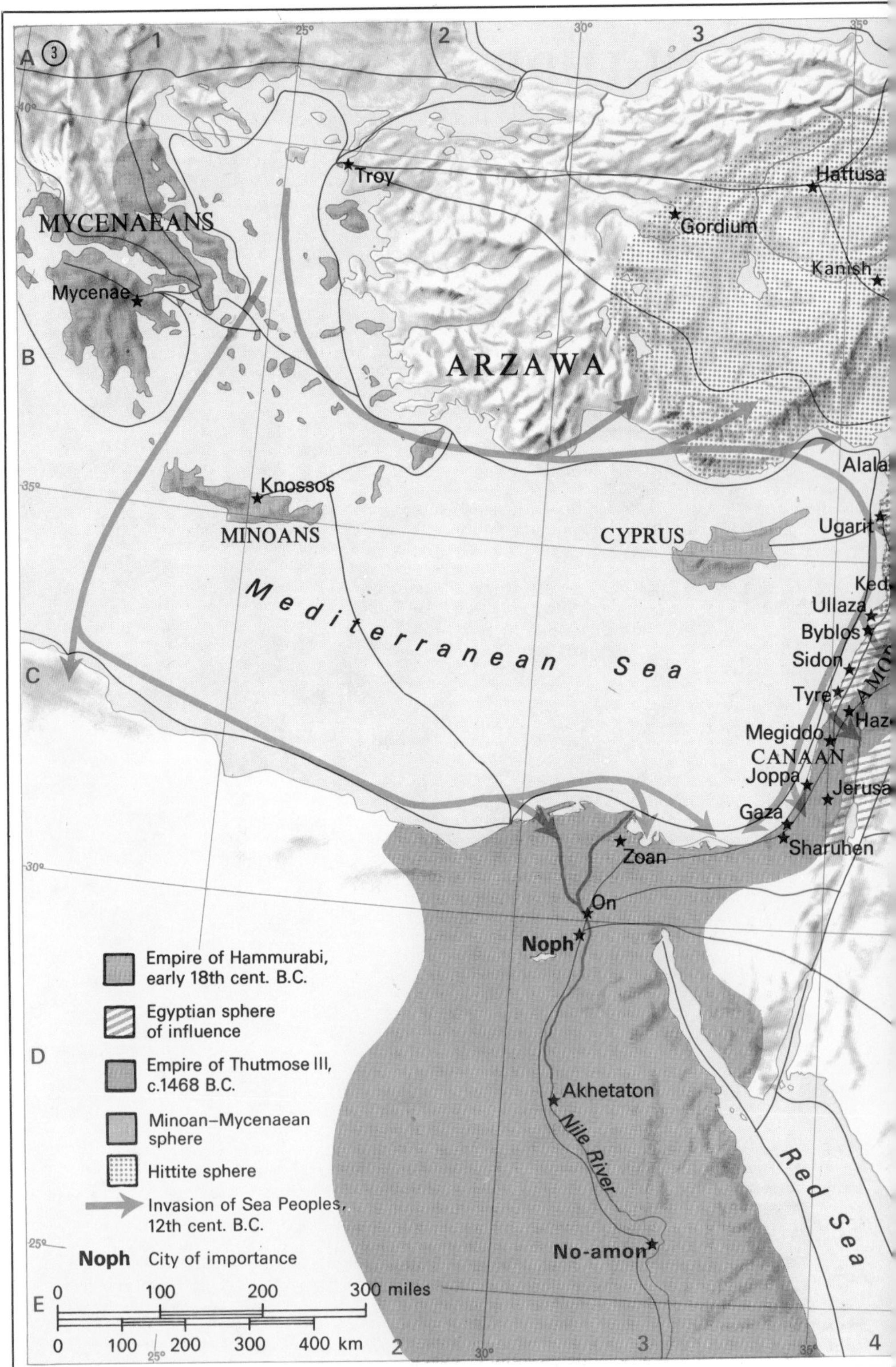

MYCENAEANS
Mycenae
Troy
Hattusa
Gordium
Kanish
ARZAWA
Knossos
MINOANS
CYPRUS
Alalakh
Ugarit
Ullaza
Byblos
Sidon
Tyre
Megiddo
CANAAN
Joppa
Gaza
Sharuhen
Mediterranean Sea
Zoan
On
Noph
Akhetaton
Nile River
No-amon
Red Sea
Empire of Hammurabi, early 18th cent. B.C.
Egyptian sphere of influence
Empire of Thutmose III, c.1468 B.C.
Minoan–Mycenaean sphere
Hittite sphere
Invasion of Sea Peoples, 12th cent. B.C.
Noph City of importance
0 100 200 300 miles
0 100 200 300 400 km

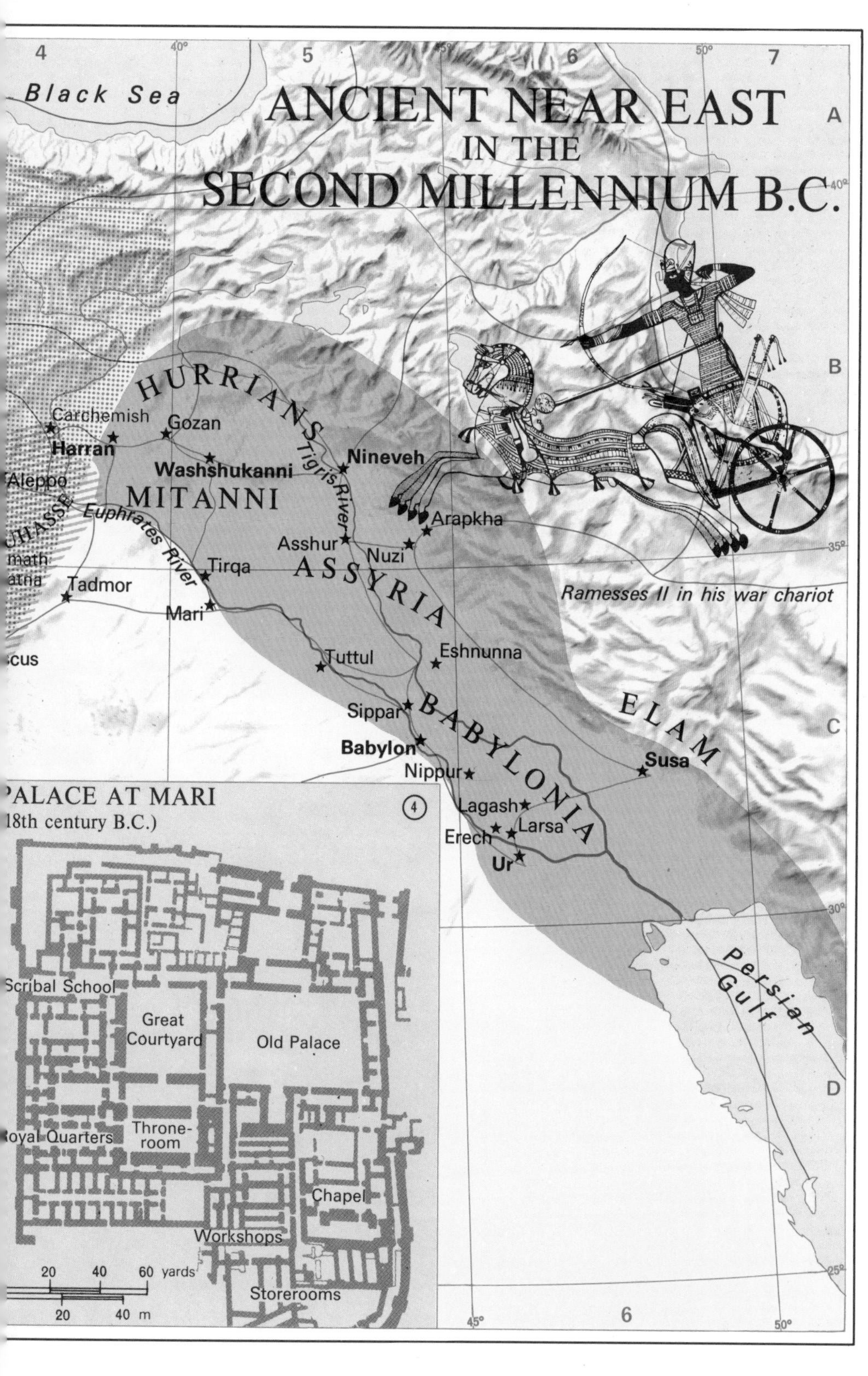

ANCIENT NEAR EAST
IN THE
SECOND MILLENNIUM B.C.
Black Sea
HURRIANS
MITANNI
ASSYRIA
BABYLONIA
ELAM
Carchemish
Harran
Gozan
Washshukanni
Nineveh
Tigris River
Euphrates River
Aleppo
Asshur
Nuzi
Arapkha
Tirqa
Tadmor
Mari
Tuttul
Eshnunna
Sippar
Babylon
Nippur
Susa
Lagash
Larsa
Erech
Ur
Persian Gulf
Ramesses II in his war chariot
PALACE AT MARI
(18th century B.C.)
Scribal School
Great Courtyard
Old Palace
Throne-room
Royal Quarters
Chapel
Workshops
Storerooms
20 40 60 yards
20 40 m

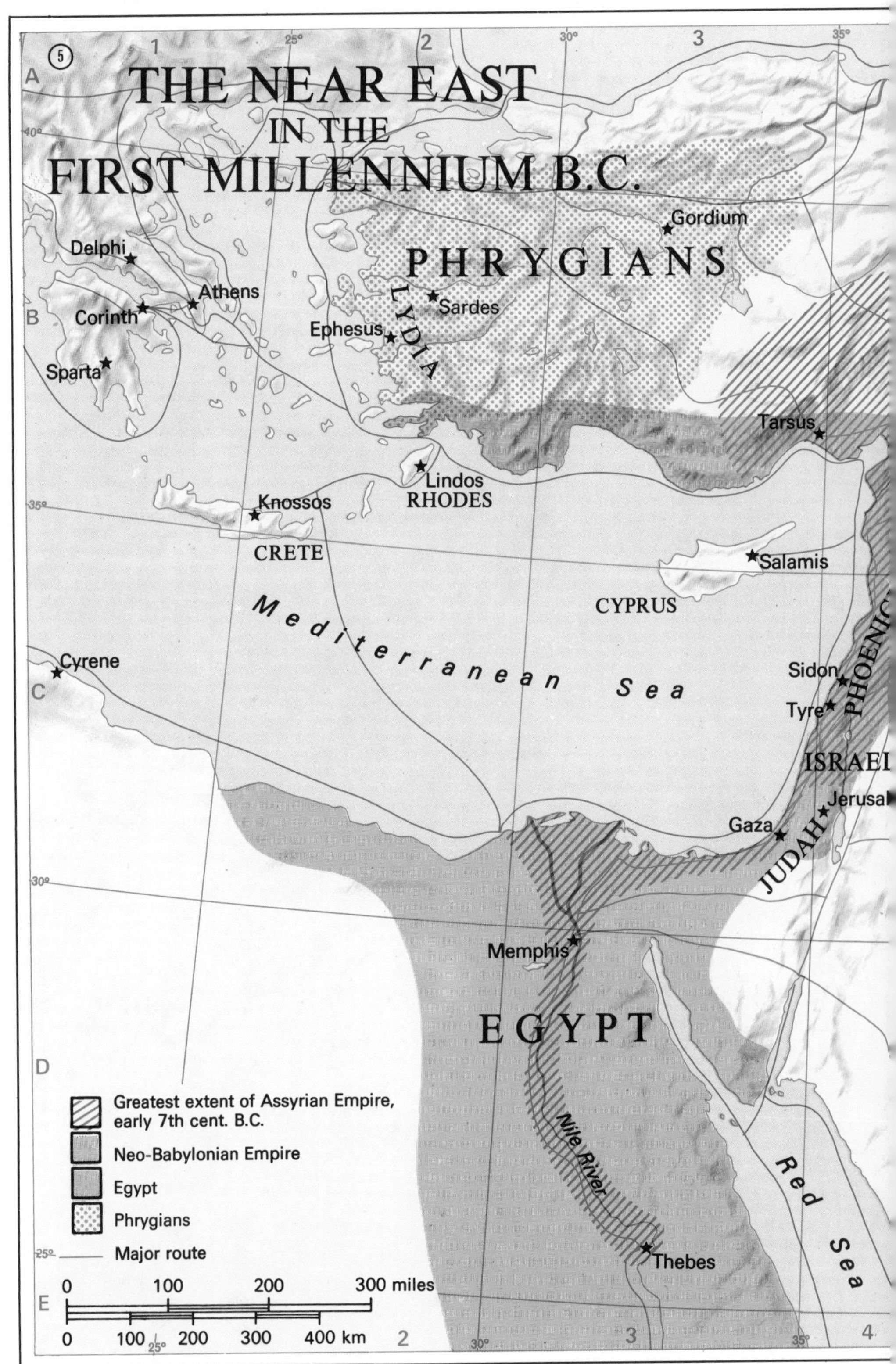

THE NEAR EAST
IN THE
FIRST MILLENNIUM B.C.
PHRYGIANS
Gordium
LYDIA
Sardes
Ephesus
Delphi
Athens
Corinth
Sparta
Tarsus
Lindos
RHODES
Knossos
CRETE
Salamis
CYPRUS
Mediterranean Sea
Cyrene
Sidon
Tyre
PHOENIC
ISRAEL
Jerusal
Gaza
JUDAH
Memphis
EGYPT
Nile River
Thebes
Red Sea
Greatest extent of Assyrian Empire, early 7th cent. B.C.
Neo-Babylonian Empire
Egypt
Phrygians
Major route
0 100 200 300 miles
0 100 200 300 400 km

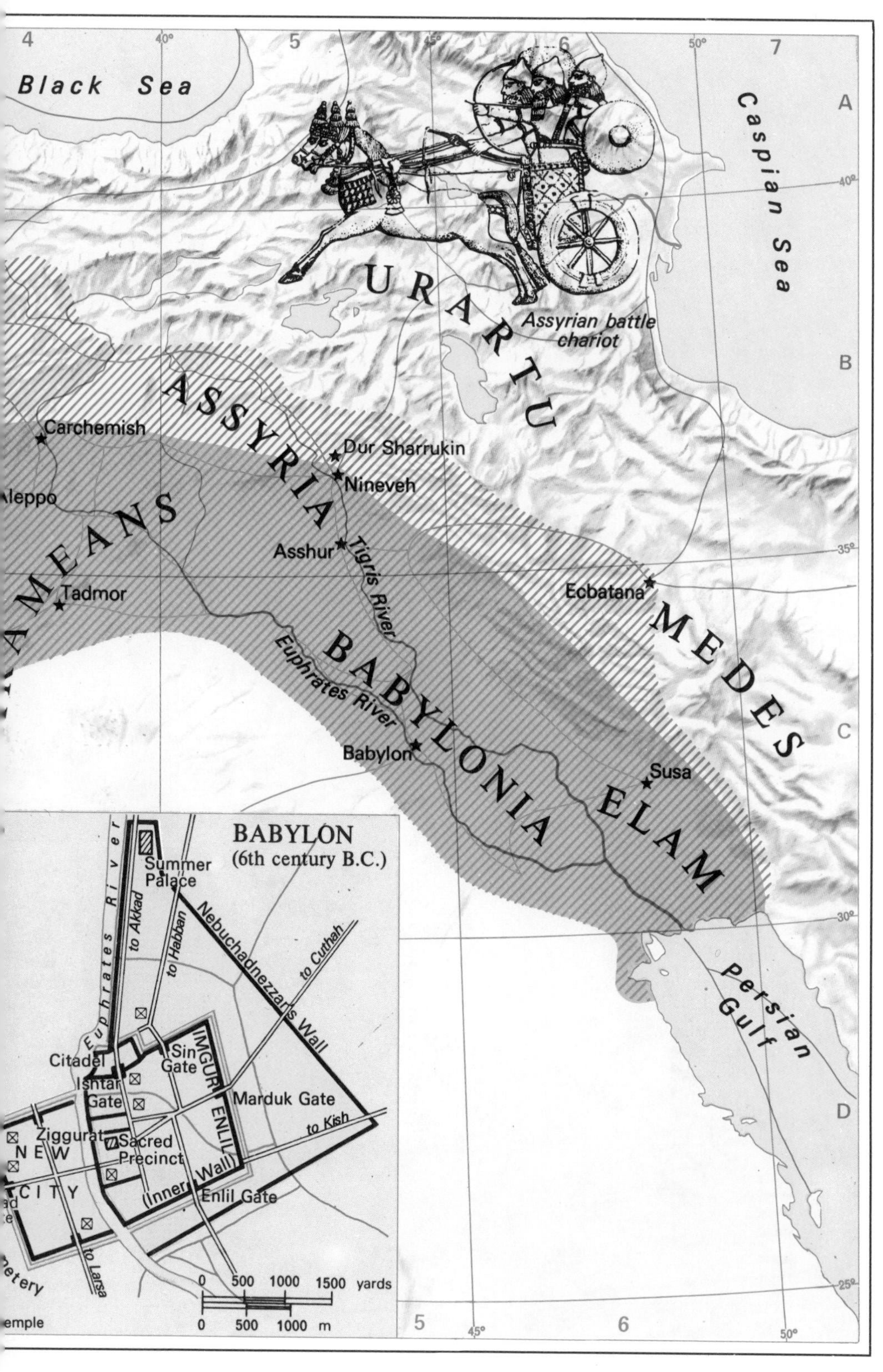
Black Sea
Caspian Sea
URARTU
Assyrian battle chariot
ASSYRIA
Carchemish
Dur Sharrukin
Nineveh
Aleppo
AMEANS
Asshur
Tigris River
Tadmor
Ecbatana
MEDES
BABYLONIA
Euphrates River
Babylon
Susa
ELAM
Persian Gulf
BABYLON
(6th century B.C.)
Summer Palace
Euphrates River
to Akkad
to Habban
Nebuchadnezzar's Wall
to Cuthah
Citadel
Sin Gate
IMGUR ENLIL
Ishtar Gate
Marduk Gate
to Kish
Ziggurat
Sacred Precinct
NEW CITY
(Inner Wall)
Enlil Gate
to Larsa
0 500 1000 1500 yards
0 500 1000 m
emple

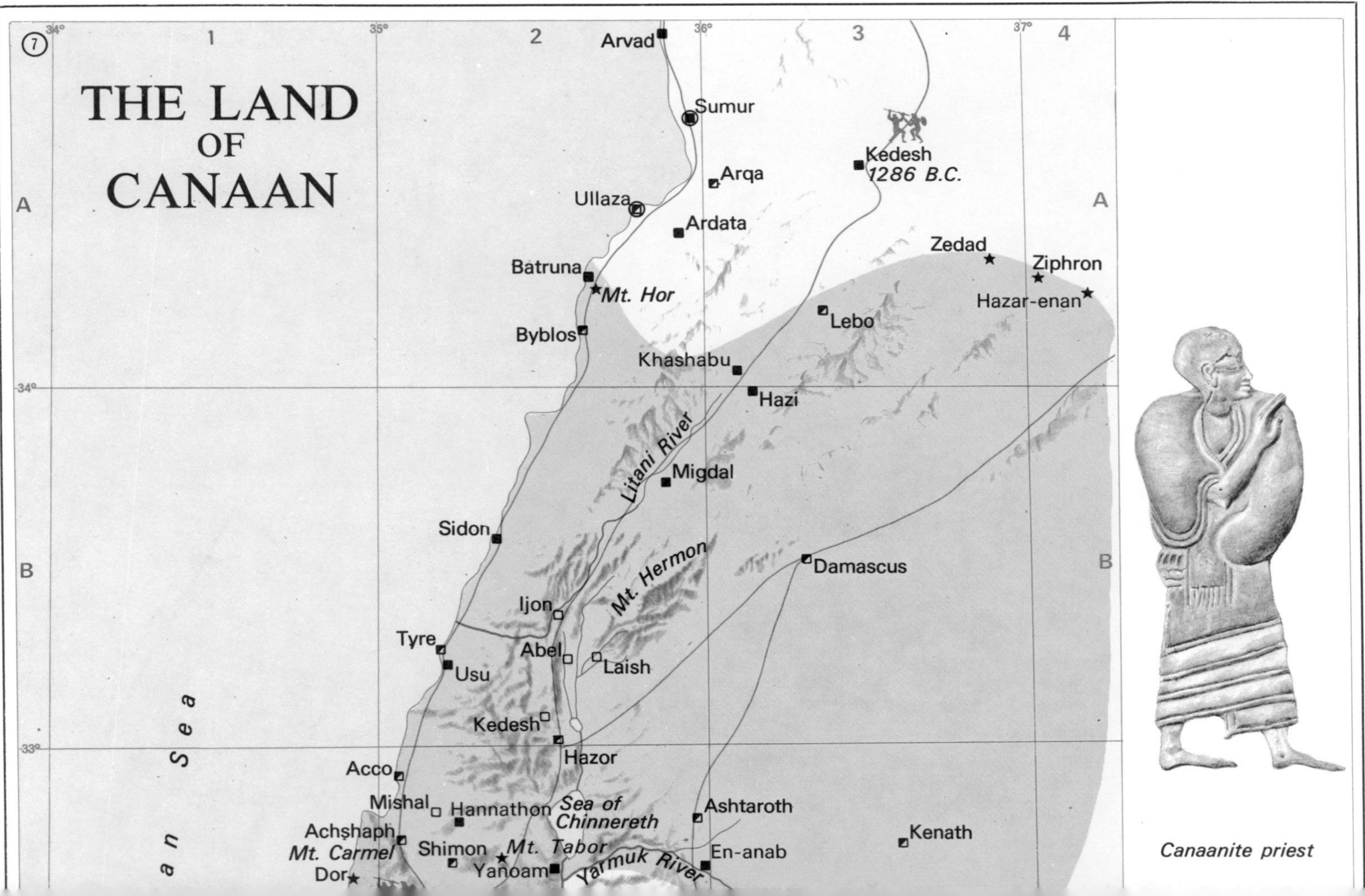

Canaanite priest

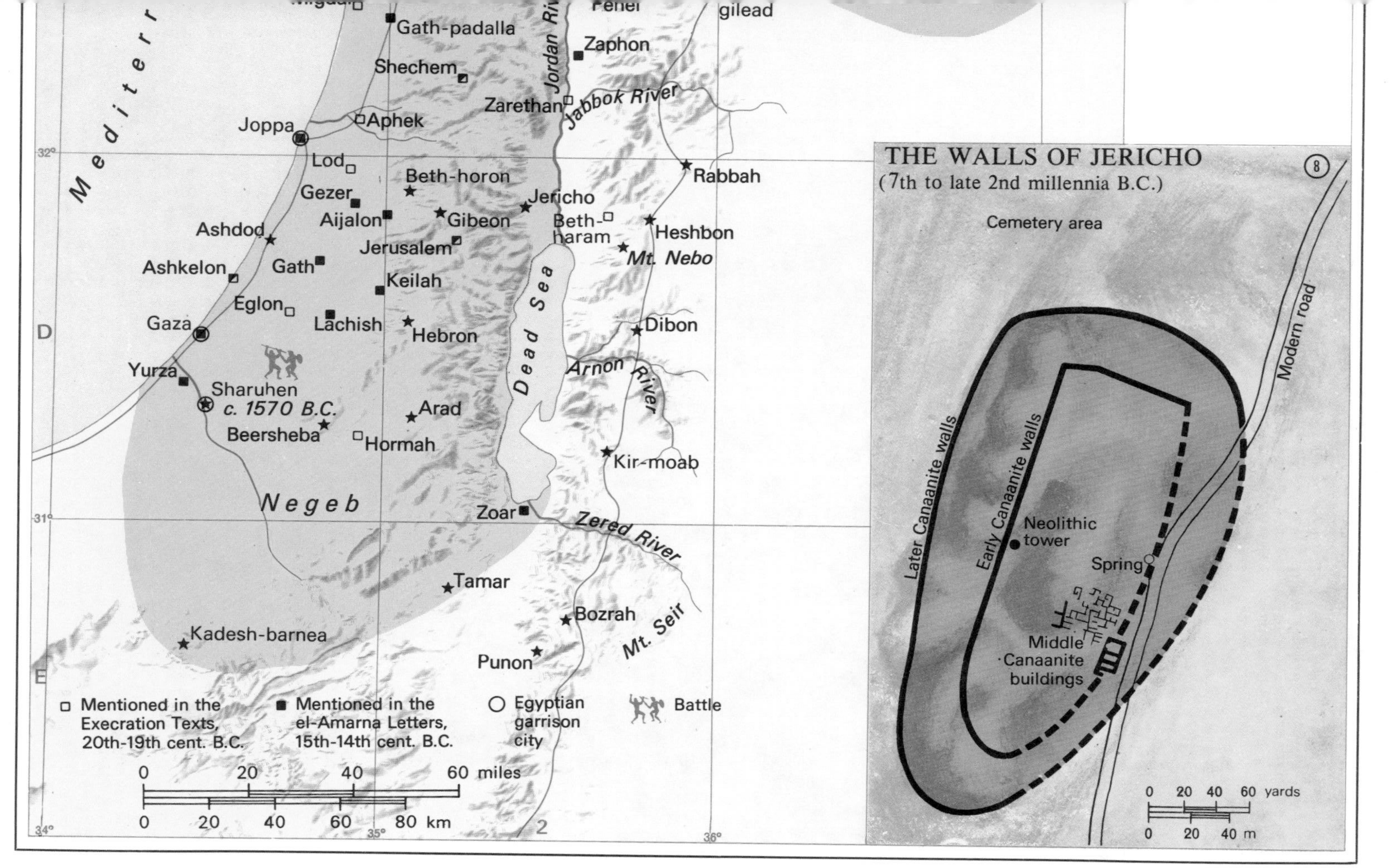
Mediterr
Gath-padalla
Zaphon
Shechem
Zarethan
Jordan Ri
Jabbok River
gilead
Joppa
Aphek
Lod
Beth-horon
Rabbah
Gezer
Jericho
Aijalon
Gibeon
Beth-haram
Heshbon
Ashdod
Jerusalem
Mt. Nebo
Ashkelon
Gath
Keilah
Dead Sea
Eglon
Gaza
Lachish
Hebron
Dibon
Yurza
Arnon River
Sharuhen
c. 1570 B.C.
Arad
Beersheba
Hormah
Kir-moab
Negeb
Zoar
Zered River
Tamar
Bozrah
Kadesh-barnea
Mt. Seir
Punon
Mentioned in the Execration Texts, 20th-19th cent. B.C.
Mentioned in the el-Amarna Letters, 15th-14th cent. B.C.
Egyptian garrison city
Battle
0 20 40 60 miles
0 20 40 60 80 km
32°
31°
34°
35°
36°
D
E
2
THE WALLS OF JERICHO
(7th to late 2nd millennia B.C.)
8
Cemetery area
Modern road
Later Canaanite walls
Early Canaanite walls
Neolithic tower
Spring
Middle Canaanite buildings
0 20 40 60 yards
0 20 40 m

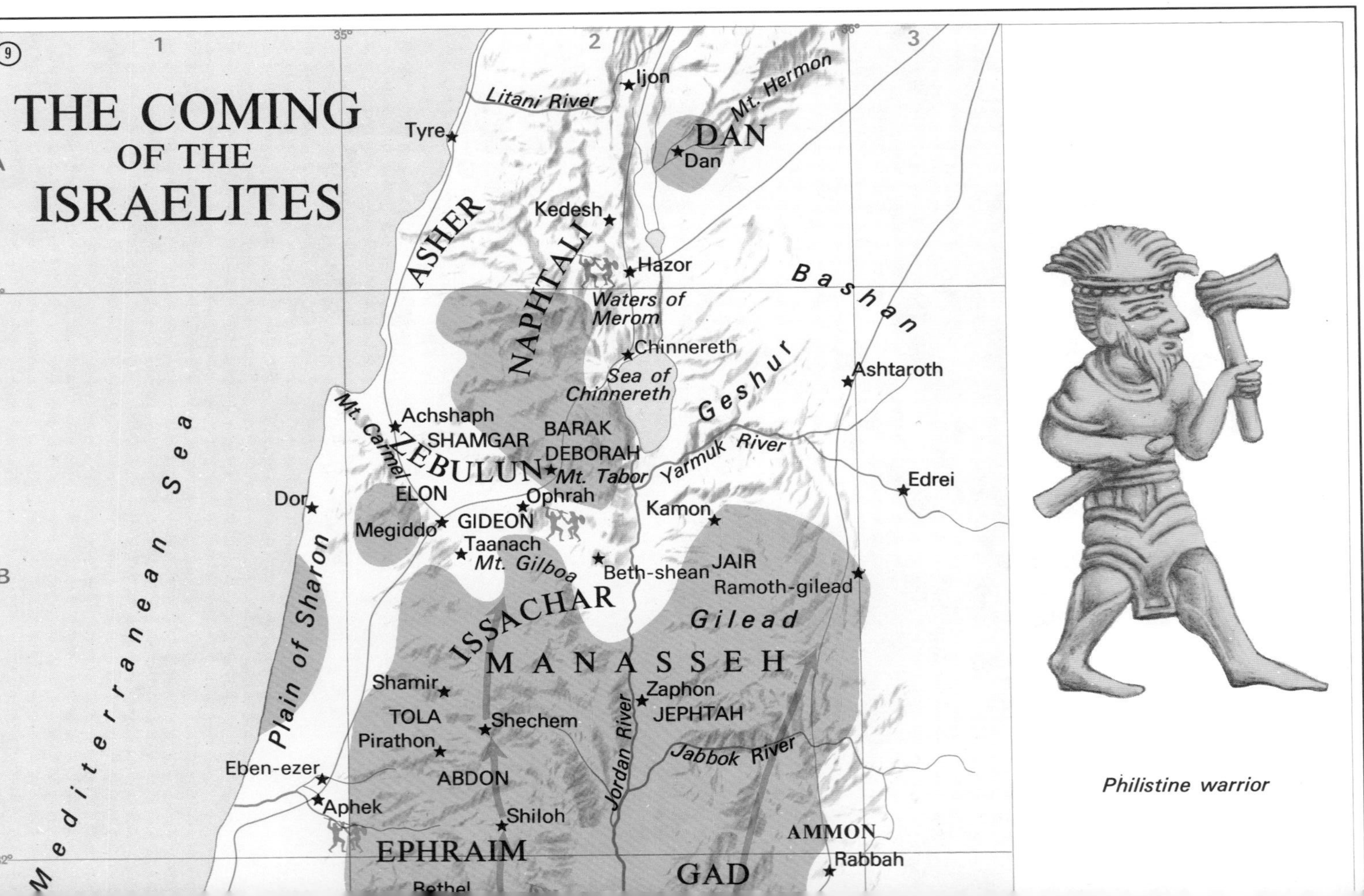

Philistine warrior

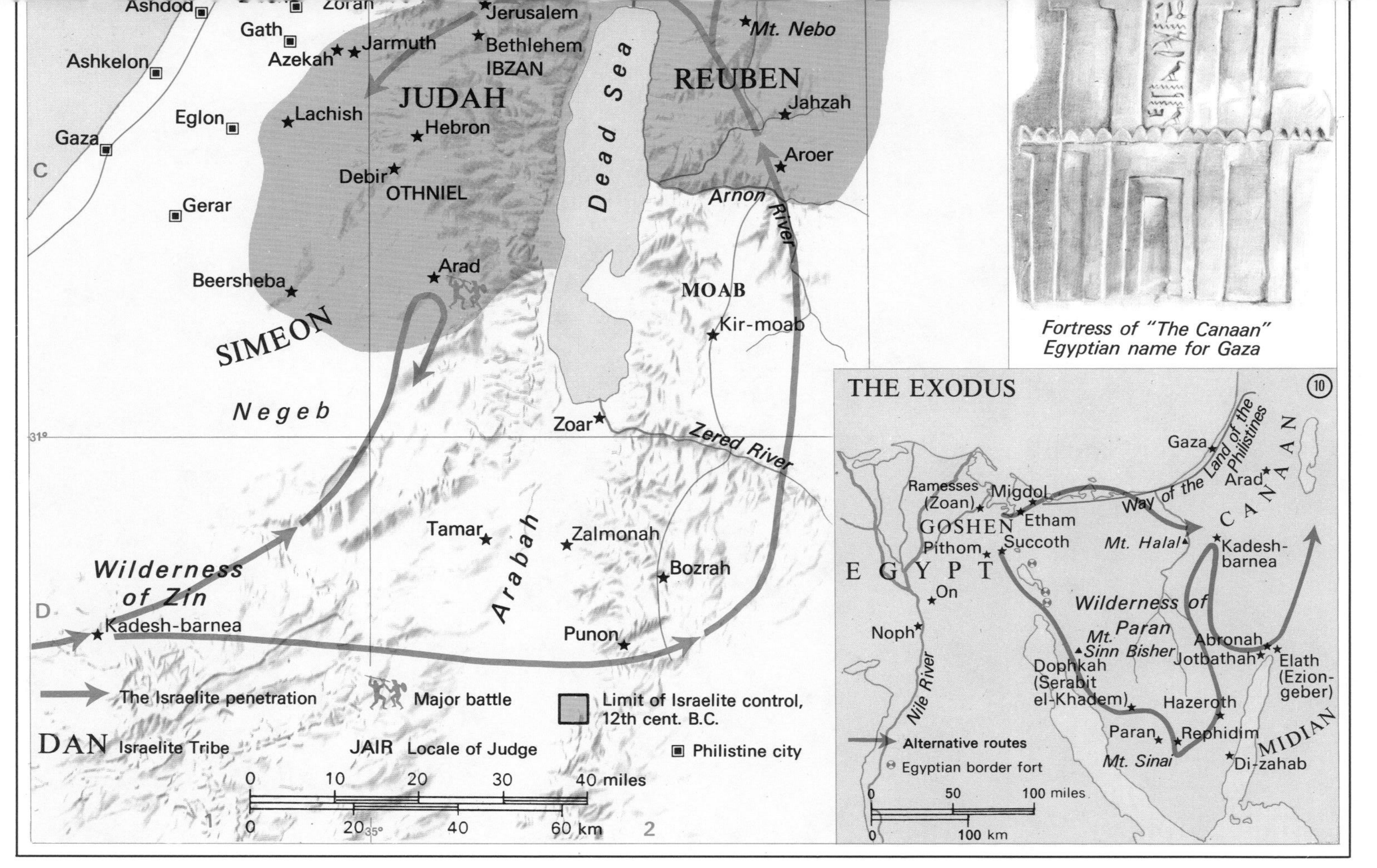

Fortress of "The Canaan"
Egyptian name for Gaza

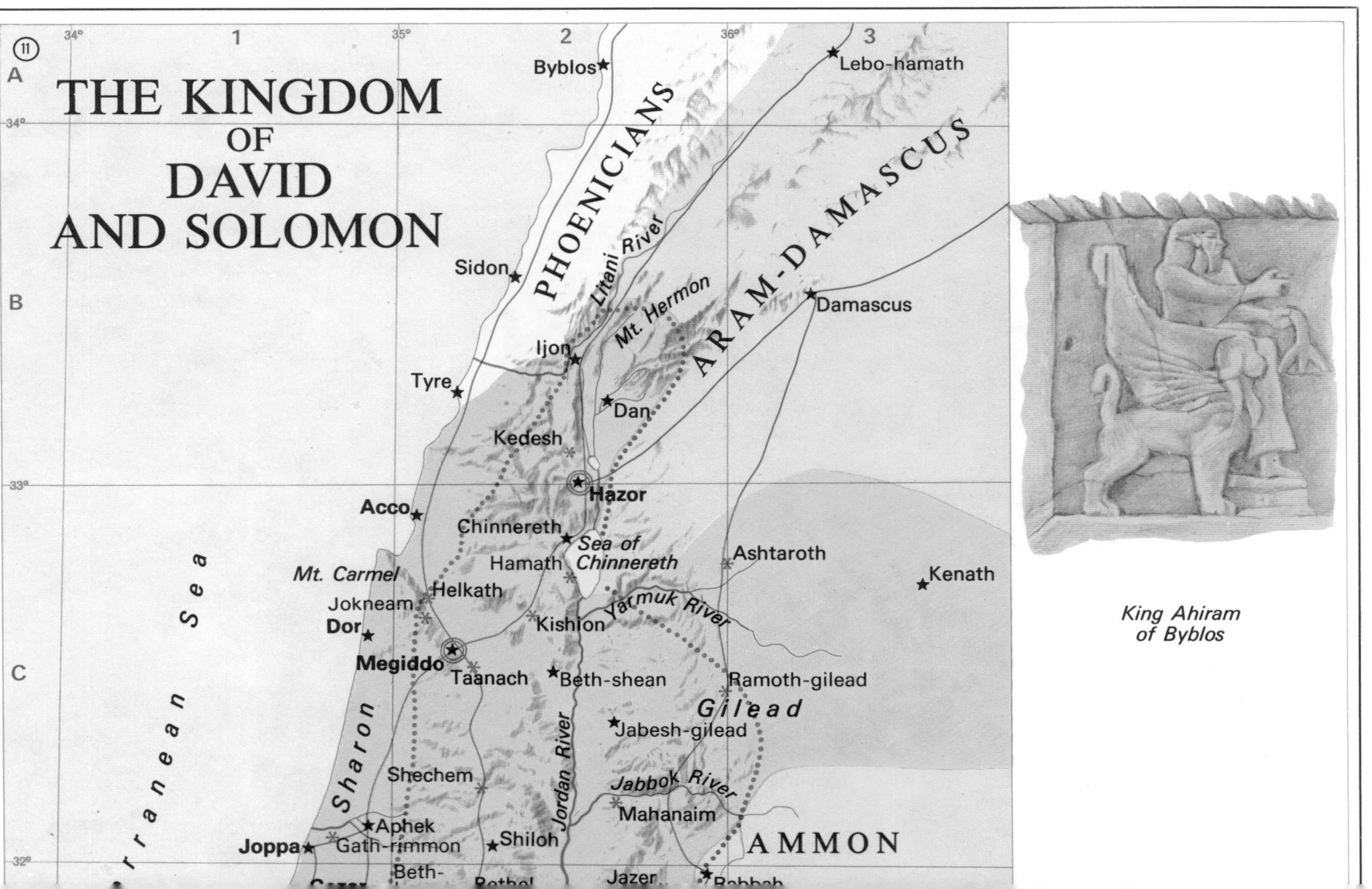

King Ahiram of Byblos

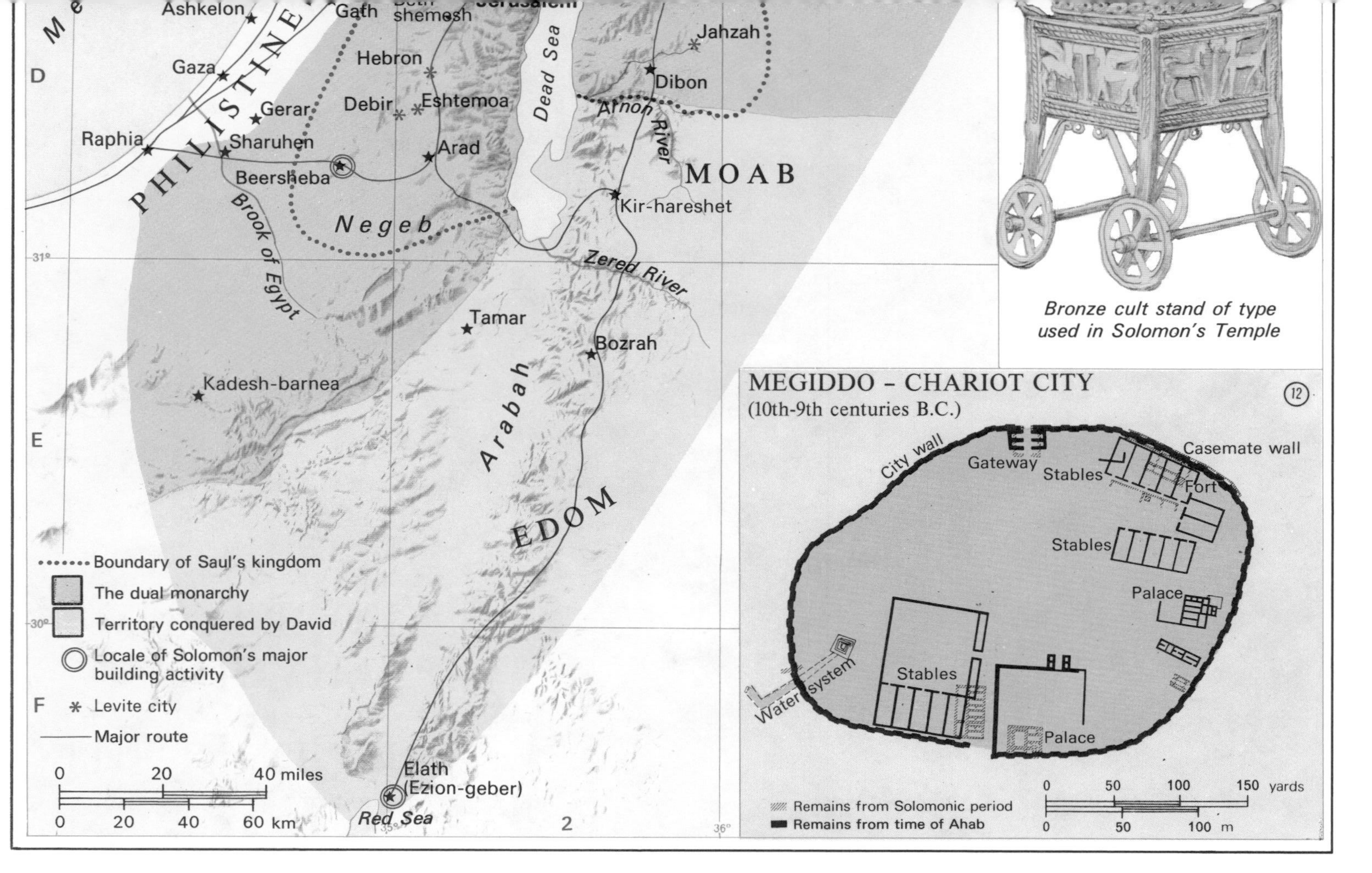

Bronze cult stand of type used in Solomon's Temple

Royal Judean seal-stamp

Seal of a high Judean official

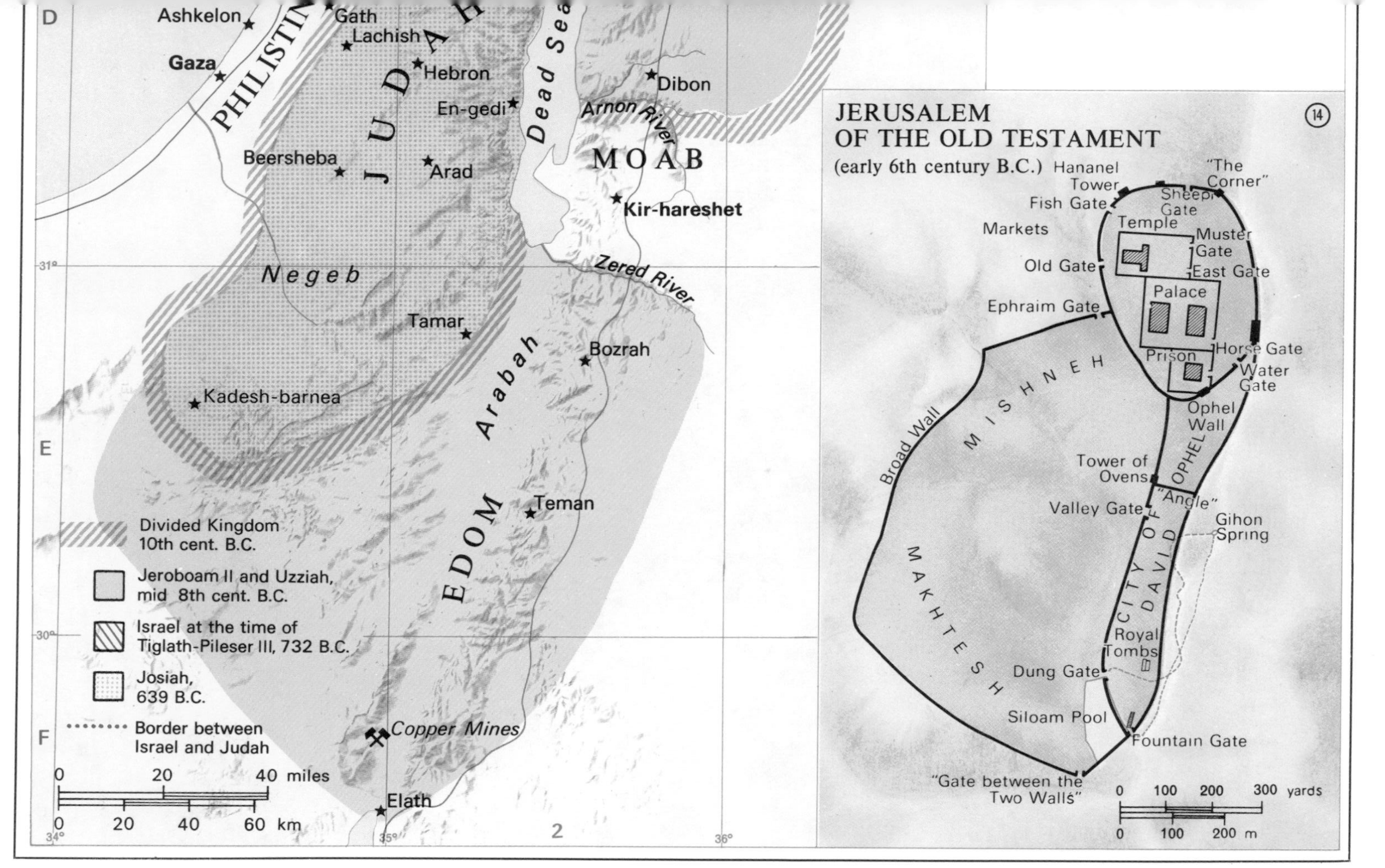

D
E
F
Ashkelon
Gaza
PHILISTIN
Gath
Lachish
Hebron
En-gedi
Beersheba
Arad
JUDAH
Dead Sea
Dibon
Arnon River
MOAB
Kir-hareshet
Zered River
Negeb
Tamar
Bozrah
Arabah
Kadesh-barnea
EDOM
Teman
Copper Mines
Elath
Divided Kingdom 10th cent. B.C.
Jeroboam II and Uzziah, mid 8th cent. B.C.
Israel at the time of Tiglath-Pileser III, 732 B.C.
Josiah, 639 B.C.
Border between Israel and Judah
0 20 40 miles
0 20 40 60 km
31°
30°
34°
35°
36°
2
JERUSALEM
OF THE OLD TESTAMENT
(early 6th century B.C.)
14
Hananel Tower
"The Corner"
Fish Gate
Sheep Gate
Markets
Temple
Muster Gate
Old Gate
East Gate
Palace
Ephraim Gate
Horse Gate
Prison
Water Gate
MISHNEH
Broad Wall
Ophel Wall
OPHEL
Tower of Ovens
"Angle"
Valley Gate
Gihon Spring
CITY OF DAVID
MAKHTESH
Royal Tombs
Dung Gate
Siloam Pool
Fountain Gate
"Gate between the Two Walls"
0 100 200 300 yards
0 100 200 m

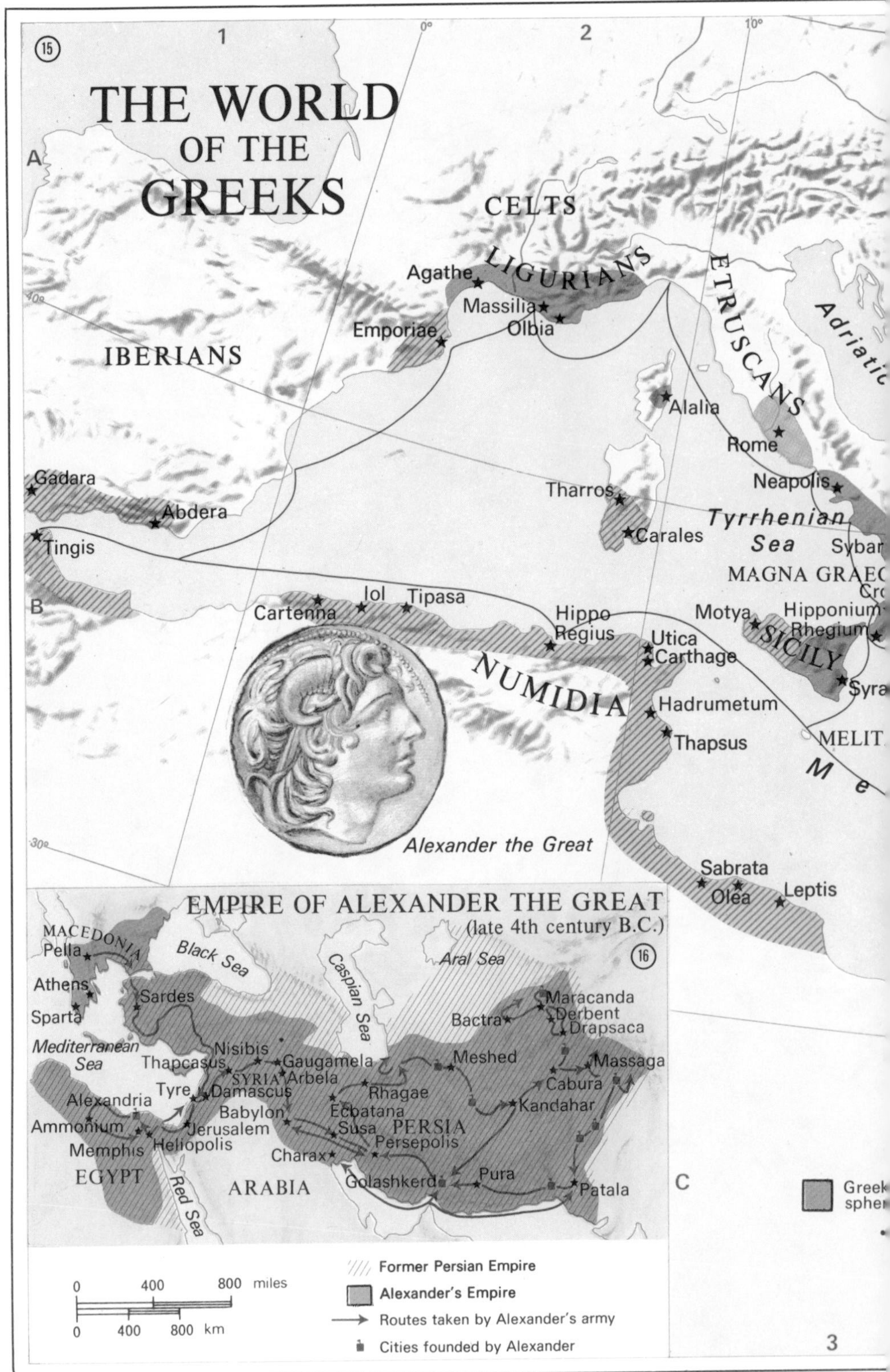
15
THE WORLD OF THE GREEKS
1
2
A
B
C
3
CELTS
LIGURIANS
IBERIANS
ETRUSCANS
Adriatic
Agathe
Massilia
Olbia
Emporiae
Alalia
Rome
Neapolis
Gadara
Abdera
Tingis
Tharros
Carales
Tyrrhenian Sea
MAGNA GRAEC
Motya
Hipponium
Rhegium
SICILY
Cartenna
Iol
Tipasa
Hippo Regius
Utica
Carthage
NUMIDIA
Hadrumetum
Thapsus
MELIT
Sabrata
Olea
Leptis
Alexander the Great
EMPIRE OF ALEXANDER THE GREAT
(late 4th century B.C.)
16
MACEDONIA
Pella
Athens
Sparta
Black Sea
Caspian Sea
Aral Sea
Sardes
Mediterranean Sea
Thapcasus
Nisibis
Gaugamela
SYRIA
Arbela
Tyre
Damascus
Alexandria
Ammonium
Jerusalem
Heliopolis
Memphis
EGYPT
Babylon
Ecbatana
Susa
Rhagae
PERSIA
Persepolis
Charax
ARABIA
Red Sea
Golashkerd
Pura
Patala
Kandahar
Cabura
Massaga
Meshed
Bactra
Maracanda
Derbent
Drapsaca
Former Persian Empire
Alexander's Empire
Routes taken by Alexander's army
Cities founded by Alexander
0 400 800 miles
0 400 800 km
Greek sphere

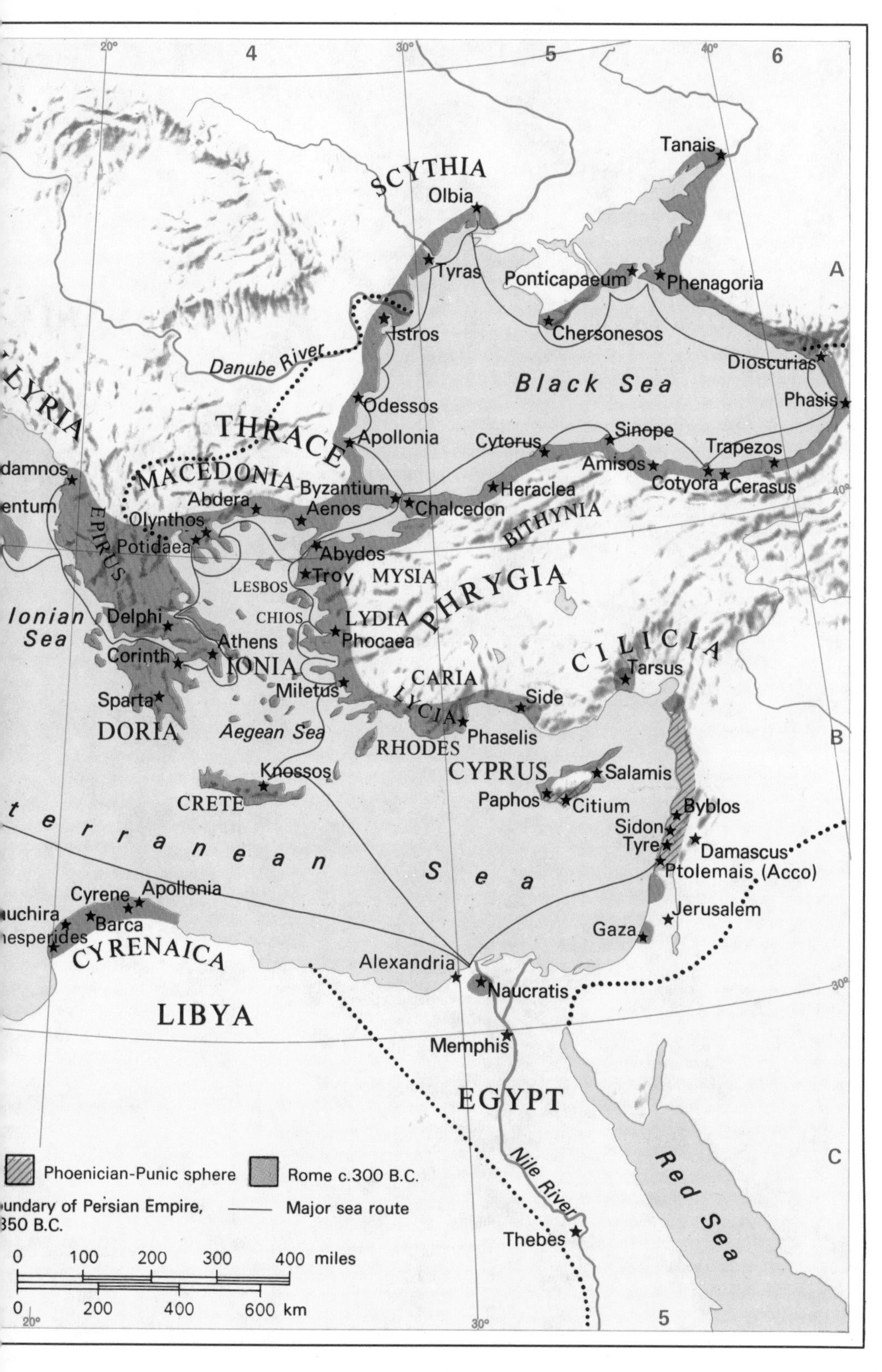

SCYTHIA
Olbia
Tanais
Tyras
Ponticapaeum
Phenagoria
Istros
Chersonesos
Danube River
Dioscurias
Black Sea
Phasis
Odessos
THRACE
Apollonia
Cytorus
Sinope
Trapezos
Amisos
Cotyora
Cerasus
MACEDONIA
Byzantium
Heraclea
Chalcedon
BITHYNIA
Abdera
Aenos
Olynthos
Potidaea
EPIRUS
Abydos
Troy
MYSIA
PHRYGIA
LESBOS
CHIOS
LYDIA
Phocaea
Ionian Sea
Delphi
Athens
Corinth
IONIA
CILICIA
Tarsus
CARIA
Miletus
Sparta
LYCIA
Side
DORIA
Aegean Sea
Phaselis
RHODES
CYPRUS
Salamis
Knossos
Paphos
Citium
CRETE
Byblos
Sidon
Tyre
Damascus
Ptolemais (Acco)
Sea
Jerusalem
Cyrene
Apollonia
Barca
CYRENAICA
Gaza
Alexandria
Naucratis
LIBYA
Memphis
EGYPT
Nile River
Red Sea
Thebes
Phoenician-Punic sphere
Rome c.300 B.C.
Major sea route
0 100 200 300 400 miles
0 200 400 600 km

17
1
2
15°
0°
North Sea
HIBERNIA
BRITANNIA
Eburacum
Lindum
A
Aquae Sulis
Londinium
Atlantic Ocean
Rhine River
GERMANIA
45°
Lutetia
GALLIA
Regina Castra
Vindobo
Mediolanum
Lugdunum
RAETIA
NORICUM
Burdigala
Vienna
Aquileia
PANN
ILLYRI
Nemausus
Genua
HISPANIA
Narbo
Massilia
ITALIA
B
Ancona
Toletum
Tarraco
Rome
Corduba
Valentia
Neapolis
Brundisium
Gades
MAURETANIA
Hippo Regius
AFRICA
Carthage
Syracuse
Medite
Leptis Magna
ROME (1st-3rd centuries A.D.)
18
Castra Praetoria
Circus of Hadrian
Tomb of Augustus
PINCIAN HILL
Mausoleum of Hadrian
QUIRINAL HILL
Baths of Diocletian
Circus of Nero
VATICAN HILL
Pantheon
VIMINAL HILL
Theater of Pompey
ESQUILINE HILL
Imperial Fora
CAPITOLINE HILL
Capitol
Baths of Trajan
Roman Forum
Colosseum
PALATINE HILL
T. Divi Claudii
Circus Maximus
CAELIAN HILL
Baths of Caracalla
AVENTINE HILL
Earliest Christian sites
0 500 1000 1500 yards
0 500 1000 m
C
2
15°

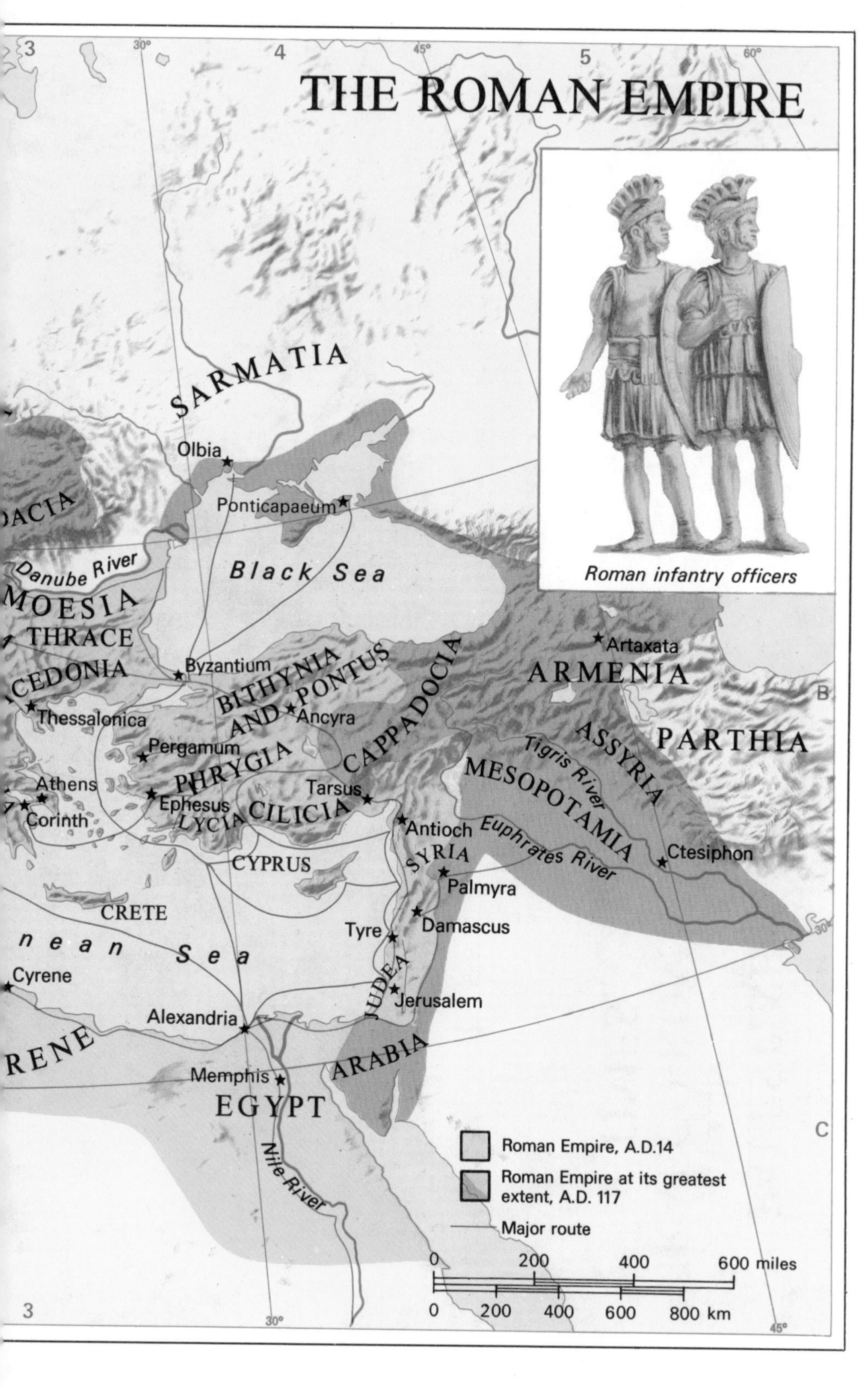
THE ROMAN EMPIRE
SARMATIA
Olbia
Ponticapaeum
DACIA
Danube River
Black Sea
MOESIA
THRACE
MACEDONIA
Byzantium
BITHYNIA AND PONTUS
Ancyra
Thessalonica
Pergamum
PHRYGIA
CAPPADOCIA
ARMENIA
Artaxata
ASSYRIA
PARTHIA
Tigris River
MESOPOTAMIA
Athens
Corinth
Ephesus
LYCIA
CILICIA
Tarsus
Antioch
Euphrates River
Ctesiphon
SYRIA
Palmyra
CYPRUS
CRETE
Damascus
Tyre
Sea
Cyrene
JUDEA
Jerusalem
Alexandria
ARABIA
Memphis
EGYPT
Nile River
Roman Empire, A.D.14
Roman Empire at its greatest extent, A.D. 117
Major route
0 200 400 600 miles
0 200 400 600 800 km
Roman infantry officers

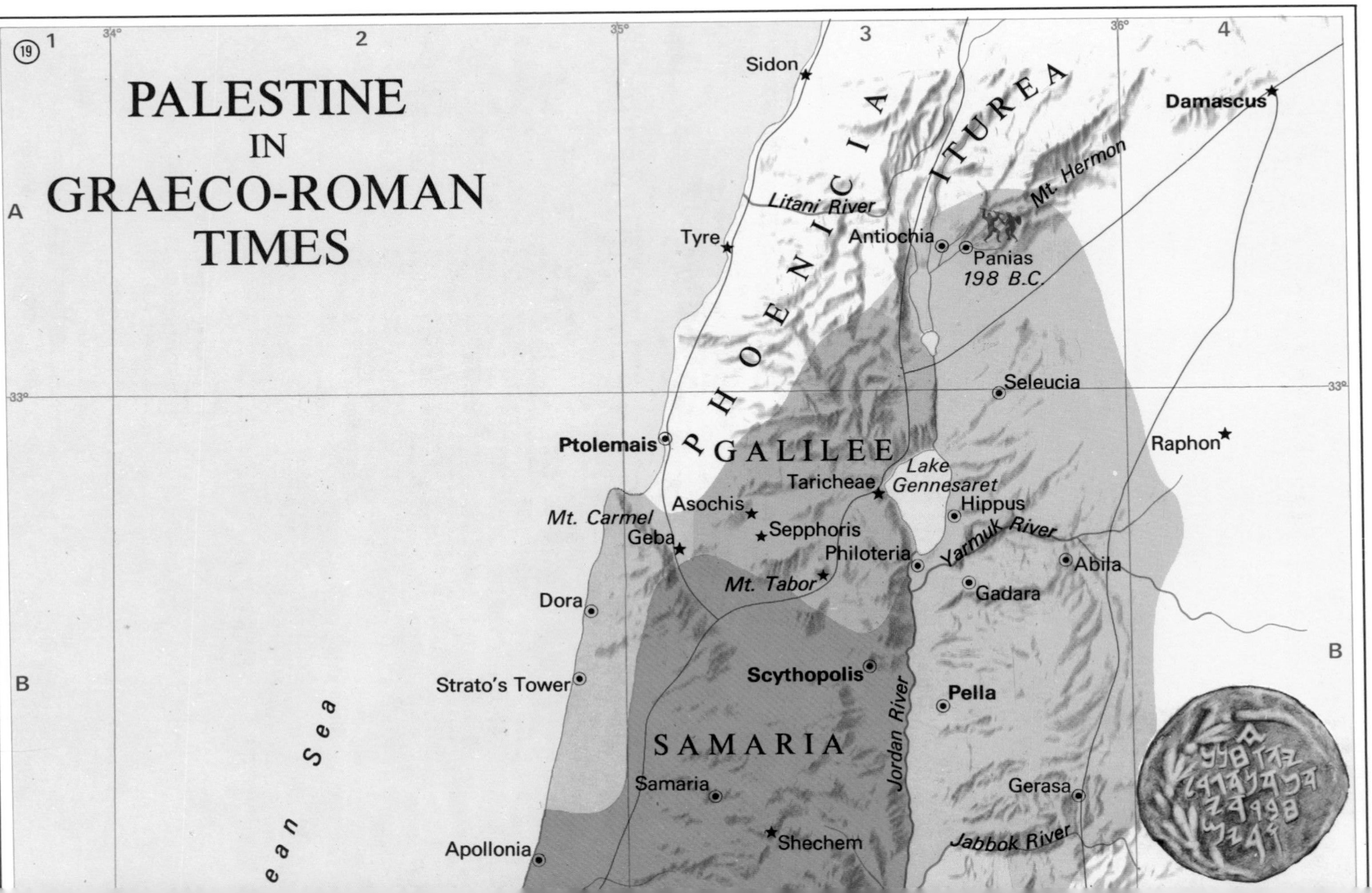

19
PALESTINE
IN
GRAECO-ROMAN
TIMES
1
2
3
4
A
B
34°
35°
36°
33°
Sidon
Tyre
Litani River
PHOENICIA
ITUREA
Mt. Hermon
Damascus
Antiochia
Panias
198 B.C.
Seleucia
Raphon
Ptolemais
GALILEE
Lake
Gennesaret
Taricheae
Asochis
Sepphoris
Mt. Carmel
Geba
Hippus
Yarmuk River
Philoteria
Abila
Mt. Tabor
Gadara
Dora
Strato's Tower
Scythopolis
Pella
Jordan River
SAMARIA
Samaria
Shechem
Gerasa
Jabbok River
Apollonia
Sea
ean

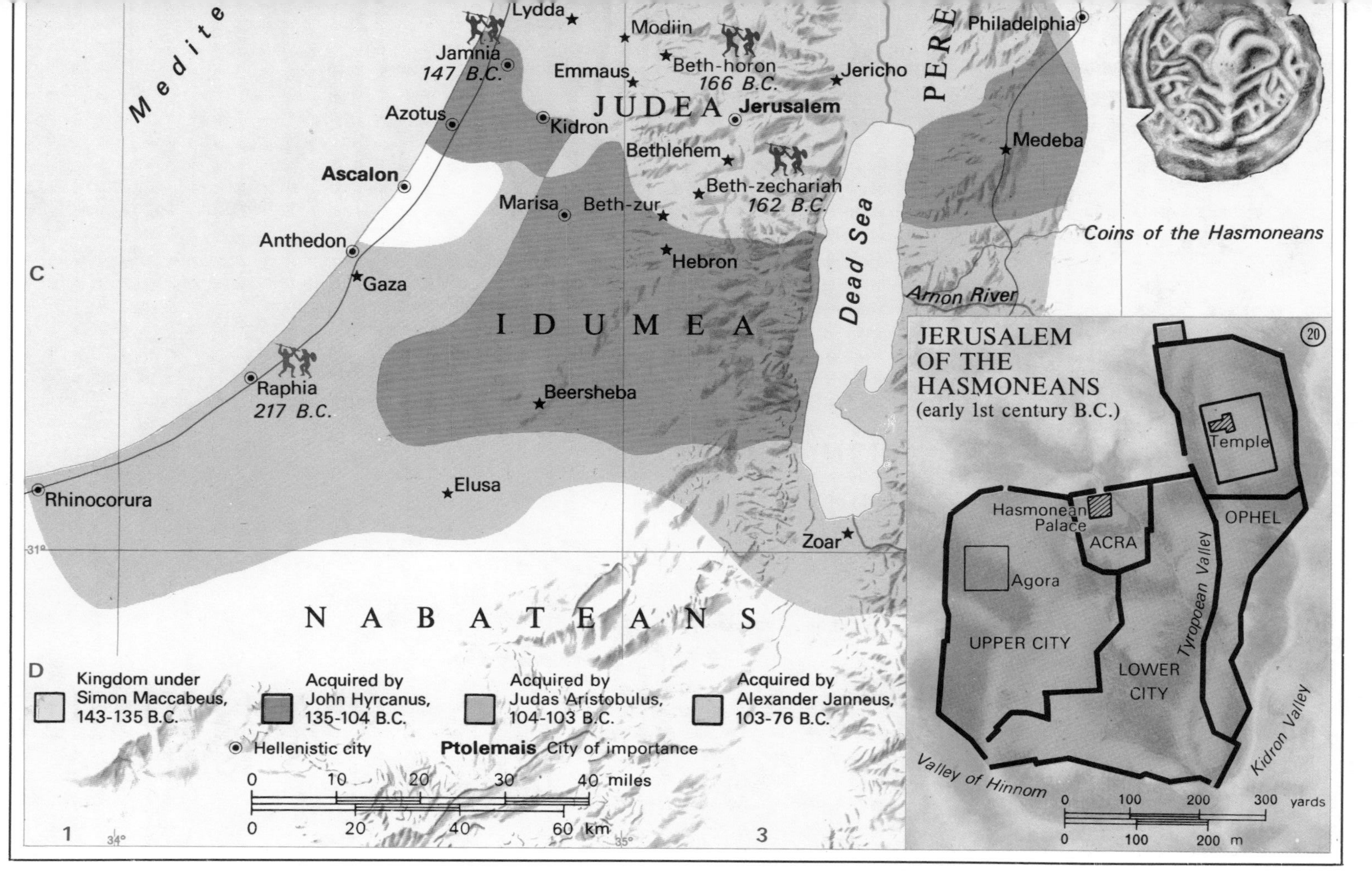
Medite
Lydda
Modiin
Jamnia
147 B.C.
Emmaus
Beth-horon
166 B.C.
Jericho
PERE
Philadelphia
Azotus
Kidron
JUDEA
Jerusalem
Medeba
Bethlehem
Ascalon
Beth-zechariah
162 B.C.
Marisa
Beth-zur
Anthedon
Hebron
Coins of the Hasmoneans
C
Gaza
Dead Sea
Arnon River
IDUMEA
Raphia
217 B.C.
Beersheba
Elusa
Rhinocorura
Zoar
31°
NABATEANS
D
Kingdom under Simon Maccabeus, 143-135 B.C.
Acquired by John Hyrcanus, 135-104 B.C.
Acquired by Judas Aristobulus, 104-103 B.C.
Acquired by Alexander Janneus, 103-76 B.C.
Hellenistic city
Ptolemais City of importance
0 10 20 30 40 miles
0 20 40 60 km
1
34°
35°
3
JERUSALEM OF THE HASMONEANS
(early 1st century B.C.)
20
Temple
Hasmonean Palace
ACRA
OPHEL
Agora
Tyropoean Valley
UPPER CITY
LOWER CITY
Kidron Valley
Valley of Hinnom
0 100 200 300 yards
0 100 200 m

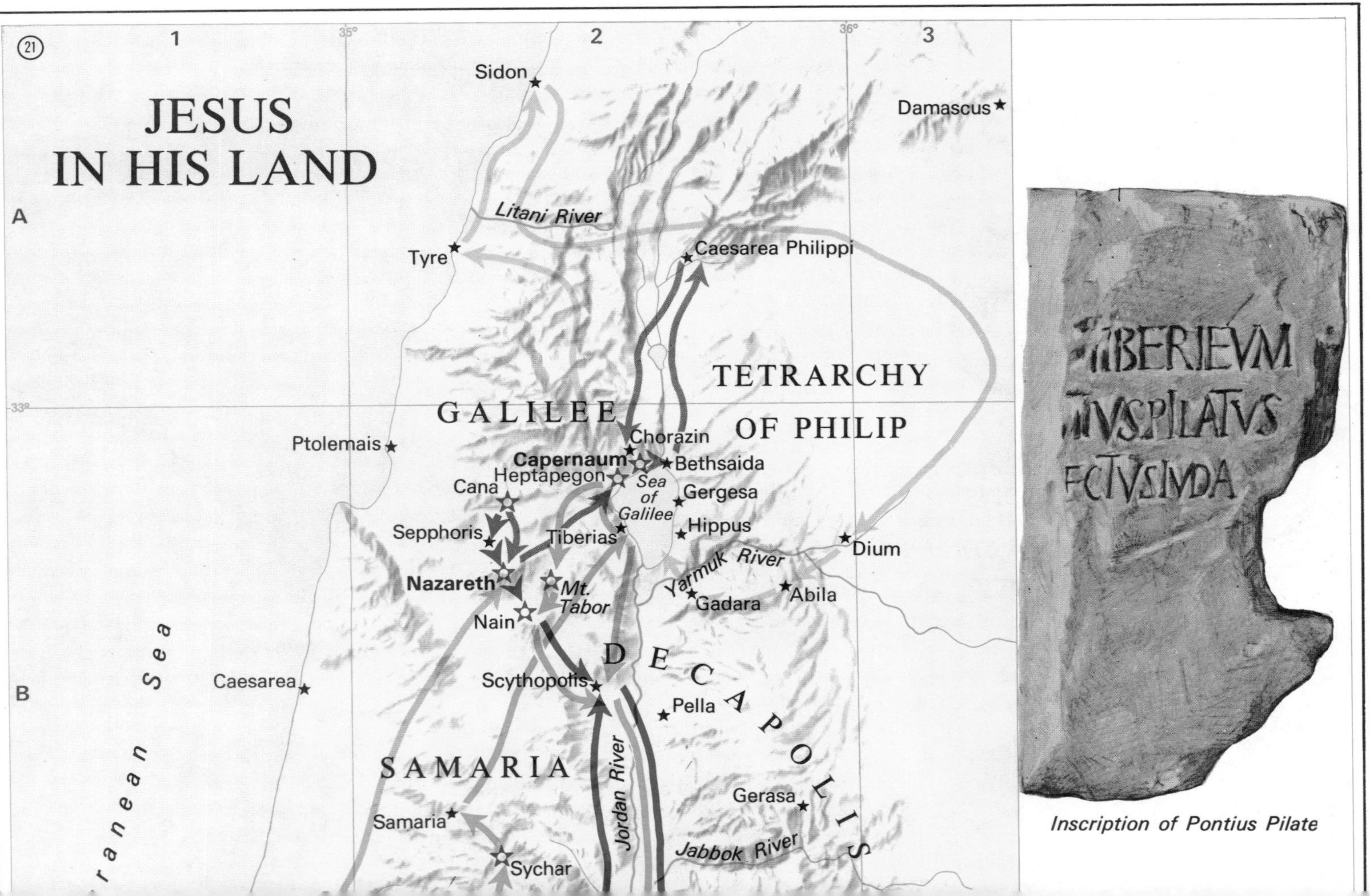

Inscription of Pontius Pilate

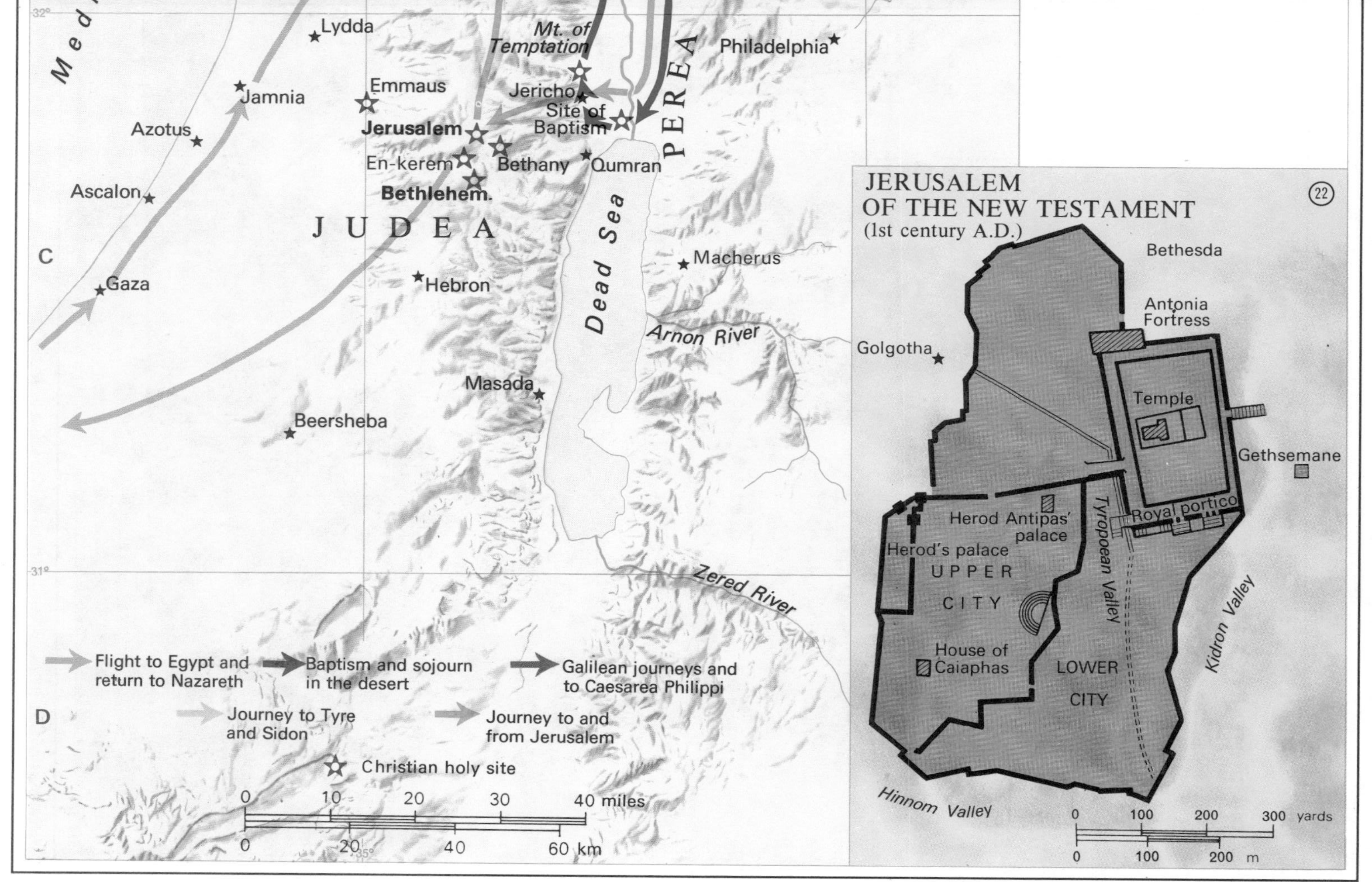

Lydda
Mt. of Temptation
PEREA
Philadelphia
Jamnia
Emmaus
Jericho
Site of Baptism
Azotus
Jerusalem
En-kerem
Bethany
Qumran
Ascalon
Bethlehem.
JUDEA
Dead Sea
Macherus
Gaza
Hebron
Arnon River
Masada
Beersheba
Zered River
C
D
Flight to Egypt and return to Nazareth
Baptism and sojourn in the desert
Galilean journeys and to Caesarea Philippi
Journey to Tyre and Sidon
Journey to and from Jerusalem
Christian holy site
0 10 20 30 40 miles
0 20 40 60 km
JERUSALEM
OF THE NEW TESTAMENT
(1st century A.D.)
22
Bethesda
Antonia Fortress
Golgotha
Temple
Gethsemane
Herod Antipas' palace
Royal portico
Herod's palace
UPPER CITY
Tyropoean Valley
Kidron Valley
House of Caiaphas
LOWER CITY
Hinnom Valley
0 100 200 300 yards
0 100 200 m

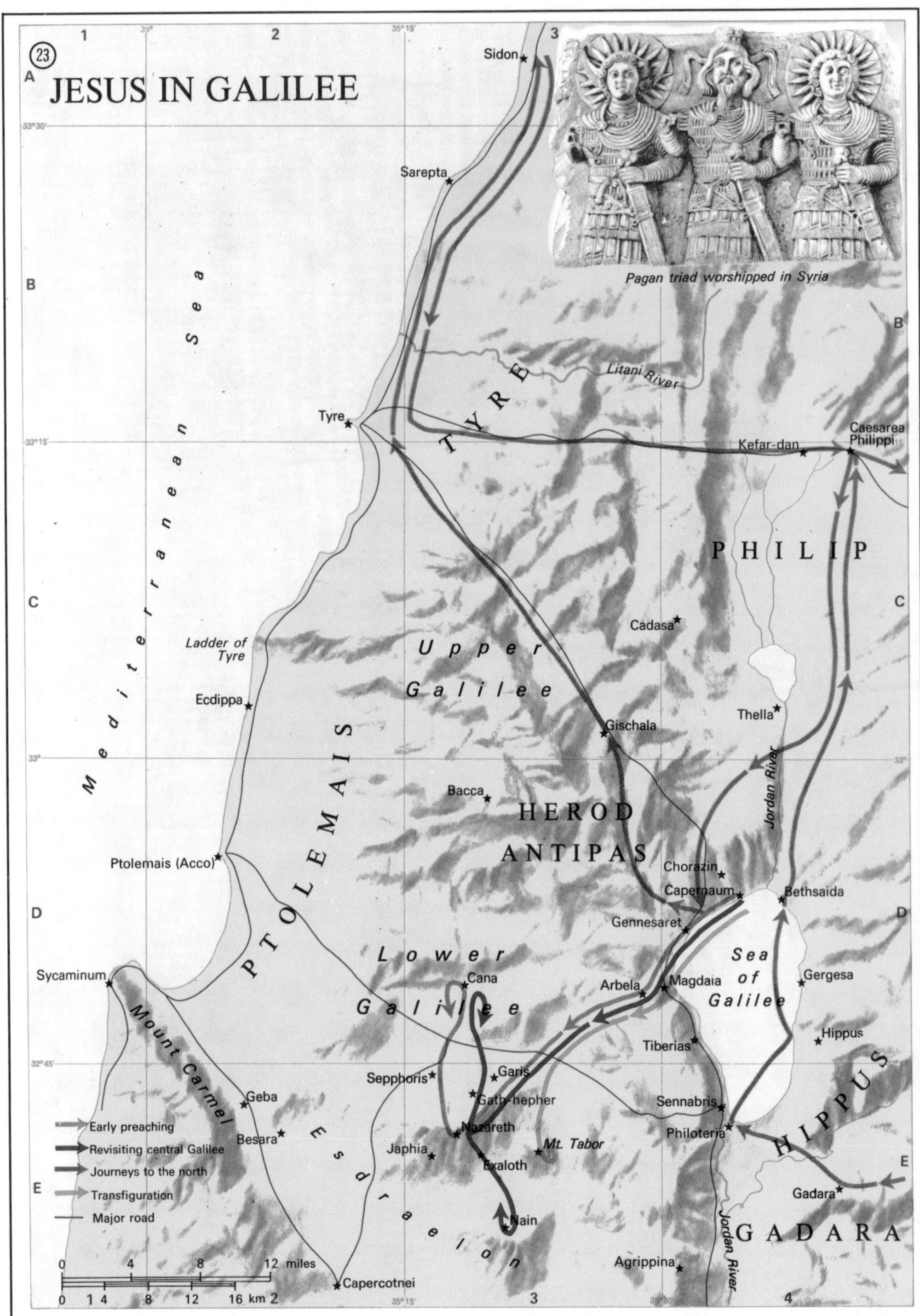
23
JESUS IN GALILEE
Pagan triad worshipped in Syria
Sidon
Sarepta
Tyre
Mediterranean Sea
Litani River
TYRE
Kefar-dan
Caesarea Philippi
PHILIP
Cadasa
Ladder of Tyre
Upper Galilee
Ecdippa
Gischala
Thella
Jordan River
PTOLEMAIS
Bacca
HEROD ANTIPAS
Ptolemais (Acco)
Chorazin
Capernaum
Bethsaida
Gennesaret
Lower Galilee
Sea of Galilee
Sycaminum
Cana
Arbela
Magdaia
Gergesa
Mount Carmel
Tiberias
Hippus
Sepphoris
Garis
Gath-hepher
Geba
Sennabris
Nazareth
Philoteria
HIPPUS
Besara
Japhia
Mt. Tabor
Exaloth
Esdraelon
Gadara
Nain
GADARA
Agrippina
Capercotnei
Early preaching
Revisiting central Galilee
Journeys to the north
Transfiguration
Major road
0 4 8 12 miles
0 1 4 8 12 16 km

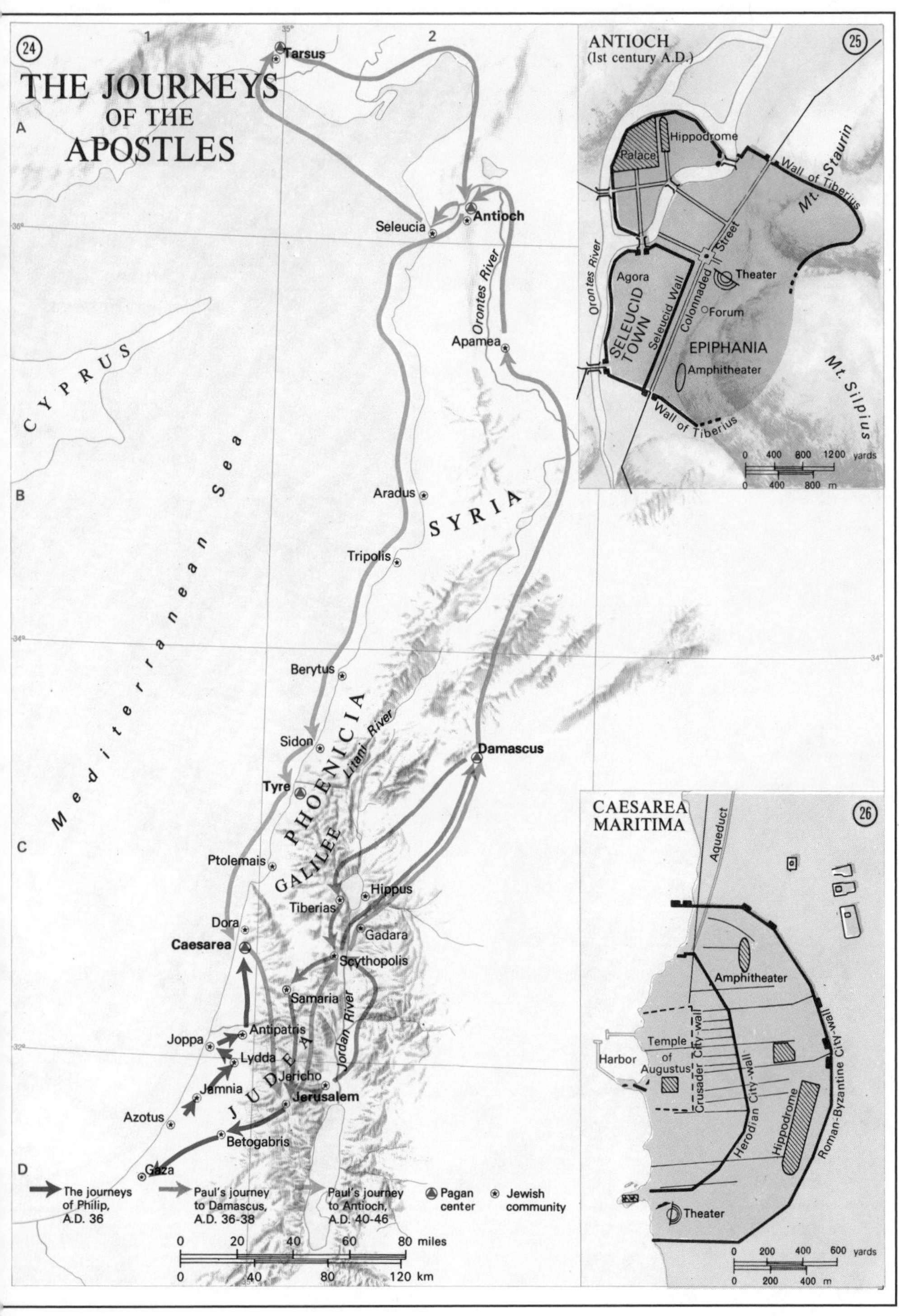

24
THE JOURNEYS OF THE APOSTLES
Tarsus
Seleucia
Antioch
Orontes River
Apamea
CYPRUS
Mediterranean Sea
Aradus
SYRIA
Tripolis
Berytus
Sidon
PHOENICIA
Litani River
Damascus
Tyre
Ptolemais
GALILEE
Hippus
Tiberias
Dora
Gadara
Caesarea
Scythopolis
Samaria
Jordan River
Antipatris
Joppa
Lydda
Jamnia
Jericho
JUDEA
Jerusalem
Azotus
Betogabris
Gaza
The journeys of Philip, A.D. 36
Paul's journey to Damascus, A.D. 36-38
Paul's journey to Antioch, A.D. 40-46
Pagan center
Jewish community
0 20 40 60 80 miles
0 40 80 120 km
ANTIOCH
(1st century A.D.)
25
Hippodrome
Palace
Wall of Tiberius
Mt. Staurin
Orontes River
Colonnaded Street
Agora
Theater
Seleucid Wall
Forum
SELEUCID TOWN
EPIPHANIA
Amphitheater
Mt. Silpius
Wall of Tiberius
0 400 800 1200 yards
0 400 800 m
CAESAREA MARITIMA
26
Aqueduct
Amphitheater
Temple of Augustus
Harbor
Crusader City-wall
Herodian City-wall
Hippodrome
Roman-Byzantine City-wall
Theater
0 200 400 600 yards
0 200 400 m

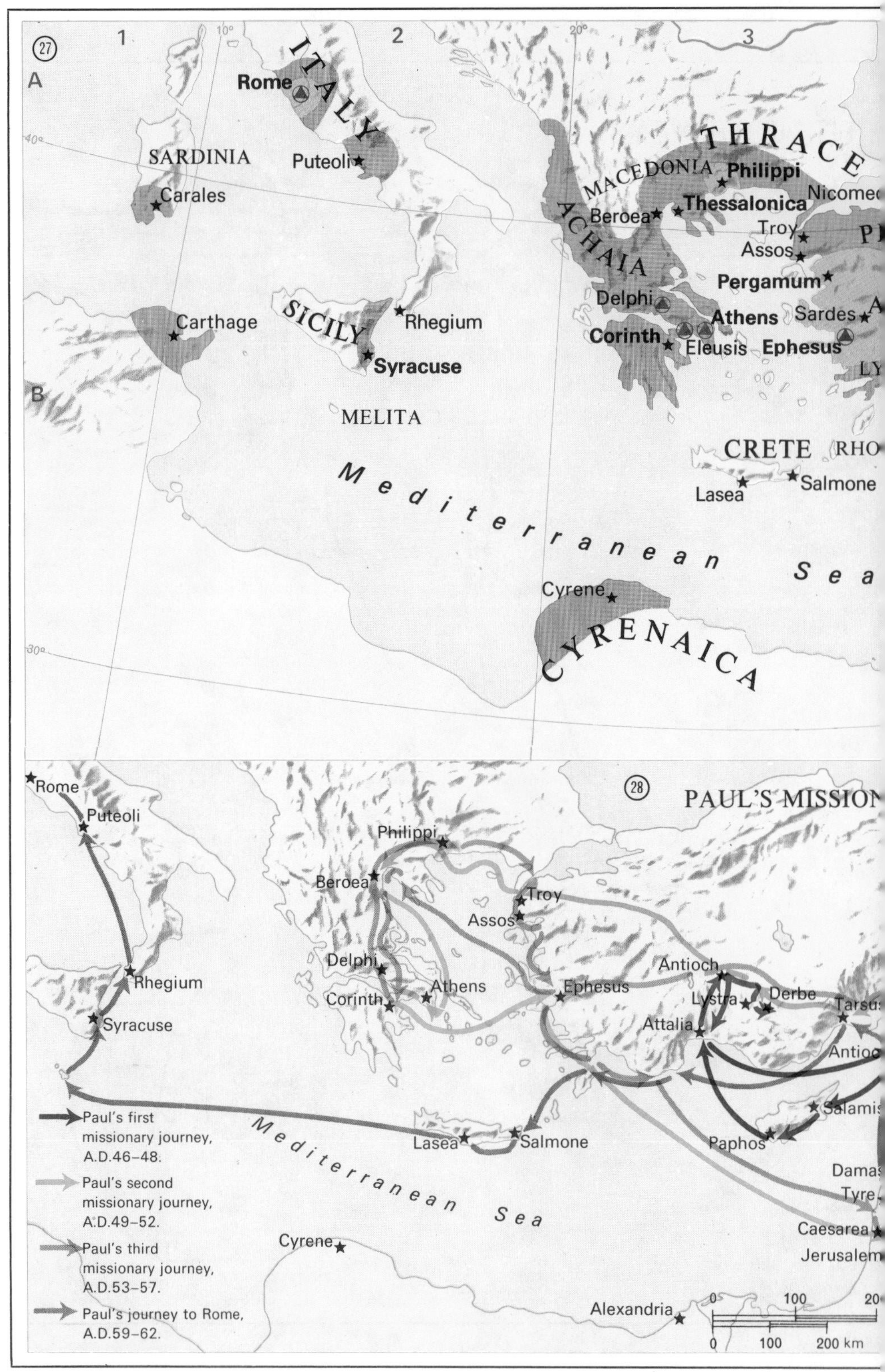

27
ITALY
Rome
Puteoli
SARDINIA
Carales
THRACE
MACEDONIA
Philippi
Thessalonica
Beroea
ACHAIA
Troy
Assos
Pergamum
Delphi
Athens
Sardes
Corinth
Eleusis
Ephesus
Carthage
SICILY
Rhegium
Syracuse
MELITA
CRETE
Lasea
Salmone
Mediterranean Sea
Cyrene
CYRENAICA
28
PAUL'S MISSION
Rome
Puteoli
Philippi
Beroea
Troy
Assos
Delphi
Athens
Corinth
Ephesus
Antioch
Lystra
Derbe
Attalia
Rhegium
Syracuse
Salamis
Paphos
Lasea
Salmone
Mediterranean Sea
Cyrene
Caesarea
Jerusalem
Alexandria
Paul's first missionary journey, A.D.46–48.
Paul's second missionary journey, A.D.49–52.
Paul's third missionary journey, A.D.53–57.
Paul's journey to Rome, A.D.59–62.
0 100 200 km

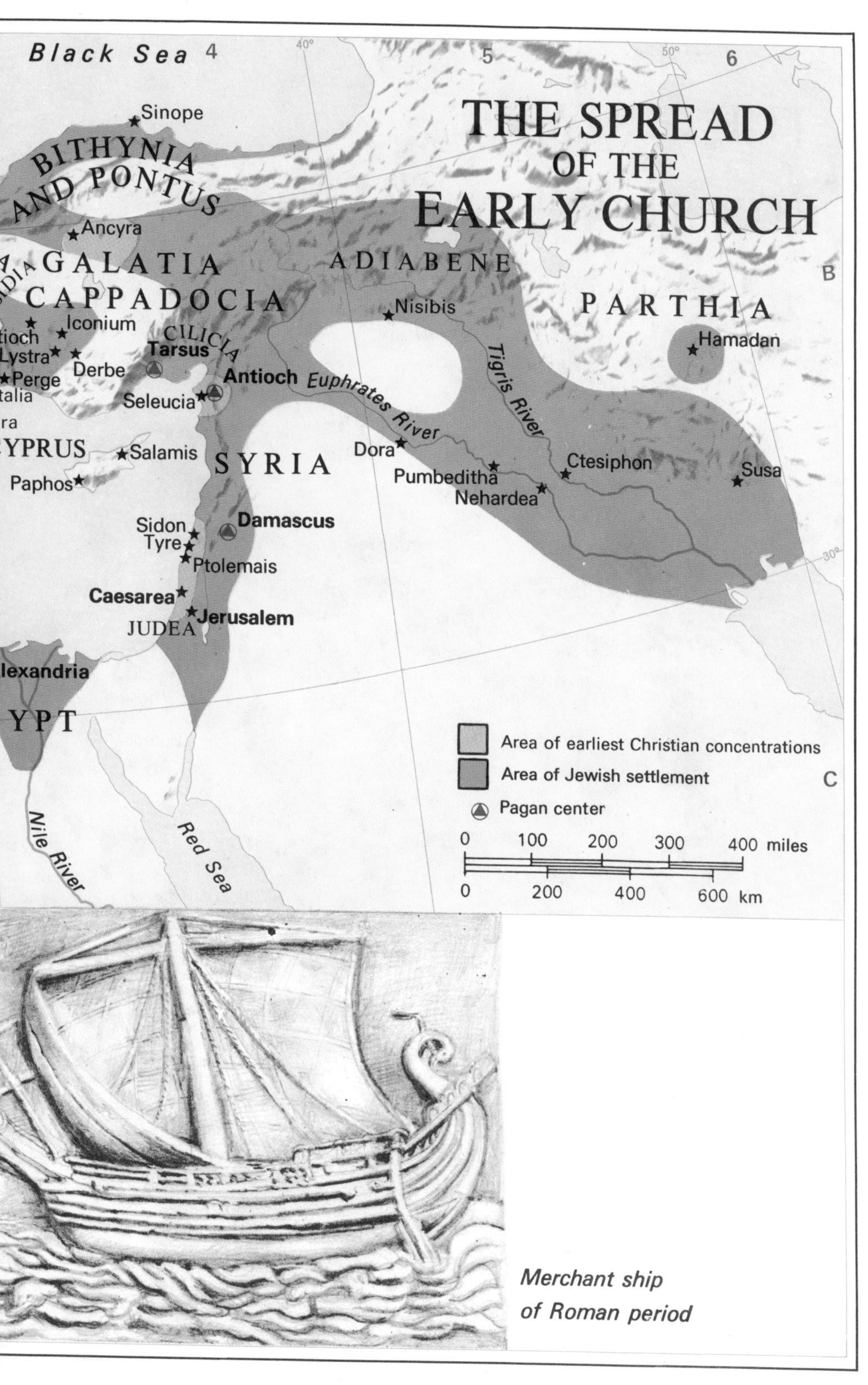
THE SPREAD OF THE EARLY CHURCH
Black Sea
Sinope
BITHYNIA AND PONTUS
Ancyra
GALATIA
CAPPADOCIA
ADIABENE
PARTHIA
Nisibis
Iconium
Lystra
Derbe
Perge
Tarsus
CILICIA
Antioch
Seleucia
Euphrates River
Tigris River
Hamadan
CYPRUS
Salamis
Paphos
SYRIA
Dora
Pumbeditha
Nehardea
Ctesiphon
Susa
Sidon
Tyre
Damascus
Ptolemais
Caesarea
Jerusalem
JUDEA
Alexandria
Nile River
Red Sea
Area of earliest Christian concentrations
Area of Jewish settlement
Pagan center
0 100 200 300 400 miles
0 200 400 600 km

Merchant ship of Roman period

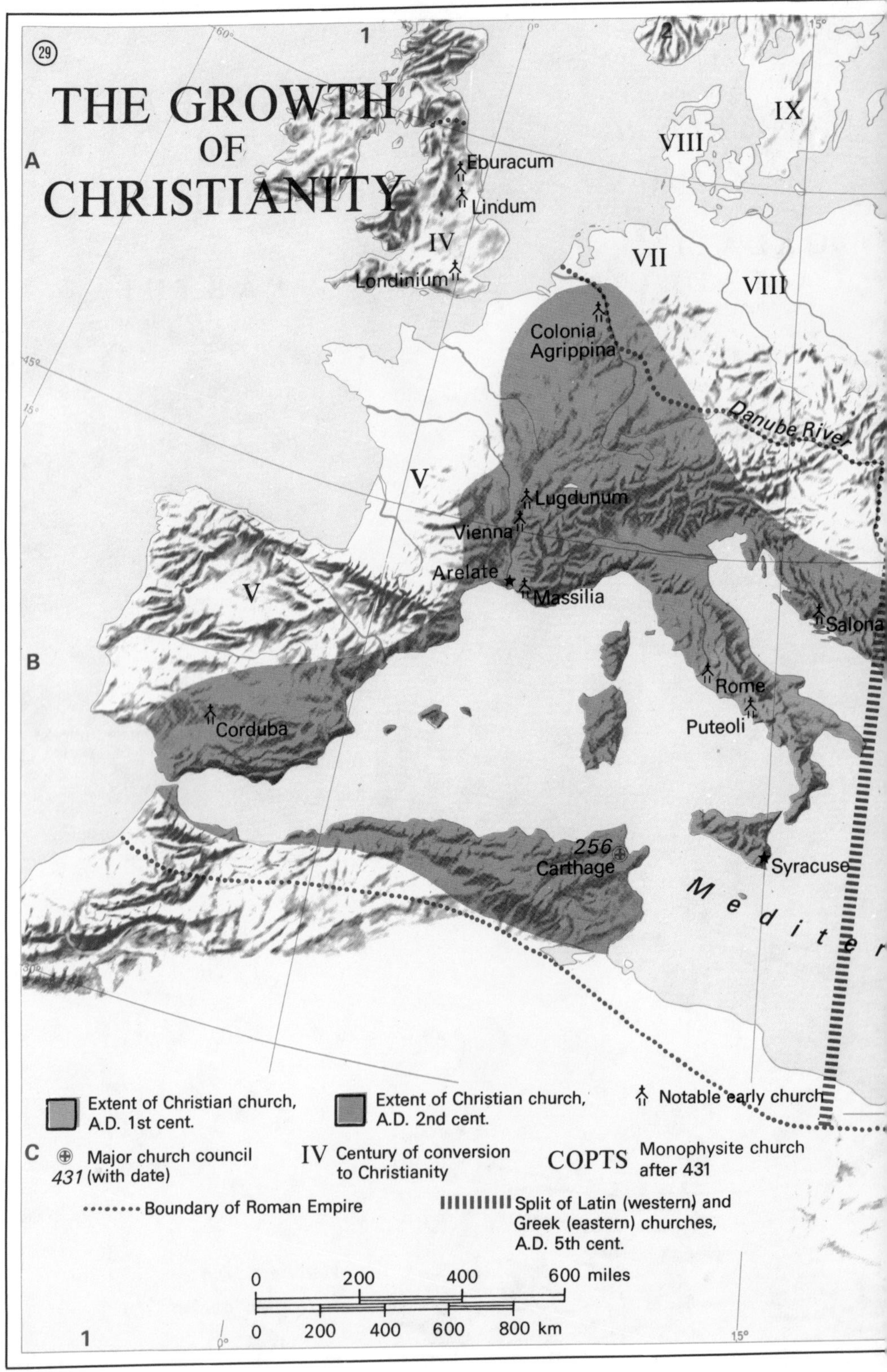
29
THE GROWTH OF CHRISTIANITY
1
2
A
B
C
IX
VIII
Eburacum
Lindum
IV
Londinium
VII
VIII
Colonia Agrippina
Danube River
V
Lugdunum
Vienna
Arelate
Massilia
V
Salona
Rome
Puteoli
Corduba
256
Carthage
Syracuse
Mediter
Extent of Christian church, A.D. 1st cent.
Extent of Christian church, A.D. 2nd cent.
Notable early church
Major church council
431 (with date)
IV Century of conversion to Christianity
COPTS Monophysite church after 431
Boundary of Roman Empire
Split of Latin (western) and Greek (eastern) churches, A.D. 5th cent.
0
200
400
600 miles
0
200
400
600
800 km
1

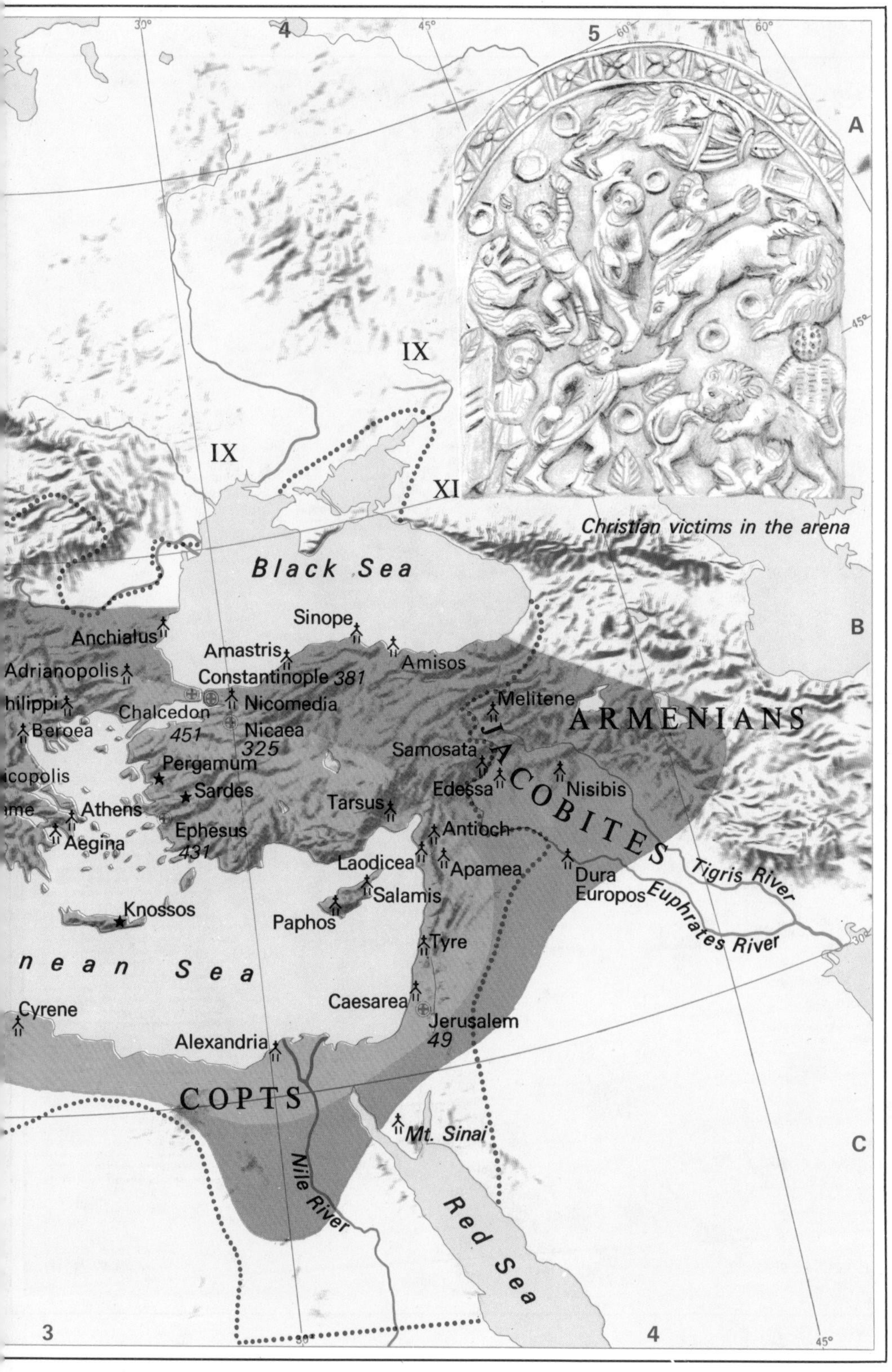

Christian victims in the arena

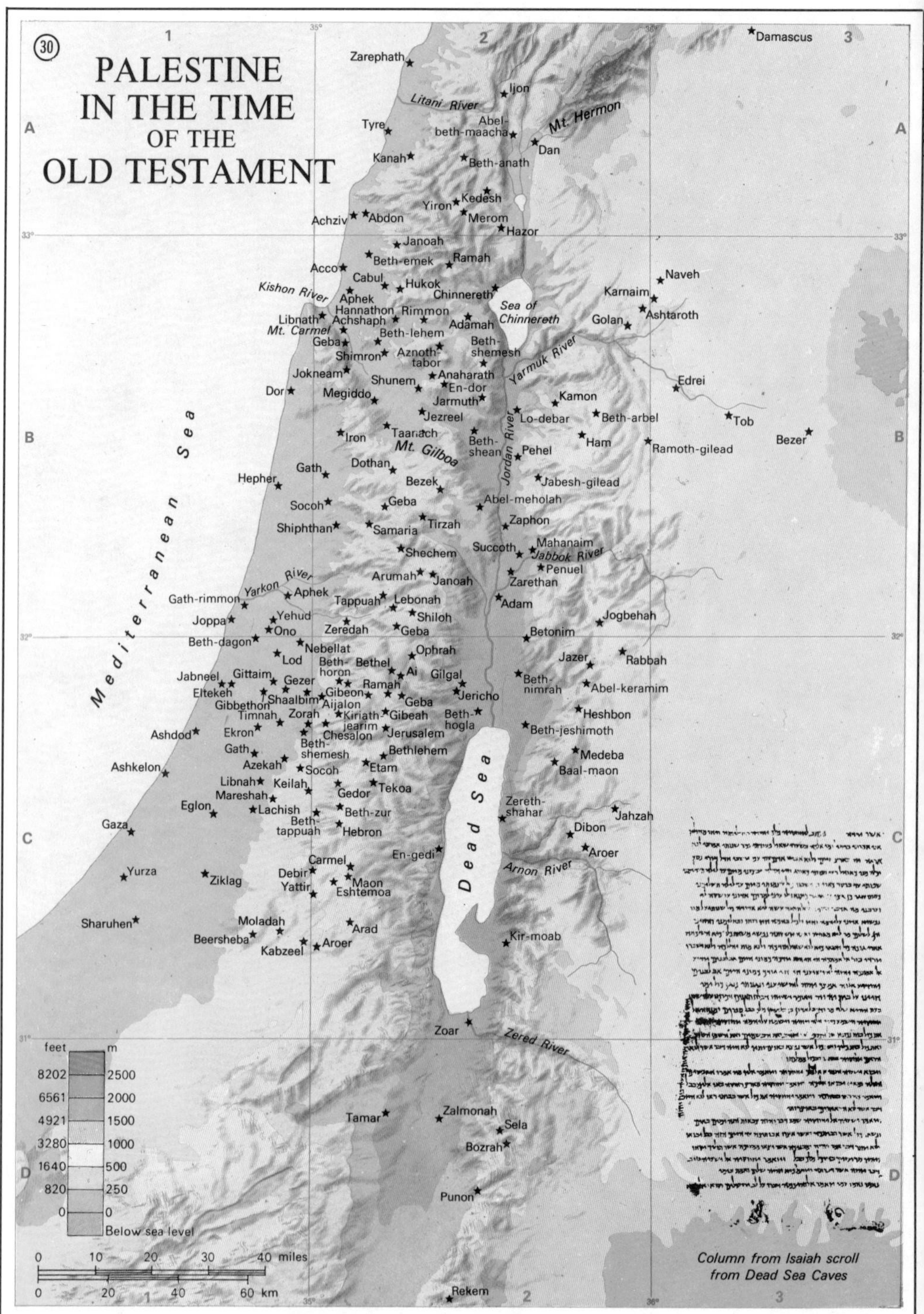
30
PALESTINE IN THE TIME OF THE OLD TESTAMENT
Mediterranean Sea
Dead Sea
Sea of Chinnereth
Damascus
Zarephath
Tyre
Kanah
Ijon
Abel-beth-maacha
Dan
Mt. Hermon
Litani River
Beth-anath
Kedesh
Yiron
Merom
Hazor
Achziv
Abdon
Janoah
Beth-emek
Ramah
Acco
Cabul
Hukok
Chinnereth
Kishon River
Aphek
Hannathon
Rimmon
Libnath
Achshaph
Mt. Carmel
Adamah
Geba
Beth-lehem
Shimron
Aznoth-tabor
Beth-shemesh
Jokneam
Shunem
Anaharath
En-dor
Dor
Megiddo
Jarmuth
Jezreel
Taanach
Iron
Mt. Gilboa
Beth-shean
Jordan River
Yarmuk River
Naveh
Karnaim
Ashtaroth
Golan
Edrei
Kamon
Lo-debar
Beth-arbel
Tob
Ham
Ramoth-gilead
Bezer
Pehel
Gath
Hepher
Dothan
Bezek
Jabesh-gilead
Socoh
Geba
Abel-meholah
Shiphthan
Samaria
Tirzah
Zaphon
Shechem
Succoth
Mahanaim
Jabbok River
Penuel
Arumah
Janoah
Zarethan
Yarkon River
Aphek
Gath-rimmon
Tappuah
Lebonah
Adam
Joppa
Yehud
Shiloh
Ono
Zeredah
Geba
Jogbehah
Betonim
Beth-dagon
Nebellat
Lod
Ophrah
Jazer
Rabbah
Beth-horon
Bethel
Ai
Jabneel
Gittaim
Gezer
Gilgal
Beth-nimrah
Abel-keramim
Eltekeh
Ramah
Gibeon
Jericho
Gibbethon
Shaalbim
Aijalon
Geba
Timnah
Zorah
Kiriath-jearim
Gibeah
Beth-hogla
Heshbon
Ashdod
Ekron
Chesalon
Jerusalem
Beth-jeshimoth
Gath
Beth-shemesh
Bethlehem
Medeba
Azekah
Socoh
Etam
Baal-maon
Ashkelon
Libnah
Keilah
Tekoa
Mareshah
Gedor
Eglon
Lachish
Beth-zur
Zereth-shahar
Jahzah
Gaza
Beth-tappuah
Hebron
Dibon
En-gedi
Aroer
Carmel
Arnon River
Yurza
Ziklag
Debir
Maon
Yattir
Eshtemoa
Sharuhen
Moladah
Arad
Beersheba
Kabzeel
Aroer
Kir-moab
Zoar
Zered River
Tamar
Zalmonah
Sela
Bozrah
Punon
Rekem
feet
m
8202
2500
6561
2000
4921
1500
3280
1000
1640
500
820
250
0
0
Below sea level
0 10 20 30 40 miles
0 20 40 60 km
Column from Isaiah scroll from Dead Sea Caves

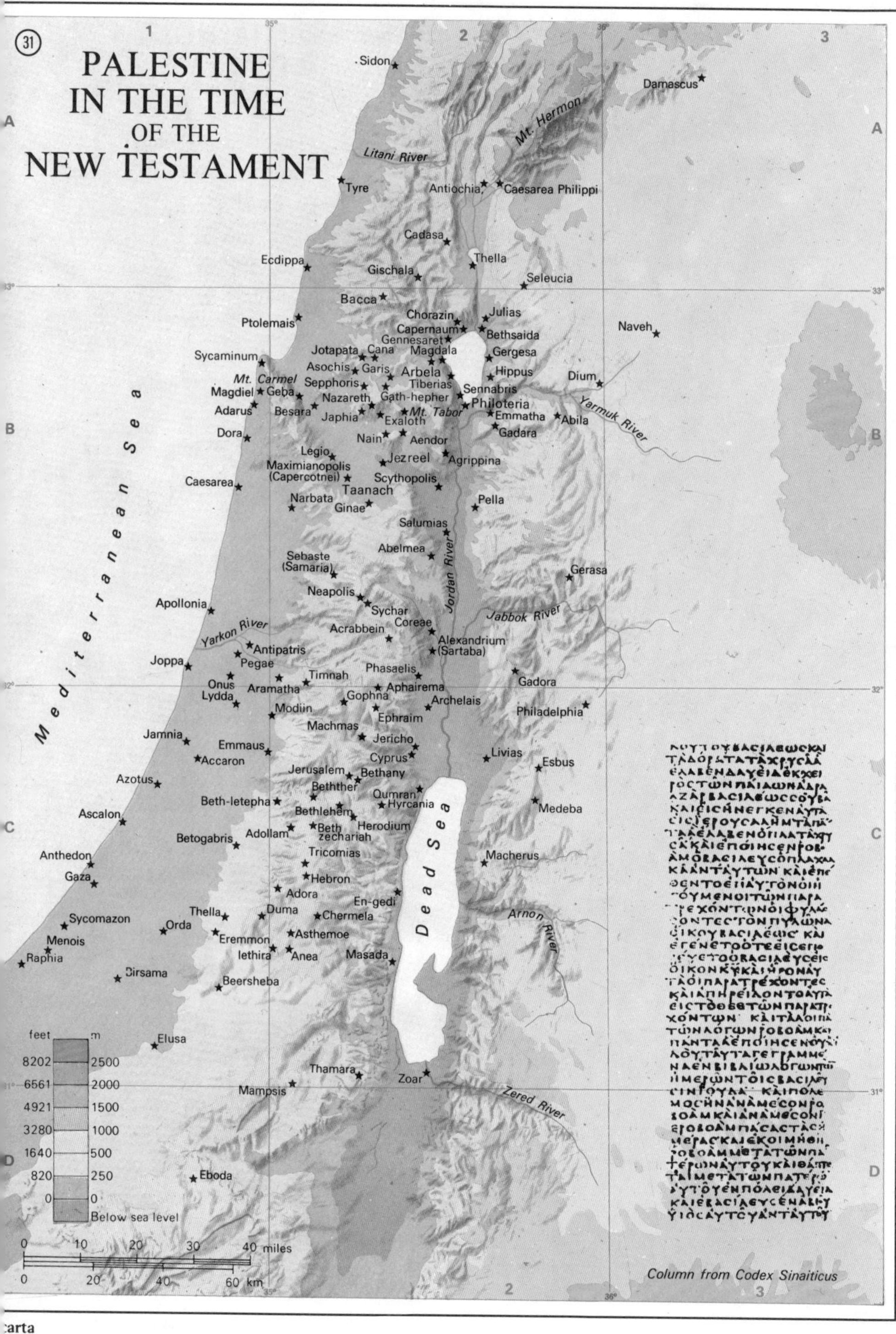
31
PALESTINE IN THE TIME OF THE NEW TESTAMENT
Sidon
Damascus
Mt. Hermon
Litani River
Tyre
Antiochia
Caesarea Philippi
Cadasa
Thella
Ecdippa
Gischala
Seleucia
Bacca
Ptolemais
Chorazin
Julias
Capernaum
Gennesaret
Bethsaida
Naveh
Sycaminum
Jotapata
Cana
Magdala
Gergesa
Asochis
Garis
Arbela
Hippus
Mt. Carmel
Sepphoris
Tiberias
Dium
Magdiel
Geba
Nazareth
Gath-hepher
Sennabris
Philoteria
Adarus
Besara
Japhia
Mt. Tabor
Emmatha
Abila
Yarmuk River
Exaloth
Gadara
Dora
Nain
Aendor
Legio
Jezreel
Agrippina
Maximianopolis (Capercotnei)
Caesarea
Scythopolis
Taanach
Narbata
Ginae
Pella
Mediterranean Sea
Salumias
Abelmea
Sebaste (Samaria)
Jordan River
Gerasa
Neapolis
Apollonia
Sychar
Jabbok River
Coreae
Acrabbein
Yarkon River
Alexandrium (Sartaba)
Antipatris
Joppa
Pegae
Phasaelis
Timnah
Onus
Aramatha
Aphairema
Gadora
Lydda
Gophna
Archelais
Modiin
Philadelphia
Ephraim
Machmas
Jamnia
Jericho
Emmaus
Cyprus
Livias
Accaron
Esbus
Jerusalem
Bethany
Azotus
Bethther
Qumran
Beth-letepha
Hyrcania
Medeba
Bethlehem
Ascalon
Herodium
Beth zechariah
Adollam
Betogabris
Dead Sea
Tricomias
Anthedon
Macherus
Gaza
Hebron
Adora
En-gedi
Sycomazon
Thella
Duma
Chermela
Arnon River
Orda
Menois
Asthemoe
Eremmon
Raphia
lethira
Anea
Masada
Birsama
Beersheba
feet
m
8202
2500
6561
2000
4921
1500
3280
1000
1640
500
820
250
0
0
Below sea level
Elusa
Thamara
Zoar
Mampsis
Zered River
Eboda
0 10 20 30 40 miles
0 20 40 60 km
Column from Codex Sinaiticus
35°
36°
33°
32°
31°
A
B
C
D
1
2
3

carta

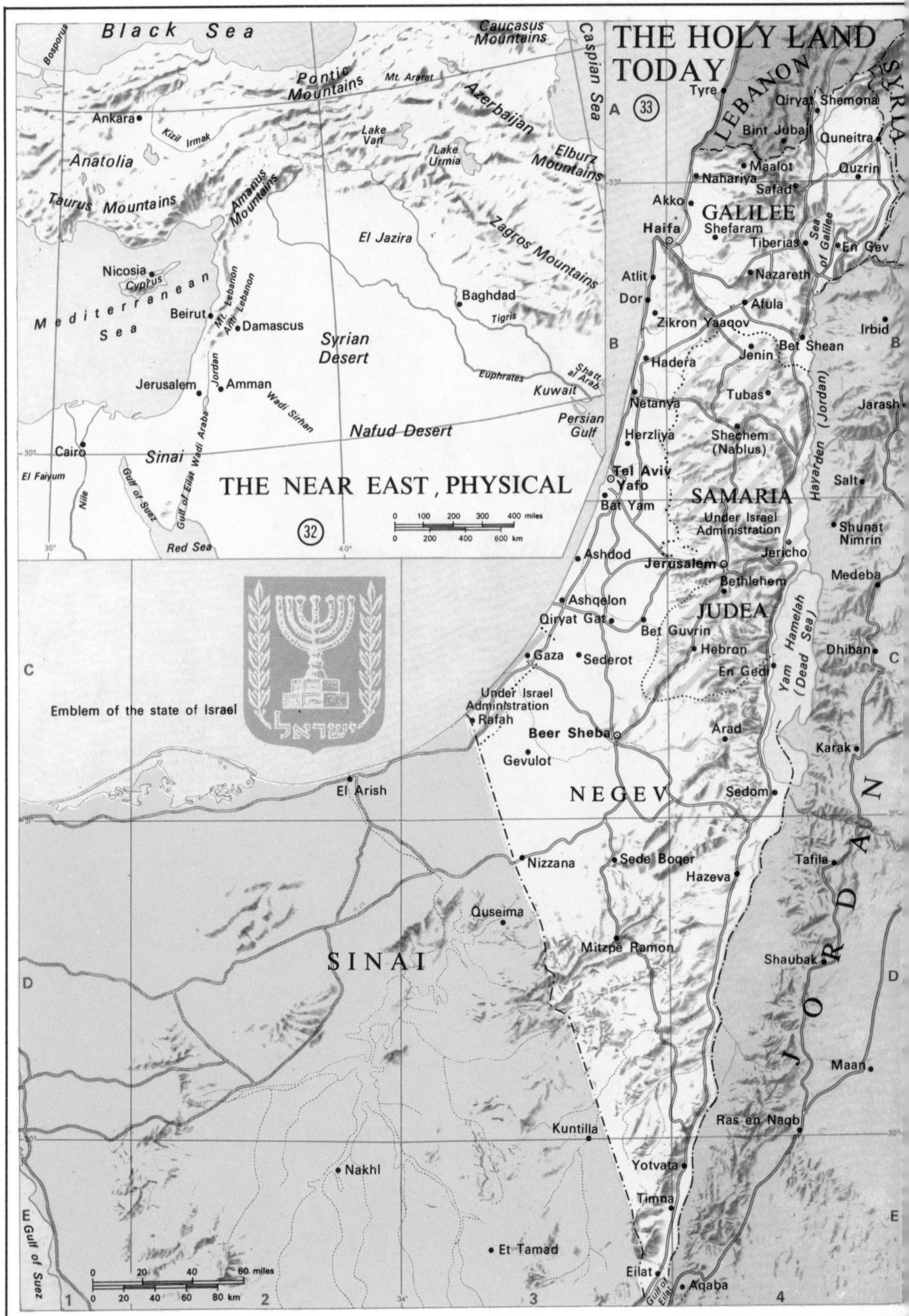
THE HOLY LAND TODAY
33
THE NEAR EAST, PHYSICAL
32
Black Sea
Bosporus
Caucasus Mountains
Caspian Sea
Pontic Mountains
Mt. Ararat
Azerbaijan
Ankara
Kizil Irmak
Lake Van
Lake Urmia
Elburz Mountains
Anatolia
Taurus Mountains
Amanus Mountains
El Jazira
Zagros Mountains
Nicosia
Cyprus
Mediterranean Sea
Mt. Lebanon
Anti-Lebanon
Baghdad
Tigris
Beirut
Damascus
Syrian Desert
Euphrates
Shatt al Arab
Jerusalem
Jordan
Amman
Kuwait
Wadi Sirhan
Persian Gulf
Nafud Desert
Cairo
Sinai
El Faiyum
Nile
Gulf of Suez
Gulf of Eilat
Wadi Araba
Red Sea
0 100 200 300 400 miles
0 200 400 600 km
Emblem of the state of Israel
ישראל
LEBANON
SYRIA
Tyre
Qiryat Shemona
Bint Jubail
Quneitra
Maalot
Quzrin
Nahariya
Safad
Akko
GALILEE
Haifa
Shefaram
Tiberias
Sea of Galilee
En Gev
Atlit
Nazareth
Dor
Afula
Zikron Yaaqov
Irbid
Bet Shean
Jenin
Hadera
Tubas
Netanya
Jarash
Herzliya
Shechem (Nablus)
Hayarden (Jordan)
Tel Aviv Yafo
Salt
Bat Yam
SAMARIA
Under Israel Administration
Shunat Nimrin
Ashdod
Jericho
Jerusalem
Bethlehem
Medeba
Ashqelon
JUDEA
Qiryat Gat
Bet Guvrin
Yam Hamelah (Dead Sea)
Gaza
Sederot
Hebron
Dhiban
En Gedi
Under Israel Administration
Rafah
Beer Sheba
Arad
Karak
Gevulot
El Arish
NEGEV
Sedom
JORDAN
Nizzana
Sede Boqer
Tafila
Hazeva
Quseima
Mitzpe Ramon
SINAI
Shaubak
Maan
Ras en Naqb
Kuntilla
Nakhl
Yotvata
Timna
Et Tamad
Eilat
Aqaba
Gulf of Eilat
Gulf of Suez
0 20 40 60 miles
0 20 40 60 80 km
A B C D E
1 2 3 4

Slack™

by Phil Simon

Award-winning author of The Age of the Platform

FOREWORD BY Cal Henderson

Founder and CTO of Slack Technologies

Slack™ For Dummies®

Published by: **John Wiley & Sons, Inc.,** 111 River Street, Hoboken, NJ 07030-5774, www.wiley.com

For general information on our other products and services, please contact our Customer Care Department within the U.S. at 877-762-2974, outside the U.S. at 317-572-3993, or fax 317-572-4002. For technical support, please visit https://hub.wiley.com/community/support/dummies.

Wiley publishes in a variety of print and electronic formats and by print-on-demand. Some material included with standard print versions of this book may not be included in e-books or in print-on-demand. If this book refers to media such as a CD or DVD that is not included in the version you purchased, you may download this material at http://booksupport.wiley.com. For more information about Wiley products, visit www.wiley.com.

Library of Congress Control Number: 2020937263

ISBN 978-1-119-66950-0 (pbk); ISBN 978-1-119-66952-4 (ePDF); ISBN 978-1-119-66951-7 (epub)

Manufactured in the United States of America

V10018630_060120

Contents at a Glance

Foreword xiii

Introduction 1

Part 1: Working Smarter and Better with Slack 7

CHAPTER 1: Why Slack Exists 9

CHAPTER 2: Getting Started with Slack 29

Part 2: Communicating Without Chaos 57

CHAPTER 3: Targeting Your Communication with Slack Channels 59

CHAPTER 4: The Wonderful World of Slack Messages 91

CHAPTER 5: Staying Informed with Notifications, Statuses, and Feeds 119

Part 3: Becoming a Slack Power User 141

CHAPTER 6: Going Deeper into Slack's Functionality 143

CHAPTER 7: Finding What You Need with Slack's Powerful Search Techniques . . . 159

CHAPTER 8: Personalizing Slack 173

CHAPTER 9: Keeping It Safe: Reviewing Slack's Security and Privacy Settings 193

Part 4: Extending Slack's Native Functionality 211

CHAPTER 10: Making Slack Hum with Robust Third-Party Apps 213

CHAPTER 11: Analyzing, Importing, Exporting, and Updating Slack User Data 245

CHAPTER 12: Integrating Slack with Popular Enterprise Systems 263

Part 5: Successfully Introducing Slack in the Workspace 275

CHAPTER 13: The Elements of Persuasion: Slack-Adoption Strategies 277

CHAPTER 14: The Inherent Risks of Deploying Slack 297

CHAPTER 15: The Future of Slack: We're Just Getting Started 315

Part 6: The Part of Tens 327

CHAPTER 16: Ten Great Slack Tips 329

CHAPTER 17: Ten or So Common Slack Myths 333

CHAPTER 18: The Top Ten or So Slack Resources 339

Index 347

Table of Contents

FOREWORD xiii

INTRODUCTION 1

About This Book 2
Foolish Assumptions 2
Icons Used in This Book 4
Beyond the Book 5
Where to Go from Here 5

PART 1: WORKING SMARTER AND BETTER WITH SLACK 7

CHAPTER 1: **Why Slack Exists** 9
Introducing Slack 9
Meeting Slack's Users and Customers 13
Understanding Why Slack Exists 14
Email: The blessing and all-too-frequent curse 15
Trapped institutional knowledge 16
Employees often can't find what they want — quickly or even at all 17
What Slack Specifically Does 18
Employer benefits 18
Employee benefits 23

CHAPTER 2: **Getting Started with Slack** 29
Reviewing Slack's Different Versions 29
Free plan 30
Standard plan 30
Plus plan 31
Enterprise Grid 31
Changing your Slack plan 31
Describing Slack's cost structure 33
Beginning Your Slack Journey with the Workspace 35
Creating a new Slack workspace 36
Signing in to an existing Slack workspace 37
Accessing your new workspace 40
Using the Slack desktop app 40
Introducing the Slack user interface 42
Summarizing Slack's Different Roles and Permissions 44
Administrative roles 44
Non-administrative roles 46

Managing member roles 47
Enterprise Grid roles and permissions......................51
Starting Your New Workspace Off on the Right Foot...............52
Expanding your existing workspace...........................52
Configuring your member profile and key account settings......54

PART 2: COMMUNICATING WITHOUT CHAOS 57

CHAPTER 3: **Targeting Your Communication with Slack Channels**..................................59
Introducing Slack Channels 60
Exploring the Different Types of Slack Channels 61
Public channels 62
Private channels 63
Multi-workspace channels 65
Shared channels 67
Creating Public and Private Channels 69
Creating your first public channel..............................70
Building an intelligent channel structure.........................73
Viewing basic channel information..............................75
Performing Channel Actions 76
Group actions...77
Individual actions..81
Adding Members to Existing Channels...........................83
Manual additions...83
Default workplace channels......................................85
Exploring Existing Public Channels...............................85
Communicating via Slack Channels 87
Posting simple channel messages 88
Understanding channel etiquette................................89

CHAPTER 4: **The Wonderful World of Slack Messages**............91
Understanding Slack Messages.....................................92
Sending a Message 92
Performing basic message actions................................94
Formatting your messages...96
Finding people in your workspace 98
Editing messages...100
Deleting messages 101
Muting conversations...101
Setting message-specific reminders..............................102
Saving DMs and channel messages 102
Pinning DMs to conversations...................................103

Creating special types of messages 104
Converting group DMs into private channels 108
Using threads to create topic-specific containers. 109
Sharing in Slack 111
Sharing files 111
Sharing messages 114
Comparing Email and Slack 116
Forwarding Email to Slack 117
Communicating Outside of Slack 117

CHAPTER 5: **Staying Informed with Notifications, Statuses, and Feeds** 119
Getting Your Arms around Notifications 120
Managing Slack notifications 120
Reviewing the different types of Slack notifications. 122
Letting Others Know Your Availability 130
Setting your status 131
Viewing your colleagues' statuses. 132
Editing your status. 133
Clearing your status 133
Setting yourself to away/active 133
Unplugging with Do Not Disturb mode 134
Configuring Device-Specific Notifications 137
Enabling notifications on mobile devices. 137
Understanding when settings collide 137
Finding Other Ways to Stay Current. 138
Receiving emails on recent activity. 138
Viewing mentions and reactions. 139

PART 3: BECOMING A SLACK POWER USER 141

CHAPTER 6: **Going Deeper into Slack's Functionality** 143
Making Calls in Slack. 143
Types of calls 144
Calls and security. 148
Sharing Your Screen in Slack 149
Presenting and viewing. 149
Drawing. 150
Saving Even More Time in Slack 150
Invoking keyboard shortcuts 151
Using commands. 152
Managing Your Life with Reminders. 153

Saving Items 155
Saving files 155
Saving messages 155
Quickly accessing your saved items 155
Creating User Groups 156

CHAPTER 7: **Finding What You Need with Slack's Powerful Search Techniques** 159
Searching for Better Search Methods 160
Performing Searches in Slack 161
Searching by workspace members. 163
Restricting searches to specific date ranges 164
Using negative keywords 165
Referencing multiple keywords. 166
Restricting search results even more 167
Searching by user reactions. 167
Searching by wildcards. 168
Searching by fuzziness 169
Searching by additional modifiers 170
Getting the Most Out of Search in Slack 170
Start small. 170
Embrace modifiers 171
Remember that results change over time .172
Be patient 172

CHAPTER 8: **Personalizing Slack** 173
Getting to Know Your Slack Options. 174
Configuring global workspace settings 175
Personalizing your Slack options. 179
Customizing User Profiles 185
Creating custom fields 186
Populating custom fields 187
Organizing Your Sidebar. 189
Using sections 189
Sorting channels 191

CHAPTER 9: **Keeping It Safe: Reviewing Slack's Security and Privacy Settings** 193
Getting Acquainted with Slack Security 194
Security and Slack's Evolution 194
Configuring Slack's Access and Security Settings 195
Confirming sign-ins via email. 195
Resetting your password 195
Viewing access logs 197

Enabling two-factor authentication 198
Additional security features 200
Enhancing Security via Slack Enterprise Grid 201
Examining Privacy in Slack 202
Message encryption 202
What data Workspace Admins can Access 204
Workspace message-retention settings 204
File-retention settings 207
Understanding Slack's Tricky Regulatory Environment 208
Restrictions on data and file retention 208
Data residency 208

PART 4: EXTENDING SLACK'S NATIVE FUNCTIONALITY 211

CHAPTER 10: Making Slack Hum with Robust Third-Party Apps 213
Understanding How Slack Has Embraced Platform Thinking 214
Comparing Public and Private Apps 215
Public apps 215
Private apps and integrations 215
Enhancing Slack with Third-Party Apps 216
Looking at app costs 216
The Slack App Directory 217
Introducing Some Popular Slack Apps 218
Polling apps 218
File- and content-sharing apps 220
Scheduling apps 221
Productivity and project-management apps 223
IFTTT Slack applets 224
Video-calling apps 225
Email apps and integrations 225
Miscellaneous apps 226
Finding and Installing Apps 227
Browsing the Slack App Directory 228
Installing a Slack app in your workspace 228
Searching for specific apps 230
Experimenting with new apps 230
Managing Apps and App Permissions 231
Approving specific apps 231
Regulating workspace apps 232
Viewing all your workspace apps 236
Enforcing your organization's app policy 236
Removing apps from your workspace 238

Disappearing apps. 239
Disabling and re-enabling preserved apps 239
Viewing app activity logs. 240
Using Workflow Builder 241
Creating workflows 241
Heeding workflow warnings 244

CHAPTER 11: **Analyzing, Importing, Exporting, and Updating Slack User Data**. 245
Analyzing Workspace Data. 246
Slack's analytics dashboard 246
Channel-specific analytics 250
Member analytics 252
Viewing Member Access Logs 253
Moving Data Around in Slack. 254
Exporting data from Slack 254
Importing data into Slack 258
Consolidating Slack workspaces 259
Avoiding mistakes when migrating data 261
Performing Mass Updates to User Data 262

CHAPTER 12: **Integrating Slack with Popular Enterprise Systems**. 263
A Brief Primer on Enterprise Systems 264
Back-office systems. 264
Front-office systems 265
Slack and Current Enterprise Systems 265
Exploring current system integrations. 268
Creating new system integrations 270
Looking forward. 274

PART 5: SUCCESSFULLY INTRODUCING SLACK IN THE WORKSPACE 275

CHAPTER 13: **The Elements of Persuasion: Slack-Adoption Strategies**. 277
A Brief Primer on Network Effects 278
Reviewing the Different Slack-Adoption Approaches. 279
The bottom-up method 279
The top-down method 280
The middle-out method 280
Making Slack Stick at Work. 281
Organization-level strategies. 281
Strategies for handling difficult employees. 286

CHAPTER 14: **The Inherent Risks of Deploying Slack** 297
Identifying the Risks of Using Slack 298
Business risks 298
Technology and security risks 304
Listing Slack's Environmental Challenges 307
Slack's financial pressures 308
Stiff competition 310
Ongoing legal and privacy concerns 311

CHAPTER 15: **The Future of Slack: We're Just Getting Started** ... 315
Increased Use of Automation and Bots 316
AI and machine learning make Slack smarter — much, much smarter 317
Slack begins to monitor employee morale and diagnose cultural issues 318
Tighter Integration with Popular Enterprise Systems 319
Better Dashboards and Analytics 319
A More Powerful Slack Work Graph 320
Continued Borrowing of Popular Features from Other Apps 322
Key Acquisitions and Partnerships 326

PART 6: THE PART OF TENS 327

CHAPTER 16: **Ten Great Slack Tips** 329
Respond Promptly to New Users' Requests, Questions, and Feedback 329
Regularly View Slack Analytics 330
Tread Lightly with New Hires 330
Establish Slack as the Default Medium for Internal Communication 330
Emphasize Slack's Carrots More Than Its Sticks 331
Keep an Eye Out for New Slack Apps 331
Tell Overly Exuberant Slack Members to Tone It Down 331
Publicize Your Status and Availability 331
Try Before You Buy 332
Know When to Turn Slack Off 332

CHAPTER 17: **Ten or So Common Slack Myths** 333
Slack Is Just Email 2.0 333
Slack Decimates the Need for Email 334
All Organizations Configure Slack in a Uniform Way 334
Slack Obviates the Need for In-Person Communication 335
Slack Solves Every Conceivable Business-Communication Problem 335
Slack Is Too Expensive for Our Company 335

Our Company Has Built a Tool That's Just as Good as Slack........336
Our Employees Don't Need Slack..............................336
Our Company Uses Slack and Nothing Else for Collaboration......337
You Can't Misuse Slack......................................338

CHAPTER 18: **The Top Ten or So Slack Resources**..................339
Slack Online Support..340
Contacting Slack..340
Browsing the Slack support site.............................340
Opening cases or making suggestions within the Slack app.....340
Finding Slack tips..340
Submitting Slack feature requests...........................341
Other Online Resources......................................341
Official resources..341
Unofficial resources..342
Developer resources...343
In-Person Resources...343
Conferences...343
Meetups...344
In-person training..345

INDEX...347

Foreword

My cofounders and I never could have imagined that our internal collaboration tool would eventually revolutionize workplace communications and change how people work. At that time, email was the default coordinating point for communications and information, but inside our company — which was split between New York City, San Francisco, and Vancouver — it was simply too slow. We wanted a better, quicker solution than email for working together and across great distances. So, like any group of engineers would, we set out to build one.

Designed to bring the tools you use and the people you work with every day into one place, Slack, we believe, is a better way of working together than email. Meaningful teamwork and engagement on Slack happens in channels, which you can read more about in Chapter 3. Channels and shared channels (between multiple organizations) represent a more efficient mechanism for workplace communication and are organized by team or projects, which helps facilitate relevant exchanges and productivity.

These channels quickly become rich, dense, searchable archives of information, giving users quick access to all the information they need in one centralized location. (You can find out more on the power of search in Slack in Chapter 7.) Slack is made even more powerful by integrating third-party apps to accomplish a range of tasks spanning all major categories of work, including project management, finance, design, customer support, and more. As you can read in Chapter 10, Slack has thousands of apps in its directory — all designed to make your workday more productive.

Even in its earliest iterations, we viewed Slack as more than a simple messaging tool. When we talk about Slack as a collaboration hub, we don't just mean people sending messages to one another, but more broadly, the work that is enabled across teams on a single platform. Slack started as a tool we built to answer our small company's needs, and it turns out those needs were pretty universal, from coffee roasters to healthcare offices to some of the world's largest financial services companies. If you're reading this book, it's likely you're in a similar situation.

I hope *Slack For Dummies* gives you strong foundational knowledge about what Slack can do to improve your workplace communications, and by reading it, you're able to pick up a few tips and tricks along the way. In the end, every business is made up of teams who are looking for a better way to work together. We're happy and grateful to be a part of your journey.

— Cal Henderson, cofounder and Chief Technology Officer, Slack Technologies, Inc.

Introduction

Not that long ago, the world's most successful organizations relied upon typewriters, landlines, inter-office memos, and secretaries. Email and even fax machines didn't exist. Back then, employees took actual vacations.

Don't believe me? Watch a few episodes of AMC's *Mad Men*. Odds are that you probably won't recognize the 1960s' world of work. Although it predates me by a few years, it's an authentic portrayal of office life back then.

The modern-day workplace is a far cry from those quaint days. Employees today are bombarded with a constant barrage of often pointless emails, text messages, meeting requests, phone calls, and information. The era of Big Data is here, and far too often multi-tasking reigns supreme. The idea of working without interruptions is foreign to many employees. Thanks to smartphones, we're almost always reachable, even when we are supposed to be on vacation.

If you're stressed while on the clock, at least take solace in the fact that you're not alone. According to a 2018 Korn Ferry survey, "Nearly two-thirds of professionals say their stress levels at work are higher than they were five years ago." (Read the study at `https://tinyurl.com/y2jxeatr`.)

Enter Slack, a tool that makes work more manageable and less overwhelming. Slack's cohesive set of powerful features allows employees to regain control of their professional lives in a number of simple yet effective ways. In addition, Slack allows you to communicate and collaborate well with your colleagues, managers, clients, partners, and vendors.

No, Slack doesn't solve every conceivable workplace problem. No software program can. Still, when used properly, Slack helps employers build valuable organizational knowledge bases, increase productivity and transparency, and often maintain an edge over their competition. Employees benefit as well in the form of less chaotic work environments, fewer emails, being able to more easily find key information, and much more.

About This Book

Slack For Dummies is the most extensive guide on how to use this powerful, flexible, affordable, and user-friendly collaboration tool. It provides an in-depth overview of Slack's most valuable features — some of which even experienced users may have overlooked since adopting it. This text goes beyond merely showing you how to install, configure, and customize Slack. It also offers practical tips on how individual users, groups, and even entire firms can get the most out of it. In short, this is the book that I wish I had when I taught myself Slack years ago.

As with all titles in the *For Dummies* series, you'll find the book's organization and flow straightforward and intuitive. The tone is conversational. Ideally, you'll have fun while concurrently learning how to use an increasingly important, popular, and useful application. I certainly had fun writing it.

Foolish Assumptions

I wrote *Slack For Dummies* with a number of different cohorts in mind:

- People who are frustrated from wasting time at work mired in their inboxes and have finally had enough.
- People who generally want to know more about how Slack works.
- Organization decision makers who (correctly) believe that their employees can collaborate and communicate better and be more productive.
- Employees at organizations that have already experimented with or purchased Slack and want to do more with it.
- People in different social or professional groups who need an easy way to communicate with fellow members, coordinate events, and the like.

REMEMBER

Slack For Dummies is geared toward everyday users, not application developers. To be sure, I mention a few resources for people who want to know more about building new apps. Make no mistake, though: This book is for normal users. If you are a proper developer and you're looking for a text on how to build Slack apps and access its application programming interfaces, unfortunately you'll have to go elsewhere.

Slack For Dummies presumes zero prior use or even knowledge of the application. Nada. If you're not exactly tech-savvy, then fret not. Perhaps you're merely curious about what this "Slack thing" can do and how you'd do it. Congratulations: You've found the right text.

I do, however, assume the following:

- » You are curious about how Slack can make your work life less chaotic.
- » You receive plenty of internal emails and sometimes struggle managing your inbox.
- » You know how to use a proper computer, whether it's a Mac or PC.
- » You can navigate mobile devices, such as smartphones or tablets.
- » At some point in your life, you've accessed the World Wide Web with an Internet browser.

I'm a firm believer in truth in advertising. By way of background, my editor and I wanted to keep this book at a reasonable length and cost. To do so, we made a few conscious decisions about its content, and I want you to know about them from the get-go.

First, the book that you're holding isn't nearly as long as *War and Peace*, but it certainly isn't slim. Please understand going in that *Slack For Dummies* does not include step-by-step directions on how to configure and tweak each and every setting or feature in any single Slack plan, never mind all four of them. Such a task is simply impractical. Even if it were, Slack adds new features on a regular basis and sometimes changes existing ones. All software companies do today. The fleas come with the dog.

Just about every other author of a contemporary book of a robust application has had to confront the same inherent tradeoff. I'm not special. Consider Greg Harvey's *Excel 2019 For Dummies* (Wiley Publishing, Inc.), a 432-page tome on Microsoft's iconic spreadsheet program. As comprehensive as that text is, it does not contain detailed examples of all Excel functions and features because it can't. Nor can it cover all of the subtle distinctions between the Excel Mac and PC versions. The same limitation applies to the equally lengthy *WordPress For Dummies* (Wiley) by Lisa Sabin-Wilson and countless others in this series.

I've deliberately chosen my battles here. *Slack For Dummies* highlights:

- » What I believe are Slack's essential and frequently used features
- » Obscure features that members *should* use — or at the very least know about — and how to intelligently use them

In some cases, I describe a feature without spending valuable space on how to actually do it because Slack makes it self-explanatory.

Second and in a similar vein, I have intentionally written all the instructions in this book to be as device-agnostic as possible. In other words, I demonstrate how to do things in Slack by using its desktop application. In some necessary cases, I do the same by accessing Slack via a browser. Put differently, I almost always demonstrate Slack's functionality using a proper computer, whether that's a PC or a Mac.

No, I'm not living in the 1970s and 1980s. (Well, maybe with my taste in music, but that's a different discussion.) I know full well that mobile devices arrived in earnest a long time ago. At times, I'll mention how you can perform a specific Slack action on a smartphone or tablet. Largely due to space considerations, however, I simply cannot replicate how to execute each Slack task on all iOS and Android versions and devices. Minor differences persist. Even if I somehow managed to pull that off in the following pages, you'd probably find half of my directions irrelevant to you. I have met very few people who use both types of devices. People typically pick one side or the other. Brass tacks: To borrow a line from Greek philosophy, in this book the needs of the many outweigh the needs of the few.

Fear not, young Jedi. The vast majority of users find Slack to be remarkably intuitive. You'll soon be able to naturally perform most of Slack's key functions on the mobile device of your choice. In the event that you're flummoxed about how to accomplish something on your phone or tablet, Slack's website contains detailed instructions on how to do whatever you want on just about whatever device you want.

Icons Used in This Book

Throughout the margins of this book are small pictures that highlight key information:

TIP

This icon highlights shortcuts that should save you some time.

WARNING

Be careful whenever you see this icon.

This icon highlights technical information that may or may not interest you. If not, then feel free to skip it.

You'll want to keep key points in mind as you work in Slack. This icon highlights those points.

Beyond the Book

In addition to what you're reading right now, this product also comes with a free access-anywhere Cheat Sheet that gives you a Slack-term glossary and a list of keyboard shortcuts. To get this Cheat Sheet, simply go to `www.dummies.com` and type *Slack For Dummies Cheat Sheet* in the Search box.

Where to Go from Here

You need not start this book on page one and continue to the end; *Slack For Dummies* isn't a novel. If you've already dabbled with this powerful collaboration tool, then you can jump around to the sections that pique your interest. I've written it in that vein.

If you're only considering hopping on the Slack train or have only heard about it, then you should start with the first two chapters. From there, you'll want to read the book in a relatively linear manner.

Regardless of where you ultimately start reading, you'll find it helpful to create a new, free Slack workspace or log into an existing one. I also recommend downloading the Slack app for your computer and at least one mobile device. I have taught myself how to use plenty of new programming languages, applications, and technologies over the years. Throughout my career, I have found that getting my hands dirty and doing the exercises myself to be invaluable.

The journey begins now.

THANK YOU

Thank you for buying *Slack For Dummies*. I hope that you find it useful, informative, and even a little entertaining. Throughout this book, I have emphasized the many *potential* benefits of Slack and how to take advantage of them.

I qualified the previous statement because Slack has never been an elixir to all corporate ills and sources of dysfunction. It never will be — nor will any technology or app, for that matter. Employees who revert to email and use Slack intermittently will fail to recognize its considerable advantages. As with any new tool, Slack's ultimate success hinges upon many factors. At the top of my list are opening your mind and setting realistic expectations for what it can and can't do.

I wish you the best of luck on your journey to communicate and collaborate better with your colleagues. Let me know if I can help.

Slack on,

Phil Simon | *www.philsimon.com*

April 28, 2020

1

Working Smarter and Better with Slack

IN THIS PART

Meet Slack

Discover the problems that Slack solves

Navigate your way around Slack

Examine Slack's different versions and roles

Create a Slack profile

IN THIS CHAPTER

» Identifying the reasons that so many employers and employees embrace Slack

» Uncovering Slack's advantages over email

» Understanding the many business problems that Slack solves

Chapter 1
Why Slack Exists

What is Slack anyway? Where did it come from? Was it the result of long-term planning, a eureka moment, or a happy accident? And what business problems can it solve, anyway?

This chapter answers these questions in spades. Further, it provides some background information about Slack.

Introducing Slack

Slack stands for *Searchable Log of All Conversation and Knowledge*. This is what many in the business world call a *backronym*: a contrived acronym. To be sure, I've seen plenty of backronyms — especially in my HR days. In this case, though, the term happens to be entirely fitting.

Slack is "where work happens." This is the pithy answer — and the one that adorns the company's website. The company's lofty mission is "to make work life simpler, more pleasant, and more productive."

I'll cut to the chase: Mission accomplished.

At a high level, Slack is a relatively new and powerful application that allows people to work, communicate, and collaborate better — one that has become increasingly popular since its launch way back in August 2013. At its core, Slack brings people together to accomplish goals through what it now calls a *workspace*. (Slack used to call this a *team*.) Figure 1-1 shows what one looks like.

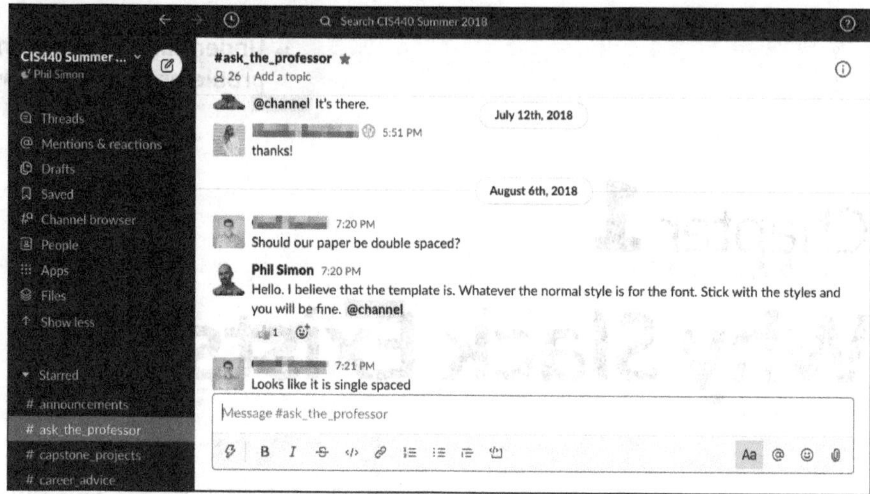

FIGURE 1-1: Slack workspace of a college professor.

If you're chomping at the bit and can't wait any longer, take an online tour of Slack by visiting `https://slack.com/features`.

Slack's popularity has exploded since its early days. As such, you may think that the idea behind Slack required years of meticulous planning and deliberation. And you'd be wrong. If you're curious about Slack's origins, check out the nearby sidebar "A happy accident: Slack's background and history." To listen to a longer version of the Slack story from the mouth of CEO and co-founder Stewart Butterfield himself, go to `bit.ly/sl-podc`.

In effect, Slack accidentally popularized — and some would argue even created — a new and colossal product category. This is no easy feat. International Data Corp labels this category the *team collaborative applications market*. The research firm estimates that worldwide spending on collaboration software is currently $16.5 billion and will reach more than $26.6 billion by 2023.

Slack is a nicely packaged set of integrated collaboration tools. In the interest of full disclosure and as Chapter 14 covers, though, other software vendors previously released somewhat comparable products.

Chapter 7 covers Slack's search functionality in depth.

A HAPPY ACCIDENT: SLACK'S BACKGROUND AND HISTORY

In 2009, Stewart Butterfield, Eric Costello, Cal Henderson, and Serguei Mourachov started a company called Tiny Speck based out of Vancouver, British Columbia. The company was building a massively multiplayer online game called *Glitch*.

After a few years of toiling away, the Tiny Speck founders realized that Glitch was never going to reach critical mass. Most startup founders have a hard time killing their darlings, but Butterfield and his cofounders could no longer ignore the obvious: It was time to abandon ship.

Don't mistake this story, though, as another example of an irresponsible startup depleting its funds. By way of background, Butterfield and his team were experienced entrepreneurs. (Butterfield's previous company, Ludicorp, had sold its photo-sharing service Flickr to Yahoo! in 2005 for roughly $25 million.) Tiny Speck managed its money well and still had plenty of *runway*, to use the parlance of Silicon Valley.

Tiny Speck's founders offered to return all their remaining funding to their investors, but the entrepreneurs first wanted to float an idea. While building Glitch, the team had cobbled together a valuable internal collaboration tool. The entrepreneurs enjoyed working with one another, and they were curious about where this new tool could go. Tiny Speck's investors agreed and let them pivot.

Slack launched the beta version of its product in August 2013. Roughly 8,000 people immediately signed up. Slack grew quickly and organically, largely thanks to marketing's holy grail: word-of-mouth.

Growth has exploded since then. With Butterfield as CEO, Slack Technologies, Inc. started trading on June 20, 2019, on the New York Stock Exchange under the apropos symbol $WORK. Its value exceeded $14 billion on February 11, 2020, after it closed a massive deal with IBM. Here are some fascinating Slack statistics:

- As of January 2020, more than 12 million people use Slack. Collectively, they send more than a billion messages every day.
- Every week and on average, an astonishing five billion actions take place on Slack. I'm talking about reading and writing messages, uploading files, commenting on them, searching for content, automating tasks, and interacting with third-party apps.

(continued)

(continued)

- Approximately half of Slack's daily active users live and work outside of the United States.
- You can find Slack users in more than 150 countries in the world.
- More than 600,000 organizations use Slack — more than 100,000 of which pay for it. Customers include Pinterest, Airbnb, CNN, Target, and Zappos.
- At least 65 percent of Fortune 100 companies pay for Slack.
- As of this writing and according to LinkedIn, 42 percent of Slack's more than 2,000 employees in its 18 offices previously worked at a top-80 tech company. By comparison, at Google that number is 58 percent.
- Nearly 22 percent of Slack employees graduated from a top-30 university. This number is second to Google's 22.3 percent.
- The accounting firm Kruze Consulting found that 60 percent of funded startups not only use Slack, but they pay for the privilege of doing so.

For more interesting Slack facts, go to `bit.ly/sl-facts`.

UNDER THE HOOD

Slack uses an impressive array of powerful, contemporary technologies, programming languages, and frameworks to work its magic. That is, it does not attempt to cram everything into a single language or framework because one size does not fit all.

According to chief technology officer Cal Henderson (and author of this book's foreword):

- Slack's web client/desktop app runs on a mix of JavaScript, ECMAScript 6 (ES6), and React.
- Slack's Android client is written in a mix of Java and Kotlin.
- Slack's iOS app relies upon both Objective C and Swift.

As for hosting, Slack engages Amazon Web Services (AWS), the world's most popular provider of cloud computing. Visit `bit.ly/slackstack` for more on the specific technologies that Slack uses.

Meeting Slack's Users and Customers

Thanks to its flexibility, Slack appeals to the smallest of startups, the largest of conglomerates, and organizations of every size in between. Firms old and new have jumped on the bandwagon.

Next, using Slack is not a binary. As you can see in Chapter 2, organizations can test its waters without making long-term financial commitments. (In this case, you *can* get a little bit pregnant.) Beyond that, individuals, groups, and departments can benefit from using Slack even if it hasn't spread throughout the entire organization — yet. To be fair, though, putting less into Slack means that employers will get less out of it.

The industries that use Slack run the gamut: technology, media, music, higher education, retail, hair salons, and restaurants. I'm hard-pressed to think of an area that Slack hasn't touched. Beyond scrappy upstarts and for-profit organizations, government agencies such as the U.S. Census Bureau and the State Department also call themselves Slack customers. Tech-savvy and tieless ex-Democratic presidential candidate Andrew Yang used it to quickly bring his new campaign volunteers up to speed. I could keep going but you catch my drift.

As for age, Slack users run the gamut. If you think that it's a tool exclusively for millennial hipsters, think again. I'm anything but a 20-something, and people far older than I use it on a daily basis.

Most fascinating to me, an increasing number of informal groups creatively use Slack to assign tasks, plan events, and communicate. I'm talking here about book clubs, hiking groups, sports leagues, and others. Then there are families. Yes, families. (Read more at `bit.ly/sl-fam3`.)

Bottom line: Slack appeals to diverse types, sizes, and compositions of formal organizations and informal groups. Every day, Slack allows millions of people to eschew outdated and ineffective communication methods. The biggest culprit: the mass email thread. Slack's ability to significantly curtail internal email represents a major reason that so many enlightened souls have embraced it.

TIP

To read detailed case studies on how different organizations and industries use Slack in creative ways, go to `bit.ly/slackwow`.

HOW I BECAME A SLACK FANBOY

In August 2016, I began my new career as a full-time college professor. I started teaching technology- and data-related subjects at ASU's W. P. Carey School of Business.

During my first year, my plate was beyond full. In no particular order, I had to familiarize myself with material for three different 400-level classes. Beyond preparing lectures, I felt compelled to overhaul most of my predecessors' opaque syllabi, assignment rubrics, and presentation slides.

Oh, I'm nowhere close to finished describing my to-do list.

I also needed to complete a number of obligatory school-specific training courses, figure out how academe works, meet with students, grade papers, design exercises to promote active learning, record videos, and become proficient at the school's learning-management system or LMS at the time (Blackboard). Oh, and I wrote a book for my analytics class.

No, I wasn't bored.

On the collaboration and communications side, like many of my colleagues, I immediately found Blackboard wanting. Given my other responsibilities, though, I wasn't about to rock the boat from the get-go. (Even if I had loved Blackboard, using another tool would have benefited my students. After all, the vast majority of my students certainly wouldn't be using an LMS after graduating.)

During my first two semesters, I experimented with some different in-class communication tools, such as Google Forms and WordPress. Ultimately, nothing really struck my fancy. Yes, those tchotchkes were useful, but they just weren't integrated. I didn't want to confuse my students. What's more, those standalone tools didn't encourage targeted communications with them.

With a year of teaching under my belt, in fall 2017, I decided to give Slack a whirl.

In a nutshell, Slack changed everything. I have proudly used it every semester since for all my classes. I have even convinced some of my hidebound colleagues to give it a shot. Not a day goes by that I don't use Slack. For the most part, my students love it.

Understanding Why Slack Exists

In hindsight, the birth of Slack was serendipitous. Lest you dismiss it, though, the problems that Slack solves are anything but trivial.

Let me start by asking you a few questions:

- How would you characterize communication and collaboration between and among people in your group, department, and company?
- How often do you experience communication-related issues?
- Do you sometimes feel overwhelmed and/or disengaged while at work?
- Does locating key documents or conversations take longer than it should?
- Have you ever wondered if there was fundamentally a better way to work?

Be honest.

If you answered no to all those questions, then feel free to skip the rest of this chapter. I'm guessing, though, that you responded *yes* to at least a few of them.

I don't know your current situation, but let me go out on a limb: Some or even most of your work-related anxiety stems from the sources I describe in the following sections. As you read them, at least take some solace in two facts:

- You're not alone in feeling this way.
- There's a light at the end of the tunnel, and its name is Slack.

Email: The blessing and all-too-frequent curse

Much of the time wasted at work stems from email or, more precisely, our misuse of email. Don't take me at my word. though.

In July 2012, the McKinsey Global Institute (MGI) released a report titled "The social economy: Unlocking value and productivity through social technologies." (Read the study at `mck.co/mgislack`.)

MGI discovered that knowledge workers spend roughly 28 percent of their work time dealing with email. The math here is downright scary: For example, if you work 50 hours per week, then you'll spend 14 of them in your inbox. (If you only clock 40 hours every week, then expect to spend about 11.2 of them in email hell.)

Alternatively, think about it this way: Thirty years ago, professionals spent zero hours sending and reading emails every week. Today, those two tasks make up nearly one-third of their workday. McKinsey urges employees to use more collaborative tools in lieu of email. The report suggests that this change would let us recapture seven to nine percent of our workweeks.

Here are the two things to remember from this report:

- Slack is one of these tools.
- In the eight years since the publication of the McKinsey report, I strongly suspect that, in most organizations, the employee email headache has only exacerbated.

Nay on the vacay

At least there's vacation, right? Imagine the thought of unplugging on a one-week sojourn in Paris or chasing golf balls in verdant Myrtle Beach.

Hmm, maybe not. Most people are unable to escape email's menacing wrath even when taking hard-earned time off.

A 2019 LinkedIn survey revealed that nearly three in five of employees on vacation admitted to checking in with their bosses or coworkers every day. Nearly one-quarter checked in three or more times per day. Employees who truly do go off the grid return with inboxes overflowing with new messages.

If you're going to be working — or just thinking about work — anyway, then why even bother taking time off? Plenty of Americans share this sentiment. In August 2019, the consumer financial services company Bankrate reported that a mere 28 percent of U.S. citizens planned to use all their allotted vacation time. In 2017, Project: Time Off found that Americans squandered 212 million days off annually.

Constant connectivity

I could keep going, but you get my point: Thanks in large part to email and constant connectivity, for many people, work has become the very definition of a no-win situation.

Trapped institutional knowledge

The near-universal use — and overuse — of email has confined a great deal of valuable organizational knowledge in the inboxes of individual employees. When employees leave a company, IT typically deactivates or deletes their email accounts. No matter the method, the result is the same: Those employees' essential files, important conversations, decisions, and institutional wisdom effectively dies.

IT'S COMPLICATED. OUR LOVE-HATE RELATIONSHIP WITH EMAIL.

Many people are critical of email as a communications medium. I'll unapologetically put myself in this camp. My 2015 book *Message Not Received: Why Business Communication Is Broken and How to Fix It* (Wiley) is in part a screed against its overuse.

But think about the utility of email for a moment. People of a certain age remember the inefficiency of life before email. I'm talking about the 1980s and early 1990s. In college, I used to photocopy letters and mail them to my friends because it was the easiest way to stay in touch with them. Business correspondence back then was hardly fast, even with the advent of fax machines. Thanks to email, those days are long gone.

More than 25 years since its widespread adoption in the corporate world, email remains remarkably powerful because of its ubiquity. When was the last time that you saw a business card without an email address? Anyone can email you about anything and vice versa — inside and outside of your company. With rare exception these days, those messages arrive both securely and instantly. Oh, and did I mention that email is essentially free?

When it comes to responses, email applications let you reply to individuals and groups without restriction — often too frequently. Everyone has done it before and recognizes the following subject line:

```
Re: Re: Re: Re: Re: Re: [insert name of topic]
```

No, email isn't perfect. No technology is. To deal with its limitations, people block certain senders, unsubscribe from newsletters, create filters and rules, and flag messages as spam.

Perhaps you've reflected on this tried-and-true model of a single, overflowing inbox with an interminable stream of context-free messages. The idea of hundreds of unread emails is unsettling, although many people store messages in different folders and sub-folders. Brass tacks: For a long time, email was probably the best that employees could do.

Thanks to Slack, that is no longer the case.

Employees often can't find what they want — quickly or even at all

At work, employees generate an enormous amount of content — much of which they can't find easily or even at all. I'm talking about Excel spreadsheets, PowerPoint presentations, contracts in Word, and other key documents. Workers often

A BLEAK PICTURE: AN OVERWORKED, DISENGAGED WORKFORCE

Employees suffering from email hell and information overload aren't exactly happy campers. The 2017 Gallup State of the American Workplace report found that a full 70 percent of workers are "actively disengaged" while on the job. The situation is downright alarming. What's the cost to U.S. companies? Oh, not much. Just anywhere from $500 to $600 billion dollars. Every year.

struggle to find key messages in their bloated inboxes. Case in point: The Findwise 2016 Enterprise Search & Findability survey found that a full one-third of responding organizations claimed that their employees experienced problems finding basic information. (Read it by visiting `bit.ly/findwise-sl`.)

The problem is so acute that an entire category of software is dedicated to helping employees find key documents and information. In basic terms, *enterprise search technology* (ESR) — also known as *enterprise search and retrieval* — allows employees to more quickly locate content while on the clock. And this is no niche market. In late 2016, Grand View Research estimates that the ESR market will reach nearly $9 billion by 2024.

Think about the irony here: As of this writing, people routinely google more than 130 *trillion* webpages in less than a second. It's an astonishing number, but they quickly find what they need and gleefully move on with their day. At the same time, untold millions of employees often can't pinpoint simple conversations or Microsoft Word documents. The words *crisis* and *opportunity* come to mind.

TIP

For a much deeper look at this problem as well as some solutions, check out *Overwhelmed: Work, Love, and Play When No One Has the Time* (Picador) by Brigid Schulte.

What Slack Specifically Does

When used correctly, Slack helps individuals, groups, and even entire organizations solve these grave workplace problems. In other words, Slack offers a number of benefits to both employers and their employees.

Employer benefits

No doubt Slack's customers realize significant benefits from using it. Fair enough, but what are those perks? The next section lists a bunch of the most important ones.

ADDRESSING THE SLACK SKEPTICS

Maybe you're saying to yourself, "Hold the phone. You really seem to love this funky new collaboration tool. Fine, but there's just one holdup: My colleagues and I already communicate well without this Slack thing for years. Why change?"

I'll give you the benefit of the doubt here: Communication at your employer isn't entirely dysfunctional. Odds are, though, that you can still reap massive rewards from using Slack.

Let me allay another concern that you may have about Slack right out of the gate: Using it requires zero technical sophistication. Nada. To use Slack, you don't have to roll up your sleeves and code. If you know how to operate a computer or a mobile app, then you can use Slack just as well as I do.

TIP

There's a world of difference between theory and practice. Sure, each of the benefits in the following sections is possible. That doesn't mean, though, that any of them is guaranteed to occur — never mind all of them. (Chapter 13 provides recommendations on how to cross the chasm between what can happen and what will happen.)

Build a permanent, comprehensive, and searchable organizational knowledge repository

Consider the following questions:

- » How much rich institutional knowledge lives in your inbox?
- » How many messages detail key, job-related interactions and decisions?
- » How much information about organizational processes is in your head and not formally documented anywhere else?

Think about these questions for a moment. I'll wait.

Now, consider what happens to those key insights if you left your company. At best, they'll remain dormant. At worst, an IT administrator deletes them forever. And the knowledge that's locked in your head? Gone forever.

Slack solves this problem far better than any email inbox does — only if employees use it, of course. Slack effectively retains an indefinite record of these valuable files, decisions, and conversations. Employees simply search Slack.

Enhance employee productivity

Slack allows employees to spend less time sending mass emails and trying to locate key documents. Where is that damn TPS report?

If you accept this premise, then it stands to reason that employees will waste less time and be more productive. I have yet to meet a single manager, company president, or CEO who didn't want her employees to be more efficient and more effective while on the clock. Slack helps employees do this in spades.

Improve employee corporate communication and collaboration

Consider organizations that rely predominantly or — heaven forbid — exclusively on in-person meetings and email back-and-forth. With rare exception, they tend to do poorly in these regards. Along with Google Docs, Dropbox, Zoom, and others, Slack is part of a new breed of tools that obviates the need for many meetings, email messages, and other old-school ways of communicating that often fail.

Facilitate remote work

Remote work is growing in popularity with no end in sight, In October 2019, the St. Louis Federal Reserve Bank found that the share of Americans who primarily work from home has risen in recent decades. A few numbers stand out:

- In 1980, a mere 0.7 percent of full-time employees worked primarily from home. By 2017, that number had risen to 3 percent.
- Seven percent of full-time workers telecommuted four days or more per month.

To read the research for yourself, see `bit.ly/ps-wfh`.

Of course, you need not be an economist to know that, over the last 20 years, the idea of working from home has gained significant traction. Few of us ever heard the term *digital nomad* in the 1990s. Then again, smartphones, powerful broadband connections, and contemporary cloud computing didn't exist.

Increase employee job satisfaction

Slack lets employees work effectively from home. As a result, everyone concerned can reap its rewards. Consider a 2013 study by the University of Melbourne and the New Zealand Work Research Institute. The two organizations discovered that employees who work at home one to three days a week are more productive than employees who need to slog into the office every day. In 2013, Stanford professor

Nicholas Bloom published a paper detailing his own findings. He found that working from home boosted employee output by 13 percent.

Beyond this study, there's no shortage of other research that has correlated remote work with higher employee job satisfaction. For example, recently Owl Labs — a video-conferencing company — released its 2019 State of Remote Work report. It confirmed that remote workers are happier and stay in jobs longer. (Read the report at `bit.ly/2oJNHOu`.)

For years now, remote work has been growing in popularity. What's more, it confers just about everyone benefits from it. Against this backdrop, you'd think that most organizations would be prepared for it. And you'd be spectacularly wrong. (If you're wondering why, see the nearby sidebar "Not remotely prepared for remote work.")

Maybe you're furrowing your brow at this point. Allowing employees to work remotely does not necessitate using Slack. That's true, but what about being able to *effectively* work outside of the office? Put differently, how can employees be productive if they lack the right tools?

Slack is particularly effective in this regard. Its powerful functionality facilitates distributed workplaces. I'm talking here about multi-user videoconferencing and screensharing, instant messaging, the ability to post meaningful status updates and availability windows, and real-time file collaboration. By providing these rich features, Slack makes it easy to accomplish things while outside of the office.

NOT REMOTELY PREPARED FOR REMOTE WORK

In 2019, Harvard Business School and Boston Consulting Group released a lengthy study called "Future Positive: How Companies Can Tap Into Employee Optimism to Navigate Tomorrow's Workplace." The two organizations surveyed 11,000 workers and 6,500 business leaders. (Read it at `hbs.me/2uDQxbc`.)

One of the study's findings is particularly apropos here: Employees consistently voiced their preference for remote, autonomous work and work-life balance. Sadly, a mere 30 percent of those surveyed indicated that their businesses were prepared to even offer it.

It's a sad state of affairs, but one that any organization can change by embracing Slack.

Allow employees to begin their jobs with less training

Slack functions in a similar way to Facebook, Twitter, LinkedIn, and other popular social networks. (For example, if you use any of those social media sites, you'll immediately grasp what the @ and # symbols do.) As such, employees won't require days or weeks of expensive, time-consuming training to get going. (Trust me: The learning curve isn't steep. The one-day, on-site class that I offer to my clients gets the ball rolling.)

REMEMBER

You don't need to fear costly training outlays. Effectively using Slack does not require sending employees away for days at a time.

Increase organizational transparency

In recent years, many organizations have become more transparent with their workforces. The benefits in this vein can be significant.

Consider 2019 research from JUST Capital. The nonprofit reviewed data from nearly 900 publicly traded U.S. companies. JUST assessed transparency and return on equity (ROE) on nine worker issues. On all but one of them, being more transparent with employees resulted in ROE boosts of anywhere between 1.2 to 3 percent. (Read the study yourself at `bit.ly/2U0j9n9`.)

For legal, ethical, and business reasons, few employers to my knowledge have embraced radical transparency. Make no mistake, though: Just being a tad more forthright with employees often improves employee perceptions of their firms' culture and their management. Sure, workers may not agree with a particular outcome or trend, but at least they're more likely to understand it.

Slack helps organizations communicate more transparently with their workforces. Compared to mass email blasts, the application does a far better job of allowing management to share information with rank-and-file employees, gather responses, and gauge them. For their part, workers can easily discuss topics and make decisions out in the open. Just as critically, Slack can publicly or privately capture why people make decisions.

REMEMBER

Organizations need not use Slack to be transparent with their workers. Using Slack just makes doing so really easy.

Help companies attract and retain top talent

Since its launch, Slack has developed a well-deserved reputation as a cool tool among many employees, especially those with hot skills. To this end, savvy recruiters sometimes play up the Slack angle when trying to lure candidates from white-hot fields, such as data science and software development.

No, by itself, the fact that Company X uses Slack won't get an applicant to take a 30-percent pay cut from a previous job or endure two-hour daily commutes. Still, positioned properly, Slack can serve as a signal to coveted candidates that Company X is a chic place to work. In turn, they may be more inclined to sign their offer letters.

Lessen voluntary employee turnover

Workers quit jobs for all sorts of personal and professional reasons. You probably know someone who was very content in her station. Maybe she even worked in her dream job. Still, her employer went bankrupt. As a result, she found herself filling out job applications online.

Don't get me wrong: Using Slack at work isn't going to make you love the job from hell. For example, what if you despise your boss and coworkers and make a fraction of what you think you should? Using Slack won't change your mind.

I have yet to see an academic study that controls for every conceivable factor driving employee satisfaction and retention. All else being equal, though, I'd bet my house on the following statement: Organizations that effectively use powerful collaboration tools such as Slack overwhelm their employees less. It stands to reason, then, that these employers are better able to retain valuable employees. It's not hard to envision lower recruiting costs, a more stable workforce, and a better culture resulting as well.

Easily train employees and diagnose issues

Slack's one-to-many screensharing functionality is ideal for holding small internal webinars, conducting formal training sessions, and more. On an individual level, this feature helps IT personnel to diagnose technical issues.

Employee benefits

What if Slack only benefited employers? That is, imagine if Slack saved organizations money and allowed them to grind more productivity out of their employees. It would still be a valuable tool, but you might justifiably be suspicious. Maybe you think that it would do nothing for you as an employee.

Fortunately, nothing could be further from the truth. Slack benefits employees just as much as — if not more than — employers in a number of key ways. To the extent that you're still a skosh skeptical, though, the following sections provide a sneak preview of how Slack can change how you work — for the better.

Tame the email beast

How many emails do you receive during a normal business day? It varies, of course. In a 2015 study from Digital Marketing Ramblings, the average office employee received 121. That number is downright unmanageable. Market research company Harris Insights & Analytics found that workers can handle a maximum of 50 per day.

Yeah, but each one of those emails really matters, right?

I beg to differ. How many relevant emails do you receive every day? I'm not talking about spam; I mean company-wide missives that, at best, only tangentially apply to you?

Slack's channel functionality (discussed at length in Chapter 3) allows you to receive only messages that you want when you want them. Think about that the next time that you're playing whack-a-mole with your inbox.

By using Slack channels (the communication containers discussed in Chapter 3), you'll reduce your dependence on email — especially from your colleagues. You may even attain the vaunted Inbox Zero: This rigorous approach to email management endeavors to keep employee inboxes empty — or almost empty — at all times.

Slack goes way beyond minimizing the sheer number of emails that employees receive, though.

PROVIDE A COMMON VIEW ON A TOPIC OR WITHIN A DEPARTMENT

Slack channels allow groups, departments, teams, and even entire firms to get easily on the same page and stay in sync. In this way, Slack promotes real group and organizational alignment. Employee inboxes provide only individual views of what's going on. Channels make it easier for groups to row in the same direction. Management consultants refer to this elusive state as *alignment*.

REALIZE THE BENEFITS OF CONTAINED DISCUSSIONS

Slack channels allow employees to hold and contain discussions in clearly defined buckets. When you don't need to spend a few seconds deciphering each message's context, you reduce your cognitive load. That's just a fancy way of saying that Slack quickly provides key information about each message.

MORE EASILY REACH CONSENSUS

Polls allow employees to vote and more easily reach key decisions. It's remarkably simple to take the temperature of a room, department, or division. Slack users can invoke polling functionality by installing any number of third-party apps. (Chapter 10 covers apps in far more detail.)

Quickly find what you need

The knowledge repository that Slack allows organizations to build doesn't just benefit your employer. (See "Build a permanent, comprehensive, and searchable organizational knowledge repository," earlier in this chapter.) I cover Slack's powerful search functionality in Chapter 7. For now, know that Slack allows employees to quickly and easily find key messages, documents, and information.

I'll conservatively claim that you spend five minutes per day trying to find relevant messages and documents. That's nearly 20 hours per year — minimum. Once you get the hang of searching in Slack, that number may well drop by 90 percent.

Consolidate notifications

In a typical workplace, you'll find employees using a bunch of disparate applications on the job. (I certainly did when I started my career as a college professor. What's more, I still do, albeit to a lesser extent since going all-in on Slack.) I'm talking about

- Email
- A file storage and sharing tool, such as Box or Dropbox
- Text messages
- Social networks, such as Facebook and LinkedIn (often for work purposes)
- Homegrown company systems
- Reporting and data-visualization tools
- Popular enterprise systems
- Some type of instant-messaging tool, such Skype and Google Hangouts
- Productivity applications from Microsoft (Office) or Google (G Suite)

Oh, and then there's the telephone. After all, many companies still provide landlines for their employees.

Yikes.

Needless to say, there's no shortage of applications that bug employees from all angles. No, Slack won't obviate the need for proper spreadsheet, database, and word-processing programs. It won't run payroll or send your CEO a P&L

statement — *at least not yet*. (Chapter 12 looks at integrations with enterprise systems. In Chapter 15, I offer predictions about how Slack will continue in this direction.)

At organizations that have embraced Slack, though, many if not most employee internal application alerts come from one single, easily controllable source: Slack. Chapter 7 discusses Slack notifications in greater detail.

Reduce workplace-related stress

I'm no psychiatrist, but riddle me this: Say that you receive fewer emails and more contextual messages. Even better, you spend less time trying to find things. Wouldn't you experience less consternation at work?

Get to know your colleagues

One of the main paradoxes of the constantly connected workplace is that employees rarely get to know many of their colleagues. For this reason, companies such as Google, Facebook, and Zappos encourage their employees to interact with each other by offering free meals and holding after-hours social gatherings.

By encouraging friendly interactions, Slack provides the same benefit. Perhaps you and a random coworker belong to the same Slack channel. Based on your online discussions, you may decide to grab a cup of coffee or videochat for a few minutes. I've had many spontaneous interactions with colleagues over Slack myself.

TIP

There's even a third-party app for forging connections with colleagues and helping new hires get acclimated to their new environs. If this sounds appealing, check out the Slack Donut app. (Chapter 10 covers apps in much more detail.)

Smoothing the acclimation process for new hires

Think about the last time that you started a new job. Consider the following questions:

- Did the HR folks or your boss inundate you with lengthy emails from day one?
- Did that onslaught of information result in your missing a key deadline or incorrectly filling out a form?
- Did you soon feel overwhelmed?

With Slack, companies don't need to pepper their new hires with myriad emails and attachments. This approach can overwhelm them. Thanks to Slack, they can simply find relevant information in appropriate channels and digest it at their own pace. They can also easily set reminders within the app, minimizing the chance of forgetting to complete a key task.

Speaking of adjusting to a new environment, since Slack is so popular, employees can frequently hit the ground running. That is, they may understand how Slack works even though many firms use it differently. The result: Many new hires will need to learn one fewer new application when they start.

A TALE OF TWO COMPANIES

Consider the following fictional dichotomy:

At the Burns Power Plant, management forbids remote work. Employees spend at least 30 percent of their day in their inboxes, and IT bans employees from using any type of collaborative software — or at least tries. Its virtual private network and firewall prohibit screensharing. Support tickets usually take days to resolve. Its systems and data are a mess. No one can find what they need when they need it. The term *inefficient* comes to mind. As a result, employees often stay late and play catchup — something that the occasional free donut just doesn't make up for.

Now imagine Burns's polar opposite: Pied Piper, a file-compression startup located in Silicon Valley. The company's management is all in on Slack. New hires quickly realize that long email chains don't fly there. Screensharing and video calls with Eastern European contractors? Check. Being able to quickly find key information? No problem. Sure, Pied Piper personnel work hard, but they go home confident that they don't have to worry about missing urgent emails.

All else being equal, at which company would you want to spend a good portion of your waking hours? Which corporate culture sounds more appealing?

IN THIS CHAPTER

» Reviewing Slack's different plans and prices

» Navigating Slack's user interface

» Creating a Slack workspace

» Exploring the different Slack roles

» Inviting others to your Slack workspace

» Configuring your profile and account settings

Chapter 2
Getting Started with Slack

Slack significantly improves how people collaborate with each other in many ways. Of course, that won't happen unless you and your colleagues understand how to use it. This chapter discusses the mechanics behind Slack. It provides details on Slack's cost, its versions and different user roles, installation, and other key attributes.

Note that this chapter covers many of Slack's robust features but does not list all of them. There are just too many of them to provide a comprehensive list.

Reviewing Slack's Different Versions

Slack offers a number of different plans to its customers. To state the obvious: the Free version is the least expensive one.

Free plan

This starter plan allows organizations and their employees to try Slack gratis. The Free version lets you take advantage of a decent amount of Slack's functionality, but members under this plan can view only a workspace's most recent 10,000 messages. (I cover workspaces later in this chapter.) Older messages are inaccessible, even in search results. What's more, Slack restricts workspaces to ten third-party apps. If you attempt to add an eleventh, you'll receive this message:

```
Workspaces on free subscriptions can only install 10 apps and your workspace has
   reached the limit. You can add [app name] if you upgrade your workspace or
   remove one of your existing apps.
```

Slack's Free version doesn't entitle you to use all third-party apps for free in perpetuity; no version does. As I cover in Chapter 10, apps don't fall under Slack's pricing model. They operate under different plans altogether.

TIP

Slack does not impose a time limit on Free plans; they do not expire.

When it comes to upgrade options, as of this writing these three exist:

- Standard plan
- Plus plan
- Enterprise Grid

Throughout the text, I collectively refer to these options as *premium plans*.

Standard plan

Slack markets its least expensive paid option, the Standard plan, to small and midsized businesses. To be fair, though, nothing prevents groups or departments at larger firms from going this route.

Features under this premium plan include guest accounts, single sign-on, multi-workspace channels, and unlimited search. (If there are 257,123 messages in your workspace, then you can search them all.) Slack also throws in group calls, screen-sharing, and unlimited apps.

For this plan, Slack charges $6.67 per person when billed yearly and slightly more per user on a monthly basis.

Plus plan

Ideal for larger firms or those with advanced administration tools, Slack's Plus plan includes all features of the Standard plan. It also sports a guarantee of at least 99.99 percent uptime, enhanced security, data-export functionality, customized message retention, higher user storage limits, and 24/7 email support. For this plan, Slack charges $12.50 per person when billed yearly and slightly more on a monthly basis.

TIP

Yes, premium Slack plans lift the ten-app restriction. Don't expect, however, to be able to use all third-party apps for free.

Enterprise Grid

Enterprise Grid represents Slack's newest, most robust, and priciest offering. The industrial-strength, all-you-can-eat plan is ideal for massive organizations that have gone all-in on Slack. Prominent customers include IBM, Target, and *The New York Times*. Enterprise Grid appeals to firms that require more granular security features, unlimited licenses, phone support, an insane 1 terabyte of storage per member, and other powerful features.

Slack doesn't list the price of Enterprise Grid plan on its website. Still, it's fair to assume two things. First, the annual fee is considerable. Second, that cost varies based on the number of users in the firm. In reality, a 20,000-employee firm may ultimately save money by purchasing Enterprise Grid. Think about the total per-user monthly fees that it would incur by paying for the Slack Plus plan.

TIP

People tend not to marry their spouses without having dated them first. Along the same lines, it's typically wise to try one of Slack's other premium plans before signing up for Enterprise Grid.

REMEMBER

Throughout this book, I focus on the features that apply to all Slack plans. When necessary, I mention key Enterprise Grid features.

Changing your Slack plan

Slack allows its customers to easily upgrade and downgrade their plans.

Upgrading

To upgrade from one Slack plan to a more robust one, follow these steps:

1. **Click on the main menu.**
2. **From the drop-down menu, select Settings & administration and then Workspace settings.**

   Slack launches a window or tab in your default browser.
3. **Click on the rocket icon on the top right-hand corner of the page.**

   Slack presents a pop-up menu with all options as well as a link to compare plans.
4. **Select your desired plan and follow the additional instructions.**

Slack walks you through the upgrade process. Once you're successful, you receive an email from Slack and a Slackbot message confirming your upgrade that resembles the one displayed in Figure 2-1.

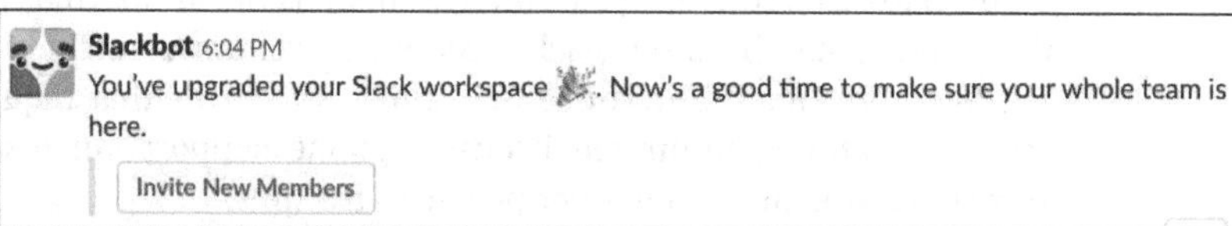

FIGURE 2-1: Slackbot upgrade confirmation message.

Upgrading your organization's Slack plan is a *binary*. That is, you can't upgrade yourself to a premium plan while keeping the other members on the free plan. This arrangement makes sense because Slack is a *team* tool, not an individual one.

Downgrading

Your firm can downgrade its Slack plan. Depending on your new plan, it will

- Lose access to certain Slack features.
- Use remaining Slack features to a more limited extent.
- Need to change channel access for existing guests.

To downgrade, follow the same instructions in the previous section but select a "lesser" plan.

For more on the specific consequences of downgrading your Slack plan, go to `bit.ly/sl-downgr`.

Describing Slack's cost structure

What if Slack magically solved every conceivable workplace and employee issue, but cost $1 million per employee per year? (It doesn't, but bear with me here.) Even if Slack could wave its magic wand, few employers would even consider it because its price would be prohibitive. Maybe professional sports teams could justify this cost.

Luckily, Slack is remarkably affordable — something that appeals to cost-conscious organizations. Because of Slack's robust functionality, the juice is more than worth the squeeze.

Starting quickly with Slack

Slack is one of many software vendors to embrace the *freemium* business model. As such, prospects can begin using Slack and many of its features within minutes and at no cost. Employees unlock additional goodies when their employers upgrade. (Parts 2 and 3 delve deeper into exactly what you can do with Slack.)

I've spent a good bit of my career seeing firsthand how executives actively resist new technologies. The reasons vary, but near the top of the list is a sometimes reasonable fear of being locked into long-term contracts and expensive consulting engagements. As I write these words, multiyear IT projects are alive and well.

Again, Slack operates under a different model. Firms can get going almost instantly. Even better, Slack does not require long-term commitments; management can opt to renew the tool every month. What if, for whatever reason, Slack doesn't take at your organization? After all, no software vendor bats a thousand. (Chapter 13 emphasizes strategies for successful adoption.) The financial harm is minimal, especially compared to traditional software purchases and implementations.

Paying only for what you use

As the nearby sidebar illustrates, Slack has wisely adopted the SaaS model. Because of this decision, its clients can more efficiently allocate their capital. The rise of cloud computing means that organizations can run Slack without owning and maintaining any hardware themselves.

This dynamic represents a sea of change from 25 years ago. As a result, if only 50 employees at Speaker City need Slack's premium features, then Slack bills the company for only 50 seats. Speaker City's CIO wouldn't need to purchase pricey servers and software, much less hire IT-support folks to keep the lights on.

A COMICALLY BRIEF HISTORY OF ENTERPRISE TECHNOLOGY

Throughout the 1980s and '90s, many organizations purchased enterprise software licenses for bulky, expensive systems. These firms paid handsomely for the rights to acquire the vendors' software, attendant consulting services, and annual support fees. The latter typically cost upwards of 20 percent of the sale price — annually to boot. The notion of paying "by the user" simply wasn't a viable pricing model back then. Needless to say, internal IT costs frequently skyrocketed, and I haven't even mentioned hardware requirements and routine upgrades.

At least firms got some bang for the buck, right? Sometimes, but not as often as you'd expect. Despite outsize costs, employees would sometimes fail to use their employer's fancy new wares, frustrating plenty of CIOs in the process. I have seen firsthand examples of what industry insiders affectionately call *shelfware*. Organizations pay ungodly sums of money for applications that effectively sat on virtual shelves.

Pricing rigidity started to soften in the late 1990s thanks to the explosion of the web. Vendors such as Salesforce.com pioneered a new pricing model: *software as a service* (SaaS). In a nutshell, organizations don't buy the software; they rent it on a monthly or annual basis. Today, myriad firms have embraced SaaS as a business model. Slack is one of many.

REMEMBER

Popular alternatives to Slack exist. Chapter 14 lists the main ones — a few of which are open-source. It's not entirely accurate to think of open-source tools as free, though. As the popular saying goes, think free speech, not free beer.

Reviewing accounting considerations

Those with accounting backgrounds should be able to differentiate between the following:

- Purchasing and deploying a SaaS tool, such as Slack
- Purchasing and deploying software in the mode prevalent 25 years ago

Organizations generally treat Slack and its ilk as an *operating expense* (OPEX). That is, the business needs to spend this money to function now and on a daily basis. At the other end of the spectrum is a *capital expense* (CAPEX), one that businesses incur to realize a potential benefit in the future. I'm no accountant, but I do know that bean counters, company presidents, and chief financial officers (CFOs) generally prefer the flexibility and lower costs of OPEX to CAPEX.

Beginning Your Slack Journey with the Workspace

What if I go old school for a moment and forget about contemporary technology? Imagine a world without computers, smartphones, apps, and even the Internet.

Think about a massive brick-and-mortar town hall meeting. Everyone can gather around for a group announcement. Most of the real action, however, takes place in an informal, decentralized manner. Attendees break out into different groups based on their interests. They engage in wildly different, meaningful, and focused discussions on the issues that most resonate with them. Everyone shares ideas and opinions. They offer meaningful solutions to problems. They reach agreement on key town issues. They vote to break deadlocks. Even better, someone in each group takes copious notes and meticulously files them. As a result, anyone can look up who said what when and why. This context is critical.

This town hall meeting is a decidedly low-tech version of Slack's starting point: the *workspace*. Formerly called a *team*, it is a cohesive amalgam of different technologies and communication tools, including:

- Channels (think chat rooms)
- Individual and group instant messaging
- Powerful search capability
- Screensharing (for customers on premium plans)
- Video calling
- And many others

What if you put all the ingredients above in a large pot and started cooking? You'd wind up with a scrumptious technological bouillabaisse called a workspace. I break down each of these individual components in subsequent chapters in this book.

TIP

Customers on Slack's Enterprise Grid plan need to know about the *organization*. This entity sits above an individual workspace; it serves as a meta-container. Think of a workspace as one big container of channels. In this vein, an org comprises all of the other containers. Of course, if your employer does not pay for Enterprise Grid, then pretend that the idea of an org doesn't exist because it doesn't.

Creating a new Slack workspace

To create a new Slack workspace, go to `https://www.slack.com/create`. You can create as many workspaces as you like but only one at a time. In my case, I belong to more than a dozen because I set one up for each of my classes every semester.

TIP

If employees at your organization already use a Slack workspace and you want to join it, skip the following steps and proceed to the next section.

Depending on what you do and how your organization uses Slack, you may belong to a number of different workspaces as I do. When I talk to people about the best ways to use Slack, I recommend that they start with one and add new ones only as needed.

Follow these directions:

1. **From `https://www.slack.com/create`, enter your email address, and click on the Next button.**

   Slack sends you a six-digit confirmation code. Don't close this browser window or tab. You need that code in the next step.

2. **Retrieve that code from your email and enter it on the page from Step 1.**
3. **Enter the name of your organization or team and press Enter or click on the Next button.**
4. **Enter the name or purpose of your workspace's project and press Enter or click on the Next button.**

   Slack creates a workspace with this name as well as the `#random` and `#general` channels. (Chapter 3 covers channels in far more depth. For now, just think of them as buckets within your workspace in which users discuss specific topics.)

5. **(Optional) Enter the email addresses of people you want to invite to this workspace.**

   You can also copy an invite link to email to anyone you like. Of course, you can skip this step and always add workspace members at a later date. Slack has now created your workspace.

6. **Click on the See Your Channel in Slack button.**

   Slack launches the workspace in a new browser tab or window. By default, Slack places your cursor in the new channel within the workspace.

7. **Click on the Finish Signing Up button.**
8. **Enter your full name and a strong password. Then click on the Next button.**

9. **Name your workspace.**

The value in this field defaults from Step 3, but you can rename it here. You can also change the first part of your workspace's URL as long as it's available. Ultimately, your workspace URL will look like this:

```
https://[workspacename].slack.com
```

TECHNICAL STUFF

URL stands for Uniform Resource Locator. Think of it as a web address.

10. **Press Enter or the click on the Next button.**

11. **(Optional) Add others' email addresses or copy a link to share with them via text, email, or any other communication tool or app.**

You can also let anyone whose email address shares your domain sign up for the app. If you invite others here, you see a confirmation page.

12. **Click on the Start the Conversation button.**

You see your new Slack workspace. You can start communicating and collaborating with others in Slack.

WARNING

If your organization has purchased Slack's Enterprise Grid plan, then it may follow a different process. That is, only Workspace Owners and Admins may be allowed to follow the preceding steps.

TIP

If you create several workspaces and decide later that you want to consolidate them, you can. See Chapter 11 for more details.

Signing in to an existing Slack workspace

Slack gives users two options when they want to log into an existing workspace:

- Requesting and receiving an email invitation
- DIY

REQUESTING AND RECEIVING AN EMAIL INVITATION

Contact the person or department responsible and ask for an email invitation. After a Workspace Owner or Admin adds you to the workspace, you will receive an invitation similar to the one shown in Figure 2-2.

Sign up by clicking on the Join Now button in the email.

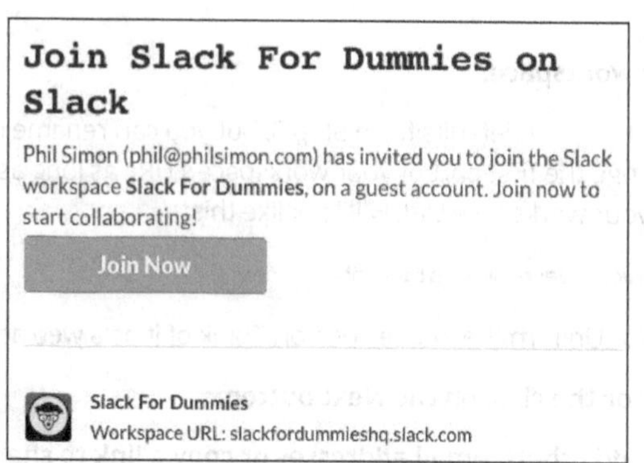

Join Slack For Dummies on Slack
Phil Simon (phil@philsimon.com) has invited you to join the Slack workspace Slack For Dummies, on a guest account. Join now to start collaborating!
Join Now
Slack For Dummies
Workspace URL: slackfordummieshq.slack.com

FIGURE 2-2: Slack workspace email invitation.

DOING IT YOURSELF

The Workspace Owner or Admin at your organization may have enabled an open signup process. If this is the case, then you don't need a person to invite you to the workspace.

For example, consider the following hypothetical example. Marillion permits anyone with a valid `@marillion.com` email to sign up. As a result, employees don't need to receive formal workspace invitations. Rather, they can just visit `https://marillion.slack.com` and sign up.

What if I am a Marillion employee, though, but I don't know the URL of my company's workspace? Slack's got me covered. I just go to `https://slack.com/signin` and click on the Find your workspace link. Slack then takes me to the page shown in Figure 2-3.

I choose the first option on Slack and enter `phil@marillion.com` as my email address. Slack attempts to verify three things:

- The email address `phil@marillion.com` does in fact exist.
- `phil@marillion.com` can indeed access an existing workspace.
- `https://marillion.slack.com` is the URL of that workspace. (In fact, you can use the same email address to join multiple workspaces, and Slack identifies them all.)

Slack indicates as much in the browser, as Figure 2-4 shows:

After Slack has verified all three of these facts, it then sends me an email that includes a unique link to the workspace. After clicking on it, I am able to do the following:

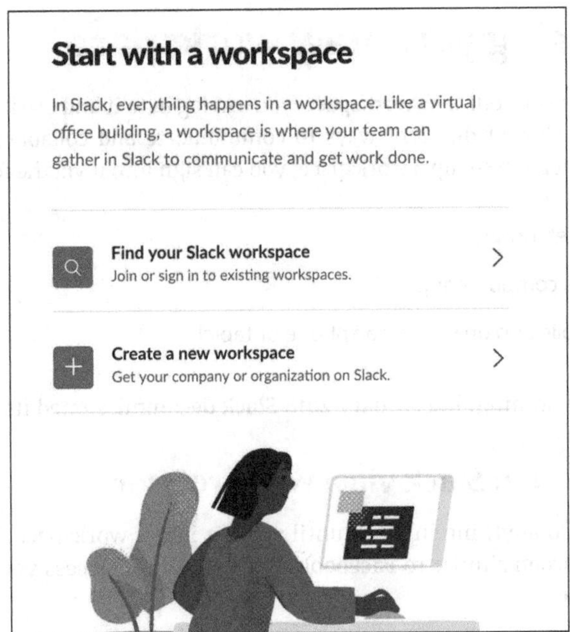
Start with a workspace
In Slack, everything happens in a workspace. Like a virtual office building, a workspace is where your team can gather in Slack to communicate and get work done.
Find your Slack workspace
Join or sign in to existing workspaces.
Create a new workspace
Get your company or organization on Slack.

FIGURE 2-3: Slack Start with a workspace page.

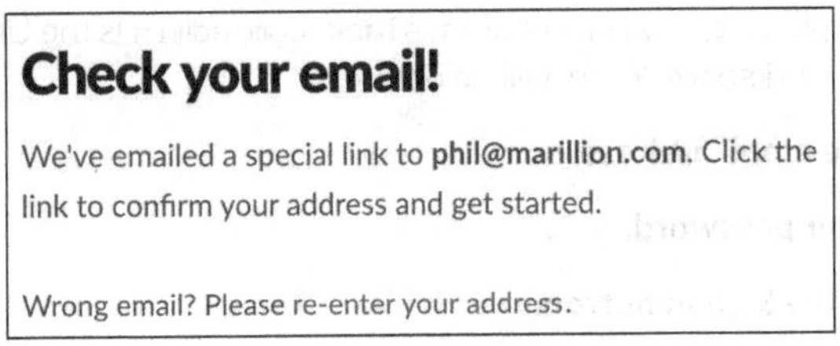

Check your email!

We've emailed a special link to **phil@marillion.com**. Click the link to confirm your address and get started.

Wrong email? Please re-enter your address.

FIGURE 2-4: Slack browser email-confirmation message.

- Create a Slack account.
- Sign in to the existing Marillion workspace.
- Start communicating with my colleagues.

I'll return to the subject adding others to your workspace later in this chapter. (See "Expanding your existing workspace.") It's imperative, though, that I cover a few other things first.

TIP

Visit `https://slack.com/signin/find` to locate any existing workspaces already associated with your email address.

Accessing your new workspace

After you create your new workspace, you can log in to it and use it. Brass tacks: Slack provides a slew of different ways to communicate and collaborate with your colleagues. After you set up a workspace, you can sign into it via the following methods:

- Any web browser
- Slack's computer app
- A mobile app on your smartphone or tablet

Apropos of nothing, in February 2018 Slack decommissioned its Apple Watch app.

Signing in to Slack via a web browser

You can't do anything in Slack until you log into a workspace. In this sense, it's a walled garden similar to Facebook. Here's how you access your workspace via a web browser:

1. **Enter your workspace's URL.**

   For example, `https://philsimon.slack.com/admin` is the URL for my personal workspace. Yours will be different.

2. **Enter the email address.**
3. **Enter your password.**
4. **Click on the Sign in button.**

As you'd expect, you can reset your password if you forgot it by clicking on the related link. Also, say that you forget the URL of your workspace. On the same page, simply type your email address. Slack sends a message containing all of the URLs for all the workspaces associated with that email address.

Using the Slack desktop app

I prefer using the app, not a web browser. I suspect that many if not most current users find it easiest to use the Slack app that corresponds to their computer's operating system. If your desktop or laptop runs MacOS, Windows, or even Ubuntu/Linux, Slack's got you covered.

TIP

Get started by going to `https://slack.com/downloads`.

Download the Slack app and install it for your computer. In this way, Slack is just like any other contemporary computer program. Of course, the exact process will hinge on your computer's specific operating system. Keep your workspace name, email address, and password handy, and you shouldn't have any problems. Once you log in to your workspace, you can start using Slack in earnest.

TIP

You may love Slack's desktop app. I certainly do. I guarantee, though, that you'll spend at least a little time using Slack in a web browser. Slack forces users to perform certain functions and configure a few settings exclusively via a browser.

Accessing Slack on mobile devices

Slack wouldn't be a very useful tool today if you could only use it on proper computers. After all, it's not 1998. Fortunately, you can any install the Slack mobile app on just about any device running a contemporary version of iOS and Android. Just follow these steps:

1. **Go to the app store on your phone or tablet.**
2. **Install Slack as you would Spotify, Facebook, or any other phone or tablet app.**
3. **Log in with your credentials.**

TIP

I recommend that you install Slack on your mobile device. If you're worried about your phone blowing up with Slack notifications, don't be. Chapter 5 covers how to customize them and keep your sanity in the process.

TIP

Slack automatically synchronizes data across devices. For example, say that you post a message in the `#announcements` channel from your Samsung Galaxy Note 10+ phone while at the gym. You immediately see the same message in Slack on your laptop — provided, of course, that you're connected to the Internet.

Meeting Slackbot

After you join a workspace, expect to meet Slackbot. Its purpose is to send you automatic tips about how to use the application. Figure 2-5 displays one of these gentle reminders about how to get the most out of Slack.

Hi, Slackbot here!
Feel free to ask me simple questions about Slack, like: How do I add a profile photo?
By the way, adding a photo will help everyone you work with! Here's a handy link or two:
Edit profile
Add apps

FIGURE 2-5: Slackbot introductory message with tips.

Introducing the Slack user interface

Slack has created an intuitive and user-friendly application that you'll love using. On a conceptual level, its user interface (UI) contains seven main design elements:

- **Sidebar:** Easily navigate Slack's views for Threads, Mentions & reactions, Drafts, Saved, Channels, People, Apps, and Files.
- **Main workspace menu:** Allows you to invoke valuable options and settings.
- **Workspace switcher:** Easily jump to different workspaces.
- **Main navigation bar:** Fixed bar for moving within a workspace, performing searches and viewing history.
- **Page header:** Fixed header that always lets you know exactly where you are in Slack.
- **Page:** The main "work area" for the selected view.
- **Detail view:** Presents more information and options for each view.

Regardless of your employer's plan and how it uses Slack, these elements exist in all workspaces. Figure 2-6 presents a conceptual overview of the Slack UI:

Figure 2-6 may look great in the abstract, but how does it translate to an actual Slack workspace? To answer that question, I present Figure 2-7.

By way of overview, three useful Slack buttons always appear in its main navigation bar. As such, you can access them in all Slack views. Each of these buttons works like comparable features on your favorite web browser:

- **Previous button (left arrow):** Takes you to your previous screen.
- **Next button (right arrow):** If you clicked on Previous, then click here to go forward.
- **History (clock):** View your most recent locations.

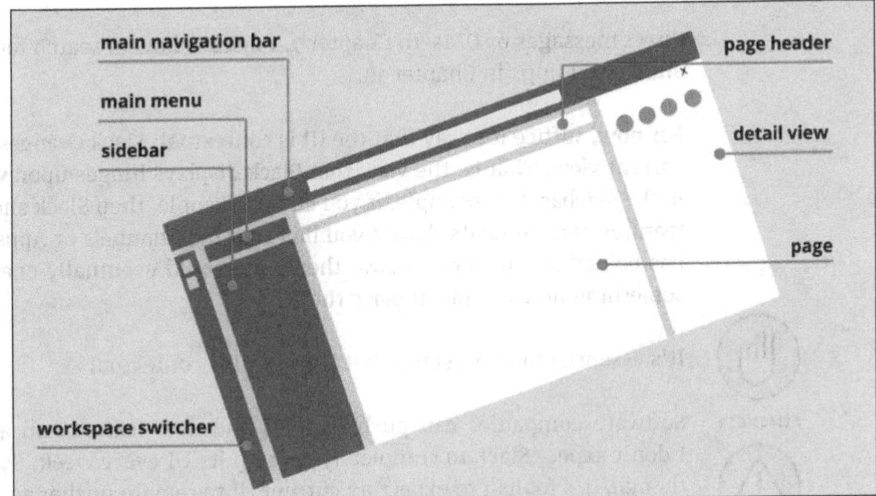

FIGURE 2-6: High-level diagram of the UI of a Slack workspace.

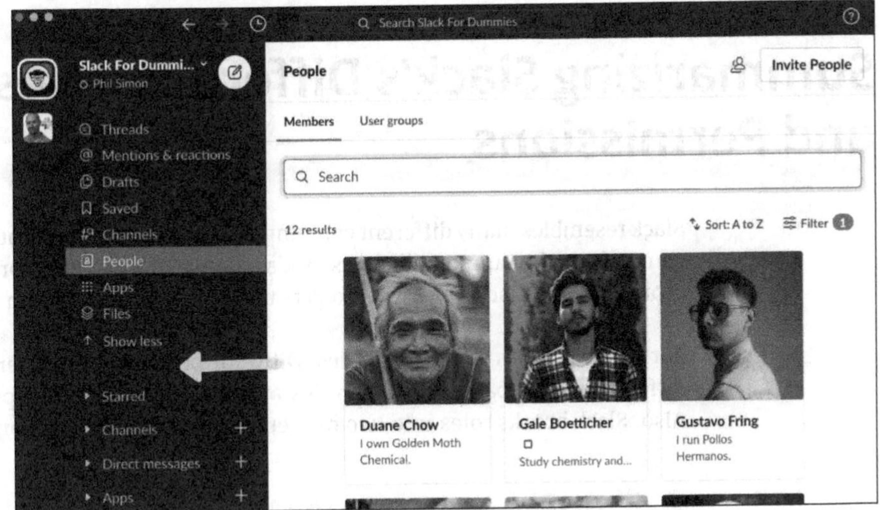

FIGURE 2-7: Sample Slack workspace with People view selected in sidebar.

These buttons help you easily navigate Slack. Get used to them.

To make things as easy as possible to understand, I inserted a yellow arrow in Figure 2-7 that highlights a narrow bar in the sidebar — one that you won't find in Slack. In this text, I refer to the two halves of the sidebar separated by that horizontal bar. The top half of the sidebar lies above it; the bottom half lies below it.

Don't let Figures 2-6 and 2-7 overwhelm you. I devote significant space in the forthcoming pages to Slack's robust features. For example, Chapter 4 addresses direct messages or DMs. In Chapter 7, I discuss how to search for specific content, and I cover apps in Chapter 10.

For now, suffice it to say that the UI is contextual: Slack changes based upon your current view. That is, the view that Slack displays hinges upon what you selected in the sidebar. For example, if you click on People, then Slack shows you different features and elements than if you had selected Channels or Apps. Finally, if Slack has bolded one of these views, then you should eventually check it out because something new has taken place there.

REMEMBER

It's essential to understand that Slack's UI is contextual.

WARNING

Software companies can push updates and new features on a daily basis. No, I don't expect Slack to completely revamp its UI every week. By the same token, though, it's foolish to expect its current UI to remain unchanged for the next five years.

Summarizing Slack's Different Roles and Permissions

Slack resembles many different contemporary applications on a number of levels — some of which you most likely use today. Consider user roles for a moment. They represent how Slack governs who gets to do what within a given workspace.

For starters, roles are not binaries. Ditto for permissions. Different users can do different things based on their roles and the organization's specific Slack plan. Also, Slack breaks roles into two buckets: administrative and non-administrative.

Administrative roles

This section describes Slack's three different administrative roles for all plans save for Enterprise Grid. (See the section "Enterprise Grid roles and permissions" later in this chapter.)

Primary Workspace Owner

Slack initially designates the person who creates the workspace as the *Primary Owner*. This special type of Owner technically outranks any other Workspace Owner and sits atop the pecking order. Primary Owners can do everything that Workspace Owners can do as well as the following tasks:

- Demote Workspace Owners
- Transfer the role of Primary Owner to someone else
- Delete workspaces

Note that Slack bills an organization's Primary Owner, not each of its employees. That is, individual members need not provide their credit card information to Slack.

An organization can assign only one Primary Owner per workspace at a time, although an existing Primary Owner can designate someone else. (The idea of designating multiple Primary Owners just doesn't make sense.) To determine your organization's Primary Owner, follow these steps:

1. **Click on the main menu.**
2. **From the drop-down menu, select Settings & administration and then Workspace settings.**

   Slack launches a new window or tab in your web browser.
3. **On the left side of the page, click on About this workspace.**
4. **Click on the Admins & Owners tab.**

Workspace Owners

Slack grants Workspace Owners the next highest workspace privileges. Permissions here include managing members, administering channels, setting security controls, exporting data, and handling other essential administrative tasks. Slack allows you to assign multiple individuals to the role of Workspace Owner although only one person can occupy the role of Primary Owner.

This begs the question: Which people at your employer should occupy the role of Workspace Owner? The answer depends on many factors, but typical examples include

- Company presidents and founders
- At large organizations, senior leaders and/or department heads — for example, a chief marketing office (CMO) may serve in this role for her company's marketing workspace
- For a semester-long college class, the professor teaching the course
- For informal groups or families, the person or people who started the workspace

Workspace Admins

While they aren't exactly slouches, Workspace Admins wield less power than Workspace Owners do. For example, they can't view billing statements, but they can still do quite a bit. Specifically, they can manage members, perform additional actions on channels, and handle other key administrative tasks. Finally, a Workspace Admin may also restrict others' rights to install third-party apps.

TIP

Slack does not limit the number of Owners and Admin accounts that you can assign to a workspace. Make sure that you trust each of them, though. To borrow an oft-used line from *Spiderman*, "With great power comes great responsibility."

Non-administrative roles

Relatively few people in your firm will be Workspace Owners and Admins. The vast majority of Slack users at your employer will occupy the following non-administrative roles.

Members

Members belong to existing workspaces but lack the administrative rights of Workspace Owners and Admins. Their privileges generally include sending messages as well as joining, creating, and posting in channels. You may allow them to invite guests to your workspace. (Chapter 8 details more about locking down the tasks that they can perform.)

Let's say that you've invited Steve to your workspace but he hasn't accepted your invitation yet. Technically, Slack considers him an *invited* member, but that's not an official role. Slack places a square icon to the left of the person's name in the bottom half of the sidebar.

TIP

Slack places circle icons next to members' names in the bottom half of the sidebar.

REMEMBER

Roles are workspace-specific. You may be a member of one workspace but an Admin or Owner of another.

Guests

You hire Marie, an independent contractor. You want her to hold a single one-day training session at your company. Should you add her as a full Slack member? Is the juice worth the squeeze? Should your organization pay Slack's monthly user fee for her to use it? Maybe, but Slack provides some options for this scenario.

Under Slack's premium plans, Workspace Admins, Workspace Owners, and members can create and manage two types of guest accounts:

- Multichannel guests
- Single-channel guests

MULTI-CHANNEL GUESTS

Multi-Channel Guests (MCGs) can join the channels that the inviting workspace member has previously designated.

TIP

Slack places squares to the left of MCGs names in the bottom half of the sidebar.

REMEMBER

Under the Plus and Standard plans, Slack charges monthly or annual fees for all members. For example, if your workspace consists of an admin, seven members, and two MCGs, then Slack charges you for all ten users. In this scenario, nobody rides for free.

SINGLE-CHANNEL GUESTS

When Single-Channel Guests (SCGs) join a Slack workspace, they belong to one predetermined channel. That is, SCGs can't join random ones. On the pricing front, only customers under premium plans can add SCGs. Slack caps this number at five per paid workspace member. For example, the Bluth Company pays for six user licenses. As such, a maximum of 30 total SCGs can join its workspace.

TIP

Slack places sideways triangle-shaped icons to the left of the names of SCGs in the bottom half of the sidebar.

Managing member roles

Slack realizes that things change over time. As long as your role permits and someone with greater privileges hasn't disabled the feature, you can elevate or downgrade members' roles in Slack.

WARNING

Tread lightly when promoting members to Owners and Admins. Your role may not permit you to demote them later. As a result, you'd have to involve someone else.

If you want to change someone's current role, follow these steps:

1. **Click on the main menu.**
2. **From the drop-down menu, select Settings & administration.**

3. **From the sub-menu that appears on the right, select Manage members.**

   Slack launches a new window or tab in your web browser.

4. **Click on the ellipsis on the right that corresponds to that member.**
5. **Click on Change account type.**
6. **Click on the radio button to the left of the new role.**
7. **Click on the green Save button.**

REMEMBER

Members and guests can't alter their own roles — never mind the roles of others. That is, they can't elevate themselves to Owners or Admins or demote themselves. A workspace member already in an administrative role needs to make this change.

Changing guest access

Slack provides a few different options for handling guests. For example, Workspace Owners and Admins can do the following:

- Demote members to single- or multichannel guests
- Upgrade guests to members

For example, say that Steven owns Porcupine Tree Music (PTM), a quirky London-based music store that uses Slack. He frequently hires subcontractors for different reasons. Steven always invites them to the PTM workspace as SCGs. In the workspace, they coordinate details about events, payments, and other details.

One of Steven's subcontractors is Gavin. He holds a few drum clinics at PTM, and they go well. Gavin's got mad chops. Steven decides to hire Gavin as a full-time employee. Gavin gleefully accepts. To quote Homer Simpson, "Done and done."

Slack wouldn't be very flexible if Steven had to create a new account for guests such as Gavin. Fortunately, he doesn't need to do so. Steven can merely upgrade Gavin's account from SCG to member with all the accoutrements associated with his new status.

To upgrade a SCG to a member, simply follow the steps in the section "Managing member roles" earlier in this chapter.

WARNING

Depending on what you're trying to accomplish, you may need to change a member's role twice. For example, I have added Gale Boetticher as a SCG in my workspace, but now I want to make him an admin. I first have to make him a member before Slack lets me upgrade his role to an admin. In other words, in this case, there's no direct path between the two roles.

Deactivating member accounts

Say that a Slack guest just isn't working out. As the Slack admin, I want to remove the person as a guest and revoke access to my workspace. Follow these steps:

1. **Click on the main menu.**
2. **From the drop-down menu, select Settings & administration and then Workspace settings.**
3. **From the sub-menu that appears on the right, select Manage members.**

   Slack launches a new window or tab in your web browser.
4. **Click on the ellipsis on the far right that corresponds to the member you want to remove.**
5. **Click on Deactivate account.**

   Slack warns you that this action deactivates Gale from the workspace, but active members are still able to view his contributions.
6. **Click on the red Deactivate button.**

   The person is no longer an active member.

Note that Slack wisely grays out the names of deactivated members in the People view. You don't see them appear in the sidebar. See Figure 2-8.

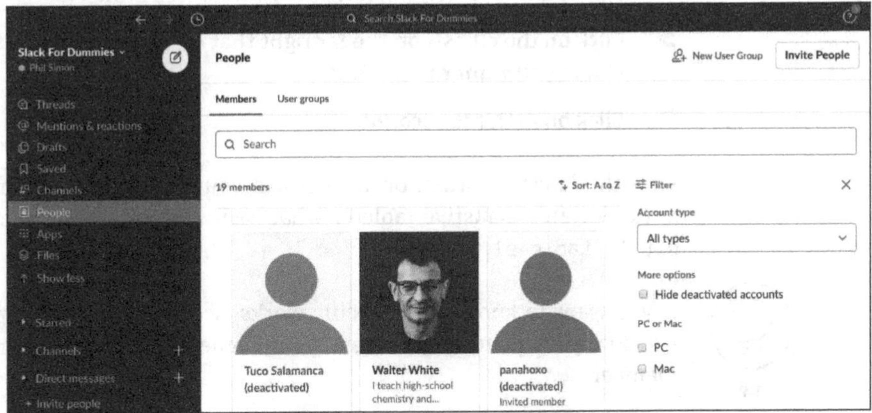

FIGURE 2-8: Deactivated accounts in the People view.

Slack disables the ability to send new messages to deactivated members. You can try, but you won't succeed.

Deleting member accounts

Before deactivation and if their settings permit, individual members can delete direct messages (DMs) and files. However, Slack doesn't let even workspace Owners and Admins delete entire members' accounts and histories — and it's not hard to understand why. After all, Slack stands for Searchable Log of All Conversation and Knowledge. The operative word here is *All*.

What if your firm fired an employee for engaging in inappropriate workplace behavior? For obvious reasons, HR would just as soon purge that employee from all records à la George Orwell's classic book *1984*. For legal reasons, though, Slack doesn't let even Workspace Owners rewrite history. At some point, a court, lawyer, or regulatory body may compel an organization to turn over information. As a company, Slack doesn't want to expose itself to liability. (For more details on this subject, see the nuanced discussion on exporting data in Chapter 11.)

Reactivating member accounts

Say that you want to reactivate a member's account after deactivating it. Simply go to the same member dashboard and follow these steps:

1. **Click on the main menu.**
2. **From the drop-down menu, select Settings & administration and then Manage members.**

   Slack launches a new window or tab in your web browser.
3. **Click on the ellipsis on the far right that corresponds to the member whom you want to reactivate.**
4. **Click on Activate account.**

Find the latest information on guest accounts and permissions at `bit.ly/sl-ch2x`. For an exhaustive table of what each role can and cannot do in Slack, see `bit.ly/table-sl`.

TIP

If you want to know your specific workspace role, go to your profile. Slack lists it below your picture and above your name. If you see nothing, then you're a member.

Transferring primary workspace ownership

If you're a Workspace Owner, then you can transfer primary ownership to a fellow Workspace Owner. Perhaps you're taking on a new role in the company or you're leaving for greener pastures.

WARNING

This move is immediate, and you can't reverse it by yourself.

Enterprise Grid roles and permissions

Slack's robust Enterprise Grid offering provides for additional administrative roles that transcend individual workspaces. In other words, on Slack's other plans, the Workspace Owner serves as its king or queen. With Enterprise Grid, however, two roles — Org Owner and Org Admins — effectively outrank the Workspace Owner.

Primary Org Owner

This individual retains the highest level of permissions. No one else can transfer ownership of the org. The person in this role can also do everything that Org Owners can do.

Org Owners

Think of Org Owners as seconds in command. As such, they can do the following:

- Determine an organization's app-management policies for all workspaces.
- Choose which settings individual Workspace Owners can enable and disable. (If you can't perform a "normal" task as a Workspace Owner under the Enterprise Grid plan, it's probably because an Org Owner has disabled that functionality.)
- Configure single security and access settings such as single sign-on and two-factor authentication. (Chapter 9 offers much more detail.)
- Configure single sign-on (SSO).

Org Admins

Org Admins can do almost everything that Org Owners can do with a few exceptions. For example, they can't override a workspace's app-management policy. For a comprehensive table of what Org Admins and Owners can and can't do, see `bit.ly/eg-slack`.

Starting Your New Workspace Off on the Right Foot

The Slack workspace is an unparalleled collaboration and communication tool. This chapter concludes by highlighting two critical things to do after you have created your workspace. First, you should invite others to join it. Second, you'll want to let your future Slack-mates know a bit about you.

Expanding your existing workspace

A recurring theme in this book is that Slack is a team tool, not an individual one. In case you forgot, you can invite members to your workspace when you create it. (See the section "Creating a new Slack workspace" earlier in this chapter.)

Your Slack workspace(s) will likely morph in ways that you don't expect. Mine certainly have. At some point, it will make sense to add new members. Invariably others will need to join in your reindeer games.

Fortunately, you don't have to put on your swami hat. You need not try to predict who'll benefit from your workspace in the future. Put differently, Slack makes it remarkably simple to add new members *after* your workspace is up and running.

Inviting others to your workspace

To invite others to your existing workspace, launch the Slack desktop app and follow these steps:

1. **Click on People in the sidebar.**
2. **Click on the white Invite People button.**

   Slack launches a new window.
3. **Select the person's role.**

   Note that the next steps will vary a bit based upon the specific role. In this example, I'll add a member.
4. **Enter the email addresses and, optionally, the names of the people you'd like to invite.**

   By default, Slack provides lines for two new members. You can Add Another or Add Many at Once. Just click on those links.
5. **(Optional) Set the specific channels to that new members will join if and when they accept your invitation.**

6. **(Optional) Compose a personalized message.**
7. **Click on the green Send Invitations button.**

When adding either type of new guest, Slack prompts you with the dialog box shown in Figure 2-9.

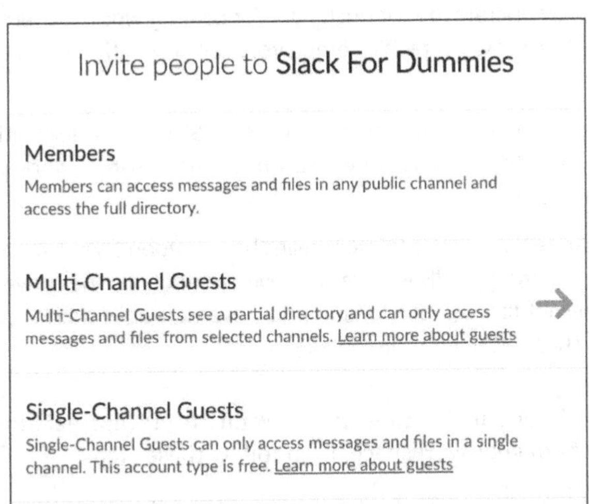

Invite people to Slack For Dummies
Members
Members can access messages and files in any public channel and access the full directory.
Multi-Channel Guests
Multi-Channel Guests see a partial directory and can only access messages and files from selected channels. Learn more about guests
Single-Channel Guests
Single-Channel Guests can only access messages and files in a single channel. This account type is free. Learn more about guests

FIGURE 2-9: Slack guest-account options.

Select the desired guest account. (Guests can't invite other guests to the workspace.)

TIP

In real life, you probably don't want your houseguests hanging around forever. Slack offers two options for deactivating guest accounts. (I told you that Slack was intuitive.) First, you can always manually disable a guest account whenever you want. Second, Slack allows you to automatically and preemptively deactivate a guest account after a fixed period of time or even on a specific date.

Restricting who can invite others to your workspace

Out of the box, Slack allows all members to invite others to join individual workspaces. (Guests lack this capability.) In October 2019, Slack smartly added some nuance to this feature. That is, Workspace Owners and Admins can limit a members' ability to invite other members to their companies' workspaces.

The reasons for adding a little friction to the workspace-signup process are manifold. Here are four:

- An organization uses a number of different workspaces for different reasons. As such, it wants to ensure that its employees, partners, and vendors join the proper ones.
- A firm may operate in an industry and/or country whose government imposes strict privacy laws over which employees can view different types of information.
- A budget-conscious small business pays for Slack's Standard or Plus plan. As a result, it wants to monitor how many members are in its workspace to limit its monthly costs.
- A human resources department relies heavily upon a workspace. As such, its discussions typically involve sensitive information. The conversations are certainly not fit for public consumption, even in public channels. (Chapter 3 covers channels in far more detail.)

Regardless of your motivation, if you want to prevent existing members from adding others to your workspace, then follow these steps:

1. **Click on the main menu.**
2. **From the drop-down menu, select Settings & administration and then Workspace settings.**

   Slack launches a window or tab in your default browser.
3. **Click on the Permissions tab at the top of the page.**
4. **Look for the word Invitations and then click on the white Expand button.**
5. **Check the box to require admin approval for invitations.**

   Optionally, you can determine the channel to which Slack sends invitations requests.
6. **Click on the green Save button.**

Configuring your member profile and key account settings

REMEMBER

Slack wants to be the place where work happens. It follows, then, that Slack needs to let members provide basic information about who they are and what they do.

Slack answers the call here by allowing members to create detailed profiles. Fields include email address, profile picture, phone number, and other key work-related information. Figure 2-10 shows the top part of my public workspace profile:

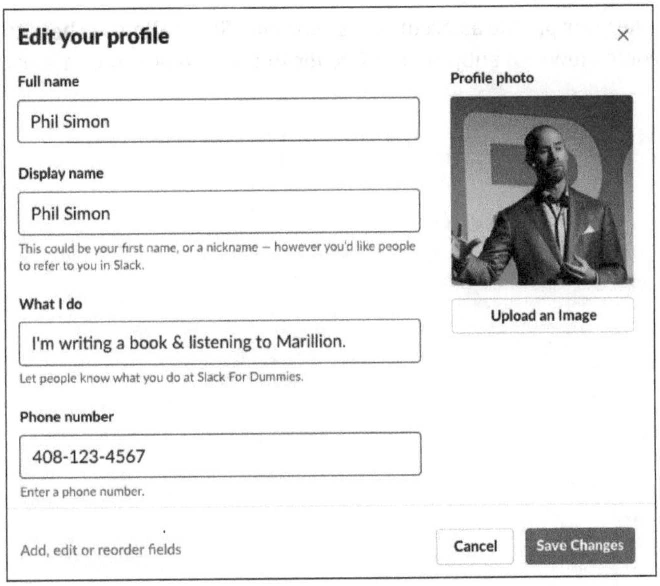

FIGURE 2-10: My Slack profile.

Note that more information exists under the buttons in Figure 2-10. To personalize your Slack profile, follow these steps:

1. **Click on the main menu.**
2. **From the drop-down menu, select View profile.**
3. **Click on the green Edit Profile button.**
   - *Profile photo:* This option is self-explanatory.
   - *Email address:* This is the email address that you use to sign in to Slack. Based upon your role and permissions, you may not be able to change it.
   - *Time zone*: Slack uses your time zone to send summary and notification emails (unless you have unsubscribed from them). With this information, Slack identifies times in your activity feeds and schedules reminders.
   - *Language: Choose language that you'd prefer to use when interacting with Slack.*
4. **Click on the green Save Changes button.**

To be sure, you can customize your profile in many other meaningful ways. For instance, customers of premium Slack plans can add a slew of different fields, such as manager name and Twitter and LinkedIn profiles. Chapter 8 delves much deeper into these options.

TIP

Make your profile as accurate as possible. Slack allows others to find you using the People view— a subject that I cover in more depth in Chapter 4.

2 Communicating Without Chaos

IN THIS PART

Create different types of channels

Target your communication

Send individual and group direct messages

Review and customize Slack notifications

» Introducing the concept of a Slack channel

» Describing the different types of Slack channels

» Creating, joining, and naming channels

» Performing additional channel actions

» Posting messages in channels

Chapter 3
Targeting Your Communication with Slack Channels

I'll bet that your relationship with email is complicated. Mine certainly is. You may lament the fact that you're always playing whack-a-mole with your inbox. At the same time, though, how else would you exchange messages with your colleagues, partners, customers, and vendors? Perhaps you've wondered if there's a legitimate alternative to email. After all, it's 2020.

If so, then you're in luck because Slack turns the traditional inbox model on its head. It offers superior options for communicating that leave email in the dust.

Let me be clear: Slack does not portend the death of email. If used properly, however, Slack will reduce the size of your inbox and reduce the rate at which it grows. You may even break your email addiction.

This chapter introduces one of Slack's pillars for promoting effective business communication and collaboration: channels.

Introducing Slack Channels

Think of Slack *channels* as individual buckets that promote discussion about a particular topic or set of topics. (I cover workspaces in Chapter 2.) Channels are big containers of information that you can make as specific or general as you like. Slack lets you customize channels until your heart's content.

At a high level, Slack users send and receive messages in two places:

- Within individual channels — the topic of this chapter.
- Outside channels via individual and group direct messages or DMs. The next chapter covers this subject.

Forget Slack for a moment. When employees join a company, the IT department creates email inboxes for them to send and receive messages. If Derrick leaves for greener pastures, then his inbox effectively dies.

Slack channels differ from email in this regard. They existed before Derrick arrived. Crucially, they will continue to exist after he leaves the company. Figure 3-1 shows how workspaces, channels, and direct messages all tie together.

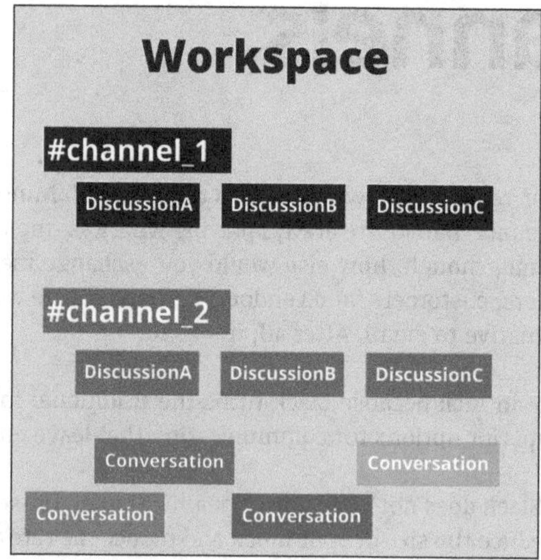

FIGURE 3-1: The basic Slack workspace communication structure.

Discussions take place inside of channels — the topic of this chapter. However, you need not debate everything in a channel. You can exchange thoughts and ideas with your colleagues via direct messages (DMs). Slack calls a string of DMs outside of channels *conversations*. Note that Figure 3-1 intentionally omits shared and multi-workspace channels for the sake of simplicity.

Slack channels allow you to keep discussions relevant to a particular topic. As such, you are able to accomplish a number of critical goals:

- You help others and yourself stay focused and organized. Channels allow people to subscribe only to their areas of personal and professional interest. That is, you can safely ignore topics that don't matter to you.
- Because Slack channels provide valuable context, you reduce the amount of time that you will need to process each message. (Given how many emails people currently receive every day, even a few seconds per message helps.)
- By using channels, you make finding information much easier. Slack users can restrict their searches to specific channels, if they like. (Chapter 7 explores Slack's native search functionality.)

When you create a new workspace, Slack automatically adds two public channels to it: `#general` and `#random`. By default, any member can post in `#general`. After that, as long as your role permits, you can set up and join as many or as few channels as you like. Slack roles restrict what users can do. (See Chapter 2 for more details.) You can also view the other members of public channels, and they can view you.

Exploring the Different Types of Slack Channels

As of this writing, Slack allows for four different types of channels depending on their plans:

- Public
- Private
- Multi-workspace channels (for Enterprise Grid customers only)
- Shared

Conceptually, each type of channel serves the same general purpose. In its simplest form, a channel represents a customizable container for discussions with others in the Slack universe. The differences are subtle but important. For instance, the primary differences between public and private channels lie in privacy settings and the ability for others to discover and join it.

REMEMBER

Regardless of the type of channel, only workspace members can access the information inside of it. Put differently, even public Slack channels aren't available to the general public.

Public channels

I want to introduce the idea of a public channel by keeping it as simple as possible:

- They generally exist within a specific Slack workspace. Exceptions to this rule occur when you share a channel with another organization. I'll get to these special types of channels at the end of this section.
- Other than single-channel guests, by default anyone in a workspace can join public channels. Of course, someone in an administrative role can disable this setting.
- Other than guests, anyone in a workspace can create public channels.

How can you use public channels? The applications are limitless. Figure 3-2 shows some of channels for a fictitious company.

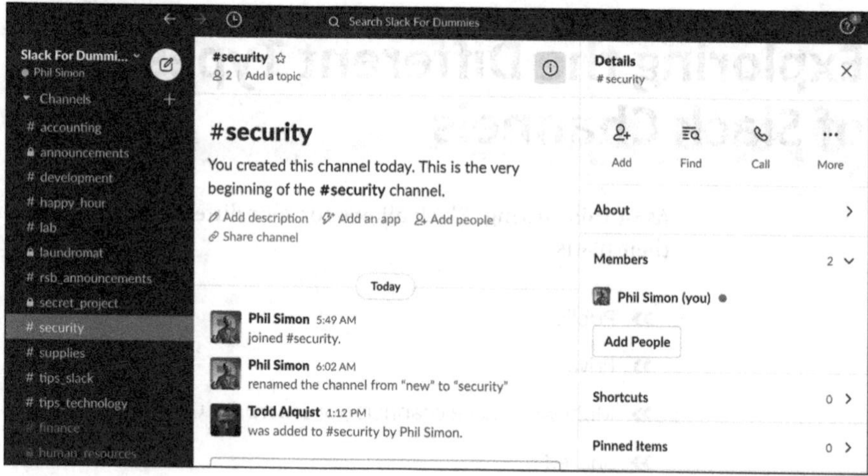

FIGURE 3-2: Workplace with channels.

The key point is this: Each channel serves a different purpose.

Here's a real-world example of how I use channels. As a college professor, I currently teach three sections of Introduction to Information Systems. In Slack, I use more than two dozen public channels for each class very semester. Examples include the following channels:

- **Each homework assignment:** I call these #hw1, #hw2, and so on.
- **General questions:** Students usually use #ask_the_professor if their questions that don't relate to specific homework assignments.
- **Writing tips:** I post tips in — wait for it — the #writing_tips channel.

No, you won't find any channels related to human resources or finance here. I could go on, but you get my point: Channels are very flexible.

TIP

I cover private channels in the following section, but note here that I use those as well. For example, over the course of the semester, I need to communicate with different teams of students about their specific projects. Only the members of #team_18 need to see my feedback for them. A public channel here just doesn't make sense.

Private channels

Like public channels, private channels also exist under a specific workspace. Public and private channels fundamentally serve the same purpose: to share context-specific information with a group of people. Any member in a Slack workspace can join — and contribute to — a public channel. The only exception to the latter is if the Workspace Owner or Admin has limited channel posting rights.

For example, an organization may create public channels for #company_news or #system_issues. The rationale here is simple: All employees should be able to view this critical company information. For confidential discussions in #payroll_issues, #research, and #hr_staffing_plans, however, discussions probably aren't fit for public consumption.

Unlike public channels, private channels appear only in users' channel directories if they are already a member of that private channel. Put differently, if you're not a member, then in theory you wouldn't know that a private channel even existed.

Unlike public channels, private ones require invitations to join. That is, you cannot browse private channels and join them.

GETTING THE HANG OF PUBLIC CHANNELS

My biggest gripe with the idea of a single, all-encompassing inbox is that one size does not fit all. Again, here's where Slack shines. You can create as many channels in each workspace as you like. As a result, employees can target their communication to others with far greater precision. Slack channels allow you to effectively segment messages to different groups of people. When people use Slack channels properly, they will annoy your colleagues less often with irrelevant messages.

Here are a couple examples of how Slack channels can build employee community while avoiding chatter that some prefer to ignore:

Scenario #1: What's for lunch?

Employees at a small marble manufacturer — call it Marillion Fabricators — often order lunch. A few times each week, someone will post a poll in the #general channel with different options, such as Chinese, pizza, or subs.

Lucy and Derek always bring their meals to work because of their dietary restrictions: Lucy is a vegan, and Derek is a pescatarian. As much as they would like to mute or leave the #general channel, they cannot. Sometimes Marillion employees post important company- and teamwide messages there. As a result, a few times per week, they'll see notifications that mean nothing to them. Slack in this case distracts them from their work and wastes some of their time.

The solution: Marillion should create and use a #lunch channel. That way, only employees who are interested can view those messages. Those who don't belong to the channel haven't missed a beat.

Scenario #2: Workplace humor

It's equally wise for employees to post only messages that are germane to a channel's purpose.

At Marillion Fabricators, Steve and Mark enjoy a good laugh at the office. A few times per week, they'll post a funny video or meme in #announcements. It's nothing inappropriate, and their intentions are benign. Ian and Pete, though, don't care much for humor on the clock. They are nice guys, but they are usually heads-down throughout the day.

Marillion creates a #humor channel, but Steve and Mark opt not to use it; they continue to post their hilarity in #announcements. In the process, they distract others. This is just bad form.

I'll bet that you can envision plenty of different scenarios in which segmenting messages would save employees time at your organization. If so, then you've grasped the main idea behind channels.

WARNING

You can leave a public channel at any time and rejoin at your leisure. However, if you leave a private channel, an existing member will need to invite you back.

This begs the question: How do you know if a particular channel to which you belong is public or private? If you see a lock icon to the left of the channel name, then it is private.

Returning to Figure 3-2, notice how the `#announcements` channel is private, but the `#supplies` and `#tips_slack` channels are public.

Note how `#secret_project` appears above the fray. This happens because I marked it as a favorite by clicking on the star icon. It then turns blue. Click on the icon again, and the channel will appear with the others because it ceases to be a favorite.

REMEMBER

When you add users to private channels, they will be able to see the entire history of all previous communications.

Multi-workspace channels

What if your organization uses Slack but different departments set up separate workspaces? Employees want to be able to send messages, share files, and collaborate within the same channel. Slack makes such scenarios possible though *multi-workspace channels* (MWCs).

TIP

You can skip this section if you're not using or considering Enterprise Grid.

TECHNICAL STUFF

Of course, a company could always try to fuse together multiple workspaces. Chapter 11 has more to say about that.

Say that you work in your company's finance department. You want to share a channel with your peers in accounting, even though the two groups use different workspaces. Follow these steps:

1. **Click on the channel name in the sidebar of the finance workspace.**
2. **Click on the information (i) icon in the top right-hand corner.**

   Slack displays a four-pane tab with the word Details above it.
3. **Click on the More icon on the far right.**

   Slack displays a panel underneath the icon.
4. **Click on Additional options.**

MULTI-WORKSPACE CHANNELS AT OCTAVARIUM UNIVERSITY

The Rudess School of Business (RSB) at Octavarium University lets each college create and independently operate its own Slack workspace. This means that professors in the Department of Information Systems and Psychology Department each play in their own sandboxes. (Sadly, professors in the schools' marketing, finance, HR, and management departments haven't embraced Slack yet.) Score one for autonomy, right?

But Jordan, the president of the university, needs to send all employees in both departments a message. Based on what you've learned so far, he has to post that message twice — once in channels in each department's workspace. Right?

Not exactly.

Slack's MWC eliminates the need for this redundancy. In this case, Workspace Owners at Octavarium create an MWC that transcends each of the individual workspaces for the two departments. They christen it #RSB_announcements. From this point forward, Jordan only needs to post an announcement once in that MWC, and members of both workspaces will be able to view it. Depending on their notification preferences, employees in each college would see it even though they belong to separate workspaces.

(In case you're wondering, the references in this example relate to the pro-metal band Dream Theater.)

5. **Select Add to other [organization name] workspaces.**

   Here you will locate the accounting workspace.

   Slack presents a search box with default text that reads Type a Team Name.

6. **Type a few letters of the workspace name with which you want to share this channel. When the workspace pops up, select it.**

7. **Click on the green Review Changes button.**

   Slack warns you if the same workspace name already exists in the "target" workspace. If that's the case, then rename the channel. I typically add an underscore when this happens. For example, `@announcements` becomes `@announcements_`.

   Slack confirms that all members of both workspaces will be able to join this channel. What's more, they will be able to see the channel's history and files.

8. **Click on the green Save Changes button.**

   Members of the finance workspace now may join the MWC, view its content, and contribute on their own.

Expect Slack to take a few minutes to make the channel available in the other workspace. In my experience, the process isn't instantaneous. Once Slack completes this process, you will see an overlapping circles icon to the right of the channel. Everyone will know that the channel now effectively exists in *both* workspaces.

Multi-workspace channels work really well for organizations that meet two conditions. Specifically, these large firms have purchased Slack's Enterprise Grid and rely upon multiple workspaces.

With Enterprise Grid, others can add you to a MWC without your consent at any point. If the MWC is public, then you can leave it if you like and rejoin it later. If the MWC is private, then you can leave it but you'll need another invite to rejoin it.

Shared channels

We live in a collaborative world. At some point, you may well want to use Slack to work with people from other organizations and third-parties that also use Slack. Examples here include vendors, clients, and partners. What if you want to share a specific channel with them? Wouldn't doing so allow you to seamlessly collaborate with them?

Customers of premium plans can choose to share channels with external organizations. (For a common scenario on why you would do this, see the sidebar, "Using shared channels to connect with partners" elsewhere in this chapter.)

Slack now allows up to ten different organizations to share the same channel. Of course, all organizations need to belong to a premium Slack plan. To share a channel with an external organization, follow these steps:

1. **In the sidebar, click on the name of the channel that you want to share with another organization.**
2. **Click on the information (i) icon in the top right-hand corner.**

   Slack displays a four-pane tab with the word Details above it.
3. **Click on the More icon on the far right.**
4. **From the drop-down menu, click Additional options.**
5. **Click on Share with another organization.**
6. **Copy the link that Slack generates so that you can share it with the person in the external organization.**
7. **Click on the green Done button.**

   You can email that link to the contact at the other organization. Alternatively, you can share the channel with another workspace that you own.

USING SHARED CHANNELS TO CONNECT WITH PARTNERS

Every year, Octavarium University welcomes corporate recruiters to its campus visits. Recruiters hold information sessions, participate in job fairs, and interview potential employees. For their part, students polish their resumes and get gussied up. They aspire to land jobs, start the next chapters of their lives, and gradually pay off their considerable student debt.

In the past, Octavarium's different career services departments posted all of this information on the school's website. While helpful, this approach doesn't lend itself to true conversations. As a result, recruiters with questions would send emails or fill out web forms. Octavarium folks answered the same questions dozens of times.

Because Slack has become engrained at Octavarium, the career services folks would like to make this process as seamless as possible. They'd like to create `#octavarium_job_info`, a single shared channel for *all* employers who visit its campus. The goal would be to easily convey details about upcoming events, logistics, and frequently asked questions for the recruiting season. The shared channel would eliminate the need to send the same email to dozens or hundreds of recruiters at different companies. Recruiters with simple questions would turn to Slack, not emails and web forms. This practice would also foster a sense of community among the recruiters, some of whom may become chummy and recognize each other when they descend upon the Octavarium campus.

8. **Paste that link into your web browser's address bar and hit Enter.**
9. **Select the workspace with which you want to share that channel.**

   Slack asks you to review and accept the channel's invitation.

   If the "receiving" workspace is on the Slack Free plan, then Slack will prompt you to start a trial to a premium plan. You'll have 14 days to kick the tires on this paid feature.
10. **Click on the green Accept Invitation box.**

    Slack has now successfully shared your channel with another organization's workspace. Slack now places two overlapping diamonds to the right of the channel to indicate that it's shared. Also, Slackbot notifies all invitees that they now belong to the channel. Note that if the invitee doesn't belong to a premium plan, then Slackbot notify will post a message with upgrade instructions.

TIP

If your organization is using Enterprise Grid, then one of its Org Owners or Admins may need to approve your request to share a channel with an external organization.

Creating Public and Private Channels

You create as many channels as you like. Each channel requires a unique name. That is, you can't create two `#development` channels within the same workspace. Also, you'll want to give your channels descriptive names. For example, you don't want to christen your company's marketing channel `#payroll`. Put differently, there's a big difference between *can* and *should*. When naming channels, common sense goes a long way.

Next, understand that Slack bans certain words in channel names. Table 3-1 lists Slack's current reserved words by language.

TABLE 3-1 Reserved Slack Words as of April 1, 2020

Language	Forbidden Words
Brazilian Portuguese	aquí, canais, canal, eu, general, geral, grupo, mí, todos
English	archive, archived, archives, all, channel, channels, create, delete, deleted-channel, edit, everyone, general, group, groups, here, me, ms, slack, slackbot, today, you
French	chaîne/chaine, général/general, groupe, ici, moi, tous
Spanish	aquí, canal, general, grupo, mí, todos

If you attempt to create a channel using one or more of the terms in Table 3-1, you see the following message:

```
That name is already taken by a channel, username, or user group.
```

TIP

When you create a channel Slack, carefully avoid the terms referenced in Table 3-1, and still receive a similar message. Chances are that Slack has added the word after this book's publication. You can view the most updated list of reserved terms by going to `bit.ly/sl-ch-nm` as well as banned Japanese symbols.

Creating your first public channel

Now you know more about the concept of a channel and some restrictions on names. It's time to create a simple one. The following steps walk you through creating a public channel in your Slack workspace.

I'm intentionally showing you how to create a basic channel in the following section. In reality, though, you'll want to put some thought into how you and others name and describe the channels in your workspace. (For more on this, see the section "Building an intelligent channel structure" later in this chapter.)

1. **Click on the plus icon next to Channels in the Slack sidebar.**

   Slack displays the window in Figure 3-3.

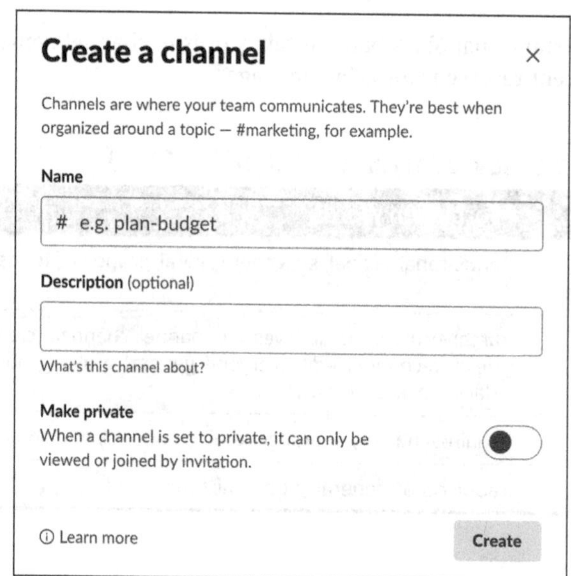
Create a channel
Channels are where your team communicates. They're best when organized around a topic — #marketing, for example.
Name
e.g. plan-budget
Description (optional)
What's this channel about?
Make private
When a channel is set to private, it can only be viewed or joined by invitation.
Learn more
Create

FIGURE 3-3: Slack prompt for creating a new channel.

2. **Enter a name for your channel.**

   Keep the following rules and suggestions in mind:

   - The current character minimum is 1; the maximum is 80.
   - I'm a fan of underscores to separate words. For example, `#marketing_team` is a better channel name than `#marketingteam`.
   - You can't use blank spaces and capital letters.

- Slack will gently suggest adding an existing prefix to your channel to help organize it. (For more on this, see the section "Adding channel prefixes" later in this chapter.)
- Remember that Slack restricts certain words (refer to Table 3-1).

Brass tacks: As long as you adhere to Slack's naming conventions, you can proceed to the next step.

3. **(Optional) Add a description to your channel.**

   Ideally, the description illustrates the conversations that should take place here. In addition, the clearer the channel's purpose, the less likely people are to post inappropriate messages in it. For more information on this topic, see the section "Defining each channel's purpose" later in this chapter.

4. **Ignore the Make private toggle.**

   After all, we're creating a private channel in this example.

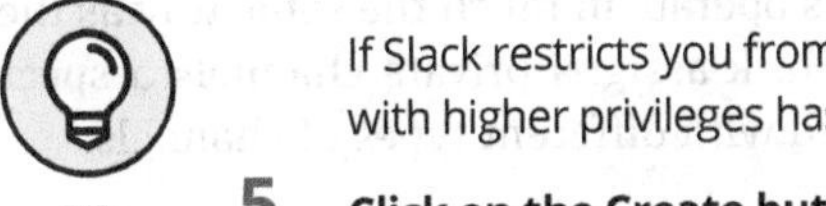

TIP

   If Slack restricts you from creating a public channel, then it's because someone with higher privileges has restricted people in your role from doing so.

5. **Click on the Create button.**
6. **(Optional) Slack will next display a screen that allows you to send channel invitations to current workspace members and user groups.**

Chapter 6 covers user groups. For now, just think of them as groups of users. Slack displays a pane like the one in Figure 3-4.

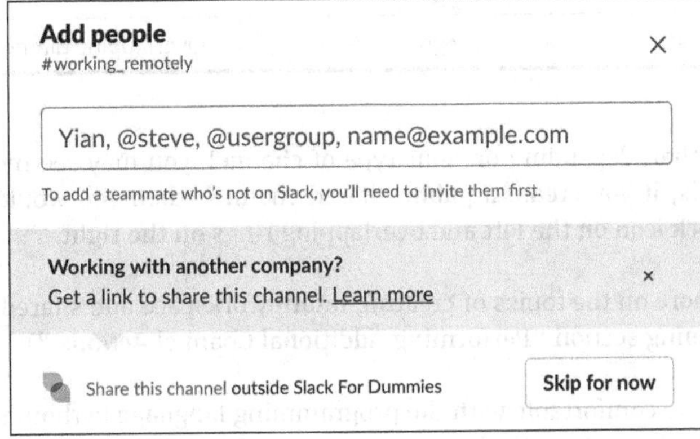

FIGURE 3-4: Slack prompt for adding members to a new channel.

» If you want to invite others, then do so. Then click on the green Done button when you're finished.

» If not, then click on the white Skip for now button. You can always add new members later. (See the section "Adding Members to Existing Channels" later in this chapter.)

After creating the new channel, Slack assigns a hashtag (#) to precede it. What's more, Slack automatically adds you to the channel although you can easily leave it.

It's best to be consistent when naming your channels. For example, say that channels containing helpful information at your organization start with #tips_, such as in `#tips_slack`.

To create a private channel, simply follow these with the exception of step number four: You'll want to move the "Private toggle" to the right. It will then turn green. Beyond this, private channels operate in much the same way as their public brethren. Note, however, that Slack assigns private channels a special icon. Table 3-2 shows the icons associated with different types of channels.

TABLE 3-2 **Slack Channel Icons and Descriptions**

Type of Channel	Icon Position	Icon Description
Public (regular)	Left	Hashtag or number sign
Private (regular)	Left	Padlock
Multi-workspace	Right	Overlapping rings or circles
Shared	Right	Overlapping diamonds

Note that, depending on your type of channel, you may see more than one icon. That is, if you create a public shared channel, then you would see two icons: a padlock icon on the left and overlapping rings on the right.

For more on the topics of creating multi-workspace and shared channels, see the upcoming section "Performing Additional Channel Actions.")

If you're comfortable with the programming language Python, then you can write scripts that automatically create as many channels as you like. That is, you need not create a bunch of channels individually. Say that you routinely need to create the same set of channels. This method can save you a great deal of time.

Building an intelligent channel structure

Slack won't prevent you from misnaming channels or entering inaccurate descriptions of the purposes that you want them to serve. As a result, you'll want to put some thought into how you structure channels in your workspace — and coach others to do the same. To this end, here's some advice.

Regardless of the type of channel that you create, each one should serve a different purpose. That's the whole point of channels. Trying to shoehorn every type of workplace message, question, poll, or announcement into a single channel or two just doesn't make sense. And forget cost, if that's what you're thinking; Slack charges by the user, not by the channel.

Defining each channel's purpose

The way in which you structure your channels hinges upon many factors. Perhaps most important are the types of communication that take place within your organization. Think about what each channel's purpose will be.

Large organizations typically create channels for `#hr`, `#finance`, `#it`, `#development`, and `#marketing` — and maybe multiple channels for each function. Others have created an `#ask_the_ceo` channel that apes Reddit's famous ask-me-anything (AMA) feature. An Italian restaurant won't use this structure. Unless you work in education, I doubt that you'll create many `#homework` channels. Again, your channels will depend on your organization's and employees' specific communication and collaboration needs.

A little forethought about how to structure the channels in your organization's Slack workspace(s) will save you a good bit of time down the road. Beyond that, smart naming is less apt to confuse users — some of whom may not share your zeal for Slack. Constantly changing channel names and purposes is bound to wreak havoc throughout a firm.

BEGINNING WITH THE END IN MIND

In his books, professor and efficiency guru Steven Covey stressed the benefits of beginning with the end in mind. Sure, it's a bit pithy, but in this case, there's some truth to that axiom. Yes, you always correct mistakes. In this case, you can create new channels and rename existing ones. Beyond that, you can use Slack's data-import and -export tools detailed in Chapter 11.

WARNING

Be wary of channel overload, especially for new users. They may become confused, post information in incorrect channels, and/or eventually stop using Slack altogether.

Workspace Owners or Admins may want to create and promote a channel dedicated to gathering all users' requests for new channels. Think of it as a meta-channel.

Adding channel prefixes

If you're thinking that adding dozens or even hundreds of channels can become hard to manage, you're absolutely right. What's more, if your colleagues create new channels willy-nilly, then your workspace's channel structure will start to become confusing. It's only a matter of time.

Fortunately, Slack channel prefixes can help in this regard. At a high level, they serve as internal guidelines for naming channels and help organize workspaces — especially large ones.

Slack provides a number of predefined prefixes, but you can create your own. By adding a set of standard prefixes such as `help`, `team`, `news`, `tips`, or `class`, workspace members can keep channel names descriptive and consistent throughout the organization.

The number of available prefixes hinges on your Slack plan. Workspaces on the Free plan create a maximum of six. For organizations on premium plans, that number is 99.

To add a new channel prefix, follow these steps:

1. **Click on the main menu.**
2. **From the drop-down menu, select Settings & administration and then Workspace settings.**

   Slack displays a sub-menu on the immediate right.
3. **Select Customize "workspace name."**

   Slack launches a new window or tab in your default web browser.
4. **Click on the tab on the far right labeled Channel Prefixes.**

   You see Slack's predefined prefixes along with descriptions of them. If you want to delete an existing prefix, just click on the X icon to its right.
5. **Click on the Add Prefix button at the bottom of the page.**

   Slack launches a new window.

6. **Enter a prefix with a maximum of ten characters.**
7. **Enter a description that informs workspace members of how to use it.**
8. **Click on the green Save button.**

   Slack now lists your new channel prefix with the rest of them.

TIP

Chapter 8 introduces sections, Slack's slick new way of organizing channels.

You may be chomping at the bit to invite others to your channels. If so, then jump to the section "Adding Members to Existing Channels" later in this chapter. I would recommend, however, that you take the time to understand some of the specific features of Slack channels before blasting out invitations right now.

Viewing basic channel information

To see an overview of a particular channel, follow these steps:

1. **Click on the channel in the bottom half of the sidebar.**
2. **Click on the circled-i icon.**

After doing this, Slack displays the channels' Detail view, which are four icons in a new pane on the right-hand side:

- **Add:** Invite others to a channel.
- **Find:** Search for information in the channel. (You won't find much material in a new channel, but that will change over time.)
- **Call:** Hold a call with channel members. (Chapter 6 explains this topic.)
- **More:** Provides additional options to manage the channel.

Underneath the set of icons are collapsible elements:

- **About:** Provides the channel's current topic, description, creation date, and the name of the person who created it.
- **Members:** View existing members and easily invite more.
- **Shortcuts:** Create a channel-specific automation through Workflow Builder. (I discuss this topic in Chapter 10.)

» **Pinned Items:** Pin a specific message to the top of the channel to maximize its visibility.

» **Shared files:** Displays files that channel members have uploaded for others to view. You don't need to scroll through dozens or hundreds of messages trying to find a file.

Note that Slack displays a number to the right of each item. As a result, you can quickly begin the process of absorbing information about the channel. Put all of these items together and you get something similar to Figure 3-5.

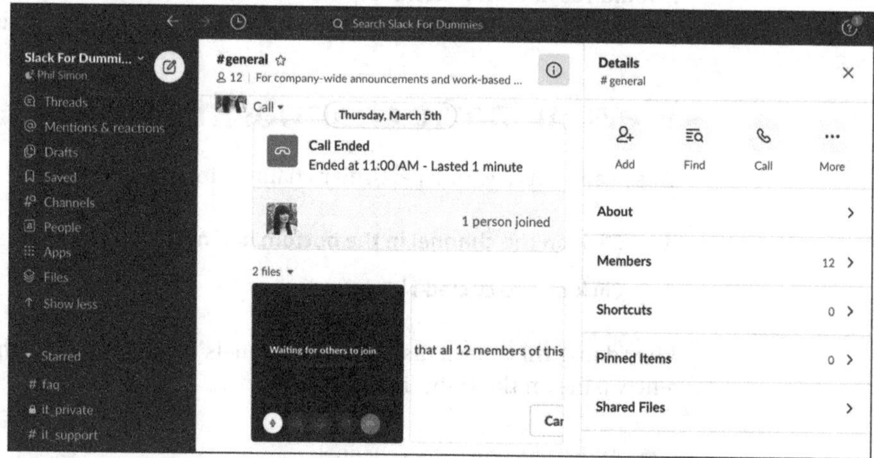

FIGURE 3-5: Channel icons and containers.

New channel members should review this information to get a sense of what to expect from it. You don't want to appear foolish in front of your new channel-mates.

Performing Channel Actions

Slack provides plenty of valuable tools to manage your organization's channels. By taking the time to understand what they do, you can avoid making rookie mistakes and confusing the people in your workspace.

Slack's channel settings and options provide many powerful ways to customize them and your overall experience. Note that, in some cases, your role may prohibit you from doing one of the things that I describe in this section. To perform the actions in this section, follow these steps:

1. **Click on the channel whose settings you want to customize.**
2. **Click on the information (i) icon in the top right-hand corner.**

   Slack displays a four-pane tab with the word Details above it. Now you'll be able to perform a number of both group and individual actions within a channel.

Group actions

Depending on their roles, Slack also allows users to perform a number of important group-related channel actions. Note that these actions don't just affect you; they affect everyone else in the channel and potentially the workspace.

To perform the channel-specific group tasks in this section, follow each of the following steps to begin the process:

1. **Click on the channel whose settings you want to customize.**
2. **Click on the information (i) icon in the top right-hand corner.**

   Slack displays a four-pane tab with the word Details above it.

Changing the channel's topic

You may have entered a topic when you initially created your channel. (See the section "Creating Basic Public and Private Channels" earlier in this chapter.) Regardless, you may want to update it. To do so, follow the first two steps at the top of the section "Group actions" and then these steps:

1. **Click on the About tab.**
2. **Click on Edit; it is underneath Topic.**

   Enter the new topic that you'd like people to discuss.
3. **Click on the green button labeled Set Topic.**

Changing the channel's description

This process is nearly identical to the prior one. Follow the first two steps at the top of the section "Group actions" and then these steps:

1. **Click on the About tab.**
2. **Click on Edit; it is underneath Description.**

   Enter or update the general purpose of the channel.
3. **Click on the green button labeled Update description.**

Managing posting permissions

For customers on Slack's Plus and Enterprise plans, Slack allows Workspace Owners and Admins to limit which members post in which channels. (On the Free and Standard plans, this option only appears in `#general`.)

For example, a large company wisely wants to lock down the `#announcements` channel and effectively make it read-only. That is, members can read others' messages but they can't post their own *in this channel*.

This process is nearly identical to the prior one. Follow the first two steps at the top of the section "Group actions" and then these steps:

1. **Click on the More icon.**
2. **From the drop-down menu, click Manage Posting Permissions.**

   From the list, select the group of people who can post in this channel. Slack lets you be very specific here.
3. **Click on the green Save button.**

Once you do this, people not permitted to post in the channel will see an eyeglasses icon and the words "Read only" at the bottom of the channel. In this case, Slack hides the message box.

Archiving channels

Archiving or retiring a channel removes it from the list of active ones in your Slack workspace. An archived channel is effectively closed for new activity. Follow the first two steps at the top of the section "Group actions" and then these:

1. **Click on the More icon.**
2. **From the drop-down menu, click Additional options.**
3. **Click on Archive this channel.**
4. **Click on the green button labeled Yes, archive the channel.**

TIP

An empty channel is effectively worthless. Say that there's no activity for six months. It's best to post a note in the channel that you're going to archive it unless you hear otherwise. Gangster tip: include `@channel in the message` to notify all members of the channel whether they are active or not. (Chapters 4 and 7 detail different notification options.)

If you want to restore an archived channel, follow these steps:

1. **Click on the Channel view in the top half of the sidebar.**
2. **Click on the name of the channel that you want to resurrect.**

   Slack displays four icons below the channel name on the right-hand side of the screen.

3. **Click on the Unarchive button.**

TECHNICAL STUFF

If you're comfortable with the programming language Python, you can write scripts that automatically archive groups of Slack channels if no one is posting in them.

Making a public channel private

If you decide that a public channel should be private, then you're in luck. Slack will let Workspace Owners and Admins convert public channels to private ones. Again, regular users don't possess adequate security.

Even Workspace Owners and Admins, though, cannot do the opposite for privacy reasons. That is, by design they cannot turn private channels into public ones. Follow the first two steps at the top of the section "Group actions" and then these:

1. **Click on the More icon.**
2. **From the drop-down menu, click Additional options.**
3. **Click on Change to a Private Channel.**
4. **Slack reminds you that you can't undo this change. You'll see a red button that reads Change to Private. Click on it.**
5. **Again, Slack warns you that this change is permanent. A Change to Private button appears. Click on it.**

   Your channel is now private. You'll see a lock icon to the left of its name in your workspace.

After you do this, Slack posts a message in the channel to minimize surprises among existing members.

Renaming channels

This action is self-explanatory. Everyone in the channel remains, as does all of its content. To rename a channel, follow the first two steps at the top of the section "Group actions" and then these:

1. **Click on the More icon.**
2. **From the drop-down menu, click Additional options.**
3. **Click on Rename channel.**
4. **Type the new name of the existing channel.**
5. **Click on the green Rename channel button.**

All channel members will see a channel message indicating the new name unless you delete that message. (See Chapter 4 for more information on deleting messages.)

Deleting channels

This action is permanent; make sure that you want to proceed. Note that members cannot perform this action. To delete an existing channel, follow the first two steps at the top of the Group Actions section and then these:

1. **Click on the More icon.**
2. **From the drop-down menu, click Additional options.**
3. **Click on Delete this channel.**
4. **Click on the box to the immediate left of Yes, Permanently delete this channel.**
5. **Click on the red Delete Channel button.**

REMEMBER

Deleting an individual message in a channel differs from deleting the entire channel. In the latter scenario, all messages go poof forever.

TECHNICAL STUFF

If you're comfortable with the programming language Python, then can you write scripts that magically delete channels *en masse*. For an example of such a script, see `bit.ly/sl-ch-delete`.

Pinning an item to a channel

What if you want to make it easy for channel members to see an important announcement or event? Slack lets you pin a conversation to the top of a channel. Ideally, pinning one increasing the chances that people will read it. You may already be familiar with this feature because Facebook, Twitter, and other social networks allow users to do the same thing.

To pin a message to the top of a channel, follow these steps:

1. **Mouse over an existing message posted in that channel.**

   Slack displays a menu.

2. **Click on the ellipsis icon to the far right.**
3. **Click on Pin to channel.**

Note that Slack won't let you pin simple messages such as "Dennis joined the channel." Also, if you want to unpin an item, follow the first two steps above and click Un-pin from channel.

Expanding the audience for your channels

Much like your business needs, your Slack workspace will evolve over time. Slack lets you turn your "regular" channel into a more robust one: either a multi-workspace channel or a shared one. (For more information on these subjects, see the section "Exploring the Different Types of Slack Channels" earlier in this chapter.)

Organizations on the Enterprise Grid plan can take advantage of one other powerful channel-management option: They can move channels to different workspaces. This action ports the channel over to a new workspace while retaining its valuable history and knowledge. (Visit `bit.ly/sl-move2` for more information on this topic.)

Individual actions

To some extent, Slack lets you customize users interaction with channels. Note that these actions in this section only affect you; they do not affect everyone else in the channel.

Starring a channel

If you want a channel to appear above the other channels in the bottom half of the sidebar, then you can easily star it. To star a channel, follow these steps:

1. **Click on the name of the channel that you want to star.**
2. **Click on the white star to the right of the channel name.**

   It's at the top of the screen underneath the search bar.

   Slack turns the star blue.

Note that starring a channel is a personal choice, not a global one. For example, in Figure 3-6, `#faq` is one of my favorite channels, but it may well not be one of Skyler's or Gustavo's.

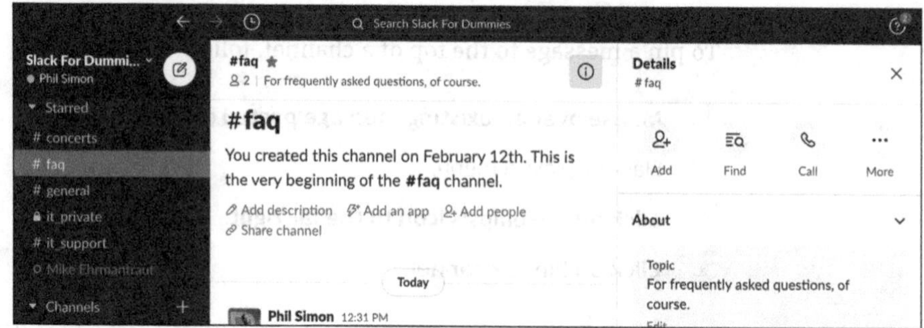

FIGURE 3-6: Starred `#faq` channel.

Simply click on the star again if you want to remove it from your favorite channels.

Jumping to a date

By clicking here, you can view the activity in that channel — if any — that took place on that date. Follow the first two steps at the top of the section "Group actions" and then these:

1. **Click on the More icon.**
2. **From the drop-down menu, click on Jump to date.**
3. **Click on the calendar date.**

Note that Slack only lets you navigate to a date if activity took place on it. That is, if no one in a channel posted anything on July 18th, then Slack won't present that date as an option.

Leaving channels

Say that you no longer care about the content in a particular channel. Maybe you find `#tech_news` too noisy. Muting seems like a separation but you want a divorce. Simply leave the channel. If it's a public channel, then you can rejoin it later on. On a desktop computer, do the following:

1. **Click on the channel that you want to leave.**
2. **Click on the information (i) icon in the top right-hand corner.**

   Slack displays a four-pane tab with the word Details above it.
3. **Click on the More icon on the far right.**

   Slack displays a panel underneath the icon
4. **From the drop-down list, click on Leave [channel name] at the bottom.**

   The process for saying *adios* to private channels involves a few more steps. Follow the first four steps and then you get a warning that you won't be able to rejoin the channel on your own — that is, someone else will need to re-invite you to the channel. Then, if you wish to proceed, take this last step:

5. **Click Yes, Leave the private channel.**

REMEMBER

Once you leave the private channel, you're out for good. You will have to ask a current channel member to re-add you if you change your mind.

Reducing channel noise

By default, Slack alerts you to all activity that takes place in your channels. You can, however, silence especially noisy channels to different degrees. Chapter 5 covers notifications in far more detail. For now, suffice it to say that your two measures are:

- Muting a channel
- Setting channel notifications

Adding Members to Existing Channels

A channel with only one member serves no purpose. Remember that Slack is a group tool, not an individual one. To this end, Slack provides two ways to add members to channels: manually and automatically via default channels.

Manual additions

Channels are living, breathing things. That is, unlike inboxes, they don't die when employees leave the company. At some point, you'll want to add workplace members to an existing channel. In other words, you don't want to wait for people to join specific channels on their own. Here's how to add members individually:

1. **In the lower half of the sidebar, click on the channel to which you want to add new members.**
2. **Click on the information (i) icon in the top right-hand corner.**

   Slack displays additional information in a new pane. Underneath About, you'll see Members.
3. **Click on Members.**

4. **Click on the white Add People button.**

   If you're adding a member to a private channel, then Slack will display the following message:

   ```
   Anyone you add will be able to see all of the channel's contents.
   ```

5. **(Optional) Click on the green Continue button.**
6. **In the new pane, type a few letters of that person's name.**

   You can repeat this process if you'd like to add more than one person to the channel.

7. **Click on the green Add button.**

   Those members now belong to the Slack channel.

That's great, but what if you want to add hundreds or thousands of users to an existing channel? Selecting them individually would take far too long.

Good news: In November 2019, Slack made it much easier to add users to channels *en masse*. Just follow these steps:

1. **Create a spreadsheet with the email addresses of each person you want to add to a channel.**
2. **Copy those email addresses.**
3. **In the lower half of the sidebar, click on the channel to which you want to add new members.**
4. **Click on the information (i) icon in the top right-hand corner.**

   Slack displays additional information in a new pane. Underneath About, you see Members.

5. **Click on Members.**
6. **Click on the white Add People button.**
7. **In the window, paste those email addresses.**

   The current limit is 1,000 at once. Slack verifies that those emails are valid and that they correspond to members in the existing workspace. In the event of issues, you can simply delete the email address in question and proceed with the rest.

TIP

Say that you change your mind and no longer want to invite someone from your pasted list. Just click on the X to the right of the person's name. Slack removes that member from the mass add. In other words, you won't have to start from scratch.

8. **Click on the green Add button.**

   Those members are now part of the Slack channel.

Default workplace channels

You can always add new members to existing public channels, either via pasting email addresses or selecting them one by one.

What if you know the public channels that you want *all* new workspace members to join? Slack makes these "auto-adds" simple. Owners and Admins can define default public channels that new workspace members will automatically join. This method represents the easiest way to add users to public channels *en masse*. Follow these steps:

1. **Click on the workspace name in the upper-left corner.**
2. **From the drop-down menu, select Settings & administration and then Workspace settings.**

   Slack takes you to the first tab on the page labeled Settings.
3. **Click on the Expand button to the right of Default Channels.**
4. **Click in the box that appears and select the public channels that all new workspace members will automatically join.**
5. **Press Tab and click on the Save button.**

   Voilà! New Slack members now automatically join the channels that you just selected, as Figure 3-7 shows.

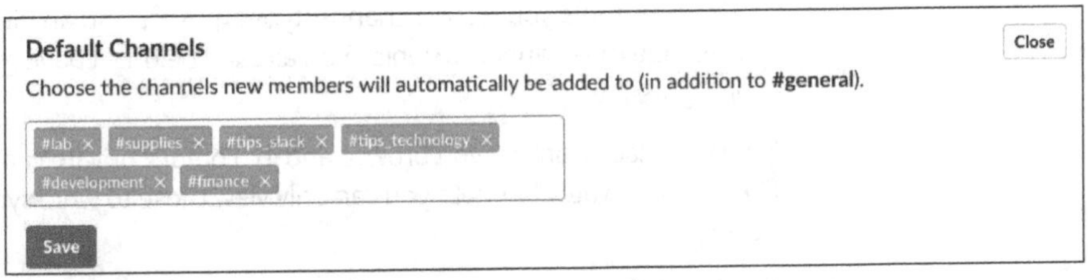

Default Channels

Choose the channels new members will automatically be added to (in addition to **#general**).

#lab × #supplies × #tips_slack × #tips_technology × #development × #finance ×

Save

Close

FIGURE 3-7: Setting default Slack channels for workspace members.

Exploring Existing Public Channels

If your organization has just started experimenting with Slack, then your colleagues may not have created many public channels. Over time, however, that will change. People will create public channels devoted to different topics.

Say that you are curious about what others in your organization are discussing. To browse existing public channels, follow these steps:

1. **Click on the Channels view in the top of the sidebar.**

   You can now browse all available public channels as well as the private channels to which you already belong, as Figure 3-8 shows.

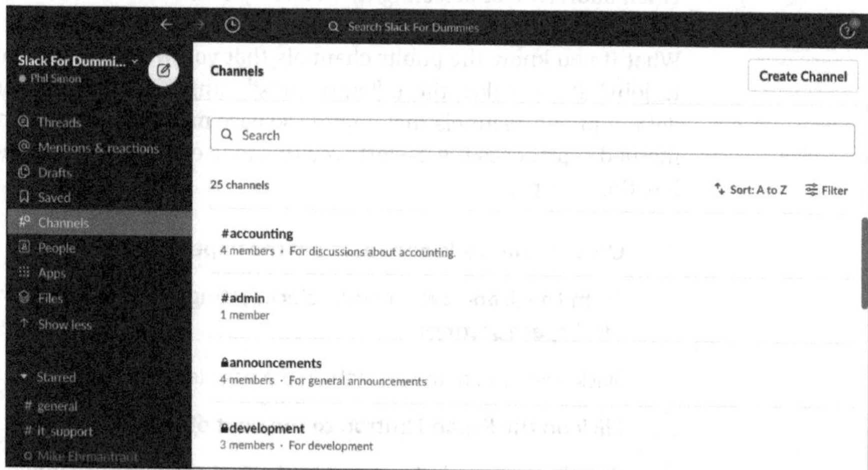

FIGURE 3-8: Viewing existing channels in a Slack workspace.

   The sheer number of channels may overwhelm you. Fortunately, Slack provides two useful ways to let users easily discover channels of interest:

   - *Sort:* Slack lets you filter by channel date, number of members, and alphabetical order.
   - *Filter:* Slack lets you restrict channel types: private and archived. You can also hide the channels to which you already belong. I have done the latter in Figure 3-9.

   Note that Slack won't let you browse and join others' private channels. By filtering on private channels, you can only view those to which you *already* belong.

2. **(Optional) Click on the channel that you want to preview before joining.**

   Slack displays four new icons in a pane on the right-hand side:

   - Preview
   - Join
   - Find
   - More

When you click on the Preview button, Slack displays the messages in the channel. You haven't joined yet; you just want to kick the tires. Previewing a channel helps you get a feel for the types of discussions already taking place there. Click on Find to search the channel for specific keywords.

3. **If you decide that you want to be a member of this channel, then click on the Join button.**

   You are now a member of this public channel. Access it in your sidebar.

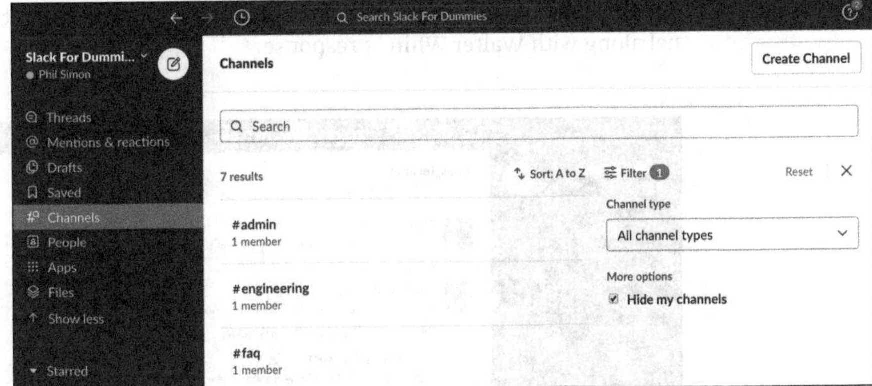

FIGURE 3-9: Browsing a filtered list of public Slack channels to which I don't belong.

TIP

Say that you already know the name of the channel you want to join. Go to any existing channel or send yourself a direct message (DM). (Chapter 4 covers DMs in much more depth.) Type */join* followed by the channel's name and hit enter. For example, if you type */join* `#marketing`, Slack skips the channel preview and automatically adds you to this channel. You can then read members' previous messages and post your own.

TIP

Say that you're joining an existing channel. Take a few minutes to read its purpose as well as a few topics. Also, if it's a relatively small or targeted channel, briefly introduce yourself to others in the channel.

Communicating via Slack Channels

Although a channel is a powerful tool, it is really only a means to an end. That is, channels only to disseminate information and interact with others. Now that you know more about channels, it's time to discuss sending messages in them. (Note that Chapter 4 covers messages in far more detail.)

TIP

It's a virtual certainty that you will spend far more time interacting with people in channels than creating and maintaining them.

Posting simple channel messages

To post simple messages in Slack channels, simply go to the bottom of a channel and type whatever you like in the message prompt. Hit enter and you're done. (Chapter 4 covers creating messages in far more detail.)

Figure 3-10 shows a simple message that I posted in the `#tips_technology` channel along with Walter White's response.

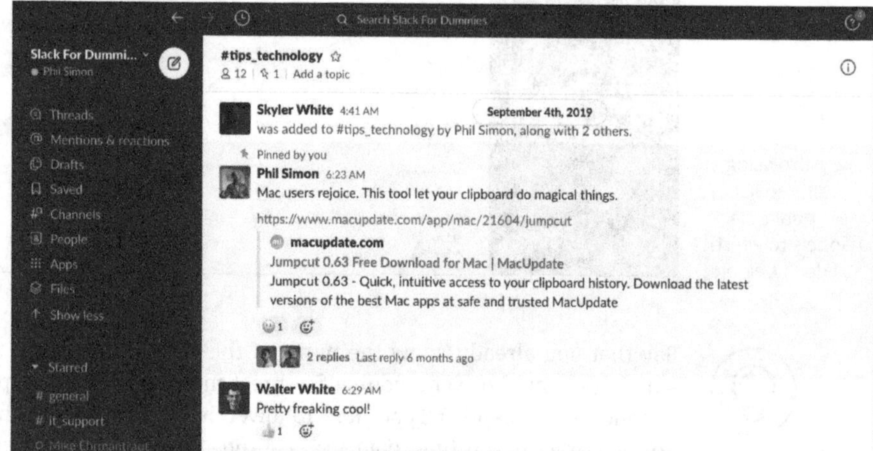

FIGURE 3-10: Simple Slack channel message with response.

REMEMBER

Messages and responses in Slack channels aren't private. That is, everyone in the channel can view the interaction. If you want to send private messages, then you'll have to use direct messages. (Again, see Chapter 4.)

You can mention your fellow workspace channel members by using the @ symbol. All other channel members can respond to any message that you post in a channel. They can include emojis, URLs, and even animated gifs in their responses.

TIP

Here are a few more tips:

- If you want to alert every member in a channel that you've sent or responded to a message, simply type `@channel`.

- Workspace Owners and Admins can delete others' messages in public channels. It's wise to follow up with the offender and explain why his message was inappropriate. Ideally, this intervention will prevent a recurrence.
- To guide the channel's discussion, set a topic. Learn more at `bit.ly/sl-topic`.

Understanding channel etiquette

Now you know a great deal about how to create Slack channels and post messages and snippets in them. It's time to discuss Slack etiquette.

If you grab a drink or six with a group of long-time friends or visit Top Golf, odds are that you're going to act in a certain way. Consider a different situation, though. Assume that you're out to lunch during a day-long job interview. You want to make a good impression with people you don't know — your potential future colleagues and bosses. As a result, you should overdress and behave in a more formal manner. Context matters.

The same holds true with Slack channels: Not all of them are created equal. What passes for acceptable behavior in one may be entirely inappropriate in another.

For example, some good-natured banter or ribbing in the `#humor` channel isn't likely to ruffle your colleagues' feathers — especially if you've known them for a while. Routinely being a wiseacre and trolling others in `#product_ideas`, though, isn't likely to fly.

Here are some other tips to keep in mind:

- Read the room. Err on the side of formality at first, especially if you're new to the company and/or channel.
- The more members in a channel, the less frequently you should post in it.
- Use your head when posting in channels. Think about the channel's purpose.

» Formatting your messages

» Posting messages in channels

» Sharing files with others

» Finding your colleagues

» Comparing Slack to email

Chapter 4
The Wonderful World of Slack Messages

Slack is a remarkably flexible and powerful tool on many levels. For example, Chapter 3 covers how you can use public and private channels to solicit information from — and provide targeted information to — others in your workspace. To be sure, that's useful. Still, you may be wondering if the channel is the only way to interact with your colleagues and partners in Slack.

The answer is a resounding no.

Slack's management understands that channels frequently don't represent the only — let alone the best — way for people to communicate with each other. To this end and as this chapter demonstrates, Slack lets you send discrete, direct messages to individuals and groups. Even better, threads let you lump messages together into a single unit and respond when and until your heart's content.

Understanding Slack Messages

Within a given workspace, you can send anyone a direct message (DM) about anything and respond. (Whether the recipient responds is another matter.) You can also post messages in channels. Much like with email, Slack lets users attach files to their messages. Share links, jokes, MP3s, videos, and whatever else you like.

Sending a Message

To send a message in Slack, follow these steps:

1. **Click on the message icon at the top of your workspace.**

   You can also click on the plus sign next to Direct messages in the lower part of the sidebar.

2. **From the drop-down menu, either type a few letters of the person's name or scroll down until you find him or her.**

   Slack displays a screen similar to Figure 4-1.

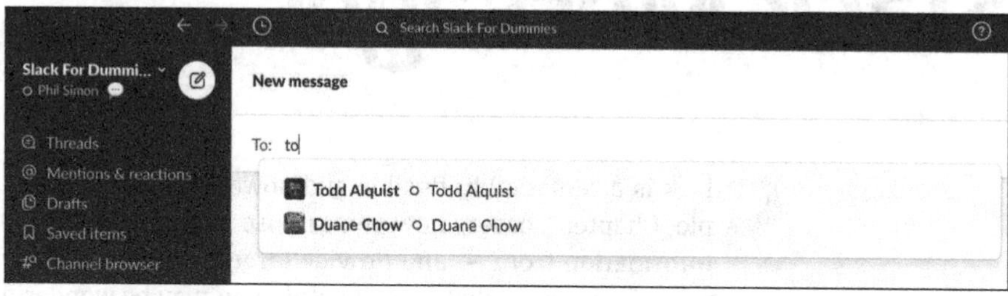

FIGURE 4-1: Composing a simple DM to send to a colleague.

   Once you enter a person's name, hit the tab button on your keyboard. Your cursor begins blinking in the message line.

TIP

   The process for posting a message to a channel is identical to sending a DM. The only difference is the recipient: a channel, not a person or group of people.

3. **(Optional) To attach a file to your message, click on the paperclip icon in the lower right-hand corner of the screen.**

   From there, you can attach a file in a way similar to how you add attachments to email messages. To easily share a file on your computer in a message, drag it from your desktop or a folder into Slack's message window. Either way, Slack attaches the file you chose or dragged to your message after you've clicked the green Upload button.

4. **(Optional) Click on the @ icon if you'd like to mention another workspace member in your message.**
5. **(Optional) Click on the emoji icon and select one if you want to spice up your message or add a reaction.**
6. **Press the Enter key on your keyboard.**

TIP

After you send a message, Slackbot alerts you if the recipient has paused notifications. By clicking on notify them anyway, Slack attempts to alert the individual. (Chapter 5 covers notifications in more depth.)

By default, the bottom half of the Slack sidebar shows you the people with whom you've most recently interacted. Of course, you can send a message to any workspace member at any point.

You can also send DMs to multiple members. You follow the same process covered in the preceding steps. Instead of choosing one recipient in Step 2, though, select as many recipients as you like as Figure 4-2 displays.

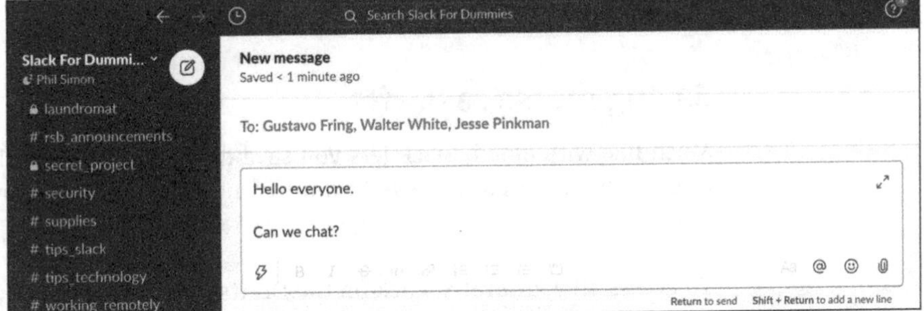

FIGURE 4-2: Selecting recipients for a group DM.

Figure 4-3 shows the results of a group DM.

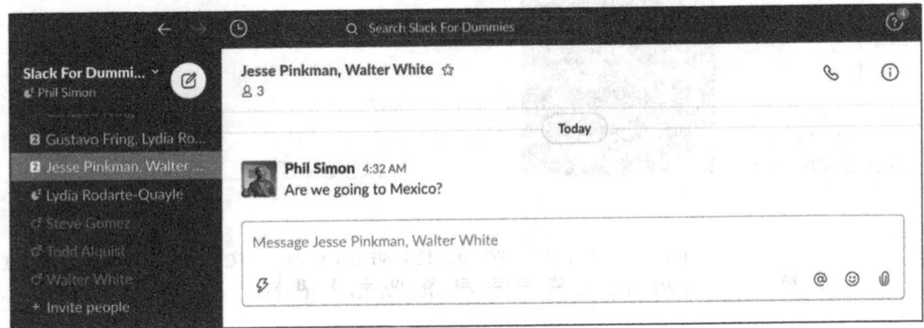

FIGURE 4-3: Example of a group DM.

After you send a group DM, the recipients appear under Direct messages in the sidebar. What's more, Slack usefully displays a number to the left of the group to indicate how many members belong to your group DM.

If you want to leave yourself a note or just paste some text from another application, you're in luck: Slack lets you send yourself DMs as you see in Figure 4-4. Simply select yourself as the recipient in Step 2 in the preceding directions.

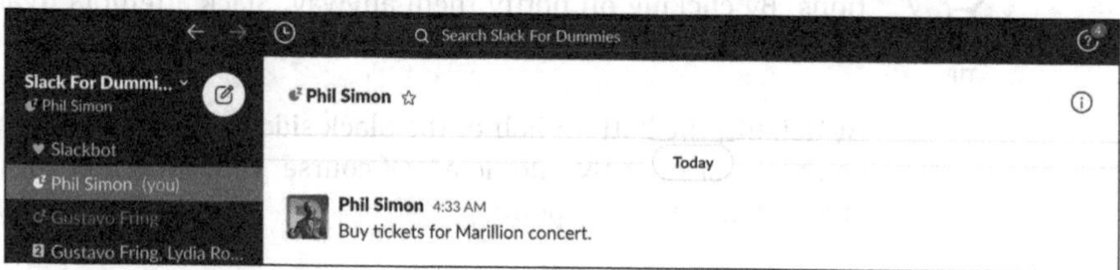

FIGURE 4-4: Example of DM sent to yourself.

Performing basic message actions

Slack lets you do much more than send simple messages to your peers. Rather, you have plenty of tools at your disposal.

Saving message drafts

Much like with email, Slack lets you save drafts of DMs. Simply enter some text into the message pane. Move to a different pane and Slack saves your text as a draft.

To access all your drafts, click on the Drafts view at the top of your workspace as you see in Figure 4-5. Return to your drafts whenever you like.

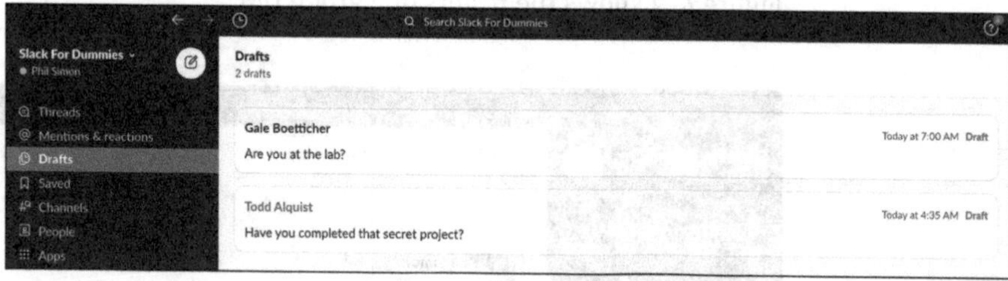

FIGURE 4-5: Slack Drafts view.

Slack bolds the word Drafts when you have created one or more. If you have not saved any drafts, then Slack won't do this.

Marking messages as read or unread

At some point you've probably used your email program's "Mark as read" feature. Slack offers the same ability in both channels and conversations. To mark a read message as unread, follow these steps:

1. **Hover over the message.**

   Three dots appear next to the message along with the message More actions.

2. **Click on Mark unread.**

   When you mark a previously read message as unread, Slack bolds the name of the person or channel name in the sidebar. The visual indicator reminds you that the ball is in your court.

Understanding Slack conversations

Broadly speaking, *conversations* refer to a series of either individual or group direct messages (DMs). Put differently, a conversation is an exchange of DMs with other workspace members that takes place outside of a channel. That last part is critical.

By default, Slack automatically creates a conversation when you exchange a DM with one or more workspace members. You can view all of your conversations in the bottom half of the sidebar under the Direct messages view.

Referencing public channels in DMs

While not a requirement, it is a good practice to reference public channel names in your DMs when appropriate. Do this by including the infamous hashtag before the channel name. Slack automatically creates a blue hyperlink to a *public* channel, but not private ones. Table 4-1 displays what happens when you use hashtags in Slack.

TABLE 4-1 Referencing Channel Names in DMs

Action	Results
Send a DM with a hashtag preceding the name of a public channel — for example, `#finance`.	`The term #finance` appears linked in blue. All members with access can click on `#finance` to open it.
Send a DM with a hashtag preceding the name of the private channel — for example, `#secret_project`.	`#secret_project` won't appear linked in blue. Members can't click on the channel's name to open it.

For example, Figure 4-6 references the #supplies channel. Following this practice makes it easy for the recipient(s) to navigate to the referenced public channel.

FIGURE 4-6: Example of DM referencing a public channel.

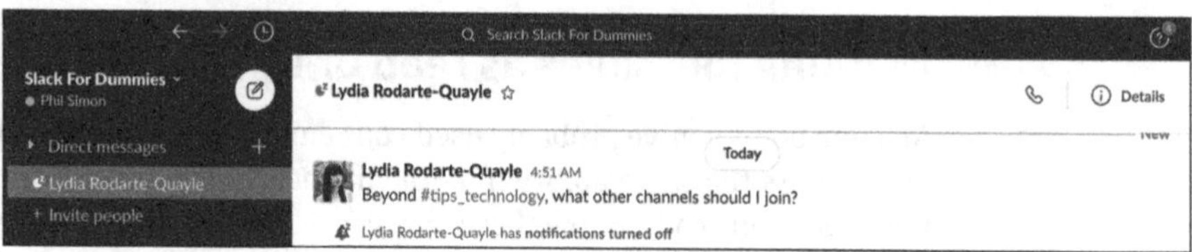

Formatting your messages

Perhaps you want to emphasize certain elements of your DMs to individuals or within channels. For instance, Elaine Benes of *Seinfeld* fame wants to go beyond merely inserting explanation points to accentuate her points.

Fortunately, Slack offers plenty of options if you want to spice the format of your message. Slack easily allows users to do each of the following:

- Create numbered and bulleted lists.
- Italicize and bold text.
- Insert code from different programming languages.
- And more.

At a high level, Slack offers two options for sprucing up your messages: a visual or WYSIWYG editor and keyboard shortcuts.

REMEMBER

WYSIWYG stands for "what you see is what you get."

Using Slack's WYSIWYG editor

Prettying up your text is remarkably intuitive. In this vein, Slack resembles word-processing programs such as Microsoft Word. For instance, to bold a block of text, simply select the words and hit the 'B' icon underneath the text section and *voilà*! Ditto for italicizing text. Table 4-2 presents all of Slack's visual formatting options from left to right.

TABLE 4-2 Formatting Slack DMs via the WYSIWYG Editor

Icon	Operation
Lightning bolt	Invokes a number of shortcuts not specific to formatting *per se*, but useful as I'll describe later.
B	Bolds the text.
I	Italicizes the text.
Strikethrough	Applies strikethrough format to the text.

Icon	Operation
</>	Applies code style to the existing text.
Link	Hyperlink text. That is, your text directs to a URL.
Numbers	Creates a numbered list.
Bullets	Creates a bulleted list.
Blockquote	Indents text to indicate that you're quoting another source or person.
Code block	Inserts an entirely new block of code.
Aa	Hides the text-formatting options.
@	Mentions someone.
☺	Adds an emoji.
Paperclip	Attaches a file to message.

Saving time with keyboard shortcuts

If you're more of a shortcut person, then you're in luck as well. Slack lets you disable the rich-text formatting options by clicking on the letter icon. Table 4-3 shows you how to format DMs using keyboard shortcuts.

TABLE 4-3 Formatting Slack DMs via Keyboard Shortcuts

Format	Keyboard Combination
Start a new paragraph	Press Shift + Enter as many times as you like.
Bold	Place asterisks at the start and end of the text.
Italics	Place underscores at the start and end of the text.
Strikethrough	Place tildes (~) at the start and end of the text.
Quoting a sentence	Place an angled bracket (>) at the start of the text.
Quoting multiple sentences	Place angled brackets (>) at the start of the text.
Inline code	Place backticks (`) at the start and end of the text. Three backticks formats a block of text.
Bulleted lists	Press Shift + 8 and then press Shift + Enter/ Return. Also, you can type [asterisk-space] or [hyphen-space], and the formatting auto-adjusts to a bulleted list.
Numbered lists	Mac users: Type Cmd + Shift + 7. PC users: Type Ctrl + Shift + 7. Also, you can type [numeral one-period-space]. Slack auto-adjusts the message formatting to a numbered list.

You don't need to memorize these shortcuts if you prefer using the WYSIWYG editor.

TIP

Regardless of whether you're a mouse or keyboard person, you can mix and match your styles in Slack messages. If you want to use bulleted lists, bold text, and a snippet of code in the same message, knock yourself out.

Finding people in your workspace

You'll send plenty of DMs in Slack to different people. This begs the question: How can you find your colleagues? You won't need to leave Slack and search your company's email directory. Slack conveniently lets you find fellow workspace members in several ways.

1. **Click on the People view in the top half of the sidebar.**

   Slack shows you something similar to Figure 4-7.

2. **Type some letters of the person's name in the search bar or just scroll down until you see the person's name or photo.**

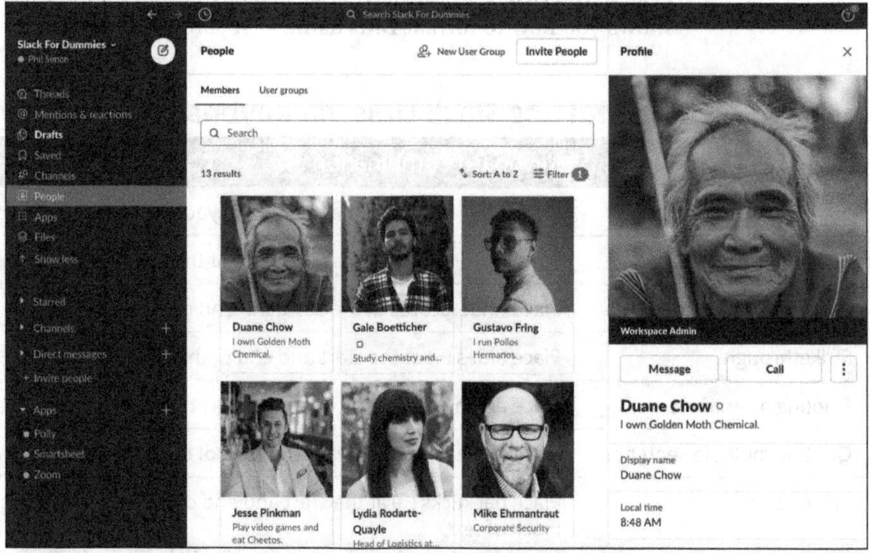

FIGURE 4-7: Slack's People view.

When you click on a person's name, Slack displays his or her profile. In Figure 4-7, I clicked on Duane's name and Slack placed a bar underneath his photo indicating his role: Workspace Admin. Slack does this with all user roles save for member. (See Chapter 2 for more information on roles.)

The People view lets you sort by name, but there are plenty of other ways to quickly find the right person in your workspace. Here's one of my favorites: You can filter by role and even deactivated users by following these steps:

1. **Click on the People view in the top half of the sidebar.**
2. **Click on the filter icon next to the search bar and go nuts.**

You can filter by account type or whether the person uses Slack on a PC or a Mac. You can also hide deactivated accounts.

TRUST BUT VERIFY

The fictitious Fizbo Apparel specializes in clown costumes. (Yes, this is a *Modern Family* reference.) The 3,000-employee company pays for Slack's Enterprise Grid plan.

Mitchell works in sales but wants to check with marketing about an upcoming company promotion for clown feet. (Folks from these two departments often don't coordinate their efforts well.) Mitchell looks at Slack People view and discovers that Cameron is running the relevant marketing campaign and rattles off a DM to his colleague.

Four days go by, and Mitchell hasn't heard boo from Cam. Mitchell's team is starting to become agitated. It needs an answer. What happened?

It turns out that even though Cam appears in the People view, he doesn't use it. As a result, he never received the message.

Clearly, you want to avoid these types of real-life scenarios from occurring. If you're uncertain if a colleague uses Slack, then do one of the following:

- Search public channels. If you see that your colleague participates in public discussions, then you can be confident that she uses Slack. (Learn more about Slack's search capabilities in Chapter 7.)
- Call, email, or, even better, drop by your colleagues' desks and ask them whether they use Slack.

Once you know that specific colleagues use Slack, just send them normal DMs without worrying about whether they went unread.

As Ronald Reagan said, "Trust but verify." If you don't, you may end up looking like a clown.

REMEMBER

Enterprise Grid workspaces work just a little bit differently than they do with other Slack plans. For example, in all other Slack plans, you see only the profiles of members in your individual workspace. That's not the case with Enterprise Grid, though. You can filter workspace members as well organization members.

WARNING

In large firms, being able to view all employees in the Slack workspace or organization is both a blessing and a curse. Just like with email, if you're not careful, you can send a DM to the wrong person. (I have done this myself with the Enterprise Grid plan.) Before pressing the Enter key, consider double-checking the person's profile to ensure that you have the right recipient, especially if your query is sensitive in nature.

TIP

Just because you find a colleague's name in the People view doesn't necessarily mean that the person uses Slack. This problem is particularly acute in big companies that pay for the Enterprise Grid plan.

Slack lets you do far more than send and read simple text DMs. You can edit DMs, delete them, set reminders, pin individual ones to conversations, and much more.

Editing messages

People send billions of emails every day and occasionally make mistakes. After you send an email, though, it's out there for good unless you catch the mistake quickly and try to recall it. Not a month goes by that I don't catch an error in my email and need to respond to my own response.

Compared to email, Slack wins here hands down. If you make a mistake, you don't need to send yet another message to everyone. After you send a DM, you can edit it afterward. To do so, just follow these steps:

1. **Hover over a message from a colleague and three dots appear on the right in a pop-up menu.**
2. **Select Edit message.**
3. **Make whatever edits to the message you like.**
4. **Click on the green Save Changes button.**

   Slack saves your changes.

Note: Slack appends the text "(edited)" to the end of your initial message.

REMEMBER

For obvious reasons, Slack prohibits even Owners and Admins from editing others' messages — anonymously or otherwise. Talk about opening Pandora's box!

Deleting messages

Who hasn't accidentally clicked on Reply All to an email and regretted it five minutes later? Recalling a message may not work before others have seen it. Indeed, the mere fact that you try to recall the message may make others more inclined to read it. Slack again offers superior functionality to email.

To delete one of your messages, follow these steps:

1. **Hover your mouse over the message that you want to eradicate.**

   Three horizontal dots and the More actions icon appear.

2. **Click on Delete message.**

   Slack confirms that you want to obliterate the message for good.

3. **Click on the Delete button to complete the kill.**

   The message disappears from Slack for good.

Just because you delete a DM doesn't mean that someone else hasn't already seen it. Shaking your head? When it comes to deleting individual emails, Outlook's message-recall functionality is no fail-safe either.

Workspace Owners and Admins can delete others' messages in public channels. I have had to do so several times with students who have posted inappropriate messages in channels.

Muting conversations

Say that you want Slack to stop pestering you with notifications about an especially noisy individual or group conversation. You easily mute it by following these steps:

1. **Click on the conversation that you want to mute.**
2. **Click on the information (i) icon in the top right-hand corner.**

   Underneath the profile image of the person with whom you're conversing, Slack displays a three-pane tab below the word Details.

3. **Click on the More tab on the right.**
4. **From the drop-down menu, click on Mute conversation.**

To restore proper notifications for the muted conversation, repeat this process but click on Unmute Conversation in Step 4.

Say that I have muted a conversation with Lydia, and she sends me another DM. Slack won't notify me. It will, however, place a red numerical badge next to her name in my sidebar. If she sends me three messages, then a red 3 will appear.

TIP

I mute conversations on a regular basis. Lest I forget to check in, I set reminders to revisit specific conversations after the discussion has died down.

Setting message-specific reminders

Odds are that you use reminders in real life. Perhaps you use a sticky note or a full-blown reminders app on your smartphone. Regardless of your tool of choice, you don't want to forget critical things like anniversaries, paying taxes, and, in my case, the Netflix premier of *El Camino*. (*Breaking Bad* is my favorite show.)

Say that you are working on a coding project. Gilfoyle sent you yet another DM. Unfortunately, you just don't have time to deal with him right now. To remind yourself about a specific DM, follow these steps:

1. **Mouse over a DM or channel message.**
2. **Click on the three horizontal dots.**

   Slack displays the words More actions.
3. **Click on Remind me about this.**

   Slack displays a pop-up window that offers you a number of options from 20 minutes to next week.
4. **Select the time and/or date that you want Slack to send you a reminder about the message.**

   Slack notifies you about the message with a notification at the time specified in Step 4.

TIP

Feel free to snooze a reminder when it goes off, just like your alarm clock.

Saving DMs and channel messages

With so many messages in a workspace, are you skeptical about keeping tabs on the critical ones? Beyond the powerful search techniques described in Chapter 7, Slack allows you to easily access your most important content. When you save a message, Slack places it in its Saved view. If saving in Slack seems similar to bookmarking websites and pages in your web browser, trust your instincts.

TIP

It's a bit of a misnomer to call this process *saving*. Slack saves everything posted in your workspace by default unless you delete it.

To save a DM or channel message, follow these steps.

1. **Hover over a message that you'd like to save.**

   Slack displays a menu with five icons.

2. **Click on the white bookmark icon.**

   It is the second one from the right.

   Slack turns the bookmark icon red.

   You can now find a shortcut to the item in your Saved view in the top half of the sidebar.

As Figure 4-8 shows, Slack's Saved view displays items in reverse chronological order from the date that you saved them. Slack does not sort these messages by the date that the sender originally sent or posted them.

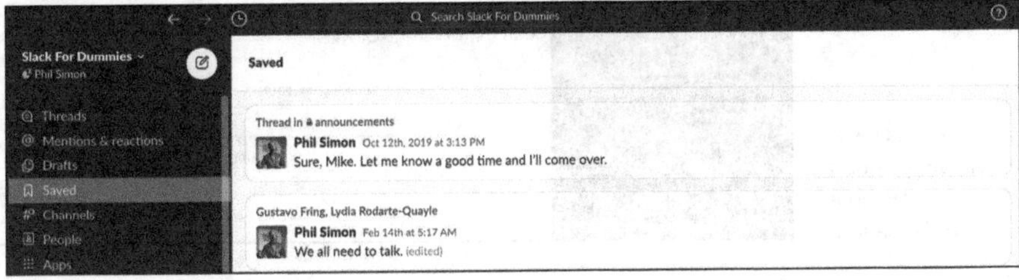

FIGURE 4-8: Slack saved a DM.

To unsave an item, click on the red bookmark for the saved item. The message's bookmark icon returns to its original white color. Slack does *not* delete the message; it just ceases to appear in your Saved view.

Pinning DMs to conversations

In any given Slack workspace, you'll mostly likely interact with some people more than others. Over the course of months or years, you may have hundreds or even thousands of conversations with your colleagues about many different things. All messages are certainly not created equal. For example, a major group or department decision counts more than a simple thank you to your peer.

Alas, Slack lets users easily identify key DMs within a conversation. You can pin DMs to conversations. As such, you'll be able to easily view the most important content in the conversation's details pane.

To pin a comment to a conversation:

1. **Hover your mouse over the DM you that want to pin to the conversation.**
2. **Click on Pin to this conversation.**

   Slack automatically pins the message to the top of the conversation.

Slack lets you pin DMs to individual conversations. Figure 4-9 shows a pinned DM within a conversation:

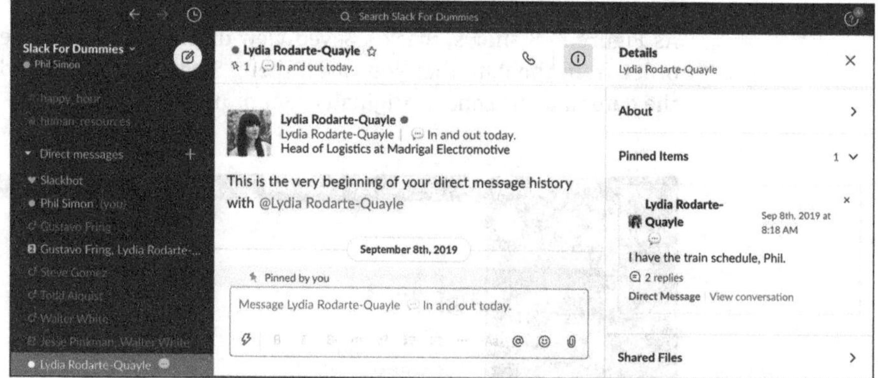

FIGURE 4-9: Viewing pinned DMs in a conversation.

To unpin a message from the larger conversation, repeat the preceding steps but in Step 2, click on Un-pin from this conversation. You can also click on the X in the upper right-hand corner of the message. Note that removing the pin does not delete the DM.

Creating special types of messages

To be sure, you'll get a great deal of mileage out of sending simple DMs and posting comments to discussions in channels. However, Slack recognizes that sometimes users need to send something other than text-based responses.

Welcome to the world of posts and snippets.

Creating rich-text messages with posts

Slack posts are similar to simple messages, but they allow users to apply richer formatting. The post functionality lets users create, edit, and share fully formatted documents directly in Slack. Posts represent a great way to collaborate on relatively simple long-form content. To be fair, though, you won't be saying goodbye to Google Docs and Microsoft Word anytime soon. Examples of posts include project plans, meeting notes, articles, and drafts of blog posts. Slack posts show a green document icon to their immediate left after a user publishes one.

To create a proper post in a Slack channel, follow these steps:

1. **Click on a channel in the sidebar.**
2. **In the message window in the lower left-hand corner, click on the lightning bolt icon.**

   Slack displays a new menu.
3. **Click on Create a post.**

   Slack launches a new window that you'll use to create your post.
4. **Add a title and any other formatting.**

   You can also add simple and formatted text, headers, bullet points, URLs, code, and more goodies.

   After you type text in the main window, highlight it and mouse over it to see all of your formatting options.
5. **When you are finished creating your post, click on the white Share button at the top of the screen.**

   Slack displays self-explanatory options around sharing the post, letting others edit it, creating a link, and adding comments. Figure 4-10 displays those options:
6. **When you are finished, click on the green Share button.**

   Your post looks something like the one in Figure 4-11.

REMEMBER

You can view existing posts on your Slack mobile apps, but you'll need to use Slack on a proper computer to create and edit them. You can view, create, edit, and delete regular channel messages, though, on any device you like.

Adding code and text snippets

In Slack, Snippets represent a quick and simple way to share bits of code, configuration files, or log files with channel members. Slack's native ability to easily share code represents one of the major reasons that software engineers are so fond of Slack.

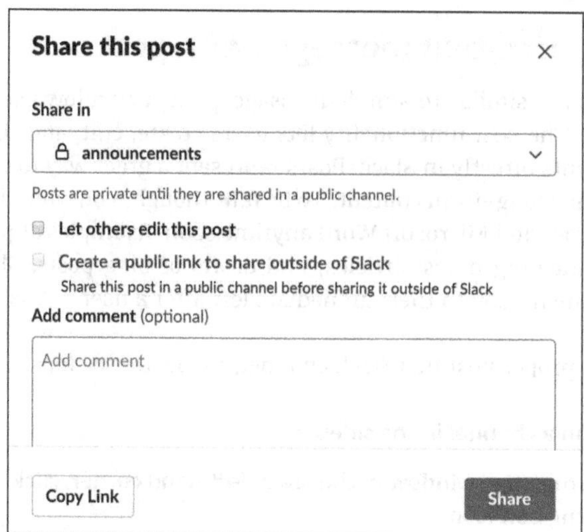

FIGURE 4-10: Sample post options.

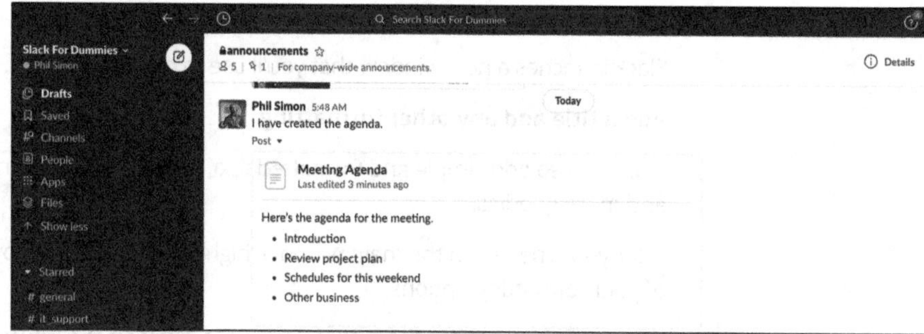

FIGURE 4-11: Sample Slack rich-text post.

Creating both types of snippets is nearly identical to creating a rich-text message. To create a proper post in a Slack channel, follow these steps:

1. **Click on a channel in the sidebar.**
2. **In the message window in the lower left-hand corner, click on the lightning bolt icon.**

   Slack displays a new menu.
3. **Click on Create a Code or text snippet.**

   Slack launches a new window.
4. **Use the new window to create your snippet.**

5. **(Optional) At the top of the page, add a title for your snippet and the type of snippet.**

TIP

If you create a code snippet, Slack attempts to determine the programming language that you're using. If Slack doesn't get it right, then just specify the language yourself from the drop-down menu.

6. **Enter your text or code in the main window under the Content heading.**

   Highlight text and mouse over it to see all your formatting options.

7. **(Optional) Enter a message that introduces your snippet to your intended audience.**

8. **When you are finished creating your snippet, enter your snippet's audience.**

   It may be a channel, an individual, or several folks.

   Slack displays self-explanatory options around sharing the snippet.

9. **When you are finished, click on the green Create Snippet.**

   Slack automatically places line numbers to the left of each line in a snippet. Figure 4-12 displays an example of a code snippet.

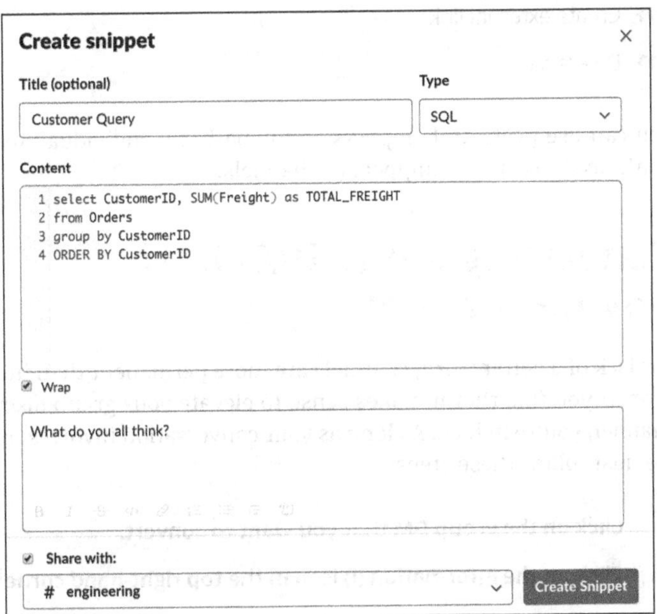

FIGURE 4-12: Sample Slack code snippet.

You can download a text snippet, view raw versions, and/or leave comments. After creating one, Slack places a white icon with a capital T to its immediate left. When you click on it, you can view the snippet's content.

Mouse over a current snippet in a channel. Slack displays these options:

- Collapse or expand (depending on the length of your snippet)
- Download
- Edit
- Share

Click on the ellipsis icon, and Slack displays these options as well:

- View details
- Copy link to file
- Save
- View raw
- Create external link
- Delete file

REMEMBER

You can use posts and snippets as the basis for individual and group DMs. You don't need to confine snippets to channels.

Converting group DMs into private channels

For lack of a better word, channels are more permanent than individual and group DMs. If you find that it makes sense to elevate your group discussion to a proper channel, you're in luck. As long as your conversation involves more than two people, just follow these steps:

1. **Click on the group DM that you want to convert.**
2. **Click on the information (i) icon in the top right-hand corner.**

   Underneath the profile images of the people with whom you're conversing, Slack displays a three-pane tab.
3. **Click on the More icon.**

4. **From the drop-down menu, click on Convert to a private channel.**
5. **Confirm that you want to create the channel by clicking on the green Yes, Continue button.**

   Slack creates a new private channel. Everyone in it can view all message history and shared files. You cannot go back.
6. **Enter a name for the channel and click on the green Convert to a private channel button.**

   Slack moves all the prior DMs into a new private channel.

REMEMBER

For privacy reasons, you cannot turn a series of group DMs into a public channel.

TIP

Using threads to create topic-specific containers

A Slack thread represents a reply or series of replies *to a specific DM* or an in-channel interaction. Slack's rationale for threads is to allow users to engage in more focused discussions around a single topic — one that can take place separately from other messages in a conversation or channel. Although similar in concept, Slack *threads* operate a bit differently than DM-based conversations in several ways.

First, unlike conversations, you can create threads from discussions that take place either within or outside of channels. (See the section "Understanding Slack conversations" earlier in this chapter.) In other words, Slack allows users to create and view threads *regardless of where they take place*. When you start one, Slack provides notifications of new responses at the top of the workspace under the Threads header in the sidebar. If you're following ten threads from six channels and four different conversations, then you can scan them all in one place. Put differently, through threads, you don't need to hunt down each response in ten different places.

Second, threads are certainly useful but they are entirely optional. Unlike conversations, Slack doesn't automatically start them for you.

Reviewing examples of threads

The types of threads run the gamut. Here a few:

- Tech-support teams use the `#hardware_issues` channel to discuss a problem with a server or route. Rather than lump everything into that single channel, they thread the discussion within that channel about problems with a particular piece of equipment.

- HR folks often talk about company policies and the discussion sometimes gets into the nitty-gritty. A thread on the implications of offering paid family leave makes a great deal of sense.
- Gus and Walt are having an animated discussion (outside of a channel) about a key business strategy. Each creates a thread in his Slack workspace to receive alerts about the other's latest response.
- Four partners in a consulting firm are providing specific feedback on a deck of PowerPoint slides. By creating a thread, you keep all comments organized.
- As a college professor, I create an `#ask_the_professor` channel for my classes every semester. That's a big bucket, to be sure. Students will usually ask me questions about the textbook that we're using, such as
  - What version of the textbook do I have to buy?
  - Can I share the textbook with my roommate?
  - Can I buy the electronic version?

  Of course, I answer all of these questions on my syllabi, but I digress. I'll turn each of these queries into a channel thread. For simple yes or no questions, however, a thread rarely makes sense. Still, there's really no downside to using them.

Creating, following, and viewing threads

To start a thread in Slack, follow these directions:

1. **Hover over a message.**

   Slack presents a floating menu with icons with the words More actions.
2. **Mouse over the second icon from the left and click on Start a thread.**

TIP

Slack makes it easy to view threads in the full context of their channels.

1. **Hover over a message in the thread.**

   Slack presents a floating menu with icons and the words More actions.
2. **Mouse over the second icon from the left and click on the Open in channel icon that appears.**
3. **To view all threads, click on the Threads view in the top half of your sidebar underneath the workspace name.**

TIP

As you use Slack, you'll soon realize that not all discussions and content are created equal; you'll invariably view some discussions as more important than others. For example, a software engineer, VP of human resources, and finance manager will all keep their eyes on different discussions. Threads are invaluable in this regard.

Unfollowing threads

If you want to disengage from an individual thread, then simply unfollow it as follows:

1. **Hover over a message in a thread that you currently follow.**
2. **Click on the three vertical dots on the far right.**

   Slack presents the words More actions.
3. **At the top of the new menu, select Unfollow thread.**

Note that you can't mute threads nor can you delete them. After you unfollow a thread, Slack no longer shows you those red badges *for that thread* under the Threads header in the sidebar. Of course, you still might see badges from threads that you are following if someone calls you out.

TIP

I'm a fan of threads, but many people only use them on a case-by-case basis. If the majority of your interactions are discrete, then they may not make sense for you. If, however, you find yourself routinely going back and forth with people about a specific topic, then a thread is the perfect vehicle for tracking updates to a particular discussion.

Sharing in Slack

I've made this point several times already but it bears repeating: Slack is a group tool, not an individual one. Aside from sending DMs and posting messages in channels, you'll often share content with your colleagues. At a high level, Slack lets you share files and messages. I'll start with the former.

Sharing files

At some point in your Slack journey, you'll want to share documents that you've created in other applications with your colleagues and maybe even with yourself. Typical examples include spreadsheets, documents, photos, and presentations.

Slack's new Files view makes this a snap. To upload a file that you intend to share, follow these steps:

1. **Click on Files in the sidebar.**
2. **Click on the white Upload a File button in the upper right-hand corner.**

   Slack prompts you to locate the file on the computer.
3. **Find the file and upload it.**

   You can do this in the same way as you do with email attachments. It's probably the Open button, but the exact name will hinge upon your computer's operating system.
4. **(Optional) From the prompt, enter a message about the file.**
5. **(Optional) Click on the blue Add file link to add another file.**

   Slack allows you to upload multiple files at a time.
6. **(Optional) From the drop-down menu, choose the channel, group of users, or app with which you want to share the file(s).**

   Again, you can share files with yourself — and no one else.
7. **Click on the green Upload button.**

Play around with Slack's powerful search options here. Specifically, you can

- Use the Files search bar to find specific documents.
- Sort existing shared files by name and date.
- Filter files by type, date range, and/or member who shared the file with you.

As Figure 4-13 displays, Slack's Files view allows you to easily access the files that you've shared — and that others have shared with you.

Note that you can also use Slack's main search bar at the very top of the workspace to find workspace files. Chapter 7 covers search in far more detail.

Copying links to existing Slack files

As another option, Slack allows users to create links to individual files that you've posted in public channels. Slack intends for you to share these links with existing workspace members. Follow these steps:

FIGURE 4-13: Slack Files view.

1. **Hover your mouse over the file.**

   Three horizontal dots and the More actions icon appear.

2. **Click on Copy link to file.**
3. **Share the file link in a channel or direct message.**

REMEMBER

Note that this process creates a private link. Even outsiders who obtain access to that URL can't view the page. Only members of the Slack workspace can view the link.

Creating external links to files posted in channels

Say that you upload a file to a channel. Now you want to share a link to that file within Slack with someone who does not belong to the workspace. You can do so by following these steps:

1. **Hover your mouse over the file or message.**

   Three horizontal dots and the More actions icon appear.

2. **Click on Create external link.**
3. **Share that link with another person via email, text, or another method you like.**

REMEMBER

Only you can create external URLs for files that you've shared. Others cannot.

If you change your mind about letting others view this link, then you can easily revoke it:

1. **Hover your mouse over the file.**
2. **Click on View external link.**

3. **Click on the Revoke button.**

   Slack warns you that others are now unable to access the link.

4. **Click on the Revoke it button.**

People who visit the now-disabled link will see a white page that reads, "The requested file could not be found."

TIP

Does an outsiders' ability to view files in Slack scare you in general? Slack has you covered. Workspace Owners and Admins can disable members' ability to generate external links. Chapter 10 covers workspace administration in more detail.

Sharing messages

You will frequently post messages to Slack channels. But what if you need to bring others into the loop? Fortunately, Slack allows you to reshare messages in a number of different ways.

Sharing messages from one public channel to another

For example, what if you spend half of your time working in marketing and the other half in IT? In effect, you work as a liaison between the two departments. Not surprisingly, you belong to both the `#marketing` and `#IT` *public* Slack channels. This distinction is critical.

In this example, you want to let people from one department know about a decision that people in the other department have made. The following steps show you how to share messages from one public channel to another:

1. **Mouse over the message that you want to share.**
2. **Click on the rightward arrow that appears.**
3. **Under the words Share with, search for channel with which you want to share the message.**

   Optionally, you can add a few words about this DM à la forwarding an email with introductory comments.

4. **Click on the green Share button.**

   You have now shared your message with members of the other channel.

REMEMBER

You can share messages from public channels to private ones but not vice versa.

Sharing files from existing messages

Along with messages, Slack allows you to easily reshare files — that is, to share a document that you have already shared with someone else. (Presumably, this document is yours.) Think of it as the equivalent of forwarding an attachment that you sent.

To share a file from an existing message that you have sent:

1. **Mouse over the file that someone has sent you in Slack.**
2. **Click on the rightward arrow that appears.**
3. **Under Share with, click on the destination for the shared file.**

   The destination can be a person or a channel. You see a familiar prompt.

4. **(Optional) Add a message to provide some context around the file.**
5. **Click on the green Share button.**

REMEMBER

Slack does not allow you to quickly share an attachment that someone has shared with you. Of course, you can always download the file and share it as your own.

REMEMBER

Keep in mind basic workplace etiquette. Don't share messages or files with others unless your reason is legitimate.

Sharing private DMs

For obvious reasons, Slack doesn't allow you to share others' private messages. Try, and Slack displays a message like the one shown in Figure 4-14.

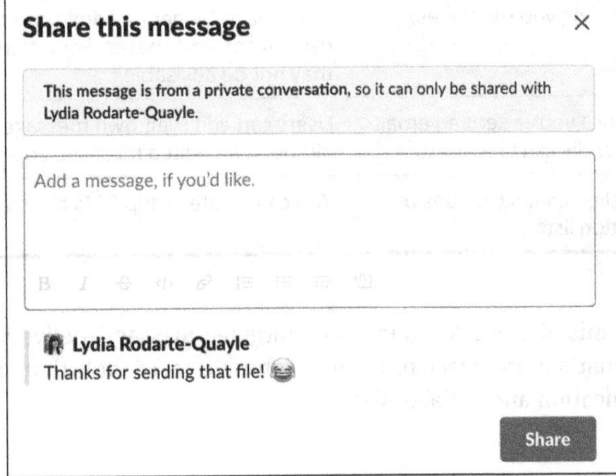

FIGURE 4-14: Slack message forbidding a user from sharing a private DM.

The same holds true for a message posted in a private channel. You can't share that message with other channels. You can only "share" it with the sender.

TIP

Of course, it's not hard to circumvent this restriction. Take a screenshot of the message and forward it to whomever you like.

Comparing Email and Slack

Slack's rich message functionality shares many traits with email. Table 4-4 highlights some of the major differences between email and Slack.

TABLE 4-4 Email versus Slack DMs

Attribute	Email	Slack DMs
Timing	Asynchronous.	Can be real-time if someone happens to be active in the workspace.
Availability	Completely open to anyone in the world with your email address, including bad actors.	Restricted to those in your workspace with the exceptions of shared and multi-workspace channels.
Privacy	Zero. You can forward a message to anyone inside or outside your organization.	Enhanced. Slack limits message- and file-forwarding both inside and outside of your workspace.
Message context	Generally lacking unless you configure advanced email filters, rules, and folders.	When used properly, much greater through public and private channels.
Muting users	You can easily block someone from sending you messages.	Slack lets you mute conversations but not users; a Workspace Owner or Admin can remove disruptive users from workspaces. For different reasons, that may not be advisable.
Edit capability	None; once you've sent an email, you generally can't retract it.	Users can edit their own messages after the fact although an edited message appears.
Group messages	Often called contact groups or distribution lists.	You can create group DMs or private channels.

Make no mistake: Slack is a far more targeted message-delivery mechanism than email. What's more, Slack provides a cohesive set of tools that enhance workplace communication and collaboration.

Forwarding Email to Slack

What happens if an internal conversation with your colleagues starts over email, but you'd like to move it to Slack? (Kudos to you for recommending Slack, by the way.)

Through any number of third-party apps, as long as everyone on the email chain can access your workspace, you can effectively move any Outlook or Gmail message to Slack for good. Simply forward the message to a unique Slack-specific email address. Slackbot delivers the email to a designated channel or DM. From there, you can continue the discussion in Slack.

Chapter 10 explores apps in more detail, but for more information about apps that support this particular feature, see `bit.ly/sfd-em`.

Although I understand the benefits of email-to-Slack apps, I view the feature as a half-measure; I don't use it for several conscious and related reasons. First, it implies that I will accept email from my students and will respond. I don't. I insist that all of my students communicate with me via Slack and nothing else. Second, by separating church and state, I know that all student communication for a specific class takes place in a specific Slack workspace. Period.

What works for me may not work for you. I know full well that you may not be able to force your peers to use Slack, let alone your superiors. (Chapter 13 offers some valuable persuasion techniques.) In this case, installing an email-to-Slack app and using it may make more sense in your case.

Communicating Outside of Slack

Here's a decidedly low-tech reminder about Slack: For two reasons, it's unlikely that you'll be able to use it exclusively and bid *adieu* to email forever.

First, everyone in a small organization may not use Slack — and that goes double for a large one. As a college professor, I use Slack as it's intended: as my default home for all student communication. As a writer, Slack trainer, and speaker, I try to do the same with all of my clients and vendors, but I don't always get my way.

This Slack-centric approach works with my students. Sometimes, however, I have to make exceptions to my "everything in Slack rule." Consider two scenarios:

- The dean of the business school does not use Slack. She sends me an email requesting some information. If I tell her that I only communicate via Slack, I risk offending her. I have to bite my tongue and respond to her email. (Yes, a little piece of me dies inside.)
- Occasionally, I have to respond to student grade appeals from the director of academic affairs. Guess what? Unfortunately, he doesn't use Slack either. In this case, it might as well not even exist.

On a different level, what if everyone at an organization uses Slack? That doesn't mean that absolutely every message or file necessarily belongs there. Put differently, it may not be possible or even wise to record all interactions in Slack. I'm not an attorney nor do I play one on TV, but potential exceptions may fall into the following buckets:

- Intellectual property
- Legal matters
- Confidential or highly sensitive corporate information
- Employee-discipline and health-related matters

Ideally, though, the percentage of messages that you send in Slack will increase over time as more people in your organization use it.

TIP

Check with the powers that be at your employer about whether you should be documenting sensitive matters in Slack — or anywhere else for that matter.

THE SLACK LEARNING CURVE

As you learn in this chapter, Slack affords users plenty of options on how to communicate. Sure, there's some overlap. For example, you can send the same message to people in multiple ways. A group direct message may serve the same purpose as private channel.

Let me put your mind at rest: At some point, you'll make a mistake — just like you have with email. You'll post a message in the wrong channel or send Elaine a DM when you really wanted to send it to George. Fret not: The Slack police won't come to your door.

» Setting your workplace status

» Taking a break with Do Not Disturb mode

» Notifying all channel and workspace members

» Configuring device-specific notifications

Chapter 5
Staying Informed with Notifications, Statuses, and Feeds

Odds are that you'll spend a great deal of time in Slack writing messages and reading others' responses. You'll share files with your colleagues, make comments on them, and participate in internal polls. (Ideally, these activities collectively mean that you'll spend far less time in your inbox.)

But how will you know that someone needs your help or input? Slack sends workspace members notifications about individual and group DMs, updates to channels, keywords, and more.

Perhaps you think an unfettered Slack will quickly become overwhelming. That is, you'll merely transfer your senses of information-overload and constant-distraction from email to Slack. You'll just go from chronically checking one application to checking another. What's the real benefit here?

To be sure, this position is an understandable and fairly common one. Trust me, though: You're mistaken. Slack is the antithesis of email's never-ending, egalitarian inbox. It allows you to prioritize the types of notifications that you'll receive, when you'll receive them, and on what device.

Take that, email!

This chapter covers how to configure notifications in Slack. In these pages, you discover how to customize your Slack alerts — even on different devices. If you want to go completely off the grid, that's easy to achieve in Slack, too.

Getting Your Arms around Notifications

At a high level, Slack notifications call attention to all the things in a workspace that interest you. To be fair, that's potentially a big bucket. More specifically, you can set notifications when any or all of the following events take place:

- Someone sends you a DM
- Someone mentions you in a channel by using `@username`
- Someone mentions `@everyone` in a channel
- Someone uses one of your keywords
- Slackbot reminds you to do something

Of course, you can tweak all of these settings. That is, when each of these five things happens, Slack doesn't have to notify you. Slack gives users unparalleled ability to control your alerts.

Managing Slack notifications

When you first install Slack and join a workspace, out-of-the-box Slack notifies you only when someone sends you a DM or mentions you in a channel by using your username.

By default, any unread workspace activity will cause Slack to display an indicator, or what Slack and other apps these days term a *badge*. The two types of Slack's badges are

» **Dot:** Signifies general unread activity in one of your Slack workspaces.

» **Number in a red circle:** Someone has done one of the following:

- Sent you a direct message
- Mentioned you or posted in a pubic channel to which you belong
- Used one of your keywords in a pubic channel to which you belong

Figure 5-1 displays my workspace with badges and unread activity.

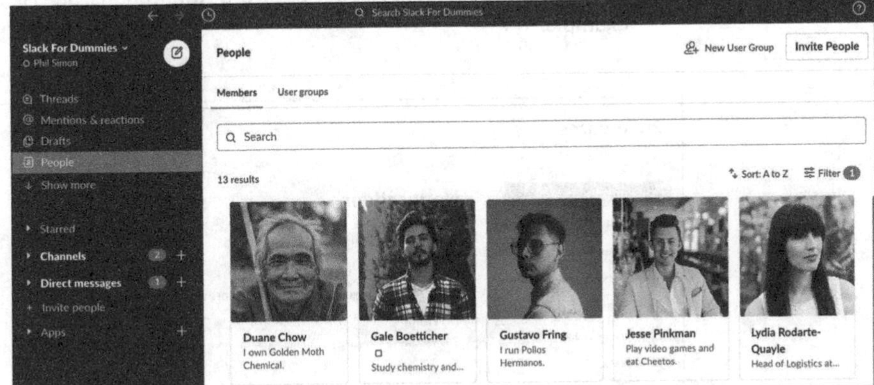

FIGURE 5-1: Slack workspace with badges and unread activity.

If you belong to multiple workspaces, then you may be worried about missing messages in one while working in the other. Don't be. As Figure 5-2 displays, Slack displays a numerical badge to the left of the sidebar indicating that new activity has taken place in the other workspace.

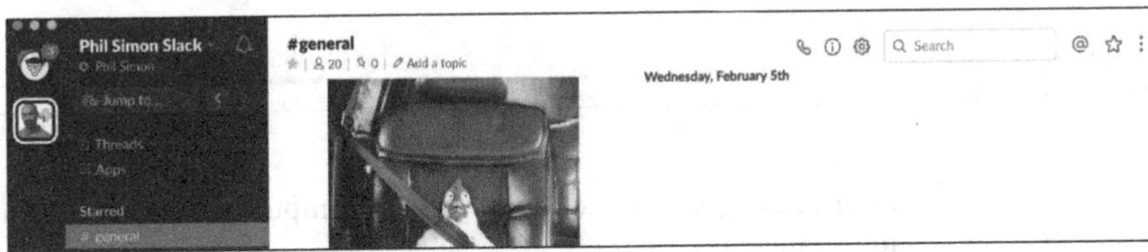

FIGURE 5-2: Slack badge indicator from another workspace.

Note that Figure 5-2 displays Slack's previous UI.

That's not to say that Slack will bother you if you want to be left alone. Later in this chapter, I explain how you can easily pause workspace notifications at any point via Do Not Disturb (DND) mode.

Reviewing the different types of Slack notifications

In Slack, notifications represent an umbrella term covering a number of different types of alerts. At a high level, you can view the settings for your workspace notifications by following these steps:

1. **Click on the main menu.**
2. **From the drop-down menu, click on Preferences.**

   At the top of the screen, you see the word Notifications. See Figure 5-3 for an example.

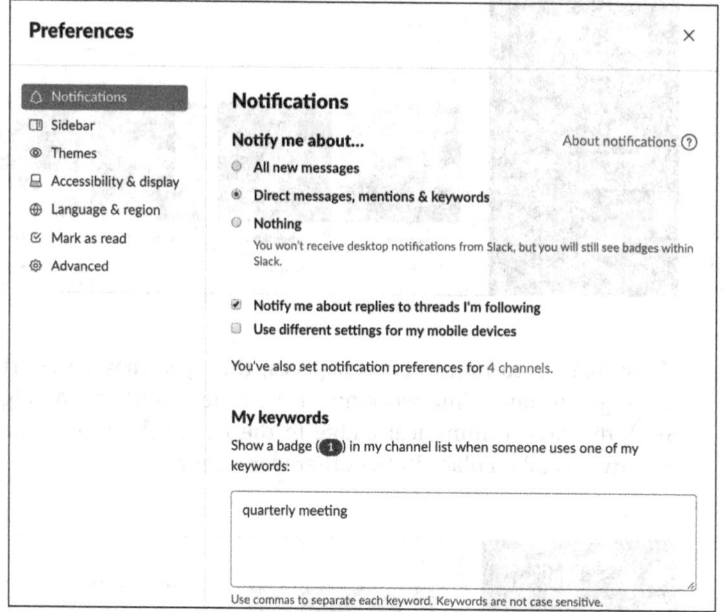

FIGURE 5-3: Slack workspace notification panel.

By accessing this panel via a proper computer, you determine where all of the magic happens.

Before going too far down the rabbit hole, remember this maxim: There's no one correct or best way to enable each of Slack's different notifications. Play around with them until you find a system that works for you. You want to balance receiving important alerts in a timely manner with keeping your sanity.

WHY I MUTE AT LEAST 50 CHANNELS EVERY SEMESTER

Each semester I teach four classes. I mandate that my 200 or so students use Slack to communicate with me and highly recommend that they use it on their group projects. After I assign them to their groups, I invite them to private channels — one channel per group. In any given semester, I'm a casual member of 50 channels.

I encourage my students to use these channels to plan meetings, coordinate work, and debate ideas with their teammates. These are important activities, but I don't need to see 50 badges as students internally discuss these topics. I don't want to leave these channels because I may have to answer a group-specific question or remind slackers (pun intended) that they all have to contribute to their projects.

What to do?

I mute each of these channels. I post a message in it telling them that if they want to reach me, they should use `@profsimon`. When another member references my handle, Slack puts a red badge to the right of my muted channel but, importantly, does not notify me. Eventually, I see the badge and promptly chime in.

Channel-specific notifications

Say that you belong to a public or private channel but only want to check in it periodically. That is, you don't need to receive regular notifications from a particular channel, but don't want to leave it altogether. Fortunately, Slack provides two ways to control your notifications from a particular channel.

MUTING A CHANNEL

If you'd like to remain in a channel but don't want to receive any notifications at all, then this feature is just the ticket for you. Muting a channel is a particularly valuable feature, and I use it frequently.

To mute a channel, follow these steps:

1. **Click on the name of the channel that you want to mute.**

   Slack displays a new pane on the right-hand side of the screen.

2. **Click on the More icon and Slack displays a number of options.**
3. **Click on the Mute #*[channel name]* button.**

TIP

Set regular reminders to check in on muted channels. (Chapter 6 covers reminders in more depth.)

After you mute a channel, Slack grays it out in the sidebar and places it below the non-muted ones. That is, it will no longer be the color of the unmuted channels. In Figure 5-4, I have muted the `#finance` and `#human_resources` channels.

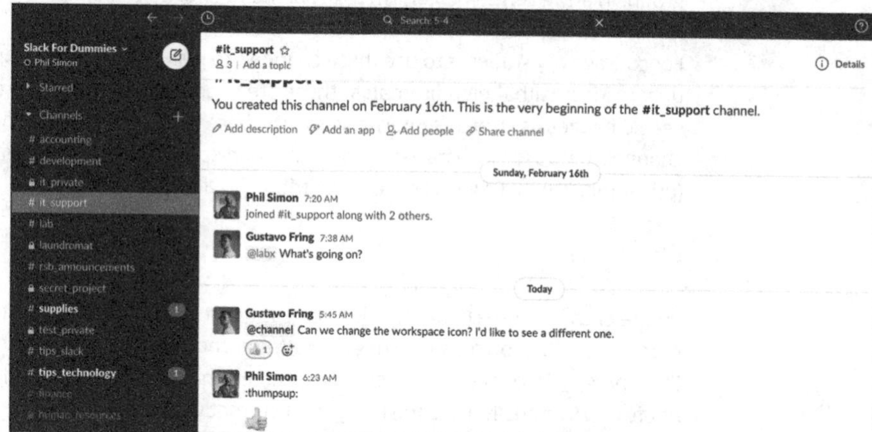

FIGURE 5-4: Example of muted Slack channels.

REMEMBER

Muting a channel is not the same as muting a conversation with a person. A workspace member can still send me a DM or correspond with me in another channel. This action only applies the activity that takes place within the channel.

REMEMBER

Say that you have muted a channel and someone mentions you in it. In this case, Slack displays a red badge in the channel. It's a subtle way of reminding you to check it. At the same time, though, Slack doesn't interrupt you with a notification.

SETTING CHANNEL NOTIFICATIONS

Slack lets you customize which channel alerts you receive and, even better, the devices on which you receive them. To tweak your channel notifications with a greater level of granularity than muting, follow these steps:

1. **In the bottom half of the sidebar, click on the name of the channel whose notification settings you'd like to change.**
2. **Click on the Details button at the top right-hand corner of the screen.**

   Slack displays a new pane on the right-hand side of the screen.

3. **Click on Notifications.**

   From here, you can ignore additional mentions and tweak the channel's notifications on your desktop and mobile device. For example, say that you don't want to receive desktop notifications from a particular channel but you want to receive @mentions on your mobile phone. If that's the case, check the boxes in Figure 5-5.

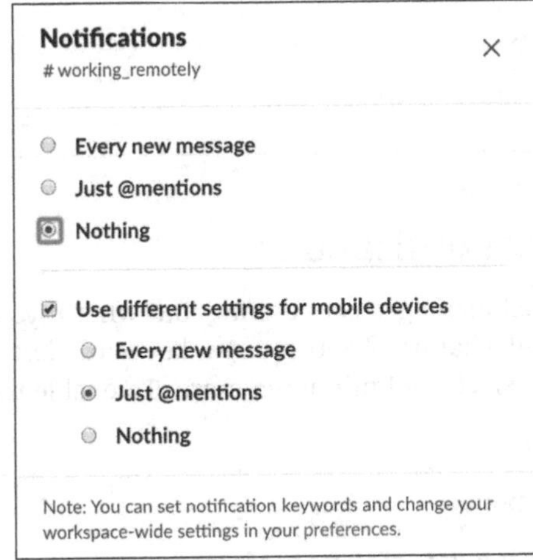

FIGURE 5-5: Example of customized channel notifications.

REMEMBER

If you fail to enable notifications from the Slack app in your phone's settings, then you won't receive them.

In a nutshell, you can configure Slack to send you different types of notifications from different channels on different devices. This is yet another example of how Slack leaves email in the dust.

Fine, but what if you want to view all your channels' notification settings in a single place? You don't have to hunt and peck. Again, Slack has you covered:

1. **Click on the main menu.**
2. **From the drop-down menu, click on Preferences.**
3. **Click on Notifications and scroll down to the very bottom of the page.**

Figure 5-6 presents a composite view of channel notifications.

Click on the X next to a channel setting. Slack then resets the channel's notifications to its default state.

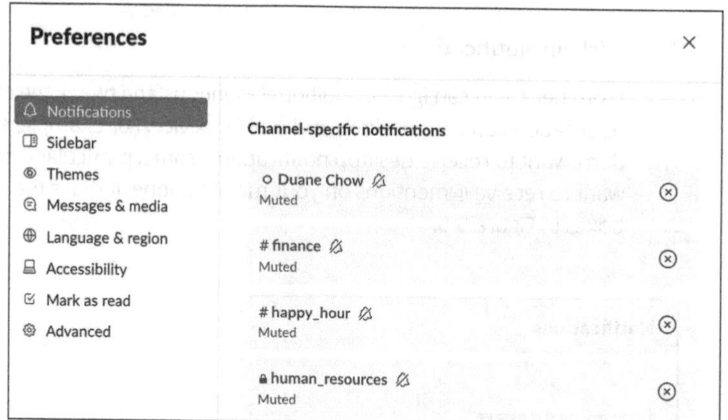

FIGURE 5-6: Slack composite view of channel notifications.

Keyword-specific notifications

Keeping track of channel messages is one thing, but what if you want to follow a term or phrase across *all* channels? Setting up a keyword alert for every channel would be cumbersome. Slack couldn't agree more. To enable these notifications, follow these directions:

1. **Click on the main menu.**
2. **From the drop-down menu, click on Preferences.**
3. **Click on Notifications and scroll down to My keywords.**
4. **Enter the keywords for which you want to receive alerts.**
5. **Click on the X in the upper right-hand corner of the screen.**

   Slack then displays a red badge in your channel list when someone uses one of your keywords in that specific channel (see Figure 5-7). For example, I want to know when anyone in my workspace uses the term *quarterly meeting*. In the notification preference panel, I simply enter that term.

When someone uses this phrase in a public channel of which I am a member, Slack notifies me. Note, however, that I won't receive notifications when others use that term in private DMs and private channels. This alert would be a clear violation of Slack's user privacy. (Chapter 9 has plenty more to say about that topic.)

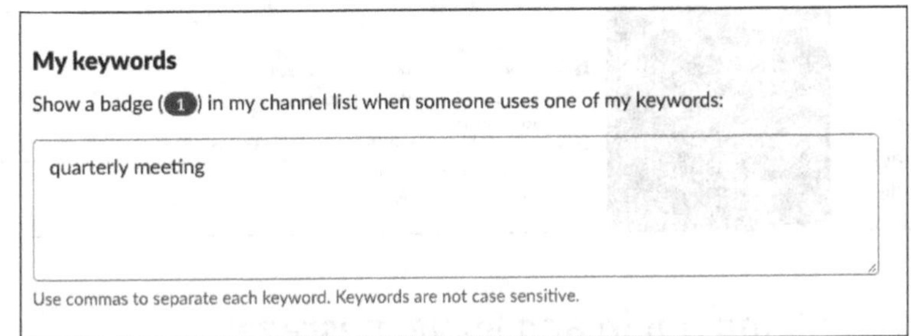

FIGURE 5-7: Slack workspace keyword alert setting for *quarterly meeting*.

DMs from individuals and groups

When a Slack user or group of users send you a DM, Slack sends you a notification. You can view unread messages underneath the channels, as Figure 5-8 shows.

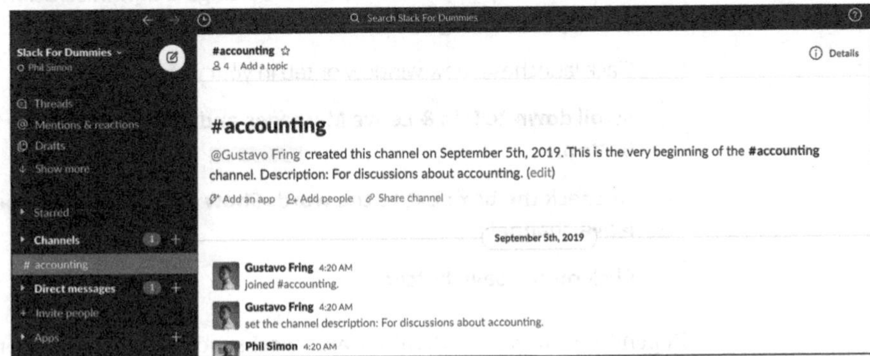

FIGURE 5-8: Slack unread DMs.

Missed calls

What if a colleague calls you but you aren't able to answer? In this case, Slack places a badge next to that person's name in the sidebar. If a colleague calls a channel and you miss it, Slack bolds the channel name in the sidebar. You see a notification that you missed a call. (Chapter 6 explains calls in more detail.)

DM reminders

Chapters 4 and 6 also cover reminders in more detail. For now, suffice it to say that you can easily set them. For example, at 3:51 p.m. on Friday, Steve sends you a DM but you're busy. You quickly set a reminder to see that message at 8:30 a.m. on Monday. At that point, Slackbot reminds you about his DM, such as the one in Figure 5-9.

FIGURE 5-9: Simple Slack reminder notification.

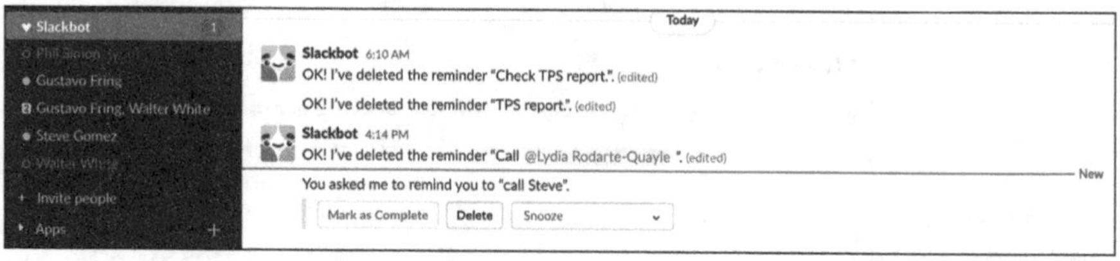

Member join and leave messages

If you work at a big company, then you probably want to disable Slack notifications when members join and leave company-wide public channels. If so, then follow these steps:

1. **Click on the main menu.**
2. **From the drop-down menu, select Settings & administration and then Workspace settings.**

   Slack launches a new window or tab in your default browser.
3. **Scroll down to Join & Leave Messages and click on the white Expand button.**
4. **Uncheck the box next to the words Show a message when people join or leave channels.**
5. **Click on the Save button.**

Depending on your individual and workspace settings, Slack may still display notifications in certain cases. (I cover customizing your workspace in Chapter 8.) Examples include

- Small public channels
- Private channels
- When somebody accepts an invitation from a member of an existing private channel

TIP

Carefully think about the notifications that you need to receive. Ideally, each one really matters.

Threads and notifications

Chapter 1 describes the chief conceit of email at work — specifically that all messages are equally important to all employees all the time. As you well know, nothing could be further from the truth; different things matter to different employees at different times. One size never fits all.

COST AND NEW MEMBER NOTIFICATIONS

If you're the primary workspace owner, then Slack's monthly cost may be at the top of your mind. Slack notifies Workspace Owners and Admins when regular members invite others to a Slack workspace — and they accept.

For the Standard and Plus plans, remember that Slack charges by the user. (Chapter 2 details Slack's different plans and their costs.) In these cases, Workspace Owners and Admins should pay attention to new member notifications. Organizations using Slack's Free and Enterprise Grid plans need not worry about the cost implications of adding new workspace members.

In Chapter 4, I describe how users can create threads that stitch together individual comments and questions into a cohesive entity. What's more, you can follow or unfollow them at your leisure. If you're keeping tabs on a thread, then Slack places a red badge next to Threads at the top of your workspace (see Figure 5-10).

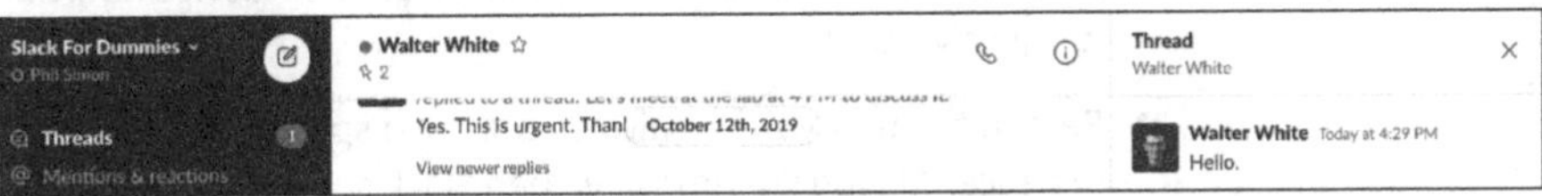

FIGURE 5-10: Slack notification of new activity in thread.

Concurrently notifying multiple users

You probably receive mass emails just about every day at your job. Maybe a few of these messages really do apply to you. As for the rest, you rightfully dismiss them as irrelevant. Mass email blasts may only mildly annoy you. Still, you likely tolerate them because they represent the only way to alert everyone in a department or company of an announcement or event. After all, generally speaking, it's better to let too many people know than too few, right?

Slack makes it easy to alert both workspace and channel members en masse. Table 5-1 provides some quick tips to get the attention of a bunch of people. By using these handles, you don't need to look everyone up in the workspace and add them to a group DM — a major timesaver to be sure. What's more, you don't need to mercilessly pepper your colleagues with unrelated messages.

WARNING

Say that you post a message in a channel with six or more members. What's more, your message includes `@channel` or `@everyone`. By default, Slack asks you to confirm your message before you send it unless a Workspace Owner or Admin has already disabled this warning.

TABLE 5-1 **@-Symbol Notification Tricks**

Callout	Purpose
`@here`	Notifies only active channel members
`@usergroup`	Notifies only the members of a particular user group
`@channel`	Notifies all members of a channel, active or not
`@everyone`	Notifies every person in the #general channel; as its name suggests, using this notifies everyone in the workspace

In addition, keep the following pointers in mind:

WARNING

- `@channel` does not work in a thread. If you want a bunch of people to see your response to a question, then post a link to the message in the desired channel.
- If you use one of the callouts in Table 5-1 in a thread, then a red badge appears in the sidebars of relevant members with one caveat: Depending on how individual members have configured their device notifications, they may not receive alerts.
- Remember that you can always call out a specific user by user name. For instance, if I type @ianmosley, then Slack shoots Ian a notification.
- See `bit.ly/sl-not` for more information on Slack's desktop notifications. Slack allows you to customize their sounds, appearance, and more.

Letting Others Know Your Availability

Anyone in your workspace can call you or send you DMs at any point. Still, you'll want to let others know about availability. Put differently, just because others can contact you doesn't mean that you want to receive notifications from them.

For example, what if someone needs to go off the grid? Say that Skyler is out of the office because she is giving birth to her new daughter, Holly. Company president Ted is considerate. He doesn't want to send her urgent DMs and become upset when she doesn't respond. (Yes, these are all *Breaking Bad* references.)

Fortunately, Slack makes it both easy and even fun to set your status — indefinitely or for a predetermined period of time. Slack statuses put the longstanding email "out of office" auto-response to shame. Note, however, that Slack can't stop someone from ignoring your status and peppering you with urgent queries if you're vacationing in Belize. No app can.

Setting your status

Set your status by following these steps:

1. **Click on the main menu and then on Update your status.**

   You see something similar to Figure 5-11.

   Figure 5-11 shows some default statuses that Slack easily lets you set, although you can customize these as needed:

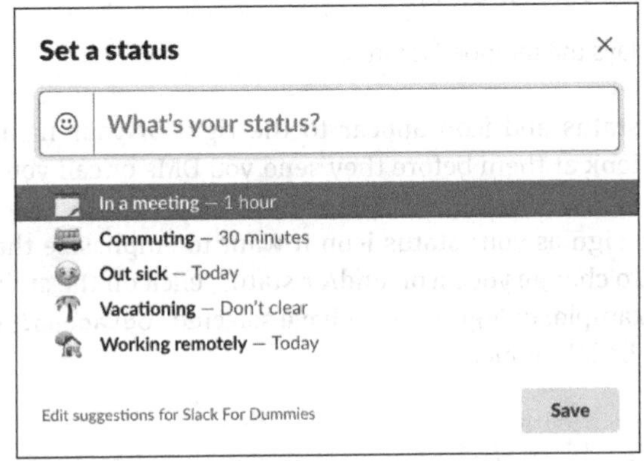

FIGURE 5-11: Slack default statuses.

2. **Click on Set a Status, which appears underneath your name.**
3. **Enter a custom status or select an existing one.**

   If you like, pick an emoji that describes your status.

   Now everyone in the workspace can view your status.

TIP

   If you know the name of the emoji that you want to include in a message, you can also type `:[emoji name]:` and press Enter. For example, `:slack:` produces the Slack emoji.

   If you do select an existing status then Slack inserts an icon to its left. You can override that icon with whatever you like.

4. **Click on the Save button.**

By letting others know your status, you can start the process of maintaining your sanity. You can also opt not to receive notifications at all via Slack's Do Not Disturb mode, but I'll get to that shortly.

Viewing your colleagues' statuses

From time to time, you will want to view your colleagues' statuses. To this end, do one of the following:

1. **If you have recently exchanged DMs with the person, then click on the member's name in the sidebar under Direct messages.**

   If Jesse has set a status, then it appears at the top of the workspace to the immediate right of his name.

2. **If not, then click on People in the sidebar.**

   Slack displays the member's status underneath his name.

3. **If you see a white callout or emoji to the right of a person's name in the sidebar, then mouse over it.**

   Slack displays the member's status.

Your custom status and icon appear to the right of your name in the sidebar. Ideally, users look at them before they send you DMs or call you.

TIP

Use a red stop sign as your status icon if want to emphasize the fact that you're unreachable. To change your icon and/or status, click on the smiley-face icon and go nuts. For example, in Figure 5-12 I have selected `:octagonal_grid:` to indicate that I want to be left alone.

USER STATUS AND ENTERPRISE GRID

Slack sets user status at the account level. As a result, under Slack's Enterprise Grid, an individual's status transcends a given workspace in an organization. For instance, say that you're a member of two workspaces within the same organization: A and B. When you set your status as "Off the grid" in Workspace A, your status cascades to Workspace B. That is, under this plan, you don't have to set your status individually for every workspace to which you belong.

If you're a member of different workspaces for *different* organizations, then your status does not cascade from one workspace to another. In this scenario, Slack rightly views your accounts as separate. In this case, if you wanted to synchronize your status, you'd have to set it separately in each workspace.

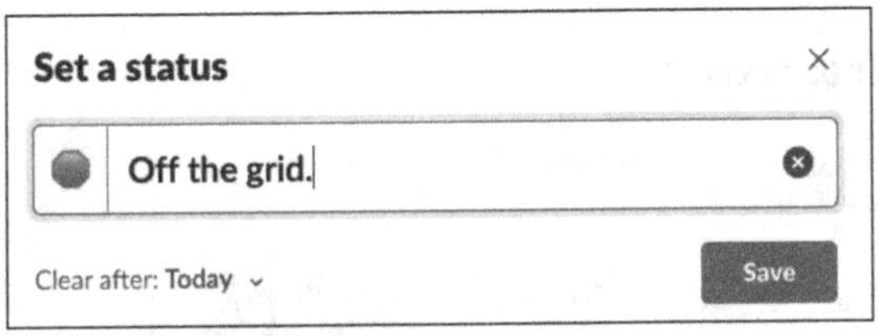

Set a status

Off the grid.

Clear after: Today

Save

FIGURE 5-12: Slack status with red stop-sign emoji.

Editing your status

Slack recognizes that you do different things throughout the day or week, so your status invariably changes. As such, you can and should set different statuses. For example, you may not want to be disturbed if you're in an important meeting. On the other hand, you may be relatively free on Tuesday afternoon.

A Slack status is meant to be temporary. At some point, you will want to change it. Follow these steps:

1. **Click on the main menu.**
2. **Enter your new status in the white text box below your name.**

Clearing your status

To remove your status altogether, follow these steps:

1. **Click on the main menu.**
2. **At the top of the drop-down menu, click on Clear status.**

Your status is now blank.

Setting yourself to away/active

When you indicate that you're away, Slack grays out your name in the sidebar. This way, your colleagues see that you're unavailable. Of course, just like email, they can still send you messages, but they shouldn't expect an immediate response.

To indicate that you are away, follow these steps:

1. **Click on the main menu.**
2. **From the drop-down menu, select Change. If you're active, then Slack flips your status to inactive and vice versa.**

When you return to a workspace after indicating that you're away, Slack asks you whether you want to let your colleagues know that you are now available. Of course, the option is yours. Figure 5-13 shows such a screen.

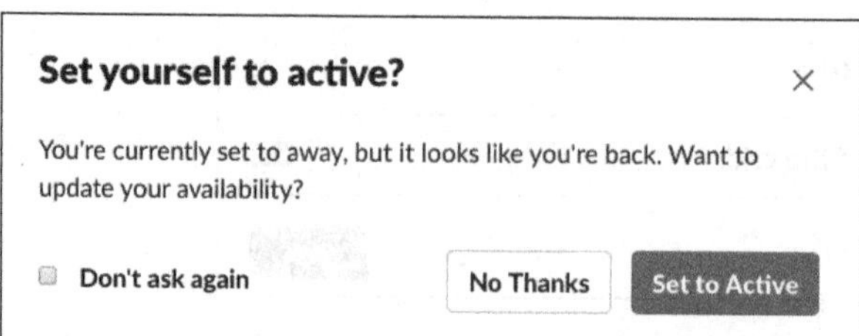

FIGURE 5-13: Slack prompt when returning from away status.

TIP

If your organization uses Enterprise Grid, then setting yourself as away applies to all of the workspaces to which you belong. For more on this topic, see the sidebar "User status and Enterprise Grid," earlier in this chapter.

Unplugging with Do Not Disturb mode

What if you worked at a software company called *Initech*? (Yes, this is an *Office Space* reference.) Your boss Bill has requested that you complete your monthly TPS reports. You start working on them, and you don't want anyone nagging you in Slack.

By enabling DND mode, Slack won't send you any notifications until you've disabled it or your DND period expires. Thanks to DND mode, you can keep Slack open and work without fear of Michael and Samir interrupting you. (Slack won't stop annoying colleagues from tapping you on the shoulder, though.)

If you attempt to call someone in DND mode, then Slack displays a message that the person doesn't want to be disturbed. In other words, Slack nixes your call.

TIP

Think of DND as snoozing; you're taking a break for a predetermined amount of time and telling others as much.

Setting a DND schedule

Here's how you set your default hours during which you don't want to receive Slack notifications:

1. **Click on the main menu.**
2. **From the drop-down menu, select Pause notifications.**

   Slack displays a sub-menu to your immediate right.
3. **Click on Do Not Disturb Schedule from the drop-down menu.**
4. **Pick the times during which you'd like Slack to disable notifications.**
5. **Press the Esc key on your keyboard or click on X in the upper right-hand corner of the screen.**

Manually activating DND mode

To pause notifications apart from your normal schedule, follow these steps:

1. **Click on the main menu.**
2. **From the drop-down menu, mouse over Do Not Disturb.**

   Slack displays a sub-menu to your immediate right.

3. **From the available options, choose how long you want to be left alone.**

After you have done this, Slack puts a small *z* next to your name at the top of the workspace until your specified window elapses.

Deactivating or adjusting DND mode

If you want to deactivate DND mode, then follow these steps:

1. **Click on the main menu.**
2. **From the drop-down menu, mouse over Pause notifications.**

   Slack displays a sub-menu to your immediate right.

3. **Click on Resume notifications now or, if you want to adjust your time frame, click on Adjust Time.**

   Slack removes the small *z* next to your name at the top of the workspace.

DND works both ways. If you see a small z next to the left of someone's name in the sidebar, then that person has enabled DND mode.

As of this writing, Slack doesn't let users create separate DND schedules for weekends. Slack's customers have requested this feature for a while now. I'm no soothsayer, but I suspect that the company will release it at some point in the future.

Great, you're thinking. Thanks to DND, you can easily tell the world to bugger off. Still, crises may arise that require someone to reach you — even if you prefer not to be disturbed unless an emergency arises. Once again, Slack has got you covered.

Sending urgent DMs

Slack lets users send urgent messages to folks who have enabled DND mode. That is, recipients receive notifications despite the fact that they're presumably busy.

What if Walt needs to send me a message, but I've enabled DND mode? I'm busy writing this book and rocking out to Marillion — both of which are important to me. Before sending me a message, Walt sees a green DND icon next to my name.

Ideally, my status deters him from interrupting me for the time being, but that's not necessarily the case. Walt types his message and presses Enter on his keyboard. Slackbot informs Walt that I don't want to be bothered right now. (See Figure 5-14.) Walt, however, is undeterred; he can't wait. Things are about to break bad, and he must reach me.

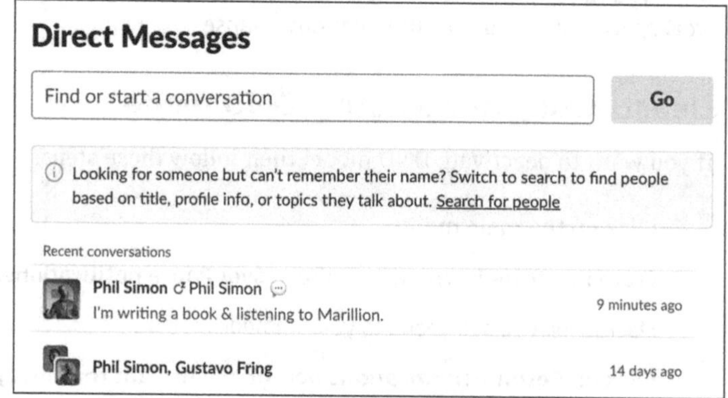

FIGURE 5-14: Slack DM options showing member DND icon.

After seeing the message in Figure 5-15, Walt clicks on Click here. At this point, Slack sends me a notification. I can respond if I want.

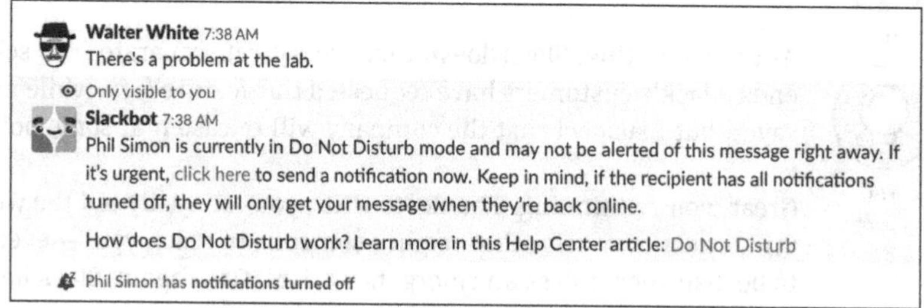

FIGURE 5-15: Overriding the DND status to send an urgent message.

Of course, I can always ignore Walt's messages. If I do, then Slack tells me that I missed critical messages while I had DND mode activated.

What if I want to ignore all notifications — from Walt or anyone in the workspace? In other words, I want to ensure that no one bothers me for any reason. Maybe I'm trying to focus, or I'm on the golf course. My recourse is simple: I can quit the Slack app. Problem solved.

TIP

Don't be afraid to use DND mode or quit Slack altogether. Nowhere is it written that you have to immediately respond to notifications — in Slack or any other tool, for that matter. As Chris Hoffman astutely writes for *The New York Times*, "Slack shouldn't be ever-present in every minute of your life." (View the article at bit.ly/2k9EFs8.)

Configuring Device-Specific Notifications

Slack recognizes that you may want different devices to send you different notifications. For example, you may want to see a wider array of alerts on your desktop because you're working. (Of course, for that very reason, you may want to see fewer.) On your phone, you may elect not to be bothered at all.

Again, your configuration choices are your own. Customize to your heart's content.

Enabling notifications on mobile devices

Chapter 2 explains how you can access Slack on any device you like — although you can only perform certain functions while using a web browser. I have installed the Slack app on my smartphone and my iPad. If you'd like to do the same, then have at it. You can also set notifications on the mobile app of your choice.

TIP

Visit bit.ly/sl-mob for far more information on mobile notifications.

Understanding when settings collide

Certain Slack settings may conflict with those on your computer, web browser, or your mobile device. Consider the following example.

I'm working on an urgent project. At 9 p.m., I open the Slack app on my iPhone. I disable Slack's DND mode, but I have set my iPhone's native DND functionality to automatically kick in at 10 p.m. until 6 a.m. In this case, my iPhone's DND mode beats its Slack counterpart. As a result, I won't receive others' DMs.

Here's another plausible scenario. Say that I am using a friend's computer. I log in to my Slack workspace via my web browser, but I don't enable its desktop notifications. I then launch Microsoft Word and work on a manuscript. Slack does not notify me of new activity in the browser.

I can think of other situations, but it's best to implement a notification system that works for you. You don't want irrelevant alerts bothering you any more than you want to miss key ones. Play around. You'll land on your own Goldilocks principle.

Finding Other Ways to Stay Current

Before concluding this chapter, here are two other useful, optional, and unobtrusive ways that Slack allows you to stay current.

Receiving emails on recent activity

What if you haven't accessed your workspace for a few weeks? (A pox on you if you haven't.) Slack by default sends you an email that summarizes the workspace messages and activity that you've missed if you've been inactive for 14 days. Figure 5-16 shows an example.

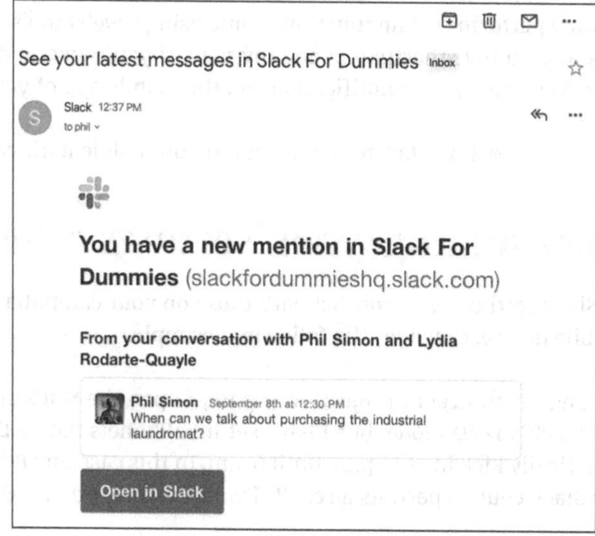

FIGURE 5-16: A Slack email to an inactive member summarizing missed activity.

If you don't find these emails useful, then you can opt out of them. Simply click on the *unsubscribe* link at the bottom of one of the emails.

TIP

I understand why Slack sends these messages and can see their benefits. Still, I always unsubscribe from these emails if I join a new workspace. Reverting to email defeats the whole purpose of Slack. After all, one of its chief benefits is that it reduces the time that you waste in your inbox.

Viewing mentions and reactions

As an added tool to keep track of everything that's going on in a workspace, Slack provides the ability to easily view all of your mentions in a single, consolidated view. These mentions include

- Your name
- Your notification keywords
- Your `@channel` mentions (optional)
- Your reactions (optional)
- Your user groups (optional)

Slack's feed eliminates the need for you to search individual channels and conversations for content related to you. At a high level, this stream is akin to the familiar news feeds of LinkedIn, Twitter, and Facebook. Even better, Slack lets you toggle this view on and off. To view your personalized mentions and reactions in Slack, follow these steps:

1. **Click on Mentions & reactions in the sidebar.**

   Slack displays a pane on the right, as Figure 5-17 shows:

   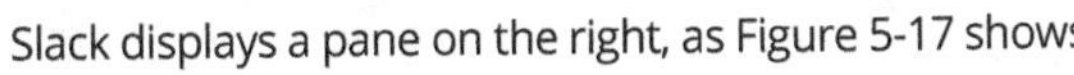

   TECHNICAL STUFF

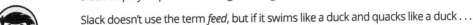

   Slack doesn't use the term *feed*, but if it swims like a duck and quacks like a duck . . .

   Note a few things about Figure 5-17. First, Slack presents user mentions in reverse chronological order. Second, Slack preserves the content from your previous view in the middle of the app. In my case, I was catching up in the `#accounting` channel before clicking on Mentions & reactions. That's why Slack displays that channel in Figure 5-17.

   Say that you find the view in Figure 5-17 to be too busy. You'd prefer to see a dedicated screen of mentions involving you. No bother.

2. **Click on the icon to the immediate left of the X in the upper right-hand corner.**

   As Figure 5-18 shows, Slack now displays a full-screen view of your feed.

TIP

Click on the filter icon in the upper-right hand corner to restrict the types of mentions that Slack shows.

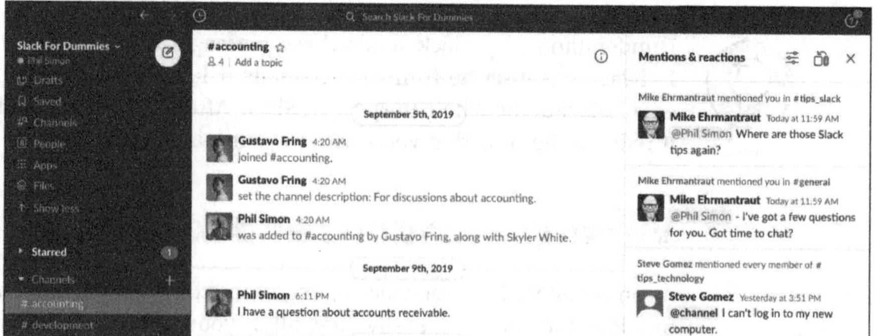

FIGURE 5-17: Slack Mentions & reactions on right-hand side.

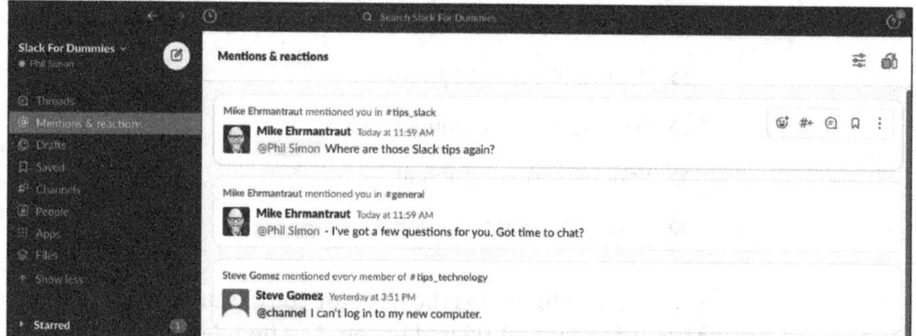

FIGURE 5-18: Slack full-screen view of Mentions & reactions.

3

Becoming a Slack Power User

IN THIS PART

Facilitate collaboration through Slack's powerful features

Find exactly what you need using Slack's powerful search options

Customize Slack's look, feel, and functionality

Review Slack's options for workplace administration

Keep your content safe and private in Slack

» Sharing your screen with your colleagues

» Using shortcuts and commands

» Setting reminders and saving items in Slack

Chapter 6
Going Deeper into Slack's Functionality

I'll bet that a good portion of your job consists of typing and reading messages. Odds are that you're in front of your keyboard more often than not.

Still, the world of work involves more than just typing and reading messages. Employees sometimes talk to their colleagues individually or as a group. (Whether they listen as carefully as they should is another matter.) They participate in meetings. People work both independently and as part of teams. They share their screens with others to accomplish a task or diagnose a problem.

In the past, employees have had to cobble together a slew of disparate tools that typically didn't work all that well. Thanks to Slack, however, those days are gone. This chapter describes some of Slack's most powerful communication and collaboration features. By using them, you'll get the most out of Slack.

Making Calls in Slack

As of this writing, more than 12 million people know that Slack is the perfect place to unify their internal communications. Part 2 of this book describes how to post messages in Slack channels and send DMs to your colleagues. Foolish is the soul, though, who believes that the only way to exchange information with another person is via text. In fact, sometimes it's simpler, better, and even downright necessary to talk to someone in real time.

Types of calls

At a high level, Slack allows for three types of calls:

- Calling individual members
- Engaging in group calls with specific people
- Calling Slack channels and letting members pick up as they wish

If you haven't put your face on yet or want some privacy, then you need not activate video. Slack doesn't require you to turn it on to take the call.

Making person-to-person calls

To initiate a call in Slack to someone else, follow these steps:

1. **Click on the name of the person you'd like to call.**
2. **Click on the Call button in the person's profile underneath the person's photo.**

   Slack attempts to notify the person that you're calling.

If the person doesn't want to be disturbed, then Slack tells you as much. (Chapter 5 details Slack notifications.)

TIP

If your network connection leaves a bit to be desired, turn off the video.

You may be able to take video calls on a computer by using a browser and not Slack's PC or Mac app. As of this writing, you can do as much with Chrome but not with Safari. In this book, I stick with using Slack on a PC or Mac.

Figure 6-1 shows a sample call with available icons.

Once on the call, Slack displays seven icons. From left to right, they are

- **The gears icon controls call settings:** Slack allows you to optionally name the call. You can also control your audio and video settings.

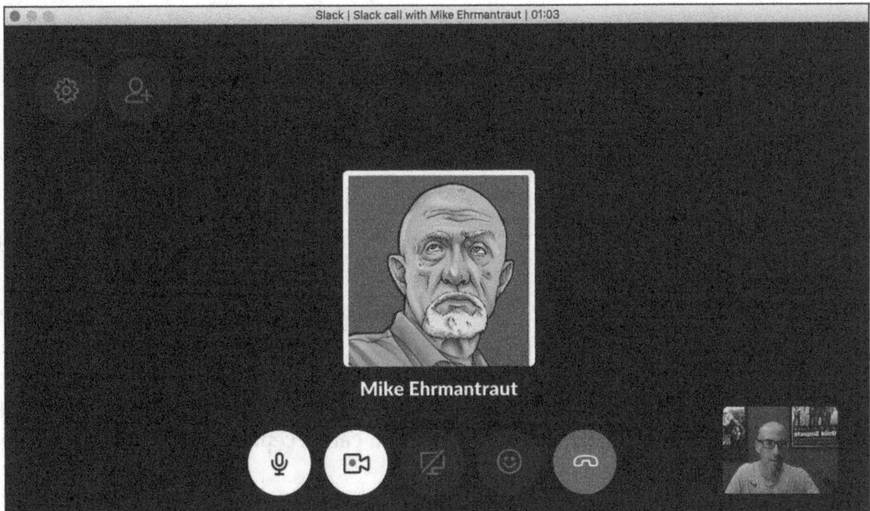

FIGURE 6-1: Slack sample video call with icons.

- **A person + icon:** By clicking here and entering a name from the list, Slack notifies the person that you'd like him to join the call. Note that it is an invitation. Slack doesn't force the invitee to hop on the call. At present, Slack supports a maximum of 15 concurrent participants per call.

  If you'd like to share the call's link, simply copy it and post it in a channel or send it to whomever you like as a DM. (You can you do other things in Slack while on the call.) Interested parties can click on the link and join the call as long as they don't exceed Slack's 15-person limit.

- **Microphone:** Hit this button if you need to mute your audio. Slack displays a muted microphone icon to the left of your face. Click on the button again to unmute it.
- **Video camera:** Click on this icon to enable and disable video.
- **Share screen:** If your organization pays for a premium plan, you can share your screen with others on the call. Slack disables sharing by default, and you'll see a red diagonal line across this icon until you enable it. Click on it to share your screen and click on it again to stop.
- **Add emojis and short text messages to the call:** You can send and receive short messages with call participants. Perhaps you need to run a quick poll, tell everyone you're stepping out for a moment, or just send a quick thumbs-up emoji.
- **Hang up call:** Just like you would in real life.

In August 2019, Slack enhanced its video-calling functionality in a number of ways. Here are the highlights:

- You can view a call's details before getting on it.
  - When people join a group call, user avatars appear.
  - Slack marks calls with timestamps to show you when they began.

TIP

Go to `bit.ly/sl-cl` to see a list of keyboard shortcuts available for Slack calls.

In case you're wondering, you need not be in front of a proper computer to take a call in Slack. Screen sharing, however, is a different matter. As Figure 6-2 shows, via the Slack mobile app, you can accept calls by clicking on the green button.

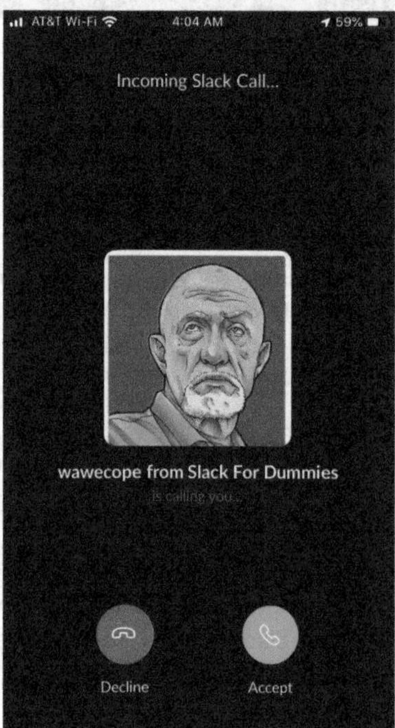

FIGURE 6-2: Accepting a Slack call on an iPhone.

Holding a group call

Group calls function largely in the same manner as person-to-person calls (see the preceding section). In fact, you can easily turn the latter into the former by sharing the call link with other people and having them jump on. That is, you need not hang up on the first call to initiate the second.

For example, James and John are discussing musical arrangements, but they need Mike's input. They can simply send Mike the call link and wait for him to join.

Calling a Slack channel

In some instances, you know exactly whom you want to call and what you need to discuss. Other times, though, things are more open-ended. For example, as a college professor, I hold formal office hours twice per week. Beyond that, on occasion I hold general review sessions. I don't know which students are going to attend. My online students may never walk through my door because they may live anywhere on the planet. I'd like to open my virtual door and let anyone "walk" in.

Slack intelligently allows workspace members on premium plans to call private and public channels but no one in particular. Channel members can answer that call if they like. Think of it as a conference call without the nine-digit codes and confused people trying to figure out how to work the software. With channel calls, workspace members can easily come and go as they please.

Here's how to initiate a channel call:

1. **In the sidebar, click on the name of the channel that you want to call.**
2. **Click on Details in the upper right-hand corner.**

   Slack presents four icons underneath Details.
3. **Click on the Call icon. It is the second from the right.**

   Slack confirms that you want to start the channel call.
4. **Click on the green Start Call button.**

   After you do, you see something similar to Figure 6-3.

   Note that only channel members are able to join.
5. **Wait for others to join the call.**

   You can always post a message in the relevant channel about the call and include the call link — in this case, `@general`. Depending on members' notification settings, Slack may bold the channel for them indicating new activity as you see Figure 6-4.

   Members can simply click on the green Join button to hop on.
6. **End the call when you finish.**

   Slack automatically posts a message to the channel notifying everyone that the call took place and has ended. Of course, you can delete that message, if you like (see Figure 6-5).

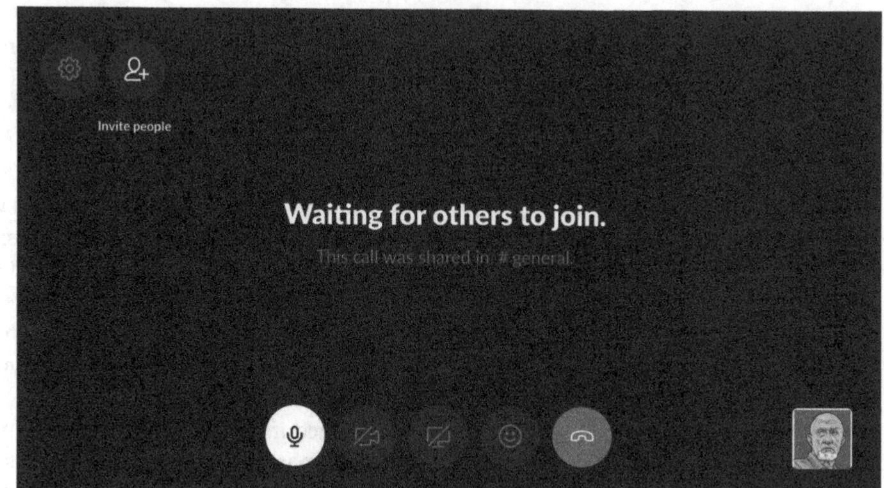

FIGURE 6-3: Slack #general channel call without participants.

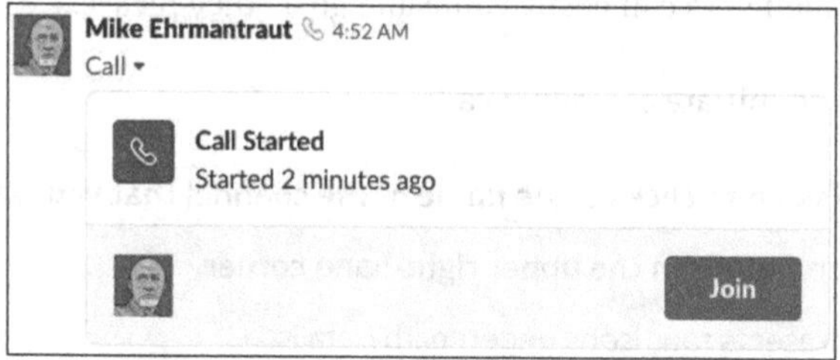

FIGURE 6-4: Slack notification in #general channel of new call.

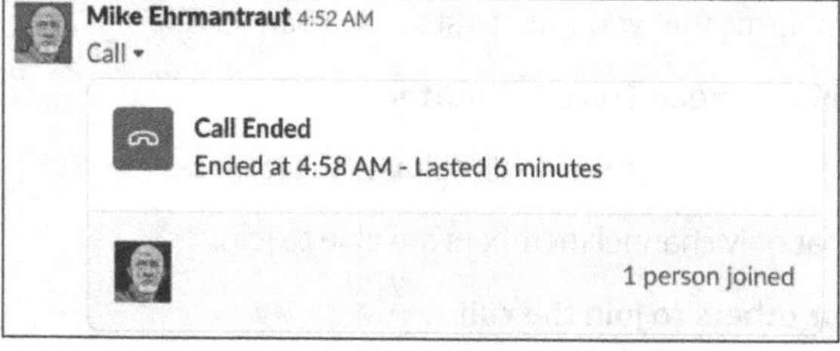

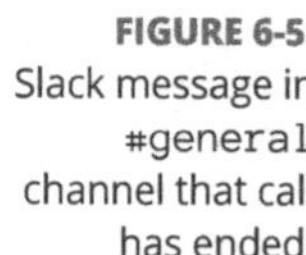

FIGURE 6-5: Slack message in #general channel that call has ended.

WARNING

Be careful here. By calling a public channel, any and every member of the workspace can join. If you're discussing sensitive company matters, then you may not want to use this feature unless you trust every member of the channel.

Calls and security

Slack doesn't record or store member calls. It does, however, keep performance-related *metadata* on each call. (Metadata is simply data about data.) For example, Slack tracks which users participated on the call, their location, and the time that a call ends. By keeping track of this metadata, Slack can improve future call quality and reduce latency.

As Chapter 9 discusses, Slack uses end-to-end encryption to ensure that all communication remains safe from prying eyes. For more on how Slack ensures the confidentiality of each call, go to `bit.ly/slcallz`.

If you need to record a call in Slack, however, you're in luck. Zoom and other third-party apps offer this valuable feature. (Chapter 10 describes apps in more detail.)

Sharing Your Screen in Slack

Screen-sharing technology isn't exactly new, and it would be downright silly for Slack not to include it in its offering. With a simple click of your mouse, Slack's premium customers can share their screens and vice versa. Provided that everyone is connected to the Internet at a reasonable speed, latency should be minimal.

TIP

You can't share your screen whole on a mobile app or web browser. You need to download the Slack desktop app. (See Chapter 2 for more details on this topic.)

Presenting and viewing

It's not hard to envision a number of useful screen-sharing scenarios:

- Firing up PowerPoint or Google Slides to give a webinar.
- Diagnosing a technical error.
- Showing someone a cool software tip.
- Providing specific feedback on a design.

Of course, you need not be the one sharing. You can view others' screens if they let you. Unfortunately, you can't control your colleague's computer through native Slack. The company nixed this feature in July 2019. If you want to "drive," you'll have to use a third-party tool such as Zoom (again, discussed in Chapter 10.)

Drawing

While you are presenting, you may benefit from letting call participants mark up your screen. Others may need to highlight specific formulas on your spreadsheet, lines in your code, and features in a software application. Fortunately, Slack allows people on the call to scribble or highlight important details on your screen.

When you enable screen sharing, Slack displays two additional icons:

- **Draw on your own screen:** By clicking on the pencil icon, you can draw on your own screen for others to see. Simply click your mouse and drag it to highlight text on your screen.
- **Let others draw on your screen:** Click on the icon with three pencils to let others draw on your screen. Note that Slack erases these scribbles after a few seconds.

TIP

Slack lets you change the color of your highlighter pen while screen-sharing. On a Mac, hold down the ⌘ key. On a PC, do the same with the Ctrl key.

Saving Even More Time in Slack

Screen sharing is just one of the different ways that Slack allows you to work more efficiently. Keyboard shortcuts and commands are optional, but they allow users to save a good bit of time.

POWER USERS AND POWER LAWS

Many contemporary business applications follow a power or Pareto law, named after the Italian polymath Vilfredo Pareto. Put simply, roughly 80 percent of a program's users take advantage of a mere 20 percent of its functionality. Case in point: Microsoft has conducted usability studies that have proven as much. The vast majority of Excel and Word users know only the basics; relatively few have monkeyed with each application's advanced features. Perhaps I'm wrong here, but I suspect that Slack is similar in this regard.

By applying the knowledge from Parts 3 and 4, you can put yourself squarely in that 20 percent — not a bad place to be.

Invoking keyboard shortcuts

In the 1970s, relatively few people used computers. Those who did primarily interacted with them via terminals. Even today, mouse-free green screens still exist in many large organizations that are lamentably tied to legacy systems. For the most part, though, the average worker today interacts with proper computers via a mouse and different applications' graphical user interfaces (GUIs).

I'm willing to bet that you use Microsoft Office. After all, more than 1.2 billion people do. I'll also wager that you have learned a decent number of shortcuts over the years. For example, press ⌘ + C on a Mac or Ctrl + C on a PC to copy text. Do the same with ⌘ + V on a Mac or Ctrl + C on a PC to paste the text that you just copied. These shortcuts work for Word, Excel, and PowerPoint. Other Office shortcuts include

- S for save
- Z for undo
- N for a new document

Sure, it takes time to learn these shortcuts, but the juice is typically worth the squeeze. Some studies have shown that you can save eight days per year by embracing these timesavers — a fact not lost on Slack. To this end, Slack provides a boatload of shortcuts for its computer app.

For example, in the Slack app you want to quickly invoke its preferences. Press ⌘ + on a Mac or Ctrl + , on a PC, and Slack displays its preferences, as shown in Figure 6-6.

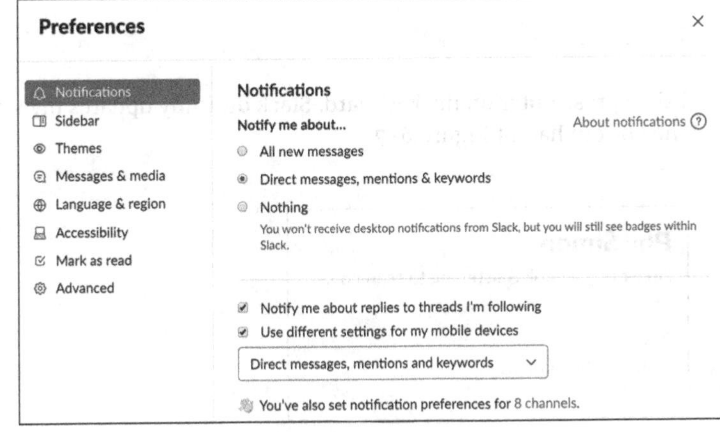

FIGURE 6-6: Viewing Slack preferences via keyboard shortcut from computer app.

TIP

Check out the full list of Slack keyboard shortcuts for all operating systems by going to `bit.ly/short-sl`. Do yourself a favor, though: Don't attempt to learn all of Slack's shortcuts at once. After you have become more comfortable using Slack, review the list. Try to learn one or two per week.

WARNING

The settings on your computer's operating system may conflict with certain Slack shortcuts. For example, say that I want to switch Slack workspaces on my MacBook Pro. Slack allows me to do this by concurrently pushing the ⌘ key and the number of the desired workspace. Unfortunately, this shortcut doesn't work for me because I've already configured that same shortcut on my Mac to switch to different desktops. Of course, I could always change my existing MacBook Pro's shortcuts. For me, though, it's just not worth reprogramming my brain.

Using commands

Perhaps you've used your computer's command-line interface before. PC folks use the command prompt. Their Mac counterparts can access the Terminal.

Are these folks Luddites? Hardly. Plenty of hardcore computer users eschew the mouse in certain instances for one simple reason: They can perform many tasks faster by typing commands compared with using a mouse to navigate menus.

Slack's founders are well aware of the benefits of command-line interfaces. (In interviews, CEO Stuart Butterfield has described how early Slack employees were fans of Internet Relay Chat, a communication application that dates back to 1988.) As such, Slack offers users the ability to quickly perform many functions via text-based commands.

Exhibit A: You can set your status in Slack by typing `/status` in any window. I type

```
/status Eating breakfast.
```

I then press Enter on my keyboard. Slack dutifully updates my status, as shown in the bottom half of Figure 6-7.

Phil Simon ○

I'm writing a book & listening to Marillion.

Status

Eating breakfast

Until 11:59 PM

FIGURE 6-7: My current Slack status.

Of course, as I mention in Chapter 2, I could have achieved the same result by following these steps:

1. **Click on the main menu.**
2. **Clicked in the white textbox underneath my name.**
3. **Type the words** Eating breakfast.
4. **Press Enter on my keyboard or click on the green Save button.**

TIP

Again, Slack often gives users multiple ways to accomplish the same task. If you're more comfortable using your mouse and Slack's menus, then knock yourself out.

Not to get all meta, but my favorite Slack shortcut provides a list of shortcuts.

```
/shortcuts
```

All the Slack shortcuts appear on the right-hand side of the app. Pretty neat.

TIP

Visit `bit.ly/sl-slash` to view a list of all of Slack's built-in slash commands.

Managing Your Life with Reminders

With so much going on at work, forgetting to do something is easy. In this vein, Slack makes it simple to set quite a few types of reminders.

REMEMBER

Chapter 4 covers message-specific reminders. The reminders in this section don't apply to a specific DM, conversation, or channel message.

For example, say that I need to speak to J.R. today at 6:50 am about a coding project. Like me, he's an early riser. In Slack, I click in any message window and type the text in Figure 6-8.

```
/remind me to call JR today at 6:50 am
```

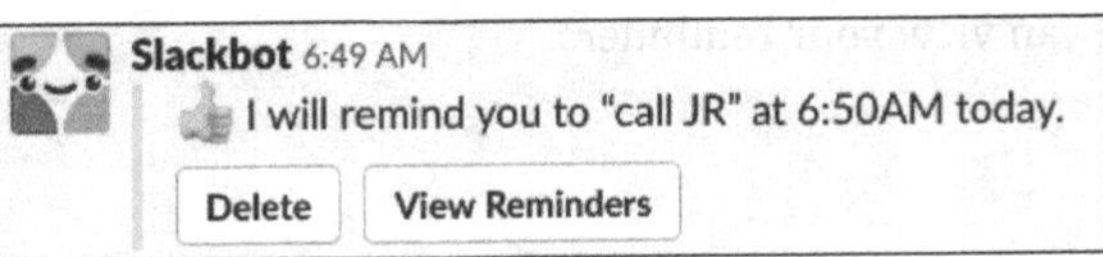
Slackbot 6:49 AM
I will remind you to "call JR" at 6:50AM today.
Delete
View Reminders

FIGURE 6-8: Slackbot reminder confirmation.

At 6:50 am, Slack reminds me to call J.R. as Figure 6-9 displays.

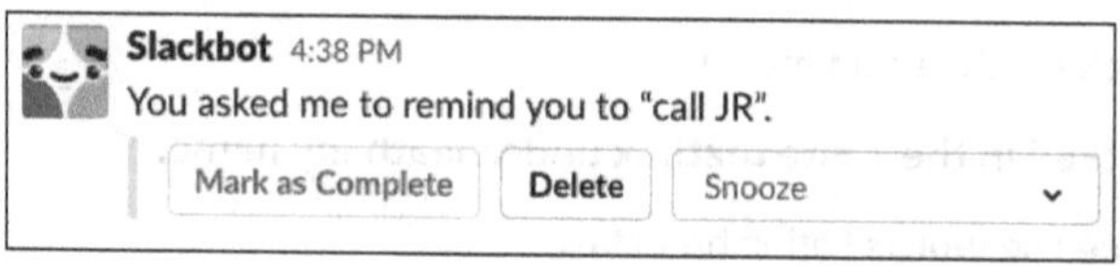

FIGURE 6-9: Slackbot reminder.

At this point, Slack presents me with a number of different options:

- Mark as complete
- Delete
- Snooze

If I select the third option, Slackbot sends a quick message confirming when it will send another reminder.

Slack's newest version allows you to create a reminder by clicking on the lightning-bolt icon in the message window. This launches an intuitive wizard.

Table 6-1 presents some particularly helpful reminders.

TABLE 6-1 Slack Reminder Shortcuts

Shortcut	Results
/remind me to *[do something]* at *[some time]*	Slack does exactly what you'd expect here.
/remind list	Returns a list of the reminders that you have set.
/remind help	Provides help text about Slack's reminder functionality.

If you mute a conversation because you don't want to deal with someone or something right now, it's wise to set a reminder to unmute it in the future.

No one else can view your reminders.

Saving Items

You're probably working on any number of different things at any given time. Sadly, few people today have the luxury of focusing on only one thing while on the clock. What if you could view a simple list of important files, messages, and things that you need to do? Starred items allow you to search less, focus on your most important tasks, and work more efficiently in Slack.

Chapter 4 covers how you can send group and individual DMs as well.

Saving files

With so many files flying around Slack, it can be challenging to keep track of them. (Chapter 7 covers search.) Fortunately, Slack lets you star files and easily access those that you've deemed especially important. Simply follow these directions:

1. **Mouse over a file.**
2. **Click on the three horizonal dots labeled More actions.**
3. **Click on Save.**

   Your file now appears in the Saved view. By default, Slack lists your saved files in reverse chronological order of when you saved them, not when the person posted them.

Saving messages

You can mark messages as favorites as well. To do this, you'll use a similar process that you use to mark files as favorites:

1. **Mouse over a DM or channel message.**

   A bookmark icon to the left of the three horizontal dots.

2. **Click on the bookmark icon and it turns red.**

   The message now appears in your Saved view.

Quickly accessing your saved items

To access your starred items, simply click on Saved in the left-hand side of the sidebar. Figure 6-10 shows you an example of what you see.

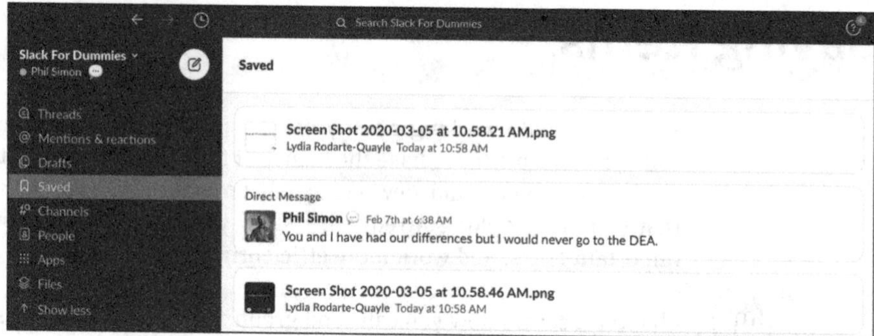

FIGURE 6-10: Slack Saved view.

Say that you no longer want a message or file to appear in your starred items. Just click on the star icon again. Slack removes the star but not the item itself.

TIP

Click on a link at the bottom of each starred item to immediately go to the DM or conversation in the relevant channel.

Creating User Groups

Although optional, user groups serve a number of valuable purposes in Slack. First, Workspace Owners and Admins can use them to add members to different public and private channels *en masse*. Techies usually need to see different information than accountants do. In higher education, nontenured professors usually don't need to view messages meant for their tenure-track brethren. Second, user groups make it easy to alert a subset of members within a single channel or group DM.

USER GROUPS: A DETAILED EXAMPLE

Tim is the newly promoted VP of national sales at Omnicorp. In total, he manages 50 different sales managers. He wants to send a message to the eight store managers in the eastern district. Tim creates a user group called `@eastern_sales_mgrs` and adds those eight managers to it. He posts a message in the entire `#sales_mgrs` channel but tags `@eastern_sales_mgrs`. After that, each of the eight managers in the `@eastern_sales_mgrs` user group sees a numbered badge next to the `#sales_mgrs` channel. The other 42 do not.

Note that, depending on their individual notification settings, Slack bolds the `#sales_mgrs` channel for all 50 members indicating that there are new messages.

Slack reserves user groups for premium plans, and they exist within a workspace. You can't share them across different ones. To create one, follow these steps:

1. **Click on the People view in the top half of the sidebar.**
2. **Click on New User Group at the top of the screen.**

   Slack displays a window like the one in Figure 6-11.

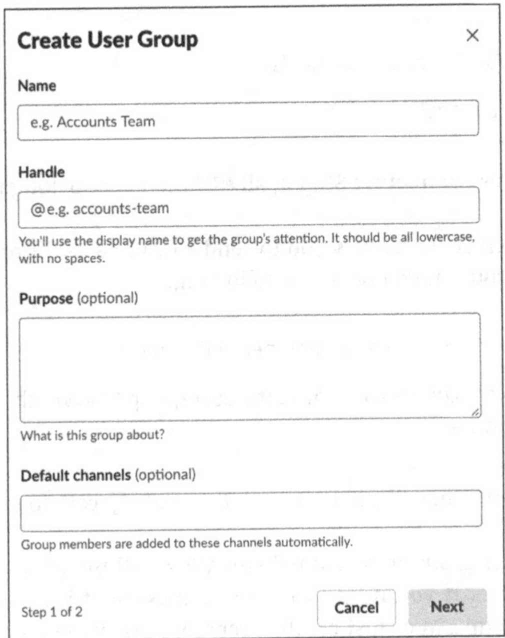

FIGURE 6-11: Slack user group initial prompt.

3. **Enter a name for the user group.**

   The handle cannot match that of another user group. Spaces are fine here.
4. **Enter a handle for the user group.**

   The handle cannot match that of a current workspace member, channel, or other user group. You need to use all lowercase letters without spaces.
5. **(Optional) Enter a purpose for the user group.**
6. **(Optional) Enter the new channels to which Slack will add members of this user group.**

   Type a few letters of the channel name and Slack auto-populates it.
7. **Click on the green Next button.**

8. **Search by name and add workspace members to your user group.**

   Type a few letters of the person's name and Slack auto-populates it.

9. **Click on the green Create Group button.**

Note that adding channels to user groups is cumulative. As a simple example, at puppet maker Sanitarium, all employees join five public channels by default. Chief Information Officer (CIO) Lars creates a new user group `@IT` with three default channels:

- » Two new public IT-related channels
- » One private channel

Once Lars finishes completing Step 9, all `@IT` members belong to eight channels.

At this time, Slack doesn't allow you to send a DM to a user group. To circumvent this limitation, you can do one of the following:

- » Create a group DM with each member of the user group.
- » Create a private channel and invite the user group to it, which will add all members at once.

Irrespective of your role, Slack does not let you add guests to user groups.

REMEMBER

Mentioning a user group in a channel still allows all members in that channel to view that message. If you need to restrict a message to the members of a user group, send a group DM or just create a separate private channel for those folks.

» **Restricting search results by date ranges**

» **Refining your results via keywords and negative keywords**

» **Using wildcards in your searches**

» **Getting the most out of your search results**

Chapter **7**

Finding What You Need with Slack's Powerful Search Techniques

Say that you actually follow the advice in this book. You are really picking up what I'm putting down. More specifically, you are using Slack as your organization's central communication and collaboration hub and knowledge repository. Along these lines, you are abiding by my default "everything belongs in Slack" rule. If these two statements are true, then it's essential that Slack lets you easily and quickly find exactly what you need.

Once again, Slack has got you covered. This chapter describes the many ways in which Slack lets you locate DMs, channel messages, different types of files, and your colleagues. After explaining the different clubs in your bag, I end with recommendations on how to most effectively find what you need in Slack.

Searching for Better Search Methods

For all sorts of reasons, Chapter 1 makes the case for Slack over email as a communication and collaboration tool. Most germane to this chapter, though, is the stark reality that people often can't find the files and messages that they need. When they do locate key documents or messages, it often takes them far too long.

Don't believe me, though.

In 2001, research firm International Data Corporation (IDC) found that the average knowledge worker spent two and a half hours searching for information. *Not per week, but per day.*

Fine, but that was nearly two decades ago. Things must have improved since then, right?

Not by that much. An oft-cited McKinsey report from 2012 revealed that that number had dropped to 1.8 hours per day or 9.3 hours per week. (Read the entire report by visiting `https://mck.co/2NhRP1G`.)

What is the true number for the average employee at your company? I don't know, but I'm sure that the answer varies. Some employees name and organize their files far more intelligently than others. Smart Microsoft Outlook users dutifully place their emails in orderly folders. For their part, Gmail users embrace the application's superior method of applying multiple tags to each message.

Part of the general "content discovery" problem stems from one simple fact: Employees typically need to visit many different applications to find work-related documents, messages, directories, and information. These tools include

- **Email applications:** Outlook and Gmail are the big kahunas here.
- **Key files:** You probably keep essential information in certain Microsoft Word and Excel documents on your hard drive.
- **Current enterprise systems:** You may need to look up information on purchases, sales, employees, vendors, partners, or other transactions.
- **Pieces of paper and sticky notes:** I bet that you've got at least one of these items on your desk or computer monitor.
- **Social networks:** For many reasons, you may network or communicate with others in LinkedIn, Facebook, Twitter, or all three.
- **Different instant-message tools:** Examples may include Skype, iMessage, Signal, WhatsApp, and Snap.

» **External hard drives and portable USB drives:** Many folks wisely abide by this maxim: Better to have it twice or thrice than not at all.

» **Standalone apps on mobile devices:** For example, I keep my travel plans in TripIt, my reading list in Pocket, and my passwords in Dashlane.

» **File-storage services:** Examples include Dropbox, Google Drive, and others.

Against this backdrop, riddle me this: Is it any wonder that employees often can't find what they want, let alone quickly?

Brass tacks: There's no single tool that searches every different device, service, and application that employees use — and that includes Slack. No, Slack won't magically read the handwritten notes on your desk. Still, by using it as your primary communication and collaboration hub, you can vastly reduce the amount of time that you spend looking for key conversations and documents.

Performing Searches in Slack

There's a good bit of functionality to unpack with Slack search. As such, it's important to walk before you run. Access the search console by following these steps:

1. **Click on the search bar in the main navigation bar of your workspace.**

   Slack shows you your most recent searches. By clicking on one of them, Slack returns the results from a previous search.

2. **If you want to conduct a new search, then type a term and press Enter on your keyboard.**

   Slack returns the results that match your query broken down into four tabs:

   - Messages
   - Files
   - Channels
   - People

It's that simple, although I cover more advanced search techniques later in this chapter.

If you're familiar with modern search engines, then you understand the general concept of search terms or keywords. To demonstrate this concept in a Slack search, Figure 7-1 shows a quick search on the word "icon."

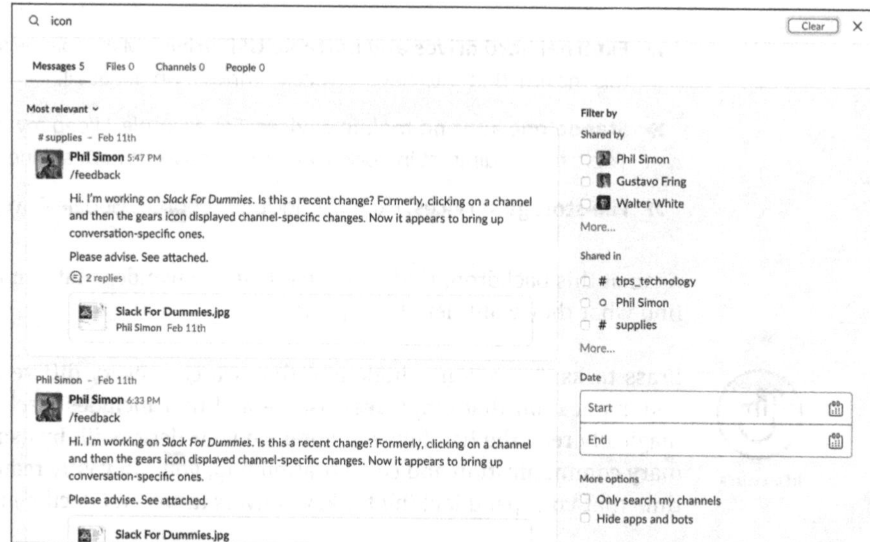

FIGURE 7-1: Slack search results on the word "icon."

Note a few things about Figure 7-1. First, Slack places a useful zero indicator next to each tab for which it could not find results from a query. In this case, Slack found five messages related to "icon" but no files, channels, or people. Second, Slack highlights the search term to provide immediate context to my query. You need not scroll through a long DM to see exactly where someone used your search term. Finally, by default, Slack displays all relevant results in reverse chronological order. If you want to change the displayed results to the most relevant results, simply click on the drop-down list below Messages.

TIP

Under Slack's Free, Standard, and Plus plans, users can search only one workspace at a time, which may entail performing the same search multiple times — that is, once per workspace. Enterprise Grid customers can concurrently search multiple workspaces if they use them.

Slack has borrowed a page from Google and other search engines. As Figure 7-1 shows, Slack provides a series of tabs at the top of the results for the following:

- **Messages:** Slack returns a list of messages that contain the keyword.
- **Files:** Slack returns a list of files that meet one of three criteria:
  - Members have uploaded files to public channels that contain the keyword.
  - Members have uploaded files to private channels that you belong to and that contain the keyword.
  - Members have uploaded files to private DMs that include you and that contain the keyword.

Slack also allows you to restrict your searches to specific file types. For example, if you want to filter your search for images, simply check that box. Slack ignores all PDFs, presentations, videos, and the like.

- **Channels:** Slack returns a list of channel-specific results. In other words, this tab displays the intersection(s) of the keyword(s) and the channel name, description, or any topics of conversation. By default, Slack displays the most relevant results. Other options include date created (newest to oldest), name (A to Z), and members (most to least).
- **People:** Slack returns a list of members whose names match the search term or those who have used the term to describe their current status. You can restrict members by Owners, Admins, Members, guests, and deactivated accounts. You can even restrict by the type of computer that the person uses (PC or Mac).

TIP

Slack limits users of its Free plan to the most recent 10,000 messages. Members on paid plans can search *all* messages in a workspace. That is, there is no limit.

TECHNICAL STUFF

Under the hood, Slack's search runs largely on *term frequency-inverse document frequency* or *TF-IDF*, a kind of artificial intelligence prototype invented way back in 1957. To be sure, this technology still works, but it's not the most contemporary way to search. (For more, visit `bit.ly/efink`.)

In addition to simple searches, Slack offers no shortage of ways to limit or expand your queries to aid in finding exactly what you need.

Searching by workspace members

Don't get me wrong: A simple search often returns exactly what you want, but Slack offers many additional search modifiers to return even more precise results.

For example, I want to restrict my search results on the word "icon" to those including a person — in this case, Walter White. By checking his name in Filter by, Slack removes results from other workspace members. See Figure 7-2.

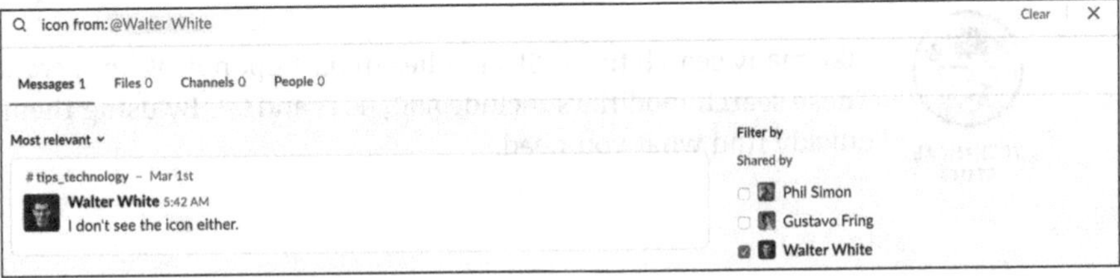

FIGURE 7-2: Slack search results on the word "icon" restricted by member name.

TIP

Mouse over a search result. If the words "View in channel" appear, then click on that link to go directly to that message in that channel. In this key way, Slack provides important context to each message in its search results.

TIP

Say that you want to restrict your results to only messages that a specific person has sent. Simply type `from@`*`username`* in the search box. You can do this with your own messages as well. For example, `from:@Phil Simon` tells Slack that I only want to view content that I generated.

Restricting searches to specific date ranges

You can also limit my results to channels and DMs. Even better, you can use date ranges to drill down even more, as I have done in Figure 7-3.

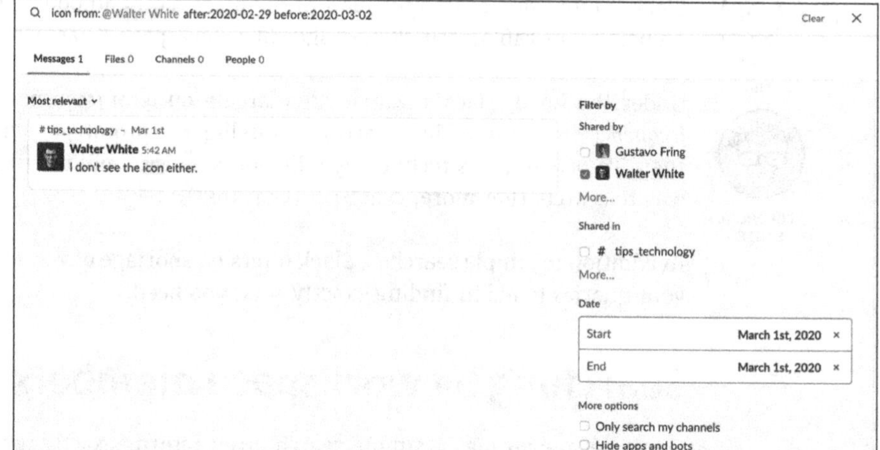

FIGURE 7-3: Slack search results on the word "icon" restricted by member name and date.

It's important to note a few things here. First, Slack updates the search bar at the top of the console to reflect the updated search criteria. If you happen to know the shortcuts for date and person, you can just type those values. Second, each of these values makes your search more specific and exclusive. You're combining keywords and other conditions to restrict the results, not expand them.

TECHNICAL STUFF

Like many search tools, Slack relies in part upon *Boolean operators* or just *Booleans*. These search modifiers include `AND`, `NOT`, and `OR`. By using them correctly, you can quickly find what you need.

Using negative keywords

You can also easily modify an existing search to exclude a particular term. In Figure 7-4, I exclude all results that include the word "changes."

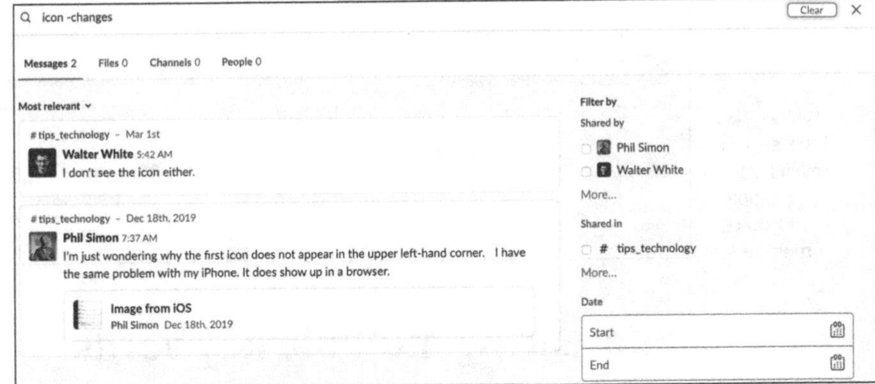

FIGURE 7-4: Slack search results using a regular and negative keyword.

Contrast the results from Figures 7-1 and 7-4. The latter excludes messages with the word "changes."

At this point, I hope that you're beginning to understand the immense power of simple Booleans. In the context of Slack, they allow users to pinpoint their search results with far greater accuracy. The end result: You save a great deal of time.

This begs the question, though, what if you don't remember specifics around a specific DM? For example, what if you don't remember who sent you a DM about a meeting? Fear not: Booleans again come to the rescue. Figure 7-5 shows an advanced search with quite a bit going on.

In English, Slack is searching for all workspace content that meets each of the following conditions:

- The content contains "meeting" but not "faculty"
- Content created between February 28, 2020 and March 1, 2020
- DM shared by either Gustavo Fring or Walter White

Slack will answer your search queries, no matter how specific they are. In this context, say that Jesse sent me a message containing the word "faculty." The DMs would *not* appear in Slack's search results for this particular query.

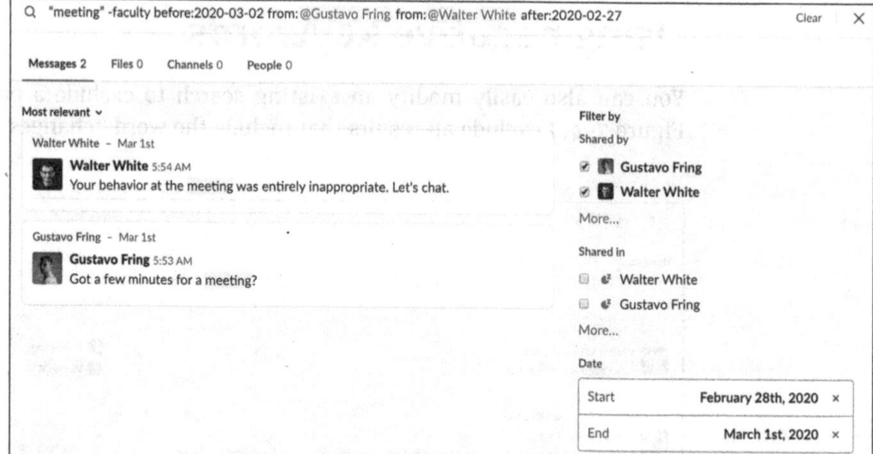

FIGURE 7-5: Slack search results from multiple workspace members.

Referencing multiple keywords

What if you wanted to reference multiple keywords or a string of text? For example, I want to find all messages and files with the phrase "TPS report." As you can see in Figure 7-6, using quotes comes in especially handy.

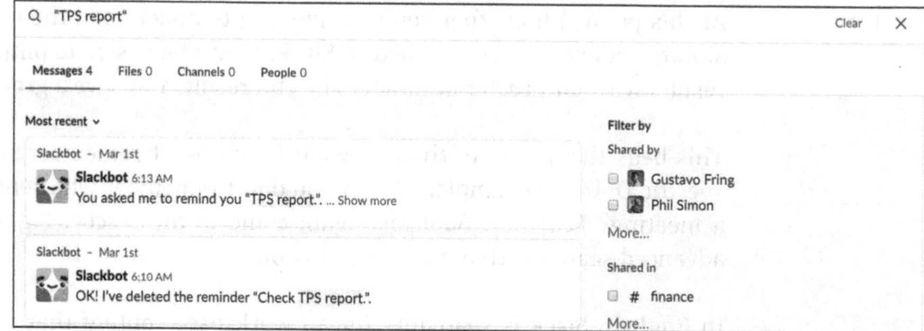

FIGURE 7-6: Slack search results containing multi-keyword phrase.

By putting quotes around those words, I've told Slack that I'm only interested in results that contain both of them in that order. That is, Slack is looking for "TPS" followed by "report." In Figure 7-7, I switch the order of those terms. As a result, I see exactly what I expect — nothing:

If you omit the quotes, then Slack returns results that include both keywords, even if they aren't next to each other. Figure 7-8 displays the results of such a query.

Q "report TPS"

Clear X

Messages 0 Files 0 Channels 0 People 0

No results

Slack couldn't find any messages related to your search. You may want to try...

- Using different keywords.
- Checking for typos.
- Adjusting your filters.

Filter by

Shared by

More...

Shared in

More...

FIGURE 7-7: Slack search results containing a reversed multi-keyword phrase.

FIGURE 7-8: Slack search results containing multiple keywords without quotes.

Restricting search results even more

Did you notice how Figure 7-8 contains messages from workspace members as well as Slackbot? Lest you think that Slack has made an error, these results actually make sense: After all, I didn't tell Slack *not* to include them. Remember what Slack stands for: It is a Searchable Log of *All* Communication and Knowledge. But what if I don't want to see messages from bots? And what if I want to view only content from the channels to which I belong?

REMEMBER

As I discuss in Chapter 3, you don't need to belong to *every* public channel in a workspace. Only join the ones that pertain to your job or group.

Again, Slack makes this search a snap. Simply check the two boxes in the lower right-hand corner of the search console, as Figure 7-9 shows.

Searching by user reactions

When I first started using Slack, I was skeptical about emojis. Today, though, I recognize their value. A simple thumbs-up can quickly acknowledge that you agree or understand something. In this case, an emoji supplants the "I agree" message, a true scourge of email life.

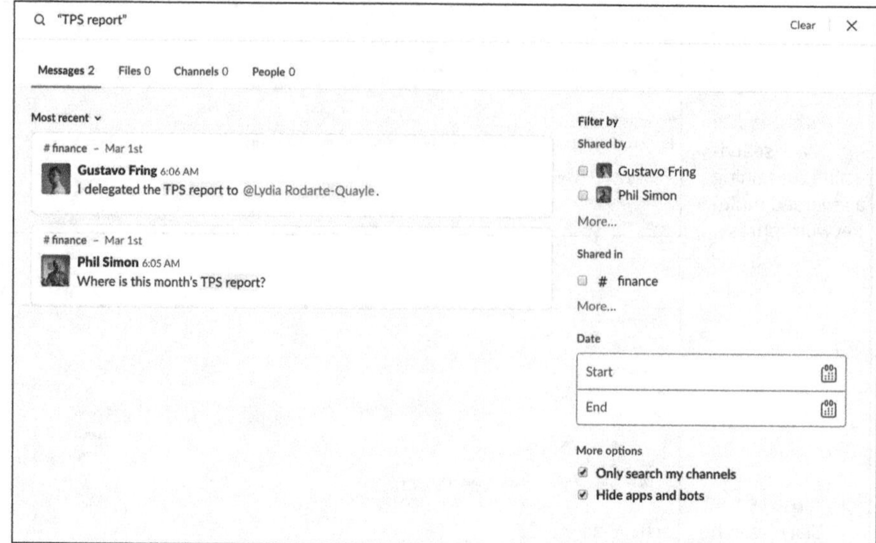

FIGURE 7-9: Slack search results from just my channels and omitting bots.

Say that you want to search for only messages that contain emojis. For example, simply type `has:reaction`, as I did in Figure 7-10.

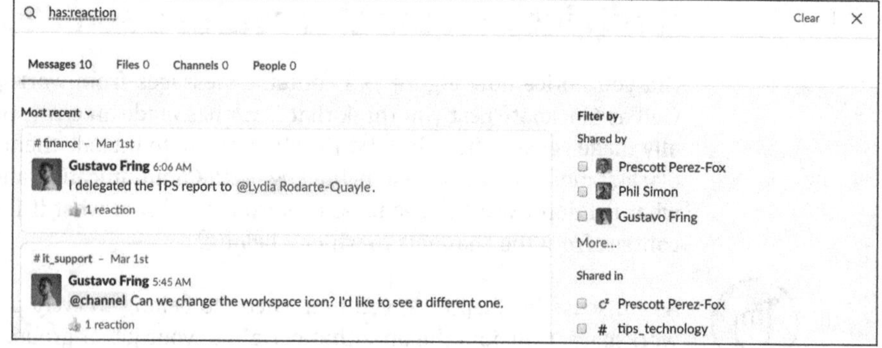

FIGURE 7-10: Slack search results for messages with emojis.

TIP

You can also limit your search results in many creative ways. For example, search for `has:link` if you only want to see messages with links.

Searching by wildcards

What if you don't know the precise term for which you're searching? You do know, however, that it starts with the letter G. Again, Slack makes this a breeze by allowing you to insert a * after the letter or letters. Figure 7-11 shows such a search.

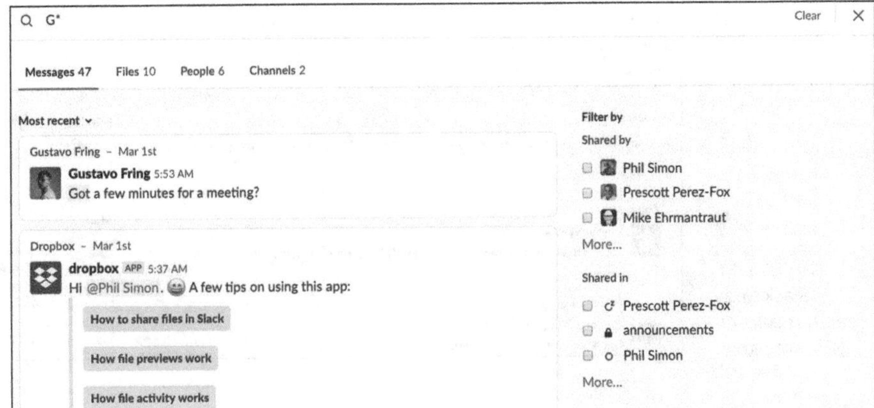

FIGURE 7-11: Slack search results with wildcard following a text string.

As Figure 7-11 demonstrates, Slack returns all results that contain a word starting with *G*. What's more, you can apply the same logic in reverse. That is, you can search for terms ending in a certain combination of characters, as I've done in Figure 7-12.

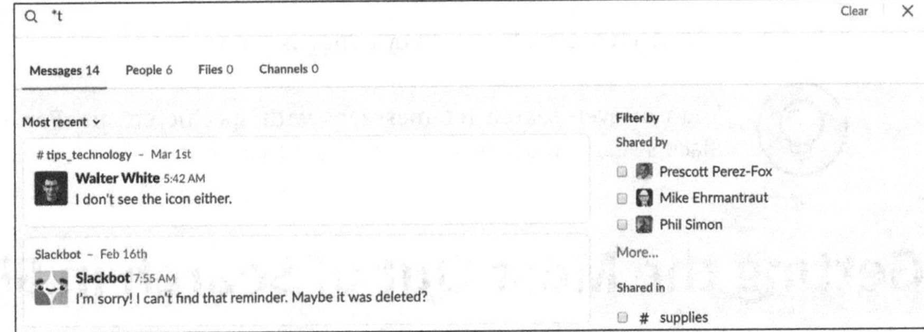

FIGURE 7-12: Slack search results with wildcard preceding text string.

Searching by fuzziness

Over the years, Slack search has improved its search functionality considerably, perhaps most notably with respect to *fuzzy search*. In this way, Slack now more closely resembles Google, Bing, DuckDuckGo, and other search engines that know what you intended to type. For example, you type "meetng" in the Slack search bar instead of "meeting." Slack dutifully returns highlighted terms based upon its best guess of what you meant, not what you typed. In this case, Slack thinks that you meant *meeting*, not *meetng*. Figure 7-13 displays the results.

REMEMBER

There are degrees of fuzziness and Slack's search functionality can't read your mind, especially in new workspaces. Expect Slack to return better results from fuzzy searches in the future.

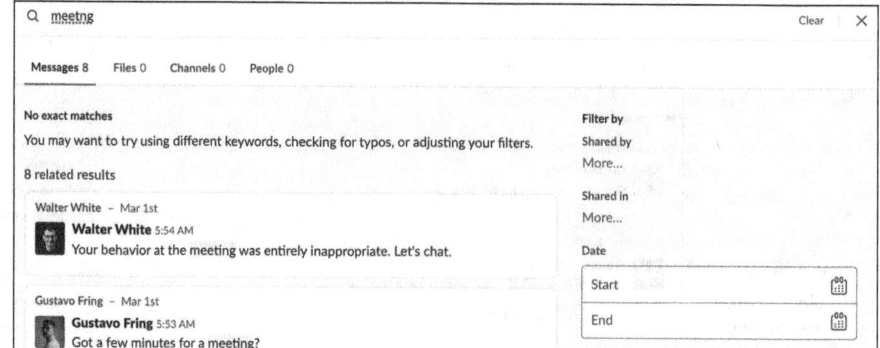

FIGURE 7-13: Slack fuzzy search results on "meetng."

Searching by additional modifiers

At the risk of overwhelming you with Slack's robust features, note that Slack allows you to search by

- Pinned content by using `has:pin`
- Starred content by using `has:star`
- Content containing links by using `has:link`

TIP

You can even search for messages with specific emojis. For a complete list of Slack's search modifiers, see `bit.ly/slack-mod`.

Getting the Most Out of Search in Slack

Here are some valuable tips on how to intelligently search for content in Slack.

Start small

In Figure 7-5, earlier in this chapter, I gradually and deliberately added constraints to my initial search. That is, I didn't start by specifying a bunch of criteria from the get-go. I ran a simple search and tweaked it from there. I recommend doing the same, especially if you're new to Slack. An example will illustrate my point here.

Say that you run a basic search for the word "lugubrious." As you'd expect, Slack returns nothing for that obscure word. Put differently, no one has ever used that wonderful word in any of the following in Slack's

» Public channels
» Private channels to which you belong
» Individual or group DMs involving you

Pepe and Homer are two of your more learned colleagues. As such, they routinely include 50-cent words such as "lugubrious" in their DMs, but you'd never know it. Slack search results do not include other members' private conversations. (See Chapter 9 for more on Slack's privacy settings.)

Because a search on "lugubrious" returns nothing in this case, further limiting your search is meaningless and a waste of time. For example, you restrict that same search to `#announcements` during the time before June 2019. You already know the answer to your query: nothing. Zilch. Put differently, if Slack can't locate the term in the entire workspace, then limiting your search to an individual channel and a time period won't change a thing. (These are examples of `AND` Booleans.)

Note, however, that including `OR` Booleans may indeed return more results. If you are searching for instances of the words "lugubrious" or "meeting," then Slack will most likely display some results.

Embrace modifiers

As your employees at your firm use Slack in lieu of email, many times you'll experience the opposite problem: Your search will return far more results than you can handle. For this reason, using the modifiers that I reference in this chapter is smart. Examples here run the gamut:

» Say that you're looking for a PDF. Check that box under the Files tab.
» Use a date range to limit the scope of your search. Start by being too inclusive rather than too exclusive.
» Refine your results with negative keywords.
» Apply quotes and wildcards after you receive a decent number of results.
» Combine keywords and additional modifiers as needed.

TIP

Keep a list of your frequent searches in a message draft or DM yourself with them.

Remember that results change over time

In Slack, search results represent a snapshot. In other words, they're not permanent. For example, in the `#suggestions` channel, you see how Gabriel and Benicio have proposed playing a practical joke on Kevin. (Yes, I'm looking at a poster of the classic flick *The Usual Suspects* as I write these words.)

On a Monday, you may search for joke in the `#suggestions` to see their banter. On Tuesday, though, that same search returns nothing. What happened?

Perhaps a Workspace Owner or Admin removed the content. Maybe Gabriel and Benicio got cold feet and decided to delete their messages. Who knows? The point is that search results in Slack are *dynamic.* They change over time.

Be patient

Think about the following two workspaces:

- A small company uses a Slack workspace. Its 15 employees send on average 30 messages per day and rarely share files with one another.
- A large hospital consists of 1,500 employees who send on average 75 messages per day and frequently share files.

Which one is going to contain more data?

It's not even close.

By extension, as its currently built, Slack will need a bit more time to process and return the results from the second workspace. (In Chapter 15, I make a prediction about how Slack will enhance its search functionality in the near future.)

IN THIS CHAPTER

» Customizing your Slack workspace

» Administering your workspace options

» Tweaking your personal Slack preferences

» Customizing user profiles

» Organizing your channels into sections.

Chapter 8
Personalizing Slack

For two reasons, Slack's management truly understands the need for customization. First, an organizations' specific collaboration and communication needs vary and change over time. The needs of a hospital system don't overlap that much with those of a Thai restaurant. Beyond that, what works today may not work tomorrow.

Second, the idea that everyone within a single organization works in an identical manner is patently absurd, but this isn't news to you. In your careers, you've probably observed many different types of workers. At the extremes, stereotypical HR folks and IT folks approach tasks from very different mindsets. Employees in finance and accounting tend to be more meticulous and conservative than big-picture product and marketing people. Toss in age, cultural, and personality differences, and you can see how an overly rigid, one-size-fits-all productivity tool may appease some people and frustrate others.

Brass tacks: A one-size-fits-all approach simply wouldn't work. Fortunately, Slack is a remarkably customizable tool.

This chapter begins by reviewing Slack's global administrative settings — those that workspace members can't override. It then moves to the individual settings and preferences that Slack users can change and concludes with a section on custom fields.

Getting to Know Your Slack Options

At a high level, Slack allows for two different levels of customizations:

- **Group:** Workspace Owners and Admins can change global settings, such as which members can post in which channels, file-retention policies, call settings, and much more.
- **Individual:** Regular members can tweak how they want Slack to look, act, and feel. (Chapter 5 describes how you can customize when and how Slack notifies you, but that's just the tip of the iceberg.) No, you can't change everything, but you can certainly make plenty of useful tweaks.

To set or change many of the settings that I describe in this chapter, you'll have to use a browser on your computer. The reason is straightforward: Slack limits what you can do on its desktop and mobile apps. There's one little wrinkle, though, that sometimes lets you circumvent this restriction and may save you some time. For details, see the nearby sidebar "Managing your workspace from a browser on your mobile device."

MANAGING YOUR WORKSPACE FROM A BROWSER ON YOUR MOBILE DEVICE

You already use an app on your tablet or smartphone to browse the web. It may be Firefox, Chrome, Safari, Opera, Brave, or something else. When you open a new tab on these browser apps and visit a web page like `www.rush.com`, by default you see a mobile version of that page. If it's a responsive website, then the page will look good. If not, then it won't. (How do you know? If you have to horizontally scroll to view information on that page, then it's not responsive.)

What if you need to change a Slack workspace setting and can't get to a proper computer? Here's the good news: You're probably in luck. Depending on your device, operating system, and browser of choice, you may be able to make that change by following these steps:

1. **Go to the URL of your slack workspace and add "/admin".**
2. **On your browser app, request the page's desktop site.**

   The exact process will vary based on the app. If you're unsure, then google it.

You may now be able to access Slack as if you were using a proper computer. If so, then you should be able to perform actions that Slack's native mobile app prohibits.

Although Workspace Owners and Admins can't tweak every setting, they can personalize their organizations' workspaces to a considerable degree. People in *all* roles, however, can modify some of their individual settings.

Configuring global workspace settings

Workspace Owners and Admins can configure certain settings for the entire workspace. For good reason, Slack prohibits regular members from overriding the settings in this section.

Changing the workspace name and URL

Sometimes companies change their names. (Slack itself is a case in point and, early in its history, Facebook famously dropped the "the.") What once sounded good now feels a bit dated or less relevant. Also, companies merge and get acquired. To this end, you may decide to rename your workspace name and URL. Here's how:

1. **Click on the main menu.**
2. **From the drop-down menu, select Settings & administration and then Workspace settings.**
3. **Scroll down to Workspace Name & URL and click on the button to its immediate right.**
4. **Type the new workspace name and URL.**

   REMEMBER

   You can only change the first part of the domain; *slack.com* is locked.
5. **Click on the green button.**

TIP

You can understand why Slack locks down this setting. Imagine if every workspace member could change this setting. It would result in utter chaos.

Customizing the workspace icon

The workspace icon appears at the top of the Slack sidebar. To change the icon, follow the first two steps in the section "Changing the workspace name and URL" earlier in this chapter. Continue as follows:

1. **Click on the main menu.**
2. **From the drop-down menu, select Settings & administration and Customize [workspace name].**

   Slack launches a new tab in your default Web browser.
3. **Click on the Workspace Icon tab.**

4. **Underneath the words Upload a New Icon, select the file from your computer and click on the green Upload Icon button.**
5. **Crop the icon as needed and then click on the green Crop Icon button.**

Setting workspace-app permissions

From the get-go, Slack allows any workspace member to install third-party apps and custom integrations. (Chapter 10 demonstrates how many companies and even independent developers have built cool and useful ways to extend Slack's native functionality.)

It's not hard to envision scenarios, though, in which an organization wants to restrict this feature or disable it altogether. Security and privacy (discussed in more detail in Chapter 9) certainly come to mind, although I can think of more prosaic reasons. For example, consider a company that uses Slack's Free plan. As such, it cannot install more than ten apps in its workspace. If employees can install whatever apps they want whenever they want, the firm will quickly reach its limit.

By enabling app approval, Workspace Owners and Admins restrict the ability of regular members to install certain apps in the workspace. After following the first two steps in the section "Changing the workspace name and URL" earlier in this chapter, continue as follows:

1. **Click on the Permissions tab. Scroll down to Apps & Custom Integrations and click on the URL immediately underneath it.**

   At the top is a section called Approve apps.

2. **Toggle the Approve Apps switch to the right if you want to restrict members from installing apps on their own.**

   Slack offers a number of other granular user and notification options. For example you can prohibit users from downloading apps outside of the Slack App Directory.

Chapter 10 delves further into the topic of third-party apps.

TIP

Slack provides a boatload of useful app-related options here, including mandating that users submit comments about why they want to install a particular app.

Setting membership options

Slack offers two ways to allow members to join a given workspace. Workspace Owners can either

» **Restrict the workspace to people who have formally received an email invitation.**

» **Allow anyone with a given email address domain to sign up for an account.**

The second option is more common for organizations that have enrolled in the Enterprise Grid plan. Can you imagine having to manually invite 30,000 employees to a new channel?

To control who can join your workspace, follow the first two steps in the section "Changing the workspace name and URL" earlier in this chapter. Continue as follows:

1. **Underneath the Settings tab, click under the Join This Workspace tab and click on the white Expand button.**

   Slack presents you with two options:

   - Allow invitations
   - Allow invitations, and approve invitations for any email address from these domains

   The second option requires you to input an email address from one or more domains.

2. **Click on the green Save button.**

Managing who can send workspace invitations

All Slack members can invite people to join a workspace. The only exception is a guest. Either for cost, privacy, or security reasons, though, perhaps you as a Workspace Owner or Admin want to approve new members. After following the first two steps in the section "Changing the workspace name and URL" earlier in this chapter, continue as follows:

1. **Underneath the Permissions tab, go to Invitations and click on the white Expand button.**
2. **Check the Require admin approval box and then click on the green Save button.**

Tailoring additional administrative settings and permissions

Slack offers the ability to perform a wide variety of administrative functions and set workspace permissions. At a high level, access them by following these steps:

1. **Click on the main menu.**
2. **From the drop-down menu, select Settings & administration and then Workspace settings.**

Slack launches a window or tab in your default browser. You see options including

- **Workspace language:** Offers an increasing number of different languages.
- **Default channels:** Govern which ones new members join here apart from `#general`.
- **Display name guidelines:** Create a custom message to guide new members in how to display their names.
- **Name display:** Set whether members' full or shorter names will appear.
- **Email display:** Show or hide whether this field appears in member profiles.
- **Do Not Disturb:** Set default DND hours. Note that employees can override them. (See Chapter 5 for more on this subject.)
- **Hide your workspace URL from external sites' logs:** Hide information that companies use to track the source of their inbound web traffic. If you'd like to hide this field, then employees at those companies won't know that your workspace members are visiting content on their sites.
- **Calls:** Enforce workspace-specific rules here. (Chapter 6 covers how to make calls in Slack.)
- **Message retention and deletion:** Specify how long your firm wants to retain employee messages. (See Chapter 9 for more on this topic.)
- **File retention and deletion:** Specify how long your organization wants to retain employee files uploaded to Slack. (See Chapter 9 for more on this topic.)
- **Delete workspace:** Use to obliterate your workspace and all of its content. (*Note:* Archiving a workspace is a less permanent solution.)

TIP

Visit `bit.ly/slack-wa` to view the comprehensive list of workspace settings and permissions.

Managing channels

By default, Slack lets everyone but guests create their own public channels. For whatever reason, settings like these may not agree with you. Fortunately, Slack provides robust channel-management tools.

To effect these changes, follow the first two steps in the section "Changing the workspace name and URL" earlier in this chapter. Continue as follows:

1. **Click on the Permissions tab at the top of the page.**
2. **Look for Channel Management and then click on the white Expand button.**
3. **Make whatever changes you like, including determining which roles can do the following:**
   - Create public and private channels.
   - Archive channels.
   - Remove members from public channels.
   - And much more.
4. **Click on the green Save button.**

Play around with Slack's different options here. The decisions that you make will profoundly affect how your colleagues use Slack.

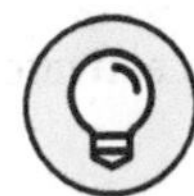

Under the Enterprise Grid plan, Org Admins and Owners prevent Workspace Admins from even seeing some of these options, let alone overriding them.

Err on the side of openness at the start of your Slack journey. The organization that excessively locks down in effect discourages employees from using it. (Chapter 13 includes other tips to promote successful Slack adoption in the workplace.)

Personalizing your Slack options

You may not like your workspace's logo or app-approval process. If that's the case, then you're welcome to make your case to the Workspace Owner or stew in silence. At least take solace in the fact that you can customize many of your Slack settings.

If you don't see one of the following options, then your Workspace Owner or Admin has disabled the options for full members.

You set many of your preferences in this section following these steps:

1. **Click on the main menu.**
2. **From the drop-down menu, select Preferences.**

After doing this, Slack displays the member preference window in Figure 8-1.

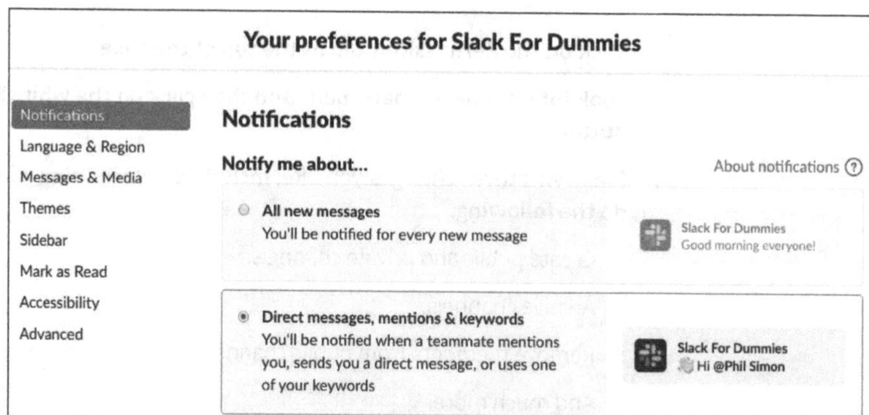

FIGURE 8-1: Slack member preference window.

From this window, Slack provides plenty of options.

Enabling dark mode

Like many apps of late, Slack has joined the dark-mode craze. To activate it for your computer's Slack app, follow these steps:

1. **Click on the main menu.**
2. **From the drop-down menu, click on Preferences.**
3. **Click on Themes.**
4. **Check or uncheck Sync with OS setting.**

   If you leave Sync with OS setting checked, Slack inherits the setting from your smartphone app. (OS here stands for *operating system*.)
5. **Click on Dark.**

REMEMBER

If you don't see these options, odds are that you downloaded the Slack app directly from `slack.com/downloads`, not the Apple or Windows app store.

Selecting a Slack theme

Perhaps you aren't enamored with Slack's default color scheme, and dark mode just doesn't do it for you. You can pick a theme that works for you or, even better, create your own. Follow these steps:

1. **Click on the main menu.**
2. **From the drop-down menu, click on Preferences.**
3. **Click on Themes and scroll down.**

4. **Select the existing theme that you want to apply or customize your theme.**

   Unless you've selected dark mode (see the preceding section), the colors immediately change.

5. **If you're satisfied with the preview, then click on the X in the top-right corner.**

You can even share your theme with the Slack community. Click on the link under Feeling Adventurous and go nuts.

Tweaking Slack's sidebar

The sidebar is where many Slack users immediately look after the application launches. After all, depending on your notification settings, the sidebar alerts you to items such as

- New channel activity
- DMs from others
- Optionally, members joining or leaving channels

Figure 8-2 shows the options that you can set in the sidebar.

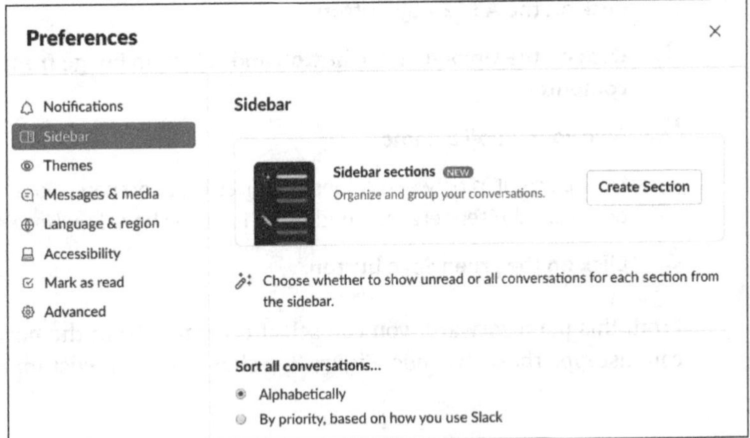

FIGURE 8-2: Slack sidebar options.

For example, you can elect for the sidebar to show you everything, unread messages and starred conversations, or unread messages only.

TIP

Certain Slack settings are only accessible via a web browser. That is, you can't perform every Slack function via its desktop or mobile app.

REMEMBER

What if you want to change an individual setting, but you're not a Workspace Owner or Admin? Unfortunately, you may be out of luck. Only administrative roles can globally configure certain settings and permissions in Slack. As such, non-administrative members may not be able to override them. (Chapter 2 discusses roles in far more detail.)

You can personalize Slack in plenty of other ways.

Creating custom emojis

If you want to express yourself with your own emoji, just follow these steps:

1. **Click on the message icon.**

   Slack launches a new message window. (Chapter 4 covers messages in far more detail.)

2. **Click on the smiley face.**

   Slack launches the emoji window.

3. **Click on the Add Emoji button.**
4. **Click on the Upload Image button and select an image from your computer.**
5. **Give your emoji a name.**

   Slack places it in between colons and gives it a short code. For instance, I added one called :heisenberg: as a nod to my favorite show, *Breaking Bad*.

6. **Click on the green Save button.**

From this point forward, you can select the emoji from the normal picker or you can just type the short code. Figure 8-3 shows my new custom emoji.

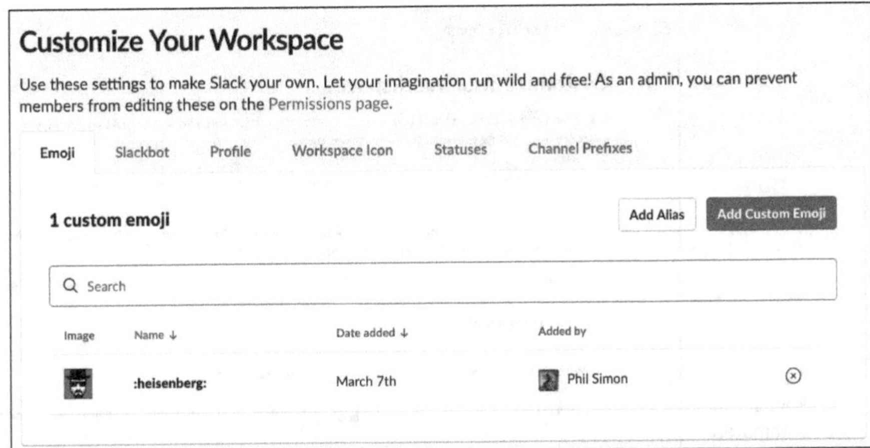

FIGURE 8-3: Slack custom emoji.

Customizing Slackbot

Slack lets users create automated responses based upon keywords or phrases in public and private channels. One potential application here is a frequently asked questions list. Alternatively, you can flag profanity or certain words. To set up custom, word-based responses, follow these steps:

1. **Click on the main menu.**
2. **From the drop-down menu, select Settings & administration and then Workspace settings.**

   Slack displays a sub-menu on the immediate right.
3. **Select Customize "workspace name."**

   This step launches a window or tab in your default web browser.
4. **Click on the Slackbot tab.**

   It is the second tab from the left.
5. **Underneath the words When someone says, enter the word that you want to flag.**

   Use your imagination. In Figure 8-4, I show one simple keyword.

   For example, your company discourages people from talking about politics in the office. (I can't think of a better way to polarize an employee base today.) As such, as Figure 8-4 displays, you configure the following rule in Slack.

   I ignore the rule and post a message containing the dreaded *p-word*. Figure 8-5 demonstrates my custom automated Slackbot response in action.

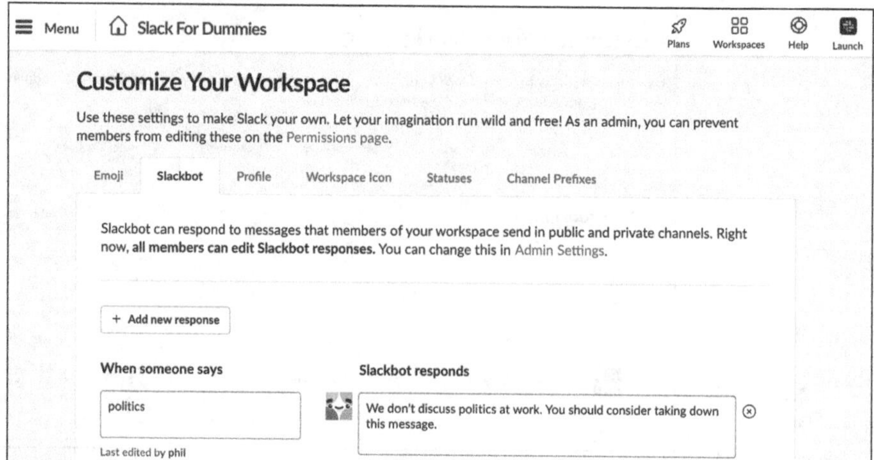

FIGURE 8-4: Slackbot setup for automated response.

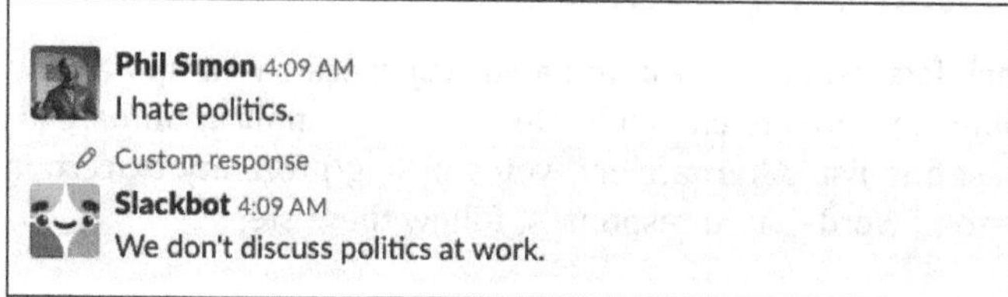

Phil Simon 4:09 AM
I hate politics.
Custom response
Slackbot 4:09 AM
We don't discuss politics at work.

FIGURE 8-5: Slackbot automated response in action.

6. **Underneath the words Slackbot responds, enter the automated response that workspace members will receive if they type the offending word or phrase.**
7. **Click on the green Save response button.**

I create one for my students every semester linked to the word "syllabus." When students type it, Slackbot immediately displays its URL. Easy peasy.

REMEMBER

Slackbot doesn't delete the offending message in the channel. Also, for privacy reasons, Slack doesn't enforce these rules in private DMs. Talk about creepy.

REMEMBER

As of this writing, Slackbot responses are workspace specific. Enterprise Grid customers can't define them at the organization level.

Setting custom workspace statuses and times

Status is a key field in Slack because it indicates your availability to your colleagues. (Chapter 2 covers status in more detail.) This setting lets you create suggested statuses along with icons and default times for them to expire. To modify default status expiration times, just follow these steps:

1. **Click on the main menu.**
2. **From the drop-down menu, select Settings & administration and then Workspace settings.**

   Slack displays a sub-menu on the immediate right.
3. **Select Customize "workspace name."**

   This step launches a window or tab in your default web browser.
4. **Click on the Status tab.**

   Slack provides a number of common statuses and default times.

   For example, by default the "Out sick" status clears after today.
5. **From the drop-down next to the status you want to change, select the new default time.**
6. **Click on the green Save button.**

Customizing User Profiles

Slack is anything but boring. In fact, it's downright fun to use. To this end, profiles that merely include employee name, rank, serial number, and email address doesn't exactly scream fun. Why not let employees include a little personal information about themselves — or at least give them the option? Fun facts and interesting tidbits can grease the wheels for social interactions and build camaraderie in the workplace.

REMEMBER

Chapter 2 explains how to populate Slack's default profile fields. Collectively, they help workspace members understand what their colleagues do.

Once again, Slack makes this type of customization easy. Customers on premium plans can create custom profile fields. That is, members aren't restricted to populating the standard fields included under Slack's Free plan.

At a high level, Workspace Owners and Admins can add two types of custom fields. First, Slack presents commonly used fields such as:

- Address
- Birthday
- Start date

Second, you can also let employees enter links or handles for personal accounts for popular web services. The usual suspects include LinkedIn, Facebook, Twitter, and GitHub — a particularly popular site for coders.

Creating custom fields

What if you don't like Slack's list of suggestions? Simply create your own fields. Options here include text, a list of options, date picker, link, and person picker. The process is remarkably self-explanatory:

1. **Click on the main menu.**
2. **From the drop-down menu, select Settings & administration and then Workspace settings.**

   Slack displays a sub-menu on the immediate right.
3. **Select Customize "workspace name."**

   This step launches a window or tab in your default web browser.
4. **Go to the Profile tab and click on Edit your workspace's profile fields.**
5. **Click on the white button that reads Create a custom field.**

   Slack takes you to the field-creation page.
6. **Select the type of field that you'd like to create.**

   TIP

   The person picker option allows people to enter their manager from a list of existing Slack members. The field also allows you to list your direct reports. This field can be invaluable when trying to track someone down or resolve an issue.
7. **Under the word Label, enter one for the new field and an optional hint.**
8. **Click on the green Create button.**

What does a Slack profile of a man with a brooding intensity look like? Figure 8-6 shows one with some custom fields.

TIP

Say that your company pays for the Enterprise Grid plan. As such, it wants to easily manage settings for all workspaces. Org Owners and Admins can determine global settings on custom fields that apply downward to all workspaces. If they do, then Owners and Admins for individual workspaces can't override these global settings on their own.

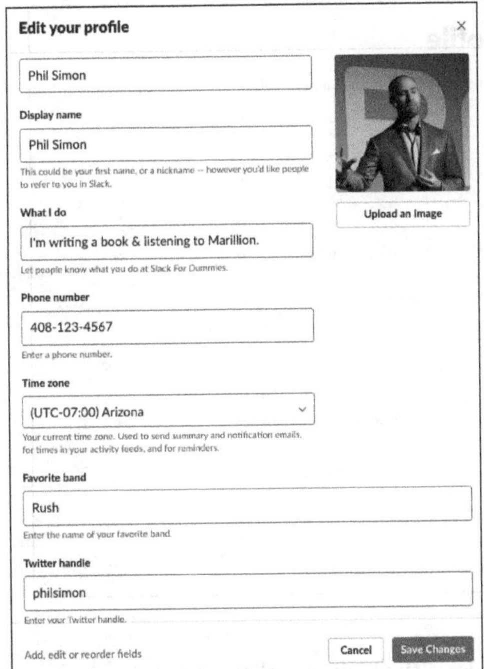

FIGURE 8-6: Slack profile of a man with a brooding intensity and custom fields.

Populating custom fields

Slack provides a great deal of flexibility in this area, but you should wield this sword carefully.

First, use your judgment. Don't use a Slack profile to replicate each and every field in your organization's human resource information system (HRIS). You'll overwhelm employees who merely want to find basic information on their colleagues. Choose wisely.

Second, what if you add a few new custom fields and want employees to populate them themselves? In this scenario, it's best to post a message in a company-wide channel. (Chapter 11 mentions a more efficient but technically demanding way of doing this for many fields with large employee populations.)

Place fields in an intelligent order. For example, phone number should appear above favorite band. You don't want a key piece of information displaying at the end of a long profile; others are more prone to miss it. Figure 8-7 displays my profile with the custom fields that I have created for my workspace.

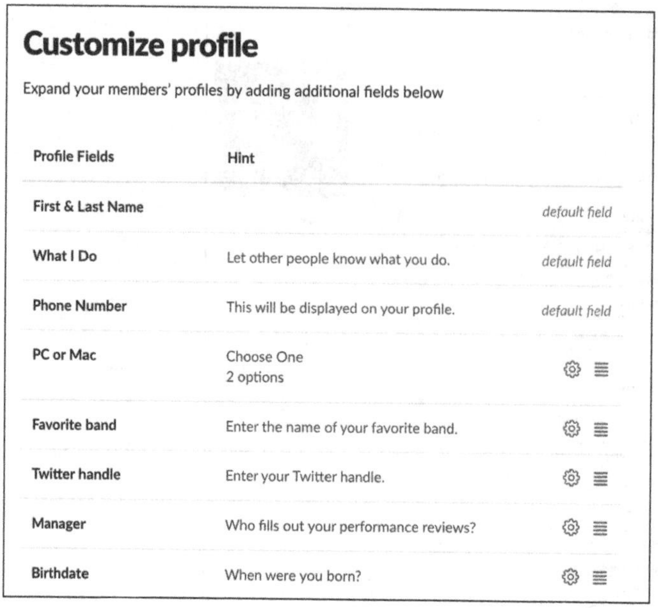

Customize profile

Expand your members' profiles by adding additional fields below

Profile Fields	Hint	
First & Last Name		*default field*
What I Do	Let other people know what you do.	*default field*
Phone Number	This will be displayed on your profile.	*default field*
PC or Mac	Choose One 2 options	
Favorite band	Enter the name of your favorite band.	
Twitter handle	Enter your Twitter handle.	
Manager	Who fills out your performance reviews?	
Birthdate	When were you born?	

FIGURE 8-7: Slack custom fields in a user profile.

If you want to reorder a field, simply click on the line icon on the right of it and drag it up or down.

Just because you can add a custom field doesn't mean that you should. Depending on where you live, a firm can expose itself to legal liability if it allows or requires employees to publicly display certain types of data. No, adding a voluntary field for Twitter handle or favorite band doesn't violate any law — unless the latter happens to be Nickelback. (I'm kidding.) Double-check with your HR department or in-house attorney, though, about whether it's wise to let employees enter personal information in Slack. Suspect fields include the following:

- Home address
- Social-security number or employee identification number
- Citizenship
- Any type of personal phone number
- Marital or disability status
- Ethnicity
- Full birthdate (including year born)

Visit `bit.ly/slack-cf` to learn more about custom fields.

Organizing Your Sidebar

As you use Slack, you may find yourself routinely communicating in dozens of different public and private channels. Ditto for individual and group DMs. I'll be the first to admit that, past a certain point, scrolling throughout all of this content can become time-consuming. The word *cumbersome* also comes to mind.

Fortunately, since its founding in 2013, Slack has constantly improved its product. One of the questions that its leadership has recently asked is: How can Slack let its users most efficiently find what they need without becoming overwhelmed?

The current version of Slack includes a new, optional, and very useful tool specifically designed to let users easily manage the content in their sidebars: the section.

Using sections

At a high level, sections allow you to easily place important channels and conversations into custom, collapsible buckets. In concept, they resemble the folder-management tools that people use on their computers every day. Think File Explorer for Windows and Finder for MacOS.

TIP

By default, Slack includes a section for Starred items.

Creating a new sidebar section

To create a new section, follow these steps:

1. **In the bottom half of the sidebar, mouse over either Starred or Channels.**

   Slack displays three vertical dots.

2. **From the sub-menu that appears, select Create New Section.**
3. **Enter a name for your section and, optionally, an emoji.**

   Slack provides a few canned suggestions for channel names. As Figure 8-8 shows, I have named my section "Important" and have added an exclamation mark as my emoji.

4. **Click on the green Create button.**

   I've created the Important section, but there's nothing in it yet.

5. **Drag and drop whatever channels and conversations into your new section.**

I have added the `#accounting`, `#development`, and `#laundromat` channels into my section as well as a group DM with Gustavo and Lydia, as Figure 8-8 shows. Before you release the mouse, Slack wisely places a white box around the enter section into which you'll be adding your new channel or conversation. This nice touch minimizes the chance that you place something in the wrong section.

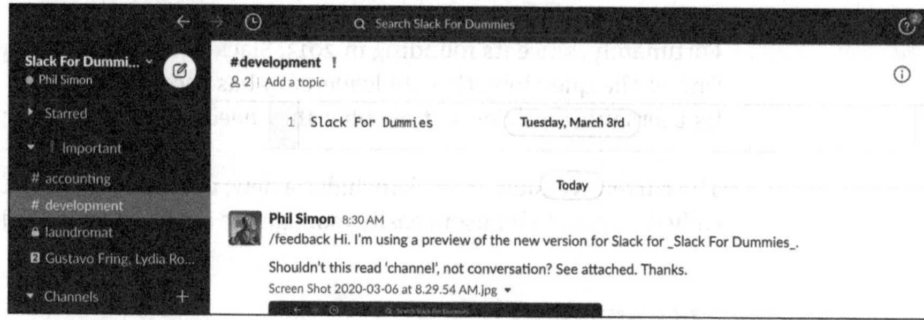

FIGURE 8-8: Slack custom section named Important.

By default, Slack sorts content in sections in alphabetical order by channels first and then by conversation.

REMEMBER

A channel can only belong to one section; you can't put it in more than one.

Slack restricts custom sidebar sections to customers on premium plans only but not by role. That is, everyone from guests to Primary Owners can use sections — and everyone in between. Also, users create their own sections; sections are not global.

Say that you want to collapse the channels and conversations in your section to save space and minimize scrolling. Simply click on the triangle to the left of the section name. Click again to expand the section. And don't think that you have to constantly expand and contract sections to stay informed of their notifications. Slack makes sure that you won't miss notifications for content in your section. (Chapter 5 discusses notifications in more depth.)

Say that I have contracted my Important section and Lydia posts a message in the `#development` channel. (Note that I have not muted that channel.) Slack bolds the entire section in white as Figure 8-9 displays.

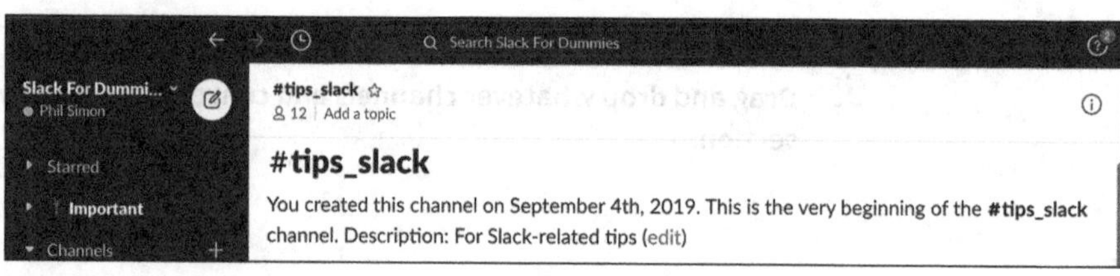

FIGURE 8-9: Slack notification of activity in channel collapses Important section.

Moving sidebar sections

Once you get the hang of sections, you'll probably create a bunch. You may want to place certain sections in a specific order. Follow these steps to move sections:

1. **Click on the section that you want to move.**
2. **Drag and drop your section where you want it to go.**

   Slack displays a white line previewing where your section will reside when you've finished moving it.
3. **Release your mouse.**

   Note that you can't place sections in the top half of the sidebar.

Renaming a sidebar section

Say that I want to rename my Important section to something a bit more colorful. Follow these directions:

1. **Right-click on the section name.**

   Slack displays a sub-menu.
2. **Click on the first option: Rename Important.**

   Of course, your section name will depend upon what you initially named it.
3. **Enter the new name for your section and, optionally, a new emoji.**
4. **Click on the green Save button.**

   Slack provides some other neat sidebar features. Play around with them. Organizing your workspace content is a breeze.

Sorting channels

By default, Slack presents public channels in the sidebar in alphabetical order and then private channels in the same way. If you like, you can let Slack automatically arrange your channels by priority or what the company calls *scientific sorting*.

To change how Slack sorts your channels and conversations, follow these steps:

1. **Click on the main menu.**
2. **From the drop-down menu, select Preferences.**

   Slack displays a new pane.

3. **Click on Sidebar.**
4. **On the right-hand side of the pane, click on Sort All Conversations.**
5. **Select the desired option.**

TIP

Be on the lookout for even more useful future Slack enhancements. For example, by the time this book hits the shelves, you should be able to customize the width of your sidebar.

IN THIS CHAPTER

» Configuring Slack's security and account settings

» Reviewing Slack's different privacy settings

» Examining Slack's message- and file-retention policies

Chapter 9

Keeping It Safe: Reviewing Slack's Security and Privacy Settings

At a bare minimum, Slack lets you and your coworkers easily share content in a far more targeted way than email ever could. Take this argument to its logical conclusion: Employees can contribute to a comprehensive and easily searchable knowledge repository. I can think of few more prized assets for any organization in the Information Age.

But what if this asset quickly turned into a massive liability? That is, what if organizations couldn't secure all of their sensitive employee communication, intellectual property, and key documents from prying eyes and bad actors? Put differently, creating a comprehensive trove of knowledge is downright dangerous if firms couldn't lock it down. Without substantial safeguards in place, organizations and employees would be justifiably loathe to hop on the Slack train.

It's time to cover Slack's most important security and privacy controls.

Getting Acquainted with Slack Security

Allow me to start by stating the obvious: No application, system, individual, firm, or data source is entirely secure. Hackers are remarkably clever, and organizations are always playing defense. Always. Former Cisco Systems CEO John Chambers summed it up perfectly when he said, "There are two types of companies: those who have been hacked, and those who don't yet know they have been hacked."

That's not to say that organizations are powerless against black hats. As I tell my students when I cover enterprise security, there are plenty of surefire ways to decrease the chances that bad actors cause chaos in an organization. They include updating software in a timely manner, requiring strong passwords, enabling two-factor authentication, educating employees, and using firewalls and virtual private networks (VPNs).

WARNING

Slack doesn't protect organizations from employees who refuse to follow basic security protocols. Nothing can.

Security and Slack's Evolution

As I covered in Chapter 1, in 2014 Slack's management decided to change the company's focus from a video game to a collaboration tool. At the time, there was no guarantee that its new direction would ultimately bear fruit. Put differently, in the company's early days with only a handful of employees, it was fair for everyone to ask, "Why devote its limited time and money on security to a communication tool that relatively few people use?"

Well, we're not in Kansas anymore for two reasons. First, since 2014, Slack has become far more popular. (That's one reason that you're reading this book. You won't find any *For Dummies* books for niche products.) Second, a long with popularity, Slack has increased in importance. Customers use the collaboration tool to perform a burgeoning number of essential company functions.

Slack has responded on both fronts. Since its nascent days, the company has spent considerable resources on beefing up its security features. In a way, it had no choice. Consider what would happen if Slack's management failed to take security considerations seriously. Many organizations would dismiss using it outright and opt for another collaboration and communication tool. (Chapter 3 describes how Slack faces plenty of competition.) For years now, Slack has not been the only pretty girl at the ball.

WARNING

There is no such thing as "complete" or "total" security with any app or system. Slack is no exception to this rule.

TIP

It's better for an IT department to adopt and formally sanction tools such as Slack rather than fight them. The former stratagem poses fewer security risks.

Configuring Slack's Access and Security Settings

At a high level, Slack provides two types of measures for protecting workspace data:

- **Customer-driven measures:** Security-related measures that Slack's customers can take.
- **Slack-driven measures:** Security features that exist whether its customers activate them or not. That is, Slack ships them with the app.

If you're thinking that different organizations may require vastly disparate levels of security, trust your instincts. A government agency that possesses sensitive citizen and infrastructure information requires greater controls than your local pizzeria or vintage clothing store. To this end, Slack provides a wide array of powerful security options — all of which I can't possibly cover in this book.

Confirming sign-ins via email

Say that you attempt to log into a Slack workspace from an unrecognized browser. Slack wants to ensure that it is really you and not a black hat. As such, expect to receive a confirmation email similar to the one shown in Figure 9-1.

Resetting your password

From time to time, people forget their passwords. Like just about every application these days, Slack easily lets you reset it.

TIP

Create complex passwords. Store all of your login credentials in a secure password manager, such as Dashlane, LastPass, 1Password, or others.

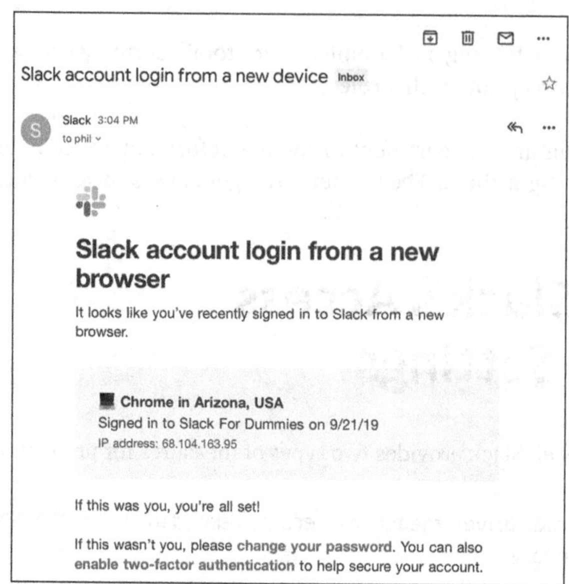

FIGURE 9-1: Slack email confirmation.

While signed out of Slack

Follow these directions to reset your password if you can't log into your Slack workspace:

1. **Go to `http://slack.com/signin`.**
2. **Enter your workspace URL and click on the green Continue button.**

   (See Chapter 2 for more information on this topic.)
3. **Below the sign-in form and underneath the green Sign in button, click on Forgot password.**

   Slack takes you to a page that requires you to input your email address.
4. **Enter your email address.**

   Make sure that it's the same one that Slack has on file.
5. **Click on the green Get Reset Link button.**

   Slack sends you an email with a link. Check your inbox.

   TIP

   If your email is tied to multiple workspaces, then Slack's email will contain links to all of them. Put differently, your login credentials may apply to more than one workspace.
6. **In the email, click on the Choose a New Password button.**
7. **Enter your new password and then confirm it.**
8. **If they both match, then click on the green Change my password button.**

While signed in to Slack

If you're still logged into Slack and forgot your password, then follow these steps:

1. **Click on the main menu.**
2. **Choose View profile from the menu.**

   Slack opens your profile on the right side of your screen.
3. **Click on the three vertical dots that appear below your profile picture.**
4. **Click on Account settings.**

   Slack opens a window or tab in your computer's default browser.
5. **Click on the expand button to the right of Password.**

   If you don't see this option, then your company requires single sign-on to sign in to Slack.

   REMEMBER

   In a nutshell, single sign-on or SSO allows people in an organization to log into disparate applications, systems, and web services via a single set of credentials.
6. **Type your current password and then enter your new password.**
7. **Click on the green Save Password button.**

Viewing access logs

Like many software vendors, Slack generates access logs for its customers. Collectively, these records of user activity and changes provide organizations with information on who did what and when. Access logs can be invaluable when investigating instances of misuse or hacks or even identifying problems. See Figure 9-2 for a sample access log.

To view an access log, follow these steps:

1. **Click on the main menu.**
2. **From the drop-down menu, select Settings & administration and then Workspace settings.**

   Slack shows you the data to which you have access.

   Slack opens your profile on the right side of your screen.

   At the right of the page, you see the words Access Logs.
3. **(Optional) If you'd like, you can download the data that Slack displays here as a comma-separated value (CSV) file by clicking on the white Download Access Logs button and saving the file.**

Guests are only able to view their own activity. Workspace Owners and Admins can see far more information about who logged in, the device used, the time of day, the Internet Protocol (IP) address, and when.

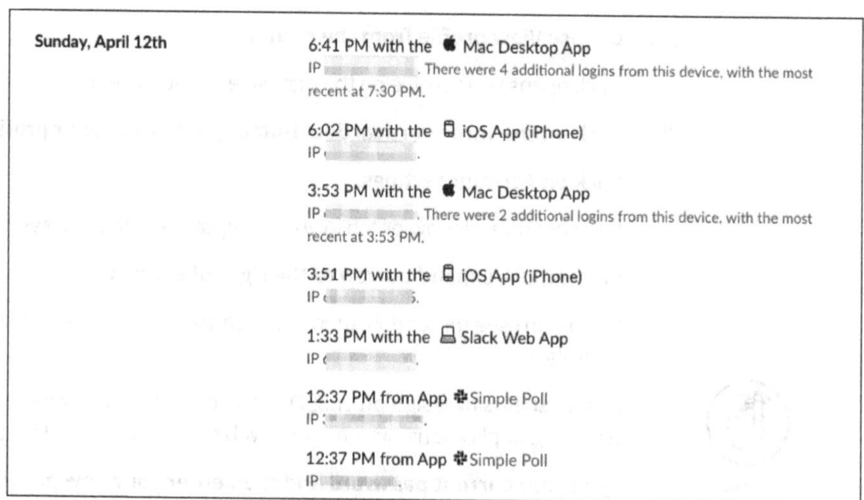

FIGURE 9-2: Example of a simple Slack access log.

Enabling two-factor authentication

What happens if someone gains access to your email address and password? It's not hard to imagine an unsavory sort posting horrible messages and lascivious photos in Slack under your name. In a professional context, such behavior may result in your suspension, demotion, or even termination.

Like many companies, Slack wants to minimize the chance that these events happen. To this end, Slack encourages its customers to activate an additional security measure called *two-factor authentication* — usually abbreviated as *2FA*. Rolled out in March 2015, 2FA adds an additional level, or *factor*, to signing in — hence its name. What's more, organizations can opt to deploy this individually or require all Slack workspace members to use it to sign in.

To set up 2FA, make sure that you have your phone handy and follow these steps.

1. **Download a Time-Based, One-Time Password (TOTP) app.**

   Popular ones include Google Authenticator, Duo Mobile, or Authy. (I have used the first two and found them to be intuitive. iPhone fans can also use the 1Password app.)

2. **Go to `my.slack.com/account/settings` and log in, if prompted.**

3. **Click on the white Expand button under the item labeled Two-Factor Authentication.**
4. **Click on the Set Up Two-Factor Authentication button.**

WARNING

If you don't see this option, then someone in your organization with greater permissions has disabled it. For example, a Workspace Owner may have required single sign-on and 2FA. The organization also may have prohibited Admins and members from disabling this feature.

5. **Elect how you'd like to receive authentication codes.**

You can use choose to receive a SMS text message or use one of the authentication apps mentioned in Step 1. If you want to receive a SMS text message, proceed to Step 6. Otherwise, skip to Step 7.

TIP

To paraphrase Walter White in one of my favorite *Breaking Bad* scenes, I prefer option B: I use an authentication app. If you do as well, then continue to Step 6.

Check your inbox. Slack sends you an email similar to the one displayed in Figure 9-3.

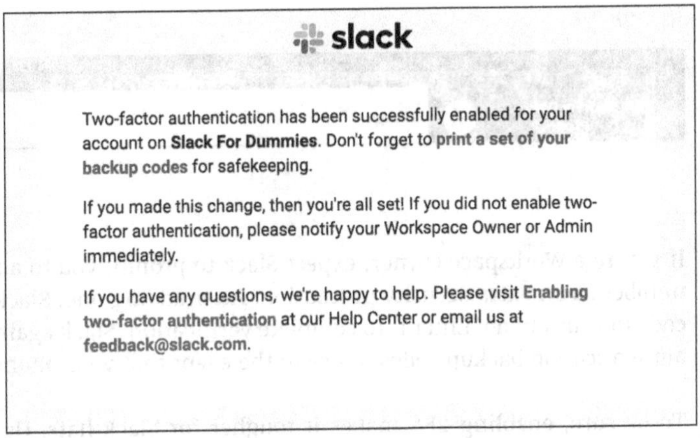

slack

Two-factor authentication has been successfully enabled for your account on **Slack For Dummies**. Don't forget to **print a set of your backup codes** for safekeeping.

If you made this change, then you're all set! If you did not enable two-factor authentication, please notify your Workspace Owner or Admin immediately.

If you have any questions, we're happy to help. Please visit **Enabling two-factor authentication** at our Help Center or email us at **feedback@slack.com**.

FIGURE 9-3: Slack email confirming individual 2FA activation.

6. **Verify your activation using the one-time code texted to you.**

To do so, select your country from the menu and enter your complete mobile phone number. Remember to include your area code. Slack sends a six-digit verification code to your device. Enter this code in your browser on the Slack 2FA configuration page and then click on the gray Verify code and enable button. Slack then sends you a text message that contains a one-time authentication code.

You'll need to enter these codes whenever you sign in to your workspace after having logged out. When you enter the code, Slack takes you to the workspace.

TIP

I encourage you to click on the link to view your specific workspace backup codes. Either print them or save them in a file on your computer or phone. If you lose your secondary device, then those codes will let you log back into your Slack workspace. Note that you can use each code only once.

7. **Alternatively, verify your account using an authentication app.**

   To do so, open your preferred authenticator app on your smartphone, click on the + icon on the app, and scan the barcode in the browser.

   In your browser, enter the code that appears at the bottom of the app. You have succeeded in enabling 2FA. Slack sends you an email indicating as much.

REMEMBER

Only customers on premium plans can switch authentication methods.

Say that you've been using Slack without enabling 2FA. A yellow triangle icon appears over your workspace icon to the left of the sidebar, as shown in Figure 9-4. This means that you have to sign back in. Once you do, that yellow icon disappears.

FIGURE 9-4: Slack workspace icon indicating that member needs to sign in again after enabling 2FA.

TIP

If you're a Workspace Owner, expect Slack to prompt you to add a backup phone number as an extra security precaution. After adding one, Slack sends a six-digit code to your phone. Enter it to complete verification. Slack again displays your ten authentication backup codes to use in the event that your phone disappears.

WARNING

To be sure, enabling 2FA makes it tougher for black hats. Unfortunately, some hackers have even figured out how to circumvent it — and not just for Slack. Scammers who successfully pull off SIM swaps seize control of someone's account and can more easily commit fraud. This technique involves targeting 2FA vulnerabilities.

Additional security features

Slack also provides granular security and access options including

» **Manage session duration:** Perhaps your company wants people to log in to Slack every week or every month.

» **Whitelist workspaces:** This option prevents employees on a company network from signing on to unapproved workspaces.

» **Enable and tweak single sign-on or (SSO):** Slack's options here include resetting all sessions, changing SSO provider, and more.

» **Reset all workspace passwords:** This option is especially useful in the event of an organization-wide breach.

You'll sooner find a real-life Easter bunny than a completely secure application. Think of security as an ongoing process, not a discrete outcome.

For more information on Slack's additional security settings and how to configure them, see `bit.ly/2McnGkf`.

Enhancing Security via Slack Enterprise Grid

Slack's newest and most expensive plan offers a number of enhanced security options for large organizations. I touch upon many of them throughout this book, but I want to call specific attention to one of them here.

Slack Enterprise Key Management or EKM offers its most security conscious customers an extra layer of protection against bad actors. Customers on the Enterprise Grid plan have the ability to configure settings at a remarkably granular level.

EKM accomplishes this objective by offering additional encryption keys to unlock access to different features. For example, Workspace Owners and Admins can control access to specific channels, messages, and files. They can also just as easily revoke their access. Finally, EKM provides Owners and Admins with enhanced member-activity logs showing who did what when and where they accessed data within Slack.

It's not hard to envision beneficial applications of EKM. Perhaps CYE Industries doesn't want Larry to share an especially sensitive file with others. Maybe Cheryl wants to know exactly where and on what device Larry accessed that file. CYE's management can even revoke Larry's access to that file for a predetermined period of time.

No, Enterprise Grid isn't cheap. However, consider the benefits for large organizations in healthcare and financial services and other highly regulated industries. These customers are often willing to pay for Slack's premium security features. As such, EKM is right up their alley.

Examining Privacy in Slack

If the last few years have taught us anything, it's that we have reached a turning point with respect to privacy: Companies can no longer treat it as an afterthought.

Case in point: Facebook, the social network with 2.5 billion monthly active users. Wunderkind CEO Mark Zuckerberg has long emphasized "connecting the world" over user privacy. The company's recent claims that it now supports intelligent privacy regulation indicate that it may finally be taking a markedly different approach with how it treats user data.

It's an understatement to claim that balancing competing interests with privacy is extremely challenging. The potential for conflict is real and nuanced. For example, Slack's customers may want the unfettered ability to view and export all messages and files in their workspaces. (Chapter 11 covers exporting data in more detail.) For their part, employees may be reluctant to use Slack if Big Brother is watching. What to do?

Fortunately, Slack provides a number of safeguards designed to protect user data.

TIP

If you want to view Slack's formal and lengthy privacy policy, head over to `https://slack.com/privacy-policy`. Note that your employer's privacy policy may conflict with Slack's. If you violate your company's rule, the "Slack let me do it" excuse probably won't fly with your boss and the HR department.

Message encryption

Forget Slack for a moment. Generally speaking, people who send encrypted messages via Signal or other secure messaging apps need not worry about prying eyes. Say that bad actors intercept those messages. It doesn't matter: the content is indecipherable gobbledygook. (The technical term here is *ciphertext*.)

Slack uses *end-to-end encryption* on all DMs as well as all content posted in public and private channels. As a result, no third-party can intercept them while they're in transit — that is, moving from sender to recipient. Let me be crystal clear: Slack users can rest assured that their messages remain secure.

That doesn't mean, though, that Workspace Owners can never access members' private messages. And here's where things get a bit more nuanced.

For starters and by default, Slack prohibits Workspace Owners and Admins from accessing others' content in private channels and DMs. (Public channels are a different story.

REMEMBER

A Workspace Owner who belongs to a private channel can view the content in that channel.

Still, scenarios exist in which organizations may need to access private employee correspondence. Examples here include meeting legitimate legal, law enforcement, or regulatory requirements.

Slack doesn't grant these requests for access willy-nilly. To acquire private employee information, Workspace Owners need to submit an application to Slack, and the company needs to approve it.

REMEMBER

Say that Slack approves an organization's request and grants this level of access. Only then could Workspace Owners conceivably share this erstwhile private information with colleagues, regulators, attorneys, and law-enforcement officials.

Second, your organization's billing plan is also a factor here. All things being equal, Org Owners and Admins may be able to obtain data from private channels and DMs if Slack grants them approval. (Chapter 11 has much more to say about the limitations and process of exporting data from Slack.)

TIP

Slack doesn't allow workspace members to natively circumvent its own encryption process. That is, Slack does not ship with a simple button that lets users disable this feature. However, it's not difficult for workspace members to use independent file-encryption utilities and achieve the same effect. For example, I can create a message using a simple text editor, save the file, and encrypt it with Encrypto or a similar tool. I can then send the encrypted file as a DM to whomever I like. Sure, this process involves a bit more work on my end, but there's a benefit: Even in the unlikely event that a Workspace Owner gains access to my private DMs, she wouldn't be able to open this document.

REMEMBER

You may be concerned about security and privacy in Slack because you're new to it. Fair enough, but in Slack, your colleagues can only view your public messages. The only exceptions to this rule are a data breach and extenuating circumstances requiring the aforementioned application and Slack's approval.

What data Workspace Admins can Access

You may be understandably concerned about the content that Workspace Owners can view. Here's how to find out who can view and download what in Slack:

1. **Go to `slack.com/account/team` and log in to your workspace.**

   Slack displays a simple three-tab web page.

2. **Click on the Retention and Exports tab on the right.**

3. **Scroll down to What data can my admins access.**

   Slack displays information on how long the workspace stores conversation history and the type of data that Admins can access.

4. **Read which types of messages Workspace Owners can potentially view and export.**

   At a minimum, Workspace Owners can view and export messages in *public* channels. They may also be able to do the same with private messages and channels under extenuating circumstances. Again, the organization needs to submit an application to Slack.

A few notes are in order here. First, hold your outrage. It's downright silly to claim that senior management and auditors should never be able to access critical organizational communications under any circumstances at all. Do a simple Google search of the Tyco, Enron, WorldCom, and Wells Fargo scandals. All of these financial crimes left plenty of digital breadcrumbs. If company auditors hadn't been asleep at the wheel, maybe these companies wouldn't have fallen so far from grace.

Second, this ability should not be a revelation to you, nor should it discourage you from using email over Slack. Make no mistake: IT folks at your company can already access your work emails. If you think otherwise, then you're sorely mistaken.

Finally, just because Workspace Owners may be able to view this information doesn't necessarily mean that they will.

TIP

When introducing Slack, be forthright about your company's privacy policy. You don't want employees forgoing the tool because they're spooked.

Workspace message-retention settings

How long do you want to keep messages in your Slack workspace? Do you want to hold on to them indefinitely? Alternatively, do you want to purge them once they reach a certain age?

I'd argue for the first option, but perhaps your company legitimately needs to delete older messages. Workspace Owners and Admins can establish message-retention settings for their workspaces by following these steps:

1. **Click on the main menu.**
2. **From the drop-down menu, select Settings & administration and then Workspace settings.**

   Slack launches a window or tab in your default browser.

3. **Under the Settings tab, scroll down to Message Retention & Deletion.**
4. **Click on the white Expand button to the right.**
5. **Select the desired settings for public and private channels and DMs.**

   Note that you can apply different settings to different items. Options here include

   - Keeping everything
   - Keeping all messages but not tracking message revisions
   - Deleting messages and their revisions after a certain period of time
   - Letting workspace members override these settings

6. **If desired, select the box to allow workspace members to override these settings and click on the green Save button.**

TIP

For Enterprise Grid customers, Org Owners and Admins can easily configure these settings for all of their workspaces. What's more, if you don't see these options, someone above you has disabled them for your workspace.

Setting message retention policies for a specific channel

On occasion, organizations want to override global message-retention settings for specific channels. Perhaps conversations in one channel are particularly important or sensitive and need to go poof.

Say that you want to *routinely* purge channel messages after a certain period of time. That is, you don't want to have to remember to delete them after three months or whatever. If your role permits, then follow these steps:

1. **Click on the channel whose settings you want to customize.**
2. **Click on the information (i) icon in the top right-hand corner.**

   Slack displays a four-pane tab with the word Details above it.

3. **Click on the More icon on the far right.**

   Slack displays a new pane underneath your mouse.

4. **From the drop-down list, click on Edit message retention.**
5. **Select the box for Use custom retention settings for this conversation.**

   This step allows Slack to automatically delete messages after a fixed time period. In other words, you can override Slack's global options for all channels in the workspace.

6. **Enter the number of days or years after which Slack will delete messages and their revisions.**

   The maximum at present is 100 years.

7. **Click on the Save button.**

WARNING

   Slack warns you that there's no going back. Not even Slack will be able to retrieve messages that you delete after this period.

8. **Select the radio button next to Yes, apply these new settings and then click on the red Apply Settings button.**

Override message retention settings for individual DMs and conversations

Sometimes we no longer need to view old messages. Of course, you can manually delete them as needed. (See Chapter 4 for additional actions that you can perform on DMs and conversations.) But what if you want a conversation with a colleague to disappear at some point in the future?

1. **Click on the conversation whose settings you want to customize.**
2. **Click on the information (i) icon in the top right-hand corner.**

   Slack displays a three-pane tab with the word Details above it.

3. **Click on the More icon on the far right.**

   Slack displays a panel underneath our mouse.

4. **Click on Edit message retention.**
5. **Click on the radio-box Use custom retention settings for this conversation.**
6. **Click on the green Save button.**
7. **Under the text Delete messages and their revisions after: enter the number of days or years that Slack should store this conversation.**

8. **Click on the green Save button.**

   Slack warns you that you are overriding your workspace's default message-retention settings for this conversation.

9. **Click on the Yes, apply these new settings box.**
10. **Click on the red Apply Settings button.**

WARNING

Think carefully before you noodle with Slack's message-retention settings. One of Slack's primary benefits is that it allows users and organizations to create a comprehensive knowledge repository. Scheduling the deletion of content by definition means that you and your colleagues will be able to access less of that knowledge and correspondence. What's more, as I describe in Chapter 15, less data impedes Slack's ability to learn about your workforce and how it communicates.

REMEMBER

If you are one of a number of Workspace Owners and Admins, then check with your colleagues before changing this setting. In my career, I have seen employees fired for purging enterprise data without consulting senior management.

File-retention settings

Remember that Slack's default content setting is inclusion. That is, Slack keeps all employee and guest files forever in workspace. Yes, Slack retains user content even if the individual leaves the company and/or the workspace. Of course, you can easily modify that setting:

1. **Click on the main menu.**
2. **From the drop-down menu, select Settings & administration and then Workspace settings.**
3. **Under the Settings tab, scroll down to File Retention & Deletion.**
4. **Click on the white Expand button to the right.**

   Your two options are

   - *Keep all files:* This option is the default.
   - *Keep all files, only for a set number of days*: If you enter a value here, then Slack warns you that it will automatically delete files when their age hits that value. Click on the red Confirm Settings button.

WARNING

Again, be careful here. Slack enforces whatever settings you select here. Say that you aggressively purge files and then decide that you want to retrieve them five years later. Tough noogies. You're out of luck. I always err on the side of inclusion. In the immortal words of Franz Kafka, "Better to have and not need than to need and not have."

Understanding Slack's Tricky Regulatory Environment

When it comes to privacy, we all have our own opinions. Maybe you believe that we should finally rein in the unfettered power of Google, Facebook, and other tech leviathans. Alternatively, you might opt for a more *laissez-faire* approach: It should be an individuals' responsibility to make informed decisions about the data they put out there. Perhaps you fall somewhere in between these two poles.

Regardless of your convictions, one thing is certain: All companies must abide by legislation in the countries in which they do business. Slack is no exception to this rule. This chapter closes with a few thoughts on how Slack is navigating key privacy issues in a tricky regulatory environment. Current privacy legislation may not affect your organization at the moment. It's a good bet, though, that at some point it will.

Restrictions on data and file retention

If you live and work in Europe, then you've most likely heard of General Data Protection Regulation (GDPR). At a high level, this 2018 legislation represents the European Union's most recent attempt to restrict what companies do with its citizens' data. The EU takes privacy far more seriously than the United States does, but that's a topic for a much longer conversation over beers.

Slack is committed to helping its European customers understand and comply with GDPR. For more information on this topic, see `https://slack.com/gdpr`.

Don't be surprised if more countries follow the EU's lead by passing more meaningful privacy legislation in the near future. I'm not clairvoyant, but I suspect that forthcoming privacy laws will impact your organization's ability to retain Slack messages and files in the years to come.

Data residency

Like many contemporary tech companies, Slack embraced cloud computing as a foundational technology from the get-go. (See Chapter 1 for more information about Slack's technology stack.) In layman's terms, this choice confers significant benefits to its users: They can access Slack and its data wherever they are as long as they are connected to the Internet. Thanks to cloud computing, Slack works anywhere, whether you're working at your desk in Manhattan, embarrassing yourself on the golf course, or visiting museums in Timbuktu. People of a certain age remember when such convenience was a pipe dream.

In a practical way, then, users may not even know — much less care about — the physical location in which their organization's Slack's data ultimately resides. Legally, though, that exact location is starting to matter a great deal. Increasingly governments around the world are passing laws mandating where companies can store their citizens' data. To wit, many large employers now have to deal with *data residency*: Laws may require them to physically store and process customer, user, and employee data within the borders of a specific country. What's more, fines for violating data residency statutes can be substantial, especially in the EU. In response, many multinational organizations are beginning to define their own policies in this vein.

Again, Slack's got you covered. Customers on Slack's Plus and Enterprise Grid plans can easily port their data to physical locations in different countries if the legal or regulatory need arises. For more on this subject, visit `bit.ly/slack-dr`.

4

Extending Slack's Native Functionality

IN THIS PART

Enhance Slack's power through third-party apps and custom integrations

Analyze, import, and export Slack data

Integrate Slack with your organization's current enterprise systems

IN THIS CHAPTER

» Understanding how Slack has embraced platform thinking

» Reviewing the different types of Slack apps

» Extending Slack's power via third-party apps

» Installing, removing, and disabling apps

» Building simple apps with Workflow Builder

Chapter 10
Making Slack Hum with Robust Third-Party Apps

To be sure, Slack's out-of-the-box functionality by itself helps millions of employees communicate better and increase their productivity. You can send targeted messages, make video calls, and perform other tasks. (For more information on these exciting features, see Parts 2 and 3.) Slack's power users know full well, though, that they can do a great deal more by taking advantage of others' creations.

This chapter describes useful and complementary Slack tools for polling, file-sharing, scheduling, and much more. You learn how easy it is to extend the power of native Slack. Put differently, if Slack has already impressed you, you ain't seen nothin' yet.

Understanding How Slack Has Embraced Platform Thinking

In a way, Slack closely resembles Amazon, Apple, Facebook, Google, Twitter, and Automattic (the company behind WordPress). Slack has built a true platform — and I don't make the claim lightly. (I'll spare you my entire rant on the subject. Suffice it to say, though, plenty of posers misuse that powerful term.)

In its simplest form, an open application programming interface, or *API*, allows different web services and applications to easily talk to each other. More formally, an API is a set of protocols and tools that lets developers more easily build software and add features. I find it best to think of APIs as hooks that connect different web services. They work under the hood, if you like.

Slack has embraced the power of APIs. The company has succeeded where most of its brethren has failed: It has created a vibrant ecosystem of external developers that are doing amazing things. Mark my words: This is no easy feat.

Slack's APIs allow its own developers to integrate a variety of different tools and services. What's more, the company's open APIs let nearly 600,000 active, registered, and external developers extend the power of native Slack in new and interesting ways. This chapter introduces you to many of those creations.

As a daily Slack user, of course, you don't need to know anything about its technical underpinnings. While useful, that knowledge isn't essential for you to work effectively within Slack. Trust me on two things, though:

- Slack users frequently interact with APIs whether they know it or not.
- Slack wouldn't work nearly as well without APIs.

Brass tacks: You don't need to be a developer to take advantage of the power of Slack's APIs.

Here's further proof that Slack understands the power of building a vibrant ecosystem of developers. The company has established a partnership with some of the leading venture-capital firms in the world. Collectively, they're investing in promising companies that will make Slack more powerful and improve the world of work. Visit `bit.ly/31QNs1Y` to learn more about the Slack Fund.

At the Slack October 2019 developer conference (Spec), the company announced the launch of an even more sophisticated app toolkit. As useful as apps are today, they'll only grow in power and sophistication in the future. I was there and saw firsthand that developers were downright giddy. Visit `bit.ly/sl-tools` to learn more.

Comparing Public and Private Apps

At a high level, Slack apps fall into two different buckets: public and private.

Public apps

As of this writing, Slack users can install more than 2,000 third-party public apps that "live" on top of its core software. Even better, that number grows just about every day. Developers design these apps as global services. That is, any company using Slack can install and benefit from these public apps.

Slack apps certainly overlap with one another. Each of the 2,000 apps isn't unique. For example, plenty provide polling, calendar integration, file sharing, and more.

It's a safe bet that this number will continue to rise as Slack gains in popularity. (Maybe this book can help in that regard. Fingers crossed.)

Private apps and integrations

To be sure, plenty of developers make their living by creating and selling public apps. As Slack has grown, however, an increasing number of its larger customers have decided to develop and deploy their own apps outside of the Slack App Directory. (To my knowledge, Slack hasn't released specific data on private apps and integrations.)

Companies' reasons for creating their own tchotchkes vary, but sometimes existing public apps just don't cut it. They may not meet an organization's specific needs or the app's paid version may be too pricey. Alternatively, a company may not want to risk giving a third-party access to sensitive information. If a company's management has the desire and resources to build a better mousetrap, then it certainly can. As of this writing, Slack's customers have built an astonishing 500,000 private apps to do a wide variety of things. Many of them allow Slack to connect to the very enterprise systems that I mention in Chapter 12.

If a public or private Slack app becomes problematic, contact the developer and open a support ticket. Make sure to include screenshots, videos, information about your computer's operating system, and the context behind when you experienced the problem. By providing this information, you'll increase the chances that the app's developers will be able to diagnose and ultimately resolve the issue. To paraphrase *Jerry Maguire*, help them help you.

REMEMBER

Developers can always create private apps and elect not to submit them to the Slack App Directory. This decision may hurt the visibility of their apps. On the other hand, Slack doesn't need to review and approve them for people to use them.

Enhancing Slack with Third-Party Apps

At a high level, Slack apps perform different functions around communication, collaboration, automation, and more. Beyond my own recommendations, I encourage you to explore them on your own. You can find all public apps in the Slack App Directory at `https://slack.com/apps`.

Like many companies that have launched app stores, Slack vets each individual app before making it available to the public. The company wants to ensure that third-party apps adhere to its terms of service. More specifically, public apps should not

- Conflict with or break core Slack functionality
- Collect and distribute user data
- Send spam
- Violate a nation's privacy laws
- Introduce malware

To minimize frustration and reduce the time required to approve developers' apps, Slack provides clear guidelines and extensive documentation. I'll spare you most of the details here, but an important one concerns how frequently approved apps should send reminders and messages to workplace members. Overly talkative or salesy apps run the risk of irritating Slack customers and users — something that, for obvious reasons, Slack strives to avoid.

Looking at app costs

As for pricing, developers of most public apps let Slack members kick the tires for free — as long as their assigned roles allow them to install new apps. (Some apps are currently free for unlimited use.) Put differently, almost all developers offer at least a trial period or limited app functionality to encourage app usage and, ultimately, proper purchases. You may recognize this approach as the freemium business model because it has been prevalent for years. In fact, you've probably encountered it at some point in your life.

To learn more about the freemium business model, check out Chris Anderson's excellent book *Free: The Future of a Radical Price* (Hyperion).

TIP

It's unwise to buy every app under the sun, but don't be afraid to pay for useful apps. I'm well aware of corporate budgets, but foolish is the firm that adopts a strict policy against paying for tools that help make employees more productive.

The Slack App Directory

Before you go about installing apps and using apps, it helps to know a bit more about the ones that are currently available in the Slack App Directory.

As you can see in Figure 10-1, Slack offers no shortage of cool apps and useful ways to find them.

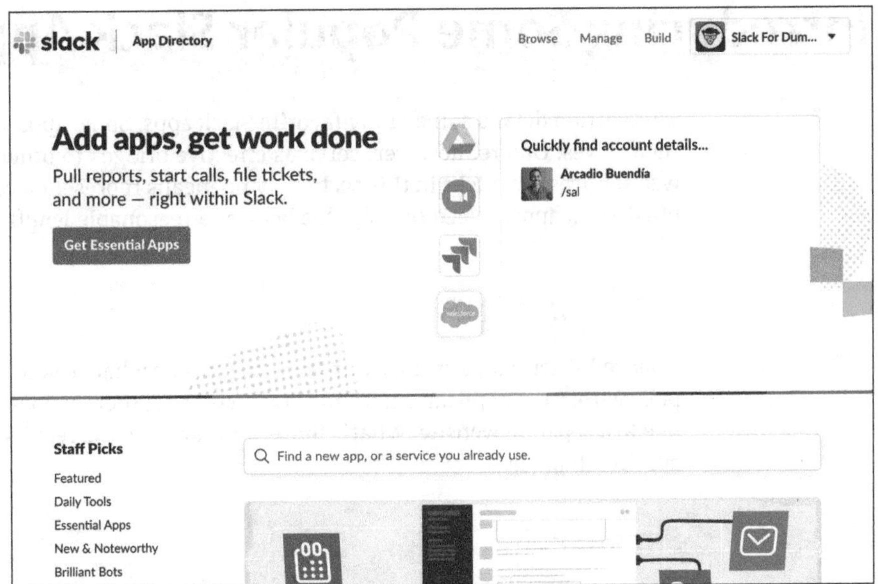

FIGURE 10-1: The Slack App Directory.

The generic link for the Slack App Directory is

```
https://www.slack.com/apps
```

TIP

Click on the green Get Essential Apps button to view the apps that Slack considers — wait for it — essential.

If you're anxious to get started, then knock yourself out. Poke around until your heart's content. For those of you who want a more formal introduction to the Slack App Directory, fear not. A bit later in the chapter, I describe how to easily locate cool apps here in the section "Finding and Installing Apps."

WARNING

Slack conducts a brief review of all apps before placing them in its App Directory. The company neither sanctions nor certifies individual apps, though. *Caveat emptor.*

WARNING

Third-party apps take the core Slack application in interesting directions, but Slack itself doesn't *directly* support them. What's more, Slack takes no legal responsibility for their actions if things break bad. Should you encounter a problem with an external app, your only recourse is to contact the developer or company directly. In this way, Slack works the same way as any mainstream app store.

Introducing Some Popular Slack Apps

This section details some of my favorite Slack apps. Some apps are über-useful by themselves. Others, however, serve as effective bridges to other applications and web services. My picks in this section by no means represent a comprehensive list of all Slack apps. I need to keep this book at a reasonable length, though.

Polling apps

Nuanced discussions in Slack are one thing, but what if you want to run quick polls within the application? Thanks to a few apps, there's no need to send someone to a separate website. What's more, you can view the results of the poll within specific channels.

Simple Poll

```
https://simplepoll.rocks
```

```
https://slack.com/apps/A0HFW7MR6-simple-poll
```

For quick one-question polls, Simple Poll is the way to go. This app also allows you to turn a message into a poll with one click. If you like, you can anonymize polls so that no one knows who voted for each option — including the member who created the poll. For example, I was curious about how my students felt on how I use PowerPoint. Figure 10-2 shows the results of a poll that I conducted.

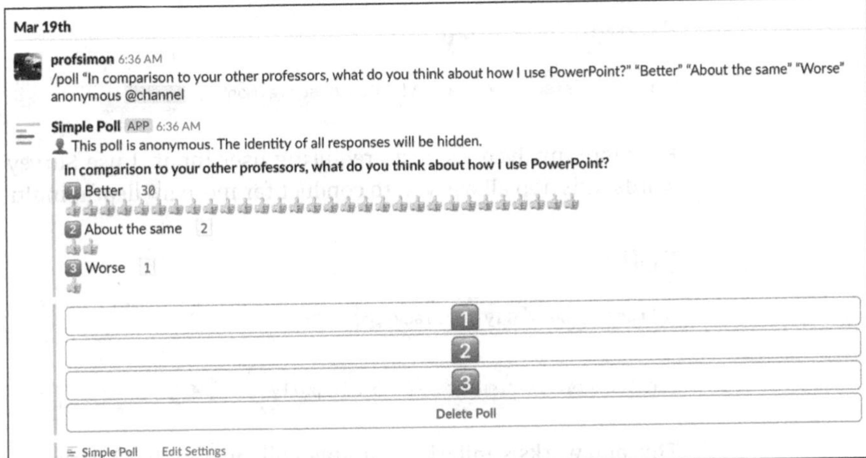

FIGURE 10-2: Example of a Simple Poll on student reaction to how I use PowerPoint in the classroom.

Note that the app limits your workspace responses to 100 per month under its free plan. Also note that Simple Poll is an example of an app that one person in a workspace can install and everyone can then use.

Slido

```
https://slack.com/apps/A4BCD103T-slido
```

It's certainly useful to collect information via traditional single- or even multi-question polls. But what if you need a way to publicly filter on which questions to answer?

For example, Heather Brunner is the CEO of WordPress hosting company WPEngine. (For more on how her company uses Slack, see the sidebar "WP Engine learns to walk before it runs" in Chapter 13.) Brunner holds a weekly one-hour all-hands meeting at the company's headquarters in Austin, Texas. She wants to answer her employees' most pressing questions. Fair enough, but how can she do so in the most transparent way possible?

Slido is ideal for situations such as these. Unlike other polling apps, Slido allows for crowdsourced questions and upvoting à la Reddit. WPEngine employees vote for their choices directly in Slack and suggest new ones. The most popular queries automatically rise to the top. In this way, Slido operates much like Reddit's upvoting feature.

Survey Monkey

```
https://slack.com/apps/A4JEUJH4M-surveymonkey
```

For more involved requests requiring user input, I use Survey Monkey. In other words, this app allows you to conduct far more in-depth, multi-question surveys.

Polly

```
https://www.polly.ai/slack-poll
```

```
https://slack.com/apps/A04E6JX41-polly
```

This app works similarly to Simple Poll, an app that I describe earlier in this section. I use it if I reach my monthly limit on Simple Poll's free plan.

File- and content-sharing apps

Google Drive and Dropbox are two of my favorite third-party Slack apps. They make my fellow Slack users and me more productive.

Google Drive

```
https://slack.com/apps/A6NL8MJ6Q-google-drive
```

Emailing attachments back and forth seems so 1999. As a result, I am a vocal advocate for Google Docs. (If only I could get all my colleagues to join me here, but I digress . . .)

The Google Drive app allows you to grant access to Google Sheets, Docs, and Slides directly in Slack. Once installed, you'll receive notifications on new comments, files, and access requests on your Google Docs — and you never have to leave Slack. Emails about others' comments go *poof*.

Dropbox

```
https://slack.com/apps/AES7B2V7D-dropbox
```

I've been using Dropbox since 2008. In a word, I find it indispensable. Slack's Dropbox app allows members to preview files right within their Slack workspaces. They can also comment on files in Dropbox and view others' comments in Slack.

I don't use Microsoft OneDrive and Box, but you can install Slack apps for these file-sharing utilities by following their intuitive processes. (For more information on installing apps, see the section "Installing an app in Slack" in this chapter.)

Pocket

```
https://app.getpocket.com
```

```
https://slack.com/apps/A95LNTTQQ-pocket
```

What if someone posts an interesting article, video, or podcast in Slack, and you would like to read it later? Pocket lets you save content to read or watch from your mobile device or computer, even if you're offline (after you've synced it). I've used Pocket long before I started noodling with Slack and absolutely love it. It helps me stay informed without creating a bunch of bookmarks in my browser.

Scheduling apps

Several apps make scheduling a breeze — and integrate tightly with Slack as well.

GOOGLE CALENDAR

```
https://slack.com/apps/ADZ494LHY-google-calendar
```

Slack's Google Calendar app is pretty useful. It allows users to do the following:

- Automatically sync their Slack statuses with their calendars
- Allow teammates to see their availability for meetings
- Receive and respond to event invites
- Receive notifications when an event is starting soon or when its details change
- Join Google Hangouts, Meet, or Zoom calls with a single click
- View a daily reminder of your upcoming events in your Google calendar within Slack

DOODLE BOT

```
https://slack.com/apps/AFA5VQJKX-doodle-bot
```

Every day I shake my head when I hear about people from different companies incessantly emailing each other to schedule a simple meeting. It's downright ridiculous.

You may not be able to access the calendars of your company's partners, clients, vendors, or applications. If this is the case, then you'll love Doodle. At a high level, it allows you to suggest meeting times for people — no matter where they are. The Doodle app allows you to effectively administer meeting requests within Slack.

MESSAGE SCHEDULER

```
https://slack.com/apps/AJ0QX9THD-message-scheduler
```

By default and as I cover in Chapter 4, Slack sends messages as soon as you press Enter or Return in the message window. But what if you want to schedule your message for later? Message Scheduler allows you to send Slack messages in the future to any person or channel.

TIP

Other apps provide nearly identical functionality. I discuss one (IFTTT) in the section "IFTTT Slack applets" later in this chapter. As you'll quickly discover, app developers often independently land on the same opportunities and features.

YouCanBook.me

```
https://www.youcanbook.me
```

You probably realized by this point that I loathe inefficiency and maddening email chains in particular. For this reason, YouCanBook.me (YCBM) is a godsend. It lets others easily schedule meetings. That is, it obviates the need for a litany of "How about Wednesday at 11?" emails and responses. Simply set your available times and dates and direct people to your own YCBM page. People can book whatever slot they like, and everyone receives email confirmations. Even better, YCBM automatically creates appointments on the host's calendar.

No, YouCanBook.me doesn't directly link to Slack as of this writing, but fret not: That's where Zapier comes in. (For more information on this topic, see Chapter 12.) As of this writing, Zapier allows users to connect Slack with more than 1,500 apps — all without writing a single line of code. And yes, YouCanBook.me is one of those magic 1,500 apps. (See `bit.ly/YCBMslack` for more information on how to integrate Slack with YouCanBook.me.)

TIP

Once you've got your arms around Slack, consider revisiting Zapier. It is certainly useful software. To be fair, though, Zapier can be a little overwhelming at first — especially if you're new to Slack. Baby steps.

Productivity and project-management apps

Used properly, those who only take advantage of Slack's native functionality can be vastly more productive. Double that when you tie Slack to powerful productivity and project management tools such as Trello, Todoist, and Workast.

Trello

```
https://slack.com/apps/A074YH40Z-trello
```

```
https://trello.com/platforms/slack
```

Google "Slack project management." The search engine returns nearly 40 million results. As much as I love Slack, though, I don't use it to directly manage meaty group projects. That's not to say, that Slack can't facilitate communication among members on those projects. It certainly does.

I generally find Gantt charts confusing. For a few years now, I've used Trello to manage group projects — and I encourage my students to do the same. You can easily create task-specific cards. What's more, you can assign those cards to students working on different tasks of a database or a website-redesign project.

The good news is that Trello plays nicely with Slack. Put simply, after installing the Trello Slack app, the two seamlessly send information back and forth and remain in sync. For example, if you want to attach Slack conversations to individual Trello cards, you can. As Trello writes it on its website, you can steer the ship from Slack with "no boating license required." Boom!

Todoist

```
https://slack.com/apps/A0NSTB8R3-todoist
```

Trello works well for group projects, but what if you want to keep track of things that you — and you alone — need to do?

Enter Todoist, my go-to productivity app. For the past six years, I have used it to ensure that I stayed on top of all sorts of personal and professional responsibilities. In Slack, after I install the app, I can add a simple item by invoking the `/todoist` command. The task will magically appear in the Todoist app on all of my devices.

Workast

```
https://slack.com/apps/A0HBTUUPK-workast
```

Slack's native reminders get the job done, but Workast (see Chapter 12) can serve as a reminder app on steroids. With Kanban boards, custom tags, and templates, Workast is much more powerful than Slack's native reminder functionality. You may decide that it's worth paying for.

IFTTT Slack applets

```
https://ifttt.com/slack
```

If This Then That (IFTTT) is a free web-based service that allows users to create simple conditional statements called *applets*. (Up until 2016, IFTTT called them *recipes*.) As of this writing, you can connect more than 300 different apps and devices. Services include Amazon Alexa, Facebook, Twitter, and Fitbit.

For example, what if you wanted to save every photo that you post on Instagram to your Dropbox account? Do you want to ask Alexa to find your lost smartphone? Would you like the day's weather to magically appear in Google Calendar?

Can you automate similar tasks with Slack? No, I just wanted to tease you.

I'm kidding. Table 10-1 displays just a few of the creative ways that people have embraced automation and linked Slack to different services and applications.

TABLE 10-1 Cool IFTTT Applets

Description	URL
Add blog posts to the `#general` Slack channel	ift.tt/sfd-1
Post whiteboard notes in Slack	ift.tt/sfd-2
Gently remind employees that expenses are due at the end of the month	ift.tt/sfd-3
Notify tech support employees of a new client issue; send incoming SMS help requests to your organization's Slack `#help` channel	ift.tt/sfd-4

IFTTT automates each of these tasks. Say adios to forgetting to post weekly channel reminders. Saving a few minutes here and there really adds up.

How do you know if an applet ran? As Figure 10-3 shows, IFTTT alerts you with notifications on your mobile device.

FIGURE 10-3: IFTTT mobile-app notification.

TIP

For more on how to build your own applets with little technical knowhow, visit `https://www.ifttt.com/slack`.

Video-calling apps

Slack lets you share your screen with others and hold video calls. (See Chapter 6 for more information on this subject.) At some point you might think: Why would anyone need to go elsewhere?

Two reasons: Numbers and existing software licenses for other tools.

As of this writing, Slack limits the number of concurrent call and screen-sharing participants to 15 on premium plans. Slack eventually hopes to increase that number in the future. Until then, organizations that require larger numbers can purchase a Zoom license. Zoom (`bit.ly/slack-zm`) is a popular video-calling and screen-sharing app that millions of people use — inside and outside of Slack. Depending on the plan, Zoom lets you simultaneously reach a maximum of 1,000 people.

If Zoom doesn't do it for you, then consider Cisco's WebEx, Fuze, Adobe Connect, or Skype for Business (Microsoft's replacement for Lync). These tools also enable webinars and screen-sharing.

TIP

You can change Slack's default calling app unless someone at your organization locks it down and prevents you from doing so.

Email apps and integrations

Email apps and integrations can be especially useful. They can quickly move conversations from email to where they probably should have been all along: Slack. Of course, no app forces people to use Slack.

Customers on the premium plans can use this native Slack email *integration* at (bit.ly/email-l) to do a number of cool things. For example, say that you want Slack to automatically send customer-lead queries to a workspace `#sales_leads` channel? Slack handles these types of notifications via a special email addresses. You can probably think of many more valuable applications of this particular app.

Slack for Outlook (`bit.ly/sfd-outl`) allows Outlook users to easily move conversations and their context to a Slack DM or channel of your choosing. Not to be outdone, Slack for Gmail (`bit.ly/sl-gmail`) does exactly what you'd expect.

Miscellaneous apps

A few other apps are particularly useful but don't fall into a single neat category.

Zendesk

```
https://slack.com/apps/A9WFQ3M0B-zendesk
```

Many organizations rely upon Zendesk to manage their internal and customer support issues. By tying it to Slack, IT folks become aware of issues much quicker. Of course, you can't resolve these issues without reporting them first.

Giphy

```
https://slack.com/apps/A0F827J2C-giphy
```

I like animated gifs. There. I said it.

TIP

Giphy serves as an example of how Slack's app installation process differs a bit from app to app. In this case, Giphy asks you to select the gif ratings. You can restrict this to G or PG (just like movie ratings). By doing so, you prohibit people from posting naughty gifs that are not safe for work — or *NSFW*, as the kids say.

Guru

```
https://slack.com/apps/A0FHVR2R0-guru
```

With so many different messages flying around Slack, it can be difficult to locate accurate, current, and official information — even with the advanced search tips that Chapter 7 covers.

Enter Guru. The app allows users to capture, aggregate, and categorize institutional knowledge by creating cards. Think of Guru as an easy way to manage and communicate the most important knowledge at your organization.

Donut

```
https://slack.com/apps/A11MJ51SR-donut
```

Whether you work remotely or in an office, you may not know many of your colleagues. Maybe you're an introvert and value your solitude. If you want to meet your peers, though, Donut encourages employees to interact with each other in person or remotely.

Finding and Installing Apps

Say that you like some of my recommended apps. Fortunately, Slack makes turning them on remarkably simple with one catch: The process for installing apps is not entirely consistent. That is, as of this writing, there is no one single, universal set of steps to follow if you want to install a workspace app. Case in point: require one workspace member to install it for everyone to use it. In other cases, individual users need to install the app in their workspace app for it to work.

Because apps do different things, I suspect that there will never be a universal installation process. For example, when you install Google Drive, Slack logically asks you to sign in with your Google credentials. As a result, the app knows who you are and which documents you've created. Also, some apps ask you from the get-go if you want to restrict them to specific channels. Don't worry, though. As I demonstrate in this section, installing a workspace app is intuitive.

TIP

It's probably wise to stick with sanctioned apps in Slack's App Directory. If you have a compelling reason to circumvent it, just remember that you're introducing additional risk to the organization. Of course, Workspace Owners and Admins can lock down this setting. (See the "Limiting workspace apps" section in this chapter for more information on this topic.)

TIP

As a Workspace Owner or Admin, your role probably permits you to install third-party apps in your Slack workspace. (This statement may not be true if your firm is on the Enterprise Grid.) If your organization is new to Slack, though, you should take it easy at first with apps for several reasons. First, you don't want to overwhelm newbies. Second, some Slack apps perform similar and even identical functions. (Chapter 13 provides more tips on successfully rolling out Slack.)

REMEMBER

If you don't see the menus and steps in the following section, then a Workspace Owner or Admin has limited your rights to manage and install apps in your workspace.

Browsing the Slack App Directory

To view the available apps for Slack workspaces, you'll need to visit the Slack App Directory. Follow these directions to locate useful apps and ultimately to install them in your workspace.

1. **Click on the Apps view in the top half of the sidebar.**
2. **Click on the green Browse App Directory button.**

   Slack takes you to your workspace's App Directory page in a new tab or window in your default web browser. For example, mine is:

   ```
   https://slackfordummieshq.slack.com/apps
   ```

Underneath Staff Picks on the left, you can easily browse apps by category. At present, Slack includes buckets for

- Featured
- Daily Tools
- Essential Apps
- New & Noteworthy
- Brilliant Bots

TIP

It's not a bad idea to bookmark this page in your web browser.

Installing a Slack app in your workspace

After browsing the Slack App Directory, you will eventually find one that you want to install in your workspace. Follow these steps:

1. **Click on the name of the app that you'd like to install.**
2. **Click on either the green Add button or the white Add to Slack button, depending on which one you see.**

   Slack confirms that you want to grant access to the app.
3. **Click on the green Add *[name of app]* app button or the green Allow button if you want to proceed.**

REMEMBER

The process for installing different Slack apps isn't entirely consistent.

4. **Confirm that you want to grant access to the app.**

   After successfully installing an app, Slackbot sends you a DM telling you that your new app is now active. Yours will look something like the one shown in Figure 10-4.

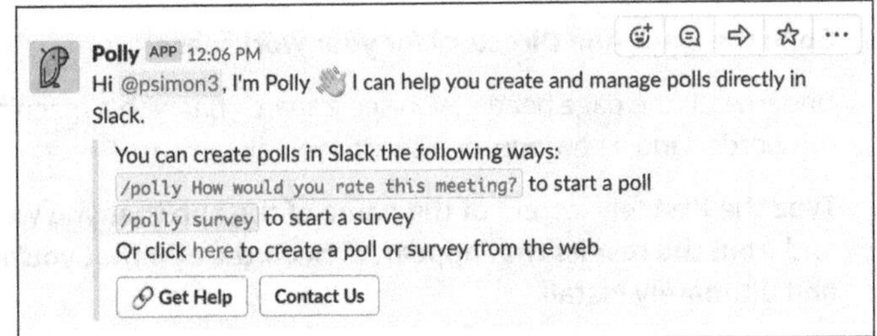

FIGURE 10-4: Slackbot in-app confirmation message for the poll application Polly.

You and others in your workspace can now start using your new app.

Slack wants to ensure that nothing untoward is taking place in your workspace. After installing an app, Workspace Owners and Admins can expect to receive a confirmation email, such as the one in Figure 10-5.

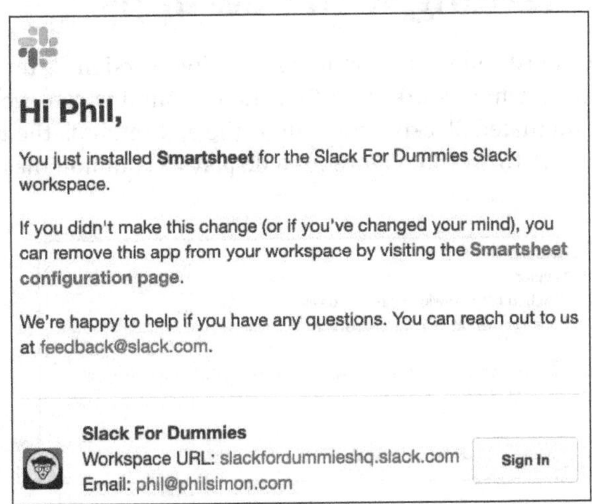

FIGURE 10-5: Slack email confirming installation of the Smartsheet app.

TIP

You can access certain apps such as Giphy within a channel by clicking on the lightning bolt icon in the message window.

Searching for specific apps

Just like in brick-and-mortar retail stores, browsing is fine when you're just poking around. Put differently, when you browse, you just want to see what's available. Sometimes, however, you know exactly what you want. Follow these directions to find and install a specific app in your workspace:

1. **Go to the Slack App Directory for your workspace.**

   Underneath the page header, you see a search bar with a magnifying glass and the words "Find a new app, or a service you already use."

2. **Type the first few letters of the name of the app that you want to install and from the results that appear, click on the app that you'd like to view and ultimately install.**

3. **Install the app as described in the earlier "Installing an App in Slack" section.**

Much like a simple channel, each app exists within an individual workspace. If you want to use an app in two workspaces, then you'll have to install it twice. Even for Enterprise Grid customers, the idea of a shared app does not currently exist.

Experimenting with new apps

Many, if not most, apps offer some type of free version. After kicking the tires on an app for a while, Workspace Owners and Admins can eventually expect to receive an automated Slackbot note. In it, the app reminds the user that the trial period is coming to an end. Figure 10-6 displays a common message:

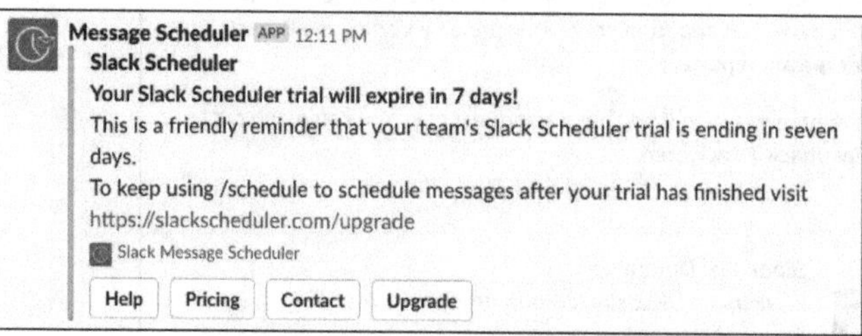

FIGURE 10-6: Slackbot message indicating expiration of trial period of Slack `Message Scheduler` app.

Depending on whether you found the app useful, click on the button that best indicates what you'd like to do.

WARNING

Keep an eye out for new apps, but resist the urge to overdo it as you start your firm's Slack journey. Installing five apps that essentially do the same thing generally isn't wise because it will confuse users. What's more, if your company is on Slack's Free plan, then you'll quickly hit the limit of ten apps.

Managing Apps and App Permissions

Now you have installed some apps in your workspace. You're ready to make Slack really hum. It makes sense, though, to understand a bit more about the mechanics behind these new tchotchkes before releasing them into the wild.

WARNING

In this chapter, I focus on managing apps for Slack's Free, Standard, and Plus plans. For its Enterprise Grid customers, Slack provides Org Owners and Admins with a separate Admin Dashboard. At a high level, this enterprise-strength tool facilitates managing apps and permissions for all workspaces in an organization. Visit `bit.ly/eg-apps2` for more information on this topic.

Approving specific apps

To be sure, apps extend Slack's core functionality in all sorts of cool ways. Left unfettered, though, the Wild Wild West may result. That is, if anyone can install anything, bad things could potentially happen. It's understandable, then, for an organization to restrict apps on two levels:

- The specific apps that members can install
- Which roles and members can install new workspace apps

I'll start by exploring the first option. To whitelist a specific app for your workspace, follow these instructions:

1. **Go to the app's home page in your Slack App Directory.**

   The specific page varies based upon your workspace name and the name of the app.

   On the right side of the page, Slack displays the text "Manage app for entire workspace?"

2. **Click on the Approve button.**

   Slack displays a message that reads, "Any member can install and configure this app."

THE CASE FOR LIMITING APPS: TWO SEINFELD EXAMPLES

At a high level and out of the box, Slack allows all Members to install and uninstall apps from a workspace at their leisure. It's not difficult to imagine scenarios, however, in which an organization does not want to grant its employees so much freedom in Slack.

Let's start with blacklisting certain apps from a workspace. The CEO of the fictitious Kramerica Industries does not want employees to install social apps such as Twitter. The rationale is straightforward: their random thoughts on Twitter aren't germane to the workplace.

On the other side of the coin, management may not want to let employee uninstall certain workspace apps. For example, Vandelay Industries purchased an enterprise Zoom license for video calling. As such, its management does not want employees using other, non-sanctioned video-calling apps. To this end, Vandelay "locks down" the Zoom app such that only a Workspace Owner or the person and/or the person who installed the app can remove it for a particular individual.

REMEMBER

Just because an app is approved for use in your workspace does not mean that members must install it for themselves — much less use it. For example, say that a Workspace Owner approves Google Drive. Geddy isn't a fan of the app and chooses not to install it. He prefers Dropbox for file storage. Put differently, users aren't obligated to use an app if it doesn't serve any purpose for them.

Regulating workspace apps

To be sure, sometimes it makes sense to whitelist specific apps. By the same token, however, you may want to restrict others in your workspace from installing an app.

Restricting specific apps

You can restrict an app if you don't want other users to be able to remove or add new instances of the app. To restrict an app, follow these instructions:

1. **Go to the app's home page in the Slack App Directory.**

   The specific page varies based upon your workspace name and the name of the app.

   On the right side of the page, Slack displays the text "Manage app for entire workspace?"

2. **Click on the Restrict button.**
3. **From the prompt, click on the red Restrict App button.**

   Slack displays a message that reads, "Members are restricted from installing this app."

Viewing a list of restricted workspace apps

To view a list of all apps banned in your workspace, follow these directions:

1. **Go to your workspace's Slack App Directory.**
2. **Click on Manage at the top of the page.**
3. **Click on Restricted; it's underneath Approved.**

   Slack displays all the blacklisted apps in your workspace.

Restricting which workspace members can install apps

You might consider the idea of whitelisting apps to be too draconian and bureaucratic. Remember that Slack is a remarkably flexible tool, though. As such, it allows Workspace Owners and Admins to restrict roles and even individual members from installing new apps. You can do quite a bit more with these features, but I'll give you one simple example.

For example, Jesse is a member in my workspace. That is, he's not a Workspace Owner and I don't want to "promote" him to an administrative role. Still, I trust him and want him to be able to install apps as he sees fit. As such, I'll follow these steps to make him an *App Manager*:

1. **Go to your workspace's Slack App Directory.**
2. **Click on Manage and then on App Management Settings on the left-hand side of the page.**

   Slack displays a window similar to the one in Figure 10-7.
3. **Make any changes.**

   For example, I can restrict the apps that workspace members can install in the workspace. In this example, though, I want to let Jesse manage apps even though he's not a Workspace Owner.

   Under Select App Managers to manage apps, I select the second option: Workspace Owners and selected members or groups.

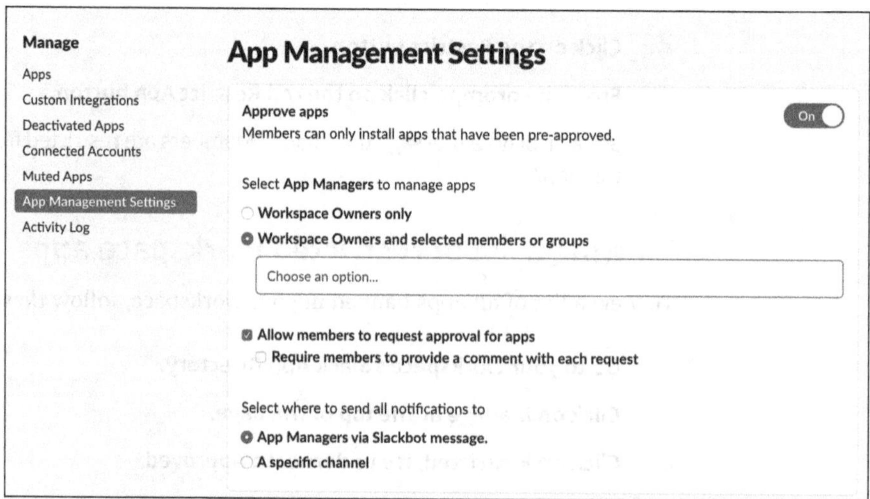

FIGURE 10-7: Slack App Management Settings.

TIP

Note that App Manager is not a full-fledged role in Slack à la Workspace Owner. You won't find it in Chapter 2. It's just a term to describe users with the equivalent of app superpowers.

4. I start typing the first few letters of Jesse's name. Slack shows his name in a blue outline.

That's it. Now Jesse can install apps even though he occupies a non-administrative role in Slack. As for the rest of the members in this example, Slack forbids them from installing unapproved apps. Should they try, Slack prompts those users with a message similar to the one shown in Figure 10-8.

After a member fills out the form, Slack notifies Workspace Owners and Admins of the request. They can decide what to do from there.

The App Management Settings menu allows Workspace Owners and Admins to set additional options around apps and security. Examples include

- You can route member app requests to an existing channel.
- You can restrict members from installing private apps. That is, they can only install apps from Slack's public App Directory.
- Say that you change your mind and want to allow other workspace members to install their own apps. From this page, you can make whatever changes you like.

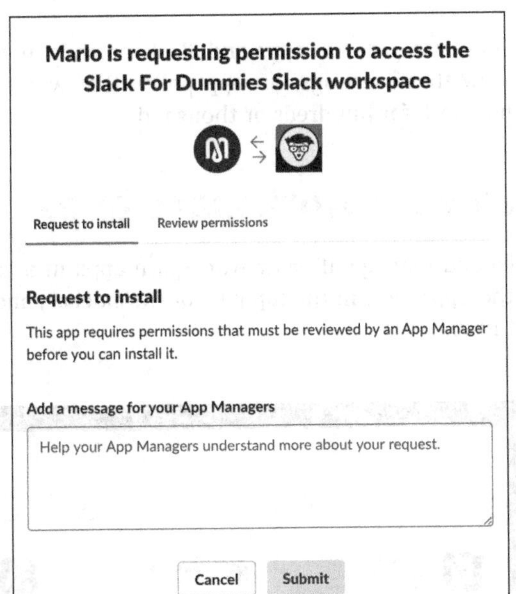

FIGURE 10-8: Slack app rejection message for Marlo, a meeting-feedback app.

Brass tacks: If a regular member cannot install an app in your workspace, it is because of one or more of the following reasons:

- Someone in your organization has specifically restricted the app.
- No one has whitelisted the app for your workspace.
- Her role doesn't let her install apps. (For example, she is a guest.)
- She needs to request permission from someone in an administrative role.

SCOPES

At a high level, *scopes* govern the specific things that apps can do. After installing a third-party app, you can review its scopes in the App Directory under the Manage heading. Examples of app scopes include the following abilities:

- Reading data from Slack
- Writing data to Slack
- Storing that data

If you're not comfortable with what an app does, then simply uninstall it.

TIP

As you become more familiar with apps and Slack expands in your organization, remember to review these settings. An app policy that works for a handful of employees may not work for hundreds or thousands.

Viewing all your workspace apps

Slack lets you see and manage all your workspace apps in a consolidated view. Simply click on the Apps view in the top part of the sidebar, and you see a figure similar to Figure 10-9.

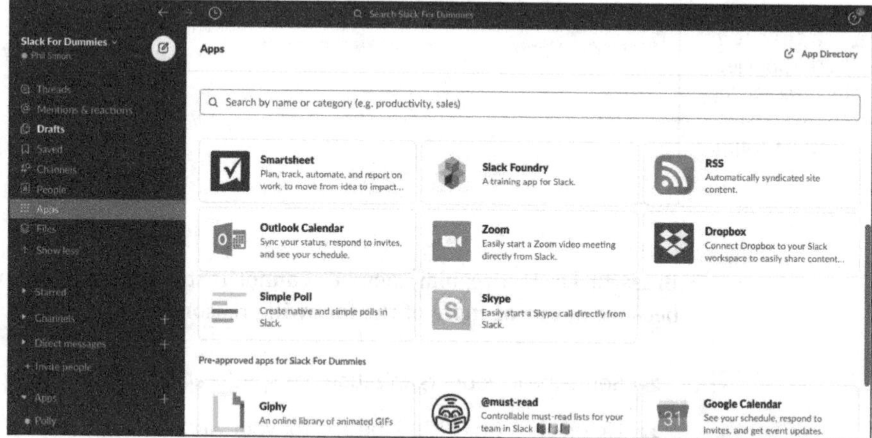

FIGURE 10-9: Slack Apps view.

Enforcing your organization's app policy

Slack's App Management Settings provide enormous flexibility for crafting the right policy for your organization. Here's one scenario on how a policy plays out with Slack members.

At Madrigal Electromotive, members can only install pre-approved apps. Lydia is the head of logistics. Her Slack role is member; she is not a Workspace Admin. Madrigal pays for Google Apps, not Microsoft Office. Importantly, Madrigal has neither restricted or approved the Microsoft Outlook Calendar app.

Lydia attempts to install the Microsoft app. Because of the current workspace settings, she'll see the message in Figure 10-10.

After she fills out the form, she'll see the grayed out text box "Request Submitted" if she views the app's page in the Slack App Directory. Slack immediately rattles off a Slackbot message to the Workspace Admin. Figure 10-11 displays that message. In English, Lydia wants to install the Outlook Calendar app and needs me to sanction it.

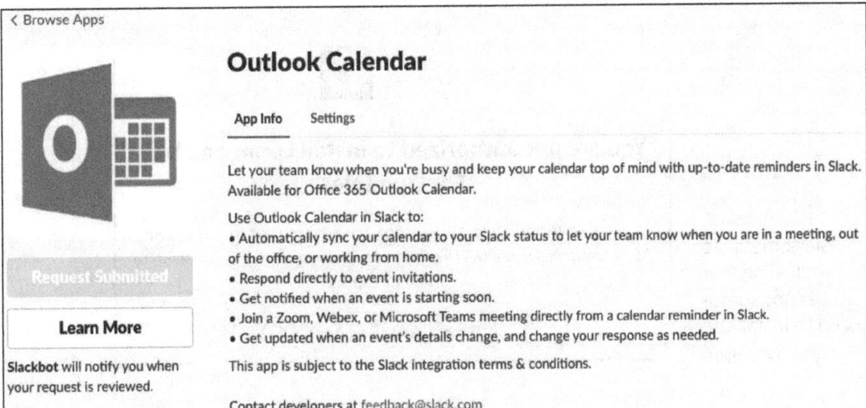

FIGURE 10-10: Slack message when member attempts to install the Outlook Calendar app.

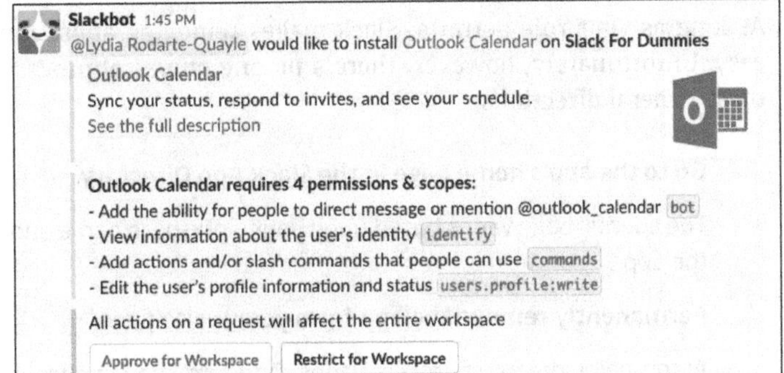

FIGURE 10-11: Slackbot message notifying Workspace Admin of member app-installation attempt.

At this point, Slack provides the Workspace Owner with two options:

1. **Approve the app request:** In this case, other members can now use the Outlook Calendar app.
2. **Restrict the app request:** If I go this route, then Slack places the Outlook Calendar app on my workspace's restricted list. (Of course, I can easily change this setting later by going back to my workspace's Manage Apps page.)

Just to finish the story, because Madrigal doesn't use Microsoft Office, I'll deny Lydia's request. Common courtesy dictates that I then send her a DM explaining why I denied her request.

Here's another scenario: Madrigal specifically restricts Loom — an app that easily allows people to create videos on computers. When Lydia attempts to install it, Slack presents her with a message as shown in Figure 10-12.

You are not authorized to install Loom on Slack For Dummies

Loom is restricted for this workspace. Please reach out to one of your App Managers if you would like additional information or to ask them to install this app.

Browse Approved Apps

FIGURE 10-12: Slack message indicating that user is not authorized to install the Loom app.

Removing apps from your workspace

As long as your role permits, Slack makes removing apps from your workspace easy. Unfortunately, however, there's no one universal process to follow. Follow these general directions:

1. **Go to the app's home page in the Slack App Directory.**

   The specific page varies based upon your workspace name and the name of the app.

2. **Permanently remove the app from your workspace.**

   At this point, the exact process varies. Odds are, though, that you'll do one of the following:

   - Click on the red Remove App button, usually at the bottom of the page. Slack asks you whether you're sure that you want to do this. (Click on the red Remove App button.)
   - Click on the white Remove button at the top of the page. Slack asks, "Are you sure you want to remove this configuration? (If so, then click on the green Yes button.)

Visit `bit.ly/ra-app` to watch a quick video of both processes for removing apps.

TIP

Make sure to inform members in your workspace or channel that you're removing an existing app. A simple message in a popular and public Slack channel will do the trick. Don't forget to use `@channel`. As usual, a little communication typically goes a long way.

REMEMBER

If you remove an app, then it will no longer properly function. For example, removing the Simple Poll means that people will no longer be able to vote on polls created prior to its removal.

What if you suspect an app of doing something questionable or downright nefarious? Maybe you think that it is collecting and storing data that it shouldn't. Perhaps it is conflicting with Slack's native functionality. If this is the case, then you can simply report it and, if necessary, uninstall it. Slack provides each public app with a home page on `slack.com`. On each page, you'll see a clickable link to report an app for "inappropriate content or behavior."

Disappearing apps

What if you're a regular Slack user and you really enjoy using a third-party app? Maybe it saves you a great deal of time. For several reasons, there's no guarantee that it will be there for you tomorrow. First, your organization's Workspace Owner or Admin may remove it from the workspace. Second, even if your organization benefits from using a particular app, external developers aren't obligated to maintain it and keep it available in perpetuity. Lastly, even if no one has removed it from your workspace, apps on occasion may mysteriously stop working.

TIP

Popular Slack apps tend not to just vanish overnight. I have never seen it happen in all of my years using Slack. If you can no longer access an app in your organization's workspace, contact your Workspace Owner or Admin to find out what happened.

TIP

If you need support for a third-party app, do not open a case with Slack support. You'll need to go to the app's home page.

Disabling and re-enabling preserved apps

Slack owns and maintains certain critical apps — even though those apps rely upon different companies' products and services. As of this writing, some of the most prominent examples of Slack's *preserved apps* include Skype, Visual Studio Team Services, and Giphy. Some Slack apps — including these 20 preserved ones — offer two options that fall somewhere between installing an app and removing it altogether: disabling and re-enabling.

The easiest way to find out if Slack has preserved an app is to visit `bit.ly/presapps`.

WARNING

It's unlikely to happen, but a company can sever access to its own API and render a preserved Slack app inoperable.

Think of disabling an app as the equivalent of a trial separation. Say that an app offers this option and you want take advantage of it. Let's say that you're sick of all of the animated gifs flying around via Giphy. (How you could be is beyond me, but I digress.) Follow these directions:

1. **Locate the app in the Slack App Directory.**
2. **Click on the Disable button in the upper-right corner of the app's webpage, as Figure 10-13 displays.**

   Slack prompts you to confirm your choice.
3. **Click on the green OK button.**

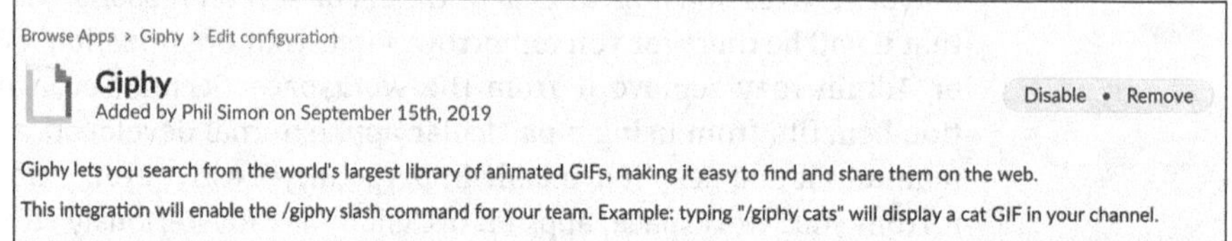
Browse Apps › Giphy › Edit configuration
Giphy
Added by Phil Simon on September 15th, 2019
Disable • Remove
Giphy lets you search from the world's largest library of animated GIFs, making it easy to find and share them on the web.
This integration will enable the /giphy slash command for your team. Example: typing "/giphy cats" will display a cat GIF in your channel.

FIGURE 10-13: Disabling the Giphy Slack app.

Note that disabling an app allows you to preserve the app's data if and when you decide to reactivate it. Removing an app altogether does not.

WARNING

Just as with removing apps, proper Slack etiquette mandates that you inform the workspace that you have disabled one of them.

Say that you change your mind and want to re-enable this app down the road. Just return to the app's home page. Click on the Enable button and confirm again. The app resumes functioning.

Viewing app activity logs

What if you and other Workspace Owners and Admins have installed and uninstalled many apps in your workspace over the course of months or years? For whatever reason, you need to know who did what and when. To obtain this information, just follow these steps:

1. **Click on the App view in Slack.**
2. **Click on the App Directory link at the top of the page.**

   Slack launches a new tab or window in your default web browser.
3. **On the left side of the page, click on Activity Log.**

   Slack displays a log of all app activity in your workspace. The log resembles the one shown in Figure 10-14.

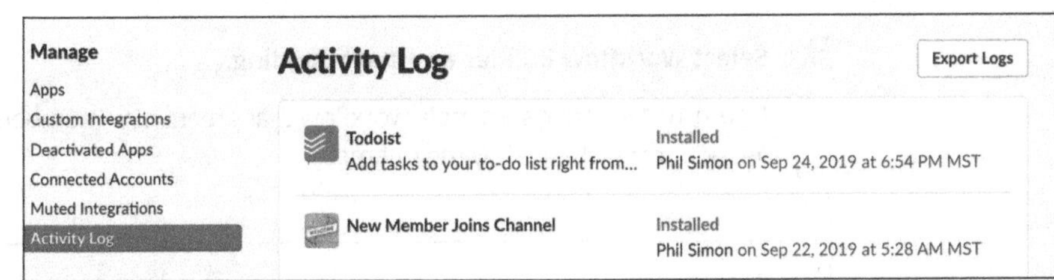

FIGURE 10-14: Slack log for app-related workspace activity.

If you want to export this data, click on the Export Logs button. (For more on Slack's extensive data exporting options, see Chapter 11.)

Using Workflow Builder

Maybe thinking about apps has got you all hopped up. You can barely contain yourself and want to build your own apps. There's just one problem — and it's a biggie: You don't know the first thing about how to code.

Without a coding background, it can take months to learn the ins and outs of a programming language. Your learning curve will depend on your experience, willingness to commit, natural ability, and other factors.

You don't care, though. You'd like to start messing around with apps now — even if it's on a limited basis.

Fortunately, Slack's got you covered once again.

Creating workflows

Launched in April 2019, Slack's Workflow Builder lets users on premium plans automate basic tasks and create useful forms. For example, say that you want to build a rudimentary app that automatically welcomes newly hired employees to a particular channel.

Start by launching Slack's Workflow Builder and following these steps:

1. **Click on the menu icon.**
2. **From the drop-down menu, select Tools.**

   Slack displays a sub-menu on the immediate right.

3. **Select Workflow Builder and start building.**

   Figure 10-15 displays a simple workflow that greets new members of the `#slack_tips` channel by their names.

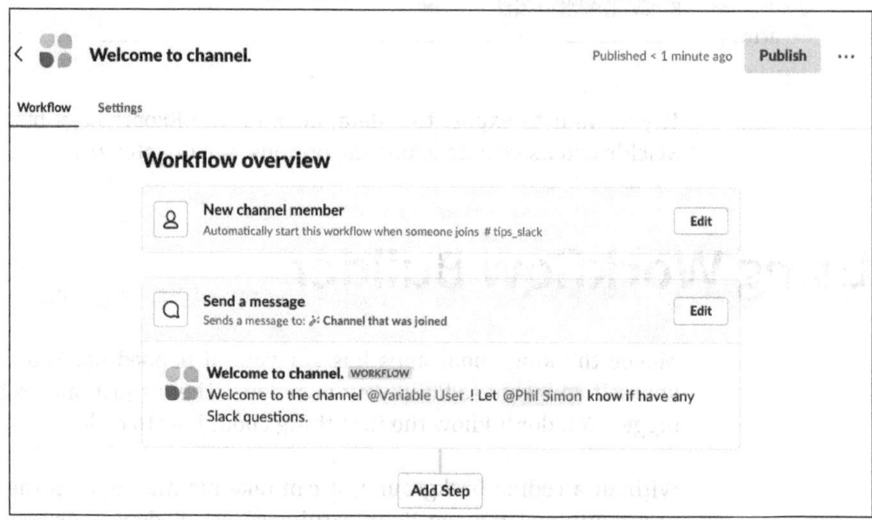

FIGURE 10-15: Workflow Builder example.

After Lydia joins `#slack_tips`, Slack automatically posts the custom message shown in Figure 10-16 welcoming her aboard.

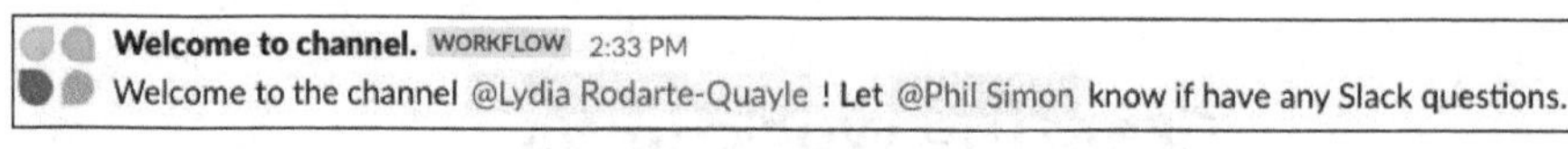

FIGURE 10-16: Workflow Builder message welcoming new member to `#slack_tips`.

Pretty cool, right? That simple workflow runs automatically — as it should. That is, my colleagues don't need to access it for themselves. It's not hard to imagine other scenarios, though, that require others to start a process when an event happens.

Say that I am the head of IT at my small company. From time to time, employees experience technical issues with their computers. If they send me emails or even Slack DMs, then they may omit key information from their messages — ultimately making it more difficult for me to help them.

In these cases, I want all employees to fill out a standard form that collects valuable information, such as the type of computer they use and the specific problem that they are having. To this end, I use Workflow Builder to create a form and add a shortcut to `#it_support`. Figure 10-17 displays what users will see when they click on the lightning-bolt icon.

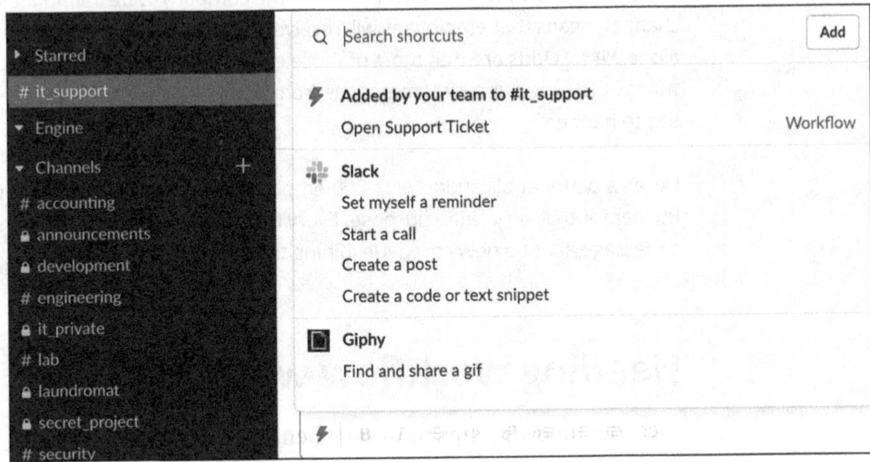

FIGURE 10-17: Workflow Builder shortcut to IT-support form.

When users click on the "Open Support Ticket" shortcut, the Slack workflow launches the form that starts the process of resolving the user's computer issues.

To create a shortcut for your workflow in a particular channel, follow these steps:

1. **Click on the channel in the lower half of the sidebar.**
2. **In the message pane, click on the lightning-bolt icon.**
3. **At the top of the pop-up, click on the white Add button.**

   Slack starts the wizard for Workflow Builder.

TIP

From here you can go nuts. Learn more about the steps involved in creating the increasing number of workflows by visiting `bit.ly/slack-wb`.

Regardless of the type of workflow you've created, after you add one to an individual channel, Slack turns the lightning-bolt icon in the message pane blue for that channel. Users can easily see the workflow from the pop-up menu.

Now that you know the basics of Workflow Builder, start experimenting. Even better, you can start a workflow and invite fellow workspace members to collaborate on it. Features such as these shouldn't surprise anyone at this point. After all, Slack is the ultimate collaboration tool.

SLACK, AUTOMATION, AND USING YOUR BRAIN

NIN Music is a fictitious 40,000-employee organization with 10 percent annual turnover. Every year, roughly 4,000 employees start at NIN roughly — 16 per work day. In this case, unleashing Workflow Builder in the company-wide `#announcements` public channel means that employees will receive 16 messages every day about new hires alone. Yikes! Odds are that most of those employees won't care and, most important, will start to tune out critical messages from that Slack channel. Trust me: You don't want this to happen.

Here's a better application. NIN's 200-employee marketing department uses Workflow Builder for that very same purpose. Every few weeks, members of `#marketing` receive a message about a new colleague joining their department. In this case, less is more.

Heeding workflow warnings

Keep the following tips in mind when creating workflows:

- In the original *Jurassic Park*, Jeff Goldblum's character Dr. Ian Malcolm famously says with his inimitable cadence, "Your scientists were so preoccupied with whether or not they could, they didn't stop to think if they should." The same principle applies when creating workflows.
- Try Workflow Builder on a small channel until you get the hang of it.
- If your organization downgrades from a premium plan to the Free one, then its employees won't be able to use previously created workflows.

Slack collects data on how early adopters are using Workflow Builder. The company's exciting product roadmap includes many enhancements to it. Expect Slack to significantly enhance the types of things that users can automate over the next few years. In two years, users will marvel at what Workflow Builder lets non-technical users do. Given Slack's rich functionality and the data that it collects, the possibilities are vast.

IN THIS CHAPTER

» Analyzing user data in Slack

» Getting data into and out of Slack

» Fusing Slack workspaces

» Updating Slack user data *en masse*

Chapter 11

Analyzing, Importing, Exporting, and Updating Slack User Data

Employees who routinely use Slack generate data — lots and lots of data. Rather than let that data just accumulate in the background, though, Slack offers ways to analyze that data, back it up, move it around, and even bring it life.

This chapter details Slack's native data-related features: analytics, data visualization, and the movement of data to and from workspaces.

What if you're not interested in doing any of these data-related things with Slack just yet? Maybe you're not a data person. I get it, but I still wouldn't skip this chapter. It's essential to know what you and others can and can't do with all the information housed in Slack.

Analyzing Workspace Data

Via its analytics dashboard, Slack lets you view data about your workspace, its channels, and its members. Your individual access hinges upon your role as well as your organization's Slack plan. People with more senior roles under a premium plan can do more with Slack data than regular Members under the Free plan.

REMEMBER

Members under Slack's Free plan can view some valuable information, but customers on premium plans can go far deeper.

Slack's analytics dashboard

Data-driven companies such as Slack recognize the value of providing users with valuable insights. Access Slack's analytics dashboard by following these steps:

1. **Click on the main menu and choose Tools and then Analytics.**
2. **Play around with the different options on channels, members, timeframes, and more.**

   Your specific options will vary based upon your role and your firm's plan. Figure 11-1 displays an example.

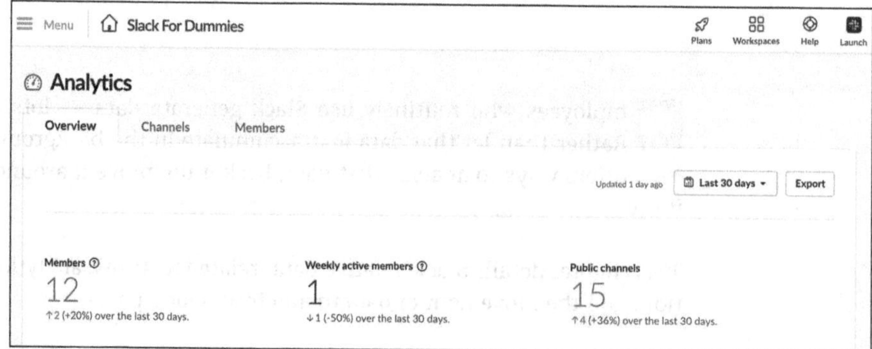

FIGURE 11-1: Slack analytics dashboard.

You can immediately view workspace-specific stats that fall under the usage umbrella, including

- Messages sent (and your plan's limit, if any)
- The total size of all of the files (and your plan's limit, if any)
- The apps that you've installed (and your plan's limit, if any)

TIP

Consider an organization using two different Slack workspaces. As of this writing, even its Owners and Admins can't view a consolidated, multi-workspace view here or anywhere else. Put differently, they can only switch between workspace views.

Active members

When you scroll down in the Slack analytics dashboard, you can view a chart that displays active members by week, as Figure 11-2 shows.

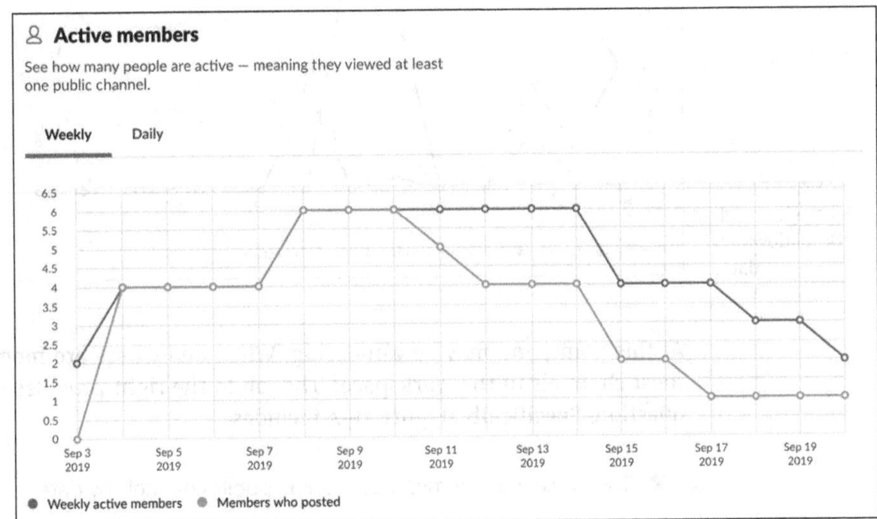

FIGURE 11-2: Slack chart showing active members (Standard plan).

Click on the Daily tab to the immediate left of Weekly to view daily numbers or "drill down," as some folks say.

Public and private

In Slack's analytics dashboard, you can scroll down to see a chart that contains the following information about your workspace:

- » The percentage of messages read in public channels by date
- » The percentage of messages read in private channels by date
- » The percentage of messages read in DMs by date

Figure 11-3 displays a breakdown of messages read by date.

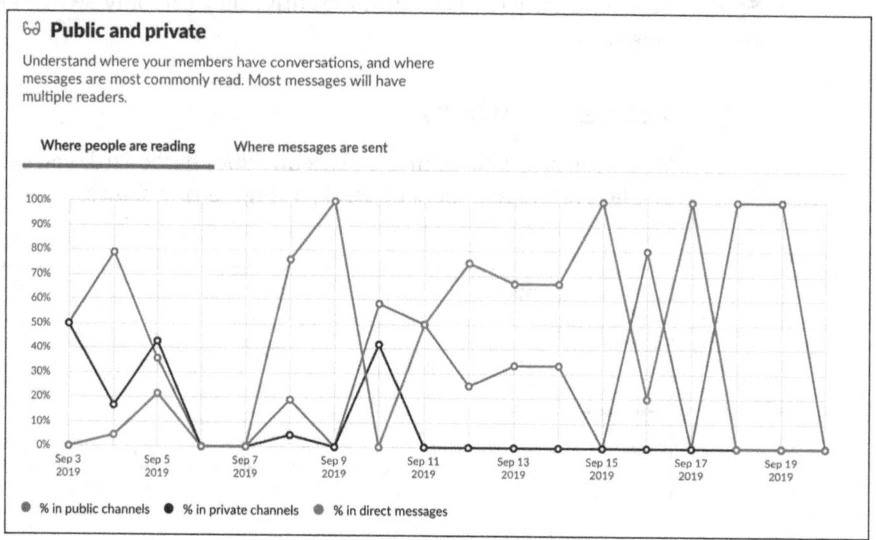

FIGURE 11-3: Messages read: Breakdown by date.

At this point, you may be wondering: When and where are members posting the most channels in the workspace? The tab to the right provides an answer to that question. Specifically, Figure 11-4 includes

- The percentage of messages sent in public channels by date
- The percentage of messages sent in private channels by date
- The percentage of messages sent in DMs by date

TIP

Note that Figures 11-3 and 11-4 display *aggregate* numbers. For example, you can't tell whether Neil and Alex exchanged 42 private messages on September 3rd, much less the specific subjects the two were discussing.

Messages and files

Say that you want to know how many messages and files workspace members are sharing. Slack customers on premium plans can view graphs that display the total number of messages sent and files uploaded in a given workspace in a graph similar to Figure 11-5.

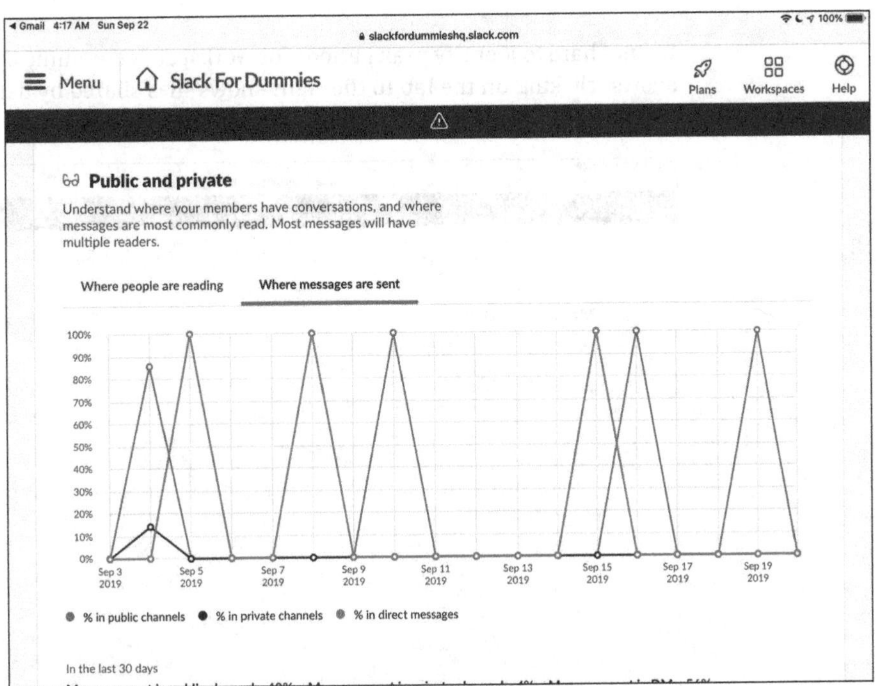

FIGURE 11-4: Breakdown of messages sent by date.

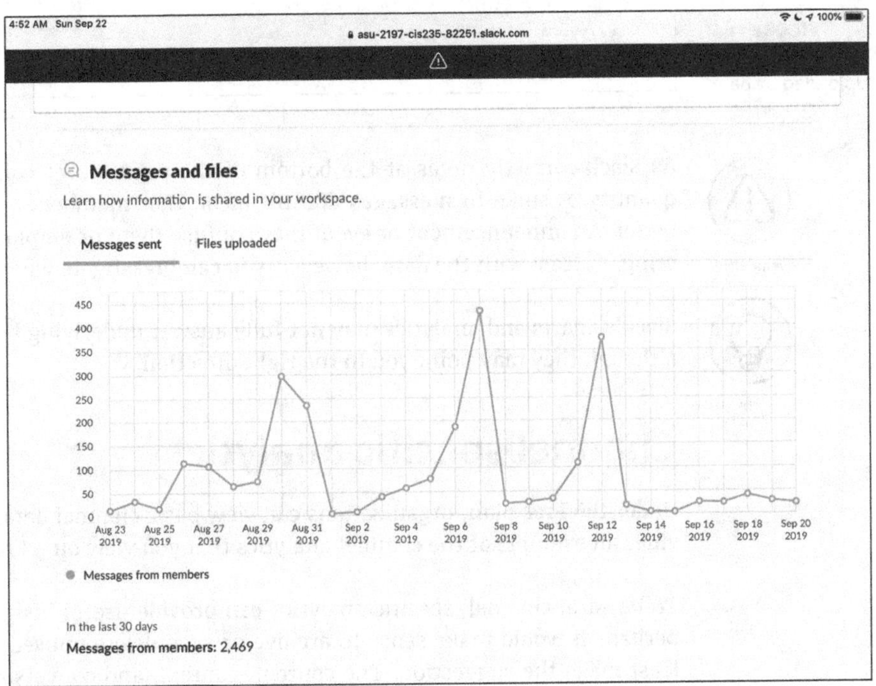

FIGURE 11-5: Total workspace messages sent by date.

It's not hard to identify peak periods for workspace communication. As Figure 11-6 shows, clicking on the tab to the right shows files shared by date.

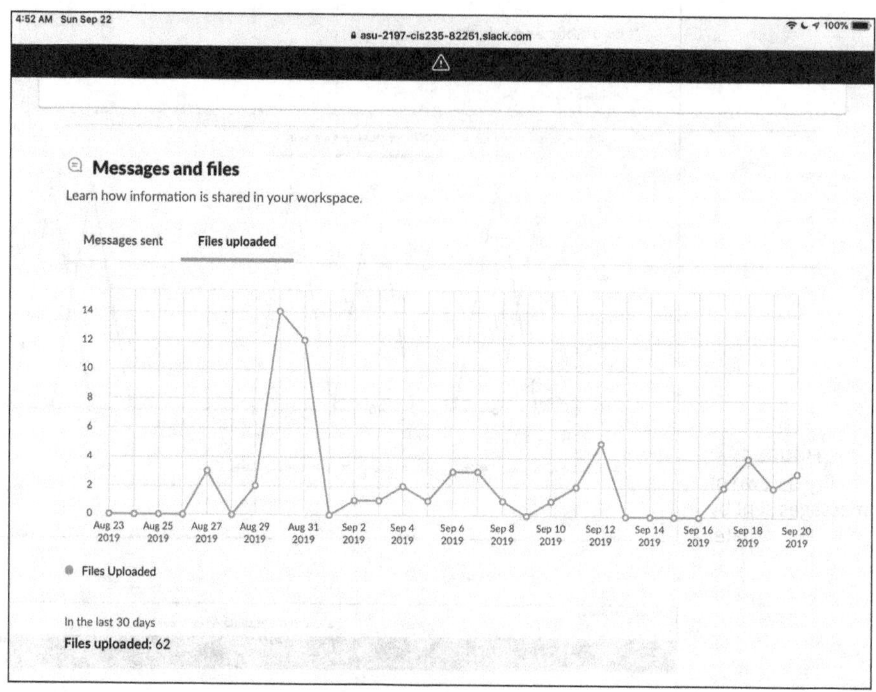

FIGURE 11-6: Workspace files uploaded by date.

WARNING

As Slack correctly notes at the bottom of the page, never confuse quality with quantity. A spike in messages doesn't mean that members are communicating better. An announcement or event may confuse them or employees may be bickering. At least with the data, however, you can investigate what's going on.

TIP

Slack's charts and analytics may not fully answer underlying business questions, although they may point you in the right direction.

Channel-specific analytics

Under the Free plan, organizations can view basic channel data. Figure 11-7 provides an example of the channel analytics that you view on a Free plan.

To be sure, channel-specific analytics can provide useful insights. For example, perhaps it would make sense to archive or even delete unused channels — or at least make the suggestion. The content, context, and conversations in channels naturally evolve over time; some may effectively go dark. On the other end of the spectrum, this data may show that a broad channel is far too noisy. Maybe segmenting it or creating a new, more specific channel makes sense in this case.

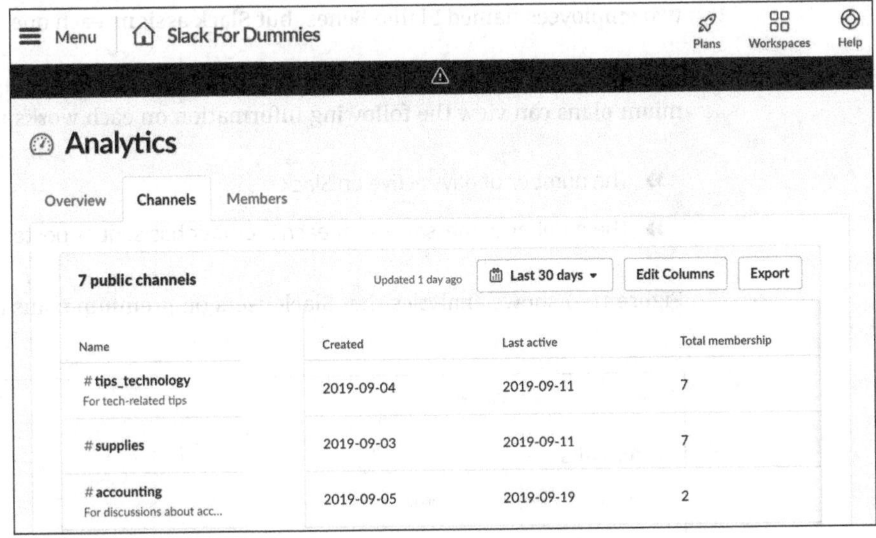

FIGURE 11-7: Slack channel analytics (Free plan).

You don't need to be a data scientist, though, to wonder what other fields may yield valuable insights on how employees at your organization communicate. Fortunately, organizations on premium plans can view enhanced analytics such as those in Figure 11-8.

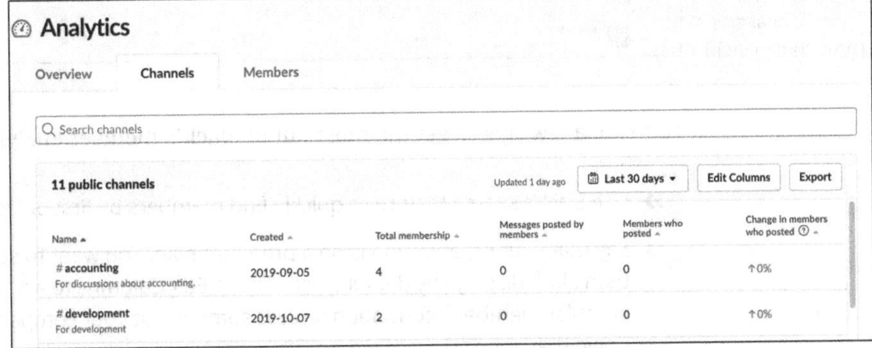

FIGURE 11-8: Slack channel analytics (premium plans).

TIP

Clicking on the white Export column generates a comma-separated values (CSV) file. Download the file and analyze the data in Microsoft Excel or Tableau.

Member analytics

Under the Free plan, Slack displays basic information on Members, including unique user ID, user name, and email address. (Yes, your workspace may contain two employees named Elaine Benes, but Slack assigns each one a unique user ID.)

As long as members' individual privileges permit, customers under Slack's premium plans can view the following information on each workspace member:

- The number of days active on Slack
- The number of messages that each member has sent or posted

Figure 11-9 shows analytics that Slack users on premium plans can see.

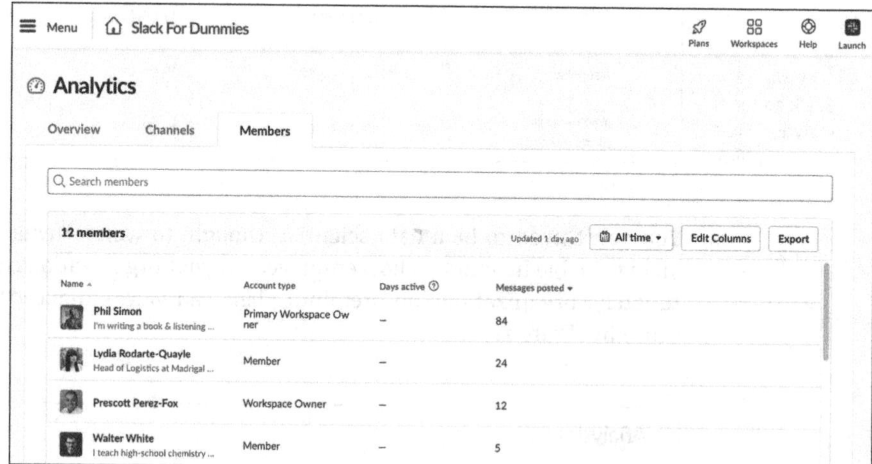

FIGURE 11-9: Slack member analytics (premium plans).

Here are a few tips to get the most out of Slack's member analytics:

- Use Slack's search feature to quickly find members by first or last name.
- Say that your organization is on a premium plan. You want to see more fields than Slack displays by default. Just click on Edit Columns to add even more granular member information (unless someone at your company has locked down that ability).
- You can do much more with analytics by installing different third-party apps. You may want to read the terms of service, though. Slack is not responsible if developers access your organization's data and things break bad. (See Chapter 10 for more information on this subject.).

Viewing Member Access Logs

Somethings seems off in your Slack account. You don't recall posting a message in a channel, let alone sharing a file. Perhaps you suspect foul play or just want to check whether you're going senile.

By keeping access logs, Slack makes it easy for you to the view following information related to your workspace logins:

- The time and date that you logged in to your workspace.
- Where you were when you logged in. No, Slack doesn't know that you were in your living room or celebrating your 52nd birthday at a Denny's in Albuquerque, New Mexico. Slack shows you the Internet Protocol or IP address used to access your account. (IP addresses correlate with physical locations.)
- The device you used to log in to your account. It may be via a web browser, smartphone app, or a desktop app.

To view a sample member access log, follow these steps:

1. **Click on the main menu.**
2. **From the drop-down menu, select Settings & administration and then Workspace settings.**
3. **On the right-hand side of the page, click on Access Logs.**

   Slack displays a log similar to Figure 11-10.

REMEMBER

For more on this subject, see "Viewing access logs" in Chapter 9.

Anyone who possesses a modicum of knowledge about enterprise security will tell you that this information helps forensics folks investigate breaches and other issues.

But what about Workspace Owners and Admins? They may well need to view more than just their own Slack activity, including their colleagues' activity. Slack lets them view the following information on all workspace members:

- The times and dates at which each workspace member signed in to Slack
- The IP addresses they used to log in
- The devices that the members used to access their account

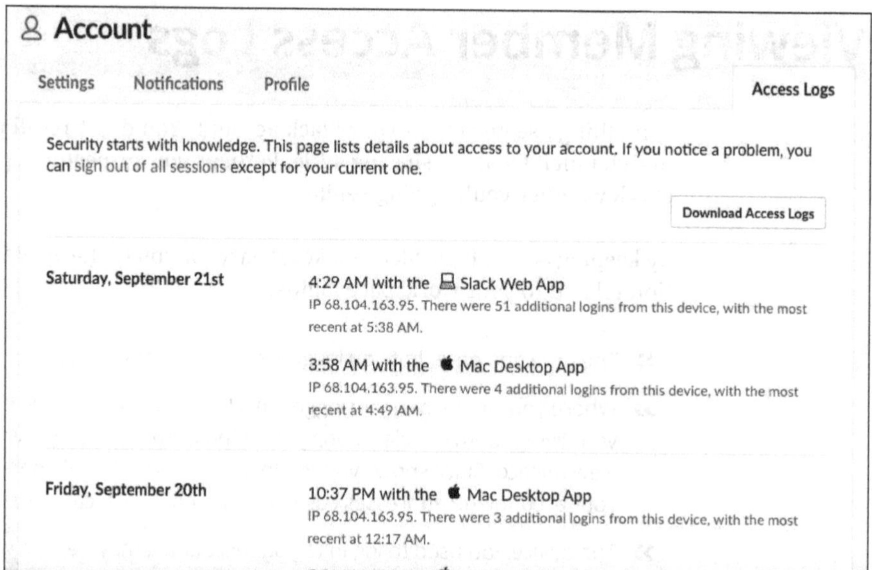

FIGURE 11-10: Slack daily access log.

TIP

You can export simple access logs from Slack to conduct additional analysis. However, user activity represents a small fraction of the information that you can export. (See the next section for more information on this subject.)

Moving Data Around in Slack

This era is nothing if not data-driven. Sometimes organizations wisely back up their data, provide it upon request to a third party, or decide to migrate it into a different application.

Slack's management has long recognized this reality. To this end, Slack offers a number of powerful ways to export, import, and generally manipulate data.

Exporting data from Slack

Slack offers users three types of powerful data exporting capabilities:

- Standard Export
- Corporate Export
- Discovery API export mechanism

Note that your workspace role governs whether you can access these tools.

Standard Export

If you're a Workspace Owner or Admin, then you can export all messages and file links posted in public channels. Slack makes this option available for customers on all plans, including the Free one. Note that the Standard Export excludes DMs and messages posted in private channels.

To perform a Standard Export, follow these steps:

1. **Click on the main menu.**
2. **From the drop-down menu, select Settings & administration and then Workspace settings.**

   Slack then directs you to a URL specific to your workspace.
3. **Click on the white button labeled Import/Export Data at the top right-hand corner of the page.**
4. **Click on the Export tab.**

   You see a screen similar to Figure 11-11.

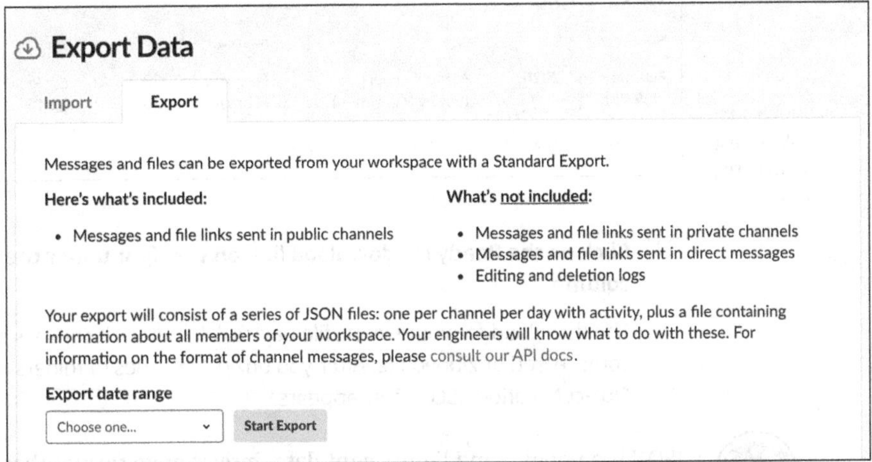

FIGURE 11-11: Slack Export Data options.

5. **Select a date range.**

   Slack provides a number of different date-based export options. You can select one of the predefined ones or enter a custom date range.
6. **Click on the Start Export button.**

   Slack begins processing your export file. When it's ready, Slack sends you an email with a downloadable link. Also, Slackbot sends you a DM containing the same link. It resembles Figure 11-12.

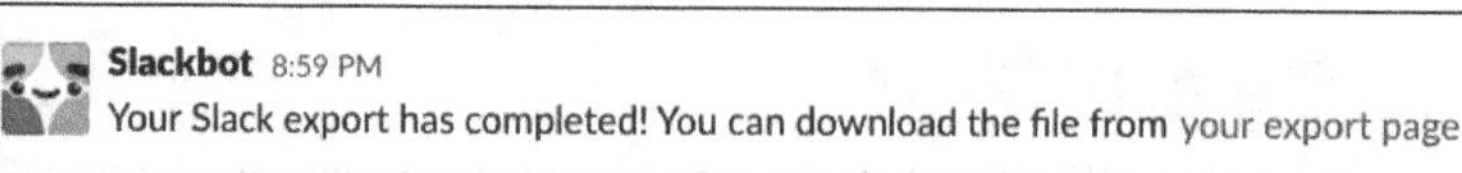

Slackbot 8:59 PM
Your Slack export has completed! You can download the file from your export page.

FIGURE 11-12: Slackbot DM with data export download link.

7. **Click on the link in Slackbot's DM.**

   Slack takes you back to your workspace's unique data-export page.

TIP

   Larger files take longer for both Slack to generate and you to download. If hundreds of employees at your organization have been using Slack for months or years, this process may take hours. Ditto if they regularly upload large files to the workspace.

8. **Scroll down the page.**

   If you have exported data before, then Slack displays a section titled "Past Exports."

9. **Click on the link to download the export file.**

   You'll see something similar to Figure 11-13.

Past Exports

Started on	Type	Date range	Status	
February 2nd, 2020 8:59 PM	Manual export (Set by Phil Simon)	February 1, 2020 – February 2, 2020	Ready for download (8KB)	⊗

Exports will be permanently removed 10 days after they are downloaded.

FIGURE 11-13: Slack past exports.

10. **Click on the Ready for download link on the right under the Status column.**

    The download for your export file begins. Ultimately, it consists of a single compressed or zipped file. After you unzip it, a series of folders and JavaScript Object Notation (JSON) files appears.

TECHNICAL STUFF

JSON is a popular and lightweight data-interchange format that people can easily read. What's more, machines can easily parse and generate JSON files.

Figure 11-14 shows the JSON files from my *Slack For Dummies* workspace.

As Figure 11-14 shows, Slack generates one JSON file per public channel per day with activity. (If no channel activity occurred on a given day, Slack doesn't generate an empty JSON file. Slack also includes a file containing data about all members of your workspace.) This method includes individual and group DMs.

Name	Date Modified	Size	Kind
▼ accounting	Today at 5:12 PM	--	Folder
2019-09-05.json	Today at 5:12 PM	933 bytes	JSON file
2019-09-09.json	Today at 5:12 PM	863 bytes	JSON file
2019-09-19.json	Today at 5:12 PM	826 bytes	JSON file
channels.json	Today at 5:12 PM	5 KB	JSON file
▶ general	Today at 5:12 PM	--	Folder
integration_logs.json	Today at 5:12 PM	10 KB	JSON file
▶ lab	Today at 5:12 PM	--	Folder
▶ supplies	Today at 5:12 PM	--	Folder
▶ test	Today at 5:12 PM	--	Folder
▶ tips_slack	Today at 5:12 PM	--	Folder
▶ tips_technology	Today at 5:12 PM	--	Folder
users.json	Today at 5:12 PM	22 KB	JSON file

FIGURE 11-14: Unzipped files from Slack Standard Export.

Figure 11-15 displays an example of one of these JSON files.


```
[
    {
        "user": "UMTA9PH41",
        "type": "message",
        "subtype": "channel_join",
        "ts": "1567682406.000200",
        "text": "<@UMTA9PH41> has joined the channel"
    },
    {
        "user": "UMTA9PH41",
        "type": "message",
        "subtype": "channel_purpose",
        "ts": "1567682406.000300",
        "text": "<@UMTA9PH41> set the channel purpose: For discussions about
        accounting.",
        "purpose": "For discussions about accounting."
    },
```


FIGURE 11-15: JSON data from a Slack Standard Export file.

WARNING

If you're thinking that you'll just open these files in Excel and your favorite spreadsheet program will understand them, think again. JSON is an entirely different file format than both .XLSX and .CSV.

Corporate Export

If your organization pays for Slack's Plus plan, then this option is available to Workspace Owners under limited circumstances. Note that your firm will need to submit an application to Slack. That is, Corporate Export isn't available by default.

It includes content from everything in the Slack workspace: public and private channels and direct messages.

REMEMBER

If a Workspace Owner or Admin enables Corporate Export for a workspace after Slack grants approval, then Standard Export is not available.

Discovery API export mechanism

What if a government agency, law firm, or compliance entity compels English paper company Wernham Hogg to turn over information on internal company communication? That is, the company needs to fulfill several different security, legal, and compliance obligations.

To meet this legitimate request, mercurial office manager David Brent needs to export or archive its Slack data in a way that the previous export options doesn't allow. In this scenario, Slack as a company finds itself squarely in the middle of organizations with conflicting interests.

If you think that the potential for abuse exists here, trust your instincts. To this end, Slack doesn't treat enhanced export requests willy-nilly. Rather, it mandates that an organization — in this case, Wernham Hogg — follow its own internal practices. Beyond that requirement, Slack ensures that the individuals and organization are legally entitled to request and view this information.

Slack approves these requests on a case-by-case basis, and only if Wernham Hogg meets two conditions. For starters, Slack makes the Discovery Export API available only to designated Org Owners under its Enterprise Grid plan. Second, customers must use pre-approved third-party apps and for only a number of limited purposes. Put differently, Slack will deny applications from nosy employees who lack sufficient documentation to justify their invasive requests.

For more detailed information on exporting in Slack, see `bit.ly/slack-de`.

REMEMBER

The content of your workspace's export files stems directly from its message- and file-retention policies. For example, consider an organization that automatically deletes content from public channels after six months. As a result, an export today omits messages from a year ago. (For more on this subject, see Chapter 9.)

Importing data into Slack

Slack recognizes that your organization may have used different collaboration tools in the past. That is, the ideas of reducing internal email and building an internal knowledge base may not have dawned upon you because you use *Slack For Dummies*.

To this end, Slack provides a number of data-portability tools. At a high level, the goal is to facilitate an organizations' efforts to import data from other collaboration tools into one of a Slack workspace.

Table 11-1 lists some of the external collaboration tools that you can bring into Slack.

TABLE 11-1 **Slack Import Options for Third-Party Tools**

Name	What Slack Allows You to Import
Flowdock	The app's message history and files
Campfire	The app's message history and files
CSV or text file	Data in a custom format. (Note that you may need to spend time mapping fields and cleaning up your data.)
ChatWork	The app's message history and files

Slack sends you an email once it begins the import process.

TIP

As of this writing, there is no simple, quick, and reliable way to migrate from Microsoft Teams to Slack — nor is the opposite true. Coincidence? I think not. After all, why would one company make it easy for its customers to move to the competition? I'm certain, though, that motivated and well-compensated software engineers have used Teams' own data-exporting tools to successfully bring a good chunk of data into a Slack workspace — or will very soon.

TIP

Say that you're planning a data migration (including bringing third-party data into Slack). Consider the brilliantly reflexive Hofstadter's Law: It always takes longer than you expect, even when you take into account Hofstadter's Law.

Consolidating Slack workspaces

When I hold Slack training sessions, my clients are brimming with curiosity. They typically want to pick my brain about the best ways to configure the application. You know by now that Slack is very flexible. Occasionally, though, that flexibility can act as a curse. Understandably, no one wants to make the wrong decision.

During these conversations, it's usually only a matter of time before someone asks me: How many workspaces should our organization create?

For several reasons, my default answer is always one. First, you can create as many public and private channels in a single workspace as you like. (See Chapter 3 for more information on this topic.) There really isn't a compelling reason to segment employees any further. (As Chapter 9 discusses, Enterprise Grid customers can customize security at a remarkably granular level within a given workspace.)

Second, Slack's default ability to analyze member data is workspace-specific. That is, access logs and usage statistics don't transcend workspaces. In this sense, no Slack entity is above the workspace. (Chapter 2 covers this topic in more detail.)

TECHNICAL STUFF

If you're technically inclined, you can attempt to merge export files from different workspaces for additional analysis. Depending on your chops, maybe you can even automate that process. I performed similar work for my clients before becoming a college professor. If you know what you're doing, it's not that hard. Regardless, this feat would involve extra and unnecessary work if your organization had simply created a single workspace from the get-go.

Third, firms that decide to fuse together disparate workspaces may encounter data-migration problems. Generally speaking, the process of extracting, transforming, and loading data (ETL) is simpler in theory than in practice.

I should know. I spent a good part of my consulting career helping organizations extract, cleanse, and move data from one system to another.

People who, for whatever reason, set up multiple workspaces and subsequently change their minds are in luck: Slack makes consolidating data from multiple workspaces easy. A fictitious example may clarify how to execute this process:

Employees at Satriani General Hospital love using Slack. Its HR and payroll departments, however, each use separate workspaces. For a long time, it's been a problem. Lately it has exacerbated. Among the many issues: HR clerks process employee raises, status changes, and transfers but sometimes forget to enter them in their HRIS in a timely manner. Urgent last-minute emails and phone calls typically make matters worse. As a result, about one-quarter of the time employees don't see their raises on their paychecks. This issue irritates the payroll manager and her staff because employees always tear into them.

At a meeting, the HR clerks pledge not to fall behind on their work. Both departments agree to communicate better in person and virtually via a single Slack workspace. To this end, they ask IT to consolidate the two workspaces. (Creating a new one just wasn't necessary. Satriani's payroll workspace will absorb the HR one.) Once IT completes that process, employees from both departments will use the newly named Payroll&HR workspace. Everybody wins.

Joe works in IT and he handles the migration. He completes the following high-level steps, ideally late at night or on the weekend when no one is using either workspace:

1. **Export the data from the HR workspace.**
2. **Upload the HR export file of the Slack workspace.**

   Slack provides two options here. First, if the export file is small enough, members can just upload it by clicking on the link. Because of the size of the HR file in this case, that method is just not going to fly for Joe.

   Joe must take advantage of Slack's second option. He uploads the file to a secure, cloud-based file-sharing service. (Several years ago, Satriani purchased an enterprise-wide Dropbox license). After uploading it, he copies the file's link.
3. **Choose which members to import.**

   Slack offers several options on how to handle importing workspace members. Because two employees may share the same name, Slack tries matching employees by email address because it is a unique field.
4. **Choose which channels to import and set their options.**

   Again, Slack provides plenty of alternatives here.
5. **Review the summary.**
6. **If you're satisfied with the results, begin the import.**

   Slack sends you an email once it has finished importing the data.

TIP

I intentionally simplified the migration process for the sake of space. Make no mistake: Slack provides many options during each of the preceding steps. To view detailed instructions and more information, see `bit.ly/2ksSDW3`.

TIP

To watch a straightforward four-minute video in which I import data from one workspace into another, visit `bit.ly/2kxmlJz`.

Avoiding mistakes when migrating data

When dealing with any data migration in any system, certain truths always hold:

» You must communicate to your colleagues exactly what you're doing, why, and when you'll be doing it. Slack is no exception to this rule.

  Consider the following: Employees continue to send messages and upload files after IT has downloaded the import file. Guess what? Those new messages won't appear in the new, consolidated workspace.

- Next, don't immediately delete old workspaces after your migration. You can't unring that bell. It's better to archive them in the event that an issue creeps up down the road. I wouldn't hold on to them forever, though. Six months is a reasonable time.
- Finally, a Slack-to-Slack migration should go smoothly. After all, the source and target systems are one and the same. Should and will, though, are two very different things — particularly if you're dealing with a large amount of data. Hope for the best, but prepare for the worst.

Performing Mass Updates to User Data

Chapter 8 covers how customers of the Plus and Enterprise Grid plans can add their own custom fields. To be sure, the reasons will vary. For the most part, though, these fields help members better understand their colleagues and their roles.

As for populating these fields, getting 40 employees in a workspace to add their favorite bands or Twitter handles to their profiles shouldn't take much effort. A polite request in a public channel should do the trick. But what if a 4,000-employee company wants to add six custom fields per Slack member? That seems like an awful lot of data entry, and the chance for error is significant.

Fortunately, Slack supports two similar methods for Workspace Owners and Admins to tackle this data problem *en masse*:

- **Users can access a powerful application programming interface (API) for identity management — the System for Cross-domain Identity Management (SCIM API).** At a high level, SCIM is an open protocol that uses cloud computing to automate the exchange of personal data between different information systems or domains. For example, if you want to move a bunch of names, email addresses, or phone numbers from system A to system B, you can use SCIM.

  TECHNICAL STUFF

  For much more on this topic, see `bit.ly/2n6ezqQ` and `bit.ly/slack-prov`.
- **Say that your organization isn't using an identity provider with built-in SCIM provisioning capabilities. In this case, you'll need to create a custom solution with the SCIM API.** For much more on this topic, see `https://api.slack.com/scim`.

» Discovering how Slack fits in

» Recognizing how Slack can extend the power of enterprise systems

Chapter 12
Integrating Slack with Popular Enterprise Systems

You can use third-party apps to extend Slack's native functionality. (See Chapter 10 for more on this subject.) Slack doesn't just need to be a place for sharing screens, exchanging DMs, calling colleagues, and reaching consensus on important organizational issues. It can do so much more.

This chapter illustrates the significant benefits that organizations can realize if they go even deeper with Slack. You learn about some initial integrations between Slack and back- and front-office systems. Depending on which systems your organization runs, you may be able to perform an increasing number of everyday business functions from right within Slack — and have that data magically flow into your employer's system(s) of record.

A Brief Primer on Enterprise Systems

At a high level and irrespective of size, organizations typically use two types of systems:

- Back-office systems
- Front-office systems

WARNING

Maybe your organization's Slack journey is just beginning, and it is experiencing some growing pains. In this case, it may not be ready to take advantage of the integrations in this chapter right now. That's understandable. Still, I recommend that you at least skim this chapter. To paraphrase the iconic investor Warren Buffett, by knowing what's possible, you can start planting seeds that will eventually grow into trees.

Back-office systems

You may never have heard the term *back-office system*. I assure you, though, that it exists at your employer in one form or another. These applications also go by the collective moniker *enterprise resource planning* or *ERP* systems. At a high level, they serve a number of invaluable operations and business-administration functions. Specific ERP activities include

- Paying employees and tracking their benefits
- Tracking employee promotions, training, and company property
- Handling key accounting and finance responsibilities, such as accounts payable, accounts receivable, and invoice processing
- Running standard financial reports, such as trial balances, profit and loss (P&L) statements, and different types of aging reports
- Issuing standard regulatory and compliance reports to government agencies and tax authorities
- Managing physical inventory and the supply chain
- Tracking employee expenses and issuing reimbursements

No one would rightfully call these business functions *sexy*. Steve Jobs never announced them on stage in front of millions of awestruck people. Make no mistake, though: All firms have to effectively complete these essential activities — or outsource them to third parties that do. The need for this basic blocking and tackling holds true for hospitals, hardware stores, restaurants, bookstores, and chic clothing shops. The lone possible exception to the preceding list is supply chain management (SCM). For example, companies such as Twitter, Spotify, and LinkedIn (now part of Microsoft) don't manufacture physical products. As such, there's no tangible inventory for them to manage.

Front-office systems

The counterpart to a back-office system is — wait for it — a *front-office system.* Firms use this type of system to manage their customers, prospects, and sales. Without front-office applications, an organization can't effectively track its customer pipeline, project revenue, determine which of its sales reps are the most productive, award sales commissions, determine their best advertising sources, anticipate customer needs, and effectively cross-sell or upsell customers. You know, little things.

Front-office systems typically fall into the following four buckets:

- Customer relationship management (CRM)
- Sales force automation (SFA)
- Customer support
- Field service management (FSM)

Depending on the industry, these application categories may overlap a tad. What's more, while just about all organizations of a certain size rely upon proper CRM systems, the same may not apply to the other three buckets. For example, SFA is particularly popular, if not downright essential, for pharmaceutical companies but less so for a footwear maker or your dentist or local butcher. I guarantee you that your Internet service provider (ISP) uses FSM software to track its technicians' on-site visits. Neither your butcher nor your dentist visits your home.

Slack and Current Enterprise Systems

If Slack is indeed where work happens, then couldn't the collaboration tool ultimately replace back- and front-office systems?

For several reasons, the answer is no. I can't envision a realistic scenario in which Slack in all its glory even attempts to replace either type of system.

First, enterprise systems allow organizations to manage critical business functions. The usual suspects include payroll, benefits, accounts receivable, accounts payable, inventory tracking, CRM, and others. Many large firms implemented ERP and CRM systems decades ago — usually with decidedly mixed results as I write in my first book *Why New Systems Fail* (Cengage).

High-profile system failures run the gamut. You may have heard of debacles such as the 2013 launch of Healthcare.gov. These disasters don't just affect government agencies, though. In 1999, Hershey attempted to implement a new supply-chain system. In a word, it bombed. The company lost $100 million in candy sales and filed a few lawsuits against its partners. More recently, car-rental company Hertz sued consulting firm Accenture for $32 million over a botched website redesign. I could cite IT-project failures all day long. Against this backdrop, rare is the chief information officer (CIO) or chief technology officer (CTO) who is willing to spend millions of dollars to replace enterprise systems that, while long in the tooth, still work.

Second, it's folly to claim that all enterprise systems are created equal. Some are far more modern and app-friendly than others. Sure, every organization needs to pay its employees and track its accounts payable, but how each accomplishes these compulsory feats is anything but standard. Consider the vastly different types of systems that organizations use today to keep the lights on:

- **Legacy systems:** These relics often run off of mainframe computers written in antediluvian programming languages such as COBOL. Believe me: The ugly green screen ain't dead yet.
- **Custom-built systems:** Sometimes CXOs aren't happy with the offerings of major software vendors. They decide to build their own back- and front-office systems — a decision that often turns out to be regrettable. In my experience, their successors often live with the consequences of these decisions. One of the biggest gaffes: thinking that software development is a core organizational competency when it most certainly is not.

  I have seen this movie before. Twenty years ago, I used to work at the pharmaceutical giant Merck. The company's IT staff built deficient homegrown HR systems that routinely frustrated many people, especially me. I would often ask: Why did Merck's management go this route? Does Microsoft manufacture its own aspirin?
- **Commercial-off-the-shelf client-server applications:** The on-premise COTS model was all the rage in the 1990s and 2000s. A company buys, configures, and maintains servers and purchases enterprise software such as Oracle, SAP, or Infor to run off of them. If this approach sounds expensive to you, then trust your instincts. (Many companies have since ported these same applications to the cloud.)

- **Outsourced systems to third parties:** Many small and midsized companies don't want to deal with the headaches of buying, deploying, configuring, and maintaining their own back-office systems. As a result, they pay vendors to perform these tasks for them.

  That's right. Good old-fashioned outsourcing is alive and well. Case in point: Why does the U.S. government routinely solicit employment data from Automatic Data Processing, Inc. (ADP)? Because the payroll-outsourcing company knows if companies are hiring. After all, ADP serves more than 700,000 clients in 113 countries. Kronos, Paychex, and Ceridian also provide comparable services. And then there are professional employer organizations (PEOs) that handle the full range of back-office services. Why outsource just the payroll process when you can outsource an entire department?

- **More contemporary, cloud-based applications:** Thanks to the explosion of cloud computing, several vendors — including Slack — have adopted the software-as-a-service (SaaS) model. (For more on SaaS, see Chapter 1.) The most prominent examples include Salesforce (CRM) and Workday (ERP).

It would take quite a bit of doing for Slack to develop a viable solution that would replace any of these key enterprise systems, never mind all of them. Brass tacks: Slack isn't going to be playing in this sandbox anytime soon. But don't think that Slack and its developers are ignoring you altogether.

REMEMBER

Even Slack's most vociferous advocates — and I put myself firmly in this camp — understand this reality: Slack complements vital enterprise systems but doesn't replace them. Slack's own management would agree with that statement.

With respect to enterprise systems, Slack's top brass is keenly aware of both of the following:

- The fragmented state of the enterprise-technology industry
- The reluctance of most management teams to disrupt their organizations' fragile systems

At the same time, though, Slack's actions indicate that it senses a legitimate business opportunity regarding enterprise systems. Rather than supplant ERP and CRM applications altogether, why couldn't Slack do the following for its clients?

- Enhance their existing enterprise systems
- Make their employees' lives easier
- Simplify their business processes

» Increase their levels of automation
» Reduce the amount of paperwork that they have to complete

Put differently, couldn't Slack complement their customers' enterprise systems?

Before answering, let me reiterate a key point that I make in Chapter 10: Slack's management has embraced platform thinking. Slack wants third-party developers and startups to take its core product in new and exciting directions — including with enterprise systems. In this vein, some ambitious companies are starting to do interesting things. One burgeoning area involves building digital bridges that connect essential but often clunky ERP and CRM systems to a lighter, more modern, more user-friendly application.

Yes, I'm talking about Slack.

Now back to my earlier question: To both Slack and its development community, the answer is a resounding yes. A few simple examples will prove my point.

REMEMBER

Beyond the simple examples I describe in the next section, make no mistake: Increased Slack automation and more integrations with contemporary enterprise systems are coming soon.

Exploring current system integrations

I'll start by describing a few of Slack's nascent integrations with enterprise systems. You may not be terribly impressed with the following examples but remember a few things as you're reading:

» Slack integration with specific enterprise systems is fairly new.
» The following examples represent just the tip of the iceberg.
» Slack continually forges new partnerships with large software vendors.
» Early adopters have built private Slack integrations for their own systems.
» Startups are feverishly working on new ways to enhance Slack.

Employees requesting time off

Think about how your employer handles most employee HR requests. I'll wager that a good percentage of worker-initiated queries are manual. For example, at some companies today, employees still need to manually fill out forms requesting time off. Others have to email their managers and ask for permission.

Perhaps this process doesn't irk you. After all, how often do you ask your boss to take a vacation, much less a leave of absence? But wouldn't it be easier to request time off in Slack?

TIP

Third-party Slack apps such as Vacation Tracker and Time.bot accomplish the same thing. As of this writing, though, these standalone tools don't integrate with existing enterprise systems.

Employees submitting expenses via Slack

Business trips often don't go as expected. Watch the 1987 flick *Planes, Trains and Automobiles* and see whether you can relate. When you finally arrive home exhausted, you probably dread submitting your expenses. Twenty bucks says that your company's expense forms and internal approval process leave more than a bit to be desired.

What if you could submit your expenses via Slack? If you use Expensify and your company has enabled its Slack integration, then you are already saving yourself some time in this regard.

THE DIFFERENCE BETWEEN SLACK APPS AND CUSTOM INTEGRATIONS

While people often lump apps and customer integrations together, there are some technical differences between them. They are more important for developers to understand but give this a read if you like:

- **Apps**: At a high level, an *app* is a wrapper of sorts around a particular set of features and components. Developers build apps and then distribute them. With the right permissions, users can easily install apps in their workspaces — not just the ones on which developers originally created them. Apps effectively generally connect Slack workspaces to external web services like Dropbox, Google Drive, and the like.
- **Custom integrations:** In a way, integrations serve the same fundamental purpose as apps. The latter, however, generally plug into an organization's internal systems. When thinking about integrations, it's natural to ask the question: Integrates with what?

Don't sweat it if this distinction isn't entirely clear to you. If you're new to Slack, this minutiae won't encumber your use of Slack one bit. What's more, Slack seems to be phasing out the term *custom integration* in lieu of the more modern term *app*. (See `bit.ly/slckcust`.)

Creating new system integrations

What do you do for a living? You probably spend a good deal of time at work in front of a computer — and rarely do you request time off and submit expenses. Think for a moment about your job. What are the ways in which you routinely interact with enterprise systems? Depending on your role, you may need to do one or more of the following:

- » Open requisitions for new department or company positions
- » Generate offer letters for applicants
- » Sign up for in-person or online training
- » Write reports for your technically challenged colleagues
- » Fill out requisition forms for goods or services
- » After receiving approval, submit purchase orders
- » Pay vendors for goods or services provided
- » Close your company's books on a quarter or year

In many instances, completing these activities involves executing several redundant or superfluous steps — even if your company has implemented state-of-the-art enterprise systems.

See whether the following scenario sounds familiar. Performing essential parts of your job regularly involves

- » Sending a series of internal emails.
- » Waiting for email approval before taking the next step — especially if you need to process exceptions or exceed thresholds.
- » Switching back-and-forth among different applications.
- » Entering the same data in different systems or multiple times in the same system. (Few things rankle me more.)
- » Looking up data in a Microsoft Excel spreadsheet or standalone Access database.
- » Following up with people who have ignored your initial messages.
- » Doing *all* of these tasks.

Did I just eerily describe your work day to a *t*?

I am not judging you. Really. A certain degree of inefficiency on the job may not bother you much or even at all. After all, work isn't supposed to be fun, right?

Fair enough, but many rank-and-file employees would like to streamline their organizations' cumbersome internal processes. Doing so would save time, minimize duplicate data entry, and reduce errors. Even if you're comfortable with the status quo, consider this point: Few things excite execs in the corner office more than the ability to save money.

To be fair, performing each of the preceding tasks entirely within Slack may not be possible yet — let alone advisable down the road. For privacy, audit, and regulatory reasons, you still may need to follow the same less-than-ideal business processes even if your firm uses Slack in innovative ways. Still, for many activities in enterprise systems, there may be a better way to get something done. In this vein, Slack may prove to be just the ticket.

Integrating Slack with enterprise systems

Depending on your company's particular systems, your organization can take advantage of three different types of automation options in Slack.

- **Use native Slack integrations:** Enterprise-software vendors are hard at work building functions that link to Slack right out of the box. As such, you may be able to use them with minimal effort.
- **Use third-party integrations:** Tray.io, Workato, and Zapier are well-funded startups that focus on application integration and automation. No, they don't work exclusively with Slack. Each company, though, has built impressive integrations that serve as Slack bridges to many mainstream ERP and CRM systems.
- **Build your own custom bridges:** Failing one of these two options, IT staff at your company can develop their own bespoke integrations — or hire outside developers to do the same. As a starting point, consider Slack's developer tools. (For more on this topic, see the developer resources in Chapter 18 as well as `https://api.slack.com`.)

To paraphrase the Fleetwood Mac song, What if you go your own way? Slack benefits from a vibrant community of tech-savvy users and talented third-party developers. Many of these folks are downright effusive about their successes and often surprisingly candid about their failures. You can learn a good deal from talking to them about their creations and experiences, either online or in person.

Some of the largest enterprise-software vendors have built native Slack integrations. Others have encouraged startups to do the same — or at least not stood in their way.

Note that I'm listing the vendors in this section in alphabetical order.

REMEMBER

I obviously don't know which systems your organization runs. If this chapter is starting to overwhelm you, then feel free to skip the rest of it. You can return to it once you've gained your footing with Slack.

INFOR

Thanks to a spate of acquisitions, Infor has grown to become one of the world's largest enterprise-software vendors. At present, its products don't natively integrate with Slack, but that's where automation startup Tray.io comes in. The latter lets users build Infor-to-Slack connectors. Read more about it at `bit.ly/trayinfor`.

Not to be outdone, Workato's HTTP Connector allows for tight Infor-Slack integrations. For more, see `bit.ly/infor-workato`.

MICROSOFT DYNAMICS

Microsoft's ERP and CRM offering has undergone a number of facelifts over the years. You can use a number of automation tools to integrate Dynamics with Slack:

- **Tray.io:** For more information, see `bit.ly/ms-crm-tray`
- **Workato:** For more information, see `bit.ly/workato-msd`
- **Zapier:** For more information, see `bit.ly/zap-slack-ms`

Note that I'm intentionally omitting Microsoft's ubiquitous productivity suite. For the purposes of this chapter, Office 365 doesn't qualify as an enterprise system.

ORACLE

For decades, Oracle has been one of the world's five largest software companies. Over the years, the company has gobbled up nearly 140 firms as of this writing according to Crunchbase. Examples include the CRM outfit Siebel and the ERP vendors PeopleSoft and NetSuite. Translation: Oracle isn't going anywhere — and Slack's management and developers are acutely aware of this fact.

Along these lines, Slack and Oracle announced a significant partnership in October 2017. The Oracle Intelligent Bot Platform helps both developers and nontechnical users build smart bots. Read more about the program at `bit.ly/2ohKF3A`.

REMEMBER

A *bot* is a simple application that automates repetitive tasks.

Oracle customers should also consider taking Workato for a test drive. You can immediately download and install more than 100 pre-built recipes or templates for Oracle's E-Business Suite. They each automate a task for a different business function. Read about what you can do at `bit.ly/ora-slk-wrk`.

SALESFORCE

Salesforce is the world's largest pure-play CRM vendor. The company pioneered the popular SaaS model when it launched in 1999. To call cofounder and CEO Marc Benioff a trailblazer is the acme of understatement. Today Salesforce offers a number of different native integrations with Slack. For example, new Salesforce accounts can automatically trigger Slack notifications.

The Salesforce AppExchange is rife with apps that automatically connect to different enterprise technologies — and Slack is no exception here. For more information, see `bit.ly/slack-integ`.

SAP

The conservative German multinational software company is also among the oldest and largest in the world. One early and particularly useful SAP integration is its Concur Expense bot for Slack. Beyond that, Tray.io and Workato both connect SAP to Slack in interesting ways. For more, see the following URLs:

```
https://tray.io/connectors/sap-erp-slack-integrations
```

```
https://www.workato.com/integrations/sap_erp+slack
```

WORKDAY

Founded in late 2005 by PeopleSoft vet Dave Duffield and launched early the next year, Workday specializes in financial and human-capital management software. Much like Salesforce.com and Slack itself, the company embraced cloud computing and SaaS from its inception. Customers don't own Workday; they merely rent it.

No shocker: Workday's modern system architecture allows it to offer an ever-increasing number of useful Slack bridges. As of this writing, they include

- Employee time-off requests and peer feedback
- Enhanced coworker look-up tools
- Rapid and role-based Slack channel assignment

More are coming. Bet on it.

ZENDESK

Zendesk is the industry leader in customer service and support ticketing. As of this writing, it sports more than 200,000 clients in 30 countries. If you've ever called or emailed customer support, you've most likely received an email from Zendesk. (Check your inbox if you're curious.)

Zendesk is a natural fit for Slack integrations. If a company uses both applications, then its support employees shouldn't need to constantly check their inboxes. Zendesk integrations let tickets, comments, and updates automatically appear in Slack. For more on this subject, see `bit.ly/zdslack`.

WARNING

What if you didn't see your firm's enterprise systems in the previous section? Maybe the reason is that it runs 25-year-old, highly customized back- and front-office systems. Odds are that you won't find *existing* tools that will let those systems easily talk to Slack. Of course, your IT department can always try to build them.

Don't view Slack integrations with the aforementioned enterprise systems as a binary. There are levels. Consider two intentionally polarized scenarios:

- **Company A:** Uses the latest versions of both Workday and Salesforce.
- **Company B:** Relies upon a patchwork of kludgy legacy systems.

All else being equal, Company A will be able to use Slack to automate far more tasks than its counterpart.

But what if you don't work at Company A? No bother. Firms need not run the latest and greatest cloud-based ERP and CRM solutions to integrate with Slack. Generally speaking, though, the older its enterprise system, the less likely a firm will be able to enjoy the considerable fruits of Slack integrations.

TECHNICAL STUFF

As I was finishing the manuscript to this book, Slack launched a simple yet powerful way for developers to connect Workflow Builder (discussed in Chapter 10) to external systems. To read more, visit `bit.ly/sl-wbhk`.

Looking forward

Chapter 15 delves much deeper into Slack's bright future. For now, though, know that the number, variety, and power of Slack enterprise-system integrations will only increase for the foreseeable future. No, no company can totally eliminate inefficiency. Also, complete automation inheres its own risks. People still matter.

Still, it's not hard to read the tea leaves. Advances in automation and machine learning are letting organizations at least partially streamline many cumbersome, time-consuming, and error-prone business processes. It's happening as you read these words. Slack is poised to play an integral role in this important shift.

5

Successfully Introducing Slack in the Workplace

IN THIS PART

Increase the chances that Slack sticks in your organization

Appreciate the challenges, risks, and limitations of using Slack

Peer into Slack's exciting future

IN THIS CHAPTER

» **Understanding the importance of network effects**

» **Reviewing the different ways to drive Slack adoption in the workplace**

» **Getting others on the Slack train**

» **Dealing with Slack naysayers and stubborn employees**

Chapter 13
The Elements of Persuasion: Slack-Adoption Strategies

I'm going to go out on a limb here: If you have read any chapters in this book, they've energized you. You're now thinking about all of the ways that Slack can improve how *you* work, how it can make *you* productive, and how it can help *you* take control of *your* professional life.

If that's the case, then I'm ecstatic.

I hate to rain on your parade, but there's just one problem. Unfortunately, it's a big one: Success with Slack is not only or even primarily about *you*. To realize its benefits throughout your organizations, your colleagues need to embrace it as well. Make no mistake: Slack does not exist in a vacuum — and therein lies the rub.

This chapter offers advice on how to get your colleagues to share your excitement about Slack. Ideally, this feeling will translate into usage, and your company will reap its rewards.

A Brief Primer on Network Effects

A *network effect* is a concept rooted in the intersection of economic theory and telecommunications, but I won't take you too far down that road here. For now, think of network effects simply as powerful, virtuous cycles that offer major benefits to companies and users alike. Still with me? When a network effect exists, the value of a product or service increases in proportion to the number of people using it.

Does the concept still seem a bit vague or theoretical? Fine, I'll make it a bit more concrete. Trust me: I'll be returning to Slack shortly.

TECHNICAL STUFF

Larger networks aren't just more valuable than smaller ones; they're *exponentially* more valuable. George Gilder built on the work of Internet pioneer Robert Metcalfe to coin the phrase *Metcalfe's Law*: the effect of a telecommunications network is proportional to the square of the number of connected users of the system. Put simply, a network consisting of two members is worth four units, not two. A network with three members isn't worth three; it's worth nine. A four-member network is worth 16, and so on. Make no mistake: This law is a really big deal.

THE BIRTH OF AMAZON

In 1994, Jeff Bezos quit working at the hedge fund D.E. Shaw, moved to Seattle, and started one of the Web's first e-commerce companies. (Yes, I vividly remember its inception, and I'm dating myself.) These events occurred long before his grand idea became the everything store — the title of Brad Stone's excellent book on the company. At that time, Amazon's comparatively modest ambition was to become the world's largest bookstore. Nothing else.

Bezos understood then — as he surely does now — the remarkable power of network effects. In his case, if Amazon could become the default destination for buying books online, then good things would happen for the company, himself, and his employees. Specifically, more publishers, vendors, and partners would sell their books on Amazon because that's where people shopped. In turn, even more people would purchase their books on Amazon. This virtuous cycle would continue indefinitely and ultimate generate enormous economic value.

It turns out that Bezos's 1994 intuition was spot-on. As of this writing, Amazon's market capitalization exceeds $1 trillion. Even after Bezos's recent and historically expensive divorce, he remains the richest person on the planet.

Think that Amazon represents the sole example of a contemporary network effect? Think again? The leaders at Facebook, Google, Apple, Uber, LinkedIn, Microsoft, Twitter, and many other tech behemoths intimately grasp the power of network effects. They have taken steps to strengthen those networks that, in part, explain current and forthcoming legislation. Take away network effects, and those companies would be worth a fraction of their current values.

Just like Amazon and Facebook, organizations that use Slack can benefit from network effects. That is, as more employees use Slack, firms benefit more from it. This truism makes Slack a more valuable tool than if only a few employees in an company dabble in it.

Slack is not an individual tool; it is a group one. As such, the benefits that you and your organization ultimately accrue from it hinge upon its successful adoption and use. Put differently, its outputs are a direct function of its inputs. More of the latter yields more of the former.

REMEMBER

Simon's First Law of Slack: The more that you and your firm put into Slack, the more that you'll get out of it.

Reviewing the Different Slack-Adoption Approaches

Slack works best when as many people as possible in your organization use it. (See the preceding section for more information on this topic.) To this end, your colleagues need to quickly get on the Slack bus.

Here are three high-level adoption approaches. Note that they are not mutually exclusive — especially at large organizations. It's not hard to imagine a firm concurrently employing two of the following methods.

The bottom-up method

In this informal scenario, entry-level and often tech-savvy employees in an organization start using Slack — maybe even under the radar. Fed up with email hell, folks don't ask for permission. They get wind of Slack, perhaps while gabbing at lunch or walking by a colleague's desk and seeing this weird application on someone's screen. In other words, Slack organically takes root at a firm. I suspect that this approach is common at large companies.

The top-down method

A bigwig mandates that employees at her company or department begin using Slack. She insists that her underlings use it; if they don't play ball, she'll be showing them the door. In theory, this demand trickles down to the lower layers of the organization. Problem solved, right?

Maybe.

I've learned a few things about change management in my days. The top-down approach works with varying degrees of success. Sure, forcing employees to adopt new technologies can work. Generally speaking, though, "want to" beats "have to" any day of the week and twice on Sunday. Put differently, it's typically better to encourage folks to move in a particular direction than to twist their arms. You can lead a horse to water, but you can't make him drink.

At the same time, though, management can't exhibit infinite patience with hidebound employees. Again, when only part of the organization uses Slack, the tool isn't nearly as effective. As a result, the employer won't realize the benefits outlined in Chapter 1 — certainly not to the same extent.

The middle-out method

Employees wedged somewhere between entry-level and the corner office adopt Slack. Adoption first grows laterally. Slack then moves to other groups or departments. Eventually, Slack starts spreading up and down the org chart.

RUMINATIONS ON SLACK AND FIELDS

Some lucky organizations start using Slack from day one, knock it out of the park, and never look back. In this context, they are green fields. They rarely deal with formidable employee resistance that often derails any effort to effect change in the workplace.

Odds are, though, that your work environment predates Slack. That is, your firm is a brown field rife with cultural baggage. Maybe it attempted to introduce Slack-like tools in the past and experienced limited success or even outright failure. The words *organ rejection* come to mind.

Does this scenario sound familiar to you? If so, then I'll bet that some employees will struggle with Slack at your firm — or any new collaboration tool for that matter. Put differently, no application or technology exists in a vacuum. Foolish is the soul who believes otherwise. Remember this point when you're rolling out Slack.

Making Slack Stick at Work

Management at your organization has purchased one of Slack's premium plans and wants to deploy it. Now everyone will use it. Sounds simple, right?

Unfortunately, nothing could be further from the truth.

When it comes to deploying new technologies, the business landscape is littered with technology failures. (Chapter 12 references prominent examples such as Hershey and Healthcare.gov.) Much like hacking, though, the vast majority of IT project failures fly under the radar. As I know from more than a decade as an enterprise-systems consultant, success with new applications is hardly assured.

Most failed corporate IT projects have historically followed the *Waterfall method* — a rigid, sequential approach to deploying software rooted in the 1950s. As a result, these endeavors typically

- Exceed their initial budgets — often by ghastly amounts
- Take far longer than anticipated
- Don't deliver the expected benefits
- All of the above

There's no simple ten-step formula or panacea for guaranteeing that an organization will thrive with Slack — or with any new technology for that matter.

Still, that's not to say that a firm can't stack the deck in its favor. To that end, the following sections cover some change-management tips that should help your employer minimize the chance that Slack fails. My suggestions fall into two buckets: organizational and individual. Collectively, they give companies the best chance at making Slack stick for good.

Organization-level strategies

To the extent that your current position allows, try applying a number of organizational-level approaches. This section details my favorites.

Know thyself

For all sorts of reasons beyond the scope of this book, a decades-old manufacturer just can't operate at the same speed as a ten-person tech startup founded last month. All things being equal, the larger and more mature the organization, the longer that it will take for new tools such as Slack to take root.

Aim for little victories

As a general rule, mature organizations that make the most out of new technologies generally don't try to boil the ocean. They eschew the inflexible Waterfall method. Instead, they follow more flexible approaches. For this reason, Agile software-development methods, such as Scrum, have exploded in popularity.

With regard to Slack, foolish is the management team that does the following:

- » Ignores its own history and culture
- » Impulsively buys an Enterprise Grid license on Monday morning
- » Starts building their own private apps on Tuesday

Depending on the organization, its culture, and the composition of its workforce, it may be best to introduce Slack gradually and build from there.

TIP

Successful software companies these days tend to release new features in regular increments; very rarely do they opt to launch everything in one big batch. Consider applying that same approach to Slack.

Maybe you're skeptical of adopting a cautious approach. If Slack is so great, then why not rip the bandage right off? If you're leaning this way, then consider this point: Perhaps the company that uses Slack to the fullest possible extent is Slack itself. (Silicon-Valley types refer to this practice as *eating your own dogfood.*) As the yarn in the nearby sidebar illustrates, even Slack proceeds at an intelligent pace.

#SLACK-ON-SLACK

Slack created and uses `#slack-on-slack`, an internal channel that lets employees submit their ideas on how to improve the application or solve a problem. (Note that Slack distinguishes suggesting new features from reporting bugs.)

In the words of Slack's VP of Business Technology Stephen Franchetti, "Focusing exclusively on big wins means momentum is invisible to frontline employees. We need their grassroots support so that they keep sharing ideas and know that there's a reasonable chance we're going to do something about it." (Visit `bit.ly/slack-iv4` to read the entire interview.)

As the kids say, true dat.

Communicate those victories

As a company, Slack isn't exactly shy about letting its employees know the progress that it's making. After all, one of Slack's principal benefits is that it allows management to be transparent with employees. (See Chapter 1 for more.)

TIP

If management wants employees to suggest ideas for improvement and innovate, then it must really listen to their ideas. This advice holds true even if the company can't implement those suggestions.

TIP

At some point, someone may ask you why you consider Slack to be an essential piece of software. Here's a short, direct answer: Employees are typically overwhelmed and disengaged while on the clock. Slack helps solve that problem.

Interview and hire people who use Slack or comparable tools

It's essential that new hires keep an organization's Slack momentum going. All of them. Every worker who refuses to use Slack makes the tool less valuable to the company and its employees.

Fair point, but isn't it best to determine whether applicants are willing to use Slack before hiring them? After all, knowing whether potential new hires are really telling the truth is an age-old conundrum. No one is clairvoyant. Still, a few progressive companies have cracked the code. If you're interested in finding out more here, see the nearby sidebar "How smart tech companies weed out posers."

WP ENGINE WALKS BEFORE IT RUNS

Based out of Austin, Texas, WP Engine provides premium hosting services. The 900-employee company's careful approach to introducing Slack has paid big dividends.

I spoke with Lauren Cox, the company's director of internal communications. When deploying Slack, WP Engine started with a measured approach. For example, it intentionally limited the number of public channels. Management didn't want to overwhelm employees and create chaos. It also didn't insist upon universal employee usage.

Cox also told me that Slack has exceeded the company's expectations. She cites how it has caused internal email to plummet. What's more, employees can in engage in more targeted conversations than they did when they used previous tools.

HOW SMART TECH COMPANIES WEED OUT POSERS

What if you're a rock-star, cocky programmer proficient at writing elegant code? Your specialties are JavaScript and Python. You decide to interview for a senior software developer position at Google. You're just brimming with confidence.

Don't think for a minute that your interviews will consist exclusively of theoretical questions such as "If you were an animal, what type would you be?" or "Where do you see yourself in five years?"

On the contrary, you're going to have to roll up your sleeves and show your coding chops — in real time and in front of an audience. Expect Google's hiring managers to watch you think through a thorny coding problem. What's more, either on a computer or a white board, you'll have to write the specific lines of code that addresses that problem. If you struggle doing this exercise, then you're not nearly as adroit as you claim. Don't hold your breath waiting to receive an offer.

Many tech companies today follow a similar screening process, especially for technical positions. For example, consider Automattic — the company behind WordPress, the content-management system that powers one-third of the Web. As my friend and author Scott Berkun writes in *The Year Without Pants* (Jossey-Bass), potential hires complete a small coding project at $25 per hour. If their code doesn't compile and/or current Automattic employees dislike interacting with these candidates, then Automattic will cut a check and continue its search with other applicants.

Use Slack during the hiring process

Can you apply a similar technique to the one described in the sidebar when sussing out an employee's Slack skills? The short answer is yes.

The following example demonstrates exactly how to do so. (Astute readers will recognize the *Better Call Saul* references.)

Howard is a partner at the law firm HHM. This is not your average bunch of lawyers: Employees do just about everything via Slack.

Howard needs to fill the open position of junior associate. He interviews Jimmy who hits all the right notes. When it comes to Slack, Jimmy claims to be a power user, but Howard is meticulous. He wants answers to the following questions:

» Does Jimmy really possess mad Slack skills and a willingness to use them? Or, as Howard suspects, is Jimmy embellishing how he has used Slack in the past?

» Is Jimmy just a bit too perfect?

Howard decides to invite Jimmy to Slack as a guest — something that he learned how to do in Chapter 2. (Go, Howard!) What's more, he instructs HHM's HR folks to communicate with Jimmy during the recruiting process only in Slack. That is, recruiters avoid the temptation to respond to any emails that Jimmy may send. In fact, if Jimmy is as adept at Slack as he claims, then why is he sending emails in the first place now that he's a workspace member?

This approach accomplishes a number of important goals. First, it serves as a litmus test. If Jimmy refuses to use Slack or uses it incorrectly, then maybe he's not all that he claims to be. If Jimmy resists using Slack, then Howard was right after all: Jimmy is all hat and no cattle. Second, it teaches Jimmy an important lesson: At HHM, Slack serves as an essential tool. Should the law firm hire him, then Jimmy will already have learned this lesson.

TIP

Never rely upon applicants being completely forthright during the interview process. It's not worth the risk. How many candidates will say no and cost themselves the job? What if the candidates claim to regularly use collaborative tools but really despise them? If you suspect that a candidate is uncomfortable with Slack, trust your instincts.

Recognize Slack's learning curve

To be sure, different employees pick up new software packages and tools at different speeds. I have seen this movie many times.

Some employees repeatedly make the same mistake when using a new system. In this case, additional training is futile. Others naturally gravitate toward new tchotchkes and soon become their company's *de facto* experts.

Yes, Slack is intuitive to use, but not all employees will agree. Nonetheless, they will have to learn to effectively use it if the organization is really committed to it.

No, Slack isn't terribly difficult to pick up. Still, your colleagues may need more than a few minutes to grasp its idea and to use it properly.

TIP

If an employee struggles with Slack, try to exhibit patience — especially early on.

YOUR COLLEAGUES ARE (PROBABLY) NOT CHRIS

My friend and colleague Chris works as a professor of information systems at Arizona State University. We became chummy because our offices were adjacent. He has spent his career developing complex applications and debugging code for large companies. Truth be told, he is ten times the coder that I am.

In August 2019, I signed the contract to write *Slack For Dummies*. At a department-wide meeting just a few days after, I caught up with Chris over lunch. I mentioned my new writing project. He seemed genuinely intrigued — or at least he was trying to humor me.

Chris had never used Slack. He had, however, noodled with Discord, an open-source alternative. I explained Slack to him and drew a simple workspace diagram with channels on a whiteboard.

It took him all of about four minutes to get it. Again, because of his background and experience with a comparable application, Chris has hit the ground running with Slack.

The larger point is that success on the job increasingly requires near-constant learning. This reality is particularly acute today, and it will only accelerate in the future. As I tell my students every semester, they're not finished learning when they pass my class or even receive their diplomas. Not to get all meta, but at college, students ideally learn how to learn.

Play the FOMO card

Many people experience anxiety because something important is happening without their knowledge. For this reason, they'll constantly check their smartphones and social-media accounts. I'm talking about the fear of missing out (FOMO).

With respect to Slack, you can use FOMO to your advantage. Tell reluctant employees that they are missing out on great conversations, important updates, valuable tips, and more. Put differently, it's where all of the cool kids hang out.

Strategies for handling difficult employees

Oh, if only effectively managing employees was so easy. Newfangled management theories abound, but dozens of exceptions belie every so-called rule. For this reason, management remains a discipline, not a true science with immutable laws. To this end, I present some ways of dealing with recalcitrant employees.

MEET THE NEW BOSS . . .

During my days as an enterprise-system consultant, I often trained groups of employees on how to use new HR and payroll applications. (I was a certified consultant in Lawson Software's HR suite back when that was a thing.) I didn't know my clients' legacy systems, and they were unfamiliar with Lawson. Many were miffed to boot that they were switching systems.

I found it best to find a middle ground with my clients and students. That is, I would demonstrate how Lawson handled the following essential actions:

- Enrolling employees in benefit plans
- Running payroll for thousands of employees
- Correcting mistakes and processing adjustments

I would then answer their specific questions. More often than not, light bulbs started going off. They came to understand that Lawson wasn't so different from their current systems after all. In fact, it contained similar or even identical functionality. Sometimes I'd even drop the lyric from The Who song "Won't Get Fooled Again." That reference usually made them smile.

Ease the transition with email-to-Slack apps

Chapters 4 and 10 describe apps that bring emails directly into Slack with a few mouse clicks. Yes, it's a half-measure, but one that arguably makes sense when dealing with skeptical or change-resistant employees. With this population, you often have to tread lightly.

If one of these apps helps them get the hang of Slack, then it serves a valuable purpose. Ideally, after a while, they'll take off the training wheels.

Remind older workers that they've used Slack-like tools before

Remind folks of a certain age that Slack really isn't so new after all. That is, they have probably used applications that have mimicked some of Slack's functionality. Because of that, it should be relatively easy for them to translate that knowledge into Slack proficiency.

Slack builds on the functionality of tools that many senior employees have probably used at home — if not on the clock. Table 13-1 displays some of the more popular pure instant-message (IM) applications that preceded Slack.

TABLE 13-1 Pre-Slack IM and Collaboration Tools

Name	Description
IRC	Internet Relay Chat launched in August 1988. To be sure, some people continue to swear by it (in large part, because it uses channels similarly to how Slack does). Regardless, it's not nearly as popular as it used to be.
Gmail chat	Rather than just email someone, Google allows users to send IMs to their contacts.
ICQ	The Israeli-based IM and Voice over Internet Protocol (VoIP) client arrived in 1996. At one point, more than 40 million people used it every day, although that number has waned in recent years.
AIM	AOL's IM tool arrived when the Web was taking off. It survived until December 2017. RIP, AIM.
Yahoo! Messenger	Released in 1998, the advertisement-supported IM client enjoyed a 20-year run. It was very popular during the company's halcyon days.
Skype	Launched in 2003 and now part of Microsoft, Skype is a telecommunications application that lets users primarily make audio and video calls. It remains popular.

By now, you know that Slack lets users do quite a bit more than send DMs. Referencing the tools in Table 13-1 allows you to find a *lingua franca* with new Slack neophytes. This technique usually bridges the gap. It can reduce their resistance, disarm them, and open their minds to using Slack.

Know thy enemy

A decade ago, I developed a simple three-pronged theory of the technology adoption based on my consulting experiences. Call it *Simon's Law of Change Management*. Three groups of people are in the world:

- People who get it.
- People who don't get it but want to get it.
- People who don't get it and don't want to get it.

Try to identify the group to which a person belongs. Focus on the first two. Try to convert as many as you can from the second group into the first. Ignore the third as much as possible. They'll never pick up what you're putting down. Ever. Ultimately, people in the third group will only frustrate you. You may need to part ways with particularly stubborn folks who undermine your organization's efforts to embrace Slack.

Offer carrots

People generally don't respond well to threats at work. I like to think that I've learned a thing or six during my stints in the corporate and academic worlds. At the top of the list is that employees prefer to voluntarily change, not have management force change upon them.

FINDING INSPIRATION AT THE GYM

At my old gym, I often saw an 80-something man on a treadmill. For that reason alone, I admired him. I'd occasionally look in his direction and see him reading different books. I put another check in the octogenarian's column. Finally, I caught a few glimpses of the books' covers. He routinely read about programming and new software applications.

As I've said many times, I want to be that guy if I last that long. I always want to care for my body and, just as important, my mind.

Unfortunately, far too many people hate change — especially at work. As I know from more than a decade of helping companies implement new technologies, old habits die hard.

TIP

"Want to" is usually a better approach than "have to."

In this vein, here are a few ways to nudge employees in the right direction.

ANSWER THE WIIFM QUESTION

As Chapter 1 demonstrates, Slack offers a number of considerable benefits to employers and employees alike. Taylor, an occasionally aloof employee in his mid-40s, doesn't really care about Slack's organizational advantages.

Against this backdrop, what should Dave — Taylor's manager — do? (Yes, these are Foo Fighters' references.)

In this case, Dave should focus on the employee side of the coin. He needs to remind Taylor how Slack can help him do his job. In other words, Dave should answer the following question from Taylor's perspective: *What's in it for me?* Specifically, Dave needs to explain to Taylor that Slack will let him

- Receive fewer emails, especially pointless ones
- Reduce the number of applications that bug him with different alerts
- Find key documents quicker
- Regularly leave the office at a normal hour because he'll be able to work more efficiently

REMEMBER

Slack lets employees tame the email beast — especially with their colleagues. To be sure, using Slack doesn't mean that your inbox will be irrevocably empty. Experienced Slack users know, however, that targeted messages allow them to keep their focus. That benefit doesn't necessarily mean, though, that others will recognize Slack's benefits, let alone will adopt it for themselves.

No, the carrot-based approach may not work. (Again, managing people is no picnic.) Hopefully, if Dave emphasizes these results with Taylor, then they will resonate with him. Because of that, he'll up his Slack game.

GENTLY REMIND EMPLOYEES ABOUT THE REAL WORLD

Depending on your age, you may remember the halcyon days in which people spent their entire professional lives with a single company. I'm talking about stable 40-year careers at single companies, such as IBM or General Motors.

Those days are largely gone and have been for decades. The Bureau of Labor Statistics reported in 2015 that baby boomers typically worked in about 12 different jobs during their careers. (See `bit.ly/2keMjkU` for more.) Brass tacks: Odds are that any one employee's current job and employer won't be her last.

How does this relate to getting employees to embrace Slack? How can you use these facts to nudge employees who lack your zeal for the application?

Here's a little technology-adoption trick that I've used throughout my career. I'll frame it in the form of a conversation:

> **Slack-resistant employee (SRE):** I just don't want to use Slack. I like the way that I work now. Why do I have to learn something new? You can't teach this old dog new tricks.
>
> **You:** First of all, old dog? Please. (Pro tip: Guess an age that's easily ten years lower than what you really think.) Second, are you sure that you're going to work here forever? Your kids often switch jobs. What happens if you need to move? What if life happens? Even if you're content here, consider this: Companies sometimes downsize, get acquired, or even go under.
>
> **SRE:** *(Flattered at the age remark; her defenses disarmed.)* What do you mean?
>
> **You:** At some point, you may have to look for another job. We all might. Many companies are deploying Slack and tools just like it. Knowledge and use of it will distinguish you from other candidates if you have to find a new place to work. What's more, it will show recruiters that you're willing to embrace change. That would probably help you, right?
>
> **SRE:** Interesting points. Okay, I'll give it a shot.
>
> **You:** Excellent. Slack is easy to learn. If I can do it, then anyone can. Plus, from what I know of you, it will be a piece of cake. Let me know if I can help. I want you to be successful.
>
> *And scene. . . (Bow to audience.)*

FAILING TO GET MY FRIENDS ON THE SLACK BANDWAGON

Every year, five of my college friends and I get together to play 3-on-3 basketball over the course of a long weekend in a different city. Yeah, we take our hoops pretty seriously. How seriously?

For starters, we wear custom jerseys. We rent an indoor court to avoid any weather-related issues. We record the seven-game series, watch the video when we get home, keep statistics, and laugh at how poorly we generally play. Over the past few years, we've even hired a proper referee. Of course, the ref dons a black-and-white shirt and brings a whistle.

If you think that the trip and related activities necessitate a good deal of planning, you're correct. I haven't even mentioned other logistics, such as arranging lodging and keeping track of flights, arrival and departure times, and shared expenses. Brass tacks: Plenty of other coordination activities go into these trips.

The way that our group plans these events has rankled me for years, not that I'm shy about my displeasure. For a while, we inconsistently used a private Facebook group. That ceased to be an option in early 2018 when I quit the social network once and for all.

Needless to say, our group communication would benefit from using Slack. If you emphatically agree with me and we ever meet, the first drink is on me.

A few years ago, I floated the idea of using Slack to my friends and set up a workspace. Unfortunately, only my friend Mike joined me in advocating for it; the other four knuckleheads outvoted us. Score one for the Luddites.

To this day, we continue to rely upon a tsunami of texts to communicate and exchange plans. (Maybe giving each of them a copy of this book will finally result in change.) As a result, the six or us generally don't know who's arriving when, although we send the same text multiple times.

Every time that I get a new and redundant text, a little piece of me dies inside. Finding key information this way isn't remotely efficient. If this were 1998, then I'd be able to accept our dysfunctional communication methods. Knowing that there's a much better way to coordinate our weekends but being unable to use it drives me bonkers.

Calm blue oceans . . .

Yes, this admittedly transparent technique appeals to people's vanity. Still, it can be surprisingly effective. (Have you ever offended someone by underestimating that person's age?) During my consulting career, I often employed it. More often than not, it has proven fruitful. To be fair, this trick is unlikely to pay dividends with stubborn employees who are close to retirement.

As I painfully discovered a few years ago, it can even be tough to convince your supposedly tech-savvy friends to change their ways. (See the nearby sidebar "Failing to get my friends on the Slack bandwagon.")

LESSONS LEARNED FROM A CASUAL SLACK LAUNCH

Empire State Indivisible (ESI) strives to create more engagement in the democratic process. Researching this book, I spoke with ESI cofounder Ricky Silver about how his organization uses Slack. Silver relayed to me ESI's early struggles with the collaboration tool.

By way of background, ESI's onboarding process for new members is vexing. The organization has learned that taking immediate and direct action is crucial to start new members off on the right foot. From day one, ESI used Slack as its organizing tool. Like anything, though, a tool is only as good as the people who use it.

ESI launched its Slack workspace without any structure and norms. What's more, its leadership hadn't spent any energy defining its goals. As a result, Silver describes ESI's early Slack workspace as a free-for-all and a bit of a disaster. Put differently, Slack's power and flexibility left ESI's leadership completely unprepared. To its credit, however, ESI's leadership quickly recognized the problem. As a result, it made the following changes:

- **More defined public channels:** Allowed members to communicate and collaborate around specific actions and issues.
- **A designated channel for banter and conversation:** Led to a more engaged community.
- **Private channels for leadership to plan, organize, and finalize actions:** Gave the organization's top brass a place to discuss issues before rolling them out to the team.

The changes have made Slack a more effective tool at ESI. Silver reports that Slack has allowed ESI to simplify its onboarding process. It has also significantly improved membership retention and engagement. Most important, its activist action has skyrocketed.

Most people have been working — albeit with different levels of efficiency — for a long time. Many people are stubbornly stuck in their ways.

WARNING

Expect some level of resistance to Slack, especially from stubborn employees at large companies.

Judiciously wield the sticks

Say that you've exhausted all of your carrots. If you're in a position of authority at your employer, it's time to bring out the sticks.

Your firm is all in on Slack. It is where work takes place. Period. Yet, absentminded folks conveniently forget or ignore this fact. Sure, everyone makes mistakes from time to time, but repeat offenders warrant stern warnings. I know of a few companies that have fired recalcitrant employees because they routinely refused to use key organizational tools — including Slack.

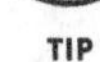

TIP

Hold employees accountable for reverting to email.

TIP

If all else fails, here's your last resort. Remind Stubborn Stu or Headstrong Helen that employee choice and freedom are not absolute. Far from it. The First Amendment has never existed inside of a company's walls. Say whatever you like; unless you blow a whistle, report an OSHA violation, or do something along those lines, your words and actions can cost you your job.

I hate to end this section on such a grim note, but I'm not wrong. Think about it: Very few people get to choose all the tools that their employers use. I certainly don't. Most workers have to live with others' technology and management decisions to continue collecting their paychecks. Ultimately, however, all individuals can exercise the ultimate choice. As Alec Baldwin's Blake chillingly says in the superb movie *Glengarry Glen Ross*, "You don't like it? Leave."

REMEMBER

No matter what you do, you may not be able to compel disobedient colleagues to use Slack.

Spread the Slack gospel at work

On a more positive note, the following sidebars offer tips for people who fall into my first two groups in my admittedly simplistic theory of the world:

- People who get it.
- People who don't get it but want to get it.

WHAT TO DO IF YOU BECOME YOUR COMPANY'S SLACK CHAMPION

What if you become the go-to person on Slack at your organization? Maybe this book even helped you attain Grand Master status. As a result, people come to you with questions and see you as a way to help them understand Slack and solve the problems covered in Chapter 1.

I'm willing to bet that your new status will help you in your current and future jobs.

At the risk of being immodest, I currently find myself in that role at ASU. To my knowledge, I was one of the first professors there to have adopted Slack back in 2017. What's more, I started advocating for it internally and loudly. After googling "Slack in the classroom," plenty of folks contacted me for additional advice. Finally, I wrote this book.

While flattering, as I know from personal experience, being your employer's resident Slack expert can also pose challenges. After all, it's probably not your explicit responsibility to teach your colleagues how to use Slack and answer all their questions. You've got a day job.

In my case, my current position as a college professor requires me to wear many hats. I teach eight classes per academic year, meet with students, serve on department committees, grade papers, and do other professorial things.

Along these lines, consider doing the following:

- Strike a balance between doing your day job and helping your peers hone their Slack skills.
- If you get sucked into long email threads, gently remind others that Slack is a better medium for this type of thing. Offer to spend some time with them — via Slack's methods no less.
- Carve out a few minutes to coach others who seem to be open to using Slack.
- Participate in Slack-related discussions on public channels.

The fact that you're already realizing Slack's benefits inside your organization gives you a great deal of street cred. Try to maintain or increase it while not sacrificing any of your daily obligations.

TEACHING OTHERS HOW TO FISH

I frequently recommend books to my students during class lectures and my informal interactions with them. What can I say? I'm an avid reader, and I enjoy it when they reciprocate. So many books, so little time.

In the 2019 fall semester, one of my more engaged students asked me a question — via Slack, of course. He wanted to know if I could create a separate public channel for book recommendations. Call him *John* here.

I reminded John that his current Slack role permits him to create channels all by himself. He didn't need my permission. I told him to go for it and let me know if he had any problems.

A few minutes later, he created the new public channel `#books_to_read`. I immediately joined it and posted links to some of my favorite business, technology, and analytics texts. I also gave him props in the channel for starting it. (No sense in taking credit for his idea.) Next, I posted a message in `#announcements` inviting all students to join it as well. Within a few hours, several other bibliophiles joined the channel. I also sent John a private DM with the screenshot of the text in this very sidebar. To add a cherry on top, I added it as a default public channel in my class workspace the following semester.

I hope that this brief yarn imparted a few key lessons about how to promote Slack adoption throughout the organization:

- Encourage others to fish for themselves. It's risky to concentrate all knowledge of any enterprise application in one employee's hands.
- Take advantage of Slack's decentralized, many-to-many nature.
- Offer support as needed.

IN THIS CHAPTER

» Considering the business and technology risks of deploying Slack

» Evaluating Slack's legal and financial challenges

Chapter 14
The Inherent Risks of Deploying Slack

I'm a really big fan of Slack — maybe even a bit obsessed. I gravitated to Slack instantly. With rare exception, my students and clients have, too.

I'm no Pollyanna, though. My career in enterprise technology has been nothing if not instructive. At the top of my list of lessons learned, success is hardly guaranteed whenever an organization introduces a new technology. It's downright naïve to ignore the risks of deploying any application, and Slack is no exception to this rule. Put differently, just because more than 12 million people have embraced it doesn't mean that employees at your company will as well.

In this chapter, I explain some of the inherent risks of deploying Slack in a work environment. Note that I've grouped them into a number of natural buckets. In some cases, I provide guidance on how to overcome these risks. In other cases (with a nod to the lovable Martin Prince on *The Simpsons*), I'll be blunt: There are no easy answers, and your company's mileage with Slack may vary.

Identifying the Risks of Using Slack

A modern business can't function without using technology. No news here. Case in point: Consider your favorite food-truck proprietor or the hip artisan baker at your local farmers' market. I'd wager that these decidedly non-technical folks rely upon high-tech payment technologies, such as Square or Apple Pay or Google Pay. Brass tacks: All companies are tech companies. Some just haven't realized it yet.

Trying to separate business and technology risks is a fool's errand: Today the two are inextricably intertwined. Keep that in mind as you read the following sections.

Business risks

By purchasing and deploying any new application, an organization faces inherent risks. In the case of Slack, its rewards far outweigh the potential downsides. Still, it would be remiss of me to ignore the real business or cultural risks of deploying it.

Capriciously adding Slack into the fray

As a collaboration tool, Slack stands on the shoulders of its ancestors. In fact, many software vendors offered respectable collaboration tools long before Slack's 2013 launch. At a high level, Slack's predecessors fall into two buckets, although there's certainly some overlap between the two:

- Pure Instant-Message (IM). (For more on this, see Table 14-1)
- General collaboration and project management

Table 14-1 displays some of the major collaboration applications that preceded Slack. Note that I'm intentionally omitting LinkedIn, Facebook, Twitter, and other pure-play social networks. Ditto for retired ones, such as Google+.

Plenty of employees at large, mature organizations have used at least some of the tools in Table 14-1. Indeed, some folks continue to use them. Ditto for small businesses and medium-sized ones. Against this backdrop, it is unrealistic to expect all employees in a multinational corporation to immediately forgo their favorite tried-and-true collaboration tools and adopt Slack just because an executive said so, especially in an era of *bring your own device* (BYOD).

TABLE 14-1 Pre-Slack Collaboration Tools

Name	Description
SharePoint	Launched in 2001, SharePoint served mainly as a document-management and storage system. Yes, it could do other things, but users often complained about its general clunkiness. (Google "SharePoint sucks" if you doubt me on this one.)
Yammer	Yammer arrived as an independent product in 2008. Microsoft acquired it in 2012 for $1.2 billion. In March 2019, Microsoft effectively rolled its functionality into Microsoft Teams.
Hipchat	A favorite of developers, this Atlassian application provided internal private online chat, IM, and other collaborative tools. Atlassian sold its core intellectual property to Slack and discontinued it in February 2019.
Basecamp	The user-friendly collaboration and project-management tool still sports a passionate client base 15 years after its debut. Basecamp is the flagship product of the company formerly known as 37signals.
Jive	Founded in 2001, Jive's collaboration suite of tools survived until Aurea acquired it in June 2017.
Ning	Cofounded by Marc Andreessen and Gina Bianchini and launched in October 2005, Ning lets anyone create a private social network or community with a few mouse clicks. Now part of Mode Media, Ning is technically still around, but that could change at any point.
Asana	The web and mobile application helps teams organize, track, and manage their work. Ex-Facebook employee Justin Rosenstein started the company in 2008 and released the product in 2012.

Still, think about one of Slack's major selling points and the reasons for its increasing popularity: It allows employers to build — and employees to access — a single, searchable knowledge repository. Throw in the ability to analyze vast troves of data discussed in Chapter 11 and the network effects discussed in Chapter 13. Your firm is well on the path to making the most out of its Slack investment.

Bottom line: Challenges aside, the benefits of entering into an exclusive, monogamous relationship with Slack more than justify the effort. Firms that haphazardly add Slack to an already bloated list of collaboration tools risk bifurcating their institutional knowledge even more. For all sorts of reasons, firms should use only one application if they want to fully reap its full benefits.

TIP

Don't look at any new enterprise technology in a vacuum. Yes, you can download Slack and be up and running within minutes. For large organizations looking to get as much bang for the buck as possible, though, it's wise to carefully review existing business tools and processes. This advice is especially valuable if your employer is considering Enterprise Grid.

THE PERILS OF ADDING TECHNOLOGY WITHOUT A STRATEGY

By 2011, the recession stemming from the 2008 sub-prime mortgage crisis had started to ebb. Emboldened CIOs began experimenting with what was then a relatively new technology: cloud computing. With Amazon Web Services (AWS), the company offered a far more efficient and cost-effective way of provisioning critical pieces of IT infrastructure. Yet, at the end of their fiscal years, many CIOs were surprised to learn that they were somehow spending more on information technology (IT) after embracing cloud computing.

How could this situation possibly compute? (Pun intended.)

The answer was simple: In many instances, large companies merely added cloud-computing services to their already complicated IT frameworks and systems. That is, they didn't retire anything. Hence, their overall IT costs surged.

Believing that Slack can do it all

Think about the killer business applications that you use on a daily basis. Forget personal apps for a moment.

I'm guessing that email and Excel are at or near the top of your list.

I'll come clean: I frequently use these tools, too. Like you, I'll send a colleague an email. (In my case, Slack adoption among college professors is lamentably far from universal.) I don't send company-wide announcements, but you might. On the Excel side, most folks have used it to build a simple model or track a list of customers or events. They then analyze the data and build simple visualizations.

That's why these tools exist. They help people do their jobs and get things done more efficiently. And there's absolutely nothing untoward going on here.

The problem is that far too many professionals use these applications as Swiss Army knives. They become proficient at a particular tool and use it for purposes for which it wasn't intended. If you only have a hammer, you view everything as a nail:

- That 20-email thread isn't helping anyone resolve the issue; it has long stopped being even remotely useful. Hitting "Reply All" only confuses others more. It's time to pick up the phone and talk to one another.

» The 50-tab, macro-laden, 80MB workbook that you email as an attachment to colleagues for updates every month reached its breaking point years ago. It's high time to port it over to another application — preferably a proper system that people can access online.

In this way, Slack is no different from email and Excel. I have no doubt that Slack will continue to evolve and add new, exciting features. (See Chapter 15 for some of my predictions about future improvements.) Still, people who fail to ground their expectations in reality are bound to be disappointed with its results.

Trying to placate all employees

It's virtually impossible for everyone in even a small organization to agree on "the best" tool. That statement applies double for large organizations. In my consulting career, I saw plenty of heated arguments among bigwigs. And the turmoil doesn't end at the executive level. After a firm adopts a new system or tool, often unhappy campers loudly pine for the days of the old one. Brass tacks: You're never going to make every employee happy — especially at large companies.

Chapter 13 covers many ways to persuade reluctant employees to adopt Slack. Rather than rehash those points here, suffice it to say that there's a nonzero chance that Slack just won't take root at your company for whatever reason — even if you follow all of my advice. To quote the iconic line from *Cool Hand Luke*, "Some men you just can't reach."

TIP

The larger the organization, the more resistance to Slack you can expect.

Adjusting to an overhauled Slack user interface

Chapter 2 provides an overview of the Slack UI. You may have found it as initially intuitive as I do. Alternatively, you may consider it confusing, or — to use a technical term — *meh*. Regardless of your first impression, if you work with Slack every day, it won't take long for you to become adept at using it.

But what if Slack suddenly and dramatically overhauls its UI? Along these lines, consider the story in the nearby sidebar "Microsoft: A cautionary UI tale."

I would bet my house that Slack would ever release a version with such a jarring redesign as Office 2007 or Windows 8. (See the nearby sidebar for more information on this subject.) It's absurd, though, to claim that Slack will never alter its UI in a significant way. In point of fact, in the spring of 2020, Slack released a new and improved version of its desktop app. Yes, I had to rewrite some sections of *Slack For Dummies* and take some new screenshots. Still, within a few minutes, I was able to adjust to Slack's new look and feel.

MICROSOFT: A CAUTIONARY UI TALE

Microsoft Office has long held the position of the leading suite of productivity tools. (The present number of worldwide users rests at 1.2 billion as of this writing.) It's a remarkable number.

I remember using Excel as a sophomore at Carnegie Mellon way back in 1991. Fast forward 29 years: Not a week goes by in which I don't use the spreadsheet application for some reason. Sometimes I have worked in Excel every day for months on end.

That's not to say that Excel has remained constant — or any part of the Office suite, for that matter. Another vendor would have surely surpassed Microsoft if the company had not enhanced early versions of Excel.

For my money, the most pronounced change in the productivity suite took place with Microsoft's release of Office 2007. Microsoft replaced the familiar — dare I say, loved? — menu items: File, Edit, View, Insert, and others. In its place, Microsoft added a contextual ribbon that would change its elements based upon what users were doing in a particular application.

Think about it. Microsoft revamped how hundreds of millions of people interacted with Excel, PowerPoint, Word, and Access — most of whom used these applications at work. Oodles of people unexpectedly struggled to perform basic functions while on the job. Case in point: Some Excel power users couldn't figure out how to sort data.

I understood and even shared their outrage. In October 2010, I penned a popular blog post called "Why Microsoft Access 2007 Sucks." Trust me: I wasn't alone in my consternation.

I saw the Office 2007 debacle play out firsthand in 2011 on a consulting gig at Bassett Medical Center in bucolic Cooperstown, New York — not much more than a solid five-iron away from the Baseball Hall of Fame. Bassett's IT folks had delayed the Office upgrade for years because they didn't want to deal with the inevitable employee blowback. This approach worked for a few years, but the clock had expired. Microsoft had finally pulled the plug on Office 2003 for good. Confused Bassett employees beset the hospital's help desk with calls. Chaos ensued.

Lest you think that Microsoft learned its lesson, the company released Windows 8 on October 26, 2012. The new operating system shipped with one of its iconic features missing. Microsoft had removed the Start button from the taskbar — the very same Start button that had adorned the lower-left corner of PCs since Windows 95. (Cue the Rolling Stones' song "Start Me Up.")

How did Windows users view the omission? Forgive me, but I'll answer my own question with a question. Guess which "new" feature Microsoft added when it released Windows 8.1 nearly one year to the day later?

You may be thinking that upgrading Slack versions is a moot point. After all, can't you decide all by yourself whether you move to a future, possibly less user-friendly version of Slack?

Well, yes and no. On one hand, Slack can't send hired goons to force customers to upgrade. On the other, application upgrades usually contain valuable new features. Arguably more important for the purposes of this discussion, they include security patches and fixes. At some point, refusing to move to the most current version of any application will eventually come back to bite you. Laggards can introduce significant security and compliance risks to their employers.

WARNING

Indefinitely postponing any application or system upgrade — Slack or otherwise — is a dangerous half-measure.

On a different level, it's not as if deploying a Slack competitor, such as Microsoft Teams, inoculates your company against a similar dilemma. In fact, you may face an even more radical UI change than any future Slack one. There are only a few ways for a firm to *completely* control all aspects of an application's UI:

- To independently build the application and host it. Does your employer possess the financial and human resources to pull off these tasks?
- To pay an independent software vendor (ISV) to do the same — often at far greater expense and risk. (Again, IT projects tend to fail.)

To my knowledge, only one company has built anything remotely close to Slack for and by itself. Headquartered in Toronto, Canada, I discovered Klick Health while researching my 2015 book *Message Not Received* (Wiley). Klick has been building its customized, internal operating system — Genome — *for nearly 20 years.*

TIP

Any time that you purchase or rent an application from a software vendor, you incur certain risks. As I'm fond of saying, the fleas come with the dog. Don't let the remote possibility of an unpleasant future upgrade prevent your company and its employees from realizing the essential and manifold benefits that Slack offers.

Acting inappropriately in Slack

We shape our buildings and afterwards our buildings shape us.

— WINSTON CHURCHILL

Slack offers remarkable, even unparalleled, flexibility as a collaboration and communications tool. Add in an increasing panoply of powerful third-party apps, and the world is your oyster. As a result, there's no one "right" Slack recipe.

Paradoxically, though, I can think of plenty of objectively idiotic ways to use Slack. Here's a partial list:

- Creating duplicate and redundant channels for essentially the same content or subject
- Excluding key members from important group discussions
- Relying upon the Free plan when the company clearly needs to upgrade
- Using Slack exclusively to send text messages when it's clearly time for old-fashioned, in-person conversations
- Being too formal or informal in Slack for the organization's culture
- Sending inappropriate content in Slack
- Using Slack to slam and intimidate colleagues

And the preceding list isn't comprehensive — not even close. Think of all the ways that you can offend your peers in a world *without* Slack. (Perish the thought!) As a parallel, the advents of social networks and smartphones certainly introduced new problems, but they also exacerbated existing ones.

Just like with any application, you decide how you want to use it. Churchill's quote applies to Slack as well. If someone is crossing the line in Slack, though, blame the Indian, not the arrow.

Technology and security risks

Again, business and technology challenges go hand in hand. Here are the major technology and security risks of using Slack. Note, however, that I could swap out Slack with just about any contemporary software company in the following section. The same risks apply to just about all of them.

Confronting vendor lock-in

Stick around the enterprise-software world long enough, and you'll eventually encounter the following situation: Your organization finds itself stuck using a particular vendor's wares. *Vendor lock-in* takes place when a company wants to move away from a specific application or system. For many reasons, though, it simply can't.

Compared to traditional software applications, vendor lock-in with Slack is less likely for several reasons. First, Slack adopted *Software as a Service* (SaaS) as its business model. (See Chapter 1.) Customers that pay monthly or annual fees typically aren't as reluctant to change applications because they haven't invested millions of dollars up front. Second, as Chapter 11 covers, Slack allows Owners to easily export public workspace data.

WARNING

There's no guarantee that Slack export files will play nicely with other collaboration tools. Moving from Slack to one of the applications mentioned in Table 14-1 may be much messier and time-consuming than you expect.

At some point, your organization may decide to break up with Slack to see other people. For two reasons, you may find the split difficult. First, employees by and large love using it. Second, the vendor behind your employer's replacement may make it harder to extricate data than Slack ever did.

Slack and system uptime

For customers on the Plus plan and above, Slack guarantees system uptime of 99.99 percent. I did the math. This provision means that, in a given year, Slack will go offline for a maximum of about nine hours.

To be sure, that 99.99 number is impressive, but not unique. That level has been fairly common in the tech world for years. For example, cloud-computing juggernauts Amazon Web Services (AWS), Microsoft Azure, and Google all guarantee similar uptime percentages on their websites.

TECHNICAL STUFF

Fun fact: As I mentioned in Chapter 1, Slack runs on AWS.

For many reasons, and in no particular order, it's in Slack's best interests to minimize its downtime:

- It doesn't want to risk alienating current or potential customers.
- If Slack fails to meet its 99.99 percent goal, then customers can apply for service credits against future use and charges.
- It's a publicly traded company. Enough said.
- System-availability issues have a tendency to pop up and even trend on social networks these days — or, as the kids say, go viral. I have not met Slack CEO Stuart Butterfield yet, but I suspect that he could do without the negative publicity.

TIP

Grizzled tech veterans like myself know that any web-based system or service will experience downtime at some point. It's only a matter of time. The mere fact that system outages make the news today proves how rarely they take place. (Don't believe me? Google "2012 Netflix Christmas outage" or "AWS fat finger 2017.") Put differently, these bumps are the exceptions that prove the rule: Cloud computing is extremely reliable and has been for well over a decade.

BUG BOUNTIES

As many of its contemporaries do, Slack enlists the help of the hacker community through a bug-bounty program. That is, Slack offers financial rewards to technically inclined people who discover system vulnerabilities and report them to the company — as opposed to doing nefarious things with them. The higher the severity, the greater the payoff.

Hackers breach Slack

If you pay attention to the news, you know that sophisticated hackers consistently breach websites, financial institutions, government agencies, and social networks. For example, in 2015 black hats disabled Square's credit-card encryption features. These events are surely unsettling. Might the same thing happen to Slack?

It already has. In March 2015, Slack announced that bad actors had accessed some of its infrastructure, including a database that stored about 1 percent of its user credentials at the time — 65,000 to be exact. In response, Slack acted appropriately: Its management acknowledged the incident, alerted affected users, fixed the issue, and took steps to shore up its systems against future attacks.

So that means that Slack is now *completely* impenetrable, right?

Hardly.

Big companies serve as big targets for hackers. Unfortunately, all companies face this reality in modern life. Let me be clear: There's nothing fundamentally unsafe about using Slack. As I discuss in Chapter 9, the company abides by the industry's best security practices as the nearby sidebar "Bug bounties" illustrates.

REMEMBER

No application or technology is entirely secure — even those currently in use at your company.

Key Slack features suddenly cease to work

Never forget that Slack is software. As such, sometimes features will break. Others work on one device, operating system, or browser but may not perform as expected on another — at least temporarily. (By the way, if you think that privately built and hosted systems never experience technical issues, think again.)

In my three-plus years using Slack, I have found its support to be excellent — and I've dealt with many software vendors in my time. I received timely responses to what were ultimately non-issues. A few times I opened a case when I didn't understand a technical feature. Only once did I report a legitimate bug. My rep was unable to provide a solution, although she mentioned that Slack already knew about this particular "undocumented feature." (Postscript: A Slack update squashed the bug for good a few months later.)

Slack almost always works exactly as advertised for many reasons — one of which is its use of automated testing frameworks (ATFs). (As I know from personal experience, the process of manually running individual tests is inefficient, time-consuming, boring, and prone to user errors.) Collectively, ATFs minimize the chance that new Slack features cause problems. They are also par for the course today in the software world because they work.

Third-party developers want to be confident that their newly released or updated apps perform as intended. To this end, in 2017, Slack launched Steno, a useful command-line utility that lets developers record and replay interactions with the Slack API.

Terminated employees remain active in Slack workspaces

Chapter 9 discusses Slack's optional but useful single sign-on (SSO) option. By way of review, SSO makes Slack more secure. From an employees' point of view, SSO simplifies how they access Slack and many other organizational apps.

Employers that forgo SSO need to ensure that they deactivate terminated employees' Slack accounts. You don't want Disgruntled Debbie wreaking havoc in Slack long after the company has shown her the door.

Listing Slack's Environmental Challenges

To paraphrase the iconic line from John Donne, no company is an island. Just like any other publicly traded company, Slack attempts to appease a wide array of disparate constituents. In no particular order, they include different countries' regulatory bodies, stockholders, its board of directors, its existing management, current customers, prospects, formal partners, the media, external developers, rank-and-file employees, the community at large, and possibly labor unions.

Try making even half of those groups happy on a mildly controversial issue. Good luck with that.

You don't have to hold an M.B.A. or be an expert on corporate governance to understand that plenty of deep conflict exists within these groups, never mind between and among them. Juggling all these relationships and responsibilities is no small chore. For primarily this reason, CEOs make the big bucks.

At some point, Slack management will make decisions that placate one group and anger another. (Amazon, Google, Microsoft, Twitter, Facebook, and just about every company of import does the same on a regular basis. Way it goes . . .) For example, Slack may delay or scuttle the release of a highly anticipated feature in one country because it doesn't want to incur the wrath of privacy-conscious European regulators. In this case, Slack would be making a calculated bet that this gambit is the right one.

Don't let the possibility of future disappointment dissuade your company from adopting Slack. Its benefits are far too important. Beyond that, if you can name a single firm from any industry that faces zero risks and challenges, dinner is on me.

Slack's financial pressures

Slack is no longer the scrappy upstart or the new kid on the block. Slack became a publicly traded company on June 20, 2019 with the apropos stock symbol of $WORK. Three months later, it had shed nearly one-third of its value. As of this writing, Slack has yet to turn a profit — hardly a rare occurrence for new tech companies. Its ambitious competitors are acutely aware of the multibillion-dollar opportunity in collaboration software described in Chapter 1.

The need to reach profitability results in company layoffs and slower product development

Yes, Slack is still in its embryonic stage, but make no mistake: It can't continue to lose money forever. At some point, investors will insist upon profits — and employee layoffs could represent one of its main levers to meet that objective. If a workforce reduction happens, then highly paid developers could see the door. (For a parallel example, see the nearby sidebar "Uber's honeymoon comes to an end.")

Playing this scenario out, Slack would then not innovate as fast and as much as some of its deep-pocketed competitors — particularly Microsoft with its Teams app. Slack would then fall behind.

No, I can't predict the stock market. Warren Buffet doesn't envy my investment track record. Based upon Slack's current financial position and other factors, I just don't foresee widespread layoffs happening anytime soon. Ditto for a slower rate of product development. Still, no one can definitively rule out either scenario out.

UBER'S HONEYMOON COMES TO AN END

After the ride-hailing giant's record $5.24 billion loss in the second quarter of 2019, Uber laid off 435 people. These folks didn't work in cost centers, such as the HR and finance departments. No, employees from Uber's engineering and product departments found themselves newly unemployed. (I have little doubt that most of them quickly found jobs.)

Not long after, California passed a law requiring ride-hailing companies to reclassify their drivers from independent contractors to full-time W-2 employees. This move isn't just about semantics: It represents an existential threat to the business models of Uber, Lyft, and others. Oh, and then there's the money factor: Hundreds of millions of dollars in annual employee-related expenses and taxes. In response, Uber's lawyers claimed that the law didn't apply because it was "a technology platform for several different types of digital marketplaces."

I wrote a book about technology platforms, and Uber's argument is patently ridiculous. Still, the headline here is that, when faced with financial pressures, even tech companies may let some of their most valuable assets go.

A potential Slack acquisition

It's not hard to envision a large tech company gobbling up the company at a premium — especially if Slack's financial pressures on the latter mount. Perhaps Oracle? Indeed, multibillion-dollar acquisitions litter the contemporary tech landscape. Case in point: In June 2019, Salesforce announced that it had acquired data-visualization vendor Tableau for nearly $16 billion. To be sure, it was a massive deal, but only one in a spate of acquisitions of analytics firms.

Slack's management has routinely insisted that it isn't on the block. I have no reason to believe otherwise. Still, as a publicly traded company, a sale isn't completely under its management's control. Again, you need not be Warren Buffett to know that not every firm successfully resists a hostile takeover.

Even in the unlikely event of an acquisition, it's all but assured that Slack's new owner would leave it largely untouched for a long time. Moreover, years down the road, I can't imagine a scenario in which its potential buyer would fail to support legacy Slack versions.

How can I be so sure? Again, I have seen this movie. Current customers would react strongly to massive changes to the application and consider defecting. No company wants to irritate its customers. What's more, there's no shortage of less Slack alternatives. Finally, Microsoft high-profile UI blunders certainly left an impression with tech companies.

WILL SLACK REMAIN INDEPENDENT?

Will a large tech behemoth make Slack a takeover target?

I have no idea. For several reasons, though, one natural potential suitor is Apple. The purveyor of high-end hardware is flush with cash, sporting more than $200 billion on its balance sheet as of January 2020. Beyond its deep pockets, Apple has increasingly diversified its business over the past two years. That is, CEO Tim Cook has embraced services with their recurring revenue streams. Apple will add to its Music, Arcade, and TV+ offerings. Slack's intuitive UI and passionate fans certainly jibe with Apple's brand and simple design aesthetic.

Stiff competition

Slack's unexpected and meteoric success has spawned plenty of imitators. That is, it is no longer the only game in town. Some of Slack's competitors are quite popular and sport zealous customer bases.

Established software vendors and eager startups have recently joined the fray. Some of the big players in the market for enterprise collaboration tools include Google Currents (previously known as Google+ for G Suite), Mattermost, Workplace by Facebook, Ryver, and Discord. Most of these tools resemble Slack's appearance and mimic at least some of its robust functionality.

And the field continues to become more crowded. In late September 2019, the file-sharing company Dropbox launched Spaces. At a high level, the former file-sharing company is attempting to reinvent itself as a full-fledged collaboration tool. Whether Dropbox succeeds is anyone's guess. Still, one thing is certain: It faces an uphill battle, especially against Slack, Microsoft Teams, and other entrenched players.

Microsoft has bundled Teams with other products in its Office suite, including Excel, PowerPoint, and Word. In November of 2019, Microsoft announced that more than 20 million people use Microsoft Teams every day. By this measure, Teams claims more daily active users than Slack does. The tech news site VentureBeat reported in March 2019 that Teams is Microsoft's fastest-growing product ever — high praise indeed for a software company founded 45 years ago.

It's conceivable that a Slack rival builds a better mousetrap — maybe even a considerably better one. In other words, despite its significant lead over its competition, no one can guarantee that Slack will indefinitely remain the industry leader — especially with Microsoft nipping at its heels.

SLACK VERSUS TEAMS

Like many organizations, this book's publisher (Wiley) uses Microsoft Teams internally and with authors. As I wrote *Slack For Dummies*, I frequently interacted with my Wiley folks via Teams to share drafts of chapters, provide updates, and answer questions. Yes, through Teams — and ironically not Slack — I communicated with my editor and the production folks to make this book a reality. (Make no mistake: Publishing a book is a group effort.) To be sure, Slack and Teams are not identical; the latter took a few minutes to figure out, but it wasn't that hard.

For the most part, the conceptual differences between Teams and Slack are minor. The two tools do similar things, but a little differently. To borrow an analogy from Vincent Vega in *Pulp Fiction*, it's akin to a McDonald's Quarter Pounder: in Holland, they call it a Royale with Cheese.

Truth be told, I prefer Slack to Teams for several reasons. First, Slack's graphical user interface (GUI) is far more intuitive. It's not even close. Teams is just a basic GUI slapped on top of Microsoft's legacy SharePoint product. Second, Slack's developer community is far more robust. (See Chapter 10 for more information on this topic.) Brass tacks: Yes, Teams is free for Microsoft Office 365 customers. As always, though, you get what you pay for.

When it comes to internal communication and collaboration, though, any application mentioned in this chapter blows email out of the water.

Ongoing legal and privacy concerns

Say that you live somewhere in the U.S. Consider the following three scenarios:

- You send your husband a text on your company-issued phone while connected to your company's WiFi network.
- You send a colleague an email using your employer's hardware, software, and network.
- You post a message in your company's new favorite tool: Slack.

In which scenario do you have a legal expectation of privacy?

The answer may depend on the country and/or state in which you live and work. Don't be surprised, though, if it is "none of the above." Courts in the United States have routinely held that employees using corporate software applications, such as email, lack any expectation of privacy unless management says otherwise.

As Lisa Guerin, Esq. writes on Nolo.com, "Employers have a lot of leeway to monitor employee emails." (Read her article at `bit.ly/21OfpIu`.)

In the immortal words of The Dude in *The Big Lebowski*, "Well, that's just, like, your opinion, man."

Fair enough, but Guerin is no outlier here. Reporter Sarah Krouse concurs with her assessment. As she explained in a July 2019 piece for *The Wall Street Journal*, many people think that their work messages are private. In point of fact, nothing could be further from the truth. (Read the article at `https://on.wsj.com/2kNjuMP`.)

TIP

Of course, the fact that employers *can* read their employees' private messages doesn't necessarily mean that they will; it's just not illegal for them to do so. If you have questions about your employer's privacy policies, talk to someone in your HR department before sending that risqué photo at work.

Slack, privacy, and ownership of content

If you create a document at work, then who owns it? What if you brainstorm an idea on the clock and email it to your manager?

In each of these scenarios, you don't own the content; your employer does. Again, courts have routinely ruled as much. What about content that you create in Slack, though? Because Slack is new, maybe it's flying under the legal system's radar.

No dice.

In April 2018, Slack announced a major update to its privacy policy. Employers can now read their employees' private DMs without asking or even telling them. (Read an informative article on the announcement at `https://nbcnews.to/2kl00io`.)

REMEMBER

Say that you're looking for a mainstream collaboration tool that lets you do and say whatever you want to whomever you want without any consequences and privacy restrictions. I've got news for you: You are more likely to see a unicorn.

Other interested parties

You may think employees personally and permanently "own" all the content that they post in Slack. After all, they created it, right?

In all but the most extenuating circumstances, they do not. Slack is an organizational communication and collaboration tool. The operative word in the last sentence is *organizational*.

Apart from a nosy Slack Workspace Owner or Admin or your Big Brother boss, courts, lawyers, and regulatory agencies might compel an employer to turn over employee messages in Slack. Specific examples include when

- An attorney or government agency needs to investigate claims of harassment, theft of trade secrets, or corporate espionage.
- A government agency requires financial-services firms to store internal correspondence for a fixed period of time.
- A court decrees that Slack must provide information stemming from a lawsuit or investigation.
- Former employees request copies of the information that their ex-employers keep about them. These scenarios fall under the purview of the European Union's General Data Protection Regulation (GDPR).

Hold your outrage

Wait a second. If you create content in Slack at work, then you don't own it and it's not necessarily private?

You're mad as hell, and you're not going to take it anymore, right? Maybe you're yelling "Attica!" à la Al Pacino in *Dog Day Afternoon.*

Relax. Count to ten.

I haven't reviewed all the dense legal jargon of every software vendor's terms of service in Table 14-1 — also known as *end-user license agreements* (EULAs). (That's my personal definition of hell, but I digress.) What's more, I'm no lawyer.

Still, I'll bet you a steak dinner that these companies' EULAs are very similar, if not nearly identical, to Slack's. Remember that the Slack legal team isn't trying to irk its customers and deter future ones from signing up. Far from it. Its legal department just needs to thread a tiny needle.

Chapter 11 covers Slack's different data-export options. Remember that Slack intentionally complicates organizations' efforts to retrieve and view their employees' private messages. Those who think that Slack makes it easy for colleagues to spy on one another are sorely mistaken.

Say that you're a privacy hawk and want to keep something completely secret. The solution is simple: Don't share it on any work-related tool or network. Your benevolent boss and occasional golf buddy Barry may not want to hand over your DMs to interested parties, but ultimately the decision may not be his to make.

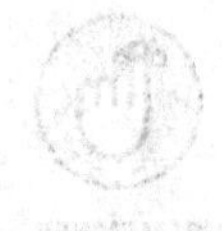

» **Making Slack smarter with AI and machine learning**

» **Integrating Slack more tightly with enterprise systems**

» **Improving search, dashboards, insights, and analytics**

» **Continuing to borrow features from competing apps**

» **Forging new partnerships**

Chapter 15
The Future of Slack: We're Just Getting Started

Consider how websites, smartphones, social networks, voice-recognition tools, and search engines have advanced over the past decade. It's folly to think that Slack will stand still and not improve on a number of different levels. That's doubly true given the formidable competition that Slack faces from both hungry startups and deep-pocketed leviathans, including Microsoft, Google, Dropbox, and Facebook.

No, I don't own a crystal ball. I'm not clairvoyant, I haven't seen Slack's internal product roadmap, and I haven't hacked the emails of Slack's top brass. (I didn't try. Really.) Still, I did a good bit of research for this book. Toss in my knowledge of the tech industry, consulting experience, and my time using Slack. Bottom line: I'm comfortable offering a number of careful predictions about where Slack is going — at least in the near term. Such prognostications are the goal of this chapter.

Increased Use of Automation and Bots

Slack already uses bots to automate reminders and allow users to easily contact technical support. Third parties have already created free or freemium apps that automate tasks such as scheduling meetings, receiving updates to Google Analytics, and many other things. Expect Slack to continue moving in this direction. Deeper automation, more sophisticated bots, and *robotic process automation* are coming.

At a high level, robotic process automation allows computers to learn how to automatically perform tasks. Put differently, a business process can run without input from a human being.

I'll keep my discussion about Slack automation limited, but a few things are going on here. First, Chapter 13 introduces you to Slack's vibrant development community. These folks started out by creating fairly simple automation apps. As of late, though, some have graduated to making more sophisticated ones. Case in point: In 2015, Howdy.ai launched Slack's first commercially available bot app. The teachable app/bot let users automatically check in for meetings via Slack and, later, Microsoft Teams. Yes, Howdy would improve over time. What's more, its Botkit allowed other developers to build their own chat bots.

Second, Amazon, Google, Microsoft, and other tech heavyweights have shrewdly pounced on many chat, automation, and AI startups. For example, in January 2020, Apple bought artificial-intelligence (AI) startup Xnor.ai for a reported $200M. Returning to Howdy, Microsoft monitored its functionality, development, and popularity for about a year. After taking it for a test drive and haggling over numbers, Microsoft acquired Howdy in November 2018.

These highly publicized acquisitions accelerate the efforts of startups and third-party developers to build their own apps. No one wants to be looking for a chair when the music stops playing. The result is a virtuous cycle of rapid innovation — one from which Slack is poised to benefit in a big way.

AI and machine learning make Slack smarter — much, much smarter

If one of Slack's major competitors purchased a hot startup, expect Slack's management to pay close attention. Like any responsible executive team, Slack's C-suite is not just trying to meet current customer needs. Rather, it is trying to anticipate customer needs five or ten years down the road. In other words, expect Slack to follow the advice of hockey legend Wayne Gretzky: It will skate to where the puck is going to be, not where it is now.

TECHNICAL STUFF

Although some people use the terms interchangeably, *machine learning* is in fact a subset of AI.

In this vein, there's arguably no more important opportunity for Slack than increasing the application's core intelligence. Forget returning simple and specific search results when people ask for them. (See Chapter 7 for more on this subject.) I'm talking about accurately and proactively forecasting what users will want and need, perhaps before even they know it themselves.

Did I just blow your mind?

Slack has hired a number of key individuals with deep expertise in technologies such as machine learning to make its flagship product exponentially smarter. Collectively, these folks are working to

- **Enhance Slack's search capabilities:** The goal is to more quickly return search results with dramatically greater accuracy.
- **Prioritize your unread messages:** Which ones are most likely to matter to each user and why?
- **Turn Slack into intimate, always-on personal assistant:** Which messages and content matter most to you right now? After answering that question, Slack would then brief you on what you need to know.

Brass tacks: When it comes to what Slack can do, we are in the first inning. In five years, I have little doubt that Slack's customers will look back at the 2020 version and see it as a necessary precursor for some truly amazing features.

IMPROVED SEARCH

Search for something on Google and Amazon, and you'll likely find what you want — often on the first try. There's a very good reason that these queries are so damn accurate: Their search technology is state-of-the-art. As Eli Finkelshteyn, cofounder of constructor.io, notes, each company eschews dated search methods, most notably TF-IDF. (See Chapter 7 for more on this subject.) In their stead, these behemoths rely upon modern machine-learning search methods that adjust based upon users' behavior and, increasingly, their underlying intent. As a result, their searches improve over time. Make no mistake: This is a really big deal.

To be sure, search in Slack has improved since its inception. Long-time users such as myself can attest to this fact. At the same time, though, search in Slack is not nearly as powerful and accurate as it can be — and, I'd argue, should be. As competitors continue to make inroads with their own integrated collaboration tools, search could differentiate one product from another.

I suspect that the bigwigs inside Slack recognize the current opportunity to expand search. Expect Slack to completely rewrite its internal search engine and adopt a more current and sophisticated approach — one based upon machine learning.

Slack begins to monitor employee morale and diagnose cultural issues

In the near future, I expect Slack to become even more useful on a number of levels. Imagine the following:

- What if Slack could monitor overall employee morale at an organization by analyzing the sentiment in DMs and channels?
- What if Slack could ascertain specific group problems?
- What if Slack could identify problematic employees and nudge HR folks to step in?

Does this seem far-fetched? Don't dismiss these possibilities. They are coming, and possibly soon. Companies are using advanced technologies to understand and mine our conversations. The most powerful of the lot include *natural language processing (NLP)*, *text analysis*, and *sentiment analysis*.

Tighter Integration with Popular Enterprise Systems

Generally speaking, employees responsible for deploying, configuring, customizing, and maintaining enterprise resource planning (ERP) systems are particularly risk averse. The mindset is almost always, "If it ain't broke, don't fix it." Many organizations manage their payroll, HR, and finances in a way that works but isn't exactly efficient. (See Chapter 11 for an all-too-real example.) As such, they typically don't want to rock the boat by altering their business processes and the systems behind them, let alone gumming up the works with new technologies. I have seen this play out more times than I can count.

Slack already plays nicely with mainstream ERP systems, such as Workday, Oracle, Salesforce, and others. (See Chapter 12 for more on this topic.) These bridges to ERP systems are merely starting points. The cat is out of the bag.

Expect more conservative firms and departments to eventually become more comfortable with the idea behind Slack. Second, more Slack case studies will surface. As a result, an increasing number of organizations will cross the chasm, to paraphrase Geoffrey Moore's bestselling book (HarperCollins). In response, the types, depths, and number of Slack apps and integrations will expand in new, fascinating ways far beyond what Chapter 10 covers.

Better Dashboards and Analytics

Slack members generate a great deal of data — all of which the application captures unless someone actively deletes it. Thank the vast decline in data storage costs over the last four decades. Against this backdrop, Workspace Owners and Admins can access an unprecedented trove of valuable data on what takes place at their firms.

Yes, Slack provides the ability to view, analyze, export, and import that data — subject to some reasonable restrictions that Chapter 9 covers. Still, these abilities represent just the tip of the iceberg. With respect to data analysis, I humbly offer two Slack data-related predictions:

- **Slack launches much better tools to analyze and understand basic member data:** Slack will soon provide better interactive tools that allow nontechnical employees to engage in true data discovery. That is, Slack will go beyond just supplying static line and bar graphs on member activity. In the future, users with sufficient rights will be able to use Slack to effectively ask and answer increasingly complex questions.

» **Slack begins providing automatic, data-based suggestions:** Slack will at some point begin providing non-obvious recommendations and insights akin to what many new best-of-breed business-intelligence (BI) applications now do. Slack will ultimately take a page from Tableau and Microsoft PowerBI. It will nudge managers to look at activity in certain channels, departments, or even among a group of employees.

A More Powerful Slack Work Graph

In April 2017, Slack cofounder and CEO Stewart Butterfield spoke at the Forbes CIO Summit in Half Moon Bay, California. In his talk, he gave a scintillating hint of his company's ambitious plans for the future. Yes, automation of simple, mind-numbing tasks can save Slack users valuable time. That's a given. Slack's stockpile of member data, though, will ultimately bring a heck of a lot more to the party.

Why can't Slack do for work what Facebook has done for social networks? (At least the positive aspects, anyway.) Why can't Slack build a work graph? What if Slack can be, to quote the Slack CEO himself, your "always-on chief of staff?"

Impossible, right?

Wrong. Slack's rock-star developers have been building a work graph for at least the last several years. The potential applications and value of such a tool are vast — so much so that it could prove to be a point of significant differentiation against Microsoft Teams and other competitors. What's more, even if a competitor developed a comparable set of features, Slack's superior trove of data would give it a substantial edge.

As Slack grows, it continues to aggregate unprecedented and highly detailed information about how, when, where, and with whom we work. (Make no mistake: Even anonymized data can be valuable.) To paraphrase Ron Burgundy, this functionality is kind of a big deal with a number of different implications.

Sure, employees' formal titles matter. You'll never hear me say otherwise. Still, official roles in and of themselves often don't indicate employees' true influence within a department or an organization, never mind within an ad hoc group of peers. With so much data at its disposal, I can see Slack launching a specific network-based feature that would allow its customers to garner a far deeper understanding of their organizations' essential *informal* networks. That tool would offer invaluable recommendations on all sorts of culture-, personnel-, project- and organization-related matters. It would indeed serve as an always-on chief of staff. The sky is the limit.

THE POWER OF FACEBOOK'S SOCIAL GRAPH

You may have heard of Facebook's vaunted social graph. At a high level, it is a visual representation of all the connections on its 2.5 billion member social network. Thanks to its massive trove of user data, Facebook's social graph can represent in vast detail how people, groups, and interests are related. The company can then detect largely hidden and unexpected links, patterns, and preferences. It can make eerily relevant product, friend, person, and movie recommendations. (For more on this topic, see the discussion on network effects in Chapter 13.)

What would such a tool look like? Apart from Facebook's social graph, check out Santiago Ortiz's creation based upon Twitter data:

Visit `bit.ly/sick-viz` to watch an amazing video of this visualization.

HUDSUCKER INDUSTRIES

Amy is a business analyst at Hudsucker Industries. She earns $40,000 per year. Amy's relatively junior title, modest salary, and lack of experience belie her true value to the firm: Her colleagues routinely ask her questions and involve her in key projects — ones that go far beyond her job description. To everyone's credit, Hudsucker uses Slack throughout the organization.

Yes, Amy is far closer to the bottom of the Hud org chart than the top, but she's no ordinary cog in the machine; she is a key node in Hudsucker's informal work network. Her manager Norville often praises her work.

Out of the blue, a rival company offers Amy a position with more responsibility, a better title, and a 20 percent raise. Rather than just dismiss it out of hand, Norville uses Slack to view Amy's real role, import, and value in the Hudsucker network. The latter number is more like $60,000. Norville immediately sees and understands the extent to which employees rely upon her. It doesn't take him long to realize her outsize value to the company and matches Amy's offer.

No, Norville may ultimately not be able to retain Amy's services, but at least he can make that decision with all of the relevant information. I would bet that well under 1 percent of all HR departments do anything remotely close to this type of analysis when deciding if and how to counter the potential defection of a key employee.

In a way, whether Slack users could view the work graph themselves is a moot point. The more important question is "What could organizations do with this superpower?" I can think of dozens of ways. Consider the simple, movie-inspired example in the following sidebar.

Imagine a tool that answers questions that people didn't even think to ask. What if Slack alerts you to a key fact or trend that you hadn't recognized?

Continued Borrowing of Popular Features from Other Apps

In today's world of consumer technology, companies repeatedly "borrow" features from competing products. And by borrow, I mean steal.

Exhibit A: Remember when Snap (the company behind Snapchat) launched *stories*? The feature let users post photo and video slideshows that disappeared after 24 hours. Snap users loved it. Not long after, Facebook aped the feature and didn't even bother renaming it. Staying with the world's largest social network, Zuck liked Twitter hashtags so much that his company implemented them in June 2013. I could keep going. Trust me, though: The same type of appropriation is pervasive in the world of enterprise software as well.

As it should, Slack will continue to closely eye competitors, such as Microsoft, Google, Dropbox, and others. Absent any type of patent, it's a safe bet that Slack will implement reasonable facsimiles of their new functionality if and when they become popular. For example, if Microsoft Teams launches an exciting new feature, Slack will strongly consider adopting it — and vice versa, as the sidebar "Microsoft embraces privates channels," illustrates.

MICROSOFT EMBRACES PRIVATE CHANNELS

In August 2019, I started working on the manuscript of this book in earnest. At that time, Microsoft Teams lacked the equivalent of Slack's private channels. In a move that should surprise exactly no one, Microsoft added that popular feature in late 2019. Ultimately, the arms race in collaboration software benefits users like you and me.

TIP

Consider the following: Your organization uses Slack. One day you hear about how Microsoft Teams introduced a new must-have feature. My advice is not to immediately abandon Slack. Odds are that Slack is well aware of Teams' shiny new toy. Next, it's a good bet that third-party developers are already working on a similar tchotchke. Failing that, you can always build your own private Slack apps. (See Chapter 10 for more on this topic.)

Slack management will continue to monitor which apps are gaining the most traction for ideas about how to improve its core product. To be fair, as I write in my 2011 book *The Age of the Platform* (Motion Publishing), this practice is common in the tech world. Amazon, Apple, Facebook, Google, and other companies have engaged in this practice for a long time. If an app is particularly useful, these companies will often build similar functionality for themselves.

BOOMERANG: ANOTHER CAUTIONARY TALE

Even before I had heard of the term, I long practiced *Inbox Zero*: I simply don't let emails endlessly accumulate in my inbox. (My use of Slack has been invaluable in this regard.)

In my pre-Slack days, sometimes I'd receive an email, but I didn't want to deal with it for a few days or even a week. Creating a separate reminder for an email was too much of a hassle. What to do?

Enter Boomerang, a premium Gmail extension that let me designate when a message would automatically return to my inbox. I loved it. I happily paid the $50 annual fee.

A few years ago, though, I let my subscription lapse. Google had added a new snooze button to each message. Snoozing essentially served the same purpose as Boomerang. I would bet my house that each of the following happened at the company:

- Management was irate when it learned of this new Gmail feature.
- After calming down, its top brass thought long and hard about whether to continue developing Gmail extensions in the future.
- Its sales took a major hit, if not plummeted.

Slack knows that it has to tread lightly with its developer community. If it consistently apes the features of its most popular third-party apps, then it runs the risk of cannibalizing the market for those developers' apps. Taking this scenario to its logical conclusion, app developers would then become justifiably upset. In turn, they would take their considerable talents to other platforms, including Slack's competition. (If you think that this scenario never plays out, then think again. Twitter is an excellent case study in how *not* to treat its ecosystem of developers.)

MY WISH LIST FOR NEW SLACK FEATURES

As much as I love Slack, I can think of many ways that it can improve.

Templates

For starters, I'd be shocked if Slack doesn't introduce workspace templates at some point. For example, I am a college professor who uses Slack each semester. As such, I create fresh workspaces for each of my four classes. As a result, I have to add the same 25 or so channels and install my favorite apps. (Yes, I run a Python script that largely automates the channel-creation process, but many professors lack the technical knowledge to do this. Relatively few want to get their hands this dirty.) Next, I have to manually configure many workspace and channel settings. Finally, I have to install apps and do a few other things that Chapter 8 covers.

Yes, it is a tad time-consuming. To me, though, Slack's juice is well worth its squeeze.

If I could wave my magic wand, Slack would let me create and deploy workspace templates. Mine would consist of predefined channels, settings, and apps. I could then apply that template to new workspaces. (Note that I don't need to port over the *content* of each public channel. I would just bring over each empty channel along with its purpose and individual settings.)

I'd like to tweak the template as needed. I suspect that other professors would as well. What's more, I can easily imagine plenty of people in different industries and companies that would benefit from that feature.

A Slack penalty box

Although Slack lets you mute conversations with individual users and groups, I want to do more. That is, I want to be able to permanently or temporarily block users who go over the line in Slack. (A few times, I have wanted to silence especially aggressive, entitled, and oblivious students. (Calm blue oceans, I know.) Admins' only recourse is to remove people from individual channels and, in the extreme, workspaces. Putting them in some sort of Slack penalty box would serve as an invaluable middle ground. To be fair, though, I can see a downside to my proposal. To the extent that the organization uses Slack as it should, that purgatory status may encumber those very knuckleheads from doing their jobs.

Channel-specific statuses

Moving on, this next wish may be overkill, but many users would benefit from being able to set channel-specific statuses. In my case, at the end of a semester, I'm usually heads-down grading. As such, I want to set an off-the-grid status to my 150 or so students. At the same time, I want my grading assistants to know that they can communicate with me via the private `#grading` channel. Yes, I can send them a group DM, but they may not have to read it.

New tools for adding members to channels

Next, I'd like the ability to add users to multiple channels via a grid as opposed to one at a time. Yes, Slack lets Workspace Owners and Admins set default channels not only globally, but by user group. Still, creating user groups for the sole purpose of adding them to different default channels seems suboptimal.

A few of my tech-savvy colleagues want to easily add members to channels in bulk. Rather than just pasting in email addresses from an Excel worksheet, for example, it would be useful to add users by values defined in custom fields. For instance, with a few clicks, an Owner or Admin could add all employees with the job title of "manager" listed in their Slack profile to a `#manager` channel. I can think of oodles of other applications of such a feature.

User-specific notifications

I'd like Slack to let me set alerts for when specific users become active. This idea is not revolutionary. Skype has shipped with this feature for as long as I can remember.

Slack's API allows for this type of event-based alert. At present, though, the company has not built this into its core product. Perhaps it's holding off because of legitimate privacy concerns.

Screen sharing with Slack support

Slack support is awesome. When diagnosing technical issues, though, I'd like to be able to share my screen with Slack's support reps. I would hazard to guess Slack deliberately imposes this restriction because of concerns over network security. As anyone who has ever shared a screen with vendor support folks knows, though, screen sharing often expedites error resolution.

Key Acquisitions and Partnerships

Slack's talented developers make the product better every day. Sometimes improvements take the form of newly released features. Other times they enhance Slack's performance by tweaking its underlying code or thwarting potential cyber malefactors. (See Chapter 1 for some interesting stats on the smart cookies who proudly call themselves Slack employees.) That's not to say, though, that all future Slack enhancements will stem exclusively from the efforts of its own coders.

Slack isn't exactly cash poor. At of the end of October 2019, it sported nearly $800 million in cash and short-term investments according to its publicly filed balance sheet. (View the company's financial statements at `yhoo.it/3eIj3ua`.) Even if you halved that number, I wouldn't be too worried about the company's financial solvency. (See Chapter 1 for more on this subject.) Over the next several years, I expect Slack to follow a similar playbook to other nascent tech companies and focus on growth over profits.

I don't possess any foreknowledge here, but I suspect that the company will make several targeted acquisitions to meet its growth imperative and offer exciting new features. The usual suspects include startups that have developed interesting, complementary, or tangential technologies. (See the Microsoft Howdy example in the "Increased Use of Automation and Bots" section earlier in this chapter for a parallel.) These deals are often as much about the startup's engineering talent as the product itself. Business folks today refer to these moves as *acquihires*.

Perhaps these acquisitions would result in Slack morphing into a software bundle akin to Microsoft Office — the most popular productivity suite in the world. New York University Stern School of Business marketing professor and serial entrepreneur Scott Galloway certainly thinks so. His history of making accurate tech-related predictions is downright uncanny. Case in point: He predicted that Amazon would gobble up Whole Foods and The We Company would nix its planned 2019 IPO. Galloway believes that Slack may ultimately need to be more than a cool collaboration tool to remain viable in the long term.

Beyond strategic acquisitions, I'd be astonished if Slack doesn't cement new agreements with software vendors beyond the ones described in Chapter 12.

Don't think for one minute that Slack's management is hurting for ideas. As I hope this book illustrates, Slack is an incredibly powerful, useful, flexible, and affordable tool. And here's the best part: Slack is just getting started.

6

The Part of Tens

IN THIS PART

Discover valuable tips to get the most out of Slack

Understand the most common misconceptions that people hold about Slack

Extend your knowledge even more with useful Slack resources

IN THIS CHAPTER

» Getting started quickly with Slack

» Making Slack stick in your organization

» Maximizing the short- and long-term benefits of using Slack

Chapter 16
Ten Great Slack Tips

In this chapter, I offer ten quick tips on getting started with Slack, getting it to stick in your organization, and maximizing its benefits. No, it's not a comprehensive list of what to do and not to do, but I have condensed much of my advice into a top-ten list.

Respond Promptly to New Users' Requests, Questions, and Feedback

Fundamentally, Slack isn't an individual tool; *it's a group one.* Many employees will have legitimate questions about using Slack at your organization. Others will make suggestions about how to use Slack differently or better.

Don't ignore or, even worse, reflexively dismiss those ideas. Respond promptly to feedback. You'll get more mileage out of Slack when more people at your firm use it.

Regularly View Slack Analytics

Chapter 11 shows you how to use Slack to view the most and least active workspace members and channels. With respect to users, you can easily see the number of messages that each user has sent as well as their days active. (Doing this does not violate members' privacy; you cannot read their messages.)

For example, YYZ rolled out Slack a year ago. During that time, Geddy has posted a mere four messages in it. What's more, Slack calculates that he's been active for only one day. Equipped with this information and depending on his particular job, I wouldn't show him the door. It's best to tap him on the shoulder and talk to him about why he's invisible on Slack. Maybe something deeper is going on at work or at home.

Tread Lightly with New Hires

New employees may become overwhelmed trying to consume a year's worth of material in a bunch of channels. It's preposterous to expect them to digest thousands of messages, documents, decisions, and content in public channels within a week of starting their jobs.

TIP

New employees would do well to go to each channel's highlights to see the most important discussions.

Establish Slack as the Default Medium for Internal Communication

To get the most bang for your buck, the default communication method for an organization, group, or department should be Slack. Sure, Slack may not make sense when sending messages to employees at different companies. In the Slack universe, the idea that, within the walls of any given company, Fernando from finance routinely emails Max in marketing is absurd.

Emphasize Slack's Carrots More Than Its Sticks

"Want to" almost always beats "have to." If employees give you static about using Slack, emphasize the former first and the latter only if necessary.

Keep an Eye Out for New Slack Apps

New productivity apps arrive all the time. Every month or so, poke around the Slack App Directory to see what new tchotchkes developers have released. You can bet that some new ones will be worth exploring.

Tell Overly Exuberant Slack Members to Tone It Down

No one likes a loud mouth or a troll. Many people have worked with knuckleheads who always had to have the last word on an email chain. I'm sure that you've met a few people who couldn't leave well enough alone.

A negative or aggressive employee may act as a bully on Slack and discourage others from using it. This behavior can be particularly troublesome when new employees join and organizations begin using Slack.

WARNING

If someone goes over the line, it's imperative to nip the trend in the bud. Respectful disagreement with someone in a public manner is fine, but outright hostility and inappropriate comments are unacceptable in any environment — and that includes a Slack workspace.

Publicize Your Status and Availability

Just like with email out-of-the-office (OOO) message, you don't want people expecting to hear from you in Slack when you're snorkeling in Belize or just off the grid. Let other users know your status availability.

Try Before You Buy

Sadly, some of your colleagues may not share your enthusiasm for Slack. After all, no technology sports a 100-percent adoption rate, and Slack is no exception. Before waiting for management to sign up for a company-wide premium plan, consider taking Slack's Free version for a spin with your group, team, or department.

Know When to Turn Slack Off

You may find it peculiar to end this list of Slack tips by telling you to stop using it. You read right, though. You don't want to be a slave to any tool — and that certainly includes Slack. I'm taking the lead here from Slack's succinct and refreshing company mantra: Work hard and go home.

IN THIS CHAPTER

- Debunking conceptual and communication myths about Slack
- Clarifying organizational myths about Slack

Chapter 17

Ten or So Common Slack Myths

In this chapter, I dispel some of the most common myths about what Slack can do and how to make it stick inside your organization.

Slack Is Just Email 2.0

If you read any part of this book, you know that Slack isn't just email under a different name. Next time you hear someone spew that nonsense, please recommend this book. I'll send some good vibes your way.

Yes, Slack and email overlap to a degree. Make no mistake, though: Slack obliterates email. Slack is a far more powerful internal collaboration tool. What's more, it allows employees to do fundamentally different things than Outlook, Gmail, or whatever email client employees use at your organization.

Brass tacks: To paraphrase the erudite comedian Gary Gulman, claiming that Slack only allows you to send messages is tantamount to calling a Lexus convertible a cup holder. You are severely underestimating what it can do.

TIP

This myth has nothing to do with general intelligence. One of my colleagues is an award-winning professor and smart cookie who knows most contemporary programming languages cold. Yet, when the two of us talk about Slack, he routinely (and incorrectly) dismisses it as *email 2.0*.

Slack Decimates the Need for Email

Slack and email will continue to coexist, although the former means far less of the latter. Many organizations have successfully adopted Slack and reaped its benefits. Employees there rarely, if ever, use email as their primary medium for internal communications. The same does not hold true externally. This distinction is big.

To put it kindly, many outsider emails aren't exactly welcome. You may remember Bill Gates's 2004 claim that spam will go the way of the Dodo by 2006. More than 15 years later, it's fair to call reports of spam's death grossly exaggerated.

Yes, spam is annoying but hardly the only problem associated with external emails. Hackers use increasingly sophisticated and blended techniques on unsuspecting users. Email is one of their most potent arrows in their quivers.

So why do all but a few oddball organizations print email addresses on all employee business cards? Because of the same network effects discussed in Chapter 13. Even for organizations that use Slack, email remains a critical method of reaching outsiders. It is really the only universal medium for work communication. Restricting the ability to potential clients, partners, and employees to contact your organization causes more problems than it solves.

All Organizations Configure Slack in a Uniform Way

Negative. There is no one right way to configure Slack. One of Slack's primary strengths is its flexibility. A small group of friends will configure and use it differently than a 20,000-employee organization. Ditto for colleges and hospitals.

TIP

Early on, experiment with different configurations of private, public, and multi-workspace channels. Play with shared channels as well. See whether user groups make sense for you. Slack settings that work well for one person, department, group, or organization may just not fit with another.

Slack Obviates the Need for In-Person Communication

No, no, a thousand times no: Slack doesn't replace in-person communication. Misunderstandings take place that often call for people to actually speak to each other — ideally in the same physical room. Just because your organization uses Slack doesn't change this fact. It never will.

Slack Solves Every Conceivable Business-Communication Problem

Ha! Slack is no panacea for poor individual and group communication. As I write in *Message Not Received* (Wiley), no tool is. Colleagues sometimes misinterpret messages or motives. (See the previous myth for one way to minimize these misunderstandings.)

Slack Is Too Expensive for Our Company

Hogwash. Any organization can begin using Slack for free at any time. Should it decide to move to a paid plan, Slack requires minimal up-front cost.

Rather than thinking exclusively about out-of-pocket expenditures, though, contemplate the implicit costs of overwhelmed and miserable employees. How much does your organization spend backfilling roles? How many times has an employee spent dozens of hours creating a document from scratch when a facsimile already existed but he didn't know about it?

If you don't consider these legitimate business costs, then you're just plain wrong. Used properly, Slack more than pays for itself.

TIP

If employees aren't ready for the changes that Slack requires, then your organization probably shouldn't buy it.

Our Company Has Built a Tool That's Just as Good as Slack

No, it hasn't built a tool as good as Slack.

Remember that Slack's *raison d'être* is to create a best-of-breed communication and collaboration tool. That's it. The company isn't working on anything else. Why else would the company's name be the same as its flagship product?

Consider a parallel between two popular business applications: Microsoft Excel and Tableau. Most people are familiar with the former. With respect to data visualization, Excel lets you create decent charts and graphs. As I've learned in the nearly 30 years that I've used it, Excel can do so much more.

On the other hand, Tableau focuses on data-visualization software. As such, it can do things that Microsoft's ubiquitous spreadsheet program simply cannot.

Now it's time to return to the world of collaboration software. The notion that a few or a few dozen capable IT employees at your firm can cobble together a tool that does just about everything that Slack does is utter nonsense. Nah, make that laughable. Even if that were true, consider the fact that Slack's own developers are constantly working on ways to extend its core offering. I mean right now.

Even if your internal tool segments messages via channels and offers video-calling screen-sharing, there's no way that you're building a work graph. (See Chapter 15 for more on this topic.)

Let me drive one final nail in the coffin of your "we built a comparable tool to Slack" argument: At this very moment, third-party developers are making Slack better by creating useful apps and extensions. Are they doing that with your firm's homegrown tool?

Our Employees Don't Need Slack

You can't see it right now, but I'm furrowing my brow. I hate to break it to you, but people who think that their colleagues effectively "collaborate" exclusively via email are misguided or downright delusional. They just don't know the meaning of the word.

I'd bet heavily against employees forgoing Slack simply because management has not sanctioned it. This goes double if you work for a large firm.

Consider the following example:

Elliot is the Chief Information Officer at Grey Matter, a fictitious 20,000-employee chemical company. (Yes, I'm dropping another *Breaking Bad* reference.) For the last six months, his team has been evaluating whether to dip its toe in the Slack pond. Elliot believes that no one is currently using Slack at Grey Matter.

For several reasons, Elliot is probably wrong.

Odds are that more than a few Grey Matter employees are currently using Slack — or something like it. After all, it's 2020, not 1998. For a long time, we've been living in an era of *bring your own device* (BYOD) and *Shadow IT*. As for the latter, it simply means that untold numbers of workers routinely use personal software applications while on the clock.

Coupled with Slack's Free plan, employees don't need the permission of their corporate overlords to use it or many other unsanctioned tools, for that matter. Blocking network access to Slack doesn't help because employees can simply use their personal data plans from carriers such as AT&T, Verizon, and T-Mobile. Confiscating employee phones will cause far more problems than it solves.

Our Company Uses Slack and Nothing Else for Collaboration

It isn't necessarily true that your organization is using only Slack to collaborate. In the BYOD era, I'm more than a little skeptical, but don't believe me:

In God we trust, all others must bring data.

— W. EDWARDS DEMING

Mio is a startup that sells software that stitches together different communication and IM tools. In June 2019, the company published the results of a survey of 200 IT decision-makers at organizations ranging in size from hundreds to hundreds of thousands of employees. (Read it yourself at `bit.ly/sl-mil`.) Its findings shouldn't shock anyone familiar with the complicated world of enterprise IT.

More than 90 percent of businesses polled reported using at least two messaging apps. Some use even more. In two-thirds of the organizations surveyed, employees used both Slack and Microsoft Teams. A common example: Company X uses Microsoft Teams but acquires Company Y — a smaller one that relies upon Slack.

You Can't Misuse Slack

Slack is just like any tool: You can use it constructively and destructively. As you know from reading this book, millions of people use Slack every day in many creative ways. For starters, Slack lets them improve the way that they work and communicate with their colleagues. It'd be silly to claim, though, that you can't use Slack in an inimical manner.

First, on an individual level, distraction while on the clock is a serious problem. In 2018, online learning platform Udemy conducted a study and found that nearly 75 percent of workers reported feeling distracted on the job. One in six claimed to feel *constantly* distracted. (Read the study at `http://bit.ly/udemy-dis`.)

A great deal of scientific research proves that constantly interrupting our work by multi-tasking makes us far *less* productive. Keep this fact in mind as you use Slack. Brass tacks: It's counterproductive to *constantly* check it throughout the day.

Second, Slack can pose an organizational problem. In researching this book, I discovered a few companies that have used Slack as a weapon. In her piece "Emotional Baggage," Zoe Schiffer of The Verge tells the fascinating tale of how senior management at luggage startup Away used Slack to intimidate its own employees. (Read it at `bit.ly/bad-slack`.) That's right: Employees at Away actually *feared* using Slack because it represented an extension of a toxic culture.

The lesson here is that it's essential to draw boundaries at work — even if your employer uses Slack.

» **Attending official and unofficial Slack events**

Chapter 18

The Top Ten or So Slack Resources

Ideally, you find *Slack For Dummies* helpful and are discovering a lot about the application. I hope that your head is spinning — in a good way. That is, you are thinking about innovative and interesting ways to use Slack at work and maybe even at home.

If so, then I have achieved my main objective with this book. I am sending good thoughts your way.

Still, no book of any reasonable length can possibly cover every feature of a robust and dynamic collaboration and communication tool — especially one that consistently releases exciting new features. To that end, this chapter offers resources for you to expand your knowledge of Slack, stay abreast of new developments, and deal with issues as they arise. It's folly to think that they never will.

I have divided the resources in this chapter into natural buckets: slack online support, other online resources, and in-person resources.

Slack Online Support

From time to time, you'll need to open a case with Slack support. Perhaps you're experiencing a technical issue, or you're not sure about how something works. I haven't met too many people who enjoy the back-and-forth with tech support folks, but at least Slack makes getting help easy.

Contacting Slack

```
https://my.slack.com/help/requests/new
```

Start here if you want to report a bug or chat with a support rep.

Browsing the Slack support site

```
https://get.slack.help/hc/en-us
```

This site is clean, intelligently laid out, and remarkably robust.

Opening cases or making suggestions within the Slack app

Start a message to anyone or in any channel by typing the following in Slack

```
/feedback
```

This invokes special functionality designed to quickly contact Slack support *within the app*. For example, while researching this book, I discovered an issue with sorting workspaces on my iPad. I submitted a support request to Slack support and included a video showing the error in action.

TIP

You can submit feedback to Slack by sending a message in a channel or group message as well. Your message goes to Slack, not the others in your channel or user group. Just remember to start your message with `/feedback`.

REMEMBER

Only members of the Enterprise Grid plan qualify for real-time phone support.

Finding Slack tips

```
https://slack.com/slack-tips
```

In this book, I have provided some of my favorite Slack tips. By no means, though, did I include a comprehensive list. Plus, my favorites may not completely overlap with yours. If you'd like to learn some more ways to save time and do cool things, head to this website.

Submitting Slack feature requests

You can certainly use `/feedback` to report bugs or ask questions as I have many times. This feedback ultimately makes Slack better. Perhaps the defining characteristic of contemporary technology platforms is that the number of people using it improves its utility for everyone else. Slack is no exception here.

REMEMBER

If you thought of a way to make Slack better in some way, then the company wants to hear it. Simply start a message with `/feedback` and detail your suggestion.

Other Online Resources

Unfortunately, if you're looking for additional help with Slack, you're confined to the limited resources in the previous section. It turns out that there's really nowhere else to go.

I'm kidding.

I'm just getting started.

Official resources

Each of the resources in this section falls under Slack's corporate umbrella. That is, Slack sanctions them.

- **Slack App Directory** (`https://slack.com/apps`): To be sure, Slack's native functionality by itself helps employees be more productive. Power users understand, though, that you can do a great deal more by taking advantage of others' complementary creations. The Slack App Directory lists the most popular and newest ways to extend Slack.
- **Slack webinars** (`https://slack.com/events/webinars`): Slack offers many live and on-demand webinars. Each delves deeper into topics such as security, shared channels, and administrative controls.

» **Slack's official blog** (`https://slackhq.com`)**:** *Several People Are Typing* is the name of Slack's blog. Here you can read articles, case studies, product announcements, and other goodies designed to help you get the most out of Slack.

» **Slack's official YouTube channel** (`bit.ly/sl-yt-3`): Slack publishes a slew of informative videos, customer-success stories, and conference highlights here.

» **Slack on Twitter** (`https://twitter.com/slackhq`)**:** Follow this account for product announcements, blog posts, and general news.

» **Slack Status on Twitter** (`https://twitter.com/slackstatus`)**:** Slack uses this account to apprise customers of network outages and other technical problems. Note that tweeting at *`@slackstatus`* does not open a support ticket. Use one of the other methods mentioned in this chapter.

» **Slack Champion Network** (`bit.ly/schamps-2`): This Slack workspace allows you to connect and interact with other Slack "champions." The focus here is on large organizations. Here you can discover best practices for launching and driving the adoption of Slack. I'm a member myself, and I really enjoy the interactions with all sorts of smart cookies.

» **Slack Platform Community** (`https://slackcommunity.com`)**:** If you like to build things and are interested in the future of work, then this is the place for you. Chapters are popping up all over the world.

Unofficial resources

The following independent resources lie outside Slack's corporate umbrella. This doesn't mean that they're not helpful. Far from it. It just means that they operate independent of Slack.

» **LinkedIn groups:** From Slack fans to bot developers, there's no shortage of specific groups devoted to using and improving it. Start at `bit.ly/sl-lig` but feel free to poke around. More spring up all the time.

» **Online training:** You can find a variety of Slack-specific courses on sites such as Udemy, Lynda, Coursera, and YouTube.

» **Reddit for Slack** (`https://www.reddit.com/r/Slack`): If you're looking for vibrant discussions, you could do much worse than going to r/Slack.

WARNING

Note that redditors can be a feisty bunch if you violate Reddit norms. Make sure to read the rules for each subreddit.

» **Existing Slack workspaces** (bit.ly/cool-slack-workspc): Depending on your interests, you can find many existing private social networks and collaboration spaces. You may want to connect and interact with fellow marketers, HR folks, entrepreneurs, musicians, fathers, or even *Star Wars* geeks.

Developer resources

Remember from the Introduction that *Slack For Dummies* is not geared toward developers. Throughout this book, I've kept that promise. Still, here are a few technical resources if you'd like to learn more about building your own Slack apps:

» Head over to https://api.slack.com to find oodles of developer documentation looking to build your own apps. You'll find information on all of Slack's APIs.

» Slack runs a rich blog specifically for developers. Find technical announcements, tips, discussions, and more at bit.ly/slack-devblog.

» Slack's newly enhanced Block Kit allows developers to expedite the process of creating powerful Slack apps. It offers app templates, a message builder, and other neat features. For more information, see bit.ly/block-kit.

In-Person Resources

The world of work has significantly changed since the *Mad Men* days. People perform plenty of tasks electronically that used to require a physical presence. Although you can learn just about anything you like over the Internet these days, sometimes you benefit going old school. Yes, I'm talking about attending an event in a physical building. Thankfully, Slack and its community offer plenty of options here.

Conferences

Slack holds its own conferences and makes its presence felt at industry-wide galas. The following sections offer information on how to meet Slack folks in person.

Frontiers

```
https://www.slackfrontiers.com
```

Slack's annual Frontiers conferences feature oodles of breakout sessions from everyday users and proper developers. You can learn how employees in different industries are using Slack. If you're technically inclined, you can learn how to build your own Slack apps.

Spec

```
https://slack.com/spec
```

Spec brings together Slack's global community of developers, partners, and customers. The conference features sessions tailored for people who

- » Already create custom integrations for their organizations.
- » Want to know more about extending what Slack can do.
- » Build their entire businesses on Slack.

I attended the Spec 2019 Conference in San Francisco in October 2019. It's no understatement to say loads of smart cookies are developing cool apps for Slack. The energy was downright infectious.

Miscellaneous tech conferences

Like many software vendors, Slack often rents booths at popular tech events. These conferences typically take place in large cities, such as Tokyo and London.

TIP

Visit https://slack.com/events for a current list of the company's official events.

Meetups

```
https://www.meetup.com/topics/slack
```

Over the years, millions of people have attended Meetups all across the globe. *Meetups* are informal get-togethers for just about every conceivable interest: politics, tennis, book clubs, hiking — you name it. (Note that the We Company acquired Meetup in 2017.)

If you want to meet fellow Slack users in Paris, New York, or wherever, then this is just the ticket for you.

In-person training

```
bit.ly/sl-trn
```

If you want to hold your own Slack training event, have at it. The preceding link provides information if you want to develop a private training class for your company.

Creating your own custom course and training materials is easier said than done. You may lack the time or, even after reading *Slack For Dummies*, sufficient expertise with Slack. If you want an experienced trainer to help employees at your organization get the most out of Slack, I'm game. I started training employees in corporate settings in 1997, fresh out of grad school. If you want to reach me at, hit me up `bit.ly/phil-slack`. (OK. That's enough with the shameless plugs).

Index

Symbols and Numerics

(hashtag), 72
@ symbol, 88, 93, 97
1Password, 195, 198
37signals, 299

A

Accenture, 266
access logs, 197–198, 253–254
acquihires, 326
acquisitions, 309–310, 326
Adobe Connect, 225
adoption strategies, 277–295
  becoming go-to person at work, 294
  bottom-up method, 279
  deployment, 281–293
  middle-out method, 280–281
  network effects, 278–279
  top-down method, 280
ADP (Automatic Data Processing, Inc.), 267
Age of the Platform, The (Simon), 323
Agile software-development, 282
AI (artificial intelligence), 316–317
AIM, 288
Airbnb, 12
Amazon, 278–279, 316, 323, 326
Amazon Alexa, 224
Amazon Web Services (AWS), 12, 299, 305
analytics, 246–252
  active members, 247
  channel-specific analytics, 250–251
  dashboard for, 246–247
  file sharing, 248–250
  future of, 319–320
  member analytics, 252
  messages sent, 248–250
  public and private messages, 247–248
  regularly reviewing, 330
Anderson, Chris, 217
Andreessen, Marc, 299
app activity logs, 240–241
App Manager role, 233–234
Apple, 279, 310, 316, 323
apps. *See* third-party apps
Arizona State University (ASU), 14, 286, 294
artificial intelligence (AI), 316–317
Asana, 299
Atlassian, 299
Aurea, 299
Authy, 198
automated testing frameworks (ATFs), 307
Automatic Data Processing, Inc. (ADP), 267
Automattic, 284
availability. *See* status and availability
Away, 338
AWS (Amazon Web Services), 12, 299, 305

B

Bankrate, 16
Basecamp, 299
Bassett Medical Center, 302
Benioff, Marc, 273
Berkun, Scott, 284
Bezos, Jeff, 278
Bianchini, Gina, 299
Blackboard, 14
Block Kit, 343
blog posts, 224
Bloom, Nicholas, 21
bookmarking messages, 102–103, 155–156
Boolean operators, 164, 171
Boomerang, 323
Boston Consulting Group, 21

bots
defined, 272
increased use of, 316
not including in search, 167–168
Oracle Intelligent Bot Platform, 272
SAP Concur Expense bot, 273
Slackbot, 41–42, 183–184, 230
Box, 221
bring your own device (BYOD) era, 298, 337
Brunner, Heather, 219
bug-bounty program, 306
Bureau of Labor Statistics, 290
Butterfield, Stewart, 10–11, 152, 320
BYOD (bring your own device) era, 298, 337

C

calls, 143–149
to channels, 147–148
group calls, 146–147
missed, 127
person-to-person calls, 144–146
emojis, 145
ending, 145
initiating, 144
inviting people to, 144
keyboard shortcuts, 146
muting, 144
naming calls, 144
screen sharing, 145–146
settings, 144–145
text, 145
video, 144–146
recording, 149
rules for, 225
security and encryption, 148–149
video calls, 144–146, 225
Campfire, 259
capital expenses (CAPEX), 34
Carnegie Mellon, 302
Ceridian, 267
Chambers, John, 193–209
@channel callout, 129–130
channels, 24, 59–89. *See also* file sharing
adding members to
automatically, 85
in bulk, 84–85
individually, 83–84
analytics, 247–251
archiving (retiring), 78
benefits of, 61
bookmarking messages, 102–103, 155
changing topic of, 77
channel overload, 74
clearly defined discussions, 24
code and text snippets, 105–108
communicating via, 87–89
alerting everyone, 88
deleting messages, 89
etiquette, 89
mentioning people with @ symbol, 88
posting messages, 88
setting topics, 89
communication structure, 60
contained discussions, 24
default, 85, 178
defined, 60
deleting, 80
descriptions, 71
changing, 77
defining purpose of channels, 73–74
direct messages vs., 61
group actions, 77–81
hashtag (#), 72
including in sidebar sections, 190
jumping to specific dates, 82
leaving, 82–83
message retention and deletion, 205–206
moving to different workspaces, 81
multi-workspace channels, 65–67
converting channels to, 81
identifying, 67, 72
leaving/rejoining, 67
purpose of, 65–66
setting up, 65–66

muting, 83
naming, 69–72
notifications, 83, 123–126
accessing settings, 125–126
missed calls, 127
muting, 123–124
resetting to default, 125
setting, 124–126
when members join/leave, 128
overview, 24
pinning items to, 76, 80–81
posting permissions, 78
posts (rich-text messages), 105–106
prefixes, 74
adding, 74–75
number of, 74
predefined, 74
private channels, 63, 65
analytics, 247–249
characteristics of, 63
converting group messages to private, 108–109
creating, 70–72
examples of, 63
identifying, 65, 72
leaving/rejoining, 65, 82–83
privacy issues, 203
sharing messages from, 115–116
providing for alignment, 24
public channels, 62–64
analytics, 247–249
characteristics of, 62
creating, 70–72
default, 85
examples of, 63–64
exploring, 85–86
#general channel, 61
identifying, 65, 72
inviting people to, 71–72
joining, 87
leaving/rejoining, 65
making private, 79
notifications when members join/leave, 128
previewing, 86–87
proper use of, 64
#random channel, 61
referencing in DMs, 95–96
sharing files via links, 112–113
sharing messages from, 114
renaming, 80
reserved words, 69
restoring archived, 79
restricting searches to, 167–168
saving messages, 102–103
scripting to create multiple, 72
scripting to delete multiple, 80
shared, 67–69
converting channels to, 81
examples of, 68
identifying, 72
number of organizations, 67
sharing, 67–69
sharing files, 76
sorting in sidebar sections, 191–192
starring, 81–82
threads, 109–111
viewing information about, 75–76
ChatWork, 259
ciphertext, 202
Cisco WebEx, 225
cloud computing, 12, 33, 208–209, 262, 267, 273, 300, 305
CNN, 12
code and text snippets, 105–108
creating, 106–107
downloading, 108
formatting, 97
programming language, 107
sharing, 107
title, 107
viewing raw version, 108
collaboration software
adding Slack to long list of collaboration tools, 298–299
Slack as only collaboration tool, 337–338
spending on, 10
command-line interface, 152–153

commercial-off-the-shelf (COTS) model, 266
content ownership, 312
Cook, Tim, 310
Costello, Eric, 11
Covey, Steven, 73
Cox, Lauren, 283
Crunchbase, 272
customer relationship management (CRM), 265–268, 271–274
customer support, 226, 265, 274

D

dark mode, 180
Dashlane, 195
data migration, 254–262
  avoiding mistakes, 261–262
  consolidating workspaces, 259–261
  exporting data, 254–258
    Corporate Export, 257–258
    Discovery API export mechanism, 258
    Standard Export, 255–257
  importing data, 258–259
data residency, 209
data-related features, 245–262
  access logs, 253–254
  analytics, 246–252
    active members, 247
    channel-specific analytics, 250–251
    dashboard for, 246–247
    file sharing, 248–250
    member analytics, 252
    messages sent, 248–250
    public and private messages, 247–248
  data migration, 254–262
    avoiding mistakes, 261–262
    consolidating workspaces, 259–261
    exporting data, 254–258
    importing data, 258–259
  mass updates to user data, 262
deployment risks, 297–313
  business risks, 298–304
    adding Slack to long list of collaboration tools, 298–299
    adjusting to user interface updates, 301, 303
    believing Slack can do everything, 300–301
    improper use of Slack, 303–304
    trying to placate all employees, 301
  environmental risks, 307–313
    acquisition possibilities, 309–310
    competition, 310
    need for profitability, 308
    privacy issues, 311–313
  tech and security risks, 304–307
    hackers, 306
    system uptime, 305
    technical issues, 306–307
    terminated employees remaining active, 307
    vendor lock-in, 304–305
deployment strategies, 281–293
  handling difficult employees, 286–293
    accountability, 293
    appealing to vanity, 290, 292–293
    carrots vs. sticks, 288–293
    email-to-Slack apps, 287
    real-world career changes, 290
    similarity to older tools, 287–288
    stubborn people who won't embrace Slack, 288
    "what's in it for me?" question, 289–290
  organizational-level strategies, 281–286
    communicating victories, 283
    fear of missing out (FOMO), 286
    knowing the organization, 281
    learning curve, 285–286
    new hires that use Slack, 283
    small victories, 282
    using Slack during hiring process, 284–285
  Waterfall method, 281
Detail view, 42–43, 75–76
digital nomads, 20
direct messages (DMs), 91–118. *See also* file sharing
  analytics, 247–249
  attaching files, 92, 97
  bookmarking, 102–103, 155
  channels vs., 61
  code and text snippets, 105–108

conversations, 61, 95, 206–207
deleting, 101
editing, 100
emojis, 93, 97
finding people, 92, 98–100
determining if someone uses Slack, 99–100
by device type, 99
by role, 99
formatting, 96–97
bold text, 96–97
bulleted lists, 97
code blocks, 97
code style, 97
hyperlink text, 97
italicized text, 96–97
with keyboard shortcuts, 97
new paragraphs, 97
numbered lists, 97
quotes, 97
strikethrough text, 96–97
with WYSIWYG editor, 96–97
group messages
converting to private channels, 108–109
sending, 93–94
marking as read/unread, 95
mentioning people with @ symbol, 93, 97
message retention and deletion, 206–207
notifications, 127
muting, 101–102
overriding notification pausing, 93
reminders, 101–102, 127–128
overriding Do Not Disturb mode, 135–136
pinning to conversations, 103–104
posts (rich-text messages), 105–106
referencing public channels in, 95–96
saving, 102–103
saving drafts, 94
sending, 92–93
sending to yourself, 94
sharing, 115–116
threads, 109–111
Discord, 285, 310
Do Not Disturb (DND) mode, 133–136
adjusting, 135
deactivating, 135
defined, 134
manually activating, 135
overriding for urgent messages, 135–136
setting default hours, 134, 178
Donut, 26, 226–227
Doodle Bot, 221–222
downgrading Slack plans, 32
Dropbox, 220–221, 310, 322
Duffield, Dave, 273
Duo Mobile app, 198

E

ECMAScript 6 (ES6), 12
EKM (Enterprise Key Management), 201–202
email, 15–16, 300–301
amount of time spent on, 15
apps for integrating, 287
attributes of, compared to Slack, 116
checking on vacation, 16
confirming sign-ins via, 195–196
dealing with imperfections of, 17
difficulty finding information, 17–18
forwarding to Slack, 117
number received daily, 24
receiving about recent Slack activity, 138–139
Slack channels as alternative to, 24, 59
third-party apps and integration, 225
utility of, 17
emojis
customized, 182–183
restricting searches to messages containing, 167–168, 170
end-user license agreements (EULAs), 313
Enterprise Grid plan, 31
creating workspaces, 37
custom user profile fields, 186
data residency, 209
exporting data, 258
finding people, 100

Enterprise Grid plan *(continued)*
message retention and deletion, 205
moving channels to different workspaces, 81
organization entity, 35
phone support, 340
roles, 51
searching, 162
security, 201–202
status and availability, 132
third-party app management and permission, 231
workspace customization options, 179
Enterprise Key Management (EKM), 201–202
enterprise resource planning (ERP), 264, 267–268, 271–272, 274, 319
enterprise search technology (enterprise search and retrieval [ESR]), 18
enterprise system integration, 263–274
apps vs., 269
back-office systems, 264–265
creating, 270–274
automation options, 271–272
Infor, 272
Microsoft Dynamics, 272
Oracle, 272
Salesforce, 273
SAP, 273
Workday, 273
Zendesk, 273–274
current, 268–269
employee expense submittals, 269
employee time-off requests, 268–269
front-office systems, 265
future of, 319
Slack as complement to, but not replacement for, 265–268
ERP (enterprise resource planning), 264, 267–268, 271–272, 274, 319
ES6 (ECMAScript 6), 12
ETL (extracting, transforming, and loading data), 260
EULAs (end-user license agreements), 313
@everyone callout, 129–130
exporting data, 254–258
Corporate Export, 257–258
Discovery API export mechanism, 258
Standard Export, 255–257
extracting, transforming, and loading data (ETL), 260

F

Facebook, 26, 202, 224, 279, 320–321, 322–323
field service management (FSM), 265
file sharing, 111–115
analytics, 248–250
creating links to files, 112–114
revoking links, 113–114
sharing with people outside workplace, 113
sharing with public channel members, 112–113
from existing messages, 115
filtering files, 112
finding files, 112
sorting files, 112
third-party apps for, 220–221
uploading files, 112
Finkelshteyn, Eli, 318
Fitbit, 224
Flickr, 11
Flowdock, 259
Franchetti, Stephen, 282
Free plan
analytics, 246, 250–252
exporting data, 255
number of apps, 176, 231
number of messages, 163
number of workspaces, 74
overview, 30
searching, 162
workflows, 244
Free: The Future of a Radical Price (Anderson), 217
freemium business model, 33, 216–217
Frontiers conferences, 344
FSM (field service management), 265
Fuze, 225
fuzzy search, 169–170

G

Galloway, Scott, 326
Gallup State of the American Workplace report, 18
Gates, Bill, 333–334
General Data Protection Regulation (GDPR), 208
Genome, 303
Gilder, George, 278
Giphy, 226, 229
Glitch game, 11
Gmail, 225, 323
Gmail chat, 288
Google, 12, 26, 279, 305, 316, 322–323
Google Analytics, 316
Google Authenticator, 198
Google Calendar, 221
Google Currents, 310
Google Drive, 220, 227
Google Forms, 14
Grand View Research, 18
Guerin, Lisa, 312
Guest role, 46–47
  adding guests, 52–53
  changing access, 48
  deactivating, 53
  Multi-Channel Guests, 47
  permissions, 50
  Single-Channel Guests, 47
Guru, 226

H

Harvard Business School, 21
hashtag (#), 72
Healthcare.gov, 266
help resources, 339–345
  blog, 342
  Champion Network, 342
  conferences, 343–344
  contacting Slack, 340
  developer resources, 343
  existing workspaces, 343
  feature requests, 341
  feedback, 340
  LinkedIn groups, 342
  Meetups, 344–345
  online training, 342
  in-person training, 345
  Platform Community, 342
  Reddit, 342
  Slack App Directory, 341
  support site, 340
  tips, 340–341
  Twitter, 342
  webinars, 341
  YouTube channel, 342
Henderson, Cal, 11–12
@here callout, 130
Hershey, 266
Hertz, 266
Hipchat, 299
Hoffman, Chris, 137
Howdy.ai, 316

I

IBM, 11, 31
ICQ, 288
IDC (International Data Corporation), 10, 160
If This Then That (IFTTT) applets, 224–225
importing data, 258–259
Infor, 266, 272
instant-message (IM) applications, 287–288
institutional/organizational knowledge
  building repository, 19
  finding, 17–18, 25
International Data Corporation (IDC), 10, 160
Internet Relay Chat (IRC), 288

J

Java, 12
JavaScript, 12
JavaScript Object Notation (JSON) files, 256–257
Jive, 299
JUST Capital, 22

K

keyboard shortcuts
for formatting, 97
full list of, 151, 153
Office shortcuts, 151
for person-to-person calls, 146
viewing preferences, 151
Klick Health, 303
Korn Ferry, 1
Kotlin, 12
Kronos, 267
Krouse, Sarah, 312
Kruze Consulting, 12

L

languages, 55
LastPass, 195
Lawson Software, 287
LinkedIn, 12, 16, 279, 342
links
file sharing via, 112–114
revoking links, 113–114
sharing with people outside workplace, 113
sharing with public channel members, 112–113
hyperlink text, 97
restricting searches to messages containing, 168, 170
Ludicorp, 11
Lyft, 309

M

machine learning, 317–318
Mattermost, 310
MCGs (Multi-Channel Guests), 47
McKinsey, 15, 160
Meetups, 344–345
Member role, 46
access logs, 253–254
analytics, 252
deactivating, 49
deleting, 50
permissions, 46
reactivating, 50
mentions
notifications, 120–121, 124–125
using @ symbol, 88, 93, 97
viewing, 139–140
Merck, 266
Message Not Received (Simon), 17, 303
Message Scheduler, 222
Metcalfe, Robert, 278
Metcalfe's Law, 278
Microsoft, 279, 316, 322
Microsoft Azure, 305
Microsoft Dynamics, 272
Microsoft Excel, 300–302, 336
Microsoft Office, 302, 310, 326
Microsoft OneDrive, 221
Microsoft Outlook, 225
Microsoft Teams, 259, 303, 310–311, 316, 322–323, 338
Mio, 337
Mode Media, 299
Moore, Geoffrey, 319
Mourachov, Serguei, 11
Multi-Channel Guests (MCGs), 47

N

natural language processing (NLP), 318
NetSuite, 272
network effects, 278–279
New York Times, 31, 137
New York University Stern School of Business, 326
New Zealand Work Research Institute, 20
Ning, 299
NLP (natural language processing), 318
Nolo.com, 312
notifications, 83, 119–130
accessing settings, 122
alerting everyone, 129–130
alerting specific people, 130
badges, 120–121
channel-specific, 123–128

accessing settings, 125–126
muting, 123–124
resetting to default, 125
setting, 124–126
when members join/leave, 128
consolidating through Slack, 25–26
default, 120, 125
device-specific, 137–138
conflicts between, 137–138
mobile devices, 137
direct messages, 127
Do Not Disturb mode, 137
missed calls, 127
muting, 101–102, 123
overriding notification pausing, 93
reminders, 101–102, 127–128
threads, 128–129
viewing mentions and reactions, 139–140

O

Objective C, 12
1Password, 195, 198
operating expenses (OPEX), 34
Oracle, 266, 272, 319
Org Admin role, 51
app management and permissions, 231
custom user profile fields, 186
external channel sharing, 69
privacy and accessing content, 203
retention and deletion, 205
Org Owner role, 51
app management and permissions, 231
custom user profile fields, 186
exporting data, 258
external channel sharing, 69
privacy and accessing content, 203
retention and deletion, 205
organization entity, 51
Ortiz, Santiago, 321
outsourcing, 267
Overwhelmed (Schulte), 18
Owl Labs, 20–21

P

Pareto, Vilfredo, 150
Pareto laws, 150
passwords
password managers, 195
resetting, 40, 195–196
all workspace passwords, 201
while signed in, 197
while signed out, 196
Paychex, 267
PeopleSoft, 272, 273
PEOs (professional employer organizations), 267
pinning
direct messages to conversations, 103–104
items to channels, 76, 80–81
restricting searches to pinned content, 170
Pinterest, 12
Plus plan
data residency, 209
exporting data, 257
fees, 31, 47, 129
overview, 31
posting permissions, 78
searching, 129
system uptime, 305
Pocket, 221
polling apps, 24–25, 219–220
Polly, 220
Simple Poll, 218–219
Slido, 219
Survey Monkey, 220
Polly, 220
posts (rich-text messages), 105–106
Primary Org Owner role, 51
Primary Owner role, 44–45
defined, 44
designating, 45
determining, 45
permissions, 45
transferring, 50

privacy, 202, 311–313
  end-to-end encryption, 202–203
  regulatory environment, 208–209
  retention and deletion, 204–207
    files, 178, 207
    messages, 178, 204–207
private channels, 63, 65
  analytics, 247–249
  characteristics of, 63
  converting group messages to private, 108–109
  creating, 70–72
  examples of, 63
  identifying, 65, 72
  leaving/rejoining, 65, 82–83
  privacy issues, 203
  sharing messages from, 115–116
productivity and project-management apps, 223–224
  Todoist, 223
  Trello, 223
  Workast, 224
professional employer organizations (PEOs), 267
public channels, 62–64
  analytics, 247–249
  characteristics of, 62
  creating, 70–72
  default, 85
  examples of, 63–64
  exploring, 85–86
  #general channel, 61
  identifying, 65, 72
  inviting people to, 71–72
  joining, 87
  leaving/rejoining, 65
  making private, 79
  notifications when members join/leave, 128
  previewing, 86–87
  proper use of, 64
  #random channel, 61
  referencing in DMs, 95–96
  sharing files via links, 112–113
  sharing messages from, 114
Python, 72, 80

R

React, 12
reactions
  adding, 93
  searching by, 167–168
  viewing, 139–140
recommendation engines, 320
recruitment, 22–23
Reddit, 342
reminders
  message-specific, 101–102, 127–128
  setting, 153–154
  shortcuts for, 154
remote work
  facilitating, 20
  job satisfaction, 20–21
  rising amount of, 20
rich-text messages (posts), 105–106
robotic process automation, 316
roles, 44–55
  adding guests, 52–53
  administrative, 44–46
    Primary Owner, 44–45, 50
    Workspace Admins, 46
    Workspace Owners, 45
  changing, 47–48
  configuring profiles and account settings, 54–55
  deactivating guest accounts, 53
  deactivating member accounts, 49
  deleting member accounts, 50
  in Enterprise Grid plan, 51
    Org Admins, 51
    Org Owners, 51
    Primary Org Owner, 51
  non-administrative, 46–49
    Guests, 46–48, 52–53
    Members, 46, 49
  reactivating member accounts, 50
  restricting who can invite others, 53–54
  workspace-specific nature of, 46
Rosenstein, Justin, 299
Ryver, 310

S

SaaS (software-as-a-service) model, 33–34, 267, 273, 304
sales force automation (SFA), 265
Salesforce, 34, 267, 273, 319
SAP, 266, 273
SCGs (Single-Channel Guests), 47
scheduling apps, 221–222
  Doodle Bot, 221–222
  Google Calendar, 221
  Message Scheduler, 222
  YouCanBook.me, 222
Schiffer, Zoe, 338
Schulte, Brigid, 18
scientific sorting, 191
SCIM (System for Cross-domain Identity Management) API, 262
SCM (supply chain management), 265
screen sharing, 149–150
  during calls, 145–146
  drawing, 150
  presenting, 149–150
Scrum, 282
searching, 159–172
  difficulty finding information, 17–18, 160–161
  for files, 112
  keyword searches, 161–172
    Boolean operators, 164, 171
    dynamic nature of results, 172
    fuzzy search, 169–170
    multiple keywords, 166–167
    negative keywords, 165–166, 171
    not including apps and bots in, 167–168
    order of results, 162
    patience, 172
    quotes, 166–167, 171
    restricting to messages containing emojis, 167–168, 170
    restricting to messages containing links, 168, 170
    restricting to pinned content, 170
    restricting to specific date ranges, 164, 171
    restricting to starred content, 170
    restricting to workplace members, 163–164
    restricting to your channels, 167–168
    tabbed results, 162–163, 171
    technology behind, 163
    wildcards, 168–169, 171
  machine learning, 318
  for people, 92, 98–100
  for workspaces, 38–39
security, 193–202
  confirming sign-ins via email, 195–196
  Enterprise Key Management, 201–202
  hackers, 306
  resetting passwords, 195–196
    all workspace passwords, 201
    while signed in, 197
    while signed out, 196
  session duration, 200
  single sign-on, 201
  terminated employees remaining active, 307
  two-factor authentication, 198–200
  viewing access logs, 197–198
  vulnerability, 194
  whitelisting workspaces, 201
sentiment analysis, 318
session duration, 200
Several People Are Typing blog, 342
SFA (sales force automation), 265
Shadow IT, 337
SharePoint, 299, 310
shelfware, 34
sidebar
  collapsing sections, 190
  creating new sections, 189–190
  customizing, 181–182
  moving sections, 191
  overview, 42–43
  renaming sections, 191
  sorting channels, 191
Siebel, 272
Simple Poll, 218–219
single sign-on (SSO), 201, 307
Single-Channel Guests (SCGs), 47
Skype, 288
Skype for Business, 225

Slack, 1, 326. *See also* adoption strategies; channels; deployment risks; deployment strategies; roles; workspaces
attributes of, compared to email, 116
author's introduction to, 14
backronym, 9
benefits to employees, 23–27
acclimation process, 26–27
consolidating notifications, 25–26
controlling email, 24–25
finding information, 25
getting to know colleagues, 26
stress reduction, 26
benefits to employers, 18–23
attracting and retaining talent, 22–23
employee corporate communication and collaboration, 20
employee productivity, 20
job satisfaction, 20–21
knowledge repository, 19
lessening turnover, 23
organizational transparency, 22
remote work, 20
training, 22–23
communicating outside of, 118
customizing, 173–188
dark mode, 180
emojis, 182–183
levels of, 174
personal preferences, 179–185
sidebar, 181–182
Slackbot, 183–184
status and availability, 184–185
themes, 180–181
user profiles, 185–188
workspaces, 175–179
documenting sensitive matters in, 118
employees of, 12
forwarding email to, 117
frameworks and programming languages, 12
future of, 315–326
acquisitions and partnerships, 326
analytics, 319–320
borrowing features from other apps, 322–324
cultural issue diagnosis, 318
dashboards, 319
employee morale monitoring, 318
enterprise system integration, 319
machine learning, 317–318
robotic process automation, 316
wish list for new features, 324–325
work graphs, 320–322
help resources, 339–345
history of, 10–11
launch of, 11
making mistakes with, 118
myths about, 333–338
our internal tool is just as good, 336
Slack as only collaboration tool, 337–338
Slack can't be misused, 338
Slack eliminates need for email, 334
Slack eliminates need for in-person communication, 335
Slack is email 2.0, 333–334
Slack is too expensive, 335
Slack solves all problems, 335
universal configuration, 334
we don't need Slack, 336–337
online tour of, 10
plans, 29–34
cost structure, 33–34
downgrading, 32
Enterprise Grid plan, 31
Free plan, 30
Plus plan, 31
Standard plan, 30
upgrading, 31–32
predecessors of, 298–299
problems tackled by, 14–18
constant connectivity, 16
difficulty finding information, 17–18, 160–161
time spent on email, 15–16
trapped institutional knowledge, 16
realistic expectations for, 6
receiving emails about recent Slack activity, 138–139
skeptics of, 19

statistics regarding, 11–12
tips for, 329–332
carrots vs. sticks, 330
expectations for new hires, 330
new productivity apps, 330
responding promptly to new users, 329
reviewing analytics, 330
Slack as default medium, 330
status and availability, 331
testing before buying, 332
troublesome behavior, 331
turning Slack off, 332
user interface, 42–44, 181–182, 301, 303
users of
ages of users, 13
case studies about, 13
companies and industries, 12–13
families, 13
informal groups, 13
number of daily actions, 11
number of users, 11
Slack App Directory, 215–218, 341
browsing, 228
Get Essential Apps button, 217
installing apps from, 228–229
searching, 230
Slack desktop app, 40–41
Slack Fund, 214
Slack mobile apps, 41
Slack Technologies, Inc., 11
Slackbot
custom, word-based responses, 183–184
purpose of, 41–42
third-party app trial periods, 230
#slack-on-slack internal channel, 282
Slido, 219
Snap, 322
software-as-a-service (SaaS) model, 33–34, 267, 273, 304
Spaces, 310
Spec developer conference, 214, 344
Square, 306
SSO (single sign-on), 201, 307
St. Louis Federal Reserve Bank, 20
Standard plan, 30
Stanford University, 20
starring
channels, 81–82
files, 155
messages, 155
restricting searches to starred content, 170
viewing saved items, 155–156
status and availability, 130–137, 331
clearing status, 133
customized, 184–185
customized statuses, 131
default expiration times, 184–185
default statuses, 131
Do Not Disturb mode, 133–136
adjusting, 135
deactivating, 135
defined, 134
manually activating, 135
overriding for urgent messages, 135–136
setting default hours, 134
editing status, 133
in Enterprise Grid plan, 132
indicating you are active, 133
indicating you are away, 133
red stop sign, 132
setting status, 131
setting via command-line interface, 152
viewing others' status, 132
Steno, 307
supply chain management (SCM), 265
Survey Monkey, 220
Swift, 12
synchronization, 41
System for Cross-domain Identity Management (SCIM) API, 262
system uptime, 305

T

Tableau, 309, 336
Target, 12, 31

team collaborative applications market, 10
teams. *See* workspaces
term frequency-inverse document frequency (TF-IDF), 163, 318
text analysis, 318
themes, 180–181
third-party apps, 213–244, 333
activity logs, 240–241
APIs, 214
approving, 231–232
disabling and re-enabling, 239–240
Donut, 226–227
email, 225–226
email integration, 287
employee time-off requests, 269
enforcing policy regarding, 236–238
enterprise system integrations vs., 269
experimenting with, 230–231
file- and content-sharing, 220–221
Dropbox, 220–221
Google Drive, 220
Pocket, 221
Giphy, 226
Guru, 226
IFTTT Slack applets, 224–225
password managers, 195
permissions for, 176
polling, 219–220
Polly, 220
Simple Poll, 218–219
Slido, 219
Survey Monkey, 220
preserved, 239–240
pricing, 216–217
productivity and project-management, 223–224
Todoist, 223
Trello, 223
Workast, 224
public vs. private apps, 215–216
removing, 238–239
restricting, 232–233
restricting who can install, 233–236
scheduling, 221–222
Doodle Bot, 221–222
Google Calendar, 221
Message Scheduler, 222
YouCanBook.me, 222
scopes, 235
Slack App Directory, 217–218
browsing, 228
installing apps from, 228–229
searching, 230
two-factor authentication, 176
vetting and guidelines for, 216
video-calling, 225
viewing and managing, 236
viewing list of restricted, 233
Workflow Builder, 241–244
Zendesk, 226
37signals, 299
threads, 109–111
conversations vs., 109
creating, 110
defined, 109
examples of, 109–110
following, 110
notifications, 128–129
unfollowing, 111
viewing, 110
time zones, 55
Time-Based, One-Time Password (TOTP) apps, 198
Time.bot, 269
Tiny Speck, 11
Todoist, 223
training
employees through Slack, 23
employees to use Slack, 22
transparency, 22
Tray.io, 271–273
Trello, 223
Twitter, 224, 279, 322, 342

U

Uber, 279, 309
Udemy, 338

University of Melbourne, 20
upgrading Slack plans, 31–32
U.S. Census Bureau, 13
U.S. State Department, 13
user groups, 156–158
  adding members to, 158
  creating, 157–158
  example of, 156
  handles, 157
  naming, 157
  purpose of, 156
user interface, 42–44
  changing views, 44
  contextual nature of, 44
  Detail view, 42–43
  history, 42
  main navigation bar, 42–43
  main workspace menu, 42–43
  navigation bar, 42
  page, 42–43
  page header, 42–43
  sidebar, 42–43, 181–182
  updates to, 301, 303
  workspace switcher, 42–43
user profiles, 185–188
  configuring, 54–56
  custom fields
    adding, 185–187
    legal issues, 188
    populating, 187–188
  finding and displaying, 98–100
  mass updates to user data, 262
  profile photos, 55
@usergroup callout, 130

V

vacation connectivity, 16
Vacation Tracker, 269
vendor lock-in, 304–305
Verge, The, 338
video-calling apps, 225

W

W. P. Carey School of Business, 14
Wall Street Journal, 312
Waterfall method, 281
We Company, The, 326, 344
web browsers, signing in to Slack via, 40
whiteboard notes, 224
whitelisting workspaces, 201
Whole Foods, 326
Why New Systems Fail (Simon), 266
WordPress, 14
work graphs, 320–322
Workast, 224
Workato, 271–273
Workday, 267, 273, 319
Workflow Builder, 241–244, 274
  creating shortcuts to workflows, 243
  creating workflows, 241–242
  warnings regarding, 244
Workplace by Facebook, 310
Workspace Admin role
  access logs, 253–254
  adding custom user profile fields, 185
  app activity logs, 240
  changing guest access, 48
  channel dedicated to new channel requests, 74
  converting public channels to private, 79
  deleting others' messages, 89, 101
  disabling file sharing, 114
  exporting data, 255–258
  limiting which members can invite, 53
  limiting which members can post, 63, 78
  mass updates to user data, 262
  new member notifications, 129
  overview, 46
  permissions, 46
  privacy and accessing content, 203–204
  third-party app permissions, 227, 229, 234
  user groups, 156
  viewing access logs, 198
  workspace customizations, 175–179

Workspace Owner role
access logs, 253–254
adding custom user profile fields, 185
app activity logs, 240
changing guest access, 48
channel dedicated to new channel requests, 74
converting public channels to private, 79
deleting others' messages, 89, 101
disabling file sharing, 114
exporting data, 255–258
limiting which members can invite, 53
limiting which members can post, 63, 78
mass updates to user data, 262
new member notifications, 129
overview, 45
permissions, 45
privacy and accessing content, 203–204
third-party app permissions, 227, 229, 234
transferring primary workspace ownership, 50
two-factor authentication, 200
user groups, 156
viewing access logs, 198
who should have, 45
workspace customizations, 175–179
workspaces, 35–40
call rules, 178
consolidating, 259–261
creating, 36–37
customizing, 175–179
default channels, 178
default Do Not Disturb hours, 178
defined, 10, 35
deleting, 178
expanding existing, 51–54
inviting people to, 52–53
restricting who can invite, 53–54, 177
file retention and deletion, 178, 207
finding, 38–39
icon, changing, 175
inviting people to, 36
language of, 178
managing from mobile devices, 174
membership options, 176–177
message retention and deletion, 178, 205, 207
name of
changing, 175
creating, 37
overview, 35
personal email display, 178
personal name display, 178
signing in to existing, 37–41
requesting and receiving email invitations, 37–38, 176–177
through open signup process, 38–39, 176–177
via desktop app, 40–41
via mobile apps, 41
via web browser, 40
third-party app permissions, 176
town hall meeting analogy, 35
URL of
changing, 37, 175
hiding, 178
whitelisting, 201
WP Engine, 219, 283

X

Xnor.ai, 316

Y

Yahoo! 11
Yahoo! Messenger, 288
Yammer, 299
Year without Pants, The (Berkun), 284
YouCanBook.me (YCBM), 222
YouTube, 342

Z

Zapier, 222, 271–272
Zappos, 12, 26
Zendesk, 226, 273–274
Zoom, 149, 225
Zuckerberg, Mark, 202

About the Author

Phil Simon is a frequent keynote speaker, Slack trainer, and recognized technology authority. He is the award-winning author of eight previous books on management, technology, and analytics. *Slack For Dummies* arrives in August of 2020. His contributions have appeared on The Harvard Business Review, *The New York Times*, CNBC, and many other prominent media outlets. Since 2016, he has taught information systems, data visualization, analytics, and business intelligence at Arizona State University's W. P. Carey School of Business.

You can find out more about his work at `www.philsimon.com`.

Dedication

"Suddenly, you were gone

From all the lives you left your mark upon"

—Rush, "Afterimage"

In memory of Neil Peart (September 12, 1952 – January 7, 2020)

Author's Acknowledgments

Kudos to Team Wiley: Steve Hayes, Kelly Ewing, and Prescott Perez-Fox.

My agent, Matt Wagner, helped seal the deal on book number nine. *Slack For Dummies* wouldn't exist without his help.

A tip of the hat to the people who keep me grounded and listen to my rants: Alan Simon, Luke Fletcher, Terri Griffith, Mike Frutiger, Dalton Cervo, Rob Hornyak, David Sandberg, Bob Schoenfeld, Chris Olsen, Greg Dawson, Steve Katz, Michael Viola, Joe Mirza, Chris McGee, Scott Berkun, Alan Berkson, Andrew Botwin, John Andrewski, Jennifer Zito, Mark Frank, Thor Sandell, Rob Metting, Jason Horowitz, Mark Cenicola, Karen Gill, Brian and Heather Morgan, Steve Putnam, Josh Bernoff, Hina Arora, and Marc Paolella.

A tip of the hat to all Slack employees and developers. Collectively, you are changing how people work and allowing us to reclaim a sense of balance. You have made a real difference in many lives. Specific props to Sam McEvans, Cal Henderson, and Andy Pflaum.

For decades of incredible music, a tip of the hat to the members of Rush (Geddy, Alex, and Neil) and Marillion (h, Steve, Ian, Mark, and Pete). Your songs and message continue to inspire millions of discerning fans. I am proud to call myself one of them.

Vince Gilligan, Peter Gould, Bryan Cranston, Aaron Paul, Dean Norris, Anna Gunn, Bob Odenkirk, Betsy Brandt, Jonathan Banks, Giancarlo Esposito, RJ Mitte, Michael Mando, Rhea Seehorn, Michael McKean, and the rest of the *Breaking Bad* and *Better Call Saul* teams have made me want to do great work.

Finally, to my parents. I'm not here without you.

Publisher's Acknowledgments

Executive Editor: Steve Hayes

Project Editor: Kelly Ewing

Technical Editor: Prescott Perez-Fox

Sr. Editorial Assistant: Cherie Case

Production Editor: Mohammed Zafar Ali

Cover Image: © Rawpixel/Getty Images

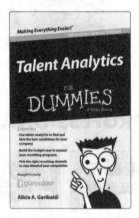

PERSONAL ENRICHMENT

9781119187790
USA $26.00
CAN $31.99
UK £19.99

9781119179030
USA $21.99
CAN $25.99
UK £16.99

9781119293354
USA $24.99
CAN $29.99
UK £17.99

9781119293347
USA $22.99
CAN $27.99
UK £16.99

9781119310068
USA $22.99
CAN $27.99
UK £16.99

9781119235606
USA $24.99
CAN $29.99
UK £17.99

9781119251163
USA $24.99
CAN $29.99
UK £17.99

9781119235491
USA $26.99
CAN $31.99
UK £19.99

9781119279952
USA $24.99
CAN $29.99
UK £17.99

9781119283133
USA $24.99
CAN $29.99
UK £17.99

9781119287117
USA $24.99
CAN $29.99
UK £16.99

9781119130246
USA $22.99
CAN $27.99
UK £16.99

PROFESSIONAL DEVELOPMENT

9781119311041
USA $24.99
CAN $29.99
UK £17.99

9781119255796
USA $39.99
CAN $47.99
UK £27.99

9781119293439
USA $26.99
CAN $31.99
UK £19.99

9781119281467
USA $26.99
CAN $31.99
UK £19.99

9781119280651
USA $29.99
CAN $35.99
UK £21.99

9781119251132
USA $24.99
CAN $29.99
UK £17.99

9781119310563
USA $34.00
CAN $41.99
UK £24.99

9781119181705
USA $29.99
CAN $35.99
UK £21.99

9781119263593
USA $26.99
CAN $31.99
UK £19.99

9781119257769
USA $29.99
CAN $35.99
UK £21.99

9781119293477
USA $26.99
CAN $31.99
UK £19.99

9781119265313
USA $24.99
CAN $29.99
UK £17.99

9781119239314
USA $29.99
CAN $35.99
UK £21.99

9781119293323
USA $29.99
CAN $35.99
UK £21.99

Small books for big imaginations

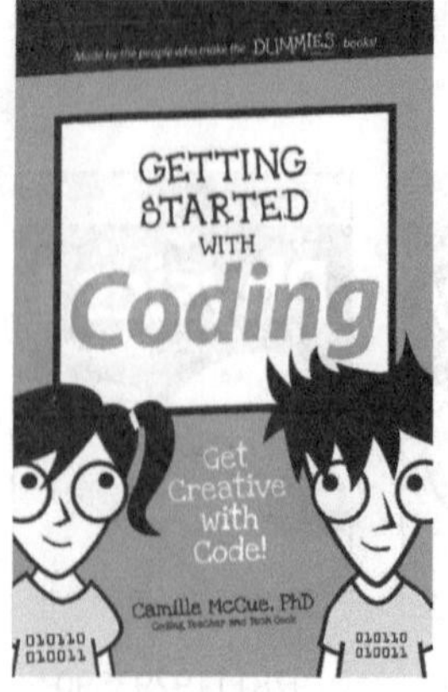

9781119177173
USA $9.99
CAN $9.99
UK £8.99

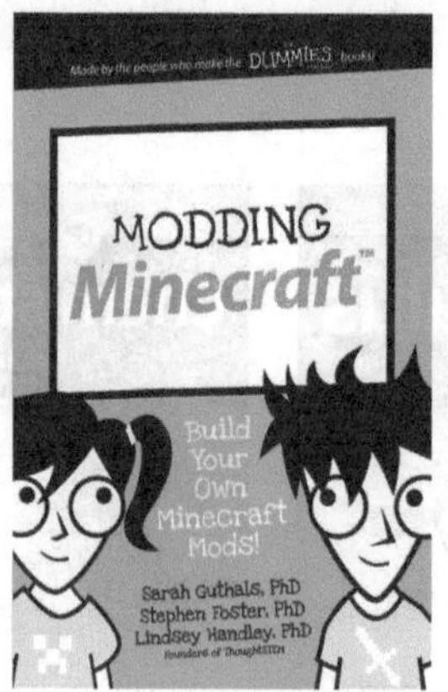

9781119177272
USA $9.99
CAN $9.99
UK £8.99

9781119177241
USA $9.99
CAN $9.99
UK £8.99

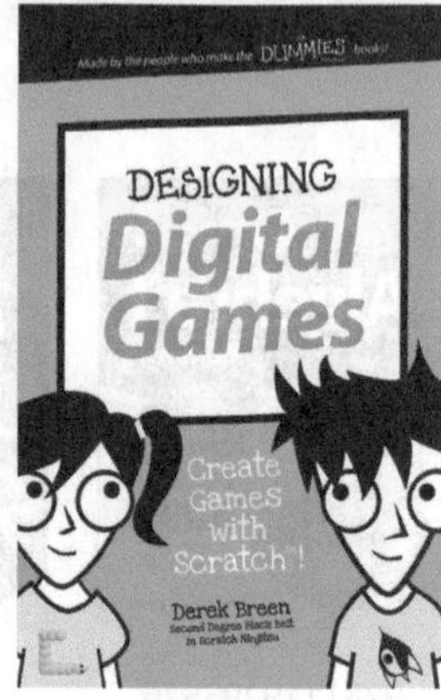

9781119177210
USA $9.99
CAN $9.99
UK £8.99

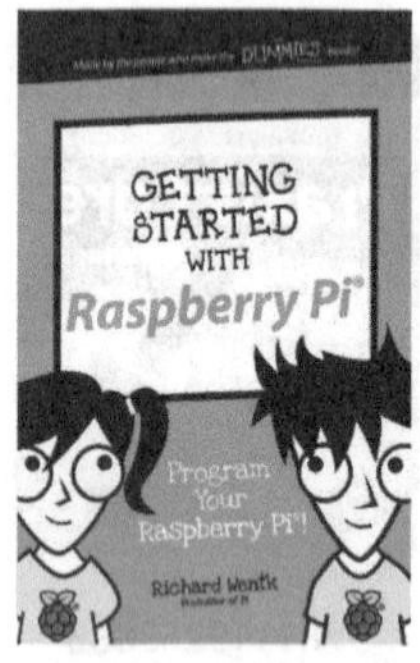

9781119262657
USA $9.99
CAN $9.99
UK £6.99

9781119291336
USA $9.99
CAN $9.99
UK £6.99

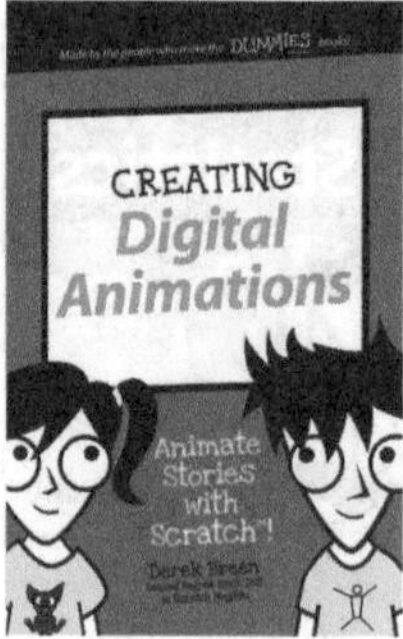

9781119233527
USA $9.99
CAN $9.99
UK £6.99

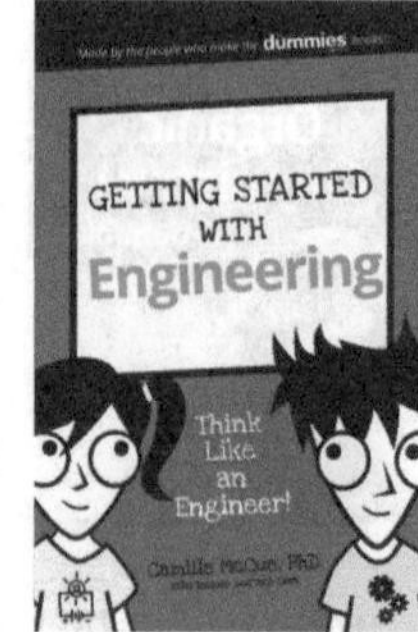

9781119291220
USA $9.99
CAN $9.99
UK £6.99

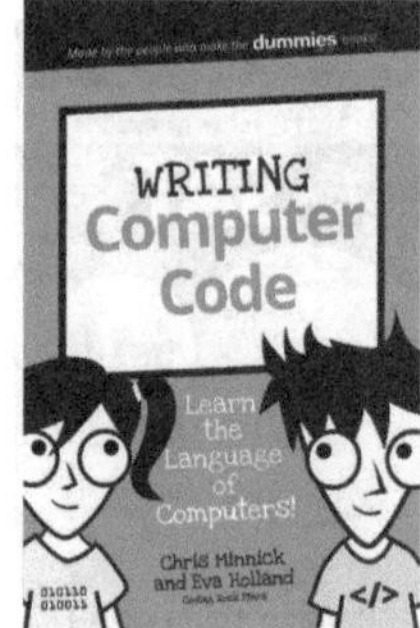

9781119177302
USA $9.99
CAN $9.99
UK £8.99

Unleash Their Creativity

dummies.com

dummies®
A Wiley Brand